The 114th Congress, 2015–16*

United States House of Representatives

Democrats: 186   Republicans: 244   Undecided: 5   2014 Election Results: Republicans gained at least 10 seats.*

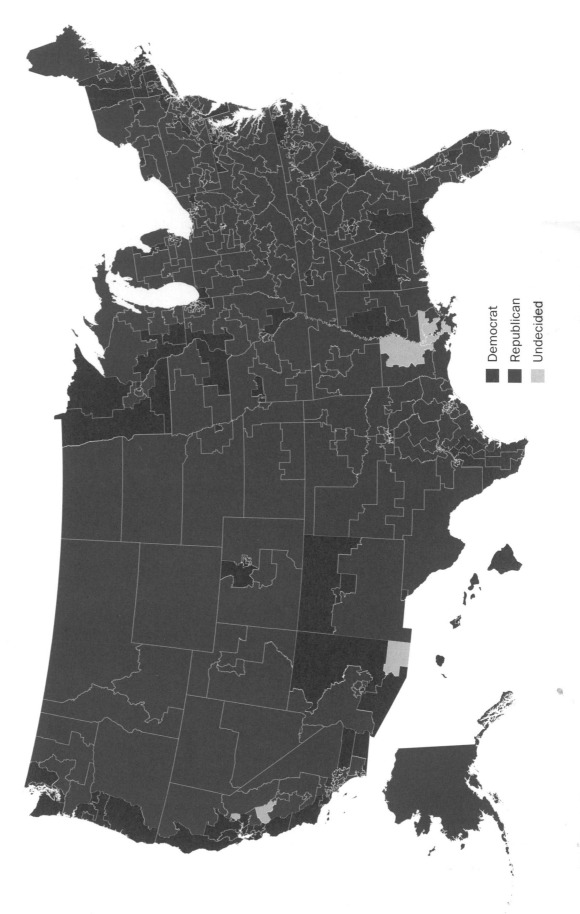

Democrat

Republican

Undecided

United States Senate

Democrats: 44   Republicans: 54   Independents: 2   **2014 Election Results:** Republicans gained 9 seats.*

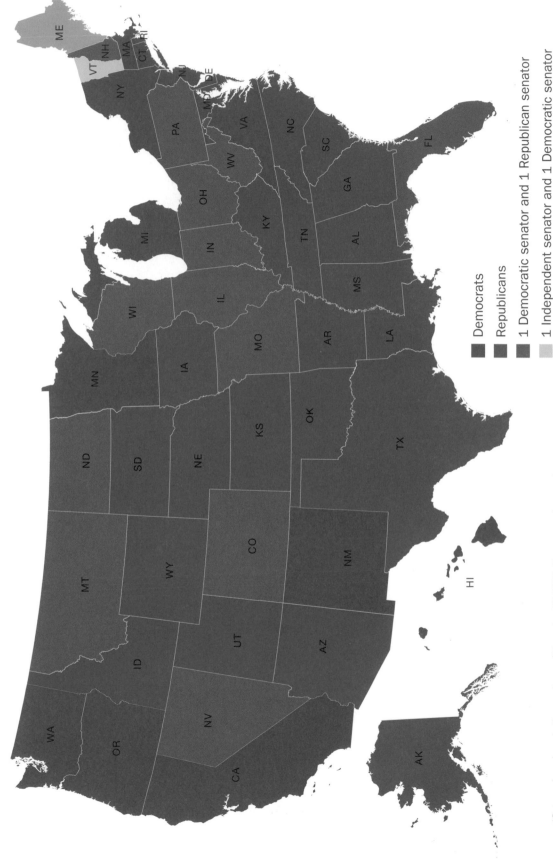

Democrats
Republicans
1 Democratic senator and 1 Republican senator
1 Independent senator and 1 Democratic senator
1 Independent senator and 1 Republican senator

*Data are based on election results as of November 18, 2014. House races in several states remained undecided pending recounts and runoff elections.

TENTH EDITION

We the People

AN INTRODUCTION TO AMERICAN POLITICS

TENTH EDITION

We the People

AN INTRODUCTION TO AMERICAN POLITICS

Benjamin Ginsberg
THE JOHNS HOPKINS UNIVERSITY

Theodore J. Lowi
CORNELL UNIVERSITY

Margaret Weir
UNIVERSITY OF CALIFORNIA AT BERKELEY

Caroline J. Tolbert
UNIVERSITY OF IOWA

 W. W. NORTON & COMPANY
NEW YORK   LONDON

W. W. Norton & Company has been independent since its founding in 1923, when William Warder Norton and Mary D. Herter Norton first published lectures delivered at the People's Institute, the adult education division of New York City's Cooper Union. The firm soon expanded its program beyond the Institute, publishing books by celebrated academics from America and abroad. By mid-century, the two major pillars of Norton's publishing program—trade books and college texts—were firmly established. In the 1950s, the Norton family transferred control of the company to its employees, and today—with a staff of four hundred and a comparable number of trade, college, and professional titles published each year—W. W. Norton & Company stands as the largest and oldest publishing house owned wholly by its employees.

Editor: Lisa Camner McKay
Project Editor: Christine D'Antonio
Editorial Assistants: Sarah Wolf and Samantha Held
Manuscript Editor: Nina Hnatov
Managing Editor, College: Marian Johnson
Managing Editor, College Digital Media: Kim Yi
Senior Production Supervisor, College: Ashley Horna
Media Editor: Toni Magyar
Media Editorial Assistant: Michael Jaoui
Marketing Manager, Political Science: Erin Brown
Art Director: Rubina Yeh
Text Design: Lissi Sigillo
Photo Editor: Evan Luberger
Photo Researcher: Julie Tesser
Permissions Manager: Megan Jackson
Permissions Clearing: Elizabeth Trammell
Information Graphics: Kiss Me I'm Polish LLC, New York
Composition: Graphic World, Inc.
Manufacturing: Courier—Kendallville

Permission to use copyrighted material is included in the credits section of this book, which begins on page A89.

978-0-393-93703-9

W. W. Norton & Company, Inc., 500 Fifth Avenue, New York, N.Y. 10110
www.wwnorton.com

W. W. Norton & Company Ltd., Castle House, 75/76 Wells Street, London W1T 3QT

1 2 3 4 5 6 7 8 9 0

To Sandy, Cindy, and Alex Ginsberg
Angele, Anna, and Jason Lowi
Nicholas Ziegler
Dave, Jackie, Eveline, and Eddie Dowling

contents

2 ● The Founding and the Constitution 38

3 ● Federalism 76

4 ● Civil Liberties 114

5 ● Civil Rights 156

PART II   Politics

6 ● Public Opinion   206

9 ● Political Parties 340

PART III   Institutions

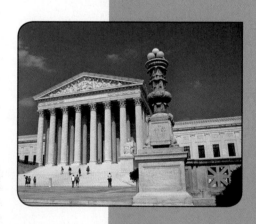

PART IV   Policy

16 ● Government and the Economy   640

18 ● Foreign Policy and Democracy   724

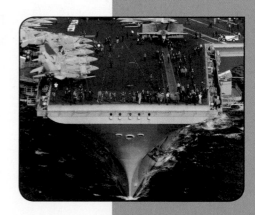

● Appendix

preface

This book has been and continues to be dedicated to developing a satisfactory response to the question more and more Americans are asking: Why should we be engaged with government and politics? Through the first nine editions, we sought to answer this question by making the text directly relevant to the lives of the students who would be reading it. As a result, we tried to make politics interesting by demonstrating that students' interests are at stake and that they therefore need to take a personal, even selfish, interest in the outcomes of government. At the same time, we realized that students needed guidance in how to become politically engaged. Beyond providing students with a core of political knowledge, we needed to show them how they could apply that knowledge as participants in the political process. The "Plug In" sections in each chapter help achieve that goal.

As events from the last several years have reminded us, "what government does" can be a matter of life and death. Recent events have reinforced the centrality of government in citizens' lives. The U.S. government has fought two wars abroad, while claiming sweeping new powers at home that could compromise the liberties of its citizens. America's role in the world is discussed daily both inside and outside the classroom. Moreover, the Internet has opened up new avenues to participation and mobilization. Reflecting all of these trends, this new Tenth Edition shows more than any other book on the market (1) how students are connected to government; (2) how digital media are changing (or not changing) the way Americans experience politics; and (3) why students should think critically about government and politics. These themes are incorporated in the following ways:

- **New "Politics and Your Future" chapter conclusions give students direct, personal reasons to care about politics.** These sections focus on the political opportunities and challenges that students will face in their lives as a result of emerging social, political, demographic, and technological change. The conclusions reprise the important point made in the chapter introductions that *government matters* and prompt students to consider how political change will impact their futures.

- **New "Plug In" sections show students how to make a difference in politics.** These boxes replace the older "Get Involved" sections with succinct, realistic steps today's students can take—online and off—to to *inform* themselves, *express* themselves, *connect* with others, and *act* in politically meaningful ways.

- **New content on how digital media are changing politics is now incorporated throughout the text.** With the Ninth Edition, we added "Digital Citizens" boxes to explore the ways that new information technologies are shaping how we experience politics. In this Tenth Edition, the coverage of digital politics has been integrated into the body of the text, in recognition of the fact that digital media have become an integral part of American politics.

- **New "America Side by Side" boxes use data figures and tables to provide a comparative perspective.** These one-page boxes appear in every chapter and replace the older "America in the World" text boxes with a more visual presentation of comparative data. By comparing political institutions and behavior across countries, students gain a better understanding of how specific features of the American system shape politics.

- **"Who Are Americans?" infographics ask students to think critically about how Americans from different backgrounds experience politics.** These sections use bold, engaging graphics to present a statistical snapshot of the nation related to each chapter's topic. Critical-thinking questions in each unit and related exercises on the StudySpace website give students a chance to compare their own views and experiences and consider the political implications. The "Who Are Americans?" PowerPoint slides include enhanced versions of the graphics for use in lectures.

- **Chapter introductions focus on "What Government Does and Why It Matters."** In recent decades, cynicism about "big government" has dominated the political zeitgeist. But critics of government often forget that governments do a great deal for citizens. Every year, Americans are the beneficiaries of billions of dollars of goods and services from government programs. Government "does" a lot, and what it does matters a great deal to everyone, including college students. At the start of each chapter, this theme is introduced and applied to the chapter's topic. The goal is to show students that government and politics mean something to their daily lives.

- **"For Critical Analysis" questions are incorporated throughout the text.** "For Critical Analysis" questions in the margins of every chapter prompt students' own critical thinking about the material in the chapter, encouraging them to engage with the topic. And the questions that accompany each "Who Are Americans?" unit ask students to consider how Americans from various backgrounds experience politics.

We continue to hope that our book will itself be accepted as a form of enlightened political action. This Tenth Edition is another chance. It is an advancement toward our goal. We promise to keep trying.

acknowledgments

W e are pleased to acknowledge the many colleagues who had an active role in criticism and preparation of the manuscript. Our thanks go to:

First Edition Reviewers

Sarah Binder, Brookings Institution
Kathleen Gille, Office of Representative David Bonior
Rodney Hero, University of Colorado at Boulder
Robert Katzmann, Brookings Institution
Kathleen Knight, University of Houston
Robin Kolodny, Temple University
Nancy Kral, Tomball College
Robert C. Lieberman, Columbia University
David A. Marcum, University of Wyoming
Laura R. Winsky Mattei, State University of New York at Buffalo
Marilyn S. Mertens, Midwestern State University
Barbara Suhay, Henry Ford Community College
Carolyn Wong, Stanford University
Julian Zelizer, State University of New York at Albany

Second Edition Reviewers

Lydia Andrade, University of North Texas
John Coleman, University of Wisconsin at Madison
Daphne Eastman, Odessa College
Otto Feinstein, Wayne State University
Elizabeth Flores, Delmar College
James Gimpel, University of Maryland at College Park
Jill Glaathar, Southwest Missouri State University
Shaun Herness, University of Florida
William Lyons, University of Tennessee at Knoxville
Andrew Polsky, Hunter College, City University of New York
Grant Reeher, Syracuse University
Richard Rich, Virginia Polytechnic
Bartholomew Sparrow, University of Texas at Austin

Third Edition Reviewers

Bruce R. Drury, Lamar University
Andrew I. E. Ewoh, Prairie View A&M University
Amy Jasperson, University of Texas at San Antonio

Loch Johnson, University of Georgia
Mark Kann, University of Southern California
Robert L. Perry, University of Texas of the Permian Basin
Wayne Pryor, Brazosport College
Elizabeth A. Rexford, Wharton County Junior College
Andrea Simpson, University of Washington
Brian Smentkowski, Southeast Missouri State University
Nelson Wikstrom, Virginia Commonwealth University

Fourth Edition Reviewers

M. E. Banks, Virginia Commonwealth University
Lynn Brink, North Lake College
Mark Cichock, University of Texas at Arlington
Del Fields, St. Petersburg College
Nancy Kinney, Washtenaw Community College
William Klein, St. Petersburg College
Dana Morales, Montgomery College
Christopher Muste, Louisiana State University
Larry Norris, South Plains College
David Rankin, State University of New York at Fredonia
Paul Roesler, St. Charles Community College
J. Philip Rogers, San Antonio College
Greg Shaw, Illinois Wesleyan University
Tracy Skopek, Stephen F. Austin State University
Don Smith, University of North Texas
Terri Wright, Cal State, Fullerton

Fifth Edition Reviewers

Annie Benifield, Tomball College
Denise Dutton, Southwest Missouri State University
Rick Kurtz, Central Michigan University
Kelly McDaniel, Three Rivers Community College
Eric Plutzer, Pennsylvania State University
Daniel Smith, Northwest Missouri State University
Dara Strolovitch, University of Minnesota

Dennis Toombs, San Jacinto College–North
Stacy Ulbig, Southwest Missouri State University

Sixth Edition Reviewers

Janet Adamski, University of Mary Hardin–Baylor
Greg Andrews, St. Petersburg College
Louis Bolce, Baruch College
Darin Combs, Tulsa Community College
Sean Conroy, University of New Orleans
Paul Cooke, Cy Fair College
Vida Davoudi, Kingwood College
Robert DiClerico, West Virginia University
Corey Ditslear, University of North Texas
Kathy Dolan, University of Wisconsin, Milwaukee
Randy Glean, Midwestern State University
Nancy Kral, Tomball College
Mark Logas, Valencia Community College
Scott MacDougall, Diablo Valley College
David Mann, College of Charleston
Christopher Muste, University of Montana
Richard Pacelle, Georgia Southern University
Sarah Poggione, Florida International University
Richard Rich, Virginia Tech
Thomas Schmeling, Rhode Island College
Scott Spitzer, California State University–Fullerton
Dennis Toombs, San Jacinto College–North
John Vento, Antelope Valley College
Robert Wood, University of North Dakota

Seventh Edition Reviewers

Molly Andolina, DePaul University
Nancy Bednar, Antelope Valley College
Paul Blakelock, Kingwood College
Amy Brandon, San Jacinto College
Jim Cauthen, John Jay College
Kevin Davis, North Central Texas College
Louis DeSipio, University of California–Irvine
Brandon Franke, Blinn College
Steve Garrison, Midwestern State University
Joseph Howard, University of Central Arkansas
Aaron Knight, Houston Community College
Paul Labedz, Valencia Community College
Elise Langan, John Jay College
Mark Logas, Valencia Community College
Eric Miller, Blinn College
Anthony O'Regan, Los Angeles Valley College
David Putz, Kingwood College
Chis Soper, Pepperdine University
Kevin Wagner, Florida Atlantic University
Laura Wood, Tarrant County College

Eighth Edition Reviewers

Andrea Aleman, University of Texas at San Antonio
Stephen Amberg, University of Texas at San Antonio

Steve Anthony, Georgia State University
Brian Arbour, John Jay College, CUNY
Greg Arey, Cape Fear Community College
Ellen Baik, University of Texas–Pan American
David Birch, Lone Star College–Tomball
Bill Carroll, Sam Houston State University
Ed Chervenak, University of New Orleans
Gary Church, Mountain View College
Adrian Stefan Clark, Del Mar College
Casey Clofstad, University of Miami
Annie Cole, Los Angeles City College
Greg Combs, University of Texas at Dallas
Cassandra Cookson, Lee College
Brian Cravens, Blinn College
John Crosby, California State University–Chico
Scott Crosby, Valencia Community College
Courtenay Daum, Colorado State University, Fort Collins
Paul Davis, Truckee Meadows Community College
Peter Doas, University of Texas–Pan American
Vida Davoudi, Lone Star College–Kingwood
John Domino, Sam Houston State University
Doug Dow, University of Texas–Dallas
Jeremy Duff, Midwestern State University
Heather Evans, Sam Houston State University
Hyacinth Ezeamii, Albany State University
Bob Fitrakis, Columbus State Community College
Brian Fletcher, Truckee Meadows Community College
Paul Foote, Eastern Kentucky University
Frank Garrahan, Austin Community College
Jimmy Gleason, Purdue University
Steven Greene, North Carolina State University
Jeannie Grussendorf, Georgia State University
M. Ahad Hayaud-Din, Brookhaven College
Virginia Haysley, Lone Star College–Tomball
Alexander Hogan, Lone Star College–CyFair
Glen Hunt, Austin Community College
Mark Jendrysik, University of North Dakota
Krista Jenkins, Fairleigh Dickinson University
Carlos Juárez, Hawaii Pacific University
Melinda Kovas, Sam Houston State University
Paul Labedz, Valencia Community College
Boyd Lanier, Lamar University
Jeff Lazarus, Georgia State University
Jeffrey Lee, Blinn College
Alan Lehmann, Blinn College
Julie Lester, Macon State College
Steven Lichtman, Shippensburg University
Mark Logas, Valencia Community College
Fred Lokken, Truckee Meadows Community College
Shari MacLachlan, Palm Beach Community College
Guy Martin, Winston-Salem State University
Fred Monardi, College of Southern Nevada
Vincent Moscardelli, University of Connecticut
Jason Mycoff, University of Delaware
Sugmaran Narayanan, Midwestern State University
Adam Newmark, Appalachian State University
Larry Norris, South Plains College

Anthony Nownes, University of Tennessee, Knoxville
Elizabeth Oldmixon, University of North Texas
Anthony O'Regan, Los Angeles Valley College
John Osterman, San Jacinto College–Central
Mark Peplowski, College of Southern Nevada
Maria Victoria Perez-Rios, John Jay College, CUNY
Sara Rinfret, University of Wisconsin, Green Bay
Andre Robinson, Pulaski Technical College
Paul Roesler, St. Charles Community College
Susan Roomberg, University of Texas at San Antonio
Ryan Rynbrandt, Collin County Community College
Mario Salas, Northwest Vista College
Michael Sanchez, San Antonio College
Mary Schander, Pasadena City College
Laura Schneider, Grand Valley State University
Ronee Schreiber, San Diego State University
Subash Shah, Winston-Salem State University
Mark Shomaker, Blinn College
Roy Slater, St. Petersburg College
Scott Spitzer, California State University–Fullerton
Debra St. John, Collin College
John Vento, Antelope Valley College
Eric Whitaker, Western Washington University
Clay Wiegand, Cisco College
Walter Wilson, University of Texas at San Antonio
Kevan Yenerall, Clarion University
Rogerio Zapata, South Texas College

Ninth Edition Reviewers

Amy Acord, Lone Star College–CyFair
Milan Andrejevich, Ivy Tech Community College
Steve Anthony, Georgia State University
Phillip Ardoin, Appalachian State University
Gregory Arey, Cape Fear Community College
Joan Babcock, Northwest Vista College
Evelyn Ballard, Houston Community College
Robert Ballinger, South Texas College
Mary Barnes-Tilley, Blinn College
Robert Bartels, Evangel University
Nancy Bednar, Antelope Valley College
Annie Benifield, Lone Star College–Tomball
Donna Bennett, Trinity Valley Community College
Amy Brandon, El Paso Community College
Mark Brewer, The University of Maine
Gary Brown, Lone Star College–Montgomery
Joe Campbell, Johnson County Community College
Dewey Clayton, University of Louisville
Jeff Colbert, Elon University
Amanda Cook-Fesperman, Illinois Valley Community College
Kevin Corder, Western Michigan University
Kevin Davis, North Central Texas College
Paul Davis, Truckee Meadows Community College
Terri Davis, Lamar University
Jennifer De Maio, California State University, Northridge

Christopher Durso, Valencia College
Ryan Emenaker, College of the Redwoods
Leslie Feldman, Hofstra University
Glen Findley, Odessa College
Michael Gattis, Gulf Coast State College
Donna Godwin, Trinity Valley Community College
Precious Hall, Truckee Meadows Community College
Sally Hansen, Daytona State College
Tiffany Harper, Collin College
Todd Hartman, Appalachian State University
Virginia Haysley, Lone Star College–Tomball
David Head, John Tyler Community College
Rick Henderson, Texas State University–San Marcos
Richard Herrera, Arizona State University
Thaddaus Hill, Blinn College
Steven Holmes, Bakersfield College
Kevin Holton, South Texas College
Robin Jacobson, University of Puget Sound
Joseph Jozwiak, Texas A & M–Corpus Christi
Casey Klofstad, University of Miami
Samuel Lingrosso, Los Angeles Valley College
Mark Logas, Valencia College
Christopher Marshall, South Texas College
Larry McElvain, South Texas College
Elizabeth McLane, Wharton County Junior College
Eddie Meaders, University of North Texas
Rob Mellen, Mississippi State University
Jalal Nejad, Northwest Vista College
Adam Newmark, Appalachian State University
Stephen Nicholson, University of California, Merced
Cissie Owen, Lamar University
Suzanne Preston, St. Petersburg College
David Putz, Lone Star College–Kingwood
Auksuole Rubavichute, Mountain View College
Ronnee Schreiber, San Diego State University
Ronald Schurin, University of Connecticut
Jason Seitz, Georgia Perimeter College
Jennifer Seitz, Georgia Perimeter College
Shannon Sinegal, The University of New Orleans
John Sides, George Washington University
Thomas Sowers, Lamar University
Jim Startin, University of Texas at San Antonio
Robert Sterken, University of Texas at Tyler
Bobby Summers, Harper College
John Theis, Lone Star College–Kingwood
John Todd, University of North Texas
Delaina Toothman, The University of Maine
David Trussell, Cisco College
Ronald Vardy, University of Houston
Linda Veazey, Midwestern State University
John Vento, Antelope Valley Community College
Clif Wilkinson, Georgia College
John Wood, Rose State College
Michael Young, Trinity Valley Community College
Tyler Young, Collin College

Tenth Edition Reviewers

Stephen P. Amberg, University of Texas at San Antonio
Juan F. Arzola, College of the Sequoias
Thomas J. Baldino, Wilkes University
Christina Bejarano, University of Kansas
Paul T. Bellinger, Jr., University of Missouri
Melanie J. Blumberg, California University of Pennsylvania
Matthew T. Bradley, Indiana University Kokomo
Jeffrey W. Christiansen, Seminole State College
McKinzie Craig, Marietta College
Christopher Cronin, Methodist University
Jenna Duke, Lehigh Carbon Community College
Francisco Durand, University of Texas at San Antonio
Carrie Eaves, Elon University
Paul M. Flor, El Camino College Compton Center
Adam Fuller, Youngstown State University
Christi Gramling, Charleston Southern University
Sally Hansen, Daytona State College
Mary Jane Hatton, Hawai'i Pacific University
David Helpap, University of Wisconsin–Green Bay
Theresa L. Hutchins, Georgia Highlands College
Cryshanna A. Jackson Leftwich, Youngstown State University
Ashlyn Kuersten, Western Michigan University
Kara Lindaman, Winona State University
Timothy Lynch, University of Wisconsin–Milwaukee

Larry McElvain, South Texas College
Corinna R. McKoy, Ventura College
Eddie L. Meaders, University of North Texas
Don D. Mirjanian, College of Southern Nevada
R. Shea Mize, Georgia Highlands College
Nicholas Morgan, Collin College
Matthew Murray, Dutchess Community College
Harold "Trey" Orndorff III, Daytona State College
Randall Parish, University of North Georgia
Michelle Pautz, University of Dayton
Michael Pickering, University of New Orleans
Donald Ranish, Antelope Valley College
Glenn W. Richardson, Jr., Kutztown University
    of Pennsylvania
Jason Robles, Colorado State University
Ionas Aurelian Rus, University of Cincinnati–Blue Ash
Robert Sahr, Oregon State University
Kelly B. Shaw, Iowa State University
Captain Michael Slattery, Campbell University
Michael Smith, Sam Houston State University
Maryam T. Stevenson, University of Indianapolis
Elizabeth Trentanelli, Gulf Coast State College
Ronald W. Vardy, University of Houston
Timothy Weaver, University of Louisville
Christina Wolbrecht, University of Notre Dame

We are also grateful to Holley Hansen, of Oklahoma State University, who contributed to the "America Side by Side" boxes, and to Gabrielle Ellul for research assistance.

Perhaps above all, we wish to thank those at W. W. Norton. For its first five editions, editor Steve Dunn helped us shape the book in countless ways. Ann Shin carried on the Norton tradition of splendid editorial work on the Sixth through Ninth Editions. Our current editor, Lisa McKay, has brought smart ideas and a keen editorial eye to this Tenth Edition. For our Coursepack and other instructor resources for the book, Toni Magyar has been an energetic and visionary editor. Nina Hnatov copyedited the manuscript, and our superb project editor Christine D'Antonio devoted countless hours keeping on top of myriad details. Ashley Horna has been dedicated in managing production. We thank Julie Tesser for finding new photos. Finally, we wish to thank Roby Harrington, the head of Norton's college department.

Benjamin Ginsberg
Theodore J. Lowi
Margaret Weir
Caroline J. Tolbert

November 2014

TENTH EDITION

We the People

AN INTRODUCTION TO AMERICAN POLITICS

Most Americans share the core political values of liberty, equality, and democracy and want their government and its policies to reflect these values. However, people often disagree on the meaning of these values and what government should do to protect them.

American Political Culture

WHAT GOVERNMENT DOES AND WHY IT MATTERS Americans sometimes appear to believe that the government is an institution that does things *to* them and from which they need protection. Students may wonder why they have to fill in long, often complicated forms to apply for financial assistance. They may frown when they see the payroll tax deducted from their small paycheck. Like Americans of all ages, they may resent municipal "red-light" cameras designed to photograph traffic violators—and send them tickets.

Although most people complain about something that government does *to* them, most everyone wants the government to do a great deal *for* them. Some of the services that people expect from government are big-ticket items, such as providing national security and keeping the nation safe from terrorist attacks. We all know that government pays for and directs the military. Students attending a state university know that state and federal public dollars help support their education.

Yet many of the other services that government provides are far less visible, and often it is not even clear that government plays a role at all. For example, students grabbing a quick bite to eat between classes take it for granted that their hamburger will not contain bacteria that might make them sick. Without federal inspection of meat, however, chances of contracting food-borne illnesses would be much higher and the everyday task of eating would be much riskier. Driving to school would not be possible if not for the tens of billions of dollars spent each year on road construction and maintenance by federal, state, and municipal authorities. Like most Americans, young people expect to get reliable information about the weather for the week ahead and warnings about dangerous events such as hurricanes. The National Weather Service and the National Hurricane Center both provide reliable forecasts for such simple calculations as whether to bring an umbrella to more significant calculations made by airlines and air traffic control to get travelers safely where they need to go. These daily decisions don't seem to involve government but in fact they do. Indeed, most Americans would not be here at all if it were not for federal immigration policies, which set the terms for entry into the United States and for obtaining citizenship.

government institutions and procedures through which a territory and its people are ruled

Government is the term generally used to describe the formal institutions through which a land and its people are ruled. As the government seeks to help and protect its citizens, it faces the challenge of doing so in ways that are true to the key American political values of liberty, equality, and democracy. Most Americans find it easy to affirm all three values in principle. In practice, however, matters are not always so clear; these values mean different things to different people, and they often seem to conflict. This is where politics comes in. **Politics** refers to conflicts and struggles over the leadership, structure, and policies of governments. As we will see in this chapter and throughout this book, much political conflict concerns policies and practices that seem to affirm one of the key American political values but may contradict another.

politics conflict over the leadership, structure, and policies of governments

chaptergoals

- Explore Americans' attitudes toward government (pp. 5–9)
- Describe the role of the citizen in politics (pp. 9–13)
- Define government and forms of government (pp. 13–17)
- Show how the social composition of the American population has changed over time (pp. 17–24)
- Analyze whether the U.S. system of government upholds American political values (pp. 24–31)

● What Americans Think about Government

Explore Americans' attitudes toward government

Since the United States was established as a nation, Americans have been reluctant to grant government too much power, and they have often been suspicious of politicians. But over the course of the nation's history, Americans have also turned to government for assistance in times of need and have strongly supported the government in periods of war. In 1933 the power of the government began to expand to meet the crises created by the stock market crash of 1929, the Great Depression, and the run on banks of 1933. Congress passed legislation that brought the government into the businesses of home mortgages, farm mortgages, credit, and relief of personal distress. More recently, when the economy threatened to fall into a deep recession in 2008 and 2009, the federal government stepped in to shore up the financial system, oversee the restructuring of the ailing auto companies, and inject hundreds of billions of dollars into the faltering economy. Today the national government is an enormous institution with programs and policies reaching into every corner of American life. It oversees the nation's economy; it is the nation's largest employer; it provides citizens with a host of services; it controls the world's most formidable military; and it regulates a wide range of social and commercial activities.

Much of what citizens have come to depend on and take for granted as somehow part of the natural environment is in fact created by government. Take the example of a typical college student's day, throughout which that student relies on

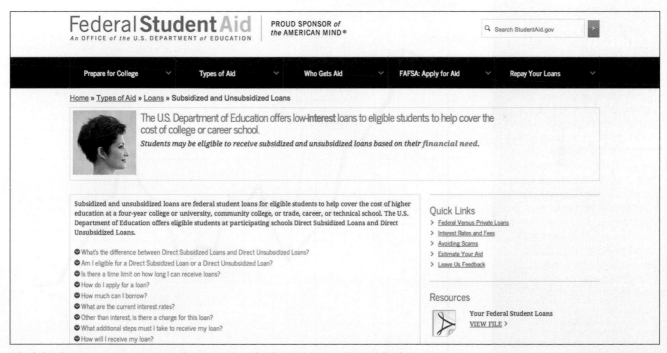

The federal government maintains a large number of websites that provide useful information to citizens on such topics as loans for education, civil service job applications, the inflation rate, and how the weather will affect farming. These sites are just one way in which the government serves its citizens.

a host of services and activities organized by national, state, and local government agencies. The extent of this dependence on government is illustrated by Table 1.1 on page 7.

Trust in Government

Ironically, even as popular dependence on the government has grown, the American public's view of government has turned more sour. Public trust in government has declined, and Americans are now more likely to feel that they can do little to influence the government's actions. The decline in public trust among Americans is striking. In the early 1960s, three-quarters of Americans said they trusted government most of the time. By 2013, only 19 percent of Americans expressed trust in government; 68 stated that they did not trust government most of the time[1] (see Figure 1.1). Different groups vary somewhat in their levels of trust: African Americans and Latinos express more confidence in the federal government than do whites. But even among the most supportive groups, considerably more than half do not trust the government.[2] These developments are important because politically engaged citizens and public confidence in government are vital for the health of a democracy.

In the aftermath of the September 11, 2001, terrorist attacks, a number of studies reported a substantial increase in popular trust in government.[3] This view, expressed during a period of national crisis, may have been indicative less of a renewed *trust* in government to do the right thing than of a fervent *hope* that it would.

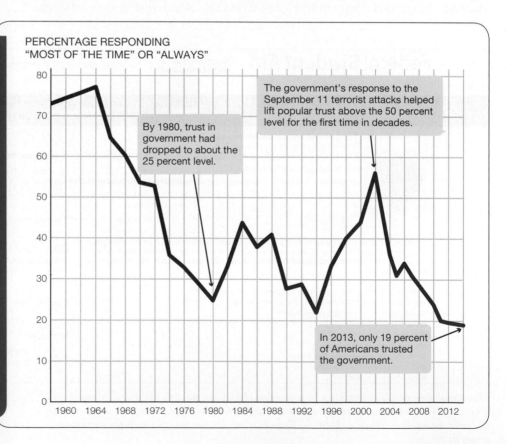

FIGURE 1.1

Trust in Government, 1958–2013

Participants in these polls were asked if they trusted the government to "do the right thing" always, most of the time, only some of the time, or never.

Since the 1960s, general levels of public trust in government have declined. What factors might help to account for changes in the public's trust in government? Why has confidence in government dropped again since September 11, 2001?

SOURCES: The American National Election Studies, 1958–2004; Pew Research Center, www.people-press .org/2013/10/18/trust-in-government -nears-record-low-but-most-federal -agencies-are-viewed-favorably (accessed 5/14/14).

PERCENTAGE RESPONDING "MOST OF THE TIME" OR "ALWAYS"

By 1980, trust in government had dropped to about the 25 percent level.

The government's response to the September 11 terrorist attacks helped lift popular trust above the 50 percent level for the first time in decades.

In 2013, only 19 percent of Americans trusted the government.

TABLE 1.1

The Presence of Government in the Daily Life of a Student at "State University"

TIME OF DAY	SCHEDULE
7:00 AM	Wake up. Standard time set by the national government.
7:10 AM	Shower. Water courtesy of local government, either a public entity or a regulated private company. Brush your teeth with toothpaste whose cavity-fighting claims have been verified by a federal agency. Dry your hair with an electric dryer manufactured according to federal government agency guidelines.
7:30 AM	Have a bowl of cereal with milk for breakfast. "Nutrition Facts" on food labels are a federal requirement, pasteurization of milk required by state law, freshness dating on milk based on state and federal standards, recycling the empty cereal box and milk carton enabled by state or local laws.
8:30 AM	Drive or take public transportation to campus. Air bags and seat belts required by federal and state laws. Roads and bridges paid for by state and local governments, speed and traffic laws set by state and local governments, public transportation subsidized by all levels of government.
8:45 AM	Arrive on campus of large public university. Buildings are 70 percent financed by state taxpayers.
9:00 AM	First class: Chemistry 101. Tuition partially paid by a federal loan (more than half the cost of university instruction is paid for by taxpayers), chemistry lab paid for with grants from the National Science Foundation (a federal agency) and smaller grants from business corporations made possible by federal income tax deductions for charitable contributions.
Noon	Eat lunch. College cafeteria financed by state dormitory authority on land grant from federal Department of Agriculture.
12:47 PM	Felt an earthquake! Check the U.S. Geological Survey at www.usgs.gov to see that it was a 3.9 on the Richter scale.
2:00 PM	Second class: American Government 101 (your favorite class!). You may be taking this class because it is required by the state legislature or because it fulfills a university requirement.
4:00 PM	Third class: Computer Lab. Free computers, software, and Internet access courtesy of state subsidies plus grants and discounts from IBM and Microsoft, the costs of which are deducted from their corporate income taxes; Internet built in part by federal government. Duplication of software prohibited by federal copyright laws.
6:00 PM	Eat dinner: hamburger and french fries. Meat inspected for bacteria by federal agencies.
7:00 PM	Work at part-time job at the campus library. Minimum wage set by federal, state, or local government, books and journals in library paid for by state taxpayers.
8:15 PM	Go online to check the status of your application for a federal student loan (FAFSA) on the Department of Education's website at studentaid.ed.gov.
10:00 PM	Go home. Street lighting paid for by county and city governments, police patrols by city government.
10:15 PM	Watch TV. Networks regulated by federal government, cable public-access channels required by city law. Weather forecast provided to broadcasters by a federal agency.
10:45 PM	To complete your economics homework, visit the Bureau of Labor Statistics at www.bls.gov to look up unemployment levels since 1972.
Midnight	Put out the trash before going to bed. Trash collected by city sanitation department, financed by "user charges."

In response to the terrorist attacks of September 11, 2001, Americans rallied around government officials and offered unprecedented support. Is support for the government during times of crisis at odds with Americans' distrust of government at other times?

political efficacy the ability to influence government and politics

And, indeed, by 2004, trust in government had fallen to near its pre-September 11 level.[4] Several factors contributed to the decline in trust. Revelations about the faulty information that led up to the war in Iraq and ongoing concern about the war had increased Americans' distrust of government. In March 2007, 54 percent of those surveyed believed that the Bush administration had deliberately misled the American public about whether Iraq had weapons of mass destruction.

By 2013 intense partisan conflict further undermined trust in government. The public watched with dismay as political differences over taxing and spending led to repeated threats to shut down the federal government. In the fall of 2011, after a bitter congressional battle over raising the national debt limit—usually a routine matter—only 10 percent of Americans trusted government to do the right thing always or most of the time, the lowest level of trust ever recorded.[5] When political differences over the Affordable Care Act, a new social program supported by President Obama to reform the American health care system, led to a government shutdown in 2013 and yet another dramatic showdown over raising the national debt limit, public trust once again dipped to historically low levels.

Does it matter if Americans trust their government? For the most part, the answer is yes. As we have seen, most Americans rely on government for a wide range of services and laws that they simply take for granted. But long-term distrust in government can result in public refusal to pay taxes adequate to support such widely approved public activities. Low levels of confidence may also make it difficult for government to attract talented and effective workers to public service.[6] The weakening of government as a result of prolonged levels of distrust may ultimately harm the United States' capacity to defend its national interest in the world economy and may jeopardize its national security. Likewise, a weak government can do little to assist citizens who need help in weathering periods of sharp economic or technological change.

Political Efficacy

Another important trend in American views about government has been a declining sense of **political efficacy**, the belief that ordinary citizens can affect what government does, that they can make government listen to them. In 2014, 78 percent of Americans said that elected officials don't care what people like them think; in 1960, only 25 percent felt so shut out of government.[7] Accompanying this sense that ordinary people can't be heard is a growing belief that government is not run for the benefit of all the people. In 2012, 57 percent of the public disagreed with the idea that the "government is really run for the benefit of all the people."[8] These views are widely shared across the age spectrum.

This widely felt loss of political efficacy is bad news for American democracy. The feeling that you can't affect government decisions can lead to a self-perpetuating cycle of apathy, declining political participation, and withdrawal from political life. Why bother to participate if you believe it makes no difference? Yet the belief that you can be effective is the first step needed to influence government. Not every effort of ordinary citizens to influence government will succeed, but without any such efforts, government decisions will be made by a smaller and smaller circle of powerful people. Such loss of broad popular influence over government actions undermines the key feature of American democracy—government by the people.

● Citizenship: Knowledge and Participation

Describe the role of the citizen in politics

The first prerequisite for achieving an increased sense of political efficacy is knowledge. Political indifference is often simply a habit that stems from a lack of knowledge about how your interests are affected by politics and from a sense that you can do nothing to affect politics. But political efficacy is a self-fulfilling prophecy: if you think you cannot be effective, chances are you will never try. Most research suggests that people active in politics have a high sense of their own efficacy. This means they believe they can make a difference—even if they do not win all the time. Most people do not want to be politically active every day of their lives, but it is essential to American political ideals that all citizens be informed and able to act.

Even though the Internet has made it easier than ever to learn about politics, the state of political knowledge in the United States today is spotty. Most Americans know little about current issues or debates. Numerous surveys indicate that the majority of Americans have significant gaps in their political knowledge. For example, in 2013 only 28 percent of those surveyed could identify Justice Anthony Kennedy as the Supreme Court's swing vote and only 47 percent knew the share of congressional seats held by women. On the other hand, the public is more knowledgeable about politicians and individuals who have been prominent in the national media. For example, when shown pictures of public figures, 52 percent could identify Florida senator Marco Rubio and 77 percent could identify Edward Snowden, the National Security Agency contractor accused of leaking classified information (see Table 1.2). But rather than dwell on the widespread political ignorance of many Americans, we prefer to view this as an opportunity for the readers of this book. Those of you who make the effort to become more knowledgeable will be much better prepared to influence the political system regarding the issues and concerns that you care most about.

After September 11, many commentators noted a revival in Americans' sense of citizenship, as manifested by ubiquitous flag displays and other demonstrations of patriotic sentiment. There seems to be little doubt that millions of Americans experienced a renewed sense of identification with their nation. Citizenship, however, has a broader meaning than just patriotism.

Political Knowledge and Trust in Government

In every country, citizens rely on government to provide certain services. But the relationship between a government and its people can vary, as does the level of trust a people have in their government. Trust in government may encourage citizens to pay taxes, engage in civic behavior, or join the government workforce. Lack of trust can make it hard for government officials to achieve public goals by reducing support for spending on public programs. Lack of trust may also cause citizens to be cynical about government and lead them to disengage from public life. In this sense, lack of trust can undermine democracy.

At the extreme, lack of trust can lead to social unrest and even revolution.

How much do levels of trust in government vary across countries? Which group is more likely to trust in government, the general population or the informed public? Many of the democracies in the table below, including the United States, have lower levels of trust in government than China, a nondemocratic country. Why would Americans be less trusting of their government than citizens of China, whose government is much less open to public scrutiny?

Country	Percentage Who Trusts Government among General Public	Percentage Who Trusts Government among Informed Public	Difference	Type of Government
China	70	80	−10	Communist state
India	64	71	−7	Parliamentary federal republic
Brazil	51	55	−4	Presidental federal republic
United States	45	59	−14	Presidental federal republic
Germany	44	55	−11	Parliamentary federal republic
Turkey	43	42	1	Republican parliamentary democracy
United Kingdom	43	53	−10	Constitutional monarchy
Poland	34	48	−14	Parliamentary republic
Russia	30	36	−6	Nondemocratic federation

NOTE: The data for the general population are based on 1,000 responses (adults age 18 years and older) per country surveyed. The data for informed publics are based on 500 responses each in China and the United States and 200 responses each in other countries; respondents are adults ages 25–64 who are college educated and in the top 25 percent of household income for their age bracket in their country, and who report significant engagement in business and policy news.

SOURCE: Edelman Trust Barometer Survey, 2013, http://edelmaneditions.com/wp-content/uploads/2013/01/EMBARGOED-2013-Edelman-Trust-Barometer -Global-Deck_FINAL.pdf (accessed 1/14/14).

TABLE 1.2

What Americans Know about Government

RESPONDENTS WHO	PERCENTAGE
Knew that only citizens can vote in federal elections	49
Knew how much of a majority is required for the U.S. Senate and House to override a presidential veto	39
Knew that Chief Justice John Roberts Jr. is generally considered a conservative	47
Believed that the government spends more on Social Security than on foreign aid	29
Could identify Florida senator Marco Rubio (from a photo)	52
Could identify Justice Anthony Kennedy as the Supreme Court's swing vote (from a photo)	47
Could identify National Security Agency leaker Edward Snowden (from a photo)	77

SOURCES: Center for Information and Research on Civic Learning and Engagement, www.civicyouth.org/wp-content /uploads/2013/01/What-Young-Adults-Know-Fact-Sheet-20131.pdf (accessed 10/14/13); Pew Research Center for the People and the Press, www.people-press.org/files/legacy-pdf/11-7-11%20Knowledge%20Release.pdf (accessed 6/8/12); and Pew Research Center for the People and the Press, www.people-press.org/2013/09/05/what-the-public -knows-in-words-pictures-maps-and-graphs/ (accessed 10/14/13).

Beginning with the ancient Greeks, citizenship has meant membership in one's community. Citizenship entailed involvement in public discussion, debate, and activity designed to improve the welfare of the community. Our meaning for **citizenship** derives from the Greek ideal: enlightened political engagement.[9] To be politically engaged in a meaningful way, citizens require resources, especially political knowledge and information. Democracy functions best when citizens are informed. But citizenship in the full sense, as understood first by the ancient Greeks, goes beyond an occasional visit to a voting booth. A good citizen must be politically engaged and have the knowledge needed to participate in political debate.

citizenship informed and active membership in a political community

The Necessity of Political Knowledge

Political knowledge means more than having a few opinions to offer a pollster or to guide your decisions in a voting booth. It is important to know the rules and strategies that govern political institutions and the principles on which they are based, but it is more important to know them in ways that relate to your own interests. Citizens need knowledge in order to assess their interests and to know when to act on them. Knowledgeable citizens are more attentive to and engaged in politics because they understand how and why politics is relevant to their lives.

Without political knowledge, no citizen can be aware of her interests or her stake in a political dispute. In 2013 the federal government experienced a partial shutdown when the House of Representatives vowed not to approve a bill funding the government for the next fiscal year unless the Affordable Care Act was delayed or

for critical analysis

Many studies seem to show that most Americans know very little about government and politics. Can we have democratic government without knowledgeable and aware citizens?

defunded. Informally known as Obamacare, the Affordable Care Act was a major legislative achievement that the administration was very unlikely to delay or defund. How many voters paid enough attention to the discussion to be able to distinguish the initial reasons for the shutdown? How many had enough of an understanding of the complex health care act to determine whether it was in their interest or not? Various public and private interest groups devote enormous time and energy to understanding alternative policy proposals and their implications so they will know which policies to support and which to oppose. Interest groups understand something that every citizen should also understand: effective participation requires knowledge.

Citizens need political knowledge also to identify the best ways to act on their interests. If your street is rendered impassable by snow, what can you do? Is snow removal the responsibility of the federal government? Is it a state or municipal responsibility? Knowing that you have a stake in a clear road does not help much if you do not know that snow removal is a city or a county responsibility and if you cannot identify the municipal agency that deals with the problem. Americans are fond of complaining that government is not responsive to their needs, but in some cases, it is possible that citizens simply lack the information they need to present their problems to the appropriate government officials.

Citizens need political knowledge also to ascertain what they cannot or should not ask of politicians and the government. We need to balance our need for protection and service with our equally pressing need for liberty. Particularly during periods when the nation's safety is threatened, Americans may be inclined to accept increased governmental intrusion into their lives in the name of national security. Since 2001, for example, Americans have accepted unprecedented levels of governmental surveillance and the erosion of some traditional restrictions on police powers in the name of preventing terrorism. It remains to be seen whether this exchange of liberty for the promise of security was a wise choice. Political knowledge, therefore, includes knowing the limits on (as well as the possibilities for) pursuing one's own individual interests through political action. This is, perhaps, the most difficult form of political knowledge to acquire.

When the federal government partially shut down in October 2013, millions of citizens were affected, including visitors who were turned away from the Statue of Liberty. Citizens need political knowledge to understand how such events affect their lives and what policies promote their interests.

Digital Citizenship

As more and more of our social, workplace, and educational activities have migrated online, so too have opportunities for political knowledge and participation, creating a new concept of "digital citizenship." Digital citizenship is the ability to participate in society online, and it is increasingly important in politics. A 2012 Pew survey found that 75 percent of Americans read the news online and more than 6 in 10 look up political information online. People also seek out government information online; 67 percent visit a local, state, or federal government website.[10] Digital citizenship benefits individuals, but it also provides advantages to society as a whole. Digital citizens are more likely to be interested in politics and to discuss politics with friends, family, and coworkers than individuals who do not use online political information. They are also more likely to vote and participate in other ways in elections.

By contrast, individuals without Internet access or the skills to participate in politics and the economy online are being left further behind. Exclusion from participation online is referred to as the digital divide (which we discuss further in Chapters 5 and 8). Lower-income and less-educated Americans, racial and ethnic minorities, and the elderly are all less likely to have Internet access. For some, location is the barrier: the limits of network infrastructure mean that many rural residents have a difficult time getting Internet access. But for many, cost is the barrier to access. Internet access and digital literacy are critical for full participation in American politics in the twenty-first century. In much the same way that higher levels of education and literacy promoted democracy and economic growth in the nineteenth century, the Internet has the potential to benefit society as a whole and to facilitate political participation of individuals within society. At the same time, the rise of the Internet raises new questions about who is able to participate and whether digital politics is changing the traditional dynamics of American politics.

for critical analysis

Just as all Americans have the right to a public education and to be taught to read and write, should all Americans have access to the Internet and be taught skills to access and use information online?

● Government

Define government and forms of government

As we saw in the introduction to this chapter, government refers to the formal institutions through which a land and its people are ruled. To govern is to rule. A government may be as simple as a tribal council that meets occasionally to advise the chief, or as complex as the vast establishments, with their procedures, laws, and bureaucracies, found in many large countries today. In the history of civilization, governments have not been difficult to establish. There have been thousands of them. The hard part is establishing a government that lasts. Even more difficult is developing a stable government that is compatible with liberty, equality, and democracy.

Is Government Needed?

Americans have always harbored some suspicion of government and have wondered how extensive a role it should play in their lives. Thomas Jefferson famously observed that the best government was one that "governed least." Generally speaking, a government is needed to provide those services, sometimes called "public goods," that all citizens need but are not likely to be able to provide adequately for themselves. These might include defense against foreign aggression, maintenance of public order, a stable currency, enforcement of contractual obligations and property rights, and a guarantee of some measure of social justice. These are goods that benefit everyone but that no individual or group on its own can afford to supply. Government, with its powers to tax and regulate, is typically viewed as the best way to provide public goods. However, there is often disagreement about which public goods are essential and how they should be provided. The precise extent to which government involvement in American society is needed has been debated throughout the nation's history and will continue to be a central focus of political contention.

autocracy a form of government in which a single individual—a king, queen, or dictator—rules

oligarchy a form of government in which a small group—landowners, military officers, or wealthy merchants—controls most of the governing decisions

democracy a system of rule that permits citizens to play a significant part in the governmental process, usually through the election of key public officials

constitutional government a system of rule in which formal and effective limits are placed on the powers of the government

authoritarian government a system of rule in which the government recognizes no formal limits but may nevertheless be restrained by the power of other social institutions

totalitarian government a system of rule in which the government recognizes no formal limits on its power and seeks to absorb or eliminate other social institutions that might challenge it

Forms of Government

Governments vary in their structure, their size, and the way they operate. Two questions are of special importance in determining how governments differ: Who governs? And how much government control is permitted?

Some nations are governed by a single individual—a king or dictator, for example. This state of affairs is called **autocracy**. Where a small group—perhaps landowners, military officers, or wealthy merchants—controls most of the governing decisions, that government is said to be an **oligarchy**. If more people participate and have some influence over decision making, that government is a **democracy**.

Governments also vary considerably in terms of how they govern. In the United States and a small number of other nations, governments are limited as to what they are permitted to control (substantive limits) and how they go about it (procedural limits). Governments that are limited in this way are called **constitutional governments**, or liberal governments. In other nations, including many in Latin America, Asia, and Africa, though the law imposes few real limits, the government is nevertheless kept in check by other political and social institutions that it is unable to control and must come to terms with—such as autonomous territories, an organized religion, organized business groups, or organized labor unions. Such governments are generally called **authoritarian**. In a third group of nations, including the Soviet Union under Joseph Stalin, Nazi Germany, perhaps prewar Japan and Italy, and North Korea today, governments not only are free of legal limits but also seek to eliminate those organized social groups that might challenge or limit their authority. These governments typically attempt to dominate or control every sphere of political, economic, and social life and, as a result, are called **totalitarian** (see Figure 1.2).

Americans have the good fortune to live in a nation in which limits are placed on what governments can do and how they can do it. Many of the world's people do not live in a constitutional democracy. By one measure, just 43 percent of the

Who governs	Type of government
One person	Autocracy
Small group (e.g., landowners, military officers, or wealthy merchants)	Oligarchy
Many people	Democracy

Limits on government	Type of government
Codified, legal substantive and procedural limits on what government can or cannot do	Constitutional
Few legal limits; some limits imposed by social groups	Authoritarian
No limits	Totalitarian

FIGURE 1.2
Forms of Government

global population (those living in 90 countries) enjoy sufficient levels of political and personal freedom to be classified as living in a constitutional democracy.[11] And constitutional democracies were unheard of before the modern era. Prior to the eighteenth and nineteenth centuries, governments seldom sought—and rarely received—the support of their subjects. The available evidence strongly suggests that ordinary people often had little love for the government or for the social order. After all, they had no stake in it. They equated government with the police officer, the bailiff, and the tax collector.[12]

Beginning in the seventeenth century, in a handful of Western nations, two important changes began to take place in the character and conduct of government. First, governments began to acknowledge formal limits on their power. Second, a small number of governments began to provide ordinary citizens with a formal voice in public affairs—through the vote. Obviously, the desirability of limits on government and the expansion of popular influence were at the heart of the American Revolution in 1776. "No taxation without representation," as we shall see in Chapter 2, was fiercely asserted from the beginning of the Revolution through the Founding in 1789. But even before the Revolution, a tradition of limiting government and expanding participation in the political process had developed throughout western Europe.

America's Founders were influenced by the English thinker John Locke (1632–1704). Locke argued that governments need the consent of the people.

Limiting Government

The key force behind the imposition of limits on government power was a new social class, the bourgeoisie, which became an important political force in the sixteenth and seventeenth centuries. *Bourgeois* is a French word for "freeman of the city," or *bourg*. Being part of the bourgeoisie later became associated with being "middle class" and with involvement in commerce or industry. In order to gain a share of control of government, joining or even displacing the kings, aristocrats, and gentry who had dominated government for centuries, the bourgeoisie sought to change existing institutions—especially parliament—into instruments of real political participation. Parliaments had existed for centuries, but were generally aristocratic institutions. The bourgeoisie embraced parliaments as means by which they could exert the weight of their superior numbers and growing economic advantage on their aristocratic rivals. At the same time, the bourgeoisie sought to place restraints on the capacity of governments to threaten these economic and political interests by placing formal or constitutional limits on governmental power.

Although motivated primarily by the need to protect and defend their own interests, the bourgeoisie advanced many of the principles that would define the central underpinnings of individual liberty for all citizens—freedom of speech, freedom of assembly, freedom of conscience, and freedom from arbitrary search and seizure. The work of political theorists such as John Locke (1632–1704) and, later, John Stuart Mill (1806–73) helped shape these evolving ideas about liberty and political rights. However, it is important to note that the bourgeoisie generally did not favor democracy as we know it. They were advocates of electoral and representative institutions, but they favored property requirements and other restrictions so as to limit participation to the middle and upper classes. Yet once these institutions of politics and the protection of the right to engage in politics were established, it was difficult to limit them to the bourgeoisie.

John Stuart Mill (1806–73) presented a ringing defense of individual freedom in his famous treatise On Liberty. *Mill's work influenced Americans' evolving ideas about the relationship between government and the individual.*

Access to Government: The Expansion of Participation

The expansion of participation from the bourgeoisie to ever-larger segments of society took two paths. In some nations, popular participation was expanded by the Crown or the aristocracy, which ironically saw common people as potential political allies against the bourgeoisie. Thus in nineteenth-century Prussia, for example, it was the emperor and his great minister Otto von Bismarck who expanded popular participation in order to build political support among the lower orders.

In other nations, participation expanded because competing segments of the bourgeoisie sought to gain political advantage by reaching out and mobilizing the support of working- and lower-class groups that craved the opportunity to take part in politics—"lining up the unwashed," as one American historian put it.[13] To be sure, excluded groups often agitated for greater participation. But seldom was such agitation by itself enough to secure the right to participate. Usually, expansion of voting rights resulted from a combination of pressure from below and help from above.

The gradual expansion of voting rights by groups hoping to derive some political advantage has been typical of American history. After the Civil War, one of the chief reasons that Republicans moved to enfranchise newly freed slaves was to use the support of the former slaves to maintain Republican control over the defeated southern states. Similarly, in the early twentieth century, upper-middle-class Progressives advocated women's suffrage because they believed that women were likely to support the reforms espoused by the Progressive movement.

Influencing the Government through Participation: Politics

Expansion of participation means that more and more people have a legal right to take part in politics. *Politics* is an important term. In its broadest sense, it refers to conflicts over the character, membership, and policies of any organization to which people belong. As Harold Lasswell, a famous political scientist, once put it, politics is the struggle over "who gets what, when, how."[14] Although politics is a phenomenon that can be found in any organization, our concern in this book is narrower. Here, *politics* will be used to refer only to conflicts and struggles over the leadership, structure, and policies of governments. The goal of politics, as we define it, is to have a share or a say in the composition of the government's leadership, how the government is organized, or what its policies are going to be. Having a share is called having **power** or influence.

Politics can take many forms, including everything from blogging and posting opinion pieces online, sending emails to government officials, voting, lobbying legislators on behalf of particular programs, and participating in protest marches and even violent demonstrations. A system of government that gives citizens a regular opportunity to elect the top government officials is usually called a **representative democracy**, or **republic**. A system that permits citizens to vote directly on laws and policies is often called a **direct democracy**. At the national level, America is a representative democracy in which citizens select government officials but do not vote on legislation. Some states and cities, however, have provisions for direct legislation through popular initiative and ballot referendum. These procedures allow citizens to collect petitions requiring an issue to be brought directly to the voters for a decision. In 2014 more than 158 initiatives appeared on state ballots, dealing with matters that ranged from taxes and raising the minimum wage to legalizing marijuana. Many hot-button issues are decided by initiatives. For example, in 2006, Michigan voters approved a measure that prohibits public institutions such as the University of Michigan from giving preferential treatment on the basis of race; in Colorado in 2010,

power influence over a government's leadership, organization, or policies

representative democracy (republic) a system of government in which the populace selects representatives, who play a significant role in governmental decision making

direct democracy a system of rule that permits citizens to vote directly on laws and policies

voters passed a referendum that called on the state to sue the federal government to enforce immigration laws. Often, broad public campaigns promote controversial referenda, attempting to persuade voters to change existing laws. For example, in 2014, four states—Alaska, Arkansas, Nebraska, and South Dakota—voted to raise the state minimum wage. Marijuana legalization was also on several state ballots. In Oregon, Alaska, and the District of Columbia voters approved measures legalizing recreational marijuana use, whereas voters in Florida turned down a measure to legalize medical marijuana. In a bid to reduce the prison population, voters in California approved a measure to make some crimes—including shoplifting, forgery, and writing bad checks, when the amounts at stake are less than $950—misdemeanors rather than felonies.

Groups and organized interests do not vote (although their members do), but they certainly do participate in politics. Their political activities usually consist of such endeavors as providing funds for candidates, lobbying, and trying to influence public opinion. The pattern of struggles among interests is called group politics, or **pluralism**. Americans have always been ambivalent about pluralist politics. On the one hand, the right of groups to press their views and compete for influence in the government is the essence of liberty. On the other hand, Americans often fear that organized groups may sometimes exert too much influence, advancing special interests at the expense of larger public interests. (We return to this problem in Chapter 11.)

pluralism the theory that all interests are and should be free to compete for influence in the government; the outcome of this competition is compromise and moderation

Sometimes, of course, politics does not take place through formal channels at all but instead involves direct action. Direct action politics can include either violent politics or civil disobedience, both of which attempt to shock rulers into behaving more responsibly. Direct action can also be a form of revolutionary politics, which rejects the system entirely and attempts to replace it with a new ruling group and a new set of rules. In recent years in the United States, groups ranging from animal-rights activists to right-to-life advocates to the Occupy Wall Street protesters have used direct action to underline their demands. Many forms of peaceful direct political action are protected by the U.S. Constitution. The country's Founders knew that the right to protest is essential to the maintenance of political freedom, even where the ballot box is available.

● Who Are Americans?

Show how the social composition of the American population has changed over time

While American democracy aims to give the people a voice in government, the meaning of "we the people" has changed over time. Who are Americans? Through the course of American history, politicians, religious leaders, prominent scholars, and ordinary Americans have puzzled over and fought about the answer to this fundamental question. Since the Founding, the American population has grown from 3.9 million in 1790, the year of the first official census, to 318 million in 2014. As the American population has grown, it has become more diverse on nearly every dimension imaginable.[15] (See the "Who Are Americans?" feature on page 19.)

At the time of the Founding, when the United States consisted of 13 states arrayed along the Eastern Seaboard, 81 percent of Americans counted by the census traced their roots to Europe, mostly England and northern Europe; nearly 20 percent were of African origin, the vast majority of whom were slaves.[16] Only 1.5 percent of the black population was free. There was also an unknown number of Native Americans, the original inhabitants of the land, not counted by the census because the government did not consider them Americans. The first estimates of

Native American societies, with their own forms of government, existed for thousands of years before the first European settlers arrived. By the time this photo of Red Cloud and other Sioux warriors was taken, around 1870, Native Americans made up about 1 percent of the American population.

Native Americans and Hispanics in the mid-1800s showed that each group made up less than 1 percent of the total population.[17]

Fast-forward to 1900. The country now stretched across the continent, and waves of immigrants, mainly from Europe, boosted the population to 76 million. In 1900 the United States was predominantly composed of whites of European ancestry, but this number now included many from southern and eastern as well as northern Europe; the black population stood at 12 percent. Residents who traced their origin to Latin America or Asia each accounted for less than 1 percent of the entire population.[18] The large number of new immigrants was reflected in the high proportion of foreign-born people in the United States: the foreign-born population reached its height at 14.7 percent in 1910.[19]

Immigration and Ethnic Diversity

As the European-origin population grew more diverse, anxiety about Americans' ethnic identity mounted. In 1900 the author of a *New York Times* front-page article answered his own question—"Are the Americans an Anglo-Saxon People?"—in the affirmative.[20] But the growing numbers of immigrants from southern and eastern Europe who were crowding into American cities spurred heated debates about how long Anglo-Saxons could dominate. Much as today, politicians and scholars argued about whether the country could absorb such large numbers of immigrants. Concerns ranged from whether their political and social values were compatible with American democracy to whether they would learn English to alarm about the diseases they might bring into the United States.

The distinct ethnic backgrounds and language differences of the new immigrants were not the only characteristics that worried the Anglo-Saxon natives; immigrant religious affiliations also aroused concern. The first immigrants to the United States were overwhelmingly Protestant, many of them fleeing religious persecution. The arrival of Germans and Irish in the mid-1800s began to shift that balance with increasing numbers of Catholics. Even so, in 1900, four in five Americans were still Protestants. The large-scale immigration of the early twentieth century threatened to reduce the proportion of Protestants significantly. The eastern European immigrants pouring into the country, especially those from Russia, were heavily Jewish;

An Increasingly Diverse Nation

Since the Founding, the American people have become increasingly diverse. This diversity and the changes in the population have frequently raised challenging questions in American politics.

Race

	1790*	1900*	2010

👤 = 1 million people

1790*
White 81%
Black 19%

1900*
White 88%
Black 12%
Other 1%

2010
White 64%
Black 12%
Hispanic 16%
Asian 5%
Native American 1%
Other 0.2%
2 or more races 2%

TOTAL POPULATION =   3,929,214   75,994,575   308,745,538

Geography

	1790	1900	2010

1790
Northeast 50%   South 50%

50%
50%

1900
Northeast 28%   Midwest 35%
South 32%   West 5%

28%
35%
5%
32%

2010
Northeast 18%   Midwest 22%
South 37%   West 23%

18%
22%
23%
37%

Age

	1900	2010

1900
0–19   44%
20–44   38%
45–64   14%
65 +   4%

2010
0–19   27%
20–44   34%
45–64   23%
65 +   13%

for critical analysis

1. The 2010 census showed that the populations of the South and the West continued to grow more rapidly than the Northeast and Midwest. What are some of the political implications of this trend?

2. Today, Americans over age 37 outnumber Americans under 37—and older adults are more likely to participate in the political process. What do you think this means for the kinds of issues and policies taken up by the government?

* The 1790 census does not accurately reflect the population because it only counted blacks and whites. It did not include Native Americans or other groups. The 1900 census did not count Hispanic Americans.

SOURCE: U.S. Census Bureau, www.census.gov (accessed 8/16/12).

In the 1900s, many immigrants entered the United States through New York's Ellis Island, where they were checked for disease before being admitted. Today, individuals hoping to immigrate to the United States often apply for a visa at the U.S. consulate in their home country before traveling to the United States, where the U.S. Customs and Border Protection checks their identity and legal status.

the southern Europeans, especially Italians, were Catholic. A more religiously diverse country challenged the implicit Protestantism embedded in many aspects of American public life. For example, religious diversity introduced new conflicts into public schooling, as Catholics sought public funding for parochial schools and dissident Protestant sects lobbied to eliminate Bible reading and prayer in the schools.

Anxieties about immigration sparked intense debate. Should the numbers of immigrants entering the country be limited? Should restrictions be placed on the types of immigrants to be granted entry? After World War I, Congress responded to the fears swirling around immigration with new laws that sharply limited the number who could enter the country each year. It also established a new National Origins quota system, based on the nation's population in 1890, before the wave of immigrants from eastern and southern Europe arrived.[21] Supporters of ethnic quotas hoped to turn back the clock and revert to an earlier America in which northern Europeans dominated. The new system set up a hierarchy of admissions: northern European countries received generous quotas for new immigrants, whereas eastern and southern European countries were granted very small quotas. These restrictions ratcheted down the numbers of immigrants so that by 1970, the foreign-born population in the United States reached an all-time low of 5 percent.

Immigration and Race

Official efforts to use racial and ethnic criteria to restrict the American population were not new but had been used to draw boundaries around the American community from the start. The very first census, as just mentioned, did not count Native Americans; in fact, no Native Americans became citizens until 1924. Although the Constitution infamously declared that each slave would count as three-fifths of a person for purposes of apportioning representation among the states, most people of African descent were not officially citizens until 1868, when the Fourteenth Amendment to the Constitution conferred citizenship on the freed slaves.

Over half a century earlier, the federal government had sought to limit the nonwhite population with a 1790 law stipulating that only free whites could become naturalized citizens. Not until 1870 did Congress lift the ban on the naturalization of nonwhites. In addition to the restrictions on blacks and Native Americans, restrictions applied to Asians as well. The Chinese Exclusion Act of 1882 outlawed the entry of Chinese laborers to the United States. These provisions were not lifted until 1943, when China became America's ally during World War II. Additional barriers enacted after World War I meant that virtually no

Asians entered the country as immigrants until the 1940s. People of Hispanic origin do not fit simply into the American system of racial classification. In 1930, for example, the census counted people of Mexican origin as nonwhite but reversed this decision a decade later—after protests by the Mexican-origin population and the Mexican government. Only in 1970 did the census officially begin counting persons of Hispanic origin, noting that they could be any race.[22]

Twenty-First-Century Americans

Race and Ethnicity By 2000, immigration had profoundly transformed the nation's racial and ethnic profile once again. The primary cause was Congress's decision in 1965 to lift the tight restrictions of the 1920s, allowing for much-expanded immigration from Asia and Latin America (see Figure 1.3). One consequence of the shift has been the growth in the Hispanic, or Latino, population. Census figures for 2012 show that the total Hispanic proportion of the population is now 17 percent; the

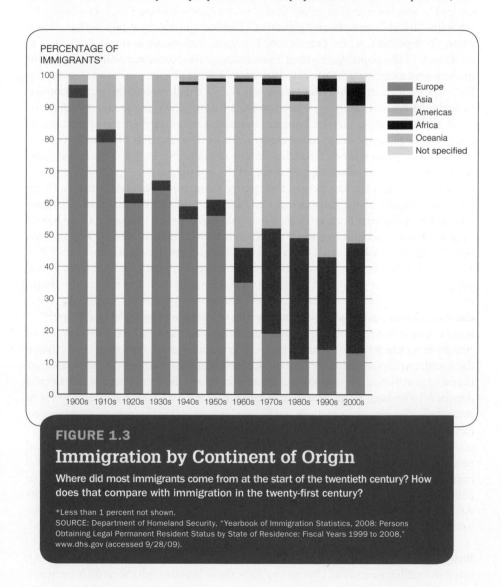

FIGURE 1.3

Immigration by Continent of Origin

Where did most immigrants come from at the start of the twentieth century? How does that compare with immigration in the twenty-first century?

*Less than 1 percent not shown.
SOURCE: Department of Homeland Security, "Yearbook of Immigration Statistics, 2008: Persons Obtaining Legal Permanent Resident Status by State of Residence: Fiscal Years 1999 to 2008," www.dhs.gov (accessed 9/28/09).

In 1965, Congress loosened restrictions on immigration, allowing millions of people from Latin America and Asia to enter the country in the decades that followed. By 2002, Hispanics were the largest minority group in the United States. Here, Antonio Villaraigosa campaigns to become the first Latino mayor of Los Angeles in 130 years. He won the election and served as mayor for eight years.

black, or African American, population is 13 percent of the total population. Asians make up 5 percent of the population. European Americans account for less than two-thirds of the population—their lowest share ever. Moreover, nearly 2.5 percent of the population now identifies itself as of "two or more races," a new category that the census added in 2000.[23] Although it is only a small percentage of the population, the multiracial category points toward a future in which the traditional labels of racial identification may be blurring, marking a major shift in the long-standing American tradition of strict racial categorization. The blurring of racial categories poses challenges to a host of policies—many of them put in place to remedy past discrimination—that rely on racial counts of the population.

Large-scale immigration means that many more residents are foreign born. In 2012, 13 percent of the population was born outside the United States, a figure comparable to foreign-born rates at the turn of the previous century.[24] Over half of the foreign born came from Latin America and the Caribbean—almost 1 in 10 from the Caribbean, nearly 4 in 10 from Central America (including Mexico), and 1 in 15 from South America.[25] Those born in Asia constituted the next-largest group, making up over one-quarter of foreign-born residents. In sharp contrast to the immigration patterns of a century earlier, fewer immigrants came from Europe. By 2012, less than 12 percent of those born outside the United States came from Europe.[26]

These figures represent only legally authorized immigrants. One new feature of American society in recent years is the very large number of immigrants who live in the country without legal authorization. Estimates put the number of undocumented immigrants at almost 12 million, the majority of whom are from Mexico and Central America.[27] The large unauthorized population became a flashpoint for controversy as states and cities passed a variety of conflicting laws regarding illegal immigrants' access to public services. Some states have offered driver's licenses to undocumented immigrants, while others have sought to bar them from public services, such as education and emergency health care, both of which are constitutionally guaranteed to unauthorized immigrants.[28] In 1982 the Supreme Court ensured access to education when it ruled in *Plyler v. Doe* that Texas could not deny funding for undocumented students.[29] In 1986, Congress guaranteed emergency medical care to all people regardless of immigration status when it passed the Emergency Medical Treatment and Active Labor Act (EMTALA).

Religion The new patterns of immigration combined with differences in birth rates and underlying social changes to alter the religious affiliations of Americans.

In 1900, 80 percent of the American adult population was Protestant; by 2012 only 48 percent of Americans identified themselves as Protestants.[30] Catholics made up 22 percent of the population, and Jews accounted for 1.8 percent. A small Muslim population had also grown, with over 0.8 percent of the population. One of the most important shifts in religious affiliation during the latter half of the twentieth century was the percentage of people who professed no organized religion: in 2012, 20 percent of the population was not affiliated with an organized church. These changes suggest an important shift in American religious identity; although the United States thinks of itself as a "Judeo-Christian" nation—and indeed was 95 percent Protestant, Catholic, or Jewish from 1900 to 1968—by 2012, this number had fallen to 75 percent of the adult population.[31]

Age As America grew and its population expanded and diversified, the country's age profile shifted with it. In 1900 only 4 percent of the population was over age 65. As life expectancy increased, the number of older Americans grew with it: by 2012, nearly 14 percent of the population was over 65. The percentage of children under the age of 18 also changed; in 1900 this group comprised 43 percent of the American population; by 2012, children 18 and under had fallen to just under a quarter of the population.[32] Another way to think about the age of Americans is that in 1800, the median age of the population was 16 years; by 1900 it was 22.9 years, and by 2012 it was 37.4 years. Even though the median age of Americans has increased, Americans tend to be younger than citizens of many industrialized countries, mainly because of the large immigrant population in the United States. In most European countries, the median age was above 41.2 in 2011.[33] But an aging population poses challenges to the United States as well. As the elderly population grows and the working-age population shrinks, questions arise about how we will fund programs for the elderly such as Social Security.

Geography Over the nation's history, Americans have changed in other ways, moving from mostly rural settings and small towns to large urban areas. The idealization of country life in American culture traces its roots to the long period in which the majority of Americans lived in rural areas. Before 1920, less than half the population lived in urban areas; today 80.7 percent of Americans do.[34] Critics charge that the American political system—created when America was a largely rural society—underrepresents urban areas. The constitutional provision allocating each state two senators, for example, overrepresents sparsely populated rural states and underrepresents urban states, where the population is far more concentrated. In addition to becoming more urban over time, the American population has shifted regionally. During the past 50 years especially, many Americans left the Northeast and Midwest and moved to the South and Southwest. As congressional seats have been reapportioned to reflect the population shift, many problems that particularly plague the Midwest and Northeast, such as the decline in manufacturing jobs, receive less attention in national politics.

Socioeconomic Status Americans have fallen into diverse economic groups throughout American history. For much of American history most people were relatively poor working people, many of them farmers. A small wealthy elite, however, grew larger in the 1890s, in a period called "the gilded age." The top 1 percent and the top 10 percent of earners accounted for a growing share of the national income. By 1928, nearly one-quarter of the total annual income went to the top 1 percent of earners; the top 10 percent took home 46 percent of total annual income. After the New Deal in the 1930s, a large middle class took shape and the share going to those at the top dropped sharply. By 1976, the top 1 percent took home only 9 percent of the national annual income. Since then, however, economic inequality has once again widened as a tiny group of super-rich has emerged. By 2012, the top 1 percent earned 20 percent of annual income and the top 10 percent took home more than half of the total national income, the highest ever recorded.[35] At the same time, the incomes of the broad middle class have largely stagnated.[36] And 15 percent of the population remains below the official poverty line. As the middle class has frayed around the edges, the numbers of poor and near poor have swelled to nearly a third of the population.[37] (See Figure 1.4.)

Population and Representation The shifting contours of the American people have regularly raised challenging questions about our politics and governing arrangements. Population growth has spurred politically charged debates about how the population should be apportioned among congressional districts. These conflicts have major implications for the representation of different regions of the country and for the balance of representation between urban and rural areas. Population growth has also transformed the close democratic relationship between congressional representatives and their constituents envisioned by the framers. For example, the framers stipulated that the number of representatives in the House of Representatives "shall not exceed one for every thirty Thousand" constituents; today the average member of Congress represents 721,641 constituents.[38] Immigration and the cultural and religious changes it entails provoked heated disputes 100 years ago and still spark passionate debate today. The different languages and customs that immigrants bring to the United States trigger fears that the country is changing in ways that may undermine American values and alter fundamental identities. The large number of unauthorized immigrants in the country today makes these anxieties even more acute. Yet a changing population has been one of the constants of American history. Indeed, each generation has confronted the myriad political challenges associated with answering the question anew, "Who are Americans?"

● American Political Culture

> **Analyze whether the U.S. system of government upholds American political values**

Underlying and framing political life in the United States are agreements on basic political values but disagreements over the ends or goals of government. Most Americans affirm the values of liberty, equality, and democracy. Values shape citizens' views of the world and define their sense of what is right and wrong, just and unjust, possible and impossible. If Americans shared no values, they would have difficulty communicating, much less agreeing on a common system of government and politics. However, sharing broad values does not guarantee political consensus. We can agree on principles but disagree over their application or how they are to be balanced. Much of the debate over the role of government has been over what government should do and how far it should go to reduce the inequalities within our society and political system while still preserving essential liberties.

Even though Americans have disagreed over the meaning of such political ideals as equality, they still agree on the importance of those ideals. The values, beliefs, and attitudes that form our **political culture** and hold together the United States and its people date back to the time of the founding of the Union.

political culture broadly shared values, beliefs, and attitudes about how the government should function. American political culture emphasizes the values of liberty, equality, and democracy

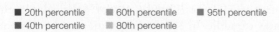

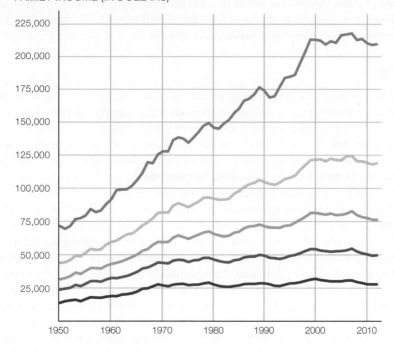

FAMILY INCOME (IN DOLLARS)*

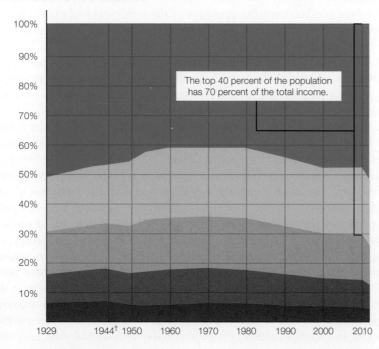

SHARE OF TOTAL INCOME

> The top 40 percent of the population has 70 percent of the total income.

FIGURE 1.4

Income in the United States

The top graph shows that while the income of most Americans has risen only slightly since 1950, the income of the richest Americans (the top 5 percent) has increased dramatically. The lower graph shows the portion of all income in the United States that goes to each group, with an increasing share going to the richest Americans in recent years. What are some of the ways that this shift might matter for American politics? Does the growing economic gap between the richest groups and most other Americans conflict with the political value of equality?

*Dollar values are given in constant 2012 dollars, which are adjusted for inflation so that we can compare a person's income in 1950 with a person's income today.
†Data for 1929–44 are not strictly comparable to later data because of differences in calculating procedures.
SOURCE: U.S. Census Bureau, Current Population Survey, www.census.gov/hhes /www/income/data/historical/inequality /index.html (accessed 1/14/14).

The essential documents of the American Founding—the Declaration of Independence and the Constitution—enunciated a set of political principles about the purposes of the new republic. In contrast with many other democracies, in the United States these political ideals did not just remain words on dusty documents. Americans actively embraced the principles of the Founders and made them central to the national identity. Let us look more closely at three of these ideals: liberty, equality, and democracy.

Liberty

No ideal is more central to American values than liberty. The Declaration of Independence defined three inalienable rights: "Life, Liberty and the pursuit of Happiness." The preamble to the Constitution likewise identified the need to secure "the Blessings of Liberty" as one of the key reasons for drawing up the Constitution. For Americans, **liberty** means both personal freedom and economic freedom. Both are closely linked to the idea of **limited government**.

The Constitution's first 10 amendments, known collectively as the Bill of Rights, above all preserve individual personal liberties and rights. In fact, the word *liberty* has come to mean many of the freedoms guaranteed in the Bill of Rights: freedom of speech and writing, the right to assemble freely, and the right to practice religious beliefs without interference from the government. Over the course of American history, the scope of personal liberties has expanded, as laws have become more tolerant and as individuals have successfully used the courts to challenge restrictions on their individual freedoms. Far fewer restrictions exist today on the press, political speech, and individual moral behavior than in the early years of the nation. Even so, conflicts persist over how personal liberties should be extended and when personal liberties violate community norms. For example, a number of cities have recently passed "sit-lie" ordinances, which limit the freedom of individuals to sit or lie down on sidewalks. Designed to limit the presence of the homeless and make city streets more attractive to pedestrians, the ordinances have also been denounced as infringements on individual liberties.

The central historical conflict regarding liberty in the United States was about the enslavement of blacks. The facts of slavery and the differential treatment of the races have cast a long shadow over all of American history. In fact, scholars today note that the American definition of freedom has been formed in relation to the concept of slavery. The right to control one's labor and the right to receive rewards for that labor have been central elements of our definition of freedom precisely because these freedoms were denied to slaves.[39]

In addition to personal freedom, the American concept of liberty means economic freedom. Since the Founding, economic freedom has been linked to capitalism, free markets, and the protection of private property. Free competition, unfettered movement of goods, and the right to enjoy the fruits of one's labor are all essential aspects of economic freedom and American capitalism.[40] In the first century of the republic, support for capitalism often meant support for the doctrine of laissez-faire (literally, "leave alone" in French). **Laissez-faire capitalism** allowed very little room for the national government to regulate trade or restrict the use of private property, even in the public interest. Americans still strongly support capitalism and economic liberty, but they now also endorse some restrictions on economic freedoms to protect the public. Today, federal and state governments

liberty freedom from governmental control

limited government a principle of constitutional government; a government whose powers are defined and limited by a constitution

laissez-faire capitalism an economic system in which the means of production and distribution are privately owned and operated for profit with minimal or no government interference

Patrick Henry's famous "Give me liberty or give me death" speech demanded freedom at any cost and has resonated with Americans throughout the nation's history.

deploy a wide array of regulations in the name of public protection. These include health and safety laws, environmental rules, and workplace regulations.

Not surprisingly, fierce disagreements often erupt over what the proper scope of government regulation should be. What some people regard as protecting the public, others see as an infringement on their own freedom to run their businesses and use their property as they see fit. For example, many business leaders opposed the Affordable Care Act, the health care reform legislation informally known as Obamacare, because it requires businesses with over 50 employees to provide health coverage for their employees and establishes standards about which health services should be covered by the insurance. In addition, the law requires that insurers pay for access to contraceptive care. From the perspective of the law's supporters, this provision simply ensures that women have access to basic health care. Many businesses, however, opposed the law as unwanted government intrusion. And some businesses strongly denounced the requirement to cover contraception, in particular, as a violation of their fundamental liberties to run their businesses as they see fit.

More recently, concerns about liberty have arisen in relation to the government's efforts to combat terrorism and protect the nation's security. These concerns escalated in 2013 when Edward Snowden, a former National Security Agency contractor, leaked top secret documents from the National Security Administration (NSA) to the press. The NSA is a national security agency charged with protecting the United States by monitoring electronic data flows—including radio, email, and cellular telephone calls—for foreign threats. The leaked documents revealed that the American government was listening in on the private communications of foreign governments, including many American allies, such as Germany and Brazil. The leaks also revealed information about domestic surveillance: the NSA had access to Americans' Facebook, Google, Apple, and Yahoo! accounts, among many other electronic data sources. It was using this "metadata" to track the connections among people, searching for suspicious ties. The revelation that the NSA had been collecting this information for three years without public knowledge set off a storm of controversy since the NSA is supposed to monitor foreign communications, not track Americans.

Concerns about terrorism leave us with an extraordinary dilemma. On the one hand, we treasure liberty, but on the other hand, we recognize that the lives of thousands of Americans have already been lost and countless others are threatened by terrorism. Can we reconcile liberty and security? Liberty and order? In previous national emergencies, Americans accepted restrictions on liberty with the understanding that these would be temporary. But because the threat of terrorism has no clear end point, doubts have grown about whether special government powers that infringe on liberties should be continued.

Equality

The Declaration of Independence declares as its first "self-evident" truth that "all men are created equal." As central as it is to the American political creed, however, equality has been an even less well-defined ideal than liberty, because people interpret "equality" in different ways. Few Americans have wholeheartedly embraced the ideal of full equality of results, but most Americans share the ideal of **equality of opportunity**—that is, the notion that each person should be given a fair chance to go as far as his or her talents will allow. Yet it is hard for Americans to reach agreement on what constitutes equality

equality of opportunity a widely shared American ideal that all people should have the freedom to use whatever talents and wealth they have to reach their fullest potential

Americans struggle to define how equality of opportunity can be provided at the same time as individual liberty. One area of debate is in education. Does the fact that New Jersey spends on average $15,968 per student each year, while North Carolina spends on average $8,312 per student, mean that there is not an equality of opportunity for school children?

political equality the right to participate in politics equally, based on the principle of "one person, one vote"

of opportunity. Must *past* inequalities be remedied in order to ensure equal opportunity in the *present*? Should inequalities in the legal, political, and economic spheres be given the same weight? In contrast to liberty, which requires limits on the role of government, equality implies an *obligation* of the government to the people.[41]

Americans do make clear distinctions between political equality and social or economic equality. **Political equality** means that members of the American political community have the right to participate in politics on equal terms. Beginning from a very restricted definition of political community, which originally included only propertied white men, the United States has moved much closer to an ideal of political equality that can be summed up as "one person, one vote." Broad support for the ideal of political equality has helped expand the American political community and extend to all the right to participate. Although considerable conflict remains over whether the political system makes participation in it harder for some people and easier for others, and whether the role of money in politics has drowned out the public voice, Americans agree that all citizens should have an equal right to participate and that government should enforce that right.

In part because Americans believe that individuals are free to work as hard as they choose, they have always been less concerned about social or economic inequality. Many Americans regard economic differences as the consequence of individual choices, virtues, or failures. Because of this, Americans tend to be less supportive than most Europeans of government action to ensure economic equality. Yet when major economic forces, such as the Great Depression of the 1930s, affect many people, or when systematic barriers appear to block equality of opportunity, Americans support government action to promote equality. Even then, however, they have endorsed only a limited government role designed to help people get back on their feet or to open up opportunity.

Because equality is such an elusive concept, many conflicts have arisen over what it should mean in practice. Americans have engaged in three kinds of controversies about the public role in addressing inequality. The first is determining what constitutes equality of access to public institutions. In 1896 the Supreme Court ruled in *Plessy v. Ferguson* that "separate but equal" accommodation for blacks and whites was constitutional.[42] In 1954, in a major legal victory for the civil rights movement, the Supreme Court's decision in *Brown v. Board of Education* overturned the "separate but equal" doctrine (see Chapter 5).[43] Today, new questions have been raised about what constitutes equal access to public institutions. Some argue that the unequal financing of public schools in cities, suburbs, and rural districts is a violation of the right to equal education. To date, these claims have not been supported by the federal courts, which have rejected the notion that the unequal economic impacts of public policy outcomes are a constitutional matter.[44] Lawsuits arguing a right to "economic equal protection" stalled in 1973 when the Supreme Court ruled that a Texas school-financing law did not violate the Constitution even though the law affected rich and poor students differently.[45]

A second debate concerns the public role in ensuring equality of opportunity in private life. Although Americans generally agree that discrimination should not be tolerated, people disagree over what should be done to ensure equality of opportunity (see Table 1.3). Controversies about affirmative action programs

TABLE 1.3

Equality and Public Opinion

Americans believe in some forms of equality more than others. How do these survey results reflect disagreement about what equality means in practice?

STATEMENT	PERCENTAGE WHO AGREE
Male and female citizens of the United States have equal rights.	97
Our society should do what is necessary to make sure that everyone has an equal opportunity to succeed.	86
Homosexuals should have equal rights in terms of job opportunities.	87
It should be legal for gay and lesbian couples to get married.	50
The fact that some are rich and some are poor is an acceptable part of the economic system.	52
We should make every possible effort to improve the position of blacks and other minorities even if it means preferential treatment (according to whites).	22
We should make every possible effort to improve the position of blacks and other minorities even if it means preferential treatment (according to blacks).	62

SOURCES: Pew Global Attitudes Project Poll, www.ropercenter.uconn.edu/data_access/ipoll/ipoll.html; Pew Research Center for the People and the Press and for the Public, "Trends in American Values, 1987–2012, Partisan Polarization Surges in Bush, Obama Years," June 4, 2012, p. 104; Princeton Survey Research Associates International/Newsweek Poll, www.ropercenter.uconn.edu/data_access/ipoll/ipoll.html; Polling Report.com, Gallup, pollingreport.com/civil.html; and Pew Research Center for the People and the Press and for the Public, www.peoplepress.org/2012/03/02/for-the-public-its-not-about-class-warfare-but-fairness (all accessed 6/9/12).

reflect these disputes. Supporters of affirmative action claim that such programs are necessary to compensate for past discrimination in order to establish true equality of opportunity today. Opponents maintain that affirmative action amounts to reverse discrimination and that a society that espouses true equality should not acknowledge gender or racial differences. The question of the public responsibility for private inequalities is central to gender issues. The traditional view, still held by many today, takes for granted that women should bear special responsibilities in the family. In this perspective, the challenges women face in the labor force due to family responsibilities fall outside the range of public concern. In the past 30 years especially, these traditional views have come under fire as advocates for women have argued that private inequalities *are* a topic of public concern.[46]

A third debate about equality concerns differences in income and wealth. Unlike in other countries, income inequality has not been an enduring topic of political controversy in the United States, which currently has the largest gap in income and wealth between rich and poor citizens of any developed nation. But Americans have generally tolerated great differences among rich and poor citizens, in part because of a pervasive belief that mobility is possible and that economic success is the product of individual effort.[47] This tolerance for inequality

for critical analysis

Economic inequality among Americans has been widening since at least the 1970s. Many politicians and news commentators say that inequality is threatening the middle class. Is there any evidence that the American public is worried about the growth in inequality?

Beginning in 2011, the Occupy movement drew attention to increasing inequality in the United States, arguing that the gap between the top 1 percent of earners and the other 99 percent was unfair.

is reflected in America's tax code, which is more advantageous to wealthy taxpayers than that of almost any other Western nation. Indeed, tax changes enacted in recent years have sharply reduced the tax burdens of upper-income Americans. Debate about taxes surfaced throughout the Obama presidency and during the 2012 election. President Obama defended the need to raise the tax rate of Americans earning more than $250,000 a year to support programs that benefit the middle class.[48] Even so, opposition among Republicans—and some Democrats—meant that tax rates increased a small amount only on those making more than $400,000 a year. The issue of inequality emerged in a new dramatic way in late 2011, when the Occupy Wall Street movement mounted protests across the country. Motivated by concerns about inequality, the movement did not develop a clear policy agenda, but concerns about inequality received new prominence. Polls showed that Americans believed that government should aim to reduce economic inequality. In 2014, 42 percent of Americans strongly agreed that the government should work to substantially reduce the gap between the rich and poor; only 20 percent strongly disagreed. More Americans expressed concern about the power of the rich, with 77 percent agreeing that there was too much power in the hands of a few rich people and large corporations.[49]

Democracy

The essence of democracy is the participation of the people in choosing their rulers and the people's ability to influence what those rulers do. In a democracy, political power ultimately comes from the people. The idea of placing power in the hands of the people is known as **popular sovereignty**. In the United States, popular sovereignty and political equality make politicians accountable to the people. Ideally, democracy envisions an engaged citizenry prepared to exercise its power over rulers. As we noted earlier, the United States is a representative democracy, meaning that the people do not rule directly but instead exercise power through elected representatives. Forms of participation in a democracy vary greatly, but voting is a key element of the representative democracy that the American Founders established.

American democracy rests on the principle of **majority rule** with **minority rights**. Majority rule means that the wishes of the majority determine what government does. The House of Representatives—a large body elected directly by the people—was designed in particular to ensure majority rule. But the Founders feared that popular majorities could turn government into a "tyranny of the majority" in which individual liberties would be violated. Concern for individual rights has thus been a part of American democracy from the beginning. The rights enumerated in the Bill of Rights and enforced through the courts provide an important check on the power of the majority.

Despite Americans' deep attachment to the *ideal* of democracy, many questions can be raised about our *practice* of democracy. The first is the restricted definition of the political community during much of American history. Property restrictions on the right to vote were eliminated by 1828; in 1870 the Fifteenth Amendment to the Constitution granted African Americans the vote, although later exclusionary

popular sovereignty a principle of democracy in which political authority rests ultimately in the hands of the people

majority rule, minority rights the democratic principle that a government follows the preferences of the majority of voters but protects the interests of the minority

for critical analysis

In the United States, do citizens make the decisions of government, or do they merely influence them?

practices denied them that right; in 1920 the Nineteenth Amendment guaranteed women the right to vote; and in 1965 the Voting Rights Act finally secured the right of African Americans to vote.

Just securing the right to vote does not end concerns about democracy, however. The organization of electoral institutions can have a significant impact on access to elections and on who can get elected. During the first two decades of the twentieth century, states and cities enacted many reforms, including strict registration requirements and scheduling of elections, that made it harder to vote. The aim was to rid politics of corruption, but the consequence was to reduce participation. Other institutional decisions affect which candidates stand the best chance of getting elected (see Chapter 10).

A further consideration about democracy concerns the relationship between economic power and political power. Money has always played an important role in elections and governing in the United States. Many argue that the pervasive influence of money in American electoral campaigns today undermines democracy. With the decline of locally based political parties that depend on party loyalists to turn out the vote, and the rise of political action committees, political consultants, and expensive media campaigns, money has become the central fact of life in American politics. Money often determines who runs for office; it can exert a heavy influence on who wins; and some argue that it affects what politicians do once they are in office.[50]

Low turnout for elections and a pervasive sense of apathy and cynicism characterized American politics for much of the past half-century. The widespread interest in the 2008 election and the near-record levels of voter turnout, which, at 61.7 percent, was the highest turnout since 1980, reversed this trend.[51] Nine million voters registered and voted for the first time in 2008, including near-record numbers of voters under the age of 24.[52] Volunteers found ways to become personally involved in politics. Although turnout in 2012 did not match 2008, these developments were a hopeful sign for those wishing to revitalize American democracy.

Although most barriers to voting have been removed for Americans ages 18 and up, many people do not vote. In the 2014 election approximately 36 percent of eligible citizens turned out at the polls.

American Political Culture
and Your Future

Americans express mixed views about government. Almost everyone complains about government at one time or another but in the past two decades, general trust in government has declined significantly. Despite mounting distrust, when asked about particular government activities or programs, a majority of Americans are more than likely to support the activities that government undertakes. These conflicting views reflect the tensions in American political culture: there is no perfect balance between liberty, equality, and democracy. In recent years, finding the right mix of government actions to achieve these different goals has become especially troublesome. Some charge that government initiatives designed to promote equality infringe on individual liberty, while others point to the need for government to take action in the face of growing inequality. Sharp political debate over competing goals alienates many citizens who react by withdrawing from politics. Yet, in contrast to totalitarian and authoritarian forms of government, democracy rests on the principle of popular sovereignty. No true democracy can function properly without knowledgeable and engaged citizens.

The remarkable diversity of the American people represents a great strength for American democracy as well as a formidable challenge. The shifting religious, racial and ethnic, and immigration status of Americans throughout history has always provoked fears about whether American values could withstand such dramatic shifts. The changing face of America also sparks hopes for an America that embodies its fundamental values more fully. Only after a bloody civil war was slavery abolished and African Americans guaranteed citizenship and voting rights. In the early 1900s, as European immigrants flocked to American cities, fears about the stability of American democracy mounted, leading to a cutoff of immigration. The portrait of Americans shifted again after 1965, when new laws permitted more immigrants from Latin America, Asia, and Africa to enter the country. Each wave of demographic change has presented new questions about the role of government in promoting a democracy that values both liberty and equality.

Demographic changes will continue to raise thorny new questions in the coming decades. For example, as the American population grows older, programs for the elderly are expected to take up an increasing share of the federal budget. Yet to be successful, a nation must invest in its young people. And, as any college student knows, the cost of college has risen in recent years. Many students drop out as they discover that the cost of college is too high. Or they graduate and find themselves saddled with loans that will take decades to pay back. Yet, in a world of ever-sharper economic competition, higher education has become increasingly important for individuals seeking economic security. Moreover, an educated population is critical to the future prosperity of the country as a whole. Are there ways to support the elderly and the young at the same time? Is it fair to cut back assistance to the elderly, who have worked a lifetime for their benefits? If we decrease assistance to the elderly, will they stay in the labor market and make the job hunt for young people even more difficult? As these trade-offs suggest, there are no easy answers to the demographic changes that will unfold in the coming years. Undoubtedly, these questions will provoke heated political conflict, as politicians and interest groups propose different strategies for supporting the young in an aging country. Informed participation of the American public, especially the participation of young people, is the only way to ensure that the steps taken to address these challenges best reflect the will of the people.

plugin

Inform

Learn about the demographic diversity of your local area by entering your zip code on the U.S. Census website (http://factfinder2.census.gov/). How does your community compare to the American population as a whole?

Express

Make a list of the most important political values you hold. How do they fit into broader American values?

Connect

See what people across the country are thinking about government and politics at the Pew Research Center's website. Do you think officials in Washington, D.C., pay attention to the public's views?

Act

Rock the Vote helps young people express their political power by organizing concerts, registration drives, and other events. Consider attending or volunteering for one of the events listed for your state at www.rockthevote.com/get-involved/.

studyguide

What Americans Think about Government

Explore Americans' attitudes toward government (pp. 5–9)

While Americans have always been hesitant about granting government too much power, they have frequently relied on it during times of national crisis and have become increasingly dependent on it to provide important services. Over the last few decades, Americans' trust in government and their sense of political efficacy have declined significantly. Low levels of trust and efficacy may threaten American democracy by weakening the government and reducing the public's willingness to participate in political life.

Key Terms

government (p. 4)

politics (p. 4)

political efficacy (p. 8)

Practice Quiz

1. *Political efficacy* is the belief that
   a) government is wasteful and corrupt.
   b) government operates efficiently.
   c) government has grown too large.
   d) government cannot be trusted.
   e) one can influence what government does.

2. Americans' trust in their government
   a) rose significantly between 1964 and 1980.
   b) increased immediately following September 11, 2001, but declined shortly thereafter.
   c) declined immediately after the September 11 attacks but has risen dramatically since 2004.
   d) has never been studied.
   e) has remained the same over the last 50 years.

Citizenship: Knowledge and Participation

Describe the role of the citizen in politics (pp. 9–13)

Citizenship requires political knowledge. When citizens know about politics, they are better able to understand their interests and to identify the best way to act on those interests. Most Americans, however, do not know much about politics.

Key Term

citizenship (p. 11)

Practice Quiz

3. Generally speaking, Americans
   a) know very little about current political issues but are able to identify some high-profile political leaders.
   b) know a great deal about current political issues but are not able to identify high-profile political leaders.
   c) know very little about current political issues and are never able to identify high-profile political leaders.
   d) know a great deal about current political issues and are able to identify high-profile political leaders.
   e) are extremely engaged with politics and trust the government to do what is right.

4. What is *digital citizenship*?
   a) a new initiative to expand online voter registration
   b) the ability to vote online
   c) the ability to progress through a path to citizenship through an online program
   d) the ability to participate in society online
   e) a new initiative by the government to provide daily updates online

Government

Define government and forms of government (pp. 13–17)

There are many different kinds of government. Prior to the modern era, governments accepted almost no limits on their behavior and provided citizens with few opportunities to participate in public affairs. Today, numerous countries, including the United States, are constitutional democracies. America's democracy provides citizens with the chance to elect top officials at all levels of government and even allows them to vote directly on laws in many states and localities.

Key Terms

autocracy (p. 14)

oligarchy (p. 14)

democracy (p. 14)

constitutional government (p. 14)

authoritarian government (p. 14)

totalitarian government (p. 14)

power (p. 16)

representative democracy (republic) (p. 16)

direct democracy (p. 16)

pluralism (p. 17)

Practice Quiz

5. What is the basic difference between an autocracy and an oligarchy?
   a) the extent to which the average citizen has a say in government affairs
   b) the means of collecting taxes and conscripting soldiers
   c) the number of people who control governing decisions
   d) the size and political influence of the military
   e) They are fundamentally the same thing.

6. When the government is formally limited in what it can control and how it controls it, this is known as
   a) totalitarianism.
   b) authoritarianism.
   c) constitutional government.
   d) autocracy.
   e) oligarchy.

7. Although not present at the national level, a number of states and cities permit citizens to vote directly on laws and policies. What is this form of rule called?
   a) a republic
   b) representative democracy
   c) direct democracy
   d) pluralism
   e) laissez-faire capitalism

8. *Pluralism* is a theory that says
   a) the means of economic production should be privately owned and operated without interference from the government.
   b) all interests in a society should be free to compete for influence over governmental decisions.
   c) government should always follow the preferences of the majority while also protecting the rights of those in the minority.
   d) American political culture should emphasize the values of liberty, equality, and democracy.
   e) one ruler should dominate all spheres of social, political, economic, and cultural life.

Who Are Americans?

> **Show how the social composition of the American population has changed over time (pp. 17–24)**

The United States is defined, in part, by its ever growing and changing population. During the last 200 years, America has become more racially, ethnically, geographically, and religiously diverse. Immigration has been an important reason for the country's shifting demographics, and it has frequently sparked intense debate about the nature of American identity and American democracy.

Practice Quiz

9. The percentage of foreign-born individuals living in the United States
   a) has increased significantly since reaching its low point in 1970.
   b) has decreased significantly since reaching its high point in 1970.
   c) has remained the same since 1970.
   d) has not been studied since 1970.
   e) has never been less than the percentage of native-born individuals living in the United States.

10. As a percentage of the total population in the United States, which age group has increased the most dramatically from 1900 to 2010?
    a) children
    b) young adults, ages 20–30
    c) adults, ages 30–44
    d) the elderly
    e) The percentage for each group has remained about the same.

American Political Culture

Most Americans express strong support for liberty, equality, and democracy. Agreement on these basic values does not mean, however, that political debate in the United States is without conflict. Questions about how to apply and balance the different elements of American political culture have motivated disagreements throughout the country's history.

Key Terms

political culture (p. 24)

liberty (p. 26)

limited government (p. 26)

laissez-faire capitalism (p. 26)

equality of opportunity (p. 27)

political equality (p. 28)

popular sovereignty (p. 30)

majority rule, minority rights (p. 30)

Practice Quiz

11. Which of the following is *not* related to the American conception of liberty?
    a) freedom of speech
    b) economic freedom
    c) freedom of religion
    d) freedom of assembly
    e) All of the above are related to liberty.

12. The principle of political equality can be best summed up as
    a) "equality of results."
    b) "equality of opportunity."
    c) "one person, one vote."
    d) "equality between the sexes."
    e) "leave everyone alone."

13. Which of the following is an important principle of American democracy?
    a) popular sovereignty
    b) majority rule
    c) limited government
    d) minority rights
    e) All of the above are important principles of American democracy.

14. Which of the following is *not* part of American political culture?
    a) belief in equality of results
    b) belief in democracy
    c) belief in individual liberty
    d) belief in free competition
    e) belief in equality of opportunity

15. Which of the following restrictions on voting have been repealed over the last 200 years in the United States?
    a) property, gender, and race
    b) gender only
    c) race only
    d) property only
    e) race and gender only

For Further Reading

Dahl, Robert. *How Democratic Is the American Constitution?* New Haven, CT: Yale University Press, 2002.

Dalton, Russell. *The Good Citizen: How a Younger Generation Is Reshaping American Politics.* Rev. ed. Washington, DC: CQ Press, 2008.

Delli Carpini, Michael X., and Scott Keeter. *What Americans Know about Politics and Why It Matters.* New Haven, CT: Yale University Press, 1996.

Fischer, Claude S., and Michael Hout. *A Century of Difference: How America Changed in the Last One Hundred Years.* New York: Russell Sage Foundation, 2006.

Hibbing, John R., and Elizabeth Theiss-Morse. *Stealth Democracy: Americans' Belief about How Government Should Work.* New York: Cambridge University Press, 2002.

Hochschild, Jennifer L. *Facing Up to the American Dream: Race, Class, and the Soul of the Nation.* Princeton, NJ: Princeton University Press, 1995.

Huntington, Samuel. *Who Are We? The Challenges to America's National Identity.* New York: Simon & Schuster, 2004.

Lasswell, Harold. *Politics: Who Gets What, When, How.* New York: Meridian Books, 1958.

McCarty, Nolan, Keith T. Poole, and Howard Rosenthal. *Polarized America: The Dance of Ideology and Unequal Riches.* Cambridge, MA: MIT Press, 2008.

Mettler, Suzanne. *The Submerged State: How Invisible Government Policies Undermine American Democracy.* Chicago: University of Chicago Press, 2011.

Nye, Joseph S., Jr., Philip D. Zelikow, and David C. King, eds. *Why People Don't Trust Government*. Cambridge, MA: Harvard University Press, 1997.

Page, Benjamin I., and Lawrence R. Jacobs. *Class War? What Americans Really Think about Economic Inequality*. Chicago: University of Chicago Press, 2009.

Putnam, Robert. *Making Democracy Work: Civic Traditions in Modern Italy*. Princeton, NJ: Princeton University Press, 1993.

Tocqueville, Alexis de. *Democracy in America*. Translated by Phillips Bradley. New York: Knopf, Vintage Books, 1945; orig. published 1835.

Zakaria, Fareed. *The Future of Freedom*. New York: W. W. Norton, 2003.

Recommended Websites

American Democracy Project
www.aascu.org/programs/adp
This is an effort by the Association of State Colleges and Universities to increase political engagement among college students. See what opportunities are available for you to become politically active.

Americans for Informed Democracy
www.aidemocracy.org
A nonpartisan organization that promotes democracy and seeks to build a new generation of globally conscious leaders. Find out how you can be politically active and coordinate a town hall meeting on campus, attend a leadership retreat, or publish your opinions on democracy.

DiversityInc
http://diversityinc.com
This site is dedicated to the promotion of American diversity and education. Here you can read about the issues that directly affect American minorities

For Democracy
www.fordemocracy.com
Most Americans know little about our government. Log on to this independent site to find a plethora of information on the history of American democracy and related current events.

Future of Freedom Foundation
www.fff.org
This organization promotes individual liberty, free markets, private property, and limited government. Find out how some people are trying to protect freedom in the United States.

Institute for Learning Technologies
www.ilt.columbia.edu/publications/digitext.html#
Columbia University's Institute for Learning Technologies provides general information on early political thinkers such as Aristotle, Hobbes, Locke, and Rousseau. Take a moment to read some of the writings on topics such as popular sovereignty, democracy, and limited government.

Mobilize.org
http://mobilize.org
This all-partisan network is dedicated to educating, empowering, and energizing young people. Find out how politics affects America's youth and what they are doing about it by being engaged and active.

U.S. Census Bureau
www.census.gov
The website for the Census Bureau offers a statistical look at our country's population and economy. Check out some of the statistics to get a better idea of American diversity.

When the framers of the Constitution met in 1787, they set out to establish a political system that would protect liberty and place limits on government. They also believed a powerful government required a broad popular base. However, they debated how best to protect liberty and how to balance democracy with other concerns.

The Founding and the Constitution

WHAT GOVERNMENT DOES AND WHY IT MATTERS The framers of the U.S. Constitution knew why government mattered. In the Constitution's preamble, the framers tell us that the purposes of government are to promote justice, to maintain peace at home, to defend the nation from foreign foes, to provide for the welfare of the citizenry, and, above all, to secure the "blessings of liberty" for Americans. The remainder of the Constitution spells out a plan for achieving these objectives. This plan includes provisions for the exercise of legislative, executive, and judicial powers and a recipe for the division of powers among the federal government's branches and between the national and state governments. The framers' conception of why government matters and how it is to achieve its goals has been America's political blueprint for more than two centuries.

Often, Americans become impatient with the Constitution, as the constitutional separation of powers often seems to be a recipe for inaction and "gridlock" when America's major institutions of government are controlled by opposing political forces. This has led to bitter fights that sometimes prevent government from delivering important services. In 2011 and again in 2013, the House and Senate could not reach agreement on a budget for the federal government or a formula for funding the public debt. For 16 days in October 2013, the federal government partially shut down, and so permit offices across the country no longer took in fees, contractors stopped receiving checks, research projects stalled, and some 800,000 federal employees were sent home on unpaid leave—at a cost to the economy of $3.1 billion.

The framers, however, believed that a good constitution not only created a government with the capacity to act forcefully but also promoted compromise and deliberation, sometimes delaying action until tempers cooled and a variety of viewpoints could be heard. Every form of government has strengths and weaknesses. The cost of compromise and deliberation encouraged by such constitutional arrangements as the separation of powers might sometimes be gridlock, but the benefit may be a government compelled to take a variety of interests and viewpoints into account when it formulates policies.

The story of America's Founding and the Constitution is generally presented as something both inevitable and glorious: it was inevitable that the American colonies would break away from Great Britain to establish their own country; and it was glorious in that the country established the best of all possible forms of government under a new constitution. In reality, though, America's successful breakaway from Britain was by no means assured, and many of the Constitution provisions were highly controversial.

America's long-standing values of liberty, equality, and democracy were all major themes of the founding period and are all elements of the U.S. Constitution. However, the Constitution was a product of political bargaining and compromise, formed in very much the same way political decisions are made today. As this chapter will show, the Constitution reflects high principle as well as political self-interest, and also defines the relationship between American citizens and their government.

chaptergoals

- Describe the events that led to the Declaration of Independence and the Articles of Confederation (pp. 41–45)

- Analyze the reasons for the failure of the Articles of Confederation (pp. 45–51)

- Explain how the Constitution attempted to improve America's governance, and outline the major institutions established by the Constitution (pp. 51–59)

- Present the controversies involved in the struggle for ratification (pp. 60–64)

- Trace how the Constitution has changed over time through the amendment process (pp. 64–68)

● The First Founding: Interests and Conflicts

Describe the events that led to the Declaration of Independence and the Articles of Confederation

Competing ideals and principles often reflect competing interests, and so it was in Revolutionary America. The American Revolution and the American Constitution were outgrowths and expressions of a struggle among economic and political forces within the colonies. Five sectors of society had interests that were important in colonial politics: (1) the New England merchants; (2) the southern planters; (3) the "royalists"—holders of royal lands, offices, and patents (licenses to engage in a profession or business activity); (4) shopkeepers, artisans, and laborers; and (5) small farmers. Throughout the eighteenth century, these groups were in conflict over issues of taxation, trade, and commerce. For the most part, however, the southern planters, the New England merchants, and the royal office and patent holders—groups that together made up the colonial elite—were able to maintain a political alliance that held in check the more radical forces representing shopkeepers, laborers, and small farmers. After 1760, however, by seriously threatening the interests of New England merchants and southern planters, British tax and trade policies split the colonial elite, permitting radical forces to expand their political influence, and set in motion a chain of events that culminated in the American Revolution.[1]

British Taxes and Colonial Interests

During the first half of the eighteenth century, Britain ruled its American colonies with a light hand. Evidence of British rule was hardly to be found outside the largest towns, and the enterprising colonists had found ways of evading most of the taxes nominally levied by the distant British regime. Beginning in the 1760s, however, the debts and other financial problems confronting the British government forced it to search for new revenue sources. This search rather quickly led to the Crown's North American colonies, which, on the whole, paid remarkably little in taxes to their parent country. The British government reasoned that a sizable fraction of its debt was, in fact, attributable to the expenses it had incurred in defense of the colonies during the French and Indian War, which ended in 1763, driving France from North America. The British also considered the cost of the continuing protection that British forces were giving the colonists from Indian attacks and that the British navy was providing for colonial shipping. Thus, during the 1760s, Britain sought to impose new, though relatively modest, taxes on the colonists.

Like most governments of the period, the British regime had limited ways in which to collect revenues. The income tax, which in the twentieth century became the single most important source of governmental revenues, had not yet been developed. In the mid-eighteenth century, governments relied mainly on tariffs, duties, and other taxes on commerce, and it was to such taxes, and to the Stamp Act, that the British turned during the 1760s.

British colonists in America shipped many goods back to England, such as furs obtained by trading with Native Americans. The British government claimed that the colonists should pay more in taxes in light of the protection their shipments received from the British navy and the expenses Britain incurred defending the colonies.

The Stamp Act, and other taxes on commerce, such as the Sugar Act of 1764, which taxed sugar, molasses, and other commodities, most heavily affected the two groups in colonial society whose commercial interests and activities were most extensive—the New England merchants and the southern planters. United under the famous slogan "No taxation without representation," the merchants and planters sought to organize opposition to these new taxes. In the course of the struggle against British tax measures, the planters and merchants broke with their royalist allies and turned to their former adversaries—the shopkeepers, small farmers, laborers, and artisans—for help. With the assistance of these groups, the merchants and planters organized demonstrations and a boycott of British goods that ultimately forced the Crown to rescind most of its hated new taxes.

From the perspective of the merchants and planters, this was a victorious conclusion to their struggle with the mother country. They were anxious to end the unrest they had helped arouse, and they supported the British government's efforts to restore order. Indeed, most respectable Bostonians supported the actions of the British soldiers involved in the Boston Massacre—the 1770 killing of five colonists by British soldiers who were attempting to repel an angry mob gathered outside the Town House, the seat of the colonial government. In their subsequent trial, the soldiers were defended by John Adams, a pillar of Boston society and a future president of the United States. Adams asserted that the soldiers' actions were entirely justified, provoked by "a motley rabble of saucy boys, negroes and mulattoes, Irish teagues and outlandish Jack tars." All but two of the soldiers were acquitted.[2]

Despite the efforts of the British government and the better-to-do strata of colonial society, it proved difficult to bring an end to the political strife. The more radical forces representing shopkeepers, artisans, laborers, and small farmers, who had been mobilized and energized by the struggle over taxes, continued to agitate for political and social change. These radicals, whose leaders included Samuel Adams, a cousin of John Adams, asserted that British power supported an unjust political and social structure within the colonies, and began to advocate an end to British rule.[3]

Political Strife and the Radicalization of the Colonists

The political strife within the colonies was the background for the events of 1773–74. In 1773 the British government granted the politically powerful East India Company a monopoly on the export of tea from Britain, eliminating a lucrative form of trade for colonial merchants. To add to the injury, the East India Company sought to sell the tea directly in the colonies instead of working through the colonial merchants. Tea was an extremely important commodity during the 1770s, and these British actions posed a serious threat to the New England merchants. Together with their southern allies, the merchants once again called on their radical adversaries for support. The most dramatic result was the Boston Tea Party. In three other colonies, antitax Americans succeeded in blocking the unloading of taxed tea, which then had to be returned to Britain. The royal governor of Massachusetts, however, refused to allow three shiploads of unsold tea to leave Boston Harbor. Anti-British radicals seized this opportunity: on the night of December 16, 1773, a group led by Samuel Adams, some of them hastily "disguised" as Mohawk Indians, boarded the three vessels and threw the entire cargo of 342 chests of tea into the harbor.

The British helped radicalize colonists through bad policy decisions in the years before the Revolution. For example, Britain gave the ailing East India Company a monopoly on the tea trade in the American colonies. Colonists feared that the monopoly would hurt colonial merchants' business and protested by throwing East India Company tea into Boston Harbor in 1773. Americans today commemorate this protest against oppressive British rule by re-enacting the events of the Boston Tea Party.

This event was of decisive importance in American history. The merchants had hoped to force the British government to rescind the Tea Act, but they did not support any further demands and did not seek independence from Britain. Samuel Adams and the other radicals, however, hoped to provoke the British government to take actions that would alienate its colonial supporters and pave the way for a rebellion. This was precisely the purpose of the Boston Tea Party, and it succeeded. By dumping the East India Company's tea into Boston Harbor, Adams and his followers goaded the British into enacting a number of harsh reprisals. Within five months after the incident in Boston, the British House of Commons passed a series of acts that closed the port of Boston to commerce, changed the provincial government of Massachusetts, provided for the removal of accused persons to Britain for trial, and, most important, restricted movement to the West—further alienating the southern planters, who depended on access to new western lands. These acts of retaliation confirmed the worst criticisms of British rule and helped radicalize Americans. Radicals such as Samuel Adams and Christopher Gadsden (of South Carolina) had been agitating for more-violent measures against the British. But ultimately they needed Britain's political repression to create widespread support for independence.

Thus, the Boston Tea Party set in motion a cycle of provocation and retaliation that in 1774 resulted in the convening of the First Continental Congress—an assembly of delegates from all parts of the country—that called for a total boycott of British goods and, under the prodding of the radicals, began to consider the possibility of independence from British rule. The eventual result was the Declaration of Independence.

The Declaration of Independence

In 1776, more than a year after open warfare had commenced in Massachusetts, the Second Continental Congress appointed a committee consisting of Thomas Jefferson of Virginia, Benjamin Franklin of Pennsylvania, Roger Sherman of Connecticut, John Adams of Massachusetts, and Robert Livingston of New York to

for critical analysis

Conflicts over taxes did not end with the American Revolution. Why is tax policy almost always controversial? What differences and similarities are there between the debates over taxes in the 1760s and today?

draft a statement of American independence from British rule. The Declaration of Independence, written by Jefferson and adopted by the Second Continental Congress, was an extraordinary document both philosophically and politically. In philosophic terms, the Declaration was remarkable for its assertion that certain rights—the "unalienable rights" that include life, liberty, and the pursuit of happiness—could not be abridged by governments. In the world of 1776, a world in which some kings still claimed to rule by divine right, this was a dramatic statement. This philosophical view was heavily influenced by the works of the philosopher John Locke, one of England's foremost liberal theorists of the seventeenth century. In his treatises on government, widely read by educated colonists, Locke asserted that all individuals were equal and possessed a natural right to defend their own lives, liberties, and possessions. Individuals created governments to help them protect these rights, and if a government failed in its duties, the citizenry had the right to alter or abolish it. In political terms, the Declaration was remarkable because, despite the differences of interest that divided the colonists along economic, regional, and philosophical lines, it identified and focused on grievances, aspirations, and principles that might unify the various colonial groups. The Declaration was an attempt to identify and articulate a history and set of principles that might help forge national unity.[4]

The purpose of the Declaration of Independence was to explain to the world why the colonists had rebelled against the British and sought self-government. The Declaration's pronouncement that "We hold these truths to be self-evident, that all men are created equal" remains a powerful principle of American democracy. Every year, Americans celebrate the signing of the Declaration on the Fourth of July.

Articles of Confederation
America's first written constitution; served as the basis for America's national government until 1789

confederation a system of government in which states retain sovereign authority except for the powers expressly delegated to the national government

The Articles of Confederation

Having declared their independence, the colonies needed to establish a governmental structure. In November 1777 the Continental Congress adopted the **Articles of Confederation**—the United States' first written constitution. Although it was not ratified by all the states until 1781, it was the country's operative constitution for almost 12 years, until March 1789.

The first goal of the Articles was to limit the powers of the central government. The relationship between the national government and the states was called a **confederation**; as provided under Article II, "each state retains its sovereignty, freedom, and independence," much like the contemporary relationship between the United Nations and its member states. The central government was given no president or any other presiding officer. The entire national government was vested in a Congress, with execution of its few laws to be left to the individual states. And the Articles gave Congress very little power to exercise. Its members were not much more than delegates or messengers from the state legislatures: their salaries were paid out of the state treasuries; they were subject to immediate recall by state authorities; and each state, regardless of its size, had only one vote. All 13 states had to agree to any amendments to the Articles.

Under the Articles of Confederation, Congress was given the power to declare war and make peace, to make treaties and alliances, to coin or borrow money, and to regulate trade with the Native Americans. It could also appoint the senior officers of the U.S. Army, but the national government had no army for those officers to command, because the nation's armed forces were composed of the state militias. Moreover, the central government could not prevent one state from discriminating against other states in the competition for foreign commerce. These extreme limits on the power of the national government made the Articles of Confederation hopelessly impractical.[5]

● The Second Founding: From Compromise to Constitution

Analyze the reasons for the failure of the Articles of Confederation

The Declaration of Independence and the Articles of Confederation were not sufficient to hold the new nation together as an independent and effective nation-state. A series of developments following the armistice with the British in 1783 highlighted the shortcomings of the Articles of Confederation.

First, many of the new country's leaders worried that the Articles of Confederation would not allow the United States to conduct its foreign affairs successfully, as the federal government was unable to enforce existing treaties and there was no national military. Furthermore, competition among the states for foreign commerce allowed the European powers to play the states off one another, which created confusion on both sides of the Atlantic. At one point during the winter of 1786–87, John Adams of Massachusetts, a leader in the independence struggle, was sent to negotiate a new treaty with the British, one that would cover disputes left over from the war. The British government responded that since the United States under the Articles of Confederation was unable to enforce existing treaties, it would negotiate with each of the 13 states separately. At the same time, the United States faced a threat from Spain, which still held vast territories in North and South America. Without a national military, the nation's borders were difficult to protect against this potentially hostile foreign power.

Second, the Articles of Confederation allowed for only a weak federal government, with state governments retaining most of the powers of government. This situation became alarming to well-to-do Americans, in particular New England merchants and southern planters, when "radical" forces began to exert considerable influence in a number of state governments. The colonists' victory in the Revolutionary War had not only ended British rule but also significantly changed the balance of political power within the new states. As a result of the Revolution, one key segment of the colonial elite—the royal land, office, and patent holders—was stripped of its economic and political privileges. In fact, many of these individuals, along with tens of thousands of other colonists who considered themselves loyal British subjects, left for Canada after the British surrender. And although the prerevolutionary elite was weakened, the prerevolutionary radicals were better organized than ever and now controlled such states as Pennsylvania and Rhode Island, where they pursued economic and political policies that struck terror in the hearts of the prerevolutionary political establishment. In Rhode Island, for example, between 1783 and 1785, a legislature dominated by representatives of small farmers, artisans, and shopkeepers had instituted economic policies, including drastic currency inflation, that frightened business and property owners throughout the country. Of course, the central government under the Articles of Confederation was powerless to intervene. Similarly, the Pennsylvania government engaged in land redistribution, to the chagrin of property owners.

However, the Articles of Confederation were by no means a complete failure. The Congress of the Confederation agreed upon two laws that helped to shape American history. These were the Land Ordinance of 1785 and the Northwest Ordinance of 1787. The Land Ordinance established the principles of land surveying and land ownership that governed America's westward expansion. Under the Northwest Ordinance, the individual states agreed to surrender their western land claims, which opened the way for the admission of new states to the Union.

These legislative successes were not adequate to sustain the fledgling federal government, however. During the 1780s, the political and economic position of the new American states deteriorated. Europe's great powers—Britain, France, and Spain—hurt colonial commerce by adopting mercantilist policies that excluded American trade while political unrest within the 13 new states further undermined trade and investment. Something had to be done.

The Annapolis Convention

The continuation of international weakness and domestic economic turmoil led many Americans to consider whether their newly adopted form of government might not already require revision. In the fall of 1786, many state leaders accepted an invitation from the Virginia legislature for a conference of representatives of all the states, to be held in Annapolis, Maryland. Delegates from only five states actually attended, so nothing substantive could be accomplished. Still, this conference was the first step toward what is now known as the second founding. The one positive result that came out of the Annapolis Convention was a carefully worded resolution calling on the Congress to send commissioners to Philadelphia at a later time "to devise such further provisions as shall appear to them necessary to render the Constitution of the Federal Government adequate to the exigencies of the Union."[6] But the resolution did not necessarily imply any desire to do more than improve and reform the Articles of Confederation.

In the winter of 1787, Daniel Shays led a makeshift army against the federal arsenal at Springfield to protest heavy taxes levied by the Massachusetts legislature. The rebellion proved the Articles of Confederation too weak to protect the fledgling nation.

Shays's Rebellion

It is quite possible that the Constitutional Convention of 1787 in Philadelphia would never have taken place at all except for a single event that occurred during the winter following the Annapolis Convention: Shays's Rebellion.

Daniel Shays, a former army captain, led a mob of farmers in a rebellion against the government of Massachusetts. The purpose of the rebellion was to prevent foreclosures on their debt-ridden land by keeping the county courts of western Massachusetts from sitting until after the next election. The state militia dispersed the mob, but for several days in February 1787, Shays and his followers terrified the state government by attempting to capture the federal arsenal at Springfield, provoking an appeal to the Congress to help restore order. Within a few days, the state government regained control and captured 14 of the rebels. Later that year, a newly elected Massachusetts legislature granted some of the farmers' demands.

The effects of the incident lingered and spread. Washington summed it up: "I am mortified beyond expression that in the moment of our acknowledged independence we should by our conduct verify the predictions of our transatlantic foe, and render ourselves ridiculous and contemptible in the eyes of all Europe."[7]

The Congress under the Confederation had been unable to act decisively in a time of crisis. This provided critics of the Articles of Confederation with precisely the evidence they needed to push the Annapolis resolution through the Congress. Thus, the states were asked to send representatives to Philadelphia to discuss constitutional revision. Seventy-four delegates were chosen. Of these, 55 would actually attend the convention, representing every state except Rhode Island, and 39 would eventually sign the newly drafted Constitution.

The Constitutional Convention

The delegates who convened in Philadelphia in May 1787 had political strife, international embarrassment, national weakness, and local rebellion fixed in their minds. Recognizing that these issues were symptoms of fundamental flaws in the Articles of Confederation, the delegates soon abandoned the plan to revise the Articles and committed themselves to a second founding—a second, and ultimately successful, attempt to create a legitimate and effective national system of government. This effort would occupy the convention for the next five months.

A Marriage of Interest and Principle For years, scholars have disagreed about the motives of the Founders in Philadelphia. Among the most controversial views of the framers' motives is the "economic interpretation" put forward by the historian Charles Beard and his disciples.[8] According to Beard's account, America's Founders were a collection of securities speculators and property owners whose only aim was personal enrichment. From this perspective, the Constitution's lofty principles were little more than sophisticated masks behind which the most venal interests sought to enrich themselves.

Contrary to Beard's approach is the view that the framers of the Constitution *were* concerned with philosophical and ethical principles. Indeed, they sought to devise a system of government consistent with the dominant philosophical and moral principles of the day. But in fact, these two views belong together; the Founders' interests were reinforced by their principles. The convention that drafted the American Constitution was chiefly organized by the New England merchants and southern planters. Although the delegates representing these groups did not all hope to profit personally from an increase in the value of their securities, as Beard would have it, they did hope to benefit in the broadest political and economic sense by breaking the power of their radical foes and establishing a system of government more compatible with their long-term economic and political interests. Thus, the framers sought to create a new government capable of promoting commerce and protecting property from radical state legislatures and populist forces hostile to the interests of the commercial and propertied classes.

The Great Compromise The proponents of a new government fired their opening shot on May 29, 1787, when Edmund Randolph of Virginia offered a resolution that proposed corrections and enlargements in the Articles of Confederation. The proposal, which showed the strong influence of James Madison, was not a simple motion. Rather, it provided for virtually every aspect of a new government.

The portion of Randolph's motion that became most controversial was called the **Virginia Plan**. This plan provided for a system of representation in the national legislature based on the population of each state or the proportion of each

Virginia Plan a framework for the Constitution, introduced by Edmund Randolph, that called for representation in the national legislature based on the population of each state

When the framers of the Constitution met in 1787, they set out to establish a political system that would protect liberty and place limits on government. They also believed that a powerful government required a broad popular base. However, they debated how best to protect liberty and how to balance democracy with other concerns, such as efficient government.

New Jersey Plan a framework for the Constitution, introduced by William Paterson, that called for equal state representation in the national legislature regardless of population

Great Compromise the agreement reached at the Constitutional Convention of 1787 that gave each state an equal number of senators regardless of its population, but linked representation in the House of Representatives to population

state's revenue contribution to the national government, or both. (Randolph also proposed a second chamber of the legislature, to be elected by the members of the first chamber.) Since the states varied enormously in size and wealth, the Virginia Plan was thought to be heavily biased in favor of the large states.

While the convention was debating the Virginia Plan, opposition to it began to mount as more delegates arrived in Philadelphia. William Paterson of New Jersey introduced a resolution known as the **New Jersey Plan**. Its main proponents were delegates from the less-populous states, including Delaware, New Jersey, Connecticut, and New York, who asserted that the more populous states—Virginia, Pennsylvania, North Carolina, Massachusetts, and Georgia— would dominate the new government if representation were to be determined by population. The smaller states argued that each state should be equally represented in the new regime regardless of the state's population.

The issue of representation threatened to wreck the entire constitutional enterprise. Delegates conferred, factions maneuvered, and tempers flared. James Wilson of Pennsylvania told the small-state delegates that if they wanted to disrupt the union, they should go ahead. The separation, he said, could "never happen on better grounds." Small-state delegates were equally blunt. Gunning Bedford of Delaware declared that the small states might, if forced, look elsewhere for friends. "The large states," he said, "dare not dissolve the confederation. If they do the small ones will find some foreign ally of more honor and good faith, who will take them by the hand and do them justice." These sentiments were widely shared. The union, as Oliver Ellsworth of Connecticut put it, was "on the verge of dissolution, scarcely held together by the strength of a hair."

The outcome of this debate was the Connecticut Compromise, also known as the **Great Compromise**. Under the terms of this compromise, in the first chamber of Congress—the House of Representatives—the representatives would be apportioned according to the population in each state. This, of course, was what delegates from the large states had sought. But in the second branch—the Senate—each state would have equal representation regardless of its size; this provision addressed the concerns of small states. This compromise was not immediately satisfactory to all

Who Benefits from the Great Compromise?

The Great Compromise attempted to balance power between large and small states in the new Congress. The figure shows the difference in representation for states in the House and Senate in the first Congress (1789–91). In the Senate each state has equal representation, which in the first Congress meant each had 1/13 of all seats. In the House the number of seats apportioned to each state is based on population; thus, the larger states have more representation.

Representation in the First Congress

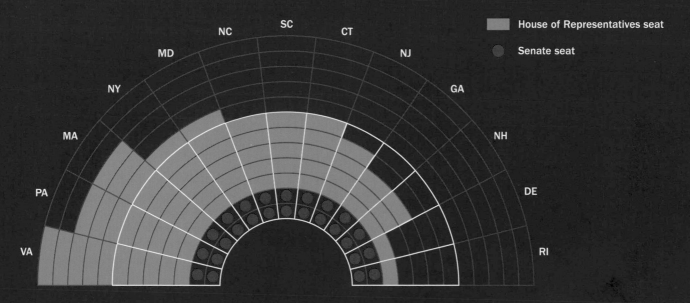

House of Representatives seat

Senate seat

State Populations, 1790*

1.	Virginia	747,610
2.	Pennsylvania	433,373
3.	North Carolina	393,751
4.	Massachusetts	378,787
5.	New York	340,120
6.	Maryland	319,728
7.	South Carolina	249,073
8.	Connecticut	237,946
9.	New Jersey	184,139
10.	New Hampshire	141,885
11.	Georgia	82,548
12.	Rhode Island	68,825
13.	Delaware	59,096

* These numbers represent the total number of persons in each state according to the 1790 census (including free white males, free white females, "all other free persons," and slaves). For the purpose of representation in the first Congress, the framers calculated the number of representatives per state in 1787 based on population estimates, which counted each slave as three-fifths of a person. This calculation is why the representation in the first Congress does not match perfectly with the total population counts reported here.

SOURCE: U.S. Census Bureau, www.census.gov (accessed 8/16/12); U.S. House of Representatives, www.history.house.gov/Institution/Apportionment/Apportionment (accessed 4/11/14).

for critical analysis

1. At the Constitutional Convention, large states supported the Virginia Plan, which would have made the whole Congress look like the House. Small states supported the New Jersey Plan, which would have made the whole Congress look like the Senate. How would each group have benefited from its favored plans?

2. What are the advantages of equal representation by states? What are the drawbacks? In your opinion, do the advantages outweigh the disadvantages?

the delegates. Indeed, two of the most vocal members of the small-state faction, John Lansing and Robert Yates of New York, were so angered by the concession that their colleagues had made to the large-state forces that they stormed out of the convention. In the end, however, most of the delegates preferred compromise to the breakup of the Union, and the plan was accepted.

The Question of Slavery: The Three-Fifths Compromise Many of the conflicts that emerged during the Constitutional Convention were reflections of the fundamental differences between the slave and the nonslave states—differences that pitted the southern planters against the New England merchants and would almost destroy the Republic in later years. In the midst of debate over large versus small states, James Madison observed,

> The great danger to our general government is the great southern and northern interests of the continent, being opposed to each other. Look to the votes in Congress, and most of them stand divided by the geography of the country, not according to the size of the states.[9]

More than 90 percent of the country's slaves resided in five states—Georgia, Maryland, North Carolina, South Carolina, and Virginia—where they accounted for 30 percent of the total population. In some places, slaves outnumbered nonslaves by as many as 10 to 1. If the Constitution were to embody any principle of national supremacy, some basic decisions would have to be made about the place of slavery in the general scheme. Madison hit on this point on several occasions as different aspects of the Constitution were being discussed. For example, he observed,

> It seemed now to be pretty well understood that the real difference of interests lay, not between the large and small but between the northern and southern states. The institution of slavery and its consequences formed the line of discrimination. There were five states on the South, eight on the northern side of this line. Should a proportional representation take place it was true, the northern side would still outnumber the other: but not in the same degree, at this time; and every day would tend towards an equilibrium.[10]

Three-Fifths Compromise
the agreement reached at the Constitutional Convention of 1787 that stipulated that for purposes of the apportionment of congressional seats, every slave would be counted as three-fifths of a person

Northerners and southerners eventually reached agreement through the **Three-Fifths Compromise**. The seats in the House of Representatives would be apportioned according to a "population" in which five slaves would count as three free persons. The slaves would not be allowed to vote, of course, but the number of representatives would be apportioned accordingly.

The issue of slavery was the most difficult one faced by the framers, and it nearly destroyed the Union. Although some delegates believed slavery to be morally wrong, an evil and oppressive institution that made a mockery of the ideals and values espoused in the Constitution, morality was not the issue that caused the framers to support or oppose the Three-Fifths Compromise. Whatever they thought of the institution of slavery, most delegates from the northern states opposed counting slaves in the distribution of congressional seats. James Wilson of Pennsylvania, for example, argued that if slaves were citizens, they should be treated and counted like other citizens. If, on the other hand, they were property, then why should not other forms of property be counted toward the apportionment of representatives? But southern delegates made it clear that they would never agree to the new government if the northerners refused to give in. William R. Davie of North Carolina heatedly said that it was time

Despite the Founders' emphasis on liberty, the new Constitution allowed slavery, counting each slave as three-fifths of a person in apportioning seats in the House of Representatives. In this 1792 painting, Liberty Displaying the Arts and Sciences, *the books, instruments, and classical columns at the left contrast with the kneeling slaves at the right—illustrating the divide between America's rhetoric of liberty and equality and the realities of slavery.*

"to speak out." He asserted that the people of North Carolina would never enter the Union if slaves were not counted as part of the basis for representation. Without such agreement, he asserted ominously, "the business was at an end." Even southerners such as Edmund Randolph of Virginia, who conceded that slavery was immoral, insisted on including slaves in the allocation of congressional seats. Eventually, the North and South compromised on the issue of slavery and representation. Indeed, northerners even agreed to permit a continuation of the odious slave trade in order to keep the South in the Union. But in due course, the disparate interests of the North and the South could no longer be reconciled and a bloody civil war was the reslult.

● The Constitution

Explain how the Constitution attempted to improve America's governance, and outline the major institutions established by the Constitution

The political significance of the Great Compromise and the Three-Fifths Compromise was to reinforce the unity of the mercantile and planter forces that sought to create a new government. The Great Compromise reassured those who feared that a new governmental framework would reduce the importance of their own local or regional influence. The Three-Fifths Compromise temporarily defused the rivalry between the merchants and planters. Their unity secured, members of the alliance supporting the establishment of a new government moved to fashion a constitutional framework consistent with their economic and political interests.

In particular, the framers sought a new government that, first, would be strong enough to promote commerce and protect property from radical state legislatures such as Rhode Island's. This became the constitutional basis for national control over commerce and finance, and for the establishment of national judicial supremacy and the effort to construct a strong presidency. See Table 2.1 for a comparison of the Articles of Confederation to the Constitution. Second, the framers sought to prevent what they saw as the threat posed by the "excessive democracy" of the state and national governments under the Articles of Confederation. This led to such constitutional principles as bicameralism (division of the Congress into two chambers), **checks and balances**, staggered terms in office, and indirect election (selection of the president by an **electoral college** rather than directly by voters and election of senators by state legislatures). Third, the framers, lacking the power to force the states or the public at large to accept the new form of government, sought to identify principles that would help secure support. This became the basis of the constitutional provision for direct popular election of representatives and, subsequently, for the addition of the **Bill of Rights** to the Constitution. Finally, the framers wanted to be certain that the government they created did not pose an even greater threat to its citizens' liberties and property rights than did the radical state legislatures they feared and despised. To prevent the new government from abusing its power, the framers incorporated principles such as the **separation of powers** and **federalism** into the Constitution. Below, we assess the major provisions of the Constitution's seven articles to see how each relates to these objectives.

If the Declaration of Independence drew its philosophical inspiration from John Locke, the Constitution drew upon the thought of the French political philosopher Baron de la Brède et de Montesquieu (1689–1755). In Montesquieu's view, the powers of government must be divided in order to prevent any one group or institution from exercising tyrannical control over the nation. Montesquieu recommended a tripartite division, placing the executive, legislative, and judicial powers in different governmental bodies. He claimed that such a tripartite division had worked very well in the Roman Republic and in Britain. The delegates to America's Constitutional Convention referred frequently to Montesquieu's writings in devising America's new governmental structure.

The Legislative Branch

In Article I, Sections 1–7, the Constitution provided for a Congress consisting of two chambers: a House of Representatives and a Senate. Members of the House of Representatives were given two-year terms in office and were to be elected directly by the people. Members of the Senate were to be appointed by the state legislatures (this was changed in 1913 by the Seventeenth Amendment, which instituted direct election of senators) for six-year terms. These terms were staggered so that the appointments of one-third of the senators would expire every two years. The Constitution assigned somewhat different tasks to the House and Senate. Though the approval of each body was required for the enactment of a law, the Senate alone was given the power to ratify treaties and approve presidential appointments. The House, on the other hand, was given the sole power to originate revenue bills.

The character of the legislative branch was directly related to the framers' major goals. The House of Representatives was designed to be directly responsible to the people in order to encourage popular consent for the new Constitution and to help

checks and balances mechanisms through which each branch of government is able to participate in and influence the activities of the other branches; major examples include the presidential veto power over congressional legislation, the power of the Senate to approve presidential appointments, and judicial review of congressional enactments

electoral college the electors from each state who meet after the popular election to cast ballots for president and vice president

Bill of Rights the first 10 amendments to the U.S. Constitution, ratified in 1791; they ensure certain rights and liberties to the people

separation of powers the division of governmental power among several institutions that must cooperate in decision making

federalism a system of government in which power is divided, by a constitution, between a central government and regional governments

TABLE 2.1

Comparing the Articles of Confederation and the Constitution

MAJOR PROVISIONS	ARTICLES OF CONFEDERATION	CONSTITUTION
Executive Branch	None	President of the United States
Judiciary	No federal court system. Judiciary exists only at state level.	Federal judiciary headed by a Supreme Court
Legislature	Unicameral legislature with equal representation for each state. Delegates to the Congress of the Confederation were appointed by the states.	Bicameral legislature consisting of Senate and House of Representatives. Each state is represented by two senators while apportionment in the House is based on each state's population. Senators are chosen by the state legislatures for six-year terms (changed to direct popular election in 1913) and members of the House by popular election.
Fiscal and economic powers	The national government is dependent upon the states to collect taxes. The states are free to coin their own money and print paper money. The states are free to sign commercial treaties with foreign governments.	Congress given the power to levy taxes, coin money, and regulate international and interstate commerce. States prohibited from coining money or entering into treaties with other nations.
Military	The national government is dependent upon state militias and cannot form an army during peacetime.	The national government is authorized to maintain an army and navy.
Legal supremacy	State constitutions and state law are supreme.	National Constitution and national law are supreme.
Constitutional amendment	Must be agreed upon by all states.	Must be agreed upon by three-fourths of the states

enhance the power of the new government. At the same time, to guard against "excessive democracy," the power of the House of Representatives was checked by the Senate, whose members were to be appointed by the states for long terms rather than elected directly by the people. The purpose of this provision, according to Alexander Hamilton, was to avoid "an unqualified complaisance to every sudden breeze of passion, or to every transient impulse which the people may receive."[11] Staggered terms of service in the Senate, moreover, were intended to make that body even more resistant to popular pressure. Since only one-third of the senators would be selected at any given time, the composition of the institution would be protected from changes in popular preferences transmitted by the state legislatures. This would prevent what James Madison called "mutability in the public councils arising from a rapid succession of new members."[12] Thus, the structure of the legislative branch was designed to contribute to governmental power, to promote popular consent for the new government, and at the same time to place limits on the popular political currents that many of the framers saw as a radical threat to the economic and social order.

The issues of power and consent were important throughout the Constitution. Section 8 of Article I specifically listed the powers of Congress, which include the authority to collect taxes, borrow money, regulate commerce, declare war, and maintain an army and navy. By granting Congress these powers, the framers indicated very clearly that they intended the new government to be far more

Article I of the Constitution establishes the structure of Congress and lists certain specific powers of Congress. The language of the Constitution reflects the framers' desire to create a government that was powerful enough to be effective but not so powerful that it would threaten individual liberty.

expressed powers specific powers granted by the Constitution to Congress (Article I, Section 8) and to the president (Article II)

elastic clause Article I, Section 8, of the Constitution (also known as the necessary and proper clause), which enumerates the powers of Congress and provides Congress with the authority to make all laws "necessary and proper" to carry them out

bicameral having a legislative assembly composed of two chambers or houses; distinguished from *unicameral*

influential than its predecessor. At the same time, by defining the new government's most important powers as belonging to Congress, the framers sought to promote popular acceptance of this critical change by reassuring citizens that their views would be fully represented whenever the government exercised its new powers.

As a further guarantee to the people that the new government would pose no threat to them, the Constitution implied that any powers not listed were not granted at all. This is the doctrine of **expressed powers**: the Constitution grants only those powers specifically expressed in its text. But the framers intended to create an active and powerful government, and so they also included the necessary and proper clause, sometimes known as the **elastic clause**, which signified that the expressed powers were meant to be a source of strength to the national government, not a limitation on it. In response to the charge that they intended to give the national government too much power, the framers included language in the Tenth Amendment stipulating that powers not specifically granted by the Constitution to the federal government were reserved to the states or to the people. As we will see in Chapter 3, the resulting tension between the elastic clause and the Tenth Amendment has been at the heart of constitutional struggles between federal and state powers.

The Executive Branch

The Articles of Confederation had not provided for an executive branch, and the framers viewed this omission as a source of weakness. Accordingly, the Constitution provided for the establishment of the presidency in Article II. As Alexander Hamilton commented, the presidential article aimed toward "energy in the Executive." It did so in an effort to overcome the natural tendency toward stalemate that was built into the **bicameral** legislature and into the separation of powers among the three branches. The Constitution afforded the president a measure of independence from the people and from the other branches of government—particularly the Congress.

In line with the framers' goal of increased power to the national government, the president was granted the unconditional power to accept ambassadors from other countries; this amounted to the power to "recognize" other countries. The president was also given the power to negotiate treaties, although their acceptance required the approval of the Senate by a two-thirds vote. The president was given the unconditional right to grant reprieves and pardons, except in cases of impeachment. And the president was provided with the power to appoint major departmental personnel, convene Congress in special session, and veto congressional enactments. (The veto power is formidable, but it is not absolute, since Congress can override it by a two-thirds vote.)

The framers hoped to create a presidency that would make the federal government rather than the states the agency capable of timely and decisive action to deal with public issues and problems—hence the "energy" that Hamilton hoped to impart to the executive branch.[13] At the same time, however, the framers sought to help the presidency withstand excessively democratic pressures by creating a system of indirect rather than direct election through a separate electoral college.

The Judicial Branch

In establishing the judicial branch in Article III, the Constitution reflected the framers' preoccupations with nationalizing governmental power and checking radical democratic impulses while preventing the new national government itself from interfering with liberty and property.

Under the provisions of Article III, the framers created a court that was literally a supreme court of the United States, and not merely the highest court of the national government alone. The most important expression of this intention was granting the Supreme Court the power to resolve any conflicts that might emerge between federal and state laws. In particular, the Supreme Court was given the right to determine whether a power was exclusive to the national government, concurrent with the states, or exclusive to the states. In addition, the Supreme Court was assigned jurisdiction over controversies between citizens of different states. The long-term significance of this provision was that as the country developed a national economy, it came to rely increasingly on the federal judiciary, rather than on the state courts, for the resolution of disputes.

Judges were given lifetime appointments to protect them from popular politics and from interference by the other branches. This, however, did not mean that the judiciary would remain totally impartial to political considerations or to the other branches, for the president was to appoint the judges, and the Senate to approve the appointments. Congress would also have the power to create inferior (lower) courts, change the jurisdiction of the federal courts, add or subtract federal judges, and even change the size of the Supreme Court.

No explicit mention is made in the Constitution of **judicial review**—the power of the courts to render the final decision when there is a conflict of interpretation of the Constitution or of laws between the courts and Congress, the courts and the executive branch, or the courts and the states. The Supreme Court eventually assumed the power of judicial review. Its assumption of this power, as we shall see in Chapter 15, was based not on the Constitution itself but on the politics of later decades and the membership of the Court.

judicial review the power of the courts to review and, if necessary, declare actions of the legislative and executive branches invalid or unconstitutional; the Supreme Court asserted this power in *Marbury v. Madison* (1803)

National Unity and Power

Various provisions in the Constitution addressed the framers' concern with national unity and power, including Article IV's provisions for comity (reciprocity) among states and among citizens of all states. Each state was prohibited from discriminating against the citizens of other states in favor of its own citizens. The Supreme Court was charged with deciding in each case whether a state had discriminated against goods or people from another state. The Constitution restricted the power of the states in favor of ensuring enough power to the national government to give the country a free-flowing national economy.

The framers' concern with national supremacy was also expressed in Article VI, in the **supremacy clause**, which provided that national laws and treaties "shall be the supreme Law of the Land." This meant that all laws made under the "Authority of the United States" would be superior to all laws adopted by any state or any other subdivision, and the states would be expected to respect all treaties made under that authority. The supremacy clause also bound the officials of all governments—state and local as well as federal—to take an oath of office to support the national Constitution. This meant that every action taken by the

supremacy clause Article VI of the Constitution, which states that laws passed by the national government and all treaties are the supreme law of the land and superior to all laws adopted by any state or any subdivision

Comparing Systems of Government

The U.S. Constitution is the world's oldest, but as other nations have developed constitutions in more recent years, they haven't always followed the American model. There is tremendous variation among systems of government around the world, even among democracies. For example, most constitutions provide for a unitary system of government, with most powers centralized at the national level, rather than federalism.

All of the countries listed below share power among three branches of government—an executive, a legislature, and a judiciary. However, the amount of power that each branch has varies. Note that in some countries, no one branch has a high degree of power. In the United States, the system of checks and balances keeps power distributed among the branches (see Figure 2.2). In Israel and the United Kingdom, which lack written constitutions, the branches of government have even less power than those in the United States.

The U.S. Constitution is also relatively short, creating a basic governmental framework but relying on experience and the courts to flesh out original document. It is important to note that as a constitution develops through usage and interpretation, its provisions may take new shape. For example, as defined in the U.S. Constitution (and shown here), presidential power seems low relative to the power of the Congress. Over time, however, presidential power has grown, as Congress has delegated significant powers, such as the war power, to the president, and as presidents have claimed additional powers. Other constitutions may provide more specific details, leaving less to interpretation, but the powers each branch has in practice may differ from the words of the constitution.

Country	Written Constitution?	Year in Effect	Length (in Words)	Federal or Unitary System	Strength of Executive	Strength of Legislature	Judicial Independence
Brazil	Yes	1988	51,368	Federal	High	Medium	Medium
France	Yes	1958	10,180	Unitary	High	Medium	Low
India	Yes	1950	146,385	Federal	Medium	Low	Medium
Israel	No	—	—	Unitary	Low	Low	Medium
Senegal	Yes	2001	10,866	Unitary	High	Medium	Low
South Africa	Yes	1997	43,062	Unitary	Medium	Medium	High
United States	Yes	1789	7,762	Federal	Low	Medium	Medium
United Kingdom	No	—	—	Unitary	Low	Low	Low

SOURCE: Comparative Constitutions Project, "Characteristics of National Constitutions," http://comparativeconstitutionsproject.org/ccp-rankings/ (accessed 2/21/14).

U.S. Congress would have to be applied within each state as though the action were in fact state law.

Amending the Constitution

The Constitution established procedures for its own revision in Article V. Its provisions are so difficult that Americans have successfully availed themselves of the amending process only 17 times since 1791, when the first 10 amendments were adopted. Many other amendments have been proposed in Congress, but fewer than 40 of them have even come close to fulfilling the Constitution's requirement of a two-thirds vote in Congress, and only a fraction have gotten anywhere near adoption by three-fourths of the states. Article V also provides that the Constitution can be amended by a constitutional convention. Occasionally, proponents of particular measures, such as a balanced-budget amendment, have called for a constitutional convention to consider their proposals. Whatever the purpose for which it was called, however, such a convention would presumably have the authority to revise America's entire system of government.

Ratifying the Constitution

The rules for the ratification of the Constitution were set forth in Article VII. Nine of the 13 states would have to ratify, or agree to, the terms in order for the Constitution to be formally adopted.

Constitutional Limits on the National Government's Power

Although the framers sought to create a powerful national government, they also wanted to guard against possible misuse of that power. To that end, the framers incorporated two key principles into the Constitution—federalism and the separation of powers. A third set of limitations, in the form of the Bill of Rights, was added to the Constitution to help secure its ratification when opponents of the document charged that it paid insufficient attention to citizens' rights.

The Separation of Powers No principle of politics was more widely shared at the time of the 1787 Founding than the principle that power must be used to balance power. As noted earlier, the French political theorist Baron de Montesquieu believed that this balance was an indispensable defense against tyranny. His writings, especially his major work, *The Spirit of the Laws,* "were taken as political gospel" at the Philadelphia Convention.[14] Although the principle of the separation of powers was not explicitly stated in the Constitution, the entire structure of the national government was built precisely on Article I, the legislature; Article II, the executive; and Article III, the judiciary (see Figure 2.1).

However, separation of powers is nothing but mere words on parchment without a method to maintain that separation. The method became known by the popular label "checks and balances" (see Figure 2.2). Each branch is given not only its own powers but also some power over the other two branches. Among the most familiar checks and balances are the president's veto as power over Congress and Congress's power over the president through its control of appointments to high executive posts and to the judiciary. Congress also has power over the president

for critical analysis

How does the separation of powers limit the national government's power? What are the consequences for the ability of the federal government to govern?

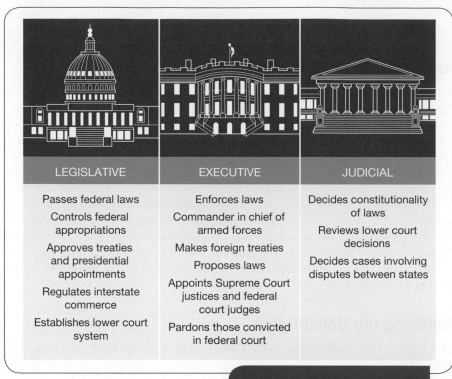

LEGISLATIVE	EXECUTIVE	JUDICIAL
Passes federal laws	Enforces laws	Decides constitutionality of laws
Controls federal appropriations	Commander in chief of armed forces	Reviews lower court decisions
Approves treaties and presidential appointments	Makes foreign treaties	Decides cases involving disputes between states
Regulates interstate commerce	Proposes laws	
Establishes lower court system	Appoints Supreme Court justices and federal court judges	
	Pardons those convicted in federal court	

FIGURE 2.1

The Separation of Powers

with its control of appropriations (the spending of government money) and (by the Senate) the right of approval of treaties. The judiciary was assumed to have the power of judicial review over the other two branches.

Another important feature of the separation of powers is the principle of giving each of the branches a distinctly different constituency. Theorists such as Montesquieu called this a "mixed regime," with the president chosen, indirectly, by electors; the House, by popular vote; the Senate (originally), by state legislatures; and the judiciary, by presidential appointment. By these means, the occupants of each branch would tend to develop very different outlooks on how to govern, different definitions of the public interest, and different alliances with private interests.

Federalism Compared with the confederation principle of the Articles of Confederation, federalism was a step toward greater centralization of power. The delegates agreed that they needed to place more power at the national level, without completely undermining the power of the state governments. Thus, they devised a system of two sovereigns—the states and the nation—with the hope that competition between the two would be an effective limitation on the power of both.

Executive over Legislative

Can veto acts of Congress

Can call Congress into a special session

Carries out, and thereby interprets, laws passed by Congress

Vice president casts tie-breaking vote in the Senate

Legislative over Judicial

Can change size of federal court system and the number of Supreme Court justices

Can propose constitutional amendments

Can reject Supreme Court nominees

Can impeach and remove federal judges

LEGISLATIVE

Legislative over Executive

Can override presidential veto

Can impeach and remove president

Can reject president's appointments and refuse to ratify treaties

Can conduct investigations into president's actions

Can refuse to pass laws or to provide funding that president requests

Judicial over Legislative

Can declare laws unconstitutional

Chief justice presides over Senate during hearing to impeach the president

JUDICIAL

Executive over Judicial

Nominates Supreme Court justices

Nominates federal judges

Can pardon those convicted in federal court

Can refuse to enforce Court decisions

Judicial over Executive

Can declare executive actions unconstitutional

Power to issue warrants

Chief justice presides over impeachment of president

EXECUTIVE

FIGURE 2.2

Checks and Balances

The Bill of Rights Late in the Philadelphia Convention, a motion was made to include a list of citizens' rights in the Constitution. After a brief debate in which hardly a word was said in its favor and only one speech was made against it, the motion was almost unanimously turned down. Most delegates sincerely believed that since the federal government was already limited to its expressed powers, further protection of citizens was not needed. The delegates argued that the states should adopt bills of rights because their greater powers needed greater limitations. But almost immediately after the Constitution was ratified, a movement arose to adopt a national bill of rights. This is why the Bill of Rights, adopted in 1791, comprises the first 10 amendments to the Constitution rather than being part of the body of it. (We will have a good deal more to say about the Bill of Rights in Chapter 4.)

● The Fight for Ratification

Present the controversies involved in the struggle for ratification

The first hurdle faced by the Constitution was ratification by state conventions of delegates elected by the people of each state. This struggle for ratification was carried out in 13 separate campaigns. Each involved different people, moved at a different pace, and was influenced by local and national considerations. Two sides faced off throughout the states, however, calling themselves **Federalists** and **Antifederalists** (see Table 2.2). The Federalists (who more accurately should have called themselves "Nationalists," but who took their name to appear to follow in the revolutionary tradition) supported the Constitution and preferred a strong national government. The Antifederalists opposed the Constitution and preferred a federal system of government that was decentralized; they took their name by default, in reaction to their better-organized opponents. The Federalists were united in their support of the Constitution, whereas the Antifederalists were divided over possible alternatives to the Constitution.

During the struggle over ratification of the Constitution, Americans argued about great political issues and principles. How much power should the national government be given? What safeguards would most likely prevent the abuse of power? What institutional arrangements could best ensure adequate representation for all Americans? Was tyranny of the many to be feared more than tyranny of the few?

Federalists those who favored a strong national government and supported the Constitution proposed at the American Constitutional Convention of 1787

Antifederalists those who favored strong state governments and a weak national government, and who were opponents of the Constitution proposed at the American Constitutional Convention of 1787

Federalists versus Antifederalists

During the ratification struggle, thousands of essays, speeches, pamphlets, and letters were presented in support of and in opposition to the proposed Constitution.

TABLE 2.2

Federalists versus Antifederalists

	FEDERALISTS	ANTIFEDERALISTS
Who were they?	Property owners, creditors, merchants	Small farmers, frontiersmen, debtors, shopkeepers, some state government officials
What did they believe?	Believed that elites were most fit to govern; feared "excessive democracy"	Believed that government should be closer to the people; feared concentration of power in hands of the elites
What system of government did they favor?	Favored strong national government; believed in "filtration" so that only elites would obtain governmental power	Favored retention of power by state governments and protection of individual rights
Who were their leaders?	Alexander Hamilton, James Madison, George Washington	Patrick Henry, George Mason, Elbridge Gerry, George Clinton

---

The best-known pieces supporting ratification were the 85 essays written between the fall of 1787 and the spring of 1788 under the name of "Publius," by Alexander Hamilton, James Madison, and John Jay. These **Federalist Papers**, as they are collectively known today, defended the principles of the Constitution and sought to dispel fears of a national authority. The Antifederalists published essays of their own, arguing that the new Constitution betrayed the Revolution and was a step toward monarchy. Among the best of the Antifederalist works were the essays, usually attributed to the New York State Supreme Court justice Robert Yates, that were written under the name of "Brutus" and published in the *New York Journal* at the same time the *Federalist Papers* appeared. The Antifederalist view was also ably presented in the pamphlets and letters written by a former delegate to the Continental Congress and future U.S. senator, Richard Henry Lee of Virginia, using the pen name "The Federal Farmer." These essays highlight the major differences of opinion between Federalists and Antifederalists. Federalists appealed to basic principles of government in support of their nationalist vision. Antifederalists cited equally fundamental precepts to support their vision of a looser confederacy of small republics.

Representation One major area of contention between the two sides was the question of representation. The Antifederalists asserted that representatives must be "a true picture of the people . . . [possessing] the knowledge of their circumstances and their wants."[15] This could be achieved, argued the Antifederalists, only in small, relatively homogeneous republics such as the existing states. In their view, the size and extent of the entire nation precluded the construction of a truly representative form of government. As Brutus put it, "Is it practicable for a country so large and so numerous . . . to elect a representation that will speak their sentiments? . . . It certainly is not."[16]

Federalists, for their part, saw no reason that representatives should be precisely like those they represented. In the Federalist view, one of the great advantages of representative government over direct democracy was precisely the possibility that the people would choose as their representatives individuals possessing ability, experience, and talent superior to their own. In Madison's words, rather than serving as a mirror or reflection of society, representatives must be "[those] who possess [the] most wisdom to discern, and [the] most virtue to pursue, the common good of the society."[17]

Tyranny of the Majority A second important issue dividing Federalists and Antifederalists was the threat of **tyranny**—unjust rule by the group in power. Both opponents and defenders of the Constitution frequently affirmed their fear of tyrannical rule. Each side, however, had a different view of the most likely source of tyranny and, hence, of the way in which to forestall the threat.

From the Antifederalist perspective, the great danger was the tendency of all governments—including republican governments—to become gradually more and more "aristocratic" in character, wherein the small number of individuals in positions of authority would use their stations to gain more and more power over the general citizenry. In essence, the few would use their power to tyrannize the many. For this reason, Antifederalists were sharply critical of those features of the Constitution that divorced governmental institutions from direct responsibility to the people—institutions such as the Senate, the executive, and the federal judiciary. The last, appointed for life, presented a particular threat: "I wonder if the

Federalist Papers a series of essays written by Alexander Hamilton, James Madison, and John Jay supporting ratification of the Constitution

for critical analysis

The Antifederalists worried that the size and diversity of the United States made democratic government impossible. In what ways might a large heterogeneous population limit democracy and enhance democracy?

tyranny oppressive government that employs cruel and unjust use of power and authority

"No taxation without representation" was a rallying cry of the American revolution. The new American government was certainly more representative than the former British rule. The debate over appropriate representation has never been fully resolved, however. Today, residents of Washington, D.C., pay federal income taxes but are not represented in the House or Senate. Presidents Bill Clinton and Barack Obama took a position on the issue by using these D.C. license plates on presidential vehicles.

limited government a principle of constitutional government; a government whose powers are defined and limited by a constitution

world ever saw . . . a court of justice invested with such immense powers, and yet placed in a situation so little responsible," protested Brutus.[18]

The Federalists, too, recognized the threat of tyranny, but they believed that the danger particularly associated with republican governments was not aristocracy but majority tyranny. The Federalists were concerned that a popular majority, "united and actuated by some common impulse of passion, or of interest, adverse to the rights of other citizens," would endeavor to "trample on the rules of justice."[19] From the Federalist perspective, it was precisely those features of the Constitution that the Antifederalists attacked as potential sources of tyranny that actually offered the best hope of averting the threat of oppression. The size and extent of the nation, for instance, was for the Federalists a bulwark against tyranny, because a majority would have difficulty uniting in a large and populous nation.

Governmental Power A third major difference between Federalists and Antifederalists was the issue of governmental power. Both opponents and proponents of the Constitution agreed on the principle of **limited government**. They differed, however, on the fundamentally important question of how to place limits on governmental action. Antifederalists favored limiting and enumerating the powers granted to the national government in relation both to the states and to the people at large. To them, the powers given the national government ought to be "confined to certain defined national objects."[20] Otherwise, the national government would "swallow up all the power of the state governments."[21] Antifederalists bitterly attacked the supremacy clause and the elastic clause of the Constitution as unlimited and dangerous grants of power to the national government.[22] Antifederalists also demanded that a bill of rights be added to the Constitution to place limits on the government's exercise of power over the citizenry.

Federalists favored the construction of a government with broad powers to defend the nation against foreign foes, guard against domestic strife and insurrection, promote commerce, and expand the nation's economy. Antifederalists shared some of these goals but still feared governmental power. In reply, Federalists such as Hamilton acknowledged that every power could be abused but argued that the way to prevent misuse of power was not by depriving the government of the powers needed to achieve national goals but by adopting the Constitution's internal checks and controls. As Madison put it, "the power surrendered by the people is first divided between two distinct governments (state and national), and then the portion allotted to each subdivided among distinct and separate departments. Hence, a double security arises to the rights of the people. The different governments will control each other, at the same time that each will be controlled by itself."[23] The Federalists' concern with avoiding unwarranted limits on governmental power led them to oppose a bill of rights, which they saw as nothing more than a set of unnecessary restrictions on the government.

The Federalists acknowledged that abuse of power remained a possibility but felt that the risk had to be taken because of the goals to be achieved. "The very idea of power included a possibility of doing harm," said the Federalist John Rutledge during the South Carolina ratification debates. "If the gentleman would show the power that could do no harm," Rutledge continued, "he would at once discover it to be a power that could do no good."[24] This aspect of the debate between the Federalists and the Antifederalists, perhaps more than any other, continues to reverberate through American politics. Should the nation limit the federal government's power to tax and spend? Should Congress limit the capacity of federal agencies to issue new regulations? Should the government endeavor to create new rights for minorities, the disabled, and others? Though the details have changed, these are the same great questions that have been debated since the Founding.

Reflections on the Founding

The final product of the Constitutional Convention would have to be considered an extraordinary victory for the groups that had most forcefully called for the creation of a new system of government to replace the Articles of Confederation. Antifederalist criticisms did force the Constitution's proponents to accept the addition of a bill

of rights designed to limit the powers of the national government. In general, however, it was the Federalist vision of America that triumphed. The Constitution adopted in 1789 created the framework for a powerful national government that for more than 200 years has defended the nation's interests, promoted its commerce, and maintained national unity. In one notable instance, the national government fought and won a bloody war to prevent the nation from breaking apart. And despite this powerful government, the system of internal checks and balances has functioned reasonably well, as the Federalists predicted, to prevent the national government from tyrannizing its citizens.

Of course, the groups whose interests were served by the Constitution in 1789, mainly the merchants and planters, are not the same groups that benefit from the Constitution's provisions today. Once incorporated into law, political principles often take on lives of their own and have consequences that were never anticipated by their original champions. Indeed, many of the groups that benefit from constitutional provisions today did not even exist in 1789. Who would have thought that the principle of free speech would influence the transmission of data on the Internet? Who would have predicted that commercial interests that once sought a powerful government might come, two centuries later, to denounce governmental activism as "socialism"? Perhaps one secret of the Constitution's longevity is that it did not confer permanent advantage on any one set of economic or social forces.

Although they were defeated in 1789, the Antifederalists present us with an important picture of a road not taken and of an America that might have been. Would Americans in the eighteenth century have been worse off if they had been governed by a confederacy of small republics linked by a national administration with severely limited powers? Were the Antifederalists correct in predicting that a

Although there was much acrimonious debate and necessary compromise as the new Constitution was written, this print suggests that farmers, artisans, and "gentlemen" alike supported it after its ratification. The national motto "e pluribus unum" reinforces this message, Latin for "out of many, one."

for critical analysis

Do you agree with Rutledge that a power that can do no harm can also do no good? How can a system of government maximize the ability of government to do good while minimizing the possibility of harm?

government given great power in the hope that it might do good would, through "insensible progress," inevitably turn to evil purposes? Two hundred years of government under the federal Constitution are not necessarily enough to answer these questions definitively.

The Citizen's Role and the Changing Constitution

Trace how the Constitution has changed over time through the amendment process

The Constitution has endured for more than two centuries as the framework of government. But it has not gone unchanged. Without change, the Constitution might have become merely a sacred text, stored under glass.

The Constitution assigns citizens an indirect but important role in this process of change. Figure 2.3 outlines the ways in which the Constitution might be amended and all of these involve citizens through the election of members of Congress and state legislatures or, hypothetically, through the election of delegates to national and state constitutional conventions. Thus far, all the amendments to the U.S. Constitution have been first approved by the Congress and then by the state legislatures. No national convention has been called since the Philadelphia Convention of 1787 and Congress has submitted all proposed amendments to the state legislatures for ratification. Amending the Constitution may be difficult, but it is ultimately controlled by institutions elected by the people. Of course, the courts also modify the Constitution and adapt it to changing circumstances. Federal judges are not elected, but they are appointed by the president with the advice and consent of the Senate, and judicial appointments have become an important issue in presidential elections. Many voters are aware that their presidential ballots may also help to shape the character of the Supreme Court and other federal courts.

Amendments: Many Are Called; Few Are Chosen

The inevitable need for change was recognized by the framers of the Constitution, and provisions for **amendment** were incorporated into Article V. Four methods of amendment are described:

amendment a change added to a bill, law, or constitution

1. Passage in House and Senate by two-thirds vote; then ratification by majority vote of the legislatures of three-fourths (now 38) of the states.

2. Passage in House and Senate by two-thirds vote; then ratification by conventions called for the purpose in three-fourths of the states.

3. Passage in a national convention called for by Congress in response to petitions by two-thirds of the states; ratification by majority vote of the legislatures of three-fourths of the states.

4. Passage in a national convention (as in method 3); then ratification by conventions called for the purpose in three-fourths of the states.

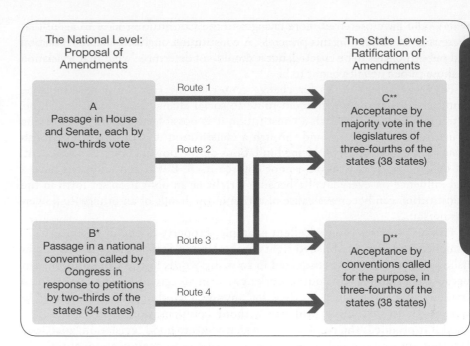

The National Level:
Proposal of
Amendments

The State Level:
Ratification of
Amendments

A
Passage in House
and Senate, each by
two-thirds vote

Route 1

Route 2

C**
Acceptance by
majority vote in the
legislatures of
three-fourths of the
states (38 states)

B*
Passage in a national
convention called by
Congress in
response to petitions
by two-thirds of the
states (34 states)

Route 3

Route 4

D**
Acceptance by
conventions called
for the purpose, in
three-fourths of the
states (38 states)

FIGURE 2.3

Four Ways the Constitution Can Be Amended

*This method of proposal has never been employed. Thus amendment routes 3 and 4 have never been attempted.

**For each amendment proposal, Congress has the power to choose the method of ratification, the time limit for consideration by the states, and other conditions of ratification. The movement to repeal Prohibition in the Twenty-First Amendment was the only occasion in which route 2 was used successfully.

Figure 2.3 illustrates each of these possible methods. Since no amendment has ever been proposed by national convention, however, methods 3 and 4 have never been employed. And method 2 has been employed only once (the Twenty-First Amendment, which repealed the Eighteenth Amendment, or Prohibition). Thus, method 1 has been used for all the others.

The Constitution has proved to be extremely difficult to amend. In the history of efforts to amend it, the most appropriate characterization is "many are called; few are chosen." Since 1789, more than 11,000 amendments have been formally offered in Congress. Of these, Congress officially proposed only 29, and 27 of these were eventually ratified by the states. Two of these—Prohibition and its repeal—cancel each other out, so that for all practical purposes, only 25 amendments have been added to the Constitution since 1791.

Which Were Chosen? An Analysis of the Twenty-Seven

There is more to the amending difficulties than the politics of campaigning and voting. It would appear that only a limited number of changes can actually be made to the Constitution. Most efforts to amend the Constitution have failed because they were simply attempts to use the Constitution as an alternative to legislation for dealing directly with a specific public problem.

The 25 successful amendments, on the other hand, are concerned with the structure or composition of government (see Table 2.3). This is consistent with the dictionary, which defines *constitution* as the makeup or composition of something. And it is consistent with the concept of a constitution as "higher law," because the whole point and purpose of a higher law is to establish a framework within which government and the process of making ordinary law can take place. Even those

for critical analysis

It is very difficult to amend the Constitution. Should the amendment process be made easier? Would the American system of government be more democratic if the Constitution could be revised more easily?

who would have preferred more changes to the Constitution have to agree that there is great wisdom in this principle. A constitution ought to enable legislation and public policies to be enacted, but it should not determine what that legislation or those public policies ought to be.

For those whose hopes for change center on the Constitution, it must be emphasized that the amendment route to social change is, and always will be, extremely limited. Through a constitution it is possible to establish a working structure of government, and through a constitution it is possible to establish basic rights of citizens by placing limitations on the powers of that government. Of course, the Constitution cannot enforce itself. But it can and does have a real influence on everyday life because a right or an obligation set forth in the Constitution can become a cause of action in the hands of an otherwise power-less person.

Private property is an excellent example. Property is one of the most fundamental and well-established rights in the United States; but it is well established not because it is recognized in so many words in the Constitution, but because legislatures and courts, working within an agreed-upon constitutional framework, have made it a crime for anyone, including the government, to trespass or to take away property without compensation. A constitution is good if it produces the cause of action that leads to good legislation, good case law, and appropriate police behavior. A constitution cannot eliminate power. But its principles can be a citizen's dependable defense against the abuse of power.

The Equal Rights Amendment (ERA) is an example of an amendment that almost succeeded. The proposed amendment guaranteed equality under the law for women and made gender discrimination illegal. The ERA was ratified by 35 state legislatures but failed to get the 38 necessary to equal three-fourths of the states.

TABLE 2.3

Amendments to the Constitution

AMENDMENT	PURPOSE	YEAR PROPOSED	YEAR ADOPTED
I	*Limits on Congress:* Congress is not to make any law establishing a religion or abridging speech, press, assembly, or petition freedoms.	1789	1791
II, III, IV	*Limits on Executive:* The executive branch is not to infringe on the right of people to keep arms (II), is not arbitrarily to take houses for a militia (III), and is not to engage in the search or seizure of evidence without a court warrant swearing to belief in the probable existence of a crime (IV).	1789	1791
V, VI, VII, VIII	*Limits on Courts:* The courts are not to hold trials for serious offenses without provision for a grand jury (V), a petit (trial) jury (VII), a speedy trial (VI), presentation of charges (VI), confrontation of hostile witnesses (VI), immunity from testimony against oneself (V), and immunity from more than one trial for the same offense (V). Neither bail nor punishment can be excessive (VIII), and no property can be taken without just compensation (V).	1789	1791
IX, X	*Limits on National Government:* All rights not enumerated are reserved to the states or the people.	1789	1791
XI	Limited jurisdiction of federal courts over suits involving the states.	1794	1795
XII	Provided separate ballot for vice president in the electoral college.	1803	1804
XIII	Eliminated slavery and eliminated the right of states to allow property in persons.	1865	1865
XIV	(Part 1) Provided a national definition of citizenship.**	1866	1868
XIV	(Part 2) Applied due process of Bill of Rights to the states.	1866	1868
XV	Extended voting rights to all races.	1869	1870
XVI	Established national power to tax incomes.	1909	1913
XVII†	Provided direct election of senators.	1912	1913
XIX	Extended voting rights to women.	1919	1920
XX	Eliminated "lame duck" session of Congress.	1932	1933
XXII	Limited presidential term.	1947	1951
XXIII	Extended voting rights to residents of the District of Columbia.	1960	1961
XXIV	Extended voting rights to all classes by abolition of poll taxes.	1962	1964
XXV	Provided presidential succession in case of disability.	1965	1967
XXVI	Extended voting rights to citizens ages 18 and over.	1971	1971††
XXVII	Limited Congress's power to raise its own salary.	1789	1992

*These amendments also impose limits on the law-enforcement powers of federal, state, and local executive branches.

**In defining *citizenship*, the Fourteenth Amendment actually provided the constitutional basis for expanding the electorate to include all races, women, and residents of the District of Columbia. Only the "eighteen-year-olds' amendment" should have been necessary, since it changed the definition of citizenship. The fact that additional amendments were required following the Fourteenth suggests that voting is not considered an inherent right of U.S. citizenship. Instead, it is viewed as a privilege.

†The Eighteenth Amendment, ratified in 1919, outlawed the sale and transportation of liquor. It was repealed by the Twenty-First Amendment, ratified in 1933.

††The Twenty-Sixth Amendment holds the record for speed of adoption. It was proposed on March 23, 1971, and adopted on July 5, 1971.

The Twenty-Sixth Amendment holds the record for speed of adoption. The amendment addressed an issue of representation, when 18-, 19-, and 20-year-olds were drafted to serve in the military during the Vietnam War but could not vote for Congress or the president who enacted the policies that affected their lives and deaths.

The Supreme Court and Constitutional Amendment

Although the process of constitutional amendment outlined in Article V has seldom been used successfully, another form of constitutional revision is constantly at work in the United States. This is, of course, judicial interpretation of the Constitution and its amendments by the Supreme Court as it reviews cases. In some instances, the Court may give concrete definition to abstract constitutional principles. For example, the Constitution's Fifth Amendment asserts in general terms that individuals accused of crimes are entitled to procedural rights. The Supreme Court, in a series of decisions, established principles giving effect to those rights. Every viewer of television crime programs knows that, upon being arrested, individuals must receive Miranda warnings informing them of their right to refuse to speak and their right to counsel. These required warnings are the result of a 1966 Supreme Court decision interpreting the meaning and implications of the Fifth Amendment.

In some instances, the Supreme Court does more than interpret or flesh out constitutional provisions: it seems to modify or augment the text itself. For example, in decisions in 1965 and 1973 on birth control and abortion, respectively, the Court said that Americans were constitutionally entitled to a right of privacy. The Constitution does not explicitly mention the right to privacy; it is derived from the Fourteenth Amendment and several provisions in the Bill of Rights.

Of course, much of the Supreme Court's power is itself based on constitutional interpretation rather than on the text of the document. The Supreme Court claims the power of judicial review—the power to render the final decision when there is a conflict of interpretations of the Constitution or federal law among the courts, Congress, the executive branch, or the states. Nowhere does the Constitution mention this power. In a number of early cases, however, the Supreme Court asserted that the Constitution gave it the power of judicial review, and this interpretation has prevailed, enhancing the Court's power. Some commentators denounce constitutional amendment by the judiciary and demand that judges limit themselves to "strict construction" of the Constitution, adhering closely to the words of the document's text. Proponents of the idea of the *living Constitution*, on the other hand, assert that the Constitution is subject to change as conditions warrant, and they argue that the judiciary is the institution best qualified to adjust the Constitution's principles to new problems and times. Advocates of strict construction and champions of the living Constitution disagree about the desirability of constitutional amendment by the courts, but both acknowledge its reality.

The Constitution
and Your Future

The Constitution's framers placed individual liberty ahead of all other political values, a concern that led many of the framers to distrust both democracy and equality. They feared that democracy could degenerate into a majority tyranny in which the populace, perhaps led by rabble-rousing demagogues, trampled on liberty. As for equality, the framers were products of their time and place; our contemporary ideas of racial and gender equality would have been foreign to them. The framers were concerned primarily with another manifestation of equality: they feared that those without property or position might be driven by what some called a "leveling spirit" to infringe on liberty in the name of greater economic or social equality. Indeed, the framers believed that this leveling spirit was most likely to produce demagoguery and majority tyranny. As a result, the basic structure of the Constitution—separated powers, internal checks and balances, and federalism—was designed to safeguard liberty, and the Bill of Rights created further safeguards for liberty. At the same time, however, many of the Constitution's other key provisions, such as indirect election of senators and the president, and the appointment of judges for life, were designed to limit democracy and, hence, the threat of majority tyranny.

By championing liberty, however, the framers virtually guaranteed that democracy and even a measure of equality would sooner or later evolve in the United States. Liberty promotes the growth of political activity and the expansion of political participation as in James Madison's famous phrase, "Liberty is to faction as air is to fire."[25] Where they have liberty, more and more people, groups, and interests will almost inevitably engage in politics and gradually overcome whatever restrictions might have been placed on participation. Indeed, this is precisely what happened in the early years of the American republic. During the Jeffersonian period, political parties formed. During the Jacksonian period, many state suffrage restrictions were removed and popular participation greatly expanded. Over time, liberty is conducive to democracy.

Liberty is sometimes confused with the absence of government. The framers of the Constitution, though, saw liberty as a purpose or goal of government, not the result of governmental absence. The government they created was designed to "secure the Blessings of Liberty" by maintaining order, keeping the peace, and intervening where necessary to allow citizens to conduct their affairs in safety and freedom. Every generation of Americans ponders and reconsiders the work of the men who framed the Constitution.

Unfortunately, liberty can never be taken for granted. It is the duty of each generation to guard its liberty from that which may threaten it. Today, for example, expanding programs of government surveillance may pose a threat to political liberty, as government agencies appear to be recording Americans' emails and phone conversations at an unprecedented level. But our history tells us that citizens' privacy is a prerequisite for effective popular political action, as those who disagree with the groups in power need privacy to plan, organize, and mobilize, lest their plans be anticipated and disrupted. Even in the mundane realm of partisan politics, the efforts of the party not in power can certainly be compromised if the government becomes privy to its plans. For instance, in the not-so-distant past, the administration of Republican Richard Nixon thought its surveillance activities of its opposition could help it to undermine Democratic campaign plans in 1972.

Known political dissidents, moreover, always face some risk of official reprisal. Accordingly, at least some citizens may refrain from acting on their political beliefs for fear that they will draw attention to themselves and become targets for tax audits or other

for critical analysis

What are the U.S. Constitution's greatest strengths? What are its most pronounced weaknesses? If you were revising the Constitution today, what would you change? Why?

Dr. Martin Luther King, Jr., was a leader of a movement embracing nonviolent opposition to racist public policies. While today most everyone would agree that this is a laudable goal, his activities earned him the suspicions and surveillance of the FBI.

government efforts to find evidence of criminality, cupidity, or other misconduct that can be used against them. This is a realistic concern given a recent past in which agents of the FBI, seeking to compile damaging information on civil rights leader Dr. Martin Luther King, Jr., secretly taped King's phone calls and meetings. More recently, in an echo of Richard Nixon's demand that the Internal Revenue Service (IRS) investigate individuals on his "enemies list," so-called Tea Party groups and other conservative organizations claimed that they were the targets of special scrutiny from the IRS. Privacy for political activities is, like the secret ballot, an important element of political freedom.

This notion of the relationship between privacy and freedom of political expression is at the heart of the Constitution's Fourth Amendment, prohibiting unreasonable searches. While many currently see the Fourth Amendment as related to evidence gathering in mundane criminal cases, the framers were well aware of the fact that government intrusions into private homes were often aimed at identifying papers, manuscripts, and books that might point to nascent efforts to foment political discontent.[26] Individuals whose private papers evinced dissenting political opinions might then be prosecuted for the crime of seditious libel, that is, criticism of Crown officials, to forestall any public expressions of their views. As Justice Brennan wrote for a unanimous court in the 1961 case of *Marcus v. Search Warrant*, "The Bill of Rights was fashioned against the background of knowledge that unrestricted power of search and seizure could also be an instrument for stifling liberty of expression."[27] In her dissent in a recent case, Justice Ginsburg called attention to this original purpose and meaning of the Fourth Amendment as an instrument for protecting liberty of political expression. Thus, as you continue to read this book, ask yourself what you can do to secure the framers' sacrifices and vision. The question of what form of government oversight we ought to tolerate changes over time as technological advances create new opportunities to collaborate with like-minded political actors as well as new opportunities for surveillance. It is the nature of democracy that the party in power today may not be in power tomorrow, thus privacy and liberty in political expression remain a concern for everyone.

plugin

Inform

Watch the video "The Constitution, the Articles, and Federalism: Crash Course U.S. History #8" on YouTube, then read the Articles of Confederation and the Constitution (both found in the Appendix to this book) to see the differences for yourself.

Express

Imagine that you are a delegate to the Constitutional Convention. What would you include in (or exclude from) the document, and why?

Connect

Choose a proposed constitutional amendment that you support (find a list at USConstitution.net) then search online to find the websites of interest groups working to pass that amendment.

Act

Search for "constitutional amendment" on Congress.gov to see what amendments have recently been proposed in Congress, and contact your representatives (via the "Members" tab) to let them know your views on a proposed amendment.

studyguide

The First Founding: Interests and Conflicts

Describe the events that led to the Declaration of Independence and the Articles of Confederation (pp. 41–45)

Dissatisfaction with British tax policies and discontent over retaliatory acts of political repression radicalized many colonists during the 1770s to push for independence from British rule. By identifying widely shared grievances, goals, and principles, the Declaration of Independence helped forge a sense of national unity among diverse elements in colonial society. The first written constitution of the United States, the Articles of Confederation, left most governmental powers in the hands of the states and placed strong limits on the powers of the national government.

Key Terms

Articles of Confederation (p. 44)

confederation (p. 44)

Practice Quiz

1. How did the British attempt to raise revenue in the North American colonies?
   a) income tax
   b) taxes on commerce
   c) expropriation and government sale of land
   d) government asset sales
   e) requests for voluntary donations

2. In their fight against British taxes, such as the Stamp Act and the Sugar Act of 1764, New England merchants allied with which of the following groups?
   a) artisans, southern planters, and laborers
   b) southern planters only
   c) laborers only
   d) artisans only
   e) southern planters and laborers only

3. The first governing document in the United States was
   a) the Declaration of Independence.
   b) the Articles of Confederation.
   c) the Constitution.
   d) the Bill of Rights.
   e) the Virginia Plan.

4. Where was the execution of laws conducted under the Articles of Confederation?
   a) the presidency
   b) the Congress
   c) the states
   d) the federal bureaucracy
   e) the federal judiciary

The Second Founding: From Compromise to Constitution

Analyze the reasons for the failure of the Articles of Confederation (pp. 45–51)

International weakness, domestic economic problems, and the national government's inability to act decisively in response to Shays's Rebellion led to a constitutional convention to replace the Articles of Confederation. The convention's delegates were deeply divided on the issues of representation in the national government and slavery. The Great Compromise and the Three-Fifths Compromise temporarily reconciled these divisions and allowed the Founders to move forward with creating a new constitutional framework for the United States.

Key Terms

Virginia Plan (p. 47)

New Jersey Plan (p. 48)

Great Compromise (p. 48)

Three-Fifths Compromise (p. 50)

Practice Quiz

5. Which of the following was *not* a reason that the Articles of Confederation seemed inadequate?
   a) the lack of a single voice in international affairs
   b) weakness of the national government
   c) persistent economic turmoil among states
   d) the power of radical forces in several states
   e) the power of radical forces in Congress

6. Which event led directly to the Constitutional Convention by providing evidence that the government created under the Articles of Confederation was unable to act decisively in times of national crisis?
   a) the Boston Tea Party
   b) the Boston Massacre
   c) Shays's Rebellion
   d) the Annapolis Convention
   e) the War of 1812

7. The draft constitution that was introduced at the start of the Constitutional Convention was authored by Edmund Randolph but showed the strong influence of
   a) William Patterson.
   b) Benjamin Franklin.
   c) James Madison.
   d) George Clinton.
   e) Thomas Jefferson.

8. Which state's proposal embodied a principle of representing states in the Congress according to their size and wealth?
   a) New Jersey
   b) Maryland
   c) Rhode Island
   d) Virginia
   e) Connecticut

9. The agreement reached at the Constitutional Convention that determined how slaves would be counted for the purposes of taxation and representation in the House of Representatives was called the
   a) Connecticut Compromise.
   b) Three-Fifths Compromise.
   c) Great Compromise.
   d) Virginia Plan.
   e) New Jersey Plan.

The Constitution

Explain how the Constitution attempted to improve America's governance, and outline the major institutions established by the Constitution (pp. 51–59)

The Founders sought to create a stronger national government than existed under the Articles of Confederation. In particular, they hoped that the new constitution would promote commerce, protect private property, and avoid the perils of "excessive democracy." The Founders' concern with national power was expressed most clearly in the supremacy clause of Article VI. The national government, however, did not have unlimited power, and there were significant limits placed on it through the separation of powers, federalism, and the Bill of Rights.

Key Terms

checks and balances (p. 52)

electoral college (p. 52)

Bill of Rights (p.52)

separation of powers (p. 52)

federalism (p. 52)

expressed powers (p. 54)

elastic clause (p. 54)

bicameral (p. 54)

judicial review (p. 55)

supremacy clause (p. 55)

Practice Quiz

10. Which mechanism was instituted in the Congress to guard against "excessive democracy"?
    a) bicameralism
    b) staggered terms in office
    c) checks and balances
    d) selection of senators by state legislatures
    e) all of the above

11. Which of the following best describes the Supreme Court as understood by the Founders?
    a) the principle check on presidential power
    b) arbiter of disputes within the Congress
    c) the body that would choose the president
    d) a figurehead commission of elders
    e) a supreme court of the nation and its states

12. How is the goal of the separation of powers actually carried out?
    a) enforcement by the Supreme Court
    b) the system of checks and balances
    c) the supremacy clause
    d) the Bill of Rights
    e) Article I

The Fight for Ratification

Before the Constitution could go into effect, it had to be ratified by 9 of the 13 states. In the debate over ratification, the Federalists supported the Constitution and the Antifederalists opposed it. The three major areas of disagreement between Federalists and Antifederalists were the question of representation, the threat of tyranny of the majority, and the extent of government power.

Key Terms

Federalists (p. 60)

Antifederalists (p. 60)

Federalist Papers (p. 61)

tyranny (p. 61)

limited government (p. 62)

Practice Quiz

13. Which of the following were the Antifederalists most concerned with?
    a) interstate commerce
    b) the protection of property
    c) the distinction between principles and interests
    d) abolishing slavery
    e) the potential for tyranny in the central government

The Citizen's Role and the Changing Constitution

The amendment process outlined in Article V of the Constitution creates significant hurdles to change that have rarely been cleared in American history. Attempts to solve specific social problems through the use of a constitutional amendment have been particularly unsuccessful at winning the support required to change the country's basic governing document. The Supreme Court, however, has provided new meaning and new substance to the Constitution on countless occasions during the last 200 years through their decisions on important cases.

Key Term

amendment (p. 64)

Practice Quiz

14. Which of the following best describes the process of amending the Constitution?
    a) It is difficult and has rarely been used successfully to address specific public problems.
    b) It is difficult and has frequently been used successfully to address specific public problems.
    c) It is easy but has rarely been used successfully to address specific public problems.
    d) It is easy and has frequently been used successfully to address specific public problems.
    e) It is easy, but it has never been used for any purpose.

For Further Reading

Ackerman, Erin, and Benjamin Ginsberg. *A Guide to the United States Constitution,* 2nd ed. New York: W. W. Norton, 2011.

Amar, Akhil Reed. *America's Constitution: A Biography.* New York: Random House, 2006.

Beard, Charles. *An Economic Interpretation of the Constitution of the United States.* New York: Macmillan, 1913.

Beeman, Richard. *Plain, Honest Men: The Making of the American Constitution.* New York: Random House, 2010.

Breyer, Stephen G. *Active Liberty: Interpreting Our Democratic Constitution.* New York: Knopf, 2005.

Dahl, Robert A. *How Democratic Is the American Constitution?* 2nd ed. New Haven, CT: Yale University Press, 2002.

Ellis, Joseph. *American Creation: Triumphs and Tragedies at the Founding of the Republic.* New York: Knopf, 2007.

Fiske, John. *The American Revolution.* Amazon Digital Services, 2012.

Hamilton, Alexander, James Madison, and John Jay. *The Federalist Papers.* Edited by Isaac Kramnick. New York: Viking, 1987.

Holton, Woody. *Unruly Americans and the Origins of the Constitution.* New York: Hill and Wang, 2007.

Jensen, Merrill. *The Articles of Confederation.* Madison: University of Wisconsin Press, 1963.

Keller, Morton. *America's Three Regimes.* New York: Oxford University Press, 2009.

Lewis, Anthony. *Freedom for the Thought That We Hate: A Biography of the First Amendment.* New York: Basic Books, 2008.

Main, Jackson Turner. *The Social Structure of Revolutionary America.* Princeton, NJ: Princeton University Press, 1965.

Rossiter, Clinton. *1787: Grand Convention.* New York: Macmillan, 1966.

Storing, Herbert, ed. *The Complete Anti-Federalist.* 7 vols. Chicago: University of Chicago Press, 1981.

Recommended Websites

The American Civil Liberties Union
www.aclu.org
> The ACLU is committed to protecting, for all individuals, the freedoms found in the Bill of Rights. This sometimes controversial organization constantly monitors the government for violations of liberty and encourages its members to take political action.

Archiving Early America
www.earlyamerica.com
> Revolutionary Americans were motivated by a variety of competing ideals, principles, and interests. Visit this website to learn more about the early colonists and the founding of our government.

Constitution Finder
http://confinder.richmond.edu
> Is the American Constitution a model for the world? Explore the constitutions of many different nations and see what elements of the U.S. Constitution can be found in the governing documents of other countries.

Find Law
http://findlaw.com/casecode/state.html
> The Find Law website provides all 50 states' constitutions. Click on your state and try to identify such constitutional principles as bicameralism, staggered terms of office, checks and balances, and separation of powers.

The National Archives
www.archives.gov
> This government site provides information about and actual digital images of such founding documents as the Declaration of Independence, the U.S. Constitution, and the Bill of Rights.

The National Constitution Center
www.constitutioncenter.org
> The National Constitution Center in Philadelphia maintains a website that provides in-depth instructional analysis of the U.S. Constitution. Check out the Interactive Constitution function and follow the document from its Preamble through the Twenty-Seventh Amendment.

Oyez
www.oyez.org
> This website for U.S. Supreme Court media has an excellent search engine for finding information on Supreme Court cases. See how the Court has interpreted the Constitution over time.

The PBS Liberty! Series
www.pbs.org/ktca/liberty
> The PBS *Liberty!* series on the American Revolution offers an in-depth look at the Revolutionary War and includes information on historical events such as the Constitutional Convention.

The Supreme Court of the United States
www.supremecourtus.gov
> The website for the U.S. Supreme Court provides information on recent decisions. Take a moment to read some oral arguments, briefs, or opinions.

Federalism is at the center of a national debate over marijuana policy: while marijuana remains illegal under federal law, some states permit marijuana for medicinal or recreational use. At the heart of federalism lies the question, what level of government should make policy in a given issue area?

Federalism

3

WHAT GOVERNMENT DOES AND WHY IT MATTERS In 1996, voters in California approved a new law legalizing the cultivation, possession, and use of marijuana for medical purposes. As the idea spread, other states followed suit. By 2014, 23 states and the District of Columbia had approved medical marijuana. In these states, medical clinics selling marijuana have popped up in many cities. With a doctor's prescription, patients can purchase marijuana for personal use. In 2012, two states went even further. Voters in Washington state and Colorado approved measures to legalize the recreational use of marijuana. The laws gave adults over the age of 21 the right to buy limited amounts of marijuana. The following year, Colorado voters agreed to place hefty tax on marijuana sales. And in the 2014 elections, ballot measures in Alaska, Oregon, and Washington, D.C., also legalized recreational use of marijuana.

States routinely devise their own laws on a wide variety of topics but the marijuana laws passed over the past two decades are extraordinary because marijuana remains a controlled substance under federal law, making it illegal to grow, sell, or possess marijuana for medical or recreational purposes. States began to legalize marijuana in defiance of clear federal prohibitions.

The federal response to the states has shifted over time. As state laws began to loosen restrictions on marijuana, the federal government at first sought to assert its authority. The federal Drug Enforcement Agency staged raids on marijuana clinics and even searched individual homes to enforce the federal law prohibiting marijuana. In 2005, the Supreme Court ruled that these federal actions were constitutional. The Court affirmed the federal government's right to prohibit marijuana even as a growing number of state laws moved in the opposite direction. By 2013, however, the Justice Department, bowing to the states, announced a change of course. The department stated that it would not challenge state laws so long as the states maintained a close watch over their marijuana markets. Instead the federal government would focus its enforcement efforts on specific issues, including trafficking by gangs, sales to minors, and selling across state lines. Washington's governor, Jay Inslee, issued a joint statement with the state's attorney general noting that the decision "reflects a balanced approach by the federal government that respects the states' interests in implementing these laws and recognizes the federal government's role in fighting illegal drugs and criminal activity."[1]

The debates about marijuana policy engage one of the oldest questions in American government: What is the responsibility of the federal government and what is the responsibility of the states? When should there be uniformity across the states and when is it better to let states adopt their own laws based on the needs and desires of their population, which may result in a diverse set of laws across the country? Which approach serves the common good?

The United States is a federal system, in which the national government shares power with lower levels of government. Throughout American history, lawmakers, politicians, and citizens have wrestled with questions about how responsibilities should be allocated across the different levels of government. Some responsibilities, such as international relations, clearly lie with the federal government. Others, such as divorce laws, are controlled by state governments. In fact, most of the rules and regulations that Americans face in their daily lives are set by state and local governments. However, many government responsibilities are shared in American federalism and require cooperation among local, state, and federal governments. The debate about "who should do what" remains one of the most important discussions in American politics.

chaptergoals

- Describe what the Constitution says about the powers of the national government and of the states (pp. 79–85)

- Consider how the relationship between the federal and state governments has changed over time (pp. 85–91)

- Trace developments in the federal framework leading to a stronger national government (pp. 92–99)

- Analyze the developments in the federal framework since the 1970s (pp. 99–107)

● Federalism in the Constitution

Describe what the Constitution says about the powers of the national government and of the states

The Constitution has had its most fundamental influence on American life through **federalism**. Federalism can be defined as the division of powers and functions between the national government and the state governments. Governments can organize power in a variety of ways. One of the most important distinctions is between unitary and federal governments. In a **unitary system**, the central government makes the important decisions, and lower levels of government have little independent power. In such systems, lower levels of government primarily implement decisions made by the central government. In France, for example, the central government was once so involved in the smallest details of local activity that the minister of education boasted that by looking at his watch he could tell what all French schoolchildren were learning at that moment because the central government set the school curriculum. In a federal system, by contrast, the central government shares power or functions with lower levels of government, such as regions or states. Nations with diverse ethnic or language groupings, such as Switzerland and Canada, are most likely to have federal arrangements. In federal systems, lower levels of government often have significant independent power to set policy in some areas, such as education and social programs, and to impose taxes. Yet the specific ways in which power is shared vary greatly: no two federal systems are exactly the same.

The United States was the first nation to adopt federalism as its governing framework. With federalism, the framers sought to limit the national government by creating a second layer of state governments. By granting a few "expressed powers" to the national government and reserving all the rest to the states, the original Constitution recognized two sovereigns: state governments and the federal government. Table 3.1, which you first saw in Chapter 1, now indicates which level of government has responsibility for the actions that affect our everyday lives.

The Powers of the National Government

As we saw in Chapter 2, the **expressed powers** granted to the national government are found in Article I, Section 8, of the Constitution. These 17 powers include the power to collect taxes, coin money, declare war, and regulate commerce. Article I, Section 8, also contains another important source of power for the national government: the **implied powers** that enable Congress "to make all Laws which shall be necessary and proper for carrying into Execution the foregoing Powers." Not until several decades after the Founding did the Supreme Court allow Congress to exercise the power granted in this **necessary and proper clause**, but as we shall see later in this chapter, this doctrine allowed the national government to expand considerably the scope of its authority, although the process was a slow one. In addition to these expressed and implied powers, the Constitution affirmed the power of the national government in the supremacy clause (Article VI), which made all national laws and treaties "the supreme Law of the Land."

federalism a system of government in which power is divided, by a constitution, between a central government and regional governments

unitary system a centralized government system in which lower levels of government have little power independent of the national government

expressed powers specific powers granted by the Constitution to Congress (Article I, Section 8) and to the president (Article II)

implied powers powers derived from the necessary and proper clause of Article I, Section 8, of the Constitution; such powers are not specifically expressed, but are implied through the expansive interpretation of delegated powers

necessary and proper clause Article I, Section 8, of the Constitution, which provides Congress with the authority to make all laws "necessary and proper" to carry out its expressed powers

TABLE 3.1

The Presence of Federal, State, and Local Government in the Daily Life of a Student at "State University"

TIME	SCHEDULE	LEVEL OF GOVERNMENT
7:00 AM	Wake up. Standard time set by the national government.	Federal and state
7:10 AM	Shower. Water courtesy of local government, either a public entity or a regulated private company.	Local
7:18 AM	Brush your teeth with toothpaste whose cavity-fighting claims have been verified by a federal agency.	Federal
7:30 AM	Have a bowl of cereal with milk for breakfast. "Nutrition Facts" on food labels are a federal requirement, pasteurization of milk required by state law, freshness dating on milk based on state and federal standards.	Federal and state
7:57 AM	Recycle the empty cereal box and milk carton.	State or local
8:30 AM	Drive or take public transportation to campus. Air bags and seat belts required by federal and state laws. Roads and bridges paid for by state and local governments, speed and traffic laws set by state and local governments, public transportation subsidized by all levels of government.	Federal, state, and local
8:45 AM	Arrive on campus of large public university. Buildings are 70 percent financed by state taxpayers.	State
9:00 AM	First class: Chemistry 101. Tuition partially paid by a federal loan (more than half the cost of university instruction is paid for by taxpayers), chemistry lab paid for with grants from the National Science Foundation (a federal agency) and smaller grants from business corporations made possible by federal income tax deductions for charitable contributions.	Federal
2:00 PM	Second class: American Government 101 (your favorite class!). You may be taking this class because it is required by the state legislature or because it fulfills a university requirement.	State
4:00 PM	Third class: Computer Lab. Free computers, software, and Internet access courtesy of state subsidies plus grants and discounts from IBM and Microsoft, the costs of which are deducted from their corporate income taxes; Internet built in part by federal government. Duplication of software prohibited by federal copyright laws.	Federal and state
6:00 PM	Eat dinner: hamburger and french fries. Meat inspected for bacteria by federal agencies.	Federal
7:00 PM	Work at part-time job at the campus library. Minimum wage set by federal government; some states set a higher minimum. Books and journals in library paid for by state taxpayers.	Federal, state
8:15 PM	Go online to check the status of your application for a federal student loan (FAFSA) on the Department of Education's website at studentaid.ed.gov.	Federal
10:00 PM	Go home. Street lighting paid for by county and city governments, police patrols by city government.	Local
10:15 PM	Watch TV. Networks regulated by federal government, cable public-access channels required by city law. Weather forecast provided to broadcasters by a federal agency.	Federal, local
10:45 PM	To complete your economics homework, visit the Bureau of Labor Statistics at www.bls.gov to look up unemployment levels since 1972.	Federal
Midnight	Put out the trash before going to bed. Trash collected by city sanitation department, financed by "user charges."	Local

The Powers of State Government

One way in which the framers sought to preserve a strong role for the states was through the Tenth Amendment to the Constitution. The Tenth Amendment states that the powers that the Constitution does not delegate to the national government or prohibit to the states are "reserved to the States respectively, or to the people." The Antifederalists, who feared that a strong central government would encroach on individual liberty, repeatedly pressed for such an amendment as a way of limiting national power. Federalists agreed to the amendment because they did not think it would do much harm, given the powers of the Constitution already granted to the national government. The Tenth Amendment is also called the "**reserved powers** amendment," because it aims to reserve powers to the states.

reserved powers powers, derived from the Tenth Amendment to the Constitution, that are not specifically delegated to the national government or denied to the states

The most fundamental power that the states retain is that of coercion—the power to develop and enforce criminal codes, to administer health and safety rules, and to regulate the family via marriage and divorce laws. These issues touch closely on state and local values, which the founders saw as appropriately differing from state to state (see Figure 3.1). The states also have the power to regulate individuals' livelihoods; if you're a doctor or a lawyer or a plumber or a barber, you must be licensed by the state. Even more fundamentally, the states have the power to define private property—private property exists because state laws against trespass define who is and is not entitled to use a piece of property. If you own a car, your ownership isn't worth much unless the state is willing to enforce your right to possession by making it a crime for anyone else to drive your car without your consent. These are fundamental matters, and the powers of the states regarding these domestic issues are much greater than the powers of the national government, even today.

A state's authority to regulate these fundamental matters is commonly referred to as the **police power** of the state and encompasses the state's power to regulate the health, safety, welfare, and morals of its citizens. Policing is what states do—they coerce you in the name of the community in order to maintain public order. And this was exactly the type of power that the Founders intended the states, not the federal government, to exercise.

police power power reserved to the state government to regulate the health, safety, and morals of its citizens

In some areas, the states share **concurrent powers** with the national government, whereby they retain and share some power to regulate commerce and affect the currency—for example, by being able to charter banks, grant or deny corporate charters, grant or deny licenses to engage in a business or practice a trade, regulate the quality of products or the conditions of labor, and levy taxes. Wherever there is a direct conflict of laws between the federal and the state levels, the issue will most likely be resolved in favor of national supremacy.

concurrent powers authority possessed by *both* state and national governments, such as the power to levy taxes

States' Obligations to One Another

The Constitution also creates obligations among the states. These obligations, spelled out in Article IV, were intended to promote national unity. By requiring the states to recognize actions and decisions taken in other states as legal and proper, the framers aimed to make the states less like independent countries and more like components of a single nation.

Article IV, Section 1, calls for "Full Faith and Credit" among states, meaning that each state is normally expected to honor the "public Acts, Records, and judicial

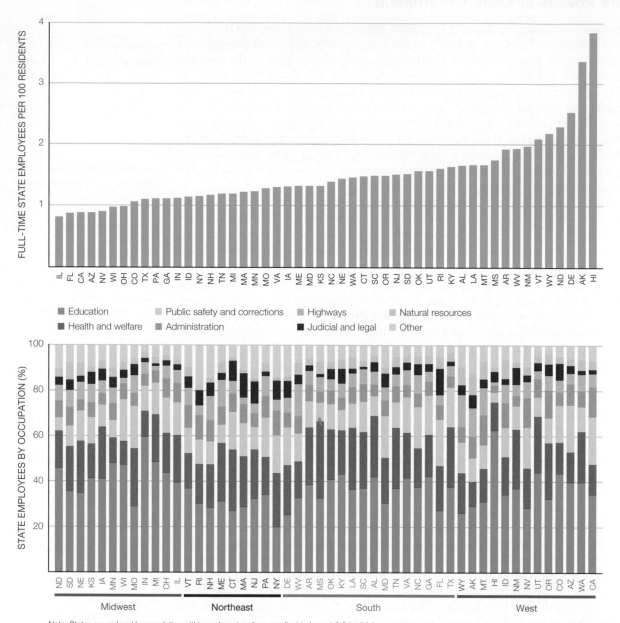

FIGURE 3.1

State Governments and Local Priorities

The Founders believed that local needs and values varied from state to state, and thus they left many powers and responsibilities to state governments rather than the national government. State governments vary in their relative size (how many state employees per 100 residents) and in the percentage of state workers employed in functions such as education, health and welfare, and public safety. How might these differences reflect differing needs and values?

SOURCE: U.S. Census Bureau, Survey of Government and Payroll, www.census.gov/govs/apes/ (accessed 1/14/14).

Proceedings" that take place in any other state. So, for example, if a person has a restraining order placed on a stalker or batterer in one state, other states are required to enforce that order as if they had issued it.

This **full faith and credit** clause notwithstanding, if a practice is against their "strong public policy," states are not obligated to recognize it—even if it has been sanctioned by other states. A look at the history of interracial marriage, for example, offers some perspective on how much leeway states have to recognize marriages performed in other states. In 1952, 30 states prohibited interracial marriage. Many of the states that prohibited interracial marriage also refused to recognize such marriages performed in other states.[2] For example, in the 1967 *Loving v. Virginia* case, which successfully challenged the ban on interracial marriage, the Lovings (a black woman and a white man) were married in the District of Columbia. However, when they returned to their home state of Virginia, which prohibited interracial marriage, the state refused to recognize them as a married couple.[3]

Until recently, same-sex marriage was in a similar position to interracial marriage half a century ago. Thirty-five states had passed "defense of marriage acts" or had adopted constitutional amendments that defined marriage as a union between one man and one woman only. Anxious to show its disapproval of gay marriage, Congress passed the Defense of Marriage Act in 1996, which declared that states would not have to recognize a same-sex marriage from another state. The act also said that the federal government would not recognize same-sex marriage—even if it were legal under state law—and that same-sex marriage partners would not be eligible for the federal benefits, such as Medicare and Social Security, normally available to spouses.[5] In 2013, however, the Supreme Court in *Windsor v. the United States* struck down the Defense of Marriage Act in part, requiring that same-sex married couples receive equal treatment on issues relating to taxes, inheritance, and other federal laws.[6] After *Windsor*, many state courts struck down the state bans on same-sex marriage. As of November 2014, 35 states and the District of Columbia recognize same-sex marriage, and 15 states ban it. The *Windsor* decision also opened the door for same-sex couples to receive federal benefits on the same terms as heterosexual married couples. Even so, most states that do not permit same-sex marriage also do not recognize same-sex marriages performed in other states. And, although the president ordered federal agencies to change their regulations to comply with the ruling, questions remained about whether same-sex married couples would receive equal treatment in social programs run jointly by states and the federal government. For example, health care for low-income Americans is funded by the federal and state governments, but the federal government left it up to the states to decide whether to provide benefits to legally married eligible same-sex couples.

Article IV, Section 2, known as the "comity clause," also seeks to promote national unity. It provides that citizens enjoying the **privileges and immunities** of one state should be entitled to similar treatment in other states. What this has come to mean is that a state cannot discriminate against someone from another state or give special privileges to its own residents. For example, in the 1970s, when Alaska passed a law that gave residents preference over

full faith and credit clause
provision from Article IV, Section 1 of the Constitution requiring that the states normally honor the public acts and judicial decisions that take place in another state

privileges and immunities clause
provision, from Article IV, Section 2, of the Constitution, that a state cannot discriminate against someone from another state or give its own residents special privileges

Should same-sex marriages performed in one state by legally recognized in another state? The Supreme Court ruled that the federal government must respect same-sex marriages performed in states where the practice is legal, but not all states perform such marriages or recognize those performed in other states.

nonresidents in obtaining work on the state's oil and gas pipelines, the Supreme Court ruled the law illegal because it discriminated against citizens of other states.[7] The comity clause also regulates criminal justice among the states by requiring states to return fugitives to the states from which they have fled. Thus, in 1952, when an inmate escaped from an Alabama prison and sought to avoid being returned to Alabama on the grounds that he was being subjected to "cruel and unusual punishment" there, the Supreme Court ruled that he must be returned according to Article IV, Section 2.[8] This example highlights the difference between the obligations among states and those among different countries. For example, in 2013, Russia refused to extradite Edward Snowden, a government contractor who leaked important intelligence documents about U.S. government spying. Although the Justice Department stated that it would not seek the death penalty for Snowden, Russia declined to hand Snowden over to American authorities. The Constitution clearly forbids states from doing something similar.

States' relationships with one another are also governed by the interstate compact clause (Article I, Section 10), which states that "No State shall, without the Consent of Congress . . . enter into any Agreement or Compact with another State." The Court has interpreted the clause to mean that states may enter into agreements with one another, subject to congressional approval. Compacts are a way for two or more states to reach a legally binding agreement about how to solve a problem that crosses state lines. In the early years of the republic, states turned to compacts primarily to settle border disputes. Today compacts are used for a wide range of issues but are especially important in regulating the distribution of river water, addressing environmental concerns, and operating transportation systems that cross state lines.[9] One unusual use of the interstate compact is the effort to enact the National Popular Vote compact. Initiated after George W. Bush won the presidency without winning the popular vote, the compact aims to make the popular vote, not the electoral college results, the criterion for victory. In signing the compact, a state agrees to award all its electoral college votes to the winner of the national popular vote. By 2014, with 10 states and the District of Columbia supporting the compact, the movement had obtained 61 percent of the 270 electoral votes needed for it to be effective.[10]

TABLE 3.2

90,107 Governments in the United States

TYPE	NUMBER
National	1
State	50
County	3,031
Municipal	19,519
Townships	16,360
School districts	12,880
Other special districts	38,266

SOURCE: U.S. Census Bureau, www2.census.gov/govs/cog/g12_org.pdf (accessed 11/02/13).

Local Government and the Constitution

Local government occupies a peculiar but very important place in the American system (see Table 3.2). In fact, the status of American local government is probably unique in world experience. First, it must be pointed out that local government has no status in the U.S. Constitution. *State* legislatures created local governments, and *state* constitutions and laws permit local governments to take on some of the responsibilities of the state governments. Local governments have always been subject to ultimate control by the states. This imbalance of power means that state governments could legally dissolve local governments or force multiple local governments to consolidate into one large locality.

Most states amended their own constitutions to give their larger cities **home rule**—a guarantee of noninterference in various areas of local affairs. But local governments enjoy no such recognition and have no protected standing at all in the federal Constitution.[11]

Local governments became administratively important in the early years of the Republic because the states possessed little administrative capability. They relied on local governments—cities and counties—to implement state laws. Local government was an alternative to a statewide bureaucracy.

home rule power delegated by the state to a local unit of government to manage its own affairs

● The Changing Relationship between the Federal Government and the States

Consider how the relationship between the federal and state governments has changed over time

At the time of the Founding, the states far outstripped the federal government in their power to influence the lives of ordinary Americans. In the system of shared powers between the states and the federal government, the states were most active in economic and social regulation, while Washington took a much more hands-off approach. Even so, the federal government gradually expanded its powers in the wake of important Supreme Court decisions. However, it was not until the New Deal in the 1930s that the federal government gained vast new powers.

Restraining National Power with Dual Federalism

As we have noted, the Constitution created two layers of government: the national government and the state governments. The consequences of this **dual federalism** are fundamental to the American system of government in theory and in practice; they have meant that states have done most of the fundamental governing. For evidence, look at Table 3.3, which lists the major types of public policies by which Americans were governed for the first century and a half under the Constitution. We call it the "traditional system" because it prevailed for much of American history and because it closely approximates the intentions of the framers of the Constitution.

dual federalism the system of government that prevailed in the United States from 1789 to 1937 in which most fundamental governmental powers were shared between the federal and state governments

Under the traditional system, the national government was quite small compared with both the state governments and the governments of other Western nations. Not only was it smaller than most governments of that time, but in fact it was also very narrowly specialized in the functions it performed. The national government built or sponsored the construction of roads, canals, and bridges (internal improvements). It provided cash subsidies to shippers and shipbuilders and distributed free or low-priced public land to encourage western settlement and business ventures. It placed relatively heavy taxes on imported goods (tariffs), not only to raise revenues but also to protect "infant industries" from competition from the more advanced European enterprises. It protected patents and provided for a common currency, which encouraged and facilitated enterprises and to expand markets.

What do these functions of the national government reveal? First, virtually all the functions were aimed at assisting commerce. It is quite appropriate to

TABLE 3.3

The Federal System: Specialization of Governmental Functions in the Traditional System, 1789–1937

NATIONAL GOVERNMENT POLICIES (DOMESTIC)	STATE GOVERNMENT POLICIES	LOCAL GOVERNMENT POLICIES
Internal improvements	Property laws (including slavery)	Adaptation of state laws to local conditions
Subsidies	Estate and inheritance laws	Public works
Tariffs	Commerce laws	Contracts for public works
Public land disposal	Banking and credit laws	Licensing of public accommodation
Patents	Corporate laws	Assessible improvements
Currency	Insurance laws	Basic public services
	Family laws	
	Morality laws	
	Public health laws	
	Education laws	
	General penal laws	
	Eminent domain laws	
	Construction codes	
	Land-use laws	
	Water and mineral laws	
	Criminal procedure laws	
	Electoral and political party laws	
	Local government laws	
	Civil service laws	
	Occupations and professions laws	

refer to the traditional American system as a "commercial republic." Second, virtually none of the national government's policies directly coerced citizens. The emphasis of governmental programs was on assistance, promotion, and encouragement—the allocation of land or capital to meet the needs of economic development.

Meanwhile, state legislatures were also actively involved in economic regulation during the nineteenth century. In the United States, then and now, private property exists only in state laws and state court decisions regarding property, trespass, and real estate. American capitalism took its form from state property and trespass laws, and from state laws and court decisions regarding contracts, markets, credit, banking, incorporation, and insurance. Laws concerning slavery were a subdivision of property law in states where slavery existed. The practice of important professions, such as law and medicine, was (and is) illegal except as provided for by state law. To educate or not to educate a child has been a

In 1815, President James Madison called for a federally funded program of "internal improvements," which was one of the few policy roles for the national government during the first half of the nineteenth century. By improving transportation through the construction of roads and canals, the government fostered the growth of the market economy and boosted federal power.

decision governed more by state laws than by parents. It is important to note also that until recent decades, virtually all criminal laws—regarding everything from trespass to murder—have been state laws. Since 1970, there has been a considerable growth in the number of federal criminal laws adopted by Congress, many of which overlap existing state laws.[12] Roughly 40 percent of the federal criminal statutes passed since the Civil War were enacted between 1970 and 1998.[13]

All this (and more, as shown in the middle column of Table 3.3) demonstrates that most of the fundamental governing in the United States was done by the states. The contrast between national and state policies, as shown by Table 3.3, demonstrates the difference in the power vested in each. The list of items in the middle column could actually have been made longer. Moreover, each item on the list is a category of law that fills many volumes of statutes and court decisions.

By allowing state governments to do most of the fundamental governing, the Constitution saved the national government from many policy decisions that might have proven too divisive for a large and very young country. There is little doubt that if the Constitution had provided for a unitary rather than a federal system, the war over slavery would have come in 1789 or not long thereafter rather than in 1861; and if it had come that early, the South might very well have seceded and established a separate, slaveholding nation. In helping the national government remain small and aloof from the most divisive issues of the day, federalism contributed significantly to the political stability of the nation, even as the social, economic, and political systems of many of the states and regions of the country were undergoing tremendous, profound, and sometimes violent, change.[14] The most fundamental impact of federalism on the way the United States is governed comes not from any particular provision of the Constitution but from the framework itself, which has determined which level of government does what and, through that, the political development of the country. As we shall see, some important aspects of federalism have changed, but the federal framework has survived two centuries and a devastating civil war.

Federalism and the Slow Growth of the National Government's Power

As the nation grew, disputes arose about the powers of the federal government versus the powers of the states. In the first several decades after the Founding, the Supreme Court decided several critical cases that expanded federal powers and facilitated trade across the states. These decisions removed barriers to trade in the new nation and laid the groundwork for a national economy. However, by the end of the nineteenth century, as reformers began to enact laws regulating businesses though such measures as child labor restrictions, the Court took a much more restrictive view of federal power. Not until well into the New Deal, in 1937, did the federal government gain the expansive powers it exercises today.

The Supreme Court's early decisions to expand federal power rested on its pronational interpretation of Article I, Section 8, of the Constitution. That article enumerates the powers of Congress, including the power to tax, raise an army, declare war, and establish post offices, and "to regulate commerce with foreign nations, and among the several States and with the Indian tribes." This **commerce clause** would later form the basis for expansive federal government control over the economy but its scope initially remained unclear.

The court's early decisions began to define national power by favoring federal control over the economy when there was a conflict between the states and the federal government. The first and most important such case was *McCulloch v. Maryland* (1819), which involved the question of whether Congress had the power to charter a national bank—an explicit grant of power nowhere to be found in Article I, Section 8.[15] Chief Justice John Marshall answered that this power could be "implied" from other powers that were expressly delegated to Congress, such as the "powers to lay and collect taxes; to borrow money; to regulate commerce; and to declare and conduct a war." Marshall's decision rested on "the necessary and proper clause" of Article I, Section 8, which gave Congress the power to enact laws "necessary and proper" for executing its substantive powers.

By allowing Congress to use the necessary and proper clause to interpret its delegated powers expansively, the Supreme Court created the potential for an unprecedented increase in national government power. Marshall also concluded that whenever a state law conflicted with a federal law (as in the case of *McCulloch v. Maryland*), the state law would be deemed invalid since the Constitution states that "the Laws of the United States . . . shall be the supreme Law of the Land." Both parts of this great case are pro-national, yet Congress did not immediately seek to expand the policies of the national government.

Another major case, *Gibbons v. Ogden* (1824), reinforced this nationalistic interpretation of the Constitution. The important but relatively narrow issue was whether the state of New York could grant a monopoly to Robert Fulton's steamboat company to operate an exclusive service between New York and New Jersey. Chief Justice Marshall argued that New York state did not have the power

commerce clause Article I, Section 8, of the Constitution, which delegates to Congress the power "to regulate commerce with foreign nations, and among the several States and with the Indian tribes"; this clause was interpreted by the Supreme Court in favor of national power over the economy

In 1916 the national government passed the Keating-Owen Child Labor Act, which excluded from interstate commerce all goods manufactured by children under age 14. The act was ruled unconstitutional by the Supreme Court, and the regulation of child labor remained in the hands of state governments until the 1930s.

to grant this particular monopoly, and so Marshall had to define what Article I, Section 8, meant by "commerce among the several states." He insisted that the definition was "comprehensive," extending to "every species of commercial intercourse." However, this comprehensiveness was limited "to that commerce which concerns more states than one." *Gibbons* is important because it established the supremacy of the national government in all matters affecting what later came to be called "interstate commerce."[16] But the precise meaning of interstate commerce would remain uncertain during several decades of constitutional discourse. Backed by the implied-powers decision in *McCulloch* and by the broad definition of "interstate commerce" in *Gibbons*, Article I, Section 8, was a source of power for the national government as long as Congress sought to facilitate commerce through subsidies, services, and land grants.

Later in the nineteenth century, though, any effort of the national government to *regulate* commerce in such areas as fraud, the production of substandard goods, the use of child labor, or the existence of dangerous working conditions or long hours was declared unconstitutional by the Supreme Court as a violation of the concept of interstate commerce. Such legislation meant that the federal government was entering the factory and the workplace—local areas—and was attempting to regulate goods that had not yet passed into interstate commerce. To enter these local workplaces was to exercise police power—a power reserved to the states. No one questioned the power of the national government to regulate businesses that intrinsically involved interstate commerce, such as railroads, gas pipelines, and waterway transportation. But well into the twentieth century the Supreme Court used the concept of interstate commerce as a barrier against most efforts by Congress to regulate local conditions.

This aspect of federalism prevailed during an epoch of tremendous economic development, the period between the Civil War and the 1930s. It gave the American economy a freedom from federal government control that closely approximated the ideal of free enterprise. The economy was never entirely free, of course; in fact, entrepreneurs themselves did not want complete freedom from government. They needed law and order. They needed a stable currency. They needed courts and police to enforce contracts and prevent trespass. They needed roads, canals, and railroads. But federalism, as interpreted by the Supreme Court for 70 years after the Civil War, made it possible for business to have its cake and eat it, too: entrepreneurs enjoyed the benefits of national policies facilitating commerce and were protected by the courts from policies regulating commerce by protecting the rights of consumers and workers.[17]

All this changed after 1937, when the Supreme Court issued a series of decisions that laid the groundwork for a much stronger federal government. Most significant was the Court's dramatic expansion of the commerce clause. By throwing out the old distinction between interstate and intrastate commerce, the Court converted the commerce clause from a source of limitations to a source of power for the national government. The Court upheld acts of Congress protecting the rights of employees to organize and engage in collective bargaining, regulating the amount of farmland in cultivation, extending low-interest credit to small businesses and farmers, and restricting the activities of corporations dealing in the stock market. The Court also upheld many other laws that contributed to the construction of the "welfare state."[18] With these rulings, the Court decisively signaled that the era of dual federalism was over. In the future, Congress would have very broad powers to regulate activity in the states.

The Changing Role of the States

As we have seen, the Constitution's commerce clause contained the seeds of a very expansive national government. However, for much of the nineteenth century, federal power remained limited. The Tenth Amendment was used to bolster arguments in favor of **states' rights**, which in their extreme version claimed that the states did not have to submit to national laws whenever they believed the national government had exceeded its authority. Prior to the Civil War, sharp differences between the North and the South over tariffs and slavery gave rise to arguments supporting nullification. Most fully articulated by John C. Calhoun, vice president under Andrew Jackson and later a senator from South Carolina, the doctrine of nullification proposed that states were not bound by federal laws that they considered unconstitutional. Such arguments were voiced less often after the Civil War, but the Supreme Court continued to use the Tenth Amendment to strike down laws that it thought exceeded national power, including the Civil Rights Act passed in 1875.

states' rights the principle that the states should oppose the increasing authority of the national government; this principle was most popular in the period before the Civil War

In June 1933, Congress passed the National Industrial Recovery Act, which gave employees the right to engage in collective bargaining with employers over wages and working conditions. Before Roosevelt's New Deal, labor law was largely a state affair, and employees faced significant barriers to organize and promote their interests.

In the early twentieth century, however, reformers began to press for national regulations to limit the power of large corporations and to preserve the health and welfare of citizens. The Supreme Court approved some of these laws, but it struck down others, including a law combating child labor. The Court stated that the law violated the Tenth Amendment because only states should have the power to regulate conditions of employment. By the late 1930s, however, the Supreme Court had approved such an expansion of federal power that the Tenth Amendment appeared irrelevant. The desire to promote equal working conditions across the country had elevated the federal government over the states. In fact, in 1941, Justice Harlan Fiske Stone declared that the Tenth Amendment was simply a "truism," that it had no real meaning.[19]

Yet the idea that some powers should be reserved to the states did not go away. One reason is that groups with substantive policy interests often support states' rights as a means for achieving their policy goals. For example, in the 1950s, southern opponents of the civil rights movement revived the idea of states' rights to support racial segregation. In 1956, 96 southern members of Congress issued a "Southern Manifesto" in which they declared that southern states were not constitutionally bound by Supreme Court decisions outlawing racial segregation. They believed that states' rights should override individual rights to liberty and formal equality. With the eventual triumph of the civil rights movement, the slogan of "states' rights" became tarnished by its association with racial inequality.

The 1990s saw a revival of interest in the Tenth Amendment and important Supreme Court decisions limiting federal power. Much of the interest in the Tenth Amendment stemmed from conservatives who believed that a strong federal government encroached on individual liberties. They believed such freedoms were better protected by returning more power to the states through the process of devolution. In 1996, Bob Dole, the Republican presidential candidate, carried a copy of the Tenth Amendment in his pocket as he campaigned, pulling it out to read it aloud at rallies.[20] The Supreme Court's 1995 ruling in *United States v. Lopez* fueled further interest in the Tenth Amendment.[21] In that case, the Court, stating that Congress had exceeded its authority under the commerce clause, struck down a federal law that barred handguns near schools. This was the first time since the New Deal that the Court had limited congressional powers in this way. In 1997 the Court again relied on the Tenth Amendment to limit federal power in *Printz v. United States*.[22] The decision declared unconstitutional a provision of the Brady Handgun Violence Prevention Act that required state and local law-enforcement officials to conduct background checks on handgun purchasers. The Court declared that this provision violated state sovereignty guaranteed by the Tenth Amendment because it required state and local officials to administer a federal regulatory program.

Thus, the expansion of the power of the national government has not left the states powerless. State governments continue to make important laws. No better demonstration of the continuing influence of the federal framework can be offered than that in the middle column of Table 3.2 is still a fairly accurate characterization of state government today. In each of these domains, however, states must now share power with the federal government.

for critical analysis

How have Supreme Court decisions affected the balance of power between the federal government and the states? Has the Supreme Court favored the federal government or the states?

In 1995 the Supreme Court ruled that the Gun-Free School Zones Act was an unconstitutional application of the commerce clause, leaving this area of regulation to the states. In striking down a federal law, the Supreme Court ruled that regulating guns near schools is a state prerogative. Some states have restrictions, whereas others do not.

● Who Does What? Public Spending and the Expanding Federal Framework

Trace developments in the federal framework leading to a stronger national government

Questions about how to divide responsibilities between the states and the national government first arose more than 200 years ago, when the framers wrote the Constitution to create a stronger union. But they did not solve the issue of who should do what. There is no "right" answer to that question; each generation of Americans has provided its own answer. In recent decades, many Americans have grown distrustful of the federal government and have supported giving more responsibility to the states.[23] Even so, they still want the federal government to set standards, promote equality, and provide security.

In political debates about the division of responsibility, some people argue for a strong federal role to set national standards, whereas others say the states should do more. These two goals are not necessarily at odds. The key is to find the right balance. In this section we will look at how the balance has shifted, and then we will consider current efforts to reshape the relationship between the national government and the states.

The New Deal

The door to increased federal action opened when states proved unable to cope with the demands brought on by the Great Depression of the 1930s. Before this national economic catastrophe, states and localities took responsibility for addressing the needs of the poor, usually through private charity. But the extent of the need created by the depression quickly exhausted local and state capacities. By 1932, 25 percent of the workforce was unemployed. The jobless lost their homes and settled into camps all over the country, called "Hoovervilles," after President Herbert Hoover. Elected in 1928, the year before the depression hit, Hoover steadfastly maintained that the federal government could do little to alleviate the misery caused by the depression. It was a matter for state and local governments, he said.

Yet demands mounted for the federal government to take action. In Congress, some Democrats proposed that the federal government finance public works to aid the economy and put people back to work. Other members of Congress introduced legislation to provide federal grants to the states to assist them in their relief efforts. Most of these measures failed to win congressional approval or were vetoed by President Hoover.

When Franklin Delano Roosevelt took office in 1933, he energetically threw the federal government into the business of fighting the depression through a number of proposals known collectively as the New Deal. He proposed a variety of temporary measures to provide federal relief and work programs. Most of the programs he proposed were to be financed by the federal government but administered by the states. In addition to these temporary measures, Roosevelt presided over the creation of several important federal programs designed to provide future economic security for Americans. The New Deal signaled the rise of a more active national government.

The National School Lunch Program, established by President Harry Truman in 1946, provides nutritious, low-cost lunches to children every day. This program is funded by federal grants to the states.

Federal Grants

For the most part, the new national programs that the Roosevelt administration developed did not directly take power away from the states. Instead, Washington typically redirected states by offering them **grants-in-aid**, whereby Congress appropriates money to state and local governments on the condition that the money be spent for a particular purpose defined by Congress (see Figure 3.2). Franklin Roosevelt's New Deal expanded the range of grants-in-aid into social programs, providing grants to the states for financial assistance to poor children. Congress added more grants after World War II, creating new programs to help states fund activities such as providing school lunches and building highways. Sometimes the national government required state or local governments to match the national contribution dollar for dollar, but in some programs, such as the

grants-in-aid programs through which Congress provides money to state and local governments on the condition that the funds be employed for purposes defined by the federal government

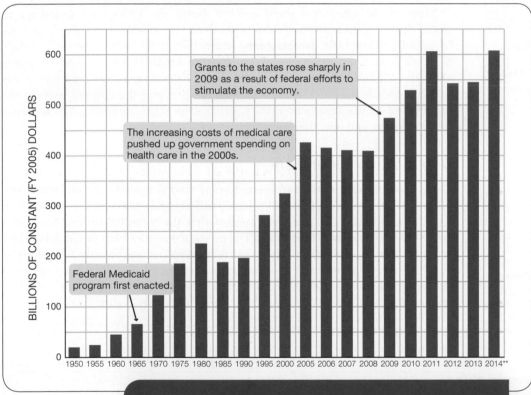

FIGURE 3.2

Historical Trend of Federal Grants-in-Aid,* 1950–2014

Spending on federal grants-in-aid to the states and local governments has grown dramatically since 1990. These increases reflect the growing public expectations about what government should do. What has been the most important cause of the steady increase in these grants?

*Excludes outlays for national defense, international affairs, and net interest.
**Estimate.

SOURCE: U.S. Budget for Fiscal Year 2015, www.whitehouse.gov/omb/budget/Historicals (accessed 5/15/14).

development of the interstate highway system, the congressional grants provided 90 percent of the cost of the program.

These types of federal grants-in-aid are also called **categorical grants** because the national government determines the purposes, or categories, for which the money can be used. For the most part, the categorical grants created before the 1960s simply helped the states perform their traditional functions.[24] During the 1960s, however, the national role expanded and the number of categorical grants increased dramatically. For example, during the 89th Congress (1965–66) alone, the number of categorical grant-in-aid programs grew from 221 to 379.[25] The *value* of categorical grants also has risen dramatically, increasing from $2.3 billion in 1950 to an estimated $607 billion in 2014. The grants authorized during the 1960s announced national purposes much more strongly than did earlier grants. One of the most important—and expensive—was the federal Medicaid program, which provides states with grants to pay for medical care for the poor, the disabled, and many nursing home residents.

Many of the categorical grants enacted during the 1960s were **project grants**, which require state and local governments to submit proposals to federal agencies. In contrast to the older, **formula grants**, which used a formula (composed of such elements as need and state and local capacities) to distribute funds, the project grants made funding available on a competitive basis. Federal agencies would give grants to the proposals they judged to be the best. In this way, the national government acquired substantial control over which state and local governments got money, how much they got, and how they spent it.

Cooperative Federalism

The growth of categorical grants created a new kind of federalism. If the traditional system of two sovereigns performing highly different functions could be called dual federalism, historians of federalism suggest that the system since the New Deal could be called **cooperative federalism**. The political scientist Morton Grodzins characterized this as a move from "layer cake federalism" to "marble cake federalism,"[26] in which intergovernmental cooperation and sharing have blurred a once-clear distinguishing line, making it difficult to say where the national government ends and the state and local governments begin (see Figure 3.3). Figure 3.4 demonstrates the financial basis of the "marble cake" idea.

categorical grants congressional grants given to states and localities on the condition that expenditures be limited to a problem or group specified by law

project grants grant programs in which state and local governments submit proposals to federal agencies and for which funding is provided on a competitive basis

formula grants grants-in-aid in which a formula is used to determine the amount of federal funds a state or local government will receive

cooperative federalism a type of federalism existing since the New Deal era in which grants-in-aid have been used strategically to encourage states and localities (without commanding them) to pursue nationally defined goals; also known as *intergovernmental cooperation*

FIGURE 3.3

Dual versus Cooperative Federalism

In layer cake federalism, the responsibilities of the national government and state governments are clearly separated. In marble cake federalism, national policies, state policies, and local policies overlap in many areas.

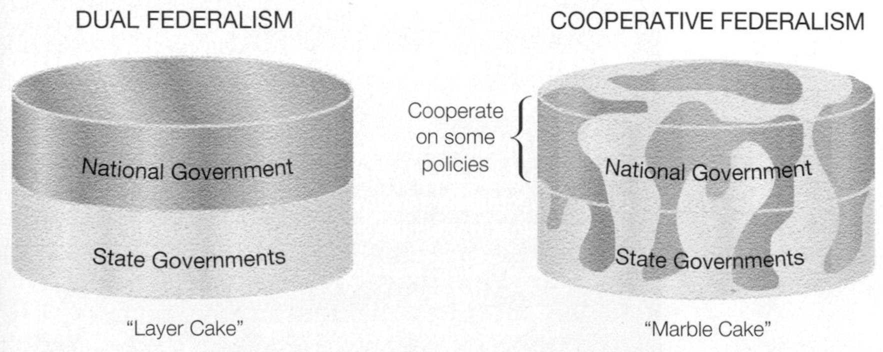

DUAL FEDERALISM

National Government

State Governments

"Layer Cake"

Cooperate on some policies

COOPERATIVE FEDERALISM

National Government

State Governments

"Marble Cake"

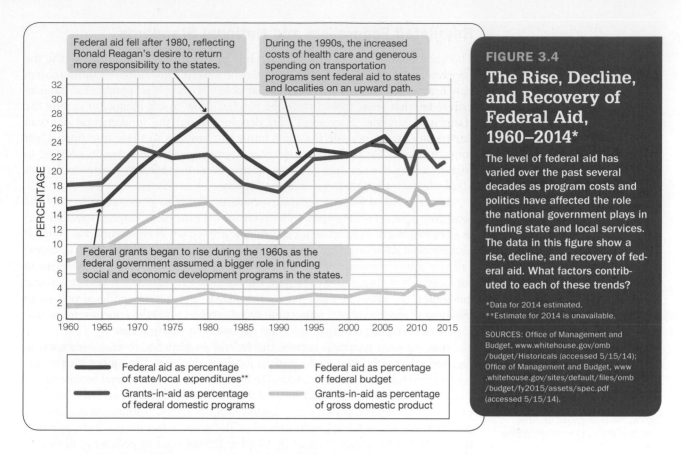

FIGURE 3.4

The Rise, Decline, and Recovery of Federal Aid, 1960–2014*

The level of federal aid has varied over the past several decades as program costs and politics have affected the role the national government plays in funding state and local services. The data in this figure show a rise, decline, and recovery of federal aid. What factors contributed to each of these trends?

*Data for 2014 estimated.
**Estimate for 2014 is unavailable.

SOURCES: Office of Management and Budget, www.whitehouse.gov/omb/budget/Historicals (accessed 5/15/14); Office of Management and Budget, www.whitehouse.gov/sites/default/files/omb/budget/fy2015/assets/spec.pdf (accessed 5/15/14).

Federal aid fell after 1980, reflecting Ronald Reagan's desire to return more responsibility to the states.

During the 1990s, the increased costs of health care and generous spending on transportation programs sent federal aid to states and localities on an upward path.

Federal grants began to rise during the 1960s as the federal government assumed a bigger role in funding social and economic development programs in the states.

Federal aid as percentage of state/local expenditures**

Grants-in-aid as percentage of federal domestic programs

Federal aid as percentage of federal budget

Grants-in-aid as percentage of gross domestic product

For a while in the 1960s, however, it appeared as if the state governments would become increasingly irrelevant to American federalism. Many of the new federal grants bypassed the states and instead sent money directly to local governments and even to local nonprofit organizations. The theme heard repeatedly in Washington was that the states simply could not be trusted to carry out national purposes.[27]

One of the reasons that Washington distrusted the states was the way African American citizens were treated in the South. The southern states' forthright defense of segregation, justified on the grounds of states' rights, helped tarnish the image of the states as the civil rights movement gained momentum. The national officials who planned the War on Poverty during the 1960s pointed to the racial exclusion practiced in the southern states as a reason for bypassing state governments. The political scientist James Sundquist described how this thinking affected the War on Poverty: "In the drafting of the Economic Opportunity Act, an 'Alabama syndrome' developed. Any suggestion within the poverty task force that the states be given a role in the administration of the act was met with the question, 'Do you want to give that kind of power to [then–Alabama governor] George Wallace?'"[28]

Yet even though many national policies of the 1960s bypassed the states, other new programs, such as Medicaid—the health program for the poor—relied on state governments for their implementation. In addition, as the national government expanded existing programs run by the states, states had to take on more responsibility. These new responsibilities meant that the states were playing a very important role in the federal system.

Regulated Federalism and National Standards

The question of who decides what each level of government should do goes to the very heart of what it means to be an American citizen. How different should things be when one crosses a state line? In what policy areas is it acceptable for states to differ? In what areas should states be similar? How much inequality among the states is acceptable? Supreme Court decisions about the fundamental rights of American citizens provide the most important answers to these questions. Over time, the Court has pushed for greater uniformity across the states. In addition to legal decisions, the national government uses two other tools to create similarities across the states: grants-in-aid and regulations.

Grants-in-aid, as we have seen, are incentives: Congress gives money to state and local governments if they agree to spend it for the purposes Congress specifies. But as Congress began to enact legislation in new areas, such as environmental policy, it also imposed additional regulations on states and localities. Some political scientists call this a move toward **regulated federalism**.[29] The national government began to set standards of conduct or to require the states to set standards that met national guidelines. The effect of these national standards is that state and local policies in the areas of environmental protection, social services, and education are more uniform from coast to coast than are other nationally funded policies.

Some national standards require the federal government to take over areas of regulation formerly overseen by state or local governments. Such **preemption** occurs when state and local actions are found to be inconsistent with federal requirements. In some cases, federal laws and regulations are more stringent than state laws. For example, as federal regulations proliferated after the 1970s, Washington increasingly preempted state and local action in many different policy areas. These preemptions required the states to abide by tougher federal rules in policies as diverse as air and water pollution, occupational health and safety, and access for the disabled. The regulated industries often oppose such laws because they increase the cost of doing business. After 1994, when Republicans retook control of Congress, the federal government used its preemption power in business's favor, limiting the ability of states to tax and regulate industry. For example, the Internet Tax Freedom Act (ITFA), first enacted by Congress in 1998 and subsequently renewed, prohibits states and localities from taxing Internet access services.

Congress is not the only federal body that can preempt the states; federal regulatory agencies can also issue rules that override state law. One controversial case involved a 2006 Food and Drug Administration drug-labeling rule preempting state laws that allow individuals to sue drug companies in state courts. Opponents—many of them trial lawyers—charged that such rules amounted to "stealth preemption" that "will deprive consumers of their right to hold negligent corporations accountable for injuries caused by defective products."[30] Supporters claimed that the rules were a proper use of federal authority. Although the Republicans came to power promising to grant more responsibility to the states, they ended up reducing state control in many areas by preemption.

State and local governments often contest federal preemptions. For example, in 2001, Attorney General John Ashcroft declared that Oregon's law permitting doctor-assisted suicide was illegal under federal drug regulations. The state, a physician, a pharmacist, and several terminally ill state residents challenged Ashcroft's rule, and in January 2006 the Supreme Court ruled in a 6–3 vote that the attorney general did not have the authority to outlaw the Oregon law.[31] Individuals have also challenged federal preemption. In 2009 the Supreme Court ruled against a

regulated federalism a form of federalism in which Congress imposes legislation on states and localities, requiring them to meet national standards

preemption the principle that allows the national government to override state or local actions in certain policy areas; in foreign policy, the willingness to strike first in order to prevent an enemy attack

drug manufacturer and in favor of a woman whose arm had to be amputated after she was improperly injected with a drug designed to counter nausea.[32] Although the drug company knew that such complications could arise, it argued that it was not responsible for the amputation because federal regulations did not require it to warn against this danger in labeling the drug. The Court, however, found the company liable for the damage. In its decision, the Court made it clear that federal regulations could not preempt state consumer protections and that states had the power to adopt stricter protections than those of the federal government.

In 2009, after only a few months in office, President Obama reversed the Bush administration's use of federal regulations to limit state laws. Under the new policy, federal regulations should preempt state laws only in extraordinary cases. The president directed agency leaders to review the regulations that had been put in place over the past 10 years and consider amending them if they interfered with the "legitimate prerogatives of the states."[33] But as we will see, the Obama administration did use its power of preemption to challenge state immigration laws, charging that states were making laws in a domain reserved for federal authority.

The growth of national standards has created some new problems and has raised questions about how far federal standardization should go. One problem that emerged in the 1980s was the increase in **unfunded mandates**— the product of a Democratic Congress that wanted to achieve liberal social objectives and Republican presidents who opposed increased social spending. Between 1983 and 1991, Congress mandated standards in many policy areas, including social services and environmental regulations, without providing additional funds to help the states meet those standards. Altogether, Congress enacted 27 laws that imposed new regulations or required states to expand existing programs.[34] For example, the 1973 Rehabilitation Act prohibited discrimination against the disabled in programs that were partly funded by the federal government. The new law required state and local governments to make public transit accessible to disabled people with wheelchair lifts in buses, elevators in train stations, and special transportation systems where needed. These requirements were estimated to cost state and local governments $6.8 billion over 30 years.[35] But Congress did not supply additional funding to help states meet these new requirements; the states had to shoulder the increased financial burden themselves.

States and localities quickly began to protest the cost of unfunded mandates. Although it is very hard to determine the exact cost of federal regulations, the Congressional Budget Office estimated that between 1983 and 1990, new federal regulations cost states and localities between $8.9 and $12.7 billion.[36] States complained that mandates took up so much of their budgets that they were not able to set their own priorities. These burdens became part of a rallying cry to reduce the power of the federal government—a cry that took center stage when a Republican Congress was elected in 1994. One of the first measures the new Congress passed was an act to limit the cost of unfunded mandates, the Unfunded Mandates Reform Act (UMRA). Under this law, the Congressional Budget Office must assess the cost of any mandate that it believes would exceed the threshold established in UMRA ($73 million in 2012, adjusted for inflation). Bills that would impose sizable costs on the private sector must also be assessed. The goal is to ensure that Congress knows how much it is expecting of state and local governments and the private sector. Congress must identify funding sources for bills that exceed the threshold established

unfunded mandates regulations or conditions for receiving grants that impose costs on state and local governments for which they are not reimbursed by the federal government

The federal government frequently passes laws that impose mandates on the states, such as the 2012 Federal Aviation Agency Modernization and Reform Act, which requires commercial airports to submit plans for emergency situations to the FAA. The costs to the states of this requirement did not exceed the threshold in the UMRA.

Government Spending in Federal and Unitary Systems

Both federalism and unitary systems are common among the countries of the world. The key difference between the two systems is in the amount of power that is reserved for state and local governments: federal systems give considerable autonomy to their subnational units, whereas unitary systems tend to be highly centralized.

The graphs here show the percentage of total government revenue that is spent by the central government, state governments, and local governments. The central government of France, a unitary country, spends a larger percentage than

Switzerland, Mexico, and the United States, all federal countries. South Korea is a unitary country where local governments operate under a great deal of autonomy, carrying out many of the state's administrative functions. As a result, local government spending in South Korea is comparable to some federal systems. This example shows that while the distinction between federalism and unitary systems is important, it is not the only factor in determining who holds power in a country.

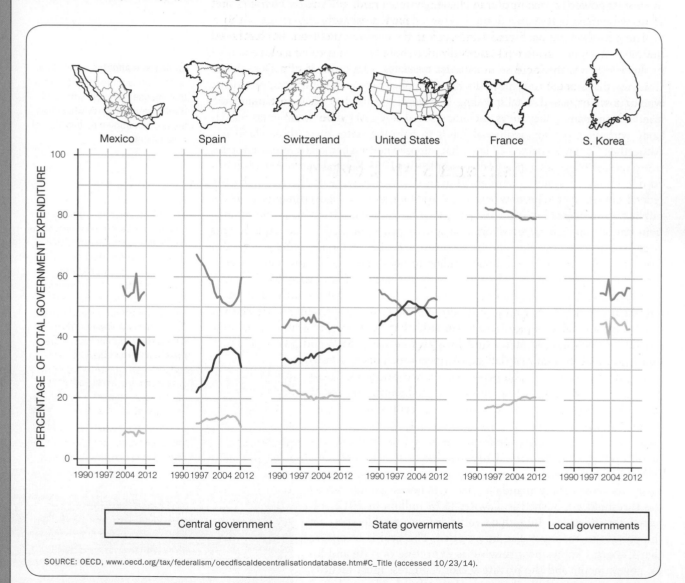

SOURCE: OECD, www.oecd.org/tax/federalism/oecdfiscaldecentralisationdatabase.htm#C_Title (accessed 10/23/14).

in UMRA. Of all public laws enacted since 1996, fewer than 5 percent have included private-sector mandates with costs estimated to exceed the threshold, while less than 1 percent have contained intergovernmental mandates (mandates on state or local governments) with such costs. [37]

New national problems inevitably raise the question of "Who pays?" Recently, concern about unfunded mandates has arisen around health care reform. The major health care reform enacted during Obama's first two years as president, the Affordable Care Act of 2010, called for a major expansion of Medicaid. But because Medicaid is partly funded by the states, any major increase in the number of Medicaid recipients could impose a significant fiscal burden on the states. Although the law provided additional federal aid to support the new requirements, the Medicaid provisions became a target for state challenges to the health care law. One of the central claims in the 26 states' lawsuits charged that the federal government did not have the power to withhold Medicaid funds from states that did not implement the new expansions.[38] The Supreme Court ultimately ruled that states could decline to expand Medicaid coverage without losing their existing Medicaid funds. After the Court's decision, 25 states, all led by Republican governors, announced that they would not implement the expanded coverage. Some began to reconsider this decision. By mid-2014, 27 states had decided to expand Medicaid, 5 states were debating the question, and 19 had decided to not expand Medicaid. It is clear that the Court's decision injected a whole new set of issues into the question of "Who pays?"

for critical analysis

Should states be required to implement unfunded mandates? How much of the funding should the federal government provide for policies or standards that it sets?

New Federalism and State Control

Analyze the developments in the federal framework since the 1970s

In 1970 the mayor of Oakland, California, told Congress that his city had 22 separate employment and training programs but that few poor residents were being trained for jobs that were available in the local labor market.[39] National programs had proliferated as Congress enacted many small grants, but little effort was made to coordinate or adapt programs to local needs. Today many governors argue for more state and local control over such national grant programs. They complain that national grants do not allow for enough local flexibility and instead take a "one-size-fits-all" approach.[40] These criticisms point to a fundamental challenge in American federalism: how to get the best results for the money spent. Do some divisions of responsibility between states and the federal government work better than others? Since the 1970s, as states became more capable of administering large-scale programs, the idea of **devolution**—transferring responsibility for policy from the federal government to the states and localities—has become popular.

Proponents of more state authority have looked to **block grants** as a way of reducing federal control. Block grants are federal grants that allow the states considerable leeway in spending federal money. President Nixon led the first push for block grants in the early 1970s, as part of his **New Federalism**. Nixon's approach consolidated programs in the areas of job training, community development, and social services into three large block grants. These grants imposed some conditions on states and localities as to how the money should be spent, but not the narrow regulations contained in the categorical grants. In addition, Congress provided an important

devolution a policy to remove a program from one level of government by delegating it or passing it down to a lower level of government, such as from the national government to the state and local governments

block grants federal grants-in-aid that allow states considerable discretion in how the funds are spent

New Federalism attempts by presidents Nixon and Reagan to return power to the states through block grants

new form of federal assistance to state and local governments, called **general revenue sharing**. Revenue sharing provided money to local governments and counties with no strings attached; localities could spend the money as they wished. In enacting revenue sharing, Washington acknowledged both the critical role that state and local governments play in implementing national priorities and their need for increased funding and enhanced flexibility in order to carry out that role (see Figure 3.5). Reagan's version of New Federalism also looked to block grants. Like Nixon, Reagan wanted to reduce the national government's control and return power to the states. But unlike Nixon, whose block grants increased federal spending, Reagan's block grants cut federal funding by 12 percent. His view was that the states could spend their own funds to make up the difference, if they chose to do so. Revenue sharing was also eliminated during the Reagan administration, leaving localities to fend for themselves. In all, Congress created 12 new block grants between 1981 and 1990.[41]

The Republican Congress elected in 1994 took this strategy even further, making substantial cuts in federal programs as well as supporting block grants. Their biggest success was the 1996 welfare reform law, which delegated to states important new responsibilities. Most of the other major proposed block grants or spending reductions, however, failed to pass Congress or were vetoed by President Clinton. The Republican congressional leadership had found that it was much easier to promise a "devolution revolution" than to deliver on that promise.[42]

Neither block grants nor reduced federal funding have proven to be magic solutions to the problems of federalism. For one thing, there is always a trade-off between accountability—that is, whether the states are using funds for the purposes intended—and flexibility. If the objective is to have accountable and efficient government, it is not clear that state bureaucracies are any more efficient or more capable than national agencies. In Mississippi, for example, the state Department of Human Services spent money from the child care block grant for office furniture and designer salt and pepper shakers that cost $37.50 a pair. As one Mississippi

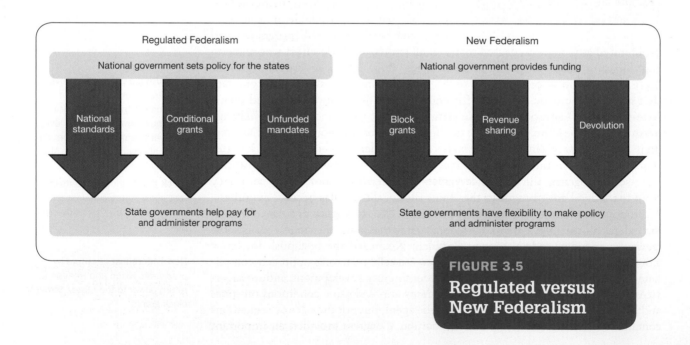

Regulated Federalism

National government sets policy for the states

National standards — Conditional grants — Unfunded mandates

State governments help pay for and administer programs

New Federalism

National government provides funding

Block grants — Revenue sharing — Devolution

State governments have flexibility to make policy and administer programs

FIGURE 3.5

Regulated versus New Federalism

state legislator said, "I've seen too many years of good ol' boy politics to know they shouldn't [transfer money to the states] without stricter controls and requirements."[43] Even after block grants were created, Congress reimposed regulations in order to increase the states' accountability.

At times the federal government has also moved to limit state discretion over spending in cases where it thinks states are too generous. For example, in 2007, President Bush issued regulations that prevented states from providing benefits under the State Children's Health Insurance Program (SCHIP) to children in families well above the poverty line. The Bush administration also barred states from providing chemotherapy to illegal immigrants, who are guaranteed emergency medical treatment under Medicaid.[44] These new rules embroiled states and the federal government in sharp conflicts over state discretion in spending decisions, once the hallmark of New Federalism.

Devolution: For Whose Benefit?

As Figure 3.6 indicates, federalism has changed dramatically over the course of American history. Finding the right balance among states and the federal government is an evolving challenge for American democracy, and since the expansion of the national government in the 1930s, questions about "who does what" have frequently provoked conflict. Why does such an apparently simple choice set off such highly charged political debate? One reason is that many decisions about federal-versus-state responsibility have implications for who benefits from government action.

Let's consider the benefits of federal control versus devolution in the realm of **redistributive programs**—programs designed primarily for the benefit of the poor. Many political scientists and economists maintain that states and localities should not be in charge of redistributive programs. They argue that since states and local

redistributive programs economic policies designed to control the economy through taxing and spending, with the goal of benefiting the poor

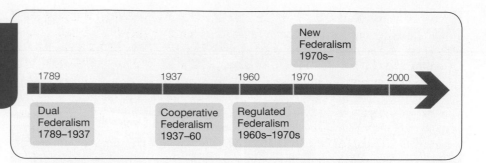

New Federalism
1970s–

1789   1937   1960   1970   2000

Dual Federalism 1789–1937   Cooperative Federalism 1937–60   Regulated Federalism 1960s–1970s

governments have to compete with one another, they do not have the incentive to spend their money on the needy people in their areas. Instead, they want to keep taxes low and spend money on things that promote economic development.[45] In this situation, states might engage in a "race to the bottom": if one state cuts assistance to the poor, neighboring states will institute similar or deeper cuts both to reduce expenditures and to discourage poorer people from moving to their states. As one New York legislator put it, "The concern we have is that unless we make our welfare system and our tax and regulatory system competitive with the states around us, we will have too many disincentives for business to move here. Welfare is a big part of that."[46]

In 1996, when Congress enacted major welfare reform, it followed a different logic. By changing welfare from a combined federal-state program into a block grant to the states, Congress gave the states more responsibility for programs that serve the poor. Supporters of the change hoped to reduce welfare spending and argued that states could act as "laboratories of democracy" by experimenting with many different approaches in order to find those that best met the needs of their citizens.[47] As states altered their welfare programs in the wake of the new law, they did indeed design diverse approaches. For example, Minnesota adopted an incentive-based approach that offers extra assistance to families that take low-wage jobs, while six other states imposed very strict time limits on receiving benefits, allowing welfare recipients less than the five-year limit in the federal legislation. After the passage of the law, welfare rolls declined dramatically. On average, they declined by more than half from their peak in 1994; in 12 states the decline was 70 percent or higher. Politicians have cited these statistics to claim that the poor have benefited from greater state control of welfare, yet most studies have found that the majority of those leaving welfare remain in poverty.

In some decisions about federalism, local concerns are overridden in the name of the national interest. The question of speed limits, traditionally a state and local responsibility, provides an example. In 1973, at the height of the oil shortage, Congress passed legislation to withhold federal highway funds from states that did not adopt a maximum speed limit of 55 miles per hour in order to reduce fuel consumption. Although Congress had not formally taken over the authority to set speed limits, the power of its purse was so important that every state adopted the new speed limit. As the crisis faded, concern about energy conservation diminished. The national speed limit lost much of its support, even though it was found to have reduced the

In 1995, Congress removed its speed limit restrictions and allowed states to raise the limit above 55 miles per hour without losing federal highway funds. As a result, speed limits went up on many highways

number of traffic deaths. In 1995, Congress repealed the penalties for higher speed limits, and states once again became free to set their own speed limits. Many states with large rural areas raised their maximum to 75 miles per hour; Montana initially set unlimited speeds in its rural areas during daylight hours. Research indicates that the number of highway deaths has indeed risen in the states that increased the limits.[48]

Because the division of responsibility in the federal system has important implications for who benefits, few conflicts over state-versus-national control will ever be settled once and for all. New evidence about the costs and benefits of different arrangements provides fuel for ongoing debates about what are properly the states' responsibilities and what the federal government should do. Likewise, changes in the political control of the national government usually provoke a rethinking of responsibilities as new leaders seek to alter federal arrangements for the benefit of the groups they represent.

Federalism since 2000

Over the past 15 years, the political polarization between Republicans and Democrats that has characterized national politics and divided states has been played out through the federal system as well. This does not mean that all decisions about federalism have divided along political lines. But many of the most controversial issues in American politics—including the appropriate size of public social spending, the rights and benefits of immigrants (legal as well as undocumented), government response to global climate change, and questions about whether and how government should regulate business and moral behavior—have been fought through the federal system. Politicians of all stripes have regularly turned to the federal government to override policies they don't like that were made at the state level. The reverse is also true: when the federal government proves unable or unwilling to act, activists and politicians instead try to achieve their goals in states and localities. Sometimes, states seek to go their own way regardless of federal law. It is often then up to the courts to decide which level of government should have the final say. In many cases, the federal government has succeeded in advancing its policy agenda on the states. However, the era since 2000 has been marked by a considerable amount of back-and-forth between the states and the federal government as debates over federalism have become politically prominent.

Although conservatives proclaim their preference for a small federal government and their support for more state autonomy, in fact they often expand the federal government and limit state autonomy. During the presidency of George W. Bush, the growth of government, the activist, free-spending Republican Congress, and a series of Supreme Court rulings supporting federal power over the states made it clear that conservatives do not always support small government; nor do they always favor returning power to the states. Once in power, many conservatives discovered not only that they needed a strong federal government to respond to public demands but also that they could use federal power to advance conservative policy goals.

For President Bush, the importance of a strong federal government dawned with force after the terrorist attacks in 2001. Aware that the American public was looking to Washington for protection, Bush worked with Congress to pass the USA PATRIOT Act, which greatly increased the surveillance powers of the federal government. A year later he created the enormous new federal Department of Homeland Security. Democrats supported the president in both initiatives.

President Bush, with the support of Democrats, also expanded federal control and increased spending in policy areas far removed from concerns about security.

The 2001 No Child Left Behind Act introduced unprecedented federal intervention in public education, traditionally a state and local responsibility. New, detailed federal testing requirements and provisions stipulating how states should treat failing schools were major expansions of federal authority in education. When a number of states threatened to defy some of the new federal requirements, Bush's Department of Education relaxed its tough stance and became more flexible in enforcing the act. The Obama administration increased flexibility even more by granting waivers to 43 states. The waivers released the states from the federal mandates around school accountability and performance, replacing them with state measures. But in other ways, Obama increased federal authority over schools. In 2009, the administration introduced a new competitive grant program called "Race to the Top." States were required to apply for the funds; states that had adopted the administration's favored reforms were best positioned to win. This meant that many states adopted teacher evaluation strategies promoted by the administration as well as the common core curriculum and the testing program associated with it. By 2014, 44 states and the District of Columbia had adopted the Common Core curriculum.

In the Supreme Court, too, many decisions began to support a stronger federal role over the states. This was surprising to many observers, because in the 1990s it had appeared that the Rehnquist Court was embarked on a "federalism revolution" designed to return more power to the states. Instead, in several key decisions, the Court reaffirmed the power of the federal government. Decisions to uphold the federal Family and Medical Leave Act and the Americans with Disabilities Act asserted federal authority against state claims of immunity from the acts. In one important 2005 case, the Court upheld the right of Congress to ban medical marijuana, even though 11 states had legalized its use. Overturning a lower court ruling that said Congress did not have authority to regulate marijuana when it had been grown for noncommercial purposes in a single state, the Supreme Court ruled that the federal government did have the power to regulate use of all marijuana under the commerce clause.[49] Even so, as we have seen, by 2014, 23 states and the District of Columbia had legalized medical marijuana. Amid this legal confusion, a medical marijuana industry began to flourish in states that allowed medical use of the drug. In 2012, Colorado and Washington went further by legalizing recreational marijuana even though it is a prohibited substance by federal law. Alaska, Oregon, and the District of Columbia joined them in 2014. Although the federal government has not endorsed these laws, it has made prosecution of marijuana in these states a low priority.

The move to a stronger federal role has not been uniform, however; in some cases the Supreme Court has granted more authority to the states. One closely watched federalism case in 2006 was the challenge to Oregon's "right to die" law, discussed earlier, which allows doctors to prescribe lethal doses of medicine for terminally ill patients who request it. Challengers claimed the law was illegal because Congress has the right to outlaw such use of drugs under the Controlled Substances Act, which regulates prescription drugs. In a 6–3 decision, the Court ruled in Oregon's favor.[50] Despite the ruling, only Washington state followed in Oregon's footsteps to make physician-assisted suicide legal.

On some issues, the majority of the states have pressed the federal government to act, but it has not responded. One issue on which most states would like the federal government to establish uniform law is Internet sales. Current law requires Internet retailers to collect sales tax on online purchases only when the business has a physical presence in the buyer's state. This has become a major issue for states, most of which rely on sales taxes for a significant part of their revenue. States were projected to lose $23 billion in 2012 from Internet sales on which no

Who Benefits from Federal Spending?

Federal Grants to State and Local Governments, 2011

Health $293 billion	Income security $114 billion	Education $89 billion	Transportation $61 billion	Other $50 billion

Although Americans often think they pay a lot in federal taxes, they receive much in return in the form of federal money for state and local programs. Federal outlays for grants to state and local governments have grown from $13.2 billion in 1940 to $514.6 billion in 2011 (in constant dollars).

Fiscal Transfers between the States and the Federal Government, 1990–2009

Net contributors
(contributed more in federal taxes than the state received in federal spending)

- $0–99 billion
- $100–299 billion
- $300–499 billion
- $500–1,000 billion

Net recipients
(received more in federal spending than the state contributed in taxes)

- $0–49 billion
- $50–99 billion
- $100–299 billion
- $300–600 billion

SOURCES:
Congressional Budget Office,
www.cbo.gov/sites/default/files/
cbofiles/attachments/
43967_FederalGrants.pdf;
Economist, www.economist.com/
blogs/dailychart/2011/08/
americas-fiscal-union (accessed
3/20/14).

NEW YORK

VIRGINIA
$592.9 billion

Every U.S. state contributes to the federal government through the federal taxes paid by the state's citizens, and every state receives money from federal spending. Federal spending is a broad category that includes the federal grants described above as well as spending on military bases and federal procurement. Not every state receives the same amount from the federal government, however. In the 20-year period from 1990 to 2009, 19 states contributed more in federal taxes than they received in federal spending, and the other 31 received more in federal spending than they contributed in federal taxes. The largest net contributor was New York, and the largest net recipient was Virginia.

for critical analysis

1. What are some of the benefits of federal grants to state and local governments?

2. What is the rationale behind transfers from one state to another? Is it fair that some states pay more in federal taxes than they receive? What might explain why some states are net recipients and some net contributors?

taxes were collected.[51] In 2013, the Senate—with support from both Democrats and Republicans—passed the Marketplace Fairness Act, which would require online retailers to collect state sales taxes. However, in the House, some Republicans opposed the measure as a tax increase. The future of the legislation remains in doubt.

The tug-of-war between the federal and state governments for policy control is particularly evident in the field of immigration. Faced with federal inaction on immigration reform, states and localities have forged their own policies. Some states, such as Arizona and Georgia, have adopted policies more restrictive than those of the federal government, while other states, such as California and Connecticut, have enacted laws to limit cooperation with federal immigration authorities. In the first half of 2013, state legislatures enacted 377 laws and resolutions related to immigration, exceeding the number passed in all of 2012.[52] Many state and local laws that govern immigration are not controversial, but others raise critical questions about what is the federal role and what are the responsibilities of state and local governments. In April 2010, Arizona enacted an extremely controversial immigration measure requiring immigrants to carry identity documents and requiring police to ask about immigration status when they stop drivers they suspect of being illegal immigrants. The federal Department of Justice joined several other groups in challenging the law. In the words of then–Attorney General Eric Holder, "It is clearly unconstitutional for a state to set its own immigration policy."[53] In 2012 the Supreme Court overturned three of four provisions in Arizona's law. But it ruled in favor of the most divisive provision, which allows state police to check the immigration status of anyone stopped or arrested.[54]

Even as the federal government challenged overly restrictive state immigration laws, it launched an additional program, Secure Communities, in which state and local authorities must check the fingerprints of people being booked into jail

The federal government brought Arizona to court over law SB1070, which imposed strict requirements on immigrants. The Supreme Court found that three provisions of the law were preempted by federal law, meaning Arizona did not have the authority to make the regulation. However, the controversial "show me your papers" provision of the law was upheld.

against a Homeland Security database. If the fingerprints find a match in the database, it is up to the federal Immigration and Customs Enforcement agents to take further action. The law led to a record number of deportations in 2009 and 2010. Some states have objected to the program, and Illinois, New York, and Massachusetts pulled out of the agreement with the federal government on the grounds that the law was detaining too many undocumented immigrants who had never committed a crime. Despite these objections, the federal government has declared that participation of state and local law-enforcement authorities is mandatory.[55]

In other ways, the Obama White House signaled that it would allow the states more leeway for action than they had under the Bush administration. This was particularly true in the domains of social policy and the environment when states sought to enact laws more stringent than those of the federal government. In the memo reversing the Bush policy of preemption, the White House noted, "Throughout our history, State and local governments have frequently protected health, safety, and the environment more aggressively than has the national Government."[56] Its new policy aimed to keep the federal government from infringing on these more aggressive state actions.

The most significant Obama law to affect the states was the 2010 health care overhaul. As we have seen, one controversial part of that legislation required states to expand their Medicaid programs to cover more low-income residents and to offer them additional services. The Supreme Court's ruling that the federal government could not impose all-or-nothing conditions on the states—implement the expansion or lose all Medicaid funding—represented a sharp departure from the past. The ruling has far-reaching potential to change the federal government's power to impose conditions on the states when it supplies the funds. The other controversial provision of the Affordable Care Act was the "individual mandate," the requirement that individuals without health care insurance be required to purchase such insurance. The 26 states suing the federal government charged that Congress exceeded its power under the commerce clause when it enacted the mandate. They charged that Congress had no power to force individuals to purchase a product and argued that the act set up a "slippery slope" in which Congress could force individuals to make other purchases. As one judge (who upheld the law) asked, "Would it be unconstitutional to require people to buy broccoli?" In defending the law, the federal government argued that the complex interactions of the health care market made the individual mandate constitutional under Congress's power to regulate commerce among the states.[57] From the moment a person is born, he or she is part of the health care economy. Even if a person does not have health insurance, federal law requires that hospitals provide treatment in an emergency. Those costs are borne by all of the people who do pay for health insurance. Taking a more narrow view of the health care market, the Court rejected this argument on the grounds that the federal government cannot regulate economic inactivity, that is, the failure to purchase health insurance. Instead, it found that the Affordable Care Act could be justified by Congress's power to tax. The law requires individuals who do not receive insurance from their employers or their parents, and are not eligible for Medicaid, to purchase insurance or pay a penalty. The Court reasoned that the penalty could be considered a tax, and in that sense, passed constitutional muster. The complex and surprising decision marked a new era in American federalism. The Court placed limits on two of the key powers that have expanded the reach of the federal government since the New Deal—the power to regulate commerce and the power to spend for the general welfare. The decision will surely invite challenges to federal power in diverse areas, possibly including education programs, the drinking age, and environmental regulations.

for critical analysis

Why is the 2010 Affordable Care Act controversial? How did the Supreme Court's decision about the law reflect the principles of federalism?

Federalism
and Your Future

It is often argued that liberals prefer a strong federal government because they value equality more than liberty. Conservatives are said to prefer granting more power to states and localities because they care most about liberty. Although this greatly oversimplifies liberal and conservative views, such arguments underscore the reality that ideas about federalism are linked to different views about the purposes of government. For what ends should government powers be used? What happens when widely shared national values conflict in practice? The connections between federalism and our fundamental national values have made federalism a focus of political contention throughout our nation's history.

In recent years, sharp differences in Americans' views on many economic and social issues have been reflected in the federal system. Nearly half of the 50 states have legalized medical marijuana, while two have gone further and legalized recreational marijuana. Thirty-five states have legalized same-sex marriage. More states are likely to change their laws on marijuana and same-sex marriage, but differences across the states are likely to persist for many years. Half of the states welcomed the expansion of Medicaid, the program that provides medical assistance to the poor. The other half, concerned about costs and the growing role of government in the economy, has declined to implement the expansion. Some states actively welcome immigrants and seek to opt out of restrictive federal laws; other states go beyond the federal government in enacting restrictive immigration laws.

For young people, these differences across the states provoke important questions about the future. Our history of federalism means that we are comfortable with the idea that states should have the freedom to enact laws that best serve their residents, within the bounds set by Congress and the courts. We expect states to act as "laboratories of democracy" that try out new policies. But the great variation across the states today poses questions that will have to be answered in the coming decades. Is the federal government endangering people by allowing states to legalize marijuana? Is it fair to a same-sex couple married in New Jersey that their marriage would not be recognized if they moved to Texas? Each generation confronts a different set of questions about how much variation across the states is appropriate. Are some of the issues on which the states differ fundamental rights that should be uniform across the country? Is it important to preserve state choice on most matters? As today's youth help to answer these questions in the coming decades, they will be remaking American federalism.

American federalism remains a work in progress. As public problems shift and as local, state, and federal governments change, questions about the relationship between American values and federalism naturally emerge. The different views that people bring to this discussion suggest that federalism will remain a central issue in American democracy.

for critical analysis

What would be the advantages and disadvantages of a unitary system in which the federal government had all the power? What would be the advantages and disadvantages of a fully decentralized system in which the states had all the power?

Will states attempt to change the drinking age in the future? The federal government required states to set the drinking age at 21 or risk losing federal highway funds, but some people feel this decision should be left to the states.

plugin

Inform

Watch the cartoon "Federal Powers vs. State Powers" on YouTube.

Express

Think about a current issue—such as gun laws, health care, same-sex marriage, or marijuana—that puts state power in contention with national power. Write out your stance on whether the issue should be addressed at the national or state level.

Connect

Find your state-level representatives on your state legislature's website. Most websites also list recent legislation and upcoming votes. Look for bills related to issues that interest you.

Act

Consider emailing your representatives in the state legislature or U.S. Congress about the issue(s) you identified and why you think the state or the national government should address it. Contact information is available on the state legislature website or House.gov and Senate.gov.

studyguide

Federalism in the Constitution

Describe what the Constitution says about the powers of the national government and of the states (pp. 79–85)

While the Founders wanted a national government that was stronger than it had been under the Articles of Confederation, they also wanted to preserve the autonomy of the states. The necessary and proper clause, the supremacy clause, and the specific powers granted to Congress in Article I demonstrate the nation-centered focus of the Constitution. The Tenth Amendment, which grants all undelegated powers to the states, shows the state-centered focus of the Constitution. The Constitution also includes some concurrent powers that are shared by both the federal government and state governments.

Key Terms

federalism (p. 79)

unitary system (p. 79)

expressed powers (p. 79)

implied powers (p. 79)

necessary and proper clause (p. 79)

reserved powers (p. 81)

police power (p. 81)

concurrent powers (p. 81)

full faith and credit clause (p. 83)

privileges and immunities clause (p. 83)

home rule (p. 85)

Practice Quiz

1. Which term describes the sharing of powers between the national government and the state governments?
   a) home rule
   b) separation of powers
   c) federalism
   d) checks and balances
   e) unitary system

2. Which amendment to the Constitution stated that the powers not delegated to the national government or prohibited to the states were "reserved to the states"?
   a) First Amendment
   b) Fifth Amendment
   c) Tenth Amendment
   d) Fourteenth Amendment
   e) Twenty-Sixth Amendment

3. A state government's authority to regulate the health, safety, and morals of its citizens is frequently referred to as
   a) the reserved power.
   b) the police power.
   c) the expressed power.
   d) the concurrent power.
   e) the implied power.

4. Which constitutional clause has been central in debates over gay and lesbian marriage because it requires that states normally honor the public acts and judicial decisions of other states?
   a) privileges and immunities clause
   b) necessary and proper clause
   c) interstate commerce clause
   d) preemption clause
   e) full faith and credit clause

5. Many states have amended their constitutions to guarantee that large cities will have the authority to manage local affairs without interference from state government. This power is called
   a) home rule.
   b) devolution.
   c) preemption.
   d) states' rights.
   e) New Federalism.

The Changing Relationship between the Federal Government and the States

Consider how the relationship between the federal and state governments has changed over time (pp. 85–91)

The relative importance of states and the federal government has changed significantly over time. During the first 100 years of American history, the national government was small and focused on assisting commerce. Beginning in the 1930s, the Supreme Court dramatically expanded the power of the federal government through its expansive interpretation of the commerce clause. The growing power of the national government has not, however, left the states powerless and state governments continue to make important laws.

Key Terms

dual federalism (p. 85)

commerce clause (p. 88)

states' rights (p. 90)

Practice Quiz

6. The relationship between the states and the national government from 1789 to 1937 is known as
   a) unitary government.
   b) New Federalism.
   c) dual federalism.
   d) cooperative federalism.
   e) regulated federalism.

7. In which case did the Supreme Court create the potential for increased national power by ruling that Congress could use the necessary and proper clause to interpret its delegated powers broadly?
   a) *United States v. Lopez*
   b) *Printz v. United States*
   c) *Marbury v. Madison*
   d) *McCulloch v. Maryland*
   d) *Gibbons v. Ogden*

8. In 1937 the Supreme Court laid the groundwork for a stronger federal government by issuing a number of decisions that
   a) dramatically narrowed the definition of the commerce clause.
   b) dramatically expanded the definition of the commerce clause.
   c) struck down the supremacy clause.
   d) struck down the privileges and immunities clause.
   e) struck down the full faith and credit clause.

Who Does What? Public Spending and the Expanding Federal Framework

Trace developments in the federal framework leading to a stronger national government (pp. 92–99)

The Great Depression effectively ended the traditional system of dual federalism in which the states and the federal government performed very different functions. Political debates continue about the division of responsibility between states and the national government in search of the right balance. The New Deal, federal grants, and cooperative and regulated federalism are all part of the shift in power and responsibility.

Key Terms

grants-in-aid (p. 93)

categorical grants (p. 94)

project grants (p. 94)

formula grants (p. 94)

cooperative federalism (p. 94)

regulated federalism (p. 96)

preemption (p. 96)

unfunded mandates (p. 97)

Practice Quiz

9. One of the most powerful tools by which the federal government has attempted to get the states to act in ways that are desired by the federal government is
   a) defending states' rights.
   b) general revenue sharing.
   c) providing grants-in-aid.
   d) requiring licensing.
   e) granting home rule.

10. The form of regulated federalism that allows the federal government to take over areas of regulation formerly overseen by states or local governments is called
    a) project grants.
    b) preemption.
    c) devolution.
    d) categorical grants.
    e) formula grants.

11. When state and local governments must conform to costly federal regulations or conditions in order to receive grants but do not receive reimbursements for their expenditures it is called
    a) a reciprocal grant.
    b) an unfunded mandate.
    c) general revenue sharing.
    d) a concurrent grant.
    e) a counterfunded mandate.

New Federalism and State Control

Analyze the developments in the federal framework since the 1970s (pp. 99–107)

Today, American federalism includes elements of cooperative, coercive, and "new" federalism. Most of the important public policy issues in recent years, including controversies about government spending, immigration, climate change, health care, and economic regulation, are debated and addressed through the United States' unique system of federalism.

Key Terms

devolution (p. 99)

block grants (p. 99)

New Federalism (p. 99)

general revenue sharing (p. 100)

redistributive programs (p. 101)

Practice Quiz

12. The process of returning more of the responsibilities of governing from the national level to the state level is known as
    a) devolution.
    b) dual federalism.
    c) incorporation.
    d) home rule.
    e) preemption.

13. To what does the term *New Federalism* refer?
    a) the era of federalism initiated by President Roosevelt during the late 1930s
    b) the national government's regulation of state action through grants-in-aid
    c) the type of federalism relying on categorical grants
    d) efforts to return more policy-making discretion to the states through the use of block grants
    e) the recent emergence of local governments as important political actors

14. A notable example of the process of giving the states more responsibility for administering government programs is
    a) campaign finance reform.
    b) prison reform.
    c) Social Security.
    d) welfare reform.
    e) trade reform.

For Further Reading

Bensel, Richard. *Sectionalism and American Political Development: 1880–1980.* Madison: University of Wisconsin Press, 1984.

Bowman, Ann O'M., and Richard C. Kearney. *The Resurgence of the States.* Englewood Cliffs, NJ: Prentice-Hall, 1986.

Derthick, Martha. *Keeping the Compound Republic: Essays on American Federalism.* Washington, DC: Brookings Institution Press, 2001.

Elazar, Daniel. *American Federalism: A View from the States.* 3rd ed. New York: Harper & Row, 1984.

Feiock, Richard C., and John T. Scholz, *Self-Organizing Federalism: Collaborative Mechanisms to Mitigate Institutional Collective Action Dilemmas.* New York: Cambridge University Press, 2009.

Gerston, Larry N. *American Federalism: A Concise Introduction.* Armonk, NY: M.E. Sharpe, 2007.

Grodzins, Morton. *The American System*. Chicago: Rand McNally, 1974.

Johnson, Kimberly S. *Governing the American State: Congress and the New Federalism, 1877–1929*. Princeton, NJ: Princeton University Press, 2007.

Kettl, Donald. *The Regulation of American Federalism*. Baltimore: Johns Hopkins University Press, 1987.

Pierceson, Jason. *Same-Sex Marriage in the United States: The Road to the Supreme Court*. Lanham, MD: Rowman and Littlefield Publishers, 2013.

Robertson, David Brian. *Federalism and the Making of America*. New York: Routledge, 2011.

Van Horn, Carl E. *The State of the States*. 4th ed. Washington, DC: CQ Press, 2005.

Recommended Websites

Constitution Finder
http://confinder.richmond.edu

Governments can organize power in either unitary or federal systems. Examine the constitutions of different countries throughout the world and try to identify how those governments organize power.

Council of State Governments
www.csg.org

This organization provides information on a variety of state-federal policy areas. See what current issues concerning federalism are of prime importance to the state governments on this site.

Governing.com
www.governing.com

See what state-federal issues are important to your local government officials on the website for *Governing* magazine.

National Conference of State Legislatures
www.ncsl.org
National Governors Association
www.nga.org

These are two of the largest organizations dedicated to representing state and local government interests at the federal level.

Oyez: U.S. Supreme Court Media
www.oyez.org

Read here about one of the most important U.S. Supreme Court decisions regarding the division of federal and state power in the case of *McCulloch v. Maryland*.

Pew Center for the States
www.pewstates.org

The Pew Center for the States provides nonpartisan reporting and research, advocacy, and technical assistance to help states deliver better results and achieve long-term fiscal health by investing in programs that provide the strongest returns.

Urban Institute
www.newfederalism.urban.org

New Federalism gives state governments more flexibility to make public policy and administer programs. The Urban Institute's "Assessing the New Federalism" policy center takes a statistical look at the success and failure of recent government programs.

U.S. Census Bureau
www.census.gov

The Census Bureau maintains one of the largest collections of data about social and economic conditions of the nation's 50 states.

World Federalist Movement
www.wfm.org

This international organization is dedicated to the division of power and authority among all local, state, and international governmental agencies. Generally, it promotes federalism and constitutional democracy throughout the world.

The Bill of Rights protects Americans from government surveillance and searches without reasonable cause. The limits on individual privacy have been a source of contestation and judicial action throughout U.S. history.

Civil Liberties

WHAT GOVERNMENT DOES AND WHY IT MATTERS Today in the United States, we often take for granted the liberties contained in the Bill of Rights. In fact, few people in recorded history, including many American citizens before the 1960s, have enjoyed such protections. For more than 170 years after its ratification by the states in 1791, the Bill of Rights meant little to most Americans. As we shall see in this chapter, guaranteeing the liberties articulated in the Bill of Rights to all Americans required a long struggle. As recently as the early 1960s, criminal suspects in state cases did not have to be informed of their rights, some states required daily Bible readings and prayers in their public schools, and some communities regularly censored books that they deemed to be obscene.

Often, the government presents restraints on liberty, particularly in such realms as speech, assembly, and privacy, as necessary to protect the nation's security. Today, for example, many Americans seem to accept the necessity of full-body scans at airports and electronic surveillance of our email and phone conversations as necessary to protect the nation against attack. Yet, the framers of the Constitution may have had qualms about such invasions of privacy. To the framers, political freedom required that citizens be protected from government surveillance and searches into citizens' private affairs. Indeed, this concern for privacy lies at the heart of the Constitution's Fourth Amendment, which prohibits "unreasonable searches and seizures."

Many people today see the Fourth Amendment as related to appropriate manners of gathering evidence in mundane criminal cases. And this in itself is important, as anyone who has been falsely accused of a crime can aver. But the framers were well aware of the fact that government intrusions into private homes were often aimed at identifying papers or manuscripts that might point to an individual's efforts to foment political discontent against the current political order.[1] Such individuals might find themselves the target of government surveillance, investigation, or even prosecution. As Justice Brennan wrote for a unanimous Supreme Court in the 1961 case *Marcus v. Search Warrant*, "The Bill of Rights was fashioned against a background of knowledge that unrestricted power of search and seizure could also be an instrument for stifling liberty of expression."[2]

Thomas Jefferson said that a bill of rights "is what people are entitled to against every government on earth." Note the wording: *against government.* Civil liberties are *protections from* improper government action. Some of these restraints are substantive liberties, which put limits on *what* the government shall and shall not have power to do—such as establishing a religion or seizing private property without just compensation. Other restraints are procedural liberties, which deal with *how* the government is supposed to act. Civil liberties require a delicate balance between governmental power and governmental restraint. The government must be kept in check, with strict limits on its powers; yet, at the same time, the government must be given enough power to defend liberty and its benefits from those who seek to deprive others of them. This chapter will explore how this balance is struck. We will see how the Supreme Court, an inherently undemocratic institution, is especially important in establishing the balance. In a sense, civil liberties can be thought of as limits on democracy. They are the "minority rights" in the principle of "majority rule with minority rights." The rights enumerated in the Bill of Rights and enforced through the courts can provide an important check on the power of the majority.

chapter goals

- Explain the origins and evolution of the civil liberties in the Bill of Rights as they apply to the federal government and the states (pp. 117–22)
- Describe how the First Amendment protects freedom of religion (pp. 122–25)
- Describe how the First Amendment protects free speech (pp. 125–34)
- Explore whether the Second Amendment means people have a right to own guns (pp. 134–37)
- Explain the major rights that people have if they are accused of a crime (pp. 137–44)
- Assess whether people have a right to privacy under the Constitution (pp. 144–49)

A Brief History of the Bill of Rights

Explain the origins and evolution of the civil liberties in the Bill of Rights as they apply to the federal government and the states

When the first Congress under the newly ratified Constitution met in late April of 1789, the most important item of business was the consideration of a proposal to add a bill of rights to the Constitution. Such a proposal had been turned down with little debate in the waning days of the Philadelphia Constitutional Convention in 1787, not because the delegates were against rights, but because, as the Federalists, led by Alexander Hamilton, later argued, it was "not only unnecessary in the proposed Constitution but would even be dangerous."[3] First, according to Hamilton, a bill of rights would be irrelevant to a national government that was given only delegated powers in the first place. To put restraints on "powers which are not granted" could provide a pretext for governments to claim more powers than were in fact granted: "For why declare that things shall not be done which there is no power to do?"[4] Second, the Constitution was to Hamilton and the Federalists a bill of rights in itself, containing provisions that amounted to a bill of rights without requiring additional amendments (see Table 4.1). For example, Article I, Section 9, included the right of **habeas corpus**, which prohibits the government from depriving a person of liberty without an open trial before a judge.

Despite the power of Hamilton's arguments, when the Constitution was submitted to the states for ratification, Antifederalists, most of whom had not been delegates in Philadelphia, picked up on the argument of Thomas Jefferson (who also had not been a delegate) that the omission of a bill of rights was a major imperfection of the new Constitution. The Federalists conceded that to gain ratification they would have to make an "unwritten but unequivocal pledge" to add a bill of rights that would include a confirmation (in what would become the Tenth Amendment) of the understanding that all powers not expressly delegated to the national government or explicitly prohibited to the states were reserved to the states.[5]

habeas corpus a court order demanding that an individual in custody be brought into court and shown the cause for detention

TABLE 4.1

Rights in the Original Constitution (Not in the Bill of Rights)

CLAUSE	RIGHT ESTABLISHED
Article I, Sec. 9	Guarantee of habeas corpus
Article I, Sec. 9	Prohibition of bills of attainder
Article I, Sec. 9	Prohibition of ex post facto laws
Article I, Sec. 9	Prohibition against acceptance of titles of nobility, etc., from any foreign state
Article III	Guarantee of trial by jury in state where crime was committed
Article III	Treason defined and limited to the life of the person convicted, not to the person's heirs

bill of attainder a law that declares a person guilty of a crime without a trial

ex post facto laws laws that declare an action to be illegal after it has been committed

TABLE 4.2

The Bill of Rights

Amendment I: Limits on Congress	Congress cannot make any law establishing a religion or abridging freedoms of religious exercise, speech, assembly, or petition.
Amendments II, III, IV: Limits on the Executive	The executive branch cannot infringe on the right of the people to keep arms (II), cannot arbitrarily take houses for militia (III), and cannot search for or seize evidence without a court warrant swearing to the probable existence of a crime (IV).
Amendments V, VI, VII, VIII: Limits on the Judiciary	The courts cannot hold trials for serious offenses without provision for a grand jury (V), a trial jury (VII), a speedy trial (VI), presentation of charges and confrontation by the accused of hostile witnesses (VI), and immunity from testimony against oneself and immunity from trial more than once for the same offense (V). Furthermore, neither bail nor punishment can be excessive (VIII), and no property can be taken without "just compensation" (V).
Amendments IX, X: Limits on the National Government	Any rights not enumerated are reserved to the state or the people (X), and the enumeration of certain rights in the Constitution should not be interpreted to mean that those are the only rights the people have (IX).

Bill of Rights the first 10 amendments to the U.S. Constitution, ratified in 1791; they ensure certain rights and liberties to the people

civil liberties areas of personal freedom constitutionally protected from government interference

"After much discussion and manipulation . . . at the delicate prompting of Washington and under the masterful prodding of Madison," the House of Representatives adopted 17 amendments; of these, the Senate adopted 12. Ten of the amendments were ratified by the necessary three-fourths of the states on December 15, 1791; from the start, these 10 were called the **Bill of Rights** (see Table 4.2).[6] The protections against improper government action contained in the Constitution and the Bill of Rights represent important **civil liberties**.

Nationalizing the Bill of Rights

The First Amendment provides that "Congress shall make no law . . ." But this is the only amendment in the Bill of Rights that addresses itself exclusively to the national government. For example, the Second Amendment provides that "the right of the people to keep and bear Arms, shall not be infringed." And the Fifth Amendment says, among other things, that "no person shall . . . be twice put in jeopardy of life or limb" for the same crime. Since the First Amendment is the only part of the Bill of Rights that is explicit in its intention to put limits on Congress and therefore on the national government, a fundamental question inevitably arises: Do the remaining provisions of the Bill of Rights put limits only on the national government, or do they limit the state governments as well?

The Supreme Court first answered this question in 1833 by ruling that the Bill of Rights limited only the national government and not the state governments.[7] But in 1868, when the Fourteenth Amendment was added to the Constitution, the question arose once again. The Fourteenth Amendment reads as if it were meant to impose the Bill of Rights on the states:

> No *State* shall make or enforce any law which shall abridge the privileges or immunities of citizens of the United States; nor shall any *State* deprive any person of life, liberty, or property, without due process of law; nor deny to any person within its jurisdiction the equal protection of the laws [emphasis added].

This language sounds like an effort to extend the Bill of Rights in its entirety to all citizens, wherever they might reside.[8] Yet this was not the Supreme Court's interpretation of the amendment for nearly 100 years. Within five years of ratification of the Fourteenth Amendment, the Court was making decisions as though the amendment had never been adopted.[9]

The only change in civil liberties during the first 50-odd years following the adoption of the Fourteenth Amendment came in 1897, when the Supreme Court held that the due process clause of the Fourteenth Amendment did in fact prohibit states from taking property for a public use without just compensation.[10] However, the Supreme Court had selectively "incorporated" into the Fourteenth Amendment only the property protection provision of the Fifth Amendment and no other clause of the Fifth or any other amendment of the Bill of Rights. In other words, although according to the Fifth Amendment, "due process" applied to the taking of life and liberty as well as property, only property was incorporated into the Fourteenth Amendment as a limitation on state power.

No further expansion of civil liberties via the Fourteenth Amendment occurred until 1925, when the Supreme Court held that freedom of speech is "among the fundamental personal rights and 'liberties' protected by the due process clause of the Fourteenth Amendment from impairment by the states."[11] In 1931 the Court added freedom of the press to that short list of freedoms protected by the Bill of Rights from state action; in 1939 it added freedom of assembly.[12]

But that was as far as the Court was willing to go. The Constitution, as interpreted by the Supreme Court in *Palko v. Connecticut*, left standing the framework in which the states had the power to determine their own laws on a number of fundamental issues. In that case, a Connecticut court had found Frank Palko guilty of second-degree murder and sentenced him to life in prison. Unhappy with the verdict, the state of Connecticut appealed the conviction to its highest court, won the appeal, got a new trial, and then succeeded in getting Palko convicted of first-degree murder. Palko appealed to the Supreme Court on what seemed an open-and-shut case of double jeopardy, which is prohibited by the Fifth Amendment. Yet, although the majority of the Court agreed that this could indeed be considered a case of double jeopardy, they decided that double jeopardy was *not* one of the provisions of the Bill of Rights incorporated into the Fourteenth Amendment as a restriction on the powers of the states. It took more than 30 years for the Court to nationalize the constitutional protection against double jeopardy. Because Frank Palko lived in the state of Connecticut rather than in a state whose constitution included a guarantee against double jeopardy, he was eventually executed for the crime.

The *Palko* case established the principle of **selective incorporation**, by which the provisions of the Bill of Rights were to be considered one by one and selectively applied as limits on the states through the Fourteenth Amendment. In order to make clear that "selective incorporation" should be narrowly interpreted, Justice Benjamin Cardozo, writing for an 8–1 majority, asserted that although many rights have value and importance, some rights do not represent a "principle of justice so rooted in the traditions and conscience of our people as to be ranked as fundamental." He went on to remark that if the Fourteenth Amendment has absorbed such rights as freedom of thought and speech, "the process of absorption has had its source in the belief that neither liberty nor

Philadelphia, Pennsylvania   December 15, 1791

Congress Adds a Bill of Rights to the Federal Constitution

10 AMENDMENTS TO GUARANTEE INDIVIDUAL RIGHTS

Madison leads the fight for passage

The promise of a Bill of Rights was instrumental to securing ratification of the Constitution. One amendment adopted by the House and Senate in 1791 was finally ratified by the states in 1992. This amendment stipulates that no law changing salaries of Congress members can take effect until after an election has intervened.

selective incorporation the process by which different protections in the Bill of Rights were incorporated into the Fourteenth Amendment, thus guaranteeing citizens protection from state as well as national governments

justice would exist if they were sacrificed."[13] *Palko* left states with most of the powers they had possessed even before the adoption of the Fourteenth Amendment, such as the power to engage in searches and seizures without a warrant, to deprive accused persons of trial by jury, to deprive accused persons of their right to confront adverse witnesses, and to prosecute accused persons more than once for the same crime.[14] Few states chose to use these kinds of powers, but some states did, and the power to do so was available for any state whose legislative majority or courts so chose.

So, until 1961, only the First Amendment and one clause of the Fifth Amendment had been clearly incorporated into the Fourteenth Amendment as binding on the states as well as on the national government.[15] After that, one by one, most of the important provisions of the Bill of Rights were incorporated into the Fourteenth Amendment and applied to the states. Table 4.3 shows the progress of this revolution in the interpretation of the Constitution.

TABLE 4.3

Incorporation of the Bill of Rights into the Fourteenth Amendment

These cases are significant because they represent the first instance that the Supreme Court acknowledged that the selected provision or amendment was binding on the states. In some cases this meant the Supreme Court overturned the state or local law under contention. In other cases, the Court held that the law did not violate the Constitution and so the law was upheld.

SELECTED PROVISIONS AND AMENDMENTS	INCORPORATED	KEY CASE
Eminent domain (V)	1897	*Chicago, Burlington, and Quincy R.R. v. Chicago*
		The city of Chicago was required to compensate a railroad company for seizing its property for the purpose of widening a city road.
Freedom of speech (I)	1925	*Gitlow v. New York*
		Upheld Gitlow's conviction for "criminal anarchy" for publishing a left-wing manifesto. The Court held the First Amendment allowed the states to suppress speech directly advocating the overthrow of the government.
Freedom of press (I)	1931	*Near v. Minnesota*
		Overturned Minnesota's permanent injunction against those who created a "public nuisance" by publishing, selling, or distributing a "malicious, scandalous and defamatory newspaper, magazine or other periodical" as an infringement on freedom of the press.
Free exercise of religion (I)	1934	*Hamilton v. Regents of the University of California*
		Students filed suit to protest mandatory military training at the University of California on religious grounds. The Court upheld the right of California to mandate that its students receive military training as permissible under the First Amendment's free exercise of religion clause.
Freedom of assembly (I) and freedom to petition the government for redress of grievances (I)	1937	*DeJonge v. Oregon*
		DeJonge's conviction for addressing a meeting of the Communist Party was overturned as an infringement on freedom of assembly.

SELECTED PROVISIONS AND AMENDMENTS	INCORPORATED	KEY CASE
Nonestablishment of state religion (I)	1947	*Everson v. Board of Education* Applying the establishment clause, the Court found that using taxpayer money to bus students to private religious schools did not constitute establishing a religion because busing was a "separate" function from the school's religious purpose.
Freedom from warrantless search and seizure (IV) ("exclusionary rule")	1961	*Mapp v. Ohio* The Court overturned the conviction of Dollree Mapp for possession of obsecene materials because the evidence was obtained in violation of the Fourth Amendment's requirement of a warrent for conducting a search.
Freedom from cruel and unusual punishment (VIII)	1962	*Robinson v. California* The Court overturned a California law imposing a 90-day jail sentence on persons found guilty of "addiction to the use of narcotics" as cruel and unusual punishment for what amounted to illness.
Right to counsel in any criminal trial (VI)	1963	*Gideon v. Wainwright* Gideon requested a lawyer at his trial for a felony crime, but was denied under Florida law. The Supreme Court held the right to counsel in the Sixth Amendment applied to the states, so Gideon got a new trial with counsel.
Right against self-incrimination and forced confessions (V)	1964	*Malloy v. Hogan* Malloy was imprisoned for contempt after refusing to answer questions about gambling activities on grounds it might implicate him. The Supreme Court held the Fifth Amendment secures defendants against self-incrimination so Malloy could not be forced to testify.
Right to remain silent (V)	1964	*Escobedo v. Illinois* Police denied repeated requests by Escobedo to see his lawyer during interrogation; Escobedo eventually incriminated himself in a murder. The Court held Escobedo's Sixth Amendment rights to counsel and to the right to remain silent were violated.
Right to counsel and to remain silent (V)	1966	*Miranda v. Arizona* Miranda was questioned by police and signed a statement of confession without being informed of his right to counsel and protection from self-incrimination. The Court held defendants in police custody must be informed of their rights.
Right against double jeopardy (V)	1969	*Benton v. Maryland* Benton was tried twice for the same crime of larceny. The Supreme Court held "double jeopardy" as impermissible under the Fifth Amendment.
Right to bear arms (II)	2010	*McDonald v. Chicago* The Supreme Court struck down a Chicago firearms ordinance making it extremely dificult to own a gun within city limits as violating the Second Amendment.

The best way to examine the Bill of Rights today is the simplest way: to take the major provisions one at a time. Some of these provisions are settled areas of law; others are not. The Court can reinterpret any one of them at any time.

● The First Amendment and Freedom of Religion

> Describe how the First Amendment protects freedom of religion

Congress shall make no law respecting an establishment of religion, or prohibiting the free exercise thereof; or abridging the freedom of speech, or of the press; or the right of the people peaceably to assemble, and to petition the Government for a redress of grievances.

The Bill of Rights begins by guaranteeing freedom of religion, and the First Amendment provides for that freedom in two distinct clauses: "Congress shall make no law [1] respecting an establishment of religion, or [2] prohibiting the free exercise thereof." The first clause is called the "establishment clause," and the second is called the "free exercise clause."

Separation between Church and State

establishment clause the First Amendment clause that says that "Congress shall make no law respecting an establishment of religion"; this law means that a "wall of separation" exists between church and state

The **establishment clause** and the idea of "no law" regarding the establishment of religion could be interpreted in several possible ways. One interpretation, which probably reflects the views of many of the First Amendment's authors, is that the government is prohibited from establishing an official church. Official state churches, such as the Church of England, were common in the eighteenth century and were viewed by many Americans as inconsistent with a republican form of government. Indeed, many American colonists had fled Europe to escape persecution for having rejected state-sponsored churches. A second possible interpretation is the view that the government may not take sides among competing religions but is not prohibited from providing assistance to religious institutions or ideas as long as it shows no favoritism. The United States accommodates religious beliefs in a variety of ways, from the reference to God on U.S. currency to the prayer that begins every session of Congress. These forms of religious establishment have never been struck down by the courts. The third view regarding religious establishment, which for many years dominated Supreme Court decision making in this realm, is the idea of a "wall of separation" between church and state—Jefferson's formulation—that cannot be breached by the government. For two centuries, Jefferson's words have had a powerful impact on our understanding of the proper relationship between church and state in America.

Despite the seeming absoluteness of the phrase "wall of separation," there is ample room to disagree on how high the wall is. One area of contestation over the appropriate boundary between church and state is in public education. For example, the Court has been consistently strict in cases of school prayer, striking down such practices as Bible reading,[16] nondenominational prayer,[17] a moment of silence for meditation, and pregame prayer at public sporting events.[18] In each of these cases, the Court reasoned that school-sponsored religious observations, even of an apparently nondenominational character, are highly suggestive of school sponsorship and therefore violate the prohibition against establishment of religion.

And although the Court has consistently disapproved of government financial support for religious schools, even when the purpose has been purely educational and secular, it has permitted certain direct aid to students of such schools in the form of busing, for example. In 1971, after 30 years of cases involving religious schools, the Court attempted to specify some criteria to guide its decisions and those of lower courts, indicating, for example, in a decision invalidating state payments for the teaching of secular subjects in parochial schools, circumstances under which the Court might allow certain financial assistance. The case was *Lemon v. Kurtzman*; in its decision, the Supreme Court established three criteria to guide future cases—what came to be called the **Lemon test**. The Court held that government aid to religious schools would be accepted as constitutional if (1) it had a secular purpose, (2) its effect was neither to advance nor to inhibit religion, and (3) it did not entangle government and religious institutions in each other's affairs.[19]

The First Amendment affects everyday life in a multitude of ways. Because of the amendment's ban on state-sanctioned religion, the Supreme Court ruled in 2000 that student-initiated public prayer in school is illegal. Pregame prayer at public schools violates the establishment clause of the First Amendment.

Although these restrictions make the *Lemon* test hard to pass, imaginative authorities are finding ways to do so, and the Supreme Court has demonstrated a willingness to let them. For example, in 1995 the Court narrowly ruled that a student religious group at the University of Virginia could not be denied student activities funds merely because it was a religious group espousing a particular viewpoint about a deity. The Court called the denial "viewpoint discrimination" that violated the free speech rights of the group.[20]

In 2004 the question of whether the phrase "under God" in the Pledge of Allegiance violated the establishment clause was brought before the Court. Written without any religious references in 1892, the pledge had long been used in schools. But in 1954, in the midst of the Cold War, Congress voted to change the pledge in response to the "godless Communism" of the Soviet Union. The revised version read, "I pledge allegiance to the flag of the United States of America and to the Republic for which it stands, one nation *under God*, indivisible, with liberty and justice for all."

Ever since the change was made, there has been a steady murmuring of discontent from those who object to an officially sanctioned profession of belief in a deity as a violation of the establishment clause of the First Amendment. In 2003, Michael A. Newdow, the atheist father of a kindergarten student, brought suit against the local California school district. Newdow argued that the reference to God turned the daily recitation of the pledge into a religious exercise. A federal court ruled that although students were not required to recite the pledge at all, having to stand and listen to "under God" still violated the First Amendment's establishment clause. The case was appealed to the Supreme Court, and on June 14, 2004—exactly 50 years to the day after the adoption of "under God" in the pledge—the Court ruled that Newdow lacked a sufficient personal stake in the case to bring the complaint. This inconclusive decision by the Supreme Court left "under God" in the pledge while keeping the issue alive for possible resolution in a future case.

Another realm of contestation over the meaning of the establishment clause is in public displays of religious symbols, such as city-sponsored nativity scenes in

Lemon test a rule articulated in *Lemon v. Kurtzman* that government action toward religion is permissible if it is secular in purpose, neither promotes nor inhibits the practice of religion, and does not lead to "excessive entanglement" with religion

Does the display of the Bible's Ten Commandments in a state or county courthouse violate the First Amendment's separation of church and state? In 2005 the Supreme Court said yes, it does, and this display in McCreary, Kentucky, was removed.

commercial or municipal areas. This realm remains contested in part because the Supreme Court's rulings on such cases have been inconclusive, as demonstrated by two 2005 cases involving displays of the Ten Commandments. In *Van Orden v. Perry*, the Court decided by a 5–4 margin that a display of the Ten Commandments outside the Texas state capitol did not violate the Constitution.[21] However, in *McCreary County v. American Civil Liberties Union of Kentucky*, decided at the same time and also by a 5–4 margin, the Court determined that a display of the Ten Commandments inside two Kentucky courthouses was unconstitutional.[22] Justice Stephen Breyer, the deciding vote in the two cases, said that the display in *Van Orden* had a secular purpose, whereas the displays in *McCreary* had a purely religious purpose. The key difference between the two cases is that the Texas display had been exhibited in a large park for 40 years with other monuments related to the development of American law without any objections raised until this case, whereas the Kentucky display was erected much more recently and initially by itself, suggesting to some justices that its posting had a religious purpose. But most observers saw little difference between the two cases. Even Breyer was hard-pressed to explain his shifting votes, except to say that *Van Orden* was a "borderline" case. Obviously, the issue of government-sponsored displays of religious symbols has not been settled.

Free Exercise of Religion

free exercise clause the First Amendment clause that protects a citizen's right to believe and practice whatever religion he or she chooses

The **free exercise clause** protects the right to believe and to practice whatever religion one chooses; it also protects the right to be a nonbeliever. The precedent-setting case involving free exercise is *West Virginia State Board of Education v. Barnette* (1943), which involved the children of a family of Jehovah's Witnesses who refused to salute and pledge allegiance to the American flag on the grounds that their religious faith did not permit it. Three years earlier, the Court had upheld such a requirement and had permitted schools to expel students for refusing to salute the flag. But the entry of the United States into a war to defend democracy, coupled with the ugly treatment to which the Jehovah's Witnesses' children had been subjected, induced the Court to reverse itself and to endorse the free exercise of religion even when it may be offensive to the beliefs of the majority.[23]

Although the Supreme Court has been fairly consistent and strict in protecting the free exercise of religious belief, it has taken pains to distinguish between religious beliefs and *actions* based on those beliefs. The 1940 case of *Cantwell v. Connecticut* established the "time, place and manner" rule. The case arose from the efforts of two Jehovah's Witnesses to engage in door-to-door fund-raising. Americans are free to adhere to any religious beliefs, but the time, place, and manner of their exercise are subject to regulation in the public interest.[24]

In another case, two Native Americans had been fired from their jobs for ingesting peyote, a cactus banned as an illegal drug. They claimed that they had been fired from their jobs unlawfully because the use of peyote was a religious sacrament protected by the free exercise clause. The Court disagreed with their claim in an important 1990 decision,[25] but Congress supported the claim and went on to engage in an unusual controversy with the Court, involving the separation of powers and the proper application of the separation of church and state. Congress reversed the Court's 1990 decision with the enactment of the Religious Freedom Restoration Act of 1993 (RFRA), forbidding any federal agency or state government from restricting a person's free exercise of religion unless the federal agency or state government demonstrates that its action "furthers a compelling government interest" and "is the least restrictive means of furthering that compelling governmental interest." One of the first applications of RFRA was to a case brought by St. Peter's Catholic Church against the city of Boerne, Texas, which had denied permission to the church to enlarge its building because the building had been declared a historic landmark. The case went to federal court on the argument that the city had violated the church's religious freedom as guaranteed by Congress in RFRA. The Supreme Court declared RFRA unconstitutional, but on grounds rarely utilized, if not unique to this case: Congress had violated the separation of powers principle, infringing on the powers of the judiciary by going so far beyond its lawmaking powers that it ended up actually expanding the scope of religious rights rather than just enforcing them. The Court thereby implied that questions requiring a balancing of religious claims against public policy claims were reserved strictly to the judiciary.[26]

for critical analysis

Despite the establishment clause, the United States still uses the motto "In God We Trust" and calls itself "one nation, under God." This Indiana license plate was introduced in 2007. Do you think its reference to God is a violation of the separation of church and state?

● The First Amendment and Freedom of Speech and of the Press

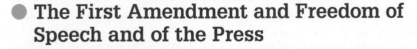

Describe how the First Amendment protects free speech

Congress shall make no law . . . abridging the freedom of speech, or of the press.

Freedom of speech and of the press have a special place in American political thought. To begin with, democracy depends on the ability of individuals to talk to one another and to disseminate information. It is difficult to conceive how democratic politics could function without free and open debate. Such debate, moreover, is seen as an essential mechanism for determining the quality or validity of competing ideas. As Justice Oliver Wendell Holmes said in 1919, "The best test of truth is the power of the thought to get itself accepted in the competition of the market. . . . That at any rate is the theory of our Constitution."[27] What is sometimes called the "marketplace of ideas" receives a good deal of protection from the courts. In 1938 the Supreme Court held that any legislation that attempts to restrict speech "is to be subjected to a more exacting judicial scrutiny . . . than are most other types of legislation."[28] This higher standard of judicial review came to be called "strict scrutiny."

The doctrine of strict scrutiny places a heavy burden of proof on the government if it seeks to regulate or restrict speech. Americans are assumed to have the right to speak and to broadcast their ideas unless some compelling reason can be identified to stop them. But strict scrutiny does not mean that speech can never be regulated. Over the past 200 years, the courts have scrutinized many different forms of speech and constructed different principles and guidelines for each. According to the courts, although virtually all speech is protected by the Constitution, some forms of speech are entitled to a greater degree of protection than others.

Political Speech

Political speech was the activity of greatest concern to the framers of the Constitution, even though some found it the most difficult form of speech to tolerate. Within seven years of the ratification of the Bill of Rights in 1791, Congress adopted the infamous Alien and Sedition Acts, which, among other things, made it a crime to say or publish anything that might tend to defame or bring into disrepute the government of the United States.

The first modern free speech case arose immediately after World War I. It involved persons who had been convicted under the federal Espionage Act of 1917 for opposing U.S. involvement in the war. The Supreme Court upheld the Espionage Act and refused to protect the speech rights of the defendants on the grounds that their activities—appeals to draftees to resist the draft—constituted a **"clear and present danger"** to national security.[29] This is the first and most famous "test" for when government intervention or censorship can be permitted.

It was only after the 1920s that real progress toward a genuinely effective First Amendment was made. Since then, political speech has been consistently protected by the courts even when it has been deemed "insulting" or "outrageous." Here is the way the Supreme Court put it in one of its most important statements on the subject, in the 1969 case *Brandenburg v. Ohio*:

> The constitutional guarantees of free speech and free press do not permit a State to forbid or proscribe advocacy of the use of force or of law violation *except where such advocacy is directed to inciting or producing imminent lawless action and is likely to incite or produce such action* [emphasis added].[30]

In other words, as long as speech falls short of actually inciting action, it cannot be prohibited, even if it is hostile to or subversive of the government and its policies. This decision came in the case of a Ku Klux Klan leader, Charles Brandenburg, who had been arrested and convicted of advocating "revengent" action against the

"clear and present danger" test
test to determine whether speech is protected or unprotected, based on its capacity to present a "clear and present danger" to society

president, Congress, and the Supreme Court, among others, if they continued "to suppress the white, Caucasian race." Although Brandenburg was not carrying a weapon, some of the members of his audience were. Nevertheless, the Supreme Court reversed the state courts and freed Brandenburg while also declaring Ohio's Criminal Syndicalism Act unconstitutional because it punished persons who "advocate, or teach the duty, necessity, or propriety [of violence] as a means of accomplishing industrial or political reform"; or who publish materials or "voluntarily assemble . . . to teach or advocate the doctrines of criminal syndicalism." The Supreme Court argued that the statute did not distinguish "mere advocacy" from "incitement to imminent lawless action." It would be difficult to go much further in protecting freedom of speech.

Another area of political speech that has recently received much attention is the First Amendment status of monetary contributions to political campaigns. Campaign finance reform laws of the early 1970s, arising out of the Watergate scandal, sought to put severe limits on campaign spending. In the 1976 case *Buckley v. Valeo*, a number of important provisions were declared unconstitutional on the basis of a new principle that spending money by or on behalf of candidates is a form of speech protected by the First Amendment.[31] (For more details, see Chapter 10.)

The issue came up again in 2003 with passage of a new and still more severe campaign finance law, the Bipartisan Campaign Reform Act (BCRA). In *McConnell v. Federal Election Commission*, the 5–4 majority seriously reduced the area of speech protected by the *Buckley v. Valeo* decision by holding that Congress was well within its power to put limits on campaign spending. The Court argued that "the selling of access . . . has given rise to the appearance of undue influence [that justifies] regulations impinging on First Amendment rights . . . in order to curb corruption or the appearance of corruption."[32] In the *McConnell* case, the Court also upheld BCRA's limitations on "issue advertising." The act prohibited political advocacy groups from running ads that mentioned a candidate within 30 days of a primary election and 60 days of a general election. This ban was justified with the argument that wealthy special interests could affect election outcomes with last-minute ad campaigns. However, in its 2007 decision in the case of *Federal Election Commission v. Wisconsin Right to Life*, the Court reversed itself, declaring that such ads were protected speech and could not be prohibited so long as they focused mainly on issues and were not simply appeals to vote for or against a specific candidate.[33]

Even more recently, in the 2010 case of *Citizens United v. Federal Election Commission*, the Supreme Court declared that the First Amendment prohibited BCRA's ban on corporate funding of independent political broadcasts aimed at electing or defeating particular candidates.[34] In its 5–4 decision, the Supreme Court ruled that the Constitution prohibits the government from regulating political speech and that therefore the government could not ban this type of political spending by corporations. In 2014 the Court again expanded its protection of campaign expenditures under the First Amendment by overturning aggregate limits restricting how much money a donor may contribute.[35] The Court's decisions in both cases have been controversial. Republicans hailed the decisions as a victory for free speech, while Democrats denounced the decisions. President Obama called *Citizens United* "a major victory for big oil, Wall Street banks, health insurance companies, and the other powerful interests that marshal their power every day in Washington to drown out the voices of everyday Americans."[36]

Fighting Words and Hate Speech

Freedom of speech does have limits, however. Speech can also lose its protected position when it moves toward the sphere of action. "Expressive speech," for example, is protected until it moves from the symbolic realm to the realm of actual conduct—to direct incitement of damaging conduct with the use of so-called **fighting words**. In 1942 a man called a police officer a "goddamned racketeer" and "a damn Fascist," and was arrested and convicted of violating a state law forbidding the use of offensive language in public. When his case reached the Supreme Court, the arrest was upheld on the grounds that the First Amendment provides no protection for such offensive language because such words "are no essential part of any exposition of ideas."[37] This decision was reaffirmed in the important 1951 case of *Dennis v. United States* when the Supreme Court held that

> there is no substantial public interest in permitting certain kinds of utterances: the lewd and obscene, the profane, the libelous, and the insulting or "fighting" words— those which by their very utterance inflict injury or tend to incite an immediate breach of the peace.[38]

for critical analysis

Is there speech that should be banned because it does not contribute to the exchange of ideas? How do we determine what speech should be protected because it contributes to this exchange and what speech does not?

Since that time, however, the Supreme Court has reversed almost every conviction based on arguments that the speaker had used "fighting words."

In recent years, the increased activism of minority and women's groups has prompted a movement against words that might be construed as offensive to members of a particular group. Scores of universities have attempted to develop speech codes to suppress utterances deemed to be racial or ethnic slurs. Similar developments have taken place in large corporations, both public and private, with many successful complaints and lawsuits alleging that the words of employers or their supervisors created a "hostile or abusive working environment." The Supreme Court has held that a "hostile working environment" results from "sexual harassment," including "unwelcome sexual advances, requests for sexual favors, and other *verbal* or physical conduct of a sexual nature [emphasis added]."[39] A fundamental free speech issue is involved in these regulations of hostile speech.

Many jurisdictions have drafted ordinances banning hate speech—forms of expression designed to assert hatred toward one or another group, be they African Americans, Jews, Muslims, or others. Such ordinances seldom pass constitutional muster. The leading Supreme Court case in this realm is the 1992 decision in *R.A.V. v. City of St. Paul.*[40] Here, a white teenager was arrested for burning a cross on the lawn of a black family in violation of a municipal ordinance that banned cross burning. The Court ruled that such an ordinance must be *content neutral*— that is, it must not prohibit actions directed at some groups but not others. The statute in question prohibited only cross burning—which is typically directed at African Americans. Since a statute banning all forms of hateful expression would be deemed overly broad, the *R.A.V.* standard suggests that virtually all hate speech is constitutionally protected.

Student Speech

One category of conditionally protected speech is the speech of high school students in public schools. In 1986 the Supreme Court backed away from a broad protection of student free speech rights by upholding the punishment of a high school student for making a sexually suggestive speech. The Court opinion held that such speech interfered with the school's goal of teaching students the limits of socially acceptable behavior.[41] Two years later the Supreme Court took another conservative step by restricting students' speech and press rights even further, defining them as part of the educational process and not to be treated with the same standard as adult speech in a regular public forum.[42] A later case involving high school students is the 2007 case of *Morse v. Frederick*.[43] This case dealt with the policies of Juneau-Douglas High School in Juneau, Alaska. In 2002 the Olympic torch relay had passed through Juneau on its way to Salt Lake City for the opening of the Winter Olympics. As the torch passed Juneau-Douglas High, a senior, Joseph Frederick, unfurled a banner reading "BONG HITS 4 JESUS." The school's principal promptly suspended Frederick, who then brought suit for reinstatement, alleging that his free speech rights had been violated. Like most of America's public schools, Juneau High prohibits assemblies or expressions on school grounds that advocate illegal drug use, saying that some federal aid is contingent on this policy. Civil libertarians, of course, see such policies as restricting students' right to free speech. Speaking for the Court's majority, Chief Justice Roberts said that the First Amendment did not require schools to permit students to advocate illegal drug use.

The Supreme Court has ruled that high school students' speech can be restricted. In a 2007 case involving a student who displayed the banner at left, the Court found that the school principal had not violated the student's right to free speech by suspending him.

Commercial Speech

Commercial speech, such as newspaper or television advertisements, does not have full First Amendment protection because it cannot be considered political speech. Initially considered to be entirely outside the protection of the First Amendment, commercial speech today is subject to limited regulation. For example, the prohibition of false and misleading advertising by the Federal Trade Commission is an old and well-established power of the federal government. The Supreme Court has upheld city ordinances prohibiting the posting of all commercial signs on public property (as long as the ban is total, so that there is no hint of selective censorship).[44]

However, the gains far outweigh the losses in the effort to expand the protection of commercial speech under the First Amendment. "In part, this reflects the growing appreciation that commercial speech is part of the free flow of information necessary for informed choice and democratic participation."[45] For example, in 1975 the Supreme Court struck down a state statute making it a misdemeanor to sell or circulate newspapers encouraging abortions; the Court ruled that the statute infringed on constitutionally protected speech and on the right of the reader to make informed choices.[46] On a similar basis, the Court reversed its own earlier decisions upholding laws that prohibited dentists and other professionals from advertising their services. For the Court, medical service advertising was a matter of health that could be advanced by the free flow of information.[47] And in a 2001 case, the Court ruled that a Massachusetts ban on all cigarette advertising violated the First Amendment right of the tobacco industry to advertise its products to adult consumers.[48] These instances of commercial speech, significant in themselves, are all the more significant because they indicate the breadth and depth of the freedom existing today to direct appeals to a large public, not only to sell goods and services but also to mobilize people for political purposes.

Symbolic Speech, Speech Plus, and the Rights of Assembly and Petition

The First Amendment treats the freedoms of religion and political speech as equal to the freedoms of assembly and petition—speech associated with action. For this reason, the long record of Supreme Court cases largely protects an individual's right to symbolic speech, assembly, and petition. Freedom of speech and freedom of assembly are closely related by the "public forum doctrine." In the 1939 case of *Hague v. Committee for Industrial Organization*, the Court declared that the government may not prohibit speech-related activities such as demonstrations or leafleting in public areas traditionally used for that purpose, though, of course, the government may impose rules designed to protect the public safety so long as these rules do not discriminate against particular viewpoints.[49]

Generally, the Supreme Court has sought to protect actions that are designed to send a political message. For example, the Court held unconstitutional a California statute making it a felony to display a red Communist flag "as a sign, symbol or emblem of opposition to organized government."[50] Although today there are limits on how far one can go with actions that convey a message symbolically, the protection of such actions is very broad. Thus, although the Court upheld a federal statute making it a crime to burn draft cards to protest the Vietnam War, on the grounds that the government had a compelling interest in preserving draft cards as part of the conduct of the war itself, the Court also deemed the wearing of black armbands to school a protected form of assembly for symbolic action.

Another example is the burning of the American flag as a protest. In 1984, at a political rally held during the Republican National Convention in Dallas, Texas, a political protester burned an American flag, thereby violating a Texas statute that prohibited desecration of a venerated object. In a 5–4 decision, the Supreme Court declared the Texas law unconstitutional on the grounds that flag burning was expressive conduct protected by the First Amendment.[51] Since 1995 the House of Representatives has seven times passed a resolution for a constitutional amendment to ban this form of expressive conduct, but each time, the Senate has failed to go along.[52]

In the 2011 case of *Snyder v. Phelps*, the Court sought to protect another form of symbolic speech. Members of the Westboro Baptist Church had frequently demonstrated at military funerals, claiming that the deaths of the soldiers were a sign that God disapproved of the acceptance

The Supreme Court has interpreted the freedom of speech as extending to symbolic acts of political protest, such as flag burning. On several occasions—most recently in 2006—a resolution for a constitutional amendment to ban flag burning has passed in the House of Representatives but has never found enough support in the Senate.

of homosexuality in the United States. The father of a soldier killed in Iraq brought suit against the church and its pastor, claiming that the demonstrators had caused him and his family severe emotional distress. The Supreme Court ruled, however, that the First Amendment protected free speech in a public place against such suits.[53]

Closer to the original intent of the assembly and petition clause is the category of **"speech plus"**—following speech with physical activity such as picketing, distributing leaflets, and other forms of peaceful demonstration or assembly. Such assemblies are consistently protected by courts under the First Amendment; state and local laws regulating such activities are closely scrutinized and frequently overturned. But the same assembly on private property is quite another matter, and can in many circumstances be regulated. For example, the directors of a shopping center can lawfully prohibit an assembly protesting a war or supporting a ban on abortion. Assemblies in public areas can also be restricted under some circumstances, especially when the assembly or demonstration jeopardizes the health, safety, or rights of others. This condition was the basis of the Supreme Court's decision to uphold a lower court order that restricted the access that abortion protesters had to the entrances of abortion clinics.[54]

"speech plus" speech accompanied by conduct such as sit-ins, picketing, and demonstrations; protection of this form of speech under the First Amendment is conditional, and restrictions imposed by state or local authorities are acceptable if properly balanced by considerations of public order

Freedom of the Press

For all practical purposes, freedom of speech implies and includes freedom of the press. With the exception of the broadcast media, which are subject to federal regulation, the press is protected under the doctrine against **prior restraint**. Beginning with the landmark 1931 case of *Near v. Minnesota*, the U.S. Supreme Court has held that, except under the most extraordinary circumstances, the First Amendment of the Constitution prohibits government agencies from seeking to prevent newspapers or magazines from publishing whatever they wish.[55] Indeed, in the case of *New York Times v. United States* (the so-called Pentagon Papers case), the Supreme Court ruled that the government could not block publication of secret Defense Department documents furnished to the *New York Times* by an opponent of the Vietnam War who had obtained the documents illegally.[56] In a 1990 case, however, the Supreme Court upheld a lower court order restraining Cable News Network (CNN) from broadcasting tapes of conversations between the former Panamanian dictator Manuel Noriega and his lawyer, supposedly recorded by the U.S. government. By a vote of 7 to 2, the Court held that CNN could be restrained from broadcasting the tapes until the trial court in the Noriega case had listened to the tapes and decided whether their broadcast would violate Noriega's right to a fair trial.[57]

prior restraint an effort by a governmental agency to block the publication of material it deems libelous or harmful in some other way; censorship; in the United States, the courts forbid prior restraint except under the most extraordinary circumstances

Another press freedom issue that the courts have often been asked to decide is the question of whether journalists can be compelled to reveal their sources of information. Journalists assert that if they cannot ensure their sources' confidentiality, the flow of information will be reduced and press freedom effectively curtailed. Government agencies, however, aver that names of news sources may be relevant to criminal or even national security investigations. More than 30 states have "shield laws," which, to varying degrees, protect journalistic sources. There is, however, no federal shield law. The Supreme Court has held that the press has no constitutional right to withhold information in court.[58] In 2005 a *New York Times* reporter, Judith Miller, was jailed for contempt of court for refusing to tell a federal grand jury the name of

a confidential source in a case involving the leaked identity of the CIA analyst Valerie Plame. Plame's husband, Joseph Wilson, had been critical of the Bush administration's Iraq policies.

In addition to prosecuting journalists for refusing to reveal their sources, the government may seek to prosecute individuals who leak information to the press. During the Obama presidency, seven individuals have been charged or prosecuted for disclosing classified information. These cases included Pfc. Bradley Manning, an army intelligence analyst sent to prison for providing classified documents to WikiLeaks, which published many of the documents, and Edward Snowden, an employee of the National Security Agency (NSA) who fled the country to escape arrest after revealing the details of NSA domestic spying operations. Another whistle-blower, Thomas Drake, was prosecuted after revealing the details of financial improprieties at the NSA to a *Baltimore Sun* reporter. Many journalists have been sharply critical of the Obama administration for its unprecedented efforts to halt whistle-blowing.[59]

Libel and Slander Some speech is not protected at all. If a written statement is made in "reckless disregard of the truth" and is considered damaging to the victim because it is "malicious, scandalous, and defamatory," it can be punished as **libel**. If such a statement is made orally, it can be punished as **slander**.

Most libel suits today involve freedom of the press, and the realm of free press is enormous. Historically, newspapers were subject to the law of libel, which provided that newspapers that printed false and malicious stories could be compelled to pay damages to those they defamed. In recent years, however, American courts have greatly narrowed the meaning of libel and made it extremely difficult, particularly for politicians or other public figures, to win a libel case against a newspaper. In the important 1964 case of *New York Times v. Sullivan*, the Court held that to be deemed libelous, a story about a public official not only had to untrue but also had to result from "actual malice" or "reckless disregard" for the truth.[60] In other words, the newspaper had to print false and malicious material deliberately. In practice, it is nearly impossible to prove that a paper *deliberately* printed maliciously false information, and it is especially difficult for a politician

libel a written statement made in "reckless disregard of the truth" that is considered damaging to a victim because it is "malicious, scandalous, and defamatory"

slander an oral statement made in "reckless disregard of the truth" that is considered damaging to the victim because it is "malicious, scandalous, and defamatory"

or other public figure to win a libel case. Essentially, the print media have been able to publish anything they want about a public figure.

However, the Court has opened up the possibility for public officials to file libel suits against the press. The Court has held that the press was immune to libel suits only when the printed material was "a matter of public concern."[61] In other words, a newspaper would have to show that the public official was engaged in activities that were indeed *public*. This principle has made the press more vulnerable to libel suits, but it still leaves an enormous realm of freedom for the press. For example, the Reverend Jerry Falwell, the leader of the Moral Majority, lost his libel suit against *Hustler* magazine even though the magazine had published a cartoon of Falwell showing him having drunken intercourse with his mother in an outhouse. A unanimous Supreme Court rejected a jury verdict in favor of damages for "emotional distress" on the grounds that parodies, no matter how outrageous, are protected because "outrageousness" is too subjective a test and thus would interfere with the free flow of ideas protected by the First Amendment.[62]

With the emergence of the Internet as an important communications medium, the courts have had to decide how traditional libel law applies to Internet content. In 1995 the New York courts held that an online bulletin board could be held responsible for the libelous content of material posted by a third party. To protect Internet service providers, Congress subsequently enacted legislation absolving them of responsibility for third-party posts. The federal courts have generally upheld this law and declared that service providers are immune from suits regarding the content of material posted by others.[63]

Obscenity and Pornography If libel and slander cases can be difficult because of the problem of determining the truth of statements and whether those statements are malicious and damaging, cases involving pornography and obscenity can be even trickier. Not until 1957 did the Supreme Court confront this problem, and it did so with a definition of obscenity that may have caused more confusion than it cleared up. In writing the Court's opinion, Justice William Brennan defined obscenity as speech or writing that appeals to the "prurient interest"—that is, whose purpose is to excite lust, as this appears "to the average person, applying contemporary community standards." Even so, Brennan added, the work should be judged obscene only when it is "utterly without redeeming social importance."[64] Instead of clarifying the Court's view, Brennan's definition actually caused more confusion. In 1964, Justice Potter Stewart confessed that, although he found pornography impossible to define, "I know it when I see it."[65]

The vague and impractical standards that had been developed meant ultimately that almost nothing could be banned on the grounds that it was pornographic and obscene. An effort was made to strengthen the restrictions in 1973, when the Supreme Court expressed its willingness to define pornography as a work that (1) as a whole, is deemed prurient by the "average person" according to "community standards"; (2) depicts sexual conduct "in a patently offensive way"; and (3) lacks "serious literary, artistic, political, or scientific value." This definition meant that pornography would be determined by local rather than national standards. Thus, a local bookseller might be prosecuted for selling a volume that was a best-seller nationally but that was deemed pornographic locally.[66] This new definition of standards did not help much either, and not long after 1973, the

Court began again to review all such community antipornography laws, reversing most of them.

In recent years, the battle against obscene speech has targeted "cyberporn"—pornography on the Internet. Opponents of this form of expression argue that it should be banned because of the easy access children have to the Internet. The first major effort to regulate the content of the Internet occurred in 1996, when Congress passed the Telecommunications Act. Attached to it was an amendment, called the Communications Decency Act (CDA), designed to regulate the on-line transmission of obscene material. The constitutionality of the CDA was immediately challenged in court by a coalition of interests led by the American Civil Liberties Union (ACLU). In the 1997 case of *Reno v. ACLU*, the Supreme Court struck down the CDA, ruling that it suppressed speech that "adults have a constitutional right to receive," and that governments may not limit the adult population to messages that are fit for children. Supreme Court justice John Paul Stevens described the Internet as the "town crier" of the modern age and said that the Internet was entitled to the greatest degree of First Amendment protection possible.[67] In 2003, Congress enacted the PROTECT Act, which outlawed efforts to sell child pornography via the Internet. The Supreme Court upheld this act in the 2008 case of *United States v. Williams*, in which the majority said that criminalizing efforts to purvey child pornography did not violate free speech guarantees.[68]

In 2000 the Supreme Court extended the highest degree of First Amendment protection to cable (not broadcast) television. In *United States v. Playboy Entertainment Group*, the Court struck down a portion of the 1996 Telecommunications Act that required cable TV companies to limit the broadcast of sexually explicit programming to late-night hours. In its decision, the Court noted that the law already provided parents with the means to restrict access to sexually explicit cable channels through various blocking devices. Moreover, such programming could come into the home only if parents decided to purchase such channels in the first place.[69]

Closely related to the issue of obscenity is the matter of violent broadcast content. Can a state or the federal government prohibit broadcasts or publications deemed to be excessively violent? Here, too, the Court has generally upheld freedom of speech. For example, in the 2011 case of *Brown v. Entertainment Merchants Association*, the Court struck down a California law banning the sale of violent video games to children, saying that the law violated the First Amendment.[70]

● The Second Amendment and the Right to Bear Arms

Explore whether the Second Amendment means people have a right to own guns

A well regulated Militia, being necessary to the security of a free State, the right of the people to keep and bear Arms, shall not be infringed.

The point and purpose of the Second Amendment is the provision for militias; they were to be the backing of the government for the maintenance of local public order. "Militia" was understood at the time of the Founding to be a military or police resource for state governments, and militias were specifically distinguished from armies and troops, which came within the sole constitutional jurisdiction of Congress.

Thus, the right of the people "to keep and bear Arms" is based on and associated with participation in state militias. The reference to citizens keeping arms underscored the fact that in the 1700s, state governments could not be relied on to provide firearms to militia members, so citizens eligible to serve in militias (white males between the ages of 18 and 45) were expected to keep their own firearms at the ready. In the late nineteenth century, some citizens sought to form their own *private* militias, but the Supreme Court cut that short with a ruling that militias are a military or police resource of state governments.[71]

The judicial record of Second Amendment cases is far sparser than for First Amendment cases, and for almost 60 years, the Court made no Second Amendment decisions. In the absence of a ruling that would apply to the entire country, localities across the country have very different gun ownership standards, the result of a patchwork of state and local laws (see Figure 4.1). For instance, in Wyoming, there is no ban on owning any type of gun, there is no waiting period to purchase a firearm, and individuals are not required to obtain a permit for carrying a concealed weapon. In California, in contrast, the possession of assault weapons is banned, there is a 10-day waiting period to purchase a firearm, and a permit is required to carry a concealed weapon.

The Court's silence on the application of the Second Amendment ended in 2008, when the Supreme Court made the first of two rulings in favor of expansive rights of gun ownership by individuals. In the case *District of Columbia v. Heller*, at issue was a strict Washington, D.C., law that banned handguns. In a 5–4 decision, the Court ruled that the Second Amendment provides a constitutional right to keep a loaded handgun at home for self-defense, a view that had long been subject to debate. In the majority opinion, Justice Antonin Scalia stated that the decision was not intended to cast doubt on all laws limiting firearm possession, such as the prohibition on gun ownership by felons or the mentally ill.[72] The District of Columbia is an entity of the federal government, and the

The mass shooting of 20 children in Newtown, Connecticut, prompted calls for legislation to limit the availability of guns. Opposition to such laws on Second Amendment grounds has prevented any significant national legislation since 1994.

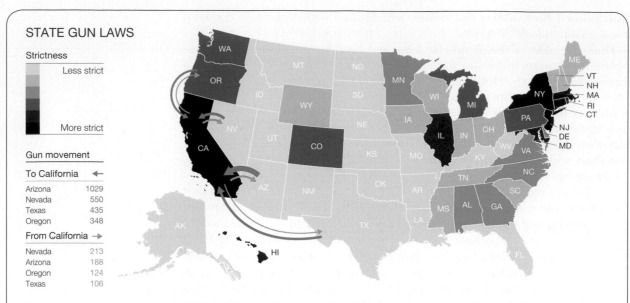

STATE GUN LAWS

Strictness

Less strict → More strict

Gun movement

To California ←

Arizona	1029
Nevada	550
Texas	435
Oregon	348

From California →

Nevada	213
Arizona	188
Oregon	124
Texas	106

The strictness of state gun laws is based on an analysis of laws aimed at preventing gun violence, such as background checks on all gun sales, permit-to-purchase requirements, and limiting handgun purchases to one a month. The arrows show the inflow and outflow of guns to and from California in 2012. The thickness of the arrow indicates the volume of guns that were used in crimes and tracked by the ATF.

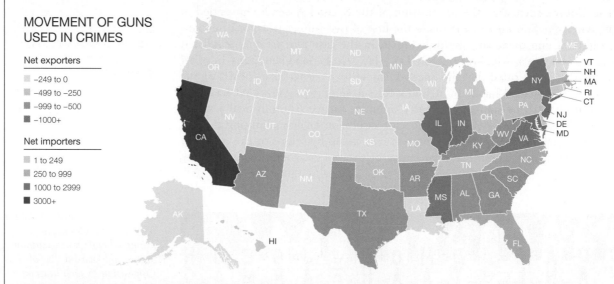

MOVEMENT OF GUNS USED IN CRIMES

Net exporters

- –249 to 0
- –499 to –250
- –999 to –500
- –1000+

Net importers

- 1 to 249
- 250 to 999
- 1000 to 2999
- 3000+

This figure maps the total number of guns imported to the state minus the total number of guns exported from the state in 2012. So negative numbers mean that the state exports more guns than it imports.

FIGURE 4.1

Guns Laws and Gun Trafficking

Although state gun laws must conform to the Second Amendment as interpreted by the U.S. Supreme Court, laws concerning gun sales and ownership vary widely from state to state. It is much more difficult to buy a gun in, say, New York or California than in Texas or Kentucky. However, there are few barriers to moving guns from one state to another. The Bureau of Alcohol, Tobacco, and Firearms (ATF) traces guns used in crimes and tracks their movement across states. How do gun laws appear to be related to the movement of guns used in crimes?

SOURCES: Brady Campaign to Prevent Gun Violence, http://bradycampaign.org/?q=programs/million-mom-march/state-gun-laws (accessed 1/14/14); U.S. Bureau of Alcohol, Tobacco, Firearms, and Explosives, www.atf.gov/sites/default/_les/assets/statistics/tracedata-2012/source-recovery-by-state.xlsx (accessed 1/14/14).

Court did not indicate that its ruling applied to state firearms laws. However, in the 2010 case of *McDonald v. Chicago*, the Supreme Court applied the Second Amendment to the states, making this decision the first new incorporation decision by the Court in 40 years. The case concerned a Chicago ordinance that made it extremely difficult to own a gun within city limits, and the Court's ruling had the effect of overturning the law.[73]

Despite these rulings, the debate over gun control continues to loom large in American politics today. A recent series of tragic shootings (including the killing of 20 elementary school students in Newtown, Connecticut, and 12 audience members at an Aurora, Colorado, movie theater) kept the issue of gun laws firmly on the national agenda.

● Rights of the Criminally Accused

Explain the major rights that people have if they are accused of a crime

Except for the First Amendment, most of the battle to apply the Bill of Rights to the states has been fought over the various protections granted to individuals who are accused of a crime, who are suspects in the commission of a crime, or who are brought before the court as a witness to a crime (Table 4.4). The Fourth, Fifth, Sixth, and Eighth amendments, taken together, are the essence of the **due process of law**, even though these precise words for this fundamental concept do not appear until the end of the Fifth Amendment. In the next sections, we will look at specific cases that illuminate the dynamics of this important constitutional issue. The procedural safeguards that we will discuss may seem remote to most law-abiding citizens, but they help define the limits of government action against the personal liberty of every citizen. Many Americans believe that "legal technicalities" are responsible for setting many actual criminals free. In many cases, this is absolutely true. In fact, setting defendants free is the very purpose of the requirements that constitute due process. One of America's traditional and most strongly held juridical values is that "it is far worse to convict an innocent man than to let a guilty man go free."[74] In civil suits, verdicts rest on "the preponderance of the evidence," but in criminal cases, guilt has to be proven "beyond a reasonable doubt"—a far higher standard. The provisions for due process in the Bill of Rights were added in order to improve the probability that the standard of "reasonable doubt" would be respected.

due process of law the right of every individual against arbitrary action by national or state governments

The Fourth Amendment and Searches and Seizures

> The right of the people to be secure in their persons, houses, papers, and effects, against unreasonable searches and seizures, shall not be violated, and no Warrants shall issue, but upon probable cause, supported by Oath or affirmation, and particularly describing the place to be searched, and the persons or things to be seized.

The purpose of the Fourth Amendment is to guarantee the security of citizens against unreasonable (i.e., improper) searches and seizures. In 1990 the Supreme Court summarized its understanding of the Fourth Amendment brilliantly and

exclusionary rule the ability of courts to exclude evidence obtained in violation of the Fourth Amendment

succinctly: "A search compromises the individual interest in privacy; a seizure deprives the individual of dominion over his or her person or property."[75] But how are we to define what is reasonable and what is unreasonable?

The 1961 case of *Mapp v. Ohio* illustrates one of the most important of the principles that have grown out of the Fourth Amendment—the **exclusionary rule**, which prohibits evidence obtained during an illegal search from being introduced in a trial. Acting on a tip that Dollree (Dolly) Mapp was harboring a suspect in a bombing incident, several policemen forcibly entered Mapp's house, claiming they had a warrant to look for the bombing suspect. The police did not find the bombing suspect but did find some materials connected to a local numbers racket (an illegal gambling operation) and a quantity of "obscene materials," in violation of an Ohio law banning possession of such materials. Although no warrant was ever produced, the evidence that had been seized was admitted by a court, and Mapp was charged and convicted of illegal possession of obscene materials.

By the time Mapp's appeal reached the Supreme Court, the issue of obscene materials had faded into obscurity, and the question before the Court was whether any evidence produced under the circumstances of the search of her home was admissible. The Court's opinion affirmed the exclusionary rule: under the Fourth Amendment (applied to the states through the Fourteenth Amendment), "all evidence obtained by searches and seizures in violation of the Constitution . . . is inadmissible."[76] This means that even people who are clearly guilty of the crime of which they are accused must not be convicted if the only evidence for their conviction was obtained illegally. This idea was expressed by Supreme Court justice Benjamin Cardozo nearly a century ago, when he wrote that "the criminal is to go free because the constable has blundered."

The exclusionary rule is the most dramatic restraint imposed by the courts on police behavior because it rules out precisely the evidence that produces a conviction; it frees those people who are *known* to have committed the crime of which they have been accused. Thus, in recent years the Court has softened the application of the exclusionary rule, and federal courts have relied on its discretionary use, whereby they make a judgment as to the "nature and quality of the intrusion." It is thus difficult to know ahead of time whether a defendant will or will not be protected from an illegal search under the Fourth Amendment.[77] In 2006, in the case of *United States v. Grubbs*, the Supreme Court ruled that the police could conduct searches using such "anticipatory warrants"—warrants issued when the police know that incriminating material is not yet present but have reason to believe that it will eventually arrive at a particular premises.[78] The warrants are held until the police are ready to conduct their search. In some instances, such as during an arrest, the authorities can conduct searches without obtaining any warrants at all.

The Fourth Amendment is also at issue in the controversy over mandatory drug testing. Such tests are most widely applied to public employees, and in 1989

the Supreme Court upheld the U.S. Customs Service's drug-testing program for its employees.[79] That same year, the Court approved drug and alcohol tests for railroad workers if they were involved in serious accidents.[80] Since then, more than 40 federal agencies have initiated mandatory employee drug tests, giving rise to public appeals against the general practice of "suspicionless testing" of employees, in violation of the Fourth Amendment. A 1995 case, in which the Court upheld a public school district's policy requiring all students participating in interscholastic sports to submit to random drug tests, surely contributed to the efforts of federal, state, and local agencies to initiate random and suspicionless drug and alcohol testing.[81]

The most recent cases suggest, however, that the Court is beginning to consider limits on the war against drugs. In 2001 the Court found it unconstitutional for police to use trained dogs in roadblocks set up to look for drugs in cars. Unlike drunk-driving roadblocks, where public safety is directly involved, narcotics roadblocks "cannot escape the Fourth Amendment's requirement that searches be based on suspicion of individual wrongdoing."[82] In a decisive 8–1 decision in 1997, the Court applied the Fourth Amendment as a shield against "state action that diminishes personal privacy" in cases that do not involve high-risk or safety-sensitive tasks.[83] And in 2013, the Court held that the use of a drug-sniffing dog on the front porch of a home constituted a search that violates the Fourth Amendment in the absence of consent of a warrant. The majority opinion, written by Justice Antonin Scalia, rested on traditional property notions."[84]

Changes in technology have also had an impact on Fourth Amendment jurisprudence. In the 2012 case of *United States v. Jones*, the Court held that prosecutors violated Jones's rights when they attached a GPS device to his Jeep and monitored his movements for 28 days.[85] On the other hand, in *Maryland v. King*, the Court upheld DNA testing of arrestees without the need for individualized suspicion. Writing for the majority, Justice Anthony Kennedy characterized DNA testing as an administrative tool for identifying the arrestee and thus legally indistinguishable from photographing and fingerprinting.[86] As new technologies develop, the Court will continue face the question of what constitutes a reasonable search.

The policing tactic of "stop and frisk" is intended to protect communities from violent crime. But opponents view it as invasion of privacy and unreasonable search without sufficient cause. Furthermore, opponents charge that such tactics damage the relationship between the police and the community.

grand jury jury that determines whether sufficient evidence is available to justify a trial; grand juries do not rule on the accused's guilt or innocence

double jeopardy the Fifth Amendment right providing that a person cannot be tried twice for the same crime

Fourth Amendment issues have also been raised by aggressive police tactics, particularly the tactic known as "stop and frisk." This is a tactic in which the police confront an individual whom they believe to be acting "suspiciously," question the individual, and conduct a search for weapons. The practice was reviewed by the Supreme Court in the 1968 case of *Terry v. Ohio* and the Court then held that if an officer had "probable cause" to believe the individual was armed, such a search was permitted.[87] In recent years, some police departments, most notably the New York City police, have made stop and frisk a routine practice, searching thousands and thousands of individuals whom they deemed to look suspicious. The police aver that this aggressive tactic has reduced crime rates. In August 2013 a federal judge, Shira Scheindlin, noted that most police stops occurred in minority communities and amounted to a form of racial profiling. The judge's order ending the practice, however, was stayed by a federal appeals court that removed Judge Scheindlin from the case and accused her of improper bias. The entire matter is currently being litigated.

The Fifth Amendment

No person shall be held to answer for a capital, or otherwise infamous crime, unless on a presentment or indictment of a Grand Jury, except in cases arising in the land or naval forces, or in the Militia, when in actual service in time of War or public danger; nor shall any person be subject for the same offence to be twice put in jeopardy of life or limb; nor shall be compelled in any criminal case to be a witness against himself, nor be deprived of life, liberty, or property, without due process of law; nor shall private property be taken for public use, without just compensation.

Grand Juries The first clause of the Fifth Amendment, the right to a **grand jury** to determine whether a trial is warranted, is considered "the oldest institution known to the Constitution."[88] Grand juries play an important role in federal criminal cases. However, the provision for a grand jury is the one important civil liberties provision of the Bill of Rights that was not incorporated into the Fourteenth Amendment to apply to state criminal prosecutions. Thus, some states operate without grand juries. In such states, the prosecuting attorney simply files a "bill of information" affirming that there is sufficient evidence available to justify a trial. If the accused person is to be held in custody, the prosecutor must take the available information before a judge to determine that the evidence shows probable cause.

Double Jeopardy "Nor shall any person be subject for the same offence to be twice put in jeopardy of life or limb" is the constitutional protection from **double jeopardy**, or being tried more than once for the same crime. The protection from double jeopardy was at the heart of the *Palko* case in 1937, which, as we saw earlier in this chapter, also established the principle of selective incorporation of the Bill of Rights. In the *Palko* case, the Supreme Court ruled that the Fifth Amendment's prohibition of double jeopardy did not apply to the states. However, in the 1969 case of *Benton v. Maryland*, the Court expressly overruled *Palko* and declared that the double jeopardy clause did, in fact, apply to the states.[89] In this case, the state of Maryland sought to try a defendant, John Benton, for larceny even though he had previously been acquitted by a jury.

Maryland's constitution did not prohibit such a proceeding and, at the second trial, Benton was convicted. The Supreme Court, however, ruled that the second trial violated Benton's rights under the U.S. Constitution. Double jeopardy now joined those rights "incorporated" via the Fourteenth Amendment.

Self-Incrimination Perhaps the most significant liberty found in the Fifth Amendment, and the one most familiar to the many Americans who watch television crime shows, is the guarantee that no citizen "shall be compelled in any criminal case to be a witness against himself." The most famous case concerning self-incrimination is one of such importance that Chief Justice Earl Warren assessed its results as going "to the very root of our concepts of American criminal jurisprudence."[90] Twenty-three-year-old Ernesto Miranda was sentenced to between 20 and 30 years in prison for the kidnapping and rape of an 18-year-old woman. The woman had identified him in a police lineup, and after two hours of questioning, Miranda confessed, subsequently signing a statement that his confession had been made voluntarily, without threats or promises of immunity. These confessions were admitted into evidence, served as the basis for Miranda's conviction, and also served as the basis for the appeal of his conviction all the way to the Supreme Court. Following one of the most intensely and widely criticized decisions ever handed down by the Supreme Court, Ernesto Miranda's case produced the rules the police must follow before questioning an arrested criminal suspect. The reading of a person's "Miranda rights" became a standard scene in every police station and on virtually every dramatization of police action on television and in the movies. *Miranda* advanced the civil liberties of accused persons not only by expanding the scope of the Fifth Amendment clause covering coerced confessions and self-incrimination but also by confirming the right to counsel (discussed later). The Supreme Court under Burger and Rehnquist considerably softened the *Miranda* restrictions, but the **Miranda rule** still stands as a protection against egregious police abuses of arrested persons. However, in the 2010 case of *Berghuis v. Thompkins*, the Supreme Court introduced an important qualification to the Miranda rule.[91] In a 5–4 decision, the Court said that statements made by suspects who did not expressly waive their

Miranda rule the requirement, articulated by the Supreme Court in *Miranda v. Arizona*, that persons under arrest must be informed prior to police interrogation of their rights to remain silent and to have the benefit of legal counsel

The case of Ernesto Miranda resulted in the creation of Miranda rights, which must be read to those arrested to make them aware of their constitutional rights.

DEFENDANT	LOCATION

SPECIFIC WARNING REGARDING INTERROGATIONS

1. YOU HAVE THE RIGHT TO REMAIN SILENT.

2. ANYTHING YOU SAY CAN AND WILL BE USED AGAINST YOU IN A COURT OF LAW.

3. YOU HAVE THE RIGHT TO TALK TO A LAWYER AND HAVE HIM PRESENT WITH YOU WHILE YOU ARE BEING QUESTIONED.

4. IF YOU CANNOT AFFORD TO HIRE A LAWYER ONE WILL BE APPOINTED TO REPRESENT YOU BEFORE ANY QUESTIONING, IF YOU WISH ONE.

SIGNATURE OF DEFENDANT	DATE
WITNESS	TIME

☐ REFUSED SIGNATURE   SAN FRANCISCO POLICE DEPARTMENT   PR.9.1.4

rights (usually by signing a form) could be used against them. The dissenting justices feared that this decision might open the way for police abuses and misleading claims.

Eminent Domain The other fundamental clause of the Fifth Amendment is the "takings clause," which extends to each citizen a protection against the "taking" of private property "without just compensation." Although this part of the Fifth Amendment is not specifically concerned with protecting persons accused of crimes, it is nevertheless a fundamentally important instance where the government and the citizen are adversaries. The power of any government to take private property for public use—a power essential to the very concept of sovereignty—is called **eminent domain**. The Fifth Amendment puts limits on that inherent power through procedures that require a showing of a public purpose and the provision of fair payment for the taking of someone's property. This provision is now universally observed in all U.S. principalities, but it has not always been meticulously observed.

The first modern case confronting the issue of public use involved a mom-and-pop grocery store in a run-down neighborhood of the District of Columbia. In carrying out a vast urban redevelopment program, the city government took the property as one of a large number of privately owned lots to be cleared for new housing and business construction. The owner of the grocery store took the government to court on the grounds that it was an unconstitutional use of eminent domain to take property from one private owner and eventually to turn that property back, in altered form, to another private owner. In 1945 the store owner lost the case. The Supreme Court's argument was a curious but very important one: the "public interest" can mean virtually anything a legislature says it means. In other words, since the overall slum clearance and redevelopment project was in the public interest, according to the legislature, the eventual transfers of property were justified.[92] This principle was reaffirmed in the 2005 case of *Kelo v. City of New London*, where the Court held that the city could seize land from one private owner and transfer it to another as part of a redevelopment plan.[93]

The Sixth Amendment and the Right to Counsel

> In all criminal prosecutions, the accused shall enjoy the right to a speedy and public trial, by an impartial jury of the State and district wherein the crime shall have been committed, which district shall have been previously ascertained by law, and to be informed of the nature and cause of the accusation; to be confronted with the witnesses against him; to have compulsory process for obtaining witnesses in his favor, and to have the Assistance of Counsel for his defence.

Like the exclusionary rule of the Fourth Amendment and the self-ncrimination clause of the Fifth Amendment, the "right to counsel" provision of the Sixth Amendment is notable for sometimes freeing defendants who seem to be guilty as charged. Other provisions of the Sixth Amendment, such as the right to a speedy trial and the right to confront witnesses before an impartial jury, are less controversial in nature.

Gideon v. Wainwright (1963) is the perfect case study because it involved a disreputable person who seemed patently guilty of the crime of which he was convicted. In and out of jails for most of his 51 years, Clarence Earl Gideon received a five-year sentence for breaking and entering a poolroom in Panama City, Florida.

eminent domain the right of government to take private property for public use

While serving time in jail, Gideon became a fairly well-qualified "jailhouse lawyer," made his own appeal on a handwritten petition, and eventually won the landmark ruling on the right to counsel in all felony cases.[94]

The right to counsel has been expanded during the past few decades, even as the courts have become more conservative. For example, although at first the right to counsel was met by judges assigning lawyers from the community as a formal public obligation, now most states and cities have created an office of public defender; these state-employed professional defense lawyers typically provide poor defendants with much better legal representation. In addition, defendants have the right to appeal a conviction on the grounds that the counsel provided by the state was deficient. For example, in 2003 the Supreme Court overturned the death sentence of a Maryland death row inmate, holding that the defense lawyer had failed to inform the jury fully of the defendant's history of "horrendous childhood abuse."[95] Moreover, the right to counsel extends beyond serious crimes to any trial, with or without a jury, that holds the possibility of imprisonment.[96]

The Eighth Amendment and Cruel and Unusual Punishment

> Excessive bail shall not be required, nor excessive fines imposed, nor cruel and unusual punishment inflicted.

Virtually all the debate over Eighth Amendment issues focuses on the last clause of the amendment: one of the greatest challenges in interpreting this provision consistently is that what is considered "cruel and unusual" varies from culture to culture and from generation to generation.

In 1972 the Supreme Court overturned several state death-penalty laws, not because they were cruel and unusual but because they were being applied unevenly—that is, blacks were much more likely than whites to be sentenced to death, and the poor more likely than the rich, and men more likely than women.[97] Very soon after that decision, a majority of states revised their capital punishment provisions to meet the Court's standards, and the Court reaffirmed that the death penalty could be used if certain standards were met.[98] Since 1976, the Court has consistently upheld state laws providing for capital punishment, although the Court also continues to review death-penalty appeals each year.

Between 1976 and mid-2014, states executed 1,384 people. Most of those executions occurred in southern states, with Texas leading the way at 515. As of 2014, 32 states had statutes providing for capital punishment for specified offenses, a policy supported by a majority of Americans, according to polls. On the other hand, 18 states bar the death penalty, and since the end of the 1990s, both the number of death sentences and the number of executions have declined annually.[99]

Despite the seeming popularity of the death penalty, the debate has become, if anything, more intense. Many death-penalty supporters assert its deterrent effects on other would-be criminals. Although studies of capital crimes usually fail to demonstrate any direct deterrent effect, this failure may be due to the lengthy delays—typically years and even decades—between convictions and executions. A system that eliminates undue delays might enhance deterrence. And deterring even one murder or other heinous crime, proponents argue, is ample justification for such laws.

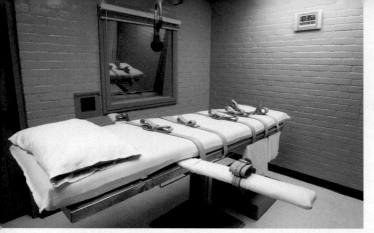

Thirty-two states currently have the death penalty for the most serious crimes. Although a majority of Americans support the death penalty, it has always been controversial and is sometimes seen as a violation of the Eighth Amendment.

Death-penalty opponents are quick to counter that the death penalty has not been proved to deter crime, either in the United States or abroad. In fact, America is the only Western nation that still executes criminals. If the government is to serve as an example of proper behavior, say foes of capital punishment, it has no business sanctioning killing when incarceration will similarly protect society. Furthermore, execution is time-consuming and expensive—more expensive than life imprisonment—precisely because the government must make every effort to ensure that it is not executing an innocent person. Curtailing legal appeals would make the possibility of a mistake too great. And although most Americans do support the death penalty, people also support life imprisonment without the possibility of parole as an alternative. Race also intrudes in death-penalty cases: people of color are disproportionately more likely than whites charged with identical crimes to be given the ultimate punishment.

The Supreme Court has long struggled to establish principles to govern executions. In recent years, the Court has issued a number of death-penalty opinions, declaring that death was too harsh a penalty for the crime of rape of a child[100] and invalidating a death sentence for a black defendant after the prosecutor improperly excluded African Americans from the jury.[101] The Court also upheld Kentucky's policy of execution by lethal injection despite arguments that this form of execution was likely to cause considerable pain.[102]

The question of cruel and unusual punishment goes beyond the death penalty. Federal courts have on occasion held that overcrowding and other dangerous conditions within prisons, such as inadequate food, medical care, and sanitation, may constitute cruel and unusual punishment. Also, prison officials employing threats and beatings against inmates may be guilty of violating this Eighth Amendment right.[103] The Court has also been concerned with punishments meted out to the mentally disabled and to juveniles. In a recent case, the Court held that life imprisonment without parole for a juvenile, even one convicted of murder, constituted cruel and unusual punishment.[104] The "Who Are Americans?" feature takes a look at the U.S. prison population.

● The Right to Privacy

right to privacy the right to be left alone, which has been interpreted by the Supreme Court to entail individual access to birth control and abortions

> **Assess whether people have a right to privacy under the Constitution**

A **right to privacy** was not granted in the Bill of Rights, but a clause in the Fourth Amendment provides for "the right of the people to be secure in their persons, houses, papers, and effects, against unreasonable searches and seizures." In a 1928 case, Justice Louis Brandeis argued in a dissent that the Fourth Amendment should be extended to a more general principle of "privacy in the home."[105] Another step in this direction was taken when several Jehovah's Witnesses directed their children not to salute the flag or say the Pledge of ance in school because the first of the Ten

Who Is in Prison?

Despite the many freedoms protected by the Bill of Rights, the United States imprisons more of its people than any other country. Although African Americans make up only about 13 percent of the total U.S. population, they make up 38 percent of the prison population. Incarceration rates by state range from a low of 145 per 100,000 residents in Maine to a high of 893 per 100,000 residents in Louisiana.*

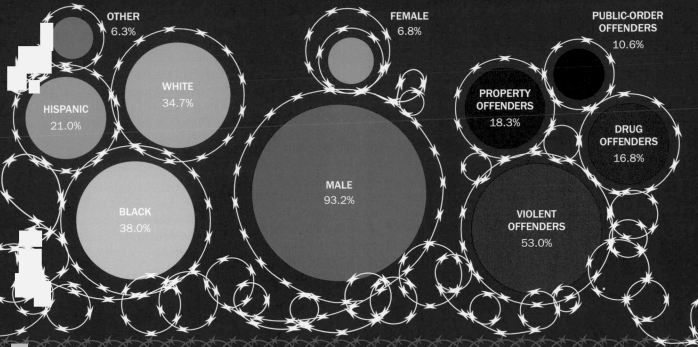

OTHER 6.3%
HISPANIC 21.0%
WHITE 34.7%
BLACK 38.0%
FEMALE 6.8%
MALE 93.2%
PROPERTY OFFENDERS 18.3%
PUBLIC-ORDER OFFENDERS 10.6%
DRUG OFFENDERS 16.8%
VIOLENT OFFENDERS 53.0%

*Violent offenses include murder, manslaughter, rape/sexual assault, robbery, and aggravated or simple assault. Property offenses include burglary, motor vehicle theft, and fraud. Drug offenses include trafficking and possession. Public order offenses include weapons, drunk driving, and indecency.

Incarceration Rates by State

Number of incarcarcerated individuals per 100,000 residents

- 145–299
- 300–399
- 400–499
- 500–599
- 600–900
- Data not available

145
378
499
358
213
184
242
211
199
190
379
434
357
441
276
333
247
282
398
261
448
360
242
392
440
440
378
451
351
325
518
489
357
583
315
648
438
494
458
717
650
542
601
893
524
401
273

for critical analysis

1. Due process guarantees the same legal protections to anyone accused of a crime. However, studies have shown that African Americans and Hispanics are more likely to be jailed—and jailed for longer—than whites convicted of similar crimes. Is this a violation of civil liberties?

2. Some people have argued that prison terms for relatively minor drug offenses violate the Eighth Amendment's ban on cruel and unusual punishment. What do you think?

for critical analysis

Read the Third, Fourth, Fifth, and Ninth amendments in the appendix at the end of this book. In your opinion, do American citizens have a right to privacy?

Commandments prohibits the worship of "graven images." They lost their case in 1940, but the Supreme Court, reversing itself in 1943, held that the 1940 case had been "wrongly decided" and recognized "a right to be left alone" as part of the free speech clause of the First Amendment.[106] Another small step was taken in 1958, when the Supreme Court recognized "privacy in one's association" in its decision that the state of Alabama could not use the membership list of the National Association for the Advancement of Colored People (NAACP) in state investigations.[107]

Birth Control

The sphere of privacy was formally recognized in 1965, when the Court ruled that a Connecticut statute forbidding the use of contraceptives violated the right of marital privacy. Estelle Griswold, the executive director of the Planned Parenthood League of Connecticut, was arrested by the state of Connecticut for providing information, instruction, and medical advice about contraception to married couples. She and her associates were found guilty as accessories to the crime and fined $100 each. The Supreme Court reversed the lower court decisions and declared the Connecticut law unconstitutional because it violated "a right of privacy older than the Bill of Rights—older than our political parties, older than our school system."[108] Justice William O. Douglas, author of the majority decision in the *Griswold* case, argued that this right of privacy is also grounded in the Constitution, because it fits into a "zone of privacy" created by a combination of the Third, Fourth, and Fifth amendments. A concurring opinion, written by Justice Arthur Goldberg, attempted to strengthen Douglas's argument by adding that "the concept of liberty . . . embraces the right of marital privacy though that right is not mentioned explicitly in the Constitution [and] is supported by numerous decisions of this Court . . . and *by the language and history of the Ninth Amendment* [emphasis added]."[109]

Abortion

The right to privacy was confirmed and extended in 1973 in an important Supreme Court decision: *Roe v. Wade*. This decision established a woman's right to seek an abortion and prohibited states from making abortion a criminal act.[110] The Burger Court's decision in *Roe* took a revolutionary step toward establishing the right to privacy. It is important to emphasize that the preference for privacy rights and for their extension to include the rights of women to control their own bodies was not something the Supreme Court invented in a vacuum. Most states did not regulate abortions in any fashion until the 1840s, at which time only 6 of the 26 existing states had any regulations governing abortion. In addition, many states had begun to ease their abortion restrictions well before the 1973 *Roe* decision, although in recent years a number of states have reinstated some restrictions on abortion.

By extending the umbrella of privacy, this sweeping ruling dramatically changed abortion practices in America. In addition, it galvanized and nationalized the abortion debate. Groups opposed to abortion, such as the National Right to Life Committee, organized to fight the liberal new standard, while abortion rights groups have sought to maintain that protection. While the Supreme Court has continued to affirm a woman's right to seek an abortion, the Court has since qualified that right, as the legal standard shifted against abortion rights supporters. In *Webster v. Reproductive Health Services* (1989), the Court narrowly upheld (by a 5–4 majority) the constitutionality

One of the most important cases related to the right to privacy was Roe v. Wade, *which established a woman's right to seek an abortion. However, the decision has remained highly controversial, with opponents arguing that the Constitution does not guarantee this right.*

of restrictions on the use of public medical facilities for abortion.[111] And in the 1992 case of *Planned Parenthood of Southeastern Pennsylvania v. Casey*, another 5–4 majority of the Court upheld *Roe* but narrowed its scope, refusing to invalidate a Pennsylvania law that significantly limits freedom of choice. The Court's decision defined the right to an abortion as a "limited or qualified" right subject to regulation by the states as long as the regulation does not constitute an "undue burden."[112] In the 2006 case of *Ayotte v. Planned Parenthood of Northern New England*, the Court held that a law requiring parental notification before a minor could obtain an abortion was not an undue burden.[113] And in the 2007 *Gonzales v. Carhart* decision, the Court effectively upheld the federal partial-birth abortion ban, which outlaws a particular type of abortion procedure.[114]

Homosexuality

In the last three decades, the right to be left alone began to include the privacy rights of homosexuals. One morning in Atlanta, Georgia, in the mid-1980s, a police officer came to the home of Michael Hardwick to serve a warrant for Hardwick's arrest for failure to appear in court to answer charges of drinking in public. One of Hardwick's unknowing housemates invited the officer to look in Hardwick's room, where he found Hardwick and another man engaging in "consensual sexual behavior" and then proceeded to arrest him under Georgia's laws against heterosexual and homosexual sodomy. Hardwick filed a lawsuit against the state, challenging the constitutionality of the Georgia law, and won his case in the federal court of appeals. The state of Georgia, in an unusual move, appealed the court's decision to the Supreme Court. In 1986 the majority of the Court reversed the lower court decision, holding against Hardwick on the grounds that "the federal Constitution confers [no] fundamental right upon homosexuals to engage in sodomy," and that therefore there was no basis to invalidate "the laws of the many states that still make such conduct illegal and have done so for a very long time."[115]

Seventeen years later, and to almost everyone's surprise, in *Lawrence v. Texas* (2003) the Court overturned *Bowers v. Hardwick* with a dramatic pronouncement

Civil Liberties around the World

Civil liberties are protected differently around the world. Interestingly, laws protecting freedom of expression and belief tend to be stronger than laws protecting other civil liberties, while the right to an established and equitable system of rule of law tends to be weakest, as the graph here shows. Freedom of association and organization also tends to receive weaker protection, especially in today's climate of fear of terrorism, when governments are concerned with identifying and disrupting terrorist organizations. Why might freedom of belief and expression be more strongly developed than other civil liberties?

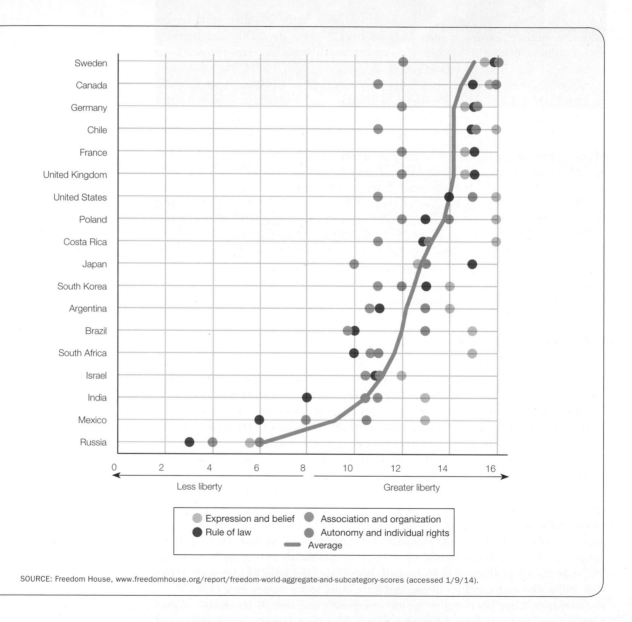

SOURCE: Freedom House, www.freedomhouse.org/report/freedom-world-aggregate-and-subcategory-scores (accessed 1/9/14).

that gays are "entitled to respect for their private lives"[116] as a matter of constitutional due process. Drawing from the tradition of negative liberty, the Court maintained, "In our tradition the State is not omnipresent in the home. And there are other spheres of our lives and existence outside the home, where the State should not be a dominant presence." Explicitly encompassing lesbians and gay men within the umbrella of privacy, the Court concluded that the "petitioners are entitled to respect for their private lives. The State cannot demean their existence or control their destiny by making their private sexual conduct a crime."[117] This decision added substance to the "right of privacy."[118]

The Right to Die

Another area ripe for litigation and public discourse is the so-called right to die. A number of highly publicized physician-assisted suicides in the 1990s focused attention on whether people have a right to choose their own death and to receive assistance in carrying it out. Can this become part of the privacy right? Or is it a new substantive right? The Supreme Court has not definitively answered this question. However, the Court refused to intervene in the well-publicized case of Terri Schiavo, a woman who suffered irreversible brain damage and was kept alive in a vegetative state via a feeding tube for 15 years. During this period, Schiavo's husband wanted to withdraw life support, citing his wife's wishes, while her parents wanted support continued indefinitely. The case was heard multiple times in the Florida state courts and the federal courts. In 2005, Schiavo's husband finally prevailed, and she was removed from life support and subsequently died. In the 2006 case of *Gonzales v. Oregon*, the Supreme Court did intervene to uphold a law allowing doctors to use drugs to facilitate the deaths of terminally ill patients who requested such assistance.[119] Thus, although the Court has not ruled definitively on the right-to-die question, it does not seem hostile to the idea.

Civil Liberties
and Your Future

Among the major civil liberties questions facing Americans today and into the future is the matter of government surveillance. Government eavesdropping on communications, travel, and personal conduct has become a fact of American life. Revelations in the summer of 2013 of extensive electronic surveillance by the National Security Agency (NSA) of Americans' phone and Internet communications caused considerable consternation in Congress and in the news media. Such surveillance, however, is not a new phenomenon in the United States. As early as 1920, the Cipher Bureau, remembered today as the "Black Chamber," an office jointly funded by the army and the State Department, secretly inspected telegrams in the Western Union system.

Today, the Black Chamber seems a quaint relic of a long-forgotten past as Americans find themselves subject to more or less constant government surveillance via electronic interception of telephone calls, examination of email communications and social media postings, to say nothing of ubiquitous security cameras now tied to crowd-scanning software, traffic monitoring, airport searches, and so forth. And, while the Black Chamber sifted through transcripted

National Intelligence Director James Clapper and other defense officials testified before Congress following revelations in 2013 of extensive government surveillance programs. Electronic monitoring allows the government to gather vast quantities of data from private communications.

telegrams by hand, peering at their contents, today the work is done by sophisticated computer software that allows the government to process and analyze enormous quantities of data, looking for possible indications of illicit activity among seemingly disparate bits of information.

Many Americans seem satisfied to believe that they are the beneficiaries rather than the potential victims of government surveillance. Those who have nothing to hide, goes the saying, have nothing to fear. This view is, of course, rather naive. As law professor Daniel Solove shows, surveillance can entrap even the most innocent individuals in a web of suspicions and allegations from which they may find it extremely difficult to extricate themselves.

Be that as it may, to couch the issue of government surveillance purely in terms of the conflict between security and privacy interests is to miss the larger question of political power in which this debate is embedded. Popular government requires that citizens possess a good deal of knowledge about the actions of the state. Knowledge is necessary to permit citizens to evaluate rulers' claims and to hold rulers accountable for their conduct. In essence, citizens must undertake their own surveillance of the government and its officials as a precondition for exerting influence over them. This idea is captured in the ancient Athenian practice of the audit (*euthyna*) in which all civil and military officials were periodically required to undergo detailed public examinations of their actions. The results might then be debated in the popular assembly (*ecclesia*), which was open to all male citizens who had performed the requisite period of military service. In this way, surveillance through the audit directly empowered the citizenry.

At the same time, citizens' ability to exercise power also requires that they have considerable protection from the state's scrutiny. To begin with, those intent on expressing anything but support for the groups in power need privacy to plan, organize, and mobilize lest their plans be anticipated and disrupted. Terrorists are hardly the only ones who need privacy. Even in the mundane realm of partisan politics, the efforts of the party-out-of-power can certainly be compromised if the government becomes privy to its plans. Known political dissidents, moreover, always face some risk of official reprisal. Accordingly, at least some citizens may refrain from acting upon their political beliefs for fear that they will draw attention to themselves and become targets for tax audits and other government efforts to find evidence of criminality, fraud, or other misconduct that can be used against them.

Thus, popular government requires a combination of government transparency and citizen privacy. To exercise influence over it, citizens must know what the government is doing. At the same time, citizens seeking to exercise influence over the government need protection from retaliation and intimidation. Unfortunately, however, the direction of American politics today seems to be diverging from these ideals. Today, indeed, the government keeps more and more of its activities secret while the citizenry has less and less privacy. These problems will continue to grow as surveillance technologies become more sophisticated and we, as citizens, will be challenged to adapt eighteenth-century constitutional protections to twenty-first-century issues. How have new technologies affected the government's ability to monitor its citizens? What are your expectations of privacy in your email conversations, your plane tickets, your reading habits?

plug

Inform

Read the Bill of Rights, which is included in the Appendix to this book. Then, learn about how civil liberties apply in the digital age by reading the "Know Your Rights" page on the Electronic Frontier Foundation's website (www.eff.org).

Express

Imagine you are a legislative staffer. Draft a policy memo on the extent of government surveillance of American citizens. Should there be limits on government surveillance in the fight against terrorism?

Connect

Visit the American Civil Liberties Union (ACLU) website and consider signing up for their mailing list. Which issues interest you?

Act

Click the "Take Action" link on the EFF's website or the "Action" link on the ACLU's site, to sign a petition or learn about other ways to get involved in current civil liberties issues.

studyguide

A Brief History of the Bill of Rights

> **Explain the origins and evolution of the civil liberties in the Bill of Rights as they apply to federal government (pp. 117–22)**

Although some of the framers believed that a bill of rights was unnecessary and potentially dangerous, the Federalists made a pledge to add one in order to secure support for the Constitution during the ratification process. During the first hundred years of American history, the Bill of Rights was interpreted to limit only the actions of the federal government. One by one, most of the important provisions of the first 10 amendments have eventually been incorporated into the Fourteenth Amendment and applied to the states.

Key Terms

habeas corpus (p. 117)

bill of attainder (p. 117)

ex post facto laws (p. 117)

Bill of Rights (p. 118)

civil liberties (p. 118)

selective incorporation (p. 119)

Practice Quiz

1. From 1789 until the end of the nineteenth century, the Bill of Rights put limits on
   a) the national government only.
   b) the state government only.
   c) both the national and state governments.
   d) neither the national nor the state government.
   e) political parties and interest groups.

2. Which of the following rights was *not* included in the original Constitution?
   a) prohibition of bills of attainder
   b) prohibition of ex post facto laws
   c) guarantee of habeas corpus
   d) guarantee of trial by jury in the state where the crime was committed
   e) None. They were all included in the original Constitution.

3. The process by which some of the liberties in the Bill of Rights were applied to the states (or nationalized) is known as
   a) preemption.
   b) selective incorporation.
   c) judicial activism.
   d) civil liberties.
   e) establishment.

4. Which of the following provisions of the Bill of Rights was incorporated in 2010?
   a) the right to counsel in any criminal trial
   b) the right against self-incrimination
   c) freedom from unnecessary searches and seizures
   d) freedom to petition the government for redress of grievance
   e) the right to bear arms

The First Amendment and Freedom of Religion

> **Describe how the First Amendment protects freedom of religion (pp. 122–25)**

Two parts of the First Amendment touch on religious freedom: the establishment clause and the free exercise clause. The courts have been somewhat inconsistent in determining how solid the establishment clause's "wall of separation" between church and state actually is in practice. While the courts have been more consistent in protecting the free exercise of religious beliefs, they have taken pains to distinguish between religious beliefs and actions based on those beliefs.

Key Terms

establishment clause (p. 122)

Lemon test (p. 123)

free exercise clause (p. 124)

Practice Quiz

5. The Supreme Court's ruling in *Lemon v. Kurtzman*, which led to the *Lemon* test, concerned the issue of
    a) school desegregation.
    b) aid to religious schools.
    c) cruel and unusual punishment.
    d) obscenity.
    e) prayer in school.

The First Amendment and Freedom of Speech and of the Press

Describe how the First Amendment protects free speech (pp. 125–34)

Given the importance of freedom of speech and of the press to the functioning of democratic government, Americans are assumed to have the right to speak and broadcast their ideas unless there is some compelling reason to stop them. According to the courts, although virtually all speech is protected by the Constitution, some forms of speech are entitled to a greater degree of protection than others. Libel, slander, and speech that incites lawless action are examples of speech that can be limited by the government.

Key Terms

"clear and present danger" test (p. 126)

fighting words (p. 128)

"speech plus" (p. 131)

prior restraint (p. 131)

libel (p. 132)

slander (p. 132)

Practice Quiz

6. Which of the following protections is *not* contained in the First Amendment?
    a) the establishment clause
    b) the free exercise clause
    c) freedom of the press
    d) the right to peaceably assemble
    e) All of the above are First Amendment protections.

7. The judicial doctrine that places a heavy burden of proof on the government when it seeks to regulate or restrict speech is called
    a) judicial restraint.
    b) judicial activism.
    c) habeas corpus.
    d) prior restraint.
    e) strict scrutiny.

8. Which of the following describes a written statement made in "reckless disregard of the truth" that is considered damaging to a victim because it is "malicious, scandalous, and defamatory"?
    a) slander
    b) libel
    c) speech plus
    d) fighting words
    e) expressive speech

The Second Amendment and the Right to Bear Arms

Explore whether the Second Amendment means people have a right to own guns (pp. 134–37)

The Second Amendment granted Americans the right "to keep and bear Arms" in order to provide for state militias. Prior to 2010, the Second Amendment was not incorporated. In *McDonald v. Chicago*, the Supreme Court asserted that the right to bear arms applies to both state governments and the federal government.

Practice Quiz

9. In *McDonald v. Chicago*, the Supreme Court ruled that
    a) states can require citizens to own firearms.
    b) federal grants can be used to support the formation of state militias.
    c) felons can be prevented from purchasing assault rifles.
    d) the Second Amendment applies to states as well as the federal government.
    e) the Second Amendment applies only to the federal government and not to states.

Rights of the Criminally Accused

The essence of the Constitution's due process of the law is found in the Fourth, Fifth, Sixth, and Eighth amendments. The Fourth Amendment protects individuals from unreasonable searches and seizures. The Fifth Amendment provides individuals with the right to a grand jury, protection from double jeopardy, and a guarantee against self-incrimination. The Sixth Amendment provides the right to legal counsel, the right to a speedy trial, and the right to confront witnesses before an impartial jury. The Eighth Amendment protects individuals against "cruel and unusual" punishment.

Key Terms

due process of law (p. 137)

exclusionary rule (p. 138)

grand jury (p. 140)

double jeopardy (p. 140)

Miranda rule (p. 141)

eminent domain (p. 142)

Practice Quiz

10. The Fourth, Fifth, Sixth, and Eighth amendments, taken together, define
    a) freedom of religion.
    b) due process of law.
    c) free speech.
    d) the right to bear arms.
    e) civil rights of minorities.

11. In *Mapp v. Ohio*, the Supreme Court ruled that
    a) evidence obtained from an illegal search could not be introduced in a trial.
    b) the government must provide legal counsel for defendants who are too poor to provide it for themselves.
    c) persons under arrest must be informed prior to police interrogation of their rights to remain silent and to have the benefits of legal counsel.
    d) the government has the right to take private property for public use if just compensation is provided.
    e) a person cannot be tried twice for the same crime.

12. Which famous case deals with the Sixth Amendment's guarantee of the right to counsel?
    a) *Roe v. Wade*
    b) *Mapp v. Ohio*
    c) *Gideon v. Wainwright*
    d) *Terry v. Ohio*
    e) *Miranda v. Arizona*

The Right to Privacy

A right to privacy is never explicitly mentioned in the Constitution. In fact, it was not until 1965 that the Supreme Court interpreted the Third, Fourth, Fifth, and Ninth amendments to create a constitutional "zone of privacy." The right to privacy has since been used to strike down laws limiting access to birth control, outlawing abortion, and criminalizing gay and lesbian sexual activity.

Key Term

right to privacy (p. 144)

Practice Quiz

13. In which case was a right to privacy related to the use of birth control first formally recognized by the Court?
    a) *Griswold v. Connecticut*
    b) *Roe v. Wade*
    c) *Lemon v. Kurtzman*
    d) *Planned Parenthood v. Casey*
    e) *Baker v. Carr*

14. In which case did the Supreme Court rule that state governments no longer had the authority to make private sexual behavior a crime?
    a) *Texas v. Johnson*
    b) *Webster v. Reproductive Health Services*
    c) *Gonzales v. Oregon*
    d) *Lawrence v. Texas*
    e) *Bowers v. Hardwick*

For Further Reading

Barendt, Eric. *Freedom of Speech.* 2nd ed. New York: Oxford University Press, 2007.

Brandon, Mark. *The Constitution in Wartime.* Durham, NC: Duke University Press, 2005.

Cash, Arthur. *John Wilkes: The Scandalous Father of Civil Liberties.* New Haven, CT: Yale University Press, 2007.

Cook, Byrne. *Reporting the War: Freedom of the Press from the American Revolution to the War on Terror.* New York: Palgrave Macmillan, 2007.

Domino, John. *Civil Rights and Liberties in the 21st Century.* 3rd ed. New York: Longman, 2009.

Dworkin, Ronald. *Justice in Robes.* Cambridge, MA: Belknap Press, 2006.

Fisher, Louis. *Military Tribunals and Presidential Power.* Lawrence: University Press of Kansas, 2005.

Friendly, Fred W. *Minnesota Rag: The Dramatic Story of the Landmark Supreme Court Case That Gave New Meaning to Freedom of the Press.* New York: Vintage, 1982.

Glendon, Mary Ann. *Rights Talk: The Impoverishment of Political Discourse.* New York: Free Press, 1991.

Lewis, Anthony. *Freedom for the Thought That We Hate: A Biography of the First Amendment.* New York: Basic Books, 2010.

Lewis, Anthony. *Gideon's Trumpet.* New York: Random House, 1964.

O'Brien, David M. *Constitutional Law and Politics: Civil Rights and Civil Liberties.* 8th ed. Vol. 2. New York: W. W. Norton, 2011.

Solove, Daniel. *Nothing to Hide: The False Tradeoff between Privacy and Security.* New Haven, CT: Yale University Press, 2011.

Sundby, Scott. *A Life and Death Decision: A Jury Weighs the Death Penalty.* New York: Palgrave Macmillan, 2007.

Waldron, Jeremy. *The Harm in Hate Speech.* Cambridge, MA: Harvard University Press, 2012.

Recommended Websites

The American Civil Liberties Union (ACLU)
www.aclu.org
> The ACLU is committed in protecting for all individuals the freedoms found in the Bill of Rights. This sometimes controversial organization constantly monitors the government for violations of liberty and encourages its members to take political action.

Electronic Privacy Information Center
http://epic.org/privacy
> For an extensive list of privacy issues, go to the web page for the Electronic Privacy Information Center. Here you will find civil liberties concerns as they relate to all forms of information technology, including the Internet.

The Free Expression Network
www.freeexpression.org
> The Free Expression Network is an organization "dedicated to preserving the right to free expression." On its website you can find links to important First Amendment issues and organizations.

Freedom Forum
www.freedomforum.org
> Freedom of speech and freedom of the press are considered critical in any democracy; however, only some kinds of speech are fully protected against restrictions. Freedom Forum is a nonpartisan agency that investigates and analyzes such First Amendment restrictions.

National Abortion and Reproductive Rights Action League
www.naral.org

National Right to Life Committee
www.HRIC.org
> The National Abortion and Reproductive Rights Action League and the National Right to Life Committee are two of the nation's largest interest groups weighing in on the abortion issue. See what these opposing groups have to say about privacy rights.

Religious Freedom Page
http://religiousfreedom.lib.virginia.edu
> The establishment clause of the U.S. Constitution has been interpreted to mean a "wall of separation" between government and religion. On the Religious Freedom Page you can find information on a variety of issues pertaining to religious freedom in the United States and around the world.

U.S. Supreme Court Media
www.oyez.org
> This website for U.S. Supreme Court media has a great search engine for finding information on cases affecting civil liberties, such as *Lemon v. Kurtzman*, *Miranda v. Arizona*, *Mapp v. Ohio*, and *New York Times v. Sullivan*, to name a few.

Debates over civil rights date to the country's founding. Today, one of the major contests over civil rights concerns same-sex marriage. As in the past, the Supreme Court has played a key role in determining what civil rights are protected by law.

Civil Rights

WHAT GOVERNMENT DOES AND WHY IT MATTERS In this chapter, we will turn from a discussion of civil liberties to an examination of civil rights. Rights and liberties are related but are not one and the same. Civil liberties are limitations on the power of the government. The concept of civil liberties defines certain spheres of activity, such as speech or worship, in which the government's authority to interfere with individuals is limited. Civil rights, on the other hand, are the rules governing who may participate in the political process and regulating the ways in which the government may or may not treat its citizens. As we shall see, among the most important rights guaranteed by the American Constitution are "equal protection" under the law and "due process" of law, concepts that will be at the heart of this chapter. Civil liberties and civil rights are both aspects of political freedom and while specific rights may conflict with particular liberties, in a broad sense rights and liberties reinforce each other. The Constitution's Bill of Rights includes both rights and liberties.

As in the case of civil liberties, Americans agree with the basic principle of civil rights but quarrel frequently over their application. The question of who has the constitutional right to do what underlies some of the major controversies of American history. Fifty years ago, the African American struggle for equal rights took center stage. Many goals of the civil rights movement that once aroused bitter controversy are now widely accepted as part of the American commitment to equal rights. But even today the question of what is meant by "equal rights" is hardly settled.

One contemporary example of a contest over civil rights is the issue of same-sex marriage. Some say that all Americans, regardless of gender preference or sexual orientation, should have the right to obtain a state marriage license. Others declare that states should only sanction opposite-sex marriages. As of November 2014, 35 states and the District of Columbia allow same-sex marriages, and 15 define marriage as a union between one man and one woman. At the federal level, the Supreme Court in 2013 struck down portions of the Defense of Marriage Act, which had defined "marriage" and "spouse" to apply only to heterosexual unions.[1] The Court said that if a state allows same-sex marriage, same-sex couples are entitled to the same federal health, tax, and other benefits as heterosexual couples. This ruling, however, does not force states to make marriage licenses available to same-sex couples. The question of whether same-sex couples do or do not have a constitutional right to marriage is far from settled and sure to generate further debate in the years to come.

Ideas about civil rights do not change easily; advocates who have challenged barriers to civil rights often struggled against strong resistance. This chapter will show how inequalities between races and genders were tolerated and even enforced by law during much of our country's history. Although the United States was founded on the ideals of liberty, equality, and democracy, its history of civil rights reveals a gap between these principles and actual practice. This history also demonstrates how the struggle to attain those ideals has helped narrow this gap. The election of Barack Obama as the nation's first black president is a testament to the successes of those struggles but does not by itself alter persistent social and economic differences across racial lines.

chaptergoals

- Trace the legal developments and social movements that expanded civil rights (pp. 159–78)

- Describe how different groups have fought for and won protection of their civil rights (pp. 178–95)

- Contrast arguments for and against affirmative action (pp. 195–99)

● The Struggle for Civil Rights

Trace the legal developments and social movements that expanded civil rights

In the United States the history of slavery and legalized racial **discrimination** against African Americans coexists uneasily with a strong tradition of individual liberty. Indeed, for much of our history Americans have struggled to reconcile such exclusionary racial practices with our notions of individual rights. With the adoption of the Fourteenth Amendment in 1868, **civil rights** became part of the Constitution, guaranteed to each citizen through "equal protection of the laws." This **equal protection clause** launched a century of political movements and legal efforts to press for racial equality.

For African Americans, the central fact of political life for most of American history has been a denial of full citizenship rights. By accepting the institution of slavery, the Founders embraced a system fundamentally at odds with the "Blessings of Liberty" promised in the Constitution. Their decision set the stage for two centuries of African American struggles to achieve full citizenship.

For women as well, electoral politics was a decidedly masculine world. Until 1920, not only were women barred from voting in national politics but electoral politics was closely tied to such male social institutions as lodges, bars, and clubs. Yet the exclusion of women from this political world did not prevent them from engaging in public life. Instead, women carved out a "separate sphere" for their public activities. Emphasizing female stewardship of the moral realm, women became important voices in social reform well before they won the right to vote.[2] Prior to the Civil War, women played leading roles in the abolitionist movement.

discrimination the use of any unreasonable and unjust criterion of exclusion

civil rights obligation imposed on government to take positive action to protect citizens from any illegal action of government agencies and of other private citizens

equal protection clause provision of the Fourteenth Amendment guaranteeing citizens "the equal protection of the laws." This clause has been the basis for the civil rights of African Americans, women, and other groups

African American men won the right to vote after the Civil War, and many former slaves began registering and voting in state elections as early as 1867. This political influence soon evaporated in the face of Jim Crow laws and the end of Reconstruction.

Slavery and the Abolitionist Movement

No issue in the nation's history so deeply divided Americans as that of slavery. The importation and subjugation of Africans kidnapped from their native lands was a practice virtually as old as the country itself: the first slaves brought to what became the United States arrived in 1619, a year before the Plymouth colony was established in Massachusetts. White southerners built their agricultural economy (especially cotton production) on a large slave labor force. By 1840 nearly half of the populations of Alabama and Louisiana consisted of black slaves. Even so, only about a quarter of southern white families owned slaves.

Slavery was so much a part of southern culture that efforts to restrict or abolish the institution were met with fierce resistance. Despite the manifest cruelties of the slave system, southerners referred to it merely as their "peculiar institution." This quaint label meant little to slavery's opponents, however, and an abolitionist movement grew and spread among northerners in the 1830s (although abolitionist sentiment could be traced back to the prerevolutionary era). Slavery had been all but eliminated in the North by this time, although relatively few northerners favored outright abolition. In fact, most whites held attitudes toward blacks that would be considered racist today.

Motivated in large part by religious and moral beliefs that slavery was wrong, the abolitionist movement spread primarily through local organizations in the North. Antislavery groups coalesced in New York, Ohio, New Hampshire, Pennsylvania, New Jersey, and Michigan. In addition, the movement spawned two political parties: the staunchly antislavery Liberty Party and the larger but more moderate Free Soil Party, which sought primarily to restrict slavery from spreading into new western territories. Some opponents of slavery took matters into their own hands, aiding in the escape of runaway slaves along the Underground Railroad. Private homes and churches scattered throughout the Northeast, once used to hide blacks on their trips to Canada, attest to the involvement of local citizenry. In the South, a similar, if contrary, fervor prompted mobs to break into post offices in order to seize and destroy antislavery literature.

In 1857, the Supreme Court inflamed this tense atmosphere with its infamous decision in *Dred Scott v. Sanford*. Dred Scott was a slave who had been taken by his owner to the free state of Illinois and the territory of Wisconsin, where slavery was forbidden by the 1820 Missouri Compromise. Scott sued for his freedom, arguing that his residence in a free territory meant he was a free man. The Court, however, disagreed, holding that slaves—indeed, all blacks—were not citizens of the United States. Scott had no due process rights because, as a slave, he was his master's permanent property, regardless of his master's having taken him to a free state or territory.[3] This decision "roused passions as never before,"[4] splitting the country deeply over the issue of slavery. The emotional power of the slavery issue was such that it precipitated the nation's bloodiest conflict, the Civil War. From the ashes of the Civil War came the Thirteenth, Fourteenth, and Fifteenth amendments, which would redefine civil rights from that time on.

The Link to the Women's Rights Movement

The quiet upstate New York town of Seneca Falls played host to what would later come to be known as the starting point of the modern women's movement.

Although a few women could vote in the early American republic, such as these New Jersey women who satisfied state property qualifications, laws were soon enacted to block women from the ballot box. At the beginning of the nineteenth century, no American woman could legally vote.

Convened in July 1848 and organized by the activists Elizabeth Cady Stanton and Lucretia Mott, the Seneca Falls Convention drew 300 delegates to formulate plans for advancing the political and social rights of women.

The centerpiece of the convention was its Declaration of Sentiments and Resolutions. Patterned after the Declaration of Independence, the Seneca Falls document declared, "We hold these truths to be self-evident: that all men and women are created equal" and "The history of mankind is a history of repeated injuries and usurpations on the part of man toward woman, having in direct object the establishment of an absolute tyranny over her." The most controversial provision of the declaration, nearly rejected as too radical, was the call for the right to vote for women. Although most of the delegates were women, about 40 men participated, including the renowned abolitionist Frederick Douglass.

The link to the antislavery movement was not new. Stanton and Mott had attended the World Anti-Slavery Convention in London in 1840 but had been denied delegate seats because of their sex. This rebuke helped precipitate the 1848 convention in Seneca Falls. The movements for women's rights and the abolition of slavery were also closely linked with the temperance movement (because alcohol abuse was closely linked to male abuses of women).

The convention and its participants were subjected to widespread ridicule, but similar conventions were organized in other states, and in the same year as the Seneca Falls Convention, New York State passed the Married Women's Property Act in order to restore the right of married women to own property.

The Civil War Amendments to the Constitution

The hopes of African Americans for achieving full citizenship rights initially seemed fulfilled when three constitutional amendments were adopted after the Civil War: the **Thirteenth Amendment** abolished slavery, the **Fourteenth Amendment**

Thirteenth Amendment one of three Civil War amendments; it abolished slavery

Fourteenth Amendment one of three Civil War amendments; it guaranteed equal protection and due process

guaranteed equal protection under the law, and the **Fifteenth Amendment** guaranteed voting rights for blacks. Protected by the presence of federal troops, African American men were able to exercise their political rights immediately after the war. Between 1869 and 1877, blacks were elected to many political offices: 2 black senators were elected from Mississippi and a total of 14 African Americans were elected to the House of Representatives. African Americans also held many state-level political offices. As voters and public officials, black citizens found a home in the Republican Party, which had secured the ratification of the three constitutional amendments guaranteeing black rights. After the war, the Republican Party continued to reach out to black voters as a means to build party strength in the South.[5]

This political equality was short-lived, however. The national government withdrew its troops from the South and turned its back on African Americans in 1877, when Reconstruction ended. In the Compromise of 1877, southern Democrats agreed to allow the Republican candidate, Rutherford B. Hayes, to become president after a disputed election. In exchange, northern Republicans dropped their support for the civil liberties and political participation of African Americans. After that, southern states erected a "Jim Crow" system of social, political, and economic inequality that made a mockery of the promises in the Constitution. The first **Jim Crow laws** were adopted in the 1870s, in each southern state, to criminalize intermarriage of the races and to segregate trains and depots. These were promptly followed by laws segregating all public accommodations, and within 10 years all southern states had adopted laws segregating the schools.

Jim Crow laws laws enacted by southern states following Reconstruction that discriminated against African Americans

Immediately after the Civil War, when male ex-slaves won the franchise, some women pressed for the right to vote at the national level, but politicians in both parties rejected women's suffrage as disruptive and unrealistic. Women also started to press for the vote at the state level in 1867, when a referendum to give women the vote in Kansas failed. Frustration with the general failure to win reforms accelerated suffrage activism. In 1872, Susan B. Anthony and several other women were arrested in Rochester, New York, for illegally registering and voting in that year's national election. (The men who allowed the women to register and vote were also indicted; Anthony paid their expenses and eventually won presidential pardons for them.) At Anthony's trial, Judge Ward Hunt ordered the jury to find her guilty without deliberation. Yet Anthony was allowed to address the court, saying, "Your denial of my citizen's right to vote is the denial of my right of consent as one of the governed, the denial of my right of representation as one of the taxed, the denial of my right to a trial of my peers as an offender against the law."[6] Hunt assessed Anthony a fine of $100 but did not sentence her to jail. She refused to pay the fine.

forcritical**analysis**

What does "separate but equal" mean? What were the consequences of this policy for Southern society and for blacks' civil rights?

Civil Rights and the Supreme Court: "Separate but Equal"

Resistance to equality for African Americans in the South led Congress to adopt the Civil Rights Act of 1875, which attempted to protect blacks from discrimination by proprietors of hotels, theaters, and other public accommodations. But the Court declared the legislation unconstitutional on the grounds that the act sought to protect blacks against discrimination by *private* businesses, whereas the Fourteenth Amendment, according to the Court's interpretation, was intended to protect

The 1896 Supreme Court case of Plessy v. Ferguson *upheld legal segregation and created the "separate but equal" rule, which fostered national segregation. Overt discrimination in public accommodations was common.*

individuals from discrimination only against actions by *public* officials of state and local governments.

In the infamous case of *Plessy v. Ferguson* (1896), the Court went still further by upholding a Louisiana statute that *required* segregation of the races on trolleys and other public carriers (and, by implication, in all public facilities, including schools). Homer Plessy, a man defined as "one-eighth black," had violated a Louisiana law that provided for "equal but separate accommodations" on trains and levied a $25 fine on any white passenger who sat in a car reserved for blacks or on any black passenger who sat in a car reserved for whites. The Supreme Court held that the Fourteenth Amendment's equal protection clause was not violated by racial distinction as long as the facilities were equal, thus establishing the **"separate but equal" rule** that prevailed through the mid-twentieth century. People generally pretended that segregated accommodations were equal as long as some accommodation for blacks existed. The Court said that although "the object of the [Fourteenth] Amendment was undoubtedly to enforce the absolute equality of the two races before the law, . . . it could not have intended to abolish distinctions based on color, or to enforce social, as distinguished from political, equality, or a commingling of the two races upon terms unsatisfactory to either."[7] What the Court was saying in effect was that the use of race as a criterion of exclusion in public matters was not unreasonable.

"separate but equal" rule doctrine that public accommodations could be segregated by race but still be considered equal

Organizing for Equality

The creation of a Jim Crow system in the southern states and the lack of a legal basis for "equal protection of the laws" prompted the beginning of a long process in which African Americans built organizations and devised strategies for asserting their constitutional rights.

The National Association for the Advancement of Colored People One such strategy sought to win political rights through political pressure and litigation. This approach was championed by the National Association for the Advancement of Colored People (NAACP), established in 1909 by a group of black and white reformers that included W. E. B. Du Bois, one of the twentieth century's most influential and creative thinkers on racial issues. Because the northern black vote was so small in the early 1900s, the NAACP relied primarily on the courts to press for black political rights. After the 1920s it built a strong membership base, with some strength in the South, which would be critical when the civil rights movement gained momentum in the 1950s.

Women's Organizations and the Right to Suffrage The 1886 unveiling in New York Harbor of the Statue of Liberty, depicting liberty as a woman, prompted women's rights advocates to call it "the greatest hypocrisy of the nineteenth century," in that "not one single woman throughout the length and breadth of the Land is as yet in possession of political Liberty."[8] Suffragists used the occasion of the Constitution's centennial in 1887 to protest the continued denial of their rights. For these women, the centennial represented "a century of injustice."

The climactic movement toward suffrage had been formally launched in 1878 with the introduction of a proposed constitutional amendment in Congress. Parallel efforts were made in the states. Many states granted women the right to vote before the national government did; western states with less entrenched political systems opened politics to women earliest. When Wyoming became a state in 1890, it was the first state to grant full suffrage to women. Colorado, Utah, and Idaho all followed suit in the next several years. Suffrage organizations grew—the National American Woman Suffrage Association (NAWSA), formed in 1890, claimed 2 million members by 1917—and staged mass meetings, parades, petitions, and protests. NAWSA organized state-by-state efforts to win the right for women to vote. Members of a more militant group, the National Woman's Party, staged pickets and got arrested in front of the White House to protest President Wilson's opposition to a constitutional amendment granting women this right. When the Nineteenth Amendment was ratified in 1920, women were finally guaranteed the right to vote.

Women have had the right to vote in the United States for less than 100 years. The women who fought for this basic political right were often ridiculed as man-haters, as depicted in this cartoon. Of course, the suffragettes believed both men and women should enjoy the same political rights.

Litigating for Equality after World War II

The shame of discrimination against black military personnel during World War II, plus revelations of Nazi racial atrocities, moved President Harry S. Truman finally to bring the problem of racial discrimination to the White House and national attention, with the appointment in 1946 of the President's Commission on Civil Rights. In 1948 the commission submitted its report, *To Secure These Rights*, which laid bare the extent of the problem and its consequences. The report also revealed the success of experiments with racial integration in the armed forces during World War II, to demonstrate to southern society that it had nothing to fear. But the commission recognized that the national government had no clear constitutional authority to pass and implement civil rights legislation. It proposed tying such legislation to the commerce power described in Article I of the Constitution, which allows Congress to regulate interstate commerce, although it was clear that discrimination was not itself related to the flow of interstate commerce.[9] The committee even suggested using the treaty power as a source of constitutional authority for civil rights legislation.[10]

The Supreme Court had begun to change its position on racial discrimination before World War II by being stricter about the criterion of equal facilities in the "separate but equal" rule. In 1938, for example, the Court rejected Missouri's policy of paying the tuition of qualified blacks to out-of-state law schools rather than admitting them to the University of Missouri Law School.[11]

After the war, modest progress resumed. In 1950 the Court rejected Texas's claim that its new "law school for Negroes" afforded education equal to that of the all-white University of Texas Law School, anticipating its future civil rights rulings by opening the question of whether *any* segregated facilities could be truly equal.[12] But in ordering the admission of blacks to all-white state law schools, the Supreme Court did not directly confront the "separate but equal" rule. The same had been true in 1944, when the Supreme Court struck down the southern practice of "white primaries," which legally excluded blacks from participation in the nominating process. Here the Court simply recognized that primaries could no longer be regarded as the private affairs of the parties but were an integral aspect of the electoral process, making parties "an agency of the State." Therefore any practice of discrimination against blacks was "state action within the meaning of the Fifteenth Amendment."[13] The most important pre-1954 decision was probably *Shelley v. Kraemer*, in which the Court ruled against the widespread practice of "restrictive covenants" whereby the seller of a home added a clause to the sales contract requiring the buyer to agree never to sell the home to any non-Caucasian, non-Christian, and so on. The Court ruled that such covenants could not be judicially enforced, since the Fourteenth Amendment prohibits any organ of the state, including the courts, from denying equal protection of its laws.[14]

Although none of those pre-1954 cases confronted "separate but equal" and the principle of racial discrimination as such, they were extremely significant to black leaders in the 1940s and gave them encouragement to believe that at last they had an opportunity and enough legal precedent to change the constitutional framework itself. Much of this legal work was done by the Legal Defense and Educational Fund of the NAACP. Until the late 1940s, lawyers working for the Legal Defense Fund had concentrated on winning small victories within the existing framework. Then, in 1948, the Legal Defense Fund upgraded its approach by simultaneously filing suits in different federal districts and through each level of schooling, with complaints ranging from unequal provision of kindergarten for blacks to unequal sports and science facilities in all-black high schools. After nearly two years of these mostly

The NAACP was formed in 1909 to promote the political rights of blacks. In the decades following, the NAACP expanded its membership significantly and played an important role in the civil rights movement of the 1950s and '60s.

Brown v. Board of Education
the 1954 Supreme Court decision that struck down the "separate but equal" doctrine as fundamentally unequal; this case eliminated state power to use race as a criterion of discrimination in law and provided the national government with the power to intervene by exercising strict regulatory policies against discriminatory actions

successful equalization suits, the lawyers decided the time was ripe to confront the "separate but equal" rule head-on, but they felt they needed some heavier artillery to lead the attack. Their choice was the African American lawyer Thurgood Marshall, who had been fighting, and often winning, equalization suits since the early 1930s. Marshall was pessimistic about the readiness of the Supreme Court for a full confrontation with segregation itself and the constitutional principle sustaining it. But the unwillingness of Congress after the 1948 election to consider fair-employment legislation seems to have convinced Marshall that the courts were the only hope.

During the next four years there emerged a clear indication that the Supreme Court itself was willing to take more civil rights cases on appeal. Yet this was no guarantee that the Court would reverse *on principle* the separate-but-equal precedent of *Plessy v. Ferguson*. All through 1951 and 1952, as cases were winding slowly through the lower-court litigation maze, intense discussions and disagreements arose among NAACP lawyers as to whether a full-scale assault on *Plessy* was good strategy, or whether it might not be better to continue with specific cases alleging unequal treatment and demanding relief with a Court-imposed policy of equalization.[15]

In the fall of 1952, the Court had on its docket cases from Delaware, Kansas, South Carolina, Virginia, and the District of Columbia challenging the constitutionality of school segregation. Of these, the case filed in Kansas became the one chosen by the NAACP. It seemed to be ahead of the pack in its district court, and it had the advantage of being located in a state outside the Deep South.[16]

Oliver Brown, the father of three girls, lived "across the tracks" in a low-income, racially mixed Topeka neighborhood. Every school day, Linda Brown took the school bus to the Monroe Elementary School, for black children, about a mile away. In September 1950, Oliver Brown took Linda to the all-white Sumner School, which was closer to home, to enter her into the third grade, in defiance of state law and local segregation rules. When they were refused, Brown took his case to the NAACP, and soon thereafter, the case **Brown v. Board of Education** was born. In mid-1953 the Court announced that the several cases on their way up would be reargued within a set of questions having to do with the intent of the Fourteenth Amendment. Almost exactly a year later, the Court responded to those questions in one of the most important decisions in its history.

In deciding the *Brown* case, the Court, to the surprise of many, basically rejected as inconclusive all the learned arguments about the intent and the history of the Fourteenth Amendment and committed itself instead to considering only the consequences of segregation:

> Does segregation of children in public schools solely on the basis of race, even though the physical facilities and other "tangible" factors may be equal, deprive the children of the minority group of equal educational opportunities? We believe that it does. . . . We conclude that in the field of public education the doctrine of "separate but equal" has no place. Separate educational facilities are inherently unequal.[17]

The *Brown* decision altered the constitutional framework in two fundamental respects. First, after *Brown*, the states no longer had the power to use race as a criterion of discrimination in law. Second, the national government from then on had the power (and eventually the obligation) to intervene with strict regulatory policies against the discriminatory actions of state or local governments, school boards, employers, and many others in the private sector.

Civil Rights after *Brown v. Board of Education*

Brown v. Board of Education withdrew all constitutional authority to use race as a criterion of exclusion, and it signaled more clearly the Court's determination to use the **strict scrutiny** test in cases related to racial discrimination. This meant that the burden of proof would fall on the government to show that the law in question *was* constitutional—not on the challengers to show the law's *un*constitutionality.[18] Although the use of strict scrutiny would give an advantage to those attacking racial discrimination, the historic decision in *Brown v. Board of Education* was merely a small opening move. First, most states refused to cooperate until sued, and many ingenious schemes were employed to delay obedience (such as paying the tuition for white students to attend newly created "private" academies). Second, even as southern school boards began to cooperate by eliminating their legally enforced (**de jure**) school segregation, extensive actual (**de facto**) school segregation remained, in the North as well as in the South, as a consequence of racially segregated housing that could not be addressed by the 1954–55 *Brown* principles. Third, discrimination in employment, public accommodations, juries, voting, and other areas of social and economic activity were not directly touched by *Brown*.

strict scrutiny a test used by the Supreme Court in racial discrimination cases and other cases involving civil liberties and civil rights that places the burden of proof on the government rather than on the challengers to show that the law in question is constitutional

de jure literally, "by law"; refers to legally enforced practices, such as school segregation in the South before the 1960s

de facto literally, "by fact"; refers to practices that occur even when there is no legal enforcement, such as school segregation in much of the United States today

"Massive resistance" among white southerners attempted to block the desegregation efforts of the national government. For example, at Little Rock Central High School in 1957, an angry mob of white students prevented black students from entering the school.

for critical analysis

Describe the changes in American society between the *Plessy v. Ferguson* and the *Brown v. Board of Education* decisions. How have changes in civil rights policy since the *Brown* case impacted society?

School Desegregation, Phase One

Although the District of Columbia and some of the school districts in the border states began to respond almost immediately to court-ordered desegregation, the states of the Deep South responded with a carefully planned delaying tactic commonly called "massive resistance" by the more demagogic southern leaders and "nullification" and "interposition" by the centrists. Either way, southern politicians stood shoulder to shoulder to declare that the Supreme Court's decisions and orders were without effect. The legislatures in these states enacted statutes ordering school districts to maintain segregated schools and state superintendents to terminate state funding wherever there was racial mixing in the classroom. Some southern states violated their own long traditions of local school autonomy by centralizing public school authority under the governor or the state board of education, and they gave themselves the power to close the schools and to provide alternative private schooling wherever local school boards might be inclined to obey the Supreme Court.

Most of these plans of "massive resistance" were tested in the federal courts and were struck down as unconstitutional.[19] But southern resistance was not confined to legislation. For example, in Arkansas in 1957, Governor Orval Faubus mobilized the Arkansas National Guard to intercede against enforcement of a federal court order to integrate Little Rock Central High School, and President Eisenhower was compelled to deploy U.S. troops and place the city under martial law. This action by the federal government underlined that a right was at issue. The Supreme Court considered the Little Rock confrontation so historically important that the opinion it rendered in that case was not only agreed to unanimously but was, unprecedentedly, signed personally by every one of the justices.[20] The end of massive resistance, however, became simply the beginning of still another southern strategy. "Pupil placement" laws authorized school districts to place each pupil in a school according to a variety of academic, personal, and psychological considerations, never mentioning race at all. This put the burden of transferring to an all-white school on the nonwhite children and their parents, making it almost impossible for a single court order to cover a whole district, let alone a whole state. This delayed desegregation awhile longer.[21]

The 1955–56 Montgomery bus boycott began with the arrest of Rosa Parks, who refused to give up her seat for a white man. The boycott lasted a year and drew national attention to the cause of civil rights.

Social Protest after *Brown*

Ten years after *Brown*, fewer than 1 percent of black school-age children in the Deep South were attending schools with whites.[22] A decade of frustration made it fairly obvious to all observers that adjudication alone would not succeed. The goal of "equal protection" required positive, or affirmative, action by Congress and by administrative agencies. And given massive southern resistance and a generally negative national public opinion toward racial integration, progress would not be made through courts, Congress, or federal agencies without intense, well-organized support. Figure 5.1 shows the increase in the number of civil rights demonstrations for voting rights and public accommodations during the years following *Brown*. The number of organized demonstrations began to mount slowly but surely after *Brown v. Board of Education*. Only a year after *Brown*, black citizens in Montgomery, Alabama, challenged

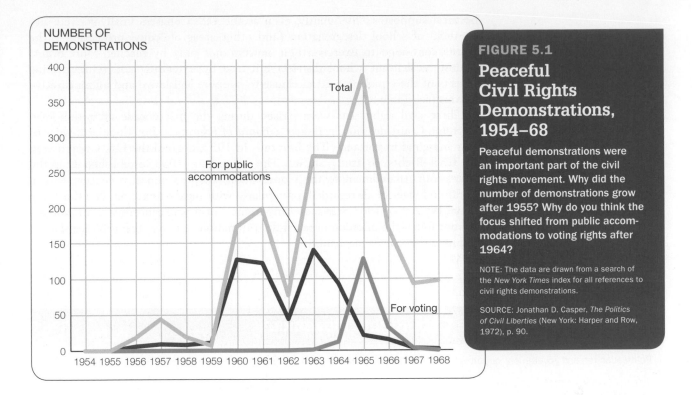

NUMBER OF DEMONSTRATIONS

Total

For public accommodations

For voting

FIGURE 5.1

Peaceful Civil Rights Demonstrations, 1954–68

Peaceful demonstrations were an important part of the civil rights movement. Why did the number of demonstrations grow after 1955? Why do you think the focus shifted from public accommodations to voting rights after 1964?

NOTE: The data are drawn from a search of the *New York Times* index for all references to civil rights demonstrations.

SOURCE: Jonathan D. Casper, *The Politics of Civil Liberties* (New York: Harper and Row, 1972), p. 90.

the city's segregated bus system with a yearlong boycott. The boycott began with the arrest of Rosa Parks, who refused to give up her seat for a white man. A seamstress who worked with civil rights groups, Parks eventually became a civil rights icon, as did one of the ministers leading the boycott, Martin Luther King, Jr. After a year of private carpools and walking, Montgomery's bus system desegregated, but only after the Supreme Court ruled the system unconstitutional. By the 1960s the many organizations that made up the civil rights movement had accumulated experience and built networks capable of launching large-scale direct-action campaigns against southern segregationists. The Southern Christian Leadership Conference, the Student Nonviolent Coordinating Committee, and many other organizations had built a movement that stretched across the South, using the media to attract nationwide attention and support. The image of protesters being beaten, attacked by police dogs, and set upon with fire hoses did much to win broad sympathy for the cause of black civil rights and to discredit state and local governments in the South. In the massive March on Washington in 1963, the Reverend Martin Luther King, Jr., staked out the movement's moral claims in his famous "I Have a Dream" speech. Steadily, the movement created intense pressure for a reluctant federal government to take more assertive steps to defend black civil rights.

The Civil Rights Acts

It is important to observe here the mutual dependence of the courts and legislatures: the legislatures need constitutional authority to act, and the courts need legislative and administrative assistance to implement court orders and focus political support. Consequently, even as the U.S. Congress finally moved into the field of school desegregation (and other areas of "equal protection"), the courts continued to exercise their powers, not only by placing court orders against recalcitrant school districts but also by extending and reinterpreting aspects of the equal protection clause to support legislative and administrative actions (see Table 5.1).

Three civil rights acts were passed during the first decade after the 1954 Supreme Court decision in *Brown v. Board of Education*. But these acts were of only marginal importance. The first one, in 1957, created the U.S. Commission on Civil Rights, to study abuses. The second, in 1960, established that the Fourteenth Amendment to the Constitution, adopted almost a century earlier, could no longer be disregarded, particularly with regard to voting. The third, the Equal Pay Act of 1963, was more important, but it was concerned with women, did not touch the question of racial discrimination, and, like the 1960 legislation, had no enforcement mechanisms.

TABLE 5.1

Cause and Effect in the Civil Rights Movement

Political action and government action worked in tandem to produce dramatic changes in American civil rights policies.

JUDICIAL AND LEGAL ACTION	POLITICAL ACTION
1954 *Brown v. Board of Education*	**1955** Montgomery, Alabama, bus boycott
1956 Federal courts order school integration; of special note is one ordering Autherine Lucy admitted to the University of Alabama, with Governor Wallace officially protesting	
1957 Civil Rights Act creating Civil Rights Commission; President Eisenhower sends 101st Airborne Division paratroops to Little Rock, Arkansas, to enforce integration of Central High School	**1957** Southern Christian Leadership Conference (SCLC) formed, with Martin Luther King, Jr., as president
1960 First substantive Civil Rights Act, primarily voting rights	**1960** Student Nonviolent Coordinating Committee formed to organize protests, sit-ins, freedom rides
1961 Interstate Commerce Commission orders desegregation on all buses and trains, and in terminals	
1961 JFK favors executive action over civil rights legislation	
1963 JFK shifts, supports strong civil rights law; JFK's assassination; LBJ asserts strong support for civil rights	**1963** Nonviolent demonstrations in Birmingham, Alabama, lead to King's arrest and his "Letter from Birmingham Jail"
	1963 March on Washington
1964 Congress passes historic Civil Rights Act covering voting, employment, public accommodations, education	
1965 Voting Rights Act	**1965** King announces drive to register 3 million blacks in the South
1966 War on Poverty in full swing	**Late 1960s** Movement diverges: part toward litigation, part toward community action programs, part toward war protest, part toward more militant "Black Power" actions

By far the most important piece of legislation passed by Congress concerning equal opportunity was the Civil Rights Act of 1964. It not only put some teeth in the voting rights provisions of the 1957 and 1960 acts but also went far beyond voting to attack discrimination in public accommodations, segregation in the schools, and, at long last, the discriminatory conduct of employers in hiring, promoting, and laying off their employees. Discrimination against women was also included, extending the important 1963 provisions. The 1964 act seemed bold at the time, but it was enacted fully 10 years after the Supreme Court had declared racial discrimination "inherently unequal" under the Fifth and Fourteenth amendments. And it was enacted long after blacks had demonstrated that discrimination was no longer acceptable.

Public Accommodations After the passage of the 1964 Civil Rights Act, public accommodations quickly removed some of the most blatant forms of racial discrimination. Signs defining "colored" and "white" restrooms, water fountains, waiting rooms, and seating arrangements were removed, and a host of other practices that relegated black people to separate and inferior arrangements was ended. In addition, the federal government filed more than 400 antidiscrimination suits in federal courts against hotels, restaurants, taverns, gas stations, and other "public accommodations."

Many aspects of legalized racial segregation—such as separate Bibles to swear in black and white witnesses in the courtroom—seem like ancient history today. But the issue of racial discrimination in public settings is by no means over. In 1993, six African American Secret Service agents filed charges after a Denny's restaurant in Annapolis, Maryland, failed to serve them; white Secret Service agents at a nearby table had received prompt service. Similar charges citing discriminatory service at Denny's restaurants surfaced across the country. Faced with evidence of a pattern of systematic discrimination and numerous lawsuits, Denny's paid $45 million in damages to plaintiffs in Maryland and California in what is said to be the largest settlement ever in a public accommodations case.[23] In addition to the settlement, the chain vowed to expand employment and management opportunities for minorities in its restaurants. Other forms of racial discrimination in public accommodations are harder to challenge, however. For example, there is considerable evidence that taxicabs often refuse to pick up black passengers.[24] Such practices may be common, but they are difficult to prove and remedy through the law.

School Desegregation, Phase Two The 1964 Civil Rights Act also declared discrimination by private employers and state governments (school boards, etc.) illegal, and then went further to provide for administrative agencies to help the courts implement these laws. Title IV of the act, for example, authorized the executive branch, through the Justice Department, to implement federal court orders to desegregate schools, and to do so without having to wait for individual parents to bring complaints. Title VI of the act vastly strengthened the role of the executive branch and the credibility of court orders by providing that federal grants-in-aid to state and local governments for education must be withheld from any school system practicing racial segregation. Title VI became the most effective weapon for desegregating schools outside the South because the situation in northern communities was subtler and more difficult to address. In the South, the problem was segregation by law coupled with overt resistance to the national government's efforts to change the situation. In contrast, outside the South, segregated facilities were the outcome of hundreds of thousands of housing choices made by individuals and families. Once racial residential patterns emerged, racial homogeneity, property values, and neighborhood schools and churches were defended by real estate agents, neighborhood organizations, and the like. Thus, in order to eliminate discrimination nationwide, the 1964 Civil Rights Act gave (1) the president, through the Justice Department's Office for Civil Rights, the power to withhold federal education grants;[25] and (2) the attorney general of the United States the power to initiate suits (rather than having to await complaints) wherever there was a "pattern or practice" of discrimination.[26]

In the decade following the 1964 Civil Rights Act, the Justice Department brought legal action against more than 500 school districts. During the same period, administrative agencies filed lawsuits against 600 school districts, threatening to suspend federal aid to education unless real desegregation steps were taken.

Busing One step taken toward desegregation was busing children from poor urban school districts to wealthier suburban ones. In 1971 the Supreme Court held that state-imposed desegregation could be brought about by busing children across school districts.[27] But the decision went beyond that, adding that under certain limited circumstances even racial quotas could be used as the "starting point in shaping a remedy to correct past constitutional violations," and that pairing or grouping schools and reorganizing school attendance zones would also be acceptable.

Three years later, however, this principle was severely restricted when the Supreme Court determined that only cities found guilty of deliberate and de jure racial segregation would have to desegregate their schools,[28] effectively exempting most northern states and cities from busing because school segregation in northern cities is generally the de facto result of segregated housing and thousands of acts of private discrimination against blacks and other minorities.

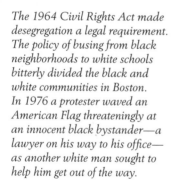

The 1964 Civil Rights Act made desegregation a legal requirement. The policy of busing from black neighborhoods to white schools bitterly divided the black and white communities in Boston. In 1976 a protester waved an American Flag threateningly at an innocent black bystander—a lawyer on his way to his office— as another white man sought to help him get out of the way.

Boston provides a good illustration of the agonizing problem of making further progress in civil rights in the schools under the constitutional framework established by these decisions. Boston school authorities were found guilty of deliberately building school facilities and drawing school districts "to increase racial segregation." After vain efforts by Boston school authorities to draw up an acceptable plan to remedy the segregation, federal judge W. Arthur Garrity ordered an elaborate desegregation plan of his own, involving busing between the all-black neighborhood of Roxbury and the nearby white, working-class community of South Boston. The city's schools were so segregated and uncooperative that even the conservative administration of President Richard Nixon had already initiated a punitive cutoff of funds. But even many liberals criticized Judge Garrity's plan as being badly conceived for involving two neighboring communities with a history of tension and mutual resentment. The plan did work well at the elementary school level but proved explosive at the high school level, generating a continuing crisis for the city of Boston and for the whole nation.[29]

The prospects for further school integration diminished with a 1991 Supreme Court decision holding that lower federal courts could end supervision of local school boards if they could show "good faith" compliance with court orders to desegregate and could show that "vestiges of past discrimination" had been eliminated "to the extent practicable."[30] It is not necessarily easy for a school board to prove that the new standard has been met, but this was the first time since *Brown* and the 1964 Civil Rights Act that the Court had opened the door at all to retreat.

In 2007 the Court's ruling in *Parents Involved in Community Schools v. Seattle School District No. 1* limited school integration measures still further. By making race one factor in assigning students to schools, the cities of Seattle, Washington, and Louisville, Kentucky, had hoped to achieve greater racial balance across the public schools. The Court ruled that these plans (even though the cities had voluntarily adopted them) were unconstitutional because they discriminated against white students on the basis of race. Many observers described the decision as the end of the *Brown* era because it eliminated one of the few public strategies left to promote racial integration. Others argued that Justice Anthony Kennedy's concurring opinion, which recognized the harm of racial isolation, may provide the basis for new efforts to promote integration in the future.[31]

Outlawing Discrimination in Employment Despite the agonizingly slow progress of school desegregation, some progress was made in other areas of civil rights during the 1960s and '70s. Voting rights were established and fairly quickly began to revolutionize southern politics. Service on juries was no longer denied to minorities. But progress in the right to participate in politics and government dramatized the relative lack of progress in the economic domain, where battles over civil rights were increasingly being fought.

The federal courts and the Justice Department entered this area through Title VII of the Civil Rights Act of 1964, which outlawed job discrimination by all private and public employers, including governmental agencies (such as fire and police departments) that employed more than 15 workers. We have already seen (in Chapter 3) that the Supreme Court gave "interstate commerce" such a broad definition that Congress had the constitutional authority to cover discrimination by virtually any local employers.[32] Title VII makes it unlawful

for critical **analysis**

Brown v. Board of Education led to the end of de jure segregation. However, de facto segregation remains in many areas, including housing and schooling. Should there be legal or social efforts to address de facto segregation?

to discriminate in employment on the basis of color, religion, sex, or national origin, as well as race.

Title VII delegated some of the powers to enforce fair-employment practices to the Justice Department's Civil Rights Division and others to a new agency created in the 1964 act, the Equal Employment Opportunity Commission (EEOC). By executive order, these agencies had the power of the national government to revoke public contracts for goods and services and to refuse to engage in contracts with any private company that could not guarantee that its rules for hiring, promotion, and firing were nondiscriminatory. And in 1972, President Nixon and a Democratic Congress cooperated to strengthen the EEOC by giving it authority to initiate suits rather than wait for grievances.

But one problem with Title VII was that the complaining party had to show that deliberate discrimination was the cause of the failure to get a job or a training opportunity. Rarely, of course, does an employer explicitly admit discrimination on the basis of race, sex, or any other illegal reason. Recognizing this, the courts have allowed aggrieved parties (the plaintiffs) to make their case if they can show that an employer's hiring practices had the *effect* of exclusion. A leading case in 1971 involved a "class action" by several black employees in North Carolina attempting to show with statistical evidence that blacks had been relegated to only one department in the Duke Power Company, which involved the least desirable manual-labor jobs, and that they had been kept out of contention for better jobs because the employer had added attainment of a high school education and the passing of specially prepared aptitude tests as qualifications for higher jobs. The Supreme Court held that although the statistical evidence did not prove intentional discrimination, and although the requirements were race-neutral in appearance, their effects were sufficient to shift the burden of justification to the employer to show that the requirements were a "business necessity" that bore "a demonstrable relationship to successful performance."[33] The ruling in this case was subsequently applied to other hiring, promotion, and training programs.[34]

Voting Rights Although 1964 was the *most* important year for civil rights legislation, it was not the only important year. In 1965, Congress significantly strengthened legislation protecting voting rights by barring literacy and other tests as a condition for voting in six southern states[35] by setting criminal penalties for interference with efforts to vote and by providing for the replacement of local registrars with federally appointed registrars in counties designated by the attorney general as significantly resistant to registering eligible blacks to vote. The right to vote was further strengthened with ratification in 1964 of the Twenty-Fourth Amendment, which abolished the poll tax, and in 1975 with legislation permanently outlawing literacy tests in all 50 states and mandating bilingual ballots or oral assistance for Spanish speakers; Chinese, Japanese, Korean, and Native Americans; and Alaska natives.

In the long run, the laws extending and protecting voting rights could prove to be the most effective of all the great civil rights legislation because the progress in black political participation produced by these acts has altered the shape of American politics. In 1965, in the seven states of the Old Confederacy covered by the Voting Rights Act (VRA), 29.3 percent of the eligible black residents were registered to vote, compared with 73.4 percent of the white residents (see Table 5.2). Mississippi was the extreme case, with 6.7 percent black and 69.9 percent white registration. By 1972 the gap between black and white registration in the seven

TABLE 5.2

Registration by Race and State in Southern States Covered by the Voting Rights Act (VRA)

The VRA had a direct impact on the rate of black voter registration in the southern states, as measured by the gap between white and black voters in each state. Further insights can be gained by examining changes in white registration rates before and after passage of the Voting Rights Act and by comparing the gaps between white and black registration. Why do you think registration rates for whites increased significantly in some states and dropped in others? What impact could the increase in black registration have had on public policy?

	BEFORE THE ACT*			AFTER THE ACT* 1971–72		
	WHITE %	BLACK %	GAP** %	WHITE %	BLACK %	GAP %
Alabama	69.2	19.3	49.9	80.7	57.1	23.6
Georgia	62.6	27.4	35.2	70.6	67.8	2.8
Louisiana	80.5	31.6	48.9	80.0	59.1	20.9
Mississippi	69.9	6.7	63.2	71.6	62.2	9.4
North Carolina	96.8	46.8	50.0	62.2	46.3	15.9
South Carolina	75.7	37.3	38.4	51.2	48.0	3.2
Virginia	61.1	38.3	22.8	61.2	54.0	7.2
TOTAL	73.4	29.3	44.1	67.8	56.6	11.2

*Available registration data as of March 1965 and 1971–72.
**The gap is the percentage-point difference between white and black registration rates.

SOURCE: U.S. Commission on Civil Rights, *Political Participation* (1968), Appendix VII: Voter Education Project, attachment to press release, October 3, 1972.

states was only 11.2 points, and in Mississippi the gap had been reduced to 9.4 points. At one time, white leaders in Mississippi had attempted to dilute the influence of this growing black vote by **gerrymandering** districts to ensure that no blacks would be elected to Congress. But the black voters changed Mississippi before Mississippi could change them. In 1988, 11 percent of all elected officials in Mississippi were black—still well below the percentage of blacks in the state's voting-age population, which was 32 percent in 1990, but progress nonetheless. Mississippi's blacks had made significant gains (as they had in other Deep South states) as elected state and local representatives, and Mississippi was one of only eight states in the country in which a black judge presided over the highest state court. (Four of the eight were Deep South states.)[36]

Several provisions of the 1965 act were scheduled to expire in 2007. However, in 2006, responding to charges that black voters still faced discrimination at the polls, Congress renewed the act for another 25 years. Pressure for renewal of the act had been intense since the disputed 2000 presidential election. The U.S. Commission on Civil Rights conducted hearings on the election in Florida, at which black voters testified about being turned away from the polls and wrongly purged from the voting rolls, and about the unreliable voting technology in their neighborhoods. On the basis of this testimony and after an analysis of the vote, the commission charged that there had been extensive racial discrimination.[37]

gerrymandering the apportionment of voters in districts in such a way as to give unfair advantage to one racial or ethnic group or political party

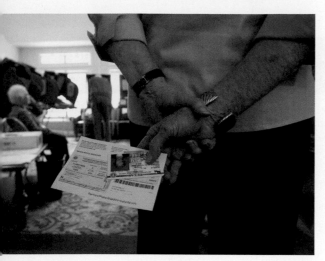

One of the most contentious areas of voting rights today are voter ID laws. Proponents say ID requirements prevent fraud, while opponents argue the rules purposely keep the poor and minorities, who are less likely to have picture IDs, from the polls.

Most recently, Texas has come under fire for gerrymandering congressional districts that discriminate against Latino voters. Due to population growth, most of it among Latinos, Texas gained four new congressional seats after the 2010 census. The heavily Republican state legislature drew a map designed to ensure that three of the new seats would go to Republican candidates. However, a coalition of minority groups and the Justice Department contested the map in court, charging that it failed to create a sufficient number of majority-minority districts. After extensive legal wrangling, the new redistricting plan included three majority-minority districts.[38]

The 1965 Voting Rights Act had also required some state and local governments to obtain federal preclearance before making any changes to their voting laws or practices. The designation of which jurisdictions needed preclearance was based upon a formula that calculated each jurisdiction's history of past voting discrimination. In the 2013 case *Shelby County v. Holder*, the Supreme Court overturned the formula, saying it was based on data more than 40 years old.[39] The Court did not strike down the idea of preclearance, but with no formula, preclearance cannot be employed unless Congress enacts a new metric. The Obama administration was critical of the decision but there seemed little possibility that Congress would take action to devise a new preclearance formula.

A new area of controversy in the realm of voting rights concerns so-called voter ID laws. Some 30 states have enacted legislation requiring voters to show positive identification at the polls. In 2014, seven of these states required photo IDs. Republicans generally support such laws, arguing that they deter voter fraud. Democrats generally oppose such laws, countering that they are particularly burdensome to poor and minority voters, who they say are less likely than others to possess such IDs. Several studies of this question have been conducted but have produced inconclusive results. Cases have been brought in several states challenging the laws on equal protection grounds. The laws have been upheld by some courts and struck down by others. In 2008 the Supreme Court upheld the constitutionality of Indiana's voter ID law, affirming the states' "valid interest" in improving election procedures and deterring fraud.[40] On the other hand, in 2013 the Supreme Court struck down an Arizona law requiring that individuals produce proof of U.S. citizenship in order to register to vote. Writing for the majority, Justice Scalia said that Arizona's new law was preempted by federal regulation that requires states to "accept and use" a simple registration form provided by the federal government.[41] Given the political controversy over voter ID laws, it seems likely that the Court will be asked to rule yet again on the question.

Housing The Civil Rights Act of 1964 did not address housing, but in 1968, Congress passed another civil rights act specifically to outlaw housing discrimination. Called the Fair Housing Act, the law prohibited discrimination in the sale or rental of most housing—eventually covering nearly all the nation's housing. Housing was among the most controversial of discrimination issues because of deeply entrenched patterns of residential segregation across the United States. Such segregation was not simply a product of individual choice. Local housing authorities deliberately segregated public housing, and federal guidelines had

sanctioned discrimination in Federal Housing Administration mortgage lending, effectively preventing blacks from joining the exodus to the suburbs in the 1950s and '60s. Nonetheless, Congress had been reluctant to tackle housing discrimination, fearing the tremendous controversy it could arouse. But just as the housing legislation was being considered in April 1968, the civil rights leader Martin Luther King, Jr., was assassinated; this tragedy brought the measure unexpected support in Congress.

Although it pronounced sweeping goals, the Fair Housing Act had little effect on housing segregation because its enforcement mechanisms were so weak. Individuals who believed they had been discriminated against had to file suit themselves. The burden was on the individual to prove that housing discrimination had occurred, even though such discrimination is often subtle and difficult to document. Although local fair-housing groups emerged to assist individuals in their court claims, the procedures for proving discrimination constituted a formidable barrier to effective change. These procedures were not altered until 1988, when Congress passed the Fair Housing Amendments Act. This new law put more teeth in the enforcement procedures and allowed the Department of Housing and Urban Development (HUD) to initiate legal action in cases of discrimination.[42]

Other attempts to challenge residential segregation had similarly mixed success. HUD tried briefly in the early 1970s to create racially "open communities" by withholding federal funds to suburbs that refused to accept subsidized housing. Confronted with charges of "forced integration" and bitter local protests, however, the administration quickly backed down. Efforts to prohibit discrimination in lending have been somewhat more promising. Several laws passed in the 1970s required banks to report information about their mortgage lending patterns, making it more difficult for them to engage in **redlining**, the practice of refusing to lend to entire neighborhoods. The 1977 Community Reinvestment Act required banks to lend in neighborhoods in which they do business. Through vigorous use of this act, many neighborhood organizations have reached agreements with banks that, as a result, have significantly increased investment in some poor neighborhoods.

Even so, racial discrimination in home mortgage lending remains a significant issue. In 2007 the issue of predatory lending—offering loans well above

redlining a practice in which banks refuse to make loans to people living in certain geographic locations

market rates, often with complex provisions that borrowers do not understand—attracted nationwide attention as the number of home foreclosures skyrocketed. Several lawsuits charged that these loans were particularly targeted at minority borrowers. In 2009, civil rights organizations; several states, including California, Illinois, Massachusetts, and New York; and some cities, including Baltimore, filed charges against banks and other lenders claiming they had illegally discriminated against African American and Latino home buyers. Minority home buyers, the suits charged, had been offered subprime mortgage products with higher interest rates, in contrast to whites with similar income levels, who were offered loans at lower interest rates. By 2012 some of these lawsuits had resulted in the largest financial settlements ever issued for lending discrimination. In announcing one settlement, the Justice Department vowed to "vigorously pursue those who would take advantage of certain Americans because of their race, national origin, gender or disability," noting that such discrimination "betrays the promise of equal opportunity that is enshrined in our Constitution and our legal framework."[43]

Marriage The Civil Rights Act of 1964 was also silent on the question of interracial marriage, which 16 states continued to outlaw in 1967. In that year, the Supreme Court ruled in *Loving v. Virginia* that such state laws were unconstitutional. The case concerned a Virginia couple, a white man and a black woman, who married in Washington, D.C., where such unions were legal. When they moved back to Virginia, which outlawed interracial marriage, authorities charged the couple with violating Virginia law. The Lovings moved back to Washington, D.C., and challenged the Virginia law. Nine years later the Supreme Court struck down state laws banning marriage on the basis of racial classifications. In so doing, the Court declared marriage "one of the 'basic civil rights of man,' fundamental to our very existence and survival."[44]

● Extending Civil Rights

> **Describe how different groups have fought for and won protection of their civil rights**

Even before equal-employment laws began to have a positive effect on the economic situation of blacks, something equally dramatic began happening: the extension of civil rights to other groups. The right not to be discriminated against was being successfully claimed by the other groups listed in Title VII of the 1964 Civil Rights Act, those defined by sex, religion, or national origin, and eventually by still other groups defined by age or sexual orientation. This extension of civil rights has become the new frontier of the civil rights struggle.

Once racial discrimination began to be seen as an important civil rights issue, other groups rose to demand recognition and active protection of their civil rights. Under Title VII, any group or individual can try, and in fact is encouraged to try, to convert goals and grievances into questions of rights and of the deprivation of those rights. A plaintiff must establish only that his or her membership in a group is an unreasonable basis for discrimination—that is, that the unequal treatment cannot be proven to be a "job-related" or otherwise clearly reasonable and relevant decision. In the United States today, the list of individuals and groups claiming illegal discrimination is lengthy.

Levels of Scrutiny under the Equal Protection Clause

Before we examine the civil rights movements of the past 60 years, it is useful to take a moment to describe how the courts have analyzed laws in cases where an individual or group has claimed discrimination. As has already been made clear, the courts have been a very important actor in the contest for rights protections. Recall that civil rights are the rules governing who may participate in the political process and regulating the ways in which the government may or may not treat its citizens. The equal protection clause of the Fourteenth Amendment does not require that everyone be treated equally. State and federal laws often create classifications allowing some but not other individuals to engage in activities or receive benifits. States, for example, allow only those with certain qualifications to engage in various occupations (such as medical professions) and set a minimum age for driving automobiles, voting, and consuming alcohol. Courts generally recognize the need for such systems of classification. Some systems of classification, on the other hand, such as those based on race, gender, or religion, raise serious constitutional questions. When dealing with challenges to state-imposed systems of classification, the courts employ a three-tiered approach, placing a greater burden of proof on the government to defend some types of classificatory schemes than others. The three tiers are often called "levels of scrutiny."

First Level The first and lowest level of scrutiny is applied by the courts to most state and federal regulatory schemes, such as motor vehicle and occupational licensing, laws setting a minimum age for the purchase of alcohol and cigarettes, and so forth. Here, the courts will generally apply the "rational basis test." Under this level of scrutiny, the burden of proof is on the plaintiff to show that there is no rational basis, whatsoever, for the goverment's rules. Such a showing is extremely difficult and few plaintiffs succeed. For example, in the case of *FCC v. Beach Communications*, a cable television provider challenged a Federal Communications Commission ruling dertermining which cable operators did and did not require local government franchises to operate their systems. The Supreme Court said that whether the FCC's decision was correct or not, it had a rational basis and did not infringe upon fundamental constitutional rights.[45]

Second Level The next level of judicial review of state action under the equal protection clause is called "intermediate or (exacting) scrutiny." Here, there is a greater burden on the government to show that its classification scheme is not only rational but that it also serves an important interest. Courts generally apply intermediate scrutiny to laws that afford differential treatment to men and women or that discriminate against the inheritance and property rights of illegitimate children. In recent years, federal courts have applied **intermediate scrutiny** in cases involving sexual orientation. For example, in the 2013 case of *Windsor v. United States* the Second Circuit Courts of Appeals employed *intermediate scrutiny* in holding that the federal Defense of Marriage Act, which applied the terms *marriage* and *spouse* only to heterosexual unions, served no legitimate state interest.[46]

intermediate scrutiny a test used by the Supreme Court in gender discrimination cases that places the burden of proof partially on the government and partially on the challengers to show that the law in question is unconstitutional

The U.S. Supreme Court affirmed the decision but did not indicate which level of scrutiny it had applied.

Third Level   The highest level of scrutiny employed by the courts, "strict scrutiny," places the burden of proof on the government to show that discrimination serves a "compelling interest," that the law is "narrowly tailored to achieve that goal," and that the government has used the "least restrictive means" for achieving its compelling interest. Strict scrutiny generally applies to laws that discriminate on the basis of race, religion, or national origin. These are termed *suspect classifications*. Strict scrutiny also applies to laws that hinder the exercise of fundamental rights, such as access to the courts or the right to vote. When a federal court employs strict scrutiny, the government is seldom able to meet its burden of proof. All race-based classifications are automatically subject to strict scrutiny.[47]

Women and Gender Discrimination

Title VII provided a valuable tool for the growing women's movement in the 1960s and '70s. In fact, in many ways the law fostered the growth of the women's movement. The first major campaign of the National Organization for Women (NOW) involved picketing the EEOC for its refusal to ban sex-segregated employment advertisements. NOW also sued the *New York Times* for continuing to publish such ads after the passage of Title VII. Another organization, the Women's Equity Action League (WEAL), pursued legal action on a wide range of sex-discrimination issues, filing lawsuits against law schools and medical schools for discriminatory admission policies, for example.

Building on these victories and the growth of the women's movement, feminist activists sought an "Equal Rights Amendment" (ERA) to the Constitution. The proposed amendment was short: its substantive passage stated that "equality of rights under the law shall not be denied or abridged by the United States or by any State on account of sex." The amendment's supporters believed that such a sweeping guarantee of equal rights was a necessary tool for ending all discrimination against women and for making gender roles more equal. Opponents charged

Political equality did not end discrimination against women in the workplace or in society at large. African Americans' struggle for civil rights in the 1950s and '60s spurred a parallel equal rights movement for women in the 1960s and '70s.

that the amendment would be socially disruptive and would introduce changes (such as unisex restrooms) that most Americans did not want. The amendment easily passed Congress in 1972 and won quick approval in many state legislatures, but it fell three states short of the 38 needed to ratify it by the 1982 deadline.[48]

Despite the failure of the ERA, efforts to stop gender discrimination expanded dramatically as an area of civil rights law. In the 1970s the conservative Burger Court (under Chief Justice Warren Burger) helped establish gender discrimination as a major and highly visible civil rights issue. Although the Supreme Court refused to treat gender discrimination as the equivalent of racial discrimination,[49] it did make it easier for plaintiffs to file and win suits on the basis of gender discrimination by applying an "intermediate" level of review to these cases, as described earlier.[50]

Equality in Education One major step was taken in 1992, when the Court decided in *Franklin v. Gwinnett County Public Schools* that violations of Title IX of the 1972 Education Act could be remedied with monetary damages.[51] Title IX forbade gender discrimination in education, but it initially sparked little litigation because of its weak enforcement provisions. The Court's 1992 ruling that monetary damages could be awarded for gender discrimination opened the door for more legal action in the area of education. The greatest impact has been in the areas of sexual harassment (the subject of the *Franklin* case) and in equal treatment of women's athletic programs. The potential for monetary damages has made universities and public schools take the problem of sexual harassment more seriously. And in the two years after the *Franklin* case, complaints to the Education Department's Office for Civil Rights about unequal treatment of women's athletic programs nearly tripled. In several high-profile legal cases, some prominent universities were ordered to create more women's sports programs, prompting many other colleges and universities to follow suit in order to avoid potential litigation.[52] In 1997 the Supreme Court refused to hear a petition by Brown University challenging a lower-court order that the university establish strict sex equity in its athletic programs. The Court's decision meant that in colleges and universities across the country, varsity athletic positions for men and women must reflect the schools' overall enrollment numbers.[53] By 2012, 40 years after Title IX was first enacted, it was clear that the ruling had a major impact on college athletic programs. But advocates for gender equality note that many differences between men and women students continue to exist. They point to gender barriers in important fields such as science, technology, engineering, and math, which women students are much less likely to enter.[54]

In 1996 the Supreme Court made another important decision about gender and education by putting an end to all-male schools supported by public funds. It ruled that the Virginia Military Institute's (VMI) policy of not admitting women was unconstitutional.[55] Along with the Citadel, an all-male military college in South Carolina, VMI had never admitted women in its 157-year history. VMI argued that the unique educational experience it offered (including intense physical training and the harsh treatment of freshmen) would be

The integration of women in the U.S. military has been a slow process. Only in 2013 did then–Secretary of Defense Leon Panetta announce that the military would lift its official ban on women serving in combat. This decision in part reflected the reality that female service members frequently found themselves in combat in Iraq and Afghanistan.

for critical analysis

Has Title IX created equality in men's and women's college athletic programs? Should there be public efforts to encourage more female students to enter well-paid fields such as science and technology, or is that mainly a matter of individual choice?

destroyed if women students were admitted. The Court, however, ruled that the male-only policy denied "substantial equality" to women. Two days after the ruling, the Citadel announced that it would accept women. VMI considered becoming a private institution in order to remain all-male, but in September 1996, the school's board finally voted to admit women. Even without formal barriers to entry, the experience of the new female cadets at these schools was not easy. The first female cadet at the Citadel, Shannon Faulkner, won admission in 1995 under a federal court order but quit after four days. Of the four women admitted to the Citadel after the Supreme Court decision, two quit within months. They charged harassment from male students, including attempts to set the female cadets on fire.[56]

Sexual Harassment Courts began to find sexual harassment to be a form of sex discrimination during the late 1970s. Most such law has been developed by courts through interpretation of Title VII of the 1964 Civil Rights Act. In 1986 the Supreme Court recognized two forms of sexual harassment. One type is "quid pro quo" harassment, which involves an explicit or strongly implied threat that submission is a condition of continued employment. The second is harassment that creates offensive or intimidating employment conditions amounting to a "hostile environment."[57] Employers and many employees have complained that "hostile environment" sexual harassment is too ambiguous. When can an employee bring charges? When is the employer liable? In 1986 the Court said that sexual harassment may be legally actionable even if the employee did not suffer tangible economic or job-related losses in relation to it. In 1993 the Court said that sexual harassment may be legally actionable even if the employee did not suffer tangible psychological costs as a result.[58] In two 1998 cases, the Court further strengthened the law when it said that whether or not sexual harassment results in economic harm to the employee, an employer is liable for the harassment if it was committed by someone with authority over the employee—by a supervisor, for example. But the Court also said that an employer may defend itself by showing that it had a sexual harassment prevention and grievance policy in effect.[59]

Sexual harassment remains an issue today. Recently, a number of cases of sexual harassment of female members of the U.S. military have come to light. These cases have led to several court-martials of both officers and noncommissioned officers. Some observers argue that the problem is systemic, however, and have urged the military to enact reforms that would hopefully have the effect of stemming the abuse of women in the military.

Equality in Employment Women have also pressed for civil rights in employment. In particular, women have fought against pay discrimination, which occurs when a male employee is paid more than a female employee of equal qualifications in the same job. In the 1960s, pay discrimination was common. After the Equal Pay Act of 1963 made such discrimination illegal, women's pay slowly moved toward the level of men's pay. In 2007 this movement received a setback when the Supreme Court ruled against a claim of pay discrimination. The case, *Ledbetter v. Goodyear Tire and Rubber Co.*, involved a woman supervisor named Lily Ledbetter, who learned late in her career that she was being paid up to 40 percent less than male supervisors, including those with less seniority. Ledbetter filed a grievance with the EEOC, charging sex discrimination.[60] The Supreme Court denied her claim, ruling that according to the law, workers must

Have Women Achieved Equal Rights?

Title VII of the 1964 Civil Rights Act prohibits gender discrimination, and the Supreme Court has consistently upheld the principle that women should have the same rights as men. Since 1960, the United States has made great strides toward gender equality in some areas but, as the data show, still has a long way to go in other areas.

Education

Percentage of college students who are women

Politics

Percentage of members of Congress who are women

Percentage of state legislators who are women

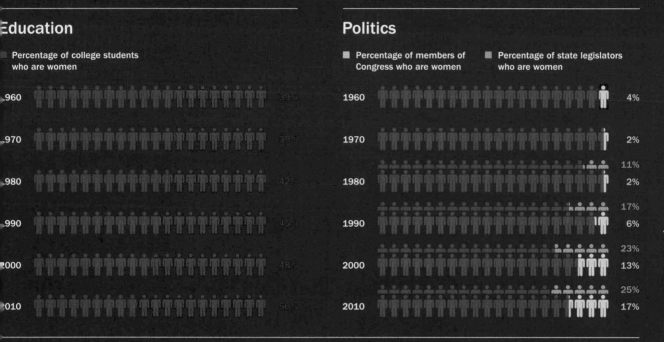

Education		Politics (Congress)	Politics (Legislators)
1960	39%		4%
1970	39%		2%
1980	42%	11%	2%
1990	45%	17%	6%
2000	48%	23%	13%
2010	56%	25%	17%

Based on the median weekly earnings for full-time workers (which excludes self-employed and full-time workers who work only part of the year), in 2012 women earned 80.9 percent as much as men. In 1979 women earned 62.3 percent as much as men.

Median Weekly Earnings by Race and Gender

White		African American		Latino		Asian American	
Men	Women	Men	Women	Men	Women	Men	Women
$879	$710	$665	$559	$592	$521	$1,055	$770

23 of 500
There are 23 female Fortune 500 CEOs.

26%
The proportion of women presidents of colleges and universities is 26 percent.

$431,000
Over a 40-year working career, the average woman loses $431,000 as the result of the wage gap.

for critical analysis

1. How much do each of these factors—education, political office, and income— say about gender equality in the United States?

2. While most Americans support the principle of equal opportunity for all groups, there is disagreement over how much the government should do to ensure equal outcomes. Discuss the difference between equal opportunity and equal outcomes in the context of women's rights.

SOURCES: Bureau of Labor Statistics, www.bls.gov/cps/tables.htm; American Progress, www.americanprogress.org/issues/labor/news/2012/04/16/11391/the-top-10-facts-about-the-wage-gap/; Catalyst, www.catalyst.org/knowledge/women-ceos-fortune-1000; Chronicle of Higher Education, http://chronicle.com/article/Who-Are-College-Presidents-/131138/ (accessed 3/19/14).

file their grievance 180 days after the discrimination occurs. Many observers found the ruling unfair because workers often do not know about pay differentials until well after the initial decision to discriminate has been made. Justice Ruth Bader Ginsburg, the only female member of the Court at the time, marked her disagreement by reading her dissent aloud, a rare occurrence. In January 2009 the Lily Ledbetter Fair Pay Act became the first bill that President Obama signed into law. The new law gave workers expanded rights to sue in cases, such as Ledbetter's, when an employee learns of discriminatory treatment well after it has started.

The fight against gender discrimination as an important part of the civil rights struggle has coincided with the rise of women's politics as a discrete movement in American politics. As with the struggle for racial equality, the relationship between changes in government policies and political action suggests that, to a great degree, changes in government policies produce political action. The inclusion of gender as a protected class in the 1964 Civil Rights Act prompted women to take steps to press for their rights where they were denied in education and employment. The "Who Are Americans?" feature on page 183 considers the progress on women's rights.

Latinos

The labels *Latino* and *Hispanic* encompass a wide range of groups with diverse national origins, distinctive cultural identities, and particular experiences. As a result, civil rights issues for them have varied considerably by group and by place. For example, the early political experiences of Mexican Americans were shaped by race and by region. In 1848, under the Treaty of Guadalupe Hidalgo, Mexico ceded to the United States territory that now comprises Arizona, California, New Mexico, and parts of Colorado, Nevada, and Utah, as well as extending the Texas border to the Rio Grande. Although the treaty guaranteed full civil rights to the residents of these territories, Mexican Americans in fact experienced ongoing discrimination, which they sought to remedy through the courts. In 1898 the courts reconfirmed Mexican Americans' formal political rights, including the right to vote. In many places, however, and especially in Texas, Mexican Americans were segregated and prevented from voting through such means as the white primary and the poll tax.[61] Texas established separate schools for Mexicans, a practice also common in Southern California. In the housing markets, Mexicans were often banned by restrictive covenants from buying or renting houses in many neighborhoods.

The earliest Mexican American independent political organizations included the League of United Latin American Citizens (LULAC), founded in 1929, and the GI Forum, created in 1948. Both groups worked to stem discrimination against Mexican Americans. LULAC pursued a legal strategy like the NAACP's to eliminate the segregation of Mexican American students. One of its earliest victories came in 1931, when it successfully challenged a Texas school district's decision to establish separate schools for Anglos and Mexicans.[62] LULAC also litigated the 1947 *Mendez v. Westminster* case, which overturned school segregation in Orange County, California. This case was an important precursor to *Brown v. Board of Education*, and many of the same actors were involved. For example, Thurgood Marshall of the NAACP, the lead attorney on *Brown* (and later a Supreme Court justice), filed a brief supporting desegregation in the *Mendez* case. Moreover, Earl Warren, the California governor who signed the legislation outlawing school segregation there after the *Mendez* decision, served as chief justice when the Supreme

Court ruled on *Brown* seven years later. By the late 1950s the first Mexican American was elected to Congress, and four others followed in the 1960s.

In the 1960s a new kind of Mexican American political movement was born. A central inspiration for political mobilization emerged from the United Farm Workers union and its charismatic leader, César Chávez. In an era of unprecedented economic prosperity, California's farmworkers, mainly Mexican migrants, remained poorly paid and lacked basic rights for fair treatment on the job. Employing novel tactics such as the national grape boycott, the union drew Americans' attention to the plight of farmworkers and the injustices that confronted Mexican migrants and Mexican Americans in the fields. Chávez, whose hunger strikes and inspirational speeches kept the movement in the public eye, came to symbolize the quest for Mexican American civil rights more broadly.[63] The fields were not the only focus of conflict. In the late 1960s, Mexican American students, inspired by the black civil rights movement, launched boycotts of high school classes in East Los Angeles, Denver, and San Antonio. Students in colleges and universities across California joined in as well. Among their demands were bilingual education, an end to discrimination, and more cultural recognition.

Since that time, Latino political strategy has developed along two tracks. One is a traditional ethnic group path of voter registration and voting along ethnic lines. The second is a legal strategy using the various civil rights laws designed to ensure fair access to the political system. The Mexican American Legal Defense and Education Fund (MALDEF), founded in 1968, has played a key role in designing and pursuing the latter strategy.

Immigrants and Civil Rights Since the 1960s, rights for Latinos have been intertwined with immigrant rights. For much of American history, legal immigrants were treated much the same as citizens. But growing immigration—including an estimated 300,000 unauthorized immigrants per year—and mounting economic insecurity have undermined this sense of equality. Groups of voters across the country now strongly support drawing a sharper line between immigrants and citizens. The Supreme Court has ruled that unauthorized immigrants are eligible for education and emergency medical care but can be denied other social benefits. The movement to deny benefits to noncitizens gathered steam in California, which experienced sharp economic distress in the early 1990s and has the highest levels of immigration of any state. In 1994, California voters approved Proposition 187, denying unauthorized immigrants all services except emergency medical care. Supporters of the measure hoped to discourage unauthorized immigration and to pressure those already in the country to leave. Opponents contended that denying basic services to unauthorized immigrants risked creating a subclass of residents in the United States whose poor health and lack of education would threaten all Americans. In 1994 and 1997 a federal court declared most of Proposition 187 unconstitutional, affirming previous rulings that unauthorized immigrants should be granted public education.

Questions about the rights of unauthorized immigrants became especially contentious in 2007. That year, Congress considered a complex compromise bill—running some 761 pages long—that attempted to accomplish three goals: increase border security to reduce illegal immigration; provide unauthorized immigrants who had been in the country for at least five years with a pathway to legal citizenship; and ensure employers an adequate supply of temporary immigrant workers through a guest worker program. The compromise failed in the face of opposition from conservatives, which disliked the provision for creating a path to legal citizenship, and from liberals, which opposed the proposed guest worker program.

In the aftermath of the failed legislation, unauthorized immigration has continued to be a hot-button political issue. One priority for advocacy groups has been the issue of undocumented immigrants who came to the United States as young children, were raised in the United States, and have no real ties to the nation in which they were born. One proposed piece of legislation to benefit such individuals is the Development, Relief, and Education Act for Alien Minors, known as the DREAM Act. This proposal would provide a route to permanent residency for such individuals via military service or college attendance. The DREAM Act was first introduced in Congress in 2001 but has been defeated every year on the ground that it would encourage illegal immigration. Absent legislation, the Department of Homeland Security has instituted its own policy, "Deferred Action for Childhood Arrivals" (DACA), instructing immigration officials to take no action to deport law-abiding individuals who entered the United States illegally as children.

Efforts to curb illegal immigration have led to civil rights violations of legal immigrants. Latino organizations opposed the Immigration Reform and Control Act of 1986 because it imposed sanctions on employers who hire undocumented workers. Such sanctions, they feared, would lead employers to discriminate against Latinos. These suspicions were confirmed in a 1990 report by the General Accounting Office that found employer sanctions had created a "widespread pattern of discrimination" against Latinos and others who appear foreign.[64]

Another ongoing issue is federal cooperation with local and state law enforcement agencies to enforce federal immigration laws. Programs first initiated by the Department of Homeland Security in the final years of the George W. Bush

administration led to immigrant "sweeps," which rounded up Latinos, many of whom were legal immigrants or even American citizens. A broad coalition of civil rights organizations opposed the program for engaging in racial profiling and violating civil rights, and the congressional Hispanic Caucus called on the new president to end it. Yet, the Obama administration's Secure Communities program, which initially sought to focus on major drug offenders, violent criminals, and those already in prison, has come under fire for illegally detaining citizens and legal immigrants. Secure Communities requires state and local police to run the fingerprints of individuals they have arrested against the Department of Homeland Security's immigration database. If the individual is not a U.S. citizen and is not in the database, Immigration and Customs Enforcement is notified.[65]

Finally, as we saw in Chapter 3, a number of states, including Arizona, Utah, South Carolina, Indiana, Georgia, and Alabama passed very strict immigration laws within the past few years. Civil rights groups have contested the laws in court, and the federal Justice Department has instituted its own legal challenges. Arizona's 2010 law provided the inspiration for these far-reaching state measures. Arizona's law required immigrants to carry identity documents with them at all times, made it a crime for an undocumented immigrant to apply for a job, gave the police greater powers to stop anyone they suspected of being an unauthorized immigrant, and required them to check the immigration status of a person they detain if they suspect that person is an unauthorized immigrant. The Justice Department challenged the law on the grounds that the federal government was responsible for making immigration law, not the states. The Supreme Court's 2012 decision was a partial victory for the federal government. The court struck down three parts of the Arizona law on the grounds that they preempted federal responsibility. These included the provision that immigrants carry identity papers, that undocumented immigrants cannot apply for jobs, and that police can stop persons they suspect of being undocumented immigrants. The Court let stand the provision that required local police to check the immigration status of an individual detained for other reasons, if they had grounds to suspect that the person was in the country illegally. Opponents of the police checks vowed to challenge that part of the law on the grounds that it led to illegal racial profiling.[66]

Race, Immigration, and Poverty

In the United States, a history of institutionalized discrimination helps explain why poverty[a] is highest in the African American community, reinforcing the race as one of the most important social divides in the United States. For many European countries, immigration is the primary social divide, with newer migrants facing the most significant economic challenges. In the United Kingdom, for instance, the highest rates of poverty are found among recent immigrant communities from Southeast Asia, particularly from Pakistan and Bangladesh. Language, education, and demographic differences between majority and minority populations help explain some of this variation, but discrimination in hiring plays a significant role.[b]

Reflecting this idea that immigration rather than race or ethnicity is the main social divide in Europe, Germany primarily distinguishes between migrant and nonmigrant populations in its 2011 census and economic reporting. In Germany, the "migrant" category includes all foreign-born noncitizens, foreign-born citizens,[c] _and_ any citizen with at least one parent who migrated after 1955. While it comprises only one-fifth of Germany's total population, the migrant community makes up a considerable percentage of low-income families: migrants have over twice the rate of poverty than the nonmigrant community.

However, poverty in Europe still has a racial or ethnic component, especially among the migrant population. Since World War II, most of Germany's migrant population was composed of its Turkish minority (which also includes Kurdish immigrants from Turkey). Concern that these migrants have failed to properly integrate into German society has sparked a heated debate in mainstream politics and has become a rallying cry for a resurgence of discriminatory right-wing extremism.[d]

Percentage of group living in poverty

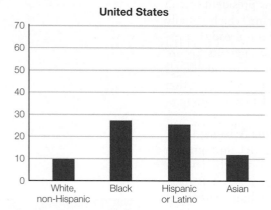

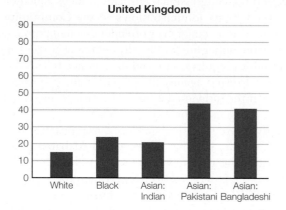

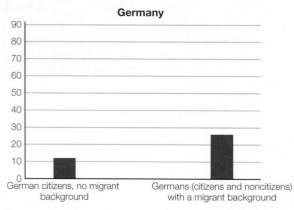

SOURCES: U.S. Census Bureau Briefs, Overview of Race and Hispanic Origin (2010), p. 4; U.S. Census Bureau Report: Income, Poverty, and Health Insurance Coverage in the United States (2012); pp. 13–15, www.census.gov/prod/2013 pubs/p60-245.pdf (accessed 10/22/14); 2011 UK Census, www.ons.gov.uk/ons/rel/census/2011-census /key-statistics-and-quick-statistics-for-local-authorities-in-the-united-kingdom—part-1/rft-ks201uk.xls (accessed 6/19/14); and Statistisches Bundesamt (Census 2011), www.destatis.de/DE/PresseService/Presse/Pressemitteilungen/2013/05/PD13_188_121.html (accessed 6/19/14).

[a]Poverty is measured differently from country to country. The United States uses a measure of "absolute" poverty, which is a calculation on whether an individual has enough to meet his basic needs. Most wealthy countries, including all the members of the European Union, instead use a measure of "relative" poverty, which compares an individual's income to others in his society.
[b]Rajeev Syal, "Undercover Job Hunters Reveal Huge Race Bias in Britain's Workplaces," _The Guardian_, October 17, 2009, www.theguardian.com/money/2009/oct/18 /racism-discrimination-employment-undercover (accessed 10/22/14).
[c]This group includes non-Germans and German ethnics that have migrated from Eastern Europe and the former Soviet Union.
[d]"Right-Wing Extremism: Germany's New Islamophobia Boom," _Der Spiegel_, March 5, 2014, www.spiegel.de/international/germany/islamophobic-hate-groups-become-more -prominent-in-germany-a-956801.html (accessed 10/22/14).

Asian Americans

Like the term *Latino*, the label *Asian American* encompasses a wide range of people from very different national backgrounds who came to the United States at different moments in history. As a consequence, Asian Americans have had very diverse experiences.

The early Asian experience in the United States was shaped by a series of naturalization laws dating back to 1790, the first of which declared that only white aliens were eligible for citizenship. Chinese immigrants began arriving in California in the 1850s, drawn by the boom of the gold rush, but they were immediately met with virulent antagonism. In 1870, Congress declared Chinese immigrants ineligible for citizenship; in 1882 the first Chinese Exclusion Act suspended the entry of Chinese laborers.

At the time of the Exclusion Act, the Chinese community was composed predominantly of single male laborers, with few women and children. The few Chinese children in San Francisco were initially denied entry to the public schools; only after parents of American-born Chinese children pressed legal action were the children allowed to attend public school. Even then, however, they were segregated into a separate Chinese school. American-born Chinese children could not be denied citizenship, however; this right was confirmed by the Supreme Court in 1898, when it ruled in *United States v. Wong Kim Ark* that anyone born in the United States was entitled to full citizenship.[67] Still, new Chinese immigrants were barred from the United States until 1943, after China had become a key wartime ally and Congress repealed the Chinese Exclusion Act and permitted Chinese residents to become citizens.

The earliest Japanese immigrants, who came to California in the 1880s, at the height of the anti-Chinese movement, faced similar discrimination. Like Chinese immigrants, Japanese immigrants were ineligible to become citizens because of their race. During the first part of the twentieth century, California and several other western states enacted laws that denied Japanese immigrants the right to own property. The denial of basic civil rights to Japanese Americans culminated in the decision to forcibly remove Americans of Japanese descent as well as Japanese noncitizen residents from their homes and confine them in internment camps during World War II. After the Japanese government launched its attack on Pearl Harbor, America's Japanese residents and citizens were suspected of disloyalty. Some 120,000 individuals of Japanese descent or heritage, including 90,000 American citizens, were forcibly relocated from their homes to 10 internment camps located in California, Idaho, Utah, Arizona, Wyoming, Colorado, and Arkansas. Conditions in the camps were poor and characterized by overcrowding, food rationing, and primitive sanitary facilities. Despite a vigorous legal challenge, the Supreme Court ruled that the internment was constitutional on the grounds of military necessity.[68] In 1944, President Roosevelt rescinded the order that began the internment process and closed the camps. Many of the internees, however, had suffered property losses and health problems during the period of internment and would never recover from its effects. Not until the Civil Liberties Act of 1988 did the federal government formally acknowledge this denial of civil rights as a "grave injustice" that had been "motivated largely by racial prejudice, wartime hysteria, and a failure of political leadership."[69] Along with a formal apology from the president, Congress issued each surviving internee a $20,000 check.

Asian immigration increased rapidly after the 1965 Immigration Act, which lifted discriminatory quotas. In spite of this and other developments, limited English

Asian immigrants faced discrimination throughout much of American history. During World War II, Americans of Japanese descent were forced from their homes and confined in internment camps. At the time, the Supreme Court supported this denial of civil rights as a necessary security measure.

proficiency barred many new Asian American (in addition to Latino) immigrants from full participation in American life. Two developments in the 1970s, however, established rights for language minorities. In 1974 the Supreme Court ruled in *Lau v. Nichols*, a suit filed on behalf of Chinese students in San Francisco, that school districts have to provide education for students whose English is limited.[70] It did not mandate bilingual education, but it established a duty to provide instruction that the students could understand. As we saw earlier, the 1970 amendments to the Voting Rights Act permanently outlawed literacy tests in all 50 states and mandated bilingual ballots or oral assistance for those who speak Chinese, Japanese, Korean, Spanish, or Native American or Alaskan languages.

Native Americans

The political status of Native Americans was left unclear in the Constitution. But by the early 1800s the courts had defined each of the Indian tribes as a nation. As members of Indian nations, Native Americans were thus declared noncitizens of the United States. The political status of Native Americans changed in 1924, when congressional legislation granted citizenship to all persons born in the United States. A variety of changes in federal policy toward Native Americans during the 1930s paved the way for a later resurgence of their political power. Most important was the federal decision to encourage Native Americans on reservations to establish local self-government.[71] Since the 1920s and '30s, Native American tribes have sued the federal government for illegal land seizures; both monetary reparations and land have been awarded as damages, but only in small amounts. Native American tribes have been more successful in winning federal recognition of their sovereignty. Sovereign status has, in turn, allowed them to exercise greater self-determination.

The Native American political movement gathered force in the 1960s as Native Americans began to use protest, litigation, and assertion of tribal rights to improve their situation. The federal government responded to the rise in Native American activism with the Indian Self-Determination and Education Assistance Act, which began to give Native Americans more control over their own land.[72]

As a language minority, Native Americans also benefited from the 1975 amendments to the Voting Rights Act and the *Lau* decision, which established the right of Native Americans to be taught in their own languages. This marked quite a change from the boarding schools by the Bureau of Indian Affairs, where members of Native American tribes were forbidden to speak their own languages until reforms began in the 1930s. In addition to these language-related issues, Native Americans have sought to expand their rights on the basis of their sovereign status. Most significant in economic terms was a 1987 Supreme Court decision that freed Native American tribes from most state regulations prohibiting gambling. The establishment of casino gambling on Native American lands has brought a substantial flow of new income to desperately poor reservations.

Disabled Americans

The concept of rights for the disabled began to emerge in the 1970s as the civil rights model spread to other groups. The seed was planted in a little-noticed provision of the 1973 Rehabilitation Act, which outlawed discrimination against individuals on the basis of disabilities. As in many other cases, the law itself helped give rise to the movement demanding rights for the disabled.[73] Inspired by the NAACP's use of a Legal Defense Fund, the disability movement founded a Disability Rights Education and Defense Fund to press its legal claims. The movement achieved its greatest success with the passage of the Americans with Disabilities Act (ADA) of 1990, which guarantees equal employment rights and access to public businesses for the disabled and prohibits discrimination in employment, housing, and health care. Claims of discrimination in violation of this act are considered by the EEOC. The impact of the law has been far-reaching, as businesses and public facilities have installed ramps, elevators, and other devices to meet the act's requirements.[74]

Gay Men and Lesbians

In less than 50 years, the lesbian, gay, bisexual, and transgender (LGBT) movement has become one of the largest civil rights movements in contemporary America. For much of the country's history, any sexual orientation other than heterosexuality was considered "deviant" and many states criminalized sexual acts considered to be "unnatural." Homosexuals were often afraid to reveal their sexual orientation for fear of reprisals, including being fired from their jobs, and the police in many cities raided bars and other establishments where it was believed that homosexuals gathered. While no formal restrictions existed on their political participation, homosexuals faced the possibility of ostracization, discrimination, and even prosecution.[75]

The contemporary gay rights movement began in earnest in the 1960s. In 1962, Illinois became the first state to repeal its sodomy laws. The movement drew national attention in 1969, when patrons at the Stonewall Inn in Greenwich Village, New York, a popular gay bar, rioted when police attempted to raid the establishment. The first gay pride parade was held in New York City the following year to commemorate the anniversary of the Stonewall riots, and gay pride parades now take place in dozens of cities across the country.

Gay rights drew national attention again in 1993, when President Bill Clinton confronted the question of whether gays should be allowed to serve in the military. As a candidate, Clinton had said he favored lifting the ban on homosexuals in the military. The issue set off a huge controversy in the first months of Clinton's presidency. After nearly a year of deliberation, the administration enunciated a compromise: its "Don't Ask, Don't Tell" policy allowed gay men and lesbians to serve in the military as long as they did not openly proclaim their sexual orientation or engage in homosexual activity. The administration maintained that the ruling would protect gay men and lesbians against witch-hunt investigations, but many advocates of gay men and lesbians expressed disappointment, charging the president with reneging on his campaign promise. After nearly 20 years of challenges, President Obama signed an executive order repealing "Don't Ask, Don't Tell," and beginning in September 2011, gay men and lesbians could serve openly in the military.

But until 1996, there was no Supreme Court ruling or national legislation explicitly protecting gay men and lesbians from discrimination. In the first gay rights case it decided, *Bowers v. Hardwick*, the Court ruled against a right to privacy that would protect consensual homosexual activity.[76] After the *Bowers* decision, the gay rights movement sought suitable legal cases to test the constitutionality of discrimination against gay men and lesbians, much as the black civil rights movement had done in the late 1940s and '50s. As one advocate put it, "lesbians and gay men are looking for their *Brown v. Board of Education*."[77] Test cases stemmed from local ordinances restricting gay rights (including the right to marry), allowing job discrimination, and affecting family law issues such as adoption and parental rights. In 1996 the Supreme Court, in *Romer v. Evans*, explicitly extended fundamental civil rights protections to gay men and lesbians by declaring unconstitutional a 1992 amendment to the Colorado state constitution that prohibited local governments from passing ordinances to protect gay rights.[78] In its decision, the Court highlighted the connection between gay rights and civil rights.

Finally, in *Lawrence v. Texas* (2003), the Court overturned *Bowers* and struck down a Texas statute criminalizing certain intimate sexual conduct between consenting partners of the same sex.[79] A victory for gay men and lesbians every bit as significant as *Roe v. Wade* was for women, *Lawrence v. Texas* extends the right to privacy to sexual minorities.

However, this decision does not undo the various exclusions that deprive gay men and lesbians of full civil rights, including the right to marry. In 1993, Hawaii's supreme court declared the state's ban on same-sex marriage discriminatory, raising the possibility that such marriages could become legal. In Washington, D.C., the Republican congressional majority responded with the Defense of Marriage Act, which defined marriage as the union of a man and a woman for purposes of federal law and benefits, such as Social Security.

Other states then took up the issue of same-sex marriage. A significant victory came in 2004, when the Supreme Judicial Court of Massachusetts ruled that under that state's constitution, same-sex couples were entitled to marry. As of November 2014, 35 states and the District of Columbia had passed laws that allowed such couples to marry. In 2012 voters for the first time approved same-sex marriage at the ballot box, with measures winning a majority in Maine, Maryland, and

Partners for 40 years, Edith Windsor and Thea Spyer were married in 2007. When Thea passed away in 2009, Edith had to pay over $300,000 in taxes because the federal government did not recognize her marriage under the terms of DOMA. In 2013, Edith won her Supreme Court case, which cleared the way for the federal government to recognize same-sex marriages.

Washington state. Some of these laws, however, have faced challenges. In California, voters repealed a law allowing same-sex marriage five months after its passage. Lower courts subsequently declared the California vote as unconstitutional discrimination. The case was appealed, by opponents of same-sex marriage, to the Supreme Court, which ruled that these groups did not have standing to bring the case, thus the lower-court ruling stands and same-sex marriage was once again allowed in California.

As described in the chapter introduction, the Supreme Court issued another important ruling on behalf of the right to marry in 2013, finding that Section 3 of the federal Defense of Marriage Act violated the equal liberty of persons under the Fifth Amendment in denying thousands of federal benefits to married same-sex couples that it granted to married opposite-sex couples. The majority wrote for the Court, "DOMA writes inequality into the entire U.S. Code."[80] In the wake of the ruling, the Obama administration directed his Cabinet to review relevant federal statutes to ensure that the decision was implemented. The Federal government subsequently expanded recognition of same-sex marriages for the purpose of federal benefits and legal proceedings, such as survivor benefits, bankruptcies, tax purposes, and immigration. Despite this change at the national level, considerable variation in LGBT civil rights policies continues to exist at the state level (see Figure 5.2).

Gay rights advocates won a significant victory of a different kind in national politics. New legislation extended the definition of hate crimes to include crimes against gay and transgender people. Such legislation had been sought since the 1998 murder of Matthew Shepard, a Wyoming college student who was brutally slain because of his sexual orientation. The new law allows for tougher penalties when a crime is designated a hate crime. In another win in 2013, the Senate approved a law that bans discrimination in the workplace based on sexual orientation and gender identity, with a vote of 64 to 32 in which 10 Republicans joined 54 Democrats. The House did not take up the bill, however, so it has not yet become law. Like other minorities fighting for civil rights, the LGBT community is organized politically to support such measures. The Human Rights Campaign is the primary national political action committee (PAC) focused on gay rights; it provides campaign financing and volunteers to work for political candidates endorsed by the group. The movement has also formed legal-rights organizations, including the Lambda Legal Defense and Education Fund.

for critical analysis

Political conflicts over same-sex marriage have been carried out in the courts, in state legislatures, in Congress, and in elections. What are some of the decisions that have been reached in each of these different decision-making arenas? Where should decisions about same-sex marriage be made?

FIGURE 5.2

Attitudes and Policies toward Gay Rights

This figure allows you to compare public opinion on gay rights in each state with that state's policies on gay rights. In which states is the public most supportive of gay rights? In which states is the opinion the least supportive? Is there a relationship between public opinion on gay rights and that state's policies on gay rights? Political scientists have found not only that public opinion influences policy, but also that policy can influence public opinion.

SOURCES: Jeffrey Lax and Justin Phillips, "Gay Rights in the States: Public Opinion and Policy Responsiveness," *American Political Science Review* 103, no 3 (2009): 367–86, Table 1; Movement Advancement Project, www.lgbtmap.org/equality-maps/legal_equality_by_state (accessed 1/14/14).

PUBLIC OPINION ON GAY RIGHTS

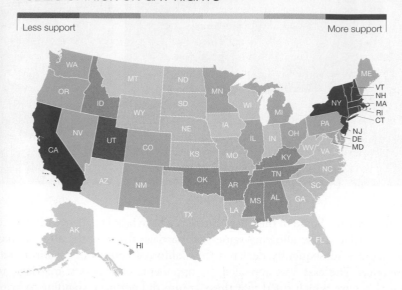

Support in public opinion is a statewide average based on the percentage of people who expressed support for gay marriage, second-parent adoption, hate crime protection for gays, or other policies related to gay rights (in a 2009 study).

STATE POLICIES ON GAY RIGHTS

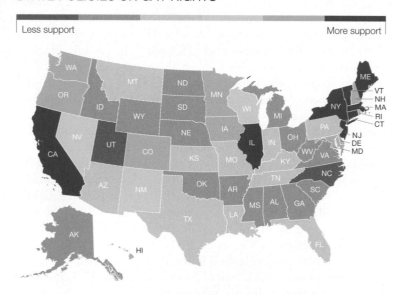

State-level policies are rated as most supportive if state laws (as of 2013) provided for same-sex marriage, second-parent adoption, hate crime protection for gays, and protections from discrimination in housing and employment; state policies are rated as least supportive if they provided for none of these.

Do the Poor Have Civil Rights?

One category often omitted from discussions of rights is the poor. Yet, America's poor have also struggled for recognition as a group with rights that should be protected. From the colonial period until the early nineteenth century, state income and property restrictions excluded the poor from voting and officeholding. In modern times, advocates have argued that the poor have a right (a claim upon government action) to education, health care, and other social benefits. Such rights are guaranteed in many European constitutions. And, in the United States, various social policies discussed in Chapter 17 appear to recognize such rights.

One area in which there is currently a disparity is in access to high-speed Internet. A 2013 Pew survey found that among those who earn less than $30,000 per year, only 54 percent have high-speed Internet access at home. This compares with 88 percent of those making at least $75,000 a year.[81] As more and more economic and political activity moves online, including job listings and applications for government services, this disparity has the potential to reinforce inequalities.

Affirmative Action

> **Contrast arguments for and against affirmative action**

The politics of rights has spread to increasing numbers of groups in American society since the 1960s. The relatively narrow goal of equalizing opportunity by eliminating discriminatory barriers evolved into the far broader goal of **affirmative action**, compensatory action to overcome the consequences of past discrimination. Affirmative action policies take race or some other status into account in order to provide greater opportunities to groups that have previously been at a disadvantage due to discrimination.

affirmative action government policies or programs that seek to redress past injustices against specified groups by making special efforts to provide members of those groups with access to educational and employment opportunities

President Lyndon Johnson put the case emotionally in 1965: "You do not take a person who, for years, has been hobbled by chains . . . and then say you are free to compete with all the others, and still just believe that you have been completely fair."[82] Johnson issued executive orders directing agency heads and personnel officers to pursue a policy of minority employment in the federal civil service and in companies doing business with the government. But affirmative action did not become a prominent goal of the national government until the 1970s.

Affirmative action also took the form of efforts by the agencies in the Department of Health, Education, and Welfare to shift their focus from "desegregation" to "integration."[83] Federal agencies, sometimes with court orders and sometimes without them, required school districts to present plans for busing children across district lines, for closing certain schools, and for redistributing faculties as well as students, or face the loss of grants-in-aid from the federal government. The guidelines constituted preferential treatment to compensate for past discrimination, and without this legislatively assisted approach to integration, there would certainly not have been the dramatic increase in the number of black children attending integrated classes.

Affirmative action was also initiated in the area of employment opportunity. The EEOC has often required plans whereby employers must attempt to increase the number of their minority employees, and the Department of Labor's Office of Federal Contract Compliance Programs has used the threat of contract revocation for the same purpose. These programs did not require the use of formal quotas.

The Supreme Court and the Burden of Proof

Efforts by the executive, legislative, and judicial branches to shape the meaning of affirmative action today tend to center on one key issue: What is the appropriate level of review in affirmative action cases—that is, on whom should the burden of proof be placed, the plaintiff, to show that discrimination has not occurred, or the defendant, to show that discrimination has occurred? Affirmative action was first addressed formally by the Supreme Court in the case of Allan Bakke (see Table 5.3). Bakke, a white male, brought suit against the University

TABLE 5.3

Supreme Court Rulings on Affirmative Action

CASE	COURT RULING
Regents of the University of California v. Bakke, 438 U.S. 265 (1978)	Affirmative action upheld, but quotas and separate admission for minorities rejected; burden of proof on defendant
Wards Cove v. Atonio, 490 U.S. 642 (1989)	All affirmative action programs put in doubt: burden of proof shifted from defendant to plaintiff (victim), then burden of proof shifted back to employers (defendants)
St. Mary's Honor Center v. Hicks, 113 S. Ct. 2742 (1993)	Required victim to prove discrimination was intentional
Adarand Constructors v. Peña, 515 U.S. 200 (1995)	All race-conscious policies must survive "strict scrutiny," with burden of proof on government to show the program serves "compelling interest" to redress past discrimination
Hopwood v. Texas, 78 F3d 932 (5th Cir., 1996)	Race can *never* be used as a factor in admission, even to promote diversity (Supreme Court refusal to review limited application to the Fifth Circuit—Texas, Louisiana, Mississippi)
Gratz v. Bollinger, 123 S. Ct. 2411 (2003)	Rejection of a "mechanical" point system favoring minority applicants to University of Michigan as tantamount to a quota; *Bakke* reaffirmed
Grutter v. Bollinger, 123 S. Ct. 2325 (2003)	Upheld race-conscious admission to Michigan Law School, passing strict scrutiny with diversity as a "compelling" state interest, as long as admission was "highly individualized" and not "mechanical," as in *Gratz*

of California at Davis Medical School on the grounds that, in denying him admission, the school had discriminated against him on the basis of his race. (That year, the school had reserved 16 of 100 available slots for minority applicants.) Bakke argued that his grades and test scores had ranked him well above many students who had been accepted at the school and that the only possible explanation for his rejection was that he was white, whereas those others accepted were black or Latino. In 1978, Bakke won his case before the Supreme Court and was admitted to the medical school, but the Court stopped short of declaring affirmative action unconstitutional. The Court rejected the procedures at the University of California because its medical school had used both a quota *and* a separate admissions system for minorities. The Court accepted the argument that achieving "a diverse student body" was a "compelling public purpose," but found that the method of a rigid quota of student slots assigned on the basis of race was incompatible with the Fourteenth Amendment's equal protection clause. Thus, the Court permitted universities (and presumably other schools, training programs, and hiring authorities) to continue to take minority status into consideration, but severely limited the use of quotas to situations (1) in which previous discrimination had been shown, and (2) where quotas were used more as a guideline for social diversity than as a mathematically defined ratio.[84]

For nearly a decade after *Bakke*, the Supreme Court was tentative and permissive about efforts by universities, corporations, and governments to experiment with affirmative action programs.[85]

But in 1995 the Supreme Court's ruling in *Adarand Constructors v. Peña* further weakened affirmative action. This decision stated that race-based policies, such as preferences given by the government to minority contractors, must survive strict scrutiny, placing the burden on the government to show that such affirmative action programs serve a compelling government interest and are narrowly tailored to address identifiable past discrimination.[86] President Clinton responded to the *Adarand* decision by ordering a review of all government affirmative action policies and practices, and adopted an informal policy of trying to "mend, not end" affirmative action.

ADMISSIONS

IT'S HIS FAULT!

DAUGHTER of ALUM   SON of BIG DONOR   SOCCER PLAYER   RAISED in DISTANT STATE   MINORITY   DIDN'T GET IN

Affirmative action remains very controversial in the United States. This cartoon makes the point that admissions offices use a number of preference categories in order to achieve their goal of a diverse class, and minority status is just one of many such categories.

This betwixt-and-between status of affirmative action was how things stood in 2003, when the Supreme Court took two cases against the University of Michigan. The first suit, *Gratz v. Bollinger* (Lee Bollinger, the university president), challenged the University of Michigan's undergraduate admissions policy and practices, alleging that by using a point-based ranking system that automatically awarded 20 points (out of 150) to African American, Latino, and Native American applicants, the university discriminated unconstitutionally against white students of otherwise equal or superior academic qualifications. The Supreme Court agreed, 6–3, arguing that something tantamount to a quota was involved because undergraduate admissions lacked the necessary "individualized consideration" and had employed instead a "mechanical one," based too much on the favorable minority points.[87] The Court's ruling in *Gratz v. Bollinger* was not surprising, given *Bakke*'s (1978) holding against quotas and given recent decisions calling for strict scrutiny of all racial classifications, even those that are intended to remedy past discrimination or promote future equality.

The second case, *Grutter v. Bollinger*, broke new ground. Barbara Grutter sued the law school on the grounds that it had discriminated in a race-conscious way against white applicants with equal or superior grades and law boards. A precarious 5–4 decision for the first time aligned the majority of the Supreme Court with Justice Powell's lone plurality opinion in *Bakke*. Powell had argued that (1) diversity in education is a compelling state interest, and (2) race could be constitutionally considered as a plus factor in admissions decisions. In *Grutter*, the Court reiterated Powell's holding and, applying strict scrutiny to the law school's policy, found that the law school's admissions process was narrowly tailored to the school's compelling state interest in diversity because it gave a "highly individualized, holistic review of each applicant's file" in which race counted but was not used in a "mechanical" way.[88] The Court's ruling that racial categories can be deployed to serve a compelling state interest put affirmative action on stronger ground. The Court reaffirmed its decision in *Grutter* in 2013 when it decided *Fisher v. University of Texas*, in which a white student challenged the use of race as one factor among many in the admissions decision. In a 7–1 decision, the Court sent the case back to the District Court with instructions to apply "strict scrutiny" to the school's policy, as articulated in *Grutter*.[89]

The election of Barack Obama as the country's first black president raised questions about whether America's racial problems had been solved and whether policies such as affirmative action were still needed. Does the election of an African American as president mean we are closer to achieving racial equality?

Referenda on Affirmative Action

The courts have not been the only center of action: during the 1990s, challenges to affirmative action also emerged in state and local politics. One of the most significant state actions was the passage by referendum in 1996 of the California Civil Rights Initiative, also known as Proposition 209. Proposition 209 outlawed affirmative action programs in the state and local governments of California, thus prohibiting those governments from using race or gender preferences in their decisions about hiring, contracting, or university admissions. Following a heated political battle, the measure passed with 54 percent of the vote, including 27 percent of the black vote, 30 percent of the Latino vote, and 45 percent of the Asian American vote.[90] In 1997 the Supreme Court refused to hear a challenge to the new law. Proposition

209 was framed as a civil rights initiative: "the state shall not discriminate against, or grant preferential treatment to, any individual or group on the basis of race, sex, color, ethnicity, or national origin."

Different wording can produce quite different outcomes. A 1997 ballot initiative asked Houston voters whether they wanted to ban affirmative action in city contracting and hiring, not whether they wanted to end preferential treatment. Fifty-five percent of Houston voters decided in favor of affirmative action.[91] In 2006, 58 percent of Michigan voters supported a measure, modeled after California's Proposition 209, to amend the state constitution by outlawing affirmative action in public education, contracting, and employment. Although University of Michigan officials initially declared that they would continue to use affirmative action criteria in the admissions process until all legal appeals were exhausted, in early 2007 the university announced that it would stop using affirmative action procedures in admissions. Buoyed by their success in Michigan, affirmative action opponents planned to place similar initiatives on the ballot in the other 17 states that provide for constitutional amendment via voter referendum. However, in 2008 they succeeded in gaining sufficient signatures to bring the measure before voters only in Colorado, where the initiative failed to obtain voter approval, and Nebraska, where voters approved the measure. In 2014 the Supreme Court upheld the Michigan affirmative action ban. This decision emboldened anti–affirmative action groups to renew their efforts to place affirmative action on state ballots.[92]

Civil Rights
and Your Future

The election of Barack Obama as the nation's first black president fueled discussions about whether America's racial problems had been solved. Polls taken just before Obama's inauguration revealed a sharp upturn in positive views about progress toward racial equality, but the euphoria about racial equality did not last for long. After Obama's election, the proportion of those believing that racism against blacks was widespread dropped somewhat. Even so, in October 2009, nearly three-quarters of blacks and close to half of all whites continued to view racism against blacks as a widespread problem.[93]

Such beliefs indicate that the election of a black president will not make the debate about civil rights and affirmative action disappear, because Americans hold fundamentally different views about whether and how the government should recognize racial distinctions. At the risk of gross oversimplification, we can divide those with differing views into two groups, and label them liberals and conservatives.[94] Conservatives argue, first, that rights in the American tradition are *individual* rights, and affirmative action violates this concept by concerning itself with "group rights," an idea said to be alien to the American tradition. Second, conservatives argue that the Constitution is "color-blind" and that any discrimination, even if it is called positive or benign, must inevitably rely on quotas and thus ultimately violate the equal protection clause.

Liberals agree that rights ultimately come down to individuals but argue that since the essence of discrimination is the unreasonable and unjust exclusion of *an entire group* from something valuable the society has to offer, discrimination itself has to be attacked on a group basis. Despite progress toward racial equality, liberals argue that race still matters. They can also cite Supreme Court history, because the first definitive interpretation of the Fourteenth Amendment by the Court, in 1873, stated that

> the existence of laws in the state where the newly emancipated Negroes resided, which discriminated with gross injustice and hardship against them *as a class*, was the evil to be remedied by this clause [emphasis added].[95]

As to the conservative argument concerning quotas, the liberal response is that the Supreme Court has already accepted ratios (a form of quota) that are admitted as evidence to prove a "pattern or practice of discrimination" sufficient to reverse the burden of proof—to obligate the employer to show that there was *not* an intent to discriminate. Further, benign quotas have often been used by Americans both to compensate for some bad action in the past or to provide some desired distribution of social characteristics—that is, diversity. For example, a long-respected policy in the United States is the "veterans' preference" by which the government automatically gives extra consideration in hiring to persons who have served in the country's armed forces. And the goal of social diversity has long justified "positive discrimination," especially in higher education—the very institution where conservatives have most adamantly argued against positive quotas for blacks and women. For example, all the Ivy League schools and many other private colleges and universities regularly and consistently reserve admissions places not only for students from minority groups but also for the children of loyal alumni and of their own faculty, even when, in a pure competition based solely on test scores and high school records, many of those same students would not have been admitted. These practices certainly underscore the liberal argument that affirmative or compensatory action for minorities is not alien to American experience. Because our nation has a history of slavery and legalized racial discrimination, and because discrimination continues to exist (although it has declined), the question of racial justice, more than any other issue, highlights the difficulty of reconciling our values to our practice.

For the past several decades, the civil rights revolution, a revolution that began with African Americans, has broadened to include women and Latinos and to address such matters as sexual orientation and immigration status. As our nation becomes more and more diverse, equal protection of the laws will become more and more important. If we are to succeed and prosper as a nation, we must be inclusive. The tumultuous history of civil rights in America demonstrates that exclusion is a recipe for national calamity. It also demonstrates that struggles for civil rights often take a long time, beginning with political action by a small group of committed individuals and often ending with legislation and legal decisions from the highest court in the country. What civil rights battles now appear on the country's horizon? What can and should be done to remedy past wrongs that have current consequences, such as when past discrimination results in an economic underclass for a racial or ethnic minority? And, most fundamentally, how does a country based on the democratic principle of majority rule ensure that the civil rights of minorities are protected?

plug**in**

Inform

Watch the short video "Women in the 19th Century: Crash Course U.S. History #16" on YouTube to learn more about the history of women's rights.

Express

Record a video of your own speech about any current social, political, or economic inequalities that you believe violate civil rights. Explain how you think the government should address the problem.

Connect

Visit the website of the Leadership Conference on Civil and Human Rights, a coalition of over 200 organizations working on rights issues, and consider following the group on Twitter.

Act

Click the "Take Action" tab on the Leadership Conference's website to find links to petitions, advice on contacting your members of Congress about current rights issues, opportunities to join a group or volunteer, or ways to participate in a demonstration.

studyguide

The Struggle for Civil Rights

> **Trace the legal developments and social movements that expanded civil rights (pp. 159–78)**

Discrimination against individuals on the basis of their race and gender was tolerated and even enforced by government policy throughout much of American history. With the adoption of the Fourteenth Amendment in 1868, civil rights became a part of the Constitution. The political struggles of African Americans and women have narrowed the gap between Americans' belief in equality and the reality of life in the United States, but they have not eliminated it.

Key Terms

discrimination (p. 159)

civil rights (p. 159)

equal protection clause (p. 159)

Thirteenth Amendment (p. 161)

Fourteenth Amendment (p. 161)

Fifteenth Amendment (p. 162)

Jim Crow laws (p. 162)

"separate but equal" rule (p. 163)

Brown v. Board of Education (p. 166)

strict scrutiny (p. 167)

de jure (p. 167)

de facto (p. 167)

gerrymandering (p. 175)

redlining (p. 177)

Practice Quiz

1. When did civil rights become part of the Constitution?
   a) in 1789 at the Founding
   b) with the adoption of the Fourteenth Amendment in 1868
   c) in 2008 when Barack Obama was elected president
   d) with the adoption of the Nineteenth Amendment in 1920
   e) in the 1954 *Brown v. Board of Education* decision

2. Which of the following could be described as a Jim Crow law?
   a) a law forcing blacks and whites to ride on separate trains
   b) a law criminalizing interracial marriage
   c) a law requiring blacks and whites to attend different schools
   d) a law segregating all public accommodations, such as hotels, restaurants, and theaters
   e) All of the above are examples of Jim Crow laws.

3. Which civil rights case established the "separate but equal" rule?
   a) *Plessy v. Ferguson*
   b) *Grutter v. Bollinger*
   c) *Brown v. Board of Education*
   d) *Regents of the University of California v. Bakke*
   e) *Adarand Constructors v. Peña*

4. Which of the following organizations established a Legal Defense Fund to challenge segregation?
   a) the Association of American Trial Lawyers
   b) the National Association of Evangelicals
   c) the National Association for the Advancement of Colored People
   d) the Student Nonviolent Coordinating Committee
   e) the Southern Christian Leadership Council

5. *Massive resistance* refers to efforts by southern states during the late 1950s and early 1960s to
   a) build public housing for poor blacks.
   b) defy federal mandates to desegregate public schools.
   c) give women the right to have an abortion.
   d) bus black students to white schools.
   e) stage large-scale protests against Jim Crow laws.

6. Which of the following made discrimination by private employers and state governments illegal?
   a) the Fourteenth Amendment
   b) the Fifteenth Amendment
   c) *Brown v. Board of Education*
   d) the 1964 Civil Rights Act
   e) *Regents of the University of California v. Bakke*

7. The Voting Rights Act of 1965 significantly extended and protected voting rights by doing which of the following?
   a) barring literacy tests as a condition for voting in six southern states
   b) requiring all voters to register two weeks before any federal election
   c) eliminating all federal-level registration requirements
   d) allowing voters to sue election officials for monetary damages in civil court
   e) All of the above are parts of the Voting Rights Act.

Extending Civil Rights

> **Describe how different groups have fought for and won protection of their civil rights (pp. 178–95)**

In the 1970s the civil rights model created by African Americans began to spread beyond racial and ethnic groups to include groups defined by sex, religion, national origin, age, and sexual orientation. For many of these groups, government polices played an important role in giving rise to movements that demanded equal treatment.

Key Term

intermediate scrutiny (p. 179)

Practice Quiz

8. The judicial test that places the burden of proof on government to show that a race-based policy serves a compelling government interest and is narrowly tailored to address identifiable past discrimination is called
   a) strict scrutiny.
   b) intermediate scrutiny.
   c) limited scrutiny.
   d) de facto segregation.
   e) de jure segregation.

9. Which of the following is *not* an example of an area in which women have made progress since the 1970s in guaranteeing certain civil rights?
   a) sexual harassment
   b) integration into all-male publicly supported universities
   c) more equal funding for college women's varsity athletic programs
   d) the passage of the Equal Rights Amendment
   e) None. These are all examples of areas in which women have made progress.

10. The Supreme Court's decision in *Mendez v. Westminster* was significant because it
    a) served as a precursor for *Brown v. Board of Education* by ruling that the segregation of Anglos and Mexican Americans into separate schools was unconstitutional.
    b) determined that anyone born in the United States was entitled to full citizenship.
    c) allowed school districts to achieve racial integration through busing.
    d) held that public accommodations could be segregated by race but still be equal.
    e) eliminated state power to use race as a criterion for discrimination in law.

11. Which of the following civil rights measures dealt with access to public businesses and accommodations?
    a) the 1990 Americans with Disabilities Act and the 1964 Civil Rights Act
    b) the 1964 Civil Rights Act only
    c) the 1990 Americans with Disabilities Act only
    d) the Equal Rights Amendment only
    e) the Equal Rights Amendment and the 1964 Civil Rights Act

12. Which of the following cases represents the *Brown v. Board of Education* case for lesbians and gay men?
    a) *Bowers v. Hardwick*
    b) *Lau v. Nichols*
    c) *Romer v. Evans*
    d) *Regents of the University of California v. Bakke*
    e) There has not been a Supreme Court ruling explicitly protecting lesbians and gay men from discrimination.

Affirmative Action

Contrast arguments for and against affirmative action (pp. 195–99)

Affirmative action policies take race or some other status into account in order to provide greater educational and employment opportunities to groups that have been discriminated against. The Supreme Court has ruled that the government must show evidence that affirmative action programs serve a compelling government interest and are narrowly tailored to address identifiable past discrimination in order to be ruled constitutional. In recent years, challenges to affirmative action have also emerged at the state and local levels.

Key Term

affirmative action (p. 195)

Practice Quiz

13. In which case did the Supreme Court find that rigid quotas are incompatible with the equal protection clause of the Fourteenth Amendment?
    a) *Regents of the University of California v. Bakke*
    b) *Korematsu v. United States*
    c) *Brown v. Board of Education*
    d) *United States v. Nixon*
    e) *Immigration and Naturalization Service v. Chadha*

14. The Supreme Court's decision in *Grutter v. Bollinger* was significant because
    a) it stated that race can never be used as a factor in university admissions.
    b) it stated that diversity is a compelling state interest and that university admissions that take racial categories into account are constitutional as long as they are highly individualized.
    c) it outlawed quotas and separate university admission standards for members of minority groups.
    d) it rejected mechanical point systems that favor minority applicants in university admissions.
    e) it declared that affirmative action policies would no longer be subject to strict scrutiny from the courts.

For Further Reading

Ackerman, Bruce. *We the People.* Vol. 3: *The Civil Rights Revolution.* Cambridge, MA: Harvard University Press, 2014.

Becker, Jo. *Forcing the Spring: Inside the Fight for Marriage Equality.* New York: Penguin, 2014.

Chen, Anthony S. *The Fifth Freedom: Jobs, Politics, and Civil Rights in the United States, 1941–1972.* Princeton, NJ: Princeton University Press, 2009.

Garrow, David J. *Bearing the Cross: Martin Luther King and the Southern Christian Leadership Conference: A Personal Portrait.* New York: Morrow, 1986.

Greenberg, Jack. *Crusaders in the Courts: How a Dedicated Band of Lawyers Fought for the Civil Rights Revolution.* New York: Basic Books, 1994.

Katznelson, Ira. *When Affirmative Action Was White: The Untold Story of Racial Inequality in Twentieth-Century America.* New York: W. W. Norton, 2006.

McClain, Paula D., and Joseph Stewart Jr. *"Can We All Get Along?" Racial Minorities in American Politics.* 4th ed. Boulder, CO: Westview Press, 2005.

Mink, Gwendolyn. *Hostile Environment: The Political Betrayal of Sexually Harassed Women.* Ithaca, NY: Cornell University Press, 2000.

Nichols, Walter. *The Dreamers: How the Undocumented Youth Movement Transformed the Immigrant Rights Debate.* Stanford, CT: Stanford University Press, 2013.

Rosales, Francisco. *Chicano! The History of the Mexican American Civil Rights Movement.* Houston: Arte Público Press, 1997.

Rosenberg, Gerald N. *The Hollow Hope: Can Courts Bring About Social Change?* Chicago: University of Chicago Press, 1991.

Russell, Nancy. *Freedom Is Not Enough: The Opening of the American Workplace.* Cambridge, MA: Harvard University Press, 2006.

Valelly, Richard. *The Voting Rights Act.* Washington, DC: CQ Press, 2005.

Recommended Websites

ADA Home Page
www.ada.gov

The Americans with Disabilities Act (ADA), enacted in 1990, guarantees equal employment rights and access to public businesses for the physically disabled. The U.S. Department of Justice maintains this website, which offers general information on ADA standards, changes in regulation, and policy enforcement.

Equal Employment Opportunity Commission (EEOC)
www.eeoc.gov

This website provides information on the federal agency and current employment laws. At this site you can even find out how someone might file a harassment or discrimination charge against an employer.

Equality Now
www.equalitynow.org

This is an organization dedicated to ending gender discrimination around the world. Read about how this group is fighting for the rights of women in Africa or campaigning against female genital mutilation and sex trafficking.

Federal Bureau of Investigation
www.fbi.gov/hq/cid/civilrights/hate.htm

Civil rights violations fall under the jurisdiction of the Federal Bureau of Investigation. Find out what steps the FBI is taking to combat the problem of hate crimes and view some comprehensive statistical data.

Feminist Majority Foundation
www.feminist.org
National Organization for Women
www.now.org

These leading women's rights groups continue to fight for gender equality and equal rights.

The Martin Luther King, Jr., Research and Education Institute
http://mlk-kpp01.stanford.edu

Dr. Martin Luther King, Jr., was a key leader in the fight for civil rights and desegregation. At this website you can find Dr. King's important speeches and papers, as well as other information about social injustice.

Gay and Lesbian Alliance against Defamation (GLAAD)
www.glaad.org
Human Rights Campaign (HRC)
www.hrc.org

These two prominent interest groups are dedicated to equal rights for lesbians and gay men and ending gender discrimination.

League of United Latin American Citizens (LULAC)
www.lulac.org

LULAC has worked to stem discrimination against Mexican Americans since World War II and is now the largest and oldest Latino organization in the United States. See what this group is doing to guarantee racial equality based on the Fourteenth Amendment's equal protection clause.

Mexican American Legal Defense and Education Fund (MALDEF)
www.maldef.org

MALDEF is the leading nonprofit Latino litigation, advocacy, and educational outreach institution in the United States. At this site, you will learn about litigation and other activities that MALDEF has initiated related to the rights of Latinos and of immigrants more generally.

NAACP
www.naacp.org

The NAACP is one of the oldest and largest civil rights organizations that is dedicated to equal rights and putting an end to racial discrimination. This group was particularly influential in the landmark case *Brown v. Board of Education*, which led to the desegregation of public schools.

U.S. Commission on Civil Rights
www.usccr.gov

The U.S. Commission on Civil Rights was created by Congress in the late 1950s and continues to investigate complaints of discrimination in American society.

U.S. Supreme Court Media
www.oyez.org

This website has a good search engine for finding information on such landmark civil rights cases as *Plessy v. Ferguson*, *Brown v. Board of Education*, *Lawrence v. Texas*, and *United States v. Wong Kim Ark*, to name only a few.

How closely should the government follow public opinion? Public opinion on important topics like health care and taxes is often sharply divided. In other cases, citizens seem to lack the political knowledge necessary to have informed opinions. These circumstances make it difficult for lawmakers to follow the will of the people.

Public Opinion

WHAT GOVERNMENT DOES AND WHY IT MATTERS The "consent of the governed"—demanded in the Declaration of Independence—is critical for the functioning of a democracy. We expect the government to pay attention to public opinion, and research has shown that public opinion does indeed have a significant impact on public policy, especially foreign policy.[1] However, many Americans have very little knowledge about government, and their opinions about what government should do are often shifting and inconsistent.

One striking characteristic of contemporary America is economic inequality. Economic inequality in the United States is increasing; by some measures, it is the highest it has been since 1928. Political scientist Larry Bartels has shown that the gap between the super-rich and everyone else has increased since the mid-1980s and continues to grow.[2] Between 1993 and 2012, the income of the top 1 percent of Americans grew 86 percent, while the income of the other 99 percent grew less than 7 percent.[3] The median household income of Americans has remained about the same for nearly a decade. Meanwhile, Americans in the upper fifth of the income distribution now earn nearly 17 times as much as those in the lowest fifth. The United States has some of the highest economic inequality in the world.[4]

Are Americans aware of this growing economic inequality, and what do they think about it? Public opinion polls can offer an answer. While most Americans appear to acknowledge the large gap between the rich and the poor in the United States, it is not clear whether the public is aware of *changes* in income inequality. Polls show that the public's attitude toward growing income inequality has remained mostly unchanged since the 1980s. Less than half of Americans (47 percent) thought the gap between the rich and the poor was a serious problem in 2013.[5] (See the "Who Are Americans?" feature on page 233.)

Furthermore, partisanship (see Chapter 9) appears to have a big effect in shaping public opinion on this issue. While 92 percent of Democrats agreed with the statement that "today it's really true that the rich just get richer while the poor get poorer," just 56 percent of Republicans agreed with the statement. The social class of the respondent also shapes public opinion. Of those who describe themselves as lower class, 84 percent agreed that the rich are getting richer, compared with 66 percent of those in the upper class. Those in the upper class also reported being more satisfied and happier.

What does public opinion on inequality mean for American politics? If many Americans are unaware that income inequality is growing, then they may not demand different policies, such as increases in the minimum wage or increased taxation on the wealthy to support government assistance for the poor. Informed public opinion is crucial in order for citizens to have their preferences heard by elected officials. Low levels of political interest or knowledge may be one reason Americans disagree about fundamental aspects of social and economic conditions.

chaptergoals

- Define public opinion, and identify broad types of values and beliefs Americans have about politics (pp. 209–16)

- Explain the major factors that shape specific individual opinions (pp. 217–25)

- Explore when and why public opinion changes and what role political knowledge plays (pp. 225–32)

- Describe the major forces that shape public opinion (pp. 232–36)

- Analyze the relationship between public opinion and government policies (pp. 236–39)

- Describe basic survey methods and other techniques researchers use to measure public opinion (pp. 240–49)

● Defining Public Opinion

The term **public opinion** refers to the attitudes that people have about issues, events, elected officials, and, of course, politics and policy. It is useful to distinguish between values and beliefs on the one hand and attitudes and opinions on the other. **Values (or beliefs)** constitute a person's basic orientation to politics. Values underlie deep-rooted goals, aspirations, and ideals that shape an individual's perceptions of political issues and events. Liberty, democracy, and equality of opportunity, for example, are basic political values held by most Americans.

Another useful term for understanding public opinion is *ideology*. **Political ideology** refers to a complex set of beliefs and values that, as a whole, form a general philosophy about government. For example, many Americans believe that governmental solutions to problems are inherently inferior to solutions offered by the private sector. The Tea Party movement, for example, advocates private-sector solutions to the problems that face society. Such a general belief may, in turn, lead individuals to form negative views of specific government programs even before they know much about them.

An **attitude (or opinion)** is a specific view about a particular issue, person, or event. An individual may have an attitude toward American policy in Iraq or an opinion about economic inequality in America. The attitude or opinion may have emerged from a broad belief about military intervention or about the role of government in the economy, but the opinion itself is very specific. Some attitudes may be short-lived and can change based on changing circumstances or new information.

When we think of public opinion, we often think in terms of differences of opinion. The media are fond of reporting political differences between Democrats and Republicans, blacks and whites, men and women, the young and the old, and so on. Certainly Americans differ on many issues, and often these differences do seem to be associated with race, religion, gender, age, or other social characteristics. For example, opinion polls show that roughly half of Americans sympathize with the Tea Party movement and half with the Occupy Wall Street movement. Those who support Occupy Wall Street have very different beliefs regarding the cause of the poor economy (that banks and elected officials are held captive by corporate interests) from those of people supporting the Tea Party (that government regulation is strangling the private sector, preventing an economic rebound). While both Occupy Wall Street and the Tea Party are populist economic movements, they have very different underlying opinions, attitudes, and ideologies about the economy and government.

Factors such as race, gender, income, age, religion, and region—which not only affect individuals' interests but also shape their experiences and upbringing—do influence Americans' beliefs and opinions. For example, individuals whose incomes differ substantially have correspondingly different views on the desirability of any number of important economic and social programs, including government health care programs. In general, the poor, who are the chief beneficiaries of these programs, support them more strongly than do those who are wealthier and pay more of the taxes that fund the programs. Blacks and whites have different views on issues that touch upon civil rights and race relations (such as affirmative action)—reflecting differences of interest and experience. There are also gender differences

public opinion citizens' attitudes about political issues, leaders, institutions, and events

values (or beliefs) basic principles that shape a person's opinions about political issues and events

political ideology a cohesive set of beliefs that forms a general philosophy about the role of government

attitude (or opinion) a specific preference on a particular issue

Attitudes may change over time based on new information, but many Americans who doubted President Obama's U.S. citizenship did not change their views even as ample evidence of his citizenship became available. Finally, the White House published the president's "long-form" birth certificate in 2011.

in views expressed by men versus women, especially on foreign policy questions, where women appear to be much more concerned with the dangers of war. Political attitudes are also strongly influenced by partisanship (Republican versus Democrat; see Chapter 9) and ideology (conservative versus liberal).

Today there is a renewed understanding that opinions about issues and politics have emotional underpinnings as well.[6] Emotional responses to candidates or policies run the gamut from strongly positive to strongly negative, and these emotions are traditionally measured by survey questions asking if a candidate (or individual, event, or issue) makes the respondent feel angry, fearful, anxious, or enthusiastic. Contrary to the idea that public opinion is purely rational, feelings are complicated and often irrational; once individuals become emotionally attached to particular beliefs, they tend to hold on to them even in the face of contradictory information. Using emotions as a guide, individuals will form opinions quickly in response to current events.[7]

As an example, more than halfway through Barack Obama's first presidential term, nearly one in five (almost 20 percent) of Americans believed that he had been born outside the United States and thus, as a noncitizen, was ineligible for the presidency. Among Republicans, those doubting the president's citizenship numbered more than two in five.[8] This belief persisted even as the verified details of Obama's personal life were widely available and included ample evidence of his American citizenship. To counter the widespread misperception, the White House eventually posted to the Internet a photograph of President Obama's "long-form" birth certificate, showing that he was born in a hospital in Honolulu, Hawaii, on August 4, 1961, at 7:24 PM.[9] In over two centuries since the Founding, a sitting president had never before been forced to prove his citizenship publicly.

Political Values

liberty freedom from governmental control

Despite their differences, most Americans share a common set of values, including a belief in the principles, if not always the actual practice, of liberty, equality, and democracy. The United States was founded on the principle of individual **liberty**. Americans have always voiced strong support for the idea of liberty, and typically support the notion that governmental interference with individuals' lives and property should be kept to a minimum. Liberty remains as important in contemporary politics as it was during the Founding era. An example is the growing

concern with civil liberties related to privacy and security of personal information. A 2013 Pew survey found that more than 50 percent of Americans believe the federal courts fail to provide adequate restraints on telephone, email, and Internet data the government collects as part of its antiterrorism policies.[10] This public opinion data underscores the fact that government surveillance is of increasing concern to most Americans and that the value of liberty matters.

Similarly, **equality of opportunity** has always been an important theme in American society. Most Americans believe that all individuals should be allowed to seek personal and economic success. Moreover, Americans generally believe that such success should be the result of individual effort and ability, rather than family connections or other forms of special privilege. Quality public education is one of the most important mechanisms for obtaining equality of opportunity in that it allows individuals, regardless of personal or family wealth, a chance to get ahead. Today, Internet access is emerging as an important form of equality of opportunity by providing online access to job opportunities, news, politics, commerce, and other benefits of digital citizenship.[11] Economic opportunity, defined as a good job and a decent standard of living, is a core value in American politics.

Most Americans also believe in **democracy**. They believe that every citizen should have the opportunity to take part in the nation's governmental and policy-making processes and to have some say in determining how they are governed, including the right to vote in elections.[12] (See Chapter 8 for a discussion of rules affecting voting in elections.) Figure 6.1 shows there is consensus among Americans on fundamental values: for instance, 86 percent believe society should do what it takes to ensure equality of opportunity, and 70 percent believe Americans shouldn't have to give up freedom in order to protect their security.

Obviously, the political values that Americans espouse have not always been put into practice. For 200 years, Americans embraced the principles of equality of opportunity and individual liberty while denying them in practice to generations of African Americans. Yet the strength of the principles ultimately helped overcome practices that deviated from those principles. Proponents of slavery and, later, of segregation were defeated in the arena of public opinion because their practices differed so sharply from the fundamental principles accepted by most Americans.

equality of opportunity a widely shared American ideal that all people should have the freedom to use whatever talents and wealth they have to reach their fullest potential

democracy a system of rule that permits citizens to play a significant part in the governmental process, usually through the election of key public officials

for critical analysis

The news often focuses on issues on which public opinion is sharply divided, but in fact there are many issues on which Americans largely agree. What other issues or values do you think have strong consensus among Americans?

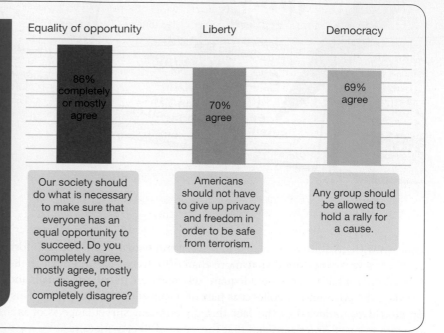

FIGURE 6.1

Americans' Support for Fundamental Values

Americans support equality of opportunity, liberty, and democracy in principle, but do they always support these values in practice? What limits, if any, do you think Americans favor when it comes to equality, liberty, and democracy?

SOURCES: Pew Research Center for the People and the Press Values Survey, www.people-press.org /question-search/?qid=1811658&pid=51&ccid =50#top (accessed 2/5/14). Pew Center/USA Today Poll, January 15–19, 2014, www.pewresearch .org/fact-tank/2014/01/22/most-young-americans -say-snowden-has-served-the-public-interest/ (accessed 2/5/2014). First Amendment Center, www .firstamendmentcenter.org (accessed 10/22/12).

Equality of opportunity

86% completely or mostly agree

Our society should do what is necessary to make sure that everyone has an equal opportunity to succeed. Do you completely agree, mostly agree, mostly disagree, or completely disagree?

Liberty

70% agree

Americans should not have to give up privacy and freedom in order to be safe from terrorism.

Democracy

69% agree

Any group should be allowed to hold a rally for a cause.

Yet even when there is broad agreement over principles, practical *interpretations* of principles can differ. For example, in contemporary politics Americans' fundamental commitment to equality of opportunity has led to divisions over affirmative action programs, with both proponents and opponents citing their belief in equality of opportunity as the justification for their position. Proponents of these programs see them as necessary to ensure equality of opportunity, whereas opponents believe that affirmative action is a form of preferential treatment that violates basic American values[13] (see Chapter 5).

Political Ideology

As we noted earlier, Americans share broadly in their fundamental political values, but the application of these values to specific policies varies quite a bit. The set of underlying orientations, ideas, and beliefs through which we come to understand and interpret politics is called a *political ideology*. Ideologies take many different forms. Some people may view politics primarily in religious terms. During the course of European political history, for example, Protestantism and Catholicism were often political ideologies as much as they were religious creeds. Each set of beliefs included not only elements of religious practice but also distinct ideas about secular authority and political action.

In America today, a variety of ideologies compete for attention and support. **Libertarianism**, for example, argues that government is wasteful and interferes with free markets and society, and so it should be limited to as few spheres of activity as possible. In 2012, Republican presidential candidate Ron Paul, a staunch libertarian, gained support among many young voters for his opposition to foreign wars and his support of civil liberties and smaller government, including legalization of marijuana. While Libertarians believe in less government intervention in economic and social realms, **socialists**, on the other hand,

libertarianism a political ideology that emphasizes freedom and voluntary association with small government

socialism a political ideology that emphasizes social ownership and strong government

argue that more government is necessary to promote justice and to reduce economic and social inequality. Although many Americans subscribe to libertarianism, socialism, and other ideologies in part, most Americans describe themselves as either liberals or conservatives, or some shade of the two. Like the political ideologies already described, liberalism and conservatism comprise beliefs about the role of the government, preferences regarding specific public policies, and ideas about which groups in society should exercise power and how they should do so (see Boxes 6.1 and 6.2).

The definitions of both *liberal* and *conservative* have changed over time. To some extent, contemporary liberalism and conservatism can be seen as differences in emphasis with regard to the fundamental American political values of liberty and equality. For liberals, equality is the most important of the core values. Liberals encourage government action in such areas as college admissions and business practices to enhance race, class, and gender equality of opportunity. They also support programs and redistributive taxation to promote equality of opportunity. For conservatives, on the other hand, liberty is the core value. Conservatives oppose many efforts of the government, however well intentioned, to interfere in private life and the marketplace.

Liberalism In classical political theory, a **liberal** was someone who favored individual initiative and was suspicious of the motives of government and of its ability to manage economic and social affairs—a definition akin to that of today's libertarian. The proponents of a larger and more active government called themselves progressives. In the early twentieth century, many liberals and progressives coalesced around the doctrine of "social liberalism," which held that government action might be needed to preserve individual liberty. Today's liberals are social liberals rather than classical liberals.

Although liberalism and conservatism are the most common political ideologies in the United States today, other ideologies, such as libertarianism, offer different perspectives on the role of government, policy issues, and society. For example, libertarians advocate a smaller role for government, less involvement overseas, and more freedom for businesses.

liberal today this term refers to those who generally support social and political reform; governmental intervention in the economy and more economic equality; expansion of federal social services; and greater concern for consumers and the environment

---

BOX 6.1

Profile of a Liberal: Senator Elizabeth Warren

- Supports stricter environmental protections.

- Favors expanded health coverage for all Americans.

- Advocates increased funding for education.

- Supports same-sex marriage.

- Supports abortion rights and birth control.

- Supports an increase in the minimum wage.

- Supports more equitable tax policy that benefits middle class Americans and imposes higher taxes on corporations.

BOX 6.2

Profile of a Conservative: Senator Chuck Grassley

- Wants to trim the size of the federal government.

- Wants to diminish government regulation of business.

- Supports harsher treatment of criminals.

- Opposes implementation of medical marijuana laws.

- Favors green energy laws including wind turbines.

- Opposes many affirmative action programs.

- Favors tax cuts.

In contemporary politics being a liberal has come to mean supporting political and social reform, government intervention in the economy, the expansion of federal social services and health care, more vigorous efforts on behalf of the poor and minorities, and greater concern for consumers and protecting the environment. Liberals generally support abortion rights and rights for gays and lesbians, and are concerned with protecting the rights of people accused of crimes. Liberals oppose state involvement in religious institutions and state sanction of religious expression. In international affairs, liberals often support arms control, aid to poor nations, and international organizations such as the United Nations and the European Union; liberals generally oppose the development and testing of nuclear weapons, and the use of American troops to influence the affairs of developing nations. Many liberals are opposed to military wars, but under President Obama many liberals have tolerated military interventions in other countries.

conservative today this term refers to those who generally support the social and economic status quo and are suspicious of efforts to introduce new political formulae and economic arrangements; conservatives believe that a large and powerful government poses a threat to citizens' freedom

Conservatism By contrast, **conservatives** believe strongly that a large government poses a threat to the freedom of individual citizens and specifically to free markets and democracy. Ironically, today's conservatives espouse the views of classical liberalism. Today, conservatives generally oppose the expansion of governmental activity, asserting that solutions to social and economic problems can and should be developed in the private sector. Thus many conservatives are opposed to increasing taxes, preferring to cut government spending instead. Conservatives particularly oppose efforts to impose government regulation on business, maintaining that regulation frequently leads to economic inefficiency, is costly, and can ultimately lower the entire nation's standard of living by making U.S. manufactured products more expensive and less competitive. In terms of social policy, many conservatives support school prayer and traditional family arrangements, and are concerned about law and order; conservatives generally oppose abortion, same-sex marriage, and the use of mandatory school busing to achieve the racial integration of schools. In international affairs, conservatism has come to mean support for military intervention and the maintenance of American military power.

Mixing Ideologies Both liberalism and conservatism are far from monolithic ideologies, and most Americans consider themselves moderates, with shades of liberal or conservative values. Public opinion often trends with the policy preferences of elites. Many conservatives support at least some government social programs. Republican president George W. Bush called himself a "compassionate conservative," to indicate that he favored programs that assist the poor and needy. In contrast, many staunch conservatives joined the rising Tea Party movement in 2009 to protest President Obama's efforts to expand the role of the federal government, especially in health care. Conservative ideologies range from moderates to Tea Party conservatives who hold much more critical views of government's role in the economy and society.

And while President Obama is liberal in supporting health care reform and other social programs, he has been criticized by those on the left for extending the tax policies of his Republican predecessor, George W. Bush, which benefited the affluent, for expanding U.S. military involvement in Afghanistan and other countries, and for historic deportations of illegal immigrants. In short, some of Obama's domestic, economic, and foreign policies are associated with conservatives, and some with liberals. The real political world is far too complex to be seen simply in terms of a struggle between liberals and conservatives. Political candidates who claim to be moderates in a large number of policy areas, such as President Obama and Governor Chris Christie, tend to overlap with the ideologies of the majority of Americans, and thus often win elections.

Figure 6.2 shows that the percentage of Americans who consider themselves moderates, liberals, or conservatives has remained relatively constant for the past

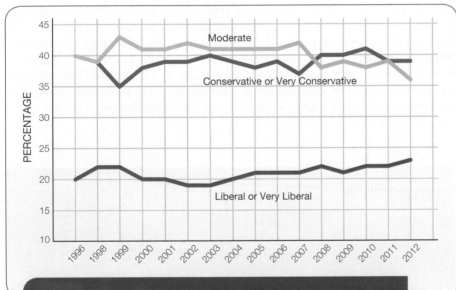

FIGURE 6.2

Americans' Ideology

More Americans identify themselves as "conservatives" than "liberals." During the period shown in this figure, however, Americans have had two Democratic presidents and have several times elected Democratic majorities to a house of Congress. What might account for this apparent discrepancy? What role do moderates play in the electorate? How stable is Americans' ideology over time?

SOURCE: Pew Research Center for the People and the Press, www.pewresearch.org/data
-trend/political-attitudes/political-ideology/ (accessed 2/5/14).

15 years. Pew surveys indicate that as of 2012, 39 percent of Americans considered themselves conservatives, 37 percent moderates, and 23 percent liberals. These numbers have remained virtually unchanged since the 1990s.

Trust in Government

One of the most important measures of public opinion in a democracy is trust in government. High levels of political trust create legitimacy for democratic government, while very low levels can cause concern. Many scholars and political pundits argue that Americans are becoming more and more disenchanted with traditional political institutions; public approval of congress reached a low of only 10 percent in 2014. "Critical citizens" are characterized by high expectations of democracy as an ideal and yet low evaluations of the actual performance of government.[14]

Why does public opinion in the form of trust matter? Declining trust has been linked to declines in political participation and voting. Low confidence in government and elected officials is related to the perception that the government is unable to solve problems, spend money in an effective or efficient way, or represent the interests and policy preferences of average voters.[15]

The Pew Research Center has tracked trust in the federal government from 1958 to 2013 by asking this question on national surveys: "How much of the time do you trust the government in Washington?"[16] The percentage of Americans who indicate they trust the government "just about always or most of the time" has fallen from 73 percent of Americans in 1960 when Eisenhower was president to just 19 percent of Americans in 2013 under President Obama. These trends in low trust in government are exhibited across party lines. By 2013, only 10 percent of Republicans indicated they trusted government some or all of the time, compared with 17 percent of Independents and 28 percent of Democrats. (When Republicans hold the White House, slightly more Republicans trust government than Democrats.) Very low trust in government is a defining feature of contemporary American politics.

for critical analysis

In a democracy, the people elect their representatives. Yet Americans say they do not trust their democratic institutions of government much of the time. Why might this be? Are people voting for representatives whom they do not trust, or might there be another explanation for the low levels of trust?

Midterm elections—elections for Congress in years when the president is not on the ballot—often see only 40 percent of eligible voters turn out. In 2014 only about 36 percent cast a ballot. But by not voting, individuals are missing an opportunity to change government and elect more trustworthy representatives.

● How We Form Political Opinions

Explain the major factors that shape specific individual opinions

Few individuals possess ideologies so cohesive that they will automatically shape all their opinions. Most people have at least some conflicting underlying attitudes. Most conservatives support some federal programs—defense, national security, or tax deductions for businesses, for example—and wish to see them, and hence the government, expanded. Many liberals favor American military intervention in other nations for what they deem to be humanitarian purposes but generally oppose American military intervention in the affairs of other nations. Let's explore what we know about how public opinion is formed.

Political Socialization and Public Opinion

People's attitudes about political issues and elected officials tend to be shaped by their underlying political beliefs and values. For example, an individual who has negative feelings about government intervention in America's economy and society would probably be predisposed to oppose the development of new social and health care programs. Similarly, someone who distrusts the military would likely be suspicious of any call for the use of U.S. troops. The processes through which these underlying political beliefs and values are formed are collectively called **political socialization**.

Probably no nation, and certainly no democracy, could survive if its citizens did not share some fundamental beliefs. If Americans had few common values or perspectives, it would be very difficult for them to reach agreement on particular issues. In contemporary America, some elements of the socialization process tend to produce differences in outlook, whereas others promote similarities. The **agents of socialization** that foster differences in political perspectives include the family and social networks, membership in social groups, party affiliation, education, self-interest, and political environment.

Of course, no brief list of the agents of socialization can fully explain the development of a given individual's basic political beliefs. In addition to the factors that are important for everyone, experiences and influences that are unique to each individual also play a role in shaping political orientation. An early encounter with a single member of another racial group, for example, can have a lasting impact on an individual's view of the entire group. A highly salient political event, such as the Vietnam War or September 11, can leave an indelible mark on a person's political consciousness. And some deep-seated personality characteristic, such as paranoia, may strongly influence the formation of someone's political beliefs. One recent experiment revealed that individuals displaying measurably higher physiological reactions to sudden noises and threatening visual images were more likely to favor defense spending, capital punishment, patriotism, and the Iraq War. That is, people who tend to be more fearful appear to support policies that protect the existing social structure from both external and internal threats.[17]

Furthermore, new research finds that many of our political beliefs may have a genetic basis and thus be "hard-wired." While it is common knowledge that genes predispose individuals to be tall or short, blonds or brunettes, brown- or blue-eyed,

political socialization the induction of individuals into the political culture; learning the underlying beliefs and values on which the political system is based

agents of socialization social institutions, including families and schools, that help to shape individuals' basic political beliefs and values

new research finds that to a surprising degree our genes also shape our political beliefs and public opinions. Using data from a large sample of twins, scholars found that our genes may contribute to half of our self-identified ideology (in other words, to why people are liberal or conservative). Individual experiences and social factors explain most of the remaining variation in individuals' political attitudes. While more research needs to be done, and while our genes influence attitudes in combination with environmental factors, the genetic predisposition of political beliefs is important and gaining attention. Beyond genes and personality traits, let us look at some of the most important agencies of socialization that do affect individuals' beliefs.[18]

The Family and Social Networks Most people acquire their initial orientation to politics from their families. As might be expected, differences in family background tend to produce divergent political perspectives. Although relatively few parents spend much time directly teaching their children about politics, political conversations occur in many households, and children tend to absorb the political views of parents and other caregivers, often without realizing it. Studies find, for example, that party preferences are initially acquired at home. Children raised in households in which the primary caregivers are Democrats tend to become Democrats, whereas children raised in homes where their caregivers are Republicans tend to favor the Republican Party.[19] Similarly, children reared in politically liberal households are more likely than not to develop a liberal outlook, whereas children raised in politically conservative settings are likely to see the world through conservative lenses. (Obviously not all children absorb their parents' political views. Two of the late Republican president Ronald Reagan's three children, for instance, rejected their parents' conservative values and became active on behalf of Democratic candidates.) Moreover, even those children whose views are initially shaped by parental values may change their minds as they mature and experience political life for themselves.

Children are socialized into political environments in ways large and small, from attending political rallies with their parents to hearing off-hand comments at the dinner table. What political opinions did you learn from your parents?

Social networks influence our opinions on many issues, from tax cuts to same-sex marriage. We learn and absorb the opinions of friends and family from their words as well as their actions, such as displaying logos or memes associated with a particular movement.

Nevertheless, family, friends, coworkers, and neighbors are an important source of political orientation for nearly everyone. Political scientist Betsy Sinclair argues that individuals are "social citizens" whose political opinions and behavior are significantly shaped by peer influence, including friends and family.[20] Sinclair shows that social networks can and do have the power to change an individual's opinion. When members of a social network express a particular political opinion or belief, Sinclair finds, others notice and conform, particularly if their conformity is likely to be highly visible. The conclusion is that basic political acts are surprisingly subject to social pressures.

Online social networks such as Facebook and Twitter likely increase the role of peers in shaping public opinion. One example of the influence of social networks on opinion is the widely shared Facebook meme of an equal sign against a red background, used to symbolize support for same-sex marriage rights. Many individuals changed their profile picture on Facebook to this symbol of marriage equality in June 2013 to share their support for this issue at the same time that the U.S. Supreme Court was deciding two controversial court cases affecting gay and lesbian marriage rights. This social media discussion was associated with upticks in public support for gay marriage rights nationally. As of 2013, polls show 51 percent of Americans favor recognizing the right of gays and lesbians to marry, while 42 percent oppose, a change from 2011 when a majority of Americans opposed same-sex marriage.[21]

Race Another important source of political values are the social groups to which individuals belong. Social groups include those to which individuals belong involuntarily (national, religious, gender, and racial groups, for example) as well as those they join willingly (political parties, labor unions, the military, and environmental, educational, and occupational groups).

Membership in a particular group can give individuals experiences and perspectives that shape their view of political and social life. In American society, for example, the experiences of blacks and whites can differ significantly. Blacks are a minority and have been victims of persecution and discrimination throughout American history. Blacks and whites also have different occupational opportunities, often live in separate communities, and may attend separate schools. Such differences tend to produce distinctive political outlooks. Many black Americans perceive other blacks as members of a group with a common identity and a shared political interest in overcoming persistent racial and economic inequality. Political scientists refer to this phenomenon as "linked fate": African Americans see their fate as linked to other members of the black community.[22] This linked fate acts as a sort of filter through which black Americans evaluate information and determine their own opinions and policy preferences.

FIGURE 6.3

Perception of Fair Treatment across Racial Groups

In the United States, racial groups may not perceive race relations in precisely the same way. How, according to the data in this figure, do blacks and whites differ in their views on race relations? Which group is more likely to think that race relations are good? What factors help to account for these differences in perception?

*12 percent of white and 13 percent of black respondents answered "don't know."

SOURCES: Pew Research Center, www.pewresearch .org/fact-tank/2013/08/28/the-black-white -and-urban-rural-divides-in-perceptions-of-racial -fairness/(accessed 2/5/14). Pew Research Center, www.people-press.org/2012/03/30 /blacks-view-of-law-enforcement-racial-progress -and-news-coverage-of-race/ (accessed 2/5/14). Pew Research Center,www.pewresearch.org/fact -tank/2013/09/06/incarceration-gap-between -white-and-blacks-widens/ (accessed 2/5/14).

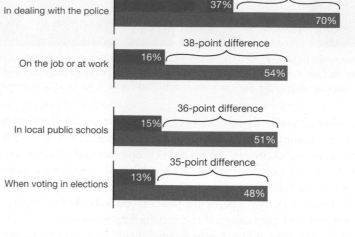

TREATMENT BLACKS RECEIVE

Percentage saying blacks in their community are treated less fairly than whites:

In dealing with the police — 37% / 70% — 33-point difference

On the job or at work — 16% / 54% — 38-point difference

In local public schools — 15% / 51% — 36-point difference

When voting in elections — 13% / 48% — 35-point difference

NEWS COVERAGE OF BLACKS

News coverage of blacks is:*

Too negative — 31% / 58% — 27-point difference

Fair — 48% / 28% — 20-point difference

Too positive — 9% / 1% — 8-point difference

■ White respondents   ■ Black respondents

That black and white Americans form distinct political outlooks is reflected in public opinion on the extent of racism in the United States (see Figure 6.3). Indeed, according to a CNN poll, 47 percent of white respondents thought racism fairly or very common, while 49 percent thought it was rare in the United States. Among African Americans, on the other hand, fully 86 percent thought racism was common and only 12 percent said it was rare, almost a 40-point difference between blacks and whites.[23]

Differences in public opinion among blacks and whites may be based on views of the role of race in the criminal justice system. Eighty percent of African Americans say blacks and other minorities do not get equal treatment under the law; the number of whites giving this response is just 40 percent. A 2013 survey found that nearly 9 in 10 African Americans said the shooting of an African American Florida teenager was unjustified and were opposed to the verdict of not guilty for the white shooter, George Zimmerman. In contrast, only 33 percent of whites believed the shooting of the African American teenager was unjustified.[24] Some analysts have found that African Americans who belong to black organizations are likely to differ more from whites in their political orientations than are blacks who don't belong to such organizations.[25]

Interestingly, Hispanic Americans, who have also been victims of racism in the United States, are less likely than African Americans to see America as a racist society; in a 2008 survey, 52 percent of Hispanic Americans and 55 percent of white Americans said that race relations in the United States were generally good. Only 29 percent of black Americans agreed.[26] Yet group consciousness can also apply to Latinos, and under some circumstances will influence policy attitudes. Level of acculturation plays a key role, as those who are first-generation immigrants are more likely to receive information geared toward Latinos (Spanish-language news, for example), which affects the political information they receive. Second- and third-generation Latinos have attitudes more consistent with non-Hispanic whites.

Gender Men and women have important differences of opinion as well. Reflecting differences in social roles and occupational patterns, women tend to oppose military intervention more than men, are more likely than men to favor policies to protect the environment, and are more supportive of government social and health care programs (see Table 6.1). Perhaps because of these differences

TABLE 6.1

Disagreements among Men and Women on Public Policy Issues

On many policy issues, there is an approximately 10-point gap between the opinions of men and women. What might explain this consistent difference?

POLICY	MEN	WOMEN	GENDER GAP
Agree that same-sex marriage should be legal in all/most cases	40	53	13 points
Agree that religious institutions that object to contraceptives should be given an exemption from insurance mandate	54	42	12 points
Believe that government does not do enough for poor people	52	62	10 points
Believe the best way to ensure peace is through good diplomacy	53	62	9 points
Believe the country should do whatever it takes to protect the environment	67	75	8 points

SOURCE: Pew Research Center, www.people-press.org/2012/03/29/the-gender-gap-three-decades-old-as-wide-as-ever/ (accessed 2/5/14).

on issues, women are more likely than men to vote for Democratic candidates. This tendency of men's and women's opinions to differ is known as the **gender gap**.

Differences in political knowledge may play a role in explaining differences in opinion. For example, research suggests that females are more politically knowledgeable about school politics than men, but are less politically knowledgeable regarding other levels of politics. If, however, there is a female Congress member, women in that district are as likely as men to be able to name their senator. Female representation at all levels of government positively relates to women's political efficacy and ability to name their representatives.

Religion Religion is an important predictor of opinion on a wide range of issues, particularly those involving morality or family. Religious individuals are usually defined in surveys as frequent church attenders and those who indicate religion and prayer is important in their lives. Among religious groups, white Evangelical Christians and Catholics tend to have more conservative views on moral issues than Protestants, mainline Christians, and individuals of other denominations. Religion is important in understanding opinions on same-sex marriage, abortion rights, marriage, gambling, and home schooling, with Catholics and Evangelical Christians much more likely to oppose abortion rights and oppose extending marriage to gays and lesbians, for example. White Evangelicals and weekly churchgoers are much more likely to hold conservative views and be Republican, while black Protestants, Hispanic Catholics, Jews, and the religiously unaffiliated are more likely to hold liberal views and favor the Democratic Party.

Party Affiliation Political party membership is one of the most important factors affecting political orientation.[27] We can think of partisanship as red- or blue-tinted glasses that color opinion on a vast array of issues. Partisans tend to rely on party leaders and the media for cues on the appropriate positions to take on major political issues.[28] Walter Lippmann, an influential political commentator of the mid-twentieth century, argued that public opinion is but an echo of elite positions on policy issues, and many others studying public opinion agree.

In recent years, partisan realignment in the South and congressional redistricting have reduced the number of conservative Democrats and all but eliminated liberal Republicans from the Congress and from positions of prominence in the party. As a result, the leadership of the Republican Party has become increasingly conservative whereas that of the Democratic Party has become more liberal, and this is reflected in public opinion. Geographic sorting also contributes to mass polarization, where liberals choose to live in neighborhoods, cities, counties, and states that are more liberal, while conservatives move to areas with populations with more conservative views. These factors contribute to the differences we see in opinion among those living in the suburbs versus central cities.

According to recent studies, differences between Democratic and Republican partisans on a variety of political and policy questions are greater today than during any other period for which data are available. On issues of national security, for example, Republicans have become very "hawkish," whereas Democrats have become quite "dovish." In an October 2003 survey, 85 percent of Republicans but only 39 percent of Democrats thought that America's war against Iraq was a good idea.[29] Gaps on social and economic issues are just as broad. An example is the showdown between congressional Republicans and Democrats over the

gender gap a distinctive pattern of voting behavior reflecting the differences in views between women and men

for critical analysis

Political scientists have observed "geographic sorting" in the United States, where liberals live in areas with other liberals, and conservatives live in areas with other conservatives. Is the area where you live strongly liberal, conservative, or evenly mixed? What are the political consequences of geographic sorting?

federal budget (which led to the 2013 government shutdown) and whether to raise the debt ceiling. In the fall of 2013, the parties disagreed over how much money the government should spend in its next budget, with Republicans demanding various cuts to President Obama's Affordable Care Act and Democrats refusing. As a result, the federal government partially shut down for over two weeks.

Despite the rift between the "red" (Republican-leaning) and "blue" (Democratic-leaning) states that seems deeper than ever, political scientist Morris Fiorina and colleagues refute the common belief that Americans are deeply divided in their fundamental political views, showing that on a broad range of issues, ranging from homosexuality to abortion, most Americans hold moderate opinions.[30] While political elites and members of Congress may be highly polarized, there is general agreement among most Americans—even on those issues thought to be most divisive. And opinion polls appear to support this, as most Americans self-identify as moderates. Thus evidence of partisan polarization in public opinion is mixed: some see deep divisions, while others see evidence of popular consensus.

Self-Interest Another way that membership in social groups can affect political beliefs is through what might be called objective political interests. On many economic issues, for example, the interests of the rich and the poor differ significantly. Inevitably, these differences in interests will produce differences in political outlook. The framers of the Constitution thought that the inherent gulf between the rich and the poor would always be the most important source of conflict in political life. More recently, the Occupy Wall Street protesters have decried the chasm between the 99 percent of income earners and the top 1 percent. Struggles over unemployment benefits, minimum wage, job creation, tax policy, health care and welfare policy, Social Security, the bailout of the banks, and so forth are fueled by differences in interest between wealthier and poorer Americans. Latinos consider the issue of immigration to be significantly more important than non-Latinos, while African Americans are more supportive of affirmative action programs than nonblacks. Difference in public opinion on these issues is influenced by group self-interest.[31]

However, some researchers find that people don't necessarily translate broad concerns about inequality or their own economic self-interest into specific policy preferences.[32] For instance, two-thirds of Americans favored the 2001 federal tax cuts supported by President George W. Bush, even though the tax disproportionately benefited the very wealthy, and would therefore likely increase economic inequality. The poor, middle class, and affluent alike favored the tax cuts. Political scientist Larry Bartels concludes that the public does not seem able to translate a concern for economic self-interest into policy preferences that would benefit average citizens.[33]

Differences in interest also exist among the generations, not just among economic classes. Senior citizens and younger Americans have very different views on such diverse issues as the war on drugs, Social Security, and criminal justice. The young, for example, are much more accepting of legalization of marijuana than older citizens, presumably because the young are more likely to use this substance recreationally.

Nevertheless, group membership can never fully explain a given individual's political views. One's unique personality and life experiences may produce political views very different from those of the group to which one might nominally

Students from the University of California and California State University protested in 2010 against proposed budget cuts to higher education. Their group membership (as students) and self-interest (in a quality education) may have informed their opinion on this issue.

belong. Some African Americans are conservative Republicans, and the occasional wealthy businessperson is also very liberal. Group membership is conducive to particular outlooks, but it is not determinative.

Education After family and social groups, education can be a third important source of differences in political perspectives. Indeed, education may be the great equalizer. Governments use public education to try to teach all children a common set of civic values; it is mainly in school that Americans acquire their basic belief in liberty, equality, and democracy. In history classes, students are taught that the Founders fought for the principle of liberty. In the course of studying such topics as the Constitution, the Civil War, and the civil rights movement, students are taught the importance of equality. Research finds education to be a strong predictor of tolerance for racial minorities.[34] Through participation in class elections and student government, students are taught the virtues of democracy. These lessons are repeated in every grade, and in a variety of contexts. It is no wonder they constitute such an important element in Americans' beliefs.

At the same time, differences in formal education are strongly associated with differences in political outlook. In particular, those who attend college are often exposed to modes of thought that will distinguish them from their friends and neighbors who do not pursue college diplomas. Education is one of the most important factors in predicting who engages in behaviors that increase political knowledge, such as regularly following the news and participating in politics (discussed in a later section).[35]

Political Environment A fourth set of factors that shape political attitudes and values are the conditions under which individuals and groups are recruited into and become involved in political life. Although political beliefs are influenced by family background and group membership, the content and character of these views is, to a large extent, determined by political circumstances. For example, the baby-boom generation that came of age in the 1960s was exposed to both the Vietnam War itself and also widespread antiwar protests on college campuses and in urban areas throughout the nation. As a result, this generation has generally opposed foreign wars.

Similarly, the views held by members of a particular group can shift drastically over time, as political circumstances change. For example, American white southerners were staunch members of the Democratic Party from the Civil War through the 1960s. As Democrats, they became key supporters of liberal New Deal and post–New Deal social programs that greatly expanded the size and power of the American national government. The 1960s mark the beginning of the South's move from the Democratic to the Republican camp—mainly because of white southern opposition to the Democratic Party's integrationist racial policies and because of determined Republican efforts to win white southern support. Since the 1960s a majority of southern whites have shifted to the Republican Party. Now southern whites provide a solid base of support for efforts to scale back social programs and sharply reduce the size and power of the national government—hence

for critical analysis

An individual's family, social networks, group membership, party affiliation, education, self-interest, and political environment can influence his or her political perspectives. What influences in your life have affected your political opinions and beliefs?

the popularity of the Tea Party movement in the South.[36] It was not a change in the character of white southerners but a change in the political environment in which they found themselves that induced this major shift in partisanship in the South.

Another example of public opinion change can be seen in the evolving political environment in the West. California's Republican governor in the 1970s, Ronald Reagan, went on in the 1980s to become one of the most admired Republican presidents, ushering in the tax revolt and deregulating many government policies. But since the 1990s, California, once a Republican stronghold, has become solidly Democratic. Some argue that the shift began with a series of ballot measures targeting racial and ethnic minorities and endorsed by the Republican Party in the 1990s, including immigration, affirmative action, and bilingual education. These ballot measures triggered a backlash, especially among Latinos, who had previously participated in politics in very low numbers. In the 1990s, registration and voting by Latinos increased dramatically, and favored Democratic political candidates and more liberal public policy. With Latinos and blacks combined making up more than 50 percent of California's population, this demographic environmental change moved California to a solid Democratic state.[37] In this case, immigration and demographic change, two environmental factors, caused public opinion in the nation's largest state to change over time. Some predict even Texas, a solidly Republican state, may turn "blue"—a Democratic state—in the next decade given that Latinos make up 40 percent of the state's population and Latinos tend to vote in high proportion for Democratic candidates.

The terrorist attacks of September 11, 2001, certainly influenced public opinion in the months immediately following the attacks and likely also had a long-term effect on many Americans' basic political beliefs.

In sum, public opinion cannot be inferred simply from the character of groups or the political climate of an era. Any group's political outlooks and orientations are shaped by the political circumstances in which that group finds itself, and those outlooks can change as circumstances change. The generation of American students now coming of political age after the September 11 terrorist attacks will have a very different view of the use of American military power from that of their parents—members of a generation that reached political consciousness during the 1960s, when opposition to the Vietnam War and military conscription was, for many, a defining political stance.

● Stability of Opinion and Political Knowledge

Explore when and why public opinion changes and what role political knowledge plays

The section above described numerous agents of socialization that influence an individual's opinion, including group identity and membership, self-interest, education, and political environment. These factors are relatively constant: one's level of education or the political environment in which one comes of age, for instance, are generally set by early adulthood. However, these are not the only influences on an individual's opinion. Notably, individuals encounter new information from political leaders and the media throughout their lives. What role does such political knowledge and information play in forming opinions?

One of the most important studies of how public opinion is formed is by political scientist John Zaller.[38] Zaller believes that opinion formation is based on an individual's memory. An individual receives information and decides whether to accept or reject that information based on his political knowledge. When asked about his opinion on a topic, the individual selects the most relevant or most recently acquired and accepted information from his "bucket" of information. Citizens with more political knowledge can differentiate between information that fits with their beliefs or does not fit—and then correctly accept or reject it. This explanation of public opinion formation implies that the information received from elites and elected officials plays a significant role in priming public opinion. This, Zaller concluded, means that the public's opinions are often unstable and unreliable, because elite sources provide competing information and they focus on different messages at different times. As a result, public opinion is merely a reflection of whatever recent elite message (or media story) an individual has stored in her short-term memory. One should thus expect a fair amount of variability in people's responses to survey questions.

Another way of understanding how individuals form public opinion is the online-processing model, advanced by the political scientist Milton Lodge and colleagues.[39] According to Lodge, an individual keeps a running tally of information and uses that tally to decide which candidate to vote for or to form an opinion on a policy issue. However, by the time an individual actually votes or voices an opinion on a specific issue, she may have forgotten some of the older information included in her decision-making process. This leads to the misconception that voters are uninformed, when in fact their opinion is informed but they have not retained all of the facts used to form that opinion. This model also implies a large role for elite information, but does not necessarily suggest that opinion is unstable.

If public opinion is easily manipulated, this would not be encouraging for democracy, which relies on citizens to play a significant part in the governmental process. But other research has shown that individuals are quite stable and rational in their policy attitudes.[40]

To take a closer look at the questions of whether and how public opinion changes, consider the issues of abortion and the economy (see Figure 6.4). Pew Research Center tracks public opinion over time with annual surveys asking identical survey questions. Some opinions are relatively stable: support for abortion has remained virtually unchanged over the past decade, with 54 percent saying abortion should be legal in all or most cases and 40 percent saying illegal in all or most cases, on average. Opinions about the economy and personal finances, however, experienced a gradual change triggered by the financial crisis in 2008. In 2004 roughly half of Americans described their personal finances as poor or fair and

The public is constantly exposed to competing messages from political elites. Viewers of NBC's popular show Meet the Press *hear different facts and points of view from Democratic senator Kirsten Gillibrand and Republican representative Mike Rogers. Political scientists study the effect of competing messages on public opinion.*

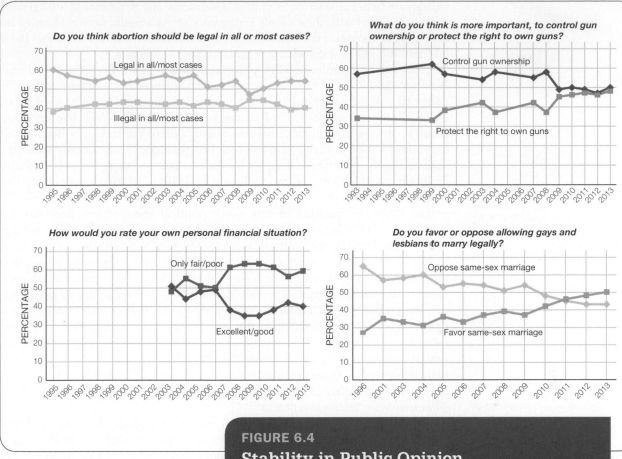

Do you think abortion should be legal in all or most cases?

Legal in all/most cases

Illegal in all/most cases

What do you think is more important, to control gun ownership or protect the right to own guns?

Control gun ownership

Protect the right to own guns

How would you rate your own personal financial situation?

Only fair/poor

Excellent/good

Do you favor or oppose allowing gays and lesbians to marry legally?

Oppose same-sex marriage

Favor same-sex marriage

FIGURE 6.4

Stability in Public Opinion

Public opinion on some issues has stayed stable in the last two decades, while opinion on other issues has shifted. What might explain why opinion on personal finance and same-sex marriage has changed, while opinion on abortion has stayed relatively constant?

SOURCE: Pew Research Center, www.pewresearch.org/data-trend/domestic-issues/abortion/; www.pewresearch.org/data-trend/domestic-issues/gun-control/; www.pewresearch.org /data-trend/national-conditions/personal-finances/; www.pewresearch.org/data-trend /domestic-issues/attitudes-on-gay-marriage/ (accessed 5/1/14).

half described their finances as good or excellent. However, public opinion began to shift in 2008. As of 2013, 6 in 10 Americans describe their personal finances as poor or fair, a 10-point shift. Opinion on same-sex marriage has changed even more. In 1996, 65 percent of Americans opposed marriage for gays and lesbians. As of 2013, only 43 percent opposed same-sex marriage. Notice that when public opinion has shifted, the shift has occurred fairly steadily in one direction; it doesn't simply jump around.[41]

Political Knowledge and Public Opinion

What best explains whether citizens are generally consistent in their political views or inconsistent and open to the influence of others? In general, knowledgeable citizens are better able to evaluate new information and determine if it is relevant to and consistent with their beliefs and opinions.[42] As a result, better-informed individuals can recognize their political interests and act consistently to further those interests. But political knowledge is generally low in America.[43]

Using public opinion surveys, political scientist Adam Berinsky found that certain segments of the population may lack sufficient knowledge of public policy to give informed opinions. When asked about preferences toward social welfare policy, for instance, disadvantaged groups are more likely than any other group to abstain from giving answers—mainly due to the lack of politically relevant information available to those with few resources. This not only leads to a potential underreporting of support for welfare policy among the poor, but also limits the political voice of those who are most likely to support social welfare policies.[44]

This raises the question of how much political knowledge is necessary for one to act as an effective citizen. In an important study of political knowledge in the United States, the political scientists Michael X. Delli Carpini and Scott Keeter found that the average American exhibits little knowledge of political institutions, processes, leaders, or policy debates.[45] Many Americans cannot even name their own congressional representatives. Does this ignorance of key political facts matter? Delli Carpini and Keeter also found that political knowledge is not evenly distributed throughout the population. Those with higher education, income, and occupational status, and who are members of social or political organizations, are more likely to know about and be active in politics. As a result, individuals with a disproportionate share of income and education also have a disproportionate share of knowledge and influence and thus are better able to get what they want from government.

Latino voters provide an illustration of the relationship between political knowledge and public opinion. Republican president George W. Bush made a concerted effort to attract Latino voters, and was rewarded with about 40 percent of the Latino vote in the 2004 elections. However, in the 2012 election, Republican presidential candidate Mitt Romney had the support of only 30 percent of Latinos, in part due to his opposition to immigration and his promise to repeal the Patient Protection and Affordable Care Act.[46] Romney's harsh rhetoric on these subjects did not resonate with this large and growing minority population. In a June 2011 Latino Decisions tracking poll, three-quarters of Latinos wanted the federal government not to deport young people who would be eligible for the DREAM Act (Development, Relief, and Education for Alien Minors).[47] Obama took a step in this direction with an executive order implementing parts of the DREAM Act in 2012; he also won a majority of the Latino vote. Latinos have a high level of political knowledge about the issue of immigration, and Obama's and Romney's different policies shaped their opinions of the candidates and their voting behavior in the 2012 elections.

Shortcuts and Cues Because being informed politically requires a substantial investment of time and energy, most Americans seek to acquire political information and to make political decisions "on the cheap" by making use of shortcuts for political evaluation and decision making rather than engaging in a lengthy process of information gathering. Researchers have found that individuals rely on cues from party elites and the media to aid in attitude formation.[48] Other "inexpensive" ways to become informed involve taking cues from trusted friends, relatives, colleagues, and perhaps religious leaders. Political scientists Richard Lau and David Redlawsk argue that most public opinion is formed by taking cues from trusted political elites: elected officials, the media, and interest groups.[49] By means of these informational shortcuts, average citizens can form political opinions that are, in most instances, consistent with their underlying preferences. They call this "voting correctly." Research shows that even individuals with low levels of political knowledge are able to make relatively informed political choices by relying on these voter cues. It is generally accepted by scholars in political science that people rely on shortcuts in forming public opinion on politics and public policy.[50]

The public's reliance on elite cues has taken on new significance in today's era of elite polarization. As the political parties and elected officials have become increasingly polarized, has this change affected the way that citizens arrive at their opinions? Political scientists James Druckman, Erik Peterson, and Rune Slothuus have found stark evidence that polarized political environments change how citizens make decisions and form opinions. Notably, polarization between the parties means that party endorsements (such as of an issue or candidate) have a larger impact on public opinion formation than they used to. At the same time, polarization decreases the impact of other information on public opinion—that is, party polarization may actually reduce levels of political knowledge. Thus, elite polarization may have negative implications for public opinion formation.[51] Interestingly, though, individuals with the most interest in news and public affairs are also the most partisan in their opinions (see Figure 6.5). For instance, while 12 percent of Republicans who follow the news "hardly at all" somewhat approve of the job President Obama is doing, only 2 percent of Republicans who follow the news "most of the time" somewhat approve. For Democrats, the trend is reversed.

Skim and Scan Another factor affecting political knowledge is the *form* in which people consume information. The transformation of political information in the digital era has had a profound effect on the way the news is reported and how citizens obtain information about politics. A 2012 survey conducted by the Pew Internet and American Life Project found that 36 percent of social networking site users say those sites are important for their political information, and more than three in four Americans read the news online or seek political information online.[52] Recent research also indicates a trend in journalism toward shorter articles and flashier headlines. Americans today are likely to read the news by scanning and skimming multiple headlines online, in bits and bytes, rather than by reading long news articles. Or as Nicholas Carr asks in his bestselling book *The Shallows: What the Internet Is Doing to Our Brains*, "Is Google making us stupid?" The answer from a review of scientific data conducted by Carr and another author is, in part, yes.[53]

Nicholas Carr's study details the decline in the deep processing that underpins "mindful knowledge acquisition, inductive analysis, critical thinking, imagination, and reflection."[54] He argues that although the Internet may seem to be making us smarter by virtue of giving us access to more data faster than ever, it also threatens the type of intelligence that is measured by depth of thought rather than sheer speed. The habits of browsing, scanning, and reading in a nonlinear fashion have undermined the capacity to immerse oneself in longer works of writing, such as books. Carr argues that throughout the history of human evolution, the ways in which we obtain information have actually

FIGURE 6.5

Political Knowledge and Public Opinion

Individuals who are more interested in news and follow public affairs tend to hold more extreme opinions. Democrats who describe themselves as very interested in news and public affairs are more likely to strongly approve of how President Obama is doing his job (as shown by the larger dark green bar) and less likely to disapprove (as shown by the smaller dark orange bar), as compared with Democrats who say they are not interested in news. For Republicans, those who describe themselves as very interested are more likely to strongly disapprove of how President Obama is doing his job (larger orange bar) than Republicans who say they are not interested in news and public affairs. In the lower graph, we see a similar pattern in opinion on global climate change.

SOURCE: CCES Common Content. 2010, http://projects.iq.harvard.edu/cces/book/common-content (accessed 10/30/14).

PRESIDENT OBAMA

Do you approve of the way President Obama is doing his job?

- Strongly disapprove
- Somewhat disapprove
- Somewhat approve
- Strongly approve

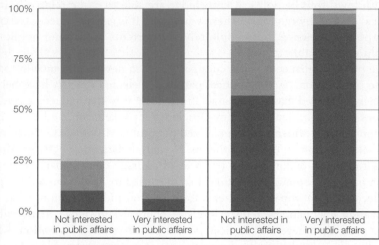

CLIMATE CHANGE

From what you know about global climate change or global warming, which one of the following statements comes closest to your opinion?

- Global climate change is not occurring; this is not a real issue.
- Concern about global climate change is exaggerated. No action is necessary.
- We don't know enough about global climate change, and more research is necessary before we take any actions.
- There is enough evidence that climate change is taking place, and some action should be taken.
- Global climate change has been established as a serious problem, and immediate action is necessary.

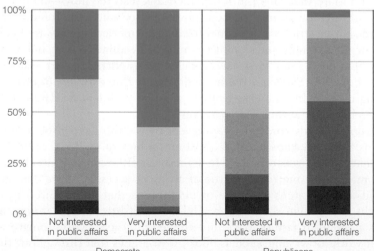

changed our brain processes. The technologies we employ to find, store, and share information can literally reroute our neural pathways. The rise of digital media is actually changing the way we think.

Extending this logic to politics, the implications are that public opinion will be less rational and more erratic, as individuals will lack a carefully developed understanding on which to base their opinions, despite the overwhelming volume of information about politics online. This trend might explain the significant percentage of Americans who believe political stories that are untrue or based on misinformation, such as the claim that President Obama is not a U.S. citizen. However, as we've seen in this chapter, some research indicates that most individuals use simple cues and shortcuts to process political information. If this is correct, scanning and skimming headlines might provide a reasonable way to be informed about politics without extensive time or effort.

Costs to Democracy? If political scientists are correct in their findings that many citizens base their opinions (and votes) on inadequate knowledge and an overreliance on cues from political elites, this raises a critical question: If political knowledge is necessary for effective citizenship, how does a general lack of such knowledge affect the way we govern ourselves?

Although understandable and, perhaps, inevitable, low levels of political knowledge and engagement weaken American democracy in two ways. First, those who lack political information cannot effectively defend their own political interests and can easily become losers in political struggles. The presence of large numbers of politically inattentive or ignorant individuals means that political power can more easily be manipulated by political elites, the media, and wealthy special interests that seek to shape public opinion.

Second, if knowledge is power, then a lack of knowledge can contribute to growing political and economic inequality. When individuals are unaware of their interests or how to pursue them, it is virtually certain that political outcomes will not favor them. One of the most important areas of government policy is taxation. As discussed in the introduction to this chapter, America has one of the largest gaps between the rich and the poor of any nation in the world. But rather than raise taxes, over the past several decades, the United States has substantially reduced the rate of taxation levied on its wealthiest citizens. Most recently, tax cuts signed into law by George W. Bush in 2001, and extended by President Obama, provided a substantial tax break mainly for the top 1 percent of the nation's wage earners. Political scientist Larry Bartels has shown that, surprisingly, most Americans favored the tax cuts, including millions of middle- and lower-middle-class citizens who did not stand to benefit from the tax policy. Additionally, 40 percent of Americans had no opinion at all regarding the Bush tax cuts. The explanation for this odd state of affairs appears to be a lack of political knowledge. Millions of individuals who were unlikely to derive benefit from President Bush's tax policy thought they would. Since most Americans think they pay too much in taxes, they favored the policy, even if the wealthy benefited much more than the middle class. (See the "Who Are Americans?" feature for public opinion on inequality.)

Bartels has employed the cartoon character Homer Simpson to explain how people don't realize what is in their economic interest: Homer wants a tax cut, and even if he gets only $1 and Mr. Burns, his boss, takes home $1,000, Homer still wants his dollar in savings.[55] But Homer is misguided in wanting his dollar in

In 2012 the billionaire Warren Buffett argued that it was not right that he—one of the richest people in the world—paid a lower tax rate than his secretary, Debbie Bosanek (pictured here). However, many Americans may not understand how changes in the tax code will affect them.

tax savings: the overall lost tax revenues, collected mainly from the wealthy, would have funded programs that benefit middle-class taxpayers like Homer. Upper-bracket taxpayers, who are more informed and knowledgeable, are more likely to see to it that their economic self-interest aligns with government policy—and vice versa. This example illustrates that basic political knowledge matters in American politics.

● The Media, Government, and Public Opinion

> **Describe the major forces that shape public opinion**

When individuals attempt to form opinions about particular political issues, events, and personalities, they seldom do so in isolation. Typically, they are confronted with—sometimes bombarded by—the efforts of a host of individuals and groups seeking to persuade them to adopt a particular point of view. In the approach to the 2012 presidential election, someone trying to decide what to think about Barack Obama or Mitt Romney could hardly avoid an avalanche of opinions expressed through the media, in meetings, or in conversations with friends. The **marketplace of ideas** is the interplay of opinions and views that takes place as competing forces attempt to persuade as many people as possible to accept a particular position on a particular issue. Given this constant exposure to the ideas of others, it is virtually impossible for most individuals to resist some modification of their own beliefs. Three forces that play important roles in shaping opinions in the marketplace are the government, private groups, and the news media.[56]

marketplace of ideas the public forum in which beliefs and ideas are exchanged and compete

Government and the Shaping of Public Opinion

All governments try to influence, manipulate, or manage their citizens' beliefs. But the extent to which public opinion is actually affected by governmental public relations can be limited. Often, governmental claims are disputed by the media, by interest groups, and at times even by opposing forces within the government itself.

This hasn't stopped modern presidents from focusing a great deal of attention on shaping public opinion to boost support for their policy agendas. Franklin Delano Roosevelt promoted his policy agenda directly to the American people through his famous "fireside chats" radio broadcasts. A hallmark of the Clinton administration was the employment of techniques such as those used in election campaigns to bolster popular enthusiasm for White House initiatives. The president established a political "war room" similar to the one that operated in his campaign headquarters, where representatives from all departments met daily to discuss and coordinate the president's public-relations efforts.[57]

The George W. Bush administration developed an extensive public-relations program to bolster popular support for the president's policies, including the administration's war against terrorism. These efforts included presidential speeches, media appearances by administration officials, numerous press conferences, and thousands of press releases presenting the administration's views.[58] Using the runway of an aircraft carrier as his stage, a confident Commander in Chief Bush, dressed in military fatigues, proclaimed the end of the Iraq War in 2003.

Who Thinks Economic Inequality Is a Problem?

Percentage who said there are "strong" or "very strong" conflicts between rich and poor

An individual's ideology and party identification may influence his or her opinions on specific issues. As this study showed, the percentage of Americans concerned about economic inequality was rougly similar for all income groups. However, the differences between liberals and conservatives, and between Democrats and Republicans, were more significant.

By income

< $20,000	64%
$20,000–40,000	66%
$40,000–75,000	71%
> $75,000	67%

By ideology

Conservative	55%
Moderate	68%
Liberal	79%

By party

Republican	55%
Independent	68%
Democrat	73%

for critical analysis

1. Do the findings in this study show that opinions are shaped by economic self-interest? Why or why not?

2. Which ideological group and which party are most likely to support government action to address inequality? Are the other groups not concerned about inequality? Use the data to explain your answers.

SOURCE: Pew Research Center, "Rising Share of Americans See Conflict between Rich and Poor," January 11, 2012, www.pewsocialtrends.org/2012/01/11/rising-share-of-americans-see-conflict-between-rich-and-poor/ (accessed 5/10/12).

His statement was premature by nearly a decade, but it effectively maintained public support for the Iraq War effort.

Like its predecessors, the Obama administration has sought to shape public opinion in the United States and abroad, relying upon the power of the president's oratorical skills to build support for his administration's initiatives in domestic and foreign policy. But Obama's White House is unique in using social media to promote the president's policy agenda. President Obama has been as theatrical as Bush and Reagan, but largely through digital media and social media. Facebook posts promote his policies, campaign, and serve to personalize the president.

One realm in which presidential messages seem to routinely impact public opinion is foreign policy. Because most Americans have relatively low levels of knowledge about foreign policy, political elites have more influence in shaping opinion on such matters.[59] As will be described in more detail in Chapter 18, the president plays a key role in deciding and implementing U.S. foreign policy, particularly in moments of crisis. One prominent example is the decision to invade Iraq, which was strongly endorsed by President George W. Bush. In this case, other elected officials agreed, and in 2002 Congress passed the Joint Resolution to Authorize the Use of United States Armed Forces Against Iraq. Public opinion in favor of invading Iraq remained above 50 percent between June and November of 2002, according to Gallup polls. By the time the invasion occurred, in March 2003, after months of presidential messages, public support had reached over 70 percent.[60]

Interest Groups and the Shaping of Public Opinion

The ideas that become prominent in political life are developed and spread not only by government officials but also by important economic and political groups searching for issues that will advance their causes. One especially notable example is the abortion issue, which has inflamed American politics over the past 30 years. The notion of a fetal "right to life," whose proponents seek to outlaw abortion and overturn the Supreme Court's 1973 *Roe v. Wade* decision, was developed by conservative politicians who saw the issue of abortion as a means of uniting Catholic and Protestant conservatives and linking both groups to the Republican Party.[61] To advance their cause, leaders of the right-to-life movement sponsored well-publicized Senate hearings at which testimony, photographs, and other exhibits were presented to illustrate the violent results of abortion procedures. At the same time, publicists for the movement produced leaflets, articles, books, and films such as *The Silent Scream* to highlight the agony and pain ostensibly felt by the "unborn" when they were being aborted. All this underscored the movement's claim that abortion was nothing more or less than the murder of more than a million innocent human beings annually in the United States. Finally, Catholic and evangelical Protestant religious leaders were organized to denounce abortion from their church pulpits and, increasingly, from their electronic pulpits on the Christian Broadcasting Network (CBN) and the various other television forums available for religious programming. Religious leaders have also organized demonstrations, pickets, and disruptions at abortion clinics throughout the nation.[62] The abortion rights issue remains a potent one.

Ideas are marketed most effectively by groups with access to financial resources, public or private institutional support, and sufficient skill or education to select, develop, and draft ideas that will attract interest and support. The development and

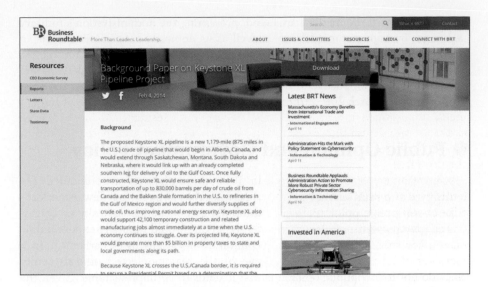

promotion of conservative themes and ideas in recent years have been greatly facilitated by the millions of dollars that conservative corporations and business organizations such as "Super PACs" (see Chapter 10), the U.S. Chamber of Commerce, and the Public Affairs Council spend each year on public information. In much the same way, liberal organizations vie for public attention armed with ample financial assets, access to the media, and well-honed skills in creating, communicating, and using ideas. In recent decades, various left-leaning public interest groups, relying heavily on voluntary contributions of time, effort, and money from their members, have organized in parallel with the rise of such institutions on the right. Through groups such as Common Cause, the National Organization for Women, MoveOn.org, the World Wildlife Federation, and Sierra Club, liberal intellectuals and professionals have been able to apply their organizational skills and educational resources to developing and promoting their ideas.[63]

The News Media and the Shaping of Public Opinion

The media are among the most powerful forces operating in the marketplace of ideas. As we shall see in Chapter 7, the mass media are not simply neutral messengers for ideas developed by others. Instead, the media are very much opinion makers in their own right and have an enormous impact on popular attitudes. For example, for the past 40 years since the publication of the Pentagon Papers by the *New York Times* and the exposure of the Watergate scandal led by the *Washington Post*, the national news media have relentlessly investigated personal and official wrongdoing on the part of politicians and public officials. The continual media presentation of corruption in government has undoubtedly contributed to the cynicism toward and distrust of government that prevails in much of the general public, as discussed above.

At the same time, the ways in which media coverage interprets or "frames" specific events can have a major impact on popular responses and opinions about these events.[64] Given the critical importance of media framing to the way the public perceives the news, the Bush administration went to great lengths to persuade broadcasters to follow its lead in their coverage of both terrorism and America's response to terrorism in the months following the September 11, 2001, attacks.

for critical **analysis**

Does it matter what news sources an individual reads? How can the news influence public attitudes on issues of public policy?

For the most part, the media acquiesced, presenting the administration's military campaigns in Afghanistan and Iraq, as well as its domestic antiterrorist efforts, in a positive light. Even supposedly liberal newspapers such as the *New York Times*, which had strongly opposed Bush in the 2000 election, praised his leadership and published articles supportive of the president's bellicose rhetoric against the Iraqi regime prior to March 2003, when President Bush ordered the invasion of Iraq.

● Public Opinion and Government Policy

Analyze the relationship between public opinion and government policies

In 1960 the authors of a book titled *The American Voter* argued that few Americans think about politics ideologically or consistently, so one would naturally expect public opinion to vary, as discussed earlier.[65] In fact, one of the reasons elected officials sometimes do not follow public opinion is that it tends to be unpredictable. Given the general lack of political knowledge among voters, the sometimes volatile nature of public opinion, and the difficulty of measuring the public will accurately, it's little wonder that politicians are sometimes unable, or unwilling, to act solely on the basis of public opinion. John Zaller's explanation of how Americans form specific opinions calls into question whether government leaders should consult public opinion at all when they make policy decisions—but consulting public opinion is their democratic duty. So how responsive is government policy to public opinion?

Government Responsiveness to Public Opinion

Studies generally suggest that elected officials are influenced by the preferences of the public. For example, political scientists Benjamin Page and Robert Shapiro have studied the relationship between macro-level changes in opinion toward various political issues and the policy outcomes that most closely correspond to the issues.[66] The results show that shifts in public opinion on particular issues do in fact tend to lead to changes in public policy. This is especially true when there are wide swings in opinion regarding particularly high-profile issues that are relatively simple. Other researchers have found similar evidence that government policy generally does track public opinion. By measuring public opinion over time, political scientists Gerald Wright, Robert Erikson, and John McIver have found, unsurprisingly, that states where conservative opinions predominate tend to adopt more conservative laws, and states with more liberal public opinion adopt more liberal policies.[67] One such example is in health care. A July 2009 Pew survey found that 65 percent of Americans favored a law "requiring all Americans to have health insurance, and government aid for those unable to afford it."[68] The federal government adopted the Affordable Health Care Act for America in 2010, which required health insurance for all citizens.

However, there is reason to question whether prevailing public opinion causes politicians to make policies that reflect the general will, or whether government policy in fact causes changes in public opinion. The relationship between government policy and opinion may be dynamic, wherein policy responds to opinion but opinion also shifts based on new government policies.[69] Recent studies of whether government policy can affect public opinion have found policy to have

To what extent do political leaders listen to the opinions of their constituents? To what extent should they listen? *Is Calvin's father right that leaders should do what they believe is right, not what the public wants?*

an effect on opinion in various policy areas, such as the environment, health care, welfare reform, the death penalty, and smoking bans. For example, researchers found that in states that adopted smoking bans, public opinion then shifted to become more critical of cigarette smoking than in states without such bans.[70] Scholars have suggested a number of possible mechanisms to explain this process. New policy may expose the public to new ideas, causing opinion to change. Or, experience with a (successful or unsuccessful) policy gives the public new information. A policy might act as a "signal" of a moral or ethical view (such as a smoking ban acting as a "signal" that smoking should be stigmatized).

Today, same-sex marriage is one of the most prominent policies engaging opinion on morality and civil rights. Opinion polls show that support for same-sex marriage is increasing. Might it be that state policies send a signal either legitimizing it (in states recognizing same-sex marriage) or stigmatizing it (in states that prohibit same-sex marriage)? Whereas only 27 percent of Americans favored same-sex marriage in 1996, support is now well over 50 percent.[71] Some new research suggests that opinion favoring marriage rights is increasing more quickly in states that have legalized same-sex marriage than in other states. This is an example where state policy may play an important role in changing public opinion.

Of course, sometimes public opinion and policy do not align. At times, officials act on their own preferences if they believe it will benefit government or society, and studies have indeed shown that lawmakers typically do use their own judgment when making policy choices.[72] The bailout of the banks in 2008, for example, was carried out despite polls showing that a majority of Americans opposed this policy. When elected officials pursue policies not aligned with centrist opinion, it is often because they view particular groups of the electorate as more important than others. Inevitably, loyal voting blocs or interest groups that regularly contribute to a candidate may have their interests more closely represented than the general public.[73]

Does Everyone's Opinion Count Equally?

In a democracy, it is assumed that elected representatives should implement the policies favored by the people, and in a general sense this happens in the United States. But when policy issues are more complicated, the public is likely to have less of a voice. Further, citizens who are more affluent and more educated may have a disproportionate influence over politics and public policy decisions. This has been shown when comparing the responsiveness of elected officials to low- and high-income individuals, voters and nonvoters, and whites and minorities. The view that some groups in a society have more influence over the political process is not new, but it is quite a departure from the traditional pluralist view of all citizens having equal access to the political sphere—the democratic ideal outlined by the scholar Robert Dahl (see Chapter 11).

How do more affluent and educated citizens manage to wield outsize influence over policy makers? One way is obvious: they vote at higher rates and they are more likely to contribute money to political campaigns. As we will discuss in Chapter 8, voters and individuals making political contributions tend to be more affluent and educated than nonvoters. Indeed, there is some evidence supporting the common, but generally untested, assumption that voters are better represented than nonvoters. In a comparative study of the roll-call votes of U.S. senators, political scientists John Griffin and Brian Newman demonstrate that elected officials are indeed responsive to the policy preferences (and public opinion) of voters, but not to those of nonvoters.[74]

Another constituency whose opinions seem to carry more weight is the wealthy. Research has found that U.S. senators from both the Republican and Democratic parties are less likely to respond to the opinions of low-income constituents than to those of constituents with higher incomes.[75] Senate votes on such varied issues as the minimum wage, civil rights, and abortion are more likely to reflect the opinions of the upper-income constituency. Additionally, some research indicates that, when weighing the opinions of those who vote and have high levels of political knowledge, senators are still more responsive to the rich. The influence of affluent Americans may explain government policies such as tax cuts for the ultrawealthy, failure to increase the minimum wage, and the elimination of the inheritance tax which contribute to inequality between the ultrarich and average Americans.[76]

As an alternative to analyzing legislative votes, political scientist Martin Gilens has used survey results to confirm that those with higher incomes are more likely to have their policy preferences represented by actual policies.[77] He considers public opinion surveys on a wide variety of policy issues conducted over 20 years and compares the responses of upper- and lower-income groups with related federal policy outcomes. Gilens found a relationship between what the public wants and what the government actually does, albeit with a strong bias toward the status quo. But when Americans with different income levels differ in their policy preferences, actual policies strongly reflect the preferences of the most affluent and show little or no relationship to the preferences of poor or middle-income Americans. Robert Dahl may be right when he argues that every American citizen has an equal right to voice opinions in the political arena, but his critics are also right to point out that some voices receive a very attentive listening while others are hardly heard at all.

Although the American political system is open to everyone, some voices are more likely to be listened to than others, such as those of the wealthy. Robert Wolf, a former chief executive at the bank UBS, raised more than $500,000 for Obama's 2012 reelection campaign and is a member of the president's Council on Jobs and Competitiveness.

Opinion on the Economy and the Environment

Economic growth and climate change are two important policy issues in countries around the globe. Unlike some issues, which may be on a nation's agenda at one moment but then fade from view, maintaining robust economic growth is almost always a top government priority. But there may be tradeoffs between promoting the economy and other goals such as protecting the environment. The environment often suffers from pollution and other consequences of economic development; at the same time, environmental regulations may slow economic growth if they impose costs on businesses.

A World Values Survey asked individuals around the world which was more important to them: protecting the environment, even if it means sacrificing economic growth, or promoting economic growth, even if it means sacrificing the environment. What might explain the differences in public opinion on this issue across countries?

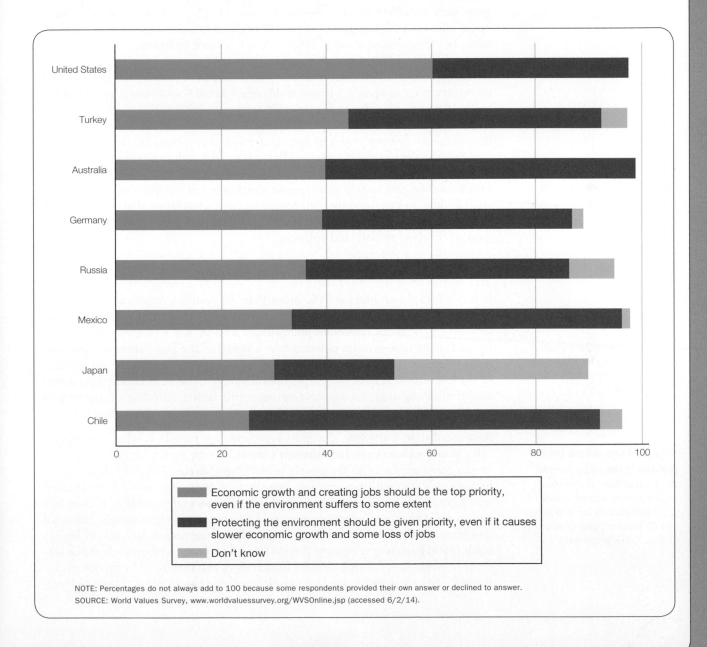

Legend:
- Economic growth and creating jobs should be the top priority, even if the environment suffers to some extent
- Protecting the environment should be given priority, even if it causes slower economic growth and some loss of jobs
- Don't know

NOTE: Percentages do not always add to 100 because some respondents provided their own answer or declined to answer.

SOURCE: World Values Survey, www.worldvaluessurvey.org/WVSOnline.jsp (accessed 6/2/14).

● Measuring Public Opinion

Describe basic survey methods and other techniques researchers use to measure public opinion

As recently as 50 years ago, American political leaders gauged public opinion by the presence of crowds at meetings and their applause. This direct exposure to the people's views did not necessarily produce accurate knowledge of public opinion. It did, however, give political leaders confidence in their public support—and therefore confidence in their ability to govern by consent.

Abraham Lincoln and Stephen Douglas debated each other seven times during the summer and autumn of 1858, two years before they became presidential nominees. Their debates took place before audiences in parched cornfields and courthouse squares. A century later, the presidential debates, although seen by millions, take place in television studios, before a few reporters, technicians, and audiences instructed not to applaud or make noise. Only rarely, such as in the grassroots or "retail" politics of the Iowa caucuses or New Hampshire presidential primary, can politicians gauge the public's response directly.[78] Retail politics is where candidates meet citizens face-to-face to discuss politics.[79]

As Chapter 7 on the media illustrates, the media convey information to millions of people, but the media are not yet as efficient at getting information back to leaders, although the rise of social media, such as Facebook and Twitter, has created improved feedback for elected officials. Today public officials make extensive use of **public-opinion polls** to help them decide whether to run for office, what policies to support, how to vote on important legislation, and what types of appeals to make in their campaigns. All recent presidents and other major political figures have worked closely with polls and pollsters.

public-opinion polls scientific instruments for measuring public opinion

Measuring Public Opinion from Surveys

It is not feasible to interview the more than 300 million Americans residing in the United States on their opinions of who should be the next president or what should be done about important policy issues such as how to improve the economy and create jobs. Instead, pollsters take a **sample** of the population and use it to make inferences (e.g., extrapolations and educated guesses) about the preferences of the population as a whole. For a political survey to be an accurate representation of the population, it must meet certain requirements, including an appropriate sampling method, a sufficient sample size, and the avoidance of selection bias.[80]

sample a small group selected by researchers to represent the most important characteristics of an entire population

Representative Samples The most representative sample is what statisticians call a **simple random sample (or probability sample)**. To take such a sample, one would need a complete list of all the people in the United States, and individuals would be randomly selected from that list. Imagine that everyone's name were entered into a lottery, with names then drawn blindly from an enormous box. If everyone had an equal chance of selection, we would have a truly random sample. Since we don't have a complete list of all Americans, pollsters use census data, lists of households (for in-person or telephone surveys), and telephone numbers (telephone surveys) to create lists, drawing samples from regions and then neighborhoods within regions. Just as in a simple random sample, everyone has an equal chance of being

simple random sample (or probability sample) a method used by pollsters to select a representative sample in which every individual in the population has an equal probability of being selected as a respondent

selected for the survey. Rolls of registered voters are often used in political surveys designed to predict the outcome of an election.

Another method of drawing samples of the national population is a technique called **random digit dialing** of landline and cell phone numbers, but not business phones or inoperative home telephones. A computer random number generator is used to produce a list of 10-digit telephone numbers. Given that 95 percent of Americans have telephones (cell phones or landlines), this technique usually results in a random national sample. Until recently, opinion polls did not include cell phone numbers, but because so many young people, urban residents, lower-income groups, and other demographic groups don't have landlines, cell phone numbers are included in many opinion polls. It allows almost every citizen a chance of being included in the survey. Telephone surveys are fairly accurate, cost-effective, and flexible in the type of questions that can be asked. Websites such as RealClearPolitics.com list the results of every political survey released each day; during elections, this can be as many as 20 different surveys daily. Every week, the opinions of Americans regarding candidates and public policies are measured, as well as opinions on a vast array of products (toothpaste), entertainment (movie star romances), and even college political science textbooks!

random digit dialing a polling method in which respondents are selected at random from a list of 10-digit telephone numbers, with every effort made to avoid bias in the construction of the sample

Sample Size A sample must be large enough to provide an accurate representation of the population. Surprisingly, though, the size of the population being measured doesn't matter, only the size of the *sample*. A survey of 1,000 people is just as effective for measuring the opinions of all Texans (26 million residents) as the opinions of all Americans (over 314 million residents).

Flipping a coin shows how this works. After tossing a coin 10 times, the number of heads and tails may not be close to 5 and 5. After 100 tosses of the coin, though, the percentage of heads should be close to 50 percent, and after 1,000 tosses, very close to 50 percent (assuming it is a fair coin). In fact, after 1,000 tosses there is a 95 percent chance that the number of heads will be somewhere between 46.9 percent and 53.1 percent. This 3.1 percent variation from 50 percent is called the sampling error or margin of error. The chance that the sample used does not accurately represent the population from which it is drawn is called the **sampling error (or margin of error)**. It is the amount of error we can expect with a typical 1,000-person survey. Normally, samples of 1,000 people are considered sufficient for accurately measuring public opinion through the use of surveys.

sampling error (or margin of error) polling error that arises based on the small size of the sample

Larger sample sizes can yield more accurate predictions of the opinions of a population, but there is a trade-off in terms of cost, since it is also more expensive to poll more people. Why is a sample size of only 1,000 generally accepted as adequately representative of much larger populations? Consider the "diminishing returns" of sampling more and more people. The sample error from a sample of 500 people is 4.4 percent. With 1,000 respondents, it drops to 3.1 percent, and with 1,500 to 2.5 percent. That is, the smaller and smaller gains in accuracy have to be weighed against the steadily increasing costs of polling more and more people. The consensus among statisticians and pollsters is that the optimal trade-off point is 1,000—hence 1,000 is the "gold standard."

When an election poll of 1,000 people indicates that 51 percent of voters surveyed favor the Republican candidate, say, Mitt Romney, and 49 percent support the Democratic candidate, Barack Obama, the outcome is considered too close to call because the difference, 2 percent, is within the margin of error. That is, a figure of 51 percent really means that between 48 and 54 percent of voters in the population *probably* favor the Republican, while a figure of 49 percent indicates that between 46 and 52 percent of all voters *probably* support the Democrat. Thus, in this example, a 52-to-48 percent Democratic victory would still be consistent with polls predicting a 51-to-49 percent Republican triumph.

Survey Design and Question Wording Even with reliable sampling procedures and a large sample, surveys may fail to reflect the true distribution of opinion within a target population. One frequent source of measurement error is the wording of survey questions. The precise words used in a question can have an enormous impact on the answers it elicits. The reliability of survey results can also be adversely affected by poor question format, faulty ordering of questions, poor vocabulary, ambiguity of questions, or questions with built-in biases.

Often, seemingly minor differences in the wording of a question can convey vastly different meanings to respondents and thus produce quite different response patterns (see Box 6.3). For example, for many years the University of Chicago's National Opinion Research Center has asked respondents whether they think the federal government is spending too much, too little, or about the right amount of money on "assistance for the poor." Answering the question posed this way, about two-thirds of all respondents seem to believe that the government is spending too little. However, the same survey also asks whether the government spends too much, too little, or about the right amount for welfare. When the word *welfare* is substituted for "assistance for the poor," about half of all respondents indicate that too much is being spent.[81]

Internet Surveys Today, pollsters are increasingly turning to the use of online surveys, often using similar techniques to those of telephone surveys. But Internet surveys can be more efficient, less costly, and more accurate than standard phone surveys, and they include larger samples of young people and yield more accurate results within age cohorts. Many surveys you will find online do not use probability sampling (random sampling), and thus are not representative of the American population. Instead, they reflect those willing to take a quiz online, or on Facebook.

Knowledge Networks (KN) and YouGov are leaders in Internet polling using random sampling methods in which respondents complete surveys online instead of being interviewed on the phone. KN has a large population of respondents (hundreds of thousands of individuals) identified using probability sampling, so the sample is representative of the American population in terms of age, education, income, gender, race, political interest, region, partisanship, and other attributes. Individuals without Internet access are given free subscriptions and, if necessary, a computer or WebTV; those with Internet access are given free subscriptions to complete the surveys. If a client commissions a survey, KN randomly draws a sample of, say, 1,000 respondents from its population of online respondents. Because respondents have agreed to complete a number of surveys in exchange for free Internet access, they are more likely to complete the surveys.

Other polling companies, such as YouGov, use different methods for conducting Internet surveys, often by using statistical weights to make the surveys generally representative of the American population.[82] Internet surveys such as the Cooperative Congressional Election Study (CCES) can have very large samples, up to 50,000 people. In the future, Internet surveys may be more representative of the American population than traditional telephone surveys, and may replace telephone surveys entirely, especially given falling response rates and the growing number of households without landline phones but using cell phones exclusively.

THE SITUATION

The public's desire for tax cuts can be hard to measure. In 2000, pollsters asked what should be done with the nation's budget surplus and got different results depending on the specifics of the question.

THE QUESTION

President Clinton has proposed setting aside approximately two-thirds of an expected budget surplus to fix the Social Security system. What do you think the leaders in Washington should do with the remainder of the surplus?

VARIATION 1

Should the money be used for a tax cut, or should it be used to fund new government programs?

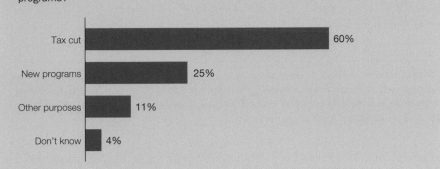

Tax cut	60%
New programs	25%
Other purposes	11%
Don't know	4%

VARIATION 2

Should the money be used for a tax cut, or should it be spent on programs for education, the environment, health care, crime fighting, and military defense?

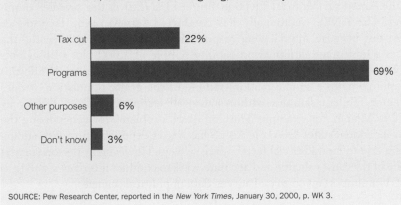

Tax cut	22%
Programs	69%
Other purposes	6%
Don't know	3%

SOURCE: Pew Research Center, reported in the *New York Times*, January 30, 2000, p. WK 3.

Critics of Internet surveys contend that the samples may still be biased by not including enough respondents from groups that are more likely to be off-line, especially non–English speakers, Latinos, African Americans, the elderly, and the poor. Online surveys may include more "politicos," or respondents who are interested in politics, than the normal population. Proponents contend that minorities and the poor are increasingly online, via mobile access, and that the samples are representative of the American population. Because Internet surveys have proved

Because not everyone has Internet access at home, obtaining a representative sample for an online survey can be difficult. However, polling companies such as YouGov are developing methods to improve accuracy, and online surveys may eventually offer a more efficient and affordable alternative to telephone surveys.

to be accurate in forecasting elections, and some argue they are more accurate than random digital telephone surveys, Internet surveys are likely here to stay.

Face-to-Face Surveys With more than 60 years' experience studying American politics, the American National Election Studies (ANES) is the premier omnibus survey. The ANES traditionally has conducted surveys using face-to-face interviews, but because interviewing respondents in person is very costly, the ANES uses a multistage, stratified probability sample of 2,000-plus respondents from regions of the country (what they call primary sampling units). While this method approximates a simple random sample of the entire population, it does not guarantee random samples within states; all respondents from Iowa may be from Des Moines, for example. This can cause problems for generalizing the results for individual states. Even the ANES has begun experimenting with adding Internet surveys to its traditional face-to-face surveys. However, in-person surveys remain one of the most valuable and accurate ways to conduct interviews, and thus the ANES is an important source of survey data in political science.

Framing Experiments within Surveys

Surveys are increasingly drawing on experimental techniques in which one group of respondents is given a treatment, or unique question wording, and responses are compared with a control group of respondents that does not receive the treatment. For example, the widespread tendency to base survey responses on the way questions are worded or "framed" provides a way to measure public opinion—through what are called framing experiments. Because of the media's power to shape public opinion, framing experiments are an important tool for measuring how the media and government shape political attitudes.

Researchers often use framing experiments (in surveys or laboratory experiments) to understand how subtle changes in the structure of political information can result in the expression of different political opinions. In one experiment, individuals in one group were exposed to a frame arguing that affirmative action is necessary to correct past discrimination, while those in a second group received a competing frame arguing that affirmative action gives African Americans special treatment. Not surprisingly, those in the first group showed greater support for affirmative action than did those in the second group for the same policies. By using a treatment and control group design, framing experiments provide more leverage in assessing cause and effect in measuring changes in public opinion.

The researchers Dennis Chong and Jamie Druckman have extended how we measure framing effects on public opinion by testing the effect of competing frames to create more realistic models of real-world political debate, where citizens are exposed to multiple perspectives on candidates and political issues.[83] Such competing frames can be expected to have different effects in shaping public opinion on a policy. In the marketplace of ideas, it matters crucially whether, say, the wealthiest Americans are characterized as the "super-rich" and "1 percenters," or alternatively as "business leaders" and "job creators." Framing experiments help researchers understand how public opinion changes in the face of new information. Framing by the media, political groups, or candidates matters because individuals often form opinions based on the latest information and arguments they are exposed to—what is "on the top of their heads"—and as a result, public-opinion polls often merely measure whatever recent elite cues (or media stories) individual respondents happen to have stored in their short-term memory.[84] Thus framing experiments are an important way to understand how public opinion moves in response to political elites and the mass media.

When Polls Are Wrong

The history of polling over the past century contains many instances of getting it wrong and learning valuable lessons in the process. As a result, polling techniques have grown more and more sophisticated, and pollsters have a more and more nuanced understanding of how public opinion is formed and how it is revealed.

Social Desirability Effects Political scientists have found that survey results can be inaccurate when the surveys include questions about sensitive issues for which individuals do not wish to share their true preferences. For example, respondents tend to overreport voting in elections and the frequency of their church attendance. Why? These activities are deemed socially appropriate, so even if the respondents did not vote or do not attend church regularly, they may feel social pressure to do so, and thus they may respond inaccurately on a survey. Political scientist Adam Berinsky calls this the **social desirability effect**, whereby respondents report what they expect the interviewer wishes to hear or whatever they think is socially acceptable, rather than what they actually believe or know to be true.[85] On other topics, respondents may feel self-conscious and so choose not to answer. This happens with questions about people's income.

Questions that ask directly about race or gender are particularly problematic. Social desirability makes it difficult to learn voters' true opinions about touchy subjects such as racial attitudes, because respondents hide their preferences from the interviewer for fear of social retribution (against what might be deemed

social desirability effect
the effect that results when respondents in a survey report what they expect the interviewer wishes to hear rather than what they believe

"politically incorrect" opinions). Berinsky, for example, found respondents in surveys didn't want to admit that they opposed school integration and would not vote for the black candidate, and therefore abstained from answering the question. Measuring public opinion can be a challenge; measuring opinions incorrectly can bias the findings. However, surveys using experiments can be designed to tap respondents' latent or hidden feelings about sensitive issues without directly asking them to express overt opinions.

Selection Bias The importance of accurate sampling was brought home early in the history of political polling. A 1936 *Literary Digest* poll predicted that the Republican candidate, Alf Landon, would defeat the Democratic incumbent, Roosevelt, in that year's presidential election. The actual election, of course, ended in a Roosevelt landslide. The main problem with the survey was what is called **selection bias** in drawing the sample. The pollsters had relied on telephone directories and automobile registration rosters to produce the survey sample. During the Great Depression, though, only wealthier Americans owned telephones and automobiles. Thus, the millions of working-class Americans who constituted Roosevelt's base of support were excluded from the sample.

Selection bias was also at play in preelection polls in the 2012 presidential election, when Gallup significantly overestimated Latino support for the Republican candidate, suggesting a close race between the Republican candidate, Mitt Romney, and the Democratic candidate, President Obama. Blogger Nate Silver, however, predicted Obama would win the election by a comfortable margin. His estimates were based on aggregating information from many different public opinion polls. Polls designed to measure the opinions of Latinos, such as Latino Decisions, estimated that 7 in 10 Latinos would vote for Democrat Obama over the Republican candidate. The election returns showed that 7 in 10 Latinos did indeed vote Democratic in 2012, and the Gallup numbers were incorrect because of selection bias (i.e., they had too few Latinos in their sample and therefore their predictions were inaccurate). As Figure 6.6 shows, Gallup was not the only polling organization to underestimate Obama's support in the 2012 election.

In recent years, the issue of selection bias has been complicated by the fact that growing numbers of individuals refuse to answer pollsters' questions, or they use such devices as answering machines and caller ID to screen unwanted callers. As noted previously, the increasing number of Americans who use cell phones (including many who do not have a landline at all) may be a problem in surveys that only include landline phone numbers. Individuals most likely to rely on cell phones alone include the young, urban residents, the poor, and minorities. These individuals would be less likely to be contacted if a telephone survey did not include cell phone numbers.

Additionally, response rates for surveys—the percentage of calls attempted that are completed—have been falling steeply. Response rates for the Pew Research Center's highly respected surveys, for example, are less than 15 percent. If pollsters could be certain that those who responded to their surveys simply reflected the views of those who refused to respond, there would be no problem. Some studies, however, suggest that the views of respondents and nonrespondents can differ, especially along social class lines. Upper-class individuals are often less willing to respond to surveys or less likely to be at home than their working-class counterparts, which can bias telephone surveys. And women are significantly more

selection bias (surveys) polling error that arises when the sample is not representative of the population being studied, which creates errors in overrepresenting or underrepresenting some opinions

for critical analysis

Is it important that public opinion polls be accurate? How might polls fail to be accurate? What are the consequences if polls are systematically inaccurate?

Actual vote margin for Obama

FIGURE 6.6

Accuracy of Final Preelection Polls, 2012

A large number of news organizations conducted polls to predict the outcome of the 2012 election. For how many of these polls was the actual result within their margin of error, assuming a sample size of 1,000 and a margin of error of plus or minus 3.1 percent? What might explain why some respected organizations, like Gallup and NPR, were so far off the mark?

SOURCE: John Sides, themonkeycage.org/2012/11/07/the-accuracy-of-the-final-national polls (accessed 5/28/13). Data from Pollster.
CREDIT: Graph: "The Accuracy of the Final National Polls," by John Sides. November 7, 2012. http://themonkeycage.org/2012/11/07/the-accuracy-of-the-final-national-polls/. Reprinted with permission.

PREDICTED MARGIN FOR OBAMA

likely to answer telephone surveys than men. Additionally, as discussed, most young people and a majority of minorities do not have landline phones, only cell phones, and are often excluded from telephone surveys. This can lead to incorrect inferences of public opinion.

Push Polling Push polling introduces a different type of bias into public-opinion polling. **Push polls** are not scientific polls, as just discussed, and are not intended to yield accurate information about a population. Instead, they involve asking a respondent a loaded question about a political candidate

push poll a polling technique in which the questions are designed to shape the respondent's opinion

Though public opinion is important, it is not always easy to interpret, and polls often fail to predict accurately how Americans will vote. In 1948, election-night polls showed Thomas Dewey defeating Harry S. Truman for the presidency. The Chicago News Tribune *trusted the polls and incorrectly printed a banner headline proclaiming Dewey the winner, which a triumphant Truman displayed when he won the election by a margin of approximately 4 percent.*

designed to elicit the response sought by the pollster and, simultaneously, to shape the respondent's perception of the candidate in question. One of the most notorious uses of push polling occurred in the 2000 South Carolina Republican presidential primary, in which George W. Bush defeated John McCain and went on to win the presidency. Callers working for Bush supporters asked conservative white voters if they would be more or less likely to vote for McCain if they knew he had fathered an illegitimate black child. Because McCain often campaigned with a daughter whom he and his wife had adopted from Mother Teresa's orphanage in Bangladesh, many voters accepted the premise of the "poll." This push poll was often cited by McCain as one of the political smear tactics that made him reluctant to expose his family to the stresses of the 2008 presidential race. More than 100 consulting firms across the nation now specialize in push polling.[86] Push polls may be one reason Americans are becoming increasingly skeptical about the practice of polling and increasingly unwilling to answer pollsters' questions.[87]

The Bandwagon Effect By influencing perceptions, public opinion polls can even influence political realities. In fact, sometimes polling can even create its own reality. The so-called **bandwagon effect** occurs when polling results influence people to support the candidate marked as the probable victor. This is especially true in the presidential nomination process, where there may be multiple candidates within one party vying to be the party's nominee. Todd Donovan and his coauthors found that the change in national media coverage received by a candidate before and after the Iowa caucuses, the first nominating event, was a major predictor of how well the candidate would do in the New Hampshire primary (the second nominating

bandwagon effect a shift in electoral support to the candidate whom public opinion polls report as the front-runner

event) and in presidential primaries nationwide, controlling for other factors, including money and standing in the polls.[88] A candidate who has "momentum"—that is, one who demonstrates a lead in the polls—usually finds it considerably easier to raise campaign funds than a candidate whose poll standing is poor. And with these additional funds, poll leaders can often afford to pay for television time and other campaign activities that will generate positive media attention and thus cement their advantage.

Public Opinion, Democracy,
and Your Future

This chapter has focused on the role of public opinion in American politics. A major purpose of democratic government, with its participatory procedures and representative institutions, is to ensure that political leaders will heed the public will. And, indeed, a good deal of evidence suggests that they do. There are many instances in which public policy and public opinion do not coincide, but often the government's actions are consistent with citizens' preferences, at least in the most general sense.[89]

Some political scientists argue, however, that government policy is much less responsive to public opinion on the issues that really count, and that when the interests of elites are at stake, government officials are much more likely to represent the opinions of the affluent than the poor.[90]

New technology may be able to help. The migration of politics online has greatly expanded the amount of information available and the ease of becoming informed. And as we will see in Chapter 7, online media are more diverse than traditional media. Given this new media environment, we might expect public opinion to be more accurate, even about the nuances of public policy. Digital citizenship offers the promise of a more informed electorate, with citizens having multiple venues in which to translate their opinions into political action and demand improved representation from political leaders.

At the same time, the Internet raises new concerns about the accuracy and consistency of public opinion. As Chapter 7 will show, Americans may become trapped in a "filter bubble" in which they are exposed only to news consistent with their political preferences. There are Internet vandals, or "bomb throwers," who defame other people and their opinions in ways that may negatively color public opinion. Misinformation—rumor masked as legitimate news—may be more common, especially in blogs, as the confusion regarding Barack Obama's country of birth illustrates. Some research finds that the gap between the haves and the have-nots in terms of political knowledge actually increases with the availability of more information. The implications are significant, given the explosion of political coverage online. The research suggests that with more information, public opinion may actually be less consistent.[91]

The Internet may be reshaping what is public opinion. The effects of new media—vast and still unfolding—include the wide dissemination of public opinion polls and the rise of Internet polling. Do new media make public opinion more or less important? Do they make elected officials more or less responsive to the citizens? Time will tell.

Of course, technological change will continue; the media of 2040 will not be the same as the media of 2015. Young adults will face a changing media environment just as their parents did. Such technological evolution may bring yet further changes to our understanding of the relationship between public opinion, government, and the media. New media may make it easier than ever for citizens to stay informed about the actions of their elected leaders, or new media may make it easier for leaders to learn about their constituents' preferences. What can citizens do to stay informed and make their views known amidst a changing media and political environment?

plugin

Inform

Read about the specific methods used by the pollsters who provide information about public opinion. For example, read the page "How does Gallup polling work?" on gallup.com.

Express

Take the Political Compass test at www.politicalcompass.org or the Pew Research Center's poltical typology quiz at www.people-press.org. These sites rate your political ideology based on your opinions.

Connect

Look up polling results for an issue that you care about to see how your opinion compares with others'. Consider checking poll aggregators like pollingreport.com or realclearpolitics .com for multiple polls on a range of topics. Pay attention to whether public opinion on your issue has changed over time.

Act

Post a survey question about a political issue on SurveyMonkey or Facebook and send to your classmates. How do the results of your poll compare to national public opinion on the same issue?

studyguide

Defining Public Opinion

Define public opinion, and identify broad types of values and beliefs Americans have about politics (pp. 209–16)

Public opinion refers to the attitudes that people have about issues, events, elected officials, and public policy. Individuals' attitudes are shaped by their underlying political beliefs and values. Despite differences in opinion on many issues, most Americans share a common set of values, including a belief in the principles of liberty, equality, and democracy.

Key Terms

public opinion (p. 209)

values (or beliefs) (p. 209)

political ideology (p. 209)

attitude (or opinion) (p. 209)

liberty (p. 210)

equality of opportunity (p. 211)

democracy (p. 211)

libertarianism (p. 212)

socialism (p. 212)

liberal (p. 213)

conservative (p. 214)

Practice Quiz

1. The term *public opinion* is used to describe
   a) the speeches and writings made by a president during his or her term in office.
   b) the analysis of events broadcast by news reporters during the evening news.
   c) the beliefs and attitudes that people have about issues.
   d) decisions of the Supreme Court.
   e) any political statement that is made by a citizen outside of his or her home.

2. Today, the term _____ refers to an ideology that supports social and political reform, greater economic equality, and expansion of government social services.
   a) libertarianism
   b) liberalism
   c) conservatism
   d) democracy
   e) moderate

3. When asked about their political ideology, more Americans describe themselves as _____ than _____.
   a) libertarian; liberal
   b) liberal; conservative
   c) conservative; liberal
   d) liberal; moderate
   e) socialist; conservative

How We Form Political Opinions

Explain the major factors that shape specific individual opinions (pp. 217–25)

A number of factors, including the family, membership in social groups, education, self-interest, and the political environment, help form people's underlying political beliefs and values in a process called *political socialization*.

Key Terms

political socialization (p. 217)

agents of socialization (p. 217)

gender gap (p. 222)

Practice Quiz

4. The process by which Americans learn political beliefs and values is called
   a) brainwashing.
   b) propaganda.
   c) indoctrination.
   d) political socialization.
   e) political development.

5. Which of the following is an agent of socialization?
   a) the family
   b) social groups
   c) education
   d) political environment
   e) All of the above are agents of socialization.

Stability of Opinion and Political Knowledge

Explore when and why public opinion changes and what role political knowledge plays (pp. 225–32)

Because being politically informed requires a substantial investment of time and energy, most Americans know relatively little about the political world. Most people acquire political information and make political decisions by relying on cues from party elites, trusted acquaintances, and the mass media. However, inadequate knowledge can prevent individuals from effectively defending their political interests.

Practice Quiz

6. Which factor best explains whether individuals are generally consistent in their political views or inconsistent and open to the influence of others?
   a) annual income
   b) age
   c) political knowledge
   d) party affiliation
   e) ideology

7. The fact that the public is inattentive to politics and must frequently rely on informational shortcuts has which of the following effects?
   a) It strengthens democracy by providing politicians with more freedom to act on a wider variety of issues.
   b) It strengthens democracy by increasing the number of people who participate in politics.
   c) It weakens democracy by making it easier for various institutions and political actors to manipulate the political process.
   d) It weakens democracy by making every citizen equally empowered to produce outcomes that are consistent with their interests on every issue.
   e) It has no effect on democracy.

The Media, Government, and Public Opinion

Describe the major forces that shape public opinion (pp. 232–36)

When individuals form opinions about specific issues, events, and politicians, they do not do so in isolation. They are bombarded by the efforts of many individuals and groups seeking to persuade them. Government officials and interest groups rely on messaging and a variety of media to get their messages across to citizens. The news media also serve as a powerful force in creating opinion and influencing popular attitudes.

Key Term

marketplace of ideas (p. 232)

Practice Quiz

8. Which of the following are the most important external influences on how political opinions are formed in the marketplace of ideas?
   a) the government, private groups, and the news media
   b) the unemployment rate, the Dow Jones industrial average, and the NASDAQ composite
   c) random digit dialing surveys, push polls, and framing experiments
   d) the Constitution, the Declaration of Independence, and the *Federalist Papers*
   e) the legislative branch, the executive branch, and the judicial branch

Public Opinion and Government Policy

> **Analyze the relationship between public opinion and government policies (pp. 236–39)**

In a democracy, elected officials should pursue policies that are favored by the public. Although there are many instances where government policy differs from the desires of the public, research has shown that there is generally a strong connection between what government does and what people want. Research has also shown, however, that more affluent and more educated citizens have a disproportionate influence over policy decisions.

Practice Quiz

9. One reason that more affluent and educated individuals have greater influence over policy is that
   a) they are most concerned with complex issues.
   b) they represent the interests of most other groups.
   c) they are more likely to vote and make campaign contributions.
   d) they tend to advocate for major changes.
   e) they tend to support the status quo.

Measuring Public Opinion

> **Describe basic survey methods and other techniques researchers use to measure public opinion (pp. 240–49)**

Surveys can provide a very accurate description of public opinion on an issue if they employ an appropriate sampling method and include a sufficient sample size. In addition to the characteristics of the sample, the reliability of surveys is also determined by the ordering and wording of the questions pollsters choose to ask.

Key Terms

public-opinion polls (p. 240)

sample (p. 240)

simple random sample (or probability sample) (p. 240)

random digit dialing (p. 241)

sampling error (or margin of error) (p. 241)

social desirability effect (p. 245)

selection bias (surveys) (p. 246)

push poll (p. 247)

bandwagon effect (p. 248)

Practice Quiz

10. Which of the following is the term used in public-opinion polling to denote the small group representing the opinions of the whole population?
    a) control group
    b) sample
    c) micropopulation
    d) respondents
    e) median voters

11. A *push poll* is a poll in which
    a) the questions are designed to shape the respondent's opinion rather than measure the respondent's opinion.
    b) the questions are designed to measure the respondent's opinion rather than shape the respondent's opinion.
    c) the questions are designed to reduce measurement error.
    d) the sample is chosen to include only undecided or independent voters.
    e) the sample is not representative of the population it is drawn from.

12. A familiar polling problem is the *bandwagon effect*, which occurs when
    a) the same results are used over and over again.
    b) polling results influence people to support the candidate marked as the probable victor in a campaign.
    c) polling results influence people to support the candidate who is trailing in a campaign.
    d) background noise makes it difficult for a pollster and a respondent to communicate with each other.
    e) a large number of people refuse to answer a pollster's questions.

For Further Reading

Althaus, Scott. *Collective Preferences in Democratic Politics.* New York: Cambridge University Press, 2003.

Asher, Herbert. *Polling and the Public: What Every Citizen Should Know*, 8th Ed Washington, D.C.: CQ Press, 2011.

Bartels, Larry. *Unequal Democracy.* Princeton, NJ: Princeton University Press, 2008.

Berinsky, Adam. *Silent Voices: Public Opinion and Political Participation in America.* Princeton, NJ: Princeton University Press, 2005.

Clawson, Rosalee, and Zoe Oxley. *Public Opinion: Democratic Ideals and Democratic Practice.* Washington, DC: CQ Press, 2008.

Delli Carpini, Michael, and Scott Keeter. *What Americans Know about Politics and Why It Matters.* New Haven, CT: Yale University Press, 1997.

Erikson, Robert, Michael MacKuen, and James Simson. *The Macro Polity.* New York: Cambridge University Press, 2002.

Fiorina, Morris. *Culture War: The Myth of a Polarized America.* New York: Longman, 2005.

Gallup, George. *The Pulse of Democracy.* New York: Simon and Schuster, 1940.

Ginsberg, Benjamin. *The Captive Public: How Mass Opinion Promotes State Power.* New York: Basic Books, 1986.

Griffin, John, and Brian Newman. *Minority Report: Evaluating Political Equality in America.* New York: Cambridge University Press, 2008.

Hutchings, Vincent. *Public Opinion and Democratic Accountability: How Citizens Learn about Politics.* Princeton University Press, 2005.

Lau, Richard, and David Redlawsk. . *How Voters Decide: Information Processing in an Election Campaign.* New York: Cambridge University Press, 2006.

Lee, Taeku. *Mobilizing Public Opinion.* Chicago: University of Chicago Press, 2002.

Nicholson Stephen. *Voting the Agenda: Candidates, Elections, and Ballot Propositions.* Princeton, NJ: Princeton University Press, 2005.

Norrander, Barbara, and Clyde Wilcox. *Understanding Public Opinion.* Washington, DC: CQ Press, 2009.

Zaller, John. *The Nature and Origins of Mass Opinion.* New York: Cambridge University Press, 1992.

Recommended Websites

American Association for Public Opinion Research
www.aapor.org
This website is one of the premier academic sites for public opinion data on a host of political and social topics.

Gallup
www.gallup.com
The Gallup Organization has been involved in the scientific study of public opinion for more than 70 years and is highly regarded. This website contains public-opinion data archives, video archives, and international polls.

The Political Compass
www.politicalcompass.org
A political ideology is a cohesive set of beliefs that form a general philosophy about government; however, people are often unsure if they are liberal, moderate, or conservative. Go to the website for the Political Compass and take the test to see whether it helps you identify your ideology.

Polling Report
http://pollingreport.com
This independent, nonpartisan resource tracks trends in American public opinion. On this site you will find countless political opinion polls by the major media outlets, all in one place.

Public Agenda
www.publicagenda.org
Measuring public opinion from surveys can be problematic. Often samples contain selection bias, or surveys have measurement error. Public Agenda is an organization that studies public opinion on major policy issues. Its website contains critiques of public opinion.

ThisNation.com
www.thisnation.com/socialization.html
The process through which underlying political beliefs and values are formed is called political socialization. This civic-minded web page offers a brief discussion of political socialization with some related web links.

Political candidates who receive positive news coverage gain momentum, which helps them attract campaign contributions and endorsements and eventually win votes. The influence of the media on political campaigns is just one example of its important role in American democracy.

The Media

7

WHAT GOVERNMENT DOES AND WHY IT MATTERS One area in which our government's role is intended to be minimal is the realm of the news media. The Constitution's First Amendment guarantees freedom of the press, and most Americans believe that a free press is an essential condition for both liberty and democratic politics. Today the media play a central role in American politics, not only in setting the agenda of topics that Americans think about and discuss, but also in swaying opinions on political issues, politicians, and candidates.

Political candidates who receive positive news coverage gain momentum, pick up political endorsements, attract campaign contributions, and win support from voters.[1] In the 2008 campaign for the Democratic Party's presidential nomination, Barack Obama exceeded the media's expectations with his early win in the Iowa caucuses, in which he upset the front-runner, Hillary Clinton. Obama's unexpected victory earned him increased press attention and eventually led the first African American president to the White House.[2] But candidates who disappoint media expectations see their political endorsements, campaign contributions, and polling numbers dwindle. The influence of the media on political candidates is just one example of the media's vitally important role in American democracy.

The rise of the Internet has brought important changes to the media industry, journalism, and their influence on politics. In fact, the Internet is fundamentally altering the media's role in politics and American democracy. Just 20 years ago the majority of Americans got their political news from a daily newspaper, from radio, or by watching the local evening news and the national evening news from one of the three major networks (ABC, CBS, and NBC). Today America is becoming a nation of "digital citizens"—daily Internet users who turn to the Internet for politics and news.[3] The Pew Research Center reports that 86 percent of American adults use the Internet, up from 14 percent in 1995. Among Internet users in 2012, 3 in 4 read the news online and 6 in 10 go online for information about politics and campaigns.[4] More Americans now read the news online than read a print newspaper, and those reading online news are more likely to vote and participate in politics in other ways.[5] Today mainstream media must compete with niche media outlets that tailor news to their readers and viewers, and Americans increasingly find political content via blogs and social media such as Facebook and Twitter. Reading news articles linked to social media platforms is increasingly common: in 2013, more than 7 in 10 online adults used a social networking site, and as a result, hearing about news from friends and family via social media is a growing trend.

The sharing of information and opinions is critical to democracy. Discussing the right of press freedom, Thomas Jefferson wrote, "The basis of our government being the opinion of the people, the very first object should be to keep that right; and were it left to me to decide whether we should have a government without newspapers or newspapers without a government, I should not hesitate a moment to prefer the latter."[6] In the twenty-first century, newspapers and other traditional media have been joined by today's digital media as an essential component of American democracy.

chaptergoals

- Describe trends in the role of print and broadcast media in providing political information (pp. 259–66)

- Explain how the Internet has transformed the news media (pp. 267–79)

- Analyze the ways the media can influence public opinion and politics (pp. 279–84)

- Explain how politicians and others try to shape the news (pp. 284–89)

- Trace the evolution of rules that govern broadcast media (pp. 289–91)

● Traditional Media

Describe trends in the role of print and broadcast media in providing political information

The American news media are among the world's freest and most diverse. Americans have literally thousands of available options in political reporting. The wide variety of newspapers, newsmagazines, broadcast media, and online sources (blogs) regularly present information that is at odds with the government's claims, and editorial opinions are sharply critical of high-ranking officials. The freedom to speak one's mind is one of the most cherished of American political values. Without the media's investigations, citizens would be forced to rely entirely on the information provided by politicians and the government, and would be deprived of an indispensable opportunity to evaluate issues carefully and form reasoned opinions.

Americans get their news from three main sources: print media (newspapers and magazines), **broadcast media** (radio and television), and, increasingly, the Internet. For the first time, online sources have become a major source of news for Americans, just behind television viewership. The Pew Research Center's 2013 biennial media attitudes survey found that half of the public now cites the Internet as a main source for national and international news. Television (69 percent) remains the public's top source for news. Only 28 percent of Americans use newspapers and 23 percent use radio as their main news source. This picture is very different than that of a decade ago, when 44 percent said newspapers were their main source for news and just 24 percent used the Internet as a primary source. The percentage turning to television for news has changed little over the past decade (see Figure 7.1).[7]

Each of these three sources has distinctive characteristics. We discuss trends in print and broadcast media in this section, and in the next section, we will take a close look at the emergence of online news and how it is changing the media industry and the way Americans get political news.

> **broadcast media** television, radio, or other media that transmit audio and/or video content to the public

The circulation and newsstand sales of traditional newspapers and news magazines has fallen in the last decade. However, because the remaining audience includes political elites and politically engaged citizens, they remain important forums in the marketplace of ideas.

Print Media

Newspapers are the oldest medium for the dissemination of the news that continues to serve in that role today. Though no longer the primary news source for most Americans, newspapers remain important because they are influential among the political elite, who rely on the detailed coverage provided by the print media to inform and influence their views about important public matters. The print media may have a smaller audience than their newer cousins in broadcasting, but they have an especially influential audience.

The emergence of newspapers (and later radio and television networks) as mass-production businesses driven primarily by the profit motive had major implications for the role of the media in politics in the late nineteenth and early twentieth centuries. For example, the development of standardized reporting and writing practices and the dominant norm of "objectivity" in political news coverage was due in large part to this shift in the structure

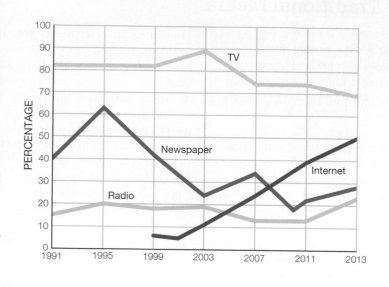

FIGURE 7.1

Americans' Main Sources for News

The media landscape for news has seen remarkable shifts in a short period of time. Twenty years ago, more than 80 percent of Americans watched news on television and more than half read news in a newspaper. Today, fewer Americans watch news on TV and just over a quarter read the newspaper. What media source has gained rather than lost its audience?

SOURCE: Pew Research Center, www.people-press .org/2013/08/08/amid-criticism-support-for-medias -watchdog-role-stands-out (accessed 4/27/14).

of media organizations. The owners of large newspaper companies, concentrated in urban areas, determined that the best way to make a profit was to appeal to as broad an audience as possible, which meant not alienating potential readers who held political views located somewhere within a broad left-right ideological mainstream. This, in turn, required methods to train and "discipline" reporters to produce a standardized, seemingly neutral news product. In fact, early specialized journalism schools, as well as major journalism prizes, were founded largely with money from the very media moguls (Joseph Pulitzer, William Randolph Hearst) who owned the first large news corporations, and whose earlier business practices did so much to tarnish the image of political journalism. In contrast, online news, as discussed in the next section, is much less likely to be objective and value neutral like traditional journalism.

These journalistic practices were successful in attracting audiences, and for a long time, most cities and towns in the country had their own newspaper. However, the long reign of newspapers as cultural and political outlets now appears to be waning, and for most traditional newspapers, recent decades have been ruinous. Competition from broadcast media and, more recently, free content online, combined with simultaneous declines in advertising revenue and circulation levels, have undermined the traditional business model of newspapers, bringing financial disaster to traditional print media.[8] Daily newspaper print circulation has declined from 62 to 49 million nationwide over the past 20 years, while advertising revenue at print newspapers has dropped dramatically since 2006 (see Figure 7.2).[9] As a result, newspapers have had to make dramatic cutbacks; estimates indicate the size of newsroom staff is down 30 percent since 2000 industrywide. These cutbacks have affected papers both big and small. The *Los Angeles Times* has reduced its news staff by half over the past decade, while others have sought bankruptcy protection, including the *Chicago Tribune*, the *Minneapolis Star Tribune*, and the *Philadelphia Inquirer*. And many others, such as the *Rocky*

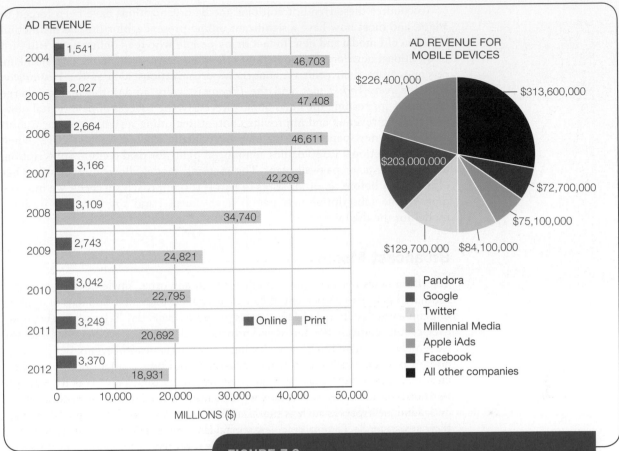

AD REVENUE

Year	Online	Print
2004	1,541	46,703
2005	2,027	47,408
2006	2,664	46,611
2007	3,166	42,209
2008	3,109	34,740
2009	2,743	24,821
2010	3,042	22,795
2011	3,249	20,692
2012	3,370	18,931

MILLIONS ($)

AD REVENUE FOR MOBILE DEVICES

$226,400,000 · $313,600,000 · $72,700,000 · $75,100,000 · $84,100,000 · $129,700,000 · $203,000,000

- Pandora
- Google
- Twitter
- Millennial Media
- Apple iAds
- Facebook
- All other companies

FIGURE 7.2

Advertising Revenue

Media is a business, not a branch of government, and so media rely on subscription and advertising money to fund their services. As newspapers' readership declined, their advertising revenue fell sharply. Some of this money shifted to online advertising, including ads for mobile devices. In 2012 total ad revenue for mobile devices was $2.6 billion, with 72 percent going to just six companies.

SOURCE: The Pew Research Center's Project for Excellence in Journalism, http://stateofthemedia .org/2013/overview-5/overview-infographic and http://stateofthemedia.org/2013/newspapers -stabilizing-but-still-threatened/newspapers-by-the-numbers (accessed 4/27/14).

Mountain News, have gone out of business altogether. Newspapers have also cut costs by closing their foreign bureaus and their offices in Washington, D.C.

The effects of a decade of newsroom cutbacks are evident in the political sphere. During the 2012 presidential election, a Pew report revealed that campaign reporters were acting primarily as megaphones, rather than as investigators, of the claims made by the candidates. This meant less reporting by journalists to interpret the claims made by the candidates. And readers noticed this shift: Pew found that nearly a third of U.S. adults stopped turning to a news outlet because it no longer provided them with the quality of news they were used to receiving.[10]

To counter these trends, traditional media organizations have been forced to adapt, and most now have a significant online presence, blurring the distinction between old media and new. In fact many people who read online news still turn to traditional news organizations, but to their online versions. Faced with shrinking revenues from their print versions, news organizations such as the *Washington Post*, the *New York Times*, and the *Economist* were among the first to charge customers for reading the news online. Recently, the success of paid digital news is increasing revenue and improving content, including reviving long-form journalism. The newspaper industry may have finally righted itself in 2012, when 450 of the nation's 1,380 dailies announced plans for paid content subscription, micropayments, or paywall plans. The metered model allows a certain number of free visits before requiring users to pay. If this approach succeeds, we may see more online subscription newspapers in the future, and a more viable business model for the digital press.

Broadcast Media

Television news reaches more Americans than any other single news source. It is estimated that over 95 percent of Americans have a television, and tens of millions of people watch national and local news programs every day. Television news, however, covers relatively few topics and provides little depth of coverage. It serves the extremely important function of alerting viewers to issues and events, but generally doesn't provide much more than a series of sound bites—brief quotes and short characterizations of the day's events, often little more than a few seconds in length. Furthermore, broadcast media do very little of their own reporting, instead relying on leading newspapers such as the *New York Times* and the *Washington Post* to set their news agenda. For example, sensational charges that President Bill Clinton had had an affair with a White House intern were reported first by the Drudge Report, a popular news aggregation website, and then picked up by the *Washington Post* and *Newsweek* before being trumpeted around the world by the broadcast media. Print and online media, as written text, also provide more detailed and complete information than radio or television media, offering a better context for analysis. (Figure 7.3 summarizes how local TV coverage has shifted over time and how it compares with newspaper coverage.)

Because they are aware of the character of television news coverage, politicians and others often seek to manipulate the news by providing the media with sound bites that will dominate news coverage for at least a few days. Twenty-four-hour news stations such as Cable News Network (CNN) offer more detail and commentary than the networks' half-hour evening news shows. Even CNN and the others, however, offer more headlines and sound bites than analysis, especially during their prime-time broadcasts. Politicians generally consider local broadcast news a friendlier venue than the national news. National reporters are often inclined to criticize and question, whereas local reporters are more likely to accept the pronouncements of national leaders at face value.

Radio news is essentially a headline service. In the short time they devote to news (usually five minutes per hour), radio stations announce the day's major events without providing much detail. All-news stations assume that most listeners are in their cars and that, as a result, the people in the audience change throughout the day as listeners reach their destinations. Thus, rather than use their time to flesh out a given set of stories, they repeat the same stories each hour to present

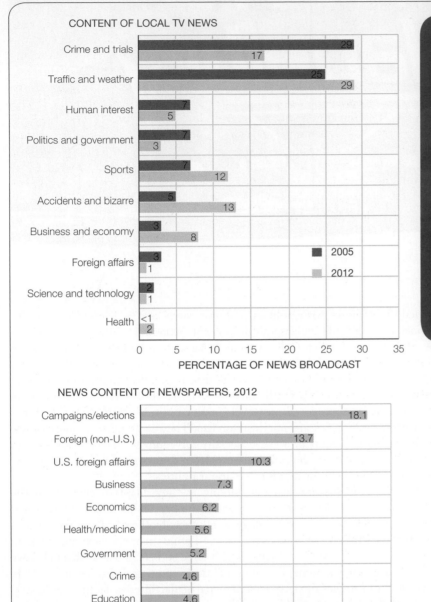

CONTENT OF LOCAL TV NEWS

Category	2005	2012
Crime and trials	29	17
Traffic and weather	25	29
Human interest	7	5
Politics and government	7	3
Sports	7	12
Accidents and bizarre	5	13
Business and economy	3	8
Foreign affairs	3	1
Science and technology	2	1
Health	<1	2

PERCENTAGE OF NEWS BROADCAST

NEWS CONTENT OF NEWSPAPERS, 2012

Category	Percentage
Campaigns/elections	18.1
Foreign (non-U.S.)	13.7
U.S. foreign affairs	10.3
Business	7.3
Economics	6.2
Health/medicine	5.6
Government	5.2
Crime	4.6
Education	4.6
Other domestic affairs	3.9

PERCENTAGE OF NEWS CONTENT

FIGURE 7.3

How Local News Coverage Has Changed

Coverage of crime and politics has decreased significantly, while traffic, weather, business, and accidents have all increased. In 2012 only 3 percent of local news coverage was dedicated to political news.

Compare the content of local TV news with that of newspapers. How do they differ?

SOURCES: The Pew Research Center's Project for Excellence in Journalism, http://stateofthemedia .org/2013/overview-5/overview-infographic (accessed 4/27/14); The Pew Research Center's Project for Excellence in Journalism, http://stateofthemedia.org/2013/newspapers -stabilizing-but-still-threatened/newspapers-by-the -numbers (accessed 4/27/14).

them to new listeners. In the 1990s radio talk shows became important sources of commentary and opinion. A number of conservative radio hosts, such as Rush Limbaugh and Sean Hannity, have huge audiences and have helped to mobilize support for conservative political causes and candidates. In the political center or left center, National Public Radio is a coveted source for moderate talk radio and provides in-depth political reporting, while the now-defunct Air America hoped to achieve on the left what Limbaugh had achieved on the right.

Major media personalities like conservative talk show host Sean Hannity make use of radio, television, and the Internet to reach as large an audience as possible. His radio show is heard by approximately 13.5 million Americans each week, making him an influential political commentator.

Comedy talk shows with political content, such as *The Daily Show* or *The Late Show*, have become increasingly important, attracting millions of television viewers. Comedian Stephen Colbert went so far as to establish a political action committee (PAC) during the 2012 presidential primaries and to enter the Republican primary in his home state of South Carolina in an effort to draw attention to problems with current campaign finance laws. These shows use humor, sarcasm, and social criticism to cover almost every major political event. Yet talk shows that cover political topics are not just for fun. They have become increasingly important sources of political news, especially for younger viewers. Pew surveys show that many Americans get political news from these shows and that followers of comedic talk shows are well informed about politics.[11]

The broadcast media are also diversifying as they adapt to changes in the American population, especially the growing number of Latinos. California and Texas are both projected to become majority Hispanic by the middle of the twenty-first century. In both states, as well as others, the Latino-oriented television channels Telemundo, Univision, and MSN Latino attract large audiences. These channels have Spanish-language programming, including political reporting and other news. They also may focus on topics or perspectives of particular interest to their audience. Coverage of the Arizona and Alabama illegal immigration laws, for example, in Hispanic media outlets was significantly different from that of mainstream media. News outlets aimed at other ethnic groups have also become common in many areas. As America has become more multicultural, multiethnic television—a form of niche media—has broadened news media.

Mass Media Ownership

One noteworthy feature of the traditional media in the United States is the growing concentration of its ownership. The United States boasts approximately 1,400 daily newspapers, 2,000 television stations, and more than 13,000 radio stations (20 percent of which are devoted to news, talk, or public affairs). Despite these substantial numbers overall, the number of traditional news-gathering sources operating nationally is actually quite small—several wire services, four broadcast networks, two elite newspapers, three newsmagazines, and a smattering of other sources, such as the national correspondents of a few large local papers and several small, independent radio networks. More than three-fourths of the daily newspapers in the United States are owned by large media conglomerates such as the Hearst, McClatchy, and Gannett corporations. Much of the national news that is published by local newspapers is provided by one wire service, the Associated Press, while additional coverage is provided by services run by several major newspapers, including the *New York Times* and the *Chicago Tribune*. More than 500 of the nation's television stations are affiliated with one of the four networks and carry that network's evening news programs. Dozens of others carry PBS (Public Broadcasting System) news. Several hundred local radio stations also carry network news or National Public Radio news broadcasts.

At the same time, though, there are only five truly national newspapers: the *Wall Street Journal*, the *Christian Science Monitor* (only online), *USA Today*, the *New York Times*, and the *Washington Post*. National news is also carried to millions of Americans by magazines though they are declining in readership. Beginning in the late 1980s, CNN became another major news source for Americans, especially after its coverage of the Persian Gulf War. However, the number of news sources—those doing actual news gathering, not simply relying on news reporting by others—has remained essentially the same, or has declined. Some of the most popular online news outlets are electronic versions of the conventional print or broadcast media.

The trend toward less variety in traditional media has been accelerated by changes in media ownership, which became possible in large part due to the relaxation of government regulations in the 1980s and '90s. The enactment of the 1996 Telecommunications Act opened the way for additional consolidation in the media industry, and a wave of mergers and consolidations has further reduced the field of independent media across the country. For example, the Australian press baron Rupert Murdoch owns the Fox network plus a host of radio, television, and newspaper properties around the world, known collectively as News Corporation, the world's second-largest media conglomerate. In 2007, Murdoch won control of the *Wall Street Journal*, consolidating his position as one of the world's most powerful publishers. News Corporation owns 800 media companies in more than 50 countries and has a net worth of $5 billion. A small number of giant corporations now control a wide swath of media holdings, including television networks, movie studios, record companies, cable channels and local cable providers, book publishers, magazines, and newspapers. Clear Channel Communications, for example, a Texas-based media conglomerate, owns 850 radio stations—by far the largest number controlled by a single company. These developments have prompted questions about whether enough competition exists among the media to produce a truly diverse set of views on political and corporate matters, or even whether the United States has become a prisoner of media monopolies.[12]

As major newspapers, television stations, and radio networks fall into fewer and fewer hands, the risk increases that politicians and citizens who express less-popular or minority viewpoints will have difficulty finding a public forum. Examples include 2012 Republican presidential candidate Ron Paul, who despite favorable showing in early nominating events, such as the Iowa caucuses and

What are the consequences for the marketplace of ideas when several large companies own huge segments of the media market? Clear Channel Communications owns major radio stations across the country, including stations in Los Angeles, St. Louis, Houston, and New York.

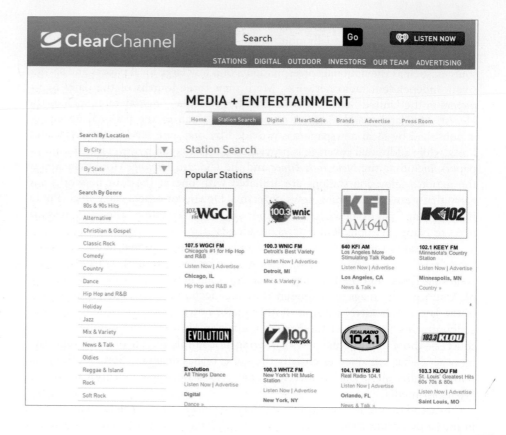

media monopoly the ownership and control of the media by a few large corporations

the New Hampshire primary, received little national media coverage because his libertarian ideas were outside the mainstream of his political party. **Media monopolies** may also be a reason for the relatively scant mainstream media coverage of the Occupy Wall Street protests, which sought to bring attention to the issue of growing income inequality. (See Chapter 8 for more discussion of the Occupy movement.) Increasingly, these groups turn to the Internet to express their views. Ultimately, media are private corporations whose business is to sell audiences to advertisers, not to supply news or entertainment. This complicates the essential role media play in democracy.

One negative consequence of media concentration may be a steadily growing distrust of the press. The political scientist Jonathan Ladd argues that from the 1950s through the 1970s, competition in American party politics and the media industry reached historic lows.[13] When competition later intensified in both of these realms, the public's distrust of the institutional media grew, leading the public to resist the mainstream press's reporting and to turn toward alternative partisan media outlets—those expressly favored by Republicans or Democrats. As a result, public opinion and voting behavior are now increasingly shaped by partisan media, such as Fox News on the right and MSNBC on the left. While it is not possible to suppress party and media competition in the twenty-first century, and certainly not in a new media environment, Ladd argues that we need new ways to augment the public's political knowledge. In an age of digital media, it is more important than ever for citizens to find and evaluate information.

New Media and Online News

Explain how the Internet has transformed the news media

The twenty-first century has already experienced a profound transformation of the media. The impact of the Internet in mass communication parallels that of the printing press in nineteenth-century America, which saw the rise of the **penny press** and widespread literacy.[14] Today, even as the newspaper business struggles for its life, readership of online news has soared. The Internet has become the medium of choice for all age groups below 50 years old to consume entertainment, news, and information about politics (see Figure 7.4). In 2000, just 35 percent of adult Internet users said they looked for news or information about politics or the upcoming campaigns online. As of 2012, that number had risen to over 60 percent.[15] Among young adults, the number is even higher: 70 percent of 18- to 29-year-olds say that the Internet is their main source of news. Beside online-only newspapers, other forums include news websites, blogs, social media, YouTube, and Twitter. **News aggregators**, such as Google News and Real Clear Politics, provide links to thousands of stories covered in the news each day, as well as the latest public opinion polls and their own synthesis of the headline news.

The Internet is particularly convenient for obtaining news, and formats for doing so are becoming more diverse and interactive. A Pew 2012 Election Survey found 48 percent of Internet-using registered voters watched news reports online about the presidential election, and 40 percent watched previously recorded videos of a candidate speech, press conference, or a debate. Watching online videos to understand a political issue was equally common. News about politics

penny press cheap, tabloid-style newspaper produced in the nineteenth century, when mass production of inexpensive newspapers first became possible due to the steam-powered printing press; a penny press cost one cent compared with other papers, which cost more than five cents

news aggregator an application or feed that collects web content such as news headlines, blogs, podcasts, online videos, and more in one location for easy viewing

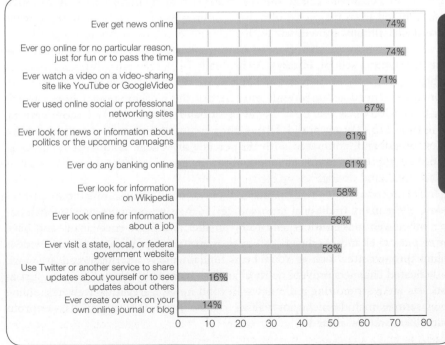

FIGURE 7.4

What Americans Use the Internet For

Obtaining news is one of the major reasons that Americans go online.

SOURCE: Pew Research Project, Internet Use over Time, www.pewinternet.org/data-trend /internet-use/internet-use-over-time (accessed 4/27/14).

The rise of new media has made it easier for Americans with Internet access to get political news, but one in five Americans is still completely offline. For example, there are neighborhoods in large cities like Chicago where over 80 percent of households lack broadband access.

digital citizen a daily Internet user with high-speed home Internet access and the technology and literacy skills to go online for employment, news, politics, entertainment, commerce, and other activities

is often humorous, and 37 percent watched a video parodying a political issue. Watching online campaign ads is common, with this activity reported by one in three Internet users. Streaming live videos is a growing substitute for television for some, as 28 percent of this population watched a live video online of a candidate speech or debate. Presidential addresses are now regularly streamed live, and millions tune in to hear the president in this format.[16] (See the "Who Are Americans?" feature for more information on where Americans get their news and who watches online news videos.)

The rise of digital media has changed the way that people get information and share it, affecting everything from political activism, political campaigns, public opinion, and more. Online media are more diverse and have created a more democratic and participatory press, one in which citizens and nonprofit organizations now play a prominent role. No longer relegated to the letters-to-the-editor section found in most print publications, readers can now post comments online, upload videos, and participate in a community providing feedback on almost all online news articles. Online media, by representing a wider range of political views than traditional media, have created a more democratic press and vibrant media environment.

The term *digital citizenship* refers to the ability to participate in society and politics online. In much the same way that education and literacy promoted democracy and economic growth in the nineteenth century, today's Internet has the potential to benefit society as a whole and facilitate political participation by individuals within society. Like education, the Internet helps provide the information and skills needed for democratic engagement and economic opportunity.[17] It facilitates social inclusion through greater access to political information and news.[18]

However, regular and effective use of the Internet requires high-speed access, technical skills, and literacy to evaluate and use information online.[19] Individuals without the access or skills to use the Internet may be increasingly uninformed and excluded from the world of politics online. As of 2013, 7 in 10 Americans were **digital citizens**, individuals with high-speed access at home (beyond mobile access), and more than 8 in 10 Americans used the Internet in some location (e.g., home, school, library). As of 2013, 74 percent of whites, 62 percent of blacks, but only 56 percent of Latinos are digital citizens by this definition (home high-speed access). While only half of the working poor (those earning less than $30,000 a year) had home broadband, 9 out of 10 of those earning more than $75,000 a year did. Fifty-eight percent of high school graduates have home broadband, compared with 90 percent of college graduates.[20] This suggests that there are significant inequalities in access to digital media, what is called the digital divide.[21]

In this section we look at the major types of online news available to citizens today. While many traditional news sources, such as newspapers, now publish online, other web news outlets tend to be smaller and more specialized, and have lower personnel and overhead costs than mainstream publishers. Sharing videos online through sites such as YouTube is fundamentally altering broadcast news, as dedicated channels provide political analysis, commentary, and comedy, just as podcasts are restructuring radio news. Beyond news aggregation websites, online news sources include niche journalism, citizen journalism and blogs, nonprofit journalism, and social media.

Where Do Americans Get Their News?

Demographics of News Audiences

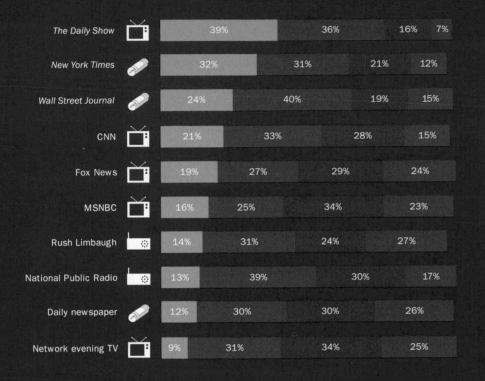

Source	18–29	30–49	50–64	65+
The Daily Show	39%	36%	16%	7%
New York Times	32%	31%	21%	12%
Wall Street Journal	24%	40%	19%	15%
CNN	21%	33%	28%	15%
Fox News	19%	27%	29%	24%
MSNBC	16%	25%	34%	23%
Rush Limbaugh	14%	31%	24%	27%
National Public Radio	13%	39%	30%	17%
Daily newspaper	12%	30%	30%	26%
Network evening TV	9%	31%	34%	25%

Age (in years)

18–29　　30–49　　50–64　　65+

In a democracy like the United States, people need information to understand current issues and the government's actions. But not all Americans get their news from the same place. Sources for news vary by medium (print, TV, radio, and Internet) as well as source (e.g., *The Daily Show*, Fox News).

NOTE: Figures may not add to 100 percent due to rounding.

Who Watches News Videos Online?

Age

18–29	48%
30–49	43%
50–64	27%
65+	11%

Income

< $30,000	25%
$30,000–49,999	34%
$50,000–74,999	36%
> $75,000	57%

Education

High school diploma or less	22%
Some college	43%
College or graduate degree	53%

SOURCES: Pew Research Center, www.people-press.org/2012/09/27/section-4-demographics-and-political-views-of-news-audiences (accessed 4/28/14); Pew Research Center, www.journalism.org/files/2014/03/News-Video-on-the-Web.pdf (accessed 4/28/14).

for critical analysis

1. Are there differences between how younger adults and older adults get their news? What might be some consequences of such differences?

2. How has digital media affected how Americans get their news?

Niche Journalism

niche journalism news reporting devoted to a targeted portion (subset) of a journalism market sector or for a portion of readers/viewers based on content or ideological presentation

In the gap opened by the decline of traditional print media, the last decade has seen the rise of **niche journalism** and specialty publications. Bloomberg News, one of the most successful specialty online sources, has hundreds of thousands of readers paying a large annual fee for detailed business-related news. In politics, Roll Call, The Hill, the National Journal, Congressional Quarterly, Salon, the Huffington Post, Real Clear Politics, and Politico, the niche leader, have detailed political reporting inside the Beltway (that is, in Washington, D.C., which is encircled by freeways). Niche journalism feeds citizens' interest in politics across the full range of the political spectrum. These niche outlets are supplemented by a rich array of international and foreign online news sources.

News consumers have shifted from a few general-purpose sources, such as the evening television news and a local newspaper, to a large number of niche publications and specialized sources: business news from one source; weather from another; sports, politics, and commentary from others. The radio has long been a primary medium for information about local traffic, but today Google Maps on smartphones provides up-to-the-minute traffic information and routing with the touch of a screen. Sports fans once depended on local evening news for information about their favorite teams but now find it online through a variety of niche media outlets, including EPSN online and Deadspin. The rise of niche journalism has fundamentally changed how Americans consume news and what they read.

Citizen Journalism and Blogs

The old media system was dominated by professional journalists, trained in journalism schools, who served as gatekeepers in determining what was front-page news and how political events were to be interpreted. This system had benefits and costs: the quality was high, but the diversity of opinions was relatively low. The media's gatekeeper role continues, but the incredible diversity of online media is changing journalism and the very nature of "news coverage." Online news is creating a new generation of whistle-blowers, enhancing the media's traditional role as a watchdog for the people against government corruption.

citizen journalism news reported and distributed by citizens, rather than professional journalists and for-profit news organizations

A distinguishing feature of the digital media is **citizen journalism**, which is interactive and participatory. Citizen journalism includes news reporting and political commentary by ordinary citizens, and even crisis coverage from eyewitnesses on the scene. Because it involves a wider range of voices in gathering news and interpreting political events, contemporary news reporting and commentary are more democratic. Magnifying the power of the Internet is the near-universal availability of digital cameras on cell phones, which gives millions of Americans the capacity to photograph or film events. At the same time, Internet sites such as YouTube permit users to upload video clips that can be viewed by hundreds of thousands of subscribers or relayed by the mainstream media for even wider dissemination. When a citizen using a mobile phone captured video of police pepper-spraying peaceful Occupy Wall Street demonstrators at the University of California–Davis in November 2011, it became headline news; the video was viewed by millions and fueled mounting concerns about police brutality toward the Occupy protesters.

In 2011 an ordinary citizen recorded video of police pepper-spraying peaceful Occupy protesters at the University of California–Davis. This video was widely shared on the Internet and the story became headline news.

Citizen journalism is enhanced by the ease with which anyone can start a blog. There are thousands of blogs, covering virtually every topic imaginable, and a large share of these include political news and commentary on local, national, and world events. Many blogs are citizen-run and are more interactive and representative of the diversity of American views than traditional news, which generally reflects the priorities of political elites. A number of blogs, such as the Daily Kos, FiveThirtyEight, and the Monkey Cage have thousands of loyal readers who regularly critique stories presented by the print and broadcast media. These online discussion and comment forums create a community for readers, further interpreting the news.

Twitter is also an important tool for citizen journalism. While only 5 to 7 percent of Americans use Twitter for politics, these users tend to be public opinion leaders, and Twitter is the preferred social media platform for political elites and candidates. A study of millions of Twitter messages about Obama during the 2012 presidential election found that the *Washington Post* was the only traditional media corporation cited in the top 10 most frequently cited websites. The other nine most-cited sites were blogs, YouTube videos, and other alternative online sources. Thus social media and citizen journalism are not replicating traditional media, but are giving political activists a new voice in shaping the news.

Citizen journalism supplements the work of professional journalists in many important ways. The diversity of online media has created new opinion leaders, new voices, and even, at times, improved information. In recent years, for example, bloggers have uncovered major factual errors in media reports and forced the networks and newspapers to issue corrections. Sharp-eyed bloggers have proven adept at recognizing faked or Photoshopped photographs in news stories—for example, pointing out that major news outlets, including the *New York Times*, the *Los Angeles Times*, Reuters, and the Associated Press, had presented doctored photos in their reports from Iraq, Afghanistan, and the Israeli-Palestinian conflict.[22] Because bloggers do not have strict editorial boards, they can post a story within minutes. This ability to scoop the mainstream media often means that bloggers are now the ones framing stories about political candidates, and candidates have only minutes to respond to accusations before the story breaks in the mainstream media.[23] By sharply lowering the technological and financial barriers that previously prevented all but a few individuals and interests from reaching mass audiences, blogs increase the ability of ordinary people to engage in effective political action. (In Chapter 8, we will take a closer look at the Internet's effects on political participation.)

To be sure, the open, freewheeling nature of blogging often means that there is little of the traditional quality control employed by "respectable," institutional old media. Because they do not face the burden of fact-checking required for the mainstream media, even well-meaning bloggers can post false information. This could be one reason why misinformation about some political issues is higher among blog readers than those reading online news from the mainstream press.[24]

Nonprofit Journalism

As traditional news organizations have cut budgets and especially investigative journalism, political information is increasingly emanating from universities, think tanks, nonprofit organizations, and private foundations. Think tanks such as the Brookings Institution, the Cato Institute, the Hoover Institution, the Heritage Foundation, and the Center for American Progress provide information, blogs, and analysis on current events to influence public debate. Universities have expanded their public outreach, encouraging faculty to explain their findings for a general audience; as a result, university faculty are increasingly cited in the mainstream media, and many are bloggers themselves. Community-based nonprofit newspapers are supported by local foundations seeking to fill the void in local news as local papers close their doors. The Kaiser Family Foundation was early in creating *Kaiser Health News*. The Bill and Melinda Gates Foundation, established by Microsoft founder Bill Gates, provides extensive funding to National Public Radio. A Pew Research Center report estimated that, in 2006–10, $14 million in nonprofit funding was spent in new media. But this represents only one-tenth of the $1.6 billion in print newspaper revenue lost during this same period.[25]

Social Media

Social media, such as Twitter and Facebook, are important players in news and political communication. Some 73 percent of online adults used a social networking site of some kind as of 2013 (the percentage increases to 90 percent among 18- to 29-year-olds). Facebook is the dominant social networking

social media web- and mobile-based technologies that are used to turn communication into interactive dialogue among organizations, communities, and individuals; social media technologies take on many different forms including blogs, Wikis, podcasts, pictures, video, Facebook, and Twitter

platform in sheer numbers of users, but 42 percent of online adults use multiple social networking sites.[26]

Both Facebook and Twitter are online networking forums that allow users to share content, news stories, photos, and videos with others, from a handful of close friends to thousands of people. Because they are more personalized and interactive than anonymous news organizations, social media are becoming an increasingly popular means for Americans to receive political information from the candidates and interest groups they support. In turn, candidates for political office, political organizations, and interest groups have been quick to adopt Facebook and Twitter as means of communicating with their supporters and providing them a continual feed of new information. In 2007 one of the founders of Facebook helped the Obama presidential campaign establish a Facebook page. The site's fund-raising section allowed visitors to set personal fund-raising goals and invite other registered friends to help them reach those goals. The Obama site attracted more than a million visitors during the 2008 campaign for the Democratic presidential nomination.[27] As of 2014, Obama's page had 40 million followers. Obama is the first American president for whom social media has played a significant role in politics and governing.

As the name "social media" suggests, social networking is a key feature of the dissemination of news through social media platforms. A majority of social media users follow links to full news stories after learning about a story from friends and family. And both Facebook and Twitter have contributed to political mobilization and information sharing by creating virtual social networks where groups of like-minded individuals can quickly and easily share information. Twitter was the communication tool of choice for organizing the Occupy Wall Street demonstrations in 2011, as thousands of Americans camped out in cities across the United States to protest growing income inequality between the top 1 percent of American income earners and the bottom 99 percent. (See Figure 7.5 for more on social media and political engagement.)

Benefits of Online News

So why have new media become so popular? Americans may prefer online news because of (1) the convenience of getting the news online, (2) the up-to-the-moment currency of the information available online, (3) the depth of the information available online, and (4) the diversity of online viewpoints.[28] At the same time, changes to the media arising from the rapid proliferation of the Internet have raised a multitude of concerns, as we will see in the section "Concerns about Online News."

Convenience Information online is convenient and always available for those who have regular access to the Internet at home or, increasingly, through mobile devices such as smartphones. Pew surveys show that nearly half of those who use online news and political information cite its convenience.[29] Google News, for example, reports the headline news (domestic and international) from thousands of sources updated by the minute, with 24-hour-a-day convenience, providing access to information with much more depth than that found when tuning in to the national evening news on television. Because political knowledge is central to the formation of political attitudes, the convenience of

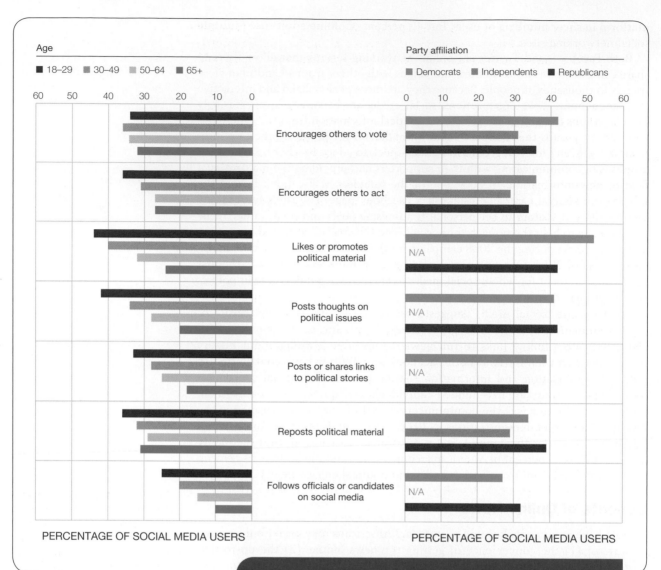

Age

- 18–29
- 30–49
- 50–64
- 65+

Party affiliation

- Democrats
- Independents
- Republicans

Encourages others to vote

Encourages others to act

Likes or promotes political material — N/A

Posts thoughts on political issues — N/A

Posts or shares links to political stories — N/A

Reposts political material

Follows officials or candidates on social media — N/A

PERCENTAGE OF SOCIAL MEDIA USERS

PERCENTAGE OF SOCIAL MEDIA USERS

FIGURE 7.5

Social Media and Political Engagement

Many Americans who use social media websites and Twitter use those social media websites to participate in politics. The graph shows the percentages of users who report having used social media for specific political activities. Across all types of activities, younger people are more likely to use social media to participate. Democrats and Republicans vary in their use of social media depending on the activity. Do either Democrats or Republicans appear more likely overall to use social media for political purposes?

SOURCE: Pew Research Internet Project, www.pewinternet.org/2012/10/19/social-media-and-political-engagement (accessed 4/27/14).

online news may lead to a more informed and engaged citizenry. Use of online political information is associated with more interest in politics, greater knowledge of politics, and a greater likelihood of discussing politics with friends and family.[30]

Currency One of the fundamental changes ushered in by an era of online news is the speed with which local, national, and international events are covered, as well as the scope of coverage. Major news stories regularly break first online, and are later reported through print newspapers and television. Social media have accelerated even further the speed with which news travels around the globe. For example, news of Osama bin Laden's death in May 2011 spread rapidly through text messaging, smartphones, and social media outlets such as Facebook and Twitter even before it could be verified by traditional media.

Depth Online news provides more information than the 60-second sound bites found in television and radio news. By blending more-detailed treatment of topics with the visual and emotive appeal of streaming videos, the Internet shares qualities both of print media (promoting knowledge) and of the visual aspects of television (promoting interest and engagement).[31] The multimedia capacity of the Internet notwithstanding, most websites still rely heavily upon written text, and most political "web surfing" consists mainly of reading, which facilitates greater recall of information and, in turn, encourages the acquisition of political knowledge.[32]

Diversity Online sources are much more diverse than those found in the traditional media, and this diversity may lead to an increase in political knowledge

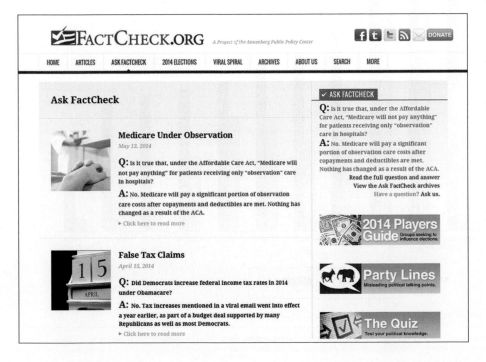

The Internet has facilitated both diversity and specialization in news media. Websites such as FactCheck.org exist solely for the purpose of evaluating statements made by U.S. politicians. The site corrects misinformation every day, such as incorrect claims about how the Affordable Care Act works.

Internet Use and Political News

Internet access is increasing around the world, and it is transforming the way that some populations are learning about politics. As the graph shows, developing countries have seen some of the largest increases in Internet use in recent years. For example, while Internet use grew by 7 percent in the United States and about 5 percent in Norway between 2008 and 2012, it nearly quintupled in South Africa and doubled in many other developing or newly industrialized countries.

As we see in this chapter (and in the next chapter on political participation), the Internet provides new opportunities for people to learn about politics and become informed participants in the political process. However, within countries, not all groups have equal access to the Internet and even those who do have access may not use it to become more informed about politics. A study of media use in the European Union found that those who are more educated and those employed full time are more likely to use the Internet for news than other groups.[a] In the developing world, this trend is even more extreme, as Internet access is often limited to the highly educated, the wealthy, or the middle class living in urban centers. Studies also show that in the developing world (as in the developed world) use of the Internet for political news competes with use for entertainment and social networking.[b]

Will increasing internet access help people in developing and newly industrialized countries become more informed and effective participants in the political process? Or will it reinforce existing inequalities between the rich and the poor, and between the highly educated and less educated? Should we be concerned about the same patterns in the United States? Why or why not?

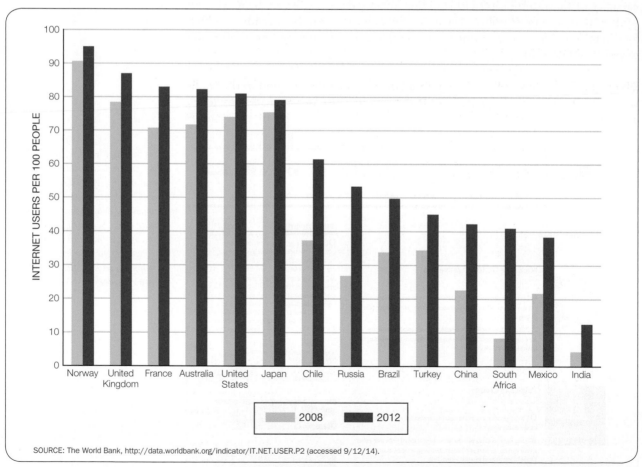

SOURCE: The World Bank, http://data.worldbank.org/indicator/IT.NET.USER.P2 (accessed 9/12/14).

[a] European Commission, "Media Use in the European Union," March 2012, http://ec.europa.eu/public_opinion/archives/eb/eb76/eb76_media_en.pdf (accessed 9/12/14).
[b] Pew Research Global Attitudes Project, "Emerging Nations Embrace Internet, Mobile Technology," February 13, 2014, http://www.pewglobal.org/2014/02/13/emerging-nations-embrace-internet-mobile-technology/ (accessed 9/12/14).

and interest.[33] While major players online certainly do include mainstream outlets (such as websites sponsored by television networks and major newspapers in the United States),[34] the Internet remains populated by a wide range of information sources. By making foreign media such as the British Broadcasting Company (BBC) and Al Jazeera television easily available, the Internet has reduced the importance of physical proximity and created a truly global shared culture. Millions went online to watch live broadcasts of Egyptian citizens protesting for democratic freedoms in 2011. By including links to columns by ideological liberals, moderates, conservatives, and libertarians, sites such as Real Clear Politics highlight the diversity of political news online. Such a vast array of voices, of course, means that online sources also can provide questionable information, misinformation, or outright lies—just as can happen in mainstream media and even presidential debates. To verify media reports found in both traditional and online media, there are new websites, such as FactCheck.org and PolitiFact.com, devoted exclusively to checking the veracity of political claims.

Decentralization and Local News A long-standing concern of scholars of traditional media has been the "nationalization of the news" that results when most political news emanates from inside the Washington, D.C., Beltway, to the detriment of local news coverage. Ten years ago the dominance of national wire services, such as the Associated Press, and budget constraints by local newspapers resulted in a dearth of relevant local news reporting. New media have decentered the political news. Online local newspapers, blogs, city and local government websites and Facebook pages, community newsletters, email listservs, social media, and other new sources have made local news and local political news more available than in previous decades. Almost every city government has a Facebook page and website, which publish news and events, as well as offer services. A 2011 Pew survey found over 50 percent of Americans use the Internet to get community or neighborhood news.[35] Readily available local news coverage may engage citizens in politics in their communities.

Concerns about Online News

While online news holds significant promise for improving access to the political information citizens need, the shift toward online media has also given rise to several major concerns. These potential disadvantages include a decline in investigative journalism, uneven quality in news content, and negative effects on knowledge and tolerance.

Loss of Investigative Power In a democracy, the press is expected to be a watchdog for the people and to inform citizens about government abuses of power. Stated another way, democracies depend on news organizations to inform the people about current events and help citizens hold their leaders accountable for their actions. The greatest challenge for contemporary news organizations is to generate enough revenue to finance traditional investigative journalism.[36] This activity requires more time and resources than other aspects of the news, and it may be the most important. When readers paid subscription fees to read the news, circulation was high and advertising provided sufficient revenue to allow newspapers and, later, broadcasters to cover both basic news (weather, sports, business) and political events. Revenue from publishing basic news would subsidize political analysis and investigative journalism. By breaking apart mainstream news organizations, online news may actually reduce the media's ability to engage in the kind of sustained, in-depth reporting that is critical to the media's watchdog role and thus to the health of American democracy.

More Variation in the Quality of News As already noted, the growing diversity of online news has led to substantial variation in the quality of available information. Multiple perspectives certainly do provide citizens with a well-stocked marketplace of ideas, but the freewheeling nature of the Internet also means that hate speech, unsubstantiated rumors, and factual errors can overwhelm thoughtful, original, and civic-oriented voices. And while viral media may elevate the watchdog function of the media, the misinformation and unsubstantiated rumors that are part of viral media can substitute for objective truth as claims are widely repeated. This is especially so in anonymous online forums. Political scientist Dianne Bystrom has noted that "the online universe of political commentary operates outside traditional media editorial boundaries and is sometimes incisive but often offensive and unsubstantiated."[37]

Political candidates and political leaders are particularly susceptible to attack when negative stories go viral and spread quickly without the traditional media filters of fact checking and respect for the privacy of public figures. This can have real consequences; for example, scholars have found that Hillary Clinton's 2008 presidential campaign was hurt by negative and arguably sexist discussion on the blogs.[38] False rumors that President Obama was not a natural-born citizen and therefore not eligible to be president under Article II of the U.S. Constitution spread rapidly on the Internet and spilled over into mainstream news. These "birther movement" conspiracy theories alleged that Obama was born in Kenya, not Hawaii, and that his birth certificate was a forgery. Extensive media coverage of the birther movement allowed what many viewed as an attack against a sitting president to become headline news, something that may not have occurred in a pre-Internet era. Belief in these theories has persisted, despite Obama's preelection release of his official long-form birth certificate from Hawaii in 2008, the posting of a copy of his birth certificate online, and confirmation by the Hawaii Department of Health based on the original documents.

Potential Effects on Knowledge and Tolerance Perhaps the greatest concern about politics in the digital age goes to the heart of modern democracy: Do online media ultimately help or hinder progress toward the ideal of a well-informed citizenry that can govern itself effectively? The very diversity of online news may actually *lower* tolerance for social and political diversity. Most bloggers do not abide by traditional media's principle of objective journalism, in which both sides of an argument are reported. Instead, the specialization of information online and on cable television means that liberals and conservatives alike can turn to specialized websites and television channels that cater to their underlying assumptions and that avoid exposing readers/viewers to information that might challenge their preconceived beliefs.[39] Even the active nature of the online experience can contribute to the compartmentalization of the electorate. On the Internet, an individual must seek out information, compared with the passive process of simply watching or listening to television.[40] The natural tendency to select online news that conforms with our own beliefs is exacerbated by the way search engines cater to our individual preferences—what one scholar has called the "filter bubble," which screens out exposure to information that might challenge or broaden our worldview.[41]

The benefits and possibilities created by digital media for the American political process may well outweigh these concerns about accuracy, reliability, ethical practices, and depth of reporting. If the new media are to create a more informed democratic process, citizens must have "information literacy," or the ability to find and evaluate information.[42] Greater access to information online makes education and critical thinking among citizens more important than ever before.

● Media Influence

Analyze the ways the media can influence public opinion and politics

The content and character of news and public affairs programming—what the media choose to present and how they present it—can have far-reaching political consequences. The media can shape and modify, if not fully form, the public's perception of events, issues, and institutions. Media coverage can rally support for, or intensify opposition to, national policies on matters as weighty as health care, the economy, or international wars. Media disclosures can greatly enhance, or fatally damage, the careers of public figures, as discussed earlier. At the same time, the media are influenced by the individuals or groups who are subjects of the news. The president, in particular, has the power to set the news agenda through speeches and actions. All politicians, for that matter, seek to shape or manipulate their media images by cultivating good relations with reporters and through news leaks and staged news events.

In recent American political history, the media have played a central role in many major events. For example, the media were a critically important factor in the civil rights movement of the 1950s and '60s. Television images showing peaceful civil rights marchers attacked by club-swinging police helped to generate sympathy among northern whites for the civil rights struggle and greatly increased the pressure on Congress to bring an end to segregation.[43] To take a second example, the media were instrumental in compelling the Nixon administration to negotiate an end to American involvement in the Vietnam War. Beginning in 1967 the media, reacting in part to a shift in elite opinion, portrayed the war as misguided and unwinnable, and as a result helped turn popular sentiment against continued American involvement.[44]

The media were also central actors in the Watergate affair, the cluster of scandals that ultimately forced President Richard Nixon, the landslide victor in the 1972 presidential election, to resign from office in disgrace just two years later. A relentless series of investigations launched by the *Washington Post*, the *New York Times*, and the television networks led to disclosures of the various abuses of which

During the 1960s, civil rights protesters learned a variety of techniques designed to elicit sympathetic media coverage. Television images of police brutality in Alabama led directly to the enactment of the 1965 Civil Rights Act.

Nixon was guilty, ultimately forcing him to choose between resignation and almost certain impeachment.

More recently, the media were crucial actors in the U.S. decision to invade Iraq in March 2003, despite the fact that Iraq had not invaded a neighboring country or attacked the United States. In the wake of the September 11 terrorist attacks, harsh media coverage of Iraqi leader Saddam Hussein, combined with White House claims that Iraq was harboring weapons of mass destruction (WMDs), led 70 percent of Americans to approve of the invasion of Iraq. (It was later determined that, in fact, Iraq did not have any WMDs. The news media, including the *New York Times*, issued a public apology to readers for some of its coverage of claims of Iraqi WMDs.) The Pew Research Center reported in a 2003 survey that individuals getting the news from mainstream American media were more supportive of the Iraq invasion, while those relying on foreign news coverage, political comedy shows, or online news were more likely to oppose the invasion.

Conservatives have long charged that the liberal biases of reporters and journalists result in distorted news coverage.[45] While journalists may lean in a Democratic direction, journalists generally defend their professionalism, insisting that their personal political leanings do not affect the way they perform their jobs.[46] Moreover, those who decry "the liberal media" seldom acknowledge the partisan or ideological leanings of media owners. Rupert Murdoch, the CEO of News Corporation (the parent company of Fox News and the *Wall Street Journal*), is a politically active conservative. Philip Anschutz, owner of the *Examiner* newspapers in San Francisco, Washington, and other cities, has been a major financial contributor to the Republican Party and to GOP candidates, including George W. Bush. As discussed in detail in the previous section, the diversity of online news sources, however, may mean that debates about liberal or conservative bias in the mainstream media are becoming less important.

How the Media Influence Politics

Traditional and digital media influence American politics in a number of important ways.[47] The power of all media collectively, both traditional and online, lies in their ability to shape what issues Americans think about (agenda setting) and what opinions Americans hold about those issues (framing and priming).

Agenda Setting and Selection Bias The first source of media power is **agenda setting**; that is, the media help to set the agenda for political discussion. Agenda setting involves identifying the issues that will receive attention by the media, which means that some things are deemed important while others are not. Groups and forces that wish to bring their ideas before the public in order to generate support for policy proposals or political candidacies must secure media coverage. If the media are persuaded that an idea is newsworthy, then they may declare it an "issue" that must be confronted or a "problem" to be solved, thus clearing the first hurdle in the policy-making process. If, on the other hand, an idea lacks or loses media appeal, its chance of resulting in new programs or policies is diminished.

After September 11, President George W. Bush had little difficulty convincing the media that terrorism and his administration's efforts to forestall further terrorist attacks merited a dominant place on the national agenda. Not surprisingly, the American-led military campaigns in Afghanistan and Iraq dominated the news throughout 2002 and 2003. Some stories have such overwhelming significance that the main concern of political leaders is not whether a story will receive attention—wars and natural disasters always receive attention—but whether the leaders themselves will figure prominently and positively in media accounts. This was certainly true in 2005, when Hurricane Katrina struck the Gulf Coast. There was no question that this storm and the damage it caused would be on the national agenda; the question was how the press and the public would apportion blame and credit. As the story took shape, the media found little to praise in the belated, haphazard emergency and relief efforts. Local, state, and national leaders were all faulted for the region's lack of preparedness and a botched relief plan, with the Bush administration and the Federal Emergency Management Agency (FEMA) receiving the largest share of blame for these failures. In 2008–09, the news agenda was dominated by the global financial crisis and the severe economic recession that ensued. More recently, the Affordable Care Act and national health insurance has dominated national headlines. Yet many important issues are not on the media's agenda, such as growing income inequality and legislative reform. Likewise, these issues are often absent from major policy discussions.

In many instances, the media serve as conduits for agenda-setting efforts by competing groups and forces. Occasionally, however, journalists themselves are instrumental in setting the agenda of political discussion. The Watergate scandal that destroyed Nixon's presidency was in some measure initiated and driven by the *Washington Post* and the national television networks.

Because the media are businesses, and because the media seek to attract the largest possible audiences, they naturally tend to cover stories with dramatic or entertainment value, giving less attention to important stories that are less compelling. News coverage often focuses on crimes and scandals, especially those involving prominent individuals. This **selection bias** means that the media may provide less information about important political issues that the public depends upon. For example, the Democratic partisan predisposition of many

agenda setting the power of the media to bring public attention to particular issues and problems

selection bias (news) the tendency to focus news coverage on only one aspect of an event or issue, avoiding coverage of other aspects

journalists did not prevent a media frenzy in January 1998 when reports surfaced that President Clinton (a Democrat) might have had an affair with a White House intern. It was the Republicans' turn in 2012 when the extramarital affairs of presidential candidates Herman Cain and Newt Gingrich made headlines. Partisanship and ideology notwithstanding, the age-old journalistic instinct for sensational stories to tell often trumps both the media's responsibility to inform the public about what really matters and the public's responsibility to demand that from the media.

What the mainstream media decide to report on and what they ignore has important implications. For example, the mainstream media provided little coverage of the Bush tax cuts of 2001 and 2003 (or their extension under President Obama in 2008), although they dramatically increased the federal budget deficit and widened the gap between the super-rich and most other Americans in terms of wealth. It is not surprising that public opinion polls showed 40 percent of Americans had no opinion on whether they favored the massive tax cuts in 2001.[48] Access to the print and broadcast media is such an important political resource that political forces that lack media access, such as the Occupy Wall Street protestors, have only a very limited opportunity to influence the political process. The selection bias of traditional media run by professional journalists, however, may be balanced out by the diversity of media sources available online, especially the growing influence of social media and blogs.

Framing The language and context in which the media presents the news, known as **framing**, can determine how the American people interpret political events. Knowing this, politicians take care to choose language that presents their ideas in the most favorable light possible. Public opinion on politics naturally changes with facts, but few citizens read legislation, so when forming opinions about policy and politics, the public relies on media coverage. This means that arguments made by elected officials and other political actors, or frames, are critical to the process of forming opinions. Political elites have some (but certainly not complete) freedom to determine the dimensions along which policies will be debated, and the frames and arguments elites use can have a powerful influence on how the public interprets events and policy.

For example, the Obama administration labeled its health care initiative the Patient Protection and Affordable Care Act, thus framing the proposal as a matter of compassionate responsibility and good economic sense. As the bill was debated in Congress, early press coverage framed it as "health care reform." Sensing that Americans generally approve of the idea of "reform," Republican opponents of the legislation chose language that framed it quite differently. The law's provisions for limiting excessive medical testing were labeled as "health care rationing," for example, and proposals to create committees to advise patients about end-of-life care were called "death panels." Other opponents called it Obamacare. The language used by Democrats and Republicans framed the debate in different terms: the Democrats framed is as achieving the positive goal of reform, while the Republicans framed it as achieving the negative outcome of rationing.

Priming A third important way the media can shape political events is known as **priming**, which is related to framing. Priming involves "calling attention to some

for critical analysis

How do the media distort political reality? How do politicians use the media for their own purposes? What are the consequences for American democracy when the electorate is informed through such a filter? How might the quality of political information in America be improved?

matters while ignoring others."[49] As a result, the public will be *primed* to use certain criteria when evaluating a politician or an issue, and ignore other criteria. For example, the media's intensive focus on terrorism and security in the wake of the September 11, 2001, terrorist attacks primed the public to evaluate President Bush's performance in office based on his ability to defend the nation from terrorism. The public was less likely to assess President Bush based on his ability to manage the economy at the time, as people were not primed to be thinking about the economy. This situation was quite different in 2008, when a serious economic recession received much more extensive media coverage than national security. In the 2008 presidential election, the economy was an important lens through which the public evaluated the candidates, more important than national security.

In the case of political candidates, the media's focus on which candidate "has momentum" and "is winning the horse race" can prime the public to evaluate the candidates based on their likelihood to win the election rather than on other criteria, such as their positions on policy issues. For example, after Barack Obama won the 2008 Iowa caucuses in the Democratic primaries, the media declared that he had momentum, as his fund-raising and poll numbers had exceeded early projections.[50] Nothing Hillary Clinton was able to do seemed to deprive Obama of the coveted momentum the media had granted him. Momentum soon becomes a feedback loop by which media attention generates public enthusiasm, which in turn garners further media attention.

The way that a story is reported in the news can influence how the audience interprets the event. After Hurricane Sandy hit the mid-Atlantic coast, for instance, the media could write a story focusing on the government's failure to respond in a timely matter or on the government's successful relief efforts. Both stories may be correct—but they leave the reader or viewer with a very different impression.

In 2004 controversial measures banning same-sex marriage were placed on 13 statewide ballots as referenda by Republican state lawmakers or as initiatives by conservative interest groups sympathetic to the Republican Party. All 13 ballot measures were approved by voters. The well-coordinated, high-profile campaigns urging passage of the measures garnered extensive media coverage in these states and may have primed citizens to vote for the Republican presidential incumbent, George W. Bush. One study found that citizens residing in one of the states with such ballot measures were more likely to rank the issue of gay marriage as very important in the presidential election, tracking a higher volume of media coverage, compared with voters in the 37 states that didn't vote on this issue. When evaluating the 2004 presidential candidates, voters in these 13 states who believed that the issue of same-sex marriage was very important were more likely to vote for the Republican candidate. The research suggests that the ballot measures on a same-sex-marriage ban may have helped re-elect President Bush in the 2004 election.[51]

Media and Public Knowledge

In general, individuals who frequently consume political news are more likely to be interested in politics, have political knowledge, and to vote in elections. There are several reasons why exposure to political information increases participation in politics. Exposure to political news increases political knowledge, which in turn increases turnout because people know whom to vote for and are more likely to perceive differences between candidates. Learning from exposure to political information on cable television news and online news also increases people's interest in electoral campaigns, which in turn, affects voter turnout.[52]

The media in all its varying forms—traditional and online—leads to a more informed public, and growing gaps between the informed and uninformed.[53] A puzzle remains, however. Despite the dramatic rise in political information and the diversity of the media, average levels of political knowledge in the population have remained constant for the last few decades.[54] One widely discussed reason has been proposed by Cass Sunstein (2001). He argues that individuals "customize" the political information they receive through their choice of news outlets to follow.[55] This leads to a polarized news environment in which media users are unlikely to encounter information that challenges their partisan viewpoints. This is related to the filter bubble, discussed above. (See Figure 7.6 for a breakdown of political knowledge by news audience.)

● News Coverage

Explain how politicians and others try to shape the news

News coverage, or the content of the news, comes from numerous sources. Government departments, politicians, corporations, interest groups, and others issue press releases to draw attention to an issue and tell their side of the story. Journalists also gain information through investigative journalism and media leaks.

Press Releases

Each year, thousands of press releases are seamlessly incorporated into daily news reports. These press releases are written by advocates or publicists and distributed to the media in the hope that journalists will publish them, under the journalists' own bylines, with little or no revision. The originator of the press release, or news release, was a well-known New York public-relations consultant named Ivy Lee. In 1906 a train operated by one of Lee's clients, the Pennsylvania Railroad, was involved in a serious wreck. Lee quickly wrote a story about the accident that presented the railroad in a favorable light, and he distributed the account to reporters. Many papers published Lee's slanted story as their own objective account of the events, and the railroad's reputation for quality and safety remained untarnished.

Consistent with Lee's example, today's press release presents facts and perspectives that serve an advocate's interests but is written in a way that mimics the factual news style of the paper, periodical, or television news program to which the press release has been sent. A well-designed press release can be nearly impossible to distinguish from an actual news story. Newspapers, of course, understand that, in publishing press releases, they are allowing themselves to be used, but they have a strong financial incentive to publish material that, in effect, allows them to fill their pages at little cost. The White House regularly issues press releases—for example, in preparation for a State of the Union address or major legislation supported by the president. Polling companies, such as Gallup, use press releases to share the results of election surveys.

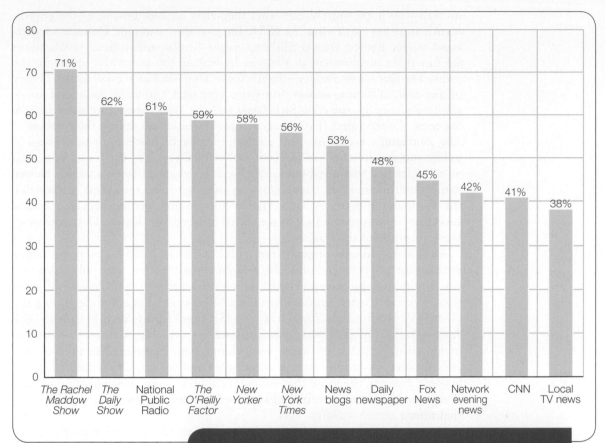

FIGURE 7.6

Where Well-Informed Americans Get News

In 2012 the Pew Research Center surveyed the public with a short quiz on current events. Overall, just 14 percent of Americans got all four questions right. Those who got three to four questions right reported getting their news from a variety of sources, as shown in the graph.

SOURCE: Pew Research Center, www.people-press.org/2012/09/27/section-4-demographics-and-political-views-of-news-audiences (accessed 4/28/14).

The capacity of news subjects to influence the news is hardly unlimited. Media consultants and issues managers may shape the news for a time, but it is generally not difficult for the media to penetrate the smoke screens thrown up by news sources if they have a reason to do so. For example, in 2013, the mainstream media exposed the "Bridgegate" scandal, involving corruption and a cover-up by staffers in the office of New Jersey governor Chris Christie.

Media Leaks

The media may also report information that is leaked by government officials. A **leak** is the disclosure of confidential information to the news media. Leaks may emanate from a variety of sources, including "whistle-blowers," lower-level

leak a disclosure of confidential information to the news media

officials who hope to publicize what they view as their bosses' or the government's improper activities. In 1971, for example, a minor Defense Department staffer named Daniel Ellsberg sought to discredit official justifications for America's involvement in Vietnam by leaking top-secret documents to the press. The Pentagon Papers—the Defense Department's own secret history of the war, differing widely from the Pentagon public pronouncements—were published by the *New York Times* and the *Washington Post* after the U.S. Supreme Court ruled that the government could not block their release.[56] The Pentagon's credibility was severely damaged, hastening the erosion of public support for the war. In 2005, President George W. Bush was infuriated when he learned that a still-unidentified source, presumed to be a whistle-blower, had leaked information concerning the president's secret orders authorizing the National Security Agency (NSA) to conduct clandestine, warrantless surveillance of suspected terrorists. Bush ordered the Justice Department to launch a probe of the leak.

Most leaks, though, originate not with low-level whistle-blowers but rather with senior government officials, prominent politicians, and political activists. Journalists are likely to regard high-level sources of confidential information as valuable assets whose favor must be retained. For example, during the George W. Bush administration, Lewis "Scooter" Libby, Vice President Dick Cheney's chief of staff, was apparently such a valuable source of leaks to so many journalists that his name was seldom even mentioned in the newspapers, despite his prominence in Washington and his importance as a decision maker.[57] Further, the more that recipients of leaked information strive to keep their sources secret, the more difficulty other journalists will have in checking that information's validity.

New technology and online media have taken the cat-and-mouse game of leaks to a new level. WikiLeaks, an independent nonprofit organization dedicated to publishing classified information, posts leaked documents to its website and uses an anonymous drop-box system so leakers cannot be identified. In recent years, WikiLeaks has released thousands of secret government documents involving instances of government corruption, war crimes in Afghanistan and Iraq, torture at the Guantánamo Bay detention camp, maps of U.S. military drone attacks on civilians around the world, and numerous embarrassing private communiqués sent by U.S. diplomats abroad.

WikiLeaks shared its treasure trove of leaked government documents with major international papers, including the *New York Times*. In July 2007 gunners aboard two U.S. Army helicopters killed over a dozen people, including two Reuters news staffers, in the Iraqi suburb of New Baghdad. When Reuters subsequently learned that the U.S. military had video footage of the attack, it tried to obtain the video through the Freedom of Information Act, but without success. The video was leaked to WikiLeaks, however, which released it in April 2010. Shot through an Apache helicopter gunsight, the video clearly shows the slaying of a wounded Reuters employee and his would-be rescuers; it led to a worldwide storm of condemnation of U.S. military action in the Iraq War.

In 2013, Edward Snowden, a former employee of the Central Intelligence Agency (CIA) and contractor for the NSA, disclosed thousands of classified digital documents to journalists and international media in what has been called the most significant leak in U.S. history. The leaks disclosed widespread global

surveillance programs by the U.S. government working with telecommunication companies. The world learned the NSA was searching millions of email and instant messaging contact lists and tracking and mapping the locations of cell phones. For revealing the mass surveillance programs, Snowden has been called a hero, a whistle-blower, a dissident, and a traitor. The leaks garnered intense media attention and sparked heated public debate over government surveillance and privacy of information for individuals.

Critics of WikiLeaks and Snowden argue that posting government documents online is not journalism, that governments must have some secrets, and that the release of some government documents may jeopardize American soldiers and their local allies by revealing their identities. The whistle-blower behind the Pentagon Papers, Daniel Ellsberg, defended WikiLeaks, arguing that it has played a vital role in informing the public of government wrongdoings in terms of foreign policy.

Leaks of classified information have sparked significant debate over what the government should classify as "secret" and what deserves to be public knowledge. After Edward Snowden leaked thousands of classified documents, he fled the United States to escape arrest and prosecution. His actions have been both defended and denounced.

Adversarial Journalism

The political power of the news media vis-à-vis the government has greatly increased in recent years through the growing prominence of "adversarial journalism," a form of reporting in which the media adopt a skeptical or even hostile posture toward the government and public officials.

During the nineteenth century, American newspapers were subordinate to the political parties. Newspapers depended on official patronage (legal notices and party subsidies) for their financial survival and were controlled by party leaders. (A vestige of that era survived into the twentieth century in such newspaper names as the *Springfield Republican* and the *St. Louis Globe-Democrat*.) At the turn of the twentieth century, with the development of commercial advertising, newspapers became financially independent, making possible the emergence of a formally nonpartisan press.

Presidents were the first national officials to make use of the opportunities presented by this development. By communicating directly to the electorate through newspapers and magazines, Theodore Roosevelt and Woodrow Wilson established political constituencies for themselves, independent of party organizations, and thereby strengthened their own power relative to that of Congress. President Franklin Delano Roosevelt used the radio, most notably in his famous fireside chats, to reach out to voters throughout the nation and to make himself the center of American political life. Roosevelt was also adept at developing close personal relationships with reporters, which enabled him to obtain favorable news coverage despite the fact that, in his day, a majority of newspaper owners and publishers were staunch conservatives. Following Roosevelt's example, subsequent presidents have all sought to use the media to enhance their popularity and power. John F. Kennedy, for example, used televised news conferences to mobilize public support for his domestic and foreign policy initiatives.

During the 1950s and early 1960s a few members of Congress also made successful use of the media, especially television, to mobilize national support for their causes. Senator Joseph McCarthy of Wisconsin made himself a powerful national figure through his well-publicized investigations of alleged Communist

for critical analysis

Before he left office in June 2007, the longtime British prime minister Tony Blair called the news media a "feral beast." Why are many politicians hostile to media? Do you share their views?

This famous photograph of the aftermath of a napalm attack was one of many media images that shaped the American public's views on the Vietnam War. Media accounts critical of the war helped to turn public opinion against it and hastened the withdrawal of American troops.

infiltration of key American institutions. However, through the mid-1960s, the executive branch continued to generate the bulk of news coverage, and the media became a cornerstone of presidential power.

The Vietnam War shattered this amicable relationship between the press and the presidency. During the early stages of U.S. involvement, American officials in Vietnam who disapproved of the way the war was being conducted leaked to reporters information critical of administrative policy. Publication of this material infuriated the White House, which pressured publishers to block its release—on one occasion, President Kennedy went so far as to ask the *New York Times* to reassign its Saigon correspondent. However, the national broadcast media and especially the two leading national newspapers, the *Washington Post* and the *New York Times*, discovered an audience for critical coverage and investigative reporting among segments of the public skeptical of administration policy. As the Vietnam War dragged on, adverse media coverage fanned antiwar sentiment. Moreover, growing opposition to the war among liberals encouraged some members of Congress to break with the White House, by then occupied by Lyndon Johnson. In turn, these shifts in popular and congressional sentiment emboldened journalists and publishers to continue to present news reports critical of the war. Gradually a generation of journalists developed a commitment to adversarial journalism, and a constituency emerged that would rally to the defense of the media whenever it came under attack from the White House.

As for the national media, aggressive use of the techniques of investigation, publicity, and exposure allowed them to enhance their autonomy and carve out a prominent place for themselves in American government and politics. Without investigative journalism, would we have known of Bill Clinton's extramarital affair or of the illegal break-in to the Democratic Party headquarters in the Watergate Building by Nixon's "Committee to Re-elect the President" and the White House's subsequent cover-up of the scandal? Or would we not have known that Iraq did not have weapons of mass destruction (WMDs), despite claims to the contrary by then-President George W. Bush? Without aggressive media coverage, would important questions be raised about the conduct of American foreign and domestic policy, including drone attacks, torture, and civil liberty violations? It is easy to criticize the media for their aggressive tactics, but would our democracy function effectively without the critical role of the press? Independent media are needed as the watchdogs of American politics.

New media has ushered in a new watchdog of government wrongdoing. Recent leaks showed the world that the American government and press sometimes concealed news, including war crimes against civilians and the use of torture by American forces. One advantage of new media is that they are less likely to be co-opted by the government. A website controlled by an Australian citizen, with web servers in many nations worldwide, including Iceland, WikiLeaks is indicative of the lawless environment that now characterizes the new media, and of how the new media are challenging even traditional media, taking the adversarial role of the press to new heights.

for critical analysis

In wartime, can media criticism of government action aid the nation's enemies? Should there be limits on media criticism of the government during time of war? Or does criticism actually enhance the nation's strength?

● Regulation of the Media

Trace the evolution of rules that govern broadcast media

In many countries, such as China, the government exercises strict control over traditional media content. In others, the government owns the broadcast media (for example, the BBC in Britain) but does not tell the media what to say.

In the United States, the print and online media are essentially free from government interference. The broadcast media, on the other hand, are subject to federal regulation. American radio and television are regulated by the Federal Communications Commission (FCC), an independent agency established in 1934. Radio and TV stations must have FCC licenses, which must be renewed every five years. Licensing provides a mechanism for allocating radio and TV frequencies to prevent broadcasts from interfering with and garbling one another. License renewals are almost always granted automatically by the FCC. Indeed, renewal requests are now filed by postcard.

Through regulations prohibiting obscenity, indecency, and profanity, the FCC has also sought to prohibit radio and television stations from airing explicit sexual and excretory references between 6 A.M. and 10 P.M., the hours when the audience is most likely to include children. Generally speaking, FCC regulation applies only to the over-the-air broadcast media. It does not apply to cable television, the Internet, or satellite radio. As a result, explicit sexual content and graphic language that would run afoul of the rules on broadcast television are regularly available on cable channels. A number of bills have been introduced in recent congresses to extend the rules to apply to cable TV and satellite radio, but none has succeeded so far.

For more than 60 years, the FCC sought not only to regulate but also to promote competition in the broadcast industry, but in 1996, Congress passed the

Federal Communications Commission (FCC) regulations prohibit obscenity, indecency, and profanity in American television and radio broadcasts. The radio personality Howard Stern incurred millions of dollars in FCC fines before moving to satellite radio, which is not regulated by the FCC.

equal time rule the requirement that broadcasters provide candidates for the same political office equal opportunities to communicate their messages to the public

right of rebuttal a Federal Communications Commission regulation giving individuals the right to have the opportunity to respond to personal attacks made on a radio or television broadcast

fairness doctrine a Federal Communications Commission requirement for broadcasters who air programs on controversial issues to provide time for opposing views; the FCC ceased enforcing this doctrine in 1985

Telecommunications Act, a broad effort to end most regulations in effect since 1934. The legislation loosened restrictions on media ownership and allowed telephone companies, cable television providers, and broadcasters to compete with one another to provide telecommunication services. Following the passage of this act, mergers between telephone and cable companies and different entertainment media produced a greater concentration of media ownership than had been possible since regulation of the industry began in 1934.

The Telecommunications Act of 1996 included an attempt to regulate the content of material transmitted over the Internet. This law, known as the Communications Decency Act, made it illegal to make "indecent" sexual material on the Internet accessible to those under age 18. The act was immediately denounced by civil libertarians and became the subject of lawsuits. In 1997 the Supreme Court ruled that the Communications Decency Act was an unconstitutional infringement of the right to freedom of speech guaranteed by the First Amendment (see Chapter 4).

Although the government's ability to regulate the content of the Internet is limited, the FCC has used its licensing power to impose several regulations that can affect the political content of radio and TV broadcasts. The first of these is the **equal time rule**, under which broadcasters must provide to candidates for the same political office equal opportunities to communicate their messages to the public. If, for example, a television station sells commercial time to a state's Republican gubernatorial candidate, it may not refuse to sell time to the Democratic candidate for the same office. Under the terms of the Telecommunications Act, during the 45 days before an election, broadcasters are required to make time available to candidates at the lowest rate charged for that time slot.

The second regulation affecting the content of broadcasts is the **right of rebuttal**, which requires that individuals be given the opportunity to respond to personal attacks. In the 1969 case of *Red Lion Broadcasting Company v. FCC*, for example, the U.S. Supreme Court upheld the FCC's determination that a radio station was required to provide a liberal author with an opportunity to respond to a conservative commentator's attack that the station had aired.[58] For many years, a third important federal regulation was the **fairness doctrine**. Under this rule, broadcasters who aired programs on controversial issues were required to provide time for opposing views. In 1985, however, the FCC stopped enforcing the fairness doctrine on the grounds that there were so many radio and television stations—to say nothing of newspapers and newsmagazines—that in all likelihood many different viewpoints were already being presented without each station being required to try to present all sides of every argument. Critics of this FCC decision charged, and continue to charge, that in many media markets the number of competing viewpoints is actually quite small. During the past several years, Democratic members of Congress have sought to revive the fairness doctrine in response to what they see as the "unfairness" of conservative talk radio.

The rise of online media challenges our thinking about regulation of the media, as it is more difficult—some say impossible—to regulate political content online. The United Nations recently declared that access to the Internet is a human right.[59] While this declaration came in response to threats by authoritarian governments against Internet access—the Egyptian government, for example, disabled Internet access for the entire nation during protests in 2011—the UN's position demonstrates the significance of information technology in modern life.[60] The U.S. government does have the power to regulate the Internet if a website infringes U.S. copyright law. In January 2012 the U.S. Department of Justice shut down a website, Megaupload, that ran services for file storing and viewing, alleging the site violated copyright law.

The Media, Democracy,
and Your Future

The free media are essential to democratic government. Ordinary citizens depend on the media to investigate wrongdoing, publicize and explain governmental actions, evaluate programs and politicians, and bring to light matters that might otherwise be known to only a handful of governmental insiders. In short, without free and active media, democratic government would be virtually impossible. Citizens would have few means through which to know or assess the government's actions—other than the claims or pronouncements of the government itself. Moreover, without active (indeed, aggressive) media, citizens would be hard-pressed to make informed choices among competing candidates at the polls.

Today's media are not only adversarial but also increasingly partisan. Blogs, niche media, social media, and other Internet outlets, of course, are often unabashedly partisan. To some extent, increasing ideological and partisan stridency is an inevitable result of the expansion and proliferation of news sources. When the news was dominated by three networks and a handful of national papers, each sought to appeal to the entire national audience. This required a moderate and balanced tone so that consumers would not be offended and transfer their attention to a rival network or newspaper. Today, there are so many news sources that few can aim for a broad-based national audience. Instead, each targets a partisan or ideological niche and aims to develop a strong relationship with consumers in that audience segment by catering to their biases and predispositions.

The media can make or break reputations, help to launch or destroy political careers, and build support for or rally opposition to programs and institutions.[61] Wherever there is so much power, at least the potential exists for its abuse or overly zealous use. All things considered, free media are so critically important to the maintenance of a democratic society that Americans must be prepared to take the risk that the media will occasionally abuse their power. Governmental controls that would prevent the media from misusing their power would also certainly destroy freedom. The ultimate beneficiaries of free and active media are the American people.

Has the rise of citizen journalism, social media, and the Internet fundamentally changed how political information is gathered and distributed? As more and more Americans go online to read the news and learn about politics, even the definition of "journalist" is being challenged. Are Twitter feeds from protestors on the ground in Egypt or in an Occupy Wall Street camp examples of citizen journalism? In an era of online news, regular citizens create content and distribute the news through personal pages and blogs. Is this real news or just social media gossip on a global scale? Wikipedia, the free online encyclopedia founded by Jimmy Wales, has millions of pages compiled by legions of volunteers and provides relatively unbiased content on virtually every political topic imaginable. Social media (Facebook, Twitter, and countless others), Wikipedia, and all Wiki-type sites involve people working collaboratively to write and create information and transmit knowledge. Is Wikimedia the future of the media?

In the twenty-first century, political campaigns are covered wall to wall by the Internet; on newspapers' sites updated throughout the day; and on blogs, tweets, social media, and cable television. There is no doubt that the new digital media are more diverse, more representative of multiple viewpoints, more interactive and participatory, and, to many, more interesting than traditional news media. Time will tell whether the shift to online news strengthens or harms American democracy.

plug

Inform

Compare how a current political news story is reported by two or more sources, such as national TV news (ABC, CBS, or NBC), cable news (CNN, MSNBC, or Fox News), newspapers (in print or online), or other online sources (such as the Drudge Report or the Huffington Post).

Express

Where do you get your news? List the sources of news you regularly use. Are you satisfied with the type of political news coverage they provide?

Connect

Visit a watchdog site like Factcheck.org to see whether the claims politicians and interest groups make via the media are accurate.

Act

Share two political news stories that interest you via Facebook or other social media.

studyguide

Traditional Media

Describe the trends in the role of print and broadcast media in providing political information (pp. 259–66)

Americans have traditionally gotten their political information from broadcast media (radio and television) and print media (newspapers and magazines). Television reaches the largest audience but provides little depth of coverage. Radio news is essentially a headline service that alerts listeners to important events without providing much detail. Newspapers, by contrast, are read by political elites for their in-depth coverage and are important in setting the agenda of the broadcast media.

Key Terms

broadcast media (p. 259)

media monopoly (p. 266)

New Media and Online News

Explain how the Internet has transformed the news media (pp. 267–79)

Online political information includes online-only newspapers, news aggregation websites, niche journalism, citizen journalism, nonprofit journalism, blogs, and social media. The convenience, currency, and diversity of online news have led many Americans to prefer it to more traditional sources. Changes arising from the emergence of the Internet have also raised concerns that online news may produce a decline in investigative journalism, a decrease in the quality of news content, and a reduction in political knowledge and tolerance.

Key Terms

penny press (p. 267)

news aggregator (p. 267)

digital citizen (p. 268)

niche journalism (p. 270)

citizen journalism (p. 270)

social media (p. 272)

Practice Quiz

1. _____ play an important role in American politics because they are influential among the political elite.
   a) Academic journals
   b) Newspapers
   c) Facebook posts
   d) Political cartoons
   e) YouTube videos

2. Most daily newspapers and local television stations are owned by
   a) a small number of giant corporations.
   b) the national government.
   c) local companies.
   d) private individuals.
   e) the employees who run them.

Practice Quiz

3. Digital citizenship requires
   a) a subscription of one or more online newspapers.
   b) high-speed internet access and the skills to use and evaluate online information.
   c) the use of a social media account.
   d) maintaining a political blog.
   e) registering one's computer with the government.

4. News reporting that is targeted in its content toward a narrow segment of the population is called
   a) nonprofit journalism.
   b) for-profit journalism.
   c) niche journalism.
   d) citizen journalism.
   e) adversarial journalism.

5. Which of the following is *not* a reason that Americans may prefer online news?
   a) the convenience of getting news online
   b) the up-to-the-moment currency of the information available online
   c) the depth of the information available online
   d) the diversity of online viewpoints
   e) the accuracy and objectivity compared to traditional media outlets

Media Influence

The content and character of news programming can have far-reaching political consequences. In recent American political history, the media have played a central role in numerous major events, such as the civil rights movement of the 1950s and '60s, the Vietnam War, and the Watergate affair. The power of the media lies in their ability to shape what issues Americans think about (agenda setting) and what opinions Americans hold about those issues (framing and priming).

Key Terms
agenda setting (p. 281)

selection bias (news) (p. 281)

framing (p. 282)

priming (p. 282)

Practice Quiz

6. The media's powers to determine what becomes a part of political discussion and to shape how political events are interpreted are known as
   a) media consolidation and selection bias.
   b) issue definition and protest power.
   c) agenda setting and framing.
   d) the illusion of saliency and the bandwagon effect.
   e) the equal time rule and the right of rebuttal.

7. Which of the following best describes the media's role in the Watergate affair?
   a) They played a central role in reporting on President Nixon's resignation but did little to reveal his abuses of power while he was president.
   b) They played a central role in President Nixon's decision to resign from the presidency by revealing his abuses of power to the public.
   c) They played a central role in disproving claims that President Nixon had abused his power while in office.
   d) They played almost no role in the Watergate affair because they were legally prohibited from discussing ongoing police investigations.
   e) They played almost no role in the Watergate affair because they refused to investigate claims that President Nixon had abused his power.

News Coverage

Press releases, leaks, and the tradition of adversarial journalism are important in determining the content of news coverage. Leaks, which are confidential pieces of information disclosed to members of the media, have driven press coverage on issues ranging from foreign policy to government corruption. Also incorporated into daily news coverage are thousands of press releases authored by advocates of influential political interests. Adversarial journalism, a form of reporting in which the media adopt a skeptical or even hostile posture toward public officials, has increased the political power of the press in recent years.

Key Term
leak (p. 285)

Practice Quiz

8. Which of the following best describes the media's use of press releases?
   a) Press releases are never incorporated into daily news reports because it is illegal under federal law.
   b) Press releases are never incorporated into daily news reports because reporters view the information they contain as biased and politically motivated.
   c) Thousands of press releases are incorporated into daily news reports every year because press releases allow news organizations to fill their pages at little cost.
   d) Press releases are rarely incorporated into daily news reports because reporters view the information as biased and politically motivated.
   e) Every press release written by a political party, interest group, candidate, or government official is incorporated into daily news reports because reporters view the information as newsworthy.

9. Most leaks originate with
    a) low-level government whistle-blowers.
    b) senior government officials, prominent politicians, and political activists.
    c) members of the public who witness misbehavior.
    d) ambassadors from foreign countries.
    e) members of the media.

10. *Adversarial journalism* refers to
    a) the recent shift in American society away from general purpose sources of information and toward narrowly focused niche sources.
    b) an era in American history when political parties provided all of the financing for newspapers.
    c) a form of reporting in which the media adopt a skeptical or even hostile posture toward the opinions and behaviors of their audience.
    d) a form of reporting in which the media adopt an accepting and friendly posture toward the government and public officials.
    e) a form of reporting in which the media adopt a skeptical or even hostile posture toward the government and public officials.

11. Which event shattered the amicable relationship between the press and the presidency?
    a) September 11, 2001
    b) the Vietnam War
    c) Watergate
    d) World War II
    e) the Monica Lewinsky affair

Regulation of the Media

Trace the evolution of rules that govern broadcast media (pp. 289–91)

Although American print and online media are free from government interference, broadcast media are subject to significant federal regulation. Radio and television stations in the United States are licensed by the Federal Communications Commission. The FCC has used its licensing power to impose several regulations, such as the equal time rule, the right of rebuttal, and the fairness doctrine, that affect the political content of radio and television broadcasts.

Key Terms

equal time rule (p. 290)

right of rebuttal (p. 290)

fairness doctrine (p. 290)

Practice Quiz

12. In general, FCC regulations apply only to
    a) cable television.
    b) Internet websites.
    c) over-the-air broadcast media.
    d) satellite radio.
    e) newspapers and magazines.

13. The now-defunct requirement that broadcasters provide time for opposing views when they air programs on controversial issues was called
    a) the equal time rule.
    b) the free speech doctrine.
    c) the fairness doctrine.
    d) the right of rebuttal.
    e) the response rule.

For Further Reading

Ansolabehere, Stephen, and Shanto Iyengar. *Going Negative*. New York: Simon & Schuster, 1997.

Carr, Nicholas. *The Shallows: What the Internet Is Doing to Our Brains*. New York: W. W. Norton & Company, 2011.

De Zengotita, Thomas. *Mediated: How the Media Shapes Our World and the Way We Live in It*. New York: Bloomsbury, 2006.

Fenton, Tom. *Bad News: The Decline of Reporting, the Business of News, and the Danger to Us All*. New York: Harper Collins, 2005.

Fox, Richard, and Jennifer Ramos. *iPolitics: Citizens, Elections and Governing in the New Media Era*. New York: Cambridge University Press, 2011.

Hamilton, James T. *All the News That's Fit to Sell*. Princeton, NJ: Princeton University Press, 2004.

Iyengar, Shanto, and Donald Kinder. *News That Matters: Television and American Public Opinion*. Chicago: University of Chicago Press, 2010.

Jamieson, Kathleen, and Paul Waldman. *The Press Effect*. New York: Oxford University Press, 2004.

Mossberger, Karen, Caroline Tolbert, and Ramona McNeal. *Digital Citizenship: The Internet, Society and Participation*. Cambridge, MA: MIT Press, 2008.

Pariser, Eli. *The Filter Bubble: What the Internet Is Hiding from You*. New York: Penguin, 2011.

Weaver, David, et al. *The American Journalist in the 21st Century: U.S. News People at the Dawn of a New Millennium.* New York: Erlbaum, 2006.

West, Darrell. *The Next Wave: Using Digital Technology to Further Social and Political Innovation.* Washington, DC: Brookings Institution Press, 2011.

Recommended Websites

Accuracy in Media
www.aim.org
> This nonprofit, watchdog group attempts to ensure accuracy in media reporting by identifying botched or slanted stories and then "setting the record straight."

Federal Communications Commission
www.fcc.gov
> The FCC is an independent regulatory agency established by the U.S. government in 1934 to regulate the broadcast media. On the official FCC website you can read about the rules and regulations that affect the media, along with other current topics of interest.

Journalism.org
www.journalism.org
> This nonprofit, nonpolitical site, sponsored by the Project for Excellence in Journalism, examines the overall performance of the press as providers of information. Their aim is to help both consumers and producers of the news.

National Newspaper Association
www.nnawes.org
> The NNA is one of the oldest and largest professional associations in the print media today. As ownership of major newspapers falls into fewer and fewer hands, the NNA is trying to protect, promote, and enhance America's community newspapers.

Newseum
www.newseum.org
> Newseum is the web page for an interactive museum of news journalism. On this site you can browse the front pages of over 500 daily national and international newspapers and explore the galleries and theaters of the news museum in Washington, D.C.

The Pew Research Center for the People and the Press
http://people-press.org
> This independent survey research organization studies attitudes toward the press and numerous political issues.

For much of the country's history, large groups of Americans were denied the right to vote. Most restrictions on voting have been eliminated for Americans age 18 and older, but voter turnout remains relatively low, especially among young voters. Will the rise of online politics increase participation?

POLLING PLACE
投票站 CASILLA ELECTORAL
投票所 LUGAR NG BOTOHAN
투표소 PHÒNG PHIẾU

Political Participation and Voting

WHAT GOVERNMENT DOES AND WHY IT MATTERS President Barack Obama was re-elected to a second term as president of the United States in the 2012 election against Republican challenger Mitt Romney. In defeating Romney, Obama won nearly every battleground state, including Colorado, Iowa, New Hampshire, Ohio, Virginia, and Wisconsin. The outcome of the presidential race was ultimately determined by Florida, however, the fourth largest state in terms of population. Florida is one of the most important battleground states because of its large number of Electoral College votes and because the numbers of Republicans and Democrats in the state are roughly equal, making it fiercely competitive every four years. What also made Florida unusual in 2012 was the large number of votes cast early, prior to Election Day. Early voting made a difference in 2012 even though new state rules had limited it.

Nationwide, 25 percent of all votes were early votes, cast either in person or absentee (mail ballots). According to political scientist Michael McDonald, 4.5 million of Florida's 8.4 million total votes (53 percent) were cast early in 2012.[1] Early voting is a form of convenience voting: it allows citizens to vote in alternative ways, on their own schedule, rather than requiring that all votes be cast in person, only on Election Day. As of 2014, 33 states allow early voting in which any qualified voter may cast a ballot in person during a designated period prior to Election Day. No explanation or justification is required. Fourteen states do not allow early voting and an explanation is required for an absentee ballot. (The remaining three states vote solely by mail.)[2] Early voting mattered in Florida and other states in the 2012 presidential race in part because Obama's campaign took advantage of early voting laws, employing a sophisticated voter registration database to call, message, and email supporters until they confirmed that a ballot had been cast.

Some scholars argue that early voting is *the* election reform of the twenty-first century; political scientist Paul Gronke calls it "a quiet revolution."[3] But in 2012 the Republican-controlled Florida state legislature significantly reduced the number of days allowed for early voting from 14 days prior to the election to 8. The change eliminated some weekend polling hours when many African Americans voted after church, with transportation provided by their congregation to and from the polls. Which voters were negatively affected by this election rule change? New research by political scientists Michael Herron and Daniel Smith analyzed the complete Florida voter rolls for 2008 and 2012 and found that limiting early voting can have a negative effect on minority turnout.[4] Obama still won Florida, but the change to early voting rules impacted the election.

Because the race in Florida was so close, *who* turned out to vote mattered a great deal. Early voting is not an esoteric election rule, but a core part of how elections are conducted in modern electoral campaigns and even more important in pivotal battleground states. In recent elections voting rules have emerged as an issue in battleground states, highlighting that who votes, how they vote, and where they vote is critically important in who wins elected office and holds political power in the United States.

chaptergoals

- Describe the major forms of traditional and online participation in politics (pp. 301–10)

- Describe the patterns of participation among major demographic groups (pp. 310–20)

- Explain the factors in the political environment that influence whether individuals vote or not (pp. 321–27)

- Explain the effect of electoral laws on voting (pp. 327–33)

Forms of Political Participation

Describe the major forms of traditional and online participation in politics

We can think of political participation as falling into two major categories. Traditional participation in politics includes voting, of course, as well as attending campaign events, party business meetings, and fund-raisers. It also includes volunteering, canvassing, displaying campaign signs, contacting elected officials and contributing to candidates and parties, or even challenging a law in court. Even protests and demonstrations can be considered age-old forms of participatory politics. Many, but not all, are face-to-face forms of participation in politics.

In addition to traditional participation there is a growing online world of digital politics—not just the exchange of information, but also fund-raising and voter mobilization. Some observers contend that digital politics is just a new way of engaging in traditional politics, while others argue that it is fundamentally different. There may be some truth to both arguments, but it is clear that digital politics is increasingly intertwined with traditional participation and is changing participation in important ways that may increase engagement in politics overall. We will see in this chapter that digital and traditional participation are combining to broaden the ways Americans participate in politics.

Traditional Political Participation

Traditional political participation refers to a wide range of activities designed to influence government, politics, and policy. For most citizens today, voting is the most common form of participation in politics. Yet ordinary people took part in politics long before the advent of the election or any other formal mechanism of popular involvement in political life. If there is any natural or spontaneous form of popular political participation, it is not the election but the riot. In fact, for much of American history, fewer Americans exercised their right to vote than participated in urban riots and rural uprisings, as voting for a long time was limited to white, male, landowning citizens. Civil unrest played an important role in American politics in the 1960s and '70s. As recently as 1999, protests helped labor unions and other opponents of trade liberalization slow the pace of change in the rules governing world trade.

traditional political participation activities designed to influence government including voting and face-to-face activities such as protesting or volunteering for a campaign

The vast majority of Americans, of course, reject rioting or violence for political ends, but peaceful **protest** is protected by the First Amendment and is generally recognized as a legitimate and important form of political activity. During the height of the civil rights movement in the 1960s, hundreds of thousands of Americans took part in peaceful protests to demand social and political rights for African Americans. More recently, peaceful marches and demonstrations have been employed by a host of groups, including opponents of the war in Iraq and anti-tax Tea Party activists. The Occupy Wall Street movement that began in September 2011 in New York City's Financial District used peaceful demonstrations to protest high unemployment, undue corporate influence on government, and growing inequality between the super-rich and the middle class—or, in the lingo of the Occupy Wall Street movement, the 1 percent versus the 99 percent of Americans. The protests in New York sparked similar Occupy movements, and their tent cities, across America. One reason people participate in public protests is to attract media

protest participation that involves assembling crowds to confront a government or other official organization

People can express political views and even influence political outcomes by engaging in protest. One advantage of protest is its visibility: through media attention, protesters can raise awareness, attract like-minded individuals to join their ranks, and put pressure on politicians.

attention, raise public awareness, and ultimately impact politicians and the policies they enact. Opinion polls suggest that the Occupy movement has been especially successful at least in raising awareness of income inequality. For example, a Pew Research Center survey found that in 2012, two-thirds of Americans (66 percent) believed there were "very strong" or "strong" conflicts between the rich and the poor—an increase of 19 percentage points since 2009.[5]

Elections are the hallmark of political participation in a democracy, of course. In addition to voting, citizens can give money to politicians or political organizations, volunteer in campaigns, contact political officials, sign petitions, attend public meetings, join organizations, display campaign signs and pins, write letters to the editor, publish articles, attend rallies, or lobby their representatives in Congress; they can even sue the government or run for elected office. They can also join interest groups, which are discussed in Chapter 11. Such activities differ from voting because they can communicate much more detailed information to public officials than voting can. Voters may support a candidate for many reasons, but their actual votes do not indicate specifically what they like and don't like, nor do they tell officials how intensely voters feel about issues. By volunteering for a political campaign, writing to their member of Congress, or attending a protest, people can convey much more specific information. For that reason, people often find these other political activities more satisfying than voting.[6] However, these other forms of political action generally require more time, effort, and/or money than voting. As a result, as Figure 8.1 shows, the percentage of the population that participates in elections other than to vote is relatively low.

Participation through Voting Whether voting is as effective or satisfying as protest (online or off-line) and other forms of political action is an open question. It is clear, however, that for most Americans, voting remains one of the most important forms of political activity. The right to vote gives ordinary Americans a more equal chance to participate in politics than almost any other form of political activity. Voting is especially important because this act selects the officials who make the

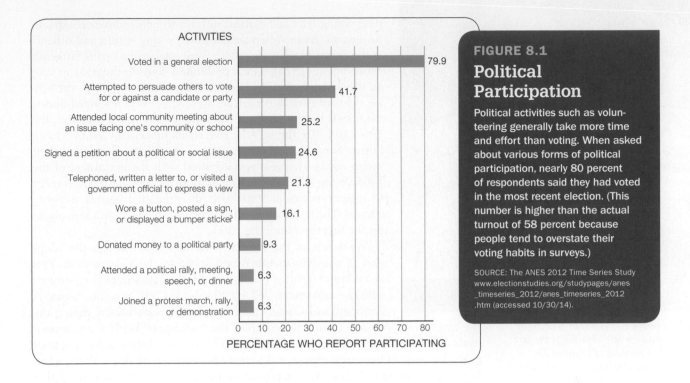

ACTIVITIES

Activity	Percentage
Voted in a general election	79.9
Attempted to persuade others to vote for or against a candidate or party	41.7
Attended local community meeting about an issue facing one's community or school	25.2
Signed a petition about a political or social issue	24.6
Telephoned, written a letter to, or visited a government official to express a view	21.3
Wore a button, posted a sign, or displayed a bumper sticker	16.1
Donated money to a political party	9.3
Attended a political rally, meeting, speech, or dinner	6.3
Joined a protest march, rally, or demonstration	6.3

PERCENTAGE WHO REPORT PARTICIPATING

FIGURE 8.1

Political Participation

Political activities such as volunteering generally take more time and effort than voting. When asked about various forms of political participation, nearly 80 percent of respondents said they had voted in the most recent election. (This number is higher than the actual turnout of 58 percent because people tend to overstate their voting habits in surveys.)

SOURCE: The ANES 2012 Time Series Study www.electionstudies.org/studypages/anes _timeseries_2012/anes_timeseries_2012 .htm (accessed 10/30/14).

laws that the American people must follow, including laws compelling them to pay taxes. Voting is the single most important political act for most Americans, and it is the most common way that individuals involve themselves in politics.

The right to vote, or **suffrage**, is a legal right. During the colonial and early national periods of American history, suffrage was generally restricted to white males over the age of 21. Many states further limited voting to those who owned property or paid more than a specified amount of annual tax. The Founders gave to the state legislatures the authority to regulate congressional elections, a decision that would have profound consequences for voting rights throughout American history. Until the early 1900s, state legislatures elected U.S. senators, and there were no direct elections for members of the Electoral College (who in turn elect the president), so elections for the U.S. House as well as state and local offices were the primary venue for citizen participation in government.

During the nineteenth and early twentieth centuries, the right to vote was not distributed equally across the American population. The states often acted to restrict expanding suffrage, initially through poll taxes (fees to vote) and literacy tests designed to curtail immigrant voting in northern cities controlled by political machines, and later imported to the southern states to disenfranchise African Americans and uneducated whites during the Jim Crow era. Voter eligibility requirements often varied greatly from state to state. Some states openly prevented the right to vote on the basis of race; others did not. Some states required property ownership for voting; others had no such restrictions. Most states mandated lengthy residency requirements, which meant that persons moving from one state to another sometimes lost their right to vote for as much as a year.[7]

Over the past two centuries of American history, a dominant trend has been federal statutes, court decisions, and constitutional amendments designed to override

suffrage the right to vote; also called *franchise*

for critical analysis

Describe the expansion of suffrage in the United States since the Founding. Why might the government have denied participation to so many for so long? What forces influenced the expansion of voting rights?

During the Vietnam War, some young people objected to the fact that they could be drafted to serve in the military and sent to fight a war when they were not yet old enough to vote for the politicians making the decision. The Twenty-Sixth Amendmented lowered the voting age from 21 to 18. Is 18 the right age limit, in your opinion?

turnout the percentage of eligible individuals who actually vote

state voting laws and expand suffrage to nonlandowners, African Americans, Asian Americans, women, young adults, and others.[8] In the South, black voting rights were established by the Fifteenth Amendment (1870), which prohibited denying the right to vote on the basis of race. Despite the Fifteenth Amendment, the voting rights of African Americans were effectively rescinded during the 1880s by the states of the former Confederacy. During the 1950s and '60s, through the civil rights movement led by Martin Luther King, Jr., and others, African Americans demanded their voting rights. This goal was achieved with the enactment of the 1965 Voting Rights Act, which authorized the federal government to register voters in states that discriminated against minority citizens. The result was the re-enfranchisement of southern blacks for the first time since the 1860s.

Women won the right to vote in 1920, through the adoption of the Nineteenth Amendment to the Constitution. This amendment resulted primarily from the activism of the women's suffrage movement, led by Elizabeth Cady Stanton, Susan B. Anthony, and Carrie Chapman Catt, among others, during the late nineteenth and early twentieth centuries. The "suffragists" held rallies, demonstrations, and protest marches for more than half a century before achieving their goal. The cause of women's suffrage was ultimately advanced by World War I, when President Woodrow Wilson and members of Congress became convinced that women would be more likely to support the war effort if they were granted the right to vote.

The most recent expansion of the right to vote in the United States, the Twenty-Sixth Amendment, lowered the voting age from 21 to 18. It was ratified during the Vietnam War, in 1971. Unlike black suffrage and women's suffrage, which came about in part because of the demands of groups that had been deprived of the right to vote, the Twenty-Sixth Amendment was intended to channel the disruptive protest activities of students involved in the anti–Vietnam War movement into peaceful participation at the ballot box.

Current Trends in Voter Turnout Today voting rights are granted to all American citizens ages 18 and older, although some states revoke this right from those who have committed a felony or are mentally incompetent. (This will be discussed in detail below.) Although eligibility to vote is now almost universal for citizens ages 18 and older, America's actual rate of voting participation, or **turnout**, is somewhat low. Only half of eligible Americans vote in presidential elections, and turnout for midterm elections (elections that fall between presidential elections) is typically much lower, around 33 percent of eligible voters. Turnout in state and local races, especially those that do not coincide with national contests, is typically much lower.[9] This means that less than a third of eligible Americans are choosing to participate in elections that impact local issues, including education and public works.

Participation in U.S. presidential elections dropped significantly after 1960, when 64 percent of eligible voters cast ballots. In 1996 participation reached a modern low when only 52 percent of eligible voters went to the polls. Since then, though, overall trends have improved somewhat. In 2004 major efforts to get out the vote brought turnout to over 60 percent—the first significant increase in voting in 40 years. The trend continued in 2008, when nearly 62 percent of the population eligible to vote did so, a modern-day record, and in the 2006 and 2010 midterm elections, turnout

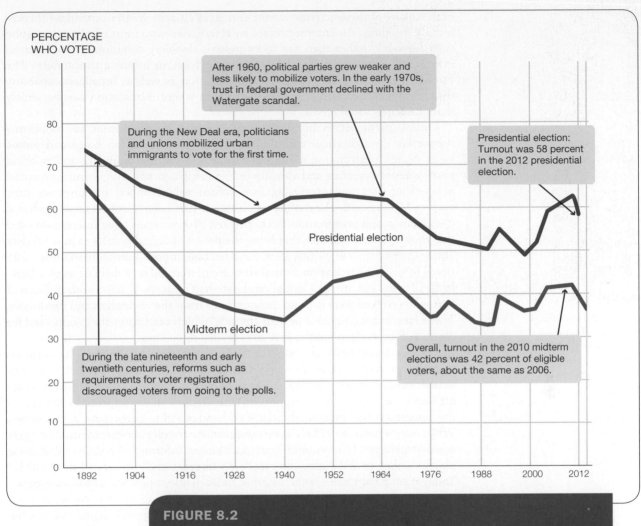

PERCENTAGE WHO VOTED

After 1960, political parties grew weaker and less likely to mobilize voters. In the early 1970s, trust in federal government declined with the Watergate scandal.

During the New Deal era, politicians and unions mobilized urban immigrants to vote for the first time.

Presidential election: Turnout was 58 percent in the 2012 presidential election.

Presidential election

During the late nineteenth and early twentieth centuries, reforms such as requirements for voter registration discouraged voters from going to the polls.

Midterm election

Overall, turnout in the 2010 midterm elections was 42 percent of eligible voters, about the same as 2006.

FIGURE 8.2

Voter Turnout in Presidential and Midterm Elections, 1892–2014

Since the 1890s, participation in elections has declined substantially. One pattern is consistent across time: more Americans tend to vote in presidential election years than in years when only congressional and local elections are held. What are some of the reasons that participation rose and fell during the last century?

SOURCES: Erik Austin and Jerome Clubb, *Political Facts of the United States since 1789* (New York: Columbia University Press, 1986); United States Election Project, www.electproject.org (accessed 11/12/14).

rose to more than 40 percent. Turnout in 2012 declined slightly to 58 percent, and the 2014 midterms saw a turnout of 36 percent of eligible voters (see Figure 8.2).

Online Political Participation

Online political participation is rapidly changing the way Americans experience politics. While traditional forms of participation remain important, the Internet gives citizens greater access to political information about campaigns and candidates and, at least potentially, a greater role in politics than ever before. Many forms of online participation build on traditional forms of participation, but the Internet

online political participation
activities designed to influence government using the Internet, including visiting a candidate's website, organizing events online, or signing an online petition

makes many of these activities easier and gives citizens greater potential for community building. The Internet offers an active, two-way form of communication with feedback, rather than the more passive, one-way communication involved in reading printed newspapers, watching television, or listening to the radio. The Internet allows person-to-person communication as well as broadcast capability through online text, video, and visual images where information can be widely shared, such as social media.

Online participation in elections includes discussing issues or mobilizing supporters through email and Twitter, posting comments on blogs and online news stories, contributing money to candidates, visiting candidate and political party websites, creating and viewing online campaign ads, campaigning on social networking sites, and organizing face-to-face neighborhood meetings on sites, such as Meetup.com. The mobile revolution is particularly important for political mobilization and organization. Sixty percent of Americans have Internet-enabled cell phones, or smartphones, that bring the power of digital politics to new heights. Today online forms of participation have become more common than most traditional forms of participation, in that they are performed on a daily or weekly basis. In 2012 every serious presidential candidate had a Facebook page, with millions of fans who received weekly if not daily updates from the campaigns and candidates. These fans, in turn, signaled to their "friends" which candidates they supported for elected office, making politics part of everyday discussion.

With each successive election, the Internet creates new platforms for communication and mobilization about politics. In 2008, Democratic candidates in particular built comprehensive Internet strategies that did more than just duplicate off-line efforts to mobilize supporters, and citizens made unprecedented use of the Internet to learn about candidates and issues and to participate in campaigns. While only 4 percent of likely voters went online for election information in 1996, a full 61 percent of Americans reported looking at information online or discussing politics online in 2012 according to Pew's Internet and American Life Project.[10] Today most Americans use the Internet to learn about political candidates, policy issues, or to express their views.[11]

Recent survey data from Pew illustrates how widespread digital politics has become. Sixty-six percent of social media users—or 39 percent of American adults—have engaged in some form of civic or political activity using social media as of 2012. More than one in three social media users have encouraged others to vote, and roughly the same percentage have shared their own thoughts or comments on politics using social media.[12] Roughly the same percentage of Democrats, Republicans, and independents use social media for politics. Notably, the young (ages 18–29) are significantly more likely than middle-age and older respondents to use social media for politics. If these trends are sustained, they may result in greater overall levels of political interest and activity. Those who benefit most from online politics are likely to be those who are most active online, including the young.[13] Because young Americans tend to move from place to place more often than citizens ages 40 years and older, traditional "snail mail" campaigns are less likely to reach them. Thus candidates and political campaigns are turning more and more to digital politics to reach young Americans.

Does Online Participation Lead to Offline Participation? An important question is whether online political participation influences offline participation, especially voting. Political participation requires that people be motivated and have an interest in the outcome of the election. They must have the knowledge or capacity to understand how to participate, and they must be mobilized.[14] Digital technology encourages information-gathering and interaction among users by combining features of traditional media in content and interpersonal communication for discussion and mobilization. Because of this combination of information and interactivity, the Internet has the potential to promote interest in politics and increase participation. The Occupy Wall Street movement is a good example of the intersection of online and traditional participation. The movement started with one simple email sent to 90,000 individuals in July 2011. Only 2,000 people originally showed up. But videos of young people being arrested by the police were posted online and quickly went viral. Within weeks, organizers in cities across the United States had used Twitter and email to organize their own protests. One month after the movement's humble beginnings, Occupy Wall Street's Twitter account had over 85,000 followers, and in the first week of October 2011 approximately 400,000 people visited their website *per day*, making Occupy Wall Street the first mass protest in the United States built on new media.

A growing body of research indicates that activities such as reading the news online, commenting on blogs, sending or receiving political emails, or using social media for politics increase the likelihood that someone will not only vote but also contribute to political campaigns and candidates, attend campaign meetings, volunteer, engage in community activities, and even contact elected officials.[15] Online participation is also linked with discussing politics with friends or family, having an interest in politics, and being politically knowledgeable.

Researchers who study this subject have suggested a number of possible reasons online politics may foster participation. First, information, which is necessary for effective political participation, is easier to obtain online and is available 24 hours a day for those who have Internet access. The Internet is increasingly compared with the invention of the printing press, which stimulated the demand for greater literacy in society.[16] Second, online news may "accidentally" engage individuals who otherwise would not be involved in politics at all. The political scientist Doris Graber has referred to the "accidental" mobilization of the electorate through the election news coverage that many Americans were exposed to by default when there were only a few television networks.[17] The Internet has created a new version of the "accidental mobilization" of those who are greeted by political information when they open their email, check Facebook, or conduct online searches—sometimes politics finds the individual, rather than the other way around.[18] Candidates regularly place political ads on social media sites and in Google searches. Individuals may be exposed to these ads and learn about politics, even if their motives for being online do not involve politics. Some research shows that individuals with low to moderate interest in politics, who are frequently online, are more likely to participate than individuals with low interest who are not online.[19]

Third, digital media have unique characteristics that enhance participation. The Internet and streaming video combine the qualities of print media that promote knowledge with the visual aspects of television that generate interest, engagement, and emotion.[20] News online covers events and issues with the same immediacy as television, but with the in-depth treatment that is typical of newspapers. Emotional responses to political candidates or issues learned in online media have been shown to trigger interest in politics and engagement.[21] In 2012, for example, Senate candidate

Like the traditional "I Voted" stickers, political messages shared on social media may remind and encourage others to participate too. In 2012, Facebook users could click an "I Voted" button to announce that they had cast a ballot.

Elizabeth Warren became a national sensation overnight with a video in which she passionately rebutted the idea that taxing the wealthy is "class warfare." Her campaign video was viewed more than 100,000 times on YouTube in one week.

Fourth, online politics lowers the barriers for entry, making it easier for people to participate in ways that require less effort. By its very nature online politics occurs in ways that are less location dependent than traditional politics: *community* takes on a very different meaning in an online context compared with a voter's actual neighborhood precinct or a local political party office. The Internet facilitates participation that is potentially broad, but with looser connections among participants than in more traditional networks of coworkers or neighbors.[22] While this may promote more extensive organizing efforts, it also encourages forms of participation that are low intensity and sporadic, possibly attracting individuals with only moderate political interest.

Thus participation online may be broader, but also less intense, possibly leading more people to participate in ways that require less effort. Forwarding an email to a friend, posting a link on Facebook, or uploading a brief comment to a local newspaper website is an individual act that doesn't require commitment to organizational membership. However, it may improve political knowledge, interest, and participation. The political scientist Bruce Bimber has shown that some interest groups are responding to this new political climate of sporadic participation by focusing more outreach on the web and by making it possible for individuals to support a specific issue or campaign without making a commitment to membership in the organization as a whole.[23] If citizens with low interest can become engaged in politics online, this will widen the pool of people participating in politics.

Finally, the Internet enables new forms of political expression through blogs, videos, social media, and websites.[24] This expressive capacity of the technology can lead to increased citizen involvement in politics, much of it through citizen journalism. The scholar Russell Dalton argues that participation is in the process of changing to include norms of citizenship that are more expressive than voting.[25] For many citizens, becoming a "fan" or follower of a candidate online is a first step toward active participation in politics.

For all these reasons, digital media may foster a new kind of community building that has the potential to reverse the trends in voter turnout and political participation, which have been declining over the past four decades. Explanations for these trends vary, but many analysts cite reduced trust in government, failures of the party system, and a diminishing stock of what Robert Putnam, author of *Bowling Alone*, calls social capital—community networks that motivate political participation.[26] By making political information, discussion, communication, and online mobilization easier, the Internet may help Americans grow a new kind of social capital, one based on shared political experiences in cyberspace.[27]

Online Protest against SOPA and PIPA Online protests to preserve Internet freedom provide a striking example of how new media can be used to mobilize traditional participation in politics (in this case, contacting members of Congress). Media "content producers" have long complained of severe economic losses due to online piracy—the illegal downloading of music, movies, TV shows, and other copyrighted material posted by foreign piracy websites. Early in 2012, at the urging of media companies and industry associations, legislation designed to clamp down on U.S.-based websites that facilitated international piracy was brought before Congress. These proposed laws, known as SOPA and PIPA,[28] represented an attempt to extend U.S. copyright laws beyond U.S. borders.

In 2012 an online protest prompted Congress to reconsider legislation designed to regulate the Internet and protect intellectual property rights. Numerous major websites "went dark" to draw attention to the issue, and Google displayed a black censorship bar along with a link to an online petition against the proposed law.

In what became characterized as a duel pitting Hollywood against Silicon Valley, proponents of the antipiracy legislation, including the U.S. Chamber of Commerce and the motion picture industry, said that SOPA and PIPA were necessary to prevent digital thievery. While acknowledging that online piracy was a problem, the technology industry objected to provisions that would have held them liable for policing any website they linked to that might contain pirated content, such as a video or song. Google, for example, links to millions and millions of websites. More generally, opponents of SOPA and PIPA said that the proposals would allow government censorship of the Internet and would damage free and open online communication. They argued that the legislation could stifle innovation and job creation in the twenty-first-century economy, especially among small businesses reliant on the Internet.

At least initially, the bills had broad bipartisan support and appeared destined to be enacted into law. Then, on January 18, 2012, more than a 100 websites launched a coordinated protest—the largest online protest in history. It included a 24-hour shutdown of the online encyclopedia Wikipedia, a nonprofit organization and one of the top 10 most-visited websites worldwide. Users were redirected to a black screen providing information on the bills and links for users to click on to contact their member of Congress. According to Wikipedia, in one day there were 160 million visits to the site, and more than 4 million people accessed the information about contacting their member of Congress. (To put this figure in perspective, remember that there are 314 million citizens in the United States.). Google users, meanwhile, faced a black censorship bar blocking the Google logo and a link reading "Tell Congress: Please don't censor the web!" The search engine directed users to a petition opposing the bills; 10 million people signed the petition in 24 hours. Craigslist, Facebook, Twitter, and hundreds of other tech giants participated as well, either blacking out their content or posting information about the issue in order to raise awareness.[29] Yahoo, Microsoft, and many other major Internet companies opposed the legislation with public statements.

To be sure, this was a different form of protest: quiet compared with a traditional street rally, but loud in its impact on the media industry and government. Overnight, protest as a tool was transformed as people turned from traditional constituent lobbying techniques (scripted calls and form letters) and toward the use of new media. Members of Congress faced a barrage of phone calls, emails, and tweets from concerned citizens voicing opposition to the antipiracy laws. In response, at least eight members of Congress publicly changed their position on the legislation within the day, many more withdrew their support in the following days, and the bills' momentum was stalled and eventually tabled. As former senator Chris Dodd said, "No Washington player can safely assume that a well-wired, heavily financed legislative program is safe from a sudden burst of Web-driven populism. . . . This is altogether a new effect."[30]

Are There Drawbacks to Online Participation? Traditional political participation and online participation are not mutually exclusive, of course. Many people are equally comfortable in both worlds, using the Internet to facilitate organizing face-to-face neighborhood meetings or seek out information about a local campaign event or where to vote. Political candidates find campaigning online particularly attractive because it is cost-efficient and can reach a wide audience of prospective voters.

As we described in Chapter 1, digital citizens are daily Internet users, requiring regular access to the technology, and the skills to use the technology, including language skills.[31] A barrier to participation in politics online then is the digital divide—defined as those without high-speed home or mobile access. Those on the wrong side of the divide tend to be poorer, lower educated, African American and Latino, and older. This creates new inequalities as the world of politics moves online.[32] Nearly one-third of Americans lack high-speed Internet access at home, although a growing number of Americans connect to the Internet through mobile devices such as cell phones, even if they lack home access, especially racial minorities and the young.[33] However, one in five Americans remains offline as of 2014. Racial minorities and the poor are more likely to cite affordability and cost as reasons for lacking Internet access at home compared with other groups. A lack of skills is a primary reason for being off-line for Latinos, while a lack of interest is the primary reason among the elderly.[34] Inequality in access to information online is an important public policy issue, separating the digital "haves" from the "have-nots."

Despite these limitations, perhaps the most transformative aspect of digital media is how they affect not the participation of ordinary citizens, but rather that of candidates and parties. Running for office can be enormously expensive, but new media may level the playing field by reducing candidate reliance on money from corporations, special interests, and wealthy donors. Despite recent Supreme Court rulings against legislative attempts to limit the influence of money in politics,[35] digital media holds promise of reinvigorating a more grassroots and participatory democracy.[36] This in turn may allow political leaders to better represent the people, rather than special interests.

● Who Participates?

Describe the patterns of participation among major demographic groups

A common starting point for understanding who votes and who does not is to consider that individuals face a number of costs and benefits related to their decision to become involved in politics, just as in any other activity in life. According to such an analysis, an individual is likely to participate only if the benefits of voting in an election outweigh the costs.[37] One benefit associated with voting, for instance, may be the favorable policies that might result from having one's preferred candidate or party in office, which the potential voter weighs against the slim likelihood of his or her vote actually influencing the outcome of the election. Another benefit of voting is the sense of pride gained from fulfilling one's civic duty. The costs related to voting can include the time and resources needed to cast a ballot and gather political information and become informed. This may in part explain why the poor and the less educated are less likely to vote.

Beyond the costs and benefits of voting, political scientists have focused on understanding the individual in her political environment and how contextual factors affect whether or not that person decides to cast a ballot on Election Day. A simple example is headline news stories declaring an early winner in the exit polls in presidential elections. If a candidate is proclaimed the winner, there is little incentive for individuals to vote; in fact not voting then becomes rational. This occurs every four years when voters on the West Coast, located in a time zone three hours later than that of the East Coast, learn that the presidential race is effectively over. Turnout in California and other western states naturally plummets. The political environment can also positively impact voter turnout. For instance, citizens living in presidential battleground states are exposed to a torrent of candidate campaigns ads, candidate visits, and grassroots mobilization efforts. These individuals are more knowledgeable about presidential elections, more interested in the campaign, and have a higher probability of voting than residents of states that are "safe" for either the Republican Party, such as Texas, or the Democratic Party, such as California. What state an individual lives in matters for participation in politics.

The factors that organize our understanding of voting in elections can be grouped into three general categories: (1) a person's social and demographic background and attitudes about politics; (2) the political environment in which elections take place, such as campaigns that seek to mobilize voters and whether an election is contested among two political candidates, and finally; (3) the state electoral laws that shape the electoral process. We examine each in turn.

Socioeconomic Status

One of the most important and consistent findings from surveys about participation is that Americans with higher levels of education, more income, and higher-level occupations—collectively, what social scientists call higher **socioeconomic status**— participate much more in politics than do those with less education and less income.[38] Education level is the single most important factor in predicting not only whether an individual will vote but also most kinds of participation. Income is an important factor (not surprisingly) when it comes to making contributions. People who are more affluent have the money, time, and capacity to participate effectively in the political system. These characteristics are also related to attitudes toward politics. Higher levels of political interest and psychological involvement in politics, such as political efficacy, are associated with individuals higher on the socioeconomic scale.[39]

Figure 8.3 shows the differences in voter turnout linked to ethnic group, education level, employment status, and age. Just 49 percent of those with only a high school diploma voted in the recent presidential election, compared with 72 percent of college graduates.

socioeconomic status status in society based on level of education, income, and occupational prestige

for critical analysis

As voter turnout has declined since its peak in the late 1800s, inequality in political participation has become more severe. Why are upper-income Americans more likely to be voters than lower-income Americans?

FIGURE 8.3

The Percentage of Americans Who Voted, 1976–2012

Voting rates vary substantially by race and ethnicity, education, employment status, and age. Which groups have the highest rates of voter turnout? Among which groups has participation increased the most since 1992?

SOURCES: U.S. Census Bureau, "Reported Voting and Registration by Race, Hispanic Origin, Sex, and Age Groups: November 1964 to 2008"; "Reported Voting and Registration by Region, Educational Attainment, and Labor Force: November 1964 to 2008," www.census.gov (accessed 4/24/14).

PERCENTAGE OF POPULATION
REPORTING THEY VOTED

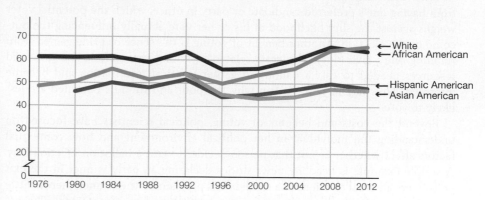

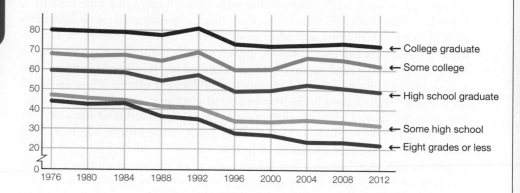

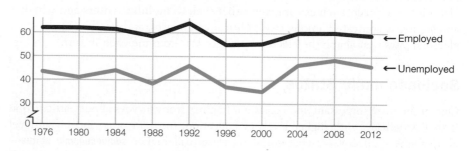

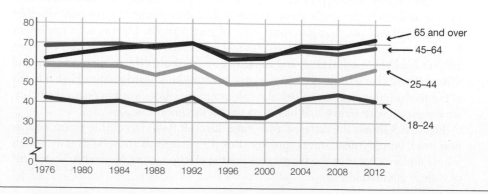

Age and Participation

Older people have much higher rates of participation than young people. In the 2008 presidential elections, youth turnout was at its highest level in decades, with 44 percent of those ages 18 to 24 voting (turnout rates were 41 percent for this age group in 2012). However, this figure is still far lower than the number of older (65 and over) voters who turned out: an estimated 70 percent of those voters cast ballots in 2008.[40] Moreover, in midterm elections, youth turnout has historically been extremely low. In 2010, for example, only 10 percent of the people who voted were young voters, compared with 19 percent in 2012.

One reason younger people vote less is that political campaigns have rarely targeted young voters. A study of political advertising found that 64 percent of campaign television advertising was directed at people over 50. Only 14.2 percent of advertising was aimed at 18- to 34-year-olds.[41] Another reason that political campaigns target older voters is that the elderly are better organized to participate than young people. The most important organization representing the elderly is AARP (formerly the American Association of Retired People), which has a membership of 40 million. AARP's ability to mobilize many thousands of individuals to weigh in on policy proposals has made the organization one of the most powerful in Washington. Young people have no comparable organization.

Since the early 1990s, several campaigns have been designed to increase the participation of young voters. Rock the Vote, which began in 1990, uses musicians and actors to urge young people to vote. It has spawned other initiatives aimed at young voters, including Rap the Vote and Rock the Vote a lo Latino. More recently, the Obama campaign made young voters central to its electoral strategy in 2008 and 2012. The campaign posted videos on YouTube and used social media to reach out to young people. It sought to increase participation of young voters through a major voter registration campaign on college campuses. Obama won 60 percent of the youth vote, compared with Mitt Romney's 36 percent. In 2008 Obama won 66 percent of younger voters.[42]

for critical analysis

When the Twenty-Sixth Amendment changed the voting age from 21 to 18 in 1971, observers expected that the youth vote would add a significant new voice to American politics. Why has the youth vote turned out to be less important than was hoped? What changes would engage more young people in the political system?

At this Rock the Vote concert, musicians such as Pharrell Williams, from the band N*E*R*D, performed to support efforts to get young people to vote. Particularly since 2000, campaigns like Rock the Vote have contributed to increases in the youth vote.

Relatively low voter turnout by the young has implications for the policies addressed by government at the local, state, and federal levels. Young people share older Americans' concerns about the economy and national security, but they tend to have more positive views about the role of government and express support for stronger environmental laws, funding for public education and colleges, and more tolerance for personal freedoms than older people do. They also are more likely to oppose military intervention overseas.[43] And although young people are less likely to engage in politics than older generations, they do have a strong interest in community service. One recent survey found that 19 percent of young people are involved in community service projects, with numbers higher among those with college experience.[44] Another survey found that 57 percent of young people felt that they could have a role in solving the problems in their community. Yet that same survey revealed cynicism about politics, with 61 percent of young people responding that "politics is a way for the powerful to keep themselves powerful."[45] The distinctive attitudes of the young, often called Millennials, suggest that higher levels of political participation by this group (which is numerically larger than the politically significant Baby Boomers) could influence politics.

African Americans

As we saw earlier in Chapter 5, in the South during much of the twentieth century, the widespread use of the poll tax, literacy tests, and other measures such as the white primary deprived African Americans (and many poor whites) of the right to vote. This system of legal segregation meant that black Americans in the South had few avenues for participating in politics. Through a combination of protest, legal action, and political pressure, the civil rights movement compelled a reluctant federal government to enforce black civil and political rights.

The victories of the civil rights movement made blacks full citizens and stimulated a tremendous growth in the number of black public officials at all levels of government as blacks exercised their newfound political rights. The movement drew on an organizational base and network of communication rooted in black churches, the NAACP, and black colleges. By voting as a cohesive bloc, African American voters began to wield considerable political power. When such legal barriers as the poll tax and the white primary were removed in the 1960s, black political participation shot up, with rates of turnout approaching those of southern whites as early as 1968.[46]

The increase in the number of black elected officials, in turn, had positive effects on the level of participation. One study of black political participation, for example, found that African Americans in cities run by a black mayor were more likely to vote, participate in campaigns, and contact public officials.[47] African Americans are also more likely to vote when residing in states with increased representation in the state legislature, as measured by the percentage of black lawmakers.[48] African Americans represented by a black member of Congress are more likely to vote in elections and to have a sense of efficacy—the belief that the government is responsive to them—and have higher levels of political knowledge.[49]

With Barack Obama running in 2008 as the first black major-party candidate for president, African American interest in the election surged. Exit polls indicated that 95 percent of African Americans who voted cast ballots for Obama. The 2008 and 2012 elections also witnessed a significant increase in minority participation and marked an end to the long-standing gap in the level of black and white voter turnout. The black-white gap went from 7 percent in 2004 to 1 percent in 2008 (see Figure 8.3).[50]

Yet despite these successes, racial segregation remains a fact of life in the United States, and new problems have emerged. Most troubling is the persistence of black urban poverty, now coupled with deep social and economic isolation.[51] These conditions, often called concentrated poverty, raise new questions about African American political participation. As the previous section on socioeconomic status described, participation (for blacks as well as whites) is highly correlated with more income, higher levels of education, and higher-level occupations. The persistence of black urban poverty is thus a troubling indicator that participation may remain low in this group, with the result that their interests will not be represented as effectively in politics.

On the other hand, African Americans who have a shared sense of collective identity, a concept called *linked fate*, are more likely to vote and participate politically. Political scientist Michael Dawson argues black-linked fate is a major predictor of political behavior. Dawson uses the construct of *linked fate* to measure the degree to which African Americans believe that their own self-interests are linked to the interests of the race.[52] That is, the experiences of African Americans with race and racial discrimination in the United States, including a history of slavery, unify their personal interests to seeking candidate and policies that benefit their racial group. Black civic, community, religious, and political organizations are also important in increasing political participation for this group.

Latinos

For many years, analysts called the Latino vote "the sleeping giant" because Latinos as a group had relatively low levels of participation in politics. One important reason for this was the low rate of naturalization, which meant that many Latinos, as noncitizens, were not eligible to vote. Among those who were eligible to vote, registration and turnout rates were relatively low.

Today politicians and political parties view Latinos as a political group of critical importance, as they have become the largest minority in the United States. Rapid population growth, increased political participation, and uncertain party attachment all magnify the importance of the Latino vote.[53] The Latino population stood at 54 million people as of 2013, or 17 percent of Americans, making Hispanics significantly more numerous than African Americans.[54] In large states such as California and Texas, Latinos are approaching 50 percent of the population. Although Latino registration and turnout are still significantly lower than those of whites and African Americans, these numbers have been steadily increasing. In 2008 a record 9.75 million Hispanics voted, accounting for 7.4 percent of the total national vote.[55] In 2012 it was 8.4 percent.

Latinos have tended to favor the Democrats in national elections, though not as strongly or consistently as African Americans. Indeed, many Republicans believe that the tendency of Latino voters to be more socially conservative on issues of marriage, abortion, and religion than other groups within the Democratic Party provides the GOP with an opportunity to attract support from this growing constituency. However, Republican opposition to immigration reform has prompted Latinos to return to their more typical Democratic voting patterns. In addition, the Obama administration aggressively reached out to Spanish-speaking media in an effort to connect to Latino voters: it held the first bilingual White House press briefing and partnered with Spanish-language networks Univision and Telemundo to broadcast White House events. In 2012, Obama and his challenger Mitt Romney both tried to appeal to Latino voters, but according to exit polls, Obama won 70 percent of the Latino vote.

for critical analysis

How significant a factor was the Latino vote in the 2012 election? Why does the percentage of eligible Latinos voting still lag behind that of other groups?

A recent study finds traditional explanations of vote choice based on economic evaluations and other predictors fail to take into account factors important to Latino voters, including perceptions of shared ethnic identity. Latinos in the United States have been especially concerned with changes in U.S. immigration policy, and responses to immigration policy might act to create a more cohesive Latino collective identity, like linked fate for African Americans discussed above. Using national public opinion polls of Latinos, political scientists Loren Collingwood, Matt Barreto, and Sergio Garcia-Rios evaluate Barack Obama's and Mitt Romney's cross-racial mobilization of Latino voters during the 2012 presidential election. They find that the candidates' policy stances vis-à-vis immigration and their ability to convey care and concern to the Latino community are important factors that shape Latino vote choice.[56]

Similar to African Americans, Latinos are also more likely to vote when residing in states with increased representation in the state legislature, as measured by the percentage of Latino lawmakers, or in a district with a Latino Congress member.[57] This phenomenon is commonly referred to as descriptive representation—when individuals are represented in government by officials of their same race, ethnicity, or gender. When meaningful descriptive representation occurs, minority groups may have a greater ability to affect policy outcomes, thus incorporating minority populations and their concerns and interests into the political system. Descriptive representation may also confer symbolic benefits, such as reducing levels of political alienation among racial and ethnic minorities.[58]

Asian Americans

Asian Americans are a smaller group than whites, Latinos, or African Americans, comprising 6 percent of the U.S. population in 2013. However, in particular states, such as California, home to 33 percent of the nation's Asian population, the group has become an important political presence. In terms of socioeconomic status, Asian Americans have education and income levels closer to those of whites than of Latinos or African Americans. Asians are less likely to vote than whites or African Americans.

No one national group dominates among the Asian American population, and their diversity has impeded the development of group-based political power. This diversity means that Asian Americans often have different political concerns, stemming from their different national backgrounds and experiences in the United States. Historically, these groups have united most effectively around common issues of ethnic discrimination or anti-Asian violence, federal immigration policies, and discriminatory mortgage loan practices.

Turnout rates among Asian Americans have been generally lower than those of other groups, though they have been gradually increasing: in 2008, 47.6 percent of Asian Americans turned out to vote, their second-highest percentage turnout since the census began tracking their participation in 1990.[59] In terms of political orientation, Asian Americans are a diverse group, but they have been moving, along with other minority groups, toward the Democratic Party in recent elections. Although a majority of Asian Americans voted Republican in the early 1990s, in the 2000s they have been voting increasingly Democratic,[60] and 73 percent of Asian Americans voted to re-elect Barack Obama in 2012.

Who Voted in 2012?

All American citizens ages 18 and over are eligible to vote in the United States, regardless of race, gender, educational attainment, or income. However, not all groups vote at the same rate, and as a result, the voting population in 2012 is not a mirror image of the population as a whole. These data show the composition of those who voted in the 2012 election compared to the group's proportion in the population as a whole. Thus, while young adults (ages 18–24) make up 12.7 percent of the American population, they made up only 8.6 percent of voters.

ANNUAL INCOME

	Percentage of citizen population (18+)	Percentage of total voters
< $20,000	9.1%	6.8%
$20,000–49,999	23.0%	21.3%
$50,000–74,999	16.9%	**18.0%**
$75,000–99,999	11.3%	**13.0%**
$100,000–149,999	11.6%	**14.1%**
$150,000+	9.3%	**11.8%**
Income not reported	18.8%	15.0%

AGE

	Percentage of citizen population (18+)	Percentage of total voters
18–24	12.7%	8.6%
25–44	34.3%	30.0%
45–64	34.9%	**39.1%**
65–74	10.2%	**12.9%**
75+	7.8%	**9.4%**

EDUCATION

	Percentage of citizen population (18+)	Percentage of total voters
Less than high school	10.2%	6.2%
High school graduate	30.4%	25.9%
Some college or associate's degree	30.1%	**31.3%**
Bachelor's degree	19.3%	**23.5%**
Advanced degree	10.0%	**13.1%**

GENDER

	Percentage of citizen population (18+)	Percentage of total voters
Men	47.8%	46.3%
Women	52.2%	**53.7%**

ETHNICITY

	Percentage of citizen population (18+)	Percentage of total voters
White (non-Hispanic)	71.1%	**73.8%**
African American	12.5%	**13.4%**
Asian	3.8%	2.9%
Hispanic	10.9%	8.4%
Other	1.7%	1.5%

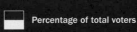

Percentage of citizen population (18+)

Percentage of total voters

SOURCE: U.S. Census Bureau, www.census.gov/hhes/www/socdemo/voting/publications/p20/2012/tables.html (accessed 5/26/14).

for critical analysis

1. Which groups are overrepresented among the voting population? Which groups are underrepresented?

2. What might explain why some groups vote in large numbers (relative to the size of the group in the total population) while other groups vote in small numbers?

NOTE: These numbers reflect U.S. citizens only, not total U.S. population. Voting is self-reported and thus may be higher than the actual numbers of who voted.

Gender and Participation

gender gap a distinctive pattern of voting behavior reflecting the differences in views between women and men

Today women register and vote at rates similar to or higher than those of men. The ongoing significance of gender issues in American politics is best exemplified by the **gender gap**—a distinctive pattern of male and female voting decisions—in electoral politics. Women tend to vote in higher numbers for Democratic candidates, whereas Republicans win more male votes. In 1980 men voted heavily for the Republican candidate, Ronald Reagan; women divided their votes between Reagan and the incumbent Democratic president, Jimmy Carter. Since that election, gender differences have emerged in congressional and state elections as well. The gender gap runs around 10 points in presidential elections.

Behind these voting patterns are differing assessments of key policy issues. Women are more likely than men to oppose military activities, especially war, and are more likely to support social spending. In 2003, 79 percent of men supported the Iraq War, for example, compared with 65 percent of women—a 14-point difference.[61] On social programs, women tend to want stronger action from government: 45 percent of men were content with the quality of public education, whereas only 39 percent of women were.[62] These differences do not mean that all women vote more liberally than all men.

One key development in gender politics in recent years is the growing number of women in elective office (see Figure 8.4), an increasingly significant form of descriptive representation. Journalists dubbed 1992 the "Year of the Woman" because so many women were elected to Congress: women doubled their numbers in the House and tripled them in the Senate. By 2009 women held

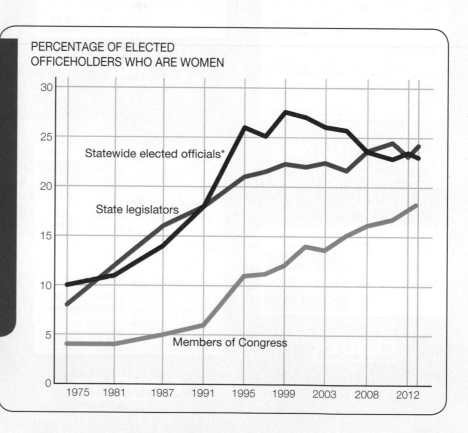

FIGURE 8.4

Increase in Number of Women in Elective Office, 1975–2013

The number of women holding elected office has always been larger in state offices than in Congress. When did the percentage of women elected to office begin to rise more rapidly?

*Governors, attorneys general, etc.
SOURCES: Cynthia Costello, Shari Miles, and Anne J. Stone., eds., *The American Woman, 2001–2002* (New York: W.W. Norton, 2002), p. 328; and Center for American Women and Politics, www.cawp.rutgers.edu (accessed 4/26/14).

PERCENTAGE OF ELECTED OFFICEHOLDERS WHO ARE WOMEN

Statewide elected officials*

State legislators

Members of Congress

17.2 percent of the seats in the House of Representatives, including that held by the first female Speaker of the House, Nancy Pelosi. A total of 17 women served in the 100-member Senate in 2009–11, which represented an all-time high for an institution that had had only 38 female senators in its entire history.[63] Following the 2014 elections, at least 20 women served in the Senate, including Joni Ernst (R-Iowa) and Tammy Baldwin (D-Wisc.). Baldwin is also the first openly gay person elected to the Senate. The number of women was expected to rise to 21, the most ever, if Mary Landrieu won the runoff election in Louisiana. In 2014 at least 79 women were elected to the House of Representatives, or 18 percent of the body. Women have been elected to the House of Representatives from 44 of the 50 states.

Recent research has shown that one key to increasing the number of women in political office is to encourage more women to run for political office. Although women are just as likely to win an election as men, women are less likely to run for office, even if they are equally qualified. They are also disadvantaged as candidates not because they are women, but because male candidates are more likely to have the advantage of incumbency.[64] Organizations supporting female candidates have worked to encourage more women to run for office and have supported them financially. In addition to the bipartisan National Women's Political Caucus (NWPC), the Women's Campaign Fund (WCF), and EMILY's List ("Early Money Is Like Yeast—it helps raise the dough") provide prochoice Democratic women with early campaign financing, which is critical to establishing electoral momentum.

Why does the gender gap matter? Although women in public office by no means take uniform positions on policy issues, surveys show that, on the whole, female legislators are more supportive of women's rights and education and health care spending, and are more attentive to children's and family issues.[65]

Religious Identity

Religious identity plays an important role in American life. For many citizens, religious groups provide an organizational infrastructure for political participation, especially around issues of special group concern. Black churches, for example, were instrumental in the civil rights movement, and black religious leaders continue to play important roles in national and local politics. Jews have also been active as a group in politics, but less through religious bodies than through a variety of social action agencies, including the American Jewish Congress, the American Jewish Committee, and the Anti-Defamation League.

For most of American history, religious language, symbols, and values have been woven deeply into the fabric of public life. Until the mid-twentieth century, public school students generally began the day with prayers or Bible readings; city halls displayed crèches during the Christmas season. But over the past 35 years, a variety of court decisions has greatly reduced this kind of overt religious influence on public life. In 1962 the Supreme Court ruled in *Engel v. Vitale* that prayer in public schools was unconstitutional—that government should not be in the business of sponsoring official prayers.[66] These decisions helped to spawn a countermovement of religious activists seeking to roll back these decisions and restore the prominent role of religion in civic life. The mobilization of religious organizations and other groups that aim to reintroduce their moral views into the public sphere has been one of the most significant political developments of the past two and a half decades. Some of the most divisive conflicts in politics today, such as those over abortion and same-sex marriage, hinge on differences over religious and moral beliefs. These divisions

Rev. Jerry Falwell helped to organize evangelical Christians into a powerful political force in the 1980s, and religion continues to heavily inform political participation today. At this appearance with Falwell, President Ronald Reagan announced his support for a ban on abortions, tougher laws against child pornography, and voluntary prayer.

have become so salient that they now constitute a major clash of cultures, with repercussions throughout the political system and across many different areas of policy.

One of the most significant drivers of this new politics has been the mobilization of white evangelical Protestants into a cohesive political force. The Moral Majority, the first broad-based political organization of evangelical Christians, was founded in 1979 and quickly rose to prominence in the 1980 election when it aligned with the Republican Party, eventually backing Ronald Reagan for president. Over the next few years, evangelicals strengthened their movement by registering voters and mobilizing them with sophisticated, state-of-the-art political techniques such as direct-mail campaigns and telephone hotlines. Their success was evident in the 1984 election, when 80 percent of evangelical Christian voters cast their ballots for Reagan. The 1988 election was a turning point in the political development of the Christian right. The televangelist Pat Robertson ran for president, and, although his candidacy was unsuccessful, his effort laid the groundwork for future political strength. Robertson's supporters gained control of some state Republican parties and won positions of power in others. With this new organizational base and sharply honed political skills, Robertson formed a new organization, the Christian Coalition, which capitalized on its ability to mobilize a large grassroots base to become one of the most important groups in American politics during the 1990s.

President George W. Bush was closely aligned with religious conservatives, and the religious right played an important role in mobilizing voters to support him in the 2000 and 2004 elections. Many analysts viewed Bush's Office of Faith-Based and Community Initiatives (whose programs were generally known as faith-based initiatives), which sought to funnel government assistance to religious groups engaged in charitable work, as a way to reward conservative Christian groups for supporting his candidacy. In fact, conservative religious groups spoke out against the initiative at first because they feared that government control would accompany federal dollars.[67]

But individual-level factors are not the only explanations for voter turnout or other forms of political participation. Our incomplete understanding of participation is evident when we compare voting across countries. For example, if more political resources lead to a greater likelihood of voting, why does the United States, one of the most prosperous countries in the world, have such a dismal history of participation? And Americans have become more educated over the past century, with more people finishing high school and attending college; so, given the well-documented links between educational attainment and voting, why has participation declined during this period?[68] These puzzles mean we need to look beyond the socioeconomic characteristics of individuals and to the larger political environment in which participation occurs.

● Political Environment and Participation

Explain the factors in the political environment that influence whether individuals vote or not

However important such individual factors as age and socioeconomic class may be in determining political participation, political environments have increasingly proven to be even more significant. Whether or not people have resources, feel engaged, or are recruited to participate in politics depends very much on their social setting—what their parents are like, whom they know, what associations they belong to. In the United States, churches are one important social institution for helping foster political participation. Through their church activities people learn the civic skills that prepare them to participate in the political world more broadly. However, Robert Putnam argues that, over the past five decades, America has experienced a collapse of community organizations (or social capital), which may explain low participation. Younger generations are less likely to be engaged in community organizations that are involved in politics than, say, generations that came of age during World War II.

Still, arguments about long-term declines in community involvement may not give enough attention to the actual political environments where politics takes place. Participation depends not only on what people think politics has to offer them and their communities, but also on whether citizens are motivated and mobilized to participate and on whether there are formal obstacles in the election system.

Mobilization

A critical aspect of political environments is whether people are mobilized—by parties, candidates, campaigns, interest groups, and social movements. A recent comprehensive study of the decline in political participation in the United States found that half of the drop-off could be accounted for by reduced **mobilization** efforts.[69] People become much more likely to participate when someone—especially someone they know—asks them to get involved.

A series of experiments conducted by the political scientists Donald Green and Alan Gerber demonstrate the importance of personal contact for mobilizing voters. Evaluating the results of several get-out-the-vote drives, Gerber and Green showed that face-to-face interaction with a canvasser greatly increased the chances that the person contacted would go to the polls. They estimated that personal contact boosted voter turnout by 9.8 percent. The impact of direct mail was much smaller, causing only a 0.6 percent increase in voting.[70] Impersonal calls from a phone bank had no measurable effect on voter turnout. Green and Gerber also evaluated the impact of mobilization on young voters by studying a series of get-out-the-vote campaigns

mobilization the process by which large numbers of people are organized for a political activity

People are more likely to turn out to vote if someone asks them face-to-face. Direct mail and impersonal phone calls are less likely to have an effect on turnout.

conducted near college campuses during the 2000 election. In these campaigns, phone contacts that were chattier and more informal than standard phone-bank messages increased turnout by an estimated 5 percent. Face-to-face contact again proved even more powerful, increasing turnout by 8.5 percent.[71] Recent research has shown that text messaging has a positive impact on youth turnout. In 2008 one study showed that sending text messages to young voters on the day before a presidential primary election increased turnout by 2.1 percent; sending messages on the day of the election increased turnout by 4.6 percent.[72] Social networks also matter. In a large experiment involving 61 million users of Facebook, political scientists said that turnout in the 2010 midterm election increased by 340,000 additional people (who otherwise would not have voted). Importantly, the closest Facebook friends had the most influence in getting users to vote, thus online and offline networks both played a role in mobilizing voters.[73]

In previous decades, political parties and social movements relied on personal contact to mobilize voters. As we will see in Chapter 9, during the nineteenth century, American political party machines employed hundreds of thousands of workers to organize and mobilize voters as well as bring them to the polls. The result was an extremely high turnout rate, typically more than 90 percent of eligible voters.[74] But political party machines began to decline in strength at the beginning of the twentieth century, and by now have, for the most part, disappeared. By the late twentieth century, political parties had become essentially fund-raising and advertising organizations rather than mobilizers of people. Without party workers to encourage eligible voters to go to the polls, and even bring them there if necessary, many of them will not participate. Nevertheless, competitive presidential elections since 2000 have once again motivated both parties to build strong grassroots organizations to reach voters and turn them out on Election Day. In the 2004 elections, Republicans were more successful in their organizational efforts than Democrats. Republicans built an organization with more than 1.4 million volunteers who were trained to make calls, go door to door to register voters, write letters to the editor in support of President Bush, post blogs online, and phone local radio call-in shows.

During the 2008 campaign, though, the Democrats built a more extensive organization to contact and turn out voters than did Republicans. Barack Obama's campaign made mobilization a centerpiece of its strategy from the start. Inspired by Obama's own experience as a community organizer, the campaign sought to organize a base of volunteers to go door to door seeking support for their candidate. Many of Obama's crucial primary victories, including his initial win in Iowa and his later success in states that, like Iowa, used the caucus system to select presidential candidates, relied on direct voter mobilization. These victories in primaries and caucuses led the Obama campaign to create a nationwide organization of paid staff and volunteers for the general election, rather than focusing on battleground states as his predecessors had done. The expansion of the electorate through mobilization became a central pillar of the Obama strategy. The campaign opened more than 700 offices in the battleground states, where paid staff coordinated the work of tens of thousands of volunteers. The Internet, as discussed earlier, played a significant role in this mobilization strategy. In contrast, the McCain campaign put less emphasis on building an organization of paid staff and volunteers, relying instead on traditional voter mobilization tactics and the battleground-state strategy that had worked four years earlier for George W. Bush.

for critical analysis

Why do efforts toward direct mobilization seem to be more successful than television advertising in promoting voter turnout? How is the Internet becoming an important tool for increasing political participation?

Analyses of the 2008 election have suggested that the Democrats' organization and mobilization helped Barack Obama win the White House. By mobilizing support in places where Democrats had not seriously contended in the past, including largely Republican states such as Indiana, the Obama campaign expanded the electoral map. In 2012, Obama swept almost all of the battleground states besides North Carolina. The marriage of technology, money, early voting, and field organization that the Obama campaign assembled for the 2008 campaign was repeated in 2012, and will surely be imitated in future elections.

In the past, social movements, such as the labor movement in the 1930s and the civil rights movement of the 1960s, played an important role in mobilizing people into politics. Since then, social movements, interest groups, and political parties have generally reduced their efforts at direct mobilization, although some—such as the labor movement, the Christian right, and the Tea Party movement—have revived direct mobilization in recent years. The Tea Party movement in particular has engaged in widespread grassroots mobilization and micro-targeting, where voters from different demographic groups received varying campaign messages emphasizing different issues.[75] Overall, however, while the number of interest groups has grown dramatically, the connection that most members have to such groups often extends no further than their checkbooks.

Electoral Competition

To be motivated to vote, individuals must be interested in the election and knowledgeable about the candidates. An important factor, often overlooked in analyzing political participation, is whether elections are competitive, that is, whether there are at least two parties (and their candidates) actively contesting a position in government.[76] Competitive elections, and the campaign spending and mobilization efforts that go along with them, have been identified as playing an important role in turnout rates in the United States and cross-nationally.[77] Conversely, limited exposure to competitive elections may be one reason for the lower levels of turnout recorded since the 1960s. In many congressional, statewide, and local races, a candidate (often the incumbent) runs unopposed or is expected to win by such a large margin that the challenger's chances are virtually nil. When congressional districts are drawn to favor one political party over another—what is termed *gerrymandering*—election outcomes can be highly lopsided in favor of one candidate over another. This is a primary reason why most members of Congress win elections by landslides—that is, by overwhelming margins.

One political scientist, Todd Donovan, uses a baseball analogy to explain the importance of competitive elections in mobilizing people to participate in politics: "People watch a game to see their team win, or because of interest in an important game. Perfect scoring is meaningless if only one team takes the field, and attendance will suffer if two teams are playing that no one can cheer for."[78] When candidates and political parties spend more effort and money to compete for an elected office, more information becomes available to voters in the form of media ads, newspaper coverage, door-to-door campaigns, online campaigns, and more. Electoral competition may reduce the cost to individuals of becoming informed, leading to higher turnout. Conversely, if elections are uncompetitive or uncontested, they generate little political information. Without active campaigns, individuals have fewer opportunities to be interested in an election, and may have less motivation to vote.[79] Under these conditions, the cost of being informed and actually voting is high.

The American states vary dramatically in the competitiveness of presidential elections, congressional elections, gubernatorial elections, and substantive ballot measures. Some U.S. House districts are so uncompetitive that a single candidate often runs in an uncontested election; in some states, up to one-third of congressional races are uncontested in some election years.[80] With only one name appearing on the election ballot, there is little incentive for a rational citizen to vote, as voting will not affect the outcome. On average over the past 40 years, only two dozen U.S. House races have been very competitive every two years, producing a victory margin of 5 percentage points or less by the winning candidate over the losing candidate—for example, the winning candidate gets 52 percent of the vote and the losing candidate 48 percent. Many studies have shown that more electoral competition and increased campaign spending on the part of candidates lead to higher voter turnout.[81]

An important source of variation in electoral competition is America's unique structure for presidential elections. No other country uses an electoral college to mediate between a national or direct vote for presidential candidates and the actual winner. To win, a U.S. presidential candidate must receive a majority of the votes in the electoral college. Each state is given a set number of votes in the electoral college based on the size of their congressional delegation. (The electoral college is covered in more detail in Chapter 10.) Some citizens reside in highly competitive battleground states, such as Ohio, Florida, and Pennsylvania. These states are defined by high levels of competition between the parties, with half the voters affiliating with the Republicans and half with the Democrats. Most Americans, however, live in non-battleground states (also called "safe" states) such as California, New York, and Texas, where one of the major parties is generally assured of victory in presidential elections. Every four years, residents of battleground states get smothered with attention from candidates and media, while citizens in states with few electoral votes or where one political party has a solid majority barely get noticed. Hence, presidential elections are often decided by a relatively small number of voters in America's dozen or so battleground states.[82] One study found that voter turnout in battleground states is higher than in non-battleground states and less skewed in terms of participation by the poor and young. Furthermore, the poor in battleground states are more interested in politics than the poor in non-battleground states.[83] Since the number of battleground states has been decreasing, fewer and fewer Americans are exposed to high-intensity presidential campaigns, which may be another reason for lower levels of turnout since the 1960s (see Figure 8.5).

Even the structure for nominating presidential candidates has implications for participation in government. Selecting presidential candidates involves a sequence of statewide primary elections and caucuses; the early phase of this process is dominated by a handful of small-population states. The resulting privileged position of Iowa and New Hampshire, sites of the nation's first caucus and first primary election, respectively, can boost political participation. Similarly, studies have shown that citizens residing in early-voting states, such as Iowa, New Hampshire, or the "Super Tuesday" states (the two dozen states

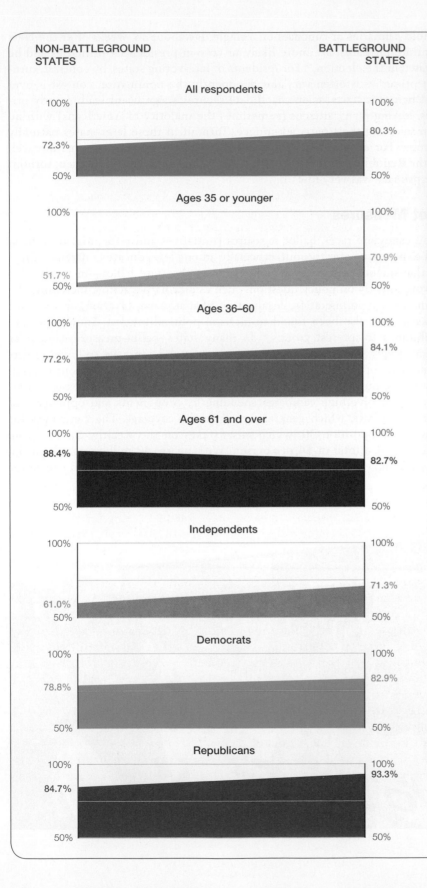

All respondents

72.3%

80.3%

Ages 35 or younger

51.7%

70.9%

Ages 36–60

77.2%

84.1%

Ages 61 and over

88.4%

82.7%

Independents

61.0%

71.3%

Democrats

78.8%

82.9%

Republicans

84.7%

93.3%

FIGURE 8.5

Electoral Competition and Voter Turnout

Presidential campaigns focus their resources on competitive battleground states, where the number of Republicans and Democrats is close enough that either party stands a chance of winning the state's electoral votes. Competitive states are awash in TV advertisements and volunteers, while voters in non-battleground states may not see a single ad for a presidential candidate. What are the effects of such mobilization efforts? The graphs compare the voter turnout of various groups in the 2012 presidential election in battleground states and non-battleground states.* Why do you think some groups are more affected by mobilization efforts and electoral competition than others?

*Battleground states in 2012 were Arizona, Colorado, Florida, Georgia, Iowa, Michigan, Minnesota, Missouri, North Carolina, Nevada, New Hampshire, Ohio, Pennsylvania, Virginia, and Wisconsin. In these states, Romney's and Obama's shares of the vote were separated by less than 10 percentage points.
SOURCE: American National Election Study, 2012 Time Series Study, http://electionstudies .org/studypages/anes_timeseries_2012 /anes_timeseries_2012.htm; and Federal Elections Commission, www.fec.gov/pubrec/fe2012 /federalelections2012.pdf (both accessed 6/9/14).

that hold primaries or caucuses on a single day about six weeks after the New Hampshire primary), are more likely to vote in presidential primaries and be interested in the election.[84] For residents of late-voting states, by contrast, turnout in primaries is often very low. Frequently the nomination contest is over almost before it starts, as one candidate secures a significant lead in early primaries, leaving many citizens (sometimes the majority of Americans) with no role in selecting their party's nominee. Turnout in these later states naturally plummets. For example, California's 2012 primary election was in June, well after the Republican nominee, Mitt Romney, had already been chosen; turnout in the primary was very low.

Ballot Measures

Beyond candidate races, ballot measures (initiatives and referenda) have been found to increase voter turnout, especially among less educated citizens.[85] Elections that include controversial initiatives on the state ballot—in which citizens vote directly on policy questions such as affirmative action, increasing the minimum wage, immigration, legalization of marijuana, taxation, or same-sex marriage—have also been found to increase political interest, knowledge, and contributions to interest groups.[86] In many states, ballot-measure campaigns are increasingly important for mobilizing voters and can have spillover effects on candidate races.[87] When citizens are asked to vote directly on controversial policy issues, public awareness of politics and policy debates increases. Initiatives often involve high campaign spending by proponents and opponents of the proposed laws, which generates mass media coverage. The campaigns for and against Proposition 30, which raised taxes on the wealthy in California in 2012, spent a total of $4 per person. With nearly 40 million people in the state, spending on the ballot measure was extremely high. A second reason for

Voters often turn out in higher numbers when there are controversial initiatives on the state ballot. In 2012 groups for and against Proposition 30, which raised taxes on the wealthy in California, spent over $100 million on media and mobilization campaigns. One result was that the campaigns raised awareness of the initiative and the election.

increased participation is that simply being asked to vote on issues—salient or otherwise—can increase participation. This has been called the "educative effects" of direct democracy, as voters are forced to make a yes or no binary choice on the policy issue.[88]

The most robust empirical finding of the educative effects of ballot measures is the positive impact of direct democracy on voter turnout. Scholars have found that statewide initiatives on the ballot increases turnout in elections, especially in lower-profile, midterm elections, but also in U.S. presidential elections and in cross-national contexts. Salient initiatives have also been shown to be associated with increased political knowledge and interest, political efficacy, and membership in citizen interest groups.

The 2004 presidential election illustrates the impact of ballot initiatives on turnout. That year, laws banning same-sex marriage appeared on the ballot in 13 states. Scholars have found that the ballot-measure campaigns and media attention increased the importance of marriage as an issue when voters evaluated the 2004 presidential candidates in these states. The issue was also a more important factor in voting for the president in the 13 states where marriage was on the ballot than in the states without such ballot-measures. That is, same-sex marriage ballot measures may have helped re-elect George W. Bush in the 2004 presidential elections by priming voters to make the issue of same-sex marriage more important, which had the effect of benefiting the Republican candidate over the Democratic candidate.[89] These studies point to ballot-measure campaigns providing the motivation to engage citizens to participate in politics.

● State Electoral Laws and Participation

Explain the effect of electoral laws on voting

As stipulated by the Constitution, the states retain control of voter registration and voting itself. This decentralized system continues to create wide variation in the laws governing elections and voting, as well as participation in politics.[90] Voter turnout in presidential elections in the last decade ranges from a high of over 70 percent of eligible voters in Minnesota to 45 percent in Mississippi, a 25-point difference. State electoral laws can create formal barriers to voting—costs to be weighed against the potential benefits of voting—that can reduce participation.

Registration Requirements

An important factor reducing voter turnout in the United States is our nation's unique state-by-state patchwork of registration rules. In most other democracies in the world, citizens are automatically registered to vote, but the United States requires a two-step process: registering to vote and then voting. In every American state but North Dakota, individuals who are eligible to vote must register with the state election board before they are actually allowed to vote, although a handful of states now allow this to occur on Election Day itself. Registration requirements were introduced at the end of the nineteenth century in response to the demands of reformers. Historical Progressive reformers hoped to make voting more difficult, both to reduce multiple voting and other forms of corruption and to discourage immigrant and working-class voters from going to the polls so political parties would be more responsive to middle-class voters and professionals. In some states, registration requirements reduced voter turnout by as much as 50 percent. Once voters are registered, they participate at very high levels—80 to 90 percent of those registered have voted in recent elections.

Registration requirements particularly reduce voting by the young, those with less education, and the less affluent because registration requires a greater degree of political involvement (a cost) than does the act of voting itself. Those with relatively little education may become interested in politics once the issues of a particular campaign are debated by the candidates, but by then it may be too late for them to register, especially if they live in states that require registration up to a month before the election. And because young people tend to change residences more often than older people, registration requirements place a greater burden on them. As a result, registration requirements not only diminish the size of the electorate but also tend to create an electorate that is, on average, better educated, more affluent, and composed of fewer young people and minorities than the citizenry as a whole (see Figure 8.6). In Europe, there is typically no registration burden on the individual voter; voter registration is handled automatically by the government. This is one reason that voter turnout rates in Europe are higher than those in the United States.

Voter Identification Requirements A relatively recent barrier is a requirement that voters provide proof of identity. Thirty-one states require all voters to show some form of ID before voting at the polls. Eight states require a photo ID, while another eight request photo ID but may count the vote with nonphoto ID under some circumstances. In the remaining states, nonphoto forms of ID are acceptable.[91] Voter identification laws in the states may disproportionately reduce voter turnout of certain groups.[92]

The issue of whether to require voters' proof of identity has become bitterly partisan. Proponents of such measures, mainly Republicans, insist that the possibility of voter fraud threatens "the sanctity of the vote"; opponents, mainly Democrats, counter that there have been almost no significant instances of voter fraud in the modern era and that the new photo ID laws are actually designed to suppress the vote of segments of the population most likely to vote for Democrats but also least likely to have photo ID—racial minorities, the elderly, and the poor.

A recent study by political scientists Rene Rocha and Tetsuya Matsubayashi sought to understand what factors drive states to adopt voter ID laws and how these laws in turn affect voter turnout of whites and minorities. Their argument is grounded in the power-threat, or backlash, hypothesis that posits that states with higher minority populations will be more likely to adopt election rules with more stringent requirements establishing eligibility to vote, including voter ID laws. Using data from all 50 states, the authors find that Republican governments increase the likelihood that a new law requiring citizens to have a photo ID in order to vote will be passed; however, this effect is weakened by the size of the minority group in the state.[93] But, state-level data from 1980 through 2010 offers little evidence for the claim that minority and Latino turnout is uniquely affected by voter ID regulations. Instead, *overall* turnout is reduced with more stringent ID laws. This finding stands in contrast to some arguments that voter ID laws disproportionately hurt participation rates of minorities. Instead, it suggests that while adoption of

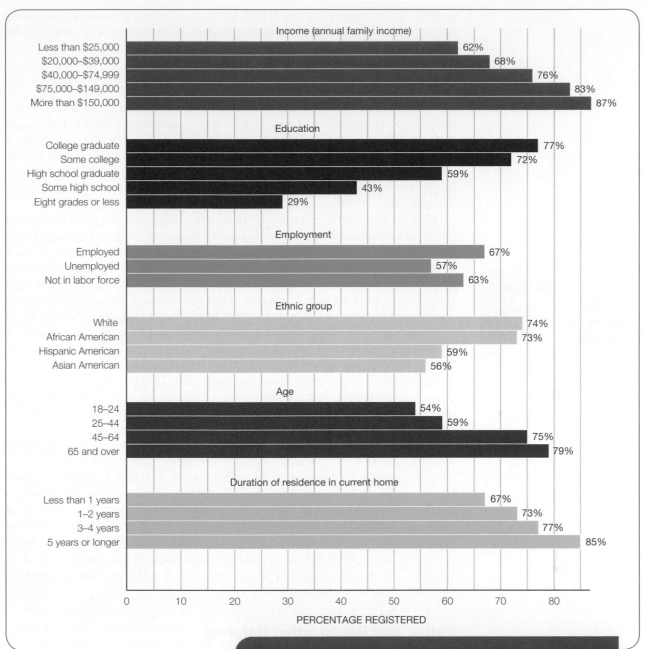

Income (annual family income)

Less than $25,000	62%
$20,000–$39,000	68%
$40,000–$74,999	76%
$75,000–$149,000	83%
More than $150,000	87%

Education

College graduate	77%
Some college	72%
High school graduate	59%
Some high school	43%
Eight grades or less	29%

Employment

Employed	67%
Unemployed	57%
Not in labor force	63%

Ethnic group

White	74%
African American	73%
Hispanic American	59%
Asian American	56%

Age

18–24	54%
25–44	59%
45–64	75%
65 and over	79%

Duration of residence in current home

Less than 1 years	67%
1–2 years	73%
3–4 years	77%
5 years or longer	85%

PERCENTAGE REGISTERED

FIGURE 8.6

Voter Registration Rates by Social Group, 2012

Some political analysts argue that registration requirements depress turnout. The percentage of the population that is registered to vote varies according to education level, employment status, race and ethnicity, and age. Are people with a lower income more or less likely to register to vote? Are less educated people more or less likely to register? Would the rates of participation among these groups change if registration requirements were altered?

SOURCES: U.S. Census Bureau, "Voting and Registration in the Election of 2012," www.census .gov/hhes/www/socdemo/voting/publications/p20/2012/tables.html (accessed 5/24/14).

voter ID policy may be (indirectly) related to race, its specific consequences seem not to be. At the same time, the seeming impact on participation of voter ID rules does undercut popular democracy.

Other Formal Barriers

A barrier to voting that has grown more important in recent years is the restriction on the voting rights of people who have committed a felony. Forty-eight states and the District of Columbia prohibit prison inmates who are serving a felony sentence from voting.[94] In 36 states, felons on probation or parole are not permitted to vote. There are also numerous restrictions on the voting rights of felons who have served their sentences. In 11 states, a felony record can result in a lifetime ban on voting.

With the sharp rise in incarceration rates in the 1980s and '90s, these restrictions have had a significant impact on voting rights. By one estimate, 5.3 million people (2.4 percent of the voting-age population) have lost their voting rights as a result of these restrictions. Further, such restrictions disproportionately affect minorities because 60 percent of the prison population is African American or Latino, though these groups make up only 25 percent of the population. One in eight black men cannot vote because of a criminal record. In the states that deny the vote to all ex-felons, nearly one in three black men has lost the right to vote.[95] The impact of felon disenfranchisement has been especially strong in the South. Concern over the impact of these voting restrictions has led to campaigns to restore voting rights to people who have committed a felony. Since 1997, 19 states have reduced voting restrictions for people with a felony record.[96] Such reforms may have an important impact on politics: one study showed that if all people with felony records had been allowed to vote, Al Gore would have won the 2000 election.[97]

Another barrier to voting has received less attention. In the United States, elections are held on Tuesdays—regular working days. In most European countries, by contrast, elections are held on Sundays or holidays. In some countries, such as India, polls remain open for several days. Holding elections on working days may make it difficult for some people to vote due to the demands of work and family. The United States has addressed this problem somewhat by expanding the use of absentee ballots, early voting, and voting by mail. Some reformers have called for an Election Day holiday, as is commonly used in Europe. This would underscore the importance of voting in America, making democratic participation a priority.

Voting and Registration Reforms

Election reform efforts over the past quarter-century have focused mainly on making voter registration and voting easier and more convenient. These reforms are based on the premise that reducing the cost of voting (in the sense of cost-benefit analysis) should increase voter turnout.[98] Leveraging the natural variation in the American states, scholars have studied the effects of early voting, Election Day registration, and absentee (mail) voting laws, among other such reforms.[99] **Election Day registration** (EDR) combines the two-step process of voting—registering to vote and casting a ballot on Election Day—into one. On the same day, citizens can both register to vote and actually cast a ballot. Ten states plus the District of Columbia have EDR laws. (California is the most

forcriticalanalysis

Why is voter turnout so low in the United States? What are the consequences of low voter turnout?

Election Day registration the option in some states to register on the day of the election, at the polling place, rather than in advance of the election

Voter Turnout in Comparison

Over the past 20 years, voter turnout in U.S. national elections has hovered around 45 percent of the voting-age population. While the number is significantly higher in presidential elections than during midterm elections,[a] turnout in the United States still lags behind the voter participation numbers in many democracies. In Australia, for instance, almost 80 percent of the voting-age population participated in its 2013 parliamentary election.[b]

So why does voter turnout vary so much from country to country? Part of the explanation rests in how we calculate who is eligible to vote. In some countries, it is not enough just to be of voting age. For example, in the United States, noncitizens and ex-felons are denied voting rights. If we exclude those populations from the base when calculating what percentage of people voted, turnout is several percentage points higher.[c]

Another part of the explanation has to do with the rules governing elections and whether they make it easier for citizens to vote—or penalize those who do not vote. In many democracies, citizens are automatically registered to vote when they reach a certain age; in contrast, U.S. citizens have to register to vote and reregister whenever they move residences. Many countries hold their elections on a Sunday, send their ballots through the mail, or declare their election day a national holiday, meaning that fewer voters have to choose between going to work or going to the polls. Voting is also compulsory in some countries. Australia, for instance, charges a $20 fee (about $17 in U.S. dollars) unless a citizen can provide a good excuse for why they did not vote.[d] These factors and others help explain why turnout is lower in the United States than in many other countries.

Average Turnout in National Elections, 1990–2013

Country	Voting-Age Population Turnout (%)	Compulsory Voting	Weekend or Holiday Voting
Australia	82.3	Yes	Yes
Turkey	79.3	Yes	Yes
Brazil	78.3	Yes	Yes
Germany	71	No	Yes
South Africa	65.6	No	Yes
Japan	64.4	No	Yes
United Kingdom	64.3	No	No
India	61.5	No	Yes
Canada	56.7	No	No
Mexico	54.6	Yes	Yes
France	51.6	No	Yes
United States	45	No	No
Switzerland	37.9	No	Yes

SOURCE: International Institute for Democracy and Electoral Assistance (IDEA), http://www.idea.int/vt/ (accessed 8/11/14).

[a]International Institute for Democracy and Electoral Assistance (IDEA), "Voter Turnout Data for the United States," www.idea.int/vt/countryview.cfm?id=231 (accessed 9/3/14).
[b]IDEA, "Voter Turnout Data for Australia," www.idea.int/vt/countryview.cfm?id=15 (accessed 9/3/14).
[c]Michael P. McDonald, "National General Election VEP Turnout Rates, 1789–Present," updated 6/11/14, www.electproject.org/national-1789-present (accessed 9/3/14).
[d]Juliet Lapidos, "Doing Democracy Right: Why Are Other Countries So Much Better at Conducting Elections Than We Are?" *Slate*, October 17, 2008, www.slate.com/articles/news_and_politics/how_they_do_it/2008/10/doing_democracy_right.html (accessed 9/3/14).

Voting by mail is a form of convenience voting that facilitates voting for those who may find it difficult to make it to the polls—for instance, because they live in a rural area, work long hours, have child care responsibilities, or do not have easy access to transportation. Several states in the West allow anyone who wishes to vote by mail to do so; in the East, voting by mail is usually only permitted for specific reasons.

recent adopter, in 2013, but has not yet implemented EDR.)[100] Proposals to adopt EDR have been considered in other states, but are often opposed because of concerns (whether legitimate or not) of Election Day fraud and noncitizens voting. Recent efforts on EDR do not all point in one direction however: North Carolina recently passed a bill that ended EDR.

As might be expected, in states that do not require registration (North Dakota) or that allow registration on the day of the election (Colorado, Connecticut, Idaho, Iowa, Maine, Minnesota, Montana, New Hampshire, North Carolina, Wisconsin, and Wyoming), not only is voter turnout higher than the national average but younger and less affluent voters turn out in larger percentages.[101] That is, there is lower political inequality. On average, EDR increases turnout by 5 percent, with all other factors held constant.[102] One of the most sophisticated studies, conducted by political scientist Michael Hamner, measured change in voter turnout after the statewide adoption of EDR, comparing turnout rates with those of similar states without EDR. The study controlled for the possibility that states adopting registration reforms may have higher turnout rates in the first place and a political culture that supports citizen participation. The results of Hamner's study indicate EDR does increase turnout, but the effects are modest. The largest effects of EDR laws are in modifying the composition of the electorate; turnout among the young, the less educated, and the poor is significantly higher in the states allowing citizens to register to vote on the same day as the election, compared to states with longer registration requirements.[103] Thus the real effect of state election reforms may be in altering *who* turns out to vote, rather than *how many* turn out.

New portable voter registration requirements in some states, for example, eliminate the need to reregister after changing residences and may reduce the bias of the electorate by removing one barrier to participation by young people and others who tend to move frequently.[104] In 1998, Oregon voters adopted a ballot measure to create a system for voting exclusively by mail, thus eliminating polling places altogether. Individual voters fill in their ballot at home and place it in the mail or in drop boxes throughout the state. Washington State followed suit a few years later, and the majority of Californians and citizens of other Western states now cast votes using **permanent absentee ballots**, which are mailed.[105] In Colorado, a state that promotes absentee voting, 77 percent of the vote was cast via absentee ballot in 2012.[106] Twenty-seven states and the District of Columbia allow "no excuse" absentee voting, which means any voter can request an absentee ballot without providing a justification. (See inside the back cover of your textbook to find voter registration requirements in your state.) The western states tend to have higher voter turnout than other parts of the country besides the Midwest, making it difficult to disentangle whether mail voting or regional political culture drives higher turnout.

Another reform that has been adopted by many states is **early voting**, which allows registered voters to cast a ballot at their regular polling place up to 40 days before the election. The effects of early voting laws on turnout and the demographic composition of who votes is not yet clear.[107] One study from Oregon found that voting by mail increased voter turnout, but only among those groups already predisposed to vote; early voting reinforces higher turnout among the upper class and older citizens, and nonvoting among the lower class.[108] However, as discussed in the introduction, other research suggests that early voting does increase turnout among groups that are traditionally less likely to vote, including minorities.

The political scientist Adam Berinksy provides an explanation for these seemingly contradictory findings that overall voter turnout has not increased despite efforts to make voting easier and more convenient. He suggests that making voting more convenient (e.g., early voting and absentee voting) simply reinforces the behavior of those most likely to vote. These reforms do not lower the costs of voting enough to engage those with few political resources, but instead lower the costs enough for the upper classes to vote more consistently. Of all the reforms, EDR has shown the most promise for increasing turnout in general and in addressing inequalities in who votes. But overall voter turnout isn't the only outcome that matters; *who* votes also impacts outcomes. One estimate put the number of early votes at one-third of the national total in 2008, with Obama outperforming his Republican opponent, John McCain, in early-voting ballots.[109] Thus state election laws allowing early voting may have helped Obama win office in 2008.[110] Obama wisely made early voting a key part of his campaign in 2008 and again in 2012, encouraging his supporters to vote early and thus avoid problems that occur on Election Day, such as long lines, poor weather, or malfunctioning voting machines.

Political Participation
and Your Future

The American political community has expanded over the course of history, with new groups winning and asserting political rights. This expansion has brought American politics more closely into line with the fundamental values of liberty, equality, and democracy. But for much of the twentieth century, the electoral system in the United States failed to mobilize an active citizenry, giving rise to an uneven pattern of political participation that gives some people more of a voice in politics than others and thus goes against the American values of equality and democracy. Since 2000 a series of highly competitive presidential elections has spurred political campaigns to pay more attention to drawing greater numbers of voters into the political process, but many Americans still do not participate in politics.

permanent absentee ballots the option in some states to have a ballot sent automatically to your home for each election, rather than having to request an absentee ballot each time

early voting the option in some states to cast a vote at a polling place or by mail before the election

Naturally enough, one of the most important factors in sustaining participation is a sense of political efficacy, the feeling that average citizens can help shape what government actually does. One important study found that elected officials respond more to the preferences of voters than nonvoters, confirming long-held assumptions that the affluent, more educated, and older citizens have more voice in politics and public policy.[111] A study by the political scientist Larry Bartels showed that senators (both Republicans and Democrats) are much less responsive to the policy preferences of low-income citizens—who are also less likely to be active voters.[112] If the voices of only the more affluent are heard during election time, the issues that concern lower-income Americans may not find a place at the top of the political agenda.

What would it take to increase political engagement among citizens of all backgrounds? Several recent developments promise to give a greater number of people more of a voice in American government. Over the past few decades innovative states have led the way by reforming and modernizing America's patchwork election system, with reforms ranging from EDR to early and mail voting, and even portable registration that eliminates altogether the need to reregister after moving to a new residence. Hawaii registers all high school students to vote, while permanent voter registration, akin to voting systems used in European countries, is increasingly a popular reform at the state level. Some states, such as Iowa, use nonpartisan boards to draw legislative districts, which tend to boost competition in congressional and state legislative races. Increased competition, in turn, often results in a more informed and energized electorate, thus increasing turnout. Drawing on the American states as laboratories of democracy allows policy makers to test what works and what does not. Reforms found to be successful at the state level may be adopted at the national level: for example, Congress debated legislation to create early voting nationally in 2008.

If more Americans voted, the policies adopted by their governments would be more representative of the majority preferences in this country. What other innovations might the states implement to encourage or enable more people to vote? How useful might it be to end registration requirements, particularly for young voters, who are the most mobile? Already, military personnel deployed overseas are allowed to vote by email in some states. Would you support vote-by-email?

The explosive growth in online communication as a means of organizing political participation has been especially apparent during recent elections. New technologies have supplied political leaders and candidates with new avenues for reaching out to citizens and have given citizens novel (and even enjoyable) ways to learn about and engage with politics. As we have learned, individuals who learn about politics online are more likely to vote and participate in politics in myriad other ways. Astonishingly diverse online news sources have given rise to new opinion leaders and new voices. Whatever promise digital politics holds for increasing political participation, it also raises the same fundamental questions that have arisen with every major new development in America's political history: How can citizens turn participation in politics into meaningful representation in government? And how, in turn, can representation result in public policies that reflect the needs of the greatest number of American citizens?

For much of American history, formal barriers restricted the right to vote and created a pattern of unequal participation in politics. Today, most of those barriers have been eliminated, but voter turnout remains relatively low, especially among young voters. In 2008 these voters cast their ballots at a polling station in a fraternity house near the UCLA campus.

plug**in**

Inform

Find out what's on the ballot in upcoming elections in your state/district, by entering your address at vote411.org (a website from the League of Women Voters).

Express

Write a list of reasons individuals may not vote. In your view, are these obstacles necessary? Consider emailing the editor of your school paper to share your opinion.

Connect

Register to vote. Find the forms, registration deadlines, polling locations, and other information by using the state-by-state URLs listed inside the back cover of this book.

Act

Cast your vote on Election Day. Consider encouraging others to vote too. Research shows that people are likely to turn out to vote if a friend or family members asks them to.

studyguide

Forms of Political Participation

Describe the major forms of traditional and online participation in politics (pp. 301–10)

Political participation refers to a wide range of activities designed to influence government, politics, and policy. These activities fall into two major categories: traditional political participation, which includes voting, volunteering, and contributing to a candidate; and online political participation, which refers to a newer set of activities carried out through the Internet, such as posting comments on a social media site or visiting a political party's website. Voting is the most common form of political participation, but voter turnout is relatively low today in the United States.

Key Terms

traditional political participation (p. 301)

protest (p. 301)

suffrage (p. 303)

turnout (p. 304)

online political participation (p. 305)

Practice Quiz

1. Which of the following is not a form of traditional political participation?
   a) volunteering in a campaign
   b) attending an abortion-rights rally
   c) contributing to the Democratic Party
   d) voting in an election
   e) uploading a political video to YouTube

2. Which group won voting rights most recently?
   a) 18- to 20-year-olds
   b) Asian Americans
   c) white property owners
   d) women
   e) African Americans

3. The *digital divide* means
   a) some citizens watch television news and some do not.
   b) newspapers rarely publish the same stories on their websites that they do in their print editions.
   c) few politicians maintain websites once they are elected to office.
   d) not all citizens have equal access to the Internet.
   e) people who learn about politics online are less informed than those who learn about it through traditional media.

Who Participates?

Describe the patterns of participation among major demographic groups (pp. 310–20)

Race, gender, age, and religious affiliation are associated with different levels and types of political participation. Generally speaking, whites, older people, and women vote most frequently. In recent elections, African Americans, Latinos, women, and young people have been more likely to support Democratic candidates than whites, males, and older people.

Key Terms

socioeconomic status (p. 311)

gender gap (p. 318)

Practice Quiz

4. Which of the following statements most accurately characterizes the rates of political participation among different age groups?
   a) Older people have much lower rates of participation than young people.
   b) Older people have much higher rates of participation than young people.
   c) Both older people and younger people participate in politics at extremely low rates.
   d) Both older people and younger people participate in politics at extremely high rates.
   e) There is no consistent pattern because sometimes younger people participate more than older people and sometimes older people participate more than younger people.

5. Currently, African Americans
   a) almost never participate in politics.
   b) consistently support the Republican Party in elections.
   c) vote at much lower rates than they did 15 years ago.
   d) vote differently from one another based on income.
   e) are more likely to participate when they feel a shared sense of collective identity.

6. In recent years, participation among Latino Americans
   a) has declined.
   b) has remained about the same.
   c) has steadily increased.
   d) has surpassed voting rates for African Americans.
   e) has not been tracked and is nearly impossible to estimate.

7. One reason that there are fewer women than men in elected office is that
   a) there is a limit set by the Constitution on the number of women who can serve in the House of Representatives.
   b) fewer women are eligible to run for office under the rules created by state and local governments.
   c) women are less attentive to politics than men.
   d) women are less likely to run for office than men.
   e) women are less likely to win elections than men.

Political Environment and Participation

Explain the factors in the political environment that influence whether individuals vote or not (pp. 321–27)

Three general factors in the political environment influence whether individuals vote or not: (1) People mobilized by political parties, candidates, campaigns, interest groups, and social movements are more likely to participate than those who are not. (2) In competitive elections, there are more opportunities for individuals to become interested in and informed about the race, as each side campaigns intensely to get its message out to the public. (3) People may also make the effort to turn out if state ballot measures address issues that are important to them.

Key Term
mobilization (p. 321)

Practice Quiz

8. Which of the following techniques is considered most effective in mobilizing voters?
   a) mass mailings
   b) robo-calls
   c) phone calls made by volunteers
   d) face-to-face contact
   e) television advertisements

9. On average over the last 40 years, how many U.S. House races have been very competitive in each election?
   a) 0
   b) 24
   c) 100
   d) 217
   e) 435

State Electoral Laws and Participation

Explain the effect of electoral laws on voting (pp. 327–33)

As stated in the Constitution, states retain control of voter registration and voting. In practice, there is wide variation in the laws governing elections and voting from state to state. Voter-registration requirements and other barriers, such as ID requirements, may reduce participation. States have experimented with reforms, such as Election Day registration and early voting, to make it easier to vote.

Key Terms
Election Day registration (p. 330)
permanent absentee ballots (p. 333)
early voting (p. 333)

Practice Quiz

10. Voter-registration requirements and processes are determined and controlled by
    a) local governments.
    b) the federal government.
    c) the U.S. Constitution.
    d) the states.
    e) an independent organization.

11. Which of the following factors is *not* currently an obstacle to voting in the United States?
    a) registration requirements
    b) that elections occur on Tuesdays
    c) the restriction of voting rights for people who have committed a felony
    d) literacy tests
    e) restrictions in some states on absentee voting

12. In states that do not require registration or that allow registration on the day of the election,
  a) voter turnout rates are more than double that of other states.
  b) no significant difference in voter turnout has been measured.
  c) younger and less affluent voters turn out in larger percentages.
  d) voter fraud has been measured at much higher levels.
  e) younger and less affluent voters turn out in lower numbers.

For Further Reading

Bimber, Bruce, and Richard Davis. *Campaigning Online: The Internet in U.S. Elections*. Oxford, UK: Oxford University Press, 2003.

Cain, Bruce E., Todd Donovan, and Caroline J. Tolbert, eds. *Democracy in the States: Experiments in Election Reform*. Washington, DC: Brookings Institution Press, 2008.

Crenson, Matthew A., and Benjamin Ginsberg. *Downsizing Democracy: How America Sidelined Its Citizens and Privatized Its Public*. Baltimore: Johns Hopkins University Press, 2004.

Dalton, Russell J. *The Good Citizen: How a Younger Generation Is Reshaping American Politics*. Washington, DC: CQ Press, 2008.

Donovan, Todd, and Shawn Bowler. *Reforming the Republic: Democratic Institutions for the New America*. Upper Saddle River, NJ: Pearson/Prentice Hall, 2004.

Green, Donald P., and Alan S. Gerber. *Get Out the Vote! How to Increase Voter Turnout*. Washington, DC: Brookings Institution Press, 2004.

Griffin, John D., and Brian Newman. *Minority Report: Evaluating Political Equality in America*. Chicago: University of Chicago Press, 2008.

Hahn, Hahrie. *Moved to Action: Motivation, Participation, and Inequality in American Politics*. Stanford, CA: Stanford University Press, 2009.

Hanmer, Michael J. *Discount Voting: Voter Registration Reforms and Their Effects*. New York: Cambridge University Press, 2009.

Lewis-Beck, Michael S., William G. Jacoby, Helmut Norpoth, and Herbert F. Weisberg. *The American Voter Revisited*. Ann Arbor: University of Michigan Press, 2008.

Manza, Jeff, and Christopher Uggen. *Locked Out: Felon Disenfranchisement and American Democracy*. New York: Oxford University Press, 2006.

McDonald, Michael P., and John Samples, eds. *The Marketplace of Democracy: Electoral Competition and American Politics*. Washington, DC: Brookings Institution Press, 2006.

Mossberger, Karen, Caroline Tolbert, and Ramona McNeal. *Digital Citizenship: The Internet, Society and Participation*. Cambridge, MA: MIT Press, 2008.

Nicholson, Steven P. *Voting the Agenda: Candidates Elections and Ballot Propositions*. Princeton, NJ: Princeton University Press, 2005.

Patterson, Thomas E. *The Vanishing Voter: Public Involvement in an Age of Uncertainty*. New York: Vintage, 2003.

Piven, Frances Fox, and Richard Cloward. *Why Americans Don't Vote*. New York: Pantheon, 1988.

Putnam, Robert D. *Bowling Alone: The Collapse and Revival of American Community*. New York: Simon and Schuster, 2000.

Rosenstone, Steven J., and John Mark Hansen. *Mobilization, Participation and Democracy in America*. New York: Macmillan, 1993.

Smith, Daniel, and Caroline Tolbert. *Educated by Initiative: The Effects of Direct Democracy on Citizens and Political Organizations in the American States*. Ann Arbor: University of Michigan Press, 2004.

Verba, Sidney, Kay Lehman Schlozman, and Henry Brady. *Voice and Equality: Civic Voluntarism in American Politics*. Cambridge, MA: Harvard University Press, 1995.

Recommended Websites

CQ MoneyLine
http://moneyline.cq.com/pml/home.do
  Campaign contributions are a form of political participation that is both necessary and controversial. This website uses data from the Federal Election Commission (FEC) to publish the names of those who give elected officials campaign money and those who may be receiving preferential treatment.

Declare Yourself
http://declareyourself.com
  Statistics on political participation show that older people are much more likely to vote than are young people. Declare Yourself is a national nonpartisan, nonprofit campaign dedicated to closing the intergenerational divide by energizing and empowering a new movement of young voters.

League of Women Voters
www.lwv.org

Established in 1920 as part of the women's suffrage movement, the League of Women Voters encourages informed and active participation in government.

Project Vote
www.projectvote.org

Since 1982, Project Vote has worked to increase the participation of low-income, minority, youth, and other marginalized and underrepresented voters. The organization sponsors voter registration drivers, get-out-the-vote programs, and monitors election laws across the states. As a community organizer, Barack Obama worked for Project Vote, registering voters in Chicago.

Project Vote Smart
www.votesmart.org

This nonpartisan site is dedicated to providing citizens with information on political candidates and elected officials. Here you can easily view candidates' biographical information, positions on issues, and voting records, so that you can make an informed choice on Election Day.

U.S. Census Bureau: Voting and Registration
www.census.gov/population/www/socdemo/voting.html

The U.S. Census Bureau collects statistics on voting and registration by various demographic and socioeconomic characteristics. See if you can find differences in voter turnout by race, age, sex, or socioeconomic status.

At their 2012 national convention, Republicans formally nominated Mitt Romney and Paul Ryan as their presidential and vice presidential candidates. While many Americans express frustration over partisan conflict, political parties play an important role in organizing American politics and government.

Political Parties

WHAT GOVERNMENT DOES AND WHY IT MATTERS In the United States, political parties help the government to respond to the needs and desires of its citizens. Political parties organize the mass public, who, as individuals, might lack the resources and knowledge to compete with wealthy elites and interest groups for a voice in politics. Strong parties and vigorous party competition make it more likely that elected officials will represent the views and wishes of the American people. Democracy is promoted when parties mobilize large numbers of individuals to participate in the political arena and to vote. Compared with interest groups, which generally pursue narrow policy objectives, political parties are capable of mobilizing much more of the electorate to win control of government.

Political parties are a core feature of the American political system. They provide guideposts for citizens and politicians alike by helping to organize the political world and simplify complex policy debates. For example, individual partisanship is the most important factor in predicting whom Americans vote for. In Congress, parties are key in setting the terms of policy conflict; they exercise significant influence over the votes of members of Congress on many important issues.

But what happens when the parties become deeply divided? Political scientist Sean Theriault argues that political parties in Congress are more polarized today than they have been at any time during the past 100 years.[1] Although there are many ways to measure polarization, one way is to look at how often members of Congress vote along straight party lines, with all Republicans voting together and all Democrats voting together. In contrast with earlier eras, Democrats and Republicans now vote along party lines on almost all legislation. Two major changes have contributed to today's extreme party polarization. First, the parties' constituencies (the mass public) are more politically and ideologically divided than they used to be. The voters who elect members of Congress are more partisan because of gerrymandered legislative districts (see Chapter 10) and geographic sorting, where voters increasingly segregate themselves into conservative and liberal communities, cities, and neighborhoods.[2] Second, lawmakers have given more power to their party leaders, who demand that party members vote with the party more frequently.

Today, over 90 percent of the votes in Congress are passed with unanimous party-line voting.[3] An example of this party polarization can be seen in the debate over President Obama's Affordable Care Act of 2009. The bill passed the House with 84 percent support from Democrats and won all 60 Democratic votes in the Senate, but there was nearly unanimous opposition to the legislation among Republican party members. Republican opposition stemmed from both policy and political concerns. Most Republicans prefer policy approaches that require less government regulation of the market and less public spending. As the opposition party, Republicans were also aware that a major policy win would likely strengthen Democrats. Republican Party leaders mobilized staunch opposition to the Democratic health care reform proposals in both the House and the Senate. In the end, only one Republican in the House voted for the health care reform bill.

In 2014, Gallup reported that just 1 in 10 Americans approve of the way Congress is doing its job.[4] Can America's politicians govern the nation under these conditions of extreme party polarization and growing distrust from the American public? Are the major political parties fulfilling their role in American democracy?

chaptergoals

- Define political parties and their functions in politics (pp. 343–47)
- Explain the roles that parties play in elections (pp. 347–49)
- Describe how the major American parties are structured at the national, state, and local levels (pp. 350–53)
- Explain how parties organize legislative business and influence policy (pp. 353–56)
- Identify the reasons for and sources of party identification (pp. 356–62)
- Describe how the party system in the United States has changed over time and its main features today (pp. 362–77)

What Are Political Parties?

Define political parties and their functions in politics

Political parties, like interest groups, are organizations that seek influence over government. Ordinarily, they can be distinguished from interest groups on the basis of their orientation. A party seeks to control the government by electing its members to office. As we will see in Chapter 11, interest groups do not control the operation of government and its personnel, but rather try to influence government policies.

political parties organized groups that attempt to influence the government by electing their members to important government offices

Although the Founders did not envision the rise of political parties and President Washington was elected the nation's first president without association with a political party, parties quickly became a core feature of the American political system and of governments in most nations in the world. Parties and **partisanship** organize the political world and simplify complex policy debates for citizens and elected officials alike. Parties also play central roles in mobilizing citizens to vote and ensuring that the public voice is heard in policy making.

partisanship identification with or support of a particular party or cause

In the United States today, the relationship between parties and government is complex. Political parties have been the chief points of contact between government, on the one side, and individual citizens and interest groups, on the other. Through organized political parties, citizens and groups can gain some control over governmental policies. Simultaneously, the government often seeks to organize and influence important groups in society through political parties to win elections and gain political power. All political parties have this dual character: they are instruments through which citizens and government attempt to influence each other.

In a landmark book written over 50 years ago, political scientist E. E. Schattschneider advocated for a political system run by party politics.[5] To be an equal democracy where rich and poor, educated and noneducated, young and old, and white and minority are represented, there must be competitive and responsible political parties that provide real choices to the electorate so that the public can participate in the government's decision-making process. Parties, he believed, are able to mobilize more people than interest groups because they can expand the "scope of conflict" or the policy debate to include most or all of the electorate through elections. While interest groups benefit from focusing on narrow policy issues, political parties must expand political conflict to the public arena and focus on a range of policy issues from the economy to foreign policy in order to win elections.

It is not enough, however, to simply have political parties. The solution to an unequal democracy where the affluent and educated are more likely to vote and have more voice in government decisions is to have "competitive" and "responsible" political parties. Schattschneider believed that when political parties compete with one another to win elections, they have incentives to continually expand policy debates to include nonvoting members of the electorate in order to gain a majority of voters and win the election. This strategy was evident in the extremely competitive 2000, 2004, 2008, and 2012 presidential elections, with widespread voter mobilization campaigns on the part of the Democratic and Republican parties. Voter turnout in 2008 was at the highest level since 1960 largely because of the get out the vote campaign drives organized by the political parties.

At party organization meetings like this one, political parties try to be "large tents" that represent the interests of diverse segments of the population—elderly retirees, young college students, unemployed steel mill workers, millionaire hedge fund managers. However, some observers believe that the parties today respond more to the interests of the affluent than to other groups.

Another key aspect of Schattschneider's argument is having responsible parties. To create a more equal democracy, political parties must act "responsibly" by continually informing the public of current political issues that are in their best interest. And once in power, political parties must enact policies that represent their members' interests, rather than responding to the demands of interest groups. In this idealized view, competitive and responsible parties can help to increase voter turnout, creating more equal representation for those in lower socioeconomic classes.

However, some political scientists argue that Schattschneider's vision is far from the reality. For example, there is evidence that political parties are skewed toward the preferences of the affluent. Political scientist Larry Bartels has found that, on economic issues, both the Democratic and Republican parties are more responsive to the preferences of the upper and middle class and both parties ignore the policy preferences of the lower class. Analyzing Senate roll-call votes, he found that the Democrats are more responsive to the middle class than Republicans are, but neither party represents the policy preferences of the poor, measured by the bottom third of the income distribution. In fact, Bartels argues that political parties are not only more responsive to the rich, but that the rich benefit more from governmental policies compared with the less affluent.[6] Related research suggests that the reason for this trend is because the affluent provide campaign contributions to elected officials that strongly influence their voting decisions.[7]

These recent studies show that, although we have a competitive two-party system in which the Republicans and Democrats compete in closely contested presidential elections, lower-income citizens with lower levels of voter turnout have little representation by the parties, except when their preferences converge (or overlap) with the preferences of more affluent citizens.[8]

As long as political parties have existed, they have been criticized for introducing selfish, "partisan" concerns into public debates and national policy. Yet political parties are extremely important to the proper functioning of a democracy. As we will see, parties increase participation in politics, provide a central cue for citizens to cast informed votes, and organize the business of Congress and governing. Some argue that the problem in America today is that political elites in Congress and the parties are too polarized along liberal and conservative lines, whereas the majority of Americans hold moderate opinions and values, and thus Congress and the parties do a poor job representing the citizens.[9] Others argue that the rules governing our election system need to be updated—what is called "election reform"—so that there are more than two major political parties and representation of the citizens can be improved.[10]

How Do Political Parties Form?

Historically, parties form in one of two ways. The first, which could be called "internal mobilization," occurs when political conflicts prompt officials and competing factions within government to mobilize popular support. This is precisely what happened during the early years of the American Republic. Competition in Congress between northeastern merchants and southern farmers led first the southerners and then the northeasterners to attempt to organize their supporters. The result was the foundation of America's first national parties: the Jeffersonians or Antifederalists, whose primary base was in the South, and the Federalists, whose strength was greatest in the New England states.

The second way that parties form is called "external mobilization," which takes place when a group of politicians outside government organizes popular support to win governmental power. For example, during the 1850s, a group of state politicians who opposed slavery, especially the expansion of slavery in America's territorial possessions, built what became the Republican Party by constructing party organizations and mobilizing popular support in the Northeast and West.

America's two major parties now, of course, are the Democrats and the Republicans. Both trace their roots back over 150 years to the nineteenth century, and both have evolved over time. Since they were formed, the two major parties have undergone significant shifts in their policy positions and their membership. These changes have been prompted both by issues and events (economic change, the civil rights movement, etc.) and by demographic and social developments in the United States. One of the most recent changes is the growth of the Latino population and voting in presidential elections, with Latinos strongly favoring the Democratic Party in 2012. The parties continue to compete with each other to win support among voters and interest groups for political office, different policies, and enduring political power. Because of this, it is important to understand the parties in relation to each other. (The development of the party system in U.S. history will be discussed later in the chapter.)

The Two-Party System in America

Over the past 200 years, Americans' conception of political parties has changed considerably. In the early years of the Republic, parties were seen as threats to the social order, and were referred to as factions. In the *Federalist Papers*, both Alexander Hamilton and James Madison condemned "factions" that pursued narrow self-interest over the broader well-being of the nation as a whole.[11] In his 1796 Farewell Address, President George Washington warned his countrymen to shun partisan politics. Nonetheless, a **two-party system** emerged early in the history of the new Republic. Beginning with the Federalists and the Jeffersonian Republicans

two-party system a political system in which only two parties have a realistic opportunity to compete effectively for control

Two-Party Systems and Multi-Party Systems

The American political system is dominated by two political parties, the Republicans and the Democrats. But the number of political parties in a country is not always two. The number varies depending on the electoral rules in place. Countries such as the United States and the United Kingdom, which use first-past-the-post systems (in which the candidate with the most votes wins the seat), tend to have two dominant parties. The membership of the U.S. Congress includes only the 2 major parties; likewise, while the United Kingdom's House of Commons has 10 parties represented, it is still dominated by its 2 largest parties.

The Netherlands, meanwhile, uses a proportional representation system (in which seats are apportioned based on the share of votes a party receives) that has led to 3 major parties, with 11 parties total in the legislature. In proportional representation systems like the Netherlands, voters select parties to represent them *nationally* rather than candidates to represent their *region*, and parties receive roughly the same percentage of seats in parliament as they received in the election. Thus, the legislature tends to more accurately resemble how the national electorate voted. The party representation in the 2013 Dutch parliament is almost identical to the 2012 national vote, whereas in the United States and the United Kingdom, the largest parties tend to be overrepresented while the smaller parties lose out.

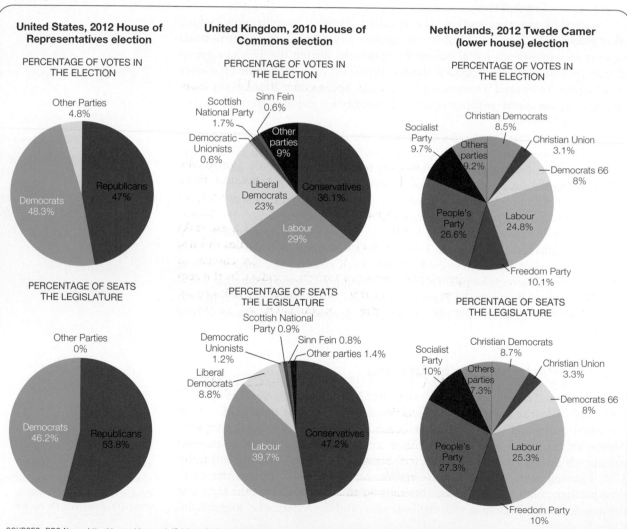

United States, 2012 House of Representatives election

PERCENTAGE OF VOTES IN THE ELECTION

- Other Parties 4.8%
- Democrats 48.3%
- Republicans 47%

PERCENTAGE OF SEATS THE LEGISLATURE

- Other Parties 0%
- Democrats 46.2%
- Republicans 53.8%

United Kingdom, 2010 House of Commons election

PERCENTAGE OF VOTES IN THE ELECTION

- Scottish National Party 1.7%
- Sinn Fein 0.6%
- Democratic Unionists 0.6%
- Other parties 9%
- Liberal Democrats 23%
- Conservatives 36.1%
- Labour 29%

PERCENTAGE OF SEATS THE LEGISLATURE

- Scottish National Party 0.9%
- Sinn Fein 0.8%
- Democratic Unionists 1.2%
- Other parties 1.4%
- Liberal Democrats 8.8%
- Conservatives 47.2%
- Labour 39.7%

Netherlands, 2012 Twede Camer (lower house) election

PERCENTAGE OF VOTES IN THE ELECTION

- Socialist Party 9.7%
- Christian Democrats 8.5%
- Christian Union 3.1%
- Others parties 9.2%
- Democrats 66 8%
- People's Party 26.6%
- Labour 24.8%
- Freedom Party 10.1%

PERCENTAGE OF SEATS THE LEGISLATURE

- Socialist Party 10%
- Christian Democrats 8.7%
- Christian Union 3.3%
- Others parties 7.3%
- Democrats 66 8%
- People's Party 27.3%
- Labour 25.3%
- Freedom Party 10%

SOURCES: BBC News, http://news.bbc.co.uk/2/shared/election2010/results/; Federal Election Commission, www.fec.gov/pubrec/fe2012/federalelections2012.pdf; *Washington Post,* www.washingtonpost.com/wp-srv/special/politics/election-map-2012/house/; NSD European Election Database, www.nsd.uib.no/european_election _database/country/netherlands/parliamentary_elections.html (accessed 6/2/14).

in the late 1780s, two major parties have dominated national politics, although *which* particular two parties has changed with the times and issues. This two-party system today includes Democrats and Republicans.

Unlike many other countries in the world that use a proportional representation system, in which seats are allocated to political parties based on their share (percentage) of the total vote cast in the election, the United States uses geographic single-member districts combined with a winner-take-all system. It doesn't matter, for example, if the contest for a House seat is won with 20 percent or 80 percent of the total vote, the candidate with the largest number of votes (a plurality) in that district wins the seat in Congress. That is why the system is "winner take all": unlike in proportional systems, runners-up do not gain representation. The U.S. system is also called "first past the post" because the candidate with the most votes wins the election, even if she did not win a majority of the popular vote. In the United States, proportional representation systems are uncommon, especially above the local level, and are absent at the national level.

Voters thus have an incentive not to vote for small or third party candidates for fear of "wasting" their vote, as only one party (usually one of the two largest parties) can win the election. Concern about wasting one's vote on third parties is called the spoiler effect. The winner-take-all system has helped create our two-party-dominant system, and third parties have historically not won seats in Congress or the presidency. Third parties are discussed in more detail later in this chapter. What is important to remember is America's election rules create our two-party system. If the rules were to change, the number of political parties would likely change as well.

for critical analysis

What rules governing the American electoral process promote a two-party system? How might different rules impact the party system?

Functions of Political Parties

Parties play important roles in the facilitation of democratic processes. In the United States, citizens take for granted that leaders will run for office, that there will be competition among candidates, that they will have the opportunity to learn about candidates and issues from campaigns, and that once in office, political leaders will work together to make policy and govern. Each of these tasks is complex, however, and would be all the more so if political parties did not exist. Parties mobilize citizens in the electorate to vote, they offer choices to voters in elections, and they provide organization for officeholders. In the sections that follow, we describe several democratic functions that parties serve. We then consider parties in government, parties as organizations, and parties in the electorate.

● Parties, Voter Mobilization, and Elections

Explain the roles that parties play in elections

Parties have always been central to the electoral process, and in recent years they have taken on a renewed role in recruiting candidates, coordinating campaigns, mobilizing voters, and raising money.[12] Parties succeed when they win elections, and thus we begin with parties and elections.

Recruiting Candidates

One of the most important but least noticed party activities is the recruitment of candidates for local, state, and national office. Each election year, candidates must be found for thousands of state and local offices as well as congressional seats. When they do not have an incumbent running for re-election, party leaders attempt to identify strong candidates and to interest them in entering the campaign.

An ideal candidate will have an unblemished record and the capacity to raise enough money to mount a serious campaign, especially if a candidate must challenge an incumbent. Party leaders are usually not willing to provide financial backing to candidates who are unable to raise substantial funds on their own. For a U.S. House seat, this can mean several hundred thousand dollars; for a Senate seat, a serious candidate must be able to raise several million dollars. Often party leaders have difficulty finding attractive candidates and persuading them to run. Candidate recruitment is problematic in an era when political candidates must assume that their personal lives will be intensely scrutinized in the press and even subjected to mudslinging campaigns by their opponents.[13] In fact one study found that over 20 percent of House races are uncontested (meaning there is only one candidate from one party on the ballot) because challenging incumbents in Congress and winning is so difficult. Incumbents in the House have on average more than double the amount of money that challengers have for their campaigns, while Senate incumbents have on average 50 percent more. Studies have also found that women candidates are less likely to run for political office than men unless they have sufficient financial resources for their campaign.

Nominations

nomination the process by which political parties select their candidates for election to public office

Nomination is the process by which a party selects a single candidate to run for each elective office. Parties want only one candidate on the ballot so that members of the same party do not take votes from one another, allowing the other party's candidate to win. Imagine, for instance, if in 2008, the presidential election had had

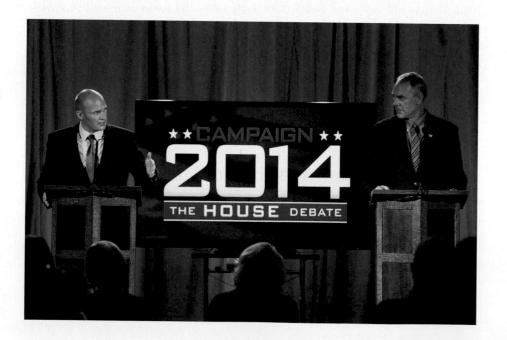

With no incumbent running for Montana's at-large House district in 2014, the Democrats nominated John Lewis (left), a former congressional aide, and the Republicans nominated Ryan Zinke (right), a state senator.

three candidates: Democrat Barack Obama, Democrat Hillary Clinton, and Republican John McCain. In all likelihood, Obama and Clinton would have split the Democratic vote, and McCain would have won. So parties undertake an internal process of nomination to settle on one candidate who will be on the ballot. The party nomination process varies from state to state and office to office, and Democrats and Republicans have different rules as well, but often the process involves a primary election among multiple candidates from the same party. Party members then vote in this primary election to select just one candidate.

Mobilizing Voters and the Ground Game

The general election period begins immediately after the nominations. Throughout American history, this has been a time of glory for the political parties, whose popular base of support is fully displayed. All the paraphernalia of party committees (signs, bumper stickers, buttons, social media slogans, YouTube ads) are on display, and committee members are activated into local party workforces. The first step involves voter registration. There was a time when party workers were responsible for virtually all of this kind of electoral activity, but they have been supplemented by civic groups such as the League of Women Voters, unions, and Chambers of Commerce. Even so, the parties frequently mail notices, call voters, and knock on doors to ensure citizens are registered. Those who have registered have to decide on Election Day if they will actually go to the polling place, stand in line, and vote for the various candidates and referenda on the ballot. If they are voting by mail in one of the states that allow this, they have to request the ballot, fill it out, and return it (see Chapter 8).

Political parties, candidates, and campaigning can make a big difference in persuading citizens to vote. Voter mobilization, once an art, has now become a science. In recent years, the two major parties have developed an extensive database on millions of potential voters, which allows the parties to bring their search for votes, contributions, and campaign volunteers to named individuals. Using these vast computerized databases, data mining, social media, and other new techniques such as micro-targeting, modern political campaigns can predict who you will vote for (sometimes even before you do)—and they are extremely effective at turning out the voters who are most likely to vote for their candidates. Micro-targeting means focusing on individuals in small, homogenous groups (e.g., suburban housewives), rather than using geographic data for a precinct or county, to measure the effectiveness of campaign messages. This technique enables political parties to identify small groups based on specific characteristics and to help tailor their candidates' strategies and messages to these groups.

Big data and more targeted messages have revolutionized how parties and candidates conduct voter-mobilization drives. It doesn't matter, after all, which party has more support if that party's voters stay home on Election Day. In 2008 the Obama campaign learned that face-to-face and in-person contacts are much more effective than mailings or robocalls in getting out the vote.[14] The lessons of 2008 were improved on in 2012 as both parties built even larger databases (the Democrats names theirs Narwhal, and the Republicans responded by dubbing theirs Orca) to tap into in developing their messages and turning out the vote. Although both parties used big data, the Democrats and the Obama campaign built a more effective network, while Romney and the Republicans still ran a more traditional top-down campaign (see Chapter 10).

Convincing voters to actually show up to cast a ballot on Election Day is one of the hardest tasks that the parties face. Research by political scientists and the campaigns themselves has shown that face-to-face, in-person contacts are much more effective than mailings, robocalls, or TV advertising in mobilizing voters.

Parties as Organizations

party organization the formal structure of a political party, including its leadership, election committees, active members, and paid staff

caucus (political) a normally closed meeting of a political or legislative group to select candidates, plan strategy, or make decisions regarding legislative matters

national convention a national institution that nominates the party's presidential and vice-presidential candidates, establishes party rules, and writes and ratifies the party's platform

> Describe how the major American parties are structured at the national, state, and local levels

In the United States **party organizations** exist at virtually every level of government (see Figure 9.1). These organizations are usually committees made up of a number of active party members. State law and party rules prescribe how such committees are constituted. Usually committee members are elected at local party meetings, called **caucuses**, or as part of the regular primary election. The best-known examples of these committees are at the national level: the Democratic National Committee and the Republican National Committee.

National Convention

At the national level, the party's most important institution is the **national convention**. The convention, held every four years, is attended by delegates from each of the states; as a group, they nominate the party's presidential and vice-presidential candidates, draft the party's campaign platform for the presidential race, and approve changes in the rules and regulations governing party procedures. Before World War II, presidential nominations occupied most of the time, energy, and effort expended at the national convention. The nomination process required days of negotiation and compromise among state party leaders and often required many ballots before a nominee was selected. In recent years, however, presidential candidates have been chosen by winning enough delegate support in state primary elections and caucuses to win the official nomination on the first ballot. The actual convention has become symbolic.

The convention's other two tasks, determining the party's rules and its platform, remain important. Party rules can determine the influence of competing factions

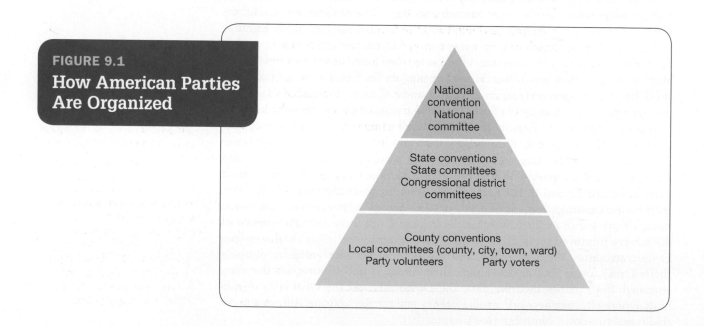

FIGURE 9.1
How American Parties Are Organized

National convention
National committee

State conventions
State committees
Congressional district committees

County conventions
Local committees (county, city, town, ward)
Party volunteers   Party voters

within the party and can also increase or decrease the party's chances for electoral success. In 1972, for example, the Democratic National Convention adopted a new set of rules favored by the party's liberal wing. Under these rules, state delegations to the Democratic Convention were required to include women and members of minority groups in rough proportion to those groups' representation among the party's membership in that state. Liberals correctly calculated that women and African Americans would generally support liberal ideas and candidates. The rules also called for the use of the proportional representation voting system, which liberals thought would give them an advantage by allowing the election of more women and minority delegates. The Republican Party used proportional representation voting for the first time in the 2012 presidential nomination, which had the effect of lengthening the nomination process and making it more difficult for Romney to emerge as the eventual party nominee. It is unclear whether the Republicans will continue to use proportional representation in 2016 since they lost the White House in 2012.

Today, the parties use their national conventions more to provide entertaining television than substantive policy. While the party platforms do not usually attract much interest, they are important statements of party doctrine that can be evaluated by voters when deciding for whom to vote.

The convention also approves the party **platform**. Platforms are often dismissed as documents filled with platitudes that voters seldom read. To some extent this criticism is well founded. Not one voter in a thousand so much as glances at the party platform, and even the news media pay little attention to the documents. Furthermore, the parties' presidential candidates make little use of the platforms in their campaigns; usually they prefer to develop and promote their own themes. Nonetheless, the platform can be an important document. The platform should be understood as a contract in which the various party groups attending the convention state their terms for supporting the ticket. Party platforms should be seen more as internal party documents than as public pledges.

platform a party document, written at a national convention, that contains party philosophy, principles, and positions on issues

National Committee

Between conventions, each national political party is technically headed by its national committee. For the Democrats and Republicans, these are called the Democratic National Committee (DNC) and the Republican National Committee (RNC), respectively. Much of what these national committees do is raise campaign funds for party candidates; given that elections in the United States are more expensive than any country in the world, this is a big job. The national committees also head off factional disputes within the party, and endeavor to enhance the party's media image. The actual work of each national committee is overseen by its chairperson. During every election cycle prior to the enactment of the campaign finance reforms of 2002, the DNC and RNC each raised tens of millions of dollars of so-called **soft money**, which could be used to support party candidates throughout the nation. The 2002 Bipartisan Campaign Reform Act (BCRA), sometimes known as the McCain-Feingold bill, outlawed this practice. To circumvent BCRA, however, each party has established a set of "shadow parties." These are **527 committees**, groups organized to promote and publicize political issues. As such, they can claim tax-exempt status under Section 527 of the Internal Revenue Code, which defines and provides tax-exempt status for nonprofit political advocacy groups.

Under the law, 527 committees can raise and spend unlimited amounts of money as long as their activities are not coordinated with those of the formal party organizations and if the aim is to inform the public and increase voter turnout. Although

soft money money contributed directly to political parties and other organizations for political activities that is not regulated by federal campaign spending laws; in 2002 federal law prohibited unregulated donations to national party committees

527 committees nonprofit independent groups that receive and disburse funds to influence the nomination, election, or defeat of candidates. Named after Section 527 of the Internal Revenue Code, which defines and grants tax-exempt status to nonprofit advocacy groups

some 527 committees are actually independent, many are directed by former Republican and Democratic party officials and run shadow campaigns on behalf of the parties.[15] In the 2008 and 2012 election cycles, nonprofit organizations formed specifically to support particular candidates became an additional source of soft money. In 2010 the Supreme Court's decision in *Citizens United v. Federal Election Committee* again changed the terms for campaigning. As we will see in Chapter 10, the amount of money spent in the 2012 presidential campaign broke new records because the Court decision allowed unlimited corporate and union contributions to political campaigns.[16]

When a party controls the White House, that party's national committee chair is appointed by the president. Typically, this means that the party's national committee becomes little more than an adjunct to the White House staff. For a first-term president, the committee devotes the bulk of its energy to the re-election campaign. The national committee chair of the party not in control of the White House is selected by the committee itself and usually takes a broader view of the party's needs, raising money and performing other activities on behalf of the party members in Congress and in the state legislatures.

Congressional Campaign Committees

Each party also forms House and Senate campaign committees to raise funds for House and Senate election campaigns. Their efforts may or may not be coordinated with the activities of the national committees. Within the party that controls the White House, the national committee and the congressional campaign committees are often rivals, since both groups are seeking donations from the same people but for different candidates: the national committee seeks funds for the presidential race, while the congressional campaign committees approach the same contributors for support for the congressional contests. In recent years, the Republican Party has attempted to coordinate the fund-raising activities of all its committees. Republicans have also sought to give the GOP's national institutions the capacity to invest funds in those close congressional, state, and local races where they can do the most good. The Democrats soon followed suit.

State and Local Party Organizations

Each of the two major parties has a central committee in each state. The parties traditionally also have county committees and, in some instances, state Senate district committees, judicial district committees, and, in the case of larger cities, citywide party committees and local assembly district "ward" committees. Congressional districts may have party committees. Some cities also have precinct committees. Precincts are not districts from which any representative is elected but instead are legally defined subdivisions of wards that are used to register voters and set up ballot boxes or voting machines.

During the nineteenth and early twentieth centuries, many cities, counties, and occasionally even a few states had such well-organized parties that they were called **machines**, whose leaders were called "bosses." The famous old machines of New York, Chicago, and Boston relied on "precinct captains" and a fairly tight group of party members around them. Precinct captains were usually members of long standing in neighborhood party clubhouses, which were important social centers and places for distributing favors to constituents.[17] Traditional party machines depended heavily on

machines strong party organizations in late nineteenth- and early twentieth-century American cities; these machines were led by "bosses" who controlled party nominations and patronage

patronage, their power to control government jobs. With thousands of jobs to dispense, party bosses were able to recruit armies of political workers, who in turn mobilized millions of voters. Voting for the party could mean the guarantee of a government job, such as a police officer, firefighter, or garbage collector. The party machines also helped immigrants process paperwork for citizenship and even distributed free turkeys on Thanksgiving, all in exchange for support for the party on Election Day.

Some of the major reform movements in American history, such as the progressive movement, were motivated by the excessive powers and abuses of these party machines and their bosses. Few, if any, machines are left today. With civil service reform, party leaders no longer control many government jobs. Nevertheless, state and local party organizations are very active in recruiting candidates and conducting voter registration drives. In addition, under current federal law, state and local party organizations can spend unlimited amounts of money on "party-building" activities such as voter registration and get-out-the-vote drives (though in some states such practices are limited by state law). As a result, for many years the national party organizations, which had enormous fund-raising abilities but were restricted by law in how much they could spend on candidates, transferred millions of dollars to the state and local organizations. The state and local parties, in turn, spent this soft money to promote national, state, and local political activities. In this process, local organizations became linked financially to the national parties and American political parties became somewhat more integrated and nationalized than ever before. At the same time, the state and local party organizations came to control large financial resources and play important roles in elections despite the collapse of the old patronage machines.[18]

Political parties used to be ruled by powerful local "bosses" who handed out jobs and favors in exchange for loyalty on Election Day. The cartoon shows New York boss Richard Croker controlling the Democratic Party organization (the donkey) with his pit bulls. Today, parties engage in party-building by organizing voter registration drives.

Parties in Government

> **Explain how parties organize legislative business and influence policy**

When the dust of the campaign has settled, does it matter which party has won? It does. Especially when the parties are sharply divided ideologically, as they have been in recent years, the party that controls government can make significant changes by moving policy in new directions.

patronage the resources available to higher officials, usually opportunities to make partisan appointments to offices and to confer grants, licenses, or special favors to supporters

Parties and Policy

One of the most familiar complaints about American politics is that the two major parties try to be all things to all people, and are therefore indistinguishable from each other. But since the 1980s, important differences emerged between the positions of Democratic and Republican party leaders on a number of key issues, and these differences are still apparent today. For example, the national leadership of the Republican Party supports maintaining high levels of military spending, cuts in social programs, tax relief for upper-income voters, tax incentives for businesses, and the "social agenda" backed by members of conservative religious denominations. The

Beginning in the 1980s the Republican Party sought to expand its base by focusing on social issues that mattered to conservative religious voters. In 2012, Republican presidential candidate Mitt Romney spoke at Liberty University, an evangelical university founded by religious leader Jerry Falwell.

national Democratic leadership, on the other hand, supports expanded social welfare spending, national health care, cuts in military spending, increased regulation of business, and a variety of consumer and environmental programs. In the current era of party polarization, the Republican and Democatic Parties in Congress often face a stalemate over economic matters, such as the federal budget and whether to raise the debt ceiling. The result has been repeated government shutdowns as the government runs out of money to pay federal employees until a new budget deal is reached.

These distinctions reflect differences in philosophy and in the core constituencies to which the parties seek to appeal. The Democratic Party at the national level seeks to unite organized labor, the poor and working class, members of racial minorities, and liberal upper-middle-class professionals. The Republicans, by contrast, appeal to business, upper-middle- and upper-class groups in the private sector, white working-class voters, military families, and religious and social conservatives. Rural and suburban areas provide more votes for the Republicans, while urban areas are dominated by Democrats.

Often party leaders will seek to develop issues they hope will add new groups to their party's constituent base. During the 1980s, for example, under the leadership of Ronald Reagan, the Republicans devised a series of "social issues," including support for school prayer, opposition to abortion, and opposition to affirmative action, designed to cultivate the support of white southerners. This effort was extremely successful in increasing Republican strength in the once solidly Democratic South. In the 1990s, under the leadership of Bill Clinton, who called himself a "new Democrat," the Democratic Party sought to develop new social programs designed to solidify the party's base among working-class and poor voters, and new, somewhat more conservative economic programs aimed at attracting the votes of middle- and upper-middle-class voters. In 2000, George W. Bush labeled himself a "compassionate conservative" to signal to the Republican base that he was a conservative while seeking to reassure moderate and independent voters that he was not an opponent of federal social programs.

As these examples suggest, parties do not always support policies just because their constituents favor these policies. Instead, party leaders can play the role of

for critical analysis

How do parties attract the popular support they need to win elections?

policy entrepreneurs, seeking ideas and programs that will expand their party's base of support while eroding that of the opposition. It is one of the essential characteristics of party politics in America that a party's programs and policies often lead, rather than follow, public opinion. Like their counterparts in the business world, party leaders seek to identify and develop "products" (programs and policies) that will appeal to the public. The public, of course, has the ultimate voice. With its votes it decides whether or not to "buy" new policy offerings.

Parties in Congress

Congress depends more on the party system than is generally recognized, as the parties form the basic organization for running Congress. For one thing, the speakership of the House is essentially a party office. All the members of the House take part in the election of the Speaker. But the actual selection is made by the **majority party**—the party that holds a majority of seats in the House. (The other party is known as the **minority party**.) When the majority party caucus presents a nominee to the entire House, its choice is then invariably ratified in a straight vote along party lines. The committee system of both houses of Congress is also a product of the two-party system. For example, each party is assigned a quota of members for each committee, depending on the percentage of total seats held by the party. As we shall see in Chapter 12, the assignment of individual members to committees is a party decision. Each party has a "committee on committees" to make such decisions. Granting permission to transfer to another committee is also a party decision, as is advancement up the committee ladder toward the chair. Since the late nineteenth century, most advancements have been automatic—based on the length of continual service on the committee. This seniority system has existed only because of the support of the two parties, however, and either party can depart from it by a simple vote.

The importance of parties in Congress became especially evident in the months after the Republicans won control of Congress in 1994. The Republican leadership was able to maintain nearly unanimous support among party members on vote after vote as it sought to implement the GOP's legislative agenda, and Democrats were rarely able to match the Republicans' strong party discipline. After 2006, however, when Democrats won back the Congress, they showed considerably more party discipline than they had in past decades. After Obama's election, Republican members of Congress also showed remarkable party discipline in their united party-line opposition to the president's major initiatives, ranging from economic stimulus to major health care reform, which led Democrats to decry the GOP as "the party of No." We revisit the role of parties in Congress today when we discuss party polarization later in this chapter.

President and Party

Strong presidents with broad popular support can depend on party ties to get their legislation enacted in Congress. Yet there has been a trade-off in using the party machinery to support the president's legislative agenda and building it to support the party in congressional elections. The political scientist Daniel Galvin argues that since the Eisenhower presidency, Republicans have paid much more attention to party building than have Democrats.[19] Given their party's minority status in the electorate for much of the past 50 years, Republican presidents have sought to enhance the party's capabilities to mobilize voters and win elections. George W. Bush's adviser Karl Rove hoped to build a strong party apparatus that would ensure a permanent Republican majority. Democratic presidents have put much less energy into building the party apparatus, focusing instead on their legislative agenda and their own re-election. It was only after their 2004 election defeat that Democrats began to pour their energies into building a stronger party. Under the chairmanship of Howard Dean, a previous presidential candidate and a former Vermont governor, the Democratic National Committee invested heavily in new technology and in creating party-mobilizing capabilities in states across the country, not just the traditionally "blue" states that have reliably voted Democratic.

The Obama campaign was able to use this party machinery as a springboard for its own mobilizing organization, Obama for America. With detailed information about Democratic Party activists, Obama for America's database became, in turn, an important political resource for the mobilizing capacities of the Democratic Party. After Obama took office, the organization was renamed Organizing for America (OFA) and became an independent project of the Democratic National Committee. During Obama's first year in office, the president used OFA to mobilize grassroots support for his legislative agenda. For example, OFA took a very active part in lobbying members of Congress to support health care reform. OFA provides training for volunteers to learn how to become organizers and it has established offices in nearly every state.

● Party Identification

party identification an individual voter's psychological ties to one party or another

Identify the reasons for and sources of party identification

One reason why parties are so important is that individual voters tend to develop **party identification** with one of the political parties. Party identification has been compared with wearing blue- or red-tinted glasses: they color voters' understanding of politics in general, and are the most important cue in how to vote in elections. That is, most Republicans vote for Republican Party candidates, and most Democrats vote for Democratic Party candidates. Approximately one-third of Americans are Republicans, one-third are Democrats, and one-third are independent of either party. However, most independents "lean" toward one of the major parties, and political scientists often consider independents who "lean" as identifying with that party. The number of people identifying as Democrats has outnumbered Republican identifiers for a long time, but the gap is narrower today than it used to be (see Figure 9.2).

Although it is an emotional tie, party identification also has a rational component. Voters generally form attachments to the party that reflects their views and interests. Once those attachments are formed, however, they are likely to persist and even be handed down to children, unless some very strong factors convince individuals that their party is no longer serving their interests. In some sense, party identification is similar to brand loyalty in the marketplace: consumers choose a brand of automobile for its appearance or mechanical characteristics and stick with it out of loyalty, habit, and unwillingness to reexamine their choices, but they may eventually change if the old brand no longer serves their interests.

On any general-election ballot, there are likely to be only two or three candidacies where the nature of the office and the characteristics and positions of the

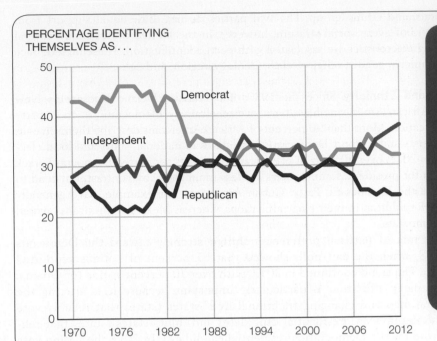

PERCENTAGE IDENTIFYING THEMSELVES AS . . .

FIGURE 9.2

Americans' Party Identification, 1970–2012

Over time, the Democrats have lost strength as more Americans identified themselves as Republicans and independents. In the past 10 years, however, the Democrats have held steadily and the number of Republicans has declined while the number of Americans identifying as independent of either party has increased to an all-time high. Why do you think this is?

SOURCE: Pew Research Center, www.people-press.org/2012/06/01/trend-in-party-identification-1939-2012/ (accessed 6/24/14).

candidates are well known to voters. But what about the choices for judges, the state comptroller, state legislative seats, the state attorney general, and many other elected positions? Parties and campaigns help by providing information when voters must choose among obscure candidates. Without knowledge of local races or judges, most voters fall back on their partisanship, voting for Republican candidates or Democratic candidates for these positions. Some states allow a straight ticket voting option, where individuals may check one box to cast a ballot for all the Republican or Democratic party candidates up and down the ballot, from local to national offices.

Party identification gives citizens a stake in election outcomes that goes beyond the particular race at hand. This is why strong party identifiers are more likely to go to the polls and, of course, are more likely than others to support the party with which they identify. **Party activists** are drawn from the ranks of the strong identifiers. Activists are those who not only vote but also contribute their time and effort to party affairs. No party could succeed without the thousands of volunteers who undertake the tasks needed to keep the organization going. Many party activists devote their time to politics because they have strong beliefs on particular policy issues. Across a range of issues, the views of Democratic activists are more liberal than those of Democratic voters, whereas the views of Republican activists are more conservative than those of Republican voters.

party activists partisans who contribute time, energy, and effort to support their party and its candidates

Group Affiliations

The Democratic and Republican parties are currently America's only truly national parties. They are the only political organizations that draw support from most regions of the country and from Americans of every racial, economic, religious, and ethnic group. The two parties do not draw equal support from members of every social stratum, however. In the United States today, several group characteristics are associated with party identification. These include race and ethnicity, gender, religion, class, ideology, region, and age.

Race and Ethnicity Since the 1930s and Franklin Delano Roosevelt's New Deal, African Americans have been overwhelmingly Democratic in their party identification. More than 90 percent of African Americans describe themselves as Democrats and support Democratic candidates in national, state, and local elections. In 2012, over 90 percent of African Americans supported Democrat Barack Obama for president. Latino voters are less monolithic, by contrast, but tend to support the Democratic Party. Cuban Americans, for example, have generally leaned Republican in their party affiliations, whereas Mexican Americans favored the Democrats.

This mix of partisan preferences shifted strongly toward the Democrats in 2008, when the exit polls showed that 67 percent of Latinos supported Obama. The trend continued in 2012, with over 70 percent voting for Obama. Latino party affiliation is particularly important because it is altering the electoral map and changing traditional "red" states (states that reliably vote for the Republican presidential candidate) and "blue" states (states that reliably vote for the Democratic presidential candidate). In 2012 the Latino vote in swing states such as Florida and Colorado helped bring the Democrats to victory. Asian Americans have been divided in past elections, but in 2012, 73 percent of Asian Americans voted for Barack Obama, and 26 percent voted for Mitt Romney, according to exit polls. Presidential voting often defines party identification.

The affiliation of African Americans and Latinos with the Democratic Party can be traced to the party's historical policy positions. The Democrats were the party of the civil rights movement, desegregation, and affirmative action policies that solidified African American support for the party. Democrats also generally

Both the Democratic and Republican parties have sought to expand their membership by appealing to Latinos, the fastest growing ethnic group in the country. Recently, the Democrats have been more successful because they are more supportive of immigration and government services for immigrants.

favor social welfare policies that help low-income African Americans. Similarly, Democrats tend to be supportive of a more lenient immigration policies than Republicans. Support for immigration is key to Latino voters favoring the Democratic Party by wide margins in recent elections.

Gender Women are somewhat more likely to support Democrats than Republicans, and men are somewhat more likely to support Republicans, in surveys of party affiliation. This reflects the fact that women and the Democratic Party tend to prioritze health, education, and social services, while men and the Republican Party tend to prioritize fiscal and economic issues and national security. This difference is known as the **gender gap**. The gender gap has varied between 6 and 11 percent since 1992. For example, George W. Bush's first election, in 2000, had a sizable gender gap: he received 53 percent support among men and 43 percent among women. In 2004 the gender gap decreased slightly, with 55 percent of men voting for Bush compared with 48 percent of women. In 2008 the gap remained on the small side, with 56 percent of women and 49 percent of men supporting Barack Obama for president, but it widened again in 2012, with 55 percent of women supporting Obama as compared with just 45 percent of men.[20]

gender gap a distinctive pattern of voting behavior reflecting the differences in views between women and men

Religion Jews are among the Democratic Party's most loyal constituent groups and have been since the New Deal. Nearly 90 percent of all Jewish Americans describe themselves as Democrats. Catholics were also once a strongly pro-Democratic group but have been shifting toward the Republican Party since the 1970s, when the party focused on abortion and other social issues deemed to be important to Catholics. Protestants are more likely to identify with the Republicans than the Democrats. Evangelical Protestants, in particular, have been drawn to the Republicans' conservative stands on social issues, such as marriage and abortion. The importance of religious conservatives to the Republican Party became more evident after 2000, when George W. Bush awarded federal grants and contracts to religious groups. By using so-called faith-based groups as federal contractors, Bush sought to ensure that these groups would have a continuing stake in Republican success. Religious conservatives, particularly white born-again Christians, overwhelmingly supported President Bush in 2004, accounting for one-third of his votes. Almost 80 percent of white born-again Christians voted for President Bush. The 2004 election results also revealed that how religious a person is, as measured by frequency of attendance at religious services, has a larger impact on voting than his or her specific religion. Voters who attended religious services weekly were more likely to vote for Bush, regardless of their religion, than were voters who were less observant. In 2008 and 2012, white evangelical Christians continued to vote overwhelmingly Republican.[21]

Class The patterns of class voting that emerged from the New Deal of the 1930s were simple: upper-income Americans were considerably more likely to affiliate with the Republicans, whereas lower-income Americans were far more likely to identify with the Democrats. This divide is reflected in the differences between the two parties on economic issues. In general, the Republicans support cutting taxes and social spending—positions that reflect the interests of the wealthy. The Democrats, however, favor increasing social spending and in some cases raising taxes on the wealthy—a position consistent with the interests of less-affluent Americans. But beginning in the 1970s, many white working-class voters, concerned with moral issues and racial liberalism, started voting Republican, and have remained in the Republican Party.

Analysts disagree about the trend of class voting, because there is no widely accepted definition of class. When the electorate is divided into thirds on the basis of income, the relationship between lower-income voters and Democratic allegiance remains strong. When class is measured by education, however, white workers without a college degree have voted heavily for Republicans in recent elections.[22]

Ideology Ideology and party identification are very closely linked. Most individuals who describe themselves as conservatives identify with the Republican Party, whereas most who call themselves liberals support the Democrats. This division has increased in recent years as the two parties have taken very different positions on social and economic issues. Before the 1970s, when party differences were more blurred, it was not uncommon to find Democratic conservatives and Republican liberals. Both of these species are rare today. Yet important differences remain between conservatives and liberals. Economic conservatives care most about reducing government regulation and taxes. Social conservatives are concerned about social issues such as abortion and same-sex marriage. The Republican Party includes both groups, but at times the interests of these two kinds of conservatives conflict. Likewise, many Democrats who are economic liberals, in favor of government programs and raising taxes, are conservative when it comes to matters such as same-sex marriage.

Region After the 2000 election, red and blue maps appeared showing the regional distribution of the vote. Democrats, represented as "Blue America," were clustered on the coasts and the upper Midwest and across the northern states. Republicans, represented as "Red America," were concentrated in the Mountain West, the Southwest, and the South.

The explanations for these regional variations are complex. Between the Civil War and the 1960s, the "Solid South" was a Democratic bastion. Today the South is solidly Republican. Southern Republicanism has come about because conservative white southerners identify the Democratic Party with the civil rights movement, racial liberalism, and with liberal positions on abortion, environmental protection, rights for same-sex couples, and other social issues. Republican strength in the South is also related to the weakness of organized labor in these regions, and to the dependence of the two regions on military programs supported by the Republicans. Democratic strength in the Northeast and Midwest is a function of the continuing influence of organized labor in the large cities of these regions, and of the regions' large populations of minority and elderly voters, who benefit from Democratic social programs. The coastal West, especially California, shifted toward the Democrats in the 1990s, in part because of the growing importance of the Latino vote (see Figure 9.3).[23]

Age Age is another factor associated with partisanship. In 2008 the shift toward the Democratic Party affected all age groups, but it was particularly strong among young voters. Polls showed that, while older voters preferred Democrats by 11–12 percent, those born after 1977 favored Democrats by 24 percent. There is nothing about a particular numerical age that leads to a particular party loyalty. Rather, individuals from the same age cohort are likely to have

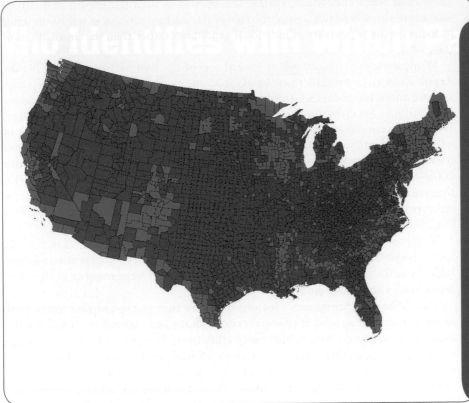

Presidential Vote by County, 2012

In 2012, Democrat Barack Obama won more votes than Republican Mitt Romney nationwide, especially in counties in the Northeast, upper Midwest (Chicago), and the West Coast. The Republicans dominated in most counties in the center of the country. Although the map shows more "red" counties than "blue," covering a greater geographic area, Obama and the Democrats won many of the most populous counties and several of the states with the most votes in the electoral college (see Chapter 10).

SOURCE: Politico, www.politico .com/2012-election/map/# /President/2012/ (accessed 11/11/14).

experienced a similar set of events during the period when their party loyalties were formed. Thus, Americans between the ages of 50 and 64 came of political age during the Cold War, Vietnam, and civil rights eras. Apparently, among voters whose initial perceptions of politics were shaped during this period, more responded favorably to the role played by the Democrats, who were antiwar and pro-civil rights, than to the actions of the Republicans. Young people who came of age during the Bush presidency have the strongest Democratic Party identification of any age group. Young people have distinct policy preferences that overlap with the Democratic Party, including strong support for same-sex relationships, legalization of marijuana, environmental protection, and more economic equality.

Recent Trends in Party Affiliation

After the 1960s, many analysts began to express concern that American parties had become too weak to play their vital role in converting popular political participation into effective government. These scholars noted such trends as a decline in partisan attachment within the electorate, the growth in the numbers of voters identifying as independents, and a rise in so-called split-ticket voting. This overall trend, sometimes termed **dealignment**, was seen as a product of growing social diversity and educational attainment, which made voters less reliant on parties to

for critical analysis

What are the major components of each party's political coalition? What factors tie these groups to their respective parties?

dealignment a movement away from the major political parties; a decline in partisan attachment

The character of a nation's party system can have profound consequences for the types of issues and policies that reach the nation's political agenda, and for critically important issues such as the distribution of wealth and economic inequality. For example, the contemporary American political parties mainly compete for the support of different groups of middle- and upper-class Americans. As a result, issues that concern the middle and upper classes, such as the environment, health care, retirement benefits, and taxation, are very much on the political agenda, whereas issues that concern working-class and poorer Americans, such as welfare and housing, receive short shrift from both parties.[27]

Over the course of American history, changes in political forces and alignments have produced six distinctive party systems.

The First Party System: Federalists and Jeffersonian Republicans

The first party system emerged in the 1790s and pitted the Federalists against the Jeffersonian Republicans. The Federalists spoke mainly for New England merchants and supported a program of protective tariffs to encourage manufacturing, assumption of the states' Revolutionary War debts, the creation of a national bank, and resumption of commercial ties with Britain. The Jeffersonians, led by southern agricultural interests, opposed these policies and instead favored free trade, the promotion of agricultural over commercial interests, and friendship with France. The Federalists sought, unsuccessfully, to use the force of law against the Jeffersonians by enacting the Alien and Sedition acts to outlaw criticism of the government. These acts, however, proved virtually impossible to enforce, and the Jeffersonians gradually expanded their base from the South into the Middle Atlantic states. In the election of 1800, Jefferson defeated the incumbent Federalist president, John Adams, and led his party to power. Over the following years, the Federalists gradually weakened. The party disappeared altogether after the pro-British sympathies of some Federalist leaders during the War of 1812 led to charges of treason against the party.

From the collapse of the Federalists until the 1830s, America had only one political party, the Jeffersonian Republicans, who gradually came to be known as the Democrats. This period of one-party politics had an absence of party competition. Throughout this period, however, there was intense factional conflict within the Democratic Party, particularly between the supporters and opponents of General Andrew Jackson, America's great military hero of the War of 1812. Jackson's opponents united to deny him the presidency in 1824, but Jackson won elections in 1828 and 1832. Jackson's support was in the South and West, and he generally espoused a program of free trade and policies that appealed to those regions.

The Second Party System: Democrats and Whigs

During the 1830s, groups opposing Jackson united to form a new political force, the Whig Party—thus giving rise to the second American party system. Both the Democrats and the Whigs built party organizations throughout the nation, and both sought to enlarge their bases of support by expanding the right to vote. They increased the number of eligible voters through the elimination of property restrictions and other barriers to voting—at least voting by white males.

Support for the new Whig Party was stronger in the Northeast than in the South and West and stronger among merchants than among small farmers. Hence, in some measure, the Whigs were the successors of the Federalists. Yet conflict between the two parties revolved more around personalities than policies. The Whigs were a diverse group united more by opposition to the Democrats than by agreement on programs. In 1840 the Whigs won their first presidential election under the leadership of General William Henry Harrison, a military hero known as "Old Tippecanoe." The Whig campaign carefully avoided issues—since the party could agree on almost none—and emphasized the personal qualities and heroism of the candidate. The Whigs also invested heavily in campaign rallies and entertainment to win the hearts, if not exactly the minds, of the voters. The 1840 campaign came to be called the "hard cider" campaign because of the practice of using food and especially drink to win votes.

During the late 1840s and early 1850s, conflicts over slavery produced sharp divisions within both the Whig and the Democratic parties, despite the efforts of party leaders to develop compromises. By 1856 the Whig Party had all but disintegrated under the strain, and many Whig politicians and voters, along with antislavery Democrats, joined the new Republican Party, which pledged to ban slavery from the western territories. In 1860 the Republicans nominated Abraham Lincoln for the presidency. Lincoln's victory strengthened southern calls for secession from the Union and, soon thereafter, for all-out civil war.

The Civil War and Post–Civil War Party System: Republicans and Democrats

During the course of the war, President Lincoln depended heavily on Republican governors and state legislatures to raise troops, provide funding, and maintain popular support for a long and bloody military conflict. The secession of the South had stripped the Democratic Party of many of its leaders and supporters, but the Democrats remained politically competitive throughout the war and nearly won the 1864 presidential election because of war weariness on the part of the northern public. With the defeat of the Confederacy in 1865, some congressional Republicans sought to convert the South into a Republican bastion through a program of Reconstruction that enfranchised newly freed slaves. This Reconstruction program collapsed in the 1870s as a result of disagreement within the Republican Party in Congress and violent resistance by southern whites. With the end of Reconstruction, the former Confederate states regained full membership in the Union and full control of their internal affairs. Throughout the South, African Americans were deprived of political rights, including the right to vote, despite post–Civil War constitutional guarantees to the contrary. The post–Civil War South was solidly Democratic in its political affiliation, and with a firm southern base, the national Democratic Party was able to confront the Republicans on a

In the 1830s the Whig Party emerged as the Democrats' main rival. This drawing depicts a Whig rally and parade during the 1840 election, which became known as the "hard cider" campaign.

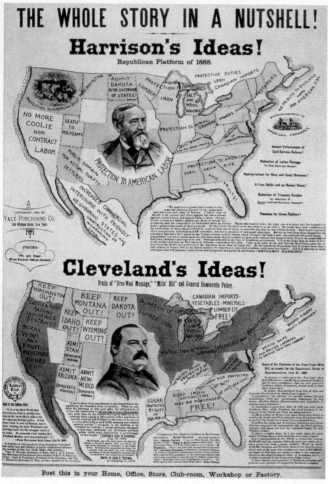

Following the Civil War, the Republican Party remained dominant in the North. This poster supporting Republican Benjamin Harrison in the 1888 election promises protective tariffs and other policies that appealed to the industrial states in the North.

more or less equal basis. From the end of the Civil War to the 1890s, the Republican Party remained the party of the North, with strong business and middle-class support, while the Democrats were the party of the South, with support also from working-class and immigrant groups.

The System of 1896: Republicans and Democrats

During the 1890s, profound and rapid social and economic changes led to the emergence of a variety of protest parties, including the Populist Party, which won the support of hundreds of thousands of voters in the South and West. The Populists appealed mainly to small farmers but also attracted western mining interests and urban workers. In the 1892 presidential election, the Populist Party carried four states and elected governors in eight. In 1896 the Populist Party effectively merged with the Democrats, who nominated William Jennings Bryan, a Democratic senator with pronounced Populist sympathies, for the presidency. The Republicans nominated the conservative senator William McKinley. In the ensuing campaign, northern and midwestern businesses made an all-out effort to defeat what they saw as a radical threat from the Populist-Democratic alliance. When the dust settled, the Republicans had won a resounding victory. The GOP ("Grand Old Party"), or Republican Party, had carried the more heavily populated northern and midwestern states and confined the Democrats to their smaller bases of support in the South and far West. For the next 36 years, the Republicans were the nation's majority party, carrying 7 of 9 presidential elections and controlling both houses of Congress in 15 of 18 contests. The Republican Party of this era was very much the party of American business, advocating low taxes, high tariffs on imports, and a minimum of government regulation. The Democrats were far too weak to offer much opposition. Southern Democrats, moreover, were too concerned with maintaining the region's autonomy on issues of race to challenge the Republicans on other fronts.

The New Deal Party System: Reversal of Fortune

Soon after the Republican presidential candidate Herbert Hoover won the 1928 presidential election, the nation's economy collapsed. The Great Depression, which produced unprecedented economic hardship, stemmed from a variety of causes, but from the perspective of millions of Americans, the Republican Party did not do enough to promote economic recovery. In 1932, Americans elected Franklin Delano Roosevelt and a solidly Democratic Congress. Roosevelt developed a program for economic recovery that he dubbed the "New Deal." Under the auspices of the New Deal, the size and reach of America's national government increased substantially. The federal government took responsibility for economic management and social welfare to an extent that was unprecedented in American history. Roosevelt designed many of his programs specifically to expand the political base of the Democratic Party. He rebuilt and revitalized the party around a nucleus of unionized workers, upper-middle-class intellectuals and professionals, southern farmers, Jews, Catholics, and African Americans—the so-called New Deal coalition that made the Democrats the nation's majority party for the next 36 years. Groping for a response to the New Deal, Republicans often wound up supporting popular New Deal programs such as Social Security in what was sometimes derided as "me too" Republicanism. Even the relatively conservative administration of Dwight D. Eisenhower in the 1950s left the principal New Deal programs intact.

The New Deal coalition was severely strained during the 1960s by conflicts over civil rights and the Vietnam War. The struggle over civil rights initially divided northern Democrats who supported the civil rights cause from white southern Democrats who defended the system of racial segregation. Subsequently, as the civil rights movement launched a northern campaign aimed at securing access to jobs and education and an end to racial discrimination in such realms as housing, northern Democrats also split, often along income lines. The struggle over the Vietnam War further divided the Democrats, with upper-income liberal Democrats strongly opposing the Johnson administration's decision to greatly expand the numbers of U.S. troops fighting in Southeast Asia. These schisms within the Democratic Party provided an opportunity for the GOP, which returned to power in 1968 under the leadership of Richard Nixon.

The Contemporary American Party System

The Republican Party widened its appeal in the second half of the twentieth century. In 1964, for example, the Republican presidential candidate Barry Goldwater argued in favor of substantially reduced levels of taxation and spending, less government regulation of the economy, and the elimination of many federal social programs. Though Goldwater was defeated by Lyndon Johnson, the ideas he espoused continued to be major themes for the Republican Party. It took Richard Nixon's "southern strategy" to give the GOP the votes it needed to end Democratic dominance of national politics. Nixon appealed to disaffected white southerners, and with the help of the independent candidate and former Alabama governor George Wallace, he sparked the shift of voters that gave the party a strong position in all the states of the former Confederacy. The movement of white southerners to the Republican Party was in part because of opposition to desegregation of the South and to the civil rights movement supported by Democratic leaders, including President Kennedy. During the 1980s, under the leadership of President Ronald Reagan, Republicans added two additional important groups to their coalition. The first were religious conservatives who were offended by Democratic support for abortion and gay rights and by alleged Democratic disdain for traditional cultural and religious values. The second were working-class whites who were drawn to Reagan's tough approach to foreign policy and his positions against affirmative action.

Richard Nixon's "southern strategy" helped broaden the Republican Party's base in the late 1960s and the 1970s by appealing to white southerners. Here, Nixon meets supporters in Georgia in 1973.

While Republicans built a political base around economic and social conservatives and white southerners, the Democratic Party maintained its support among a majority of unionized workers and upper-middle-class intellectuals and professionals. Democrats also appealed strongly to racial minorities. The 1965 Voting Rights Act had greatly increased black voter participation in the South and helped the Democratic Party retain some House and Senate seats in southern states. And whereas the Republicans appealed to social conservatives, the Democrats appealed strongly to Americans concerned with abortion rights, gay rights, women's rights, environmentalism, and other progressive social causes.

Despite the success of Republican presidential candidates in attracting votes from groups previously associated with the Democratic Party, Republicans generally did not do as well at the state and local levels until the 1990s, when conservative religious groups made a concerted effort to expand their influence within the Republican Party. This effort led to conflict between these members of the "religious right" and more traditional fiscal Republicans, whose major concerns were economic matters such as taxes and federal regulation of business. The two factions of the party came together when the Republicans won both houses of Congress in 1994 (the first time in almost half a century). The Republicans retained control of Congress in 1996, despite President Clinton's re-election in that year. In 2000, George W. Bush united the party's centrist and right wings behind a program of tax cuts, education reform, military strength, and family values.

However, by 2006, the public's disapproval of the Bush administration and the war in Iraq led to major losses for Republicans in both houses of Congress. Campaigning during the worst financial crisis since the 1930s and burdened with a president whose approval ratings had sunk to historic lows, Republicans fared poorly in the 2008 elections. With the party in disarray, contending factions sought to redefine a strategy that would allow Republicans to regain the White House.

In 2008, Democrats reached beyond their base by appealing to moderate voters and independents in states that had once been Republican strongholds, and they won control of Congress as well as the presidency for the first time since 1995. However, the continuation of sharp partisan differences in Congress signaled that intense party conflict would continue to characterize American politics. Republicans won control of the House of Representatives in 2010, and although Obama was re-elected to the presidency in 2012, control of Congress remained divided through 2014, when Republicans won majorities in both houses.

This history of the party system has focused on parties at the national level. However, as discussed earlier, parties operate at the local and state levels as well, serving the same functions as at the federal level. While support for political parties at the local and state levels tends to follow national-level patterns, there are also differences. The ideology of Republican candidates in Massachusetts, for instance, is more liberal than national-level Republican candidates. Massachusetts has one of the most liberal populations in the country. As a result, there are no Republican members of the Massachusetts delegation to the U.S. House, but 17 percent of the state legislature is Republican (see Figure 9.4). Some states have an even bigger gap between state and national

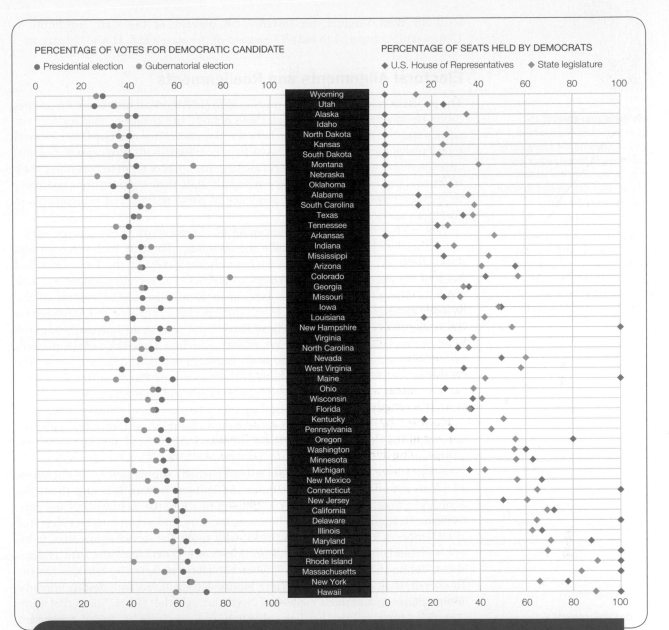

PERCENTAGE OF VOTES FOR DEMOCRATIC CANDIDATE
● Presidential election ● Gubernatorial election

PERCENTAGE OF SEATS HELD BY DEMOCRATS
◆ U.S. House of Representatives ◆ State legislature

Wyoming
Utah
Alaska
Idaho
North Dakota
Kansas
South Dakota
Montana
Nebraska
Oklahoma
Alabama
South Carolina
Texas
Tennessee
Arkansas
Indiana
Mississippi
Arizona
Colorado
Georgia
Missouri
Iowa
Louisiana
New Hampshire
Virginia
North Carolina
Nevada
West Virginia
Maine
Ohio
Wisconsin
Florida
Kentucky
Pennsylvania
Oregon
Washington
Minnesota
Michigan
New Mexico
Connecticut
New Jersey
California
Delaware
Illinois
Maryland
Vermont
Rhode Island
Massachusetts
New York
Hawaii

FIGURE 9.4

Party Support Representation

The states are listed here by the percentage of the public that identifies as Democratic, from the least (Wyoming) to the most (Hawaii). The overall pattern in presidential elections (shown on the left) reflects party identification in the states quite closely. Races for governor follow the same pattern, with a few notable exceptions. We might expect representation in state legislatures and the U.S. house (shown on the right) to follow the same pattern, but here we see even more variation. While Democrats generally hold more seats in the more Democratic states, the percentage of seats often differs significantly from the Democratic presidential vote and from public opinion. For example, Ohio has roughly equal numbers of Democratic and Republican voters, and 52 percent of Ohioans voted for Obama in 2012, but only 25 percent of Ohio's delegation to the U.S. House and 37 percent of the state legislature was Democratic

Sources: The Council of State Governments, Book of the States 2013, Table 3–3; Office of the Clerk, U.S. House of Representatives. Member data: http://clerk.house.gov/member_info.excel-labels-113.xls: The Council of State Governments, Book of the States 2013, Table 6–7 (data are from the most recent gubernatorial election prior to December 2012): U.S. National Archives and Records Administration, www.archives.gov/federal-register/electoral-college/2012/popular-vote.html: Gallup, State of the States, www.gallup.com/poll/125066/state-states.aspx (accessed 10/30/14).

level. In West Virginia, for instance, 58 percent of the state legislature is Democratic, compared to only 33 percent of the state's U.S. House delegation.

Electoral Alignments and Realignments

The points of transition between party systems in American history are sometimes called **electoral realignments**. During these periods, the coalitions that support the parties and the balance of power between the parties are redefined. In historical terms, realignments occur when new issues, combined with economic or political crises, mobilize new voters and persuade large numbers of them to reexamine their traditional partisan loyalties and permanently shift their support from one party to another. Figure 9.5 charts the sequence of party systems and realignments in American history.

Although scholars dispute the timing of realignments, there is some agreement that five have occurred since the Founding. The first took place around 1790–1800, when the Jeffersonian Republicans defeated the Federalists and became the dominant force in American politics. The second realignment took place in about 1828, when the Jacksonian Democrats seized control of the White House and the Congress. In the third period of realignment, centered on 1860, the newly founded Republican Party, led by Abraham Lincoln, won power, in the process destroying the Whig Party, which had been one of the nation's two major parties since the 1830s. Many northern voters who had supported the Whigs or the Democrats on the basis of their economic stands shifted their support to the Republicans as slavery replaced tariffs and economic concerns as the central item on the nation's political agenda. Many southern Whigs shifted their support to the Democrats. The new sectional alignment of forces that emerged was solidified by the trauma of the Civil War and persisted almost to the turn of the century.

In the 1890s, this alignment was at least partially supplanted by an alignment of political forces based on economic and cultural factors, bringing about the fourth electoral realignment. In the election of 1896, the Republican candidate, William McKinley, emphasizing business, industry, and urban interests, defeated the Democrat, William Jennings Bryan, who spoke for sectional interests, farmers, and fundamentalism. Republican dominance lasted until the fifth realignment, during the period 1932–36, when the Democrats, led by Franklin Delano Roosevelt, took control of the White House and Congress and, despite sporadic interruptions, maintained control of both through the 1960s. Since that time, American party politics has been characterized primarily by **divided government**, wherein the presidency is controlled by one party while the other party controls one or both houses of Congress.

Such periods of electoral realignment in American politics have had extremely important policy consequences. Realignments occur when new issue concerns, coupled with economic or political crises, weaken the established political elite and permit new groups of politicians to create coalitions of forces capable of capturing and holding the reins of governmental power. The construction of new governing coalitions during these realigning periods has effected major changes in American governmental institutions and policies. Each period of realignment was a turning point in American politics. The choices made by the national electorate during these periods helped shape the course of American political history for the following generation.[28]

electoral realignment the point in history when a new party supplants the ruling party, becoming in turn the dominant political force; in the United States, this has tended to occur roughly every 30 years

divided government the condition in American government wherein the presidency is controlled by one party while the opposing party controls one or both houses of Congress

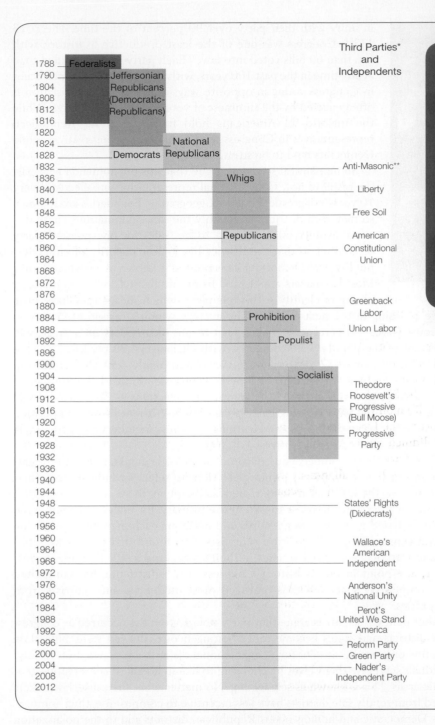

FIGURE 9.5

How the Party System Evolved

During the nineteenth century, the Democrats and the Republicans emerged as the two dominant parties in American politics. As the American party system evolved, many third parties emerged, but few of them remained in existence for very long.

*Or in some cases, fourth parties; most of these parties lasted through only one term.

**The Anti-Masonics had the distinction of being not only the first third party but also the first party to hold a national nominating convention and the first to announce a party platform.

Party Polarization

A distinguishing feature of the contemporary party system is **party polarization**. Polarization in Congress is measured by party unity in roll-call votes. In 2013, for example, Republicans in the House voted with their fellow Republican colleagues on 92 percent of roll-call votes. Similarly, Democrats in Congress voted

party polarization the division between the two major parties on most policy issues, with members of each party unified around their party's positions with little crossover

Increasing ideological polarization in Congress has been accompanied by an erosion of professional civility. At this House Oversight and Government Reform Committee hearing in 2014, the committee chair ordered the microphone of a committee member from the opposing party turned off.

in unity with their party over 90 percent of the time. The 2013 113th Congress was one of the least productive in history, with less than 60 bills voted into law.[29] Each party is more unified than at any time in the past 100 years, with Democrats and Republicans in Congress voting in opposite ways on many laws. Legislation is often enacted by the slimmest of vote margins in Congress. While the majority of Americans hold moderate views, Republican representatives in Congress tend to be strong conservatives while Democrats tend to be strong liberals.

Some political scientists argue that this phenomenon is in part the result of how Congressional representatives are elected. Every 10 years, congressional district geographic boundaries are redrawn so that each district has roughly the same population. These districts are increasingly drawn to be "safe" for one political party or another so that the district has a clear majority of either Republicans or Democrats. This process is known as gerrymandering. Most lawmakers are elected from safe districts, where a majority of voters identify with their party, which means they have little chance of losing in the next election. The average winning margin of victory in the House is over 40 percentage points. That means incumbents, on average, win 70 percent of the popular vote compared with challengers' 30 percent.[30] Of the 435 House races in 2012, only 23 were considered highly contested or toss-up races, measured by a vote margin of 5 percent or less.[31] In 2014 the number of toss-up House races was about 17. Uncompetitive elections in Congress and safe seats are associated with growing party polarization. Without facing competition from the other party during general elections, Congress members are increasingly strong liberals or strong conservatives.

Because of these homogeneous partisan districts, lawmakers face the greatest threats in their own party's primary elections to select a candidate for office. This can have the effect of moving Congress members more to the ideological extremes of their party in order to win in the primary. By analyzing members of the House based on their voting records and assigning each member a "score" on a liberal-conservative scale, political scientists have found that today's Republicans and Democrats are further apart in their scores (and hence their ideologies) than at any point in recent history. Congressional redistricting has eliminated most competitive seats and thus removed most moderates and centrists from both parties.

Other political scientists argue that party polarization has occurred as congressional districts and states become more homogeneous (the red state, blue state phenomenon), not because of how congressional districts are drawn, but because individuals segregate themselves by choosing to live in liberal or conservative geographic areas. This is known as self-sorting. No matter what the cause, lawmakers elected from solidly safe districts have less incentive to compromise, thus homogeneous Democratic and homogeneous Republican districts add to the polarization of the political parties.

As Congress became more ideologically extreme, members gave more power to their party leaders, who changed the rules in Congress so that the majority could control the legislative process more easily, making party polarization worse. Political scientist Barbara Sinclair has shown that the percentage of bills in the House that are debated using restrictive rules has grown over the last 30 years.[32] At the same time that the ability to debate legislation on the floor of the House is restricted, individual members exercise less personal choice in deciding how to vote. In the Senate, which has unlimited debate over legislation, the situation isn't much better. The filibuster, whose use was once relegated to a handful of major national issues in a given Congress, has become a routine weapon of obstruction, applied even to widely supported bills or presidential nominations. The same goes for the confirmation process, where even noncontroversial appointments are blocked in the Senate.

Accompanying the rising party polarization has been a breakdown of civility in Congress. Members of polarized parties engage in name calling and ad hominem attacks (attacking the ethics of a person). This fuels the negative view that most Americans have of Congress.[33] Approval of Congress in 2014 stood at approximately 13 percent of the American public, up just slightly from a record low of 9 percent in November 2013.[34] This extreme party polarization has led not only to low approval of government but also to an inability of Congress to compromise and adopt policies that would benefit the majority of Americans.

This polarization among the parties in Congress does not match the ideology of the American public. Imagine if we could line up all 317 million Americans on a continuum from the most liberal on the left to the most conservative on the right. There would be far fewer very strong liberals and very strong conservatives than moderates. The majority of Americans would fall somewhere in between, somewhat just left of center or just right of center. Opinion polls show that the distribution of ideology in the United States represents a single hump (like a one-humped camel), with the majority of Americans holding a moderate ideology. Now imagine lining up the members of Congress on the same continuum from most liberal to most conservative. Few lawmakers would fall in the middle, with the majority either to the far left (strong Democrat) or the far right (strong Republican)—essentially a two-humped camel. This suggests that party polarization in Congress has created a Congress that does not match the aggregate ideology of the American public.

Should we believe the media pundits who tell us that Americans are deeply divided between the red states and the blue states? Is the American population really polarized on hot-button moral, economic, and cultural issues? Many political scientists believe that in fact most Americans are moderates in terms of their opinions on major issues.[35] However, this issue continues to be debated.

Third Parties

Although the United States has a two-party-dominant system, the country has always had more than two parties. Typically, **third parties** in the United States have represented social and economic interests that for one or another reason were not given voice by the two major parties.[36] Such parties have had a good deal of influence on ideas and elections in the United States. The Populists, a party centered in the rural areas of the West and Midwest, and the Progressives, spokesmen for the urban middle classes in the late nineteenth and early twentieth centuries, are the most important examples in the past 100 years. More recently, H. Ross Perot, who ran in 1992 as an independent and in 1996 as the Reform Party's nominee, won the votes of almost one in five Americans.

Because third parties almost always lose at the national level, such parties exist as a protest movement against the two parties or to promote specific issues. Third

third parties parties that organize to compete against the two major American political parties

TABLE 9.1

Parties and Candidates in 2012

CANDIDATE	PARTY	VOTE TOTAL	PERCENTAGE OF VOTES
Barack Obama	Democratic	65,915,796	51.06
Mitt Romney	Republican	60,933,500	47.20
Gary Johnson	Libertarian	1,275,971	0.99
Jill Stein	Green	469,628	0.36
Virgil Goode	Constitution	122,308	0.09

SOURCE: Federal Election Commission, www.fec.gov (accessed 6/24/14).

parties often are sources of new ideas and party realignment. Third parties also profoundly affect American elections, as they take votes from the two major parties, often swinging the election in favor of the Democrats or the Republicans. In the extremely close 2000 presidential election, for example, third-party candidate Ralph Nader won just 3 percent of the popular vote, but that was enough to swing the election to Republican George W. Bush. While the majority of Americans favored the Democratic Party in 2000, having a third party in the race split the Democratic vote, so the party lost the White House. Most Nader voters would have preferred Al Gore over George Bush, but by voting for Nader they inadvertently enabled Bush to win. The same thing happened in 1992 and 1996, but this time it was the conservative vote that was split between two parties. H. Ross Perot's Reform Party won roughly 19 percent of the popular vote in 1992 (the highest third-party vote share since Teddy Roosevelt), which allowed Democrat Bill Clinton to win the presidency with just 43.0 percent of the popular vote (to Republican George H. W. Bush's 37.4 percent). Sometimes the margins are even smaller: in Florida in 2012, Barack Obama was .05 percent ahead of Mitt Romney, but Libertarian Party candidate Gary Johnson won .05 percent of the popular vote, likely from voters who otherwise would have supported Romney. Because of these losses, leaders in both major political parties fear third-party challenges in presidential elections.

Table 9.1 lists the top candidates in the presidential election of 2012, including the top third-party and independent candidates who ran. In addition to the candidates listed in Table 9.1, the Socialist Party, the Prohibition Party, and several other parties nominated candidates for the presidency in 2012. However, third parties did not play a significant role in the outcome in 2012.

Third Parties at the State and Local Levels Third-party and independent candidacies also arise at the state and local levels. In New York, the Liberal and Conservative parties have been on the ballot for decades. In 1998, Minnesota elected a third-party governor, the former professional wrestler Jesse Ventura. The

Libertarian and Green parties in particular run candidates in many state and local elections. In 2012 independent candidates won Senate races in Maine and Vermont.

Obstacles Facing Third Parties Americans usually assume that only candidates nominated by one of the two major parties have any chance of winning an election. Thus, a vote cast for a third-party or independent candidate is often seen as a vote wasted. Voters who would prefer a third-party candidate may feel compelled to vote for the major-party candidate whom they regard as the "lesser of two evils," to avoid wasting their votes in a futile gesture.

Under federal election law, only parties that receive more than 5 percent of the national presidential vote are entitled to federal funds. The Reform Party qualified by winning 8.2 percent in 1996. Ralph Nader, the Green Party candidate in 2000, hoped to win the 5.0 percent of the vote that would entitle the Green Party to federal funds, but failed to achieve that threshold.

As discussed earlier, third-party prospects are also hampered by America's single-member district system for allocating seats. In many other nations, several individuals can be elected to represent each legislative district—a system of multiple-member districts, which are more favorable to minor-party candidates. Add to that the plurality, or winner-take-all, system of voting discussed earlier in this chapter, where candidates need to win more votes than in countries using the proportional representation system. (In a proportional system, parties can earn seats in government with 15–20 percent of the popular vote.) This higher American threshold discourages minor parties.[37]

The Influence of Third Parties Although the Republican Party was the only American third party to make itself permanent (by replacing the Whigs), other third parties have enjoyed an influence far beyond their electoral size. This is because large parts of their programs were adopted by one or both of the major parties, which sought to appeal to the voters mobilized by the new party, and so expand their own electoral strength. The Democratic Party, for example, became a great deal more liberal when it adopted most of the Progressive program early in the twentieth century. Many socialists felt that President Roosevelt's New Deal had adopted most of their party's program, including old-age pensions, unemployment compensation, an agricultural marketing program, and laws guaranteeing workers the right to organize into unions. This kind of influence explains the short lives of third parties. Their causes are usually eliminated when the major parties absorb their programs and draw their supporters into the mainstream.

Although it is not technically a political party, the Tea Party movement had a considerable impact on the Republican Party primaries in 2010, when Tea Party candidates defeated several incumbents and candidates endorsed by Republican Party leaders. Some high-profile Tea Party candidates, including Rand Paul (R-Ky.), then went on to win office in the 2010 midterm elections. In total, the Tea Party succeeded in electing about 32 percent of their candidates in 2010—not a huge percentage, but a strong showing for a newly organized group. The Tea Party's electoral influence was felt again in the 2014 midterm elections. Notably, Representative Eric Cantor, who was the House Majority Leader for the Republican Party, lost his primary election to David Brat, a Tea Party candidate, 45 percent to 55 percent. *The New York Times* called the loss "one of the most stunning primary election upsets in congressional history."[38] Although it took the name Tea Party and sponsored a national convention, the Tea Party movement is not a formal party. It is an organized challenge to incumbents by the most conservative wing of the Republican Party.[39]

Election Reform and Third Parties In part because third parties have become increasingly common in American politics, despite election rules favoring a two-party system, one-third of all winning presidential candidates since the Civil War have been elected with a plurality (simply more votes than any other candidate) but not a majority (more than 50 percent of all votes) of the national popular vote.[40] When one considers those voting for the losing major-party presidential candidate and a losing third-party candidate (e.g., Perot, Nader), a majority of Americans who cast a vote for president in recent elections are on a "losing side" about a third of the time. If the party that wins the presidency in one out of three elections is not favored by a majority of voters, that calls into question the legitimacy of our election system. Some scholars suggest that the failure to secure majorities may continue in the future with the rise of independent candidates and dissatisfaction with the two major political parties.[41]

Some proponents of election reform argue that two major parties are not sufficient to represent the varied interests of America's 317 million people, and that more political parties would improve representation. Forms of proportional representation, multiple-member districts, or instant run-off voting would increase the probability of third-party representation in American politics. State ballot access laws are another major impediment for third parties. Third parties often fail to meet criteria to get on the ballot, such as registration fees or petition requirements in which a certain number of voters must sign a petition in order for the third party or independent candidate to gain ballot access. States with lower access hurdles, such as Minnesota, have more third-party candidates. Those who

Green Party candidate Jill Stein ran for president in 2012 and received less than 1 percent of the vote. Although minor-party candidates do not have much chance of winning the presidency or seats in Congress, their campaigns can affect the issues that the major parties put on their agendas.

favor a stronger role for third parties argue that states should make it easier to get on the ballot. Supporters of the current system, on the other hand, contend that America's two-party system creates stability in governing and prevents the need for a coalition government, where multiple small parties work together to form a majority to govern.

Ranked Choice Voting An example of an election reform that may reduce party polarization and increase opportunities for third parties is ranked choice voting (RCV). Ranked choice voting is a ballot form used in countries around the world. Rather than casting a single vote for one's most preferred choice, a voter ranks candidates from the most preferred to least preferred (usually the top three) on the ballot, putting a "1" by the first choice, a "2" by the second choice, and so on. If a candidate wins a majority of first-place votes (50 percent plus one), the candidate is declared the winner and second- or third-place votes are not counted. But if the top candidate does not receive a majority of the votes cast, the candidate with the fewest first-choice votes is eliminated, and those voters' ballots are redistributed to their second-choice candidates. The ballots are recounted; if the leading candidate has a majority of votes cast, a winner is declared. The process is repeated until a majority winner is declared. This system eliminates the "spoiler" effect that occurs when votes for a third-party or minor candidate are discarded.

Research suggests that RCV leads to more civility in political campaigns and cooperation among candidates who seek to be a voter's second choice if they cannot be a first choice. RCV is a form of instant run-office voting in that it guarantees that the winner of an election has support from a majority of those voting in the election, rather than a plurality. RCV is used in many countries around the world, but in the United States only a handful of local districts use RCV (including San Francisco and Oakland, California; Cambridge, Massachusetts; and Minneapolis, Minnesota). Successful local experiments in election reform may open the doors to use of this process at the state or even national level.

Political Parties
and Your Future

Political parties are bulwarks of liberty and freedom. As noted earlier, in the first years of the Republic, it was not the Constitution or the courts that preserved free speech in the face of Federalist efforts to silence the government's critics; it was the vigorous opposition of the Jeffersonian Republicans. To this day, the presence of an opposition party is a fundamentally important check on attempts by those in power to skirt the law and infringe on citizens' liberties. Competition among the political parties is also a key factor in stimulating voter turnout. Competition gives citizens an incentive to vote and politicians an incentive to get them to vote.[42] As early as the 1790s, political parties used diverse techniques to mobilize voters, many of which remain familiar today: "mass meetings, barbecues, stump-speaking, festivals of many kinds, processions and parades, runners and riders, door-to-door canvassing, the distribution of tickets and ballots, . . . free transportation to the polls, outright bribery and corruption of other kinds."[43]

Parties in the United States are considered to be ground-up organizations, meaning that they get their power from the members of the mass public who support them at the local level. However, until fairly recently, political party bosses controlled the party platform, the party message, and often, through early money to candidates, who held elected office and who won the nomination for president.

While this elite-driven process still occurs today, the process of party formation and many aspects of party politics have been turned upside down with the digital revolution in communication. Four resources that political parties use to contest and win elections (time, money, expertise, and organization) have all been altered by the Internet. New media are decentralizing party power, as citizens can volunteer and give money to the party of their choice without ever being contacted by a party official. Online fund-raising allows millions of donors to give small contributions to parties, and new media allow the party to spread its message far and wide online. This is beneficial for parties because more people are involved, but at the same time, there are more divergent opinions that must be recognized and appeased. No longer can party leaders craft their own message and relay it to the field; they must also listen to what their supporters want. If the party does not appeal to the mass public, members of the mass public will form their own groups, or even competing parties.

The question remains, however, what influence these new groups and parties will have on politics given current U.S. election rules. Will the ability of the mass public to make their desires known to party leaders mean that party leaders pay more attention to these preferences? Is the two-party system the optimal system for American politics, or would electoral reforms encourage more parties to form and, hence, more choice for voters?

Parties help to crystallize a world of possible government actions into a set of distinct choices. In so doing, they make it easier for ordinary citizens to understand politics, evaluate candidates, and make their own choices.

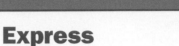
plugin

Inform

Visit the websites of the Republican and Democratic national committees (democrats.org and gop.com), as well as websites of a couple of minor parties—such as the Green Party or the Libertarian Party—that interest you. Read about their platforms, typically found under a tab for "Issues" or "About Our Party."

Express

Which elements of the major and minor parties' policy platforms appeal to you? Draft your own "party platform" with the issues and policy positions that are most important to you.

Connect

Follow the Democratic Party, the Republican Party, and/or a minor party on Twitter or Facebook.

Act

Volunteer your time to at the local or state headquarters for the major or minor party whose policy positions best match your own. You can find office locations and volunteer opportunities on the parties' websites.

study**guide**

What Are Political Parties?

Define political parties and their functions in politics (pp. 343–47)

A political party is an organization that seeks influence over government by electing its members to office. Although some people are critical of political parties, they are extremely important to the functioning of a democracy because they increase participation in politics, provide a central cue for citizens to cast informed votes, and organize the business of Congress and governing.

Key Terms

political parties (p. 343)

partisanship (p. 343)

two-party system (p. 345)

Practice Quiz

1. A political party is different from an interest group in that a political party
   a) seeks to control the entire government by electing its members to office and thereby controlling the government's personnel.
   b) seeks to control only limited, very specific functions of government.
   c) is entirely nonprofit.
   d) has a much larger membership.
   e) has a much smaller membership.

Parties, Voter Mobilization, and Elections

Explain the roles that parties play in elections (pp. 347–49)

Because parties succeed when they win elections, parties have a large role in recruiting candidates, coordinating campiagns, mobilizing voters, and raising money.

Key Term

nomination (p. 348)

2. Parties today are important in the electoral process in
   a) recruiting and nominating candidates for office.
   b) financing all of the campaign's spending.

   c) providing millions of volunteers to mobilize voters.
   d) creating a responsible party government.
   e) changing the electoral laws to make voting easier.

3. A major innovation in voter mobilization in the 2008 and 2012 elections was
   a) the parties' use of direct mail.
   b) party efforts to register voters.
   c) the parties' use of enormous databases of potential voters.
   d) the parties' distribution of signs and buttons.
   e) a focus on persuasion, rather than turnout.

Parties as Organizations

Describe how the major American parties are structured at the national, state, and local levels (pp. 350–53)

Party organizations exist at virtually every level of government in the United States, and they play an important role in structuring electoral competition. At the national level, for example, party organizations assemble conventions every four years that nominate the party's presidential and vice-presidential candidates, draft the party's campaign platform for the presidential race and approve changes in the rules governing party procedures. Similarly, at the state and local levels, party organizations are active in recruiting candidates to run for office and in conducting voter registration and get-out-the-vote drives.

Key Terms

party organization (p. 350)

caucus (political) (p. 350)

national convention (p. 350)

platform (p. 351)

soft money (p. 351)

527 committees (p. 351)

machines (p. 352)

patronage (p. 353)

Practice Quiz

4. Which of the following is *not* determined at a party's national convention?
   a) the party's candidate for president
   b) the party's candidate for vice president
   c) the party's campaign platform for the presidential race
   d) the congressional committees party representatives will be assigned to
   e) the rules and regulations governing party procedures

5. The Bipartisan Campaign Reform Act outlawed
   a) patronage.
   b) caucuses.
   c) hard money.
   d) soft money.
   e) party machines.

6. Through which mechanism did party leaders in the late nineteenth and early twentieth centuries maintain their control?
   a) civil service reform
   b) soft money contributions
   c) machine politics
   d) electoral reform
   e) political action committees

Parties in Government

Explain how parties organize legislative business and influence policy (pp. 353–56)

Political parties exert a great deal of influence over public policy, the structure of Congress, and the behavior of presidents. The sharp ideological divisions between Democrats and Republicans in recent years mean that election outcomes matter greatly for the kinds of laws that government enacts. Many of the most important organizational features of Congress, such as the role of the House Speaker, the committee system, and seniority, also depend on the party system. In order to overcome their minority status in the electorate, Republican presidents have spent significantly more time mobilizing voters than Democratic presidents.

Key Terms

policy entrepreneur (p. 355)

majority party (p. 355)

minority party (p. 355)

Practice Quiz

7. By identifying problems and proposing policies that will expand their party's base of support, party leaders can act as
   a) party bosses.
   b) convention delegates.
   c) patrons.
   d) policy entrepreneurs.
   e) party activists.

8. Which of the following features of the House of Representatives is determined by a vote of the whole membership rather than by decisions within each party?
   a) the assignments of individual members to particular committees.
   b) advancement up the committee ladder.
   c) the ability of individual members to transfer from one committee to another.
   d) the use of the seniority system for determining committee chairs.
   e) selection of the Speaker of the House.

Party Identification

Party identification refers to the psychological and emotional attachments people have to one of the political parties. In contemporary American politics, a wide variety of group characteristics, including race, ethnicity, gender, religion, class, ideology, region, and age, are associated with an individual's party identification. Party loyalties in the United States are currently in a state of flux, and roughly one-third of Americans identify themselves as independents rather than as Democrats or Republicans.

Key Terms

party identification (p. 356)

party activists (p. 357)

gender gap (p. 359)

dealignment (p. 361)

Practice Quiz

9. The decline in partisan attachment in the electorate is referred to as
   a) polarization.
   b) independentification.
   c) unalignment.
   d) realignment.
   e) dealignment.

Party Systems

A nation's party system refers to the organization of the parties within the country, the balance of power between and within party coalitions, the parties' social and institutional bases, and the issues and policies around which party competition is organized. Over the course of American history, changes in political forces and alignments have produced six distinctive party systems. Although third parties have occasionally influenced election outcomes and placed new ideas on the political agenda, numerous factors limit their long-term success and they have rarely been able to win elections at the national level.

Key Terms

electoral realignment (p. 370)

divided government (p. 370)

party polarization (p. 371)

third parties (p. 373)

Practice Quiz

10. Which party was founded as a political expression of the antislavery movement?
    a) American Independent
    b) Prohibition
    c) Republican
    d) Democratic
    e) Whig

11. The periodic episodes in American history in which an "old" dominant political party is replaced by a "new" dominant political party are called
    a) constitutional revolutions.
    b) party turnovers.
    c) governmental realignments.
    d) presidential elections.
    e) electoral realignments.

12. Historically, when do realignments occur?
    a) typically, every 20 years
    b) whenever a minority party takes over Congress
    c) when large numbers of voters permanently shift their support from one party to another
    d) in even-numbered years
    e) in odd-numbered years

13. Third parties have influenced national politics mainly by
    a) electing their candidates to the presidency.
    b) electing their candidates to Congress.
    c) supporting the major parties' platforms.
    d) promoting specific issues and ideas.
    e) preventing realignments.

For Further Reading

Aldrich, John H. *Why Parties? A Second Look.* Chicago: University of Chicago Press, 2011.

Bartels Larry. *Presidential Primaries and the Dynamics of Public Choice.* Princeton, NJ: Princeton University Press, 1988.

Burnham, Walter Dean. *Critical Elections and the Mainsprings of American Politics.* New York: W. W. Norton, 1970.

Cohen, Marty, David Karol, Hans Noel, and John Zaller. *The Party Decides: Presidential Nominations before and after Reform.* Chicago: University of Chicago Press, 2008.

Donovan, Todd, and Shaun Bowler. *Reforming the Republic: Democratic Institutions for the New America.* Englewood Cliffs, NJ: Prentice Hall, 2003.

Green, Donald, Bradley Palmquist, and Eric Schickler. *Partisan Hearts and Minds: Political Parties and the Social Identities of Voters.* New Haven, CT: Yale University Press, 2002.

Maisel, L. Sandy. *Political Parties and Elections: A Very Short Introduction.* New York: Oxford University Press, 2007.

McCarty, Nolan, Keith Poole, and Howard Rosenthal. *Polarized America: The Dance of Ideology and Unequal Riches.* Cambridge, MA: MIT Press, 2006.

Polsby, Nelson W. *The Consequences of Party Reform.* New York: Oxford University Press, 1983.

Redlawsk, David, Caroline Tolbert, and Todd Donovan. *Why Iowa? How Caucuses and Sequential Elections Improve the Presidential Nominating Process.* Chicago: University of Chicago Press, 2011.

Schattschneider, E. E. *The Semi-Sovereign People.* New York: Harcourt Brace, 1960.

Shefter, Martin. *Political Parties and the State: The American Historical Experience.* Princeton, NJ: Princeton University Press, 1994.

Recommended Websites

D.C.'s Political Report
www.dcpoliticalreport.com/Disclaimer.htm
Here you can find almost every organization that identifies itself as a political party, including such obscure groups as the American Beer Drinker's Party or the Scorched Earth Party.

Democratic Party
www.dnc.org

Republican Party
www.GOP.com, www.rnc.org
These are the official websites for the Democrats and Republicans. Compare the platforms of the two main U.S. parties and see whether there's "not a dime's worth of difference" between the two of them.

Green Party
www.gp.org

Libertarian Party
www.lp.org
The Green Party and Libertarian Party are two of the largest and most successful third parties in recent years. Find out what these parties are trying to accomplish.

National Annenberg Election Survey
http://annenbergpublicpolicycenter.org
Individual voters tend to develop psychological ties to one party or another. The National Annenberg Election Survey (NAES) uses survey data to track party identification by state every two years. Find out if your state has more Democratic or Republican identifiers.

Campaigns are the mechanism through which candidates for political office attempt to persuade individuals to vote for them on Election Day. Electoral rules affect how and where candidates campaign, which means some groups of potential voters receive much more attention from candidates than others.

10

Campaigns and Elections

WHAT GOVERNMENT DOES AND WHY IT MATTERS Election rules are not neutral. Like those in games or sports, election rules shape strategy. When the NBA moved the 3-point line farther from the basket, teams had to adjust their shooting and scoring strategy. Similarly, there are thousands of rules governing elections in the United States that influence the behavior of candidates, parties, interest groups, and citizens.

One of the most important "rules of the game" in U.S. elections is the electoral college. The president of the United States is the winner of the electoral college—the first to earn 270 of the college's 538 votes—rather than the winner of the national popular vote (the candidate who receives the most votes from citizens at the ballot box). Electors in the electoral college are allocated to each state on the basis of the size of the state's congressional delegation. Thus North Dakota has 3 votes in the electoral college (2 senators plus 1 representative), and California has 55 (2 senators plus 53 representatives). Washington, D.C., also gets 3 electoral votes.

The electoral college and most elections in the United States are governed by plurality, or winner-take-all, rules. With only two exceptions, each state awards *all* of its electors to the candidate who receives the most votes in the state. Thus, Obama received all 55 of California's electoral votes though he won only 60 percent of the votes in the state.

The electoral college system and the winner-take-all rule have a profound effect on how presidential candidates campaign, effectively forcing candidates to spend their resources on a small number of competitive battleground states. Battleground, or swing, states are those in which Democrats and

Republicans are roughly even in the population. Because "candidates see the world in terms of amassing 270 electoral votes,"[1] they focus not on winning the most individual votes but rather on winning the electoral votes of states that are not considered safely Republican or safely Democratic. States with a higher proportion of Democrats, who can be expected to vote for Democratic candidate Jones, do not merit any attention from Republican candidate Smith, because Smith knows that Jones will get all of the state's electoral votes, even if Smith wins 45 percent of the vote to Jones's 55 percent. By the same token, Democrat Jones will not campaign in states with a high proportion of Republicans.

Meanwhile, residents of battleground states get smothered with attention from the candidates and media, as presidential candidates vie for that state's electoral college votes. In 2012, Democratic candidate Barack Obama spent a total of $404 million on television ads; of this total, $173 million was spent in Florida (a state with 19 million people), where hundreds of thousands of ads aired. Virtually no television ads aired in states that were considered safely Democratic like California, with nearly 38 million people, or states that were considered safely Republican like Texas, with 26 million people.

Research has shown that citizens residing in battleground states are more interested in politics, more knowledgeable, and more likely to vote, even among the poorest residents who tend to have the lowest levels of participation in politics. These citizens are immersed in active campaigns. In contrast, the majority of Americans live in states that are "safe" for either the Democratic or Republican presidential candidate. Without electoral competition in safe states, the needs and concerns of the residents may well be ignored. But changing the rules of the game is difficult. In this chapter, we learn about the rules governing elections and why they matter.

chaptergoals

- Describe the major rules and procedures of elections in the United States (pp. 387–98)
- Explain how campaigns are typically conducted (pp. 398–407)
- Describe how candidates raise the money they need to run (pp. 407–14)
- Identify the major factors that influence voters' decisions (pp. 415–18)
- Analyze the strategies, issues, and outcomes of the 2012 and 2014 elections (pp. 418–25)

Elections in America

Describe the major rules and procedures of elections in the United States

Elections are a remarkable feature of democratic government: every few years, the citizens are provided the means with which to overthrow the government and select new leaders. In the United States, tens of thousands of political offices at the local, state, and national level are subject to popular election. Although Americans do not often vote directly on policy, they exert tremendous influence over political outcomes through the regular selection of their leaders. By allowing citizens to hold their elected representatives accountable for their actions, elections are at the very heart of democracy.

Elections do not just happen spontaneously, rather, they are highly routinized events, subject to specific rules. In the American federal system, the responsibility for running elections is decentralized, resting largely with state and county governments. State laws specify who may vote, how they vote, and where they vote. Furthermore, electoral rules provide a process for individuals who wish to appear on the ballot and how they can campaign. Elections are

Elections are the most important way that Americans participate in politics. Some of the rules for American elections have been in place since the Founding, while others have evolved over time. This painting shows Election Day in Philadelphia in 1815.

midterm elections congressional elections that do not coincide with a presidential election; also called *off-year elections*

primary elections elections held to select a party's candidate for the general election

general election a regularly scheduled election involving most districts in the nation or state, in which voters select officeholders; in the United States, general elections for national office and most state and local offices are held on the first Tuesday following the first Monday in November in even-numbered years (every four years for presidential elections)

closed primary a primary election in which voters can participate in the nomination of candidates, but only of the party in which they are enrolled for a period of time prior to primary day

open primary a primary election in which the voter can wait until the day of the primary to choose which party to enroll in to select candidates for the general election

majority system a type of electoral system in which, to win a seat in the parliament or other representative body, a candidate must receive a majority of all the votes cast in the relevant district

runoff election a "second round" election in which voters choose between the top two candidates from the first round

plurality system a type of electoral system in which, to win a seat in the parliament or other representative body, a candidate need only receive the most votes in the election, not necessarily a majority of votes cast

administered by state, county, and city election boards that are responsible for establishing and staffing polling places and verifying the eligibility of individuals who come to vote. National presidential elections take place every four years, on the first Tuesday in November; congressional elections are held every two years, also on the first Tuesday in November. Congressional elections that do not coincide with a presidential election are sometimes called **midterm elections**. Localities and states can choose when to hold their elections. Most Americans have the opportunity to vote in three or four elections each year. Voting in elections is the most common form of participation in American politics.

Election season begins with **primary elections**, which are held to select each party's candidates for the general election. In the case of local and statewide offices, the winners of primary elections face one another as their parties' nominees in the general election. A primary election is like a prelim in a sporting event. It is used to select the best candidate to represent the political party in the general election. Thus primary elections are races where Democrats compete against Democrats and Republicans against Republicans (except in states that have "top two primaries" in which candidates from all parties run against one another and the top two face each other in the general election; California and Washington State use this method). The primary is followed by the **general election**, the decisive electoral contest. The winner of the general election is elected to office for a specified term.

America is one of few nations in the world to hold primary elections. In most countries, nominations are controlled by party officials, as they once were in the United States. The primary system was introduced at the turn of the twentieth century by reformers who hoped to weaken the power of party leaders by taking candidate nominations out of their hands. Under the laws of some states, only registered members of a political party may vote in a primary election to select that party's candidates. This is called a **closed primary**. Other states allow all registered voters to choose on the day of the primary in which party's primary they will participate. This is called an **open primary**.

What It Takes to Win

On the surface, the basic idea of how an election works may seem simple: voters select their preferred candidate on the ballot and then votes are counted up. But there are actually many possible variations on how people vote and how the votes are counted. In some countries, a candidate must receive an absolute majority (50 percent plus 1) of all the votes cast in the relevant district in order to win the election. This type of electoral system is called a **majority system**. In the United States, it is used in primary elections by a few southern states. Majority systems usually include a provision for a **runoff election** between the two top candidates, because if the initial race draws several candidates, there is little chance that any one will receive a majority.

In other nations, as in the United States, candidates for office need not win an absolute majority of the votes cast to win an election. Instead, victory is awarded to the candidate who receives the most votes, regardless of the actual percentage this represents. A candidate receiving 50 percent, or 30 percent, or even 20 percent, of the popular vote can win if no other candidate receives more votes. This type of electoral system is called a **plurality system** and is used in most elections in the United States.

Most European nations and advanced democracies employ a third type of electoral system, called **proportional representation**. Under proportional rules, competing political parties are awarded legislative seats in rough proportion to the percentage of popular votes that each party won. A party that wins 30 percent of the vote will receive roughly 30 percent of the seats in the parliament or other representative body. Proportional representation benefits smaller groups or minor parties because it usually allows a party to win legislative seats with fewer votes than would be required under a majority or plurality system. A party that wins 10 percent of the national vote might win 10 percent of the parliamentary seats. In the United States, by contrast, a party that wins 10 percent of the vote would probably win no seats in Congress. Because they give small parties little chance of success, plurality and majority systems tend to reduce the number of competitive political parties. This is one of the reasons that the United States has only two significant political parties (see Chapter 9 for more on the two-party system in the United States).

proportional representation
a multiple-member district system that allows each political party representation in proportion to its percentage of the total vote

The Ballot

Before the 1890s, voters cast ballots according to political parties. Each party printed its own ballots, listed only its own candidates for each office, and employed party workers to distribute the ballots at the polls. Because voters had to choose which party's ballot to use, it was very difficult for a voter to cast anything other than a **straight-ticket vote**. The advent of a new, neutral ballot at the turn of the twentieth century brought a significant change to electoral procedure. The new ballot (called the Australian ballot or long-form ballot) was prepared and administered by the government rather than the political parties. Each ballot was identical and included the names of all candidates for office. This ballot reform made it possible for voters to make their choices on the basis of the individual rather than the collective merits of a party's candidates.

Because all candidates for the same office now appeared on the same ballot, voters were no longer forced to choose straight-ticket voting. This gave rise to the

straight-ticket voting selecting candidates from the same political party for all offices on the ballot

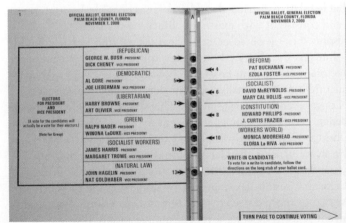

Some of the devices that have been used to record votes in the United States are notably prone to errors that can affect election results. For example, in 2000 in Florida's Palm Beach County, some voters were confused by the "butterfly ballot" (left), which made it difficult to match candidates and votes. In the 2012 and 2014 elections, many of the nation's voters cast their ballots on electronic touch-screen machines. Critics of touch-screen voting systems, however, question the machines for their accuracy and security against fraud.

phenomenon of split-ticket voting in American elections, where voters may vote for a Democrat for Senate and a Republican for governor. If a voter supports candidates from more than one party in the same election, he or she is said to be casting a split-ticket vote. Voters who support only one party's candidates are casting a straight-ticket vote.

The actual ballots used by voters vary from county to county across the United States. Some counties employ paper ballots, while most use mechanical voting machines or computerized systems. Not surprisingly, the controversy surrounding Florida's presidential vote in 2000 led to a closer look at the different ballot forms and voting systems in use in the country, and it became apparent that some of them produced unreliable results. When many counties moved to introduce computerized voting systems, critics warned that they might be vulnerable to unauthorized use or "hacking." During the 2008 Ohio primaries, a software error was discovered that potentially affected electronic voting machines used in 34 states. The machine's manufacturer moved to correct the error before the November national elections, and the 2008, 2010, 2012, and 2014 elections produced few complaints about electronic voting.

Legislative Elections and Electoral Districts

The boundaries for some elected offices are straightforward: all eligible U.S. citizens 18 years or older may vote for president; all eligible residents of Pennsylvania may vote for Pennsylvania's governor and senators. Other political offices, such as members of the House of Representatives and many state legislatures, are elected from geographic legislative districts whose boundaries are drawn by the states. The boundaries for congressional and state legislative districts are usually redrawn every 10 years in response to population changes, as determined by the U.S. Census. This redrawing of district boundaries is called **redistricting**. The geographic shape of district boundaries is influenced by several factors. Some of the most important influences have been federal court decisions. In the 1963 case of *Gray v. Sanders*, and in the 1964 cases of *Wesberry v. Sanders* and *Reynolds v. Sims*, the Supreme Court held that legislative districts within a state must include roughly equal populations, so as to accord with the principle of "one person, one vote."[2] During the 1980s the Supreme Court also declared that legislative districts should, insofar as possible, be contiguous, compact, and consistent with existing political subdivisions.[3]

Despite these legal cases, state lawmakers who are responsible for drawing the district boundaries routinely seek to influence electoral outcomes to favor one political party over another (or incumbents over challengers) in drawing electoral districts for Congress and state legislatures. This strategy is called **gerrymandering**, named for a nineteenth-century Massachusetts governor, Elbridge Gerry, who was alleged to have designed a district in the shape of a salamander to promote his party's interests. The principle behind gerrymandering is simple: different populations of voters in districts can produce different electoral results. For example, by dispersing the members of a particular group across two or more districts, state legislators can dilute that group's voting power and prevent it from electing a representative in any district. (In the lingo of gerrymandering, this is called "cracking.") Alternatively, by concentrating the members of a party in as few districts as possible, state lawmakers can try to ensure that their opponents will elect as few representatives as possible. (This is referred to as "packing.") The widespread practice of gerrymandering has created many safe districts

redistricting the process of redrawing election districts and redistributing legislative representatives. This happens every 10 years to reflect shifts in population or in response to legal challenges in existing districts

gerrymandering the apportionment of voters in districts in such a way as to give unfair advantage to one racial or ethnic group or political party

The drawing of electoral districts is always a matter of controversy, with opponents accusing one another of "gerrymandering"— drawing district boundaries in such a way as to serve a particular group's interests. The original gerrymander was a districting plan attributed to the Massachusetts governor Elbridge Gerry (1744–1814) that had the shape of a salamander.

in Congress, where incumbents rarely face a serious challenger, even though there are elections every two years in the House. This is one reason most members of Congress are elected in landslide elections, and why 98 percent of incumbents are re-elected. When their districts are redrawn, incumbents are often more vulnerable.

The federal government has supported congressional districts made up primarily of minority group members, a practice intended to increase the number of African Americans and Latinos elected to public office. The Supreme Court has viewed this effort as constitutionally dubious, however. Beginning with the 1993 case of *Shaw v. Reno*, the Court has generally rejected efforts to create such **majority-minority districts**.[4] The Court has asserted that districting based exclusively on racial criteria is unlawful.

Presidential Elections

While many of the rules related to presidential elections and congressional elections are the same, presidential elections have special features. As discussed in the introduction, the president is technically elected by the electoral college, not by popular vote. Second, presidential candidates from the two major parties are officially nominated at the parties' national conventions, following state primary elections and caucuses to select delegates to the conventions. While primary elections are also used to select candidates in congressional and other types of elections, the national convention delegate system for nominating candidates is unique to presidential elections.

Nominating Presidential Candidates: Primaries and Caucuses Before the general election, the parties must select candidates to represent the parties in the general election. The process starts with primary elections and **caucuses** (essentially a party business meeting) that are held by the major political parties to choose a candidate who will face the nominee from the other major party during the general election. Most states hold primary elections, but about one-third use caucuses instead. The most famous caucuses are those in Iowa, the first state to select presidential candidates in the calendar year. Citizens attending local caucuses typically elect delegates to statewide conventions, at which delegates to the national party conventions are then chosen. The New Hampshire primary is the second election in the presidential nomination process. Both the Iowa caucus and New Hampshire primary are characterized by **grassroots politics**, where presidential candidates spend a great deal of time in the state to meet with voters face-to-face. Like the general elections, early primaries and caucuses tend to be highly contested, with high levels of campaign spending and mobilization (get-out-the-vote) drives.

The primaries and caucuses traditionally begin in January of a presidential election year and end six months later, in June (see Table 10.1). Early voting states, such as Iowa and New Hampshire, are important because they can help candidates secure media attention, campaign contributions, and increased standing in the polls, or what is called "momentum." Candidates spend months courting voter support in these two states. A candidate who performs better than expected in Iowa and New Hampshire will usually be able to win public support and media coverage for subsequent races. A candidate who fares poorly in these two states may be written off as a loser, and drop out of the race. Iowa and New Hampshire play a disproportionate role in picking presidential candidates for the two major parties because they are the first states to cast votes in the primaries and caucuses. Today, the presidential

for critical analysis
How do district boundaries affect elections for the U.S. House and state legislatures? Should districts be drawn based on partisan considerations or other criteria?

majority-minority district a gerrymandered voting district that improves the chances of minority candidates by making selected minority groups the majority within the district

caucus (political) a normally closed political party business meeting of citizens or lawmakers to select candidates, elect officers, plan strategy, or make decisions regarding legislative matters

grassroots politics political campaigns that operate at a local level, often using face-to-face communication to generate interest and momentum by citizens

TABLE 10.1

The 2012 Primaries and Caucuses Calendar

January 3	**Iowa** Republican and Democratic caucuses
January 10	**New Hampshire** presidential primary
January 21	**Nevada** Democratic caucuses
	South Carolina Republican primary
January 28	**South Carolina** Democratic primary
January 31	**Florida** presidential primary (*nonbinding* for the Democrats)
February 4	**Maine** Republican caucuses
	Nevada Republican caucuses
February 7	**Colorado** Republican caucuses
	Minnesota Republican caucuses
	Missouri presidential primary (*nonbinding* for the Republicans)
February 26	**Maine** Democratic caucuses
February 28	**Arizona** presidential primary (*nonbinding* for the Democrats)
	Michigan presidential primary (*nonbinding* for the Democrats)
March 3	**Washington** Republican caucuses
March 6 ("Super Tuesday")	**Alaska** Republican district conventions
	American Samoa Democratic caucuses
	Colorado Democratic caucuses
	Georgia presidential primary
	Idaho Republican caucuses
	Massachusetts presidential primary
	Minnesota Democratic caucuses
	North Dakota Republican caucuses
	Ohio consolidated presidential/state primary
	Oklahoma presidential primary
	Tennessee presidential primary
	Vermont presidential primary
	Virginia presidential primary
	Wyoming Republican caucuses
March 7	**Hawaii** Democratic caucuses
March 10	**Guam** Republican caucuses
	Kansas Republican caucuses
	U.S. Virgin Islands Republican caucuses
March 11	**Maine** Democratic caucuses
March 13	**Alabama** presidential primary
	American Samoa Republican caucuses
	Hawaii Republican caucuses

March 13 (cont'd)	**Mississippi** presidential primary
	Utah Democratic caucuses
March 17	**Missouri** Republican caucuses
March 18	**Puerto Rico** Republican caucuses
March 20	**Illinois** presidential primary
March 24	**Louisiana** presidential primary
March 31	**Arizona** Democratic caucuses
April 3	**District of Columbia** presidential primary
	Maryland presidential primary
	Texas presidential primary
	Wisconsin presidential primary
April 9–16	**Alaska** Democratic precinct caucuses
April 14	**Idaho** Democratic caucuses
	Kansas Democratic caucuses
	Nebraska Democratic caucuses
	Wyoming Democratic caucuses
April 15	**Washington** Democratic caucuses
April 24	**Connecticut** presidential primary
	Delaware presidential primary
	New York presidential primary
	Pennsylvania presidential primary
	Rhode Island presidential primary
May 5	**Florida** Democratic caucuses
	Guam Democratic caucuses
	Michigan Democratic caucuses
May 8	**Indiana** presidential primary
	North Carolina presidential primary
	West Virginia presidential primary
May 15	**Nebraska** Republican presidential primary
	Oregon presidential primary
May 22	**Arkansas** presidential primary
	Kentucky presidential primary
June 5	**California** presidential primary
	Montana presidential primary
	New Jersey presidential primary
	New Mexico presidential primary
	North Dakota presidential primary
	South Dakota presidential primary
June 26	**Utah** Republican presidential primary

SOURCE: National Conference of State Legislatures, www.ncsl.org/research/elections-and-campaigns/2012-presidential-primary-calendar.aspx (accessed 6/20/14).

nomination has become "front-loaded," with states vying with one another to increase their political influence by holding their nominating processes earlier in the calendar year in order to receive more attention from candidates and the media.

As we saw in Chapter 7, if Barack Obama had not won in Iowa, most commentators believe he would not have been able to go on to capture the Democratic nomination for president in 2008. One study found that the change in mass media coverage that candidates receive before and after the Iowa caucuses predicts how well they will do in the New Hampshire primary, and in presidential primaries nationwide measured by vote share.[5] It is not winning the Iowa caucuses that matters, but doing better than expected by the media. President Carter came in second (after "undecided") in the 1976 Iowa caucuses, for example, but beat media expectations and used this success to propel his nomination to the White House. With the rise of the Internet, media coverage of early nominating events is even greater, and may further increase the importance of states holding early primaries and caucuses.[6]

As noted in Chapter 9, the Democratic Party requires that state presidential primaries allocate delegates on the basis of proportional representation; Democratic candidates win delegates in rough proportion to their percentage of the primary vote. The Republican Party does not require proportional representation, but most states have now written proportional representation requirements into their election laws. A few states use the winner-take-all system, by which the candidate with the most votes wins all the party's delegates in that state. When the primaries and caucuses are concluded, it is usually clear which candidates have won their parties' nominations.

Nominating Presidential Candidates: Party Conventions For more than 50 years after America's founding, presidential nominations were controlled by each party's congressional caucus—all the party's members in the House and the Senate. Critics referred to this process as the "King Caucus" and charged that it did not fairly represent the views of party members throughout the nation. Thus the "King Caucus" process was replaced by the system of national conventions. As it developed over the next century, the convention became the decisive institution in the presidential nominating processes of the two major parties. The convention was a deliberative body in which party groups argued, negotiated, and eventually reached a decision. The convention was composed of delegates from each state. The size of a state's delegation depended on the state's population, and each delegate was allowed one vote for the purpose of nominating the party's presidential and vice-presidential candidates.

Between the 1830s and World War II, national convention delegates were generally selected by a state's party leaders. Usually the delegates were public officials, political activists, and party notables from all regions of the state, representing most major party factions. Typically, many votes were needed before the nomination could be decided. Often deadlocks developed among the most powerful party factions, and state leaders would be forced to compromise, sometimes choosing a little-known candidate. Among the more famous "dark horse" nominees were James Polk in 1844 and Warren Harding in 1920. Although he was virtually unknown, Polk won the Democratic nomination when it became clear that none of the more established candidates could win. Similarly, Harding,

Iowa caucus-goers were the first to vote in the 2012 presidential primaries. The United States is one of few nations in the world to hold primary elections and caucuses.

for critical analysis

Is it fair that two relatively small states (in terms of population) such as Iowa and New Hampshire should have such outsize influence in picking presidents?

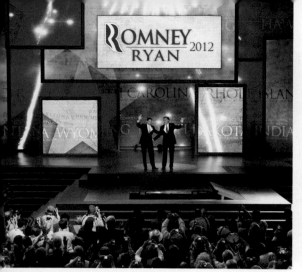

Although the party's nominees for the president and the vice president are "officially" announced at the party conventions, they are actually selected much earlier through caucuses and primary elections. In 2012, Mitt Romney and Paul Ryan formally accepted the Republican nomination at the national convention.

party platform a party document, written at a national convention, that contains party philosophy, principles, and policy positions

delegate a representative who votes according to the preferences of his constituency

electoral college the presidential electors from each state who meet after the general election to cast ballots for president and vice president

another political unknown, won the Republican nomination after the major candidates had fought one another to a standstill.

Over time, reformers came to view the convention as a symbol of rule by party elites. Around the turn of the twentieth century, many states adopted direct primary elections to choose presidential candidates, in which average citizens would have a voice in picking presidents. Today, as we saw earlier in this chapter, the nomination is determined in a series of primary elections and local party caucuses held in virtually all 50 states during the months prior to the party's national convention. These primaries and caucuses determine how each state's convention delegates will vote. Candidates now arrive at the convention knowing who has enough delegate support in hand to assure a victory in the first round of balloting. State party leaders no longer serve as power brokers, and the party's presidential and vice-presidential choices are made relatively quickly.

Even though the party convention no longer controls presidential nominations, it still has a number of important tasks. The first of these is the adoption of party rules concerning such matters as convention delegate selection and future presidential primary elections. In 1972, for example, the Democratic convention adopted rules requiring convention delegates to be broadly representative of the party's membership in terms of race and gender. The Democratic Party refused to seat several state delegations that were deemed not to meet this standard. Another important task for the convention is the drafting of a **party platform**, a statement of principles and pledges around which the delegates can unite.

Today, convention **delegates** are generally political activists with strong positions on social and political issues. In states such as Michigan and Iowa, party caucuses choose many of the delegates who will actually attend the national convention. In most of the remaining states, primary elections determine how a state's delegation will vote. Delegate votes won in primary elections are apportioned to candidates on the basis of proportional representation. Thus, a candidate who received 30 percent of the vote in the California Democratic primary would receive roughly 30 percent of the state's delegate votes at the party's national convention.

Once the nominations have been settled and most other party business has been resolved, the presidential and vice-presidential nominees deliver acceptance speeches. These speeches are opportunities for the nominees to begin their formal general election campaigns on a positive note, and they are usually meticulously crafted to make as positive an impression on the electorate as possible.

The Electoral College The presidential election differs from other elections in another important way as well: the voters do not directly elect the president. In the early history of popular voting, nations often made use of indirect elections. In these elections, voters would choose the members of an intermediate body. These members would, in turn, select public officials. The assumption underlying such a process was that ordinary citizens were not qualified to choose their leaders and could not be trusted to do so directly. The last vestige of this procedure in America is the **electoral college**, the group of electors who formally select the president and vice president of the United States.

When Americans go to the polls on Election Day, they are technically not voting directly for presidential candidates although they mark ballots for one presidential and vice presidential candidate. Instead, voters within each state are choosing among slates of electors selected by each state's party and pledged, if elected, to support that party's presidential candidate. These are indirect elections. To win, a presidential candidate must receive a majority of the votes in the electoral college, which are awarded to states based on the size of their congressional delegation (senators plus representatives).[7] The system protects the interests of small-population states, as the advantages in representation that small states have in the U.S. Senate are carried over to the presidential election process. In each state (except Maine and Nebraska), the party candidate who wins the popular vote wins all the electoral college votes for that state, using winner-take-all rules.[8] The presidential candidate with a majority of votes in the electoral college—not necessarily the candidate with the most votes from the people—becomes president. No other country uses an electoral college to mediate between a national or direct/popular vote for presidential candidates and the winner.

On all but three occasions since 1824, the electoral vote has simply ratified the nationwide popular vote. Since electoral votes are won on a state-by-state basis, it is mathematically possible for a candidate who receives a nationwide popular plurality to fail to carry states whose electoral votes would add up to a majority. Thus, in 1876, Rutherford B. Hayes was the winner in the electoral college despite receiving fewer popular votes than his rival, Samuel Tilden. In 1888, Grover Cleveland received more popular votes than Benjamin Harrison, but received fewer electoral votes. The third instance happened in 2000. Support for changing the election rules has been gaining momentum since that election, which was followed by a lengthy legal battle over re-counting votes in Florida that ultimately ended with the U.S. Supreme Court's decision in *Bush v. Gore*.[9] The decision resolved the dispute in Florida, which handed George W. Bush the presidency. Even though the Democratic candidate, Vice President Al Gore, had won 500,000 more votes nationwide, Republican George W. Bush won a majority of the electoral college and was elected president. This controversial election created ripple effects in motivating efforts to reform American elections.

Calls for eliminating the electoral college and using a national popular vote for president are widespread, as surveys show that more than three in four Americans would prefer such a direct election for the president.[10] Replacing the electoral college with another system would require a constitutional amendment that most agree would be extremely difficult to pass. However, reform is still possible, since the Constitution allows states to choose the method of selecting presidential electors. One example of a recent attempt to reform the electoral college is the National Popular Vote plan, which has been introduced and adopted in a number of state legislatures.[11] Under the proposed rule change, a state's electoral college votes would go to the candidate who won the national popular vote, not the candidate with a plurality of votes in that specific state. States would enter a compact with other states making the same change, which would go into effect when a number of states representing a majority in the electoral college (270 electoral votes) approved it. The reform would effectively bypass the electoral college without the need for an amendment to the U.S. Constitution. As of 2014, 10 states plus Washington, D.C., representing 165 electoral votes, had enacted the bill into law. Replacing the electoral college with a national popular vote would dramatically alter the influence of states and change the nature of presidential campaigns. Competition would no longer be confined to a few large battleground states, such as Florida, Ohio, and Pennsylvania, but would likely focus more on urban areas where the most votes are found.[12]

Another limitation of the electoral college is that the president of the United States may not have wide popular support. Few democracies in the world elect a president who does not win a majority of the popular vote. Since the Civil War, one-third

Replacing the electoral college with the popular election of the president would have a significant impact on how campaigns are waged. Presidential candidates would have a greater incentive to campaign in large population centers, like San Francisco and Houston. Opponents worry that less populated rural areas would be ignored.

of all winners of the electoral college have been elected with a plurality (less than 50 percent) rather than a majority of the national popular vote.[13] This happens when a third-party candidate receives votes as well. If the third-party candidate is more closely aligned ideologically with the losing major-party candidate, then a majority of the citizens do not support the winning presidential candidate. This situation has happened on several occasions. Notably, President Lincoln won just over 40 percent of the popular vote in a four-way tie to be president in 1860 on the brink of the Civil War, and President Clinton was elected with just 43 percent of the popular vote in 1992. Some suggest that the failure to secure a majority may continue in the future with the rise of independent voters and dissatisfaction with the two major political parties.[14]

Direct-Democracy Elections

Beyond presidential and congressional elections, 24 states also provide for the initiative process, as we saw in Chapter 1. **Ballot initiatives** allow citizens to circulate petitions to place policy change or proposed laws directly on the ballot for a popular vote. If a ballot measure receives majority support, it becomes law. Controversial issues frequently appear on the ballot of states with the initiative process—for example, proposals to ban same-sex marriage, raise the minimum wage, legalize marijuana, and reform the election process. In recent years, voters in several states have voted to cut taxes, prohibit social services for illegal immigrants, end affirmative action, protect open space and the environment, and prevent offshore drilling. At the turn of the twentieth century, ballot initiatives were used to grant women suffrage (the right to vote), prevent child labor, limit the work day to eight hours, and allow voters to elect U.S. senators directly (rather than having them chosen by state legislatures). Ballot initiative campaigns often involve high spending by proponents and opponents, and mass media campaigns that can rival that of congressional and presidential candidates within a state. All 50 states have the legislative **referendum**, in which the state legislature refers laws to the voters for a popular vote. Referendum votes are required for changes to state constitutions.

The initiative and the referendum are examples of what is called direct democracy. They allow voters to govern directly without intervention by government

ballot initiative a proposed law or policy change that is placed on the ballot by citizens or interest groups for a popular vote

referendum the practice of referring a proposed law passed by a legislature to the vote of the electorate for approval or rejection

officials or the political parties. The validity of ballot measure results, however, is subject to judicial action. If a court finds that an initiative violates the state or national constitution, it can overturn the result. This happened in 2012 when the federal courts overturned California's Proposition 8 banning same-sex marriage.[15] In Washington state, the state Supreme Court overturned a ballot initiative requiring that all measures to raise taxes pass with a two-thirds majority in the state legislature, a requirement not found in the state's constitution.[16]

Ballot initiatives not only change policy but also appear to affect political behavior. One study found that states with initiatives on the ballot have higher voter turnout over time. Citizens living in direct-democracy states report more interest in politics, and are more likely to discuss politics. Why is this so? If electoral rules offer people more opportunities to participate in decisions, those rules may have an "educative" effect on those people.[17] Representative democracy allows citizens to vote on who gets to make political decisions; ballot propositions go further, offering voters the possibility of directly making public policy. When they have more opportunities to act politically, citizens may learn to participate more, and come to believe their participation has meaning.

Elections with policy issues on the ballot provide information to voters in the form of political campaigns and attention in the mass media. Ballot measures concerning controversial policy issues such as same-sex marriage, raising taxes for the wealthy, nonpartisan redistricting, and immigration rights generate their own campaigns, with television, newspaper, and Internet ads; professional campaign consultants; and mobilization drives that contact potential voters.[18] Hundreds of initiatives and referenda appear on state election ballots every two years. Initiative campaigns can pump millions of dollars into the American states each election. In the 2002 elections, almost $9.00 per capita was spent on initiative campaigns in Arizona, more than the amount spent on any single candidate race in the state. Ballot measures and their associated campaigns often draw more media attention and spending than prominent candidate races. And initiatives are increasingly common: more initiatives and referenda have appeared on state ballots in the last 30 years than at any other time in American history, outside of the Progressive era. In 2014, an unusually low year, 158 measures appeared on statewide election ballots. Hot-button topics on statewide ballots included raising the minimum wage, legalizing marijuana, abortion, education funding, gambling, guns, immigration, insurance, redistricting, raising taxes, cutting taxes, and voting rights.

In addition, ballot measures can have spillover effects, shaping both the national agenda and evaluations of and voting for gubernatorial and congressional candidates.[19] The tax revolt in the late 1970s, with initiatives and referenda on many state ballots lowering taxes, may have contributed to Republican Ronald Reagan's successful bid for the White House in 1980. Ballot measures banning same-sex marriage placed on the ballot of 13 states may have primed voting for the Republican presidential candidate in the 2004 election, George W. Bush. In 2006 coordinated ballot measures in multiple states raising the minimum wage may have influenced voters to focus on the economy, and increased voting for Democrats in Congress and for Democratic governors. Placing issues on the ballot as part of an effort to influence candidate elections is a relatively new, but important, strategy for political campaigns. Such effects on candidate races highlight just how important issue elections are in American politics.

Eighteen states also have legal provisions for **recall** elections, which allow voters to remove governors and other state officials from office prior to the expiration of their

recall a procedure to allow voters to remove state officials from office before their terms expire by circulating petitions to call a vote

terms. In California, for example, if 12 percent of those who voted in the last general election sign petitions demanding a special recall election, one must be scheduled by the state board of elections. In 2003 many California voters blamed Governor Gray Davis for the state's $38 billion budget deficit, allowing his opponents to secure enough signatures to force a vote. In October 2003, Davis became only the second governor in American history to be recalled by his state's electorate. (In 2012, Wisconsin governor Scott Walker won a highly visible recall election, keeping his position.) Federal officials, such as the president and members of Congress, are not subject to recall.

● Election Campaigns

Explain how campaigns are typically conducted

A **campaign** is an effort by political candidates (and their supporters) to win the backing of donors, political activists, and voters in their quest for political office. Campaigns precede every primary and general election. Because of the complexity of the campaign process, and because of the amount of money that candidates must raise, presidential campaigns usually begin almost two years before the November presidential elections. The campaign for any office consists of a number of steps. Candidates must first organize an exploratory committee consisting of supporters who will help them raise funds and bring their names to the attention of the media and potential donors. This step is relatively easy for a candidate currently in office, known as an **incumbent**. Incumbents usually are already well known and have little difficulty attracting supporters and contributors—unless of course they have been subject to damaging publicity while in office.

campaign an effort by political candidates and their supporters to win the backing of donors, political activists, and voters in their quest for political office

incumbent a candidate running for re-election to a position that he or she already holds

Advisers

The next step in a typical campaign involves recruiting advisers and creating a formal campaign organization (see Figure 10.1). Most candidates, especially for national or

Candidates for national office hire professional campaign advisers to guide their campaigns and direct volunteers. Here, Mitt Romney collaborates with senior adviser Kevin Madden and chief strategist Stuart Stevens during a strategy meeting en route to a campaign event in Ohio in 2012.

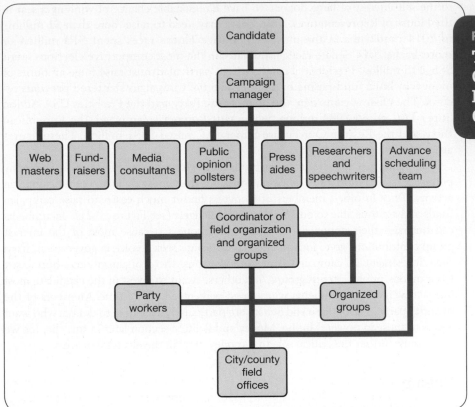

FIGURE 10.1
The Typical
Organization of a
National Political
Campaign

statewide office, will need a campaign manager, a media consultant, a pollster, a financial adviser, and a press spokesperson, as well as a staff director to coordinate the activities of volunteer and paid workers. For a local campaign, candidates generally need hundreds of workers, both professionals and volunteers. State-level campaigns call for thousands of workers, and presidential campaigns require tens of thousands of workers nationwide.

Virtually all serious contenders for national and statewide office retain the services of professional campaign consultants. Increasingly, candidates for local office, too, have come to rely on professional campaign managers. Consultants offer candidates the expertise necessary to conduct accurate opinion polls, produce television commercials, organize direct-mail campaigns, and make use of sophisticated computer analyses. Professional political consultants have taken the place of the old-time party bosses who once controlled political campaigns, and naturally they prefer to work for candidates who seem to have a reasonable chance of winning. Most consultants who direct campaigns specialize in politics, although some are drawn from the ranks of corporate advertising or public relations, and they may work with commercial clients in addition to politicians.

Fund-Raising

Modern national political campaigns are fueled by enormous amounts of money. Together with their advisers, candidates must begin serious fund-raising efforts at an early stage in the campaign, usually by appealing both to the altruism of small donors and to the self-interest of large donors. To have a reasonable chance of winning a seat in the House of Representatives, a candidate may need to raise more than $1 million; in 2014 candidates in the most competitive House races spent $10 million or more. In the 2014 Senate races, candidates in the most competitive elections spent $85–115 million. Presidential candidates in particular must raise huge amounts of money. In 2012 fund-raising by the presidential campaigns shattered previous records. The Obama campaign, the Democratic Party, and the Priorities USA Action Super PAC raised $934 million, while Mitt Romney's campaign, the Republican Party, and the Restore Our Future Super PAC raised $881 million. These figures are unprecedented.

Candidates generally begin raising funds long before they face an election, and many politicians spend more time soliciting donations than engaging in any other campaign activity. Once in office, members of Congress find it much easier to raise campaign funds and are thus able to outspend their challengers (see Figure 10.2).[20] Incumbents can out-raise their opponent by significant amounts because most of the interest group contributions go to incumbents. These groups seek a voice in government from their investment in campaign contributions; thus, these organizations—businesses, labor unions, public interest groups, and others—want to invest in the candidate most likely to win, and incumbents win a large percentage of the time. Members of the majority party in the House and Senate are particularly attractive to donors who want access to those in power.[21] In the "Money and Politics" section later in this chapter, we will discuss further the critical role that money plays in the electoral process.

Polling

Virtually all contemporary campaigns for national and statewide office, and many local campaigns, make extensive use of opinion polling. To be competitive, a candidate must collect voting and poll data to assess the electorate's opinions and past behavior. Polls, conducted throughout most political campaigns, provide the basic information that candidates and their staff use to craft campaign strategies—that is, to select issues, assess the candidates' strengths and weaknesses and those of the opposition, and measure voter responses to the campaign. The themes, issues, and messages that candidates present during a campaign are generally based on polls and small face-to-face sessions with voters, called "focus groups." In recent years, pollsters have become central figures in most national campaigns, and some have continued as advisers to their clients after they've won the election.

Campaign Strategy

For those candidates lucky enough to survive the nominating process, the last hurdle is the general election (see Figure 10.3). There are essentially two types of general election in the United States today. The first type is the organizationally driven, labor-intensive election. Candidates campaign in local elections and many congressional elections by recruiting large numbers of volunteers to hand out leaflets and organize rallies. The candidates make appearances at receptions, community group meetings, local rallies, and even in shopping malls and on busy street corners. Generally, local and congressional campaigns depend less on issues and policy proposals and more on hard work designed to make the candidate more visible than his opponent. Statewide campaigns, some congressional races, and of course the national presidential election fall into the second category: the media-driven, capital-intensive electoral campaign.

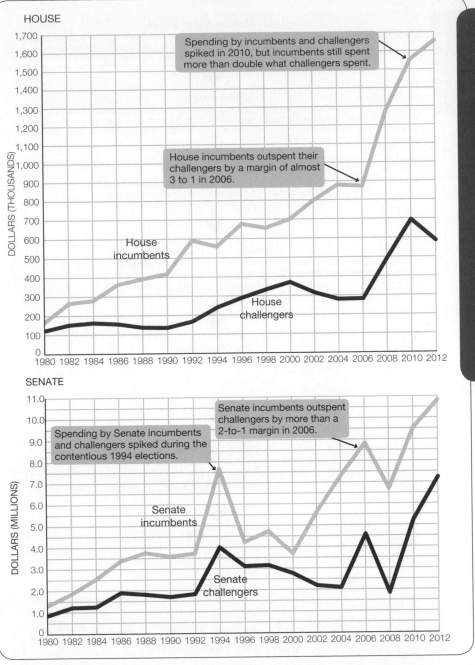

HOUSE

Spending by incumbents and challengers spiked in 2010, but incumbents still spent more than double what challengers spent.

House incumbents outspent their challengers by a margin of almost 3 to 1 in 2006.

House incumbents

House challengers

SENATE

Spending by Senate incumbents and challengers spiked during the contentious 1994 elections.

Senate incumbents outspent challengers by more than a 2-to-1 margin in 2006.

Senate incumbents

Senate challengers

FIGURE 10.2

Average House and Senate Campaign Expenditures, 1980–2012

The average amount spent by House and Senate incumbents to secure re-election has risen sharply in recent years, whereas spending by challengers has remained more stable. What would you expect to see as a consequence of this trend? Is legislation needed to level the playing field?

SOURCES: Norman J. Orstein, Thomas E. Mann, and Michael J. Malbin, eds., *Vital Statistics on Congress, 2001–2002* (Washington, DC: American Enterprise Institute, 2002), 87, 93; and Campaign Finance Institute, www.brookings.edu /vitalstats (accessed 6/20/14).

All campaigns must decide on a campaign strategy: What will their main message be? How will they allocate their resources? Which voters will they target? The electoral college, discussed above, is one election rule that influences the campaign strategy of presidential candidates by forcing candidates to focus on a handful of battleground states, while ignoring the rest of the country. Battleground states are those in which Democrats and Republicans are roughly even in the population. (They are also called swing states because they "swing" in their support between the Republican and Democratic parties from election to election.) The 2012

FIGURE 10.3

Electing the President: Steps in the Process

Formation of an Exploratory Committee
Formed 18 to 24 months before the election, this committee begins fund-raising and bringing the candidate's name to the attention of the media and influential groups.

Fund-Raising
Presidential candidated must develop fundraising strategies, hire expert fundraisers, and quickly build a subtantial "war chest" early on to show they are serious contenders.

Campaigning
Months before the primaries, candidates begin meetings with local leaders, public appearances, ad campaigns, and other strategies.

Primaries and Caucuses
Candidates need to do well in early contests such as Iowa and New Hampshire in order to build momentum and win their party's nomination. Party debates give candidates an opportunity to impress large television audiences.

The Convention
The Democratic and Republican parties hold national conventions in September prior to the November general election. The party's nominees for president and vice president are "officially" announced.

The General Election Campaign
In the months leading up to the November election, candidates focus on battleground or swing states as they aim to win at leat 270 votes in the electoral college. They run television ads and use new media to reach voters. They must continue to raise money throughout this process.

The Debates
In October, the major party candidates engage in several televised debates along with one vice presidential debate.

The General Election
On the Tuesday following the first Monday in November, voters in each state cast ballots. In most states, the candidate who wins the most votes in the state wins all of the state's votes in the electoral college.

The Electoral College
The electors meet in their state capitals in December, and their votes are officially counted in January.

The Inauguration
The president is officially inaugurated on January 20.

presidential candidates focused their television advertising in media markets reaching voters in just 10 competitive swing states. Combined, the Democratic candidate Obama and Republican Romney spent nearly $1 billion on television ads. Of this total, $173 million was spent in one state (Florida), where hundreds of thousands of ads aired. The candidates spent $151 million in Virginia, $150 million in Ohio, $97 million in North Carolina, $73 million in Colorado, and $57 million in Iowa. Virtually no television ads aired in the nation's largest population states of California and New York (safe for the Democratic candidate) or Texas (safe for the Republican candidate). In presidential races, residents of battleground states get most of the attention from the candidates and media, while citizens in noncompetitive states barely get noticed. This race to 270 electoral college votes profoundly effects the campaign strategy of presidential candidates, political parties, and the behavior of citizens, who are much more likely to vote if they live in a swing state.[22]

Contemporary political campaigns rely on a number of communications tools to reach the voters they want to target and bid for their support. These tools include the media, debates, and microtargeting.

The Media Extensive use of the broadcast media, television in particular, is the hallmark of the modern political campaign. Candidates endeavor to secure as much positive news and feature coverage as possible. This type of coverage is called *free media* because the cost of air time is borne by the media themselves. Candidates can secure free media coverage by participating in newsworthy events. Incumbents introduce legislation, sponsor hearings, undertake inspection tours of the sites of fires and floods, meet with delegations of foreign dignitaries, and so on, to capture the attention of the television cameras. Challengers announce new policy proposals, visit orphanages and senior centers, and demand that their opponents agree to a series of debates. Generally speaking, incumbents have the advantage in securing free media time.

The 1992 presidential campaign introduced two new media techniques that are still important today: the talk show interview and the "electronic town hall meeting." Candidates used interviews on television and radio talk shows to reach the large audiences drawn to this popular entertainment program format. The **town hall meeting** format allows candidates the opportunity to interact with ordinary citizens, thus showing the candidates' concern with the views and needs of the voters. Both talk show appearances and town hall meetings allow candidates to deliver their messages to millions of Americans without the input of journalists or commentators who might criticize or question the candidates' assertions.

In addition to pursuing free media coverage, candidates spend millions of dollars for *paid media* time, in the form of television and radio ads as discussed in the previous section. Many of these ads consist of 15-, 30-, or 60-second **spots (advertisements)** that deliver a candidate's message to a target audience before uninterested or hostile viewers can tune it out. Examples of extremely effective spots include George H. W. Bush's 1988 "Willie Horton" ad, which implied that Bush's opponent, Michael Dukakis, coddled criminals, and Lyndon Johnson's 1964 "daisy" ad, which suggested that Johnson's opponent, Barry Goldwater, would lead the United States into nuclear war. Television spots are used to establish candidate name recognition, create a favorable image of the candidate and a negative image of the opponent, link the candidate with desirable groups in the community, and communicate the candidate's stands on selected issues.

town hall meeting an informal public meeting in which candidates meet with ordinary citizens. Allows candidates to deliver messages without the presence of journalists or commentators

spot (advertisement) a 15-, 30-, or 60-second television campaign commercial that permits a candidate's message to be delivered to a target audience

Often in the later stages of a campaign, candidates will "go negative," putting out ads attacking their opponents' character by exposing sordid incidents or unsavory associations. Though voters consistently say they reject so-called negative campaigning, attacks such as the 1988 "Willie Horton" ad can be devastatingly effective in the heat of a closely contested race, even when the ads are misleading or patently false. The targets of these attacks are forced to issue denials and use valuable campaign time defending themselves rather than promoting their ideas.

Journalists, voters, and scholars frequently complain that such ads undermine elections and even democratic government itself. The argument is that voters are turned off by the negativity of politics and the media, and in turn are uninformed about politics and less likely to vote. Americans tend to see negative campaign ads as just that: negative. But political scientist John Geer has found that negative campaigns are more effective than positive campaigns in shaping voter decisions. He argues that when political candidates attack each other, raising doubts about each other's views and qualifications, voters benefit.[23] Negative ads are more likely to address important policy differences between candidates and provide supporting evidence. Positive ads tend to focus on candidates' personal characteristics rather than issues, and do not provide any supporting evidence regarding the candidates' claims. Thus voters may learn more from negative ads than positive ads.

In addition to ads sponsored by the candidates, numerous campaign ads are sponsored by the political parties and by political advocacy groups seeking to influence the outcome of the election. As discussed in Chapter 4, the 2003 Bipartisan Campaign Reform Act (BCRA) prohibited advocacy groups from running ads that mentioned a candidate's name within 30 days of a primary election and 60 days of a general election. The purpose of the ban was to prevent well-heeled groups from conducting ad blitzes just before an election, thus possibly distorting the results. In its 2007 decision in *Federal Election Commission v. Wisconsin Right to Life*, the Supreme Court struck down the ad ban as an unconstitutional restriction on speech.[24] Following the 2010 *Citizens United* decision, interest groups can form Super PACs and run unlimited campaign ads for or against candidates, as long as the organizations are "independent" of the candidate's campaign. This decision prevented the spending limits in BCRA from playing a significant role in election campaigns.

Debates Public debates were a critical part of the democratic process of ancient Greece, where they were both a vital form of public entertainment and the principal means of what today would be called "voter education." Many successful American politicians, such as Abraham Lincoln, came to prominence largely because of their skill as debaters. Today, both presidential and vice-presidential candidates hold debates, as do candidates for statewide and even local offices. Debates give voters the opportunity to see how the candidates fare in direct, face-to-face exchanges outside the "campaign bubble" of stage-managed public appearances and carefully scripted speeches. Candidates who can "think on their feet" may be seen as demonstrating the kind of on-the-spot decision making that is more like actual governing than anything else they do in a campaign.

Televised presidential debates began with the famous 1960 Kennedy-Nixon clash. Kennedy's strong performance in the debate and the perception of many voters that the youthfully vigorous Kennedy "looked presidential" were major factors in bringing about his victory over the much better-known Richard Nixon. In 1984, Ronald

Reagan was able to dispel misgivings that some voters had about his age with a well-timed joke about the "youth and inexperience" of his Democratic rival, Senator Walter Mondale. Indeed, candidates can make or break their campaigns with the strength of their debate performances, including even unconscious gestures and the nuances of their facial expressions. President George H. W. Bush was thought to have "lost" a 1992 debate when he was seen nervously glancing at his watch while his opponent, Bill Clinton, was speaking. In the 2012 presidential primaries, the Republicans held a dozen nationally televised debates, more than ever before, with real consequences for the presidential chances of a number of candidates. Before the debates, Texas governor Rick Perry was considered the ideal candidate to take the White House, given his policy positions and standing within the party. But a number of high-profile gaffes during the debates—including one in which he could not remember the name of one of the U.S. government departments he wished to eliminate if he were elected—turned voters off. Candidates spend a great deal of time preparing for debate appearances, rehearsing their responses to likely questions and devising gambits to catch their opponents off guard. But because debates force candidates to react spontaneously, many voters believe that they provide the most important and revealing moments of a campaign.

Micro-targeting The media and debates allow candidates to communicate their policy goals and promises to voters. While this is efficient for campaigns, it is also blunt: different voters care about different issues, after all. As we saw in Chapter 9, the idea behind micro-targeting is to send different campaign ads or messages to different demographic groups of voters and potential voters. Suburban "soccer moms," for instance, would be targeted with different ads than rural "cowboy dads."

Republican president George W. Bush is credited with successfully using micro-targeting in the 2000 and 2004 presidential elections. His campaign focused on wedge issues—issues where a voter's preferences diverge from those of her political party. By targeting such voters with messages focusing on Bush's position on the wedge issue, the campaign hoped to convince these voters to cast a ballot for Bush rather than his opponent.[25]

Micro-targeting became more sophisticated during the 2008 presidential campaign, as Democrats built an extensive organization to contact and turn out voters. In 2008, Obama's campaign assigned every voter in the country a pair of scores based on the likelihood that the person would (1) cast a ballot and (2) support Obama. These scores were derived from an unprecedented volume of ongoing survey work. Every week, in each battleground state, the campaign conducted 5,000 to 10,000 short telephone interviews that quickly gauged a voter's preferences and 1,000 long-form traditional interviews. To estimate individual-level scores, statistical algorithms looked for patterns in these opinions and the many other data points the campaign had assembled for every voter—as many as 1,000 variables each, drawn from voter registration records, consumer data warehouses, and past campaign contacts. With this mountain of information, the campaign could then use different, carefully targeted messages for different demographic, regional, and ideological groups to persuade them to turn out and vote for Obama.[26] The Obama campaign repeated this strategy in 2012. Because of micro-targeting, millions of Americans heard from other Americans about issues that mattered the most to them. Some argue those conversations were more powerful than the millions of dollars spent on TV ads.

Contemporary presidential campaigns gather large amounts of data on potential voters in order to effectively tailor campaign messages to specific demographics. Armed with this data, volunteers for both the Romney and Obama campaigns made thousands and thousands of phone calls to urge individuals to support their candidate on Election Day in 2012.

Once campaigns have identified specific groups of voters, they reach out via face-to-face contacts, phone calls, mailings, and social media to reach their target audiences. Personal contact is thought to be extremely effective. Staffs of paid or volunteer callers, using computer-assisted dialing systems and prepared scripts, also place calls to deliver their candidate's message. The targeted groups are generally those identified by polls as either uncommitted or weakly committed, and even strong supporters of the candidate who are contacted simply are encouraged to vote. In 2008 and 2012 the presidential campaigns of both parties also placed hundreds of thousands of automated "robocalls" urging voters to support their candidates.

Direct mail is both a vehicle for communicating with voters and a mechanism for raising funds. After obtaining the appropriate mailing lists, candidates usually send pamphlets, letters, and brochures describing themselves and their views to voters believed to be sympathetic. Often the letters sent to voters are personalized. The recipient is addressed by name in the text, and the letter appears actually to have been signed by the candidate. Of course, these "personal" letters and even the signatures are generated by a computer. In addition to its use as a political advertising medium, direct mail has also become an important source of campaign funds. Computerized mailing lists permit campaign strategists to pinpoint individuals whose interests, background, and activities suggest that they may be potential donors to the campaign. Research suggests direct mail and robocalls are not very effective, while in-person and phone contacts are effective.[27]

The Internet has also become a major weapon in modern political campaigns. Today, every presidential campaign and most campaigns for Congress and major state offices develop an Internet strategy for fund-raising, generating interest in the candidate, mobilizing supporters, and getting out the vote. (See Chapters 7 and 8 for more on this.) These sites help build enthusiasm and are potent fund-raising tools. One reason the Internet is such an effective means of organizing presidential campaigns is because of cost: the Internet allows the organization of volunteers at a fraction of the cost of traditional campaigns. Obama's campaign took advantage of free advertising on YouTube rather than relying exclusive on television ads. Online political videos may be more effective than television ads because viewers make a conscious choice to watch them, instead of having their television program interrupted by an unwanted ad. Obama's YouTube video ads in the 2008 election were watched for 14.5 million hours. By comparison, purchasing 14.5 million hours on broadcast TV would have cost an estimated $47 million. According to reports released by the Pew Research Center soon after the election, in 2012 fully 55 percent of registered voters watched political videos online, including news reports about the election, debates, humorous and parody videos, and political ads.[28]

Certainly "people power" remains important in modern political campaigns. Candidates continue to use the political services of tens of thousands of volunteers, especially for grassroots get-out-the-vote drives. Still, even the recruitment of campaign workers has become a job for electronic technology. Employing a technique called "instant organization," paid staff use phone banks to contact potential campaign workers in areas targeted by a computer (which they also do when contacting potential voters, as discussed earlier). Volunteer workers are recruited from among those called.

for critical analysis

Do American political campaigns help voters make a decision? Or do they produce more confusion than enlightenment?

● Money and Politics

Describe how candidates raise the money they need to run

During the nineteenth century, national political campaigns in the United States employed millions of people. Indeed, as many as 2.5 million individuals did political work during the 1880s.[29] Most of these workers, however, were volunteers, so the direct cost of campaigns was relatively low. For example, in 1860, Abraham Lincoln spent only $100,000—which was approximately twice the amount spent by his chief opponent, Stephen A. Douglas.

Campaign tasks that were once performed by masses of party workers with some cash now require fewer personnel but a great deal more money, for the new political style depends on surveys, computers, and other electronic communication methods. The modern political campaign is enormously expensive. A 60-second spot on prime-time network television costs hundreds of thousands of dollars each time it is aired. Polling expenses in a statewide race can easily reach or exceed the six-figure mark. Campaign consultants can charge substantial fees. A serious national direct-mail campaign requires at least $1 million in "front-end cash" to pay for mailing lists, printing, envelopes, and postage.[30]

In the nineteenth century, labor-intensive campaigns allowed parties whose chief support came from groups nearer the bottom of the social scale to use their numerical superiority as a partial counterweight to the institutional and economic resources more readily available to the opposition. The capital-intensive campaign of the modern era, by contrast, has given a major boost to the political fortunes of candidates whose supporters are able to furnish the large sums now needed to compete effectively.[31]

Candidates with the most campaign dollars often win, and that was certainly the case with President Obama, who in 2008 out-fund-raised his Republican opponent, John McCain. It was also the case with Republican Mitt Romney, who out-fund-raised his Republican challengers in 2012, including Newt Gingrich and Rick Santorum. Dominated by expensive technology, therefore, electoral politics has become a contest in which the wealthy and powerful have a decided advantage. The 2012 presidential election shattered previous records for campaign spending: spending by candidates, political parties, and interest groups on the congressional and presidential races was $6 billion combined in 2012, as compared with $5.3 billion in 2008 and $4.2 billion in 2004. Figure 10.4 shows how the presidential candidates spent the money they raised in 2012.

The Courts and Campaign Spending

The United States is rare among democracies in allowing candidates to raise unlimited sums of money to spend on their campaigns. In most democratic countries, publically financed campaigns are the norm; in such a system, candidates or parties are provided with a set amount of money to spend by the government. In the United States, candidates are not subject to such restrictions, and they raise ever-increasing amounts of money from private individuals, corporations, and interest groups. Reformers have long been concerned about the potential for corruption that exists when candidates are actively soliciting private interests for funding. In an attempt to limit the influence of private money, the federal government has adopted a number of laws to limit and regulate contributions to political campaigns. But three Supreme Court cases adopted over a 40-year period have slowly dismantled most of these restrictions.

The first major case, *Buckley v. Valeo* (1976) was a landmark Supreme Court case that struck down several provisions of the Federal Election Campaign Act of 1974, a law that limited campaign expenditures, independent expenditures by individuals and groups, and expenditures by a candidate from personal funds. The decision introduced the idea that money (in this case, campaign contributions) counts as "speech" under the First Amendment and that candidates could spend unlimited amounts of their own money on their own campaign. However, the Court left intact the provision of the law that sets limits on individuals' campaign contributions.[32]

In 2010 the U.S. Supreme Court ruled in *Citizens United v. Federal Election Commission* that the government could not restrict independent expenditures by corporations or unions to political campaigns.[33] (Independent expenditures are sums of money spent to influence a campaign but are not allowed to coordinate with a candidate's official campaign.) The Court said restrictions on independent expenditures violated the First Amendment. With this decision, the United States entered a new era of campaign finance in which corporations and unions can spend unlimited sums. *Citizens United* permitted individuals and organizations to form committees, called super political action committees (Super PACs), which could raise unlimited amounts of money to run advertising for and against candidates so long as their efforts were not coordinated with those of the candidates[34] (see Chapter 11). This resulted in a significant increase in campaign spending in the 2010 midterm election and unprecedented spending in the 2012 presidential election. Obama, the Democratic National Committee, and its affiliated Super PACs spent $1.11 billion in 2012, while Romney, the Republican National Committee, and its affiliated Super PACs spent $928 million, or almost $1 billion, swamping previous general election totals.

In 2014 the Supreme Court removed additional limits on individuals' campaign contributions in its decision in *McCutcheon et al. vs FEC*.[35] The decision extended arguments that limits on political contributions to violate First Amendment

SPENDING BY OBAMA, DEMOCRATIC PARTY, AND DEMOCRATIC SUPER PACS

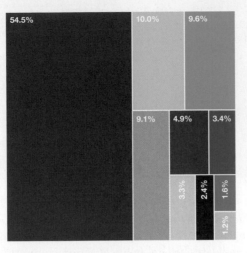

Category	Total spent (millions $)
■ Advertising	580.1
■ Mail	97.3
■ Fund-raising	106.4
■ Payroll	102.3
■ Administration	52.0
■ Travel	35.7
■ Polling	34.9
■ Events	25.3
■ Consultants	13.2
■ Lists	16.8
TOTAL	$1,064.0

SPENDING BY ROMNEY, REPUBLICAN PARTY, AND REPUBLICAN SUPER PACS

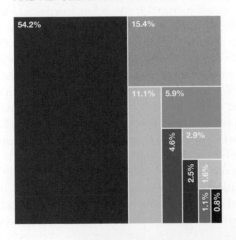

Category	Total spent (millions $)
■ Advertising	$470.3
■ Mail	$133.4
■ Fund-raising	$96.2
■ Payroll	$50.8
■ Administration	$21.3
■ Travel	$39.6
■ Polling	$14.2
■ Events	$7.0
■ Consultants	$24.7
■ Lists	$9.6
TOTAL	$867.1

FIGURE 10.4

How Presidential Campaigns Spent Money, 2012

Presidential candidates and the groups that support them spend nearly half of their money on advertising. However, advertising is not the only major expense. The cost of raising money is itself a major line item in the campaign budget.

SOURCE: *Washington Post*, www.washingtonpost.com/wp-srv/special/politics /campaign-finance (accessed 6/4/14).

In 2014, Shaun McCutcheon successfully challenged the federal limit on the amount of money any one individual can donate to political campaigns and candidates. However, many people worry that recent Supreme Court decisions overturning campaign spending limits reinforce the influence of the very affluent in American politics at the expense of everyone else.

freedoms, arguments that had appeared in both *Buckley* and *Citizens United*. The case challenged the two-year cap on the amount of money an individual could give to federal candidates, federal political action committees, and political party committees (set at $117,000 in the 2012 election cycle). The Court decision held that there was no evidence that the government's restrictions on total campaign contributions prevented corruption—in other words, that there was no evidence that making campaign contributions to large numbers of candidates lead to the donor controlling the actions of elected officials. Thus, the Court held, such restrictions were not justified. Chief Justice John Roberts wrote for the majority, "The government may no more restrict how many candidates or causes a donor may support than it may tell a newspaper how many candidates it may endorse." The Court let stand the limit on the amount of money that an individual can give to any one candidate in a two-year election cycle (currently set at $2,600).

As the Court struggles to balance free speech with preventing political corruption, the sum of these three court decisions tips the scale in favor of speech. Opponents raise concerns that unlimited spending by wealthy donors, corporations, and other organizations could worsen existing corruption in American politics. This concern is bolstered by a number of new studies finding that members of Congress make decisions that represent the interests of wealthy campaign donors, not average voters.[36]

Sources of Campaign Funds

Although restrictions remain on how money is raised and spent on elections, there is today a great deal of latitude on where money comes from and what it is used for. Campaigns have at least six potential sources of funds.

Individual Donors Politicians spend a great deal of time asking people for money. Money is solicited via direct mail, through the Internet, over the phone, and in numerous face-to-face meetings. Under federal law, individuals may donate as much as $2,600 per candidate per election, $5,000 per PAC per calendar year, $32,400 per national party committee per calendar year, and $10,000 to state and local committees per calendar year. (There is no limit to the number of candidates or PACs that an individual can give to, however—a result of the Supreme Court's decision

Campaign Laws in Comparison

Electoral campaigns are more expensive in the United States than any other country, with only India even approaching the same amount of spending.[a] Both are large federal countries, so spending is high partly because these countries have multiple levels of government to elect. However, critics have argued that the amount of money in these campaigns creates an unfair advantage for certain candidates, increases the importance (and political influence) of large campaign donors, and potentially undermines the quality of democracy in both countries.

Some countries have sought to address corruption issues and improve political accountability by creating rules that limit campaign contributions or campaign spending. Japan sets very strict limits on campaign contributions and some limits on spending; the United Kingdom, in contrast, does not limit contributions but has strict rules on spending.

Some countries also allow qualified parties and/or candidates free or subsidized access to media, which reduces the need to raise huge sums. In Norway, political advertising (which is where most U.S. campaign money goes) is banned on television and radio, and the election itself only runs about two weeks. Most campaign money—roughly 74 percent[b]—comes from public funds made available to all parties by the Norwegian government.

	Donor Limits	Spending Limits	Availability of Public Funding	Access to Free/ Subsidized Media	Cost of a Recent Election
United States	Strong Annual limits on individual and group contributions	Weak Political parties have limits, but there are no limits on candidates or outside groups.	Only during campaigns	No	$7.1 billion (2012)
India	None	Very weak No bans on party spending; candidate spending is poorly enforced	None	Yes All political parties (but not all candidates) are guaranteed equal access.	$4.9 billion (2014 projection)
Japan	Strong Annual limits regarding individual and group contributions	Very weak No spending limits on parties, some limits on candidates	Regularly available	Yes Political parties receive media access; candidates receive access for some elections. Bans on online campaigning	$780 million (2009)
United Kingdom	None	Strong Spending limits are set at a fixed amount that varies by region.	Regularly available	Yes Political parties, not candidates, receive free media access.	$91 million (2010)
Norway	None	None	Regularly available	No Political commercials are banned.	Roughly $6.5 million (2013)

SOURCES: The International Institute for Democracy and Electoral Assistance Political Finance Database, www.idea.int/political-finance (accessed 7/18/14).
Cost data are from the U.S. Federal Election Commission, "FEC Summarizes Campaign Activity of the 2011–2012 Election Cycle," revised March 27, 2014, www.fec.gov/press/press2013/20130419_2012-24m-Summary.shtml; Gottipati and Singh, "India Set to Challenge U.S. for Election-Spending Record"; and Thompson, "International Campaign Finance: How Do Countries Compare?" Norway's election spending is estimated based on reporting of the 2013 election campaign contributions from Statistics Norway, "Election Campaign Contribution, 2013," September 25, 2013, www.ssb.no/en/valg/statistikker/valgkamp (accessed 7/18/14).

[a]Sruthi Gottipati and Rajesh Kumar Singh, "India Set to Challenge U.S. for Election-Spending Record," Reuters, March 9, 2014, www.reuters.com/article/2014/03/09/us-india-election-spending-idUSBREA280AR20140309 (accessed 7/18/14).
[b]Nick Thompson, "International Campaign Finance: How Do Countries Compare?" CNN World, March 5, 2012, www.cnn.com/2012/01/24/world/global-campaign-finance (accessed 7/18/14).

in *McCutcheon*.)[37] The "Who Are Americans?" feature looks at the characteristics of donors and nondonors to political campaigns.

political action committee (PAC) a private group that raises and distributes funds for use in election campaigns

Political Action Committees (PACs) PACs are organizations established by corporations, labor unions, or interest groups to channel the contributions of their members into political campaigns. Under the terms of the 1971 Federal Election Campaign Act, which governs campaign finance in the United States, PACs are permitted to make larger contributions to any given candidate than individuals are allowed to make. Moreover, allied or related PACs often coordinate their campaign contributions, greatly increasing the amount of money a candidate actually receives from the same interest group. More than 4,500 PACs are registered with the Federal Election Commission (FEC), which oversees campaign finance practices in the United States. Nearly two-thirds of all PACs represent corporations, trade associations, and other business and professional groups. Many congressional and party leaders have established PACs, known as leadership PACs, to provide funding for their political allies. (PACs are discussed further in Chapter 11.)

527 committees nonprofit independent groups that receive and disburse funds to influence the nomination, election, or defeat of candidates. Named after Section 527 of the Internal Revenue Code, which defines and provides tax-exempt status for nonprofit advocacy groups

Independent Spending: 527, 501c(4), and Super PAC Committees Committees known as **527s** and **501c(4)s** are independent groups that are currently not covered by the campaign-spending restrictions imposed in 2002 by the BCRA. These groups, named for the sections of the tax code under which they are organized, can raise and spend unlimited amounts on political advocacy as long as their efforts are not coordinated with those of any candidate's campaign. A 527 is a group established specifically for the purpose of political advocacy, whereas a 501c(4) is a nonprofit group, such as an environmental or other public interest group, that also engages in advocacy. A 501c(4) may not spend more than half its revenue for political purposes. Yet, unlike a 527, a 501c(4) is not required to disclose where it gets its funds or exactly what it does with them. As a result, it has become a common practice for wealthy and corporate donors to route campaign contributions far in excess of the legal limits through 501c(4)s. Outside spending via 527s and 501c(4)s played an unprecedented role in the 2012 presidential race, as groups ran extensive television ads. Priorities USA Action Super PAC raised $64 million to support Democrats, while the Restore Our Future Super PAC raised $132 million to help Republicans. The top-spending Super PACs were primarily those advocating against Obama, including American Crossroads ($85 million), the Republican National Committee ($41 million), and Americans for Prosperity ($34 million). Super PACs on both sides relied on very large contributions.

501c(4) committees nonprofit groups that also engage in issue advocacy. Under Section 501c(4) of the federal tax code such a group may spend up to half its revenue for political purposes

Political Parties Before 2002 most campaign dollars took the form of "soft money," unregulated contributions to the national parties nominally to assist in party building or voter registration efforts rather than for particular campaigns. Federal campaign finance legislation crafted by senators John McCain and Russell Feingold and enacted in 2002 sought to ban soft money by prohibiting the national parties from receiving contributions from corporations, unions, or individuals and preventing them from directing such funds to their affiliated state parties. However, it did not reduce the overall importance of money in politics, and political parties continue to play a major role in financing political campaigns. Under federal rules, a national political party committee may make

Who Donates to Political Campaigns?

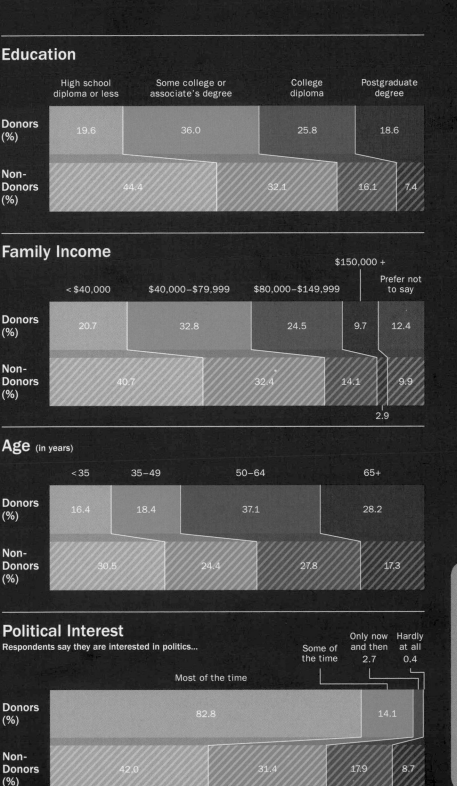

Education

	High school diploma or less	Some college or associate's degree	College diploma	Postgraduate degree
Donors (%)	19.6	36.0	25.8	18.6
Non-Donors (%)	44.4	32.1	16.1	7.4

Family Income

	< $40,000	$40,000–$79,999	$80,000–$149,999	$150,000 +	Prefer not to say
Donors (%)	20.7	32.8	24.5	9.7	12.4
Non-Donors (%)	40.7	32.4	14.1	2.9	9.9

Age (in years)

	< 35	35–49	50–64	65+
Donors (%)	16.4	18.4	37.1	28.2
Non-Donors (%)	30.5	24.4	27.8	17.3

Political Interest

Respondents say they are interested in politics...

	Most of the time	Some of the time	Only now and then	Hardly at all
Donors (%)	82.8	14.1	2.7	0.4
Non-Donors (%)	42.0	31.4	17.9	8.7

Political campaigns are funded in large measure by donations. In the 2012 election cycle, individual donations to candidates and campaigns totaled approximately $981 million. Over two-thirds of this amount came from small donations of less than $200 each. The graphic here shows the demographic profiles of those who donated to a candidate, campaign, or political organization and those who did not. Those who are older, are more educated, and are more interested in politics are more likely to donate.

SOURCES: Federal Election Commission, www.fec.gov/disclosurep/pnational.do (accessed 6/9/14) and 2012 Cooperative Congressional Election Study, Common Content; Ansolabehere, Stephen; Schaffner, Brian, 2012, "CCES Common Content, 2012," http://hdl.handle.net/1902.1/21447 UNF:5:mMbfa1Vn45NxO7I6aZPicg== CCES [Distributor] V5 [Version]

for critical analysis

1. What characteristics describe those who are most likely to give money to campaigns? Does the pattern of who gives money to campaigns surprise you? Why or why not?

2. If you wanted to make a prediction about whether a specific person is likely to give money to a candidate or a campaign, what one demographic question would you ask him or her?

unlimited "independent expenditures" advocating support for its own presidential candidate or advocating the defeat of the opposing party's candidate as long as these expenditures are not coordinated with the candidate's own campaign. A national party committee may also spend up to $19 million in coordination with its presidential candidate's campaign even if its candidate has accepted public funding. Thus, for example, even though John McCain accepted full public funding for his 2008 presidential bid, the national Republican Party helped fund McCain's advertising up to the federal limit.

Public Funding The Federal Election Campaign Act also provides for public funding of presidential campaigns, as discussed above. As they seek a major-party presidential nomination, candidates become eligible for public funds by raising at least $5,000 in individual contributions of $250 or less in each of 20 states. Candidates who reach this threshold may apply for federal funds to match, on a dollar-for-dollar basis, all individual contributions of $250 or less they receive. Currently, candidates who accept matching funds may spend no more than $42 million, including the matching funds, in their presidential primary campaigns. The funds are drawn from the Presidential Election Campaign Fund. Taxpayers may contribute $3 to this fund, at no additional cost to themselves, by checking a box on the first page of their federal income tax returns. Major-party presidential candidates receive a lump sum (about $91 million in 2012) during the summer prior to the general election. They must meet all their general expenses from this money. Third-party candidates are eligible for public funding only if they received at least 5 percent of the vote in the previous presidential race. This stipulation effectively blocks pre-election funding for third-party or independent candidates, although a third party that wins more than 5 percent of the vote can receive public funding after the election.

Under current law, no candidate is required to accept public funding for either the nominating races or general presidential election. Candidates who do not accept public funding are not affected by any expenditure limits. In 2008, John McCain accepted public funding for the general election campaign, receiving $84 million, but Barack Obama declined, choosing to rely on his own fundraising prowess. Obama was ultimately able to outspend McCain by a wide margin. Candidates who accept public funding may not engage in fund-raising for their own campaigns. Neither major party candidate accepted public financing in 2012. As a result, many observers believe that the 2008 race may be the last time that a major-party candidate will forgo his own fund-raising in favor of public funding. Candidates who accept public funding may not engage in fund-raising for their own campaigns.

The Candidates Themselves On the basis of the Supreme Court's 1976 decision in *Buckley v. Valeo*, the right of individuals to spend their *own* money to campaign for office is a constitutionally protected matter of free speech and is not subject to limitation.[38] Thus, extremely wealthy candidates often contribute millions of dollars to their own campaigns. The New Jersey Democrat Jon Corzine, for example, spent approximately $60 million of his own funds in a successful U.S. Senate bid in 2000 and another $40 million when he ran for governor of New Jersey in 2005. The only exception to the *Buckley* rule concerns presidential candidates who accept federal funding for their general election campaigns. Such individuals are limited to $50,000 in personal spending.

● How Voters Decide

Identify the major factors that influence voters' decisions

Whatever the capacity of those with the money and power to influence the electoral process, it is the millions of individual decisions on Election Day that ultimately determine electoral outcomes. Sooner or later the choices of voters weigh more heavily than the schemes of campaign advisers or the leverage of interest groups.

Three factors influence voters' decisions at the polls: partisan loyalty, issues and policy preferences, and candidate characteristics.

Partisan Loyalty

Partisan loyalty was considerably stronger during the 1940s and '50s than it is today, but even now most voters feel a certain sense of identification or kinship with the Democratic or Republican party. This sense of identification is often handed down from parents to children and is reinforced by social and cultural ties. Partisan identification predisposes voters in favor of their party's candidates and against those of the opposing party (see Figure 10.5). At the level of the presidential contest, issues and candidate personalities may become very important, although even here many Americans supported Mitt Romney or Barack Obama in the 2012 race only because of partisan loyalty. But partisanship is more likely to assert itself in the less visible races, where issues and the candidates are not as well known. State legislative races, for example, are often decided by voters' party ties. Once formed, voters' partisan loyalties seldom change. Voters tend to keep their party affiliations unless some crisis causes them to reexamine the bases of their loyalties and to conclude that they have not given their support to the appropriate party. During these relatively infrequent periods of electoral change, millions of voters can change their party ties. For example, at the beginning of the New Deal era,

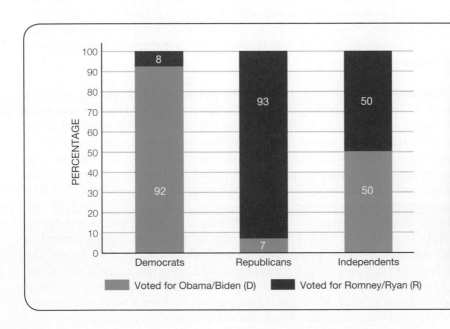

FIGURE 10.5

The Effect of Party Identification on the Vote, 2012

In 2012 more than 90 percent of Democrats and Republicans supported their party's presidential candidate. Should candidates devote their resources to converting voters who identify with the opposition or to winning more support among independents? What factors might make it difficult for candidates to simultaneously pursue both courses of action?

between 1932 and 1936, millions of former Republicans transferred their allegiance to Franklin Roosevelt and the Democrats.

Issues and Policy Preferences

Policy preferences are a second factor influencing voters' choices at the polls. Voters may cast their ballots for the candidate whose position on economic issues they believe to be closest to their own, or the candidate who has what they believe to be the best record on foreign policy. Issues are more important in some races than others. If candidates articulate and publicize very different positions on important policy issues, voters are more likely to be able to identify and act on whatever policy preferences they may have.

The ability of voters to make choices on the basis of policy preferences is diminished, however, if competing candidates do not differ substantially or do not focus their campaigns on policy matters. Very often, candidates deliberately take the safe course and emphasize positions that will not offend any voters. Thus, they often trumpet their opposition to corruption, crime, and inflation—things favored, presumably, by few voters. Such a strategy, though perfectly reasonable, makes it extremely difficult for voters to make their issue or policy preferences the basis for their choices at the polls.

Voters' issue choices usually involve a mix of their judgments about the past behavior of competing parties and candidates and their hopes and fears about candidates' future behavior. Political scientists call choices that focus on future behavior **prospective voting**, whereas those based on past performance are called **retrospective voting**. To some extent, whether prospective or retrospective evaluation is more important in a particular election depends on the strategies of competing candidates. Candidates always endeavor to define the issues of an election in terms that will serve their interests. Incumbents running during a period of prosperity will seek to take credit for the economy's happy state and will define the election as revolving around their record of success. This strategy encourages voters to make retrospective judgments. By contrast, an insurgent running during a period of economic uncertainty will tell voters it is time for a change and ask them to make prospective judgments. Thus, Bill Clinton focused on change in 1992 and prosperity in 1996, and through well-crafted media campaigns was able to define voters' agenda of choices.

The Economy As we identify the strategies and tactics employed by opposing political candidates and parties, we should keep in mind that the best-laid plans of politicians often go awry. Election outcomes are affected by a variety of forces that candidates for office cannot fully control. Among the most important of these forces is the condition of the economy. If voters are satisfied with their economic prospects, they tend to support the party in power, while voter unease about the economy tends to favor the opposition. Thus, George H. W. Bush lost in 1992 during an economic downturn even though the American-led victory in the Gulf War had briefly given him a 90 percent favorable rating in the polls just one year earlier. And Bill Clinton won in 1996 during an economic boom even though voters had serious concerns about his moral fiber. As we shall see later in this chapter, the 2008 financial crisis gave Barack Obama and the Democrats a significant advantage. Over the past quarter-century, the Consumer Confidence Index, calculated by the Conference Board, a business research group, has been a fairly accurate predictor of presidential outcomes. The index is based on surveys asking voters how

prospective voting voting based on the imagined future performance of a candidate or political party

retrospective voting voting based on the past performance of a candidate or political party

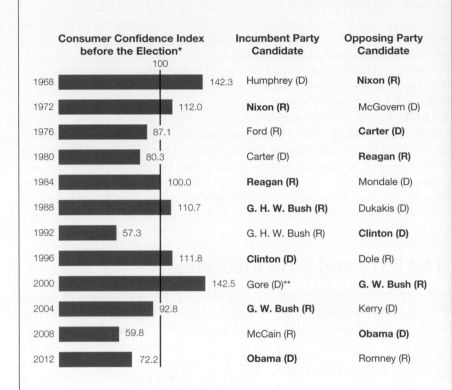

FIGURE 10.6

Consumer Confidence and Presidential Elections

Since 1968 the Consumer Confidence Index has been a fairly reliable predictor of incumbents' political fortunes. Was the result of the 2012 election consistent with this trend? What issues other than the economy influenced the 2012 election?

*Survey was bimonthly prior to 1977 so figures for 1968, 1972, and 1976 are for October and they are for September from 1983 on.

**Gore won the popular vote but Bush was elected by the electoral college.

NOTE: A score above 100 means most people are optimistic about the economy. A score below 100 means most people are pessimistic about the economy. The candidate who won the election appears in bold.

SOURCE: The Conference Board, www .conference-board.org/data/consumerdata .cfm (accessed 11/3/14).

Consumer Confidence Index before the Election* / **Incumbent Party Candidate** / **Opposing Party Candidate**

Year	Index	Incumbent Party Candidate	Opposing Party Candidate
1968	142.3	Humphrey (D)	**Nixon (R)**
1972	112.0	**Nixon (R)**	McGovern (D)
1976	87.1	Ford (R)	**Carter (D)**
1980	80.3	Carter (D)	**Reagan (R)**
1984	100.0	**Reagan (R)**	Mondale (D)
1988	110.7	**G. H. W. Bush (R)**	Dukakis (D)
1992	57.3	G. H. W. Bush (R)	**Clinton (D)**
1996	111.8	**Clinton (D)**	Dole (R)
2000	142.5	Gore (D)**	**G. W. Bush (R)**
2004	92.8	**G. W. Bush (R)**	Kerry (D)
2008	59.8	McCain (R)	**Obama (D)**
2012	72.2	**Obama (D)**	Romney (R)

optimistic they are about the future of the economy. It would appear that a generally rosy view, indicated by a score over 100, augurs well for the party in power. An index score under 100, suggesting that voters are pessimistic about the economy's trend, suggests that incumbents should worry about their own job prospects (see Figure 10.6). The 2012 elections deviated from this pattern, with Obama re-elected despite a Consumer Confidence Index score of 72.2 before the election. But the probability of re-election is high for incumbent presidents, as discussed below, and Obama used the same successful grassroots mobilization ground game in 2008 as in 2012 to turn out loyal supporters, drawing on a very well-funded campaign.

Candidate Characteristics

Candidates' personal attributes always influence voters' decisions. Some political analysts claim that voters prefer tall candidates to short ones, candidates with shorter names to candidates with longer names, and candidates with lighter hair to candidates with darker hair. Perhaps these rather frivolous criteria do play some role. But the more important candidate characteristics that affect voters' choices are race, ethnicity, religion, gender, geography, and social background. In general, voters may be proud to see someone of their ethnic, religious, or geographic background in a position of leadership, and they may presume that such candidates are likely to have views and perspectives close to their own. This is why, for many years, politicians sought to "balance the ticket," making certain that their party's ticket included members of as many important groups as possible.

Just as candidates' personal characteristics may attract some voters, they may repel others. Some voters are prejudiced against candidates from certain ethnic, racial, or religious groups. And for many years, voters were reluctant to support the candidacies of women, although this appears to be changing. Indeed, the fact that in 2008 the Democratic candidate was a black man and the Republican vice-presidential candidate a woman indicates the increasing diversity of candidates for public office.

Voters also pay attention to candidates' personality characteristics, such as "decisiveness," "honesty," and "vigor." In recent years, integrity has become a key election issue. In the 2012 election, Obama's opponents painted him as a weak leader, unable to turn the economy around, defend American industries from China's rising economic power, or defend the nation's interests globally. Romney's opponents said he only cared about the super-rich, at the expense of the working class. He was also portrayed as anti-minority and, ina particular, anti-Latino, as his rhetoric was harsh on illegal immigrants in terms of "self" deportation. However, voters seemed less concerned with these matters than with the ability of the candidates to deal with the nation's economic woes.

for critical analysis

What factors influence voters' choices? What factors matter most to you when you decide how to cast your ballot?

● The 2012 and 2014 Elections

Analyze the strategies, issues, and outcomes of the 2012 and 2014 elections

In the fall of 2012, more than 123 million Americans went to the polls to select a president, members of Congress, governors, and numerous other officials. Voters re-elected Barack Obama to the presidency and confirmed the Democratic Party's control of the Senate and the Republican Party's majority in the House of Representatives. Obama won more than 62 million votes, or roughly 51 percent, while his Republican challenger, Mitt Romney, had received about 59 million votes, or 48 percent. Though the president's margin of victory was about 5 percentage points less than in 2008, it was enough to give him 332 electoral votes to win the constitutionally mandated electoral college majority. The president's solid margin of victory was built on a coalition of women, working-class voters, and minority voters in several key battleground states. Despite the billions of dollars spent by candidates and the hoopla of the campaign, the 2012 election was decided more by demographic realities than political rhetoric.

Generally speaking, incumbent presidents have a substantial advantage when they seek re-election to a second term. During the course of American history, incumbent presidents standing for re-election have won about 70 percent of the time. Furthermore, Obama had won office handily in 2008 over his Republican rival, Senator John McCain. Obama had promised "Change we can believe in," and energized legions of young supporters who saw Obama as an energetic politician who would pursue a progressive social agenda and bring an end to America's wars in the Middle East. Many liberal voters had also been eager to elect America's first black president and thus make a break with the nation's long and unhappy history of racial discrimination. Despite this advantage of incumbency and the optimism his 2008 campaign inspired, the re-election of President Barack Obama in 2012 was never a foregone conclusion.

Once in office, Obama in his first term was eager to make good on his promise of change. He worked to bring an end to the war in Iraq and to wind down the war in Afghanistan, but was only modestly successful. In the realm of domestic policy, between 2008 and 2010, with the cooperation of a Congress controlled by the

Democrats, the president succeeded in bringing about a massive overhaul of America's health care system. Under the terms of what came to be known as "Obamacare," tens of millions of previously uninsured Americans would be required to purchase federally subsidized health insurance policies through state insurance exchanges. Despite some initial doubt, the Supreme Court upheld the main provisions of Obamacare in 2012. The president also signed into law a major new program, the Dodd-Frank Wall Street Reform and Consumer Protection Act, aimed at protecting the nation's financial system from a future crisis like the one that nearly brought about a global financial catastrophe in 2008–09. The act provided for tighter regulation of banks, prohibitions on some risky investment activities, and protections for consumers and borrowers. The president also signed a $700 billion economic stimulus bill to create jobs and spur investment and growth.

Despite the successes claimed by President Obama and his allies, Democrats lost control of the House of Representatives in the 2010 midterm elections. It is often the case that the president's party loses some seats in the midterm elections, but in 2010 the Democrats received a much larger drubbing than usual, losing 60 seats and ceding control of the House to the Republicans. In Senate races, the GOP failed to win enough seats to take control, but with 46 seats, had enough votes to sustain filibusters if necessary. What Obama and the Democrats had viewed as major accomplishments were seen by conservative Republican voters as a series of disasters. These voters saw Obamacare as a costly government takeover of a major industry and an unwarranted intrusion into the lives of Americans. These same voters saw financial reform as a policy that would strangle America's financial services industry. With encouragement and momentum from the Tea Party movement, conservatives defeated numerous members of Congress who had supported Obama and left the president with a Republican House of Representatives that vowed to block any new presidential initiatives. Over the next two years, the president and Congress engaged in acrimonious battles over the federal budget and the federal government's borrowing power (the debt limit) that twice brought the U.S. government to the brink of financial ruin before last-minute compromises temporarily averted disaster.

All the while, the nation's economy, which had been battered by the 2007–08 recession, was showing only tepid signs of recovery. For much of the president's first term, unemployment remained in the uncomfortably high 8–9 percent range; the housing market was weak; a number of major financial institutions seemed tottering on the edge of failure; and job seekers, including hundreds of thousands of recent college graduates, found themselves unemployed or underemployed. Against this backdrop, President Obama's re-election hardly seemed assured. However, the Republicans needed to find a candidate who could defeat the president and appeal to the various factions of their party.

The Republican Nomination Process in 2012

As we saw in Chapter 9, America's two major political parties have witnessed an ideological realignment in the past 40 years that has made both parties more ideologically consistent: the Republican Party is the party of conservatives while the Democratic Party is consistently the party of liberals. However, the growing ideological split between the two parties has not meant that each party is ideologically uniform. In 2012 the Republican nomination was sharply contested by several candidates representing different factions in the party. Former Massachusetts governor and successful

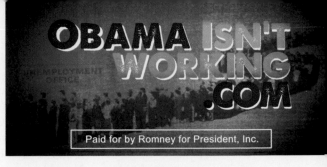

Paid for by Romney for President, Inc.

In 2012, the Romney campaign and other Republican groups attacked Obama's handling of the economy. As a sitting president presiding over a somewhat shaky economy, with unemployment uncomfortably high, Obama's re-election was not a given. In response, the president pointed to the government's investment in infrastructure, a policy he supported and that creates jobs, as well as economic indicators that were finally moving in the right direction.

financier Mitt Romney spoke for fiscal conservatives. Former Pennsylvania senator Rick Santorum and Minnesota congresswoman Michele Bachmann were the champions of the social conservatives. Texas congressman Ron Paul spoke for libertarians, who desire less government in both social and economic realms, and former House Speaker Newt Gingrich represented neoconservatives. Several other candidates, who lacked significant bases of support, including business executive Herman Cain, Texas governor Rick Perry, former Utah governor and ambassador Jon Huntsman, former New Mexico governor Gary Johnson, and former Minnesota governor Tim Pawlenty, sought to stake out positions that might attract supporters if the front-runners faltered. (Divisions among the Democrats were relatively inconsequential for the simple reason that the party's presidential nominee was a given: like it or not, all the party's factions had to accommodate themselves to President Obama.)

In 2011–12 the Republican hopefuls engaged in a series of televised debates where each argued that he (or she) would be best able to defeat the Democrats. Gradually, candidates who found themselves unable to attract strong support dropped out of the race, and by February 2012 only four remained: Gingrich, Paul, Romney, and Santorum. Over the next several months, these four candidates faced one another in a series of Republican primaries and caucuses. Romney's superior organization and financial base made him the front-runner. The GOP's social and religious conservatives, though, were unenthusiastic about the former Massachusetts governor. Some saw him as a liberal in Republican clothing while others, particularly evangelical Protestants, were unhappy about the idea of a member of the Mormon faith leading the party. These groups gave their support to Rick Santorum, who eventually carried 11 states and more than 20 percent of the primary vote. By spring 2012 Romney had clearly won the delegate votes needed for the nomination, and Santorum suspended his campaign. Romney carried 42 states and territories, and Santorum 11.

Having won the Republican nomination, Romney moved to reassure the party's social conservatives that he was worthy of their enthusiastic support in the general election. Conservatives would not jump to the Obama camp, but anything less than enthusiastic participation in the campaign on the part of social conservatives would doom the GOP's ticket to defeat. Accordingly, Romney endorsed a party platform that would appeal to this group. Its provisions included a constitutional amendment to ban abortion; elimination of government-funded family planning programs, with the exception of abstinence training; and a program of detention for "dangerous" aliens. Other provisions included partial privatization of the Medicare program, elimination of the federal income tax, and an end to various forms of federal regulation. Yet, many conservatives remained unconvinced about Romney. Radio talk show hosts such as Glenn Beck and Michael Savage continued to attack the Massachusetts governor.

The 2012 General Election

In recent years, the bedrock base of GOP support has consisted of reasonably affluent, educated, middle-aged, middle-class white men living in suburban and rural areas. The Democrats, on the other hand, have been able to rely upon the votes of a majority of women, less affluent Americans, urban residents, younger voters, African Americans, and, increasingly, Hispanic voters. While there are certainly poor Republicans and affluent Democrats, this split approaches a classic division between the "have mores" and "have lesses." Romney alluded to this division when he said, in what he thought to be a closed-door meeting with Republican donors, that 47 percent of Americans paid few taxes, depended on government handouts, and would never vote for him. When news of Romney's comments leaked, Republicans sought to contain the damage but did not necessarily dispute the accuracy of Romney's analysis.

While America consists of 50 states, presidential elections are usually fought in only 9 or 10 states. This is so because some states are solidly Republican (sometimes called the red states) while others are solidly Democratic (known as the blue states). The states of the Deep South, for example, are so securely in the Republican camp that Democratic presidential candidates hardly bother to campaign there. Most of the states of the Northeast and West Coast, on the other hand, are committed to the Democrats and receive little attention from the GOP. In 2012 opinion polls indicated that only 8 of the 50 states were actually toss-ups. These were Colorado, Florida, Iowa, Nevada, New Hampshire, Ohio, Virginia, and Wisconsin. Here the Obama and Romney campaigns and their various supporters spent hundreds of millions of dollars on television and online advertising, phone banks, voter registration drives, and rallies as well as numerous candidate visits. While voters in many states would hardly have reason to notice the presidential contest, voters in the battleground states could hardly turn on their television sets or answer their phones without being urged to support Obama or Romney.

Of course, while most campaigning was undertaken on a state-by-state basis, the candidates did face one another in one major set of national forums. Some research suggests candidate performance during the debates results in short-term swings in public opinion, but does not have long-term effects on support for the presidential candidates; rather, such factors such as incumbency and the state of economy loom much larger. Nevertheless, presidential debates typically draw a wide audience and educate the public about the candidates. There were three nationally televised presidential debates in 2012 plus one vice-presidential debate. The first presidential debate was watched by 67 million people and was more remarkable for style than substance. The candidates discussed the economy, the federal deficit, Social Security, and the Affordable Care Act, with Romney criticizing Obama's record and the president defending his accomplishments. In terms of style, however, Obama and Romney differed sharply. Governor Romney seemed alert and aggressive, making points assertively and methodically as he accused the president of increasing the nation's debt, failing to bolster the economy, and undermining the private sector in favor of government-run programs. The president, in contrast, appeared disengaged. In the wake of the first debate, the national polls suggested that the race was neck and neck. The president improved his performance in the next two debates and was generally judged to have been the winner, as was Vice President Biden in his confrontation with Republican vice-presidential candidate Paul Ryan.

Obama responded to Romney's assertions in the debates by redoubling his efforts in battleground states, with speeches and campaign commercials labeling Romney a multimillionaire who was out of touch with ordinary Americans and who sent American jobs overseas. The Obama campaign argued that Romney had favored allowing Detroit to go bankrupt, despite the potential loss of hundreds of thousands of jobs. Obama also coined the term *Romnesia*, to suggest that Romney continually changed positions for reasons of expedience and expected voters to forget what his previous positions had been. These efforts succeeded in shoring up Obama's

Romney's remark—made at a private fund-raiser—that 47 percent of Americans were dependent on government and not worth his campaign's time offended many Americans. The issue highlighted the division of the electorate into "have mores" and "have lesses."

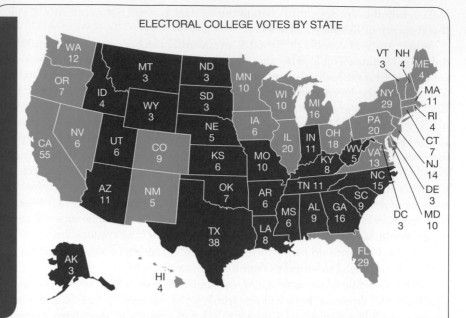

ELECTORAL COLLEGE VOTES BY STATE

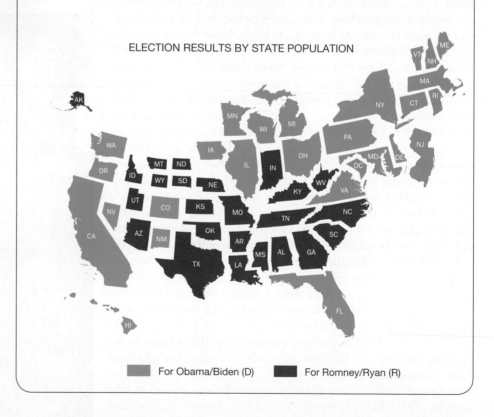

ELECTION RESULTS BY STATE POPULATION

For Obama/Biden (D)   For Romney/Ryan (R)

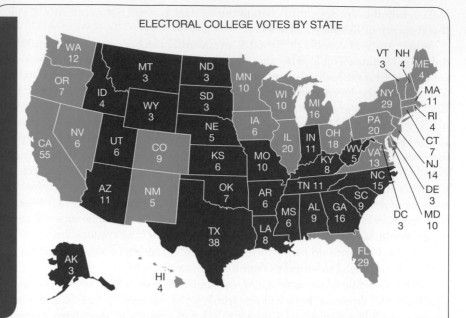

FIGURE 10.7

The 2012 Presidential Election Results

Barack Obama defeated Mitt Romney in the 2012 presidential election, winning 332 votes in the electoral college (62 percent of the total). The top map shows who won each state; there, red seems to dominate. However, if we adjust the map to show each state in proportion to its population, blue states—those won by Obama—clearly dominate.

SOURCE: *Washington Post*, www.washingtonpost.com/wpsrv/special/politics/election-map-2012/president/ (accessed 6/8/14).

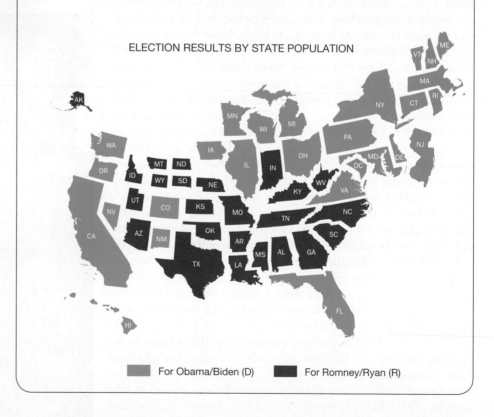

support among working-class Americans. According to exit polls, the president won 63 percent of the votes of those whose family incomes were less than $30,000 per year and 57 percent of those who earned between $30,000 and $49,000 per year.

The Obama campaign also redoubled its efforts among women voters. In recent years, women have tended to give a majority of their votes to the Democrats, producing a so-called gender gap in the electoral arena. Democratic ads reminded women that it was the Democratic Party that supported such issues as equal pay. Foolish remarks on rape and abortion by GOP senatorial candidates in Indiana and Missouri were highlighted by the Democrats to underscore Republican insensitivity to women's concerns. On Election Day, 55 percent of women voters supported Obama, while Romney received the votes of 52 percent of America's men.

Finally, Obama campaign workers were determined to ensure high levels of turnout among minority voters, who potentially could be decisive in several battleground states. African American voters were a loyal Democratic constituency and could be counted upon to turn out for the president. But the Democrats had been making enormous efforts to bring Asian and Latino voters into their camp. Latinos are the most rapidly growing group in the American population and were responsible for about 10 percent of the votes cast in 2012. The Democratic Party had made a major effort to court Latinos on such issues as immigration and, in 2012, Democrats had pushed for ballot initiatives in a number of states that offered undocumented young Latinos who had been raised in the United States the opportunity to attend public colleges at the in-state tuition rate. These so-called "American Dream" referenda not only cemented the relationship between the Democratic Party and the Latino community, but also helped bring Latinos to the polls in large numbers. This strategy proved extremely successful. Not only did Obama capture 93 percent of the African American vote, but he also won approximately 70 percent of the Latino vote across the country. Among whites, by contrast, Romney received 58 percent of the vote.

Taken together, working-class voters, women, and minority constituents gave Obama the votes he needed for victory. This "one-two-three punch" was particularly important in the battleground states (see Figure 10.7). Astonishingly, President Obama carried all the battleground states, and in each one, exit polls suggested that the critical margin was provided by low-income groups, minorities, and women.

The 2014 Midterm Elections

In 2014 Republicans needed to pick up six additional seats to win a majority in the U. S. Senate, and thus control of both houses of Congress. In fact, the GOP gained nine Senate seats, giving it a solid majority. The Republicans also deepened their advantage in the House of Representatives. Immediately after the election, it was clear that the party had won at least 10 additional seats in the House (pending recounts or run-offs in several districts), taking a majority with approximately 244 of the 435 seats, or 55 percent. After six years of Democrats in the White House and eight in majority control in the Senate, party power in the United States flipped to Republican control of Congress.

What explains Republicans' wins in 2014? First, midterm elections tend to favor the Republican Party because the lower voter turnout for midterm elections means that there is a larger proportion of white, older, and affluent voters (who tend to support the Republican Party) as compared to the electorate in higher-turnout presidential elections, which include more young, minority, and less affluent voters (who are more likely to favor the Democrats). The election of 2014 had the lowest voter turnout in a midterm election since World War II; only 36 percent of eligible voters cast a ballot.

Second, President Obama's low approval rating in 2014 contributed to the outcome of the elections, which were widely understood as a referendum on the party of the president. Third, the president's party generally tends to lose seats in midterm elections, giving up some seats that the party gained in the presidential election. This loss is because of the "coattails effect" that occurs in presidential elections: the success of the candidate who wins the presidency helps fellow party members get elected to Congress. Then, in midterm elections, the electorate often reacts against the ideological position and policies of the president's party and supports candidates from the other party. This trend is especially strong when one party has controlled the presidency for two consecutive terms. From 1950 through 2010, there have been seven midterm elections that took place when one party had controlled the presidency for two consecutive terms (during the presidencies of Truman, Eisenhower, Johnson, Reagan, Clinton, and George W. Bush). In these elections, the incumbent president's party lost an average of 29 seats in the House and 6 seats in the Senate. The election results from 2014 fit this pattern.

While the Democrats' losses in Congress may have been expected, the enormous increase in campaign spending was not. A record total of $3.6 billion was spent in the 2014 midterm elections, primarily on 36 Senate races—the most money ever spent on a midterm (non-presidential) election in U.S. history, according to the Center for Responsive Politics.[39] In comparison, the 2012 presidential race between Obama and Romney cost just over $2 billion in total spending by the candidates, parties, and outside groups.

Just a handful of states had highly competitive U.S. Senate races in 2014, and the lion's share of all campaign spending and television advertising was focused on these races. Senate races in North Carolina and Iowa were among the most competitive. The North Carolina 2014 Senate race was the most expensive Senate race in history with $115 million in total spending. Spending by outside groups not affiliated with the candidates or parties (independent expenditures) accounted for $690 million dollars nationwide, the most ever in a midterm election. The majority of this campaign spending was used for radio and television advertising, much of it negative campaign ads. In Iowa, national groups spent millions to affect the race for an open Senate seat, making it the most expensive non-presidential race in the state's history ($85 million); 57,000 political ads aired on television over two months.[40] The small state allowed the campaigns and affiliated outside groups to saturate the airwaves, running back to back political advertisements.

Senate races were also competitive in Kansas, Colorado, Alaska, Georgia, and New Hampshire, with the winning candidate predicted to win by less than 5 percentage points. In the majority of states, however, Senate races were uncompetitive, with the winning candidate predicted to win by a landslide. The least competitive Senate race was in Alabama, where the Republican incumbent ran unchallenged; his probability of winning was 100 percent. Oklahoma and

Wyoming were the second least competitive Senate races, with the Republican candidate predicted to win by a margin of over 30 percentage points.

In House races, a record total of $119 million was spent by the Republican Party, its outside groups, and candidates, and $110 million by the Democratic Party, its outside groups, and candidates. The most expensive House race in terms of independent expenditures was in California's District 7 with a total of $13.3 million spent, followed by Minnesota's District 6 ($12.4 million) and Arizona's District 1 ($11.7 million). These off-the-charts numbers represent a post–*Citizens United* political universe, where groups or corporate interests not affiliated with the candidate campaigns can spend unlimited dollars to influence election outcomes. These trends appear to set the stage for exploding spending in the 2016 presidential election, and they raise concerns that the special interests with the most money will determine outcomes in elections.

As in 2012, early voting was significant in 2014. Ninety million people voted early, or 41 percent of those eligible to do so. Nationwide, 27.5 percent of votes were cast prior to Election Day, up from 25 percent in 2010.[41] Republican congressional candidates improved on their ground game in 2014, with more grassroots organizing, more direct mailings, and a stronger online presence using hybrid media—the intermingling of traditional media (television, radio, and print) and online media (especially social media).

Many commentators described 2014 as a "Republican wave," as the party also won a majority of the nation's governorships. Although the 2014 election was good for Republicans, it was also good for groups supporting a higher minimum wage. Voters in five states endorsed minimum wage increases on Election Day. Significantly, minimum wage initiatives carried the day even in states where Republicans won statewide offices, including Arkansas, Nebraska, and South Dakota.

Campaigns, Elections,
and Your Future

As this chapter has described, one of the key features of American elections is campaign funding. The size of a candidate's campaign war chest affects her ability to micro-target voters with campaign messages, purchase television ads, hire staff and organize volunteers for voter mobilization drives, and open field offices, which, in turn, affects who wins public office. Thus the laws that govern how candidates can raise funds and who can give money are important "rules of the game" that impact election results.

The important role played by private funds in American elections affects the balance of power among contending economic and citizen groups. Politicians need large amounts of money to campaign successfully for major public office. This fact inevitably ties their interests to the interests of the individuals and groups that can provide this money: the affluent and business interests. In a nation as large and diverse as the United States, to be sure, campaign contributors represent many different groups and, often, clashing interests. The fact remains, however, that those with more money will be able to give more; and once in office, elected officials can be expected to represent the interests of those who supported them.

Two trends in campaign finance may play a role in how elections are funded in the future and, thus, who is elected to office and what policies are enacted. On the one hand, recent decisions by the Supreme Court have overturned federal laws that sought to set some limits on who could give and how much they could give. The laws existed in hopes of limiting the influence of affluent interests over the electoral process and government. But the Court has held that giving money is (in some circumstances) a form of political speech that is essential to the country's democratic process. Will moneyed interests continue to play a large role in the election process? What new laws may be needed to make the rules of the game fair? Will campaign spending increase to the point that the citizens of tomorrow enact reform for public financing or free media for qualified candidates?

The Internet is an increasingly important tool in fund-raising. Building on Obama's success in raising money online in 2008, his 2012 campaign introduced a new iPhone app and other new tools for soliciting donations.

The other trend suggests that there is still power in large numbers of small donors. Like other aspects of the political process, campaign donations continued to go digital in 2012. Thirteen percent of American adults donated to one of the presidential candidates in 2012, a higher than average percentage. There are partisan differences in how donations were made: 57 percent of Democratic campaign donors gave online or via email in 2012, compared with just 34 percent of Republican donors. In 2012 the Federal Election Commission allowed political campaigns to accept campaign contributions via text message, and again, Democrats were more likely to contribute using the new technology. The ease and ubiquity of digital media has facilitated political donations to an extent not seen before. As new technologies emerge, will citizens continue to make small donations in large numbers, providing a counterweight to the small number of large donors who give hundreds of thousands of dollars?

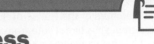

plugin

Inform

Check out 270towin.com, a website that shows how the electoral college system influences presidential campaign strategy. Click states on the 2016 map to see how their electoral votes could change the outcome. How competitive was your state in 2012, 2008, and 2004?

Express

Should some aspects of American elections be reformed? For example, should campaign donations and/or spending be limited more strictly? Should the electoral college be abolished?

Connect

Follow a congressional or presidential candidate on social media, such as Facebook or Twitter. Observe the issues his or her posts address.

Act

Volunteer for a political campaign, and help support a presidential, congressional, or local candidate. Candidate websites have information about getting involved.

studyguide

Elections in America

Describe the major rules and procedures of elections in the United States (pp. 387–98)

American elections are subject to many specific rules. The responsibility for administering elections rests mainly with states and counties, and most elections in the United States today use the Australian ballot and operate under a plurality, rather than majority or proportional representation, system. Unlike members of the House of Representatives, who are elected through a direct vote from districts that are redrawn every 10 years, presidents are elected indirectly by the electoral college.

Key Terms

midterm elections (p. 388)

primary elections (p. 388)

general election (p. 388)

closed primary (p. 388)

open primary (p. 388)

majority system (p. 388)

runoff election (p. 388)

plurality system (p. 388)

proportional representation (p. 389)

straight-ticket vote (p. 389)

redistricting (p. 390)

gerrymandering (p. 390)

majority-minority district (p. 391)

caucus (political) (p. 391)

grassroots politics (p. 391)

party platform (p. 394)

delegate (p. 394)

electoral college (p. 394)

ballot initiative (p. 396)

referendum (p. 396)

recall (p. 397)

Practice Quiz

1. A closed primary is a primary election in which
   a) one's vote is kept private.
   b) only registered members of the party may vote.
   c) only registered members of the party may run.
   d) only two candidates are allowed to run.
   e) voting is conducted by mail.

2. To win under the plurality system used in most American elections a candidate must receive
   a) more than 50 percent of the popular vote.
   b) more than 50 percent in the runoff election.
   c) more than two-thirds of the popular vote.
   d) more than 75 percent of the popular vote.
   e) the most votes, regardless of the percentage.

3. When a voter casts a ballot for a party's presidential candidate and then "automatically" votes for the rest of that party's candidates, it is referred to as
   a) primary voting.
   b) one-way voting.
   c) proportional representation.
   d) straight-ticket voting.
   e) split-ticket voting.

4. If a state has 10 members in the U.S. House of Representatives, how many votes in the electoral college does that state have?
   a) 2
   b) 10
   c) 12
   d) 20
   e) The number of votes cannot be determined from this information.

Election Campaigns

Explain how campaigns are typically conducted (pp. 398–407)

In order to successfully run for national or statewide office, candidates must create formal campaign organizations that employ a campaign manager, a media consultant, a pollster, a financial adviser, a press spokesperson, and a staff director. Campaigns must decide on a message and a strategy for communicating that message to the voters they want to target.

Key Terms

campaign (p. 398)

incumbent (p. 398)

town hall meeting (p. 403)

spot (advertisement) (p. 403)

Practice Quiz

5. An incumbent is a candidate who
   a) does not currently hold office.
   b) has the support of both major parties.
   c) already holds the office he or she is running for.
   d) won the primary election.
   e) has been nominated at the party convention.

6. Since 1980, the average amount of money that House incumbents raise to secure re-election has
   a) been surpassed by the average amount of money spent by challengers.
   b) declined to zero after the passage of the Bipartisan Campaign Reform Act in 2003.
   c) remained the same as the average amount spent by challengers since 1980.
   d) increased at a greater rate than the average amount spent by challengers.
   e) decreased at a greater rate than the average amount spent by challengers.

Money and Politics

Describe how candidates raise the money they need to run (pp. 407–14)

Modern political campaigns in the United States are enormously expensive, and candidates with the most money often win. Supreme Court cases over the past 40 years have removed many restrictions on campaign finance. Candidates finance their campaigns with money from individual donors, political action committees, political parties, independent 527 and 501c(4) groups, and the candidates' own bank accounts. The Federal Elections Campaign Act also provides for public funding of presidential campaigns.

Key Terms

political action committee (PAC) (p. 412)

527 committees (p. 412)

501c(4) committees (p. 412)

Practice Quiz

7. In *Buckley v. Valeo*, the Supreme Court ruled that
   a) PAC donations to campaigns are constitutionally protected.
   b) candidates cannot spend any of their own money to run for office.
   c) the right of individuals to spend their own money to campaign is constitutionally protected.
   d) the political system is corrupt.
   e) the entire Federal Elections Campaign Act is unconstitutional.

8. In the 2012 presidential election, public funding
   a) was accepted by both major-party candidates.
   b) was accepted by Barack Obama only.
   c) was accepted Mitt Romney only.
   d) was declined by both major-party candidates.
   e) was not available.

How Voters Decide

Identify the major factors that influence voters' decisions (pp. 415–18)

Three factors influence the decisions that voters make at the polls: partisan loyalty; issues and policy preferences; and candidate characteristics. Partisan attachments do not change frequently and are an important influence on which candidates a voter chooses to support. Voters may also consider the past and future behavior of competing parties and candidates. A candidate's race, ethnicity, religion, gender, and social background are also weighed by voters on Election Day.

Key Terms

prospective voting (p. 416)

retrospective voting (p. 416)

Practice Quiz

9. Partisan loyalty
   a) is often handed down from parents to children.
   b) changes frequently.
   c) is currently much stronger than it was in the 1940s and 1950s.

d) is mandated in states with closed primaries.
e) has little impact on voting in congressional and state-level elections.

10. When a voter decides which candidate to vote for based on past performance, the voter is engaged in
    a) prospective voting.
    b) retrospective voting.
    c) the coattail effect.
    d) candidate-centered voting.
    e) ticket splitting.

11. The Consumer Confidence Index
    a) measures how business leaders rate the federal government's regulation of the economy during election years.
    b) was a federal government program designed to increase economic growth during the Reagan administration.
    c) has been an inaccurate predictor of presidential outcomes.
    d) has been a fairly accurate predictor of presidential outcomes.
    e) is based on government reports of objective economic indicators.

The 2012 and 2014 Elections

Analyze the strategies, issues, and outcomes of the 2012 and 2014 elections (pp. 418–25)

In the 2012, voters re-elected Barack Obama to the presidency, and Democrats retained control of the Senate while Republicans retained control of the House of Representatives. Throughout the 2012 campaigns both parties argued that they had a better plan for addressing the economic challenges facing the nation and other issues. In the 2014 midterm elections, low turnout and frustration with the Democratic Party helped the Republicans win majorities in both Houses of Congress.

Practice Quiz

12. The biggest issue in the 2012 national elections was
    a) same-sex marriage.
    b) energy policy.
    c) abortion.
    d) the economy.
    e) Medicare.

13. During the 2012 Republican primaries, which faction within the party did Romney represent?
    a) social conservatives
    b) fiscal conservatives
    c) neoconservatives
    d) paleoconservatives
    e) extreme conservatives

14. In 2012, Romney and the Republicans received a majority of votes from
    a) whites, Asian Americans, and young voters.
    b) whites, Latinos, and women.
    c) whites, men, and more affluent voters.
    d) African Americans, women, and more affluent voters.
    e) African Americans, Latinos, and young voters.

For Further Reading

Abramson, Paul, John Aldrich, and David Rohde. *Change and Continuity in the 2008 Elections*. Washington, DC: CQ Press, 2009.

Ackerman, Bruce, and Ian Avres. *Voting with Dollars*. New Haven, CT: Yale University Press, 2004.

Browning, Graeme. *Electronic Democracy.* New York: Cyberage, 2002.

Ginsberg, Benjamin, and Martin Shefter. *Politics by Other Means: Institutional Conflict and the Declining Significance of Elections in America.* New York: W. W. Norton, 1999.

Heilemann, John, and Mark Halperin. *Game Change: Obama and the Clintons, McCain and Palin, and the Race of a Lifetime.* New York: Harper, 2010.

Maass, Matthias. *The World Views of the 2008 U.S. Presidential Election*. New York: Palgrave, 2009.

Nelson, Michael, ed. *The Elections of 2008.* Washington, DC: CQ Press, 2009.

Polsby, Nelson, Aaron Wildavsky, and David Hopkins. *Presidential Elections.* 12th ed. New York: Rowman and Littlefield, 2007.

Raymond, Allen, and Ian Spiegelman. *How to Rig an Election.* New York: Simon & Schuster, 2008.

Schier, Steven. *You Call This an Election?* Washington, DC: Georgetown University Press, 2003.

Wayne, Stephen. *Is This Any Way to Run a Democratic Election?* 3rd ed. Washington, DC: CQ Press, 2007.

Recommended Websites

Center for Voting and Democracy
www.fairvote.org
> The Center for Voting and Democracy is dedicated to open access to voting, equal representation, and a voice for all Americans. Read about some of their electoral reform proposals such as runoff elections, proportional representation, and alternatives to the electoral college.

The Color of Money
www.colorofmoney.org
> Campaign funding affects the balance of power among contending social groups in America. Politicians are tied to groups that provide them with the large amounts of money needed to campaign for major office. This website examines federal campaign contributions with a focus on race and ethnicity to show how campaign money has the potential to skew government policy decisions.

ElectionMail.com
www.electionmail.com
> Are you thinking about running for office? Whether you aspire to be student government president or president of the United States, here you can find links to affordable political printing, including political brochures, campaign literature, and campaign signs.

Federal Election Commission
www.fec.gov
> The Federal Election Commission (FEC) is an independent government agency that was created in 1975 to administer and enforce the Federal Election Campaign Act (FECA). At the official FEC website you can read about the rules and regulations that govern the financing of federal elections and other topics of interest.

JibJab.com
www.jibjab.com
> This website became famous for its political video clips during the 2004 presidential campaign. For a good laugh check out some of the political jokes or rummage through the video archives to find one of the original Bush or Kerry clips.

MultiEducator.com
www.multied.com/elections/
> MultiEducator's History Central website features a major section on elections. Here you can find the history of every U.S. national election, including popular and electoral votes, turnout, and a map of the states carried by each competing candidate.

National Archives and Records Administration
www.archives.gov/federal-register/electoral-college/index.html
> The U.S. National Archives and Records Administration's Electoral College page is a great resource on presidential elections. Find answers to frequently asked questions about our electoral system, read about how electors vote, or try predicting who will win the next presidential election with the electoral college calculator.

OpenSecrets.org
www.opensecrets.org
> Campaign funds come from a variety of sources, including individual donors, political action committees (PACs), self-contributions, independent spending, parties, and public funding. At this site you can research funding for all federal officials, including your own members of Congress.

Project Vote Smart
www.votesmart.org
> Project Vote Smart is a nonpartisan site dedicated to providing citizens with information on political candidates and elected officials. Here you can easily view a candidate's biographical information, position on issues, and voting record, so that you can make an informed choice on Election Day.

Voter Information Services
www.vis.org
> Voter Information Services (VIS) is a nonpartisan, nonprofit organization dedicated to helping interested citizens learn about their elected members of Congress. Here you can obtain a Congressional Report Card for your members of Congress and find out where they stand on the issues.

The use of "fracking" to recover gas has brought environmental groups into conflict with the energy industry. Both sides have tried to influence government regulations related to fracking.

Groups and Interests

11

WHAT GOVERNMENT DOES AND WHY IT MATTERS For the past several years, environmental groups and the nation's energy industry have been locked in a struggle over the issue of "hydraulic fracking." This is a method for recovering natural gas trapped in shale formations deep beneath the earth's surface. The energy industry, which stands to make enormous profits from extracting the gas, asserts that fracking is the key to achieving American energy independence. Environmental groups, on the other hand, argue that fracking produces greenhouse gas emissions, undermines air quality, and contaminates drinking water while discouraging investment in cleaner, renewable forms of energy.

Despite these environmental concerns, large sections of the United States, including tracts in New York, Pennsylvania, and Ohio, are being fracked for their natural gas. Environmental groups appear to be losing the battle. Why? The energy industry, organized in groups such as the Natural Gas Alliance, the Independent Petroleum Association of America, and the American Gas Association, has deployed an army of nearly 800 lobbyists, including former members of Congress and other former high-ranking government officials, to promote their cause on Capitol Hill and in the state capitals. The industry has also spent tens of millions of dollars on advertising and campaign contributions—filling the coffers of Democrats and Republicans alike. Even President Obama, a self-proclaimed environmentalist, declared in his 2011 State of the Union address that natural gas produced in America was an important part of America's energy future.

The case of fracking exemplifies the power of interest groups in action. Tens of thousands of organized groups have formed in the United States, ranging from civic associations to huge nationwide groups such as the National Rifle Association (NRA), whose chief cause is opposition to restrictions on gun ownership, and Common Cause, a public interest group that advocates for such issues as limits on campaign spending. Despite the array of interest groups in American politics, however, not all interests are represented equally, and the results of competition among various interests are not always consistent with the common good. In this chapter we will examine the nature and consequences of interest group politics in the United States.

chaptergoals

- Describe the major types of interest groups and whom they represent (pp. 435–42)

- Describe how interest groups and social groups organize (pp. 442–48)

- Analyze why the number of interest and advocacy groups has grown in recent decades (pp. 448–49)

- Explain how interest groups try to influence government and policy (pp. 449–63)

● Defining Interest Groups

Describe the major types of interest groups and whom they represent

Alexis de Tocqueville, a famous nineteenth-century French writer, once wrote that America was "a nation of joiners."[1] This defining characteristic of American political life has not changed since Tocqueville made his observation. Americans are much more likely to join political and social organizations than people in other countries, and America has more organized interest groups than other nations. Many believe this unique trend has a positive impact on democracy. But others worry that the power wielded by these groups can dominate Congress and the political process at the expense of average citizens and the public welfare.

The framers of the U.S. Constitution also feared the power that could be wielded by organized interests. Yet they believed that interest groups thrived because of liberty—the freedom that all Americans enjoy to organize and to express their views. If the government were given the power to regulate or in any way to forbid efforts by organized interests to interpose themselves in the political process, it would in effect have the power to suppress liberty. The solution to this dilemma was presented by James Madison in the *Federalist Papers* no. 10:

> Take in a greater variety of parties and interests [and] you make it less probable that a majority of the whole will have a common motive to invade the rights of other citizens. . . . [Hence the advantage] enjoyed by a large over a small republic.[2]

According to Madison, a good government encourages multitudes of interests so that no single interest, which he called a "faction," can ever tyrannize (or consistently dominate) the others. Expanding the arena of contestation from local to state government, and from state to the federal government, should make it more likely that there are overlapping and cross-cutting interests (or factions) where a majority cannot systematically tyrannize a minority. The basic assumption is that all the competing interests will regulate one another, producing balance.[3]

Today, this Madisonian principle is called **pluralism**. Pluralism is a theory of democracy based on the balancing of interests in society via groups that compete for policy outcomes from government. While an interest group may lose on one issue, it may win on the next, and overall the vast majority of society will be represented in government. According to pluralist theory, all interests are and should be free to compete for influence. Moreover, according to pluralist doctrine, the outcome of this competition is compromise and moderation, since no group is likely to be able to achieve any of its goals without accommodating itself to some of the views of its many competitors.[4]

Some observers believe that the pluralist vision is realized in America's political system. Political scientist Robert Dahl, for example, argues that a pluralist system where interest groups compete against one another for representation by elected officials will benefit all groups by allowing groups representing a minority to beat an apathetic majority on issues that are especially important (or salient) to the minority.[5]

An **interest group** is an organized group of people that makes policy-related appeals to government. This definition of interest groups includes membership organizations (citizen groups) as well as businesses, corporations, universities, unions, and other institutions that restrict membership to particular occupational groups

pluralism the theory that all interests are and should be free to compete for influence in the government; the outcome of this competition is compromise and moderation

interest group individuals who organize to influence the government's programs and policies

Although public school teachers are a minority of the total population, they are an influential interest group in many states because they are highly informed and act as a group in support of issues related to their profession, including teachers' salaries.

or other categories of persons. Individuals form groups to increase the chance that their views will be heard and their interests treated favorably by the government. Interest groups are sometimes referred to as "lobbies," "special interests," or "pressure groups." They are also sometimes confused with political action committees (PACs), which are groups that raise and distribute money for use in election campaigns (see Chapter 10). Many interest groups create PACs in their name to be the money-giving arm of the interest group. For example, the National Rifle Association PAC donates money to political candidates and officeholders on behalf of the National Rifle Association, which represents the interests of gun owners. One final distinction is that interest groups are also different from political parties: interest groups tend to concern themselves with the *policies* of government; parties tend to concern themselves with the *personnel* of government in that parties organize to win elected office and interest groups do not.

The number of interest groups in the United States is enormous, and millions of Americans are members of one or more groups, at least to the extent of paying dues or attending an occasional meeting. By representing the interests of such large numbers of people and encouraging political participation, organized groups can and do enhance American democracy. Organized groups educate and mobilize their members for elections and grassroots lobbying efforts, thus encouraging participation in politics. Groups lobby members of Congress and the executive, engage in litigation, and generally represent their members' interests in the political arena. Interest groups also monitor government programs to make certain that these programs do not adversely affect their members. In all these ways, organized interests can be said to promote democratic politics.

Because not all interests are represented equally, interest group politics works to the advantage of some and the disadvantage of others, and not all organized interests are successful. Organized interest groups in the United States are predominantly economic groups: groups working on behalf of businesses and industry far outweigh citizen groups in terms of their number of registered lobbyists in Washington, D.C., and state capitals, and in their financial resources to influence government and elections. The ability of economic groups to mobilize resources often results in legislative victories. Examples of such groups include the oil and gas industries, telecommunication firms, pharmaceutical companies, and trial lawyers.

But even large groups that are well represented in Washington are sometimes defeated in political struggle. On January 18, 2012, the Recording Industry Association of American (RIAA) received a political blow when antipiracy legislation it promoted in Congress—known as SOPA and PIPA—was defeated by a massive online protest. Thousands of websites blacked out their content to protest the proposed legislation that threatened free speech and Internet freedom. Wikipedia reports more than 162 million people viewed its protest banner and Google collected over 7 million signatures to boycott companies and supporting the legislation.

Common Types of Interest Groups

Economic and Corporate Groups Interest groups come in as many shapes and sizes as the interests they represent. The most obvious are groups with a direct economic interest in governmental policy. Businesses and corporations make up over 41 percent of those registered to lobby in Washington, with trade associations comprising another 22 percent and labor unions just 2 percent of groups registered to lobby.[6] Trade associations are generally supported by groups of producers or manufacturers in a particular economic sector, such as the National Association of Manufacturers, American Fuel and Petrochemical Manufacturers, the Recording Industry Association of America, and the American Farm Bureau Federation. Trade associations care about broad industrywide issues that are important to them, and they lobby and make financial contribution to gain access to elected officials. In addition to these broadly representative groups, specific companies, such as Dow Chemical, Dupont, AT&T, Apple, Microsoft, Comcast, Exxon, and General Motors, may be active in Washington on certain issues that are of particular concern to them. Combined, over 6 in 10 groups lobbying in Washington represent businesses, corporations, or trade associations.

Which industry contributes the most to federal candidates? The website Open Secrets lists the top industries contributing to members of the 113th Congress in 2013 (see Table 11.1). Interestingly, nearly the same industries rank among the top funders for both Democrat and Republican members of Congress.

Labor Groups Labor organizations are equally active lobbyists as corporate economic groups. The AFL-CIO, the United Mine Workers, and the Teamsters all lobby on behalf of organized labor. In recent years, groups have arisen to further the interests of public employees, the most significant among these being the American Federation of State, County, and Municipal Employees (AFSCME). However, according to one study, labor unions represent just 2 percent of the total number of interest groups registered to lobby in Washington.[7]

While other economic groups far outweigh unions in sheer number in the nation's capital, average spending on lobbying and campaign contributions tells a somewhat different picture. Unions in fact have the highest average PAC spending, followed by businesses and corporate groups, then professional associations. While there may be fewer organized unions, they wield influence through lobbying efforts and targeted contributions to political campaigns.

Wealthy corporate interest groups usually find it easier to gain attention from elected officials than do other types of groups. Here, Maine governor Paul LePage speaks at a news conference to discuss a report from the Pharmaceutical Research and Manufacturers of America (PhRMA), an interest group representing biopharmaceutical companies and researchers.

TABLE 11.1

Top Industries Contributing to Members of Congress, 2013

RANK	INTEREST GROUP	TOTAL ($)	PERCENTAGE TO DEMOCRATS	PERCENTAGE TO REPUBLICANS
1	Lawyers/law firms	14,888,218	70	30
2	Retired	11,848,809	46	54
3	Securities/investments	11,531,593	46	54
4	Health professionals	10,814,554	38	62
5	Insurance	9,389,222	38	62
6	Real estate	9,182,372	47	53
7	Leadership PACs	8,576,885	44	56
8	Oil and gas	6,463,740	16	84
9	Pharmaceuticals/health products	5,645,953	42	58
10	Lobbyists	5,602,638	50	50
11	Electric utilities	5,330,949	36	64
12	Commercial banks	5,140,048	31	69
13	TV/movies/music	4,706,207	60	39
14	Building trade unions	4,191,283	83	17
15	Manufacturing distribution (miscellaneous)	4,055,258	34	66

SOURCE: Center for Responsive Politics, www.opensecrets.org/industries/mems.php (accessed 12/16/13).

Professional Associations Professional lobbies such as the American Bar Association and the American Medical Association (AMA) have been particularly successful at furthering their members' interests in state and federal legislatures. Professional associations comprise 9 percent of the total number of groups lobbying in Washington. Financial institutions, represented by organizations such as the American Bankers Association and the National Savings and Loan League, although often less visible than other lobbies, also play an important role in shaping legislative policy.

Citizen Groups (or Public Interest Groups) Recent years have witnessed the growth of a powerful "public interest" lobby, purporting to represent the general good rather than its own economic interests. **Citizen groups** have been most

citizen groups groups that claim they serve the general good rather than only their own particular interests

visible in the consumer protection and environmental policy areas, although public interest groups cover a broad range of issues. Citizen groups comprise only 14 percent of the groups registered to lobby in Washington. However, a survey of 315 lobbyists and government officials about 98 randomly selected policy issues found that citizen groups were more likely to be mentioned as being influential in the debate than any other type of group.[8]

The Natural Resources Defense Council, the Sierra Club, the National Civic League, and Common Cause are all examples of public interest groups. Claims to represent *only* the public interest should be viewed with caution, however: it is not uncommon to find decidedly private interests seeking to hide behind the term *public interest*. For example, the benign-sounding Partnership to Protect Consumer Credit is a coalition of credit card companies fighting for less federal regulation of credit abuses, and Project Protect is a coalition of logging interests promoting increased timber cutting.[9]

Ideological Groups Closely related to and overlapping with public interest groups are ideological groups, organized in support of a particular political or philosophical perspective. The National Right to Life and the Christian Coalition, for example, promote conservative values and social goals, such as opposing same-sex marriage. The National Taxpayers Union campaigns to reduce the size of the federal government. Liberal-leaning groups, including EMILY's List and MoveOn.org, support causes such as women's representation and increasing the minimum wage.

Public-Sector Groups The perceived need for representation on Capitol Hill has generated a public-sector lobby in the past several years, including the National League of Cities, the National Conference of State Legislatures, the National Governor's Association, and the "research" lobby. The latter group comprises think tanks and universities that have an interest in obtaining government funds for research and support, and it includes such diverse institutions as Harvard University, the Brookings Institution, and the American Enterprise Institute. Indeed, universities have expanded their lobbying efforts even as they have reduced faculty positions and course offerings.[10] These groups represent 12 percent of the total number of groups lobbying in Washington.

What Interests Are Not Represented?

It is difficult to categorize unrepresented interests precisely because they are not organized and are not able to represent to government their identity and their demands. The political scientist David Truman referred to these interests as "potential interest groups."[11] And he is undoubtedly correct that at any time, as long as there is freedom, any interest shared by a lot of people can develop through "voluntary association" into a genuine interest group that can demand, usually successfully. But the fact remains that many widely shared interests are not represented by organized groups. Two such "potential" groups are the homeless and the poor. Both groups have shared interests in policy outcomes, such as job programs and affordable housing. But the groups lack organization through which to press these concerns.[12]

Unequal Representation and the Upper-Class Bias of Group Membership
Despite the benefits of interest groups in terms of mobilizing and educating the

Interest Group Membership

In his famous 1835 work *Democracy in America,* the French thinker Alexis de Tocqueville stated that "In no country in the world has the principle of association been more successfully used, or more unsparingly applied to a multitude of different objects, than in America."[a] Since then, a multitude of scholars have noted that the United States is a "nation of joiners," with more people active in various groups than almost any other country in the world.

Why is group membership higher in the United States than in many other countries? Part of the explanation has to do with demographics and economics. People who are employed full time, more educated, and wealthier are more likely to join voluntary organizations.[b] This finding helps explain why membership is lower in developing countries like Turkey or Chile, where much of the population still lacks the time and resources to make joining more feasible. Americans also tend to believe that participation in community affairs is an important part of good citizenship, an idea that some scholars say is related to the institutions of American government and the nature of the Constitution.[c]

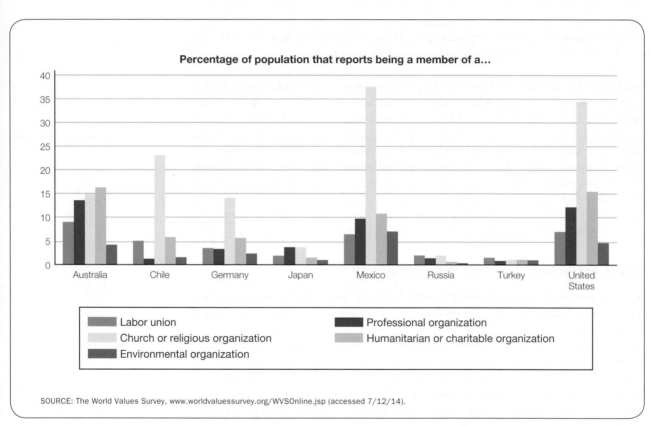

Percentage of population that reports being a member of a...

Legend:
- Labor union
- Church or religious organization
- Environmental organization
- Professional organization
- Humanitarian or charitable organization

SOURCE: The World Values Survey, www.worldvaluessurvey.org/WVSOnline.jsp (accessed 7/12/14).

[a]Alexis de Tocqueville, *Democracy in America* (New York: W. W. Norton, 2007), chap. 12.
[b]James E. Curtis, Edward G. Grabb, and Douglas E. Baer, "Voluntary Association Membership in Fifteen Countries: A Comparative Analysis," *American Sociological Review* 57, no. 2 (1992): 139–52.
[c]Gabriel Almond and Sidney Verba, *The Civil Culture: Political Attitudes and Democracy in Five Nations* (Newbury Park, CA: Sage Publications, 1989), p. 127.

Not all groups organize to promote their common interests. Those who are well-educated and well-off financially are more likely to have the time, money, and skills needed to organize and mobilize an interest group. One result is that the needs of such groups as the homeless are often not heard in political debate.

public and the arguments in favor of pluralism, there are concerns about the influence of special interests in the United States. One long-standing critic is E. E. Schattschneider, who argued in a famous quote, "The flaw in the pluralist heaven is that the heavenly chorus sings with a strong upper-class accent."[13] Critics contend pressure politics, or interest group politics, is heavily skewed in favor of corporate, business, and upper-class groups, leaving those with lower socioeconomic status less able to participate in and influence politics.

This is because membership in interest groups is not randomly distributed in the population. People with higher incomes, higher levels of education, and management or professional occupations are much more likely to become members of groups than are those who occupy the lower rungs on the socioeconomic ladder.[14] Well-educated, upper-income business and professional people are more likely to have the time, money, concerns, and skills needed to play a role in a group or association. Moreover, for business and professional people, group membership may provide personal contacts and access to information that can help advance their careers. At the same time, of course, corporate entities—businesses and the like—usually have ample resources to form or participate in groups that seek to advance their interests.

The result is that interest group politics in the United States tends to have a pronounced upper-class bias. Certainly, many interest groups and political associations have a working- or lower-class membership—labor organizations or welfare-rights organizations, for example—but the vast majority of interest groups and their members are drawn from the middle and upper-middle classes. In general, the "interests" served by interest groups are the interests of society's "haves." Even when interest groups take opposing positions on issues and policies, the conflicting positions they espouse usually reflect divisions among upper-income strata rather than conflicts between the upper and lower classes. When the political system is run by interest groups, democracy will be unequal since interest groups primarily cater to those with high socioeconomic status.

Schattschneider believed that in order to have equal representation in government America needed strong competitive, responsible political parties willing and able to mobilize the lower classes and nonvoters. That is, citizens from the bottom rungs of the socioeconomic ladder must be organized on the massive scale associated with political parties. Competitive political parties provide alternative choices so that the public can participate in the government's decision-making process.

for critical analysis

What interest groups are you familiar with, from personal experience or the news? Whose interests do those groups represent?

While interest groups benefit from a limited scope, political parties must expand political conflict to the public arena to win elections. When political parties compete with one another to win elections, they have incentives to continually expand political discussion to nonvoting members of the electorate to gain a majority of voters. Finally, political parties must also act "responsibly" by informing the public of salient political issues in the public interest, not narrow economic interests.

By representing broad public interests not represented by economic interest groups, competitive parties should bring more equal representation to democracy. Thus, the relative importance of political parties and interest groups in American politics has far-ranging implications for the distribution of political power in the United States, and for how well the interests of America's lower and middle classes are represented. (To be fair, some public interest groups, membership groups, and netroots groups, discussed below, seek to educate and inform the public and bring in new members.)

netroots grassroots online activist organizations that have redefined membership and fund-raising practices and streamlined staff structure

● How Groups Organize

Describe how interest groups and social groups organize

Although interest groups are many and varied, most share certain key organizational components. These include leadership, money, an agency or office, and members.

Leadership and decision-making structure is critical for group organization. For some groups, this structure is very simple. For others, it can be quite elaborate and involve hundreds of local chapters that are melded into a national apparatus. Interest group leadership is, in some respects, analogous to business leadership. Political entrepreneurs initially organize interest groups with a strong commitment to a particular set of goals. Such entrepreneurs see the formation of a group as a means both for achieving those goals and for enhancing their own influence in the political process. And just as is true in the business world, successful groups often become bureaucratized; a paid professional staff replaces the initial entrepreneurial leadership. In the 1960s, for example, Ralph Nader led a ragtag band of consumer advocates (Nader's Raiders) in a crusade for product safety that resulted in the enactment of numerous laws and regulations, such as the requirement that all new cars be equipped with seat belts. Today, Nader remains active in the consumer movement, and his loosely organized band of raiders has been transformed into a well-organized and well-financed phalanx of interlocking groups led by professional staff.

New **netroots** or online advocacy groups often have a streamlined staff structure with little bureaucracy. However, entrepreneurship may be even more important in the world of organizing online. As computer scientist Clay Shirky explains in *Here Comes Everybody*, the Internet has given rise to a proliferation of online organizations without formal organizing structures: Shirky asks what happens when the Internet and social media allow peole to do things together without traditional formal organizations.[15] Examples include Wikipedia, whose content is provided by volunteers from around the world. But the real impact of the digital

The consumer activist Ralph Nader successfully established a network of consumer advocacy groups that has endured for 50 years. One of his earliest campaigns was to support mandatory airbags in cars.

media revolution is not politics without groups but is the advent of new forms of organization. Leadership remains a priority for online organizations. Shirky explains that a small group of leader-organizers will contribute the vast majority of effort necessary to make the group a success. Entrepreneurship and leadership are important for all interest groups, but especially so for those with little staff and formal organization, as the leader holds the organization together.

The second key organizational component of interest groups is a financial structure capable of sustaining the organization and funding the group's activities. Because the cost of maintaining online organizations is lower than for traditional groups, more and varied types of netroots will be able to form and succeed. Most interest groups rely on membership dues or voluntary contributions from sympathizers. Many also sell some ancillary services to members, such as insurance and vacation tours. In addition, many groups establish an agency that actually carries out the group's tasks. This may be a research organization, a public relations office, or a lobbying office in Washington or a state capital.

Finally, almost all interest groups must attract and keep members, whether membership is defined formally or informally. Groups must persuade individuals to invest the money, time, energy, or effort required to take part in the group's activities. Members play a larger role in some groups than in others. In **membership associations**, group members actually serve on committees and engage in projects. In the case of labor unions, members pay significant dues and attend rallies or march in picket lines; in the case of political or ideological groups, members may participate in demonstrations and protests. In another set of groups, **staff organizations**, a professional staff conducts most of the group's activities; members are called on only to pay dues and make other contributions. Among the well-known public interest groups, some, such as the National Organization for Women (NOW), are membership groups; others, such as Defenders of Wildlife and the Children's Defense Fund, are staff organizations.

The "Free-Rider" Problem Whether they need individuals to volunteer or merely to write checks, both types of groups need to recruit and retain members. Yet many groups find this task difficult, even when it comes to recruiting members who agree strongly with the group's goals. Why? As the economist Mancur Olson explains, the benefits of a group's success are often broadly available and cannot be denied to nonmembers.[16] Such benefits can be called **collective goods**. This term is usually associated with certain government benefits, but it can also be applied to beneficial outcomes of interest group activity.

Olson offers this example: suppose a number of private property owners live near a mosquito-infested swamp. Each owner wants this swamp cleared. But if one or a few of the owners were to clear the swamp alone, their actions would benefit all the other owners as well, without any effort on the part of those other owners. Each of the inactive owners would be a **free rider** on the efforts of the ones who cleared the swamp. Thus, there is a disincentive for any of the owners to undertake the job alone. Since the number of concerned owners is small in this particular case, they might eventually be able to organize themselves to share the costs as well as to enjoy the benefits of clearing the swamp.

But suppose the number of interested people is increased. Suppose the common concern is not the neighborhood swamp but polluted air or groundwater involving thousands or even millions of residents. National defense is the most obvious collective good whose benefits are shared by all residents, regardless of the taxes they pay or the support they provide. As the number of involved persons increases, or as the size

membership association
an organized group in which members play a substantial role, sitting on committees and engaging in group projects

staff organization a type of membership group in which a professional staff conducts most of the group's activities

collective goods benefits sought by groups that are broadly available and cannot be denied to nonmembers

free riders those who enjoy the benefits of collective goods but did not participate in acquiring or providing them

of the group increases, the free-rider phenomenon becomes more of a problem. The group would no doubt be more influential if all concerned individuals were active members—if there were no free riders. This collective action problem is one of the major reasons why many groups do not form.

Why Join Groups? Individuals do not have much incentive to become active members and supporters of a group that is already working more or less on their behalf. To overcome this free-rider problem, groups can offer members "selective benefits" available only to group members. These benefits can be informational, material, solidary, or purposive. Of course, groups sometimes offer combinations of benefits. A community association, for example, can offer its members a sense of belonging (solidary benefit), involvement in community decision making (purposive benefit), and reduced rates on homeowners' insurance (material benefit) or a community swimming pool (material benefit). Table 11.2 gives some examples of the range of benefits in each of these categories.

Informational benefits are the most widespread and important category of selective benefits offered to group members. Information is provided through online communication such as email, conferences, training programs, and newsletters and other periodicals sent automatically to those who have paid membership dues. **Material benefits**

informational benefits special newsletters, periodicals, training programs, conferences, and other information provided to members of groups to entice others to join

material benefits special goods, services, or money provided to members of groups to entice others to join

---

TABLE 11.2

Selective Benefits of Interest Group Membership

CATEGORY	BENEFITS
Informational benefits	Conferences
	Professional contacts
	Publications
	Coordination among organizations
	Research
	Legal help
	Professional codes
	Collective bargaining
Material benefits	Travel packages
	Insurance
	Discounts on consumer goods
Solidary benefits	Friendship
	Networking opportunities
Purposive benefits	Advocacy
	Representation before government
	Participation in public affairs

SOURCE: Adapted from Jack Walker, Jr., *Mobilizing Interest Groups in America: Patrons, Professions, and Social Movements* (Ann Arbor: University of Michigan Press, 1991), p. 86.

include anything that can be measured monetarily, such as gifts, discount purchasing, shared advertising and, perhaps most valuable of all, health and retirement insurance. **Solidary benefits** include the friendship and networking opportunities that membership provides. Extremely important to many of the newer citizen groups and netroots is "consciousness raising," including the satisfaction of working toward a common goal with like-minded individuals. One example of this can be seen in the claims of many women's organizations that active participation conveys to each member an enhanced sense of her own value and a stronger ability to advance individual as well as collective rights. Members of associations based on ethnicity, race, or religion also derive solidary benefits from interacting with individuals they perceive as sharing their own backgrounds, values, and perspectives.

A fourth type of benefit involves the appeal of the purpose of an interest group. An example of these **purposive benefits** is businesses joining trade associations to further their economic interests. Similarly, individuals join consumer, environmental, or other civic groups to pursue goals important to them. Many of the most successful interest groups of the past 20 years have been citizen groups or public interest groups organized largely around shared ideological goals, including government reform, election and campaign reform, civil rights, economic equality, "family values," and even opposition to government itself.

solidary benefits selective benefits of group membership that emphasize friendship, networking, and consciousness raising

purposive benefits selective benefits of group membership that emphasize the purpose and accomplishments of the group

The Internet and Interest Groups

How interest groups foster participation in politics and sustained collective action by citizens is changing because of the Internet. Political scientist and former vice president of the Sierra Club David Karpf argues in a new book that digital media and social media have created a new kind of interest group politics in America that has revolutionized political advocacy. New netroots political associations, such as the liberal-leaning MoveOn.org and conservative-leaning Americans for Prosperity, have arisen in the past decade to play an increasingly important role in citizen participation in politics. These grassroots online activist organizations have redefined membership and fund-raising practices via innovative methods for communicating with their members, measuring the opinions of their members, and moving their members into action—both in terms of influencing public opinion and working on behalf of the organization.[17]

Traditional interest groups are expensive to organize (which is one reason why group membership has an upper-class bias), and they rely on professional advocates and direct mail. They are also slow to change. By contrast, netroots associations are relatively inexpensive to organize and are quick to adapt to an ever-changing world of politics. Rather than requiring an annual membership fee to join, like traditional interest groups, membership in netroots is free and is defined by receiving emails/communication from the group or working on behalf of the group. Targeted fund-raising drives over local, state, or federal government legislation, a salient event, or an election is how the organization raises funds to maintain the organization, rather than through annual dues. While most traditional interest groups are focused on a single issue—for instance, the Sierra Club seeks protection of the environment while AARP (formerly the American Association of Retired Persons) lobbies on behalf of the elderly—netroots associations are often issue generalists that have a wide umbrella of issues for which they lobby.

Netroots groups are less expensive to organize because they have a streamlined staff structure with fewer staff who often work from virtual offices. In contrast,

MoveOn.org pioneered a new model of interest group membership and operations. Founded in 1998 and claiming 2 million members, MoveOn seeks to leverage technology to lower the barriers to political participation. This model has since been replicated by other interest groups

traditional interest groups must maintain offices in Washington, D.C., and other regional locations. The modified staff structure of netroots groups engages in different work routines that prioritize communication with members through email, Twitter, and other digital platforms rather than mailing expensive glossy newsletters or engaging in direct lobbying of members of Congress. Netroots associations employ grassroots strategies to pressure elected officials, including using online media to organize rallies, fund-raising events, letter-writing campaigns, boycotts, and protests. Membership and fund-raising practices that were pioneered by MoveOn.org have spread across the political advocacy system to more traditional interest groups. Netroots groups may improve representation for citizens, counteracting the disproportionate influence of business and corporate interests in Washington.

Netroots organizations may also differ from traditional groups in the types of benefits they offer members, as the cases of MoveOn and AARP illustrate.

MoveOn and the Benefits of Membership Rather than offering members material selective incentives to join the group, online activist groups like MoveOn offer informational selective benefits to members via daily or weekly news updates and solidary benefits of volunteering or donating money on behalf of the organization. Unlike mainstream media, netroots are decidedly partisan in the information they provide members. In addition netroots associations offer their members purposive benefits—the knowledge that one is contributing to a dearly held cause. Purposive benefits may be the most important of all in maintaining the new online citizen advocacy groups.

AARP and the Benefits of Membership One group that has been extremely successful in recruiting members and mobilizing them for political action is

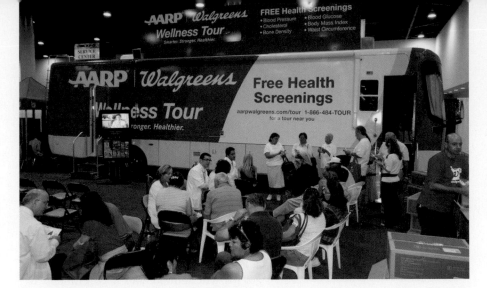

AARP is one of the largest interest groups in the country. One way that AARP attracts members is through selective benefits, such as hotel discounts, affordable health insurance, credit and identity theft protection, and free health tests, like this one in Miami Beach, Florida. These benefits attract members who remain invested in AARP's success because they enjoy tangible benefits from membership.

AARP. The organization was founded as the American Association of Retired Persons in 1958 as a result of the efforts of a retired California high school principal, Ethel Percy Andrus, to find affordable health insurance for herself and the thousands of members of the National Retired Teachers Association (NRTA). For the insurer, it provided an expanded market; for Andrus, it was a way to serve the ever-growing elderly population, whose problems and needs were expanding along with their numbers and their life expectancy. Today, AARP is a large and powerful organization with 38 million members and an annual income of $900 million. In addition, the organization receives $90 million in federal grants. Its national headquarters in Washington, D.C., staffed by nearly 3,000 full-time employees, is so large that it has its own zip code. Its monthly periodical, *AARP: The Magazine*, has a circulation larger than that of America's leading newsmagazines.

How did this large organization overcome the free-rider problem and recruit 38 million older people as members? First, no other organization has ever more successfully provided the selective benefits necessary to overcome the free-rider problem. It helps that AARP began as an organization to provide affordable health insurance for aging members rather than as an organization to influence public policy. But that fact only strengthens the argument that members need short-term individual benefits if they are to invest effort in a longer-term and less concrete set of benefits. As AARP evolved into a political interest group, its leadership added more selective benefits for individual members. It provided guidance against consumer fraud, offered low-interest credit cards, evaluated and endorsed products that were deemed valuable to members, and provided auto insurance and a discounted mail-order pharmacy.

The resources of AARP are so extensive that its leadership has been able to mobilize itself on issues of importance to the group. One of its most successful methods of mobilization for political action is the "telephone tree," with which AARP leaders can quickly mobilize thousands of members for and against proposals that affect Social Security, Medicare, and other questions of security for the aging. A "telephone tree" in each state enables the state AARP chair to phone all of the AARP district directors, who then can phone the presidents of the dozens of local chapters, who can call their local officers and individual members. Within 24 hours, thousands of individual AARP members can be contacting local, state, and national officials to express their opposition to proposed legislation. It is no wonder that AARP is respected and feared throughout Washington. Other

for critical analysis

Why aren't college students organized more effectively as an interest group? What issues would such a group advocate? What might be some impediments to the creation of a National Organization of College Students?

organizations have borrowed strategy from AARP, creating digital versions of the telephone tree using social media and email to allow members to contact their elective representatives over important policy issues.

● The Growth of Interest and Advocacy Groups

> **Analyze why the number of interest and advocacy groups has grown in recent decades**

Interest groups and concerns about them are not new phenomena. As long as there is government, as long as government makes policies that add value or impose costs, and as long as there is liberty to organize, interest groups will abound; and if government expands, so will interest groups. There was, for example, a spurt of growth in the national government during the 1880s and '90s, arising largely from the first government efforts at economic intervention to fight large monopolies and to regulate some aspects of interstate commerce. In response, a parallel spurt of growth occurred in national interest groups, including the imposing National Association of Manufacturers (NAM) and numerous other trade associations. Many groups organized around specific agricultural commodities as well. This period also marked the beginning of the expansion of trade unions as interest groups. Later, in the 1930s, interest groups with headquarters and representation in Washington began to grow significantly, concurrent with that decade's historic and sustained expansion within the national government (see Chapter 3).

Over the past half-century there has been an even greater increase both in the number of interest groups seeking to play a role in the American political process and in the extent of their opportunity to influence that process. Interest and advocacy groups have become much more numerous, more active, and more influential in American politics, with lobby groups and Super PACs playing major roles in Congress and in electoral politics. This explosion of interest group activity has two basic origins: first, the expansion of the role of government during this period, and second, the coming-of-age of a new and dynamic set of political forces in the United States—forces that have relied heavily on "public interest" groups to advance their causes.

The Expansion of Government

Modern governments' extensive economic and social programs have powerful politicizing effects, often sparking the organization of new groups and interests. The activities of organized groups are usually viewed in terms of their effects on governmental action. But interest group activity is often as much a consequence as an antecedent of governmental programs. Even when national policies begin as responses to the appeals of pressure groups, government involvement in any area can be a powerful stimulus for political organization and action by those whose interests are affected.

For example, during the 1970s, expanded federal regulation of the automobile, oil, gas, education, and health care industries impelled each of these interests to increase substantially its efforts to influence the government's behavior. These efforts, in turn, spurred the organization of other groups to augment or counter the activities of the first.[18] Similarly, federal social programs have sparked political organization. For example, federal programs and court decisions in such areas as abortion and school prayer were one factor leading to the rise of fundamentalist religious groups. Thus, the expansion of government in recent decades has also stimulated increased group activity and organization.

Like the federal government, the states too have expanded their scope of government, and have likewise witnessed a growth in the number and diversity of interest groups. But interest group activity isn't uniform across the states, and scholars have measured this activity in a variety of sophisticated ways. One study used the number of trade associations to stand in for the number of interest groups for the years 1990–2005. The researcher found that large-population, affluent states with higher per capita income and higher government expenditures have more trade associations than other states. These large-population, affluent states legislate on more policy areas, and thus activate the business community to lobby to protect their economic interests. Economists call this rent seeking.[19]

Public interest groups often advocate for interests that are not addressed by traditional lobbies. For example, in addition to many other activities, the Public Interest Research Group (PIRG) publishes an annual toy safety report to help protect consumers and to encourage policy makers to address problems in this area.

Growth of Public Interest Groups in the 1960s and '70s

The second factor accounting for the explosion of interest group activity was the emergence of a new set of forces in American politics that can collectively be called the New Politics movement, which began in the 1960s and '70s. For this group of upper-middle-class professionals and intellectuals, the civil rights and antiwar movements were formative political experiences. They formed groups to crusade against racial discrimination and the Vietnam War, and this experience taught them the political efficacy of organized group activity to affect politics. In more recent years, these men and women have focused attention on issues such as environmental protection, women's rights, rights for gay men and lesbians, and nuclear disarmament.

Members of this movement founded or strengthened public interest groups such as Common Cause, the Sierra Club, the Environmental Defense Fund, and NOW. Such groups were able to influence the media, Congress, and even the judiciary, and enjoyed a remarkable degree of success during the late 1960s and early 1970s in securing the enactment of environmental, consumer, and occupational health and safety legislation. Technology aided in the rise and success of these public interest groups. In the 1970s and '80s, computerized direct-mail campaigns allowed public interest groups to reach hundreds of thousands of potential sympathizers and contributors. Today, the Internet and digital platforms such as social media, Twitter, email, and blogs serve the same function even more efficiently, giving rise to a new generation of activist online groups. Email allows relatively small groups to identify their adherents and mobilize them throughout the nation.

● Interest Group Strategies

Explain how interest groups try to influence government and policy

Interest groups work to improve the likelihood that their policy interests will be heard and treated favorably by all branches and levels of the government. The quest for political influence or power takes many forms.

Insider strategies include access to key decision makers, lobbying, and litigating cases in courts. Outsider strategies include going public and using electoral politics. These strategies do not exhaust all the possibilities, but they paint a broad picture of ways that groups use their resources in the fierce competition for power (see Figure 11.1).

Many groups employ a mix of insider and outsider strategies. For example, environmental groups such as the Sierra Club lobby members of Congress and key congressional staff members; participate in bureaucratic rule making by offering comments and suggestions to agencies on new environmental rules; and bring lawsuits under various environmental acts such as the Endangered Species Act, which authorizes groups and citizens to come to court if they believe the act is being violated. At the same time, the Sierra Club attempts to influence public opinion through media campaigns and to influence electoral politics by supporting candidates who it believes share its environmental views and by opposing candidates it views as foes of environmentalism. While most groups win sometimes and lose sometimes when advocating for their policy goals, in general groups that are well organized and have resources, including citizens groups, are more effective.

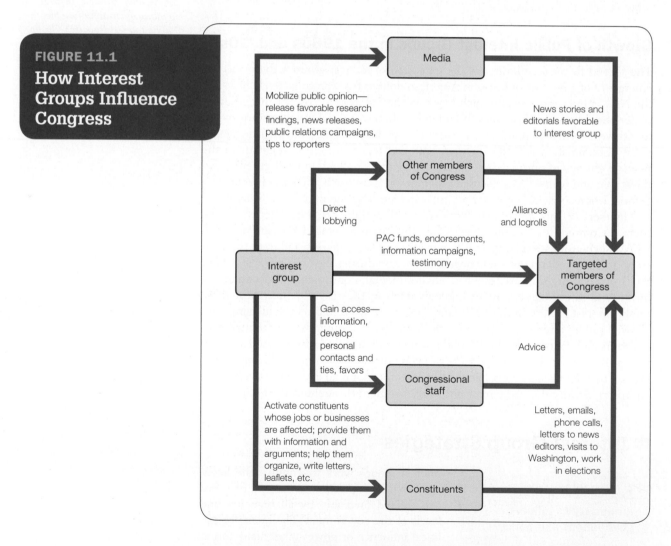

FIGURE 11.1

How Interest Groups Influence Congress

Direct Lobbying

Lobbying is an attempt by a group to influence the policy process through persuasion of government officials. Most Americans tend to believe that interest groups exert their influence through direct contact with members of Congress, but lobbying encompasses a broad range of activities that groups engage in with all sorts of government officials and the public as a whole.

The 1946 Federal Regulation of Lobbying Act defines a lobbyist as "any person who shall engage himself for pay or any consideration for the purpose of attempting to influence the passage or defeat of any legislation of the Congress of the United States." The 1995 Lobbying Disclosure Act requires all organizations employing lobbyists to register with Congress and to disclose whom they represent, whom they lobby, what they are looking for, and how much they are paid. Approximately 12,000 lobbyists are currently registered.[20]

Lobbying involves a great deal of activity on the part of someone speaking for an interest, and lobbyists attempt to influence the policy process in a variety of ways.[21] Lobbyists first and foremost provide information to lawmakers about their interests and the legislation at hand. They communicate this information to lawmakers, administrators, and committee staff members with facts about pertinent issues. They often testify on behalf of their clients at congressional committee and agency hearings. Lobbyists talk to reporters, place ads in newspapers, and organize letter-writing, phone call, and email campaigns. They also play an important role in fund-raising, helping to direct clients' contributions to certain members of Congress and presidential candidates. See Figure 11.2 for an illustration of several interest groups' involvement in politics.

Lobbying Congress Traditionally, the term *lobbyist* referred mainly to individuals who sought to influence the passage of legislation in the Congress. The First Amendment to the Constitution provides for the right to "petition the Government for a redress of grievances." But as early as the 1870s, *lobbying* became the common term for petitioning. And since petitioning cannot take place on the floor of the House or Senate, petitioners must therefore confront members of Congress in the lobbies of the legislative chamber—hence the term *lobbying*.

Sophisticated lobbyists win influence by providing information about policies to busy members of Congress. Although interest groups do not necessarily buy votes, they do buy time, expertise, and influence. Studies have found that those interest groups providing the most money to representatives are more likely to be consulted by that representative and asked to provide information and expertise in discussing a bill pertaining to that group's area of interest. This, in essence, gives interest groups a voice in shaping how legislation is written, and while it cannot ensure votes for laws preferred by the group, by participating in the policy process, organized interests are influencing policy.

The influence of lobbyists, in many instances, is based on personal relationships and the behind-the-scenes services they are able to perform for lawmakers. Many of Washington's top lobbyists have close ties to important members of Congress or were themselves important political figures, thus virtually guaranteeing that their clients will have direct access to congressional leaders. Some important lobbyists have more than a business relationship to lawmakers: quite a few, in fact, are married to prominent political figures. For example, Linda Daschle of LHD and Associates is the wife of former Senate majority leader Tom Daschle, and Hadassah

lobbying a strategy by which organized interests seek to influence the passage of legislation by exerting direct pressure on government officials

for critical analysis

Under U.S. law, lobbyists are required to register with Congress and disclose information about whom they represent and how much they are paid. What purpose does this law serve? Which groups are most likely to support such a rule?

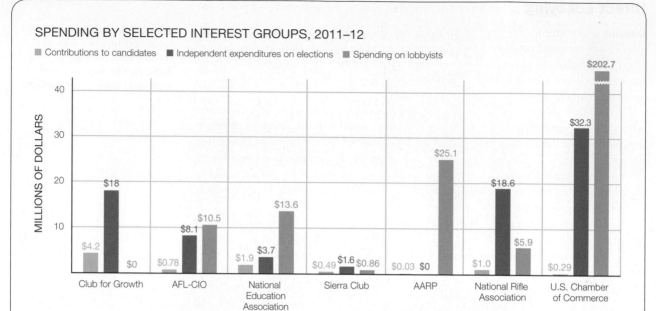

SPENDING BY SELECTED INTEREST GROUPS, 2011–12

■ Contributions to candidates   ■ Independent expenditures on elections   ■ Spending on lobbyists

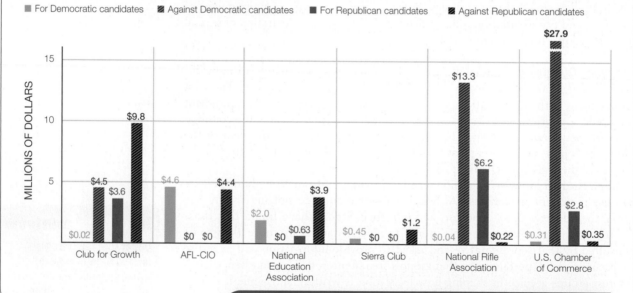

SPENDING ON ADS FOR/AGAINST CANDIDATES BY SELECTED GROUPS, 2011–12*

■ For Democratic candidates   ▨ Against Democratic candidates   ■ For Republican candidates   ▨ Against Republican candidates

FIGURE 11.2

Interest Group Spending

Interest groups are one mechanism through which Americans' voices are heard. Organized interests play a large role in structuring candidate and party support, financing campaigns, and lobbying Congress on the issues important to group members. But as the examples shown here illustrate, interest groups vary in how much money they give directly to candidates, how much they spend on advertising, during elections, and how much they spend on lobbying.

*AARP is not included in this figure because it did not have any independent expenditures on elections.
SOURCE: Open Secrets' Organizational Profiles, www.opensecrets.org/orgs (accessed 4/19/14).

Lieberman, wife of Senator Joseph Lieberman, was for many years a lobbyist for the pharmaceutical industry.

Through their lobbyists, interest groups also have substantial influence in setting the legislative agenda. They help to craft specific language in legislation and build coalitions and comprehensive campaigns around particular policy issues.[22] These coalitions do not rise from the grassroots but instead are put together by Washington lobbyists who launch comprehensive campaigns that combine simulated grassroots activity with information and campaign funding for members of Congress.

What happens to interests that do not engage in extensive lobbying? They often find themselves "Microsofted," that is, marginalized in the political process. In 1998 the software giant was facing antitrust action from the Justice Department and had few friends in Congress. One member of the House, Representative Billy Tauzin (R-La.), told Microsoft's chair, Bill Gates, that without an extensive investment in lobbying, the corporation would continue to be "demonized." Gates responded by quadrupling Microsoft's lobbying expenditures and hiring lobbyists with strong ties to Congress. The result was congressional pressure on the Justice Department resulting in a settlement of the Microsoft suit on terms favorable to the company.

Similarly, in 1999, members of Congress advised Wal-Mart that its efforts to win approval to operate savings and loans in its stores were doomed to failure if the retailer did not greatly increase its lobbying efforts. "They don't give money. They don't have congressional representation—so nobody here cares about them," said one influential member. Like Microsoft, Wal-Mart learned its lesson, hired more lobbyists, and got what it wanted.[23] By 2005, Wal-Mart had become a seasoned political player, creating a "war room" in its Arkansas headquarters. Staffed by a phalanx of veteran political operatives from both parties, the war room is the nerve center of the giant retailer's lobbying and public-relations efforts.[24] Today, Wal-Mart spends more than $5 million a year on its lobbying efforts.[25]

Lobbying the President So many individuals and groups clamor for the president's time and attention that only the most skilled and best-connected members of the lobbying community can hope to influence presidential decisions. Typically, a president's key political advisers and fund-raisers will include individuals with ties to the lobbying industry who can help their friends gain access to the White House.

During the 2008 presidential campaign, Barack Obama said, "Lobbyists won't find a job in my White House." Soon after his election, however, Obama appointed David Axelrod as his senior adviser. Before joining the Obama campaign and administration, Axelrod was a partner in ASK Public Strategies, a consulting group that had helped the giant Illinois utility Commonwealth Edison obtain a major rate hike. At least 30 other senior Obama administration officials have a lobbying background.[26] The lobbying industry is so much a part of Washington that it probably would have been impossible for the president to keep his campaign pledge.

Lobbying the Executive Branch Even when an interest group is very successful at getting its bill passed by Congress and signed by the president, the prospect of full and faithful implementation of that law is not guaranteed. Often a group and its allies do not pack up and go home as soon as the president turns their lobbied-for new law over to the appropriate agency. In some respects, interest group access to the executive branch is promoted by federal law. The Administrative Procedure Act, first enacted in 1946 and frequently amended in subsequent years, requires most federal agencies to provide notice and an opportunity for comment before

Interest groups may also try to influence the president's decisions. In 2009, President Obama met with business leaders to discuss how a new health care policy would affect their employees' health insurance plans.

implementing proposed new rules and regulations. This "notice and comment rule making" is designed to allow interests an opportunity to make their views known and to participate in the implementation of federal legislation that affects them. In 1990, Congress enacted the Negotiated Rulemaking Act to encourage administrative agencies to engage in direct and open negotiations with affected interests when developing new regulations. These two pieces of legislation—which have been strongly enforced by the federal courts—have played an important role in opening the bureaucratic process to interest group influence. Today, few federal agencies would consider attempting to implement a new rule without consulting affected interests, known in Washington as "stakeholders."[27]

Iron Triangles For the most part, access to decision makers does not require bribes or other forms of illegal activity. In many areas, interest groups, government agencies, and congressional committees routinely work together for mutual benefit. The interest group provides campaign contributions for members of Congress, and it lobbies for larger budgets for the agency. The agency, in turn, provides government contracts for the interest group and constituency services for friendly members of Congress. The congressional committee or subcommittee, meanwhile, supports the agency's budgetary requests and the programs the interest group favors. This so-called **iron triangle** has one angle in an executive branch program, another angle in a Senate or House legislative committee or subcommittee, and a third angle in some highly stable and well-organized interest group. The angles in the triangular relationship are mutually supporting and can last over a long period of time, especially if a committee member has considerable seniority in Congress. An interest cannot feel comfortable about its access to Congress until it has one or more of its

iron triangle the stable, cooperative relationship that often develops among a congressional committee, an administrative agency, and one or more supportive interest groups; not all of these relationships are triangular, but the iron triangle is the most typical

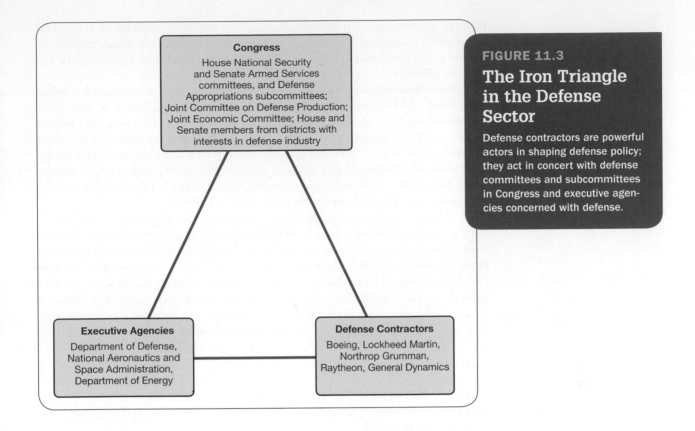

Congress

House National Security
and Senate Armed Services
committees, and Defense
Appropriations subcommittees;
Joint Committee on Defense Production;
Joint Economic Committee; House and
Senate members from districts with
interests in defense industry

Executive Agencies

Department of Defense,
National Aeronautics and
Space Administration,
Department of Energy

Defense Contractors

Boeing, Lockheed Martin,
Northrop Grumman,
Raytheon, General Dynamics

FIGURE 11.3

The Iron Triangle in the Defense Sector

Defense contractors are powerful actors in shaping defense policy; they act in concert with defense committees and subcommittees in Congress and executive agencies concerned with defense.

"own" people with 10 or more years of continuous service on the relevant committee or subcommittee. Figure 11.3 illustrates an important iron triangle in recent American political history: that of the defense industry.

A number of important policy domains, such as the environment and welfare, are controlled not by highly structured and unified iron triangles but by broader **issue networks**. These networks consist of like-minded politicians, consultants, public officials, political activists, and interest groups that care about the issue in question. Activists and interest groups recognized as being involved in the issue (the stakeholders) are customarily invited to testify before congressional committees or give their views to government agencies considering action in their domain. Issue networks and iron triangles may be overlapping and coexist.

issue network a loose network of elected leaders, public officials, activists, and interest groups drawn together by a specific policy issue

Regulating Lobbying

Sometimes the actions of lobbyists are outside of the law. In 2005 a prominent Washington lobbyist, Jack Abramoff, was indicted on numerous charges of fraud and violations of federal lobbying laws. During the investigation of his activities, it was revealed that Abramoff, along with his associate Michael Scanlon, had collected tens of millions of dollars from several American Indian tribes that operated lucrative gambling casinos. (Indian gambling is currently a $16 billion industry in the United States.) What Abramoff provided in exchange was access to key Republican members of Congress, who helped his clients shut down rival casino operators. Abramoff was closely associated with several House members, including the former House majority leader Tom DeLay. Millions of tribal dollars found their way into the campaign war chests of Abramoff's friends in Congress. Thus, through a well-connected lobbyist, money had effectively purchased access and influence. Abramoff and several of his associates subsequently pleaded guilty to federal bribery and fraud charges, and Abramoff was sentenced to more than five years in prison.

Because lobbyists are so influential in Washington, D.C., Congress has tried to limit their role by adopting stricter guidelines for lobbyists. However, the effectiveness of the new rules is unclear. For example, businesses may no longer deduct lobbying costs as a business expense. Trade associations must report to members the proportion of their dues that goes toward lobbying, and that proportion of the dues may not be reported as a business expense. The most important new regulation was the 1995 Lobbying Disclosure Act, which expanded the definition of the organization and individuals that must register to lobby.

In 1996, Congress passed legislation limiting the size of gifts to its own members: no gift could be worth more than $50, and no member could receive more than $100 from a single source. It also banned the practice of honoraria for giving speeches, which special interests had used to supplement congressional salaries. In 2007 congressional Democrats secured the enactment of a new package of ethics rules designed to fulfill their 2006 campaign promise to bring an end to lobbying abuses. The new rules prohibited lobbyists from paying for most meals, trips, parties, and gifts for members of Congress. Lobbyists were also required to disclose the amounts and sources of small campaign contributions they collected from clients and "bundled" into large contributions. And interest groups were required to disclose the funds they used to rally voters to support or oppose legislative proposals. According to the *Washington Post*, however, within a few weeks, lobbyists had learned how to circumvent many of the new rules, and lobbying firms were as busy as ever.[28]

Using the Courts

Interest groups sometimes turn to litigation when they lack access or when they feel they have insufficient influence to change a policy. Interest groups can use the courts to affect public policy in at least three ways: (1) by bringing suit directly on behalf of the group itself, (2) by financing suits brought by individuals, or (3) by filing a companion brief as an amicus curiae (literally "friend of the court") to an existing court case (see Chapter 15 for a discussion of amicus curiae briefs).

Among the best-known illustrations of using the courts for political influence is found in the history of the NAACP. The most important of these court cases was, of course, *Brown v. Board of Education of Topeka, Kansas*, in which the U.S. Supreme Court held that legal segregation of the schools was unconstitutional.[29] Later, extensive litigation accompanied the women's rights movement in the 1960s and the movement for rights for gays and lesbians in the 1990s.

The 1973 Supreme Court case of *Roe v. Wade*, which took away a state's power to ban abortions, sparked a controversy that brought conservatives to the fore on a national level.[30] Since 1973, conservative groups have made extensive use of the courts to whittle away at the scope of the privacy doctrine initially defined by the Supreme Court in *Roe v. Wade*. They obtained rulings, for example, that prohibit the use of federal funds to pay for voluntary abortions. And in 1989, right-to-life groups were able to use the case of *Webster v. Reproductive Health Services* to restore the right of states to place restrictions on abortion, thus undermining the *Roe v. Wade* decision (see Chapter 4).[31] The *Webster* case brought more than 300 interest groups on both sides of the abortion issue to the Supreme Court's door. On the other side of the political spectrum, the American Civil Liberties Union (ACLU) regularly uses litigation to challenge state and federal laws that restrict the rights of individuals and groups. This includes recent successful challenges to laws ending affirmative action in the states.

Litigation involving large businesses is voluminous in such areas as taxation, antitrust, interstate transportation, patents, and product quality and standardization. Often a business is brought to litigation against its will by virtue of initiatives taken against it by other businesses or by government agencies. But many individual businesses bring suit themselves to influence government policy, and business groups also frequently use the courts because of the number of government programs applied to them. Major corporations and their trade associations pay tremendous amounts of money each year in fees to the most prestigious Washington law firms. Much of this money is used to keep the best and most experienced lawyers prepared to represent the corporations in court or before administrative agencies when necessary.

Mobilizing Public Opinion

Going public is a strategy that attempts to mobilize the widest and most favorable climate of opinion, and is a favored strategy of citizen groups and netroots or online activist groups. Many groups consider it imperative to maintain this climate at all times. As early as the 1930s, political analysts were distinguishing between the "old lobby" of direct group representation before Congress and the "new lobby" of public-relations professionals addressing the public at large as a way to ultimately reach Congress.[32]

One of the best-known ways of going public is the use of **institutional advertising**. A casual scanning of major mass-circulation magazines, newspapers, and television ads will provide numerous examples of expensive and well-designed ads by the major oil companies, automobile and steel companies, other large corporations, and trade associations. The ads show how much these organizations are doing for the country, for the protection of the environment, or for the defense of the American way of life. The purpose of the ads is to create and maintain a positive association between an organization and the community at large in the hope of drawing on these favorable feelings as needed for specific political campaigns later on.

Citizen groups and online netroots organizations rely heavily on mobilizing the public opinion of their members via social media, Twitter campaigns, and targeted email messages. On any given day a new viral media story may become headline news, and in most cases an interest group is behind the story. Such groups span the ideological spectrum from liberal to conservative, and can wield significant pressure on elected officials to act.

Protests and Demonstrations Many groups resort to going public because they lack the resources, the contacts, or the experience to use other political strategies. The sponsorship of boycotts, sit-ins, mass rallies, and marches by Martin Luther King, Jr.'s Southern Christian Leadership Conference (SCLC) and

When the Food and Drug Administration required cigarette packages to carry new warning labels such as these, a coalition of tobacco companies sued the government, claiming the labels violated First Amendment rights. The companies won their suit. In response, anti-cigarette groups such as the Campaign for Tobacco-Free Kids are urging the FDA to develop new warnings.

institutional advertising
advertising designed to create a positive image of an organization

In 2013 protesters marched on Capitol Hill in Washington, D.C., to protest the government's surveillance programs of its citizens. The march was organized by StopWatching.Us, a coalition of more than 100 public advocacy groups that span the ideological spectrum, to gain media attention and urge lawmakers to action.

related organizations during the 1950s and '60s is one of the most significant and successful cases of going public to create a more favorable climate of opinion by calling attention to abuses. The success of these events inspired similar efforts by women's groups. Organizations such as NOW used public strategies in their drive for legislation and in their efforts to gain ratification of the Equal Rights Amendment. The 2010 GOP takeover of the House of Representatives began with the spontaneous self-organization of the Tea Party movement in 2009 as an angry response to the Obama administration's health care initiatives. In 2011 the Occupy Wall Street movement sparked demonstrations across America and around the world, giving voice to those who are outraged by economic inequality.

grassroots mobilization a lobbying campaign in which a group mobilizes its membership to contact government officials in support of the group's position

Grassroots Mobilization Another form of going public is **grassroots mobilization**, in which a lobby group mobilizes its members and their families throughout the country to write or email their elected representatives in support of the group's position. Among the most effective users of the grassroots effort in contemporary American politics is the religious right. Networks of evangelical churches have the capacity to generate hundreds of thousands of letters, phone calls, and emails to Congress and the White House. For example, the religious right was outraged when President Clinton announced soon after taking office that he planned to end the military's ban on gay and lesbian soldiers. The Reverend Jerry Falwell, an evangelical leader, called on viewers of his television program to dial a telephone number that would add their names to a petition urging Clinton to retain the ban on gays in the military. Within a few hours, 24,000 people had called to support the petition.[33]

Grassroots campaigns have been so effective in recent years that a number of Washington consulting firms have begun to specialize in this area. In 2007, for example, a grassroots firm called Grassfire.org led the drive to kill the immigration reform bill supported by President Bush and a number of congressional Democrats that would have legalized the status of many illegal immigrants. Grassfire.org used the Internet and talk radio programs to generate a campaign that yielded 700,000 signatures on petitions opposing the bill. The petitions, along with tens of thousands of phone calls, letters, and emails generated by Grassfire and several other groups, led to the bill's defeat in the U.S. Senate.[34]

A notorious online grassroots organization is Anonymous. Anonymous is a loosely associated network of activists and hackers that specializes in online protests. Some consider the group to be outside of the law, while others consider them freedom fighters or digital Robin Hoods. The group's website describes it as "an internet gathering" with a decentralized organizational structure that operates on ideas rather than directives. The group became known for a series of well-publicized hacks and distributed denial-of-service (DDoS) attacks on government, religious organizations (specifically, the Church of Scientology), and corporate websites. Anonymous prioritizes Internet freedom and has mounted protests against anti–digital piracy campaigns by motion picture and recording industry trade association and by government; recently the organization has been active in promoting the rights of gays and lesbians. Anonymous, like other online organizations that do not engage in cyber attacks, prioritizes mobilizing public opinion over insider strategies, such as lobbying, and has been especially effective in mounting citizen protests.

Sometimes, what initially appears to be an upswelling of grassroots mobilization is not in fact a genuine grassroots campaign but instead represent "Astroturf lobbying" (a play on the name of the artificial grass used on many sports fields). Such campaigns, often using email, have increased in frequency in recent years, as members of Congress have grown more and more skeptical of Washington lobbyists and far more attentive to demonstrations of support for a particular issue by their actual constituents.

Using Electoral Politics

In addition to attempting to influence members of Congress and other government officials, interest groups also seek to use the electoral process to elect the right legislators in the first place and to ensure that those who are elected will owe them a debt of gratitude for their support. If we view matters in perspective, groups invest more resources in lobbying than in electoral politics. Nevertheless, financial support and campaign activism can be important tools for organized interests.

Political Action Committees By far the most common electoral strategy employed by interest groups is that of giving financial support to political parties or specific candidates running for office. But such support can easily cross the threshold into outright bribery. Therefore, Congress has occasionally attempted to regulate this strategy. For example, the Federal Election Campaign Act of 1971 (amended in 1974) requires that each candidate or campaign committee itemize the full name and address, occupation, and principal business of each person who contributes more than $100. These provisions have been effective up to a point, resulting in numerous indictments, resignations, and criminal convictions in the aftermath of the 1972 Watergate scandal.

The Watergate scandal was triggered by the illegal entry of a group of clandestine agents employed by the president's re-election committee into the office

for critical analysis

Do you think petitions are likely to be effective in shaping government policy, or do elected officials still respond primarily to well-established business interests, rather than citizen groups? Are online petitions more for show than for substance?

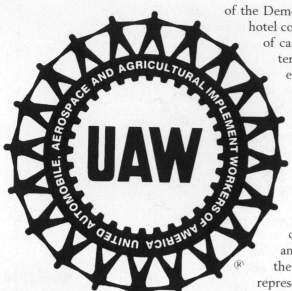

The labor union UAW is a major donor to Super PACs. In the 2012 election cycle, it donated $11.8 million to various Super PACs.

political action committee (PAC) a private group that raises and distributes funds for use in election campaigns

Super PAC an independent political action committee that may raise unlimited sums of money from corporations, unions, and individuals but is not permitted to contribute to or coordinate directly with parties or candidates

of the Democratic National Committee in the Watergate apartment and hotel complex. An investigation quickly revealed numerous violations of campaign finance laws, involving millions of dollars in unregistered cash from corporate executives to President Nixon's re-election committee. Reaction to Watergate produced further legislation on campaign finance in 1974 and 1976, but the effect was to restrict individuals rather than interest-group campaign activity. In the 2013–14 election cycle, individuals may contribute no more than $2,600 to any candidate for federal office in any primary or general election. A **political action committee (PAC)**, however, can contribute $5,000, provided it contributes to at least five different federal candidates each year. (Campaign finance regulations are discussed in more detail in Chapter 10.) Beyond this, the laws permit corporations, unions, and other interest groups to form PACs and to pay the costs of soliciting funds from private citizens for the PACs. In other words, PACs operate in the electoral arena by representing interest groups. The option to form a PAC was made available by law in the early 1970s. Before then it was difficult, if not downright illegal, for corporations, including unions, to get directly involved in elections by supporting parties and candidates.

The flurry of reform legislation of the 1970s attempted to reduce the influence that special interests have over elections, but the effect has been almost the exact opposite. Electoral spending by interest groups has been increasing steadily. The number of PACs has also increased significantly—from 480 in 1972 to more than 5,500 in 2012. Opportunities for legally influencing campaigns are now widespread. In the 2014 election, groups reported independent expenditures totaling $780 million, of which $339 million was from Super PACs, $39 million from trade associations, and only $1.7 million from unions. Political parties spent $228 million. These numbers do not include all outside spending, since certain kinds of ads are not required to be reported to the government.[35]

Given the enormous costs of television commercials, polls, computers, and other elements of contemporary political technology, most politicians are eager to receive PAC contributions and are at least willing to give a friendly hearing to the needs and interests of contributors. Most politicians probably will not simply sell their services to the interests that fund their campaigns, but there is some evidence that interest groups' campaign contributions do influence the overall pattern of political behavior in Congress and in the state legislatures. (See the "Who Are Americans?" feature for one depiction of who is represented by PACs.)

Concern about PACs grew through the 1980s and '90s, creating a constant drumbeat for reform of federal election laws. Proposals to abolish PACs were introduced in Congress on many occasions, with perhaps the most celebrated being the McCain-Feingold bill, which became the Bipartisan Campaign Reform Act (BCRA) of 2002. When originally proposed in 1996, McCain-Feingold was aimed at reducing or eliminating PACs. But in a stunning about-face, when campaign finance reform was adopted in 2002, it did not restrict PACs in any significant way. Rather, it eliminated unrestricted "soft money" donations to the national political parties.

One consequence of this reform, as seen in Chapter 10, was the creation of a host of new organizations, which includes 527 committees, organizations created to promote particular ideas or candidates, and **Super PACs,** formally called

Who Is Represented by PACs?

In the presidential election cycles of 2000, 2004, 2008, and 2012, political action committees (PACs) spent a grand total of $1.4 billion to elect and defeat political candidates. PACs representing labor groups spent the most, followed closely by the financial sector. For many sectors, the amount donated to Democratic candidates and Republican candidates was fairly even.

PAC Contributions to Federal Candidates, 2000–12

Democratic candidates   Republican candidates

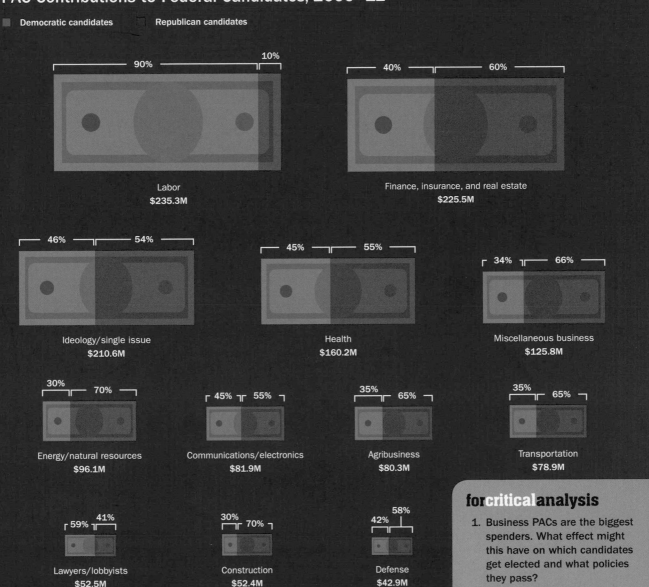

Labor
$235.3M — 90% / 10%

Finance, insurance, and real estate
$225.5M — 40% / 60%

Ideology/single issue
$210.6M — 46% / 54%

Health
$160.2M — 45% / 55%

Miscellaneous business
$125.8M — 34% / 66%

Energy/natural resources
$96.1M — 30% / 70%

Communications/electronics
$81.9M — 45% / 55%

Agribusiness
$80.3M — 35% / 65%

Transportation
$78.9M — 35% / 65%

Lawyers/lobbyists
$52.5M — 59% / 41%

Construction
$52.4M — 30% / 70%

Defense
$42.9M — 42% / 58%

for critical analysis

1. Business PACs are the biggest spenders. What effect might this have on which candidates get elected and what policies they pass?

2. Which party benefits the most from PAC donations? Why do you think this is?

SOURCES: Open Secrets, www.opensecrets.org/pacs/ (accessed 4/12/14)

The amount of money spent by organized interests on elections has increased dramatically in the last decade. This cartoon raises the concern that influence in government is for sale and only the extremely wealthy can buy it.

"independent expenditure-only committees," which were created for the purpose of promoting whatever candidacies their organizers wish. Super PACs may raise unlimited sums of money from corporations, unions, and individuals but are not permitted to contribute to or coordinate directly with parties or candidates. This change has had the effect of strengthening interest groups and weakening parties. As long as a group's campaign expenditures are not coordinated with those of a candidate's campaign, the group is free to spend as much money as it wishes. Such expenditures are viewed as "issue advocacy" and are protected by the First Amendment. The Supreme Court's landmark decision, *Citizens United v. Federal Election Commission* (2010) dramatically increased the flow of money from interest groups, 527s, and Super PACs into politics and electoral campaigns. *Citizens United* removed restrictions on corporate and union political spending, freeing business to back whatever politicians it chose.[36] Individuals and organizations can give an unlimited amount to Super PACs. In the 2010 congressional elections, Super PACs spent $60 million. In 2014, Super PACs spent $339 million on House and Senate races.[37]

Campaign Activism Financial support is not the only way that organized groups seek influence through electoral politics. Sometimes activism can be even more important than campaign contributions. Campaign activism on the part of conservative groups played a very important role in bringing about the Republican capture of both houses of Congress in 1994. For example, Christian Coalition activists played a role in many races, including those in which Republican candidates were not strongly identified with the religious right. One postelection study suggested that more than 60 percent of the more than 600 candidates supported by the Christian right were successful in state, local, and congressional races in 1994, especially in the South.[38] In many congressional districts, Christian Coalition efforts were augmented by grassroots campaigns launched by the NRA, which had been outraged by Democratic support for gun-control legislation. Both groups are well organized at the local level and were able to mobilize their members across the country to participate in congressional races. In the 2012 presidential elections, prochoice groups mobilized their supporters to turn out and vote for Democratic candidate Obama via telephone get-out-the-vote drives.

Ballot Initiatives Another political tactic that interest groups sometimes use is sponsorship of ballot initiatives at the state level. The initiative, a device adopted by half the states around 1900, allows proposed laws to be placed on the general election ballot and submitted directly to the state's voters, bypassing the state legislature and the governor. The initiative was originally promoted by late-nineteenth-century Populists as a mechanism that would allow the people to govern directly—an antidote to interest group influence in the legislative process.

Some studies have suggested that, ironically, many initiative campaigns today are actually sponsored by interest groups seeking to circumvent legislative opposition to their goals. In recent years, for example, initiative campaigns have been sponsored by the insurance industry, automobile industry, trial lawyers' associations, and tobacco companies.[39] The success of business groups promoting antitax initiatives and conservative activists seeking to ban same-sex marriage has led liberal activists to develop their own initiative campaign. In 1998, liberal activists established the Ballot Initiative Strategy Center (BISC) to provide national coordination for these efforts, which led to successes such as the 2010 Oregon campaign for Propositions 66 and 67, which increased taxes for corporations and high-income wage earners. The role of interest groups in initiative campaigns should come as no surprise, since such campaigns can cost millions of dollars.

While businesses may sponsor ballot initiatives, such measures are much more likely to be rejected by voters on Election Day than initiatives sponsored by citizen groups. In an important study by political scientist Elisabeth Gerber, she finds that citizens groups and unions are the most effective at sponsoring ballot measures, whereas businesses, trade associations, and professional associations are more effective at lobbying state legislatures. The implication is that mechanisms of direct democracy, like the initiative process, favor citizen interests while lobbying favors economic interests.[40]

for critical analysis

Describe the different techniques of influence that organized interests employ. When is one technique preferable to another?

Interests Groups
and Your Future

We would like to think that government policies are products of legislators representing the public interest. The truth of the matter is that few programs and policies ever reach the public agenda without the vigorous efforts of important national interest groups. In the realm of economic policy, social policy, and international trade policy, the activity of interest groups is of critical importance.

James Madison wrote that "liberty is to faction as air is to fire."[41] By this he meant that the organization and proliferation of interests are inevitable in a free society. As long as competition among different interests were free, open, and vigorous—that is, as long as pluralism thrived—there would be some balance of power among them, and no one interest would be able to dominate the political or governmental process.

Indeed, there is considerable competition among organized groups in the United States. Prochoice and antiabortion forces, for example, continue to be locked in a bitter struggle. Nevertheless, interest group politics is not as balanced as Madisonian theory and pluralism might suggest. Although the weak and poor do occasionally become organized to assert their interests, interest group politics is generally a form of political competition best suited to the wealthy and powerful.

Moreover, although groups sometimes organize to promote broad public concerns, they more often represent relatively narrow, selfish interests. Small groups seeking narrow interests can be organized much more easily than large and diffuse collectives. The members of relatively small groups—say, bankers or hunting enthusiasts—are usually able to recognize their shared interests and the need to pursue them in the political arena. Members of large and diffuse groups—say, consumers or the unemployed—often find it difficult to recognize their shared interests or the need to engage in collective action to achieve them.[42]

As this chapter has shown, major changes to political or social institutions can have a significant impact on the number and identity of interest groups. One of the major social trends of our time is demographic change. Notably, the baby boomers, a large generation of Americans born in the period after World War II (from 1946 to 1964) are now reaching retirement and old age. Elderly Americans are highly organized and are represented by interest groups, such as AARP, that lobby government for benefits, including health care subsidies, to keep the cost of their medical care low. Because resources are limited, however, benefits to elderly Americans may come at the expense of social goals that may be more important to other generations. Today's college students are part of the millennial generation, born 1980–2001, who are more numerous than baby boomers. Young people are most affected by the cost of a college education and the job opportunities that exist when they graduate, rather than health care, since the young tend to be relatively healthy but need education and experience. Yet it is difficult to organize college students and the millennial generation on a national or statewide scale to lobby government to spend more on higher education or job opportunities. Why are young people's interests poorly represented and elderly people better represented? Could new organizational opportunities from netroots help young people organize?

Interest groups sometimes seem to have a greater impact than voters on the government's policies and programs, especially through financial contributions to political candidates. Yet, before we decide that we should do away with interest groups, we should think carefully: If there were no organized interests, would the government pay more attention to ordinary voters? Would young people be better or worse off if there were no interest groups in the United States? Or would the government simply pay less attention to everyone? In his work *Democracy in America*, Alexis de Tocqueville argued that the proliferation of groups promoted democracy by encouraging governmental responsiveness. Does group politics foster democracy or impede democracy? It does both.

plugin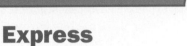

Inform

Find out which groups give the most money to your representatives in Congress by clicking "Congress" at www.opensecrets.org/politicians. You can look up your representatives by zip code.

Express

Imagine you are an aide to a member of Congress. Write a brief policy memo for or against more regulation of lobbying.

Connect

Find an interest group that appeals to you at votesmart.org/interest-groups, then follow that group on Facebook or Twitter.

Act

Join an interest group that works on behalf of a cause you support. Consider forming a campus chapter at your college or university.

studyguide

Defining Interest Groups

Describe the major types of interest groups and whom they represent (pp. 435–42)

An interest group is an organized group of people that makes policy-related appeals to government. Common types of interest groups include economic and corporate groups, labor groups, and citizen (or public interest) groups. Well-educated, upper-income, professional people are more likely to have the time, money, and skills to participate in interest groups.

Key Terms

pluralism (p. 435)

interest group (p. 435)

citizen groups (p. 439)

Practice Quiz

1. The theory that competition among organized interests will produce balance and compromise, with all the interests regulating one another is
   a) pluralism.
   b) elite power politics.
   c) democracy.
   d) socialism.
   e) libertarianism.

2. Groups that claim to serve the general good, rather than their own particular interests are
   a) membership associations.
   b) citizen groups.
   c) professional associations.
   d) ideological groups.
   e) public-sector groups.

How Groups Organize

Describe how interest groups and social groups organize (pp. 442–48)

Almost all interest groups share a similar set of organizational components, including leadership, money, an office, and members. In order to overcome the free-rider problem, interest groups attempt to provide their potential members with informational, material, and purposive benefits. New online advocacy groups known as *netroots organizations* have established new approaches to organization and membership.

Key Terms

netroots (p. 442)

membership association (p. 443)

staff organization (p. 443)

collective goods (p. 443)

free riders (p. 443)

informational benefits (p. 444)

material benefits (p. 444)

solidary benefits (p. 445)

purposive benefits (p. 445)

Practice Quiz

3. To overcome the free-rider problem, groups
   a) lobby Congress.
   b) litigate.
   c) provide selective benefits.
   d) provide collective goods.
   e) go public.

4. Friendship and networking are examples of
   a) purposive benefits.
   b) informational benefits.
   c) solidary benefits.
   d) material benefits.
   e) member dues.

5. Discount purchasing and health insurance are examples of
   a) purposive benefits.
   b) informational benefits.
   c) solidary benefits.
   d) material benefits.
   e) member dues.

The Growth of Interest and Advocacy Groups

In recent decades there has been a significant growth in the number of interest groups seeking to influence the American political process. One reason for this change has been the dramatic expansion of the role of American government over the last four decades. Another reason for this change has been the emergence of a new set of political forces in the United States called the "New Politics" movement.

Practice Quiz

6. Which of the following is an important reason for the enormous increase in the number of groups seeking to influence the American political system?
   a) the decrease in the size and activity of government during the last few decades
   b) the increase in the size and activity of government during the last few decades
   c) the increase in the amount of soft money in election campaigns in recent decades
   d) the increase in legal protection provided to interest groups as a result of the Supreme Court's evolving interpretation of the First Amendment
   e) the increase in the number of people identifying themselves as an independent in recent decades

7. Which types of interest groups are most often associated with the New Politics movement?
   a) political action committees
   b) professional associations
   c) government groups
   d) labor groups
   e) public interest groups

Interest Group Strategies

Interest groups take action to improve the probability that their policy interests will be treated favorably by all branches and all levels of government. These actions often take many different forms. Insider strategies include direct lobbying, cultivating access to decision makers, and using the court system. Outsider strategies include mobilizing public opinion and using electoral politics.

Key Terms

lobbying (p. 451)

iron triangle (p. 454)

issue network (p. 455)

institutional advertising (p. 457)

grassroots mobilization (p. 458)

political action committee (PAC) (p. 460)

Super PAC (p. 460)

Practice Quiz

8. Which of the following best describes the federal government's laws regarding lobbying?
   a) Federal law allows lobbying but only on issues related to taxation.
   b) Federal law allows lobbying but only if the lobbyists receive no monetary compensation for their lobbying.
   c) Federal law strictly prohibits any form of lobbying.
   d) Federal law requires all organizations employing lobbyists to register with Congress and to disclose whom they represent, whom they lobby, what they are looking for, and how much they are paid.
   e) There are no laws regulating lobbying because the federal government has never passed any legislation on the legality of the activity.

9. A loose network of elected leaders, public officials, activists, and interest groups drawn together by a public policy issue is referred to as
   a) an issue network.
   b) a public interest group.
   c) a political action committee.
   d) pluralism.
   e) an iron triangle.

10. Which of the following is a way that interest groups use the courts to influence public policy?
    a) supplying judges with solidary benefits
    b) joining an issue network
    c) creating an iron triangle
    d) forming a political action committee
    e) filing amicus curiae briefs

11. Which of the following are examples of the "going public" strategy?
    a) free riding, pluralism, and issue networking
    b) donating money to political parties, endorsing candidates, and sponsoring ballot initiatives
    c) institutional advertising, grassroots advertising, and protests and demonstrations
    d) providing informational benefits, providing solidary benefits, and providing material benefits
    e) filing an amicus brief, bringing a lawsuit, and financing those who are filing a lawsuit

12. Which of the following is *not* an activity in which interest groups frequently engage?
    a) starting their own political party
    b) litigation
    c) sponsoring ballot initiatives at the state level
    d) lobbying
    e) contributing to campaigns

13. Following the *Citizens United* decision in 2010, electoral spending by interest groups and Super PACs
    a) declined significantly.
    b) declined slightly.
    c) remained roughly the same.
    d) increased slightly.
    e) increased dramatically.

For Further Reading

Ainsworth, Scott. *Analyzing Interest Groups*. New York: W. W. Norton, 2002.

Alexander, Robert, ed. *The Classics of Interest Group Behavior*. New York: Wadsworth, 2005.

Baumgartner, Frank, Jeffrey M. Berry, Beth L. Leech, David C. Kimball, and Marie Hojnacki. *Lobbying and Policy Change: Who Wins, Who Loses and Why*. Chicago: University of Chicago Press, 2009.

Berry, Jeffrey. *Interest Group Society*. 5th ed. New York: Longman, 2008.

Cigler, Allan J., and Burdett A. Loomis, eds. *Interest Group Politics*. 7th ed. Washington, DC: CQ Press, 2006.

Dahl, Robert. *A Preface to Democratic Theory*. Chicago: University of Chicago Press, 1956.

Esterling, Kevin. *The Political Economy of Expertise*. Ann Arbor: University of Michigan Press, 2004.

Goldstein, Kenneth. *Interest Groups, Lobbying, and Participation in America*. New York: Cambridge University Press, 2008.

Kaiser, Robert. *So Damn Much Money: The Triumph of Lobbying and the Corrosion of American Government*. New York: Vintage, 2010.

Karpf, David. *The MoveOn Effect: The Unexpected Transformation of American Political Advocacy*. New York: Oxford University Press, 2012.

Lessig, Lawrence. *Republic, Lost: How Money Corrupts Congress—and a Plan to Stop It*. New York: Twelve/Hachette Book Group, 2011.

Lowi, Theodore J. *The End of Liberalism: The Second Republic of the United States*. 2nd ed. New York: W. W. Norton, 1979.

Moe, Terry M. *The Organization of Interests: Incentives and the Internal Dynamics of Political Interest Groups*. Chicago: University of Chicago Press, 1980.

Nownes, Anthony. *Total Lobbying: What Lobbyists Want and How They Try to Get It*. New York: Cambridge University Press, 2006.

Olson, Mancur, Jr. *The Logic of Collective Action: Public Goods and the Theory of Groups*. Cambridge, MA: Harvard University Press, 1965.

Rozell, Mark, Clyde Wilcox, and David Madland. *Interest Groups in American Campaigns*. Washington, DC: CQ Press, 2005.

Shirky, Clay. *Here Comes Everybody: The Power of Organizing Without Organizations*. New York: Penguin Press, 2008.

Strolovitch, Dara. *Affirmative Advocacy: Race, Class, and Gender in Interest Group Politics*. Chicago: University of Chicago Press, 2007.

Recommended Websites

AARP
www.aarp.org
AARP (formerly the American Association of Retired Persons) is one of the largest and most significant interest groups in the United States. Read about the history of this organization, its group benefits, and how it is affecting political issues and elections.

AFL-CIO Legislative Alert Center
www.aflcio.org/issues/legislativealert
Created in 1955, the AFL-CIO represents more than 10 million working men and women. See how this influential labor group is active and involved in political issues.

American Civil Liberties Union
www.aclu.org

American Conservative Union
www.conservative.org
The American Civil Liberties Union and the American Conservative Union are two of the nation's largest and most influential ideological interest groups. See what these opposing groups have to say about our government and current political issues.

American Israel Public Affairs Committee (AIPAC)
www.aipac.org
Due to globalization, interest groups cannot limit their activities to one country. Decisions made in Washington, D.C., can affect countries around the world. The American Israel Public Affairs Committee (AIPAC) works with Republicans and Democrats to maintain a strong relationship between the United States and Israel.

MoveOn
www.moveon.org
This progressive interest group is dedicated to bringing ordinary citizens back into the political process and electing liberal members of government. See how this group uses electoral politics, via political action committees and campaign activism, to achieve its agenda.

National Rifle Association (NRA)
www.nra.org

Coalition to Stop Gun Violence
www.csgv.org

Brady Campaign to Prevent Gun Violence
www.bradycampaign.org
Lobbying is an attempt by a group to influence the policy process by persuading government officials. These three groups employ a variety of lobbying techniques on the issue of gun control.

U.S. PIRG (United States Public Interest Research Group)
www.uspirg.org
This public interest group stands up for ordinary citizens. Its special emphasis is on consumer rights and the environment. U.S. PIRG mobilizes public opinion via institutional advertising, social movements, and grassroots efforts. PIRG chapters can be found in most states and at many colleges and universities.

World Wildlife Fund
www.wwf.org
The World Wildlife Fund is dedicated to protecting nature. They provide information to policy makers about conservation and advocate policies to help preserve the natural environment.

In addition to its lawmaking powers, Congress plays a critical role in American democracy as a representative institution. The members of Congress—100 senators and 435 representatives—represent the voices of the people across America. Yet some observers worry that Congress does not represent all voices equally.

Congress

WHAT GOVERNMENT DOES AND WHY IT MATTERS As 2013 drew to a close, the price of milk threatened to skyrocket. The cause? Members of Congress could not agree on a farm bill. The bill, which provides subsidies for farmers and funds for the Supplemental Nutrition Assistance Program (SNAP or food stamps) for the needy, usually wins support from both Democrats and Republicans. But in 2013, the Republican House passed a bill that would reduce SNAP benefits by $4 billion a year, while the Democratic Senate enacted a bill with a cut of only $400 million, a tenth of the size of the Republican cut.[1] As months passed, the two chambers could not reconcile their differences. Yet, the farm bill touched not only SNAP recipients and farmers; failure to pass a farm bill would be widely felt as expiring dairy subsidies affected the price of milk for all Americans. Recognizing the widespread consequences of the stalemate, the House ultimately accepted a much smaller cut in food stamps and the sharp increase in diary prices was averted.

On other issues, such as immigration reform, Congress proved unable to reach agreement. Congress last passed comprehensive immigration reform in 1986 and, despite many differences, a growing chorus of voices agreed that it was time for the federal government to again take action. Some groups favor tighter border controls, arguing that illegal immigration puts a burden on basic social services, such as health care, that benefit all Americans. Those in favor of tighter borders needed federal action. On the other side, "Dreamers"—undocumented young people brought to the United States as children—pushed Congress to create a pathway to citizenship for the more than 11 million undocumented immigrants already in the country. Without such legislation, many young people are unable to seek educational and job opportunities in the country they grew up in. And employers, ranging from farmers to high-tech entrepreneurs, complained that our system for admitting immigrants posed large burdens on business and needed to be updated. In 2013 the Senate responded to these pressures with a comprehensive immigration bill. The bill reflected a compromise on the major elements of reform, including a pathway to citizenship for the undocumented, large sums for improved border security, and an overhaul of the procedures for admitting new legal immigrants, including workers. However, the House could not reach agreement on a bill and the push for comprehensive immigration reform ultimately died.

Congress has vast authority over many aspects of American life. Laws related to federal spending, taxing, and regulation all pass through Congress. While the debates over these laws may seem hard to follow because they are complex and technical or because heated, partisan struggles distract from the substance of the issue, it is important for the American people to learn about what Congress is doing. As the examples of the farm bill and immigration reform indicate, actions taken—or not taken—in Congress affect the everyday experiences we take for granted. With its power to spend and tax, Congress also affects the choices that people face and the opportunities they can expect in life. With so much information about Congress available on the Internet, it is not hard to get beyond the heated rhetoric and simplistic headlines and ask your own questions about a proposed law. How will it affect my life and the lives of people I care about? What is the impact on my country? Making laws is often compared with making sausage, because it is such a complex and often messy process. Even so, it is vital for citizens to monitor what Congress does because the laws it passes are so central to their lives.

chaptergoals

- Describe who serves in Congress and how they represent their constituents (pp. 473–86)

- Explain how party leadership, the committee system, the staff system, and caucuses help structure congressional business (pp. 486–92)

- Outline the steps in the process of passing a law (pp. 492–97)

- Analyze the factors that influence which laws Congress passes (pp. 497–507)

- Describe Congress's influence over other branches of government (pp. 507–11)

Congress: Representing the American People

Describe who serves in Congress and how they represent their constituents

Congress is the most important representative institution in American government. Each member's primary responsibility is to the district, to his or her **constituency**, not to the congressional leadership, a party, or even Congress itself. Yet the task of representation is not a simple one. Views about what constitutes fair and effective representation differ, and constituents may have very different expectations of their representatives. Members of Congress must consider these diverse views and expectations as they represent their districts.

constituency the residents in the area from which an official is elected

House and Senate: Differences in Representation

The framers of the Constitution provided for a **bicameral** legislature—that is, a legislative body consisting of two chambers. As we saw in Chapter 2, the framers intended each of these chambers, the House of Representatives and the Senate, to serve a different constituency. Members of the Senate, appointed by state legislatures for six-year terms, were to represent society's elite. Today, members of both House and Senate are elected directly by the people. The 435 members of the House are elected from districts apportioned according to population; the 100 members of the Senate are elected by their states, with two senators from each. Senators continue to have much longer terms in office and usually represent much larger and more diverse constituencies than do their counterparts in the House (see Table 12.1).

bicameral having a legislative assembly composed of two chambers or houses, distinguished from *unicameral*

The House and Senate play different roles in the legislative process. In essence, the Senate is the more deliberative of the two bodies—the forum in which any and all ideas that senators raise can receive a thorough public airing. The House is the more centralized and organized of the two bodies—better equipped to play a routine role in the governmental process. In part, this difference stems from the

TABLE 12.1

Differences between the House and the Senate

	HOUSE	SENATE
Minimum age of member	25 years	30 years
U.S. citizenship	At least 7 years	At least 9 years
Length of term	2 years	6 years
Number representing each state	1–53 per state (depends on population)	2 per state
Constituency	Local	Local and statewide

different rules governing the two bodies. These rules give House leaders more control over the legislative process and allow House members to specialize in certain legislative areas. The rules of the much smaller Senate give its leadership relatively little power and discourage specialization.

Both formal and informal factors contribute to differences between the two chambers of Congress. Differences in the length of terms and requirements for holding office, specified by the Constitution, generate differences in how members of each body develop their constituencies and exercise their powers of office. For the House, the small size and relative homogeneity of their constituencies and the frequency with which they must seek re-election make House members more attuned to the legislative needs of local interest groups. The result is that members of the House most effectively and frequently serve as the agents of well-organized local interests with specific legislative agendas—for instance, used-car dealers seeking relief from regulation, labor unions seeking more favorable legislation, or farmers looking for higher subsidies. Because House members seek re-election every two years, they are interested in doing what their constituents want right *now*.

Senators, on the other hand, serve larger and more heterogeneous constituencies. As a result, they are somewhat better able than members of the House to act as the agents for groups and interests organized on a statewide or national basis. Moreover, with longer terms in office, senators have more time to consider "new ideas" or to bring together new coalitions of interests rather than simply serving existing ones.

Trustee versus Delegate Representation

For the Founders, Congress was the national institution that best embodied the ideals of representative democracy. But what is the role of a representative? A member of Congress can interpret her job as representative in two different ways: as a **delegate**, acting on the express preferences of her constituents; or as a **trustee**, more loosely tied to constituents and empowered to make the decisions she thinks best. The delegate role appears to be the more democratic because it forces representatives to heed the desires of their constituents. But this requires the representative to be in constant touch with constituents; it also requires constituents to follow each policy issue very closely. The problem with this form of representation is that most people do not follow every issue so carefully; instead they focus only on the issue or issues of particular interest to them. Many people are too busy to get the information necessary to make informed judgments even on issues they care about. Thus, adhering to the delegate form of representation runs the risk that the voices of only a few active and informed constituents get heard. Although it seems more democratic at first glance, the delegate form of representation may actually open Congress up to even more influence by special interests.

When congressional members act as trustees, on the other hand, they may not pay sufficient attention to the wishes of their constituents. In this scenario, the only

delegate a representative who votes according to the preferences of his or her constituency

trustee a representative who votes based on what he or she thinks is best for his or her constituency

For its first 128 years, Congress was a decidedly masculine world. In 1917, Jeanette Rankin (R-Mont.; pictured back row, far right) became the first woman to serve in Congress. A total of 297 women have served as U.S. representatives or senators, while 11,804 men have served.

way the public can exercise influence is by voting every two years for representatives and every six years for senators. In fact, most members of Congress take this electoral check very seriously. They try to anticipate the wishes of their constituents even when they don't know exactly what those wishes are, because they know that unpopular decisions can be used against them in the coming election.

Sociological versus Agency Representation

We have become so accustomed to the idea of representative government that we tend to forget what a peculiar concept representation really is. A representative claims to act or speak for some other person or group. But how can one person be trusted to speak for another? How do we know that those who call themselves our representatives are actually speaking on our behalf, rather than simply pursuing their own interests?

There are two circumstances under which one person reasonably might be trusted to speak for another. The first occurs if the two individuals are so similar in background, character, interests, and perspectives that anything said by one would very likely reflect the views of the other as well. This principle is at the heart of what is sometimes called **sociological representation**—the sort of representation that takes place when representatives have the same racial, gender, ethnic, religious, or educational backgrounds as their constituents. The assumption is that sociological similarity helps to promote good representation; thus the composition of a properly constituted representative assembly should mirror the composition of society.

The second circumstance under which one person might be trusted to speak for another occurs if the two are formally bound together so that the representative is in some way accountable to those he is supposed to represent. If representatives can somehow be punished for failing to speak properly for their constituents, then we know they have an incentive to provide good representation even if their own personal backgrounds, views, and interests differ from the backgrounds of those they represent. This principle is called **agency representation**—the sort of representation that takes place when constituents have the power to hire and fire their representatives.

Both sociological and agency representation play a role in the relationship between members of Congress and their constituencies.

The Social Composition of the U.S. Congress The extent to which the U.S. Congress is representative of the American people in a sociological sense can be seen by examining social characteristics of the House and Senate today. For example, the religious affiliations of members of both the House and Senate are overwhelmingly Protestant—the distribution is very close to the proportion in the population at large (the Protestant category comprises more than 15 denominations). Catholics are the second-largest category of religious affiliation, and Jews a much smaller, third category.[2] Religious affiliations directly affect congressional debate on a limited range of issues where different moral views are at stake, such as abortion.

African Americans, women, Latinos, and Asian Americans have increased their congressional representation in the past two decades, but for most of American history, few members of Congress came from these groups (see Figure 12.1). Even with recent increases, the representation of minorities in Congress is still

sociological representation a type of representation in which representatives have the same racial, gender, ethnic, religious, or educational backgrounds as their constituents; it is based on the principle that if two individuals are similar in background, character, interests, and perspectives, then one can correctly represent the other's views

agency representation a type of representation in which a representative is held accountable to a constituency if he or she fails to represent that constituency properly; this is incentive for good representation when the personal backgrounds, views, and interests of the representative differ from those of his or her constituency

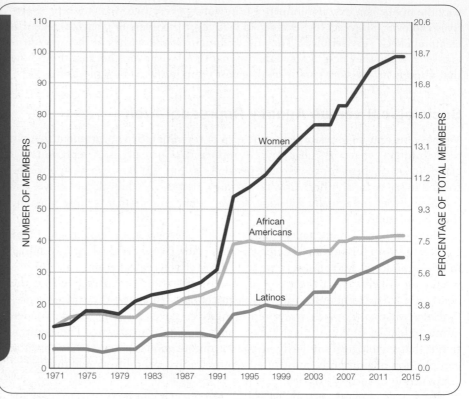

FIGURE 12.1

Women, African Americans, and Latinos in the U.S. Congress, 1971–2014

Congress has become much more socially diverse since the 1970s. After a gradual increase from 1971 to 1990, the number of women and African American members grew quickly during the first half of the 1990s. How closely does the number of female, African American, and Latino representatives reflect their proportion of the total U.S. population?

SOURCES: Harold W. Stanley and Richard G. Niemi, eds., *Vital Statistics on American Politics 2003–2004* (Washington, DC: CQ Press, 2003), 207, Table 5–2; and Jennifer E. Manning, *Membership of the 113th Congress: A Profile*, Congressional Research Service 7-5700, January 13, 2014, www.fas.org/sgp/crs /misc/R42964.pdf (accessed 2/24/14).

not comparable to their proportions in the general population. After the Democrats won a majority in the House in November 2006, Nancy Pelosi (D-Calif.) became the first female Speaker of the House and held that position through 2010. Following the 2012 elections, the 113th Congress (2013–14) included 79 women in the House of Representatives and 20 women in the Senate, an all-time high. Since many important contemporary national issues cut along racial and gender lines, pressure for reform in the representative process is likely to continue until all groups are fully represented.

The occupational backgrounds of members of Congress have always been a matter of interest because so many issues split along economic lines that are relevant to occupations and industries. The legal profession is the dominant career of most members of Congress prior to their election. Public service or politics is also a significant background, with many members coming from positions in state and local government. In addition, many members of Congress have important ties to business and industry.[3] Moreover, members of Congress are much more highly educated than most Americans. More than 9 in 10 members hold university degrees, and close to half of them have law degrees.[4] This is not a portrait of the U.S. population. Congress is not a sociological microcosm of American society. (See the "Who Are Americans?" feature.)

Can Congress still legislate fairly or take account of a diversity of views and interests if it is not a sociologically representative assembly? The task is certainly much more difficult. Yet there is reason to believe it can. Representatives, as we shall see shortly, can serve as the agents of their constituents even if they do not precisely mirror their sociological attributes. Yet sociological representation is a matter of some importance, even if it is not an absolute prerequisite for fair

Who Are the Members of Congress?

Gender

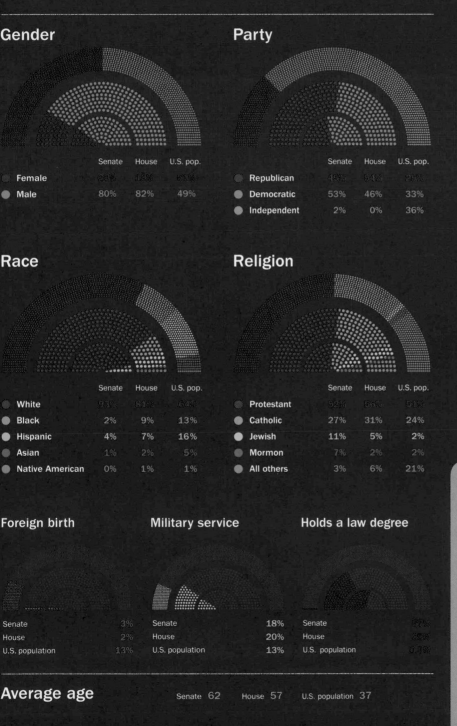

	Senate	House	U.S. pop.
Female	20%	18%	51%
Male	80%	82%	49%

Party

	Senate	House	U.S. pop.
Republican	45%	54%	25%
Democratic	53%	46%	33%
Independent	2%	0%	36%

Key

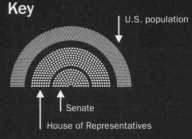

U.S. population

Senate

House of Representatives

Although the number of women, African Americans, and Latinos in Congress has increased in recent decades, Congress is still much less diverse than the American population. Members of Congress are predominantly male, white, Protestant Christian, and most commonly come from a professional and educational background as lawyers. These data compare the 113th Congress, which took office in 2013, with the U.S. population as a whole.

Race

	Senate	House	U.S. pop.
White	93%	81%	64%
Black	2%	9%	13%
Hispanic	4%	7%	16%
Asian	1%	2%	5%
Native American	0%	1%	1%

Religion

	Senate	House	U.S. pop.
Protestant	52%	56%	51%
Catholic	27%	31%	24%
Jewish	11%	5%	2%
Mormon	7%	2%	2%
All others	3%	6%	21%

Foreign birth

Senate	3%
House	2%
U.S. population	13%

Military service

Senate	18%
House	20%
U.S. population	13%

Holds a law degree

Senate	57%
House	45%
U.S. population	0.4%

Average age

| Senate 62 | House 57 | U.S. population 37 |

for critical analysis

1. Does it matter if the backgrounds of members of Congress reflect the population as a whole? Can members still represent their constituents effectively if they do not come from similar backgrounds?

2. Visit www.house.gov and www.senate.gov to identify your representatives in Congress and visit their web pages. How similar are their backgrounds to yours? How closely do their policy positions, as expressed on their web pages, match your own?

SOURCE: Congressional Research Service, www.fas.org/sgp/crs/misc/R42964.pdf; U.S. Census Bureau, www.census.gov/population/age/data/2012comp.html (accessed 3/19/14).

To more effectively promote a legislative agenda that addresses issues that disproportionately affect racial and ethnic minority groups, members of Congress from those groups have formed caucuses. Here, members of the Congressional Black Caucus discuss economic opportunity at a town meeting in Miami Gardens, Florida.

legislation by members of the House and Senate. At the least, the social composition of a representative assembly is important for symbolic purposes: to demonstrate to groups in the population that the government takes them seriously. If Congress is not representative symbolically, then its own authority, and indeed that of the entire government, is reduced.[5]

Representatives as Agents A good deal of evidence indicates that whether or not members of Congress share their constituents' sociological characteristics, they *do* work very hard to speak for their constituents' views and to serve their constituents' interests. The idea of representative as agent is similar to the relationship of lawyer and client. True, the relationship between the member of Congress and an average of 710,767 "clients" in the district, or the senator and millions of "clients" in the state, is very different from that of the lawyer and client. But the criteria of performance are comparable. One expects at the very least that each representative will constantly seek to discover the interests of the constituency and take those interests into account as he governs. Whether members of Congress always represent the interests of their constituents is another matter, as we will see later in this chapter.[6]

There is constant communication between constituents and congressional offices, and the volume of email from constituents and advocacy groups has grown so large so quickly that congressional offices have struggled to find effective ways to respond in a timely manner.[7] At the same time, members of Congress have found new ways to communicate with constituents. They have created websites describing their achievements, established a presence on social networking sites, and issued e-newsletters that alert constituents to current issues. Many also have set up blogs and used Twitter accounts to establish a more informal style of communication with constituents.

The seriousness with which members of the House attempt to behave as representatives can be seen in the amount of time they spend on behalf of their constituents. One way to measure the amount of time members of Congress devote to constituency service (called "casework") is to look at the percentage of personal House and Senate staff (personal staff being non-committee member staff) assigned to district and state offices. In 1972, 22.5 percent of House members' personal staff were located in district offices; by 2005 the number had grown to 50.7 percent.[8] For the Senate, the staff in state offices grew from 12.5 percent in 1972 to 39 percent in 2005. The service that these offices provide is not merely a matter of handling correspondence. It includes talking to constituents, providing them with minor services, presenting special bills for them, attempting to influence decisions by regulatory commissions on their behalf, helping them apply for federal benefits, such as Social Security and Small Business Administration loans, and assisting them with immigration cases. For example, Representative Michael Capuano's (D-Mass.) website notes that his office helped a young man from the former Soviet Union secure travel documents to attend an international mathematics competition and win a gold medal for the United States, expedited a refugee constituent's application to bring his wife to the United States, and petitioned the federal government to grant political asylum to a young man who was at risk of being deported to a war-torn African country where he faced persecution.[9]

In many districts, there are two or three issues on which constituents have such pronounced opinions that representatives feel they have little freedom of choice. For example, representatives from districts that grow wheat, cotton, or tobacco probably will not want to exercise a great deal of independence on relevant agricultural legislation. In oil-rich states such as Oklahoma and Texas, senators and members of the House are likely to be leading advocates of oil interests. For one thing, representatives are probably fearful of voting against their district interests; for another, the districts are unlikely to have elected representatives who would *want* to vote against them. On the other hand, on many issues, constituents do not have very strong views, and representatives are free to act as they think best. Foreign policy issues often fall into this category.

The influence of constituencies is so pervasive that both parties have strongly embraced the informal rule that nothing should be done to endanger the re-election chances of any member. Party leaders obey this rule fairly consistently by not asking any member to vote in a way that might conflict with a district interest.

The Electoral Connection

The sociological composition of Congress and the activities of representatives once they are in office are very much influenced by electoral considerations. Three factors related to the U.S. electoral system affect who gets elected and what they do once in office. The first factor concerns who decides to run for office and which candidates have an edge over others. The second issue is that of incumbency advantage. Finally, the way congressional district lines are drawn can greatly affect the outcome of an election. Let us examine more closely the impact that these considerations have on representation.

Who Runs for Congress Voters' choices are restricted from the start by who decides to run for office. In the past, decisions about who would run for a particular elected office were made by local party officials. A person who had a record of service to the party, or who was owed a favor, or whose "turn" had come up, might be nominated by party leaders. Today, few party organizations have the power to slate candidates in this way. Instead, parties try to ensure that well-qualified candidates run for Congress. During the 1990s, the Republican Party developed "farm teams" of local officials who were groomed to run for Congress. Their success led Democrats to attempt a similar strategy. Even so, the decision to run for Congress is a personal choice, and one of the most important factors determining who runs for office is an individual candidate's ambition.[10] A potential candidate may also assess whether he can attract enough money to mount a credible campaign. The ability to raise money depends on connections with other politicians, interest groups, and national party organizations.

Features distinctive to each congressional district also affect the field of candidates. For example, the way the congressional district overlaps with state legislative boundaries may affect a candidate's decision to run. A state-level legislator who is considering running for the U.S. Congress is more likely to assess her prospects favorably if her state district coincides with the congressional district (because the voters will already know her).

incumbency holding the political office for which one is running

Incumbency Incumbency plays a very important role in the American electoral system and in the kind of representation citizens get in Washington. Once in office, members of Congress gain access to an array of tools they can use to stack the deck in favor of their re-election. The most important of these is constituency service: taking care of the problems and requests of individual voters. Through such services and through regular newsletter mailings, incumbents seek to establish a "personal" relationship with their constituents. The success of this strategy is evident in the high rates of re-election for congressional incumbents: as high as 98 percent for House members and 90 percent for members of the Senate in recent years (see Figure 12.2). It is also evident in what is called "sophomore surge"—the tendency for candidates to win a higher percentage of the vote when seeking subsequent terms in office. In 2014 approximately 95 percent of incumbents in the House and 79 percent in the Senate were re-elected.[11] Furthermore, incumbents often win by large margins: in 2012 only 64 of the 435 House races were decided by a margin of less than 10 percent. The average margin of victory across all congressional contests was 31.85 percent.[12]

Incumbency can help a candidate by scaring off potential challengers. In many races, potential candidates may decide not to run because they fear that the incumbent simply has too much money or is too well liked or too well-known, or that a

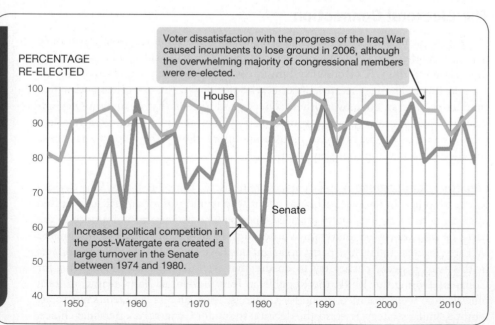

FIGURE 12.2

The Power of Incumbency

Members of Congress who run for re-election have a very good chance of winning. Has the incumbency advantage generally been greater in the House or in the Senate? What are the consequences of the incumbency advantage for who serves in Congress?

SOURCES: Norman J. Ornstein et al., eds., *Vital Statistics on Congress, 1999–2000* (Washington, DC: AEI Press, 2000), pp. 57–58; and authors' update.

PERCENTAGE RE-ELECTED

Voter dissatisfaction with the progress of the Iraq War caused incumbents to lose ground in 2006, although the overwhelming majority of congressional members were re-elected.

House

Senate

Increased political competition in the post-Watergate era created a large turnover in the Senate between 1974 and 1980.

district's partisan leanings are too unfavorable. The efforts of incumbents to raise funds to ward off potential challengers start early. A Connecticut Democrat, Joe Courtney, won his seat in 2006 by a very small margin, with only 91 more votes than his opponent. He began fund-raising for the 2008 election even before he was sworn in for his first term. In addition, the Democratic Congressional Campaign Committee placed him on its "Frontline team," a group of the 29 most vulnerable Democrats. The Democratic leadership took special efforts to raise the profile of these members of Congress. For example, Courtney and others in the Frontline team received high-profile speaking assignments on the floor of Congress and were appointed to key congressional committees. In 2008, Courtney won his seat by a comfortable margin, and he was easily re-elected in 2010, 2012, and 2014.[13]

The advantage of incumbency thus tends to preserve the status quo in Congress. This fact has implications for the social composition of Congress. For example, incumbency advantage makes it harder for women to increase their numbers in Congress because most incumbents are men. Women who run for open seats—that is, seats for which there are no incumbents—are just as likely to win as male candidates.[14] Supporters of **term limits** argue that such limits are the only way to get new faces into Congress. They believe that incumbency advantage and the tendency of many legislators to view politics as a career mean that very little turnover will occur in Congress unless limits are imposed on the number of terms a legislator may serve.

term limits legally prescribed limits on the number of terms an elected official can serve

Yet the percentage of incumbents who are returned to Congress after each election also depends on how many members decide to run again. Because each year some members decide to retire, turnover in Congress is greater than the re-election rates of incumbents suggest. On average, 10 percent of the House and Senate decide to retire each election.

The precarious economy and the backlash against the party in power made 2008 and 2010 difficult election years for some incumbents. Democrats felt particularly vulnerable in 2010, given that their party controlled the presidency and both houses of Congress in a year when economic woes contributed to strong anti-incumbent sentiment.[15] Even with retirements, 54 incumbent Democratic members of the House and two incumbent Democratic senators lost their seats in 2010, including two who lost in the primaries. Incumbents fared better in the 2012 elections. In the House, 13 incumbents lost primary races and 27 incumbents lost their seats in the general election; while one incumbent senator lost in the primaries and one lost the general election. In 2014, 45 members of the House and 11 members of the Senate did not run for re-election (due to retiring, running for a different office, resigning, appointment to a different office, or death). Republicans candidates fared well in 2014. Only 3 Republican House incumbents lost their elections, compared to 10 Democrats. In the Senate races, no Republicans lost, compared to 5 Democratic senators. The Republicans' victories handed them control of the Senate.

Apportionment and Redistricting The final factor affecting who wins a seat in Congress is the way congressional districts are drawn. Every 10 years, state legislatures must redraw congressional districts to reflect population changes. Because the number of congressional seats has been fixed at 435 since 1929, redistricting is a zero-sum process; in order for one state to gain a seat, another must lose one. The process of allocating congressional seats among the 50 states is called **apportionment**. States with population growth gain additional seats; states with a population decline or with less population growth lose seats. Over the past several decades, the shift of the American population to the South and the West has greatly increased the size of

apportionment the process, occurring after every decennial census, that allocates congressional seats among the 50 states

the congressional delegations from those regions (see Figure 12.3). This trend continued after the 2010 census. Texas emerged as the biggest winner, with a gain of four additional seats, while Florida added two seats and Arizona, Georgia, Nevada, South Carolina, Utah, and Washington each added one seat.[16] Latino voters are nearly three times as prevalent in states that gained seats than in states that lost seats, suggesting that the growth of Latino population is a major factor in the American political landscape.[17]

States that gain or lose seats must then redraw their congressional district borders. Not surprisingly, **redistricting** is a highly political process: districts are shaped to create an advantage for the party with a majority in the state legislature, which controls the redistricting process in most states. In this complex process, those charged with drawing districts use sophisticated computer technologies to come up with the most favorable district boundaries. Redistricting can create open seats and may pit incumbents of the same party against one another, ensuring that one of them will lose. Redistricting can also give an advantage to one party by clustering voters with some ideological or sociological characteristics in a single district, or by separating those voters into two or more districts. The manipulation of electoral districts to serve the interests of a particular group is known as **gerrymandering** (see Chapter 10).

Some analysts claim that Republicans have benefited from partisan gerrymandering since the 2010 redistricting cycle, because the GOP controlled the majority of state legislatures at the time. To support this argument, they point to the 2012 congressional election, in which the GOP maintained its majority in the House despite winning 1.4 million fewer votes than Democratic House candidates.[18] But others question whether districting that favors Republicans is a product of deliberate gerrymandering. They argue that these districts may reflect the natural clustering of Democrats in urban areas, not deliberate bias.[19] Even so, concern about partisan gerrymandering has led some states to take redistricting power away from state legislatures and give it to independent commissions. In the 2010 redistricting

redistricting the process of redrawing election districts and redistributing legislative representatives; this happens every 10 years to reflect shifts in population or in response to legal challenges to existing districts

gerrymandering the apportionment of voters in districts in such a way as to give unfair advantage to one racial or ethnic group or political party

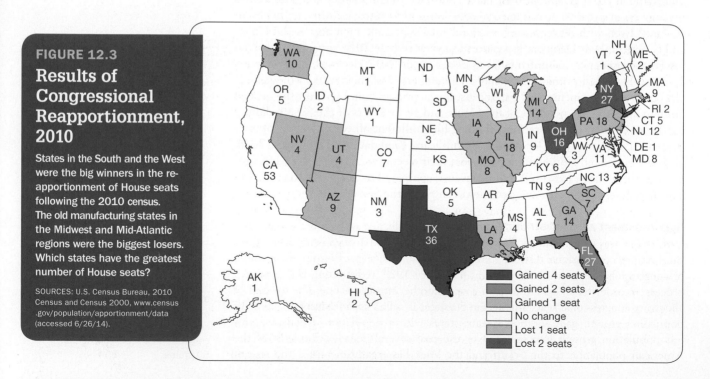

FIGURE 12.3

Results of Congressional Reapportionment, 2010

States in the South and the West were the big winners in the reapportionment of House seats following the 2010 census. The old manufacturing states in the Midwest and Mid-Atlantic regions were the biggest losers. Which states have the greatest number of House seats?

SOURCES: U.S. Census Bureau, 2010 Census and Census 2000, www.census .gov/population/apportionment/data (accessed 6/26/14).

Gained 4 seats
Gained 2 seats
Gained 1 seat
No change
Lost 1 seat
Lost 2 seats

Redrawing legislative districts is a difficult task because it has implications for who will be elected. Here, the attorney for Arizona's Independent Redistricting Commission discusses a possible layout with a city council member from Casa Grande. Arizona gained one congressional seat following the 2010 census.

cycle, seven states—California, Arizona, Hawaii, Idaho, New Jersey, Washington, and Montana—required district lines to be drawn by commissions.[20]

As we saw in Chapter 10, since the passage of the 1982 amendments to the Voting Rights Act of 1965, race has become a major, and controversial, consideration in drawing voting districts. These amendments, which encouraged the creation of districts in which members of racial minorities have decisive majorities, have greatly increased the number of minority representatives in Congress. After the 1991–92 redistricting, the number of predominantly minority districts doubled, rising from 26 to 52. Among the most fervent supporters of the new minority districts were white Republicans, who used the opportunity to create more districts dominated by white Republican voters. These developments raise thorny questions about representation. Some analysts argue that the system may grant minorities greater sociological representation but has made it more difficult for minorities to win substantive policy goals, but others dispute this argument.[21]

In the case of *Miller v. Johnson* (1995), the Supreme Court limited racial redistricting by ruling that race could not be the predominant factor in creating electoral districts.[22] The distinction between race being the "predominant" factor and its being one factor among many is very hazy. As a result, concerns about redistricting and representation have not disappeared.[23] Questions about minority representation emerged in 2011 in Texas, which gained four new seats as a result of reapportionment. The Republican legislature drew a map that advantaged Republicans in three of those districts. But the plan drew a legal challenge on the grounds that it underrepresented Hispanic voters, who accounted for most of the state's population growth. Although federal judges drew a map more favorable to minorities (and Democrats), the Supreme Court ruled that the state did not have to use the map drawn by judges. The state ultimately agreed to a map that added two Latino-dominated districts. However, federal courts ruled that this map also weakened Latino and African American political power by creating too few minority districts. The future of race in redistricting became more uncertain after the 2013 Supreme Court decision in *Shelby County v. Holder*. That decision invalidated a section of the Voting Rights Act requiring that the Justice Department approve the redistricting plans of jurisdictions with a history of racial discrimination.[24] Many Democrats expressed disappointment with the decision, fearing that the previously covered states, several of which are controlled by Republican majorities, might try to redraw district lines to partisan ends and further bias districts toward Republicans.[25] Because the drawing of district boundaries affects incumbents as well as the field of candidates who decide to run for office, it continues to be a key battleground on which political parties fight about the meaning of representation.

Direct Patronage

As agents of their constituents, members of Congress have numerous opportunities to provide direct benefits, or **patronage**, for their districts. The most important such opportunity for direct patronage is in so-called **pork-barrel** legislation, which specifies a project to be funded within a particular district. Many observers of Congress argue that pork-barrel bills are the only ones that some members are serious about moving toward actual passage, because they are seen as so important to members' re-election bids.

A common form of pork-barreling is the "earmark," by which members of Congress insert into bills language that provides special benefits for their own constituents. When the Democrats took over Congress in 2007, they vowed to limit the use of earmarks, which had grown from 1,439 per year in 1995 to 15,268 in 2006. More troubling, earmarks were connected to congressional scandals. For example, the Republican House member Randy "Duke" Cunningham (R-Calif.) was sent to jail in 2005 for accepting bribes by companies hoping to receive earmarks in return.[26] The House passed a new rule requiring that those representatives supporting each earmark identify themselves and guarantee that they have no personal financial stake in the requested project. A new ethics law applied similar provisions to the Senate. The new requirements appear to have had some impact: the 2007 military bill, for example, passed with only half the dollar amount of earmarks as the military bill passed in 2006 contained. But in the midst of the sharp economic downturn in 2009, Congress passed an economic stimulus bill that contained more than 8,000 earmarks. In many cases, Republicans and some Democrats who voted against the bill were later happy to take credit from their constituents for the earmarks they had placed in it. In his 2010 State of the Union address, President Obama called for Congress to publish a list of all earmark requests on a single website. Congress not only failed to enact such legislation, but in 2010 it set a new record by passing 11,320 earmarks worth $32 billion. Still, in 2011 the House and the Senate agreed to a two-year moratorium on earmarks in spending bills and renewed the ban in 2012 for the 113th Congress.[27] Despite the moratorium, some members of Congress charged that special provisions were creeping back into legislation, and a few members of Congress supported making the moratorium permanent.[28]

Highway bills are a favorite vehicle for congressional pork-barrel spending. A 2005 highway bill was full of such items, containing more than 6,000 projects earmarked for specific congressional districts. These measures often have little to do with transportation needs, instead serving as evidence for constituents that congressional members can bring federal dollars back home. Perhaps the most extravagant item in the 2005 bill—and the one least needed for transportation—was a bridge in Alaska designed to connect a barely populated island to the town of

Ketchikan, population just under 8,000. At a cost that could soar to $2 billion, the bridge would have replaced an existing five-minute ferry ride. Alaska's representative, Don Young (R), proudly claimed credit. After Hurricane Katrina, "the bridge to nowhere" became a symbol of wasteful congressional spending. Sensitive to this criticism, Congress removed the earmarks for the bridge from the final legislation.

There are a few other types of direct patronage (see Figure 12.4). One important form of constituency service is intervention with federal administrative agencies on behalf of constituents. Members of the House and Senate and their staff spend a great deal of time on the telephone and in administrative offices seeking to secure favorable treatment for constituents and supporters. For example, members of Congress can assist senior citizens who are having Social Security or Medicare benefit eligibility problems. Most members of Congress have a "constituent services" section on their websites, providing information about what they can and cannot do to assist their constituents. For example, Representative Paul Ryan's (R-Wisc.) website puts it this way: "one of the most important jobs I have is to provide assistance to my constituents. Providing help with a problem involving a federal agency or helping obtain an American flag flown over the U.S. Capitol are only a few examples of the number of services that I provide to those I represent."[29]

A different form of patronage is the **private bill**. Unlike a public bill, which is supposed to deal with general rules and categories of behavior, people, and institutions, a private bill proposes to grant some kind of relief, special privilege, or exemption to the person named in the bill. As many as 75 percent of all private bills introduced (and one-third of those that pass) are concerned with obtaining citizenship for foreign nationals who do not have resident status in the United States. Private legislation is a congressional privilege that can be abused, but it is impossible to imagine members of

private bill a proposal in Congress to provide a specific person with some kind of relief, such as a special exemption from immigration quotas

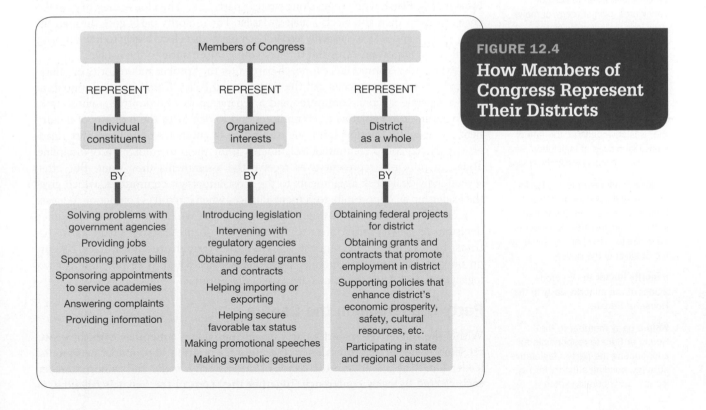

FIGURE 12.4

How Members of Congress Represent Their Districts

Members of Congress

REPRESENT — Individual constituents — BY

- Solving problems with government agencies
- Providing jobs
- Sponsoring private bills
- Sponsoring appointments to service academies
- Answering complaints
- Providing information

REPRESENT — Organized interests — BY

- Introducing legislation
- Intervening with regulatory agencies
- Obtaining federal grants and contracts
- Helping importing or exporting
- Helping secure favorable tax status
- Making promotional speeches
- Making symbolic gestures

REPRESENT — District as a whole — BY

- Obtaining federal projects for district
- Obtaining grants and contracts that promote employment in district
- Supporting policies that enhance district's economic prosperity, safety, cultural resources, etc.
- Participating in state and regional caucuses

Congress completely giving up one of the easiest, cheapest, and most effective forms of patronage available to them. It can be defended as an indispensable part of the process by which members of Congress seek to fulfill their role as representatives. And obviously they like the privilege because it helps them win re-election.

● The Organization of Congress

> **Explain how party leadership, the committee system, the staff system, and caucuses help structure congressional business**

The U.S. Congress is not only a representative assembly, it is also a legislative body. To exercise its power to make laws, Congress must first bring about something close to an organizational miracle. The building blocks of congressional organization include the political parties, the committee system, congressional staff, the caucuses, and the parliamentary rules of the House and Senate. Each of these factors plays a key role in the organization of Congress and in the process through which Congress formulates and enacts laws.

Party Leadership in the House

Every two years, at the beginning of a new Congress, the members of each party gather to elect their House leaders. House Republicans call their gathering the **conference**. House Democrats call theirs the **caucus**. The elected leader of the majority party is later proposed to the whole House and is automatically elected to the position of **Speaker of the House**, with voting along straight party lines. The House majority conference or caucus then also elects a **majority leader**. The minority party goes through the same process and selects a **minority leader**. Each party also elects a **whip** to line up party members on important votes and to relay voting information to the leaders.

Next in order of importance for each party after the Speaker and majority or minority leader is what Democrats call the Steering and Policy Committee—Republicans have a separate steering committee and a separate policy committee—whose tasks are to assign new legislators to committees and to deal with the requests of incumbent members for transfers from one committee to another. At one time, party leaders strictly controlled committee assignments, using them to enforce party discipline. Today, in principle, representatives receive the assignments they want. But often several individuals seek assignments to the most important committees, which gives the leadership an opportunity to cement alliances when it resolves conflicting requests.

Generally, representatives seek assignments that will allow them to influence decisions of special importance to their districts. Representatives from farm districts, for example, may request seats on the Agriculture Committee.[30] Seats on powerful committees such as Ways and Means, which is responsible for tax legislation, and Appropriations are especially popular.

Party Leadership in the Senate

Within the Senate, the majority party usually designates a member with the greatest seniority to serve as president pro tempore, a position of primarily ceremonial leadership. Real power is in the hands of the majority leader and minority leader, each elected by party conference. Together they control the Senate's calendar, or

conference a gathering of House Republicans every two years to elect their House leaders; Democrats call their gathering the caucus

caucus (political) a normally closed meeting of a political or legislative group to select candidates, plan strategy, or make decisions regarding legislative matters

Speaker of the House the chief presiding officer of the House of Representatives; the Speaker is the most important party and House leader, and can influence the legislative agenda, the fate of individual pieces of legislation, and members' positions within the House

majority leader the elected leader of the majority party in the House of Representatives or in the Senate; in the House, the majority leader is subordinate in the party hierarchy to the Speaker of the House

minority leader the elected leader of the minority party in the House or Senate

whip a party member in the House or Senate responsible for coordinating the party's legislative strategy, building support for key issues, and counting votes

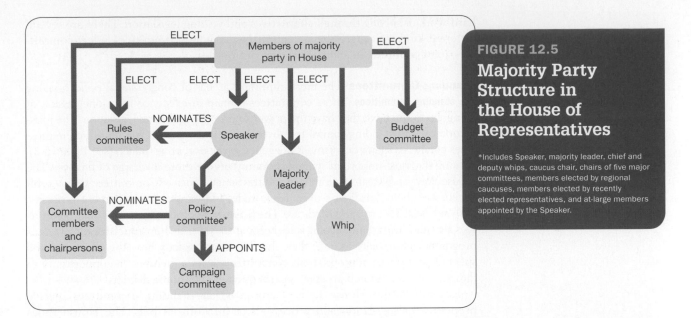

FIGURE 12.5

Majority Party Structure in the House of Representatives

*Includes Speaker, majority leader, chief and deputy whips, caucus chair, chairs of five major committees, members elected by regional caucuses, members elected by recently elected representatives, and at-large members appointed by the Speaker.

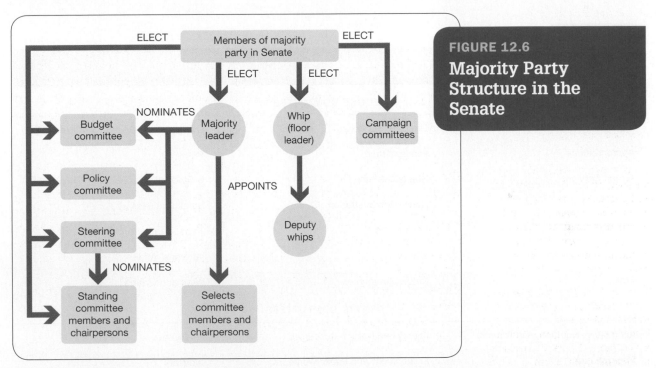

FIGURE 12.6

Majority Party Structure in the Senate

agenda for legislation. Each party also elects a policy committee, which advises the leadership on legislative priorities. The structure of majority party leadership in the House and the Senate is shown in Figures 12.5 and 12.6.

The Committee System

The committee system is central to the operation of Congress. At each stage of the legislative process, Congress relies on committees and subcommittees to do the hard work of sorting through alternatives and writing legislation. There are several different kinds of congressional committees: standing committees, select committees, joint committees, and conference committees.

Standing Committees The most important arenas of congressional policy making are **standing committees**. These committees remain in existence from one session of Congress to the next; they have the power to propose and write legislation. The jurisdiction of each standing committee covers a particular subject matter, which in most cases parallels a major department or agency in the executive branch (see Table 12.2). Among the most important standing committees are those in charge of finances. The House Ways and Means Committee and the Senate Finance Committee are powerful because of their jurisdiction over taxes, trade, and expensive entitlement programs such as Social Security and Medicare. The Senate and House Appropriations committees also play important ongoing roles because they decide how much funding various programs will actually receive; they also determine exactly how the money will be spent. A seat on an appropriations committee allows a member the opportunity to direct funds to a favored program—perhaps one in her home district.

Except for the House Rules Committee, all standing committees receive proposals for legislation and process them into official bills. The House Rules

standing committee a permanent committee with the power to propose and write legislation that covers a particular subject, such as finance or agriculture

TABLE 12.2

Permanent Committees of Congress

HOUSE COMMITTEES

Agriculture	Financial Services	Oversight and Government Reform
Appropriations	Foreign Affairs	Rules
Armed Services	Homeland Security	Science, Space, and Technology
Budget	House Administration	Small Business
Education and the Workforce	Intelligence	Transportation and Infrastructure
Energy and Commerce	Judiciary	Veterans' Affairs
Ethics	Natural Resources	Ways and Means

SENATE COMMITTEES

Agriculture, Nutrition, and Forestry	Energy and Natural Resources	Intelligence
Appropriations	Environment and Public Works	Judiciary
Armed Services	Finance	Rules and Administration
Banking, Housing, and Urban Affairs	Foreign Relations	Small Business and Entrepreneurship
Budget	Health, Education, Labor, and Pensions	Veterans' Affairs
Commerce, Science, and Transportation	Homeland Security and Governmental Affairs	

Committees hold hearings to gather information for legislation. The committee on Homeland Security was set up as a select committee in the wake of 9/11 and is now a permanent committee. In February 2014, the committee listened to testimony from U.S. Homeland Security secretary Jeh Johnson on his analysis of challenges and priorities facing his department.

Committee decides the order in which bills come up for a vote on the House floor and determines the specific rules that govern the length of debate and opportunity for amendments. The Senate, which has less formal organization and fewer rules, does not have a rules committee.

Select Committees **Select committees** are usually not permanent and usually do not have the power to present legislation to the full Congress. (The House and Senate Select Intelligence committees are permanent, however, and do have the power to report legislation, which means they can send legislation to the full House or Senate for consideration.) These committees hold hearings and serve as focal points for the issues they are charged with considering. Congressional leaders form select committees when they want to take up issues that fall outside the jurisdictions of existing committees, to highlight an issue, or to investigate a particular problem. Examples of select committees investigating political scandals include the Senate Watergate Committee of 1973, the committees set up in 1987 to investigate the Iran-Contra affair, and the Whitewater Committee of 1995–96. Select committees set up to highlight ongoing issues have included the House Select Committee on Hunger, established in 1984, and the House Select Committee on Energy Independence and Global Warming, created in 2007 but abolished in 2011, when Republicans assumed control of the House. In 2003 an important select committee, the House Select Committee on Homeland Security, was created to oversee the new Department of Homeland Security. Unlike most select committees, this one had the ability to present legislation. Initially the committee had only temporary status. It was made a regular permanent committee in 2005.

Joint Committees **Joint committees** involve members from both the Senate and the House. There are four such committees: economic, taxation, library, and printing. These joint committees are permanent, but they do not have the power to present legislation. The Joint Economic Committee and the Joint Taxation Committee have often played important roles in collecting information and holding

select committees (usually) temporary legislative committees set up to highlight or investigate a particular issue or address an issue not within the jurisdiction of existing committees

joint committees legislative committees formed of members of both the House and Senate

hearings on economic and financial issues. In 2011, Congress created the Joint Select Committee on Deficit Reduction and, in an unusual move, gave the committee the power to write and report legislation. Informally known as "the supercommittee," the committee was charged with coming up with $1.2 trillion in debt reduction. Formed after a contentious debate about raising the debt limit (usually a routine matter), the super-committee proved unable to come to an agreement and disbanded less than four months after it was created.

conference committees joint committees created to work out a compromise on House and Senate versions of a piece of legislation

Conference Committees Finally, **conference committees** are temporary committees whose members are appointed by the Speaker of the House and the presiding officer of the Senate. These committees are charged with reaching a compromise on legislation once it has been passed by the House and the Senate. Conference committees play an extremely important role in determining the laws that are actually passed, because they must reconcile any differences in the legislation passed by the House and Senate.

When control of Congress is divided between two parties, each is guaranteed significant representation in conference committees. When a single party controls both houses, the majority party is not obligated to offer such representation to the minority party. In 2003, Democrats complained that Republicans took this power to the extreme by excluding them and adding new provisions to legislation at the conference committee stage. Democrats even prevented several conference committees from convening to protest their near exclusion from conference committees on major energy, health care, and transportation laws. After they returned to power in 2007, the Democrats also largely bypassed the conference committees; when their early efforts to reach compromises in committee were derailed by partisan differences, the Democrats began making closed-door agreements between top leaders in the House and the Senate. Although the process facilitated compromises across the two chambers, it meant that important changes to bills were made in private, without the transparency that would have been part of the conference committee process. After 2010, Congress continued to avoid conference committees. Instead, the Republican House and Democratic Senate exchanged amendments as they sought to reach agreement on the final version of a bill, a practice known informally as "ping pong."[31]

seniority the ranking given to an individual on the basis of length of continuous service on a committee in Congress

Politics and the Organization of Committees Within each committee, hierarchy has usually been based on **seniority** determined by years of continuous service on that particular committee. In general, each committee is chaired by the most senior member of the majority party. But the principle of seniority is not absolute. When the Republicans took over the House in 1995, they violated the principle of seniority in the selection of key committee chairs. House Speaker Newt Gingrich defended the new practice, saying, "You've got to carry the moral responsibility of fielding the team that can win or you cheat the whole conference."[32] Since then, Republicans have continued to depart from the seniority principle, often choosing committee chairs on the basis of loyalty or fund-raising abilities rather than seniority. In 2007, Democrats returned to the seniority principle for choosing committee chairs but altered traditional practices in other ways by offering freshmen Democrats choice committee assignments to increase their chances of re-election.[33]

Over the years, Congress has reformed its organizational structure and operating procedures. Most changes have been made to improve efficiency, but some reforms have also been a response to political considerations. In the 1970s, for example, Congress increased the number of subcommittees and gave greater autonomy to subcommittee chairs. (Subcommittees are responsible for considering a specific subset of issues under a committee's jurisdiction.) By enhancing subcommittee power and allowing more members to chair subcommittees and appoint subcommittee staff, the reforms undercut the power of committee chairs. Yet the reforms of the 1970s created new problems for Congress: power became more fragmented, making it harder to reach agreement on legislation. The Republican leadership of the 104th Congress (1995–97), seeking to reverse this fragmentation of congressional power and concentrate more authority in the party leadership, reduced the number of subcommittees and limited the time committee chairs could serve to three terms. They made good on this in 2001, when they replaced 13 committee chairs.

As a consequence of these changes, committees no longer have the central role they once held in policy making. Furthermore, sharp partisan divisions have made it difficult for committees to deliberate and bring bipartisan expertise to bear on policy making as in the past. With committees less able to engage in effective decision making, they typically do not deliberate for very long or call witnesses, and it has become more common in recent years for party-driven legislation to go directly to the floor, bypassing committees altogether.[34] Nonetheless, committees continue to play an important role in the legislative process, especially on issues that are not sharply partisan.[35]

The Staff System: Staffers and Agencies

The congressional institution second in importance only to the committee system is the staff system. Every member of Congress employs many staff members whose tasks include handling constituent requests and, to a large extent, dealing with legislative details and the activities of administrative agencies. Staffers often bear the primary responsibility for formulating and drafting proposals, organizing hearings, dealing with administrative agencies, and negotiating with lobbyists. Indeed, legislators typically deal with one another through staff, rather than through direct personal contact. Staffers even develop policy ideas, draft legislation, and, in some instances, have a good deal of influence over the legislative process. Representatives and senators together employ roughly 11,500 staffers in their Washington and home offices. In addition, Congress employs more than 2,000 committee staffers.[36] These individuals make up the permanent staff that stays attached to every House and Senate committee regardless of turnover in Congress and that is responsible for organizing and administering the committee's work, including doing research, scheduling, organizing hearings, and drafting legislation. Committee staffers can play key roles in the legislative process.

One example of the importance that members of Congress attach to committee staffers was the conflict over hiring a new staff director for the House Ethics Committee in 2005. The Committee on Ethics has the power to investigate members for unethical practices and can issue reprimands or censures when it finds that members have violated House rules. In 2010, with allegations of ethics violations swirling around several prominent House members, including long-serving representative Maxine Waters (D-Calif.), and the successful censuring of Charles Rangel (D-N.Y.), then the powerful chairman of the Ways and Means Committee, the committee on Ethics was at the center of congressional conflict. But following a series of tumultuous shakeups in which the staff director resigned and two deputy attorneys were effectively

Members of Congress rely heavily on their personal staffs and on committee staffs, who often play an important role in the legislative process.

fired over allegations of mishandling the Waters investigation, the committee was at a standstill for more than four months as Republicans and Democrats struggled to agree on an acceptable staff director replacement.[37]

Not only does Congress employ personal and committee staff, but it has also established **staff agencies** designed to provide the legislative branch with resources and expertise independent of the executive branch. These agencies enhance Congress's capacity to oversee administrative agencies and to evaluate presidential programs and proposals. They include the Congressional Research Service, which performs research for legislators who wish to know the facts and competing arguments relevant to policy proposals or other legislative business; the Government Accountability Office, through which Congress can investigate the financial and administrative affairs of any government agency or program; and the Congressional Budget Office, which assesses the economic implications and likely costs of proposed federal programs.

Informal Organization: The Caucuses

In addition to the official organization of Congress, an unofficial organizational structure also exists: the caucuses. **Caucuses** are groups of senators or representatives who share certain opinions, interests, or social characteristics. A large number of caucuses are composed of legislators representing particular economic or policy interests, such as the Travel and Tourism Caucus, the Steel Caucus, the Mushroom Caucus, and Concerned Senators for the Arts. Legislators who share common backgrounds have organized caucuses such as the Congressional Black Caucus, the Congressional Caucus for Women's Issues, and the Hispanic Caucus. All these caucuses seek to advance the interests of the groups they represent by promoting legislation, encouraging Congress to hold hearings, and pressing administrative agencies for favorable treatment. In recent years, some caucuses have evolved into powerful lobbying organizations, well funded by interest groups. For example, the Sportsmen's Caucus receives funds from a nonprofit foundation that itself benefits from donations from the National Rifle Association, sports equipment manufacturers, and firearms manufacturers. In 2010 conservative Republicans in the House and Senate formed the Tea Party Caucus to advance antispending policies.

● Rules of Lawmaking: How a Bill Becomes a Law

> **Outline the steps in the process of passing a law**

The institutional structure of Congress is a key factor in shaping the legislative process. A second and equally important set of factors is the rules of congressional procedure. These rules govern everything from the introduction of a **bill** through its submission to the president for signing (see Figure 12.7). Not only do these regulations influence the fate of every bill, but they also help determine the distribution of power in the Congress.

Committee Deliberation

The first step in getting a law passed is drafting legislation. Members of Congress, the White House, and federal agencies all take roles in developing and drafting

staff agencies legislative support agencies responsible for policy analysis

caucuses (congressional) associations of members of Congress based on party, interest, or social group, such as gender or race

bill a proposed law that has been sponsored by a member of Congress and submitted to the clerk of the House or Senate

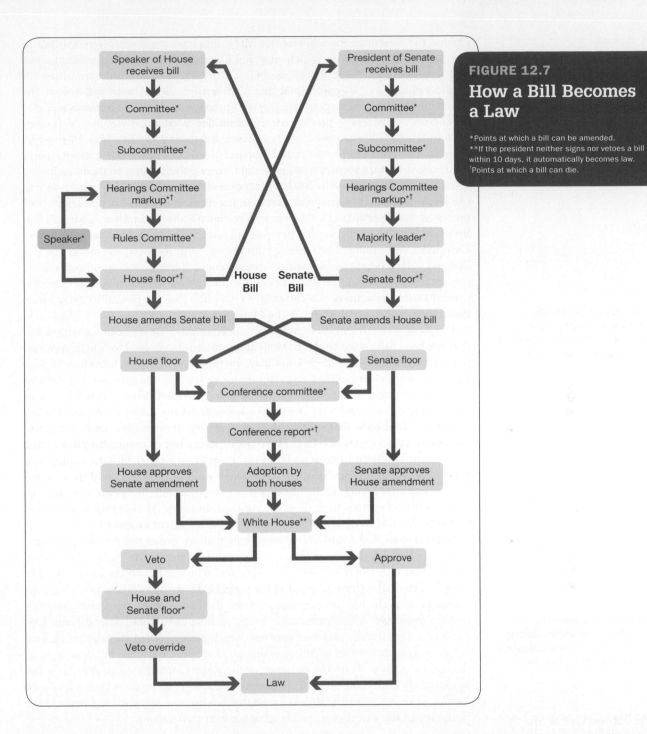

FIGURE 12.7

How a Bill Becomes a Law

*Points at which a bill can be amended.
**If the president neither signs nor vetoes a bill within 10 days, it automatically becomes law.
†Points at which a bill can die.

Speaker of House receives bill → **Committee*** → **Subcommittee*** → **Hearings Committee markup*†** → **Rules Committee*** → **House floor*†**

Speaker*

President of Senate receives bill → **Committee*** → **Subcommittee*** → **Hearings Committee markup*†** → **Majority leader*** → **Senate floor*†**

House Bill **Senate Bill**

House amends Senate bill **Senate amends House bill**

House floor **Senate floor**

Conference committee*

Conference report*†

House approves Senate amendment **Adoption by both houses** **Senate approves House amendment**

White House**

Veto **Approve**

House and Senate floor*

Veto override

Law

initial legislation. Bills can originate in the House or the Senate but only the House can introduce "money bills," those that spend or raise revenues. The framers' inserted this provision in the Constitution because they believed that the chamber closest to the people should exercise greater authority over taxing and spending. The bill is then officially submitted by a senator or representative to the clerk of the House or Senate and referred to the appropriate committee for deliberation.

During the course of its deliberations, the committee typically refers the bill to one of its subcommittees, which may hold hearings, listen to expert testimony, and amend the proposed legislation before referring it to the full committee for consideration. The full committee may then accept the recommendation of the subcommittee or hold its own hearings and prepare its own amendments.

The next steps in the process are the **committee markup** sessions, in which committees rewrite bills to reflect changes discussed during the hearings. In the partisan fighting that has characterized Congress in recent years, the minority party has charged that its members are often not given enough time to study proposed legislation before markup. In 2003 conflict over this issue drew the Capitol police to the House and almost resulted in a fistfight among representatives when Democrats protested their treatment by the House Ways and Means Committee. Charging that they had been given a complex pension bill only 10 hours before markup, House Democrats walked out. The ensuing commotion, with Republicans calling the police and a Democratic congressman threatening a Republican, presented a sorry spectacle for the evening news. Although Democrats lost a resolution to censure the committee for its actions, the committee chair, Bill Thomas (R-Calif.), later broke down in tears as he apologized on the House floor.

Frequently, the committee and subcommittee do little or nothing with a bill that has been submitted to them. Many bills are simply allowed to "die in committee" without serious consideration. Often, members of Congress introduce legislation that they neither expect nor even desire to see enacted into law but present mainly to please a constituency group by taking a stand. Many such bills are of narrow interest or stand little chance of passing given the political climate. For example, in 2009 Bobby Rush (D-Ill.) introduced a bill to establish a national registry for firearms. As with most bills that are not reported out of committee, Rush's bill attracted little serious interest and only one cosponsor.[38] These bills die a quick and painless death. Other pieces of legislation have ardent supporters and die in committee only after a long battle. But in either case, most bills are never reported out of the committees to which they are assigned. In a typical congressional session, 95 percent of the roughly 8,000 bills introduced die in committee.

In the House, the relative handful of bills that are presented out of committee must pass one last hurdle within the committee system—the Rules Committee, which determines the rules that will govern action on the bill on the House floor. In particular, the Rules Committee allots the time for debate and decides to what extent amendments to the bill can be proposed from the floor. A bill's supporters generally prefer a **closed rule**, which puts severe limits on floor debate and amendments. Opponents of a bill usually prefer an **open rule**, which permits potentially damaging floor debate and makes it easier to add amendments that may cripple the bill or weaken its chances for passage. Thus, the outcome of the Rules Committee's deliberations can be extremely important, and the committee's hearings can be an occasion for sharp conflict. In recent years, the Rules Committee has become less powerful because the House leadership exercises so much influence over its decisions.

Debate

The next step in getting a law passed is debate on the floor of the House and Senate. Party control of the agenda is reinforced by the rule giving the Speaker of the House and the president of the Senate the power of recognition during debate on a bill. Usually the chair knows the purpose for which a member intends to

committee markup the session in which a congressional committee rewrites legislation to incorporate changes discussed during hearings on a bill

closed rule a provision by the House Rules Committee limiting or prohibiting the introduction of amendments during debate

open rule a provision by the House Rules Committee that permits floor debate and the addition of new amendments to a bill

speak well in advance of the occasion. Spontaneous efforts to gain recognition are often foiled. For example, the Speaker may ask, "For what purpose does the member rise?" before deciding whether to grant recognition.

In the House, virtually all the time allotted by the Rules Committee for debate on a given bill is controlled by the bill's sponsor and by its leading opponent. In almost every case, these two people are the committee chair and the ranking minority member of the committee that processed the bill—or those they designate. These two participants are, by rule and tradition, granted the power to allocate most of the debate time in small amounts to members who are seeking to speak for or against the measure. Preference in the allocation of time goes to the members of the committee whose jurisdiction covers the bill.

Filibuster In the Senate, the leadership has much less control over floor debate. Indeed, the Senate is unique among the world's legislative bodies for its commitment to unlimited debate. Once given the floor, a senator may speak as long as he wishes. On a number of memorable occasions, senators have used this opportunity to prevent action on legislation that they opposed. Through this tactic, called the **filibuster**, small minorities or even one individual in the Senate can force the majority to give in. Filibusters can be ended by a Senate vote to cut off debate, called **cloture**. From 1917 to 1975, it took two-thirds of the Senate or 67 votes to end a filibuster. In 1975 the Senate changed the rules to three-fifths of the Senate or 60 votes needed for cloture. The threat of a filibuster ensures that, in crafting legislation and proposing judicial appointments, the majority takes into account the viewpoint of the political minority.

For much of American history, senators only rarely used the filibuster, though during the 1950s and '60s, opponents of civil rights legislation often used filibusters to block its passage. In the last 20 years, the filibuster has become so common that observers routinely note that it takes 60 votes to get anything passed in the Senate. The 110th Congress (2007–08) set a new record, with 112 cloture votes (the vote to end a filibuster). The 113th Congress (2013–14) broke the record, with 178 cloture votes as of November 2014. In contrast, the 109th Congress (2005–06) held only 54 cloture votes.[39]

In 2013 the Democratic Senate leader Harry Reid (Nev.) mobilized his party to alter the filibuster rules for the first time in many decades. Frustrated by the repeated failure of the Senate to vote on many of the president's nominees to fill positions in the executive branch—including judgeships to important federal courts—Reid invoked what senators had come to call "the nuclear option," a change to the filibuster rules. Under the new rules, nominees for positions in the executive branch and the federal courts—except the Supreme Court—cannot be filibustered. This means that they can be approved by a simple majority vote. Not surprisingly, the two parties had different views on the decision. Reid defended it as necessary, due to what he called "unbelievable, unprecedented obstruction." Republicans denounced the new rule, stating, in the words of Pat Roberts (R-Kan.), "We have weakened this body permanently."[40]

Amendments and Holds The filibuster is not the only technique used to block Senate debate. Under Senate rules, members have virtually unlimited ability to propose amendments to a pending bill. Each amendment must be voted on before the bill can come to a final vote. The introduction of new amendments can be stopped only by unanimous consent. This, in effect, can permit a determined minority to filibuster by amendment, indefinitely delaying the passage of a bill.

Once a senator is granted the floor, Senate rules permit him to speak for as long as he wishes. Although "talking filibusters" are rare today, in 2013 Senator Rand Paul (R-Ky.) spoke continuously for 13 hours about the legality of potential drone strikes on U.S. soil.

filibuster a tactic used by members of the Senate to prevent action on legislation they oppose by continuously holding the floor and speaking until the majority backs down; once given the floor, senators have unlimited time to speak, and it requires a vote of three-fifths of the Senate to end a filibuster

cloture a rule or process in a legislative body aimed at ending debate on a given bill; in the U.S. Senate, 60 senators (three-fifths) must agree in order to impose a time limit and end debate

Senators can also place "holds," or stalling devices, on bills to delay debate. Senators place holds on bills when they fear that openly opposing them will be unpopular. Because holds are kept secret, the senators placing the holds do not have to take public responsibility for their actions. There have been several efforts to eliminate holds. In 1997 opponents of this practice introduced an amendment that would have required publicizing the identity of the senator putting a bill on hold. But when the Senate voted on the measure, the proposal to end the practice of anonymous holds had "mysteriously disappeared."[41] Although no one took credit for killing the measure, it was evident that the majority of senators wanted to maintain the practice. In 2007 reformers succeeded in passing the Honest Leadership and Open Government Act. Although the new law did not eliminate holds, it contained provisions requiring senators who imposed a hold to identify themselves in the *Congressional Record* after six days and state the reasons for the hold.[42] Even with this provision, senators continued to impose holds on legislation and especially on presidential appointees. Senator Lindsey Graham (R-S.C.) aroused the ire of the White House in 2013 for threatening to use holds on all of President Obama's nominees unless the administration made survivors of the 2012 terrorist attack on the U.S. mission in Benghazi, Libya, available to Congress for questioning.[43]

Voting Once a bill is debated on the floor of the House and the Senate, the leaders schedule it for a vote on the floor of each chamber. By this time, congressional leaders know what the vote will be; leaders do not bring legislation to the floor unless they are fairly certain it is going to pass. As a consequence, it is unusual for the leadership to lose a bill on the floor. On rare occasions, the last moments of the floor vote can be very dramatic, as each party's leadership puts its whip organization into action to make sure that wavering members vote with the party. In September 2008 the House of Representatives surprisingly rejected a $700 billion bank rescue plan, which led the Dow Jones Industrial Index to decline nearly 7 percent in a single day—one of the biggest drops in recent history. As the *New York Times* reported, lawmakers were "almost speechless" on hearing that the bill had not passed; not only did the White House and the congressional leadership of both parties expect the bill to prevail, albeit narrowly, but so did even its most ardent opponents. As the end of the voting period drew close, it was clear that the bill was going down to defeat, with 205 votes for the bill and 228 against. (A few days later, the House passed a revised version of the bill by 263 to 171 votes.)[44]

Conference Committee: Reconciling House and Senate Versions of Legislation

Getting a bill out of committee and through both houses of Congress is no guarantee that the bill will be enacted into law; it must be considered by a conference committee. Frequently, bills that begin with similar provisions in both chambers emerge with little resemblance to each other. Alternatively, a bill may be passed by one chamber but undergo substantial revision in the other chamber. In such cases, a conference committee composed of the senior members of the committees or subcommittees that initiated the bill may be required to iron out differences between the two now-dissimilar pieces of legislation. Sometimes members or leaders will let objectionable provisions pass on the floor, knowing that they will get the chance to make changes in conference. Usually, conference committees meet behind closed doors. Agreement requires a majority of each of the two delegations. Legislation that emerges successfully from a conference committee is more often a compromise than a clear victory for one side. In recent years, as we have seen, polarization in Congress has led to much less reliance on conference committees. Instead, leaders exchange amendments in the hope of reaching agreement.

When a bill comes out of conference, it faces one more hurdle. Before it can be sent to the president for signing, the House-Senate conference committee's version of the bill must be approved on the floor of each chamber. Usually such approval is given quickly. Occasionally, however, a bill's opponents use this round of approval as one last opportunity to defeat a piece of legislation.

Presidential Action

The final step in passing a law is presidential approval. Once adopted by the House and Senate, a bill goes to the president, who may choose to sign the bill into law or veto it. If the president does not sign the bill or veto it within 10 days, and Congress is in session, the bill automatically becomes law. The **veto** is the president's constitutional power to reject a piece of legislation. To veto a bill, the president returns it unsigned within 10 days to the house of Congress in which it originated. If Congress adjourns during the 10-day period, and the president has taken no action, the bill is also considered to be vetoed. This latter method is known as the **pocket veto**. The possibility of a presidential veto affects how willing members of Congress are to push for different pieces of legislation at different times. If they think a proposal is likely to be vetoed they might shelve it until a later time.

A presidential veto may be overridden by a two-thirds vote in both the House and Senate. A veto override says much about the support that a president can expect from Congress, and it can deliver a stinging blow to the executive branch. Presidents will often back down from a veto threat if they believe that Congress will override the veto.

How Congress Decides

Analyze the factors that influence which laws Congress passes

What determines the kinds of legislation that Congress ultimately produces? According to the simplest theories of representation, members of Congress respond to the views of their constituents. In fact, the process of creating a legislative agenda, drawing up a list of possible measures, and deciding among them is a very complex one, in which a variety of influences from inside and outside government play important roles. External influences include a legislator's constituency and various interest groups. Influences from inside government include party leadership, congressional colleagues, and the president. Let us examine each of these influences individually and then consider how they interact to produce congressional policy decisions.

for critical analysis

Two of Congress's chief responsibilities are representation and lawmaking. How do these responsibilities support and reinforce each other? How might they also conflict with each other?

veto the president's constitutional power to turn down acts of Congress; a presidential veto may be overridden by a two-thirds vote of each house of Congress

pocket veto a presidential veto that is automatically triggered if the president does not act on a given piece of legislation passed during the final 10 days of a legislative session

Constituency

Because members of Congress, for the most part, want to be re-elected, we would expect the views of their constituents to be a primary influence on the decisions that legislators make. Yet constituency influence is not so straightforward. In fact, most constituents pay little attention to politics and often do not even know what policies their representatives support. Nonetheless, members of Congress spend a lot of time worrying about what their constituents think, because they realize that the choices they make may be scrutinized in a future election and used as ammunition by an opposing candidate. Because of this possibility, members of Congress do try to anticipate their constituents' policy views, especially if they think that voters will take them into account during elections.[45] In this way, constituents may affect congressional policy choices even when there is little direct evidence of their influence. In October 1998, for example, 31 House Democrats broke party ranks and voted in favor of an impeachment inquiry against President Clinton because they believed a "no" vote could cost them re-election that November. In 2002 the White House successfully pressed to schedule the vote authorizing the use of force in Iraq right before the midterm elections to pressure members to vote for it. At the time, 53 percent of Americans favored invading Iraq and 40 percent opposed such a move.[46]

Representatives spend a lot of time meeting with constituents in their districts to explain how they have helped their district and learn what issues their constituents care about. Such meetings are often informal events at local restaurants or fairs.

Interest Groups

Interest groups are another important external influence on congressional policies. Members of Congress pay close attention to interest groups for a number of reasons: interest groups can mobilize constituents, serve as watchdogs on congressional action, and supply candidates with money. When members of Congress are making voting decisions, those interest groups that have some connection to constituents in particular members' districts are most likely to be influential, and those groups with the ability to mobilize followers in many congressional districts may be especially influential. In recent years, Washington-based interest groups with little grassroots strength have recognized the importance of locally generated activity. Accordingly, they have sought to simulate grassroots pressure with so-called Astroturf lobbying (see Chapter 11). Such campaigns encourage constituents to sign form letters, postcards, or emails, which are then sent to congressional representatives. Lobbying campaigns set up toll-free telephone numbers for a system in which simply reporting your name and address to the listening computer will generate a letter to your congressional representative. One Senate office estimated that such organized campaigns to demonstrate "grassroots" support account for two-thirds of the mail the office received. As such campaigns increase, however, they become less influential, because members of Congress are aware of how rare real constituent interest actually is.[47]

Many interest groups now also use legislative "scorecards" that rate how members of Congress vote on issues of importance to that group. A high or low rating by an important interest group may provide a potent weapon in the next election. Interest groups can increase their influence over a particular piece of legislation by signaling their intention to include it in their scoring. Among the most influential groups that use scorecards, often posting them on their websites for members and the public to see, are the National Federation of Independent Business, the AFL-CIO, National Right to Life, the League of Conservation Voters, and the National Rifle Association.

Interest groups also have substantial influence in setting the legislative agenda and in helping to craft specific language in legislation. Today, sophisticated lobbyists win influence by providing information about policies to busy members of Congress. In the 2009–10 health reform effort, the biotechnology firm Genentech ghostwrote statements that more than a dozen members of Congress placed into the *Congressional Record*. Genentech's role came to light when it became evident that some members had used the exact same language in their entries.[48] In recent years, interest groups have also begun to build broader coalitions and comprehensive campaigns around particular policy issues. These coalitions do not rise from the grass roots but instead are put together by Washington lobbyists, who launch comprehensive lobbying campaigns that combine simulated grassroots activity with information and campaign funding for members of Congress.

Close financial ties between members of Congress and interest group lobbyists often raise eyebrows because they suggest that interest groups get special treatment in exchange for political donations. Concerns about the influence of lobbyists in Congress mounted in the early 2000s when Republicans launched the K Street Project, named after the street in Washington where many high-powered lobbyists have offices. The K Street Project placed former Republican staffers in key lobbying positions and ensured a large and steady flow of corporate cash into Republican coffers. Congressional relationships to lobbyists came under close scrutiny when

for critical analysis

How does congressional ethics legislation address concerns about corruption? Why is it important that lawmakers identify the earmarks they add to legislation?

the lobbyist Jack Abramoff, a self-proclaimed big supporter of the K Street Project, pleaded guilty in early 2006 to charges of conspiracy, mail fraud, and tax evasion.

Concern over such corruption led Congress to enact new ethics legislation in 2007. The new law sets new restrictions on the gifts lobbyists can bestow on lawmakers and limits privately funded travel. The law also prohibits members of Congress from lobbying for two years after they retire and requires lawmakers to identify the earmarks they insert in legislation. Further, it aims to shine light on the practice of "bundling," whereby lobbyists assemble money from a number of clients to make a single political donation. Now lobbyists are required to disclose the names of the individual contributors to these political donations. Although the new law provides additional transparency, revealing more about the relationship between lobbyists and members of Congress, it is widely viewed as lacking sufficient authority to go after those who are suspected of ethics violations.[49] Moreover, the large sums of cash raised by "Super PACs"—discussed in Chapter 10—have introduced a whole new set of questions about the role of special interests in politics, especially because donors to Super PACs can remain anonymous. Although they cannot openly coordinate with candidates, Super PACs can endorse candidates by name and are often run by people close to the candidates they support. In 2012 Super PACs poured unprecedented sums of money into the race for president, but they also targeted key congressional contests in an effort to affect the balance of power between the parties in Congress.[50] This pattern continued in 2014, when Super PACs made donations totaling $33 million to congressional candidates. Interest group allies of both parties mobilized to influence outcomes in the 2014 midterms.

Party

In both the House and Senate, party leaders have a good deal of influence over the behavior of their party members. This influence, sometimes called "party discipline," was once so powerful that it dominated the lawmaking process. In the late 1800s, party leaders could often command the allegiance of more than 90 percent of their members. A vote in which half or more of the members of one party take one position while at least half of the members of the other party take the opposing position is called a **party unity vote**. At the beginning of the twentieth century, nearly half of all **roll-call votes** in the House of Representatives were party votes. For much of the twentieth century, the number of party votes declined as bipartisan legislation became more common. The 1990s witnessed a return to strong party discipline as partisan polarization drew sharper lines between Democrats and Republicans, and congressional party leaders aggressively used their powers to promote party discipline. In 2005 party discipline was close to its all-time high.

Typically, party unity is greater in the House than in the Senate. House rules grant greater procedural control of business to the majority party leaders, which gives them more influence over House members. In the Senate, however, the leadership has few sanctions over its members. The former Senate minority leader Tom Daschle once observed that a Senate leader seeking to influence other senators has as incentives "a bushel full of carrots and a few twigs."[51]

Though it has not reached nineteenth-century levels, party unity has been on the rise in recent years because the divisions between the parties have deepened on many high-profile issues such as abortion, health care, and financial reform (see Figure 12.8). Party unity scores rise when congressional leaders try

party unity vote a roll-call vote in the House or Senate in which at least 50 percent of the members of one party take a particular position and are opposed by at least 50 percent of the members of the other party

roll-call vote a vote in which each legislator's yes or no vote is recorded as the clerk calls the names of the members alphabetically

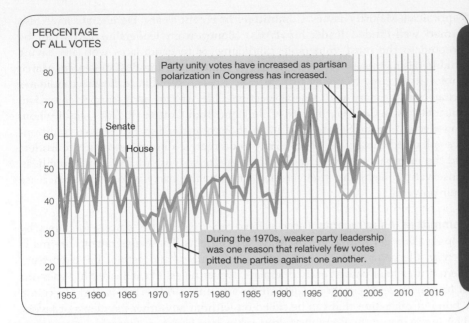

PERCENTAGE OF ALL VOTES

Party unity votes have increased as partisan polarization in Congress has increased.

Senate

House

During the 1970s, weaker party leadership was one reason that relatively few votes pitted the parties against one another.

80
70
60
50
40
30
20

1955 1960 1965 1970 1975 1980 1985 1990 1995 2000 2005 2010 2015

FIGURE 12.8

Party Unity Votes by Chamber

Party unity votes are roll-call votes in which a majority of one party lines up against a majority of the other party. Party unity votes increase when the parties are polarized and when the party leadership can enforce discipline. Why did the percentage of party unity votes decline in the 1970s? Why has it risen in recent years?

SOURCES: CQ Roll Call's Vote Studies, http://media.cq.com/votestudies (accessed 6/9/14).

to put a partisan stamp on legislation. For example, in 1995, then-Speaker Newt Gingrich sought to enact a Republican "Contract with America" that few Democrats supported. The result was more party unity in the House than in any year since 1954. Since then, the polarization of political parties has resulted in very high party unity scores. In 2013, House Democrats voted with the majority 88 percent of the time, close to their all-time high of 92 percent in 2008. In 2013, Senate Democrats set a record for party unity by voting with their caucus 94 percent of the time. Republicans were also very united. In 2013, House Republicans voted with their party 92 percent of the time, their all-time high; Senate Republicans voted with their party 86 percent of the time.[52]

To some extent, party unity is based on ideology and background. Republican members of the House are more likely than Democrats to have been elected by rural or suburban districts. Democrats are likely to be more liberal on economic and social questions than their Republican colleagues in both houses. These differences certainly help to explain roll-call divisions between the two parties. Ideology and background, however, are only part of the explanation for party unity. The other part has to do with party organization and leadership. Among the resources that party leaders have at their disposal to reward loyal members who vote with the party are (1) leadership PACs, (2) committee assignments, (3) access to the floor, (4) the whip system, (5) logrolling, and (6) the presidency.

Leadership PACs Leaders have increased their influence over members in recent years with aggressive use of leadership political action committees. Leadership PACs are organizations that members of Congress use to raise funds that they then distribute to other members of their party running for election. Republican congressional leaders pioneered the aggressive use of leadership PACs to win their congressional majority in 1995, and the practice has spread widely since that time. The former House majority leader Tom DeLay was especially aggressive in raising funds, creating several important PACs, including Americans for a Republican Majority (ARMPAC), Retain Our Majority Program (ROMP), and the

Republican Majority Issues Committee. In recent years, Democrats have also formed well-funded leadership PACs. Money from leadership PACs can be directed to the most vulnerable candidates or to candidates who are having trouble raising money. For example, in 2014, the leadership PAC of Senator Marco Rubio (R-Fla.) spent money to help conservative Republican Senate candidates facing close primary and general elections. He was an early supporter of Joni Ernst (R-Iowa), Cory Gardner (R-Colo.), and Tom Cotton (R-Ark.), all of whom won election to the Senate in 2014. Although leadership PACs have traditionally enhanced the power of the party and created a bond between the leaders and the members who receive their help, aggressive use of PACs by Republican conservatives highlights their use for wings of the party who want to increase their power.[53]

Committee Assignments Party leaders can create debts among members by helping them get favorable committee assignments. These assignments are made early in the congressional careers of most members and cannot be taken from them if they later balk at party discipline. Nevertheless, if the leadership goes out of its way to get the right assignment for a member, this effort is likely to create a bond of obligation that can be called on without any other payments or favors. This is one reason the Republican leadership gave freshmen favorable assignments when the Republicans took over Congress in 1995. When Nancy Pelosi assumed the position of Speaker in 2007, she sought to spread power more widely by limiting the number of committees that any one member could chair. She also gave freshmen representatives access to key committees that would raise their political stature.[54] By offering attractive committee assignments to members in competitive races, especially to new members, she sought to boost her party's chances in the next elections. And she engendered loyalty to the party among its new members.

As Speaker of the House, John Boehner attempted to keep his party unified, despite disagreements between the Tea Party members and other Republicans. These disagreements were pronounced in debates over the federal government's 2014 budget.

Access to the Floor The most important everyday resource available to the parties is control over access to the floor. With thousands of bills awaiting passage and most members clamoring for access in order to influence a bill or publicize themselves, floor time is precious. In the Senate, the leadership allows ranking committee members to influence the allocation of floor time (who will speak for how long); in the House, the Speaker, as head of the majority party (in consultation with the minority leader), allocates large blocks of floor time. Thus, floor time is allocated in both houses of Congress by the majority and minority leaders. More important, the Speaker of the House and the majority leader in the Senate possess the power of recognition. This seemingly insubstantial authority is, in fact, quite formidable and can be used to stymie a piece of legislation completely or frustrate a member's attempts to speak on a particular issue. Because the power is significant, members of Congress usually attempt to stay on good terms with the Speaker and the majority leader to ensure they will continue to be recognized.

As House Speaker, Nancy Pelosi was particularly generous in offering freshmen Democrats and other especially vulnerable Democrats an opportunity to speak on the floor. When Republicans assumed control of the House in 2010, they likewise ensured that the voices of freshmen Republicans were heard on the House floor.[55]

The Whip System Some influence accrues to party leaders through the whip system, which is primarily a communications network for conveying the leaders' wishes and plans to the members. Between 12 and 20 assistant and regional whips are selected to operate at the direction of the majority or minority leader and the whip. They poll all the members to learn their intentions on specific bills, enabling the leaders to know if they have enough support to allow a vote as well as whether the vote is so close that they will need to put pressure on undecided members. In those instances, the Speaker or a lieutenant will go to a few party members who have indicated they will switch if their vote is essential—an expedient that the leaders try to limit to a few times per session.

The whip system helps maintain party unity in both houses of Congress, but it is particularly critical in the House of Representatives because of the large number of legislators whose positions and votes must be accounted for. The majority and minority whips and their assistants must be adept at inducing compromise among legislators who hold widely differing viewpoints. The whips' personal styles and their perception of their function significantly affect the development of legislative coalitions and the compromises that emerge. As Republican House whip from 1995 to 2002, Tom DeLay established a reputation as an effective vote counter and a tough leader, earning the nickname the Hammer. DeLay also expanded the reach of the whip, building alliances with Republicans outside Congress, particularly those in ideological and business-oriented groups. Since Republicans retook control of the House following the 2010 elections, the whip operation has been faced with significant challenges from the large number of freshmen members of Congress. An unusually high number of members (87) were freshmen, 40 percent of whom had never held elected office before, calling themselves "citizen politicians."

Logrolling An agreement between two or more members of Congress who have nothing in common except the need for support is called **logrolling**. The agreement states, in effect, "You support me on bill X, and I'll support you on another bill of your choice." Since party leaders are the center of the communications networks in the two chambers, they can help members create large logrolling coalitions. Hundreds of logrolling deals are made each year, and although there are no official record-keeping books, it would be a poor party leader whose whips did not know who owed what to whom. In some instances, logrolling produces strange alliances. A most unlikely alliance emerged in Congress in October 1991, an alliance that one commentator dubbed "the corn for porn plot."[56] The alliance joined Senate supporters of the National Endowment for the Arts (NEA) with senators seeking limits on the cost of grazing rights on federal lands. The NEA, which provides federal funding to the arts, had been under fire from the conservative senator Jesse Helms (R-N.C.) for funding some controversial artists whose work Helms believed to be indecent. In an effort to block federal support for such works, Helms attached a provision to the NEA's funding that would have prohibited the agency from awarding grants to any work that in a "patently offensive way" depicted "sexual or excretory activities or organs." Supporters of the NEA condemned such restrictions as a violation of free speech and pointed out that many famous works of art could not have been funded under such restrictions. When it appeared that the amendment would pass, NEA supporters offered western senators a deal. In exchange for voting down the Helms amendment, they would eliminate a planned hike in grazing fees. Republican senators from 16 western states switched their votes and defeated the Helms amendment. Although Helms called his defeat the product of "back-room deals and parliamentary flimflam," his amendment was simply the victim of the time-honored congressional practice of logrolling.[57]

logrolling a legislative practice whereby agreements are made between legislators in voting for or against a bill; vote trading

The Presidency Of all the influences that maintain the clarity of party lines in Congress, the influence of the presidency is probably the most important. Indeed, the office is a touchstone of party discipline in Congress. Since the late 1940s, under President Harry Truman, presidents each year have identified a number of bills that they want to be considered part of their administration's program. By the mid-1950s, both parties in Congress began to look to the president for these proposals, which became the most significant part of Congress's agenda. The president's support is a criterion for party loyalty, and party leaders are able to use it to rally some members. Since 2011, with the presidency in Democratic hands and the House of Representatives controlled by Republicans, party polarization has limited the president's agenda-setting powers. Instead, his proposals have become targets for congressional opponents.

When Congress Can't Decide

We've considered the major factors that influence congressional decisions, but what happens if Congress as a whole can't decide and fails to act? By the end of 2013, the 113th Congress was on track to be the least productive Congress in modern history. The 112th Congress had held the record but in 2013, Congress enacted fewer than 60 new laws, making it the least productive single year on record. The previous record low was in 1995, when just 88 laws were enacted.[58]

Indeed, many high-profile bills ended in failure throughout 2012 and 2013. In 2012, when Republican leader John Boehner attempted to strike a "grand bargain" with President Obama over taxes and spending—one very favorable to Republicans—conservative Republicans in the House rejected it as not going far enough. The political standoff that resulted included regular threats of a government shutdown and resulted in the decision by rating agency Moody's to downgrade the U.S. credit rating. The impasse continued into 2013 when House Republicans refused to pass a bill funding government operations or extending

Passing legislation is difficult. Efforts to pass immigration reform in 2013 ultimately failed, even though the Senate passed a bill that was supported by House Minority Leader Nancy Pelosi (D-Calif.) and the Congressional Hispanic Caucus. Opposition from House Republicans meant the bill was not brought for a vote in the House, however.

Public Opinion of the Legislature

The U.S. Congress suffers from low approval ratings: very few Americans approve of the way Congress is handling its job. Are all legislatures equally unpopular? The World Values Survey has asked respondents around the world for their level of confidence in their legislative branch of government. In the United States, Japan, Australia, Chile, and Mexico, citizens report a low degree of confidence in their legislatures. Only in Turkey does a majority of the public report "a great deal" or "quite a lot" of confidence in the legislature. Mexico is notable in that 38 percent of the public reports having no confidence in the legislature.

In democracies, the legislature is usually expected to be the branch of government that is closest to the people. So why do people around the world consistently report low levels of confidence in the legislature? One explanation might be cultural change: younger generations may be less deferential to authority and more skeptical of governmental power than older generations. Others have pointed to corruption scandals affecting members of legislatures as a possible cause.[a] Perhaps the most convincing argument is reflected in the adage, "familiarity breeds contempt." As legislatures become more and more transparent in their operations, the media are able to report easily on the conflict and controversy that legislatures engage in when attempting to pass legislation. As a result of all this (often negative) media attention, the public has developed a negative attitude about legislative institutions.[b]

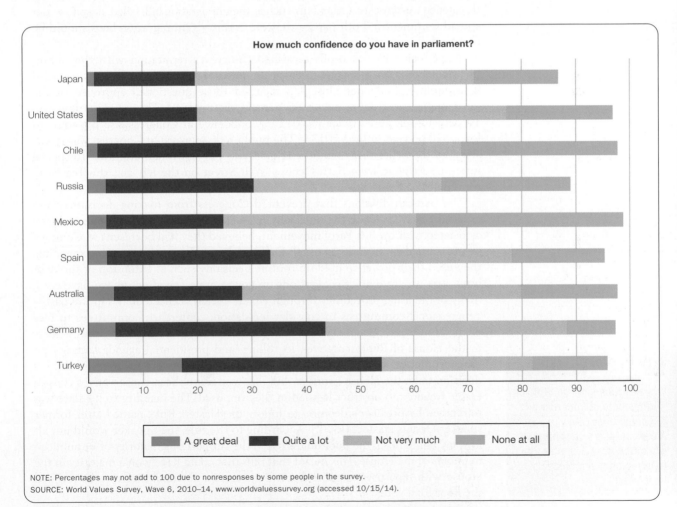

How much confidence do you have in parliament?

Legend: A great deal · Quite a lot · Not very much · None at all

NOTE: Percentages may not add to 100 due to nonresponses by some people in the survey.

SOURCE: World Values Survey, Wave 6, 2010–14, www.worldvaluessurvey.org (accessed 10/15/14).

[a]Pippa Norris, ed., *Critical Citizens: Global Support for Democratic Governance?* (New York: Oxford University Press, 1999).

[b]See Richard E. Neustadt, "The Politics of Mistrust" in *Why People Don't Trust Government*, ed. Joseph S. Nye, Jr., Philip D. Zelikow, and David C. King (Cambridge, MA: Harvard University Press, 1997), and Russell J. Dalton, *Democratic Challenges, Democratic Choices: The Erosion of Political Support in Advanced Industrial Democracies* (New York: Oxford University Press, 2004).

the debt ceiling unless the spending bill included language delaying implementation of the Affordable Care Act (ACA).[59] As a consequence, the federal government shut down for the first time in almost two decades. Despite House Speaker John Boehner's warnings to the Republican conference that the GOP would be blamed for the shutdown and his attempts to negotiate with Senate Democrats and the White House to reopen the government, House Republicans stood firm on their insistence to tie any deal to delaying the ACA.[60] As Representative Steve Pearce (R-N.M.) argued, "At times, you must act on principle and not ask what cost, what are the chances of success."[61] Eventually, with public ire rising over the continued shutdown, the House voted to pass a Senate bill—which contained virtually no concessions to the GOP—to reopen the government and extend the debt limit for four months, just hours before the United States was set to cross the debt-ceiling deadline.[62] Democrats and Republicans succeeded in averting a second showdown over the debt ceiling when both sides agreed on a budget deal in late 2013.

Deliberation on many other bills also entailed prolonged stalemates or failure. As we have seen, the House initially rejected the farm bill, usually a bipartisan measure. A bill passed only at the last minute when the price of milk threatened to skyrocket. Other bills, such as the immigration bill, failed, despite widespread sentiment in both parties that the country's immigration laws should be overhauled.

These legislative stand-offs tarnished Congress's reputation with the public. In November 2013, Congress received the lowest levels of approval ever recorded in a public opinion poll. Just 9 percent of those questioned approved of the job Congress was doing, while 86 percent disapproved. The previous low was 10 percent, registered twice in 2012.[63] Confidence in Congress also hit a record low of 10 percent in June 2013.[64] The public's disapproval of Congress was intensified by the belief that members of Congress pay too much attention to special interests, a charge from both Occupy Wall Street on the left and the Tea Party movement on the right.

The partisan divisions that prevented Congress from making decisions were especially acute because the unusually large class of freshmen Republicans, many associated with the Tea Party movement, believed they had been sent to Congress to put an end to business as usual. Dedicated to reducing government spending, they used their power to hold up routine decisions, such as extension of the debt limit, as a way to extract concessions on government spending. As we have seen, many of the usual procedures through which Congress enacted laws in the past—congressional committees to consider legislation, conference committees to reconcile House and Senate versions of legislation, a whip system to support leaders in the House of Representatives, logrolling, and presidential agenda setting—no longer function when Congress is so divided. Moreover, Speaker Boehner's decision to let the House "work its will" allowed Republican conservatives considerable freedom to obstruct legislation they opposed. The inability to legislate was reinforced by Boehner's decision to follow the Hastert Rule, named after former speaker Dennis Hastert (R-Ill.). According to the rule, the Speaker would not allow any bill to reach the floor unless it had the support of a majority of Republican members of the House. This meant that bills that could have won a majority in the House with bipartisan support from Democrats and Republicans never reached the floor for a vote.

By the end of 2013, the Speaker appeared to have become fed up with opposition of many members of his party to compromise. As it seemed that the conservative members of his party were prepared to reject yet another compromise on the budget and risk another showdown, Boehner praised the deal that had been struck with Democrats. At the same time he chastised conservative groups outside Congress, such as the Club for Growth and Heritage Action, that opposed it. Boehner blamed these groups for the earlier government shutdown and charged that they were "pushing our members in places where they don't want to be."[65] The Congress passed a modest compromise bill, averting a prolonged stand-off.

Congressional Polarization Congress's inability to decide reflects the deep ideological differences that separate the two parties. Efforts to measure the ideological distance between the two parties show that since the mid-1970s, Republicans and Democrats have been diverging sharply and are now more polarized than at any time in the last century. Democrats have become more liberal and Republicans have become more conservative on issues related to the economy and the role of government.[66] But as Figure 12.9 shows, the Republican Party has experienced the greatest ideological shift, becoming sharply more conservative. Moreover, because congressional districts are increasingly homogeneous in their ideology—in part due to gerrymandering but mainly because of natural clustering of the population—most members of Congress are in safe seats. Their constituents will not punish them for failing to compromise. Moreover, active mobilization by organizations on the right, such as the Club for Growth, mean that Republican members of Congress who support compromises might be punished. These outside organizations have financed alternative candidates to challenge members who vote against the organizations' positions. Boehner's rebuke of these groups may signal more possibilities for compromise in the future.

However, congressional polarization is here to stay so long as voters elect representatives with sharply different views about what government should and shouldn't do. Until there is more agreement about the role of government and the best way to manage the budgetary challenges that face the country, congressional stand-offs on major legislation will remain a regular feature of American politics.

for critical analysis

How does polarization contribute to congressional gridlock? How has the use of congressional procedures made it more difficult to enact legislation in recent years?

● Beyond Legislation: Other Congressional Powers

Describe Congress's influence over other branches of government

In addition to the power to make the law, Congress has at its disposal an array of other instruments through which to influence the process of government. The Constitution gives the Senate the power to approve treaties and appointments. And Congress has a number of other powers through which it can share with the other branches the capacity to administer the laws.

Oversight

Oversight, as applied to Congress, refers to the effort to oversee or to supervise how the executive branch carries out legislation. Oversight is carried out by committees

oversight the effort by Congress, through hearings, investigations, and other techniques, to exercise control over the activities of executive agencies

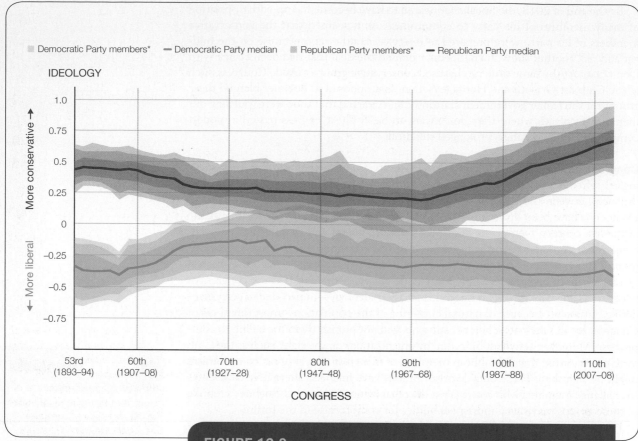

Democratic Party members* — Democratic Party median Republican Party members* — Republican Party median

IDEOLOGY

FIGURE 12.9

Polarization in Congress

In recent decades Democrats and Republicans in Congress are increasingly polarized, as Democrats have become more liberal and Republicans more conservative. One way of measuring polarization is to estimate the ideology of members of Congress based on their roll call votes, and then graph the ideologies of each party's members. As the graph shows, polarization was lower in the 1940s and 1950s, with some Democrats and some Republicans even overlapping in their ideologies.

*The lightest shade represents the range of ideologies of party members in the 5th–95th percentiles. The next lightest shade represents the 10th–90th percentiles. The darkest shade represents the 25th–75th percentiles.

SOURCE: Voteview, http:/;voteview .com/dwnominate.asp (accessed 4/21/14).

---

appropriations the amounts of money approved by Congress in statutes (bills) that each unit or agency of government can spend

or subcommittees of the Senate or the House, which conduct hearings and investigations to analyze and evaluate bureaucratic agencies and the effectiveness of their programs. Their purpose may be to locate inefficiencies or abuses of power, to explore the relationship between what an agency does and what a law intends, or to change or abolish a program. Most programs and agencies are subject to some oversight every year during the course of hearings on **appropriations**, the funding of agencies and government programs.

Committees or subcommittees have the power to subpoena witnesses, administer oaths, cross-examine, compel testimony, and bring criminal charges for contempt (refusing to cooperate) and perjury (lying under oath). Hearings and investigations are similar in many ways, but they differ on one fundamental point. A hearing is usually held on a specific bill, and the questions asked are usually intended to build a record with regard to that bill. In an investigation, the committee or subcommittee does not begin with a particular bill, but examines a broad area or problem and then concludes its investigation with one or more proposed bills.

In recent years, congressional oversight power has increasingly been used as a tool of partisan politics. The Republican Congress aggressively investigated President Clinton, racking up 140 hours of sworn testimony on whether the president had used the White House holiday card list for partisan purposes. By contrast, the Republican-controlled Congress failed to scrutinize seriously the actions of the Bush administration during Bush's first six years in office. The investigation into the abuse of prisoners in Iraq's Abu Ghraib prison, for example, entailed only 12 hours of sworn testimony. Moreover, the few oversight hearings that the Republican Congress held sought mainly to support the leadership's policy goals—during a hearing on Arctic oil drilling, for example, much testimony was devoted to the benefits of such drilling. Congress also convened oversight hearings on issues that had nothing to do with the executive branch, such as the high-profile hearings on steroid use in Major League Baseball in 2005 and 2008.[67]

When the Democrats took control of Congress in 2007, congressional oversight increased dramatically. To highlight the importance of oversight, Democrats renamed the House Government Reform Committee, calling it the Committee on Oversight and Government Reform, and added four new subcommittees dedicated to oversight. They also hired more than 200 new investigative staffers.[68] Armed with these resources, Congress stepped up the number of oversight hearings: during its first six months in power, the Democratic Congress held 942 oversight hearings, compared with 579 for the same period when Republicans controlled Congress in 2005.[69] Congressional leaders are quite aware of oversight hearings as political tools. Since 2010, the Republican House has used the oversight power to highlight the politically weak points in President Obama's record, holding extensive hearings on the Affordable Care Act and on the militant attack of the American consulate in Benghazi, Libya that resulted in American deaths.[70]

Congress may call on members of the executive branch and others to testify at hearings. Here, former Internal Revenue Service (IRS) official Lois Lerner appears at a House Oversight and Government Reform Committee hearing on whether the IRS targeted groups based on their political beliefs.

Advice and Consent: Special Senate Powers

The Constitution has given the Senate another special power, one that is not based on lawmaking. The president has the power to make treaties and to appoint top executive officers, ambassadors, and federal judges—but only "with the Advice and Consent of the Senate" (Article II, Section 2). For treaties, two-thirds of those present must concur; for appointments, a simple majority is required.

The power to approve or reject presidential requests includes the power to set conditions. In fact, the Senate only occasionally exercises its power to reject

executive agreement an agreement, made between the president and another country, that has the force of a treaty but does not require the Senate's "advice and consent"

impeachment the formal charge by the House of Representatives that a government official has committed "Treason, Bribery, or other high Crimes and Misdemeanors"

The Senate possesses the power to impeach federal officials. In American history, 16 federal officials have been impeached, including two presidents. In 1998 the House impeached President Bill Clinton for lying under oath about his affair with White House intern Monica Lewinsky.

treaties and appointments, and despite recent debate surrounding judicial nominees, only a handful of judicial nominees have been rejected by the Senate during the past century, whereas hundreds have been approved. However, the recent increase in use of the filibuster to block judicial nominees led the Democratic Senate to bar the filibuster in deliberations about judicial and executive branch appointments.

Most presidents make every effort to take potential Senate opposition into account in treaty negotiations with foreign powers. Instead of treaties, presidents frequently resort to **executive agreements** that do not need Senate approval. The Supreme Court has held that such agreements are equivalent to treaties.[71] In the past, presidents sometimes concluded secret agreements without informing Congress of the agreements' contents, or even their existence. For example, American involvement in the Vietnam War grew in part out of a series of secret arrangements made between American presidents and the South Vietnamese during the 1950s and '60s. Congress did not even learn of the existence of these agreements until 1969. In 1972, Congress passed the Case Act, which requires that the president inform Congress of any executive agreement within 60 days of its having been reached. This provides Congress with the opportunity to cancel agreements it opposes. In addition, Congress can limit the president's ability to conduct foreign policy through executive agreement by refusing to appropriate the funds needed to implement an agreement. In this way, for example, Congress can modify or even cancel executive agreements to provide American economic or military assistance to foreign governments.

Impeachment

The Constitution also grants Congress the power of impeachment over the president, vice president, and other executive officials. **Impeachment** means to charge a government official (president or otherwise) with "Treason, Bribery, or other high Crimes and Misdemeanors" and bring him before Congress to determine guilt. Impeachment is thus like a criminal indictment in which the House of Representatives acts like a grand jury, voting (by simple majority) on whether the accused ought to be impeached. If a majority of the House votes to impeach, the impeachment trial moves to the Senate, which acts like a trial jury by voting whether to convict and forcibly remove the person from office (which requires a two-thirds majority of the Senate). The impeachment power is a considerable one; its very existence in the hands of Congress is a highly effective safeguard against the executive tyranny so greatly feared by the framers of the Constitution. The House has initiated impeachment proceedings more than 60 times in U.S. history. Fewer than 20 officials were ultimately impeached, and only 8—all federal judges—were convicted by the Senate and removed from office.[72]

Controversy over Congress's impeachment power has arisen over the grounds for impeachment, especially the meaning of "high Crimes and Misdemeanors." A strict reading of the Constitution suggests that the only impeachable offense is an actual crime. But a more common working definition is that "an impeachable offense is whatever the majority of the House of Representatives considers it to be at a given moment in history."[73] In other words, impeachment, especially impeachment of a president, is a political decision.

The political nature of impeachment was very clear in the two instances of presidential impeachment that have occurred in American history. In the first, in 1867, President Andrew Johnson, a southern Democrat who had battled a congressional Republican majority over Reconstruction, was impeached by the House but saved from conviction by one vote in the Senate. In 1998 the House impeached President Bill Clinton on two counts, for lying under oath and obstructing justice during the investigation into his sexual affair with the White House intern Monica Lewinsky. The vote was highly partisan, with only five Democrats voting for impeachment on each charge. In the Senate, where a two-thirds majority was needed to convict the president, only 45 senators voted to convict on the first count of lying and 50 voted to convict on the second charge of obstructing justice. As in the House, the vote for impeachment was highly partisan, with all Democrats and only five Republicans supporting the president's ultimate acquittal.

for critical analysis

Under what circumstances should Congress exercise its power of impeachment? Why has impeachment been used so rarely in U.S. history?

Congress
and Your Future

Much of this chapter has described the major institutional components of Congress and has shown how they work as Congress makes policy. But what do these institutional features mean for how Congress represents the American public? Does the organization of Congress promote the equal representation of all Americans? Or are there institutional features of Congress that allow some interests more access and influence than others?

As we noted at the beginning of this chapter, Congress instituted a number of reforms in the 1970s to make itself more accessible and to distribute power more widely within the institution. These reforms sought to respond to public views that Congress had become a stodgy institution ruled by a powerful elite that made decisions in private. We have seen that these reforms increased the number of subcommittees, prohibited most secret hearings, and increased the staff support for Congress. These reforms spread power more evenly throughout the institution and opened new avenues for the public to contact and influence Congress.

But the opening of Congress ultimately did not benefit the broad American public as reformers had envisioned. In fact the congressional reforms enacted during the 1970s actually made Congress less effective and, ironically, more permeable to special interests. Open committee meetings made it possible for sophisticated interest groups to monitor and influence every aspect of developing legislation. The unanticipated, negative consequences of these reforms highlighted the trade-off between representation and effectiveness in Congress.[74] Efforts to improve representation by opening Congress up made it difficult for Congress to be effective.

When Congress is ineffective, American democracy suffers. As we have seen in this chapter, prolonged stalemates in Congress have led to a reduction in

America's credit rating and a costly government shutdown. Moreover, Americans have lost confidence in Congress as it has lurched from crisis to crisis. Is it time for some major changes to make Congress work better? Disillusionment with congressional gridlock has led some to say that the United States should become a parliamentary system, where the winning party can enact the legislation it promised in its party platform. Such a system is more accountable to voters and less prone to stalemate. But Americans would have to jettison the presidency and become a unicameral body to operate as a true parliamentary system, like that of Britain.

Short of such major institutional transformations, are there changes that would make Congress work better? One measure that might lead to more bipartisan agreement—the appointment of citizen commissions to draw district lines—has been adopted in some states. If this practice became more widespread, it is possible that it would lead to election of more moderate candidates, making it easier to compromise in Congress. Changes in the way Congress conducts its business could also promote more bipartisan decision making. For example, House Speaker John Boehner decided that he would only bring legislation to the floor if a majority of Republicans supported it. The "Hastert Rule," as this practice is called, after former speaker Dennis Hastert, is not a formal rule of Congress, rather it is a norm that Boehner decided to implement. It is a practice that could easily be abandoned, allowing bipartisan majorities to enact legislation. Another significant change—eliminating the filibuster in the Senate—would heighten partisan differences but ease gridlock. As we have seen, the Senate voted to eliminate the filibuster for executive branch appointments and judicial candidates (except for the Supreme Court) in 2013. Abandoning the filibuster altogether would allow legislation to move more smoothly through the Senate. Will any of these changes—or other measures—be adopted? Each carries risks to political parties and to politicians. Yet, gridlock carries political risks as well, as the public grows frustrated with congressional inaction on important policy areas. What areas of public policy might suffer if Congress continues its inability to decide? How politicians weigh these different choices will shape how—and whether—Congress fills its central position in American democracy.

plugin

Inform

Find out who represents your state in the Senate (by entering your state at www.senate.gov) and in the House of Representatives (by entering your zip code at www.house.gov).

Express

Look up your representative's recent voting record in the *Washington Post*'s U.S. Congress Votes Database (http://projects.washingtonpost.com/congress/113/). Make a list of five issues he or she voted on, and state whether you would have voted the same way on behalf of your district.

Connect

Follow your members of Congress on social media. Pay attention to which issues they address in their posts, and consider posting a comment if you have an opinion.

Act

Let your member of Congress know about issues that are important to you by sending them an email and encouraging friends and family to do so as well. Members' email addresses are given on their web pages.

studyguide

Congress: Representing the American People

Describe who serves in Congress and how they represent their constituents (pp. 473-86)

A member of Congress's primary responsibility is to his or her district and to his or her constituency. The House and Senate operate according to a different sets of rules and play different roles in the legislative process. Although members of Congress often do not share their constituents' sociological characteristics, they do work hard to speak for their constituents' views and to serve their constituents' interests. Generally speaking, there are three factors related to the U.S. electoral system that affect who gets elected and what they do once in office: who decides to run for Congress, the incumbency advantage, and the way congressional districts are drawn.

Key Terms

constituency (p. 473)

bicameral (p. 473)

delegate (p. 474)

trustee (p. 474)

sociological representation (p. 475)

agency representation (p. 475)

incumbency (p. 480)

term limits (p. 481)

apportionment (p. 481)

redistricting (p. 482)

gerrymandering (p. 482)

patronage (p. 484)

pork-barrel (or pork) (p. 484)

private bill (p. 485)

Practice Quiz

1. Because they have larger and more heterogeneous constituencies, senators
   a) have less freedom to consider "new ideas" or to bring together new coalitions of interests.
   b) are more attuned to the needs of localized interest groups.
   c) care more about re-election than House members.
   d) can better represent the national interest.
   e) face less competition in elections than House members.

2. What type of representation is described when constituents have the power to hire and fire their representative?
   a) agency representation
   b) sociological representation
   c) democratic representation
   d) trustee representation
   e) economic representation

3. Sociological representation is important in understanding the U.S. Congress because
   a) members often vote on the basis of their religion.
   b) Congress is a microcosm of American society.
   c) most people vote for people who are just like them.
   d) the composition of Congress is symbolically important for the authority of the government.
   e) there is a distinct "congressional sociology."

4. Some have argued that the creation of minority congressional districts has
   a) made it easier to draw districts.
   b) lessened the sociological representation of minorities in Congress.
   c) made it more difficult for minorities to win substantive policy goals.
   d) been a result of the media's impact on state legislative politics.
   e) lessened the problem of pork-barrel politics.

5. One way members of Congress can work as agents of their constituents is by
   a) providing direct patronage.
   b) taking part in a party vote.
   c) joining a caucus.
   d) supporting term limits.
   e) spending time on fund-raising for their re-election campaign.

The Organization of Congress

> **Explain how party leadership, the committee system, the staff system, and caucuses help structure congressional business (pp. 486–92)**

Congress is not only a representative body but also a lawmaking institution. The political parties, the committee system, congressional staff, the caucuses, and the parliamentary rules of the House and Senate play key roles in the process through which Congress formulates and enacts law. The committee system is particularly important to the legislative process because Congress relies on committees and subcommittees to do the difficult work of sorting through alternatives and writing bills.

Key Terms

conference (p. 486)

caucus (political) (p. 486)

Speaker of the House (p. 486)

majority leader (p. 486)

minority leader (p. 486)

whip (p. 486)

standing committee (p. 488)

select committees (p. 489)

joint committees (p. 489)

conference committees (p. 490)

seniority (p. 490)

staff agencies (p. 492)

caucuses (congressional) (p. 492)

Practice Quiz

6. Which of the following types of committees includes members of both the House and the Senate?
   a) standing committee
   b) select committee
   c) conference committee
   d) rules committee
   e) No committees include both House members and senators.

7. A series of reforms instituted by Congress in the 1970s, including an increase in the number of subcommittees and greater autonomy for subcommittee chairs, was intended to
   a) reduce the power of committee chairs.
   b) increase the power of committee chairs.
   c) secure re-election for all committee chairs.
   d) end the filibuster.
   e) guarantee the electoral defeat of all committee chairs.

Rules of Lawmaking: How a Bill Becomes a Law

> **Outline the steps in the process of passing a law (pp. 492–97)**

The rules of congressional procedure influence the fate of every bill and determine the distribution of power in Congress. Debate over bills is much less restricted in the Senate than in the House, and the filibuster gives tremendous power to individual senators. The president's veto power also exerts an important influence on Congress's lawmaking because the possibility of a presidential veto affects how willing members of Congress are to push for different pieces of legislation.

Key Terms

bill (p. 492)

committee markup (p. 494)

closed rule (p. 494)

open rule (p. 494)

filibuster (p. 495)

cloture (p. 495)

veto (p. 497)

pocket veto (p. 497)

Practice Quiz

8. The difference between a closed rule and an open rule in the House is
   a) a closed rule puts severe limits on floor debate and amendments, whereas an open rule permits floor debate and makes amendments easier.
   b) an open rule puts severe limits on floor debate and amendments, whereas a closed rule permits floor debate and makes amendments easier.
   c) a closed rule allows journalists and members of the public to listen to debates about a bill, whereas an open rule prevents journalists and members of the public from listening to debates about the bill.
   d) an open rule allows journalists and members of the public to listen to debates about a bill, whereas a closed rule prevents journalists and members of the public from listening to debates about the bill.
   e) a closed rule prevents the federal judiciary from declaring a bill unconstitutional once passed, whereas an open rule allows the federal judiciary to declare a bill unconstitutional.

9. Which of the following is not a technique that can be used to block debate about a bill in the Senate?
   a) filibuster
   b) caucus
   c) the introduction of new amendments
   d) cloture
   e) placing holds on bills

How Congress Decides

Analyze the factors that influence which laws Congress passes (pp. 497–507)

A variety of influences from inside and outside government play a role in congressional decision making. External influences include the policy preferences of the legislator's constituency and the lobbying of various interest groups. Party leaders within Congress use committee assignments, access to the floor, the whip system, logrolling, and the president's support to influence how representatives behave.

Key Terms

party unity vote (p. 500)

roll-call vote (p. 500)

logrolling (p. 503)

Practice Quiz

10. Members of Congress take their constituents' views into account because
    a) most constituents pay close attention to what's going on in Congress.
    b) members are not allowed to consider internal influences.
    c) most constituents are well informed about the policy choices made in Congress.
    d) members worry that their voting record will be scrutinized at election time.
    e) they can be impeached if they go against their constituents' policy preferences.

11. Which of the following is not a resource that party leaders in Congress use to create party discipline?
    a) leadership PACs
    b) committee assignments
    c) access to the floor
    d) the whip system
    e) roll-call votes

12. An agreement between members of Congress to trade support for each other's bills is known as
    a) oversight.
    b) filibuster.
    c) logrolling.
    d) patronage.
    e) cloture.

Beyond Legislation: Other Congressional Powers

Describe Congress's influence over the other branches of government (pp. 507–11)

Congress has many other powers than simply lawmaking. Using hearings, investigations, and other techniques, Congress exercises control over the agencies of the executive branch. Under the Constitution, the president can only make treaties and appoint top executive officers, ambassadors, and federal judges "with the Advice and Consent of the Senate." The Constitution also grants Congress the power of impeachment over the president, vice president, and other executive officials.

Key Terms

oversight (p. 507)

appropriations (p. 508)

executive agreement (p. 510)

impeachment (p. 510)

Practice Quiz

13. When Congress conducts an investigation to explore the relationship between what a law intended and what an executive agency has done, it is engaged in
    a) oversight.
    b) advice and consent.
    c) appropriations.
    d) executive agreement.
    e) direct patronage.

14. Which of the following statements about impeachment is not true?
    a) The president is the only official who can be impeached by Congress.
    b) Impeachment means to charge a government official with "Treason, Bribery, or other high Crimes and Misdemeanors."
    c) The House of Representatives decides by simple majority vote whether the accused ought to be impeached.
    d) The Senate decides whether to convict and remove the person from office.
    e) There have only been two instances of impeachment in American history.

For Further Reading

Adler, E. Scott. *Why Congressional Reforms Fail*. Chicago: University of Chicago Press, 2002.

Binder, Sarah. *Minority Rights, Majority Rule: Partisanship and the Development of Congress*. Cambridge, MA: Cambridge University Press, 1997.

Dodd, Lawrence C., and Bruce I. Oppenheimer, eds. *Congress Reconsidered*. 10th ed. Washington, DC: CQ Press, 2012.

Dodson, Debra L. *The Impact of Women in Congress*. New York: Oxford University Press, 2006.

Fenno, Richard F. *Homestyle: House Members in Their Districts*. Boston: Little, Brown, 1978.

Fiorina, Morris. *Congress: Keystone of the Washington Establishment*. 2nd ed. New Haven, CT: Yale University Press, 1989.

Fowler, Linda, and Robert McClure. *Political Ambition: Who Decides to Run for Congress?* New Haven, CT: Yale University Press, 1989.

Koger, Gregory. *Filibustering: A Political History of Obstruction in the House and Senate*. Chicago: University of Chicago Press, 2010.

Lee, Frances E. *Beyond Ideology: Politics, Principles, and Partisanship in the U.S. Senate*. Chicago: University of Chicago Press, 2009.

Mann, Thomas E., and Norman J. Ornstein. *It's Even Worse Than It Looks: How the American Constitutional System Collided with the New Politics of Extremism*. New York: Basic Books, 2012.

Mayhew, David R. *Congress: The Electoral Connection*. New Haven, CT: Yale University Press, 1974.

Palmer, Barbara, and Denise Simon. *Breaking the Political Glass Ceiling: Women and Congressional Elections*. 2nd ed. New York: Routledge, 2008.

Redman, Eric. *The Dance of Legislation*. Seattle: University of Washington Press, 2001.

Schickler, Eric, and Frances E. Lee. *The Oxford Handbook of the American Congress*. New York: Oxford University Press, 2011.

Wawro, Gregory J., and Eric Schickler. *Filibuster: Obstruction and Lawmaking in the U.S. Senate*. Princeton, NJ: Princeton University Press, 2006.

Recommended Websites

Cook Political Report
www.cookpolitical.com

The Cook Political Report, by Charlie Cook, is a nonpartisan analysis of electoral politics. Check out current House and Senate races for an in-depth analysis of past elections and previews of future congressional elections.

Library of Congress: Thomas
http://thomas.loc.gov

The Library of Congress's "Thomas" website is a superb place to find information about the U.S. Congress. Roll-call votes, current legislation, the full text of the *Congressional Record*, and committee reports are just a few of the archives you will find.

National Committee for an Effective Congress
www.ourcampaigns.com

Congressional redistricting is the process of redrawing House districts every 10 years to account for shifts in population. For information about redistricting in your state, log on to the Redistricting Resource Center, provided by the National Committee for an Effective Congress.

Roll Call
www.rollcall.com

Roll Call, the newspaper of Capitol Hill, provides daily coverage on the members, legislation, and events taking place in and around the U.S. legislature.

The Sunlight Foundation and Taxpayers for Common Sense
http://earmarkwatch.org

Earmarks are language that members of Congress insert in legislation that dedicates funds for specific uses, many whose broad benefits can be questioned. The Sunlight Foundation and Taxpayers for Common Sense are two watchdog groups that have joined forces to publish a database of congressional earmarks. Earmarks can be searched by state, congressional sponsor, recipient, and description of the project.

U.S. House of Representatives
www.house.gov

U.S. Senate
www.senate.gov

These are the official websites for the U.S. House of Representatives and the U.S. Senate. Here you can find information on your members of Congress, key congressional leaders, bills currently under consideration, and legislative committees.

One of the president's important roles is to serve as commander in chief of the armed forces. Times of war and national emergency have often served to strenghten the office of the presidency.

The Presidency

WHAT GOVERNMENT DOES AND WHY IT MATTERS By 2016, President Barack Obama will be able to look back despite his two terms as president and point to a solid record of policy triumphs, often despite determined Republican opposition. Under the president's leadership, the nation's health care system was significantly redesigned so that, beginning in 2014, health insurance was offered to 32 million previously uninsured Americans. With the president's signature in 2010, the Dodd-Frank Wall Street Reform and Consumer Protection Act imposed a major set of new regulations on the financial services sector, whose practices had been blamed for the "Great Recession" of 2008. The president brought most American troops home from Iraq and Afghanistan. Terrorist mastermind Osama bin Laden was killed by U.S. special operations troops. And, in pitched battles with congressional Republicans, the president forced Congress to end the 2013 government shutdown, agree to an increase in the national debt limit, and accept several of his most controversial judicial and executive branch nominees. This last victory came when Senate Democrats were able to eliminate the Senate's historic filibuster rule, which had allowed Republicans to prevent debate on the president's nominations.

These policy triumphs reflect the considerable power of contemporary presidents. But President Obama also suffered a number of significant failures. His efforts to bring about immigration reform were blunted, as were his attempts to induce Congress to enact gun control legislation. Some of the president's actions, such as his agreement to reduce economic sanctions against Iran in exchange for an Iranian promise to slow the development of nuclear weapons, remained highly controversial. With the departure of American forces, Iraq descended into chaos and sectarian violence. Even the president's health care triumph was tempered by the errors, mismanagement, and confusion surrounding the rollout of the program in 2014. Thus despite Obama's efforts and notable policy successes, the president and the nation continued to confront major problems including budget deficits, unemployment, failing schools, and challenges abroad. The president's powers are not without limit.

President Obama's record of successes and failures is a reflection of the strengths and limits of the institution. Obama inherited a presidency considerably more powerful than the institution imagined by the framers of the U.S. Constitution, as well as problems vastly more complex.

In this chapter, we examine the foundations of the American presidency and assess the origins and character of presidential power in the twenty-first century. National emergencies are one source of presidential power, but presidents are also empowered by democratic political processes and, increasingly, by their ability to control and expand the institutional resources of the office. But as we will see, presidential power is not without limit.

chaptergoals

- Explain the role of the president in the American political system (pp. 521–22)

- Understand the expressed, delegated, and inherent powers of the presidency (pp. 523–35)

- Identify the institutional resources presidents have to help them exercise their powers (pp. 535–40)

- Explain how modern presidents have become even more powerful (pp. 540–50)

● Establishing the Presidency

Explain the role of the president in the American political system

The presidency was established by Article II of the Constitution, which begins by asserting, "The executive power shall be vested in a President of the United States of America." Article II describes the manner in which the president is to be chosen and defines the basic powers of the presidency. By vesting the executive power in a single president, the framers were emphatically rejecting proposals for various forms of collective leadership. Some delegates to the Constitutional Convention had argued in favor of a multiheaded executive or an "executive council" in order to avoid undue concentration of power in the hands of one individual. Most of the framers, however, wanted to provide for "energy" in the executive, and they thought that a unitary executive would be more energetic than some form of collective leadership. They believed that a powerful executive would help protect the nation's interests vis-à-vis other nations and promote the federal government's interests relative to the states.

The presidential selection process defined by Article II resulted from a struggle between those delegates who wanted the president to be selected by, and thus be responsible to, Congress and those delegates who preferred that the president be elected directly by the people. Direct popular election would create a more independent and more powerful presidency. With the adoption of a scheme of indirect election through an electoral college, with electors to be selected by the state legislatures (and close elections to be resolved in the House of Representatives), the framers hoped to achieve a "republican" solution: a strong president responsible to state and national legislators rather than directly to the electorate. This indirect method of electing the president probably did dampen the power of most presidents in the nineteenth century.

The framers' idea that electors would be chosen by the state legislatures gave way during the nineteenth century to various systems of popular selection of the electors. This made the presidency a more democratic institution and the president more directly responsible to the American people than to the states. Today, in 48 of the 50 states, the candidate who wins the state's popular vote wins all the electoral

The election of the American president does not formally conclude on Election Day in November. In December, electors from each state cast their votes for president. The state electoral votes are then counted in January in the House of Representatives, which announces the victor.

college votes for that state. The presidential candidate with a majority of votes in the electoral college—not necessarily the candidate with the most votes from the people—becomes president. The number of electors per state is equal to its number of delegates in the House and Senate, thus small states are overrepresented in the electoral college. As a result, the electoral college system can sometimes distort the outcomes of presidential races, although it does not undermine the principle of popular selection of the nation's leaders.

caucus (political) a normally closed political party business meeting of citizens or lawmakers to select candidates, elect officers, plan strategy, or make decisions regarding legislative matters

The presidency was strengthened somewhat in the 1830s with the introduction of the national convention system of nominating presidential candidates. Until then, presidential candidates had been nominated by their party's congressional delegates through a **caucus** system, derisively called "King Caucus" because any candidate for president was beholden to the party's leaders in Congress both for the party's nomination and for their support in the presidential election. The national nominating convention arose outside Congress in order to provide some representation for a party's voters who lived in districts where they were in the minority. The political party in each state made its own provisions for selecting delegates to attend the presidential nominating convention, and in virtually all states, the selection was dominated by the party leaders. (Only in recent decades have state laws intervened to regularize the selection process and to provide, in all but a few instances, for open election of delegates.) The convention system quickly became the most popular method of nominating candidates for all elective offices and remained so until well into the twentieth century, when it succumbed to the criticism that it was undemocratic and dominated by a few leaders in a "smoke-filled room." But during the nineteenth century, the convention system was seen as a victory for democracy against the congressional elite. Furthermore, the national convention gave the presidency a base of power independent of Congress.

This additional independence did not immediately transform the presidency into the office familiar to us today, but the national convention did begin to open the presidency to larger social forces and newly organized interests in society. In other words, it gave the presidency a broad popular base that would eventually demand and support increased presidential power. Improvements in the telegraph, the telephone, and other forms of mass communication enabled individuals to share their complaints and allowed national leaders (especially presidents and presidential candidates) to reach out directly to the people. Eventually, though more slowly, the presidential selection process began to be further democratized with the adoption of primary elections through which millions of ordinary citizens were given an opportunity to take part in the presidential nominating process by popular selection of convention delegates.

But despite political and social conditions favoring the enhancement of the presidency, the development of presidential government as we know it today did not mature until the middle of the twentieth century. For a long period, even as the national government began to grow, Congress was careful to keep a tight rein on the president's power. The real turning point in the history of American national government came during the administration of Franklin Delano Roosevelt. Roosevelt greatly enlarged the bureaucracies of the executive branch, created the Executive Office of the President, and expanded presidential responsibility for the nation's budget. Roosevelt also led by example in the use of executive orders in place of legislation and executive agreements in place of treaties, reducing the congressional role in domestic and foreign policy, and subsequent presidents have continued both practices. Since FDR and his "New Deal" of the 1930s, every president has been strong whether or not he was committed to the goal of a strong presidency.

The Constitutional Powers of the Presidency

Understand the expressed, delegated, and inherent powers of the presidency

Whereas Section 1 of Article II of the Constitution explains how the president is to be chosen, Sections 2 and 3 outline the powers and duties of the president. These two sections identify two sources of presidential authority. Some presidential powers, called the **expressed powers** of the office, are specifically established by the language of the Constitution. For example, the president is authorized to make treaties, grant pardons, and nominate judges and other public officials. These specifically defined powers cannot be revoked by Congress or any other agency without an amendment to the Constitution. Other expressed powers include the authority to receive ambassadors and the command of the military forces of the United States.

The list of expressed presidential powers is brief, but these expressed powers have become the foundation of a second set of presidential powers, the so-called **implied powers** of the office. An implied power is one that can be considered necessary to allow the president to exercise his expressed power. For example, the Constitution expressly gives the president the power to appoint "all other officers of the United State . . . which shall be established by law." Article II does not, however, expressly grant the president the power to remove such officials from office. From the earliest years of the Republic, though, presidents claimed that the removal power was implied by the appointment power. In 1926 the U.S. Supreme Court affirmed this idea in the case of *Myers v. United States*.[1]

In addition to the president's expressed and implied powers, Article II declares that the president "shall take Care that the Laws be faithfully executed." Since the laws are enacted by Congress, this language implies that Congress is to delegate to the president the power to implement or execute its will. Powers given to the president by Congress are called **delegated powers**. In principle, Congress delegates to the president only the power to identify or develop the means through which to carry out its decisions. So, for example, if Congress determines that air quality should be improved, it might delegate to a bureaucratic agency in the executive branch the power to identify the best means of bringing about such an improvement as well as the power to implement the actual cleanup process. In practice, of course, decisions about how to clean the air are likely to have an enormous impact on businesses, organizations, and individuals throughout the nation. By delegating power to the executive branch, Congress substantially enhances the importance of the presidency. In most cases, Congress delegates power to bureaucratic agencies in the executive branch rather than to the president, but as we shall see, contemporary presidents have found ways to capture a good deal of this delegated power for themselves.

expressed powers specific powers granted by the Constitution to Congress (Article I, Section 8) and to the president (Article II)

implied powers powers necessary to allow presidential exercise of expressed powers

delegated powers constitutional powers that are assigned to one governmental agency but that are exercised by another agency with the express permission of the first

Expressed Powers

The president's expressed powers, as defined by Sections 2 and 3 of Article II, fall into several categories:

1. *Military*. Article II, Section 2, provides for the power as "Commander in Chief of the Army and Navy of the United States, and of the Militia of the several States, when called in to the actual Service of the United States."

2. *Judicial.* Article II, Section 2, also provides the power to "grant Reprieves and Pardons for Offences against the United States, except in Cases of Impeachment."

3. *Diplomatic.* Article II, Section 2, further provides the power "by and with the Advice and Consent of the Senate to make Treaties." Article II, Section 3, provides the power to "receive Ambassadors and other public Ministers."

4. *Executive.* Article II, Section 3, also authorizes the president to see to it that all the laws are faithfully executed; Section 2 gives the chief executive power to appoint, remove, and supervise all executive officers and to appoint all federal judges.

5. *Legislative.* Article I, Section 7, and Article II, Section 3, give the president the power to participate authoritatively in the legislative process.

commander in chief the role of the president as commander of the national military and the state National Guard units (when called into service)

Military Power The president's military powers are among the most important exercised by the chief executive. The position of **commander in chief** makes the president the highest military authority in the United States, with control of the entire defense establishment. The president is also head of the nation's intelligence network, which includes not only the Central Intelligence Agency (CIA) but also the National Security Council (NSC), the National Security Agency (NSA), the Federal Bureau of Investigation (FBI), and a host of less well-known but very powerful international and domestic security agencies.

Military Sources of Domestic Power The president's military powers extend into the domestic sphere. Article IV, Section 4, provides that the "United States shall [protect] every State . . . against Invasion . . . and . . . domestic Violence." Congress has made this an explicit presidential power through statutes directing the president as commander in chief to discharge these obligations.[2] The Constitution restrains the president's use of domestic force by providing that a state legislature (or governor when the legislature is not in session) must request federal troops before the president can send them into the state to provide public order. Yet this proviso is not absolute. First, presidents are not obligated to deploy national troops merely because the state legislature or governor makes such a request. More important, the president may deploy troops in a state or city without a specific request from the state legislature or governor if the president considers it necessary to maintain an essential national service during an emergency, enforce a federal judicial order, or protect federally guaranteed civil rights.[3]

One historic example of the unilateral use of presidential emergency power, even when the states don't request it, is the decision by President Dwight D. Eisenhower in 1957 to send troops into Little Rock, Arkansas, against the wishes of the state of Arkansas, to enforce court orders to integrate Little Rock's Central High School. The governor of Arkansas, Orval Faubus, had posted the Arkansas National Guard at the entrance to Central High School to prevent the court-ordered admission of nine black students. After an effort to negotiate with Governor Faubus failed, President Eisenhower reluctantly sent 1,000 paratroopers to Little Rock; they stood watch while the black students took their places in the all-white classrooms.

In most instances of domestic disorder, whether from human or from natural causes, presidents tend to exercise unilateral power by declaring a "state of emergency," thereby making available federal grants, insurance, and direct assistance. In 2005, President Bush declared a state of emergency to allow the

One of the president's responsibilities is the maintenance of public order. After Hurricane Katrina devastated the Gulf Coast in 2005, President Bush declared a federal state of emergency in Louisiana and sent troops to the region to rescue residents, provide food and medicine, and keep order.

Federal Emergency Management Agency (FEMA) to coordinate the government's response to Hurricane Katrina, an immense storm that devastated the city of New Orleans, resulting in approximately 1,830 deaths. Chaos reigned in the days immediately following the storm, including looting and violence. Bush sent some 22,000 federal troops to bolster local efforts to restore order and offer aid.

Judicial Power The presidential power to grant reprieves, pardons, and amnesty involves power over all individuals who may be a threat to the security of the United States. Presidents may use this power on behalf of a particular individual, as did Gerald Ford when he pardoned Richard Nixon in 1974 "for all offenses against the United States which he . . . has committed or may have committed." Or they may use it on a large scale, as did President Andrew Johnson in 1868, when he gave full amnesty to all southerners who had participated in the "Late Rebellion," and President Carter in 1977, when he declared an amnesty for all the draft evaders of the Vietnam War. This power of life and death over others helped elevate American presidents to the level of earlier conquerors and kings, before whom supplicants might come to make their pleas for mercy.

Diplomatic Power The president is America's "head of state," its chief representative in dealings with other nations, having the power to make treaties for the United States (with the advice and consent of the Senate). When President George Washington received Edmond Genêt ("Citizen Genêt") as the formal emissary of the revolutionary government of France in 1793 and had his cabinet officers and Congress back his decision, he established a greatly expanded interpretation of the power to "receive Ambassadors and other public Ministers," extending it to the power to "recognize" other countries. That power gives the president the almost unconditional authority to review the claims of any new ruling groups in order to determine whether they indeed control the territory and population of their country, so that they can commit it to treaties and other agreements.

In recent years, presidents have expanded the practice of using executive agreements instead of treaties to establish relations with other countries.[4] An **executive agreement** is exactly like a treaty because it is a contract between two countries, but it does not require Senate approval. There are actually two types of executive

executive agreement an agreement, made between the president and another country, that has the force of a treaty but does not require the Senate's "advice and consent"

As head of state, the president is America's chief representative in dealings with other countries. In 2013, Obama met with Chinese president Xi Jinping to discuss a common approach to North Korea and cyber security, two important issues on the U.S. national security agenda.

agreements. One is the executive-congressional agreement. For this type of agreement, the president will submit the proposed arrangement to Congress for a simple majority vote in both houses, usually easier for presidents to win than the two-thirds approval of the Senate that is required for a treaty. The other type of executive agreement is the sole executive agreement, which is simply an understanding between the president and a foreign state and is not submitted to Congress for approval. In the past, sole executive agreements were used to flesh out commitments already made in treaties or to arrange for matters well below the level of policy. Since the 1930s, however, presidents have entered into sole executive agreements on important issues when they were uncertain about their prospects for securing congressional approval. For example, the General Agreement on Tariffs and Trade (GATT), one of the cornerstones of U.S. international economic policy in the post–World War II era, was based on an executive agreement. The courts have held that executive agreements have the force of law, as though they were formal treaties.

Executive Power The Constitution focuses executive power and legal responsibility on the president. The famous sign on President Truman's desk, "The Buck Stops Here," was not merely an assertion of Truman's personal sense of responsibility but also his recognition of the legal and constitutional responsibility of the president. The most important basis of the president's power as chief executive is found in Article II, Section 3, of the Constitution, which stipulates that the president must see that all the laws are faithfully executed, and Section 2, which provides that the president will appoint, remove, and supervise all executive officers, and appoint all federal judges (with Senate approval). The power to appoint the principal executive officers and to require each of them to report to the president on subjects relating to the duties of their departments makes the president the true chief executive officer (CEO) of the nation. The president is subject to some limitations, because the appointment of all such officers, including ambassadors, ministers, and federal judges, is subject to a majority approval by the Senate. But these appointments are at the discretion of the president, and the loyalty and the responsibility of each appointee are presumed to be directed toward the president.

executive privilege the claim that confidential communications between a president and close advisers should not be revealed without the consent of the president

Another component of the president's power as chief executive is **executive privilege**, the claim that confidential communications between a president and close advisers should not be revealed without presidential consent. Presidents have made this claim ever since George Washington refused a request from the House of Representatives to deliver documents concerning negotiations of an important treaty. Washington refused (successfully) on the grounds that, first, the House was not constitutionally part of the treaty-making process, and second, diplomatic negotiations required secrecy.

Although many presidents have claimed executive privilege, the concept was not tested in the courts until the 1971 "Watergate" affair. President Richard Nixon refused congressional demands that he turn over secret White House tapes that congressional investigators suspected would establish his complicity in illegal activities. In *United States v. Nixon* (1974), the Supreme Court ordered Nixon to turn over the tapes.[5] The president complied with the order and was forced to resign from office. The *United States v. Nixon* case is often seen as a blow to presidential power, but in actuality, the Court's ruling recognized for the first time the

legal validity of executive privilege, though holding that it did not apply in this particular instance. Subsequent presidents have cited *United States v. Nixon* in support of their claims of executive privilege. The Obama administration has invoked executive privilege once, in response to congressional demands for records from Attorney General Eric Holder relating to Operation Fast and Furious, an arms-trafficking sting operation that went awry, with federal agents losing track of hundreds of guns they sold to suspected gun smugglers.

Legislative Power The president plays a role not only in the administration of government but also in the legislative process. Two constitutional provisions are the primary sources of the president's power in the legislative arena. The first of these is the portion of Article II, Section 3, providing that the president "shall from time to time give to the Congress Information of the State of the Union, and recommend to their Consideration such Measures as he shall judge necessary and expedient." Delivering a "State of the Union" address may at first appear to be little more than the president's obligation to make recommendations for Congress's consideration. But as political and social conditions began to favor an increasingly prominent presidential role, each president, especially since Franklin Delano Roosevelt, began to rely on this provision in order to become the primary initiator of proposals for legislative action in Congress and the most important single participant in legislative decision making, as well as the principal source for public awareness of national issues.[6]

The second of the president's legislative powers is the veto power assigned by Article I, Section 7.[7] The **veto** is the president's constitutional power to reject acts of Congress (see Figure 13.1), making the president the most important single legislative leader.[8] No bill vetoed by the president can become law unless both the House and Senate override the veto by a two-thirds vote. In the case of a **pocket veto**, Congress does not have the option of overriding the veto, but must reintroduce the bill in the next session. Usually, if a president is presented with a bill and does not sign it within 10 days, it automatically becomes law. But this is true only while Congress is in session. If a president chooses not to sign a bill presented within the last 10 days of a legislative session, and Congress is out of session when the 10-day limit expires, instead of becoming law, the bill is vetoed.

Use of the veto varies according to the political situation each president confronts. George W. Bush did not find it necessary to use his veto power until 2007, when the Democrats took control of both houses of Congress. During his last two years in office, Bush vetoed 10 bills, including legislation designed to prohibit the use of harsh interrogation tactics, saying it "would take away one of the most valuable tools in the war on terror."[9] President Obama, who has had a Democratic majority in the Senate since taking office, has used his veto power only twice during his first six years in office. Since the time of George Washington, presidents have used their veto power 2,564 times, and on only 110 occasions has Congress overridden them. As shown in Figure 13.2, the number of presidential vetoes is higher when Congress is controlled by the opposite party.

Though not explicitly, the Constitution provides the president with the power of **legislative initiative**—the president's implied power to bring a legislative agenda before Congress. The framers of the Constitution clearly saw legislative initiative as one of the keys to executive power. "Initiative" implies the ability to formulate

The Supreme Court's decision in United States v. Nixon *is often seen as a blow to presidential power because Nixon was required to turn over secret tapes related to the Watergate scandal, despite his claims of executive privilege. Here, Nixon points to transcripts of the tapes that he is turning over to House impeachment investigators.*

veto the president's constitutional power to turn down acts of Congress; a presidential veto may be overridden by a two-thirds vote of each house of Congress

pocket veto a presidential veto that is automatically triggered if the president does not act on a given piece of legislation passed during the final 10 days of a legislative session

for critical analysis

How might the anticipation of a veto affect the behavior of Congress? And how might the anticipation of a congressional override affect the president's behavior?

legislative initiative the president's inherent power to bring a legislative agenda before Congress

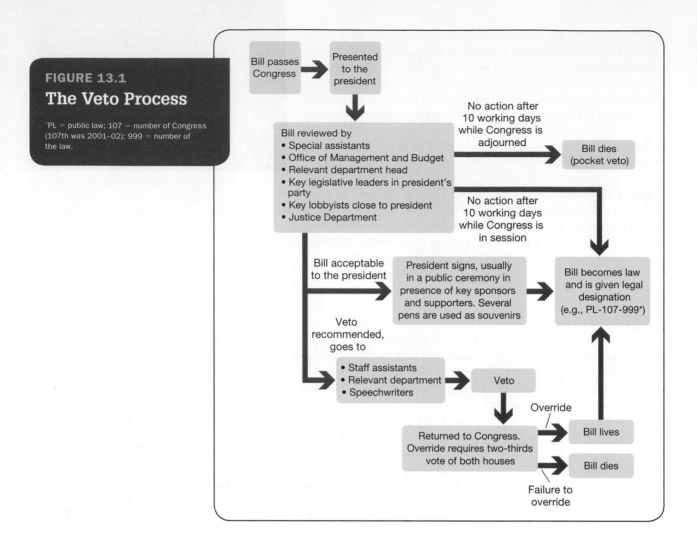

FIGURE 13.1

The Veto Process

*PL = public law; 107 = number of Congress (107th was 2001–02); 999 = number of the law.

Bill passes Congress → Presented to the president

Bill reviewed by
- Special assistants
- Office of Management and Budget
- Relevant department head
- Key legislative leaders in president's party
- Key lobbyists close to president
- Justice Department

No action after 10 working days while Congress is adjourned → Bill dies (pocket veto)

No action after 10 working days while Congress is in session

Bill acceptable to the president

President signs, usually in a public ceremony in presence of key sponsors and supporters. Several pens are used as souvenirs

Bill becomes law and is given legal designation (e.g., PL-107-999*)

Veto recommended, goes to
- Staff assistants
- Relevant department
- Speechwriters

Veto

Returned to Congress. Override requires two-thirds vote of both houses

Override → Bill lives

Failure to override → Bill dies

proposals for important policies, and the president, as an individual with a great deal of staff assistance, is able to initiate decisive action more frequently than Congress, with its large assemblies that have to deliberate and debate before taking action. With some important exceptions, Congress depends on the president to set the agenda of public policy. For example, Congress has come to expect the president to propose the government's budget. And quite clearly, initiative confers the power of being able to set the terms of discourse in the making of public policy.

For example, during the weeks immediately following September 11, George W. Bush took many presidential initiatives to Congress, and each was given almost unanimous support—from commitments to pursue Al Qaeda, remove the Taliban, and reconstitute the Afghanistan regime, all the way to almost unlimited approval for mobilization of both military force and the power to regulate American civil liberties. President Obama emphasized health care for all Americans by making the Afforadable Care Act the centerpiece of his legislative initiative.

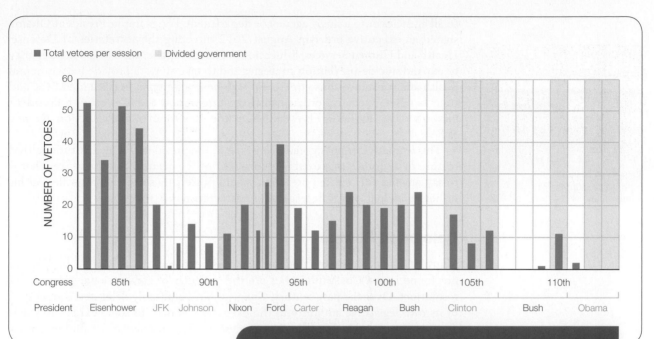

■ Total vetoes per session   ■ Divided government

NUMBER OF VETOES

Congress — 85th — 90th — 95th — 100th — 105th — 110th

President — Eisenhower — JFK — Johnson — Nixon — Ford — Carter — Reagan — Bush — Clinton — Bush — Obama

FIGURE 13.2

The Presidential Use of the Veto

One of the president's checks over the legislative branch is the use of the veto. The use of the veto has varied considerably over the course of American history. The bars in the graph show the number of vetoes each president made per session of Congress. What is the overall trend for vetoes? Why might this be? What is the relationship between the number of vetoes and whether Congress is controlled by the same party as the president (unified government) or the opposite party (divided government)?

NOTE: Congress changed party control mid-sessions in 1953–54 and 2001. The first president Bush shown here is George H. W. Bush (101st and 102nd Congresses); the second is George W. Bush (107th–110th Congresses).
SOURCE: The American Presidency Project, www.presidency.ucsb.edu/data/vetoes.php (accessed 4/21/14).

The president's initiative does not end with congressional policy making and the making of laws in the ordinary sense of the term. The president has still another legislative role (in all but name) within the executive branch. This is designated as the power to issue **executive orders**. The executive order is first and foremost simply a normal tool of management, a power that virtually any CEO has to make "company policy"—rules-setting procedures, etiquette, chains of command, functional responsibilities, and so on. But evolving out of this normal management practice is a recognized presidential power to promulgate rules that have the effect and the formal status of legislation. Most presidential executive orders provide for the reorganization of structures and procedures or otherwise direct the affairs of the executive branch—to be applied either across the board

executive order a rule or regulation issued by the president that has the effect and formal status of legislation

to all agencies or to a single agency or department. For example, President Obama signed an executive order in August 2012 directing the secretaries of Defense, Health and Human Services, Education, Veterans Affairs, and Homeland Security to expand suicide-prevention strategies and to take steps to provide better mental health and substance abuse treatment services for veterans, service members, and their families. Executive orders can also establish new agencies, as with President Nixon's order in 1970–71 establishing the Environmental Protection Agency (EPA).

for critical analysis

Although Congress passes laws, the president has influence too. What is the president's role in the legislative process?

This legislative or policy leadership role of the presidency is an institutionalized feature of the office that exists independent of the occupant of the office. That is to say, anyone duly elected president would possess these powers regardless of his or her individual energy or leadership characteristics.[10]

Delegated Powers

Many of the powers exercised by the president and the executive branch are not found in the Constitution but are the products of congressional statutes and resolutions. Over the past century, Congress has voluntarily delegated a great deal of its own legislative authority to the executive branch. To some extent, this delegation of power has been an almost inescapable consequence of the expansion of government activity in the United States since the New Deal. Given the vast range of the federal government's responsibilities, Congress cannot execute and administer all the programs it creates and the laws it enacts. Inevitably, Congress must turn to the hundreds of departments and agencies in the executive branch or, when necessary, create new agencies to implement its goals. Thus, for example, in 2002, when Congress sought to protect America from terrorist attacks, it established a Department of Homeland Security with broad powers in the realms of law enforcement, public health, and immigration. Similarly, in 1970, when Congress enacted legislation designed to improve the nation's air and water quality, it assigned the task of implementing its goals to the new EPA, created by President Nixon's executive order and empowered by Congress to set and enforce air- and water-quality standards.

As they implement congressional legislation, federal agencies collectively develop thousands of rules and regulations and issue thousands of orders and findings every year. Agencies interpret Congress's intent, promulgate rules aimed at implementing that intent, and issue orders to individuals, firms, and organizations to impel them to conform to the law. When it establishes an agency, Congress sometimes grants it only limited discretionary authority, providing very specific guidelines and standards that must be followed by the administrators charged with the program's implementation. Take the Internal Revenue Service (IRS), for example. Most Americans view the IRS as a powerful agency whose dictates can have an immediate and sometimes unpleasant impact on their lives. In fact, congressional tax legislation is very specific and detailed, leaving little to the discretion of IRS administrators.[11] The agency certainly develops numerous rules and procedures to enhance tax collection. It is Congress, however, that establishes the structure of the tax liabilities, tax exemptions, and tax deductions that determine each taxpayer's burdens and responsibilities.

In most instances, though, congressional legislation is not very detailed. Often, Congress defines a broad goal or objective and delegates enormous discretionary power to administrators to determine how that goal is to be achieved. Agency

Presidential Powers

Many countries around the world have a president at the head of government. But the powers of the president are not constant from country to country. This chapter has described the constitutional powers of the American president in detail. The table here compares these powers to the powers of the presidents of France, Germany, and South Africa.

Both Germany and South Africa have parliamentary systems of government, meaning that the most powerful executive position is the prime minister (who is the leader of and is elected by the legislature and thus part of the legislative branch). In Germany the most powerful position is held by the chancellor while the president plays a mostly ceremonial role, similar to the United Kingdom's queen. South Africa's president is actually more analogous to a prime minister, as he leads the legislature (and is elected by it) and runs the government, but the position also involves a ceremonial role. Finally, France's system is called "semi-presidential," which is an executive system that divides power between a president and a prime minister, who have different but (theoretically) equal powers.

Looking at these different countries, in which system does the president appear to have the most power in shaping the politics within his or her country?

	Type of Executive System	Elected by	Legislative Power	Power to Appoint Justices	Power to Declare War	Power to Call New Parliamentary Elections	Term Limits
United States	Presidential	Electoral college (indirectly by the voters)	Can sign or veto legislation Responsible for enacting legislation	Yes	No	No	Two four-year terms
France	Semi-presidential	The voters	Appoints prime minister, but cannot dismiss him/her Can sign bills or send them back to the parliament for reconsideration Can initiate referendum	Yes	No	Yes	Two consecutive five-year terms
Germany	Parliamentary	The parliament*	Can sign law but only on behalf of the chancellor Position is largely ceremonial	No	No**	Yes	Two five-year terms
South Africa	Parliamentary	The parliament	Can sign bills or send them back to the parliament for reconsideration Considerable legislative powers	Yes	Yes	Yes	Two five-year terms

*Germany's president is elected by a special federal convention, which includes all the members of Germany's Bundestag (lower house of parliament), as well as an equal number of representatives sent by the regional legislatures.

**One of the most famous clauses of the German constitution is their neutrality requirement; the country may only maintain weapons for defensive purposes

SOURCES: Basic Law for the Federal Republic of Germany, 1949: www.gesetz-eim-internet.de/englisch_gg/englisch_gg.html; Constitution of the Republic of South Africa, 1996: www.gov.za/documents/constitution/1996/a108-96.pdf; Constitution of the Fifth Republic, 1958: www.assemblee-nationale.fr/english/ (all accessed 10/16/14).

administrators have enormous discretionary power to draft rules and regulations that have the effect of law. Indeed, the courts treat these administrative rules like congressional statutes. For all intents and purposes, when Congress creates an agency such as the Department of Homeland Security, giving it a broad mandate to achieve some desirable outcome, it transfers its own legislative power to the executive branch.

During the nineteenth and early twentieth centuries, Congress typically wrote laws that provided fairly clear principles and standards to guide executive implementation. For example, the 1923 tariff act empowered the president to increase or decrease duties on certain manufactured goods in order to reduce the difference in costs between domestically produced products and those manufactured abroad. The act authorized the president to make the final determination, but his discretionary authority was quite constrained. The statute listed the criteria the president was to consider, fixed the permissible range of tariff changes, and outlined the procedures to be used to calculate the cost differences between foreign and domestic goods. When an importer challenged a particular executive decision as an abuse of delegated power, the Supreme Court had no difficulty finding that the president was merely acting in accordance with Congress's directives.[12]

At least since the New Deal, however, Congress has tended to give executive agencies broad mandates and to draft legislation that offers few clear standards or guidelines for implementation by the executive. For example, the 1933 National

The influence of the president and the executive branch is widespread, as the executive is responsible for the implementation of many laws that Congress passes. These delegated powers extend to health care, as the executive branch orchestrated the health insurance enrollment process for millions of Americans under the Affordable Care Act. They also extend to consumer safety when the Consumer Product Safety Commission issues recalls for hazardous products like this surge protector, which could overheat, smoke, and melt.

Industrial Recovery Act gave the president the authority to set rules to bring about fair competition in key sectors of the economy without ever defining what the term meant or how it was to be achieved.[13] This pattern of broad delegation became typical in the ensuing decades. The 1972 Consumer Product Safety Act, for example, authorizes the Consumer Product Safety Commission to reduce unreasonable risk of injury from household products but offers no suggestions to guide the commission's determination of what constitutes reasonable and unreasonable risks or how these are to be reduced.[14] This means the executive branch, under the president's direction, has wide discretion to make rules that impact American citizens and businesses. A recent example of the executive branch's role is the 2011 Affordable Care Act. After the law passed, several members of Congress admitted that they did not fully understand how the act would work and were depending upon the Department of Health and Human Services (HHS), the agency with primary administrative responsibility for the act, to explain it to them. The case of the Affordable Care Act is fairly typical. As administrative scholar Jerry L. Nashaw has observed, "Most public law is legislative in origin but administrative in content."[15]

This shift from the nineteenth-century pattern of relatively well-defined congressional guidelines for administrators to the more contemporary pattern of broad delegations of congressional power to the executive branch is, to be sure, partially a consequence of the great scope and complexity of the tasks that America's contemporary government has undertaken. During much of the nineteenth century, the federal government had relatively few

Who Are America's Presidents?

American presidents have all been men and have all been Christians. Until the election of Barack Obama in 2008, they had all been white. As the data show, a majority of presidents have come from the southeastern United States, with Virginia producing the most American presidents, especially in the nation's first decades.

Race

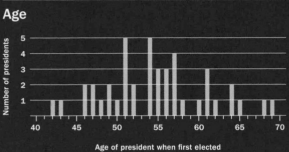

White **42**   African American **1**

Religion

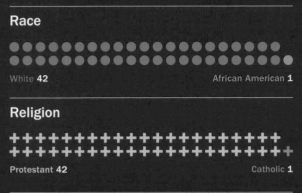

Protestant **42**   Catholic **1**

Party*

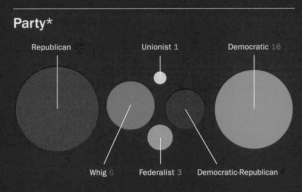

Republican
Unionist 1
Democratic 16
Whig 6
Federalist 3
Democratic-Republican

Age

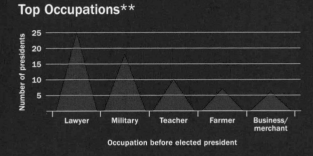

Age of president when first elected

Top Occupations**

Occupation before elected president

Lawyer   Military   Teacher   Farmer   Business/merchant

Region†

Presidents

- ○ 0
- ● 1
- ● 2
- ● 4
- ● 7
- ● 8

NOTE: Grover Cleveland served as America's 22nd and 24th presidents. He is counted only once in the demographic data here, thus the total number of people who have served as U.S. president is 43.

*Some presidents switched parties during their political careers, thus the numbers sum to more than 43.

**This chart reflects the top nonpolitical careers of U.S. presidents. (All presidents except Washington had previous political and/or public service experience.) Presidents may have had more than one occupation, and some occupations do not appear on this list, thus the numbers do not sum to 43.

† Andrew Jackson was born in the Waxhaw area, on the North Carolina–South Carolina border.

SOURCES: Roper Center, www.ropercenter.uconn.edu/elections/common/pop_vote.html; David Leip, http://uselectionatlas.org/RESULTS/; the American Presidency Project, www.presidency.ucsb.edu/showelection.php?year=1840; Miller Center, University of Virginia, http://millercenter.org/president (accessed 3/17/14).

for critical analysis

1. Why do you think all presidents have been Christian men and all but one have been white? Do you think this is likely to change in coming years?

2. Why do you think so many presidents have come from the South and the East? What electoral or historical factors may have produced this trend?

domestic responsibilities, and Congress could pay close attention to details. Today, the operation of an enormous executive establishment and literally thousands of programs under varied and changing circumstances requires that administrators be allowed some considerable measure of discretion to carry out their jobs. Nevertheless, the end result is to shift power from Congress to the executive branch.

Inherent Powers

inherent powers powers claimed by a president that are not expressed in the Constitution but are inferred from it

Presidents have claimed a fourth source of power beyond expressed, implied, and delegated powers. These are powers not specified in the Constitution or the law but are "powers over and beyond those expressly granted in the Constitution or reasonably to be implied from express grants."[16] Referred to as the **inherent powers** of the presidency, they are most often asserted by presidents in times of war or national emergency. Yet not all powerful presidents claimed inherent powers.

For example, after the fall of Fort Sumter and the outbreak of the Civil War, President Abraham Lincoln issued a series of executive orders for which he had no clear legal authority. Without even calling Congress into session, Lincoln combined the state militias into a 90-day national volunteer force, called for 40,000 new volunteers, enlarged the regular army and navy, diverted $2 million in unspent appropriations to military needs, instituted censorship of the U.S. mail, ordered a blockade of southern ports, suspended the writ of habeas corpus in the border states, and ordered the arrest by military police of individuals whom he deemed to be guilty of engaging in or even merely contemplating treasonous actions.[17] Lincoln asserted that these extraordinary measures were necessary to confront this crisis. When Congress convened in July, he reported his actions to it, saying that they could only be legal if Congress passed a law making them so, which it did. Even though Lincoln never claimed inherent powers, his example was used by later presidents as justification.[18]

War and Inherent Presidential Power The Constitution gives Congress the power to declare war. Presidents, however, have gone a long way toward capturing this power for themselves. Congress has not declared war since June 1942,[19] but since then, American military forces have engaged in numerous campaigns throughout the world under the orders of the president. When North Korean forces invaded South Korea in June 1950, Congress was actually prepared to declare war, but President Harry S. Truman asserted that the president and not Congress could decide when and where to deploy America's military might. Truman dispatched American forces to Korea without a congressional declaration, and in the face of the emergency, Congress felt it had to acquiesce, and approved money to finance the conflict. This became the pattern for future congressional-executive relations in the military realm: the wars in Vietnam, Bosnia, Afghanistan, and Iraq, and a host of lesser conflicts, were all fought without declarations of war. Approximately 102,000 U.S. troops have died in these military engagements, with half of that total occurring during the Vietnam War.

War Powers Resolution a resolution of Congress that the president can send troops into action abroad only by authorization of Congress, or if American troops are already under attack or serious threat

In 1973, Congress responded to presidential unilateralism by passing the **War Powers Resolution** over President Richard M. Nixon's veto. This resolution reasserted the principle of congressional war power, required the president to inform Congress of any planned military campaign, and stipulated that forces must be withdrawn within 60 days if there is no specific congressional authorization for their continued deployment. Presidents, however, have generally ignored the War Powers Resolution, claiming inherent executive power to defend the nation. Thus, President George W. Bush responded to the September 2001 attacks by Islamic terrorists by organizing a major military campaign to overthrow the Taliban regime in Afghanistan, which had sheltered the terrorists. In 2003, Bush ordered the invasion of Iraq, which he accused of posing a threat to the United States. U.S. forces overthrew the government of the Iraqi dictator, Saddam Hussein, and occupied the country. In both instances, Congress passed resolutions approving the president's actions, but the president was careful to assert that he did not need congressional authorization. The War Powers Resolution was barely mentioned on Capitol Hill and was ignored by the White House. President Obama, for his part, has made frequent use of special operations forces and unmanned aerial vehicles (or drones) to conduct military operations. Congress has not been consulted.

Military emergencies have typically also led to expansion of the domestic powers of the executive branch. This was true during the First and Second World Wars and has been true in the wake of the "war on terror" as well. Within a month of the September 11, 2001, attacks, the White House had drafted and Congress had enacted the USA PATRIOT Act, expanding the power of government agencies to engage in domestic surveillance activities, including electronic surveillance, and restricting judicial review of such efforts. The act also gave the attorney general greater authority to detain and deport aliens suspected of having terrorist affiliations. The following year, Congress created the Department of Homeland Security, combining offices from 22 federal agencies into one huge new cabinet department that would be responsible for protecting the nation from attack and responding to natural disasters. As an executive agency, the Department of Homeland Security is overseen by the president.

for critical analysis

Presidents have expressed, delegated, and inherent sources of power. Which of the three do you think most accounts for the powers of the presidency?

● The Presidency as an Institution

Identify the institutional resources presidents have to help them exercise their powers

The framers of the Constitution, as we saw, created a unitary executive because they thought this would make the presidency a more energetic institution. Nevertheless, since the ratification of the Constitution, the president has been joined by thousands of officials and staffers who work for, assist, or advise the chief executive (see Figure 13.3). Collectively, these individuals could be said to make up the institutional presidency and to give the president a capacity for action that no single individual, however energetic, could duplicate. The first component of the institutional presidency is the president's Cabinet.

The Cabinet

In the American system of government, the **Cabinet** is the traditional but informal designation for the heads of all the major federal government departments. The Cabinet has no constitutional status. Unlike in Great Britain and many other parliamentary countries, where the cabinet *is* the government, the American Cabinet is not a collective body. It meets but makes no decisions as a group. Each appointment must be approved by the Senate, but cabinet members are not responsible to the Senate or to Congress at large.

Cabinet the secretaries, or chief administrators, of the major departments of the federal government; Cabinet secretaries are appointed by the president with the consent of the Senate

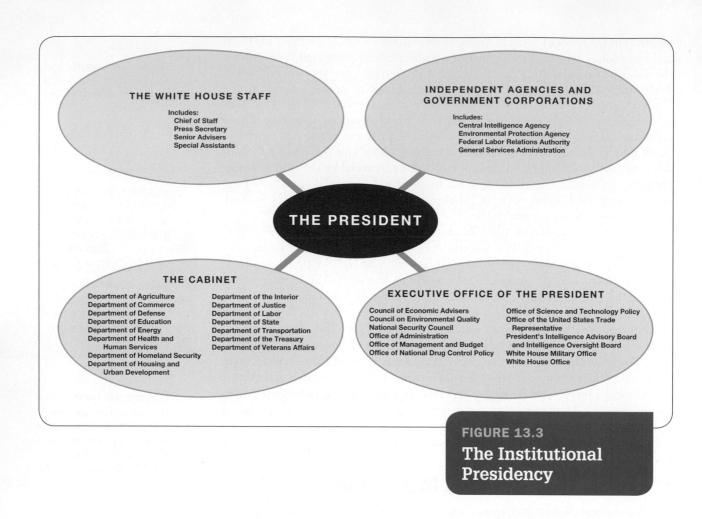

FIGURE 13.3

The Institutional Presidency

Since cabinet appointees generally have not shared political careers with the president or with one another, and since they may meet literally for the first time only after their selection, this motley collection of appointees is unlikely to form an effective governing group. Although President Clinton's insistence on a cabinet diverse enough "to look like America" could be considered an act of political wisdom, it virtually guaranteed that few of his appointees had ever spent much time working together or even knew the policy positions or beliefs of the other appointees.[20]

Some presidents have relied more heavily on an "inner cabinet." This includes the **National Security Council (NSC)**. The NSC, established by law in 1947, is composed of the president, the vice president, the secretary of state, the secretary of defense, and other officials invited by the president. It has its own staff of foreign policy specialists run by the special assistant to the president for national security affairs. For these highest appointments, presidents often turn to people from outside Washington, usually longtime associates. The inner Cabinet also can include the ranking officials of the White House staff.

National Security Council (NSC)
a presidential foreign policy advisory council composed of the president, the vice president, the secretary of state, the secretary of defense, and other officials invited by the president

The White House Staff

The **White House staff** is composed mainly of analysts and advisers.[21] Although many of the top White House staff members are given the title "special assistant" for a particular task or sector, the judgments and advice they are supposed to provide are a good deal broader and more generally political than those coming from the Executive Office of the President or from the cabinet departments. The members of the White House staff also tend to be more closely associated with the president than are other presidentially appointed officials.

From an informal group of fewer than a dozen people (popularly called the **Kitchen Cabinet**) and no more than four dozen at its height during the Roosevelt presidency in 1937, the White House staff has grown substantially.[22] Richard Nixon employed 550 people in 1972. President Carter, who found so many of the trappings of presidential power distasteful, and who publicly vowed to keep his staff small and decentralized, built an even larger and more centralized staff. President Clinton reduced the White House staff by 20 percent, but a large White House staff is still essential. In Obama's second term, the White House staff numbered approximately 450. In the spirit of transparency, the White House lists their names, position, and salary on the White House website.[23]

The Executive Office of the President

Created in 1939, the **Executive Office of the President (EOP)** is a major part of what is often called the "institutional presidency"—the permanent agencies that perform defined management tasks for the president. Somewhere between 1,500 and 2,000 highly specialized people work for EOP agencies.[24] The importance of each agency in the EOP varies according to the personal orientation of each president. The most important and the largest EOP agency is the Office of Management and Budget (OMB). Its roles in preparing the national budget, designing the president's program, reporting on agency activities, and overseeing regulatory proposals connect the OMB to every conceivable presidential responsibility. The status and power of the OMB have grown in importance with each successive president, and the director of the OMB is now one of the most powerful officials in Washington. At one time the process of budgeting was a "bottom-up" procedure, with expenditure and program requests passing from the lowest bureaus through the departments to "clearance" in the OMB and thence to Congress, where each agency could be called in to explain what its "original request" was before the OMB revised it. Now the budgeting process is "top-down": the OMB sets the terms of discourse for agencies as well as for Congress.

The staff of the Council of Economic Advisers (CEA) constantly analyzes the economy and economic trends in order to help the president anticipate events, rather than waiting and reacting to them. The Council on Environmental Quality was designed to do for environmental issues what the CEA does for economic issues. The NSC—the "inner Cabinet" mentioned earlier—is composed of designated cabinet officials who meet regularly with the president to give advice on the large national security picture. The staff of the NSC assimilates and analyzes data from all intelligence-gathering agencies (CIA, etc.). Other EOP agencies perform more specialized tasks.

White House staff analysts and advisers to the president, each of whom is often given the title "special assistant"

Kitchen Cabinet an informal group of advisers to whom the president turns for counsel and guidance; members of the official Cabinet may or may not also be members of the Kitchen Cabinet

Executive Office of the President (EOP) the permanent agencies that perform defined management tasks for the president; created in 1939, the EOP includes the OMB, the CEA, the NSC, and other agencies

The Vice Presidency

The vice presidency is a constitutional anomaly even though the office was created along with the presidency by the Constitution. The vice president exists for two purposes only: to succeed the president in case of death, resignation, or incapacity and to preside over the Senate, casting a tie-breaking vote when necessary.[25]

The main value of the vice president as a political resource for the president is electoral. Traditionally, presidential candidates choose running mates who can win the support of at least one state (preferably a large one) that may not otherwise support the ticket. It is very doubtful that John Kennedy would have won in 1960 without his vice-presidential candidate, Lyndon Johnson, and the contribution Johnson made to winning in Texas. Another traditional guideline holds that the vice-presidential nominee should provide some regional balance and, wherever possible, ideological or ethnic balance as well. In 2008, Barack Obama chose Senator Joseph Biden of Delaware to be his running mate for a number of reasons. To begin with, Biden is Catholic and has blue-collar origins. Obama believed correctly that Biden would appeal to these important groups in such must-win states as Pennsylvania and Ohio. Perhaps even more important, Biden possesses enormous foreign policy experience and chaired the Senate Foreign Relations Committee. The Republicans had often pointed to Obama's lack of experience in the international realm as indicating that he was not ready to be president; Democrats hoped that Biden's presence on the ticket would put the "experience" issue to rest.

As the institutional presidency has grown in size and complexity, most presidents of the past 25 years have sought to use their vice presidents as a management resource after the election. President Clinton, for example, relied greatly on his vice president, Al Gore, to oversee the National Performance Review (NPR), an ambitious program to "reinvent" the way the federal government conducts its affairs. President George W. Bush granted unprecedented power and responsibility to his vice president, Dick Cheney, who helped shape the "war on terror." In the Obama White House, Vice President Biden is said to be regarded as the "skeptic-in-chief."[26] Biden's role is to question and criticize policy recommendations made to the president—until, of course, the president makes a decision, at which point the vice president falls loyally into step.

The vice president is also important because, in the event of the death or incapacity of the president, he or she will succeed to the nation's highest office. During the course of American history, eight vice presidents have had to replace presidents who died in office. One vice president, Gerald Ford, found himself at the head of the nation when President Richard Nixon was forced to resign as a result of the Watergate scandal. During the 2004 vice-presidential debates, Dick Cheney sought to distinguish himself from the Democratic vice-presidential nominee, John Edwards, by averring that he, unlike the less-experienced Edwards, had been chosen for his ability to serve as president if that became necessary.

Until the ratification of the Twenty-Fifth Amendment in 1965, the succession of the vice president to the presidency was a tradition, launched by John Tyler when he assumed the presidency after William Henry Harrison's death, rather than a constitutional or statutory requirement. The Twenty-Fifth Amendment codified

Presidential candidates often choose their vice presidential running mates to gain a specific electoral advantage. Barack Obama's choice of Joe Biden helped to alleviate criticism of Obama's lack of foreign policy experience. Since taking office, Biden has played an important role in U.S. foreign policy. For example, in 2014 he met with the acting Ukrainian prime minister following Russia's annexation of Crimea, formerly a Ukrainian province.

this tradition by providing that the vice president would assume the presidency in the event of the chief executive's death or incapacity and setting forth the procedures that would be followed. In the event that both the president and vice president are killed, the Presidential Succession Act of 1947 establishes an order of succession, beginning with the Speaker of the House and continuing with the president pro tempore of the Senate and the Cabinet secretaries. This piece of legislation, adopted during the Cold War and prompted by fear of a nuclear attack, has taken on new importance in an age of global terrorism.

The First Spouse

The president serves as both chief executive and chief of state—the equivalent of Great Britain's prime minister and monarch rolled into one, simultaneously leading the government and representing the nation at official ceremonies and functions.

Because they are generally associated exclusively with the head-of-state aspect of America's presidency, presidential spouses are usually not subject to the same sort of media scrutiny or partisan attack as that aimed at the president. Traditionally, most first ladies have limited their activities to the ceremonial portion of the presidency: greeting foreign dignitaries, visiting other countries, and attending important national ceremonies.

Some first spouses, however, have had considerable influence over policy. Franklin Roosevelt's wife, Eleanor, was widely popular, but also widely criticized for her active role in many elements of her husband's presidency. During the 1992 campaign, Bill Clinton often implied that his wife would be active in the

First Lady Michelle Obama has focused attention on children's health with her "Let's Move!" campaign. This campaign emphasizes physical activity and healthy eating to combat childhood obesity. In Iowa, more than 10,000 school-aged children joined Michelle Obama for an exercise class.

administration; he joked that voters would get "two for the price of one." And indeed, after the election, Hillary Clinton took a leading role in many policy areas, most notably heading the administration's health care reform effort. She also became the first first lady to seek public office on her own, winning a seat in the U.S. Senate in 2000 and then running for president in 2008. Later, President Obama named Clinton secretary of state, a position Clinton saw as a possible stepping stone to the presidency. Barack Obama's wife, Michelle, is a lawyer and served for a number of years as a senior administrator at the University of Chicago's Pritzker School of Medicine. Michelle Obama has emerged as a visible and active administration figure, as when she launched an anti–childhood obesity campaign in 2010.

At one time, historians and journalists liked to debate the question of strong versus weak presidents. Some presidents, such as Abraham Lincoln and FDR, were called "strong" for their leadership and their ability to guide the nation's political agenda. Others, such as James Buchanan and Calvin Coolidge, were seen as "weak" for failing to develop significant legislative programs and seeming to observe rather than shape political events. Today, the strong-versus-weak categorization has become moot. *Every president is strong*, not so much as a function of personal charisma or political savvy but as a reflection of the increasing power of the presidency. Let us see how this came about.

● The Contemporary Bases of Presidential Power

> **Explain how modern presidents have become even more powerful**

During the nineteenth century, Congress was America's dominant institution of government, and members of Congress sometimes treated the president with disdain. Today, however, no one would assert that the presidency is unimportant. Presidents seek to dominate the policy-making process and claim the power to lead the nation in time of war. The expansion of presidential power over the course of the past century has come about not by accident but as the result of an ongoing effort by successive presidents to enlarge the powers of the office.

Generally, presidents can expand their power in two ways: through popular mobilization and through the administration. First, presidents may use popular appeals to create a mass base of support that will allow them to dominate their political foes, a tactic called "going public."[27] Second, presidents may seek to bolster their control of established executive agencies or to create new administrative institutions and procedures that will reduce their dependence on Congress and give them a more independent governing and policy-making capability. Perhaps the most obvious example of this is the use of executive orders to achieve policy goals in lieu of seeking to persuade Congress to enact legislation.

Presidents have a third tool: their political party. Each president has relied on his own party to implement his legislative agenda. President Obama, for instance, relied on Democrats in the Senate to help his approvals to the federal judiciary win appointment. However, the president does not control his party; party members have considerable autonomy. Moreover, in America's system of separated powers, the president's party may be in the minority in Congress and unable to do much for the chief executive's programs. Consequently, although their party is valuable to chief executives, it has not been a fully reliable presidential tool. As a result, contemporary presidents are more likely to use the two other methods, popular mobilization and executive administration, to achieve their political goals.

Going Public

In the nineteenth century, it was considered inappropriate for presidents to engage in personal campaigning on their own behalf or in support of programs and policies. When Andrew Johnson broke this unwritten rule and made a series of speeches vehemently seeking public support for his Reconstruction program, even some of his supporters were shocked at what they saw as his lack of decorum and dignity. The president's opponents cited his "inflammatory" speeches in one of the articles of impeachment drafted by the Congress.[28]

In the twentieth century, though, popular mobilization became a favored weapon in the political arsenals of most presidents. The first to make systematic use of appeals to the public were Theodore Roosevelt and Woodrow Wilson, but the president who used public appeals most effectively was Franklin Delano Roosevelt. FDR was "firmly persuaded of the need to form a direct link between the executive office and the public."[29] Roosevelt developed a number of tactics for forging such a link. He often embarked on speaking trips around the nation to promote his programs. On one such tour, he told a crowd, "I regain strength just by meeting the American people."[30] In addition, FDR made effective use of a new electronic medium, the radio, to reach millions of Americans. In his famous "fireside chats," the president's voice could be heard in every living room in the country, discussing programs and policies and generally assuring Americans that Franklin Delano Roosevelt was aware of their difficulties and working diligently toward solutions.

Roosevelt was also an innovator in the realm of what now might be called press relations. When he entered the White House, FDR faced a mainly hostile press, typically controlled by conservative members of the business establishment.[31] To circumvent the editors and publishers who were generally unsympathetic to his goals, the president worked to cultivate the reporters who covered the White House. Roosevelt made himself available for biweekly press conferences where he offered candid answers to reporters' questions and made certain to make important policy announcements that would provide the reporters with significant stories for their papers.[32] Roosevelt was the first president to designate a press secretary, Stephen Early, who was charged with organizing the press conferences and making certain that reporters observed the informal rules distinguishing those presidential comments that could be attributed directly to the president from those that were off the record.

President Franklin Delano Roosevelt's direct appeals to the American people allowed him to "reach over the heads" of congressional opponents and force them to follow his lead because their constituents demanded it.

Every president since FDR has sought to craft a public-relations strategy that would emphasize the incumbent's strengths and maximize his popular appeal. For John F. Kennedy, handsome and quick-witted, the televised press conference was an excellent public-relations vehicle. Johnson and Nixon lacked Kennedy's charisma, but both were effective television speakers, usually reading from a prepared text. Bill Clinton made extensive use of televised town meetings—carefully staged events that gave the president an opportunity to appear to consult with rank-and-file citizens about his goals and policies without having to face the sorts of pointed questions preferred by reporters.

One Clinton innovation was to make the White House Communications Office an important institution within the EOP. The Communications Office became responsible not only for responding to reporters' queries but also for developing and implementing a coordinated communications strategy—promoting the president's policy goals, developing responses to adverse news stories, and making certain that a favorable image of the president would, insofar as possible, dominate the news. George W. Bush relied heavily on material crafted by the Communications Office, whereas Barack Obama often relies on his own formidable speaking abilities.

Going Public Online President Obama has also been the first to make full use of a new communication medium—in this case, the Internet. Drawing on the interactive tools of the web, Obama's 2008 and 2012 campaigns changed the way politicians organize supporters, advertise to voters, defend against attacks, and communicate with their constituents.[33] The Internet has not only changed the way modern presidents campaign but also how they govern. The Whitehouse.gov website keeps the president's constituents abreast of his policy agenda with a weekly streaming video address by the president, press briefings, speeches and remarks, a daily blog, photos of the president, the White House schedule, and other information. Virtually everything the president does is recorded online. YouTube airs Obama's press conferences and public appearances on a daily basis. Every presidential address is now streamed live online.

Circumventing television and other traditional media, the Internet allows the president to broadcast his policy ideas directly to the citizens. In March 2012, Obama broke new media ground again, appearing on Bill Simmons's "B.S. Report" (a regular series of podcasts on ESPN's website) in the first-ever podcast with a sitting U.S. president. Obama's Facebook page personalizes the president's connection with his constituents and the causes they care about. In early 2014, Obama had 42 million Twitter followers. Websites, podcasts, Facebook, and other new media forums facilitate direct communication between the president and the people, creating a virtual network of constituents. Like FDR in the 1930s and '40s, and Kennedy in the 1960s, Obama may have changed how presidents govern for some time to come.

The Limits of Going Public Some presidents have been able to make effective use of popular appeals to overcome congressional opposition. Popular support, though, has not been a firm foundation for presidential power: the public is notoriously fickle. After America's triumph in the 1990 Persian Gulf War, President George H. W. Bush scored a remarkable 90 percent approval rating in the polls. Two years later, however, after the 1991 budget

for critical analysis

What are the advantages and disadvantages of presidents governing via digital media? How do these pros and cons compare with "going public" in the age of television?

crisis, Bush's support plummeted, and the president was defeated in his bid for re-election. His son, President George W. Bush, maintained an approval rating of over 70 percent for more than a year following the September 11 terrorist attacks. By the end of 2005, however, President Bush's approval rating had dropped to 39 percent as a result of the growing unpopularity of the Iraq War, the administration's inept handling of hurricane relief, and a number of White House scandals, including the conviction of Vice President Cheney's chief of staff on charges of lying to a federal grand jury. Between the time President Obama took office in January 2009 and July 2014, his public approval ranged from a high of 65 percent in May 2009 to a low of 40 percent in the summer of 2011.[34] Such declines in popular approval during a president's term in office are nearly inevitable and follow a predictable pattern.[35] Both before and after they are elected, presidents generate popular support by promising to undertake important programs that will contribute directly to the well-being of large numbers of Americans. Almost without exception, presidential performance falls short of promises and popular expectations, leading to a decline in public support and the ensuing weakening of presidential influence.[36] It is a rare American president, such as Bill Clinton, who exits the White House more popular than when he went in.

The Administrative Strategy

Contemporary presidents have increased the administrative capabilities of their office in three ways. First, they have enhanced the reach and power of the EOP. Second, they have sought to increase White House control over the federal bureaucracy. Third, they have expanded the role of executive orders and other instruments of direct presidential governance. Taken together, these three components of what might be called the White House "administrative strategy" have given presidents a capacity to achieve their programmatic and policy goals even when they are unable to secure congressional approval. Indeed, some recent presidents have been able to accomplish a great deal with remarkably little congressional, partisan, or even public support.

The Growth of the EOP The EOP has grown from six administrative assistants in 1939 to several hundred employees working directly for the president in the White House office, along with some 2,500 individuals staffing the several divisions of the Executive Office. The creation and growth of the White House staff gives the president an enormously enhanced capacity to gather information, plan programs and strategies, communicate with constituencies, and exercise supervision over the executive branch. The staff multiplies the president's eyes, ears, and arms, becoming a critical instrument of presidential power.[37]

In particular, the OMB serves as a potential instrument of presidential control over federal spending and hence a mechanism through which the White House has greatly expanded its power. The OMB has the capacity to analyze and approve all legislative proposals, not only budgetary requests, emanating from all federal agencies before being submitted to Congress. This procedure, now a matter of routine, greatly enhances the president's control over the entire executive branch. All legislation originating in the White House as well as all executive orders also go through the OMB.[38] Thus, through one White House agency, the president has the means to exert major influence over the flow of money and the shape and content of national legislation.

Regulatory Review A second tactic that presidents have used to increase their power and reach is the process of regulatory review, through which presidents have sought to seize control of rule making by the agencies of the executive branch (see also Chapter 14). Whenever Congress enacts a statute, its actual implementation requires the promulgation of hundreds of rules by the agency charged with administering the law and effecting the will of Congress. Some congressional statutes are quite detailed and leave agencies with relatively little discretion. Typically, however, Congress enacts a relatively broad statement of legislative intent and then delegates to the appropriate administrative agency the power to fill in many important details.[39] In other words, Congress typically says to an administrative agency, "Here is the problem: deal with it."[40] The discretion that Congress delegates to administrative agencies has provided recent presidents with an important avenue for expanding their own power.

For example, President Clinton believed the president had full authority to order agencies of the executive branch to adopt such rules as the president thought appropriate. During the course of his presidency, Clinton issued 107 directives to administrators ordering them to propose specific rules and regulations. Republicans, of course, denounced Clinton's actions as a usurpation of power.[41] However, after President George W. Bush took office, he made no move to surrender the powers Clinton had claimed—quite the contrary. Bush vigorously continued the Clinton-era practice of issuing presidential directives to agencies, spurring them to issue new rules and regulations. Obama's first regulatory director, Cass Sunstein, not only issued a number of major regulatory directives to federal agencies but also launched a "look back" program. Under this program, the administration sought to eliminate several hundred existing federal rules it deemed obsolete.[42]

Governing by Decree: Executive Orders A fourth mechanism through which contemporary presidents have sought to enhance their power to govern unilaterally is through the use of executive orders and other forms of presidential decrees, including executive agreements, national security findings and directives, proclamations, reorganization plans, signing statements, and a host of others.[43] Executive orders have a long history in the United States and have been the vehicles for a number of important government policies, including the purchase of Louisiana, the annexation of Texas, the emancipation of the slaves, the internment of Japanese Americans, the desegregation of the military, the initiation of affirmative action, and the creation of important federal agencies, among them the EPA and the FDA.[44] (See Figure 13.4.)

Although wars and national emergencies produce the highest volume of executive orders, such presidential actions also occur frequently in peacetime. In the realm of foreign policy, unilateral presidential actions in the form of executive agreements have virtually replaced treaties as the nation's chief foreign policy instruments.[45] Presidential decrees, however, are often used for purely domestic purposes. In November 2104, President Obama issued executive orders that would protect some 4 million undocumented immigrants from the threat of deportation. These orders provoked an outcry from congressional Republicans who declared that the president had exceeded his constitutional authority.

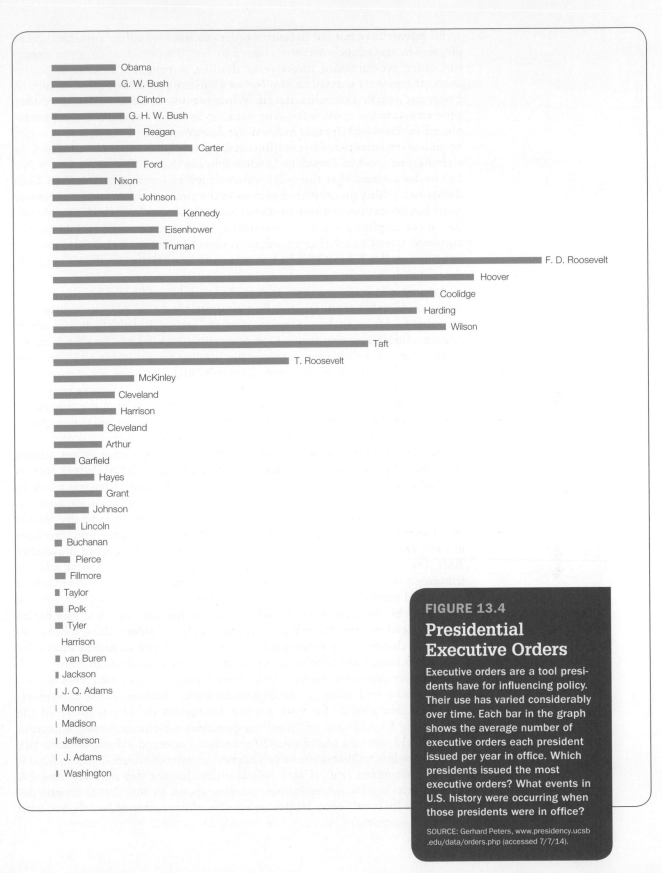

Obama
G. W. Bush
Clinton
G. H. W. Bush
Reagan
Carter
Ford
Nixon
Johnson
Kennedy
Eisenhower
Truman
F. D. Roosevelt
Hoover
Coolidge
Harding
Wilson
Taft
T. Roosevelt
McKinley
Cleveland
Harrison
Cleveland
Arthur
Garfield
Hayes
Grant
Johnson
Lincoln
Buchanan
Pierce
Fillmore
Taylor
Polk
Tyler
Harrison
van Buren
Jackson
J. Q. Adams
Monroe
Madison
Jefferson
J. Adams
Washington

FIGURE 13.4
Presidential Executive Orders

Executive orders are a tool presidents have for influencing policy. Their use has varied considerably over time. Each bar in the graph shows the average number of executive orders each president issued per year in office. Which presidents issued the most executive orders? What events in U.S. history were occurring when those presidents were in office?

SOURCE: Gerhard Peters, www.presidency.ucsb.edu/data/orders.php (accessed 7/7/14).

Presidents may not use executive orders to issue whatever commands they please. The use of such decrees is bound by law. If a president issues an executive order, proclamation, directive, or the like, in principle he does so pursuant to the powers granted to him by the Constitution or delegated to him by Congress, usually through a statute. When presidents issue such orders, they generally state the constitutional or statutory basis for their actions. For example, when President Truman ordered the desegregation of the armed services, he did so pursuant to his constitutional powers as commander in chief. In a similar vein, when President Lyndon Johnson issued Executive Order No. 11246, he asserted that the order was designed to implement the 1964 Civil Rights Act, which prohibited employment discrimination. Where an executive order has no statutory or constitutional basis, the courts have held it to be void. The most important such is *Youngstown Co. v. Sawyer* (1952).[46] Here, the Supreme Court ruled that President Truman's seizure of the nation's steel mills during the Korean War had no statutory or constitutional basis and was thus invalid.

A number of court decisions, though, have established broad boundaries that leave considerable room for presidential action. For example, the courts have held that Congress might approve presidential action after the fact or, in effect, ratify presidential action through "acquiescence" by not objecting for long periods of time or by continuing to provide funding for programs established by executive orders. Further, the courts have indicated that some areas, most notably the realm of military policy, are presidential in character, allowing presidents wide latitude to make policy by executive decree. Thus, within the very broad limits established by the courts, presidential orders can be important policy tools.

President George W. Bush did not hesitate to use executive orders, issuing more than 300 between his inauguration and the end of 2008. During his first months in office, Bush issued orders prohibiting the use of federal funds to support international family-planning groups that provided abortion counseling services, and limiting the use of embryonic stem cells in federally funded research projects. Throughout his administration, Bush made very aggressive use of executive orders in response to the threat of terrorism. In November 2001, for example, he issued a directive authorizing the creation of military tribunals to try noncitizens accused of involvement in acts of terrorism against the United States.

During his time in office, President Obama has also issued a number of executive orders, many of which rescinded Bush-era orders. Thus, Obama ordered the closing of the Guantánamo prison and ordered an end to what were deemed unlawful methods of interrogation of terror suspects. In June 2012, Obama issued an order designed to halt the deportation of undocumented immigrants who had come to the United States as children. These individuals would become eligible for work permits. Immigrant rights groups hailed the order while Republicans criticized the president for circumventing Congress. And in 2013, Obama issued over 20 executive orders to enhance federal gun regulations. In all, Obama issued 164 executive orders between 2009 and 2013, from the mundane (e.g., closing federal offices for the day on December 24, 2012) to the significant, as in the examples above. In July 2014, Obama declared that he would soon be issuing a series of executive orders to deal with illegal immigration.

In 2013, Obama issued an executive order to prepare the United States for the impacts of climate change. Here, scientists use time-lapse cameras to document and analyze the rate at which this Alaskan glacier is shrinking

Signing Statements To negate congressional actions to which they objected, recent presidents have made frequent and calculated use of presidential **signing statements** when signing bills into law.[47] The signing statement is an announcement made by the president, at the time of signing a congressional enactment into law, that offers the president's interpretation of the law and usually innocuous remarks predicting the many benefits the new law will bring to the nation. Occasionally, presidents have used signing statements to point to sections of the law they have deemed improper or even unconstitutional, and to instruct executive branch agencies how to execute the law.[48] President Harry Truman, for example, accompanied his approval of the 1946 Hobbs Anti-Racketeering Act with a message offering his interpretation of ambiguous sections of the statute and indicating how the federal government would implement the new law.[49]

Presidents have made signing statements throughout American history, though many were not recorded and did not become part of the official legislative record. Ronald Reagan's attorney general, Edwin Meese, is generally credited with transforming the signing statement into a routine tool of presidential direct action.[50] Meese believed that carefully crafted signing statements would provide a basis for action by executive agencies and, perhaps even more important, would become part of the history and context of a piece of legislation if and when judicial interpretation became necessary. Indeed, to make certain of this, Meese reached an agreement with the West Publishing Company to include them in its authoritative texts of federal legislation.[51]

signing statements
announcements made by the president when signing bills into law, often presenting the president's interpretation of the law

With the way thus paved, Reagan, followed by George H. W. Bush, Clinton, George W. Bush, and Obama, proceeded to use detailed and artfully designed signing statements—prepared by the Department of Justice—to reinterpret congressional enactments. George W. Bush issued 161 signing statements. Within these 161 statements, however, Bush inserted nearly 1,200 specific signing statement provisions—more than twice as many provisions as all past presidents combined—using them to rewrite the law on numerous occasions. As a candidate, Obama criticized Bush's prolific use of signing statements but did not entirely abandon the practice as president. In his first five years in office, Obama issued 25 signing statements containing 74 specific provisions.[52] In 2013, for example, President Obama signed a defense appropriation bill that included, among numerous other provisions, restrictions on transferring detainees out of military prisons in Afghanistan and Guantánamo Bay, Cuba. Obama said many portions of the bill were needed, but he attached a signing statement claiming that he had the constitutional power to override the section of the law that imposed the transfer restrictions.

Presidential Nonenforcement of Laws

A final instrument of direct presidential governance is nonenforcement of statutes with which they disagree. Congress may make the law but presidents implement and enforce it. If the president decides that a particular law is not to his liking and refuses to enforce it, Congress may find that its intent is stymied. President Obama, for example, declared that his administration would not defend the federal Defense of Marriage Act in the courts and would refrain from enforcing several immigration laws. More recently, the president suspended enforcement of portions of the Affordable Care Act when the rollout of "Obamacare" produced public confusion. Since the president is the nation's chief law enforcer, refusal to enforce a law can become a unilateral negation of its effects.

The Advantages of the Administrative Strategy

Through the course of American history, party leadership and popular appeals have played important roles in presidential efforts to overcome political opposition, and both continue to be instruments of presidential power. Reagan's tax cuts and Clinton's budget victories were achieved with strong partisan support. George W. Bush, lacking the oratorical skills of Reagan or Roosevelt, nevertheless made effective use of sophisticated communications strategies to promote his agenda. Yet, as we have seen, in the modern era parties have waned in institutional strength, and the effects of popular appeals have often proven evanescent. The limitations of the alternatives have increasingly impelled presidents to try to expand the administrative capabilities of the office and their own capacity for unilateral action as means of achieving their policy goals. And in recent decades, the expansion of the Executive Office, the development of regulatory review, and the use of executive orders and signing statements have given presidents a substantial capacity to achieve significant policy results despite congressional opposition to their legislative agendas.

In principle, perhaps, Congress could respond more vigorously to unilateral policy making by the president than it has. Certainly, a Congress willing to impeach a president should have the mettle to overturn his or her administrative directives. But the president has significant advantages in such struggles with Congress.

In battles over presidential directives and orders, Congress is on the defensive, reacting to presidential initiatives. The framers of the Constitution saw "energy," or the ability to take the initiative, as a key feature of executive power.[53] When the president takes action by issuing an order or an administrative directive, Congress must respond through the cumbersome and time-consuming law-making process, overcome internal divisions, and enact legislation that the president may ultimately veto. Moreover, as the political scientist Terry Moe has argued, in such battles Congress faces a significant collective action problem: members are likely to be more sensitive to the substance of a president's actions and its short-term effects on their constituents than to the more general long-term implications of presidential power for the vitality of their institution.[54]

The Limits of Presidential Power

Though the "administrative strategy" has provided presidents with a host of new powers, presidents are not dictators or kings. Their power continues to be limited by Congress and, especially, by the congressional power of the purse. In 2011 and again, in 2013, Congress demonstrated that its control over federal spending and borrowing papers could force the president to pay attention to the legislative branch. In the budget battle of 2013, Republicans used their control of the House of Representatives to shut down most government agencies for more than two weeks until a budgetary compromise was reached. So long as Congress controls the purse strings, the president must pay attention to its wishes.

Remember, too, that the president is not omnipotent. Decisions made by leaders in foreign nations who do not answer to the president affect America's economic health to say nothing of the nation's security. And, while the public frequently blames or rewards the president for economic performance; as discussed in Chapter 10, the Consumer Confidence Index, a measure of how optimistic consumers are about the future of the economy, is a very good indicator of a sitting president's chances for re-election. But the president's actual impact on the economy is limited. Unemployment and inflation, two important indicators of economic health, are subject to macroeconomic conditions that can never be fully within the president's control, such as consumer demand and the productivity of workers.

The president is also limited in the implementation of his legislative agenda when the opposing party is in control of the House and Senate. As Figure 13.5 shows, presidential success on congressional votes is much higher when his party is in the majority in Congress. In periods of divided government, when one or both houses of Congress are controlled by the opposition party, the president has much more difficulty implementing his agenda. Immigration reform is one example. After his re-election in 2012, President Obama made immigration reform a key policy goal. In June 2013, the Senate, with a Democratic majority, passed a bill that Obama supported. Among other provisions, the bill provided a pathway to citizenship for undocumented immigrants. However, the House, controlled by the Republicans, never allowed the bill to come to a vote.

While presidents are more powerful today than they were 200 years ago, they are still subject to constitutional checks and balances. This process can lead to frustration, such as the 2013 government shutdown.

FIGURE 13.5

Presidential Success on Congressional Votes, 1953–2013*

Presidents have more success in Congress when their party is in the majority. Can you identify the periods when presidents had majority support in Congress and when they did not?

*Percentages based on votes on which presidents took a position.
SOURCE: Congressional Quarterly, "CQ's Roll Call Vote Studies," http://media.cq.com/votestudies (accessed 3/17/14).

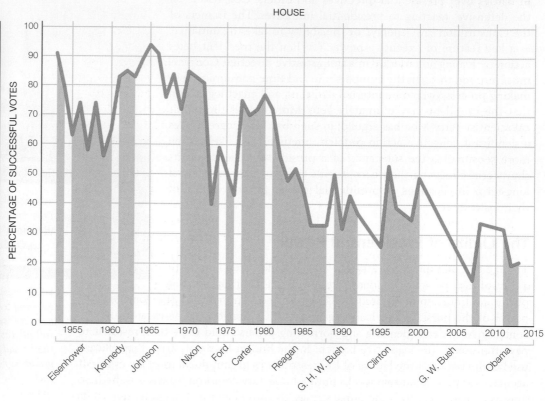

HOUSE

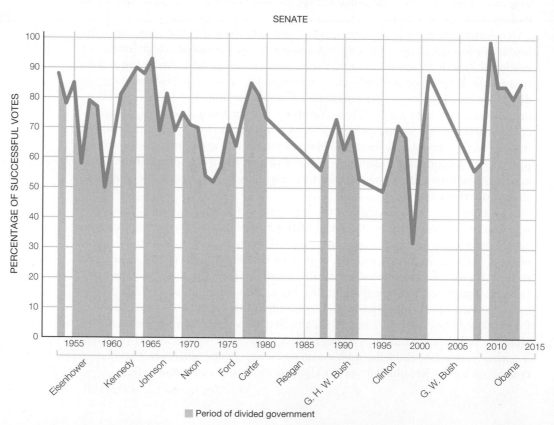

SENATE

■ Period of divided government

Presidential Power
and Your Future

The framers of the Constitution created a system of government in which the Congress and the executive branch were to share power. At least since the New Deal, however, the powers of Congress have waned, whereas those of the presidency have expanded dramatically. There is no doubt that Congress continues to be able to confront presidents and even, on occasion, hand the White House a sharp rebuff. During the 2011 debt crisis, for instance, President Obama was unable to force House Republicans to accept his plan for dealing with the nation's deficits and was compelled to accede to many of the GOP's demands in order to prevent a potentially disastrous default on government debt.

In the larger view, however, presidents' occasional defeats, however dramatic, have to be seen as temporary setbacks in a gradual but decisive shift toward increased presidential power. Louis Fisher, a leading authority on the separation of powers, recently observed that in what are arguably the two most important policy arenas, national defense and the federal budget, the powers of Congress have been in decline for at least the past 50 years. The last time Congress exercised its constitutional power to declare war was June 1942, and yet, since that time, American forces have been committed to numerous conflicts around the world by order of the president. The much-hailed 1973 War Powers Resolution, far from limiting presidential power, actually allowed the president considerably more discretionary authority than what was granted by the Constitution, which seems to require congressional authorization before troops can be deployed for even one day. The War Powers Resolution gave the president the authority to deploy forces abroad for 60 days without congressional authority. And presidents have ignored even this stipulation.

As to spending powers, the framers of the Constitution conceived the "power of the purse" to be Congress's most fundamental prerogative. For more than a century this power was jealously guarded by powerful congressional leaders such as Taft-era House speaker "Uncle" Joe Cannon, who saw congressional control of the budget as a fundamental safeguard against "Prussian-style" militarism and autocracy. Since the New Deal, however, successive Congresses have yielded to steadily increasing presidential influence over the budget process. In 1939, Congress allowed Franklin Delano Roosevelt to take a giant step toward presidential control of the nation's purse strings when it permitted him to bring the Bureau of the Budget (BoB) into the newly created EOP. Roosevelt and his successors used the BoB (now called the OMB) effectively to seize the nation's legislative and budgetary agenda. In 1974, Congress attempted to respond to Richard Nixon's efforts to further enhance presidential control of spending when it enacted the Budget and Impoundment Control Act, legislation centralizing Congress's own budgetary process and apparently reinforcing congressional power. Yet, less than 10 years later, Congress watched as President Ronald Reagan essentially seized control of the congressional budget process. Subsequently, Congress has surrendered more and more power to the president.

What might the growth of executive power mean to students reading this book today? It might mean that policies they favor can more easily become the law of the land. Congress works slowly while the president can work quickly—making law by the stroke of a pen. Some advocates, for example, have asserted that President Obama can issue executive orders legalizing the status of America's estimated 11 million undocumented immigrants even though Congress has failed to enact legislation on immigration reform. Presidential strength works both ways, however: for those who oppose a particular policy or have qualms about some aspect of it, the stroke of the presidential pen might seem hasty and autocratic. Proponents of quick and unilateral presidential action should be careful what they wish for. They may not always welcome the action.

Today's students should also consider one of the chief concerns about presidential power expressed by the framers of the Constitution. The framers feared that executives were often too ready to go to war. Legislatures, they thought, were more likely to consider the costs and sacrifices entailed by war. Accordingly, the war power was given to Congress to "leash the dogs of war." The framers possessed a good deal of practical experience and their views merit consideration. Does presidential unilateralism or congressional deliberation offer better protection from the dogs of war so feared by the framers? In an era of significant international tension and trouble spots, including Iran, North Korea, Iraq, Syria, Libya, and Ukraine, the ease with which the country's leaders enter armed conflict may be a real concern.

A powerful presidency, a weak Congress, and a partially apathetic electorate make for a dangerous mix. Presidents have increasingly asserted the right to govern unilaterally and now appear able to overcome most institutional and political constraints. Presidential power, to be sure, can be a force for good. To cite one example from the not-so-distant past, it was President Lyndon Johnson, more than Congress or the judiciary, who faced up to the task of smashing America's racial apartheid system. Yet, as the framers knew, unchecked power is always dangerous. Americans of the founding generation feared that unchecked presidential power would lead to *monocracy*, a republican form of monarchy without a king. Inevitably, we will pay a price for our undemocratic politics.

plugin

Inform

Watch a few recent presidential speeches, including this year's State of the Union address, on YouTube. What problems does the president consider most pressing? What solutions does he propose?

Express

Make a list of powers claimed by modern presidents that are not in the Constitution. Explain why you think the president should or should not have each of these powers.

Connect

Follow the president and/or vice president on social media. What issues are highlighted in posts from the past week? What solutions are proposed?

Act

Create a petition at whitehouse.gov (currently found under the "Participation" tab) regarding an issue you care about, and try to get as many signatures as possible. Can you get past the threshold necessary for an official White House response?

study guide

Establishing the Presidency

Explain the role of the president in the American political system (pp. 521–22)

The framers of the Constitution debated whether executive authority should be concentrated in the hands of one individual and whether this individual should be elected directly by the people. The decision to establish a single president, rather than some form of collectively led executive, was intended to provide for "energy" in the executive. The framers settled on an indirect system of selecting the president (the electoral college) that would make the president responsible to state and national legislators rather than to the public. It was not until the emergence of the national convention system in the 1830s that the presidency obtained the broad popular base needed to increase presidential power.

Key Term

caucus (political) (p. 522)

Practice Quiz

1. Which article of the Constitution describes the basic powers of the presidency and the means of selecting presidents?
   a) Article I
   b) Article II
   c) Article III
   d) Article IV
   e) Article V

2. The Founders chose to select the president through indirect election in order to
   a) increase the strength and influence of political parties.
   b) build an imperial presidency that would overwhelm the power of Congress.
   c) force the president to be responsive to the will of the people.
   d) make the president responsible to the state and national legislatures.
   e) create a more independent chief executive.

The Constitutional Powers of the Presidency

Understand the expressed, delegated, and inherent powers of the presidency (pages 523–35)

Presidents have three kinds of powers: expressed, delegated, and inherent. The president's expressed powers, as defined by Article II of the Constitution, include military, judicial, diplomatic, executive, and legislative powers. The expressed powers also entail a set of implied powers, which can be considered necessary in order to carry out the expressed powers. The president's delegated powers are not found in the Constitution but are, instead, the product of congressional statutes and resolutions. The president's inherent powers grow from "the rights, duties and obligations of the presidency" that presidents often assert during times of war and national crisis.

Key Terms

expressed powers (p. 523)
implied powers (p. 523)
delegated powers (p. 523)
commander in chief (p. 524)
executive agreement (p. 525)
executive privilege (p. 526)

veto (p. 527)
pocket veto (p. 527)
legislative initiative (p. 527)
executive order (p. 529)
inherent powers (p. 534)
War Powers Resolution (p. 534)

Practice Quiz

3. Which of the following does *not* require the advice and consent of the Senate?
   a) an executive agreement
   b) a treaty
   c) appointment of ambassadors
   d) Supreme Court nominations
   e) All of the above require the advice and consent of the Senate.

4. What did the Supreme Court rule in *United States v. Nixon*?
   a) Nixon had to turn his secret White House tapes over to congressional investigators because presidents do not have the power of executive privilege.
   b) Nixon did not have to turn his secret White House tapes over to congressional investigators because, in general, presidents have the power of executive privilege.

   c) Nixon had to turn his secret White House tapes over to congressional investigators but, in general, presidents have the power of executive privilege.

   d) Nixon did not have to turn his secret White House tapes over to congressional investigators but, in general, presidents do not have the power of executive privilege.

   e) All presidents are immune from criminal investigations and cannot, therefore, be tried in any court of law.

5. What are the requirements for overriding a presidential veto?
   a) 50 percent plus one vote in both houses of Congress
   b) two-thirds vote in both houses of Congress
   c) two-thirds vote in the Senate only
   d) three-fourths vote in both houses of Congress.
   e) A presidential veto cannot be overridden by Congress.

6. When the president issues a rule or regulation that reorganizes or otherwise directs the affairs of the executive branch, such as the directives that established the Executive Office of the President and the Environmental Protection Agency, it is called
   a) an executive agreement.
   b) an executive order.

   c) an executive mandate.
   d) administrative oversight.
   e) legislative initiative.

7. Which of the following military and war powers does the Constitution *not* assign to the president?
   a) command of the army and navy of the United States
   b) the power to declare war
   c) command of the state militias
   d) the power to make treaties
   e) The Constitution assigns all of the powers above to the president.

8. The War Powers Resolution of 1973 was an act passed by Congress that
   a) required the CIA to collect intelligence on all Americans born in a foreign country.
   b) outlawed presidential use of executive agreements.
   c) created the National Security Council.
   d) granted the president the authority to declare war.
   e) stipulated military forces must be withdrawn within 60 days in the absence of a specific congressional authorization for their continued deployment.

The Presidency as an Institution

Identify the institutional resources presidents have to help them exercise their powers (pp. 535–40)

The institutionalized presidency is made up of the Cabinet, the White House staff, the Executive Office of the President, the vice presidency, and the First Spouse. Through their advice and assistance, these thousands of individuals give the president a capacity for action that he could never have by himself. When coupled with the president's formal powers, the institutionalized presidency makes the chief executive an important player in the country's policy-making process.

Key Terms

Cabinet (p. 535)

National Security Council (NSC) (p. 536)

White House staff (p. 537)

Kitchen Cabinet (p. 537)

Executive Office of the President (EOP) (p. 537)

Practice Quiz

9. The Office of Management and Budget is part of
   a) the Executive Office of the President.
   b) the White House staff.
   c) the Kitchen Cabinet.

   d) the Congressional Budget Office.
   e) the Bureau of Economic Analysis.

10. Approximately how many people work for agencies within the Executive Office of the President?
   a) 25 to 50
   b) 700 to 1,000
   c) 1,500 to 2,000
   d) 4,500 to 5,000
   e) 25,000 to 30,000

11. Which of the following statements about vice presidents is *not* true?
   a) The vice president succeeds the president in case of death, resignation, or incapacitation.
   b) The vice president casts the tie-breaking vote in the Senate when necessary.
   c) The vice president serves as an honorary member of the Supreme Court.
   d) Eight vice presidents have had to replace American presidents who died in office.
   e) Presidential candidates often select a vice presidential candidate who is likely to bring the support of a state that would not otherwise support the ticket.

The Contemporary Bases of Presidential Power

Although Congress was the dominant institution in the American political system throughout the nineteenth century, modern presidents have expanded the policy-making power of their office in a number of ways. While some presidents have relied primarily on the support of party members to advance their legislative goals, contemporary presidents more commonly turn to popular mobilization and executive administration in pursuing policy change.

Key Term

signing statements (p. 547)

Practice Quiz

12. What are two ways that presidents can expand their power?
    a) avoiding popular appeals and loosening their control of executive agencies
    b) using popular appeals and bolstering their control of executive agencies
    c) using popular appeals and loosening their control of executive agencies
    d) avoiding popular appeals and bolstering their control of executive agencies
    e) weakening national partisan institutions and bolstering their control of executive agencies

13. The Supreme Court case *Youngstown Co. v. Sawyer* was significant because
    a) it showed that the courts would never invalidate an executive order.
    b) it showed that the courts would invalidate executive orders that have no statutory or constitutional basis.
    c) it asserted that pocket vetoes were unconstitutional.
    d) it upheld the notion of executive privilege.
    e) it struck down the Budget and Impoundment Control Act.

14. When the president makes an announcement about his interpretation of a congressional enactment that he is signing into law, it is called
    a) a signing statement.
    b) a line item veto.
    c) an executive order.
    d) legislative initiative.
    e) regulatory review.

For Further Reading

Barber, James David. *The Presidential Character.* Englewood Cliffs, NJ: Prentice-Hall, 1992.

Crenson, Matthew, and Benjamin Ginsberg. *Presidential Power: Unchecked and Unbalanced.* New York: W. W. Norton, 2007.

Draper, Robert. *Dead Certain: The Presidency of George Bush.* New York: Free Press, 2007.

Edwards, George. *Why the Electoral College Is Bad for America.* New Haven, CT: Yale University Press, 2004.

Genovese, Michael, Todd Belt, and William Lammers. *The Presidency and Domestic Policy.* Boulder, CO: Paradigm, 2013.

Goldsmith, Jack. *The American Presidency: Power and Constraint.* New York: W. W. Norton, 2012.

Hayes, Stephen F. *Cheney: The Untold Story of America's Most Powerful and Controversial Vice President.* New York: HarperCollins, 2007.

Lowi, Theodore J. *The Personal President: Power Invested, Promise Unfulfilled.* Ithaca, NY: Cornell University Press, 1985.

Maraniss, David. *Barack Obama.* New York: Simon and Schuster, 2013

Milkis, Sidney. *The American Presidency: Origins and Development.* Washington, DC: CQ Press, 2011.

Nelson, Michael. *The Presidency and the Political System.* Washington, DC: CQ Press, 2013

Neustadt, Richard E. *Presidential Power: The Politics of Leadership from Roosevelt to Reagan.* Rev. ed. New York: Free Press, 1990.

Pfiffner, James. *Understanding the Presidency.* 6th ed. New York: Longman, 2010.

Skowronek, Stephen. *The Politics Presidents Make: Leadership from John Adams to Bill Clinton.* Cambridge, MA: Belknap Press of Harvard University Press, 1997.

Yoo, John. *The Powers of War and Peace.* Chicago: University of Chicago Press, 2005.

Recommended Websites

Almanac of Policy Issues: War Powers Resolution
www.policyalmanac.org/world/archive/war_powers _resolution
.shtml

The War Powers Resolution was passed in 1973 to define and limit the president's power during times of war. Read the full text of the resolution on this website.

The American Presidency Project
www.americanpresidency.org

Directed by Gerhard Peters and John T. Woolley at UC Santa Barbara, this site contains over 88,000 documents related to the study of the presidency, including party platforms, candidates' remarks, statements of administration policy, documents released by the Office of the Press Secretary, and election debates. This site is also an excellent resource for data related to the study of the presidency.

Dave Leip's Atlas of U.S. Presidential Elections
www.uselectionatlas.org

For information on upcoming and past presidential elections, refer to this website. Experiment with the electoral college calculator to see how your state could affect the electoral outcome.

The National Archives: Executive Branch
www.archives.gov/executive

Research official executive branch documents at the Executive Branch website, provided by the U.S. National Archives and Records Administration.

Vicepresidents.com
www.vicepresidents.com

This website is dedicated to providing lots of interesting facts and archives about vice presidents, along with some lively humor.

The White House
www.whitehouse.gov

This is the official website of the White House. Here you can read about current presidential news, the president's Cabinet, executive orders, and presidential appointments.

White House Historical Association
www.whitehousehistory.org

The White House Historical Association is dedicated to the understanding, appreciation, and preservation of the White House. At its website you can find historical facts and take a detailed online tour of the numerous rooms and the property.

The White House: Past First Ladies
www.whitehouse.gov/history/firstladies/

The first lady is an important resource for the president in his role as head of state. Read about the current and past first ladies on this website.

Government bureaucracies affect ordinary Americans in countless ways. For example, the Environmental Protection Agency (EPA) proposes and enforces regulations that protect Americans' health and the environment. Here, an EPA worker vacuums a gasoline-like substance that contains the cancer-causing chemical benzene from the South Platte River, north of Denver, Colorado.

14

Bureaucracy in a Democracy

WHAT GOVERNMENT DOES AND WHY IT MATTERS Americans depend on government bureaucracies to accomplish the most spectacular achievements as well as the most mundane. Yet they often do not realize that public bureaucracies are essential for providing the services they use every day and rely on in emergencies. On a typical day, a college student might check the weather forecast, drive on an interstate highway, mail the rent check, drink from a public water fountain, check the calories on the side of a yogurt container, attend a class, log on to the Internet, and meet a relative at the airport. Each of these activities is possible because of the work of a government bureaucracy: the U.S. Weather Service, the U.S. Department of Transportation, the U.S. Postal Service, the Environmental Protection Agency, the Food and Drug Administration, the student loan programs of the U.S. Department of Education, the Advanced Research Projects Agency (which developed the Internet in the 1960s), and the Federal Aviation Administration. Without the ongoing work of these agencies, many of these common activities would be impossible, unreliable, or more expensive. Even though bureaucracies provide essential services that all Americans rely on, they are often disparaged by politicians and the general public alike as "big government," and come into public view only when they are charged with fraud, waste, and abuse.

In emergencies, the national perspective on bureaucracy and, indeed, on "big government" shifts. After the September 11 terrorist attacks, all eyes turned to Washington. The federal government responded by strengthening and reorganizing the bureaucracy to undertake a whole new set of responsibilities designed to keep America safe. In the biggest government reorganization in over half a century, Congress created the Department of Homeland Security in 2002. The massive new department merged 22 existing agencies into a single department employing nearly 170,000 workers.

As we shall see in this chapter, Americans have a love-hate relationship with the federal bureaucracy. This ambivalence sometimes prompts politicians to promise that they will slash the federal bureaucracy. Yet they rarely follow through on such promises. Because Americans rely on government in so many aspects of their lives, significant reductions in the federal bureaucracy would create disruptions that no one wishes to experience.

chaptergoals

- Define bureaucracy, and describe the basic features of the executive branch (pp. 561–69)

- Describe the major goals we expect federal agencies to promote (pp. 569–80)

- Evaluate some of the ways politicians have tried to make the bureaucracy more efficient (pp. 580–87)

- Explain why it is often difficult to control the bureaucracy (pp. 587–91)

● Bureaucracy and Bureaucrats

Define bureaucracy, and describe the basic features of the executive branch

Bureaucracy is nothing more nor less than a form of organization, a complex structure of offices, tasks, and rules. *Bureau*, a French word, can mean either "office" or "desk." *Cracy* is from the Greek word for "rule" or "form of rule." Taken together, *bureau* and *cracy* produce an interesting definition: bureaucracy is rule by offices and desks. Each member of an organization has an office, meaning both a place and a set of responsibilities. That is, each "office" comprises a set of tasks that are specialized to the needs of the organization, and the person holding that office (or position) performs those specialized tasks. Specialization and repetition are essential to the efficiency of any organization. Therefore, when an organization is inefficient, it is often because it is not "bureaucratized" enough! But bureaucracies do not only perform specialized tasks that require routine action. As we shall see, they also undertake politically controversial tasks that require them to exercise a great deal of discretion and professional judgment. In many areas of policy, Congress writes laws that are very broad, and it is up to the bureaucracy to define what the policy will mean in practice. The decisions that bureaucrats make, often based on professional judgments, can themselves become politically contentious.

> **bureaucracy** the complex structure of offices, tasks, rules, and principles of organization that are employed by all large-scale institutions to coordinate the work of their personnel

At its best, bureaucracy ensures fair, accountable administration overseen by professionals. Consider the contrast with patrimonial systems of administration. In these systems, people are treated differently depending on their ties to the ruler. Those with close ties can expect better treatment than those who are out of favor. In bureaucracies, by contrast, rules are applied to all people in the same way. Moreover, bureaucracies require that interactions be documented. Documentation allows those who feel they have been treated unfairly to challenge bureaucracies, creating more accountability. Finally, administration by professionals ensures that bureaucracies benefit from the skills and professional norms of their workers.

Both routine and exceptional tasks require the organization, specialization, and expertise found in bureaucracies. To provide services, government bureaucracies employ specialists such as meteorologists, doctors, and scientists. To do their jobs effectively, these specialists require resources and tools (ranging from paper to complex computer software), they have to coordinate their work with others (for example, traffic engineers must communicate with construction engineers), and there must be effective outreach to the public (for example, doctors must be made aware of health warnings). Bureaucracy is a means of coordinating the many different parts that must work together for the government to provide useful services.

What Bureaucrats Do

"Government by offices and desks" conveys to most people a picture of hundreds of office workers shuffling millions of pieces of paper. There is a lot of truth in that image, but we have to look more closely at what papers are being shuffled and why. More than 70 years ago, an astute observer defined bureaucracy as "continuous routine business."[1] Almost any organization succeeds by reducing its work to routine tasks performed by different specialists. But with specialization, one worker's output becomes another worker's input, making the timing of such relationships essential and therefore requiring these workers to stay in communication with one another. In fact, bureaucracy was the first information network.

Bureaucrats Implement Laws Congress is responsible for making the laws, but in most cases legislation only sets the broad parameters for government action. Bureaucracies are responsible for filling in the blanks by determining how the laws should be implemented. This requires bureaucracies to draw up detailed rules that guide the process of **implementation** and also to play a key role in enforcing the laws. Congress needs the bureaucracy to engage in rule making and implementation for several reasons. One is that bureaucracies employ people who have much more specialized expertise in specific policy areas than do members of Congress. Decisions about how to achieve many policy goals—from managing the national parks to regulating air quality to ensuring a sound economy—rest on the judgment of specialized experts. A second reason that Congress needs bureaucracy is that because updating legislation can take many years, bureaucratic flexibility can ensure that laws are administered in ways that take new conditions into account. Finally, members of Congress often prefer to delegate politically difficult decision making to bureaucrats.

implementation the efforts of departments and agencies to translate laws into specific bureaucratic rules and actions

Bureaucrats Make Rules One of the most important activities that government agencies do is issue rules that provide more detailed and specific indications of what a given congressional policy will actually mean. For example, the Clean Air Act empowers the Environmental Protection Agency (EPA) to assess whether current or projected levels of air pollutants pose a threat to public health, determine whether motor vehicle emissions are contributing to such pollution, and create rules designed to regulate these emissions. Under the George W. Bush administration, the EPA claimed it did not have the authority to regulate a specific group of pollutants commonly referred to as "greenhouse gases" (for example, carbon dioxide). In 2007 the Supreme Court ruled that the EPA did have that authority and had to provide a justification for not regulating such emissions.[2] In the first year of the Obama administration, the agency ruled that greenhouse gases posed a threat to public health and that the emissions from new motor vehicles contributed to greenhouse gas pollution.[3] The agency then imposed new emission standards for automobiles, which would raise the average fuel economy for new vehicles to 35.5 miles per gallon starting in 2016, a standard later boosted to 54.4 miles per gallon by 2025.[4] Not only will this finding by the EPA have a significant effect on the automobile industry, but it could also lead to far-reaching regulations in the future governing all industries that generate greenhouse gases. Not surprisingly, the agency's findings soon faced legal challenges by industries affected by the ruling.[5]

An example of a bureaucratic rule that affects the many Americans who drive cars is fuel economy standards. Higher fuel economy saves drivers money, helps the environment, and reduces dependence on oil. Opponents argue it may also increase the cost of cars and burden auto companies, which employ many Americans.

The rule-making process is thus a highly political one. Once a new law is passed, the relevant agency studies the legislation and proposes a set of rules to guide implementation. These proposed rules are then open to comment by anyone who wishes to weigh in. Representatives for the regulated industries and advocates of all sorts commonly submit comments. But anyone who wishes to can go to the website www.regulations.gov to read proposed rules, enter comments, and view the comments of others. Once rules are approved, they are published in the *Federal Register* and have the force of law.

During the 1970s and '80s, the length of time required to develop an administrative rule from a proposal to actual publication in the *Federal Register* (when it takes on full legal status) grew from an average of 15 months to an average of 35 to 40 months. Inefficiency? No. Most of the increased time is attributable to new procedures requiring more public notice, more public hearings in Washington and elsewhere, more cost-benefit analysis, and stronger legal obligations to prepare "environmental impact statements" demonstrating that the proposed rule or agency action will not have an unacceptably large negative impact on the human or physical environment.[6] Thus, a great deal of what is popularly decried as the lower efficiency of public agencies can be attributed to the political, judicial, legal, and public-opinion restraints and extraordinarily high expectations imposed on public bureaucrats. If a private company such as Microsoft were required to open up all its decision processes and management practices to full view by the media, its competitors, and all interested citizens, Microsoft—despite its profit motive and the pressure of competition—would likely appear far less efficient, perhaps no more efficient than public bureaucracies.

Bureaucrats Enforce Laws In addition to rule making, bureaucracies play an essential role in enforcing the laws, thus exercising considerable power over private actors. For example, in 2013, the auto manufacturers Hyundai and Kia reached a settlement with the EPA after the agency, which monitors fuel economy tests for all vehicles sold in the United States, found that the companies overstated the mileage claims for their cars. Hyundai and Kia agreed to reimburse nearly 1 million customers for the shortfall in the fuel economy, totaling approximately $400 million.[7]

Bureaucrats Innovate A good case study of the important role agencies can play is the story of how ordinary federal bureaucrats created the Internet. Yes, it's true: what became the Internet was developed largely by the U.S. Department of Defense, and defense considerations still shape the basic structure of the Internet. In 1957, immediately following the profound American embarrassment over the Soviet Union's launching of Sputnik, the first satellite to orbit the earth, Congress authorized the establishment of the Advanced Research Projects Agency (ARPA) to develop, among other things, a means of maintaining communications in the event of a strategic attack on the existing telecommunications network (the telephone system). Since the telephone network was highly centralized and therefore could have been completely disabled by a single attack, ARPA developed a decentralized, highly redundant network with an improved probability of functioning after an attack. The full design, called by the acronym ARPANET, took almost a decade to create. By 1971 around 20 universities were connected to the ARPANET. The forerunner to the Internet was born.[8]

The Merit System: How to Become a Bureaucrat Although they face more inconveniences than their counterparts in the private sector, public bureaucrats are rewarded in part with greater job security than employees of most private organizations. More than a century ago the federal government attempted to imitate business by passing the Civil Service Act of 1883, which was followed by almost universal adoption of equivalent laws in state and local governments. These laws required that appointees to public office be qualified for the job to which they

The Department of State's foreign service officer corps represents U.S. interests abroad. To become a foreign service officer, you must take a both a written and oral exam. Approximately 75 percent of the 20,000 or so applicants who take the exam each year do not pass.

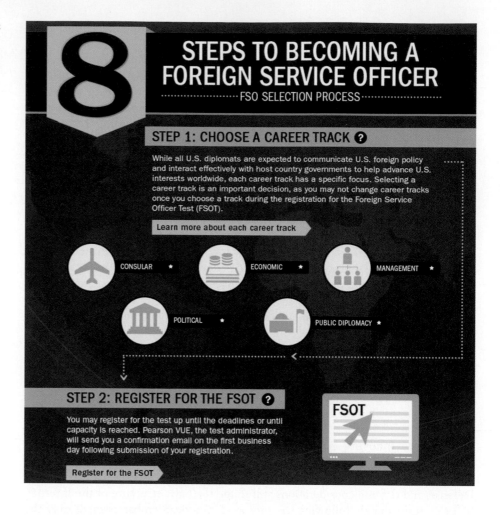

8 STEPS TO BECOMING A FOREIGN SERVICE OFFICER

FSO SELECTION PROCESS

STEP 1: CHOOSE A CAREER TRACK ?

While all U.S. diplomats are expected to communicate U.S. foreign policy and interact effectively with host country governments to help advance U.S. interests worldwide, each career track has a specific focus. Selecting a career track is an important decision, as you may not change career tracks once you choose a track during the registration for the Foreign Service Officer Test (FSOT).

Learn more about each career track

CONSULAR ★ ECONOMIC ★ MANAGEMENT ★

POLITICAL ★ PUBLIC DIPLOMACY ★

STEP 2: REGISTER FOR THE FSOT ?

You may register for the test up until the deadlines or until capacity is reached. Pearson VUE, the test administrator, will send you a confirmation email on the first business day following submission of your registration.

Register for the FSOT

FSOT

merit system a product of civil service reform, in which appointees to positions in public bureaucracies must objectively be deemed qualified for those positions

were appointed. This policy came to be called the **merit system**; its goal was not merely to put an end to political appointments under the "spoils system" but also to create a system of competitive examinations through which the very best candidates were to be hired for every job. At the higher levels of government agencies, including such posts as cabinet secretaries and assistant secretaries, many jobs are filled with political appointees and are not part of the merit system.

As a further safeguard against political interference (and to compensate for the lower-than-average pay given to public employees), merit-system employees (genuine civil servants) were given legal protection against being fired without a show of cause. Reasonable people may disagree about the value of such job security and how far it should extend in the civil service, but the justifiable objective of this job protection, cleansing bureaucracy of political interference while upgrading performance, cannot be disputed.

The Size of the Federal Service

How many people does it take to make rules, implement laws, enforce laws, and innovate in all the areas that the government touches, from aviation safety to national defense to environmental protection to public health? For decades, politicians from both parties have asserted that the federal government is too big. Ronald Reagan led the way in 1981 with his assertion that government was the problem, not the solution. Fifteen years later President Bill Clinton abandoned the traditional Democratic defense of government, declaring that "the era of big government is over." President George W. Bush voiced similar sentiments when he accepted his party's nomination for president in 2000, proclaiming, "Big government is not the answer!" President Obama struck a different tone. Addressing Congress on the topic of health care reform, he noted that while Americans had a "healthy skepticism about government," they also believed that "hard work and responsibility should be rewarded by some measure of security and fair play" and recognized "that sometimes government has to step in to help deliver that promise."[9] Despite fears of bureaucratic growth getting out of hand, however, the federal service has hardly grown at all during the past 35 years; it reached its peak postwar level in 1968, with 3.0 million civilian employees plus an additional 3.6 million military personnel (a figure swollen by the war in Vietnam). The number of civilian federal employees has since fallen to less than 2.8 million in 2012; the number of military personnel totals 1.4 million.[10]

The growth of the federal service over the past 50 years is even less imposing when placed in the context of the total workforce and when compared with the size of state and local public employment. Figure 14.1 indicates that since 1950,

for critical analysis

How has the size of the federal service changed over the past six decades? How are calls for smaller government related to the size of the federal service?

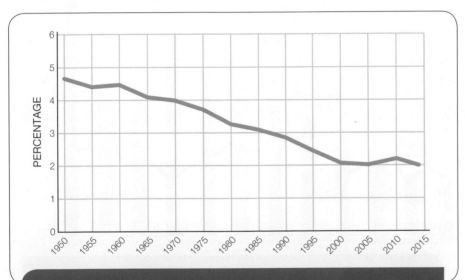

FIGURE 14.1

Employees in the Federal Service as a Percentage of the National Workforce, 1950–2013

Since 1950, the ratio of federal employment to the total workforce has gradually declined. Today federal employees make up less than 2 percent of the total workforce in the United States. Even at its height, federal employees made up less than 6 percent. What do these numbers suggest about the size of the federal government today?

NOTE: Employment numbers are for December of each year.
SOURCE: Bureau of Labor Statistics, Current Employment Statistics, http://bls.gov/webapps/legacy/cesbtab1.htm (accessed 3/20/14).

the ratio of federal employment to the total workforce has in fact has *declined* slightly in the past 60 years. Meanwhile, state and local employment has grown: in 1950 there were 4.3 million state and local civil service employees (about 6.5 percent of the country's workforce). In 2014 there were close to 20 million state and local employees (nearly 15 percent of the nation's employed workforce).[11] Federal employment, in contrast, exceeded 6 percent of the workforce only during World War II, and almost all of that temporary growth was military.

Another useful comparison is illustrated in Figure 14.2. Although the dollar increase in federal spending shown by the bars looks impressive, the trend line indicating the relation of federal spending to the gross domestic product (GDP) remained close to what it had been in 1960. This changed in 2009, when the recession pushed spending up dramatically, as the federal government sought to stimulate

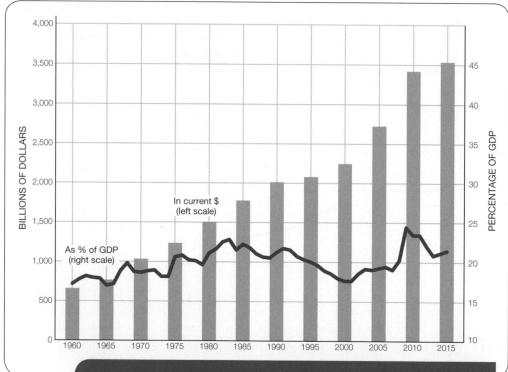

FIGURE 14.2

Annual Federal Outlays, 1950–2015*

As the bars in the figure indicate, when measured in dollars, federal government spending has gone up over time, from $423 billion in 1950 to over $3 trillion in 2013. (The amounts here are measured in constant 2009 dollars, which means the numbers have been adjusted for inflation.) But as the red line shows, federal spending as a percentage of gross domestic product has moved up and down just slightly over time. Thus while government spending has grown, it has basically kept pace with the growing size of the U.S. economy.

*Data for 2014 and 2015 are estimated.
SOURCE: Office of Management and Budget, Table 1.3—Summary of Receipts, Outlays, and Surpluses or Deficits (-) in Current Dollars, Constant (FY 2009) Dollars, and as Percentages of GDP: 1940–2019, www.whitehouse.gov /omb/budget/historicals (accessed 3/20/2014).

the economy, and spending rose on other recession-related programs, such as unemployment insurance. After 2009 the budget also reflected the costs of the wars in Iraq and Afghanistan, which had not been included in the recent economic Bush administration's budgets.

In sum, the national government is indeed "very large," but it has not been growing any faster than the economy or society. Bureaucracy keeps pace with society, despite people's seeming dislike of it, because the control towers, the prisons, the Social Security system, and other essential elements of modern-day society cannot be operated without bureaucracy. Indeed, the recent growth of government spending does not reflect a growth in the federal bureaucracy but rather an increase in payments to individuals for valued social programs such as Social Security and Medicare (which provides health care for people over 65), and a temporary boost in federal grants to the states to help them weather the recent economic recession.

Although the federal executive branch is large and complex, everything about it is commonplace because its many bureaucracies touch so many aspects of daily life. Government bureaucracies implement the decisions made through the political process. Public bureaucracies are powerful because politicians, and the people delegate vast power to them to make sure that society's collective needs are addressed, providing most citizens with the freedom to pursue their private ends.

The Organization of the Executive Branch

Cabinet **departments**, agencies, and bureaus are the operating parts of the bureaucratic whole. At the top is the head of the department, who in the United States is called the "secretary" of the department.[12] Below the secretary and the deputy secretary is a second tier of "undersecretaries," who have management responsibilities for one or more operating agencies. Those operating agencies are the third tier of the department, yet they are the highest level of responsibility for the actual programs around which the entire department is organized. This third tier is generally called the "bureau level." Each bureau-level agency usually operates under a statute, enacted by Congress, that set up the agency and gave it its authority and jurisdiction. The names of these bureau-level agencies are often quite well known to the public—the Forest Service and the Food Safety and Inspection Service, for example. These are the so-called line agencies, those that deal directly with the public. Sometimes these agencies are officially called "bureaus," such as the Federal Bureau of Investigation (FBI), which is part of the third tier of the Department of Justice. But bureau is also the conventional term for this level of administrative agency, even though many agencies or their supporters have preferred over the years to adopt a more politically palatable designation, such as "service" or "administration." Each bureau is, of course, even further subdivided into divisions, offices, or units—all are parts of the bureaucratic hierarchy.

Not all government agencies are part of cabinet departments. Some **independent agencies** are set up by Congress outside the departmental structure altogether, even though the president appoints and directs the heads of these agencies. Independent agencies usually have broad powers to provide public services that are either too expensive or too important to be left to private initiatives. Some examples of independent agencies are the National Aeronautics and Space Administration (NASA), the Central Intelligence Agency (CIA), and the EPA. **Government corporations** are a third type of government agency but are more like private businesses in performing and charging for a market service, such as transporting railroad passengers (Amtrak).

department the largest subunit of the executive branch; the secretaries of the 15 departments form the Cabinet.

independent agency agency that is not part of a cabinet department

government corporation government agency that performs a market-oriented public service and raises revenues to fund its activities

Bureaucracy in Comparison

As one of the world's largest and most populous countries, the United States has a vast bureaucracy to run government programs and services. However, as a percentage of the labor force, the number of government employees in the United States is not especially high. As the first graph below shows, the size of government bureaucracies, relative to each country's work force, varies widely. For example, the Norwegian government employs roughly 30 percent of the labor force, whereas only around 6 percent of Japanese workers work for the government.

We can also see differences in whether most government employees work at the national level or the subnational level in each country. In the United States, most government employees work at the state or local level, rather than the national level. In other countries like Italy or Turkey, most bureaucrats work for the national government. What do you think accounts for these differences? How does federalism influence American bureaucracy, and what differences do we see in countries like France that do not have federalist systems?

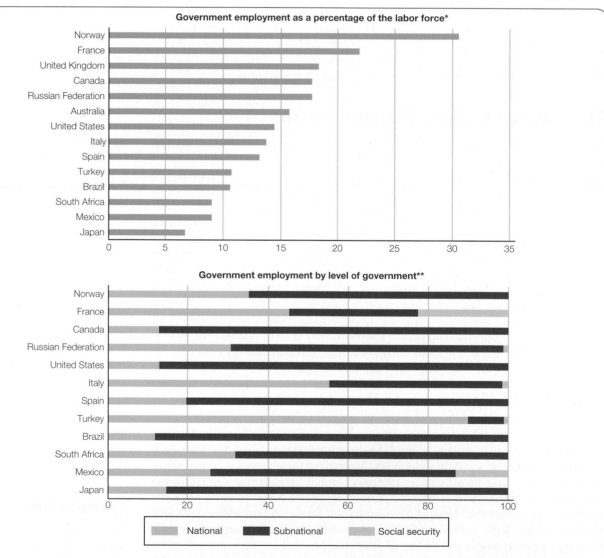

*Data are 2011 estimates. Germany, Norway, and the United Kingdom: Data are for 2010 instead of 2011. Japan, Mexico, Brazil and the Russian Federation: 2009 instead of 2011. France and South Africa: 2006 instead of 2011.

**Data are for 2011. Data on the United Kingdom and Australia are not available.

SOURCE: OECD, *Government at a Glance 2013*, http://www.oecd-ilibrary.org/governance/government-at-a-glance-2013_gov_glance-2013-en (accessed 6/30/14).

NASA, an independent agency of the federal government, was established by President Eisenhower in 1958. Its mission is "To reach for new heights and reveal the unknown so that what we do and learn will benefit all humankind."

Yet a fourth type of agency is the independent regulatory commission, given broad discretion to make rules. The first regulatory agencies established by Congress, beginning with the Interstate Commerce Commission in 1887, were set up as independent regulatory commissions because Congress recognized that regulatory agencies are "mini-legislatures," whose rules are exactly the same as legislation but require the kind of expertise and full-time attention that is beyond the capacity of Congress. Until the 1960s most of the regulatory agencies set up by Congress, such as the Federal Trade Commission (1914) and the Federal Communications Commission (1934), were independent regulatory commissions. But beginning in the late 1960s and the early 1970s, all new regulatory programs, with two or three exceptions (such as the Federal Election Commission), were placed within existing departments and made directly responsible to the president. After the financial crisis that began in 2008, Congress passed legislation to improve regulation of banks and other nonbank financial institutions. The legislation also created an important new regulatory agency, the Consumer Financial Protection Bureau. The bureau enforces consumer protection laws; for example, regulating bank practices that affect credit cards and mortgages. The agency aims to eliminate deceptive practices and act as the voice of consumers. Its website (www.consumerfinance.gov) also takes complaints from consumers and provides easy to understand information on many topics, including student debt repayment.

Goals of the Federal Bureaucracy

Describe the major goals we expect federal agencies to promote

The different agencies of the executive branch can be classified into three main groups by the services they provide to the American public. The first category of agencies provides services and products that seek to promote the public welfare. The second group of agencies works to promote national security. The third group provides services that help maintain a strong economy. Let us look more closely at what each set of agencies offers to the American public.

The National Institutes of Health is an example of a federal bureaucracy that promotes the public welfare by conducting cutting-edge biomedical research. NIH research has helped doctors to treat diabetes and cardiovascular disease, among many other illnesses. This scientist is studying pancreatic beta cells, which play a role in diabetes

regulatory agency a department, bureau, or independent agency whose primary mission is to impose limits, restrictions, or other obligations on the conduct of individuals or companies in the private sector

Promoting the Public Welfare

One of the most important activities of the federal bureaucracy is to promote the public welfare. Americans often think of government welfare as a single program that goes only to the very poor, but in fact a number of federal agencies provide services, build infrastructure, and enforce regulations designed to enhance the well-being of the vast majority of citizens. Departments that have important responsibilities for promoting the public welfare in this sense include the Department of Housing and Urban Development, the Department of Health and Human Services, the Department of Veterans Affairs, the Department of the Interior, the Department of Education, and the Department of Labor. Ensuring the public welfare is also the main activity of agencies in other departments, such as the Department of Agriculture's Food and Nutrition Service, which administers the federal school lunch program and the Supplemental Nutrition Assistance Program (formerly known as food stamps). In addition, multiple independent regulatory agencies enforce regulations that aim to safeguard the public health and welfare.

The Department of Health and Human Services (HHS) administers the program that comes closest to the popular understanding of welfare: Temporary Assistance for Needy Families (TANF). Yet this program is one of the smallest activities of the department. HHS also oversees the National Institutes of Health (NIH), which is responsible for cutting-edge biomedical research, and for two major health programs of the federal government: Medicaid, which provides health care for low-income families and for many elderly and disabled people; and Medicare, which is the health insurance available to most elderly people in the United States.

A different notion of the public welfare but one highly valued by most Americans is provided by the National Park Service, under the Department of the Interior. First created in 1916, the National Park Service is responsible for the care and upkeep of national parks. Since the nineteenth century, Americans have seen protection of the natural environment as an important public goal and have looked to federal agencies to implement laws and administer programs that preserve natural areas and keep them open to the public.

The federal bureaucracy also promotes public welfare through the watchdog activities of many **regulatory agencies**. These include the Food and Drug Administration (FDA), within the Department of Health and Human Services, the Occupational Safety and Health Administration (OSHA), in the Department of Labor, as well as numerous independent regulatory commissions, such as the Consumer Product Safety Commission, the FCC, and the EPA. An agency or commission is regulatory if Congress delegates to it relatively broad powers over a sector of the economy or a type of commercial activity and authorizes it to make rules within that jurisdiction. Rules made by regulatory agencies have the force and effect of law. Figure 14.3 shows how much the federal government spent on selected regulatory agencies in 2012, though these are just a few of the many agencies involved in regulatory activities.

Often working behind the scenes, regulatory agencies seek to promote the welfare of all Americans. The EPA, for example, works to protect public health by ensuring the provision of clean and safe drinking water. Just as the agency sets standards to limit emissions from automobiles in order to protect the public from air pollutants, as we saw earlier, the EPA also sets national water quality standards to protect against

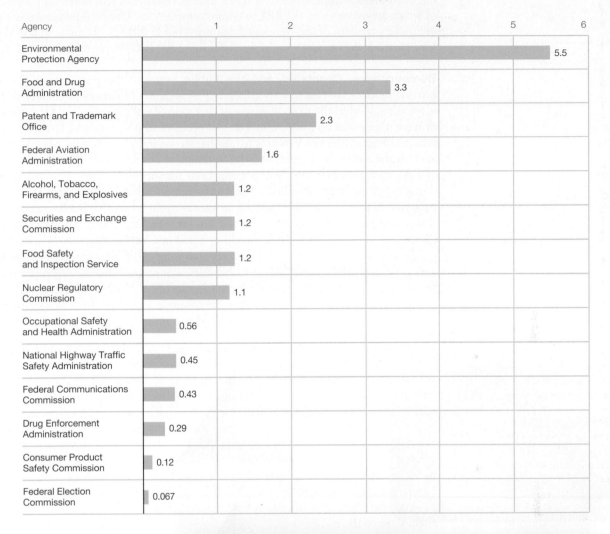

BILLIONS ($)

Agency						
	1	2	3	4	5	6

Environmental Protection Agency — 5.5

Food and Drug Administration — 3.3

Patent and Trademark Office — 2.3

Federal Aviation Administration — 1.6

Alcohol, Tobacco, Firearms, and Explosives — 1.2

Securities and Exchange Commission — 1.2

Food Safety and Inspection Service — 1.2

Nuclear Regulatory Commission — 1.1

Occupational Safety and Health Administration — 0.56

National Highway Traffic Safety Administration — 0.45

Federal Communications Commission — 0.43

Drug Enforcement Administration — 0.29

Consumer Product Safety Commission — 0.12

Federal Election Commission — 0.067

FIGURE 14.3

Spending on Regulation by Selected Agencies

One way bureaucratic agencies promote the public welfare is by regulating the activities of individuals or companies. There are costs and benefits associated with regulation. Calculating the benefits (in such terms as food-borne illnesses avoided or traffic accidents prevented) is difficult, but regulatory agencies' expenditures offer one way to look at costs. This figure shows the expenditures of selected agencies that regulate activities in a variety of areas. Do any of the data here surprise you, either because of how much or how little is spent by a certain agency?

SOURCE: Susan Dudley and Melinda Warren, http://regulatorystudies.columbian.gwu.edu/files/downloads/2014_Regulators_Budget.pdf (accessed 8/26/14).

contaminants that may pose health risks. The safety standards apply to the more than 170,000 public water systems around the country that support our access to safe drinking water and are implemented by states, local governments, and water suppliers—all of which are overseen by the EPA to ensure compliance.[13] Unsafe drinking water may seem like a concern of less-developed countries, but in 2014, a chemical spill in West Virginia made the tap water undrinkable for some 300,000 people for at least five days.

Bureaucracies, Clienteles, and the Public Some of the public agencies that provide services are tied to a specific group or segment of American society that is often thought of as the main clientele of that agency. For example, the Department of Agriculture was established in 1862 to promote the interests of farmers. Likewise, the Department of Veterans Affairs has strong links to veterans' organizations such as the American Legion and the Veterans of Foreign Wars. The Department of Education relies on teachers' organizations for support. Figure 14.4 is a representation of this type of politics. This configuration is known as an iron triangle, a pattern of stable relationships among an agency in the executive branch, a congressional committee or subcommittee, and one or more organized groups of agency clientele. (Iron triangles were discussed in detail in Chapter 11.)

These relationships with particular clienteles are often important in preserving agencies from political attack. During his 1980 campaign, Ronald Reagan promised to dismantle the Department of Education as part of his commitment to get government "off people's backs." After his election, Reagan even appointed a secretary of the department who was publicly committed to eliminating it. Yet by the end of his

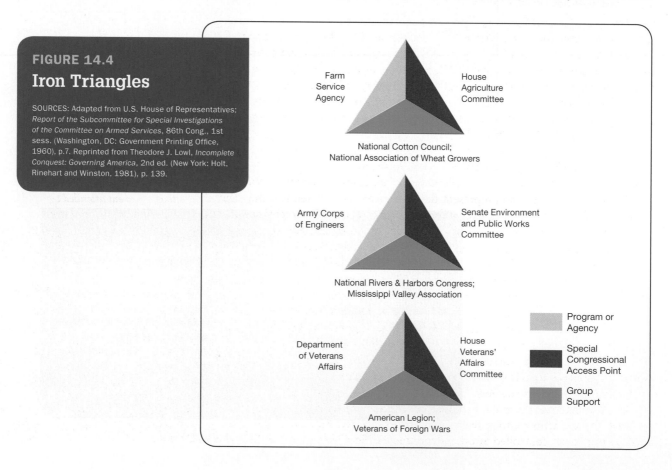

FIGURE 14.4

Iron Triangles

SOURCES: Adapted from U.S. House of Representatives; *Report of the Subcommittee for Special Investigations of the Committee on Armed Services*, 86th Cong., 1st sess. (Washington, DC: Government Printing Office, 1960), p.7. Reprinted from Theodore J. Lowl, *Incomplete Conquest: Governing America*, 2nd ed. (New York: Holt, Rinehart and Winston, 1981), p. 139.

Farm Service Agency

House Agriculture Committee

National Cotton Council; National Association of Wheat Growers

Army Corps of Engineers

Senate Environment and Public Works Committee

National Rivers & Harbors Congress; Mississippi Valley Association

Department of Veterans Affairs

House Veterans' Affairs Committee

American Legion; Veterans of Foreign Wars

Program or Agency

Special Congressional Access Point

Group Support

administration, the Department of Education was still standing and barely touched. In 1995 the Republican Congress vowed to eliminate the Department of Education, along with two other departments, but it, too, failed. The educational constituency of the department (its clientele) mobilized to save it each time. Teachers unions and educational administrators formed a powerful alliance to defend the department.

Nevertheless, the ability of clientele groups to get their way is not automatic, as agencies have to balance limited resources, competing interests, and political pressures. For example, the Department of Veterans Affairs long resisted the efforts of Vietnam veterans to be compensated for exposure to Agent Orange, a chemical defoliant used extensively during the Vietnam War. Veterans charged that exposure to Agent Orange had left them with a variety of diseases ranging from cancer to severe birth defects in their children. Only after decades of lobbying, lawsuits, and federally sponsored studies did the Department of Veterans Affairs provide assistance to affected veterans.

for critical analysis

What is the impact of iron triangles on government services in the United States? Do the ties among agencies, congressional committees, and organized groups promote the efficient provision of government services?

Providing National Security

One of the remarkable features of American federalism is that the most vital agencies for providing security for the American people (namely, the police) are located in state and local governments. But some agencies vital to maintaining national security are located in the national government, and they can be grouped into two categories: (1) agencies to confront threats to internal national security and (2) agencies to defend American security from external threats. The departments of greatest influence in these two areas are Homeland Security, Justice, Defense, and State.

Agencies for Internal Security The task of maintaining domestic security changed dramatically after the terrorist attacks of September 11, 2001. The creation of the Department of Homeland Security in late 2002 signaled the high priority that domestic security would now have. The orientation of domestic agencies shifted as well, as agencies geared up to prevent terrorism, a very different task from their former charge of investigating crime. With this shift in responsibility came broad new powers, many of them controversial, including the power to detain terrorist suspects and to engage in extensive domestic intelligence gathering about possible terrorists.

Before September 11, most of the effort put into maintaining internal national security took the form of legal work related to prosecuting federal crimes. The largest and most important unit of the Justice Department is the Criminal Division. Lawyers in the Criminal Division represent the U.S. government when it is the plaintiff enforcing federal criminal laws, except for those cases (about 25 percent) specifically assigned to other divisions or agencies. Criminal litigation is handled by U.S. attorneys, who are appointed by the president. There is one U.S. attorney in each of the 94 federal judicial districts; he or she supervises the work of a number of assistant U.S. attorneys.

The Civil Division of the Justice Department deals with litigation in which the United States is the defendant being sued for injury and damages allegedly inflicted by a government official or agency. The missions of the other divisions of the Justice Department—Antitrust, Civil Rights, Environment and Natural Resources, and Tax—are described by their names.

In 2002 the new Department of Homeland Security joined the Justice Department as the major bureaucracy charged with domestic security. The department took over some of the security-oriented agencies previously controlled by other departments. (See Table 14.1

The Department of Homeland Security is tasked with the broad goal of keeping America safe. Its 240,000 employees work in jobs as diverse as aviation security, emergency response, and chemical facility inspection. DHS also provided security at MetLife Stadium for the 2014 Super Bowl, an event attended by approximately 82,000 people.

TABLE 14.1

Department of Homeland Security

SELECTED OFFICES	FUNCTION	2014 BUDGET, IN MILLION $	ESTIMATED NUMBER OF EMPLOYEES
Department Mangement and Operations	Provides leadership, direction, and management to DHS	728	1,939
Analysis and Operations	Provides intelligence analysis, information sharing, incident management support, and situational awareness	300	850
Office of Inspector General	Conducts and supervises audits, inspections, special reviews, and investigations of the department's programs and operations	139	681
U.S. Customs and Border Protection (CBP)	Responsible for securing America's borders to protect the United States against terrorist threats and prevent the illegal entry of inadmissible persons and contraband, while facilitating lawful travel, trade, and immigration	12,377	60,952
U.S. Immigration and Customs Enforcement (ICE)	The principal investigative arm of DHS	5,611	19,332
Transportation Security Administration (TSA)	Provides security for the nation's transportation system	7,305	55,704
Coast Guard	Safeguards our nation's maritime Interests and natural resources on our rivers, in U.S. ports, on the high seas, and in the maritime domain around the world	10,438	50,926
U.S. Secret Service	Protects national leaders and safeguards the nation's financial infrastructure and payment systems	1,839	6,572
Office of Health Affairs (OHA)	Advises, promotes, integrates, and enables a safe and secure workforce and nation in pursuit of national health security	127	99
Federal Emergency Management Agency (FEMA)	Manages and coordinates the federal response to and recovery from major domestic disasters and emergencies of all types	13,780	12,098

SOURCE: U.S. Department of Homeland Security, "Budget-in-Brief, Fiscal Year 2015," www.dhs.gov/sites/default/files/publications/FY15BIB.pdf (accessed 3/20/14).

for a look inside the DHS.) Growing pains were evident in Homeland Security's first years. Different bureaucratic cultures, now part of a single operation, quickly became embroiled in turf battles with one another and with the FBI (which remained in the Justice Department) as the two departments attempted to sort out their respective responsibilities. These early problems signaled deeper challenges that the Department of Homeland Security has continued to face throughout its existence. DHS has been unable to establish itself as a strong institutionally coherent presence capable of coordinating government action. Part of the problem is that the DHS portfolio of responsibilities is both large and vague. It is responsible for all kinds of internal security including terrorist attacks, border security, natural disasters, and food safety. At times the agency has emphasized one or the other of these responsibilities, so that the overarching goal of "homeland security" has failed to gain traction. In addition, the agency failed to establish strong links with state and local agencies whose activities remain critical to its on-the-ground capabilities.

for critical analysis

Why was the Department of Homeland Security created? What problems has the new department faced?

Agencies for External National Security Two departments occupy center stage in maintaining external national security: the departments of State and Defense.

The State Department's primary mission is diplomacy. As the most visible public representative of American diplomacy, the secretary of State works to promote American perspectives and interests in the world. For example, in 2013, Secretary of State John Kerry made a closely watched stop in Egypt, the first visit by a high-ranking American official since a coup by the Egyptian military deposed the country's first democratically elected president. Kerry hoped to defuse anti-American sentiment and underscore American support for democracy in that country. Although diplomacy is the primary task of the State Department, diplomatic missions are only one of its organizational dimensions. As of 2014 the State Department comprised 35 bureau-level units, each under the direction of an assistant secretary.[14]

These bureaus support the responsibilities of the elite foreign-service officers (FSOs), who staff U.S. embassies around the world and who hold almost all the most powerful positions in the department below the rank of ambassador.[15] The ambassadorial positions, especially the plum positions in the major capitals of the world, are filled by presidential appointees, many of whom get their posts by having been important donors to victorious political campaigns.

Despite the importance of the State Department in foreign affairs, fewer than 20 percent of all U.S. government employees working abroad are directly under its authority. By far the largest number of career government professionals working abroad are under the authority of the Defense Department.

In 2002 the Defense Department created the U.S. Northern Command, a regional command charged with ensuring homeland defense, directing military operations inside the nation's borders, and providing emergency backup to state and local governments, which are the first responders to any security disaster. The creation of a regional command within the United States was an unprecedented move, breaching a long-standing line between domestic law enforcement and foreign military operations. As the creation of a military capacity within the United States suggests, addressing the threat of terrorism calls for greater coordination of internal and external security. In 2004 the National Commission on Terrorist Attacks upon the United States (the 9/11 Commission) issued a widely read report that revealed that different departments of the American government had information that, if handled properly, might have prevented the attacks of September 11, 2001.[16] The 9/11 Commission's work prompted a major reorganization of the fragmented intelligence community.

In 2005 a new office, the Office of the Director of National Intelligence, took over responsibility for coordinating the efforts of the 16 different agencies that gather intelligence. The DNI reports directly to the president each morning.

National Security and Democracy Of all the agencies in the federal bureaucracy, those charged with providing national security most often come into conflict with the norms and expectations of American democracy. Two issues in particular arise as these agencies work to ensure the national security: (1) the trade-offs between respecting the personal rights of individuals versus protecting the general public, and (2) the need for secrecy in matters of national security versus the public's right to know what the government is doing. Needless to say, Americans often disagree about what activities the government should be able to pursue to defend U.S. national security.

When national security is at stake, federal agencies have taken actions that are normally considered incompatible with individual rights. For example, during World War II thousands of American citizens of Japanese descent were interned in camps due to national security concerns. Although the Supreme Court approved this action, the federal government has since acknowledged that it constituted unjustified discrimination and has offered reparations to those who were interned.

With the advent of the war on terrorism, the government gained unprecedented powers to detain foreign suspects, carry out wiretaps and searches, conduct secret military tribunals, and build an integrated law enforcement and intelligence system. Congress hastily enacted many of these sweeping provisions of the Patriot Act several weeks after the terrorist attacks, with little debate. Since then, extensive doubts about the broad powers of the Patriot Act have spread. When Congress debated renewing the Patriot Act in 2005–06, these concerns about individual liberties threatened to block renewal. The act that was finally approved in 2006 did include modest revisions, such as exempting most libraries from having to turn over users' records to the government. Nonetheless, many in Congress felt the safeguards to individual liberties did not go far enough.

Protecting national security often requires the government to conduct its activities in secret. Yet, as Americans have come to expect a more open government in the past three decades, many believe that federal agencies charged with national security keep too many secrets from the American public. As one critic put it, "the United States government must rest, in the words of the Declaration of Independence, on 'the consent of the governed.' And there can be no meaningful consent where those who are governed do not know to what they are consenting."[17] The effort to make information related to national security more available to the public began in 1966 with the passage of the Freedom of Information Act (FOIA). Strengthened in 1974 after Watergate, the act allows any person to request classified information from any federal agency. The information obtained through the Freedom of Information Act often reveals unflattering or unsuccessful aspects of national security activities. One private organization, the National Security Archive, makes extensive use of FOIA requests to obtain information about the activities of national security agencies. The National Security Archive has published many of these documents on its website and maintains an archive in Washington, D.C., that is open to the public. For example, the organization's website contains "The Torture Archive," a searchable database of documents related to the detention of individuals in the Global War on Terror and the authorized use of torture by the American government.

The tension between secrecy and democracy sharpened dramatically with the threat of terrorism. Access under the FOIA was curtailed, and the range of information

deemed sensitive has greatly expanded. Some analysts worried that secrecy would prevent Congress from carrying out its basic oversight responsibilities. They also claimed that much of the secrecy had nothing to do with national security. The day after President Obama's election, he launched a process that would culminate in an Open Government Directive. He also instructed federal agencies that they should administer the FOIA law liberally: when in doubt, err on the side of openness. In 2011 the Department of Justice created the website www.foia.gov so that the public could learn more about the FOIA process. The site presents data about the number of FOIA requests by agency and the size of the backlog in processing those requests (see Figure 14.5). And in the most substantive change, at the end of his first year in office, Obama issued an executive order designed to promote more rapid declassification of secret documents.

The Obama administration's campaign to make government more transparent was challenged, however, by national security contract worker Edward Snowden's leak of sensitive national security documents in 2013. The Snowden documents exposed the extent, and potential illegality, of the National Security Agency's (NSA) global surveillance operations. Following the revelation that the NSA was collecting private data on millions of Americans and foreign nationals—not only tracking phone calls but also email messages, web browser history, and personal contacts—concern mounted among the American public, government watchdog groups, and representatives in Congress, while foreign allies threatened to suspend cooperation on global antiterrorism efforts.[18] President Obama responded to the growing outrage by appointing an independent, five-member panel of intelligence experts to assess the NSA's activities. Three months later, in December 2013, the panel determined that the NSA's massive data collection "made only a modest contribution to the nation's security" and recommended among dozens of other reforms, that the government stop the collection program and relinquish the files to a third party.[19] While the Obama administration publicly endorsed many of the panel's findings and outlined changes to the surveillance program—including requiring the agency to obtain prior court approval to access calling records[20]—it remains to be seen whether its proposed reforms will succeed in winning back public trust.

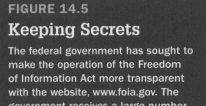
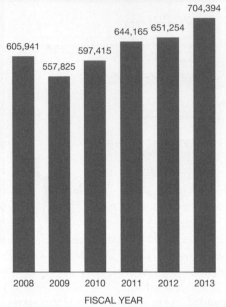

REQUESTS RECEIVED

605,941   557,825   597,415   644,165   651,254   704,394

2008   2009   2010   2011   2012   2013

FISCAL YEAR

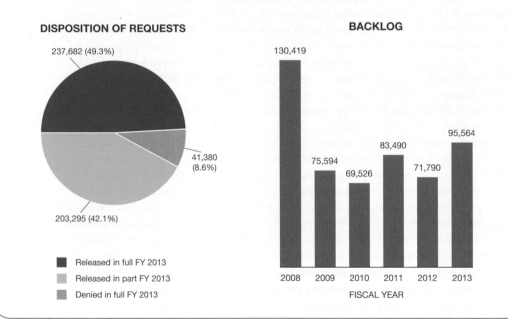

DISPOSITION OF REQUESTS

237,682 (49.3%)

41,380 (8.6%)

203,295 (42.1%)

■ Released in full FY 2013
■ Released in part FY 2013
■ Denied in full FY 2013

BACKLOG

130,419

75,594   69,526   83,490   71,790   95,564

2008   2009   2010   2011   2012   2013

FISCAL YEAR

Maintaining a Strong Economy

In our capitalist economic system, the government does not directly run the economy. Yet many federal government activities are critical to maintaining a strong economy. Foremost among these are the agencies responsible for fiscal and monetary policy. Other agencies, such as the Internal Revenue Service (IRS), collect private resources into use for public purposes. Tax policy may also strengthen the economy through decisions about whom to tax, how much, and when. Finally, the federal government, through such agencies as the Department of Transportation, the Commerce Department, and the Energy Department, may directly provide services or goods that bolster the economy.

Fiscal and Monetary Agencies Fiscal policy can refer to any government policy having to do with public finance. However, Americans often reserve *fiscal* for taxing and spending policies and use *monetary* for policies having to do with banks, credit, and currency.

While the responsibility for making fiscal policy lies with Congress, the administration of fiscal policy occurs primarily in the Treasury Department. In addition to collecting income, corporate, and other taxes, the Treasury also manages the national debt: $17 trillion in 2014.[21] The Treasury Department is also responsible for printing U.S. currency, but currency is only a tiny proportion of the entire money economy. Most of the trillions of dollars used in the transactions of the private and public sectors of the U.S. economy exist virtually—in computerized accounts rather than actual currency.

A key monetary agency is the **Federal Reserve System**, which is headed by the Federal Reserve Board. The Federal Reserve System (called simply the Fed) has authority over the interest rates and lending activities of the nation's most important banks. Congress established the Fed in 1913 as a clearinghouse responsible for adjusting the supply of money and credit to the needs of commerce and industry in different regions of the country. The Fed is also responsible for ensuring that banks do not overextend themselves, a policy that guards against bank failures during a sudden economic scare, such as occurred in 1929. The Treasury and the Federal Reserve took center stage when a string of bank failures threatened economic catastrophe in 2008. These agencies designed a $700 billion bailout package and convinced Congress that a rapid response was needed to avert a worldwide depression. Although the Treasury and the Federal Reserve sprang into action when economic calamity loomed, critics charged that the crisis could have been prevented if these agencies had exercised more regulatory oversight over the financial sector during the previous decade. In 2010 the Congress and the president created the Financial Stability Oversight Council to identify systemwide risks to the financial sector. As part of its duties, the council devised a rule to identify "systemically important" nonbank financial companies that would pose a grave threat to U.S. financial stability in the event that they failed and prompts stiffer regulatory oversight of those companies.[22]

Revenue Agencies One of the first actions Congress took under President George Washington was to create the Department of the Treasury, and probably its oldest function is the collection of taxes on imports, called tariffs. Now part of the Department of Homeland Security, federal customs agents are located at every U.S. seaport and international airport to oversee the collection of tariffs. But far and away the most important of the **revenue agencies** is the IRS, a bureau within the Treasury Department.

The IRS is the government agency that Americans love to hate. As one expert put it, "probably no organization in the country, public or private, creates as much clientele *dis*favor as the Internal Revenue Service. The very nature of its work brings it into an adversarial relationship with vast numbers of Americans every year [emphasis added]."[23] Taxpayers complain about the IRS's needless complexity, its lack of sensitivity and responsiveness to individual taxpayers, and its overall lack of

fiscal policy the government's use of taxing, monetary, and spending powers to manipulate the economy

Federal Reserve System a system of 12 Federal Reserve banks that facilitates exchanges of cash, checks, and credit; regulates member banks; and uses monetary policies to fight inflation and deflation

revenue agency an agency responsible for collecting taxes. Examples include the Internal Revenue Service for income taxes; the U.S. Customs Service for tariffs and other taxes on imported goods; and the Bureau of Alcohol, Tobacco, Firearms and Explosives for collection of taxes on the sale of those particular products

efficiency. Such complaints led Congress to pass the IRS Restructuring and Reform Act of 1998, which instituted a number of new protections for taxpayers.

The politics of the IRS is interesting because, although thousands upon thousands of corporations and wealthy individuals have a strong and active interest in American tax policy, key taxation decisions are set by agreements among the president, the Treasury Department, and the leading members of the two tax committees in Congress, the House Ways and Means Committee and the Senate Finance Committee. External influence is not spread throughout the 50 states but is much more centralized in the majority political party, a few key figures in Congress, and a handful of professional lobbyists. Suspicions of unfair exemptions and favoritism are widespread, and they do exist, but these exemptions come largely from Congress, *not* from the IRS itself.

Economic Development Agencies Federal agencies also conduct programs designed to strengthen particular segments of the economy or to provide specific services aimed at strengthening the entire economy. Created in 1889, the Department of Agriculture is the fourth-oldest cabinet department. Its initial mission, to strengthen American agriculture by providing information about effective farming practices, reflected the enormous importance of farming in the American economy. Through its Agricultural Extension Service, the Department of Agriculture established an important presence in rural areas throughout the country. It also built strong support for its activities among the nation's farmers and at the many land-grant colleges, where agricultural research has been conducted for over 100 years.

At first glance, the Department of Transportation, which oversees the nation's highway and air traffic systems, may seem to have little to do with economic development. But effective transportation is the backbone of a strong economy. The interstate highway system, for example, is widely acknowledged as a key factor in promoting economic growth in the decades after World War II. The Small Business Administration, in the Department of Commerce, provides loans and technical assistance to small businesses across the country.

For one picture of how the federal government prioritizes these goals, see the "Who Are Americans?" feature, which shows the number of employees of major executive departments.

● Can the Bureaucracy Be Reformed?

> **Evaluate some of the ways politicians have tried to make the bureaucracy more efficient**

When citizens complain that government is too bureaucratic, what they often mean is that government bureaucracies seem inefficient and waste money. The epitome of such bureaucratic inefficiency in the late 1980s was the Department of Defense, which was revealed to have spent $640 apiece for toilet seats and $435 apiece for hammers. In 2013, the Internal Revenue Service was faulted for putting on expensive conferences for its employees in Anaheim, California, and Las Vegas.[24] Many citizens also have negative personal experience with the federal government: mountains of forms to fill out, lengthy waits, and unsympathetic service. Why can't government do better? many citizens ask.

Who Are "Bureaucrats"?

Executive Branch Employees, 2013 (in thousands)

Cabinet departments

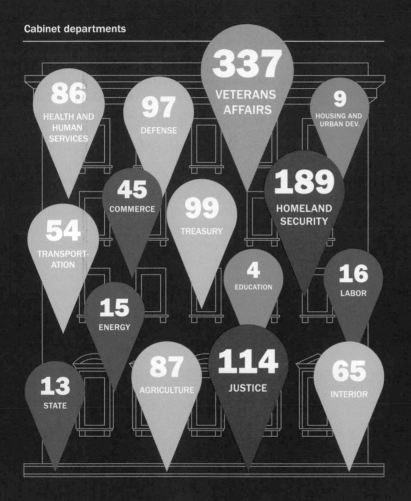

86 HEALTH AND HUMAN SERVICES

97 DEFENSE

337 VETERANS AFFAIRS

9 HOUSING AND URBAN DEV.

45 COMMERCE

99 TREASURY

189 HOMELAND SECURITY

54 TRANSPORT-ATION

4 EDUCATION

16 LABOR

15 ENERGY

13 STATE

87 AGRICULTURE

114 JUSTICE

65 INTERIOR

Independent agencies

1 NATIONAL SCIENCE FOUNDATION

62 SOCIAL SECURITY

12 GENERAL SERVICES ADMIN.

2 GOVERNMENT PRINTING OFFICE

17 E.P.A

18 NASA

1 FEDERAL TRADE COMMISSION

5 OFFICE OF PERSONNEL MANAGEMENT

Number of employees

- < 10,000
- 10,000–49,999
- 50,000–99,999
- 100,000–199,999
- > 200,000

Location, 2013

440 22% WASHINGTON, D.C., AREA

1,557 78% — OTHER

SOURCE: U.S. Office of Personnel Management, www.fedscope.opm.gov/employment.asp (accessed 5/9/14).

Contrary to popular notions of "paper pushers," the people who work in the federal bureaucracy perform a range of tasks essential to the functioning of American society. Nearly 2 million executive branch employees are involved in protecting the nation's security, managing the economy, and promoting public welfare through various means, including environmental protection and health and safety regulations. Most federal employees work outside the Washington, D.C., area.

for critical analysis

1. Which category of departments and agencies—security, economic, or public welfare—employs the most people? Why?

2. With 2 million people working for the executive branch, mostly outside of the Washington, D.C., area, how can Congress and the president be sure that they are serving the public's interests?

Do these frustrations mean that bureaucracy needs to be reformed? In a sense, bureaucracy is always in need of reform. Technological change and a dynamic private sector mean that public bureaucracies must always be looking for ways to take advantage of innovations to improve their performance. When bureaucracies fail to implement timely reforms, they can appear out of date and provoke frustration among citizens who rely on them. For example, the application of new technologies and innovative management strategies in the private sector during the 1980s made government agencies look even more lumbering and inefficient by comparison. People were coming to expect faster service and more customer-friendly interactions in the private sector. Yet, reforms may be more difficult to implement in the public sector because it is held to much higher standards of accountability than are private companies. Speedy service delivery can be hindered by the need to act in accordance with the multiple rules and regulations that govern bureaucracies. Moreover, the practices of bureaucracies are much more carefully scrutinized by watchdogs than is the private sector. The IRS conferences that attracted negative press are, in fact, common practice in the private sector, where they are rarely questioned. The tension between accountability and responsiveness, played out in the public eye, make reform both necessary and challenging for bureaucracies.

The government has sought to find various ways to make the federal bureaucracy more efficient. The key strategies used to promote reform include reinventing bureaucratic procedures, termination, devolution, and privatization. In general, Democratic administrations have aimed to make the existing bureaucracy work more effectively, whereas Republican administrations have sought to sideline the bureaucracy, especially by contracting out government work to private companies.

In 1993, President Clinton launched the National Performance Review (NPR)—part of his promise to "reinvent government"—to make the federal

In recent decades there have been several attempts to "reinvent" government. In 1993, President Bill Clinton and Vice President Al Gore established the National Performance Review to reinvent government. Gore promoted this on David Letterman's show, where he railed against the government's procurement requirements, which even specified the number of pieces into which a government ashtray may shatter.

bureaucracy more efficient, accountable, and effective. The NPR sought to prod federal agencies into adopting flexible, goal-driven practices. Clinton promised that the result would be a government that would "work better and cost less." Virtually all observers agreed that the NPR made substantial progress. Its original goal was to save more than $100 billion over five years, in large part by cutting the federal workforce by 12 percent (more than 270,000 jobs) by the end of 1999. In fact, by 2000, $136 billion in savings were already assured through legislative or administrative action, and the federal workforce had been cut by 426,200.[25] The streamlining of government business procedures did help make government work more effectively, but it did not institute the more sweeping approach to reform demanded by some political leaders. These leaders have instead pursued efforts to terminate, devolve, or contract out government functions.

Termination

The only *certain* way to reduce the size of the bureaucracy is to eliminate programs through termination, a rare occurence. Even in the 12 years of the Reagan and George H. W. Bush administrations, both of which proclaimed a strong commitment to the reduction of the national government, not a single national government agency or program was terminated. In the 1990s, Republicans did succeed in eliminating two small agencies.

The overall difficulty in terminating bureaucracy is a reflection of Americans' love-hate relationship with the national government. As antagonistic as Americans may be toward bureaucracy in general, they benefit from the services being rendered and the protections being offered by particular bureaucratic agencies. They fiercely defend their favorite agencies while perceiving no inconsistency in their hostility toward the bureaucracy in general. A good case in point is the agonizing problem of closing military bases in the wake of the end of the Cold War with the former Soviet Union, when the United States no longer needed so many bases. Since every base was in some congressional member's district, it proved impossible for Congress to decide to close any of them. Consequently, beginning in 1988, Congress established the Defense Base Closure and Realignment Commission (BRAC) to decide on base closings, allowing Congress only an up or down vote on the commission's proposals.[26] Five different BRAC reports, the most recent in 2005, have formed the basis for closing bases and modifying the operations in the remaining bases.

Elected leaders have come to rely on a more incremental approach to downsizing the bureaucracy. Much has been done by budgetary means, reducing the budgets of all agencies across the board by small percentages and cutting some less-supported agencies by larger amounts. Yet these changes are still incremental, leaving the existence of agencies unaddressed.

Devolution

The next most effective approach to genuinely reducing the size of the federal bureaucracy is **devolution**, downsizing the federal bureaucracy by delegating the implementation of programs to state and local governments. Devolution often alters the pattern

devolution a policy to remove a program from one level of government by delegating it or passing it down to a lower level of government, such as from the national government to the state and local governments

Americans may desire smaller government in the abstract, but they defend the agencies that affect them. Closing military bases in the United States has proved particularly controversial. Both citizens and local politicians mobilized across the country to urge the Base Closure and Realignment Commission not to close military bases in their localities.

of who benefits most from government programs. Opponents of devolution in social policy, for example, charge that it reduces the ability of the government to remedy inequality. They argue that state governments, which cannot run deficits as the federal government does, and which have more limited taxing capabilities, will inevitably cut spending on programs that serve low-income residents. They point to the State Children's Health Insurance Program (SCHIP), which was created in 1997 to extend health insurance to low-income children. When the economy was booming, states added children to the rolls and some states even extended benefits to the children's parents. But by 2002, as states faced significant budget crises, many cut back on SCHIP. Although the federal government was initially able to compensate for state funding problems, states have found it difficult to keep pace with the rising number of children without health insurance.

Often the central aim of devolution is to provide more efficient and flexible government services. Yet by its very nature, devolution entails variation across the states. In some states, government services may improve as a consequence of devolution. In other states, services may deteriorate as the states use devolution as an opportunity to cut spending and reduce services. This has been the pattern in the implementation of the welfare reform passed in 1996, the most significant devolution of federal government social programs in many decades. Some states, such as Wisconsin, have used the flexibility of the reform to design innovative programs that respond to clients' needs; other states, such as Idaho, have virtually dismantled their welfare programs. The recession that began in 2008 provided the first real evidence about what increased state flexibility meant for low-income Americans. Studies showed that the number of people on public assistance rose by 14 percent even as the unemployment rate increased by 88 percent between 2007 and 2010.[27] Moreover, states varied widely in how they responded: for example, although the unemployment rate rose by 146 percent in Arizona—increasing from 4 percent at the end of 2007 to almost 10 percent in 2010—public assistance rolls actually fell by 48 percent. In Oregon, by contrast, public assistance cases rose by 70 percent although unemployment grew by only 41 percent. The overall lack of growth and state variation in welfare contrasts sharply with the rise in food stamp recipients during 2008–09, a program run by the federal government. Food stamp recipients grew by 45 percent between 2009 and 2010 and pulled an estimated 9 percent of Americans out of poverty in 2009.[28] Critics argued that devolution gave the states too much flexibility in designing their own welfare programs and that the result has been a program unable to assist the poor when they need it most.

This is the dilemma that devolution poses. Up to a point, variation can be considered one of the virtues of federalism. But in a democracy, it is inherently dangerous to have large variations in the provisions of services and benefits.

Privatization

Most of what is called privatization is the provision of government goods and services by private contractors under direct government supervision. Except for top-secret strategic materials, virtually all military hardware, from boats to bullets, is produced on a privatized basis by private contractors. Research services worth billions of dollars are bought under contract by governments from universities and from ordinary industrial corporations and private "think tanks." **Privatization**

for critical analysis

Dissatisfied citizens have supported a range of bureaucratic reforms, including termination of agencies, devolution of responsibility to lower levels of government, and privatization. Are such reforms likely to make the bureaucracy more responsive to public wishes?

privatization a formerly public service that is now provided by a private company but paid for by the government

One strategy to carry out the tasks of government is privatization. The U.S. military and Department of Defense contract many services to companies such as Booz Allen Hamilton, which provides systems for personnel management, program support, and assessment, among other services.

simply means that a formerly public activity is picked up under contract by a private company or companies. But such programs are still very much government programs—paid for by government and supervised by government. Privatization downsizes the government only in that the workers providing the service are no longer counted as part of the government bureaucracy.

President George W. Bush made privatization a central component of his effort to reform the federal bureaucracy. He introduced new procedures that would subject more than 800,000 federal jobs, nearly half the federal civilian workforce, to competitive outsourcing. If it were determined that a company could do the job more efficiently, the work would be contracted out. Under Bush, government outsourcing grew dramatically as the government sought to staff the new Department of Homeland Security and pursue wars in Afghanistan and Iraq without increasing the numbers of federal employees. One estimate of the growth of contracting showed that at the end of the Cold War in 1990, there were three and a half contractors and grantees (those working with a grant from the federal government) for every civil servant; by 2005 the buildup connected with national security had altered the ratio to five and a half contractors and grantees for every civil servant.[29] Payments for federal contracts grew from $209 billion in 2000 to $537 billion in 2011.[30] Although military contracts account for much of the growth, contracting is common throughout the federal bureaucracy. In fact, contracting is now so widespread that it has been called a "virtual fourth branch of government."[31]

The central aim of privatization is to reduce the cost of government. Depending on how it is conducted, competitive outsourcing may not lead to extensive privatization; instead, competition may improve government performance by forcing federal agencies to reexamine how they can do their work more efficiently. When private contractors can perform a task as well as government can, but for less money, taxpayers win. But private firms are not necessarily more efficient or less costly than government, especially when there is little competition among private firms and when public bureaucracies are not granted a fair chance to bid in the contracting competition. Less than half of existing contracts were subject to open competition (Figure 14.6).[32] When private firms have a monopoly on service provision, they may be less efficient than government and more expensive. In fact, there is no good evidence that privatization saves the government money.

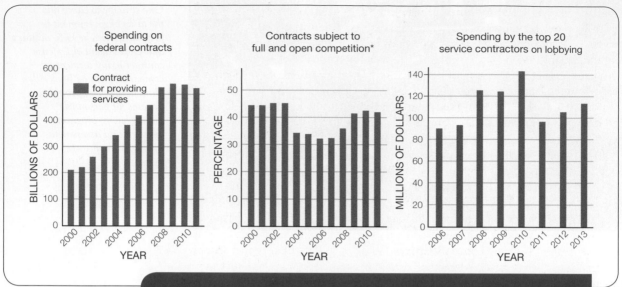

Spending on federal contracts

BILLIONS OF DOLLARS (y-axis: 0 to 600)
YEAR (x-axis: 2000 to 2010)

Contract for providing services

Contracts subject to full and open competition*

PERCENTAGE (y-axis: 0 to 50)
YEAR (x-axis: 2000 to 2010)

Spending by the top 20 service contractors on lobbying

MILLIONS OF DOLLARS (y-axis: 0 to 140)
YEAR (x-axis: 2006 to 2013)

FIGURE 14.6

Outsourcing the Government

As spending on federal contracts has grown, the number of contracts subject to open competition initially declined but later rose again. The rise in spending by private contractors on lobbying and campaign contributions raises questions about improper political influence on government contracting decisions.

*Includes both new contracts and payments against existing contracts.
SOURCES: Fedspending.org. "Summary of Federal Spending: Financial Assistance and Procurement," www.fedspending.org (accessed 6/22/14); Fedspending.org, "Federal Contract Awards by Extent of Competition," www.fedpending.org (accessed 6/22/14; Federal Procurement Data System—Next Generation, Top 100 Contractors Report. www.fpds.gov/fpdsng_cms/index.php/en/reports/62-top-100-contractors-report (accessed 7/2/14); Center for Resposive Politics, www.opensecrets.org (accessed 7/2/14).

Concerns about adequate government oversight and accountability of private contractors has escalated as the scale of contracting has dramatically increased. Consider the use of private contractors in Iraq and Afghanistan. Congressional hearings revealed massive cost overruns by KBR (formerly a subsidiary of Halliburton, the firm that former vice president Dick Cheney headed), which held $9 billion in no-bid contracts to provide services ranging from supplying fuel for the military to preparing cafeteria meals in Iraq. Army auditors have challenged $1.9 billion of KBR's bills as improper, citing violations ranging from unserved meals to inflated gas prices.[33] In 2013, the national security leaks by Edward Snowden and a mass shooting at the Washington Navy Yard, a U.S. military base, both by government contractors, raised fresh concerns about the outsourcing of government and prompted Congress to pass legislation calling for a review of contractors' security clearances.[34]

In most aspects of government activity, contract employees work side by side with government employees in what has been called a "blended workforce."[35] Many agencies that rely on technical expertise, such as the National Oceanographic and Atmospheric Administration, routinely rely on contractors. But although federal regulations forbid the outsourcing of "inherently governmental work," no clear line separates governmental and nongovernmental work. For example, in 2006 the General Services Administration hired a private firm, CACI International, to help it examine cases of fraud by other private contractors. Not only did the private contract workers hired by the GSA in this case cost double what their public counterparts cost, but they were engaged in oversight of other private contractors, a clear conflict of interest.[36]

As alarm over the activities of contractors has grown, there have been several efforts to increase accountability. In 2002 the federal government created a centralized database to record how well contractors have performed. The aim of the database is to provide a resource for agencies as they offer new contracts. However, research by the Government Accountability Office (GAO) showed that after seven years, the database was poorly documented and was seldom used in agency decision making.[37] As part of the 2009 National Defense Authorization Act, Congress called for the creation of an additional database that will keep track of contractors who commit legal or contractual violations,[38] though government transparency groups have complained that the new database also suffers from poor documentation.[39] In 2008 Congress also responded to the concerns about contractors by creating a "Commission on Wartime Contracting." Its final report sharply criticized the use of private contractors, estimating that the practice had wasted between $31 and $60 billion during the wars in Afghanistan and Iraq. It made numerous recommendations for reform but noted that successful reforms would require congressional action and funding for new oversight capabilities.[40]

Some members of Congress have sought far-reaching regulations on contractors. For example, Senator Chuck Schumer (D-N.Y.) and Representative Chris Van Hollen (D-Md.) proposed legislation in 2010 that would prohibit government contractors from making political contributions.[41] Members of Congress have also proposed forbidding contractors from performing sensitive functions in war settings, including interrogations, security, and intelligence functions. Proposals for such major reforms, however, are difficult to enact given the political connections of many federal contractors.

The Obama administration has sought to address the concerns about contracting in several ways. In July 2009 the White House Office of Management and Budget (OMB) took steps to reduce the government's reliance on outside contractors. Departments and agencies were told to cut contract spending by 7 percent over the next two years.[42] By 2011 the administration announced that for the first time in 13 years, spending on outside contractors had declined.[43] The White House also drafted an executive order requiring government contractors to disclose their political donations, though Congress blocked those efforts by passing a federal spending bill in 2014 that prohibits any funding to require contractors to provide campaign disclosures.[44]

for critical analysis

Private firms play a significant role in providing government services, including both internal and external security. What are the advantages and disadvantages of relying on private firms to provide essential services? Can government provide adequate oversight of these private companies?

● Managing the Bureaucracy

Explain why it is often difficult to control the bureaucracy

By their very nature, bureaucracies pose challenges to democratic governance. Although bureaucracies provide the expertise needed to implement the public will, they can also become entrenched organizations that serve their own interests. The public's task is neither to retreat from bureaucracy nor to attack it, but to take advantage of its strengths while making it more accountable to the demands of democratic politics and representative government.

We must return to James Madison's observation "You must first enable the government to control the governed; and in the next place oblige it to control itself."[45] Today, after more than 200 years, millions of employees, and trillions of dollars since the Founding, the problem is the same. Now, though, the process has a name, administrative accountability, which implies that some higher authority will guide and judge the actions of the bureaucracy. The highest authority in a democracy is *demos* ("the people"), and the guidance for bureaucratic action is the popular will. But that ideal of accountability must be translated into practical terms by the president and Congress.

The President as Chief Executive

In 1937, President Franklin Roosevelt's Committee on Administrative Management officially addressed a plea that had been growing increasingly urgent: "The president needs help." The national government had grown rapidly during the preceding 25 years, but the structures and procedures necessary to manage the burgeoning executive branch had not yet been established. The response to the call for "help" for the president initially took the form of three management policies: (1) All communications and decisions that related to executive policy decisions must pass through the White House; (2) In order to cope with such a flow, the White House must have an adequate staff of specialists in research, analysis, legislative and legal writing, and public affairs; and (3) The White House must have additional staff to ensure that presidential decisions are made, communicated to Congress, and carried out by the appropriate agency.

Making the Managerial Presidency The story of the modern presidency can be told largely as a series of responses to the plea for managerial help. Indeed, each expansion of the national government into new policies and programs in the twentieth century was accompanied by a parallel expansion of the president's management authority.[46]

President Jimmy Carter, in particular, was probably more preoccupied with administrative reform and reorganization than any other twentieth-century president. His reorganization of the civil service will long be recognized as one of the most significant contributions of his presidency. The Civil Service Reform Act of 1978 was the first major revamping of the federal civil service since its creation in 1883. The 1978 act created the Merit Systems Protection Board (MSPB) to defend competitive merit recruitment and promotion from political encroachment. A separate Federal Labor Relations Authority (FLRA) was set up to administer collective bargaining and to address individual personnel grievances. The third new agency, the Office of Personnel Management (OPM), was created to manage recruiting, testing, training, and the retirement system. The Senior Executive Service—a top management rank for civil servants—was also created to recognize and foster "public management" as a profession and to facilitate the movement of "super-grade" career officials across agencies and departments.[47]

Carter also tried to impose a stringent budgetary process on all executive agencies. Called "zero-based budgeting," it was a method of budgeting from the bottom up whereby each agency was required to rejustify its entire mission rather than merely its next year's increase. Zero-based budgeting did not succeed, but the effort was not lost on President Reagan. From Carter's "bottom-up" approach, Reagan went to a "top-down" approach, whereby the initial budgetary decisions would be made in the White House and the agencies would be required to abide by those decisions. This process converted the OMB into an agency of policy determination and presidential management.[48] President George H. W. Bush took Reagan's centralization strategy even further in using the White House staff instead of cabinet secretaries for managing the executive branch.[49]

President Clinton was often criticized for the way he managed his administration. His loose approach to administration even included all-night "bull sessions," complete with pizza. Yet, as we have seen, Clinton also inaugurated one of the most systematic efforts "to change the way government does business" in his NPR. Heavily influenced by the theories of management consultants who prized decentralization, customer responsiveness, and employee initiative, Clinton sought to infuse these new practices into government.[50]

George W. Bush was the first president with a degree in business. His management strategy followed a standard business school dictum: select skilled subordinates and delegate responsibility to them. Bush followed this model closely in his appointment of highly experienced officials to cabinet positions and in his selection of Dick Cheney for vice president. But critics contended that the Bush administration's distrust of the bureaucracy led the administration to exercise inappropriate political control. Political appointees occupied high agency positions that allowed them to suppress the work of agency experts when they threatened to undercut the administration's political goals.

The Obama administration has sought to reinvigorate federal agencies, which reflects the Democrats' greater support for strong government institutions. Obama's approach to the managerial presidency features a deep belief in the importance of scientific expertise in government service. The president's appointments to head key regulatory agencies, including the EPA, OSHA, and the FDA, reflected this conviction. Some of the new agency leaders were well-known academic experts; others had won recognition for their achievements in state or local administrative settings.

Decades of reform have increased the managerial capacity of the presidency, but such reforms themselves do not ensure democratic accountability—presidents must put their managerial powers to use. Although Ronald Reagan was an enormously popular president, he was faulted for his disengaged management style. During his administration, the National Security Council staff was not prevented from running its own policies toward Iran and Nicaragua for at least two years (1985–86) after Congress had explicitly restricted activities toward Nicaragua and the president had forbidden negotiations with Iran. The Tower Commission, appointed to investigate the Iran-Contra affair, concluded that "at no time did [President Reagan] insist upon accountability and performance review."[51] In 2008, Congress held hearings to investigate the financial crisis. Members grilled banking and insurance executives and the former chairman of the Federal Reserve, Alan Greenspan. Greenspan, once hailed as a financial wizard, memorably admitted that inadequate regulation of lending practices had played a role in causing the crisis.

Congressional Oversight

Congress is constitutionally essential to responsible bureaucracy because ultimately the key to bureaucratic responsibility is legislation. When a law is passed and its intent is clear, the accountability for implementation of that law is also clear. Then the president knows what to "faithfully execute," and the responsible agency

Congress holds hearings to determine whether federal agencies are successfully performing their jobs. After a shooting at the Navy Yard in 2013, the Senate Homeland Security and Governmental Affairs Committee interviewed administrators from the Office of Personnel Management, Office of Management and the Budget, Government Accountability Office, and Office of the Director of National Intelligence on procedures for government clearances and background checks.

oversight the effort by Congress, through hearings, investigations, and other techniques, to exercise control over the activities of executive agencies

for critical analysis

What are some of the important topics on which Congress has held oversight hearings? What did Congress try to achieve by holding oversight hearings?

understands what is expected of it. But when Congress enacts vague legislation, agencies must resort to their own interpretations. The president and the federal courts often step in to tell agencies what the legislation intended. So do the most intensely interested groups. Yet when everybody from president to courts to interest groups gets involved in the actual interpretation of legislative intent, to whom and to what is the agency accountable?

Congress's answer is **oversight**. The more power Congress has delegated to the executive, the more it has sought to re-involve itself in directing the interpretation of laws through committee and subcommittee oversight of each agency. The standing committee system in Congress is well suited to oversight, inasmuch as most of the congressional committees and subcommittees have jurisdictions roughly parallel to one or more departments and agencies, and members of Congress who sit on these committees can develop expertise equal to that of the bureaucrats. The exception is the Department of Homeland Security, whose activities are now overseen by more than 20 committees. One of the central recommendations of the 9/11 Commission—as yet unimplemented—was to create a single committee with oversight of the Department of Homeland Security.

The most visible indication of Congress's oversight efforts is the use of public hearings, before which bureaucrats and other witnesses are summoned to discuss and defend agency budgets and past decisions. In 2013 and 2014, for example, Congress held high-profile hearings on topics as diverse as the attack on the American mission in Benghazi, Libya; reform of the Postal Service; and security concerns about the Department of Health and Human Services' new Healthcare.gov website.

The data drawn from systematic studies of congressional committee and subcommittee hearings and meetings show quite dramatically that Congress has tried through oversight to keep pace with the expansion of the executive branch. The annual number of oversight hearings has grown over time as the bureaucracy has expanded. Oversight hearings in both the Senate and the House increased dramatically in the 1970s in the aftermath of the Watergate scandal. In recent years, oversight has become a topic of substantial political concern. After the Republicans took over Congress in 1995, they concentrated their oversight power on investigating scandal. When George W. Bush became president in 2001, congressional oversight virtually disappeared. In the words of the congressional scholars Thomas Mann and Norman Ornstein, Republican members of Congress saw "themselves as field lieutenants in the president's army far more than they [did] as members of a separate and independent branch of government."[52] In Mann and Ornstein's view, Congress's failure to exercise its oversight role led to poor government performance and bureaucracies that were not accountable to the American people. After winning back Congress in 2006, the Democrats revived the oversight role, holding hearings on such issues as the use of government contractors in the Iraq and Afghanistan wars and the Troubled Asset Relief Program (TARP), which was instituted to help bail out the banks in 2008. When Republicans took control of the House in 2010, oversight hearings focused on the Democratic administration's programs, such as the Consumer Financial Protection Bureau and, in 2013, the troubled rollout of the Affordable Care Act.

Individual members of Congress can also carry out oversight inquiries. Such standard congressional "casework" can address significant questions of public responsibility even when they are motivated only by the demands of an individual constituent. Oversight also encompasses the communications between congressional staff and agency staff. In addition, Congress has created for itself three large agencies whose obligations are to engage in constant research on matters related to the executive branch. These are the GAO, the Congressional Research Service (CRS), and the Congressional Budget Office (CBO), each designed to give Congress information independent of the information it can get directly from the executive branch through hearings and other communications.[53] Another source of information for oversight is directly from citizens through the FOIA, which, as we have seen, gives ordinary citizens the right to gain access to agency files and agency data. Nevertheless, the information citizens gain through FOIA can be made effective only through the institutionalized channels of congressional committees and, though rarely, through public interest litigation in the federal courts.

The increasing use of federal contractors raises new questions about democratic accountability. When government work is outsourced, federal monitoring is essential to ensure that funds are spent in accordance with the public will and to confirm that the costs are fair. Yet government contracting is now so extensive that such monitoring has become extremely difficult. Even with monitoring, accountability may be hard to achieve; many of the mechanisms of democratic accountability do not apply to private firms that contract to perform public work. For example, private corporations can resist FOIA requests, and they are not constrained by the same ethics rules as public employees. Moreover, because private firms do not have to disclose information about their operations in the same way that public bureaucracies do, Congress has much more limited oversight. The move to privatization clearly presents major challenges to democratic accountability.

One of the most troubling aspects of outsourcing is that private contractors donate millions of dollars each year to political campaigns and lobbying. As Figure 14.6 shows, the top 20 federal contractors have substantially increased their spending on lobbying in recent years. These expenditures raise troubling questions about how assertive members of Congress are likely to be in scrutinizing the business practices of important political donors or in moving activities from the private to the public sector.

for critical analysis

Through elected officials (the president and Congress), the public can achieve some control over the bureaucracy. What are the relative advantages and disadvantages of presidential and congressional control of the bureaucracy?

Bureaucracy
and Your Future

Americans' views about the federal government bureaucracy present something of a paradox. On the one hand, the public expresses dislike for "big government," exemplified by bureaucracy. From this perspective, the federal government is too large, inherently wasteful, and at odds with individual freedom. On the other hand, Americans support many government programs and have high expectations for government. Indeed, high expectations lead many Americans to blame bureaucrats when the country faces problems, such as the prolonged economic downturn of recent years. One consequence of these divergent views is that public discussion about bureaucracy is often high on emotion and short on facts.

Arguments contending that the federal government is too large ignore the fact that the number of government employees has not grown disproportionately large when compared with the size of the American workforce. Charges that government wastes the taxpayers' money must also be put into perspective. As we have seen in this chapter, outsourcing government activities to private contractors does not offer a remedy for wasteful spending. In fact, private firms may be more wasteful than the public sector unless there is strong government oversight of private activities. Finally, it is true that bureaucratic rules often limit the freedom of individuals and corporations. But the laws that bureaucracies implement were enacted by our elected representatives in Congress. They are, in fact, the product of our democratic political system. As these considerations suggest, building a bureaucracy that reflects American values is not a simple task. Adequate congressional oversight is one important part of the solution because a bureaucracy that is shielded from the public eye may wind up pursuing its own interests rather than those of the public. Even so, an administration whose every move is subject to intense public scrutiny may be hamstrung in its efforts to carry out the public interest. Finding the right balance between bureaucratic autonomy and public scrutiny is a central task of creating an effective government; it requires both presidential and congressional vigilance to build an effective and responsive bureaucracy.

The emergence of "big data" is likely to change the way bureaucracies operate in the future. Big data refers to very large data sets that compile information on a wide range of topics including climate, traffic, health, and the NSA's huge database of phone calls and use of social media. Big data has the potential to improve government performance by linking sources of information that were previously unconnected. It also will allow the government to analyze information that was stored as text or went uncollected. Advances in government's ability to implement programs in public health, food safety, and transportation are only the beginning of what big data promises. At the same time, however, big data poses a threat to individual privacy, as the revelations about the NSA's data suggests. As bureaucracies tap into the promise of big data to create more effective programs, a close public eye on the implications for the right to privacy will be needed. How might big data improve the government's delivery of services in the future? What additional safeguards might be needed to protect individuals' privacy?

plugin

Inform

Learn about the role of the American bureaucracy at www.ushistory.org /gov/8.asp.

Express

Identify three federal or state bureaucratic institutions that have directly affected your life—such as the DMV, the IRS, the FAA, the FDA, or any of the other agencies mentioned in this chapter. Write a couple of sentences about your interaction with each agency and whether it performed its role well in your experience.

Connect

Find at least one federal agency's Facebook page and see what types of information members of the bureaucracy are posting. Consider posting a response if the rules and regulations being discussed affect you.

Act

Share information from a federal agency's website, such as the Department of Education's Federal Student Aid page or the Department of Justice's FOIA page, with friends or classmates, along with your thoughts on why it is important.

studyguide

Bureaucracy and Bureaucrats

> **Define bureaucracy, and describe the basic features of the executive branch (pp. 561–69)**

Bureaucracy is defined as the complex structure of offices, tasks, and rules that private and public organizations use to coordinate the work of their personnel. The federal executive branch is composed of cabinet departments, independent agencies, government corporations, and independent regulatory commissions. Although many people express concerns that the national government is too large, the federal service has actually grown very little over the last 35 years. Through their rule making and enforcement decisions, the federal service touches on many important aspects of daily life.

Key Terms
bureaucracy (p. 561)

implementation (p. 562)

merit system (p. 564)

department (p. 567)

independent agency (p. 567)

government corporation (p. 567)

Practice Quiz

1. What task must bureaucrats perform if Congress charges them with enforcing a law through explicit directions?
   a) constitutional revisions
   b) implementation
   c) interpretation
   d) lawmaking
   e) quasi-judicial decision making

2. State and local laws similar to the Civil Service Act of 1883 require that appointees to public office
   a) pledge an oath of loyalty to the United States.
   b) be qualified for the job to which they are appointed.
   c) not belong to any political party.
   d) cannot be fired for any reason.
   e) cannot serve more than four years.

3. Which of the following best describes the size of the federal service in the past 35 years?
   a) rampant, exponential growth
   b) no change in size
   c) decrease in the number of federal employees as a percentage of the work force
   d) major growth as compared to the growth of the economy and the society
   e) the federal service has been eliminated in favor of more state government employees

4. Which of the following are *not* part of the executive branch?
   a) Cabinet departments
   b) government corporations
   c) independent regulatory commissions
   d) agencies
   e) All of the above are parts of the executive branch.

5. Which of the following is an example of a government corporation?
   a) National Aeronautics and Space Administration
   b) Amtrak
   c) Social Security Administration
   d) National Science Foundation
   e) Federal Express

Goals of the Federal Bureaucracy

> **Describe the major goals we expect federal agencies to promote (pp. 569–80)**

The federal bureaucracy promotes the public welfare through a diverse set of services, products, and regulations. Some federal agencies, such as the Department of Defense, the Department of Justice, and the Department of Homeland Security, protect the country against internal and external security threats. Other federal agencies, such as the Federal Reserve System and the Internal Revenue

Service, promote the public's welfare by helping maintain a strong economy.

Key Terms
regulatory agency (p. 570)

fiscal policy (p. 579)

Federal Reserve System (p. 579)

revenue agency (p. 579)

Practice Quiz

6. A stable relationship between a bureaucratic agency, a clientele group, and a legislative committee is called
   a) a standing committee.
   b) a conference committee.
   c) a cabinet.
   d) an issue network.
   e) an iron triangle.

7. Americans refer to government policy about banks, credit, and currency as
   a) interstate commerce policy.
   b) deficit policy.
   c) fiscal policy.
   d) monetary policy.
   e) regulatory policy.

Can the Bureaucracy Be Reformed?

Evaluate some of the ways politicians have tried to make the bureaucracy more efficient (pp. 580–87)

Many Americans express frustration with the performance of the federal bureaucracy. As a result, politicians have frequently explored various methods of making the federal bureaucracy more efficient. In general, politicians have attempted four strategies to promote bureaucratic reform: "reinventing" government, termination of programs, devolution, and privatization.

Key Terms

devolution (p. 583)
privatization (p. 584)

Practice Quiz

8. Which president instituted the bureaucratic reform of the National Performance Review?
   a) Richard Nixon
   b) Lyndon Johnson
   c) Jimmy Carter
   d) Bill Clinton
   e) George W. Bush

9. Devolution refers to
   a) the gradual decline in efficiency that always comes when government begins to implement a new program.
   b) moving all or part of a program from the public sector to the private sector.
   c) a policy of reducing or eliminating regulatory restraints on the conduct of individuals or private institutions.
   d) a policy to remove a program from one level of government by passing it down to a lower level of government.
   e) reducing the overall number of regulatory agencies in the federal bureaucracy.

10. Which of the following is *not* a way in which the bureaucracy might be reduced?
    a) devolution
    b) termination
    c) privatization
    d) eminent domain
    e) None of the above are ways in which the bureaucracy might be reduced.

11. Which of the following best describes the changes in government contracting since 2000?
    a) Spending on government contracts has decreased while the number of government contracts subject to open competition has increased.
    b) Spending on government contracts has decreased while the number of government contracts subject to open competition has decreased.
    c) Government contracting ended in 2000 as a result of the Supreme Court's decision in *Immigration and Naturalization Service v. Chadha*.
    d) Spending on government contracts has increased while the number of government contracts subject to open competition has decreased.
    e) Spending on government contracts has increased while the number of government contracts subject to open competition has increased.

Managing the Bureaucracy

Explain why it is often difficult to control the bureaucracy (pp. 587–91)

The federal bureaucracy provides the expertise that is needed to implement the law. However, parts of the bureaucracy can also become entrenched organizations that serve their own interests rather than the public will.

While the emergence of the "managerial presidency" during the twentieth century has given the president more authority over the bureaucracy, presidents have sometimes used their managerial capacities to limit rather than promote democratic accountability. Congress can exert control over the federal bureaucracy by enacting specific legislation and engaging in vigorous oversight.

Key Term

oversight (p. 590)

Practice Quiz

12. The executive branch is kept accountable to the public mainly by
    a) the judiciary.
    b) direct, popular election of top bureaucrats.
    c) the president and Congress.
    d) the media.
    e) administrative adjudication.

13. The concept of *oversight* refers to the effort made by
    a) Congress to make executive agencies accountable for their actions.
    b) the president to make executive agencies accountable for their actions.
    c) the president to make Congress accountable for its actions.
    d) the courts to make executive agencies responsible for their actions.
    e) the states to make the executive branch accountable for its actions.

14. Which of the following agencies were created by Congress to engage in research on problems taking place in or confronted by the executive branch?
    a) Government Accountability Office, Congressional Research Service, Congressional Budget Office
    b) Department of Justice, Department of the Interior, Department of the Treasury
    c) Congressional Oversight Organization, Bureau of Government Performance, National Performance Review Association
    d) Office of Management and Budget, Council of Economic Advisors, Oversight and Government Reform
    e) Government Accountability Office, National Performance Review, Troubled Asset Relief Program

For Further Reading

Aberbach, Joel D., and Mark A. Peterson, eds. *Institutions of American Democracy: The Executive Branch* (Institutions of American Democracy Series). New York: Oxford University Press, 2006.

Arnold, Peri E. *Making the Managerial Presidency: Comprehensive Organization Planning.* Princeton, NJ: Princeton University Press, 1986.

Gormley, William, and Stephen Balla. *Bureaucracy and Democracy: Accountability and Performance.* 3rd ed. Washington, DC: CQ Press, 2012.

Kettl, Donald F. *System under Stress: The Challenge to 21st Century Government.* 3rd ed. Los Angeles: Sage/CQ Press , 2014.

Kettl, Donald F., and James W. Fesler. *The Politics of the Administrative Process.* 4th ed. Washington, DC: CQ Press, 2008.

Light, Paul C. *A Government Ill Executed: The Decline of the Federal Service and How to Reverse It.* Cambridge, MA: Harvard University Press, 2008.

Verkuil, Paul. *Outsourcing Sovereignty: Why Privatization of Government Functions Threatens Democracy and What We Can Do about It.* New York: Cambridge University Press, 2007.

Weiner, Tom. *Legacy of Ashes: The History of the CIA.* New York: Doubleday, 2007.

Wildavsky, Aaron. *The New Politics of the Budget Process.* 2nd ed. New York: HarperCollins, 1992.

Wilson, James Q. *Bureaucracy: What Government Agencies Do and Why They Do It.* New York: Basic Books, 1989.

Recommended Websites

Central Intelligence Agency
www.cia.gov

The Central Intelligence Agency (CIA) is one of several bureaucracies responsible for providing national security. A major problem facing this clandestine agency is how to provide security and meet the public's right to know what the government is doing. At the official website for the CIA, see what questions are often asked.

Department of Homeland Security
www.dhs.gov

The Department of Homeland Security was created after 9/11 to promote bureaucratic communication and domestic security. See what the department is doing to protect America from foreign threats.

Federal Emergency Management Agency
www.fema.org

In the aftermath of Hurricane Katrina, the Federal Emergency Management Agency (FEMA) became infamous for its role in the disaster relief efforts. View the disaster history of your state and see what FEMA is currently doing to prevent disasters and assist Americans in need.

Official U.S. Executive Branch Websites
www.loc.gov

This resource page at the Library of Congress website provides links to every federal department, independent agency, and regulatory commission in the federal bureaucracy.

Project on Government Oversight
www.pogo.org

The Project on Government Oversight is an independent, nonprofit organization that seeks to make government more accountable by investigating corruption and misconduct. Originally set up to focus on the military, this organization now examines all types of government bureaucracies.

Reason Foundation
reason.org/areas/topic/privatization

The Reason Foundation is dedicated to promoting libertarian principles and limited government. Their website includes studies and opinion pieces on a range of policy issues, including many related to the size and effectiveness of the federal bureaucracy.

U.S. Agency for International Development
www.usaid.gov

In 1961 Congress created the U.S. Agency for International Development (USAID) to provide economic and social development assistance to foreign countries. Often criticized for promoting American values and foreign policy objectives, USAID is currently involved in numerous global issues.

The Supreme Court is America's highest court. Although often viewed as the least political of the three branches, the Court's rulings touch on major political issues and affect ordinary Americans in many ways, from health care to immigration to free speech.

The Federal Courts

15

WHAT GOVERNMENT DOES AND WHY IT MATTERS The judicial branch of the U.S. federal government is headed by the Supreme Court. Many Americans view the Supreme Court as aloof and apolitical, because unlike the president and members of Congress, the judges who sit on the Supreme Court are appointed, not elected. Thus they do not need to raise money or campaign the way that other politicians do. But the issues that the Supreme Court decides are often as political as those voted on in the House and Senate, and the Supreme Court is often asked to hear questions that touch the lives of ordinary Americans, including students, in a very direct and meaningful way. One recent example, from 2007, is the case of *Morse v. Frederick*.[1] This case dealt with the policies of Juneau-Douglas High School in Juneau, Alaska. In 2002 the Olympic torch relay passed through Juneau on its way to Salt Lake City for the opening of the Winter Olympics. As the torch passed Juneau-Douglas High, a senior, Joseph Frederick, unfurled a banner that read, "Bong Hits 4 Jesus." The school's principal promptly suspended Frederick, who then brought suit for reinstatement, alleging that his right to freedom of speech had been violated.[2]

Like most of America's public schools, Juneau-Douglas High prohibits on school grounds any assemblies or expressions that advocate illegal drug use. Schools say that some federal aid is contingent on this policy. Civil libertarians see such policies as restricting students' right to free speech—a right that has been recognized by the Supreme Court since a 1969 case in which it ruled that an Iowa public school could not prohibit students from wearing antiwar armbands. Unfortunately for Joseph Frederick, today's Supreme Court has a more conservative cast than it did in 1969. Speaking for the

Court's majority, Chief Justice John G. Roberts said that the First Amendment did not require schools to permit students to advocate illegal drug use. This decision affected not only Joseph Frederick but also millions of other students whose views might be seen as inappropriate by school administrators. Far from being a remote institution, the Supreme Court's reach includes every public school in America.

Every year, nearly 25 million cases are tried in American courts, and one American in every nine is directly involved in litigation. Cases can arise from disputes between citizens, from efforts by government agencies to punish wrongdoing, or from citizens' efforts to prove that their rights have been infringed on as a result of government action—or inaction. Many critics of the U.S. legal system assert that Americans have become too litigious (ready to use the courts for all purposes). But the heavy use that Americans make of the courts is also an indication of the extent of conflict in American society. And given the existence of social conflict, it is far better that Americans seek to settle their differences through the courts than resort to violence or otherwise take matters into their own hands. The framers of the American Constitution called the Supreme Court the "least dangerous branch" of American government. Today, though, it is not unusual to hear the Court described as an all-powerful "imperial judiciary." Before we can understand this transformation and its consequences, we must look in some detail at America's judicial process.

chaptergoals

- Identify the general types of cases and types of courts in our legal system (pp. 601–6)

- Describe the different levels of federal courts and their functions (pp. 606–12)

- Explain how the Supreme Court exercises the power of judicial review (pp. 612–20)

- Describe the process the Supreme Court follows in the exercise of its power of judicial review (pp. 620–28)

- Consider the personal and political influences on judges and the courts (pp. 628–34)

● The Legal System

Identify the general types of cases and types of courts in our legal system

Originally, a "court" was the place where a sovereign ruled—where the king or queen governed. Settling disputes between citizens was part of governing. In modern democracies, courts and judges have taken over the power to settle conflicts by hearing the facts on both sides and deciding which side possesses the greater merit. But since judges are not kings, they must have a basis for their authority. That basis in the United States is the Constitution and the law. Courts decide cases by hearing the facts on both sides of a quarrel and applying the relevant law or principle to the facts. This can be a sensitive matter because courts have been given the authority to settle disputes between not only citizens but also citizens and the government itself, where the courts are obliged to maintain the same neutrality and impartiality as they do in disputes involving two citizens. This is the essence of the "rule of law": that "the state" and its officials must be judged by the same laws as the citizenry.

Cases and the Law

Court cases in the United States proceed under two broad categories of law: criminal law and civil law, each with myriad subdivisions.

Cases of **criminal law** are those in which the government charges an individual with violating a statute that has been enacted to protect public health, safety, morals, or welfare. In criminal cases, the government is always the **plaintiff** (the party that brings charges) and alleges that a criminal violation has been committed by a named **defendant**. Most criminal cases arise in state and municipal courts and involve matters ranging from traffic offenses to robbery and murder. Although the great bulk of criminal law is still a state matter, a large and growing body of federal criminal law deals with matters ranging from tax evasion and mail fraud to acts of

criminal law the branch of law that regulates the conduct of individuals, defines crimes, and specifies punishment for criminal acts

plaintiff the individual or organization that brings a complaint in court

defendant the one against whom a complaint is brought in a criminal or civil case

In criminal cases, the government charges an individual with violating a statute protecting health, safety, morals, or welfare. Most such cases arise in state and municipal courts. Here, an Illinois county court hears testimony in a murder case.

terrorism and the sale of narcotics. Defendants found guilty of criminal violations may be fined or sent to prison.

civil law the branch of law that deals with disputes that do not involve criminal penalties

Cases of **civil law** involve disputes among individuals, groups, corporations, and other private entities, or between such litigants and the government, in which no criminal violation is charged. Unlike in criminal cases, the losers in civil cases cannot be fined or sent to prison, although they may be required to pay monetary damages for their actions. In a civil case, the one who brings a complaint is the plaintiff and the one against whom the complaint is brought is the defendant. The two most common types of civil cases involve contracts and torts. In a typical contract case, an individual or corporation charges that it has suffered because of another's violation of a specific agreement between the two. For example, the Smith Manufacturing Corporation may charge that Jones Distributors failed to honor an agreement to deliver raw materials at a specified time, causing Smith to lose business. Smith asks the court to order Jones to compensate it for the damage it allegedly suffered. In a typical tort case, one individual charges that he has been injured by another's negligence or malfeasance. Medical malpractice suits are one example of tort cases. Another important area of civil law is administrative law, which involves disputes over the jurisdiction, procedures, or authority of administrative agencies. A plaintiff may assert, for example, that an agency did not follow proper procedures when issuing new rules and regulations. A court will then examine the agency's conduct in light of the Administrative Procedure Act, the legislation that governs agency rule making.

precedent prior case whose principles are used by judges as the basis for their decision in a present case

In deciding cases, courts apply statutes (laws) and legal **precedents** (prior decisions). State and federal statutes, for example, often govern the conditions under which contracts are and are not legally binding. Jones Distributors might argue that it was not obliged to fulfill its contract with the Smith Manufacturing Corporation because actions by Smith, such as the failure to make promised payments, constituted fraud under state law. Precedents established in previous cases also guide courts' decisions in new cases. Attorneys for a physician being sued for malpractice might search for prior instances in which courts ruled that actions similar to those of their client did not constitute negligence. Such precedents are applied under the doctrine of **stare decisis**, a Latin phrase meaning "let the decision stand."

stare decisis literally, "let the decision stand"; the doctrine that a previous decision by a court applies as a precedent in similar cases until that decision is overruled

If a case involves the actions of the federal government or a state government, a court may also be asked to examine whether the government's conduct was consistent with the Constitution. In a criminal case, for example, defendants might assert that their constitutional rights were violated when the police searched their property. Similarly, in a civil case involving federal or state restrictions on land development, plaintiffs might assert that government actions violated the Fifth Amendment's prohibition against taking private property without just compensation. Thus, both civil and criminal cases may raise questions of constitutional law.

Types of Courts

In the United States, systems of courts have been established both by the federal government and by the governments of the individual states. Both systems have several levels, as shown in Figure 15.1. More than 97 percent of all court cases in the United States are heard in state courts. The overwhelming majority of criminal cases, for example, involve violations of state laws prohibiting such actions as murder, robbery, fraud, theft, and assault. If such a case is brought to trial, it will be heard in a state **trial court**, in front of a judge and sometimes a jury, who will determine whether

trial court the first court to hear a criminal or civil case

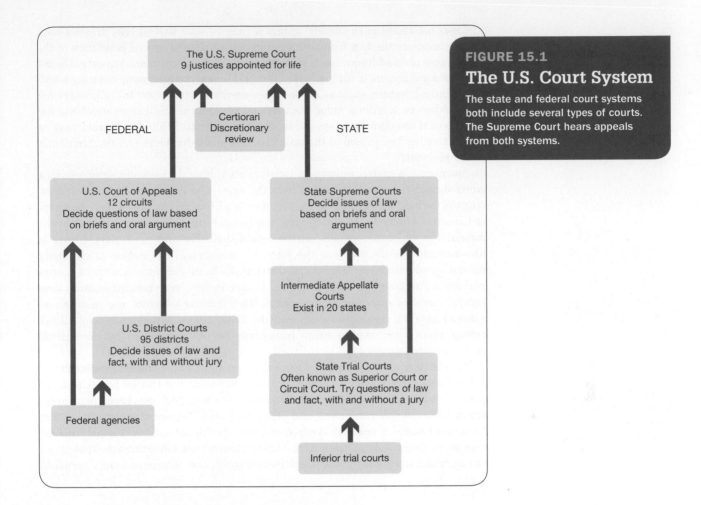

FIGURE 15.1

The U.S. Court System

The state and federal court systems both include several types of courts. The Supreme Court hears appeals from both systems.

the defendant violated state law. If the defendant is convicted, she may appeal the conviction to a higher court, such as a state **court of appeals**, and from there to a court of last resort, usually called the state's **supreme court**. The government is not entitled to appeal if the defendant is found not guilty in a criminal case.

Similarly, in civil cases, most litigation is brought in the courts established by the state in which the activity in question took place. For example, a patient bringing suit against a physician for malpractice would file the suit in the appropriate court in the state where the alleged malpractice occurred. The judge hearing the case would apply state law and state precedent to the matter at hand. (There is some variation in court structure among the 50 states.) In a civil case, such as malpractice, either side may appeal the verdict if they lose.

The party filing an appeal, known as an appellant, usually must show that the trial court made a legal error in deciding the case. Appeals courts do not hear witnesses or examine additional evidence and will only consider new facts under unusual circumstances. Thus, for example, a physician who loses a malpractice case might appeal on the basis that the trial court misapplied the relevant law or incorrectly instructed the jury. It should be noted that in both criminal and civil matters, most cases are settled before trial through negotiated agreements between the parties. In criminal cases these agreements are called **plea bargains**.

court of appeals a court that hears appeals of trial court decisions

supreme court the highest court in a particular state or in the United States. This court primarily serves an appellate function

plea bargain a negotiated agreement in a criminal case in which a defendant agrees to plead guilty in return for the state's agreement to reduce the severity of the criminal charge or prison sentence the defendant is facing

jurisdiction the sphere of a court's power and authority

Cases are heard in the federal courts if they involve federal laws, treaties with other nations, or the U.S. Constitution; these areas are the official **jurisdiction** of the federal courts. In addition, any case in which the U.S. government is a party is heard in the federal courts. If, for example, an individual is charged with violating a federal criminal statute, such as evading the payment of income taxes, charges are brought before a federal judge by a federal prosecutor. Civil cases involving the citizens of more than one state and in which more than $75,000 is at stake may be heard in either the federal or the state courts, usually depending on the preference of the plaintiff.

But even if a matter belongs in federal court, how do we know which federal court should exercise jurisdiction over the case? The jurisdiction of each federal court is derived from the U.S. Constitution and federal statutes. Over the years, as Congress enacted statutes creating the federal judicial system, it specified the jurisdiction of each type of court it established. For the most part, Congress has assigned jurisdictions on the basis of geography. The nation is currently, by statute, divided into 94 judicial districts. Each of the 94 U.S. district courts, including one court for each of three U.S. territories, exercises jurisdiction over federal cases arising within its district. The judicial districts are, in turn, organized into 11 regional circuits and the D.C. circuit (see Figure 15.2). Each circuit court exercises appellate jurisdiction over cases heard by the district courts within its region.

original jurisdiction the authority to initially consider a case. Distinguished from appellate jurisdiction, which is the authority to hear appeals from a lower court's decision

Article III of the Constitution gives the Supreme Court **original jurisdiction** in a limited variety of classes including (1) cases between the United States and one of the 50 states, (2) cases between two or more states, (3) cases involving foreign ambassadors or other ministers, and (4) cases brought by one state against citizens of another state or against a foreign country. Article III assigns original jurisdiction in all other federal cases to the lower courts that Congress was authorized to establish. Importantly, the Constitution gives the Supreme Court appellate

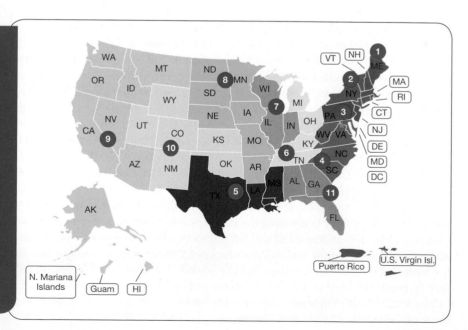

FIGURE 15.2

Federal Appellate Court Circuits

The 94 federal district courts are organized into 12 regional circuits: the 11 shown here, plus the District of Columbia, which has its own circuit. Each circuit court hears appeals from lower federal courts within the circuit. A 13th federal circuit court, the U.S. Court of Appeals for the Federal Circuit, hears appeals from a number of specialized courts such as the U.S. Court of Federal Claims.

SOURCE: www.uscourts.gov/court_locator .aspx (accessed 7/27/10).

jurisdiction in all federal cases. Courts of original jurisdiction are the courts that are responsible for discovering the facts in a controversy and creating the record on which a judgment is based. In courts that have appellate jurisdiction, judges receive cases after the factual record is established by the trial court. Ordinarily, new facts cannot be presented before appellate courts.

Geography, however, is not the only basis for federal court jurisdiction. Congress has also established several specialized courts that have nationwide original jurisdiction in certain types of cases. These include the U.S. Court of International Trade, created to deal with trade and customs issues, and the U.S. Court of Federal Claims, which handles damage suits against the United States. Congress has also established a court with nationwide appellate jurisdiction, the U.S. Court of Appeals for the Federal Circuit, which hears appeals involving patent law and those arising from the decisions of the trade and claims courts. Other federal courts assigned specialized jurisdictions by Congress include the U.S. Court of Appeals for Veterans Claims, which exercises exclusive jurisdiction over cases involving veterans' claims, and the U.S. Court of Military Appeals, which deals with questions of law arising from trials by court martial.

With the exception of the claims court and the Court of Appeals for the Federal Circuit, these specialized courts were created by Congress on the basis of the powers the legislature exercises under Article I, rather than Article III, of the Constitution. Article III is designed to protect judges from political pressure by granting them life tenure and prohibiting reduction of their salaries while they serve. The judges of Article I courts, by contrast, are appointed by the president for fixed terms of 15 years and are not protected by the Constitution from salary reduction. As a result, these "legislative courts" are generally viewed as less independent than the courts established under Article III of the Constitution. The three territorial courts (for Guam, the U.S. Virgin Islands, and Northern Mariana Islands) were also established under the provisions in Article I, and their judges are appointed for 10-year terms.

The appellate jurisdiction of the federal courts extends to cases originating in the state courts. In both civil and criminal cases, a decision of the highest state court can be appealed to the U.S. Supreme Court by raising a federal issue. A defendant who appeals a lower-court decision in federal court might assert, for example, that they were denied the right to counsel or were otherwise deprived of the **due process of law** guaranteed by the federal Constitution, or they might assert that important issues of federal law were at stake in the case. The U.S. Supreme Court is not obligated to accept such appeals, and will do so only if it believes that the matter has considerable national significance. In addition, in criminal cases, defendants who have been convicted in a state court may request a **writ of habeas corpus** from a federal district court. Sometimes known as the "Great Writ," habeas corpus is a court order to the authorities to release a prisoner deemed to be held in violation of his legal rights. In 1867 its distrust of southern courts led Congress to authorize federal district judges to issue such writs to prisoners who they believed had been deprived of constitutional rights in state court. Generally speaking, state defendants seeking a federal writ of habeas corpus must show that they have exhausted all available state remedies and must raise issues not previously raised in their state appeals. Federal courts of appeals and, ultimately, the U.S. Supreme Court have appellate jurisdiction for federal district court habeas decisions.

Although the federal courts hear only a small fraction of all the civil and criminal cases decided each year in the United States, their decisions are extremely

due process of law the right of every individual against arbitrary action by national or state governments

writ of habeas corpus a court order that the individual in custody be brought into court and shown the cause for detention; habeas corpus is guaranteed by the Constitution and can be suspended only in cases of rebellion or invasion

important. It is in the federal courts that the Constitution and federal laws that govern all Americans are interpreted and their meaning and significance established. Moreover, it is in the federal courts that the powers and limitations of the increasingly powerful national government are tested. Finally, through their power to review the decisions of the state courts, it is ultimately the federal courts that dominate the American judicial system.

● Federal Courts

Describe the different levels of federal courts and their functions

In 2010 federal district courts (the lowest federal level) received 361,323 cases. Though large, this number is approximately 3 percent of the number of cases heard by state courts (see Figure 15.3). The federal courts of appeal listened to 55,992 cases in 2010, and about 15 percent of the verdicts were appealed to the U.S. Supreme Court. Most of the cases filed with the Supreme Court are dismissed without a ruling on their merits. The Court has broad latitude to decide what cases it will hear, and generally listens to only those cases it deems to raise the most important issues. Only 76 cases were given full-dress Supreme Court review in 2011–12.[3]

Federal Trial Courts

Most of the cases of original federal jurisdiction are handled by the federal district courts. Although the Constitution gives the Supreme Court original jurisdiction in several types of cases, such as those affecting ambassadors and those in which a state is one of the parties, most original jurisdiction goes to the lowest courts—the trial courts.

The 94 federal district court are staffed by 679 federal district judges. District judges are assigned to district courts according to the workload; the busiest of these courts may have as many as 28 judges. Only one judge is assigned to each case, except where statutes provide for three-judge courts to deal with special issues. The routines and procedures of the federal district courts are essentially the same as those of the lower state courts, except that federal procedural requirements tend to be stricter. States, for example, do not have to provide a grand jury, a 12-member trial jury, or a unanimous jury verdict. Federal courts must follow all these procedures.

Federal Appellate Courts

Roughly 20 percent of all lower-court cases, along with appeals from some federal agency decisions, are subsequently reviewed by federal appeals courts. As noted, the country is divided geographically into 11 regional circuits and the D.C. circuit, each of which has a U.S. Court of Appeals. A 13th appellate court, the U.S. Court of Appeals for the Federal Circuit, has a subject matter, rather than a geographical, jurisdiction.

Except for cases selected for review by the Supreme Court, decisions made by the appeals courts are final. Because of this finality, certain safeguards have been built into the system. The most important is the provision of more than

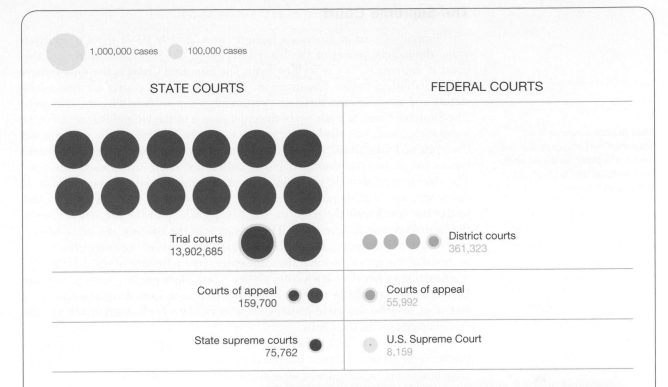

1,000,000 cases   100,000 cases

STATE COURTS   FEDERAL COURTS

Trial courts
13,902,685

District courts
361,323

Courts of appeal
159,700

Courts of appeal
55,992

State supreme courts
75,762

U.S. Supreme Court
8,159

FIGURE 15.3

Caseloads of American Courts

This figure shows the total incoming caseloads of U.S. courts in 2010 (the most recent year for which complete state court data are available). More than 99 percent of the cases heard in American courts every year are heard in state courts. At both the federal and the state levels, lower court decisions can be appealed to the appropriate court of appeals. Why do you think a larger percentage of federal district court decisions are appealed, as compared with state trial court decisions?

SOURCES: National Center for State Courts and the Court Statistics, www.courtstatistics.org/ (accessed 5/26/14); Supreme Court, www.supremecourt.gov/publicinfo/year-end/2010year-endreport.pdf (accessed 5/26/14).

one judge for every appeals case. Each court of appeals has from 6 to 28 permanent judgeships, depending on the workload of the circuit. Although normally three judges hear appealed cases, in some instances a larger number of judges sits together en banc.

Another safeguard is provided by the assignment of a Supreme Court justice as the circuit justice for each of the 12 circuits. The circuit justice deals with requests for special action by the Supreme Court. The most frequent and best-known action of circuit justices is that of reviewing requests for stays of execution when the full Court is unable to do so—primarily during the summer, when the Court is in recess.

The Supreme Court

The Supreme Court is America's highest court. Article III of the Constitution vests "the judicial power of the United States" in the Supreme Court, and this court is supreme in fact as well as form. The Supreme Court is the only federal court established by the Constitution. The lower federal courts are created by statute and can be restructured or, presumably, even abolished by the Congress. The Supreme Court is made up of the chief justice of the United States and eight associate justices. The **chief justice** presides over the Court's public sessions and conferences. In the Court's actual deliberations and decisions, however, the chief justice has no more authority than her colleagues. Each justice casts one vote. The chief justice, though, is always the first to speak and vote when the justices deliberate; voting then proceeds in order of seniority. In addition, if the chief justice has voted with the majority, she decides which of the justices will write the formal opinion for the court. The character of the opinion can be an important means of influencing the evolution of the law beyond the mere affirmation or denial of the appeal on hand. To some extent, the influence of the chief justice is a function of her own leadership ability. Some chief justices, such as the late Earl Warren, have been able to lead the court in a new direction. In other instances, forceful associate justices, such as the late Felix Frankfurter, are the dominant figures on the Court.

The Constitution does not specify the number of justices who should sit on the Supreme Court; Congress has the authority to change the Court's size. In the early nineteenth century, there were six Supreme Court justices; later there were seven. Congress set the number of justices at nine in 1869, and the Court has remained that size ever since. In 1937, President Franklin Delano Roosevelt, infuriated by several Supreme Court decisions that struck down New Deal programs, asked Congress to enlarge the Court so that he could add a few sympathetic justices to the bench. Although Congress balked at Roosevelt's "court packing" plan, the Court gave in to FDR's pressure and began to take a more favorable view of his policy initiatives. The president, in turn, dropped his efforts to enlarge the Court.

chief justice justice on the Supreme Court who presides over the Court's public sessions and whose official title is chief justice of the United States

The number of justices varied during the first 80 years of American history, but has held at nine since 1869. The justices hear and decide all cases as a group. Despite ideological differences, in recent years approximately half of all cases were decided by a unanimous vote of 9 to 0.

How Judges Are Appointed

Federal judges are appointed by the president and confirmed by the Senate. They are generally selected from among the more prominent or politically active members of the legal profession. Many federal judges previously served as state court judges or state or local prosecutors. Before the president makes a formal nomination, however, the senators from the candidate's own state must indicate that they support the nominee. This is an informal but seldom violated practice called **senatorial courtesy**. If one or both senators from a prospective nominee's home state belong to the president's political party, the president will almost invariably consult them and secure their blessing for the nomination. Because the president's party in the Senate will rarely support a nominee opposed by a home-state senator from its ranks, this arrangement gives these senators virtual veto power over appointments to the federal bench in their own states. Senators also see nominations to the judiciary as a way to reward important allies and contributors in their states. If the state has no senator from the president's party, the governor or members of the state's House delegation may make suggestions. The practice of "courtesy" generally does not apply to Supreme Court appointments, only to district and circuit court nominations.

Federal appeals court nominations follow much the same pattern. Since appeals court judges preside over jurisdictions that include several states, however, senators do not have so strong a role in proposing potential candidates. Instead, potential appeals court candidates are generally suggested to the president by the Justice Department or by important members of the administration. The senators from the nominee's own state are still consulted before the president will formally act.

There are no formal qualifications for service as a federal judge. In general, presidents endeavor to appoint judges who possess legal experience and good character and whose partisan and ideological views are similar to their own. Once the president has formally nominated an individual, the nominee must be considered by the Senate Judiciary Committee and confirmed by a majority vote in the full Senate. In recent years, a good deal of partisan conflict has surrounded judicial appointments. Senate Democrats have sought to prevent Republican presidents from appointing conservative judges while Senate Republicans have worked to prevent Democratic presidents from appointing liberal judges. During the early months of the Obama administration, Republicans were able to slow the judicial appointment process through filibusters and other procedural maneuvers so that only three of the president's 23 nominations for federal judgeships were confirmed by the Senate.[4] Some of Obama's allies urged the president to take a more aggressive stance, or risk allowing Republicans to block what had been considered a key Democratic priority. In November 2013 the Senate voted 52 to 48 to end the use of the filibuster against all executive branch and judicial nominees exept those to the Supreme Court. By the beginning of his sixth year in office, the president had secured the appointment of 184 new district court judges and 44 new appeals court judges.[5]

Supreme Court Appointments While political factors play an important role in the selection of district and appellate court judges, they are decisive when it comes to Supreme Court appointments. Because the high court has so much

senatorial courtesy the practice whereby the president, before formally nominating a person for a federal judgeship, seeks the indication that senators from the candidate's own state support the nomination

influence over American law and politics, virtually all presidents have made an effort to select justices who share their political philosophies.

Five of the nine current justices as of 2014 were appointed by Republican presidents (Table 15.1). This conservative majority, consisting of Chief Justice Roberts and justices Alito, Kennedy, Scalia, and Thomas, has propelled the Court in a more conservative direction in a variety of areas. In 2009 and 2010, for example, in a series of 5–4 decisions, the Court overturned limits on corporate campaign spending, ruled that the Federal Communications Commission was justified in penalizing the use of expletives on the airwaves, and blocked a suit against former attorney general John Ashcroft by a terrorist suspect alleging that the suspect had been mistreated in prison. In 2011 and 2012, however, Chief Justice Roberts responded to charges that the Court's decisions were political rather than judicial by joining the liberal bloc in two important cases. The first was the Court's decision to invalidate portions of an Arizona law designed to identify and apprehend illegal aliens.[6] The second was the Court's 5–4 decision to uphold the Affordable Care Act, President Obama's major legislative achievement. Critics had charged that the Act's requirement that all Americans purchase health insurance was unconstitutional. Roberts wrote that this requirement was just another federal tax.[7]

In recent decades, Supreme Court nominations have come to involve intense partisan struggle. Typically, after the president has named a nominee, interest groups opposed to the nomination mobilize opposition in the media, among the public, and in the Senate. When President George H. W. Bush proposed the conservative judge Clarence Thomas for the Court, for example, liberal groups launched a campaign to discredit Thomas. After extensive research into his

TABLE 15.1

Supreme Court Justices, 2014 (in Order of Seniority)

NAME	YEAR OF BIRTH	PRIOR EXPERIENCE	APPOINTED BY	YEAR OF APPOINTMENT
Antonin Scalia	1936	Law professor, federal judge	Reagan	1986
Anthony Kennedy	1936	Federal judge	Reagan	1988
Clarence Thomas	1948	Federal judge	G. H. W. Bush	1991
Ruth Bader Ginsburg	1933	Federal judge	Clinton	1993
Stephen Breyer	1938	Federal judge	Clinton	1994
John Roberts, Jr. (*Chief Justice*)	1955	Federal judge	G. W. Bush	2005
Samuel Alito	1950	Federal judge	G. W. Bush	2006
Sonia Sotomayor	1954	Federal judge	Obama	2009
Elena Kagan	1960	Solicitor general	Obama	2010

Who Are Federal Judges?

One factor among many that presidents may take into account when selecting judicial nominees is diversity. The number of Supreme Court justices is relatively small, so it is easy to count the number of African Americans (2), women (4), and Hispanics (1) who have served as Supreme Court justices. How diverse is the rest of the federal judiciary? The first section below shows the racial, ethnic, and gender composition of the lower federal courts.

Federal Judges in 2013, by Race and Gender

 = 20 federal judges

White men 2862

African American men 148

Hispanic men 86

Asian American men 24

White women 285

African American women 50

Hispanic women 30

Asian American women 10

Appointments to Federal Courts, by Administration

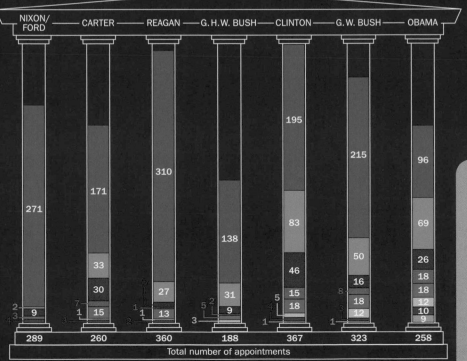

Legend:
- White men
- White women
- African American men
- African American women
- Hispanic men
- Hispanic women
- Asian American men
- Asian American women

NIXON/FORD — CARTER — REAGAN — G.H.W. BUSH — CLINTON — G.W. BUSH — OBAMA

	NIXON/FORD	CARTER	REAGAN	G.H.W. BUSH	CLINTON	G.W. BUSH	OBAMA
	271	171	310	138	195	215	96
		33			215...		69
		30	27	31	83	50	26
					46	16	18
	9	15	13	9	15 / 18	18 / 12	18 / 12 / 10 / 9
Total	289	260	360	188	367	323	258

Total number of appointments

SOURCE: Federal Judicial Center, http://www.fjc.gov/history/home.nsf/page/judges_diversity.html (accessed 5/22/14).

for critical analysis

1. Would you describe the federal judiciary as diverse? Does racial, ethnic, and gender diversity of federal judges matter? Why or why not?

2. What similarities and differences do you notice among the judicial appointments of the presidents shown? What might account for the differences in terms of the diversity of their appointees?

In 2009, President Obama's first nominee to the Supreme Court, Sonia Sotomayor, was sworn in. Although a large Democratic majority in the Senate all but guaranteed that Sotomayor would be confirmed, Republican senators asked her questions for weeks on her approach to the law.

background, opponents of the nomination were able to produce evidence suggesting that Thomas had sexually harassed a former subordinate, Anita Hill. Thomas denied the charge. After contentious Senate Judiciary Committee hearings, highlighted by testimony from both Thomas and Hill, Thomas narrowly won confirmation.

Likewise, conservative interest groups carefully scrutinized Bill Clinton's somewhat more liberal nominees, hoping to find information about them that would sabotage their appointments. During his two opportunities to name Supreme Court justices, Clinton was compelled to drop several potential appointees because of information unearthed by political opponents.

In 2009, when President Obama nominated federal Judge Sonia Sotomayor to replace retiring justice David Souter, conservatives denounced Sotomayor as a "reverse racist" because of her support for affirmative action. Many Republican senators, however, were reluctant to oppose a Hispanic nominee. For several years the GOP has made efforts to attract America's rapidly growing Hispanic population. Republicans feared that opposing Sotomayor would undermine these efforts.[8] In 2010, Republicans severely criticized Obama's nomination of Elena Kagan, solicitor general and former Harvard law dean, to replace retiring justice John Paul Stevens. Kagan was, nevertheless, confirmed by the Senate.

● The Power of the Supreme Court: Judicial Review

judicial review the power of the courts to review and, if necessary, declare actions of the legislative and executive branches invalid or unconstitutional; the Supreme Court asserted this power in *Marbury v. Madison* (1803)

> **Explain how the Supreme Court exercises the power of judicial review**

The term **judicial review** refers to the power of the judiciary to examine and, if necessary, invalidate actions undertaken by the legislative and executive branches if it finds them unconstitutional. The term is sometimes also used to describe the scrutiny that appellate courts give to the actions of trial courts, but, strictly speaking, this is an improper use. A higher court's examination of a lower court's decisions might be called "appellate review," but it is not judicial review.

Judicial Review of Acts of Congress

Because the Constitution does not give the Supreme Court the power of judicial review over congressional enactments, the Court's exercise of it is something of a usurpation. It is not known whether the framers of the Constitution opposed judicial review, but "if they intended to provide for it in the Constitution, they did so in a most obscure fashion."[9] Disputes over the intentions of the framers were settled in 1803 in the case of *Marbury v. Madison.*[10] This case arose after Thomas Jefferson replaced John Adams in the White House. Jefferson's secretary of state, James Madison, refused to deliver an official commission to William Marbury, who had been appointed to a minor office by Adams and approved by the Senate just before Adams left the presidency. Marbury petitioned the Supreme Court to order Madison to deliver the commission. Jefferson and his followers did not believe that the Court had the power to undertake such an action and might have resisted the order. Chief Justice John Marshall was determined to assert the power of the judiciary but knew he must avoid a direct confrontation with the president. Accordingly, Marshall turned down Marbury's petition but gave as his reason the unconstitutionality of the legislation upon which Marbury had based his claim. Thus, Marshall asserted the power of judicial review but did so in a way that would not provoke a battle with Jefferson. The Supreme Court's decision in this case established the power of judicial review. The Court said:

> It is emphatically the province and duty of the Judicial Department [the judicial branch] to say what the law is. Those who apply the rule to particular cases must, of necessity, expound and interpret that rule. If two laws conflict with each other, the Courts must decide on the operation of each. . . . So, if a law [e.g., a statute or treaty] be in opposition to the Constitution, if both the law and the Constitution apply to a particular case, so that the Court must either decide that case conformably to the law, disregarding the Constitution, or conformably to the Constitution, disregarding the law, the Court must determine which of these conflicting rules governs the case. This is of the very essence of judicial duty.

The Court's legal power to review acts of Congress has not been seriously questioned since 1803. One reason for that is that the Supreme Court makes a self-conscious effort to give acts of Congress an interpretation that will make them constitutional. For example, in its 2012 decision upholding the constitutionality of the Affordable Care Act, the Court agreed with the many legal scholars who had argued that the Congress had no power under the Constitution's commerce clause to order Americans to purchase health insurance. But, rather than invalidate the act, the Court declared that the law's requirement that all Americans purchase insurance was actually a tax and, thus, represented a constitutionally acceptable use of Congress's power to levy taxes.[11]

In more than two centuries, the Court has concluded that only 175 acts of Congress directly violate the Constitution.[12] These cases are often highly controversial. For example, in 2007 and 2014, the high court struck down a key portion of the bipartisan Campaign Reform Act, through which Congress had sought to regulate spending in political campaigns[13] The Court found that provisions of the act limiting political advertising violated the First Amendment. These cases are unusual in that Congress rarely overturns acts of Congress.

Judicial Review of State Actions

The power of the Supreme Court to review state legislation or other state action and to determine its constitutionality is neither granted by the Constitution nor inherent in the federal system. But the logic of the **supremacy clause** of Article VI of the Constitution, which declares the Constitution itself and laws made under its authority to be the supreme law of the land, is very strong. Furthermore, in the Judiciary Act of 1789, Congress conferred on the Supreme Court the power to reverse state constitutions and laws whenever they are clearly in conflict with the U.S. Constitution, federal laws, or treaties.[14] This power gives the Supreme Court appellate jurisdiction over all the millions of cases that American courts handle each year.

supremacy clause Article VI of the Constitution, which states that laws passed by the national government and all treaties are the supreme law of the land and superior to all laws adopted by any state or any subdivision

Judicial Review across the Globe

In 1946 only about a quarter of democracies had a court that possessed judicial review; by 2006 almost 90 percent did.[a] The type of judicial review varies by county. The United States has concrete judicial review, which means that a specific case must be brought to the Supreme Court before it can declare a law unconstitutional. Other countries, such as France, have abstract judicial review, which means the constitutional court does not have to wait for a specific court case in order to declare a law unconstitutional. Instead, the court usually responds to a request by an elected official, such as a member of parliament or local government, in ruling whether a law is unconstitutional. Some countries, such as Germany and South Africa, possess both types of judicial review.

Not all democracies have judicial review. For example, the judiciary in the United Kingdom officially lacks this power. The United Kingdom is one of the few remaining democracies with parliamentary sovereignty, meaning that, while local laws can be declared unconstitutional, no court can overturn a law passed by the national parliament. British courts can rule a law passed by parliament as "incompatible" with European Union law or other treaty obligations, but this does not automatically strike the law down. Instead, the law stays "on the books" and the parliament is asked to reconsider the law and amend it so it does not contradict other laws.[b]

Country/Court	Concrete Review	Abstract Review	What Can Be Reviewed
United States *Supreme Court*	Yes	No	• National legislation • Actions of other national government institutions (e.g., executive orders) • State and local laws • Lower court decisions and appeals
India *Supreme Court*	Yes	No	• National legislation • Actions of other national government institutions • State and local laws • Lower court decisions and appeals • Past judgments by the Supreme Court
Germany *Federal Constitutional Court*	Yes	Yes	• National legislation • Actions of other national government institutions • State and local laws • Constitutional amendments • Election law violations
South Africa *Constitutional Court*	Yes	Yes	• National legislation • Actions of other national government institutions • Local laws • Lower court decisions and appeals
France *Constitutional Council*	Limited*	Yes	• National legislation *prior to being signed into law* • Legislation pertaining to cases before the other high courts
United Kingdom *Supreme Court** *	No	No	• Actions of other government institutions ("secondary legislation") • Local laws

*A 2009 reform allows some concrete review. For more information, see Ordinance No. 58-1067 at www.conseil-constitutionnel.fr/conseil-constitutionnel/root/bank_mm/ anglais/en_ordinance_58_1067.pdf (accessed 9/12/14).
**Prior to 2009, the role of the "high court" was performed by the United Kingdom's House of Lords (the 12 "Law Lords").

[a]David S. Law and Mila Versteeg, "The Evolution and Ideology of Global Constitutionalism," *California Law Review*, 99, no. 5 (2010): 1163–1257.
[b]United Kingdom Judicial Office, "About the Judiciary: Judges and Parliament," www.judiciary.gov.uk/about-the-judiciary/the-judiciary-the-government-and-the-constitution/jud-acc-ind/judges-and-parliament/ (accessed 9/12/14).

In 2011 the Supreme Court struck down a California law that regulated the sale of violent video games to children, saying it violated the First Amendment. California state senator Leland Yee, who proposed the ban, held up some of the games the law would have regulated.

The supremacy clause of the Constitution not only established the federal Constitution, statutes, and treaties as the "supreme Law of the Land," but also provided that "the Judges in every State shall be bound thereby, any Thing in the Constitution or Laws of the State to the Contrary notwithstanding." Under this authority, the Supreme Court has frequently overturned state constitutional provisions or statutes, state court decisions, and local ordinances it deems to contravene rights or privileges guaranteed under the federal Constitution or federal statutes.

The civil rights arena abounds with examples of state laws that the Supreme Court has overturned because the statutes violated guarantees of due process and equal protection contained in the Fourteenth Amendment to the Constitution. For example, in the 1954 case of *Brown v. Board of Education*, the Court overturned statutes from Kansas, South Carolina, Virginia, and Delaware that either required or permitted segregated public schools, ruling that such statutes denied black schoolchildren equal protection under the law.[15] In 2003 the Court ruled that Texas's law criminalizing sodomy violated the right to liberty protected by the due process clause.[16]

State statutes in other areas of law are equally subject to challenge. Many of the Supreme Court's recent decisions overturning state law have come in cases concerning criminal punishments and campaign finance. For example, in 2012 the Court struck down Alabama and Arkansas statutes that mandated a sentence of life in prison without possibility of parole for minors who were found guilty of homicide. The Court held this statute violated the Eighth Amendment's prohibition of cruel and unusual punishment.[17] Also in 2012, the court overturned a Montana law that barred corporate expenditures in support or opposition to a political candidate or party as a violation of the First Amendment.[18]

One realm in which the Court constantly monitors state conduct is the area of law enforcement. As we saw in Chapter 4, over the years, the Supreme Court has developed a number of principles regulating police conduct to ensure that the police do not violate constitutional liberties. These principles, however, must often be updated to keep pace with changes in technology. In a 2012 decision, the Supreme Court found that police use of a GPS tracker—a device invented more than two centuries after the adoption of the Bill of Rights—constituted a "search" as defined by the Fourth Amendment. In the case of *United States v. Jones*, the Court ruled that the police were prohibited from attaching a global-positioning device to a car belonging to a suspected drug dealer without first obtaining a valid warrant.[19]

Judicial Review of Federal Agency Actions

Although Congress makes the law, as we saw in Chapters 12 and 14, it can hardly administer the thousands of programs it has enacted and must therefore delegate power to the president and to a huge bureaucracy to achieve its purposes. For example, if Congress wishes to improve air quality, it cannot possibly anticipate all the conditions and circumstances that may arise with respect to that general goal. Inevitably, Congress must delegate to the executive substantial discretionary power to make judgments about the best ways to bring about improved air quality in the face of changing circumstances. Thus, over the years, almost any congressional program will result in thousands upon thousands of pages of administrative regulations developed by executive agencies nominally seeking to implement the will of the Congress.

Delegation of power to the executive poses a number of problems for Congress and the federal courts. If Congress delegates broad authority to the president, it risks seeing its goals subordinated to and subverted by those of the executive branch.[20] If Congress attempts to limit executive discretion by enacting precise rules and standards to govern the conduct of the president and the executive branch, it risks writing laws that do not conform to real-world conditions and that are too rigid to be adapted to changing circumstances.[21]

Over the past two centuries, the issue of delegation of power has led to a number of court decisions regarding the scope of the delegation. Courts have also been called on to decide whether the regulations adopted by federal agencies are consistent with Congress's express or implied intent.

As presidential power expanded during the New Deal era, one indication of increased congressional subordination to the executive was the enactment of laws that contained few, if any, principles limiting executive discretion. Congress enacted legislation, often at the president's behest, that gave the executive virtually unfettered authority to address a particular concern. For example, the Emergency Price Control Act of 1942 authorized the executive to set "fair and equitable" prices without spelling out what those terms might mean.[22] Although the Court initially challenged these delegations of power to the president during the New Deal, it retreated from its position when faced with a confrontation with President Franklin Delano Roosevelt. Perhaps as a result, no congressional delegation of power to the president since then has been struck down as impermissibly broad. Particularly in recent years, the Supreme Court has found that so long as federal agencies developed rules and regulations "based upon a permissible construction" or "reasonable interpretation" of Congress's statute, the judiciary would accept the views of the executive branch. Generally, the courts give considerable deference to administrative agencies as long as those agencies engage in a formal rule-making process as prescribed by the various statutes governing agency rule making. This principle was recently reaffirmed in the

2014 case of *Chamber of Commerce of the United States v. Environmental Protection Agency*. The Supreme Court was unwilling to overturn a "reasonable" agency interpretation of the Clean Air Act, even though the interpretation did not precisely conform to the language of the statute.[23]

Judicial Review and Presidential Power

The federal courts are also called on to review the actions of the president. On many occasions, members of Congress as well as individuals and groups have challenged presidential orders and actions in the federal courts. In recent years, the federal bench has, more often than not, upheld assertions of presidential power in such realms as foreign policy, war and emergency powers, legislative power, and administrative authority. In June 2004, however, the Supreme Court ruled on three cases involving President George W. Bush's antiterrorism initiatives and claims of executive power, and in two of the three cases appeared to place some limits on presidential authority.

One important case was *Hamdi v. Rumsfeld*.[24] Yaser Esam Hamdi, apparently a Taliban soldier, was captured by American forces in Afghanistan and brought to the United States, where he was incarcerated at the Norfolk Naval Station. Hamdi was classified as an enemy combatant and denied civil rights, including the right to counsel, despite the fact that he had been born in Louisiana and held American citizenship. In June 2004 the Supreme Court ruled that Hamdi was entitled to a lawyer and "a fair opportunity to rebut the government's factual assertions." Thus the Supreme Court did assert that presidential actions were subject to judicial scrutiny and that the Court could place some constraints on the president's power. But at the same time, the Court affirmed the president's single most important claim: the unilateral power to declare individuals, including U.S. citizens, "enemy combatants," who could be

The courts have the authority to settle disputes between not only individuals and other private entities but also individuals and the government. In recent "enemy combatant" cases, the Supreme Court has ruled on presidential power as it relates to the rights of prisoners held at the U.S. base in Guantánamo, Cuba. In 2008 demonstrators dressed as Guantánamo detainees protested outside the Court.

detained by federal authorities under adverse legal circumstances. Several of the justices intimated that once designated an enemy combatant, a U.S. citizen might be tried before a military tribunal, without the normal presumption of innocence.

In the 2006 case of *Hamdan v. Rumsfeld*, Salim Hamdan, a Taliban fighter, was captured in Afghanistan and held at the Guantánamo Bay naval base. The Bush administration planned to try Hamdan before a military commission authorized by a 2002 presidential order. The Supreme Court ruled that the commissions created by the president planned to use procedures that would violate federal law and U.S. treaty obligations.[25] President Bush responded by demanding that Congress rewrite the law. Congress quickly obliged and enacted the Military Commissions Act, which gave the president statutory authority for his actions. In Section 7 of the act, Congress declared that Guantánamo prisoners could not bring habeas corpus petitions to federal courts to seek their release. In the 2008 case of *Boumediene v. Bush*, however, the Supreme Court struck down Section 7 and declared habeas corpus to be a fundamental right.[26] Judicial review of presidential actions is not limited to presidential war powers and the realm of terrorism. In 2013 the Fourth U.S. Circuit Court of Appeals ruled that President Obama violated the Constitution when he made so-called recess appointments to the National Labor Relations Board in order to avoid the need to secure Senate confirmation. Recess appointments are customarily used only when the Senate adjourns at the end of the year, but the president made the appointments in question when the Senate was on a short break. In June 2014 the Supreme Court ruled that a Senate recess of less than 10 days was "presumptively too short" to justify a recess appointment. In this case, the Senate had only recessed for 3 days.[27]

Judicial Review and Lawmaking

Much of the work of the courts involves the application of statutes to the particular case at hand. Over the centuries, judges have also developed a body of rules and principles of interpretation that are not grounded in specific statutes. This body of judge-made law is called **common law**. For example, tort law, which determines whether one person is liable for causing harm to another, is based more upon cases and precedents than statute.

The appellate courts, however, are in another realm. Their rulings can be considered laws, but they govern the behavior only of the judiciary. The written opinion of an appellate court is about halfway between common law and statutory law. As in common law, the opinion is judge-made and draws heavily on the precedents of previous cases. But, as in statutory law, it tries to articulate the rule of law controlling the case in question and future cases like it. It differs from a statute in that a statute addresses itself to the future conduct of citizens, whereas a written opinion addresses itself mainly to the future willingness or ability of courts to take cases and render favorable opinions. Decisions by appellate courts affect citizens by opening or closing access to the courts.

A specific case illustrates the distinction. Before the Second World War, one of the most insidious forms of racial discrimination was the "restrictive covenant," a clause in a contract whereby the purchasers of a house agreed that if they later decided to sell the home, they would sell only to a Caucasian. When a case finally reached the Supreme Court in 1948, the Court ruled unanimously that citizens had a right to discriminate with restrictive covenants in their sales contracts but that the courts could not enforce those contracts. Its argument was that enforcement would

for critical **analysis**

During his 2005 confirmation hearings, senators asked Chief Justice Roberts why the Supreme Court was more willing to declare acts of Congress unconstitutional than it was to confront the president on the constitutionality of his actions. What reasons might you identify?

common law law made through court precedent rather than legislative enactments

constitute violation of the Fourteenth Amendment provision that no state shall "deny to any person within its jurisdiction equal protection under the law."[28] The Court was thereby predicting what it would and would not do in future cases of this sort. Most states have now enacted statutes that forbid homeowners from placing such covenants in sales contracts.

Many areas of civil law have been constructed in the same way: by judicial messages to other judges, some of which are eventually codified into legislative enactments. An example of great concern to employees and employers is that of liability for injuries sustained at work. Courts have sided with employees so often that it has become virtually useless for employers to fight injury cases. It has become "the law" that employers are liable for such injuries, without regard to claims of negligence. But the law in this instance is simply a series of messages to lawyers that they should advise their corporate clients not to appeal injury decisions. In recent years, the Supreme Court has also been developing law in the realm of sexual harassment in the workplace. In a 2006 case, for example, the Court said that a victim of sexual harassment who was transferred from her job could sue her employer even though the company disciplined the perpetrator when the harassment was reported.[29]

The appellate courts cannot decide what types of behavior will henceforth be a crime. They cannot directly prevent the police from forcing confessions from suspects or intimidating witnesses. In other words, they cannot directly change the behavior of citizens or eliminate abuses of government power. What they can do, however, is make it easier for mistreated persons to gain redress.

In redressing wrongs, the appellate courts—and even the Supreme Court itself—often call for a radical change in legal principle. Changes in race relations, for example, would probably have taken a great deal longer if the Supreme Court had not rendered the 1954 decision *Brown v. Board of Education*, which redefined the rights of African Americans.

Similarly, the Supreme Court interpreted the doctrine of the separation of church and state so as to alter significantly the practice of religion in public institutions. For example, in a 1962 case *Engel v. Vitale*, the Court declared that a once widely observed ritual—the recitation of a prayer by students in a public school—was unconstitutional under the establishment clause of the First Amendment.[30] Almost all the dramatic changes in the treatment of criminals and of persons accused of crimes have been made by the appellate courts, especially the Supreme Court. The Supreme Court brought about a veritable revolution in the criminal process with three cases over less than five years: *Gideon v. Wainwright*, in 1963, established the obligation of state courts to provide legal counsel to defendants who could not afford their own attorneys.[31] *Escobedo v. Illinois*, in 1964, gave suspects the right to remain silent and the right to have counsel present during questioning. But the *Escobedo* decision left confusions that allowed differing decisions to be made by lower courts.[32] In *Miranda v. Arizona*, in 1966, the Supreme Court cleared up these confusions by setting forth what is known as the Miranda rule: arrested people have the right to remain silent, the right to be informed that anything they say can be held against them, and the right to counsel before and during police interrogation (see Chapter 4).[33] In 2000 the Supreme Court considered overruling *Miranda* in

Due process of law is an area in which federal courts have played a critical role in "making law" since the 1960s. In 2012 the Supreme Court heard the case of Evan Miller, who was tried as an adult on murder charges for a crime he allegedly committed when he was 14 years old and was sentenced to life without parole. The Court ruled that a life-without-parole sentence for a 14-year-old violates the Eighth Amendment's prohibition against cruel and unusual punishment.

Dickerson v. United States, but it decided that the wide acceptance of Miranda rights in the legal culture was "adequate reason not to overrule" it.[34]

One of the most significant changes brought about by the Supreme Court was the revolution in legislative representation unleashed by the 1962 case of *Baker v. Carr*.[35] In this landmark case, the Supreme Court held that it could no longer avoid reviewing complaints about the apportionment of seats in state legislatures. Following that decision, the federal courts went on to force reapportionment of all state, county, and local legislatures in the country.

● The Supreme Court in Action

Describe the process the Supreme Court follows in the exercise of its power of judicial review

Given the millions of disputes that arise every year, the job of the Supreme Court would be impossible if it were not able to control the flow of cases and its own caseload. Over the years, the courts have developed specific rules that govern which cases within their jurisdiction they will and will not hear. In order to be heard by the courts, cases must meet certain criteria that are initially applied by the trial court but may be reconsidered by appellate courts. These rules of access can be broken down into three major categories: case or controversy, standing, and mootness.

Article III of the Constitution and Supreme Court decisions define judicial power as extending only to "cases and controversies." This means that the case before a court must be an actual controversy, not a hypothetical one, with two truly adversarial parties. The courts have interpreted this language to mean that they do not have the power to render advisory opinions to legislatures or agencies about the constitutionality of proposed laws or regulations. Furthermore, even after a law is enacted, the courts will generally refuse to consider its constitutionality until it is actually applied.

standing the right of an individual or organization to initiate a court case, on the basis of their having a substantial stake in the outcome

Parties to a case must also have **standing**—that is, they must show that they have a substantial stake in the outcome of the case. The traditional requirement for standing has been to show injury to oneself; that injury can be personal, economic, or even aesthetic, such as a neighbor's building a high fence that blocks one's view of the ocean. In order for a group or class of people to have standing (as in class-action suits), each member must show specific injury. This means that a general interest in the environment, for instance, does not provide a group with sufficient basis for standing.

mootness a criterion used by courts to screen cases that no longer require resolution

The Supreme Court also uses a third criterion in determining whether it will hear a case: that of **mootness**. In theory, this requirement disqualifies cases that are brought too late—after the relevant facts have changed or the problem has been resolved by other means. The criterion of mootness, however, is subject to the discretion of the courts, which have begun to relax the rules of mootness, particularly in cases where a situation that has been resolved is likely to come up again. In the abortion case *Roe v. Wade*, for example, the Supreme Court rejected the lower court's argument that because the pregnancy in question had already come to term, the case was moot. The Court agreed to hear the case because no pregnancy was likely to outlast the lengthy appeals process.[36]

Putting aside the formal criteria, the Supreme Court is most likely to accept cases that involve conflicting decisions by the federal circuit courts, cases that present important questions of civil rights or civil liberties, and cases in which the federal government is the appellant. Ultimately, however, the question of which cases to accept can come down to the preferences and priorities of the justices. If a group of justices believes that the Court should intervene in a particular area of policy or politics, they are likely to look for a case or cases that will serve as vehicles for judicial intervention. For many years, the Court was not interested in considering challenges to affirmative action or other programs designed to provide particular benefits to minorities. In recent years, however, several of the Court's more conservative justices have been eager to push back the limits of affirmative action and racial preference, and have therefore accepted a number of cases that would allow them to do so. In the 2014 case of *Schuette v. Coalition to Defend Affirmative Action*, for example, the Court ruled that a Michigan ballot initiative that resulted in a ban on racial preferences in college admissions was constitutional. The decision paved the way for other states to prohibit the use of race as a factor in college admissions.[37]

Writs Most cases reach the Supreme Court through a **writ of certiorari**. Certiorari is an order to a lower court to deliver the records of a particular case to be reviewed for legal errors. The term *certiorari* is sometimes shortened to *cert*, and cases deemed to merit certiorari are referred to as "certworthy." An individual who loses in a lower federal court or state court and wants the Supreme Court to review the decision has 90 days to file a petition for a writ of certiorari with the clerk of the U.S. Supreme Court. Petitions for thousands of cases are filed with the Court every year (see Figure 15.4).

writ of certiorari a decision of at least four of the nine Supreme Court justices to review a decision of a lower court; *certiorari* is Latin, meaning "to make more certain"

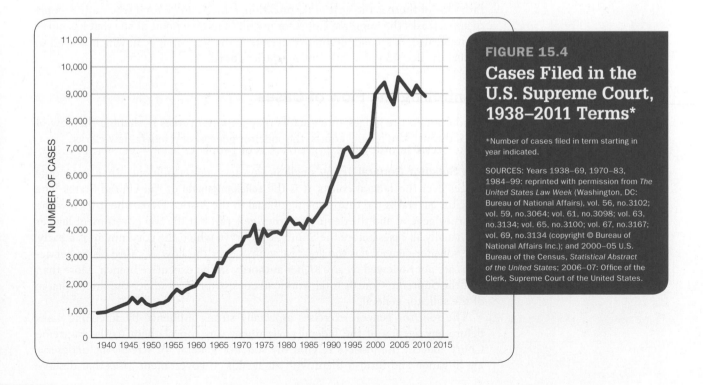

FIGURE 15.4

Cases Filed in the U.S. Supreme Court, 1938–2011 Terms*

*Number of cases filed in term starting in year indicated.

SOURCES: Years 1938–69, 1970–83, 1984–99: reprinted with permission from *The United States Law Week* (Washington, DC: Bureau of National Affairs), vol. 56, no.3102; vol. 59, no.3064; vol. 61, no.3098; vol. 63, no.3134; vol. 65, no.3100; vol. 67, no.3167; vol. 69, no.3134 (copyright © Bureau of National Affairs Inc.); and 2000–05 U.S. Bureau of the Census, *Statistical Abstract of the United States*; 2006–07: Office of the Clerk, Supreme Court of the United States.

Since 1972 most of the justices have participated in a "certiorari pool" in which their law clerks work together to evaluate the petitions. Each petition is reviewed by one clerk, who writes a memo for all the justices participating in the pool, summarizing the facts and issues and making a recommendation. Clerks for the other justices add their comments to the memo. After the justices have reviewed the memos, any one of them may place any case on the "discuss list," which is circulated by the chief justice. If a case is not placed on the discuss list, it is automatically denied certiorari. Cases placed on the discuss list are considered and voted on during the justices' closed-door conference.

For certiorari to be granted, four justices must be convinced that the case satisfies Rule 10 of the Rules of the U.S. Supreme Court. Rule 10 states that certiorari is not a matter of right but is to be granted only when there are special and compelling reasons. These include conflicting decisions by two or more circuit courts, conflicts between circuit courts and state courts of last resort, conflicting decisions by two or more state courts of last resort, decisions by circuit courts on matters of federal law that should be settled by the Supreme Court, and a circuit court decision on an important question that conflicts with Supreme Court decisions. It should be clear from this list that the Court will usually take action under only the most compelling circumstances—when there are conflicts among the lower courts about what the law should be, when an important legal question has been raised in the lower courts but not definitively answered, or when a lower court deviates from the principles and precedents established by the high court. Few cases are able to gain the support of four justices needed for certiorari. In recent sessions, although thousands of petitions were filed, the Court has granted certiorari to barely more than 80 petitioners each year—about 1 percent of those seeking a Supreme Court review.

A handful of cases reach the Supreme Court through avenues other than certiorari. One of these is the writ of certification, which can be used when a U.S. court of appeals asks the Supreme Court for instructions on a point of law that has never been decided. A second alternative avenue is the writ of appeal, which is used to appeal the decision of a three-judge district court.

Controlling the Flow of Cases

In addition to the judges, other actors play important roles in shaping the flow of cases through the federal courts: the solicitor general and federal law clerks.

The Solicitor General If any single person has greater influence than individual judges over the federal courts, it is the **solicitor general** of the United States. The solicitor general is the third-ranking official in the Justice Department (below the attorney general and the deputy attorney general) but the top government lawyer in virtually all cases before the Supreme Court in which the government is a party. The solicitor general has the greatest control over the flow of cases; his or her actions are not reviewed by any higher authority in the executive branch. More than half the Supreme Court's total workload consists of cases under the direct charge of the solicitor general.

The solicitor general exercises especially strong influence by screening cases before any agency of the federal government can appeal them to the Supreme Court; indeed, the justices rely on the solicitor general to "screen out undeserving litigation and furnish them with an agenda to government cases that deserve

solicitor general the top government lawyer in all cases before the Supreme Court where the government is a party

serious consideration."[38] Agency heads may lobby the president or otherwise try to circumvent the solicitor general, and a few of the independent agencies have a statutory right to make direct appeals, but without the solicitor general's support, these requests are seldom reviewed by the Court. Congress has given only a few agencies, including the Federal Communications Commission, the Federal Maritime Commission, and in some cases the Department of Agriculture (even though it is not an independent agency), the right to appeal directly to the Supreme Court without going through the solicitor general.

The solicitor general can enter a case even when the federal government is not a direct litigant by writing an **amicus curiae** ("friend of the court") brief. A friend of the court is not a direct party to a case but has a vital interest in its outcome. Thus, when the government has such an interest, the solicitor general can file an amicus brief or a federal court can invite such a brief because it wants an opinion in writing. Other interested parties may file briefs as well.

amicus curiae literally, "friend of the court"; individuals or groups who are not parties to a lawsuit but who seek to assist the Supreme Court in reaching a decision by presenting additional briefs

In addition to exercising substantial control over the flow of cases, the solicitor general can shape the arguments used before the federal courts. Indeed, the Supreme Court tends to give special attention to the way the solicitor general characterizes the issues. The solicitor general is the person who appears most frequently before the Court and, theoretically at least, is the most disinterested. The credibility of the solicitor general is not hurt when several times each year he comes to the Court to withdraw a case with the admission that the government has made an error.

Law Clerks Every federal judge employs law clerks to research legal issues and assist with the preparation of opinions. Each Supreme Court justice is assigned four clerks, almost always honors graduates of the nation's most prestigious law schools. A clerkship with a Supreme Court justice is a great honor and generally

Federal judges, including Supreme Court justices, rely on their clerks for research and help in preparing opinions. Serving as a law clerk to a Supreme Court justice is a prestigious position. Three current justices—Roberts, Breyer, and Kagan—clerked for a Surpeme Court justice early in their careers.

indicates that the fortunate individual is likely to reach the very top of the legal profession. The work of the Supreme Court clerks is a closely guarded secret, but it is likely that some justices rely heavily on their clerks for advice in writing opinions and in deciding whether the Court should hear specific cases. In a recent book, a former law clerk to the late justice Harry Blackmun charged that Supreme Court justices yielded "excessive power to immature, ideologically driven clerks, who in turn use that power to manipulate their bosses."[39]

Lobbying for Access: Interests and the Court

At the same time that the Court exercises discretion over which cases it will review, groups and forces in society often seek to persuade the justices to listen to their problems. Lawyers representing interest groups try to choose the proper client and the proper case, so that the issues in question are most dramatically and appropriately portrayed. When possible, they also pick a district or jurisdiction with a sympathetic judge in which to bring the case. Sometimes they even have to wait for an appropriate political climate. They must also attempt to develop a proper record at the trial court level, one that includes some constitutional arguments and even, when possible, errors on the part of the trial court.

One of the most effective strategies that litigants use in getting cases accepted for review by the appellate courts is to bring the same type of suit in more than one circuit (that is, to develop a "pattern of cases"), in the hope that inconsistent treatment by two different courts will improve the chance of a Supreme Court review. The two most notable users of the pattern-of-cases strategy in recent years have been the National Association for the Advancement of Colored People (NAACP) and the American Civil Liberties Union (ACLU). For many years, the NAACP (and its Defense Fund—now a separate group) has worked through local chapters and with many individuals to encourage litigation on issues of racial discrimination and segregation. Sometimes it distributes petitions to be signed by parents and filed with local school boards and courts, deliberately sowing the seeds of future litigation. The NAACP and the ACLU often encourage private parties to bring suit and then join the suit as amici curiae.

In many states, it is considered unethical and illegal for attorneys to engage in "fomenting and soliciting legal business in which they are not parties and have no pecuniary right or liability." The NAACP was sued by the state of Virginia in the late 1950s in an attempt to restrict or eliminate its efforts to influence the pattern of cases. The Supreme Court reviewed the case in 1963, recognized that the strategy was being used, and held that the NAACP strategy was protected by the First and Fourteenth amendments, just as other forms of speech and petition are protected.[39]

Thus, many pathbreaking cases are eventually granted certiorari because repeated refusal to review one or more of them would amount to a rule of law just as much as if the courts had handed down a written opinion. In this sense, the flow of cases, especially the pattern of significant cases, influences the behavior of the appellate judiciary.

The Supreme Court's Procedures

The Supreme Court's decision to accept a case is the beginning of what can be a lengthy and complex process (see Figure 15.5). After a petition is filed and certiorari is granted, the Court considers the reasoning on both sides as presented in briefs and oral argument, the justices discuss the case in conference, and opinions are carefully drafted.

The Preparation First, the attorneys on both sides must prepare **briefs**, written documents in which the attorneys explain why the Court should rule in favor of their client. Briefs are filled with referrals to precedents specifically chosen to show that other courts have frequently ruled in the same way the attorneys are requesting that the Supreme Court rule. The attorneys for both sides muster the most compelling precedents they can in support of their arguments.

> **briefs** written documents in which attorneys explain, using case precedents, why the court should find in favor of their client

As the attorneys prepare their briefs, they often ask sympathetic interest groups for their help. These groups are asked to file amicus curiae briefs that support the claims of one or the other litigant. In a case involving separation of church and state, for example, liberal groups such as the ACLU and People for the American Way are likely to be asked to file amicus briefs in support of strict separation, whereas conservative religious groups are likely to file amicus briefs advocating increased public accommodation of religious ideas. Often dozens of briefs will be filed on each side of a major case. Amicus filings are one of the primary methods used by interest groups to lobby the Court. By filing these briefs, groups indicate to the Court where they stand and signal to the justices that they believe the case to be an important one.

Oral Argument The next stage of a case is **oral argument**, in which attorneys for both sides appear before the Court to present their positions and answer the justices' questions. Each attorney has only a half hour to present her case, and this time includes interruptions for questions. Certain members of the Court, such as Justice Antonin Scalia, are known to interrupt attorneys dozens of times. Others, such as Justice Clarence Thomas, seldom ask questions. For an attorney, the opportunity to argue a case before the Supreme Court is a singular honor and a mark of professional distinction. It can also be a harrowing experience, as when justices interrupt a carefully prepared presentation. Nevertheless, oral argument can be very important to the outcome of a case. It allows justices to understand better the heart of the case and to raise questions that might not have been addressed in the opposing sides' briefs. It is not uncommon for justices to go beyond the strictly legal issues and ask opposing counsel to discuss the implications of the case for the Court and the nation at large.

> **oral argument** the stage in the Supreme Court procedure in which attorneys for both sides appear before the Court to present their positions and answer questions posed by justices

The Conference Following oral argument, the Court discusses the case in its Wednesday or Friday conference, a strictly private meeting that no outsiders are

April 19, 2013

The Chamber of Commerce filed a petition for a writ of certiorari in the case *Chamber of Commerce of the United States of America, et al. v. Environmental Protection Agency, et al.*

May 2013

Filing of briefs and amicus curiae briefs in support of the petitioner, including the Institute for Trade, Standards, and Sustainable Development and Nobel Prize–winning economist Thomas C. Shelling

July 2013

Brief of the solicitor general on behalf of the Environmental Protection Agency (the respondent)

August 7, 2013

The case is distributed for conference.

October 15, 2013

The petition (certiorari) is granted.

November 25, 2013

Date for oral argument is set for February 24, 2014.

December 2013

Briefs and amicus curiae briefs are filed on behalf of petitioner.

January 2014

Briefs and amicus curiae briefs are filed on behalf of respondent.

February 24, 2014

Oral argument of one hour

June 2014

Decision

FIGURE 15.5

Time Line of a Supreme Court Case

This calendar of events in the case of *Chamber of Commerce v. Environmental Protection Agency* illustrates the steps of the process a case goes through as it moves through the Supreme Court. The total time from petition to the Supreme Court to the decision is just over one year, although the initial case was filed years ago in a lower court.

The Supreme Court allocates just one hour to hear oral arguments, even in difficult and contentious cases. Attorneys for both sides must make their arguments succinctly and respond to questions from the nine justices, which are often very pointed.

permitted to attend. The chief justice presides over the conference and speaks first; the other justices follow in order of seniority. The justices discuss the case and eventually reach a decision on the basis of a majority vote. If the Court is divided, a number of votes may be taken before a final decision is reached. As the case is discussed, justices may try to influence or change one another's opinions. At times, this may result in compromise decisions.

Opinion Writing After a decision has been reached, one of the members of the majority is assigned to write the **opinion**. This assignment is made by the chief justice or by the most senior justice in the majority if the chief justice is on the losing side. The assignment of the opinion can make a significant difference to the interpretation of a decision. Every opinion of the Supreme Court sets a major precedent for future cases throughout the judicial system. Lawyers and judges in the lower courts will examine the opinion carefully to ascertain the Supreme Court's intent. Differences in wording and emphasis can have important implications for future litigation. Thus, in assigning an opinion, the justices must give serious thought to the impression the case will make on lawyers and on the public, and to the probability that one justice's opinion will be more widely accepted than another's.

One of the more dramatic instances of this tactical consideration occurred in 1944, when Chief Justice Harlan F. Stone chose Justice Felix Frankfurter to write the opinion in the "white primary" case *Smith v. Allwright*. The chief justice believed that this sensitive case, which overturned the southern practice of prohibiting black participation in nominating primaries, required the efforts of the most brilliant and scholarly jurist on the Court. But the day after Stone made the assignment, Justice Robert H. Jackson wrote a letter to Stone urging a change of assignment and arguing that Frankfurter, a foreign-born Jew from New England, would not win the South with his opinion, regardless of its brilliance. Stone accepted the

opinion the written explanation of the Supreme Court's decision in a particular case

advice and substituted Justice Stanley Reed, an American-born Protestant from Kentucky and a southern Democrat in good standing.[41]

Once the majority opinion is drafted, it is circulated to the other justices. Some members of the majority may agree with both the outcome and the rationale but wish to emphasize or highlight a particular point. For that purpose, they draft a concurring opinion, called a *regular concurrence*. In other instances, one or more justices may agree with the majority decision but disagree with the rationale presented in the majority opinion. These justices may draft *special concurrences*, explaining their own rationale for the decision and how it differs from the majority's rationale.

Dissent Justices who disagree with the majority decision of the Court may choose to publicize the character of their disagreement in the form of a **dissenting opinion**. The dissenting opinion is generally assigned by the senior justice among the dissenters. Dissents can be used to express irritation with an outcome or to signal to defeated political forces in the nation that their position is supported by at least some members of the Court. Ironically, the most dependable way an individual justice can exercise a direct and clear influence on the Court is to write a dissent. Because there is no need to please a majority, dissenting opinions can be more eloquent and less guarded than majority opinions. The current Supreme Court often produces 5–4 decisions, with dissenters writing long and detailed opinions that, they hope, will help them persuade a swing justice to join their side on the next round of cases dealing with a similar topic. During the Court's 2006–07 term, Justice Ruth Bader Ginsburg was so unhappy about the majority's decisions in a number of cases that she twice violated her own long-standing practice and read forceful dissents from the bench, thus underscoring her disagreement with current legal trends and pointing the way toward other possibilities.

Dissent plays a special role in the work and impact of the Court because it amounts to an appeal to lawyers all over the country to keep bringing similar cases. Therefore, an effective dissent influences the flow of cases through the Court and the arguments that lawyers will use in later cases. Even more important, dissent points out that although the Court speaks with a single opinion, it is the opinion only of the majority—and one day the majority might go the other way.

dissenting opinion a decision written by a justice in the minority in a particular case in which the justice wishes to express his or her reasoning in the case

● Explaining Supreme Court Decisions

> Consider the personal and political influences on judges and the courts

The Supreme Court makes its mark on American politics and society through the decisions it hands down. But judicial decision making does not take place in a vacuum, of course. Like other actors in government, justices are influenced by institutional concerns, prior experience, and personal philosophy. In addition, the Court as a whole is affected by the overarching political system in which it plays a role. Over time, that role has shifted as a result of political developments both inside and outside the Court.

Influences on Supreme Court Decision Making

The Supreme Court explains its decisions in terms of law and precedent. But it is the Court itself that decides what the laws actually mean and what importance the precedent will actually have. Throughout its history, the Court has shaped and reshaped the law. In the late nineteenth and early twentieth centuries, for example, the Supreme Court held that the Constitution, law, and precedent permitted racial segregation in the United States. Beginning in the late 1950s, however, the Court found that the Constitution prohibited segregation on the basis of race and indicated that the use of racial categories in legislation was always suspect. By the 1970s and '80s, the Court once again held that the Constitution permitted the use of racial categories—when such categories were needed to help members of minority groups achieve full participation in American society. Since the 1990s, the Court has retreated from this position, too, indicating that governmental efforts to provide extra help to racial minorities could represent an unconstitutional infringement on the rights of the majority.

Institutional Interests The Supreme Court's justices are acutely aware of the Court's place in history and they care about protecting the Court's power and reputation. This desire to protect the institutional integrity of the Court can sometimes influence judicial thinking. During the 1930s, for example, the Supreme Court became embroiled in a political struggle with President Franklin Roosevelt over his "New Deal" programs. During the 1935–36 term, the Court struck down several of the president's initiatives in a series of 5–4 votes. Furious, the president responded by proposing a court-reform plan that would have increased the size of the Court to as many as 15 justices. Roosevelt hoped to pack the Court with his own appointees and, thus, win future cases over New Deal programs. Justice Owen Roberts, who had been one of the five justices voting against the president's initiatives, made a sudden reversal, voting in favor of an important New Deal policy he had been expected to oppose. The media dubbed Roberts' shift "The switch in time that saved nine."

Such institutional concerns are not isolated incidents, however. More recently, Chief Justice John Roberts seemed to have institutional concerns in mind when he surprised fellow conservatives by casting the deciding vote in favor of the constitutionality of the Affordable Care Act in 2012. Roberts had been widely expected to oppose the president's health care reform effort. However, the Court's conservative majority had come under increasing political fire for its positions on such matters as campaign finance and affirmative action. Roberts, according to one commentator, saw himself as "uniquely entrusted with the custodianship of the court's legitimacy, reputation, and stature" and was determined to show that the Court stood above mere political ideology.[42]

Political and Governmental Experience When justices take their places on the Court, they bring to the bench decades of prior career experience as lawyers, public officials, judges on lower courts, and so forth. This prior experience helps to shape their understanding of government and politics and plays a role in their decision making. One area in which prior experience seems to be important is the question of congressional versus presidential power. None of today's justices has ever served in Congress or a state legislature. The last justice to have done so was retired Justice Sandra Day O'Connor, who had previously served as a member of the Arizona state legislature. The past experience of the current justices have made them more familiar with the operations of the executive branch and so they tend to give the president and the agencies of the executive branch considerable deference, seldom reversing presidential or agency decisions. Congress, on the other hand, is alien territory to the justices. Though they show deference to Congress, they are more inclined to look askance at congressional than executive actions.

Members of Congress have noticed the Court's occasional disdain for their institution. During the Senate's 2005 confirmation hearings for Chief Justice John Roberts, then-chairman of the Senate Judiciary Committee, the late Senator Arlen Specter (R-Pa.), said, "I take umbrage at what the Court has said and so do my colleagues . . . Do we have your commitment that you won't characterize your method of reasoning as superior to ours?" Roberts gave a noncommittal reply.[43]

Activism and Restraint Judicial philosophy also plays a role in the decisions of all judges, including those on the Supreme Court. One element of judicial philosophy is the issue of activism versus restraint. Over the years, some justices have believed that courts should interpret the Constitution according to the stated intentions of its framers and defer to the views of Congress when interpreting federal statutes. Justice Felix Frankfurter, for example, advocated judicial deference to legislative bodies and avoidance of the "political thicket" in which the Court would entangle itself by deciding questions that were essentially political rather than legal in character. Advocates of **judicial restraint** are sometimes called "strict constructionists," because they look strictly to the words of the Constitution in interpreting its meaning.

The alternative to restraint is **judicial activism**. Activist judges such as Chief Justice Earl Warren believed that the Court should go beyond the words of the Constitution or a statute to consider the broader societal implications of its decisions. Activist judges sometimes strike out in new directions, promulgating new interpretations or inventing new legal and constitutional concepts when they believe these to be socially desirable. For example, Justice Harry Blackmun's opinion in *Roe v. Wade* was based on a constitutional right to privacy that is not found in the words of the Constitution but was, rather, from the Court's prior decision in *Griswold v. Connecticut*.[44] Blackmun and the other members of the majority in the *Roe* case argued that the right to privacy was implied by other constitutional provisions. In this instance of judicial activism, the Court knew the result it wanted to achieve and was not afraid to make the law conform to the desired outcome.

Activism and restraint are sometimes confused with liberalism and conservatism. For example, conservative politicians often castigate "liberal activist" judges and call for the appointment of conservative jurists who will refrain from reinterpreting the law. To be sure, some liberal jurists are activists and some conservatives have been advocates of restraint, but the relationships are by no means synonymous. Indeed, the Rehnquist court, dominated by conservatives, was among the most activist courts in American history, particularly in such areas as federalism and election law. The Roberts court is continuing along the same route. For example, in the 2014 case of *McCutcheon vs. Federal Election Commission*, the Court struck down one of the major remaining elements of Congress's efforts to regulate campaign finance. The court's five more conservative justices said that limits on how much individuals could contribute in any given election were a restraint on free speech.[45] This decision could be described as "activist" because it broadens the interpretation of "speech" and overturns congressional legislation that has significant public support. As the examples of these conservative courts illustrate, a judge may be philosophically conservative and believe in strict construction of the Constitution but also be jurisprudentially activist and believe that the courts must play an active and energetic role in policy making, if necessary striking down acts of Congress to ensure that the intent of the framers is fulfilled.

judicial restraint judicial philosophy whose adherents refuse to go beyond the clear words of the Constitution in interpreting the document's meaning

judicial activism judicial philosophy that posits that the Court should go beyond the words of the Constitution or a statute to consider the broader societal implications of its decisions

for critical analysis

In its 2010 decision in *McDonald v. Chicago*, the Supreme Court applied the doctrine of selective incorporation and ruled that the Second Amendment right to bear arms applies to the states as well as to the federal government. What is "selective incorporation"? What is its significance in American constitutional history?

Political Ideology and Partisanship The philosophy of activism versus restraint is sometimes a smokescreen for political ideology, and indeed, the liberal or conservative attitudes or partisan leanings of justices play an important role in their decisions.[46] In the past, liberal judges have often been activists, willing to use the law to achieve social and political change, whereas conservatives have been associated with judicial restraint. Interestingly, however, in recent years some conservative justices who have long called for restraint have actually become activists in seeking to undo some of the work of liberal jurists.

From the 1950s to the 1980s, the Supreme Court took an activist role in such areas as civil rights, civil liberties, abortion, voting rights, and police procedures. For example, the Supreme Court was more responsible than any other governmental institution for breaking down America's system of racial segregation. Since that time, however, the conservative justices appointed by presidents Ronald Reagan, George H. W. Bush, and George W. Bush have become the dominant bloc on the Court and, as we saw earlier, have moved the Court to the right on a number of issues, including affirmative action and abortion.

The political struggles of recent years amply illustrate the importance of judicial ideology. Is abortion a fundamental right or a criminal activity? How much separation must there be between church and state? Does application of the Voting Rights Act to increase minority representation constitute a violation of the rights of whites? The answers to these and many other questions cannot be found in the words of the Constitution. They must be located, instead, in the hearts and minds of the judges who interpret that text.

Judicial philosophy, ideology, institutional interest, and prior experience all influence the thinking of justices. In the end, however, the Supreme Court is a court of law and must pay heed to statutes and legal precedent. A decision that cannot be justified by law and precedent cannot be issued. To ignore the law would be to undermine the rule of law and to destroy the constitutional structure in which the Supreme Court occupies such a prominent place.

Judicial Power and Politics

One of the most important institutional changes to occur in the United States during the past half-century has been the striking transformation of the role and power of the federal courts, and of the Supreme Court in particular. Understanding how this transformation came about is the key to understanding the contemporary role of the courts in America.

Traditional Limitations on the Federal Courts For much of American history, the power of the federal courts was subject to a number of limitations.[47] To begin with, unlike other governmental institutions, courts cannot exercise power on their own initiative. Judges must wait until a case is brought to them before they can make authoritative decisions. Traditionally, moreover, courts were constrained by judicial rules of standing that limited access to the bench. Claimants who simply disagreed with governmental action or inaction could not obtain access to the courts, which was limited to individuals who could show that they were specifically affected by the government's behavior in some area. This limitation on access diminished the judiciary's capacity to forge links with important political and social forces.

Second, courts were traditionally limited in the character of the relief they could provide. In general, courts acted only to offer relief or assistance to individuals and not to broad social classes, again inhibiting the formation of alliances between the courts and important social forces.

Third, courts lacked enforcement powers of their own and were compelled to rely on executive or state agencies to ensure compliance with their edicts. If the executive or state agencies were unwilling to assist the courts, judicial enactments could go unheeded, as when President Andrew Jackson declined to enforce Chief Justice John Marshall's 1832 order to the state of Georgia to release two missionaries it had arrested on Cherokee lands. Marshall asserted that the state had no right to enter the lands without the Cherokees' assent.[48] Jackson is reputed to have said, "John Marshall has made his decision, now let him enforce it."

Fourth, federal judges are, of course, appointed by the president (with the consent of the Senate). As a result, the president and Congress can shape the composition of the federal courts and ultimately, perhaps, the character of judicial decisions. Finally, Congress has the power to change both the size and jurisdiction of the Supreme Court and other federal courts. In many areas, federal courts obtain their jurisdiction not from the Constitution but from congressional statutes. On a number of occasions, Congress has threatened to take matters out of the Court's hands when it was unhappy with the Court's policies.[49] For example, in 1996, Congress enacted several pieces of legislation designed to curb the jurisdiction of the federal courts. One of these laws was the Prison Litigation Reform Act, which limits the ability of federal judges to issue "consent decrees," under which the judges could take control of state prison systems. As to the size of the Court, on one memorable occasion that we mentioned earlier, presidential and congressional threats to expand the size of the Supreme Court—Franklin Delano Roosevelt's "court packing" plan—encouraged the justices to drop their opposition to New Deal programs.

As a result of these limitations on judicial power, through much of their history the chief function of the federal courts was to provide judicial support for executive agencies and to legitimize acts of Congress by declaring them to be consistent with constitutional principles. Only on rare occasions have the federal courts dared to challenge Congress or the executive branch.[50]

Two Judicial Revolutions Since the Second World War, however, the role of the federal judiciary has been strengthened and expanded. There have been two judicial revolutions in the United States since then. The first and more visible of these was the substantive revolution in judicial policy. As we saw earlier in this chapter and in Chapters 4 and 5, in many policy areas, including school desegregation, legislative apportionment, and criminal procedure, and in obscenity, abortion, and voting rights, the Supreme Court was at the forefront of a series of sweeping changes in the role of the U.S. government and, ultimately, the character of American society.[51]

At the same time that the courts were introducing important policy innovations, they were also bringing about a second, less visible revolution. During the 1960s and '70s, the Supreme Court and other federal courts instituted a series of changes in judicial procedures that fundamentally expanded the power of the courts in the United States.

First, the federal courts liberalized the concept of standing to permit almost any group that seeks to challenge the actions of an administrative agency to bring its case before the federal bench. In 1971, for example, the Supreme Court ruled that public interest groups could use the National Environmental Policy Act to challenge the actions of federal agencies by claiming that the agencies' activities might have adverse environmental consequences.[52]

Congress helped to make it even easier for groups dissatisfied with government policies to bring their cases to the courts by adopting Section 1983 of the U.S. Code, which permits the practice of "fee shifting"—that is, allowing citizens who successfully bring a suit against a public official for violating their constitutional rights to collect their attorneys' fees and costs from the government. Thus, Section 1983 encourages individuals and groups to bring their problems to the courts rather than to Congress or the executive branch. These changes have given the courts a far greater role in the administrative process than ever before. Many federal judges are concerned that federal legislation in areas such as health care reform will create new rights and entitlements that give rise to a deluge of court cases. "Any time you create a new right, you create a host of disputes and claims," warned Barbara Rothstein, chief judge of the federal district court in Seattle, Washington.[53]

Second, the federal courts broadened the scope of relief to permit themselves to act on behalf of broad categories or classes of persons in "class-action" cases, rather than just on behalf of individuals.[54] A **class-action suit** is a procedural device that permits large numbers of persons with common interests to join together under a representative party to bring or defend a lawsuit. One example of a class-action suit is the case of *In re Agent Orange Product Liability Litigation*, in which a federal judge in New York certified Vietnam War veterans as a class with standing to sue a manufacturer of herbicides for damages allegedly incurred from exposure to the defendant's product while in Vietnam.[55] The class potentially numbered in the tens of thousands.

Third, the federal courts began to employ so-called structural remedies, in effect retaining jurisdiction of cases until the court's mandate had actually been implemented to its satisfaction.[56] The best known of these instances was federal judge W. Arthur Garrity, Jr.'s effort to operate the Boston school system from his bench in order to ensure its desegregation. Between 1974 and 1985, Judge Garrity issued 14 decisions relating to different aspects of the Boston school desegregation plan that had been

class-action suit a legal action by which a group or class of individuals with common interests can file a suit on behalf of everyone who shares that interest

Today, the Supreme Court is frequently at the center of major political issues. In 2014 it decided the case of Burwell v. Hobby Lobby, *in which arguments for religious freedom under the First Amendment came into play. The Court decided that employers with religious objections were not required to provide employees with no-cost access to contraception.*

developed under his authority and put into effect under his supervision.[57] In 1985, as a result of a suit brought by the NAACP five years earlier, federal judge Leonard B. Sand imposed fines that would have forced the city of Yonkers, New York, into bankruptcy if it had refused to accept his plan to build public housing in white neighborhoods. Twenty-two years and $1.6 million in fines later, in 2007, the city finally gave in to the judge's ruling.

Through these three judicial mechanisms, the federal courts paved the way for an unprecedented expansion of national judicial power. In essence, liberalization of the rules of standing and expansion of the scope of judicial relief drew the federal courts into linkages with important social interests and classes, while the introduction of structural remedies enhanced the courts' ability to serve these constituencies. Thus, during the 1960s and '70s, the power of the federal courts expanded in the same way the power of the executive expanded during the 1930s: through links with constituencies, such as civil rights, consumer, environmental, and feminist groups, that staunchly defended the Supreme Court in its battles with Congress, the executive, and other interest groups.

for critical analysis

In what ways are courts, judges, and justices shielded from politics and political pressure? In what ways are they vulnerable to political pressure? Are the courts an appropriate place for politics?

The Federal Judiciary
and Your Future

In the original conception of the framers, the judiciary was to be the institution that would protect individual liberty from the government. As we saw in Chapter 2, the framers believed that in a democracy the great danger was what they termed "tyranny of the majority"—the possibility that a popular majority, "united or actuated by some common impulse or passion," would "trample on the rules of justice."[58] The framers hoped that the courts would protect liberty from the potential excesses of democracy. And for most of American history, the federal courts' most important decisions were those that protected the freedoms—to speak, worship, publish, vote, and attend school—of groups and individuals whose political views, religious beliefs, or racial or ethnic backgrounds made them unpopular.

Today, Americans of all political persuasions seem to view the courts as useful instruments through which to pursue their goals rather than protectors of individual rights. Conservatives want to ban abortion and help business maintain its profitability, whereas liberals want to promote school integration and help enhance the power of workers in the workplace. These may all be noble goals, but they present a basic dilemma for students of American government. If the courts are simply one more set of policy-making institutions, who is left to protect the liberty of individuals?

Students should realize that the decisions made by the Supreme Court today will have important consequences for their lives and futures. The Court's campaign-finance decisions will have consequences for who will govern the nation you inherit. The Court's decisions in the realm of equal protection will have an impact on your life and career chances. The Court's decisions in the realm of immigration will affect who will and will not be able to call themselves Americans. The Court's decisions in the realm of presidential war powers may or may not send some of you to distant battlefields. The Supreme Court is not an abstract entity in far-off Washington. It reaches directly into your life.

plug**in**

Inform

Watch the Standard Deviants' five-minute "Judicial Branch Intro" on YouTube for a review of which features of the court system were established in the Constitution versus the Judiciary Act.

Express

Identify one Supreme Court decision that affects your life, and explain how. For ideas, search www.uscourts .gov for their "Landmark Supreme Court Cases about Students" page.

Connect

Visit www.uscourts.gov/Court_Locator .aspx, and find your nearest federal court. What does this court do? Find a link to your state's judicial/court system home page by searching online or through www.ncsc.org/Information -and-Resources/Browse-by-State/ State-Court-Websites.aspx. What do state and local courts in your area do?

Act

Do you have a legal question? You can ask a question about court procedures and the law on the FindLaw website, browse answers to many common questions, and even find legal counsel.

study guide

The Legal System

Identify the general types of cases and types of courts in our legal system (pp. 601–6)

American court cases proceed under two broad categories of law: criminal law and civil law. There are court systems at both the federal and state level in the United States. While state courts hear only cases involving questions of state law, the federal courts decide cases addressing federal laws, treaties with other nations, and the Constitution.

Key Terms

criminal law (p. 601)

plaintiff (p. 601)

defendant (p. 601)

civil law (p. 602)

precedent (p. 602)

stare decisis (p. 602)

trial court (p. 602)

court of appeals (p. 603)

supreme court (p. 603)

plea bargain (p. 603)

jurisdiction (p. 604)

original jurisdiction (p. 604)

due process of law (p. 605)

writ of habeas corpus (p. 605)

Practice Quiz

1. What is the name for the body of law that involves disputes between private parties?
   a) civil law
   b) privacy law
   c) plea bargains
   d) household law
   e) common law

2. By which term is the practice of the courts to uphold precedent known?
   a) habeas corpus
   b) certiorari
   c) stare decisis
   d) rule of four
   e) senatorial courtesy

3. Where do most trials in America take place?
   a) state courts
   b) appellate courts
   c) federal courts
   d) federal circuit courts
   e) the Supreme Court

4. Which of the following is not included in the original jurisdiction of the Supreme Court?
   a) cases between the United States and one of the 50 states
   b) cases brought by one state against citizens of another state or against a foreign country
   c) cases involving challenges to the constitutionality of state laws
   d) cases between two or more states
   e) cases involving foreign ambassadors or other ministers

5. The term "writ of habeas corpus" refers to
   a) a court order that an individual in custody be brought into court and shown the cause for his or her detention.
   b) a criterion used by courts to screen cases that no longer require resolution.
   c) a decision of at least four of the nine Supreme Court justices to review a decision of a lower court.
   d) a short, unsigned decision by an appellate court, usually rejecting a petition to review the decision of a lower court.
   e) a brief filed by the solicitor general when the federal government is not a direct litigant in a Supreme Court case.

Federal Courts

Describe the different levels of federal courts and their functions (pp. 606–12)

The federal courts hear a very small percentage of the cases decided in the United States each year. Presidents typically nominate judges for the federal judiciary who are prominent members of the legal profession and who share their partisan and ideological views. The importance of appointments to the federal judiciary has made the confirmation process in the Senate increasingly contentious in recent years.

Key Terms

chief justice (p. 608)

senatorial courtesy (p. 609)

Practice Quiz

6. Under what authority is the number of Supreme Court justices decided?
   a) the president
   b) the chief justice
   c) the Department of Justice
   d) Congress
   e) the Constitution

7. The formal requirements for service as a federal judge include
   a) experience as a state-level judge.
   b) a minimum age of 30.
   c) a minimum of 10 years' legal experience.
   d) a neutral political background.
   e) There are no formal requirements for service as a federal judge.

The Power of the Supreme Court: Judicial Review

> **Explain how the Supreme Court exercises the power of judicial review (pp. 612–20)**

The U.S. Supreme Court has the power to review the constitutionality of acts of Congress and the federal executive branch, as well as state actions. Although this power is not explicitly provided for in the Constitution, the Supreme Court asserted the power of judicial review in its 1803 *Marbury v. Madison* decision, and this power has generally been accepted since then.

Key Terms

judicial review (p. 612)

supremacy clause (p. 613)

common law (p. 618)

Practice Quiz

8. The Supreme Court's decision in *Marbury v. Madison* was important because
   a) it invalidated state laws prohibiting interracial marriage.
   b) it ruled that the recitation of prayers in public schools is unconstitutional under the establishment clause of the First Amendment.
   c) it established that arrested people have the right to remain silent, the right to be informed that anything they say can be held against them, and the right to counsel before and during police interrogation.
   d) it provided an expansive definition of *commerce* under the interstate commerce clause.
   e) it established the power of judicial review.

9. The U.S. Supreme Court's power to review state actions comes from
   a) the Constitution.
   b) *Hamdi v. Rumsfeld* and *Hamdan v. Rumsfeld*.
   c) the supremacy clause and the Judiciary Act of 1789.
   d) certiorari and amicus curiae.
   e) The Supreme Court does not have the power to review state actions.

The Supreme Court in Action

> **Describe the process the Supreme Court follows in the exercise of its power of judicial review (pp. 620–28)**

Most cases reach the Supreme Court by a writ of certiorari. The Supreme Court is most likely to grant a writ of certiorari to cases that involve conflicting decisions by the federal circuit courts, cases that present important questions of civil rights or civil liberties, and cases in which the federal government is the appellant. Much of the Supreme Court's power in the American political system comes from its power to invalidate actions taken by the legislative and executive branches of government if these actions violate the Constitution.

Key Terms

standing (p. 620)

mootness (p. 620)

writ of certiorari (p. 621)

solicitor general (p. 622)

amicus curiae (p. 623)

briefs (p. 625)

oral argument (p. 625)

opinion (p. 627)

dissenting opinion (p. 628)

10. Which of the following influence the flow of cases heard by the Supreme Court?
    a) the attorney general and the Secretary of State
    b) the solicitor general and law clerks
    c) the president and Congress
    d) state legislatures
    e) the federal district and circuit courts

11. Which government official is responsible for arguing the federal government's position in cases before the Supreme Court?
    a) the vice president
    b) the attorney general
    c) the chief justice
    d) the U.S. district attorney
    e) the solicitor general

12. Which of the following is a brief submitted to the Supreme Court by someone other than one of the parties in the case?
    a) amicus curiae
    b) habeas corpus
    c) solicitor general
    d) ex post brief
    e) de jure brief

Explaining Supreme Court Decisions

> **Consider the personal and political influences on judges and the courts (pp. 628–34)**

Throughout most of American history, the federal courts avoided confrontations with the other branches of government and worked primarily to provide support for executive actions and congressional laws by declaring them to be consistent with constitutional principles. During the 1960s and '70s, the federal courts liberalized the concept of standing, broadened the scope of relief courts could provide, and began to employ structural remedies. As a result of these changes, the power of the federal court system expanded dramatically.

Key Terms

judicial restraint (p. 630)
judicial activism (p. 630)
class-action suit (p. 633)

Practice Quiz

13. Which of the following would *not* be accurately characterized as a traditional limitation on the power of the federal courts?
    a) The president shapes the federal judiciary through the appointment process.
    b) Courts lack enforcement powers of their own and are compelled to rely on executive or state agencies to ensure compliance with their rulings.
    c) Congress has the power to change both the size and jurisdiction of the federal courts.
    d) Courts can act to offer relief or assistance to broad social classes but not to specific individuals.
    e) Courts cannot exercise power on their own initiative and must wait for cases to be brought to them.

14. How have changes in judicial policy areas and judicial procedure affected the power of the federal judiciary since World War II?
    a) Strong involvement in sweeping policy change has expanded the courts' power, but changes in procedure have sought to limit judicial power.
    b) Changes in procedure have expanded the courts' power, but the courts have played only minor roles in policy change.
    c) Both policy and procedure changes have expanded judicial power.
    d) Both policy and procedure changes have lessened judicial power.
    e) Judicial policy and judicial procedure have remained largely unchanged since World War II.

For Further Reading

Baum, Lawrence. The Supreme Court. 11th ed. Washington, DC: CQ Press, 2012.

Block, Frederick. *Disrobed: An Inside Look at the Life and Work of a Federal Trial Judge.* New York: Westlaw, 2012.

Cross, Frank. *Decision Making in the U.S. Courts of Appeals.* Stanford, CA: Stanford University Press, 2007.

Dorsen, David. *Henry Friendly, Greatest Judge of His Era.* Cambridge, MA: Harvard University Press, 2012.

Epstein, Lee. *Constitutional Law for a Changing America.* Washington, DC: CQ Press, 2007.

Greenhouse, Linda. *The U.S. Supreme Court: A Very Short Introduction.* New York: Oxford University Press, 2012.

Hall, Kermit L., James W. Ely Jr., and Joel B. Grossman. *The Oxford Companion to the Supreme Court of the United States.* 2nd ed. New York: Oxford University Press, 2005.

McClosky, Robert, and Sanford Levinson. *The American Supreme Court.* Chicago: University of Chicago Press, 2004.

O'Brien, David M. *Storm Center: The Supreme Court in American Politics.* 8th ed. New York: W. W. Norton, 2008.

Peppers, Todd, and Artemus Ward. *In Chambers: Stories of Supreme Court Law Clerks and Their Justices,* Charlottesville, VA: University of Virginia Press, 2012.

Posner, Richard. *Reflections on Judging.* Cambridge, MA: Harvard University Press, 2013

Raskin, Jamin B. *We the Students: Supreme Court Decisions for and about Students.* Washington, DC: Congressional Quarterly Press, 2003.

Rosenberg, Gerald. *The Hollow Hope: Can Courts Bring About Social Change?* Chicago: University of Chicago Press, 1991.

Rossum, Ralph. *Antonin Scalia's Jurisprudence.* Lawrence: University Press of Kansas, 2006.

Stevens, John Paul. *Five Chiefs: A Supreme Court Memoir.* Boston: Little, Brown, 2011.

Sunstein, Cass. *Are Judges Political?* Washington, DC: Brookings Institution Press, 2006.

Toobin, Jeffrey. *The Nine: Inside the Secret World of the Supreme Court.* New York: Anchor Books, 2008.

Toobin, Jeffrey. The Oath: The Obama White House and the Supreme Court. New York: Anchor Books, 2013.

Whittington, Keith. *Political Foundations of Judicial Supremacy: The President, the Supreme Court, and Constitutional Leadership in U.S. History.* Princeton, NJ: Princeton University Press, 2008.

Recommended Websites

Concourts
www.concourts.net
The U.S. Supreme Court has the responsibility for examining and interpreting the Constitution. The Concourts website assumes a comparative perspective and looks at systems of constitutional review in over 150 countries.

FindLaw
www.findlaw.com
FindLaw's website provides answers to most legal questions and helps individuals find legal counsel.

Justice Talking
www.justicetalking.org
Justice Talking is a public radio program that examines current legal issues and important court cases.

Legal Information Institute
www.law.cornell.edu
The Legal Information Institute at Cornell University is a wonderful website for conducting legal research.

Office of the Solicitor General
www.usdoj.gov/osg
The solicitor general conducts litigation on behalf of the U.S. Supreme Court and has a tremendous amount of control over the cases that it hears. See what cases are currently being considered by this powerful official of the Justice Department.

U.S. Courts
www.uscourts.gov
The U.S. court system consists of trial, appellate, and supreme courts. The U.S. Courts website provides a look at the different types of courts in the federal judiciary.

U.S. Supreme Court
www.supremecourtus.gov
The website for the U.S. Supreme Court provides information on recent decisions. Take a moment to read some oral arguments, briefs, or court opinions.

U.S. Supreme Court Media
www.oyez.com
The website for U.S. Supreme Court Media has a great search engine for finding information on such landmark cases as *Marbury v. Madison, Miranda v. Arizona,* and *Roe v. Wade.*

The federal government spent nearly a trillion dollars in response to the economic crisis that began in 2008, but unemployment remained a problem in the years that followed. At this hiring fair in New York, long lines of job seekers awaited the opportunity to find work.

Government and the Economy

16

WHAT GOVERNMENT DOES AND WHY IT MATTERS Many of the students reading this book, and the members of their families, were affected by the global economic crisis that began in 2008. Families lost homes and jobs. Students have been financially pressed, with many unable to afford college tuition. Recent graduates have been unable to find full-time employment. For many, the American dream of prosperity suddenly seemed beyond reach.

Since the 1930s, Americans have counted on the federal government to ensure a prosperous economy. Political leaders have a wide variety of tools they can use to improve economic performance. Among the most widely used are public spending, tax cuts, and interest rate changes, all of which aim to stimulate economic activity or reduce inflation. Policy makers also employ regulations to influence competition among firms. Political leaders' choice of economic tools depends on their perceptions about what the most pressing economic problem is, beliefs about which tools are most likely to be effective, and considerations about who is likely to benefit from a particular economic policy and who is likely to be hurt. Although economic policy is a highly technical field, the choice of policy tools is fundamentally a political decision.

In 2008, with the financial sector seemingly on the brink of collapse, the federal government launched a series of major interventions designed to prop up failing banks and insurance companies. It was not just financial institutions that faced collapse. As the economic instability spread, Washington bailed out other distressed industries, ending up as a major stakeholder in both the financial sector and the auto industry. The federal government also passed a sweeping package in 2009 to help stimulate the economy, save jobs, and make longer-term investments to help build future prosperity. As the economic crisis began to ebb, however, Congress struggled to implement enduring reforms to the financial regulatory system. Banks argued that the crisis had been resolved and cautioned that too much regulation would impede the economic recovery. On the other hand, some government officials warned that not enough was being done to rein in use of the risky financial instruments that had caused the crisis in the first place. Consumer advocates pressed for more aggressive government regulation of mortgage lenders and credit card issuers to protect borrowers.

These developments raise fundamental questions about the role of the government in the economy. On one side of the spectrum are those who believe that the government should have a minimal role in the economy. Government's main purpose should be to set and enforce rules that ensure economic stability. In this perspective, the government is sometimes called the "night watchman state."[1] At the other end of the spectrum are those who want to see the state actively engaged in shaping economic outcomes. Not only should the government promote economic growth, according to this perspective, but it should also step in to protect individuals from economic harm. The government's role in the economy should be active, to shape the kind of society we want.

American economic policy has historically reflected the belief that individual liberty is the key to a thriving economy. In this view, the government's role is to set the basic rules that govern economic transactions and then stand back and let individuals engage in the market. However, periodically Americans have demanded restrictions on market freedoms to protect the public. An array of laws governing competition and protecting consumers and the environment is the consequence of these democratic demands. Although Americans are often uneasy with the idea of government intervention into the market, they show little support for unravelling existing regulations.

chaptergoals

- Identify the broad reasons government gets involved in the economy (pp. 643–51)

- Explore why economic policy is often controversial (pp. 651–59)

- Describe how the government uses monetary, fiscal, and regulatory policies to influence the economy (pp. 659–72)

- Explain why the government tries to balance economic prosperity with policies that protect the environment (pp. 673–77)

● The Goals of Economic Policy

Identify the broad reasons government gets involved in the economy

The job of this and the next chapter is to step beyond the politics and the institutions to look at the goals of government: the public policies. **Public policy** can be defined simply as an officially expressed purpose or goal backed by a sanction (a reward or a punishment). Public policy can be embodied in a law, a rule, a regulation, or an order. This chapter will focus on policies aimed at the economy.

At the most basic level, government makes it possible for the economy to function efficiently by setting the rules for economic exchange and punishing those who violate those rules. Among the most important rules for the economy are those that define property rights, contracts, and standards for goods. This kind of government rule making allows markets to expand by making it easier for people who do not know each other to engage in economic transactions: they no longer have to rely only on personal trust to do business. Likewise, government helps markets expand by creating money and standing behind its value. Money allows diverse goods to be traded and greatly simplifies economic transactions. Without government involvement in providing and standardizing a national currency, it would be very difficult to purchase such basic items as groceries: imagine a world in which different stores used different currencies, or in which you needed to trade something you made yourself for your groceries. This would be a major impediment to economic exchange!

Government involvement in the economy now extends far beyond these basic market-creating functions. As we shall see in this section, government has become involved in many aspects of the economy in order to promote the public well-being. Of course, there is often vigorous disagreement about the extent to which government should intervene in the economy. Further, beliefs about which forms of government intervention in the economy are most necessary and most effective have changed over time. Although the policies have changed, government intervention in the economy has, for nearly a century, sought to achieve four fundamental goals: (1) to promote economic stability, (2) to stimulate economic growth, (3) to promote business development, and (4) to protect employees and consumers.

public policy a law, rule, statute, or edict that expresses the government's goals and provides for rewards and punishments to promote those goals' attainment

At the most basic level, government's role in the economy is to make it easier for markets to function. The government sets rules for doing business, creates money, and backs its value—functions that influence even the simplest economic transactions, such as buying groceries at a typical farmer's market.

Promoting Stable Markets

One of the central reasons for government involvement in the economy is to protect the welfare and property of individuals and businesses. Maintaining law and order is one of the most important ways government can protect welfare and property. The federal government has also enacted laws designed to protect individuals and businesses in economic transactions. Federal racketeering laws, for example, aim to end criminal efforts to control businesses through such illegal means as extortion and kickbacks.

Another reason that Congress began to adopt national business regulatory policies was that companies felt burdened by the inconsistent regulations across the various states. Companies often preferred a single, national regulatory authority, no matter

The interstate highway system is an important public good provided by the government to support the economy. While almost everyone benefits from the highway system, no single participant could afford to provide it alone.

public goods goods or services that are provided by the government because they either are not supplied by the market or are not supplied in sufficient quantities

gross domestic product (GDP) the total value of goods and services produced within a country

how burdensome, because it would ensure consistency throughout the United States; the companies could thereby treat the nation as a single market.[2]

The government also promotes economic stability by providing **public goods**. This term refers to facilities the state provides because no single participant can afford to provide those facilities. The provision of public goods may entail supplying the physical marketplace itself—such as the commons in New England towns or the provision of an interstate highway system to stimulate the trucking industry. The provision of public goods is essential to market operation, and the manner in which the government provides these goods will affect the market's character.

Promoting Economic Prosperity

In addition to setting the basic conditions that allow markets to function, governments may actively intervene in the economy to promote economic growth. Although the idea that government should stimulate economic growth can be traced back to Alexander Hamilton's views about promoting industry, it was not until the twentieth century that the federal government assumed such a role.

Measuring Economic Growth Since the 1930s the federal government has carefully tracked national economic growth by measuring it in several different ways. The two most important measures are the gross national product (GNP), which is the market value of the goods and services produced in the economy, and the **gross domestic product (GDP)**, the same measure but excluding income from foreign investments. In the late 1990s the American economy grew at a rate of over 4 percent a year, considered high by modern standards (see Figure 16.1). Growth was slower during the 2000s, averaging 1.9 percent annually. This was largely the result of two recessions: one in the early 2000s and the second that began in 2008. In the middle part of the decade (2003–07), the economy grew at a strong 2.8 percent annually.[3] As Figure 16.1 shows, the recession that began in 2008 led to negative economic growth in 2008 and 2009, and growth since that time has been sluggish.

The engine of American economic growth has shifted over the centuries. In the 1800s the nation's rich endowment of natural resources was especially important in propelling growth. Manufacturing industries became the driving force of economic growth during the late nineteenth century as mass production made it possible to manufacture goods at a pace that was once unimaginable. In more recent times, the high-technology boom fostered unanticipated and vigorous economic growth that made the United States the envy of the world. Despite these very different economic engines, the basic prerequisites of growth were similar in each case: strong investment, technological innovation, and a productive workforce. Throughout the nation's history, the federal government has adopted policies to promote each of these conditions needed to sustain economic growth.

The most fundamental way that government affects investment is by promoting business, investor, and consumer confidence. When businesses fear political instability, unpredictable government action, or widespread disregard of the law, they are unlikely to invest. When consumers are insecure about the future, they are unlikely to spend.

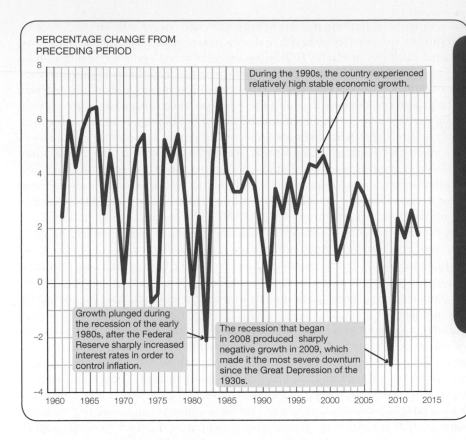

PERCENTAGE CHANGE FROM
PRECEDING PERIOD

During the 1990s, the country experienced relatively high stable economic growth.

Growth plunged during the recession of the early 1980s, after the Federal Reserve sharply increased interest rates in order to control inflation.

The recession that began in 2008 produced sharply negative growth in 2009, which made it the most severe downturn since the Great Depression of the 1930s.

FIGURE 16.1

Changes in Real Gross Domestic Product, 1960–2013

The rates of growth in gross domestic product have varied over time. They were particularly volatile during the 1980s as the economy first plunged into recession and then rapidly recovered with high rates of growth. What was the pattern of growth during the last five presidential election years?

SOURCE: Bureau of Economic Analysis, "Percent Change from Preceding Period in Real Gross Domestic Product," www.bea.gov (accessed 5/1/2014).

The federal government also promotes investment through its regulation of financial markets. The most important federal agency in this regard is the Securities and Exchange Commission (SEC), created after the stock market crash of 1929. The SEC requires companies to disclose information about the stocks and bonds they are selling, inform buyers of the investment risks, and protect investors against fraud. In this way the SEC helps maintain investor confidence and a strong supply of capital for American business. The SEC came in for harsh criticism during the financial crisis in 2008. Analysts pointed to weak SEC oversight and regulation as an important factor in the near collapse of the financial sector. Major financial reforms enacted in 2010 substantially beefed up the SEC's enforcement capabilities and require the agency to take the lead in implementing many of the key regulations.[4]

Public investment is another important source of growth in the American economy. In the 1930s and again in the late 1970s the federal government promoted public investment as a means to spark economic growth. Some kinds of public investment promote growth as a by-product of other, more central objectives. One of the most important of these is spending on the nation's defense. Many analysts credited the rise in military spending associated with the war in Iraq with helping to spur economic growth in 2003.

The second important condition for economic growth is innovation. The federal government has sought to support innovation in a variety of ways. One of the most important is through the National Science Foundation. Created in 1950, the National Science Foundation supports basic research across a range of fields in order to advance fundamental knowledge that may be broadly useful.[5] Federal government sponsorship of health research began in the late 1800s. Today, the National Institutes of Health (NIH) conducts basic and applied research in biomedicine. The Human Genome Project—the effort to map the basic genetic structure of human life—was initiated by government researchers and only later taken up by private corporations. Recently, the NIH has taken the lead in basic research to counter bioterrorism. Its efforts to understand the biology of various infectious agents and to develop vaccines are expected to produce important new knowledge about the human immune system. Research sponsored by the military has long been an important source of innovation for the American economy. Such key twentieth-century innovations as radar and nuclear power stemmed from military research. And as we saw in Chapter 14, military research also created the technology for the twenty-first century with ARPANET, the precursor to the Internet.

A third fundamental condition for economic growth is a sufficient and productive workforce. Federal immigration policy has played a key role in ensuring an adequate supply of labor throughout American history. Immigration laws routinely give special priority to workers who have skills that are in demand among American employers. Immigrants with nursing degrees, for example, have long received special priority.

Today, a productive workforce is a highly educated workforce. Education, as we will see in Chapter 17, is primarily the responsibility of state and local governments. The federal government, however, supports the development of a productive workforce with a variety of programs to promote higher education, such as educational grants, tax breaks, and loans. The federal government also sponsors a limited array of job-training programs that focus primarily on low-skilled workers. Some analysts argue that the federal government must do much more to support the development of a highly skilled workforce if the United States is to sustain economic growth in the future.

Full Employment Before the 1930s, neither the federal nor the state governments sought to promote full employment. Unemployment was widely viewed as an unfortunate occurrence that government could do little to alter. The New Deal response to the prolonged and massive unemployment of the Great Depression changed that view. The federal government put millions of people back to work on public projects sponsored by such programs as the Works Progress Administration (WPA). The bridges, parks, and buildings they constructed can still be seen across the United States today. The federal government viewed these programs as temporary measures, however. As the buildup for World War II boosted the economy and unemployment melted away, the employment programs were dismantled.

The New Deal and government wartime spending, however, showed that government could help ensure full employment. Public expectations changed as well: after the war, Americans looked to the federal government to reduce unemployment. Moreover, economic theory now supported their expectations. John Maynard Keynes's theories that government could boost employment by stimulating demand had become very influential.

Federal policy placed the most emphasis on achieving full employment during the 1960s. Keynesian economists in the Council of Economic Advisers persuaded President Kennedy to enact the first tax cut designed to stimulate the economy and promote full employment.[6] The policy was widely seen as a success,

How Are Americans Employed?

Occupations and Average Annual Wages

Sales and related occupations

13,646,450 $37,520

Food preparation and serving-related occupations

11,218,710 $21,430

Transportation and material moving occupations

8,635,940 $33,200

The government uses the policy tools at its disposal to promote a number of economic goals, including economic growth, full employment, and business development. The approximately 128.3 million Americans employed across various occupations benefit from these policies. But Americans are employed in diverse occupations with different needs and substantially different wages, which makes national employment policy complex.

- Number of employees
- Average annual wage

Education, training, and library occupations

8,409,060 $50,870

Health care practitioners and technical occupations

7,514,980 $72,730

Business and financial operations occupations

6,178,070 $68,740

Construction and extraction occupations

4,956,770 $44,630

Community and social service occupations

1,890,410 $43,830

Arts, design, entertainment, sports, and media occupations

1,725,670 $53,850

Legal occupations

1,002,330 $98,380

Farming, fishing, and forestry occupations

409,590 $24,300

SOURCE: Bureau of Labor Statistics, www.bls.gov/oes/2011/may/oes_nat.htm#13-0000 (accessed 5/9/14).

for critical analysis

1. What are the major occupational sectors in the American economy? How do wages differ across occupations?

2. Does government economic policy help some sectors of the economy more than others? Does it matter what the dominant occupations are?

One reason unemployment rose after 2008 was that numerous companies went out of business. The Circuit City chain, which had already begun layoffs before the economic crisis, closed all 500 of its stores by early 2009.

inflation a consistent increase in the general level of prices

categorical grants congressional grants given to states and localities on the condition that expenditures be limited to a problem or group specified by the law

and unemployment declined to a low of 3.4 percent in 1968. Favorable economic conditions in the 1990s reduced unemployment to record lows once again.

The worldwide economic recession of 2008 led to the loss of over 8 million American jobs. The Obama administration and Congress responded by passing a sweeping stimulus package called the American Recovery and Reinvestment Act in 2009, to help encourage economic growth, save existing jobs, and make longer-term investments that would encourage job creation, such as in weatherization projects and clean-technology construction. Despite these actions, the unemployment rate, still over 6 percent in 2014, remained stubbornly high years after the economy began growing again. The so-called jobless recovery left policy makers divided over how the government could best promote job creation.

Low Inflation During the 1970s and early 1980s, **inflation**, a consistent increase in the general level of prices, was one of America's most vexing problems. Rising prices harm consumers, especially those on a fixed income such as the elderly. Inflation also undermines the entire economy because it creates uncertainty about future prices, making investors cautious. Inflation was finally reduced from its historic highs of nearly 20 percent down toward 2 and 3 percent a year by the mid-1980s. Since that time, inflation has remained low. Even so, economic policy makers watch prices closely for any sign of inflation.

Promoting Business Development

During the nineteenth century, the national government promoted the development of important markets that eventually contributed significantly to U.S. GDP. National roads and canals were built to tie states and regions together. National tariff policies promoted domestic markets by restricting imported goods; a tax on an import raised its price and weakened its ability to compete with similar domestic products. The national government also heavily subsidized the railroad system. Until the 1840s, railroads were thought to be of limited commercial value. But between 1850 and 1872, Congress granted more than 100 million acres of public-domain land to railroad interests, and state and local governments pitched in an estimated $280 million in cash and credit. Before the end of the century, 35,000 miles of track existed, almost half the world's total at the time.

Railroads were not the only clients of federal support for the private markets. Many sectors of agriculture began receiving federal subsidies during the nineteenth century. Agriculture remains highly subsidized to this day. In 2005, 40 percent of farms in the United States received subsidies; by 2006 the total subsidy was estimated at more than $20 billion. One of the many criticisms of the farm subsidy program is that it disproportionately supports large-scale farmers rather than small family farmers. The list of farm subsidy recipients includes many large corporations.

The national government also promotes business development indirectly through **categorical grants** (see Chapter 3), whereby the federal government offers grants to states on condition that the state (or local) government undertake a particular activity. Thus, in order to use motor transportation to improve national markets, a 900,000-mile national highway system was built during the 1930s, based on a formula whereby the national government would pay 50 percent of the cost if the state provided the other 50 percent. Over 20 years, beginning in the late 1950s, the federal government constructed an additional 45,000 miles of interstate highways. In this program, the national government agreed to pay 90 percent of the

Since the early nineteenth century, the government has been an important promoter of business development in the United States. Beginning around 1850, federal, state, and local governments gave railroad companies the land on which to lay tracks and financial aid to construct the railroads. Railroads received additional land from the government, which they could sell at low prices to attract settlers to build along their lines.

construction costs on the condition that each state provide 10 percent of the costs of any portion of a highway built within its boundaries.[7] The tremendous growth of highways was a major boon to the automobile and trucking industries.

The federal government supports specific business sectors with direct subsidies, loans, and tax breaks. In 1953 the Small Business Administration (SBA) was created to offer loans, loan guarantees, and disaster assistance to small businesses. Recognizing that such businesses often find it harder to obtain financing and to recover from unexpected events such as fires, the federal government has provided assistance where the market would not. Today, the SBA provides more than $45 billion in such assistance to small businesses.

Among the many contemporary examples of policies promoting private industry, Sematech may be the most instructive. Sematech is a nonprofit research and development (R&D) consortium of major U.S. computer microchip manufacturers, set up in 1987 to work with government and academic institutions to reestablish U.S. leadership in semiconductor manufacturing. (The United States appeared to be in danger of losing out to the Japanese in this area during the 1980s.) The results of its research were distributed among the consortium members.[8] For nine years, industry and government together spent $1.7 billion to make the American microchip industry the leader in the world. The government contributed about half of the total expenditures. In 1997 federal funding was phased out. Industry leaders, convinced they no longer needed federal support, themselves initiated the break with government. At a critical moment, the federal government had stepped in to save the chip industry; it stepped out once that goal had been achieved.

Since September 11, 2001, the federal government has taken on a major role in promoting technological innovation related to national security. Even before the September 11 terrorist attacks, the CIA had set up its own venture capital firm, In-Q-Tel (the Q stands for a character in the James Bond movies), to invest in high-tech start-ups whose work could enhance intelligence efforts. More recently, the federal government has aimed to support the alternative energy industry. The Energy Policy Act of 2005 greatly increased the number and cost

The government promotes technological innovation and business growth in specific sectors. For example, businesses that provide renewable energy sources, such as wind power, have benefited from significant federal tax credits and loans in recent years.

of tax credits and loan programs for renewable and efficient energy technologies. As the recession hit, Washington stepped up its efforts to support the alternative energy industry, seeing it as a way to expand economic growth in an emerging sector. The Emergency Economic Stabilization Act of 2008 and the American Recovery and Reinvestment Act of 2009 expanded subsidies and created a new program allowing companies to receive a one-time cash grant in lieu of tax credits. Between 2013 and 2017, the federal government is projected to spend roughly $40 billion in tax-related support (including $17.2 billion for grants in lieu of tax credits) for the production of renewable energy, as well as an additional $10 billion to support energy efficiency and alternative technology vehicles.[9]

Protecting Employees and Consumers

Stable relations between business and labor are important elements of a productive economy. During the latter half of the nineteenth century, strikes over low wages or working conditions became a standard feature of American economic life. In fact, the United States has one of the most violent histories of labor relations in the world. Yet for most of American history, the federal government did little to regulate relations between business and labor. Local governments and courts often weighed in on the side of business by prohibiting strikes and arresting strikers.

As the economic depression enveloped the United States in the 1930s, plummeting wages and massive strikes for union recognition prompted Congress to pass the 1935 National Labor Relations Act, which set up a new framework for industrial relations. The new law created a permanent agency, the National Labor Relations Board (NLRB), charged with overseeing union elections and collective bargaining between labor and industry. The federal government weighed in further on the side of organized labor in 1938, when it passed the Fair Labor Standards Act, which created the minimum wage. Because it is not indexed to inflation, the value of the minimum wage declines if it is not raised periodically. Since 1938 conflicts over increasing the minimum wage have been a regular feature of American politics.

During the 1950s and '60s, the federal government played an active role in industrial relations. The Department of Labor and occasionally even the president directly intervened in labor-management disputes to ensure peaceful industrial relations. Although Democrats were generally seen as more supportive of labor, both parties sought to achieve a balance between business and labor that would promote a strong, stable economy.

President Reagan made a decisive break with this tradition of compromise in 1981, when he fired striking air traffic controllers (who were federal employees) and hired permanent replacements to take their jobs. Politicians are now much less likely to intervene in labor relations.

Economic policies also protect consumers. The idea that the federal government should protect consumers emerged in the first decade of the 1900s. Upton Sinclair's graphic exposé of the meatpacking industry, *The Jungle* (1906), galvanized public concern about unsanitary food processing. These concerns prompted the U.S. Department of Agriculture to inspect packing plants and the meat they produced, stamping approved meats with the now-familiar "USDA" certification. Similar concern about the safety of food, drugs, and cosmetics led to the creation of the Food and Drug Administration in 1927.

The movement for consumer protection took off again in the 1960s. The consumer advocate Ralph Nader's 1965 book *Unsafe at Any Speed* helped spark new demands for federal action. Nader's book showed that design flaws in the Corvair, a popular car model, had caused deaths that could have been prevented. Nader's book not only led to the demise of the Corvair but also mobilized calls for more federal action to protect consumers. The first response was the 1966 National Traffic and Motor Vehicle Safety Act, which gave the Department of Transportation responsibility for ensuring vehicle safety. Federal responsibility for consumer safety expanded in 1972, when Congress created the Consumer Product Safety Commission, an independent agency that informs consumers about hazards associated with products and works with industry to set product standards. In cases where safety concerns are severe, the commission will see that such products are recalled. Through the Consumer Product Safety Commission, the Department of Transportation, and the Food and Drug Administration, the federal government continues to play an active role in protecting the public from unsafe products.

In recent years, federal agencies have been very active in ensuring auto safety. Especially serious were charges that General Motors had hidden a problem related to its ignition system, which had caused 13 deaths. Some charged that the flaw may have caused even more fatalities. General Motors recalled 2.6 million cars but its failure to act earlier triggered a number of government investigations. The Justice Department launched an investigation about whether the company intentionally misled consumers. In addition, the new head of GM was called to testify before Senate and House panels about allegations that the company had failed to act even though it knew about the problems with the ignition system. Congressional investigators also probed why a federal agency, the National Highway Traffic Safety Administration, had failed to act, when it first learned of the defects.[10] The charges reveal the challenges involved in ensuring consumer safety when the government agencies charged with protecting the public do not take swift action.

The National Highways Traffic Safety Administration (NHTSA) is one government agency that protects consumers, in part by ensuring that vehicles are safe. However, the NHTSA failed to act on complaints about a serious flaw in some GM cars that led to numerous accidents before the cars were recalled in 2014.

for critical analysis

What does the American government do to ensure that the products Americans buy are safe? What challenges does it face in making certain that products are safe?

The Politics of Economic Policy Making

Explore why economic policy is often controversial

All politicians want a healthy economy, but they often differ in their views about how to attain it. Addressing economic challenges and maintaining a strong economy are extremely important to political leaders. As presidents from Herbert Hoover (who presided over the beginning of the Great Depression of the 1930s) to Jimmy Carter (who faced double-digit inflation) discovered, voters will punish politicians for poor economic performance. In the 50 years that followed the Great Depression and the federal government's first big steps into the economy, politicians from both parties agreed that the government played an important role in ensuring a strong economy. They did not always agree about what priorities should guide economic policy. Democrats generally expressed more concern about unemployment than did Republicans, who focused more on reducing budget deficits. In the 1980s, however, the differences between the parties on economic policy became much more fundamental. While Democrats and Republicans alike embraced a smaller role for the government in the economy, growing numbers of Republicans began to reject the idea that government should intervene in the economy at all. Instead, they argued that a free market was the best way to ensure economic prosperity. Democrats continued to believe that economic prosperity required government action.

Should the Government Intervene in the Economy?

Until 1929 most Americans believed that government had little to do with actively managing the economy. The world was guided by the theory—called laissez-faire economics—that the economy, if left to its own devices, would produce full employment and maximum production. This traditional view of the relationship between government and the economy crumbled in 1929 before the stark reality of the Great Depression of 1929–33. Some misfortune befell nearly everyone. Around 20 percent of the workforce became unemployed, and few of these individuals had any monetary resources or the old family farm to fall back on. Banks failed, wiping out the savings of millions who had been prudent enough or fortunate enough to have any. Thousands of businesses closed, throwing middle-class Americans onto the bread lines alongside unemployed laborers and dispossessed farmers. The Great Depression proved to Americans that the economic system was not, in fact, perfectly self-regulating, as had been generally believed.

Demands grew for the federal government to act. In Congress, some Democrats proposed that the federal government finance public works to aid the economy and put people back to work. Other members introduced legislation to provide federal grants to the states to assist their relief efforts.

When President Franklin Delano Roosevelt took office in 1933, he energetically threw the federal government into the business of fighting the Depression. He proposed a variety of temporary measures to provide federal relief and work programs. Most of the programs he proposed were to be financed by the federal government but administered by the states. In addition to these temporary measures, Roosevelt presided over the creation of several important federal programs designed to provide future economic security for Americans. Since that time, the public has held the government, and the president in particular, responsible for ensuring a healthy economy.

One of the main ways that the federal government sought to keep the economy healthy was through decisions about taxing and spending in accordance with the ideas of the British economist John Maynard Keynes. **Keynesians** argue that by pumping money into the economy, particularly by running deficits during periods of recession, government can stimulate demand and create a cycle of increased production and jobs that will pull the economy out of recession. Governments can do this by increasing public spending through such measures as public works or public employment, or by temporary tax cuts. Tax cuts will allow workers to keep more of their earnings; their increased spending power will boost consumption and increase demand.[11]

After World War II, Republicans and Democrats broadly agreed that Keynesian ideas could best guide economic policy. By the 1960s Keynesians believed that economic policy did not need to provoke political controversy because they could ensure ongoing prosperity by "fine-tuning" the economy. Democrats and Republicans often disagreed about how much the government should do to alleviate unemployment or inflation but they shared a pragmatic view that government intervention could solve economic problems. President Richard Nixon, a Republican, reflected the strong consensus behind Keynesian ideas when he remarked in 1971, "Now I am a Keynesian." The question about whether and how government should intervene in the economy appeared settled.

Keynesians followers of the economic theories of John Maynard Keynes, who argued that the government can stimulate the economy by increasing public spending or by cutting taxes

Partisan Divisions over the Government Role in the Economy By the 1980s the broad consensus about the role of the government in the economy had evaporated. Growing numbers of Republicans began to reject the idea that government could help ensure economic prosperity. Instead, they argued that freeing markets from government intervention would produce the best economic results. As Ronald Reagan put it in his first inaugural address, "Government is not the solution to our problem, government is the problem."[12]

Thus the ideas of **laissez-faire capitalism** began to make a comeback in American politics. These arguments were first elaborated in the late 1700s by the great Scottish economist Adam Smith. Smith believed that most government involvement in the economy (such as the government-authorized monopolies that dominated trade in his day) suppressed economic growth. Instead, he argued that competition among free enterprises would unleash economic energy, fostering growth and innovation. In his view, the self-seeking behavior of individuals, when subject to the discipline of market competition, would create products that consumers wanted at the best possible price. Smith praised "the invisible hand" of the market, by which he meant that millions of individual economic transactions together create a greater good—far better than the government could create. Smith believed that the government role should be restricted to national defense, establishing law and order (including the protection of private property), and providing basic public goods (such as roads) that facilitate commerce.

Although only a few politicians would entirely remove government from the economy, Republicans draw on the ideas of laissez-faire economics as they argue for significant reductions in the government's role. Many Democrats, on the other hand, continue to believe that government has an important role to play in promoting a strong economy. This fundamental disagreement between the parties over the appropriate role of government underlies the fierce contemporary political debates over the government role in taxes, spending, and economic regulation.

Taxes Today some of the most intense conflicts between Democrats and Republicans concern taxes. As Republicans embraced the idea that reducing the role of government in the economy would promote investment and spur economic growth, they made tax cuts their highest priority. Rejecting Keynesian ideas, they adopted the idea of **supply-side economics**. This approach maintains that lower tax rates create incentives for more productive and efficient use of resources. When individuals know they can keep more of their earnings, they are more likely to be productive workers and creative investors. In this perspective, low taxes are not just a temporary measure to stimulate the economy; taxes should remain low at all times to ensure a growing economy.

Because no one really likes to pay taxes, Republican support for tax cuts creates a political dilemma for Democrats. How can they defend taxes? Polls show that most of the time—although not always—a majority of Americans think that their taxes are too high.[13] Aware of the

laissez-faire capitalism an economic system in which the means of production and distribution are privately owned and operated for profit with minimal or no government interference

supply-side economics an economic theory that posits that reducing the marginal rate of taxation will create a productive economy by promoting levels of work and investment that would otherwise be discouraged by higher taxes

"Supply-siders" argue that reducing tax rates will spur economic growth, as people are able to spend and invest more of their money. In the 1980s, President Ronald Reagan— shown here holding an oversize tax form—sought to simplify the tax laws and reduce taxes.

political damage that might come from opposing tax cuts, many Democratic members of Congress have supported tax cuts. But because most Democrats favor higher levels of public spending than do Republicans, they ultimately need taxes to fund government programs. To resolve this political problem, Democrats have sought to increase taxes on the wealthy. One reliable finding in public opinion polls is that the majority of Americans agree that upper-income people are not paying their fair share of taxes.[14] Raising taxes on the wealthy involves boosting taxes on investment income, which accounts for a much greater share of the income for the wealthy. By making the rich the target for tax increases and highlighting the special tax loopholes they enjoy, Democrats hope to turn the politics of taxes to their advantage.

Spending and Deficits Government spending is another area where the two parties have locked horns. Contending that the federal government has become too big, Republicans argue for reduced government spending. In their view, big government is not only wasteful, it is also a drag on the economy. Moreover, Republicans argue, excessive spending creates deficits, which can harm the economy. It is not hard to convince Americans that government spending is wasteful or that government is too big or that deficits are bad. When asked, a majority of Americans regularly say they would prefer a smaller government with fewer services.[15]

Yet, polls reveal little support for cutting specific government programs (see Figure 16.2).[16] In fact, the public shows the strongest support for the most expensive government programs. Social Security, which provides pensions to the elderly, and Medicare, which supplies health insurance for the elderly, are both politically popular. Only the most ardent spending foes among Republicans have argued for cutting these programs. Indeed, in 2003 Republicans agreed to a major expansion in Medicare spending by adding a prescription drug benefit to the program. The popularity of these programs reflects the fact that government provides real benefits to real people. President Obama has articulated the position that the government should help to provide what individuals cannot provide for themselves. Democrats therefore support government spending on education, infrastructure, health care, and other public programs. Taking away these programs will deny economic opportunities to Americans, they believe, and in so doing, will hurt the national economy.

Because neither party wishes to cut big, expensive, popular programs and because tax increases have been so difficult to enact, budget deficits have grown periodically over the past three decades. Democratic critics point to rising deficits as proof that supply-side economics does not work; they argue that the economy would be better off without tax cuts. Some go further, arguing that Republicans deliberately reduced taxes in order to win support for spending cuts. This strategy, called "starving the beast," suggests that spending cuts would become more popular in the face of rising deficits.[17]

Because it is politically difficult to raise taxes or reduce big spending programs, most cuts have fallen on smaller programs, often those adminsitered by the states. As we will see, this is what happened in 2013 after a Republican and Democratic standoff over the deficit led to a set of cuts applied to smaller programs. Unusually, in 2013 these spending reductions also applied to military spending. The unpopularity of the cuts and a declining deficit led Congress to soften the impact of spending reductions in 2014.

for critical analysis

How does government spending hurt the economy? How does government spending help the economy?

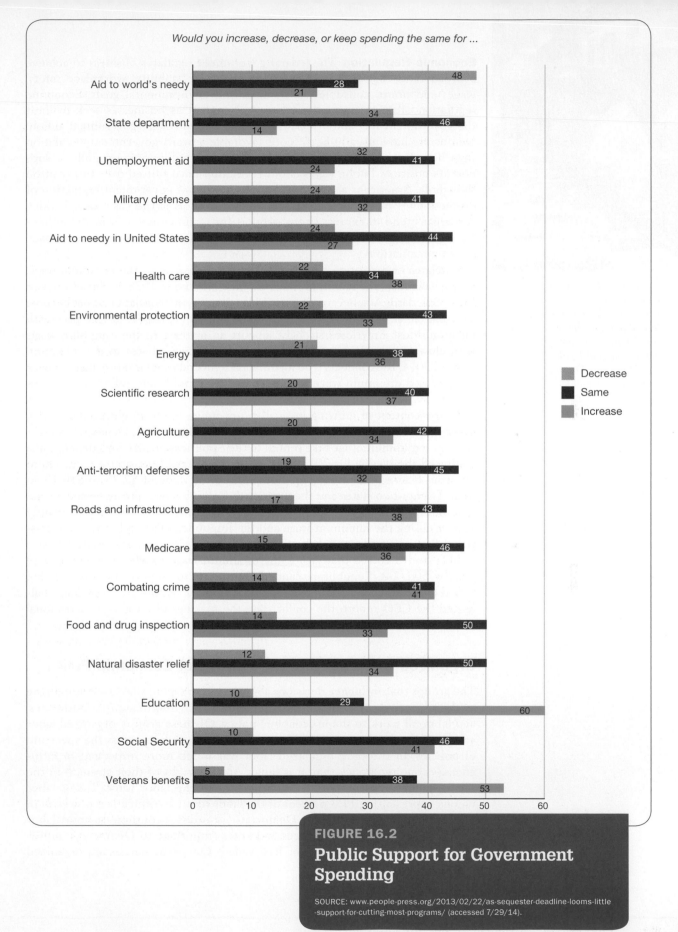

Would you increase, decrease, or keep spending the same for ...

	Decrease	Same	Increase
Aid to world's needy	48	28	21
State department	34	46	14
Unemployment aid	32	41	24
Military defense	24	41	32
Aid to needy in United States	24	44	27
Health care	22	34	38
Environmental protection	22	43	33
Energy	21	38	36
Scientific research	20	40	37
Agriculture	20	42	34
Anti-terrorism defenses	19	45	32
Roads and infrastructure	17	43	38
Medicare	15	46	36
Combating crime	14	41	41
Food and drug inspection	14	50	33
Natural disaster relief	12	50	34
Education	10	29	60
Social Security	10	46	41
Veterans benefits	5	38	53

FIGURE 16.2

Public Support for Government Spending

SOURCE: www.people-press.org/2013/02/22/as-sequester-deadline-looms-little-support-for-cutting-most-programs/ (accessed 7/29/14).

As of early 2014, the federal minimum wage was $7.25. Democrats in Congress argued that minimum-wage workers, like these restaurant employees, could not live on so little, and 22 states already required businesses to pay a higher minimum wage. However, Republicans worried that raising the federal minimum wage would increase unemployment.

Economic Regulation The federal government regulates business to achieve a broad range of objectives, including economic stability, workplace safety, wages and hours, consumer satisfaction, and environmental goals. Economic regulation often attracts intense political conflict as businesses seek to limit the government role and other interests press for stronger government action. Democrats have usually been more favorable toward government regulation than have Republicans. Each party can point to public opinion polls to support its position. Public views about regulation have shifted over time but on the whole, Americans agree with the statement that government regulation of business does more harm than good.[18] However, as is the case for spending, Americans tend to express strong support for maintaining or even strengthening current regulations. Only a small percentage of Americans want to roll back existing regulations.

One area of regulation that sharply divides the parties is the minimum wage. As we have seen, the minimum wage was first enacted in 1938 as part of the Fair Labor Standards Act. Because it is not indexed to rise with inflation, it has become a regular target of political conflict, as supporters aim to raise it to keep pace with inflation. Most Americans strongly support an increase in the minimum wage, with close to three-quarters of Americans supporting a boost in the minimum wage in 2014. Respondents who identify as Democrats are far more likely to back an increased minimum wage but about half of Republicans polled also express support.[19]

In the context of growing inequality, upcoming midterm elections in 2014, and a federal minumum wage that had not risen since 2007, Democrats sought to make a minimum wage hike central to their political agenda. President Obama embraced the idea in his 2014 State of the Union Address, urging Congress to raise the federal minimum wage from its current value of $7.25 to $10.10 an hour. Twenty-two states and the District of Columbia had already enacted state minimum wages higher than the federal wage. But with business adamantly against raising the minimum wage and the Republican base split, most congressional Republicans opposed the increase. When a Congressional Budget Office (CBO) study showed that raising the minimum wage to $10.10 would reduce jobs by 500,000, Republicans faulted Democrats for supporting a policy that would cut jobs when unemployment was still high.[20] Although Democrats challenged the CBO report, the conflict had the makings of a classic congressional stalemate. (See Figure 16.3.)

Organized Interests and the Politics of Economic Policy

The groups that influence decisions about economic policy are as wide-ranging as the objectives of policy. Consumer groups, environmentalists, businesses, and labor all work to shape economic policy. Of these groups, organized labor and business are the most consistent actors that weigh in across the spectrum of policies. In the past, organized labor was much more important in influencing economic policy than it is today. At the height of their strength in the 1950s, unions represented some 35 percent of the labor force. Today, labor unions, representing 11.3 percent of the labor force, are much less powerful in influencing economic policy.[21] Democratic presidents continue to court labor because unions control resources and votes important to Democratic politicians, but labor's overall power has waned. On particular issues, organized

MINIMUM WAGE

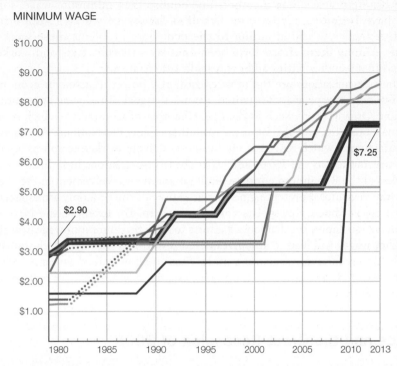

MINIMUM WAGE ADJUSTED FOR INFLATION (2013 DOLLARS)

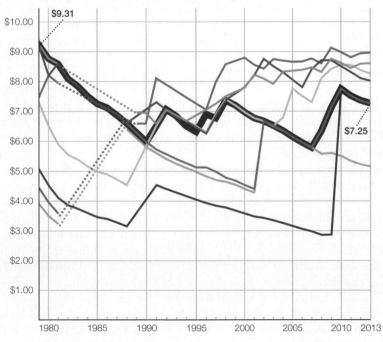

FIGURE 16.3

The Minimum Wage, 1979–2013

The federal government and most U.S. states have minimum wage laws. The minimum wage has increased over time across the United States (see top graph). However, near-constant inflation during this time period has reduced the real value of these wages, so the purchasing power of the minimum wage has declined. Illinois, Oregon, and Vermont have had some of the highest minimum wages in the country. Georgia, Texas, and Kansas have had minimum wages that are among the lowest. How do the data in these graphs relate to arguments for or against a higher federal minimum wage?

NOTE: Department of Labor data are not available for all states for all years. A dotted line indicates a gap of more than two years in the data.

SOURCES: Department of Labor Wage and Hour Division, www.dol.gov/whd/state/stateMinWageHis.htm (accessed 6/4/14); Consumer Price Index, www.bls.gov/data (accessed 6/4/14).

labor can still exercise significant influence. For example, labor played a key role in Congress's decision to increase the minimum wage in 2007 and was a key advocate of boosting the federal minimum wage to $10.10 an hour in 2014. Although most union members make more than minimum wage, some unions have begun to advocate on behalf of low-wage workers, supporting innovative tactics to call attention to the economic problems these workers confront. Among these efforts have been one-day strikes by fast-food workers launched in a hundred cities and protests in other cities.[22]

Business organizations are the most consistently powerful actors in economic policy. Business groups are most united around the goal of reducing government regulation. Organizations, such as the U.S. Chamber of Commerce, which represents small business, and the Business Roundtable and the National Association of Manufacturers, which represent big business, actively worked to roll back government regulation in the 1970s and '80s. These organizations have been strong supporters of the Republican efforts to limit government involvement in the economy. Business groups representing particular sectors of the economy are especially active on issues that are of special concern to them. For example, the National Restaurant Association has denounced efforts to raise the minimum wage, warning that higher wages will lead to automation and fewer jobs. The high-tech industry regularly argues in favor of granting more visas to allow skilled foreign workers into the country. Other industry groups, particularly in agriculture, lobby to retain subsidies that they have enjoyed for decades.

Politics and the Great Recession of 2008

for critical **analysis**

The role of government in the economy has waxed and waned over time. What circumstances might prompt greater government involvement? What circumstances might suggest a smaller governmental role?

The severe economic downturn that began in 2008, often called the "Great Recession," provoked unprecedented government intervention into the economy. As the near-collapse of the financial sector in 2008 reverberated throughout the U.S. (and world) economy, thousands of Americans lost their homes, banks refused to lend, and unemployment rose. The federal government, first under George W. Bush and then under Barack Obama, initiated large-scale government interventions in the hope of staving off the downward economic spiral. These included emergency measures to bail out failing companies, short-term stimulus to get the economy moving again, and proposals for regulations that would prevent similar financial meltdowns in the future. However, support for these measures wavered as fear of rising deficits, exploding long-term debt, and, more abstractly, "big government" grew.

Propping up the financial sector presented an economic challenge for federal officials. President Bush found he could not count on support from congressional Republicans when he sought to enact a major bailout for the financial sector. A bipartisan group in Congress ultimately approved a $700 billion emergency "bailout" in October 2008 (known as the Troubled Asset Relief Program, or TARP), which the Treasury Department drew on to infuse major financial institutions with capital. It was not just major banking institutions that faced ruin. Auto companies, teetering on the edge of bankruptcy, also received major infusions of cash from the federal government.[23] By late 2010 the economy had stabilized sufficiently that many of the financial institutions that had received funds under TARP were able to pay the federal government back. The CBO estimated that TARP would end up costing taxpayers $34 billion, far less than the initial $700 billion.[24]

Congress also passed a sweeping package in 2009 to help stimulate the economy, save jobs (particularly in the public sector), and make longer-term investments that would help stimulate economic growth. The $789 billion American Recovery and Reinvestment Act (more commonly known as the "stimulus" bill of 2009) contained a number of measures to stimulate growth in the short term and prevent drastic cuts to public services. Among the most important measures in the act were reductions in individual and business taxes by $288 billion in order to generate more spending and job hiring. The measure also spent $195.5 billion on aid, health insurance subsidies, and job training for low-income and unemployed workers, and $44.5 billion designed to limit teacher layoffs and cutbacks in local school districts. The rest of the investments not only aimed to create new jobs in the short term but also sought to be long-term investments in infrastructure and education that would help future growth. The act reflected Keynesian logic that called for public investment during periods of economic downturn.

Although only some Republicans and Democrats had balked at supporting the financial bailout package in 2008, by early 2009 a sharp partisan rift had become evident. No Republicans in the House and only three in the Senate voted to support the 2009 stimulus package. Republicans denounced the House measure as overly tilted toward spending rather than tax cuts. But even when Senate Democrats added significant new tax cuts to the bill, most Republicans still opposed it. While Democrats defended the measure as an infusion of funds needed to prevent a depression, Republicans denounced it as wasteful spending and made their opposition a defining stance toward the Obama administration. Mounting unemployment complicated the political judgments about the stimulus; despite the injection of public funds into the economy, national unemployment rose to a seasonally adjusted rate of 9.6 by September 2010, with rates much higher in some states.[25] The nonpartisan CBO estimated that ARRA increased the number of full-time jobs by as many as 2 million.[26] Yet because unemployment remained high, ARRA did not get much credit from the public for helping the economy, and it attracted considerable criticism for contributing to the budget deficit. When Congress considered a second stimulus bill focused on job-creation, it succeeded in enacting a relatively small job-creation package worth $15 billion, most of which consisted of tax credits for businesses that hired new employees.[27]

The American Recovery and Readjustment Act provided $787 billion to support economic growth following the recession that began in 2008. Among other provisions, the act included funding for projects that would help keep Americans employed during the downturn.

● The Tools of Economic Policy

Describe how the government uses monetary, fiscal, and regulatory policies to influence the economy

The U.S. economy is no accident; it is the result of specific policies that have expanded American markets and sustained massive economic growth. The Constitution provides that Congress shall have the power

To lay and collect Taxes, . . . to pay the Debts and provide for the common Defence and general Welfare; . . . To borrow Money; . . . To coin Money [and] regulate the Value thereof.

These clauses of Article I, Section 8, are the constitutional sources of the fiscal and monetary policies of the national government. The Constitution says nothing, however, about *how* these powers can be used, although the way they are used shapes the economy. As it works to meet the multiple goals of economic policy, the federal government relies on a broad set of tools that has evolved over time. Let us now turn to the actual tools designed to accomplish the goals of economic policy. As we will see, decisions about which tools to use are not simply technical choices, they are highly political decisions that reflect political conflicts over whether the government should act at all and if so, which tools to use and when to use them.

Monetary Policies

monetary policies efforts to regulate the economy through the manipulation of the supply of money and credit; America's most powerful institution in this area of monetary policy is the Federal Reserve Board

Monetary policies manipulate the growth of the entire economy by controlling the availability of money to banks. With very few exceptions, banks in the United States are privately owned and locally operated. Until well into the twentieth century, banks were regulated, if at all, by state legislatures. Each bank was granted a charter, which gave it permission to make loans, hold deposits, and make investments within that state. Although more than 25,000 banks continue to be chartered by the states, they are less important in the overall financial picture than they used to be, as the most important banks now are members of the federal banking system.

Federal Reserve System a system of 12 Federal Reserve banks that facilitates exchanges of cash, checks, and credit; regulates member banks; and uses monetary policies to fight inflation and deflation

Federal Reserve System But banks did not become the core of American capitalism without intense political controversy. The Federalist majority in Congress, led by Alexander Hamilton, did in fact establish a Bank of the United States, in 1791, but it was vigorously opposed by agrarian interests, led by Thomas Jefferson, who feared that the interests of urban, industrial capitalism would dominate such a bank. The Bank of the United States was terminated during the administration of Andrew Jackson, but the fear of a central, public bank lingered eight decades later, when, in 1913, Congress established an institution, the **Federal Reserve System**, to integrate private banks into a single national system. The Federal Reserve System did not become a central bank in the European tradition but rather is composed of 12 Federal Reserve banks, each located in a major commercial city. The Federal Reserve banks are not ordinary banks; they are banker's banks that make loans to other banks, clear checks, and supply the economy with currency and coins. They also play a regulatory role over the member banks. Every national bank must be a member of the Federal Reserve System and must follow national banking rules. State banks and savings and loan associations may also join if they accept national rules. At the top of the system is the Federal Reserve Board—"the Fed"—comprising 7 members appointed by the president (with Senate confirmation) for 14-year terms. The chairman of the Fed is selected by the president from among the 7 members of the board for a 4-year term. In all other concerns, however, the Fed is an independent agency (see Chapter 14) inasmuch as its members cannot be removed during their terms except "for cause," and the president's executive power does not extend to them or their policies. Nonetheless, observers charged the longtime Federal Reserve chairman, Alan Greenspan, with being attentive to politics, for example, in his endorsement of President George W. Bush's tax cuts. In his 2005 confirmation hearings to head the Fed, the economist Ben Bernanke promised Congress that he would be "strictly independent of all political influences."[28]

The major advantage that a bank gains from being in the Federal Reserve System is that it can borrow from the system. This enables banks to expand their loan

The chair of the Federal Reserve is one of the most important people in Washington, as the Fed plays an important role in maintaining a strong national economy. At her confirmation hearing in 2013, Janet Yellen discussed the role of the Fed in reducing unemployment and in keeping inflation at approximately 2 percent a year.

operations continually, as long as there is demand for loans in the economy. On the other hand, it is this very access of member banks to the Federal Reserve System that gives the Fed its power: the ability to expand and contract the *amount of credit* available in the United States.

The Fed can affect the total amount of credit through the interest (called the **federal funds rate**) that member banks charge one another for loans. If the Fed significantly decreases the federal funds rate, making it cheaper to borrow money, this can give a boost to a sagging economy. In the steep recession that began in 2008, the Fed acted aggressively. By December 2008 it had cut rates nine times from a high in September 2007 of 4.75 percent to a historically low percentage rate close to zero. Moreover, the Federal Reserve kept interest rates at that same low level well into 2014, in an attempt to encourage lending again and thus economic growth.[29] If the Fed raises the federal funds rate, it can put a brake on the economy, because the higher rates make it more expensive to borrow money. This makes it more difficult for new businesses to get loans, for instance.

Although the Federal Reserve is responsible for ensuring high employment as well as price stability, it has been particularly important in fighting inflation. During the late 1970s and early 1980s, with inflation at record high levels, Federal Reserve chairman Paul Volcker aggressively raised interest rates in order to dampen inflation. Although his actions provoked a sharp recession, they raised the stature of the Fed, demonstrating its ability to manage the economy. Because the Fed is so closely associated with inflation fighting, Senate Democrats pressed Ben Bernanke, President George W. Bush's nominee to head the Fed, to indicate at his nomination hearings that he would view maximum employment as a goal of equal importance to that of fighting inflation. In 2014, Janet Yellen, the new head of the Fed, vowed to continue the focus on employment.

for critical analysis

Why is the Federal Reserve so important to economic policy?

federal funds rate the interest rate on loans between banks that the Federal Reserve Board influences by affecting the supply of money available

Another power of the Fed is called **open-market operations**, whereby the Fed buys and sells government securities. When the Fed buys government securities in the open market, it is pumping money into the economy and stimulating economic activity; when it sells securities, it is applying brakes to the economy.

Fostering Investment The federal government also provides insurance to foster credit and encourage private capital investment. The Federal Deposit Insurance Corporation (FDIC) insures bank deposits up to $250,000. Another important promoter of investment is the federal insurance of home mortgages through the Department of Housing and Urban Development (HUD). By guaranteeing mortgages, the government can reduce the risks that banks run in making such loans, thus allowing banks to lower their interest rates and making such loans more affordable to middle- and lower-income families. Such programs have enabled millions of families that could not otherwise have afforded it to finance the purchase of a home.

This system began to unravel in the first decade of the 2000s, with the growth of the subprime market for lending. This market made home loans available to people who could not otherwise have afforded to buy a home. At the same time, however, it created new instabilities in the market by offering risky loans that would become more costly due to adjustable interest rates. The slowing housing market in 2007 set off a wave of foreclosures as many homeowners discovered that they could not pay back their loans. After the recession hit in 2008, many more Americans lost their homes to foreclosures: by 2012 nearly 3 million homes had been lost. Estimates showed that another 3 million homes could be foreclosed over the next three years.[30]

The foreclosure crisis in turn sent shock waves through the financial system, as investment banks found themselves holding worthless loans. One casualty of the home loan meltdown was the Wall Street investment bank Bear Stearns, which faced bankruptcy early in March 2008. Seeking to limit the harm to the broader economy that such a bankruptcy would cause, Fed chairman Bernanke arranged for Bear Stearns to be bought, at bargain-basement prices, by JPMorgan Chase, another investment bank. In making this move, Bernanke was exercising powers of the Federal Reserve Act that had not been used since the 1930s.[31] After the firm Lehman Brothers collapsed in 2008 and several other investment banks and insurance companies moved closer to insolvency, the Federal Reserve also provided billions of dollars to banks so that they could continue to lend money for student loans, auto loans, and residential mortgages. In all, the Fed gave nearly $400 billion in emergency loans to financial institutions.[32]

Although many were impressed by the swift action undertaken by the Fed, critics charged that its supervision of the banking system prior to the crisis had been too lax. This led to an unusually contentious set of Senate confirmation hearings for Chairman Bernanke, whom President Obama had renominated in 2009. Most Democrats prefer that the Federal Reserve take a strong stand in regulating banks and in prioritizing the problem of unemployment. Republicans, on the other hand, fear that excessive regulation will limit economic growth. Republicans are more likely to see unemployment as a problem of workers who lack appropriate job skills, rather than a problem that requires more stimulus of the economy.

Fiscal Policies

Fiscal policy includes the government's taxing and spending powers. Personal and corporate income taxes, which raise most of the U.S. government's revenues, are the most prominent examples. Although the direct purpose of an income tax is to raise revenue, each tax has a different impact on the economy, and government can attempt to plan for that impact.

Taxation During the nineteenth century, the federal government received most of its revenue from a single tax, the **tariff**. It also relied on excise taxes, which are taxes levied on specific products, such as tobacco and alcohol. As federal activities expanded in the 1900s, the federal government added new sources of tax revenue. The most important was the income tax, proposed by Congress in 1909, ratified by the states, and added to the Constitution in 1913 as the Sixteenth Amendment. The income tax is levied on individuals and corporations. With the creation of the Social Security system in 1935, social insurance taxes became an additional source of federal revenue.

Before World War II, individual income taxes accounted for only 14 percent of federal revenues.[33] The need to raise revenue for World War II made the income tax much more important. Congress expanded the base of the income tax so that most Americans paid income taxes after World War II. Figure 16.4 shows several notable shifts that have occurred in taxes since 1960. Social insurance taxes now compose a much greater share of federal revenues, rising from 15.9 percent of revenues in 1960 to an estimated 34 percent in 2014. Receipts from corporate income taxes declined over the same period, dropping from 23.2 percent of receipts in 1960 to 11.1 percent in 2014. The share of the federal individual income tax has remained fairly stable; it was 44.0 percent in 1960 and estimated at 46.2 percent in 2014.

One of the most important features of the American income tax is that it is a "progressive," or "graduated," tax, with the heaviest burden carried by those most able to pay. A tax is called **progressive** if the rate of taxation goes up with

tariff a tax on imported goods

progressive taxation taxation that hits upper income brackets more heavily

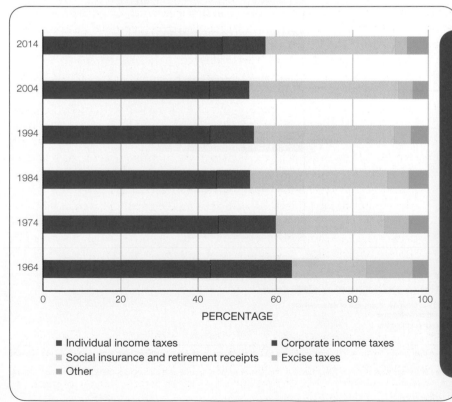

FIGURE 16.4

Federal Revenues by Type of Tax

The federal government collects revenue from a variety of different taxes. Most important is the individual income tax, which has accounted for approximately 45 percent of federal revenue over the past 50 years. Revenues from corporate income tax have fallen considerably over this time period, from 20.9 percent in 1964 to 11 percent in 2014. In the same period, taxes for social insurance and retirement have grown substantially. Does the federal government draw more of its revenue from progressive taxes or regressive taxes?

SOURCE: Office of Management and Budget, "Percentage Composition of Receipts by Source: 1934–2019," The Budget for Fiscal Year 2015, www.whitehouse.gov (accessed 4/2/14).

Chart legend:
- Individual income taxes
- Corporate income taxes
- Social insurance and retirement receipts
- Excise taxes
- Other

X-axis: PERCENTAGE (0, 20, 40, 60, 80, 100)
Y-axis years: 2014, 2004, 1994, 1984, 1974, 1964

Tax Rates around the World

How do tax rates in the United States compare to those in other countries? Focusing just on personal income taxes, different countries have different tax rates depending on income, and individuals may receive tax relief if they are married or have children. As the first figure here shows, U.S. income tax rates (federal plus average state income taxes) are slightly below average when compared to other countries in the Organization for Economic Cooperation and Development (OECD).

However, when we look at the total tax burden as a share of the country's economy (GDP), the tax burden in the United States is significantly less than in other wealthy countries. The second figure shows how the United States compares to selected OECD countries and the average for all OECD countries. When we compare total tax revenue as a percentage of GDP,[a] Chile and Mexico are the only OECD members that have a lower tax burden than the United States.[b]

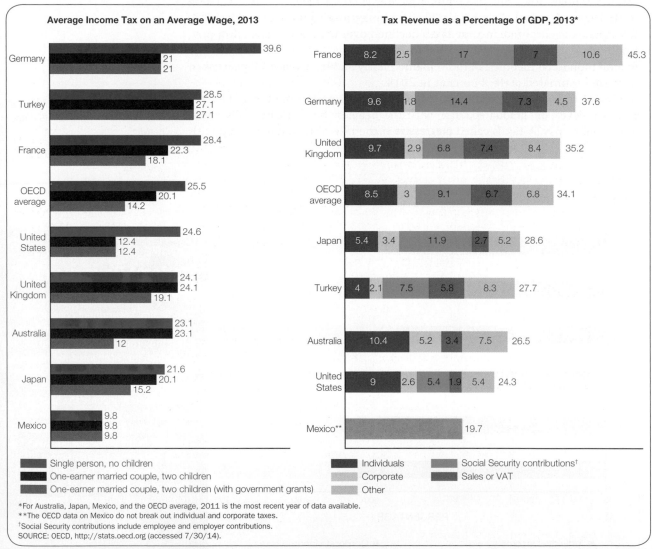

Average Income Tax on an Average Wage, 2013

Germany: 39.6 / 21 / 21
Turkey: 28.5 / 27.1 / 27.1
France: 28.4 / 22.3 / 18.1
OECD average: 25.5 / 20.1 / 14.2
United States: 24.6 / 12.4 / 12.4
United Kingdom: 24.1 / 24.1 / 19.1
Australia: 23.1 / 23.1 / 12
Japan: 21.6 / 20.1 / 15.2
Mexico: 9.8 / 9.8 / 9.8

- Single person, no children
- One-earner married couple, two children
- One-earner married couple, two children (with government grants)

Tax Revenue as a Percentage of GDP, 2013*

France: 8.2 / 2.5 / 17 / 7 / 10.6 — 45.3
Germany: 9.6 / 1.8 / 14.4 / 7.3 / 4.5 — 37.6
United Kingdom: 9.7 / 2.9 / 6.8 / 7.4 / 8.4 — 35.2
OECD average: 8.5 / 3 / 9.1 / 6.7 / 6.8 — 34.1
Japan: 5.4 / 3.4 / 11.9 / 2.7 / 5.2 — 28.6
Turkey: 4 / 2.1 / 7.5 / 5.8 / 8.3 — 27.7
Australia: 10.4 / 5.2 / 3.4 / 7.5 — 26.5
United States: 9 / 2.6 / 5.4 / 1.9 / 5.4 — 24.3
Mexico**: 19.7

- Individuals
- Corporate
- Other
- Social Security contributions[†]
- Sales or VAT

*For Australia, Japan, Mexico, and the OECD average, 2011 is the most recent year of data available.
**The OECD data on Mexico do not break out individual and corporate taxes.
[†]Social Security contributions include employee and employer contributions.
SOURCE: OECD, http://stats.oecd.org (accessed 7/30/14).

[a]Since larger, wealthier economies generate more tax revenue than smaller and poorer countries, controlling for GDP gives us a more comparable measure of tax burdens across different types of economies.
[b]OECD.StatExtract, "All-In Average Personal Income Tax Rates at Average Wage by Family Type," Table I.6, http://stats.oecd.org/index.aspx?DataSetCode=TABLE_I6 (accessed 7/31/14).

each higher income bracket. A tax is called **regressive** if people in lower income brackets pay a higher proportion of their income toward the tax than people in higher income brackets. For example, a sales tax is deemed regressive because everybody pays at the same rate, so that people who make less money end up paying a greater share of their income in sales taxes than do people who make more money. The Social Security tax is another example of a regressive tax. In 2014, Social Security law applied a tax of 6.2 percent on the first $117,000 of income for the retirement program and an additional 1.45 percent on all income (without limit) for Medicare benefits, for a total of 7.65 percent in Social Security taxes. This means that a person earning an income of $117,000 pays $8,950 in Social Security taxes, a rate of 7.65 percent. But someone earning twice that income, $234,000, pays a total of $11,267 in Social Security taxes, a rate of 4.55 percent. As one's income continues to rise, the amount of Social Security taxes also rises (until the cap is reached), but the rate, or the percentage of one's income that goes to taxes, declines. As part of the Affordable Care Act, high earners (individuals making over $200,000 and couples earning more than $250,000) faced an additional Medicare tax of 0.9 percent on all of their income.

regressive taxation taxation that hits lower income brackets more heavily

Although the primary purpose of the graduated income tax is, of course, to raise revenue, an important second objective is to collect revenue in such a way as to reduce the disparities of wealth between the lowest and the highest income brackets. We call this a policy of **redistribution**. Another policy objective of the income tax is the encouragement of the capitalist economy by rewarding investment. The tax laws allow individuals or companies to deduct from their taxable income any money they can justify as an investment or a "business expense"; this gives an incentive to individuals and companies to spend money to expand their production, their advertising, or their staff, and reduces the income taxes that businesses have to pay. These kinds of deductions are called incentives or "equity" by those who support them; others call them **loopholes**. The tax reforms of the 1980s actually closed a number of important loopholes in U.S. tax laws. But others still exist—on home mortgages and on business expenses, for example—and others will likely return, because there is a strong consensus among members of Congress, both Democrats and Republicans, that businesses often need such incentives. The differences between the two parties focus largely on which incentives are justifiable.[34]

redistribution a policy whose objective is to tax or spend in such a way as to reduce the disparities of wealth between the lowest and the highest income brackets

loophole incentive to individuals and businesses to reduce their tax liabilities by investing their money in areas the government designates

The tax reform laws of 1981 and 1986 significantly reduced the progressiveness of the federal income tax. In the 1960s the highest tax bracket applied a 91 percent tax to income over $200,000 (which is the equivalent to $1.5 million in today's dollars).[35] Drastic rate reductions were instituted in 1986, however. The Tax Reform Act of 1986 established five tax brackets, ranging from a 15 percent tax on those in the lowest income bracket to 39.6 percent on those in the highest income bracket.

Taxes became a controversial issue again during the George W. Bush administration. After passing major cuts in income tax rates in 2001, President Bush proposed, and Congress passed, a sweeping new round of cuts in 2003. Bush's plan was intended to promote investment by reducing taxes on most stock dividends, to spur business activity by offering tax breaks to small businesses, and to stimulate the economy by reducing the tax rates for all taxpayers. In 2006, Congress extended the rate reductions on dividends and capital gains, a move that estimates showed would cost the treasury $70 billion over five years. The argument for the tax cuts was largely a supply side argument: the cuts would make for a prosperous economy. Opponents charge that it made no sense to cut taxes since the benefits of the tax cuts went primarily to the wealthy. Critics also charge that the tax cuts caused the federal budget, which was in surplus when Bush took office, to fall into deficit.[36]

TABLE 16.1

Taxable Income Brackets and Rates, 2014

This table shows the federal tax rates that Americans pay on their income. The United States has a progressive tax system in that the tax rate goes up on Americans with more income.

TAX RATE %	INDIVIDUALS	MARRIED COUPLES FILING JOINTLY	HEAD OF HOUSEHOLD FILERS
10	$0 to $9,075	$0 to $18,150	$0 to $12,950
15	$9,076 to $36,900	$18,151 to $73,800	$12,951 to $49,400
25	$36,901 to $89,350	$73,801 to $148,850	$49,401 to $127,550
28	$89,351 to $186,350	$148,851 to $226,850	$127,551 to $206,600
33	$186,351 to $405,100	$226,851 to $405,100	$206,601 to $405,100
35	$405,101 to $406,750	$405,101 to $457,600	$405,101 to $432,200
39.60	$406,751+	$457,601+	$432,201+

SOURCE: Tax Foundation, http://taxfoundation.org/article/2014-tax-brackets# ftn1 (accessed 5/6/14).

for critical analysis

What are the multiple goals of tax policy in America? How else might some of these goals be achieved? In what ways is the tax system in the United States progressive? In what ways is it regressive?

President Obama and the Democratic leadership proposed extending the tax cuts for everyone with annual incomes under $250,000; those making more would have their income taxes revert back to the rates in the 1990s. Republicans preferred to extend the tax cuts for everyone. In late 2010, Congress agreed to a two-year extension of the cuts until December 2012. As the new deadline loomed in 2012, many analysts warned that the pending expiration of the tax cuts, which might amount to as much as $500 billion in additional taxes, coupled with $100 billion in federal spending cuts to which Congress and the president had previously agreed, could push the still-faltering U.S. economy over a "fiscal cliff" if they came to pass. After a series of complex negotiations stretching over three years, Congress struck a deal to raise income taxes on couples making over $450,000 a year from 35 percent to 39.6 percent. (See Table 16.1 for the tax brackets in 2014. The brackets go up every year to keep pace with inflation.)

Spending and Budgeting The federal government's power to spend is one of the most important tools of economic policy. Decisions about how much to spend affect the overall health of the economy. They also affect every aspect of American life, from the distribution of income to the availability of different modes of transportation to the level of education in society.

The president and Congress have each created institutions to assert control over the budget process. The Office of Management and Budget (OMB) in the Executive Office of the president is responsible for preparing the president's budget. This budget contains the president's spending priorities and the estimated costs of the president's policy proposals. It is viewed as the starting point for the annual debate over the budget. When different parties control the presidency and Congress, the president's budget may have little influence on the budget that is ultimately adopted. Members of the president's own party also may have different priorities.

Congress has its own budget institutions. Congress created the Congressional Budget Office (CBO) in 1974 so that it could have reliable information about the costs and economic impact of the policies it considers. At the same time, it set up a budget process designed to establish spending priorities and to consider individual expenditures in light of the entire budget. A key element of the process is the annual budget resolution, which designates broad targets for spending. By estimating the costs of policy proposals, Congress hoped to control spending and reduce deficits. When the congressional budget process proved unable to hold down deficits in the 1980s, Congress established stricter measures to control spending, including "spending caps" that limit spending on some types of programs.

Not surprisingly, the fight for control over spending is one of the most contentious in Washington, as interest groups and politicians strive to determine the priorities and appropriate levels of spending. Decisions about spending are made as part of the annual budget process. During the 1990s, when the federal **budget deficit** first became a major political issue and when parties were deeply split on spending, the budget process became the focal point of the entire policy-making process. With the rapid swing from budget surpluses in 2000 to record deficits by 2003, deficits once again emerged as a political issue (Figure 16.5). This time, however, Republican leaders, who had made deficits the focal point of politics in the mid-1990s, largely dismissed their importance. As House majority leader Tom DeLay put it, "The Soviet Union had a balanced

budget deficit amount by which government spending exceeds government revenue in a fiscal year

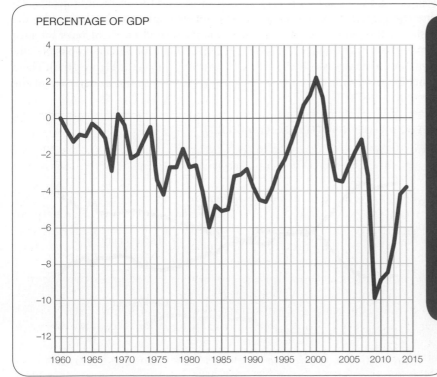

PERCENTAGE OF GDP

FIGURE 16.5

U.S. Budget Deficits and Surpluses, 1960–2014*

The federal deficit grew substantially during the 1980s under President Reagan. During the 1990s, the budget deficit declined significantly but then grew dramatically after 2001. When was the last time that the federal budget showed a surplus? Why did the budget deficit grow so much after 2001?

*Data for 2014 are estimated.
SOURCE: Office of Management and Budget, "Summary of Receipts, Outlays, and Surpluses or Deficits (−) as Percentages of GDP: 1930–2019," *The Budget for Fiscal Year 2015, Historical Tables,* www.whitehouse.gov (accessed 4/2/14).

budget. Well, you can raise taxes until you balance it, but the economy will go into the toilet."[37]

The deficit once again drove the economic policy agenda between 2010 and 2013, when Republicans in the House of Representatives and Democrats in the Senate and White House engaged in a contentious series of battles over the federal deficit and President Obama's economic policies.[38] The impasse stemmed from Republicans' insistence that the deficit, which had grown substantially in the aftermath of the Great Recession, be reduced primarily through spending cuts, while Democrats pushed for deficit reduction through a mix of spending cuts and tax increases for the wealthiest Americans. The resolution to the standoff, the Budget Control Act of 2011, achieved $1 trillion in deficit reduction over 10 years, all through spending cuts, but also scheduled additional, automatic across-the-board "sequestration" cuts beginning in 2013 if a bipartisan "Supercommittee" failed to reach a deal securing an additional $1.2 trillion in deficit reduction. To the frustration of all, the Supercommittee failed to agree on a new deficit reduction plan. In March 2013 sequestration cuts finally came into effect after Congress and the White House failed to cancel the cuts. A period of high-stakes back-and-forth negotiation over the debt finally came to an end in October 2013 when another failure to agree on the terms of raising the debt ceiling—with Republicans demanding a one-year delay in the implementation of the Affordable Care Act, further spending cuts on social programs, and negotiations on entitlements reform, and Democrats insisting on a clean, no-strings-attached increase in the debt limit—led to a shutdown of the federal government for the first time in almost two decades.[39] The government reopened after 16 days with a resolution cleanly raising the debt limit and funding the government for another two years.

A very large and growing proportion of the annual federal budget is **mandatory spending**, expenditures that are, in the words of the OMB, "relatively uncontrollable." Interest payments on the national debt, for example, are determined by the actual size of the national debt. Legislation has mandated payment rates for such programs as retirement under Social Security, retirement for federal employees, unemployment assistance, Medicare, and farm price supports (see Figure 16.6). These payments increase with the cost of living; they increase as the average age of the

mandatory spending federal spending that is made up of "uncontrollables," budget items that cannot be controlled through the regular budget process

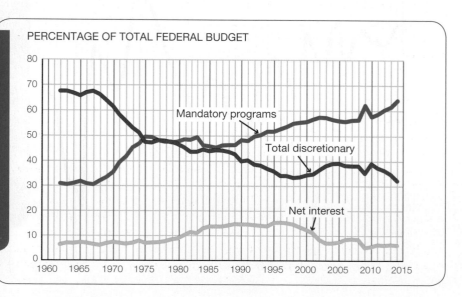

FIGURE 16.6

Mandatory Spending, Discretionary Spending, and Net Interest, 1962–2014*

*Data for 2014 are estimated.
SOURCE: Office of Management and Budget, "Percentage Distribution of Outlays by Budget Enforcement Act Category: 1962–2019," *The Budget for Fiscal Year 2015*, www.whitehouse. gov (accessed 4/3/14).

PERCENTAGE OF TOTAL FEDERAL BUDGET

Mandatory programs

Total discretionary

Net interest

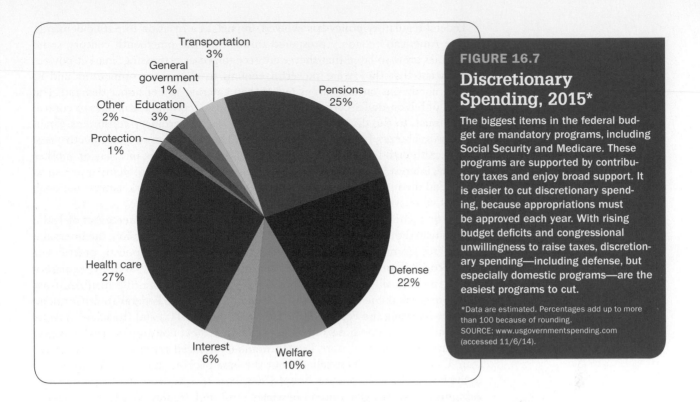

FIGURE 16.7

Discretionary Spending, 2015*

The biggest items in the federal budget are mandatory programs, including Social Security and Medicare. These programs are supported by contributory taxes and enjoy broad support. It is easier to cut discretionary spending, because appropriations must be approved each year. With rising budget deficits and congressional unwillingness to raise taxes, discretionary spending—including defense, but especially domestic programs—are the easiest programs to cut.

*Data are estimated. Percentages add up to more than 100 because of rounding.
SOURCE: www.usgovernmentspending.com (accessed 11/6/14).

population goes up; they increase as national and world agricultural surpluses go up. In 1970, 38.5 percent of the total federal budget was made up of these **uncontrollables**; in 1975, 52.5 percent fell into that category; and by 2012 around 65 percent was in the uncontrollable category. This means that the national government now can do very little **discretionary spending** that will allow it to counteract fluctuations in the business cycle. (Figure 16.7 shows discretionary spending in 2015.)

Government spending as a fiscal policy works fairly well when deliberate deficit spending is used to stop a recession and to speed up the recovery period, but it does not work very well in fighting inflation, because elected politicians are often politically unable to make the drastic expenditure cuts and tax hikes necessary to balance the budget, much less to produce a budgetary surplus.

Regulation and Antitrust Policy

Americans have long been suspicious of concentrations of economic power. Federal economic regulation aims to protect the public against potential abuses by concentrated economic power in two ways. First, the federal government can establish conditions that govern the operation of big businesses to ensure fair competition. For example, it can require a business to make information about its activities and account books available to the public. Second, the federal government can force a large business to break up into smaller companies if it finds that the business has established a **monopoly**. This is called **antitrust policy**. In addition to economic regulation, the federal government engages in social regulation. Social regulation establishes conditions on businesses in order to protect workers, the environment, and consumers.

uncontrollables budgetary items that are beyond the control of budgetary committees and can be controlled only by substantive legislative action in Congress; some uncontrollables, such as interest on the debt, are beyond the power of Congress, because the terms of payments are set in contracts

discretionary spending federal spending on programs that are controlled through the regular budget process

monopoly a single firm in a market that controls all the goods and services of that market; absence of competition

antitrust policy government regulation of large businesses that have established monopolies

Federal regulatory policy has evolved, in part, as a reaction to public demands. As the American economy prospered throughout the nineteenth century, some companies grew so large that they were recognized as possessing "market power." This meant that they were powerful enough to eliminate competitors and to impose conditions on consumers rather than catering to consumer demand. The growth of billion-dollar corporations led to collusion among companies to control prices, much to the dismay of smaller businesses and ordinary consumers. Small businesses, laborers, farmers, and consumers all began to clamor for protective regulation. Although the states had been regulating businesses in one way or another all along, interest groups turned to Washington as economic problems appeared to be beyond the reach of the individual state governments. If markets were national, there would have to be national regulation.[40]

The first national regulatory policy was the Interstate Commerce Act of 1887, which created the first national independent regulatory commission, the Interstate Commerce Commission (ICC), designed to control the monopolistic practices of the railroads. Three years later, the Sherman Antitrust Act extended regulatory power to cover all monopolistic practices. The ICC and the Sherman Antitrust Act were strengthened in 1914 with the enactment of the Federal Trade Commission Act (creating the Federal Trade Commission, or FTC) and the Clayton Antitrust Act. At the same time, public demands to protect consumers led the federal government to enact a more limited number of social regulations. As we have seen, Upton Sinclair's best-seller about the meatpacking industry, *The Jungle*, led to the Federal Meat Inspection Act of 1906. Two decades later, the Food and Drug Administration was given broad powers to test and regulate products viewed as essential to public health.

The modern era of comprehensive national regulation began in the 1930s. Most of the regulatory programs of the 1930s were established to regulate the conduct of companies within specifically designated sectors of American industry. For example, the jurisdiction of one agency was the securities industry; the jurisdiction of another was the radio (and eventually television) industry. Others included banking, coal mining, and agriculture. At this time, Congress also set the basic framework of American labor regulation, including the rules for collective bargaining and the minimum wage.

When Congress turned once again to regulatory policies in the 1970s, it became still bolder, moving beyond the effort to regulate specific industrial sectors and toward regulating aspects of the entire economy. The scope or jurisdiction of such agencies as the Occupational Safety and Health Administration (OSHA), the Consumer Product Safety Commission (CPSC), and the Environmental Protection Agency (EPA) is as broad as the entire economy, indeed the entire society.

Despite occasional high-profile regulatory cases such as the one against Microsoft in the 1990s, the trend since the late 1970s has been against regulation. Over the years, businesses complained about the burden of the new regulations they confronted, and many economists began to argue that excessive regulation was hurting the economy. In the 1980s, Congress and the president responded with a wave of **deregulation**. For example, President Reagan went about the task of changing the direction of regulation by way of "presidential oversight." Shortly after taking office, he gave the OMB authority to review all executive branch proposals for new regulations. By this means, Reagan reduced the total number of regulations issued by federal agencies, dropping

deregulation a policy of reducing or eliminating regulatory restraints on the conduct of individuals or private institutions

American farmers have long benefited from government subsidies. Agricultural subsidies are designed to help farmers stay in business even when the markets for their crops are less favorable, so that the country can rely on a steady food supply.

the number of pages in the *Federal Register* from 74,000 in 1980 to 49,600 in 1987.[41]

The financial crisis that began in 2008 put regulation on the agenda once again. As the economic emergency subsided, Congress began to consider long-term reform of the financial industry. A central question was how to create regulations that would prevent excessive risk taking by investors, seen as the principal cause of the recession. The complex reform that Congress enacted in 2010 (the Dodd-Frank Wall Street Reform and Consumer Protection Act) included a range of new regulations on the financial industry. It created a Consumer Financial Protection Bureau, placed under the auspices of the Federal Reserve but independent of it. The new agency has a broad mandate to regulate consumer financial products, such as mortgages and credit cards, to ensure that they are fair and competitive. The reform also created a new Financial Stability Oversight Council, headed by the Treasury secretary, with responsibility for identifying risks to the economy before they spread.

Subsidies and Contracting

Subsidies and contracting are the carrots of economic policy. Their purpose is to encourage people to do something they might otherwise not do or to get people to do more of what they are already doing. Sometimes the purpose is merely to compensate people for something done in the past.

Subsidies **Subsidies** are simply government grants of cash or other valuable commodities, such as land. Although subsidies are often denounced as "giveaways," they have played a fundamental role in the history of government in the United States. Subsidies were the dominant form of public policy of the national government and the state and local governments throughout the nineteenth century. They continue to be an important category of public policy at all levels of government. The first planning document ever written for the national government, Alexander Hamilton's *Report on Manufactures*, was based almost entirely on Hamilton's assumption that American industry could be encouraged by federal subsidies and that these were not only desirable but constitutional.

subsidies government grants of cash or other valuable commodities, such as land, to an individual or an organization; used to promote activities desired by the government, reward political support, or buy off political opposition

The thrust of Hamilton's plan was not lost on later policy makers. Subsidies in the form of land grants were given to farmers and to railroad companies to encourage western settlement. Substantial cash subsidies have traditionally been given to shipbuilders to help build the commercial fleet and to guarantee the use of the ships as military personnel carriers in times of war. The effect of any subsidy has to be measured somewhat indirectly in terms of what people *would be doing* if the subsidy were not available. For example, many thousands of people settled in lands west of the Mississippi only because land subsidies were available. Similarly, hundreds of research laboratories exist in universities and corporations only because certain types of research subsidies from the government are available to fund them.

Policies using the subsidy technique continued to be plentiful in the twentieth century and into the twenty-first, even after the 1990s, when there was widespread public and official hostility toward subsidies. For example, in 2007 the annual value of corporate subsidies, not including agriculture, was estimated at more than $92 billion.[42] Politicians have always favored subsidies because subsidies can be treated as "benefits" that can be spread widely in response to many demands that might otherwise produce profound political conflict. Subsidies can, in other words, be used to buy off the opposition.

Contracting Like any corporation, a government agency must purchase goods and services by contract. The law requires open bidding for a substantial proportion of these contracts because government contracts are extremely valuable to businesses in the private sector and because the opportunities and incentives for abuse surrounding contracting are very great. But contracting is more than a method of buying goods and services. It is also an important technique of policy, because government agencies are often authorized to use their **contracting power** as a means of encouraging corporations to improve themselves, helping to build up whole sectors of the economy, and encouraging certain desirable goals or behavior, such as equal employment opportunity. For example, the infant airline industry of the 1930s was nurtured by the national government's lucrative contracts to carry airmail. A more recent example is the use of government contracting to encourage industries, universities, and other organizations to engage in research and development on a wide range of issues in basic and applied science.

Military contracting has long been a major element in government spending. So tight was the connection between defense contractors and the federal government during the Cold War that as he was leaving office, President Eisenhower warned the nation to beware of the powerful "military-industrial complex." After the Cold War, as military spending and production declined, major defense contractors began to look for alternative business activities to supplement the reduced demand for weapons. For example, Lockheed Martin, the nation's largest defense contractor, began to bid on contracts related to welfare reform. Since the terrorist attacks of 2001, however, the military budget has been awash in new funds, and military contractors are flooded with business. President Bush increased the Pentagon budget by more than 7 percent a year, requesting so many weapons systems that one observer called the budget a "weapons smorgasbord."[43] Military contractors geared up to produce not only weapons for foreign warfare but also surveillance systems to enhance domestic security.

contracting power the power of government to set conditions on companies seeking to sell goods or services to government agencies

The Environment and the Economy

Explain why the government tries to balance economic prosperity with policies that protect the environment

One of the most important reasons that the government intervenes in the economy is to protect the environment. Although federal interest in environmental conservation stretches back to the 1900s, federal regulation of industry grew more extensive with the rise of the modern environmental movement in the 1970s. By then the consequences of economic growth that paid little attention to environmental impact were evident all over America. Cleveland's Cuyahoga River, long a dumping ground for industrial waste, had caught fire in 1969, and the burning river became an especially vivid symbol of environmental neglect. The first "Earth Day," in 1970, highlighted the new ecological concerns, which became a major feature of American politics in subsequent decades.[44]

A wave of new laws wrote environmental goals into policy. The 1969 National Environmental Policy Act (NEPA), the Clean Air Act amendments of 1970, the 1972 Clean Water Act, and the 1974 Safe Drinking Water Act together established a new set of goals and procedures for protecting the environment. These acts are properly considered part of economic policy because they affect virtually every aspect of the economy. NEPA, for example, requires federal agencies to prepare an environmental impact statement for every major development project they propose. In this way, environmental impacts routinely become factored into considerations about whether a particular project is feasible or desirable.

Environmental disasters have often drawn attention to new environmental hazards and have prompted greater federal regulation. For example, during the mid-1970s the residents of the Love Canal neighborhood in Buffalo, New York, discovered that their neighborhood had been built on a toxic waste dump. Many of the chemicals in the soil were suspected carcinogens. At federal and state cost, residents were moved to new homes. Partly as a result of this highly publicized incident, Congress passed legislation to facilitate cleanup of hazardous waste sites.

Yet government action and corporate liability are often bitterly contested issues in this area. Protecting the environment presents policy makers with difficult trade-offs. Compliance with environmental regulations can be very costly. Moreover, critics maintain that federal standards are sometimes too high. How clean should the air be? What is the difference between pure drinking water and safe drinking water? Who should bear the costs of protecting the environment? Not only do citizens, consumers, and businesses take different perspectives on these questions but the goals themselves often present a moving target. As new scientific evidence shows (or fails to find evidence for) new or suspected environmental hazards, conflicts emerge over the proper role of government.

The Debate on Climate Change

Nowhere have these conflicts been more acute than in the debate over climate change. A large and growing body of scientific evidence suggests that greenhouse gas emissions from cars, power plants, and other human-made sources are causing temperatures on earth to rise.[45] The projected environmental consequences are dire: melting polar ice caps, extreme weather, droughts, fire, rising sea levels, and disease. All would have profound economic consequences. Yet these projections come with

Former vice president Al Gore's 2006 film, An Inconvenient Truth, *attracted broad attention to the issue of climate change. The film won an Academy Award, and Gore was a co-recipient of the Nobel Peace Prize for his efforts to raise public awareness.*

considerable uncertainty. How likely are most catastrophic scenarios? Should we prepare for the most damaging outcomes or only the most likely outcomes of climate change?[46] These questions are important because the costs of transforming the world's carbon-based technologies through lower energy use and newer green technologies are enormous. These questions are especially salient for the United States, which has the world's largest economy and is responsible for 25 percent of the world's greenhouse gas emissions but has only 10 percent of the world's population.[47] And because the United States relies so heavily on fossil fuels for its energy sources, the effort to reduce carbon emission requires a major shift in how we obtain and use energy.

As scientists have learned more about the effects of human activity on the climate, the issue of climate change has risen on the national agenda. For example, in 2007, 84 percent of Americans reported believing that human activity was at least a contributing factor in climate change.[48] However, the economic recession and political controversy over climate change seemed to shift public perceptions about the existence and importance of climate change. In 2010 only 57 percent of America reported believing that global climate change was happening at all, with just 50 percent of respondents "very" or "somewhat" worried about climate change. In another survey, respondents ranked climate change last in importance in a list of 21 top public policy issues.[49] In the same survey, just over half of the public said they would support protecting the environment over stimulating the economy, while 36 percent chose the economy.[50] The Obama administration made climate change an important focus of attention and encouraged federal agencies to move aggressively on this issue. In 2009 the EPA began to set standards so that it could, for the first time ever, regulate greenhouse gas emissions under the Clean Air Act. The administration also proposed creating a new Climate Service that would centralize the collection and analysis of data on climate change across the world. The new attitude was epitomized by Commerce secretary Gary Locke, who noted in his announcement of the planned Climate Service that "whether we like it or not, climate change represents a real threat."[51]

for critical analysis

What are some of the policies that can be used to address climate change? Which policies have the best chance of being enacted?

Environmental Policies

Policy makers charged with devising approaches to climate change have identified three basic policy approaches. The first is mitigation, or reduction, of greenhouse gas emissions. The second is large-scale research and development to promote alternative technologies. The third consists of measures that allow us to adapt to a warmer climate. Each of these strategies entails potentially gargantuan costs in the form of higher energy prices, subsidies to industry, infrastructure projects, and relocation decisions. When specific policy proposals are discussed and these costs become apparent, the consensus for addressing climate change breaks down.

Mitigation: Reducing Emissions The mitigation approach, which seeks to reduce greenhouse gas emissions, has garnered the most attention from policy makers. Two proposed policies that aim to achieve this goal, both controversial, are tougher standards for auto fuel mileage and higher taxes on gasoline. Although the public strongly supports higher gas-mileage standards, auto companies resisted such standards for nearly 30 years after they were first put in place in the early 1970s. In 2009 the EPA announced that it would set standards for greenhouse gas emissions for automobiles under the Clean Air Act, raising the fuel economy standards for new vehicles to 35.5 miles per gallon beginning in 2016.[52] As for proposals to increase gasoline taxes, public opinion polls routinely show that a majority of Americans oppose a tax on gasoline as a way to reduce emissions, and few politicians want to sponsor such an unpopular policy.[53]

Proponents of reducing carbon emissions pinned their hopes on a "cap-and-trade" system as the most politically feasible strategy to achieve their goal. This

One approach to addressing climate change is reducing emissions—from factories, power plants, and cars. Capping emissions can be controversial if it imposes costs on businesses and ultimately on consumers, but recent cap-and-trade proposals may offer a more efficient way to reduce pollution.

approach sets a target for carbon emissions for each industry but allows companies to trade "carbon credits" with one another. This market-based system is attractive to political leaders because it achieves its goals by creating incentives for private actors and allows them flexibility as they seek to reduce emissions. More than 23 large firms, including leading automakers, have joined environmentalists in a coalition called the U.S. Climate Action Partnership (USCAP) to press for a cap-and-trade system to reduce carbon emissions.[54] In 2009 the House of Representatives passed a landmark cap-and-trade bill aimed at reducing greenhouse gas emissions. However, opposition from some Democrats and most Republicans in the Senate made further movement toward final passage of cap-and-trade legislation unlikely. New signs of progress emerged, however, in early 2010, with three senators of both parties—Senators John Kerry (D-Mass.), Joseph Lieberman (I-Conn.), and Lindsey Graham (R-S.C.)—proposing legislation that would apply carbon controls to specific sectors of the economy rather than setting the overall national target envisioned by the cap-and-trade scheme.[55] One of the central elements of the proposal was a requirement that power plants limit their emissions, with the cap becoming more stringent over the next decade. Another key provision was the imposition of a carbon tax on gasoline, with the money raised being used to fund alternative fuel vehicle technologies such as electric cars.[56] Though this proposal was not enacted, its central ideas continue to be the focus of congressional discussion.

Promoting Alternative Technologies Many analysts and politicians prefer a second strategy for addressing the problems associated with fossil fuels, one that centers on increased research and development to promote alternative technologies. President Obama came out strongly in favor of a comprehensive energy and climate change bill that would, among other things, provide funding and large tax incentives for the production and adoption of clean-energy technologies. He also warned that the United States was falling behind other countries, including China, in the production of clean-energy products, arguing that this industry would be a vital source of millions of new jobs over the next few decades.[57] The 2009 Recovery Act allocated nearly $30 billion to support alternative energy technology investment and to improve energy efficiency.

Green technologies may prove to be a boon for the American economy. Because highly skilled labor is required to produce most such technologies, America has a competitive advantage over many other countries. Furthermore, a move toward green technologies could significantly improve American national security. Indeed, some argue that reducing the use of fossil fuels and adopting more fuel-efficient technologies would take money away from regimes that support terrorism against the United States.

Adaptation Policies A final approach to climate change is adaptation to a warmer climate. Adaptation would entail a diverse set of policies, including establishment of green corridors, pest and disease control, water conservation to deal with drought, and new infrastructure such as seawalls to cope with rising sea levels.[58] Many scientists believe that deliberate adaptation has to be part of any approach to climate change because even if we take major steps to mitigate carbon emissions and pour resources into developing new technologies, climate change has already arrived.

Many aspects of a deliberate adaptation strategy would be difficult to implement in the market-oriented, decentralized context of the United States. Although some European countries, such as the low-lying Netherlands, are relocating people as part of their adaptation strategy, American politicians have little stomach for initiating such controversial measures. Moreover, the combination of conservation and new infrastructure requires considerable public resources and broad coordination across multiple public agencies. Both are hard to achieve in the context of American politics. For example, the environmentally sensitive Sacramento Delta is extremely vulnerable to rising sea levels. The delta, a swath of land that lies below sea level, is economically important because it supplies much of Northern California, including California agribusiness, with water. Yet decisions about what happens in the delta involve more than 200 government agencies.[59]

Global climate change poses a difficult economic challenge for the United States. It presents the opportunity for American industry to take the lead in developing green technologies, placing the nation's economic prosperity on a fundamentally new base. Yet it also calls for government to enforce the reduction of carbon emissions and adapt current practices to a changing world. Many industries have expressed support for action to address climate change, but such a major economic transformation creates winners and losers. Firms, such as the auto companies, whose profits are jeopardized and workers whose jobs are threatened by change have successfully blocked bold action in the past. The diffuse long-term harms that climate change poses are hard to pit against the specific concentrated costs that industries face today. Nonetheless, growing recognition that climate change is real and poses potentially catastrophic consequences ensures that economic policy and environmental policy will be ever more closely intertwined in the future.

Economic Policy
and Your Future

For three decades, a sharp partisan debate has driven the politics of economic policy. Most Republicans have pressed for freer markets and less government while most Democrats have defended the need for market regulation and more government intervention in the economy. The partisan divisions have made it difficult for policy makers to come to terms with an economy that has changed radically since the debate over more or less government commenced during the Reagan years. The American economy is now far more open to the rest of the world and many American firms do most of their production in China and other developing economies, not in the United States. At the same time, the distribution of economic gains in the United States has shifted upward. As the debate about more or less government has led to a series of policy stalemates among politicians, the income of the American middle class has stagnated and the gains going to the top 1 percent have soared.[60]

Everyone agrees that economic policy should address the needs of the next generation and indeed, frequently refer to the future to defend their views about economic policy. Yet, the Great Recession and the divisive politics of economic policy have cut short the debate about how federal economic policy can be re-oriented to promote future growth and, at the same time, ensure that all Americans have the opportunity to benefit from that growth. To consider the needs of future generations requires shifting the debate over economic policy from "more or less government" to "what kind of government?" Should spending priorities be shifted in the face of an altered global economy and wage stagnation at home? Have the last three decades shown us that less government intervention leads to greater gains for the wealthy? As the federal government has stalled over these issues, state governments of different partisan orientations have begun to take action. For example, two "red states" have taken significant steps to invest in the next generation: Tennessee made community college free to all students in the state and Oklahoma provides universal access to prekindergarten schooling. These and other state models offer important guideposts that can inform federal policy and perhaps ultimately help to break the stalemate over government's role in the economy.

plugin

Inform

Check the newspaper or a news website to see what economic policies are in the news. Look for stories on taxes, employment, regulation of businesses, economic inequality, and economic growth.

Express

Write a list of how you expect economic policies to affect your life in the next five years.

Connect

Follow the Federal Reserve on Facebook. Post a question or comment if any of the topics interest you.

Act

Join an organization that promotes fiscal responsibility in government, such as the Concord Coalition, or one that promotes economic justice, such as the Sargent Shriver National Center on Poverty Law (www.povertylaw.org).

studyguide

The Goals of Economic Policy

Identify the broad reasons government gets involved in the economy (pp. 643–51)

Public policies, which are officially expressed goals backed by rewards or punishments, can be embodied in laws, rules, regulations, or orders. In contemporary societies, government makes it possible for the economy to function efficiently by setting the rules for economic exchange and punishing those who violate the rules. Through a variety of different policies, the U.S. government has pursued four economic goals over the last century: to promote economic stability, to stimulate economic growth, to promote business development, and to protect employees and consumers.

Key Terms

public policy (p. 643)

public goods (p. 644)

gross domestic product (GDP) (p. 644)

inflation (p. 648)

categorical grants (p. 648)

Practice Quiz

1. Which of the following is *not* one of the reasons that government is involved in the economy?
   a) to guarantee economic equality
   b) to promote economic stability
   c) to stimulate economic growth
   d) to promote business development
   e) to protect employees and consumers

2. The total value of goods and services produced within a country is referred to as
   a) the Gross National Product.
   b) the Gross Domestic Product.
   c) the Dow Jones Industrial Average.
   d) the federal funds rate.
   e) the Gini coefficient.

3. Inflation refers to
   a) a lack of change in the general level of prices.
   b) a tax on imported goods.
   c) a consistent increase in the general level of prices.
   d) a consistent decrease in the general level of prices.
   e) an increase in the interest rate on loans between banks.

The Politics of Economic Policy Making

Explore why economic policy is often controversial (pp. 651–59)

Although all politicians want a healthy economy, they often have different views about how to attain it and what the priorities of economic policy should be. The three schools of economic thought that have been most influential with American policy makers, interest groups, and members of the public are Keynesianism, laissez-faire capitalism, and supply-side economics. Government spending is controversial, but there is usually little public support for cutting specific programs. Consumer groups, environmentalists, businesses, and labor all work to shape economic policy.

Key Terms

Keynesians (p. 652)

laissez-faire capitalism (p. 653)

supply-side economics (p. 653)

Practice Quiz

4. The argument for laissez-faire capitalism was first elaborated by
   a) Ben Bernake.
   b) Milton Friedman.
   c) Alan Greenspan.
   d) James Madison.
   e) Adam Smith.

5. Which of the following economic perspectives argues for an ongoing role for government in the economy?
   a) Keynesianism
   b) laissez-faire
   c) libertarianism
   d) monetarism
   e) rational expectations

6. Republicans in government typically favor
   a) more government spending.
   b) an increase in the minimum wage.

c) a greater role for government in the economy
d) a smaller role for government in the economy.
e) no role for government in the economy.

The Tools of Economic Policy

Describe how the government uses monetary, fiscal, and regulatory policies to influence the economy (pp. 659–72)

The sustained growth of the American economy is the result of specific policies enacted by the U.S. government. The Constitution gives the federal government the power to set monetary and fiscal policies. Monetary policy in the United States is determined primarily by the Federal Reserve Board. Most of the U.S. government's revenues come from personal and corporate income taxes, and most of the federal government's budget is now made up of mandatory, rather than discretionary, spending.

Key Terms

monetary policies (p. 660)

Federal Reserve System (p. 660)

federal funds rate (p. 661)

open-market operations (p. 662)

fiscal policy (p. 662)

tariff (p. 663)

progressive taxation (p. 663)

regressive taxation (p. 665)

redistribution (p. 665)

loophole (p. 665)

budget deficit (p. 667)

mandatory spending (p. 668)

uncontrollables (p. 669)

discretionary spending (p. 669)

monopoly (p. 669)

antitrust policy (p. 669)

deregulation (p. 670)

subsidies (p. 671)

contracting power (p. 672)

Practice Quiz

7. Monetary policy seeks to influence the economy through
   a) taxing and spending.
   b) privatizing and nationalizing selected industries.

c) the availability of credit and money.
d) foreign exchange of currency.
e) administrative regulation.

8. Monetary policy is handled largely by
   a) Congress.
   b) the Department of the Treasury.
   c) the federal judiciary.
   d) the Federal Reserve System.
   e) the president.

9. A situation in which the government attempts to affect the economy through taxing and spending is an example of
   a) a reserve requirement.
   b) an expropriation policy.
   c) a monetary policy.
   d) a fiscal policy.
   e) eminent domain.

10. A tax that places a greater burden on those who are better able to afford it is called
    a) regressive.
    b) progressive.
    c) inflationary.
    d) a flat tax.
    e) voodoo economics.

11. A policy whose objective is to tax or spend in such a way as to reduce the disparities of wealth between the highest and lowest income brackets is called
    a) antitrust policy.
    b) deregulation.
    c) discretionary spending.
    d) equalization.
    e) redistribution.

12. Which of the following statements best describes the U.S. budget deficit?
    a) The budget deficit grew substantially in the 1980s and declined substantially in the 1990s before rising sharply again in the 2000s.
    b) The budget deficit declined substantially in the 1980s and grew substantially in the late 1990s into the 2000s.
    c) The budget deficit grew consistently between 1980 and the present.

d) The budget deficit declined consistently between 1980 and the present.
e) The budget deficit has remained exactly the same since 1980.

13. Which of the following statements best describes spending in the federal budget?
a) Mandatory and discretionary spending now make up approximately equal parts of the total budget.
b) Mandatory spending has been outlawed, and the total budget is now made up of discretionary spending.
c) Mandatory spending is now a much larger percentage of the total budget than discretionary spending.
d) Discretionary spending has been outlawed, and the total budget is now made up of mandatory spending.
e) Discretionary spending is now a much larger percentage of the total budget than mandatory spending.

The Environment and the Economy

Explain why the government tries to balance economic prosperity with policies that protect the environment (pp. 673–77)

The federal government frequently regulates industry in order to protect the environment. One of the most important environmental issues currently facing the U.S. government is climate change. Policy makers charged with devising approaches to the problem of climate change have identified three basic approaches: mitigation of greenhouse emissions, promotion of alternative energy technologies, and adaptation to a warmer climate.

Practice Quiz

14. A cap-and-trade system is an example of which kind of policy approach to global warming?
a) adaptation to a warmer climate
b) Not in My Backyard (NIMBY)
c) mandatory spending
d) mitigation
e) promoting alternative technologies

For Further Reading

Baldwin, Robert, Martin Cave, and Martin Lodge. *Understanding Regulation.* New York: Oxford University Press, 2012.

Bernanke, Ben S. *The Federal Reserve and the Financial Crisis.* Princeton, N.J. Princeton University Press, 2013.

Blanchard, Olivier, Paul Romer, Michael Spence, and Joseph Stiglitz. *In the Wake of the Crisis: Leading Economists Reassess Economic Policy.* Cambridge, MA: MIT Press, 2012.

Frank, Robert H. *Falling Behind: How Rising Inequality Harms the Middle Class.* Berkeley: University of California Press, 2007.

Friedman, Milton, and Walter Heller. *Monetary versus Fiscal Policy.* New York: W. W. Norton, 1969.

Hacker, Jacob S., and Paul Pierson. *Winner-Take-All Politics: How Washington Made the Rich Richer—and Turned Its Back on the Middle Class* (New York: Simon and Schuster, 2010).

Harris, Richard A., and Sidney M. Milkis. *The Politics of Regulatory Change.* 2nd ed. New York: Oxford University Press, 1996.

Jacobs, Lawrence, and Theda Skocpol, eds. *Inequality and American Democracy: What We Know and What We Need to Learn.* New York: Russell Sage Foundation, 2005.

McCarty, Nolan, Keith T. Poole, and Howard Rosenthal. *Political Bubbles: Financial Crises and the Failure of American Democracy.* Princeton, NJ: Princeton University Press, 2013.

Page, Benjamin I., and Lawrence R. Jacobs. *Class War: What Americans Really Think about Economic Inequality.* Chicago: University of Chicago Press, 2009.

Schick, Allen. *The Federal Budget: Politics, Policy, Process.* 3rd ed. Washington, DC: Brookings Institution Press, 2007.

Stein, Robert M., and Kenneth N. Bickers. *Perpetuating the Pork Barrel: Policy Subsystems and American Democracy.* New York: Cambridge University Press, 1995.

Stiglitz, Joseph E. *The Price of Inequality: How Today's Divided Society Endangers Our Future.* New York: W. W. Norton, 2013.

Waterhouse, Benjamin C. *Lobbying America: The Politics of Business from Nixon to NAFTA.* Princeton, NJ: Princeton University Press, 2014.

Wells, David. *The Federal Reserve System.* Jefferson, NC: McFarland, 2004.

Recommended Websites

Board of Governors of the Federal Reserve System

www.federalreserve.gov

The Federal Reserve System consists of 12 banks that use monetary policy to fight inflation and deflation. Visit the Fed's official website to see how it is working to maintain a strong economy.

Citizens for Tax Justice

www.ctj.org

Review federal, state, and local tax laws at the website of Citizens for Tax Justice. This nonprofit organization is dedicated to educating ordinary citizens about tax laws and reducing the tax burden on low- and middle-income Americans.

National Bureau of Economic Research

www.nber.org

The National Bureau of Economic Research is a nonprofit, nonpartisan organization dedicated to creating a better understanding of the economy. Take a minute to review some of its free research publications.

Tax Foundation

www.taxfoundation.org/research/topic/9.html

The Tax Foundation is a respected organization that has been providing Americans with information about tax policy for more than 50 years. Click on your state to learn about current tax and spending policies.

Treasury Direct

www.treasurydirect.gov/govt/govt.htm

Treasury Direct, part of the U.S. Department of the Treasury, provides a statistical look at federal, state, and public debt.

U.S. Census Bureau: The 2010 Statistical Abstract

www.census.gov/compendia/statab/brief.html

The Annual Statistical Abstract, provided by the U.S. Census Bureau, makes available an abundance of statistics on education, welfare, housing, employment, and agriculture.

U.S. Department of Commerce

www.commerce.gov

The U.S. Department of Commerce promotes domestic and international commerce to foster economic progress. Review the initiatives and programs designed to encourage economic development.

Health care is an area of social policy that has been controversial. Although most Americans support universal access to health care, they disagree about the best way to ensure high-quality health care. As Congress considered various proposals in 2009 and 2010, the debate heated up

Social Policy

WHAT GOVERNMENT DOES AND WHY IT MATTERS Social policies promote a range of public goals. The first is to protect against the risks and insecurities that most people face over the course of their lives. These include illness, disability, temporary unemployment, and the reduced earning capability that comes with old age. Most spending on social welfare in the United States goes to programs that serve these purposes, such as Social Security and medical insurance for the elderly. These programs are widely regarded as successful and popular. Although large projected deficits in both programs have generated conflict, they are the least controversial areas of social spending.

Comprehensive health care reform is more controversial. Most Americans support universal access to health care, but when it comes to specific proposals, they often express doubts. Democrats experienced the public ambivalence about health care reform after they enacted major changes to the system in 2010. The Affordable Care Act is complex legislation that many people find hard to understand. Some parts of it are clearly popular, such as the provision that allows young people to remain on their parents' insurance until they reach the age of 26 and full coverage of many preventive health services for adults and children. Other features, such as the requirement that everyone purchase insurance, with federal assistance, remain unpopular. When the Supreme Court ruled that most of the act, including the individual mandate, was constitutional, the public remained divided. Even after the act was fully implemented in 2014, the public was split, with 46 percent of Americans holding unfavorable views of the legislation and 38 percent holding favorable views. Nearly two years after its enactment, Americans could not agree about the role government should play in ensuring health care for all.[1]

Two other goals of social policy have also been controversial: promoting equality of opportunity and assisting the poor. Although Americans admire the ideal of equal opportunity, there is no general agreement about what government should do to address inequalities: groups that have suffered from past inequality generally support much more extensive government action to promote equality of opportunity than do others. Yet most Americans support some government action, especially in the area of education.

The third goal of social policy, to alleviate poverty, has long generated controversy in the United States. Americans take pride in their strong work ethic and prize the value of self-sufficiency. As a result, the majority of Americans express suspicion that the able-bodied poor will not try hard enough to support themselves if they are offered too much assistance or if they receive the wrong kind of assistance. Yet Americans also recognize that poverty may be the product of past inequality of opportunity. Since the 1960s, a variety of educational programs and income-assistance policies have sought to end poverty and promote equal opportunity. Much progress has been made toward these goals. However, the disproportionate rates of poverty among minorities suggest that our policies have not solved the problem of unequal opportunity. Likewise, the high rates of child poverty challenge us to find new ways to assist the poor.

American social policy reflects the nation's views about which risks should be borne by the individual and which should be shared by society as a whole. As such, social policy reflects public wishes, as would be expected in a democracy. However, Americans often have quite different views about how social policy should advance the value of equality. A majority now believes that America has grown too unequal, and there is broad consensus that equality of opportunity is not only desirable but also an essential part of American culture. There is much less agreement about which social policies are needed to reduce the gulf between the rich and the poor and to promote equality of opportunity.

chaptergoals

- **Trace the history of government programs designed to help the poor (pp. 687–98)**
- **Describe how education, health, and housing policies try to promote equality of opportunity (pp. 698–710)**
- **Explain how contributory and noncontributory programs benefit different groups of Americans (pp. 710–17)**

● The Welfare State

Trace the history of government programs designed to help the poor

For much of American history, local governments and private charities were in charge of caring for the poor. During the 1930s, when this largely private system of charity collapsed in the face of widespread economic destitution, the federal government created the beginnings of an American welfare state. The idea of the welfare state was new; it meant that the national government would oversee programs designed to promote economic security for all Americans—not just for the poor. The American system of social welfare comprises many different policies enacted over the years since the Great Depression. Because each program is governed by distinct rules, the kind and level of assistance available vary widely.

The History of the Social Welfare System

America has always had a welfare system, but until 1935 it was almost entirely private, composed of an extensive system of voluntary donations through churches and other religious groups, ethnic and fraternal societies, communities and neighborhoods, and philanthropically inclined wealthy individuals. Most often it was called "charity," and although it was private and voluntary, it was thought of as a public obligation.

There were great variations in the generosity of charity from town to town, but one thing seems to have been universal—the tradition of distinguishing between two classes of poor: the "deserving poor" and the "undeserving poor." The deserving poor were widows and orphans and others rendered dependent by some misfortune, such as the death or serious injury of the family's breadwinner in the course of war or honest labor. The undeserving poor were able-bodied persons unwilling to work, transients new to the community, and others of whom, for various reasons, the community did not approve. This private charity was a very subjective matter: the givers and their agents spent a great deal of time and resources examining the qualifications, both economic and moral, of the seekers of charity.

Before the Great Depression, much of the private charity was given in cash, called "outdoor relief." But because of fears that outdoor relief spawned poverty rather than relieving or preventing it, many communities set up settlement houses and other "indoor relief" institutions. Some of America's most dedicated and unselfish citizens worked in the settlement houses, and their efforts made a significant contribution to the development of the field of social work.

A still-larger institution of indoor relief was the police station, where many of America's poor sought temporary shelter. But even in the severest weather, the homeless could not stay in police stations for many nights without being jailed as vagrants.[2] Indeed, the settlement houses and the police departments were not all that different in their approaches, since social workers in those days tended to consider "all social case work [to be] mental hygiene."[3] And even though not all social workers were budding psychiatrists, "it was true that they focused on counseling and other preventive techniques, obscuring and even ignoring larger structural problems."[4]

The severe limitations on financing faced by private charitable organizations and settlement houses slowly produced a movement by many groups toward public

During the depression, the government took a more active role in helping poor and struggling Americans. Here, people line up to receive free bread.

responsibility for some of these charitable or welfare functions. Workers' compensation laws were enacted in a few states, for example, but the effect of such laws was limited because they benefited only workers injured on the job, and of them, only those who worked for certain types of companies. A more important effort, one that led more directly to the modern welfare state, was public aid to mothers with dependent children. Beginning in Illinois in 1911, the movement for mothers' pensions spread to include 40 states by 1926. Initially such aid was viewed as simply an inexpensive alternative to providing "indoor relief" to mothers and their children. Moreover, applicants not only had to pass a rigorous means test but also had to prove they were deserving, because the laws provided that assistance would be given only to individuals who were deemed "physically, mentally, and morally fit." In most states, a mother was deemed unfit if her children were illegitimate.[5]

In effect, these criteria proved to be racially discriminatory. Many African Americans in the South and ethnic immigrants in the North were denied benefits on the grounds of "moral unfitness." Furthermore, local governments were allowed to decide whether to establish such pension programs. In the South, many counties with large numbers of African American women refused to implement assistance programs.

Despite the spread of state government programs to assume some of the obligation to relieve the poor, the private sector remained dominant until the 1930s. Even as late as 1928 only 11.6 percent of all relief granted in 15 of the largest cities came from public funds.[6] Nevertheless, the various state and local public experiences provided guidance and precedents for the national government's welfare system.

The traditional approach, dominated by the private sector, with its severe distinction between deserving and undeserving poor, crumbled in the face of the stark reality of the Great Depression in 1929. During the depression, misfortune became so widespread and private wealth shrank so drastically that private charity was out of the question, and the distinction between deserving and undeserving became impossible to draw. Around 20 percent of the workforce immediately became unemployed; this figure grew as the depression stretched into years. Moreover, few of these individuals had any monetary resources or any family farm on which to fall back. Banks failed, wiping out the savings of millions who had been fortunate enough to have any savings at all. Thousands of businesses failed as well, throwing middle-class Americans onto the bread lines along with unemployed laborers, dispossessed farmers, and those who had never worked in any capacity whatsoever. The Great Depression proved to Americans that poverty could be a result of imperfections in the economic system as well as of individual irresponsibility. It also forced Americans to drastically alter their standards regarding who was deserving and who was not.

Once poverty and dependency were accepted as problems inherent in the economic system, a large-scale public policy approach was not far away. By the time the Roosevelt administration took office in 1933 the question was not whether there was to be a public welfare system but how generous or restrictive that system would be.

Foundations of the Welfare State

The founding of the modern welfare state in the United States occurred with the passage of the Social Security Act of 1935. This act created two separate categories of welfare: contributory and noncontributory.

Contributory Programs The category of welfare programs financed by taxation can justifiably be called "forced savings"; these programs force working Americans to contribute a portion of their earnings to provide income and benefits for present-day retirees, with the understanding that younger workers will one day provide for them in the same way. These **contributory programs** are what most people have in mind when they refer to **Social Security** or social insurance. Under the original contributory program, old-age insurance, the employer and the employee were each required to pay equal amounts, which in 1937 were set at 1 percent of the first $3,000 in wages, to be deducted from the paycheck of each employee and matched by the same amount from the employer. This percentage has increased over the years; the contribution in 2014 was 7.65 percent subdivided as follows: 6.2 percent on the first $117,100 of income for Social Security benefits, plus 1.45 percent on all earnings for Medicare.[7] Starting in 2014, households earning over $250,000 a year paid an extra 0.9 percent in Medicare taxes due to a provision in the Affordable Care Act.

Social Security may seem to be a rather conservative approach to welfare. In effect, the Social Security tax, as a forced saving, sends a message that people cannot be trusted to save voluntarily to take care of their own needs. But in another sense, it is quite radical. Social Security is not real insurance; workers' contributions do not accumulate in a personal account, as they would in an annuity. Consequently, contributors do not receive benefits in proportion to their contributions, and this means that a redistribution of wealth is occurring. The formula by which Social Security benefits are calculated aims to provide lower-income workers with a higher proportion of their contributions than higher-income workers receive. This is because the goal of Social Security is to ensure a basic income to all workers once they retire. Research has shown, however, that due to different mortality rates and other factors, the system does not end up redistributing from well-off to less well-off workers as intended by the formula. The system does redistribute to women, who earn less than men, have fewer years in the workforce (and hence tend to contribute less to Social Security than do men), and live longer than men.[8] In the short term, Social Security redistributes money from the young to the old: the taxes of current workers are paying for the benefits received by retirees.

Congress increased Social Security benefits every two or three years during the 1950s and '60s. In 1972, Congress decided to end the grind of biennial legislation to increase benefits by establishing **indexing**, whereby benefits paid out under contributory programs would be modified annually by **cost-of-living adjustments (COLAs)**

contributory programs social programs financed in whole or in part by taxation or other mandatory contributions by their present or future recipients

Social Security a contributory welfare program into which working Americans contribute a percentage of their wages and from which they receive cash benefits after retirement or if they become disabled

indexing periodic process of adjusting social benefits or wages to account for increases in the cost of living

cost-of-living adjustments (COLAs) changes made to the level of benefits of a government program based on the rate of inflation

The Supplemental Nutrition Assistance Program (SNAP) helps needy people buy food. The program is sometimes still called "food stamps," but today recipients use a government-provided debit card that is accepted at most grocery stores.

designed to increase benefits to keep up with the rate of inflation. But of course Social Security taxes (contributions) also increased after almost every benefit increase. This made Social Security, in the words of one observer, "a politically ideal program. It bridged partisan conflict by providing liberal benefits under conservative financial auspices."[9] In other words, conservatives could more readily yield to the demands of the well-organized and ever-growing constituency of elderly voters if benefit increases were automatic; liberals could cement conservative support by agreeing to finance the increased benefits through increases in the regressive Social Security tax, paid into a special Social Security fund, rather than out of the general revenues coming from the more progressive income tax, which are paid into the Treasury. (See Chapter 16 for a discussion of regressive and progressive taxes.)

The biggest single expansion in contributory programs since 1935 was the establishment in 1965 of **Medicare**, which provides substantial medical services to elderly persons who are already eligible to receive old-age, survivors', and disability insurance under the original Social Security system.

Noncontributory Programs Programs to which beneficiaries do not have to contribute—**noncontributory programs**—are also known as "public assistance programs," or, more commonly, as "welfare." Until 1996 the most important noncontributory program was Aid to Families with Dependent Children (AFDC)—originally called Aid to Dependent Children—which was founded in 1935 by the original Social Security Act. In 1996, Congress abolished AFDC and replaced it with the Temporary Assistance for Needy Families (TANF) block grant. Eligibility for public assistance is determined by **means testing**, a procedure that requires applicants to show a financial need for assistance. Between 1935 and 1965, the government created programs to provide housing assistance, school lunches, and food stamps to other needy Americans.

Like contributory programs, the noncontributory public assistance programs also made their most significant advances during the 1960s and '70s. The largest single category of expansion was the establishment in 1965 of **Medicaid**, a program that provides extended medical services to low-income Americans. Noncontributory programs underwent another major transformation during the 1970s in the level of benefits they provide. Besides being means tested, noncontributory programs are state based; grants-in-aid are provided by the federal government to the states as incentives to establish the programs but states retain considerable leeway to establish eligibility criteria (see Chapter 3). Thus, from the beginning there were considerable disparities in benefits from state to state. The national government sought to rectify the disparities in levels of old-age benefits in 1974 by creating the Supplemental Security Income (SSI) program to augment benefits for the elderly, the blind, and the disabled. SSI provides uniform minimum benefits across the entire nation and includes mandatory COLAs. States are allowed to be more generous if they wish, but no state is permitted to provide benefits below the minimum level set by the national government. As a result, 25 states increased their SSI benefits to the mandated level.

The TANF program is also administered by the states and, as with the old-age benefits just discussed, benefit levels vary widely from state to state (see Figure 17.1). For example, in 2013, the states' monthly TANF benefits for a family of three varied from $170 in Mississippi to $923 in Alaska.[10] Even the most generous TANF payments are well below the federal poverty line. In 2014 the poverty level for a family of three included those earning less than $19,790 a year or $1,649 a month.[11]

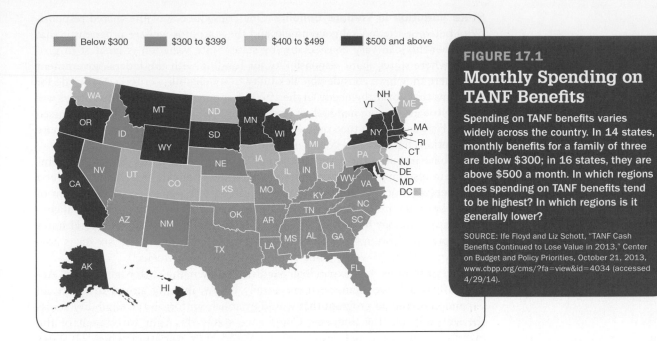

FIGURE 17.1

Monthly Spending on TANF Benefits

Spending on TANF benefits varies widely across the country. In 14 states, monthly benefits for a family of three are below $300; in 16 states, they are above $500 a month. In which regions does spending on TANF benefits tend to be highest? In which regions is it generally lower?

SOURCE: Ife Floyd and Liz Schott, "TANF Cash Benefits Continued to Lose Value in 2013," Center on Budget and Policy Priorities, October 21, 2013, www.cbpp.org/cms/?fa=view&id=4034 (accessed 4/29/14).

Map legend: Below $300 | $300 to $399 | $400 to $499 | $500 and above

The number of people receiving AFDC benefits expanded in the 1970s, in part because new welfare programs had been established during the mid-1960s: Medicaid (discussed earlier) and the **Supplemental Nutrition Assistance Program (SNAP)**, which is still sometimes called by its old name, food stamps. These programs provide what are called **in-kind benefits**—noncash goods and services that would otherwise have to be paid for in cash by the beneficiary. Because AFDC recipients automatically received Medicaid and food stamps, these new programs created an incentive for poor Americans to establish their eligibility for AFDC.

Another, more complex reason for the growth of AFDC in the 1970s was that it became more difficult for the government to terminate people's AFDC benefits for lack of eligibility. In the 1970 case of *Goldberg v. Kelly*, the Supreme Court held that the financial benefits of AFDC could not be revoked without due process—that is, a hearing at which evidence is presented.[12] This ruling inaugurated the concept of **entitlement**, a class of government benefits with a status similar to that of property (which, according to the Fourteenth Amendment, cannot be taken from people "without due process of law"). *Goldberg v. Kelly* did not provide that the beneficiary had a "right" to government benefits; it provided that once a person's eligibility for AFDC was established, and as long as the program was still in effect, that person could not be denied benefits without due process. The decision left open the possibility that Congress could terminate the program and its benefits by way of legislation. If the welfare benefit were truly a property right, Congress would have no authority to deny it.

Thus the establishment of in-kind benefit programs and the legal obstacles involved in terminating benefits contributed to the growth of the welfare state. But it is important to note that real federal spending (that is, spending adjusted for inflation) on AFDC itself did not rise after the mid-1970s. Unlike Social Security, AFDC was not indexed to inflation; without cost-of-living adjustments, the value of AFDC benefits fell by more than one-third.

Supplemental Nutrition Assistance Program (SNAP) the largest antipoverty program, which provides recipients with a debit card for food at most grocery stores; formerly known as *food stamps*

in-kind benefits noncash goods and services provided to needy individuals and families by the federal government

entitlement a legal obligation of the federal government to provide payments to individuals, or groups of individuals, according to eligibility criteria or benefit rules

State Variation in Welfare Benefits One consequence of the shared responsibility between the federal government and the states for welfare programs is that social benefits can vary considerably by state. State variation is greatest in programs where states share responsibility for funding with the federal government and where they have considerable flexibility to set eligibility criteria, as they do for programs that cover the needy. In the 1970s it appeared that the United States was moving toward a more national set of standards with the creation of SSI, discussed above. However, since that time, changes in federal laws and provisions for more state options have created considerable divergences among the states.

We have just seen the wide variation in TANF benefits across the states. Unemployment insurance is another policy in which state benefits and eligibility criteria are diverging. For most of the program's history, states provided a maximum of 26 weeks of unemployment insurance but in periods of recession, the federal government would pay for extended benefits. However, in recent years several states have opted to shorten the availability of unemployment insurance: six states now allow fewer than 26 weeks while two states allow more weeks.[13]

The provisions for expanding Medicaid under the Affordable Care Act of 2010, which we examine more closely below, initially aimed to create an expanded Medicaid program that would establish uniformity in eligibility across the states. When the Supreme Court gave states the right to opt out of the expansion, however, the result was increased state variation when 21 states opted out. States make other decisions about Medicaid eligibility that create state variation. For example, noncitizen legal immigrants are required to reside in the United States for five years before they can receive Medicaid but states can waive this requirement for children and pregnant women. Half of the states waive this requirement.[14]

The political polarization we have seen in national politics is increasingly evident in state choices about social benefits. States governed solely by Democrats or solely by Republicans take very different perspectives on social policy. The result is a patchwork that is growing more, not less, diverse.

Welfare Reform

From the 1960s to the 1990s, opinion polls consistently showed that the public viewed welfare beneficiaries as "undeserving."[15] Underlying that judgment was the belief that welfare recipients did not want to work. The Progressive-era reformers who first designed AFDC wanted single mothers to stay at home with their children. Motivated by horror stories of children killed in accidents while their mothers were off working or of children tied up at home all day in order to be kept safe, these reformers believed that it was better for the child if the mother did not work. By the 1960s, as more women entered the labor force and as welfare rolls rose, welfare recipients appeared in a more unfavorable light. Common criticisms charged that welfare recipients were taking advantage of the system, that they were irresponsible people who refused to work. These negative assessments were amplified by racial stereotypes. By 1973, 46 percent of welfare recipients were African American. Although the majority of recipients were white, media portrayals helped create the widespread perception that the vast majority of welfare recipients were black. A careful study by Martin Gilens has shown how racial stereotypes of blacks as uncommitted to the work ethic reinforced public opposition to welfare.[16]

Despite negative public sentiment toward welfare and welfare recipients, it proved difficult to reform welfare. While many reformers wanted to require work in exchange for benefits, few wished to be seen as harming children by eliminating benefits. Yet providing services, such as child care, that would enable single mothers to work would require spending substantially more on welfare. And most reformers wished to spend less, not more, on the program. Congress added modest work requirements in 1967, but little changed in the administration of welfare. A more significant reform in 1988 imposed stricter work requirements but also provided additional support services, such as child care and transportation assistance. This compromise legislation reflected a growing consensus that effective reform entailed a combination of sticks (work requirements) and carrots (extra services to make work possible). The 1988 reform also created a new system to identify the absent parent (usually the father) and enforce child-support payments.

In recent decades, welfare reform has emphasized work requirements and training for unemployed recipients. Here, an instructor provides training in using power tools as part of a Detroit-area welfare-to-work program funded by the federal government.

These reforms were barely implemented when welfare rolls rose again with the recession of the early 1990s, reaching an all-time high in 1994. Sensing continuing public frustration with welfare, when Bill Clinton was a presidential candidate he vowed "to end welfare as we know it," an unusual promise for a Democrat. Once in office, Clinton found it difficult to design a plan that would provide an adequate safety net for recipients unable to find work. One possibility, to provide government jobs as a last resort, was rejected as too expensive. Clinton's major achievement in the welfare field was to increase the Earned Income Tax Credit. This credit now allows working parents whose annual income falls below $49,078 (for a family of three or more) to file through their income tax return for an income supplement of up to $5,751, depending on their income and family size. It was a first step toward realizing Clinton's campaign promise to ensure that "if you work, you shouldn't be poor."

Congressional Republicans then proposed a much more dramatic reform of welfare, which Clinton, facing a campaign for re-election in 1996, signed. The Personal Responsibility and Work Opportunity Reconciliation Act (PRWORA) repealed AFDC. In place of the individual entitlement to assistance, the new law created block grants to the states and allowed states much more discretion in designing their cash-assistance programs to needy families. The new law also established time limits, restricting recipients to two years of assistance and creating a lifetime limit of five years. It imposed new work requirements on those receiving welfare, and it restricted most legal immigrants from receiving benefits. The aim of the new law was to reduce welfare caseloads, promote work, and reduce out-of-wedlock births. Notably, reducing poverty was not one of its stated objectives.

After this law was enacted, the number of families receiving assistance dropped by 60 percent nationwide (see Figure 17.2). The sharp decline in the number of recipients was widely hailed as a sign that the welfare reform was working. Indeed, former welfare recipients have been more successful at finding and keeping jobs than many critics of the law predicted. One important indicator of how welfare has changed is the proportion of funds it provides in cash assistance. Before the 1996 reform, assistance was provided largely in the form of a cash grant. By 2008, 70 percent of welfare funds were allocated for noncash assistance and 30 percent for cash assistance. This means that an increasing proportion of welfare funds is spent on such costs as assistance with transportation to work, temporary shelter, or

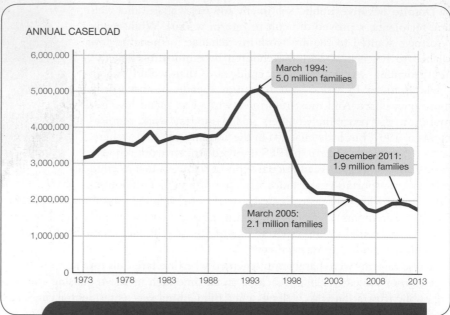

ANNUAL CASELOAD

March 1994:
5.0 million families

December 2011:
1.9 million families

March 2005:
2.1 million families

FIGURE 17.2

Welfare Caseload, 1973–2013

Welfare caseloads began to decline even before the 1996 reform. They have continued to plummet in the years since welfare reform. Welfare caseloads remained low even during the recession that began in 2008. Does the decline in the welfare caseload show that the 1996 reform was successful?

*Average monthly AFDC/TANF and SSP (separate state programs), families caseload.
SOURCE: U.S. Department of Health and Human Services, Administration for Children and Families, "Appendix Table 2:1: Average Monthly AFDC/TANF and SSP Families and Recipients, Fiscal Years 1960–2011," *TANF: Tenth Report to Congress,* December 12, 2013, www.acf.hhs .gov/sites/default/files/ofa/10th_tan_report_congress_appendix.pdf (accessed 4/29/14); U.S. Department of Health and Human Services, Administration for Children and Families, Data and Reports, Caseload Data, www.acf.hhs.gov/programs/ofa/programs/tanf/data-reports (accessed 4/29/14).

for critical analysis

Why was AFDC such an unpopular program? How did the creation of TANF alter welfare and what has it meant for TANF as an antipoverty program? Should TANF be reformed again?

one-time payments for emergencies so that people do not go on the welfare rolls. The orientation of assistance has shifted away from subsidizing people who are not in the labor force and toward addressing temporary problems that low-income people face and providing assistance that facilitates work.[17] But critics point out that most former welfare recipients are not paid enough to pull their families out of poverty. While the 1996 law has helped reduce welfare caseloads, it has done little to reduce the underlying problem of poverty.[18]

As the economy soured in 2009 and 2010, the number of people on welfare rolls began to move upward, but at a very slow rate. The American Recovery and Reinvestment Act of 2009 included a TANF Emergency Fund that provided monies for states to create subsidized jobs for low-income parents and young adults. Despite these measures, many advocates for the poor worried that the state TANF programs were not assisting enough poor families. After the Emergency Fund expired in 2011, advocates for the poor charged that, with states making deep cuts to their budgets, TANF was not keeping pace with the growth of poverty caused by the recession.[19] They contrasted it to the growth of the supplemental nutrition program (SNAP, or food stamps), whose growth closely tracked the rise in unemployment and poverty during the recession. In 2007, before the recession took hold, approximately 26.3 million individuals received SNAP benefits. By 2014, that number had risen to more than 46.9 million people a month, close to 15 percent of all Americans.[20]

How Do We Pay for the Welfare State?

Since the 1930s, when the main elements of the welfare state were first created, spending on social policy has grown dramatically. Most striking has been the growth of entitlement programs, the largest of which are Social Security and Medicare. The costs of entitlement programs grew from 26 percent of the total federal budget in 1962 to 64.1 percent by 2014. Funds to pay for these social programs have come disproportionately from increases in payroll taxes. In 1970 social insurance taxes accounted for 23 percent of all federal revenues; in 2014 they had grown to 34 percent of all federal revenues.[21] Meanwhile, since 1970, corporate taxes have fallen from 17 to 11.1 percent of all federal revenues. Because the payroll tax is regressive, low- and middle-income families have carried the burden for funding increased social spending.

Although much public attention has centered on welfare and other social spending programs for the poor, such as food stamps, these programs account for only a small proportion of social spending. For example, even at its height, AFDC made up only 1 percent of the federal budget. In recent years, Congress has tightly controlled spending on most means-tested programs, and lawmakers and government officials currently express little concern that spending on such programs is out of control. Spending on SNAP benefits rose substantially during the recession but even at these historically high rates, spending on programs for the poor is dwarfed by the costs of social insurance programs for the elderly. As Figure 17.3 shows, together the three biggest programs that assist low-income people (SNAP, Medicaid, and unemployment insurance) accounted for 2 percent of GDP in 2014 while spending on programs targeted at the elderly—Social Security and Medicare—together represented 8.4 percent of GDP.

Spending on Social Security The biggest spending increases to the welfare state have come in social insurance programs that provide benefits to the elderly. Such expenditures are hard to control because these programs are entitlements, and the government has promised to cover all people who fit the category of beneficiary. So, for example, the burgeoning elderly population will require that spending on Social Security automatically increase in the future. Furthermore, because Social Security benefits are indexed to inflation, there is no easy way to reduce benefits. Spending on medical programs (Medicare and Medicaid) has also proved difficult to control, in part because of the growing numbers of people eligible for the programs but also because of rising health care costs. Health care expenditures have risen much more steeply than inflation in recent years.

Concern about social spending has centered on Social Security because the aging of the baby-boom generation will force spending up sharply in the coming decades. In the past, there were always many more young workers than retirees receiving Social Security. That situation is changing as individuals live longer and as

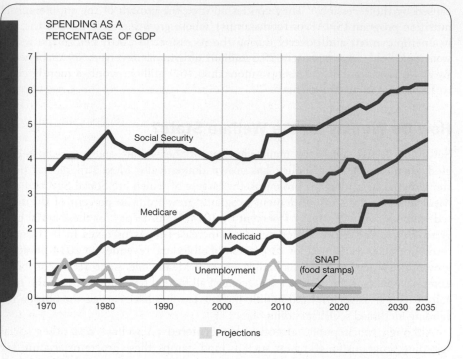

FIGURE 17.3

Size of the Welfare State

Spending on Medicare, Medicaid, and Social Security are all projected to rise as a percent of GDP. Social Security, a contributory program that provides income to the elderly, is by far the largest welfare program in the United States. Which program is the smallest?

SOURCE: Congressional Budget Office, www.cbo.gov/publication/44521 (accessed 4/29/14); Congressional Budget Office, www.cbo.gov/publication/45229 (accessed 4/29/14); Office of Management and Budget, www.whitehouse.gov/omb/budget/historicals (accessed 4/29/14).

the very large generation known as the baby boomers reaches retirement. Indeed, under current law, the Social Security Trust Fund, the special government account from which Social Security payments are made, is projected to experience a shortfall beginning in 2033.[22]

Critics also contend that Americans are not getting their money's worth from Social Security and that workers would be better off if they could take at least part of the payroll tax that currently pays for Social Security and invest it in individual accounts. They highlight unfavorable rates of return in the current system, noting, for example, that a male worker born in 2000 who is single can expect to see a return of only 0.86 percent on his Social Security contributions. This is far below stock market returns over the past decades.[23] These arguments have received less attention since the economic recession, which started in 2008, and the stock market volatility that accompanied it.

Because Social Security is such a popular program, proposed changes that might weaken it are generally greeted with suspicion, and politicians often shy away from proposing changes to the system. President George W. Bush was an exception, however, and he came to office supporting Social Security reforms, including the creation of private retirement accounts. Soon after taking office, the president appointed a Social Security Commission, whose final report prominently featured individual accounts as a reform strategy. The commission recommended three reform plans, each of which offered workers the choice of contributing a portion (ranging from 2 to 4 percent) of the payroll tax to an individual account. The worker's traditional benefits would be reduced by the amount diverted to the individual account. According to the commission, individual plans would create a better system because they would allow workers to accumulate assets and build wealth that could be passed on to their children.[24]

Given the politically volatile character of debates about Social Security, President Bush backed off from proposing any changes in the program during his first term. Nonetheless, in 2004, immediately after his re-election, Bush announced that he would make Social Security reform a centerpiece of his next administration. Although Bush did not put forth a precise plan, private accounts were at the heart of his approach to reform. During the first half of 2005, the president toured the country attempting to win support for his ideas. But he immediately faced huge opposition as unions and AARP mobilized to oppose him. AARP launched a national advertising campaign against private accounts, with slogans designed to highlight the risks and radical nature of the president's proposal: "If we feel like gambling, we'll play the slots," and "If you have a problem with the sink, you don't tear down the entire house." Senate Democrats, displaying unusual unity, closed ranks against the president's ideas. By October 2005 the president had to admit that Social Security reform was dead. When Republicans gained control of the House of Representatives in 2011, they remembered Bush's experience and refrained from proposing changes to Social Security.

Supporters of the current Social Security system contend that the system's financial troubles are exaggerated. They dispute arguments that deficits require cuts in Social Security. They point out that Social Security taxes were raised in 1983 and that the program's trust funds were officially placed "off budget," in a so-called lockbox, so that the program would be prepared to serve the aging baby-boom generation.[25] They argue that instead of saving that money, however, the federal government cut taxes on the wealthy and used Social Security taxes to finance the deficit in the federal operating budget. Advocates of the current system believe that many of Social Security's troubles could be solved by raising income taxes on the wealthy and eliminating the cap on payroll taxes. In 2014 only the first $117,000 in income was subject to the payroll tax. If this cap were lifted, these critics argue, the resulting revenues would cut the expected shortfall in the Social Security Trust Fund in half.

Supporters of the current system are also deeply skeptical about the benefits of individual accounts. They charged that President Bush presented a rosy scenario that overestimated likely gains through the stock market. When more realistic assumptions are adopted and the costs of the private accounts are considered, the critics argue, individual accounts would not provide higher benefits than the current system. Moreover, they note that individual accounts would do nothing to solve the budget crisis that Social Security will face.[26]

Finally, supporters of the present system emphasize that Social Security is not just a retirement account but also a social insurance program that provides "income protection to workers and their families if the wage earner retires, becomes disabled, or dies."[27] Because it provides this social insurance protection, supporters argue, Social Security's returns should not be compared with those of a private retirement account.

In 2010, President Obama appointed a bipartisan commission on reducing the national debt, which recommended reforms to Social Security. The commission recommended increasing Social Security taxes on the wealthy, increasing the age for receiving benefits, and gradually reducing future benefits. But in a charged political context, neither party wanted to take the initiative on reforms that would ensure that Social Security remain solvent.

The Social Security system is one of the most popular government programs, but recent reports have estimated that by 2033 it will be unable to pay full benefits. Both parties have proposed reforms to address the projected shortfall, but the issue remains highly controversial.

Spending on Medicare Although much of the public debate has focused on the costs of Social Security, most experts agree that Medicare and Medicaid pose the biggest budget challenge. The rapidly rising cost of health care—often at twice the rate of inflation—makes it much harder to control how much the government spends. Moreover, as more of the large baby-boom generation reaches 65, the costs of Medicare are expected to skyrocket. While payroll taxes are sufficient to cover Social Security payments fully until 2033, and small changes in benefits and taxes would see the program through the baby-boom retirement years, the cost challenges to Medicare are much more significant. In 2012 payroll taxes accounted for only 38 percent of all Medicare revenues; 40 percent came from general revenues.[28] In 2012, Medicare accounted for 16 percent of the federal budget, and Medicare costs present an ongoing challenge in the effort to reduce the deficit.[29]

A sweeping plan for reforming Medicare and Medicaid came from Paul Ryan (R-Wisc.), who in 2011 proposed replacing the current program with payments—called "premium support"—that could be used to help pay for private insurance. The plan called for converting Medicaid from an entitlement program, where costs are shared between the federal government and the states, to a block grant. The block grant would provide federal funds to the state but would not guarantee eligibility to some groups as does an entitlement.

An analysis of the Ryan plan by the Congressional Budget Office showed that while the plan might reduce the deficit, it would require elderly beneficiaries to pay substantially more for health care and would likely leave current Medicaid beneficiaries without health care coverage.[30] These proposals met with intense opposition from Democrats. Public opposition to the proposed Medicare changes played a significant role in Republican defeat in a 2011 special election for a normally Republican New York state district. After that defeat, Republicans backed off on their proposals to redesign Medicare and Medicaid. Even so, rising health care expenditures and budget deficits meant that the issue of controlling costs in Medicare and Medicaid will remain on the national agenda.

● Opening Opportunity

> **Describe how education, health, and housing policies try to promote equality of opportunity**

The welfare state not only supplies a measure of economic security but also provides opportunity. The American belief in **equality of opportunity** makes such programs particularly important. Programs that provide opportunity keep people from falling into poverty and offer a hand up to those who are poor. At their best, opportunity policies allow all individuals to rise as high as their talents will take them. Three types of policies are most significant in opening opportunity: education policies, health policies, and housing policies.

equality of opportunity a widely shared American ideal that all people should have the freedom to use whatever talents and wealth they have to reach their fullest potential

Education Policies

Those who understand American federalism from Chapter 3 already are aware that most of the education of the American people is provided by the public policies of state and local governments. What may be less obvious is that these education policies—especially the policy of universal compulsory public education—are the most important single force in the distribution and redistribution of opportunity in America.

For most of American history, the federal government has played only a minor role in education. In the early years of the nation, the government assisted schools through the Land Ordinance of 1785 and the Northwest Ordinance of 1787, both of which ensured that lands were set aside for public schools and their maintenance. In 1862, Congress established land-grant colleges with the Morrill Act. After World War II the federal government stepped up its role in education policy with the enactment of the GI Bill of Rights of 1944, the National Defense Education Act (NDEA) of 1958, the Elementary and Secondary Education Act of 1965 (ESEA), and various youth and adult vocational training acts since 1958. Note, however, that since the GI Bill was aimed almost entirely at postsecondary schooling, the national government did not truly enter the field of elementary education until after 1957.[31]

What finally brought the national government into elementary education was embarrassment that the Soviet Union had beaten the United States into space with the launching of Sputnik, the world's first satellite. As a result, the federal government adopted the policy under NDEA of improving education in science and mathematics. At the same time, the federal government recognized the role of education in promoting equality of opportunity. In 1965 the ESEA offered federal aid for education by allocating funds to school districts with substantial numbers of children from families who were unemployed or earning less than $2,000 a year. By the early 1970s federal expenditures for elementary and secondary education were running over $4 billion per year. Today the federal government spends $74.9 billion, 12 percent of all spending on K–12 education; states and localities each account for 44 percent of spending. Over time, however, federal education funds have become less targeted on low-income districts as Congress has failed to update the formula for allocating funds.[32]

As we saw in Chapter 5, the federal government also pursued the goal of equal opportunity in education through its support for racial desegregation. This meant dismantling the system of "separate but equal" education in the South and challenging de facto racial segregation in the North. Throughout the 1960s the Justice Department played a major role in pressing for desegregation and in monitoring progress of school integration. Yet, 50 years after the Civil Rights Act, this goal has remained elusive. Segregated patterns in housing create segregated schools unless vigorous policy interventions are implemented. However, such policies, including requirements for cross-district busing and provisions for affordable housing in affluent suburbs, have been struck down by the courts.

Ronald Reagan's administration signaled a new focus for federal education policy: the central goal of equal opportunity was replaced by the pursuit of higher standards. In 1983 the Department of Education issued A Nation at Risk, an influential report that identified low educational standards as the cause of America's declining international economic competitiveness. The report did not suggest any changes in federal policy, but it urged states to make excellence in education their primary goal. This theme was picked up again by President George H. W. Bush. Because Republicans have historically opposed a strong federal role in education, the initiatives of Reagan and Bush remained primarily advisory, but they were very influential in focusing educational reform on standards and testing, now widely practiced across the states.

U.S. Education Policy: Lagging or Leading?

The Program for International Student Assessment (PISA) conducts surveys of educational achievement around the globe, and in recent years American students have consistently scored lower in mathematics and science than students in many Asian and European countries.[a] For many education advocates, this trend is particularly worrisome, as the United States on average spends considerably more per student than many of countries that scored higher on these tests, as the graph below shows. Concerns about competitiveness have driven recent education policy decisions in the United States, including the adoption of the Common Core State Standards in most states.

However, some education experts argue that we should not be too quick to label the U.S. education system a failure. They point out that PISA results might not be truly comparable, as the selection of test-takers for the survey may be biased. For instance, the U.S. test sample includes students from across the United States who represent many social and economic backgrounds; in contrast, Shanghai's school system (which ranked #1 on the test) excludes most migrant children and poor students whose parents come from China's rural regions.[b] Compared to other developed countries, the United States has greater social inequality and a larger immigrant population, meaning that the education system includes more students from poor and disadvantaged backgrounds. If PISA scores were weighted to take demographics into account, the ranking of the United States would jump up significantly.[c]

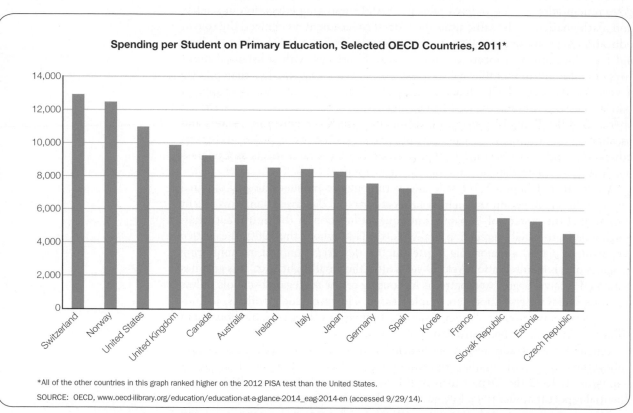

Spending per Student on Primary Education, Selected OECD Countries, 2011*

*All of the other countries in this graph ranked higher on the 2012 PISA test than the United States.

SOURCE: OECD, www.oecd-ilibrary.org/education/education-at-a-glance-2014_eag-2014-en (accessed 9/29/14).

[a]Julia Ryan, "American Schools vs. the World: Expensive, Unequal, Bad at Math," *The Atlantic*, December 3, 2013, www.theatlantic.com/education/archive/2013/12/american-schools-vs-the-world-expensive-unequal-bad-at-math/281983/ (accessed 9/29/14).
[b]Tom Loveless, "Attention OECD-PISA: Your Silence on China Is Wrong," Brookings Institution, December 11, 2013, www.brookings.edu/blogs/brown-center-chalkboard/posts/2013/12/11-shanghai-pisa-scores-wrong-loveless (accessed 9/29/14).
[c]Martin Carnoy and Richard Rothstein, "What Do International Tests Really Show about U.S. Student Performance?" Economic Policy Institute, January 28, 2013, www.epi.org/publication/us-student-performance-testing/ (accessed 9/29/14).

The federal role was substantially increased by President George W. Bush's signature education act, the No Child Left Behind Act of 2001. Supported by Democrats and Republicans, the law sought to combine the goals of higher standards and equality of opportunity. It aimed to improve standards through stronger federal requirements for testing and school accountability. Every child in grades three through eight had to be tested yearly for proficiency in math and reading. The law aimed to promote equality of opportunity with two provisions: first, for a school to be judged a success, it had to show positive test results for all subcategories of children—minority race and ethnicity, English learners, and disability—not just overall averages. Second, parents whose child is in a failing school had the right to transfer the child to a better school. Because of strong congressional opposition to creating a national test, the states were made responsible for setting standards and devising appropriate tests.

As we saw in Chapter 3, although No Child Left Behind (NCLB) initially attracted broad bipartisan support, it quickly generated considerable controversy. Many states branded it an unfunded mandate, noting that the law placed expensive new obligations on the schools to improve their performance but provided woefully inadequate resources. Teachers objected that "teaching to the test" undermined critical thinking. In some states, up to half the schools failed to meet the new standards, presenting a costly remedial challenge. Under the federal law, they were required to improve student performance by providing such new services as supplemental tutoring, longer school days, and additional summer school. Moreover, critics charged that NCLB actually undermined equality of opportunity because it ended up punishing underperforming schools—mostly those schools that bear the greatest burden for teaching the neediest students.[33]

Faced with these conflicts, the Obama administration sought a major overhaul of No Child Left Behind. But by 2011, with Congress unable to agree on new legislation, the administration initiated its own reform. The president announced that states could apply for waivers that would exempt them from some of the requirements of No Child Left Behind. Waivers would be granted if states could show that they had their own plans for improving student achievement. One requirement that had become especially troublesome was the mandate that all students be proficient in reading and math by 2014. As that date drew closer, it became apparent that few, if any, schools would meet that standard. In 2012 the administration made good on its promise and began to grant states waivers from key requirements of No Child Left Behind. By 2014, 45 states had been granted waivers from NCLB.[34]

But waivers did not signal a movement away from a standards-based approach to equality of opportunity. In fact, Obama's education initiatives have drawn many of the same criticisms that surrounded NCLB, especially the emphasis on high-stakes testing. As a condition of receiving waivers, states were required to show that they had adopted a strong set of educational standards and that they linked teacher evaluations to test results. In an effort to show that they had adopted high educational standards, most states endorsed a set of standards known as the Common Core State Standards. Drawn up by representatives of the National Governors Association and the Council of Chief State School Officers in 2010, the standards set out clear markers for student knowledge. While many educators believe that the standards could serve as a tool for promoting equality of opportunity by improving education in all schools, the testing regime associated with the Common Core drew sharp criticisms as a return to the failed policies of NCLB.[35]

for critical analysis

Why did the No Child Left Behind Act, initially passed with bipartisan support, become so controversial? Do educational standards promote equality of opportunity? Why or why not?

Education policy is the most important means of providing equal opportunity for all Americans. President Obama sought to overhaul some problematic aspects of the No Child Left Behind Act, but Congress struggled to agree on the new provisions.

The Obama administration has also put its imprint on education with its strong support for charter schools—publicly funded schools that are free from the bureaucratic rules and regulations of the school district in which they are located and free to design specialized curricula and to use resources in ways they think most effective. Since the creation of the first charter schools in Minnesota in 1990, states across the country have passed legislation to authorize them. Many states, however, proceeded slowly, establishing caps on the number of new charter schools that could be created each year. The Obama administration put its weight behind charter schools in one of its first pieces of legislation, the American Reinvestment and Recovery Act, sometimes called the stimulus bill. The act included a new $4.3 billion program called Race to the Top, which offered competitive grants to state education systems. To be eligible for the grants, states had to agree to lift the caps on the number of charter schools that could be created each year. In the end, the administration awarded sizable grants to 11 states and Washington, D.C., praising the states for proposing bold new programs for assessing teachers and overhauling failing schools.[36] Several years after the program began, it was clear that states had promised more than they could do in the limited time that the funds were provided. While the additional financing helped to shore up school budgets in a period of tremendous financial strain, systemwide improvements proved more elusive.[37]

As policy makers, politicians, and educators struggle over implementing standards and supporting alternatives models for education, such as charter schools, some critics fundamentally question the focus of these efforts.[38] These critics argue that the American schools face unprecedented challenges in educating students from impoverished families and growing numbers of English learners in a setting where the goal is to make every student college-ready. From this perspective, the solution does not lie in more testing or in charter schools but rather in providing more assistance to children in poverty, free preschool, and enhanced assistance to the schools that educate low-income students and English learners.

The federal government also plays an important role in helping to fund higher education. As in K–12 education, most funds for public systems of higher education have historically come from the states, not the federal government. However, federal programs have made a big difference in promoting equal access to higher education. Perhaps the most celebrated higher-education program of all is the GI Bill of 1944, which put higher education in reach of a whole generation of World War II veterans who never thought they would attend college. The federal government built on this role in the 1950s and '60s with the National Defense Education Act (NDEA) and the Higher Education Act (HEA). Spurred by the desire to compete with the Soviet Union in science education, the NDEA offered low-interest loans to college students. The Higher Education Act of 1965 expanded the federal role further, supplying assistance directly to colleges and offering additional need-based grants allocated to students by universities. In 1972, Congress created the Pell grant program, which offered grants (that do not need to be repaid) directly to lower-income students.

Together these programs opened the doors of higher education much more widely than ever before in American history. But over the past 40 years, as states have sharply reduced funding for higher education and college tuition has risen dramatically, these financial assistance programs have not kept pace. Whereas Pell grants had initially provided enough to pay for tuition plus room and board at a four-year public college, by 2011, they covered only 54 percent of tuition.[39] The growing costs of higher education have put college out of reach for many lower-income students and have left those who do attend college with a heavy load of debt. In the 18 years between 1992 and 2010, average student debt nearly doubled, to $22,011.[40]

Americans have long prided themselves on a system of education—at the primary, secondary, and higher-education levels—that promotes opportunity. A changing world economy that features intense competition from developing economies has put a premium on the importance of a high-skill workforce. Yet, our system of education has fallen short in delivering the benefits of a high-quality education to all children and higher education is now out of reach for many, even as it grows in importance. These challenges mean that debates about how education can best promote equal opportunity will grow even more intense in the future.

Health Policies

Until recent decades, no government in the United States (national, state, or local) concerned itself directly with individual health. But public responsibility was always accepted for *public* health. After New York City's newly created Board of Health was credited with holding down a cholera epidemic in 1867, most states created statewide public-health agencies. Within a decade, the results were obvious. Between 1884 and 1894, for example, Massachusetts's rate of infant mortality dropped from 161.3 per 1,000 to 141.4 per 1,000.[41]

The U.S. Public Health Service (USPHS) has been in existence since 1798 but was a small part of public-health policy until after World War II. Established in 1937 but little noticed for 20 years was the National Institutes of Health (NIH), an agency within the USPHS that was created to do biomedical research. Between 1950 and 2012, NIH expenditures by the national government increased from $160.0 million to $30.9 billion. NIH research on the link between smoking and disease led to one of the most visible public-health campaigns in American history. The Centers for Disease Control and Prevention (CDC), which monitors outbreaks of disease and implements prevention measures, coordinates such public-health campaigns. Subsequently, NIH's focus turned to cancer and acquired immunodeficiency syndrome (AIDS).

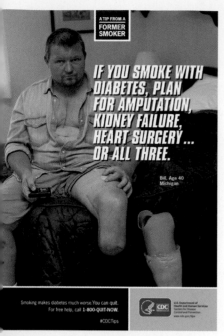

Bill, Age 40
Michigan

The National Institutes of Health played a major role in researching the link between smoking and cancer, and the Centers for Disease Control and Prevention has mounted major ad campaigns to make the public aware of the many risks associated with smoking.

As with smoking, this work on AIDS resulted in massive public-health education as well as new products and regulations. Federal programs for HIV/AIDS research, treatment, prevention, and income support had a budget of $28.3. billion in 2013, a major increase from the $2.9 billion spent in 1990.[42] President Clinton put greater emphasis on HIV/AIDS by appointing an "AIDS czar" to coordinate federal HIV/AIDS policy, and by giving this position cabinet status. Under presidents Bush and Obama, the coordinator for national HIV/AIDS policy directed the Office of National AIDS Policy as part of the White House Domestic Council. Although this federal attention to HIV/AIDS has contributed to new treatments that have saved many lives, the rates of infection have remained unchanged for the past decade.[43]

Other recent commitments to the improvement of public health are the numerous laws aimed at cleaning up and defending the environment (including the creation in 1970 of the Environmental Protection Agency) and laws attempting to improve the health and safety of consumer products (regulated by the Consumer Product Safety Commission, created in 1972).

In addition to important public-health campaigns, government now plays a significant role in providing for individual health. Health policies aimed directly at the poor include Medicaid and nutritional programs, particularly food stamps and the school lunch program. In 2013 federal grants to states for Medicaid totaled $265 billion, up from $41 billion in 1990.[44] Medicaid covers not only the poor but also people who are disabled; it also assists the elderly poor who cannot pay Medicare premiums. Because there is no provision for long-term care in the United States, Medicaid has become the de facto program financing nursing home residents when they have exhausted their savings. In fact, the disabled and elderly account for 65 percent of all Medicaid spending.[45] Medicaid is the single largest medical insurance program in the United States, covering 62 million people, a number that is expected to rise as the Affordable Care Act's expansion provisions (discussed below) are put into place.

Health Care Reform Even with the passage of the Patient Protection and Affordable Care Act in March 2010, the United States is the only advanced industrial nation without universal access to health care. Opposition from the American Medical Association, the main lobbying organization of doctors, prevented President Roosevelt from proposing national health insurance during the 1930s, when other elements of the welfare state became law. As a result, the United States developed a patchwork system: in 2012, 56 percent of the nonelderly population received health insurance through their employers, older Americans were covered through Medicare, and the poor and disabled were assisted with Medicaid.[46] However, the growing costs of employer-provided insurance means that increasing numbers of workers cannot afford it. Many small employers cannot even afford to offer benefits because they are so expensive. And both Medicaid and Medicare face severe fiscal strain due to rising costs.

President Clinton's major attempt to reshape federal health policy, and the boldest policy initiative of his administration, was his effort to reform America's health care system. In September 1993, Clinton announced a plan with two key objectives: to limit the rising costs of the American health care system and to provide universal health insurance coverage for all Americans. (More than 41 million Americans lacked health insurance.) Clinton's plan, spearheaded by the first lady, Hillary Rodham Clinton, at first garnered enormous public support and seemed likely to win congressional approval in some form. But the plan, which entailed a major expansion of federal administration of the health care system, gradually lost momentum as resistance to it took root among those who feared changes in a system that worked well for them. Although Clinton had pledged to make health care the centerpiece of his 1994 legislative agenda, no health care bill even came up for a full congressional vote that year. Following the failure of President Clinton's health care initiative, Congress passed a much smaller program expanding health insurance coverage for low-income children not already receiving Medicaid, called the State Children's Health Insurance Program.

Medicare Reform In 2003, Congress enacted a major reform of the Medicare program, which has provided health care to seniors since 1965. Most notably, Congress added a prescription drug benefit to the package of health benefits for the elderly. The high cost of prescription drugs had been an issue of growing concern to millions of older Americans. Yet the bill proved very controversial. Critics charged that the bill included a sweetheart deal with drug companies, because the legislation contained a provision prohibiting the federal government from using its purchasing power to reduce drug prices. Many Democrats also objected to the legislation because it opened the door for private health plans to play a significant role in health care provision for the elderly. They feared that the entry of such plans would significantly weaken Medicare, which has been one of the most strongly supported federal social programs. Fiscal conservatives worried about the costs of the prescription drug package. This concern escalated several months after the bill's passage, when the administration issued new, much higher cost estimates for the prescription drug benefit than the estimates presented when the bill was being debated. Adding fuel to the growing controversy over drug prices was the disclosure that the former Medicare administrator had prevented his chief actuary from releasing the higher cost estimates to Congress as it was considering the Medicare bill.

The conflict over Medicare reform highlights the problems surrounding health care more generally. A majority of Americans believe that government should ensure that all people receive adequate health care. Yet how to deliver such benefits and how to pay for them are extremely contentious issues.[47]

Health Care Legislation in 2010 After the 2008 election, the Obama administration and the Democratic Congress pressed forward with comprehensive health reform. Seeking to avoid the conflicts that broke out in Congress over the Clintons' fully formed and highly complex health reform proposal, Obama offered Congress broad principles for reform, not a detailed proposal. The administration aimed at covering most Americans who lacked health insurance with a reform strategy that built on the existing system. The plan that ultimately passed had three key features: the first was the creation of new state-based insurance exchanges where individuals could buy health insurance, along with insurance regulation that would prohibit insurers from denying benefits for a variety of reasons such as preexisting conditions. With a few exceptions, the legislation also makes insurers cover preventive medicine in full. The second provision of the ACA, known as "the individual mandate," required uninsured individuals to purchase health insurance; those who do not have insurance are subject to a fine (scheduled to rise over time) of 1 percent of yearly household income or $95, whichever was larger. The third major provision of the ACA was a set of subsidies to help the uninsured and small businesses purchase insurance as well as an expansion of the public programs Medicaid and the SCHIP. The Medicaid expansion made more people eligible for the program by opening it to people with incomes at or below 138 percent of the poverty level. This meant that individuals making up to $16,000 a year would be eligible to receive Medicaid. The reform also allowed working-aged adults without dependent children to qualify for the program for the first time. This provision was intended to provide health insurance for many of the country's uninsured. Figure 17.4 shows the projected number of insured Americans with and without the ACA in 2024.

The politics of health care reform have remained a focus of partisan contention. All the new Republican house members elected in 2010 favored repeal of the measure. Republican presidential candidate Mitt Romney likewise pledged to roll back the measure. Tea Party activists, fearful that the law involved too much government control, also mobilized against it. These activists were angered by the Supreme Court decision declaring most of the Affordable Care Act constitutional. One poll found that 82 percent of Tea Party activists wanted to continue their efforts to block the law.[48]

The rollout of the state insurance exchanges in fall 2013 further damaged public perceptions of the Affordable Care Act. Massive computer problems with the main website, heathcare.gov, meant that some applicants working through the online system were cut off after hours of effort; others could not even get started on their applications. These problems affected applicants from the 27 states that did not set up their own insurance exchanges but relied on the

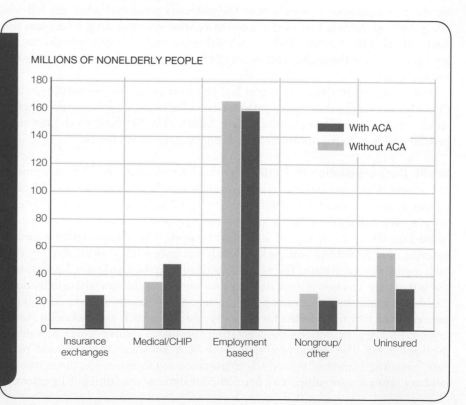

FIGURE 17.4

Projected Insurance Coverage with and without ACA, 2024

These projections by the Congressional Budget Office predict that in 2024 over 20 million people will receive health insurance through the exchanges set up by the ACA. The act would also boost the number of people receiving benefits through Medicaid and the Children's Health Insurance Program. The CBO projects that the number of uninsured people will be 30 million lower with the ACA than they would be without the ACA.

SOURCE: Congressional Budget Office, "Updated Estimates of the Effects of the Insurance Coverage Provisions to the Affordable Care Act," April 2014, www.cbo.gov/publication/45231 (accessed 4/29/14).

MILLIONS OF NONELDERLY PEOPLE

With ACA
Without ACA

Insurance exchanges | Medical/CHIP | Employment based | Nongroup/other | Uninsured

federal website. Some of the state exchanges, such as Covered California, worked largely as intended but others, such as Oregon's, failed altogether. Only after a major reworking of the online system did the federal insurance exchanges begin to work as intended. The administration gradually extended the sign-up deadline, and by April 2014 it announced that more than 8 million people had signed up through the exchanges, a number that exceeded initial expectations.[49] Even so, the disastrous launch of the insurance exchanges represented a missed opportunity for the administration to change public perceptions of the Affordable Care Act, and more Americans reported an unfavorable view of the ACA than a favorable view into 2014.[50]

The new health reform law faced challenges from state governments soon after it was enacted. Twenty-one state attorneys general filed lawsuits against the legislation on the grounds that the provision requiring individuals to purchase health insurance expanded the commerce clause beyond its constitutional limits. The states also objected to provisions that required them to expand their Medicaid programs to cover more poor people or lose the Medicaid funds that they received from the federal government. Even though the federal government will initially pay for 100 percent of the expansion and after 2016 will cover 90 percent of new costs, the states argued that the federal government had overstepped its powers in withdrawing all federal Medicaid funds if states did not comply with new coverage requirements.

The Supreme Court decided these suits in 2012, ruling that most of the act was constitutional.[51] Chief Justice John Roberts, regarded as a conservative,

Some Americans opposed the 2010 Affordable Care Act because they were concerned that decisions previously left to patients and their doctors would be made by the government.

surprised many observers by personally writing the decision that declared the individual mandate constitutional. However, the decision found that the mandate could not be justified as constitutional under the commerce clause, which the administration relied on in its arguments before the Court. Because the mandate regulated economic *inactivity* (i.e., the failure to purchase health insurance) Roberts argued that the commerce clause, which regulates economic *activity*, did not apply. Instead the Court ruled that the requirement to purchase insurance was legal under Congress's taxing powers (since, under the law, failure to purchase insurance will result in a penalty). The decision on Medicaid, the second contested feature of the act, also came as a surprise. The Court ruled that Congress did not have the power to take existing Medicaid funds away from states if they did not comply with the expansion requirements. The governors of several states including Florida and South Carolina immediately announced their intention to opt out of the expansion. Eventually 21 states decided not to expand their Medicaid programs. These state decisions left 5.7 million people who would have qualified for Medicaid without access to health care.[52]

The Affordable Care Act remains controversial. One area in particular that has attracted controversy concerns the types of services that must be covered. When the Obama administration announced a provision requiring all employers to provide contraceptive services at no cost as part of their insurance plans, it ignited a firestorm of partisan contention. Republicans charged that the administration was interfering with religious freedom; Democrats countered that Republicans were trying to take the country back to the 1950s. In fact, polls showed significant partisan division on the issue: while 62 percent of all Americans approved of the measure, and 83 percent of Democrats approved, only 42 percent of Republicans did.[53] The president's compromise proposal, which required the insurance companies, not the religious institutions, to provide contraception, did little to quell the controversy. The issue reemerged when Hobby Lobby, an arts and crafts chain store, challenged the federal law because its owners objected to requirements that their insurance cover all forms of contraception, including birth control methods they opposed on religious grounds. Pitting federal standards for equal treatment for women against business owners rights to religious freedom, the conflict reached the Supreme Court in 2014. A divided court ruled that "closely held" corporations—where the owners actively manage the companies—were exempt from provisions of law that violated their owners' religious beliefs.[54]

Housing Policies

The United States has one of the highest rates of home ownership in the world, and the central thrust of federal housing policy has been to promote home ownership. The federal government has traditionally done much less to provide housing for low-income Americans who cannot afford to buy homes.

Federal housing programs were first created during the Great Depression of the 1930s, when many Americans found themselves unable to afford housing. Through public housing for low-income families, which originated in 1937 with the Wagner-Steagall National Housing Act and subsidized private housing after 1950, the percentage of American families living in overcrowded conditions was reduced from 20 percent in 1940 to 9 percent in 1970. Federal policies made an even greater contribution to reducing "substandard" housing, defined by the U.S. Census Bureau as dilapidated houses without hot running water and without some other plumbing. In 1940 almost 50 percent of American households lived in substandard housing. By 1950 this had been reduced to 35 percent; by 1975, to 8 percent.[55]

Despite these improvements in housing standards, federal housing policy until the 1970s was largely seen as a failure. Restricted to the poorest of the poor and marked by racial segregation and inadequate spending, public housing contributed to the problems of the poor by isolating them from shopping, jobs, and urban amenities. Dilapidated high-rise housing projects stood as a symbol of the failed American policy of "warehousing the poor." By the 1980s the orientation of housing policy had changed: most federal housing policy for low-income Americans came in the form of housing vouchers (called Section 8 vouchers and now called housing choice vouchers) that provided recipients with support to rent in the private market. Although this program did not promote the same kind of isolation of the poor, it was often useless in very active housing markets, where the vouchers provided too little money to cover rental costs. Most cities and suburbs have long waiting lists to receive vouchers, and many housing authorities have closed their lists for 5 to 10 years because they have so few vouchers to hand out. The lack of affordable rental housing in the United States has become an increasingly pressing problem, made much worse by the recession that started in 2008. Neither the federal government nor the states have enacted policies that go far toward addressing this issue.

The Clinton administration at first showed a strong ideological commitment to encouraging housing policies and combating homelessness. But especially after 1994, the Clinton administration began to retreat. HUD secretary Henry Cisneros continually had to waive, virtually to the point of abandonment, a long-standing one-for-one HUD rule that provided that for every public housing unit destroyed, another would have to be built. This rule mattered because during the 1990s the main public housing program, called HOPE VI, allowed local public housing authorities to tear down the high-rise public housing that had been such a failure. In its place, city after city dismantled its old public housing projects and replaced them with new mixed-income units. The policy assumed that reducing concentrations of poverty would benefit the poor. Unfortunately, few of the original residents have been able to move into the new units.[56] The Bush administration placed less emphasis on housing policy. It proposed transforming the federal voucher program into a block grant to the states. The initiative, which never came to a vote in Congress, faced opposition from housing proponents who feared that it would greatly reduce assistance to low-income renters.

Beginning in 2007 and 2008, a home loan foreclosure crisis presented the government with a different kind of housing problem. During the housing boom of the early 2000s, many homeowners received loans that they later could not afford to repay. This was due in part to the deregulation of the mortgage industry in 1999. The deregulation allowed many new mortgage companies to form, offering loans that cost little at first but later required large payments from homeowners. This form of "predatory lending" targeted unsophisticated buyers and made it very hard for borrowers to understand the terms of the loans, which contained pages and pages of small print written in legalese. Lending standards were relaxed to the point that rising numbers of borrowers were offered "no-doc" loans, which required no documentation of the borrowers' income. As more and more Americans took out such loans, demand for housing rose, and housing prices skyrocketed. This was

Many cities have been replacing high-rise housing projects with new mixed-income units, such as these homes in New Haven, Connecticut.

the housing bubble—a bubble that was bound to burst because so many borrowers would not be able to pay back their loans. As growing numbers of homeowners began to default on their loans in 2007, banks foreclosed on their houses and the value of housing began to drop. This downward spiral set off the major recession that began in 2007. As borrowers defaulted, banks holding that debt, including the biggest banks in America, teetered on the edge of failure and threatened to destabilize the entire economy. Many of the new mortgage companies, which had grown into huge businesses, went bankrupt. As unemployment rose, more families, unable to pay their mortgages, lost their homes. Many homeowners found that their homes were "underwater," meaning the homeowners owed more on their mortgages than the mortgaged properties were now worth.

By 2014 nearly 5 million homes had been lost to foreclosure.[57] The federal government responded with a plan that would slow the rising interest rates that were the cause of the problem for some homeowners. It also created several additional programs designed to help homeowners facing foreclosure. However, these programs did not experience much success. Many argued that a program reducing the amount of principal owed on a mortgage was the only way to stem the foreclosure crisis. But banks objected to such a program, as did a significant segment of the public. Some of the opposition to this kind of homeowner bailout stemmed from different perspectives on who was responsible for the mortgage crisis. While some people blamed predatory lenders, others blamed the borrowers themselves, who had taken out loans they couldn't afford, sometimes misrepresenting their ability to pay. In fact, the Tea Party movement got its start in 2009, when Rick Santelli, a cable television reporter, launched into a passionate rant against helping troubled homeowners, who, he claimed, had only themselves to blame.[58]

The federal government and the states continued to look for ways to stem the tide of foreclosures, which remained a major barrier to economic recovery. In 2012 states announced a legal settlement with banks that required the latter to pay $26 billion to homeowners who had received foreclosure notices without proper documentation. In the rush to foreclose on homes, banks had systematically violated the legal requirements, including by employing the practice of "robo-signing," in which documents were forged or never reviewed. However, given the size of the foreclosure crisis, this settlement was unlikely to make a major impact. As the millions of families that have lost their homes struggle to get back on their feet and neighborhoods across the country grapple with vacant homes, the effects of the housing bubble will be felt for many years to come.

● Who Gets What from Social Policy?

> **Explain how contributory and noncontributory programs benefit different groups of Americans**

The two categories of social policy, contributory and noncontributory, generally serve different groups of people. We can understand much about the development of social policy by examining which constituencies benefit from different policies. The "Who Are Americans?" feature shows two of the key areas in which the government provides assistance and presents recent data on the numbers of beneficiaries and the money spent on these programs.

Who Receives Benefits from Social Programs?

Almost all Americans benefit from public welfare programs at some point in their lives. Two important programs in America's safety net are Medicaid, which provides health insurance to the poor, and unemployment insurance, which helps Americans who lose their jobs. Children make up a disproportionate number of the Medicaid enrollees.

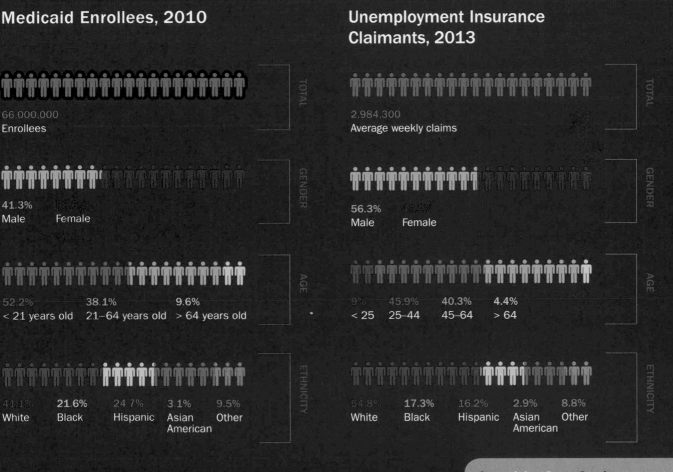

Medicaid Enrollees, 2010

TOTAL

66,000,000
Enrollees

GENDER

41.3%
Male

58.6%
Female

AGE

52.2%
< 21 years old

38.1%
21–64 years old

9.6%
> 64 years old

ETHNICITY

41.1%
White

21.6%
Black

24.7%
Hispanic

3.1%
Asian American

9.5%
Other

Unemployment Insurance Claimants, 2013

TOTAL

2,984,300
Average weekly claims

GENDER

56.3%
Male

43.5%
Female

AGE

9%
< 25

45.9%
25–44

40.3%
45–64

4.4%
> 64

ETHNICITY

54.8%
White

17.3%
Black

16.2%
Hispanic

2.9%
Asian American

8.8%
Other

for critical analysis

1. What are some of the major differences between the demographics of those on Medicaid and those receiving unemployment compensation?

2. What underlying social patterns about poverty and employment do these data suggest?

SOURCES: Centers for Medicare and Medicaid Services, www.cms.gov/Research-Statistics-Data-and-Systems/Statistics-Trends-and-Reports/ CMS-Statistics-Reference-Booklet/2013.html (accessed 5/9/14); U.S. Department of Labor, www.ows.doleta.gov/unemploy/chariu.asp (accessed 5/9/14).

The strongest and most generous programs are those in which the beneficiaries are widely perceived as deserving of assistance and also are politically powerful. Because Americans prize work, constituencies that have "earned" their benefits in some way or those who cannot work because of a disability are usually seen as most deserving of government assistance. Politically powerful constituencies are those who vote as a group, lobby effectively, and mobilize to protect the programs from which they benefit.

When we study social policies from a group perspective, we can see that the elderly and the middle class receive the most benefits from the government's social policies and that children and the working poor receive the fewest. In addition, America's social policies do little to change the fact that minorities and women are more likely than white men to be poor.

The Elderly

The elderly are the beneficiaries of the two strongest and most generous social policies: old-age pensions (what we call Social Security) and Medicare (medical care for the elderly). As these programs have grown, they have provided most elderly Americans with economic security and have dramatically reduced the poverty rate among the elderly. In 1959, before very many people over the age of 65 received social insurance, the poverty rate for the elderly was 35 percent; by 2012 it had dropped to 9 percent.[59] Because of this progress, many people call Social Security the most effective antipoverty program in the United States.[60] This does not mean that the elderly are rich, however; in 2012 the median income of elderly households was $33,848, well below the national median income.[61] The aim of these programs is to provide security and prevent poverty.

One reason that Social Security and Medicare are politically strong is that the elderly are widely seen as a deserving population. They are not expected to work, because of their age. Moreover, both programs are contributory, and a work history is a requirement for receiving a Social Security pension. But these programs are also strong because they serve a constituency that has become quite powerful. The elderly are a very large group: in 2013 there were 41.5 million Americans over the age of 65. Because Social Security and Medicare are not means tested, they are available to nearly all people over the age of 65, whether they are poor or not. The size of this group is of great political importance because the rates of voter turnout are greater among the elderly than among the rest of the population.

In addition, the elderly have developed strong and sophisticated lobbying organizations that can influence policy making and mobilize elderly Americans to defend these programs against proposals to cut them. One important and influential such organization is AARP. Originally the American Association of Retired Persons, in 1999 the organization changed its name to its initials only because 44 percent of AARP members work full or part time. AARP had more than 39 million members in 2014, amounting to one-fifth of all voters. It also has a sophisticated lobbying organization in Washington, which employs 63 lobbyists and a staff of 165 policy analysts.[62] (See Chapter 11 for more discussion of AARP's lobbying efforts.) Although AARP is the largest and the strongest

AARP has been highly effective in representing the interests of the elderly in social policy. Here, AARP members demonstrate in favor of the right to buy cheaper prescription drugs from Canada under Medicare.

organization of the elderly, other groups, such as the Alliance for Retired Americans, to which many retired union members belong, also lobby Congress on behalf of the elderly. When Congress considers changes in programs that affect the elderly, these lobbying groups pay close attention. They mobilize their supporters and work with legislators to block changes they believe will hurt the elderly.[63]

The Middle and Upper Classes

Americans don't usually think of the middle class or upper class as benefiting from social policies, but government action promotes the social welfare of the middle and upper classes in a variety of ways. First, medical care and pensions for the elderly help the middle class by relieving them of the burden of caring for elderly relatives. Before these programs existed, old people were more likely to live with and depend financially on their adult children. Many middle-class families whose parents and grandparents are in nursing homes rely on Medicaid to pay nursing home bills.

In addition, the middle and upper classes benefit from what some analysts call the shadow welfare state.[64] These are the social benefits that private employers offer to their workers: medical insurance and pensions, for example. The federal government subsidizes such benefits by not taxing the payments that employers and employees make for health insurance and pensions. These **tax expenditures**, as they are called, are an important way the federal government helps ensure the social welfare of the middle and upper classes. (Such programs are called "tax expenditures" because the federal government helps finance them through the tax system rather than by direct spending.) Another key tax expenditure that helps the well-off is the tax exemption on mortgage interest payments: taxpayers can deduct the amount they have paid in interest on a mortgage from the income they report on their tax return. By allowing these payments to be counted as deductions, the government makes home ownership less expensive.

People often don't think of these tax expenditures as part of social policy because they are not as visible as the programs that provide direct payments or services to beneficiaries. But tax expenditures represent a significant federal investment: they cost the national treasury some $1.26 trillion a year and make it easier and less expensive for working Americans to obtain health care, save for retirement, and buy homes.[65] These programs are very popular with the middle and upper classes, and Congress rarely considers reducing them. On the few occasions when public officials have tried to limit these programs—with proposals to limit the amount of mortgage interest that can be deducted, for example—they have quickly retreated. These programs are simply too popular among Americans, whose power comes from their numbers at the polling booth.

tax expenditures government subsidies provided to employers and employees through tax deductions for amounts spent on health insurance and other benefits

The Working Poor

People who are working but are poor or just above the poverty line receive only limited assistance from government social programs. This is somewhat surprising, given that Americans value work so highly. But the working poor are typically employed in jobs that do not provide pensions or health care; often they are renters because they cannot afford to buy homes. This means they cannot benefit from the shadow welfare state that subsidizes the social benefits enjoyed by most middle-class Americans. At the same time, however, they cannot get assistance through programs such as Medicaid and TANF, which are largely restricted to the nonworking poor.

Three government programs do assist the working poor: the Affordable Care Act (described earlier), the Earned Income Tax Credit (EITC), and the Supplemental Nutrition Assistance Program (or SNAP, formerly known as food stamps). The EITC was implemented in 1976 to provide poor workers some relief from increases in the taxes that pay for Social Security. As it has expanded, the EITC has provided a modest wage supplement for the working poor, allowing them to catch up on utility bills or pay for children's clothing.

Poor workers can also receive benefits from SNAP. To be eligible, households must earn below 130 percent of the poverty line (about $25,400 a year for a three-person family in 2014). The average monthly benefit for a family of three is $395 a month.[66] Food advocates, such as Feeding America, have encouraged people to take "the SNAP Challenge," in which people who do not need food stamps spend $1.50 a meal (the average for SNAP recipients) for a week. In the words of one high-profile participant, "I was hungry last week—laser-focused on how much food was left in the fridge and how many dollars were left in my wallet. I was scared about eating portions that were too big, and wasn't sure what to do if my food ran out."[67] Because the wages of less-educated workers have declined significantly over the past 15 years and minimum wages have not kept pace with inflation, the problems of the working poor remain acute.

Even though the working poor may be seen as deserving, they are not politically powerful because they are not organized. There is no equivalent to AARP for the poor. Nonetheless, because work is highly valued in American society, politicians find it difficult to cut the few social programs that help the working poor. In 1995 efforts to cut the EITC were defeated by coalitions of Democrats and moderate Republicans, although Congress did place new restrictions on food stamps and also reduced the level of spending on this type of aid.

The Nonworking Poor

The only nonworking, able-bodied poor people who receive federal cash assistance are parents who are caring for children. The primary source of cash assistance for these families was AFDC and now is the state-run TANF program, but they also rely on SNAP and Medicaid. Able-bodied adults who are not caring for children are not eligible for federal assistance other than food stamps. Many states provide small amounts of cash assistance to such individuals through programs called "general assistance," but in the past decade, many states have abolished or greatly reduced their general assistance programs in an effort to encourage these adults to work. Americans don't like to subsidize adults who are not working, but they do not want to harm children.

AFDC was the most unpopular social spending program ever undertaken by the federal government; as a result, spending on it declined after 1980. Under TANF, states receive a fixed amount of federal funds, whether the welfare rolls rise or fall. Because the number of people on welfare has declined so dramatically since 1994 (by more than 50 percent), states have had generous levels of federal resources for the remaining welfare recipients. Many states, however, have used the windfall of federal dollars to cut taxes and indirectly support programs that benefit the middle class, not the poor.[68] Welfare recipients have little political power to resist cuts to their benefits. During the late 1960s and early 1970s, the short-lived National Welfare Rights Organization sought to represent the interests of welfare recipients. But keeping the organization in operation proved difficult because its members and its

for critical analysis

Two factors that seem to influence a particular group's ability to get what it wants from social policy are (1) the perception that the group is deserving, and (2) the political organization and power of the group. How have these factors affected social policy in recent years?

constituents had few resources and were difficult to organize.[69] Because welfare recipients are widely viewed as undeserving, and because they are not politically organized, they have played little part in recent debates about welfare.

The impact of the recession has meant that record numbers of Americans are receiving food assistance through SNAP. With unemployment well above 8 percent since early 2009 and the numbers of long-term unemployment very high, nutrition assistance has been the most responsive program. In 2014 more than 46.9 million people (15 percent of the population) received SNAP benefits.[70]

Minorities, Women, and Children

Minorities, women, and children are disproportionately poor. Much of this poverty is the result of disadvantages that stem from the position of these groups in the labor market. In 2012 the poverty rate for African Americans was 27.2 percent, and for Latinos it was 25.6 percent. Both rates are more than double the poverty rate for non-Hispanic whites, which was 9.7 percent.[71] The median income for black households in 2012 was $33,321. For Hispanics it was $39,005, whereas for non-Hispanic white households the median household income was $57,009.[72] Much of this economic inequality occurs because minority workers tend to have low-wage jobs. Minorities are also more likely to become unemployed and to remain unemployed for longer periods of time than are white Americans. African Americans, for example, typically have experienced twice as much unemployment as have other Americans. The combination of low-wage jobs and unemployment often means that minorities are less likely to have jobs that give them access to the shadow welfare state. They are more likely to fall into the precarious categories of the working poor or the nonworking poor.

In the past several decades, policy analysts have begun to talk about the "feminization of poverty," or the fact that women are more likely than men to be poor.

The poor and working poor (including many single mothers with children) have little influence on government. Although organized protests representing their interests occasionally do occur, they fail to have the impact of similar protests by other groups, such as senior citizens.

This problem is particularly acute for single mothers, who are more than twice as likely to fall below the poverty line as the average American (see Figure 17.5). When the Social Security Act was passed in 1935, the main programs for poor women were Aid to Dependent Children (ADC) and survivors' insurance for widows. The framers of the act believed that ADC would gradually disappear as more women became eligible for survivors' insurance. The social model behind the Social Security Act was that of a male breadwinner with a wife and children. Women were not expected to work, and if a woman's husband died, ADC or survivors' insurance would help her stay at home and raise her children. The framers of Social Security did not envision today's large number of single women heading families. At the same time, they did not envision that so many women with children would also be working. This combination of changes helped make

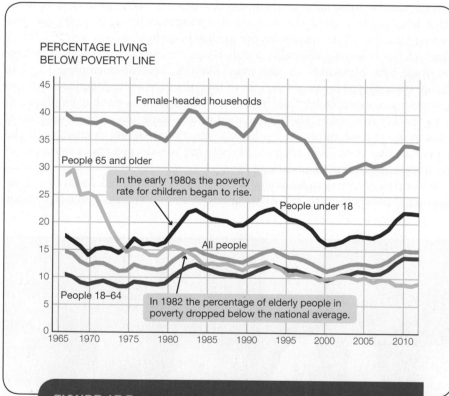

PERCENTAGE LIVING
BELOW POVERTY LINE

Female-headed households

People 65 and older

In the early 1980s the poverty rate for children began to rise.

People under 18

All people

People 18–64

In 1982 the percentage of elderly people in poverty dropped below the national average.

FIGURE 17.5

Poverty Levels in the United States, 1966–2012

Poverty rates in the U.S. population vary considerably. The rate of poverty among female-headed households declined significantly in the 1990s and has been increasing again since 2000. Which group has seen the greatest reduction in its poverty level since 1966?

SOURCE: U.S. Census Bureau, Historical Poverty Tables, "Table 2, Poverty Status, by Family Relationship, Race, and Hispanic Origin" and "Table 3, Poverty Status, by Age, Race and Hispanic Origin," www.census.gov/hhes/www/poverty/datalhistorical/people.html (accessed 4/29/14).

AFDC (the successor program to ADC) more controversial. Many people asked why welfare recipients shouldn't work, if the majority of women who were not on welfare worked. Such questions led to the welfare reform of 1996, which created TANF.

The need to combine work and child care was understood as a challenging problem for most single parents. This problem is more acute for single mothers than for single fathers, because on average, women still earn less than men and because working creates new expenses such as child care and transportation costs. Many women working in low-wage jobs do not receive health insurance as a benefit of their jobs; they must pay the cost of such insurance themselves. As a result, many poor women found that once they were working, the expenses of child care, transportation, insurance, and other needs left them with less cash per month than they would have received if they had not worked and had instead collected AFDC and Medicaid benefits. These women concluded that it was not "worth it" for them to leave AFDC and go to work. Some states are now experimenting with programs to encourage women to work by allowing them to keep some of their welfare benefits even when they are working. Although Americans want individuals to be self-sufficient, research suggests that single mothers with low-wage jobs are likely to need continuing assistance to make ends meet.[73]

One of the most troubling issues related to American social policy is the number of American children who live in poverty. The rate of child poverty in 2012 was 21.8 percent—6.8 percent higher than that of the population as a whole. These high rates of poverty stem in part from the design of American social policies. Because these policies do not generously assist able-bodied adults who aren't working, and because these policies offer little help to the working poor, the children of these adults are likely to be poor as well.

As child poverty has grown, several lobbying groups have emerged to represent children's interests; the best known of these is the Children's Defense Fund. But even with a sophisticated lobbying operation, and although their numbers are large, poor children do not vote and therefore cannot wield much political power.[74]

for critical analysis

Critics of American social policy argue that social policy does more harm than good. What negative consequences of social policy do they point to? Do you agree with their arguments?

Social Policy
and Your Future

The development of social policy in the United States reflects shifts in our views about how government can best help accomplish fundamental national goals. Until the 1930s the federal government did very little in the domain of social policy. The country's major social policy was free public education, which was established by the states and administered locally. Americans placed especially strong emphasis on education because an educated citizenry was seen as an essential component of a strong democracy.[75] Given the strength of these beliefs, it is not surprising that free public education was available in the United States well before European nations established public education systems.

Other public social policies, established from the 1930s on, have stirred up much more controversy. Liberals often argue that more generous social policies are needed if America is truly to ensure equality of opportunity. Some liberals have argued that the government needs to go beyond simply providing opportunity and should ensure more equal conditions, especially where children are concerned. Conservative critics, on the other hand, often argue that social policies that offer income support take the ideal of equality too far and, in the process, do for individuals what those individuals should be doing for themselves. From this perspective, social policies make the government too big, and big government is seen as a fundamental threat to Americans' liberties.

Where do average Americans fit in these debates? Americans are often said to be philosophical conservatives and operational liberals.[76] When asked about government social policy in the abstract, they say they disapprove of activist government—a decidedly conservative view. But when they must evaluate particular programs, Americans generally express support—a more liberal perspective. Some programs, of course, are preferred over others. Policies in which the recipients are regarded as deserving, such as programs for the elderly, receive more support than those that assist working-age people. Programs that have a reputation for effectiveness and those that require people to help themselves through work are also viewed favorably.[77] In sum, most Americans take a pragmatic approach to social welfare policies: they favor programs that work and they want to reform those that seem not to work.

Yet reform is often difficult to achieve. The most pressing social policy issue in the coming decades—the rising cost of health care—has been notoriously difficult to address. The United States spends more on health care than any other advanced nation but many Americans remain without access to care, even after the expansions in the Affordable Care Act (see Figure 17.4). The share of our economy devoted to health care rose from 7.2 percent in 1970 to 17.9 percent in 2010, and it appears to be growing again after a brief slowdown.[78] The causes of increasing health care costs are many, including new technology, administrative complexity, greater coverage for more people, and an aging population. Can we reap the advantages of our highly advanced health care system and reduce costs at the same time? While most Americans might prefer this outcome, it is very difficult to reach agreement on the reforms needed to attain this goal. The complex system that delivers health care in the United States includes powerful interests that resist changes to current arrangements. Yet the projected increase in the proportion of older Americans in coming decades makes the need to control health care costs especially urgent. What strategies might be used to initiate a national discussion of health care? What are the consequences of inaction for today's young adults? Although discussions of health care costs are often complex and technical, it is vital that more Americans engage in this debate if we are to re-create a health care system that is both affordable and effective.

plugin

Inform

Explore the poverty information on the U.S. Census Bureau's website (www .census.gov/hhes/www/poverty). Notice how poverty has changed over time.

Express

Identify some social policies that you support and some that you disagree with. Explain your view of the government's role in each of the areas you identified.

Connect

Follow the Center for Law and Social Policy, a public interest group that works "to improve the lives of low-income people," on Twitter or Facebook. Do you agree or disagree with its perspective on government policies to address poverty? Consider posting a comment.

Act

Share information about higher education policies that affect you and your fellow students. For example, the Student Aid Alliance website provides information about the federal government's role in student aid and offers several ways to take action if you are concerned.

studyguide

The Welfare State

Trace the history of government programs designed to help the poor (pp. 687–98)

Prior to the Great Depression, assistance to the poor was provided mainly by local governments and private charities. The Social Security Act of 1935 gave the federal government a much larger role and created two separate categories of welfare: contributory and noncontributory. Spending on social policy, particularly entitlement programs, has grown dramatically ever since the 1930s, and the costs have been paid primarily through payroll taxes.

Key Terms

contributory programs (p. 689)

Social Security (p. 689)

indexing (p. 689)

cost-of-living adjustments (COLAs) (p. 689)

Medicare (p. 690)

noncontributory programs (p. 690)

means testing (p. 690)

Medicaid (p. 690)

Supplemental Nutritional Assistance Program (SNAP) (p. 691)

in-kind benefits (p. 691)

entitlement (p. 691)

Practice Quiz

1. Prior to 1935, the private welfare system in the United States made a distinction between
   a) contributory and noncontributory programs.
   b) citizens and recent immigrants.
   c) the deserving poor and the undeserving poor.
   d) mandatory and discretionary spending.
   e) religious and secular assistance.

2. America's welfare state was constructed initially in response to
   a) the Civil War.
   b) World War II.
   c) political reforms of the Progressive era.
   d) the Great Depression.
   e) the growth of the military-industrial complex.

3. Which of the following is an example of a contributory program?
   a) Medicaid
   b) Medicare
   c) Temporary Assistance for Needy Families
   d) Supplemental Nutrition Assistance Program
   e) Aid to Families with Dependent Children

4. Means testing requires that applicants for welfare benefits show
   a) that they are capable of getting to and from their workplace.
   b) that they have the ability to store and prepare food.
   c) some definite need for assistance plus an inability to provide for it.
   d) that they have the time and resources to take full advantage of federal educational opportunities.
   e) that they are natural-born citizens who have never been convicted of a felony.

5. In 1996, as part of welfare reform, Aid to Families with Dependent Children was abolished and replaced by
   a) the Earned Income Tax Credit.
   b) Aid to Dependent Children.
   c) the Affordable Care Act.
   d) Supplemental Security Income.
   e) Temporary Assistance for Needy Families.

6. Which of the following are examples of in-kind benefits?
   a) Medicaid and SNAP
   b) Social Security payments and cost-of-living adjustments
   c) Medicare and unemployment compensation
   d) the GI Bill of Rights and the Equal Rights Amendment
   e) the Earned Income Tax Credit and No Child Left Behind

7. Government benefits to individuals that *cannot* be taken away without due process of the law are called
   a) cost-of-living adjustments.
   b) noncontributory programs.
   c) entitlement programs.
   d) indexing programs.
   e) tax expenditure programs.

Opening Opportunity

The federal government enacts three types of policies in order to keep people from falling into poverty and to help those who are already poor: education policies, health policies, and housing policies. Although the federal government played only a minor role in education throughout most of American history, it has become more active since the 1950s. Until the passage of the Patient Protection and Affordable Care Act in 2010, the United States was the only advanced industrial nation without universal access to health care. The federal government has concentrated most of its efforts on housing policy to promote home ownership rather than to provide housing for low-income Americans who cannot afford to buy homes.

Key Term

equality of opportunity (p. 698)

Practice Quiz

8. What event prompted the federal government to enter the field of elementary education?
   a) the Civil War
   b) the Great Depression
   c) World War II
   d) the Soviet Union's launching of Sputnik
   e) the Civil Rights movement

9. Which of the following was *not* part of the No Child Left Behind Act of 2001?
   a) a provision allowing parents whose child is attending a failing school to transfer the child to a better school
   b) a requirement that all students be proficient in reading and math by 2014
   c) a requirement that schools show positive results for all subcategories of students and not just positive overall averages
   d) a requirement that a national test be used to evaluate every student around the country
   e) a requirement that every child in grades 3 through 8 be tested yearly for proficiency in math and reading

10. A charter school is
    a) a publicly funded school that is free from the rules and regulations of local school districts.
    b) a privately funded school that is subject to the rules and regulations of local school districts.
    c) a privately funded school that is free from the rules and regulations of local school districts.
    d) a school that meets the requirements spelled out in the No Child Left Behind Act of 2001.
    e) a school created by the GI Bill of Rights of 1944.

11. Most nonelderly adults receive health insurance through
    a) Social Security.
    b) Medicare.
    c) Medicaid.
    d) their employers.
    e) local charitable organizations.

Who Gets What from Social Policy?

The federal government's social policies tend to provide the largest benefits to those groups that are politically organized and to those groups that the public perceives to be deserving of assistance. As a result, children and the poor receive the fewest benefits from the federal government and the middle class and the elderly receive the most. Government policies do little to change the fact that minorities and women are more likely than white men to be poor.

Key Term

tax expenditures (p. 713)

Practice Quiz

12. In terms of receiving benefits of social policies, what distinguishes the elderly from the working poor?
    a) The elderly are perceived as deserving, whereas the working poor are not.
    b) The elderly receive fewer benefits from the government's social policies.
    c) The elderly are more organized and more politically powerful than are the working poor.
    d) The elderly are less organized and less politically powerful than are the working poor.
    e) There is no significant difference between these two groups.

13. Who are the chief beneficiaries of the "shadow welfare state"?
    a) children
    b) the elderly
    c) the nonworking poor
    d) the working poor
    e) the middle class

14. Which two government programs provide direct assistance to the working poor?
    a) Medicaid and the Earned Income Tax Credit
    b) Temporary Assistance for Needy Families and SNAP
    c) Temporary Assistance for Needy Families and the Earned Income Tax Credit
    d) SNAP and the Earned Income Tax Credit
    e) Social Security and Medicare

15. Which of the following statements about the poverty in the United States is most accurate?
    a) African Americans have a lower poverty rate than whites.
    b) Hispanics have a lower poverty rate than whites.
    c) Hispanics have a higher poverty rate than whites.
    d) The rate of child poverty is less than the rate of adult poverty.
    e) Women are less likely than men to fall below the poverty line.

For Further Reading

Campbell, Andrea Louise. *How Policies Make Citizens: Senior Political Activism and the American Welfare State.* Princeton, NJ: Princeton University Press, 2005.

Cohen, David K., and Susan L. Moffitt, *The Ordeal of Equality: Did Federal Regulation Fix the Schools?* Cambridge, MA: Harvard University Press, 2009.

Hacker, Jacob S. *The Great Risk Shift: Why American Jobs, Families, Health Care, and Retirement Aren't Secure—and How We Can Fight Back.* New York: Oxford University Press, 2006.

Howard, Christopher. *The Welfare State Nobody Knows: Debunking Myths about U.S. Social Policy.* Princeton, NJ: Princeton University Press, 2007.

Katz, Michael. *In the Shadow of the Poorhouse: A Social History of Welfare in America.* New York: Basic Books, 1986.

Katznelson, Ira, and Margaret Weir. *Schooling for All: Race, Class, and the Democratic Ideal.* New York: Basic Books, 1985.

Light, Paul. *Artful Work: The Politics of Social Security Reform.* New York: Random House, 1985.

Marmor, Theodore R, Jerry L. Mashaw, and John Pakutka. *Social Insurance; America's Neglected Heritage and Contested Future.* Washington, DC: CQ Press, 2013.

Mettler, Suzanne. *Degrees of Inequality: How the Politics of Higher Education Sabotaged the American Dream.* New York: Basic Books, 2014.

Mettler, Suzanne. *The Submerged State: How Invisible Government Policies Undermine American Democracy.* Chicago: University of Chicago Press, 2011.

Murray, Charles. *Losing Ground: American Social Policy, 1950–1980.* New York: Basic Books, 1984.

Patterson, James T. *America's Struggle against Poverty in the Twentieth Century.* Cambridge, MA: Harvard University Press, 2000.

Skocpol, Theda. *The Missing Middle: Working Families and the Future of American Social Policy.* New York: W. W. Norton, 2000.

Soss, Joe, Richard C. Fording, and Sanford F. Schramm, *Disciplining the Poor: Neoliberal Paternalism and the Persistent Power of Race.* Chicago: University of Chicago Press, 2011.

Weir, Margaret, Ann Orloff, and Theda Skocpol, eds. *The Politics of Social Policy in the United States.* Princeton, NJ: Princeton University Press, 1988.

Recommended Websites

Center for Retirement Research
http://crr.bc.edu/index.php
Americans pay for their retirement with a mix of Social Security, employer-sponsored savings plans, and private savings. This website provides analyses of the challenges that face all aspects of the current arrangements and includes a downloadable "Social Security Fix-It Book."

Center on Budget and Policy Priorities
www.cbpp.org
The Center on Budget and Policy Priorities is a nonpartisan, liberal-leaning nonprofit organization that provides timely data and analysis of social programs that serve low-income Americans. It also studies economic and social changes that affect the well-being of low-income

people. Areas of research include the Earned Income Tax Credit, Food Assistance, Social Security, and climate change. The center focuses on state and local policies as well as national programs.

Libertarian Party
www.lp.org
Contrary to many other Americans, libertarians believe that social programs pose a threat to personal freedom and should be eliminated. Go to the Libertarian Party's website to read the organization's opinions and positions on most current social policies.

Medicare
www.medicare.gov
Health care is one of the largest and most controversial social programs in the United States. At the Medicare website, find out what services the Department of Health and Human Services provides.

Modern American Poetry: The Great Depression
www.english.uiuc.edu/maps/depression/depression.htm
The Great Depression changed American opinion about the causes of and responsibility for poverty. This website, by Carey Norton at the University of Illinois at Urbana-Champaign, provides information, statistics, and photos of this historical period as well as analysis of poems by depression-era writers.

Poverty.com
www.poverty.com
Poverty is a problem that exists in the United States and around the world. Read about how poverty, hunger, and related problems affect people in other areas of the globe.

Public Agenda
www.publicagenda.com
Public Agenda is a nonpartisan organization that tries to bridge the gap between American leaders and public opinion on current social, domestic, and foreign policy issues.

U.S. Department of Education
www.ed.gov
The U.S. Department of Education is dedicated to providing equal access to education and improving academic programs throughout America. At the department's website, you can learn about the No Child Left Behind Act and other policies.

The United States spends hundreds of billions of dollars—far more than any other country—on its military and weapons. However, Americans often disagree on when and how their government should act in international affairs, especially when it comes to deploying the U.S. military.

Foreign Policy and Democracy

18

WHAT GOVERNMENT DOES AND WHY IT MATTERS Ever since George Washington, in his Farewell Address, warned the American people "to have . . . as little political connection as possible" with foreign nations and to "steer clear of permanent alliances," Americans have been distrustful of foreign policy. But despite their distrust, the United States has been forced to pursue its national interests in the world through a variety of means, including diplomacy, economic policy, and precisely the sorts of entangling alliances with other nations and involvements with international organizations that would have troubled Washington.

To some college students, foreign policy may seem like a distant or abstract matter, but not too long ago tens of thousands of students were drafted and sent to serve in Korea and Vietnam. Even today, in the era of the all-volunteer military, thousands of recent college graduates (and numerous current college students) have served in America's military forces in Iraq and Afghanistan, and many others know someone who has been wounded or killed on distant battlefields.

War is only one aspect of American foreign policy, but America has fought a large number of wars. Though Americans like to regard themselves as a peaceful people, since our own Civil War, American forces have been deployed abroad on hundreds of occasions for both major conflicts and minor skirmishes. Writing in 1989 historian Geoffrey Perret commented that no other nation "has had as much experience of war as the United States."[1] America has not become less warlike in the years since Perret published his observation. Between 1989 and the present, American forces have fought two wars in the Persian Gulf and a war in Afghanistan, while engaging in lesser military actions

725

in Panama, Kosovo, Somalia, and elsewhere. Every year, America's military arsenal and defense budget dwarf those of other nations. America currently spends approximately $640 billion per year on its military and weapons programs—a figure that represents over one-third of the world's total military expenditure and over three times the amount spent by the People's Republic of China, the nation that currently ranks second to the United States in overall military outlays.[2] The debt we incur for these programs is likely to be paid by today's college students for their entire working lives.

Foreign policy, especially military policy, is often a major political issue in the United States. An old American adage asserts that "politics stops at the water's edge." The point of this saying is that unless we put our domestic political disunity aside and work together to protect our nation's political, economic, and security interests in the wider world, all Americans will suffer. In today's world, however, the water's edge does not neatly demarcate the difference in interests between "us" and "them." As the global economic crisis that began in 2008 revealed, "our" economic interests and "their" economic interests are intertwined. Environmental concerns are global, not national. And even in the realm of security interests, some risks and threats are shared and require international rather than national responses. Our national government, created to further our national interests, must find ways of acting internationally and striking the right balance between competition and cooperation in the international arena.

chaptergoals

- Explain how foreign policy is designed to promote security, prosperity, and humanitarian goals (pp. 727–37)

- Identify the major players in foreign-policy making, and describe their roles (pp. 738–45)

- Describe the means the United States uses to carry out foreign policy (pp. 745–54)

● The Goals of Foreign Policy

Explain how foreign policy is designed to promote security, prosperity, and humanitarian goals

The term *foreign policy* refers to the programs and policies that determine America's relations with other nations and foreign entities. Foreign policy includes diplomacy, military and security policy, international human rights policies, and various forms of economic policy, such as trade policy and international energy policy. Of course, foreign policy and domestic policy are not completely separate categories but are instead closely intertwined: America's decisions in its foreign policy impact domestic policies and outcomes. Take security policy, for example. Defending the nation requires the design and manufacture of tens of billions of dollars' worth of military hardware. The manufacture and procurement of this military equipment might provide jobs in American communities where the equipment is built, while paying for it involves raising taxes or choosing not to fund other types of programs.

Many of the basic contours of the foreign policy arena are similar to those of America's other policy domains. The nation's chief foreign-policy makers are the president, Congress, and the bureaucracy. Just as in economic and social policy, battles over foreign policy often erupt among and within these institutions as competing politicians and a variety of organized groups and rival political forces pursue their own versions of the national interest or their own narrower purposes that they seek to present as the national interest. In the foreign policy arena, the institutional powers of the presidency give presidents and their allies an advantage over political forces based in Congress, although Congress is not without resources of its own through which to influence the conduct of foreign policy. Moreover, like domestic policy matters, foreign policy issues often figure prominently in public debate and in national election campaigns as competing forces seek to mobilize popular support for their positions, or at least to castigate the opposition for the putative shortcomings of its policies.

In this section we will examine the goals of American foreign policy. Although U.S. foreign policy has a number of purposes, three main goals stand out. These are security, prosperity, and the creation of a better world. These goals overlap with one another, and each can never be pursued fully in isolation. Then, in the following sections, we will discuss the actors and institutions that shape foreign policy. Next, we will analyze the instruments that policy makers have at their disposal to implement foreign policy.

Security

To many Americans, the chief goal of the nation's foreign policy is protection of America's security in an often hostile world. Traditionally, the United States has been concerned about threats that might emanate from other countries, such as Nazi Germany during the 1940s and then Soviet Russia until the Soviet Union's collapse in the late 1980s. Today, American security policy is concerned not only with the actions of other nations but also with the activities of terrorist groups and other hostile **non-state actors**.[3] To protect the nation's security from foreign threats, the United States has built an enormous military apparatus and a complex array of

non-state actors groups other than nation-states that attempt to play a role in the international system. Terrorist groups are one type of non-state actor

intelligence-gathering institutions, such as the Central Intelligence Agency (CIA), charged with evaluating and anticipating challenges from abroad.[4]

Security is, of course, a broad term. Policy makers must be concerned with Americans' physical security. The September 11 terrorist attacks killed and injured thousands of Americans, and the government constantly fears that new attacks could be even more catastrophic. Policy makers must also be concerned with such matters as the security of America's food supplies, transportation infrastructure, and energy supplies. Many of our efforts in the Middle East, for example, are aimed at ensuring continuing American access to vital oil fields. In recent years, cyberspace has become a new security concern. The nation's dependence on computers means that the government must be alert to efforts by hostile governments, groups, or even individual "hackers" to damage computer networks or access sensitive or proprietary information. In 2014 the U.S. Department of Justice charged five Chinese military officers with cyber espionage by hacking into computer networks of U.S. companies in the nuclear and solar energy industries.

During the eighteenth and nineteenth centuries, American security was based mainly on the geographic isolation of the United States. Separated by two oceans from European and Asian powers, many Americans thought that the country's security would be best preserved by our remaining aloof from international power struggles. This policy was known as **isolationism**. In his 1796 Farewell Address, President George Washington warned Americans to avoid permanent alliances with foreign powers, and in 1823, President James Monroe warned foreign powers not to meddle in the Western Hemisphere. Washington's warning and what came to be called the Monroe Doctrine were the cornerstones of the U.S. foreign policy of isolationism until the end of the nineteenth century. The United States saw itself as the dominant power in the Western Hemisphere and, indeed, believed that its "manifest destiny" was to expand from sea to sea. The rest of the world, however, should remain at arm's length.

In the twentieth century, technology made oceans less of a barrier to foreign threats, and the world's growing economic interdependence meant that the United States could no longer ignore events abroad. At the beginning of the twentieth century, despite its isolationist sentiments, the United States entered World War I on the side of Great Britain and France when the Wilson administration concluded that America's economic and security interests would be adversely affected by a German victory. In 1941, America was drawn into World War II when Japan attacked the U.S. Pacific fleet anchored at Pearl Harbor, Hawaii. Even before the Japanese attack forced America to fight, the Roosevelt administration had already concluded that the United States must act to prevent a victory by the German-Japanese-Italian Axis alliance. Until the Japanese attack, however, President Roosevelt had not been able to overcome proponents of American isolationism, who declared that our security was best served by leaving foreigners to their own devices. With their attack, the Japanese proved that the Pacific Ocean could not protect the United States from foreign foes and effectively discredited isolationism as a security policy.

In the aftermath of World War II, the United States developed a new security policy known as **containment** to check or "contain" the growing power of the Soviet Union. By the end of the 1940s, the Soviets had built a huge empire and enormous military forces. Most threatening of all, it had built nuclear weapons and intercontinental bombers capable of attacking the United States. The United States was committed to maintaining its own military might as a means of

isolationism avoidance of involvement in the affairs of other nations

containment a policy designed to curtail the political and military expansion of a hostile power

deterrence, to discourage the Soviets from attacking the United States or its allies. Some Americans wanted a more aggressive policy, arguing that we should attack the Soviets before it was too late. Others said that we should show our peaceful intentions and attempt to placate the Soviets. This policy is called **appeasement**.

The policies that the United States actually adopted, deterrence and containment, could be seen as midway between preventive war and appeasement. A nation pursuing a policy of deterrence, on the one hand, signals its peaceful intentions, but on the other hand indicates its willingness and ability to fight if attacked. Thus, during the era of confrontation with the Soviet Union, known as the **Cold War**, the United States frequently asserted that it had no intention of attacking the Soviet Union. At the same time, however, the United States built a huge military force, including a vast arsenal of over 1,500 nuclear warheads, and frequently asserted that, in the event of a Soviet attack, it had the ability and will to respond with overwhelming force. The Soviet Union announced that its nuclear weapons were also intended for deterrent purposes. Eventually the two sides possessed such enormous arsenals of nuclear missiles that each potentially had the ability to destroy the other in the event of war. This heavily armed standoff came to be called a posture of mutually assured destruction. Eventually, this situation led to a period of "détente," in which a number of arms control agreements were signed and the threat of war was reduced.

A policy of deterrence requires not only the possession of large military forces but also that the nation pursuing such a policy convince potential adversaries that it is willing to fight. France had a large army in the 1930s, but Nazi Germany was not deterred from pursuing its expansionist goals in Europe because the German chancellor, Adolf Hitler, did not believe that the French were actually willing to fight. Thus, as part of its policy of deterrence, the United States engaged in wars in Korea, Vietnam, and elsewhere in response to what it believed to be Soviet aggression. Though the United States had no particular interests in Korea or Vietnam, American policy makers believed that if the United States did not fight in these areas, the Soviets would be emboldened to pursue an expansionist policy elsewhere, thinking that the Americans would not respond. Interventions in Korea and Vietnam were also justified by the so-called Truman Doctrine, which called for American assistance to any nation threatened by the Soviet Union and its allies.

The dissolution of the Soviet Union began in 1985, and the final collapse occurred in 1991, partly because the USSR's huge military expenditures undermined its creaky and inefficient centrally planned economy. The new Russia, though still a formidable and sometimes unfriendly power, seemed to pose less of a threat to the United States. Americans celebrated the end of the Cold War and believed that the enormous expense of America's own military forces might be reduced. Within a few years of the Soviet collapse, however, a new set of security threats emerged, requiring new policy responses. The September 11 terrorist attacks demonstrated a threat against which some security scholars had long warned: that non-state actors and so-called rogue states might acquire

During the Cold War, the United States and the Soviet Union engaged in an arms race, each acquiring nuclear weapons to deter the other from attacking.

appeasement the effort to forestall war by giving in to the demands of a hostile power

Cold War the period of struggle between the United States and the former Soviet Union lasting from the late 1940s to about 1990

The U.S. invasion of Iraq was an example of preventive war. The Bush administration argued that it had to strike Iraq first, before Iraq used weapons of mass destruction to attack American interests.

nation-states political entities consisting of a people with some common cultural experience (nation) who also share a common political authority (state), recognized by other sovereignties (nation-states)

preventive war policy of striking first when a nation fears that a foreign foe is contemplating hostile action

significant military capabilities, including nuclear weapons, and would not be affected by America's deterrent capabilities.

A policy of deterrence assumes certainty and rationality. Certainty means that a potential adversary must know for sure that the United States will reply with force if attacked. Rationality means that, to be deterred, a potential adversary must be capable of rationally assessing the risks and costs of aggression against the United States. These two assumptions, which were valid when we sought to counter the Soviet Union, may not be valid in the context of contemporary security threats. Unlike **nation-states**, which are countries with governments and fixed borders, terrorist groups are non-state actors having no fixed geographic location that can be attacked. Terrorists may believe they can attack and melt away, leaving the United States with no one against whom to retaliate. Hence, the threat of massive retaliation does not deter them. Rogue states are nations with unstable and erratic leaders who seem to pursue policies driven by ideological or religious fervor rather than careful consideration of economic or human costs. The United States considers North Korea and Iran to be rogue states.

To counter these new security threats, the George W. Bush administration shifted from a policy of deterrence to one of **preventive war**—the willingness to strike first in order to prevent an enemy attack. The United States declared that it would not wait to be attacked but would, if necessary, take action to disable terrorist groups and rogue states before they could develop the capacity to harm the United States.[5] The Bush administration's "Global War on Terror" is an expression of this notion of prevention, as was the U.S. invasion of Iraq. The United States also refused to rule out the possibility that it would attack North Korea or Iran if it deemed those nations' nuclear programs to be an imminent threat to American security interests. Accompanying this shift in military doctrines was an enormous increase in overall U.S. military spending (see Figure 18.1).

In June 2014 in a commencement address at the U.S. Military Academy at West Point, President Obama signaled a shift in American military policy. The president declared that U.S. policy had led to what he described as too many "military adventures." In the future, said the president, American policy would be based on collective action and restraint. While a military option would remain available if Americans were directly threatened, the president said that nonmilitary options, including diplomacy and economic sanctions, should always be tried first.

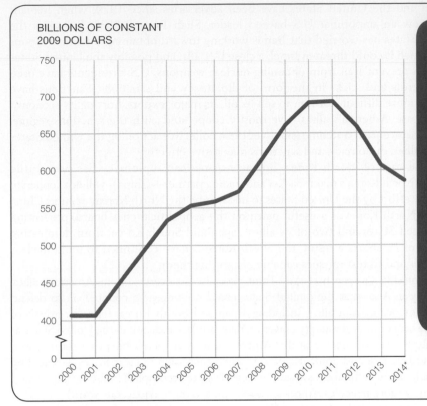

BILLIONS OF CONSTANT
2009 DOLLARS

FIGURE 18.1

U.S. Spending on National Defense since 2000

The United States has long spent large sums of money on national defense. During the 1990s the budget for national defense declined as the country enjoyed a "peace dividend" following the conclusion of the Cold War. After the attacks of September 11 and the commencement of the war on terrorism, however, national defense spending rose steadily; in a decade, spending increased by 70 percent.

*Data for 2014 are estimated.
SOURCE: Office of Management and Budget, Table 6.1, www.whitehouse.gov/omb/budget /historicals (accessed 6/12/14).

This emphasis on diplomacy, sanctions, and collective action seemed to characterize the president's responses to three major foreign policy problems encountered by the administration. These were the Russian quasi-annexation of the Crimean area of Ukraine, the Iranian nuclear program, and the North Korean effort to build missiles capable of carrying nuclear warheads.

The crisis in Crimea worsened in March 2014, when Russian forces effectively seized control of the Crimean Peninsula, an area that had been part of the Ukraine. Many of the peninsula's inhabitants were ethnic Russians and apparently preferred Russian rule. Russian prime minister Putin said Russia's actions were necessary to prevent disorder and bloodshed and to reassert Russia's historic rights to the region. Russian troops next massed along other portions of the Ukrainian border. The Obama administration urged the Russians to withdraw, announced a program of economic sanctions, and sought through diplomacy to encourage America's NATO allies to impose sanctions, as well. The result illustrated the difficulties inherent in collective action and the use of sanctions. Many of America's European allies depend on Russian energy supplies and engage in a good deal of trade with the Russians. As a result, while all agreed in principle that Russia should withdraw from Crimea, none were prepared to follow the American lead and it seemed that nothing would be done to dislodge the Russians from Crimea. Subsequently, Russian forces supported separatist groups in several other parts of the Ukraine. After one of these groups shot down a civilian airliner, European governments tightened their economic sanctions, and Russia at least temporarily reduced its level of threatening behavior toward the Ukraine.

Iran and the United States have been adversaries since 1979, when Iranians overthrew an unpopular U.S.-backed leader, Shah Reza Pahlavi. For years the United States has worried that Iran is working toward obtaining nuclear weapons with which it could threaten Israel, a close U.S. ally, and possibly the United States itself. To prevent Iran from obtaining nuclear weapons, U.S. presidents have used both carrots and sticks in the form of diplomacy and sanctions. Sanctions have made it more difficult for Iran to sell its oil, its major export, hurting its economy. In this case, America's allies have mostly cooperated with the sanctions regime. While the eventual outcome is not yet clear, collective action by the United States and its allies, diplomacy, and sanctions may prove effective.

In the case of North Korea, however, American diplomacy has been futile because North Korea's major backer and trading partner—China—will not cooperate with any effort by the United States to undermine the North Korean regime. China regards North Korea as a useful pawn on the geopolitical chessboard, preventing the United States and two of its allies, Japan and South Korea, from dominating the Sea of Japan. As a result, the North Koreans have continued to build nuclear warheads and to test missiles capable of carrying them.

The president's speech at West Point also raised concerns among America's allies, especially in Asia, that the United States could no longer be counted on to defend them. America's Asian allies, including Japan and South Korea, fear the growth of Chinese economic and military power on their borders and look to the United States as a counterweight to China. Fear that America is no longer a reliable protector may well lead the Japanese and South Koreans to build their own nuclear forces—something that each nation certainly possesses the technology to accomplish in short order. Hence, an irony: a more peaceful America may produce a more dangerous world.

In September 2014, President Obama seemed to shift away from his West Point pronouncements by ordering air strikes against Islamic militants operating in Iraq and Syria. A group calling itself ISIS (Islamic State of Iraq and Syria) was able to overrun large portions of Syria and Iraq and was deemed by the president to pose a threat to American interests. The president seemed to feel that he had shown enough restraint, and it was time to call on the military. Accordingly, in October 2014 the United States launched a series of air attacks designed to blunt the ISIS advance and to provide support for Kurdish forces and others pitted against ISIS troops.

Economic Prosperity

A second major goal of U.S. foreign policy is promoting American prosperity. America's international economic policies are intended to expand employment opportunities in the United States, to maintain access to foreign energy supplies at a reasonable cost, to promote foreign investment in the United States, and to lower the prices Americans pay for goods and services.

Among the most visible and important elements of U.S. international economic policy is trade policy. The promotion and advertising of American goods and services abroad is a long-standing goal of U.S. trade policy, and it is one of the major obligations of the Department of Commerce. Yet modern trade policy involves a complex arrangement of treaties, tariffs, and other mechanisms of policy formation. Trade policy is always complicated because most Americans benefit from a policy of free trade, which tends to reduce the cost of goods and services. One reason that consumer electronics are so inexpensive is that televisions, smartphones, and other gadgets are imported from all over the world, driving down their prices. However, many American industries and their employees are hurt by free trade if it results in factories and jobs moving abroad. Hence trade policy always produces huge political battles between those who stand to benefit and those who stand to lose from particular policies. Trade is an area where the line between domestic and foreign policy is blurred. The most important international organization for promoting trade is the **World Trade Organization (WTO)**, which officially came into being in 1995. The WTO grew out of the **General Agreement on Tariffs and Trade (GATT)**. Since World War II, GATT had brought together a wide range of nations for regular negotiations designed to reduce barriers to trade. Such barriers, many believed, had contributed to the breakdown of the world economy in the 1930s and had helped cause World War II. The WTO has 151 members worldwide, including the United States. Similar policy goals are pursued in regional arrangements, such as the **North American Free Trade Agreement (NAFTA)**, a trade treaty among the United States, Canada, and Mexico.

Working toward freer trade has been an important goal of each presidential administration since World War II. Yet as globalization has advanced, concerns about the consequences of free trade, and about the operation of the WTO in particular, have grown. Critics contend that the WTO does not pay sufficient attention to the concerns of developing nations or to such issues as environmental degradation, human rights, and labor practices, including the use of child labor in many countries. Countries in the developing world accuse the United States and Europe of hypocrisy in preaching free trade but then using patents and subsidies to protect their markets. There have been some successes on these issues, notably new WTO guidelines that allow poor countries to override expensive patents. Such patents make desperately needed drugs unavailable to most of the developing world. It has been more difficult to reach agreement on agricultural subsidies. Both the United States and Europe provide massive subsidies to their own agricultural industries. The prospects for resolving this issue are dim. The developed world has been reluctant to confront the economic dislocations and political costs of reducing the subsidies.

Agriculture and Trade One of the most controversial areas of trade liberalization is agriculture. Since 2001 the WTO trade talks—called the Doha Round because they began in Doha, Qatar, in 2001—have focused particularly on reducing trade barriers in agriculture. Since the formation of the WTO, the United States has pressured the developing world to reduce trade barriers. At the same time, however, the United States and Europe have offered heavy subsidies to their own agricultural industries. Such subsidies keep the prices high of commodities like wheat and corn, helping to ensure that farmers make a profit. Developing countries have long imposed tariffs on agricultural products to limit the entry of these artificially cheap products, which would otherwise destroy their agricultural sector. During the Doha Round, the developing world charged the richer nations with hypocrisy for demanding that poor countries lower tariffs yet refusing to reduce their agricultural subsidies. Of course, both subsidies and tariffs are harmful from the consumer's point of view, who pays higher prices for food products.

Both the United States and Europe have been reluctant to reduce subsidies and tariffs because farmers are important political constituencies. During the mid-1990s the United States

Word Trade Organization (WTO) international organization promoting free trade that grew out of the General Agreement on Tariffs and Trade

General Agreement on Tariffs and Trade (GATT) international trade organization, in existence from 1947 to 1995, that set many of the rules governing international trade

North American Free Trade Agreement (NAFTA) trade treaty among the United States, Canada, and Mexico to lower and eliminate tariffs among the three countries

Critics of the WTO—like these protesters in Indonesia—argue that it is biased toward the interests of the United States and other developed countries, and that its policies hurt developing nations.

began to cut agricultural subsidies, but in the lead-up to the 2002 elections, President Bush signed a very generous farm bill that reinstated many of these subsidies. By 2006, American farm subsidies neared record highs. U.S. trade officials have sought to persuade American farmers that the costs of reduced subsidies will be far outweighed by the benefits gained from opening new markets for their products.

Jobs and Trade Trade was also an issue in the 2008 election. During their third debate, John McCain accused Barack Obama of promoting protectionist policies, while Obama said Republicans had exported American jobs abroad and allowed an enormous trade deficit to develop. The U.S. trade deficit (a negative trade balance, meaning the country imports more than it exports) reached nearly $60 billion (see Figure 18.2), and jobs growth in the United States had been low for several years. Analysts predicted that many of the 2.8 million manufacturing jobs lost in the recession of the early 2000s would never return to the United States. Moreover, outsourcing, the practice of moving jobs to other countries, began to hit the white-collar workforce, as jobs for workers such as call center operators and computer programmers moved to India and other countries with cheaper labor forces. In 2010 the United States accused China of manipulating trade rules to its own advantage, and China, in return, accused the United States of mismanaging its own economy. In 2012, China announced that it would reduce its purchases of U.S. government securities in order to become less vulnerable to fluctuations in the value of the dollar. The United States pointed out that this might result in a reduction of its imports of Chinese goods.

FIGURE 18.2

U.S. International Trade in Goods and Services

The United States has a "trade deficit" with the rest of the world, which means it imports more goods and services from abroad than it exports. Economists argue about whether this is a problem for the U.S. economy. Some assert that a deficit means the United States is a debtor nation, living beyond its means. Others assert that the trade deficit reflects investment in American productive capabilities. Still others argue that imports as well as exports are good for the American economy.

SOURCE: U.S. Census Bureau, Foreign Trade Statistics, www.census.gov/foreign-trade /statistics/historical/exhibit_history.xls (accessed 6/12/14).

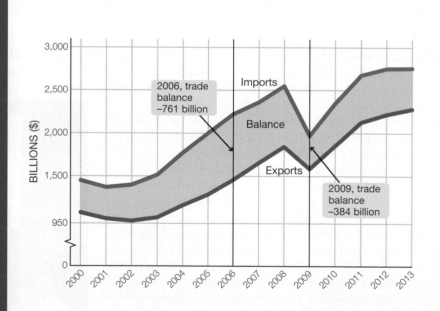

International Humanitarian Policies

A third goal of American policy is to make the world a better place for all its inhabitants. The main forms of policy that address this goal are international environmental policy, international human rights policy, and international peacekeeping. The United States also contributes to international organizations that work for global health and against hunger, such as the World Health Organization. These policies are often seen as secondary to the other goals of American foreign policy, and are forced to give way if they interfere with security or foreign economic policy. Moreover, although the United States spends billions annually on security policy and hundreds of millions on trade policy, it spends relatively little on environmental, human rights, and peacekeeping efforts. Some critics charge that America has the wrong priorities, spending far more to make war than to protect human rights and the global environment. Nevertheless, a number of important American foreign policy efforts are, at least in part, designed to make the world a better place (see Figure 18.3).

In the realm of international environmental policy, the United States supports a number of international efforts to protect the environment. These include the United Nations Framework Convention on Climate Change, an international agreement to study and ameliorate harmful changes in the global environment, and the Montreal Protocol, an agreement signed by more than 150 countries to limit the production of substances potentially harmful to the world's ozone layer. Other nations have severely criticized the United States for withdrawing from the 1997 Kyoto Protocol, an agreement setting limits on emissions of greenhouse gases from industrial countries. The United States has asserted that the Kyoto Protocol would be harmful to American economic interests. Although the United States is concerned with the global environment, national economic interests took precedence in this case. In preparation for the 2012 expiration of the Kyoto agreement, world leaders gathered in Copenhagen, Denmark, in 2009 to begin the process

One of the most basic ways that the United States promotes international humanitarian goals is by providing food, medical supplies, and other necessities to regions experiencing crises. Here, aid workers distribute food aid from the United States to refugees displaced by fighting in South Sudan.

FOREIGN ASSISTANCE BY REGION

North and South America
$2.2 billion

North Africa and Middle East
$4 billion

South and Central Asia
$5.2 billion

Europe and Eurasia
$1.2 billion

Sub-Saharan Africa
$11 billion

East Asia and the Pacific
$1.3 billion

FOREIGN ASSISTANCE BY CATEGORY (BILLIONS $)

- ■ North and South America
- ■ North Africa and Middle East
- ■ Europe and Eurasia
- ■ Sub-Saharan Africa
- ■ South and Central Asia
- ■ East Asia and Pacific
- ■ Global or unspecified*

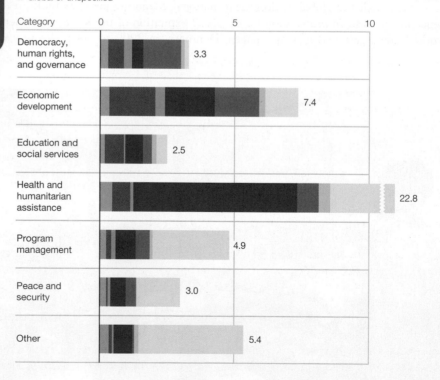

Category	Value
Democracy, human rights, and governance	3.3
Economic development	7.4
Education and social services	2.5
Health and humanitarian assistance	22.8
Program management	4.9
Peace and security	3.0
Other	5.4

of negotiating a new climate treaty. The "Copenhagen Climate Summit," however, failed to produce a binding international agreement and ended with the United States, Europe, and China blaming one another for the lack of concrete results.

The same national priorities seem apparent in the area of human rights policy. The United States has a long-standing commitment to human rights and is a party to most major international human rights agreements. These include the International Covenant on Civil and Political Rights, the UN Convention against Torture, the International Convention on the Elimination of All Forms of Racial Discrimination, and various agreements to protect children. The State Department's Bureau of Democracy, Human Rights, and Labor works cooperatively with international organizations to investigate and focus attention on human rights abuses. In 1998 the United States enacted the International Religious Freedom Act, which calls on all governments to respect religious freedom. The act lists a number of sanctions that the United States and other signatories may employ to punish nations found to be in violation.

Although the United States is committed to promoting human rights, this commitment has a lower priority in American foreign policy than the nation's security concerns and economic interests. Thus, the United States is likely to overlook human rights violations by its major trading partners, such as China, and remain silent in the face of human rights violations by such allies as Saudi Arabia. Nevertheless, human rights concerns do play a role in American foreign policy. For example, beginning in 2007 the United States has annually made available several million dollars in small grants to pay medical and legal expenses incurred by individuals who have been the victims of retaliation in their own countries for working against their governments' repressive practices. In this small way, the United States is backing its often-asserted principles.

Another form of U.S. policy designed to improve the condition of the world is support for international peacekeeping efforts. At any point in time, a number of border wars, civil wars, and guerrilla conflicts flare somewhere in the world, usually in its poorer regions. These wars often generate humanitarian crises in the form of casualties, disease, and refugees. In cooperation with international agencies and other nations, the United States funds a number of efforts to keep the peace in volatile regions and to deal with the health care and refugee problems associated with conflict. In 2013 the United States provided more than $2 billion in funding for United Nations (UN) peacekeeping operations in Haiti, the Democratic Republic of Congo, Mali, Kosovo, Lebanon, and elsewhere.[6]

As the world's wealthiest nation, the United States also recognizes an obligation to render assistance to nations facing crises and emergencies. In 2010, for example, the United States sent medical aid, food relief, and rescue teams to Haiti when that impoverished island nation was struck by a devastating earthquake, and in 2011 the United States provided support to Japan when a tsunami devastated a portion of the Japanese coast and damaged a Japanese nuclear reactor. In 2014 the United States pledged $300 million in humanitarian aid to the people of South Sudan, a population at grave risk of famine due to military conflict between government and rebel forces.

America's humanitarian policies are important. Without American efforts and funding, many international humanitarian programs would be far less successful than they are today. In general, though, security and economic interests take precedence in the eyes of U.S. policy makers over humanitarian concerns.

for critical analysis

Why does the United States pursue international humanitarian policy? Should the United States pay more attention to the human rights records of its trading partners, like China, or allies, like Saudi Arabia?

Who Makes American Foreign Policy?

> **Identify the major players in foreign-policy making, and describe their roles**

As we have seen, domestic policies are made by governmental institutions and influenced by a variety of interest groups, political movements, and even the mass media. The same is true in the realm of foreign policy. The president and his chief advisers are the principal architects of U.S. foreign policy. However, Congress, the bureaucracy, the courts, political parties, interest groups, and trade associations also play important roles in this realm. Often the president and Congress are at odds over foreign policy. When the Democrats took control of Congress in 2006, they vowed to force President Bush to end the war in Iraq. The president vowed, in turn, to resist the Democrats' efforts, and generally prevailed. Ethnic lobbies such as the pro-Israel lobby and the Armenian lobby also seek to affect foreign policy. In 2007 the Armenian lobby persuaded Congress to condemn Turkey's actions in 1915 that led to the deaths of more than a million Armenians. The president, fearing that Turkey, an important U.S. ally, would be offended, blocked the effort. Let us examine the major institutions and forces shaping American foreign policy.

The President

The Constitution assigns the president very clear powers in the realm of foreign and security policy. The president is given the power to make treaties (with the advice and consent of the Senate), appoint ambassadors, and serve as commander in chief of the army and navy of the United States. Presidents have expanded on these powers, claiming that their inherent power to defend the nation serves as the basis for presidential primacy in all matters affecting America's international interests. Since World War II, presidents have declined to ask Congress for a declaration of war as required by the Constitution and have, instead, committed American forces to foreign conflicts under their own authority.

Most American presidents have been domestic politicians who set out to make their place in history through achievements in domestic policy. A standard joke during Bill Clinton's 1992 campaign, extending well into his first year, was that he had learned his foreign policy at the International House of Pancakes. Thus, it was not unusual that Clinton's successor, George W. Bush, had virtually no foreign policy preparation prior to taking office. He had traveled very little outside the United States, and he had had virtually no foreign experience as governor of Texas.

Nonetheless, Bush was decisive in the initiatives he took to define America's national interest for his administration. Examples include revival of the controversial program to develop a nuclear missile shield ("Star Wars"); his abandonment of the Anti-Ballistic Missile (ABM) treaty, which alienated Russia; changes in policy priorities away from humanitarian and environmental goals and toward goals more specifically within the realm of national security; and turning America's concerns (by degree or emphasis) away from Europe and toward an "Asia-first" policy.

September 11 and its aftermath immensely accentuated the president's role and his place in foreign policy.[7] By 2002 foreign policy was the centerpiece of the Bush administration's agenda. In a June 1 speech at West Point, the **Bush Doctrine** of preemptive war was announced. Bush argued that "our security will require all Americans . . . to be ready for preemptive action when necessary to defend our liberty

Bush Doctrine foreign policy based on the idea that the United States should take preemptive action against threats to its national security

and to defend our lives." Bush's statement was clearly intended to justify his administration's plans to invade Iraq, but it had much wider implications for international relations and for the central role of the American president in guiding foreign policy.

By 2010, President Obama had put his own stamp on American foreign policy, altering the conduct of America's war in Afghanistan and seeking to compel the Israelis and Palestinians to accept a Middle East peace deal. Obama also sought to engage more fully America's allies, who had been miffed by the previous administration's tendency to engage in unilateral action. Thus, as mentioned above, the United States worked closely with its NATO allies in 2011 to bring an end to the Libyan dictatorship of Mu'ammar Qaddafi.

During the course of his first year in office, Obama also concluded direct U.S. military involvement in Iraq and began to withdraw American forces from Afghanistan. One of Obama's triumphs was the military raid that resulted in the killing of Osama bin Laden, who had long been sought by the United States for his role in the September 11 terrorist attacks. As we saw, however, President Obama faced a number of challenges as he neared the end of his presidency. Russian prime minister Putin had upset the international order in Europe by seizing the Crimean Peninsula. North Korea continued to test missiles, Iran had not definitively halted its nuclear weapons program, Israel and the Palestinians fought a war in Gaza, and ISIL militants sought to win control of Iraq, Syria, and Lebanon. These and, no doubt, new problems would challenge Obama's successors. Presidents have come to dominate American foreign policy but America's foreign policies are never able to cure the ills of the world.

The Bureaucracy

The major foreign policy actors in the bureaucracy are the secretaries of the departments of State, Defense, and the Treasury; the Joint Chiefs of Staff (JCS), especially the chair of the JCS; and the director of the CIA. Since 1947 a separate unit in the White House has overseen the vast foreign policy establishment for the purpose of synthesizing all the messages arising out of the bureaucracy and helping the president make his own foreign policy. This is the National Security Council (NSC). It is a "subcabinet" made up of the president, the vice president, the secretary of defense, and the secretary of state, plus others each president appoints. Since the profound shake-up of September 11, two additional key players have been added. The first of these was the secretary of the new Department of Homeland Security (DHS), composed of 22 existing agencies relocated from all over the executive branch on the theory that their expertise could be better coordinated, more rational, and more efficient in a single organization designed to fight international terrorism and domestic natural disasters. The second key player was imposed at the top as the war in Iraq was becoming a quagmire: a director of national intelligence, to collate and coordinate intelligence coming in from multiple sources and to report a synthesis of all this intelligence to the president, on a daily basis.

Since the creation of the CIA in 1947 and the Department of Defense in 1949 (replacing the Department of War), the secretary of defense and the director of the CIA have often been rivals engaged in power struggles for control of the intelligence community.[8] For the most part, secretaries of defense have prevailed in these battles, and the Defense Department today controls more than 80 percent of the nation's intelligence capabilities and funds. The creation of the position of director of national intelligence in 2005 to coordinate all intelligence activities set off new Washington power struggles as the "intelligence czar" faced opposition from both the CIA and the Department of Defense. As of 2010, the Defense Department has continued to resist cooperating with civilian intelligence agencies and has moved to expand its own intelligence capabilities at the other agencies' expense.

In addition to these top cabinet-level officials, key lower-level staff members have policy-making influence as strong as that of the cabinet secretaries, and occasionally even stronger. These include the two or three specialized national security advisers in the White House, the staff of the NSC (headed by the national security adviser), and a few other career bureaucrats in the departments of State and Defense, whose influence varies according to their specialty and to the foreign policy issue at hand. A few civilian intelligence agencies are also involved in foreign policy and national security, the most important of which are the Federal Bureau of Investigation (FBI), the U.S. Citizenship and Immigration Services, and the Internal Revenue Service (IRS).

In the wake of September 11, military and law enforcement agencies increased their role in America's foreign policy making.[9] To a significant extent, American foreign policy is driven by military and antiterrorism concerns, and the agencies deemed capable of addressing these concerns are coming to play a larger and larger role in American foreign policy. In recent years, American ambassadors have complained that they have been relegated to secondary status as the White House has looked to military commanders for information, advice, and policy implementation. For every region of the world, the U.S. military has assigned a "combatant commander," usually a senior general or admiral, to take charge of operations in that area. In many instances, these combatant commanders, who control troops, equipment, and intelligence capabilities, have become the real eyes, ears, and voices for American foreign policy in their designated regions.

Congress

Although the Constitution gives Congress the power to declare war (see Table 18.1), Congress has exercised this power on only five occasions: the War of 1812, the Mexican War (1846), the Spanish-American War (1898), World War I (1917), and World War II (1941). For the first 150 years of American history, Congress's foreign policy role was limited because the United States' role in world affairs was limited. During this time, the Senate was the only important congressional foreign policy player because of its constitutional role in reviewing and approving treaties. The treaty power is still the primary entrée of the Senate into foreign-policy making. But since World War II and the continual involvement of the United States in international security and foreign aid, Congress as a whole has become a major foreign-policy maker because most modern foreign policies require financing, which requires action by both the House of Representatives and the Senate. For example, Congress's first act after September 11, 2001, was to authorize the president to use "all necessary and appropriate force," coupled with a $40 billion emergency appropriations bill for homeland defense. And although President Bush believed he possessed the constitutional authority to invade Iraq, he still sought congressional approval, which he received in October 2002. After the Democrats took control of Congress in 2007, the Democratic leadership proposed a new resolution opposing President Bush's policies in Iraq. The president asserted that he would not be bound by such a vote.

TABLE 18.1

Principal Foreign Policy Provisions of the Constitution

	POWERS GRANTED	
	PRESIDENT	CONGRESS
War power	Commander in chief of armed forces	Provide for the common defense; declare war
Treaties	Negotiate treaties	Ratification of treaties by two-thirds majority (Senate)
Appointments	Nominate high-level government officials	Confirm president's appointments (Senate)
Foreign commerce	No explicit powers, but treaty negotiation and appointment powers pertain	Explicit power "to regulate foreign commerce"
General powers	Executive power; veto	Legislative power; power of the purse; oversight and investigation

Not only does the president need Congress to provide funding for foreign and military policy initiatives, but under the Constitution many presidential agreements with foreign nations also have to be approved by Congress. Article II, Section 2, of the Constitution declares that proposed treaties with other nations must be submitted by the president to the Senate and approved by a two-thirds vote. Because this "supermajority" is usually difficult to achieve, presidents generally prefer a different type of agreement with other nations, called an **executive agreement**. An executive agreement is similar to a treaty and has the force of law but usually requires only a plurality vote (that is, 50 percent plus one) in both houses of Congress for approval.

Another aspect of Congress's role in foreign policy is the Senate's power to confirm the president's nominations of cabinet members, ambassadors, and other high-ranking officials (such as the director of the CIA, but not the director of the NSC). A final constitutional power of Congress is the regulation of "commerce with foreign nations."

Other congressional players are the foreign policy, military policy, and intelligence committees: in the Senate, these are the Foreign Relations Committee, the Armed Services Committee, and the Homeland Security and Governmental Affairs Committee; in the House, these are the Foreign Affairs and Homeland Security Committees and the Armed Services Committee. Usually a few members of these committees who have spent years specializing in foreign affairs become trusted members of the foreign policy establishment and are influential makers of foreign policy. In fact, several members of Congress have left the legislature to become key foreign affairs cabinet members. After September 11, 2001, congressional committees conducted hearings on the failure of the intelligence agencies, but at the time, most members of

executive agreement an agreement, made between the president and another country, that has the force of a treaty but does not require the Senate's "advice and consent"

Congress were reluctant to take on these agencies or a popular president. In 2007, though, with Congress under Democratic control and the president's popularity fading, a number of congressional committees launched inquiries into the conduct of the war in Iraq and the more general operations of the intelligence and defense communities. Within weeks, congressional testimony revealed flaws in military procurement procedures, military planning, and other aspects of the administration's programs and policies. Congressional investigations and the publicity they generate are weapons Congress frequently uses to blunt presidential power. In 2014, Republicans planned to hold hearings on the 2012 attack on America's consulate in Benghazi, Libya, which resulted in the deaths of the U.S. ambassador and three other Americans. The attack came while Hillary Clinton was secretary of state and Republicans hoped to tarnish her image before the 2016 presidential election in which she would very likely be the Democratic candidate.

Interest Groups

Although the president, the executive branch "bureaucracy," and Congress are the true makers of foreign policy, the "foreign policy establishment" is a much larger arena, including what can properly be called the shapers of foreign policy: a host of unofficial, informal players who possess varying degrees of influence depending on their prestige, reputation, socioeconomic standing, and, most important, the party and ideology that are dominant at a given moment.

By far the most important category of nonofficial player is the interest group—that is, the interest group to which one or more foreign policy issues are of longstanding and vital relevance. Economic interest groups are reputed to wield the most influence, but the myths about their influence far outnumber and outweigh the realities. In fact, the influence of organized economic interest groups in foreign policy varies enormously from issue to issue and year to year. Most of these groups are "single-issue" groups and are therefore most active when their particular issue is on the agenda. On many of the broader and more sustained policy issues—such as NAFTA or the general question of American involvement in international trade—the larger interest groups, sometimes called peak associations, find it difficult to maintain tight enough control of their many members to speak with a single voice. The most systematic study of international trade policies and their interest groups concluded that the leaders of these large economic interest groups spend more time maintaining consensus among their members than they do lobbying Congress or pressuring major players in the executive branch.[10] The more successful economic interest groups, in terms of influencing foreign policy, are the narrower, single-issue groups such as the tobacco industry, which over the years has successfully kept American foreign policy from putting heavy restrictions on international trade in and advertising of tobacco products; and the computer hardware and software industries, which have successfully hardened the American attitude toward Chinese piracy of intellectual property rights.

Another type of interest group with a well-founded reputation for influence in foreign policy is made up of people with strong attachments to and identification with their country of national origin. The interest group with the reputation for the greatest influence is Jewish Americans, whose family and emotional ties to Israel make them one of the most alert and active interest groups in the whole field of foreign policy. In 2010 a dispute between Israel and the Obama administration over Israel's construction of new Jewish housing in Jerusalem led to an intense effort by American Jews to generate congressional support for Israel's position. Similarly, Americans of Irish heritage, despite having lived in the United States for two, three, or four generations, still maintain vigilance about American policies toward Ireland and Northern Ireland. Many other ethnic and national interest groups wield similar influence over American foreign policy.

These ethnic or national-origin interest groups, exhibiting a kind of dual loyalty that Americans generally welcome as a worthy sentiment, are more influential than their counterparts in other democratic countries. But there are limits, especially when national origin is coupled with or tied to countries in which a single religion is dominant. For example, Jews with strong ties to Israel and Catholics with connections to Ireland have on occasion been blocked from group influence on foreign policy because "dual loyalty" can be taken by other groups as "doubtful loyalty."[11] Nevertheless, Irish and Jewish groups, and a variety of other ethnic American interest groups, are vigorously involved in salient aspects of foreign policy, and it is an irrational or nonrational elected politician who disregards their signals. It is quite possible that the "electoral connection"[12] and the politics of representation in Congress (and the White House) are at their most intense when national origin is linked to a foreign policy issue. Many will argue that the rationality principle "need not . . . be equated with such narrowly self-serving actions."[13] However, the nationality interest is often the strongest electoral connection.

A third type of interest group, one with a reputation that has been growing in the past two decades, is devoted to human rights. Such groups are made up of people who, instead of having self-serving economic or ethnic interests in foreign policy, are genuinely concerned about the welfare and treatment of people throughout the world—particularly those who suffer under harsh political regimes. A relatively small but often quite influential example is Amnesty International, whose exposés of human rights abuses have altered the practices of many regimes around the world. In recent years, the Christian right has been a vocal advocate for the human

Amnesty International is an interest group that works to protect human rights, often by calling on powerful countries to adopt foreign policies that support those rights. In 2013, Amnesty International activists urged the American government to support a treaty to prevent the international transfer of weapons that would be used in war crimes or other violations of human rights.

rights of Christians who are persecuted in other parts of the world for their religious beliefs, most notably in China. For example, in the 1990s, the Christian Coalition joined groups such as Amnesty International in lobbying Congress to restrict trade with countries that permitted attacks against religious believers.

A related type of group with rapidly growing influence is the ecological or environmental group, sometimes collectively called "greens." Groups of this nature often depend more on demonstrations than on the usual forms and strategies of influence in Washington, such as lobbying and using electoral politics, for example. Environmental activists staged major protests at the 2009 London and 2010 Toronto international economic summits.

A final actor in the realm of foreign policy is public opinion. For the most part, public opinion is not engaged in foreign policy issues, as most Americans are concerned mainly with domestic issues. However, public opinion does begin to count when the nation is at war. Americans are often impatient with military actions that seem long and drawn out, producing costs and casualties for reasons that no longer seem clear. Presidents are aware that long wars and casualties are likely to turn public opinion against them and provide ammunition for their political foes. Fear of public opinion is one reason that presidents have favored professional military forces and technologies like drones that would reduce the immediacy of war to America's general public.

Putting It Together

What can we say about who actually makes American foreign policy? First, except for the president, the influence of players and shapers varies from case to case—this is a good reason to look with some care at each example of foreign policy in this chapter. Second, because the one constant influence is the centrality of the president in foreign-policy making, it is best to evaluate other actors and factors as they interact with the president.[14] Third, the reason influence varies from case to case is that each case arises under different conditions and with vastly different time constraints: for issues that arise and are resolved quickly, the opportunity for influence is limited. Fourth, foreign policy experts will usually disagree about the level of influence any player or type of player has on policy making.

Let's make a few tentative generalizations to frame the remainder of this chapter. First, when an important foreign policy decision has to be made under conditions of crisis, when time is of the essence, the influence of the presidency is at its strongest. Second, within these time constraints, access to the decision-making process is limited almost exclusively to the narrowest definition of the foreign policy establishment. The arena for participation is tiny; any discussion at all is limited to the officially and constitutionally designated players. To put this another way, in a crisis, the foreign policy establishment works as it is supposed to.[15] As time becomes less restricted, even when the decision to be made is of great importance, the arena of participation expands to include more government players and more nonofficial, informal players—the most concerned interest groups and the most important journalists. In other words, the arena becomes more pluralistic and, therefore, less distinguishable from the politics of domestic-policy making. Third, because there are so many other countries with power and interests on any given issue, there are severe limits on the choices the United States can make. That is, in sharp contrast to domestic politics, U.S. policy makers in the foreign policy realm are engaged not only in infighting but also in strategic interaction with policy makers in other nations; their choices are made both in reaction to and in anticipation of these strategic interactions. As one author concludes, in foreign affairs, "policy takes precedence over politics."[16] Thus, even though foreign-policy making in noncrisis situations may closely resemble the pluralistic politics of domestic-policy making, foreign-policy making is still a narrower arena with fewer participants.

● The Instruments of Modern American Foreign Policy

> **Describe the means the United States uses to carry out foreign policy**

Any government has at hand certain instruments, or tools, to use in implementing its foreign policy. An instrument is neutral, capable of serving many goals. There have been many instruments of American foreign policy, and we can deal here only with those instruments we deem most important in the modern epoch: diplomacy, the United Nations, the international monetary structure, economic aid and sanctions, collective security, military force, and arbitration. Each of these instruments will be evaluated in this section for its utility in the conduct of American foreign policy, and each will be assessed in light of the history and development of American values.

Diplomacy

We begin this treatment of instruments with diplomacy. **Diplomacy** is the representation of a government to other foreign governments. Its purpose is to promote national values or interests by peaceful means. According to Hans Morgenthau, "a diplomacy that ends in war has failed in its primary objective."[17]

diplomacy the representation of a government to other governments

The first effort to create a modern diplomatic service in the United States was made through the Rogers Act of 1924, which established the initial framework for a professional foreign service staff. But it took World War II and the Foreign Service Act of 1946 to forge the foreign service into a fully professional diplomatic corps.

Diplomacy, by its very nature, is overshadowed by spectacular international events, dramatic initiatives, and meetings among heads of state or their direct personal representatives. The traditional American distrust of diplomacy continues today, albeit in a weaker form. Impatience with or downright distrust of diplomacy has been built into not only all the other instruments of foreign policy but also the modern presidential system itself.[18] So much personal responsibility has been heaped on the presidency that presidents are reluctant to entrust any of their authority or responsibility in foreign policy to professional diplomats in the State Department and other bureaucracies.

In 2008 both parties' presidential candidates criticized the Bush administration for having failed to use diplomacy to secure greater international support for the Iraq War. Both promised to revitalize American diplomacy. President Obama appointed Hillary Clinton secretary of state in part to underline the importance

The secretary of state is America's chief diplomat. In 2014, Secretary of State John Kerry met with leaders involved in the ongoing turmoil in Iraq, including the leader of the Kurdistan region, Massud Barzani (right).

he attached to diplomacy by choosing such a prominent figure as America's chief diplomat.

The significance of diplomacy and its vulnerability to politics may be better appreciated as we proceed to the other instruments. While Americans have traditionally distrusted diplomacy, it was an instrument more or less imposed on them as the prevailing means of bargaining among nation-states in the nineteenth century. The other instruments to be identified and assessed here are instruments that Americans self-consciously crafted for themselves to take care of their own chosen place in the world affairs of the second half of the twentieth century and beyond. The instruments therefore better reflect American culture and values than diplomacy does.

The United Nations

United Nations (UN) an organization of nations founded in 1945 to be a channel for negotiation and a means of settling international disputes peaceably; the UN has had frequent successes in providing a forum for negotiation and, on some occasions, a means of preventing international conflicts from spreading; on a number of occasions, the UN has been a convenient cover for U.S. foreign policy goals

The utility of the **United Nations (UN)** to the United States as an instrument of foreign policy can be too easily underestimated because the UN is a very large and unwieldy institution with few powers and no armed forces to implement its rules and resolutions. Its supreme body is the UN General Assembly, comprising one representative of each of the 192 member states; each member representative has one vote, regardless of the size of the country. Important issues require a two-thirds-majority vote, and the annual session of the General Assembly runs only from September to December (although it can call extra sessions). It has little organization that can make it an effective decision-making body, with only six standing committees, few tight rules of procedure, and no political parties to provide priorities and discipline. Its defenders are quick to add that although it lacks armed forces, it relies on the power of world opinion—and this is not to be taken lightly. The powers of the UN devolve mainly to the organization's "executive committee," the UN Security Council, which alone has the real power to make decisions and rulings that member states are obligated by the UN Charter to implement. The Security Council may be called into session at any time, and each member (or a designated alternate) must be present at UN headquarters in New York at all times. The council is composed of 15 members: 5 are permanent (the victors of

World War II), and 10 are elected by the General Assembly for unrepeatable two-year terms. The 5 permanent members are China, France, Russia, the United Kingdom, and the United States. Each of the 15 members has only one vote, and a 9-vote majority of the 15 is required on all substantive matters. But each of the five permanent members also has a negative vote, a "veto," and one veto is sufficient to reject any substantive proposal.

The UN can serve as a useful forum for international discussions and an instrument for multilateral action. Most peacekeeping efforts to which the United States contributes, for example, are undertaken under UN auspices.

The International Monetary Structure

Fear of a repeat of the economic devastation that followed World War I brought the United States together with its allies (except the USSR) to Bretton Woods, New Hampshire, in 1944 to create a new international economic structure for the postwar world. The result was two institutions: the International Bank for Reconstruction and Development (commonly called the World Bank) and the International Monetary Fund.

The World Bank was set up to finance long-term capital. Leading nations took on the obligation of contributing funds to enable the World Bank to make loans to capital-hungry countries. (The U.S. quota has been about one-third of the total.)

The **International Monetary Fund (IMF)** was set up to provide for the short-term flow of money. After the war, the U.S. dollar replaced gold as the chief means by which the currencies of one country would be "changed into" currencies of another country for purposes of making international transactions. To permit debtor countries with no international balances to make purchases and investments, the IMF was set up to lend dollars or other appropriate currencies to such needy member countries to help them overcome temporary trade deficits.

During the 1990s the importance of the IMF increased through its efforts to reform some of the largest debtor nations and formerly Communist countries,

International Monetary Fund (IMF) an institution established in 1944 that provides loans and facilitates international monetary exchange

The United States is the most influential member of the World Bank, which provides loans and other assistance to developing countries. Here, workers in Afghanistan work to improve roads. The World Bank has provided hundreds of millions of dollars to help rebuild Afghanistan over the past decade.

to bring them more fully into the global capitalist economy. For example, in the early 1990s, Russia and 13 other former Soviet republics were invited to join the IMF and the World Bank, with the expectation that they would receive $10.5 billion from these two agencies, primarily for a currency stabilization fund. Each republic was to get a permanent IMF representative, and the IMF increased its staff by at least 10 percent to provide the expertise necessary to cope with the problems of these emerging capitalist economies.[19]

The IMF, with tens of billions of dollars contributed by its members, has more money to lend poor countries than does the United States, Europe, or Japan (the three leading IMF shareholders) individually. It makes its policy decisions in ways that are generally consonant with the interests of the leading shareholders.[20] Two weeks after September 11, 2001, the IMF approved a $135 million loan to economically troubled Pakistan, a key player in the war against the Taliban government of Afghanistan because of its strategic location. Turkey, also because of its strategic location in the Middle East, was likewise put back in the IMF pipeline.[21] The future of the IMF, the World Bank, and all other private sources of international investment will depend in part on extension of more credit to developing countries, because credit means investment and productivity. But the future may depend even more on reducing the debt that is already there from previous extensions of credit.

Economic Aid and Sanctions

Every year, the United States provides nearly $30 billion in economic assistance to other nations. Some aid has a humanitarian purpose, such as helping to provide health care, shelter for refugees, or famine relief. A good deal of American aid, however, is designed to promote American security interests or economic concerns. For example, the United States provides military assistance to a number of its allies in the form of advanced weapons or loans to help them purchase such weapons. These loans generally stipulate that the recipient must purchase the designated weapons from American firms. In this way, the United States hopes to bolster its security and economic interests with one grant. The two largest recipients of American military assistance are Israel and Egypt, American allies that fought two wars against each other. The United States believes that its military assistance allows both countries to feel sufficiently secure to remain at peace with each other.

Aid is an economic carrot. Sanctions are an economic stick. Economic sanctions that the United States employs against other nations include trade embargoes, bans on investment, and efforts to prevent the World Bank or other international institutions from extending credit to a nation against which the United States has a grievance. Sanctions are most often employed when the United States seeks to weaken what it considers a hostile regime or when it is attempting to compel some particular action by another regime. Thus, for example, in order to weaken the Castro government, the United States has long prohibited American firms from doing business with Cuba. In recent years, the United States has maintained economic sanctions against Iran and North Korea in an effort to prevent those nations from pursuing nuclear weapons programs. The United States also uses economic sanctions to advance its international humanitarian policy goals. The United States currently has sanctions in place against Sudan, Zimbabwe, Belarus, and Myanmar, four countries with records of serious violations of civil and political rights.[22]

As the Iranian example shows, unilateral sanctions by the United States usually have little effect, since the target can usually trade elsewhere, sometimes even with foreign affiliates of U.S. firms. If, however, the United States is able to persuade its allies to cooperate, sanctions have a better chance of success. International sanctions against Libya, for example, were decisive in compelling that nation to enter into negotiations with the United States over Libyan responsibility for the 1988 bombing of an airliner over Lockerbie, Scotland, that killed more than 100 Americans. The Libyans ultimately agreed to accept responsibility and pay compensation to the victims' families.

for critical analysis

There has been a good deal of debate about whether economic sanctions can convince North Korea or Iran to halt its nuclear weapons programs. What factors might help to determine the effectiveness of economic sanctions?

Collective Security

In 1947 most Americans hoped that the United States could meet its world obligations through the UN and economic structures alone. But most foreign-policy makers recognized that was a vain hope, even as they were permitting and encouraging Americans to believe it. These policy makers had anticipated the need for military entanglements at the time of drafting the original UN Charter by insisting on language that recognized the right of all nations to provide for their mutual defense independent of the UN. And almost immediately after enactment of the Marshall Plan, designed to promote European economic recovery, the White House and a parade of State and Defense Department officials followed up with an urgent request to the Senate to ratify, and to both houses of Congress to finance, mutual defense alliances.

The Senate, at first quite reluctant to approve treaties providing for national security alliances, ultimately agreed with the executive branch. The first collective security agreement was the Rio Treaty (ratified by the Senate in September 1947), which created the Organization of American States (OAS). This was the model treaty, anticipating all succeeding collective security treaties by providing that an armed attack against any of its members "shall be considered as an attack against all the American States," including the United States. A more significant break with U.S. tradition against peacetime entanglements came with the North Atlantic Treaty (signed in April 1949), which created the **North Atlantic Treaty Organization (NATO)**. The Australian, New Zealand, United States Security (ANZUS) Treaty, which tied Australia and New Zealand to the United States, was signed in September

North Atlantic Treaty Organization (NATO) an organization, comprising the United States, Canada, and most of Western Europe, formed in 1949 to counter the perceived threat from the Soviet Union

The United States joined NATO in 1949 to help counter the threat of the Soviet Union. Following the collapse of the Soviet Union in 1990, NATO remains an important institution for multilateral cooperation in international affairs.

1951. Three years later, the Southeast Asia Treaty created the Southeast Asia Treaty Organization (SEATO).

In addition to these multilateral treaties, the United States entered into a number of **bilateral treaties** (treaties between two countries), such as the treaty with Vietnam that resulted in ultimately unsuccessful American military action to protect that nation's government. As one author has observed, the United States has been a *producer* of security, whereas most of its allies have been *consumers* of security.[23]

bilateral treaties treaties made between two nations

This pattern has continued in the post–Cold War era, and its best illustration is in the Persian Gulf War, where the United States provided the initiative, the leadership, and most of the armed forces, even though its allies were obliged to reimburse over 90 percent of the cost.

It is difficult to evaluate collective security and its treaties, because the purpose of collective security as an instrument of foreign policy is prevention, and success of this kind has to be measured in terms of what did *not* happen. Critics have argued that U.S. collective security treaties posed a threat of encirclement to the Soviet Union, forcing it to produce its own collective security, particularly the Warsaw Pact.[24] Nevertheless, no one can deny the counterargument that more than 60 years have passed without a world war.

In 1998 the expansion of NATO took its first steps toward including former Warsaw Pact members, extending membership to the Czech Republic, Hungary, and Poland. Most of Washington embraced this expansion as the true and fitting end of the Cold War, and the U.S. Senate echoed this with a resounding 80-to-19 vote to induct these three former Soviet satellites into NATO. The expansion was also welcomed among European member nations, who quickly approved the move, hailing it as the final closing of the book on Yalta, the 1945 treaty that divided Europe into Western and Soviet spheres of influence after

Military Expenditures around the World

Security is an important foreign policy goal of every country. Military force is one tool of foreign policy that countries use to secure their territory and interests. In 2013 countries around the world spent approximately $1.7 trillion on military expenditures. To put this number in perspective, the total size of the world economy was about $74 trillion in 2013, according to the International Monetary Fund,[a] so military expenditures make up about 2.3 percent of the global economy.

Countries vary significantly in how much they spend on their militaries. The United States is notable for spending far more than other countries: at $640 billion, U.S. military spending represents about 38 percent of the world's total. Among democracies, France spends the second highest, at $61 billion, or just 4 percent of the world's total.

Why does the United States choose to spend so much on its military? Why do other countries, like South Korea, which sits in a much more hostile neighborhood than the United States, spend so little?

One reason that America's friends are able to limit their own military spending is that they depend upon the United States for military security. Since World War II, the United States has provided a security umbrella for much of Western Europe, Japan, and other nations, as well. America's preeminence in the realm of security gives the United States considerable influence but often leads to resentment among Americans and charges that other nations are failing to pay their fair shares. The United States, however, is a global power with security interests throughout the world, so it stands to reason that its military spending would outpace that of its allies, who generally view their interests in local or regional terms.

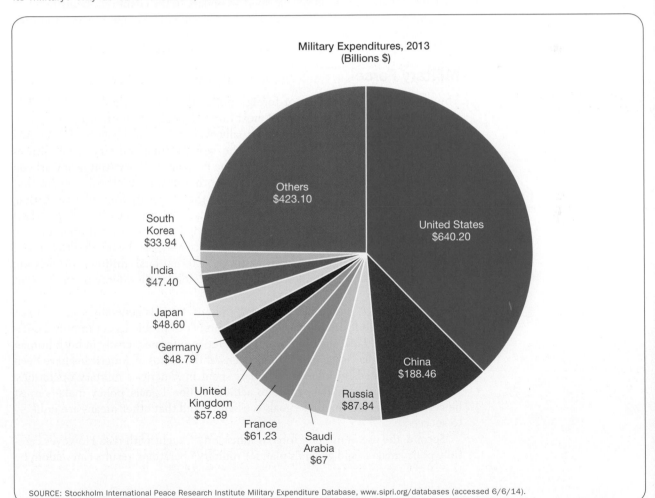

Military Expenditures, 2013 (Billions $)

- Others $423.10
- South Korea $33.94
- India $47.40
- Japan $48.60
- Germany $48.79
- United Kingdom $57.89
- France $61.23
- Saudi Arabia $67
- Russia $87.84
- China $188.46
- United States $640.20

SOURCE: Stockholm International Peace Research Institute Military Expenditure Database, www.sipri.org/databases (accessed 6/6/14).

[a]International Monetary Fund, World Economic and Financial Surveys World Economic Outlook Database, www.imf.org/external/pubs/ft/weo/2014/01/weodata/index.aspx (accessed 6/10/14).

the defeat of Germany. Expanded membership seems to have made NATO less threatening and more acceptable to Russia. Russia became a partner when the NATO-Russia Council was formed in 2002. Finally, although the expanded NATO membership (28 countries in 2012) reduces the threat to Russia, it also reduces the utility of NATO as a military alliance. The September 11, 2001, attack on the United States was the first time in its more than 50-year history that Article 5 of the North Atlantic Treaty had to be invoked; it provides that an attack on one country is an attack on all the member countries. In fighting "the war on terror," the Bush administration recognized that no matter how preponderant American power was, some aspects of U.S. foreign policy could not be achieved without multilateral cooperation. On the other hand, the United States did not want to be constrained by its alliances. The global coalition initially forged after September 11, 2001, numbered more than 170 countries. Not all joined the war effort in Afghanistan, but most if not all provided some form of support for some aspect of "the war on terror," such as economic sanctions and intelligence.

Two years later, however, the war in Iraq put this coalition to the test. The Bush administration was determined not to make its decision to go to war subject to the UN, NATO, or any other international organization. The breadth of the United States' coalition was deemed secondary to the coalition's being nonconstraining. As a result, other than the British government, no major power supported the United States' actions.

Military Force

The most visible instrument of foreign policy is, of course, military force. The United States has built the world's most imposing military, with army, navy, marine, and air force units stationed in virtually every corner of the globe. The United States is responsible for one-third of the world's total military expenditures (see the "America Side by Side" feature). The Prussian military strategist Carl von Clausewitz famously called war "politics by other means." By this he meant that nations used force not simply to demonstrate their capacity for violence. Rather, force or the threat of force is a tool nations must sometimes use to achieve their foreign policy goals. Military force may be needed to protect a nation's security interests and economic concerns. Ironically, force may also be needed to achieve humanitarian goals. For example, without international military protection, the refugees in Darfur camps would be completely at the mercy of the violent Sudanese regime.

Though force is sometimes necessary, military force is generally seen as a last resort and avoided if possible because of a number of problems commonly associated with its use. First, the use of military force is extremely costly in both human and financial terms. In the past 50 years, tens of thousands of Americans have been killed and hundreds of billions of dollars spent in America's military operations. Before they employ military force to achieve national goals, policy makers must be certain that achieving those goals is essential and that other means are unlikely to succeed.

Second, the use of military force is inherently fraught with risk. However carefully policy makers and generals plan for military operations, results can seldom be

Who Serves in the U.S. Military?

Gender

U.S. Military
14% Female
86% Male

86%

U.S. Population
51% Female
49% Male

49%

Race/Ethnicity

U.S. Military
66% White   3% Asian
16% Black   5% Other
10% Hispanic

66%

U.S. Population
64% White
13% Black
16% Hispanic
5% Asian
3% Other

64%

Education

New enlistees, 2010

U.S. Military
98% High school
graduates

98%

U.S. Population
86% High school
graduates

86%

The Department of Defense and the military are often responsible for implementing foreign policy that relates to security. Who are the men and women in the armed forces? The military has a far greater proportion of men to women than the general population, but in terms of race and ethnicity, the military is fairly similar to the United States as a whole. Residents of southern states are significantly more likely to enlist than those from other regions.

SOURCES: Department of Defense, "Population Representation in the Military Services, 2010." U.S. Census, 2010.

Geographic Origin

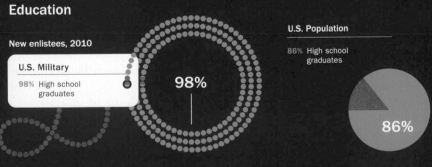

U.S. military new enlistees, 2012

12.4%
23%   19.7%
42.2%

Northeast 12.4%   Midwest 19.7%
South   42.2%   West

U.S. population

18%
23%   22%
37%

Northeast 18%   Midwest 22%
South   37%   West

for critical analysis

1. The move to an all-volunteer military in the United States in 1973 resulted in a more educated and professionalized force. However, the United States has used the draft in the past, and some countries require military service of all citizens. Can you think of some arguments for and against each approach?

2. Does it matter if some groups are more heavily represented in the armed forces than others?

fully anticipated. Variables ranging from the weather to unexpected weapons and tactics deployed by opponents may upset the most careful calculations and turn military operations into costly disasters or convert maneuvers that were expected to be quick and decisive into long, drawn-out, expensive struggles. For example, American policy makers expected to defeat the Iraqi army quickly and easily in 2003—and they did. Policy makers did not anticipate, however, that American forces would still be struggling years later to defeat the insurgency that arose in the war's aftermath.

Finally, in a democracy, any government that chooses to address policy problems through military means is almost certain to encounter political difficulties. Generally speaking, the American public will support relatively short and decisive military engagements. If, however, a conflict drags on, producing casualties and expenses with no clear outcome, the public loses patience and opposition politicians point to the government's lies and ineptitude. The wars in Korea, Vietnam, and Iraq are all examples of protracted conflicts whose domestic political repercussions became serious liabilities for the governments that initially decided to make use of military force.

Thus, military force remains a major foreign policy tool, and the United States currently possesses a more powerful and effective set of military forces than any other nation. Nevertheless, even for the United States, the use of military force is fraught with risk and is not to be undertaken lightly.

Arbitration

The final foreign policy tool we shall consider is dispute arbitration. Arbitration means referring an international disagreement to a neutral third party for resolution. Arbitration, like diplomacy, is sometimes seen as a form of "soft power" as distinguished from military force, economic sanctions, and other coercive foreign policy instruments. The United States will occasionally turn to international tribunals to resolve disputes with other countries. For example, in February 2008 the U.S. government asked the International Court of Justice to resolve a long-standing dispute with Italy over American property confiscated by the Italian government more than 40 years ago. To take another example, in 1981 the United States and Iran established an arbitral tribunal to deal with claims arising from Iran's seizure of the U.S. embassy in Tehran in 1979; the tribunal resulted in a settlement.

More important, the United States relies heavily on the work of arbitral panels to maintain the flow of international trade on which America's economy depends. U.S. firms would be reluctant to do business abroad if they could not be certain that their property and contractual rights would be honored by other nations. Arbitration helps produce that certainty. Almost every international contract contains an arbitration clause requiring that disputes between the parties will be resolved not by foreign governments but by impartial arbitral panels accepted by both sides. By the terms of the New York Convention, virtually every nation in the world has agreed to accept and enforce arbitral verdicts. The United States has incorporated the terms of the New York Convention into federal law, and U.S. courts vigorously enforce arbitral judgments. The United States may not be happy with the outcome of every arbitral proceeding, but the arbitral system is essential to America's economic interests.

Foreign Policy
and Your Future

The nineteenth-century British statesman Lord Palmerston famously said, "Nations have no permanent friends or allies; they only have permanent interests." Palmerston's comment illustrates what is sometimes known as the "realist" view of foreign policy. The realist school holds that foreign policies should be guided by the national interest (mainly security and economic interest) and that policy makers should steel themselves to the necessity of making decisions that might be viewed from the outside as cold and ruthless if they serve the nation's interests. Although many public officials have denounced such views in public—especially if they were running for office—many became realists once in power. Every one of America's post–World War II presidents, liberals and conservatives, Democrats and Republicans alike, has been willing to order young Americans into battle and to visit death and destruction on the citizens of foreign states if he believed the national interest required it.

The harsh rationality of foreign policy often clashes with America's history and ideals. U.S. democratic and liberal traditions lead Americans to hope for a world in which ideals rather than naked interests govern foreign policy and in which U.S. leaders pay heed to ideals. The ideals that Americans historically have espoused (though not always lived by) assert that U.S. foreign policies should have a higher purpose than the pursuit of self-interest and that America is to use force only as a last resort. Since the realities of U.S. foreign policy often clash with these historic ideals, American policy makers often struggle to explain their actions and avoid admitting to motivations that don't embody those ideals.

"Simply stated, there is no doubt that Saddam Hussein now has weapons of mass destruction," said Vice President Dick Cheney in 2002. When it turned out that these weapons did not exist, Assistant Defense Secretary Paul Wolfowitz explained, "For bureaucratic reasons, we settled on one issue, weapons of mass destruction [as justification for invading Iraq], because it was the one reason everyone could agree on."[25] As a candidate for the presidency, Barack Obama was praised for denouncing the Bush administration's treatment of enemy combatants. Obama was especially critical of the Guantánamo detention facility, where some alleged enemy combatants were incarcerated. Once in office, however, Obama did not rush to close the Guantánamo facility—though he continued to plan for its eventual closure.

Must America always choose between its ideals and its interests? The founders of the Republic believed that America would be different from other nations. They believed that its ideals would be its source of power; that its ideals would allow it to inspire and lead others as a "shining beacon." But international events can make it difficult to always pursue those ideals. The forces of globalization mean that it is easier than ever for small groups of extremists with violent intentions to travel to American shores and carry out their plans. On the other hand, those same forces of globalization have been the source of many positive outcomes. Greater trade reduces the price of many products for American consumers as well as those abroad. Furthermore, many scholars believe that the increasing global economic interdependence is a force for peace: it is difficult to go to war with one's major trading partners because the harm domestically would be too great. What can U.S. leaders do in the future to make sure that globalization is a positive force that promotes U.S. security and prosperity? If, in the pursuit of national power and security, our political leaders always choose narrow interests over transcendent ideals, might they be robbing America of its true source of international power and global security?

plugin

Inform

Visit a U.S. news website, such as www.cnn.com, www.nytimes.com, or www.wsj.com, and look at the top three stories in world news. What U.S. foreign policy decisions are involved in each? Who is involved in making or influencing the decisions?

Express

Make a list of ways that international affairs and foreign policy—possibly including security concerns, the global economy, or issues like the environment—affect your life.

Connect

See how people around the world view the United States at www.pewglobal .org/database. Click "Questions by Topic" and then "U.S. Image."

Act

Consider working with an interest group on a foreign policy issue you care about, such as Amnesty International (human rights), Move America Forward (supporting American troops), or Just Foreign Policy (equality and justice from a nonpartisan perspective).

The Goals of Foreign Policy

Explain how foreign policy is designed to promote security, prosperity, and humanitarian goals (pp. 727–37)

The programs and policies that determine U.S. relations with other nations and foreign entities are referred to as *American foreign policy*. The three main goals of American foreign policy are security, prosperity, and the creation of a better world. Although each of these goals is important in understanding the contours of American foreign policy, most policy makers usually give precedence to security and economic interests over humanitarian concerns.

Key Terms

non-state actors (p. 727)

isolationism (p. 728)

containment (p. 728)

appeasement (p. 729)

Cold War (p. 729)

nation-states (p. 730)

preventive war (p. 730)

World Trade Organization (WTO) (p. 733)

General Agreement on Tariffs and Trade (GATT) (p. 733)

North American Free Trade Agreement (NAFTA) (p. 733)

Practice Quiz

1. Which of the following terms best describes the American posture toward the world prior to the middle of the twentieth century?
   a) interventionist
   b) isolationist
   c) appeasement
   d) humanitarian
   e) internationalist

2. *Cold War* refers to the
   a) competition between the United States and Canada over Alaska.
   b) the years between World War I and World War II when the United States and Germany were hostile to one another.
   c) the long-standing conflict over which nation controls Antarctica.
   d) the period of struggle between the United States and the Soviet Union between the late 1940s and the late 1980s.
   e) the economic competition between the United States and Japan today.

3. Which of the following terms describes the idea that the development and maintenance of military strength discourage attack?
   a) appeasement
   b) détente
   c) deterrence
   d) containment
   e) "Minuteman" theory of defense

4. In trade policy since World War II, American presidents have generally supported
   a) ending the role of the international institutions like the GATT and the WTO.
   b) ending all farm subsidies in the United States.
   c) tight restrictions on U.S. exports.
   d) closing the borders to most imports.
   e) freer trade.

Who Makes American Foreign Policy?

Identify the major players in foreign-policy making, and describe their roles (pp. 738–45)

While the president and his chief advisers are the principal architects of U.S. foreign policy, many other actors in the American political system play an important role in determining how the United States interacts with other nations. Specifically, Congress, the bureaucracy, the courts, political parties, and interest groups all exert some influence over American foreign policy. With the exception of the president, the precise influence of each of these actors varies from case to case.

Key Terms

Bush Doctrine (p. 738)

executive agreement (p. 741)

Practice Quiz

5. *Bush Doctrine* refers to
   a) the idea that the United States should not allow foreign powers to meddle in the Western Hemisphere.
   b) the idea that the United States should avoid future wars by giving in to the demands of hostile foreign powers.
   c) the idea that the United States should take preemptive action against threats to its national security.
   d) the idea that the United States should never take preemptive action against threats to its national security.
   e) the idea that the United States should always secure international approval before taking any military action.

6. The Constitution assigns the power to declare war to
   a) the National Security Council.
   b) the president.
   c) Congress.
   d) the secretary of defense.
   e) the chief justice of the United States.

7. An agreement made between the president and another country that has the force of a treaty but requires only a majority vote (not a supermajority) in both houses of Congress for approval is called
   a) an executive order.
   b) an executive privilege.
   c) an executive agreement.
   d) a diplomatic decree.
   e) arbitration.

8. The making of American foreign policy during noncrisis moments is
   a) dominated entirely by the president.
   b) dominated entirely by Congress.
   c) dominated entirely by interest groups.
   d) dominated entirely by the Department of Defense.
   e) pluralistic, involving a large mix of both official and unofficial players.

The Instruments of Modern American Foreign Policy

Describe the means the United States uses to carry out foreign policy (pp. 745–54)

The most important tools for the United States in implementing its foreign policy in the modern era have been diplomacy, the United Nations, the international monetary structure, economic aid and sanctions, collective security, military force, and arbitration. Many of the international organizations that influence contemporary American foreign policy, such as the United Nations, the International Monetary Fund, the World Bank, NATO, and the International Court of Justice, were formed in the years immediately following World War II. As a result of the fact that the United States possesses a more powerful and effective military than any other nation, military force is a particularly important tool for American foreign policy.

Key Terms

diplomacy (p. 745)
United Nations (UN) (p. 746)
International Monetary Fund (IMF) (p. 747)
North Atlantic Treaty Organization (NATO) (p. 749)
bilateral treaties (p. 750)

Practice Quiz

9. Which of the following statements about the United Nations is *not* true?
   a) It gives every country one vote in the General Assembly.
   b) It has a powerful army to implement its decisions.
   c) The five permanent members of the UN Security Council are China, France, Russia, the United Kingdom, and the United States.
   d) It was designed to be a channel for negotiation and a means of settling international disputes peaceably.
   e) Important issues require a two-thirds majority vote in the General Assembly.

10. Which of the following are important international economic institutions created in the 1940s?
    a) the Federal Reserve System and the Council of Economic Advisers
    b) the North Atlantic Treaty Organization and the Southeast Asia Treaty Organization
    c) the International Monetary Fund and the World Bank
    d) the International Court of Justice and the Warsaw Pact
    e) the Office of Management and Budget and the General Agreement on Tariffs and Trade

11. Which of the following was dedicated specifically to the economic recovery of Western Europe after World War II?
   a) the Marshall Plan
   b) the Lend-Lease Act
   c) the General Agreement on Tariffs and Trade
   d) the North American Free Trade Agreement
   e) the International Monetary Fund

12. The North Atlantic Treaty Organization was formed by the United States,
   a) Canada, and most of Eastern Europe.
   b) Canada, and the Soviet Union.
   c) Canada, and Mexico.
   d) Canada, and most of Western Europe.
   e) Canada, and the United Kingdom.

13. Which statement best describes the military spending of the United States compared to other countries?
   a) The United States spends about the same as most other countries in the world.
   b) The United States spends significantly more than any other country in the world.
   c) The United States spends significantly more than any other country in the world except for China.
   d) The United States spends significantly less than any other country in the world.
   e) The United States spends slightly less than most other countries in the world.

For Further Reading

Art, Robert. *The Use of Force: Military Power and International Politics*. New York: Rowman and Littlefield, 2009.

Bacevich, Andrew. *The New American Militarism: How Americans Are Seduced by War*. New York: Oxford University Press, 2006.

Bacevich, Andrew. *The Limits of Power: The End of American Exceptionalism*. New York: Metropolitan Books, 2008.

Dorman, Andrew, and Joyce Kaufman, eds. *Providing for National Security*. Palo Alto, CA: Stanford University Press, 2014.

Drezner, Daniel. "The Realist Tradition in American Public Opinion." *Perspectives on Politics* (March 2008): 51–70.

Fisk, Robert. *The Great War for Civilization: The Conquest of the Middle East*. New York: Knopf, 2005.

Gaddis, John L. *The Cold War: A New History*. New York: Penguin Press, 2005.

Ginsberg, Benjamin. *The Worth of War*. New York: Prometheus, 2014.

Herring, George C. *From Colony to Superpower: U.S. Foreign Relations since 1776*. New York: Oxford University Press, 2011.

Hook, Steven. *U.S. Foreign Policy: The Paradox of World Power*. Washington, DC: CQ Press, 2010.

Ikenberry, John. *American Foreign Policy*. New York: Wadsworth, 2010.

Jentleson, Bruce W. *American Foreign Policy—The Dynamics of Choice in the 21st Century*. 5th ed. New York: W.W. Norton, 2013.

Kagan, Robert. *Dangerous Nation*. New York: Knopf, 2006.

Kaufman, Joyce. *A Concise History of U.S. Foreign Policy*. New York: Rowman and Littlefield, 2010.

Kennan, George F. *Around the Cragged Hill: A Personal and Political Philosophy*. New York: W. W. Norton, 1993.

Nasr, Vali. *The Dispensable Nation: American Foreign Policy in Retreat*. New York: Anchor, 2014.

Pillar, Paul. *Intelligence and U.S. Foreign Policy*. New York: Columbia University Press, 2011.

Recommended Websites

American Israel Public Affairs Committee
www.aipac.org

Interest groups are some of the main shapers of foreign policy. One of the top lobbies in the nation, the American Israel Public Affairs Committee (AIPAC) works to strengthen the U.S.-Israel relationship.

Foreign Policy Association
www.fpa.org

This nonprofit organization tries to generate interest in and draw attention to global issues and policies.

International Monetary Fund
www.imf.org

World Trade Organization
www.wto.org

The International Monetary Fund (IMF) and the World Trade Organization (WTO) have been considered instruments of modern American foreign policy. Read about how these organizations are trying to promote capitalism, free trade, and economic development.

National Security Council
www.whitehouse.gov/nsc/

The National Security Council was formed in 1947 and consists of senior advisers and cabinet officials who keep the president informed on all matters of national security and foreign policy.

Peterson Institute for International Economics
www.iie.com

The Peterson Institute for International Economics is dedicated to analyzing international economic policy. Take a minute to review some of the studies that have influenced the policies of such international organizations as NAFTA, the WTO, and the IMF.

United Nations
www.un.org

Founded in 1945, the United Nations promotes international peace and security. Visit the UN website for information on the General Assembly, the Security Council, economic and social development, and humanitarian issues.

U.S. Department of State
www.state.gov

The U.S. Department of State is the primary bureaucratic department for American diplomacy and national security.

U.S. Senate: Treaties
http://senate.gov/pagelayout/legislative/d_three_sections
_with_teasers/treaties.htm

The most important foreign policy task of the Senate is reviewing and approving treaties. Learn more about the Senate's treaty-making powers and find information about treaty action at this U.S. Senate website.

The Declaration of Independence

In Congress, July 4, 1776

The unanimous Declaration of the thirteen united States of America,

When in the Course of human events, it becomes necessary for one people to dissolve the political bands which have connected them with another, and to assume among the powers of the earth, the separate and equal station to which the Laws of Nature and of Nature's God entitle them, a decent respect to the opinions of mankind requires that they should declare the causes which impel them to the separation.

We hold these truths to be self-evident, that all men are created equal, that they are endowed by their Creator with certain unalienable Rights, that among these are Life, Liberty and the pursuit of Happiness.—That to secure these rights, Governments are instituted among Men, deriving their just powers from the consent of the governed.—That whenever any Form of Government becomes destructive of these ends, it is the Right of the People to alter or to abolish it, and to institute new Government, laying its foundation on such principles and organizing its powers in such form, as to them shall seem most likely to effect their Safety and Happiness. Prudence, indeed, will dictate that Governments long established should not be changed for light and transient causes; and accordingly all experience hath shewn, that mankind are more disposed to suffer, while evils are sufferable, than to right themselves by abolishing the forms to which they are accustomed. But when a long train of abuses and usurpations, pursuing invariably the same Object evinces a design to reduce them under absolute Despotism, it is their right, it is their duty, to throw off such Government, and to provide new Guards for their future security.—Such has been the patient sufferance of these Colonies; and such is now the necessity which constrains them to alter their former Systems of Government. The history of the present King of Great Britain is a history of repeated injuries and usurpations, all having in direct object the establishment of an absolute Tyranny over these States. To prove this, let Facts be submitted to a candid world.

He has refused his Assent to Laws, the most wholesome and necessary for the public good.

He has forbidden his Governors to pass Laws of immediate and pressing importance, unless suspended in their operation till his Assent should be obtained; and when so suspended, he has utterly neglected to attend to them.

He has refused to pass other Laws for the accommodation of large districts of people, unless those people would relinquish the right of Representation in the Legislature, a right inestimable to them and formidable to tyrants only.

He has called together legislative bodies at places unusual, uncomfortable, and distant from the depository of their public Records, for the sole purpose of fatiguing them into compliance with his measures.

He has dissolved Representative Houses repeatedly, for opposing with manly firmness his invasions on the rights of the people.

He has refused for a long time, after such dissolutions, to cause others to be elected; whereby the Legislative powers, incapable of Annihilation, have returned to the People at large for their exercise; the State remaining in the mean time exposed to all the dangers of invasion from without, and convulsions within.

He has endeavoured to prevent the population of these States; for that purpose obstructing the Laws for Naturalization of Foreigners; refusing to pass others to encourage their migrations hither, and raising the conditions of new Appropriations of Lands.

He has obstructed the Administration of Justice, by refusing his Assent to Laws for establishing Judiciary powers.

He has made Judges dependent on his Will alone, for the tenure of their offices, and the amount and payment of their salaries.

He has erected a multitude of New Offices, and sent hither swarms of Officers to harrass our people, and eat out their substance.

He has kept among us, in times of peace, Standing Armies without the Consent of our legislatures.

He has affected to render the Military independent of and superior to the Civil power.

He has combined with others to subject us to a jurisdiction foreign to our constitution, and unacknowledged by our laws; giving his Assent to their Acts of pretended Legislation:

For Quartering large bodies of armed troops among us:

For protecting them, by a mock Trial, from punishment for any Murders which they should commit on the Inhabitants of these States:

For cutting off our Trade with all parts of the world:

For imposing Taxes on us without our Consent:

For depriving us in many cases, of the benefits of Trial by Jury:

For transporting us beyond Seas to be tried for pretended offences:

For abolishing the free System of English Laws in a neighboring Province, establishing therein an Arbitrary government, and enlarging its Boundaries so as to render it at once an example and fit instrument for introducing the same absolute rule into these Colonies:

For taking away our Charters, abolishing our most valuable Laws, and altering fundamentally the Forms of our Governments:

For suspending our own Legislatures, and declaring themselves invested with power to legislate for us in all cases whatsoever.

He has abdicated Government here, by declaring us out of his Protection and waging War against us.

He has plundered our seas, ravaged our Coasts, burnt our towns, and destroyed the lives of our people.

He is at this time transporting large Armies of foreign Mercenaries to compleat the works of death, desolation and tyranny, already begun with circumstances of Cruelty & perfidy scarcely paralleled in the most barbarous ages, and totally unworthy the Head of a civilized nation.

He has constrained our fellow Citizens taken Captive on the high Seas to bear Arms against their Country, to become the executioners of their friends and Brethren, or to fall themselves by their Hands.

He has excited domestic insurrections amongst us, and has endeavoured to bring on the inhabitants of our frontiers, the merciless Indian Savages, whose known rule of warfare, is an undistinguished destruction of all ages, sexes and conditions.

In every stage of these Oppressions We have Petitioned for Redress in the most humble terms: Our repeated Petitions have been answered only by repeated injury. A Prince whose character is thus marked by every act which may define a Tyrant, is unfit to be the ruler of a free people.

Nor have We been wanting in attentions to our Brittish brethren. We have warned them from time to time of attempts by their legislature to extend an unwarrantable jurisdiction over us. We have reminded them of the circumstances of our emigration and settlement here. We have appealed to their native justice and magnanimity, and we have conjured them by the ties of our common kindred to disavow these usurpations, which, would inevitably interrupt our connections and correspondence. They too have been deaf to the voice of justice and of consanguinity. We must, therefore, acquiesce in the necessity, which denounces our Separation, and hold them, as we hold the rest of mankind, Enemies in War, in Peace Friends.

We, Therefore, the Representatives of the United States of America, in General Congress, Assembled, appealing to the Supreme Judge of the world for the rectitude of our intentions, do, in the Name, and by Authority of the good People of these Colonies, solemnly publish and declare, That these United Colonies are, and of Right ought to be Free and Independent States; that they are Absolved from all Allegiance to the British Crown, and that all political connection between them and the State of Great Britain, is and ought to be totally dissolved; and that as Free and Independent States, they have full Power to levy War, conclude Peace, contract Alliances, establish Commerce, and to do all other Acts and Things which Independent States may of right do. And for the support of this Declaration, with a firm reliance on the protection of divine Providence, we mutually pledge to each other our Lives, our Fortunes and our sacred Honor.

The foregoing Declaration was, by order of Congress, engrossed, and signed by the following members:

John Hancock

NEW HAMPSHIRE
Josiah Bartlett
William Whipple
Matthew Thornton

MASSACHUSETTS BAY
Samuel Adams
John Adams
Robert Treat Paine
Elbridge Gerry

RHODE ISLAND
Stephen Hopkins
William Ellery

CONNECTICUT
Roger Sherman
Samuel Huntington
William Williams
Oliver Wolcott

NEW YORK
William Floyd
Philip Livingston
Francis Lewis
Lewis Morris

NEW JERSEY
Richard Stockton
John Witherspoon
Francis Hopkinson
John Hart
Abraham Clark

PENNSYLVANIA
Robert Morris
Benjamin Rush
Benjamin Franklin
John Morton
George Clymer
James Smith
George Taylor
James Wilson
George Ross

DELAWARE
Caesar Rodney
George Read
Thomas M'Kean

MARYLAND
Samuel Chase
William Paca
Thomas Stone
Charles Carroll,
  of Carrollton

VIRGINIA
George Wythe
Richard Henry Lee
Thomas Jefferson
Benjamin Harrison
Thomas Nelson, Jr.
Francis Lightfoot Lee
Carter Braxton

NORTH CAROLINA
William Hooper
Joseph Hewes
John Penn

SOUTH CAROLINA
Edward Rutledge
Thomas Heyward, Jr.
Thomas Lynch, Jr.
Arthur Middleton

GEORGIA
Button Gwinnett
Lyman Hall
George Walton

Resolved, That copies of the Declaration be sent to the several assemblies, conventions, and committees, or councils of safety, and to the several commanding officers of the continental troops; that it be proclaimed in each of the United States, at the head of the army.

The Articles of Confederation

Agreed to by Congress November 15, 1777;
ratified and in force March 1, 1781

To all whom these Presents shall come, we the undersigned Delegates of the States affixed to our Names, send greeting. Whereas the Delegates of the United States of America, in Congress assembled, did, on the fifteenth day of November, in the Year of Our Lord One thousand Seven Hundred and Seventy seven, and in the Second Year of the Independence of America, agree to certain articles of Confederation and perpetual Union between the States of Newhampshire, Massachusetts-bay, Rhodeisland and Providence Plantations, Connecticut, New-York, New-Jersey, Pennsylvania, Delaware, Maryland, Virginia, North-Carolina, South-Carolina and Georgia in the words following, viz. "Articles of Confederation and perpetual Union between the states of Newhampshire, Massachusettsbay, Rhodeisland and Providence Plantations, Connecticut, New-York, New-Jersey, Pennsylvania, Delaware, Maryland, Virginia, North-Carolina, South-Carolina and Georgia.

Art. I. The Stile of this confederacy shall be "The United States of America."

Art. II. Each state retains its sovereignty, freedom and independence, and every Power, Jurisdiction and right, which is not by this confederation expressly delegated to the United States, in Congress assembled.

Art. III. The said states hereby severally enter into a firm league of friendship with each other, for their common defence, the security of their Liberties, and their mutual and general welfare, binding themselves to assist each other, against all force offered to, or attacks made upon them, or any of them, on account of religion, sovereignty, trade, or any other pretence whatever.

Art. IV. The better to secure and perpetuate mutual friendship and intercourse among the people of the different states in this union, the free inhabitants of each of these states, paupers, vagabonds and fugitives from Justice excepted, shall be entitled to all privileges and immunities of free citizens in the several states; and the people of each state shall have free ingress and regress to and from any other state, and shall enjoy therein all the privileges of trade and commerce, subject to the same duties, impositions and restrictions as the inhabitants thereof respectively, provided that such restriction shall not extend so far as to prevent the removal of property imported into any state, to any other state, of which the Owner is an inhabitant; provided also that no imposition, duties or restriction shall be laid by any state, on the property of the united states, or either of them.

If any Person guilty of, or charged with treason, felony, or other high misdemeanor in any state, shall flee from Justice, and be found in any of the united states, he shall, upon demand of the Governor or executive power, of the state from which he fled, be delivered up and removed to the state having jurisdiction of his offence.

Full faith and credit shall be given in each of these states to the records, acts and judicial proceedings of the courts and magistrates of every other state.

Art. V. For the more convenient management of the general interests of the united states, delegates shall be annually appointed in such manner as the legislature of each state shall direct, to meet in Congress on the first Monday in November, in every year, with a power reserved to each state, to recall its delegates, or any of them, at any time within the year, and to send others in their stead, for the remainder of the Year.

No state shall be represented in Congress by less than two, nor by more than seven Members; and no person shall be capable of being a delegate for more than three years in any term of six years; nor shall any person, being a delegate, be capable of holding any office under the united states, for which he, or another for his benefit receives any salary, fees or emolument of any kind.

Each state shall maintain its own delegates in a meeting of the states, and while they act as members of the committee of the states.

In determining questions in the united states, in Congress assembled, each state shall have one vote.

Freedom of speech and debate in Congress shall not be impeached or questioned in any Court, or place out of Congress, and the members of congress shall be protected in their persons from arrests and imprisonments, during the time of their going to and from, and attendance on congress, except for treason, felony, or breach of the peace.

Art. VI. No state without the Consent of the united states in congress assembled, shall send any embassy to, or receive any embassy from, or enter into any conference, agreement, or alliance or treaty with any King, prince or state; nor shall any person holding any office or profit or trust under the united states, or any of them, accept of any present, emolument, office or title of any kind whatever from any king, prince or foreign state; nor shall the united states in congress assembled, or any of them, grant any title of nobility.

No two or more states shall enter into any treaty, confederation or alliance whatever between them, without the consent of the united states in congress assembled, specifying accurately the purposes for which the same is to be entered into, and how long it shall continue.

No state shall lay any imposts or duties, which may interfere with any stipulations in treaties, entered into by the united states in congress assembled, with any king, prince or state, in pursuance of any treaties already proposed by congress, to the courts of France and Spain.

No vessels of war shall be kept up in time of peace by any state, except such number only, as shall be deemed necessary by the united states in congress assembled, for the defence of such state, or its trade; nor shall any body of forces be kept up by any state, in time of peace, except such number only, as in the judgment of the united states, in congress assembled, shall be deemed requisite to garrison the forts necessary for the defence of such state; but every state shall always keep up a well regulated and disciplined militia, sufficiently armed and accoutred, and shall provide and constantly have ready for use, in public stores, a due number of field pieces and tents, and a proper quantity of arms, ammunition and camp equipage.

No state shall engage in any war without the consent of the united states in congress assembled, unless such state be actually invaded by enemies, or shall have received certain advice of a resolution being formed by some nation of Indians to invade such state, and the danger is so imminent as not to admit of a delay, till the united states in congress asssembled can be consulted; nor shall any state grant commissions to any ships or vessels of war, nor letters of marque or reprisal, except it be after a declaration of war by the united states in congress assembled, and then only against the kingdom or state and the subjects thereof, against which war has been so declared, and under such regulations as shall be established by the united states in congress assembled, unless such state be infested by pirates; in which case vessels of war may be fitted out for that occasion, and kept so long as the danger shall continue, or until the united states in congress assembled shall determine otherwise.

Art. VII. When land-forces are raised by any state for the common defence, all officers of or under the rank of colonel, shall be appointed by the legislature of each state respectively, by whom such forces shall be raised, or in such manner as such state shall direct, and all vacancies shall be filled up by the state which first made the appointment.

Art. VIII. All charges of war, and all other expences that shall be incurred for the common defence or general welfare, and allowed by the united states in congress assembled, shall be defrayed out of a common treasury, which shall be supplied by the several states in proportion to the value of all land within each state, granted to or surveyed for any Person, as such land and the buildings and improvements thereon shall be estimated according to such mode as the united states in congress assembled, shall from time to time direct and appoint.

The taxes for paying that proportion shall be laid and levied by the authority and direction of the legislatures of the several states within the time agreed upon by the united states in congress assembled.

Art. IX. The united states in congress assembled, shall have the sole and exclusive right and power of determining on peace and war, except in the cases mentioned in the sixth article—of sending and receiving ambassadors—entering into treaties and alliances, provided that no treaty of commerce shall be made whereby the legislative power of the respective states shall be restrained from imposing such imposts and duties on foreigners, as their own people are subjected to, or from prohibiting the exportation of any species of goods or commodities whatsoever—of establishing rules for deciding in all cases, what captures on land or water shall be legal, and in what manner prizes taken by land or naval forces in the service of the united states shall be divided or appropriated—of granting letters of marque and reprisal in times of peace—appointing courts for the trial of piracies and felonies committed on the high seas and establishing courts for receiving and determining finally appeals in all cases of captures, provided that no member of congress shall be appointed a judge of any of the said courts.

The united states in congress assembled shall also be the last resort on appeal in all disputes and differences now subsisting or that hereafter may arise between two or more states concerning boundary, jurisdiction or any other cause whatever; which authority shall always be exercised in the manner following. Whenever the legislative or executive authority or lawful agent of any state in controversy with another shall present a petition to congress stating the matter in question and praying for a hearing, notice thereof shall be given by order of congress to the legislative or executive authority of the other state in controversy, and a day assigned for the appearance of the parties by their lawful agents, who shall then be directed to appoint by joint consent, commissioners or judges to constitute a court for hearing and determining the matter in question: but if they cannot agree, congress shall name three persons out of each of the united states, and from the list of such persons each party shall alternately strike out one, the petitioners beginning, until the number shall be reduced to thirteen; and from that number not less than seven, nor more than nine names as congress shall direct, shall in the presence of congress be drawn out by lot, and the persons whose names shall be so drawn or any five of them, shall be commissioners or judges, to hear and finally determine the controversy, so always as a major part of the judges who shall hear the cause shall agree in the determination: and if either party shall neglect to attend at the day appointed, without shewing reasons, which congress shall judge sufficient, or being present shall refuse to strike, the congress shall proceed to nominate three persons out of each state, and the secretary of congress shall strike in behalf of such party absent or refusing; and the judgment and sentence of the court to be appointed, in the manner before prescribed, shall be final and conclusive; and if any of the parties shall refuse to submit to the authority of such court, or to appear to defend their claim or cause, the court shall nevertheless proceed to pronounce sentence, or judgment, which shall in like manner be final and decisive, the judgment or sentence and other proceedings being in either case transmitted to congress, and lodged among the acts of congress for the security of the parties concerned: provided that every commissioner, before he sits in judgment, shall take an oath to be administered by one of the judges of the supreme or superior court of the state, where the cause shall be tried, "well and truly to hear and determine the matter in question, according to the best of his judgment, without favour, affection or hope of reward:" provided also, that no state shall be deprived of territory for the benefit of the united states.

All controversies concerning the private right of soil claimed under different grants of two or more states, whose jurisdictions as they may respect such lands, and the states which passed such grants are adjusted, the said grants or either of them being at the same time claimed to have originated antecedent to such settlement of jurisdiction, shall on the petition of either party to the congress of the united states, be finally determined as near as may be in the same manner as is before prescribed for deciding disputes respecting territorial jurisdiction between different states.

The united states in congress assembled shall also have the sole and exclusive right and power of regulating the alloy and value of coin struck by their own authority, or by that of the respective states—fixing the standard of weights and measures throughout the united states—regulating the trade and managing all affairs with the Indians, not members of any of the states, provided that the legislative right of any state within its own limits be not infringed or violated—establishing and regulating post-offices from one state to another, throughout all the united states, and exacting such postage on the papers passing thro' the same as may be requisite to defray the expences of the said office—appointing all officers of the land forces, in the service of the united states, excepting regimental officers—appointing all the officers of the naval forces, and commissioning all officers whatever in the service of the united states—making rules for the government and regulation of the said land and naval forces, and directing their operations.

The united states in congress assembled shall have authority to appoint a committee, to sit in the recess of congress, to be denominated "A Committee of the States," and to consist of one delegate from each state; and to appoint such other committees and civil officers as may be necessary for managing the general affairs of the united states under their direction—to appoint one of their number to preside, provided that no person be allowed to serve in the office of president more than one year in any term of three years; to ascertain the necessary sums of Money to be raised for the service of the united states, and to appropriate and apply the same for defraying the public expenses—to borrow money, or emit bills on the credit of the united states, transmitting every half year to the respective states an account of the sums of money so borrowed or emitted,—to build and equip a navy—to agree upon the number of land forces, and to make requisitions from each state for its quota, in proportion to the number of white inhabitants in such state; which requisition shall be binding, and thereupon the legislature of each state shall appoint the regimental officers, raise the men and cloath, arm and equip them in a soldier like manner, at the expense of the united states; and the officers and men so cloathed, armed and equipped shall march to the place appointed, and within the time agreed on by the united states in congress assembled: But if the united states in congress assembled shall, on consideration of circumstances judge proper that any state should not raise men, or should raise a smaller number than its quota, and that any other state should raise a greater number of men than the quota thereof, such extra number shall be raised, officered, cloathed, armed and equipped in the same manner as the quota of such state, unless the legislature of such state shall judge that such extra number cannot be safely spared out of the same, in which case they shall raise officer, cloath, arm and equip as many of such extra number as they judge can be safely spared. And the officers and men so cloathed, armed and equipped, shall march to the place appointed, and within the time agreed on by the united states in congress assembled.

The united states in congress assembled shall never engage in a war, nor grant letters of marque and reprisal in time of peace, nor enter into any treaties or alliances, nor coin money, nor regulate the value thereof, nor ascertain the sums and expenses necessary for the defence and welfare of the united states, or any of them, nor emit bills, nor borrow money on the credit of the united states, nor appropriate money, nor agree upon the number of vessels of war, to be built or purchased, or the number of land or sea forces to be raised, nor appoint a commander in chief of the army or navy, unless nine states assent to the same: nor shall a question on any other point, except for adjourning from day to day be determined, unless by the votes of a majority of the united states in congress assembled.

The congress of the united states shall have power to adjourn to any time within the year, and to any place within the united states, so that no period of adjournment be for a longer duration than the space of six Months, and shall publish the Journal of their proceedings monthly, except such parts thereof relating to treaties, alliances or military operations, as in their judgment require secrecy; and the yeas and nays of the delegates of each state on any question shall be entered on the Journal, when it is desired by any delegate; and the delegates of a state, or any of them, at his or their request shall be furnished with a transcript of the said Journal, except such parts as are above excepted, to lay before the legislatures of the several states.

Art. X. The committee of the states, or any nine of them, shall be authorised to execute, in the recess of congress, such of the powers of congress as the united states in congress assembled, by the consent of nine states, shall from time to time think expedient to vest them with; provided that no power be delegated to the said committee, for the exercise of which, by the articles of confederation, the voice of nine states in the congress of the united states assembled is requisite.

Art. XI. Canada acceding to this confederation, and joining in the measures of the united states, shall be admitted into, and entitled to all the advantages of this union: but no other colony shall be admitted into the same, unless such admission be agreed to by nine states.

Art. XII. All bills of credit emitted, monies borrowed and debts contracted by, or under the authority of congress, before the assembling of the united states, in pursuance of the present confederation, shall be deemed and considered as a charge against the united states, for payment and satisfaction whereof the said united states and the public faith are hereby solemnly pledged.

Art. XIII. Every state shall abide by the determinations of the united states in congress assembled, on all questions which by this confederation are submitted to them. And the Articles of this confederation shall be inviolably observed by every state, and the union shall be perpetual; nor shall any alteration at any time hereafter be made in any of them; unless such alteration be agreed to in a congress of the united states, and be afterwards confirmed by the legislatures of every state.

And Whereas it hath pleased the Great Governor of the World to incline the hearts of the legislatures we respectively represent in congress, to approve of, and to authorize us to ratify the said articles of confederation and perpetual union. Know Ye that we the undersigned delegates, by virtue of the power and authority to us given for that purpose, do by these presents, in the name and in behalf of our respective constituents, fully and entirely ratify and confirm each and every of the said articles of confederation and perpetual union, and all and singular the matters and things therein contained: And we do further solemnly plight and engage the faith of our respective constituents, that they shall abide by the determinations of the united states in congress assembled, on all questions, which by the said confederation are submitted to them. And that the articles thereof shall be inviolably observed by the states we respectively represent, and that the union shall be perpetual. In Witness whereof we have hereunto set our hands in Congress. Done at Philadelphia in the state of Pennsylvania the ninth day of July, in the Year of our Lord one Thousand seven Hundred and Seventy-eight, and in the third year of the independence of America.

The Constitution of the United States of America

We the People of the United States, in Order to form a more perfect Union, establish Justice, insure domestic Tranquility, provide for the common defence, promote the general Welfare, and secure the Blessings of Liberty to ourselves and our Posterity, do ordain and establish this Constitution for the United States of America.

Article I

SECTION 1

[LEGISLATIVE POWERS]

All legislative Powers herein granted shall be vested in a Congress of the United States, which shall consist of a Senate and House of Representatives.

SECTION 2

[HOUSE OF REPRESENTATIVES, HOW CONSTITUTED, POWER OF IMPEACHMENT]

The House of Representatives shall be composed of Members chosen every second Year by the People of the several States, and the Electors in each State shall have the Qualifications requisite for Electors of the most numerous Branch of the State Legislature.

No Person shall be a Representative who shall not have attained to the Age of twenty five Years, and been seven Years a Citizen of the United States, and who shall not, when elected, be an Inhabitant of that State in which he shall be chosen.

Representatives and *direct Taxes*[1] shall be apportioned among the several States which may be included within this Union, according to their respective Numbers, *which shall be determined by adding to the whole Number of free Persons, including those bound to Service for a Term of Years, and excluding Indians not taxed, three fifths of all other Persons.*[2] The actual Enumeration shall be made within three Years after the first Meeting of the Congress of the United States, and within every subsequent Term of ten Years, in such Manner as they shall by Law direct. The Number of Representatives shall not exceed one for every thirty Thousand, but each State shall have at Least one Representative; *and until such enumeration shall be made, the State of New Hampshire shall be entitled to chuse three, Massachusetts eight, Rhode-Island and Providence Plantations one, Connecticut five, New-York six, New Jersey four, Pennsylvania eight, Delaware one, Maryland six, Virginia ten, North Carolina five, South Carolina five, and Georgia three.*[3]

When vacancies happen in the Representation from any State, the Executive Authority thereof shall issue Writs of Election to fill such Vacancies.

The House of Representatives shall chuse their Speaker and other Officers; and shall have the sole Power of Impeachment.

SECTION 3

[THE SENATE, HOW CONSTITUTED, IMPEACHMENT TRIALS]

The Senate of the United States shall be composed of two Senators from each State, *chosen by the Legislature thereof,*[4] for six Years; and each Senator shall have one Vote.

Immediately after they shall be assembled in Consequence of the first Election, they shall be divided as equally as may be into three Classes. The Seats of the Senators of the first Class shall be vacated at the Expiration of the second Year, of the second Class at the Expiration of the fourth Year, and of the third Class at the Expiration of the sixth Year, so that one third may be chosen every second Year; *and if Vacancies happen by Resignation, or otherwise, during the Recess of the Legislature of any State, the Executive thereof may make temporary Appointments until the next Meeting of the Legislature, which shall then fill such Vacancies.*[5]

No Person shall be a Senator who shall not have attained to the Age of thirty Years, and been nine Years a Citizen of the United States, and who shall not, when elected, be an Inhabitant of that State for which he shall be chosen.

The Vice President of the United States shall be President of the Senate, but shall have no Vote, unless they be equally divided.

The Senate shall chuse their other Officers, and also a President pro tempore, in the Absence of the Vice President, or when he shall exercise the Office of President of the United States.

---

[1]Modified by Sixteenth Amendment.

[2]Modified by Fourteenth Amendment.

[3]Temporary provision.

[4]Modified by Seventeenth Amendment.

[5]Modified by Seventeenth Amendment.

The Senate shall have the sole Power to try all Impeachments. When sitting for that Purpose, they shall be on Oath or Affirmation. When the President of the United States is tried, the Chief Justice shall preside: And no Person shall be convicted without the Concurrence of two thirds of the Members present.

Judgment in Cases of Impeachment shall not extend further than to removal from Office, and disqualification to hold and enjoy any Office of honor, Trust or Profit under the United States: but the Party convicted shall nevertheless be liable and subject to Indictment, Trial, Judgment and Punishment, according to Law.

SECTION 4
[ELECTION OF SENATORS AND REPRESENTATIVES]
The Times, Places and Manner of holding Elections for Senators and Representatives, shall be prescribed in each State by the Legislature thereof; but the Congress may at any time by Law make or alter such Regulations, except as to the Places of chusing Senators.

The Congress shall assemble at least once in every Year, and such Meeting shall be on the first Monday in December, unless they shall by Law appoint a different Day.[6]

SECTION 5
[QUORUM, JOURNALS, MEETINGS, ADJOURNMENTS]
Each House shall be the Judge of the Elections, Returns and Qualifications of its own Members, and a Majority of each shall constitute a Quorum to do Business; but a smaller Number may adjourn from day to day, and may be authorized to compel the Attendance of absent Members, in such Manner, and under such Penalties as each House may provide.

Each House may determine the Rules of its Proceedings, punish its Members for disorderly Behaviour, and, with the Concurrence of two thirds, expel a Member.

Each House shall keep a Journal of its Proceedings, and from time to time publish the same, excepting such Parts as may in their Judgment require Secrecy; and the Yeas and Nays of the Members of either House on any questions shall, at the Desire of one fifth of those Present, be entered on the Journal.

Neither House, during the Session of Congress, shall, without the Consent of the other, adjourn for more than three days, nor to any other Place than that in which the two Houses shall be sitting.

SECTION 6
[COMPENSATION, PRIVILEGES, DISABILITIES]
The Senators and Representatives shall receive a Compensation for their Services, to be ascertained by Law, and paid out of the Treasury of the United States. They shall in all Cases, except Treason, Felony and Breach of the Peace, be privileged from Arrest during their Attendance at the Session of their respective Houses, and in going to and returning from the same; and for any Speech or Debate in either House, they shall not be questioned in any other Place.

No Senator or Representative shall, during the Time for which he was elected, be appointed to any civil Office under the Authority of the United States, which shall have been created, or the Emoluments whereof shall have been encreased during such time; and no Person holding any Office under the United States, shall be a Member of either House during his Continuance in Office.

SECTION 7
[PROCEDURE IN PASSING BILLS AND RESOLUTIONS]
All Bills for raising Revenue shall originate in the House of Representatives; but the Senate may propose or concur with Amendments as on other Bills.

Every Bill which shall have passed the House of Representatives and the Senate, shall, before it become a Law, be presented to the President of the United States: If he approve he shall sign it, but if not he shall return it, with his Objections to that House in which it shall have originated, who shall enter the Objections at large on their Journal, and proceed to reconsider it. If after such Reconsideration two thirds of that House shall agree to pass the Bill, it shall be sent, together with the Objections, to the other House, by which it shall likewise be reconsidered, and if approved by two thirds of that House, it shall become a Law. But in all such Cases the Votes of both Houses shall be determined by yeas and Nays, and the Names of the Persons voting for and against the Bill shall be entered on the Journal of each House respectively. If any Bill shall not be returned by the President within ten Days (Sundays excepted) after it shall have been presented to him, the Same shall be a Law, in like Manner as if he had signed it, unless the Congress by their Adjournment prevent its Return, in which Case it shall not be a Law.

Every Order, Resolution, or Vote to which the Concurrence of the Senate and House of Representatives may be necessary (except on a question of Adjournment) shall be presented to the President of the United States; and before the Same shall take Effect, shall be approved by him, or being disapproved by him, shall be repassed by two thirds of the Senate and House of Representatives, according to the Rules and Limitations prescribed in the Case of a Bill.

SECTION 8
[POWERS OF CONGRESS]
The Congress shall have Power

To lay and collect Taxes, Duties, Imposts and Excises, to pay the Debts and provide for the common Defence and general Welfare of the United States; but all Duties, Imposts and Excises shall be uniform throughout the United States;

To borrow Money on the credit of the United States;

---

[6]Modified by Twentieth Amendment.

To regulate Commerce with foreign Nations, and among the several States, and with the Indian Tribes;

To establish an uniform Rule of Naturalization, and uniform Laws on the subject of Bankruptcies throughout the United States;

To coin Money, regulate the Value thereof, and of foreign Coin, and fix the Standard of Weights and Measures;

To provide for the Punishment of counterfeiting the Securities and current Coin of the United States;

To establish Post Offices and post Roads;

To promote the Progress of Science and useful Arts, by securing for limited Times to Authors and Inventors the exclusive Right to their respective Writings and Discoveries;

To constitute Tribunals inferior to the supreme Court;

To define and punish Piracies and Felonies committed on the high Seas, and Offences against the Law of Nations;

To declare War, grant Letters of Marque and Reprisal, and make Rules concerning Captures on Land and Water;

To raise and support Armies, but no Appropriation of Money to that Use shall be for a longer Term than two Years;

To provide and maintain a Navy;

To make Rules for the Government and Regulation of the land and naval Forces;

To provide for calling forth the Militia to execute the Laws of the Union, suppress Insurrections and repel Invasions;

To provide for organizing, arming, and disciplining, the Militia, and for governing such Part of them as may be employed in the Service of the United States, reserving to the States respectively, the Appointment of the Officers, and the Authority of training the Militia according to the discipline prescribed by Congress;

To exercise exclusive Legislation in all Cases whatsoever, over such District (not exceeding ten Miles square) as may, by Cession of particular States, and the Acceptance of Congress, become the Seat of the Government of the United States, and to exercise like Authority over all Places purchased by the Consent of the Legislature of the State in which the Same shall be, for the Erection of Forts, Magazines, Arsenals, dock-Yards, and other needful Buildings;—And

To make all Laws which shall be necessary and proper for carrying into Execution the foregoing Powers, and all other Powers vested by this Constitution in the Government of the United States, or in any Department or Officer thereof.

SECTION 9
[SOME RESTRICTIONS ON FEDERAL POWER]
The Migration or Importation of such Persons as any of the States now existing shall think proper to admit, shall not be prohibited by the Congress prior to the Year one thousand eight hundred and eight, but a Tax or duty may be imposed on such Importation, not exceeding ten dollars for each Person.[7]

The Privilege of the Writ of Habeas Corpus shall not be suspended, unless when in Cases of Rebellion or Invasion the public Safety may require it.

No Bill of Attainder or ex post facto Law shall be passed.

No Capitation, or other direct, Tax shall be laid, unless in Proportion to the Census or Enumeration herein before directed to be taken.[8]

No Tax or Duty shall be laid on Articles exported from any State.

No Preference shall be given by any Regulation of Commerce or Revenue to the Ports of one State over those of another; nor shall Vessels bound to, or from, one State, be obliged to enter, clear, or pay Duties in another.

No Money shall be drawn from the Treasury, but in Consequence of Appropriations made by Law; and a regular Statement and Account of the Receipts and Expenditures of all public Money shall be published from time to time.

No Title of Nobility shall be granted by the United States: And no Person holding any Office of Profit or Trust under them, shall, without the Consent of the Congress, accept of any present, Emolument, Office, or Title, of any kind whatever, from any King, Prince, or foreign State.

SECTION 10
[RESTRICTIONS UPON POWERS OF STATES]
No State shall enter into any Treaty, Alliance, or Confederation; grant Letters of Marque and Reprisal; coin Money; emit Bills of Credit; make any Thing but gold and silver Coin a Tender in Payment of Debts; pass any Bill of Attainder, ex post facto Law, or Law impairing the Obligation of Contracts, or grant any Title of Nobility.

No State shall, without the Consent of the Congress, lay any Imposts or Duties on Imports or Exports, except what may be absolutely necessary for executing its inspection Laws: and the net Produce of all Duties and Imposts, laid by any State on Imports or Exports, shall be for the Use of the Treasury of the United States; and all such Laws shall be subject to the Revision and Control of the Congress.

No State shall, without the Consent of Congress, lay any Duty of Tonnage, keep Troops, or Ships of War in time of Peace, enter into any Agreement or Compact with another State, or with a foreign Power, or engage in War, unless actually invaded, or in such imminent Danger as will not admit of delay.

Article II

SECTION 1
[EXECUTIVE POWER, ELECTION,
QUALIFICATIONS OF THE PRESIDENT]
The executive Power shall be vested in a President of the United States of America. *He shall hold his Office during the Term of*

---

[7]Temporary provision.

[8]Modified by Sixteenth Amendment.

four *Years, and, together with the Vice President, chosen for the same Term, be elected, as follows*[9]

Each State shall appoint, in such Manner as the Legislature thereof may direct, a Number of Electors, equal to the whole Number of Senators and Representatives to which the State may be entitled in the Congress: but no Senator or Representative, or Person holding an Office of Trust or Profit under the United States, shall be appointed an Elector.

The electors shall meet in their respective States, and vote by ballot for two Persons, of whom one at least shall not be an Inhabitant of the same State with themselves. And they shall make a List of all the Persons voted for, and of the Number of Votes for each; which List they shall sign and certify, and transmit sealed to the Seat of the Government of the United States, directed to the President of the Senate. The President of the Senate shall, in the Presence of the Senate and House of Representatives, open all the Certificates, and the Votes shall then be counted. The Person having the greatest Number of Votes shall be the President, if such Number be a Majority of the whole Number of Electors appointed; and if there be more than one who have such Majority, and have an equal Number of Votes, then the House of Representatives shall immediately chuse by Ballot one of them for President; and if no Person have a Majority, then from the five highest on the List the said House shall in like Manner chuse the President. But in chusing the President, the Votes shall be taken by States, the Representation from each State having one Vote; A quorum for this Purpose shall consist of a Member or Members from two thirds of the States, and a Majority of all the States shall be necessary to a Choice. In every Case, after the Choice of the President, the person having the greatest Number of Votes of the Electors shall be the Vice President. But if there should remain two or more who have equal Votes, the Senate shall chuse from them by Ballot the Vice President.[10]

The Congress may determine the Time of chusing the Electors, and the Day on which they shall give their Votes; which Day shall be the same throughout the United States.

No Person except a natural born Citizen, or a Citizen of the United States, at the time of the Adoption of this Constitution, shall be eligible to the Office of President; neither shall any Person be eligible to that Office who shall not have attained to the Age of thirty five Years, and been fourteen Years a Resident within the United States.

In Case of the Removal of the President from Office, or his Death, Resignation, or Inability to discharge the Powers and Duties of the said Office, the Same shall devolve on the Vice President, and the Congress may by Law provide for the Case of Removal, Death, Resignation or Inability, both of the President and Vice President, declaring what Officer shall then act as President, and such Officer shall act accordingly, until the Disability be removed, or a President shall be elected.

---

[9]Number of terms limited to two by Twenty-Second Amendment.

[10]Modified by Twelfth and Twentieth Amendments.

The President shall, at stated Times, receive for his Services, a Compensation, which shall neither be increased nor diminished during the Period for which he shall have been elected, and he shall not receive within that Period any other Emolument from the United States, or any of them.

Before he enter on the Execution of his Office, he shall take the following Oath or Affirmation:—"I do solemnly swear (or affirm) that I will faithfully execute the Office of President of the United States, and will to the best of my Ability, preserve, protect and defend the Constitution of the United States."

SECTION 2
[POWERS OF THE PRESIDENT]
The President shall be Commander in Chief of the Army and Navy of the United States, and of the Militia of the several States, when called into the actual Service of the United States; he may require the Opinion, in writing, of the principal Officer in each of the executive Departments, upon any Subject relating to the Duties of their respective Offices, and he shall have Power to grant Reprieves and Pardons for Offences against the United States, except in Cases of Impeachment.

He shall have Power, by and with the Advice and Consent of the Senate, to make Treaties, provided two thirds of the Senators present concur; and he shall nominate, and by and with the Advice and Consent of the Senate, shall appoint Ambassadors, other public Ministers and Consuls, Judges of the supreme Court, and all other Officers of the United States, whose Appointments are not herein otherwise provided for, and which shall be established by Law: but the Congress may by Law vest the Appointment of such inferior Officers, as they think proper, in the President alone, in the Courts of Law, or in the Heads of Departments.

The President shall have Power to fill up all Vacancies that may happen during the Recess of the Senate, by granting Commissions which shall expire at the End of their next Session.

SECTION 3
[POWERS AND DUTIES OF THE PRESIDENT]
He shall from time to time give to the Congress Information of the State of the Union, and recommend to their Consideration such Measures as he shall judge necessary and expedient; he may, on extraordinary Occasions, convene both Houses, or either of them, and in Case of Disagreement between them, with Respect to the Time of Adjournment, he may adjourn them to such Time as he shall think proper; he shall receive Ambassadors and other public Ministers; he shall take Care that the Laws be faithfully executed, and shall Commission all the Officers of the United States.

SECTION 4
[IMPEACHMENT]
The President, Vice President and all civil Officers of the United States, shall be removed from Office on Impeachment for,

and Conviction of, Treason, Bribery, or other high Crimes and Misdemeanors.

Article III

SECTION 1

[JUDICIAL POWER, TENURE OF OFFICE]

The judicial Power of the United States, shall be vested in one supreme Court, and in such inferior Courts as the Congress may from time to time ordain and establish. The Judges, both of the supreme and inferior Courts, shall hold their Offices during good Behaviour, and shall, at stated Times, receive for their Services, a Compensation, which shall not be diminished during their Continuance in Office.

SECTION 2

[JURISDICTION]

The judicial Power shall extend to all Cases, in Law and Equity, arising under this Constitution, the Laws of the United States, and Treaties made, or which shall be made, under their Authority;— to all Cases affecting Ambassadors, other public Ministers and Consuls;—to all Cases of admiralty and maritime Jurisdiction;— to Controversies to which the United States shall be a Party;—to Controversies between two or more States;—*between a State and Citizens of another State;*—between Citizens of different States,— between Citizens of the same State claiming Lands under Grants of different States, *and between a State*, or the Citizens thereof, *and foreign States, Citizens or Subjects.*[11]

In all Cases affecting Ambassadors, other public Ministers and Consuls, and those in which a State shall be Party, the supreme Court shall have original Jurisdiction. In all the other Cases before mentioned, the supreme Court shall have appellate Jurisdiction, both as to Law and Fact, with such Exceptions, and under such Regulations as the Congress shall make.

The Trial of all Crimes, except in Cases of Impeachment, shall be by Jury; and such Trial shall be held in the State where the said Crimes shall have been committed; but when not committed within any State, the Trial shall be at such Place or Places as the Congress may by Law have directed.

SECTION 3

[TREASON, PROOF, AND PUNISHMENT]

Treason against the United States, shall consist only in levying War against them, or in adhering to their Enemies, giving them Aid and Comfort. No Person shall be convicted of Treason unless on the Testimony of two Witnesses to the same overt Act, or on Confession in open Court.

The Congress shall have Power to declare the Punishment of Treason, but no Attainder of Treason shall work Corruption of Blood, or Forfeiture except during the Life of the Person attainted.

Article IV

SECTION 1

[FAITH AND CREDIT AMONG STATES]

Full Faith and Credit shall be given in each State to the public Acts, Records, and judicial Proceedings of every other State. And the Congress may by general Laws prescribe the Manner in which such Acts, Records and Proceedings shall be proved, and the Effect thereof.

SECTION 2

[PRIVILEGES AND IMMUNITIES, FUGITIVES]

The Citizens of each State shall be entitled to all Privileges and Immunities of Citizens in the several States.

A Person charged in any State with Treason, Felony or other Crime, who shall flee from Justice, and be found in another State, shall on Demand of the executive Authority of the State from which he fled, be delivered up, to be removed to the State having Jurisdiction of the Crime.

No person held to Service or Labour in one State, under the Laws thereof, escaping into another, shall, in Consequence of any Law or Regulation therein, be discharged from such Service or Labour, but shall be delivered up on Claim of the Party to whom such Service or Labour may be due.[12]

SECTION 3

[ADMISSION OF NEW STATES]

New States may be admitted by the Congress into this Union; but no new State shall be formed or erected within the Jurisdiction of any other State; nor any State be formed by the Junction of two or more States, or Parts of States, without the Consent of the Legislatures of the States concerned as well as of the Congress.

The Congress shall have Power to dispose of and make all needful Rules and Regulations respecting the Territory or other Property belonging to the United States; and nothing in this Constitution shall be so construed as to Prejudice any Claims of the United States, or of any particular State.

SECTION 4

[GUARANTEE OF REPUBLICAN GOVERNMENT]

The United States shall guarantee to every State in this Union a Republican Form of Government, and shall protect each of them against Invasion; and on Application of the Legislature, or of the Executive (when the Legislature cannot be convened), against domestic Violence.

Article V

[AMENDMENT OF THE CONSTITUTION]

The Congress, whenever two thirds of both Houses shall deem it necessary, shall propose Amendments to this Constitution, or, on the Application of the Legislatures of two thirds of the

---

[11]Modified by Eleventh Amendment.

[12]Repealed by the Thirteenth Amendment.

several States, shall call a Convention for proposing Amendments, which, in either Case, shall be valid to all Intents and Purposes, as Part of this Constitution, when ratified by the Legislatures of three fourths of the several States, or by Conventions in three fourths thereof, as the one or the other Mode of Ratification may be proposed by the Congress; *Provided that no Amendment which may be made prior to the Year One thousand eight hundred and eight shall in any Manner affect the first and fourth Clauses in the Ninth Section of the first Article;*[13] and that no State, without its Consent, shall be deprived of its equal Suffrage in the Senate.

Article VI

[DEBTS, SUPREMACY, OATH]

All Debts contracted and Engagements entered into, before the Adoption of this Constitution, shall be as valid against the United States under this Constitution, as under the Confederation.

This Constitution, and the Laws of the United States which shall be made in Pursuance thereof; and all Treaties made, or which shall be made, under the Authority of the United States, shall be the supreme Law of the Land; and the Judges in every

---

[13]Temporary provision.

State shall be bound thereby, any Thing in the Constitution or Laws of any State to the Contrary notwithstanding.

The Senators and Representatives before mentioned, and the Members of the several State Legislatures, and all executive and judicial Officers, both of the United States and of the several States, shall be bound by Oath or Affirmation, to support this Constitution; but no religious Test shall be required as a Qualification to any Office or public Trust under the United States.

Article VII

[RATIFICATION AND ESTABLISHMENT]

The Ratification of the Conventions of nine States, shall be sufficient for the Establishment of this Constitution between the States so ratifying the Same.[14]

Done in Convention by the Unanimous Consent of the States present the Seventeenth Day of September in the Year of our Lord one thousand seven hundred and Eighty seven and of the Independence of the United States of America the Twelfth. *In Witness* whereof We have hereunto subscribed our Names,

---

[14]The Constitution was submitted on September 17, 1787, by the Constitutional Convention, was ratified by the conventions of several states at various dates up to May 29, 1790, and became effective on March 4, 1789.

G:[0] *WASHINGTON—*
Presidt. and deputy from Virginia

NEW HAMPSHIRE
John Langdon
Nicholas Gilman

MASSACHUSETTS
Nathaniel Gorham
Rufus King

CONNECTICUT
Wm. Saml. Johnson
Roger Sherman

NEW YORK
Alexander Hamilton

NEW JERSEY
Wil: Livingston
David Brearley
Wm. Paterson
Jona: Dayton

PENNSYLVANIA
B Franklin
Thomas Mifflin
Robt. Morris
Geo. Clymer
Thos. FitzSimons
Jared Ingersoll
James Wilson
Gouv Morris

DELAWARE
Geo: Read
Gunning Bedford jun
John Dickinson
Richard Bassett
Jaco: Broom

MARYLAND
James McHenry
Dan of St Thos. Jenifer
Danl. Carroll

VIRGINIA
John Blair—
James Madison Jr.

NORTH CAROLINA
Wm. Blount
Richd. Dobbs Spaight
Hu Williamson

SOUTH CAROLINA
J. Rutledge
Charles Cotesworth
Pinckney
Charles Pinckney
Pierce Butler

GEORGIA
William Few
Abr Baldwin

Amendments to the Constitution

Proposed by Congress and Ratified by the Legislatures of the Several States, Pursuant to Article V of the Original Constitution.

Amendments I–X, known as the Bill of Rights, were proposed by Congress on September 25, 1789, and ratified on December 15, 1791.

Amendment I

[FREEDOM OF RELIGION, OF SPEECH, AND OF THE PRESS]
Congress shall make no law respecting an establishment of religion, or prohibiting the free exercise thereof; or abridging the freedom of speech, or of the press; or the right of the people peaceably to assemble, and to petition the Government for a redress of grievances.

Amendment II

[RIGHT TO KEEP AND BEAR ARMS]
A well regulated Militia, being necessary to the security of a free State, the right of the people to keep and bear Arms, shall not be infringed.

Amendment III

[QUARTERING OF SOLDIERS]
No Soldier shall, in time of peace be quartered in any house, without the consent of the Owner, nor in time of war, but in a manner to be prescribed by law.

Amendment IV

[SECURITY FROM UNWARRANTABLE SEARCH AND SEIZURE]
The right of the people to be secure in their persons, houses, papers, and effects, against unreasonable searches and seizures, shall not be violated, and no Warrants shall issue, but upon probable cause, supported by Oath or affirmation, and particularly describing the place to be searched, and the persons or things to be seized.

Amendment V

[RIGHTS OF ACCUSED PERSONS IN CRIMINAL PROCEEDINGS]
No person shall be held to answer for a capital, or otherwise infamous crime, unless on a presentment or indictment of a Grand Jury, except in cases arising in the land or naval forces, or in the Militia, when in actual service in time of War or in public danger; nor shall any person be subject for the same offence to be twice put in jeopardy of life or limb; nor shall be compelled in any criminal case to be a witness against himself, nor be deprived of life, liberty, or property, without due process of law; nor shall private property be taken for public use, without just compensation.

Amendment VI

[RIGHT TO SPEEDY TRIAL, WITNESSES, ETC.]
In all criminal prosecutions, the accused shall enjoy the right to a speedy and public trial, by an impartial jury of the State and district wherein the crime shall have been committed, which district shall have been previously ascertained by law, and to be informed of the nature and cause of the accusation; to be confronted with the witnesses against him; to have compulsory process for obtaining witnesses in his favor, and to have the Assistance of Counsel for his defence.

Amendment VII

[TRIAL BY JURY IN CIVIL CASES]
In suits at common law, where the value in controversy shall exceed twenty dollars, the right of trial by jury shall be preserved, and no fact tried by a jury, shall be otherwise reexamined in any Court of the United States, than according to the rules of the common law.

Amendment VIII

[BAILS, FINES, PUNISHMENTS]
Excessive bail shall not be required, nor excessive fines imposed, nor cruel and unusual punishments inflicted.

Amendment IX

[RESERVATION OF RIGHTS OF PEOPLE]
The enumeration in the Constitution, of certain rights, shall not be construed to deny or disparage others retained by the people.

Amendment X

[POWERS RESERVED TO STATES OR PEOPLE]
The powers not delegated to the United States by the Constitution, nor prohibited by it to the States, are reserved to the States respectively, or to the people.

Amendment XI

[*Proposed by Congress on March 4, 1794;
declared ratified on January 8, 1798.*]
[RESTRICTION OF JUDICIAL POWER]
The Judicial power of the United States shall not be construed to extend to any suit in law or equity, commenced or prosecuted against one of the United States by Citizens of another State, or by Citizens or Subjects of any Foreign State.

Amendment XII

[*Proposed by Congress on December 9, 1803;
declared ratified on September 25, 1804.*]
[ELECTION OF PRESIDENT AND VICE PRESIDENT]
The Electors shall meet in their respective states and vote by ballot for President and Vice-President, one of whom, at least, shall not be an inhabitant of the same state with themselves; they shall name in their ballots the person voted for as President, and in distinct ballots the person voted for as Vice-President, and they shall make distinct lists of all persons voted for as President, and of all persons voted for as Vice-President, and of the number of votes for each, which lists they shall sign and certify, and transmit sealed to the seat of the government of the United States, directed to the President of the Senate;—the President of the Senate shall, in presence of the Senate and House of Representatives, open all the certificates and the votes shall then be counted;—The person having the greatest number of votes for President, shall be the President, if such number be a majority of the whole number of Electors appointed; and if no person have such majority, then from the persons having the highest numbers not exceeding three on the list of those voted for as President, the House of Representatives shall choose immediately, by ballot, the President. But in choosing the President, the votes shall be taken by states, the representation from each state having one vote; a quorum for this purpose shall consist of a member or members from two-thirds of the states, and a majority of all the states shall be necessary to a choice. And if the House of Representatives shall not choose a President whenever the right of choice shall devolve upon them, before the fourth day of March next following, then the Vice-President shall act as President, as in the case of the death or other constitutional disability of the President.—The person having the greatest number of votes as Vice-President, shall be the Vice-President, if such number be a majority of the whole number of Electors appointed, and if no person have a majority, then from the two highest numbers on the list, the Senate shall choose the Vice-President; a quorum for the purpose shall consist of two-thirds of the whole number of Senators, and a majority of the whole number shall be necessary to a choice. But no person constitutionally ineligible to the office of President shall be eligible to that of Vice-President of the United States.

Amendment XIII

[*Proposed by Congress on January 31, 1865;
declared ratified on December 18, 1865.*]

SECTION 1
[ABOLITION OF SLAVERY]
Neither slavery nor involuntary servitude, except as a punishment for crime whereof the party shall have been duly convicted, shall exist within the United States, or any place subject to their jurisdiction.

SECTION 2
[POWER TO ENFORCE THIS ARTICLE]
Congress shall have power to enforce this article by appropriate legislation.

Amendment XIV

[*Proposed by Congress on June 13, 1866;
declared ratified on July 28, 1868.*]

SECTION 1
[CITIZENSHIP RIGHTS NOT TO BE ABRIDGED BY STATES]
All persons born or naturalized in the United States, and subject to the jurisdiction thereof, are citizens of the United States and of the State wherein they reside. No State shall make or enforce any law which shall abridge the privileges or immunities of citizens of the United States; nor shall any State deprive any person of life, liberty, or property, without due process of law; nor deny to any person within its jurisdiction the equal protection of the laws.

SECTION 2
[APPORTIONMENT OF REPRESENTATIVES IN CONGRESS]
Representatives shall be apportioned among the several States according to their respective numbers, counting the whole number of persons in each State, excluding Indians not taxed. But when the right to vote at any election for the choice of electors for President and Vice-President of the United States, Representatives in Congress, the Executive and Judicial officers of a State, or the members of the Legislature thereof, is denied to any of the male inhabitants of such State, being twenty-one years of age, and citizens of the United States, or in any way abridged, except for participation in rebellion, or other crime, the basis of representation therein shall be reduced in the proportion which the number of such male citizens shall bear to the whole number of male citizens twenty-one years of age in such State.

SECTION 3
[PERSONS DISQUALIFIED FROM HOLDING OFFICE]
No person shall be a Senator or Representative in Congress, or elector of President and Vice-President, or hold any office, civil or military, under the United States, or under any State, who,

having previously taken an oath, as a member of Congress, or as an officer of the United States, or as a member of any State legislature, or as an executive or judicial officer of any State, to support the Constitution of the United States, shall have engaged in insurrection or rebellion against the same, or given aid or comfort to the enemies thereof. But Congress may by a vote of two-thirds of each House, remove such disability.

SECTION 4
[WHAT PUBLIC DEBTS ARE VALID]
The validity of the public debt of the United States, authorized by law, including debts incurred for payment of pensions and bounties for services in suppressing insurrection or rebellion, shall not be questioned. But neither the United States nor any State shall assume or pay any debt or obligation incurred in aid of insurrection or rebellion against the United States, or any claim for the loss or emancipation of any slave; but all such debts, obligations and claims shall be held illegal and void.

SECTION 5
[POWER TO ENFORCE THIS ARTICLE]
The Congress shall have power to enforce, by appropriate legislation, the provisions of this article.

Amendment XV
[*Proposed by Congress on February 26, 1869;*
declared ratified on March 30, 1870.]

SECTION 1
[NEGRO SUFFRAGE]
The right of citizens of the United States to vote shall not be denied or abridged by the United States or by any State on account of race, color, or previous condition of servitude.

SECTION 2
[POWER TO ENFORCE THIS ARTICLE]
The Congress shall have power to enforce this article by appropriate legislation.

Amendment XVI
[*Proposed by Congress on July 2, 1909;*
declared ratified on February 25, 1913.]
[AUTHORIZING INCOME TAXES]
The Congress shall have power to lay and collect taxes on incomes, from whatever source derived, without apportionment among the several States, and without regard to any census or enumeration.

Amendment XVII
[*Proposed by Congress on May 13, 1912;*
declared ratified on May 31, 1913.]
[POPULAR ELECTION OF SENATORS]
The Senate of the United States shall be composed of two Senators from each State, elected by the people thereof, for six years; and each Senator shall have one vote. The electors in each State shall have the qualifications requisite for electors of the most numerous branch of the State legislatures.

When vacancies happen in the representation of any State in the Senate, the executive authority of such State shall issue writs of election to fill such vacancies: *Provided*, That the legislature of any State may empower the executive thereof to make temporary appointments until the people fill the vacancies by election as the legislature may direct.

This amendment shall not be so construed as to affect the election or term of any Senator chosen before it becomes valid as part of the Constitution.

Amendment XVIII
[*Proposed by Congress December 18, 1917;*
declared ratified on January 29, 1919.]

SECTION 1
[NATIONAL LIQUOR PROHIBITION]
After one year from the ratification of this article the manufacture, sale, or transportation of intoxicating liquors within, the importation thereof into, or the exportation thereof from the United States and all territory subject to the jurisdiction thereof for beverage purposes is hereby prohibited.

SECTION 2
[POWER TO ENFORCE THIS ARTICLE]
The Congress and the several States shall have concurrent power to enforce this article by appropriate legislation.

SECTION 3
[RATIFICATION WITHIN SEVEN YEARS]
This article shall be inoperative unless it shall have been ratified as an amendment to the Constitution by the legislatures of the several States, as provided in the Constitution, within seven years from the date of the submission hereof to the States by the Congress.[1]

Amendment XIX
[*Proposed by Congress on June 4, 1919;*
declared ratified on August 26, 1920.]
[WOMAN SUFFRAGE]
The right of citizens of the United States to vote shall not be denied or abridged by the United States or by any State on account of sex.

Congress shall have power to enforce this article by appropriate legislation.

---

[1]Repealed by the Twenty-First Amendment.

Amendment XX

[*Proposed by Congress on March 2, 1932;
declared ratified on February 6, 1933.*]

SECTION 1
[TERMS OF OFFICE]
The terms of the President and Vice President shall end at noon on the 20th day of January, and the terms of Senators and Representatives at noon on the 3d day of January, of the years in which such terms would have ended if this article had not been ratified; and the terms of their successors shall then begin.

SECTION 2
[TIME OF CONVENING CONGRESS]
The Congress shall assemble at least once in every year, and such meeting shall begin at noon on the 3d day of January, unless they shall by law appoint a different day.

SECTION 3
[DEATH OF PRESIDENT-ELECT]
If, at the time fixed for the beginning of the term of the President, the President elect shall have died, the Vice President elect shall become President. If a President shall not have been chosen before the time fixed for the beginning of his term, or if the President elect shall have failed to qualify, then the Vice President elect shall act as President until a President shall have qualified; and the Congress may by law provide for the case wherein neither a President elect nor a Vice President elect shall have qualified, declaring who shall then act as President, or the manner in which one who is to act shall be selected, and such person shall act accordingly until a President or Vice President shall have qualified.

SECTION 4
[ELECTION OF THE PRESIDENT]
The Congress may by law provide for the case of the death of any of the persons from whom the House of Representatives may choose a President whenever the right of choice shall have devolved upon them, and for the case of the death of any of the persons from whom the Senate may choose a Vice President whenever the right of choice shall have devolved upon them.

SECTION 5
[AMENDMENT TAKES EFFECT]
Sections 1 and 2 shall take effect on the 15th day of October following the ratification of this article.

SECTION 6
[RATIFICATION WITHIN SEVEN YEARS]
This article shall be inoperative unless it shall have been ratified as an amendment to the Constitution by the legislatures of three-fourths of the several States within seven years from the date of its submission.

Amendment XXI

[*Proposed by Congress on February 20, 1933;
declared ratified on December 5, 1933.*]

SECTION 1
[NATIONAL LIQUOR PROHIBITION REPEALED]
The eighteenth article of amendment to the Constitution of the United States is hereby repealed.

SECTION 2
[TRANSPORTATION OF LIQUOR INTO "DRY" STATES]
The transportation or importation into any State, Territory, or Possession of the United States for delivery or use therein of intoxicating liquors, in violation of the laws thereof, is hereby prohibited.

SECTION 3
[RATIFICATION WITHIN SEVEN YEARS]
This article shall be inoperative unless it shall have been ratified as an amendment to the Constitution by conventions in the several States, as provided in the Constitution, within seven years from the date of the submission hereof to the States by the Congress.

Amendment XXII

[*Proposed by Congress on March 21, 1947;
declared ratified on February 27, 1951.*]

SECTION 1
[TENURE OF PRESIDENT LIMITED]
No person shall be elected to the office of President more than twice, and no person who has held the office of President or acted as President, for more than two years of a term to which some other person was elected President shall be elected to the office of the President more than once. But this Article shall not apply to any person holding the office of President when this Article was proposed by the Congress, and shall not prevent any person who may be holding the office of President, or acting as President, during the term within which this Article becomes operative from holding the office of President or acting as President during the remainder of such term.

SECTION 2
[RATIFICATION WITHIN SEVEN YEARS]
This article shall be inoperative unless it shall have been ratified as an amendment to the Constitution by the legislatures of three-fourths of the several States within seven years from the date of its submission to the States by the Congress.

Amendment XXIII

[*Proposed by Congress on June 16, 1960;
declared ratified on March 29, 1961.*]

SECTION 1

[ELECTORAL COLLEGE VOTES FOR THE DISTRICT OF COLUMBIA]
The District constituting the seat of Government of the United States shall appoint in such manner as the Congress may direct:

A number of electors of President and Vice President equal to the whole number of Senators and Representatives in Congress to which the District would be entitled if it were a State, but in no event more than the least populous State; they shall be in addition to those appointed by the States, but they shall be considered, for the purposes of the election of President and Vice President, to be electors appointed by a State; and they shall meet in the District and perform such duties as provided by the twelfth article of amendment.

SECTION 2

[POWER TO ENFORCE THIS ARTICLE]
The Congress shall have power to enforce this article by appropriate legislation.

Amendment XXIV

[*Proposed by Congress on August 27, 1962;
declared ratified on January 23, 1964.*]

SECTION 1

[ANTI-POLL TAX]
The right of citizens of the United States to vote in any primary or other election for President or Vice President, for electors for President or Vice President, or for Senator or Representative of Congress, shall not be denied or abridged by the United States or any State by reason of failure to pay any poll tax or other tax.

SECTION 2

[POWER TO ENFORCE THIS ARTICLE]
The Congress shall have power to enforce this article by appropriate legislation.

Amendment XXV

[*Proposed by Congress on July 6, 1965;
declared ratified on February 10, 1967.*]

SECTION 1

[VICE PRESIDENT TO BECOME PRESIDENT]
In case of the removal of the President from office or his death or resignation, the Vice President shall become President.

SECTION 2

[CHOICE OF A NEW VICE PRESIDENT]
Whenever there is a vacancy in the office of the Vice President, the President shall nominate a Vice President who shall take the office upon confirmation by a majority vote of both houses of Congress.

SECTION 3

[PRESIDENT MAY DECLARE OWN DISABILITY]
Whenever the President transmits to the President pro tempore of the Senate and the Speaker of the House of Representatives his written declaration that he is unable to discharge the powers and duties of his office, and until he transmits to them a written declaration to the contrary, such powers and duties shall be discharged by the Vice President as Acting President.

SECTION 4

[ALTERNATE PROCEDURES TO DECLARE AND
TO END PRESIDENTIAL DISABILITY]
Whenever the Vice President and a majority of either the principal officers of the executive departments, or of such other body as Congress may by law provide, transmit to the President pro tempore of the Senate and the Speaker of the House of Representatives their written declaration that the President is unable to discharge the powers and duties of his office, the Vice President shall immediately assume the powers and duties of the office as Acting President.

Thereafter, when the President transmits to the President pro tempore of the Senate and the Speaker of the House of Representatives his written declaration that no inability exists, he shall resume the powers and duties of his office unless the Vice President and a majority of either the principal officers of the executive department, or of such other body as Congress may by law provide, transmit within four days to the President pro tempore of the Senate and the Speaker of the House of Representatives their written declaration that the President is unable to discharge the powers and duties of his office. Thereupon Congress shall decide the issue, assembling within forty eight hours for that purpose if not in session. If the Congress, within twenty one days after receipt of the latter written declaration, or, if Congress is not in session, within twenty one days after Congress is required to assemble, determines by two-thirds vote of both Houses that the President is unable to discharge the powers and duties of his office, the Vice President shall continue to discharge the same as Acting President; otherwise, the President shall resume the powers and duties of his office.

Amendment XXVI

[*Proposed by Congress on March 23, 1971;
declared ratified on July 1, 1971.*]

SECTION 1

[EIGHTEEN-YEAR-OLD VOTE]

The right of citizens of the United States, who are eighteen years of age or older, to vote shall not be denied or abridged by the United States or by any State on account of age.

SECTION 2

[POWER TO ENFORCE THIS ARTICLE]

The Congress shall have power to enforce this article by appropriate legislation.

Amendment XXVII

[*Proposed by Congress on September 25, 1789;
declared ratified on May 8, 1992.*]

[CONGRESS CANNOT RAISE ITS OWN PAY]

No law varying the compensation for the services of the Senators and Representatives, shall take effect, until an election of representatives shall have intervened.

The Federalist Papers

No. 10: Madison

Among the numerous advantages promised by a well constructed Union, none deserves to be more accurately developed than its tendency to break and control the violence of faction. The friend of popular governments never finds himself so much alarmed for their character and fate, as when he contemplates their propensity to this dangerous vice. He will not fail therefore to set a due value on any plan which, without violating the principles to which he is attached, provides a proper cure for it. The instability, injustice, and confusion introduced into the public councils have, in truth, been the mortal diseases under which popular governments have everywhere perished, as they continue to be the favorite and fruitful topics from which the adversaries to liberty derive their most specious declamations. The valuable improvements made by the American constitutions on the popular models, both ancient and modern, cannot certainly be too much admired; but it would be an unwarrantable partiality to contend that they have as effectually obviated the danger on this side, as was wished and expected. Complaints are everywhere heard from our most considerate and virtuous citizens, equally the friends of public and private faith and of public and personal liberty, that our governments are too unstable, that the public good is disregarded in the conflicts of rival parties, and that measures are too often decided, not according to the rules of justice and the rights of the minor party, but by the superior force of an interested and overbearing majority. However anxiously we may wish that these complaints had no foundation, the evidence of known facts will not permit us to deny that they are in some degree true. It will be found, indeed, on a candid review of our situation, that some of the distresses under which we labor have been erroneously charged on the operation of our governments; but it will be found, at the same time, that other causes will not alone account for many of our heaviest misfortunes; and, particularly, for that prevailing and increasing distrust of public engagements and alarm for private rights which are echoed from one end of the continent to the other. These must be chiefly, if not wholly, effects of the unsteadiness and injustice with which a factious spirit has tainted our public administration.

By a faction I understand a number of citizens, whether amounting to a majority or minority of the whole, who are united and actuated by some common impulse of passion, or of interest, adverse to the rights of other citizens, or to the permanent and aggregate interests of the community.

There are two methods of curing the mischiefs of faction: the one, by removing its causes; the other, by controlling its effects.

There are again two methods of removing the causes of faction: the one, by destroying the liberty which is essential to its existence; the other, by giving to every citizen the same opinions, the same passions, and the same interests.

It could never be more truly said than of the first remedy, that it is worse than the disease. Liberty is to faction what air is to fire, an aliment without which it instantly expires. But it could not be a less folly to abolish liberty, which is essential to political life, because it nourishes faction, than it would be to wish the annihilation of air, which is essential to animal life, because it imparts to fire its destructive agency.

The second expedient is as impracticable, as the first would be unwise. As long as the reason of man continues fallible, and he is at liberty to exercise it, different opinions will be formed. As long as the connection subsists between his reason and his self-love, his opinions and his passions will have a reciprocal influence on each other; and the former will be objects to which the latter will attach themselves. The diversity in the faculties of men, from which the rights of property originate, is not less an insuperable obstacle to a uniformity of interests. The protection of these faculties is the first object of Government. From the protection of different and unequal faculties of acquiring property, the possession of different degrees and kinds of property immediately results; and from the influence of these on the sentiments and views of the respective proprietors, ensues a division of the society into different interests and parties.

The latent causes of faction are thus sown in the nature of man; and we see them everywhere brought into different degrees of activity, according to the different circumstances of civil society. A zeal for different opinions concerning religion, concerning Government, and many other points, as well of speculation as of practice; an attachment to different leaders ambitiously contending for pre-eminence and power; or to persons of other descriptions whose fortunes have been interesting to the human passions, have in turn divided mankind into parties, inflamed them with mutual animosity, and rendered them much more disposed to vex and oppress each other, than to co-operate for their common good. So strong is this propensity of mankind to fall into mutual animosities, that where no substantial occasion presents itself, the most frivolous and fanciful distinctions have been sufficient to kindle their unfriendly passions, and excite their most violent conflicts. But the most common and durable source of factions has been the various and unequal distribution of property. Those who hold and those who are without property have ever formed distinct interests in society. Those who are creditors, and those who are debtors, fall under a like discrimination. A landed interest, a manufacturing interest, a mercantile interest, a moneyed interest, with many lesser interests, grow up of necessity in civilized nations, and divide them into different classes, actuated by different sentiments and views. The regulation of these various and interfering interests forms the principal task of modern Legislation, and involves the spirit of party and faction in the necessary and ordinary operations of Government.

No man is allowed to be judge in his own cause, because his interest would certainly bias his judgment and, not improbably, corrupt his integrity. With equal, nay with greater reason, a body of men are unfit to be both judges and parties at the same time; yet what are many of the most important acts of legislation but so many judicial determinations, not indeed concerning the rights of single persons, but concerning the rights of large bodies of citizens; and what are the different classes of legislators but advocates and parties to the causes which they determine? Is a law proposed concerning private debts? It is a question to which the creditors are parties on one side and the debtors on the other. Justice ought to hold the balance between them. Yet the parties are, and must be, themselves the judges; and the most numerous party, or in other words, the most powerful faction must be expected to prevail. Shall domestic manufacturers be encouraged, and in what degree, by restrictions on foreign manufacturers? are questions which would be differently decided by the landed and the manufacturing classes, and probably by neither with a sole regard to justice and the public good. The apportionment of taxes on the various descriptions of property is an act which seems to require the most exact impartiality; yet there is, perhaps, no legislative act in which greater opportunity and temptation are given to a predominant party to trample on the rules of justice. Every shilling with which they overburden the inferior number is a shilling saved to their own pockets.

It is in vain to say that enlightened statesmen will be able to adjust these clashing interests and render them all subservient to the public good. Enlightened statesmen will not always be at the helm. Nor, in many cases, can such an adjustment be made at all without taking into view indirect and remote considerations, which will rarely prevail over the immediate interest which one party may find in disregarding the rights of another or the good of the whole.

The inference to which we are brought is that the *causes* of faction cannot be removed and that relief is only to be sought in the means of controlling its *effects*.

If a faction consists of less than a majority, relief is supplied by the republican principle, which enables the majority to defeat its sinister views by regular vote. It may clog the administration, it may convulse the society; but it will be unable to execute and mask its violence under the forms of the Constitution. When a majority is included in a faction, the form of popular government, on the other hand, enables it to sacrifice to its ruling passion or interest both the public good and the rights of other citizens. To secure the public good and private rights against the danger of such a faction, and at the same time to preserve the spirit and the form of popular government, is then the great object to which our enquiries are directed. Let me add that it is the great desideratum by which alone this form of government can be rescued from the opprobrium under which it has so long labored and be recommended to the esteem and adoption of mankind.

By what means is this object attainable? Evidently by one of two only. Either the existence of the same passion or interest in a majority at the same time must be prevented, or the majority, having such co-existent passion or interest, must be rendered, by their number and local situation, unable to concert and carry into effect schemes of oppression. If the impulse and the opportunity be suffered to coincide, we well know that neither moral nor religious motives can be relied on as an adequate control. They are not found to be such on the injustice and violence of individuals, and lose their efficacy in proportion to the number combined together, that is, in proportion as their efficacy becomes needful.

From this view of the subject it may be concluded that a pure Democracy, by which I mean a Society consisting of a small number of citizens, who assemble and administer the Government in person, can admit of no cure for the mischiefs of faction. A common passion or interest will, in almost every case, be felt by a majority of the whole; a communication and concert results from the form of Government itself; and there is nothing to check the inducements to sacrifice the weaker party or an obnoxious individual. Hence it is that such Democracies have ever been spectacles of turbulence and contention; have ever been found incompatible with personal security or the rights of property; and have in general been as short in their lives as they have been violent in their deaths. Theoretic politicians, who have patronized this species of Government, have erroneously supposed that by reducing mankind to a perfect equality in their political rights, they would at the same time be perfectly equalized and assimilated in their possessions, their opinions, and their passions.

A Republic, by which I mean a Government in which the scheme of representation takes place, opens a different prospect and promises the cure for which we are seeking. Let us examine the points in which it varies from pure Democracy, and we shall comprehend both the nature of the cure and the efficacy which it must derive from the Union.

The two great points of difference between a Democracy and a Republic are: first, the delegation of the Government, in the latter, to a small number of citizens elected by the rest; secondly, the greater number of citizens and greater sphere of country over which the latter may be extended.

The effect of the first difference is, on the one hand, to refine and enlarge the public views by passing them through the medium of a chosen body of citizens, whose wisdom may best discern the true interest of their country and whose patriotism and love of justice will be least likely to sacrifice it to temporary or partial considerations. Under such a regulation it may well happen that the public voice, pronounced by the representatives of the people, will be more consonant to the public good than if pronounced by the people themselves, convened for the purpose. On the other hand, the effect may be inverted. Men of factious tempers, of local prejudices, or of sinister designs, may, by intrigue, by corruption, or by other means, first obtain the suffrages, and then betray the interests of the people. The question resulting is, whether small or extensive Republics are most favorable to the election of proper guardians of the public weal; and it is clearly decided in favor of the latter by two obvious considerations.

In the first place it is to be remarked that however small the Republic may be, the Representatives must be raised to a certain number in order to guard against the cabals of a few; and that however large it may be they must be limited to a certain number in order to guard against the confusion of a multitude. Hence, the number of Representatives in the two cases not being in proportion to that of the Constituents, and being proportionally greatest in the small Republic, it follows that if the proportion of fit characters be not less in the large than in the small Republic, the former will present a greater option, and consequently a greater probability of a fit choice.

In the next place, as each Representative will be chosen by a greater number of citizens in the large than in the small Republic, it will be more difficult for unworthy candidates to practise with success the vicious arts by which elections are too often carried; and the suffrages of the people being more free, will be more likely to centre on men who possess the most attractive merit and the most diffusive and established characters.

It must be confessed that in this, as in most other cases, there is a mean, on both sides of which inconveniencies will be found to lie. By enlarging too much the number of electors, you render the representative too little acquainted with all their local circumstances and lesser interests; as by reducing it too much, you render him unduly attached to these, and too little fit to comprehend and pursue great and national objects. The Federal Constitution forms a happy combination in this respect; the great and aggregate interests being referred to the national, the local and particular to the State legislatures.

The other point of difference is the greater number of citizens and extent of territory which may be brought within the compass of Republican than of Democratic Government; and it is this circumstance principally which renders factious combinations less to be dreaded in the former than in the latter. The smaller the society, the fewer probably will be the distinct parties and interests composing it; the fewer the distinct parties and interests, the more frequently will a majority be found

of the same party; and the smaller the number of individuals composing a majority, and the smaller the compass within which they are placed, the more easily will they concert and execute their plans of oppression. Extend the sphere and you take in a greater variety of parties and interests; you make it less probable that a majority of the whole will have a common motive to invade the rights of other citizens; or if such a common motive exists, it will be more difficult for all who feel it to discover their own strength and to act in unison with each other. Besides other impediments, it may be remarked, that where there is a consciousness of unjust or dishonorable purposes, communication is always checked by distrust in proportion to the number whose concurrence is necessary.

Hence, it clearly appears that the same advantage which a Republic has over a Democracy in controlling the effects of faction is enjoyed by a large over a small republic—is enjoyed by the Union over the States composing it. Does this advantage consist in the substitution of representatives whose enlightened views and virtuous sentiments render them superior to local prejudices and to schemes of injustice? It will not be denied that the representation of the Union will be most likely to possess these requisite endowments. Does it consist in the greater security afforded by a greater variety of parties, against the event of any one party being able to outnumber and oppress the rest? In an equal degree does the increased variety of parties comprised within the Union increase this security? Does it, in fine, consist in the greater obstacles opposed to the concert and accomplishment of the secret wishes of an unjust and interested majority? Here again the extent of the Union gives it the most palpable advantage.

The influence of factious leaders may kindle a flame within their particular States but will be unable to spread a general conflagration through the other States: a religious sect may degenerate into a political faction in a part of the Confederacy; but the variety of sects dispersed over the entire face of it must secure the national Councils against any danger from that source: a rage for paper money, for an abolition of debts, for an equal division of property, or for any other improper or wicked project, will be less apt to pervade the whole body of the Union than a particular member of it; in the same proportion as such a malady is more likely to taint a particular county or district than an entire State.

In the extent and proper structure of the Union, therefore, we behold a republican remedy for the diseases most incident to Republican Government. And according to the degree of pleasure and pride we feel in being republicans ought to be our zeal in cherishing the spirit and supporting the character of federalist.

PUBLIUS
November 22, 1787

No. 51: Madison

To what expedient, then, shall we finally resort, for maintaining in practice the necessary partition of power among the several departments as laid down in the constitution? The only answer that can be given is that as all these exterior provisions are found to be inadequate the defect must be supplied, by so contriving the interior structure of the government as that its several constituent parts may, by their mutual relations, be the means of keeping each other in their proper places. Without presuming to undertake a full development of this important idea I will hazard a few general observations which may perhaps place it in a clearer light, and enable us to form a more correct judgment of the principles and structure of the government planned by the convention.

In order to lay a due foundation for that separate and distinct exercise of the different powers of government, which to a certain extent is admitted on all hands to be essential to the preservation of liberty, it is evident that each department should have a will of its own; and consequently should be so constituted that the members of each should have as little agency as possible in the appointment of the members of the others. Were this principle rigorously adhered to, it would require that all the appointments for the supreme executive, legislative, and judiciary magistracies should be drawn from the same fountain of authority, the people, through channels having no communication whatever with one another. Perhaps such a plan of constructing the several departments would be less difficult in practice than it may in contemplation appear. Some difficulties, however, and some additional expense would attend the execution of it. Some deviations, therefore, from the principle must be admitted. In the constitution of the judiciary department in particular, it might be inexpedient to insist rigorously on the principle: first, because peculiar qualifications being essential in the members, the primary consideration ought to be to select that mode of choice which best secures these qualifications; second, because the permanent tenure by which the appointments are held in that department must soon destroy all sense of dependence on the authority conferring them.

It is equally evident that the members of each department should be as little dependent as possible on those of the others for the emoluments annexed to their offices. Were the executive magistrate, or the judges, not independent of the legislature in this particular, their independence in every other would be merely nominal.

But the great security against a gradual concentration of the several powers in the same department consists in giving to those who administer each department the necessary constitutional means and personal motives to resist encroachments of the others. The provision for defence must in this, as in all other cases, be made commensurate to the danger of attack. Ambition must be made to counteract ambition. The interest of the man must be connected with the constitutional rights of the place. It may be a reflection on human nature that such devices should be necessary to control the abuses of government. But what is government itself but the greatest of all reflections on human nature? If men were angels, no government would be necessary. If angels were to govern men, neither external nor internal controls on government would be necessary. In framing a government which is to be administered by men over men, the great difficulty lies in this: You must first enable the government to control the governed; and in the next place oblige it to control itself. A dependence on the people is, no doubt, the primary control on the government; but experience has taught mankind the necessity of auxiliary precautions.

This policy of supplying, by opposite and rival interests, the defect of better motives, might be traced through the whole system of human affairs, private as well as public. We see it particularly displayed in all the subordinate distributions of power, where the constant aim is to divide and arrange the several offices in such a manner as that each may be a check on the other; that the private interest of every individual may be a sentinel over the public rights. These inventions of prudence cannot be less requisite in the distribution of the supreme powers of the State.

But it is not possible to give to each department an equal power of self-defense. In republican government, the legislative authority necessarily predominates. The remedy for this inconveniency is to divide the legislature into different branches; and to render them, by different modes of election and different principles of action, as little connected with each other as the nature of their common functions and their common dependence on the society will admit. It may even be necessary to guard against dangerous encroachments by still further precautions. As the weight of the legislative authority requires that it should be thus divided, the weakness of the executive may require, on the other hand, that it should be fortified. An absolute negative on the legislature appears, at first view, to be the natural defense with which the executive magistrate should be armed. But perhaps it would be neither altogether safe nor alone sufficient. On ordinary occasions it might not be exerted with the requisite firmness, and on extraordinary occasions it might be perfidiously abused. May not this defect of an absolute negative be supplied by some qualified connection between this weaker branch of the stronger department, by which the latter may be led to support the constitutional rights of the former, without being too much detached from the rights of its own department?

If the principles on which these observations are founded be just, as I persuade myself they are, and they be applied as a criterion to the several State constitutions, and to the federal Constitution, it will be found that if the latter does not perfectly correspond with them, the former are infinitely less able to bear such a test.

There are, moreover, two considerations particularly applicable to the federal system of America, which place that system in a very interesting point of view.

First. In a single republic, all the power surrendered by the people is submitted to the administration of a single government; and usurpations are guarded against by a division of the government into distinct and separate departments. In the compound republic of America, the power surrendered by the people is first divided between two distinct governments, and then the portion allotted to each subdivided among distinct and separate departments. Hence a double security arises to the rights of the people. The different governments will control each other, at the same time that each will be controlled by itself.

Second. It is of great importance in a republic not only to guard the society against the oppression of its rulers, but to guard one part of the society against the injustice of the other part. Different interests necessarily exist in different classes of citizens. If a majority be united by a common interest, the rights of the minority will be insecure. There are but two methods of providing against this evil: The one by creating a will in the community independent of the majority—that is, of the society itself; the other, by comprehending in the society so many separate descriptions of citizens as will render an unjust combination of a majority of the whole very improbable, if not impracticable. The first method prevails in all governments possessing an hereditary or self-appointed authority. This, at best, is but a precarious security; because a power independent of the society may as well espouse the unjust views of the major as the rightful interests of the minor party, and may possibly be turned against both parties. The second method will be exemplified in the federal republic of the United States. Whilst all authority in it will be derived from and dependent on the society, the society itself will be broken into so many parts, interests and classes of citizens, that the rights of individuals, or of the minority, will be in little danger from interested combinations of the majority. In a free government the security for civil rights must be the same as that for religious rights. It consists in the one case in the multiplicity of interests, and in the other in the multiplicity of sects. The degree of security in both cases will depend on the number of interests and sects; and this may be presumed to depend on the extent of country and number of people comprehended under the same government. This view of the subject must particularly recommend a proper federal system to all the sincere and considerate friends of republican government: Since it shows that in exact proportion as the territory of the Union may be formed into more circumscribed Confederacies, or States, oppressive combinations of a majority will be facilitated; the best security, under the republican form, for the rights of every class of citizens, will be diminished; and consequently the stability and independence of some member of the government, the only other security, must be proportionally increased. Justice is the end of government. It is the end of civil society. It ever has been and ever will be pursued until it be obtained, or until liberty be lost in the pursuit. In a society under the forms of which the stronger faction can readily unite and oppress the weaker, anarchy may as truly be said to reign as in a state of nature, where the weaker individual is not secured against the violence of the stronger: And as, in the latter state, even the stronger individuals are prompted, by the uncertainty of their condition, to submit to a government which may protect the weak as well as themselves: So, in the former state, will the more powerful factions or parties be gradually induced, by a like motive, to wish for a government which will protect all parties, the weaker as well as the more powerful. It can be little doubted that if the State of Rhode Island was separated from the Confederacy and left to itself, the insecurity of rights under the popular form of government within such narrow limits would be displayed by such reiterated oppressions of factious majorities that some power altogether independent of the people would soon be called for by the voice of the very factions whose misrule had proved the necessity of it. In the extended republic of the United States, and among the great variety of interests, parties, and sects which it embraces, a coalition of a majority of the whole society could seldom take place on any other principles than those of justice and the general good; and there being thus less danger to a minor from the will of the major party, there must be less pretext, also, to provide for the security of the former, by introducing into the government a will not dependent on the latter, or, in other words, a will independent of the society itself. It is no less certain than it is important, notwithstanding the contrary opinions which have been entertained, that the larger the society, provided it lie within a practicable sphere, the more duly capable it will be of self-government. And happily for the *republican cause*, the practicable sphere may be carried to a very great extent by a judicious modification and mixture of the *federal principle.*

PUBLIUS
February 6, 1788

The Anti-Federalist Papers

Essay by Brutus in the *New York Journal*

When the public is called to investigate and decide upon a question in which not only the present members of the community are deeply interested, but upon which the happiness and misery of generations yet unborn is in great measure suspended, the benevolent mind cannot help feeling itself peculiarly interested in the result.

In this situation, I trust the feeble efforts of an individual, to lead the minds of the people to a wise and prudent determination, cannot fail of being acceptable to the candid and dispassionate part of the community. Encouraged by this consideration, I have been induced to offer my thoughts upon the present important crisis of our public affairs.

Perhaps this country never saw so critical a period in their political concerns. We have felt the feebleness of the ties by which these United-States are held together, and the want of sufficient energy in our present confederation, to manage, in some instances, our general concerns. Various expedients have been proposed to remedy these evils, but none have succeeded. At length a Convention of the states has been assembled, they have formed a constitution which will now, probably, be submitted to the people to ratify or reject, who are the fountain of all power, to whom alone it of right belongs to make or unmake constitutions, or forms of government, at their pleasure. The most important question that was ever proposed to your decision, or to the decision of any people under heaven, is before you, and you are to decide upon it by men of your own election, chosen specially for this purpose. If the constitution, offered to your acceptance, be a wise one, calculated to preserve the invaluable blessings of liberty, to secure the inestimable rights of mankind, and promote human happiness, then, if you accept it, you will lay a lasting foundation of happiness for millions yet unborn; generations to come will rise up and call you blessed. You may rejoice in the prospects of this vast extended continent becoming filled with freemen, who will assert the dignity of human nature. You may solace yourselves with the idea, that society, in this favoured land, will fast advance to the highest point of perfection; the human mind will expand in knowledge and virtue, and the golden age be, in some measure, realised. But if, on the other hand, this form of government contains principles that will lead to the subversion of liberty—if it tends to establish a despotism, or, what is worse, a tyrannic aristocracy; then, if you adopt it, this only remaining assylum

for liberty will be shut up, and posterity will execrate your memory.

Momentous then is the question you have to determine, and you are called upon by every motive which should influence a noble and virtuous mind, to examine it well, and to make up a wise judgment. It is insisted, indeed, that this constitution must be received, be it ever so imperfect. If it has its defects, it is said, they can be best amended when they are experienced. But remember, when the people once part with power, they can seldom or never resume it again but by force. Many instances can be produced in which the people have voluntarily increased the powers of their rulers; but few, if any, in which rulers have willingly abridged their authority. This is a sufficient reason to induce you to be careful, in the first instance, how you deposit the powers of government.

With these few introductory remarks, I shall proceed to a consideration of this constitution:

The first question that presents itself on the subject is, whether a confederated government be the best for the United States or not? Or in other words, whether the thirteen United States should be reduced to one great republic, governed by one legislature, and under the direction of one executive and judicial; or whether they should continue thirteen confederated republics, under the direction and controul of a supreme federal head for certain defined national purposes only?

This enquiry is important, because, although the government reported by the convention does not go to a perfect and entire consolidation, yet it approaches so near to it, that it must, if executed, certainly and infallibly terminate in it.

This government is to possess absolute and uncontroulable power, legislative, executive and judicial, with respect to every object to which it extends, for by the last clause of section 8th, article 1st, it is declared "that the Congress shall have power to make all laws which shall be necessary and proper for carrying into execution the foregoing powers, and all other powers vested by this constitution, in the government of the United States; or in any department or office thereof." And by the 6th article, it is declared "that this constitution, and the laws of the United States, which shall be made in pursuance thereof, and the treaties made, or which shall be made, under the authority of the United States, shall be the supreme law of the land; and the judges in every state shall be bound thereby, any thing in the constitution, or law of any state to the contrary notwithstanding." It appears from these articles that there is no need of any intervention of the state governments, between the Congress and the people, to execute any one power vested in the general government, and that the constitution and laws of every state are nullified and declared void, so far as they are or shall be inconsistent with this constitution, or the laws made in pursuance of it, or with treaties made under the authority of the United States.—The government then, so far as it extends, is a complete one, and not a confederation. It is as much one complete government as that of New York or Massachusetts, has as absolute and perfect powers to make and execute all laws, to appoint officers, institute courts, declare offences, and annex penalties, with respect to every object to which it extends, as any other in the world. So far therefore as its powers reach, all ideas of confederation are given up and lost. It is true this government is limited to certain objects, or to speak more properly, some small degree of power is still left to the states, but a little attention to the powers vested in the general government, will convince every candid man, that if it is capable of being executed, all that is reserved for the individual states must very soon be annihilated, except so far as they are barely necessary to the organization of the general government. The powers of the general legislature extend to every case that is of the least importance—there is nothing valuable to human nature, nothing dear to freemen, but what is within its power. It has authority to make laws which will affect the lives, the liberty, and property of every man in the United States; nor can the constitution or laws of any state, in any way prevent or impede the full and complete execution of every power given. The legislative power is competent to lay taxes, duties, imposts, and excises;—there is no limitation to this power, unless it be said that the clause which directs the use to which those taxes, and duties shall be applied, may be said to be a limitation: but this is no restriction of the power at all, for by this clause they are to be applied to pay the debts and provide for the common defence and general welfare of the United States; but the legislature have authority to contract debts at their discretion; they are the sole judges of what is necessary to provide for the common defence, and they only are to determine what is for the general welfare; this power therefore is neither more nor less, than a power to lay and collect taxes, imposts, and excises, at their pleasure; not only [is] the power to lay taxes unlimited, as to the amount they may require, but it is perfect and absolute to raise them in any mode they please. No state legislature, or any power in the state governments, have any more to do in carrying this into effect, than the authority of one state has to do with that of another. In the business therefore of laying and collecting taxes, the idea of confederation is totally lost, and that of one entire republic is embraced. It is proper here to remark, that the authority to lay and collect taxes is the most important of any power that can be granted; it connects with it almost all other powers, or at least will in process of time draw all other after it; it is the great mean of protection, security, and defence, in a good government, and the great engine of oppression and tyranny in a bad one. This cannot fail of being the case, if we consider the contracted limits which are set by this constitution, to the late [state?] governments, on this article of raising money. No state can emit paper money—lay any duties, or imposts, on imports, or exports, but by consent of the Congress; and then the net produce shall be for the benefit of the United States: the only mean therefore left, for any state to support its government and discharge its debts, is by direct taxation; and the United States have also power to lay and collect taxes, in any way they please. Every one who has thought on the subject, must be convinced that but small sums of money can be collected in any country, by direct taxe[s], when the foederal government begins to exercise the right of taxation in all its parts, the legislatures of the several states will find it impossible to raise monies to support their governments. Without money they cannot be supported, and they must dwindle away, and, as before observed, their powers absorbed in that of the general government.

It might be here shewn, that the power in the federal legislative, to raise and support armies at pleasure, as well in peace as in war, and their controul over the militia, tend, not only to a consolidation of the government, but the destruction of liberty.—I shall not, however, dwell upon these, as a few observations upon the judicial power of this government, in addition to the preceding, will fully evince the truth of the position.

The judicial power of the United States is to be vested in a supreme court, and in such inferior courts as Congress may from time to time ordain and establish. The powers of these courts are very extensive; their jurisdiction comprehends all civil causes, except such as arise between citizens of the same state; and it extends to all cases in law and equity arising under the constitution. One inferior court must be established, I presume, in each state, at least, with the necessary executive officers appendant thereto. It is easy to see, that in the common course of things, these courts will eclipse the dignity, and take away from the respectability, of the state courts. These courts will be, in themselves, totally independent of the states, deriving their authority from the United States, and receiving from them fixed salaries; and in the course of human events it is to be expected, that they will swallow up all the powers of the courts in the respective states.

How far the clause in the 8th section of the 1st article may operate to do away all idea of confederated states, and to effect an entire consolidation of the whole into one general government, it is impossible to say. The powers given by this article are very general and comprehensive, and it may receive a construction to justify the passing almost any law. A power to make all laws, which shall be *necessary and proper*, for carrying into execution, all powers vested by the constitution in the government of the United States, or any department or officer thereof, is a power very comprehensive and definite [indefinite?], and may, for ought I know, be exercised in a such manner as entirely to abolish the state legislatures. Suppose the legislature of a state should pass a law to raise money to support their government and pay the state debt, may the Congress repeal this law, because it may prevent the collection of a tax which they may think proper and necessary to lay, to provide for the general welfare of the United States? For all laws made, in pursuance of this constitution, are the supreme law of the land, and the judges in every state shall be bound thereby, any thing in the constitution or laws of the different states to the contrary notwithstanding.—By such a law, the government of a particular state might be overturned at one stroke, and thereby be deprived of every means of its support.

It is not meant, by stating this case, to insinuate that the constitution would warrant a law of this kind; or unnecessarily to alarm the fears of the people, by suggesting, that the federal legislature would be more likely to pass the limits assigned them by the constitution, than that of an individual state, further than they are less responsible to the people. But what is meant is, that the legislature of the United States are vested with the great and uncontroulable powers, of laying and collecting taxes, duties, imposts, and excises; of regulating trade, raising and supporting armies, organizing, arming, and disciplining the militia, instituting courts, and other general powers. And are by this clause invested with the power of making all laws, *proper and necessary*, for carrying all these into execution; and they may so exercise this power as entirely to annihilate all the state governments, and reduce this country to one single government. And if they may do it, it is pretty certain they will; for it will be found that the power retained by individual states, small as it is, will be a clog upon the wheels of the government of the United States; the latter therefore will be naturally inclined to remove it out of the way. Besides, it is a truth confirmed by the unerring experience of ages, that every man, and every body of men, invested with power, are ever disposed to increase it, and to acquire a superiority over every thing that stands in their way. This disposition, which is implanted in human nature, will operate in the federal legislature to lessen and ultimately to subvert the state authority, and having such advantages, will most certainly succeed, if the federal government succeeds at all. It must be very evident then, that what this constitution wants of being a complete consolidation of the several parts of the union into one complete government, possessed of perfect legislative, judicial, and executive powers, to all intents and purposes, it will necessarily acquire in its exercise and operation.

Let us now proceed to enquire, as I at first proposed, whether it be best the thirteen United States should be reduced to one great republic, or not? It is here taken for granted, that all agree in this, that whatever government we adopt, it ought to be a free one; that it should be so framed as to secure the liberty of the citizens of America, and such an one as to admit of a full, fair, and equal representation of the people. The question then will be, whether a government thus constituted, and founded on such principles, is practicable, and can be exercised over the whole United States, reduced into one state?

If respect is to be paid to the opinion of the greatest and wisest men who have ever thought or wrote on the science of government, we shall be constrained to conclude, that a free republic cannot succeed over a country of such immense extent, containing such a number of inhabitants, and these encreasing in such rapid progression as that of the whole United States. Among the many illustrious authorities which might be produced to this point, I shall content myself with quoting only two. The one is the baron de Montesquieu, spirit of laws, chap. xvi. vol. I [book VIII]. "It is natural to a republic to have only a small territory, otherwise it cannot long subsist. In a large republic there are men of large fortunes, and consequently of less moderation; there are trusts too great to be placed in any single subject; he has interest of his own; he soon begins to think that he may be happy, great and glorious, by oppressing his fellow citizens; and that he may raise himself to grandeur on the ruins of his country. In a large republic, the public good is sacrificed to a thousand views; it is subordinate to exceptions, and depends on accidents. In a small one, the interest of the public is easier perceived, better understood, and more within the reach of every citizen; abuses are of less extent, and of course are less protected." Of the same opinion is the marquis Beccarari.

History furnishes no example of a free republic, any thing like the extent of the United States. The Grecian republics were of small extent; so also was that of the Romans. Both of these, it is true, in process of time, extended their conquests over large territories of country; and the consequence was, that their governments were changed from that of free governments to those of the most tyrannical that ever existed in the world.

Not only the opinion of the greatest men, and the experience of mankind, are against the idea of an extensive republic, but a variety of reasons may be drawn from the reason and nature of things, against it. In every government, the will of the sovereign is the law. In despotic governments, the supreme authority being lodged in one, his will is law, and can be as easily expressed to a large extensive territory as to a small one. In a pure democracy the people are the sovereign, and their will is declared by themselves; for this purpose they must all come together to deliberate, and decide. This kind of government cannot be exercised, therefore, over a country of any considerable extent; it must be confined to a single city, or at least limited to such bounds as that the people can conveniently assemble, be able to debate, understand the subject submitted to them, and declare their opinion concerning it.

In a free republic, although all laws are derived from the consent of the people, yet the people do not declare their consent by themselves in person, but by representatives, chosen by them, who are supposed to know the minds of their constituents, and to be possessed of integrity to declare this mind.

In every free government, the people must give their assent to the laws by which they are governed. This is the true criterion between a free government and an arbitrary one.

The former are ruled by the will of the whole, expressed in any manner they may agree upon; the latter by the will of one, or a few. If the people are to give their assent to the laws, by persons chosen and appointed by them, the manner of the choice and the number chosen, must be such, as to possess, be disposed, and consequently qualified to declare the sentiments of the people; for if they do not know, or are not disposed to speak the sentiments of the people, the people do not govern, but the sovereignty is in a few. Now, in a large extended country, it is impossible to have a representation, possessing the sentiments, and of integrity, to declare the minds of the people, without having it so numerous and unwieldly, as to be subject in great measure to the inconveniency of a democratic government.

The territory of the United States is of vast extent; it now contains near three millions of souls, and is capable of containing much more than ten times that number. Is it practicable for a country, so large and so numerous as they will soon become, to elect a representation, that will speak their sentiments, without their becoming so numerous as to be incapable of transacting public business? It certainly is not.

In a republic, the manners, sentiments, and interests of the people should be similar. If this be not the case, there will be a constant clashing of opinions; and the representatives of one part will be continually striving against those of the other. This will retard the operations of government, and prevent such conclusions as will promote the public good. If we apply this remark to the condition of the United States, we shall be convinced that it forbids that we should be one government. The United States includes a variety of climates. The productions of the different parts of the union are very variant, and their interests, of consequence, diverse. Their manners and habits differ as much as their climates and productions; and their sentiments are by no means coincident. The laws and customs of the several states are, in many respects, very diverse, and in some opposite; each would be in favor of its own interests and customs, and, of consequence, a legislature, formed of representatives from the respective parts, would not only be too numerous to act with any care or decision, but would be composed of such heterogenous and discordant principles, as would constantly be contending with each other.

The laws cannot be executed in a republic, of an extent equal to that of the United States, with promptitude.

The magistrates in every government must be supported in the execution of the laws, either by an armed force, maintained at the public expence for that purpose; or by the people turning out to aid the magistrate upon his command, in case of resistance.

In despotic governments, as well as in all the monarchies of Europe, standing armies are kept up to execute the commands of the prince or the magistrate, and are employed for this purpose when occasion requires: But they have always proved the destruction of liberty, and [are] abhorrent to the spirit of a free republic. In England, where they depend upon the parliament for their annual support, they have always been complained of as oppressive and unconstitutional, and are seldom employed in executing of the laws; never except on extraordinary occasions, and then under the direction of a civil magistrate.

A free republic will never keep a standing army to execute its laws. It must depend upon the support of its citizens. But when a government is to receive its support from the aid of the citizens, it must be so constructed as to have the confidence, respect, and affection of the people." Men who, upon the call of the magistrate, offer themselves to execute the laws, are influenced to do it either by affection to the government, or from fear; where a standing army is at hand to punish offenders, every man is actuated by the latter principle, and therefore, when the magistrate calls, will obey: but, where this is not the case, the government must rest for its support upon the confidence and respect which the people have for their government and laws. The body of the people being attached, the government will always be sufficient to support and execute its laws, and to operate upon the fears of any faction which may be opposed to it, not only to prevent an opposition to the execution of the laws themselves, but also to compel the most of them to aid the magistrate; but the people will not be likely to have such confidence in their rulers, in a republic so extensive as the United States, as necessary for these purposes. The confidence which the people have in their rulers, in a free republic, arises from their knowing them, from their being responsible to them for their conduct, and from the power they have of displacing them when they misbehave: but in a republic of the extent of this continent, the people in general would be acquainted with very few of their rulers: the people at large would know little of their proceedings, and it would be extremely difficult to change them. The people in Georgia and New-Hampshire would not know one another's mind, and therefore could not act in concert to enable them to effect a general change of representatives. The different parts of so extensive a country could not possibly be made acquainted with the conduct of their representatives, nor be informed of the reasons upon which measures were founded. The consequence will be, they will have no confidence in their legislature, suspect them of ambitious views, be jealous of every measure they adopt, and will not support the laws they pass. Hence the government will be nerveless and inefficient, and no way will be left to render it otherwise, but by establishing an armed force to execute the laws at the point of the bayonet—a government of all others the most to be dreaded.

In a republic of such vast extent as the United-States, the legislature cannot attend to the various concerns and wants of its different parts. It cannot be sufficiently numerous to be acquainted with the local condition and wants of the different districts, and if it could, it is impossible it should have sufficient time to attend to and provide for all the variety of cases of this nature, that would be continually arising.

In so extensive a republic, the great officers of government would soon become above the controul of the people, and abuse their power to the purpose of aggrandizing themselves, and oppressing them. The trust committed to the executive offices, in a country of the extent of the United-States, must be various and of magnitude. The command of all the troops and navy of the republic, the appointment of officers, the power of pardoning offences, the collecting of all the public revenues, and the power of expending them, with a number of other powers, must be lodged and exercised in every state, in the hands of a few. When these are attended with great honor and emolument, as they always will be in large states, so as greatly to interest men to pursue them, and to be proper objects for ambitious and designing men, such men will be ever restless in their pursuit after them. They will use the power, when they have acquired it, to the purposes of gratifying their own interest and ambition, and it is scarcely possible, in a very large republic, to call them to account for their misconduct, or to prevent their abuse of power.

These are some of the reasons by which it appears, that a free republic cannot long subsist over a country of the great extent of these states. If then this new constitution is calculated to consolidate the thirteen states into one, as it evidently is, it ought not to be adopted.

Though I am of opinion, that it is a sufficient objection to this government, to reject it, that it creates the whole union into one government, under the form of a republic, yet if this objection was obviated, there are exceptions to it, which are so material and fundamental, that they ought to determine every man, who is a friend to the liberty and happiness of mankind, not to adopt it. I beg the candid and dispassionate attention of my countrymen while I state these objections—they are such as have obtruded themselves upon my mind upon a careful attention to the matter, and such as I sincerely believe are well founded. There are many objections, of small moment, of which I shall take no notice—perfection is not to be expected in any thing that is the production of man—and if I did not in my conscience believe that this scheme was defective in the fundamental principles—in the foundation upon which a free and equal government must rest—I would hold my peace.

BRUTUS
October 18, 1787

Presidents and Vice Presidents

	PRESIDENT	VICE PRESIDENT		PRESIDENT	VICE PRESIDENT
1	George Washington *(Federalist 1789)*	John Adams *(Federalist 1789)*	12	Zachary Taylor *(Whig 1849)*	Millard Fillmore *(Whig 1849)*
2	John Adams *(Federalist 1797)*	Thomas Jefferson *(Dem.-Rep. 1797)*	13	Millard Fillmore *(Whig 1850)*	
3	Thomas Jefferson *(Dem.-Rep. 1801)*	Aaron Burr *(Dem.-Rep. 1801)*	14	Franklin Pierce *(Democratic 1853)*	William R. D. King *(Democratic 1853)*
		George Clinton *(Dem.-Rep. 1805)*	15	James Buchanan *(Democratic 1857)*	John C. Breckinridge *(Democratic 1857)*
4	James Madison *(Dem.-Rep. 1809)*	George Clinton *(Dem.-Rep. 1809)*	16	Abraham Lincoln *(Republican 1861)*	Hannibal Hamlin *(Republican 1861)*
		Elbridge Gerry *(Dem.-Rep. 1813)*			Andrew Johnson *(Unionist 1865)*
5	James Monroe *(Dem.-Rep. 1817)*	Daniel D. Tompkins *(Dem.-Rep. 1817)*	17	Andrew Johnson *(Unionist 1865)*	
6	John Quincy Adams *(Dem.-Rep. 1825)*	John C. Calhoun *(Dem.-Rep. 1825)*	18	Ulysses S. Grant *(Republican 1869)*	Schuyler Colfax *(Republican 1869)*
7	Andrew Jackson *(Democratic 1829)*	John C. Calhoun *(Democratic 1829)*			Henry Wilson *(Republican 1873)*
		Martin Van Buren *(Democratic 1833)*	19	Rutherford B. Hayes *(Republican 1877)*	William A. Wheeler *(Republican 1877)*
8	Martin Van Buren *(Democratic 1837)*	Richard M. Johnson *(Democratic 1837)*	20	James A. Garfield *(Republican 1881)*	Chester A. Arthur *(Republican 1881)*
9	William H. Harrison *(Whig 1841)*	John Tyler *(Whig 1841)*	21	Chester A. Arthur *(Republican 1881)*	
10	John Tyler *(Whig and Democratic 1841)*		22	Grover Cleveland *(Democratic 1885)*	Thomas A. Hendricks *(Democratic 1885)*
11	James K. Polk *(Democratic 1845)*	George M. Dallas *(Democratic 1845)*	23	Benjamin Harrison *(Republican 1889)*	Levi P. Morton *(Republican 1889)*

	PRESIDENT	VICE PRESIDENT		PRESIDENT	VICE PRESIDENT
24	Grover Cleveland *(Democratic 1893)*	Adlai E. Stevenson *(Democratic 1893)*	34	Dwight D. Eisenhower *(Republican 1953)*	Richard M. Nixon *(Republican 1953)*
25	William McKinley *(Republican 1897)*	Garret A. Hobart *(Republican 1897)*	35	John F. Kennedy *(Democratic 1961)*	Lyndon B. Johnson *(Democratic 1961)*
		Theodore Roosevelt *(Republican 1901)*	36	Lyndon B. Johnson *(Democratic 1963)*	Hubert H. Humphrey *(Democratic 1965)*
26	Theodore Roosevelt *(Republican 1901)*	Charles W. Fairbanks *(Republican 1905)*	37	Richard M. Nixon *(Republican 1969)*	Spiro T. Agnew *(Republican 1969)*
27	William H. Taft *(Republican 1909)*	James S. Sherman *(Republican 1909)*			Gerald R. Ford *(Republican 1973)*
28	Woodrow Wilson *(Democratic 1913)*	Thomas R. Marshall *(Democratic 1913)*	38	Gerald R. Ford *(Republican 1974)*	Nelson Rockefeller *(Republican 1974)*
29	Warren G. Harding *(Republican 1921)*	Calvin Coolidge *(Republican 1921)*	39	James E. Carter *(Democratic 1977)*	Walter Mondale *(Democratic 1977)*
30	Calvin Coolidge *(Republican 1923)*	Charles G. Dawes *(Republican 1925)*	40	Ronald Reagan *(Republican 1981)*	George H. W. Bush *(Republican 1981)*
31	Herbert Hoover *(Republican 1929)*	Charles Curtis *(Republican 1929)*	41	George H. W. Bush *(Republican 1989)*	J. Danforth Quayle *(Republican 1989)*
32	Franklin D. Roosevelt *(Democratic 1933)*	John Nance Garner *(Democratic 1933)*	42	William J. Clinton *(Democratic 1993)*	Albert Gore, Jr. *(Democratic 1993)*
		Henry A. Wallace *(Democratic 1941)*	43	George W. Bush *(Republican 2001)*	Richard Cheney *(Republican 2001)*
		Harry S. Truman *(Democratic 1945)*	44	Barack H. Obama *(Democratic 2009)*	Joseph R. Biden, Jr. *(Democratic 2009)*
33	Harry S. Truman *(Democratic 1945)*	Alben W. Barkley *(Democratic 1949)*			

glossary

affirmative action government policies or programs that seek to redress past injustices against specified groups by making special efforts to provide members of those groups with access to educational and employment opportunities

agency representation a type of representation in which a representative is held accountable to a constituency if he or she fails to represent that constituency properly; this is incentive for good representation when the personal backgrounds, views, and interests of the representative differ from those of his or her constituency

agenda setting the power of the media to bring public attention to particular issues and problems

agents of socialization social institutions, including families and schools, that help to shape individuals' basic political beliefs and values

amendment a change added to a bill, law, or constitution

amicus curiae literally, "friend of the court"; individuals or groups who are not parties to a lawsuit but who seek to assist the Supreme Court in reaching a decision by presenting additional briefs

Antifederalists those who favored strong state governments and a weak national government, and who were opponents of the Constitution proposed at the American Constitutional Convention of 1787

antitrust policy government regulation of large businesses that have established monopolies

appeasement the effort to forestall war by giving in to the demands of a hostile power

apportionment the process, occurring after every decennial census, that allocates congressional seats among the 50 states

appropriations the amounts of money approved by Congress in statutes (bills) that each unit or agency of government can spend

Articles of Confederation America's first written constitution; served as the basis for America's national government until 1789

attitude (or opinion) a specific preference on a particular issue

authoritarian government a system of rule in which the government recognizes no formal limits but may nevertheless be restrained by the power of other social institutions

autocracy a form of government in which a single individual—a king, queen, or dictator—rules

ballot initiative a proposed law or policy change that is placed on the ballot by citizens or interest groups for a popular vote

bandwagon effect a shift in electoral support to the candidate whom public opinion polls report as the front-runner

bicameral having a legislative assembly composed of two chambers or houses; distinguished from *unicameral*

bilateral treaties treaties made between two nations

bill a proposed law that has been sponsored by a member of Congress and submitted to the clerk of the House or Senate

bill of attainder a law that declares a person guilty of a crime without a trial

Bill of Rights the first 10 amendments to the U.S. Constitution, ratified in 1791; they ensure certain rights and liberties to the people

block grants federal grants-in-aid that allow states considerable discretion in how the funds are spent

briefs written documents in which attorneys explain, using case precedents, why the court should find in favor of their client

broadcast media television, radio, or other media that transmit audio and/or video content to the public

Brown v. Board of Education the 1954 Supreme Court decision that struck down the "separate but equal" doctrine as fundamentally unequal; this case eliminated state power to use race as a criterion of discrimination in law and provided the national government with the power to intervene by exercising strict regulatory policies against discriminatory actions

budget deficit amount by which government spending exceeds government revenue in a fiscal year

bureaucracy the complex structure of offices, tasks, rules, and principles of organization that are employed by all large-scale institutions to coordinate the work of their personnel

Bush Doctrine foreign policy based on the idea that the United States should take preemptive action against threats to its national security

Cabinet the secretaries, or chief administrators, of the major departments of the federal government; Cabinet secretaries are appointed by the president with the consent of the Senate

campaign an effort by political candidates and their supporters to win the backing of donors, political activists, and voters in their quest for political office

categorical grants congressional grants given to states and localities on the condition that expenditures be limited to a problem or group specified by the law

caucus (political) a normally closed meeting of a political or legislative group to select candidates, plan strategy, or make decisions regarding legislative matters

caucuses (congressional) associations of members of Congress based on party, interest, or social group, such as gender or race

checks and balances mechanisms through which each branch of government is able to participate in and influence the activities of the other branches; major examples include the presidential veto power over congressional legislation, the power of the Senate to approve presidential appointments, and judicial review of congressional enactments

chief justice justice on the Supreme Court who presides over the Court's public sessions and whose official title is chief justice of the United States

citizen groups groups that claim they serve the general good rather than only their own particular interests

citizen journalism news reported and distributed by citizens, rather than professional journalists and for-profit news organizations

citizenship informed and active membership in a political community

civil law the branch of law that deals with disputes that do not involve criminal penalties

civil liberties areas of personal freedom constitutionally protected from government interference

civil rights obligation imposed on government to take positive action to protect citizens from any illegal action of government agencies and of other private citizens

class-action suit a legal action by which a group or class of individuals with common interests can file a suit on behalf of everyone who shares that interest

"clear and present danger" test test to determine whether speech is protected or unprotected, based on its capacity to present a "clear and present danger" to society

closed primary a primary election in which voters can participate in the nomination of candidates, but only of the party in which they are enrolled for a period of time prior to primary day

closed rule a provision by the House Rules Committee limiting or prohibiting the introduction of amendments during debate

cloture a rule or process in a legislative body aimed at ending debate on a given bill; in the U.S. Senate, 60 senators (three-fifths) must agree in order to impose a time limit and end debate

Cold War the period of struggle between the United States and the former Soviet Union lasting from the late 1940s to about 1990

collective goods benefits sought by groups that are broadly available and cannot be denied to nonmembers

commander in chief the role of the president as commander of the national military and the state National Guard units (when called into service)

commerce clause Article I, Section 8, of the Constitution, which delegates to Congress the power "to regulate commerce with foreign nations, and among the several States and with the Indian tribes"; this clause was interpreted by the Supreme Court in favor of national power over the economy

committee markup the session in which a congressional committee rewrites legislation to incorporate changes discussed during hearings on a bill

common law law made through court precedent rather than legislative enactments

concurrent powers authority possessed by *both* state and national governments, such as the power to levy taxes

confederation a system of government in which states retain sovereign authority except for the powers expressly delegated to the national government

conference a gathering of House Republicans every two years to elect their House leaders; Democrats call their gathering the caucus

conference committees joint committees created to work out a compromise on House and Senate versions of a piece of legislation

conservative today this term refers to those who generally support the social and economic status quo and are suspicious of efforts to introduce new political formulae and economic arrangements; conservatives believe that a large and powerful government poses a threat to citizens' freedom

constituency the residents in the area from which an official is elected

constitutional government a system of rule in which formal and effective limits are placed on the powers of the government

containment a policy designed to curtail the political and military expansion of a hostile power

contracting power the power of government to set conditions on companies seeking to sell goods or services to government agencies

contributory programs social programs financed in whole or in part by taxation or other mandatory contributions by their present or future recipients

cooperative federalism a type of federalism existing since the New Deal era in which grants-in-aid have been used strategically to encourage states and localities (without commanding them) to pursue nationally defined goals; also known as "intergovernmental cooperation"

cost-of-living adjustments (COLAs) changes made to the level of benefits of a government program based on the rate of inflation

court of appeals a court that hears appeals of trial court decisions

criminal law the branch of law that regulates the conduct of individuals, defines crimes, and specifies punishment for criminal acts

de facto literally, "by fact"; refers to practices that occur even when there is no legal enforcement, such as school segregation in much of the United States today

de jure literally, "by law"; refers to legally enforced practices, such as school segregation in the South before the 1960s

dealignment a movement away from the major political parties; a decline in partisan attachment

defendant the one against whom a complaint is brought in a criminal or civil case

delegate a representative who votes according to the preferences of his or her constituency

delegated powers constitutional powers that are assigned to one governmental agency but that are exercised by another agency with the express permission of the first

democracy a system of rule that permits citizens to play a significant part in the governmental process, usually through the election of key public officials

department the largest subunit of the executive branch; the secretaries of the 15 departments form the Cabinet

deregulation a policy of reducing or eliminating regulatory restraints on the conduct of individuals or private institutions

devolution a policy to remove a program from one level of government by delegating it or passing it down to a lower level of government, such as from the national government to the state and local governments

digital citizen a daily Internet user with high-speed home Internet access and the technology and literacy skills to go online for employment, news, politics, entertainment, commerce, and other activities

diplomacy the representation of a government to other governments

direct democracy a system of rule that permits citizens to vote directly on laws and policies

discretionary spending federal spending on programs that are controlled through the regular budget process

discrimination the use of any unreasonable and unjust criterion of exclusion

dissenting opinion a decision written by a justice in the minority in a particular case in which the justice wishes to express his or her reasoning in the case

divided government the condition in American government wherein the presidency is controlled by one party while the opposing party controls one or both houses of Congress

double jeopardy the Fifth Amendment right providing that a person cannot be tried twice for the same crime

dual federalism the system of government that prevailed in the United States from 1789 to 1937 in which most fundamental governmental powers were shared between the federal and state governments

due process of law the right of every individual against arbitrary action by national or state governments

early voting the option in some states to cast a vote at a polling place or by mail before the election

elastic clause Article I, Section 8, of the Constitution (also known as the necessary and proper clause), which enumerates the powers of Congress and provides Congress with the authority to make all laws "necessary and proper" to carry them out

Election Day registration the option in some states to register on the day of the election, at the polling place, rather than in advance of the election

electoral college the electors from each state who meet after the popular election to cast ballots for president and vice president

electoral realignment the point in history when a new party supplants the ruling party, becoming in turn the dominant political force; in the United States, this has tended to occur roughly every 30 years

eminent domain the right of government to take private property for public use

entitlement a legal obligation of the federal government to provide payments to individuals, or groups of individuals, according to eligibility criteria or benefit rules

equal protection clause provision of the Fourteenth Amendment guaranteeing citizens "the equal protection of the laws"; this clause has been the basis for the civil rights of African Americans, women, and other groups

equal time rule the requirement that broadcasters provide candidates for the same political office equal opportunities to communicate their messages to the public

equality of opportunity a widely shared American ideal that all people should have the freedom to use whatever talents and wealth they have to reach their fullest potential

establishment clause the First Amendment clause that says that "Congress shall make no law respecting an establishment of religion"; this law means that a "wall of separation" exists between church and state

ex post facto laws laws that declare an action to be illegal after it has been committed

exclusionary rule the ability of courts to exclude evidence obtained in violation of the Fourth Amendment

executive agreement an agreement, made between the president and another country, that has the force of a treaty but does not require the Senate's "advice and consent"

Executive Office of the President (EOP) the permanent agencies that perform defined management tasks for the president; created in 1939, the EOP includes the OMB, the CEA, the NSC, and other agencies

executive order a rule or regulation issued by the president that has the effect and formal status of legislation

executive privilege the claim that confidential communications between a president and close advisers should not be revealed without the consent of the president

expressed powers specific powers granted by the Constitution to Congress (Article I, Section 8) and to the president (Article II)

fairness doctrine a Federal Communications Commission requirement for broadcasters who air programs on controversial issues to provide time for opposing views; the FCC ceased enforcing this doctrine in 1985

federal funds rate the interest rate on loans between banks that the Federal Reserve Board influences by affecting the supply of money available

Federal Reserve System a system of 12 Federal Reserve banks that facilitates exchanges of cash, checks, and credit; regulates member banks; and uses monetary policies to fight inflation and deflation

federalism a system of government in which power is divided, by a constitution, between a central government and regional governments

Federalist Papers a series of essays written by Alexander Hamilton, James Madison, and John Jay supporting ratification of the Constitution

Federalists those who favored a strong national government and supported the Constitution proposed at the American Constitutional Convention of 1787

Fifteenth Amendment one of three Civil War amendments; it guaranteed voting rights for African American men

fighting words speech that directly incites damaging conduct

filibuster a tactic used by members of the Senate to prevent action on legislation they oppose by continuously holding the floor and speaking until the majority backs down; once given the floor, senators have unlimited time to speak, and it requires a vote of three-fifths of the Senate to end a filibuster

fiscal policy the government's use of taxing, monetary, and spending powers to manipulate the economy

501c(4) committees nonprofit groups that also engage in issue advocacy; under Section 501c(4) of the federal tax code such a group may spend up to half its revenue for political purposes

527 committees nonprofit independent groups that receive and disburse funds to influence the nomination, election, or defeat of candidates; named after Section 527 of the Internal Revenue Code, which defines and provides tax-exempt status for nonprofit advocacy groups

formula grants grants-in-aid in which a formula is used to determine the amount of federal funds a state or local government will receive

Fourteenth Amendment one of three Civil War amendments; it guaranteed equal protection and due process

framing the power of the media to influence how events and issues are interpreted

free exercise clause the First Amendment clause that protects a citizen's right to believe and practice whatever religion he or she chooses

free riders those who enjoy the benefits of collective goods but did not participate in acquiring or providing them

full faith and credit clause provision from Article IV, Section 1 of the Constitution requiring that the states normally honor the public acts and judicial decisions that take place in another state

gender gap a distinctive pattern of voting behavior reflecting the differences in views between women and men

General Agreement on Tariffs and Trade (GATT) international trade organization, in existence from 1947 to 1995, that set many of the rules governing international trade

general election a regularly scheduled election involving most districts in the nation or state, in which voters select officeholders; in the United States, general elections for national office and most state and local offices are held on the first Tuesday following the first Monday in November in even-numbered years (every four years for presidential elections)

general revenue sharing the process by which one unit of government yields a portion of its tax income to another unit of government, according to an established formula; revenue sharing typically involves the national government providing money to state governments

gerrymandering the apportionment of voters in districts in such a way as to give unfair advantage to one racial or ethnic group or political party

government institutions and procedures through which a territory and its people are ruled

government corporation government agency that performs a market-oriented public service and raises revenues to fund its activities

grand jury jury that determines whether sufficient evidence is available to justify a trial; grand juries do not rule on the accused's guilt or innocence

grants-in-aid programs through which Congress provides money to state and local governments on the condition that the funds be employed for purposes defined by the federal government

grassroots mobilization a lobbying campaign in which a group mobilizes its membership to contact government officials in support of the group's position

grassroots politics political campaigns that operate at a local level, often using face-to-face communication to generate interest and momentum by citizens

Great Compromise the agreement reached at the Constitutional Convention of 1787 that gave each state an equal number of senators regardless of its population, but linked representation in the House of Representatives to population

gross domestic product (GDP) the total value of goods and services produced within a country

habeas corpus a court order demanding that an individual in custody be brought into court and shown the cause for detention

home rule power delegated by the state to a local unit of government to manage its own affairs

impeachment the formal charge by the House of Representatives that a government official has committed "Treason, Bribery, or other high Crimes and Misdemeanors"

implementation the efforts of departments and agencies to translate laws into specific bureaucratic rules and actions

implied powers powers that are not specifically expressed in the Constitution but are seen as necessary to allow presidents to exercise their expressed powers

incumbency holding the political office for which one is running

incumbent a candidate running for re-election to a position that he or she already holds

independent agency agency that is not part of a cabinet department

indexing periodic process of adjusting social benefits or wages to account for increases in the cost of living

inflation a consistent increase in the general level of prices

informational benefits special newsletters, periodicals, training programs, conferences, and other information provided to members of groups to entice others to join

inherent powers powers claimed by a president that are not expressed in the Constitution but are inferred from it

in-kind benefits noncash goods and services provided to needy individuals and families by the federal government

institutional advertising advertising designed to create a positive image of an organization

interest group individuals who organize to influence the government's programs and policies

intermediate scrutiny a test used by the Supreme Court in gender discrimination cases that places the burden of proof partially on the government and partially on the challengers to show that the law in question is unconstitutional

International Monetary Fund (IMF) an institution established in 1944 that provides loans and facilitates international monetary exchange

iron triangle the stable, cooperative relationship that often develops among a congressional committee, an administrative agency, and one or more supportive interest groups; not all of these relationships are triangular, but the iron triangle is the most typical

isolationism avoidance of involvement in the affairs of other nations

issue network a loose network of elected leaders, public officials, activists, and interest groups drawn together by a specific policy issue

Jim Crow laws laws enacted by southern states following Reconstruction that discriminated against African Americans

joint committees legislative committees formed of members of both the House and Senate

judicial activism judicial philosophy that posits that the Court should go beyond the words of the Constitution or a statute to consider the broader societal implications of its decisions

judicial restraint judicial philosophy whose adherents refuse to go beyond the clear words of the Constitution in interpreting the document's meaning

judicial review the power of the courts to review and, if necessary, declare actions of the legislative and executive branches invalid or unconstitutional; the Supreme Court asserted this power in *Marbury v. Madison* (1803)

jurisdiction the sphere of a court's power and authority

Keynesians followers of the economic theories of John Maynard Keynes, who argued that the government can stimulate the economy by increasing public spending or by cutting taxes

Kitchen Cabinet an informal group of advisers to whom the president turns for counsel and guidance; members of the official Cabinet may or may not also be members of the Kitchen Cabinet

laissez-faire capitalism an economic system in which the means of production and distribution are privately owned and operated for profit with minimal or no government interference

leak a disclosure of confidential information to the news media

legislative initiative the president's inherent power to bring a legislative agenda before Congress

***Lemon* test** a rule articulated in *Lemon v. Kurtzman* that government action toward religion is permissible if it is secular in purpose, neither promotes nor inhibits the practice of religion, and does not lead to "excessive entanglement" with religion

libel a written statement made in "reckless disregard of the truth" that is considered damaging to a victim because it is "malicious, scandalous, and defamatory"

liberal today this term refers to those who generally support social and political reform; governmental intervention in the economy and more economic equality; expansion of federal social services; and greater concern for consumers and the environment

libertarianism a political ideology that emphasizes freedom and voluntary association with small government

liberty freedom from governmental control

limited government a principle of constitutional government; a government whose powers are defined and limited by a constitution

lobbying a strategy by which organized interests seek to influence the passage of legislation by exerting direct pressure on government officials

logrolling a legislative practice whereby agreements are made between legislators in voting for or against a bill; vote trading

loophole incentive to individuals and businesses to reduce their tax liabilities by investing their money in areas the government designates

machines strong party organizations in late nineteenth- and early twentieth-century American cities; these machines were led by "bosses" who controlled party nominations and patronage

majority leader the elected leader of the majority party in the House of Representatives or in the Senate; in the House, the majority leader is subordinate in the party hierarchy to the Speaker of the House

majority-minority district a gerrymandered voting district that improves the chances of minority candidates by making selected minority groups the majority within the district

majority party the party that holds the majority of legislative seats in either the House or the Senate

majority rule, minority rights the democratic principle that a government follows the preferences of the majority of voters but protects the interests of the minority

majority system a type of electoral system in which, to win a seat in the parliament or other representative body, a candidate must receive a majority of all the votes cast in the relevant district

mandatory spending federal spending that is made up of "uncontrollables," budget items that cannot be controlled through the regular budget process

marketplace of ideas the public forum in which beliefs and ideas are exchanged and compete

material benefits special goods, services, or money provided to members of groups to entice others to join

means testing a procedure by which potential beneficiaries of a public-assistance program establish their eligibility by demonstrating a genuine need for the assistance

media monopoly the ownership and control of the media by a few large corporations

Medicaid a federally and state-financed, state-operated program providing medical services to low-income people

Medicare a form of national health insurance for the elderly and the disabled

membership association an organized group in which members play a substantial role, sitting on committees and engaging in group projects

merit system a product of civil service reform, in which appointees to positions in public bureaucracies must objectively be deemed qualified for those positions

midterm elections congressional elections that do not coincide with a presidential election; also called off-year elections

minority leader the elected leader of the minority party in the House or Senate

minority party the party that holds a minority of legislative seats in either the House or the Senate

Miranda rule the requirement, articulated by the Supreme Court in *Miranda v. Arizona*, that persons under arrest must be informed prior to police interrogation of their rights to remain silent and to have the benefit of legal counsel

mobilization the process by which large numbers of people are organized for a political activity

monetary policies efforts to regulate the economy through the manipulation of the supply of money and credit; America's most powerful institution in this area of monetary policy is the Federal Reserve Board

monopoly a single firm in a market that controls all the goods and services of that market; absence of competition

mootness a criterion used by courts to screen cases that no longer require resolution

nation-states political entities consisting of a people with some common cultural experience (nation) who also share a common political authority (state), recognized by other sovereignties (nation-states)

national convention a national institution that nominates the party's presidential and vice-presidential candidates, establishes party rules, and writes and ratifies the party's platform

National Security Council (NSC) a presidential foreign policy advisory council composed of the president, the vice president, the secretary of state, the secretary of defense, and other officials invited by the president

necessary and proper clause Article I, Section 8, of the Constitution, which provides Congress with the authority to make all laws "necessary and proper" to carry out its expressed powers

netroots grassroots online activist organizations that have redefined membership and fund-raising practices and streamlined staff structure

New Federalism attempts by presidents Nixon and Reagan to return power to the states through block grants

New Jersey Plan a framework for the Constitution, introduced by William Paterson, that called for equal state representation in the national legislature regardless of population

news aggregator an application or feed that collects web content such as news headlines, blogs, podcasts, online videos, and more in one location for easy viewing

niche journalism news reporting devoted to a targeted portion (subset) of a journalism market sector or for a portion of readers/viewers based on content or ideological presentation

nomination the process by which political parties select their candidates for election to public office

noncontributory programs social programs that provide assistance to people on the basis of demonstrated need rather than any contribution they have made

non-state actors groups other than nation-states that attempt to play a role in the international system; terrorist groups are one type of non-state actor

North American Free Trade Agreement (NAFTA) trade treaty among the United States, Canada, and Mexico to lower and eliminate tariffs among the three countries

North Atlantic Treaty Organization (NATO) an organization, comprising the United States, Canada, and most of Western Europe, formed in 1949 to counter the perceived threat from the Soviet Union

oligarchy a form of government in which a small group—landowners, military officers, or wealthy merchants—controls most of the governing decisions

online political participation activities designed to influence government using the Internet, including visiting a candidate's website, organizing events online, or signing an online petition

open-market operations methods by which the Open Market Committee of the Federal Reserve System buys and sells government securities and other investment instruments to help finance government operations and to reduce or increase the total amount of money circulating in the economy

open primary a primary election in which the voter can wait until the day of the primary to choose which party to enroll in to select candidates for the general election

open rule a provision by the House Rules Committee that permits floor debate and the addition of new amendments to a bill

opinion the written explanation of the Supreme Court's decision in a particular case

oral argument the stage in the Supreme Court procedure in which attorneys for both sides appear before the Court to present their positions and answer questions posed by justices

original jurisdiction the authority to initially consider a case; distinguished from appellate jurisdiction, which is the authority to hear appeals from a lower court's decision

oversight the effort by Congress, through hearings, investigations, and other techniques, to exercise control over the activities of executive agencies

partisanship identification with or support of a particular party or cause

party activists partisans who contribute time, energy, and effort to support their party and its candidates

party identification an individual voter's psychological ties to one party or another

party organization the formal structure of a political party, including its leadership, election committees, active members, and paid staff

party platform a party document, written at a national convention, that contains party philosophy, principles, and policy positions

party polarization the division between the two major parties on most policy issues, with members of each party unified around their party's positions with little crossover

party unity vote a roll-call vote in the House or Senate in which at least 50 percent of the members of one party take a particular position and are opposed by at least 50 percent of the members of the other party

patronage the resources available to higher officials, usually opportunities to make partisan appointments to offices and to confer grants, licenses, or special favors to supporters

penny press cheap, tabloid-style newspaper produced in the nineteenth century, when mass production of inexpensive newspapers first became possible due to the steam-powered printing press; a penny press cost one cent compared with other papers, which cost more than five cents

permanent absentee ballots the option in some states to have a ballot sent automatically to your home for each election, rather than having to request an absentee ballot each time

plaintiff the individual or organization that brings a complaint in court

platform a party document, written at a national convention, that contains party philosophy, principles, and positions on issues

plea bargain a negotiated agreement in a criminal case in which a defendant agrees to plead guilty in return for the state's agreement to reduce the severity of the criminal charge or prison sentence the defendant is facing

pluralism the theory that all interests are and should be free to compete for influence in the government; the outcome of this competition is compromise and moderation

plurality system a type of electoral system in which, to win a seat in the parliament or other representative body, a candidate need only receive the most votes in the election, not necessarily a majority of votes cast

pocket veto a presidential veto that is automatically triggered if the president does not act on a given piece of legislation passed during the final 10 days of a legislative session

police power power reserved to the state government to regulate the health, safety, and morals of its citizens

policy entrepreneur an individual who identifies a problem as a political issue and brings a policy proposal into the political agenda

political action committee (PAC) a private group that raises and distributes funds for use in election campaigns

political culture broadly shared values, beliefs, and attitudes about how the government should function; American political culture emphasizes the values of liberty, equality, and democracy

political efficacy the ability to influence government and politics

political equality the right to participate in politics equally, based on the principle of "one person, one vote"

political ideology a cohesive set of beliefs that forms a general philosophy about the role of government

political parties organized groups that attempt to influence the government by electing their members to important government offices

political socialization the induction of individuals into the political culture; learning the underlying beliefs and values on which the political system is based

politics conflict over the leadership, structure, and policies of governments

popular sovereignty a principle of democracy in which political authority rests ultimately in the hands of the people

pork barrel (or pork) appropriations made by legislative bodies for local projects that are often not needed but that are created so that local representatives can win re-election in their home districts

power influence over a government's leadership, organization, or policies

precedent prior case whose principles are used by judges as the basis for their decision in a present case

preemption the principle that allows the national government to override state or local actions in certain policy areas; in foreign policy, the willingness to strike first in order to prevent an enemy attack

preventive war policy of striking first when a nation fears that a foreign foe is contemplating hostile action

primary elections elections held to select a party's candidate for the general election

priming process of preparing the public to bring specific criteria to mind when evaluating a politician or issue

prior restraint an effort by a governmental agency to block the publication of material it deems libelous or harmful in some other way; censorship; in the United States, the courts forbid prior restraint except under the most extraordinary circumstances

private bill a proposal in Congress to provide a specific person with some kind of relief, such as a special exemption from immigration quotas

privatization a formerly public service that is now provided by a private company but paid for by the government

privileges and immunities clause provision, from Article IV, Section 2, of the Constitution, that a state cannot discriminate against someone from another state or give its own residents special privileges

progressive taxation taxation that hits upper income brackets more heavily

project grants grant programs in which state and local governments submit proposals to federal agencies and for which funding is provided on a competitive basis

proportional representation a multiple-member district system that allows each political party representation in proportion to its percentage of the total vote

prospective voting voting based on the imagined future performance of a candidate or political party

protest participation that involves assembling crowds to confront a government or other official organization

public goods goods or services that are provided by the government because they either are not supplied by the market or are not supplied in sufficient quantities

public opinion citizens' attitudes about political issues, leaders, institutions, and events

public-opinion polls scientific instruments for measuring public opinion

public policy a law, rule, statute, or edict that expresses the government's goals and provides for rewards and punishments to promote those goals' attainment

purposive benefits selective benefits of group membership that emphasize the purpose and accomplishments of the group

push poll a polling technique in which the questions are designed to shape the respondent's opinion

random digit dialing a polling method in which respondents are selected at random from a list of 10-digit telephone numbers, with every effort made to avoid bias in the construction of the sample

recall a procedure to allow voters to remove state officials from office before their terms expire by circulating petitions to call a vote

redistribution a policy whose objective is to tax or spend in such a way as to reduce the disparities of wealth between the lowest and the highest income brackets

redistributive programs economic policies designed to control the economy through taxing and spending, with the goal of benefiting the poor

redistricting the process of redrawing election districts and redistributing legislative representatives; this happens every 10 years to reflect shifts in population or in response to legal challenges in existing districts

redlining a practice in which banks refuse to make loans to people living in certain geographic locations

referendum the practice of referring a proposed law passed by a legislature to the vote of the electorate for approval or rejection

regressive taxation taxation that hits lower income brackets more heavily

regulated federalism a form of federalism in which Congress imposes legislation on states and localities, requiring them to meet national standards

regulatory agency a department, bureau, or independent agency whose primary mission is to impose limits, restrictions, or other obligations on the conduct of individuals or companies in the private sector

representative democracy (republic) a system of government in which the populace selects representatives, who play a significant role in governmental decision making

reserved powers powers, derived from the Tenth Amendment to the Constitution, that are not specifically delegated to the national government or denied to the states

retrospective voting voting based on the past performance of a candidate or political party

revenue agency an agency responsible for collecting taxes; examples include the Internal Revenue Service for income taxes; the U.S. Customs Service for tariffs and other taxes on imported goods; and the Bureau of Alcohol, Tobacco, Firearms and Explosives for collection of taxes on the sale of those particular products

right of rebuttal a Federal Communications Commission regulation giving individuals the right to have the opportunity to respond to personal attacks made on a radio or television broadcast

right to privacy the right to be left alone, which has been interpreted by the Supreme Court to entail individual access to birth control and abortions

roll-call vote a vote in which each legislator's yes or no vote is recorded as the clerk calls the names of the members alphabetically

runoff election a "second round" election in which voters choose between the top two candidates from the first round

sample a small group selected by researchers to represent the most important characteristics of an entire population

sampling error (or margin of error) polling error that arises based on the small size of the sample

select committees (usually) temporary legislative committees set up to highlight or investigate a particular issue or address an issue not within the jurisdiction of existing committees

selection bias (news) the tendency to focus news coverage on only one aspect of an event or issue, avoiding coverage of other aspects

selection bias (surveys) polling error that arises when the sample is not representative of the population being studied, which creates errors in overrepresenting or underrepresenting some opinions

selective incorporation the process by which different protections in the Bill of Rights were incorporated into the Fourteenth Amendment, thus guaranteeing citizens protection from state as well as national governments

senatorial courtesy the practice whereby the president, before formally nominating a person for a federal judgeship, seeks the indication that senators from the candidate's own state support the nomination

seniority the ranking given to an individual on the basis of length of continuous service on a committee in Congress

"separate but equal" rule doctrine that public accommodations could be segregated by race but still be considered equal

separation of powers the division of governmental power among several institutions that must cooperate in decision making

signing statements announcements made by the president when signing bills into law, often presenting the president's interpretation of the law

simple random sample (or probability sample) a method used by pollsters to select a representative sample in which every individual in the population has an equal probability of being selected as a respondent

slander an oral statement made in "reckless disregard of the truth" that is considered damaging to the victim because it is "malicious, scandalous, and defamatory"

social desirability effect the effect that results when respondents in a survey report what they expect the interviewer wishes to hear rather than what they believe

social media web and mobile-based technologies that are used to turn communication into interactive dialogue among organizations, communities, and individuals; social media technologies take on many different forms including blogs, Wikis, podcasts, pictures, video, Facebook, and Twitter

Social Security a contributory welfare program into which working Americans contribute a percentage of their wages and from which they receive cash benefits after retirement or if they become disabled

socialism a political ideology that emphasizes social ownership and strong government

socioeconomic status status in society based on level of education, income, and occupational prestige

sociological representation a type of representation in which representatives have the same racial, gender, ethnic, religious, or educational backgrounds as their constituents; it is based on the principle that if two individuals are similar in background, character, interests, and perspectives, then one can correctly represent the other's views

soft money money contributed directly to political parties and other organizations for political activities that is not regulated by federal campaign spending laws; in 2002 federal law prohibited unregulated donations to national party committees

solicitor general the top government lawyer in all cases before the Supreme Court where the government is a party

solidary benefits selective benefits of group membership that emphasize friendship, networking, and consciousness raising

Speaker of the House the chief presiding officer of the House of Representatives; the Speaker is the most important party and House leader, and can influence the legislative agenda, the fate of individual pieces of legislation, and members' positions within the House

"speech plus" speech accompanied by conduct such as sit-ins, picketing, and demonstrations. Protection of this form of speech under the First Amendment is conditional, and restrictions imposed by state or local authorities are acceptable if properly balanced by considerations of public order

spot (advertisement) a 15-, 30-, or 60-second television campaign commercial that permits a candidate's message to be delivered to a target audience

staff agencies legislative support agencies responsible for policy analysis

staff organization a type of membership group in which a professional staff conducts most of the group's activities

standing the right of an individual or organization to initiate a court case, on the basis of their having a substantial stake in the outcome

standing committee a permanent committee with the power to propose and write legislation that covers a particular subject, such as finance or agriculture

stare decisis literally, "let the decision stand"; the doctrine that a previous decision by a court applies as a precedent in similar cases until that decision is overruled

states' rights the principle that the states should oppose the increasing authority of the national government; this principle was most popular in the period before the Civil War

straight-ticket voting selecting candidates from the same political party for all offices on the ballot

strict scrutiny a test used by the Supreme Court in racial discrimination cases and other cases involving civil liberties and civil rights that places the burden of proof on the government rather than on the challengers to show that the law in question is constitutional

subsidies government grants of cash or other valuable commodities, such as land, to an individual or an organization; used to promote activities desired by the government, reward political support, or buy off political opposition

suffrage the right to vote; also called *franchise*

Super PAC an independent political action committee that may raise unlimited sums of money from corporations, unions, and individuals but is not permitted to contribute to or coordinate directly with parties or candidates

Supplemental Nutrition Assistance Program (SNAP) the largest antipoverty program, which provides recipients with a debit card for food at most grocery stores; formerly known as *food stamps*

supply-side economics an economic theory that posits that reducing the marginal rate of taxation will create a productive economy by promoting levels of work and investment that would otherwise be discouraged by higher taxes

supremacy clause Article VI of the Constitution, which states that laws passed by the national government and all treaties are the supreme law of the land and superior to all laws adopted by any state or any subdivision

supreme court the highest court in a particular state or in the United States; this court primarily serves an appellate function

tariff a tax on imported goods

tax expenditures government subsidies provided to employers and employees through tax deductions for amounts spent on health insurance and other benefits

term limits legally prescribed limits on the number of terms an elected official can serve

third parties parties that organize to compete against the two major American political parties

Thirteenth Amendment one of three Civil War amendments; it abolished slavery

Three-Fifths Compromise the agreement reached at the Constitutional Convention of 1787 that stipulated that for purposes of the apportionment of congressional seats, every slave would be counted as three-fifths of a person

totalitarian government a system of rule in which the government recognizes no formal limits on its power and seeks to absorb or eliminate other social institutions that might challenge it

town hall meeting an informal public meeting in which candidates meet with ordinary citizens; allows candidates to deliver messages without the presence of journalists or commentators

traditional political participation activities designed to influence government including voting and face-to-face activities such as protesting or volunteering for a campaign

trial court the first court to hear a criminal or civil case

trustee a representative who votes based on what he or she thinks is best for his or her constituency

turnout the percentage of eligible individuals who actually vote

two-party system a political system in which only two parties have a realistic opportunity to compete effectively for control

tyranny oppressive government that employs cruel and unjust use of power and authority

uncontrollables budgetary items that are beyond the control of budgetary committees and can be controlled only by substantive legislative action in Congress; some uncontrollables, such as interest on the debt, are beyond the power of Congress, because the terms of payments are set in contracts

unfunded mandates regulations or conditions for receiving grants that impose costs on state and local governments for which they are not reimbursed by the federal government

unitary system a centralized government system in which lower levels of government have little power independent of the national government

United Nations (UN) an organization of nations founded in 1945 to be a channel for negotiation and a means of settling international disputes peaceably; the UN has had frequent successes in providing a forum for negotiation and, on some occasions, a means of preventing international conflicts from spreading; on a number of occasions, the UN has been a convenient cover for U.S. foreign policy goals

values (or beliefs) basic principles that shape a person's opinions about political issues and events

veto the president's constitutional power to turn down acts of Congress; a presidential veto may be overridden by a two-thirds vote of each house of Congress

Virginia Plan a framework for the Constitution, introduced by Edmund Randolph, that called for representation in the national legislature based on the population of each state

War Powers Resolution a resolution of Congress that the president can send troops into action abroad only by authorization of Congress, or if American troops are already under attack or serious threat

whip a party member in the House or Senate responsible for coordinating the party's legislative strategy, building support for key issues, and counting votes

White House staff analysts and advisers to the president, each of whom is often given the title "special assistant"

Word Trade Organization (WTO) international organization promoting free trade that grew out of the General Agreement on Tariffs and Trade

writ of certiorari a decision of at least four of the nine Supreme Court justices to review a decision of a lower court; *certiorari* is Latin, meaning "to make more certain"

writ of habeas corpus a court order that the individual in custody be brought into court and shown the cause for detention; habeas corpus is guaranteed by the Constitution and can be suspended only in cases of rebellion or invasion

endnotes

Chapter 1

1. Pew Research Center, "Trust in Government Nears Record Low, but Most Federal Agencies Are Viewed Favorably," October 18, 2013, www.people-press.org/2013/10/18/trust-in-government-nears-record-low-but-most-federal-agencies-are-viewed-favorably/ (accessed 5/15/14).

2. Pew Research Center, "Trust in Government Nears Record Low."

3. The ANES Guide to Public Opinion and Electoral Behavior, "Trust the Federal Government, 1958–2008," www.electionstudies.org/nesguide/toptable/tab5a_1.htm (accessed 6/8/12).

4. ANES Guide to Public Opinion and Electoral Behavior, "Trust the Federal Government."

5. The New York Times/CBS News Poll, "Americans' Approval of Congress Drops to Single Digits," October 25, 2011, www.nytimes.com/interactive/2011/10/25/us/politics/approval-of-congress-drops-to-single-digits.html?ref=politics (accessed 6/8/12).

6. Joseph S. Nye, Jr., "Introduction: The Decline of Confidence in Government," in *Why People Don't Trust Government*, ed. Joseph S. Nye Jr., Philip D. Zelikow, and David C. King (Cambridge, MA: Harvard University Press, 1997), p. 4.

7. Pew Research Center for the People and the Press, "Political Typology Survey," January 2014, www.ropercenter.uconn.edu/data_access/ipoll/ipoll.html (accessed 7/7/14).

8. Pew Research Center for the People and the Press, "Partisan Polarization Surges in Bush, Obama Years; Trends in American Values: 1987–2012, Section 4: Values about Government and the Social Safety Net," www.people-press.org/2012/06/04/section-4-values-about-government-and-the-social-safety-net/ (accessed 6/8/12).

9. This definition is taken from Norman H. Nie, Jane Junn, and Kenneth Stehlik-Barry, *Education and Democratic Citizenship in America* (Chicago: University of Chicago Press, 1996).

10. Pew Internet and American life, "What Internet Users Do Online," February 2012 survey, http://pewinternet.org/Trend=Data=(Adults)/Online=activities=Total.uspx (accessed 6/5/12).

11. Freedom House, "Freedom in the World Report, 2013, Essay: Democratic Breakthroughs in the Balance," www.freedomhouse.org/report/freedom-world-2013/essay-democratic-breakthroughs-balance (accessed 9/25/13).

12. See Eugen Weber, *Peasants into Frenchmen: The Modernization of Rural France, 1870–1914* (Stanford, CA: Stanford University Press, 1976), chap. 5.

13. See V. O. Key, *Politics, Parties, and Pressure Groups* (New York: Crowell, 1964), p. 201.

14. Harold Lasswell, *Politics: Who Gets What, When, How* (New York: Meridian Books, 1958).

15. Susan B. Carter, Scott Sigmund Gartner, Michael R. Haines, Alan L. Olmstead, Richard Sutch, and Gavin Wright, eds., *Historical Statistics of the United States: Millennial Edition Online*, Table Aa145-184, Population, by Sex and Race: 1790–1990 (New York: Cambridge University Press, 2006). Data from 2012 available at U.S. Census Bureau, www.census.gov (accessed 2/25/12).

16. Carter et al., *Historical Statistics of the United States*, Table Aa145-184, Population, by Sex and Race: 1790–1990.

17. Carter et al., *Historical Statistics of the United States*, Table Aa145-184, Population, by Sex and Race: 1790–1990; Table Aa2189-2215, Hispanic Population Estimates.

18. U.S. Census Bureau, www.census.gov; Claude S. Fischer and Michael Hout, *A Century of Difference: How America Changed in the Last One Hundred Years* (New York: Russell Sage Foundation, 2006), p. 36.

19. Carter et al., *Historical Statistics of the United States*, Table Aa22-35, Selected Population Characteristics.

20. Fischer and Hout, *A Century of Difference*, p. 24.

21. Michael B. Katz and Mark J. Stern, *One Nation Divisible: What America Was and What It Is Becoming* (New York: Russell Sage Foundation, 2006), p. 16.

22. Carter et al., *Historical Statistics of the United States*, Table Aa145-184, Population, by Sex and Race: 1790–1990, p. 23. Karen R. Humes, Nicholas A. Jones, and Roberto R. Ramirez, "Overview of Race and Hispanic Origin: 2010," *2010 Census Briefs*, Number C210BR-02 (Washington, DC: U.S. Census Bureau, March 2011), p. 4, www.census.gov/prod/cen2010/briefs/c2010br-02.pdf (accessed 10/14/2011).

23. U.S. Census Bureau, "Annual Estimates of the Resident Population by Sex, Race, and Hispanic Origin for the United States, States, and Counties: April 1, 2010 to July 1, 2012," factfinder2.census.gov/faces/tableservices/jsf/pages/productview.xhtml?pid=PEP_2012_PEPASR6H&prodType=table (accessed 9/25/13).

24. U.S. Census Bureau, "2012 American Community Survey 1-Year Estimates: Selected Social Characteristics in the United States," factfinder2.census.gov/faces/tableservices/jsf/pages/productview.xhtml?pid=ACS_12_1YR_DP02&prodType=table (accessed 9/25/13).

25. U.S. Census Bureau, "2012 American Community Survey 1-Year Estimates: Selected Characteristics of the Foreign-Born Population by Region of Birth: Latin America," factfinder2.census.gov/faces/tableservices/jsf/pages/productview.xhtml?pid=ACS_12_1YR_S0506&prodType=table (accessed 9/25/13).

26. U.S. Census Bureau, "2012 American Community Survey 1-Year Estimates: Selected Social Characteristics in the United States," factfinder2.census.gov/faces/tableservices/jsf/pages/productview.xhtml?pid=ACS_12_1YR_DP02&prodType=table (accessed 9/25/13).

27. Michael Hoefer, Nancy Rytina, and Bryan Barker, "Estimates of the Unauthorized Immigrant Population Residing in the United States: January 2011," *Population Estimates*, Office of Immigration Statistics, Department of Homeland Security, March 2012, www.dhs.gov/sites/default/files/publications/ois_ill_pe_2011.pdf (accessed 9/25/13).

28. Anthony Faiola, "States' Immigrant Policies Diverge," *Washington Post*, October 15, 2007, p. A1.

29. *Plyler v. Doe*, 457 U.S. 202 (1982).

30. The Pew Forum on Religion and Public Life, "'Nones' on the Rise: One in Five Adults Have No Religious Affiliation," Pew Research Center, October 9, 2012, www.pewforum.org/files/2012/10/NonesOnTheRise-full.pdf (accessed 5/15/14).

31. The Pew Forum on Religion and Public Life, "'Nones' on the Rise"; Michael Lipka, "How Many Jew Are There in the United States?" Pew Research Center, October 2, 2013, www.pewresearch.org/fact-tank/2013/10/02/how-many-jews-are-there-in-the-united-states/ (accessed 5/15/14). Muslim population is from 2010. See Pew Research Religion and Public Life Project, "The Future of the Global Muslim Population," January 27, 2011, www.pewforum.org/2011/01/27/the-future-of-the-global-muslim-population/#the-americas (accessed 5/15/14).

32. U.S. Census Bureau, "Annual Estimates of the Resident Population for Selected Age Groups by Sex for the United States, States, Counties, and Puerto Rico Commonwealth and Municipios: April 1, 2010 to July 1, 2012," factfinder2.census.gov/faces/tableservices/jsf/pages/productview.xhtml?src=bkmk (accessed 9/25/13).

33. Eurostat, "Population Structure and Ageing," October 2012. epp.eurostat.ec.europa.eu/statistics_explained/index.php/Population_structure_and_ageing (accessed 9/25/13).

34. U.S. Census Bureau, "Growth in Urban Population Outpaces Rest of Nation, Census Bureau Reports," March 26, 2012, www.census.gov/newsroom/releases/archives/2010_census/cb12-50.html (accessed 9/25/13).

35. Thomas Piketty, and Emmanuel Saez, "Income Inequality in the United States, 1993–1998," *Quarterly Journal of Economics* 18 No. 1 (2003), (Tables and Figures Updated to 2012, September 2013), elsa.berkeley.edu/~saez/TabFig2012prel.xls (accessed 10/14/13).

36. U.S. Census Bureau, "Historical Income Tables, Tables F-2, F-3 and F-6."

37. "Bordering on Poverty," *New York Times* November 18, 2011, www.nytimes.com/interactive/2011/11/19/us/bordering-on-poverty.html?ref=us (accessed 10-16-13).

38. U.S. Census Bureau, "Congressional Apportionment: 2010 Apportionment Results," www.census.gov/population/apportionment/files/Apportionment%20Population%202010.pdf (accessed 9/25/13)

39. See Judith N. Shklar, *American Citizenship: The Quest for Inclusion* (Cambridge, MA: Harvard University Press, 1991).

40. Herbert McClosky and John Zaller, *The American Ethos: Public Attitudes toward Capitalism and Democracy* (Cambridge, MA: Harvard University Press, 1984), p. 19.

41. J. R. Pole, *The Pursuit of Equality in American History* (Berkeley: University of California Press, 1978), p. 3.

42. *Plessy v. Ferguson*, 163 U.S. 537 (1896).

43. *Brown v. Board of Education*, 347 U.S. 483 (1954).

44. See Rogers M. Smith, *Liberalism and American Constitutional Law* (Cambridge, MA: Harvard University Press, 1985), chap. 6.

45. The case was *San Antonio Independent School District v. Rodriguez*, 411 U.S. 1 (1973). See the discussion in Smith, *Liberalism and American Constitutional Law*, pp. 163–64.

46. See the discussion in Eileen McDonagh, "Gender Political Change," in *New Perspectives on American Politics*, ed. Lawrence C. Dodd and Calvin C. Jillson (Washington, DC: CQ Press, 1994), pp. 58–73. The argument for moving women's issues into the public sphere is made by Jean Bethke Elshtain, *Public Man, Private Woman* (Princeton, NJ: Princeton University Press, 1981).

47. Roger Lowenstein, "The Way We Live Now: The Inequality Conundrum," *New York Times Magazine*, June 10, 2007, p. 11.

48. Associated Press, "Obama: Tax Cuts Will Be Felt by April 1," February 21, 2009, www.msnbc.msn.com/id/29314485/ (accessed 9/28/09).

49. The Roper Center for Public Opinion Research, "Topics at a Glance: Poverty," www.ropercenter.uconn.edu/data_access/ipoll/ipoll.htm (accessed 5/15/14). Pew Research Center for the People and the Press and for the Public, "Trends in American Values, 1987–2012, Partisan Polarization Surges in Bush, Obama Years," June 4, 2012, www.people-press.org/2012/06/04/partisan-polarization-surges-in-bush-obama-years p. 89 (accessed 6/9/12).

50. Kevin Phillips, *Arrogant Capital: Washington, Wall Street, and the Frustration of American Politics* (Boston: Little, Brown, 1994).

51. United States Election Project, "Voter Turnout: Turnout 1980–2008," http://elections.gmu.edu/voter_turnout.htm (accessed 9/29/09).

52. Center for the Study of the American Electorate, "2008 Turnout Report: African-Americans, Anger, Fear and Youth Propel Turnout to Highest Level since 1960," news release, December 17, 2008, www.american.edu/ia/cdem/csae/pdfs/2008pdfoffinaledited.pdf (accessed 9/29/09).

Chapter 2

1. The social makeup of colonial America and some of the social conflicts that divided colonial society are discussed in Jackson Turner Main, *The Social Structure of Revolutionary America* (Princeton, NJ: Princeton University Press, 1965).

2. George B. Tindall and David E. Shi, *America: A Narrative History*, 8th ed. (New York: W. W. Norton, 2010), p. 202.

3. For a discussion of events leading up to the Revolution, see Charles M. Andrews, *The Colonial Background of the American Revolution* (New Haven, CT: Yale University Press, 1924).

4. See Carl Becker, *The Declaration of Independence* (New York: Knopf, 1942).

5. An excellent and readable account of the development from the Articles of Confederation to the Constitution will be found in Alfred H. Kelly, Winfred A. Harbison, and Herman Belz, *The American Constitution: Its Origins and Development*, 7th ed. (New York: W. W. Norton, 1991), vol. 1, chap. 5.

6. Reported in Samuel E. Morrison, Henry Steele Commager, and William Leuchtenberg, *The Growth of the American Republic* (New York: Oxford University Press, 1969), vol. 1, p. 244.

7. Quoted in Morrison et al., *The Growth of the American Republic*, vol. 1, p. 242.

8. Charles A. Beard, *An Economic Interpretation of the Constitution of the United States* (New York: Macmillan, 1913).

9. Madison's notes, along with the somewhat less complete records kept by several other participants in the convention, are available in a four-volume set. See Max Farrand, ed., *The Records of the Federal Convention of 1787*, 4 vols., rev. ed. (New Haven, CT: Yale University Press, 1966).

10. Farrand, ed., *The Records of the Federal Convention of 1787*, vol. 1, p. 476.

11. Alexander Hamilton, James Madison, and John Jay, *The Federalist Papers*, ed. Clinton L. Rossiter (New York: New American Library, 1961), no. 71.

12. *The Federalist Papers*, no. 62.

13. *The Federalist Papers*, no. 70.

14. Max Farrand, *The Framing of the Constitution of the United States* (New Haven, CT: Yale University Press, 1962), p. 49.

15. Melancton Smith, quoted in Herbert J. Storing, *What the Anti-Federalists Were For* (Chicago: University of Chicago Press, 1981), p. 17.

16. "Essays of Brutus," no. 1, in *The Complete Anti-Federalist*, ed. Herbert Storing (Chicago: University of Chicago Press, 1981).

17. *The Federalist Papers*, no. 57.

18. "Essays of Brutus," no. 15, in Storing, ed., *The Complete Anti-Federalist*.

19. *The Federalist Papers*, no. 10.

20. "Essays of Brutus," no. 7, in Storing, ed., *The Complete Anti-Federalist*.

21. "Essays of Brutus," no. 6, in Storing, ed., *The Complete Anti-Federalist*.

22. Storing, *What the Anti-Federalists Were For*, p. 28.

23. *The Federalist Papers*, no. 51.

24. Quoted in Storing, *What the Anti-Federalists Were For*, p. 30.

25. *The Federalist Papers*, no. 10.

26. Thomas P. Crocker, "The Political Fourth Amendment," *Washington University Law Review*, vol. 88, no. 2 (2010) 303–79.

27. *Marcus v. Search Warrant*, 367 U.S. 717 (1961).

Chapter 3

1. Bradley Dennis, "Obama Administration Will Not Block State Marijuana Laws, If Distribution Is Regulated," *Washington Post*, August 29, 2013, http://articles.washingtonpost.com/2013-08-29/national/41566270_1_marijuana-legalization-attorney-general-bob-ferguson-obama-administration (accessed 11/17/13).

2. Adam Liptak, "Bans on Interracial Unions Offer Perspective on Gay Ones," *New York Times*, March 17, 2004, p. A22.

3. *Loving v. Virginia* 388 U.S. 1 (1967). The Lovings were charged with violating Virginia's miscegenation laws and were sentenced to one year in jail, which would

be suspended if they left the state for 25 years. Five years later, with the assistance of the American Civil Liberties Union, the Lovings filed a motion to vacate their conviction. The Supreme Court heard the case and overturned the Lovings's conviction, finding Virginia's miscegenation law unconstitutional under the due process clause and equal protection clause of the Fourteenth Amendment.

4. ProCon.org, "35 States with Legal Gay Marriage and 15 States with Same-Sex Marriage Bans," updated November 20, 2014, http://gaymarriage.procon.org/view.resource.php?resourceID=004857 (accessed 11/21/14).

5. Ken I. Kersch, "Full Faith and Credit for Same-Sex Marriages?" *Political Science Quarterly* 112 (Spring 1997): 117–36; Joan Biskupic, "Once Unthinkable, Now under Debate," *Washington Post*, September 3, 1996, p. A1.

6. *United States v. Windsor*, 570 U.S. __ (2013).

7. *Hicklin v. Orbeck*, 437 U.S. 518 (1978).

8. *Sweeny v. Woodall*, 344 U.S. 86 (1953).

9. Patricia S. Florestano, "Past and Present Utilization of Interstate Compacts in the United States," *Publius* 24 (Fall 1994): 13–26.

10. See the discussion in www.nationalpopularvote.com (accessed 5/15/14); for a critique of the effort, see David Gringer, "Note: Why the National Popular Vote Is the Wrong Way to Abolish the Electoral College," *Columbia Law Review* 108 (January 2008): 182–230.

11. A good discussion of the constitutional position of local governments is in Richard Briffault, "Our Localism: Part I, the Structure of Local Government Law," *Columbia Law Review* 90, no. 1 (January 1990): 1–115. For more on the structure and theory of federalism, see Larry N. Gerston, *American Federalism: A Concise Introduction* (Armonk, NY: M.E. Sharpe, 2007), and Martha Derthick, "Up-to-Date in Kansas City: Reflections on American Federalism" (1992 John Gaus Lecture), *PS: Political Science and Politics* 25 (December 1992): 671–75.

12. Gary Fields and John R. Emshwiller, "As Criminal Laws Proliferate, More Are Ensnared," *Wall Street Journal*, July 23, 2011, online.wsj.com/news/articles/SB10001424052748703749504576172714184601654 (accessed 11/5/13).

13. Rachel Barkow, "Federalism and Criminal Law: What the Feds Can Learn from the States," 109 *Michigan Law Review* 519 (2011), www.michiganlawreview.org/assets/pdfs/109/4/barkow.pdf (accessed 11/5/13).

14. For a good treatment of the contrast between national political stability and social instability, see Samuel P. Huntington, *Political Order in Changing Societies* (New Haven, CT: Yale University Press, 1968), chap. 2.

15. *McCulloch v. Maryland*, 4 Wheaton 316 (1819).

16. *Gibbons v. Ogden*, 9 Wheaton 1 (1824).

17. The Sherman Antitrust Act, adopted in 1890, for example, was enacted not to restrict commerce, but rather to protect it from monopolies, or trusts, in order to prevent unfair trade practices and to enable the market again to become self-regulating. Moreover, the Supreme Court sought to uphold liberty of contract to protect businesses. For example, in *Lochner v. New York*, 198 U.S. 45 (1905), the Court invalidated a New York law regulating the sanitary conditions and hours of labor of bakers on the grounds that the law interfered with liberty of contract.

18. The key case in this process of expanding the power of the national government is generally considered to be *NLRB v. Jones & Laughlin Steel Corporation*, 301 U.S. 1 (1937), in which the Supreme Court approved federal regulation of the workplace and thereby virtually eliminated interstate commerce as a limit on the national government's power.

19. *United States v. Darby Lumber Co.*, 312 U.S. 100 (1941).

20. W. John Moore, "Pleading the 10th," *National Journal*, July 29, 1995, p. 1940.

21. *United States v. Lopez*, 14 U.S. 549 (1995).

22. *Printz v. United States*, 521 U.S. 98 (1997).

23. See the poll reported in Guy Gugliotta, "Scaling Down the American Dream," *Washington Post*, April 19, 1995, p. A21. See also John Kincaid and Richard L. Cole, "Citizens' Attitudes toward Issues of Federalism in Canada, Mexico and the United States," *Publius: The Journal of Federalism* 41, no. 1 (2011): 53–75.

24. Kenneth T. Palmer, "The Evolution of Grant Policies," in *The Changing Politics of Federal Grants*, ed. Lawrence D. Brown, James W. Fossett, and Kenneth T. Palmer (Washington, DC: Brookings Institution Press, 1984), p. 15.

25. Palmer, "The Evolution of Grant Policies," p. 6.

26. Morton Grodzins, *The American System*, ed. Daniel J. Elazar (Chicago: Rand McNally, 1966).

27. See Terry Sanford, *Storm over the States* (New York: McGraw-Hill, 1967).

28. James L. Sundquist, with David W. Davis, *Making Federalism Work* (Washington, DC: Brookings Institution Press, 1969), p. 271. George Wallace was mistrusted by the architects of the War on Poverty because he was a strong proponent of racial segregation and "states' rights."

29. See Donald F. Kettl, *The Regulation of American Federalism* (Baton Rouge: Louisiana State University Press, 1983).

30. Cindy Skrzycki, "Trial Lawyers on the Offensive in Fight against Preemptive Rules," *Washington Post*, September 11, 2007, p. D2.

31. *Gonazales v. Oregon*, 546 U.S. 243 (2006).

32. *Wyeth v. Levine*, 555 U.S. 555 (2009).

33. Philip Rucker, "Obama Curtails Bush's Policy of 'Preemption,'" *Washington Post*, May 22, 2009, p. A3.

34. See U.S. Advisory Commission on Intergovernmental Relations, *Federal Regulation of State and Local Governments: The Mixed Record of the 1980s* (Washington,

DC: Advisory Commission on Intergovernmental Relations, July 1993).

35. Robert Jay Dilger and Richard S. Beth, "Unfunded Mandates Reform Act: History, Impact, and Issues," (Washington, DC: Congressional Research Service, April 19, 2011), p.40, http://digital.library.unt.edu/ark:/67531/metadc40084/m1/1/high_res_d/R40957_2011Apr19.pdf (accessed 11/16/13).

36. U.S. Advisory Commission on Intergovernmental Relations, *Federal Regulation of State and Local Governments*, p. iii.

37. Congressional Budget Office, "A Review of CBO's Activities in 2012 under the Unfunded Mandates Reform Act," March 2013, www.cbo.gov/sites/default/files/cbofiles/attachments/44032_UMRA.pdf (accessed 11/2/13).

38. Adam Liptak, "Justices to Hear Health Care Case as Race Heats Up," *New York Times*, November 15, 2011, p. A1.

39. Quoted in Timothy Conlon, *New Federalism: Intergovernmental Reform from Nixon to Reagan* (Washington, DC: Brookings Institution Press, 1988), p. 25.

40. For the emergence of complaints about federal categorical grants, see Palmer, "The Evolution of Grant Policies," pp. 17–18. On the governors' efforts to gain more control over federal grants after the 1994 congressional elections, see Dan Balz, "GOP Governors Eager to Do Things Their Way," *Washington Post*, November 22, 1994, p. A4.

41. U.S. Advisory Commission on Intergovernmental Relations, *Federal Regulation of State and Local Governments*.

42. For an assessment of the achievements of the 104th and 105th Congresses, see Timothy Conlan, *From New Federalism to Devolution: Twenty-Five Years of Intergovernmental Reform* (Washington, DC: Brookings Institution Press, 1998).

43. Robert Frank, "Proposed Block Grants Seen Unlikely to Cure Management Problems," *Wall Street Journal*, May 1, 1995, p. 1.

44. Sarah Kershaw, "U.S. Rule Limits Emergency Care for Immigrants," *New York Times*, September 22, 2007, p. A1.

45. U.S. Committee on Federalism and National Purpose, *To Form a More Perfect Union* (Washington, DC: National Conference on Social Welfare, 1985). See also the discussion in Paul E. Peterson, *The Price of Federalism* (Washington, DC: Brooking Institution Press, 1995), esp. chap. 8.

46. Malcolm Gladwell, "Remaking Welfare: In States' Experiments, a Cutting Contest," *Washington Post*, March 10, 1995, p. 6.

47. The phrase "laboratories of democracy" was coined by Supreme Court Justice Louis Brandeis in his dissenting opinion in *New State Ice Co. v. Liebman*, 285 U.S. 262 (1932).

48. "Motor Vehicle Fatalities in 1996 Were 12 Percent Higher on Interstates, Freeways in 12 States That Raised Speed Limits," Insurance Institute for Highway Safety, press release, October 10, 1997.

49. *Gonzales v. Raich*, 545 U.S. 1 (2005). For more, see William Yardley, "New Federal Crackdown Confounds States That Allow Medical Marijuana," *New York Times*, May 8, 2011, p. A13.

50. *Gonzales v. Oregon* (2006).

51. National Conference of State Legislatures, "Collecting E-Commerce Taxes," www.ncsl.org/research/fiscal-policy/collecting-ecommerce-taxes-an-interactive-map.aspx (accessed 11/17/13).

52. National Conference of State Legislatures, "2013 Report on State Immigration Laws," www.ncsl.org/research/immigration/immgration-report-august-2013.aspx (accessed 11/3/13).

53. Associated Press, "Justice Department Sues Utah over State's Illegal Immigration Enforcement Law," *Washington Post*, November 22, 2011, www.washingtonpost.com/national/us-department-of-justice-sues-utah-over-immigration-enforcement-law/2011/11/22/gIQAJeJEmN_story.html (accessed 11/27/11).

54. *Arizona v. United States*, 11–182 (2012). Adam Liptak, "Blocking Parts of Arizona Law, Justices Allow Its Centerpiece," *New York Times*, June 25, 2012, www.nytimes.com/2012/06/26/us/supreme-court-rejects-part-of-arizona-immigration-law.html (accessed 11/3/13).

55. Julia Preston, "States Resisting Program Central to Obama's Immigration Strategy," *New York Times*, May 6, 2011, p. A18; Gretchen Gavett, "Why Three Governors Challenged Secure Communities," PBS *Frontline*, October 18, 2011, www.pbs.org/wgbh/pages/frontline/race-multicultural/lost-in-detention/why-three-governors-challenged-secure-communities (accessed 11/27/11).

56. The White House, Office of the Press Secretary, Memorandum for the Heads of Executive Departments and Agencies, Subject: Preemption, May 20, 2009, http://theusconstituion.org/blog.history/wp-content/uploads/2009/05/obama-preemption-memo-5202009.pdf (accessed 10/17/09).

57. Adam Liptak, "In Health Law, Asking Where U.S. Power Stops," *New York Times*, November 14, 2011, p. A1.

Chapter 4

1. Thomas P. Crocker, "The Political Fourth Amendment," *Washington University Law Review* 88, no. 2 (2010): 347.

2. *Marcus v. Search Warrant*, 367 U.S. 717 (1961).

3. Alexander Hamilton, James Madison, and John Jay, *The Federalist Papers*, ed. Clinton Rossiter (New York: New American Library, 1961), no. 84, p. 513.

4. *The Federalist Papers*, no. 84, p. 513.

5. Clinton Rossiter, *1787: The Grand Convention* (New York: W. W. Norton, 1987), 302.

6. Rossiter, *1787*, p. 303. Rossiter also reports that "in 1941 the States of Connecticut, Massachusetts, and Georgia celebrated the sesquicentennial of the Bill of Rights by giving their hitherto withheld and unneeded assent."

7. *Barron v. Baltimore*, 7 Peters 243, 246 (1833).

8. The Fourteenth Amendment also seems designed to introduce civil rights. The final clause of the all-important Section 1 provides that no state can "deny to any person within its jurisdiction the equal protection of the laws." It is not unreasonable to conclude that the purpose of this provision was to obligate the state governments as well as the national government to take positive actions to protect citizens from arbitrary and discriminatory actions, at least those based on race. This will be explored in Chapter 5.

9. For example, *The Slaughterhouse Cases*, 16 Wallace 36 (1883).

10. *Chicago, Burlington and Quincy Railroad Company v. Chicago*, 166 U.S. 226 (1897).

11. *Gitlow v. New York*, 268 U.S. 652 (1925).

12. *Near v. Minnesota*, 283 U.S. 697 (1931); *Hague v. C.I.O.*, 307 U.S. 496 (1939).

13. *Palko v. Connecticut*, 302 U.S. 319 (1937).

14. All of these were implicitly included in the *Palko* case as "not incorporated" into the Fourteenth Amendment as limitations on the powers of the states.

15. There is one interesting exception, which involves the Sixth Amendment right to public trial. In the 1948 case *In re Oliver*, 33 U.S. 257, the right to the public trial was, in effect, incorporated as part of the Fourteenth Amendment. However, the issue in that case was put more generally as "due process," and public trial itself was not actually mentioned in so many words. Later opinions, such as *Duncan v. Louisiana*, 391 U.S. 145 (1968), cited the *Oliver* case as the precedent for more explicit incorporation of public trials as part of the Fourteenth Amendment.

16. *Abington School District v. Schempp*, 374 U.S. 203 (1963).

17. *Engel v. Vitale*, 370 U.S. 421 (1962).

18. *Wallace v. Jaffree*, 472 U.S. 38 (1985).

19. *Lemon v. Kurtzman*, 403 U.S. 602 (1971). The *Lemon* test is still good law, but as recently as the 1994 Court term, four justices have urged that the test be abandoned. Here is a settled area of law that may soon become unsettled.

20. *Rosenberger v. Rector and Visitors of the University of Virginia*, 515 U.S. 819 (1995).

21. *Van Orden v. Perry*, 545 U.S. 677 (2005).

22. *McCreary County v. American Civil Liberties Union of Kentucky*, 545 U.S. 844 (2005).

23. *West Virginia State Board of Education v. Barnette*, 319 U.S. 624 (1943). The case it reversed was *Minersville School District v. Gobitus*, 310 U.S. 586 (1940).

24. *Cantwell v. Connecticut*, 310 U.S. 296 (1940).

25. *Employment Division, Department of Human Resources of Oregon v. Smith*, 494 U.S. 872 (1990).

26. *City of Boerne v. Flores*, 521 U.S. 507 (1997).

27. *Abrams v. United States*, 250 U.S. 616 (1919).

28. *United States v. Carolene Products Company*, 304 U.S. 144 (1938), note 4. This footnote is one of the Court's most important doctrines. See Alfred H. Kelly, Winfred A. Harbison, and Herman Belz, *The American Constitution: Its Origins and Development*, 7th ed. (New York: Norton, 1991), vol. 2, 519–23.

29. *Schenk v. United States*, 249 U.S. 47 (1919).

30. *Brandenburg v. Ohio*, 395 U.S. 444 (1969).

31. *Buckley v. Valeo*, 424 U.S. 1 (1976).

32. *McConnell v. Federal Election Commission*, 540 U.S. 93 (2003).

33. *Federal Election Commission v. Wisconsin Right to Life*, 551 U.S. 449 (2007).

34. *Citizens United v. Federal Election Commission*, 558 U.S. 50 (2010).

35. *McCutcheon v. Federal Election Commission*, 572 U.S. — (2014).

36. Arthur Delaney, "Supreme Court Rolls Back Campaign Finance Restrictions," *Huffington Post*, updated May 25, 2011, www.huffingtonpost.com/2010/01/21/supreme-court-rolls-back_n_431227.html (accessed 7/9/12).

37. *Chaplinsky v. State of New Hampshire*, 315 U.S. 568 (1942).

38. *Dennis v. United States*, 341 U.S. 494 (1951), which upheld the infamous Smith Act of 1940, which provided criminal penalties for those who "willfully and knowingly conspire to teach and advocate the forceful and violent overthrow and destruction of the government."

39. *Capital Broadcasting Company v. Acting Attorney General*, 405 U.S. 1000 (1972).

40. *R.A.V. v. City of St. Paul*, 506 U.S. 377 (1992).

41. *Bethel School District No. 403 v. Fraser*, 478 U.S. 675 (1986).

42. *Hazelwood School District v. Kuhlmeier*, 484 U.S. 260 (1988).

43. *Morse v. Frederick*, 551 U.S. 393 (2007).

44. *City Council v. Taxpayers for Vincent*, 466 U.S. 789 (1984).

45. Fisher, *American Constitutional Law*, p. 546.

46. *Bigelow v. Virginia*, 421 U.S. 809 (1975).

47. *Virginia State Board of Pharmacy v. Virginia Citizens Consumer Council*, 425 U.S. 748 (1976). Later cases restored the rights of lawyers to advertise their services.

48. *Lorillard Tobacco v. Reilly*, 533 U.S. 525 (2001).

49. *Hague v. Committee for Industrial Organization*, 307 U.S. 496 (1939).

50. *Stromberg v. California*, 283 U.S. 359 (1931).

51. *Texas v. Johnson*, 488 U.S. 884 (1989).

52. Charles Babington, "Senate Rejects Flag Desecration Amendment," *Washington Post*, June 28, 2006, www.washingtonpost.com/wp-dyn/content/article/2006/06/27/AR2006062701056.html (accessed 11/13/13).

53. *Snyder v. Phelps*, 562 U.S. — (2011).

54. For a good general discussion of speech plus, see Louis Fisher, *American Constitutional Law* (New York: McGraw-Hill, 1990), 544–46. The case upholding the buffer zone against the abortion protesters is *Madsen v. Women's Health Center*, 512 U.S. 753 (1994).

55. *Near v. Minnesota*, 283 U.S. 697 (1931).

56. *New York Times v. United States*, 403 U.S. 731 (1971).

57. *Cable News Network, Inc., v. Noriega*, 498 U.S. 976 (1990).

58. *Branzburg v. Hayes*, 408 U.S. 656 (1972).

59. Emily Bazelon, "Obama's War on Journalists: His Administration's Leak Investigations Are Outrageous and Unprecedented," *Slate*, May 14, 2013, www.slate.com /articles/news_and_politics/jurisprudence/2013/05/obama _s_justice_department_holder_s_leak_investigations _are_outrageous_and.html (accessed 11/15/14).

60. *New York Times v. Sullivan*, 376 U.S. 254 (1964).

61. Shannon Hutzler, "Protecting Informed Public Participation," Valparaiso University Law Review 41, no. 3 (Spring 2007): 1235–84.

62. *Hustler Magazine v. Falwell*, 485 U.S. 46 (1988).

63. See *Zeran v. America Online*, 129 F3d 327 (4th Cir. 1997).

64. *Roth v. United States*, 354 U.S. 476 (1957).

65. Concurring opinion in *Jacobellis v. Ohio*, 378 U.S. 184 (1964).

66. *Miller v. California*, 413 U.S. 15 (1973).

67. *Reno v. American Civil Liberties Union*, 521 U.S. 844 (1997).

68. *United States v. Williams*, 553 U.S. 285 (2008).

69. *United States v. Playboy Entertainment Group*, 529 U.S. 803 (2000).

70. *Brown v. Entertainment Merchants Association*, 564 U.S. — (2011).

71. *Presser v. Illinois*, 116 U.S. 252 (1886).

72. *District of Columbia v. Heller*, 554 U.S. 570 (2008).

73. *McDonald v. Chicago*, 561 U.S. 3025 (2010).

74. *In re Winship*, 397 U.S. 361 (1970). An outstanding treatment of due process in issues involving the Fourth through Seventh amendments will be found in Fisher, *American Constitutional Law*, chap. 13.

75. *Horton v. California*, 496 U.S. 128 (1990).

76. *Mapp v. Ohio*, 367 U.S. 643 (1961). Although Mapp went free in this case, she was later convicted in New York on narcotics trafficking charges and served 9 years of a 20-year sentence.

77. For a good discussion of the issue, see Fisher, *American Constitutional Law*, pp. 884–89.

78. *United States v. Grubbs*, 547 U.S. 90 (2006).

79. *National Treasury Employees Union v. Von Raab*, 39 U.S. 656 (1989).

80. *Skinner v. Railroad Labor Executives' Association*, 489 U.S. 602 (1989).

81. *Vernonia School District 47J v. Acton*, 515 U.S. 646 (1995).

82. *Indianapolis v. Edmund*, 531 U.S. 32 (2000).

83. *Chandler v. Miller*, 520 U.S. 305 (1997).

84. *Florida v. Jardines*, 569 U.S. __ (2013).

85. *United States* v. Jones, 132 S. 565 U.S. __ (2012).

86. *Maryland v. King*. 569 U.S. __ (2013).

87. *Terry v. Ohio*, 392 U.S. 1 (1968).

88. Edwin S. Corwin and J. W. Peltason, *Understanding the Constitution* (New York: Holt, 1967), 286.

89. *Benton v. Maryland*, 395 U.S. 784 (1969).

90. *Miranda v. Arizona*, 348 U.S. 436 (1966).

91. *Berghuis v. Thompkins*, 560 U.S. 370 (2010).

92. *Berman v. Parker*, 348 U.S. 26 (1954). For a thorough analysis of the case, see Benjamin Ginsberg, "*Berman v. Parker*: Congress, the Court, and the Public Purpose," *Polity* 4 (1971): 48–75. For a later application of the case that suggests that "just compensation"—defined as something approximating market value—is about all a property owner can hope for protection against a public taking of property, see Theodore Lowi et al., *Poliscide: Big Government, Big Science, Lilliputian Politics*, 2nd ed. (Lanham, MD: University Press of America, 1990), 267–70.

93. *Kelo v. City of New London*, 545 U.S. 469 (2005).

94. *Gideon v. Wainwright*, 372 U.S. 335 (1963).

95. *Wiggins v. Smith*, 539 U.S. 510 (2003).

96. For further discussion of these issues, see Corwin and Peltason, *Understanding the Constitution*, 319–23.

97. *Furman v. Georgia*, 408 U.S. 238 (1972).

98. *Gregg v. Georgia*, 428 U.S. 153 (1976).

99. The Clark County Prosecuting Attorney, "U.S. Executions since 1976," www.clarkprosecutor.org/html /death/usexecute.htm (accessed 12/14/11); Gallup, "Death Penalty," www.gallup.com/poll/1606/death -penalty.aspx (accessed 5/22/12); Erik Eckholm, "In Death Penalty's Steady Decline, Some Experts See a Societal Shift," *New York Times*, December 19, 2013, p. A23.

100. *Kennedy v. Louisiana*, 554 U.S. 407 (2008).

101. *Snyder v. Louisiana*, 552 U.S. 472 (2008).

102. *Baze v. Rees*, 553 U.S. 35 (2008).

103. *Hudson v. McMillan*, 503 U.S. 1 (1992).

104. *Miller v. Alabama*, 567 U.S. __ (2012).

105. *Olmstead v. United States*, 227 U.S. 438 (1928). See also David M. O'Brien, *Constitutional Law and Politics*, 6th ed. (New York: W. W. Norton, 2005), vol. 1, pp. 76–84.

106. *West Virginia State Board of Education v. Barnette* (1943).

107. *NAACP v. Alabama ex rel. Patterson*, 357 U.S. 447 (1958).

108. *Griswold v. Connecticut*, 381 U.S. 479 (1965).

109. *Griswold v. Connecticut*, concurring opinion. In 1972 the Court extended the privacy right to unmarried women: *Eisenstadt v. Baird*, 405 U.S. 438 (1972).

110. *Roe v. Wade*, 410 U.S. 113 (1973).
111. *Webster v. Reproductive Health Services*, 492 U.S. 490 (1989), which upheld a Missouri law that restricted the use of public medical facilities for abortion. The decision opened the way for other states to limit the availability of abortion.
112. *Planned Parenthood of Southeastern Pennsylvania v. Casey*, 505 U.S. 833 (1992).
113. *Ayotte v. Planned Parenthood*, 546 U.S. 320 (2006).
114. *Gonzales v. Carhart*, 550 U.S. 124 (2007).
115. *Bowers v. Hardwick*, 478 U.S. 186 (1986).
116. *Lawrence v. Texas*, 539 U.S. 558 (2003).
117. *Lawrence v. Texas* (2003).
118. It is worth recalling here the provision of the Ninth Amendment: "The enumeration in the Constitution, of certain rights, shall not be construed to deny or disparage others retained by the people."
119. *Gonzales v. Oregon*, 546 U.S. 243 (2006).

Chapter 5

1. *United States v. Windsor*, 570 U.S. 12 (2013).
2. Paula Baker, "The Domestication of Politics: Women and American Political Society, 1780–1920," American Historical Review 89 (June 1984): 620–47.
3. *Dred Scott v. Sandford*, 19 Howard 393 (1857).
4. Oscar Handlin, *America—A History* (New York: Holt, Rinehart and Winston, 1968), p. 474.
5. August Meier and Elliot Rudwick, *From Plantation to Ghetto* (New York: Hill and Wang, 1976), pp. 184–88.
6. Jill Dupont, "Susan B. Anthony," New York Notes (Albany: New York State Commission on the Bicentennial of the U.S. Constitution, 1988), p. 3.
7. *Plessy v. Ferguson*, 163 U.S. 537 (1896).
8. Dupont, "Susan B. Anthony," p. 4.
9. The prospect of a "fair employment practices" law tied to the commerce power produced the Dixiecrat break with the Democratic Party in 1948. The Democratic Party organization of the States of the Old Confederacy seceded from the national party and nominated its own candidate, the then-Democratic governor of South Carolina, Strom Thurmond, who later became a Republican senator. This almost cost President Truman the election.
10. This was based on the provision in Article VI of the Constitution that "all treaties made, . . . under the Authority of the United States" shall be the "supreme Law of the Land." The commission recognized that if the U.S. Senate ratified what became the Universal Declaration of Human Rights (a treaty), then that power could be used as the constitutional umbrella for effective civil rights legislation. The Supreme Court had recognized in *Missouri v. Holland*, 252 U.S. 416 (1920), that a treaty could enlarge federal power at the expense of the states.
11. *Missouri ex rel. Gaines v. Canada*, 305 U.S. 337 (1938).
12. *Sweatt v. Painter*, 339 U.S. 629 (1950).
13. *Smith v. Allwright*, 321 U.S. 649 (1944).
14. *Shelley v. Kraemer*, 334 U.S. 1 (1948).
15. Kermit L. Hall, *The Magic Mirror: Law in American History* (New York: Oxford University Press, 1989), pp. 322–24. See also Richard Kluger, Simple Justice (New York: Random House, Vintage Edition, 1977), pp. 530–37.
16. The District of Columbia case came up, too, but since the District of Columbia is not a state, this case did not directly involve the Fourteenth Amendment and its equal protection clause. The plaintiffs confronted the Court on the same grounds, however—that segregation is inherently unequal. Their victory in effect was "incorporation in reverse," with equal protection moving from the Fourteenth Amendment to become part of the Bill of Rights. See *Bolling v. Sharpe*, 347 U.S. 497 (1954).
17. *Brown v. Board of Education of Topeka, Kansas*, 347 U.S. 483 (1954).
18. The Supreme Court first declared that race was a suspect classification requiring strict scrutiny in the decision *Korematsu v. United States*, 323 U.S. 214 (1944). In this case, the Court upheld President Roosevelt's executive order of 1941 allowing the military to exclude persons of Japanese ancestry from the West Coast and to place them in internment camps. It is one of the few cases in which classification based on race survived strict scrutiny.
19. The two most important cases were *Cooper v. Aaron*, 358 U.S. 1 (1958), which required Little Rock, Arkansas, to desegregate, and *Griffin v. Prince Edward County School Board*, 377 U.S. 218 (1964), which forced all the schools of that Virginia county to reopen after five years of closing to avoid desegregation.
20. In *Cooper v. Aaron*, the Supreme Court ordered immediate compliance with the lower court's desegregation order and went beyond that with a stern warning that it is "emphatically the province and duty of the judicial department to say what the law is."
21. *Shuttlesworth v. Birmingham Board of Education*, 358 U.S. 101 (1958), upheld a "pupil placement" plan purporting to assign pupils on various bases, with no mention of race. This case interpreted Brown to mean that school districts had to stop explicit racial discrimination but were under no obligation to take positive steps to desegregate. For a while black parents were doomed to case-by-case approaches.
22. For good treatments of this long stretch of the struggle of the federal courts to integrate the schools, see Paul Brest and Sanford Levinson, *Processes of Constitutional Decision-Making: Cases and Materials*, 2nd ed. (Boston: Little, Brown, 1983), pp. 471–80; and Alfred H. Kelly, Winfred A. Harbison, and Herman Belz, *The American*

Constitution: Its Origins and Development, 6th ed. (New York: W. W. Norton, 1983), pp. 610–16.

23. Pierre Thomas, "Denny's to Settle Bias Cases," *Washington Post*, May 24, 1994, p. A1.

24. See Hamil Harris, "For Blacks, Cabs Can Be Hard to Get," *Washington Post*, July 21, 1994, p. J1.

25. For a thorough analysis of the Office for Civil Rights, see Jeremy Rabkin, "Office for Civil Rights," in *The Politics of Regulation*, ed. James Q. Wilson (New York: Basic Books, 1980).

26. This was an accepted way of using quotas or ratios to determine statistically that blacks or other minorities were being excluded from schools or jobs, and then, on the basis of that statistical evidence, to authorize the Justice Department to bring suits in individual cases and class-action suits. In most segregated situations outside the South, it is virtually impossible to identify and document an intent to discriminate.

27. *Swann v. Charlotte-Mecklenburg Board of Education*, 402 U.S. 1 (1971).

28. *Milliken v. Bradley*, 418 U.S. 717 (1974).

29. For a good evaluation of the Boston effort, see Gary Orfield, *Must We Bus? Segregated Schools and National Policy* (Washington, DC: Brookings Institution, 1978), pp. 144–46. See also Bob Woodward and Scott Armstrong, *The Brethren: Inside the Supreme Court* (New York: Simon and Schuster, 1979), pp. 426–27; and J. Anthony Lukas, *Common Ground* (New York: Random House, 1986).

30. *Board of Education v. Dowell*, 498 U.S. 237 (1991).

31. John A. Powell, "Segregated Schools Ruling Not All Bad: In Rejecting Seattle's Integration Bid, Top Court Majority Also Held That Avoiding Racial Isolation Is a Legitimate Public Goal," *Newsday*, July 16, 2007, p. A33.

32. See especially *Katzenbach v. McClung*, 379 U.S. 294 (1964). Almost immediately after passage of the Civil Rights Act of 1964, a case was brought challenging the validity of Title II, which covered discrimination in public accommodations. Ollie's Barbecue was a neighborhood restaurant in Birmingham, Alabama. It was located 11 blocks away from an interstate highway and even farther from railroad and bus stations. Its table service was for whites only; there was only a take-out service for blacks. The Supreme Court agreed that Ollie's was strictly an intrastate restaurant, but since a substantial proportion of its food and other supplies was bought from companies outside the state of Alabama, there was a sufficient connection to interstate commerce; therefore, racial discrimination at such restaurants would "impose commercial burdens of national magnitude upon interstate commerce." Although this case involved Title II, it had direct bearing on the constitutionality of Title VII.

33. *Griggs v. Duke Power Company*, 401 U.S. 24 (1971). See also Allan Sindler, *Bakke, DeFunis, and Minority Admissions* (New York: Longman, 1978), pp. 180–89.

34. For a good treatment of these issues, see Charles O. Gregory and Harold A. Katz, *Labor and the Law* (New York: W. W. Norton, 1979), chap. 17.

35. In 1970 this act was amended to outlaw for five years literacy tests as a condition for voting in all states.

36. Joint Center for Political Studies, *Black Elected Officials: A National Roster—1988* (Washington, DC: Joint Center for Political Studies Press, 1988), pp. 9–10. For a comprehensive analysis and evaluation of the Voting Rights Act, see Bernard Grofman and Chandler Davidson, eds., *Controversies in Minority Voting: The Voting Rights Act in Perspective* (Washington, DC: Brookings Institution Press, 1992).

37. Ford Fessenden, "Ballots Cast by Blacks and Older Voters Were Tossed in Far Greater Numbers," *New York Times*, November 12, 2001, p. A17.

38. Aaron Blake, "Texas Redistricting Case: Five Things You Need to Know," *Washington Post*, December 13, 2011, www.washingtonpost.com/blogs/the-fix/post/texas-redistricting-case-five-things-you-need-to-know/2011/12/13/gIQAdowHsO_blog.html (accessed 6/22/12); Manny Fernandez, "Federal Judges Approve Final Texas Redistricting Maps," *New York Times*, February 28, 2012, www.nytimes.com/2012/02/29/US/final-texas-redistricting-maps-approved.html (accessed 6/22/12).

39. *Shelby County v. Holder*, 570 U.S. __ (2013).

40. *Crawford v. Marion County Election Board*, 553 U.S. 181 (2008). See also David Stout, "Supreme Court Upholds Voter Identification Law in Indiana," *New York Times*, April 29, 2008, www.nytimes.com/2008/04/29/washington/28cnd-scotus.html (accessed 1/13/14).

41. *Arizona et. al. v. Inter Tribal Council of Arizona Inc.*, 570 U.S. __ (2013). See also Nina Totenberg, "Supreme Court Strikes Down Arizona Voting Law," National Public Radio, June 17, 2013, www.npr.org/2013/06/17/192790981/supreme-court-strikes-down-arizona-voting-rule (accessed 1/13/14).

42. See Douglas S. Massey and Nancy A. Denton, *American Apartheid: Segregation and the Making of the Underclass* (Cambridge, MA: Harvard University Press, 1993), chap. 7.

43. Michael Powell, "Bank Accused of Pushing Mortgage Deals on Blacks," *New York Times*, June 6, 2009; Charlie Savage, "Countrywide Will Settle a Bias Suit," *New York Times*, December 22, 2011, p. B1.

44. *Loving v. Virginia*, 388 U.S. 1 (1967).

45. *FCC v. Beach Communications*, 508 U.S. 307 (1993).

46. *Windsor v. United States*, 699 F.3d 169 2nd Cir. 2012.

47. *Adarand Contractors v. Pena*, 515 U.S. 200 (1995).

48. See Jane J. Mansbridge, *Why We Lost the ERA* (Chicago: University of Chicago Press, 1986); and Gilbert Steiner, *Constitutional Inequality* (Washington, DC: Brookings Institution Press, 1985).

49. See *Frontiero v. Richardson*, 411 U.S. 677 (1973).

50. See *Craig v. Boren*, 423 U.S. 1047 (1976).

51. *Franklin v. Gwinnett County Public Schools*, 503 U.S. 60 (1992).

52. Jennifer Halperin, "Women Step Up to Bat," *Illinois Issues* 21 (September 1995): 11–14.

53. Joan Biskupic and David Nakamura, "Court Won't Review Sports Equity Ruling," *Washington Post*, April 22, 1997, p. A1.

54. Debra DeMeis and Rosanna Hertz, "Sex, Sports, and Title IX on Campus: The Triumphs and Travails," Daily Beast, June 22, 2012, www.dailybeast.com /articles/2012/06/22/sex-sports-and-title-ix-on-campus -the-triumphs-and-travails.html (accessed 6/22/12).

55. *United States v. Virginia*, 518 U.S. 515 (1996).

56. Judith Havemann, "Two Women Quit Citadel over Alleged Harassment," *Washington Post*, January 13, 1997, p. A1.

57. *Meritor Savings Bank v. Vinson*, 477 U.S. 57 (1986). See also Gwendolyn Mink, *Hostile Environment: The Political Betrayal of Sexually Harassed Women* (Ithaca, NY: Cornell University Press, 2000), pp. 28–32.

58. *Harris v. Forklift Systems, Inc.*, 510 U.S. 17 (1993).

59. *Burlington Industries v. Ellerth*, 524 U.S. 742 (1998); *Faragher v. City of Boca Raton*, 524 U.S. 775 (1998).

60. *Ledbetter v. Goodyear Tire and Rubber Co.*, 550 U.S. 618 (2007).

61. New Mexico had a different history because not many Anglos settled there initially. (*Anglo* is the term for a non-Hispanic white, generally of European background.) Mexican Americans had considerable power in territorial legislatures between 1865 and 1912. See Lawrence H. Fuchs, *The American Kaleidoscope* (Hanover, NH: University Press of New England, 1990), pp. 239–40.

62. *Salvatierra v. Del Rio Independent School District*, 1930 (Texas).

63. On the United Farm Workers and Cesar Chavez, see Marshall Ganz, *Why David Sometimes Wins: Leadership, Organization, and Strategy in the California Farm Worker Movement* (New York: Oxford University Press, 2009); Miriam Pawel, *The Union of Their Dreams: Power, Hope and Struggle in Cesar Chavez's Farm Worker Movement* (New York: Bloomsbury Press, 2010); and Jacques E. Levy, *Cesar Chavez: Autobiography of La Causa* (Minneapolis: University of Minnesota Press, 2007).

64. Dick Kirschten, "Not Black and White," *National Journal*, March 2, 1991, p. 497.

65. Gretchen Gavett, "Controversial 'Secure Communities' Immigration Program Will Be Mandatory by 2013," www.pbs.org/wgbh/pages/frontline/race-multicultural /lost-in-detention/controversial-secure-communities -immigration-program-will-be-mandatory-by-2013 (accessed 12/3/2013).

66. *Arizona v. United States*, 567 U.S.__(2012); Robert Barnes and N. C. Aizenmann, "Supreme Court Rejects Much of Arizona Immigration Law," *Washington Post*, June 25, 2012, www.washingtonpost.com/politics/supreme-court -rules-on-arizona-immigration-law/2012/06/25 /gJQA0Nrm1V_story.html?hpid=zl (accessed 6/25/12).

67. *United States v. Wong Kim Ark*, 169 U.S. 649 (1898).

68. *Korematsu v. United States*, 323 U.S. 214 (1944).

69. Children of the Camps, "Historical Documents: The Civil Liberties Act of 1988," http://pbs.org/childofcamp /history/civilact.html (accessed 2/17/08).

70. *Lau v. Nichols*, 414 U.S. 563 (1974).

71. Not all Native American tribes agreed with this, including the Navajos. See Ronald Takaki, *A Different Mirror: A History of Multicultural America* (Boston: Little, Brown, 1993), pp. 238–45.

72. On the resurgence of Native American political activity, see Stephen Cornell, *The Return of the Native: American Indian Political Resurgence* (New York: Oxford University Press, 1990); and Dee Brown, *Bury My Heart at Wounded Knee* (New York: Holt, Rinehart, 1971).

73. See the discussion in Robert A. Katzmann, *Institutional Disability: The Saga of Transportation Policy for the Disabled* (Washington, DC: Brookings Institution Press, 1986).

74. For example, after pressure from the Justice Department, one of the nation's largest rental-car companies agreed to make special hand controls available to any customer requesting them. See "Avis Agrees to Equip Cars for Disabled," *Los Angeles Times*, September 2, 1994, p. D1.

75. For more, see Dale Carpenter, *Flagrant Conduct: The Story of* Lawrence v. Texas (New York: W. W. Norton 2012).

76. *Bowers v. Hardwick*, 478 U.S. 186 (1986).

77. Quoted in Joan Biskupic, "Gay Rights Activists Seek a Supreme Court Test Case," *Washington Post*, December 19, 1993, p. A1.

78. *Romer v. Evans*, 517 U.S. 620 (1996).

79. *Lawrence v. Texas*, 539 U.S. 558 (2003).

80. *United States v. Windsor*, 570 U.S. 12 (2013).

81. Pew Research Center's Internet and American Life Project Spring Tracking Survey, April 17–May 19, 2013, http://pewinternet.org/Reports/2013/Broadband/Findings .aspx (accessed 12/4/13).

82. From Lyndon B. Johnson, *The Vantage Point* (New York: Holt, Rinehart, and Winston, 1971), p. 166.

83. The Department of Health, Education, and Welfare (HEW) was the cabinet department charged with administering most federal social programs. In 1980, when education programs were transferred to the newly created Department of Education, HEW was renamed the Department of Health and Human Services.

84. *Regents of the University of California v. Bakke*, 438 U.S. 265 (1978).

85. See, for example, *United Steelworkers v. Weber*, 443 U.S. 193 (1979), and *Fullilove v. Klutznick*, 448 U.S. 448 (1980).

86. *Adarand Constructors v. Peña*, 515 U.S. 200 (1995).

87. *Gratz v. Bollinger*, 539 U.S. 244 (2003).

88. *Grutter v. Bollinger*, 539 U.S. 306 (2003).

89. *Fisher v. University of Texas*, 570 U.S.__(2013).

90. Michael A. Fletcher, "Opponents of Affirmative Action Heartened by Court Decision," *Washington Post*, April 13, 1997, p. A21.

91. See Sam Howe Verhovek, "Houston Vote Underlined Complexity of Rights Issue," *New York Times*, November 6, 1997, p. A1.

92. *Schuette v. Committee to Defend Affirmative Action*, 572 U.S.__(2014).

93. Frank Newport, "Little 'Obama Effect' on Views about Race Relations; Attitudes toward Race Not Significantly Improved from Previous Years," October 29, 2009, www.gallup.com/poll/123944/Little-Obama-Effect-Views-Race-Relations.aspx (accessed 10/30/09).

94. There are still many genuine racists in America, but with the exception of a lunatic fringe, made up of neo-Nazis and members of the Ku Klux Klan, most racists are too ashamed or embarrassed to take part in normal political discourse. They are not included in either category here.

95. *Slaughterhouse Cases*, 16 Wallace 36 (1873).

Chapter 6

1. See, for example, John H. Aldrich, Christopher Gelpi, Peter Feaver, Jason Reifler, and Kristin Thompson Sharp, "Foreign Policy and the Electoral Connection," *Annual Review of Political Science* 9 (2006): 477–502. John H. Aldrich, John L. Sullivan, and Eugene Borgida "Foreign Affairs and Issue Voting: Do Presidential Candidates 'Waltz before a Blind Audience'?" *American Political Science Review* 81 (1989): 123–41.

2. Larry Bartels, *Unequal Democracy: The Political Economy of the New Gilded Age* (Princeton, NJ: Princeton University Press, 2008).

3. Emmanuel Saez, "Striking It Richer: The Evolution of Top Incomes in the United States," September 3, 2013, http://elsa.berkeley.edu/~saez/saez-UStopincomes-2012.pdf (accessed 2/13/14).

4. Pew Research Center www.pewresearch.org/fact-tank/2014/01/07/5-facts-about-economic-inequality (accessed 2/13/14).

5. Pew Research Center, "The U.S.'s High Income Gap Is Met with Relatively Low Public Concern," December 6, 2013, www.pewresearch.org/fact-tank/2013/12/06/the-u-s-s-high-income-gap-is-met-with-relatively-low-public-concern/ (accessed 1/20/14).

6. M. Lodge and C. S. Taber, "Three Steps toward a Theory of Motivated Political Reasoning," in A. Lupia, M. McCubbins, and S. Popkin, eds., *Elements of Reason: Cognition, Choice, and the Bounds of Rationality* (London: Cambridge University Press, 2000); George E. Marcus, W. Russell Neuman, and Michael MacKuen, *Affective Intelligence and Political Judgment* (Chicago: University of Chicago Press, 2000); David Redlawsk, "Hot Cognition or Cool Consideration? Testing the Effects of Motivated Reasoning on Political Decision Making," *Journal of Politics* 64 (2002): 1021–44; David Redlawsk, Andrew Civettini, and Karen Emmerson, "The Affective Tipping Point: Do Motivated Reasoners Ever 'Get It'?" *Political Psychology* 31, no. 4 (2010).

7. Marcus, Neuman, and MacKuen, *Affective Intelligence and Political Judgment*.

8. David Redlawsk, "A Matter of Motivated Reasoning," *New York Times*, April 22, 2011, www.nytimes.com/roomfordebate/2011/04/21/barack-obama-and-the-psychology-of-the-birther-myth/a-matter-of-motivated-reasoning (accessed 9/7/12).

9. www.whitehouse.gov/sites/default/files/rss_viewer/birth-certificate-long-form.pdf (accessed 9/7/12).

10. Pew Research Center, "Few See Adequate Limits on NSA Surveillance Program but More Approve Than Disapprove," July 26, 2013, www.people-press.org/2013/07/26/few-see-adequate-limits-on-nsa-surveillance-program/ (accesses 3/19/14).

11. See Karen Mossberger, Caroline Tolbert, and Ramona McNeal, *Digital Citizenship: The Internet, Society and Participation* (Cambridge: MIT Press, 2008).

12. See Harry Holloway and John George, *Public Opinion* (New York: St. Martin's Press, 1986). See also Paul R. Abramson, *Political Attitudes in America* (San Francisco: Freeman, 1983).

13. See Paul M. Sniderman and Edward G. Carmines, *Reaching beyond Race* (Cambridge, MA: Harvard University Press, 1997).

14. Pippa Norris, ed., *Critical Citizens: Global Support for Democratic Government* (New York: Oxford University Press, 1999); Robert Putnam, *Bowling Alone: The Collapse and Revival of American Community*. New York: Simon & Schuster, 2000.

15. Todd Donovan and Shaun Bowler, *Reforming the Republic: Democratic Institutions for the New America*. (New York: Pearson, 2003).

16. Pew Research Center for the People and the Press, "Public Trust in Government: 1958–2013," October 18, 2013, www.people-press.org/2013/10/18/trust-in-government-interactive/ (accessed 7/2/14).

17. Douglas R. Oxley, Kevin B. Smith, John R. Alford, Matthew V. Hibbing, Jennifer L. Miller, Mario Scalora, Peter K. Hatemi, and John R. Hibbing, "Political Attitudes Vary with Physiological Traits," *Science* 321, no. 5896 (September 19, 2008): 1667–70. See also Jeffrey Mondak, *Personality and the Foundation of Political Behavior* (Cambridge: Cambridge University Press, 2010).

18. John Alford, Carolyn Funk, and John Hibbing, "Are Political Orientations Genetically Transmitted?" *American Political Science Review*, no. 2 (2005): 153–67. Pew Research Center, "Study on Twins Suggests Our Political Beliefs May Be Hard-Wired," December 9, 2013, www.pewresearch.org/fact-tank/2013/12/09/study-on-twins-suggests-our-political-beliefs-may-be-hard-wired/ (accessed 1/20/13).

19. See Angus Campbell, Philip E. Converse, Warren E. Miller, and Donald E. Stokes, *The American Voter* (New York: Wiley, 1960), p. 147.

20. Betsy Sinclair, *The Social Citizen: Peer Networks and Political Behavior* (Chicago: University of Chicago Press, 2012).

21. Pew Research Center, "In Gay Marriage Debate, Both Supporters and Opponents See Legal recognition as 'Inevitable,'" www.people-press.org/2013/06/06/in-gay-marriage-debate-both-supporters-and-opponents-see-legel-recognition-as-inevitable (accessed 3/19/14).

22. Katherine Tate, *Black Faces in the Mirror* (Princeton, NJ: Princeton University Press, 1993).

23. CNN Poll, 2009.

24. Jon Cohen, "Zimmerman Verdict: 86 Percent of African Americans Disapprove," Washington Post, July 22, 2013, www.washingtonpost.com/blogs/post-politics/wp/2013/07/22/zimmerman-verdict-86-percent-of-african-americans-disapprove/?hpid=z1 (accessed 1/20/13).

25. See also Michael C. Dawson, *Behind the Mule: Race, Class, and African American Politics* (Princeton, NJ: Princeton University Press, 1994).

26. CBS News/New York Times Poll, 2008.

27. Donald Green, Bradley Palmquist, and Eric Schickler, *Partisan Hearts and Minds: Political Parties and the Social Identities of Voters* (New Haven, CT: Yale University Press, 2002).

28. See Richard Lau and David Redlawsk, *How Voters Decide: Information Processing during an Election Campaign* (New York: Cambridge University Press, 2006).

29. David S. Broder, "Partisan Gap Is at a High, Poll Finds," *Washington Post*, November 9, 2003, p. A6.

30. Morris Fiorina, Samuel Abrams, and Jeremy Pope, *Culture War? The Myth of a Polarized America* (New York: Longman Publishers, 2004).

31. Jack Citrin, Donald Green, Christopher Muste, and Cara Wong, "Public Opinion toward Immigration Reform: The Role of Economic Motivations," *Journal of Politics* 59 (1997): 858–81; David Sears and Jack Citrin, *Something for Nothing in California* (Berkeley: University of California Press, 1982).

32. Nathan J. Kelly and Peter K. Enns, "Inequality and the Dynamics of Public Opinion: The Self-Reinforcing Link between Economic Inequality and Mass Preferences," *American Journal of Political Science* 54, no. 4 (2010): 855–70; Jacob S. Hacker and Paul Pierson, *Winner-Take-All Politics: How Washington Made the Rich Richer—and Turned Its Back on the Middle Class* (New York: Simon and Schuster, 2010).

33. Larry M. Bartels, "Homer Gets a Tax Cut: Inequality and Public Policy in the American Mind," *Perspectives on Politics* 3, no. 1 (2005): 15–31; Larry Bartels, *Unequal Democracy* (Princeton, NJ: Princeton University Press, 2008).

34. Jennifer A. Heerwig and Brian J. McCabe, "Education and Social Desirability Bias: The Case of a Black Presidential Candidate," *Social Science Quarterly* 90, no. 3 (2009): 674–86.

35. Raymond E. Wolfinger and Steven J. Rosenstone, *Who Votes?* (New Haven, CT: Yale University Press, 1980). See also Steven J. Rosenstone and John Mark Hansen, *Mobilization, Participation, and Democracy in America* (New York: Macmillan, 1993).

36. Thomas E. Mann and Norman J. Ornstein, *It's Even Worse Than It Looks: How the American Constitutional System Collided with the New Politics of Extremism* (New York: Basic Books, 2012).

37. Shaun Bowler, Gary Segura, and Stephen Nicholson, "Earthquakes and Aftershocks: Race, Direct Democracy, and Partisan Change," *American Journal of Political Science* 50 (2006): 146–59. For a more general discussion of the spillover effects of ballot measures on public opinion, see Stephen Nicholson, *Voting the Agenda: Candidates, Elections, and Ballot Propositions* (Princeton, NJ: Princeton University Press, 2005).

38. John R. Zaller, *The Nature and Origins of Mass Opinion* (New York: Cambridge University Press, 1992).

39. Milton Lodge, Kathleen McGraw, and Patrick Stroh, "An Impression-Drive Model of Candidate Evaluation." *American Political Science Review* 83, No. 2 (1989): 399–419.

40. Benjamin I. Page and Robert Y. Shapiro, *The Rational Public: Fifty Years of Trends in Americans' Policy Preferences* (Chicago: University of Chicago Press, 1995); Eugene Wittkopf, *Faces of Internationalism: Public Opinion and Foreign Policy* (Durham, NC: Duke University Press, 1990).

41. Pew Research Center, "In Gay Marriage Debate."

42. Zaller, *Nature and Origins of Mass Opinion.*

43. Carroll Glynn, Susan Herbst, Garrett J. O'Keefe, Robert Y. Shapiro, and Mark Lindeman *Public Opinion*, 2nd ed. (Boulder, CO: Westview, 2004), p. 293. See also Michael X. Delli Carpini and Scott Keeter, *What Americans Know about Politics and Why It Matters* (New Haven, CT: Yale University Press, 1996).

44. Adam J. Berinsky, "The Two Faces of Public Opinion," *American Journal of Political Science* 43, no. 4 (1999): 1209–30.

45. Delli Carpini and Keeter, *What Americans Know about Politics and Why It Matters.*

46. Matt Barreto, "Watch for 'Sí Se Puede' Signs at Obama Rallies," *New York Times*, May 23, 2012, www.nytimes.com/roomfordebate/2012/05/23/securing-the-hispanic

-vote/watch-for-si-se-puede-signs-at-obama-rallies (accessed 6/6/12).

47. Pilar Marrero, "June Tracking Poll: Immigration Is a Critical Issue for Voters," *Latino Decisions*, June 10, 2011, www.latinodecisions.com/blog/2011/06/10/june-tracking-poll-immigration-is-a-critical-issue-for-voters (accessed 6/6/12).

48. Adam J. Berinsky, "Assuming the Costs of War: Events, Elites and American Support for Military Conflict," *Journal of Politics* 69, no. 4 (2007): 975–97; Zaller, *Nature and Origins of Mass Opinion*.

49. Richard R. Lau and David P. Redlawsk, "Advantages and Disadvantages of Cognitive Heuristics in Political Decision Making," *American Journal of Political Science* 45 (October 2001): 951–71. Lau and Redlawsk, *How Voters Decide*.

50. For a discussion of the role of information in politics, see Arthur Lupia and Matthew D. McCubbins, *The Democratic Dilemma: Can Citizens Learn What They Need to Know?* (New York: Cambridge University Press, 1998). See also Shaun Bowler and Todd Donovan, *Demanding Choices: Opinion and Voting in Direct Democracy* (Ann Arbor: University of Michigan Press, 1998). See also Samuel Popkin, *The Reasoning Voter: Communication and Persuasion in Presidential Campaigns* (Chicago: University of Chicago Press, 1991); Arthur Lupia, "Shortcuts Versus Encyclopedias: Information and Voting Behavior in California Insurance Reform Elections," *American Political Science Review* 88 (1994): 63–76; and Wendy Rahn, "The Role of Partisan Stereotypes in Information Processing about Political Candidates," *American Journal of Political Science* 37 (1993): 472–96.

51. James Druckman, Erik Petersen, and Rune Slothuus, "How Elite Partisan Polarization Affects Public Opinion Formation," *American Political Science Review* 107, no. 1 (February 2013): 57–79.

52. Pew Research Center, "Social Media and Political Engagement," October 2012, www.pewinternet.org/2012/10/19/social-media-and-political-engagement (accessed 8/14/14).

53. Tony Dokoupil, "Is the Web Driving Us Mad?" *Newsweek*, July 27, 2012, http://mag.newsweek.com/2012/07/08/is-the-internet-making-us-crazy-what-the-new-research-says.html (accessed 3/19/14); Nicholas Carr, *The Shallows: What the Internet Is Doing to Our Brains* (New York: W. W. Norton, 2011).

54. Nicholas Carr, "Is Google Making Us Stupid?" *The Atlantic*, July/August 2008, http://www.theatlantic.com/magazine/archive/2008/07/is-google-making-us-stupid/306868/ (accessed 6/27/14).

55. Bartels, *Unequal Democracy*.

56. Benjamin Ginsberg, *The American Lie: Government by the People and Other Political Fables* (Boulder, CO: Paradigm, 2007).

57. Gerald F. Seib and Michael K. Frisby, "Selling Sacrifice," *Wall Street Journal*, February 5, 1993, p. 1.

58. Peter Marks, "Adept in Politics and Advertising, 4 Women Shape a Campaign," *New York Times*, November 11, 2001, p. B6.

59. John Zaller and Dennis Chiu, "Government's Little Helper: U.S. Press Coverage of Foreign Policy Crises, 1945–1991," *Political Communications* 13 (1996): 385–405

60. Gallup, "Support for Invasion of Iraq Remains Contingent on U.N. Approval," November 12, 2002, www.gallup.com/poll/7195/support-invasion-iraq-remains-contigent-un-approval.aspx (accessed 2/19/14). Pew Research Center, "Public Attitudes toward the War in Iraq: 2003–2008," www.pewresearch.org/2008/03/19/public-attitudes-toward-the-war-in-iraq-20032008 (accessed 2/19/14).

61. *Roe v. Wade*, 410 U.S. 113 (1973).

62. See Gillian Peele, *Revival and Reaction* (Oxford: Clarendon, 1985). See also Connie Paige, *The Right-to-Lifers* (New York: Summit, 1983).

63. See David Vogel, "The Public Interest Movement and the American Reform Tradition," *Political Science Quarterly* 96 (Winter 1980): 607–27.

64. See Shanto Iyengar, *Is Anyone Responsible? How Television Frames Political Issues* (Chicago: University of Chicago Press, 1991); and Shanto Iyengar, *Do the Media Govern?* (Thousand Oaks, CA: Sage, 1997).

65. Campbell, Converse, Miller, and Stokes, *The American Voter*.

66. Benjamin I. Page and Robert Y. Shapiro, "Effects of Public Opinion on Policy," *American Political Science Review* 77, no. 1 (1983): 175–90.

67. Gerald C. Wright, Rober S. Erikson, and John P. McIver, "Public Opinion and Policy Liberalism in the American States," *American Journal of Political Science* 31, no. 4 (November 1987): 980–1001.

68. Pew Research Center, "Mixed Views of Economic Polices and Health Care Reform Persist," October 8, 2009, www.people-press.org/2009/10/08/mixed-views-of-economic-policies-and-health-care-reform-persist/ (accessed 2/15/14).

69. Christopher Wlezien, "The Public as Thermostat: Dynamics of Preferences for Spending," *American Journal of Political Science*, 39 no. 4 (1995): 981–1000.

70. See Pacheco, Julianna, "Attitudinal Policy Feedback and Public Opinion: The Impact of Smoking Bans on Attitudes toward Smokers, Secondhand Smoke, and Anti-Smoking Policies," *Political Research Quarterly*, 77, no. 3 (2013): 714–34; Barbara Norrander, "The Multi-Layered Impact of Public Opinion on Capital Punishment Implementation in the American States," *Political Research Quarterly* 53, no. 4 (2000): 771–93; Suzanne Mettler and Joe Soss, "The Consequences of Public Policy for Democratic Citizenship: Bridging Policy Studies and Mass Politics," *Perspectives on Politics* 2, no. 1 (2004): 55–73;

Andrea Hetling and Monika L. McDermott, "Judging a Book by Its Cover: Did Perceptions of the 1996 U.S. Welfare Reforms Affect Public Support for Spending on the Poor?" *Journal of Social Policy* 37, no. 3 (2008): 471–87; Joe Soss, "Lessons of Welfare: Policy Design, Political Learning, and Political Action," *American Political Science Review* 93, no. 2 (1999): 363–80; Joe Soss and Sanford F. Schram, "A Public Transformed? Welfare Reform as Policy Feedback," *American Political Science Review*, 101, no. 1 (2007): 111.

71. Pew Research Center, "Changing Attitudes on Gay Marriage," June 2013, http://features.pewforum.org/same-sex-marriage-attitudes/slide2.php (accessed 1/17/14).

72. Malcolm E. Jewell, *Representation in State Legislatures* (Lexington: University Press of Kentucky, 1982).

73. Lawrence R. Jacobs and Robert Y. Shapiro, *Politicians Don't Pander: Political Manipulation and the Loss of Democratic Responsiveness* (Chicago: University of Chicago Press, 2000).

74. John Griffin and Brian Newman, "Are Voters Better Represented?" *Journal of Politics* 67 (2005): 1206–27.

75. Bartels, *Unequal Democracy*.

76. Other authors have endorsed Bartels's view that government policy exacerbates income inequality. See, for example, Jacob S. Hacker and Paul Pierson, *Winner-Take-All Politics: How Washington Made the Rich Richer—And Turned Its Back on the Middle Class* (New York: Simon and Schuster, 2010).

77. Martin Gilens, "Inequality and Democratic Responsiveness," *Public Opinion Quarterly* 69, no. 5 (2005): 778–96; and Martin Gilens, "Preference Gaps and Inequality in Representation," *PS: Political Science and Politics* 42, no. 2 (2009): 335–41.

78. David Redlawsk, Caroline Tolbert, and Todd Donovan. *Why Iowa? How Caucuses and Sequential Elections Improve the Presidential Nominating Process* (Chicago: University of Chicago Press, 2011).

79. Redlawsk, Tolbert, and Donovan, *Why Iowa?*

80. Herbert Asher, *Polling and the Public* (Washington, DC: CQ Press, 2001), p. 64.

81. Michael Kagay and Janet Elder, "Numbers Are No Problem for Pollsters, Words Are," *New York Times*, August 9, 1992, p. E6.

82. Lynn Vavreck and Douglas Rivers, "The 2006 Cooperative Congressional Election Study," *Journal of Elections, Public Opinion and Parties* 18, no. 4 (2008): 355–66. See also Simon Jackman and Lynn Vavreck, "Primary Politics: Race, Gender, and Age in the 2008 Democratic Primary," *Journal of Elections, Public Opinion and Parties* 20, no. 2 (2010): 153–86.

83. Dennis Chong and James N. Druckman, "A Theory of Framing and Opinion Formation in Competitive Elite Environments," *Journal of Communication* 57 (2007): 99–118. See also Stephen P. Nicholson and Robert M. Howard, "Framing Support for the Supreme Court in the Aftermath of *Bush v. Gore*," *Journal of Politics* 65, no. 3 (2003): 676–95; and Dennis Chong and James N. Druckman, "Framing Public Opinion in Competitive Democracies" *American Political Science Review* 101, no. 4 (2007): 637–55.

84. John R. Zaller, *The Nature and Origins of Mass Opinion* (New York: Cambridge University Press, 1992).

85. See Adam Berinsky, "The Two Faces of Public Opinion," *American Journal of Political Science* 43, no. 4 (1999): 1209–30. See also Adam Berinsky, "Political Context and the Survey Response: The Dynamics of Racial Policy Opinion," *Journal of Politics* 64, no. 2 (2002): 567–84.

86. "Dial S for Smear," *Memphis Commercial Appeal*, September 22, 1996.

87. For a discussion of the growing difficulty of persuading people to respond to surveys, see John Brehm, *Phantom Respondents* (Ann Arbor: University of Michigan Press, 1993).

88. Redlawsk, Tolbert and Donovan, *Why Iowa?*

89. Christopher Wlezien and Stuart Soroka, "The Relationship between Public Opinion and Policy," in Russell Dalton and Hans-Dieter Klingemann, eds., *Oxford Handbook of Political Behavior* (New York: Oxford University Press, 2009), pp. 799–817.

90. Gilens, "Inequality and Democratic Responsiveness"; Bartels, *Unequal Democracy*.

91. Ryan Claassen and Benjamin Highton, "Does Policy Debate Reduce Information Effects in Public Opinion? Analyzing the Evolution of Public Opinion on Health Care," *Journal of Politics* 68, no. 2 (2006): 410–20.

Chapter 7

1. Larry M. Bartels, *Presidential Primaries and the Dynamics of Public Choice* (Princeton, NJ: Princeton University Press, 1988).

2. David Redlawsk, Caroline Tolbert, and Todd Donovan, *Why Iowa? How Caucuses and Sequential Elections Improve the Presidential Nominating Process* (Chicago: University of Chicago Press, 2011).

3. Karen Mossberger, Caroline Tolbert, and Ramona McNeal, *Digital Citizenship: The Internet, Society and Participation* (Cambridge, MA: MIT Press, 2008). See also J. E. Katz and R. E. Rice, *Social Consequences of Internet Use: Access, Involvement, and Interaction* (Cambridge, MA: MIT Press, 2002).

4. Pew Internet and American Life, "Trend Data (Adults): What Internet Users Do Online," February 2012, http://pewinternet.org/Static-Pages/Trend-Data-(Adults)/Online-Activites-Total.aspx (accessed 6/12/12).

5. Caroline Tolbert and Ramona McNeal, "Unraveling the Effects of the Internet on Political Participation," *Political Research Quarterly* 56, no. 2 (2003): 175–85. See also

Bruce Bimber, "Information and Political Engagement in America: The Search for Effects of Information Technology at the Individual Level," *Political Research Quarterly* 54 (2001): 53–67; Bruce Bimber, *Information and American Democracy: Technology in the Evolution of Political Power* (Cambridge: Cambridge University Press, 2003); and Brian S. Krueger, "Assessing the Potential of Internet Political Participation in the United States," *American Politics Research* 30 (2002): 476–98.

6. Julian P. Boyd et. al., ed., *The Papers of Thomas Jefferson*. Princeton, NJ: Princeton University Press, http://press-pubs.uchicago.edu/founders/documents/amendl_speechs8.html (accessed 5/30/14).

7. Pew Research Center, "Amid Criticism, Support for Media's 'Watchdog' Role Stands Out," August 8, 2013, www.people-press.org/2013/08/08/amid-criticism-support-for-medias-watchdog-role-stands-out (accessed 4/27/14).

8. Robert McChesney and John Nichols, *The Death and Life of American Journalism: The Media Revolution That Will Begin the World Again* (New York: Nation Books, 2010).

9. Darrell West, *The Next Wave: Using Digital Technology to Further Social and Political Innovation* (Washington, DC: Brookings Institution Press, 2011).

10. Pew Journalism Project, "State ofthe News Media 2013, Overview," 2013, http://stateofthemedia.org.2013/overview-5/ (accessed 4/29/2014).

11. Pew Research Center Publications, "The Internet's Broader Role in Campaign 2008," January 11, 2008, http://pewresearch.org/pubs/689/the-internets-broader-role-in-campaign-2008; and *"The Daily Show*: Journalism, Satire or Just Laughs?" May 8, 2008, http://pewresearch.org/pubs/829/the-daily-show-journalism-satire-or-just-laughs (accessed 9/7/12).

12. For a criticism of the increasing consolidation of the media, see the essays in Patricia Aufderheide et al., *Conglomerates and the Media* (New York: New Press, 1997).

13. Jonathan M. Ladd, *Why Americans Hate the Media and How It Matters* (Princeton, NJ: Princeton University Press, 2012).

14. West, *The Next Wave*; Edward Glaeser, *Triumph of the City: How Our Greatest Invention Makes Us Richer, Smarter, Greener, Healthier, and Happier* (New York: Penguin Press, 2011).

15. Pew Internet Project, "Internet Use over Time," 2014, www.pewinternet.org/datatrend/internet-use/internet-use-over-time (accessed 4/29/2014).

16. Pew Internet Project, "Online Political Videos and Campaign 2012," November 2, 2012, www.pewinternet.org/2012/11/02/online-political-videos-and-campaign-2012 (accessed 4/29/2014).

17. Mossberger, Tolbert and McNeal, *Digital Citizenship*; Brian A. Krueger, "A Comparison of Conventional and Internet Political Mobilization, *American Politics Research* 34, no. 6 (2006): 759–76.

18. Antony Wilhelm, *Digital Nation: Toward an Inclusive Information Society* (Cambridge, MA: MIT Press, 2006); P. DiMaggio, E. Hargittai, et al., "Social Implications of the Internet," *Annual Review of Sociology* 27, no. 1 (2001): 307–36.

19. Karen Mossberger, Caroline Tolbert, and Mary Stansbury, *Virtual Inequality: Beyond the Digital Divide* (Washington, DC: Georgetown University Press, 2003); Pippa Norris, *Digital Divide: Civic Engagement, Information Poverty, and the Internet Worldwide* (New York: Cambridge University Press, 2001).

20. Pew Internet Project, "Broadband Technology Fact Sheet,"2014,www.pewinternet.org/fact-sheets/broadband-technology-fact-sheet (accessed 4/29/2014).

21. National Telecommunications and Information Administration, *Digital Nation: 21st Century America's Progress toward Universal Broadband Access* (Washington, DC: U.S. Department of Commerce, 2011).

22. See, for example, Katharine Q. Seelye and Julie Bosman, "Bloggers Drive Inquiry on How Altered Images Saw Print," *New York Times*, August 9, 2006, p. C1.

23. Richard Davis, "Interplay: Political Blogging and Journalism," in *iPolitics: Citizens, Elections, and Governing in the New Media Era*, ed. Richard L. Fox and Jennifer M. Ramos (Cambridge: Cambridge University Press, 2012), pp. 76–99.

24. Pew Research Center Publications, "State of the News Media 2010," March 15, 2010, http://pewresearch.org/pubs/1523/state-of-the-news-media-2010 (accessed 9/11/12); West, *The Next Wave*.

25. Pew Research Center, "State of the Media, 2010"; West, *The Next Wave*.

26. Pew Internet Project, "Social Media Update 2013," December 30, 2013, www.pewinternet.org/2013/12/30/social-media-update-2013 (accessed 4/29/2014).

27. Amy Schatz, "BO, UR So Gr8: How a Young Tech Entrepreneur Translated Barack Obama into the Idiom of Facebook," *Wall Street Journal*, May 26, 2007, p. 1.

28. Karen Mossberger and Caroline Tolbert, "Digital Democracy," in *Oxford Handbook of American Elections and Political Behavior*, ed. Jan Leighley (New York: Oxford University Press, 2010).

29. Tolbert and McNeal, "Unraveling the Effects of the Internet."

30. Mossberger, Tolbert, and McNeal, *Digital Citizenship*. See Richard L. Fox and Jennifer M. Ramos, eds., *iPolitics: Citizens, Elections, and Governing in the New Media Era* (Cambridge: Cambridge University Press, 2011).

31. W. R. Neuman, M. R. Just, and A. N. Crigler, *Common Knowledge: News and the Construction of Political Meaning* (Chicago: University of Chicago Press, 1992).

32. A. Healy and D. McNamara, "Verbal Learning and Memory: Does the Modal Model Still Work?" in *Annual Review of Psychology*, Vol. 47, ed. J. Spense, J. Darley, and D. Foss (Palo Alto, CA: Annual Reviews, 1996), pp. 143–72.

33. Cass Sunstein, *Republic.com* (Princeton, NJ: Princeton University Press, 2001). See also Mossberger and Tolbert "Digital Democracy."

34. Michael Margolis and David Resnick, *Politics as Usual: The Cyberspace "Revolution"* (Thousand Oaks, CA: Sage, 2000).

35 See Pew Internet and American Life, "Trend Data (Adults): What Internet Users Do Online." See also Karen Mossberger, Caroline Tolbert, and Allison Hamilton, "Measuring Digital Citizenship: Mobile Access and Broadband," *International Journal of Communication* 6 (2012): 2492–528.

36. West, *The Next Wave*; McChesney and Nichols, *The Death and Life of American Journalism*.

37. Dianne Bystrom, "Advertising, Web Sites, and Media Coverage: Gender and Communication along the Campaign Trail," in *Gender and Elections: Shaping the Future of American Politics*, 2nd ed., ed. Susan J. Carroll and Richard L. Fox (Cambridge: Cambridge University Press, 2010), pp. 239–62.

38. Regina G. Lawrence and Melody Rose, *Hillary Clinton's Race for the White House: Gender Politics and Media on the Campaign Trail* (Boulder, CO: Lynne Reinner Publishers, 2010).

39. Matthew A. Baum, "Preaching to the Choir or Converting the Flock: Presidential Communication Strategies in the Age of Three Medias," in *iPolitics*, ed. Fox and Ramos, pp. 183–205.

40. Ann Crigler, Marion Just, Lauren Hume, Jesse Mills, and Parker Hevron, "YouTube and TV Advertising Campaigns: Obama versus McCain in 2008," in *iPolitics*, ed. Fox and Ramos, pp. 103–24.

41. Eli Pariser, *The Filter Bubble: What the Internet Is Hiding from You* (New York: Penguin Press, 2011).

42. Karen Mossberger, Caroline Tolbert, and Mary Stansbury, *Virtual Inequality: Beyond the Digital Divide* (Washington, DC: Georgetown University Press, 2003).

43. David J. Garrow, *Protest at Selma: Martin Luther King, Jr., and the Voting Rights Act of 1965* (New Haven, CT: Yale University Press, 2001).

44. See Todd Gitlin, *The Whole World Is Watching* (Berkeley: University of California Press, 1980).

45. Tim Groseclose, *Left Turn: How Liberal Media Bias Distorts the American Mind* (New York: St. Martin's Press, 2011).

46. Pew Research Center Publications, "How Journalists See Journalists in 2004: Views on Profits, Performance and Politics," May 2004, http://people-press.org/files/legacy-pdf/214.pdf (accessed 9/7/2012).

47. Doris Graber, ed., *Media Power in American Politics*, 5th ed. (Washington, DC: Congressional Quarterly Press, 2006).

48. Larry Bartels, *Unequal Democracy* (Princeton, NJ: Princeton University Press, 2008).

49. Shanto Iyengar and Donald R. Kinder, *News That Matters: Television and American Opinion* (Chicago: University of Chicago Press, 1987), p. 63.

50. Redlawsk, Donovan, and Tolbert, *Why Iowa?*

51. Todd Donovan, Caroline Tolbert, and Daniel Smith, "Priming Presidential Votes with Direct Democracy," *Journal of Politics* 70, no. 4 (2008): 1217–31.

52. Larry M. Bartels and Wendy M. Rahn, "Political Attitudes in the Post-Network Era," presented at the Annual Meeting of the American Political Science Association, Washington, DC (2000); Michael X. Delli Carpini and Scott Keeter, *What Americans Know about Politics and Why It Matters* (New Haven, CT: Yale University Press, 1996); Thomas R. Palfrey and Keith T. Poole, "The Relationship between Information, Ideology, and Voting Behavior," *American Journal of Political Science* 31, no. 3 (1987): 511–30; Sidney Verba, Kay Lehman Schlozman, and Henry E. Brady, *Voice and Equality: Civic Voluntarism in American Politics* (Cambridge, MA: Harvard University Press, 1995).

53. Markus Prior, "News vs. Entertainment: How Increasing Media Choice Widens Gaps in Political Knowledge and Turnout," *American Journal of Political Science* 49, no. 3 (2005): 577–92.

54. Delli Carpini and Keeter, *What Americans Know about Politics*.

55. Cass Sunstein, *Republic.com* (Princeton, NJ: Princeton University Press, 2001).

56. *New York Times v. United States*, 403 U.S. 713 (1971).

57. Michael Massing, "The Press: The Enemy Within," *New York Review of Books*, December 15, 2005, p. 6.

58. *Red Lion Broadcasting Company v. FCC*, 395 U.S. 367 (1969).

59. United Nations General Assembly, "Report of the Special Rapporteur on the Promotion and Protection of the Right to Freedom of Opinion and Expression," 2011.

60. Andrew Chadwick, *Internet Politics: States, Citizens, and New Communication Technologies* (Oxford: Oxford University Press, 2006).

61. See Martin Linsky, *Impact: How the Press Affects Federal Policymaking* (New York: W. W. Norton, 1986).

Chapter 8

1. Michael McDonald, *United States Election Project*, http://elections.gmu/edu/early vote 2012.html (accessed 5/25/14).

2. National Conference of State Legislatures, "Absentee and Early Voting," www.ncsl.org/research/elections-and-campaigns/absentee-and-early-voting.aspx (accessed 5/24/14).

3. Paul Gronke, "Early Voting: The Quiet Revolution in American Elections," in *Law and Election Politics: The Rules of the Game*, 2nd ed., ed. Matthew Streb (Boulder, CO: Lynne Riener, 2012).

4. Michael C. Herron and Daniel A. Smith, "Race, Party, and the Consequences of Restricting Early Voting in Florida in the 2012 General Election," *Political Research Quarterly* 67, no. 3 (July 2014): 646–65.

5. Pew Research Center for the People and the Press, "No Consensus about Whether Nation Is Divided Into 'Haves' and 'Have-Nots,'" September 29, 2011, http://pewresearch.org/pubs/2109/haves-have-nots-economic-divisions (accessed 9/14/12).

6. Sidney Verba, Kay Lehman Schlozman, and Henry E. Brady, *Voice and Equality: Civic Voluntarism in American Politics* (Cambridge, MA: Harvard University Press, 2005), chap. 3, for kinds of participation, and pp. 66–67 for prevalence of local activity.

7. Michael P. McDonald, "American Voter Turnout in Historical Perspective," in *The Oxford Handbook of American Elections and Political Behavior*, ed. Jan Leighley (New York: Oxford University Press, 2010), pp. 125–43.

8. Todd Donovan and Shaun Bowler, *Reforming the Republic: Democratic Institutions for the New America* (Upper Saddle River, NJ: Pearson Education, 2004).

9. For a discussion of the decline in voter turnout over time, see Ruy A. Teixeira, *The Disappearing American Voter* (Washington, DC: Brookings Institution Press, 1992). See also Michael McDonald and Samuel Popkin, "The Myth of the Vanishing Voter" *American Political Science Review*, 95 (2001): 963–74, and Michael McDonald, "Voter Turnout," *United States Election Project*, http://elections.gmu.edu/voter_turnout.htm (accessed 9/14/12).

10. Pew Internet and American Life Project, "Trend Data (Adults): What Internet Users Do Online," April 2012, http://pewinternet.org/Trend-Data-%28Adults%29/Online-Activites-Total.aspx (accessed 7/26/12).

11. Aaron Smith, "The Internet's Role in Campaign 2008," Pew Research Center for the People and the Press, November 2008.

12. Pew Research Center, "Social Media and Political Engagement," www.pewinternet.org/2012/10/19/social-media-and-political-engagement/ (accessed 6/24/14).

13. Mossberger, Tolbert, and McNeal, *Digital Citizenship*; B. S. Krueger, "Assessing the Potential of Internet Political Participation in the United States," *American Politics Research* 30 (2002): 476–98; B. S. Krueger, "A Comparison of Conventional and Internet Political Mobilization," *American Politics Research* 34, no. 6 (2006): 759–76;

Andrew Chadwick, *Internet Politics: States, Citizens, and New Communication Technologies* (Oxford: Oxford University Press, 2006); Bruce Bimber, *Information and American Democracy: Technology in the Evolution of Political Power* (Cambridge: Cambridge University Press, 2003); and Rachel Gibson, Wainer Lusoli, and Steven Ward, "Online Participation in the UK: Testing a 'Contextualized' Model of Internet Effects," *British Journal of Politics and International Relations* 7, no. 4 (2006): 561–83.

14. Verba, Schlozman, and Brady, *Voice and Equality*.

15. Caroline Tolbert and Ramona McNeal, "Unraveling the Effects of the Internet on Political Participation," *Political Research Quarterly* 56, no. 2 (2003): 175–85; see also Bruce Bimber, "Information and Political Engagement in America: The Search for Effects of Information Technology at the Individual Level," *Political Research Quarterly* 54 (2001): 53–67; Bruce Bimber, *Information and American Democracy: Technology in the Evolution of Political Power* (Cambridge: Cambridge University Press, 2003); and Brian Krueger, "Assessing the Potential of Internet Political Participation in the United States," *American Politics Research* 30 (2002): 476–98. J. Thomas and G. Streib, "The New Face of Government: Citizen-Initiated Contacts in the Era of E-Government," *Journal of Public Administration Theory and Research* 13, no. 1 (2003): 83–102; D. V. Shah, J. Cho, William P. Eveland, and N. Kwak, "Information and Expression in a Digital Age: Modeling Internet Effects on Civic Participation," *Communication Research* 32, no. 5 (2005): 531–65; K. Kenski and N. J. Stroud, "Connections between Internet Use and Political Efficacy, Knowledge, and Participation," *Journal of Broadcasting and Electronic Media* 50, no. 2 (2006): 173–92; Arthur Lupia and G. Sin, "Which Public Goods Are Endangered? How Evolving Communication Technologies Affect the Logic of Collective Action," *Public Choice* 117 (2003): 315–31.

16. Smith, "Internet's Role in Campaign 2008." See also Darrell West, *The New Wave* (Washington, DC: Brookings Institution Press, 2011).

17. Doris Graber, *Processing the News: How People Tame the Information Tide*, 2nd ed. (New York: Longman, 1988).

18. Mossberger and Tolbert, "Digital Democracy."

19. Caroline Tolbert and Allison Hamilton, "Political Engagement and the Internet in the 2008 U.S. Presidential Election: A Panel Survey," in Eva Anduiza, Mike Jensen, and Laia Jorba, eds., *Digital Media and Political Engagement Worldwide: A Comparative Study* (Cambridge: Cambridge University Press, 2012).

20. W. R. Neuman, M. R. Just, and A. N. Crigler, *Common Knowledge: News and the Construction of Political Meaning* (Chicago: University of Chicago Press, 1992).

21. David P. Redlawsk, "Hot Cognition or Cool Consideration: Testing the Effects of Motivated Reasoning," *Journal of Politics* 64 (2002): 1021–44.

22. Manuel Castells, *The Rise of the Network Society: The Information Age: Economy, Society, and Culture* (Oxford: Blackwell, 1997).

23. Bimber, *Information and American Democracy*; Bruce Bimber and Richard Davis, *Campaigning Online: The Internet in U.S. Elections* (Cambridge: Cambridge University Press, 2003).

24. D. Stolle and M. Micheletti, "The Expansion of Political Action Repertoires: Theoretical Reflections on Results from the Nike Email Exchange Internet Campaign," American Political Science Association, Washington, DC, 2005.

25. Russell Dalton, *The Good Citizen: How a Younger Generation Is Reshaping American Politics* (Washington, DC: CQ Press, 2008).

26. Robert Putnam, *Bowling Alone: The Collapse and Revival of American Community* (New York: Simon and Schuster, 2000).

27. Karen Mossberger, Allison Hamilton, and Caroline Tolbert, "Measuring Digital Citizenship: Mobile Access and the Less Connected," *International Journal of Communication*, forthcoming. Pippa Norris, *Digital Divide: Civic Engagement, Information Poverty, and the Internet Worldwide* (New York: Cambridge University Press, 2001); Benjamin Barber, "The New Telecommunications Technology: Endless Frontier or the End of Democracy?" *Constellations* 4, no. 2 (2011): 208–28; Tolbert and McNeal, "Unraveling the Effects of the Internet"; H. Rheingold, *The Virtual Community: Homesteading on the Electronic Frontier* (Reading, MA: Addison-Wesley, 1993).

28. Acronyms for the Stop Online Piracy Act (SOPA) and the PROTECT IP Act (Preventing Real Online Threats to Economic Creativity and Theft of Intellectual Property Act, or PIPA).

29. Jenna Wortham, "A Political Coming of Age for the Tech Industry," *New York Times*, January 18, 2012, www.nytimes.com/2012/01/18/technology/web-wide-protest-over-two-antipiracy-bills.html (accessed 9/2/14).

30. Jenna Wortham, "Public Outcry over Antipiracy Bills Began as Grass-Roots Grumbling: Suddenly, Hollywood Wants to Sit Down and Talk," *New York Times*, January 20, 2012, p. B1.

31. Mossberger, Tolbert, and McNeal, *Digital Citizenship*.

32. Pippa Norris, *Digital Divide: Civic Engagement, Information Poverty, and the Internet Worldwide* (New York: Cambridge University Press, 2001). See also Karen Mossberger, Caroline Tolbert, and May Stansbury, *Virtual Inequality: Beyond the Digital Divide* (Washington, DC: Georgetown University Press, 2003).

33. Pew Research Center, "Cell Phone and Smartphone Ownership Demographics," www.pewinternet.org/data-trend/mobile/cell-phone-and-smartphone-ownership-demographics/ (accessed 5/25/14).

34. Karen Mossberger, Caroline Tolbert, and William Franko, *Digital Cities: The Internet and the Geography of Opportunity* (New York: Oxford University Press, 2012).

35. See e.g., *Citizens United v. Federal Election Commission*, 558 U.S. __ (2010) and *McCutcheon v. Federal Election Commission*, 572 U.S. __ (2014).

36. *Citizens United v. Federal Election Commission*.

37. Anthony Downs, *An Economic Theory of Democracy* (New York: Harper and Row, 1957); William H. Riker and Peter C. Ordeshook, "A Theory of the Calculus of Voting," *American Political Science Review* 62, no. 1 (1968): 25–42.

38. Angus Campbell, Philip E. Converse, Warren E. Miller, and Donald E. Stokes, *The American Voter* (New York: Wiley, 1960); Steven Rosenstone and John Mark Hansen, *Mobilization, Participation, and Democracy in America* (New York: Macmillan, 1993); Kay Lehman Scholzman, Sidney Verba, and Henry E. Brady, *The Unheavenly Chorus: Unequal Political Voice and the Broken Promise of American Democracy* (Princeton, NJ: Princeton University Press, 2012).

39. Sidney Verba and Norman H. Nie, *Participation in America: Political Democracy and Social Equality* (New York: Harper and Row, 1972).

40. Emily Hoban Kirby and Kei Kawashima-Ginsberg, "The Youth Vote in 2008," Center for Information and Research on Civic Learning and Engagement, August 17, 2009, www.civicyouth.org/?page_id=241 (accessed 11/25/09).

41. Michael DeCourcy Hinds, "Youth Vote 2000: They'd Rather Volunteer," *Carnegie Reporter* 1, no. 2 (Spring 2001): 2.

42. Tyler Kingkade, "Youth Vote 2012 Turnout," Huffington Post, www.huffingtonpost.com/2012/11/07/youth-vote-2012-turnout-exit-polls_n_2086092.html (accessed 5/24/14).

43. The OnLine NewsHour, Generation Next: Speak Up Be Heard, "Iraq, Economy Weigh on Minds of Young Voters," August 31, 2007, www.pbs.org/newshour/generation-next/demographic/youthvote_08-31.html (accessed 2/21/08).

44. Emily Hoban Kirby, Karlo Barrios Marcelo, and Kei Kawashima-Ginsberg, "Volunteering and the College Experience," Center for Information and Research on Civic Learning and Engagement, August 2009, www.civicyouth.org/?page_id=237 (accessed 11/25/09).

45. The Center of Information and Research on Civic Learning and Engagement, "Millennials Talk Politics: A Study of College Student Political Engagement," 2007, www.civicyouth.org/?page_id=250 (accessed 11/29/09).

46. Connie Cass, "'Motor Voters' Impact Slight," *Chattanooga News-Free Press*, June 20, 1997, p. A5. On the need to motivate voters see Marshall Ganz, "Motor Voter or Motivated Voter?" *American Prospect*, no. 28 (September–October 1996): 41–49. On the hopes for Motor Voter, see Frances Fox Piven and Richard A. Cloward, "Northern Bourbons: A Preliminary Report on the National Voter Registration Act," *PS: Political Science and Politics* 29, no. 1 (March 1996): 39–42. On turnout in the 1996 election, see Barbara Vobejda, "Just under Half of Possible Voters Went to the Polls," *Washington Post*, November 7, 1996, p. A3.

47. Lawrence Bobo and Franklin D. Gilliam, "Race, Sociopolitical Participation, and Black Empowerment," *American Political Science Review* 24, no. 2 (June 1990): 377–93.

48. Rene Rocha, Caroline Tolbert, Daniel Bowen, and Chris Clark, "Race and Turnout: Does Descriptive Representation in State Legislatures Increase Minority Voting?" *Political Research Quarterly* 63, no. 3 (2010): 890–907.

49. Susan Banducci, Todd Donovan, and Jeffrey Karp, "Minority Representation, Empowerment and Participation," *Journal of Politics* 66, no. 2 (2004): 534–56.

50. Mark Hugo Lopez and Paul Taylor, "Dissecting the 2008 Electorate: Most Diverse in U.S. History," Pew Research Center, April 30, 2009, www.pewhispanic .org/2009/04/30/dissecting-the-2008-electorate-most -diverse-in-us-history/ (accessed 9/14/12).

51. See William Julius Wilson, *The Truly Disadvantaged: The Inner City, the Underclass, and Public Policy* (Chicago: University of Chicago Press, 1987); and Douglas Massey and Nancy Denton, *American Apartheid: Segregation and the Making of the American Underclass* (Cambridge, MA: Harvard University Press, 1993).

52. Michael Dawson, *Black Visions: The Roots of Contemporary African-American Political Ideologies* (Chicago: University of Chicago Press, 2003).

53. Barreto, Nuño, and Sanchez, "The Disproportionate Impact of Voter ID Requirements."

54. Matt Barreto, Gary Segura, and Nathan Woods, "The Mobilizing Effect of Majority–Minority Districts on Latino Turnout," *American Political Science Review* 98 (2004): 65–75, and authors' update.

55. Douglas R. Hess and Jody Herman, "Representational Bias in the 2008 Electorate, November 2009," www .projectvote.org/reports-on-the-electorate-/440.html (accessed 11/21/09).

56. Loren Collingwood, Matt Barreto, and Sergio García-Rios, "Revisiting Latino Voting: Cross-Racial Mobilization in the 2012 Election" *Political Research Quarterly*, 67 (2014): 4.

57. John Griffin and Brian Newman, *Minority Report: Evaluating Political Equality in America* (New York: Cambridge University Press, 2008); Rodney R. Hero, *Latinos and the U.S. Political System: Two-Tiered Pluralism* (Philadelphia: Temple University Press, 1992); Daniel Bowen and Christopher Clark, "Revisiting Descriptive Representation in Congress: Assessing the Effect of Race on the Constituent-Legislator Relationship," *Political Research Quarterly* (July 2014).

58. Adrian Pantoja and Gary Segura, "Does Ethnicity Matter? Descriptive Representation in the Statehouse and Political Alienation Among Latinos," *Social Science Quarterly* 84 (2003): 441–60.

59. U.S. Census Bureau, "Resident Population by Race, Hispanic Origin Status, and Age—Projections," www .census.gov/compendia/statab/cats/population /estimates_and_projections_by_age_sex_raceethnicity. html (accessed 11/24/09).

60. U.S. Census Bureau, "Reported Voting and Registration by Race, Hispanic Origin, Sex, and Age Groups: November 1964 to 2008"; "Reported Voting and Registration by Region, Educational Attainment, and Labor Force: November 1964 to 2008," CNN National Exit Poll 2008, www.cnn.com/ELECTION/2008/results /polls/#USP00p1 (accessed 11/22/09).

61. Dan Balz and Jon Cohen, "Majority in Poll Favor Deadline for Iraq Pullout," *Washington Post*, February 27, 2007, p. A1.

62. Gallup Poll, January 2003.

63. National Conference of State Legislatures, "Women in State Legislatures: 2009 Legislative Session," www.ncsl .org/default.aspx?tabid515398 (accessed 11/25/09).

64. Kira Sanbonmatsu, "Political Parties and the Recruitment of Women to State Legislatures," *Journal of Politics* 64, no. 3 (August 2002): 791–809; Jennifer L. Lawless and Richard L. Fox, *Why Are Women Still Not Running for Public Office?* (Washington, DC: Brookings Institution Press, 2008).

65. Center for American Women and Politics, "The Impact of Women in Public Office: Findings at a Glance" (New Brunswick, NJ: Rutgers University Press, n.d.).

66. *Engel v. Vitale*, 370 U.S. 421 (1962); *Abington School District v. Schempp*, 374 U.S. 203 (1963).

67. Laurie Goodstein, "Bush's Charity Plan Is Raising Concerns for Religious Right," *New York Times*, March 3, 2001, p. A1.

68. See Richard A. Brody, "The Puzzle of Political Participation in America," in *The New American Political System*, ed. Anthony King (Washington, DC: American Enterprise Institute, 1978), chap. 8.

69. Rosenstone and Hansen, *Mobilization, Participation, and Democracy*, p. 59.

70. Alan S. Gerber and Donald P. Green, "The Effects of Canvassing, Telephone Calls, and Direct Mail on Voter Turnout: A Field Experiment," *The American Political Science Review* 94, no. 3 (September 2000): 660.

71. Donald P. Green and Alan S. Gerber, "Getting Out the Youth Vote: Results from Randomized Field Experiments," December 29, 2001, pp. 26–27, www .youngvoterstrategies.org (accessed 3/8/08).

72. Student PIRGs New Voter Project, "Text Reminders Increase Primary Youth Turnout," October 2008, www .newvotersproject.org/research/text-messaging (accessed 11/30/09).

73. Robert M. Bond, Christopher J. Fariss, James Fowler, Jason J. Jones, Adam D. I. Kramer, Cameron Marlow, and Jaime E. Settle, "A 61-Million-Person Experiment in Social influence and Political Mobilization," *Nature* 489 (2012): 295–98.

74. Erik Austin and Jerome Chubb, *Political Facts of the United States since 1789* (New York: Columbia University Press, 1986), pp. 378–79.

75. Theda Skocpol, *The Tea Party and the Remaking of Republican Conservatism* (New York: Oxford University Press, 2013).

76. Michael P. McDonald and John Samples, eds., *The Marketplace of Democracy: Electoral Competition and American Politics* (Washington, DC: Brookings Institution Press, 2006).

77. Mark N. Franklin, "Electoral Participation," in *Comparing Democracies: Elections and Voting in Global Perspective*, ed. Lawrence LeDuc, Richard G. Niemi, and Pippa Norris (Thousand Oaks, CA: Sage, 1996), pp. 216–35; G. Bingham Powell, "American Voter Turnout in Comparative Perspective," *American Political Science Review* 80, no. 1 (1986): 17–43.

78. Todd Donovan, "A Goal for Reform: Make Elections Worth Stealing," *PS: Political Science and Politics* 40, no. 4 (2007): 681–6.

79. Donovan, "A Goal for Reform"; Gary W. Cox and Michael C. Munger, "Closeness, Expenditures, and Turnout in the 1982 U.S. House Elections," *American Political Science Review* 83, no. 1 (1989): 217–31; James G. Gimpel, Karen M. Kaufmann, and Shanna Pearson-Merkowitz, "Battleground States versus Blackout States: The Behavioral Implications of Modern Presidential Campaigns," *Journal of Politics* 69, no. 3 (2007): 786–97.

80. Donovan and Bowler, *Reforming the Republic*; McDonald and Samples, *Marketplace of Democracy*; Gary Jacobson, *The Politics of Congressional Elections*, 7th ed. (New York: Longman, 2008).

81. Samuel C. Patterson and Gregory A. Caldeira, "Getting Out the Vote: Participation in Gubernatorial Elections," *American Political Science Review* 77, no. 3 (1983): 675–89; Gregory A. Caldeira and Samuel C. Patterson, "Contextual Influences on Participation in U.S. State Legislative Elections," *Legislative Studies Quarterly* 7, no. 3 (1982): 359–81; Cox and Munger, "Closeness, Expenditures, and Turnout"; Gary W. Copeland, "Activating Voters in Congressional Elections," *Political Behavior* 5, no. 4 (1983): 391–401; Robert A. Jackson, "The Mobilization of U.S. State Electorates in the 1988 and 1990 Elections," *Journal of Politics* 59, no. 2 (1997): 520–37; Thomas M. Holbrook

and Scott D. McClurg, "The Mobilization of Core Supporters: Campaigns, Turnout, and Electoral Composition in United States Presidential Elections," *American Journal of Political Science* 49, no. 4 (2005): 689–703; Andre Blais, "What Affects Voter Turnout?" *Annual Review of Political Science* 9 (2006): 111–25; Andre Blais and Agnieszka Dobrzynska, "Turnout in Electoral Democracies," *European Journal of Political Research* 33, no. 2 (2003): 239–61.

82. Jeffrey Karp and Caroline Tolbert, "Support for Nationalizing Presidential Elections," *Presidential Studies Quarterly* 40, no. 4 (2010): 771–93; Daron Shaw, *The Race to 270: The Electoral College and the Campaign Strategies of 2000 and 2004* (Chicago: University of Chicago Press, 2006).

83. Gimpel, Kaufmann, Pearson-Merkowitz, "Battleground States versus Blackout States"; Julianna Sandell Pacheco, "Political Socialization in Context: The Effect of Political Competition on Youth Voter Turnout," *Political Behavior* 30, no. 4 (2008): 415–36; Keena Lipsitz, "The Consequences of Battleground and 'Spectator' State Residency for Political Participation," *Political Behavior* 31, no. 2 (2009): 187–209.

84. David Redlawsk, Caroline Tolbert, and Todd Donovan, *Why Iowa? How Caucuses and Sequential Elections Improve the Presidential Nominating Process* (Chicago: University of Chicago Press, 2011).

85. Caroline Tolbert, Daniel C. Bowen, and Todd Donovan, "Initiative Campaigns: Direct Democracy and Voter Mobilization," *American Politics Research* 37, no. 1 (2009): 155–92.

86. Caroline Tolbert, John A. Grummel, and Daniel A. Smith, "The Effects of Ballot Initiatives on Voter Turnout in the American States," *American Politics Research* 29, no. 6 (2001): 625–48; Mark A. Smith, "The Contingent Effects of Ballot Initiatives and Candidate Races on Turnout," *American Journal of Political Science* 45, no. 3 (2001): 700–706; Caroline J. Tolbert and Daniel A. Smith, "The Educative Effects of Ballot Initiatives on Voter Turnout," *American Politics Research* 33, no. 2 (2005): 283–309; Daniel A. Smith and Caroline J. Tolbert, *Educated by Initiative: The Effects of Direct Democracy on Citizens and Political Organizations in the American States* (Ann Arbor: University of Michigan Press, 2004).

87. Stephen Nicholson, *Voting the Agenda: Candidates, Elections, and Ballot Propositions* (Princeton, NJ: Princeton University Press, 2005).

88. Daniel Smith and Caroline Tolbert, *Educated by Initiative: The Effects of Direct Democracy on Citizens and Political Organizations in the American States* (Ann Arbor: University of Michigan Press, 2004); Frederick Boehmke and Daniel Bowen, "Direct Democracy and Individual Interest Group Membership," *Journal of Politics* 72, no. 3 (2010): 659–71.

89. Todd Donovan, Caroline Tolbert, and Daniel Smith, "Priming Presidential Votes with Direct Democracy," *Journal of Politics* 70, no. 4 (2008): 1217–31.

90. Bruce E. Cain, Todd Donovan, and Caroline J. Tolbert, *Democracy in the States: Experiments in Election Reform* (Washington, DC: Brookings Institution Press, 2008).

91. National Conference of State Legislatures, "Voter Identification Requirements," www.ncsl.org/research/elections-and-campaigns/voter-id.aspx (accessed 5/24/14).

92. Matt Barreto, Stephen Nuño, and Gabriel Sanchez, "The Disproportionate Impact of Voter-ID Requirements on the Electorate—New Evidence from Indiana," *PS: Political Science & Politics* 42 (2009): 111–16.

93. Rene R. Rocha and Tetsuya Matsubayashi, "The Politics of Race and Voter ID Laws in the States: The Return of Jim Crow?" *Political Research Quarterly* 67, no. 3 (2014): 666–79.

94. The data in this paragraph are drawn from the Sentencing Project and Human Rights Watch, "Losing the Vote: The Impact of Felony Disenfranchisement Laws in the United States" (October 1998), www.sentencingproject.org/tmp/File/FVR/fd_losingthevote.pdf (accessed 2/22/08).

95. Sentencing Project, "Expanding the Vote: State Felony Disenfranchisement Reform, 1997–2008," September 25, 2008, www.sentencingproject.org/detail/news/cfm?news _id5492 (accessed 11/30/09).

96. Ryan S. King, "Expanding the Vote: State Felony Disenfranchisement Reform, 1997–2008" (Sentencing Project, September 2008), www.sentencingproject.org/doc/publications/fd_statedisenfranchisement.pdf (accessed 12/5/09).

97. Chris Uggen and Jeffrey Manza, "Democratic Contraction: Political Consequences of Felon Disenfranchisement in the United States," *American Sociological Review 2002* 67, no. 6 (2002): 777–803.

98. Benjamin Highton, "Easy Registration and Voter Turnout," *Journal of Politics* 59 (1997): 565–75; Benjamin Highton, "Voter Registration and Turnout in the United States," *Perspectives on Politics* 2, no. 3 (2004): 507–15; Michael J. Hanmer, *Discount Voting: Voter Registration Reforms and Their Effects* (New York: Cambridge University Press, 2009); Cain, Donovan, and Tolbert, *Democracy in the States*.

99. Cain, Donovan, and Tolbert, *Democracy in the States*.

100. National Conference of State Legislatures, www.nesl.org/research/elections-and-campaigns/same-day-registration.aspx (accessed 4/23/13).

101. Robert A. Jackson, Robert D. Brown, and Gerald C. Wright, "Registration, Turnout and the Electoral Representativeness of U.S. State Electorates," *American Politics Quarterly* 26, no. 3 (July 1998): 259–87. See also Benjamin Highton, "Easy Registration and Voter Turnout," *Journal of Politics* 59, no. 2 (April 1997): 565–87.

102. Highton "Easy Registration and Voter Turnout"; Stephen Knack and James White, "Election-Day Registration and Turnout Inequality," *Political Behavior* 22, no. 1 (2000): 29–44; Craig Leonard Brians and Bernard Grofman, "When Registration Barriers Fall, Who Votes? An Empirical Test of a Rational Choice Model," *Public Choice* 99 (1999): 161–76; Michael J. Hanmer, *Discount Voting: Voter Registration Reforms and Their Effects* (New York: Cambridge University Press, 2009); Mary Fitzgerald, "Greater Convenience but Not Greater Turnout: The Impact of Alternative Voting Methods on Electoral Participation in the United States," *American Politics Research* 33, no. 6 (2005): 842–67; Caroline J. Tolbert, Todd Donovan, Bridgett King, and Shaun Bowler, "Election Day Registration, Competition, and Voter Turnout," in *Democracy in the States: Experiments in Election Reform*, ed. Bruce E. Cain, Todd Donovan, and Caroline J. Tolbert (Washington, DC: Brookings Institution Press, 2008), pp. 83–98.

103. Hanmer, *Discount Voting*; Robert A. Jackson, Robert D. Brown, and Gerald C. Wright, "Registration, Turnout, and the Electoral Representativeness of U.S. State Electorates," *American Politics Quarterly* 26, no. 3 (1998): 259–87; Robert D. Brown, Robert A. Jackson, and Gerald C. Wright, "Registration, Turnout, and State Party Systems," *Political Research Quarterly* 52, no. 3 (1999): 463–79.

104. Michael P. McDonald, 2008. "Portable Voter Registration," *Political Behavior* 30, no. 4 (2008): 491–501.

105. Cain, Donovan, and Tolbert, *Democracy in the States*.

106. Michael McDonald, "2012 Early Voting Statistics," *United States Election Project*, http://elections.gmu.edu/early_vote_2012 (accessed 4/23/14).

107. Paul Gronke, Eva Galanes-Rosenbaum, and Peter Miller, "Early Voting and Turnout," *PS: Political Science and Politics* 40, no. 4 (October 2007): 639–45; Fitzgerald "Greater Convenience but Not Greater Turnout"; Adam J. Berinsky, "The Perverse Consequences of Electoral Reform in the United States," *American Politics Research* 33, no. 4 (2005): 471–91.

108. Jeffrey Karp and Susan Banducci, "Going Postal: How All-Mail Elections Influence Turnout," *Political Behavior* 22, no. 3 (2000): 223–39.

109. Democracy Corps, "The 2008 Early Voting Statistics," *United States Election Project*, http://elections.gmu.edu/early vote 2008.html (accessed 11/20/09).

110. "Voting by Mail and Turnout: A Replication and Extension," Early Voting Information Center, www.earlyvoting.net/blog/node/155 (accessed 12/5/09); Paul Gronke, Eva Galanes-Rosenbaum, and Peter Miller, "Early Voting and Turnout," *PS: Political Science and Politics* 40, no. 4 (October 2007): 639–45.

111. John Griffin, and Michael Keane, "Are Voters Better Represented?" *Journal of Politics* 67, no. 4 (2005): 1206–27.

112. Larry Bartels, *Unequal Democracy: The Political Economy of the New Gilded Age* (Princeton, NJ: Princeton University Press, 2008).

Chapter 9

1. Sean Theriault, *Party Polarization in Congress* (Cambridge: Cambridge University Press, 2008).
2. James G. Gimpel, J. Celeste Lay, and Jason E. Schuknecht, *Cultivating Democracy: Civic Environments and Political Socialization in America* (Washington, DC: Brookings Institution Press, 2003).
3. Elahe Izadi, "Congress Sets Record for Voting Along Party Lines," *National Journal*, Febuary 3, 2014, www.nationaljournal.com/congress/congress-sets-record-for-voting-along-party-lines-20140203 (accessed 4/1/14).
4. Gallup, "Congress Job Approval Starts 2014 at 13%," January 14, 2014, www.gallup.com/poll/166838/congress-job-approval-starts-2014.aspx (accessed 4/1/14).
5. E. E. Schattschneider, *The Semi-Sovereign People: A Realist's View of Democracy in America* (New York: Holt, Rinehart & Winston, 1960).
6. Larry Bartels, *Unequal Democracy: The Political Economy of the New Guilded Age* (Princeton, NJ: Princeton University Press, 2008).
7. Martin Gilens, *Affluence and Influence: Economic Inequality and Political Power in America* (Princeton, NJ: Princeton University Press, 2012).
8. Gilens, *Affluence and Influence*.
9. Morris Fiorina, Samuel Abrams, and Jeremy Pope, *Culture War? The Myth of a Polarized America* (New York: Pearson Longman, 2004).
10. Todd Donovan and Shaun Bowler, *Reforming the Republic: Democratic Institutions for the New America* (Upper Saddle River, NJ: Prentice Hall, 2003).
11. James Madison, *The Federalist Papers*, no. 10: "The Same Subject Continued: The Union as a Safeguard against Domestic Faction and Insurrection. The New York Packet. Friday, November 23, 1787," http://thomas.loc.gov/home/ histdox/fed_10.html (accessed 11/11/12).
12. Raymond J. La Raja, "Political Parties in the Era of Soft Money," in *The Parties Respond: Changes in American Parties and Campaigns*, 4th ed., ed. Sandy L. Maisel (Boulder, CO: Westview Press, 2002), pp. 163–88.
13. For an excellent analysis of the parties' role in recruitment, see Paul Herrnson, *Congressional Elections: Campaigning at Home and in Washington* (Washington, DC: CQ Press, 1995).
14. Sasha Issenberg, *Victory Lab: The Secret Science of Winning Campaigns* (New York: Crown Publishers, 2012).
15. Glen Justice, "F.E.C. Declines to Curb Independent Fund Raisers," *New York Times*, May 14, 2004, p. A16.
16. *Citizens United v. Federal Election Commission*, 558 U.S. 50 (2010).
17. See Harold Gosnell, *Machine Politics: Chicago Model*, rev. ed. (Chicago: University of Chicago Press, 1968).
18. For a useful discussion, see John Bibby and Thomas Holbrook, "Parties and Elections," in *Politics in the American States*, ed. Virginia Gray and Herbert Jacob (Washington, DC: CQ Press, 1996), pp. 78–121.
19. Daniel Galvin, *Presidential Party Building: Dwight D. Eisenhower to George W. Bush* (Princeton, NJ: Princeton, University Press, 2009).
20. Based on exit polls available at http://elections.nytimes.com/2012/results/president/exit-polls (accessed 11/12/12).
21. The Pew Forum on Religion and Public Life, "How the Faithful Voted: 2012 Preliminary Analysis," www.pewforum.org/Politics-and-Elections/How-the-Faithful-Voted-2012-Preliminary-Exit-Poll-Analysis.aspx#rr (accessed 11/12/12).
22. Christopher Shea, "Who Are You Calling Working Class?" *Boston Globe*, February 12, 2006, www.boston.com/news/globe/ideas/articles/2006/02/12/who_are_you_calling_working_class/ (accessed 2/24/08).
23. Shaun Bowler, Gary Segura, and Stephen Nicholson, "Earthquakes and Aftershocks: Race, Direct Democracy, and Partisan Change," *American Journal of Political Science* 50 (January 2006): 146–59.
24. Jeffry A. Karp and Caroline J. Tolbert, "Support for Nationalizing Presidential Elections," *Presidential Studies Quarterly* 40, no. 4 (December 2010).
25. See Morris Fiorina, "Parties and Partisanship: A Forty Year Retrospective," *Political Behavior* 24, no. 2 (June 2002): 93–115.
26. On the limited polarization among ordinary voters, see Fiorina, Abrams, and Pope, *Culture War?*; on growing partisan attachment among a subset of voters, see Alan Abramowitz and Kyle Saunders, "Why Can't We Just Get Along? The Reality of a Polarized America," *The Forum* 3, no. 2 (2005): 1–22.
27. See Matthew Crenson and Benjamin Ginsberg, *Downsizing Democracy* (Baltimore: Johns Hopkins University Press, 2002).
28. Benjamin Ginsberg, *The Consequences of Consent* (New York: Random House, 1982), chap. 4.
29. Nolan McCarty, Keith T. Poole, and Howard Rosenthal, *Polarized America: The Dance of Ideology and Unequal Richest* (Cambridge, MA: MIT Press, 2006). For 2013 data, see "Congress Sets Record for Voting along Party Lines," *National Journal*, February 3, 2014, "CQ Roll Call's Vote Studies—2013 in Review," *Congressional Quarterly*, February 3, 2014.
30. Donovan and Bowler, *Reforming the Republic*.
31. "2012 U.S. House Elections," *Washington Post*, November 19, 2013, www.washingtonpost.com/wp-srv/special/politics/election-map-2012/house (accessed 1/14/14).

32. Barbara Sinclair, *Unorthodox Lawmaking: New Legislative Processes in the U.S. Congress*, 4th ed. (Washington, DC: CQ Press, 2011).

33. John R. Hibbing and Elizabeth Theiss-Morse, *Stealth Democracy: Americans' Beliefs about How Government Should Work* (New York: Cambridge University Press, 2002).

34. Gallup, "Congress Job Approval Starts 2014 at 13%."

35. Fiorina, Abrams, and Pope, *Culture War?*

36. For a discussion of third parties in the United States, see Daniel Mazmanian, *Third Parties in Presidential Elections* (Washington, DC: Brookings Institution Press, 1974).

37. See Maurice Duverger, *Political Parties* (New York: Wiley, 1954).

38. Jonathan Martin, "Eric Cantor Defeated by David Brat, Tea Party Challenger, in G.O.P. Primary Upset," *New York Times*, June 10, 2014, www.nytimes.com/2014/06/11/us/politics/eric-cantor-loses-gop-primary.html (accessed 6/24/14).

39. Alex Isenstadt, "Tea Party Candidates Falling Short," *Politico*, March 7, 2010, www.politico.com/news/stories/0310/34041.html (accessed 3/11/10).

40. Donovan and Bowler, *Reforming the Republic.*

41. Andri Blais, *To Keep or to Change First Past the Post? The Politics of Election Reform* (New York: Oxford University Press, 2008).

42. Stanley Kelley Jr., Richard E. Ayres, and William Bowen, "Registration and Voting: Putting First Things First," *American Political Science Review* 61 (June 1967): 359–70.

43. David H. Fischer, *The Revolution of American Conservatism* (New York: Harper & Row, 1965), p. 93.

Chapter 10

1. Daron Shaw, *The Race to 270: The Electoral College and the Campaign Strategies of 2000 and 2004* (Chicago: University of Chicago Press, 2006), p. 4.

2. *Gray v. Sanders*, 372 U.S. 368 (1963); *Wesberry v. Sanders*, 376 U.S. 1 (1964); *Reynolds v. Sims*, 377 U.S. 533 (1964).

3. *Thornburg v. Gingles*, 478 U.S. 613 (1986).

4. *Shaw v. Reno*, 509 U.S. 113 (1993).

5. David Redlawsk, Caroline J. Tolbert, and Todd Donovan, *Why Iowa? How Caucuses and Sequential Elections Improve the Presidential Nomination Process* (Chicago: University of Chicago Press, 2011).

6. Redlawsk, Tolbert, and Donovan, *Why Iowa?*

7. Shaw, *Race to 270.*

8. State legislatures determine the system by which electors are selected. Almost all states use this "winner-take-all" system. Maine and Nebraska, however, provide that one electoral vote goes to the winner in each congressional district and two electoral votes go to the winner statewide.

9. *Bush v. Gore*, 531 U.S. 98 (2000).

10. Jeffrey Karp and Caroline J. Tolbert, "Explaining Support for Nationalizing Presidential Elections," Midwest Political Science Association (2009).

11. See www.nationalpopularvote.com for details (accessed 5/27/14).

12. Karp and Tolbert, *Explaining Support*; Shaw, *Race to 270.*

13. Todd Donovan and Shaun Bowler, *Reforming the Republic: Democratic Institutions for the New America* (Upper Saddle River, NJ: Pearson Press, 2003).

14. André Blais, *To Keep or to Change First Past the Post? The Politics of Electoral Reform* (Oxford: Oxford University Press, 2008).

15. Adam Nagourney, "Court Strikes Down Ban on Gay Marriage in California," *New York Times*, February 7, 2012, www.nytimes.com/2012/02/08/us/marriage-ban-violates-constitution-court-rules.html (accessed 8/21/12).

16. Peter Callaghan, "Washington State Supreme Court Rules Unconstitutional Initiatives That Require Two-Thirds Majority for Tax Hikes," *Tacoma News Tribune*, http://blog.thenewstribune.com/politics/2013/02/28/washington-state-supreme-court-rules-unconstitutional-initiatives-that-require-two-thirds-majority-for-tax-hikes/ (accessed 5/27/14).

17. Daniel Smith and Caroline J. Tolbert, *Educated by Initiative: The Effects of Direct Democracy on Citizens and Political Organizations in the American States* (Ann Arbor: University of Michigan Press, 2004).

18. Shaun Bowler, Todd Donovan, and Caroline J. Tolbert. *Citizens as Legislators: Direct Democracy in the United States* (Columbus: Ohio State University Press, 1998).

19. Stephen Nicholson, *Voting the Agenda: Candidates, Elections, and Ballot Propositions* (Princeton, NJ: Princeton University Press, 2005).

20. Stephen Ansolabehere and James Snyder, "Campaign War Chests and Congressional Elections," *Business and Politics* 2 (2000): 9–34.

21. Gary W. Cox and Eric Magar, "How Much Is Majority Status in the U.S. Congress Worth?" *American Political Science Review* 93 (1999): 299–309.

22. Shaw, *Race to 270.*

23. John Greer, *In Defense of Negativity: Attack Ads in Presidential Campaigns* (Chicago: University of Chicago Press, 2006).

24. *Federal Election Commission v. Wisconsin Right to Life, Inc.*, 551 U.S. 449 (2007).

25. D. Sunshine Hillygus and Todd G. Shields, *The Persuadable Voter: Wedge Issues in Political Campaigns* (Princeton, NJ: Princeton University Press, 2009).

26. Sasha Issenberg, *The Victory Lab: The Secret Science of Winning Campaigns*, New York: Crown. 2012

27. Alan S. Gerber and Donald P. Green, "The Effects of Canvassing, Telephone Calls, and Direct Mail on Voter Turnout: A Field Experiment," *The American Political Science Review* 94, no. 3 (September 2000): 660.

28. Pew Research Center, "Online Political Videos and Campaign 2012," November 2, 2012, www.pewinternet.org/2012/11/02/online-political-videos-and-campaign-2012/ (accessed 10/13/14).

29. M. Ostrogorski, *Democracy and the Organization of Political Parties* (New York: Macmillan, 1902).

30. Timothy Clark, "The RNC Prospers, the DNC Struggles as They Face the 1980 Election," *National Journal*, October 27, 1980, p. 1619.

31. For discussions of the consequences of this, see Thomas Edsall, *The New Politics of Inequality* (New York: W. W. Norton, 1984). See also Thomas Edsall, "Both Parties Get the Company's Money—but the Boss Backs the GOP," *Washington Post*, National Weekly Edition, September 16, 1986, p. 14; and Benjamin Ginsberg, "Money and Power: The New Political Economy of American Elections," in *The Political Economy*, ed. Thomas Ferguson and Joel Rogers (Armonk, NY: M.E. Sharpe, 1984).

32. *Buckley v. Valeo*, 424 U.S. 1 (1976)

33. *Citizens United v. Federal Election Commission*, 558 U.S. 50 (2010).

34. *Citizens United v. Federal Election Commission*.

35. *McCutcheon et al. v. Federal Election Commission*. 572 U.S. __ (2014).

36. Martin Gilens, *Affluence and Influence: Economic Inequality and Political Power in America*, (New York: Russell Sage Foundation and Princeton University Press, 2012).

37. *McCutcheon et al. v. Federal Election Commission*.

38. *Buckley v. Valeo*, 424 U.S. 1 (1976).

39. Russ Choma, "Money Won on Tuesday, but Rules of the Game Changed," Center for Responsive Politics, www.opensecrets.org/news/2014/11/money-won-on-tuesday-but-rules-of-the-game-changed/ (accessed 11/6/14).

40. Erin Murphy, "National Groups Spend Millions to Affect Iowa Senate Race," *The Gazette*, October 19, 2014, http://thegazette.com/subject/news/national-groups-spend-millions-to-affect-iowa-senate-race-20141019 (accessed 11/7/14).

41. Michael P. McDonald, "Early Voting Pulling Into the Station," *Huffington Post*, updated 11/3/14, www.huffingtonpost.com/michael-p-mcdonald/early-voting-pulling-into_b_6091452.html (accessed 11/11/14).

Chapter 11

1. Alexis de Tocqueville, *Democracy in America*, ed. J. P. Mayer and trans. George Lawrence (New York: Harper Collins, [1835-40] 1988), p. 513.

2. Alexander Hamilton, James Madison, and John Jay, *The Federalist Papers*, ed. Clinton L. Rossiter (New York: New American Library, 1961), no. 10, p. 83.

3. *The Federalist Papers*, no. 10.

4. The best statement of the pluralist view is in David Truman, *The Governmental Process* (New York: Knopf, 1951), chap. 2.

5. Robert Dahl, *A Preface to Democratic Theory* (Chicago: University of Chicago Press, 1956).

6. Frank Baumgartner, Jeffrey M. Berry, Beth L. Leech, David C. Kimball, and Marie Hojnacki, *Lobbying and Policy Change: Who Wins, Who Loses and Why* (Chicago: University of Chicago Press, 2009).

7. Baumgartner et al., *Lobbying and Policy Change*.

8. Baumgartner et. al., *Lobbying and Policy Change*.

9. Erika Falk, Erin Grizard, and Gordon McDonald, "Legislative Issue Advertising in the 108th Congress: Pluralism or Peril?" *Harvard International Journal of Press/Politics* 11, no. 4 (Fall 2006): 148–64, http://hij.sagepub.com/cgi/reprint/11/4/148 (accessed 3/2/08).

10. Betsy Wagner and David Bowermaster, "B.S. Economics," *Washington Monthly*, November 1992, pp. 19–21.

11. Truman, *The Governmental Process*.

12. For an exploration of lower-class interest groups and social movements, see Frances Piven and Richard Cloward, *Poor People's Movements* (New York: Vintage, 1978).

13. E. E. Schattschneider, *The Semisovereign People: A Realist's View of Democracy in America.* (New York: Holt, Rinehart and Winston, 1960).

14. Kay Lehman Schlozman and John T. Tierney, *Organized Interests and American Democracy* (New York: Harper and Row, 1986), p. 60.

15. Clay Shirky, *Here Comes Everybody: The Power of Organizing without Organizations* (New York: Penguin Press, 2008).

16. Mancur Olson, *The Logic of Collective Action* (Cambridge, MA: Harvard University Press, 1965).

17. David Karpf, *The MoveOn Effect: The Unexpected Transformation of American Political Advocacy* (New York: Oxford University Press, 2012).

18. John Herbers, "Special Interests Gaining Power as Voter Disillusionment Grows," *New York Times*, November 14, 1978.

19. L. Brooke Conaway, "Explaining Interest Group Activity across US States." Working Paper, 2008, myweb.clemson.edu/~maloney/download/SpringFellowships-09/Conaway/Explaining%20Interest%20Group%20Activity%20Across%20US%20States.doc (accessed 2/10/14).

20. Center for Responsive Politics, "Lobbying Database," www.opensecrets.org/lobby/ (accessed 12/17/13)

21. For discussions of lobbying, see Allan J. Cigler and Burdett A. Loomis, eds., *Interest Group Politics* (Washington, DC: CQ Press, 1983). See also Jeffrey M. Berry, *Lobbying for the People* (Princeton, NJ: Princeton University Press, 1977).

22. Marie Jojnacki, "Interest Groups' Decisions to Join Alliances or Work Alone," *American Journal of Political Science* 41 (1997): 61–87; Kevin W. Hula, *Lobbying Together: Interest*

Groups Coalitions in Legislative Politics (Washington, DC: Georgetown University Press, 1999).

23. Common Cause, "The Microsoft Playbook: A Report from Common Cause," September 25, 2000.

24. Michael Barbaro, "A New Weapon for Wal-Mart: A War Room," *New York Times*, November 1, 2005, p. 1.

25. Center for Responsive Politics, Organizational Profiles, www.opensecrets.org/orgs (accessed 10/13/14).

26. "Editorial: Obama's Lobbyists," *Washington Times*, May 7, 2009, www.washingtontimes.com/news/2009/may/07/obamas-lobbyists (accessed 9/6/12).

27. For an excellent discussion of the political origins of the Administrative Procedure Act, see Martin Shapiro, "APA: Past, Present, Future," *Virginia Law Review* 72, no. 477 (March 1986): 447–92.

28. David Kirkpatrick, "Congress Finds Ways of Avoiding Lobbyist Limits," *Washington Post*, February 11, 2007, p. 1.

29. *Brown v. Board of Education of Topeka, Kansas*, 347 U.S. 483 (1954).

30. *Roe v. Wade*, 410 U.S. 113 (1973).

31. *Webster v. Reproductive Health Services*, 492 U.S. 490 (1989).

32. E. Pendleton Herring, *Group Representation before Congress* (New York: McGraw-Hill, 1936).

33. Michael Weisskopf, "Energized by Pulpit or Passion, the Public Is Calling," *Washington Post*, February 1, 1993, p. A1.

34. Julia Preston, "Grass Roots Roared and Immigration Bill Collapsed," *New York Times*, June 10, 2007, p. A1.

35. Center for Responsive Politics, "2014 Outside Spending, by Group," www.opensecrets.org/outsidespending/summ.php?disp=O (accessed 11/12/14).

36. *Citizens United v. Federal Election Commission*, 558 U. S. 50 (2010).

37. Center for Responsive Politics, "2014 Outside Spending, by SuperPAC," www.opensecrets.org/outsidespending/summ.php?cycle=2014&chrt=V&disp=O&type=S (accessed 11/12/14).

38. Richard L. Burke, "Religious-Right Candidates Gain as GOP Turnout Rises," *New York Times*, November 12, 1994, p. 10.

39. Elisabeth R. Gerber, *The Populist Paradox* (Princeton, NJ: Princeton University Press, 1999).

40. Gerber, *The Populist Paradox*.

41. *The Federalist Papers*, no. 10.

42. Olson, *The Logic of Collective Action*.

Chapter 12

1. Associated Press, "Milk Prices Could Rise If Farm Bill Looms," *Washington Post* (December 5, 2013), www.washingtonpost.com/politics/federal_government/boehner-floats-farm-bill-extension/2013/12/05/ce3510ce-5dd0-11e3-8d24-31c016b976b2_story.html (accessed 12/10/13).

2. Jennifer E. Manning, "Membership of the 113th Congress: A Profile," Congressional Research Service, October 31, 2013, www.fas.org/sgp/crs/misc/R42964.pdf (accessed 12/1/13).

3. Manning, "Membership of the 113th Congress."

4. Manning, "Membership of the 113th Congress."

5. For a discussion, see Benjamin Ginsberg, *The Consequences of Consent* (New York: Random House, 1982), chap. 1.

6. See Kristen D. Burnett, "Congressional Apportionment" (Washington, DC: U.S. Census Bureau, November 2011), www.census.gov/prod/cen2010/briefs/c2010br-08.pdf (accessed 1/23/12). For some interesting empirical evidence, see Angus Campbell, Philip Converse, Warren Miller, and Donald Stokes, *Elections and the Political Order* (New York: Wiley, 1966), chap. 11; for more recent considerations about the relationship between members of Congress and their constituents, see Lawrence Jacobs and Robert Y. Shapiro, *Politicians Don't Pander: Political Manipulation and the Loss of Democratic Responsiveness* (Chicago: University of Chicago Press, 2000); and Larry M. Bartels, *Unequal Democracy: The Political Economy of the New Gilded Age* (Princeton, NJ: Princeton University Press, 2008).

7. Congressional Management Foundation, *Communicating with Congress: How Citizen Advocacy Is Changing Mail Operations on Capitol Hill* (Washington, DC: Partnership for a More Perfect Union at the Congressional Management Foundation, 2011), http://congressfoundation.org/storage/documents/CMF_Pubs/cwc-mail-operations.pdf (accessed 1/23/12).

8. Norman J. Ornstein, Thomas E. Mann, and Michael J. Malbin, *Vital Statistics on Congress 2008* (Washington, DC: Brookings Institution, 2009), pp. 111–12.

9. Representative Michael Capuano, "Casework Examples," www.house.gov/capuano/services/casework_examples.shtml (accessed 12/1/13).

10. See Linda Fowler and Robert McClure, *Political Ambition: Who Decides to Run for Congress* (New Haven, CT: Yale University Press, 1989); and Alan Ehrenhalt, *The United States of Ambition: Politicians, Power, and the Pursuit of Office* (New York: Three Rivers Press, 1992).

11. Data for 2014 are based on *Roll Call*, "Casualty List," www.rollcall.com/politics/casualtylist.html (accessed 11/6/14), and NPR, "Incumbents Who Lost Seats Tonight," www.npr.org/blogs/itsallpolitics/2014/11/04/361486490/incumbents-who-lost-seats-tonight (accessed 11/6/14).

12. Ballotpedia, United States Congress Elections, 2012, http://ballotpedia.org/United_States_Congress_elections,_2012 (accessed 4/17/14).

13. Michael Leahy, "House Rules," *Washington Post*, June 10, 2007, p. W12.

14. See Barbara C. Burrell, *A Woman's Place Is in the House: Campaigning for Congress in the Feminist Era* (Ann Arbor: University of Michigan Press, 1994); and David Broder, "Key to Women's Political Parity: Running," *Washington Post*, September 8, 1994, p. A17.

15. Dan Balz, "Dodd, Dorgan, and Ritter to Retire as Democrats Face a Difficult Mid-Term Year," *Washington Post*, January 7, 2010.

16. U.S. Census Bureau, "Map: Apportionment of the U.S. House of Representatives Based on the 2010 Census," *U.S. Census Bureau Congressional Apportionment*, www.census.gov/population/apportionment/data/2010_apportionment_results.html (accessed 02/6/12).

17. Pew Research Center, "The 2010 Congressional Reapportionment and Latinos," www.pewhispanic.org/2011/01/05/the-2010-congressional-reapportionment-and-latinos/ (accessed 2/24/14).

18. Greg Giroux, "Republicans Win Congress as Democrats Get Most Votes," Bloomberg, March 18, 2013, www.bloomberg.com/news/2013-03-19/republicans-win-congress-as-democrats-get-most-votes.html (accessed 12/2/13).

19. Eric McGhee, "Are the Democrats Still at a Disadvantage in Redistricting?" The Monkey Cage, July 9, 2013, themonkeycage.org/2013/07/09/are-the-democrats-still-at-a-disadvantage-in-redistricting/ (accessed 12/2/13).

20. Royce Crocker, "Congressional Redistricting: An Overview," Congressional Research Service, November 21, 2012, www.fas.org/sgp/crs/misc/R42831.pdf (accessed 12/2/13).

21. "Did Redistricting Sink the Democrats?" *National Journal*, December 17, 1994, p. 2984.

22. *Miller v. Johnson*, 515 U.S. 900 (1995).

23. Bernie Becker, "Reapportionment Roundup," *New York Times*, December 24, 2009, http://thecaucus.blogs.nytimes.com/2009/12/24/reapoortionment-roundup/(accessed 1/31/10).

24. L. Paige Whitaker, "Congressional Redistricting and the Voting Rights Act: A Legal Overview," Congressional Research Service, August 30, 2013, www.fas.org/sgp/crs/misc/R42482.pdf (accessed 12/2/13).

25. Chris Cillizza, "What the Supreme Court's Voting Rights Act Decision Means for Politics," *Washington Post*, June 25, 2013, www.washingtonpost.com/blogs/the-fix/wp/2013/06/25/what-the-voting-rights-act-decision-means-for-politics/ (accessed 12/2/13).

26. Tom Hamburger and Richard Simon, "Everybody Will Know if It's Pork," *Los Angeles Times*, January 6, 2007, p. A1.

27. Speaker of the House John Boehner, "House Republicans Renew Earmark Ban for 113th Congress," November 16, 2012, www.speaker.gov/general/house-republicans-renew-earmark-ban-113th-congress (accessed 12/1/13).

28. Jared Allen, "Lawmakers Pushing for Earmark Reform Think Obama Boosted Their Chances," *The Hill*, January 30, 2010, http://thehill.com/homenews/house/78869-lawmakers-think-obama-boosted-earmark-reform- (accessed 1/31/10); David S. Fallis, Scott Higham and Kimberly Kindy, "Congressional Earmarks Sometimes Used to Fund Projects Near Lawmakers' Properties," *Washington Post*, February 6, 2012, p. 1.

29. Paul Ryan, paulryan.house.gov/constituentservices/#.UpqzA8RJOSo (accessed 11/30/13).

30. Richard Fenno, Jr., *Home Style: House Members in Their Districts* (Boston: Little, Brown, 1978).

31. Edward Epstein, "Dusting Off Deliberation," *CQ Weekly*, June 14, 2010, pp. 1436–442. Sarah Binder, "Where Have All the Conference Committees Gone?" *The Monkey Cage* (blog), December 21, 2011, themonkeycage.org/blog/2011/12/21/where-have-all-the-conference-committees-gone/ (accessed 2/7/12).

32. Derek Willis, "Republicans Mix It Up When Assigning House Chairmen for the 108th," *Congressional Quarterly Weekly*, January 11, 2003, p. 89.

33. Rebecca Kimitch, "CQ Guide to the Committees: Democrats Opt to Spread the Power," *Congressional Quarterly Weekly*, April 16, 2007, p. 1080.

34. Richard E. Cohen, "Crackup of the Committees," *National Journal*, July 31, 1999, pp. 2210–216.

35. David W. Rohde, "Committees and Policy Formulation," in *Institutions of American Democracy: The Legislative Branch*, ed. Paul J. Quirk and Sarah A. Binder (New York: Oxford University Press, 2005), pp. 201–23.

36. Ornstein, Norman J., Thomas E. Mann, Michael J. Mablin, and Andrew Rugg, "Vital Statistics on Congress," Brookings Institution and American Enterprise Institute, July 2013, www.brookings.edu/~/media/research/files/reports/2013/07/vital%20statistics%20congress%20mann%20ornstein/vital%20statistics%20chapter%205%20%20congressional%20staff%20and%20operating%20expenses_update.pdf (accessed 11/30/13).

37. Susan Crabtree, "After Four-Month Impasse, House Ethics Taps Staff Director," Talking Points Memo, May 2, 2011, talkingpointsmemo.com/muckraker/after-four-month-impasse-house-ethics-taps-staff-director (accessed 11/30/13).

38. Donny Shaw, "The Vast Majority of Bills Go Nowhere," Sunlight Foundation, August 25, 2009, www.opencongress.org/articles/view/1180-The-Vast-Majority-of-Bills-Go-Nowhere (accessed 11/29/13).

39. U.S. Senate, Senate Actions on Cloture Motions, www.senate.gov/pagelayout/reference/cloture_motions/clotureCounts.htm (accessed 11/29/13).

40. Jeremy W. Peters, "Senate Vote Curbs Filibuster Power to Stall Nominees," *New York Times*, November 22, 2013, p. A1.

41. See Robert Pear, "Senator X Kills Measure on Anonymity," *New York Times*, November 11, 1997, p. 12.

42. Jonathan Weisman, "House Votes 411–18 to Pass Ethics Overhaul," *Washington Post*, August 1, 2007, p. A1.

43. Leigh Munsil, "Graham Won't Lift Nominee-Hold Threat over Benghazi," Politico, November 11, 2013, www.politico.com/blogs/politico-live/2013/11/graham-wont-lift-nomineehold-threat-over-benghazi-177154.html (accessed 11/30/13).

44. Carl Hulse and David M. Herszenhorn, "Defiant House Rejects Huge Bailout; Next Step Is Uncertain," New York Times, September 29, 2008, www.nytimes.com/2008/09/30/business/30cong.html?pagewanted=1&_r=1 (accessed 2/4/10); Reuters, "House Passes Bailout, Focus Shifts to Fallout," October 3, 2008, www.reuters.com/article/idUSTRE49267J20081003 (accessed 2/4/10).

45. See John W. Kingdon, Congressmen's Voting Decisions (New York: Harper and Row, 1973), chap. 3; and R. Douglas Arnold, The Logic of Congressional Action (New Haven, CT: Yale University Press, 1990).

46. Lydia Saad, "Top Ten Findings about Public Opinion and Iraq," Gallup News Service, October 8, 2002, www.gallup.com/poll/6964/top-ten-findings-about-public-opinion-iraq.aspx (accessed 6/22/14).

47. Jane Fritsch, "The Grass Roots, Just a Free Phone Call Away," New York Times, June 23, 1995, p. A1.

48. Robert Pear, "In House, Many Spoke with One Voice: Lobbyists," New York Times, November 14, 2009, p. A1.

49. Eliza Newlin Carney, "For Ethics Hawks, Congress Could Be Next," National Journal Online, February 17, 2009, www.nationaljournal.com/njonline/rg_20090217_2426.php (accessed 2/5/10).

50. Dan Eggen, "SuperPACs Target Congressional Races," Washington Post, January 29, 2012, www.washingtonpost.com/politics/super-pacs-target-congressional-races/2012/01/26/gIQAyRfnaQ_story.html (accessed 2/9/12).

51. Holly Idelson, "Signs Point to Greater Loyalty on Both Sides of the Aisle," Congressional Quarterly Weekly Report, December 19, 1992, p. 3849.

52. CQ Roll Call's Vote Studies, Average Unity Scores, media.cq.com/votestudies (accessed 4/17/14).

53. Alexander Bolton, "DeMint's Leadership PAC Battles Leaders in Fight for the Future of Senate GOP Caucus," The Hill, August 4, 2011, http://thehill.com/homenews/senate/175397-demints-leadership-pac-battles-leaders-in-fight-for-future-of-senate (accessed 1/23/12); for a list of leadership PACs, see the Open Secrets website, www.opensecrets.org/industries/indus.php?Ind=Q03 (accessed 1/23/12).

54. Kimitch, "CQ Guide to the Committees," p. 1080.

55. Leahy, "House Rules," p. W12; Marin Cogan, "Freshmen Jump Line for Floor Speeches," Politico, January 18, 2011, www.politico.com/news/stories/0111/47791.html (accessed 2/9/12).

56. James J. Kilpatrick, "Don't Overlook Corn for Porn Plot," Chicago Sun-Times, January 3, 1992, p. 23.

57. Dennis McDougal, "Cattle Are Bargaining Chip of the NEA," Los Angeles Times, November 2, 1991, p. F1.

58. Susan Davis, "Congress Hits New Productivity Lows," USA Today, November 30, 2013, www.usatoday.com/story/news/politics/2013/11/30/unproductive-congress-record-low/3691993/ (accessed 11/30/13); Dan Roberts, "Gridlocked Congress on Track for Least Productive Year in History," Guardian, December 3, 2013 (accessed 12/12/13); but see also, Pew Research Center, Drew DeSilver, "Current Congress Is Not the Least Productive in Recent History, But Close," www.pewresearch.org/fact-tank/2013/09/03/current-congress-is-not-the-least-productive-in-recent-history-but-close/ (accessed 12/12/13).

59. Jonathan Weisman and Jeremy Peters, "Government Shuts Down in Budget Impasse," New York Times, October 1, 2013, www.nytimes.com/2013/10/01/us/politics/congress-shutdown-debate.html (accessed 12/1/13).

60. Caren Bohan and Rachelle Younglai, "Boehner Warns against Shutting U.S. Government over 'Obamacare,'" Reuters, August 23, 2013, www.reuters.com/article/2013/08/23/us-usa-healthcare-republicans-idUSBRE97L15120130823 (accessed 12/1/13).

61. Ashley Parker, "Conservatives with a Cause: 'We're Right,'" New York Times, September 30, 2013, www.nytimes.com/2013/10/01/us/politics/conservatives-with-a-cause-were-right.html (accessed 12/1/13).

62. Jonathan Weisman and Ashley Parker, "Republicans Back Down, Ending Crisis Over Shutdown and Debt Limit," New York Times, October 16, 2013, www.nytimes.com/2013/10/17/us/congress-budget-debate.html (accessed 12/1/13).

63. Frank Newport, "Congressional Approval Sinks to Record Low," Gallup, November 12, 2013, www.gallup.com/poll/165809/congressional-approval-sinks-record-low.aspx (accessed 11/30/13).

64. Elizabeth Mendes, and Joy Wilke, "Americans' Confidence in Congress Falls to Lowest on Record," June 13, 2013, www.gallup.com/poll/163052/americans-confidence-congress-falls-lowest-record.aspx (accessed 11/30/13).

65. David Espo, "Budget Peace Breaks Out—after Boehner Tough Talk," Seattle Times, December 12, 2013, seattletimes.com/html/politics/2022445764_apxbudgetbattle.html (accessed 12/12/13).

66. See Geoffrey C. Layman, Thomas M. Carsey, and Juliana Menasce Horowitz, "Party Polarization in American Politics: Characteristics, Causes, and Consequences,"Annual Reivew of Political Science, no. 9 (2006): 83–110.

67. Susan Milligan, "Congress Reduces Its Oversight Role; Since Clinton, a Change in Focus," Boston Globe, November 20, 2005, p. A1; Bill Shaikin, "Clemens Is Star Attraction at Hearing," Los Angeles Times, February 12, 2008, p. D1.

68. Elizabeth Williamson, "Revival of Oversight Role Sought; Congress Hires More Investigators, Plans Subpoenas," Washington Post, April 25, 2007, p. A1.

69. Thomas E. Mann, Molly Reynolds, and Peter Hoey, "A New, Improved Congress?" New York Times, August 26, 2007, p. 11.

70. Eric Lipton and Sheryl Gay Stolberg, "Health Law Rollout Provides Rich Target for Oversight Chief," *New York Times*, November 12, 2013, www.nytimes.com/2013/11/13/us /politics/health-law-rollout-provides-rich-target-for-over sight-chief.html?_r=0 (accessed 12/12/13).

71. *United States v. Pink*, 315 U.S. 203 (1942). For a good discussion of the problem, see James W. Davis, *The American Presidency* (New York: Harper and Row, 1987), chap. 8.

72. U.S. House, "Impeachment," http://history.house.gov /Institution/Origins-Development/Impeachment/(accessed 4/18/14).

73. Carroll J. Doherty, "Impeachment: How It Would Work," *Congressional Quarterly Weekly Report*, January 31, 1998, p. 222.

74. See Kenneth A. Shepsle, "Representation and Governance: The Great Legislative Trade-off," *Political Science Quarterly* 103, no. 3 (1988): 461–84.

Chapter 13

1. *Myers v. United States*, 272 U.S. 52 (1926).

2. These statutes are contained mainly in Title 10 of the United States Code, Sections 331, 332, and 333.

3. The best study covering all aspects of the domestic use of the military is that of Adam Yarmolinsky, *The Military Establishment* (New York: Harper and Row, 1971). Probably the most famous instance of a president's unilateral use of the power to protect a state "against domestic violence" was President Grover Cleveland's dealing with the Pullman Strike of 1894. The famous Supreme Court case that ensued was *In re Debs*, 158 U.S. 564 (1895).

4. In *United States v. Pink*, 315 U.S. 203 (1942), the Supreme Court confirmed that an executive agreement is the legal equivalent of a treaty, despite the absence of Senate approval. This case approved the executive agreement that was used to establish diplomatic relations with the Soviet Union in 1933. An executive agreement, not a treaty, was used in 1940 to exchange "fifty over-age destroyers" for 99-year leases on some important military bases.

5. *United States v. Nixon*, 418 U.S. 683 (1974).

6. For a different perspective, see William F. Grover, *The President as Prisoner: A Structural Critique of the Carter and Reagan Years* (Albany: State University of New York Press, 1988).

7. A third source of presidential power is implied from the provision for "faithful execution of the laws." This is the president's power to impound funds—that is, to refuse to spend money Congress has appropriated for certain purposes. One author referred to this as a "retroactive veto power" (Robert E. Goosetree, "The Power of the President to Impound Appropriated Funds," *American University Law Review* [January 1962]). This impoundment power has been used freely and to considerable effect by many modern presidents, and Congress has occasionally delegated such power to the president by statute. But in reaction to the Watergate scandal, Congress adopted the Congressional Budget and Impoundment Control Act of 1974, which was designed to circumscribe the president's ability to impound funds by requiring that the president must spend all appropriated funds unless both houses of Congress consented to an impoundment within 45 days of a presidential request. Therefore, since 1974, the use of impoundment has declined significantly. Presidents have had either to bite their tongues and accept unwanted appropriations or to revert to the older and more dependable but politically limited method of vetoing the entire bill.

8. For more on the veto, see Robert J. Spitzer, *The Presidential Veto: Touchstone of the American Presidency* (Albany: State University of New York Press, 1989).

9. Dan Eggen, "Bush Announces Veto of Waterboarding Ban," WashingtonPost.com, March 8, 2008, www .washingtonpost.com/wp-dyn/content/article/2008/03 /08AR2008030800304.html (accessed 6/10/10).

10. For a good review of President Clinton's legislative leadership in the first session of his last Congress, see *Congressional Quarterly Weekly*, November 13, 1999, especially the cover story by Andrew Taylor, "Clinton Gives Republicans a Gentler Year-End Beating," pp. 2698–700.

11. Kenneth F. Warren, *Administrative Law*, 3rd ed. (Upper Saddle River, NJ: Prentice-Hall, 1996), p. 250.

12. *J. W. Hampton & Co. v. United States*, 276 U.S. 394 (1928).

13. 48 Stat. 200.

14. Theodore J. Lowi, *The End of Liberalism*, 2nd ed. (New York: W. W. Norton, 1979), p. 117.

15. Jerry L. Nashaw, *Greed, Chaos, and Governance: Using Public Choice to Improve Public Law* (New Haven, CT: Yale University Press, 1997), p. 106

16. *Henry C. Black, Black's Law Dictionary, 6th ed. (St. Paul, MN: West Publishing Co., 1991)*, 539.

17. James G. Randall, *Constitutional Problems under Lincoln* (New York: Appleton, 1926), chap. 1.

18. Edward S. Corwin, *The President: Office and Powers*, 4th rev. ed. (New York: New York University Press, 1957), p. 229.

19. Congress has made 11 declarations of war in its history. In June 1942, Congress declared war against Bulgaria, Hungary, and Romania, which were allies of Germany in World War II. See www.senate.gov/pagelayout/history /h_multi_sections_and_teasers/WarDeclarationsby Congress.htm (accessed 4/21/14).

20. Adam *Clymer*, "The Transition: Push for Diversity May Cause Reversal on Interior Secretary," *New York Times*, December 23, 1992, p. 1.

21. A substantial portion of this section is taken from Theodore J. Lowi, *The Personal President* (Ithaca, NY: Cornell University Press, 1985), pp. 141–50.

22. All the figures since 1967, and probably 1957, are understated, because additional White House staff members were on "detail" service from the military and other departments (some secretly assigned) and are not counted here because they were not on the White House payroll.

23. "2012 Annual Report to Congress on White House Staff," www.whitehouse.gov/briefing-room/disclosures/annual-records/2012 (accessed 12/7/13).

24. The actual number is difficult to estimate because, as with White House staff, some EOP personnel, especially in national security work, are detailed to the EOP from outside agencies.

25. Article I, Section 3, provides that "The Vice-President . . . shall be President of the Senate, but shall have no Vote, unless they be equally divided." This is the only vote the vice president is allowed.

26. David Ignatius, "A Skeptical Biden's Role," RealClear Politics.com, November 26, 2009, www.realclearpolitics.com/articles/2009/11/26/a_skeptical_bidens_role_99320.html (accessed 5/12/09).

27. Samuel Kernell, *Going Public: New Strategies of Presidential Leadership*, 3rd ed. (Washington, DC: CQ Press, 1997); also Jeffrey K. Tulis, *The Rhetorical Presidency* (Princeton, NJ: Princeton University Press, 1987).

28. Tulis, *The Rhetorical Presidency*, p. 91.

29. Sidney M. Milkis, *The President and the Parties* (New York: Oxford University Press, 1993), p. 97.

30. James MacGregor Burns, *Roosevelt: The Lion and the Fox* (New York: Harcourt, Brace, 1956), p. 317.

31. Burns, *Roosevelt*, p. 317.

32. Kernell, *Going Public*, p. 79.

33. Claire Cain Miller, "How Obama's Internet Campaign Changed Politics," *New York Times*, November 7, 2008, brts.blogs.nytimes.com/2008/11/07/how-obamas-internet-campaign-changed-politics/?_php=true&_type=blogs&_r=o (accessed 4/7/14); David Plouffe, *The Audacity to Win: The Inside Story and Lessons of Barack Obama's Historic Victory* (New York: Penguin Group, 2009).

34. Gallup, www.gallup.com/poll/124922/presidential-approval-center.aspx (accessed 3/14/14).

35. Lowi, *The Personal President*.

36. Lowi, *The Personal President*, p. 11.

37. Milkis, *The President and the Parties*, p. 128.

38. Milkis, *The President and the Parties*, p. 160.

39. The classic critique of this process is Lowi, *The End of Liberalism*.

40. Kenneth Culp Davis, *Administrative Law Treatise* (St. Paul, MN: West Publishing, 1958), p. 9.

41. For example, Douglas W. Kmiec, "Expanding Power," in *The Rule of Law in the Wake of Clinton*, ed. Roger Pilon (Washington, DC: Cato Institute Press, 2000), pp. 47–68.

42. John M. Broder, "Powerful Shaper of U.S. Rules Quits, Leaving Critics in Wake," *New York Times*, August 4, 2012, p. A1.

43. A complete inventory is provided in Harold C. Relyea, "Presidential Directives: Background and Review," Congressional Research Service Report 98–611 (Washington, DC: Library of Congress, November 9, 2001).

44. Terry M. Moe and William G. Howell, "The Presidential Power of Unilateral Action," *Journal of Law, Economics and Organization* 15, no. 1 (January 1999): 133–4.

45. Moe and Howell, "The Presidential Power of Unilateral Action," p. 164.

46. *Youngstown Sheet & Tube Co. v. Sawyer*, 346 U.S. 579 (1952).

47. Philip Cooper, *By Order of the President* (Lawrence: University Press of Kansas, 2002), p. 201.

48. Corwin, *The President*, p. 283.

49. Cooper, *By Order of the President*, p. 201.

50. Cooper, *By Order of the President*, p. 203.

51. Cooper, *By Order of the President*, p. 216.

52. Robert J. Spitzer, "Comparing the Constitutional Presidencies of George W. Bush and Barack Obama: War Powers, Signing Statements, Vetoes," *White House Studies* 12 (October 2013): 125–46; update by author.

53. Alexander Hamilton, James Madison, and John Jay, *The Federalist Papers*, ed. Clinton Rossiter (New York: New American Library, 1961), no. 70, pp. 423–30.

54. Terry Moe, "The Presidency and the Bureaucracy: The Presidential Advantage," in *The Presidency and the Political System*, ed. Michael Nelson (Washington, DC: Congressional Quarterly Press, 2002), pp. 416–20.

Chapter 14

1. Arnold Brecht and Comstock Glaser, *The Art and Techniques of Administration in German Ministries* (Cambridge, MA: Harvard University Press, 1940), p. 6.

2. Linda Greenhouse, "Justices Say E.P.A. Has Power to Act on Harmful Gases," *New York Times*, April 3, 2007, www.nytimes.com/2007/04/03/washington/03scotus.html?ex=1333339200&en=e0d0a1497263d879&ei=5124&partner=permalink&exprod=permalink (accessed 2/15/10).

3. Environmental Protection Agency, "Endangerment and Cause or Contribute Findings for Greenhouse Cases under Section 202(a) of the Clean Air Act," epa.gov/climatechange/endangerment.html (accessed 2/16/10).

4. Environmental Protection Agency, "Regulations and Standards: Vehicles/Engines," www.epa.gov/oms/climate/regulations.htm (accessed 2/16/10).

5. Juliet Eilperin, "EPA Needed More Data before Ruling on Greenhouse Gas Emissions, Report Says," *Washington Post*, September 28, 2011, www.washingtonpost.com/national/health-science/epa-needed-more-data-before-ruling-on-greenhouse-gas-emissions-report-says/2011/09/28/gIQABs2X5K_story.html (accessed 1/2/12).

6. Gary Bryner, *Bureaucratic Discretion* (New York: Pergamon Press, 1987).

7. Jerry Hirsch, "Hyundai, Kia Reach $400-Million Settlement over Inflated MPG Claims," *Los Angeles Times*, December 23, 2013, articles.latimes.com/2013/dec/23/autos/la-fi-hy-hyundai-kia-settle-mpg-lawsuit-20131223 (accessed 1/20/14).

8. This account is drawn from Alan Stone, *How America Got On-Line: Politics, Markets, and the Revolution in Telecommunications* (Armonk, NY: M. E. Sharpe, 1997), pp. 184–87.

9. "Obama's Health Care Speech to Congress," *New York Times*, September 9, 2009, www.nytimes.com/2009/09/10/us/politics/10obama.text.html (accessed 2/10/10).

10. Office of Personnel and Management, "Comparison of Total Civilian Employment of the Federal Government by Branch, Agency, and Area as of June 2012 and September 2012," Table 2, www.opm.gov/policy-data-oversight/data-analysis-documentation/federal-employment-reports/employment-trends-data/2012/september/table-2/ (accessed 1/20/14); Defense Manpower Data Center, "Active Duty Military Personnel by Service by Rank/Grade," www.dmdc.osd.mil/appj/dwp/reports.do?category=reports&subCat=milActDutReg (accessed 1/20/14).

11. U.S. Census Bureau, "Government Employment and Payrolls," www2.census.gov/govs/apes/11stlus.txt (accessed 1/20/14); Bureau of Labor Statistics, Table B-1: Employees on nonfarm payrolls by industry sector and selected industry detail, www.bls.gov/news.release/empsit.t17.htm (accessed 10/16/14).

12. There are historical reasons that American cabinet-level administrators are called "secretaries." During the Second Continental Congress and the subsequent confederal government, standing committees were formed to deal with executive functions related to foreign affairs, military and maritime issues, and public financing. The heads of those committees were called "secretaries" because their primary task was to handle all correspondence and documentation related to their areas of responsibility.

13. Environmental Protection Action, "Understanding the Safe Drinking Water Act," August 2009, water.epa.gov/lawsregs/guidance/sdwa/upload/2009_08_28_sdwa_fs_30ann_sdwa_web.pdf (accessed 1/20/14).

14. U.S. Department of State, "Department Organization Chart," www.state.gov/r/pa/ei/rls/dos/99494.htm (accessed 12/19/13).

15. For more details, consult John E. Harr, *The Professional Diplomat* (Princeton, NJ: Princeton University Press, 1972), p. 11; and Nicholas Horrock, "The CIA Has Neighbors in the 'Intelligence Community,'" *New York Times*, June 29, 1975, sec. 4, p. 2. See also Morton H. Halperin and Priscilla Clapp, with Arnold Kanter, *Bureaucratic Politics and Foreign Policy*, 2nd ed. (Washington, DC: Brookings Institution Press, 2007).

16. *The 9/11 Commission Report: Final Report of the National Commission on Terrorist Attacks upon the United States* (New York: W. W. Norton, 2004).

17. Daniel Patrick Moynihan, "The Culture of Secrecy," *Public Interest* (Summer 1997): 55–71.

18. Louise Osborne, "Europeans Outraged Over NSA Spying, Threaten Action," USA Today, October 29, 2013, www.usatoday.com/story/news/world/2013/10/28/report-nsa-spain/3284609/ (accessed 1/24/14).

19. Warren Strobel and Mark Hosenball, "White House Review Panel Proposes Curbs on Some NSA Programs," Reuters, December 18, 2013, www.reuters.com/article/2013/12/18/us-usa-surveillance-obama-idUSBRE9BG1AQ20131218 (accessed 1/24/14).

20. Mark Landler and Charlie Savage, "Obama Outlines Calibrated Curbs on Phone Spying," New York Times, January 17, 2014, www.nytimes.com/2014/01/18/us/politics/obama-nsa.html (accessed 1/24/14).

21. U.S. Department of the Treasury, "The Debt to the Penny and Who Holds It," www.treasurydirect.gov/NP/BPDLogin?application=np (accessed 2/18/10).

22. Financial Stability Oversight Council, "Designations," www.treasury.gov/initiatives/fsoc/designations/Pages/default.aspx (accessed 1/23/14).

23. George E. Berkley, *The Craft of Public Administration* (Boston: Allyn and Bacon, 1975), p. 417.

24. Lisa Rein, "IRS Conference in Anaheim Featured Gifts, other Excesses Approved by Top Officials, Report Says," *Washington Post:* June, 6, 2013, www.washingtonpost.com/blogs/federal-eye/wp/2013/06/04/irs-conference-in-anaheim-featured-gifts-other-excesses-approved-by-top-officials-report-says/ (accessed 1/31/14).

25. Vice President Gore's National Partnership for Reinventing Government, "Appendix F, History of the National Partnership for Reinventing Government Accomplishments, 1993–2000, A Summary," http://govinfo.library.unt.edu/npr/whoweare/appendixf.html (accessed 3/28/08).

26. Public Law 101–510, Title XXIX, Sections 2,901 and 2,902 of Part A (Defense Base Closure and Realignment Commission); see the 2005 commission's website, DefenseBaseClosureandRealignmentCommission,www.brac.gov (accessed 1/3/12).

27. Sheila Zedlewski and Pamela Loprest with Erika Huber, "What Role Is Welfare Playing in This Period of High Unemployment?" Urban Institute, Fact Sheet 3, August 2011, www.urban.org/UploadedPDF/412378-Role-of-Welfare-in-this-Period-of-High-Unemployment.pdf (accessed 7/4/12).

28. Sabrina Tavernise, "Food Stamps Helped Reduced Poverty Rate, Study Says," *New York Times*, April 10, 2012, A16.

29. Paul C. Light, "The New True Size of Government," Organizational Performance Initiative, Research Brief

no. 2, p. 8, Wagner School of Public Service, New York University, http://wagner.nyu.edu/performance/files / True_Size.pdf (accessed 3/11/08).

30. OMB Watch, "Total Spending by Year," FedSpending.org, www.fedspending.org/fpds/chart_total.php (accessed 1/2/12).

31. Scott Shane and Ron Nixon, "In Washington, Contractors Take On Biggest Role Ever," *New York Times*, February 4, 2007, p. A1.

32. Shane and Nixon, "In Washington, Contractors Take on Biggest Role Ever."

33. Matt Kelley, "GAO Challenges $150B Contract Awarded by Army," *USA Today*, October 31, 2007, p. 5A.

34. Marjorie Censer, "Five Provisions in the New Defense Policy Legislation for Contractors to Watch," *Washington Post*, January 5, 2014, www.washingtonpost.com/business /capitalbusiness/five-provisions-in-the-new-defense -policy-legislation-for-contractors-to-watch/2014/01/03 /f6dd00ec-6c10-11e3-a523-fe73f0ff6b8d_story.html (accessed 1/24/14).

35. Shane and Nixon, "In Washington, Contractors Take on Biggest Role Ever."

36. Shane and Nixon, "In Washington, Contractors Take on Biggest Role Ever."

37. General Accountability Office, *Federal Contractors: Better Performance Information Needed to Support Agency Contract Award Decisions*, April 2009, GAO-09-374; www .gao.gov/new.items/d09374.pdf (accessed 2/26/10).

38. Neil Gordon, "Move over FCMD, Make Way for FAPIIS," Project on Government Oversight, http: //pogoblog.typepad.com/pogo/2009/09/move-over -fcmd-make-way-for-fapiis.html (accessed 2/26/10).

39. Tom Lee, "FAPIIS May Be the Worst Government Website We've Ever Seen," Sunlight Foundation, April 19, 2011, sunlightfoundation.com/blog/2011/04/19/fapiis -may-be-the-worst-government-website-weve -ever-seen/ (accessed 1/23/14).

40. For the estimates on waste, see Commission on Wartime Contracting in Iraq and Afghanistan, *Transforming Wartime Contracting: Controlling Costs, Reducing Risks: Final Report to Congress*, p. 18, August 2011, www .wartimecontracting.gov (accessed 1/4/12).

41. Dan Egan, "Democrats Proposing New Limits on Corporate Campaign Donations," *Boston Globe*, February 12, 2010, www.boston.com/news/nation/washington /articles/2010/02/12/democrats_proposing_new_limits _oncorporate_campaign_donations/ (accessed 2/27/10).

42. Joe Davidson, "OMB Moves to Cut Outside Contractors," *Washington Post*, July 29, 2009, www.washingtonpost.com /wp-dyn/content/article/2009/07/28/AR2009072802812 .html (accessed 2/18/10).

43. Joe Davidson, "Deficit-Cutters Must Also Weigh the Cost of Contractors," *Washington Post*, February 4, 2011, www .washingtonpost.com/wp-dyn/content/article/2011/ 02/03/AR2011020306809.html?nav=emailpage (accessed 1/2/12).

44. Ed O'Keefe, "The Winners and Losers of the New Spending Bill," *Washington Post*, January 14, 2014, www .washingtonpost.com/blogs/the-fix/wp/2014/01/13 /the-winners-and-losers-of-the-new-spending-bill/ (accessed 1/23/14).

45. Alexander Hamilton, James Madison, and John Jay, *The Federalist Papers*, ed. Clinton Rossiter (New York: New American Library, 1961), no. 51, p. 322.

46. The title of this section was inspired by Peri Arnold, *Making the Managerial Presidency* (Princeton, NJ: Princeton University Press, 1986).

47. For more details and evaluations, see David Rosenbloom, *Public Administration* (New York: Random House, 1986), pp. 186–221; Charles H. Levine, with the assistance of Rosslyn S. Kleeman, *The Quiet Crisis of the Civil Service: The Federal Personnel System at the Crossroads* (Washington, DC: National Academy of Public Administration, 1986).

48. Lester Salamon and Alan Abramson, "Governance: The Politics of Retrenchment," in *The Reagan Record*, ed. John Palmer and Isabel Sawhill (Cambridge, MA: Ballinger, 1984), p. 40.

49. Colin Campbell, "The White House and the Presidency under the 'Let's Deal' President," in *The Bush Presidency: First Appraisals*, ed. Colin Campbell and Bert A. Rockman (Chatham, NJ: Chatham House, 1991), pp. 185–222.

50. See John Micklethwait, "Managing to Look Attractive," *New Statesman* 125, November 8, 1996, p. 24.

51. Quoted in I. M. Destler, "Reagan and the World: An 'Awesome Stubborness,'" in *The Reagan Legacy: Promise and Performance*, ed. Charles O. Jones, (Chatham, NJ: Chatham House, 1988), pp. 244–57. The source of the quote is *Report of the President's Special Review Board* (Washington, DC: Government Printing Office, 1987).

52. Thomas E. Mann and Norman J. Ornstein, *The Broken Branch: How Congress Is Failing America and How to Get It Back on Track* (New York: Oxford University Press, 2006), p. 155.

53. The Office of Technology Assessment (OTA) was a fourth research agency serving Congress until 1995. It was one of the first agencies scheduled for elimination by the 104th Congress. Until 1983, Congress had still another tool of legislative oversight: the legislative veto. Each agency operating under such provisions was obliged to submit to Congress every proposed decision or rule, which would then lie before both chambers for 30 to 60 days. If Congress took no action by one-house or two-house resolution explicitly to veto the proposed measure during the prescribed period, the measure became law. The legislative veto was declared unconstitutional by the

Supreme Court in 1983 on the grounds that it violated the separation of powers—the resolutions Congress passed to exercise its veto were not subject to presidential veto, as required by the Constitution. See *Immigration and Naturalization Service v. Chadha*, 462 U.S. 919 (1983).

Chapter 15

1. *Morse v. Frederick*, 551 U.S. 393 (2007).
2. Charles Lane, "Court Backs School on Speech Curbs," *Washington Post*, June 26, 2007, p. A6.
3. U.S. Courts Statistical Tables, 2012, www.uscourts.gov/statistics.aspx (accessed 9/12/14).
4. Michael A. Fletcher, "Obama Criticized as Too Cautious on Judicial Posts," *Washington Post*, October 15, 2009, www.washingtonpost.com/wp-dyn/content/article/2009/10/15/AR2009101504083.html (accessed 3/1/10).
5. Russell Wheeler, "Judicial Nominations and Confirmations after Three Years—Where Do Things Stand?" Governance Studies at Brookings, January 13, 2012, www.brookings.edu (accessed 8/27/14).
6. *Arizona v. United States*, 11–182 (2012).
7. *National Federation of Independent Business v. Sebelius*, 11–393 (2012).
8. Peter Wallsten and Richard Simon, "Sotomayor Nomination Splits GOP," *Los Angeles Times*, May 27, 2009, http://articles.latimes.com/2009/may/27/nation/na-court-access27 (accessed 3/1/10).
9. C. Herman Pritchett, *The American Constitution* (New York: McGraw-Hill, 1959), p. 138.
10. *Marbury v. Madison*, 1 Cr. 137 (1803).
11. *National Federation of Independent Business v. Sebelious*, 567 U.S. __ (2012).
12. Acts of Congress held unconstitutional in whole or in part by the Supreme Court of the United States," General Printing Office, www.gpo.gov/fdsys/pkg/GPO-CONAN-2013/pdf/GPO-CONAN-2013-11.pdf (accessed 4/20/14).
13. *Federal Election Commission v. Wisconsin Right to Life*, 551 U.S. 449 (2007).
14. This review power was affirmed by the Supreme Court in *Martin v. Hunter's Lessee*, 1 Wheat. 304 (1816).
15. *Brown v. Board of Education*, 347 U.S. 483 (1954).
16. *Lawrence v. Texas*, 539 U.S. 558 (2003).
17. *Miller v. Alabama*, 567 U.S. __, No. 10–9646, slip op. (2012).
18. *American Tradition Partnership, Inc. v. Bullock*, 564 U.S. __, No. 11-1179, slip op. (2012).
19. *United States v. Jones*, 10-1259 (2012).
20. Theodore J. Lowi, *The End of Liberalism*, 2nd ed. (New York: W. W. Norton, 1979); also David Schoenbrod, *Power without Responsibility: How Congress Abuses the People through Delegation* (New Haven, CT: Yale University Press, 1993).
21. Kenneth Culp Davis, *Discretionary Justice* (Baton Rouge: Louisiana State University Press, 1969), pp. 15–21.
22. Emergency Price Control Act, 56 Stat. 23 (January 30, 1942).
23. *Chamber of Commerce of the United States v. Environmental Protection*, No. 12-1272 (2014).
24. *Hamdi v. Rumsfeld*, 542 U.S. 507 (2004).
25. *Hamdan v. Rumsfeld*, 548 U.S. 557 (2006).
26. *Boumediene v. Bush*, 553 U.S. 723 (2008).
27. *National Labor Relations Board v. Noel Canning*, 572 U.S. __ (2014).
28. *Shelley v. Kraemer*, 334 U.S. 1 (1948).
29. *Burlington Northern v. White*, 548 U.S. 53 (2006).
30. *Engel v. Vitale*, 370 U.S. 421 (1962).
31. *Gideon v. Wainwright*, 372 U.S. 335 (1963).
32. *Escobedo v. Illinois*, 378 U.S. 478 (1964).
33. *Miranda v. Arizona*, 384 U.S. 436 (1966).
34. *Dickerson v. United States*, 530 U.S. 428 (2000).
35. *Baker v. Carr*, 369 U.S. 186 (1962).
36. *Roe v. Wade*, 410 U.S. 113 (1973).
37. *Schuette v. Coalition to Defend Affirmative Action*, 572 U.S. __ (2014).
38. Robert Scigliano, *The Supreme Court and the Presidency* (New York: Free Press, 1971), p. 162. For an interesting critique of the solicitor general's role during the Reagan administration, see Lincoln Caplan, "Annals of the Law," *New Yorker*, August 17, 1987, pp. 30–62.
39. Edward Lazarus, *Closed Chambers* (New York: Times Books, 1998), p. 6.
40. *NAACP v. Button*, 371 U.S. 415 (1963). The quotation is from the opinion in this case.
41. *Smith v. Allwright*, 321 U.S. 649 (1944).
42. Charles Krauthammer, "Why Roberts Did It," *The Washington Post*, June 29, 2012, www.washingtonpost.com/opinions/charles-krauthammer-why-roberts-did-it/2012/06/28/gjQA4X0g9V_story.html (accessed 4/22/14).
43. Matthew Crenson and Benjamin Ginsberg, *Presidential Power: Unchecked and Unbalanced* (New York: W. W. Norton, 2007), p. 316.
44. *Griswold v. Connecticut*, 381 U.S. 479 (1965).
45. *McCutcheon vs. Federal Election Commission*, 572 U.S. __ (2014).
46. R. W. Apple, Jr., "A Divided Government Remains, and with It the Prospect of Further Combat," *New York Times*, November 7, 1996, p. B6.
47. For limits on judicial power, see Alexander Bickel, *The Least Dangerous Branch* (Indianapolis, IN: Bobbs-Merrill, 1962).
48. *Worcester v. Georgia*, 6 Pet. 515 (1832).
49. See Walter Murphy, *Congress and the Court* (Chicago: University of Chicago Press, 1962).
50. Robert Dahl, "The Supreme Court and National Policy Making," *Journal of Public Law* 6 (1958): 279.

51. Martin Shapiro, "The Supreme Court: From Warren to Burger," in *The New American Political System*, ed. Anthony King (Washington, DC: American Enterprise Institute, 1978).

52. *Citizens to Preserve Overton Park v. Volpe*, 401 U.S. 402 (1971).

53. Toni Locy, "Bracing for Health Care's Caseload," *Washington Post*, August 22, 1994, p. A15.

54. See "Developments in the Law—Class Actions," *Harvard Law Review* 89 (1976): 1318.

55. *In re Agent Orange Product Liability Litigation*, 100 F.R.D. 718 (D.C.N.Y. 1983).

56. See Donald Horowitz, *The Courts and Social Policy* (Washington, DC: Brookings Institution Press, 1977).

57. *Moran v. McDonough*, 540 F2d 527 (1 Cir., 1976; *cert. denied*, 429 U.S. 1042 [1977]).

58. Alexander Hamilton, James Madison, and John Jay, *The Federalist Papers*, ed. Clinton Rossiter (New York: New American Library, 1961), no. 10, p. 78.

Chapter 16

1. Robert Nozick, *Anarchy, State and Utopia* (New York: Basic Books, 1974; reprint, Oxford: Blackwell, 2003).

2. Compare with Gabriel Kolko, *The Triumph of Conservatism* (New York: Free Press, 1963), chap. 6.

3. Bureau of Economic Analysis, "Percent Change from Preceding Period in Real Gross Domestic Product," www.bea.gov/national/nipaweb/SelectTable.asp?Popular=Y (accessed 3/5/10).

4. "Times Topics: Financial Regulatory Reform," *New York Times*, updated September 20, 2011, http://topics.nytimes.com/topics/reference/timestopics/subjects/c/credit_crisis/financial_regulatory_reform/index.html (accessed 5/16/12).

5. See David M. Hart, *Forged Consensus: Science, Technology and Economic Policy in the United States, 1921–1953* (Princeton, NJ: Princeton University Press, 1998).

6. See Margaret Weir, *Politics and Jobs: The Boundaries of Employment Policy in the United States* (Princeton, NJ: Princeton University Press, 1992).

7. The act of 1955 officially designated the interstate highways as the National System of Interstate and Defense Highways. It was indirectly a major part of President Dwight Eisenhower's defense program. But it was just as obviously a "pork-barrel" policy as any rivers and harbors legislation.

8. The members included AMD, Digital, Hewlett-Packard, IBM, Intel, Lucent, Motorola, National Semiconductor, Rockwell, and Texas Instruments.

9. Molly Sherlock, "Energy Tax Policy: Issues in the 113th Congress," Congressional Research Service, December 2013, www.fas.org/sgp/crs/misc/R43206.pdf (accessed 4/25/14).

10. Matthew L. Wald, "U.S. Agency Knew about G.M. Flaw but Did Not Act," *New York Times*, March 30, 2014, www.nytimes.com/2014/03/31/business/us-regulators-declined-full-inquiry-into-gm-ignition-flaws-memo-shows.html (accessed 4/27/14).

11. For a good summary of Keynes's ideas, see Robert Lekachman, *The Age of Keynes* (New York: McGraw-Hill, 1966).

12. Ronald Reagan, Inaugural Address, January 20, 1981, www.reaganfoundation.org/pdf/Inaugural_Address_012081.pdf (accessed 4/27/14).

13. Gallup, Taxes, www.gallup.com/poll/1714/taxes.aspx (accessed 4/27/14).

14. Gallup, Taxes.

15. Pew Research Center for the People and the Press, "Views of Government: Key Data Points," October 22, 2013, www.pewresearch.org/key-data-points/views-of-government-key-data-points/ (accessed 4/27/14).

16. Pew Research Center for the People and the Press, "As Sequester Deadline Looms, Little Support for Cutting Most Programs," www.people-press.org/2013/02/22/as-sequester-deadline-looms-little-support-for-cutting-most-programs/ (accessed 4/27/14).

17. See, for example, Paul Krugman, "The Bankruptcy Boys," *New York Times*, February 21, 2010, www.nytimes.com/2010/02/22/opinion/22krugman.html?_r=0 (accessed 4/27/14).

18. Pew Research Center for the People and the Press, "Section 2: Views of Government Regulation," February 23, 2012, www.people-press.org/2012/02/23/section-2-views-of-government-regulation/ (accessed 4/27/14).

19. Pew Research Center for the People and the Press, "Most See Inequality Growing, but Partisans Differ over Solutions," January 23, 2014, www.people-press.org/2014/01/23/most-see-inequality-growing-but-partisans-differ-over-solutions/ (accessed 4/27/14).

20. Congressional Budget Office, "The Effects of a Minimum-Wage Increase on Employment and Family Income," February 18, 2014, www.cbo.gov/publication/44995 (accessed 4/27/14).

21. Bureau of Labor Statistics, "Union Members—2013," January 24, 2014, www.bls.gov/news.release/pdf/union2.pdf (accessed 3/30/14).

22. Steven Greenhouse, "Wage Strikes Planned at Fast-Food Outlets," *New York Times*, December 1, 2013, www.nytimes.com/2013/12/02/business/economy/wage-strikes-planned-at-fast-food-outlets-in-100-cities.html?_r=0 (accessed 4/27/14).

23. David Sanger, David Herszenhorn, and Bill Vlasic, "Bush Aids Detroit, but Hard Choices Await Obama," *New York Times*, December 19, 2008, www.nytimes.com

/2008/12/20/business/20auto.html? r=3&hp (accessed 3/7/10).

24. Reuters, "CBO Raises TARP Cost Estimate to $34 Billion,"December16,2011,www.reuters.com/article/2011/12/16/us-usa-tarp-cost-idUSTRE7BF1W920111216 (accessed 7/3/12).

25. Bureau of Labor Statistics, "United States Unemployment Rate," www.tradingeconomics.com/united-states/unemployment-rate (accessed 7/3/12).

26. Congressional Budget Office, February 22, 2012, http://cbo.gov/publications/43014 (accessed 7/3/12).

27. Ben Pershing, "House Passes $15 Billion Jobs Bill," *Washington Post*, March 5, 2010, www.washingtonpost.com/wp-dyn/content/article/2010/03/04/AR2010030402757.html (accessed 3/5/10).

28. Kevin G. Hall, "Bernanke to Stay on Greenspan Path, but Not All the Way," *Seattle Times*, November 16, 2005, p. C1.

29. The Federal Reserve Board, *Intended Federal Funds Rate, 1990 to Present*, www.federalreserve.gov/fomc/fundsrate.htm (accessed 3/8/10).

30. Donna S. Robinson, "NY Fed Estimates Millions More Foreclosures Possible" *Realty Biz News*, January 13, 2012, http://realtybiznews.com/ny-fed-estimates-millions-more-foreclosures-possible-in-2012-and-2013/9878531/ (accessed 9/26/12).

31. Steven R. Weisman, "Bernanke Faces Bear Stearns Queries," *New York Times*, April 2, 2008, p. C1.

32. John Ydstie, "Federal Reserve Mulls Its Role One Year after Crisis," National Public Radio, September 14, 2009, www.npr.org/templates/story/story.php?storyId=112767144 (accessed 3/8/10).

33. Executive Office of the President of the United States, GPO Access, "Budget of the United States Government: Historical Tables Fiscal Year 2009," Table 2.2—Percentage Composition of Receipts by Source: 1934–2013, http://origin.www.gpoaccess.gov/usbudget/fy09/hist.html (accessed 5/9/08).

34. For a systematic account of the role of government in providing incentives and inducements to business, see C. E. Lindblom, *Politics and Markets* (New York: Basic Books, 1977), chap. 13. For a detailed account of the dramatic Reagan tax cuts and reforms, see Jeffrey Birnbaum and Alan Murray, *Showdown at Gucci Gulch: Lawmakers, Lobbyists, and the Unlikely Triumph of Tax Reform* (New York: Random House, 1987).

35. See Tax Foundation, *Federal Individual Income Tax Rates History, 1862–2013,* http://taxfoundation.org/article/us-federal-individual-income-tax-rates-history-1913-2013-nominal-and-inflation-adjusted-brackets (accessed 3/30/14).

36. Center on Budget and Policy Priorities, "Tax Cuts, Myths and Realities," November 16, 2007, www.cbpp.org/9-27-06tax.htm (accessed 3/20/08).

37. Jay Heflin, "House Dems Want Bush Tax Cuts to Expire, but Say It's Tough Sell," *The Hill*, February 8, 2010, http://thehill.com/homenews/house/80133-democrats-supporting-ending-tax-cut-but-see-it-as-tough-sell (accessed 3/8/10).

38. Jackie Calmes, "Demystifying the Fiscal Impasse That Is Vexing Washington," *New York Times*, November 15, 2012, www.nytimes.com/2012/11/16/us/politics/the-fiscal-cliff-explained.html; Jonathan Weisman, "Answers to Questions on Capital's Top Topic," *New York Times*, February 21, 2013, www.nytimes.com/2013/02/22/us/politics/questions-and-answers-about-the-sequester.html (accessed 4/26/14).

39. David Espo, "Shutdown Orders Issued as Congress Misses Deadline," Associated Press, October 1, 2013, bigstory.ap.org/article/health-law-challenge-threatens-government-shutdown (accessed 4/26/14).

40. For an account of the relationship between mechanization and law, see Lawrence Friedman, *A History of American Law* (New York: Simon and Schuster, 1973), 409–29.

41. The *Federal Register* is the daily publication of all official acts of Congress, the president, and the administrative agencies. A law or executive order is not legally binding until it is published in the *Federal Register*.

42. Veronique de Rugy, "Hold On to Your Wallet: The Cost of Corporate Welfare and Rent-Seeking," *National Review Online*, July 25, 2012, www.nationalreview.com/corner/312251/hold-your-wallet-cost-corporate-welfare-and-rent-seeking-veronique-de-rugy# (accessed 9/26/12).

43. James Dao, "The Nation; Big Bucks Trip Up the Lean New Army," *New York Times*, February 10, 2002, sec. 4, p. 5, www.nytimes.com/2002/02/10/weekinreview/the-nation-big-bucks-trip-up-the-lean-new-army.html?pagewanted=all (accessed 9/26/12).

44. See Samuel P. Hays, *Beauty, Health, and Permanence: Environmental Politics in the United States, 1955–1985* (Cambridge: Cambridge University Press, 1987).

45. Pew Center on Global Climate Change, "Climate Change 101: The Science and Impacts," www.pewclimate.org/docUploads/101_Science_Impacts.pdf (accessed 3/21/08).

46. See the discussion in Peter R. Orszag, "Issues in Climate Change," Congressional Budget Office, November 16, 2007, www.cbo.gov/ftpdocs/88xx/doc8819/11-16-Climate ChangeConf.pdf (accessed 3/21/08).

47. Energy Information Administration, "Greenhouse Gases, Climate Change, and Energy," www.eia.doe.gov/oiaf/1605/ggccebro/chapter1.html (accessed 3/21/08).

48. John M. Broder and Marjorie Connelly, "Public Says Warming Is a Problem, but Remains Split on Response," *New York Times*, April 27, 2007, www.nytimes.com/2007/04/27/world/americas/27iht-27poll.5466260.html (accessed 7/3/12).

49. Tam Hunt, "The Good News: Climate Change Doesn't Matter Anymore," May 31, 2011, www.renewableenergyworld.com/rea/news/article/2011/05/the-good-news-climate-change-doesnt-matter-anymore (accessed 7/2/12).

50. Hunt, "The Good News."

51. Associated Press, "Obama Proposes Agency on Climate Change," February 8, 2010, www.cbsnews.com/stories/2010/02/08/tech/main6186608.shtml (accessed 3/8/10).

52. Michael Austin, "Breaking Down the New 2016 Fuel Economy Standards," *Car and Driver*, April 2, 2010, http://blog.caranddriver.com/breaking-down-the-new-2016-fuel-economy-standards/ (accessed 9/26/12).

53. Survey by Cable News Network, conducted by Opinion Research Corporation, November 2–4, 2007, and based on telephone interviews with a national adult sample of 1,024, USORC.110707.R05L.

54. Environmental Defense Fund, "Coalition Defines Clear Path for Climate Action," www.edf.org/climate/coalition-defines-clear-path-climate-action (accessed 7/2/12).

55. Juliet Eilperin and Steven Mufson, "Senators to Propose Abandoning Cap-and-Trade," *Washington Post*, February 27, 2010, www.washingtonpost.com/wp-dyn/content/article/2010/02/26/AR2010022606084.html?hpid=topnews (accessed 3/5/10).

56. Associated Press, "Obama Proposes Agency on Climate Change," February 8, 2010, www.cbsnews.com/stories/2010/02/08/tech/main6186608.shtml (accessed 3/8/10).

57. Hendrik Hertzberg, "Cooling on Warming," *The New Yorker*, February 7, 2011, p. 21.

58. Orszag, "Issues in Climate Change," pp. 6–7.

59. Joe Palca, "California Turns to Holland for Flood Expertise," National Public Radio, January 14, 2008, www.npr.org/templates/story/story.php?storyId=18080442 (accessed 3/21/08).

60. Steven Greenhouse, "Our Economic Pickle," *New York Times*, January 13, 2013, www.nytimes.com/2013/01/13/sunday-review/americas-productivity-climbs-but-wages-stagnate.html?_r=0 (accessed 5/2/14).

Chapter 17

1. Henry J. Kaiser Family Foundation, "Health Tracking Poll: Exploring the Public's Views on the Affordable Care Act (ACA)," http://kff.org/interactive/health-tracking-poll-exploring-the-publics-views-on-the-affordable-care-act-aca (accessed 5/12/14).

2. A good source of pre-1930s welfare history is James T. Patterson, *America's Struggle against Poverty, 1900–1994* (Cambridge, MA: Harvard University Press, 1994), chap. 2.

3. Quoted in Patterson, *America's Struggle against Poverty*, p. 26.

4. Patterson, *America's Struggle against Poverty*, p. 26.

5. Patterson, *America's Struggle against Poverty*, p. 27.

6. This figure is based on a WPA study by Ann E. Geddes, reported in Merle Fainsod et al., *Government and the American Economy*, 3rd ed. (New York: W. W. Norton, 1959), p. 769.

7. Social Security, Official Social Security Website, "2014 Social Security Changes," www.socialsecurity.gov/news/press/factsheets/colafacts2014.html (accessed 5/3/14).

8. C. Eugene Steuerle, Adam Carasso, and Lee Cohen, *How Progressive Is Social Security and Why?* (Washington, DC: Urban Institute, 2004), www.urban.org/publications/311016.html (accessed 5/3/14).

9. Edward J. Harpham, "Fiscal Crisis and the Politics of Social Security Reform," in *The Attack on the Welfare State*, ed. Anthony Champagne and Edward Harpham (Prospect Heights, IL: Waveland, 1984), p. 13.

10. Liz Schott and Ife Floyd, "Tax Benefits Are Low and Have Not Kept Pace with Inflation: Benefits Are Not Enough to Meet Families' Basic Needs. Appendix 1: Changes in State TANF Benefit Levels (Single-Parent Family of Three)," *Center on Budget and Policy Priorities*, October 14, 2010, www.cbpp.org/files/10-14-10tanf.pdf (accessed 2/19/12).

11. This poverty threshold is for a household of three persons that includes two children. Department of Health and Human Services, Office of the Assistant Secretary for Planning and Evaluation, 2014 Poverty Guidelines, www.aspe.hhs.gov/poverty/14poverty.cfm (accessed 5/10/14).

12. *Goldberg v. Kelly*, 397 U.S. 254 (1970).

13. Center on Budget and Policy Priorities, "Update: Where Things Stand for the Unemployed," May 1, 2014, www.offthechartsblog.org/update-where-things-stand-for-the-unemployed-2 (accessed 5/12/14); Congress enacted extended unemployment benefits in 2009 to address the high unemployment during the recession but did not reauthorize it in late 2013.

14. Henry J. Kaiser Family Foundation, "Status of State Action on the Medicaid Expansion Decision," August 28, 2014, http://kff.org/health-reform/state-indicator/state-activity-around-expanding-medicaid-under-the-affordable-care-act/ (accessed 9/22/14).

15. See Martin Gilens, *Why Americans Hate Welfare* (Chicago: University of Chicago Press, 1999), chaps. 3, 4.

16. Gilens, *Why Americans Hate Welfare*.

17. Center for Law and Social Policy, "Analysis of Fiscal Year 2006 TANF and MOE Spending by States," http://clasp.org/WelfarePolicy/pdf/map100907us.pdf (accessed 4/9/08).

18. See the discussion of the law and the data presented in House Ways and Means Committee Print, WMCP: 106-14, 2000 Green Book, Section 7, Temporary

Assistance for Needy Families (TANF), http://frwebgate .access.gpo.gov/cgi-bin/useftp.cgi?IPaddress=162.140.64 .181&filename=wm014_07.wais&directory=/data/wais /data/106_green_book (accessed 3/26/08); Rebecca M. Blank, "Evaluating Welfare Reform in the United States," *Journal of Economic Literature* 40 (December 2002): 1105–66.

19. LaDonna Pavetti and Liz Schott, "TANF's Inadequate Response to Recession Highlights Weakness of Block-Grant Structure," (Washington, DC: Center on Budget and Policy Priorities), July 14, 2011, www.cbpp.org/cms /?fa=view&id=3534 (accessed 2/10/12).

20. Center for Budget and Policy Priorities, "Chartbook: SNAP Helps Struggling Families Put Food on the Table," April 18, 2012, www.cbpp.org/cms/?fa=view&id=3744#part5 (accessed 7/6/12); U.S. Department of Agriculture, Food and Nutrition Service, Supplemental Nutrition Assistance Program, www.fns.usda.gov/pd/34SNAPmonthly .htm (accessed 5/3/14).

21. Data for 2014 are estimates. Office of Management and Budget, "Table 8.3, Percentage Distribution of Outlays by Budget Enforcement Act Category: 1962–2019," www .whitehouse.gov/omb/budget/Historicals; Office of Management and Budget, "The President's Budget, Historical Tables: Table 2.2, Percentage Composition of Receipts by Source: 1934–2019," www.whitehouse.gov/omb/budget /Historicals (accessed 5/10/14).

22. Congressional Budget Office, "The 2013 Long-Term Projections for Social Security: Additional Information," www.cbo.gov/publication/44972 (accessed 5/3/14).

23. President's Commission to Strengthen Social Security, "Strengthening Social Security and Creating Personal Wealth for All Americans," December 21, 2001, www.csss.gov/reports/Final_report.pdf (accessed 3/26/08).

24. President's Commission to Strengthen Social Security, "Strengthening Social Security."

25. Alicia H. Munnell, "Are the Social Security Trust Funds Meaningful?" Center for Retirement Research, Boston College, May 2005, no. 30, p. 4, http://crr.bc.edu/ images /stories/Briefs/ib_30.pdf (accessed 3/25/08); see also Social Security Online, Summary of P.L. 98-21, (H.R. 1900) Social Security Amendments of 1983—Signed on April 20, 1983, www.ssa.gov/history/1983amend.html (accessed 3/25/08).

26. Christian E. Weller, "Undermining Social Security with Private Accounts," Economic Policy Institute Issue Brief, December 11, 2001, www.epi.org/content.cfm /issuebriefs_ib172; Robert Greenstein, "Social Security Commission Proposals Contain Serious Weaknesses but May Improve the Debate in an Important Respect," Center on Budget and Policy Priorities, December 26, 2001, www.centeronbudget.org/12-11-01socsec.htm (accessed 3/26/08).

27. Quoted in Jill Quadragno, "Social Security Policy and the Entitlement Debate," in *Social Policy and the Conservative Agenda*, eds. Clarence Y. H. Lo and Michael Schwartz (Malden, MA: Blackwell, 1998), p. 111.

28. Henry J. Kaiser Family Foundation, "Sources of Medicare Revenue, 2012," http://kff.org/medicare/slide/sources-of -medicare-revenue-2012 (accessed 5/3/14).

29. Henry J. Kaiser Foundation, "Medicare Spending and Financing Fact Sheet," http://kff.org/medicare/fact-sheet /medicare-spending-and-financing-fact-sheet (accessed 5/3/14).

30. Congressional Budget Office, "Long Term Analysis of a Budget Proposal by Chairman Ryan," April 5, 2011, www .cbo.gov/publication/22085 (accessed 7/6/12); See also the discussion in Kaiser Family Foundation Program on Medicare Policy, "Proposed Changes to Medicare in the 'Path to Prosperity,'" April 2011, www.kff.org/medicare /upload/8179.pdf (accessed 3/1/12).

31. There were a couple of minor precedents. One was the Smith-Hughes Act of 1917, which made federal funds available to the states for vocational education at the elementary and secondary levels. Second, the Lanham Act of 1940 made federal funds available to schools in "federally impacted areas," that is, areas with an unusually large number of government employees and/or where the local tax base was reduced by large amounts of government-owned property.

32. See the critique in Raegen T. Miller and Cynthia G. Brown, "Bitter Pill, Better Formula: Toward a Single, Fair, and Equitable Formula for ESEA Title I, Part A," (Washington, DC: Center for American Progress, February 2010), www .americanprogress.org/wp content/uploads/issues/2010/02 /pdf/bitter_pill.pdf (accessed 5/11/14).

33. David K. Cohen and Susan L. Moffitt, *The Ordeal of Equality: Did Federal Regulation Fix the Schools?* (Cambridge, MA: Harvard University Press, 2009).

34. Motoko Rich, "'No Child' Law Whittled Down by White House," *New York Times*, July 6, 2012, p. A1; U.S. Department of Education, Elementary and Secondary Education, ESEA Flexibility, www2.ed.gov/policy/elsec /guid/esea-flexibility/index.html (accessed 5/11/14).

35. For a positive view of the standards, see Sonja Brookins Santelises, "Abandoning the Common Core Is Taking the Easy Way Out," The Equity Line, http://theequityline.org /wp/2014/03/31/abandoning-the-common-core-is-taking -the-easy-way-out; for a critique see Valerie Strauss, "The Coming Common Core Melt-down," *Washington Post*, January 23, 2014, www.washingtonpost.com/blogs/answer -sheet/wp/2014/01/23/the-coming-common-core -meltdown (accessed 5/11/14).

36. Veronica DeVore, "'Race to the Top' Education Funds Awarded to 9 States and D.C.," August 24, 2010, www .pbs.org/newshour/rundown/2010/08/round-two-results -announced-for-race-to-the-top.html (accessed 7/6/12).

37. Elaine Weiss, "Mismatches in Race to the Top Limit Educational Improvement: Lack of Time, Resources, and Tools to Address Opportunity Gaps Puts Lofty State Goals Out of Reach," www.boldapproach.org/report (accessed 5/11/14).

38. One of the most vocal proponents of this viewpoint is former assistant secretary of education Diane Ravitch, *The Life and Death of the Great American School System* (New York: Basic Books, 2011).

39. Suzanne Mettler, *Degrees of Inequality: How the Politics of Higher Education Sabotaged the American Dream* (New York: Basic Books, 2014), 52–54.

40. Mettler, *Degrees of Inequality*, 52–54.

41. Morton Keller, *Affairs of State: Public Life in Nineteenth Century America* (Cambridge, MA: Belknap Press, 1977), p. 500.

42. Henry J. Kaiser Family Foundation, "U.S. Federal Funding for HIV/AIDS: The President's FY 2014 Budget Request," January 22, 2014, http://kff.org/hivaids/slide/u-s-federal -funding-for-hivaids/ (accessed 5/10/14).

43. Noam N. Levey, "Obama's HIV/AIDS Policy Hailed for Targeting Spread of Disease," *Los Angeles Times*, July 14, 2010, http://articles.latimes.com/2010/jul/14/nation/la -na-obama-aids-20100714 (accessed 3/1/12); Henry J. Kaiser Family Foundation, "The HIV/AIDS Epidemic in the United States," April 7, 2014, http://kff.org/hivaids-fact-sheet/the-hivaids-epidemic-in-the-united-states/ (accessed 5/10/14).

44. Office of Management and Budget, US Budget, Historical Tables, Table 12.3, Total Outlays for Grants to State and Local Governments, www.whitehouse.gov/omb /budget/Historicals (accessed 5/10/14).

45. Kaiser Commission on Medicaid and the Uninsured, *Medicaid: A Primer*, p. 26.

46. Henry J. Kaiser Family Foundation, "Health Insurance Coverage of the Non-Elderly, 0–64, http://kff.org/other /state-indicator/nonelderly-0-64 (accessed 5/10/14).

47. For a comparison of opinion in 1993 when the Clinton plan was considered and opinion in 2009 as reform was just beginning again, see Pew Research Center for the People and the Press, "Obama's Ratings Remain High Despite Some Policy Concerns," www.people-press .org/2009/06/18/obamas-ratings-remain-high-despite -some-policy-concerns/(accessed 7/6/12).

48. The Henry J. Kaiser Family Foundation, Kaiser Health Tracking Poll, "Early Reaction to Supreme Court Decision on the ACA," p. 3.

49. White House, "Fact Sheet: Affordable Care Act by the Numbers," www.whitehouse.gov/the-press-office/2014/04/17 /fact-sheet-affordable-care-act-numbers (accessed 5/12/14).

50. Henry J. Kaiser Family Foundation, "Health Tracking Poll: Exploring the Public's Views on the Affordable Care Act (ACA)," http://kff.org/interactive/health-tracking-poll-exploring-the-publics-views-on-the -affordable-care-act-aca (accessed 5/12/14).

51. *National Federation of Independent Business v. Sebelius*, 567 U.S. __ (2012).

52. Kaiser Family Foundation "Status of State Action."

53. "February Kaiser Health Tracking Poll," March 1, 2012, healthreform.kff.org/scan.aspx?tag=Public+Opinion (accessed 3/1/12).

54. *Sebelius v. Hobby Lobby Stores, Inc.*; the case was combined with two similar challenges: *Conestoga Wood Specialties Corp. v. Sebelius* and *Autocam Corp. v. Sebelius*.

55. John E. Schwarz, *America's Hidden Success*, 2nd ed. (New York: W. W. Norton, 1988), pp. 41–42.

56. See, for example, Lawrence Vale, "Housing Chicago: Cabrini-Green to Parkside of Old Town," http://places .designobserver.com/feature/housing-chicago-cabrini -green-to-parkside-of-old-town/32298 (accessed 3/1/12).

57. Peter Dreier, Saqib Bhatti, Rob Call, Alex Schwartz, and Gregory Squires, *Underwater America: How the So-Called Housing "Recovery" Is Bypassing Many American Communities* (Berkeley, CA: Haas Institute for a Fair and Inclusive Society, 2014), p. 8.

58. Theda Skocpol and Vanessa Williamson, *The Tea Party and the Remaking of Republican Conservatism* (New York: Oxford University Press, 2012), chap. 1.

59. U.S. Census Bureau, Historical Poverty Tables, "Table 2. Poverty Status, by Family Relationship, Race, and Hispanic Origin" and "Table 3. Poverty Status, by Age, Race and Hispanic Origin," www.census.gov/hhes/www/poverty /data/historical/people.html (accessed 4/29/14).

60. See, for example, Theodore R. Marmor, Jerry L. Mashaw, and Philip L. Harvey, *America's Misunderstood Welfare State* (New York: Basic Books, 1990), p. 156.

61. U.S. Census Bureau, Current Population Survey, 2013 Annual Social and Economic Supplement. HINC-02. Age of Householder—Households, by Total Money Income in 2012, Type of Household, Race and Hispanic Origin of Householder, www.census.gov/hhes/www /cpstables/032013/hhinc/hinc02_000.htm (accessed 5/10/14).

62. Frederick R. Lynch, "How AARP Can Get Its Groove Back," *New York Times*, June 23, 2011, www.nytimes.com/2011 /06/24/opinion/24lynch.html, and "Influence and Lobbying: AARP Lobbyists, 2011," www.opensecrets.org /lobby/clientlbs.php?id=D000023726&year=2011 (accessed 2/20/12).

63. See Andrea Louise Campbell, *How Policies Make Citizens: Senior Political Activism and the American Welfare State* (Princeton, NJ: Princeton University Press, 2005).

64. Christopher Howard, *The Hidden Welfare State: Tax Expenditures and Social Policy in the United States* (Princeton, NJ: Princeton University Press, 1999); Jacob S. Hacker, *The Divided Welfare State: The Battle over Public and Private Benefits in the United States* (New York: Cambridge University Press, 2002).

65. Office of Management and Budget, "Table 17-1: Estimates of Total Income Tax Expenditures for Fiscal Years 2010–2016," *Analytical Perspectives: Budget of the U.S. Government* (2010), www.whitehouse.gov/sites/default/files/omb/budget/fy2012/assets/spec.pdf (accessed 2/20/12).

66. Center on Budget and Policy Priorities, "Policy Basics: Introduction to the Supplemental Nutrition Assistance Program (SNAP)," March 19, 2014, www.centeronbudget.org/cms/index.cfm?fa=view&id=2226 (accessed 5/12/14).

67. "Panera CEO: On Food Stamps, I Can't Eat in My Own Restaurant," September 25, 2013, http://eatocracy.cnn.com/2013/09/25/panera-ceo-on-food-stamps-i-cant-eat-in-my-own-restaurant (accessed 5/12/14).

68. Raymond Hernandez, "Federal Welfare Overhaul Allows Albany to Shift Money Elsewhere," *New York Times*, April 23, 2000, p. 1.

69. Frances Fox Piven and Richard Cloward, *Poor People's Movements* (New York: Pantheon, 1977), chap. 5.

70. U.S. Department of Agriculture, Food and Nutrition Service, Supplemental Nutrition Assistance Program, www.fns.usda.gov/pd/34SNAPmonthly.htmwww.fns.usda.gov/snap (accessed 5/12/14).

71. Carmen DeNavas-Walt, Bernadette D. Proctor, and Jessica C. Smith, "Income Poverty and Health Insurance Coverage in the United States," U.S. Census Bureau, September 2013, www.census.gov/prod/2013pubs/p60-245 (accessed 5/12/14).

72. Carmen DeNavas-Walt, Bernadette D. Proctor, and Jessica C. Smith, "Income Poverty and Health Insurance Coverage in the United States," U.S. Census Bureau, September 2013, www.census.gov/prod/2013pubs/p60-245.pdf (accessed 5/12/14).

73. See, for example, Sharon Hayes, *Flat Broke with Children: Women in the Age of Welfare Reform* (New York: Oxford University Press, 2004).

74. U.S. Census Bureau, "Poverty: Historical Poverty Tables—People: Table 2: Poverty Status of People by Family Relationship, Race, and Hispanic Origin: 1959 to 2010," www.Census.Gov/Hhes/www/Poverty/Data/Historical/People.Html (accessed 2/20/12). For an argument that children should be given the vote, see Paul E. Peterson, "An Immodest Proposal," *Daedalus* 121, no. 4 (Fall 1992): 151–74.

75. On the relationship between education and democracy in the United States, see Ira Katznelson and Margaret Weir, *Schooling for All: Race, Class, and the Democratic Ideal* (New York: Basic Books, 1985).

76. See L. Free and Hadley Cantril, *The Political Beliefs of Americans* (New York: Simon and Schuster, 1968).

77. See Fay Lomax Cook and Edith Barrett, *Support for the American Welfare State* (New York: Columbia University Press, 1992); and Hugh Heclo, "The Political Foundations of Antipoverty Policy," in *Fighting Poverty: What Works and What Doesn't*, ed. Sheldon H. Danziger and Daniel H. Weinberg (Cambridge, MA: Harvard University Press, 1986), pp. 312–40.

78. Henry J. Kaiser Family Foundation, *Health Care Costs: A Primer*, kaiserfamilyfoundation.files.wordpress.com/2013/01/7670-03.pdf (accessed 5/12/14).

Chapter 18

1. Geoffrey Perret, *A Country Made by War* (New York: Random House, 1989), p. 558.

2. Stockholm International Peace Research Institute, "Trends in World Military Expenditure, 2013," http://books.sipri.org/files/FS/SIPRIFSI404.pdf (accessed 6/12114).

3. Rupert Smith, *The Utility of Force: The Art of War in the Modern World* (New York: Vintage, 2008).

4. D. Robert Worley, *Shaping U.S. Military Forces: Revolution or Relevance in a Post–Cold War World* (Westport, CT: Praeger Security International, 2006).

5. Colin S. Grey, "The Implications of Preemptive and Preventive War Doctrines," Strategic Studies Institute, July 2007, www.strategicstudiesinstitute.army.mil/pdffiles/pub789.pdf (accessed 8/1/14).

6. Better World Campaign How the U.S. Funds the UN, www.betterworldcampaign.org (accessed 9/19/14).

7. Matthew Crenson and Benjamin Ginsberg, *Presidential Power: Unchecked and Unbalanced* (New York: W. W. Norton, 2007).

8. Benjamin Ginsberg, *The American Lie: Government by the People and Other Political Fables* (Boulder, CO: Paradigm, 2007).

9. Paul R. Pillar, *Terrorism and American Foreign Policy* (Washington, DC: Brookings Institution Press, 2003).

10. Raymond A. Bauer, Ithiel de Sola Pool, and Lewis Anthony Dexter, *American Business and Public Policy: The Politics of Foreign Trade*, 2nd ed. (Chicago: Aldine-Atherton, 1972).

11. For a good treatment of this in regard to Irish-Catholics and Catholics in general, see Timothy Byrnes, *Catholic Bishops and American Politics* (Princeton, NJ: Princeton University Press, 1991). For a (controversial) discussion of the role of Jewish groups, see John J. Mearsheimer and Stephen M. Walt, *The Israel Lobby and U.S. Foreign Policy* (New York: Farrar, Straus and Giroux, 2007).

12. This felicitous term is from David R. Mayhew, *Congress: The Electoral Connection* (New Haven, CT: Yale University Press, 1974).

13. John H. Aldrich, *Why Parties? The Origin and Transformation of Political Parties in America* (Chicago: University of Chicago Press, 1995), p. 278.

14. A very good brief outline of the centrality of the president in foreign policy is found in Paul E. Peterson, "The President's Dominance in Foreign Policy Making," *Political Science Quarterly* 109 (Summer 1994): 215–34.

15. One confirmation of this is found in Theodore Lowi, *The End of Liberalism: The Second Republic of the United States*, 2nd ed. (New York: W. W. Norton, 1979), pp. 127–30; another is found in Stephen Krasner, "Are Bureaucracies Important?" *Foreign Policy* 7 (Summer 1972): 159–79. However, it should be noted that Krasner was writing his article in disagreement with Graham T. Allison, "Conceptual Models and the Cuban Missile Crisis," *American Political Science Review* 63, no. 3 (September 1969): 689–718.

16. Peterson, "The President's Dominance in Foreign Policy Making," p. 232.

17. Hans Morgenthau, *Politics among Nations*, 2nd ed. (New York: Knopf, 1956), p. 505.

18. See Theodore Lowi, *The Personal President: Power Invested, Promise Unfulfilled* (Ithaca, NY: Cornell University Press, 1985), pp. 167–69.

19. "IMF: Sleeve-Rolling Time," *The Economist*, May 2, 1992, pp. 98–99.

20. James Dao and Patrick E. Tyler, "U.S. Says Military Strikes Are Just a Part of Big Plan," *The Alliance*, September 27, 2001; and Joseph Kahn, "A Nation Challenged: Global Dollars," *New York Times*, September 20, 2001, p. B1.

21. Turkey was desperate for help extricating its economy from its worst recession since 1945. The Afghanistan crisis was going to hurt Turkey all the more; Turkey's strategic location helped its case with the IMF. "Official Says Turkey Is Advancing in Drive for I.M.F. Financing," *New York Times*, October 6, 2001, p. A7.

22. For information on current U.S. sanctions programs, visit U.S. Department of the Treasury, "Sanctions Programs and Country Information," www.treasury.gov /resource-center/sanctions/Programs/Pages/Programs .aspx (accessed 6/1/14).

23. George Quester, *The Continuing Problem of International Politics* (Hinsdale, IL: Dryden Press, 1974), p. 229.

24. The Warsaw Pact was signed in 1955 by Albania, Bulgaria, Czechoslovakia, Hungary, the German Democratic Republic (East Germany), Poland, Romania, and the Soviet Union. Albania later dropped out. The Warsaw Pact was terminated in 1991.

25. Ginsberg, *The American Lie*, p. 3.

answer key

Chapter 1
1. e
2. b
3. a
4. d
5. c
6. c
7. c
8. b
9. a
10. d
11. e
12. b
13. e
14. a
15. a

Chapter 2
1. b
2. a
3. b
4. c
5. e
6. c
7. c
8. d
9. b
10. e
11. e
12. b
13. e
14. a

Chapter 3
1. c
2. c
3. b
4. e

5. a
6. c
7. c
8. b
9. c
10. b
11. b
12. a
13. d
14. d

Chapter 4
1. a
2. e
3. b
4. e
5. b
6. e
7. e
8. b
9. d
10. b
11. a
12. c
13. a
14. d

Chapter 5
1. b
2. e
3. a
4. c
5. b
6. d
7. a
8. a
9. d
10. a

11. a
12. e
13. a
14. b

Chapter 6
1. c
2. b
3. c
4. d
5. e
6. c
7. c
8. a
9. c
10. b
11. a
12. b

Chapter 7
1. b
2. a
3. b
4. c
5. e
6. c
7. b
8. c
9. b
10. e
11. b
12. c
13. c

Chapter 8
1. e
2. a
3. d

4. b
5. e
6. c
7. d
8. d
9. b
10. d
11. d
12. c

Chapter 9
1. a
2. a
3. c
4. d
5. d
6. c
7. d
8. e
9. e
10. c
11. e
12. c
13. d

Chapter 10
1. b
2. e
3. d
4. c
5. c
6. d
7. c
8. d
9. a
10. b
11. d
12. d

13. b
14. c

Chapter 11
1. a
2. b
3. c
4. c
5. d
6. b
7. e
8. d
9. a
10. e
11. c
12. a
13. e

Chapter 12
1. d
2. a
3. d
4. c
5. a
6. c
7. a
8. a
9. b
10. d
11. e
12. c
13. a
14. a

Chapter 13
1. b
2. d
3. a

4. c
5. b
6. b
7. b
8. e
9. a
10. c
11. c
12. b
13. b
14. a

Chapter 14
1. b
2. b
3. c
4. e
5. b
6. e

7. d
8. d
9. d
10. d
11. d
12. c
13. a
14. a

Chapter 15
1. a
2. c
3. a
4. c
5. a
6. d
7. e
8. e

9. c
10. b
11. e
12. a
13. d
14. c

Chapter 16
1. a
2. b
3. c
4. e
5. a
6. d
7. c
8. d
9. d
10. b

11. e
12. a
13. c
14. d

Chapter 17
1. c
2. d
3. b
4. c
5. e
6. a
7. c
8. d
9. d
10. a
11. d
12. c

13. e
14. d
15. c

Chapter 18
1. b
2. d
3. c
4. e
5. c
6. c
7. c
8. e
9. b
10. c
11. a
12. d
13. b

photo credits

JANNER/MCT/Landov; p. 219 (left): © Stacy Walsh Rosenstock/Alamy; p. 219 (middle): © Stacy Walsh Rosenstock/Alamy; p. 219 (right): © Pinhole Photographic/Alamy; p. 224: AP Photo/Rich Pedroncelli; p. 225: AP Photo; p. 226 (both): William B. Plowman/NBC/NBC NewsWire via Getty Images; p. 231: Martin H. Simon/Corbis; p. 235: Business Roundtable; p. 237: Bill Watterson; p. 238: Doug Mills/The New York Times/Redux; p. 248: Bettmann/Corbis. P. 256: Sara D. Davis/Getty Images; p. 259: © Bernhard Classen/age footstock; p. 264: Paul Zimmerman/Getty Images; p. 266: Clear Channel; p. 268: Nick Suydam/Alamy; p. 271: Jasna Hodzic/The California Aggie/EPA/Newscom; p. 275: Courtesy of FactCheck.org; p. 280: Charles Moore/Black Star; p. 283 (top): WANG CHENGYUN/Xinhua/Landov; p. 283 (bottom): HANDOUT/Reuters/Landov; p. 287: Jack Plunkett/Invision/AP; p. 288: AP Photo/Nick Ut; p. 290: Shannon Stapleton/Reuters/Corbis. Chapter 8: p. 298: Hill Street Studios/Getty Images; p. 302: AP Photo/Alex Menendez; p. 304: Hulton Archive/Getty Images; p. 307: Xinhua/eyevine/Redux; p. 309: Aaron Anderer; p. 313: AP Photo; p. 320: AP Photo/Ira Schwarz; p. 321: Jim West/Alamy; p. 326: Kevork Djansezian/Getty Images; p. 332: Marc Piscotty/Getty Images; p. 334: AP Photo. Chapter 9: p. 340: Mladen Antonov/AFP/Getty Images; p. 344: © Art Directors & TRIP/Alamy; p. 348: AP Photo/Bozeman Daily Chronicle, Adrian Sanchez-Gonzalez; p. 349: AP Photo/Ed Andrieski; p. 351: BRIAN BLANCO/EPA/Landov; p. 353: © Bettmann/CORBIS; p. 354: KEVIN LAMARQUE/Reuters/Landov; p. 358: AP Photo/barackobama.com; p. 365: Granger Collection; p. 366: Granger Collection; p. 368: Nixon Presidential Library & Museum; p. 372: Chip Somodevilla/Getty Images; p. 376: AP Photo. Chapter 10: p. 384: Bloomberg via Getty Images; p. 387: Courtesy The Historical Society of Pennsylvania; p. 389 (left): Reuters/Corbis; p. 389 (right): AP Photo; p. 390: Granger Collection; p. 393: Bob Daemmrich/Alamy; p. 394: Reuters/Mike Segar/Landov; p. 396: Kristin Murphy, Deseret News; p. 398: AP Photo/Charles Dharapak; p. 406: Win McNamee/Getty Images; p. 410: © Jay Mallin/ZUMA Press/Corbis; p. 419: Alliance Images/Alamy; p. 421: Patrick Farrell/MCT/Newscom; p. 425: Daniel Acker/Bloomberg via Getty Images; p. 426: Joel Kowsky/Bloomberg/Getty Images. Chapter 11: p. 432: Courtesy Stefanie Penn Spear/ecowatch.org; p. 436: Alamy; p. 437: AP Photo/Robert F. Bukaty; p. 441: Rex Features via AP Images; p. 442: Bettmann/Corbis; p. 446: Screenshot used with permission of MoveOn.org 2014; p. 447: © Jeff Greenberg 2 of 6/Alamy; p. 449: Zunique/Newscom; p. 454: Ron Sachs/Pool/CNP/Corbis; p. 457: AP Photo/U.S. Food and Drug Administration; p. 458: JONATHAN ERNST/Reuters/Landov; p. 460: Courtesy of the UAW; p. 462: www.cartoonstock.com. Chapter 12: p. 470: JIM BOURG/Reuters/Landov; p. 474: Bettmann/Corbis; p. 478: JOE SKIPPER/Reuters/Landov; p. 483: AP Photo/Ross D. Franklin; p. 489: Alex Wong/Getty Images; p. 491: Scott J. Ferrell/Congressional Quarterly/Getty Images; p. 495: AP Photo/Senate Television; p. 498: STAFF/Reuters/Landov; p. 502: Alex Wong/Getty Images; p. 504: Alex Wong/Getty Images; p. 509: Drew Angerer/Getty Images; p. 510: William Philpott/AFP/Getty Images. Chapter 13: p. 518: JIM YOUNG/Reuters/Landov; p. 521 (left): AP Photo/Tim Roske; p. 521 (right): Chip Somodevilla/Getty Images; p. 525: JAMES NIELSEN/AFP/Getty Images; p. 526: JEWEL SAMAD/AFP/Getty Images; p. 527: AP Photo/File; p. 532 (top): LUCY NICHOLSON/Reuters/Landov; p. 532 (bottom): AP Photo/U.S. Consumer Product Safety Commission; p. 538: Sergey Starostenko/Kommersant Photo via Getty Images; p. 539: Conrad Schmidt/AFP/Getty Images; p. 541: Bettmann/Corbis; p. 547: © Ethan Welty/Aurora Photos/Corbis; p. 549: JEWEL SAMAD/AFP/Getty Images. Chapter 14: p. 558: Craig F. Walker/The Denver Post via Getty Images; p. 562: © Katharine Andriotis Photography, LLC/Editorial/Alamy; p. 564: U.S. Dept. of State; p. 569: Gene Blevins/LA Daily News/Corbis; p. 570: Richard T. Nowitz/Science Source; p. 573: John Moore/Getty Images; p. 577: FOIA.gov; p. 582: CBS/courtesy Everett Collection; p. 583: AP Photo/Ben Chrisman; p. 585: Jeffrey MacMillan/For The Washington Post via Getty Images; p. 590: Douglas Graham/CQ Roll Call/Newscom. Chapter 15: p. 598: © Melvyn Longhurst/Alamy; p. 601: AP Photo; p. 608: AP Photo/Pablo Martinez Monsivais, File; p. 612: KAREN BLEIER/AFP/Getty Image; p. 615: AP Photo; p. 617: AP Photo; p. 619: AP Photo/The Decatur Daily, Clyde Stancil; p. 623: Mark Wilson/Getty Images; p. 624: David Hume Kennerly/Getty Images; p. 627: Arthur Lien; p. 633: Chip

Somodevilla/Getty Images. **Chapter 16: p. 640:** Don Emmert/AFP/Getty Images; **p. 643:** © Robert Mullan/incamerastock/Corbis; **p. 644:** © Cameron Davidson/Corbis; **p. 648:** Brian H. Thomas/Alamy; **p. 649 (left):** Granger Collection; **p. 649 (right):** Bettmann/Corbis; **p. 650:** Tom Paiva Photography/Getty Images; **p. 651:** National Highway and Safety Administration; **p. 653:** AP Photo; **p. 656:** © Richard Levine/Alamy; **p. 659:** Justin Sullivan/Getty Images; **p. 661:** Scull/BloombergNews/Landov; **p. 671:** © Cameron Davidson/Cameron Davidson/Corbis; **p. 674:** Paramount Classics/Photofest; **p. 675:** Dennis MacDonald/Getty Images. **Chapter 17: p. 684:** AP Photo; **p. 688:** Joseph Barnell/SuperStock; **p. 690:** Tim Boyle/Getty Images; **p. 693:** Jim West imageBROKER/Newscom; **p. 697:** ©Bob Daemmrich/The Image Works; **p. 702:** Chip Somodevilla/Getty Images; **p. 704:** Centers for Disease Control; **p. 707:** Jewel Samad/AFP/Getty Images; **p. 709:** Peter Hvizdak/The Image Works; **p. 712:** © Jim West/Alamy; **p. 715:** AP Photo. **Chapter 18: p. 724:** U.S. Navy photo by Mass Communication Specialist Seaman Kyle D. Gahlau; **p. 729:** Bettmann/Corbis; **p. 730:** AP Photo; **p. 733:** BAY ISMOYO/AFP/Getty Images; **p. 735:** Giulio Petrocco/AFP/GettyImages; **p. 743:** JIM WATSON/AFP/Getty Images; **p. 746:** BRENDAN SMIALOWSKI/AFP/Getty Images; **p. 747:** AP Photo; **p. 748:** BAY ISMOYO/AFP/GettyImages; **p. 750:** Dursun Aydemir/Anadolu Agency/Getty Images.

index

Democratic National Committee (DNC), 351, 352, 356, 408
Democratic Party, 345, 358, 359, 362, 364–70; *see also* political parties
  and 2009 economic stimulus package, 659
  and 2010 election, 419
  and ACA, 708
  Asian Americans' support for, 316
  characteristics of, 222–23
  and civil rights of African Americans, 162
  congressional party unity, 500–501, *501*
  control of Congress in 2006, 738
  and economic policy, 651
  election campaign of 2010, 479
  election campaign of 2012, 418, 420–23
  and Federal Reserve, 662
  fund-raising activities of, 352
  gerrymandering, 482
  and health care reform, 342, 705, 706, 708
  and income inequality, 208
  key policy positions of, 353, 354
  and labor groups, 656, 658
  and laissez-faire economics, 653
  Latino voters and, 315, *358*, 358–59
  liberalism of, 375
  and minimum wage, 656
  mobilization efforts of, 322, 323
  organizational efforts of, 322
  party-building by, 356
  party identification, 356
  and primary delegates, 393
  and public works financing, 92
  recruitment of candidates by, 479
  and redistricting, 482–84
  and regulation, 656
  religious affiliations of members, 222
  responsiveness of, 344, 364
  tax and social spending views of, 359–60, 654
  and tax debate, 30
  white southerners in, 224
demonstrations, 457–58
Dennis v. United States, 128
department, defined, 567
deregulation, 670–71
descriptive representation, 316
deterrence, 729–30
devolution, 99, 101–3, 583–84

DHS. *See* Homeland Security, Department of
Dickerson v. United States, 141, 620
digital citizens, 258, 268; *see also* Internet
  defined, 268
  offline political participation of, 306–8
digital citizenship, 12–13
  defined, 12, 268
digital divide, 13, 268, 310
digital literacy, 13
digital media. *See* Internet
diplomacy, 745–46
diplomatic power (president), 525–26
direct-action politics, 17
direct democracy, 16, 396–98
direct elections, 521
direct lobbying, 451–53
direct mail campaigns, 406
direct patronage, 484–86
Disability Rights Education and Defense Fund, 191
disabled Americans, civil rights for, 191
discretionary spending, *668*, 669, *669*
discrimination
  against Asian Americans, 188–90
  based on sexual orientation, 191–94
  against citizens of other states, 83–84
  defined, 159
  against disabled Americans, 191
  employment, 171, 173–74
  gender, 178–84
  in housing, 176–78
  against Latinos/Hispanics, 184–87
  in lending, 177–78
  against Native Americans, 190–91
  positive, 200
  racial, 165, 167, 171–78, 618–19, 688
  against women, 171
dissenting opinion, 628
district courts, federal, 605–7
District of Columbia, 83, 142, 166, 192
  EDR laws, 330
  marijuana laws, 77
District of Columbia v. Heller, 135, 137
divided government, 370
DNA testing, 139
DNC. *See* Democratic National Committee
Dodd, Chris, 310
Dodd–Frank Wall Street Reform and Consumer Protection Act of 2010, 419, 519, 671

Doha Round, 733
Dole, Bob, 91, 374
donations (political campaigns). *See* fund-raising
Donovan, Todd, 248–49, 323
"Don't Ask, Don't Tell," 192
double jeopardy, 140–41
Douglas, Stephen, 240, 407
Douglas, William O., 146
Douglass, Frederick, 161
DREAM Act, 186, 228
Dred Scott v. Sandford, 160
drinking age, *108*
Druckman, Jamie, 229, 245
Drudge Report, 262
Drug Enforcement Agency, U.S. (DEA), 77
drug testing, 139
dual federalism, 85–88, *94*
Du Bois, W. E. B., 163–64
due process, 157
due process clause, 118, 119
due process of law, 137–44
  cruel and unusual punishment, 143–44
  double jeopardy, 140–41
  eminent domain, 142
  grand juries, 140
  right to counsel, 142–43
  searches and seizures, 137–40
  self-incrimination, 141–42
Dukakis, Michael, 403
Duke Power Company, 174

E
Early, Stephen, 541
early voting, 299–300, 333, 334
earmarks, 484–85
Earned Income Tax Credit (EITC), 693, 714
East India Company, 42–43
e-commerce, 104, 106
economic aid and sanctions, *736*, 748–49
economic crisis of 2008. *See* financial crisis and recession of 2008
economic development agencies, 580
economic equality/inequality, 23–24, *25*, 28, *233*
economic freedom, 26–27
economic growth, environmental policy vs., 239, *239*
economic growth, measuring, 644–46
Economic Opportunity Act, 95

SECOND EDITION

Governing Texas

SECOND EDITION

Governing Texas

Anthony Champagne
UNIVERSITY OF TEXAS AT DALLAS

Edward J. Harpham
UNIVERSITY OF TEXAS AT DALLAS

 W. W. NORTON & COMPANY
NEW YORK   LONDON

W. W. Norton & Company has been independent since its founding in 1923, when William Warder Norton and Mary D. Herter Norton first published lectures delivered at the People's Institute, the adult education division of New York City's Cooper Union. The firm soon expanded its program beyond the Institute, publishing books by celebrated academics from America and abroad. By mid-century, the two major pillars of Norton's publishing program—trade books and college texts—were firmly established. In the 1950s, the Norton family transferred control of the company to its employees, and today—with a staff of four hundred and a comparable number of trade, college, and professional titles published each year—W. W. Norton & Company stands as the largest and oldest publishing house owned wholly by its employees.

Editor: Peter Lesser
Project Editor: Christine D'Antonio
Editorial Assistants: Sarah Wolf and Samantha Held
Manuscript Editor: Ellen Lohman
Managing Editor, College: Marian Johnson
Managing Editor, College Digital Media: Kim Yi
Senior Production Supervisor, College: Ashley Horna
Media Editor: Toni Magyar
Media Editorial Assistant: Michael Jaoui
Marketing Manager, Political Science: Erin Brown
Art Director: Rubina Yeh
Text Design: Lissi Sigillo
Photo Editor: Evan Luberger
Photo Researcher: Donna Ranieri
Permissions Manager: Megan Jackson
Information Graphics: Kiss Me I'm Polish LLC, New York
Composition: Achorn International, Inc.
Manufacturing: Courier—Kendallville

Permission to use copyrighted material is included in the credits section of this book, which begins on page A53.

Library of Congress Cataloging-in-Publication Data

Champagne, Anthony.
Governing Texas / Anthony Champagne, University of Texas at Dallas, Edward J. Harpham, University of Texas at Dallas.—Second edition.
     pages cm
Includes bibliographical references and index.
ISBN 978-0-393-93684-1 (pbk.)
1. Texas—Politics and government.   I. Harpham, Edward J. II. Title.
JK4816.C48 2015
320.4764—dc23

2014041101

W. W. Norton & Company, Inc., 500 Fifth Avenue, New York, N. Y. 10110
www.wwnorton.com

W. W. Norton & Company Ltd., Castle House, 75/76 Wells Street, London W1T 3QT

1 2 3 4 5 6 7 8 9 0

contents

9 ● The Texas Judiciary   275

preface

Our goal in this text is to offer readers a broad understanding of the factors that are reshaping political processes and institutions in the Lone Star State in the first two decades of the twenty-first century. We are particularly concerned with explaining how the principles underlying constitutional government in Texas are being reworked in the face of new political, economic, and demographic changes. By supplementing our institutional analysis with concrete examples from everyday political life in Texas, we hope to show the reader that politics and government in Texas are not only important to their lives but endlessly fascinating as well.

Features of the Second Edition

Another, related goal of the book is to provide students with extensive pedagogical support throughout each chapter. In every chapter, several features engage students' interest and help them master the learning objectives for the topic.

- **Chapter Goals** appear at the start of the chapter and then recur at the start of the relevant sections throughout the chapter to create a more focused, active reading experience.

- **Extensive end-of-chapter review sections organized around Chapter Goals** include section outlines, practice quiz questions, key terms, and Recommended Websites, as well as information about related online resources. Students have everything they need to master the material in each section of the chapter.

- **"Who Are Texans?" infographics** engage visually oriented students with a "statistical snapshot" of the state related to each chapter's topic. These features help students grasp the political implications of demographic, political, economic, and regional diversity in Texas. Related exercises in the online coursepacks and slides in the instructor PowerPoints make it easy for instructors to bring these graphics into their online or face-to-face classrooms.

- **NEW "Texas and the Nation" infographics** enable students to compare Texas's government and politics to other states'. Critical thinking questions accompany each "Texas and the Nation" graphic and encourage students to engage deeply with the graphics and draw their own conclusions. Related exercises in the online coursepacks and slides in the PowerPoints make it easy for instructors to bring these graphics into their online or face-to-face classrooms.

- **"You Decide" boxes in every chapter** address controversial issues in Texas politics that students care about. These boxes encourage students to think beyond their knee-jerk reactions and consider all sides of the debate.

- **"What Government Does and Why It Matters" chapter introductions** draw students into the chapter by showing them why they should care about the chapter's topic.

Revisions to the Second Edition

In the second edition of *Governing Texas*, we have tried to provide students with the most up-to-date account of Texas government and politics. Every chapter was scrutinized with help from dozens of outside reviewers, and we have tried to provide the most current examples and data throughout the text. Highlights of the new edition include:

- Updated material on the 2013 legislative session and the 2014 elections throughout, including new data from the Legislative Budgeting Board

- A new graphic feature—"Texas and the Nation"—in each chapter, enabling students to look at Texas from a broader national perspective

- Updated data in the "Who Are Texans?" graphics throughout

- An expanded discussion of the Texas constitutional founding in Chapter 2

- A new appendix, featuring a group of primary source readings that complement the text, including the Texas Declaration of Independence and the Texas Ordinance of Secession

- A completely revised chapter on "Texas in the Federal System" (Chapter 3), now placed after the chapter on the Texas Constitution

- Updated chapter on interest groups, which now offers discussions of collective action and interest group capture

- Heavily revised chapter on local government, which has been moved up in the text to appear after chapters about the other institutions established by the constitution and now includes an extended discussion of the politics surrounding the provision and funding of public pensions

- New discussions of efficiency and rationality in the policy-making process in Chapter 12 on public policy

We believe that these changes will assist professors in teaching students the nuts and bolts of Texas government and politics, as well as the broad themes and issues that will shape the Lone Star State in the coming decades.

Resources for Assessment and a Dynamic Classroom Experience

The media package for *Governing Texas*, Second Edition, offers all of the tools needed for effective assessment, targeted self-study, and dynamic classroom presentations—either online or face-to-face. Features include the following.

Norton Coursepacks: Our content, your course
Rachel Bzostek, *University of Texas, Tyler*
Jeremy Duff, *Midwestern State University*
Alexander Hogan, *Lone Star College, CyFair*
Sharon Navarro, *University of Texas, San Antonio*

Easily add high-quality Norton digital media to your online, hybrid, or lecture course—all at no cost. Norton Coursepacks work with and leverage your existing Learning Management System, so there's no new system to learn, and access is free and easy. Comprehensive Coursepacks are ready to use, right from the start, but are easy to customize, using the system you already know and understand. Norton Coursepacks include exclusive multimedia content and assessment tools that are not found anywhere else, such as test banks and quizzes, interactive learning tools, and exercises covering chapter objectives and tagged to State Learning Outcomes. Every chapter includes:

- Video exercises from *The Texas Tribune* and ABC News to help students retain and apply information through current events
- **NEW** "Who Are Texans?" and "Texas and the Nation" animated infographics to guide students through interpreting data
- Simulations to get students thinking about how Texas government really works
- **NEW** "You Decide" exercises to help students engage varying views on contemporary issues
- **NEW** "By the Numbers" exercises to help students practice quantitative skills by exploring key datagraphics from the text

Norton Ebook: Same great book, a fraction of the price
Norton ebooks allow students to access the entire book and much more; they can search, highlight, and take notes with ease, as well as collaborate and share their notes with teachers and classmates. The *Governing Texas*, Second Edition, ebook can be viewed on any device—laptop, tablet, phone, even a public computer—and will stay synced between devices.

Lecture PowerPoints
Ronald Vardy, *Wharton County Junior College*
The second edition of *Governing Texas* offers fully customizable lecture slides with clicker questions, teaching ideas, and discussion questions in the instructor-only notes field. "Who Are Texans?" and "Texas and the Nation" slides feature popular infographics and pop quiz questions for the optimal lecture experience.

Art Slides
Photographs and drawn figures from the book are available for classroom use.

Instructor's Manual
Jeremy Duff, *Midwestern State University*
The Instructor's Manual includes chapter outlines, class activities, and group discussion questions. Each chapter also offers suggested video clips with links and discussion questions.

Test Bank

Sharon Navarro, *University of Texas, San Antonio*

The revised test bank assesses chapter learning goals and Texas Student Learning Outcomes, applies Bloom's Taxonomy across these goals and outcomes, and improves the overall quality and accuracy of our assessment through extensive peer review.

About the Authors

Over the past 25 years, we have worked together on a number of books that have studied various aspects of government and political life in Texas. We come to the study of Texas politics and government from two very different backgrounds.

Anthony Champagne was born in Louisiana as the French surname suggests. His mother's family, however, were pioneer farmers and ranchers in Hopkins County, Texas. It was growing up with Louisiana and Texas connections that gave him a life-long interest in politics. When he moved to the University of Texas at Dallas in 1979, he immediately visited the Sam Rayburn Library in Bonham. Sam Rayburn was one of the Texas's most influential political figures. He was elected to the U.S. House of Representatives in 1912 and served until his death in 1961. During that time, he was chairman of one of the most influential committees of the House, was Majority Leader, Speaker, and Minority Leader of the House. He is responsible for much of the major legislation in the New Deal and for his key role in the politics of the Truman, Eisenhower, and early Kennedy Administrations. A chance meeting at the Sam Rayburn Library with H. G. Dulaney, Sam Rayburn's secretary for 10 years, led to the opportunity to do over 130 oral histories with persons associated with Sam Rayburn. As a result, Champagne was completely hooked on studying Texas politics. He was particularly interested in the transformation of the state from an overwhelmingly Democratic state to a Republican bulwark. And, he was interested in how Texas changed from being a key partner with the national government in the cooperative federalism of the New Deal period to a state whose leaders are frequent critics of national power today. Political change in the state from the Sam Rayburn era to today is a key research focus of his.

Edward Harpham, in contrast, was born in Montreal to second generation Canadian parents who immigrated to the United States soon after his birth. His family's migration over the last 100 years from Sheffield to Toronto (1919) to Delaware (1952) to Texas (1978) and the industries that employed the family (auto service industry, chemical industry, and academia) mirror the demographic changes that have reshaped much of the population movement in the United States and Texas throughout the twentieth century. Trained as a political theorist with a deep interest in political economy, Harpham's move to Texas sparked an interest in how economic changes in the late twentieth century were changing the contours of the state's traditional political life in new and unexpected ways. At the heart of his work lies an abiding interest on the role that ideas play in shaping the growth and development of political institutions and public policies in the modern information age.

acknowledgments

We are grateful for the suggestions that we have received from many thoughtful and experienced government instructors across the state. For their input on the plan and execution of this book, we thank:

Jason Abbott, Hill College
Lee Almaguer, Midland College
Marcos Arandia, North Lake College
Ellen Baik, University of Texas–Pan American
Robert Ballinger, South Texas College
Annie Johnson Benifield, Lone Star College–Tomball
David Birch, Lone Star College–Tomball
Robin Marshall Bittick, Sam Houston State University
Patrick Brandt, University of Texas at Dallas
Gary Brown, Lone Star College–Montgomery
Lee Brown, Blinn College
Jonathan Buckstead, Austin Community College
Daniel Bunye, South Plains College
James V. Calvi, West Texas A&M University
Michael Campenni, Austin Community College
Larry Carter, University of Texas at Arlington
Max Choudary, Northeast Lakeview College
Mark Cichock, University of Texas at Arlington
Adrian Clark, Del Mar College
Tracy Cook, Central Texas College
Cassandra Cookson, Lee College
Leland M. Coxe, University of Texas at Brownsville
Rosalyn Crain, Houston Community College–Northwest
Sandra K. Creech, Temple College
Kevin Davis, North Central Texas College
Steve Davis, Lone Star College–Kingwood
Henry Dietz, University of Texas at Austin
Brian Dille, Odessa College
Douglas Dow, University of Texas at Dallas
Jeremy Duff, Midwestern State University
David Edwards, University of Texas at Austin
Matthew Eshbaugh-Soha, University of North Texas
Lou Ann Everett, Trinity Valley Community College
Victoria Farrar-Myers, University of Texas at Arlington
John P. Flanagan, Weatherford College
Ben Fraser, San Jacinto College
Joey Fults, Kilgore College

Frank J. Garrahan, Austin Community College
Will Geisler, Collin College
David Garrison, Collin College
Terry Gilmour, Midland College
Randy Givens, Blinn College
Donna Godwin, Trinity Valley Community College
Larry Gonzalez, Houston Community College–Southwest
Paul Gottemoller, Del Mar College
Kenneth L. Grasso, Texas State University
Heidi Jo Green, Lone Star College–CyFair
Sara Gubala, Lamar University
Yolanda Hake, South Texas College
Sabrina Hammel, Northeast Lakeview College
Jeff Harmon, University of Texas at San Antonio
Tiffany Harper, Collin College
Billy Hathorn, Laredo Community College
Ahad Hayaud-Din, Brookhaven College
Virginia Haysley, Lone Star College–Tomball
Tom Heiting, Odessa College
John Hitt, North Lake College
Kevin Holton, South Texas College
Taofang Huang, University of Texas at Austin
Casey Hubble, McLennan Community College
Glen Hunt, Austin Community College
Tammy Johannessen, Austin Community College
Doris J. Jones, Tarrant County College
Joseph Jozwiak, Texas A&M Corpus Christi
Christy Woodward Kaupert, San Antonio College
David Kennedy, Lone Star College–Montgomery
Edward Korzetz, Lee College
Melinda Kovacs, Sam Houston State University
Heidi Lange, Houston Community College–Southwest
Boyd Lanier, Lamar University
James Lantrip, South Texas College
David Lektzian, Texas Tech University
Raymond Lew, Houston Community College–Central
Bob Little, Brookhaven College

Robert Locander, Lone Star College–North Harris
Nicholas Long, St. Edward's University
George Lyon, El Paso Community College
Mitzi Mahoney, Sam Houston State University
Lynne Manganaro, Texas A&M International University
Sharon Manna, North Lake College
Bobby J. Martinez, Northwest Vista College
David McClendon, Tyler Junior College
Mike McConachie, Collin College
Elizabeth McLane, Wharton County Junior College
Phil McMahan, Collin College
Eddie Meaders, University of North Texas
Banks Miller, University of Texas at Dallas
Eric Miller, Blinn College
Patrick Moore, Richland College
Sherri Mora, Texas State University–San Marcos
Dana Morales, Lone Star College–Montgomery
Amy Moreland, Sul Ross State University
Rick Moser, Kilgore College
Mark R. Murray, South Texas College
James Myers, Odessa College
Sugumaran Narayanan, Midwestern State University
Sharon Navarro, University of Texas at San Antonio
Jalal Nejad, Northwest Vista College
Timothy Nokken, Texas Tech University
James Norris, Texas A &M International University
John Osterman, San Jacinto College
Cissie Owen, Lamar University
David Putz, Lone Star College Kingwood
Himanshin Raizada, Lamar University
Prudencio E. Ramirez, San Jacinto College
John Raulston, Kilgore College
Daniel Regalado, Odessa College
Darrial Reynolds, South Texas College

Donna Rhea, Houston Community College–Northwest
Laurie Robertstad, Navarro College
Mario Salas, University of Texas at San Antonio
Larry Salazar, McLennan Community College
Michael Sanchez, San Antonio College
Raymond Sandoval, Richland College
Gilbert Schorlemmer, Blinn College
Mark Shomaker, Blinn College
Dennis Simon, Southern Methodist University
Shannon Sinegal, Temple College
Brian William Smith, St. Edward's University
Michael Smith, South Plains College
Thomas E. Sowers II, Lamar University
John Speer, Houston Community College
Jim Startin, University of Texas at San Antonio
Andrew Teas, Houston Community College–Northwest
John Theis, Lone Star College Kingwood
Sean Theriault, University of Texas at Austin
John Todd, University of North Texas
Delaina Toothman, Texas State University
Steven Tran, Houston Community College
Homer D. Trevino, McLennan Community College
Christopher Turner, Laredo Community College
Ronald W. Vardy, University of Houston
Linda Veazey, Midwestern State University
Albert Waite, Central Texas College
David Watson, Sul Ross State University
Clay Wiegand, Cisco College
Neal Wise, St. Edward's University
Kathryn Yates, Richland College
Michael Young, Trinity Valley Community College
Tyler Young, Collin College
Rogerio J. Zapata, South Texas College

We also thank Jason Casellas of the University of Houston for his contributions to the book. Jason developed Chapters 4 and 5 on parties and elections, bringing a current perspective and important insights to these topics. Jason also revised and created new "Who Are Texans?," "Texas and the Nation," and "You Decide" features. We thank the following University of Texas at Dallas students for their assistance: Lisa Holmes, Josh Payne, Ali Charania, Alan Roderick, Basel Musharbash, Liza Miadzvedskaya, and Sachi Dave.

At W. W. Norton, Peter Lesser provided editorial guidance throughout the process of developing and publishing the book. Project editor Christine D'Antonio and editorial assistants Sarah Wolf and Samantha Held kept everything organized. Copy editor Ellen Lohman helped polish the text. Production manager Ashley Horna made sure we ended up with a high-quality book, right on schedule. Media editor Toni Magyar and associate media editor Laura Musich worked with the authors of accompanying resources to develop useful tools for students and instructors. Our sincere thanks to all of them.

Anthony Champagne
Edward J. Harpham

December 2014

SECOND EDITION

Governing Texas

In some ways state-level politics in Texas resembles national politics, but in other ways Texas's political culture is quite distinctive.

The Political Culture, People, and Economy of Texas

WHY TEXAS'S POLITICAL CULTURE MATTERS In his *Travels with Charley*, John Steinbeck once described Texas as "a state of mind . . . a mystique closely approximating a religion." Americans passionately loved or hated Texas. Steinbeck believed that Texas, despite its vast space, its varying topography, its many cultures and ways of life, had a cohesiveness that may be stronger than any other part of America. He writes, "Rich, poor, Panhandle, Gulf, city, country, Texas is the obsession, the proper study and the passionate possession of all Texans."

Certain myths define the obsession that is Texas—and Texans—in the popular imagination. The cowboy who challenges both Native American and Mexican rule, the rancher and farmer who cherish their economic independence, the wildcatter who is willing to risk everything for one more roll of the dice, and the independent entrepreneur who fears the needless intrusion of government into his life—such are the myths about Texans.

These myths extend far into the popular imagination when we think about various politicians who have led the state since its founding: the visionary Stephen F. Austin locked in a Mexican jail after presenting Texas grievances to the authorities, the military hero Sam Houston who wins the Battle of San Jacinto but is thrown out of office because of his rejection of secession, the irrepressible Ma and Pa Ferguson who both served as governors, and the larger-than-life Lyndon Baines Johnson who began his career as a schoolteacher in Cotulla, Texas, and completed it as a champion of civil rights and the poor.

The reality of Texas today, its people and its leaders, is much more complicated than the Texas of popular myths. Texas is not only the second-largest state in the Union, comprising more than 261,000 square miles; it is also the second most populous. Texas has a population of more than 26 million people, and that population is rapidly growing and becoming more and more diverse. Whites constitute a little more than 45 percent of the population, while Latinos constitute more than 38 percent. Just fewer than 12 percent of the population are African American, and roughly 4 percent are Asian. Eighty-five percent of Texans live in urban areas, with many involved in an economy driven by high-tech industry and globalization. More than a quarter of the population has a bachelor's degree. On the whole, Texans are young, with 26.8 percent under the age of 18 and 10.9 percent over the age of 65.

Texas politics today is a political community that is dominated by the Republican Party. The Democratic Party of Vice President John Nance Garner (1868–1967), Speaker of the House Sam Rayburn (1882–1961), President Lyndon Johnson (1908–1973), and Lieutenant Governor Bob Bullock (1929–1999) no longer controls the key political offices in the state. Since the mid-1990s, Texas politics and government have been largely controlled by an establishment within the Republican Party led by such individuals as President George W. Bush (b. 1946), Governor Rick Perry (b. 1950), Lieutenant Governor David Dewhurst (b. 1945), and Texas Speaker of the House Joe Straus (b. 1959). In recent years, however, this establishment has been challenged from within the party. An increasingly aggressive group of dissidents tied into the Tea Party movement have advanced hyperconservative political positions on a variety of social and economic issues, including abortion, birth control, same-sex marriage, immigration, and taxes. Led by politicians like Senator Ted Cruz (b. 1970), Lieutenant Governor Dan Patrick (b. 1956), and Attorney General Ken Paxton (b. 1962), Tea Party supporters have pushed Texas Republicans further to the right by melding a cultural conservatism on issues like abortion and gay rights to an anti-Washington rhetoric that calls for lower taxes, less government spending and regulation, and a balanced budget.

The Democratic Party, too, has moved in new directions, spurred on by new and younger leaders. Gubernatorial candidate Wendy Davis (b. 1963) gave her party a shot in the arm when she filibustered against antiabortion laws at the end of the 2013 legislative session. Likewise, the twin brothers Julian and Joaquin Castro (b. 1974) represent something new to the party and the state. Educated at Stanford and Harvard Law School, the former has served two terms as the mayor of San Antonio before moving on to a cabinet position in the Obama administration. The latter, meanwhile, has entered the U.S. House of Representatives.

Undoubtedly, Tea Party Republicans like Ted Cruz and up-and-coming Democrats like Wendy Davis and the Castro brothers will give rise to new myths about the people and politicians found in Texas. We should be careful before we fully accept any of these myths. As in the past, the reality of Texas—its people and its politics—is much more complex than the myths we spin about it. Conservative Republicans may control today's political agenda, but their long-term dominance in politics and government is not certain. Increasing racial and ethnic diversity points to a new Texas, one that looks sharply different from the one in the history books and one that appears to favor Democrats (the party preferred today by most Latinos, African Americans, and recent immigrants). The future of the state and its people will be determined in large part by the struggle between an assertive Republican majority and a resurgent Democratic minority as both try to address the various political, economic, and demographic challenges facing the state. Moving our understanding of governance and politics beyond the myths about Texas is the goal of this chapter and the book.

chaptergoals

- Describe the defining characteristics of political culture in Texas (pp. 5–7)
- Explain how Texas's geography has influenced its political culture (pp. 7–9)
- Trace the evolution of Texas's economy (pp. 10–19)
- Explain how the population of Texas has changed over time (pp. 19–26)
- Describe Texas's shift from a rural society to an urban one (pp. 26–32)

● Texas Political Culture

> **Describe the defining characteristics of political culture in Texas**

Studies of Texas politics often begin with a discussion of Texas's **political culture**. Though the concept is somewhat open ended, states do often exhibit a distinctive culture that is the "product of their entire history." Presumably the political culture of a state has an effect on how people participate in politics and how individuals and institutions interact.[1] Political scientist Daniel Elazar has created a classification scheme for state political cultures that is used widely. He uses the concepts of moralistic, individualistic, and traditionalistic to describe such cultures. These three state political cultures are contemporary manifestations of the ethnic, socioreligious, and socioeconomic differences that existed among America's original thirteen colonies.[2]

According to Elazar, **moralistic political cultures** were rooted in New England, where Puritans and other religious groups sought to create the Good Society. In such a culture, politics is the concern of everyone, and government is expected to take action to promote the public good and advance the public welfare. Citizen participation in politics is viewed as positive; people are encouraged to pursue the public good in civic activities.

Individualistic political cultures, on the other hand, originated in the middle states, where Americans sought material wealth and personal freedom through commercial activities. A state with an individualistic political culture generally places a low value on citizen participation in politics. Politics is a matter for professionals rather than for citizens, and the role of government is strictly limited. Government's role is to ensure stability so that individuals can pursue their own interests.

Traditionalistic political culture developed initially in the South, reflecting the values of the slave plantation economy (pre-1865) and its successor, the Jim Crow era (1876–1965). Rooted in preindustrial values that emphasize social hierarchy

political culture broadly shared values, beliefs, and attitudes about how the government should function and politics should operate; American political culture emphasizes the values of liberty, equality, and democracy

moralistic political culture the belief that government should be active in promoting the public good and that citizens should participate in politics and civic activities to ensure that good

individualistic political culture the belief that government should limit its role to providing order in society, so that citizens can pursue their economic self-interests

traditionalistic political culture the belief that government should be dominated by political elites and guided by tradition

The Lone Star is the symbol of Texas and reflects its individualistic political culture.

elite a small group of people that dominates the political process

for critical analysis

How would one describe Texas political culture? What patterns of Texas politics reflect its political culture?

provincialism a narrow, limited, and self-interested view of the world often associated with rural values and notions of limited government

and close interpersonal, often familial, relations among people, traditional culture is concerned with the preservation of tradition and the existing social order. In such states, public participation is limited and government is run by an established **elite**. Public policies disproportionately benefit the interests of those elites.

States can, of course, have cultures that combine these concepts. One book classified Colorado, for example, as having a "moralistic" political culture. California was classified as having a "moralistic individualistic" political culture and New York an "individualistic moralistic" culture. New Jersey was classified as "individualistic" and Georgia "traditionalistic." Florida and Kentucky were seen as "traditionalistic individualistic." Often Texas is categorized as having a "traditionalistic individualistic" political culture.[3] Taxes are kept low, and social services are minimized. Political elites, such as business leaders, have a major voice in how the state is run. In spite of the difficulty in measuring the concept of political culture in any empirical way, it is a concept widely regarded as useful in explaining fundamental beliefs about the state and the role of state government.

Yet, the political culture of a state can change over time. Texas is undergoing dramatic changes, including some change in its political culture. It is also difficult to classify the political culture of a state as large and as diverse as Texas in any one category. In fact, Texas has many different political cultures or subcultures within its borders.[4]

Three long-lasting patterns in Texas politics seem to indicate a "traditionalistic individualistic" state political culture. Indeed, political elites interested in limited government with low taxes and few social services dominate Texas politics today. It is also the case that at least some of these characteristics of state politics are undergoing rapid change. We examine these elements of Texas political culture below.

The One-Party State

For over 100 years, Texas was dominated by the Democratic Party. Winning the Democratic Party primary was tantamount to winning the general election. As we will see in later chapters, this pattern no longer holds. During the 1990s substantial competition emerged between the parties for control of the state legislature. Following redistricting in 2002 the Republicans secured a 7-vote majority in the state Senate and a 24-vote majority in the state House. Between 2002 and 2014 all major statewide elected offices were controlled by Republicans. The question today is not whether the political culture of Texas will continue to be defined by a powerful Democratic Party, but how that culture will be redefined by two forces: a powerful Republican Party in most suburban and rural areas and a resurgent Democratic Party in Texas's most urban counties.

Provincialism

A second pattern that once defined Texas political culture is **provincialism**, a narrow view of the world that is often associated with rural values and notions of limited government. The result often was an intolerance of diversity and a notion of the public interest that dismissed social services and expenditures for education. Some of the more popular politicians in Texas have stressed cornpone—a hickish rural rejection of modern urban lifestyles—intolerance, and a narrow worldview rather than policies that might offer advantages to the state as it competes with other states and with other nations. Like the one-party Democratic state, Texas provincialism has faded as a defining feature of the political culture. The growing influence of minorities, women, and gays in state politics, increasing urbanization, and Texas's relevance in the global economy have all undercut Texas's provincialism.

Business Dominance

A third, continuing pattern that has helped define Texas's political culture is its longtime dominance by business. Labor unions are rare in Texas except in the oil-refinery areas around Beaumont–Port Arthur. Other groups that might offer an alternative to a business perspective, such as consumer interests, are poorly organized and poorly funded. Business groups are major players in Texas politics, in terms of campaign contributions, organized interest groups, and lobbyists.

This chapter will investigate the economic, social, and demographic changes that transformed Texas's political culture during the twentieth century. These changes shook Texas government and politics in the 1990s and have continued to shape them in the second decade of the twenty-first century.

Ties between business and political leaders in Texas have always been strong. Here, then governor Rick Perry appears with Ralph Babb, the chief executive of Comerica Bank, to announce that Comerica would move its corporate headquarters to Dallas.

● The Land

> **Explain how Texas's geography has influenced its political culture**

Much of Texas's history and political life has been shaped by the relationship forged between its people and the land. Texas is the second-largest state in size, next to Alaska. To understand the dynamics of political life and governance in Texas demands an appreciation of the vast spaces and topography that define the state.

Perhaps the most distinctive characteristic of Texas's geography is its size. The longest straight-line distance across the state from north to south is 801 miles; the longest east–west distance is 773 miles. To put this into perspective, the east–west distance from New York City to Chicago is 821 miles, cutting across five different states. The north–south distance between New York City and Charleston, South Carolina, is 763 miles, cutting across six different states.

Distances alone do not tell the whole story of the diverse geography found in Texas. There are four distinct physical regions in Texas: the Gulf Coastal Plains, the Interior Lowlands, the Great Plains, and the Basin and Range Province (Figure 1.1).[5] The distinctive features of these regions have shaped politics in Texas in a number of important ways.

The Gulf Coastal Plains

The Gulf Coastal Plains extend from the Louisiana border and the Gulf of Mexico, along the Rio Grande up to Del Rio, and northward to the line of the Balcones Fault and Escarpment. As one moves westward, the climate becomes increasingly arid. Forests become less frequent as post oak trees dominate the landscape until they too are replaced by the prairies and brushlands of central Texas.

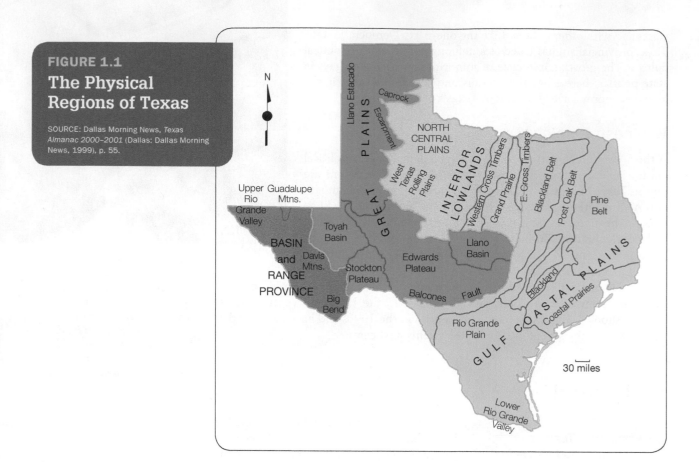

FIGURE 1.1

The Physical Regions of Texas

SOURCE: Dallas Morning News, *Texas Almanac 2000–2001* (Dallas: Dallas Morning News, 1999), p. 55.

The eastern portion of the Gulf Coastal Plains—so-called east Texas—is characterized by hilly surfaces covered by forests of pine and hardwoods. Almost all of Texas's timber production takes place here. It is also the home of some of Texas's most famous oilfields. To the west is the Blackland Belt. A rolling prairie soil made the Blackland Belt a prime farming area during the late nineteenth and early twentieth centuries. It was a major center of cotton production in Texas. Today it is the most densely populated area of the state and has a diversified manufacturing base.

The Coastal Prairies around Houston and Beaumont were the center for the post–World War II industrial boom, particularly in the petrochemical industry. Winter-vegetable and fruit production plays a major role in the Lower Rio Grande Valley, while livestock is important in the Rio Grande Plain, an area that receives less than 24 inches of rainfall on average every year and during the summer months experiences rapid evaporation.

Texas's political life grew out of the Gulf Coastal Plains. The land grants made available to Americans willing to come to Texas in the first half of the nineteenth century were located here. This region was the foundation of plantation life during the antebellum period when slavery flourished in the state. The Dallas–Fort Worth area is located in the northwestern part of this region, once a bastion of a small Republican Party. A union movement grew out of the industrialized areas along the coast, providing support to a liberal wing of the Democratic Party. For the most part, though, the Gulf Coastal Plains were dominated by rural conservative values, be they located in the Democratic Party (from 1876 to the early 1990s) or in the

Republican Party (from the 1990s to today). Urbanization and suburbanization in Houston and Dallas–Fort Worth have added new dimensions to the political life of this region. Urban areas have become increasingly Democratic, while suburban areas have become more Republican.

The Interior Lowlands

The Interior Lowlands are an extension of the interior lowlands that run down from Canada. They are bordered by the Balcones Escarpment on the east and south and the Caprock Escarpment on the west. Beginning to the west of Fort Worth, the eastern edge of the Interior Lowlands has predominantly an agricultural economy and a rural population. The western portion, meanwhile, rises from 750 to 2,000 feet in elevation. The West Texas Rolling Plains contain much level, cultivable land and are home to a large cattle-raising industry. Many of the state's largest ranches are located here. The region is dominated by conservative politics and the Republican Party.

The Great Plains

Pushing down into northwest Texas from the Rocky Mountains to the Balcones Fault, the Great Plains define the terrain in much of western Texas, rising from 2,700 feet in the east to more than 4,000 feet along the New Mexico border. The major city on the northern plains is Amarillo. Ranching and petroleum production dominate the economy. The southern plains economy centers on agriculture and cotton production, with Lubbock as the major city. Large-scale irrigation from underwater reservoirs, particularly the Ogallala Aquifer, has played a major role in the economic development of this region. A major concern of policy makers is that pumping out of the aquifer exceeds replenishment, raising questions of the viability of basing future growth on the irrigation practices of the past. We will return to a discussion of the problem of aquifer depletion in the public policy chapter (see Chapter 12).

As in East Texas, conservative political values have a home in the Interior Lowlands and the Great Plains. While representatives from this area have played a major role in the political life of the state over the last 100 years, their power has been ebbing in the face of the population pressures of Texas's expanding urban areas elsewhere.

for critical analysis
How has the diverse geography of Texas affected its development?

The Basin and Range Province

The fourth geographic region in Texas is the Basin and Range Province. Here one finds Texas's mountains in the Guadalupe Range along the border with New Mexico, which includes Guadalupe Peak (8,749 feet) and El Capitan (8,085 feet). To the southeast is Big Bend country, so named because the Rio Grande River surrounds it on three sides as the river makes its southward swing. Rainfall and population are sparse in this region.

The area running from the Basin and Range Province to the Lower Rio Grande has always had a distinctive political culture, heavily dominated by the fact that Texas and Mexico have been joined at the hip economically and demographically. In the late twentieth and early twenty-first centuries, the Border region, including El Paso, McAllen, and Brownsville, has remained a Democratic Party bastion.

● Economic Change in Texas

Trace the evolution of Texas's economy

The famous twentieth-century economist Joseph Schumpeter characterized the capitalist economic system as being a process of "creative destruction."[6] By this he meant that capitalism was an economic system that underwent periodic waves of transformation fueled by technological innovations in production and distribution. These waves of technological transformation were put into place by entrepreneurs who had visions of new ways to produce and distribute goods and services and who were willing to act on those visions. The capitalist process of creative destruction not only creates a new economic and social world; it destroys old ones. The world of railroads, steam, and steel transformed American economic and social life by nationalizing the market and making new opportunities available to businesses and individuals during the late nineteenth century. It also destroyed the local markets that had defined rural American communities since the Founding. The technological innovation tied to gasoline combustion engines, electricity, and radio restructured the American economy again in the 1920s, leaving in its wake a society and an economy that would never be the same.

Schumpeter's theory of creative destruction provides a useful way to think about the economic changes that have shaped and reshaped the Texas economy. Three great waves of technological change have helped define and redefine the Texas political economy over the last 150 years. The first centered on the production of cotton and cattle and their distribution by an extensive railroad system. The second grew out of the oil industry. The third and most recent is tied to the development of the high-tech digital economy.

Cotton

Cotton is one of the oldest crops grown in Texas.[7] Missions in San Antonio in the eighteenth century are reported to have produced several thousand pounds of cotton annually, which were spun and woven by local artisans. Serious cultivation of cotton began in 1821 with the arrival of white Americans. Political independence, statehood, and the ongoing removal of the Native American "threat" in the years before the Civil War promoted the development of the cotton industry. By the mid-nineteenth century, cotton production in Texas soared, placing Texas eighth among the top cotton-producing states in the Union. Although production fell in the years following the Civil War, by 1869 it had begun to pick up again. By 1880, Texas led all states in the production of cotton in most years.

A number of technological breakthroughs further stimulated the cotton industry in Texas. First, in the 1870s barbed wire was introduced, enabling farmers to cordon off their lands and protect their cash crop from grazing cattle. Second, the building of railroads brought Texas farmers into a national market. Finally, a newly designed plow made it easier to dig up the prairie soil and significantly increase farm productivity.

Throughout the 1870s immigrants from the Deep South and Europe flooded the prairies of Texas to farm cotton. Most of these newly arrived Texans became tenant farmers or sharecroppers. Tenants lived on farms owned by landowners, providing their own animals, tools, and seed. They generally received two-thirds of the final value of the cotton grown on the farm, while the landlords received the other third. Another form of tenant farming is sharecropping. Sharecroppers furnished only their labor but received only one-half of the value of the final product. Almost half of the state farmers were tenants by the turn of the century.[8]

Two important consequences resulted from the tenant and sharecropping system. First, it condemned many rural Texans to lives of social and economic dependency. The notorious "crop-lien" system was developed to extend credit to farmers in exchange for liens on their crops. The result often was to trap farmers in a debt cycle from which they could not escape. Second, the tenant and sharecropping system helped fuel radical political discontent in rural areas, sparking both the Grange and Populist movements. These movements played a major role in defining the style of Texas politics throughout much of the late nineteenth and early twentieth centuries.

During the late nineteenth century, in most years Texas produced more cotton than any other state. But although one-quarter of the cotton produced in the United States still comes from Texas, the importance of the cotton industry to the state's economy has declined since the 1920s. This photo shows land and machinery used to farm cotton.

Cotton production cycled up and down as farmers experienced a series of crises and opportunities during the late nineteenth and early twentieth centuries, ranging from destructive boll weevils to an increased demand brought on by World War I to a collapse in prices following the war. The general decline of the cotton culture continued after World War II. The 1930 Census reported that 61 percent of all farmers in Texas were tenant farmers. One-third of these farmers were sharecroppers. These numbers fell throughout the Great Depression and beyond. By 1987 only 12 percent of all farmers were tenants.[9]

Cattle

The history of ranching and the cattle industry parallels that of cotton in many ways.[10] The origins of ranching and the cattle industry extend back to the late seventeenth century, when the Spanish brought livestock to the region to feed their missionaries, soldiers, and civilians. Ranching offered immigrants an attractive alternative to farming during the periods of Mexican and Republic of Texas rule. In the 1830s traffic in cattle was limited to local areas. This began to change as cattle drives and railroads began opening up new markets in the east.

Following the Civil War, the cattle industry took off, expanding throughout the state. As with cotton, the invention of barbed wire helped close off the lands used for grazing. By the end of the nineteenth century, ranch lands had been transformed from open range to fenced pasturing. As a result, conflicts over land often broke out between large and small ranchers, as well as between ranchers and farmers. As cattle raising became a more specialized and efficient business, periodic conflicts broke out between employers and employees. Throughout the twentieth century, ranching remained a cyclical industry, struggling when national and international prices collapsed and thriving during upturns in the economy.

Ranching and cotton production remain important industries in the state, although increasingly dominated by big agribusiness companies. Texas normally leads the nation in livestock production. Similarly, it normally leads all other states in cotton production. Over 28 percent of the total cotton production in the United States came from Texas. In 2013 the annual cotton crop was 4.1 million bales, down from a peak in 2005 of 8.4 million bales. Production has fluctuated in recent years because of the severe drought that has plagued parts of the state.[11]

Neither cotton production nor ranching drives the Texas political economy as in the past. The number of people making a living from agriculture has dropped significantly over the last 50 years as agribusiness has pushed out the family farm

Cattle ranching is another of Texas's dominant industries. The most famous ranch in Texas is the King Ranch, shown here in 1950. Currently covering almost 1,300 square miles, it is larger than the state of Rhode Island.

and ranch. In 1940, 23 percent of the population worked on farms and ranches. Another 17 percent were suppliers to farms and ranches or helped assemble, process, or distribute agricultural products. Currently, less than 2 percent of the population lives on farms and ranches, with an additional 15 percent of the population providing support, processing, or distribution services to agriculture in Texas.[12]

A new set of technological breakthroughs challenged the nineteenth-century dominance of cotton and cattle in the early twentieth century. These breakthroughs focused not on what grew on the land, but on what lay beneath it.

Oil

Oil was first sighted in the mid-seventeenth century by Spanish explorers.[13] There was no market or demand for the product, and nothing was done to develop this natural resource. Over a century later, encouraged by a growing demand for petroleum products following the Civil War, a scattering of entrepreneurs dug wells, although they were not commercially viable. The first economically significant oil discovery in Texas was in 1894 in Navarro County near Corsicana. By 1898 the state's first oil refinery was operating at the site. Oil production had become economically viable.

What catapulted Texas into the era of oil and gas was the discovery at Spindletop on January 10, 1901. Located three miles south of Beaumont along the Gulf Coast, the Spindletop discovery produced Texas's first oil boom. The success of Spindletop encouraged large numbers of speculators and entrepreneurs to try their luck in the new business. Within three years, three major oilfields had been discovered within 150 miles of Spindletop.

Oil fever spread throughout Texas over the next decade. In north central Texas, major discoveries took place at Brownwood, Petrolia, and Wichita Falls. In the teens major discoveries were made in Wichita County, Limestone County near Mexia, and once again in Navarro County. In 1921 oil was found in the Panhandle, and by the end of the decade major oilfields were being developed all across the state. The biggest oilfield in the state was found in October 1930 in east Texas. As journalist Mary G. Ramos notes, "By the time the East Texas field was developed, Texas's economy was powered not by agriculture, but by petroleum."[14]

The oil and gas industry transformed the social and economic fabric of Texas in a number of important ways. By providing cheap oil and gas, the industry made possible a new industrial revolution in twentieth-century America that was fueled by hydrocarbons. Cheap oil provided a new fuel for transportation and manufacturing. Railroads and steamships were able to convert from coal to oil. Manufacturing plants and farms were able to operate more efficiently with a new, cheap source of energy, encouraging individuals to migrate to cities away from farms. Automobile production was encouraged, as was the building of roads. The Interstate Highway System that was built during the 1950s and 1960s changed fundamentally the transportation patterns that shaped the movements of people and goods in Texas. The triangle formed by I-35 from San Antonio to Dallas–Fort Worth, I-45 from Dallas–Fort Worth to Houston, and I-10 from Houston to San Antonio became the heartland of the Texas economy and the location of an increasing percentage of the state's population.

The oil and gas industry also sparked a rapid industrialization of the Gulf Coast region. Among the companies developing the Gulf Coast oilfields were Gulf Oil, Sun Oil, Magnolia Petroleum, the Texas Company (then Texaco, now ChevronTexaco), and Humble Oil (which later became Esso, then Exxon, and finally ExxonMobil). The refineries, pipelines, and export facilities laid the foundations for the large-scale industrialization that would take place along the Gulf Coast in the Houston–Beaumont–Port Arthur region. By 1929 in Harris County, for example, 27 percent of all manufacturing employees worked in refineries. By 1940 the capacity of all the refineries had increased fourfold.[15] The petrochemical industry continued to flourish throughout the 1960s, when demand for its products grew at the rate of 10 percent a year.

One important effect of the oil and gas boom in Texas was the development of a new rhythm to economic life in the state. There had been a natural pace to the economy when it was tied to the production of cotton and cattle. Prices of products could rise and fall, bringing prosperity or gloom to local economies. But there was a bond between the land and the people and the communities that formed around them. Oil and gas, on the other hand, introduced a boom-and-bust mentality that carried over into the communities that sprang up around oil and gas discoveries. Rural areas were often unprepared for the population explosion that followed the discovery of oil or gas. Housing was often inadequate or nonexistent. Schools quickly became overcrowded. General living conditions were poor as people sought to "make it big." The irony of the oil and gas business was that a major discovery that brought large amounts of new oil and gas to market could lead to a sudden collapse in prices. Prosperous economic times could quickly turn into local depressions. And when particular fields were tapped out, boom towns could quickly become ghost towns.

The oil and gas industry also transformed government and the role that it played in the economy. Following the Civil War, a series of attempts to regulate the railroads had largely failed. In 1890, after considerable controversy fueled by Populist anti-railroad sentiment, a constitutional amendment was passed to create an agency to regulate the railroads, the Texas Railroad Commission. This regulatory agency's powers were extended in 1917 to regulate energy. The Railroad Commission was empowered to see that petroleum pipelines were "common carriers" (that they transported all producers' oil and gas) and to promote well-spacing rules. In an attempt to bring stability to fluctuations in world oil prices brought on by the glut of oil on world markets in the 1930s and to conserve wasteful oil production, the commission won the authority to prorate oil and determine how much every oil well in Texas might produce. Through the late 1960s the Texas Railroad Commission was one of the most important regulatory bodies in the nation. It was also one of the few democratically elected regulatory agencies.

Helping to expand the power of state government in the economy through the Railroad Commission was only one effect of the oil and gas industry in Texas. It also had an important fiscal effect on state government. Beginning in 1905 the state collected oil production taxes. These rose from $101,403 in 1906 to over $1 million in 1919 and almost $6 million in 1929. For the 2014–15 biennium, it was estimated that oil production taxes, or severance taxes, would contribute $6.5 billion to the state budget, up from $5.09 billion in 2012–13, an increase of 27.6 percent. Natural gas production taxes added another $2.99 billion to the state budget, down 1.2 percent in 2012–13.[16] These numbers represented a sharp turnaround from the previous two decades, when oil and natural gas revenues had sharply fallen. As we will see in Chapter 11 on public finance in Texas, oil and natural gas production has returned to play an increasingly important role in the state's finances through the severance tax.

Much like the state coffers, higher education in Texas has benefited from the oil and gas industry. What many thought was worthless land at the time had been set aside by the state constitution of 1876 and the state legislature in 1883 to support higher education (the Permanent University Fund). As luck would have it, oil was discovered in the West Texas Permian Basin in 1923 on university land. Soon 17 wells were producing oil on that land, sparking a building boom at the University of Texas. In 1931 the income of the Permanent University Fund was split between the University of Texas at Austin and Texas A&M University, with the former receiving two-thirds and the latter one-third. In 1984 the income was opened up to all University of Texas and Texas A&M schools. Along with the royalties from other natural resources on university land, oil and gas royalties created one of the largest university endowments in the world. Today, the Permanent University Fund holds title to 2.1 million acres located in 24 counties, primarily in west Texas. In December 2012 the market value of the Permanent University Fund was calculated to be $15.881 billion.[17]

The oil and gas industry had one other effect on life in Texas that is worth noting. Fortunes were made in the industry, and those fortunes paved the way for an expansion of private philanthropy that would have a major influence in shaping Texas's culture. Among the most famous examples of this private philanthropy were the Meadows Foundations, established in 1948 to promote programs in health, education, visual arts, social services, and historical preservation. The Sid W. Richardson Foundation was founded in 1947 and supported health and education programs, as well as the development of the arts in Fort Worth. The Bass Performance Hall, which opened in May 1998, was funded by the Bass brothers, grand-nephews of the independent oilman Sid Richardson.

One can trace the rise and decline and rise again of the oil and gas industry in Texas through production figures (see Figure 1.2). Oil production in Texas seemed to peak in 1972, and there were decades of decline in the state's production. New technologies such as horizontal drilling and fracking have led to a new boom era of oil and gas production in Texas beginning in 2008 and carrying through until today. In September 2013, 2.7 million barrels of oil per day were pumped in Texas—the highest monthly record since September 1981, when such records first began to be kept. That was a 30 percent increase in production over the previous September's figures. More than one million barrels of that daily production came from the Permian Basin region in west Texas. This oilfield may be the second largest in the world. The result of this new oil boom is that oil (and gas) is emerging again as a mainstay of the Texas economy, although it is an economy that is far more diversified than in an earlier era. With the new Texas oil boom will come greater resources for the

for critical analysis

During the 1980s the price of oil fell from almost $35 a barrel to $10 a barrel, seriously harming Texas's economy. To what extent has the economy of Texas changed so that devastation in one industry will not have the effect that the failure of the oil industry did in the 1980s?

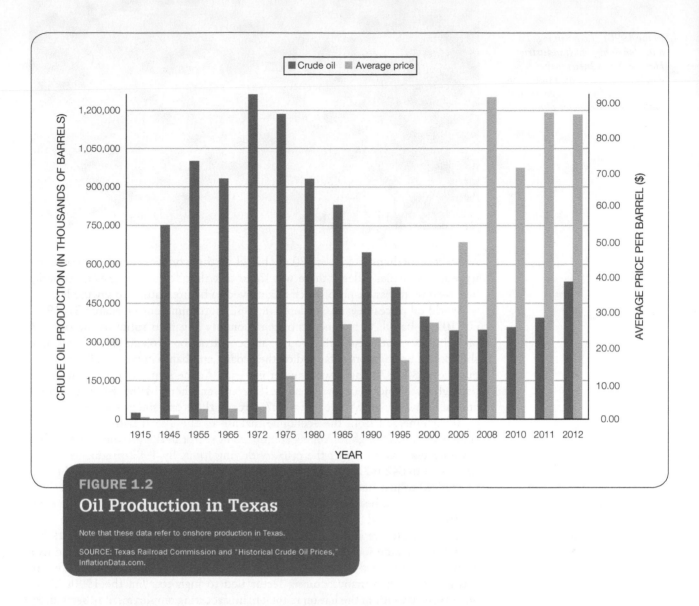

FIGURE 1.2

Oil Production in Texas

Note that these data refer to onshore production in Texas.

SOURCE: Texas Railroad Commission and "Historical Crude Oil Prices,"
InflationData.com.

Texas budget. Additionally, with the boom will come new demands for vast water supplies—an essential component of the new drilling technology—and new concerns over the effects that those new technologies will have on the environment.[18]

New industries and technologies have come to assume significant roles in plotting the state's economic future. Among the most important of these was the burgeoning high-tech industry.

High-Tech Industries

The movement out of the era of oil and gas and into that of high tech was not an easy one. World oil prices rose in 1981 to almost $35 per barrel. At the time, oil-related businesses accounted for 26 percent of the gross state product. From 1971 to 1981 the average rate of economic growth was 4.4 percent. Fueled by a booming oil-based economy and a rapidly increasing population, real estate prices shot up in urban areas such as Houston and Dallas. Projections were made that as oil

In the 1990s, Texas emerged as a leader in high-tech industries. Here, a Texas Instruments employee oversees the production of silicon wafers in the company's Dallas semiconductor plant.

prices rose, perhaps to $70 or $80 per barrel on the world market, future prosperity was inevitable. Indeed, there was some talk that Texas's oil-driven economy had become recession-proof. Such talk proved to be premature, to say the least.

World oil prices began to collapse in 1982, bottoming out on March 31, 1986, at $10 per barrel. Other sectors of the economy began to suffer as the price of oil fell. Real estate deals fell through, and construction projects slowed and then shut down. Speculators defaulted on their loans, and banks began to fail. Throughout the 1980s, 370 banks went under in Texas. At the same time, the state went through two major recessions, one in 1982 and another in 1986–87. The average annual economic growth slowed to 1.7 percent, the worst since World War II.

Texas emerged from the economic malaise of the 1980s with a transformed state economy. Though remaining an important sector in the economy, the oil and gas business was no longer the primary driving force. By 1992 production of oil had fallen to 642 million barrels worth $11.8 billion. Production continued to fall until 2000 to just under 349 million barrels worth a little over $10 billion. Over 146,000 jobs had been lost in the oil industry throughout the 1980s. By the early 1990s oil accounted for only about 12 percent of the gross state product.

In contrast to the 1980s, the 1990s were a period of rapid growth. In the 1990s, unlike in early periods of speculative booms such as the 1970s, the economy's growth was grounded in a rapidly diversifying economy. At the heart of this boom was a fast-growing manufacturing sector tied to high tech. In the 1990s, Texas went from seventh in the nation in total manufacturing employment to second. By 2013, 15 percent of the state's gross domestic product came from manufacturing. Eight percent of the workforce was employed in manufacturing.[19]

Two metropolitan areas stand out as national centers for the rapidly evolving high-tech industry. The Austin–San Marcos metropolitan area is the home of the computer giant Dell and has become a production center for computer chips, personal computers, and related computer hardware with such companies as Flextronics, Apple, Oracle, and IBM. Seven of the area's largest employers are part of the computer or semiconductor industry. The Dallas metropolitan area, particularly north of the city, is the home of a number of important electronic and electronic-equipment companies, including Texas Instruments. Houston has become known worldwide for its medical center and expanding research facilities in the medical field. A 2014 study released by the TechAmerica Foundation found that Texas was the leading tech export state with $45.1 billion in exports in 2012, up 7.3 percent from 2011. Approximately 331,000 jobs in Texas were supported by these tech exports.[20]

NAFTA

Texas's place in national and international markets has been shaped by its central location, its border with Mexico, and its sophisticated transportation infrastructure. There are 306,404 miles of highways in Texas (the most in the nation) along with 45 railroads operating on 10,405 rail miles (the most in the nation) (see Figure 1.3). There are 12 deep-water ports in Texas, including the Port of Houston, which was ranked second nationally for total trade and thirteenth globally for total cargo volume. The Dallas–Fort Worth International Airport and George Bush Intercontinental Airport in Houston ranked high on the list of the world's busiest airports and were major hubs for both national and international travel. Over 6.5 million trucks, 47.8 million personal vehicles, and 22.9 million people crossed the Texas-Mexico border in 2013.[21]

One defining feature of the Texas economy in the 1990s and 2000s was the **North American Free Trade Agreement (NAFTA)**. Signed on December 17, 1992, by Prime Minister Brian Mulroney of Canada, President Carlos Salinas de Gortari of Mexico, and President George H. W. Bush of the United States, NAFTA sought to create a free-trade zone—an area free of customs duties—in North America that was the largest of its kind in the world. Considerable controversy surrounded the passage of NAFTA, with many groups arguing that free trade would hurt U.S. workers and companies because of the cheap labor available in Mexico. An important milestone in the agreement was reached on October 19, 2001, when Mexican trucks were finally allowed to cross over into the United States with goods for U.S. markets.

North American Free Trade Agreement (NAFTA) trade treaty among the United States, Canada, and Mexico to lower and eliminate tariffs among the three countries

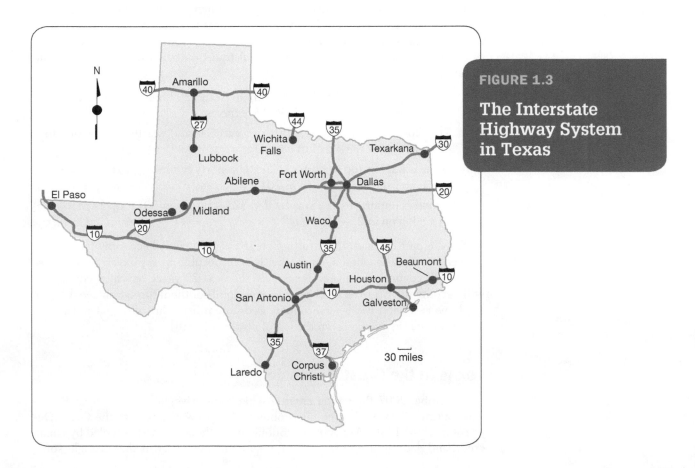

FIGURE 1.3

The Interstate Highway System in Texas

30 miles

The signing of NAFTA in 1992 created a free-trade zone in North America. Although many Texas workers were adversely affected by the availability of cheaper labor in Mexico, NAFTA appears to have had a beneficial effect on the state's economy as a whole. Here, President George H. W. Bush stands between President Carlos Salinas de Gortari of Mexico and Prime Minister Brian Mulroney of Canada at the signing ceremony.

Despite NAFTA provisions, Mexican trucks had been banned in the United States for almost 20 years because of strong labor union opposition and concerns over safety.

Today NAFTA links approximately 450 million consumers in the United States, Canada, and Mexico with a combined gross domestic product of $19.6 trillion. According to a recent Standard and Poor's study, Mexico has benefited the most from the agreement. But Texas has benefited enormously as well. NAFTA was not the only cause to the diversification of the Texas economy since the 1980s, but it has accelerated that diversification. Along the border, NAFTA has clearly had an impact in stimulating trade and transport across the state and stimulating the production of jobs. For example, Laredo, Texas—the port of entry for 40 percent of U.S.–Mexico truck transport trade—has seen its labor force increase 48 percent between 1994 and 2014, far above the 35 percent state average. International toll bridges alone accounted for 23 percent of Laredo's general fund revenue in 2012.[22]

After more than 20 years, it appears that the trade agreement has had both negative and positive impacts on Texas. A 2011 study by the Economic Policy Institute calculated that almost 683,000 jobs had been lost in the United States because of NAFTA. The study estimated that three-fifths of these jobs were in the manufacturing sector. Over 55,000 of these displaced jobs came from Texas.[23] U.S. workers generally lost their jobs because of the stiffer competition from low-wage businesses in Mexico or because plants had been relocated to Mexico. (Under federal law such workers are entitled to additional unemployment compensation.)

Although there were some losers in the movement toward free trade with Mexico and Canada, there were also big winners. The following statistics from 2013 put the importance of Texas's international trade, particularly with Mexico and Canada, into perspective:[24]

- Texas exports totaled $279.7 billion, up from $207 billion in 2012. Texas exports were 17.7 percent of all U.S. exports.
- The North American market (Mexico and Canada) was the destination for 45.4 percent of these exports.
- Mexico was the top importer of Texas exports at almost $101 billion in 2013, up from $72.7 billion in 2012.
- Canada's imports from Texas totaled $25.9 billion in 2013, up from $18.8 billion in 2010.

For the past 20 years, the information age and the global economy have transformed the Texas economic landscape. It is impossible to say exactly how these forces will continue to change Texas over the next 20 years, or which companies will become the ChevronTexacos or ExxonMobils of the information age. We can say, however, that it will be an economy as different from that of the oil and gas era as the oil and gas era was from the era of cotton and cattle.

Texas in the Great Recession

In December 2007 the nation entered what some have called "the Great Recession," a time of chronic economic problems that drew analogies to the Great Depression of the 1930s. A speculative bubble in the housing market fueled by cheap credit and poor business practices culminated in a credit crisis that brought some of America's largest banks and investment houses to their knees. Only the massive intrusion of the Federal Reserve System into credit markets in the fall of 2008 prevented the banking system from melting down. The Federal Reserve reported that between November 2007 and March 2009, 86 percent of American industries cut back production. The GNP dropped 1.7 percent and household net worth fell $11 trillion or 18 percent during the recession.[25]

Texas was one of the last states to enter the Great Recession and was one of the first to exit. Prior to the recession, Texas employment had peaked at 10.6 million in August 2008. From late 2008 through 2009, 427,600 jobs were lost in Texas to the Great Recession. By November 2011 employment had recovered to prerecession levels. By April 2014 another 829,000 jobs had been added to the Texas economy. The story at the national level was not so rosy. By the summer of 2014 jobs numbers were only beginning to approach pre–Great Recession levels. Meanwhile the unemployment rate in Texas rose to 8.2 percent and hovered there throughout most of 2010. Unemployment rates began falling in early 2011 and continued to fall for the next two years, dropping from 6.4 percent in March 2013 to 5.2 percent in April 2014.[26]

Many Texas politicians sought to take credit for Texas's performance during and after the Great Recession. Comparisons were made with big-government, high-tax states like California that suffered severely. Low taxes and low services, pro-business and free market government, an entrepreneurial spirit—all were given credit for the "Texas economic miracle."[27] But the factors that may have helped Texas get by relatively unscathed were likely more straightforward. The housing market declined much less severely in Texas than in the rest of the nation. Most of Texas did not experience the surge in real estate values found in other states like California, Nevada, Florida, and Arizona. While foreclosure rates throughout the country increased sixfold between 2005 and 2009, in Texas they rose only marginally. Texas's banking industry also appeared to have weathered the storm better than its counterparts in other states. Article 16 of the Texas Constitution, as amended in 1997, forbids consumers from using home-equity loans for credit that exceeds 80 percent of the mortgage, and this probably provided a cushion against the credit crunch. Two of the most important factors that may have helped Texas escape the worst of the Great Recession were discussed above: an increasingly diversified economy lubricated by international trade and a resurgent oil and gas industry.[28]

Texas was not hit as hard as other states by the recession that started in 2007 and deepened in 2008. However, some Texans—including these Tea Party protesters—were alarmed by the massive spending involved in the national government's stimulus efforts.

● The People of Texas

> **Explain how the population of Texas has changed over time**

The population in Texas has grown rapidly in the last 165 years. In 1850 the population stood at a little more than 210,000 people, more than one-quarter of whom were African American slaves. Texas in 1850 also was an overwhelmingly rural state. Only 4 percent of the population lived in urban areas. By 1900 the population had increased to more than 3 million people, with 83 percent continuing to live in rural areas. The 1980s began as boom years for population growth, with increases running

TABLE 1.1

The Changing Face of Texas, 1850–2012

	1850	1900	1950	1990	2012
Population	213,000	3,050,000	7,710,000	17,000,000	26,059,203
White	72%	80%	87%	61%	44.5%
African American	28%	20%	13%	12%	12.3%
Latino	NA*	NA	NA	25%	38.2%
Asian	NA	NA	NA	NA	4.2%

*NA= not available. Note that percentages do not add to 100 percent because of rounding.

SOURCES: *Statistical Abstract of the United States: 1994* (Washington, DC: U.S. Department of Commerce, Bureau of the Census, 1994); see also *Texas Almanac 2014–2015* (Denton: Texas State Historical Association, 2014), 15; 2010 U.S. Census. Other editions of the *Texas Almanac* also consulted. These are available online.

between 2.9 percent and 1.6 percent per year from 1980 through 1986. With the collapse of oil prices, however, population growth slowed significantly between 1987 and 1989 to less than 1 percent.[29]

With a recovering economy, population growth surged in the 1990s (see Table 1.1). In 1990, 17 million people resided in the state. By 2012 the number of people was estimated to be over 26 million. Almost 45 percent of the population were non-Hispanic white in 2012, down from 61 percent in 1990. A little over 11 percent were African American. Over 38 percent were Hispanic, up from 25 percent in 1990.

Three factors account for the population growth in Texas: natural increase as a result of the difference between births and deaths; international immigration, particularly from Mexico; and domestic immigration from other states. The makeup of the growth in population shifted in significant ways over the course of the decade. In 1991 almost two-thirds of population growth was accounted for by natural increases. A little more than 20 percent was a result of international immigration, while less than 14 percent resulted from domestic immigration. By 2013 natural increases accounted for only 54 percent of population growth, while international immigration accounted for about 16.8 percent and domestic immigration for about 29.7 percent.[30] In the early decades of the twenty-first century, Texas was being redefined not by native-born Texans but by individuals coming to Texas to share in and contribute to the state's diversified economy.

Whites

For most of the nineteenth and twentieth centuries, the dominant ethnic group was non-Hispanic whites. Whites in Texas comprise a wide range of European ethnic groups, including English, Germans, Scots, Irish, Czechs, and European Jews. The first wave of whites came to Texas before the break with Mexico. Encouraged by **Impresarios** such as Moses Austin and his son Stephen F. Austin, who were authorized by the Spanish and later the Mexican leaders to bring people to Texas, these newcomers sought inexpensive land. But they brought along a new set of individualistic attitudes and values about democratic government that paved the way for the Texas Revolution. Following the revolution, a new surge of white im-

Impresario an individual who promotes, organizes, or helps to finance a particular endeavor

Prior to statehood, many of Texas's whites were European immigrants. For instance, in 1844 close to 5,000 Germans arrived and soon thereafter established the towns of New Braunfels and Fredericksburg. This painting from the 1850s shows a German American family from Fredericksburg "going visiting."

migrants came from the Deep South. Like their predecessors, they sought cheap land. But they brought with them new cultural baggage: slavery. By the time of the American Civil War, this group had come to dominate the political culture of the state. Although most Texas farmers did not own slaves themselves, the vast majority supported the institution as well as secession from the Union.

Defeat in the Civil War shattered the dominance of the traditional white power structure in the state. By the end of Reconstruction, however, it had reasserted itself, establishing the three patterns that defined Texas politics for the next hundred years: the one-party Democratic state, provincialism, and business dominance. Whites continued to dominate and define Texas's political culture throughout much of the twentieth century, but by the end of that century much had changed. As a percentage of the population, white population peaked at 74 percent in 1950. This percentage began to fall, reaching 44.5 percent in 2014, and will likely continue to fall (see Figure 1.4).

Numbers alone do not tell the whole story. Whites living in Texas at the end of the twentieth century were not cut from the same cloth as those who had preceded them. A new wave of white immigration into Texas over the past 40 years has redefined the political culture of white Texans. No longer can one assume that a white Texan lives on a farm, holds culturally conservative values, and is firmly tied to the Democratic Party. On the contrary, he or she may be an urbanite or suburbanite who wasn't born in Texas and who votes Republican.

Latinos

The use of the terms *Hispanic* and *Latino* can be confusing. The terms are often used interchangeably to refer to people of Spanish descent or people from Latin America. We will use the term Latino except when referring to statistical databases such as the U.S. Census that use the term *Hispanic*.

Most Latinos in Texas are people of Mexican descent.[31] Prior to independence from Spain, this included people born of Iberian (Spanish) parents as well as mestizos (people of mixed Spanish and Native American ancestry). In the early nineteenth century, approximately 5,000 people of Mexican descent were living in Texas. Although this number fluctuated considerably over the years, by 1850 it was estimated that 14,000 Texans were of Mexican origin. Texas became for many a refuge from the political and economic instability that troubled Mexico from the late 1850s to the 1920s. Despite periodic attempts to curtail the growth of the Mexican American population in Texas, it grew from an estimated 700,000 in 1930 to 1,400,000 in 1960. The 2000 census counted 5.1 million Mexican Americans

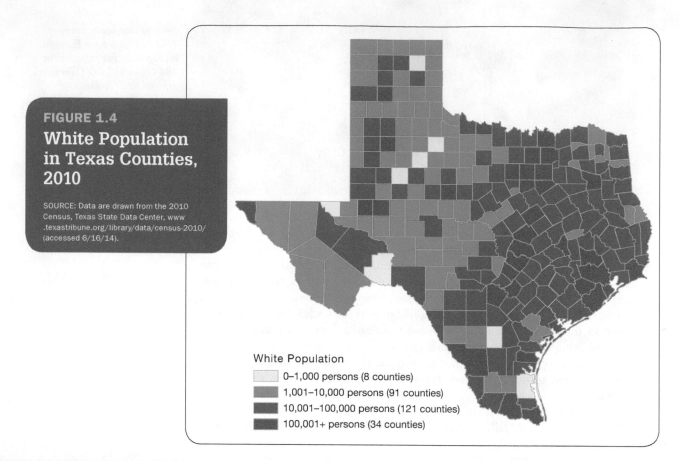

FIGURE 1.4

White Population in Texas Counties, 2010

SOURCE: Data are drawn from the 2010 Census, Texas State Data Center, www.texastribune.org/library/data/census-2010/ (accessed 6/16/14).

White Population

- ☐ 0–1,000 persons (8 counties)
- ▨ 1,001–10,000 persons (91 counties)
- ▧ 10,001–100,000 persons (121 counties)
- ■ 100,001+ persons (34 counties)

Most Latinos in Texas are Mexican American. During the first half of the twentieth century, Mexicans immigrated to Texas to work in the emerging cotton industry. This 1939 photo shows cotton pickers laboring in the sun over rows of white cotton.

living in Texas. In 2013 there were 9.97 million Latinos residing in Texas. Texas Latinos constituted almost 19 percent of all Latinos in the United States.[32]

Until 1900, Latinos were concentrated in south Texas, constituting a majority along the border with Mexico and in certain border counties of west Texas. During the first few decades of the twentieth century, Latinos migrated to northwest Texas and the Panhandle to work as laborers in the newly emergent cotton economy. Labor segregation limited the opportunities available to many Latinos before World War II. After World War II, however, many Latinos left agricultural work and took jobs in the rapidly growing urban areas of Texas. By the end of the century, Latinos constituted majorities in the cities of San Antonio and El Paso and sizable minorities in Houston, Dallas, Austin, and Fort Worth (see Figure 1.5).

The political status of Latinos in Texas has changed considerably over the past hundred years. In the nineteenth century, numerous obstacles limited their participation in the political life of the state. Voting, particularly among the lower economic classes, was discouraged or tightly controlled. The white-only primary and the **poll tax** actively discouraged voting by Latinos. Only after World War II were Latino politicians able to escape some of the strictures that had been imposed on them by the dominant Anglo political culture of the time. A more tolerant atmosphere in the growing urban areas enabled Latino politicians to assume positions of importance in the local political community. In 1956, Henry B. Gonzalez became the first Mexican American to be elected to the Texas Senate in modern times. In the mid-1960s a political movement emerged in the La Raza Unida Party, which sought to confront many of the discriminatory practices that isolated Texas Latinos

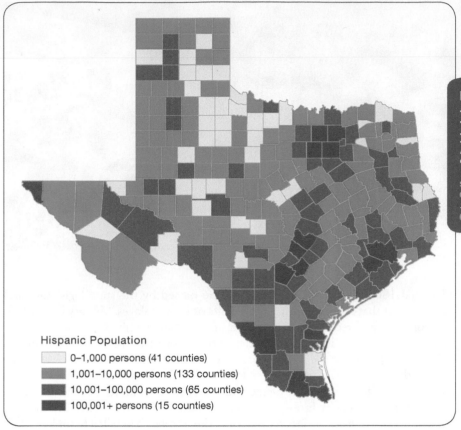

FIGURE 1.5

Hispanic Population in Texas Counties, 2010

SOURCE: Data are drawn from the 2010 Census, Texas State Data Center, www.texastribune.org/library/data/census-2010/ (accessed 6/16/14).

Hispanic Population

☐ 0–1,000 persons (41 counties)

☐ 1,001–10,000 persons (133 counties)

☐ 10,001–100,000 persons (65 counties)

☐ 100,001+ persons (15 counties)

from the political and economic mainstream. By the 1980s, Latino political leaders were playing a growing role in state politics, and Latino voters were courted heavily by both political parties. The number of Latinos elected to public office rose from 1,466 in 1986 to 2,521 in 2011. In 2013 the National Association of Latino Elected and Appointed Officials reported that 1 Latino served in the U.S. Senate from Texas, 6 Latinos represented Texas in the U.S. House of Representatives, 7 Latinos were in the Texas State Senate, and 40 Latinos were elected to the state legislature. In addition, the association reported that 2,477 Latinos served as local officials in Texas.[33]

poll tax a state-imposed tax on voters as a prerequisite for voting; poll taxes were rendered unconstitutional in national elections by the Twenty-Fourth Amendment, and in state elections by the Supreme Court in 1966.

African Americans

People of African descent were among the earliest explorers of Texas.[34] Most African Americans, however, entered Texas as slaves. Anglo Americans from the upper and lower South brought slaves with them to Texas. At first, antislavery attitudes among Spanish and Mexican authorities kept the slave population down. However, independence from Mexico lifted the restrictions on slavery, creating an incentive for southerners to expand the system of slavery westward. The number of slaves in Texas rose from 5,000 in 1830 to 11,000 in 1840 to 58,000 in 1850. By the Civil War, over 182,000 slaves lived in Texas, approximately one-third of the state's entire population.

Emancipation for African Americans living in Texas came on June 19, 1865. Emancipation, however, did not bring anything approaching equality. Between

As in most former slave states, there was initial resistance to the civil rights movement in Texas. These signs appeared in Fort Worth's Riverside section in September 1956 during a protest over a black family's moving into a previously all-white block of homes.

1865 and 1868 a series of Black Codes were passed by the state legislature and various cities that sought to restrict the rights of former slaves. Military occupation and congressional reconstruction opened up new opportunities for former slaves, who supported the radical wing of the Republican Party. Ten African American delegates helped write the Texas Constitution of 1869. Forty-three served as members of the state legislature between 1868 and 1900. The end of Reconstruction and the return to power of the Democratic Party in the mid-1870s reversed much of the progress made by former slaves in the state. In 1900 over 100,000 African Americans voted in Texas elections. By 1903 the number had fallen to under 5,000, largely because of the imposition of the poll tax in 1902 and the passage of an early version of the white-primary law in 1903. In 1923 the legislature explicitly banned blacks from voting in the Democratic primary. Segregation of the races became a guiding principle of public policy, backed by the police power of the state and reinforced by lynching and race riots against African Americans. For all intents and purposes, African Americans had become second-class citizens, disenfranchised by the political system and marginalized by the political culture.

Federal court cases in the 1940s and 1950s offered some hope of relief to African Americans living in Texas. The Supreme Court decision in *Smith v. Allwright* (1944) outlawed the white primary. *Sweatt v. Painter* (1950) guaranteed African Americans admission to Texas's graduate and professional schools. Finally, *Brown v. Board of Education* (1954) outlawed the segregation of public schools.

Political progress was much slower. The Civil Rights Act of 1964 and the Voting Rights Act of 1965 helped to open up the political system in Texas to African Americans. In 1966 a small number of African American candidates actually began to win political office in the state. In 1972, Barbara Jordan became the first African American woman to be elected to the U.S. House of Representatives from Texas.

Today the African American population is concentrated in east Texas, where the southern plantation and sharecropping systems were dominant during the nineteenth century. Large numbers of African Americans had also migrated to form sizable minorities in the urban and suburban areas of Houston and Dallas (see Figure 1.6). African American political leaders have come to play major roles in these areas as members of Congress, the state legislature, and city councils. African Americans were also elected mayors of Houston and Dallas in the late 1990s. The

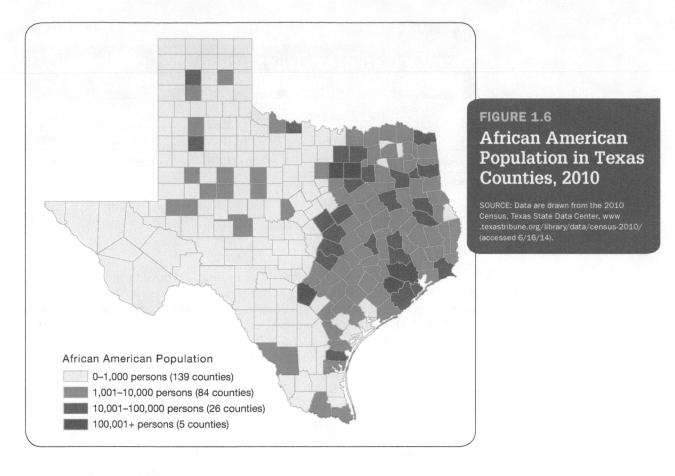

FIGURE 1.6

African American Population in Texas Counties, 2010

SOURCE: Data are drawn from the 2010 Census, Texas State Data Center, www .texastribune.org/library/data/census-2010/ (accessed 6/16/14).

African American Population

- 0–1,000 persons (139 counties)
- 1,001–10,000 persons (84 counties)
- 10,001–100,000 persons (26 counties)
- 100,001+ persons (5 counties)

political influence of African Americans in Texas has not been extended to west Texas, where few African Americans live.

Asians

Although considerably smaller than other groups, the Asian population has grown in Texas in recent years. Asians include individuals from a variety of countries, but particularly India, Vietnam, China, Pakistan, Korea, and Japan. In 2012 the U.S. Census Bureau estimated that approximately 1 million Asians resided in Texas, or about 4.2 percent of the state's population.[35] Asians tend to be concentrated in certain urban areas, particularly in West Houston and Fort Bend County, the western and northern suburbs of Dallas, Arlington, and Travis County. Sizable pockets of Asians are also found scattered along the Gulf Coast.[36]

Age

When compared with the rest of the nation, the population of Texas is relatively young. In 2012, 26.8 percent of the population were estimated to be under 18 years old, compared with 23.5 percent nationally. In addition, only 10.9 percent of the population in Texas were 65 years of age or older, compared with 13.7 percent nationally.[37] Having a relatively young population compared with those of other states presents Texas with a variety of problems and opportunities, as we shall see in later chapters.

for critical analysis

How did the population of Texas change during the 1990s? What is its racial and ethnic composition? How do these changes complicate the idea of the "typical" Texan?

TABLE 1.2

Per Capita Income in Texas and the United States, 1990–2011 (in Nominal Nonadjusted Dollars)

	1990	1995	2006	2011
United States	$19,477	$23,076	$36,276	$41,560
Texas	$17,421	$21,033	$34,257	$40,147

SOURCE: U.S. Department of Commerce, Bureau of Economic Analysis.

Poverty and Wealth

Younger populations tend to be poorer, as income and poverty statistics bear out. As noted above, the 1990s were a period of rapid economic growth in Texas. Despite this growth, however, Texas continued to lag behind the nation as a whole (see Table 1.2). Per capita income in Texas, however, rose from $17,421 in 1990 to $40,147 in 2011. Per capita income in Texas metropolitan areas was considerably higher ($41,035) when compared with Texas rural areas ($33,621). Interestingly, Sutton County, a lightly populated rural county in southwest Texas, had the highest per capita income of $79,103. This seeming anomaly is explained by the fact that it is rich in oil and natural gas. Starr County, in the southeast corner of the state along the Rio Grande, had the lowest at $19,235. Texas ranked 25th among the states in per capita income, up from 32nd in 1990.

The percentage of the population in Texas living below the poverty level—a level established by the federal government—fell from 15.7 percent to 14.9 percent between 1990 and 2004, rose to 16.9 percent in 2006, and rose to 17.9 percent in 2012. During the same period, the national poverty rate fell from 13.5 percent to 11.7 percent, rose to 13.3 percent in 2006, and rose to 15.9 percent in 2012.[38]

● Urbanization

urbanization the process by which people move from rural areas to cities

Describe Texas's shift from a rural society to an urban one

Urbanization is the process by which people move from rural to urban areas. Suburbanization is the process by which people move out of central city areas to surrounding suburban areas. Much of Texas's history is linked to ongoing urbanization. By the first decade of the twenty-first century, this process was largely complete, as 85 percent of the population now reside in urban areas (see Table 1.3). Suburbanization, however, continues as city populations spill over into surrounding suburban areas.[39]

Most Texas cities are the result of American settlement and culture.[40] The Spanish influence on urban life in Texas grew out of efforts to extend territorial control northward out of Mexico through a series of presidios (garrisons), missions (churches), and pueblos (towns). The physical organization and planning of the towns reflected this imperial mission. For example, the largest Spanish settlement was San Antonio. It was initially established as a supply depot to missions in east Texas. Later it expanded

How Is the Texas Population Changing?

The face of Texas is changing rapidly and will continue to change well into the future. The figures below show projections of how the Texas population will change over the next 40 years. The state's population will continue to grow quickly, especially as the number of Hispanic Texans increases. Further, most of the population growth in the state will happen in metropolitan areas—Dallas–Fort Worth, Houston, San Antonio, and Austin.

Race and Total Population

= 250,000 people

	1980			**2010**			**2050**	
White	66%	Latino	21%	White	45%	Latino	38%	White	28%	Latino	54%
African American	12%	Other	1%	African American	12%	Other	6%	African American	10%	Other	8%

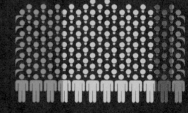

Total population =	14,229,191	25,145,561	41,311,221

Geography (projected population growth from the year 2010, by metropolitan area)

Area	2010	2020		2050	
San Antonio	2,142,508	2,481,286	+16%	3,445,603	+61%
El Paso	804,123	929,478	+16%	1,301,438	+62%
Dallas–Fort Worth	6,426,214	7,445,492	+16%	11,147,784	+73%
Houston	5,920,416	6,934,564	+17%	10,273,617	+74%
Brownsville	406,220	478,974	+18%	729,461	+80%
Austin	1,716,289	2,090,278	+22%	3,338,673	+95%
McAllen	774,769	953,069	+23%	1,589,783	+105%

for critical analysis

1. How do you think the increase in the Latino population will change the nature of Texas politics? Will it change the issues that the state government focuses on? Will it have an impact on what party wins elections in Texas?

2. Texas is traditionally associated with images of farming, ranching, and other elements of rural life. How do you think the growth of the urban population will change the image of Texas?

SOURCES: Texas State Data Center, http://txsdc.utsa.edu/;
Office of State Demographer, http://osd.state.tx.us/ (accessed 5/14/14).

TABLE 1.3

Urbanization in Texas, 1850–2010

	1850	1900	1950	2010
Urban	4%	17%	63%	85%
Rural	96%	83%	37%	15%

SOURCES: *Statistical Abstracts of the United States: 1994* (Washington, DC: U.S. Department of Commerce, Bureau of the Census, 1994); Dallas Morning News, *Texas Almanac 2001–2002* (Dallas: Dallas Morning News, 2001); U.S. Department of Agriculture, Economic Research Service. U.S. Census Bureau, "Texas: 2010, Population and Housing Unit Counts, 2010 Census of Population and Housing" (September 2012), p. 16.

as missions were established to convert local Native Americans to Christianity and farms were cultivated to feed the local population. By the early nineteenth century, San Antonio's population had reached 2,500. Other smaller settlements were located in east Texas, along the border with French and, later, American territory.

White American influence began with the arrival of Moses Austin in 1820 in San Antonio. Soon his son Stephen F. Austin followed. The Spanish offered the Austins and other impresarios grants of land to encourage the inflow of Americans into underpopulated regions of Texas. Small towns emerged as administrative units for impresario grants. There was considerably more freedom and dynamism in American urban areas than in Spanish ones. Americans brought with them a host of new interests and ideas that would transform urban life in Texas, including a new language, slavery, Protestantism, and a commitment to free enterprise and democracy. The courthouse became a central feature of many American towns, often located in the center of the town surrounded by shops.

Urbanization has transformed Texas political life. From Reconstruction through the first 50 years of the twentieth century, Texas's political life grew out of its rural-based economy based on cotton, cattle, oil, and natural gas. Today, urbanization and accompanying suburbanization are the forces driving politics in the state.

The expansion of Texas's urban life initially began along the Gulf Coast and gradually expanded west, particularly along rivers. New technologies transformed the urban landscape of Texas. Dredging technologies helped to stimulate the growth of port cities such as Houston, Galveston, Corpus Christi, and Brownsville. Railroad construction in the second half of the nineteenth century opened up new lands to urban development. In 1880 there were only 11 towns of 4,000 or more people in all of Texas. Following the rapid expansion of the railroads in the 1880s and 1890s, the number rose to 36. By 1910, when the railroad network of 13,110 miles was completed, Texas had 49 towns with a population of 4,000 or more. By 1920, 5 cities—Dallas, El Paso, Fort Worth, Houston, and San Antonio—had populations of more than 50,000. Later technological breakthroughs in transportation, such as cars and air travel, would reinforce the population grid laid out by the railroads.

The Urban Political Economy

Understanding the complexity of the government and politics in Texas today demands having some sense of how Texas's three major metropolitan areas compare with each other (see Tables 1.4 and 1.5).

Immigration in Texas

Immigration has long been an important part of Texas culture. Texas's southern border with Mexico is 1,254 miles long—longer than the border of any of the other states that share a border with Mexico. Prior to 1836 most of Texas was part of Mexico and many people living in the state were of Mexican descent. Even today, many Mexican Americans in the state can trace their lineage back to the time when Mexico controlled Texas. After the terrorist attacks of September 11, the U.S.–Mexico border tightened considerably. Traditionally, residents in border areas could cross the border easily. With increasing border and security concerns, border crossings become more difficult. One of Texas's ongoing debates is over the most effective ways to ensure border security and respect the diversity of the state's history.

In the 2014 campaign for lieutenant governor, Houston state senator Dan Patrick campaigned against the incumbent David Dewhurst by running on a platform of stopping the "illegal invasion" of immigrants into Texas. Patrick emphasized that the federal government was not enforcing border security by allowing so many immigrants into Texas. He further claimed that lack of border security has brought third world diseases into the state. In his campaign he promised to spend more state money on border security since, Patrick claimed, the federal government was not doing its job. Though Lieutenant Governor Dewhurst increased funds for border security, he could not overcome the strong Tea Party influence in the Republican primary and was trounced by Patrick in a runoff on May 27, 2014 by a nearly 2-to-1 margin.

Patrick also gained headlines by debating then San Antonio mayor Julian Castro about immigration reform. Castro accused Patrick of dog whistle politics, that is, appealing to exclusionist and racist rhetoric in order to win the election. Castro argued that there is no "invasion" of immigrants. He said that illegal immigration has dropped from its peak levels and undocumented immigrants are essential to the state's economy. Castro argued that those in the country illegally, especially those in college or serving in the military, should be allowed a path to citizenship. Patrick disagreed, claiming that those in the country illegally should go to the "back of the line" and wait their turns. He also suggested that granting citizenship to illegal immigrants would only encourage more illegal immigration. Patrick opposed "amnesty," the notion of allowing illegal immigrants the opportunity to eventually become U.S. citizens. More illegal immigration, according to Patrick, will strain the state budget on education and health care. Patrick also opposed in-state tuition for undocumented immigrants. He claimed that citizens should be given the priority and illegal immigrants should not have this benefit.

The debate in Texas mirrors the national debate regarding how best to deal with immigration. There are approximately 11 million undocumented or "illegal" immigrants in the United States, and about 2 million of those immigrants are in Texas, mostly of Latino descent and mostly from Mexico. In recent years, the number of undocumented people from Central American countries other than Mexico has grown considerably. In 2014 there was a disturbing development: a significant

The Paso del Norte Bridge between El Paso and Ciudad Juarez is the busiest cross-border footpath between the United States and Mexico.

increase in illegal immigration by children entering the United States without parents.

Some claim Patrick's views will turn off the growing Latino population because the harsh anti-immigrant rhetoric is perceived as anti-Latino. On the other hand, Patrick claimed that he supports legal immigration and just wants to stop illegal immigration. Castro and others have argued that the United States is a nation of immigrants and there must be a comprehensive way to reform the problem. They say that businesses in Texas greatly benefit from the hard work of undocumented immigrants and as long as jobs are available, immigrants will find a way to make it to the United States despite expensive border security efforts. Patrick countered that the border must be secured first before any discussion of how to deal with those in the country illegally takes place. What should Texas do about immigration?

critical thinking questions

1. Do you agree with Dan Patrick or Julian Castro? Should illegal immigrants be given a pathway to citizenship or be sent back to their country of origin?

2. Is compromise possible on immigration? Are the only two options deportations and amnesty?

TABLE 1.4

Populations of the Largest Cities in Texas, 2012

Houston (Harris County)	2,160,821
San Antonio (Bexar County)	1,382,951
Dallas (Dallas County)	1,241,162
Austin (Travis County)	842,592
Fort Worth (Tarrant County)	777,992
El Paso (El Paso County)	672,538

SOURCE: 2012 Estimates from U.S. Census Bureau.

Houston Houston, located in Harris County, is the largest city in Texas and the fourth-largest city in the United States—with a population of 2.1 million—behind New York, Los Angeles, and Chicago. Its consolidated metropolitan area encompasses eight counties, with an estimated population of 6.1 million in 2011. Houston grew by 7.5 percent during the first decade of the twenty-first century.

The city originated in 1836 out of the entrepreneurial dreams of two brothers, Augustus Chapman Allen and John Kirby Allen, who sought to create a "great interior commercial emporium of Texas."[41] The town was named after Sam Houston, the leader of Texas's army during its war of independence from Mexico. Early settlers came from the South, bringing with them the institution of slavery. As a consequence, segregation was built into the social structure from the outset. For the first half of the twentieth century, African Americans were either denied or given limited access to a variety of public services such as parks, schools, buses, restrooms, and restaurants. Although not enforced legally, residential segregation divided the city into a number of distinct racially divided neighborhoods for much of the twentieth century.

In the late nineteenth century, Houston's economic well-being depended on cotton and commerce. Railroads played an integral role in placing Houston at the hub of the Texas economy. The opening of the Houston Ship Channel further enhanced Houston's place in the state economy by helping to turn it into the second or third (depending on whose ranking is used) deep-water port in the United States. But it was oil that fundamentally transformed the Houston area in the twentieth century. Oil refineries opened along the ship channel and a petrochemical industry emerged, making Houston one of the leading energy centers in the world. Today Houston continues to rank first in the nation in the manufacture of petroleum equipment.

By 1930, Houston had become the largest city in Texas, with a population of around 292,000 people. The population continued to expand throughout the 1940s, 1950s, and 1960s, assisted by a liberal annexation policy that enabled the city to incorporate into itself many of the outlying suburban areas. Although the oil bust in the mid-1980s slowed the city's growth, that growth continued in the early twenty-first century, extending into suburban areas such as Clear Lake City and other urban areas such as Galveston.

Dallas–Fort Worth The Metroplex is an economic region encompassing the cities of Dallas and Fort Worth, as well as a number of other suburban cities, including Arlington (population 375,600), Mesquite (139,629), Garland (233,564), Richardson (103,297), Irving (225,427), Plano (272,068), McKinney (143,223), Carrollton (125,409), Grand Prairie (181,824), Frisco (128,176), and Denton (121,123).[42] The major counties in the area are Dallas, Tarrant, and Collin. The Metroplex is joined together by a number of interlocking highways running north–south and east–west, and a major international airport that is strategically located in the national air system.

Dallas was founded as a trading post in 1841, near where two roads were to be built by the Republic.[43] By the 1850s it had become a retail center servicing the rural areas. By 1870 the population had reached 3,000 people. The coming of the Houston and Texas Central Railroad in 1871 and the Texas and Pacific Railroad in 1873 made Dallas the first rail crossroads in Texas and transformed forever its place in the state's economy. Markets now beckoned east and north, encouraging

TABLE 1.5

Race and Ethnic Breakdown of Texas and Its Largest Counties, 2012

	WHITE (%)	BLACK (%)	ASIAN (%)	MULTIPLE RACE (%)	HISPANIC (%)	TOTAL
Texas	44.5%*	12.3%	4.2%	1.7%	38.2%	26,060,796
Harris	32.2	19.5	6.6	1.6	41.5	4,253,963
Dallas	32.2	22.9	5.5	31.7	38.9	2,453,907
Tarrant	50.7	15.6	5.0	2.2	27.4	1,881,445
Bexar	29.8	8.1	2.7	2.1	59.1	1,785,787
Travis	50.1	9.0	6.1	2.3	33.8	1,096,246
Collin	61.8	9.2	12.0	2.4	15.0	834,674
El Paso	13.7	3.9	1.2	1.3	81.2	828,600

*Columns may not add to 100 percent as a result of multiple counting. These are estimates projected from the 2010 Census.
SOURCE: 2010 U.S. Census.

entrepreneurs and merchants to set up shop. Cotton became a major cash crop, and the population expanded over threefold to more than 10,000 people in 1880. By the turn of the twentieth century, the city had grown to more than 42,000 people.

As with Houston, the oil economy changed the direction and scope of the city's economic life. With the discovery of oil in east Texas in 1930, Dallas became a major center for petroleum financing. By the end of World War II, the economy had diversified, making Dallas a minor manufacturing center in the nation. In the 1950s and 1960s technology companies such as Ling-Temco-Vought (LTV) and Texas Instruments were added to the industrial mix, transforming Dallas into the third-largest technology center in the nation. The high-tech boom of the 1990s was built from the corporate infrastructure laid down in the 1950s and 1960s. Dallas grew from 844,401 people in 1970 to 904,078 in 1980 to 1,241,162 in 2012.

Although they are locked together in important ways economically, Dallas and Fort Worth are as different as night and day. Whereas Dallas looks to the East and embodies a more corporate white-collar business culture, Fort Worth looks to the West. It is where the West begins in Texas.

Fort Worth originated as an army post in 1849.[44] By 1853 the post had been abandoned as new forts were located to the west. Although settlers took the fort over, population growth was slow through the early 1870s. The spark that enabled the town to begin to prosper was the rise of the cattle industry. Fort Worth was a convenient place for cowboys to rest on their cattle drives to Kansas. Cattle buyers established headquarters in the city. Gradually other businesses grew up around these key businesses. Transportation and communication links improved with the establishment of stage lines to the west and railroad lines to the north and east.

By 1900, Fort Worth was served by eight different railroad companies, many of them transporting cattle and cattle-related products to national markets. The two world wars encouraged further economic development in Fort Worth. Over 100,000 troops were trained at Camp Bowie during World War I. World War II brought an important air force base and, along with it, the aviation industry. The Consolidated Vultee Aircraft Corporation, which was later bought by General Dynamics, became the largest manufacturing concern in the city. Between 1900 and 1950 the population grew from 26,668 to 277,047. In 2012, Fort Worth's population was 777,992. The overall metropolitan area of Dallas–Fort Worth included 6.7 million people in 2011.

San Antonio San Antonio is located in Bexar County, the fourth-largest county in Texas today. San Antonio grew out of the Spanish presidio San Antonio de Bexar, which was founded in 1718.[45] In 1773 it became the capital of Spanish Texas, with a population of around 2,100 people. Because of the threats posed by Native Americans and Mexicans after the Texas Revolution, the population declined to about 800 people by 1846. On Texas's entry into the Union, however, the population took off, reaching 3,488 in 1850 and 8,235 in 1860. By the Civil War, San Antonio was the largest city in Texas.

Following the Civil War, San Antonio grew rapidly, stimulated by the building of the San Antonio Railroad in 1877. By 1880 the population had grown to more than 20,000 people, mostly Anglo Americans from southern states. The population continued to grow through the first two decades of the twentieth century, reaching 161,000 by 1920. Mexican immigration increased significantly following the Mexican Revolution of 1910 and the building of a city infrastructure that provided paved roads, utilities, water, telephones, and hospitals. By midcentury San Antonio had become a unique blend of Latino, German, and southern Anglo American cultures. Population growth slowed down in the 1930s but picked up again during World War II, reaching over 408,000 in 1950. Major military bases came to dot the landscape around San Antonio. By 1960 the population topped 587,000 people.

Today, San Antonio is Texas's second-largest city. The population of the city was estimated to be 1,382,951 in 2012, and the San Antonio metropolitan area as a whole had a population of 2,234,003, making it the thirty-first-largest metropolitan area in the country. San Antonio's population has become increasingly Hispanic. Approximately 63.2 percent of the people are Hispanic, 29 percent are Anglo American, and 6 percent are African American.[46]

Unlike Houston or Dallas, San Antonio lacks high-paying manufacturing jobs, and average metropolitan income is lower than in Houston and Dallas. The economy rests on four legs: national military bases, educational institutions, tourism, and a large medical research complex.

In some areas of Texas, Asian immigrants are a growing force. The signs behind Charles Park, president of the Asian District Development Association of Dallas, at the Asiana Plaza in Dallas attest to the changing demographic landscape of Texas.

for critical analysis

Based on the population growth, urbanization, and economic change of the last two decades, what do the next two decades hold for Texas? Which areas will grow in population, and will government be ready for that growth? What can or should government do to maintain and strengthen the economy of Texas?

● Thinking Critically about Texas's Political Culture

In this chapter, we have studied the political culture of Texas and seen how the state has been transformed by economic and demographic shifts over the past hundred years. Three great technological revolutions have reshaped the economic life of the state. The first—based on the production of agricultural products such as cotton and cattle and on the newly built railroad system—defined economic life in the latter decades of the nineteenth and early twentieth centuries. The second—based on the production of oil and the industries that oil made possible—dominated the economy well into the second half of the twentieth century. The third—the era of high tech—has transformed the state by diversifying its economy and tying it closely to the growing international economy. Accompanying and fueling these economic revolutions have been ongoing demographic changes, which have redefined who the "typical"

How Does Texas's Population Compare to Other Major States'?

Texas is more diverse than many states in the country, which has important implications for the future of the state's politics. Also, the Texas population has increased dramatically, while some states are not growing as fast. In fact many states in the Midwest such as Ohio and Pennsylvania have seen population declines in recent years.

Racial Diversity

Texas		California		Florida		New York		Ohio	
White	45%	White	40%	White	59%	White	57%	White	81%
Black	12%	Black	6%	Black	15%	Black	14%	Black	12%
Hispanic	38%	Hispanic	39%	Hispanic	22%	Hispanic	18%	Hispanic	3%
Other	4%	Other	15%	Other	4%	Other	10%	Other	4%

Percentage Change in Population by County, 2000–10

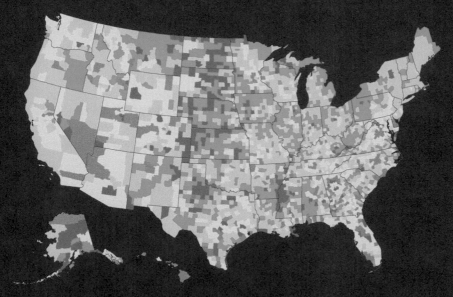

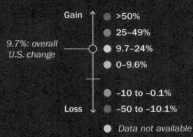

9.7%: overall U.S. change

Gain ↑
● >50%
● 25–49%
● 9.7–24%
● 0–9.6%

● –10 to –0.1%
Loss ↓ ● –50 to –10.1%
○ *Data not available*

for critical analysis

1. In what ways are California and Texas similar in terms of demographic makeup? How are they different?

2. In what ways will Texas politics change in the future based on its racial and ethnic makeup?

SOURCE: U.S. Census Current Population Survey, www.census.gov (accessed 5/14/14).

As immigration has changed the demographic profile of Texas, it has also given rise to numerous political debates. Here, protesters for immigration reform rally in San Antonio outside a hotel where U.S. Speaker of the House John Boehner held a fundraiser.

Texan is and where this person lives. No longer can it be said that a "typical" Texan is simply an extension of white American culture rooted in southern tradition. No longer does this person reside in a small town, living life close to the land much as his or her ancestors did. Like the economy, the people of Texas have been diversified. Increasing numbers of Latinos from Mexico and whites from other parts of the United States have created a new melting pot of cultures and concerns throughout the state. These cultures have come together in the big metropolitan areas across Texas.

As we have seen in this chapter, the majority of Texans today continue to view government and politics in Texas through the lens of a political culture dominated by both traditionalistic and individualistic values. There is a tendency in the political culture to defer to leaders in positions of authority. But this deferential politics is checked by a healthy suspicion of giving too much power to those in authority. As a result, in Texas, government is often perceived as something that gets in the way of our individual liberty rather than something through which we accomplish collective objectives.

Two notions of equality also play important roles in the political culture of Texas. First, there is the idea of equality of opportunity. This aspect of equality is deeply rooted in Texas's traditional individualistic political culture. The job of government is to treat individuals fairly and to ensure them a fair chance to make it on their own through their own skills and initiative. Few Texans believe that it is the task of state government to redistribute resources from the rich to the poor, ensuring some equality of result.

In addition to equality of opportunity, political equality has been an issue in Texas politics, with the growing importance of African American and Latino minorities in the state. Debates over the meaning of equal participation and representation at all levels of state government have reshaped the broad contours of political life in Texas and given rise to one of the bitterest and most controversial issues to face the state legislature in recent decades: congressional and legislative redistricting.

The ideals of democratic self-government are enshrined in various constitutions under which Texas has operated since the days of the Republic. The people are formally given a number of important roles to play in the political process, including choosing the members of all three branches of government and approving constitutional amendments. As we will see, however, the actual operations of state government and politics tend to work in seemingly undemocratic ways. Arcane rules in the legislative and executive branches allow power to concentrate in the hands of a few individuals. Elections of judges politicize their selection in a way unimaginable in national politics. Well-funded special-interest groups have been able to exert their influence on elections in Texas and to penetrate the legislative process. The rise to power of the Republican Party in the state may be best understood as the triumph of a new set of interests that have successfully displaced those attached to the traditional Democratic Party.

Texans in general and Texas political leaders in particular may be committed to the idea of democracy. The Texas Constitution may enshrine the values of democratic self-government. As we will see, however, the actual operations of Texas politics and government raise serious questions about what kind of democracy the state really is. The tension between the ideal and reality of democracy in Texas may come to play an important role in restructuring the political system as it responds to ongoing economic and demographic change in the state.

for critical analysis

In Texas political culture, governmental power is often seen as a threat to individual liberty. However, Texans also tend to value equality of opportunity and political equality for all citizens. To what extent should the Texas state government use its power to ensure equality?

Texas Political Culture

Describe the defining characteristics of political culture in Texas (pp. 5–7)

Texas political culture can best be characterized as individualistic and traditional. Texans have great pride in their state and have adopted a famous phrase, "Don't mess with Texas," for those external forces wishing to change the state's way of doing things. Texas is a low-tax state with distrust for large government programs. Business plays a major role in defining the political culture of the state.

Key Terms

political culture (p. 5)

moralistic political culture (p. 5)

individualistic political culture (p. 5)

traditionalistic political culture (p. 5)

elite (p. 6)

provincialism (p. 6)

Practice Quiz

1. In terms of area, how does Texas rank among the 50 states?
   a) first
   b) second
   c) third
   d) fifth
   e) seventh

2. *Provincialism* refers to
   a) a narrow view of the world.
   b) a progressive view of the value of diversity.
   c) a pro-business political culture.
   d) an urban society.
   e) a group of counties.

The Land

Explain how Texas's geography has influenced its political culture (pages 7–9)

Because of Texas's immense size, the state's topography is diverse, with east Texas's flat lands, west Texas's arid climate, and central Texas's hill country all representing diverse ecosystems and land patterns.

Practice Quiz

3. Which of Texas's physical regions is characterized by the presence of many of the state's largest ranches?
   a) Gulf Coastal Plains
   b) Great Plains
   c) Interior Lowlands
   d) Basin and Range Province
   e) Rio Grande Valley

4. Which of Texas's physical regions is found in the western-most part of Texas?
   a) Gulf Coastal Plains
   b) Great Plains
   c) Interior Lowlands
   d) Basin and Range Province
   e) Pine Belt

Economic Change in Texas

The Texas economy has undergone a series of technological transformations over the past 100 years. Once the Texas economy was grounded in cotton and ranching. Oil production came to play an important role in the twentieth century. Today, high technology and international trade play important roles in the state's economy. Texas appears to have weathered the Great Recession better than most other states.

Key Term

North American Free Trade Agreement (NAFTA) (p. 17)

Practice Quiz

5. Creative destruction
   a) destroys both old and new economies.
   b) creates new economies and destroys old ones.
   c) maintains old economies and creates new ones.
   d) creates and maintains old and new economies.
   e) does not affect economies.

6. Which industry controlled the politics and economy of Texas for most of the twentieth century?
   a) cotton
   b) cattle
   c) railroad
   d) oil
   e) technology

7. Which of the following statements is true?
   a) Oil production in Texas is smaller today than it was 10 years ago.
   b) Oil production no longer plays an important role in the state's economy.
   c) Oil has been almost totally drained from Texas oil fields.
   d) The Dallas–Fort Worth region has become a major producer of oil in the early twenty-first century.
   e) Fracking and horizontal drilling have reinvigorated Texas's oil industry.

8. Unlike earlier eras, the Texas economy of the twenty-first century features
   a) computers, electronics, and other high-tech products.
   b) transportation, oil and natural gas, and banking.
   c) insurance, construction, and banking.
   d) ranching, oil, and tourism.
   e) education, the military, and agriculture.

9. NAFTA refers to
   a) an oil company.
   b) an independent regulatory commission.
   c) an interstate road network.
   d) an interest group.
   e) an international trade agreement.

10. What is meant by the "Great Recession"?
    a) the post–Vietnam War era in the mid-1970s when housing prices rose
    b) the period of high inflation during the early 1980s
    c) a time of chronic economic problems beginning in late 2007 that drew analogies to the Great Depression of the 1930s
    d) the time when Democrats lost control of the Texas House for the first time since Reconstruction
    e) a period of high unemployment in the early 1990s

The People of Texas

Texas demography has changed over the last century. Once dominated by whites, Texas now has a large Latino population that, when coupled with the African American population and other minorities, now makes Texas a majority-minority state. Despite considerable overall wealth in Texas, Texans tend to be younger and poorer than the average American.

Key Terms

impresario (p. 20)

poll tax (p. 22)

Practice Quiz

11. Which of the following accounts for most of Texas's population growth?
    a) immigration
    b) natural increases as a result of the difference between births and deaths
    c) domestic immigration
    d) NAFTA
    e) movement from rural to urban areas

12. Which of the following is not true?
    a) Latinos are increasing as a percentage of the population in Dallas.
    b) More African Americans live in east Texas than west Texas.
    c) San Antonio has a larger white population than Latino.
    d) Houston's largest minority population is Latino.
    e) The Latino population in Texas has grown rapidly in recent decades.

Urbanization

Describe Texas's shift from a rural society to an urban one (pp. 26–32)

Initially a rural state, Texas has urbanized, with Houston, San Antonio, and Dallas–Fort Worth representing the largest metropolitan areas in the state. This process of urbanization has changed the state's economy from an agricultural powerhouse to a high-tech and innovative economy.

Key Term
urbanization (p. 26)

Practice Quiz

13. *Urbanization* refers to a process in which
    a) people move from rural to urban areas.
    b) people from the north and west move to Texas.
    c) people move out of urban centers to the suburbs.
    d) people move out of urban centers to rural areas.
    e) minorities assume political control of a city.

14. The three major metropolitan areas in Texas are
    a) Houston, Dallas–Fort Worth, and San Antonio.
    b) Houston, Dallas–Fort Worth, and El Paso.
    c) El Paso, Houston, and Austin.
    d) San Antonio, El Paso, and Brownsville-Harlingen-McAllen.
    e) San Antonio, El Paso, and Houston.

Recommended Websites

Business QuickFacts
http://quickfacts.census.gov/qfd/states/48000.html

Federal Reserve Bank of Texas
http://dallasfed.org/index.cfm

Handbook of Texas
www.tshaonline.org/handbook/online/

Office of the Governor, Economic Development and Tourism, Business and Industry Data Center
www.governor.state.tx.us/ecodev/divisions/bidc/

Texas Almanac
www.texasalmanac.com

Texas State Data Center and Office of the State Demographer
www.txsdc.utsa.edu

Amendments to the Texas Constitution originate in the House of Representatives and then go to voters for approval. Here, Texas Speaker of the House Joe Straus strikes the gavel as the Texas House votes to pass a proposed constitutional amendment that would boost spending for roads and bridges.

The Texas Constitution

WHY THE TEXAS CONSTITUTION MATTERS The Texas Constitution is the legal framework within which government works in Texas just as the U.S. Constitution is the legal framework for our national institutions. Perhaps even more than the U.S. Constitution, the Texas Constitution has an immediate and enormous impact on the everyday lives of Texans. There are rights guaranteed to Texans in Article 1 of the Texas Constitution that go far beyond those of the U.S. Constitution, addressing issues related to Texans' private lives. For example, Article 1, Section 7, stipulates that no money will be appropriated or drawn from the treasury that benefits a sect, religious society, or religious seminary. Section 7 clearly lists the conditions that must be met by the state if it wants to take, damage, or destroy the private property of individuals. Section 30 provides a detailed list of the rights that the victims of crime have, including the right to be treated with dignity and privacy in the criminal process and a right to confer with representatives of the prosecutor's office. Section 31 narrowly defines a marriage as consisting "only of the union of one man and one woman." Section 33 guarantees Texans a right to access and use public beaches. One could argue that each of these cases is more a matter of policy preference than constitutional right. By placing these in the Bill of Rights of the Texas Constitution, particular policy positions take on a protected status. It is more difficult to change a right enshrined in the Texas Constitution than it is to change a policy backed by statutory law.

Given the length and detail of the Texas Constitution, the amendment process assumes a central role in the political process. Every few years, the Texas Legislature presents to the voters a list of proposed amendments to the state constitution. There are some important differences between the amending process for the Texas Constitution and the U.S. Constitution. For example, voter approval is necessary for the amendments to the Texas Constitution to take effect. Moreover, since 1789 there have been only 27 amendments to the U.S. Constitution but 483 amendments to the Texas Constitution as of 2013. In 2009, 10 amendments were proposed by the state legislature and approved by voters. In 2011, 10 amendments were proposed and passed. In 2013, 9 amendments were proposed and passed.

Occasionally amendments deal with overall structural issues of government. In 1979, for example, an amendment passed giving the governor limited authority to remove appointed statewide officials. In 1995 a constitutional amendment passed that abolished the office of the state treasurer, placing its duties in the Texas Comptroller's Office. In such cases, amendments to the Texas Constitution function like those to the U.S. Constitution. At other times, though, the amendments to the Texas Constitution are a far cry from those of the U.S. Constitution. There are many more amendments to the Texas Constitution that have dealt with technical problems in the constitution, reflecting efforts to clean up specific language in the state constitution that was now out of date. In 2007 an amendment passed that eliminated the county Office of the Inspector of Hides and Animals.[1] The office had been effectively vacated with the passage of a new Agricultural Code that eliminated the office in law.[2] But the constitution needed to be brought up to date with the law. In 2013, Proposition 2 eliminated language relating to a State Medical and Education Board and a State Medical Education Fund, neither of which were operational.

Other amendments to the Texas Constitution grapple with pressing policy matters. Interestingly, the electorate is asked to give its approval of certain policy initiatives directly through the amendment process, something that is inconceivable at the national level. In 2009 amendments were passed protecting private property from certain private property takings by the state through eminent domain, establishing a National Research University Fund, and allowing members of emergency service districts to serve for four years. In 2011 amendments were passed allowing the Texas Water Development Board to issue bonds so that loans could be given to local governments for water projects and granting the City of El Paso more borrowing authority. Among the amendments passed in 2013, Amendment 6 provided for the creation of two funds to help finance important water projects in the future. Without the passage of these amendments by the electorate, effective public policy in a variety of areas central to the future of Texas would have ground to a halt. Far more than the U.S. Constitution, the Texas Constitution is involved with the nuts and bolts of public policy and must be taken into account frequently by Texas legislators seeking to address problems in new and innovative ways.

Much criticism has been lodged against the Texas Constitution as being a cumbersome document that fails to meet the needs of a modern dynamic state. Yet efforts to introduce a fundamental reform of the constitutional system of government in Texas have floundered, leaving politicians the unenviable task of bringing the constitution up to date in a piecemeal manner. The Texas Constitution remains a document much disparaged and not well understood by the population as a whole.

chaptergoals

- Identify the main functions of state constitutions (pp. 41–42)
- Describe the six Texas constitutions that preceded the current constitution (pp. 43–53)
- Explain the circumstances that led to the Texas Constitution that is still in use today (pp. 54–55)
- Analyze the major provisions of the Texas Constitution today (pp. 55–62)
- Describe modern efforts to change the Texas Constitution (pp. 63–73)

The Role of a State Constitution

Identify the main functions of state constitutions

State **constitutions** perform a number of important functions. They legitimate state political institutions by clearly explaining the source of their power and authority. State constitutions also delegate power, explaining which powers are granted to particular institutions and individuals and how those powers are to be used. They prevent the concentration of political power by providing political mechanisms that check and balance the powers of one political institution or individual officeholder against another. Finally, they define the limits of political power. Through declarations of rights, state constitutions explicitly forbid the intrusion of certain kinds of governmental activities into the lives of individuals.

constitution the legal structure of a government, which establishes its power and authority as well as the limits on that power

The idea of constitutional government in Texas since its first constitution has been heavily indebted to the larger American experience. Five ideas unite the U.S. and Texas constitutional experiences. First, political power in both the United States and Texas is ultimately derived from the people. The Preamble to the U.S. Constitution begins with the clear assertion that it is "We the People of the United States" that ordains and establishes the Constitution. Echoing these sentiments, the Preamble to the Texas Constitution proclaims that "the People of the State of Texas, do ordain and establish this Constitution." In both documents, political power is something that is artificially created through the constitution by a conscious act of the people.

Second, the U.S. and Texas constitutions feature **separation of powers**. The legislative, executive, and judicial branches of government have their own unique powers derived from the people. Each branch has its corresponding duties and obligations.

separation of powers the division of governmental power among several institutions that must cooperate in decision making

Third, the U.S. and Texas constitutions structure political power in such a way that the power of one branch is checked and balanced by the power of the other two branches. The idea of **checks and balances** reflects a common concern among the framers of the U.S. Constitution and the authors of Texas's various constitutions that the intent of writing a constitution was not just to establish effective governing institutions. Its purpose was also to create political institutions that would not tyrannize the very people who established them. In this theory of checks and balances, both the U.S. and Texas constitutions embody the ideas articulated by James Madison in *The Federalist Papers*, nos. 10, 47, and 51. There Madison argued that one of the most effective ways of preventing **tyranny** (the concentration of power in one branch) was to pit the self-interest of officeholders in one branch against the self-interest of officeholders in the other branches. Good intentions alone would not guarantee liberty in either the United States or Texas. Rather, constitutional means combined with self-interest would ensure that officeholders had an interest in preserving a balance among the different branches of government.

checks and balances the constitutional idea that overlapping power is given to different branches of government to limit the concentration of power in any one branch

tyranny according to James Madison, the concentration of power in any one branch of government

The concern for preventing the emergence of tyranny is also found in a fourth idea that underlies the U.S. and Texas constitutions: the idea of individual rights. Government is explicitly forbidden to violate a number of particular rights that the people possess. Some rights, such as freedom of speech, freedom of assembly, and freedom of religion, are guaranteed by both the U.S. Constitution and the Texas Constitution. Interesting, the Texas Constitution also guarantees other rights not found in the U.S. Constitution, such as certain victims' rights and the right to have an "efficient system of public free schools." In this the Texas Constitution can be seen as guaranteeing a broader set of rights than the U.S. Constitution.

The final idea embodied in both the U.S. and Texas constitutions is that of **federalism**. Federalism is the division of government into a central government and a series of regional governments (see Chapter 3). Both kinds of government exercise direct authority over individual citizens of the United States and of each particular state. Article IV, Section 4, of the U.S. Constitution guarantees that every state in the Union will have a "Republican Form of Government." Curiously, no attempt is made to explain what exactly a "Republican Form of Government" entails. The Tenth Amendment to the U.S. Constitution also recognizes the importance of the idea of federalism to the American political system. It reads, "The powers not delegated to the United States by the Constitution, nor prohibited by it to the States, are reserved to the States respectively, or to the people." According to the U.S. Constitution, enormous reservoirs of political power are thus derived from the people who reside in the states themselves.

However, some important differences distinguish the constitutional experience of Texas from that of the United States. Most important is the subordinate role that Texas has in the federal system. Article VI of the U.S. Constitution contains the **supremacy clause**, declaring the Constitution and the laws of the United States to be "the supreme Law of the Land." The supremacy clause requires all judges in every state to be bound by the U.S. Constitution, notwithstanding the laws or constitution of their particular state. In matters of disagreement, the U.S. Constitution thus takes precedence over the Texas Constitution. One of the major issues of the Civil War was how the federal system was to be understood. Was the United States a confederation of autonomous sovereign states that were ultimately independent political entities capable of secession (much like the current European Union)? Was the United States a perpetual union of states that were ultimately in a subordinate relationship to the central government? The results of the war and the ratification of the Fourteenth Amendment in 1868 ultimately resolved this question in terms of the latter. The idea that the United States was a perpetual union composed of subordinate states would have profound implications for constitutional government in Texas throughout the late nineteenth and twentieth centuries. The incorporation of the Bill of Rights through the Fourteenth Amendment, which made much of the Bill of Rights apply to the states, became a dominant theme of constitutional law in the twentieth century. The Fourteenth Amendment effectively placed restrictions on Texas government and public policy that went far beyond those laid out in Texas's own constitution.

Another major difference between the U.S. and Texas constitutions lies in the **necessary and proper clause** of Article I, Section 8. Section 8 begins by listing in detail the specific powers granted to Congress by the Constitution. The Founders apparently wanted to limit the scope of national government activities. But Section 8 concludes by granting Congress the power necessary to accomplish its constitutional tasks. The net effect of this clause was to provide a constitutional basis for an enormous expansion of central government activities over the next 200-plus years.

Drafters of Texas's various constitutions generally have been unwilling to grant such an enormous loophole in the exercise of governmental power. Although granting state government the power to accomplish certain tasks, Texas constitutions have generally denied officeholders broad grants of discretionary power to accomplish their goals.

federalism a system of government in which power is divided, by a constitution, between a central government and regional governments

supremacy clause Article VI of the U.S. Constitution, which states that the Constitution and laws passed by the national government and all treaties are the supreme law of the land and superior to all laws adopted by any state or any subdivision

necessary and proper clause Article I, Section 8, of the U.S. Constitution; it provides Congress with the authority to make all laws "necessary and proper" to carry out its powers

The First Texas Constitutions

Describe the six Texas constitutions that preceded the current constitution

Many myths surround the origins of Texas as a state. Some trumpet its unique origins as an independent republic that fought to attain its own independence from an oppressive regime much like the United States did. Others suggest that Texas has a certain privileged position as a state given the way that it entered the Union or that it reserved for itself a right to break up into separate states or even to leave the Union. To separate the myth from the reality, it is necessary to understand the Founding of Texas out of its war of independence with Mexico and its subsequent constitutional development.

Texas has operated under seven constitutions, one when it was part of a state under the Mexican political regime prior to Independence, one as an independent republic, one as a member of the Confederacy, and four as a state in the United States. Each was shaped by historical developments of its time and, following the first constitution, attempted to address the shortcomings of each previous constitution. In this section, we look at the six Texas constitutions that preceded the current constitution.

The Texas Founding

Political scientists refer to "the Founding" as that period in American history when the foundational principles of American political life were established, roughly the period of time from the Declaration of Independence in 1776 through the ratification of the Constitution (1790) and the Bill of Rights (1791). Texas has a founding period, but one that is much longer and more convoluted.

In the mid-eighteenth century, the American colonies had been part of a larger constitutional regime, the British Empire. Following the French and Indian War, the colonies found themselves under increasing centralized control from London, including the imposition of various unpopular taxes like the Stamp Tax. Resistance to this centralized control led to growing political tensions between Britain and the colonies, culminating in armed confrontations at Lexington and Concord. The Declaration of Independence, the Articles of Confederation, and the writing of new state constitutions along with the Treaty of Paris signaled the break with Britain and the emergence of the United States as a confederated republic, that is, a group of largely independent states joined together by a weak national organization. The inability of the Articles of Confederation to provide a strong and effective central government following the American Revolution gave rise to calls for the Constitutional Convention that met in Philadelphia in 1787 to draft the document that became the U.S. Constitution.

On the face of it, Texas's road to independence appears to mirror that of the United States. Like the United States, Texas had a period of discontent with the governing regime that culminated in a Declaration of Independence. This document cataloged grievances against Mexico and announced the establishment of a new Republic of Texas. But whereas Britain was a stable and powerful empire in the mid-eighteenth century, Mexico was not. Mexico had only recently freed itself from Spain and was experiencing a lengthy period of domestic turmoil. In addition, while the American colonies had been effective self-governing entities before the

Declaration of Independence, Texas was not. The Texas Founding encompassed a number of phases of constitutional government. These phases stretched from 1836 when Texas declared itself an independent republic to 1876 when reconstruction after the Civil War came to an end and a new state constitution was put into place.

The Constitution of Coahuila y Tejas, 1827 Despite the growing fears of American expansionism following the Louisiana Purchase, in 1803 Spanish Texas was still sparsely populated. In 1804 the population of Spanish Texas was estimated to be 3,605. In 1811, Juan Bautista de las Casas launched the first revolt against Spanish rule in San Antonio. The so-called Casas Revolt was successfully put down by the summer of 1811. The next year, a second challenge to Spanish rule took place along the border between Texas and the United States. After capturing Nacogdoches, La Bahia, and San Antonio, rebel forces under José Bernardo Gutiérrez de Lara issued a declaration of independence from New Spain and drafted a constitution. By 1813, however, this revolt had also been put down, and bloody reprisals had depopulated the state. Texas remained part of New Spain until the Mexican War of Independence.[3]

The Mexican War of Independence grew out of a series of revolts against Spanish rule during the Napoleonic Wars. Burdened by debts brought on by a crippling war with France, Spain sought to extract more wealth from its colonies. The forced abdication of Ferdinand VII in favor of Napoleon's brother Joseph in 1808 and an intensifying economic crisis in New Spain in 1809 and 1810 undermined the legitimacy of Spanish rule. Revolts broke out in Guanajuato and spread throughout Mexico and its Texas province. Although these rebellions were initially put down

This 1844 cartoon satirized congressional opposition to the annexation of Texas. Personified as a beautiful young woman, Texas is holding a cornucopia filled with flowers. Though James K. Polk, elected to the presidency in 1844, welcomes Texas, the Whig Party leader Senator Henry Clay, with arms folded, warns, "Stand back, Madam Texas! For we are more holy than thou! Do you think we will have anything to do with gamblers, horse-racers, and licentious profligates?"

by royalist forces loyal to Spain, by 1820 local revolts and guerrilla actions had helped to weaken continued royal rule from Spain. On August 24, 1821, Mexico was formally granted independence by Spain.

Because Texas was part of Mexico, the first federal constitution that it operated under was the Mexican Constitution. At the national level, there were two houses of Congress. The lower house was composed of deputies serving two-year terms. In the upper house, senators served four-year terms and were selected by state legislatures. The president and vice president were elected for four-year terms by the legislative bodies of the states. There was a supreme court, composed of 11 judges, and an attorney general. Although the Mexican Constitution mandated separate legislative, executive, and judicial branches, no attempt was made to define the scope of states' rights in the Mexican confederation. Local affairs remained independent of the central government. Although the Mexican Constitution embodied many of the ideas found in the U.S. Constitution, there was one important difference: Catholicism was established as the state religion and was supported financially by the state.[4]

Under the Mexican Constitution of 1824, the state of Coahuila and the sparsely populated province of Texas were combined into the state of Coahuila and Texas. Saltillo, Mexico, was the capital. More than two years were spent drafting a constitution for the new state. It was finally published on March 11, 1827.

The state was formally divided into three separate districts, with Texas composing the District of Bexar. Legislative power for the state was placed in a **unicameral** legislature composed of 12 deputies elected by the people. The people of the District of Bexar (Texas) elected 2 of these. Along with wide-ranging legislative powers, the legislature was also empowered to elect state officials when no majority emerged from the popular vote, to serve as a grand jury in political and military matters, and to regulate the army and militia. Executive power was vested in a governor and a vice governor, each elected by the people for a four-year term. Judicial power was placed in state courts. The Constitution of 1827 formally guaranteed citizens the right to liberty, security, property, and equality. Language in the Constitution of 1827 also supported efforts to curtail the spread of slavery, an institution of vital importance to planters who were immigrating from the American South. The legislature was ordered to promote education and freedom of the press. As in the Mexican federal constitution, Catholicism was the established state religion.[5]

unicameral comprising one body or house, as in a one-house legislature

The Constitution of the Republic of Texas, 1836

Texas's break with Mexico was in large part a constitutional crisis that culminated in separation. Americans had come to Texas for a variety of reasons. Some, like Stephen F. Austin, had come to Texas in the service of the Mexican state as *empresarios*, individuals whose goal was to encourage immigration into Texas from America through the distribution of land made available by the Mexican government. They saw themselves as Mexican citizens working with the constitutional regime of 1827. There were other American immigrants who came to Texas as part of America's move westward. They were far less committed to integrating themselves into the Mexican political community. For these people, independence from Mexico either as an independent Republic or as part of the United States was the ultimate political objective.

Recognizing the dangers to Mexican authority by Americans coming into Texas, Mexican officials made various attempts to limit the influx of new American immigrants. These restrictions, along with other grievances, led to growing discontent among Texans over their place in the Mexican federal system. Ultimately,

Texans called for political conventions in 1832 and 1833 to discuss new constitutional forms of government. Along with demands for a more liberal immigration policy for people from the United States and for the establishment of English- and Spanish-speaking primary schools, calls for separate statehood for Texas emerged from the conventions. The 1833 convention actually drafted a constitution for this newly proposed state modeled on the Massachusetts Constitution of 1780. Stephen F. Austin's attempt to bring the proposed constitution to the attention of the central government in Mexico City led to his imprisonment, which in turn pushed Texas closer to open rebellion against the central Mexican government.

On November 7, 1835, a declaration was adopted by a meeting of state political leaders at San Felipe, which stated the reasons Texans were beginning to take up arms against the Mexican government. The declaration proclaimed that Texas was rising up in defense of its rights and liberties as well as the republican principles articulated in the Mexican Constitution of 1824. It was one thing to call for a defense of republican principles under the Mexican Constitution of 1824; it was something else to call for separation from Mexico; and it was something else again to advocate separation from Mexico followed by union with the United States. In the end, the declaration was but a prelude to the formal Texas Declaration of Independence that emerged out of the Convention of 1836 held at Washington-on-the-Brazos.

Of the 59 delegates attending the Convention of 1836, only 10 had lived in Texas prior to 1830. Two had arrived as late as 1836. Thirty-nine of the delegates were from southern slave states, 6 were from the border state of Kentucky, 7 were from northern states, 3 were from Mexico (including 2 born in Texas), and 4 were from other English-speaking lands.[6] The final products of the convention—the Texas Declaration of Independence and the Constitution of 1836—reflected the interests and values of these participants.

In their own Declaration of Independence, delegates to the convention proclaimed that the federal constitutional regime they had been invited to live under by the rulers of Mexico had been replaced by a military tyranny that combined a "despotism of the sword and the priesthood." Echoing the American Declaration of Independence, they presented a long list of grievances against the central government, including the failure to provide freedom of religion, a system of public education, and trial by jury.

The Texas Declaration of Independence Like the Founders during the American Revolution, leaders of the Texas Revolution felt they needed to justify their actions in print. Written by George C. Childress and adopted by the general convention at Washington-on-the-Brazos on March 2, 1836, the Texas Declaration of Independence stated why it was necessary to separate from Mexico and create an independent republic. Not surprisingly, the document draws heavily on the ideas of John Locke and Thomas Jefferson for inspiration. The description of the role of the government, "to protect the lives, liberty, and property of the people," repeated verbatim Locke's litany of the primary reasons for establishing government. Like Jefferson's Declaration, Texas's declaration catalogs a list of grievances against the Mexican regime. According to Texas's declaration, the existing government had abdicated its duties to protect the governed and had broken the trustee relationship that binds a people to those in authority. By dissolving civil society into its original elements, the government had forced the people to assert their inalienable right of self-preservation and to take political affairs into their own hands again. The "melancholy conclusion" of Texas's declaration echoed ideas that Locke and

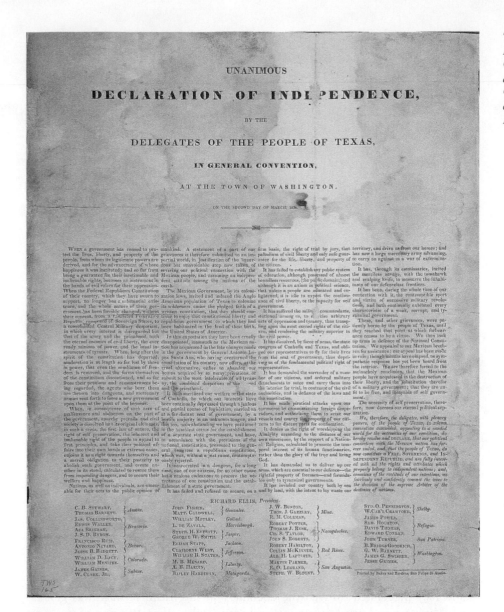

The Texas Declaration of Independence was written by George C. Childress and adopted at the Convention of 1836. Childress modeled the document on the American Declaration of Independence (see Appendix).

Jefferson would have understood well: any government that stripped a people of their liberty was unacceptable to those raised on principles of self-government. Self-preservation demanded "eternal political separation" from the very state (Mexico) that had invited them to settle in Texas (see Figure 2.1).

After declaring Texas a separate republic independent from Mexico, the convention proceeded to draft and pass a new constitution reflecting these republican sentiments. Resembling the U.S. Constitution in being brief and flexible (fewer than 6,500 words), the 1836 Constitution established an elected chief executive with considerable powers, a **bicameral** legislature, and a four-tiered judicial system composed of justice, county, district, and supreme courts.[7] Power was divided among these three branches, and a system of checks and balances was put into place. Complicated procedures were included for amending the constitution, and a bill of rights was elaborated.

bicameral having a legislative assembly composed of two chambers or houses

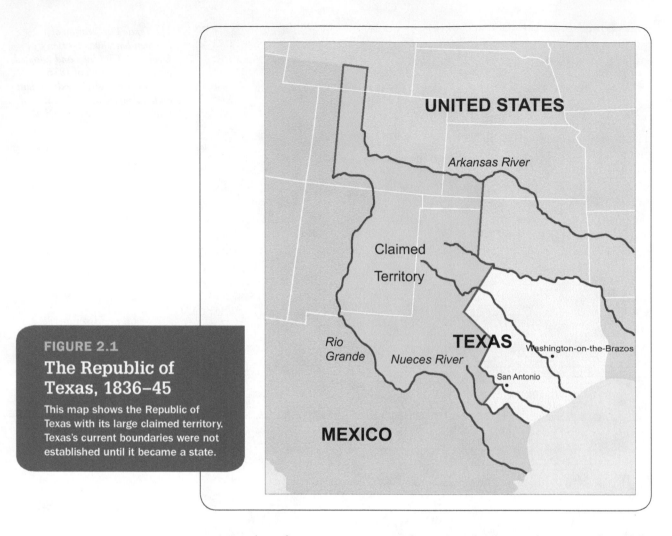

A number of important provisions from Spanish-Mexican law were adapted for the Texas Republic in the constitution, including the idea of community property, homestead exemptions and protections, and debtor relief. The values of American democracy percolated through the document. White male suffrage was guaranteed. Ministers and priests were ineligible for public office. But one of the most important aspects of the Constitution of 1836, at least from the perspective of newly immigrated Americans from the South, may have been the defense of slavery as an institution.

The Constitution of Coahuila y Tejas of 1827 had challenged, albeit unsuccessfully, the existence of slavery as an institution. Although the 1836 Constitution of the Republic of Texas outlawed the importation of slaves from Africa, it guaranteed that slaveholders could keep their property and that new slaveholding immigrants could bring their slaves into Texas with them. The results of this constitutional protection were monumental. In 1836, Texas had a population of 38,470, including 5,000 slaves. By 1850 the slave population had grown to 58,161, over one-quarter of the state's population. By 1860 there were more than 182,566 slaves, accounting for more than 30 percent of the state's population.[8] To all intents and purposes, the Constitution of 1836 not only saved slavery as an institution in Texas but also provided the protections needed for slavery to flourish.

It was one thing to declare independence from Mexico, but quite another to win independence. Only after the Battle of San Jacinto, where on April 21 Sam Houston's force of 900 men overran the 1,300-man force of Santa Anna and captured Santa Anna himself, did Texas become an independent state.[9]

The Texas State Constitution of 1845

The next phase of Texas's Founding took place from 1845 to 1861. Although the 1836 Constitution called for annexation by the United States, Texas remained an independent republic for nine years. There were concerns in the United States that if Texas were admitted to the Union, it would be as a slave state. Texas's admission to the Union could alter the delicate balance between slave and free states and further divide the nation over the sensitive subject of slavery. Additionally, it was feared that annexation by the United States would lead to war with Mexico. The defeated Mexican general and dictator Santa Anna had repudiated the Treaty of Velasco, which had ended the war between Texas and Mexico. Still claiming Texas as part of its own territory, Mexico undoubtedly would have gone to war to protect what it felt to be rightfully its own.

Hesitation over admitting Texas to the Union was overcome by the mid-1840s. On March 1, 1845, the U.S. Congress approved a resolution that brought Texas into the Union as a state. The annexation resolution had a number of interesting provisions. First, the Republic of Texas ceded to the United States all military armaments, bases, and facilities pertaining to public defense. Second, Texas retained a right to all "its vacant and unappropriated lands" as well as to its public debts. This was no small matter, because Texas claimed an enormous amount of land that extended far beyond its present state boundaries. The boundary issues were not resolved until Congress passed the Compromise of 1850 which, among other things, established Texas's boundaries in exchange for a payment from the federal government where some of the funds were used to pay Texas's debts. Finally, Texas was given permission to break up into four additional states when population proved adequate.

The lowering of the Republic flag marked Texas's annexation to the Union on March 1, 1845. A state constitution was drafted shortly thereafter to reflect Texas's new role.

On July 4, 1845, Anson Jones, fourth and final president of the Republic of Texas, called a convention in Austin to draft a state constitution. Drafters of the constitution relied heavily on the Constitution of 1836, although the final document ended up being almost twice as long. The familiar doctrines of separation of powers, checks and balances, and individual rights defined the basic design of government.

Under the Constitution of 1845, the legislature would be composed of two houses. The House of Representatives would have between 45 and 90 members, elected for two-year terms. Members were required to be at least 21 years of age. The Senate would be composed of between 19 and 33 members, elected for four-year terms. Half of the Senate would be elected every two years. As in the U.S. Constitution, revenue bills would originate in the House. Executive vetoes could be overturned by a two-thirds vote of each house. In a separate article on education, the legislature was ordered to establish a public school system and to set aside lands to support a Permanent School Fund. Another interesting power granted to the legislature was the power to select the treasurer and comptroller in a joint session.

This constitution provided for an elected governor and lieutenant governor. The governor's term was set at two years. He could serve only four years as governor in any six-year period. Among the executive powers granted to the governor were the powers to convene and adjourn the legislature, to veto legislation, to grant pardons and reprieves, and to command the state militia. The governor also had the power to appoint the attorney general, secretary of state, and district and supreme court judges, subject to the approval of the Senate.

The Constitution of 1845 established a judicial branch consisting of a supreme court composed of three judges, district courts, and lower courts deemed necessary by the legislature. Judges on the higher courts were to be appointed to six-year terms and could be removed from office subject to a two-thirds vote of both houses of the legislature.

Amending the Constitution of 1845 was difficult. After being proposed by a two-thirds vote of each house, amendments had to be approved by a majority of the voters. In the next legislature, another two-thirds vote of each house was necessary for ratification. Only one amendment was ever made to the Constitution of 1845. In 1850, an amendment was added to provide for the election of state officials who were originally appointed by the governor or by the legislature.[10]

This constitution retained some of the unusual provisions from the annexation resolution. Texas could divide itself into as many as five states and was responsible for paying its own foreign debt. It would retain title to its public lands, which could be sold to pay its debt. There was even a provision allowing Texas to fly its flag at the same height as the U.S. flag.

The Constitution of 1861: Texas Joins the Confederacy

The issue of slavery had delayed Texas's admission into the United States for nine years, until 1845. Northerners rightly feared that admission of Texas into the Union would intensify southern efforts to extend the slave system westward and would destroy the tenuous balance of power between slave and free states that had been established under the Missouri Compromise. While slavery made it difficult for Texas to get into the Union in 1848, slavery drove Texas from the Union in 1861. By 1860 slavery had become a vital institution to the Texas economy. Con-

This image shows what the Texas State capitol looked like in the 1850s. It burned in 1881. Texas's first constitution after joining the Union as a state was ratified in 1845. It lasted until 1861 when Texas seceded from the Union along with other southern states.

centrated in east Texas and along the Gulf Coast, slaves had come to constitute 30 percent of the population. However, in large sections of the state, particularly in the north and west, the economy was based on ranching or corn and wheat production rather than cotton. There slavery was virtually nonexistent. The question of whether Texas should secede was a controversial one that divided the state along regional and ethnic as well as party lines.

Pressure to secede mounted following the presidential election of Abraham Lincoln in November 1860. A staunch Unionist, Governor Sam Houston refused to convene a special session of the legislature to discuss secession. Seeking to bypass Houston, a number of influential political leaders in the state, including the chief justice of the Texas Supreme Court, called for a special convention in January 1861 to consider secession. Giving in to the pressure, Houston called a special session of the legislature in the hopes of undercutting the upcoming secession convention. The legislature, however, had other ideas, validating the call for the convention and turning its chambers over to the convention.

Lawyers and slaveholders dominated the secession convention. Lawyers composed 40 percent of the delegates; slaveholders composed 70 percent. The Texas Ordinance of Secession, produced by the convention on February 2, 1861, reflected this proslavery membership. In striking language, it proclaimed that the northern states had broken faith with Texas, particularly regarding the institution of slavery. Northerners had violated the very laws and constitution of the federal Union by appealing to a "higher law" that trampled on the rights of Texans. In language that people living in the twenty-first century find hard to understand, the Ordinance of Secession proclaimed,

> We hold as undeniable truths that the governments of the various States, and of the confederacy itself, were established exclusively by the white race, for themselves and their posterity; that the African race had no agency in their establishment; that

they were rightfully held and regarded as an inferior and dependent race, and in that condition only could their existence in this country be rendered beneficial and tolerable.[11]

Texas voters approved secession from the Union on February 23, 1861. The secession convention reconvened to enact a new constitution to guide the state as it entered the **Confederacy**. There were surprisingly few changes in the final document. This constitution was similar to the Constitution of 1845 except that references to the United States of America were replaced with references to the Confederate States of America. Public officials had to declare allegiance to the Confederacy, and slavery and states' rights were defended. A clause in the 1845 Constitution that provided for the possible emancipation of slaves was eliminated, and freeing slaves was declared illegal. But for the most part, the document accepted the existing constitutional framework. Controversial proposals, such as resuming the African slave trade, were rejected. The move out of the Union into the Confederacy may have been a radical one, but the new constitution was conservative insofar as it reaffirmed the existing constitutional order in the state.[12]

The Constitution of 1866: Texas Rejoins the Union

Defeat in the Civil War led to the institution of another state constitution in 1866. The provisional governor, Andrew Jackson Hamilton, called a constitutional convention on November 15, 1865, a little over six months after the surrender of Lee's army in Virginia. Delegates were elected on January 8, 1866, and the convention was held February 7. Few former secessionists were excluded from voting, with the result that there were strong Unionist and secessionist factions at the convention.

A number of actions were taken to bring the state into compliance with President Andrew Johnson's policy of Reconstruction, including the rejection of the right to secession, a repudiation of the war debt incurred by the state, and an acceptance of the abolition of slavery. The convention granted freedmen fundamental rights to their persons and property and gave them the right to sue and be sued as well as the right to contract with others. However, there was little support for extending suffrage to blacks, and they were banned from holding public office. The convention also made a few changes to the existing constitutional system in Texas. These changes came to be known as the Constitution of 1866.

As in the two previous constitutions, the size of the House was set between 45 and 90, and that of the Senate between 19 and 33. Terms of office remained the same as under the 1845 and 1861 constitutions, although salaries were increased. Reapportionment was to be based on the number of white male citizens, who would be counted in a census every 10 years.

The governor's salary was also increased, and the term was extended to 4 years, with a limit of 8 years in any 12-year period. The governor was also granted, for the first time, a line-item veto on appropriations. The comptroller and the treasurer were to be elected by the voters for 4-year terms.

Under the new constitution, the state supreme court was expanded from three to five judges and terms were increased to 10 years. Their salaries also were increased. The chief justice was to be selected from the five judges on the supreme court. District court judges were to be elected for 8-year terms, and the attorney general for a 4-year term.

Confederacy the Confederate States of America, those southern states that seceded from the United States in late 1860 and 1861 and argued that the power of the states was more important than the power of the central government

Voters ratified the Constitution of 1866 in June in a relatively close referendum, 28,119 to 23,400. The close vote was attributed to a widespread unhappiness with the increase in salaries of the various state officers.[13]

The Reconstruction Constitution of 1869

In 1869, Texas wrote still another constitution to meet the requirements of the Congressional Reconstruction Acts of 1867. A vote calling for a constitutional convention was ordered by General Winfield Scott Hancock, the commander of the Texas and Louisiana military district, in early 1868. Against Democratic opposition, **Radical Republicans** easily won the vote for a convention by 44,689 to 11,440. Of the 90 delegates to the convention, only 6 had served in the previous constitutional convention. Ten were blacks. The vast majority represented the interests of various wings in the Republican Party. The convention was a rancorous affair as delegates argued over a wide range of issues, including railroad charters, lawlessness in the state, and whether laws passed during the war years were legal. In the final days of the convention, delegates finally got down to the constitutional matters and the problems of accepting the Thirteenth and Fourteenth Amendments. Although delegates never completed their task of reworking the Constitution of 1866, their efforts were published under orders by military officials, without being submitted to the voters, and became the Constitution of 1869.

Radical Republicans a bloc of Republicans in the U.S. Congress who pushed through the adoption of black suffrage as well as an extended period of military occupation of the South following the Civil War

A number of features of the Constitution of 1869 stand out.[14] The U.S. Constitution was declared to be the supreme law of the land. Slavery was forbidden, and blacks were given the right to vote. Fourteenth Amendment guarantees of equality before the law were recognized. Additionally, the constitution altered the relationship among the three branches of government.

The House of Representatives was set at 90 and the Senate at 30 members. Senatorial terms were extended to six years, with one-third of the seats to be elected every biennium. Legislative sessions were to be held annually.

The most critical changes were in the executive branch and the courts. The powers of the governor were vastly expanded. Among other things, the governor was given wide-ranging appointment powers that included the power to appoint judges. The state supreme court was reduced from five to three judges. The term of supreme court judges was also lowered to nine years, with one new judge to be appointed every three years. Salaries for state officials were increased.

A Republican affiliated with the Radical faction of the party and a former Union general, Edmund Davis, governed under this constitution. Davis had vast authority, since the constitution had centralized power in the executive while reducing local governmental control. Varying interpretations exist of the government provided by Davis, though the popular perception at the time was that Davis presided over a corrupt, extravagant administration that eventually turned to the state police and the militia to attempt to maintain its regime.

In 1872 the Democrats regained control of the state government, and in 1873 the Democrat Richard Coke was elected governor. Davis attempted to maintain control over the governor's office by having his handpicked supreme court invalidate Coke's election. Davis refused to give up his office and surrounded himself with state police in the capitol building. However, when Democrats slipped past guards and gathered upstairs in the capitol building to organize a government, Davis was unable to obtain federal troops to retain him in office. Democrats were able to form a government, and Davis left office.

The Constitution of 1876

Explain the circumstances that led to the Texas Constitution that is still in use today

The final phase of Texas's Founding takes place with the passage of the Constitution of 1876. To prevent another government such as Davis's, efforts were made to write a new constitution. In 1874 a constitution was proposed and later rejected by a sitting legislature.[15] Finally, in 1875 a constitutional convention was called. Three delegates were selected by popular vote from each of the 30 senatorial districts. The final composition of the convention included 75 white Democrats and 15 Republicans, 6 of whom were black. Not one of the elected delegates had participated in the constitutional convention of 1868–69. Forty of the delegates were farmers, and 40 were members of the **Grange**, a militant farming organization that had emerged to improve the plight of farmers.

Grange a militant farmers' movement of the late nineteenth century that fought for improved conditions for farmers

The document that emerged from this convention, the Constitution of 1876, is still the basis for Texas government today. In an era of agriculture when prices and incomes were low and when little was demanded or expected from government, much in the 1876 Constitution made sense. However, one might question whether a constitution designed primarily by white males for whites in a rural agrarian society—and for the purpose of keeping the likes of Edmund Davis from ever controlling the state again—is the best foundation for government in the modern era.

The framers were committed to a constitution with four major themes. First, they wanted strong popular control of state government. Second, they believed

The example of Edmund Davis's reign motivated the revision of executive branch power in the Constitution of 1876. The framers of that constitution sought popular control of state government in order to limit the appointment powers of the governor as provided by the Constitution of 1869.

that a constitution should seriously limit the power of state government. Third, they sought economy in government. Fourth, the framers sought to promote agrarian interests, particularly those of small farmers, who formed the basis of support for the Grange movement.

Popular control of state government meant that the governor's vast appointment powers were limited by making judges and other public officials subject to election. But popular control of the government did not mean that all the electorate voted. When the framers of the 1876 Constitution thought of popular control of state government, they thought of control by white males.

In the effort to limit the powers of state government, the constitution placed great restrictions on the actions of government, restrictions that could be modified only through a complex constitutional amendment process. Executive authority was diffused among numerous officeholders, rather than concentrated in the hands of the governor. Although subsequently changed by constitutional amendment, an initial provision further limited gubernatorial power by setting a two-year term limit for the office. The legislature was part-time, ordinarily sitting for a proscribed time period every other year. This was in contrast to the 1869 Constitution, which provided that the legislature meet in annual sessions.

Economy in government was accomplished in several ways. The constitution restricted the extent of government debt and of government's power to tax. In addition, there were limits on the salaries of state officials, especially those of legislators. A major economic depression had begun in 1873, and many Texans were experiencing economic hardship. One way money was saved was by decentralizing public education. Schools were segregated, and compulsory education laws were eliminated. By having local control over education, white landowners could avoid paying taxes for the education of black students.

Texas at that time was an agricultural state. Wishing to protect agrarian interests, the framers wrote provisions protecting homesteads and restricting institutions that at that time were perceived to be harmful to farmers, such as banks and railroads. Greater responsibility was placed on local instead of state officials. There were also detailed regulations on railroad competition, freight and passenger rates, and railroad construction incentives.

Even in its earliest stages, the Texas Constitution of 1876 was a lengthy, rigid, and detailed document, and purposely so. Regulations curtailing government power were placed not in statutes where they could easily be reversed, but in the body of the constitution. The goal of this design was to ensure that the Radical Republicans and Edmund Davis would never again be able to reign and spend in Texas. They, of course, never did, although over the years the constitution became an increasingly unwieldy document.

for critical analysis

Consider the characteristics of the constitutions adopted prior to 1876. What were the major provisions of each? Which were incorporated into the present Texas Constitution? Why does the state constitution place so many limits on state government? What changes could be made to the constitution to increase its effectiveness?

● The Constitution of Texas Today

Analyze the major provisions of the Texas Constitution today

The U.S. Constitution has two great virtues: brevity and flexibility. Neither of these virtues can be said to characterize the Texas Constitution. The U.S. Constitution is limited to 7 short articles and 27 amendments, and takes up only 8 pages of the *World Almanac*. Much in the federal document is left unsaid, allowing lawmaking to be accomplished by statute. In contrast, in 2013 the Texas Constitution contained

16 articles (Table 2.1; another article that concerned Spanish and Mexican land titles was deleted from the constitution in 1969). Seven hundred and sixty-five amendments have been proposed by the legislature. Four hundred and eighty-three were approved by the electorate, while 282 have been defeated. Curiously, three amendments were proposed by the legislature, but for obscure historical reasons never voted on by the electorate.[16] Many of the articles are lengthy, complex affairs, taking up over 67 pages of text in one edition of the *Texas Almanac*. But it is not just the length that differentiates the two constitutions. There is a difference in tone. The Texas Constitution reflects the writers' fears of what government could do if the principle of **limited government** was not clearly established.

In addition to its severe limits on executive power, the Texas Constitution also addresses a number of specific policy problems directly in the text, turning what might appear to be matters of public policy into issues of constitutional authority. By granting a variety of boards and districts a special place in the constitution, the framers set out additional checks and balances that make it difficult for governors to exercise power effectively. Quite unintentionally, the Texas Constitution became a place where special interests could seek to promote and protect their own agendas, even in the face of considerable political opposition.

The contrasts in character between the federal and Texas constitutions are a direct reflection of the differences in their framers' underlying goals. The U.S. Con-

limited government a principle of constitutional government; a government whose powers are defined and limited by a constitution

TABLE 2.1

The Texas Constitution: An Overview

Article 1: The Bill of Rights

Article 2: Separation of Powers in State Government

Article 3: The State Legislature

Article 4: The Plural Executive

Article 5: The Judicial Department

Article 6: Suffrage in Texas

Article 7: Public Education in Texas

Article 8: Taxation and State Revenues

Articles 9 and 11: Concerning Local Government, Including Counties and Municipal Corporations

Article 10: Empowering the State to Regulate Railroads and to Create the Texas Railroad Commission

Article 12: Empowering the State to Create General Laws for Corporations

Article 13: Concerning Spanish and Mexican Land Titles, Now Deleted from the Constitution

Article 14: Creates the General Land Office to Deal with Registering Land Titles

Article 15: Impeachment Provisions

Article 16: General Provisions Covering a Wide Range of Topics

Article 17: Amendment Procedures

stitution was written to overcome the liabilities of the Articles of Confederation and create a government that could act effectively in the public welfare in a variety of policy areas. The Texas Constitution was written to prevent the expansion of governmental authority and the return of a system of political power that was perceived as acting against the interests of the people.

The Preamble

The preamble to the Texas Constitution is surprisingly short: "Humbly invoking the blessings of Almighty God, the people of the State of Texas do ordain and establish this Constitution." This brevity is more than made up for in what follows.

Article 1: Bill of Rights

Article I of the U.S. Constitution establishes and delegates power to the legislative branch of government. One of the overriding concerns of the Founders was to create a legislature that could act effectively in public affairs. What came to be known as the Bill of Rights—the first 10 amendments to the Constitution—was added after the original Constitution was drafted and approved.

In contrast, the Texas Constitution puts its Bill of Rights up front as Article 1, well before any discussion of the legislature, the executive, or the courts. From the beginning, the purpose of the Texas Constitution was not simply to create a set of institutions that could wield political power. It was to limit the way political power is used and to prevent it from being abused.

The Texas Bill of Rights embodies certain ideas captured in the U.S. Bill of Rights. All "free men" are declared to have free and equal rights that cannot be denied or abridged because of sex, race, color, creed, or national origin. Freedom of religious worship is guaranteed, and there will be no religious test for office. Liberty of speech and liberty of the press are guaranteed. Individuals are protected from unreasonable search and seizure, from excessive bail, from bills of attainder and ex post facto laws, and from double jeopardy. Article 1 also guarantees an individual a right to trial by jury and the right to bear arms "in the lawful defense of himself or the State; but the Legislature shall have the power, by law, to regulate the wearing of arms, with a view to prevent crime" (Article 1, Section 23).

Article 1 also contains some ideas that move beyond those guaranteed by the first 10 amendments to the U.S. Constitution. The right to **republican government**, something clearly stated in the main body of the U.S. Constitution but not in the U.S. Bill of Rights, is powerfully articulated in the first two sections of Article 1. According to Article 1 of the Texas Constitution, all political power is inherent in the people, and the people of Texas have at all times the "inalienable right to alter, reform or abolish their government in such manner as they may think expedient" (Article 1, Section 2).

republican government a representative democracy, a system of government in which power is derived from the people

The differences between the Texas Bill of Rights and the U.S. Bill of Rights are not simply matters of where best to articulate a philosophy of republican government. They also involve very concrete matters of public policy. Section 26 in the Texas Bill of Rights, for example, forbids monopolies that are contrary to the public interest, and states that the law of primogeniture and entail (a law designed to keep large landed properties together by restricting inheritance to the firstborn) will never be in effect in the state. Although monopolies remain a public concern today, primogeniture and entail do not. Section 11 in the Texas Bill of Rights grapples with the complicated issue of bail and under what specific circumstances an individual can be denied bail. Significantly, Section 11 has been the subject of three major constitutional revisions: in 1955, 1977, and 1993. Section 30, adopted in 1989, provides a long list of the "rights of crime victims," including the right to be treated fairly and with dignity, the right to be protected from the accused, and the right to restitution. Although these are important matters of public policy for Texas today, they could hardly be considered proper material for the U.S. Constitution.

Article 2: The Powers of Government

Like the U.S. Constitution, Article 2 divides the power of government in Texas into three distinct branches: the legislative, the executive, and the judicial. It also stipulates that no one in any one branch shall be attached to either of the other branches, except where explicitly permitted (as in the case of the lieutenant governor's role in the Senate). The article—one short paragraph of text—assures that a version of the separation of powers doctrine found in the U.S. Constitution will be embodied in Texas institutions.

Article 3: Legislative Department

Article 2 is one of the shortest articles in the Texas Constitution. Article 3 is the longest, comprising almost one-third of the text. Like Article I of the U.S. Constitution, Article 3 of the Texas Constitution vests legislative power in two houses: a Senate of 31 members and a House of Representatives of no more than 150 members. It stipulates the terms of office and qualifications. House members serve two-year terms, whereas senators serve four-year terms, half being elected every two years. House members must be citizens of the United States, must be at least 21 years of age, and must have resided in the state for two years and in their district for one year. Senators must be citizens of the United States, must be at least 26 years old, and must have resided in the state for five years and in their districts for one year. In addition, Article 3 provides for the selection of officers in both houses of the legislature, states when and for how long the legislature shall meet (Section 5), and explains how the legislative proceedings will be conducted (Sections 29–41) and how representative districts will be apportioned (Sections 25, 26, and 28).

Like Article 1, Texas's Bill of Rights, Article 3 moves well beyond the U.S. Constitution, putting limits on what the legislature can do. For example, it puts limits on legislators' salaries and makes it difficult to increase those salaries. Article 3 also creates a bipartisan Texas Ethics Commission whose job, among other things, is to recommend salary increases for members of the legislature and to set per diem rates for legislators and the lieutenant governor. Article 3, Section 49(a), also subjects the legislature to the actions of the comptroller of public accounts, whose duty is to prepare a report prior to the legislative session on the financial condition of the state treasury and to provide estimates of future expenditures by the state. This provision of the Texas Constitution effectively limits the state legislature to the financial calculations and endorsements of the comptroller, a check on the legislature all but unimaginable to the writers of the U.S. Constitution.

Putting constraints on certain legislative actions is only part of the story. The largest portion of Article 3 (Sections 47–64) is dedicated to addressing a variety of policy problems, including lotteries, emergency service districts, the problem of debt creation, problems surrounding the Veterans' Land Board and the Texas Water Development Board, Texas park development, the creation of a state medical education board, and even the establishment of an economic development fund in support of the now defunct superconducting supercollider.

Article 4: Executive Department

Article II of the U.S. Constitution concentrates executive power in the presidency. The desire was to create a more effective and more responsible executive than had been possible under the Articles of Confederation. The Texas Constitution lists a number of offices in the executive, legislative, and judicial branches which are specified in Table 2.2. Article 4 of the Texas Constitution states that the executive shall consist of six distinct offices: the governor, who serves as the chief executive; the lieutenant governor, who serves as the president of the Senate; the secretary of state, who keeps the official seals of the state; the comptroller of public accounts; the commissioner of the General Land Office; and the attorney general, who acts as the state's chief legal officer. With the exception of the secretary of state, who is appointed by the governor and approved by the Senate, all other offices are elected by qualified voters every four years. Besides creating a **plural executive**, Article 4 guarantees its members will have independent political bases in the electorate. This provides an additional check against any concentration of powers in the hands of any one person.

plural executive an executive branch in which power is fragmented because the election of statewide officeholders is independent of the election of the governor

Article 5: Judicial Department

Article III of the U.S. Constitution succinctly provides for a Supreme Court and empowers Congress to create any necessary lower courts. Nothing could be further from the detailed discussion of the state courts found in Article 5 of the Texas Constitution. Besides creating one supreme court to hear civil cases and one court of criminal appeals to hear criminal cases, Article 5 provides for such lesser courts as courts of appeal, district courts, commissioner's courts, and justice of the peace courts, and empowers the legislature to establish other courts as deemed necessary. It also goes into such details as the retirement and compensation of judges, the jurisdictions of the various courts, and the duties of judges; it states what to do in the case of court vacancies, and includes a series of discussions on particular issues involving the lower courts.

An even greater difference between the federal Constitution and the Texas Constitution is the crucial role the latter gives to elections. Federal judges are appointed by the executive and approved by the Senate. In Texas, the people elect state judges. Nine supreme court and nine court of criminal appeals judges are elected at large in the state. Lower court positions are elected by voters in their relevant geographic locations. Much like the U.S. Constitution, the Texas Constitution seeks to create an independent judiciary that can check and balance the other two branches of government. But it seeks an additional check as well. It wants the people to watch over the courts.

Article 6: Suffrage

Article 6 contains a short but detailed discussion about who may vote in Texas. It also empowers the legislature to enact laws regulating voter registration and the selection of electors for president and vice president.

TABLE 2.2

Major Constitutional Officers in Texas

LEGISLATIVE (ARTICLE 3)

OFFICE/POSITION	ELECTED BY/APPOINTED BY	DUTIES
Speaker of the House	Elected by House members	Leads the House
President Pro Tempore of the Senate	Elected by a Senate member	Leads Senate in absence of the Lieutenant Governor

EXECUTIVE (ARTICLE 4)

OFFICE/POSITION	ELECTED BY/APPOINTED BY	DUTIES
Governor	Elected by Texas voters for 4-year term	Chief executive of the state
Lieutenant Governor	Elected by Texas voters for 4-year term	Acts as Governor in absence of Governor and presides over Senate
Secretary of State	Appointed by the Governor by and with advice and consent of Senate	Chief election officer of Texas
Comptroller of Public Accounts	Elected by Texas voters	Chief steward of state finances
Commissioner of the General Land Office	Elected by Texas voters	Manages state assets, investments, and mineral rights from state lands and serves as chair for numerous state boards and commissions
Attorney General	Elected by Texas voters	Represents the state in cases where the state is a party

JUDICIAL (ARTICLE 5)

OFFICE/POSITION	ELECTED BY/APPOINTED BY	DUTIES
Justice of Supreme Court	9 positions elected by Texas voters for 6-year terms	Decides on civil cases reaching Texas Supreme Court
Judge of Court of Criminal Appeals	9 positions elected by Texas voters for 6-year terms	Decides on criminal cases reaching Texas court of criminal appeals
Justice of the Court of Appeal	80 justices in 14 courts of appeal elected by Texas voters for 6-year terms from multimember districts	Decides on cases reaching Texas court of appeal
District Court Judge	456 District Court judges elected by Texas voters for 4-year terms from a mixture of multi- and single-member districts	Decides on cases in Texas district court

Other county-level court officials are also elected for 4-year terms on a county or precinct basis. Municipal court judges are usually appointed.

OTHER IMPORTANT OFFICES

OFFICE/POSITION	ELECTED BY/APPOINTED BY	DUTIES
Texas Railroad Commissioner (Article 13, Section 30)	3 officers elected by Texas voters for 6-year overlapping terms	Regulates the oil and gas industry, gas utilities, pipeline safety, and surface coal and uranium mining (no longer regulates railroads)
State Board of Education Member (Article 7)	15 members elected by Texas voters from single-member districts for 4-year terms	Makes statewide policies for public schools
Agricultural Commissioner (office established under Agricultural Code, not the Constitution)	Elected by Texas voters to a 4-year term	Regulates state agriculture and administers state agriculture policy

Article 7: Education

The concerns found in the Texas Declaration of Independence over the need for public schools to promote a republican form of government are directly addressed in Article 7. Section 1 makes it a duty of the state legislature to support and maintain "an efficient system of public free schools." The Texas Supreme Court's interpretation of this provision as applying to school funding in the state has led to the current political battles over school finance. Sections 2–8 provide for their funding and the creation of a State Board of Education to oversee the operations of elementary and secondary education in the state. State universities are the subject of over half of Article 7, where detailed discussions of the funding and operations of particular state institutions are put directly into the text.

Article 8: Taxation and Revenue

The complex issue of taxation is the subject of Article 8. Once again we find a highly detailed account of several important policy issues built directly into the text of the constitution. One of the most controversial sections of the Texas Constitution centers on the issue of the income tax. Section 1 enables the legislature to tax the income of individuals and businesses. This power, however, is subject to Section 24, which was passed by the 73rd Legislature in 1993. Section 24 requires that the registered voters in the state approve a personal income tax and that the proceeds from this tax be dedicated to education and tax relief. As with other portions of the constitution, the net effect of these provisions is to curtail severely what the state legislature can do and how it is to do it. If Section 24 of Article 8 is any indication, the public fear of unresponsive and potentially tyrannical government was as alive during the 1990s as it was in 1876.

Articles 9 and 11: Local Government

These articles provide highly detailed discussions of the creation, organization, and operation of counties and municipal corporations.

Articles 10, 12, 13, and 14

These heavily revised articles deal with a series of specific topics: the railroads (10), private corporations (12), Spanish and Mexican land titles (13), and public lands (14). Article 10 empowers the state to regulate railroads and to establish the Railroad Commission. Article 12 empowers the state to create general laws creating private corporations and protecting the public and individual stockholders. Article 13, now entirely deleted from the constitution, dealt with the nineteenth-century issue of Spanish and Mexican land titles. Article 14 created a General Land Office to deal with the registration of land titles.

Article 15: Impeachment

Impeachment is, in the U.S. Constitution, one of the major checks Congress holds against both the executive and judicial branches of government. The House of Representatives holds the power to impeach an individual; the Senate is responsible for conducting trials. A two-thirds vote in the Senate following impeachment by the House leads to the removal of an individual from office.

impeachment under the Texas Constitution, the formal charge by the House of Representatives that leads to trial in the Senate and possible removal of a state official

A similar process is provided for in Article 15 of the Texas Constitution. The House has the power to impeach. The Senate has the power to try the governor, lieutenant governor, attorney general, land-office commissioner, and comptroller, as well as judges of the supreme court, the courts of appeal, and district courts. Conviction requires a two-thirds vote of the senators present. In contrast to the U.S. Constitution, the Texas Constitution rules that all officers against whom articles of impeachment are proffered are suspended from their office. The governor is empowered to appoint a person to fill the vacancy until the decision on impeachment is reached.

Despite these similarities to the impeachment procedures in the U.S. Constitution, the Texas Constitution has its own caveats. Most notably, the Texas Constitution does not explicitly define impeachable offenses in terms of "Treason, Bribery, or other high Crimes and Misdemeanors," as the U.S. Constitution does. The House and Senate (and the courts) decide what constitutes an impeachable offense.[17] In addition, the supreme court has original jurisdiction to hear and determine whether district court judges are competent to discharge their judicial duties. The governor may also remove judges of the supreme court, courts of appeal, and district courts when requested by the two-thirds vote of each legislature. Significantly, the reasons for removing a judge in this case need not rise to the level of an impeachable offense, but need only involve a "willful neglect of duty, incompetence, habitual drunkenness, oppression in office, or other reasonable cause" (Article 15, Section 8). The barriers to removing a judge by political means are thus, at least on paper, much lower in Texas than in national government.

In 1980, Section 9 was added to Article 15, providing a new way to remove officials appointed by the governor. With the advice and consent of two-thirds of the members of the Senate present, a governor may remove an appointed public official. If the legislature is not in session, the governor is empowered to call a special two-day session to consider the proposed removal.

Article 16: General Provisions

Article 16 is one of the lengthiest in the Texas Constitution and has no parallel in the U.S. Constitution. It is literally a catchall article tackling a variety of issues ranging from official oaths of office to community property to banking corporations and stock laws to the election of the Texas Railroad Commission to the state retirement systems. Here, perhaps more than anywhere else, we see the complexity and confusion of the philosophy reflected in the Texas Constitution.

Article 17: Amending the Constitution

Like the U.S. Constitution, the Texas Constitution explicitly delineates how it can be amended. Essentially, amendments undergo a four-stage process: First, the legislature must meet in either regular or special session and propose amendments. Second, these amendments must be approved by a two-thirds vote of all the members elected to each house. Third, a brief statement explaining the amendments must be published twice in each recognized newspaper in the state that meets the publication requirements for official state notices. Finally, the amendments must be approved by a majority of the state voters.

Recent Attempts to Rewrite the Texas Constitution

Describe modern efforts to change the Texas Constitution

Given the difficulty of amending the state constitution, a surprising number of amendments have been proposed since 1876. A considerable number of these have been turned down in the popular vote. As Table 2.3 shows, demands for amending the Constitution have intensified in recent years, as legislators have dealt with the problem of making changes in public policy while being constrained by an unwieldy constitutional document.

Sharpstown and the Failed Constitutional Reforms of 1974

A drive to rewrite the Texas Constitution grew out of a major stock fraud that broke in the early 1970s, involving the Sharpstown State Bank and the National Bankers Life Insurance Corporation. Following the 1970 elections, which had been dominated, as generally was the case, by the conservative wing of the Democratic Party, a suit was filed in Dallas federal court. Attorneys for the Securities and Exchange Commission alleged that a number of influential Democrats, including Governor Preston Smith, the state Democratic chairman and state banking board member Elmer Baum, Speaker of the House Gus Mutscher, and others, had been

TABLE 2.3

Amending the Texas Constitution

The Constitution of Texas has been amended 483 times since its inception in 1876.

YEARS	NUMBER PROPOSED	NUMBER ADOPTED
1876–1900	31	17
1901–20	56	21
1921–40	71	47
1941–60	78	59
1961–80	151	98
1981–2000	180	148
2001–10	79	77
2011	10	7
2013	9	9
2014	1	1
Totals	**666**	**484**

SOURCE: Texas Legislative Council and Texas Secretary of State.

The Sharpstown State Bank scandal led to a demand for a new constitution to replace the outmoded 1876 document. This cartoon, which shows Governor Dolph Briscoe regally proclaiming, "This baby has a wart . . . off with his head!" satirizes Briscoe's stance against the new constitution.

—By BOB TAYLOR, Times Herald Staff Cartoonist

"This baby has a wart...off with his head!"

bribed. By the fall of 1971 Mutscher and two of his associates had been indicted. On March 15, 1972, they were convicted and sentenced to five years' probation.

The convictions fueled a firestorm in the state to "throw the rascals out." During the 1972 elections, "reform" candidates dominated the Democratic primary and the general election. The conservative rancher-banker Dolph Briscoe became governor, but only by a plurality, making him the first governor in the history of the state not to receive a majority of the popular vote. Other reform-minded candidates such as William P. Hobby, Jr., and John Hill were successful. Hobby won the lieutenant governor's race, while Hill became attorney general, defeating the three-term Democratic incumbent Crawford C. Martin. When the smoke cleared, half of the House seats were occupied by new members, and the Senate had witnessed a higher-than-normal rate of turnover. The elections had one other outcome: an amendment was passed empowering the legislature to sit as a constitutional convention whose task would be to rewrite the Constitution.[18]

The constitutional convention met on January 8, 1974, in Austin. The idea was for the convention to draft a new constitution that would then be presented to state voters for ratification. Originally scheduled to last 90 days, the convention was extended to 150 days. Even so, it did not have enough time. Bitter politics, coupled with the intense demands of highly mobilized special interests, made it impossible to reach the necessary agreement. In the end, proponents of a new constitution failed to achieve a two-thirds majority by three votes (118 to 62, with 1 abstention).

The movement to rewrite the constitution did not die at the convention. During the next session of the legislature, eight constitutional amendments were passed that effectively would have rewritten the constitution through the normal

Which State Has the Longest Constitution?

State Constitution Length (estimated)

- ● < 19,999 words
- ● 20,000–39,999 words
- ● 40,000–59,999 words
- ● 60,000–79,999 words
- ● > 79,999 words

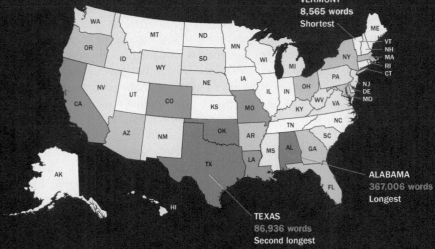

VERMONT
8,565 words
Shortest

ALABAMA
367,006 words
Longest

TEXAS
86,936 words
Second longest

The Texas Constitution is the second-longest state constitution in the United States. The framers of the Texas Constitution gave the state government very specific powers so that the government could not use ambiguity to expand its powers. As a result, the Texas Constitution requires frequent amendments to address situations not covered specifically in the original constitution. The Texas Constitution has been amended 484 times as of 2014, fourth most of any state.

Amendments Added to Constitution

- ● < 75 amendments
- ● 75–149 amendments
- ● 150–224 amendments
- ● 225–300 amendments
- ● > 300 amendments

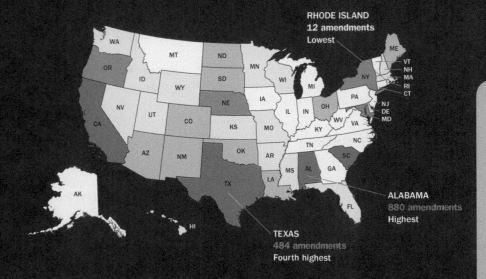

RHODE ISLAND
12 amendments
Lowest

ALABAMA
880 amendments
Highest

TEXAS
484 amendments
Fourth highest

for critical analysis

1. How would such a long and detailed state constitution achieve the framers' goal of limiting the scope and power of government in Texas?

2. The U.S. Constitution is a much shorter document than the Texas Constitution and has only 27 amendments. Why would a shorter constitution lead to fewer amendments?

SOURCE: Book of the States, 2014. Council of State Governments. Data for 2014 compiled by the authors.

for critical analysis

What was the rationale for attempting to rewrite the constitution in 1974 and 1999? What changes were proposed? Why did these attempts fail?

amendment process. Each proposal, however, was turned down by the electorate in a special election on November 4, 1975. The Constitution of 1876 remained alive, if not well.

The 1999 Ratliff-Junell Proposal

For the first time since the unsuccessful effort to revise the constitution in the mid-1970s, state senator Bill Ratliff and state representative Rob Junell, both powerhouses in the state legislature, proposed a new constitution for Texas in 1999. Ratliff argued, "It's time for Texas to have a constitution that's appropriate for the twenty-first century." They were concerned that the 1876 Constitution was too restrictive and cumbersome for modern government. It is lengthy, cluttered, and disorganized. The document had become so chaotic that in both 1999 and 2001, amendments were approved "to eliminate duplicative, executed, obsolete, archaic, and ineffective provisions" in the constitution.

Among the major Ratliff-Junell proposals was that the governor would be given the authority to appoint several state officeholders who are now elected. Additionally, the executive branch would be reorganized so that the governor would have an appointed cabinet of department heads, subject to senate confirmation, much as the U.S. president does. With that proposal, only the lieutenant governor, the attorney general, and the state comptroller would be elected.

The governor would also be given the power to appoint all appellate and district judges. Afterward, the judges would be subject to voter approval in retention elections—where they have no opponent on the ballot but where voters are asked if they wish to retain the appointed judge in office for a specified time period. Ratliff argued that the changes would make the governor more accountable for how state government works.

The legislature would remain part-time and would continue to meet in regular session every other year. It would also convene in a special 15-day "veto session," in order to consider overriding any gubernatorial vetoes from previous sessions. State senators now serve four-year terms and state representatives two-year terms. Under the proposed constitution, these terms would be increased to six years for state senators and four years for state representatives. For the first time, there would also be term limits so that representatives' service would be limited to eight regular sessions in the House or 16 years in office, and senators' service could not exceed nine regular sessions in the Senate or 18 years in office.

Although county government would remain as it is today, local voters would be given the authority to abolish their own county's obsolete offices without statewide approval through constitutional amendments.

Even as it was proposed, its sponsors realized that the revamped constitution would be tough to pass. And they were right—it did not pass, but suffered the fate of earlier efforts to change the 1876 Constitution.

Recent Amendments

In the 2013 constitutional amendment elections, voters were asked to consider nine proposed amendments. All nine of the amendments passed, although only approximately 8 percent of registered voters bothered to vote, up from 5.2 percent in the 2011 constitutional amendment elections. Despite the increase, one thing that is clear about elections that deal with constitutional amendments is that voting participation is invariably low. "Who Are Texans?" compares the percentage turnout of registered voters in November special elections on constitutional

Who Votes in Texas Elections Amending the Constitution?

Voter Turnout in Texas Constitutional Amendment Elections Compared with Turnout for Presidential Elections*

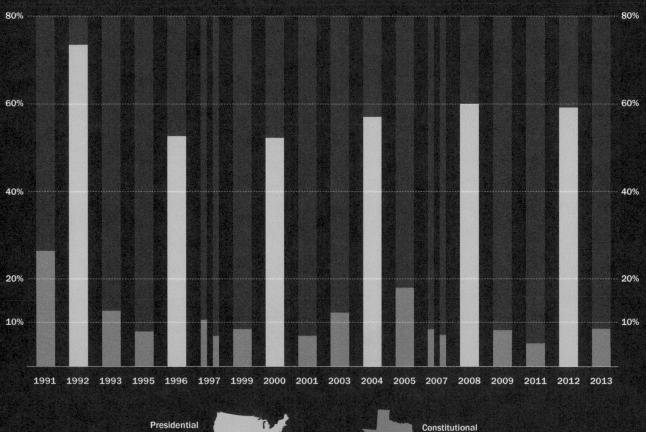

 Presidential election

 Constitutional amendment election

Since 1983, Texans have voted to amend the state's constitution dozens of times. Turnout in these elections is always low, even when well-publicized amendments are on the ballot. For example, in 2005, 17 percent of registered voters voted on Proposition 2, which banned same-sex marriage in the state.

* 1997—elections in August and November; 2007—elections in May and November.

SOURCE: Texas Secretary of State, www.sos.state.us/ (accessed 5/14/14).

for critical analysis

1. Why is turnout relatively low for elections dealing with constitutional amendments?

2. How might results change for Constitutional amendment elections if they were held during presidential election years?

amendments with the percentage turnout in presidential elections (which tend to produce the highest turnout). There are two likely reasons for the low voter turnout in constitutional amendment elections: (1) Constitutional amendment elections are usually held in "off" years when there are no elections with candidates on the ballot. Because of this, the political parties take a less active role in getting out the vote, and there are no candidates to generate voter turnout. As a result, advertising campaigns to get out the vote are frequently limited only to the activities of interest groups that support or oppose the issues on the ballot. (2) Many of the amendments are relatively insignificant to most voters.

Most of the 2013 proposed constitutional amendments listed in Table 2.4 were uncontroversial. Such was not the case in 2011 when 3 of the 10 amendments presented to the voters were turned down. The controversial ones were those that the Tea Party and other antitax groups saw as increasing the financial burden on Texans. For example, Proposition 4 was defeated because it would have expanded the ability of counties to issue bonds to finance the development of unproductive areas where those bonds were to be repaid with property tax revenues. Critics of the proposal argued that it would clear the way for new toll roads. Proposition 7 was defeated because it would have given El Paso new borrowing authority. Proposition 8 passed the legislature with bipartisan support. It would have given property owners the opportunity to opt out of agricultural or wildlife conservation property tax exemptions in favor of water conservation property tax exemptions. The Tea Party successfully opposed the proposition on the grounds that it would shift the tax burden to others.[19] While the Tea Party and other antitax groups could not defeat all of the propositions they opposed, low voter turnout enabled them to

Amendments to the state constitution affect many areas of Texans' lives. The amendments passed in 2011 included one intended to help address drought in Texas by making additional funds available to local governments for water projects.

TABLE 2.4

Passed Constitutional Amendments, 2013–14

2013

Proposition 1 (HJR 62)	The constitutional amendment authorizing the legislature to provide for an exemption from ad valorem taxation of all or part of the market value of the residence homestead of the surviving spouse of a member of the armed services of the United States who is killed in action. (Passed 73.3%)
Proposition 2 (HJR 79)	The constitutional amendment eliminating an obsolete requirement for a State Medical Education Board and a State Medical Education Fund, neither of which is operational. (Passed 74.4%)
Proposition 3 (HJR 133)	The constitutional amendment to authorize a political subdivision of this state to extend the number of days that aircraft parts that are exempt from ad valorem taxation because of their location in this state for a temporary period may be located in this state for purposes of qualifying for the tax exemption. (Passed 84.6%)
Proposition 4 (HJR 24)	The constitutional amendment authorizing the legislature to provide for an exemption from ad valorem taxation of part of the market value of the residence homestead of a partially disabled veteran or the surviving spouse of a partially disabled veteran if the residence homestead was donated to the disabled veteran by a charitable organization. (Passed 57.7%)
Proposition 5 (SJR 18)	The constitutional amendment to authorize the making of a reverse mortgage loan for the purchase of homestead property and to amend lender disclosures and other requirements in connection with a reverse mortgage loan. (Passed 84.7%)
Proposition 6 (SJR 1)	The constitutional amendment providing for the creation of the State Water Implementation Fund for Texas and the State Water Implementation Revenue Fund for Texas to assist in the financing of priority projects in the state water plan to ensure the availability of adequate water resources. (Passed 87.0%)
Proposition 7 (HJR 87)	The constitutional amendment authorizing a home-rule municipality to provide in its charter the procedure to fill a vacancy on its governing body for which the unexpired term is 12 months or less. (Passed 72.4%)
Proposition 8 (SJR 54)	The constitutional amendment repealing Article 9, Section 7, Texas Constitution, which relates to the creation of a hospital district in Hidalgo County. (Passed 62.6%)
Proposition 9 (SJR 42)	The constitutional amendment relating to expanding the types of sanctions that may be assessed against a judge or justice following a formal proceeding instituted by the State Commission on Judicial Conduct. (Passed 85.1%)

2014

Proposition 1 (SJR 1)	The constitutional amendment providing for the use and dedication of certain money transferred to the state highway fund to assist in the completion of transportation, construction, maintenance, and rehabilitation projects, not to include toll roads. (Passed 79.8%)

Proposition 2 and Same-Sex Marriage

In November 2005, Texans went to the polls to vote on Proposition 2 to amend the Texas Constitution, a measure aimed at prohibiting same sex marriages in the state. Supporters of Proposition 2 wanted the ban on such marriages enshrined in the state constitution in order to prevent any future legislation. The measure passed with nearly 76 percent of Texans voting in support of the proposition.

In 2009 a same-sex couple living in Texas who were married in 2006 in Massachusetts, where such marriages are legal, filed for divorce. Because their marriage had not been recognized in Texas, their filing for divorce was problematic. The couple sued the state, claiming that Proposition 2 violated the full faith and credit clause of the U.S. Constitution, which stipulates that licenses issued by one state must be recognized in other states. They also claimed that it violated the equal protection clause, which gives all citizens the right to equal protection under the law. A federal district court judge in Dallas agreed with the plaintiffs. In 2010 the Fifth Circuit Court of Appeals overruled the district court after an appeal from the state of Texas, claiming that Texas had the right to pass Proposition 2 and that the equal protection clause was not violated.

The U.S. Supreme Court's ruling in 2013 striking down the Defense of Marriage Act has important implications for gay marriage in Texas, however. The federal government now recognizes gay marriages, so federal benefits are now accorded to same-sex couples regardless of where they reside. In the aftermath of the U.S. Supreme Court's DOMA decision, in 2014 a federal district court in San Antonio struck down Texas's ban on same-sex marriage. That decision is currently being appealed.

The issue of same-sex marriage illustrates the trade-offs between minority

rights and majority rule in a democracy. The majority of Texans had approved Proposition 2, denying marriage rights to same-sex couples but minorities retain certain rights under the U.S. Constitution. The equal protection clause was written in order to ensure that no class of citizens would be treated differently or in a second-class manner. The U.S. Supreme Court has developed suspect classifications such as race and ethnicity so that when laws single out a group of people, they must have a compelling justification. Compelling justification means that there must be an overwhelming reason for adopting

this classification. On the other hand, classifications based on sex must have a substantial justification to be upheld. This classification demands an exceedingly persuasive justification to be used. Other classifications generally must have a rational basis. A rational justification must have a reasonable justification for using it. (We discuss these standards of review in Chapter 3.) Which standard of equal protection review should be applied to Proposition 2? Would Proposition 2 be constitutional under any of these standards of equal protection review?

Proponents of Proposition 2 use the rational basis test, arguing that it does have a rational basis—the defense of the one-flesh union between one man and one woman, that cannot exist between two men or two women. They also believe that society is better when marriages unite one man and one woman to create families with children. Families, they argue, are the cornerstone of civilization and must be protected against the spread of alternative lifestyles.

Opponents argue that gay men and lesbians wishing to enter into marriage arrangements should be allowed to do so. They argue that they should be entitled to the same tax benefits, visitation rights, and societal respect for their mutual commitment. Society, they say, should encourage monogamy and the establishment of lifelong commitments. They claim that such laws as Proposition 2 are not rational and only reflect antigay sentiment.

critical thinking questions

1. Is Proposition 2 a violation of the equal protection clause of the U.S. Constitution?

2. How do we balance the rights of minority groups, such as gays and lesbians, with the will of the majority?

In 2005 social conservatives urged Texans to vote in favor of Proposition 2, which defined marriage in Texas as the union of one man and one woman. This appeal to traditional values contributed to relatively high turnout, and Proposition 2 passed by more than a 3-to-1 margin.

exert a significant influence. Indeed, their defeat of three proposals broke the modern pattern in which amendments are routinely approved. For example, between 2001 and 2010, 77 of 79 proposed amendments were approved.

Most of the 2005 proposed constitutional amendments were, like the previously discussed propositions, of significance only to a narrow group of people. For example, one of the nine proposed amendments provided for clearing land titles in Upshur and Smith counties. Another authorized the legislature to provide for a six-year term for a board member of a regional mobility authority. Yet the turnout in this election was much higher than is typically seen in constitutional amendment elections. The reason was Proposition 2, which defined marriage in Texas as the union of one man and one woman. The proposition also prohibited the state or any political subdivision of the state from creating or recognizing any legal status identical to or similar to marriage. The proposition generated a strongly favorable vote—1,723,782 in favor versus 536,913 against. Unlike Proposition 12 in 2003, this was not an economic battle involving interests concerned with tort law; rather, this was an issue pitting social conservatives against those more sympathetic to gay rights. The strength of the social conservative vote in the state was, of course, remarkable, since the amendment carried by more than a 3-to-1 margin. Many churches and religious organizations strongly supported the proposed amendment. Their activities probably generated the relatively high voter turnout. The proposition was unusual in that people felt it was important to their lives because it affected their value systems. Although it is doubtful the amendment was necessary to support the traditional concept of marriage and although the ambiguity of the provision rejecting any legal status similar to marriage is disturbing, a significant part of the voting population apparently believed that it was important to vote their moral values, even if the proposal was largely symbolic.

Although most constitutional amendments are not of great importance, there are some notable exceptions. Table 2.5 identifies some of those amendments that,

TABLE 2.5

Some Important Constitutional Amendments

In 1894, Texans strongly supported an amendment providing for the election of railroad commissioners. In later years, when Texas became a major oil producer, the railroad commission gained the authority to regulate oil production and became the most powerful elected regulatory agency in the country.

In 1902, Texans by a huge majority backed an amendment "requiring all persons subject to a poll tax to have paid a poll tax and to hold a receipt for same before they offer to vote at any election in this state, and fixing the time of payment of said tax." The poll tax required a payment of money prior to voting. The effect was to reduce the size of the electorate, limiting the opportunity of those with lower incomes to vote.

In 1919, the same year the national prohibition amendment was ratified, Texas ratified a state prohibition amendment.

In 1935, Texans repealed statewide prohibition. In its place was a local option whereby local communities chose whether alcohol would be sold in those communities. This was two years after repeal of national prohibition.

In 1954, Texans passed an amendment requiring women to serve on juries. Previous to that, women were exempt on the grounds that they were needed at home as the center of home life.

In 1966, Texans repealed the poll tax as a voting requirement in the face of pressures from the U.S. Supreme Court and from a national constitutional amendment that eliminated the poll tax in national elections.

In 1972, Texans overwhelmingly passed a constitutional amendment "to provide that equality under the law shall not be denied or abridged because of sex, race, color, creed or national origin." This amendment was primarily seen as an equal rights amendment banning sex discrimination, since federal civil rights statutes largely dealt with discrimination on other grounds. It was the state version of a proposed sexual equal rights amendment that was never ratified and made part of the U.S. Constitution.

In 2003 a constitutional amendment promoting the tort reform agenda passed that placed limitations on lawsuits. In "civil lawsuits against doctors and health care providers, and other actions," the legislature was authorized "to determine limitations on non-economic damages."

In 2005 a constitutional amendment was passed "providing that marriage in this state consists only of the union of one man and one woman and prohibiting this state or a political subdivision of this state from creating or recognizing any legal status identical or similar to marriage." The amendment was passed in response to the movement toward the recognition of civil unions and same-sex marriage in some states.

In 2009, Texans supported an amendment establishing "the national research university fund to enable emerging research universities in this state to achieve national prominence as major research universities." The amendment was a recognition that the Texas economy would benefit by the development of nationally recognized research universities in the state.

In 2009, in reaction to a U.S. Supreme Court decision involving eminent domain—the taking of private property for public use—that was seen as unsympathetic to property rights, Texans passed an amendment "to prohibit the taking, damaging, or destroying of private property for public use unless the action is for the ownership, use, and enjoyment of the property by the State, a political subdivision of the State, the public at large, or entities granted the power of eminent domain under law or for the elimination of urban blight on a particular parcel of property, but not for certain economic development or enhancements of tax revenue purpose."

like Proposition 12 in 2003 or Proposition 2 in 2005, have had great significance in the public policy of the state.

● Thinking Critically about the Texas Constitution

In this chapter, we explored the Texas Founding and the story of constitutional government in Texas. We analyzed the seven constitutions under which Texas has been governed and explained the similarities and differences between the U.S. Constitution and Texas's current constitution (the Constitution of 1876). We also discussed attempts over the past 30 years to replace this constitution with a new one. If there is one lesson to be learned from our study, it is that the Texas Constitution matters in our everyday lives as much as, if not more than, the U.S. Constitution. The ideas of liberty and equality are enshrined in the Texas Constitution as they are in the U.S. Constitution. In some ways, the Texas Constitution does a better job of protecting liberty and providing for equality than does the U.S. Constitution. Where the Texas Constitution most fundamentally differs from the U.S. Constitution is in its view of democracy. Although championing democratic forms of government, the writers of the Texas Constitution were even more suspicious of centralized institutions of power than were the Founders of the United States. The Texas Constitution places serious constraints on the Texas Legislature's ability to act as an independent body. It creates a weak plural executive, in which executive power is limited and decentralized. Finally, the Texas Constitution subjects the courts to periodic elections. In Texas, the institutions of democracy were never meant to be too far removed from the guiding hand of the people.

A number of additional themes were emphasized in this chapter. First, Texas's current constitution is far more complex than its predecessors or the U.S. Constitution. Matters that are considered public policy in most other states often must be addressed as constitutional issues in Texas. Second, the Texas Constitution is based on a general distrust of politicians and political power. It was originally written to prevent the expansion of political power that had taken place during Reconstruction and to make sure that political power could not be centralized in a way that might hurt the liberties and civil rights of the people. By limiting and decentralizing power, the Texas Constitution makes it hard to implement and successfully administer public policies. Third, the Texas Constitution has been a difficult document to replace. Although amended 483 times, it has not been replaced by a new constitution to date and will probably not be replaced in the future. One reason for this is that mobilizing support for a wholesale reworking of the constitution has proven to be difficult. Another is that the general distrust of government and political power that gave birth to the Constitution of 1876 continues to hold sway among the citizenry.

Many people see some desirable features in the Texas Constitution. Like many state constitutions, the Texas Constitution has a Bill of Rights. Nor are all the rights in the Texas Bill of Rights merely a duplication of those in the U.S. Constitution. To some extent, the Texas Bill of Rights provides more constitutional protections than does the U.S. Constitution. State constitutions may do this under the doctrine of independent state grounds. That is, although a state constitution may provide more rights than the U.S. Constitution, it may not take away rights granted by the U.S. Constitution. One may think of the U.S. Constitution as a baseline to which states can add but not subtract protections. One of the most interesting Texas rights is an amendment adopted in 1972. It states, "Equality under the law shall not be denied or abridged because of sex, race, color, creed, or national origin." It is important to note that the amendment provides explicit protection from sex discrimination, something that is not mentioned in the U.S. Constitution. It is, in fact, a state version of the federal Equal Rights Amendment, which was almost ratified in the 1970s but which never quite received sufficient support from the states to become a part of the U.S. Constitution.

Still, in spite of its positive aspects, the Texas Constitution is a lengthy, confusing, and highly restrictive document. Yet efforts to drastically change the document seem doomed to failure. There is little public outcry over the large numbers of amendments on which voters regularly must cast ballots. Additionally, the Texas Constitution provides protections for the interests of key groups in Texas society, groups that are reluctant to give up those protections in exchange for a more flexible document.

for critical analysis

How does the supremacy clause of the U.S. Constitution affect Texas government?

The Role of a State Constitution

Identify the main functions of state constitutions (pp. 41–42)

The state constitution is the governing document of the state much in the same way the U.S. Constitution sets up the framework for the nation as a whole. Many of the ideas found in the U.S. Constitution are also found in Texas's constitutions, including republican government, separation of powers, checks and balances, and individual rights.

Key Terms

constitution (p. 41)

separation of powers (p. 41)

checks and balances (p. 41)

tyranny (p. 41)

federalism (p. 42)

supremacy clause (p. 42)

necessary and proper clause (p. 42)

Practice Quiz

1. Which idea is contained in both the U.S. and Texas constitutions?
   a) separation of powers
   b) Keynesianism
   c) laissez-faire economics
   d) *Rebus sic stantibus*
   e) none of the above

2. Which of the following is *not* an important function of a state constitution?
   a) prevents the concentration of political power
   b) delegates power to individuals and institutions
   c) allows government to intrude in the lives of businesses and individuals
   d) legitimizes political institutions
   e) limits application of the U.S. Constitution

3. Which part of the U.S. Constitution reserves power to the states?
   a) Article I
   b) Article VI
   c) First Amendment
   d) Tenth Amendment
   e) Nineteenth Amendment

4. Under the U.S. Constitution, the government of Texas is most limited by
   a) Article IV of the U.S. Constitution.
   b) the implied-powers clause and the Tenth Amendment of the U.S. Constitution.
   c) the Fourteenth Amendment of the U.S. Constitution.
   d) All matter equally.
   e) None matter.

The First Texas Constitutions

Describe the six Texas constitutions that preceded the current constitution (pp. 43–53)

Texas has had seven constitutions reflecting the concerns of the historical periods in which they were written. The Civil War and Reconstruction played a major role in shaping Texans' attitudes toward the dangers of strong state government.

Key Terms

unicameral (p. 45)

bicameral (p. 47)

Confederacy (p. 52)

Radical Republicans (p. 53)

Practice Quiz

5. The Constitution of 1861
   a) generally accepted the existing constitutional framework.
   b) guided Texas's entry into the Confederate States of America.
   c) supported slavery.
   d) defended states' rights.
   e) all of the above

6. A unique feature of the Constitution of 1869 was that
   a) it explicitly rejected the power of the federal government in Texas.
   b) fewer than 1 percent of voters opposed it.
   c) it was less than four pages long.
   d) it was never submitted to the voters.
   e) it is considered the best of Texas's constitutions.

The Constitution of 1876

The Constitution of 1876 sought to limit the powers that had been wielded under the previous constitution by Republican governor Edmund Davis. It remains, though much amended, the existing state constitution of Texas.

Key Term

Grange (p. 54)

Practice Quiz

7. A new Texas Constitution was written
   a) when Reconstruction ended.
   b) when the Compromise of 1850 was adopted.
   c) at the start of World War I.
   d) in 1999.
   e) none of the above

8. The present Texas Constitution
   a) is well organized and well written.
   b) is considered to be one of the best of the 50 state constitutions.
   c) delegates a great deal of power to the governor.
   d) severely limits the power of the governor and other state officials.
   e) all of the above

9. The Constitution of 1876 was a reaction to the Reconstruction Constitution of 1869 because
   a) the 1869 Constitution was too short.
   b) the 1869 Constitution forbade slavery.
   c) the 1869 Constitution increased state officials' salaries.
   d) the 1869 Constitution was seen as giving the governor too much power.
   e) none of the above

10. When the framers of the Constitution of 1876 wrote of "the people," they meant
    a) all adult citizens of Texas.
    b) all adult male citizens of Texas.
    c) all adult white male citizens of Texas.
    d) all citizens except carpetbaggers and scalawags.
    e) none of the above

The Constitution of Texas Today

Today's Texas Constitution is lengthy and includes over 400 amendments. It limits the power of state government and tries to prevent the concentration of power in the hands of one person.

Key Terms

limited government (56)

republican government (p. 57)

plural executive (p. 59)

impeachment (p. 61)

Practice Quiz

11. Article 1 of the Texas Constitution
    a) contains the Texas Bill of Rights.
    b) renounces the use of the death penalty.
    c) rejects the U.S. Constitution's Bill of Rights.
    d) recognizes the supremacy of the national government.
    e) accepts the principle of rapprochement.

12. The Texas Bill of Rights
    a) guarantees some rights not found in the U.S. Bill of Rights.
    b) duplicates the U.S. Bill of Rights.
    c) is unusual, since state constitutions generally do not have Bills of Rights.
    d) guarantees gay marriage.
    e) outlaws abortion.

13. The Texas Constitution requires that Texas judges
    a) be appointed by the governor.
    b) be a member of the Republican Party.
    c) be senior lawyers.
    d) be elected by the people.
    e) cannot receive campaign contributions.

Recent Attempts to Rewrite the Texas Constitution

Describe modern efforts to change the Texas Constitution (pp. 63–73)

Recent attempts to rewrite the Texas constitution have been unsuccessful. Amendments continue to be the easiest way to modify the document.

Practice Quiz

14. A new constitution for Texas
    a) is unlikely to be ratified before 2015.
    b) is scheduled for a vote in 2014.
    c) has a 50–50 chance of being ratified.
    d) has a very small chance of being written and ratified.
    e) none of the above

15. Voter turnout for constitutional amendment elections could be improved if
    a) they were held at the same time as presidential elections.
    b) there were more voter awareness of the proposed amendments.
    c) the amendments involved significant issues for voters.
    d) all of the above
    e) none of the above

Recommended Websites

Handbook of the State of Texas
www.tshaonline.org/handbook/online/

Texas Constitution
www.constitution.legis.state.tx.us/

Texas Constitutions 1824–76
http://tarlton.law.utexas.edu/constitutions/

The assurance of voting rights has been a key debate for decades. It exemplifies the tensions between federal and state government. Here U.S. Attorney General Eric Holder speaks in Houston about his opposition to recent Texas voter identification laws and his support of the Voting Rights Act of 1965.

Texas in the Federal System

3

WHY FEDERALISM MATTERS Ninety-year old Jim Wright decided that he would vote near his Fort Worth home in the November 2013 Constitutional Amendment election as he had voted in every election since 1944. He realized that the state of Texas required a valid photo identification or voter identification certificate in order to vote, so he took his driver's license and his faculty identification card from Texas Christian University where he had taught for many years and where he still had an office. However, Wright discovered he could not vote. His eyesight was poor, and so he had stopped driving a few years previously and had not renewed his driver's license when it expired in 2010. His TCU faculty identification card was not considered under Texas law to be valid photo identification. As a result, Wright was not allowed to vote. He then tried to get a voter identification card from the Department of Public Safety but was turned down there for lack of proper identification. Luckily for Wright, his secretary was able to dig through files and locate his birth certificate, and with that he was able to obtain a voter identification certificate in time to vote in the election.[1]

Interestingly, Wright was one of the best-known people in Fort Worth. He was its U.S. congressperson from 1955 to 1989 and was majority leader of the U.S. House of Representatives from 1977 to 1987. He was Speaker of the U.S. House of Representatives from 1987 to 1989. Earlier, he had fought in World War II in the Army Air Corps, where he earned the Distinguished Flying Cross. He had been elected to the Texas House of Representatives in 1946 and was the youngest mayor in Texas when he was elected mayor of Weatherford prior to being elected to Congress.[2]

Wright had been an opponent of the poll tax, which required voters to pay a tax in order to vote. He was an early advocate of the right to vote for 18-year-olds and was one of only 8 out of 22 Texas members of Congress who voted for the 1965 Voting Rights Act. The Voting Rights Act outlawed literacy and other similar devices that historically were used to disfranchise minorities. Section 5 of the act specifically prohibited covered jurisdictions from implementing changes affecting voting without first obtaining approval from the Department of Justice or from the U.S. District Court for the District of Columbia. A formula based on previous voting patterns was used to determine which jurisdictions had disenfranchised voters in the past and thus would have to have prior approval—known as preclearance—before changes in the voting laws would be allowed to go into effect. All this changed in 2013. In *Shelby County v. Holder*, the U.S. Supreme Court found the original coverage formula was outdated and was an intrusion on states' rights. Absent a new, updated coverage formula passed by Congress, states were now free to pass laws affecting voting without Justice Department or U.S. District Court approval.

For Texas, *Shelby County v. Holder* meant that a recently passed voter identification law did not require federal approval. Republicans claimed the law was passed to reduce voter fraud. Democrats claimed that the law actually was designed not to reduce almost nonexistent voter fraud, but to disfranchise many minority voters who tend to vote Democratic. It is too early to assess the impact of the law at this point, although the voter identification law certainly raises important questions about state regulation of the franchise and it does raise an important issue of federalism. What is the role of the national government versus the states in the regulation of elections? To what extent should states regulate the franchise? What role should the national government have in protecting the franchise of people who, unlike Wright, have greater difficulty in providing proper identification to vote? This chapter will examine federalism in the United States. As with the voter identification law, we shall see that the issues relating to state versus national power are important, numerous, and complex.

chapter**goals**

- Understand federalism (pp. 80–86)
- Trace the major changes in national and state power over time (pp. 86–90)
- Describe the sources of national and state power as they relate to federalism today (pp. 90–100)

Understanding Federalism

federalism a system of government in which power is divided between a central government and regional governments

Understand federalism

Federalism is a system of government in which power is divided between a central government and regional governments. At its core is decentralization of government, and in the United States, the balance in the powers of the states and national government has been the subject of intense political dispute since the American Revolution. States have always done much of the routine governance in the United States. State laws provide the regulations for birth, death, marriage, divorce, and most crime and punishment. Most commercial law is regulated by the states, and states manage education, prisons, highways, welfare, environmental issues, corporations, and professions. Many of the political conflicts in the nation have been fought over the proper roles of states versus the national government. These conflicts include disputes over the states' rights to leave the union, the power of government to regulate business, the implementation of political reforms, and responses to problems of race, poverty, and abortion.

Roughly 40 percent of the world's population lives in countries that are organized around a federal principle where there is a national government and regional governments, each of which has the authority to maintain order, make laws,

spend money, and provide services. Federalist countries include the United States, Argentina, Australia, Austria, Belgium, Brazil, Canada, Ethiopia, Germany, India, Mexico, Nigeria, Spain, and Switzerland. The European Union may be developing into a federalist system as well. Federalism exists because it is a method for bringing together smaller units to achieve larger goals—primarily the fostering of commerce and improving military security. In India, Belgium, and Spain, for example, federalism has been used to hold together nations that have serious geographical, ethnic, or cultural divisions. In these countries, the regional governments represent ethnic or religious minorities and have unique powers of self-governance. This is different from the United States, where all states have equal legal standing and authority. In other federal systems, the national government consciously attempts to redistribute the country's wealth to the poorest regions, something not done in the United States. Additionally, federalism in the United States has proven enormously flexible in comparison with other federal nations. Federalism in America has adapted to vast changes in the geographic size of America, to large increases in its population, and to changes in the racial, religious, and ethnic background of its population. It has also adapted to vast economic changes in the nation.[3]

Immediately following the United States' independence from Britain, the Articles of Confederation gave states the primary role in governance, and the national government was small and had limited powers. The relative weakness of the national government meant that the states functioned as nearly independent entities rather than as one nation. In the mid-1780s, the diversity of the states and their self-serving policies appeared to be splitting the new nation apart. An economic decline in the 1780s worsened the divisions in the country. Daniel Shays led a rebellion of Massachusetts debtors who attacked towns and burned courthouses. The new nation seemed on the precipice of revolt. George Washington criticized the state governments for the new nation's problems, saying the states' pursuit of narrow self-interest was making "the situation of this great country weak, inefficient and disgraceful." However, it was hard for the national government under the Articles of Confederation to act. The Confederation Congress had limited powers

Under the Articles of Confederation, the United States had a weak central government—states had more significant powers. This made it difficult for the United States to fund a strong military, as exemplified by terrible conditions for the troops at Valley Forge during the American revolution.

and the rules allowed a few states—in some cases a single state—to block congressional action. It took 9 states (out of 13) to enact any defense or economic policy. The Congress could not tax; it had to request money from the state governments and it could not compel payment by the states. There was no executive or court system under the Confederation. The Confederation could not defend the nation because it could not pay for an army or a navy. By 1786 the Congress was broke because states were not paying their share of expenses for the national government. Even though a majority of the states supported the Congress's efforts to tax imports, individual states objected and killed these tax proposals. Moreover, the Articles of Confederation could not be easily amended since a unanimous vote of the states was required for amendment.[4] By 1786 it was becoming clear that something had to be done to increase the power of the national government. A meeting was held in Annapolis, Maryland, in 1786 that called for a convention of states to meet in Philadelphia the following year to "render the constitution of the Federal Government adequate to the exigencies of the Union." That led to the Constitutional Convention in 1787, where 55 delegates met and designed the new U.S. Constitution.[5]

sovereign possessing supreme political authority within a geographic area

Under the U.S. Constitution, a federal system was created in which the national government was **sovereign**, deriving its power directly from the American people. Individual states were also sovereign, deriving their power from the people in their state through their state constitutions.[6] The immediate effect of the Constitution was to increase national power and to delegate to the national government distinctive powers and responsibilities such as national defense and foreign policy. State governments also had separate powers and responsibilities, such as protecting public safety. Local governments were created by state governments, and their powers are granted (and can be revoked) by state governments. Rather than being a part of a federal system, local governments were the creations of states, and continue to be so today.

State interests were protected under the new Constitution in a variety of ways, and one of the most important was that each state would get equal representation in the Senate. At the time, state legislatures chose the U.S. senators from that state, and so the senators were agents of state interests in the national government. States also retained their power to tax and to maintain a militia, and they had commercial powers, for example, the power to regulate commerce within states. The national government also had taxing authority, military powers, and commercial authority such as the power to regulate commerce between states. And it had flexible powers that could be expanded in the future through Congress's constitutional power, "To make all Laws which shall be necessary and proper for carrying into Execution the foregoing Powers, and all other Powers vested by this Constitution In the Government of the United States."[7]

In the debates over ratification of the Constitution, there was great concern that the national government had been made too powerful and that, if ratified, the Constitution would foster a centralized tyranny that would destroy the rights of the people and the states. In an effort to alleviate these concerns, the Bill of Rights was added to the Constitution in the form of the first ten amendments. The Tenth Amendment (see Table 3.1), commonly called the States' Rights Amendment, states, "The powers not delegated to the United States by the Constitution, nor prohibited by it to the States, are reserved to the States respectively, or to the people." Although James Madison personally did not believe that the Tenth Amendment was necessary, Madison urged that it be adopted. The problem with the amendment is that it does not delineate national and state powers, and rather than settle conflicts over federalism, the amendment has rather been a source of conflict over the meaning of federalism.[8]

TABLE 3.1

The Tenth Amendment (commonly called the States' Rights Amendment)

The powers not delegated to the United States by the Constitution, nor prohibited by it to the States, are reserved to the States respectively, or to the people.

Federalism in Early America

Controversy over the exact nature of the federal system divided Americans in the late 1820s and '30s. During the Nullification Crisis in 1833, South Carolina tried to assert the right to veto (or nullify) national legislation passed by Congress. Spokesmen like John C. Calhoun argued that a strong national government was a threat to the sovereignty of states, and argued for a system along the lines of the original Articles of Confederation. President Andrew Jackson responded by threatening to use military force in support of federal law. South Carolina backed down.

Although the national government had imposed its will successfully during the Nullification Crisis, the question of the exact relationship between the central government and individual states was still open. In spite of the forces of decentralization, most notably coming from the South, the Supreme Court under Chief Justice John Marshall (1801–35)—a Federalist and an appointee of President John Adams—issued a number of important opinions that promoted national power at the expense of state power. In *McCulloch v. Maryland* (1819), for example, one issue was whether Congress had the power to incorporate the Second Bank of the United States. If Congress did have the power to incorporate the Bank, the second issue was whether Maryland could tax the Bank. Writing for a unanimous Court, Marshall noted that Article I, Section 8, of the Constitution enumerated the powers of Congress (see Table 3.2). Nowhere in Article I, Section 8, is specifically found the power to incorporate a bank. However, Article I, Section 8, also contains

TABLE 3.2

Article I, Section 8, Enumerated Powers of Congress

Lay and collect taxes, duties, imposts and excises

Pay the debts

Provide for the common defense and general welfare of the United States

Borrow money

Regulate commerce with foreign nations, and among the several states, and with the Indian Tribes

Establish a uniform rule of naturalization

Establish uniform laws of bankruptcy

Coin money, regulate the value thereof, and of foreign coin

Fix the standard of weights and measures

Provide for the punishment of counterfeiting

Establish post offices and post roads

Provide for patents and copyrights

Constitute lower federal courts

Define and punish Piracy, felonies on the high seas, and offenses against the law of nations

Declare war

Grant Letters of Marque and Reprisal

Make rules concerning captures on land and water

Raise and support armies with an appropriation no more than two years

Provide and maintain a Navy

Make rules for land and naval forces

Provide for calling forth the militia to execute laws of the Union, suppress insurrections, and repel invasions

Provide for organizing, arming, disciplining, and training the militia and for governing them in the service of the United States with officers appointed by the states

Exclusive legislation over the District of Columbia

Make all laws which shall be necessary and proper for carrying into execution the foregoing powers.

a provision that Congress has the power "To make all Laws which shall be necessary and proper for carrying into Execution the foregoing powers, and all other Powers vested by this Constitution in the Government of the United States." A Bank of the United States could be a means to accomplish some of those enumerated powers, such as carrying out the power to borrow money. As a result, Congress did have the implied power to incorporate the bank, as the "necessary and proper" clause of Article I, Section 8, provided a source of implied powers for the national government. Marshall further noted in his opinion that unlike the Articles of Confederation, there was no provision of the U.S. Constitution that excluded the recognition of implied powers. He even made the case that the Tenth Amendment recognized that Congress had implied powers because it said, "The powers not delegated to the United States" rather than "The powers not *expressly* delegated to the United States." Marshall also wrote that the states did not have the power to tax the Second Bank of the United States. For the states to have that taxing power, he argued, would transfer the supremacy of the national government to the states. It was a vastly important decision favoring national power at the expense of state powers.[9]

A major power of the national government is the power to regulate interstate commerce. Gibbons v. Ogden (1824) was a key case that expanded national power. It held that Congress had the power to regulate interstate commerce, like shipping between New York and New Jersey, pictured here.

Gibbons v. Ogden (1824) was another major Marshall Court decision that expanded national power. The case dealt with a dispute over the operation of steamboats in New York waters. Robert Fulton and Robert Livingston obtained a monopoly from New York to operate steamboats in its waters, and they granted a license to Aaron Ogden to operate steamboats between New Jersey and New York. Thomas Gibbons obtained a license from the national government to operate steamboats between New Jersey and New York, and Ogden went to New York courts to get an injunction against Gibbons. Marshall wrote that one of the powers of Congress in Article I, Section 8, was the "power to regulate commerce with foreign nations, and among the several states."[10] Ogden argued that power was limited to the interchange of commodities and did not include navigation, but Marshall broadly defined commerce to include navigation and wrote that interstate commerce "cannot stop at the external boundary line of each state, but may be introduced into the interior." While the completely internal commerce of a state could be considered reserved to the states for regulation, if commerce was not completely internal to a state, it was interstate commerce and could be regulated by Congress, as the regulation of interstate commerce "does not stop at the jurisdictional lines of the several states."[11] This decision, providing a broad definition of interstate commerce, was to be the primary source of the most important regulatory power of Congress: the power to regulate interstate commerce.

Marshall was consistent in deciding cases to expand the power of the national government and weaken the power of states. However, Marshall was unwilling to make the Bill of Rights apply to the states as well as the national government. That would take the ratification of the Fourteenth Amendment in 1868. In Marshall's time, it was clear that the Bill of Rights was not a restriction on the powers of states; it was intended to limit the powers of the national government.

The Constitution was created out of a fear of disunity. Seventy-five years after the ratification of the Constitution, an observer of the American experiment with federalism would have concluded that it was a failure. America faced a massive rebellion and a war that was immensely bloody.[12] The Civil War was, in part, a struggle over the meaning of the federal system and the proper relationship between the national and the state governments. Southern states, including Texas, feared that a national government controlled by northern states would move to end slavery, an institution that they felt was essential to their social, political, and economic way of life. They saw the creation of the Confederacy as a movement back to the older confederation system embodied in the Articles of Confederation where the central government in Richmond was weak and the individual states were strong. This vision of a confederation effectively came to a close with General Lee's surrender at the Appomattox Court House.

The United States and Texas flags that fly in front of many government buildings in Texas (including Dallas's city hall, pictured here) reflect the nature of federalism. Both the national government and the state government are sovereign. The third flag is the flag of the city of Dallas.

Reconstruction the period after the Civil War when much of the South was under military occupation

dual federalism the system of government that prevailed in the United States from 1789 to 1937, in which most fundamental governmental powers were strictly separated between the federal and state governments

In 1869 the Supreme Court in the case *Texas v. White* resolved the debate over whether states can secede from the Union. The case dealt with the legality of a bond sale sponsored by Texas that had occurred under the Confederate government of Texas. In rejecting the legality of the sale of bonds, Chief Justice Salmon Chase authored the opinion which said that the Constitution "in all its provisions, looks to an indestructible Union, composed of indestructible states." Secession was void and Texas had remained a state during the Civil War. Texas had not had a lawful government during the Confederacy, and so the bond sale was void. Additionally, the Union had a right to provide Texas with a republican form of government. The national government could create a government in Texas after the war where no legitimate government existed because Article IV, Section 4, of the Constitution provided, "The United States shall guarantee to every State in this Union a Republican Form of Government."[13]

● Dual Federalism

> **Trace the major changes in national and state power over time**

Following the end of **Reconstruction** and into the early twentieth century, the Court further embraced **dual federalism**. The national government was relatively small in comparison to the states and states did most of the governing. The national government's role was more or less limited to providing for national defense and foreign policy and assisting in the development of commerce. Citizens' daily lives were chiefly affected by their state governments, not the national government.

The classic statement of dual federalism is found in *The Collector v. Day* (1870), a U.S. Supreme Court case that challenged the authority of the federal government to tax the income of a state judge. The majority opinion stated,

> The general government and the states, although both exist within the same territorial limits, are separate and distinct sovereignties, acting separately and independently of each other within their respective spheres. The former in its appropriate sphere is supreme, but the states within the limits of their powers not granted, or, in the language of the Tenth Amendment, "reserved," are as independent of the general government as that government within its sphere is independent of the states'.[14]

Using this dual federalism perspective, the Court ruled that state officers did not have to pay a federal income tax because such a tax would interfere with the autonomy of states.

Prior to the late 1930s the Supreme Court was using dual federalism to strike down regulation of the economy by the national government. Congress's power to regulate interstate commerce was narrowly defined so that it could only ban the shipment of harmful goods in interstate commerce and could only regulate the distribution of goods in interstate commerce. This meant, for example, that Congress was powerless to forbid the distribution of the products of child labor in interstate commerce, and it could not regulate the aspects of the manufacture of goods such as monopolies on production of goods or working conditions in factories.

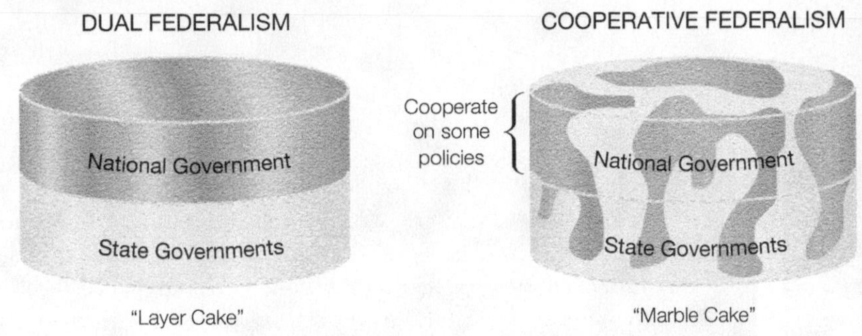

DUAL FEDERALISM

COOPERATIVE FEDERALISM

National Government

State Governments

"Layer Cake"

Cooperate
on some
policies {

National Government

State Governments

"Marble Cake"

FIGURE 3.1

Dual versus Cooperative Federalism

In layer-cake federalism, the responsibilities of the national government and state governments are clearly separated. In marble cake federalism, national policies, state policies, and local policies overlap in many areas.

This system of dual federalism was described by political scientist Morton Grodzins as **layer-cake federalism** (see Figure 3.1). Like the layers on a cake, the powers of the national government and state governments were largely separate and, one might add, the layer that was the national government's powers and responsibilities was smaller than was the layer that represented the powers and responsibilities of state governments.[15] Under layer-cake federalism, there were still clear limits to the sovereignty of states. States could not nullify national legislation, nor could they secede from the Union. But states had a major role to play in governance that was quite distinct from the role of the federal government.

layer-cake federalism a way of describing the system of dual federalism in which there is a division of responsibilities between the state and the national governments

Marble-Cake Federalism

With the presidency of Franklin Roosevelt—when America faced the Great Depression and then World War II—the relationship between the national government and the states changed dramatically. Federalism changed to what has been called **marble-cake federalism**, where the boundaries between the national government and the states became blurred. The initial form of marble cake federalism was **cooperative federalism**, where national and state governments worked together to provide services—often with joint funding of programs or state administration of programs mostly funded by the national government. In fighting the Great Depression, Roosevelt pursued a variety of such programs. The Social Security Act of 1935, for instance, changed the existing federal system in a number of fundamental ways. First, it put into place a national insurance program for the elderly (now known as Social Security) where individuals in all states were assessed a payroll tax on their wages. Upon retirement, "participants" were to receive a pension check. Second, the act put into place a series of state-federal programs to address particular social problems, including unemployment insurance, aid to dependent children, aid to the blind and disabled, and aid to impoverished elderly people. The basic model for these programs was that the federal government would make money available to states that established their own programs in these areas, provided they met specific administrative guidelines. Although the federal dollars came with these strings attached, the programs were state run and could differ from state to state. This type of funding system was common in the early days of cooperative federalism. The grants using this model were called **categorical grants**.

marble-cake federalism a way of describing federalism where the boundaries between the national government and state government have become blurred

cooperative federalism a type of federalism existing since the New Deal era in which grants-in-aid have been used to encourage states and localities (without commanding them) to pursue nationally defined goals; also known as *intergovernmental cooperation*

categorical grants congressionally appropriated grants to states and localities on the condition that expenditures be limited to a problem or group specified by law

During the 1930s, Texans were affected by unemployment and drought that had led to massive poverty across the state. The federal government stepped in to help, employing people in public works projects. Here, people make copper utensils for a Texas Hospital.

Wickard v. Filburn, decided by the Supreme Court in 1942, is probably the most extreme example of how the New Deal led to a rejection of state power when it appeared to conflict with the power of the national government. Roscoe Filburn was a small farmer in Ohio who violated a national law, the Agricultural Adjustment Act of 1938, by growing an additional 239 bushels of wheat beyond the allowable limit. For this violation, he was subject to a fine of $117.11. Filburn challenged the penalty by arguing that the federal law was unconstitutional because it was based on Congress's power to regulate interstate commerce. Filburn claimed that interstate commerce was not involved in his case because he was producing the wheat within his own state for his own use, not for interstate distribution. The Court, however, held that interstate commerce was involved: if Filburn had not grown the wheat himself, he would have had to purchase it, most likely through interstate commerce. And the cumulative effect of many farmers such as Filburn growing wheat beyond their allotment for their own use would have had a substantial influence on the price and market conditions for this commodity. The decision indicated that the power of Congress to regulate interstate commerce was remarkably broad, further eroding state autonomy in the federal system.[16]

During the New Deal period, the idea was abandoned that the Tenth Amendment was a barrier to national power and that the national government could not involve itself in areas that were reserved only to the states. As *Wickard v. Filburn* (1942) suggested, the regulatory power of the national government under the interstate commerce clause was so broad that there seemed no boundaries on national power.

In the 1960s during President Lyndon B. Johnson's Great Society, new programs were added to the Social Security Act. Medicare was established to provide health insurance for the elderly, paid for through a payroll tax on current workers. Medicaid was added to provide health care funding for individuals enrolled in the state-federal Aid to Families with Dependent Children (AFDC) program. Medicaid's funding and administration were based on the same state-federal principles as AFDC and unemployment insurance: the federal government provided funding for approved state programs. Federalism continued to evolve with the passage of civil rights legislation in the 1950s and '60s, when the role of the national government was expanded to protect the rights of minorities. In the process, the national

Federal Funds to Texas versus Other States

Many factors affect how much federal funding a state receives. Federal money can go directly to individuals, such as Social Security or Medicare. Federal money can also go to the states which then decide how best to use the funds to benefit their constituents, such as for highway funding. In the graph below, we can compare how much federal money Texas and Texans receive compared to California, Florida, New York, and Ohio.

Federal Funds Received by States, 2003–13

● Florida ● California ● Texas ● New York ● Ohio

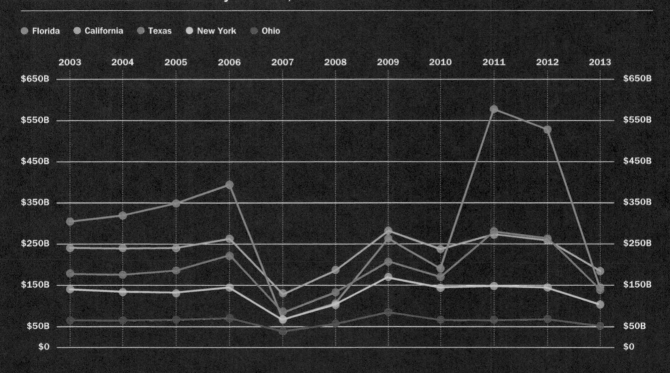

Federal Aid as Percentage of State Revenue, 2012*

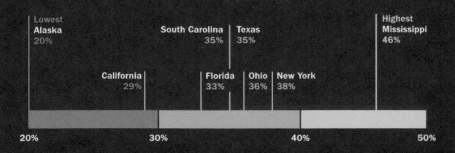

| Lowest Alaska 20% | | California 29% | | South Carolina 35% | Texas 35% | Florida 33% | Ohio 36% | New York 38% | | Highest Mississippi 46% |

20%   30%   40%   50%

for critical analysis

1. What might explain why certain states receive more funding than others at different time periods?

2. Why do you suppose Florida receives more federal funding than Texas when the population of Texas is much larger?

*Does not include programs like Social Security and Medicare that provide money directly to individuals in the states.

SOURCE: Federal funds data from usaspending.gov (accessed 5/27/14). Federal aid data from Census Bureau; Tax Foundation, Facts and Figures. Table 9. Washington, D.C., 2014.

government was often thrown into conflict with southern states such as Texas that persisted in trying to maintain a segregated society.

The broad interpretation of interstate commerce in cases such as *Wickard v. Filburn* (1942) became the foundation for much of the civil rights legislation passed during the Johnson administration.

President Richard M. Nixon briefly tried a somewhat different version of federalism that he called **New Federalism**. In an attempt to reduce federal control, Nixon introduced a funding mechanism called **block grants**, which allowed the states considerable leeway in spending their federal dollars. In the 1980s, President Ronald Reagan adopted Nixon's New Federalism as his own, and block grants became an important part of state-federal cooperation.

New Federalism's biggest success, however, was during President Bill Clinton's administration when, in 1996, major reforms were passed in welfare programs that gave the states a significant decision-making role. By the 1990s, liberals and conservatives were in agreement that welfare in America was broken. Replacing the state-federal system with a system of grants tied to federal regulations and guidelines lay at the heart of the Clinton welfare reforms, the most important since the New Deal.

● Coercive Federalism

Describe the sources of national and state power as they relate to federalism today

In recent years some national actions have been described as **coercive federalism**, where federal regulations are used to force states to change their policies to meet national goals. Until the 2012 Supreme Court decision involving the Affordable Care Act (commonly called Obamacare) struck down the provision, states were threatened with the loss of all Medicaid funding if they did not expand their Medicaid coverage to comply with the legislation. Perhaps most disturbing for states are the federal "**unfunded mandates**," which are the federal requirements that the state (or local) governments pay the costs of federal policies.[17] For example, the federal Americans with Disabilities Act requires that street curbs be accessible to wheelchairs, but the federal government does not pay for the curbs. That cost is passed on to state and local governments. Along with unfunded mandates, federal **preemption** is another aspect of coercive federalism. Preemption is where Congress passes laws and, through the Supremacy Clause of the Constitution in Article VI of the Constitution, which states, "This Constitution and the Laws of the United States which shall be made In Pursuance thereof; . . . shall be the supreme Law of the Land," Congress can pass laws that impose national priorities upon the states. The U.S. Conference of Mayors identified 10 federal mandates that cost cities about 11 percent of their budgets.[18] The National Association of Counties has identified 12 federal mandates that cost counties about 12 percent of their budgets.[19]

Preemption does not necessarily cost a state money as would unfunded mandates, though preemption will prevent the implementation of state laws. As an example, in *Arizona v. Inter Tribal Council of Arizona, Inc.* (2013), the Supreme Court rejected Arizona's requirement that voter registration officials reject any application for voter registration not accompanied by documentary evidence of citizenship. The Court held that the Arizona law was preempted by the National

---

New Federalism the attempts by Presidents Nixon and Reagan to return power to the states through block grants

block grants federal grants that allow states considerable discretion on how funds are spent

coercive federalism federal policies that force states to change their policies to achieve national goals

unfunded mandates federal requirements that states or local governments pay the costs of federal policies

preemption where the national government imposes its priorities and prevents the state from acting in a particular field

How Do Federal Funds Flow to Texas?

Federal grants provide states with money for programs that range from Medicaid and school lunches to tuberculosis control and immunization programs. As the chart below indicates, federal grants make up a majority of the money the state of Texas spends on health care and business and economic development, and a large share of the money spent on natural resources, education, and general government.

2012–13 Texas Budget

 = $1 billion

STATE FUNDS
$189B

FEDERAL FUNDS
$64.7B

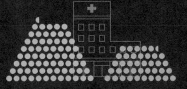

Education
S: $75.7   F: $10.2

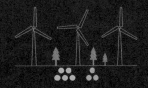

Health and human services
S: $68.6   F: $39.5

Business and economic development
S: $22.3   F: $9.4

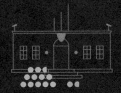

Public safety and criminal justice
S: $11.7   F: $1.8

General government
S: $4.9   F: $0.9

Natural resources
S: $4.9   F: $2.9

Other (regulatory, judiciary, legislature, general provisions)
S: $1.7   F: $0.01

for critical analysis

1. What benefits do federal grants provide to the state of Texas? What drawbacks might these grants present to the state?

2. How does the presence of so much federal money in the Texas budget affect the relationship between the state and federal governments?

SOURCE: Legislative Budget Board, www.lbb.state.tx.us (accessed 5/14/14).

Voter Registration Act of 1993 that required states to accept and use a federal registration form that did not require documentation of citizenship, but rather required a statement from the applicant that the applicant is a citizen.[20]

Preemption of a state statute by a federal statute can be removed by passage of a federal law. As a result, within hours of the Supreme Court's decision in *Arizona v. Inter Tribal Council of Arizona, Inc.*, Senator Ted Cruz of Texas introduced an amendment—that was not passed by Congress—to the Senate's immigration bill that would permit states to require documentary evidence of citizenship.[21]

States have begun to fight back against modern federalism. State officials in Mississippi, Oregon, and Texas vowed to reject attempts by the federal government to impose new gun laws.[22] Numerous sheriffs from around the country claimed that if new federal gun laws were passed, they would not enforce them. Similarly, several state leaders have been highly critical of the Affordable Care Act and have refused to initiate the health insurance exchanges under the act. State leaders have also been critical of the federal government's efforts to enforce immigration laws. Attorney General Greg Abbott as of late April 2013 has sued the Obama administration 25 times. These included lawsuits against the Affordable Care Act, several suits against the Environmental Protection Agency, a lawsuit against the Federal Energy Regulatory Commission, and lawsuits regarding redistricting and voter identification related to preclearance under the Voting Rights Act.[23] Much of this litigation and criticism of the federal government reflects the rebellion against modern federalism. As Attorney General Greg Abbott put it in defending his office's lawsuits against the federal government, "when Texas challenges the federal government, it's about more than money. It's about principles—fundamental principles enshrined in the Constitution and recently reaffirmed by the U.S. Supreme Court when it said: 'The national government possesses only limited powers; the states and the people retain the remainder. The independent power of the states serves as a check on the power of the federal government.' Defending the constitutional principles that have made the United States truly exceptional: That's priceless."[24]

As coercive federalism became more common, concerns were expressed in the last few decades of the twentieth century, particularly among conservative Republicans, that the central state was becoming too strong in the federal system. Not surprisingly, the Supreme Court rethought its doctrines on federalism still again. The effort to rethink the federal system is evident in Supreme Court decisions beginning in the 1990s. Although not dramatic reinterpretations of constitutional law, the Court's rulings did begin to place limits on Congress's ability to legislate under the interstate commerce power, and it resurrected the Tenth Amendment as a protection for the rights of states.

The Court returned to the Tenth Amendment—the so-called states' rights amendment—some of the strength that it had lost during the New Deal era. *Printz v. United States* (1997) challenged a provision of the 1993 Brady Handgun Violence Prevention Act. The Brady act required the attorney general to establish by the end of November 1998 a national database for instant background checks on anyone buying a handgun. Until the database could be finalized, the act required local law enforcement officials to verify that no handguns were sold to unqualified persons. Sheriffs in Montana and Arizona claimed that this provision was unconstitutional on the grounds that the federal government did not have the authority to command state and local officials to administer a federal program. The Supreme Court agreed that the law infringed on the rights of states, writing, "The Federal

Government may neither issue directives requiring the States to address particular problems, nor command the States' officers, or those of their political subdivisions, to administer or enforce a federal regulatory program."[25]

Major U.S. Constitutional and Statutory Restrictions on the States

The Thirteenth, Fourteenth, and Fifteenth amendments to the Constitution were ratified in the aftermath of the Civil War. The Thirteenth Amendment, of course, banned slavery and was important after the Civil War in ending slavery as a basis of the Southern economy. It was the other Civil War Amendments, the Fourteenth and Fifteenth amendments, that even today have had a dramatic effect on the nature of federalism because the Fourteenth and Fifteenth amendments provide the basis for the major constitutional and statutory restrictions on the powers of states.

Incorporation of the Bill of Rights

Even the great nationalist Chief Justice Marshall was unwilling to hold that rights in the Bill of Rights applied to the states. It was just too clear that the Bill of Rights intended to limit the powers of the national government and not state governments. The application of the Bill of Rights to the states potentially changed in 1868 with the ratification of the Fourteenth Amendment, which clearly applied to states.

Section 1 of the Fourteenth Amendment states, "All persons born or naturalized in the United States and subject to the jurisdiction thereof, are citizens of the United States and of the State wherein they reside. No State shall make or enforce any law which shall abridge the privileges or immunities of citizens of the United States; nor shall any State deprive any person of life, liberty, or property, without due process of law; nor deny to any person within its jurisdiction the equal protection of the laws." The Fourteenth Amendment was proposed by Congress in 1866 and ratified a little more than two years later when 28 of the then 37 states ratified it.

It was not until the 1890s that the Court used the Fourteenth Amendment to hold in two cases that state governments could not seize property for public use without providing just compensation under the Fifth Amendment of the U.S. Constitution.[26] Then, in *Gitlow v. People of State of New York* (1925), Justice Edward Sanford noted in what has come to be called the **Sanford dictum** that "we may and do assume that freedom of speech and of the press are among the fundamental rights and liberties protected from impairment by the states."[27] As the years passed, other rights in the Bill of Rights were held to be fundamental rights and therefore applicable to the states. With few exceptions, as the twentieth century progressed, justices adopted the theory of **selective incorporation**. That meant that the Court would select out some rights in the Bill of Rights as fundamental—so essential to the concept of ordered liberty—that those rights were incorporated (held to be part of) the "liberty" that was guaranteed in the language of the Fourteenth Amendment of the U.S. Constitution that stated that "nor shall any State deprive any person of life, *liberty* [emphasis added], or property, without due process of law." More and more rights were selected by the Court to be fundamental rights that were held to apply to the states. Most recently, in 2010 the Court held that the Second Amendment right to "keep and bear arms" applied to the states.[28] There are now very few rights in the Bill of Rights that have not been held to be fundamental—and few would argue that those rights are of much value. For example, the right to indictment by a grand jury has not been held to apply to the states, nor has the right to a jury trial in civil cases of more than $20. Nor has the Eighth Amendment provision against excessive fines and bail been held to apply to the state, or the provision in the Third Amendment that limits the quartering of soldiers in a person's home. In the years since the process of selective incorporation of the rights in the Bill of Rights began, so many rights have been selected by the Court as fundamental that near-total incorporation of all the rights in the Bill of Rights has occurred and been made to apply to the states. The result is that the freedom of states to restrict persons in those matters protected by the Bill of Rights has virtually been eliminated. Incorporation of the Bill of Rights is one of those areas where the freedom of the states to act in ways different from the national government has been virtually eliminated.

Sanford dictum held in *Gitlow v. New York* that the First Amendment right of free speech was a fundamental right that applied to the states

selective incorporation rights in the Bill of Rights that the Court believes are fundamental and are held to apply to the states as well as the national government because they are part of the "liberty" protected from state action in the Fourteenth Amendment

Herman Sweatt (right) walks with a white student at the University of Texas. Sweatt refused to attend a separate, all-black law school.

The Equal Protection Clause

With few exceptions, in the nineteenth century the equal protection clause offered little promise of being a U.S. Constitutional restriction on the states. It was not until well into the twentieth century that the equal protection clause became a useful legal instrument to combat racial discrimination by the states. In the 1930s the Court began to chip away at state laws promoting racial discrimination. In 1950 a Texas case heralded the end of segregated higher education. H. M. Sweatt was denied admission to the University of Texas Law School because he was black. He refused to attend a black law school that had been set up by Texas to provide what Texas claimed to be a separate but equal education for black Texans seeking a legal education. Texas claimed that having an all-white University of Texas Law School and a separate all-black law school provided separate but equal educations for black and white law students which complied with the interpretation of the equal protection clause by the Supreme Court in *Plessy v. Ferguson* (1896) when

Voting and Redistricting in Texas

In 1965, President Lyndon Johnson made history by signing the Voting Rights Act into law. The purpose of the legislation was to eliminate racial discrimination in voting. A somewhat controversial element of the law was Section 5, which required states covered under that provision, including Texas, to have any changes to voting procedures approved by the Department of Justice or a federal court in the District of Columbia. The rationale behind what is termed "preclearance" was to ensure that the federal government would have oversight over voting laws in states that have had histories of excluding racial minorities from the political process.

The Voting Rights Act has been renewed periodically since 1965. During that time, the Department of Justice has challenged many states, including Texas, and required them to redraw legislative districts in order to comply with the Voting Rights Act. In recent years, there has been a backlash against the Voting Rights Act by many state governments, including Texas. In 2013, Attorney General Greg Abbott challenged the Department of Justice by claiming that preclearance was a violation of Texas state sovereignty. Abbott argued that the federal government singled out Texas for preclearance and that it is not fair to make some states, but not others, comply with the law. He argued that in 2013 there is no longer a question of voter discrimination in Texas and that all states should be treated equally. He also claimed that the Voting Rights Act exceeded the bounds of federal authority. He cited the Tenth Amendment to the U.S. Constitution, which reserves powers to the states that are not specifically enumerated to the federal government in the Constitution.

While the U.S. Supreme Court did not agree with Abbott's arguments in full, it did deliver a ruling striking down

portions of the Voting Rights Act that establish a formula used to determine which states are subject to Section 5 preclearance. By the Court's striking down the formula, preclearance has been suspended for now. It is uncertain today that Congress will pass a new and constitutional formula. Civil rights groups are alarmed that without the protection of preclearance, Texas and other states will design legislative districts that will dilute the influence of minority voters and prevent them from electing candidates of their choice.

Part of the conundrum is that in Texas, most minorities are members of the Democratic Party and during redistricting, parties attempt to maximize their influence in elections. Republi-

cans claim that they are not discriminating against minorities, but against Democrats, which is perfectly acceptable and legal. However, when most minorities are Democrats, how do we know the true source of the discrimination? The courts have been reluctant to give a definitive answer, but part of the challenge is distinguishing racial discrimination (which is illegal) from political discrimination (which is legal). If it turns out that Democratic minorities are packed into heavily concentrated districts, the influence of minorities in Texas politics may be diluted as a practical matter. However one feels about the politics, Texas's redrawing of the boundaries of these districts is now considered lawful.

critical thinking questions

1. Does preclearance violate the Tenth Amendment and give the federal government too much power, or is it a necessary check on the states to make sure that minorities are not discriminated against?

2. Are there ways that Texas and the federal government can compromise on how best to ensure the rights of minorities in the electoral process?

it upheld state-required racially segregated train cars in Louisiana. Sweatt's argument was that the black law school was not equal to the University of Texas Law School but was inferior and, therefore, to require him to go to the black law school would deny him the equal protection of the laws. The Supreme Court agreed with Sweatt, pointing out that there were vast differences in the facilities as well as differences in the prestige of the schools, the reputation of the faculty, the experience of the administration, and the influence of the alumni. While the Court stopped just short of declaring the doctrine of "separate but equal" to be unconstitutional, after Sweatt, it was hard to see how the doctrine could survive.[29] The doctrine did not survive. In 1954, in *Brown v. Board of Education of Topeka*, the Supreme Court unanimously held that segregated public schools were inherently unequal.[30] The doctrine of **"separate but equal"** was dead, though there was opposition to the decision in many states including Texas that would delay for decades the end of legally created segregation in public schools.

Now when the courts are presented with an issue of racial discrimination under the equal protection clause, the courts will ask the question, "Is there a compelling governmental interest that would justify a classification based on race?" And if a compelling governmental interest does exist, can that governmental interest be achieved in a less drastic way than through a racial classification? The result of this modern-day application of equal protection to the states is that it is very difficult for a state to justify a law that classifies people based on race. This standard is commonly called **strict scrutiny**.

Any classification made by the law can be attacked on equal protection grounds. Because the equal protection clause is found in the Fourteenth Amendment, which was an amendment ratified after the Civil War to provide protection for former slaves, the equal protection clause offers the greatest protection against racial classifications. The Court has treated some other cases like racial cases; that is, the Court has used the strict scrutiny or the "compelling governmental interest" standard. However, those cases are few and far between and would generally involve a denial of a fundamental right such as the right to vote.

At one time, all classifications other than race and fundamental rights cases were judged under the equal protection clause by a very lenient standard, the **rational basis test**, in which the Court asked, "Is there a rational justification for the law?" There are almost always rational justifications for any law—administrative convenience or saving money can, for example, be rational justifications for laws. It takes an exceptionally foolish law to be determined irrational by the Court. Still, major provisions can be struck down as unconstitutional using the rational basis test. In November 2005, Texans approved a state constitutional amendment that defined marriage as being between one man and one woman. That provision was challenged in federal district court, and using the rational basis test, the judge found that the amendment was not connected to any legitimate governmental interest that justified a discriminatory law. In other words, the judge held there was no rational basis for a ban on same-sex marriage. That decision is now on appeal, but it does show that although it is much easier for plaintiffs to win a case with strict or intermediate scrutiny, even state constitutional amendments might be approved that are found to have no legitimate rational justification.[31]

In the 1970s there was a movement to use the equal protection clause to strike down statutes that discriminated on the basis of sex. In a 1976 case involving a classification based on sex, the Court ruled, "Classifications by gender must serve important governmental objectives and must be substantially related to achievement of those objectives."[32] This higher standard for sex-based classifications—

"separate but equal" an interpretation of the equal protection clause of the Fourteenth Amendment that held that states could segregate races as long as equal facilities were provided; it was overturned in 1954

strict scrutiny the most rigorous equal protection standard. It requires that the government show a compelling state interest in order to successfully defend a law that makes certain classifications such as racial classifications. Additionally, that classification must be one that is narrowly tailored by the least drastic means possible to achieve the government's objective.

rational basis test presumes that the legal classification made by the government is constitutional; all the government must show is some rational justification for the law

often called the **intermediate standard of review** or the substantial governmental interest test made it much harder for states to pass constitutional laws based on sex.

At times the Court has used the intermediate standard of review for classifications made by the law that are not classifications based on sex. For example, in *Plyler v. Doe* (1982) Texas withheld from local school boards state funds for the education of children who were "not legally admitted into the United States." Justice Brennan, writing for the Court, held, "If the State is to deny a discrete group of innocent children the free public education that it offers to other children residing within its borders, that denial must be justified by a showing that it furthers some substantial state interest. No such showing was made here."[33] That expansion of the "substantial governmental interest" test beyond gender classifications has, however, been far more random and unclear than the use of the test for gender classifications.

The equal protection clause has become one of the most powerful constitutional restrictions on states. All laws create classifications of people, and the clause provides certain standards depending on the classification made by the state that courts use to judge the legitimacy of the law. As a rough rule of thumb, a classification based on race or one affecting fundamental rights will be judged under strict scrutiny or the "compelling governmental interest" standard—a standard so demanding that the law will probably be unconstitutional. A classification based on gender will be judged by the "substantial governmental interest" standard or possibly the counterpart of this standard, the "exceedingly persuasive justification" standard that has sometimes been used by the Court to make the "substantial governmental interest test" an even more difficult barrier to governmental action. It is very likely that classifications judged under these standards will be unconstitutional as well. Other classifications—for example, classifications based on wealth—will be judged under the "rational basis" standard and, unless the classification made by the law is essentially so arbitrary that it is mindless, the law will be upheld under this standard since laws generally do have some sort of a rational justification.

State Regulation of Voting

The Voting Rights Act was passed under Congress's authority under the Fifteenth Amendment to legislate to protect the right to vote where the nation or a state might deny or restrict that right on the basis of race or color. Section 4 of the act provides a coverage formula that defines the jurisdictions covered under the act, and Section 5 of the act requires that federal officials—initially the U.S. Department of Justice—approve or preclear any changes in voting in jurisdictions that are defined in the law. Those jurisdictions include Texas. Voting changes that must be precleared include such things as the establishment of voter identification laws, redistricting of political boundaries, and changes in the times or locations of polling places. Texas has been required to preclear since 1975 and, like other covered jurisdictions, state officials have chafed over the need to secure federal approval for the changes they wish to make in voting in the state. That is why an Alabama case decided by the U.S. Supreme Court in the summer of 2013 is so important to Texas and to federalism. The case, *Shelby County, Ala. v. Holder* (2013), involved a challenge to Congress's decision to reauthorize the Voting Rights Act. Shelby County, Alabama, claimed that the act went beyond Congress's power to pass the law under the authority of the Fifteenth Amendment and that the law placed "substantial federalism costs" on the covered jurisdictions, costs that were so great that the Tenth Amendment rights of the states were violated.

intermediate standard of review primarily used for classifications in the law based on sex; for the law to be constitutional the government must show important governmental objectives and the law must be substantially related to achievement of those objectives

Shelby County as a political unit of the state of Alabama has been covered by the preclearance requirement since 1965. It viewed the act as outdated, taking the position,

> Given the federalism costs Section 5 imposes, the provision can be justified only by contemporary evidence of the kind of "unremitting and ingenious defiance" that existed when the Voting Rights Act was originally passed in 1965. . . . Insisting that the legislative record lacks "evidence of a systematic campaign of voting discrimination and gamesmanship by the covered jurisdictions," Shelby County contends that section 5's remedy is unconstitutional because it is no longer congruent and proportional to the problem it seeks to cure.[34]

Texas filed an amicus curiae or friend of the court brief in the Supreme Court litigation. Such a brief is sometimes filed by states, groups, or individuals with a strong interest in the outcome of the case but who are not the parties to the litigation. Texas's brief supported Shelby County's claim that Section 5 of the Voting Rights Act went beyond Congress's powers to pass laws under the Fifteenth Amendment and placed substantial enough costs on federalism that there was a violation of the Tenth Amendment. Texas's brief noted that the act was based on voting conditions in Texas in 1975. Unlike 1975, however, Texas now has bilingual ballots, and in every federal election between 1996 and 2004, blacks in Texas registered and voted at higher rates than whites, while Latinos in Texas registered to vote at higher rates between 1980 and 2002 than Latinos in jurisdictions not covered by Section 5. The remainder of the Texas amicus brief is essentially an argument that substantial costs to federalism are created by the preclearance requirement, and the evidence used is that preclearance has prevented the implementation of Texas's voter identification law where a voter must provide an identification—a Texas driver's license, an election identification certificate, a personal identification card issued by the state, a U.S. military identification with a photo of the prospective voter, a U.S. citizenship certificate with a photo of the prospective voter, a U.S. passport, or a Texas concealed handgun license.[35] The Texas brief argued,

> For nearly two years, the Civil Rights Division of the Department of Justice has used every weapon in its arsenal to thwart the implementation of a law that the Court has recognized as a legitimate and constitutional fraud-prevention measure. Because of section 5, the State of Texas still is unable to implement its voter-identification law—a law that Indiana and non-covered jurisdictions may enact and enforce without any interference from federal authorities.[36]

In late June 2013 the Court issued its blockbuster 5–4 decision striking down the formula for determining the states covered under the Section 5 preclearance requirement. Holding that the formula for determining coverage under the act was based on decades-old data, the Court held that Shelby County was correct in its position that the data used to determine if a jurisdiction was covered were too outdated to be valid. Congress could, of course, draft another formula to cover jurisdictions under the act, but that formula must be based on current voting conditions. The Court emphasized two important points about the federal system: (1) all states enjoy equal sovereignty, and (2) under the Tenth Amendment, states have broad power to regulate elections. Only exceptional conditions, such as the racial discrimination in voting at the time of the initial passage of the 1965 Voting Rights Act, justified intrusion on the powers and the equality of states. The Court's view was that the outdated data that determined which jurisdictions were covered under the act did not provide sufficient evidence of those exceptional conditions that justified current intrusion into state powers over voting and thus, absent a valid formula to determine which states must go through a preclearance procedure, no state had to undergo preclearance.[37] Given this decision, Texas no longer has to obtain preclearance to change aspects of its system of elections. However, the U.S. Justice Department can still sue under Section 2 of the Voting Rights Act to prohibit changes in elections that show racial discrimination. Currently the U.S. Justice Department is suing Texas under Section 2 to stop Texas's system of voter identification.

It is clear that the voter identification requirement has had some effect on some voters, such as women who have married or divorced and changed their names so that their identification does not match the voting lists or elderly persons such as former Speaker Jim Wright who no longer had a valid driver's license. However, political scientists have found that the effect of voter identification laws is not what one ordinarily suspects. As Professors Keith Bentele and Erin O'Brien have written,

> The results of a wide range of studies indicate that most registered voters do possess the forms of identification required by voter ID laws. Consequently, such laws may do little to suppress routine voters, but may serve to reduce participation among the eligible unregistered population who are much more likely to lack basic forms of required identification. It has been suggested that "the real value of restrictive voter ID may be in what we might call 'surge protection' against the kind of mobilization of new, first-time voters who very likely handed Obama his election [in 2008]."[38]

Flexibility for States under the Constitution: Independent State Grounds

Although there are restrictions on the states imposed by the Fourteenth Amendment and by statutes passed under the authority of the Fifteenth Amendment, states do have some leeway to expand rights of their citizens through a concept known as **independent state grounds**. State constitutions can provide greater constitutional guarantees to a state's citizens than the U.S. Constitution. Essentially, the rights guaranteed in the U.S. Constitution are a floor—the minimal rights that are provided—but the U.S. Constitution does not function as a ceiling on rights. State constitutions can provide additional constitutional protections. Independent state grounds are a characteristic of federalism in that states are free to add to the rights guaranteed at the national level. Some states, such as Massachusetts, have relied on their state constitutions to invalidate laws against same-sex marriage.[39] Under the U.S. Constitution, Texas's very inequitable property tax–based system for funding public education was held to be constitutional. The U.S. Supreme Court held that education was not a fundamental right and so Texas only needed a rational justification—that is, local control of schools—in order for the funding system to be upheld.[40] However, in *Edgewood v. Kirby* (1989), the Texas Supreme Court relied on the Texas Constitution to strike down the school funding system. The Court held, "Whether the legislature acts directly or enlists local government to help meet its obligation, the end product must still be what the [Texas] constitution commands—i.e., an efficient system of public free schools throughout the state."[41]

In the 1970s there was a major effort to gain ratification of an Equal Rights Amendment to the U.S. Constitution. If ratified, the key part of the amendment

independent state grounds allow states, usually under the state constitution, to expand rights beyond those provided by the U.S. Constitution

would have stated, "Equality of rights under the law shall not be denied or abridged by the United States or by any state on account of sex." Although that amendment to the U.S. Constitution was never ratified, in 1972 Texas adopted its version of the Equal Rights Amendment, which is Article 1, Section 3a, of the Texas Constitution: "Equality under the law shall not be denied or abridged because of sex, race, color, creed, or national origin." U.S. Supreme Court decisions have provided major protection against sex discrimination under the equal protection clause of the Fourteenth Amendment to the U.S. Constitution; however, it is the Texas Constitution, rather than the U.S. Constitution, that contains an explicit ban.

● Thinking Critically about Federalism

One of the most intriguing political questions is whether the new generation of leadership in Texas will be successful in creating a new relationship between the states and the national government. We have seen that federalism has significantly changed over time. Early in the country's history, the country moved from a confederation to a view that a stronger national government and weaker states were needed. The nation then fought a bloody civil war in part over whether a strong national government or a confederation was the most desirable system of government. From that perspective the country moved to dual federalism. Then, in the late 1930s, the country moved toward cooperative or marble-cake federalism. In more recent years, coercive federalism has become increasingly common. There is no reason to believe that federalism will not continue to evolve and change. Leading Texans are now wishing to return greater power to the states. They argue the national government is too distant, controlling, expensive, and unresponsive. Perhaps they are in the vanguard of a new view of federalism. At this point it is unclear—maybe they are not in the vanguard, but fighting a rearguard action for a lost cause that was the long-ago demise of dual federalism. This remains to be seen, although the key question is whether the current relationship between the states and the national government is best for resolving important policy issues or whether returning greater power to the states is the more appropriate way to solve major policy problems.

Understanding Federalism

Understand federalism (pp. 80–86)

Along with many other countries, the American system of government has divided power between national and regional or state governments. That division of power has varied over time, and America's notion of federalism has evolved through a number of forms.

Key Terms

federalism (p. 80)

sovereign (p. 82)

Practice Quiz

1. *Federalism* refers to
   a) a system of government where cities are strong.
   b) a system of government where executive power is grounded in a committee of governors.
   c) a system of government where there is a national government as well as a number of regional governments.
   d) a system of government dominated by business interests.
   e) a system of government with strong parliaments.

2. The Articles of Confederation
   a) was a loose confederation of independent states that operated in the 1820s.
   b) was never accepted by a majority of the states.
   c) derived its power directly from the state governments.
   d) replaced the U.S. Constitution of 1787.
   e) outlawed effective state constitutions.

3. The relationship between the states and the national government
   a) has been a matter of continuing controversy throughout the nation's history.
   b) was finally settled when the Articles of Confederation were rejected in favor of the U.S. Constitution.
   c) was resolved for all time by the Civil War.
   d) was resolved by Article I, Section 8, of the U.S. Constitution.
   e) was not a problem in a federal system.

4. The Supreme Court under John Marshall expanded national power partly through
   a) rejecting the Articles of Confederation.
   b) expanding the meaning of interstate commerce.
   c) expanding Congress's war-making powers.
   d) ignoring the Tenth Amendment.
   e) increasing the powers of the president.

5. Prior to the ratification of the Fourteenth Amendment, the Bill of Rights
   a) applied only to states.
   b) applied only to the national government.
   c) applied to states and the national government.
   d) was essential in protecting individual rights.
   e) was applied only in extreme cases of rights violations.

6. *McCulloch v. Maryland* (1819) was important
   a) in establishing that the national government had implied powers.
   b) in establishing that state governments had implied powers.
   c) in showing that the state and national governments could cooperate.
   d) in preventing national banks from operating.
   e) in destroying corrupt state banking systems.

Dual Federalism

Trace the major changes in national and state power over time (pp. 86–90)

American federalism has gone through major changes over the history of the country. In the late nineteenth century there was a strict division between the powers of the state and the powers of the national government. That division was called dual federalism or layer-cake federalism. During Franklin Roosevelt's New Deal, federalism was dramatically redefined and there was greater involvement of the national government in all areas of American life. Cooperative federalism or marble cake federalism became the new approach to state and national relationships. In recent times, many believe federalism has taken a new form and has become coercive, where the national government compels the state to act in ways that achieve national priorities.

Key Terms

Reconstruction (p. 86)

dual federalism (p. 86)

layer-cake federalism (p. 87)

marble-cake federalism (p. 87)

cooperative federalism (p. 87)

categorical grants (p. 87)

New Federalism (p. 90)

block grants (p. 90)

Practice Quiz

7. *Dual federalism*
   a) refers to a system of government where states do most of the governing.
   b) existed in the United States following World War II.
   c) rejected the idea that states were sovereign political entities.
   d) is the idea that there are two branches to the national legislature.
   e) drained all power from state governments.

8. Layer-cake federalism switched to marble-cake federalism
   a) after the Civil War.
   b) during World War I.
   c) during the New Deal.
   d) after the fall of the Soviet Union.
   e) because of President Ronald Reagan's efforts.

9. The use of categorical grants was a way of promoting
   a) cooperative federalism.
   b) dual federalism.
   c) coercive federalism.
   d) bipartisan federalism.
   e) civil rights.

Coercive Federalism

Describe the sources of national and state power as they relate to federalism today (pp. 90–100)

The incorporation of much of the Bill of Rights has limited the power of state governments by making them subject to restrictions under the U.S. Constitution. Additionally, the preemption doctrine has allowed the national government to prohibit state legislation in certain fields. An important constitutional provision that limits state action is the Fourteenth Amendment, particularly the equal protection clause of that amendment which prohibits discriminatory actions by state governments. Until recently, a number of jurisdictions—including Texas—were limited by the 1965 Voting Rights Act in the legislation they could pass involving the electoral process, although a recent U.S. Supreme Court decision has made it possible for Texas to pass controversial voter identification legislation. Finally, while state governments cannot reduce the rights guaranteed by the U.S. Constitution, they can expand those guarantees under the concept of independent state grounds.

Key Terms

coercive federalism (p. 90)

unfunded mandates (p. 90)

preemption (p. 90)

Sanford dictum (p. 94)

selective incorporation (p. 94)

"separate but equal" (p. 96)

strict scrutiny (p. 96)

rational basis test (p. 96)

intermediate standard of review (p. 97)

independent state grounds (p. 99)

Practice Quiz

10. Hostility to modern federalism is partly a result of
    a) dual federalism.
    b) funded mandates.
    c) unfunded mandates.
    d) Tenth Amendment interpretations.
    e) high taxes.

11. States must adhere to most of the provisions of the Bill of Rights because of a process known as
    a) inclusion of the Bill of Rights.
    b) incorporation of the Bill of Rights.
    c) expansion of the Bill of Rights.
    d) ratification of the Bill of Rights.
    e) the Sanford dictum.

12. The equal protection clause of the Fourteenth Amendment
    a) makes it difficult for states to discriminate against minorities.
    b) is rarely used by federal courts.
    c) ensures that states will continue to have a republican form of government.
    d) mandates the right to vote for all adult citizens.
    e) requires all states to have an equal number of senators.

13. The outcome of a court case involving the equal protection clause
    a) tends to be determined by the standard of review that is used.
    b) depends on how unequal the law is.
    c) depends on the skill of the lawyers.
    d) can never be predicted.
    e) is usually in favor of the state.

14. Independent state grounds
    a) allow states to provide fewer state constitutional protections.
    b) allow states to provide more state constitutional protections than the U.S. Constitution.
    c) allow states to remain independent of the national government.
    d) prevent the national government from overriding the Tenth Amendment rights of states.
    e) limit the power of the national government to pass economic regulations.

15. The national government can preempt state laws because
    a) the national government is weaker than any state.
    b) the Tenth Amendment to the Constitution specially allows state laws to be overridden by federal laws.
    c) the supremacy clause of the Constitution makes national laws supreme over state laws.
    d) the Sanford dictum established preemption.
    e) the main reason the Constitution was adopted was so that state laws could be preempted.

16. The Voting Rights Act
    a) ensured the right to vote for women.
    b) ensured the right to vote for 18-year-olds.
    c) approved photo ID requirements for voters.
    d) required that voters know how to read and write.
    e) was the major law providing the right to vote for African Americans.

Recommended Websites

Federalism in Action
www.federalisminaction.com

Freedom Works
www.freedomworks.org

Texas Conservative Coalition
www.txcc.org

TEXANS FOR OBAMA

2012 Election Precincts (VTDs)

Democrats dominated Texas politics for nearly a century, but today the Republican Party is dominant. Can Democrats turn Texas blue again? How do party politics affect Texans?

Political Parties in Texas

WHY POLITICAL PARTIES MATTER When will Texas "turn blue"? That is, when will Texas turn Democratic enabling key statewide offices to be held, once again, by members of the Democratic Party? Political pundits across the nation and in Texas have been asking this largely because of two parallel developments: the ongoing dominance of the Republican Party in the state and the state's growing minority population, which is increasingly Latino.

Following the Civil War until the election of Ronald Reagan in 1980 Texas was largely a one-party state. Conservative Democrats from rural areas dominated state politics in all branches of government. The first Republican senator from Texas since Reconstruction was John Tower, elected in an off-year election in 1961 to replace the newly elected vice president Lyndon Johnson. The first Republican governor since Reconstruction was William Clements, elected in 1978. Throughout the 1990s the state was transformed from a Democratic to a Republican bastion. With the retirement of Democratic lieutenant governor Bob Bullock at the beginning of 1999, Republicans took over complete control of all statewide offices. The control of the Texas House of Representatives shifted to the Republicans in 2002, paving the way for a redistricting fight and ultimately, in 2004, a Republican takeover of both branches of the state legislature. By 2004, Texas had become solidly Republican, a key player in the coalition of conservative interests that came to dominate the national Republican Party.

One might expect that a triumphant Republican Party might seek out new ways to appeal to the growing Latino population in the state and cement its hold over state politics by broadening its political base. After all, some conservative values—that is, opposition to abortion and to same-sex marriage—may appeal to some in the Latino community, particularly those with strong Catholic religious beliefs. Surprisingly, though, the 2014 Republican primary was filled with candidates staking out political positions that seemed against the interests of most Latino voters. For example, some of these very conservative candidates had strong anti-immigration messages and supported tighter restrictions on voting. At the very time that one might expect the Republican Party to moderate itself and adopt positions more in line with an emerging Latino electorate, the party was being driven to the right.

The election of Julian Castro as mayor of San Antonio along with the election of his twin Joaquin Castro to a congressional seat from San Antonio has led some to believe that a Democratic wind is in the air. Democrats have staked their hope in the large and growing Latino population, as most Latinos still identify with the Democratic Party. Nevertheless, there are undercurrents that raise questions about the ability of Democrats to rise to power on a Latino tsunami. Later, we will explore the problem of low voting rates among Latinos in Texas elections. In this chapter, we note that some Latino elected officials and a substantial minority of the Latino population identify as Republican. Several Latinos have won statewide office as Republicans in recent years, including Victor Carrillo to the Railroad Commission and Eva Guzman to the Texas Supreme Court. Republican and Tea Party–leaning Ted Cruz, a Cuban American, was elected to the U.S. Senate in 2012. In contrast with African Americans, who have remained solidly Democratic as a group, Latinos are more willing to cross party lines and vote for Republicans. For example, Latino votes were a factor in Republican George W. Bush's victory in the governor's races of 1994 and 1998. Bush received nearly 40 percent of the Latino vote in 1998, and his success signaled the possibility that Latinos might be gradually shifting to the Republican Party. Although a large-scale shift of Latinos toward the Republicans has not yet come to pass, and some observers doubt that it is likely, the underlying reality remains that Republicans cannot ignore a group that makes up nearly 40 percent of the state's population if they expect to continue winning elections in twenty-first-century Texas.

Whether Texas continues to be a red (Republican) or a blue (Democratic) state, it is important to understand political parties and their structure because knowledge of the rules in government is essential to advancing public policy. Because parties play such a large role in government processes, we must know how parties are organized, how candidates are selected, and how partisanship influences public policy. This chapter will address the history of political parties in Texas, the current party system, and what the future holds for the party system in the state, including some answers to the much-talked-about question of "when Texas will turn blue."

chapter**goals**

- Describe the main functions of state party organizations (pp. 106–20)
- Trace the evolution of the party system in Texas (pp. 120–27)
- Analyze how ideological divisions and demographic change affect Texas political parties (pp. 127–32)

The Role of Political Parties in Texas Politics

Describe the main functions of state party organizations

Political parties can be looked at from a number of perspectives. In the narrowest sense, a political party refers to an organization of people established to win elections. This can include people holding or running for office who identify formally with the party. It can also refer to the professionals and volunteers who actively work for the election of their party's candidates. In a broader sense, a political party can refer to those people in the electorate who identify with a particular party and vote for that party's candidates on a regular basis.

Political parties help candidates win elections and assist voters in making their electoral choices. Perhaps the most important function of parties in Texas is that they provide a label under which candidates can run and with which voters can identify. Because Texas elects large numbers of officeholders, it is unlikely that voters will be familiar with the views or the qualifications of every candidate. However, Texas voters overwhelmingly identify with or lean toward either the Republican Party or the Democratic Party.[1] Those voters use the party affiliation of the candidates as a way to decide for whom to vote. Thus, for many voters, without other information, the party label becomes the standard they apply in casting a ballot for a candidate. Voters often use the party label as a cue to the ideology of candidates. A voter may assume that, for example, a Republican candidate is a "conservative" and may vote for or against that candidate because of the ideology that a party affiliation implies.[2]

Parties to some extent help in raising money for candidates' campaigns and in assisting candidates with legal requirements and training for a campaign. They sometimes recruit candidates for political races, although in Texas any candidate may run in a party primary, and, if victorious in the primary, will become the party nominee. Parties also assist in "getting out the vote" for candidates through phone banks, door-to-door contacts, and other efforts.

Once a candidate is elected to office, party affiliation helps in organizing the government. Governors will usually appoint people who are members of their own party. Increasingly, the Texas legislature is divided by party. Public officials may also feel a greater sense of loyalty and cooperation toward other public officials of their party. After all, they often campaign together and make appearances at the same political events, and their fortunes often rise and fall together based on the popularity of the party. In that sense, the banding together of officeholders with the same party affiliation provides voters an opportunity to hold the party accountable for its policies or its failures.

Texas Parties in the National Context

States differ in terms of the strength of the political parties, and parties also tend to have less power at the state level than they do in the national government. For example, in neighboring Louisiana, the parties are relatively weak. In the Louisiana legislature, even though the majority party controls committee assignments, chairs of committees sometimes include a mix of Democrats and Republicans. This has historically also been true in Texas. The current speaker of the Texas House, Joe Straus from San Antonio, is considered a moderate Republican and owes his election to the speakership to many Democrats in the legislature who voted to elect him speaker. In recognition of their support, Straus made some Democrats committee chairs. This would never happen in the U.S. Congress, as parties are much more important in national politics. In Congress, the majority party gives leadership positions like committee chairs only to its own loyal party members.

Why might parties at the state level have less power? Tip O'Neill, the former Speaker of the U.S. House, used to say that "all politics is local," and this certainly rings true in Texas. Local issues are usually not ideological in nature. They often deal with who is most effective at creating jobs and keeping districts safe for residents. Voters in local races are therefore likely to be influenced by these concerns in

One of the most important functions of political parties is to select candidates to run for office under the party label. The Republican Party of Texas officially announced its candidates for office at its 2014 convention in Fort Worth.

partisan polarization the degree to which Republicans have become more conservative and Democrats have become more liberal

addition to hot-button issues such as abortion and same-sex marriage. This means that partisanship has been less important in running the everyday business of the state. To be sure, ideological issues might matter in certain state-level elections during some election years. **Partisan polarization**, which is the degree to which Republicans have become more conservative and Democrats have become more liberal, is beginning to become more pronounced in the Texas legislature. Partisan polarization in politics means that it is increasingly difficult for politicians to compromise on important policy issues. Compromise is often considered a sign of weakness and caving in to the other side.

Party politics in Texas is similar to party politics in some other southern states, but there are important differences. Other southern states have had historically larger African American populations than Texas. As we will discuss later, African Americans are generally loyal Democrats. They constitute nearly 30 percent of the population in Mississippi and Louisiana, for example. In Texas, African Americans are concentrated in east Texas and in the major urban areas, and represent only 12 percent of the state's population. Another major difference between Texas and some other southern states is Texas's large Hispanic population, which currently is estimated at 38 percent of the state's population. Like African Americans, Hispanics tend to be Democrats, but not to the same degree.

To a certain extent, Texas is similar to New Mexico, Arizona, and Colorado in terms of its large Hispanic population. In contrast with the Hispanic population in Arizona, however, Tejanos (Texans of Mexican descent) are more likely to have resided in the state for generations. In Arizona, the Sonora Desert region is the largest gateway for Mexican immigration, and new immigrants in Arizona exhibit political behavior that differs from that of their Tejano counterparts in many ways. For example, new immigrants are even more likely than Tejanos to identify as Democrats and to see the Democratic Party as more supportive of immigrant rights.

Public Attitudes about Parties

Texans, like many Americans, are increasingly identifying as independent. However, in practice many self-identified independents lean toward either Democratic or Republican affiliation. What is the source of these political leanings? The process of **political socialization** occurs throughout our early years, when our parents, religious leaders, teachers, and others influence our partisan identifications. Although this can change over time for many people, we often retain the same political beliefs as those of our parents. We are also profoundly shaped by our surrounding environment. Texas has a long history of state pride, independence, and conservatism. People growing up in the state are accustomed to these values and thus incorporate them into their political ideologies and partisan preferences. Visitors to the state are often surprised about how much state pride exists. For example, the very notion of a state pledge of allegiance recited by many schoolchildren is a practice that surprises people from other states.

political socialization the introduction of individuals into the political culture; learning the underlying beliefs and values on which the political system is based

How does partisan affiliation affect Texas voters? According to a May 2012 *Texas Tribune* poll, 56 percent of respondents cited party affiliation as either very or somewhat important when deciding for whom to vote. Party identification acts as an important cue that signals candidates' political views. For the most part, when we see an "R" or a "D" next to a candidate's name, we make certain assumptions about the positions the candidate takes. Of course, other characteristics of candidates matter too; in the same poll, voters also cited the candidate's record, issue positions, and character as important considerations in their voting choices.[3]

In Texas, the Republican Party has complete control of state government, and voters continue to re-elect Republicans to all levels of government. This does not mean that there is no competition within the Republican Party, however. Republican primaries often pit conservatives against moderates. An example of this was the Republican gubernatorial primary between Governor Rick Perry and Senator Kay Bailey Hutchison in 2009. Perry positioned himself to the right of Hutchison even though she had compiled a conservative voting record in the U.S. Senate since her election in 1994.

At the conservative end of the spectrum, the Tea Party movement is particularly strong in Texas. In a February 2013 *Texas Tribune* poll, nearly 20 percent of respondents said that they would vote for a Tea Party candidate if the movement organized as a third party. When asked about the Tea Party's influence on the state Republican Party, respondents were split: 31 percent felt that the Tea Party had too much influence, 18 percent thought their degree of influence was about right, and 28 percent thought that they had too little influence.[4] According to a 2012 *Texas Tribune* poll, roughly 34 percent of voters in Texas would support a generic Democratic candidate, while 45 percent would support a generic Republican candidate.[5] This leaves a substantial remainder of "swing" voters who ultimately decide elections. Since their control of state government gives Republicans a built-in advantage, it is increasingly difficult for Democrats to win statewide.

The Contemporary Republican Party in Texas

Texas Republicans are currently experiencing a major division within the party. Established pro-business Republicans have dominated state politics in recent years, but the Tea Party movement has begun to influence state legislative races as well as major statewide races.

While running for lieutenant governor in 2014, Dan Patrick positioned himself as more conservative than his opponent, fellow Republican David Dewhurst. Here, Patrick is seen campaigning with Mike Huckabee, a conservative media personality and former Arkansas governor and presidential candidate.

Consider the lieutenant governor's race in 2013. The Republican candidate, Lieutenant Governor David Dewhurst, had the endorsement of Governor Rick Perry and many of the state's political leaders. However, state senator Dan Patrick, a darling of the Tea Party movement, posed a significant challenge to Dewhurst especially in terms of grassroots support. Patrick was one of several Republicans who challenged Dewhurst because they sensed a weak candidate who lost the U.S. Senate primary in 2012 to now senator Ted Cruz. Patrick ran to the right of Dewhurst and all the other candidates, especially on his immigration positions. In a debate in early 2014, he called for an end to the "invasion" of illegal immigrants from the Southern border. In a low turnout primary in early March 2014, Patrick forced Dewhurst into a runoff by winning a plurality of 41 percent versus Dewhurst's 28 percent. In the runoff primary, Patrick overwhelmed Dewhurst, receiving 65 percent of the vote compared to 35 percent for Dewhurst. It was remarkable that an incumbent lieutenant governor would be defeated in his own party primary, but Patrick successfully positioned himself to the right of Dewhurst in an increasingly conservative party.

Patrick ran ads criticizing Dewhurst for being too moderate, a charge that is not particularly helpful in a Republican primary. Patrick took a page from Cruz's playbook by criticizing Dewhurst for being an insider and state government official with endorsements from the state's political establishment. Patrick went on to win the general election over Democrat Leticia Van de Putte, a Latina state senator from San Antonio, with 58 percent of the vote.

Texas Republicans currently hold all of the major statewide elected offices. The governor, lieutenant governor, comptroller, attorney general, members of the state supreme court, and the railroad commissioners are all Republicans. Texas Democrats have attempted to recruit challengers for these offices but have come up short. As the lieutenant governor's race demonstrates, the major competition for important statewide offices occurs during the Republican primary, much in the same way the Democratic primary used to fulfill this role when Texas was a Democratic state.

The Republican Party in Texas has not always been so powerful. Prior to 1994, Democrats held many statewide offices in Texas. Ann Richards, the state's last Democratic governor, was a proud liberal, as was former U.S. senator Ralph Yarborough, who championed the Bilingual Education Act in 1968. However, few pundits seriously thought that the Democratic candidates for the U.S. Senate seat in 2012 had a realistic chance of winning the general election in November. This is a remarkable change from only 10 years prior, when Democrat Ron Kirk was seen by Democrats as a more formidable candidate for statewide office, even though on Election Day he lost to Senator John Cornyn by double digits.

The Contemporary Democratic Party in Texas

Texas Democrats have been relegated to minority status in the state since the early 2000s. Democrats controlled the Texas House until 2002. Other southern states, such as Arkansas, still have Democratic legislatures and statewide elected officials; however, these officeholders are more conservative than the national Democratic Party. In West Virginia, for example, Democrats dominate state government, but in presidential elections, the state often votes Republican. Before 1994, Texas exhibited similar voting patterns, but now Republicans are elected to all statewide offices at the state and federal levels.

Most Texas Democrats today would be classified as liberal. The party's base is made up of African Americans, Latinos, and white liberals in urban areas. Most white liberals are located in Austin, Houston, Dallas, and San Antonio and have often moved to Texas from other parts of the country. This coalition, however, is currently not large enough to win many elections in statewide races. Most whites in the state have settled into the Republican Party, and because whites turn out to vote at much higher rates than Latinos, who are the fastest-growing minority group in the state, Republicans have won recent elections. Democrats hope to mobilize Latinos, who constitute nearly 40 percent of the state's population, to encourage them to vote. Sixty-nine percent of Texas Latinos are American citizens by birth, but a large proportion of these are under age 18 and cannot vote. Moreover, voter turnout rates among Texas Latinos are lower than the rates among their Anglo counterparts. It will require extensive efforts to register and bring Latino voters to the polls in force to change this.

No Democrat has won Texas in a presidential race since Jimmy Carter in 1976. In 2012, Republican presidential candidate Mitt Romney won 57 percent of the vote in Texas, while Barack Obama won just 41 percent. Democratic candidates also fared poorly in the U.S. Senate race to replace retiring senator Kay Bailey Hutchison; Ted Cruz, the Republican nominee, won the office easily.

This does not mean that Texas Democrats do not have influence in certain localities. In Travis County, the home of Austin, Democrats dominate city government. Other major cities, including Houston and San Antonio, have Democratic mayors and city councils. However, this influence does not extend to statewide elections.

Democrats continually try to build their presence and power in Texas. Most Democrats in Congress from Texas are either Latino or African American. Here, former president Bill Clinton appears at a campaign event with fellow democrats state representative Pete Gallego (D-Alpine, left), former San Antonio mayor (now Secretary for Housing and Urban Development) Julian Castro, and U.S. congressman Joaquin Castro (far right), during a campaign rally in San Antonio.

When Democrat Bill White, the former mayor of Houston, ran for governor in 2010, he lost to Rick Perry.

Seven of the nine Democrats representing Texas in the U.S. Congress are either Latino or African American. The first African American woman elected to Congress from Texas was Barbara Jordan, who played a major role in the investigation of Richard Nixon during the Watergate scandal. Her legacy remains strong among African Americans in Texas. Lloyd Doggett of Austin and Gene Green of Houston are the only two white Democrats representing Texas in Congress. This suggests that the majority of Texas Democrats are minorities, and, with the growth of the minority population in the state, the party makeup will become more minority and less white. This demographic change in Texas makes the state more similar to its southern neighbors. In the Deep South, the Democratic Party is mostly an African American party. This is not true in the Northeast, where more whites identify as Democrats than in the South.

Democratic and Republican Party Organization

Although many Texans proclaim that they are "registered Republicans" or "registered Democrats," Texas does not have a system of party registration. Registered voters may vote in either the Democratic or Republican primary. When they do vote in a primary, their voter registration card will be stamped "Democrat" or "Republican" to prevent them from voting in the other primary as well.

One of the most important functions of political parties is to select candidates to run for office under the party label. Today that is done through primary elections. If several candidates are running for the party nomination in a primary election, it may be that none receive a majority vote. In that case, the party will hold a runoff election to determine who will be nominated. Primaries were not always used to

How Republican Is Texas?

The South has become a solidly Republican region, and Texas is no exception to this. Indeed, former president Clinton official Paul Begala, a native Texan, once called the state "South Carolina on steroids." Since the 1960s, South Carolina has been a reliable Republican state in presidential elections. On the other hand, California has become a solidly Democratic state since the 1990s largely due to its growing Latino population and its relatively high population of white liberals. How does Texas compare to other key states on political partisanship?

Percentage of Residents Who Identify as Republicans*

Utah	Wyoming	Idaho	Kansas	Nebraska	North Dakota	Alabama	Montana	Oklahoma
62.3%	56.8%	56.0%	51.1%	50.8%	50.7%	50.3%	49.8%	48.3%

South Carolina	Mississippi	Alaska	South Dakota	Georgia	Tennessee	Indiana	Arizona	Missouri
47.0%	46.5%	46.5%	45.3%	45.1%	44.6%	44.2%	44.0%	43.8%

Colorado	Virginia	Louisiana	Kentucky	Texas	Nevada	New Hampshire	Arkansas	West Virginia
43.7%	43.4%	43.0%	42.9%	42.7%	42.5%	42.3%	42.2%	42.1%

North Carolina	Wisconsin	Iowa	Pennsylvania	Florida	Ohio	New Mexico	Oregon	Maine
41.8%	41.4%	40.3%	40.2%	40.2%	39.4%	39.4%	39.3%	37.7%

Washington	Minnesota	Michigan	New Jersey	Delaware	Connecticut	Illinois	California	Vermont
37.3%	37.3%	36.1%	35.2%	34.1%	33.9%	33.7%	33.5%	33.0%

Massachusetts	Maryland	New York	Hawaii	Rhode Island	D.C.
32.4%	32.4%	30.3%	29.6%	28.4%	13.3%

*Or who identify as independents but say they lean Republican

SOURCE: 2012 Gallup Organization.

for critical analysis

1. How does Texas compare to other states in terms of partisanship?

2. How might demographic change, especially the growing Latino population, change Texas's political preferences?

precinct the most basic level of political organization at the local level

precinct chair the local party official, elected in the party's primary election, who heads the precinct convention and serves on the party's county executive committee

county executive committee the party group, made up of a party's county chair and precinct chairs, that is responsible for running a county's primary elections and planning county conventions

county chair the county party official who heads the county executive committee

state executive committee the committee responsible for governing a party's activities throughout the state

state chair and **vice chair** the top two state-level leaders in the party

select the party nominee. During the nineteenth century, candidates were nominated at party conventions, but early in the twentieth century the state moved to the primary as a way to select candidates.

To understand how the parties are organized, think first in terms of the permanent organization of the party and then in terms of the temporary (campaign) organization (see Figure 4.1). In each election **precinct**, a **precinct chair** will be elected in the party primary. The precinct chair will head the precinct convention and will also serve on the party's **county executive committee**. In the primary, the **county chair** will also be elected. The county chair will head the county executive committee, which is composed of the chair and the precinct chairs. The main responsibility of the county executive committee is to run the county primary and plan the county conventions. There may be other district committees as well for political divisions that do not correspond to the county lines.

At the state level, there is a **state executive committee**, which includes a **state chair** and **vice chair**. These officers are selected every two years at the state party conventions. The state executive committee accepts filings by candidates for statewide office. It helps raise funds for the party, and it helps establish party policy. Both the Democratic and Republican parties also employ professional staff to run day-to-day operations and to assist with special problems that affect the party.

The temporary organization of the party includes the **precinct conventions**. The main role of the precinct conventions is to select delegates to the **county convention** and possibly to submit resolutions that may eventually become part of the party platform.

Delegates chosen by the precinct convention then go to the county conventions (or in urban areas, to district conventions). These conventions will elect delegates to the **state convention**. Both the Democratic and Republican parties hold state

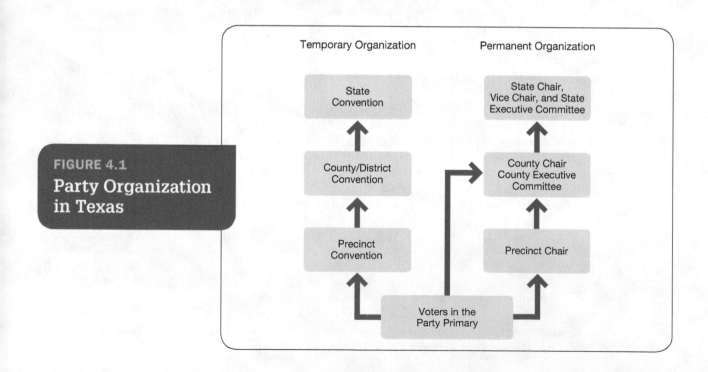

FIGURE 4.1
Party Organization in Texas

Temporary Organization

Permanent Organization

State Convention

State Chair, Vice Chair, and State Executive Committee

County/District Convention

County Chair County Executive Committee

Precinct Convention

Precinct Chair

Voters in the Party Primary

Political parties in Texas are organized at the precinct level, the county level, and the state level. This photo shows the Fayette County Republican Headquarters in La Grange.

conventions every other year. These conventions certify the nominees of the party for statewide office; adopt a platform; and elect a chair, a vice chair, and a state executive committee. In presidential election years, the state conventions select delegates for the national party conventions, elect delegates for the national party committee, and choose presidential electors, who, if the party's choice for president carries the state in the election, will formally cast the state's electoral votes for the president in the electoral college.

Conflict occurs not only between political parties but also within the parties. Battles for control of a state party have often been fought in Texas politics, where rival ideological and other interest groups have struggled to control precinct, county, and state conventions and to elect their candidates for precinct chair, county chair, and state executive committee. In the 1950s struggles for control of the Democratic Party between liberals and conservatives were fierce. There have also been calmer times in Texas politics, when involvement in the parties has been minimal and battles have been few. Sometimes, apathy has been so great that precinct conventions have been sparsely attended and offices such as precinct chair have gone unfilled.

Third Parties in Texas

In Texas, as in many other states, the two parties in power have made it difficult for third parties to gain access to the ballot. In essence, both parties agree that a third competitor is not a net positive for either party. Third-party candidates rarely win elections in Texas. In general, third-party candidates are also seen as inevitable losers at the ballot box, and voters would prefer to "go with the winner."

precinct convention a meeting held by a political party to select delegates for the county convention and to submit resolutions to the party's state platform; precinct conventions are held on the day of the party's primary election and are open to anyone who voted in that election

county convention a meeting held by a political party following its precinct conventions, for the purpose of electing delegates to its state convention

state convention a party meeting held every two years for the purpose of nominating candidates for statewide office, adopting a platform, electing the party's leadership, and in presidential election years selecting delegates for the national convention and choosing presidential electors

Dixiecrats conservative Democrats who abandoned the national Democratic Party in the 1948 presidential election

La Raza Unida Party political party formed in Texas in order to bring attention to the concerns of Mexican Americans

In Texas, third parties have emerged at certain points in history, mainly because of a particular issue. In the late nineteenth century, two farmers movements—the Grange and the Populist movements—provided alternatives to the two major political parties in various elections. In 1948 racial integration became an issue when the States' Rights Party, or **Dixiecrats**, rallied behind segregationist Strom Thurmond for president instead of Democratic Party candidate Harry Truman. Interestingly, while Thurmond carried some states, he did not carry Texas, which voted for Truman. Segregation became a third-party issue again in 1968 when Alabama governor George Wallace ran as a third-party candidate against the liberal Democratic candidate Hubert Humphrey. Echoing the success of Dixiecrat Thurmond, Wallace carried a number of southern states but failed to win Texas, which supported Humphrey. Much of Humphrey's support can be attributed to the lingering popularity of President Johnson in the state.

The civil rights movement in the 1960s planted the seeds for an independent Latino movement named **La Raza Unida**, meaning "united race." Jose Angel Gutierrez led the party at its inception, which was concentrated in Zavala County. La Raza Unida developed into a third party in Texas and was able to win races in Crystal City and other small towns in south Texas. The party was able to do this by taking advantage of nonpartisan elections in many cities and towns. Even today, many cities, such as Austin, conduct nonpartisan elections. This does not mean that the candidates running for office do not belong to political parties. It just means that their party affiliation is not listed on the ballot. Reformers in many cities pushed for this so that voters would vote on the basis of candidate qualifications rather than by political party. La Raza Unida won many of these races in Zavala County and other surrounding counties, so that at one point, the party was able to take

Independent candidates face considerable challenges in elections. Although the musician and writer Kinky Friedman's 2006 candidacy for governor attracted major media attention, Friedman received only 12.4 percent of the vote.

Third-Party Ballot Access in Texas

In Texas, as in most other states, all state legislators and members of the executive branch are members of one of the two major political parties: the Democratic Party or the Republican Party. As discussed in this chapter, the state parties hold primary elections in order to determine who their candidates will be for the general election. Voters are not necessarily limited to choosing between the two major parties. For example, third-party presidential candidate Gary Johnson, representing the Libertarian Party, appeared on the ballot in all 50 states in 2012. However, general election ballot access is difficult in Texas because of laws passed by the legislature. This results in many elections between candidates of the two major political parties.[a]

Texas requires parties that did not get 5 percent of the vote in a previous statewide race to collect a minimum number of signatures for their candidate to get on the ballot. This number must equal at least 1 percent of the total number of people who voted in the most recent gubernatorial election. Other states have similar requirements for ballot access. However, in Texas, parties that hope to qualify for inclusion on the ballot by petition are also required to notify the state that they intend to do so. This law, passed in 1993, is unique to Texas.

The intention form is usually due in January of election years.[b] Many third parties point out that this requirement discriminates against parties that are formed in the spring of election years, because by then it is too late to complete the form. If Texas had a law like this in 1912, Theodore Roosevelt could not have put his new Progressive (or "Bull Moose") Party on the ballot, because even the idea for the party did not occur to Roosevelt until he failed to get the Republican presidential nomination in June 1912.

Should Texas make it easier or more difficult for third parties to gain access to the ballot? Proponents of

Texas, like most states, makes it challenging for minor party candidates like Gary Johnson to get on the ballot.

the law argue that adding more uncertainty to the political process by allowing more names on the ballot only muddies the waters, as historical election returns indicate that one of the two major party candidates will most likely win. Adding third parties to ballots might thwart the will of the people by allowing a candidate to win without majority support. Some point to the presidential election of 2000, when Vice President Al Gore lost Florida's electoral votes and thus the election because of the presence of Green Party candidate Ralph Nader on the Florida ballot.

Opponents of the law argue that the two major political parties have joined forces to eliminate competition.[c] This leads to strict ballot access laws, requiring stringent deadlines and, in some cases, unrealistic numbers of signatures of registered voters in a given area. Opponents also argue that in a democracy, access to the ballot should be open so that voters have a true say on Election Day. Limiting the ballot to only two parties severely restricts the will of the people.

[a] Ross Ramsey, "Smaller Parties Refuse to Be Counted Out," *New York Times*, April 6, 2012, p. A19.
[b] Texas Secretary of State, www.sos.state.tx.us/elections/forms/181004.pdf (accessed 5/5/14).
[c] The Coalition for Free and Open Elections, http://cofoe.org; Ballot Access News, www.ballot-access.org (accessed 5/5/14).

critical thinking questions

1. Should every party be allowed a spot on the ballot, regardless of its chances of winning votes? Why or why not?

2. What would be the ideal way to regulate ballot access? How should access to the ballot be determined?

control of some city councils, school boards, and even the top city job of mayor. By 1972 the party nearly cost Democrat Dolph Briscoe the governorship because of the candidacy of Ramsey Muñiz. While this movement ultimately faded away, as most third-party movements do, it marked the growing influence of Latinos in the state.

In recent years, the Libertarian Party in Texas has emerged as a third-party alternative to the two major political parties. While running candidates for a wide range of offices across the state, the Libertarian Party has not been successful at the polls and had little impact on Election Day. For the most part, it has been a party of protest where people dissatisfied with politics in the state can express their discontent at the polls. Libertarians believe in limited government and can be considered fiscal conservatives and social liberals. Former U.S. representative Ron Paul of Lake Jackson, nominally a Republican, ran for president in 1988 as a Libertarian, and his isolationist views on foreign policy in particular are quite distinct from those of other Republicans. Libertarians are particularly active in some of the major cities, including Austin. While they do not win very many elections, they can influence politics in other ways. For example, the major parties may adopt some of the positions promoted by Libertarians (or members of other minor parties) in order to win their support in runoff elections.

The most recent case involving a significant threat to the major-party candidates was the 2006 election for governor. Rick Perry was seen as a vulnerable incumbent, especially during a year that was not particularly favorable for Republicans. Democrat Chris Bell, a former Houston member of Congress, won the Democratic nomination, but two major independent candidates also ran for governor. They were former comptroller Carole Keeton Strayhorn from Austin and musician and humorist Kinky Friedman, whose catchy slogan was "Why the hell not?" When all the ballots were counted, Perry was re-elected governor with 39 percent of the vote. While it is not clear that a two-way race between Bell and Perry would have ensured a Bell victory, the candidacies of Strayhorn and Friedman damaged whatever mandate Perry could claim from a victory without a majority.

Why don't people vote for third parties? In general elections, Texas employs what is known as a **"first past the post," single-member district** electoral system. Under a first past the post system, only the candidate who wins the plurality of votes, that is, the most votes, is elected. According to **Duverger's Law**, this type of voting system tends to favor a two-party system because a vote for a third-party candidate generally does not result in a win. Consider the 2006 governor's race in which Perry won with less than an outright majority. Although Friedman and Strayhorn made a good showing for third-party candidates, they still only received 12.4 percent and 18.1 percent of the vote, respectively. Even if a runoff election had occurred, it would have been between the top two vote getters, Perry and Bell. This is not to say that a vote for a third-party candidate is "wasted," because major-party candidates as well as the parties themselves can often be responsive to voters who might have voted for a third-party candidate. Winning candidates often run in future elections and would like to appeal to constituents who might not have supported them in the past.

In contrast, some other countries use a system of **proportional representation** that encourages third-party voting because even if a party wins only 10 percent of the vote in an election, it will still win 10 percent of the seats in the legislature or other

"first past the post" an election rule that states that the winner is the candidate who receives a plurality of the votes

single-member district an electorate that is allowed to elect only one representative for each district

Duverger's Law the observation that in a single-member district system of electing representatives, a two-party system will emerge

proportional representation a multimember district system that allows each political party representation in proportion to its percentage of the total vote

representative body. Voters in these countries are therefore more likely to vote for third and minor parties, because they will almost certainly be able to elect at least one of these candidates.

Many American voters believe that their votes would be wasted if they voted for a third-party candidate. This expectation is rational, as the history of elections shows that a Republican or Democrat will almost always win. Most voters logically decide that it makes more sense to vote for the major-party candidate whose ideology is closest to their own.

The Occupy and Tea Party Movements in Texas

The recent **Occupy** and **Tea Party movements** have become prominent nationwide and in Texas. Occupy has held demonstrations in Austin and other major Texas cities, protesting the influence of big banks and Wall Street on American politics. Tea Party advocates, however, have had greater influence in Texas mainly because of their libertarian antitax message, which resonates with many Texans. The implications of these antitax policies in Texas means less funding for K–12 and higher education and fewer social services, such as children's health care programs.

Tea Party organizers have not yet sought to run a third-party candidate in elections, however. Instead, they have tried to influence Republican primary elections (see Figure 4.2). They believe that they can have more influence in state politics if they become a force to be reckoned with within the Republican Party. Undoubtedly, this is a wise strategy given the history of defeat for third parties, not only in the state but nationwide. Tea Party groups have focused their efforts on key statewide races. They have campaigned against incumbents, such as Speaker Straus of San

Occupy movement political movement aimed at limiting the influence of Wall Street and big corporations in American politics; created following government bailouts in 2008

Tea Party movement created after Barack Obama's election, a political movement that advocates lower government spending, lower taxes, and limited government

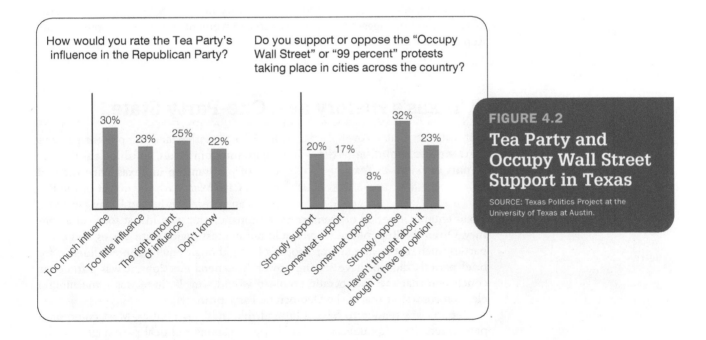

FIGURE 4.2

Tea Party and Occupy Wall Street Support in Texas

SOURCE: Texas Politics Project at the University of Texas at Austin.

The Tea Party has had a strong influence on the Republican Party. Tea Party leader Konni Burton got the Republican nomination for Wendy Davis's state senate seat in Fort Worth.

Antonio, whom they deem to be too moderate. While the Tea Party has had some success in defeating incumbents and nominating preferred candidates, it remains to be seen whether the movement will be co-opted by the Republican Party or be an independent influence. Ted Cruz's victory in the U.S. Senate runoff in July 2012 seemed to suggest that the Tea Party movement has been co-opted by the Republican Party.

● Texas's History as a One-Party State

> **Trace the evolution of the party system in Texas**

In order to understand the present partisan environment in Texas, let us look at the history of partisanship in Texas since the end of the Civil War. With the defeat of the Republican governor Edmund J. Davis in 1873, Texas entered a period of Democratic dominance that would last for over a century. Often the Republican Party would not contest major state offices, and other parties, such as the Populist or People's Party, though having some influence for brief periods, did not have staying power. In general elections, it was a foregone conclusion that the Democratic nominee would win. If there was a meaningful election contest, it was in the Democratic Party primary.

Republicans tended to have a limited role in Texas politics. Most commonly, people remained Republicans in the hope of gaining political patronage (usually local postmaster or rural mail carrier positions) when Republican presidents were in office. Some Republicans were businesspeople unhappy with the liberal policies of Democratic presidents such as Franklin Delano Roosevelt or Harry Truman. However, the Republican Party was not a threat to Democratic dominance in the state. Indeed, Republicans interested in patronage from the national government may have had an incentive to keep the Republican Party small, as the fewer the Republicans, the less the competition for patronage positions. When the father of the late senator Lloyd Bentsen first moved to the Rio Grande Valley, he visited with R. B. Creager, who was then state chairman of the Republican Party. Lloyd Bentsen, Sr., told Creager that he wanted to get involved in the Republican Party because his father had been a devoted Republican in South Dakota. Rather than welcoming Bentsen into the Republican Party, Creager told Bentsen, "You go back to Mission [Texas] and join the Democratic Party, because what's best for Texas is for every state in the union to have a two-party system and for Texas to be a one-party state. When you have a one-party state, your men stay in Congress longer and build up seniority."[6]

In 1952 and 1956, however, the Democratic governor Allan Shivers led a movement often known as the **Shivercrat movement**, which presaged a dramatic change in party alignments a quarter century later. Governor Shivers was a conservative Democrat and widely regarded as one of the most able Texas governors of the twentieth century. He supported the candidacy of the Republican Dwight Eisenhower for the presidency against the Democratic nominee, Adlai Stevenson. Stevenson opposed the Texas position on the Tidelands, offshore lands claimed by both Texas and the national government, which were believed to contain oil. Additionally, Stevenson was much more liberal than Shivers, and Eisenhower was a famous and popular hero of World War II. Governor Shivers not only supported Eisenhower for the presidency; he and all statewide officeholders except the agriculture commissioner, John White, ran on the ballot as Democrats *and* Republicans. It was an act of party disloyalty condemned by loyal Democrats such as Speaker of the U.S. House of Representatives Sam Rayburn, and it led to much tension in the Democratic Party between liberal and conservative Democrats as well as between party loyalists and the Shivercrats.

The Shivercrat movement sent a strong message that many conservative Democrats were philosophically opposed to the national Democratic Party and although they were unwilling to embrace the Republican Party fully, they found the Republican Party more compatible with their views. A pattern in voting known as **presidential Republicanism** was strengthening, whereby conservative Texas voters would vote Democratic for state offices but vote Republican for presidential candidates. With the Shivercrat movement, those conservatives were more numerous and more closely aligned with the Republican Party. To be sure, the fact that some Democratic voters supported the Republican candidate did not mean that the state would vote Republican during every presidential election. As the "Who Are Texans?" graphic shows, the fortunes of Republican presidential candidates fluctuated between 1944 and 2012. Nevertheless, presidential Republicanism would persist in Texas and other southern states until Republicans began to get elected in state and local races in the 1990s and beyond.

Still, in state elections, the Democratic Party was overwhelmingly the dominant party. There might be pockets of the state where Republicans showed strength. Traditionally, in the post–Civil War era, the "German counties" in the Texas Hill Country, which were settled by German immigrants, showed Republican leanings. Dallas County, whose voters were influenced by a powerful group of conservative businesspeople and a conservative newspaper, the *Dallas Morning News*, showed early Republican strength, electing a very conservative Republican congressperson

Shivercrat movement a movement led by the Texas governor Allan Shivers during the 1950s in which conservative Democrats in Texas supported Republican candidate Dwight Eisenhower for the presidency because many of those conservative Democrats believed that the national Democratic Party had become too liberal

presidential Republicanism a voting pattern in which conservatives vote Democratic for state offices but Republican for presidential candidates

Though Democrats dominated Texas politics for decades, presidential Republicanism grew when Democrats supported Republican presidential candidate Dwight Eisenhower, who ran for president in 1952 and 1956. Here, Eisenhower is seen campaigning in Lubbock.

in the 1950s. However, for the most part, the Democratic Party was so dominant in state elections that the Republican Party did not field opponents to the Democratic nominees.

During this era, the Democratic Party was an umbrella party that held a variety of groups and interests. Liberals and conservatives belonged to the party, as did members of labor unions, businesspeople, farmers, and city dwellers. Often liberals and conservatives within the party battled for control of the party and its offices. But when liberals and conservatives were not engaged in periodic intraparty battles, struggles that occurred with considerable regularity, what political organization existed tended to be based on personal ties and personal popularity of individual candidates.

Until about the 1940s, Texas politics was often chaotic and confused. By about the mid-1940s, however, a split between liberals and conservatives developed in the Democratic Party that focused on New Deal economic policies and civil rights measures. This liberal-conservative split became a characteristic division within the Democratic Party, and liberals and conservatives battled in the party primaries. Between the mid-1940s and the mid-1970s, the victor in these primary squabbles would then go on to win the general election. However, by the late 1970s the winner of the Democratic primary had to face a significant conservative challenge from Republicans in the general election.[7]

The Era of Conservative Democrats

After Reconstruction and through the mid-twentieth century, conservative Democrats were in control of state government. These Democratic officeholders were conservative on fiscal and racial issues and exerted a powerful influence in the region as well as in Congress. This may seem hard to fathom in today's political environment, where Democrats are seen as liberal and Republicans as conservative, but recall that the Republican Party was initially started in Illinois as an antislavery party. Conservative Democrats in the early to mid-twentieth century were not particularly favorable to policies that would make it easier for African Americans to vote or participate in civic life in an equal manner. Many southern Democrats were elected to Congress and gained seniority in the Democratic-controlled U.S. Congress. Northern Democrats, however, had always been more liberal than their southern counterparts and did not like the growing influence of the South on policy matters in Washington.

In the many contests between conservative Democrats and liberal Democrats within Texas when the Democratic Party was the only game in town, the conservatives usually won because of the sheer fact that there were more conservatives than liberals in the state. However, some liberals did emerge, such as U.S. senator Ralph Yarborough, and to some extent, President Lyndon B. Johnson. Even though the two men were political adversaries, they both held progressive views, unlike many of their white Texas counterparts. U.S. senator Lloyd Bentsen, who served the state during the 1980s, became the vice-presidential candidate for Michael Dukakis in 1988 but was unable to win the state for his running mate. Instead, Republican George H. W. Bush, who had moved to Texas from Connecticut, carried the state and the general election. The Reagan Revolution had reached Texas, and from that point on, the Democratic Party in the state shrank to become the minority party.

for critical analysis

Consider how electoral decisions could be made if candidates were not identified by party membership. Would it be more or less difficult for individuals to discover the candidates' views on the issues? Would fund-raising be more or less difficult?

When Did Texas Become Republican?

The Republican Party is the dominant party in Texas. However, this is a fairly recent development. Before the 1970s, Texans were less likely than the rest of the nation to support Republican presidential candidates. And it was only in the 1990s and the early 2000s that Republicans came to hold a majority of seats in the Texas delegation to the U.S. House and in the Texas legislature.

Republican Share of the Presidential Vote

■ Texas   ■ National

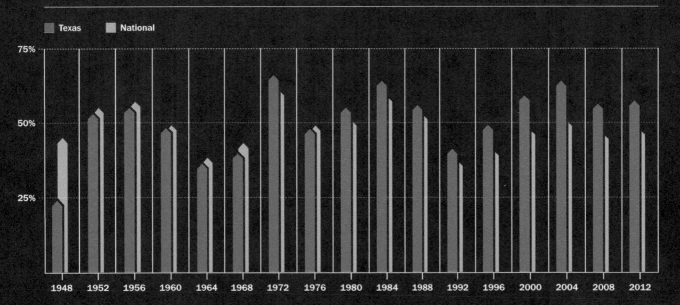

1948 1952 1956 1960 1964 1968 1972 1976 1980 1984 1988 1992 1996 2000 2004 2008 2012

Republican Share of Offices Held

Texas statewide offices

0%   100%

Texas House

10.7%   65.3%

Texas Senate

9.7%   64.5%

Texas delegation to U.S. House

                                                                     69.4%

1978 1982 1986 1990 1994 1998 2002 2006 2010 2015

SOURCES: First figure: 1948–2004 data from the CQ Elections and Voting Collection. 2008 data from the Associated Press. Second figure: 1974–2002 data from Republican Party of Texas. 2004–15 data calculated by author from election results archived at the Texas Secretary of State.

for critical analysis

1. Consider the timing of the shift toward the Republican Party in Texas. What factors contributed to this shift?

2. The figures show that in the last few elections, the growth of the Texas Republican Party has leveled out somewhat. Do you think the growth of the Texas Republican Party has stalled, or will the party's strength continue to grow in Texas?

The Growth of the Republican Party

One of the most important developments in Texas politics has been the growth of the Republican Party (see Figure 4.3). This growth can be seen along three interrelated dimensions: in terms of those who identify with the Republican Party, those who vote for Republican Party candidates in primaries and the general election, and those Republicans who have been elected to office. In the 1950s more than 60 percent of Texans identified with the Democratic Party and fewer than 10 percent identified themselves as Republicans. The remainder considered themselves independents. In the 1960s, Republican identification in Texas rose above 10 percent, Democratic identification remained above 60 percent, and identification as independents dropped slightly. The 1970s saw a decline in Democratic affiliation and an increase in Republican affiliation. Both patterns accelerated during the 1980s.[8] In 2008, Texans who identified themselves as Republicans saw a drop from 37 percent in 2004 to 33 percent, whereas Democratic Party affiliation remained steady at 30 percent.[9] A 2009 Gallup poll study identified Texas as being a competitive state with Republican leanings.[10] There is, however, clearly a difference between poll responses and election results where Texas has been and remains strongly Republican. Interestingly, when one considers competition between the two parties in terms of actual voters in the primaries or the general election, a different story emerges. Among actual voters in both primaries and general elections, Texas has become a strongly Republican state over the last decade. This conclusion is confirmed when one considers the number of Republican officeholders in the state.

In the first quarter of the twentieth century, the Republican Party was only a token party. In the state legislature, for example, Republicans never held more

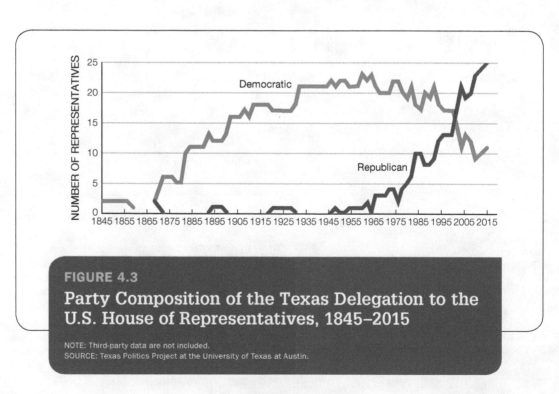

FIGURE 4.3

Party Composition of the Texas Delegation to the U.S. House of Representatives, 1845–2015

NOTE: Third-party data are not included.
SOURCE: Texas Politics Project at the University of Texas at Austin.

TABLE 4.1

Growth of the Republican Party in Texas

YEAR	U.S. SENATE	OTHER STATEWIDE	U.S. HOUSE	TEXAS SENATE	TEXAS HOUSE	COUNTY OFFICE	DISTRICT OFFICE	SCHOOL BOARD	TOTAL
1974	1	0	2	3	16	53	NA	NA	75+
1980	1	1	5	7	35	166	NA	NA	215+
1990	1	6	8	8	57	547	170	5	802
2000	2	27	13	16	72	1,233	336	10	1,709
2010	2	27	23	19	101	1,500	386	11	2,069
2012	2	27	24	19	95	NA	NA	NA	NA
2014	2	27	25	20	98	NA	NA	NA	NA

SOURCE: Republican Party of Texas.

than one seat in the Texas Senate and never more than two seats in the Texas House from 1903 to 1927. From 1927 to 1951 there were no Republicans in the Texas legislature, and then a lone Republican was elected from Dallas to serve only one term in the Texas House. It was another decade before Republicans were again elected to the legislature, when 2 served in the Texas House. Then in 1962, 6 Republicans were elected to the House from Dallas County and 1 from Midland County. By 1963 there were 10 Republicans in the Texas House and none in the Texas Senate.[11]

As Table 4.1 shows, as late as 1974 there were not many more than 75 Republican officeholders in the entire state of Texas. One of those officeholders was U.S. senator John Tower, and there were 2 Texas Republicans in the U.S. House of Representatives. No Republicans were elected to state office in statewide elections. There were only 3 Republicans in the Texas Senate and only 16 Republicans in the Texas House of Representatives. Ronald Reagan's election as president in 1980 marked a significant change in how Texans began to vote not only in presidential elections but also in state elections. The Reagan era ushered in a period when conservative Democrats began to switch to the Republican Party in record numbers. This switch became more evident at the end of the Reagan and Bush years when Texas became a Republican state not only in presidential races but also in state races. In 2014 both U.S. senators from Texas were Republican and 25 Texas members of the U.S. House of Representatives were Republican. A majority of the Texas Senate, 20 of the 31 members, and the Texas House of Representatives, 98 of the 150 members, was Republican.

It was a record of remarkable Republican growth and Democratic decline. By 1999 every statewide elected official was Republican. (This remained true in 2014 as well.) That included the governor, lieutenant governor, attorney general, comptroller, land commissioner, agriculture commissioner, all three members of the Texas Railroad Commission, and all nine members of both the Texas Supreme Court and the Texas Court of Criminal Appeals. Only 20 years earlier, William Clements was the first statewide official elected as a Republican since Reconstruction.

The Disappearance of Conservative Democrats

Blue Dog Democrats another name for conservative Democrats, mostly from the South

Conservative Democrats, also known as **Blue Dog Democrats**, are becoming an endangered species in Texas and in the rest of the South. Such Democrats never left the party they grew up in, and they have become marginalized in the national party because of their social conservatism. Many of these Democrats are opposed to abortion and same sex marriage while supportive of gun rights. These positions put them at odds with the prevailing consensus in the Democratic Party. Some of the few conservative Democrats elected to Congress in recent years even refused to support Nancy Pelosi of San Francisco as their party leader because of their divergence from her more liberal views.

By 2012 all of the conservative Democrats elected to represent Texas in the U.S. Congress had retired, switched parties, or lost their elections. For example, former congressperson Chet Edwards was a conservative Democrat who represented Crawford, the home of former president George W. Bush. In the 2010 elections, Edwards lost his bid for re-election to Republican Bill Flores, a businessman. Congressperson Ralph Hall of Rockwall switched to the Republican Party in 2004 after spending many years as a conservative Democrat. He switched parties in order to have more influence in Congress's governing party, although just two years later, the Democrats retook control of the U.S. House. In 2014, Hall decided to run for re-election despite his 91-year-old age. Hall lost in a runoff with Tea Party–backed attorney John Ratcliffe. The seat is strongly Republican, and Ratcliffe was elected to the seat.

The biggest losses for conservative Democrats came following the 2003 redistricting cycle, spearheaded by Tom DeLay. As House majority leader, DeLay wanted to take advantage of the new Republican majority in the state legislature in order to redraw congressional districts, which he thought were too favorable

Recent elections have continued the trend toward greater strength of Republicans in Texas. Even conservative Democrats—like Representative Congressman Chet Edwards from Waco, pictured here—have recently lost their seats in Congress.

to Democrats. Although controversial, DeLay was able to succeed in organizing a dramatic redistricting session, which put many conservative Democrats from Texas at risk of losing their seats.

After this episode, two Texas Democrats, Representatives Charles Stenholm and Max Sandlin, lost their seats to Republicans. Another Democrat, Jim Turner, decided not to seek re-election in his newly configured district in east Texas. Redistricting has left liberal Lloyd Doggett of Austin as the only white Democrat representing a majority white congressional district in Texas. Gene Green of Houston represents a majority-minority district.

The pattern we observe in Congress is also present at the state legislative level. Of the 74 Democrats in the Texas House of Representatives, 12 are considered conservative in research conducted by Mark Jones of Rice University. This is relative to other Democrats, not Republicans. The most conservative Democrat in the Texas House is still more liberal than the most liberal Republican.[12] In the most recent legislative session, however, Allan Ritter of Nederland, who was one of the 12 conservative Democrats, switched to the Republican Party.

In today's political environment, the influence of conservative Democrats and liberal Republicans is very limited. At the national level and in Texas, conservatives are disproportionately members of the Republican Party and liberals are members of the Democratic Party. In many races, there are a shrinking number of truly independent voters who can swing elections. Often, both parties attempt to mobilize their own bases instead of trying to reach these swing voters.

● Issues in Texas Party Politics

Analyze how ideological divisions and demographic change affect Texas political parties

Both the Democrats and the Republicans have factions within the party, and these factions emphasize different issues. For example, the Democratic Party in Texas has a large Latino base, which is very interested in the issue of immigration. The Republican Party has a strong and growing Tea Party contingent, which is making the party more antitax and fiscally conservative. In this section, we will examine some of these conflicts both between and within the major parties.

Party Unity and Disunity

All groups have opposing factions within them, and political parties are no exception. When a party becomes dominant in a state, these factional battles become particularly important because the stakes are higher for the factions of the dominant party.

When the Democratic Party was the dominant party in Texas, factional battles were common between liberals and conservatives in the party. These conflicts in the Democratic Party were especially notable during the 1950s in the struggles between the pro-Eisenhower conservative Democrats, led by Allan Shivers, and the pro-Stevenson liberal and loyalist Democrats, led by Sam Rayburn, Lyndon Johnson, and Ralph Yarborough. Now that the Republican Party is the dominant party in Texas, major factional battles have occurred for control of that party. One faction is the religious right. This group includes religious conservatives who are especially concerned with social issues such as abortion, prayer in public schools and at school events, the teaching of evolution in public schools, and the perceived decline in family values. The other major segment of the party is composed of economic conservatives. This group is primarily concerned with reduced government spending, lower taxes, and greater emphasis on free enterprise. At the end of the day, however, these factions often end up supporting their party candidate in the general election.

In the 2006 primary some Republicans, including two of the party's largest contributors in Texas, believed that some Republicans in the Texas House were too moderate and spent money to try to defeat them.[13] At least six Republican incumbents were aided by last-minute contributions from a political action committee that poured about $300,000 into their campaigns to help protect them from Republican challengers. Nevertheless, two of the six incumbents were defeated and one was thrown into a runoff.[14] The 2014 primary battle between Lieutenant Governor David Dewhurst and Senator Dan Patrick suggests that the ideological tensions in the Republican Party continue between what is essentially a conservative faction and an even more conservative faction. The latter faction has been identified with the Tea Party movement. Tea Party favorite U.S. senator Ted Cruz now has protégés: Dan Patrick in the lieutenant governor's position and Ken Paxton as attorney general. A number of the newly elected members of the state legislature are also Tea Party favorites.

To maintain its political strength, the Republican Party has to keep these factional disputes within the party. When Senator Kay Bailey Hutchison challenged Governor Rick Perry in the primary, some of Perry's appointees endorsed Hutchison. Afterward, they were asked to step down from their appointive positions. These were seen as examples of the rift that emerged between two wings of the Republican Party. For years, the Democratic Party battles between its liberal and conservative wings were kept inside the party because there was no rival party to which one of the factions could go. Eventually the Republican Party emerged as a home where many conservative Democrats felt comfortable. Conceivably, the factional disputes in the Republican Party could lead one of the factions—the more moderate Republicans—to move to the Democratic Party.

Urban, Rural, and Suburban Influences on Partisanship

As in the rest of the country, one of the major divides in political party affiliation is rural versus urban. Today's large suburban populations must be added to this equation. The growth of suburban enclaves around major cities such as the Dallas–Fort Worth metroplex, Houston, and San Antonio has profoundly changed politics. Prior to the growth of suburbia, people lived either in cities or in rural areas. Rural residents were often cattle ranchers or farmers. As cattle raising and farming became more mechanized and large companies displaced local farmers, it became less profitable to run family farms. Many rural residents relocated to urban areas to work in banks, oil companies, or other industries.

During the 1950s the federal government embarked on a major project to connect cities through an interstate highway system. One consequence of this system was that it made it easier for workers to travel to and from urban areas. For those who wanted to escape urban congestion, it became easier to move to the outskirts of the city and travel by car to their jobs. While mass transit facilitated suburban

State senator Leticia Van de Putte, of San Antonio, is one of a growing number of influential Hispanics in the Democratic Party in Texas. Here, she makes an announcement about helping indentured servants, who are brought over the border and then forced to work, often under harsh conditions, to pay off their "debt" to the traffickers who transported them.

commuting in other parts of the country, in Texas, taxpayers were unwilling to fund these infrastructure investments.

Texas's interstate highway system encouraged the process of "white flight," the mass exodus of more affluent whites from urban areas to suburban areas. This left urban areas with eroding tax bases and remaining poor minority populations, who did not have the luxury of purchasing automobiles to commute between city and suburb.

The political result of this changing demographic is that cities have become more Democratic, even in Texas, where the urban strongholds of Austin, Dallas, and Houston deliver the most Democratic votes in the state. Rural areas have remained solidly conservative and have become Republican in Texas, and suburban areas can best be described as hybrid areas with pockets of Republicans and Democrats depending on the specific area and local issues.

Another consequence is that voters tend to settle in places with like-minded people so that cities tend to attract more Democrats, and suburban and rural areas tend to attract more Republicans. This reinforces the political proclivities already established in such communities. A recent book, *Our Patchwork Nation*, by Dante Chinni and James Gimpel explores this phenomenon nationwide, arguing that different communities have distinct political characteristics.[15]

The tensions introduced by suburbanization are clearly seen in Dallas County over the last decade. As Dallas County has urbanized and the suburbs have extended to adjoining counties, Dallas County has been transformed into an urban, Democratic county. In the media coverage of the 2000 presidential election, one small judicial race in Dallas County was almost overlooked. Only one puzzled article on the race's results appeared in the *Dallas Morning News*.[16] A three-time

Republican judge, Bill Rhea, won re-election against a first-time Democratic candidate, Mary Ann Huey. That should have been no surprise. By the late 1980s the only Democrat who could win a judicial race in Dallas County was Ron Chapman, a Democratic judge who happened to share the name of the most popular disk jockey in the county.[17] In the early 1980s there had been a wholesale rush of incumbent Democratic judges to the Republican Party. Although varying explanations were given by the party switchers, perhaps the most honest and straightforward was by Judge Richard Mays: "My political philosophy about general things has nothing to do with me [sic] being a judge. . . . That's not the reason I'm switching parties. The reason I'm switching is that to be a judge in Dallas County you need to be a Republican." With Mays's switch in August 1985, 32 of the 36 district judges in Dallas County were Republicans, though none were Republicans before 1978.[18] It would, of course, not take long until all judges in Dallas County were Republican.[19]

So what was remarkable about that one district court race between a Democratic challenger and a longtime Republican incumbent, other than the fact that a Democrat had the temerity to challenge an incumbent in a Republican bastion such as Dallas County? Out of 560,558 votes cast, only 4,150 votes separated the two candidates. In other words, a three-term Republican judge with no scandal or other controversy surrounding his name won with only 50.3 percent of the vote. It is no wonder that the judge commented, "I'm thrilled to be serving again and duly humbled by the vote count."[20] Even more astounding, Judge Rhea's Democratic opponent, Mary Ann Huey, had run with no money, no political experience, and no support from the legal community. She ran in the same year that George W. Bush was the presidential nominee, with no other Democratic judicial candidates on the ballot at the county level, and with little more than audacity on her side.

Judge Rhea's humbling experience, of course, was not caused by his judicial performance but rather by demographic changes. The Republican base in Dallas County has moved to places such as Collin, Denton, and Rockwall counties. That suburban growth has changed those traditionally Democratic counties into Republican counties but has left the old Republican base—Dallas—with a larger African American and an even larger Latino population and has returned to the Democratic column that it left a little more than 20 years ago.

In the 2004 elections, George W. Bush carried Dallas County by fewer than 10,000 votes (50.72 percent), and Dallas County elected Democrats as sheriff and four countywide elected judges. The 2006 elections in Dallas County were truly a watershed in the county's politics. A Democrat was elected county judge, a Democrat was elected district attorney, and all 42 Democrats who ran for Dallas County judgeships were elected. Democrats continued their sweep of countywide elections in 2008, 2010, and 2012.

In 2008, Harris County also dramatically shifted to the Democratic column, electing a large number of Democrats to county office. It seemed to be following in Dallas County's footsteps. However, the 2010 elections moved Harris County back into the Republican column, and in 2012, Harris County was a virtual tie between Obama and Romney.

African Americans in Texas Political Parties

In Texas, African Americans are a smaller percentage of the population than in neighboring Louisiana. Approximately 12 percent of the state population is African American, and most of that population is concentrated in east Texas as well

TABLE 4.2

Turnout by Race: 2012 Presidential Year versus 2010 Statewide Election Year

	NUMBER OF ELIGIBLE VOTERS IN 2012 (IN MILLIONS)	TURNOUT OF ELIGIBLE VOTERS IN 2010 STATEWIDE ELECTION YEAR (%)	TURNOUT OF ELIGIBLE VOTERS IN 2012 PRESIDENTIAL YEAR (%)	DIFFERENCE BETWEEN 2012 AND 2010 (%)
White*	8.33	43.8%	60.9%	17.1%
African American	2.00	38.7	63.1	24.4
Asian	0.57	22.2	42.4	20.2
Hispanic	4.38	23.1	38.8	15.7
Total	15.4	36.4	53.8	17.4

*White does not include whites who identify as Hispanic.
SOURCE: U.S. Census Bureau, www.census.gov/hhes/www/socdemo/voting/publications/p20/2012/tables.html (accessed 5/19/14).

as in the major cities of Houston, Dallas, San Antonio, and Austin. Depending on the election, the vast majority of African Americans cast their votes for Democrats. This is not unusual, as African Americans in other parts of the country are similarly loyal to the Democratic Party.

The influence of African Americans in the Democratic Party in Texas is high not only because they tend to vote Democratic more than Republican but because they participate in elections more than other ethnic groups. During the 2010 statewide elections, 38.7 percent turned out to vote. During the presidential election of 2012, 63.1 percent turned out to vote. These percentages were far above the total proportion of registered voters who turned out in 2010 (36.4 percent) and in 2012 (53.8 percent). See Table 4.2.

This is not to say that all African Americans are Democrats. Former railroad commissioner Michael Williams became the first black Republican to be elected to the statewide post. The former Texas Supreme Court chief justice Wallace Jefferson is also an African American Republican and was elected by voters to his position. Other than Williams and Jefferson, only two other African Americans have been elected to statewide office in recent years.

African Americans have been elected mayors of important cities in Texas. Democrat Lee Brown became Houston's first African American mayor in 1997, and Democrat Ron Kirk became Dallas's first African American mayor in 1995. In 2002, Kirk ran for the U.S. Senate but lost to white Republican John Cornyn.

Latinos and the Future of Party Politics in Texas

The 2002 elections raised serious questions about how soon the Latino vote would transform politics in Texas. In an attempt to break the lock that the Republicans had on statewide offices, the Democratic Party put forward a "Dream Team" with Tony Sanchez, a wealthy Latino businessman from Laredo who had been an appointee of Republican governor Rick Perry and had a record of not participating

for critical analysis

What is the significance of
Latino population growth to
parties in Texas?

in many elections, running for governor alongside Ron Kirk running for the U.S. Senate and John Sharp (a former state comptroller and white conservative Democrat) running for lieutenant governor. The idea was to mobilize minority voters to vote for the Democratic ticket while holding traditional white voters. The strategy failed dismally as Sanchez lost to the Republican candidate Perry (40 percent to 58 percent), Kirk lost to the Republican Cornyn (43 percent to 55 percent), and Sharp lost to the Republican Dewhurst (46 percent to 52 percent). Especially disappointing because Sanchez was the first Latino major party nominee for governor, Latino voter turnout was only 32.8 percent. The Democratic "Dream Team" became a nightmare. Sanchez had money and spent it with abandon, but he was a poor campaigner who could not even mobilize the Latino vote.

Additionally, Democrats didn't anticipate the grassroots get-out-the-vote effort put forth by the Republicans. Republican straight-ticket voting in key urban and suburban counties across the state appeared to have outdistanced Democratic straight-ticket voting. Further, it appeared that negative campaigning, particularly directed at Tony Sanchez, may have undercut support for the Democratic ticket among traditional white conservative voters.[21]

The 2010 election has been described as a Republican tsunami running throughout the nation. Texas experienced this wave in three important ways. First, four Democratic incumbent U.S. congresspeople were defeated. Second, Republicans maintained their monopoly over statewide elected offices. Third, Republicans gained 22 seats in the Texas House. A conservative majority reasserted itself in Texas politics. Since the 2010 elections, two Latino members of the state house have switched parties. Aaron Peña of Edinburg and Jose Lozano of Kingsville became Republicans, although redistricting led Peña to retire from politics in January 2013.

Despite the final results of the 2008 and 2010 elections, few commentators were willing to dismiss the growing importance of the Latino vote in the state. One indication of that importance is that in 2010 it was estimated that Hispanics constituted about 20 percent of the registered voters in Texas.[22]

However, Latinos have not fully realized their potential voting strength. Table 4.2 shows Latino voting population figures and turnout rates in comparison to other racial and ethnic groups in the state in 2012 (a presidential year) and 2010 (a statewide election year). This is an issue that we will explore in more depth in Chapter 5. For now, we should note that Latino voters have a significantly lower turnout rate than whites and African Americans in both presidential years and statewide election years. Moreover, there are a large number of Latinos living in Texas—perhaps around two million—who are not citizens, some of whom are documented residents and many others who are not, who are not eligible to vote.[23] Such facts will likely depress the electoral power of the Latino population in Texas political parties in the short and medium run. It should be remembered, however, that many of the children of these noncitizens will be Americans by being born in the United States and thus eligible to vote. Few would be surprised if a life spent living and being educated in the United States led to higher turnout rates among younger Latinos in the future. The full impact of the Latino demographic surge on political parties may not be felt until the next generation comes of age.[24]

● Thinking Critically about Parties in Texas

We often think of conflict in politics between the Democratic and Republican parties, especially in government. While this is certainly true, conflict can also occur within political parties among different factions. These factions usually compromise to support their candidates during the general election. Political parties therefore provide a structure through which candidates strive to win office. The two major parties in Texas are the Democratic and the Republican parties, although most of the elected officials in the state are Republican. In south Texas, however, Democrats control many cities, towns, and school boards because of the large Latino population, which is overwhelmingly Democratic.

One of the most striking developments in Texas politics over the past 20 to 25 years is that one-party Democratic dominance is gone from the Texas political scene. That decline in Democratic dominance corresponds to the rise of the Republican Party in Texas. In 2014 every statewide elected officeholder in Texas was a Republican.

Currently, the most dangerous conflict within the Republican Party is the split between social conservatives and economic conservatives who have a low-taxing, low-spending agenda. This split was strikingly revealed in the primary battle between Lieutenant Governor Dewhurst and Senator Patrick. Patrick's victory in the primary may signal the triumph of the social conservatives and their increasingly powerful role in the state's politics. However, Republicans are not necessarily secure as the dominant party. It is important that the Republican Party grow and expand its base of support. One of the Republican Party's great weaknesses is its lack of support among Latinos, the fastest-growing ethnic group in Texas. If the Republicans are to continue their remarkable successes in Texas politics, they will have to make greater inroads with Latino voters. Patrick's tone of describing illegal immigration as an "invasion" makes this all the more challenging.

Democrats still have a significant base of support in urban counties with large minority populations and with older Texans and with liberals. For Texas to be a competitive two-party state, the Democrats need to win some statewide elections. The party needs to regroup and redirect its appeal to Texans. Most important, if the Democratic Party is to do more than lose elections, it must do what parties have traditionally done in states that have political machines. That is, it must get out the vote. In part, the key to success in future Texas elections is a party's ability to mobilize the Latino vote in the state.

study guide

The Role of Political Parties in Texas Politics

In Texas, political parties serve as brand labels for voters to determine whom to vote for in elections that have little or no publicity. Texas political parties also have conventions and committees that help their members organize and mobilize in elections.

Key Terms

partisan polarization (p. 108)

political socialization (p. 109)

precinct (p. 114)

precinct chair (p. 114)

county executive committee (p. 114)

county chair (p. 114)

state executive committee (p. 114)

state chair and vice chair (p. 114)

precinct convention (p. 114)

county convention (p. 114)

state convention (p. 114)

Dixiecrats (p. 116)

La Raza Unida Party (p. 116)

"first past the post" (p. 118)

single-member district (p. 118)

Duverger's Law (p. 118)

proportional representation (p. 118)

Occupy movement (p. 119)

Tea Party movement (p. 119)

Practice Quiz

1. Providing a label that helps voters identify those seeking office is an important function of
   a) the state.
   b) political parties.
   c) interest groups.
   d) regional and subregional governments.
   e) the president.

2. The process by which political parties become more distant from each other in terms of ideology is
   a) partisan convergence.
   b) partisan polarization.
   c) partisan conventions.
   d) partisan equilibrium.
   e) partisan deliverance.

3. All of the following groups constitute the Democratic Party base in Texas *except*
   a) business leaders.
   b) Latinos.
   c) African Americans.
   d) white liberals.
   e) urban residents.

4. Which minority group is the fastest growing in Texas?
   a) African Americans
   b) Latinos
   c) Asian Americans
   d) Native Americans
   e) All are growing equally.

5. In the state of Texas, the highest level of temporary party organization is the
   a) state convention.
   b) state executive committee.
   c) governor's convention.
   d) civil executive committee.
   e) speaker's committee.

6. Which of the following third parties and movements had the most success in winning elections in post–World War II Texas?
   a) La Raza Unida Party
   b) the Occupy movement
   c) the Green Party
   d) the Kinky Friedman movement
   e) the Constitution Party

Texas's History as a One-Party State

Texas has traditionally been a one-party state, meaning that one party has been in control of state politics for a long time. In the post–Civil War period, the Democrats held power in the state, but since 1994 the Republicans have won every statewide election and consequently dominate state politics.

Key Terms

Shivercrat movement (p. 121)

presidential Republicanism (p. 121)

Blue Dog Democrats (p. 126)

Practice Quiz

7. The Shivercrat movement was
   a) a group of conservative Democrats in Texas who supported Eisenhower for president.
   b) a group of liberal Democrats who supported equal rights for all Americans.
   c) a group of conservative Republicans who rejected the Obama administration.
   d) a group of liberal Republicans who rejected the Bush administration.
   e) a group of Libertarians.

8. In Texas, the Republican Party became the dominant party in
   a) the 1950s.
   b) the 1960s.
   c) the 1970s.
   d) the 1980s.
   e) the 1990s.

9. Blue Dog Democrats were
   a) northeastern Democrats with conservative views.
   b) southern Democrats with liberal views.
   c) southern Democrats with conservative views.
   d) northern Democrats with liberal views.
   e) western Democrats with liberal views.

10. Presidential Republicanism refers to which of the following?
    a) Texans voting for Republican local candidates
    b) Texans voting for Republican presidents and Democrats for state offices
    c) Texans voting for Republican presidents and Republicans for state offices
    d) Texans voting for Democratic local candidates
    e) Texans voting for third-party candidates at all levels

Issues in Texas Party Politics

Texas is a diverse state with divisions between north and south and east and west. Latinos currently constitute nearly 40 percent of the state's population and currently favor the Democratic Party, although their registration and turnout rates are lower than those of the other major demographic groups.

Practice Quiz

11. Which of the following is *not* true?
    a) Cities in Texas have become more Democratic.
    b) Cities in Texas are dominated by third parties.
    c) Rural areas of Texas are solidly Republican.
    d) Texas suburbs contain pockets of both Democrats and Republicans.
    e) Democrats dominate elections in Dallas County.

12. African Americans in Texas
    a) tend to cast their votes for Democrats.
    b) are a large part of the Republican base.
    c) vote mainly for independent candidates.
    d) constitute less than 10 percent of the population.
    e) split their votes evenly between the Democratic and Republican parties.

Recommended Websites

Libertarian Party of Texas
www.tx.lp.org

Republican Party of Texas
www.texasgop.org

Texas Democrats
www.txdemocrats.org

Texas Tribune
www.texastribune.org

Wendy Davis

Forgetting to Be Afraid

A Memoir

Elections in Texas

WHY ELECTIONS MATTER After his failed 2012 presidential run, Texas governor Rick Perry decided not to run for re-election in 2014. Perry's announcement paved the way for Attorney General Greg Abbott to seek the Republican nomination for governor. With Comptroller Susan Combs's retirement and Land Commissioner Jerry Patterson's run for attorney general, most of the statewide offices were open seats, creating a whirlwind of campaign activity. With only token opposition, Attorney General Abbott trounced his primary opponents in March 2014 and faced Democrat Wendy Davis in November 2014. Wendy Davis became a national figure when she filibustered a bill that would have tightened abortion access in Texas. Because Davis was a state senator from a moderate district in Fort Worth, state Democrats and many national Democrats saw in her an opportunity to "turn Texas blue" again.

But Davis had a monumental task before her, as no Democrat had been elected statewide in Texas since Bob Bullock had won the lieutenant governor's office in 1994. If elected, she would have become the second Democratic woman to be elected governor in Texas since World War II. (Ann Richards was Texas governor from 1991 to 1995, when she was defeated by George W. Bush.)

Davis's major challenge was to appeal to a broad segment of Texas's electorate. Some Latino leaders initially expressed concerns with her candidacy when she did not actively campaign in the Rio Grande Valley running up to the Democratic primaries. Her opponent in the primary, Reynaldo Madrigal, who did not campaign and had virtually no campaign funds, actually beat her in some south Texas counties. Some pundits argued that Davis's pro-choice notoriety may have hurt her among many religious, Catholic Latinos in the Rio Grande Valley. Whatever the case, Davis and the state Democratic Party had to attract a significant number of Latino votes in order to have a reasonable chance of winning statewide. Simply put, there were not enough white liberals in Texas for Democrats to win statewide elections.

Davis's campaign also featured a rocky start with allegations that she abandoned her children to move to Boston to attend law school. While she denies these claims, Davis has had to face charges that she put her career before her family when she decided to leave her husband and children behind in Fort Worth when she attended Harvard Law School. Defenders of Davis have noted that a male candidate would never face similar accusations and that sexism was at play in this charge. Davis was also accused of misleading voters by claiming she lived in a trailer for a longer period than she actually did and that she did not acknowledge her second husband's contributions to her law school tuition. Whatever the true story was, the controversy made it more difficult for Davis to extend her appeal beyond liberal Democrats to a broader electorate including suburban Republican women voters. These voters had played a major role in Ann Richards's successful campaign for the governorship against Clayton Williams in 1988 and had to be won if Davis were to be elected.[1]

In order for a Democrat to win a statewide race in Texas, many pundits claim that the candidate must run a flawless campaign against a flawed Republican candidate. Davis did not accomplish this against Abbott and lost. Democrats had hope in the race for lieutenant governor, however, with state senator Leticia Van de Putte. Van de Putte was a San Antonio Democrat whose Latina background was seen as a strong asset in the race, and her personal story as a pharmacist-turned-politician might appeal to a broad segment of the state's population. She faced Dan Patrick, a bombastic Republican state senator who challenged the incumbent lieutenant governor David Dewhurst for not being conservative enough. His platform stressed stopping the "invasion" of illegal immigrants and toughening up border security. Van de Putte was overwhelmed by the number of Republican votes in Texas, and Patrick won the race comfortably.

Why should it matter who is elected governor and lieutenant governor? The governor of Texas has important national stature, as we recall from George W. Bush's successful transition to the presidency. The governor has the power to set the agenda, veto legislation, and influence public policy in the state. The lieutenant governor also is a powerful position in Texas. The powers of the lieutenant governor include setting the agenda, appointing committee chairs, and presiding over the state Senate. Some governors were also former lieutenant governors, such as Rick Perry. While these high-profile elections received more attention than usual from voters, the reality is that all elections matter for public policy in Texas. Elections to the city council, school board, and state legislature also make a huge difference in our lives. Education funding, health care policy, tax policy, and environmental policy are all affected by whom we elect to represent us, whether at the national or local level.

chaptergoals

- **Describe the types of elections held in Texas and how they work (pp. 139–41)**
- **Explain how the rules for voting affect turnout among different groups of Texans (pp. 142–59)**
- **Present the main features of election campaigns in Texas (pp. 160–66)**

Features of Elections in Texas

Describe the types of elections held in Texas and how they work

Elections are the most important vehicles by which the people express themselves in the democratic process in Texas. At the national level, elections are limited to the selection of the president and vice president (via the Electoral College) and members of Congress. In Texas, however, voters select candidates for various offices in all three statewide branches of government (the legislature, executive, and judiciary) and in numerous local elections. Texans also vote for changes to the state constitution, which can alter public policy in the state. In theory, such elections are meant to enable the people to exercise some direct control over each branch. In practice, however, one-party dominance and low levels of voter participation have often told a different story, leaving the government exposed to special interests and big money.

Elections are the mechanisms people use to select leaders, authorize actions by government, and borrow money on behalf of government. In Texas, there are a multitude of elections: primary elections, general elections, city elections, school board elections, special elections, elections for community college boards and the governing boards for many special districts, and bond elections for city, county, and state governments.

Primary Elections

Primary elections are the first elections held in an electoral cycle. In Texas, they are generally held on the second Tuesday in March of even-numbered years. Primary elections determine the party's nominees for the general election. They are conducted by the political party and funded jointly by the party and the state. Essentially, parties collect filing fees from those seeking nomination and use these funds to pay for their share of holding the primary election.

primary election a ballot vote in which citizens select a party's nominee for the general election

The Democratic and Republican parties conduct primaries in all of Texas's 254 counties. Within each county, voters cast ballots in precincts. The number of voting precincts varies depending on the population of the county. Less-populated counties such as Loving and Kennedy have as few as 6 precincts, whereas Harris County contains more than 1,000 voting precincts.

Republicans seeking their party's nomination file papers and pay a filing fee to the Republican Party. Likewise, Democrats file papers and pay a filing fee to the Democratic Party. If several Republicans (or Democrats) seek the office of governor, they will campaign against each other and one will be chosen to run in the general election. Winning the primary election requires an absolute majority. The party's nominees must have more votes than all opponents combined. If no candidate receives an absolute majority, there is a **runoff primary** between the two candidates receiving the most votes. Voters who participate in the Republican Party primary cannot vote in a Democratic runoff; likewise, anyone who voted in the Democratic Party primary cannot vote in a Republican runoff. However, those who voted in neither the Democratic nor Republican primary can vote in either the Republican or Democratic runoff primary.

runoff primary a second primary election held between the two candidates who received the most votes in the first primary election if no candidate in the first primary election had received a majority

An **open primary** allows any registered voter to cast a ballot in either, but not both, primaries. There are no party restrictions. One can consider oneself a Republican and vote in the Democratic primary or can leave home intending to

open primary a primary election in which any registered voter can participate in the contest, regardless of party affiliation

vote in the Democratic primary, change one's mind, and vote in the Republican primary.

The Texas Constitution and election laws call the Texas system a **closed primary**, because one must declare one's party affiliation before voting, but in practice it is an open primary. Before receiving a primary ballot, the voter signs a roll sheet indicating eligibility to vote and pledging to support the party's candidates. By signing the roll sheet, the voter makes a declaration of party affiliation prior to voting. However, because the voter declares a party affiliation only a few moments prior to voting in the primary, the primary is closed only in the narrowest sense of the term. These declarations in no way bind a voter to support the party's candidates in future elections. Many other states have true closed primaries in that only registered party members can vote in these elections. Each state decides how it will run primary elections.

General Election

The **general election** is held the first Tuesday following the first Monday in November of even-numbered years. The Democratic Party's nominee runs against the nominee of the Republican Party. It is possible that independent and minor-party candidates will also appear on the general election ballot.

Major state officials (governor, lieutenant governor, comptroller of public accounts, attorney general, and so on) are elected in nonpresidential election years. This arrangement seeks to prevent popular presidential candidates from influencing the outcomes of Texas races. For example, it is possible that a popular Republican presidential candidate might draw more than the usual number of Republican votes, and an unusually large Republican presidential vote might swing the election for statewide candidates running under the Republican banner. Likewise, it prevents an uncommonly popular statewide candidate from influencing the presidential election. If statewide elections were held in presidential election years, a Democratic candidate for governor, for example, might influence Texas's presidential voting by increasing the number of votes for Democratic candidates in general.

General elections are held in November to select national and state officeholders. Members of city councils, school boards, and other local government entities are also selected by general elections; however, these elections usually take place outside the traditional early November time period. In many cases, this means very low voter turnout. For example, in the Austin municipal elections in May 2012, there was a record low turnout of only 10 percent of the city's registered voters. City leaders have proposed moving the election to November in the future to encourage a larger proportion of voters to participate. It is not clear whether even such a move will help. In Houston's mayoral race in November 2013, the turnout was only slightly higher at 13 percent of the city's registered voters.

Special Elections

In Texas, **special elections** are used to fill vacancies in office, to give approval to borrow money, or to ratify or reject amendments to the Texas Constitution. The dates for special elections are specified by the Texas legislature. If a Texas state senator resigns, for example, the governor will call a special election to fill the vacancy.

Texas laws require voter approval before any governmental agency in Texas can borrow money and assume long-term debt. If the local school district wants to borrow money to build a new high school and repair three elementary schools, a special election must be held. During the election, voters decide whether they will allow the school board to borrow the money.

The legislature proposes amendments to the Texas Constitution, and the voters in a special election ratify them.

Running as an Independent

It is unusual for a candidate to run for office in Texas as an independent. One reason is that there are substantial requirements for getting one's name on the ballot. Additionally, an independent candidate lacks the political support of party organizations and the advantage of having a party label on the ballot. As we saw in Chapter 4, however, in 2006, Texas had two independent candidates for governor: Kinky Friedman and former Austin mayor Carole Keeton Strayhorn, the state comptroller, who had been elected to that office as a Republican.

Both candidates were obviously hoping that an independent candidacy would attract the votes of Democrats who believed that a Democratic candidate for governor could not win in Texas. They also were hoping to get substantial votes from Republicans disaffected with the policies and performance of the Republican governor, Rick Perry. Strayhorn, in particular, seemed to have strong appeal to Democrats who usually contributed large sums to Democratic nominees. One study of Strayhorn's contributions from July through December of 2005, for example, found that 52 percent of her campaign funds were from people who had given exclusively or almost exclusively to Democrats over the previous five years.[2]

Each state decides its own requirements for getting on the ballot. Some states make it easier for independents to get on the ballot, but the process in Texas is relatively difficult. For Friedman and Strayhorn to get on the ballot, for example, they had to meet the following requirements:

1. The candidates must obtain signatures on a petition from registered voters. The signatures must equal 1 percent of the total votes in the last governor's race. This meant that Friedman and Strayhorn each had to obtain 45,540 signatures.

2. The signatures must come from registered voters who did not participate in any political party primary election.

3. Signature collection cannot begin until the day after the last primary election. In 2006 this was March 8.

4. Voters may sign only one candidate's petition. If they sign both, only the first signature provided will count.[3]

The two major political parties don't agree on much, but they do agree on keeping competitors out. Making it difficult for independents to get their names on the ballot helps ensure that the two major political parties will continue to dominate politics in the state well into the future. Elections may be open in Texas, but they work through the dominant political parties, helping to solidify their control over the political process and the major political offices in the state. The electoral performances of Friedman and Strayhorn also point to the difficulties of independent candidacy in that both of these candidates received only a small fraction of the overall vote.

Some blame the relatively low voter turnout for Texas elections on the frequency of elections and the large number of candidates. Also, state officials are not elected in presidential election years, when voter participation tends to be highest.

Participation in Texas Elections

Explain how the rules for voting affect turnout among different groups of Texans

When we think of political participation, we often think of voting. This is the most basic and fundamental duty citizens have in democracy. Other forms of political participation include signing petitions, protesting, and writing letters to the newspaper and elected officials, some of which we will discuss in this chapter and others we will discuss in later chapters. Here, we begin by examining the history of voting in the state and the regulations and procedures surrounding voting rights. Issues include who can vote, how easy it is to register to vote, and why so few Texans vote.

Earlier Restrictions on the Franchise

The franchise refers to the act of voting or the right to vote. For much of the period of one-party Democratic control that began in the late nineteenth century, there were restrictions on the franchise.

Women Women were allowed to vote in primaries and party conventions in Texas in 1918 and obtained the right to vote in all elections as a result of the **Nineteenth Amendment** to the U.S. Constitution in 1920. However, some of the most influential politicians in the state were opposed to the franchise for women. Joseph Weldon Bailey, for example, who had been Democratic leader in the U.S. House of Representatives and later the informal Democratic leader in the U.S. Senate, was an eloquent opponent of women's **suffrage**, arguing that women could not vote because they could not perform the three basic duties of citizenship: jury service, *posse comitatus* service (citizens who are deputized to deal with an emergency), and military service. He believed that women's morals dictated their beliefs and women would force their beliefs on men. The result, he felt, would be prohibition of alcohol.[4] Tinie Wells, the wife of Jim Wells, perhaps the most influential south Texas political leader of his day, was also an important and influential spokesperson for the anti–women's suffrage movement.[5] Governor "Farmer Jim" Ferguson was another opponent of women's suffrage, but when he was impeached, his successor, William P. Hobby, proved a key supporter of women's right to vote. It was Governor Hobby who called the legislature into special session in 1919 to consider the Nineteenth Amendment. Thus Texas became the ninth state and the first state in the South to ratify the women's suffrage amendment.[6]

The Poll Tax Minorities had an even tougher time gaining access to the ballot in Texas. In the early part of the twentieth century, powerful political bosses had economic power and personal influence over Latino voters. They used this power to support national politicians such as John Nance Garner. Garner represented a huge part of south Texas, which stretched from Laredo to Corpus Christi and then north almost to San Antonio. A lifelong Democrat, he began his service in the House of Representatives in 1903 and served until 1933. From 1931 to 1933, he was Speaker of the U.S. House of Representatives, and from 1933 to 1941, he was vice president of the United States. He is most famous for his quip that the vice presidency was not worth more than a bucket of warm spit. Garner was the

Nineteenth Amendment ratified in 1919, amendment guaranteeing women the right to vote

suffrage term referring to the right to vote

first Speaker from Texas and the first vice president from Texas. His south Texas political base was secured by votes that were controlled by the south Texas political bosses.[7]

One restriction on voting that affected poor people in general during this era was the **poll tax**. Enacted in 1902, it required voters to pay a tax, presumably to cover the costs of elections by the end of January in an election that took place in early November. That tax was usually between $1.50 and $1.75. It was a small sum, but it had to be paid in advance of the election, and in the first third of the century, the tax could be one, two, or even more days' wages for a farm worker. Thus, it tended to disenfranchise poorer people.

The south Texas political bosses used the poll tax to great advantage. They would purchase large numbers of poll tax receipts and provide those receipts to their supporters, who often depended on the bosses for jobs and other economic, legal, and political assistance and who therefore would vote as the bosses wanted.

Although the poll tax was made illegal in federal elections in 1964 by the passage of the Twenty-Fourth Amendment to the U.S. Constitution, it remained legal in state elections in Texas until 1966, when it was held unconstitutional.[8] After the elimination of the poll tax, Texas continued to require **early registration** for voting—registration more than nine months before the general election. Early registration was required on a yearly basis. This requirement effectively prevented migrant workers from voting. These provisions lasted until 1971, when they were voided by

poll tax a state-imposed tax on voters as a prerequisite for voting; poll taxes were rendered unconstitutional in national elections by the Twenty-Fourth Amendment, and in state elections by the Supreme Court in 1966

early registration the requirement that a voter register long before the general election; in effect in Texas until 1971

Participation in elections in Texas is low relative to that in other states. In the past, there were restrictions on the franchise. One such restriction that discouraged poor people from voting was the poll tax, which remained legal in Texas until 1966. Here, voters are asked to pay the poll tax and then vote against Pappy O'Daniel.

the federal courts.[9] Texas even prohibited anyone who was not a property owner from voting in revenue bond and tax elections until the practice was stopped by federal courts in 1975.[10] Texas also required an unusually long period of residency. Until 1970 voters had to have lived in the state for at least one year and to have lived in the county for at least six months prior to voting. This was another restriction on the franchise that was struck down by the federal courts.[11]

The White Primary The most oppressive restriction on the franchise, however, was designed to minimize the political strength of African American voters. It was the **white primary**. This practice came under scrutiny by federal courts numerous times in the 21 years between 1923 and 1944; yet each time, the Texas legislature and state parties found a way to maintain the white primary and exclude black voters. In 1923 the Texas legislature flatly prohibited African Americans from voting in the Democratic primary. Since Texas was a one-party state at this time the effect, of course, was to prevent African Americans from participating in the only "real" election contests. Texas was able to do this because of a 1921 U.S. Supreme Court decision, *Newberry v. United States*, which dealt with a federal campaign-expenditures law. In interpreting the law, the Court stated that the primary election was "in no real sense part of the manner of holding the election."[12] This cleared the way for southern states, including Texas, to discriminate against African Americans in the primaries.

In 1927, however, the Supreme Court struck down the Texas white primary law, claiming that the legal ban on black participation was a violation of the equal protection clause of the Constitution.[13] In response, the Texas legislature passed another law that authorized the political parties, through their state executive committees, to determine the qualifications for voting in the primaries. That law, of course, allowed the parties to create white primaries. The theory was that what a state could not do directly because of the Fourteenth Amendment, it could authorize political parties to do. However, in *Nixon v. Condon* (1932), the U.S. Supreme Court held that the state executive committees were acting as agents of the state and were discriminating in violation of the Fourteenth Amendment.[14] As a result, the Texas Democratic Party convention, acting on its own authority and without any state law, passed a resolution that confined party membership to white citizens. That case was also appealed to the U.S. Supreme Court, and in *Grovey v. Townsend* (1935), the Court held there was no violation of the Fourteenth Amendment. The Fourteenth Amendment requires "equal protection under the law" for individuals of all races. However, the Court said that this requirement applied only to "state action," not action by private groups. Since there was no state law authorizing the white primary, the Court believed there was no "state action," only discrimination by a private organization, the Democratic Party, which is not banned by the Fourteenth Amendment.[15] Thus, the Court upheld the white primary until 1944, when, in *Smith v. Allwright*, it decided that the operation of primary elections involved so much state action and so much public responsibility that the white primary did involve unconstitutional state action.[16]

Even with the *Smith* decision, at least one Texas county held unofficial primaries by the **Jaybird Party**. This was a Democratic political organization that excluded African Americans. The winners in the Jaybird primary then entered the regular Democratic Party primary, in which they were never defeated for county office and where they seldom had opposition. In *Terry v. Adams*, the U.S. Supreme Court finally ruled that the Jaybird primary was an integral, and the only effective, part of the elective process in the county. Thus, the Fifteenth Amendment (which deals

white primary primary election in which only white voters are eligible to participate

Jaybird Party after the white primary was ruled unconstitutional, this offshoot Democratic party preselected candidates for the Democratic primary and prohibited African Americans from participating

with the right to vote) was applicable, and the white "preprimary" primary of the Jaybird Party was ruled unconstitutional.[17]

What made the white primary restriction work for Democrats during this era was the fact that Texas was a one-party state, where elections were decided in the Democratic Party primary. If Texas had had a competitive two-party system during this era, the state might have had a more difficult time imposing and maintaining these restrictions on the franchise. In a competitive two-party system, to obtain and retain power, both parties would have to search for ways to build and increase their base of support in order to be the victorious party. In a one-party system, there is a greater incentive to restrict participation in the party in order to retain control over it. Losers in a battle for control of a one-party system essentially have no place to go. If they cannot maintain a place in the dominant party's councils, then they have no other avenue for expressing their political views.

Expanding the Franchise

At least since the 1940s there has been a gradual expansion of the franchise in Texas. Much of that expansion was brought about by litigation in the federal courts, often by African American and Latino civil rights organizations. For example, the National Association for the Advancement of Colored People (NAACP) filed lawsuits throughout the 1960s and '70s challenging laws that restricted or otherwise stunted African American political advancement. The Mexican American Legal Defense and Education Fund (MALDEF) has also been active in monitoring any changes in electoral laws and challenging them if they prevented Latino political advancement.

Federal laws also played an important role in the expansion of the franchise. The most important of these laws was the **Voting Rights Act of 1965**, which applied to Texas as a result of congressional amendments after 1975. The Voting Rights Act was a piece of legislation initially aimed at ensuring that African Americans were not discriminated against at the polls. The year prior to the passage of this bill, Congress had passed the Civil Rights Act, which was intended to ensure the equality of African Americans in terms of access to businesses, hotels, and other public facilities. President Lyndon B. Johnson signed both laws even though he knew it would damage his political popularity in the South.

The Voting Rights Act has without question had an important influence on elections in Texas. One provision of the law was to send federal examiners to southern states to register voters. In many southern states, blacks were systematically denied the ability to register to vote, much less attempt to vote. In Mississippi, only about 7 percent of blacks were registered to vote prior to 1965, but by 1967 more than 67 percent had been registered to vote. This demonstrates the success of the Voting Rights Act in its efforts to ensure equal access to the ballot.

Section 2 of the Voting Rights Act involves a nationwide prohibition against the abridgement of voting rights on the basis of race or ethnicity. Because this affects all states, some localities outside of the South have been sued in federal court alleging violations of voting rights on the basis of race or ethnicity.

The Voting Rights Act has been renewed several times since 1965, and new provisions have been added since then. For example, bilingual ballots are now required in certain areas where more than 5 percent of voters speak another language. This ensures that voters who cannot speak English are not disenfranchised. However, the Supreme Court ruled in 2013 in *Shelby County v. Holder* that a key section of the Voting Rights Act was unconstitutional, which affects a provision requiring

Voting Rights Act of 1965
important legislation passed in order to ensure that African Americans would be guaranteed the right to vote. Renewed several times since 1965, the act also prevents the dilution of minority voting strength

Supporters of the Voting Rights Act rally outside the U.S. Supreme Court. In 2013 the Court ruled that Section 5 of the Voting Rights Act—the "preclearance" provisions, which aimed to protect minority voters—was unconstitutional.

Texas to have its new districts or other changes in electoral procedures approved by the U.S. Department of Justice or a District of Columbia federal court.

Contracting the Franchise?

Highly partisan legislation passed in 2011 may make it more difficult for some people to vote. Over Democratic opposition, the Republican majority in the Texas legislature passed a voter identification law that requires a photo identification in order to vote. Republicans claimed that the photo identification requirement is necessary in order to prevent voter fraud. Democrats, in contrast, have argued that evidence of voter fraud is minimal and that the law will make it harder for low-income persons, students, and the elderly (all of whom typically support Democrats) to vote.[18] Forms of photo identification that are acceptable are a driver's license, an election identification certificate, a Department of Public Safety personal ID card, a U.S. military ID, a U.S. citizenship certificate, a U.S. passport, and a Department of Public Safety–issued concealed handgun license.[19] Photo ID cards issued by colleges and universities are not acceptable. As we noted at the beginning of Chapter 3, this law made it difficult for former Speaker of the House Jim Wright to vote in 2013. It remains to be seen if the Texas voter ID law will ultimately be upheld by the appellate courts. State political leaders, such as Governor Perry and Attorney General Abbott, have argued that Texas should not be singled out along with other southern states and subjected to the special scrutiny, and should be allowed to have a voter ID law without any approval process. The "You Decide" section takes a closer look at this issue.

Voter Identification Laws

In 2011 the Texas legislature passed a law that requires all voters to produce photo identification when they present themselves to vote in an election. Prior to the law, Texans could present a voter registration certificate, which does not carry a photograph. Under the new law, not all forms of photo identification are considered valid for voting purposes. For example, state-issued concealed weapons permits are allowed, but student identification cards are not. A voter who shows up to the polls without appropriate photo identification may cast a provisional ballot, but must return to the registrar's office with photo identification within six days to make his or her vote count.

Supporters of the law argue that requiring photo identification is necessary to ensure the integrity of the election system and assure Texans that their elections are free from fraud. They claim that fraud is often undetected and difficult to prosecute, so the absence of high rates of voter fraud prosecution does not mean that it is a problem that should be ignored. Supporters believe that having the potential of penalties for breaking the law will deter any attempts to commit fraud. They point out that one needs to show photo identification to board airplanes, conduct official business, and perform transactions with banks and other organizations. They also point to public opinion polls showing that the majority of Texans support the simple proposition that you must show photo identification to prove who you are in order to vote.

Opponents of the law claim that the measure is not really about preserving the integrity of the electoral system, but it is meant to minimize Democratic turnout in order to help the state Republican Party keep its hold on power. Those who oppose the law claim that it puts an undue burden on populations who are less likely to possess photo identification (and who often vote for

Democrats), such as elderly, disabled, minority, and poor voters, by making them go through additional steps to vote. The law does provide for free photo identification, but in some rural areas, opponents argue, the nearest Department of Public Safety office is far away and not easily accessible. In addition, opponents suggest that the law is in essence a solution in search of a problem, pointing to studies that show there is no real problem concerning voter fraud in Texas.

The question remains whether voter identification laws are on balance positive or negative. There are legitimate arguments for and against the legislation, but one thing is clear: Republicans strongly support the measure and Democrats have attempted to stop the measure. This fact alone suggests that Republicans believe they will electorally benefit from the law, while Democrats believe they will be harmed. In Wisconsin, a federal judge agreed with challengers to that state's voter ID law and declared it unconstitutional because of social science evidence suggesting that minorities were adversely affected by the new requirements. However, backers of the Texas law point to data showing that turnout in the November 2013 election was nearly double that of previous elections without the voter ID requirement, including in heavily Hispanic counties. This suggests, they argue, that the law did not adversely affect minority turnout. You decide. Should voter IDs be required for voting in Texas elections?

critical thinking questions

1. Do the arguments for the legislation outweigh the arguments against it?

2. Is there a way to compromise on this issue? If so, what would a compromise look like?

Qualifications to Vote

Today, meeting the qualifications to register to vote in Texas is relatively easy. A voter must be

1. eighteen years of age
2. a U.S. citizen
3. a resident of Texas for 30 days
4. a resident of the county for 30 days

To be eligible to vote, one must be a registered voter for 30 days preceding the election and a resident of the voting precinct on the day of the election. Two groups of citizens cannot vote even if they meet all the preceding qualifications: felons who have not completed their sentences and those judged by a court to be mentally incompetent.

motor voter law a national act, passed in 1993, that requires states to allow people to register to vote when applying for a driver's license

According to the Texas secretary of state, 71.91 percent of the state's voting age-population (13.6 million citizens) was registered to vote in 2014.[20] The **motor voter law**,[21] which allows individuals to register to vote when applying for or renewing driver's licenses, is one factor in increased registration. Public schools distribute voter registration cards as students turn 18. Cooperative efforts between the secretary of state's office and corporations also increase the number of registered voters. Most colleges and universities also have registration drives to encourage young people to register to vote.

Following the November 2012 election, a Census Bureau survey found that registration rates varied across racial and ethnic lines. Latino eligible voters registered at a 54.5 percent rate, below that of blacks (73.2 percent) and whites (73.0 percent).[22]

Low Voter Turnout

In most elections, fewer than 50 percent of U.S. citizens vote.[23] Even fewer Texans exercise their right to vote, especially young people. Texas ranks last in the nation in voter participation. Table 5.1 provides data on the abysmal turnout of registered voters in the various types of recent Texas elections. Considering the ease of registration and the ability to vote early, voter participation should be higher. Why do so few Texans vote?

A more detailed analysis reveals several factors that may contribute to low participation rates:

1. low levels of educational attainment
2. low per capita income
3. high rate of poverty
4. location in the South
5. young population
6. traditionalistic and individualistic political culture
7. candidate-centered elections and little party competition
8. lack of media attention to substantive political issues
9. large numbers of undocumented residents and felons

Education and income appear to be the two most important factors in determining whether someone votes, and this is often referred to as socioeconomic sta-

TABLE 5.1

Turnout by Registered Voters in Texas Elections

ELECTION	VOTING TURNOUT AS PERCENTAGE OF REGISTERED VOTERS
2001 special election (constitutional amendments)	6.9
2002 Democratic primary (gubernatorial)	8.4
2002 Republican primary (gubernatorial)	5.1
2002 general election (gubernatorial)	36.2
2003 special election (constitutional)	12.2
2004 Democratic primary (presidential)	6.8
2004 Republican primary (presidential)	5.6
2004 general election (presidential)	56.6
2005 special election (constitutional amendments)	18.0
2006 Democratic primary (gubernatorial)	4.0
2006 Republican primary (gubernatorial)	5.2
2006 general election (gubernatorial)	33.6
2007 November special election (constitutional amendments)	8.7
2008 general election (presidential)	59.5
2009 November special election (constitutional amendments)	8.2
2010 Democratic primary (gubernatorial)	5.2
2010 Republican primary (gubernatorial)	11.4
2010 general election (gubernatorial)	38.0
2011 November special election	5.0
2012 Republican primary (presidential)	11.3
2012 Democratic primary (presidential)	5.0
2013 November special elections (constitutional amendments)	8.6
2014 Democratic primary (gubernatorial)	4.1
2014 Republican primary (gubernatorial)	9.8
2014 general election (gubernatorial)	33.6

tus (SES). In Texas, low levels of education and high levels of poverty are both the strongest predictors of low voter participation. While college students and other young adults were mobilized by President Obama's election in 2008 and 2012, the fact remains that voter turnout among this demographic is low. In addition, the average age of Texans is less than the national average, and young people vote in smaller numbers; this may also contribute to Texas's low turnout rate.

In 2014 only 33.6 percent of registered voters cast ballots in the Texas gubernatorial election.

In the southern states that composed the Confederacy, individuals participate in smaller numbers than in other parts of the United States. Texas was part of the Confederacy, and its level of participation is consistent with lower levels of voting in the South. That said, Texas differs from most other southern states with its large Latino population, many of whom, perhaps up to 2.0 million, are not eligible to vote because either they are not registered or they are undocumented residents in the state. Moreover, the overwhelming majority of these Latinos are from Mexico and may not have been brought up in a political culture that encourages participation at the polls. As the children born and educated in America of these residents reach voting age, it is likely that registration rates and voting rates among Latinos will increase. For now, however, they remain lower than those for whites or blacks.

According to the political scientist Daniel Elazar, Texas's political culture is traditionalistic and individualistic (see Chapter 1).[24] Low levels of voting characterize these cultures. In a traditionalistic political culture, the political and economic elite discourage voting. People choose not to vote in individualistic cultures because of real or perceived corruption in government.

Interestingly, there are still other possible explanations for low voter participation in Texas. In keeping with the Texas tradition of decentralized government, there are so many elections in Texas and so many candidates for office that voters are simply overloaded with elections and candidates. Note that as shown in Table 5.1, voter participation was much higher in the general election than in the special constitutional election. If there were fewer elections, the ballot might be longer, but voter turnout would likely be higher, because more voters would be attracted to at least some races or issues on the ballot. Additionally, the practice of having elections in nonpresidential election years decreases voter turnout because the highest voter participation tends to occur for presidential elections. A third problem is that most elections in Texas involve very low-visibility offices. Voters likely know little about the candidates for these positions or the offices themselves, and such a lack of knowledge would naturally discourage voter participation. Efforts have been made in a number of states, most notably Washington, to increase voter knowledge by having the state provide biographical information about the candidates to voters, but Texas makes little effort to enhance voter knowledge of candidates. Independent groups such as the League of Women Voters often provide voter guides, but only readers of newspapers or those who actively seek these voter guides benefit from this information. Finally, some suggest that the new voter identification law will reduce voter turnout even more.

Who Votes in Texas?

Voter Turnout by Race, 2012

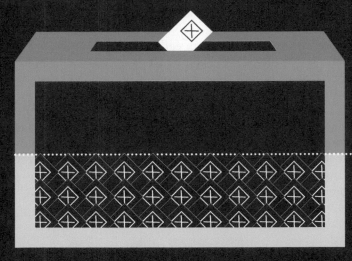

Texas Totals

**Citizen voting-
age population**
15,891,110

**Total voter
turnout***
51%

Texas is now a majority-minority state. This means that the nonwhite population exceeds the Anglo population. However, this does not mean that the majority of the state's voters are nonwhite. It is still the case that the Latino population is underrepresented compared to their population on the state's voter rolls.

◗ 10% voter turnout

White voter turnout

61%

Citizen voting-
age population
8,965,260

Latino voter turnout

39%

Citizen voting-
age population
4,209,595

African American voter turnout

63%

Citizen voting-
age population
2,029,885

Asian voter turnout

42%

Citizen voting-
age population
464,765

* Percentage of citizen voting-age population who voted in 2012

Source: Noncitizen data from U.S. Census Bureau, Current Population Survey.
Racial group data from American Community Survey, U.S. Census Bureau. Turnout data from U.S. Census Bureau.

for critical analysis

1. Which groups have the lowest percentage of eligible voters registered?

2. What can we conclude about the difference among racial/ethnic groups in regard to voter turnout in Texas?

Early Voting

early voting a procedure that allows voters to cast ballots during the two-week period before the regularly scheduled election date

Early voting is a procedure that increases the polling period from 12 hours on Election Day to an additional two weeks prior to the election. The legislature has allowed early voting in an effort to increase participation. It is designed for those who have trouble getting to the polls between 7 AM and 7 PM on Election Day. For most elections, early voting commences on the 17th day before the elections and ends four days prior to Election Day.

Voting early is basically the same as voting on Election Day. An individual appears at one of the designated polling places, presents appropriate identification, and receives and casts a ballot. Early voting has at best only modestly increased voting participation.

Predictions that Democrats would benefit from early voting did not hold true after Texas moved strongly into the Republican column. Republican candidates for the highest office on the ballot get a much larger proportion of early votes than do the Democratic candidates. In 2004, for example, 63 percent of the early votes for president in Texas were cast for George W. Bush, compared with 37 percent of the early votes for John Kerry. In 7 of the 10 elections examined, however, Republicans got a slightly smaller proportion of overall votes (votes cast in early voting plus Election Day voting) than early votes. And in 6 of the 10 elections, Democrats got a slightly larger proportion of overall votes than early votes. This suggests that early voting has been a bit more beneficial to Republicans than to Democrats, although the advantage has been very slight (Table 5.2).

TABLE 5.2

Early Voting and Overall Voting by Party in Texas

YEAR	OFFICE	EARLY/OVERALL VOTES FOR REPUBLICANS (PERCENTAGE OF TOTAL)	EARLY/OVERALL VOTES FOR DEMOCRATS (PERCENTAGE OF TOTAL)
1994	Senate	62/61%	37/38%
1996	President	52/49	45/44
1998	Governor	68/69	32/31
2000	President	63/59	35/38
2002	Senator	57/55	42/43
2004	President	63/61	37/38
2006	Senator	56/56	44/44
2008	President	54/55	45/44
2010	Governor	56/55	41/42
2012	President	59/57	40/41

SOURCE: Texas Secretary of State.

How Did Texans Vote in 2012?

Race	Pop.%	🐴 = Obama	🐘 = Romney		

National

Race	Pop.%	Obama	Romney
White	72%	39%	59%
Black	13%	93%	6%
Hispanic	10%	71%	27%
Asian	3%	73%	26%
Other	2%	58%	38%

Texas

Race	Pop.%	Obama	Romney
White	67%	25%	70%
Black	12%	88%	9%
Hispanic	21%	53%	42%
Asian			
Other			

Note: Data on Asian American voters and other groups were not available from Texas exit polls.

California

Race	Pop.%	Obama	Romney
White	55%	44%	54%
Black	8%	96%	4%
Hispanic	23%	70%	29%
Asian	12%	77%	22%
Other	3%	52%	38%

Voters in Texas are known for their conservatism and their support of the Republican Party. In 2012, while the country voted for Barack Obama over Mitt Romney by a 51–48 margin, Texas went for Romney 57–41.

In Texas, these exit polls show that Romney won in large part because he won an overwhelming share of white voters. Obama won among African American and Hispanic voters in Texas by similar numbers to what he won nationally. Romney won 70 percent of white votes in Texas, 11 points better than the 59 percent of white voters he won nationally. Compare this to California, a state with similar demographics to Texas: Romney won only 54 percent of California's white voters.

for critical analysis

1. Why do you think Romney appealed to white Texans more than he appealed to white voters in the rest of the country? How distinct does this make Texans?

2. As we've seen in earlier chapters, the Hispanic population of Texas is growing over time. How might this growth change the outcomes of future elections in Texas?

TABLE 5.3

Percentage of Registered Voters and Voting-Age Population Voting in the Republican Primaries

YEAR	REGISTERED VOTERS	PERCENTAGE OF REGISTERED VOTERS VOTING IN REPUBLICAN PRIMARIES	PERCENTAGE OF VOTING-AGE POPULATION VOTING IN REPUBLICAN PRIMARIES
2014	13,601,324	9.98%	7.18%
2012	13,065,425	11.09	7.93
2010	13,023,358	11.40	8.00
2008	12,752,417	10.68	7.68
2006	12,722,671	5.15	3.94
2004	12,264,663	5.60	4.27
2002	12,218,164	5.09	4.01
2000	11,612,761	9.70	7.78
1998	11,159,845	5.35	4.24
1996	9,698,506	10.52	7.44
1994	9,041,906	6.16	4.26

The Importance of the Republican Primary

Table 5.3 shows how important the Republican primary has become in statewide elections. That is because the winner of the Republican primary, in this era of Republican dominance in the state, will be the winner of a statewide election. For example, 11.09 percent of registered voters and only 7.93 percent of the voting-age population in Texas voted in the Republican primary in 2012, but the winner of that primary has since the 1990s become the victor in statewide elections. Of course, many of the Republican primaries for statewide offices are contested, and to be successful in winning office all that is needed is a majority of the vote in the primary. In the 2012 elections, theoretically a person could win statewide office with the votes of less than 5.546 percent of the registered voters in the state, assuming those voters cast ballots in the Republican primary.

Racial and Ethnic Variations in Voting and Participation

While Texas is a state with a larger percentage of minorities than non-Hispanic whites, this does not mean that the majority of the state's voters are minorities. For example, in the November 2014 elections, Latinos comprised only about 17 percent of the Texas electorate.[25] As a result of a variety of factors, including the large undocumented population consisting of mostly Latinos from Mexico and Latin

America and the lower rate of voter turnout for Latino citizens, non-Hispanic whites wield considerable influence in the state electorate.

Because most African Americans and Latinos tend to vote for Democrats and non-Hispanic whites tend to vote for Republicans, the balance of power in most state elections currently tilts toward Republicans. Democrats hope that as more Latinos become citizens, they will register and turn out to vote, but these hopes have yet to fully materialize.

Public Opinion Differences on Issues Public opinion on issues varies according to race and ethnicity. In a book titled *Divided by Color*, Donald Kinder and Lynn Sanders show that the views of African Americans and whites are remarkably different on issues ranging from the death penalty to affirmative action.[26] For example, according to a November 2013 *Texas Tribune* survey, 76 percent of whites supported the death penalty, while 60 percent of African Americans supported the death penalty. Significantly more African Americans, however, believe that the death penalty is often implemented for innocent citizens. In the same survey, 31 percent of African Americans believed the death penalty was implemented for innocent citizens "a great deal of the time" compared with 9 percent of whites.[27] In most cases, African Americans are more liberal than whites on political issues.

One issue with remarkable convergence on public opinion between blacks and whites is same sex marriage. In Texas, according to a June 2013 *Texas Tribune* survey, 33 percent of African Americans, 38 percent of whites, and 45 percent of Latinos supported same sex marriage.[28] This is one reason why Texas is one of several states that were able to pass a state constitutional amendment defining marriage in the state as between one man and one woman. While the gulf in public opinion is more pronounced between African Americans and whites compared to Latinos and whites, even the latter two groups differ on attitudes about public policy, especially the role of government.

Consider the issue of immigration policy. Most Latinos surveyed in Texas support the DREAM Act, a policy that would allow undocumented students who serve in the military or graduate from college to become citizens. According to a February 2014 *Texas Tribune* poll, 54 percent of whites in Texas strongly oppose this policy, especially the version that allows college graduates to become citizens.[29] For conservatives, this amounts to an unacceptable form of amnesty for illegal immigrants. In contrast, a minority of Latinos (33 percent) strongly oppose the DREAM Act. Whites are also more likely than Latinos to support restrictive immigration policies, although African Americans are just as likely to support such immigration policies.

Regarding education policy, Latinos in Texas are more likely to support a greater role for government in public education. In general, Latinos view education as a more important policy issue than their white counterparts. This could be for several reasons. First, Latinos are generally poorer and less educated than the majority white population and correctly see educational attainment as a key to success. Second, many Latinos are immigrants who view education as the ticket to the American Dream. Finally, Latinos have the highest high school dropout rates, and this reality has important ramifications for social, political, and economic advancement.

One related issue area with a significant divide in opinion between whites and Latinos is bilingual education. Most Latinos in Texas support the use of bilingual education—instruction in English and Spanish until students can transition to full English instruction. On the other hand, most Anglos oppose this policy and support total immersion in English. A May 2010 *Texas Tribune* poll shows that 55 percent of white Texans strongly supported ending bilingual education, while only 22 percent of Latinos supported this position. Forty-four percent of Latinos strongly opposed ending bilingual education, while only 15 percent of whites strongly opposed ending bilingual education.[30] This policy, along with attitudes about an English Only law for Texas, is one of the most polarized by ethnicity in the state.

Redistricting in Texas

Every 10 years, the U.S. Census is charged with counting how many people live in the United States. The process of **reapportionment** involves recalculating how many congressional districts each state will receive based on the state's population. For example, Texas gained four new congressional seats following the 2010 Census because of the explosive population growth of the state. Since the House of Representatives is capped at 435 members, other states had to lose some of their congressional seats. States such as New York lost congressional seats because their populations had increased more slowly during the previous 10 years. The state legislature is tasked with drawing new congressional districts every 10 years to comply with the new overall number of seats allowed.

In 2011 the Texas legislature drew new congressional districts (Figure 5.1A), a process called **redistricting**. This is a blatantly political procedure because the majority party uses it to retain power by creating as many friendly districts as it can. The Republicans in charge of the legislature attempted to draw as many Republican-voting districts as possible. If Democrats had been in control, they would have tried to maximize their number of seats as well. Because more than 67 percent of the population growth in Texas was a result of Latino immigration and birth rates among native-born Latinos and foreign-born Latinos, Latino leaders in the state wanted at least two of the new seats to be majority Latino. Most Latino-majority districts in the state tend not to elect Republicans, which put the Republican-led legislature in a bind.

Until a 2013 U.S. Supreme Court decision, the terms by which Texas must comply with the Voting Rights Act further complicated the situation. Section 5 of the act requires that any changes to election procedures, including the drawing of new district lines, must go through the process of **preclearance**. This means that the U.S. Department of Justice or a District of Columbia federal court must approve the new district lines in order to make sure that the voting rights of minorities are not diminished. Districts that have been created to help minorities win cannot be dismantled in order to benefit a particular political party. For the most part, it is the southern states of the old Confederacy that were subject to this provision. Texas Attorney General Greg Abbott argued that Section 5 of the act violated the Tenth Amendment to the U.S. Constitution because it singles out particular states for preclearance. The preclearance requirement is but one example of the conflict between Texas and the federal government on a number of issues (see Chapter 3). Governor Perry has frequently criticized the federal government for its regulations and mandates. Section 5 is no longer applicable to Texas because of the U.S. Supreme Court's decision in *Shelby County v. Holder*, in which the Court ruled that the formula used to determine which states are subject to preclearance

reapportionment process that takes place every 10 years to determine how many congressional seats each state will receive, depending on population shifts

redistricting the process of redrawing election districts and redistributing legislative representatives in the Texas House, Texas Senate, and U.S. House; this process usually happens every 10 years to reflect shifts in population or in response to legal challenges in existing districts

preclearance provision under Section 5 of the Voting Rights Act of 1965 requiring any changes to election procedures or district lines to be approved by the U.S. Department of Justice or the U.S. district court for the District of Columbia is unconstitutional. Congress must pass a new formula in order for Section 5 to become applicable once again. When asked whether they thought Texas should be subject to federal oversight of its elections, 41 percent of respondents said yes and 47 percent responded no in a *Texas Tribune* poll conducted in February 2013.[31]

In the 2011 redistricting round, several lawsuits were filed by different parties challenging the districts created by the Texas legislature, and the federal court stepped in (Figure 5.1B). Ultimately, the legislature and the court created one new congressional district with a majority Latino population that stretched from Bexar County to Travis County along Interstate 35. The three other new districts were designed to elect Republicans. This was accomplished by splitting Travis County, the seat of Austin, into five congressional districts in order to dilute the Democratic vote. Since most Travis County voters are white Democrats, there are no protections under the law for diluting their vote. The U.S. representative for Austin, Democrat Lloyd Doggett, was forced to run in the new Latino majority district, since the other four districts were majority Republican. Because of the federal court's lengthy process, the Texas primary was pushed back to May 29, 2012, much later than the late March date originally scheduled.

One possible solution to reforming redistricting is to take the process away from the legislature. In Texas, the state legislature decides how the district lines will be drawn, and critics often say that this is the only time when politicians choose their voters and not the other way around. Some states, such as Arizona, have taken the responsibility away from the legislature and created an independent redistricting commission. Such a commission, supporters argue, would create fairer districts in Texas without the influence of politicians who have a vested interest in protecting their seats and political parties. According to a May 2011 *Texas Tribune* poll, 40 percent of respondents voiced support in principle for such a system, while 30 percent were opposed, and 30 percent were unsure of the plan.[32] Changing the system of redistricting will be challenging because legislators of both parties greatly benefit from the ability to influence how district lines are drawn.

Contemporary Barriers to Voting

While the days of poll taxes are over, there are still barriers to voting in contemporary Texas. For example, in many cities, council members are elected at-large, meaning that there are no individual districts for the city. Consider a city that has 10 city council seats and is 20 percent African American, 25 percent Latino, and 55 percent white. In at-large races, the white majority could theoretically capture all of the city's 10 council seats. If the city had a single-member district system, there would be a distinct possibility that at least 4 of the seats would be held by minorities. Austin has an at-large system of electing city council members but is currently considering changing the system in order to provide for better geographic and racial representation.

Other tactics for preventing certain groups from voting include reducing the number of polling places in certain areas, the presence of broken voting machines, misleading information provided to voters, and voter intimidation. While such practices are becoming less frequent, there are still reports of them in every contested election.

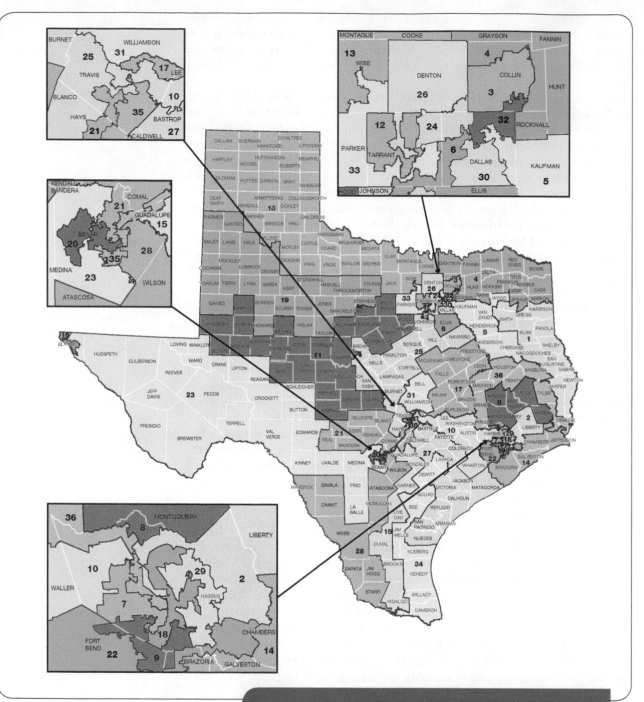

FIGURE 5.1A

Texas U.S. Congressional District Maps: Legislature Plan

The district map drawn by the Republican majority in the Texas legislature in 2011 was designed to help Republicans win as many U.S. House seats as possible. However, Latino leaders complained that the plan didn't create more Latino-majority districts.

SOURCE: Texas Legislative Council.

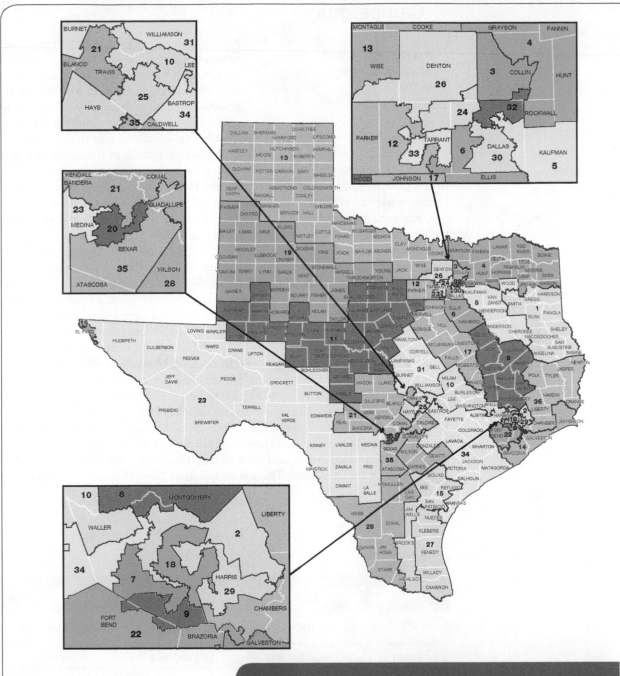

FIGURE 5.1B

Texas U.S. Congressional District Maps: Court Plan

By comparing the court-approved plan above with the Republican legislature's plan at left, we can see district lines were changed to comply with the Voting Rights Act. Note significant differences in the urban areas as well as in East Texas.

SOURCE: Texas Legislative Council.

Campaigns

Political campaigns are efforts of candidates to win support of the voters. The goal of the campaign is to attain sufficient support to win the primary election in March and the general election in November. Some campaigns last a year or more; however, the more accepted practice is to limit the campaign to a few months before the election.

In recent statewide elections, the distinguishing feature of the campaigns was the lack of emphasis on state issues, including the pressing issue of the state budget. Instead, Republicans ran against the national Democratic administration, whereas Democrats tried to distance themselves from President Obama and his policies.

Campaigns involve attempts to reach the voters through print and electronic media, the mail, door-to-door campaigning, speeches to large and small groups, coffee hours, and telephone solicitation. Costs are enormous. During the 2000s, candidates for statewide races spent as much as $39 million. A new record up to that point for campaign spending was set in the 2002 gubernatorial race, when the Democrat Tony Sanchez and the Republican Rick Perry spent a total of $88 million. In 2006 the amount raised in the gubernatorial race fell to $53.4 million, 28.7 percent of which went to the two independent candidates, Carole Keeton Strayhorn and Kinky Friedman. In 2010 total campaign contributions by Democrats seeking the governorship came to nearly $37 million and total contributions by Republicans came to nearly $55 million—an amount far larger than the $30 million raised by Republicans in 2006 because of the primary challenge to Rick Perry by Kay Bailey Hutchison. In late October 2014, Greg Abbott had spent $46.8 million to Wendy Davis's $36 million. For all statewide offices, Republican campaign contributions overwhelmed Democratic campaign contributions. Total contributions in state House and state Senate races were also far greater for Republicans than for Democrats. There is no question, then, that money is important

TABLE 5.4

Amount Raised by All Candidates in Texas, 2012*

OFFICE	DEMOCRAT ($)	REPUBLICAN ($)	THIRD-PARTY ($)
Governor	$36,994,646	$54,682,462	$0
Judicial	401,025	2,592,108	110
Other statewide	3,150,119	21,387,407	1,547
House	28,780,507	48,634,984	26,552
Senate	3,979,924	6,991,616	23,007

*Listed by political party. Excludes contributions to candidates not up for election in 2010 and one candidate for state senate who withdrew.
SOURCE: Calculated from Institute on Money in State Politics.

TABLE 5.5

Campaign Contributions in Statewide Executive Offices: Texas General Elections 2010

OFFICE	CANDIDATE	DOLLARS CONTRIBUTED	PERCENTAGE OF VOTE*
Governor	R. Perry (R)	$39,328,540	54.97%
	B. White (D)	26,291,535	42.29
Lieutenant governor	D. Dewhurst (R)	9,240,480	61.78
	L. Chavez-Thompson	958,040	34.83
Agriculture commissioner	Todd Staples (R)	1,742,941	60.82
	Hank Gilbert (D)	336,363	35.79
Attorney general	Greg Abbott (R)	5,828,370	64.05
	Barbara Radnafsky (D)	1,135,031	33.66
Comptroller	Susan Combs (R)	2,744,001	83.16
	None		
Land commissioner	Jerry Patterson (R)	864,688	61.66
	Hector Uribe (D)	102,487	35.28
Railroad commissioner	David Porter (R)	564,488	59.40
	Jeff Weems (D)	287,248	36.23

*Numbers do not add to 100 percent because of the presence of third-party candidates.
SOURCE: Institute on Money in State Politics and Texas Secretary of State.

for candidate success in Texas. Candidates must continually raise money by hosting fundraisers with donors, making phone calls to potential donors, and setting up websites that make it easy for ordinary citizens to contribute (see Tables 5.4 and 5.5).

Candidates who run in Texas for federal office, such as the U.S. Congress, are subject to federal campaign finance laws, which are stricter than state laws and which impose limits for campaign contributions, although the federal laws have been greatly weakened by U.S. Supreme Court decisions that have held parts of the federal laws to restrict free speech. Candidates for state offices, however, are subject to state laws enacted in 1991 when the Texas Ethics Commission (TEC) was established. State candidates and lobbyists must file quarterly reports with the TEC, although with the exception of judicial campaigns there are no limits to campaign contributions for state races. The state imposes a moratorium on contributions to state legislators just prior to the beginning of a legislative session.

In some places in the United States, the parties have a major role in the running of political campaigns. That is not the case in Texas. Here the candidates have the major responsibility for campaign strategy, for running their campaigns, and for raising money. At times, party leaders will try to recruit individuals to run for office, especially if no candidates volunteer to seek an office or if the candidates appear to be weak ones. For the most part, the benefit of the party to a candidate in Texas is that the party provides the party label under which the candidate runs. That

"Democratic" or "Republican" label is, of course, important to candidates because many voters use the party label in casting their votes, especially for low-visibility races. The party also contains numerous activists whom the candidate can tap for campaign tasks such as manning phone banks, preparing mailings, and posting campaign ads. Additionally, the party does provide some support for the candidate, most commonly through campaigns to get out the vote for the party's candidates. Campaigning in Texas, however, is generally left up to the candidate, and in that effort, the parties take a secondary role.

Name recognition is essential for candidates. Incumbents hold a distinct advantage in this regard. Officeholders have many ways to achieve name visibility. They can mail out news releases, send newsletters to their constituents, appear on radio talk shows, and give speeches to civic clubs. Newspaper coverage and local television news coverage of the politician can increase name recognition. Challengers have a more difficult time getting this crucial name visibility, although new media sources such as Facebook and Twitter accounts can help both incumbents and challengers gain name recognition, especially among young people.

The case of William R. Clements illustrates the importance of name recognition. In 1978, William R. Clements was a political unknown. He spent thousands of dollars of his own fortune to gain name recognition. He leased hundreds of billboards throughout the state. Each had a blue background with white letters proclaiming "CLEMENTS." In the print media, early ads bore the simple message, "ELECT CLEMENTS." The unprecedented scale of this advertising effort made Clements's name better known among the voters in Texas. This, in turn, stimulated interest in his campaign's message. Clements won the race for governor, becoming the first Republican to hold that office in Texas since the end of Reconstruction.

Payments for media ads account for the greatest expense in most campaigns. In metropolitan areas, television, radio, and print advertising are very costly. Full-page ads in metropolitan newspapers can cost as much as $40,000. Candidates for metropolitan districts in the Texas House of Representatives and Texas Senate need to reach only a small portion of the population, but they are forced to purchase ads in media sources that go to hundreds of thousands of people not represented. In rural areas, any individual ad is relatively inexpensive. However, candidates must advertise in dozens of small newspapers and radio stations, and the costs add up.

Even more important, the campaigns must be well designed. A slipup in a well-funded campaign can do great harm, as Greg Abbott discovered in his campaign for governor. While Abbott has made efforts to appeal to the Latino vote, his campaign received criticism when in February 2014 he referred to law enforcement tactics in the border region as resembling "third world country practices that erode the social fabric of our communities." A journalist for the *Monitor*, a newspaper in the Rio Grande Valley, called on Abbott to apologize for his comments. Abbott refused to apologize, saying his comments were not directed at Latinos, but rather at the lack of border security in South Texas. Abbott sought to repair his relationship with Latino voters by emphasizing his Latina wife as the imminent first Latina first lady of Texas. While this slipup did not cost him the election (he received 44 percent of the Latino vote—a healthy number for a Republican candidate), it still raised larger questions about the state's Republican Party and its relationship with the growing Latino vote.[33]

Some impressive but limited evidence indicates that television can be a very valuable tool for a Texas political candidate. On four occasions in the 1990s Republican Supreme Court candidates were challenged in the primary by candidates

Candidates for statewide office in Texas routinely spend hundreds of thousands of dollars, if not millions, on their campaigns. Though much money goes to television advertising, candidates also spend time meeting voters one-on-one, as Republican candidate Ken Paxton does here at Joe Allen's Pit Bar-B-Que in Abilene.

with little, if any, organized support and minimal funding. Yet the insurgent candidates all showed great strength in areas where the established candidates did not run television ads. Of course, there may be additional explanations for the strength of established candidates in areas where ads were shown. Perhaps the candidates worked harder in those areas or were better organized. And in some areas, candidates may have had stronger name recognition than their opponents.[34]

None of the insurgent candidates had the resources to run television ads; only the established candidates did, and only in some media markets. It was the support the established candidates received in the areas where they ran television ads that led to their victories. It is important to note that since the data all relate to the Republican primary, the effect of the political party label is controlled. If we compare the percentage difference in votes for established candidates in areas where television ads were run with votes in areas where no ads were run, the difference is remarkable: established candidates received between 12 percent and 18.5 percent more votes in media markets where they bought television time.[35]

Given the myriad factors that may explain electoral success, we should beware of imputing victory in these judicial races solely to television ads. On the other hand, the general pattern of high margins of victory in areas where television was used is so powerful that it cannot be ignored.

Important Issues in Texas Campaigns

The open gubernatorial seat in 2014 pitted Greg Abbott against Wendy Davis. With the state's economic challenges of the mid-2000s largely in the rearview mirror, both candidates fought hard to distinguish themselves on issues. Davis had become prominent because of her filibuster of an antiabortion bill in 2011, but she wanted to expand her policy portfolio beyond this one issue. Abbott had distinguished himself as attorney general of Texas by challenging the Obama administration on a host of policy issues, including the Affordable Care Act, the Voting Rights Act, and gun rights.

Education policy became an important issue in the 2014 elections when Greg Abbott proposed expanding programs for pre-kindergarten. Wendy Davis had already proposed a plan that would increase funding for this program, but Abbott criticized Davis's plan for not including measures to monitor whether the programs were working. Davis countered by accusing Abbott of hypocrisy by defending cuts to pre-Kindergarten programs in his capacity as the state's attorney general. The tenor of the education debate in 2014 is a far cry from the debates in 2010, when the debate revolved around mitigating drastic budget cuts to education in the face of a budget shortfall.

The gubernatorial campaign also highlighted issues that were not typical in previous races. Equal pay for equal work became a major issue in April 2014 when the *San Antonio Express News* revealed that female assistant attorneys general in Abbott's office were paid approximately $6,000 less on average than their male counterparts. Abbott responded by asserting that the reason for the discrepancy was that the male employees were on average more experienced. Wendy Davis pressed Abbott on whether he would support her bill guaranteeing equal pay for equal work in Texas. Abbott claimed that he supported equal pay for equal work but not her bill because of his belief that a new law was not necessary. It did not help Abbott that his surrogates fumbled some of their explanations as to why Abbott opposed the legislation. For example, Abbott supporter and Red State Women PAC chair Cari Christman claimed women were "too busy" to think about equal pay for equal work and Texas GOP chair Beth Cubriel stated that the reason women are paid less than men is because men "are better negotiators."[36] These issues have no doubt become more prominent because of Wendy Davis's presence in the gubernatorial race as the first female Democratic Party candidate for governor since Ann Richards.

Gun rights has consistently been a salient issue in Texas, especially regarding recent debates about whether firearms should be allowed on college campuses. Texas also has a concealed carry law allowing licensed individuals to carry concealed firearms throughout the state with some exceptions such as bars. Even Democrats in Texas do not take positions at odds with the pro-gun sentiment in the state. Wendy Davis surprised many when she announced that she would back a bill allowing Texans to carry unconcealed pistols on their waists. Of course, Abbott also supports the legislation, but criticized Davis for her support of allowing private individuals and businesses to block individuals from carrying pistols on their property. He also accused Davis of wanting to enact more restrictions on gun owners and compared her to former New York City mayor Michael Bloomberg, a strong gun control advocate. The National Rifle Association, the nation's leading pro-gun lobbying group, gave Abbott an A and Davis a D on their gun control policies.

Immigration policy also became a very salient issue in all of the statewide races. Republican candidates for all major elective offices pledged to enact strict border security measures and spend state resources on keeping illegal immigrants out of the state. This emphasis on immigration is a marked change from the 1990s when then governor Bush appealed to the Latino vote in the state. For example, Re-

Immigration is a major issue in Texas elections. Democrats and Republicans have called for reform, but their approaches differ strongly.

publican candidate for Agriculture Commissioner Eric Opiela ran a television ad where he appeared on a farm next to a barbed wire fence announcing that illegal immigrants need to go to the back of the line and that there should be no amnesty for illegal immigrants. He lost the Republican primary with only 17 percent of the vote. More notorious, however, in his positions on immigration was lieutenant gubernatorial candidate Dan Patrick, who said in a debate that he wanted to stop the "invasion" of illegal immigrants to Texas. Patrick challenged Lieutenant Governor David Dewhurst from the right by arguing that Dewhurst was not sufficiently conservative on this issue. Land commissioner Jerry Patterson, another candidate for lieutenant governor, accused Patrick of hypocrisy by revealing that Patrick had knowingly hired an undocumented immigrant for his sports bar business back in the 1990s. Patrick denied that he knew the individual in question was in the country illegally, but it did not seem to hurt Patrick's candidacy, as he came in first place in the Republican primary held in March 2014.

Tax policy also became a state issue, especially in the comptroller's race between Sen. Glenn Hegar (R-Katy) and Mike Collier (D-Houston). Collier, a Certified Public Accountant, ran campaign ads claiming that Hegar wanted to abolish the state property tax and increase sales taxes. Since Texas does not have a state income tax, property taxes are somewhat higher than in other states. The state relies on property taxes to fund public education and sales taxes for other state spending. Sales taxes in Texas usually average 8.25 percent on most items, with the exception of medicine and groceries. Increasing sales taxes often disproportionately affects lower-income Texans since a higher percentage of their income is spent on purchasing goods and services. Hegar ran a campaign touting his conservative credentials and his desire for lower taxes in general, and was ultimately elected comptroller of public accounts in the November election.

● Thinking Critically about Elections in Texas

Elections in Texas are essential to the state's functioning democracy. It is important to think critically about how elections are structured and who benefits from the types of districts that are created by the state legislature. Because of the single-member district system, third parties are disadvantaged in state politics, and this has important implications for how policy is made.

The state has a formal process for candidates who want to serve their fellow citizens in elective office. The candidate must first run in a party primary; then, if the candidate does not receive a majority of the votes, he or she must run in a runoff primary. Ideally, the battles of primaries and runoff primaries will be forgotten and the party will come together in support of the nominee in order to win the election. However, what often happens is that the primaries and runoffs create enormous conflicts and divisions within the party that are not healed. The opposition then exploits those party divisions so that their candidate can win the election.

Redistricting in Texas has been very controversial since the passage of the Voting Rights Act in 1965. Texas has traditionally been subject to additional constraints when it draws new district lines, and the federal courts have stepped in to make sure that the voting rights of African Americans and Latinos have not diminished. However, this is no longer the case. Until Congress acts to address the Supreme Court's ruling, Texas is no longer subject to preclearance of its legislative districts. Election results are greatly influenced by the kind of districts that are drawn, which is why it is so important to pay close attention to this process, which occurs by law at least every ten years. Districts do not just arise out of thin air; politicians create them to advance their own interests as well as their party's goals.

While Republicans have been winning statewide elections, the growing Latino population and increased diversification of the state may change this. Wendy Davis had hoped to capitalize on the changing demographics of the state in her bid for governor but could not overcome countervailing winds against her candidacy, including the state's entrenched conservatism and the national tilt in favor of Republicans. While not as strongly Democratic as African Americans, Latinos in Texas are more likely to identify as Democrats. As more Latinos register to vote and participate in state elections, Texas may once again become a competitive two-party state, but as the 2014 elections demonstrate, the Republicans currently dominate state politics.

Campaigns—especially statewide campaigns—are very expensive. For the most part, the candidates themselves must raise the money necessary to win an election. Gubernatorial campaigns can cost $40 million or more. One effect of the high cost of campaigns in Texas is that candidates are often very wealthy individuals willing to use their own money in their campaigns. Wealthy individuals, however, will not always prevail at the ballot box. Consider former lieutenant governor David Dewhurst. His bruising loss to Senator Ted Cruz in the state Republican primary for a U.S. Senate seat in 2012 left him vulnerable in his bid for re-election. Insurgent senator Dan Patrick challenged Dewhurst from the right, forced him into a runoff, and defeated him in the primary. Dewhurst had invested millions of his own money in the Senate primary and his bid for re-election.

Although Texas once tried to narrow the franchise, primarily by limiting the right to vote through poll taxes and white primaries, in recent years it has tried to expand the franchise through the motor voter law and through early voting. Yet voter participation in Texas is the lowest in the nation. Overall, voter turnout in 2014 was only 33.4 percent of eligible voters, which was less than the turnout in 2010. That is probably because of the demographics of Texas voters and Texas's political culture, but it may also be a result of the scheduling of elections in Texas, the vast number of elections, and the large number of low-visibility candidates for office. Participation in elections is important because public policies are determined by who is elected to office. For example, policies related to funding for higher education that affect all college students in Texas are dependent on elected officials and the people they appoint. It also remains to be seen whether the state's new voter identification law will have an impact on voter turnout in the state.

studyguide

Features of Elections in Texas

> **Describe the types of elections held in Texas and how they work (pp. 139–41)**

Texas allows all registered voters the choice to vote in one party primary during an election season. Should a candidate not receive a majority of votes in a primary, a runoff is held to determine who the party nominee will be. The general election ultimately decides who is elected to office.

Key Terms

primary election (p. 139)

runoff primary (p. 139)

open primary (p. 139)

closed primary (p. 140)

general election (p. 140)

special election (p. 140)

Practice Quiz

1. In a primary election,
   a) voters choose all local officials who will hold office in the following year.
   b) voters select federal officials for office.
   c) voters select their party's candidate for a general election.
   d) voters choose third-party candidates.
   e) voters cast ballots on proposed constitutional amendments.

2. Which of the following is *not* a type of election found in Texas?
   a) general
   b) primary
   c) distinguished
   d) special
   e) runoff primary

3. Officially, Texas has a
   a) joint primary.
   b) extended primary.
   c) open primary.
   d) closed primary.
   e) Jaybird primary.

4. The first Tuesday following the first Monday in November of even-numbered years is the day for which election?
   a) primary election
   b) runoff primary
   c) runoff for the general election
   d) secondary election
   e) general election

5. When are gubernatorial elections held?
   a) during presidential election years
   b) during odd-numbered years
   c) during even-numbered years that are not presidential election years
   d) every year
   e) every six months

Participation in Texas Elections

> **Explain how the rules for voting affect turnout among different groups of Texans (pp. 142–59)**

Participation in Texas elections varies by election. Turnout is lowest in party primaries, followed by elections when a presidential candidate is not on the ballot. Latinos and those of lower socioeconomic status are also less likely to vote in state elections.

Key Terms

Nineteenth Amendment (p. 142)

suffrage (p. 142)

poll tax (p. 143)

early registration (p. 143)

white primary (p. 144)

Jaybird Party (p. 144)

Voting Rights Act of 1965 (p. 145)

motor voter law (p. 148)

early voting (p. 152)

reapportionment (p. 156)

redistricting (p. 156)

preclearance (p. 156)

Practice Quiz

6. Which of the following is true?
   a) Poll taxes are legal.
   b) Women acquired the right to vote in the original 1876 Texas Constitution.
   c) The poll tax restricted the participation of poor people in the general election.
   d) You do not have to be a resident of Texas to vote in Texas.
   e) Latinos vote at higher rates than African Americans.

7. In which of the following elections is voter turnout the highest?
   a) presidential elections
   b) gubernatorial general elections
   c) city elections
   d) runoff elections
   e) off-year congressional elections

8. The two most important factors in determining whether someone will vote are

   a) income and education.
   b) education and family history of voting.
   c) income and gender.
   d) party membership and gender.
   e) ethnicity and race.

9. Who has benefited the most from early voting?
   a) Republicans
   b) Democrats
   c) All parties have benefited equally.
   d) Independents
   e) Greens

10. The procedure by which certain states, such as Texas, are required to obtain approval every time they make changes to districts is called
    a) redistricting.
    b) reapportionment.
    c) preclearance.
    d) external validation.
    e) judicial review.

Campaigns

Present the main features of election campaigns in Texas (pp. 160–66)

Because of Texas's size, statewide campaigns can be expensive. There are several major media markets, which makes television advertising very expensive. Grassroots efforts to mobilize voters are also costly because of the large territory. This means wealthy candidates are often on the ballot.

Practice Quiz

11. One distinguishing feature of the 2014 campaign in Texas was
    a) the increased presence of third-party candidates.
    b) the lack of emphasis on education policy.
    c) the candidates' focus on equal pay for equal work.
    d) the unusually low levels of money spent on media ads.
    e) the candidates' focus on welfare reforms.

12. Who is the first Republican to become Texas governor since Reconstruction?

    a) William Clements
    b) Rick Perry
    c) George W. Bush
    d) Ann Richards
    e) Kinky Friedman

13. The most costly item for most political campaigns is
    a) travel.
    b) security.
    c) fund-raising.
    d) media.
    e) food.

14. Prior to running for re-election as a lieutenant governor, David Dewhurst unsuccessfully ran for which office?
    a) state Senate
    b) U.S. Senate
    c) U.S. House of Representatives
    d) governor
    e) attorney general

Recommended Websites

Texas Secretary of State
www.sos.state.tx.us/

Texas Tribune
www.texastribune.org

Dineen Majcher (right) was frustrated with the emphasis her daughter's school placed on standardized testing. She took action by helping to create an interest group and challenging Texas's education policies.

Interest Groups and Lobbying

WHY INTEREST GROUPS MATTER Dineen Majcher had had enough. A lawyer and mother of an incoming ninth grader in a prestigious Austin high school, she couldn't believe what she was hearing. Fifteen percent of her daughter's final grade in history would come from a new mandated statewide test, one that the teacher had never seen. This struck her as unfair and unreasonable. How could students prepare for such a test? Why 15 percent of the grade? She went first to the principal to protest, but to no avail. This was after all a mandated state test, part of a 30-year effort of the education reformers to bring testing and accountability to all elementary and secondary schools across the state. So Majcher raised the ante, getting the Austin School Board to request a waiver from the State Board of Education from the "15 percent rule." The request was denied. Raising the ante again, Majcher signed up to testify at legislative committee hearings that had been called for January 2012. During the hearings Majcher met others from across Texas who were also dissatisfied with the testing movement that had dominated educational policy for over 30 years. Together these individuals established an interest group called Texans Advocating for Meaningful Student Assessment, or TAMSA. The group became known in the legislature as "Mothers Against Drunk Testing."

The goals of TAMSA were clearly articulated on its website: "to improve public education in Texas through the use of meaningful and effective student assessments that allow for more productive class-room instruction and more efficient use of public funds." On their face, these goals might seem to be relatively uncontroversial. In fact, however, they were questioning the philosophy of educational reform that had dominated the state for almost three decades.

TAMSA enabled people to join together and seek policy change in a number of ways: first, by provid-ing like-minded individuals an organizational structure for discussing problems and offering solutions; second, by providing a vehicle for working with other organizations like the Texas Association of School Administrators, who were also concerned with testing; third, by raising money to help pay for their efforts; and fourth, by educating the public and policy makers alike about the problems of testing across the elementary and secondary curriculum. TAMSA spearheaded the drive to change public policy regarding testing in the state. What had begun as a protest about unfair testing was morphing into an interest group with a clear political object.

Since the early 1980s, testing was seen to be one of the best ways to ensure accountability by identifying schools that worked and those that didn't. From 1984 to 2008, an ever-growing list of tests in a variety of subjects was created to promote accountability and reform. Under STAAR (State of Texas Assessment of Academic Readiness), students in grades 3 through 12 were subject to a list of tests, including 15 end-of-course tests that were to be included in students' final grades.

Over the years, support for reform through testing and accountability came from a variety of sources inside and outside the legislature. Leading legislators from both parties, leaders at the Texas Education Agency, and business leaders came to believe statewide testing was a key to higher performance. George W. Bush identified testing as a central part of his plan for educational reform in Texas in the '90s and placed testing at the heart of his "No Child Left Behind" initiatives when he was president in the early 2000s. Key business interests, including the Texas Association of Business, supported expanded testing, seeing the tests as a way to ratchet up the quality of poorly performing schools across the state. Not surprisingly, the businesses involved in creating the tests also came to support the tests. As the debates over reform were proceeding in the legislature, Pearson publishers had a five-year contract with the state that was estimated to be worth $462 million. Testing itself had become big business with big interests worth protecting in the state legislature.

Given the interests supporting testing and decades-old accountability initiatives, few thought at the beginning of the 2013 legislative session that change was in the wind. But it was. New legislators open to new ideas about reform were chairing the educational committees in both the House and the Senate. Entrenched interests in educational reform had lost their ability to control the agenda. On a paltry budget of under $100,000, drawing upon inexpensive social media and relying on the expertise of a few key members, TAMSA played a major role in getting the legislature to rethink what educational reform meant. In response to the efforts of TAMSA and other like-minded groups and individuals, the legislature dropped the number of end-of-year course exams from 15 to 5.

The story of Dineen Majcher and TAMSA highlights how interest groups matter in Texas politics. Interest groups provide support for existing policies in many areas of public policy, support legislators in their electoral campaigns, and help to articulate ideas from which policies can be crafted. Texas politics can be understood only with a clear understanding of the role that interest groups play in elections and in the legislative process.[1]

chaptergoals

- **Define interest groups, and describe the major ways they try to influence Texas government (pp. 173–83)**

- **Describe the role of PACs in Texas elections (pp. 183–91)**

- **Explain how ordinary individuals can influence Texas government (pp. 191–93)**

● Interest Groups in the Political Process

Define interest groups, and describe the major ways they try to influence Texas government

It is probably true that all of us have political interests, goals, or objectives that can be achieved with governmental intervention. Many of us, however, will never act to achieve those goals. A few of us may speak privately to a legislator or other official. Some of us will join with others to try to convince the government to help us achieve our interests. When we do that, we have formed an **interest group**.

In Texas, as elsewhere, interest groups assume a variety of forms. There are a wide range of interests active in national, state, and local politics that form into interest groups, including those concerned with business, labor, agriculture, the professions such as law, medicine, and accounting, government affairs such as state employees, cities, and universities, and public interest advocates such as the Sierra Club. Interest groups can be set up to serve the interests of a small number of people concerned with one particular interest, such as getting a road built in a county. They can also be established to serve the interests of a group of people with broader interests, such as those interested in reforming the school system by promoting vouchers, charter schools, home schooling, or better testing. Some interests are established to represent the common interests of various business or labor groups in the state, such as those of the real estate industry or chemical workers unions. An interest group is a "peak association" when it is an interest group organized as an umbrella organization that seeks to coordinate the various activities of member groups in a number of targeted areas.

interest group an organization established to influence the government's programs and policies

Resources and Strategies of Interest Groups

Political scientists have identified various resources that interest groups are able to mobilize in politics. First, interest groups have members. Groups can become influential because of whom they represent. The Texas Medical Association and the Texas Bar Association are excellent examples of groups representing influential people across Texas. Some people clearly are more important than others. But numbers matter, too. Politicians who ignore the concerns of broad-based evangelical groups in discussions of abortion or marriage do so at their own peril. Second, and perhaps more important than the first, interest groups have the ability to raise money. Clearly, it is advantageous to have access to a few deep-pocketed individuals when trying to raise money in support of a particular cause. But in the age of the Internet, it is also useful for there to be large numbers of members who are willing to give, if only a little.

A third resource possessed by interest groups is information about their membership and about the problems that concern their membership. In recent years, interest groups have begun to mine large databases of people who might be interested in particular policies or issues. Such information can become a valuable resource for politicians seeking to raise money or to promote a particular policy objective. Interest groups also offer advice on the best ways to address the concerns of their membership. Interest groups clearly are motivated by their self-interest, and the positions they present to legislators reflect this interest. The first drafts of bills introduced into the House or Senate often come from interest groups seeking to promote their own particular perspective. A fourth resource, one closely related to the third, is credibility. Providing information to a policy maker is important. But this must be good information if, over the longer run, an interest group or its representatives are to be taken seriously. Bad information about a problem or the concerns of a group's members can undercut an interest group's effectiveness quickly.

The resources that are available to interest groups are the foundation upon which various strategies are developed by interest groups to promote their concerns. Among the strategies that we will explore in this chapter are (1) explicit political strategies such as grassroots organizing, get-out-the-vote and electioneering campaigns, and campaign financing; (2) legislative strategies such as lobbying and testifying before legislative committees; (3) public awareness strategies such as drafting policy reports, writing editorials, and conducting educational campaigns in various public forums; and (4) supporting litigation that challenges existing policies in court. As we will see, the strategies that are adopted by various interest groups largely depend on the resources available to them at the time.

Interest Groups and Democratic Politics

The rights to associate with others and to petition government lie at the heart of the rights guaranteed by the U.S. and Texas constitutions. Having a common interest is one thing. Organizing that common interest into an effective group that can act to promote that interest is quite something else. In his seminal book *The Logic of Collective Action*, Mancur Olson analyzed a collective action problem that lies at the heart of interest-group politics: people have an interest in organizing into an interest group that effectively represents their interests in politics. But people also have an interest in getting someone else to pay for that group's organizational costs. This is the **free rider problem**. If everyone acts as a free rider, some organizations do not form to represent particular interests in politics. Ironically, the larger the common interest, the more difficult it may be to overcome the free rider problem and create effective interest groups. According to Olson's theory, a small group of insurance companies are more likely to form a powerful interest group to affect health care policy than the millions of poor people who lack quality health care. Similarly, business interests are more likely to form a common front in politics than consumers because it is easier for the business interests to overcome the costs of collective action, that is, the costs of acting together as an organized interest group.[2]

Interest groups engage in a number of activities to overcome the free rider problem. Sometimes, they offer people particular incentives to join a group. These selective benefits often cover a wide range of activities, from a subscription to a magazine, to access to special information on the Internet, to invitations to special conferences, to special discounts. For example, AAA (the American Automobile Association) organizes for road and vehicle safety and provides members with roadside assistance and travel discounts—strong incentives to join.

Interest groups also can provide people with symbolic benefits, such as listing individuals' names as sponsors of an organization or offering free buttons, hats, or T-shirts showing their support to the ongoing activities of the organization. The purpose of such activities is to strengthen the commitment an individual has to an interest group and to overcome the free rider problem.

One of the most important lessons to be drawn from the logic of collective action is that some interests do not get represented easily in the political process. Upper-class business interests are more likely to be represented than lower-class

free rider problem the incentive to benefit from others' work without making a contribution, which leads individuals in a collective action situation to refuse to work together

minority interests. A second lesson is that it is very difficult, even rare, for interest groups to emerge that protect the broad interests of large numbers of people or any vaguely defined public interest. Significantly, when such groups do emerge, as with the Grange or Prohibition movement in the nineteenth and early twentieth centuries, they can come to wield considerable power. Nevertheless, in the push and pull of everyday politics in Texas, it is more likely for narrowly targeted interests to organize effectively in defense of their interests than it is for the public as a whole to organize. Even the above-mentioned "public interest groups" are not so much advancing the public good as a whole (whatever that may be) than advocating for the views that certain individuals have about the public good.

Olson's theory provides an explanation of why it has often been claimed that business-oriented interest groups dominate the Texas legislature. Using campaign contributions, political pressure, and sometimes corruption, "the Lobby," as pro-business groups were called, was once purported to run Texas government. Some of the most influential business leaders of the state belonged to the "8F Crowd." At the Lamar Hotel in Houston, 8F was the number on a suite of rooms where George R. Brown held court. Brown was a founder of Brown and Root, one of the world's largest construction firms and until April 2007 part of the even larger Halliburton Company. He met regularly with other fabulously wealthy Texans such as Jesse Jones of Texas Commerce Bank and Tenneco, Gus Wortham of American General Insurance, and James Elkins of the Vinson and Elkins law firm. These men socialized together and worked together to promote their political interests. For 40 years they were considered the king makers in Texas politics who determined much of the important policy of state government.[3]

The 8F Crowd was, of course, an interest group—an elite, wealthy, powerful, pro-business interest group. Although the 8F Crowd is long gone from the Texas political scene, much of what it did is still done in Texas politics by other interest groups, though no modern-day group is ascribed the influence that was allegedly held by the 8F Crowd.

Nevertheless, Texas is known as a state that has long had powerful interest groups. During the Texas Constitutional Convention of 1875, an interest group played an important role. That was the Grange, a powerful farmers' organization, of which many of the constitution's framers were members. As Chapter 2 indicated, the Constitution of 1876 reflected many of the values of Grange members. It was a document for rural Texas that was pro–small farmer and opposed to a powerful state government.

With the development of a strong oil and gas industry in Texas in the first half of the twentieth century, the oil industry began playing an important role in state politics. In one-party states, interest groups often become powerful political actors, perhaps because one-party states tend to have a small number of important sectors in their economies and limited economic development. However, Texas has in the past 20 years moved from a Democratic one-party system to a competitive two-party system to a Republican-dominated system. And with an expanding Latino vote, it may soon become a more competitive two-party system again. It also now has a strong and diversified economy. Yet interest groups maintain great influence.

Lobbying, derided by some as "Austin's oldest profession," is big business in Texas. When the legislature is in session, many lobbyists can be spotted around the capitol waiting to meet with legislators. When the legislature is not in session, lobbyists are often busy with campaign activities.

Interest Groups and Policy Makers

Interest groups want something from policy makers: they want policy that is beneficial for their groups. On the other hand, policy makers benefit from developing relationships with interest groups. From those groups, the policy maker gains information, since the interest groups can provide substantial expertise in areas that are their special concern. Additionally, interest groups can provide campaign funds to the policy maker. In a state as large as Texas, with numerous media markets and with some party competition, considerable campaign funds are necessary to run and win elections. An interest group can help raise money from its membership for a candidate sympathetic to the interest group's goals. Also, interest groups can supply votes to the policy maker. They can assist in mobilizing their own groups, and they can supply campaign workers to distribute campaign leaflets and to operate phone banks to get out the vote. Interest groups can also publicize issues through press conferences, press releases, publications, conferences, and hearings and even by filing lawsuits. Finally, interest groups can engage in research and education programs. It has become increasingly common for interest groups to engage in public education programs by running advertisements in the Texas media explaining why their particular approaches to a public policy problem would be more beneficial to Texans in general.

Unlike a private citizen interested in and involved in politics, larger or better-funded interest groups have the advantages of time, money, expertise, and continuity. Although concerned citizens do have an impact on public policy in Texas, organized and well-funded interest groups have an advantage in affecting the policy process. It is difficult for a concerned citizen from Houston to spend time in Austin developing relationships with policy makers and trying to convince those policy makers to support public policies that are compatible with the individual's goals. On the other hand, if that individual joins with like-minded people to create an organized interest group, the group may have a greater likelihood of achieving policy goals. It might be possible to fund an office in Austin with a staff that could monitor events in state government on a daily basis and develop relationships with key policy makers. Additionally, although some individuals in Texas do have the money to provide substantial campaign support to policy makers, even those individuals can get more "bang for the buck" if they join with others in **bundling** their funds into a larger contribution from the interest group. The creation of an organized interest group also allows for the development of a staff. The staff can gain in-depth knowledge of an area of policy far greater than could be gained by most individuals working alone. Also, an individual may be intensely concerned with an issue in one legislative session but may find it difficult to sustain that interest over a period of many legislative sessions. The larger, better-funded, more successful organized interest groups have continuity. They are in Austin developing relationships with policy makers and presenting the views of the organization day in and day out, year in and year out. The result is that legislators and other policy makers can develop long-standing relationships with the interest groups and the groups' representatives in Austin.

On September 15, 2010, Governor Perry received a briefing on tort reform at the Austin airport. He then flew to Houston and was taken to the Petroleum Club, where he dined with the political arm of an interest group, Texans for Lawsuit Reform. He was then driven to Mach Industrial Group in Houston, where he held a press conference to discuss their endorsement.[4] It was an important day

bundling the interest-group practice of combining campaign contributions from several sources into one larger contribution from the group, so as to increase the group's impact on the candidate

for Perry—though not surprising—because he had gotten the official support of a group described as "arguably the most powerful interest group in Texas politics, in large part because of the massive amounts of money it raises from the state's business community."[5] Texans for Lawsuit Reform helped reshape the Texas Supreme Court into a more pro-business court, and it has reshaped the legislature into a more pro-business body. With Texans for Lawsuit Reform on Perry's side, he had an incredibly powerful and wealthy interest group backing him in the 2010 election. And Texans for Lawsuit Reform knew it could help re-elect a pro-business candidate to the governorship.

Types of Interest Groups and Lobbyists

Interest groups strive to influence public opinion, to make their views known to policy makers, and to elect and support policy makers who are friendly to their points of view. To accomplish these goals, interest groups usually maintain **lobbyists** in Austin who try to gain access to policy makers and communicate their objectives to them. There are several different types of lobbyists. Some interest groups have full-time staffs in Austin whose members work as lobbyists. One form of interest group is, of course, a corporation, and companies often have government relations departments that lobby for the companies' interests. Lobbyists may be employed by an interest group to deal with one issue, or they may be employed by an interest group on a regular basis. Some lobbyists represent only one client; others will represent large numbers of clients. All lobbyists, however, must be able to reach and communicate with policy makers. Corporate interest groups tend to use either government relations departments or law firms to represent their interests in Austin. Often industries have broad interests that need representation. For example, an insurance company may have one specific interest it wishes to have represented. However, the insurance industry as a whole also has a wide range of issues that need representation, and thus it will form an industrywide interest group.

Interest groups may also represent professional groups. One of the most influential professional groups in Austin is the Texas Medical Association, which represents the interests of doctors in state government. Other professional groups represent accountants, chiropractors, opticians, dentists, lawyers, and teachers.

That teachers are an important interest group suggests still another type of interest group—public-employee interest groups. Public school teachers may be the largest and most effective of these groups, but firefighters, police officers, and even justices of the peace and constables all are represented in Austin.

Some interest groups are formed with a single issue in mind. For example, an interest group may be concerned about the regulation of abortion or school vouchers or tort reform or the environment. Other interest groups are concerned with multiple issues that affect the groups. Public school teachers, for example, are concerned about job security, qualifications of teachers, health insurance, pensions, salaries, and other matters that affect the lives of their members.

Civil rights groups such as the National Association for the Advancement of Colored People, the League of United Latin American Citizens, and the Mexican American Legal Defense Fund are concerned about civil rights issues affecting the lives primarily of African Americans and Latinos. Interestingly, not only do these groups often try to influence public opinion and the legislature, but they have had notable success in representing their groups' interests through litigation, especially in the federal courts.

lobbyist an individual employed by an interest group who tries to influence governmental decisions on behalf of that group

Other public interest groups try to promote consumer, environmental, and general public issues. Examples of these groups are Public Citizen, the Sierra Club, and Common Cause. Groups such as the Sierra Club work to promote environmental interests, whereas groups such as Public Citizen and Common Cause tend to have broader interests and work to promote more open government. These groups rarely have much funding, but they often can provide policy makers with information and expertise. In addition, they can mobilize their membership to support or oppose bills, and they can publicize matters that are important to their goals.

Getting Access to Policy Makers

In order to communicate the goals of their interest groups to policy makers, lobbyists must first gain access to those policy makers. Gaining access to policy makers, of course, imposes on the time of legislators, so lobbyists will often spend significant sums entertaining them. That entertainment is one of the most criticized aspects of lobbying. But from the lobbyists' perspective, entertainment is an important tool for reaching policy makers and putting them in a congenial frame of mind. Entertainment by lobbyists can involve expensive dinners, golf, and other activities. For example, lobbyists for Texas Utilities (TXU) bought a $300 saddle for one state representative and a $200 bench for another. TXU lobbyists also treated a state senator to a trip to the Masters golf tournament and picked up the dinner tab as well. One House member received a gun as a gift, another received a jacket, and several got "deer-processing" costs paid for by these lobbyists.[6]

When Representative Lon Burnam proposed legislation to regulate consumer versions of "stun guns," the lobbyist for TASER International as a joke gave Burnam a gift of a pink "stun gun" valued at more than $150. The "stun gun" was, of course, a minor expenditure.[7] Others are much more lavish. When Governor Perry wanted to go to the Rose Bowl game, the trucking lobby picked up the costs of a private jet for $14,580. The former Texas Motor Transportation Association president who arranged the trip said, "Let's face it, if you have a way to help the sitting governor get somewhere he wants to be and to help our industry get where it needs to be, to me it becomes a no-brainer."[8] In the first two months of 2011, lobbyists spent more than $1.2 million, with much of that money going toward events, goods, and gifts for lawmakers and others in state government.[9]

Some interest groups focus on a single issue, such as abortion. When Texas passed a law requiring women to undergo a sonogram 24 hours before having an abortion, antiabortion groups applauded the measure, but some women's groups protested against it.

Texas lawmakers receive only $600 per month plus $150 a day when on legislative business, but lawmakers are permitted to use campaign contributions for expenses associated with holding office. This allows interest groups to fund significant lavish benefits for lawmakers. For example, about one-third of the spending of North Texas lawmakers—about $3.4 million of roughly $10 million in 2007–09—has gone to fund things other than campaign expenditures. Senator Florence Shapiro has used her contributions to fund a car lease for a Mercedes Benz and to pay for conference stays at the Ritz-Carlton in Palm Beach, the Venetian in Las Vegas, and the Hay-Adams in Washington, D.C. Thirty-six North Texas lawmakers spent nearly $560,000 on travel and entertainment, $470,000 on Austin living expenses, and $290,000 on food.[10]

In May 2013 there were 1,663 registered lobbyists in Texas.[11] This is a decrease from the 1,836 registered lobbyists in 2011. An analysis that was done of the lobbying reports in 2013 found these lobbyists had 2,820 clients.[12] Because of the loose nature of the Texas reporting

Andrea McWilliams is one of Texas's highest-paid and most successful lobbyists.

laws, it is unclear what these lobbyists were paid, but it was as much as $328 million in 2013.[13] Twenty-five of them reported maximum lobbying incomes of at least $1.5 million.[14]

Sometimes lobbyists have long-standing personal ties to policy makers, and those bonds can be invaluable to the lobbyists' clients. When lobbyist Andrea McWilliams celebrated her 40th birthday in California's wine country, six Texas lawmakers traveled to California for the party including the chair of the House Appropriations Committee and the chair of the Senate Public Education Committee. In McWilliams's case, the personal ties to these lawmakers were probably strengthened by the fact that she and her clients had contributed more than $206,000 to the campaigns of the six lawmakers over the past several years.[15] McWilliams was the highest-paid lobbyist with the largest number of clients in the 2013 legislative session.[16]

Access to policy makers may also be gained by building support for an issue among their constituents. Constituents may be encouraged, for example, to write or call legislators about a bill and offer their opinions. Essentially, the interest group tries to mobilize interested voters to get involved in the political process on behalf of the group's goals.

Lobbying and Government's "Revolving Door" One important way of gaining access to those in government is to employ former officials as lobbyists. A lobbyist who is a former legislator often has friends in the legislature and can use that friendship to gain access. Additionally, a former legislator often is in an exceptionally good position to understand the personal relationships and informal power centers that must be contacted to accomplish a legislative objective. As a result, some of the best-paid lobbyists in Austin are former Texas state officials and often are former legislators.

In 2010, 65 registered lobbyists were former legislators. What they have in common is knowledge of "how to pass bills, to kill them, whom to talk to, which clerks are friendly, whose birthdays are coming up—all inside stuff that makes the government machine whir."[17] Other especially valuable lobbyists have been former committee clerks for major committees and chiefs of staff of members who were on major committees.[18] Ten recently retired lawmakers were lobbyists in the 2009 legislative session. The 10 had a total of 68 lobbying contracts allowing them to generate between $2,025,000 and $3,890,000 in fees. One gets a sense of the value of these ex-legislators-turned-lobbyists from the explanation Representative Jim Pitts gave for sponsoring an amendment that was pushed by an AT&T lobbyist and former legislator, Pat Heggerty. The amendment would have forced the state to pay for rerouting phone lines for road projects. Said Representative Pitts of the amendment, "I was just trying to help Pat out."[19] The amendment later failed to pass. In 2013, 12 additional defeated or recently retired legislators became lobbyists. They reported up to $2,130,000 in income from 49 clients.[20]

It is not only former legislators who can move on to successful lobbying careers. Forty Perry aides either have left the administration to become lobbyists or have joined the administration after having been lobbyists. Some have moved back and forth from administration to lobbying in a revolving door fashion. Five of Perry's closest campaign aides have been lobbyists. Two of his ex-aides became lobbyists who headed pro-Perry PACs.[21]

One former-legislator-turned-lobbyist who reversed course and went back into the legislature is Todd Hunter. Hunter had served in the legislature from 1989 to 1997. An active lobbyist as late as 2007, he was elected to the Texas House in 2008.[22] Jerry Patterson, Texas land commissioner, was a state senator, became a lobbyist, and was able to move to his statewide office with little criticism of his role as a lobbyist. However, David Sibley, a state senator who became a lobbyist and then tried to regain his old position, caught tremendous political flak for this decision and, to a considerable degree, lost the Republican primary because of that career choice.[23] The issue of lobbying by former officials and their staffs is a significant one, as there is concern that policy decisions may be made with an eye toward future lucrative lobbying jobs.

Texas has only weak laws dealing with lobbying by former government officials. A former member of the governing body or a former executive head of a regulatory agency cannot lobby the agency for two years after leaving office. Senior employees or former officers of Texas regulatory agencies cannot ever lobby a governmental entity on matters they were involved in when employed by the government. However, there are no legal restrictions on lobbying by a former governor, former lieutenant governor, former legislator, or any former aides to these officials.[24]

What Lobbyists Do with Access Once lobbyists obtain access to policy makers, they provide information that may be useful. For example, they may explain how a bill benefits a legislator's district, or how it benefits the state, or how it is perceived as being unfair. Since the staffs of Texas legislators are small, lobbyists perform useful functions by explaining what numerous bills are intended to do. They may even write bills to be introduced by friendly legislators or write amendments to bills. Almost certainly, if a bill affects the interests of a lobbyist's client and reaches a point in the process where hearings are held on the bill, the lobbyist will arrange for testimony to be given at the hearing explaining the interest group's viewpoint on the proposed legislation.

Lobbyists do not limit their activities to the legislative process, of course. Rules proposed by the bureaucracy or the courts can affect the interests of lobbyists'

Is He a Lobbyist?

Lobbyists are individuals hired by interest groups to advocate on their behalf to state lawmakers. Organizations ranging from business groups to environmental groups to teachers' groups all employ lobbyists to advance their agendas. Not all groups technically lobby legislators. Some groups and lobbyists might occasionally interact with a legislator, but their primary goal is to advocate on behalf of their agenda in general terms.

Sometimes the actions of interest groups can blur the line between lobbying and general advocacy. This distinction is crucial because in Texas, as in many other states, laws require lobbyists to report their activities in the spirit of full disclosure so that the public can see how much money is being spent to influence legislators. Lobbyists must register with the Texas Ethics Commission (TEC), reveal their list of clients, and disclose how much they are compensated for their services. Consider the case of the interest group Empower Texans and its subsidiary known as Texans for Fiscal Responsibility. The organization is committed to promoting conservative ideals and increasing the number of conservative legislators in Texas. It has aligned with the Tea Party wing of the Republican Party in calling for reduced taxes and cuts to balance the state budget. Not surprisingly, Empower Texans and Texans for Fiscal Responsibility have refused to endorse some Republican incumbents in the state legislature, instead supporting challengers in the Republican primary who are more conservative.

In 2012 two Republicans who were not endorsed by Empower Texans and Texans for Fiscal Responsibility filed a complaint with the TEC, claiming that the head of these groups, Michael Quinn Sullivan, had lobbied during the most recent legislative session despite the fact that he was not registered. The two state representatives, Jim Keffer and Vicki Truitt, allege that Sullivan communicated with state representatives and their staff about their priorities for

Michael Quinn Sullivan
President, Texans for Fiscal Responsibility

the legislative session. In particular, they claim that the group opposed the re-election of Speaker Joe Straus within the Texas House in favor of a more conservative legislator, and they say that the group tried to influence representatives to oppose the use of the state's $9.6 billion Rainy Day Fund to balance the state budget. The complaint alleges that Empower Texans's activities went beyond merely taking public positions on these issues and crossed into the territory of active lobbying.

Keffer and Truitt also allege that Texans for Fiscal Responsibility failed to file campaign finance disclosure forms for the last quarter of 2011, as required by state law. They insist that it is hard to believe that the organization did not make contributions to politicians during this period. Because Sullivan did not register, he did not reveal who was funding his organization.

On the other side of the issue, Sullivan claims that the two legislators were simply upset that they were not endorsed by Texans for Fiscal Responsibility and did not receive campaign contributions. In particular, the organization endorsed Truitt's Republican opponent in the 2012 primary, and Sullivan actively campaigned against Truitt in the past. He argues that the timing of the complaint is suspect, coming soon before an election, and that discussions with legislators are not the primary purpose of the organization.

The TEC investigated the allegations and decided that there was insufficient evidence of lobbying. Nevertheless, they decided to pursue a hearing, which would have required Sullivan's organization to release the names of donors. In response, Sullivan sued the TEC in federal court, claiming that his organization's free speech rights were violated and that revealing donors would violate their privacy. In April 2014, however, the federal district court judge sent the case back to state court for possible adjudication. You decide. Did Sullivan and Empower Texans cross the line from advocacy to active lobbying?

critical thinking questions

1. What exactly is a lobbyist? How is lobbying different from speaking out in public in support of or against a particular issue or candidate? Why do you think Texas disclosure laws are different for lobbyists than for general advocacy groups?

2. Based on the limited information above, is Michael Quinn Sullivan a lobbyist? Should he have registered with the state? Why or why not?

clients. Lobbyists will testify at hearings on rules and try to provide information to administrators in face-to-face meetings as well.

Corruption There is always a concern that lobbyists may corrupt policy makers by bribing them in order to accomplish the interest groups' policy objectives. Early in the twentieth century, Sam Rayburn, later a famed U.S. congressperson and Speaker of the House, served in the Texas House of Representatives for six years. At that time, he was especially concerned with corruption and refused to accept free meals and entertainment from lobbyists. He called some of his fellow legislators "steak men." By that he meant that the legislators would sell their votes on a bill for a steak dinner at the Driskill Hotel in Austin. "Steak men" (and women) may still exist in Texas politics, but for the most part, lobbyists provide information, campaign contributions, and political support (or opposition) rather than bribes.

Still, from time to time lobbying does stoop to very low levels. In 1989, "Bo" Pilgrim, a large poultry producer, distributed $10,000 checks to state senators in the capitol while he was lobbying them on workers' compensation reform. Perhaps even more troubling, some senators accepted the checks until media attention forced them to reconsider. Yet this practice of offering $10,000 while asking for a senator to vote on a specific bill was not illegal under state law. A year later, the Speaker of the Texas House of Representatives, "Gib" Lewis, got in trouble for his close relationship with a law firm that specialized in collecting delinquent taxes for local governments. In 1991, Speaker Lewis was indicted for receipt of an illegal gift from the law firm. Ultimately, Lewis plea-bargained and received a minor penalty. The result of these scandals, however, was legislation that created a state ethics commission. The legislation imposed additional lobbying reporting requirements and restrictions on speaking fees that interest groups paid legislators and pleasure trips that lobbyists provided. By no means was the law a major regulation of or restriction on lobbying practices, but it did put some limits on lobbying behavior.

Who Represents Ordinary Texans?

Another problem with lobbying was well described by the director of a public-interest lobby, Craig McDonald: "Legislators are rubbing shoulders with . . . lobbyists, almost all of whom hustle for business interests. While corporate interests dominate our legislative process, there is virtually no counterbalancing lobby to represent ordinary Texans. Nowhere on the list of Texas's biggest lobby spenders will you find a single group dedicated to the interests of consumers, the environment or human services. No wonder these citizen interests repeatedly get steamrolled in Austin."[25]

Figure 6.1 classifies the interests represented by the registered lobbyists and estimates the value of those lobbying expenditures. The "Who Are Texans?" graphic looks at campaign contributions to Texas legislators. Although the categories in both are very broad, it is clear that business interests dominate in Texas government. Of course, many issues considered by Texas government may pit one business interest against another, and sometimes a business or professional organization may find itself aligned with consumer interests. For example, the Texas Trial Lawyers Association, an organization of plaintiffs' lawyers in Texas, frequently allies with consumer interests. Many of the clients of these lawyers are consumers who sue large businesses. The interests of these lawyers and their clients are especially close, since the lawyers are paid on a contingent fee basis, which means they don't receive payment unless their clients receive payment. It is also the case that lob-

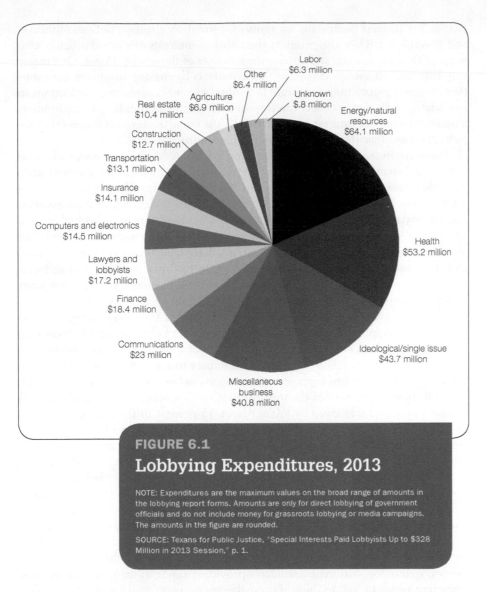

FIGURE 6.1

Lobbying Expenditures, 2013

NOTE: Expenditures are the maximum values on the broad range of amounts in the lobbying report forms. Amounts are only for direct lobbying of government officials and do not include money for grassroots lobbying or media campaigns. The amounts in the figure are rounded.

SOURCE: Texans for Public Justice, "Special Interests Paid Lobbyists Up to $328 Million in 2013 Session," p. 1.

bying is not all there is to the representation of interests in Austin. Interest groups without money may still mobilize their members in order to accomplish their objectives, or they may influence public opinion.

Still, there is no question that money does help in politics. Figure 6.1 and the data in the "Who Are Texans?" graphic provide support for concern that in this battle of mostly business interests, there may not be an objective voice, or at least a voice for the public interest, that reaches the ears of legislators.

● Another Side to Lobbying

Describe the role of PACs in Texas elections

Lobbyists in Texas represent mostly business interests, and they are active in trying to gain access to government officials and inform them of the legislative desires of their clients. But interest groups are not simply information channels between business and government. They also promote the political interests of elected officials who support their viewpoints and oppose the interests of those who do not. One major way that interest groups engage in this activity is by making campaign contributions. Interest groups may encourage individual members to make contributions to candidates, or they may collect funds from their members, bundling those funds as a donation from the interest group. When this is done, the interest group creates a **political action committee (PAC)** to make the contribution.

political action committee (PAC) a private group that raises and distributes funds for use in election campaigns

There are numerous reasons for forming a PAC. A candidate is more likely to notice a substantial contribution from a PAC than many small contributions from individual members of an interest group. Additionally, the lobbyist who delivers a substantial PAC check to a candidate can more likely gain political access than can a lobbyist who simply asks interest-group members to mail individual checks. The PAC becomes a way for the interest group to send a message to the candidate that its members care strongly enough about their agenda that they are prepared to back those goals with money. In some cases, a PAC can even serve as an intermediary to provide money to candidates that the PAC's members might not want to support publicly.

issue advocacy independent spending by individuals or interest groups on a campaign issue but not directly tied to a particular candidate

PACs may give money directly to the candidate, or they may engage in **issue advocacy** that supports the candidate but is independent of the candidate's control. The candidate does not report these independent expenditures on contribution disclosure statements. PACs may also spend money to support an issue rather than a specific candidate or to support such activities as "get-out-the-vote" campaigns. In 2008 about 55 percent of the money given to Democratic and Republican legislative candidates was given by PACs. About 45 percent of the money was given by individuals. In 2010 about 67 percent of the money given to Democratic and Republican legislative candidates was PAC money. Interestingly, however, in 2010 individuals gave more than PACs to candidates for statewide nonjudicial offices.[26]

Campaign contributions can be, to a considerable degree, divided in terms of the economic interests represented by the contributors. The "Who Are Texans?" graphic in this chapter shows that the largest contributor was the finance, insurance, and real estate sector. This sector is a major part of the Texas economy and is subject to significant state regulation. That is also true of general business, energy and natural resources, construction, and health. In contrast to business, political parties, agriculture, and even candidates providing funds to their own campaigns, labor represents a small amount of campaign spending.

Getting Out the Vote

Getting out the vote on Election Day is an important and difficult task. Both the Republican and Democratic parties spend much time and money making sure that their voters get to the polls and vote for their candidates. In recent years, get-out-the-vote efforts by both parties have involved mining so-called big databases to identify people who are likely to vote for their candidates, calling them on the phone, and visiting them at home. Battleground Texas is the latest attempt by the Democratic Party to identify potential Democratic voters, to make them familiar with Democratic positions and candidates, and to get them to vote. Similar efforts have been made by the Republican Party in recent years, particularly those identifying with the Tea Party movement.

Get-out-the-vote initiatives also can be an important part of interest-group activity. The most successful get-out-the-vote campaign run by an interest group was

Which Interest Groups Contribute the Most?

Interest groups try to achieve favorable policies not only by lobbying members of the Texas legislature directly but also by influencing who becomes members of the legislature in the first place by donating to the election campaigns of favored candidates. The chart below breaks down contributions from employees of different industries by party in 2012.

Contributions to Texas Legislature Candidates in 2012

= $250,000   Contributions to Democrats   Contributions to Republicans

86% (R)
14% (D)

58.6% (R)
41.4% (D)

87.5% (R)
12.5% (D)

Finance, insurance, and real estate
$22,124,719

Lawyers and lobbyists
$20,688,389

General business
$15,340,450

89.5% (R)
10.5% (D)

76.6% (R)
23.4% (D)

87.4% (R)
12.6% (D)

82.8% (R)
17.2% (D)

Energy and natural resources
$15,173,687

Health
$9,779,813

Construction
$9,705,427

Communications and electronics
$3,797,859

83% (R)
17% (D)

31% (R)
69% (D)

Agriculture
$3,466,073

Labor
$2,893,278

87.3% (R)
12.7% (D)

79% (R)
21% (D)

Transportation
$2,882,133

Defense
$130,872

for critical analysis

1. What industries tend to donate more to Republicans? Why do you think they do so? What industries tend to donate more to Democrats? Why do you think they do so?

2. Why do interest groups want to donate to candidates before they reach office? What goals are they trying to achieve in doing so?

SOURCE: National Institution on State Money in Politics Industry Influence,
www.followthemoney.org/database/IndustryTotals.phtml?s=TX&y=2010 (accessed 1/3/13).

that conducted by the Texas Medical Association in 1988, which sought to elect its slate of candidates to the Texas Supreme Court. Physicians were encouraged to give to TEXPAC, the medical association PAC. They were also encouraged to make individual contributions to certain candidates. Additionally, physicians were given slate cards with recommended candidates, literature endorsing candidates, and even expensively produced videotapes. They were asked not only to encourage families and friends to vote for the candidates endorsed by the medical association but also to encourage their patients to vote for them. The effort by the medical association was remarkable for its fund-raising success and for its reaching and mobilizing the grass roots.[27]

Most efforts by interest groups, however, are far less sophisticated. Generally, interest groups' PACs simply provide resources for the candidates to get out the vote. Unfortunately for the interest groups, sometimes they misjudge the political viability of the candidates they support. Backing an unsuccessful candidate results in a waste of the interest group's funds and the likely alienation of the winning candidate. In the 2010 primary campaign, Texans for Lawsuit Reform, the pro-business and pro–tort reform interest group that has had spectacular successes in forwarding its agenda over the past 15 years, suffered a remarkable failure. Although it had contributed $602,290 to 28 candidates, 53 percent of this money was spent on 4 incumbent candidates who lost their primaries, and another 28 percent of their money was spent on 3 candidates—2 of them incumbents—who were forced into a runoff election. Obviously, Texans for Lawsuit Reform thought these candidates were important for achieving its agenda, but it is questionable how desirable it is for an interest group to pump huge amounts of money into the campaigns of incumbent candidates who do not have the political strength even to win in their own party primary elections. And the high degree of financial support for candidates can be hurtful to the candidate. In one of these races, the winning candidate's main issue was that the defeated incumbent had received money from an organization known for giving huge sums to Republican candidates. This, contended the winner, was proof that the incumbent Democrat was not a real Democrat but a Republican with a Democratic label.[28]

Nevertheless, Texans for Lawsuit Reform scored impressive victories in the 2010 general election. It gave more than $550,000 to Republican Marva Beck to defeat Democratic representative Jim Dunnam and $300,000 to Republican Larry Gonzales to defeat Democrat Diana Maldonado.[29]

Defeating Opponents

Generally, incumbents have a huge advantage over challengers in an election. Since they are officeholders, they usually have greater name recognition than challengers, and it is easy for incumbents to get publicity by holding town hall meetings, by announcing the relocation of new businesses to the district, or simply by attending community events. Additionally, they usually have an established network of supporters who helped them get into office at least once previously. There are two great exceptions to incumbency advantage: (1) scandal can destroy incumbency advantage, and (2) redistricting can ruin the political base of incumbents.

Except in cases of scandal or redistricting, however, it is far safer for interest groups to try to work with incumbents. Campaign money, for example, overwhelmingly goes to incumbents. In the 2012 campaign for the Texas House of Representatives incumbents raised 4.9 times the amount raised by challengers, and in the Texas Senate incumbents raised 10.7 times the amount raised by challengers

Contributions to State Legislators: How Does Texas Compare?

Contributions to State House Candidates per Voting Eligible Person, 2012

Arkansas
$12.74
$6,494,694*

Texas
$4.59
$73,949,992*

California
$3.67
$86,572,280*

North Carolina
$2.72
$18,937,780*

New York
$1.96
$18,937,780*

Arizona
$0.95
$4,157,517*

Above $7.00		$3.00 to $3.99		$2.00 to $2.99		$1.00 to $1.99		Under $1.00	
Arkansas	$12.74	Oklahoma	$3.90	Delaware	$2.94	New York	$1.96	Arizona	$0.95
Oregon	$7.17	California	$3.67	Connecticut	$2.79	South Dakota	$1.91	North Dakota	$0.82
Wyoming	$7.13	Missouri	$3.67	North Carolina	$2.72	South Carolina	$1.85	Alabama	$0.31
		Ohio	$3.65	Kansas	$2.71	Wisconsin	$1.82	New Jersey	$0.12
		Hawaii	$3.56	Tennessee	$2.60	Minnesota	$1.70	New Hampshire	$0.09
$4.00 to $7.00		West Virginia	$3.50	Massachusetts	$2.42	Colorado	$1.66	Mississippi	$0.003
		Pennsylvania	$3.45	Michigan	$2.41	Maine	$1.54		
Alaska	$6.46	New Mexico	$3.38	Idaho	$2.40	Maryland	$1.43		
Iowa	$5.94	Washington	$3.27	Florida	$2.26	Vermont	$1.26		
Illinois	$5.51	Indiana	$3.23	Georgia	$2.20				
Texas	$4.59	Rhode Island	$3.02	Montana	$2.06				
Nevada	$4.46	Kentucky	$3.00	Utah	$2.03				

Texas has few regulations regarding how much money can be given to state legislators and candidates for the state legislature. Other states are far more restrictive in terms of how much money any one individual can give in any given year. The chart provides a state-by-state comparison of total number of dollars given to state legislature candidates in 2012.

for critical analysis

1. How does Texas compare to other states in terms of partisanship?

2. How might demographic change, especially the growing Latino population, change Texas's political preferences?

*Total amount given to candidates per state

Data not available for Louisiana, Nebraska, and Virginia.

SOURCE: Contribution data from 2012 Gallup Organization; voting eligible population data from United States Election Project, www.elections.gmu.edu/turnout_2012G.html (accessed 2/12/14).

TABLE 6.1

Average Dollars Raised by Incumbents and Challengers for the Texas Legislature, 2012

OFFICE	INCUMBENTS ($)	CHALLENGERS ($)
House	$388,719	$79,258
Senate	1,113,440	103,823

SOURCE: National Institute on Money in State Politics.

(see Table 6.1). Incumbents win elections to an overwhelming degree.[30] Some of the campaign contributions to incumbent legislators are spectacularly large. Speaker Joe Strauss, for example, received $6,551,013 in contributions—no doubt in recognition that as Speaker he was in a position to advance or hinder much legislation. Another influential legislator, Dan Branch, received $2,594,365 in contributions. In the Texas Senate in 2012, incumbent Wendy Davis faced a tough Republican challenger but outraised the challenger with $4,310,971 in contributions compared to her Republican opponent's $3,340,325.[31]

Of course, sometimes an interest group does not want to help a candidate or even pressure a candidate; it wants to defeat that candidate. This can be a risky strategy because if the candidate wins, then the interest group will be faced with not only an unfriendly public official but also one displeased with the interest group for its opposition. When that happens, the interest group will often "get well" or "get on the late train." This means that the interest group will make a substantial political contribution to the winning candidate whom it formerly opposed. Often, winning candidates have significant campaign debts after a grueling election battle, and they appreciate the late contributions of former enemies, which are offered as a way of making amends.

Although "late-train" contributions may improve the relationship between officials and interest groups, usually candidates reserve a special loyalty for those supporters who backed them early. Without support at the very beginning of a campaign, it is hard for a candidate to build an organization and get the support necessary to make a decent campaign start. That is why early supporters are so valuable. The best lobbyists start early in trying to develop relationships with candidates and with new legislators. One national PAC, EMILY's List (EMILY stands for Early Money Is Like Yeast), is funded by women and provides early campaign contributions to female candidates. Legislators remember who was with them at the beginning of their political careers—and this can be immensely beneficial to the lobby that cultivated that early relationship.[32]

Sometimes PACs give to both candidates as a way to avoid alienating either one, though the possibility remains that such dual giving will wind up alienating both. At other times, interest groups simply don't care if they alienate a candidate. The 2010 Democratic primary election between state representatives Tara Rios Ybarra and Jose Manuel Lozano highlighted the lines that can clearly separate interest groups during a campaign. Texans for Lawsuit Reform contributed $256,610 to Ybarra, which was 56 percent of her campaign funds. Ybarra lost to Lozano, who was backed by trial lawyers who were not the least bit sympathetic to the goals of Texans for Lawsuit Reform.[33]

An extraordinary battle occurred in the 2012 Republican primary where Texans for Lawsuit Reform backed railroad commissioner Elizabeth Ames Jones in her challenge to Republican state senator Jeff Wentworth. Wentworth served nearly five years in the Texas House before being elected to the state senate in 1992. He appeared to be well established and unbeatable. An early poll showed him with a large lead. But although Wentworth supported 21 of 23 bills considered by Texans for Lawsuit Reform to be "major" legislation, he angered the interest group by criticizing a 2003 constitutional amendment that limited the amounts patients could receive in medical malpractice suits. He also voted against a bill that reduced the amount of money coastal homeowners could receive after hurricanes. While Wentworth was defeated, it was not by Jones, but by Donna Campbell, who had Tea Party backing. Nevertheless, Wentworth blamed his defeat on the "mammoth $2 million-plus negative campaign launched against me by Texans for Lawsuit Reform."[34] The defeat no doubt sent a message to Republican lawmakers that they had better not cross Texans for Lawsuit Reform.

When an interest group is convinced that it cannot work with a public official, the interest group may undertake an all-out effort to defeat that official. But spending money by no means guarantees success. Dr. James Leininger is one of the biggest contributors to Republican candidates. In the 2006 election cycle, he gave over $5 million to Republican candidates in Texas, either through individual contributions or by giving to PACs that then made contributions. Leininger and some of the PACs he supports are strong supporters of school vouchers. Much of this money backed challengers to Republican incumbents who were unfavorable to vouchers. The effort was unsuccessful and the result, according to Texans for Public Justice, was a legislature "even less receptive to vouchers than its predecessor."[35]

A U.S. Supreme Court decision in 2009, *Citizens United v. Federal Election Commission*, created the opportunity to create an organization that opposed powerful incumbents without having to disclose the donors. Few wealthy Texans proved willing to openly fund political attacks on Speaker Joe Strauss and his allies, but in the 2012 election cycle, Empower Texans moved several hundred thousand dollars through its nonprofit organization and thus avoided having to disclose its political contributors. Most of this money was spent on a number of House races with the

Empower Texans is a powerful political action committee that provides money to candidates, sometimes from undisclosed donors.

biggest expenditures going to failed challenges to Speaker Strauss and to Representative Lance Gooden. The nonprofits spent about $290,000 on mailers, about $40,000 on Internet ads, and about $18,000 on robo-calls. Another nonprofit that does not have to report donors is the Texas Organizing Project, which spent a bit more than $234,000 mostly supporting Harris County sheriff Adrian Garcia and 14 other local candidates along with the Texas House campaign of Mary Ann Perez. These new funding structures where donors do not have to be reported are known as sources of **dark money**.[36]

dark money political money where the donors of the money do not have to be disclosed

Interest-Group Capture

Interest groups can sometimes have such influence over an agency of government that it is said that the interest group has "captured" that agency—meaning that the agency primarily serves the objectives of the interest group. Interest groups can develop long-term relationships with the agencies that regulate the industries that they represent in a number of ways. For example, interest groups can donate money to the election or re-election of agency officials who must seek election to their office. Subject to certain ethics rules, industries can also hire former agency officials to work for them as lobbyists. The closer the connection between the agency and the industry, the more complete is the capture.

interest-group capture government agency that serves the objectives of the interests that the agency is supposed to regulate

Such **interest-group capture** may have occurred with the Texas Railroad Commission. The Railroad Commission has the primary responsibility for regulating the oil and natural gas industry, pipelines, and coal and uranium surface-mining operations. The commission is run by three statewide elected officials who serve staggered six-year terms. Although one unsuccessful candidate for the commission included railroad safety in his campaign platform, the Railroad Commission's name is long outdated and has nothing to do with railroads.[37]

In 2010, Public Citizen, a consumer advocacy group, published a highly critical report on the commission which pointed out that at the Railroad Commission, "political spending is out of control, well over half of campaign donations coming from the very industries the commission is supposed to regulate. Real or perceived, this creates a conflict of interest. Railroad commissioner is seen as a springboard to higher elected office in the state, giving influence-peddlers more incentive to curry favor and sitting commissioners to amass campaign war chests. . . . Campaign donations coming from regulated industries present a very real problem, inserting the probability that regulatory decisions are made in favor of large donors rather than the public's interest."[38]

The Public Citizen report pointed out that by 2010, 80 percent of donations to incumbent commissioners were from the industries they regulated, which was up from 45 percent of donations to incumbents in 2001, and there had been nearly a tenfold increase in donations. Additionally, the size of individual donations had increased—in 2000, 80 percent of donations were $1,000 or more; in 2010, 92 percent of donations were $1,000 or more.[39] In the 2012 election an incumbent, Barry Smitherman, received $5,144,683 in campaign contributions, with the oil and gas industry being the largest group to make contributions. In a race for an open seat, Christi Craddick won with $2,850,158 in contributions, again with the oil and gas industry being the largest business/industrial group to make contributions.[40] Of course, that so many contributions should be from the oil and gas industry should not be surprising, since the commission is the main regulatory agency for oil and gas and other industries do not have the concerns about the commission's work that would cause those industries to make major contributions. And groups such

The Texas Railroad Commission regulates Texas's oil and gas industries. Some say that this commission has been captured by those special interests, which sometimes advocates controversial procedures like fracking.

as environmental groups do not have the resources to compete with the oil and gas industry in backing environmental candidates.

The staff of the Sunset Advisory Commission prepared a report in 2012 that attempted to deal with some of the concerns that the Texas Railroad Commission had been captured by the oil and gas industry. Among other things, the report recommended that the commission's name be changed to realistically reflect its contemporary duties: the Texas Energy Resources Commission. It also recommended that solicitation and receipt of campaign contributions by commissioners or candidates seeking the office be limited to the one- and one-half-year time frame around the election rather than having full-time fund-raising throughout the six-year term of office. It recommended that commissioners be banned from knowingly accepting contributions from those with contested cases before the commission, and it recommended that commissioners must resign their office if they become candidates for another elected office. There was also a recommendation that independent hearing examiners be used in contested cases involving oil and gas.[41]

House Speaker Pro Tem Dennis Bonnen was especially concerned that two sitting railroad commissioners had recently run for the U.S. Senate while retaining their offices and raising money from the oil and gas industry. While the efforts to reform the commission were publicly endorsed by the railroad commissioners, Bonnen claimed the commissioners were privately lobbying to weaken the proposals. The reform proposals failed in the 2013 legislature.[42]

● Individuals as Lobbyists

Explain how ordinary individuals can influence Texas government

Sometimes ordinary individuals can have a remarkable impact on public policy, although interest groups clearly have an advantage in influencing the legislative process. Nevertheless, a persistent individual with a well-reasoned argument can make a difference. For example, Tyrus Burks lost his wife and two children in a late-night electrical fire in West Dallas. Burks did not awaken in time to save them because he is deaf and did not hear the audible smoke alarm. Texas's state property code required the installation of audible smoke alarms but not visual alarms. In 2009, Burks became an advocate for a bill that would require property managers to buy and install visual smoke alarms if hearing-impaired tenants requested them and to put the alarms in visible locations such as bedrooms. Supported by state senator Royce West, the Sephra Burks Law, named for Tyrus's wife, who was also deaf, went into effect at the start of 2010. Tyrus Burks was an active lobbyist for the bill and gave legislative testimony in support of it with the aid of a sign language interpreter.

Burks's efforts benefited from the support of the Texas Apartment Association, a major interest group representing apartment property interests, who backed the bill. Burks's story was tragic and his argument was compelling. It would have been difficult for opposition to emerge against such a proposal. Still, his efforts resulted in a major victory for the deaf, who are protected by such a law requiring visual smoke alarms in only three other states and the District of Columbia.[43] Burks's achievement demonstrates that individuals can, at least sometimes, be successful lobbyists.

The problem is that relatively few Texans are engaged in the neighborhood, in their community, or in politics, and so much lobbying is left to organized interest groups with professional lobbyists. Table 6.2 provides a number of measures of civic engagement, and all show Texas is considerably lower than the national average on these measures. Texas is near the bottom of the nation in terms of measures of social connectedness that would lead to civic involvement such as discussing politics with friends or family, group involvement, frequent communication with friends and family, and even trust in all or most of the people in the neighborhood. Nor in comparison with the rest of the nation are Texans involved in volunteer activity or charitable donations. Texans tend not to contact or visit their public of-

Occasionally, ordinary individuals can have a direct influence on policy. Barbara Brown, of Plano, lobbied local government and the state legislature to get better bicycle safety laws and programs passed. Brown's son was killed in an accident while riding his bicycle.

TABLE 6.2

Measures of Texas Civic Health

	PERCENTAGE OF TEXANS AGREEING (%)	NATIONAL AVERAGE (%)	RANKING OF TEXAS AMONG THE STATES
Contacted or visited public official	9%	12%	49
Discuss politics with friends or family a few times a week or more	26	29	44
Communicate with friends and family frequently	78	79	41
Trust all or most people in the neighborhood	50	57	47
Donate $25 or more to charitable or religious organizations	47	52	43
Group involvement	38	39	37
Volunteer activity	25	27	42
Registered to vote	62	65	42
Voting	36	45	50

SOURCE: Regina Lawrence, Deborah Wise, and Emily Einsohn, Texas Civic Health Index (Austin: Annette Strauss Institute for Civic Life, 2013).

ficials, register to vote, or vote. With such low levels of civic engagement, individual effects on the Texas political process are likely to be low.[44]

Interestingly, while 52 percent of Texans in one survey claimed they were very interested in politics and public affairs and 37 percent said they were somewhat interested, Texas has the lowest proportion of actual voters of any state. Texans give all sorts of reasons for not voting, the most common reason being that Texans claim they are too busy or that work conflicts with voting and the next most common reason that they either are not interested or believe their vote does not matter.[45] Figure 6.2 provides the reasons given in 2012 when Texans were asked why they did not vote. Of course, Texas's low levels of voting participation—the lowest level in the country—means that organized interest groups fill the void in political activity and can wield vast influence in the state's political process.

● Thinking Critically about Interest Groups

Interest groups play an important role in Texas politics even though Texas is no longer a one-party state with limited economic development. Even with two major political parties and a diverse economy, Texas politics cannot be understood without also examining the role of interest groups. Interest groups in Texas have a notable pro-business flavor. Labor is weak in Texas, and its role in the political process is quite limited. Trial lawyers are an especially wealthy and important interest group that promotes liberal policies in Texas, but with the growth of the

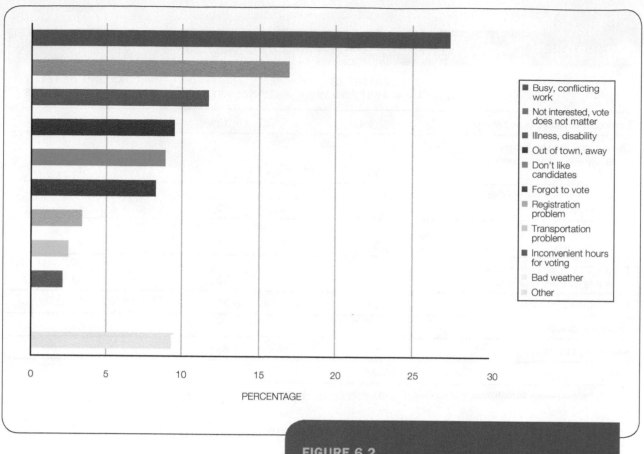

FIGURE 6.2

Reasons Texans Give for Not Voting

SOURCE: Data are reported in Regina Lawrence, Deborah Wise, and Emily Einsohn, *Texas Civic Health Index* (Austin: Annette Strauss Institute for Civic Life, 2013), p. 22.

Republican Party and tort reform interest groups, the influence of the trial lawyers has waned.

Though no single interest group or coalition of interest groups dominates Texas politics, by far most lobbyists represent business interests, and the bulk of PAC money comes from business interests. Often, of course, businesses are pitted against one another in the political process. Also, public interest, civil rights, consumer, and environmental groups may still be successful by mobilizing public opinion and influencing the media. However, there are only a few interest groups that offer alternatives to business perspectives on policy issues. Less frequently, ordinary individuals are able to influence public policy. Although they tend to be at a disadvantage in terms of money and other resources, dedicated individuals with a compelling argument sometimes succeed in lobbying for specific legislation. This is especially true when they are pursuing goals that do not put them in conflict with well-organized and well-funded interest groups.

Interest Groups in the Political Process

Define interest groups, and describe the major ways they try to influence Texas government (pp. 173–83)

Interest groups in Texas are organizations of interested citizens who band together to influence public policy. Lobbyists are hired to cultivate relationships with legislators and convince them of their clients' interests. The goal of lobbyists is to gain access to policy makers to persuade them to support the positions of the interest group.

Key Terms

interest group (p. 173)

free rider problem (p. 174)

bundling (p. 176)

lobbyist (p. 177)

Practice Quiz

1. The "8F Crowd"
   a) was a group of legislators who failed the eighth grade.
   b) was a group of extremely wealthy Texans who met in Suite 8F of the Lamar Hotel in Houston and controlled Texas politics for 40 years.
   c) were 25 legislators who boycotted the eighth session of the legislature in order to prevent the legislators from taking any action because it lacked a quorum.
   d) was made up of eight lobbyists who were close friends of the governor.
   e) were the eight most powerful officials in the state who met in Suite F of the Austin State Office Building.

2. Interest groups provide public officials with all the following *except*
   a) information.
   b) money.
   c) media coverage.
   d) votes.
   e) committee assignments.

3. The goals of interest groups include all *except*
   a) electing people to office in order to support the groups' goals.
   b) influencing those who control government.
   c) educating the public and members about issues of importance to the group.
   d) providing campaign funds for favored candidates.
   e) maintaining a heterogeneous membership.

4. Interest groups have an advantage over individuals in influencing policy because interest groups usually have
   a) more time to influence officials.
   b) greater expertise than individuals.
   c) more money to influence elections.
   d) more staff.
   e) all of the above.

5. When interest groups combine small contributions from many sources to form one large contribution, it is called
   a) bundling.
   b) compacting.
   c) cracking.
   d) polling.
   e) packing.

6. The most important thing interest groups need to be effective is
   a) the support of a majority of Texans.
   b) office space in Austin.
   c) a variety of issues on which to lobby.
   d) a large, paid staff.
   e) access to politicians.

7. Trial lawyers are which type of interest group?
   a) professional group
   b) public employee group
   c) single-issue group
   d) consumer group
   e) business group

8. Interest groups often hire former legislators as lobbyists to
   a) gain greater access to current legislators.
   b) benefit from the policy expertise of former legislators.
   c) benefit from the personal "insider" knowledge of the former legislator.
   d) all of the above.
   e) none of the above.

Another Side to Lobbying

Political action committees (PACs) are private groups that raise and distribute funds for election campaigns. Interest groups play a major role in getting out the vote. Interest-group money can play a major role in defeating as well as electing candidates.

Key Terms

political action committee (PAC) (p. 184)

issue advocacy (p. 184)

dark money (p. 190)

interest-group capture (p. 190)

Practice Quiz

9. Lobbyists are
   a) all corrupt.
   b) all unethical.
   c) important sources of information for legislators.
   d) harmful to the democratic process.
   e) never retired legislators.

10. In Texas, the most powerful interest groups represent which interests?
    a) consumer
    b) civil rights
    c) business
    d) owners of oil wells
    e) public employee

11. PACs are used to
    a) stir the public's interest in politics.
    b) raise money from individuals, which is then bundled and given to candidates.
    c) create media campaigns to influence the course of government.
    d) create grassroots campaigns.
    e) all of the above.

12. One of the most important grassroots tactics of interest groups is
    a) to gain support from all the mayors of town in a district.
    b) to get out the vote.
    c) to form political alliances with executive and legislative leaders.
    d) to lobby the judicial branch of national and state government.
    e) to interpret the needs of their members.

13. Interest groups have a hard time defeating incumbent legislators unless
    a) the legislator is involved in scandal.
    b) the legislator has been redistricted.
    c) the legislator's positions have generated overwhelming opposition in the district.
    d) all of the above.
    e) none of the above.

14. Dark money refers to
    a) money that is illegally donated to politicians for their re-election.
    b) money that cannot be used to pay typical campaign expenditures.
    c) vouchers that candidates can use to fund their campaigns.
    d) donated money that does not have to be reported by a campaign.
    e) money that is printed on special dark green paper specifically formulated for campaigns.

15. Capture theory refers to the idea that
    a) interest groups are controlled by politicians.
    b) through long-term relationships, government interests come to serve the objectives of an interest group.
    c) politicians work for the public good by controlling special interests.
    d) labor unions are controlled by business.
    e) business interests are captured by labor unions.

Individuals as Lobbyists

Citizens can lobby their legislators by calling, writing, or visiting their offices. Industries and well-financed interests can afford professional lobbyists to try to influence legislation, but legislators will listen to individual citizens, especially if they join together in large numbers.

Practice Quiz

16. Individuals have the best chance to influence public policy when they
    a) are not opposed by organized interest groups.
    b) are polite.
    c) entertain legislators.
    d) vote.
    e) live in Austin.

Recommended Websites

Texans for Public Justice
www.tpj.org

Texas Ethics Commission
www.ethics.state.tx.us/

Texas Medical Association
www.texmed.org

Texas Trial Lawyers Association
www.ttla.com/TX/

TEXPAC
www.texpac.org

Texans for Lawsuit Reform
www.tortreform.com/

When passing (or blocking) legislation in Texas, the rules matter. In 2013 state senator Wendy Davis (D-Fort Worth) staged an over 10-hour filibuster that temporarily stopped a bill restricting abortions. Eventually, in another special legislative session, the bill finally passed.

The Texas Legislature

WHY THE TEXAS LEGISLATURE MATTERS After the 83rd legislative session ended, Governor Rick Perry called a special 30-day session. The last item on the session's agenda was a bill to regulate abortion procedures, providers, and facilities: Senate Bill 5. The bill was complex, subjecting abortion providers in Texas to a number of new regulations. The most notable and significant change was a ban on the abortion of fetuses older than 20 weeks. Supporters of the bill argued that such abortions should be banned because there was evidence that fetuses of that gestational stage are capable of feeling pain. This restriction would not apply in cases in which the fetus was severely deformed or in which the life of the mother was in danger. However, in the latter scenario, the performing physician would be required to try to save the fetus's life. The bill also required abortion facilities to meet the same safety and quality standards as ambulatory surgical centers—clinics that specialize exclusively in outpatient surgical procedures. Opponents of the bill argued that this would force 37 of the state's 42 abortion clinics to either close or relocate.[1] A Senate amendment to the bill required that abortion-inducing drugs be prescribed only by physicians. Finally, all physicians who perform abortions had to have admitting privileges at a hospital less than 30 miles away from the abortion facility.

Filibusters in the Texas Senate are very different from those in the U.S. Senate. They are based on Senate Rules 4.01 and 4.03, which allow a senator to speak on a bill for as long as the senator desires without interruption. This privilege is subject to several limitations. The senator must remain standing at his or her desk for the entire time and cannot lean on anything, sit in a chair, or take any breaks. The speaker must also ensure all of his or her comments are germane to the bill. Senate rules enable other senators to call the speaker on a point of order if these rules are not followed. After a point of order is raised, the president of the Senate may sustain or overrule the point of order. This ruling can be challenged from the floor, resulting in a vote that either supports or rejects the ruling on the point of order. If the filibustering senator is successfully called on three points of order, a simple majority of the Senate may vote to prevent the senator from continuing with his or her remarks.[2] The overall effect of these rules is to make Texas senatorial filibusters "endurance contests" for individual senators.[3]

On Tuesday, June 25, 2013—the last day of the special legislative session—the main item on the agenda was Senate Bill 5. At 11:18 AM, Senator Wendy Davis of Fort Worth took the floor, intending to filibuster until the session ended at midnight. She held the floor until 10:07 PM.[4] She was called on three points of order. First, her remarks on Planned Parenthood's budget were deemed not to be germane.[5] Second, having another senator help her with her back brace violated the spirit of the rule against leaning or sitting.[6] This particular point of order was decided by a 17-to-11 vote.[7] Third, her discussion of a Texas law requiring women to have a sonogram before receiving an abortion was not germane.[8] At this point, the Senate voted 19 to 10 to finally end the filibuster.[9]

After Davis was forced to surrender the floor, other Democratic senators began raising points of order and parliamentary inquiries in an attempt to run out the last two hours of the session. At 11:45 PM, Senator Leticia Van de Putte of San Antonio made a motion to adjourn that was not recognized by the presiding senator. Van de Putte followed up with a question: "At what point must a female senator raise her hand or her voice to be recognized over her male colleagues in the room?"[10] The Senate gallery, which was packed with opponents of the bill, erupted with applause and cheers. The noise drowned out the proceedings on the floor and prevented Republicans from calling a vote until 12:02 AM— after the special session had officially ended.[11] The bill received 18 yeas and 11 nays.[12] At first, it was announced that the bill had passed. The Senate went so far as to change the date of the final vote from June 26 to June 25 on its automated bill tracking website. At 3:00 AM, however, the lieutenant governor conceded that the vote had begun too late and that the bill had failed. Yet his closing comment—"See you soon"—reflected the near-certainty that the bill would pass in the next special session.[13]

Senate Bill 5 and Wendy Davis's filibuster reveal a number of important points about Texas politics and the rules and strategies seen in the Texas legislature. Pro-life legislation is important to the Republican Party base (as pro-choice policies are important for the Democratic Party base), but such social legislation was not the mainstay of the legislative agenda in the regular legislative session. A hard push for such legislation in the regular session would have tied up other bills that had priority for the Republican majority. Instead, such controversial social legislation was saved for the special session after almost all of the legislative agenda had been handled in the regular session. There was an advantage in bringing up such legislation in a special session. For one thing, in a special session, the legislative agenda is not overwhelmed by bills. A special session is limited to the issues for which the special session is called. Additionally, it is easier for bills to pass in a special session where the regular session requirement of a two-thirds vote for Senate consideration of a bill does not apply. The disadvantage of such legislation being considered in a special session is that a session is limited to 30 days and a well-timed filibuster, such as used by Senator Wendy Davis, can block a bill where the vote comes near the end of the session. That use of the filibuster to block a bill, however, can be overcome if the governor immediately calls still another 30-day special session with the blocked bill as a key agenda item in the session.

The battle over the bill also shows the importance of symbolic politics. Politicians sometimes battle over issues important to key constituencies to build and maintain support from those constituencies but don't expect to make lasting changes. That is, Senator Davis's filibuster may well have stopped passage of the bill in the special session, but it was clear that the bill would pass in the next special session immediately after the first. And, given federal court decisions on the issue of abortion, it is likely that parts of the abortion bill are unconstitutional. One thing became clear, however: social issues provoke intense partisan battles—the old friendly and congenial Texas legislature no longer exists. The new Texas legislature is increasingly moving in the bitter partisan direction of the U.S. Congress.

chaptergoals

- Describe the bicameral organization of the legislature and the rules for membership (pp. 201–4)

- Explain when the legislature meets (pp. 204–6)

- Outline the legislative and nonlegislative powers of the legislature (pp. 206–10)

- Trace the process through which law is made in Texas (pp. 210–17)

- Describe the roles of other state officials and interested parties in shaping legislation (pp. 217–19)

- Analyze how party leadership and partisanship affect power in the legislature (pp. 219–25)

- Explain the politics of redistricting (pp. 226–29)

Structure of the Texas Legislature

Describe the bicameral organization of the legislature and the rules for membership

The Texas state legislature is the most important representative institution in the state. Members share many of the duties and responsibilities that are taken up at the national level by members of the U.S. Congress. Like members of the U.S. Congress, the members of the Texas House and Senate are responsible for bringing the interests and concerns of their constituencies directly into the democratic political processes. But the important constitutional and institutional differences between the U.S. Congress and the Texas state legislature must be taken into account if we are to understand the role that the state legislature plays in democracy in Texas.

Bicameralism

Like the U.S. Congress and all the states except Nebraska, Texas has a **bicameral** legislature, with two chambers: the Texas House of Representatives and the Texas

bicameral having a legislative assembly composed of two chambers or houses

Before becoming law in Texas, a bill must pass in both houses of the legislature. In 2013 the legislature passed a law forbidding guns on college campuses unless specifically authorized by the campus.

Senate. The Texas legislature's 150 House members and 31 senators meet in regular session for 140 days every odd-numbered year. Senators serve four-year terms, and House members serve for two years. Each represents a single-member district. Each member of the Texas House represents approximately 168,000 people. Each senator represents over 811,000 constituents. A state senator now represents more people than does a member of the U.S. House of Representatives. Elections are held in November of even-numbered years, and senators and House members take office in January of odd-numbered years.

Bicameralism creates interesting dynamics in a legislature. For one thing, it means that before a law is passed, it will be voted on by two deliberative bodies representing different constituencies. In 2009, for example, the Texas Senate passed legislation to allow college students and faculty with concealed handgun licenses to carry their firearms on campus. That legislation, however, was killed in the Texas House of Representatives.[14] In 2011 the Texas Senate again passed a bill with an amendment allowing guns on campus. In the Texas House, the bill had support from a majority of members. However, the bill failed in the House because of a successful parliamentary objection that the gun amendment was not germane to the bill it amended, which dealt with scholarships.[15] In 2013 the National Rifle Association–backed bill allowing guns on campus passed the House, but the bill died in the Texas Senate when it failed to get the two-thirds vote needed in the Senate for the bill to be brought to the floor for discussion and a vote.[16] If a bill cannot be killed in one house, it can be killed or modified in the other body.

One effect of bicameralism in Texas is that the author of a bill in one house that has been amended in the other body has the option of accepting or rejecting the amendment. If the author accepts the amendment, the bill moves forward; if the author rejects the amendment, the bill is killed.

Bicameralism allows a member of one legislative body to retaliate against a member of either body for not cooperating on desired legislation. A "local and consent" calendar in the House is usually reserved for uncontroversial bills or bills limited to a localized problem. In order for a bill to be passed from that calendar, it has to pass without the objection of any member of the House. That requirement provides a perfect opportunity for members to retaliate against other members for perceived slights.[17]

Membership

The constitutional requirements for becoming a member of the Texas legislature are minimal. A senator must be a U.S. citizen, a qualified voter, and a resident of the state for at least five years and of the district for at least one year. Additionally, the senator must be at least 26 years of age. Members of the House must be at least 21, U.S. citizens, qualified voters, and residents of the state for two years and of the district for one year. These requirements are in keeping with the political philosophy of those who wrote the Constitution of 1876. They believed holding public office required little or no formal training and should be open to most citizens.

In Texas, the typical legislator is white, male, Protestant, college educated, and affluent and has a professional or business occupation. These characteristics do not mean that others cannot be elected to the state legislature, but they do indicate that individuals with most of these informal characteristics have a distinct advantage. Members of the legislature must have jobs that allow them the flexibility to campaign for office and to work in the legislature for 140 days every other year, as well as in special legislative sessions and meetings of committees when the legislature is not in session. Thus, about one-third of the members of the legislature are attorneys. The legal profession is one of the few careers that pays well and offers the flexibility a legislator needs. Lawyers who serve in the legislature may even gain increased legal business either from interests with legislative concerns or because of the enhanced visibility of a lawyer-legislator.[18]

Republicans control both houses of the Texas legislature. In the 2015 legislative session, there were 11 Democrats and 20 Republicans in the Texas Senate and there were 52 Democrats and 98 Republicans in the Texas House of Representatives.

Legislators in Texas cannot expect to live on their legislative salaries. In keeping with the Texas constitutional tradition of a low-cost, part-time legislature, Texas representatives receive a salary of only $7,200 a year. Legislators also receive a payment of $150 a day when the legislature is in session. When the legislature is not in session, legislators may claim up to 12 days per month of **per diem** pay if they are in Austin on official business, or 16 days if they are committee chairs. The legislators themselves determine what qualifies as official business. It is common to pay expenses from officeholder expense accounts and to pocket the per diem so that it becomes a salary supplement. Legislative retirement pensions are very generous. The pension is tied to district judges' salaries, which are $125,000 a year. That salary is multiplied by the years of service of the legislator times 2.3 percent. A legislator who has served 10 years thus would qualify for a pension of $28,750 per year. A legislator serving 20 years would qualify for a pension of $57,500 per year. Lawmakers are eligible for pensions with at least 8 years of service. With 8 years of service, the lawmaker can start collecting a pension at age 60. With 10 years of service, a lawmaker can start collecting at age 50.[19]

per diem daily payment to a public official engaged in state business

Originally, per diem rates were set by the Texas Constitution, and a constitutional amendment was necessary to change this. In 1991, Texans adopted an amendment allowing the Texas Ethics Commission to propose changes in legislative salaries, which then require voter approval. To date, the commission has not recommended a salary increase. At the start of each regular session, the Ethics Commission sets the legislative per diem. In the 2011 session, with major belt-tightening throughout state government, the legislature asked the Texas Ethics Commission to reduce its scheduled per diem of $168 a day to $150.[20] One Texas legislator found a way to increase his income by billing both the state and his campaign funds for his travel expenses. Representative Joe Driver of Garland pled guilty to a third-degree felony for double billing thousands of dollars in expenses. His conviction raises questions about how closely legislators' expenses are monitored.[21] During one of the 2013 special legislative sessions which lasted 30 days, 147 Texas lawmakers collected their $150 per diem for the entire time even though a number of them did not attend the session and even though the House and Senate actually met only a few days. Eight senators and 26 House members gave written notice that they did not wish to receive the per diem when they were not in Austin.[22]

Although the "typical" member of the Texas state legislature is white and male, women and minority groups have increased their representation in recent years. For example, state representative and entrepreneur Helen Giddings has become an influential member of the House Business and Industry and Appropriations committees.

"Who Are Texans: Who Are the Members of the Texas Legislature?" shows the proportions of minorities and women serving in the legislature. Although those numbers have increased over the years, they are not in proportion to their strength in the population of Texas. Civil rights laws have increased voting by minorities, and those laws provide protection for minority political districts, though the 2013 decision of the U.S. Supreme Court overturning part of the Voting Rights Act may lead to reduced legal protection for minority districts. Thus, more minority officeholders have been elected and, as the Hispanic population in Texas increases, additional Latino legislators will be elected. Women have also had an increased role in politics, especially since the 1970s, and as a result, it is likely that additional women will be elected to legislative office.

● Sessions of the Legislature

> **Explain when the legislature meets**

Not all state legislatures meet for the same time periods. Some state legislatures meet every year like the U.S. Congress. Texas's legislature generally meets every other year unless the governor calls it to meet between regular sessions.

Regular Sessions

The Texas Constitution specifies that **regular sessions** of the Texas legislature be held for 140 days in odd-numbered years. The **biennial** legislative sessions have their origin in the nineteenth-century idea that legislative service is a part-time job and a belief that short, biennial sessions would limit the power of the legislature. For a few years, legislators were encouraged to end their work early by being paid for only 120 days of service.

Thousands of bills and resolutions are introduced into the legislature during a regular session, and the 140-day limitation places a considerable restriction on the legislature's ability to deal with this workload. In the 2013 regular legislative session, for example, 5,868 bills were introduced and 1,437 passed. If resolutions are included as well as bills, 10,630 were introduced and 5,909 were passed. The governor vetoed 26 of the bills passed by the legislature.[23] Hundreds of bills pass in the last hours of a legislative session, most with little or no debate. More die in the end-of-session crush of business because there isn't time to consider them.

Special Sessions

If the legislature does not complete its agenda before the end of the legislative session or if problems arise between regular sessions, the governor may call a **special session**. Special sessions last no more than 30 days, but there is no limit to the number of special sessions a governor can call, and the governor sets their agenda. Texas has averaged one special session a year since 1876, although years may go by with no special session, whereas in some years there may be three or four sessions.

The ability to call and set the agenda of a special session provides the governor with control over which issues are discussed and what bills are passed. In many instances, the governor, the Speaker of the Texas House, the lieutenant governor, and various committee chairs will meet to decide what will be done to solve the problem at hand. Once the leaders address the issue and develop solutions, the governor calls the special session.

Once the session begins, the governor can open it to different issues. At times, the governor bargains for a legislator's vote in return for adding to the special

regular session the 140-day period, occurring only in odd-numbered years, during which the Texas legislature meets to consider and pass bills

biennial occurring every two years

for critical analysis

Texas is the second-largest state and the second most populous state. Can a legislature that meets only 140 days every other year meet Texas's needs? Will changes in the economy make a full-time legislature necessary? Why?

special session a legislative session called by the governor that addresses an agenda set by him or her and that lasts no longer than 30 days

Who Are the Members of the Texas Legislature?

Gender

	Texas Pop.	Texas House	Texas Senate
Female	50%	21%	23%
Male	50%	79%	77%

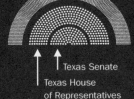

Key — Texas Population, Texas Senate, Texas House of Representatives

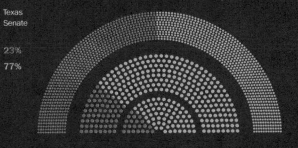

The Texas legislature is designed to be a representative body. How well does the legislature represent Texas? In many ways, the legislature does not look like Texas. The data to the left are for the Texas legislature in 2013–14. The state is evenly split between men and women, while the legislature is four-fifths male. While the state has no ethnic majority in its population, more than two-thirds of Texas legislators are white. Perhaps the biggest differences, though, relate to socioeconomic status. Over half of the members of the legislature hold graduate degrees, while only 9 percent of the population does.

Race

	Texas Pop.	Texas House	Texas Senate
White	45%	66%	70%
Black	12%	12%	7%
Hispanic	38%	21%	23%
Asian	4%	1%	0

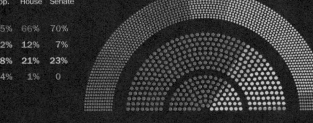

Education

	Texas Pop.	Texas House	Texas Senate
< HS diploma	19%	0	0
High school grad.	48%	7%	3%
Associate's degree	17%	3%	0
Bachelor's degree	7%	53%	39%
Graduate degree	9%	37%	58%

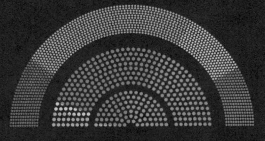

Occupation

- Business
- Attorney
- Community service
- Health care
- Education
- Other

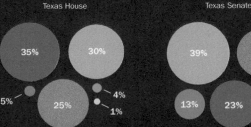

Texas House: 35%, 30%, 5%, 25%, 4%, 1%
Texas Senate: 39%, 23%, 13%, 23%, 3%

for critical analysis

1. How much do you think the racial, gender, and socioeconomic makeup of the Texas legislature matter to the type of laws that the legislature passes? If the legislature had more people of color, more women, or more middle-class members, would it pass different policies?
2. Why do you think that members of the Texas legislature come from the more educated, higher socioeconomic groups? Does the structure of the Texas legislature encourage or discourage people from particular occupations to run?

SOURCES: For Texas House, numbers calculated by author based on data from the Directory of Elected Officials of the Texas Tribune: www.texastribune.org/directory/. State demographic data calculated from the US Census Bureau American Community Survey, www.census.gov (accessed 5/14/14).

session agenda an issue of importance to that legislator. In 2003, Governor Perry called three special sessions of the legislature to address congressional redistricting. In 2004 a fourth special session was called to address school finance. In 2005, in addition to the regular session, two special sessions addressed school finance. There was also a special session in 2006, 2009, and 2011. As discussed earlier, in 2013 two special sessions were called—the second because legislation that restricted abortion in Texas was not passed in the first largely because of Senator Wendy Davis's filibuster.

Between legislative sessions, members serve on interim committees that may require a few days of their time each month. Legislators are also frequently called on to present programs to schools, colleges, and civic clubs. They supervise the staff of their district offices and address the needs of their constituents. Special sessions, interim committee meetings, speeches, and constituent services require long hours with little remuneration. Many members devote more than 40 hours a week to legislative business in addition to maintaining their full-time jobs.

When Texas was a rural, predominantly agricultural state, biennial sessions worked well; however, Texas has moved beyond this description. In the twenty-first century, Texas is a modern state with more than 80 percent of its population living in metropolitan areas. Population growth continues at a rapid rate. The state's gross domestic product exceeds that of many nations. Part-time legislators serving biennial 140-day sessions may not work well anymore in allowing the state to respond quickly and effectively to problems that arise.

Powers of the Legislature

> **Outline the legislative and nonlegislative powers of the legislature**

The Texas legislature sets public policy by passing bills and resolutions, but it also supervises the state bureaucracy through the budgetary process and the Sunset Act, an act that provides for the review and, when deemed appropriate, the termination of state agencies. This supervision is achieved using legislative and nonlegislative powers. Legislative powers consist of passing bills and resolutions. Nonlegislative powers are those functions falling outside the lawmaking function.

Legislative Powers

bill a proposed law that has been sponsored by a member of the legislature and submitted to the clerk of the House or Senate

local bill a bill affecting only units of local government, such as a city, county, or special district

special bill a bill that gives an individual or corporation a special exemption from state law

Bills Revenue bills must begin in the House of Representatives. All other bills may start in either the House or the Senate. For decades, a **bill** would be introduced in either the House or the Senate and work its way through the legislative process in that chamber. A bill introduced in the Senate would be passed by the Senate prior to going to the House. Today, it is customary for a bill to be introduced in the House and the same bill, a companion bill, to be introduced in the Senate at the same time. This simultaneous consideration of bills saves time in the legislature.

There are three classifications of bills in the Texas legislature: (1) local bills, (2) special bills, and (3) general bills. **Local bills** affect only units of local government such as a city, a county, special districts, or more than one city in a county. A local bill, for example, might allow a county to create a sports authority or to establish a community college. **Special bills** give individuals or corporations an exemption

Characteristics of Texas Legislators Compared to Other States

	Texas	California	Florida	New York	Ohio
Gender	Female 21%	Female 27%	Female 25%	Female 22%	Female 24%
	Male 79%	Male 73%	Male 75%	Male 78%	Male 76%
Race	Latino 20%	Latino 23%	Latino 29%	Latino 28%	Latino 0%
	African American 9%	African American 11%	African American 16%	African American 16%	African American 14%
Education level	H.S. diploma 2%	H.S. diploma 2%	H.S. diploma 1%	H.S. diploma 1%	H.S. diploma 4%
	Bachelor's degree 37%	Bachelor's degree 67%	Bachelor's degree 27%	Bachelor's degree 32%	Bachelor's degree 29%
	Graduate degree 49%	Graduate degree 51%	Graduate degree 56%	Graduate degree 52%	Graduate degree 49%

The Texas legislature is predominately white and male, even though the state population has become more diverse. Even though women are nearly half of the population, around the country, most legislatures are still predominantly male. The Latino and black populations in Texas combine to form nearly half of the state's residents, although this is not reflected in the legislature either. How does Texas compare to other states on the representation of women, minorities, and educational attainment?

for critical analysis

1. What can you conclude about the educational background of legislators from these states? Would you guess that their economic status is high or low?

2. Which state is most like Texas in terms of its legislative makeup? Which is least like Texas? What might explain some of the similarities and differences?

SOURCE: National Conference of State Legislators, www.ncsl.org/research/about-state-legislatures (accessed 2/20/14).

A Full-Time or Part-Time Legislature?

The Texas legislature is a part-time, citizen legislature. It meets only once every two years for 140 days. Members of the Texas House are elected for two-year terms and are paid $7,200 per year. They receive a per diem allowance for expenses while they are in session. Members of the Texas Senate are elected for four-year terms and receive the same pay. Texas's legislators generally have other forms of employment, as not many people can live on $7,200 per year. If problems demanding attention arise outside of the regular session, then the governor can call a special session to deal with a specific issue.

It is interesting to contrast the Texas legislature with a professional legislature, such as New York's. The New York legislature is considered professional because legislators are committed to being full-time representatives; they meet year-round, and members are paid $79,500 per year. The U.S. Congress is more similar to the New York legislature and can be considered a professional legislature because members of Congress serve year-round.

As a candidate for president in 2011 and 2012, former governor Rick Perry campaigned on adapting the Texas model to the U.S. Congress. Perry argued that the Founders intended a "citizen" Congress similar to the one in Texas, with members serving for only a few terms and retaining their regular employment in the private sector. This vision also fits with the principle of limited government—the principle that Congress or the legislature really should have a small role and the more they are in session, the more temptations they have to engage in corrupt practices and to pass laws restricting liberties.

Opponents argue that the Texas model is not one that should be adopted for the U.S. Congress or other

legislatures. Legislators are not any less prone to corruption under the Texas model. Under either model, lobbyists attempt to influence policy makers, and the fact that legislators have private-sector jobs does not minimize this possibility. Meeting once every two years reduces the time to deliberate and make sensible policies. In Texas, critics argue that the legislative session is rushed, and legislators rely too heavily on staff who work year-round and are more familiar with the ins and outs of policy making. The rush of completing the legislation necessary to govern the state often leaves important issues unresolved, leading to the need for more special sessions. Members who are not independently wealthy are unable to legislate effectively because they cannot just leave their jobs for

140 days at a time every two years. All of these factors result in a less productive legislature.

Your vision of the proper role of government will likely affect where you come down on this issue. Liberals, who prefer an active government, would probably prefer a full-time legislature which actively addresses social problems. Conservatives, who are not supporters of government activity in the economy, are more likely to support a minimal role for legislators so that citizens are free to make their own choices without governmental interference.

Why should citizens care about this issue? The political process matters, and how legislative institutions are designed makes a difference in terms of policy outcomes.

critical thinking questions

1. Are you more convinced by the arguments for a part-time legislature or a full-time legislature? What are the advantages and disadvantages of each approach?

2. What sorts of compromises are possible between Texas's 140-day session and a full-time approach?

from state law. A special bill could grant compensation to an individual wrongly convicted and sentenced to prison. **General bills** apply to all people and/or property in the state. General bills define criminal behavior; establish standards for divorce, child custody, or bankruptcy; and address other matters affecting people and property throughout the state. There is great variation among legislators in terms of the number of bills introduced. In the 2013 regular session of the legislature, for example, Senator John Carona introduced 132 bills, whereas Senator Sylvia Garcia introduced 8. Representative Linda Harper-Brown introduced 95 bills, and Representative Craig Goldman introduced 9.[24]

Resolutions There are three types of **resolutions** in the Texas legislature: (1) concurrent resolutions, (2) joint resolutions, and (3) simple resolutions. **Concurrent resolutions** must pass both the House and Senate, and they require the governor's signature. These resolutions involve issues of interest to both chambers. They may request information from a state agency or call on Congress for some action. Senate Concurrent Resolution 6 might, for example, call on Congress to propose an amendment requiring a balanced federal budget.

Joint resolutions require passage in both the House and Senate but do not require the governor's signature. The most common use of joint resolutions is to propose amendments to the Texas Constitution or to ratify amendments to the U.S. Constitution. Resolutions that propose amendments to the Texas Constitution require a two-thirds vote of the membership of both houses of the state legislature. Ratification of amendments to the U.S. Constitution requires a majority vote in both the Texas House and Senate.

Simple resolutions concern only the Texas House or the Senate, and they do not require the governor's signature. They are used to adopt rules, to request opinions from the attorney general, to appoint employees to office in the House or Senate, or to honor outstanding achievements by Texas residents. For example, Senate Resolution (SR) 27 could recognize the achievements of a Nobel Prize winner or the San Jacinto College baseball program for accomplishments in the National Junior College Athletic Association.

Resolutions of honor or recognition are acted on without debate and without requiring members to read the resolution. Such resolutions are mostly symbolic acts that are designed to promote goodwill with voters. However, at times these simple symbolic acts can go terribly wrong. A Fort Worth doctor was twice honored by the Texas House of Representatives as the "doctor of the day." It was then reported, to the embarrassment of the House and the legislators who introduced him to the House, that the doctor was a registered sex offender who had been convicted of having a sexual relationship with a 17-year-old female patient.[25]

Nonlegislative Powers

Nonlegislative powers include the power to serve constituents, electoral powers, investigative powers, directive and supervisory powers, and judicial powers. The functions of these powers fall outside the scope of passing bills and resolutions; however, the passage of legislation may be necessary to exercise these powers.

Legislators have the power to get things done for or in the name of **constituents**. Efforts on behalf of constituents may involve legislative activity, such as introducing a bill or voting on a resolution. Often, however, working on behalf of constituents involves nonlegislative activity, such as arranging an appointment for a constituent with a government agency that regulates some aspect of the constituent's life,

general bill a bill that applies to all people and/or property in the state

resolution an expression of opinion on an issue by a legislative body

concurrent resolution a resolution of interest to both chambers of the legislature and which must pass both the House and Senate and generally be signed by the governor

joint resolution a resolution, commonly a proposed amendment to the Texas Constitution or ratification of an amendment to the U.S. Constitution, that must pass both the House and Senate but which does not require the governor's signature

simple resolution a resolution that concerns only the Texas House or Senate, such as the adoption of a rule or the appointment of an employee, and which does not require the governor's signature

constituent a person living in the district from which an official is elected

electoral power the legislature's mandated role in counting returns in the elections for governor and lieutenant governor

investigative power the power, exercised by the House, the Senate, or both chambers jointly, to investigate problems facing the state

directive and supervisory power the legislature's power over the executive branch; for example, the legislature determines the size of appropriations for state agencies

judicial power the power of the House to impeach and of the Senate to convict members of the executive and judicial branches of state government

impeachment according to the Texas Constitution, the formal charge by the House of Representatives that leads to a trial in the Senate and possibly to the removal of a state official

writing a letter of recommendation for a constituent, or giving a speech to a civic group in the legislator's district.

Electoral powers of the legislature consist of formally counting returns in the elections for governor and lieutenant governor. This is accomplished during a joint session of the legislature when it is organized for the regular session.

Investigative powers can be exercised by the House of Representatives, by the Senate, or jointly by both bodies. The legislature can undertake to investigate problems facing the state, the integrity of a state agency, or almost anything else it wishes. A special investigative committee is established by a simple resolution creating the committee, establishing the jurisdiction of the committee, and explaining the need for the investigation. If the special committee is formed in the House, the Speaker appoints the members of the committee. The lieutenant governor appoints members for special committees in the Senate. The Speaker and the lieutenant governor share appointments if it is a joint investigation.

Directive and supervisory powers enable the legislature to have considerable control over the executive branch of government. The legislature determines the size of the appropriation each agency has to spend for the next two years. The amount of money an agency has determines how well it can carry out its goals and objectives. A review of each agency of state government takes place every 12 years.

Judicial powers include the ability of the House to impeach members of the executive and judicial branches of state government. On **impeachment**, a trial takes place in the Senate. A majority vote of the House is required to bring charges, and a two-thirds vote of senators attending is necessary to convict an individual of the impeachment charges. Unlike the U.S. Constitution, the Texas Constitution does not explicitly define what constitutes an impeachable offense. This will be determined by the House and Senate in the impeachment process itself.[26]

Each body can compel attendance at regular and special sessions. More than once, Texas Rangers have handcuffed absent members and brought them to the legislature. On rare occasions, a chamber will punish nonmembers who disrupt proceedings by imprisoning them for up to 48 hours. The House and Senate judge the qualifications of members and can expel a member for cause.

● How a Bill Becomes a Law in Texas

Trace the process through which law is made in Texas

Anyone can write a bill, but only members of the legislature can introduce a bill. Bills may be written by members of the executive branch, by lobbyists, by constituents, or by local governmental entities. Legislators may also write bills, often with the help of a legislative staff expert in drafting legislation. There are, of course, innumerable reasons for drafting and introducing a bill.

Revenue bills must start in the House of Representatives. Other bills can start in either the House or Senate. Figure 7.1 shows the flow of a bill from the time it is introduced in the Texas House of Representatives to final passage and submission to the governor. A bill introduced in the Senate would follow the same procedure in reverse. Examining this figure suggests that the process of how a bill becomes law is long, detailed, and cumbersome. However, when the process is distilled to its basic parts, there are only six steps in how a bill becomes law. For a bill that starts in the House these steps are (1) **introduction**, (2) **referral**, (3) **consideration by standing committee**, and (4) **floor action**. Steps (1) through (4) are repeated in the Senate. Step (5) is action by a **conference committee** and approval by both houses, and finally, (6) is **action by the governor**.

Introduction in the House

A legislator introduces a bill by placing copies of the bill with the clerk of the House. In the Senate, the secretary of the Senate receives the bill. The clerk or secretary numbers the bill and enrolls it by recording its number, title, caption, and sponsor in a ledger. Similar information is entered into a computer.

Rules of the legislature require that the bill be read on three separate occasions. After enrollment, the bill is read for the first time by its number, title, and caption.

Referral

After undergoing first reading, the bill is assigned to a standing committee by the Speaker. In the Senate, the lieutenant governor assigns it to a committee. Since committees in the Texas legislature have overlapping jurisdictions, the Speaker and lieutenant governor can assign a bill to a friendly committee or an unfriendly one. The committee to which a bill is assigned can determine whether the bill survives or dies in committee.

Committee Action

Every bill introduced in the Texas legislature is assigned to a **standing committee**, and the vast majority of bills die in committee. The chair of the committee kills most by pigeonholing. **Pigeonholing** means that the committee chair sets the bill aside and never brings it before the committee.

Standing committees are considered the "workhorses" of the legislature (see Table 7.1). If the bill does not die, it most likely is amended. Few bills leave the committee in the same form as they arrived. Parts of several bills can also be combined to form a single bill. Changes are made to make the bill more acceptable to the entire legislature or to meet the political desires of the leadership or members of the committee. Hearings can take place to allow experts and the public to educate committee members on the good and bad points of the bill. In the Senate, all bills reported by the committee must have a public hearing.

Floor Action

In the House, bills referred by a standing committee go next to the Calendars Committee, which, after consulting the Speaker, schedules bills for debate. The Speaker determines the length of debate in the House. Customarily, each member is allowed 10 minutes of debate. Early in the session when the agenda is not crowded, debate may last longer. Later in the session when there is a crush of legislative business, debate will be more limited. Some bills will be voted on without debate; however, important or controversial bills are usually allocated adequate time.

introduction the first step in the legislative process, during which a member of the legislature gets an idea for a bill and files a copy of it with the clerk of the House or secretary of the Senate

referral the second step in the legislative process, during which a bill is assigned to the appropriate standing committee by the Speaker (for House bills) or the lieutenant governor (for Senate bills)

consideration by standing committee the third step in the legislative process, during which a bill is killed, amended, or heard by a standing committee

floor action the fourth step in the legislative process, during which a bill referred by a standing committee is scheduled for floor debate by the Calendars Committee

conference committee a joint committee created to work out a compromise on House and Senate versions of a piece of legislation

action by the governor the final step in the legislative process, during which the governor signs, vetoes, or refuses to sign a bill

standing committee a permanent committee with the power to propose and write legislation that covers a particular subject, such as finance or agriculture

pigeonholing a step in the legislative process during which a bill is killed by the chair of the standing committee to which it was referred, as a result of his or her setting the bill aside and not bringing it before the committee

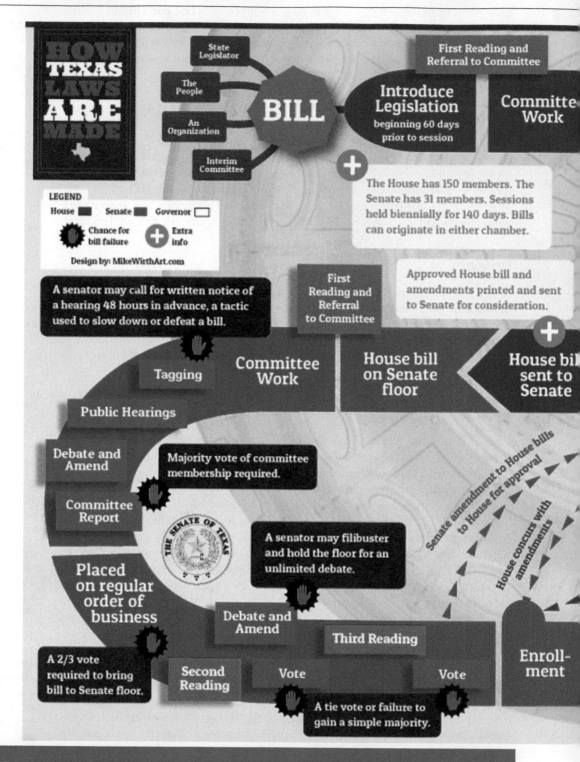

FIGURE 7.1

How a Bill Becomes a Law in Texas

Passing legislation in Texas is a complicated process. There are many points along the way where a bill can die.

SOURCE: This graphic was created for the February 2013 Issue of *Texas Co-op Power* magazine, a publication of Texas Electric Cooperatives, www. TexasCoopPower.com.

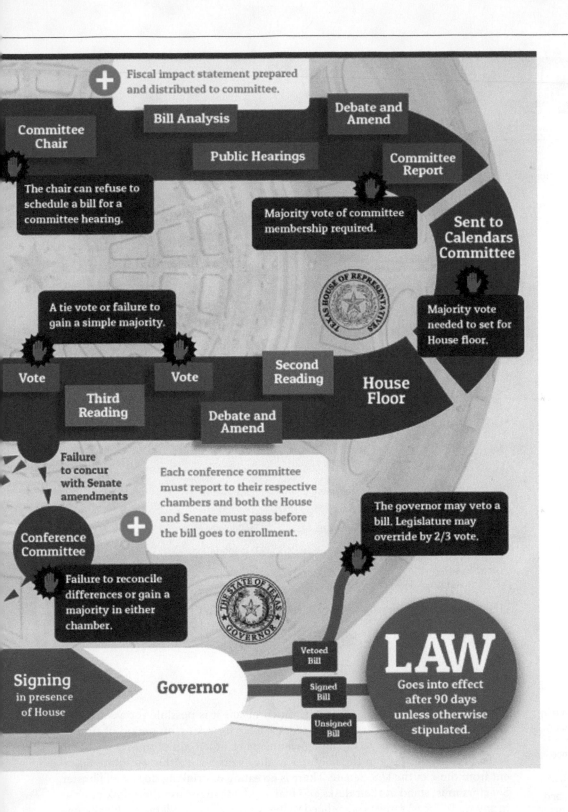

Fiscal impact statement prepared and distributed to committee.

Bill Analysis

Debate and Amend

Committee Chair

Public Hearings

Committee Report

The chair can refuse to schedule a bill for a committee hearing.

Majority vote of committee membership required.

Sent to Calendars Committee

Majority vote needed to set for House floor.

A tie vote or failure to gain a simple majority.

Second Reading

Vote

Vote

House Floor

Third Reading

Debate and Amend

Failure to concur with Senate amendments

Each conference committee must report to their respective chambers and both the House and Senate must pass before the bill goes to enrollment.

The governor may veto a bill. Legislature may override by 2/3 vote.

Conference Committee

Failure to reconcile differences or gain a majority in either chamber.

TEXAS HOUSE OF REPRESENTATIVES

THE STATE OF TEXAS GOVERNOR

Signing in presence of House

Governor

Vetoed Bill

Signed Bill

Unsigned Bill

LAW

Goes into effect after 90 days unless otherwise stipulated.

TABLE 7.1

Standing Committees of the Texas Senate and House (83rd Legislature), 2013–14

SENATE STANDING COMMITTEES

Administration	Finance	Natural Resources
Agriculture, Rural Affairs & Homeland Security	Government Organization	Nominations
Business & Commerce	Health & Human Services	Open Government
Criminal Justice	Higher Education	State Affairs
Economic Development	Intergovernmental Relations	Transportation
Education	Jurisprudence	Veterans Affairs & Military Installations

HOUSE STANDING COMMITTEES

Agriculture & Livestock	General Investigating & Ethics	Natural Resources
Appropriations	Government Efficiency and Reform	Pensions
Business & Industry	Higher Education	Public Education
Calendars	Homeland Security & Public Safety	Public Health
Corrections	House Administration	Redistricting
County Affairs	Human Services	Rules & Resolutions
Criminal Jurisprudence	Insurance	Special Purpose Districts
Culture, Recreation & Tourism	International Trade & Intergovernmental Affairs	State Affairs
Defense & Veterans' Affairs	Investments & Financial Services	Technology
Economic & Small Business Development	Judiciary & Civil Jurisprudence	Transportation
Elections	Land & Resource Management	Urban Affairs
Energy Resources	Licensing & Administrative Procedures	Ways & Means
Environmental Regulation	Local & Consent Calendars	

filibuster a tactic used by members of the Senate to prevent action on legislation they oppose by continuously holding the floor and speaking until the majority backs down. Once given the floor, senators have unlimited time to speak as long as they follow Senate rules, and it requires a vote of three-fifths of the Senate to end a filibuster

Debate in the Senate is unlimited, which means it is possible for a senator to **filibuster**. A filibuster occurs when a senator talks for a lengthy period of time in an effort to kill a bill or to obtain amendments or other compromises. There are certain rules that apply to the filibuster in the Texas Senate that are quite different from those in the U.S. Senate. There is no eating or drinking during a filibuster. Senators must stand at their desks and may not lean, sit, or use their desk or chair in any way. Remarks must be confined to the issue under consideration. Finally, one must speak in an audible voice.

In the past 72 years, there have been more than 100 filibusters. The longest filibuster was in 1977 by Senator Bill Meier, who spoke for 43 hours. Given the time constraints under which the Texas legislature operates, even the threat of a filibuster may be sufficient to kill or force changes in a bill.

Another tactic used in both the House and the Senate to prevent or delay passage of a bill is called "chubbing." Here, one or more members debate bills at length to slow down the legislative process. Like the filibuster, this is a particularly effective tactic as the legislative session draws to a close.

Sponsors of a bill are expected to gather sufficient votes to pass the bill. In fact, before the Calendars Committee schedules the bill for floor debate, sponsors often assure the committee that they have enough votes to pass the bill.

The Texas Senate has a rule that bills generally shall be considered according to the "regular order of business." This means that bills and resolutions are considered on second reading and listed in the order in which the committee report was received by the secretary of the Senate. Bills and resolutions are considered on the third reading in the order in which they were passed on the second reading. In order to conduct business, especially when dealing with legislation that is controversial, this "regular order" blocks consideration of legislation because it can be considered only if the Senate suspends this rule requiring consideration in order. A two-thirds vote is required to suspend the rules. Thus, for all practical purposes, legislation in the Senate must have two-thirds support to pass rather than a simple majority. In the 2011 legislative session, the highly partisan issue of requiring an identification document to vote was excluded from the two-thirds rule, which made it possible for Senate Republicans to pass the legislation.

Conference Committee

Bills must pass the House and Senate in exactly the same form. If the bill is different in any way, it is sent to a conference committee. Conference committees have 10 members: 5 members from the House appointed by the Speaker, and 5 members from the Senate appointed by the lieutenant governor.

Senate rules require that 2 members of the standing committee that considered the bill must be appointed. Unless specifically instructed, the conference committee cannot change parts of the bill that are the same. Changes are made and compromises reached only on parts of the bill that differ.

Once a compromise is reached, the report of the conference committee goes to the House and Senate. It can be debated in each chamber, but the report cannot be changed. It must be either accepted or rejected as is. If either chamber fails to approve the report of the conference committee, the bill is dead. Although it is possible for the conference committee to try a second time to reach a compromise, it is unusual for conference committees to do so.

If the report is accepted in both chambers of the legislature, a final copy of the bill is prepared. The Speaker of the House, the clerk of the House, the president of the Senate (lieutenant governor), and the secretary of the Senate sign the bill. Signatures of the Speaker and lieutenant governor are required by Article 3, Section 38 of the Texas Constitution. The next stop is the governor's desk.

Before a law is passed in Texas, it is voted on by the two chambers of the legislature— the House and the Senate. Here, state senators Dan Patrick (left) and Robert Nichols cast votes on a 2013 transportation bill. Raising one finger means "yes" and raising two fingers means "no."

The Governor

veto according to the Texas Constitution, the governor's power to turn down legislation; can be overridden by a two-thirds vote of both the House and Senate

post-adjournment veto a veto of a bill that occurs after the legislature adjourns, thus preventing the legislature from overriding it

line-item veto the power of the executive to veto specific provisions (lines) of an appropriations bill passed by the legislature

Former governor Rick Perry speaks to the Texas legislature. The governor can influence legislation through the veto or the line-item veto. The threat of a veto can be powerful, as legislators often try to take the governor's preferences into account and avoid a veto. Governor Perry set a record for the number of vetoes in one year: 82 in 2001.

It is the governor's responsibility to sign or **veto** legislation. During the first 130 days of a regular session, the governor has 10 days from the time a bill arrives on his or her desk to sign or veto the legislation. If the governor neither signs nor vetoes the bill in the 10 days, it becomes law without the governor's signature. In the last 10 days of a session, the governor has 20 days from the time the bill arrives on his or her desk to sign or veto the legislation. Again, if the governor does neither, it becomes law without the governor's signature. Unlike the U.S. president, who may sometimes kill a bill without signing it through what is called a "pocket veto," the Texas governor does not have this power.

The governor's veto can be overridden by a two-thirds vote of both the House and Senate. Anytime the governor vetoes a bill, he or she attaches a message explaining why it was vetoed. It is then returned to the chamber that originated the bill. If the presiding officer elects to allow a vote to override the veto, a vote is scheduled. Only two vetoes have been overridden in more than 70 years.

Many bills arrive on the governor's desk in the last few days of a session. Almost all important or controversial bills reach the governor in the waning moments of a session. If the governor wants to veto a bill that comes to him or her from day 131 to day 140, the governor simply waits until the legislature adjourns to exercise the veto. The governor's veto cannot be overridden because the legislature has adjourned. Vetoing legislation after legislative adjournment is called a **post-adjournment veto**, or a strong veto, since the legislature has no opportunity to overturn the veto. The post-adjournment veto provides the governor with an excellent bargaining tool, since the governor can threaten a veto unless changes are made in a bill.

The governor also has a **line-item veto** that allows him or her to sign a bill and draw lines through specific items, deleting them from the bill. Except for the items that the governor has deleted, the bill becomes law. In Texas, the line-item veto applies only to the state's omnibus appropriations bill. Governor Perry used the line-item veto in 2009 to reduce the state budget by $97.2 million in general revenue and $288.9 million from all funding sources.[27] In 2013, Governor Perry exercised his line-item veto on several appropriations such as a $100,000 appropriation for the William P. Hobby Jr. School of Public Affairs at the University of Houston and a $1,500,000 appropriation for the Department of Mexican-American Studies at the University of Texas at Austin. Table 7.2 provides the total number of vetoes by Texas governors since 1991.

Other Ways in Which the Governor Influences Legislation

Message power is the governor's ability to communicate with the legislature. Early in each session, the governor delivers a State of the State message that is similar to the president's State of the Union message. In this address, the governor puts forth a vision for Texas and what legislation will accomplish that vision. If the governor chooses to submit an executive budget, a letter stating why this budget should be adopted accompanies it.

Periodically, the governor will visit with legislators to gain their vote on a bill. A personal visit can be persuasive, but increasingly, it is members of the governor's paid staff who are sent on these

TABLE 7.2

Total Number of Vetoes by Texas Governors, 1991–2013

YEAR	GOVERNOR	TOTAL VETOES
2013	Perry	26
2011	Perry	25
2009	Perry	38
2007	Perry	54
2005	Perry	19
2003	Perry	48
2001	Perry	82*
1999	Bush	33
1997	Bush	37
1995	Bush	25
1993	Richards	26
1991	Richards	36

*Record number of vetoes by a Texas governor.
SOURCES: Texas Legislature, "Legislative Statistics," July 10, 2013; Legislative Reference Library of Texas, "Bill Statistics."

legislative visits. Like lobbyists for corporations and interest groups, the governor's representatives use their skills to encourage passage of bills the governor favors and to kill bills the governor opposes. However, there is a problem with this practice. The Texas Constitution forbids use of tax dollars to influence the legislature, and the governor's staff is, of course, paid through tax dollars. The governor's representatives avoid this ban by claiming they are simply providing needed information to the legislators. One should not underestimate the informal power that the governor has to influence legislation.

● Additional Players in the Legislative Process

Describe the roles of other state officials and interested parties in shaping legislation

In addition to the legislators and the governor, there are others involved in the lawmaking process during both regular and special sessions. One official, the comptroller of public accounts, has direct involvement in the legislative process, while other players are involved indirectly.

The media can influence the legislative agenda through the stories that they cover. Accordingly, legislators try to attract media attention that will support their positions. Here, Speaker Joe Straus speaks at a press conference.

The Comptroller of Public Accounts

The comptroller of public accounts issues revenue estimates to inform the legislature of the amount of money it can spend in the next two years. Texas's operating budgets must balance. The Texas Constitution forbids borrowing money to conduct the daily operations of government. The estimate provided by the comptroller sets the limit on state spending. If the legislature wants to spend more than the comptroller estimates, it must enhance revenue—that is, increase taxes and fees.

The comptroller's estimates can be political in nature. The comptroller can provide a low revenue estimate and tell the legislature that the estimate will remain low until it passes bills the comptroller wants. On passage of those bills, the comptroller can revise the estimate to increase the spending limit and allow the legislature to complete its business.

The Media

Media can determine issues of importance by the selection of stories they cover. If the media cover more stories on crime, crime and criminal justice issues will move toward the top of the legislature's agenda. A media focus on corporate fraud, rising homeowners' insurance rates, alcohol-related traffic deaths, or poor performance by Texas public school students will increase legislative attention to these issues.

The media inform the public about the issues the legislature is considering and about the job the legislature is doing during the session. Media coverage of the legislature provides the public with needed information on what is going on in Austin. Stories portraying the legislature as modern, efficient, and hardworking provide the public with a positive image of the legislature, whereas stories about legislators sleeping at their desks or killing legislation on technicalities provide a negative image.

The Courts

Federal and state courts influence the legislative agenda. In recent years, the courts' scrutiny has included the prison system, the state's treatment of patients in state mental hospitals, the funding of public education, and equality of funding for colleges and universities in South Texas. The ability to rule acts of the legislature and actions of state agencies unconstitutional gives courts significant power over issues the legislature addresses. To a remarkable degree, state and federal courts have issued decisions that have forced the Texas legislature to act in areas that the legislature would have preferred to avoid—largely because action required a significant expenditure of money. For example, many recent legislative actions directed toward criminal justice and public education are responses to court rulings.

Lobbyists

During a regular session, roughly 1,800 individuals register as lobbyists and attempt to influence the legislature. A lobbyist's responsibility is to convince legislators to support the interest the lobbyist represents. Lobbyists want legislators' votes on bills. At the least, they desire access to legislators.

The Public

Individuals can influence legislators. Legislators are evaluated at each election. If the people believe their elected officials are representing them well, legislators are re-elected. A legislator who fails to live up to expectations might not be re-elected.

The public can serve as lobbyists. Letters, email, or telephone calls urging representatives or senators to vote a certain way constitute a lobbying effort. Members of the public can also write legislation, but must convince at least one legislator to sponsor it and introduce it for consideration by the legislature.

The public and interest groups may also influence the legislature. During a special session in which the legislature dealt with tax reduction, these Houston-area realtors and others demonstrated in favor of property tax relief.

● Power and Partisanship in the Legislature

Analyze how party leadership and partisanship affect power in the legislature

Among the most powerful political figures in Texas are the leaders of the House and Senate. They play a key role in structuring the committees of the legislature, setting the state's political agenda, and passing or defeating bills.

Leadership

The **Speaker** of the Texas House of Representatives and the lieutenant governor are two of the most powerful political figures in the state. Republican representative Joe Straus of San Antonio is currently the Speaker of the House. In November 2014, Dan Patrick was elected **lieutenant governor** and will lead the Senate. The Texas House and Senate endow both officials with considerable control over the legislative process. It is fair to say that either of them can usually kill legislation they oppose, and often they have the power to pass legislation they support.

Members of the House elect the Speaker at the beginning of the regular session. Additionally, at the start of each regular session, members of the House adopt rules that give the Speaker institutional powers sufficient to control the work of the House. Speakers usually are the dominant figures in the Texas House and wield vast power.

One of the most interesting developments in modern times in the Texas legislature was the turmoil surrounding the 2002–08 speakership of Republican Tom Craddick. Craddick first challenged the Democratic Speaker "Pete" Laney and ultimately displaced Laney when the Republicans gained control of the House. Craddick worked to redistrict Texas congressional districts so as to increase substantially the number of Republicans in the Texas congressional delegation. As Speaker, Craddick was accused of micromanaging the House, of taking discretion away from committee chairs, and of insisting that members support his views on key issues even when contrary to the desires of their constituents. Republicans also

Speaker the chief presiding officer of the House of Representatives; the Speaker is the most important party and House leader, and can influence the legislative agenda, the fate of individual pieces of legislation, and members' positions within the House

lieutenant governor a statewide elected official who is the presiding officer of the Senate; the lieutenant governor is one of the most important officials in state government and has significant control over legislation in the state Senate

The Speaker of the House is one of the most powerful people in Texas politics. In 2009, Tom Craddick (left) was replaced as Speaker by Joe Straus (right).

lost seats in the Texas House between 2004 and 2006—a loss blamed in part on Craddick's leadership. The result was an open rebellion against Craddick, who was able to retain his position in the 2007 session only by resorting to a questionable parliamentary maneuver: he refused to recognize a motion to "vacate the chair," which would have caused a vote on his fate as Speaker.[28] It is doubtful that such dissension over a Speaker had occurred since Ira Evans was removed as Speaker in 1871.[29] In 2009, Craddick lost his speakership to Joe Straus, a Republican from San Antonio, who was elected Speaker by a coalition of anti-Craddick Republicans and Democrats. Straus faced opposition in every legislative session from conservatives who saw him as too moderate and as too favorable to Democrats, but Straus was able to retain his position as Speaker.

The lieutenant governor is elected statewide to a four-year term. His or her major responsibility is to serve as president of the Senate and to preside over the Senate. Unlike the Speaker, the lieutenant governor is not a member of the Senate, simply its presiding officer, who may vote only to break a tie.

At the start of each regular session, senators adopt rules that the Senate will follow for the next two years. Article 22 of the Senate Rules requires a vote of two-thirds of the members present to suspend any rule of the Senate unless the rules specify a different majority. The rules also establish the office of president pro tempore of the Senate, who is a member elected by the Senate to perform the duties of lieutenant governor in the absence or disability of the lieutenant governor. These rules also give the lieutenant governor enormous control of the work of the Senate. Among these powers granted to the lieutenant governor under the rules are

- the power to decide all questions of order on the Senate floor (subject to appeal from members)

- the power to recognize members on the floor
- the power to break a tie on a particular vote
- the power to refer bills to committees
- the power to appoint members to standing committees, subcommittees, special committees, and conference committees

Centralizing Power: Sources of the Leadership's Power

The operation of the Texas legislature is significantly different from that of the U.S. Congress. In the U.S. Congress, the leader of the president's party in the House and the Senate is the president's spokesperson in that house of Congress. Additionally, the level of partisanship is high. Committee appointments are made in such a way that the majority party controls every committee, and chairs of those committees are always members of the majority party. Each house of Congress has majority party leadership and minority party leadership. Such divisions do not exist in the Texas legislature. No member of the Texas legislature is formally known as the governor's spokesperson.

Because the governor has no leader in the legislature, the membership does not owe allegiance to party leaders in the legislature, and leadership and power have become centralized in the Speaker and lieutenant governor. The Speaker and lieutenant governor can make appointments with limited regard for party affiliation, thus ensuring that members will be loyal to them rather than to the party. The Texas legislature is not organized along party lines the way the U.S. Congress is. Committee assignments and committee chairmanship appointments cross party lines so that in the Texas House, for example, where the majority party is now Republican, a Democrat may chair an important committee and successfully sponsor important legislation. The bipartisan appointment of committee chairs, however, may be a declining tradition.

Certain factors may undermine the state legislature's tradition of nonpartisan politics. Most of the powers of the Speaker and of the lieutenant governor are granted by the rules that each chamber's membership votes on at the beginning of the legislative session. The powers of the Speaker and of the lieutenant governor could potentially be greatly reduced if the members of the legislature so chose. One could, for example, imagine a future Republican Senate that would reduce the powers of the lieutenant governor over the Texas Senate if a Democrat were elected lieutenant governor. Of course, one of the first rules that would have to change is the requirement of a two-thirds vote for a bill in the Senate to be voted on out of order. Indeed, the two-thirds rule in the state Senate encourages some degree of bipartisanship, because Republicans do not quite control two-thirds of the Senate and so need Democratic votes.

The two-thirds rule came under attack in the 2009 special session of the legislature and it continued to be criticized in 2011 and 2013, mainly because the requirement of such a large supermajority makes it difficult to pass bills that arouse partisan tensions. Democrats support the rule because with it, Democratic support is needed to pass any bill in the Senate. Some Republicans wanted to abandon the rule in order to allow their majority to pass legislation without Democratic support. Others want to weaken the requirement of a supermajority by having a three-fifths rule instead of a two-thirds rule. Still other Republicans are inclined to support the long precedent of a two-thirds requirement. At least for the time

for critical analysis

Who are the most important leaders in the Texas legislature? What are their powers? How does the battle over redistricting illustrate the party politics within the legislature?

being, the two-thirds rule remains. However, it can be easily changed at some point, as the rules of the Senate are passed by majority vote.[30]

The Republican congressional redistricting bill in 2003 led to abandonment of the two-thirds rule for that bill so that redistricting that was beneficial to Republicans could be passed. That bill would have been impossible to pass without changes in the rules that allowed passage by majority vote. In the 2009 special session of the legislature, the Texas Senate was able to pass a highly partisan bill that required voters to show identification. This occured solely because the two-thirds rule is not used in special sessions.[31] It was not until 2011, when the Texas Senate again abandoned the two-thirds rule, that the voter identification bill became law. The restrictions on abortion that were passed in the second special session of the legislature were passed because it was a special session in which the two-thirds rule in the Texas Senate is not used.

As the Texas Senate becomes more partisan, it seems likely that there will be increased use of special rule changes to allow for the passage of controversial bills, a lowering of the two-thirds supermajority requirement for passing a bill, or a complete abandonment of the two-thirds rule in favor of majority rule.

The structure of the Texas legislature and the lack of formal lines of gubernatorial authority in the legislature are very important in centralizing power in the hands of the Speaker and the lieutenant governor. However, these officials have other important sources of power as well. One of those powers—a power especially important in the Texas House—is the power of **recognition**. The Senate rule allowing unlimited debate decreases the lieutenant governor's power in this area. In the House, the Speaker controls legislative debate, including who speaks and how long debate will last. On occasion, the Speaker ignores or skips a member seeking recognition to speak. This is a signal to other members of the House that this individual has fallen from the Speaker's good graces. That ability to pick and choose among those desiring to speak on the House floor, however, allows the Speaker to structure the debate and to affect the outcome of legislation.

As mentioned earlier, the Senate has a rule that for votes to be taken on bills, the bills must be taken in order, or for a bill to be taken out of order, there must be a two-thirds vote. Given the vast powers of the lieutenant governor, on issues that are important to him, he can usually control the votes of at least one-third of the membership. Thus, if a bill is opposed by the lieutenant governor, he or she can frequently prevent it from being taken out of order for consideration.

One of the most important sources of power for the Speaker and the lieutenant governor is the committee assignment power. The committees on which legislators serve are important to individual members and to the presiding officer. For members, assignments to powerful committees increase their prestige in the legislature. Committee assignment also affects how well constituents are represented. Assigning members to standing committees is one of the most important duties of the lieutenant governor and the Speaker.

The Speaker and the lieutenant governor have major roles in appointing the membership of committees, appointing chairs of committees, and setting the legislative agenda. Party affiliation and seniority are of only moderate importance in committee assignments. The most important factor in committee assignments is the members' relationships with the presiding officer. In order to maintain control over the legislature, the Speaker and lieutenant governor use their committee assignment powers to appoint members who are loyal to them and who support their legislative agendas. When chairs and vice chairs of important committees are appointed, usually only the most loyal friends and allies of the Speaker and

recognition the power to control floor debate by recognizing who can speak before the House and Senate

TABLE 7.3

Democrats/Republicans Appointed Committee Chairs during the Speakership of Joe Straus

	2009 Dem.	2009 Rep.	2011 Dem.	2011 Rep.	2013 Dem.	2013 Rep.
Standing committees	14	20	11	25	13	24
Select committees	1	5	0	3	1	3
Joint committee	—	—	0	1	0	1
Percentage of Democrats in House	49%		33%		37%	

NOTE: We are indebted to Sachi Dave for her work on this table.
SOURCE: Legislative Reference Library and Texas Tribune.

lieutenant governor are chosen. In 2013, 6 of the 18 standing committee chairs in the Senate were Democrats. Thirteen of the 38 standing committee chairs in the House were Democrats. Speaker Straus has stated that one issue important to him when appointing chairs and members of committees is to ensure that the committees "reflect the geographic and demographic diversity of Texas."[32] At the beginning of every legislative session, members of the House are asked to submit a list of committees on which they would like to serve. The Speaker then assigns committee memberships with consideration given to the House members' seniority, their leadership skills, and their interest in particular issues. Chairs and other leadership positions are often given to more senior members with leadership skills and interests in the areas over which their committee has jurisdiction.[33] Straus, a Republican, was initially elected Speaker with Democratic votes in a successful challenge to the then Republican Speaker Tom Craddick's leadership. As Table 7.3 shows, since being elected Speaker, Straus has named Democrats to the chairs of standing committees of the House roughly in proportion to their numbers in the House. Of course some committees are more important than others, but in a purely partisan legislative body, no Democrats would be appointed chair of a committee by a Republican Speaker.

During his tenure as Republican lieutenant governor, David Dewhurst was in a far different position from Speaker Straus. Straus was elected from a House district like all other members and then was elected to the Speaker's office by the membership of the House; Dewhurst was elected to preside over the Texas Senate in a statewide election. Nevertheless, like Straus, as Tables 7.3 and 7.4 show, Dewhurst maintained a practice of appointing Democrats to chair standing committees roughly in proportion to the number of Democrats in the Texas Senate.

Not only do the Speaker and the lieutenant governor have vast committee assignment powers, but committees in the Texas legislature also have overlapping jurisdiction. Although each bill must be assigned to a committee, it can be assigned to more than one committee. Since the Speaker and the lieutenant governor assign bills to committees in their respective chambers, they use the bill assignment power to influence the fate of the bill. They can, for example, assign bills they oppose to committees they believe hostile to the bill and those they support to committees they believe will favor the bill.

TABLE 7.4

Democrats/Republicans Appointed as Committee Chairs during David Dewhurst's Tenure as Lieutenant Governor

	2003		2005		2007		2009		2011		2013*	
	Dem.	Rep.	Dem.	Rep.	Dem.	Rep.	Dem.	Rep.	Dem.	Rep.	Dem.	Rep
Standing committees	6	9	5	10	11	20	6	12	7	12	7	11
Select committees	1	1	0	3	5	10	0	2	1	1	0	2
Percentage of Democrats in Senate	39%		39%		35%		39%		39%		37%	

NOTE: We are indebted to Sachi Dave for her work on this table.

*As a result of the death of a Democratic senator, there were only 30 senators during this session.

SOURCE: Legislative Reference Library and Texas Tribune.

Since bills must pass the House and Senate in exactly the same form, the Speaker and the lieutenant governor can exercise still another important influence on policy through their power to appoint conference committees. As we have seen, if any differences exist in a bill passed by both the House and the Senate, the bill goes to a conference committee that works out the differences in the House and Senate versions. By appointing the conference committee members, the Speaker and lieutenant governor can affect the language and even the fate of the bill.

Partisan Voting in the Texas Legislature

Between 1876 and 1980, the Democratic Party controlled both houses of the Texas legislature. The last 20 years of the twentieth century saw the growth of the Republican Party in both the House and the Senate, culminating in the Republican seizure of power in both houses in 2004. As conservative Republicans replaced conservative Democrats, particularly from rural and suburban districts, more traditional ideological splits appeared along partisan lines. When Representative Straus initially gained the speakership in 2011 with liberal Democratic and moderate Republican votes, some observers felt that the partisan rhetoric might be muted. As more conservative Republicans were elected in his second term and moderate Republicans were either retired or defeated, partisan ideological fault lines appeared with a vengeance. Ideological differences between Democrats and Republicans now play a major role in legislative politics. Political journalist Paul Burka has written, "Over the past 40 years, the ideological differences between the members of the Democratic and Republican delegations in the Texas House of Representatives have increased dramatically."

It is possible to show that increasing gulf between Democrats and Republicans by using roll-call votes cast by members of the Texas House over time. If one categorizes the votes along the dimension of liberalism-conservatism such that a score of −1.00 is extreme liberal and a score of 1.00 is extreme conservative, the average score of Republicans in the Texas House in 1973 was 0.44. The average score for Democrats was 0.01. In 2009 the average Republican score was 0.67, a significant

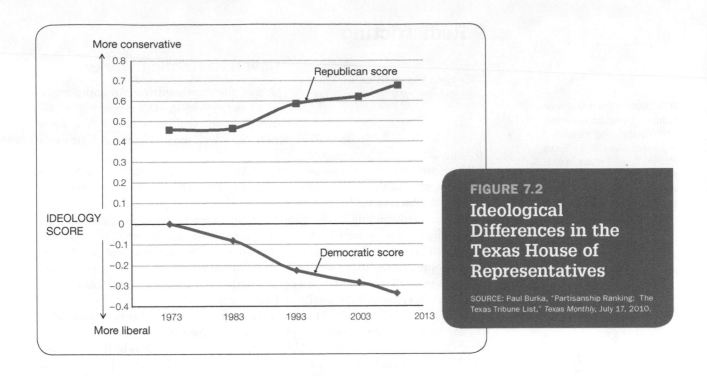

FIGURE 7.2

Ideological Differences in the Texas House of Representatives

SOURCE: Paul Burka, "Partisanship Ranking: The Texas Tribune List," *Texas Monthly*, July 17, 2010.

movement toward increased conservatism. In contrast, the Democrats in the Texas House became increasingly liberal. In 2009 the Democratic score was −0.34 (see Figure 7.2).

Another indication of the partisan gap between Democrats and Republicans in the Texas House is that in 1973, 37 percent of Democratic House members were more conservative than the most liberal Republican in the House. In 1995 only 4 percent of Democratic House members were more conservative than the most liberal Republican. Since 1999 there has been no Democrat in the House who has been more conservative than the most liberal Republican.[34] In a recent study of the 2013 Texas House, political scientist Mark Jones found that every Democrat was more liberal than any Republican.[35] Jones found the same pattern in the Texas Senate.[36] The ideological gap that exists between Democrats and Republicans makes it harder for common ground across party lines to be identified and to produce a policy consensus. In that sense, the Texas legislature is becoming more like the U.S. Congress. As sociologist Paul Starr has pointed out regarding the U.S. Congress,

> Traditionally, political parties in the United States have been broad coalitions that overlapped each other ideologically. The Republicans had included liberals . . . and the Democrats had included conservatives. But by 2009, the ideological alignment of the parties was nearly complete. . . . The growing ideological divergence between the two parties made cooperation between them more difficult.[37]

That pattern Starr saw in the U.S. Congress is now seen in the Texas legislature. With it we are seeing the end of the cooperation between Democrats and Republicans in Austin.

Redistricting

Explain the politics of redistricting

redistricting the process of redrawing election districts and redistributing legislative representatives in the Texas House, Texas Senate, and U.S. House; this usually happens every 10 years to reflect shifts in population or in response to legal challenges in existing districts

single-member district a district in which one official is elected rather than multiple officials

one-person, one-vote principle the principle that all districts should have roughly equal populations

How Redistricting Works

One of the most controversial and partisan issues is **redistricting**—the redrawing of district lines for the Texas House, the Texas Senate, and the U.S. House of Representatives, which must be done at least every 10 years, after the federal census.

There are 150 Texas House districts and 31 Texas Senate districts. One senator or one member of the House represents each district. This is called representation by **single-member districts**.

Although redistricting can be more frequent, at least after each census, the legislature draws new boundaries for each Texas House and Senate district. Newly drawn districts for the Texas House and Senate must contain an almost equal number of people in order to ensure equal representation. That requirement guarantees that each person's vote counts the same whether the vote is cast in Houston, Big Lake, El Paso, Presidio, Brownsville, or Commerce.

For much of the first half of the twentieth century, Texas and other states failed to draw new boundaries, and even after U.S. Supreme Court decisions, Texas did not do so willingly. Not until the U.S. Supreme Court's decisions in *Baker v. Carr* (1962) and *Reynolds v. Sims* (1964), compelling the legislature to draw new districts, were boundaries drawn that represented the population fairly.[38] These and subsequent decisions meant that Texas had to draw legislative districts of roughly equal populations—a concept known as the **one-person, one-vote principle**.

Congressional redistricting is also a responsibility of the legislature. Once the U.S. Congress apportions itself, the Texas legislature divides Texas into the appropriate number of congressional districts. According to the 1964 Supreme Court case *Wesberry v. Sanders*, each state's U.S. House districts must be equal in population.[39] Depending on how the districts are drawn, the representation of the two political parties in the U.S. House of Representatives can be significantly changed. Indeed, reapportionment can so change the division of the parties that control of the U.S. House of Representatives can be affected. Thus, maneuvering over redistricting is highly partisan.

In 2006 the U.S. Supreme Court upheld most of the new boundaries drawn in the Republicans' controversial redistricting but found that some of the redrawn districts failed to protect minority voting rights. Here, Governor Perry displays the new redistricting map. The new map drawn by Republicans after the 2010 census again went to federal courts.

If the legislature fails to redistrict at the first regular session after the census, the task falls to the Legislative Redistricting Board (LRB). The LRB has five ex officio members: the lieutenant governor, the Speaker of the House, the attorney general, the commissioner of the General Land Office, and the comptroller of public accounts.

When the legislature adjourns without redistricting, the LRB convenes. The LRB must meet within 90 days of legislative adjournment and complete its responsibilities within another 60 days. Even here, the influence of the Speaker and the lieutenant governor is clearly visible.

Texas redistricting plans must comply with the federal Voting Rights Act, although the U.S. Supreme Court has recently weakened that law. A federal court can temporarily redraw district lines if a redistricting violates this law by disadvantaging minority voters.

Partisan differences in the state legislature resulted in the failure to pass a redistricting plan in 2001 during its regular session, transferring the responsibility to the Republican-dominated LRB. On a split vote, the board developed redistricting plans that appeared to favor the Republican Party. The board's decision, in turn, was appealed to the federal courts. A three-judge panel, composed of two Democrats and one Republican, approved the lines drawn for the state senate, noting that the U.S. Justice Department had determined that the plan did not violate the Voting Rights Act. However, the court modified the board's plan for the House, arguing that the Department of Justice had rejected the plan because it was seen as diluting Hispanic voting strength in three areas of the state. The court felt that its role in the entire redistricting process was constrained. In their decision, the judges commented that "federal courts have a limited role in considering challenges to pre-cleared, legislatively adopted redistricting plans."[40]

The final plan approved by the court appeared to be a great victory for the Republican Party. Twenty-seven incumbent Democrats found themselves placed in districts with other Democratic incumbents. Four Democrats who chaired key committees announced that they would not seek re-election. Many observers felt that redistricting would make the Republicans the majority party in the House and would maintain their majority status in the Senate. And many doubted that the Speaker of the House, Democrat Pete Laney, would be able to mobilize the votes needed for re-election to the speakership in the next session. After the 2002 elections, these observers were proven correct.[41]

Power and Partisanship in the Redistricting Battle

Republican control of the Texas House and Senate in 2002 heralded more than simply a shift in party control of the legislature. With Republican control came a significant decline in the harmonious, bipartisan spirit that had largely governed the Texas legislature. The Republican leadership, especially House Speaker Tom Craddick, chose to govern in a more partisan fashion. Additionally, a number of Democrats in the House who saw their power slipping away chose a rebellious course. They worked to make Craddick's speakership a difficult one, obstructing Republican legislative efforts as much as possible.

This new partisan tension in the Texas legislature rose to a fever pitch in 2003 when Republicans, with the support of the Republican majority leader Tom DeLay, sought to alter the Texas congressional districts for partisan advantage. The Republican goal was to increase Republican representation in the Texas congressional delegation and, in so doing, help ensure a continuing Republican majority in the

Although the Texas legislature is not as susceptible to partisan squabbling as the U.S. Congress, flare-ups between the Democrats and Republicans do occur. For example, in this photo, Texas House Democrats celebrate their return to Texas in May 2003, after spending four days in Ardmore, Oklahoma, to kill a GOP-produced congressional redistricting plan.

U.S. House of Representatives. The Republican effort was unconventional in that it occurred in midcycle—that is, it was the second redistricting after the 2000 census. As a rule, redistricting occurs only once after each decennial census, although there is no legal requirement that this be the case.

After the 2000 census, the Texas legislature could not agree on redistricting, and a federal court devised a plan. The 2000 congressional redistricting gave the Democrats an advantage. With control of the state legislature, however, Republicans argued that the existing redistricting plan was unsatisfactory because it reflected a Democratic majority that no longer existed. Republicans wanted a plan that more clearly reflected Republican voting in Texas.[42] In 2000, Democrats won 17 congressional seats and Republicans won 13, even though Republicans won 59 percent of votes in the state and Democrats received only 40 percent. In 2002, Democrats got only 41 percent of the statewide vote, but they won 17 seats to 15 for the Republicans. In fact, since 1996, Republicans had never received less than 55 percent of the statewide vote, and Democrats never won more than 44 percent, yet Republicans were a minority in the Texas congressional delegation. With the new redistricting plan in 2004, Republicans got 58 percent of the statewide vote and elected 21 members of Congress from Texas. Democrats got 41 percent of the statewide vote and elected 11 members of Congress from Texas.[43]

The Republican congressional redistricting plan was not enacted without political turmoil, however. At the end of 2003, 51 Democrats from the state legislature walked out and gathered in Ardmore, Oklahoma, where the Texas state police did not have jurisdiction to bring them back to the state capitol. The result was that a quorum could not be reached to pass the plan. The Democratic legislators did not return to Austin until redistricting was taken off the agenda. A special legislative session was called to deal with redistricting, but the bill did not pass. In a second special session dealing with redistricting, 11 of the 12 Democratic members of the Senate fled to Albuquerque in order to prevent a Senate vote. Finally, a third special session produced a plan that passed both houses of the legislature.[44]

Most notable about the 2004 redistricting was that seven incumbent congressional Democrats were targeted for defeat. A lawsuit that challenged the redistricting on the grounds that it diluted minority votes stressed that the Democrats had been elected with minority support. The lawsuit also pointed out that these seven Democrats had either been paired so that they had to run against another incumbent or had been given a more Republican district.[45] A case before the U.S. Supreme Court challenged the extremely partisan gerrymandering of the Texas redistricting, its reduction of the strength of minority voters, and its use of the now outdated 2000 census. The Court did find that there had been a reduction in the strength of minority voters. However, the extremely partisan gerrymander and the mid-decennial redistricting using the 2000 census were upheld. For the most part, Republicans were successful in reshaping the partisan composition of the Texas delegation to the U.S. House of Representatives. However, the 2006 election led to Democratic control of the U.S. House and to a Texas congressional delegation with vastly weakened power because of the loss of key Democrats in the redistricting.[46]

The 2010 census led to another round of redistricting for the Texas legislature and the U.S. House of Representatives. The overwhelmingly Republican legislature designed a redistricting plan strongly favorable to Republicans, but the plan ran afoul of a federal court which held that minority voting rights were violated. The court ordered a redistricting plan that was more favorable to Democrats. Redistricting has seemingly become a perpetual issue before the Texas legislature. In 2013 the Texas legislature again voted on redistricting for the Texas House, the Texas Senate, and Texas's U.S. congressional districts. The legislature basically accepted the districting done by the federal courts prior to the 2012 elections, although there are legal challenges to the Texas House and the congressional district lines on the grounds that insufficient recognition of minority interests was given in developing the 2012 districts.[47]

● Thinking Critically about the Texas Legislature

The Texas legislature has undergone great changes and continues to do so. Perhaps the most significant change has been the increasing partisanship. The Texas legislature is less partisan than the U.S. Congress, but the Texas party divide was especially notable under Speaker Tom Craddick, during the redistricting battles, and during the battles over a voter identification law in 2009 and 2011. Straus's bipartisan election as Speaker in 2009 was indicative of a desire to calm down some of the partisanship in the House that had risen during the Craddick years. Tea Party supporters such as newly elected lieutenant governor Patrick, however, may be moving the legislature back into a more partisan direction.

The two-thirds rule in the Texas Senate is under attack. That rule requires considerable consensus to pass legislation from that body. If the two-thirds rule is reduced to a three-fifths rule or even majority rule, there will be renewed partisanship and rancor in the Texas Senate.

The Texas legislature seems in some ways like an archaic institution. Unless there are special sessions, it meets once every two years and is a part-time body with very limited compensation for its members. The structure of the legislature, however, has survived since the 1876 Constitution, and there seems little likelihood that the structure will soon change.

Especially notable regarding the legislature is the vast power held by the Speaker and the lieutenant governor. The 1876 Constitution showed its distrust of a powerful governor, and the result is that in Texas the governor must share political influence with two other major powers in Texas government—the Speaker and the lieutenant governor, over whom the governor exerts no formal control. Still, the revolt against Speaker Craddick does remind us that it is perilous for the Speaker to try to exert so much power that he becomes subject to rebuke from a constituency whose views he ultimately must reflect—the views of a majority of the members of the Texas House.

studyguide

Structure of the Texas Legislature

> **Describe the bicameral organization of the legislature and the rules for membership (pp. 201–4)**

The Texas legislature is bicameral. The leader of the House is the Speaker, and the lieutenant governor presides over the Texas Senate. Although the typical member of the legislature is white and male, women and minorities have increased their representation in recent years.

Key Terms

bicameral (p. 201)

per diem (p. 203)

Practice Quiz

1. There are _____ members of the Texas Senate, and state senators serve a _____ -year term.
   a) 31/4
   b) 100/6
   c) 150/2
   d) 300/6
   e) 435/2

2. Texas House members differ from Texas Senate members because
   a) House members represent smaller districts and are subject to more frequent elections.
   b) House members represent people, and senators represent counties.
   c) House members are elected from single-member districts and senators from multimember districts.
   d) House members have term limits, and senators do not have term limits.
   e) House members must live in the state for 10 years before standing for election, and senators do not have a residency requirement.

Sessions of the Legislature

> **Explain when the legislature meets (pp. 204–6)**

The Texas legislature meets once every two years for 140 days and additionally as required in special sessions called by the governor. Special sessions must have a specific purpose, such as redistricting or school finance.

Key Terms

regular session (p. 204)

biennial (p. 204)

special session (p. 204)

Practice Quiz

3. The Texas legislature meets in regular session
   a) 90 days every year.
   b) 180 days every year.
   c) 140 days each odd-numbered year and 60 days each even-numbered year.
   d) 140 days each odd-numbered year.
   e) 180 days each even-numbered year.

4. The agenda for a special session of the Texas legislature is set by the
   a) lieutenant governor and the Speaker of the House.
   b) governor.
   c) Texas Supreme Court.
   d) chair of the joint committee on special sessions.
   e) agenda-setting committee.

Powers of the Legislature

Outline the legislative and nonlegislative powers of the legislature (pp. 206–10)

The Texas legislature passes bills and resolutions and supervises the state bureaucracy through the budgetary process and sunset legislation.

Key Terms

bill (p. 206)

local bill (p. 206)

special bill (p. 206)

general bill (p. 209)

resolution (p. 209)

concurrent resolution (p. 209)

joint resolution (p. 209)

simple resolution (p. 209)

constituent (p. 209)

electoral power (p. 210)

investigative power (p. 210)

directive and supervisory power (p. 210)

judicial power (p. 210)

impeachment (p. 210)

Practice Quiz

5. The Texas legislature does not pass this type of bill or resolution:
   a) local bill
   b) special bill
   c) joint resolution
   d) concurrent resolution
   e) holiday resolution

6. Texas legislators do not
   a) provide assistance to constituents.
   b) investigate wrongdoing by federal agencies.
   c) investigate wrongdoing in state agencies.
   d) pass bills and resolutions.
   e) count election returns for governor and lieutenant governor.

How a Bill Becomes a Law in Texas

Trace the process through which law is made in Texas (pp. 210–17)

The process of a how a bill becomes a law is similar to the federal level. A key difference is the governor's use of the line-item veto by which the governor can eliminate individual appropriations or line items in the state budget. Additionally, the lieutenant governor and the Speaker of the Texas House have exceptionally strong powers. The committee system plays a major role in shaping the legislative process.

Key Terms

introduction (p. 211)

referral (p. 211)

consideration by standing committee (p. 211)

floor action (p. 211)

conference committee (p. 211)

action by the governor (p. 211)

standing committee (p. 211)

pigeonholing (p. 211)

filibuster (p. 214)

veto (p. 216)

post-adjournment veto (p. 216)

line-item veto (p. 216)

Practice Quiz

7. If a bill fails to pass the Texas House and Texas Senate in exactly the same form, the bill
   a) dies.
   b) is returned to the standing committee in the House or Senate that originally considered the bill.
   c) is sent to a conference committee.
   d) is sent to the governor, who decides which version of the bill will be signed.
   e) becomes a law.

8. The _____ provides the governor with a powerful tool with which to bargain with the legislature.
   a) ability to introduce five bills in a regular session
   b) post-adjournment veto
   c) pocket veto
   d) message power
   e) initiative

Additional Players in the Legislative Process

Describe the roles of other state officials and interested parties in shaping legislation (pp. 217–19)

Other than the two leaders in the House and the Senate, committee chairs have enormous influence in crafting legislation in Texas. The comptroller plays an important role in legislation by issuing revenue estimates to inform the legislation about the money available for the legislature to spend.

Practice Quiz

9. Which state official, in large part, determines the total amount of money the legislature may appropriate?
   a) governor
   b) lieutenant governor
   c) treasurer
   d) comptroller of public accounts
   e) attorney general

Power and Partisanship in the Legislature

Analyze how party leadership and partisanship affect power in the legislature (pp. 219–25)

The Speaker of the House and the lieutenant governor are the most important actors in the legislature. Together they help to centralize power in the legislature, and they facilitate or prevent the passage of legislation. The legislature has become increasingly partisan.

Key Terms

Speaker (p. 219)

lieutenant governor (p. 219)

recognition (p. 222)

Practice Quiz

10. The two most powerful political figures in the Texas legislature are the
    a) governor and the lieutenant governor.
    b) governor and the attorney general.
    c) Speaker of the House and the governor.
    d) Speaker of the House and the lieutenant governor.
    e) chairs of the finance committee in each house.

11. The Speaker of the Texas House is chosen
    a) in a statewide election.
    b) in a party-line vote by members of the Texas House.
    c) by a majority of the members of the House whether Democrat or Republican.
    d) by seniority in the House.
    e) by lot.

12. The lieutenant governor is the presiding officer of
    a) the Texas Senate.
    b) the governor's cabinet.
    c) the Texas legislature.
    d) the Legislative Conference committees.
    e) the Treasury.

13. The chairs of the Texas House committees are
    a) of the same party as the Speaker.
    b) selected on the basis of seniority.
    c) chosen because of their experience.
    d) both Democrats and Republicans.
    e) independents.

14. The ability of the lieutenant governor and the Speaker of the House to control the final outcome of legislation comes from their power to
    a) appoint members of conference committees.
    b) refuse to approve the work of standing committees.
    c) exercise the legislative line-item veto.
    d) change up to three lines in any bill.
    e) control floor debate.

15. In recent years, the Texas legislature has
    a) become more partisan.
    b) become less partisan.
    c) become more experienced in lawmaking.
    d) been more inclined to let the governor make policy.
    e) been more respectful of county officials.

Redistricting

One of the most partisan activities of the legislature involves redrawing of district lines for the Texas House of Representatives and the Texas Senate. New districts must be drawn at least every 10 years to reflect changes in the population of the state. This process of redistricting provides the opportunities for the dominant political party to create districts for their partisan advantage. While there are some legal and constitutional restrictions on redistricting, generally as long as the districts reflect equal populations and racial or ethnic minorities are not disadvantaged legislators have great freedom in drawing district boundaries.

Key Terms

redistricting (p. 226)

single-member district (p. 226)

one-person, one-vote principle (p. 226)

Practice Quiz

16. An important issue for the legislature at least every 10 years is
    a) adopting a budget.
    b) deciding the order of succession to the office of governor.
    c) impeaching the lieutenant governor.
    d) redistricting.
    e) electing the president.

17. Legislative districts in Texas
    a) are created by a nonpartisan commission.
    b) are designed to benefit partisan interests.
    c) are voted on in a special election.
    d) are created in a cooperative effort between the two parties.
    e) are designed by the Center for Legislative Districts every 10 years.

Recommended Websites

Chron.com—*Houston Chronicle*
www.chron.com/new/politics

Speaker of the Texas House of Representatives
www.house.state.tx.us/speaker/welcome.htm

Texas Legislative Council
www.tlc.state.tx.us

Texas Legislature Online
www.capitol.state.tx.us

Texas Lieutenant Governor
www.senate.state.tx.us/75r/LtGov/Ltgov.htm

Window on State Government (Comptroller of Public Accounts) www.window.state.tx.us

Although the governor is the most visible leader in Texas politics, Texas governors have fewer powers than governors in other states. Greg Abbott, elected in 2014, succeeded one of the more powerful governors in Texas history, Rick Perry. Will Abbott use the power of the governor's office like Perry did?

The Texas Executive Branch

8

WHY THE EXECUTIVE BRANCH MATTERS The late lieutenant governor of Texas Bob Bullock said that he did not want to be governor because he claimed that all a Texas governor did was cut ribbons. Bullock was a remarkably powerful and effective lieutenant governor, and he gave weight to the view that real power in Texas was not in the governor's office, but in the lieutenant governor's office. As one reporter put it, "Before Perry, half the stories about the doings in the state Capitol were either about the inherent weakness of the governor's office or the ancient lore about how the lieutenant governor holds the state's most powerful office."[1] After all, in Texas the governor has no cabinet, and although the governor appoints people to the various boards and commissions that run state agencies, only a third of board members come up for appointment every two years, and they cannot easily be fired.

While on paper the governor's office may appear to be weak in terms of the formal powers granted by the constitution, particularly when compared to that in other states, Texas governors can come to possess considerable power. Brian McCall, a former legislator and author of a book on the Texas executive, claims that there were Texas governors who have been real powers in the state and did not just let the state be run by the lieutenant governor, or the legislature and its leadership, or other powerful elected officials such as the attorney general or the comptroller. In spite of McCall's research, the myth persists that Texas governors are mere figureheads.[2]

How will Governor Greg Abbott wield the power of the governorship? If Abbott needs a model of a highly powerful Texas governor, he need not look further than his predecessor, Rick Perry. Perry may be the modern proof of McCall's thesis that a Texas governor could be a powerful figure in state politics and that the office of the governor matters. Perry came to the governor's office with considerable political experience. He was elected as a Democrat to the Texas House of Representatives in 1984 and served three two-year terms. In 1989 he changed parties from the Democratic to the Republican Party, and in 1990 he was elected commissioner of agriculture. In 1998 he was elected lieutenant governor, and in December 2000, upon the resignation of Governor George W. Bush to become president of the United States, Rick Perry assumed the governorship. He was elected to full terms as governor in 2002, 2006, and 2010. Perry was the longest-serving governor in Texas history. His many years in office gave him time to learn how to use the powers given to him under the Texas Constitution and to maximize his influence throughout Texas government.

Perry had failures—the most well known was his failed presidential campaign in 2012. He also failed in his effort to create the Trans-Texas Corridor, which was to be a $175 billion network of roads, railways, data lines, and pipelines stretching from Mexico to Oklahoma. He called for mandatory vaccination of young girls against the human papillomavirus that can lead to cervical cancer and faced a backlash from religious conservatives who believed the vaccine would encourage promiscuity. Supporting the effort to put Texas in the forefront of cancer research, the Cancer Prevention and Research Institute of Texas, run by his appointees, came under investigation for possible misapplication of millions of dollars in grant money.

Perry, however, exerted control over state government in a way that no other Texas governor has. He was the only governor who appointed every member of the boards and commissions that run Texas government. He used the veto power to punish political opponents in the legislature, and he successfully advocated a social agenda that greatly limited access to abortion. He successfully pushed a pro-business agenda that includes tort reform, low taxes, and business-friendly regulation. He claimed that he caused Texas to weather the Great Recession better than other states and to be a job-creating state.[3] Greg Abbott, Perry's successor, may or may not be able to mobilize the limited constitutional power of the office of the governor as effectively as Perry did. But one thing is clear: Perry's record of failures and achievements as chief executive of the state shows that governors do matter.

chaptergoals

- Describe the powers of the Texas governor and the limits of the governor's power (pp. 236–54)
- Identify the other elected officials who make up the plural executive (pp. 254–63)
- Explain the roles played by boards, commissions, and regulatory agencies (pp. 263–69)

● The Governor

Describe the powers of the Texas governor and the limits of the governor's power

At the national level, the president represents and is responsible to the people as a whole. The president is the spokesperson for the government and the people in national and international affairs. Throughout the twentieth century, various presidents parlayed the powers granted them by the U.S. Constitution into what some commentators call the "imperial presidency." The governorship in Texas is not an analogous imperial one. Compared with the president, the governor of Texas is weak. Executive power in Texas is divided among a number of separately elected officials, all of whom are elected by and responsible to the people as a whole. This plural executive has important implications for democratic life in the Lone Star State.

Although the governor of Texas is the most visible state official, Texas's governor has far less formal power than most governors. In 1983 a study of the appointment, budget, removal, and organizational powers of governors ranked Texas's governor 49th in the nation, ahead only of the governor of South Carolina.[4] In 1990 a study of gubernatorial authority in the nation also ranked Texas's governor 49th, ahead of the governor of Rhode Island.[5]

To understand the restrictions placed on the office, it is necessary to remember that the Constitution of 1876 was a reaction to the Reconstruction government that existed in Texas following the Civil War. During Reconstruction, the governor was very powerful, and many regarded state government as oppressive and corrupt. When a new constitution was drafted at the end of the Reconstruction era, Texans did their best to ensure that no state official had extensive power. The Texas Constitution of 1876 placed strict limits on the governor's ability to control the people appointed to office and almost eliminated the possibility that appointees to office could be removed. Power was further fragmented among other officeholders, who are collectively known as the plural executive. Each of these officeholders is elected and has separate and distinct responsibilities. Members of major state boards, such as the Railroad Commission and the State Board of Education, are also elected and are largely outside the control of the governor.

Governors who are successful in pushing their programs through the legislature and seeing them implemented by the bureaucracy are able to use the limited formal powers available to them, exercise their personal political power, exploit the prestige of the office of governor, and marshal various special interests to their cause. One political writer likens the office of governor to a bronco that breaks most who attempt to ride it and will be successfully handled by very few. In short, successful governors are successful politicians.[6]

Former state representative Brian McCall has written about the modern Texas governorship, arguing that Texas governors can be quite powerful in spite of the weaknesses of the office that are inherent in the Texas Constitution. He points out that governors who develop a collaborative relationship with the legislature can realize many of their goals if they are flexible, have a vision, are willing to motivate others to achieve that vision, and will work cooperatively with the legislature. McCall notes that when former governor Allan Shivers was asked about the weak governorship of Texas, he responded, "I never thought it was weak. I had all the power I needed."[7] McCall, in stressing that capable individuals could parlay the Texas governorship into a position of power, noted that only the governor has the power to call special sessions of the legislature. The governor can pardon criminals and can permit fugitives to be extradited to other states. The governor appoints people to state governing boards and commissions. Only the governor can declare martial law. Only the governor can veto acts or specific appropriations passed by the legislature. Through the traditional State of the State address delivered at the beginning of every legislative session, the governor can outline state priorities and convince others of the importance of those priorities. The governor can be a major persuasive force in mobilizing interest groups, editorial boards of newspapers, and opinion leaders to support his or her agenda.

Not all governors have the personal skills to turn the office into a powerful one. Some have been unable to develop a collaborative relationship with the legislature.

for critical analysis

What can governors do to overcome the inherent weakness of the position? What are the implications for democratic government of a weak chief executive?

George W. Bush was governor of Texas from 1995 until he was elected president of the United States in 2000. Here, Bush is seen campaigning for re-election as governor in 1998. Like Rick Perry, Bush was able to achieve a number of his political goals as governor, despite the limited powers of the office.

Others have not had the interest or the ability to develop their own vision and political agenda. Still others have been unable to accomplish their goals because of economic downturns that have limited their resources. However, McCall argues that modern governors such as John Connally, Ann Richards, and George Bush have had the persuasive skills that have enabled them to achieve major political objectives in spite of the constitutional limitations on the powers of the office.[8]

Still, even many successful governors have not acted as if the job is a demanding one. George W. Bush, according to McCall, would typically arrive at the office by eight in the morning, leave for a run and a workout at 11:40 AM, return at 1:30 PM, and play video golf or computer solitaire until 3 PM.[9] Governor Perry was so detached from the operation of state government that he did not receive a full briefing on the raid on a polygamist cult that put 400 children in protective custody and involved a half-dozen state agencies and 1,000 state personnel until five days after the event. One review of Governor Perry's schedule during the first four months of the 2011 legislative session showed that he averaged only 21 hours per week on state business and took six three-day weekends.[10]

Qualifications

Only three formal constitutional qualifications are required to become governor of Texas. Article 4 of the Texas Constitution requires the governor to (1) be at least 30 years of age, (2) be a U.S. citizen, and (3) live in Texas five years immediately before election. Texas governors have tended to be male, white, conservative, either personally wealthy or with access to wealth, Protestant, and middle-aged, and they have had considerable prior political experience.

Women compose more than 50 percent of the population of the United States and Texas, but only two women—Miriam Ferguson (1925–27, 1933–35) and Ann Richards (1991–95)—have served as governor of Texas.

William Clements's victory over John Hill in the gubernatorial campaign of 1978 was the first time since Reconstruction that a Republican had won the office.

George W. Bush was the second Republican elected governor and the first individual elected for two consecutive four-year terms.

Access to money is important because running for governor is inordinately expensive. A campaign for the governorship can cost tens of millions of dollars, and few Texans have or can raise that kind of money. The 2010 gubernatorial campaign set a record, costing about $91 million when all primary and general election candidates are considered. Tony Sanchez, the Democratic nominee for governor in 2002, spent over $66 million in that campaign, a record for an individual candidate. About $60 million of those funds came from his family's fortune in a losing effort for the governor's mansion.

Sam Kinch, a former editor of *Texas Weekly*, suggests that prior political experience is an important consideration in selecting a governor. Kinch maintains that although experience may not mean that someone will be a better governor, it does mean he or she is more likely to know how to handle the pressures of the office.[11]

Election and Term of Office

Before 1974, Texas governors served two-year terms, with most being elected to a maximum of two consecutive two-year terms. As Table 8.1 shows, there have been exceptions, such as Coke Stevenson, Price Daniel, and John Connally, who each served for six years, or Allan Shivers, who served for eight years. In 1972, Texas voters adopted a constitutional amendment changing the governor's term to four years. In 1974, Dolph Briscoe was the first governor elected to a four-year term of office. Rick Perry served as governor from 2000 through 2014, the longest tenure for a Texas governor.

Gubernatorial elections are held in off-years (years in which a president is not elected) to minimize the effect of presidential elections on the selection of the Texas governor. The Texas legislature, controlled at the time by Democrats, designed the off-year system to eliminate the possibility that a popular Republican presidential candidate would bring votes to a Republican candidate for governor. Likewise, party leaders wanted to negate the chances of an unpopular Democratic presidential candidate costing a Democratic gubernatorial candidate votes in the general election. Unfortunately, because of this timing, voter turnout in gubernatorial contests is relatively low.

Campaigns

Campaigns for governor of Texas last at least 10 months. Candidates hit the campaign trail in January of an election year to win their party's primary election in March; then they continue campaigning until the November general election. Successful candidates spend thousands of hours and millions of dollars campaigning. The money goes to pay staff salaries and for travel, opinion polls, telephone banks, direct mailings, and advertisements in print and broadcast media. Texas is so large that statewide candidates must purchase print and electronic advertisements in 19 media markets to reach every corner of the state.

In the 2010 Republican primary, Kay Bailey Hutchison spent over $14 million in her losing battle against Rick Perry. Perry spent nearly $13 million in the primary. Overall, Perry spent about $39 million and Bill White spent about

Rick Perry's 14-year tenure as Texas's governor was the longest in the state's history. Here, Perry celebrates at the victory party for his successor, Greg Abbott.

TABLE 8.1

Governors of Texas and Their Terms of Office since 1874

Richard Coke	1874–76	Miriam Ferguson	1933–35
Richard B. Hubbard	1876–79	James V. Allred	1935–39
Oran M. Roberts	1879–83	W. Lee O'Daniel	1939–41
John Ireland	1883–87	Coke Stevenson	1941–47
Lawrence S. Ross	1887–91	Beauford H. Jester	1947–49
James S. Hogg	1891–95	Allan Shivers	1949–57
Charles A. Culberson	1895–99	Price Daniel	1957–63
Joseph D. Sayers	1899–1903	John Connally	1963–69
S. W. T. Lanham	1903–07	Preston Smith	1969–73
Thomas M. Campbell	1907–11	Dolph Briscoe	1973–79*
Oscar B. Colquitt	1911–15	William Clements	1979–83
James E. Ferguson	1915–17	Mark White	1983–87
William P. Hobby	1917–21	William Clements	1987–91
Pat M. Neff	1921–25	Ann Richards	1991–95
Miriam Ferguson	1925–27	George W. Bush	1995–2000**
Dan Moody	1927–31	Rick Perry	2000–2015
Ross Sterling	1931–33	Greg Abbott	2015–

*Term changed to four years with the 1974 general election.
**Resigned to become president of the United States.
SOURCE: Dallas Morning News, *Texas Almanac and State Industrial Guide 1998–99* (Dallas: A. H. Belo, 1999).

$26 million in their campaigns. That is $14.37 for every vote Perry received and $12.48 for every vote White received. High-priced campaigns illustrate that successful candidates need personal wealth or access to wealth. At the end of October 2014, Greg Abbott had spent $46.8 million and Wendy Davis had spent about $36 million. The 2014 governor's race will not involve record expenditures but will approach $90 million in total.

Removal of a Governor

In Texas, the only constitutional method of removing a governor from office is by **impeachment** and conviction. "To impeach" means to accuse or to indict, and impeachment is similar to a true bill (indictment) by a grand jury. The Texas Constitution notes that the governor may be impeached but does not give any grounds for impeachment. Possible justifications for impeachment are failure to perform the duties of governor, gross incompetence, and official misconduct.

Impeachment begins in the Texas House of Representatives. A majority vote of the Texas House is required to impeach or to bring charges. If the House votes for

Impeachment the formal charge by the House of Representatives that leads to a trial in the Senate and the possible removal of a state official

Comparing the Governor of Texas with the Governors of Other States

Years of Republican or Democratic Advantage in Control of Governorships, 1995–2014

● More Republican ● More Democratic ● Even split

Since 1994, Texas has elected only Republicans to the governor's office. Texas's neighboring states, Louisiana and Oklahoma, also are represented by Republican governors, but they haven't always been. This chart shows which party has controlled governorship most often in each state.

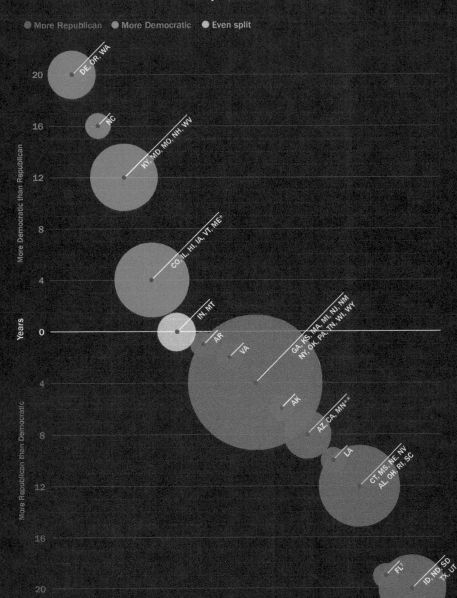

Years

More Democratic than Republican

20 — DE, OR, WA

16 — NC

12 — KY, MD, MO, NH, WV

8 — CO, IL, HI, IA, VT, ME*

4 —

0 — IN, MT / AR / VA / GA, KS, MA, MI, NJ, NM, NY, OK, PA, TN, WI, WY

4 —

8 — AK / AZ, CA, MN** / LA

12 — CT, MS, NE, NV / AL, OH, RI, SC

16 —

20 — FL† / ID, ND, SD, TX, UT

More Republican than Democratic

Geographic distribution

Republican	Democratic
● 16–20 years	● 16–20 years
● 11–15 years	● 11–15 years
● 6–10 years	● 1–10 years
● 1–5 years	
● Even split	

for critical analysis

1. Which region of the country had the most Democratic governors in the last 20 years? Why might this be?

2. Are there states whose governorship has been more Republican or more Democratic than you expected? Why?

* Independent Angus King was governor from 1995-2003.
** Independent Jesse Ventura was governor from 1999-2003.
† Charlie Christ left the Republican Party in April 2010 and held no party affiliation as governor until he left office in January 2011.

SOURCE: National Governor's Association, www.nga.org (accessed 5/23/14).

impeachment, the trial takes place in the Texas Senate. One or more members of the Texas House prosecute the case, and the chief justice of the Supreme Court of Texas presides over the impeachment proceedings. A two-thirds vote of the senators present and voting is necessary to convict. If convicted, the governor is removed from office and disqualified from holding any other state office.

Any member of the executive or judicial branch may be impeached. Once the House votes for impeachment charges against an official, that individual is suspended from office and cannot exercise any of his or her duties. Governor James Ferguson was the only Texas governor to be impeached and convicted.

Succession

The Texas Constitution provides for the lieutenant governor to become governor if the office becomes vacant through impeachment and conviction, death, resignation, or the governor's absence from the state.

In December 2000 a succession occurred when Governor George W. Bush became president-elect of the United States and resigned as governor. Lieutenant Governor Rick Perry immediately took the oath to become governor of Texas. The *Houston Chronicle* has characterized Rick Perry as "a politician who so looks the part that it's been joked that he was ordered straight from central casting."[12] Perry, a former state legislator from Haskell, was a conservative Democrat who switched to the Republican Party in 1990 and ran successfully for commissioner of agriculture. His six years in the Texas House, eight years as head of a major state agency, and two years as lieutenant governor and president of the Texas Senate provided him with a great deal more experience than any other governor of the last three decades.[13]

Should the governor leave the bounds of the state, the lieutenant governor becomes acting governor. If the governor is impeached, the lieutenant governor serves as acting governor before and during the trial. While serving as acting governor, the lieutenant governor earns the governor's daily salary, which is far better

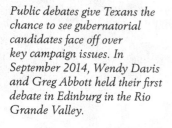

Public debates give Texans the chance to see gubernatorial candidates face off over key campaign issues. In September 2014, Wendy Davis and Greg Abbott held their first debate in Edinburg in the Rio Grande Valley.

Who Elected Governor Greg Abbott in 2014?

Greg Abbott's support was widespread across the state. He had decisive support in non-border rural counties. Although not winning in all, he polled well in most urban counties. He received surprising support from Latino voters, including those living along the border.

2014 Election Results, by County

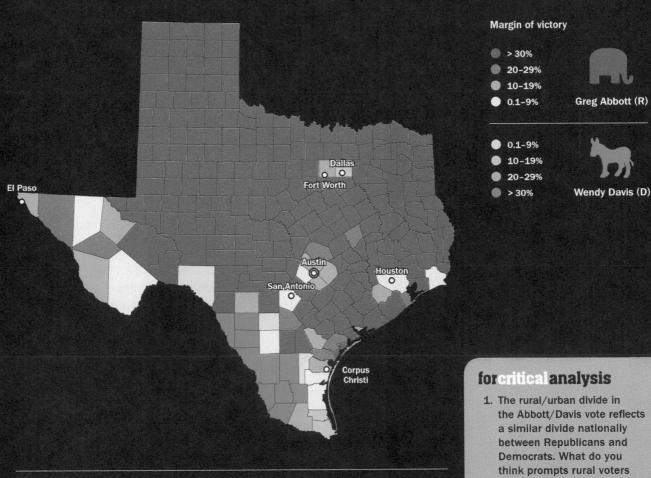

Margin of victory

- \> 30%
- 20–29%
- 10–19%
- 0.1–9%   **Greg Abbott (R)**

- 0.1–9%
- 10–19%
- 20–29%
- \> 30%   **Wendy Davis (D)**

El Paso

Dallas

Fort Worth

Austin

Houston

San Antonio

Corpus Christi

Vote Share   = Greg Abbott   = Wendy Davis

Urban and suburban		55% 45%
Rural and small town		77% 23%

SOURCE: CNN, www.cnn.com/election/2014/results/state/TX/governor (accessed 11/28/14).

for critical analysis

1. The rural/urban divide in the Abbott/Davis vote reflects a similar divide nationally between Republicans and Democrats. What do you think prompts rural voters to vote differently from urban voters?

2. Now that Abbott has won the election, do you think he will tend to favor urban or rural areas in his actions as governor? What policies might he support that will be more favorable to rural areas?

than the $20 earned as lieutenant governor. (However, a governor who is absent from the state still earns the same daily salary.)

When out of the state, the governor is legally entitled to Department of Public Safety protection. George W. Bush spent part of 1999 and 2000 campaigning to be president of the United States. During fiscal year 1999 it cost Texans an additional $2,365,000 to provide protection for the governor while he was on the presidential campaign trail.[14] In 1992, Governor Ann Richards was often out of the state campaigning for Bill Clinton, and the Texas taxpayers picked up the cost of her security detail. Governor Perry was also out of the state a great deal during his campaign for the 2012 Republican presidential nomination.

Constitutionally, the governor's office is weak. Former lieutenant governor Bill Hobby noted that about the only way he knew when he was acting governor was by a note his secretary left on his daily calendar.[15] In the first three months of 2000, Rick Perry, then lieutenant governor, served as acting governor more days than George W. Bush was in the state to serve as governor. Perry's press secretary commented that the added duties of being acting governor were not very noticeable and that those duties made little difference in Perry's schedule.[16] State government takes little notice of the governor's absences. Former Speaker of the Texas House Pete Laney has said that the governor's office is "holding court and cutting ribbons" and in 2000 commented on Governor Bush's out-of-state campaigning by saying, "I guess we've been doing pretty well without [a governor]."[17]

Legislation further defines succession from the governor to the lieutenant governor, to the president pro tempore of the Texas Senate, speaker of the house, attorney general, and the chief judges of the Texas courts of appeal in descending order.

Compensation

The governor's salary is set by the legislature. Texas pays its governor $150,000 annually. In addition to this salary, the governor receives use of an official mansion near the capitol grounds, although fire damage prevented its use as an official residence from June 2008 to the summer of 2011. Governors and the legislature often squabble about the amount of money needed for upkeep of the mansion and its grounds. The governor also receives use of a vehicle, a state-owned aircraft, and a personal staff.

Staff

The governor's staff consists of nearly 250 individuals. This includes a chief of staff, a deputy chief of staff, a general counsel, and a press secretary. A scheduler coordinates the governor's appointments, personal appearances, and work schedule. Governor Perry had 35 staff members who focus solely on policy issues.[18]

The staff keeps the governor informed about issues and problems facing the state, and it may suggest courses of action. In addition, during a four-year term, a governor makes several thousand appointments to various state posts. It is impossible for a governor to be acquainted personally with each appointee. Some of the staff find qualified individuals for each post and recommend them to the governor. Other staff members track legislation. They talk with legislators, especially key people such as committee chairpersons. The staff lets the governor know when his or her personal touch might make a difference in the outcome of legislation. For each bill that passes the legislature, a staff member prepares a summary of the bill with a recommendation that the governor sign or veto the bill.

Recent governors have used their staffs to be more accessible to the public. Governor Perry, like his immediate predecessors, wanted his staff to be no more than a phone call away from those who need assistance. In theory, individuals need only call a member of the governor's staff to receive help or find out where to go for help. The Office of the Governor has a Citizen's Assistance Hotline that handles thousands of calls each year from Texans needing assistance with their problems with state government.

Executive Powers of the Governor

Texas has a board or agency form of government. Over 400 state boards, commissions, and agencies make up the executive branch of Texas government. Agencies may be as obscure as the Texas Funeral Commission or the State Preservation Board or as well-known as the Public Utilities Commission of Texas or the Texas Department of Human Services, but each is important to its constituents. These multimember boards are the policy-making bodies for their agencies. They employ and oversee the people who operate the agencies on a daily basis.

Appointment Power The governor's power of **appointment** is the most significant executive power. It allows a degree of control over 410 governmental entities, including a wide range of agencies, commissions, and boards, as shown in Table 8.2. Governor Perry's long tenure has allowed him to appoint more than 4,000 people to these boards, and through these appointments he has been able to exert control throughout state government. One lobbyist described Perry's appointees as much different from Governor Bush's in that they "appear to be much more concerned with the larger political context and what sort of direction, either signaled or voiced, is coming from the governor's office."[19]

The power of appointment enables the governor to exercise the power of **patronage**. It permits the governor to reward supporters by appointing them to office. Most of the offices pay very little, but they do offer supporters some prestige. The governor can also use the appointment power to repay political favors by appointing friends and associates of legislators to office as well as to garner political IOUs from politicians. Most important, a governor can use the appointment power to influence agency policy. To a great degree, the effectiveness of a governor's use of the appointment power will determine the governor's success in office.

There are 410 entities to which the governor makes appointments. In some cases, the appointment power to these entities is shared with others. For example, the State Commission on Judicial Conduct regulates the ethics and behavior of Texas judges. It is governed by a 13-member commission. Six of the commission members, appointed by the Texas Supreme Court, are judges representing various court levels. Two members, appointed by the State Bar, are non-attorneys and non-judges. The governor appoints five citizen members. The Texas Ethics Commission promotes ethics rules for states officials and the commission is where campaign finance data are reported. The commission has eight members—four appointed by the governor, two appointed by the lieutenant governor, and two by the Speaker of the Texas House of Representatives. Some of the entities to which the governor makes appointments are advisory as opposed to policy-making. For example, the

appointment the power of the chief executive, whether the president of the United States or the governor of a state, to appoint persons to office

patronage the resources available to higher officials, usually opportunities to make political appointments to offices and to confer grants, licenses, or special favors to supporters

TABLE 8.2

The Governor's Appointment Power

The following are examples of some of the entities in Texas, in just four policy areas, where the governor has the power to appoint members. This power can provide the governor with significant power over policy in these areas.

WATER

Angelina and Neches River Authority, Upper, Lower Central Colorado River Authority, Brazos River Authority, Canadian River Compact Commissioner, Board of Pilot Commissioners for Galveston County Ports, Guadalupe-Blanco River Authority, Upper Guadalupe River Authority, Gulf of Mexico Fishery Management Council, Gulf States Marine Fisheries Commission, Lavaca-Navidad River Authority, Nueces River Authority, Red River Authority and Red River Compact, Sabine River Authority and Sabine River Compact, San Antonio River Authority, San Jacinto River Authority, Trinity River Authority, Sulphur River Basin Authority, Western States Water Council, Evergreen Underground Water Conservation District, and Drought Preparedness Council

HEALTH

Aging and Disability Services Council, Texas Council on Alzheimer's Disease and Related Disorders, Texas Council on Autism and Pervasive Developmental Disorders, Chronic Kidney Disease Task Force, Texas Council for Developmental Disabilities, Health Professions Council, Oversight Committee of the Cancer Prevention and Research Institute, Council on Cardiovascular Disease and Stroke, and Sickle Cell Disease Advisory Committee

LAW ENFORCEMENT

Automobile Burglary and Theft Prevention Authority, Border Security Council, Task Force to Reduce Child Abuse and Neglect, Crime Stoppers Council, Crime Victims' Institute Advisory Council, Texas Board of Criminal Justice, Homeland Security Council, Commission on Jail Standards, Juvenile Justice Advisory Board, Juvenile Probation Commission, and Commission on Law Enforcement Officer Standards and Education

PROFESSIONAL LICENSING

Texas Optometry Board, Board of Orthotics and Prosthetics, Board of Nursing, Board of Occupational Therapy Examiners, Board for the Licensure of Professional Medical Physicists, Medical Board, Board of Examiners of Marriage and Family Therapists, Board of Examiners in the Fitting and Dispensing of Hearing Instruments, Board of Podiatric Medical Examiners, Physician Assistant Board, Board of Plumbing Examiners, Board of Physical Therapy Examiners, Board of Pharmacy, Board of Veterinary Medical Examiners, Appraiser Licensing and Certification Board, Board of Architectural Examiners, Board of Chiropractic Examiners, Board of Dental Examiners, State Board of Examiners of Dietitians, and State Board for Educator Certification

governor appoints the three-member Firefighters' Star of Texas Award Advisory Committee, which considers firefighters killed or seriously injured in the line of duty for an award.

Some of these entities are both advisory and appointed by several different officers. For example, the Oil-Field Cleanup Fund Advisory Committee has 10 members. One member is appointed by the lieutenant governor, one by the presiding officer of the house committee with primary jurisdiction over energy resources, one by the lieutenant governor from the academic field of geology or economics, one by the Speaker of the Texas House of Representatives from the field of geology or economics, one by the governor, and one by the executive officer (or the officer's designee) of the Texas Oil and Gas Association, the Texas Independent Producers and Royalty Owners Association, the Panhandle Producers and Royalty Owners Association, the Permian Basin Producers Association, and the Alliance of Energy Producers. The committee meets with the Railroad Commission about oilfield cleanup issues and reports to the governor, the lieutenant governor, and the speaker about any problems in the administration of oilfield cleanup funds and about any recommendations for legislation dealing with oilfield cleanup. Oilfield cleanup is not a top priority for most Texans, but it is a vital issue for oil producers and royalty owners. Such commissions provide input to state government for specialized issues such as oilfield cleanup. There are a number of these rather obscure advisory committees where the governor has an appointive role. For example, there is the Parental Rights Advisory Panel, the Nursing Facility Administrators Advisory Committee, the Advisory Committee to the Texas Board of Criminal Justice on Offenders with Medical or Mental Impairments, the Texas Academy of Mathematics and Science Advisory Board, the Governor's Advisory Council on Physical Fitness, the Preservation Trust Fund Advisory Board, the Real Estate Research Advisory Committee, and numerous other such groups.

The governor also makes appointments to many commissions that have major policy impact. Examples include the governing boards of Texas public universities that have considerable influence over the governance and policies of universities. The governor appoints all members to the boards of regents. Additionally, the governor appoints all of the nine members to the Texas Higher Education Coordinating Board, which oversees all public postsecondary education in the state including determining when public colleges and universities start or continue offering degrees, or what core class requirements all students in state colleges or universities must take. Another major commission is the Parks and Wildlife Commission. Appointed by the governor, the commissioners run an agency responsible for the management and conservation of the state's natural resources, with particular responsibility to provide for hunting, fishing, and outdoor recreation for Texans. The governor appoints the three members of the Alcoholic Beverage Commission, which is responsible for the regulation of all aspects of alcoholic beverages within the state and which collects $200 million a year in taxes and fees on alcohol. Many of the bodies over which the governor has supervision through the appointment process deal with water (its conservation, use, control, and navigation), health and aging, law enforcement, and professional licensing.

To a great extent, Texas government is run through these many boards and commissions. These boards have three main purposes: (1) they provide the broad policy guidance and advice for the operation of Texas's executive branch; (2) they provide a place where interests can influence the executive branch—for example, the Timothy Cole Advisory Panel on Wrongful Convictions can provide information on ways to resolve some of the problems wrongfully convicted persons have in re-entering the free world after years in prison; (3) they can provide important patronage to the governor where political friends and supporters can be rewarded with positions of influence, honor, and sometimes income.

Appointment Controversies A governor, however, must exert some care in appointments. Failure to appoint responsible individuals can lead to serious political problems. In 2007 there was a scandal within the Texas Youth Commission, which has authority over institutionalized juveniles. It became clear that not only was there a widespread pattern of physical and sexual abuse of juveniles in the facilities, but authorities tried to cover up the abuse. As a result, Governor Perry's appointees had to resign from the commission, and it was necessary to reorganize the agency. When the Texas Forensic Science Commission decided to hear testimony from an arson expert who believed that Cameron Todd Willingham was convicted and executed on the basis of faulty evidence of arson in an arson-murder case, Governor Perry replaced the chairman of the commission and refused to reappoint other members of the commission. Perry was trying to avoid political embarrassment since he was in office when Willingham was executed and had denied him a reprieve even after a detailed arson report had been provided that said the evidence against Willingham was flimsy.[20]

A recent scandal involves the Cancer Prevention and Research Institute of Texas (CPRIT) and its 11-member oversight committee that is the entity's governing body. The governor, the lieutenant governor, and the speaker all appoint three members to serve staggered terms, and the attorney general and state comptroller are members of the committee. The CPRIT became involved in controversy when it approved an $11 million commercialization grant without proper review. A state audit then revealed $56 million in grants were approved without proper review and $6.8 million in advance payments were made to a statewide clinical trial network that had since filed for bankruptcy.[21] The idea behind CPRIT was a promising one. In 2007, Texas voters supported a constitutional amendment that established CPRIT and authorized the state to issue up to $3 billion in bonds to fund cancer research and prevention services in Texas. But mismanagement and scandal have hit the agency along with a criminal investigation. While members of the oversight committee have not been charged with a crime, they have not been good stewards of the agency and rather appear to be political cronies—members of the oversight committee have donated a combined $1.5 million to Governor Perry, Lieutenant Governor Dewhurst, and Speaker Straus.[22] The peer review system for cancer funding proposals has fallen apart. The eight-member scientific review council has resigned, as have many on the roster of reviewers of funding proposals. The reason: according to Nobel prize-winning biologist Phillip Sharp of MIT, who resigned as chair of the CPRIT scientific review council, "Clearly there has been pressure at the board level to do things differently" than through peer review of proposals. When such problems emerge in an agency, ultimately the officials making the appointments are accountable for the flaws of their appointees.[23]

One developing story that holds potential for embarrassing Governor Perry is the possible impeachment and criminal prosecution of University of Texas System Regent Wallace Hall. Hall, a Perry appointee, was engaged in a two-year quest to remove University of Texas president Bill Powers, who had opposed Perry and some regents over tuition rates and the roles of research and teaching. Hall used open records laws to request over 800,000 pages of material from the university. His actions potentially are a misuse of office, and he may have improperly handled sensitive information and failed to disclose key information about himself on his application to become a regent. The last impeachment in Texas was about 40 years ago involving the impeachment of Judge O. P. Carillo in 1975, so an impeachment is a rare event in the state. Additionally, criminal charges are possible with

The authority to appoint many state officials is an important executive power. In 2014, Rick Perry appointed Nandita Berry as Texas secretary of state.

or without impeachment. Perry was the appointing officer for Hall, although his departure from the governorship may protect him from the political consequences of making an appointment whose fate may be a rare removal from office and/or criminal punishment.[24]

The Senate and Gubernatorial Appointments The governor appoints people to office, but the Texas Senate must also confirm them. However, because the Senate may not meet for almost two years, the appointee takes office immediately and does not wait for Senate confirmation. An example of how the governor must consider the views of the Texas Senate in making appointments occurred with the appointment of Eleanor Kitzman as Texas insurance commissioner. Insurance commissioner is a particularly important office in Texas, since it is a single appointed office rather than a board or commission and the commissioner has regulatory authority over insurance companies that operate in Texas. Kitzman had great problems with the legislature. She was criticized for being too favorable to insurance companies. What seemed to sink her chances for approval by the Senate, however, was when Kitzman, who never blocked any large insurance premium hikes while she was commissioner, withheld insurance company profit data from the legislature. If it had not been clear before the data were withheld, it was certainly clear afterward that Kitzman would not be confirmed. Governor Perry did not even submit her name to the Senate Nominations Committee and the Senate did not vote on her nomination, which meant that she had to leave office at the end of the regular legislative session.[25]

An important limitation on the power of the governor to appoint persons to office is the informal requirement that the individual's state senator must approve the appointment. This is known as **senatorial courtesy** and applies regardless of the

senatorial courtesy the practice whereby the president, before formally nominating a person for a federal judgeship, seeks the indication that senators from the candidate's own state support the nomination; in Texas, the practice whereby the governor seeks the indication that the senator from the candidate's home supports the nomination

party affiliation of the governor, senator, or appointee. Usually, if the appointee's senator concurs in the appointment, the remainder of the Senate will agree. However, if the appointee's senator opposes the appointment, the remainder of the Senate will also oppose the appointment.

The process for removing an appointee is also complicated. A governor can remove his or her appointee who refuses to resign with the approval of two-thirds of the Texas Senate.[26] This complex procedure for the termination of members of boards and commissions, along with the practice of senatorial courtesy, can be a significant limitation on the governor's power to influence the policies of state agencies. Chairs of boards, however, serve at the pleasure of the governor and so can easily be removed if they do something that displeases the governor.

Budgetary Power Officially, the Texas governor is the state's chief budget officer. As such, governors submit an **executive budget** to the legislature. This budget suggests a plan for revenue and expenditure for Texas, but more important, it indicates the governor's priorities for the state in the next biennium.

In 1949 in an effort to gain more control over the state's budget, the legislature established the Legislative Budget Board (LBB), which is responsible for preparing a **legislative budget**. Thus, two budgets are prepared and submitted to the legislature: an executive budget by the governor and a legislative budget by the LBB. As a creation of the legislature, the LBB's budget proposal receives more consideration by the House and Senate than the governor's recommendations, and in recent years the governor's budget has fallen into disuse. Legend has it that the governor's budget has been used as a doorstop and a paperweight, and one diminutive legislator used two copies as a booster in his office chair. In 1989, Governor Clements recognized the futility of submitting an executive budget and simply endorsed the recommendations of the LBB. Ann Richards followed Clements's precedent, but Governor George Bush took a more active role in budget preparation and Governor Perry was very involved in dealing with the state's 2011 budgetary shortfall.

The governor has some control over the final appropriations bill through the use of the line-item veto; however, the governor must have the support of the legislative board to impound funds or transfer funds from one agency to another if circumstances change from the time the money was appropriated. There is one exception to the constraint on gubernatorial power to transfer funds. Under a 1993 law, the governor can declare an emergency and bypass the other legislative members of the LBB. In 2014, Governor Perry declared an emergency and shifted $38.7 million from a Department of Public Safety fund to pay for the National Guard to patrol the Texas-Mexico border. Overall, the budgetary process does not provide the governor acting alone with a highly effective means of controlling state agencies.

Military and Police Power The governor is commander in chief of the state's National Guard units when they are not under presidential orders. These units are headed by the adjutant general, who is appointed by the governor. The governor can declare martial law, which suspends most civil authority and imposes military rule over an area. Martial law can be declared in the event of a riot, flood, hurricane, tornado, or other disaster to protect lives and property. In Texas, law enforcement and police power are primarily a local responsibility, and the governor has

executive budget the state budget prepared and submitted by the governor to the legislature, which indicates the governor's spending priorities. The executive budget is overshadowed in terms of importance by the legislative budget

legislative budget the state budget that is prepared and submitted by the Legislative Budget Board (LBB) and that is fully considered by the House and Senate

for critical analysis

What are the governor's formal powers? How does the governor exercise these powers?

Deployment of the state's national guard in times of emergency is one aspect of the governor's military power. Here, Texas National Guard troops deliver relief supplies after Hurricane Ike in 2009.

few responsibilities in this area. The governor appoints, with Senate approval, the three-member Public Safety Commission that directs the work of the Department of Public Safety (DPS). The DPS is responsible for highway traffic enforcement (highway patrol), drivers' licensing, motor vehicle inspection, truck weighing stations, and the Texas Rangers. When circumstances warrant, the governor can assume command of the Rangers, an elite, highly trained force of about 150 officers with 63 support staff. If there is evidence of ongoing violence or corruption, the governor can use informal powers, the prestige of the governor's office, and appeals to the media to compel appropriate action from local law enforcement officials.

Legislative Powers of the Governor

As we saw earlier, the governor's legislative powers include message power, power of the veto, and the authority to call special sessions and set their agendas. If a governor uses these powers effectively, he or she can have considerable control over the state's legislative business, but they do not enhance his or her ability to control the executive branch of state government.

Message Power Any communication between the governor and the legislature is part of the message power. Early in each regular session, the governor delivers a State of the State message. In this speech to a joint session of the legislature, the governor explains his or her plan for the state in the coming two years. The governor may propose specific programs or simply set general goals for the state. The speech is covered by most news media, and it is often broadcast on public television and radio stations.

If the governor submits an executive budget, he or she may address the legislature on the important items in the proposed plan of spending and revenue. At the very least, the budget proposal is forwarded to the legislature with a letter briefly explaining the budget.

Lobbying by governors is part of the message power. Governors try to pass or defeat bills important to them. For example, early in 1991, Governor Ann Richards successfully lobbied for legislation that would expand higher educational opportunities in the Rio Grande Valley and that resulted in the creation of the University of Texas at Brownsville.

Although not exactly part of the governor's message power, personal connections with and the use of staff are effective ways for a governor to communicate with and influence the legislature.

Veto Power Governors of Texas can sign or **veto** legislation—but in most cases they sign legislation. Since becoming governor in 2000, Perry vetoed 301 bills.[27] Examples of bills vetoed by the governor

- a bill that would have provided state training for armed classroom teachers
- a bill aimed at preventing wage discrimination against women
- a bill that would have required Texas Railroad Commission members to resign before running for another state office
- a bill that would have made it easier for small towns to obtain the rights to run their water systems if their water rates were at least 50 percent higher than the rates in some nearby cities
- a bill that would have ordered a study of the state's curriculum standards and would have limited the number of benchmark exams school districts could administer locally
- a bill that would have reduced the power of university regents and made it more difficult for the regents to fire a university president[28]

When the governor vetoes a bill after the legislature adjourns, it is called a **post-adjournment** (or strong) **veto**. This veto is absolute, because the legislature that passed the vetoed bills no longer exists. As a result, if the governor decides to veto a bill, it stays vetoed.

Texas governors possess the **line-item veto**, which is the ability to veto individual parts of an appropriations bill. The governor signs the bill but strikes out particular lines in the bill. Items struck from the bill do not become law, but the remainder of the appropriations bill does.

In 2013, Governor Perry used the line-item veto to eliminate about $7.5 million in state funding for the prosecutors who investigate public corruption cases in the state capital. Perry claimed that the investigative unit had "lost the public confidence" as a result of the DWI conviction and unruly behavior while arrested of the Democratic district attorney of Travis County, Rosemary Lehmberg. The funding veto jeopardized the jobs of 35 employees and threatened about 400 cases being investigated. Critics of the veto claimed the veto was an effort to stop the continuing investigation into corruption in the Cancer Prevention and Research Institute that potentially could prove embarrassing to Governor Perry. The governor also vetoed a total of $29 million in spending items, many for higher education such as $2 million for the petroleum engineering program at Texas A&M International University, $1.5 million for the Department of Mexican-American Studies at UT–Austin, and smaller items at the University of North Texas, Prairie View A&M, and the University of Houston.[29]

This line-item veto allows Texas governors considerable control over appropriations to state agencies, and this power can be used by the governor to reduce state expenditures or to punish agencies or programs disfavored by the governor.[30] It is one important power of the governor that is greater than that of the president of the United States, who does not have the power to issue a line-item veto because the U.S. Supreme Court has held that such a power violates separation of powers in the U.S. Constitution.

Special Sessions Special sessions of the Texas legislature are called by the governor, last for no more than 30 days, and may consider only those items placed on the agenda by the governor. **Special sessions** are called to address critical problems as defined by the governor. The nature of special sessions allows the legislature to focus attention on specific issues.

From 1989 through 2013 the legislature met in 22 special sessions. These sessions considered the complicated and divisive issues of reform of workers' compensation laws, public school finance, reapportionment, and voter identification. The sessions ranged from 30 days to 2 days, with six of the sessions occurring in 1989–90 and five occurring from 2005 through 2011.[31] In 2013 three special sessions were called, two lasting 30 days and one lasting seven days. The issues involved redistricting, sentencing, transportation, and abortion regulation, which received the most attention.

Judicial Powers of the Governor

Texas elects each of its appellate and district court judges, but when vacancies occur because of the death, resignation, or retirement of the incumbent or as a result of creation of new courts, the governor is responsible for appointing individuals to fill these vacancies. The governor also fills vacancies (before an election) in the office of district attorney.

Once appointed to office, judges tend to remain in office. More than 95 percent of incumbents win re-election. Through this power to appoint judges, the governor has considerable influence over the Texas judicial system.

Clemency normally includes the power to issue pardons, grant paroles, and issue reprieves. The governor's power in this area is severely limited because of abuses of previous governors. Pardons can be granted only on the recommendation of the Board of Pardons and Paroles. Texas governors can neither grant nor deny paroles. Governors have the ability to grant each person condemned to death one 30-day reprieve. Additional reprieves and any other act of clemency must be recommended by the Board of Pardons and Paroles.

In December 2012, Governor Perry granted clemency to 14 persons after receiving a recommendation from the Texas Board of Pardons and Paroles. In one case, a 41-year-old man who had been convicted of public intoxication in 1988 and sentenced to pay a $215 fine was granted a full pardon. In another, a woman who had been convicted of debit card abuse in 1993 and sentenced to five years of deferred adjudication probation, a $1,500 fine, and $510 in restitution received a full pardon. In another case, a man had been convicted of assault in 1987 and theft in 1988. He had been sentenced to three months of deferred adjudication probation and a $100 fine for the assault and six months of deferred adjudication probation and a $100 fine for the theft. He received a full pardon. Interestingly, in none of these cases did the pardon release a person from imprisonment. Rather it cleared their record of a crime from years in the past.[32]

The Office and Its Occupants

People often expect governors to be able to do things they are not equipped to do. They are expected to be chief executives in more than name only despite being granted little in the way of formal power. Constitutionally and statutorily, the governor is ill-equipped to exert control over the Texas bureaucracy.

John Connally was regarded as a strong governor, whereas Dolph Briscoe was regarded as weak. In part, the difference was that Connally actively sought to lead.

As governor, he had a dynamic personality, whereas Briscoe was more retiring in his personal style and did not seek to have the impact Connally had. Allan Shivers acted as if the governor of Texas had the powers of a king and so he was considered an imperial governor. Preston Smith was described as one of the most ordinary people ever to serve as governor. Smith is seldom given credit for doing much as governor, yet he established the first actual planning organization in Texas government. Rick Perry has used his lengthy service and his appointment powers over state boards and commissions to exert unusually strong control over the operation of government.

In large part, the office of governor is what the person holding the position makes it. Whether the governor is viewed as strong or weak depends on how the governor conducts him- or herself in office, uses the position's formal power, and exercises political influence.

● The Plural Executive

Identify the other elected officials who make up the plural executive

plural executive an executive branch in which power is fragmented because the election of statewide officeholders is independent of the election of the governor

When Texans drafted a constitution in 1876, they chose to limit executive power and disperse it through several elected officials called the **plural executive**. Texans elect six of the seven people who make up the plural executive: the governor, lieutenant governor, attorney general, comptroller of public accounts, commissioner of the General Land Office, and commissioner of agriculture (see Table 8.3 and Table 8.4). The governor appoints the seventh person, the secretary of state. With the exception of the Commissioner of Agriculture whose office is created by statute, these offices are established by Article 3, Section 1, of the Texas Constitution. Except for the lieutenant governor, who receives the same salary as a legislator, salaries of members of the plural executive are set by the legislature.

TABLE 8.3

Elected Officials in Texas with Executive Responsibilities

SINGLE-ELECTED EXECUTIVES	MULTIELECTED EXECUTIVES
Governor	Railroad Commission (3 members)
Lieutenant governor	State Board of Education (15 members)
Attorney general	
Land commissioner	
Agriculture commissioner	
Comptroller	

TABLE 8.4

State Executive Officeholders, 2015

Governor	Greg Abbott (R)
Lieutenant governor	Dan Patrick (R)
Attorney general	Ken Paxton (R)
Comptroller of Public Accounts	Glenn Hegar (R)
Commissioner of the General Land Office	George P. Bush (R)
Commissioner of Agriculture	Sid Miller (R)
Railroad commissioners	Ryan Sitton (R)
	David Porter (R)
	Christi Craddick (R)
Secretary of State (appointed)	Carlos Cascos (R)

The Railroad Commission of Texas and the State Board of Education assume considerable executive authority in the state, although these offices are not formally part of the executive branch established under Article 4 of the Texas Constitution. Instead the Railroad Commission of Texas is created by the legislature under statutory law authority granted under Article 10, Section 2, of the Texas Constitution. The State Board of Education, in contrast, is created under Article 7, Section 8. This is important because the constitution allows the legislature to decide in both cases whether these offices will be appointed or elective, how large the commission or board will be, and how long terms of office will be.

If the legislature wanted to change the way that the Commissioner of Agriculture, the Railroad Commission, or the Board of Education is selected, all it would have to do is pass a new law. To change the other executive offices' term or authority would demand a constitutional amendment. The ultimate result of all these constitutional nuances is vast fragmentation of responsibility for public policy in the state.

Elections are partisan, and each member of the plural executive may choose to operate independently of the others. At times, members of the plural executive may be in competition with each other, often because of conflicting personal ambitions. That occurred when John Hill was attorney general and sought to take the governorship from Dolph Briscoe, and when Mark White was attorney general and sought the governorship from Bill Clements. Because of the difficulty of defeating incumbents, however, it is far more likely that members of the plural executive will wait for a vacancy in a more prestigious office before seeking that higher office. Champions of the plural executive believe that it limits the power of executive officials and makes these officers more accountable to the public. Opponents assert the plural executive is inefficient and does not promote good government. The governor is a member of the plural executive, but this multipart executive limits the governor's control of the executive branch because he or she has little authority over this group.

TABLE 8.5

Campaign Contributions in 2010 and the Plural Executive

OFFICE	LOSING CANDIDATE	CONTRIBUTIONS TO LOSER ($)	WINNING CANDIDATE	CONTRIBUTIONS TO WINNER ($)
Governor	B. White (D)	$26,291,535	R. Perry (R)	$39,328,540
Lieutenant governor	L. Chavez-Thompson (D)	958,040	D. Dewhurst (R)	9,240,480
Attorney general	B. Radnotsky (D)	1,135,031	G. Abbott (R)	5,828,370
Comptroller	(No Democratic candidate)	0	S. Combs (R)	2,744,001
Agriculture Commissioner	P. Gilbert (D)	336,363	T. Staples (R)	1,742,941
Land commissioner	H. Uribe (D)	102,487	J. Patterson (R)	864,688

SOURCE: National Institute on Money in State Politics.

One can get a sense of the importance of the various positions in the plural executive simply by looking at the campaign contributions received by winning candidates for these offices in the 2010 elections. Table 8.5 shows the contributions received by both the Democratic and the Republican nominees in 2010. Governor Rick Perry, the incumbent Republican, received over $39 million in contributions. In contrast, his Democratic opponent, Bill White, received much less. The incumbent Republican lieutenant governor David Dewhurst had over $9 million in contributions, compared with only about $958,000 in contributions for his opponent. The winning candidate for attorney general had nearly $6 million in contributions, the winning candidate for comptroller more than $2.7 million in contributions even though she had no Democratic opponent. The agriculture commissioner had more than $1.7 million, and the land commissioner had more than $864,000. Two things are especially notable about these figures. One is the enormous amounts of money that are contributed to candidates. The other is how lopsided the contributions are in favor of the Republican candidates. It is a sign of the strength of the Republican Party and the weakness of the Democratic Party in Texas elections that Republican candidates raise so much more money for their campaigns than do Democratic candidates.

Secretary of State

secretary of state state official, appointed by the governor, whose primary responsibility is administering elections

Strangely, given Texas's fragmentation of power, the governor does appoint the Texas **secretary of state**, even though this office is an elective one in 37 other states.[33] Though once considered a "glorified keeper of certain state records," the secretary of state is now an important officer.[34] The secretary of state has myriad responsibilities, and the appointment of a secretary of state is one of the governor's most important tasks.

As Texas's chief election official, the secretary of state conducts voter registration drives. His or her office works with organizations such as the League of Women Voters to increase the number of registered voters. The secretary of state's office also collects election-night returns from county judges and county clerks and makes the results available to the media. This service provides media and voters with a convenient method of receiving the latest official election returns in Texas.

All debt and Uniform Commercial Code filings are placed with the secretary of state's office. When any individual borrows money from a financial institution, a copy of the loan agreement is placed in the secretary of state's office.

Lieutenant Governor

The **lieutenant governor** has executive responsibilities, such as serving as acting governor when the governor is out of state and succeeding a governor who resigns, is incapacitated, or is impeached. The real power of the office of lieutenant governor, however, is derived from its place in the legislative process.

lieutenant governor the second-highest elected official in the state and president of the state Senate

According to the Texas Constitution, the lieutenant governor is the "Constitutional President of the Senate" and has the right to debate and vote on all issues when the Senate sits as a "Committee of the Whole." The Texas Constitution also grants the lieutenant governor the power to cast a deciding vote in the Senate when there is a tie. Like the Speaker of the House, the lieutenant governor signs all bills and resolutions. The constitution names the lieutenant governor to the Legislative Redistricting Board, a five-member committee that apportions the state into senatorial and house districts if the legislature fails to do so following a census. Other powers of the lieutenant governor are derived from various statutes passed by the legislature. For example, the lieutenant governor is chair of the Legislative Budget Board and is a member of a number of other boards and committees, including the Legislative Audit Committee, the Legislative Education Board, the Cash Management Committee, and the Bond Review Board.

The Texas Constitution grants the Senate the power to make its own rules, and lieutenant governors traditionally have been granted significant legislative power by the Senate itself. The Senate rules empower the lieutenant governor to decide all parliamentary questions and to use discretion in following Senate procedural rules. The lieutenant governor is also empowered to set up standing and special

In 2014, Texans elected conservative state senator Dan Patrick (left, R-Houston) to the powerful position of lieutenant governor. He defeated state senator Leticia Van de Putte (right, D-San Antonio) in the election.

committees and to appoint committee members and chairs of the committees. The Senate rules, and not just the Texas Constitution, make the lieutenant governor one of the most powerful political leaders in the state. New Senate rules passed by a future Senate could, of course, substantially alter the power possessed by the lieutenant governor.

Political Style of Lieutenant Governors Bob Bullock served as lieutenant governor of Texas from 1991 to 1999. A force in Texas politics for over 40 years, he was one of the strongest and most effective lieutenant governors Texas politics had ever seen. He took a bluff, rough, tough, head-knocking approach to leadership. He was feared and respected by friends and foes alike.

His successor, Rick Perry, brought a very different style to the office. The first Republican elected lieutenant governor in over 100 years, Perry had served two terms as the Texas commissioner of agriculture from 1985 to 1991. Prior to that, he served in the Texas House of Representatives, representing a rural west Texas district as a Democrat. His switch to the Republican Party reflected the broader movement of rural conservatives in the 1980s and 1990s. Expectations for Perry were low when he assumed office. In contrast to Bullock, Perry had a low-key style. But his style was appreciated by senators long under the demanding eye of Bob Bullock. Perry compared himself with a football player following in the footsteps of the Heisman Trophy winner Ricky Williams from the University of Texas. Like a running back imagining himself scoring a touchdown, Perry actually practiced banging a gavel in the empty Senate chamber. Perry's situation was also made more difficult by the fact that then–incumbent governor George W. Bush was actively pursuing the presidency, leaving additional jobs and uncertainties on Perry's shoulders.

Democratic senator John Whitmire, whom Perry had removed as chairman of the Senate Criminal Justice Committee, may have offered the best evaluation of Perry's leadership ability when commenting on a newspaper article that claimed Perry had lost control of the Senate during a debate over hate-crime legislation. Whitmire said, "I don't know how in the hell you say he lost control of the Senate. Was it a major difference in the way Bullock would have done it? Yeah. Serious difference. But I think members kind of appreciated the fact he didn't use his position as lieutenant governor to strong-arm members into positions that were contrary to their districts. Do I agree with all his decisions or operations, philosophy? Of course not. Essentially he was a freshman. . . . I'm sure he would be the first to tell you he learned by doing. No one's ever tried to govern us while the governor's been running for president. He had a good session."[35]

When George W. Bush became president and Lieutenant Governor Rick Perry became governor, the Senate elected one of its members to serve as lieutenant governor. That person was Bill Ratliff, a Republican from Mount Pleasant who was chairman of the powerful Senate Finance Committee. Ratliff had been in the Senate since 1989. A civil engineer, Ratliff was a strong believer in bipartisanship and was fascinated by the policy-making process. Known for his candor and moderation, he quickly alienated conservatives in his party when he named the Democratic senator Rodney Ellis of Houston as his replacement as chairman of the Finance Committee. As the presiding officer of the Senate, Ratliff oversaw a legislative session that had considerable accomplishments, such as passage of a statewide teacher health plan and the extension of Medicaid coverage to hundreds of thousands of poor children.

One poll showed Ratliff the leader in a Republican primary for lieutenant governor, and so he announced he would seek the office in the next election. However,

for critical analysis

How does the power of the lieutenant governor differ from that of the governor?

one of his opponents was Land Commissioner David Dewhurst, who claimed he would spend tens of millions of dollars of his own money in the race. Ratliff soon ran into trouble with Republican contributors whom he needed in order to compete with Dewhurst's money. Ratliff quickly discovered that his political moderation was not favored by many contributors, and with love for policy but distaste for politics, Ratliff concluded he should withdraw and not be a candidate for the office. One of his advisers suggested that Ratliff claim he was dropping out of the race because of a fatal disease. The fatal disease, noted Ratliff, was "independence and moderation."[36]

Dewhurst successfully ran for lieutenant governor in 2002 and was re-elected in 2006 and in 2010. As lieutenant governor, Dewhurst was in very different political circumstances from his two Republican predecessors, Perry and Ratliff. Republicans held a majority in the Senate throughout the Dewhurst years. Though Dewhurst pledged to work with state Democrats and appointed some as committee chairmen, partisanship became an increasingly divisive force in the state Senate under Dewhurst. Far more low-key than Bob Bullock and much less dominant a personality, Dewhurst has proven an effective lieutenant governor who unsuccessfully sought to replace Kay Bailey Hutchison as U.S. senator from Texas and was defeated in the Republican run-off primary for lieutenant governor by Dan Patrick, an ultra-conservative state senator. Patrick received 65 percent of the vote against Dewhurst in the run-off primary and won the general election with 58 percent of the vote. He will likely prove to be a more partisan and more bombastic personality than Dewhurst.

Attorney General

The **attorney general** (AG) is elected to a four-year term and acts as the chief lawyer for the state of Texas. The AG is, in effect, head of Texas's civil law firm. Currently the Texas AG oversees the work of over 700 lawyers.

attorney general elected state official who serves as the state's chief civil lawyer

The AG's office is concerned primarily with civil matters. When a lawsuit is filed against the state or by the state, the AG manages the legal activities surrounding that lawsuit. Any time a state agency needs legal representation, the AG's office represents the agency. In any lawsuit to which Texas is a party, the AG's office has full responsibility to resolve the case and can litigate, compromise, settle, or choose not to pursue the suit.

One of the more important powers of the AG's office comes from the opinion process. Any agency of state or local government can ask the AG's office for an advisory opinion on the legality of an action. The AG's office will rule on the question, and the ruling has the force of law unless overturned by a court or the legislature.

Probably the most controversial and criticized aspect of the work of the AG's office is child support collection. Almost one-half of the AG's 4,000 employees are involved in collecting child support, and they have collected more than $21 billion since Greg Abbott became AG. However, this program is the subject of intense criticism because much child support remains uncollected.

The AG's office has little responsibility in criminal law but may appoint a special prosecutor if a local district attorney asks the AG for assistance. This can happen when there is a potential conflict of interest, as, for example, if the district attorney is a friend of or works with a local official who is under criminal investigation. In one recent case, lawyers from the AG's office prosecuted a state district judge in Collin County on bribery charges.

The General Land Office is influential in large part because it awards oil and gas exploration rights for publicly owned lands. Land Commissioner George P. Bush was elected in 2014.

land commissioner elected state official who is the manager of most publicly owned lands

agricultural commissioner elected state official who is primarily responsible for enforcing agricultural laws

for critical analysis

The commissioner of agriculture, the land commissioner, the state comptroller, and the attorney general each head agencies that have significant responsibility for the operation of state government. To what extent is the public aware of these agencies and the major role they play in government?

Generally, criminal cases in Texas are prosecuted by district or county attorneys elected in each county. The county is usually responsible for the costs of the trial and for all appeals in state court. If a criminal case is appealed to the federal courts, the AG's office assumes responsibility.[37]

Commissioner of the General Land Office

The General Land Office (GLO) is the oldest state agency in Texas. Historically the **land commissioner** gave away land. Today, the GLO is the land manager for most publicly owned lands in Texas. Texas owns or has mineral interest in 13 million acres of land in the state, plus all submerged lands up to 10.35 miles into the Gulf of Mexico. All but 28 of Texas's 254 counties have some of these public lands.

The GLO also awards grazing and oil and gas exploration rights on this land. Thousands of producing oil and gas wells are found on state-owned land and are managed by the GLO. These responsibilities make the office of land commissioner quite influential. A significant portion of royalties on oil and natural gas produced by these wells goes to the Permanent School Fund and the Permanent University Fund.

The commissioner also manages the Veterans' Land Program, through which the state makes low-cost loans to Texas veterans. The program includes loans for land, housing, and home improvements. Recently, the GLO was given authority over some environmental matters. The land commissioner is responsible for environmental quality on public lands and waters, especially along the Texas coast. All of Texas's Gulf Coast beaches are publicly owned and under the jurisdiction of the GLO.

In recent years, the former commissioner of the GLO, Jerry Patterson, was involved in considerable controversy over the disposition of 9,269 acres of state land in the Christmas Mountains just north of Big Bend National Park. The Christmas Mountains land was under the control of the GLO and Patterson offered to sell the land to either public or private entities. After a public outcry over the proposed sale, the National Park Service expressed interest in accepting a donation of the land. However, Patterson, who is staunchly pro-hunting and pro-handgun, rejected the proposed donation because at the time the National Park Service banned hunting and the carrying of handguns in national parks. Finally, in 2011 the land was transferred to the Texas State University System, where it will serve as an "outdoor classroom." To satisfy Patterson's concerns, it was agreed that the land will be open to those who are licensed to carry handguns and to hunting.[38]

Commissioner of Agriculture

The **agricultural commissioner** is primarily responsible for enforcing agricultural laws. These include administration of animal quarantine laws, inspection of food, and enforcement of disease- and pest-control programs. Enforcement of the state's laws helps to ensure that Texas's farm products are of high quality and are disease free.

The Department of Agriculture checks weights and measures. Each year a representative of the department checks each motor fuel pump to make sure that it dispenses the correct amount of fuel. Scales used by grocery stores and markets are checked to guarantee that they weigh products correctly.

Farming and ranching are big business in Texas. Although a large number of small family farms exist in the state, large corporate farms increasingly dominate Texas agriculture. These large agribusinesses are greatly affected by the decisions of the commissioner. Such decisions can increase or decrease the cost of production. Changes in production costs affect the profit margins of these agribusinesses and ultimately the price consumers pay for food products.

Comptroller of Public Accounts

The **comptroller** is a powerful state official because he or she directs the collection of tax and nontax revenues and issues an evaluation and estimate of anticipated state revenues before each legislative session. Tax collection is the most visible function of the comptroller. The taxes collected by the comptroller include the general sales tax, severance tax on natural resources, business franchise tax, motor fuel tax, inheritance tax, most occupational taxes, and many minor taxes.

comptroller elected state official who directs the collection of taxes and other revenues and estimates revenues for the budgeting process

Although collecting billions in revenue is important, estimating revenues provides the comptroller with more power. These estimates, issued monthly during legislative sessions, are vital to the appropriations process because the legislature is prohibited from spending more than the comptroller estimates will be available. Final passage of any appropriations bill is contingent on the comptroller's certifying that revenues will be available to cover the monies spent in the appropriation. Because most bills require the expenditure of monies, this certification function provides the comptroller with significant power over the legislative process. If the comptroller is unable to certify that monies are available to pay for the appropriation, the legislature must reduce the appropriation or increase revenues. More than just an auditor, accountant, and tax collector, the comptroller is a key figure in the appropriations process.

In 1996 the office of state treasurer was eliminated, and the comptroller of public accounts assumed the duties of that office. Since then, the comptroller of public accounts has been the official custodian of state funds and is responsible for the safety of the state's money and for investing that money.

To ensure the safety of Texas's money, funds are deposited only in financial institutions designated by the State Depository Board as eligible to receive state monies. Deposits are required to earn as much money as possible. The more money earned as interest on deposits, the fewer tax dollars are needed.

An interesting responsibility of the comptroller is returning abandoned money and property to their rightful owners. In October of each year, the comptroller publishes a list of individuals with unclaimed property. One list included $117,000 in a forgotten savings account, a certificate of deposit for $104,000, gold coins, diamond rings, family photos, and rare baseball trading cards. Money or property that remains unclaimed goes to the state.

Accountability of the Plural Executive

Except for the secretary of state, each member of the plural executive is directly accountable to the people of Texas through elections. The plural executive is accountable to the legislature in three ways: the budgetary process, Sunset Review, and the impeachment process.

The legislature can demonstrate its satisfaction, or lack thereof, with an agency of the plural executive by the amount of money it appropriates to that agency. A significant increase in appropriations indicates an agency in good standing with the

A Plural or Single Executive?

In many ways, the Texas executive branch is similar to the federal executive branch. The governor, like the president, is the chief executive. The governor is the commander-in-chief of military forces in the state, has the power to appoint people to various administrative offices, and is responsible for making sure that the laws are faithfully executed. But unlike the president and vice-president who run on the same ticket, the governor and lieutenant governor are elected separately. Moreover, the governor of Texas does not have a cabinet that he appoints and controls. The Secretary of State is appointed by the governor, but the comptroller of public accounts, the attorney general, the land commissioner, and the agriculture commissioner (a statutory, not constitutional, office) are all elected separately. We call this a plural executive system because executive power is divided among different officeholders.

Many other states follow the federal model or single executive model, so that when the governor and lieutenant governor are elected to office together, they can appoint all of the relevant officeholders to run the executive branch. In these instances, the attorney general, the secretary of state, the agriculture commissioner, and all other "cabinet" officials are appointed by the governor and serve at his or her pleasure.

Advocates of the plural executive model, such as that used in Texas, argue that a decentralized system of power within the executive branch helps guard against abuses of power. The Texas Constitution intentionally provides for a weak governorship, and the plural executive is one way to guarantee this. If the attorney general and other statewide officials are not beholden to the governor, they will not necessarily support the governor's agenda. Supporters of the Texas model also argue that it is more democratic in that the

electorate has a larger role to play in the selection of executive officers.

Opponents of the plural executive model argue that the problem is not that the office of the governor is too powerful in Texas, but that it is too weak. The plural executive only makes it more difficult for the governor to govern effectively and creates a counterproductive tug of war among all of the separately elected officials. In the federal model, the president can decide who is best suited for a particular role and delegate power accordingly. The Texas governor, on the other hand, cannot give orders to the lieutenant governor or the attorney general, thus making it more difficult to run the state in a responsible manner.

In Texas's recent past, Republican governor George W. Bush had to work alongside Democratic lieutenant governor Bob Bullock in order to pass his legislative agenda. Some observers saw this as a positive effect of the plural executive, because it required compromise for the good of the state. Opponents of the plural executive might have seen this as a negative effect, because it undermined the power of the governor to implement his agenda. Each form of governance has its benefits and its costs for democracy.

As of 2014 all of the statewide elected officials in Texas are Republicans. However, this does not guarantee policy unity. While former attorney general (now governor) Greg Abbott and former governor Rick Perry (both pictured above) have agreed on some of the major issues, such as the state of Texas suing the federal government over the Affordable Care Act, but this cooperation is not necessarily the norm. Many observers believe that the election of Tea Partyer Dan Patrick to lieutenant governor and Ken Paxton to attorney general in 2014 may pose problems to the newly elected governor Greg Abbott. In situations with a mix of Democrats and Republicans in the plural executive, disagreement is even more common. When Republican Bill Clements was governor of Texas, for example, Democratic attorney general Mark White and he were often at odds because of differences in their political views and White's ambition to become governor.

critical thinking questions

1. Is the plural executive more democratic than the single executive model? Does it lead to more efficient and accountable government? Why or why not?

2. If you were to design a state executive branch, how would you decide whether to have a plural executive or a single executive? What are the pros and cons of each model?

legislature, whereas little or no increase in funds indicates legislative displeasure. Sunset Review can lead to reforms of an agency and even its elimination.

The Texas Constitution, not the legislature, creates most of the plural executive. Impeachment and conviction are the ultimate check on an elected official. The Texas House of Representatives can impeach an official for such things as criminal activity or gross malfeasance in office. The Texas Senate then tries the official. If convicted by the Senate, the official is removed from office.

for critical analysis
What are the effects of a plural executive on accountability in state government?

The Plural Executive and the Governor

The plural executive dilutes the ability of the governor to control state government. The governor appoints the secretary of state but has no control over other members of the plural executive. Officials are elected independently, and they do not run as a slate. They do not answer to the governor, and they do not serve as a cabinet. They tend to operate their offices as independent fiefdoms, and they jealously guard their turf. The plural executive can make state government appear as if it is going in several different directions at once. This is especially true when members of the plural executive are political rivals. For example, widely publicized tensions between Governor Rick Perry and Comptroller Carole Strayhorn led to Strayhorn's unsuccessful campaign as an independent against Perry in 2006.

With each member of the plural executive having separate and distinct responsibilities, state government and statewide planning lack cohesiveness. However, the plural executive is a product of Texas's history and environment. Like much of Texas government, it was a result of the public's negative reaction to Governor Edmund J. Davis at the close of Reconstruction.

● Boards, Commissions, and Regulatory Agencies

Explain the roles played by boards, commissions, and regulatory agencies

The state **bureaucracy** in Texas has numerous state boards, commissions, councils, and committees as well as major agencies within the plural executive that have administrative or advisory functions. In addition to the governmental bodies under the direct control of the single executives who are part of the elected plural executive, there are also bodies (1) run by multimember boards appointed by the governor and confirmed by the Senate; (2) with single executives appointed by the governor and confirmed by the Senate; (3) run by boards appointed by several persons within the plural executive or even by legislative officers, and confirmed by the Senate; and (4) run by multimember boards elected by the people. Overall, the state bureaucracy employed 308,800 in full-time equivalent positions in 2013, up from 274,776 employees in 2004.[39]

Governor Perry's lengthy service gave him enormous influence throughout state government, as he is the only Texas governor in modern history to have made every appointment in state government that a governor can make—and he also made numerous appointments to vacancies in office such as the Texas appellate courts and scores of district judgeships. State law usually sets the terms of persons on

bureaucracy the complex structure of offices, tasks, rules, and principles of organization that are employed by all large-scale institutions to coordinate the work of their personnel

state boards at four or six years. As a result, each new governor spends a great deal of time replacing holdover appointments from previous governors. With Perry's lengthy tenure as governor, however, those holdover appointments are long gone. The result, according to former state representative and author Brian McCall, is that "in this regard, [Perry] is by far the most powerful governor in Texas history. No governor has been able to do what he has done."[40]

Perry placed many of his closest advisers in key positions, which has spread not only his personal influence but also his personal political philosophy of a pro-business state government. To compare Perry's influence with previous governors, McCall noted that Governor Preston Smith in 1969 was able to appoint the entire board of regents at Texas Tech by getting an amendment inserted into a minor bill that changed the name of Texas Technological to Texas Tech University. When the name change took effect, the entire board of regents lost their positions and Smith was able to appoint the board. Perry appointed the entire boards of 17 public colleges and universities and has had a voice in selecting the chancellors of those universities.[41]

Perry also disciplined board members who have displeased him. The most notorious instance was in 2009 when he refused to reappoint three members of the Texas Forensic Science Board two days before they were to examine a flawed arson investigation. Perry also appointed a new chair of the Forensic Science Board, who abruptly canceled its meeting, and the review of the arson case never took place. In that same year, a Texas Tech regent who was a Perry appointee claimed that a former Perry staff member had told him to resign from the Board of Regents because the regent had endorsed Kay Bailey Hutchison in the Republican primary for governor.[42]

Not all of Perry's nominees were approved by the (overwhelmingly Republican) state Senate. One of his nominees for the Board of Pardons and Paroles, best known for her political activism and opposition to sex-toy parties in the Burleson, Texas, area, was turned down by the Senate with an overwhelming 27-to-4 vote against her confirmation. State senator John Whitmire, a Democrat and the chair of the Senate Criminal Justice Committee, argued that she was turned down not because the issue was a partisan one, but simply because she was not qualified for a position that considers "life and death matters."[43]

Multimember Appointed Boards

Most boards and commissions in Texas are headed by members appointed by the governor and confirmed by the Senate. Some commissioners are appointed by a variety of other people, including the lieutenant governor, the Speaker of the House, or leaders of select professional organizations like the State Bar or State Medical Association. Multimember commissions with heads appointed by the governor include innocuous agencies, such as the Bandera County River Authority, the State Seed and Plant Board, the Caddo Lake Compact Commission, and the Texas Funeral Commission. There are also better-known agencies, such as the Texas Alcoholic Beverage Commission, the Department of Parks and Wildlife, the Texas Youth Commission, and the Texas Department of Corrections. Except in the case of a major controversy, such as the sexual abuse scandal that embroiled the Texas Youth Commission in 2007, these agencies work in anonymity, although several of them have a direct effect on the lives of Texans. One such example is the Public Utilities Commission.

The Department of Parks and Wildlife is an agency in the Texas executive branch and is led by a board appointed by the governor. The department manages natural resources and fishing, hunting, and outdoor recreation in the state. Here, an employee measures fish caught near Corpus Christi.

Public Utilities Commission (PUC) More than most other agencies, the Public Utilities Commission (PUC) has a direct effect on consumers' pocketbooks. Before 1975 cities in Texas set utility rates. The PUC was established in 1975, in part to protect consumers and to curb the rate at which utility costs were increasing. The commission is responsible for setting all local telephone and some electric rates.

Local telephone rates vary from one part of Texas to another, but all rates in a service area are the same. The commission also determines the maximum charge for pay telephones and approves additional services such as caller ID, call waiting, and call forwarding. A rule that took effect in September 1999 prohibits an individual's local service from being disconnected for nonpayment of long-distance bills. Another regulation by the PUC establishes a "no call" list for phone numbers of Texas residents who do not wish to receive telemarketing calls from companies that do not have a business relationship with the phone customer.

With the introduction of retail competition to the electric industry, the PUC has had a major role in providing information to consumers and in setting requirements for providers of electric services. The PUC maintains a web site that allows electric customers to compare the costs of electricity from the various electric service providers.

Appointed Single Executives

The Texas Department of Insurance Whereas the PUC is run by a multimember body appointed by the governor and confirmed by the Texas Senate, the Texas Department of Insurance is run by one commissioner appointed by the governor for a two-year term and confirmed by the Senate. This single-member appointive system has been in effect since 1993, when governance of the agency by a three-member appointed board was abandoned in favor of single-member governance. The purpose of the Department of Insurance is to regulate the insurance market in Texas, a complicated task that affects most Texans.

In the early 2000s, Texas was faced with huge increases in the cost of homeowners' insurance brought on at least in part by major increases in insurance claims, most notably for mold damage. From the first quarter of 2000 to the fourth quarter of 2001, the number of mold claims increased from 1,050 to 14,706. Additionally, the costs of these claims increased significantly to the point that insurance payments became greater than insurance premiums. And with a declining economy during this period, insurance companies were no longer making substantial profits on their investment of insurance premiums. Homeowner premiums increased rapidly. Between 2001 and 2002 homeowners' premiums rose 21.8 percent. Some companies chose not to write any new homeowners' policies; other companies simply pulled out of the Texas market. In 1997, 166 companies were writing homeowners' policies in Texas; by 2003 only 101 companies were writing such policies.[44]

In response, the Texas Department of Insurance began to deregulate insurance coverage so that, for example, policies could be written that charged more for complete mold coverage, less for reduced mold coverage, and significantly less for no mold coverage.

The legislature also stepped into the homeowners' insurance cost issue, which by 2002–03 was reaching crisis proportions. One effect of the legislature's involvement was a "file and use" regulatory system that was implemented at the end of 2004. This system allowed insurers to institute new rates immediately after filing them with the Texas Department of Insurance. The commissioner of insurance can then disapprove of the new rates and may force the company to issue rebates to policyholders.[45] Thus, the commissioner of insurance appears to wield great power over insurance rates but only after those rates have gone into effect.

In 2007, Insurance Commissioner Mike Geeslin canceled Allstate's 5.9 percent rate hike, but Allstate got a court order allowing it to keep charging higher rates, at least temporarily. State Farm has been battling the Department of Insurance for years after ignoring an order from the commissioner to cut its rates by 12 percent.

State Farm's battle with the Texas Department of Insurance has taken on the characteristics of a marathon. The company has shown no sign of compromising with the state in its legal battle over the state's claim that it overcharged homeowners. Additionally, in 2009–10 it twice filed to increase its insurance rates and ignored the insurance commissioner's claim that customers deserved a break from increases. The result was a 35 percent boost in insurance rates for many customers in Dallas and nearby counties. State Farm has also successfully sued the Texas Department of Insurance to keep the agency from publicizing documents related to its rate increases. State Farm's obstinacy in dealing with the Insurance Commission means that for a 10-year-old brick home in north Dallas with an insured value of $150,000, the premium would average about $1,679 per year compared with the average premium charged by other companies of $1,298 per year.[46] While the department's battles with Allstate and State Farm continue, insurance companies have been reducing coverage of homes on the Texas coast out of fear that a hurricane could cause the companies major losses.[47]

Although insurance companies advocate less regulation, consumer groups argue that the insurance commissioner has inadequate powers to deal with insurance companies. Indeed, it is doubtful that the commissioner has sufficient power to force an uncooperative insurer to comply with his or her decisions. The commissioner is also faced with the seemingly intractable problem of keeping rates low and coverage available in hurricane-prone areas to which more and more people are moving.

Multimember Elected Boards

Members of two state agencies are elected by the voters: the Railroad Commission of Texas and the State Board of Education. The Railroad Commission has 3 members elected statewide to six-year terms of office. One of the 3 members is elected every two years. The Board of Education is a 15-member board elected to four-year terms from single-member districts.

Railroad Commission of Texas (RRC) At one time, the Railroad Commission of Texas (RRC) was one of the most powerful state agencies in the nation. It regulated intrastate railroads, trucks, and bus transportation and supervised the oil and natural gas industry in Texas. For most of the RRC's existence, regulation of the oil and gas industry was the RRC's primary focus.

Today the RRC is a shadow of its former self. Court decisions, deregulation of the transportation industry, other state and federal legislation, and the decline in the nation's dependence on Texas's crude oil production have diminished the commission's power. In 2005 the RRC's limited authority over railroads was transferred to the Texas Department of Transportation, so the RRC now has no authority over what was once its major reason for existence. During the RRC's heyday when Texas was a major oil producer, the commission limited production to conserve oil and to maintain prices. Because it restricted oil production, the RRC was one of the most economically significant governmental bodies on the national and international stage. As oil production shifted to the Middle East, the RRC became the model for OPEC, the Organization of Petroleum Exporting Countries, which also seeks to limit oil production to maintain prices. At one time, members of the Texas RRC wielded such vast economic power that they were among the state's most influential politicians. Renewed energy production in Texas as a result of fracking and horizontal drilling appears to again be increasing the importance of the RRC, although it will never again be a major decision-making body for world oil and gas prices. There are now simply too many major oil and gas fields outside of Texas.

State Board of Education (SBOE) The State Board of Education (SBOE) sets policy for public education (pre-kindergarten to 12th grade programs supported by the state government) in Texas. The education bureaucracy that enforces the SBOE's rules and regulations is called the Texas Education Agency (TEA). Together these two bodies control public education in Texas by determining licensing requirements for public school teachers, setting minimum high school graduation criteria for recommended or advanced curriculums, establishing standards for accreditation of public schools, and selecting public school textbooks.

Texas spends millions of dollars each year purchasing textbooks, and the state furnishes these books without charge to students. Books must meet stringent criteria, and because the state buys so many textbooks, publishers print books especially for students in Texas. Often states that spend less money on textbooks than Texas must purchase those originally printed for Texas.

The commissioner of education is appointed by the governor from a list of candidates submitted by the SBOE. He or she is administrative head of the TEA and serves as adviser to the SBOE. The commissioner of education is at the apex of the public education bureaucracy in Texas.

In recent years, the Texas SBOE has become an ideological battleground. In 2009 that conflict led the board to review how evolution was taught. In what was a partial defeat for the social conservatives, no longer would teachers be

The State Board of Education sets policy for public education, from pre-kindergarten through 12th grade. In recent years, some of the board's decisions concerning curriculums and textbooks have generated controversy.

required to teach "strengths and weaknesses" of evolution, although they would be encouraged to teach "all sides." Other battles have broken out over other aspects of educational policy. For example, one policy goal was that high school students were to learn how the cultural contributions of "people from various racial, ethnic, gender, and religious groups shape American culture." One of the leading social conservatives on the board proposed an unsuccessful amendment that would delete the words "from various racial, ethnic, gender, and religious groups." That suggested, of course, that teaching would not focus on the role of those specific groups in shaping American culture. Another amendment proposed that students be required to evaluate the contributions of significant Americans—Thurgood Marshall, Billy Graham, Newt Gingrich, William F. Buckley, Jr., Hillary Rodham Clinton, and Edward Kennedy. All passed the board except for Edward Kennedy. Other issues involve whether César Chávez was significant enough to be in social studies textbooks and whether greater emphasis should be placed on Christianity in the founding of the nation.

Although many Texas voters may not be aware of them, the battles fought within the SBOE have wide-reaching effects. They affect not only the education of Texas schoolchildren but also that of children across the nation. Because the state's textbook market is so large, the content of the textbooks used in Texas sets the tone for textbook content in other states that are less populous and therefore have smaller markets for texts.[48]

As a result of the 2010 elections, there was a power shift on the SBOE when the leader of the social conservatives who was the chair of the board was defeated. The 2012 elections created a new battle for control of the board. Because of changes in the single-member districts of the SBOE that were caused by redistricting, all members of the board were up for election.[49] The 2012 election reduced the social conservative block still further, continuing the anti–social conservative trend begun in the 2010 elections. In 2014 there were seven seats up for election. Six incumbents ran, and all six were re-elected. The result is that the SBOE's position will likely change little.

Making Agencies Accountable

In a democracy, elected officials are ultimately responsible to the voters. Appointed officials are indirectly accountable to the people through the elected officials who appoint them. Both are responsible to legislatures that determine responsibilities and appropriate money to carry out those responsibilities. In Texas, the plural executive is responsible to the legislature for its biennial funding and to the voters for re-election. The myriad state agencies look to the legislature for funding, and once every 12 years they must justify their existence to the **Sunset Advisory Commission (SAC)**.

The 12-member SAC has 5 members from the Texas Senate and 1 public member appointed by the lieutenant governor. Five members from the Texas House and 1 public member are appointed by the Speaker of the Texas House.

The Sunset Review Act created the SAC in 1977. The act established specific criteria to be considered in evaluating the continuing need for an agency. One of several laws enacted in the mid-1970s to bring more openness and accountability to Texas government, the Sunset process establishes a date on which an agency is abolished unless the legislature passes a bill for the agency to continue in operation.

During its Sunset review, an agency must, among other things, document its efficiency, the extent to which it meets legislative mandates, and its promptness and effectiveness in handling complaints, and it must establish the continuing need for its services. The review process is lengthy, lasting almost two years.

After a thorough study of an agency, the SAC recommends one of three actions to the legislature: (1) the agency continues as is, with no change in its organization or functions; (2) the agency continues but with changes (reorganization, a new focus for the agency, or merger with other agencies); or (3) the agency is abolished.

If option 1 or 2 is recommended, specific action by the legislature is required before the date of the agency's abolition. Option 1 requires specific legislation to re-create the agency in its existing form. Option 2 requires the legislature to re-create the agency with some or all of the changes recommended by the SAC. If the legislature agrees the agency should be abolished, no action is necessary. It will expire at the Sunset deadline; the sun sets and the agency is no more.

Each state agency has been through the Sunset process. The legislature has allowed the sun to set on more than 58 agencies; 12 agencies have been merged with existing bodies. Since 1978 the legislature has accepted the majority of recommendations of the SAC.

Sunset Advisory Commission (SAC) a commission created in 1975 for the purpose of reviewing the effectiveness of state agencies

for critical analysis
What is the source of power of Texas bureaucratic agencies? How are these agencies held accountable to other elected public officials or the public?

● Thinking Critically about the Executive in Texas

At the national level, the president is elected, through the Electoral College, by the people as a whole. The president is the spokesperson for the nation in the world and is the commander in chief of the armed forces. When there is a national crisis, the people look to the president for leadership. Throughout the twentieth century, the power and authority of the presidency increased significantly, often at

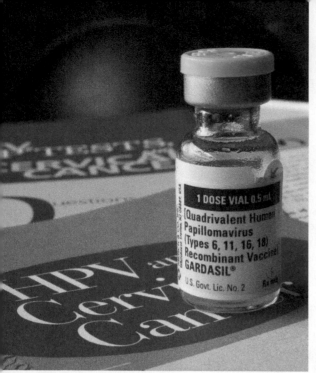

Governor Perry experienced a significant check from the legislature in 2007 after he issued an executive order for girls in Texas to be vaccinated against human papillomavirus, or HPV, a sexually transmitted disease linked to cervical cancer. The legislature passed a bill overturning the order.

the expense of Congress. American democracy has become an executive-led system, with a weak Congress and a partially demobilized electorate.

Such is not the case in Texas. The fear of a strong executive who could ignore the wishes of either the legislature or the people, as was the case during Reconstruction in Texas, led in 1876 to a constitution that created a plural executive. The governor is the chief executive officer in the state, elected directly by the popular vote of all the people of Texas. People turn to the governor for leadership and direction during times of crisis. But compared with that of the president, the power of the Texas governor is more limited. Many key executive officials, including the lieutenant governor, the attorney general, the comptroller, and the land commissioner, are elected—like the governor—directly by the people. These members of the plural executive, along with other popularly elected statewide boards and commissions, possess power and authority that under other constitutional arrangements the governor might possess. As has been noted throughout this chapter, Governor Perry's ability to accumulate power in the governor's office is unprecedented in recent history. That his successors will be able to wield the limited powers of the governor as efficiently is by no means certain.

The existence of an institutionally weak office of the governor and a plural executive has a number of important implications for democracy in Texas. First, because power and authority are divided among a number of distinct officers, no individual is fully responsible for executive initiatives in the state. Indeed, executive officials can struggle with each other for power as they seek to move the state government in different directions. Partisanship can exacerbate the natural conflict built into the executive branch in Texas. A Democratic lieutenant governor may or may not be willing to work closely with a Republican governor. But the worst clashes may be among executive officials of the same party. The fight between Governor Rick Perry and Comptroller Carole Strayhorn, both Republicans, culminating in Strayhorn's running against the incumbent governor as an independent in 2006, was an example of a fundamental truth in Texas politics: the executive does not have to speak with one voice or in harmony with itself.

A second consequence of the plural executive for democracy in Texas is that it has given rise to a powerful executive officer in the state legislature, outside the office of the governor. The lieutenant governor has become, along with the Speaker of the House, one of the two most important officials in the state legislature. The lieutenant governor, not the governor, runs the Texas Senate. The lieutenant governor, not the governor, is the executive branch's chief legislative official.

The dispersal of power and authority among a number of different executive offices in the state has a third consequence for democracy in the state. Additional points of access are created for interest groups seeking to influence government and public policy, making it easier for special interests to impose their will on the policy-making process. The 2014 elections have continued the Republican Party's firm hold over the plural executive and will have major consequences for policy and politics in Texas.

The Governor

Although the Texas governor is considered weak compared to governors of other states, the power of appointing members to boards made Governor Rick Perry the most powerful governor in state history largely because of his long tenure. Among the executive powers the governor possesses are appointment, budgetary, military, and police powers. Among his legislative powers are message and veto powers and the ability to call special sessions of the legislature.

Key Terms

impeachment (p. 240)

appointment (p. 245)

patronage (p. 245)

senatorial courtesy (p. 249)

executive budget (p. 250)

legislative budget (p. 250)

veto (p. 252)

post-adjournment veto (p. 252)

line-item veto (p. 252)

special session (p. 253)

Practice Quiz

1. Which of the following is *not* necessary to become governor of Texas?
   a) A governor must be at least 30 years of age.
   b) A governor must have lived in Texas for at least five years.
   c) A governor must be a U.S. citizen.
   d) A governor must be a lawyer.
   e) A governor must have substantial campaign funding.

2. The election for governor of Texas is held in an off-year in order to
   a) increase voter participation in elections in odd-numbered years.
   b) influence the presidential vote in Texas.
   c) decrease the likelihood of voter fraud.
   d) give governors an opportunity to campaign for presidential candidates.
   e) prevent the presidential vote in Texas from influencing the election of state officials.

3. The only constitutional method of removing the governor is
   a) *quo warranto* proceedings.
   b) *ex post facto* removal.
   c) a vote of no confidence.
   d) impeachment.
   e) impeachment and conviction.

4. The governor's most effective power in controlling the executive branch of state government is the power
   a) of the veto.
   b) of appointment.
   c) of removal.
   d) of judicial review.
   e) to create a state budget.

5. The governor's veto is absolute when it is a
   a) line-item veto.
   b) special veto.
   c) budgetary veto.
   d) post-adjournment veto.
   e) select veto.

6. The governor can grant
   a) pardons.
   b) suspended sentences.
   c) probation.
   d) retrials.
   e) parole.

The Plural Executive

Unlike the president of the United States, the governor of Texas does not appoint a cabinet. Voters in Texas elect the lieutenant governor and other major statewide offices in separate elections. This disperses power within the executive branch, which means that executive officers must compromise not only with the legislature but also within the executive branch.

Key Terms

plural executive (p. 254)

secretary of state (p. 256)

lieutenant governor (p. 257)

attorney general (p. 259)

land commissioner (p. 260)

agricultural commissioner (p. 260)

comptroller (p. 261)

Practice Quiz

7. Which member of the plural executive is appointed?
   a) secretary of state
   b) land commissioner
   c) lieutenant governor
   d) comptroller of public accounts
   e) attorney general

8. The attorney general is
   a) part of the governor's cabinet.
   b) elected independently of the governor.
   c) appointed by the Texas Supreme Court.
   d) the governor's lawyer.
   e) chosen by the State Bar of Texas.

9. The land commissioner
   a) records all property deeds.
   b) administers state land.
   c) surveys property in Texas.
   d) is appointed by the state Senate.
   e) administers Big Bend National Park.

10. Members of the plural executive are accountable to the
    a) voters and the governor.
    b) legislature and voters.
    c) constitution.
    d) state supreme court.
    e) legislature.

Boards, Commissions, and Regulatory Agencies

The governor's most important power is the ability to appoint people to boards, commissions, councils, committees, and regulatory agencies. Such institutions have important powers to interpret state regulations and make a difference in the lives of everyday Texans.

Key Terms

bureaucracy (p. 263)

Sunset Advisory Commission (SAC) (p. 269)

Practice Quiz

11. The Public Utilities Commission
    a) regulates some electric rates.
    b) regulates local phone rates.
    c) maintains a website so consumers can compare electric rates.
    d) maintains a "do not call" registry.
    e) All of the above are features of the Public Utilities Commission.

12. The Texas Department of Insurance
    a) has limited power to regulate insurance rates.
    b) collects the penalties for not buying health insurance under Obamacare.
    c) sells insurance for mold coverage.
    d) is run by a five-member elected board.
    e) All of the above are features of the Texas Department of Insurance.

13. The Railroad Commission of Texas
    a) is responsible for the safety of the state's railroads.
    b) issues bonds to support the state's transportation needs.
    c) regulates oil and gas production in Texas.
    d) approves mergers of railroads.
    e) is the most powerful agency in the state.

14. The State Board of Education
    a) has a major role in determining the books used in Texas public schools.
    b) is appointed by the legislature.
    c) reviews applications to state colleges and universities.
    d) is responsible for school property tax rates.
    e) governs local boards of education.

15. Which agency investigates the performance of state agencies and recommends whether an agency should be abolished, continued as is, or continued with changes?
    a) Legislative Budget Board
    b) Legislative Research Bureau
    c) Texas Research League
    d) Public Utilities Commission
    e) Sunset Advisory Commission

Recommended Websites

Attorney General of Texas
www.oag.state.tx.us/

Lieutenant Governor of Texas
www.ltgov.state.tx.us/

Office of the Governor
www.governor.state.tx.us/

Railroad Commission of Texas
www.rrc.state.tx.us/

Sunset Advisory Commission
www.sunset.state.tx.us/

Texas Department of Agriculture
www.agr.state.tx.us/

Texas General Land Office
www.glo.state.tx.us/

Texas Secretary of State
www.sos.state.tx.us/

Window on State Government (Comptroller's Office)
www.window.state.tx.us/

The Texas Judiciary

WHY THE JUDICIARY MATTERS The presiding judge of the Texas Court of Criminal Appeals, Sharon Keller, has cultivated a "tough on crime" image. Her campaign literature, for example, has shown a figure behind bars with the headline, "He won't be voting for Judge Sharon Keller."

However, Keller may have crossed the line in terms of her harshness toward criminal defendants on September 25, 2007. That evening, Michael Richard was scheduled to die by lethal injection. Earlier that day, the Supreme Court of the United States had agreed to hear a challenge to the constitutionality of death by lethal injection. Ordinarily, that would lead to a petition to the Court of Criminal Appeals for a stay of execution, in order to wait for the decision of the U.S. Supreme Court.

Things went terribly wrong. The lawyers for Michael Richard were working against a tight deadline for their petition, and they claimed they experienced computer problems that created a delay in preparing their documents. They called the Court of Criminal Appeals and asked that the court stay open an extra 20 minutes so that the stay of execution request could be filed. Judge Keller refused to keep the court open. In making this decision, she did not consult with other judges on the court, some of whom were working in the same building. Other judges on the court have stated that they would have stayed late to hear the appeal if they had known about it. Michael Richard was executed that evening.

Complaints were filed against Judge Keller with the State Commission on Judicial Conduct. The hearing officer, known as a special master, found plenty of blame to go around in this case. He found that the Texas Defender Service, which provided legal representation for Michael Richard, was unable to show that it actually had computer problems that made it unable to file the claim on time. In fact, the Texas Defender Service did not even contemplate filing a lethal injection claim until over two hours after the Supreme Court had agreed to hear a lethal injection case, and then it assigned a junior attorney to prepare documents, the first of which was not ready until 4:45 PM and all of which were not completed until 5:56 PM that day. Nor did the Court of Criminal Appeals escape criticism. And though Judge Keller's behavior did not, according to the special master, justify removal from office or reprimand, it "was not exemplary of a public servant." He stated, "Although [Judge Keller] says that if she could do it all over again she would not change any of her actions, this cannot be true. Any reasonable person, having gone through this ordeal, surely would realize that open communication, particularly during the hectic few hours before an execution, would benefit the interests of justice. Further, her judgment in not keeping the clerk's office open past 5:00 to allow the TDS to file was highly questionable. In sum, there is a valid reason why many in the legal community are not proud of Judge Keller's actions."[1] In the fall of 2010 a special court of review dismissed the public warning against Keller on the grounds that a warning cannot be a penalty following a formal proceeding against a judge. For many people in the state, this dismissal of the public warning against Keller may have been technically correct but politically a mistake, making it appear that judges may be unaccountable for their actions. It led to broad-based support for a constitutional amendment during the 2013 legislative session allowing for such public warnings.

Michael Richard's execution was not the only issue when Judge Keller ran for re-election in 2012. There was also her problem with the Texas Ethics Commission which had fined her $100,000—the largest fine they had ever imposed—for failing to report $2.4 million in property and income on personal financial statements that are required by the Ethics Commission.[2]

First elected in 1994, Keller was the only Court of Criminal Appeals judge who faced Democratic opposition. Her opponent, Keith Hampton, garnered endorsements or favorable mentions from all five of the major daily papers in Texas, and 52 percent of Texas lawyers favored him over Keller in a State Bar of Texas poll.

Still, Texas is a Republican state and Keller had the advantage of being an incumbent with a Republican Party label. In the election, she got 55.49 percent of the vote, which was only slightly less than the 56.64 percent of the vote that was her victory percentage in 2006 prior to the Richard execution and the Texas Ethics Commission fine. All did not go Keller's way. In the 2013 constitutional amendment election, Proposition 9 received 84.65 percent of the vote. Proposition 9 was an effort to correct the problem that led to the dismissal of the public warning against Judge Keller. The Texas Constitution did not specifically say that a disciplinary case could lead to a warning, although the state's legal code does. The amendment would correct that glitch and allow the warning.[3]

This episode highlights two reasons that judicial politics matters to each and every citizen: First, because judges are elected, judges and judicial candidates are encouraged to behave in ways that may cultivate the favor of voters even as the judges seem to sidestep notions of justice. Second, partisan judicial elections make party affiliation and incumbency especially important factors in judges' being elected to office, since voters often have little other information about judicial candidates. One reason that Texas is the death penalty capital of the nation may be that it has a partisan election system for selecting not only judges but also the district attorneys, who prosecute crimes.

chaptergoals

- Describe how the Texas court system is organized (pp. 277–82)
- Explain the legal process and the differences between criminal and civil law (pp. 282–85)
- Evaluate the process for selecting judges in Texas (pp. 285–98)
- Assess the impact of recent changes related to tort reform, litigation, and disciplining judges (pp. 298–305)

● Court Structure

Describe how the Texas court system is organized

Like the federal courts, the state and local courts in Texas are responsible for securing liberty and equality under the law. However, the democratic mechanisms put into place in Texas to select judges and to hold them accountable for their actions are quite different from those at the national level. Federal judges are appointed by the president and confirmed by the Senate. They have lifetime appointments. This means that federal judges, subject to good behavior in office, are free from the ebb and flow of democratic politics. They do not have to cater to public opinion and are empowered to interpret the law as they see fit, without fear of reprisal at the polls. In Texas, however, judges are elected to office. Although they may initially be appointed to their offices, sooner or later they are responsible to the people for their decisions in office. Election of judges brings not only the people but also interest groups into the selection and retention of judges. The influence of special interest money in judicial campaigns raises important questions about the relationship between the rule of law and the nature of democratic politics.

Texas has a large and complex court structure consisting of a hodgepodge of courts with overlapping jurisdiction (see Figure 9.1). Additionally, some courts have specialized jurisdiction, whereas others have broad authority to handle a variety of cases. At the highest level for civil cases is the **Texas Supreme Court**, which consists of nine justices, including a chief justice. This court hears civil and juvenile cases only, and at the state level, it has final appellate jurisdiction. The only requirements for being a Texas Supreme Court justice are that one must be a citizen of

Texas Supreme Court the highest civil court in Texas; consists of nine justices and has final state appellate authority over civil cases

The Texas Supreme Court is the highest civil court in Texas. The court consists of nine justices (pictured here as of 2014).

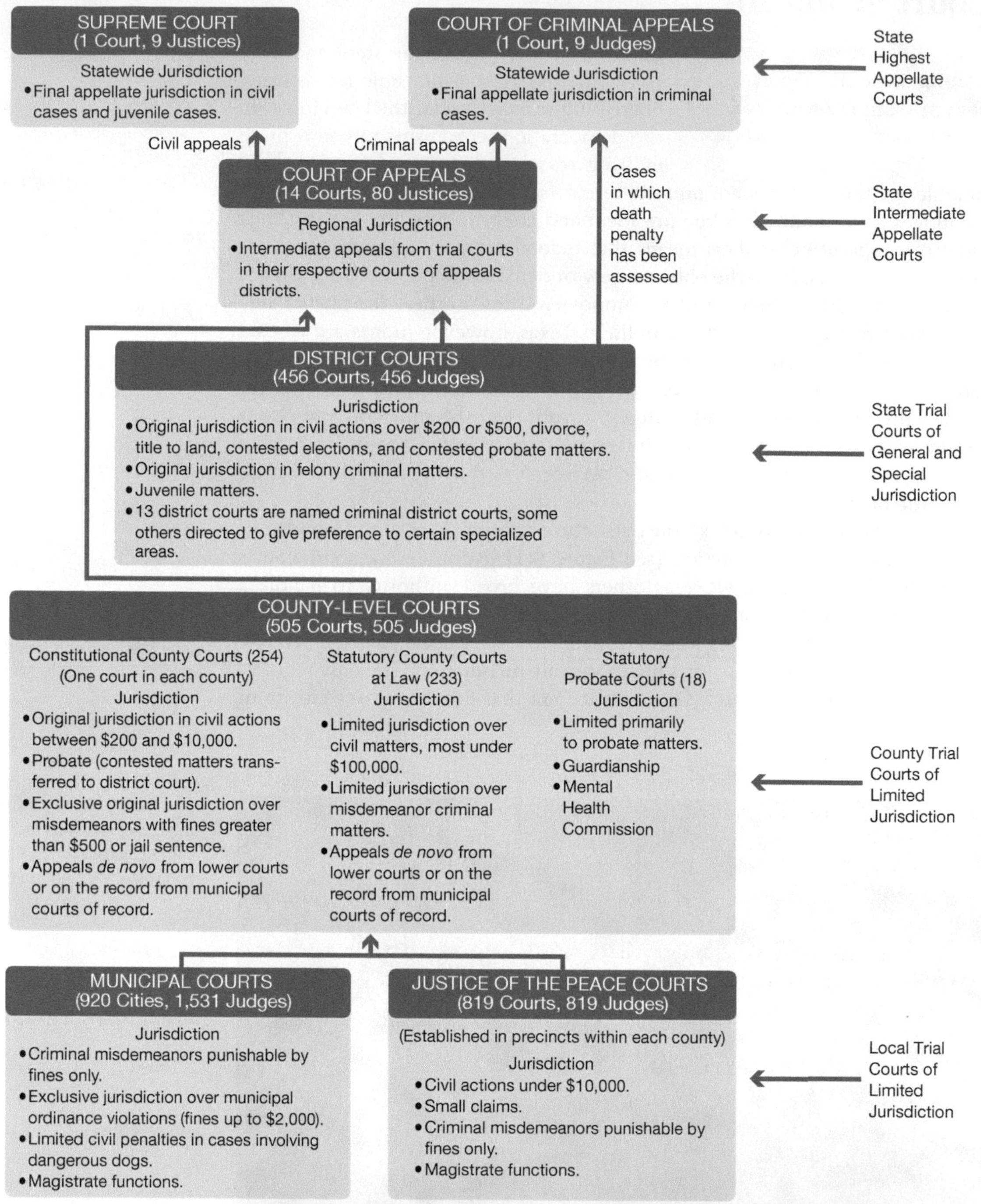

SUPREME COURT
(1 Court, 9 Justices)

Statewide Jurisdiction
• Final appellate jurisdiction in civil cases and juvenile cases.

COURT OF CRIMINAL APPEALS
(1 Court, 9 Judges)

Statewide Jurisdiction
• Final appellate jurisdiction in criminal cases.

State Highest Appellate Courts

Civil appeals   Criminal appeals

COURT OF APPEALS
(14 Courts, 80 Justices)

Regional Jurisdiction
• Intermediate appeals from trial courts in their respective courts of appeals districts.

Cases in which death penalty has been assessed

State Intermediate Appellate Courts

DISTRICT COURTS
(456 Courts, 456 Judges)

Jurisdiction
• Original jurisdiction in civil actions over $200 or $500, divorce, title to land, contested elections, and contested probate matters.
• Original jurisdiction in felony criminal matters.
• Juvenile matters.
• 13 district courts are named criminal district courts, some others directed to give preference to certain specialized areas.

State Trial Courts of General and Special Jurisdiction

COUNTY-LEVEL COURTS
(505 Courts, 505 Judges)

Constitutional County Courts (254)
(One court in each county)
Jurisdiction
• Original jurisdiction in civil actions between $200 and $10,000.
• Probate (contested matters transferred to district court).
• Exclusive original jurisdiction over misdemeanors with fines greater than $500 or jail sentence.
• Appeals de novo from lower courts or on the record from municipal courts of record.

Statutory County Courts at Law (233)
Jurisdiction
• Limited jurisdiction over civil matters, most under $100,000.
• Limited jurisdiction over misdemeanor criminal matters.
• Appeals de novo from lower courts or on the record from municipal courts of record.

Statutory Probate Courts (18)
Jurisdiction
• Limited primarily to probate matters.
• Guardianship
• Mental Health Commission

County Trial Courts of Limited Jurisdiction

MUNICIPAL COURTS
(920 Cities, 1,531 Judges)

Jurisdiction
• Criminal misdemeanors punishable by fines only.
• Exclusive jurisdiction over municipal ordinance violations (fines up to $2,000).
• Limited civil penalties in cases involving dangerous dogs.
• Magistrate functions.

JUSTICE OF THE PEACE COURTS
(819 Courts, 819 Judges)

(Established in precincts within each county)
Jurisdiction
• Civil actions under $10,000.
• Small claims.
• Criminal misdemeanors punishable by fines only.
• Magistrate functions.

Local Trial Courts of Limited Jurisdiction

FIGURE 9.1
The Structure of the Texas Court System
SOURCE: Texas Office of Court Administration.

the United States and a resident of Texas, be at least 35 years of age, and have been either a practicing lawyer or judge for at least 10 years. The term of a justice is six years, with at least three justices being elected every two years. Justices on the Texas Supreme Court are paid $150,000 a year; the chief justice receives $2,500 a year more. Supreme Court justices are elected to six-year terms.

The **Texas Court of Criminal Appeals** is the highest appeals court in the state for criminal cases. This court also has nine judges, including a presiding judge. The pay, terms, and qualifications of Court of Criminal Appeals judges are the same as for the Texas Supreme Court. Perhaps the most important task of the Court of Criminal Appeals is its jurisdiction over automatic appeals in death penalty cases.

Both the Supreme Court and the Court of Criminal Appeals have appellate jurisdiction. This means that they have the authority to review the decisions of lower courts to determine whether legal principles and court procedures were followed correctly. This authority also provides the power to order that a case be retried if mistakes were made. Texas has 14 other appellate courts, located in various parts of the state, which have both criminal and civil jurisdiction. These courts are intermediate appellate courts and hear appeals from the trial courts. Usually, before the Supreme Court or the Court of Criminal Appeals hears a case, the initial appeal has been heard by one of the **courts of appeal**. These courts have intermediate appellate jurisdiction in various regions of the state for civil, juvenile, and criminal cases. Presently, there are 80 judges who serve on the 14 courts of appeal, which range in size from 3 to 13 judges. Although there are occasions when every judge on a court of appeal will hear a case, mostly appeals at this level are heard by panels of three judges. The requirements for a court of appeal justice are the same as those for justices of the higher courts. Courts of appeal justices are paid $137,500 a year and the chief justice of each of the courts of appeal receives an additional $2,500. All of the justices on the courts of appeal are eligible for a maximum of an additional $7,500 that would be paid by a county supplement.

The major trial courts in Texas are the **district courts**. Each county has at least one district court, although rural parts of Texas may have several counties that are served by one district court. Urban counties have many district courts. Harris County (Houston), for example, has 59 district courts and Dallas County has 48. District courts usually have general jurisdiction, meaning that they hear a broad range of civil and criminal cases. However, in urban counties, some district courts with specialized jurisdiction hear only civil, criminal, juvenile, or family law matters. Those district courts having general jurisdiction would hear felony criminal cases, divorces, land disputes, election contests, and civil lawsuits. District court judges receive $125,000 a year, and they may receive up to $15,000 in additional salary a year from county supplement payments to the state salary. Currently, there are 456 district judges, 9 State Supreme Court judges, 9 court of criminal appeals judges, and 80 court of appeal judges.

Texas is unusual in having the office of **county judge** in each of its 254 counties. Not only does the county judge preside over the county commissioners' court and thus have responsibilities for administration of county government, but the county judge also presides over the county court. Often these **county courts** have jurisdiction over uncontested probate cases and over the more serious misdemeanor criminal offenses involving fines greater than $500 or a jail sentence as well as over civil cases where the amounts in dispute are relatively small, generally in the $200 to $10,000 range. The county court may also hear appeals from municipal courts or from justice of the peace courts. Thus, the county judge combines political-administrative functions with some judicial functions. However, in the more populated counties,

Texas Court of Criminal Appeals the highest criminal court in Texas; consists of nine justices and has final state appellate authority over criminal cases

courts of appeal the 14 intermediate-level appellate courts that hear appeals from district and county courts to determine whether the decisions of these lower courts followed legal principles and court procedures

district courts the major trial courts in Texas, which usually have general jurisdiction over a broad range of civil and criminal cases

county judge the person in each of Texas's 254 counties who presides over the county court and the county commissioners' court, with responsibility for the administration of county government; some county judges carry out judicial responsibilities

county courts the courts that exist in some counties that are presided over by county judges

The Texas Court of Criminal Appeals is the highest court in the state for criminal cases. Like the Texas Supreme Court, it has nine justices (pictured here as of 2014).

statutory county courts at law
courts that tend to hear less serious cases than those heard by district courts

statutory probate courts
specialized courts whose jurisdiction is limited to probate and guardianship matters

justice of the peace courts
local trial courts with limited jurisdiction over small claims and very minor criminal misdemeanors

there are county courts at law and sometimes probate courts. As a result, in the larger counties most, and sometimes all, of the county judges' judicial duties are now performed by other courts.

In larger counties, there are **statutory county courts at law**. Since the county courts at law were created by statute, often at widely different times, the jurisdiction of these courts varies significantly. Usually, the county courts at law hear appeals from justices of the peace and from municipal courts. In civil cases, they usually hear cases involving sums greater than would be heard by a justice of the peace court but less than would be heard by district courts. Typically, county courts at law hear civil cases involving less than $100,000. In comparison to the district courts, the county courts at law would hear less serious criminal offenses.

Some of the county courts at law have specialized jurisdiction; most commonly these are in the most urban counties, where some of the courts will have only civil jurisdiction and others only criminal jurisdiction. Currently there are 237 county court at law judges.

In the most urban areas of the state, the legislature has created courts known as **statutory probate courts**. These courts are highly specialized, as their primary activity involves probate matters that relate to the disposition of property of deceased persons. They may also deal with matters relating to guardianship of people unable to handle their own affairs, and they may handle mental-health commitments. In other parts of the state, depending on the statute, probate matters may be heard by the county court, the county court at law, or the district court. Currently, there are 18 statutory probate court judges.

Each county in Texas has between one and eight justice of the peace precincts, depending on population, although large urban counties have more than one judge in each precinct. Harris County, for example, has two in each of eight precincts. Within each precinct are **justice of the peace courts**. There are 819 justice of the peace courts

The boxes of evidence that the State of Texas prepared for the trial against tobacco companies in 1997 occupied an entire gym in Texarkana. In a civil case, the plaintiff bears the burden of proof and must demonstrate that the defendant is more than not likely responsible for the harm suffered by the plaintiff.

in Texas. These courts hear class C misdemeanors, which are less serious crimes. They also have jurisdiction over minor civil matters. In the past the courts functioned as small claims courts. Unfortunately, the courts used formal rules of evidence which gave a great advantage to parties represented by lawyers. As a result of a law passed in 2011, however, while suits must be for less than $10,000, the suits can be handled more informally. Rules governing suits now may not be "so complex that a reasonable person without legal training would have difficulty understanding or applying the rules."[4] Justices may issue search and arrest warrants. In counties without medical examiners, they may fulfill the administrative functions of coroners.

Justices of the peace mostly handle traffic misdemeanors. Of the more than 2.37 million cases disposed of by justice of the peace courts in 2012, more than 1.5 million were traffic and parking cases. In contrast, justice of the peace courts heard only about 391,000 civil cases.[5]

Justices of the peace have faced considerable criticism in recent years. In Dallas County, an auditor discovered 22,000 unprocessed traffic cases. The justice of the peace had failed to collect as much as $2 million in fines. Unlike any other judge in Texas except for the county judge (who is often an administrator rather than a judge), 92 percent of the 819 justices of the peace in Texas are non-lawyers, and the lack of justices' legal credentials has led to considerable debate in the state.[6] The office has its origins in medieval England and has existed in Texas since 1837, even before statehood. In the days of the frontier, justices of the peace provided legal authority where no other existed. Indeed, the famed Judge Roy Bean was a justice of the peace. The initial idea was that a justice of the peace would be a respected person in the community who was chosen for ability, judgment, and integrity. Today, as the former Texas state bar president Frank Newton has pointed out, "In almost every large metropolitan area, there are some JPs who do virtually nothing and sort of get lost in the shuffle. People don't tend to get all excited about JP elections. Most people don't know what a JP does. JP is not a very prestigious job."[7]

Municipal courts have been created by the legislature in each of the incorporated cities of the state. There are 926 cities and towns in Texas that have these courts; larger cities have multiple courts. There are 1,559 municipal court judges in the

municipal courts local trial courts with limited jurisdiction over violations of city ordinances and very minor criminal misdemeanors

ordinance a regulation enacted by a city government each of Texas's incorporated cities and towns

state. Municipal courts have jurisdiction over violations of city **ordinances** and, concurrent with justice of the peace courts, have jurisdiction over class C misdemeanors, for which the punishment for conviction is a fine. Municipal judges may issue search and arrest warrants, but they have only limited civil jurisdiction.[8] Municipal courts, like justice of the peace courts, function primarily as traffic courts. In 2012 municipal courts disposed of slightly more than 6 million cases. About 4.94 million of these cases were traffic and parking cases.[9]

Great controversy has erupted in the city of Dallas, where the city council has demanded that municipal judges—there are 11 full-time and 18 part-time municipal judges in Dallas—get tougher with offenders or lose their judicial appointments. In particular, city officials have claimed that the judges give too many trial postponements, set fines too low, and don't hold accused violators accountable for ignoring citations.[10]

● The Legal Process

Explain the legal process and the differences between criminal and civil law

Just as the Texas Supreme Court hears civil cases and the Texas Court of Criminal Appeals hears criminal cases, it is useful to think of the law as divided into these parts. **Civil law** involves a dispute, usually between private individuals over relationships, obligations, and responsibility. Though there are exceptions with a violation of the civil law, the remedy is often for the offending party to pay compensation to the injured party.

In contrast, **criminal law** involves the violation of concepts of right and wrong as defined by criminal statutes. In criminal law, the state accuses individuals of violations and, if found guilty, the violator is subject to punishment. In some cases, that punishment may involve loss of liberty or even loss of life.

In civil law, an aggrieved person will usually obtain a lawyer and file a petition that details the **complaint** against the person accused of causing the harm. The petition is filed with the clerk of court, who issues a citation against the defendant. The defendant will usually file an **answer** explaining why the allegations are not valid. Depending on the issue, the amounts of money that may be awarded as damages, and the probability of success, the aggrieved person may be able to obtain the services of a lawyer on a **contingent fee** basis. This means that the lawyer will not charge the individual if the case is lost but will obtain a portion of the damages awarded if the case is won. It is not unusual for such contingent fee arrangements to involve one-third or more of the damages award plus expenses. Lawyers who handle cases on contingent fee agreements often handle personal-injury cases and are known as trial lawyers. Traditionally, these lawyers will contribute money to judicial candidates who are sympathetic to plaintiffs. They make money only if they win, so they have a strong economic interest in supporting judicial candidates who are sympathetic to plaintiffs and to the awarding of large damages.

The person being sued either will have to hire an attorney on his or her own or, if insured, will be represented by an attorney paid for by the insurance company. Fee arrangements vary for civil defense lawyers, but often they are paid by the hour, in which case they get paid whether they win or lose. Their economic

civil law a branch of law that deals with disputes, usually between private individuals over relationships, obligations, and responsibility

criminal law the branch of law that regulates the conduct of individuals, defines crimes, and specifies punishment for criminal acts

complaint the presentation of a grievance by the plaintiff in a civil case

answer the presentation of a defendant's defense against an allegation in a civil case

contingent fee a fee paid to the lawyer in a civil case which is contingent on winning the case

incentives to contribute money to judicial campaigns may be different from the incentives trial lawyers have, but civil defense lawyers do contribute large sums to judicial campaigns in order to elect judges who support their views on tort law.

The court to which a civil case is taken depends on the type of case and the amount of money involved. Most commonly, a civil case will be settled, meaning the dispute is resolved without going to court. Settlements may, however, occur during trial, sometimes immediately before a jury renders its decision. If a case is not settled and goes to trial, it may be heard either by a judge or, if requested by either side, by a jury. Although civil jury cases do not have to be unanimous in Texas, the burden of proof is on the plaintiff. The standard of proof that the plaintiff must meet is **preponderance of the evidence**. That means that the plaintiff must show that it is more likely than not that the defendant is the cause of the harm suffered by the plaintiff.

preponderance of the evidence the standard of proof in a civil jury case, by which the plaintiff must show that the defendant is more likely than not the cause of the harm suffered by the plaintiff

Civil cases may involve tiny amounts of damages or they may involve billions of dollars, which have the potential of breaking huge corporations, such as happened in the 1980s when Pennzoil successfully sued Texaco in a dispute over the takeover of the Getty Oil Company.[11]

Civil case verdicts may, of course, be appealed. Appeals are usually from the trial court to the intermediate court of appeal and perhaps further to the state supreme court. Given the cost of appeals and the delay that is involved, it is not unusual for some settlement to be reached after the verdict but before the case goes through the appellate process. For example, a plaintiff might agree to settle for much less than the verdict in the case to avoid the expense and delay of further appeals.

Litigating a civil case is time consuming and expensive. As a result, in Texas and in other states, it is increasingly common to try to negotiate a settlement through mediation or arbitration. With arbitration, the parties to the dispute agree to present their case to a decision maker and to be bound by the decision. With mediation, the parties to the dispute try to reach a compromise resolution of the problem without going to trial. Generally, lawyers are used in mediations and arbitrations that have significant financial value, although persons assisting the parties in mediations and arbitrations do not necessarily have to be lawyers. Mediation is especially popular in civil disputes because the parties to the dispute are reaching the agreement and are not forced into a particular decision as they would be with arbitration. Mediation is also a very flexible process for resolving disputes where resolutions of disputes are contractual agreements between the opposing parties. To resolve the dispute they may agree to any legal remedy. One of the most unusual such remedies for a dispute occurred a number of years ago when Southwest Airlines and Stevens Aviation had a dispute over which company could use the slogan "Plane Smart." The two sides initially agreed to determine which company would use the slogan by having an arm-wrestling match between Southwest's and Stevens Aviation's company chairmen. Lawyers later worked out another agreement, but the company chairmen went ahead and held their arm-wrestling event.

In criminal cases, the state alleges a violation of a criminal law and is usually represented in court by a prosecutor. Some prosecutors are career prosecutors with vast trial experience. These people will often prosecute the most difficult and complex cases, such as felonies and **capital cases**. However, because the pay of prosecutors is often much lower than that of private lawyers who do litigation in the private sector, it is common for most prosecutors to be quite young and inexperienced. Once they gain trial experience, prosecutors commonly move into the private sector.

capital case a criminal case in which the death penalty is a possible punishment

Defendants may hire criminal defense attorneys, who usually charge a flat fee to handle the case. Criminal defense lawyers, of course, do not work on a contingent fee basis. Since most criminal defendants are found guilty, criminal defense lawyers often prefer to obtain as much of their fee as possible in advance of the verdict.

Some parts of Texas have public defender offices where salaried lawyers provide at least some adult indigent criminal defense services in a county. Bexar County has established the first public defender office for indigent criminal appeals. Travis County has a public defender office representing only indigents with mental impairments.[12] A public defender office represents indigents in capital cases in west Texas.[13]

In Texas, indigent criminal defendants are more commonly represented by court-appointed lawyers. These are lawyers appointed by the judge to represent a defendant. Usually, these government-paid fees are less than would be charged to nonindigent defendants. Thus, some lawyers are reluctant to fulfill court appointments; others may not put the time and energy into a court-appointed case that they would if they were privately paid; others take court appointments because they have a limited number of paying clients; and still others take court appointments to gain experience. Concern over the poor quality of legal representation provided indigent criminal defendants, especially in capital cases, led to legislation in 2001 to increase the pay and qualifications of court-appointed lawyers.

Serious crimes are **felonies**. In those cases, as well as many lesser offenses known as **misdemeanors**, prior to the trial there will be an indictment by a grand jury. In Texas, a **grand jury** consists of 12 persons who sit for two to six months. Depending on the county, a grand jury may meet only once or twice, or it may meet several times a week. Although sometimes grand juries are selected randomly from a pool of qualified citizens, mostly Texas grand jurors are chosen by a commissioner system. A district judge will appoint several grand jury commissioners, who will then select 15 to 20 citizens of the county. The first 12 who are qualified become the grand jury.[14]

Grand juries can inquire into any criminal matter but usually spend most of their time on felony crimes. They work in secret and rely heavily on the information provided by the prosecutor, though in some cases grand juries will work quite independently of the prosecutor. These grand juries are called runaway grand juries because the prosecutor has lost control of them, but such cases are very rare. If nine of the grand jurors decide a trial is warranted, they will indict a suspect. An **indictment** is also known as a "true bill." On the other hand, sometimes a grand jury does not believe a trial is warranted. In those cases, the grand jury issues a "no bill" decision.

Although a suspect has the right to trial by jury, he or she may waive that right and undergo a **bench trial** before the judge only. Most commonly, the suspect will engage in a **plea bargain**. With plea bargaining, a suspect agrees to plead guilty in exchange for a lighter sentence than might be imposed if the suspect were found guilty at trial. Approximately 97 percent of criminal convictions in Texas are the result of plea bargains.[15] If the suspect does choose trial by jury, felony juries will have 12 members; misdemeanor juries will have 6 members. There must be a unanimous verdict of guilty or not guilty. If the jurors are not unanimous, the result is a hung jury and a mistrial is declared. The prosecutor may then choose to retry the suspect. In addition to the requirement of unanimity in jury decisions, another important difference between civil and criminal cases is the standard of proof. In criminal cases, rather than the standard of preponderance of the evidence, the stan-

felony a serious criminal offense, punishable by a prison sentence or a fine; a capital felony is possibly punishable by death

misdemeanor a minor criminal offense, usually punishable by a fine or a jail sentence

grand jury jury that determines whether sufficient evidence is available to justify a trial; grand juries do not rule on the accused's guilt or innocence

indictment a written statement issued by a grand jury that charges a suspect with a crime and states that a trial is warranted

bench trial a trial held without a jury and before only a judge

plea bargain negotiated agreement in a criminal case in which a defendant agrees to plead guilty in return for the state's agreement to reduce the severity of the criminal charge or prison sentence the defendant is facing

Judge Elizabeth Coker swearing in former prosecutor Kaycee Jones as a new district judge. Coker became known as the "texting judge" when it was discovered that during a trial of a defendant accused of felony injury to a child, she texted prosecutor Jones suggesting a line of questions that the prosecutors should ask the defendant. Coker resigned while she was under investigation by the State Commission on Judicial Conduct.

dard is **beyond a reasonable doubt**. This means that the prosecutor must prove the charges against the defendant, and they must be proven to a very high standard so that a reasonable doubt of innocence does not exist.

If a guilty verdict is returned, there will be a separate hearing on the sentence, which in Texas is sometimes also determined by the jury. At the sentencing hearing, factors such as prior record and background will be considered, even though these factors could not be considered at the trial portion of the proceeding.

Of course a defendant may also appeal a verdict. Usually, the appeals are by a convicted defendant who alleges that an error in the trial may have affected the case's outcome. In rare cases, a prosecutor may also appeal. For the most part, however, criminal defendants will appeal their convictions to an intermediate appeals court and perhaps further to the Texas Court of Criminal Appeals. In capital cases, however, the appeal will be directly to the Texas Court of Criminal Appeals.

beyond a reasonable doubt the legal standard in criminal cases, which requires the prosecution to prove that a reasonable doubt of innocence does not exist

● Judicial Politics

> **Evaluate the process for selecting judges in Texas**

Although there are still generalist lawyers who handle all sorts of cases, much of the practice of law is very specialized. Thus, in the civil process, trial lawyers and civil defense lawyers tend to back opposing candidates for judgeships. It is not unusual for trial lawyers to support one candidate, often the Democrat, who is more likely to be the more liberal, or pro-plaintiff, candidate, and for the civil defense lawyers to support the Republican, who is more likely to be the conservative, or pro-defendant, candidate. The civil defense lawyers will often align themselves with business groups and with professional groups, such as medical doctors, to support judges inclined to favor the civil defense side.

In the criminal process, it is sometimes possible to see criminal defense lawyers backing one candidate and prosecutors backing the other. Some prosecutors' offices are quite political, and the prosecutors will publicly support pro-prosecution judicial candidates. They will often be aligned with victims' rights groups. Criminal defense lawyers, on the other hand, will often back one of their own in contested criminal court races.

One big difference in the campaigns of civil court judges versus criminal court judges is the amount of money involved. Enormous amounts can be involved in civil cases, and so it is worth lots of money to trial lawyers and civil defense interests to elect candidates favorable to their point of view. On the other hand, with the exception of a relatively few highly paid criminal defense lawyers, the practice of criminal law is not very lucrative. Prosecutors are on salary, and usually the salaries are not large. Criminal defense lawyers often represent clients with little money. And most criminal cases are plea-bargained. The economic incentives to contribute large sums to criminal court races don't exist. The result is that a strong candidate for the Texas Supreme Court may raise in the neighborhood of $1,000,000 for a campaign, whereas a strong candidate for the Texas Court of Criminal Appeals may raise $100,000. However, as Texas has become predominantly Republican at the statewide level, hard-fought contests between Democrats and Republicans for the Texas Supreme Court and the Texas Court of Criminal Appeals have become rare.

for critical analysis

What is the most important feature of how judges are selected in Texas? What does this feature reveal about Texas politics more broadly?

Initial Appointment of Judges by the Governor

A notable aspect of the Texas judiciary is that with the exception of municipal judges, who tend to be appointed by local governments, all judges are elected in partisan elections. Still, because the governor appoints district and appellate judges to the bench to fill vacancies prior to an election or to fill judgeships on new courts, large percentages of judges initially get on the bench through appointment. Although there has been some controversy over the relatively small number of appointments of minorities made by some governors, gubernatorial appointment has generated little additional controversy.[16] Table 9.1 shows the percentage of district and appellate judges who have initially gained their seats through appointment by the governor. Currently, about 55 percent of appellate judges and 38 percent of the trial judges initially got on the bench through appointment.[17] Still, the controversial issue in Texas judicial politics deals with how the remaining judges obtained their seats and how all judges retain their seats if they wish to remain in office. That controversy involves the partisan election of judges in Texas.

The Elections Become Highly Partisan

Until 1978 the selection of judges in partisan elections did not create much concern. Texas was overwhelmingly a Democratic state, and judges were elected as Democrats. The only real competition occurred in the Democratic primary, and with the political advantage of incumbency, judges were rarely defeated even in the primary. Competition in judicial races occurred in those relatively rare cases where there was an open seat in which no incumbent sought office. Beginning in 1978, however, changes began to occur in Texas judicial politics. William Clements, the

TABLE 9.1

Percentage of Judges Obtaining Their Position Initially through Appointment

YEAR	TRIAL COURTS* (%)	APPELLATE COURTS** (%)
1962	57%	50%
1984	67	51
1998	46	40
2001	34	38
2003	43	43
2006	43	50
2009	36	51
2011	37	52
2012	38	55

* Trial courts are the district and criminal district courts.
** Appellate courts are the supreme court, the court of criminal appeals, and the courts of appeal.
SOURCES: Anthony Champagne, "The Selection and Retention of Judges in Texas," *Southwestern Law Journal* 40 (May 1986): 66; Texas Office of Court Administration, "Profile of Appellate and Trial Judges" as of September 1, 1998, 2001, 2003, 2006, 2009, March 1, 2011, September 1, 2012.

first Republican governor since Reconstruction, was elected. The governor has the power to appoint judges to the district and higher courts when new courts have been created or when a judicial vacancy occurs as a result of death, resignation, or retirement. Unlike the previous Democratic governors who appointed members of the Democratic Party, Clements began appointing Republicans. With that advantage of incumbency and with the increasing popularity of the Republican party label, some of the Republican judges began to win re-election.

Helped by the popularity of Ronald Reagan in Texas, other Republicans began seeking judicial offices and winning. Thus, by the early 1980s, in statewide elections and in several counties in Texas, competition began to appear in judicial races. With that competition, incumbent judges began to be defeated. Sensing the growth of Republican strength, a number of Democratic judges changed to a Republican Party affiliation. From 1980 through July 24, 1985, 13 district and appellate judges changed from the Democratic to the Republican Party; 11 county court judges switched; and 5 justices of the peace changed parties. Judge Don Koons switched parties in early 1985 and explained his move to the Republican Party by saying, "I ran as a Democrat in 1982. It was a long, tough year, but we won. On the other hand, it cost a lot more money and time away from the bench to run as a Democrat. The work suffers some, and you've got to be always hustling money."[18] Koons apparently believed that with the emerging strength of the Republican Party, a switch in party affiliation would make his job more secure.

Judicial elections became more expensive because judicial candidates needed money to run meaningful campaigns. In particular, campaigns that used television advertising became very expensive because of high media costs.

Is justice for sale in Texas? Because statewide judicial races are expensive, candidates for judgeships have been forced to raise considerable amounts of money. This, in turn, has led to criticism that judicial decisions are, in effect, being bought.

Judicial candidates needed money because judicial races tend to have low-visibility campaigns in which voters are unaware of the candidates. The races tend to be overshadowed by higher-visibility races, such as the race for governor or U.S. senator. Money was needed to give judicial candidates some degree of name visibility by voters. However, in general, Texas voters do not give much money to judicial campaigns. Instead, it is lawyers, interest groups, and potential litigants who tend to be donors in judicial races.[19] That money to judicial candidates often comes from parties interested in the outcomes of cases has raised concerns about the neutrality of Texas judges who are deciding cases that involve the financial interests of persons who have given them campaign funds. A Texas poll found that 83 percent of the public thought that judges were strongly or somewhat influenced by contributions in their decisions. Ninety-nine percent of lawyers believed that campaign contributions have at least some influence on judges. Perhaps even more striking, 86 percent of judges reported that they believed campaign contributions had at least some influence on judicial decisions.[20]

Contributions for judicial races in Texas can sometimes amount to several hundred thousand dollars, especially for hotly contested district court races or appellate races. In general, however, the most expensive races are for the Texas Supreme Court.

When races are contested between Democratic and Republican candidates, a candidate can raise well over $1 million. However, hard-fought races are now rare as these statewide elections have moved into the Republican column. Because these are statewide races and because this court sets the tone of tort law

Elected or Appointed Judges?

Federal judges are appointed for life by the president, with the advice and consent of the U.S. Senate. Several states follow the federal model in which the governor appoints state judges with the advice and consent of the state senate.

In Texas, however, members of the Texas Supreme Court and the Court of Criminal Appeals, as well as all lower state courts, are elected to their posts, rather than appointed, by the voters in partisan elections. Texas is one of only seven states that elect judges in partisan elections. Thirteen states elect judges in nonpartisan elections and another two have a mix of partisan and nonpartisan aspects in their election of judges.

Is there an alternative to appointing or electing judges? Many "good government" advocates support merit selection, which several states employ and which has been suggested many times as a possible alternative to the current system in Texas. Merit selection involves a commission that vets potential judges based on their character and temperament. A group of approved judicial nominees is then presented to the governor, who appoints one as judge. After a period of time, that judge runs in a retention election. The judge does not face an opponent, but the ballot question asks voters whether the judge should be retained in office.

Supporters of the Texas model like the fact that it holds judges accountable to the electorate. This system leads criminal court judges to run campaigns touting their tough sentencing practices and "zero tolerance" for criminals. Texas model supporters maintain that the alternative is undemocratic because elites would choose judges

who would become entrenched in their positions and make rulings without any fear of public backlash. If judges are insulated from the public, then they can render decisions without accountability.

Opponents of electing judges argue that the Texas model inevitably leads to corruption because lawyers and other interests can make campaign contributions to judges, which will influence their rulings. Especially in civil cases, Texas judges could sell out to the highest bidder. According to critics of judicial elections, in criminal cases, the rights of the accused might not be taken as seriously, as the public consistently favors tough rulings and sentences on criminals. With the partisan election of judges, the best-qualified persons are not chosen because voters tend to vote based on party affiliations rather than merit.

Some Texas state legislators have proposed changing the judicial selection system. One option that some observers have suggested is a hybrid system in which Texas Supreme Court and appellate court judges would be appointed, while lower court judges would be elected. This system might be an effective compromise to ensure responsiveness at a certain level. However, changing the selection system in any way would generally require a constitutional amendment, which is not easy to implement. The larger debate revolves around whether it is possible to keep politics out of judicial selection. Gubernatorial appointments also inevitably involve political considerations. As in most political debates, there are clear trade-offs involved when deciding which approach is best. Which would you choose?

critical thinking questions

1. Should judges be elected or appointed? Is merit selection an effective compromise?

2. Should the selection system vary according to type of judge?

throughout the state, a great deal of money is needed and a great deal can be raised. Table 9.2 shows the average contribution to Texas Supreme Court candidates for each election period from 1980 through 2012. The contribution data are reported for those races that were contested by both a Republican and a Democratic candidate. In the 2000 Supreme Court elections, the Republicans were so strong that no Democrat even bothered to run for any position on the Texas Supreme Court. By 2012 the Democratic candidate against Republican incumbent Nathan Hecht could only raise a little less than $76,000. Any real battle for a position on the Texas Supreme Court is now in the Republican primary.

TABLE 9.2

Average Contributions to Texas Supreme Court Candidates*

YEAR	AVERAGE FOR ALL CANDIDATES	AVERAGE FOR WINNING CANDIDATES
1980	$155,033	$298,167
1982**	173,174	332,998
1984**	967,405	1,922,183
1986	519,309	1,024,817
1988	859,413	842,148
1990	970,154	1,544,939
1992	1,096,001	1,096,687
1994	1,499,577	1,627,285
1996	656,190	1,277,127
1998	521,519	829,794
2000	NA[†]	584,719[††]
2002[†]	425,474	568,430
2004**	394,906	548,685
2006**	995,218	1,792,523
2008	654,819	910,973
2010	438,854	744,033
2012	206,272	336,838

*Averages are reported for candidates from contested races featuring both a Republican and Democratic candidate.
** The 1982, 1984, 2004, and 2006 elections each featured only one contested race with both a Democratic and Republican candidate.
[†]No Democrats ran in the three Supreme Court elections in 2000.
[††]Average campaign contributions for the three victorious Republicans; none had a Democratic opponent.
[†]Chief Justice Tom Phillips ran for re-election and refused to accept any campaign contributions beyond his cash on hand, which amounted to $19,433. His Democratic opponent, however, raised almost no funds—$12,815. Phillips was the victor in this race, which lowers the average contributions for this year.
SOURCES: Kyle Cheek and Anthony Champagne, Judicial Politics in Texas (New York: Peter Lang, 2005), p. 38; Institute on Money in State Politics.

In spite of judicial campaigns, however, voters often know little about judicial candidates. As a result, they vote not for the best-qualified person to be a judge, but for the party label. As the Republican Party has become increasingly dominant in statewide races, it is the Republican label, rather than the qualifications or experience of judicial candidates, that has determined the outcome of judicial races. Related to the importance of party label in judicial races is the effect of top-of-the-ticket voting. In 1984 the popularity of Ronald Reagan seemed to help Texas judicial candidacies, as many voters cast straight or almost straight Republican ballots. In that year Reagan received nearly 64 percent of the presidential vote in Texas. All four Republican incumbent district judges who were challenged by Democrats won. Sixteen Democratic incumbent district judges were challenged by Republicans. Only three of those Democrats won. In contrast, in 1982, U.S. Senator Lloyd Bentsen ran for re-election. Bentsen was a very popular senator and a Democrat. His candidacy on the Democratic ballot seems to have encouraged voters to cast ballots for Democrats further down on the ticket. Bentsen received slightly more than 59 percent of the vote in Texas. In that year, 26 Republican incumbent district judges faced Democratic opposition; only 14 won. Yet 16 Democratic district judges faced opposition, and 14 won.[21]

Even voters who try to make a serious effort to learn about judicial candidates can have a hard time. In Houston, for example, voters are faced with ballots loaded with so many judicial candidates that it becomes nearly impossible to be an informed voter. In 1994 one of the most extreme examples of a long judicial ballot occurred in Harris County, where voters were faced with 45 judicial elections that were primary elections and then 8 runoff primary elections. In the general election, there were 59 contested judicial elections and 16 more elections where the judicial candidate was unopposed. In 2010, Harris County voters cast ballots in 10 contested appellate court races and 36 contested district court races. In 2012, Harris County voters faced a ballot with 11 contested appellate races and 23 contested district court races.

The Name Game

In 1994, Cathy Herasimchuk ran for the Texas Court of Criminal Appeals. In a three-way Republican primary, she won only 26 percent of the statewide vote. The candidates in the Democratic and Republican primaries who did make the runoff for that seat all had simple, easy-to-spell and easy-to-pronounce names. Herasimchuk was appointed to the Court of Criminal Appeals in 2001, but in running for election to the court in 2002, she realized she had a problem with her name. As she said, "Everybody told me you couldn't win city dog catcher with the name Herasimchuk, and they all turned out to be accurate." Herasimchuk's problems getting elected certainly had nothing to do with her credentials. She has been a Harris County prosecutor, a criminal defense lawyer, an adviser to then-governor Bush, and a law school lecturer. When she successfully ran in 2002, she did so under her maiden name—Cathy Cochran.[22]

The name game continued in the 2008 elections for judges in Harris County. Most Republican judges in that county were swept out of office, but four Republicans survived. They had all been challenged by Democrats with unusual names. As a result, the incumbent Republican judge Sharon McCally was able to defeat the Democratic challenger Ashish Mahendru; Republican judge Mark Kent Ellis defeated Democrat Mekisha Murray; Judge Patricia Kerrigan, a Republican, defeated the Democrat Andres Pereira; and Judge Joseph Halback defeated his Democratic challenger, Goodwille Pierre.[23]

Some have claimed that a Latino name will hurt candidates in Republican primaries. In reference to judicial races, for example, Justice David Medina was defeated by John Devine in the 2012 Republican runoff primary for the Texas Supreme Court, and in 2002 Justice Xavier Rodriguez was defeated in the Republican primary for the Texas Supreme Court by Steve Smith. There have been other nonjudicial Republican primary elections where persons with Latino names have been defeated by persons with non-Hispanic names. However, the victory of Ted Cruz over David Dewhurst in the 2012 Republican runoff primary for U.S. senator from Texas suggests that the assertion that there is ethnic bias in Republican primary voting may be overblown.[24]

for critical **analysis**

How does the selection process influence who becomes a judge in Texas?

Minority Representation in the Texas Judiciary

Minority groups have been concerned that countywide and larger partisan judicial races make it difficult for minorities to get elected to judgeships—and that Texas judges do not reflect the diversity of the state.

Although women do not make up 50 percent of the judiciary as they do of the population, there is a higher proportion of women in the Texas judiciary than of minorities. Women were at one time a great rarity on the bench. In 1970 only 1 percent of the nation's judiciary was female. As late as 1979 only 4 percent of the nation's judges were women.[25] In Texas, the first woman to serve as a state judge was Sarah Hughes, who was appointed in 1935 and who served as a district judge until 1961, when she was appointed to the federal bench. Famous for a number of her decisions, including one that forced Dallas County to build a new jail, she is probably best known as the judge who swore in Lyndon Johnson as president after the assassination of John F. Kennedy. In 2012, however, 42 percent of appellate judges in Texas were women, and 40 percent of district judges were women. Thirty-one percent of county court-at-law judges were female, as were 33 percent of the probate judges. Eleven percent of county judges, 35 percent of municipal judges, and 36 percent of justices of the peace were women.[26]

Different interpretations have been offered for the low numbers of minorities on the bench. The lack of racial and ethnic diversity on the bench is a nationwide problem. Ninety-two percent of the state judges in the nation are white.[27] Civil rights groups in several states with elective judiciaries, including Texas, have argued that white voters dominate countywide and larger districts and will vote against minority judicial candidates. Civil rights organizations representing Latinos and African Americans have argued that for minorities to get elected to office, there must be smaller judicial districts where minority voters make up the majority.

An alternative argument is that minority candidates in Texas, like minority voters, tend to be Democrats at a time when Republicans increasingly are winning judicial races. Thus, minorities do not get elected to judicial office because they run as Democrats.[28] Still another argument is that there are few minority judges because there are few minority lawyers and, with the exception of county judges and justices of the peace, judges in Texas must be lawyers.

The issue of minority representation on the bench has been the subject of major concern by minority and civil rights leaders in Texas. It was also the subject of prolonged federal litigation. In 1989 a case was tried in federal court in Midland. The case, *League of United Latin American Citizens v. Mattox*, was a suit against countywide election of judges in 10 of the larger counties in Texas.[29] The suit, filed by minority plaintiffs, argued that countywide election of judges diluted the strength of minority voters and violated the Voting Rights Act. The trial judge agreed with the plaintiffs and, after a political solution failed, ordered that judges be elected in nonpartisan elections from smaller judicial districts. The trial court order, however, was blocked by the Fifth Circuit, which is the federal court of appeals for the region that includes Texas.[30] The case was then appealed to the U.S. Supreme Court, along with a Louisiana case; the Supreme Court held that the Voting Rights Act did apply to judicial elections.[31] The case was then returned to the Fifth Circuit to examine whether minority voting strength was diluted and to determine the state's interest in maintaining countywide elections. Ordinarily, the federal courts of appeal do not preside as an entire group to hear cases; instead, they hear cases in panels of three judges. Such a panel decided in favor of the minority plaintiffs, and a settlement seemed to be reached with the state to have elections of judges from smaller districts in the larger counties. However, in important cases, it is sometimes possible to appeal a decision of a panel of three judges to the entire court of appeal. When this happens, the court is said to sit *en banc*. That happened when some of the defendants in the suit were unhappy with the settlement, and the entire Fifth Circuit ruled in 1993 that party affiliation of minority candidates explained the failure of minority judicial candidates to win election rather than the candidates' minority status. Thus, countywide election of judges was not illegal, and there was no legal need to reduce the size of districts from which judges were elected.[32]

Since that decision, minority leaders and minority groups have continued to express concerns about the small numbers of minority judges, but any solution that would involve smaller districts would have to result from an act of the legislature rather than the actions of a federal court. Judicial reform bills in the legislature since this decision have included provisions for smaller judicial districts, but those bills have not passed. Perhaps the strongest judicial reform bill was one backed by then-Democratic lieutenant governor Bob Bullock, who created a task force to try to develop an acceptable compromise on the judicial selection issue. The proposed

for critical analysis

Few minorities hold judicial office in Texas. Although African Americans and Hispanics make up about 50 percent of the Texas population, relatively few Texas judges belong to these groups. Offer at least three suggestions, including alternative election methods, to increase the number of minorities holding judicial office in Texas.

en banc referring to an appellate hearing with all judges participating

constitutional amendment designed by the task force passed the Texas Senate in 1995 but failed to pass the Texas House. Under the plan, all appellate judges would be appointed by the governor. District judges, on the other hand, would be chosen from county commissioner precincts in nonpartisan elections. After serving for a time, they would run countywide in **retention elections**, in which there would be a "yes" or "no" vote on their retention in office and where they would face no opponent on the ballot.

retention election an election in which voters decide whether to keep an incumbent in office by voting "yes" or "no" to retain the incumbent and where there is no opposing candidate

On the surface, the compromise seemed to offer something for almost everyone. Because the governor appointed appellate judges, judges would have greater career security and no worries about campaign funding. The business community, recognizing that Texas tended to elect conservative governors and was increasingly likely to elect conservative Republican governors, got appointed appellate judges. Nonpartisan elections would protect trial judges from party sweeps in which judges are voted out of office solely because of their party affiliation. Minorities would get smaller judicial districts for the major trial courts. But what looked like a great compromise fell through. Although African Americans supported the compromise, Latinos did not. The two largest counties in Texas—Harris and Dallas—elected a total of 96 of the 386 district judges then chosen in Texas. Under the compromise, one-fourth of Harris and Dallas county judges would be elected from each of the county commissioners' precincts in that county. Both Dallas and Harris counties had three white county commissioners and one African American. Latinos, on the other hand, elected no county commissioner and believed that the compromise would not promote the election of more Latino judges. They believed that to elect Latino judges, considerably smaller districts were needed. As a result, much Latino support was not forthcoming. Further, the political parties opposed the compromise. Nonpartisan elections might protect the interests of judges, but they weakened the political parties. Additionally, an appointive system for appellate judges reduced the number of elective offices, thereby reducing the role of the political parties. Although his powers would have increased with an appointed appellate judiciary, Governor George W. Bush opposed the compromise, probably because he did not want to oppose the Republican Party. Because the plan had the support of Lieutenant Governor Bob Bullock and because he gave the legislation priority on his legislative agenda that year, it passed the Texas Senate. However, the proposal died in the Texas House. The Bullock proposal was probably the best hope for judicial change for a long time to come.[33]

One of the business community's underlying concerns about smaller districts seemed to be a fear that small districts might create a narrower electorate for judges. That narrow electorate might in some areas prove unduly sympathetic to plaintiffs who file suit against businesses. Whatever the cause of the low number of minority judges, the lack of diversity on the bench, the role of money in judicial races, the defeat of incumbents, the importance of party label, top-of-the-ticket voting, and the "name game" have all created support for alternative judicial selection systems.

Alternative Means of Selection

Judges are selected in the United States by a variety of ways. One way is through appointment by the governor and approval by the state Senate. This method is used in Texas to select judges to new courts or courts where there has been a death, resignation, or retirement during a judicial term. It is also similar to the system for selecting federal judges, who are appointed by the president and confirmed by vote

Who Are Texas Judges?

Race and Gender of Texas Judges, 2012

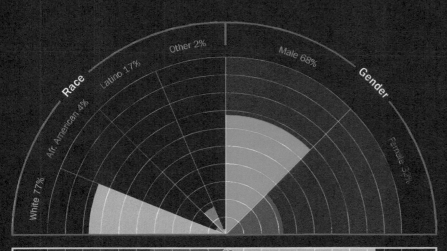

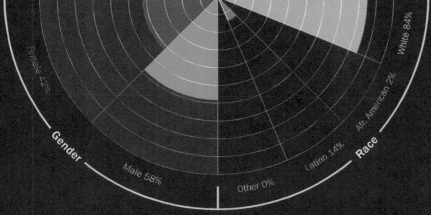

Trial Courts

Trial courts include district courts, county courts at law, and probate courts

Total judges: 663

Appellate Courts

Appellate courts include the state Supreme Court, courts of appeal, and Court of Criminal Appeals

Total judges: 97

As Texas becomes more diverse, how does the racial and ethnic composition of the state's judges reflect this new racial reality?

for critical analysis

1. Why do you think there are fewer minority judges in Texas courts than the overall minority population in the state (12% black and 38% Latino)?

2. What are some of the factors that might lead to an increase in the representation of minorities in the state's courts?

SOURCE: Texas Courts Online, www.courts.state.tx.us/pubs/AR2013/jud_branch/3-judge-profile090113.pdf (accessed 5/14/14).

of the U.S. Senate. However, this method of judicial selection is contrary to Texas's traditional distrust of a powerful chief executive. At a time when Texas governors are Republicans, it also is not a system that Democrats tend to favor.

Another system for selecting judges is nonpartisan election. Such a system for selecting judges in Texas would eliminate much of the partisan politics, but at the same time, it would make it more difficult for candidates to reach voters. This is because in a truly nonpartisan election, judicial candidates would have to run for office without the benefit of political parties. In some states that have ostensibly nonpartisan elections, such as Ohio, the parties continue to take an active role to the point that it is difficult to distinguish that type of nonpartisan system from a partisan election system. If Texas instituted a truly nonpartisan system, however, candidates would require even more campaign money to reach voters they could no longer reach through the mechanisms of the political parties.

Most commonly, however, judicial reformers argue for a system of judicial selection that is commonly called **merit selection** of judges. In this system, a blue-ribbon committee consisting of lawyers and lay people supplies to the governor the names of a small number of candidates for a judgeship. The governor makes the judicial appointment from this list, and after the judge serves for a brief time, he or she runs in a retention election. In a retention election, the incumbent does not have an opponent. Instead voters are asked whether the incumbent should be retained for another term of office. The voters then vote "yes" or "no" on the judge's retention. As might be expected in an election where one does not have an opponent, the incumbent usually wins. One study of retention elections found that only 1.6 percent of incumbent judges were defeated in retention elections.[34] Yet from time to time, interest groups will organize against a judge in a retention election and spend a great deal of money trying to defeat him or her; sometimes those efforts have been successful. One of the great concerns about merit selection is the nature of the merit selection commission, because those commissioners filter out all but a handful of prospective judges. Some are quite fearful of this centralized method of determining who should be judges, and although there is much support for merit selection in Texas, there is also much opposition.[35]

In recent years, one of the most popular reform proposals has been a system known as "appoint-elect-retain." Under this system, the governor would appoint a judge with confirmation by two-thirds of the state Senate. The governor-appointed nominee would not assume office until confirmed by the Senate, which would meet year-round for the purpose of dealing with judicial confirmations. In the first election thereafter, the judge would run in a contested nonpartisan election and subsequently in retention elections. This is, of course, a hybrid plan that encompasses aspects of gubernatorial appointment, nonpartisan election, and merit selection.

Another reform plan would have appellate vacancies filled by gubernatorial appointment with senatorial confirmation. The appellate judges would then run in nonpartisan elections followed by retention elections. In Dallas, Tarrant, and Bexar counties, district court judges would be elected from county commissioner precincts rather than from one district encompassing the entire county. Additionally, in Harris County, district judges would be elected from smaller geographic regions than county commissioner precincts. Supporters of this plan tend to believe that it would increase the number of minority judges, especially trial court judges in urban areas. Of course, this is also a hybrid plan designed to combine various reform proposals in order to gain sufficient support to become the new way Texas selects its judges.

merit selection a judicial reform under which judges would be nominated by a blue-ribbon committee, would be appointed by the governor, and, after a brief period in office, would run in a retention election

In 2009, Rick Perry appointed Eva Guzman—the first Latina woman to serve on the Texas Supreme Court—to fill a vacancy on the court. Guzman was elected to a full term in the 2010 election.

Comparing How Texas Selects Its Judges to the Rest of the Country

Judicial Selection Methods

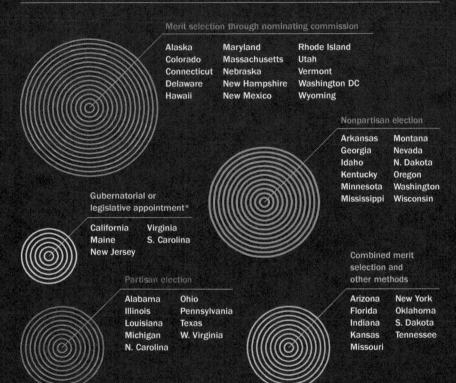

Merit selection through nominating commission

Alaska	Maryland	Rhode Island
Colorado	Massachusetts	Utah
Connecticut	Nebraska	Vermont
Delaware	New Hampshire	Washington DC
Hawaii	New Mexico	Wyoming

Nonpartisan election

Arkansas	Montana
Georgia	Nevada
Idaho	N. Dakota
Kentucky	Oregon
Minnesota	Washington
Mississippi	Wisconsin

Gubernatorial or legislative appointment*

California	Virginia
Maine	S. Carolina
New Jersey	

Combined merit selection and other methods

Arizona	New York
Florida	Oklahoma
Indiana	S. Dakota
Kansas	Tennessee
Missouri	

Partisan election

Alabama	Ohio
Illinois	Pennsylvania
Louisiana	Texas
Michigan	W. Virginia
N. Carolina	

Texas is one of nine states that choose their state judges through partisan elections. This means that voters generally decide for whom to vote based on party affiliation. With so many offices on the ballot, it is simply easier for voters to use their party affiliation as a shortcut. Not all states select judges this way. Many states employ a merit selection method through nominating commissions which make recommendations to the governor. Other states have judges selected by the governor without nominating commissions. Twelve states elect their judges in nonpartisan elections, meaning that judges' parties are not listed on the ballot. The remaining states use a combination of merit selection and other methods.

Judicial Selection Methods: A Regional View

- ● Merit selection through nominating commission
- ● Gubernatorial or legislative appointment without nominating commission
- ● Partisan election
- ● Nonpartisan election
- ● Combined merit selection and other methods

for critical analysis

1. What are the advantages of nonpartisan elections to select judges? Which method of selection do you think is the most ideal and why?

2. Are there regional patterns in how judges are selected? If so, why do you think that is?

* Without nominating commission

SOURCE: American Judicature Society, Judicial Selection in the States, http://www.judicialselection.us/ (accessed 5/14/14)

At least for the time being, however, it seems likely that not much will change in the way Texas selects its judges. Restructuring the system would be a major change, and these are always difficult to initiate. Changing might upset many voters, who like being able to vote for judges, and it would surely upset the political parties, which like having large numbers of judicial candidates running under their party label. It might also upset lawyers accustomed to the traditional ways of selecting judges and even judges who have benefited from the present system. That has led some to argue that judicial reform needs to be less drastic and more incremental. These reformers have suggested lengthening judicial terms of office on the grounds that longer terms mean fewer election contests and therefore less need for campaign money, less of a chance for defeat of incumbents, and less involvement of judges in politics. Another proposed incremental reform is to remove judges from the straight party vote. This means that a voter would actually have to cast a ballot for the judicial candidate rather than simply voting for everyone on the Republican or Democratic column by casting a straight party vote. Such a reform would remove judicial candidates from the effects of top-of-the-ticket voting. It would, of course, also reduce the votes that judges receive and lessen their dependence and reliance on the political parties. Still another suggested reform is to increase the levels of experience needed to serve on the bench. The idea is that even if judicial races are subject to the whims of voters, high qualifications for judges would mean that there would be experienced judges on the bench rather than highly inexperienced judges who won simply because they were good campaigners or because they had the right party affiliation in that election year.

Judicial Campaign Fairness Act a judicial reform that places limits on judicial campaign contributions

Perhaps the most significant judicial reform in Texas is the **Judicial Campaign Fairness Act**. Texas is the only state with a campaign finance regulation of this type. Among the most important aspects of compliance with the act are campaign contribution limitations. For example, statewide judicial candidates limit themselves to contributions of no more than $5,000 from any individual in any election. Additionally, statewide candidates can receive no more than $30,000 per election from any law firm. Although the amounts of money that can be donated are still quite high, there has been a significant reduction from contribution amounts in the 1980s when, prior to the act, some donors would give candidates $25,000, $50,000, and even more in campaign contributions. A recent strengthening of campaign contribution limits requires that if a judge receives campaign contributions from a party to a lawsuit, or if the party's lawyer had made contributions in excess of the limits in the Judicial Campaign Fairness Act, the judge would recuse him- or herself from the case.[36]

For many, the role of money in judicial campaigns is the most troubling issue in Texas judicial politics. As long as judges are elected, however, money will be necessary to run judicial campaigns, and where elections are competitive, a great deal of campaign money will be necessary.

● Issues in the Texas Court System

Assess the impact of recent changes related to tort reform, litigation, and disciplining judges

One of the most important issues in Texas has been tort reform, which is the effort to change the system for awarding damages in lawsuits where harm is claimed. Tort reform has had important effects on the Texas judiciary.

Civil Cases and Tort Reform

Figure 9.2 shows the numbers of civil cases disposed of by the courts of appeal and the trial courts in 2006, 2010, and 2012. The Texas court system is overloaded and would not be able to function adequately without the aid of visiting judges who are retired or defeated judges who continue hearing cases in order to assist with the growing caseloads.

The Texas Supreme Court sets the tone for civil cases throughout the state. Most important of those types of cases, because of the large amounts of money involved, is tort law. Tort law refers to civil cases in which one person has been harmed by the actions of another. For example, medical malpractice cases are a common type of tort case. In the early to mid-1980s, the court tended to be sympathetic to the plaintiffs' positions in tort cases. That is, the court tended to support the side in a case that was suing businesses, professionals, and insurance companies. However, in 1988 more justices began to be elected who favored the defendants in civil lawsuits. One reason for this change was that in 1988 Republican justices began to be elected, and they were more conservative than many of the previous justices, who were Democrats. Another explanation is that interest groups that were harmed by the pro-plaintiff tendencies of the court began to organize, raise and spend money, and elect justices more sympathetic to their perspective.

In the 1980s plaintiffs' lawyers—lawyers who sue businesses, professionals, and insurance companies—worked to elect pro-plaintiff justices. The tide turned, and business, professional, and insurance interests were now electing pro-defense

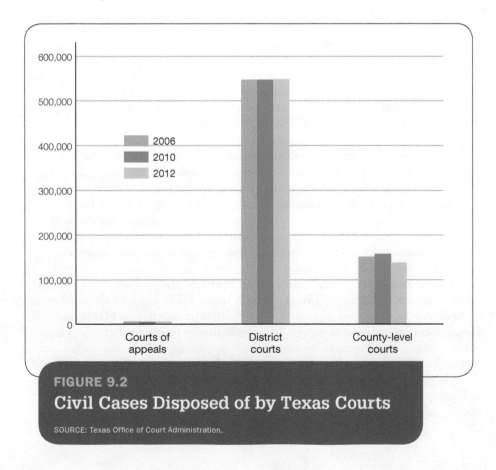

FIGURE 9.2
Civil Cases Disposed of by Texas Courts

SOURCE: Texas Office of Court Administration.

justices. In 1996–97 civil defendants won three-fourths of the time, and insurance companies won almost all their substantive cases. Physicians, hospitals, and pharmaceutical companies won all seven of their cases before the Texas Supreme Court. In 1997–98 civil defendants won 69 percent of the time.[37] However, by 1998–99 the court was not as strongly pro-defendant, perhaps because of several new justices on the court who were regarded as somewhat moderate in their judicial philosophy. In insurance cases, defendants won only 40 percent of the time, plaintiffs won 40 percent of the time, and the decision of the court was a split decision 20 percent of the time. Defendants in medical cases (typically hospitals or doctors), however, still won 100 percent of the time.[38] Most recently, the court seems to have shifted strongly in favor of civil defendants. A study of the decisions of the Texas Supreme Court in tort cases found that defendants won 87 percent of the time.[39] Still another study of the Texas courts of appeal also found a strongly pro-defendant pattern in civil matters. When plaintiffs in tort cases won at the trial court level and the defendants appealed, the appellate courts reversed the decision 49 percent of the time. When defendants in civil cases prevailed and the plaintiffs appealed, the trial court decision was reversed only 25 percent of the time. The authors of this study add, "Tort reform measures enacted by the legislature, as well as Texas Supreme Court decisions favoring tort defendants, have discouraged some . . . plaintiffs from filing suit at all."[40] It is this power of the Texas Supreme Court to set the tone in civil cases that makes that court a political battleground, since millions—even billions—of dollars can be at stake as a result of the court's decisions.

Judicial Districts

Texas judges may be elected, but Texas judges do not represent an electorate like legislators or county commissioners do. As a result, Texas judges are not subject to redistricting according to the one person–one vote standards used in districting officials in legislative bodies. The result is that Texas judicial districts are a hodgepodge of jurisdictions. Things have not changed since a 1993 report that criticized the structure of the Texas courts. That report stated,

> The framers of our current Constitution deliberately designed a system to "localize justice," establishing a multiplicity of largely autonomous conveniently located courts across the state. With the passage of time, the organization of the courts has become more, not less, cumbersome. A case may frequently be eligible for filing in more than one court, either because of overlapping geographical boundaries or overlapping subject matter jurisdiction. Courts with the same name may have different responsibilities and similar places may have quite dissimilar court structures.[41]

An illustration of this cumbersome court structure can be found in the district court structure in Anderson County in east Texas. There are four district courts in Anderson County. One of those courts also has jurisdiction in Henderson and Houston counties; one of them also has jurisdiction in Freestone, Leon, and Limestone counties; one has jurisdiction in Houston County; and the fourth has jurisdiction in Cherokee County. Bastrop County has three district courts—two of them have jurisdiction only in Bastrop County, but the third court has jurisdiction in Bastrop, Burleson, Lee, and Washington counties. Dallas County has 39 district courts—all with jurisdiction solely in Dallas County. Since district court judges have four-year terms, that means there may be roughly 20 district court judgeships on the ballot in Dallas County in any general election. Harris County has 59 district courts, which means there might be about 30 district court judgeships on the ballot in Harris County. And, of course, the number of judgeships on the ballot is even more overwhelming for voters because Dallas County also has 16 courts at law and 3 probate courts—not to mention 11 justice of the peace courts at the precinct level. Harris County has 19 courts at law in addition to the 59 district courts and 16 precinct-level justice of the peace courts. These judgeships do not include appellate courts.[42] The idea may be that state judges should be accountable to voters through elections, but when there are numerous judicial contests—and since most judicial contests are low visibility races—it is hard for a voter to cast a thoughtful ballot, but very easy to simply vote on the basis of the party affiliation of the judicial candidate.

The Role of Lawyers

Lawyers occupy a crucial role in the legal process. In order to practice law, one must be a licensed lawyer, and in order to be licensed in Texas, it is generally necessary to complete a Juris Doctor (JD) degree at a law school accredited by the American Bar Association. Usually this degree takes three years beyond the bachelor's degree if the law student attends full-time. After completing law school, it is necessary for a prospective lawyer to take the state bar exam. After passing the Texas state bar, one may be sworn as a lawyer in Texas. Texas has an integrated bar, which means that all licensed lawyers in the state must join and pay dues to the State Bar of Texas. That agency offers a variety of services to lawyers such as insurance plans, a journal, and professional meetings. Since lawyers must undergo continuing education, the state bar authorizes continuing education credit for a number of educational programs. The State Bar of Texas is unusual in that it is not only a professional organization of lawyers but also an agency of government that is charged with enforcing ethical standards for the profession. Lawyers can be disciplined for a variety of infractions ranging from serious criminal behavior, to failing to keep a client informed of the status of a legal matter, to failure to promptly pay out funds from a legal settlement. The state bar may also enforce rules against illegal efforts to generate litigation. In 2012, for example, a Houston lawyer was disciplined for permitting a non-lawyer to make a number of telephone calls from the lawyer's office to patient rooms at a large Houston hospital for the purpose of soliciting legal business for the lawyer.[43]

Illegal generation of litigation is commonly known as barratry, and the state legislature has become so concerned about lawyers' inappropriately generating legal business that in 2011 it passed new legislation that allows for a penalty of up to $10,000 and the recovery of attorney's fees. The goal of the new legislation was to prevent what is commonly known as "ambulance chasing," something that appears to continue to be a problem in spite of long-standing state bar rules against it. Some of the horror stories of barratry include people being solicited to sign contracts with lawyers for lawsuits at home, in hospitals, and even during funerals. At times the relatives of accident victims have been offered large payments to sign a contract with a particular lawyer to file a lawsuit.[44]

It is too early to assess the value of the new law in discouraging barratry, though three months after the law was passed, the first barratry lawsuit was filed against two south Texas lawyers who were accused of firing their office manager when she

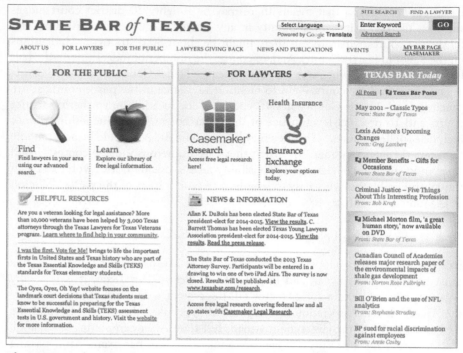

The State Bar of Texas webpage shows the variety of activities of the state bar. Every lawyer licensed to practice in Texas must be a member of the State Bar of Texas.

refused to sign a contract with them where the office manager would receive a bonus payment for illegally soliciting and referring cases to the lawyers.[45] In 2012 state representative Ronald Reynolds was arrested for the crime of barratry. Reynolds, who was a supporter of the new barratry law in 2011, was charged with illegally soliciting clients on his own and through the office of a chiropractor. The alleged scheme to solicit clients was discovered when a "runner"—a person used by an attorney to solicit clients for the attorney—approached an attorney who was involved in a car accident. The "runner" tried to get the attorney in the accident to hire Representative Reynolds to represent her, but the accident victim instead reported that solicitation to authorities.[46] That charge against Reynolds fell apart when an investigator in the case was arrested for stealing evidence in a case. But Reynolds was arrested a second time on another barratry charge for allegedly paying a man kickbacks who would examine accident reports and then approach and persuade accident victims to sign contracts for legal representation.[47]

In 2010 there were slightly more than 77,000 active lawyers in Texas and more than 1.2 million active lawyers in the United States. In Texas 30.56 active lawyers exist for every 10,000 people, and in the United States as a whole 38.42 active lawyers exist for every 10,000 people.[48] With the decline in the number of legal jobs during the Great Recession, both in Texas and nationally, there is much discussion about whether there are too many lawyers, although it seems likely that the demand for lawyers will increase with an improvement in the economy. Of course, lawyers trained in out-of-state law schools may take the bar exam and be licensed in Texas, but the state has a substantial number of law schools: the University of Texas, Texas Tech, Texas Southern, St. Mary's, South Texas, Southern Methodist University, Baylor, and Texas Wesleyan. A new law school in Dallas, the University of North Texas College of Law, opened in 2014. In spite of the weakened job market for lawyers, Texas has law schools aplenty.

The legal process in Texas relies on lawyers. Constitutional county court judges are not required to be lawyers, and justices of the peace do not have to be lawyers, but all other judges must be "learned in the law," a term found in the Texas Constitution whose meaning has come to require a law degree. Even justice of the peace courts, which in theory are informal courts where people can easily resolve their minor criminal and civil issues, often have rules of operation that would be confusing to non-lawyers. The Texas Rules of Civil Procedure and Evidence, for example, apply to civil cases in justice of the peace courts, although not when justices of the peace sit as judges in small claims courts, a distinction that itself is confusing to non-lawyers—and much of the litigation in justice of the peace courts involves lawyers who, for example, are representing businesses trying to collect debts or apartment complexes trying to evict a tenant. Of course, in civil and criminal litigation, it is possible for a layperson to pursue a case without a lawyer, but it is generally recognized that non-lawyers are at a significant disadvantage if they are without legal help in either a civil or a criminal proceeding.

State representative Ronald Reynolds supported the new barratry law in Texas only to find himself in trouble for allegedly violating that law.

Discipline of Judges

The State Commission on Judicial Conduct was created by a constitutional amendment in 1965. It is charged with investigating allegations of judicial misconduct and disability and is charged with discipline of judges. There are 13 members on the commission and they serve six-year terms. Members of the commission are unpaid. The commission also has a staff of 14. In 2011 the commission spent nearly $997,000, mostly on staff salaries. The commission is an unusual hybrid agency in that two attorney members are appointed by the state bar and the six judicial members are appointed by the Supreme Court of Texas, with one of the judicial members being an appellate judge, one a county court at law judge, one a constitutional county judge, one a district judge, one a justice of the peace, and one a municipal judge. There are five citizen members who can neither be lawyers nor be judges who are appointed by the governor. The state Senate confirms the commission members.

In dealing with disciplinary issues involving Texas judges, the commission relies on complaints from the public, from attorneys, and from members of the judiciary. In 2012 there were 1,216 complaints filed with the commission, but some are immediately dismissed for failure of the complaint to allege misconduct. A common complaint is that the person disagrees with the judge's decision, but of course this is not a violation of the Code of Judicial Conduct, which is the ethical code promulgated by the Supreme Court of Texas that is enforced by the commission along with certain legislative requirements on judges. Indeed, one of the problems of the commission is that it is responsible for enforcing requirements that the Supreme Court of Texas places on judges and laws passed by the legislature that affect judges. Potentially, there could be a conflict between the Texas Supreme Court rules and the legislatively imposed requirements, in which case it would be unclear what the commission should do. Still another problem with the commission is that because it deals with ethical issues of judges, its decision making is done behind closed doors and thus the commission lacks openness and transparency in decision making. Still, other than impeachment by the legislature or criminal prosecution of judges, both rare and extreme measures, the commission is the only mechanism for regulating ethical and legal conduct of Texas judges.[49]

In 2012 the commission imposed 49 sanctions on judges and three suspensions of judges. In addition, the commission accepted three resignations of judges who chose to resign rather than to be sanctioned. The commission can recommend public censure or removal of a judge or the judge's involuntary retirement to a seven-judge review tribunal that is composed of the chief justice of Texas and six appellate judges. The review tribunal's decision can be appealed by the affected judge to the Supreme Court of Texas. No such case occurred in 2012. Other decisions of the commission can be appealed by the affected judge to a court of review consisting of three appellate judges. Three such cases occurred in 2012.

Most of the disciplinary actions of the commission involve private sanctions of the judge. In 2012, 34 sanctions were of a private nature and consisted of the commission providing a private admonition, warning, or reprimand to the judge (admonitions are less severe sanctions than are warnings, which are less severe than are reprimands). In 13 of the private sanction cases, judges were ordered to obtain additional training. In only eight cases were sanctions made public. Five were public admonitions, one was a warning, one was a reprimand, and one was a public sanction with an order for continuing education of the judge. Public reprimands do have especially serious consequences for judges, as often when judges retire, they become visiting judges where they are paid to hear cases when sitting judges are on vacation or where dockets are overloaded and they also continue to be paid retirement income. Judges who receive a public reprimand are not allowed to serve as visiting judges.

A disproportionate share of sanctions are against justices of the peace—30 of the 49 sanctions in 2012 were against justices of the peace, 1 was against a county constitutional court judge, 1 against an appellate judge, 1 against a county court at law judge, 6 against district judges, and 10 against municipal judges.[50]

A widely publicized disciplinary case occurred against Judge William Adams. In 2012 Judge Adams, a county court of law judge in Aransas County, Texas, was suspended for a time and then disciplined by a public warning. In 2011 his adult daughter released a videotape on the Internet that depicted the judge beating her when she was 16 years old in 2004. He struck her at least 17 times, yelled profanities, and threatened additional harm to her. The release of the video led to international media coverage. In the course of the investigation of the matter, incidents were also discovered where Judge Adams appeared to display anger and a poor judicial demeanor toward some attorneys in his courtroom. The commission concluded "that Judge Adams' actions depicted in the 2004 videotape, once publicly released, cast reasonable doubt on his capacity to act impartially as a judge and interfered with the proper performance of his judicial duties." The commission also concluded "that Judge Adams' treatment of certain attorneys in his courtroom . . . fell far below the minimum standards of patient, courteous and dignified courtroom demeanor expected of judicial officials." As a result, the commission condemned Judge Adams's behavior by issuing a public warning.[51]

In another widely publicized case in 2013, Judge Elizabeth Coker (see photo on p. 285), a district court judge in Trinity, Polk, and San Jacinto counties, resigned rather than face discipline from the conduct commission. Judge Coker allegedly texted a prosecutor in the gallery during a trial when she disliked how a witness was being questioned and urged that the examining prosecutor should ask different questions that might yield greater success in the case, thus violating the neutrality expected of a judge in a case.[52]

The most widely publicized disciplinary case against a judge in recent years was the one against the presiding judge of the Texas Court of Criminal Appeals, Sharon Keller. As discussed in the introduction to this chapter, Judge Keller refused to keep the clerk's office at the court open beyond 5 PM to receive an appeal from death row inmate Michael Richard. As a result, Richard was executed later that evening. Although Keller received a public warning as a disciplinary action by the State Commission on Judicial Conduct, she was successful in her litigation against the discipline by arguing that a warning cannot be a penalty following a formal proceeding against a judge. Re-elected to another six-year term in 2012 with 55.49 percent of the vote, she remains the presiding judge of the court.

● Thinking Critically about the Judiciary in Texas

Texas elects its judges in partisan judicial elections. For many years, when the Democratic Party was dominant, Texas judicial elections were staid, low-budget, noncompetitive events. However, with the growth of the Republican Party, judicial elections became highly political, and large amounts of money have been raised for judicial candidates, especially in Texas Supreme Court races. Often these judicial races pitted business interests against candidates backed by the plaintiffs' bar because the Texas Supreme Court sets the tone of tort law in the state. These elections have calmed down in recent years as the Democratic Party has weakened and, at least in statewide races, judicial elections have become less competitive.

There have been problems in Texas judicial races, in large part because voters often don't know much about judicial candidates. As a result, voters often decide on the basis of the candidate's party affiliation or the candidate's name appeal. The result has been the election of several judicial candidates who lacked significant qualifications for the job.

Numerous efforts have been proposed to change the way judges are selected in Texas. There have been efforts to change the system of selection to "merit selection" and to nonpartisan election. Minority groups have pushed to reduce the size of judicial districts in order to increase the election of minority judges. However, no change so far has been successful. No majority coalition can agree on appropriate changes in the judicial selection system, and significant opposition to change comes from groups such as the political parties and business interests. Additionally, Texans seem satisfied with the current system of selection and seem to prefer to elect their judges. Recent injustices in the Texas criminal system do raise questions about how the system can be improved. One might speculate that a criminal justice system in which both judges and prosecutors are elected creates political pressures to gain convictions at all costs.

Texas courts handle large caseloads of both civil and criminal cases. The highest civil court in the state is the Texas Supreme Court, currently an all-Republican court elected with strong support from business interests. The court has been severely criticized for being too sympathetic to those interests. The highest criminal court in the state is the Texas Court of Criminal Appeals. That court is also an all-Republican court, which was elected with strong support from prosecutors and victims' rights groups. Perhaps its most important function is as the appellate court for the death penalty in the state.

Because the Texas court system affects the liberty and especially the pocketbooks of Texans, it will continue to be an area of concern and controversy. And the most controversial area of Texas justice will continue to be the process by which judges are selected.

Court Structure

Describe how the Texas court system is organized (pp. 277–82)

The appellate court system in Texas is divided into civil and criminal tracks with the Texas Supreme Court being the highest state-level court for civil cases and the Texas Criminal Court of Appeals being the highest for criminal cases. Texas has an intermediate appellate court system and trial courts that range from district courts for the most important criminal and civil cases, to county courts for less important criminal and civil cases, to justice of the peace and municipal courts for settling the lowest level of conflicts.

Key Terms

Texas Supreme Court (p. 277)
Texas Court of Criminal Appeals (p. 279)
courts of appeal (p. 279)
district courts (p. 279)
county judge (p. 279)
county courts (p. 279)
statutory county courts at law (p. 280)
statutory probate courts (p. 280)
justice of the peace courts (p. 280)

municipal courts (p. 281)
ordinance (p. 282)

Practice Quiz

1. The highest criminal court in the state of Texas is the
   a) Texas Supreme Court.
   b) Texas Court of Appeals.
   c) Texas Court of Criminal Appeals.
   d) county court.
   e) district court.

2. The major trial courts in Texas are the
   a) courts of appeals.
   b) justice of the peace courts.
   c) district courts.
   d) municipal courts.
   e) county courts.

3. Which of the following positions in the judiciary are filled primarily by non-lawyers?
   a) Texas Supreme Court justices
   b) district judges
   c) justices of the peace
   d) Texas Criminal Court of Appeals justices
   e) probate judges

The Legal Process

Explain the legal process and the differences between criminal and civil law (pp. 282–85)

Civil law is dramatically different from criminal law with the burden of proof relying on different standards. Plaintiffs are the initiators of legal actions in civil cases. Defendants in civil cases respond to accusations made against them. Civil cases may lead to trial or dismissal by a judge. They may also be resolved by a settlement between the parties. The state is a prosecutor in a criminal case, and the accused individual is the defendant. Criminal cases can result in a trial, a dismissal, or a plea bargain.

Key Terms

civil law (p. 282)
criminal law (p. 282)
complaint (p. 282)

answer (p. 282)
contingent fee (p. 282)
preponderance of the evidence (p. 283)
capital case (p. 283)
felony (p. 284)
misdemeanor (p. 284)
grand jury (p. 284)
indictment (p. 284)
bench trial (p. 284)
plea bargain (p. 284)
beyond a reasonable doubt (p. 285)

Practice Quiz

4. Grand juries
   a) determine the guilt of defendants.
   b) decide whether a trial of an accused is warranted.

c) agree to plea bargains.
d) recommend that defendants undergo bench trials.
e) hear appeals of convictions.

5. On conviction, the criminal's punishment is determined
   a) by the grand jury.

b) in a separate hearing by the jury or judge that determined the person's guilt.
c) by the prosecuting attorney.
d) by the prosecuting and defense attorneys.
e) by the Texas Court of Criminal Appeals.

Judicial Politics

Evaluate the process for selecting judges in Texas (pp. 285–98)

Unlike federal judges, Texas judges are elected in partisan elections. Partisan elections make judges accountable to voters, but critics claim that unqualified judges are elected solely because of their party labels. These critics advocate alternatives for choosing judges such as merit selection. Minorities are not proportionately represented, possibly in part because most judges are elected from large districts that are non-minority.

Key Terms

en banc (p. 293)

retention election (p. 294)

merit selection (p. 296)

Judicial Campaign Fairness Act (p. 298)

Practice Quiz

6. Civil defense lawyers often align themselves with
   a) business and professional groups.
   b) the grand jury.
   c) groups that support workers.
   d) judges supported by the Democratic Party.
   e) labor groups.

7. Texas's movement from being a Democratic to a Republican state led to
   a) defeats of large numbers of incumbent judges.
   b) party switching by incumbent judges.
   c) large campaign contributions to judges.
   d) election of more Republican judges.
   e) all of the above

8. In Texas, which event marked the rise of the Republican Party and partisan judicial elections?
   a) the election of President Ronald Reagan
   b) the impeachment of William Jefferson Clinton

c) the appointment of Tom Phillips as Chief Justice of the United States
d) the election of Bill Clements as governor of Texas
e) the Shivercrat movement

9. Which of the following groups has the largest number of judges?
   a) African Americans
   b) American Indians
   c) Asian Americans
   d) Latinos
   e) women

10. Elections lost as a result of party membership rather than race or ethnicity do not violate
    a) the Fifth Amendment to the U.S. Constitution.
    b) the Fair Elections Act.
    c) Article I of the Texas Constitution.
    d) *Clements v. Maddox.*
    e) the Voting Rights Act.

11. How likely is Texas to change its method of selecting judicial candidates?
    a) Texas is scheduled to change to the Missouri Plan in January 2016.
    b) extremely likely in the next two decades
    c) likely in the next decade
    d) a 50–50 chance change will soon occur
    e) unlikely

12. Which of the following sets campaign contribution limits for judicial candidates in Texas?
    a) Judicial Campaign Fairness Act
    b) Judicial Campaign Law
    c) Equal Justice Act
    d) Code of Judicial Conduct
    e) Federal Rules of Civil Procedure

Issues in the Texas Court System

Texas courts make decisions affecting Texans on a variety of issues, including the ultimate penalty of death and tort cases such as medical malpractice.

Practice Quiz

13. Philosophically, in the past few years, Texas courts became
    a) more pro-defendant in civil cases.
    b) more liberal.
    c) more pro-defendant in criminal cases.
    d) more conservative.
    e) hostile to tort reform.

14. All lawyers who regularly practice in Texas
    a) must be members of the State Bar of Texas.
    b) must have graduated from a Texas law school.
    c) must appear in court at least twice a year.
    d) must volunteer to sit on grand juries.
    e) do not need any additional training once they have a law license.

15. The State Commission on Judicial Conduct
    a) screens judicial candidates to determine if they are qualified to be judges.
    b) offers continuing education courses for judges.
    c) investigates complaints of ethical violations by judges.
    d) recommends trial judges for promotion to appellate courts.
    e) makes rules governing the conduct of judges.

Recommended Websites

The Supreme Court of Texas
www.supreme.courts.state.tx.us/

Texans for Public Justice
www.tpj.org

Texas Court of Criminal Appeals
www.cca.courts.state.tx.us/

Texas Courts Online: Texas Court Structure
www.courts.state.tx.us/

Sometimes the decisions of local governments can have dire consequences. Fifteen people, including 12 firefighters, died in an explosion and fire at a fertilizer plant in West, Texas. West had no fire code and thus the plant was not required to install sprinklers. This photo shows the memorial service for the firefighters.

10

Local Government in Texas

WHY LOCAL GOVERNMENT MATTERS On April 17, 2013, the tiny town of West, Texas, was rocked by an explosion at the local fertilizer plant. There were 15 fatalities, 200 injuries, and damage estimated at $100 million. There are estimates that $40,000 worth of sprinklers would have prevented the explosion, but the town did not have a fire code that mandated them. Under state law, both the city and the county could adopt a fire code, but they chose not to do so. Less than one week before the West explosion, state representative Walter Price testified before the County Affairs Committee that all Texas counties should be authorized to have a fire code. The proposal was opposed on the grounds that a fire code would require property owners to retrofit their buildings to comply with the code.

Only 15 counties in Texas have adopted a fire code, although 81 are allowed by state law to do so. Texas is one of just a handful of states with no statewide fire code. And there are many counties that cannot impose a fire code even if they chose to do so. For a county to have a fire code, state law requires that they have a population of more than 250,000 or that they touch a county of that size. One hundred seventy-three counties do not meet that requirement, and 85 percent of those counties do not have a full-time professional fire department anywhere in the county, although 21 of those counties do have special districts called emergency service districts that provide some fire protection. Still, Victoria County has approximately 39 million pounds of poisonous chemicals within its borders and 11 million pounds of flammable chemicals; Parmer County has 10 companies within its borders that have 2.3 million pounds of toxic anhydrous ammonia; Jasper County has a paper mill containing 83,280 pounds of chlorine dioxide. None of these counties are allowed by law to have a fire code.

Local government is generally praised for being closer to the people it serves and, therefore, being more responsive to those people than the state or national government can be. The problem is sometimes local governments do not have the power or the ability to provide adequate services for their citizens. The disaster in West raises the question of whether local governments are doing a basic job—protecting the people they serve.[1]

chapter**goals**

- Explain the importance of county government in Texas
  (pp. 312–20)

- Describe the major types of city government in Texas (pp. 320–30)

- Examine the role of special districts in Texas government
  (pp. 330–36)

- Examine the financial problems facing local government
  (pp. 337–41)

● County Government in Texas

Explain the importance of county government in Texas

Local government institutions play a major role in Texas. There are more than 4,800 general-purpose local governments, an average of about 19 per county.[2] Local government is everywhere in Texas, providing water, electricity, and sewer services, as well as police protection and public education.

All but two states have governmental units known as counties (or parishes), but Texas has 254 counties, more than any other state.[3] County government in Texas is primarily a way of governing rural areas. Because Texas is so vast, with huge areas that are sparsely populated, county government remains an important aspect of local government. As was discussed in Chapter 2, the Texas Constitution places numerous restrictions on government, and numerous provisions of the constitution place restrictions on counties. Indeed, in Texas, counties have very constricted governmental powers. Unlike city governments, county governments usually do not have powers to legislate. Because they lack much of the power of self-government, they often function primarily as an administrative arm of the state government.

Texas counties have their origins in the "municipality," which was the local governmental unit under Spanish and Mexican rule. These municipalities were large and included settlements and surrounding rural territories. In 1835, Texas was divided into 3 departments and 23 municipalities. With the Republic of 1836, the 23 municipalities became counties. By the time Texas became a state in 1845, there were 36 counties, and when Texas entered the Confederacy in 1861, there were 122 counties. The number of counties increased steadily until 1921, when the 254th county was created. The underlying goal of the proliferation of counties was that any citizen could travel to the county seat—on horseback, of course—and return home in a day. Given the sparse population of west Texas, in particular, that initial plan for county organization was eventually rejected, but it does show that Texans believed that the local center of government, the county seat, should be accessible to the people.[4]

Numerous County Offices: Checks and Balances or Built-In Problems?

As with the state government, one of the characteristics of county government in Texas is a multiplicity of elected governmental officials. Some argue that the large number of public officials at the county level is desirable because it creates a strong system of checks and balances, allowing no one official to dominate county government.[5] However, that system of checks and balances comes at a high price. There are problems of coordination of governmental activity, much as at the state level. One of the most important bodies of county elected officials is the **county commissioners' court**, which is the main governing unit in the county. Although the commissioners' court is not really a judicial court, it may have gotten its name from the Republic of Texas Constitution (1836–45), in which the county governing unit consisted of the chief justice of the county court and the justices of the peace within the county.[6]

The current structure of the county commissioners' court, shown in Figure 10.1, consists of a **county judge** and four commissioners. The county judge is elected countywide and serves for four years. He or she presides over the meetings of the commissioners' court and has administrative powers as well as judicial powers in rural counties. In those counties, the county judge hears minor criminal cases and handles some civil matters such as probate matters. In larger counties, the county judge is an administrator only, with the judicial duties of the office removed by the creation of judgeships, such as probate judgeships and county-court-at-law judgeships.

Each commissioners' court also has four **county commissioners**; each of these officials is elected from a precinct that encompasses roughly one-fourth of the population of the county. In the late 1960s one of the great issues in constitutional law involved the issue of malapportionment, the allegation that election districts did not represent equal population groupings. The malapportionment of Texas's county commissioners' courts became an important case before the U.S. Supreme Court because those precincts tended to be drawn to represent fairly equal land areas rather than equal population groupings. In *Avery v. Midland County* (1968), the U.S. Supreme Court held that the principle of "one person, one vote" applies to

county commissioners' court the main governing body of each county; has the authority to set the county tax rate and budget

county judge the person in each of Texas's 254 counties who presides over the constitutional county court and county commissioners' court, with responsibility for the administration of county government; some county judges carry out judicial responsibilities

county commissioner government official (four per county) on the county commissioners' court whose main duty is the construction and maintenance of roads and bridges

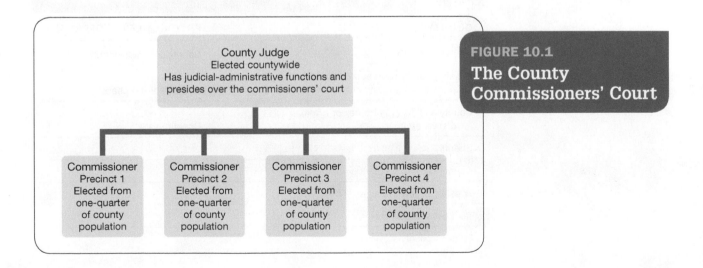

FIGURE 10.1
The County Commissioners' Court

commissioners' courts just as it applies to legislative districts. The result was that commissioners' precincts must now be drawn to reflect equal population groupings within counties.[7]

The main duty of county commissioners is the construction and maintenance of county roads and bridges; usually each commissioner provides for roadwork within his or her precinct. That aspect of a commissioner's work is, of course, very important to rural residents; it can be politically controversial and has sometimes been tinged with corruption.[8]

The commissioners' court also sets the county tax rate and the county budget. Related to its taxing and budgeting powers is its power to make contracts and pay bills. Perhaps the most important expenditure of most county commissioners' courts, other than road and bridge expenditures, is the cost of building and maintaining county jails. Indigent health care can be a significant cost for counties as well, along with, in some cases, fire protection and sanitation. Some counties also have costs associated with the maintenance of libraries and hospitals and costs for emergency welfare expenditures, such as those brought on by natural disasters or fires. The commissioners' court can appoint certain county officials, and it can hire personnel as well as fill vacancies in county offices. It also administers elections in the county.

However, as noted earlier, there are numerous elected officials in Texas counties, each with an independent power base. It seems nearly inevitable that tensions would develop between the budgetary powers of the commissioners' courts and the needs and desires of other elected county officials.

As Table 10.1 shows, other officeholders are elected at the county level and still others at the precinct level of the county. There is some variation in the numbers of officeholders, depending on the county. For example, larger counties will have more justices of the peace and more **constables** than smaller ones. In some counties, constables serve legal papers, while in others, constables also have a law-enforcement role with the authority to patrol, give tickets, and make arrests. Some

constable precinct-level county official involved with serving legal papers and, in some counties, enforcing the law

TABLE 10.1

Countywide and Precinct-Level Elected Officials

COUNTYWIDE OFFICIALS	PRECINCT-LEVEL OFFICIALS
County judge	County commissioners
Possibly county court-at-law judges, possibly probate judges, and district judges	Justices of the peace
County and district attorney or criminal district attorney	Constables
Sheriff	
County and district clerk or district clerk	
Possibly county treasurer	
Tax assessor-collector	
Possibly county surveyor	

The county commissioners' court is the main governing unit at the county level, with control over the county budget and projects such as road construction. Here, Denton County commissioner Andy Eads appears with Texas Motor Speedway president Eddie Gossage at the groundbreaking for a highway extension near the speedway.

counties use constables to check on truants from school, having found a niche area that others in law enforcement do not seem to want.

Larger counties may have probate judges, numerous district judges, and county-court-at-law judges. Smaller counties may not have probate judges or even county-court-at-law judges. Some of the smaller counties may share district judges and district attorneys with other counties. Laws setting up different offices often vary from county to county as well. As a result, some counties have county attorneys and district attorneys; others have criminal district attorneys that combine the county attorney and district attorney offices. Some counties have county clerks and district clerks; smaller counties may combine the offices in one person. Some counties have county treasurers; others do not have such an office.

Are Some Counties Too Small?

The reason for the variation in offices is not simply that laws were passed at different times, thus sacrificing uniformity among counties. It is also the case that Texas is a large, diverse state with great variation among its counties. The result is great variation in the numbers of government officials, the duties of officials, and the services provided by the different county governments. Brewster County has a population of only 9,316, but it covers a territory of 6,193 square miles, about the size of Connecticut and Rhode Island combined. Rockwall County, in contrast, has only 149 square miles and a population of 83,021. Although Harris County has a population of 4,253,700, Loving County has a population of only 71, yet Loving County covers a huge land area—nearly 677 square miles.[9] Most employed residents of Loving County work for the Loving County government. The fact that the county government is the major employer in the county may be the main justification for Loving County's continuing existence as a governmental unit—although people with taxable property may also prefer the Loving County tax structure to that of another governmental unit.[10]

County courthouses are where civil and criminal cases are heard. This photo shows the Jasper County Courthouse during the capital murder case of the men accused of the 1998 dragging death of James Byrd, Jr.

A small population may create a sense of community and closeness to local government, but it can place a terrific strain on county resources when unusual events occur.

One of the medium-size Texas counties is Jasper County in east Texas, which in 2012 had a population of 35,923. Jasper County had huge costs as a result of the capital murder trials of three men accused in the 1998 dragging death of James Byrd, Jr. Two of the three men were sentenced to death; the third got life in prison. Costs associated with the trial came to over $1.02 million. The result was such a strain on the $10 million annual county budget that the county was forced to increase property taxes by 8 percent over two years to pay for the trial. Only a massive flood in the county in the late 1970s had come close to creating a financial burden similar to that of the trial.[11]

Jasper County is not the only county struggling with a huge financial burden from capital murder trials. The basic cost of prosecuting a capital case averages $200,000 to $300,000, and that does not include the costs of indigent-defense lawyers, appeals, and trial transcripts.

The burden of the capital case on Jasper County convinced Texas lawmakers to expand a program to assist counties in paying the "extraordinary costs" of prosecuting capital murder cases. That aid program was motivated by a fear that underpopulated counties would pursue lesser charges than those carrying the death penalty to avoid incurring financial hardship. One of the sponsors of the legislation, for example, said that he had often heard concerns expressed over the cost pressures of capital trials from officials in the 17 rural counties he represented.

Polk County in east Texas (2012 population of about 45,656) estimated that it had unanticipated costs of $200,000 when the U.S. Supreme Court overturned the sentence of Johnny Paul Penry, who was convicted in the stabbing death of a

woman in 1979, and sent the case back for another trial. Even with $100,000 in aid from the state to help pay the bill, the costs of one trial tremendously burdened Polk County.[12] An even more severe situation faced tiny Franklin County (2012 population of 10,640) in 2007, when it needed to come up with a minimum of $250,000 for a murder trial.[13] Since capital murder cases were so rare in the county, the commissioners had no money at all budgeted for such a purpose. For small counties such as Polk and Franklin, expenses like these require either major cuts in other budget items or tax increases.

Very small counties in the Big Bend area of Texas are discovering that they cannot afford to prosecute the drug violations that are too small for the federal government to prosecute. In counties that have Border Patrol checkpoints, relatively minor drug cases have been prosecuted at the county level rather than by the federal government, although the federal government has provided some aid for funding these prosecutions. But Hudspeth County (2011 population of 3,423) has discovered that for every dollar it gets for handling federal border crimes and seized assets, it costs the county $2 to detain, process, and prosecute the offenders. As Hudspeth County is the site of a border checkpoint, the cost has gotten so substantial that the county has chosen to no longer prosecute the federal drug cases sent to it. Brooks County (2011 population of 7,222) had previously stopped taking the federal drug cases from its Border Patrol checkpoint because the county found the costs too great, and Kenedy County (2011 population of 437) has recently made the same decision. Part of the problem is that the federal government has decided to reimburse local authorities only for prosecution costs but not for detention costs. For small-population counties like Hudspeth County, that imposed too great a financial burden, since detention is the most expensive item in the county budget.[14]

According to the 2010 Census, 160 Texas counties have populations of fewer than 30,000, and 137 of those counties have populations of fewer than 20,000. One recent study confirmed fears that Texas has wide variations in its counties'

The county commissioners' court is also responsible for constructing and maintaining bridges, such as this one near Houston.

application of capital punishment, in part because of the costs of death penalty cases to smaller counties. Between 1976, when the U.S. Supreme Court reinstated capital punishment, and July 2011, Texas sent just over 1,060 inmates to death row. Only four of the state's most heavily populated counties—Harris, Bexar, Dallas, and Tarrant—accounted for 534 of these death sentences. By itself, Harris County, the county with the largest population, accounted for 280, or 28 percent, of the death sentences. In contrast, 135 Texas counties with relatively small populations have not sent an inmate to death row in 1976–2011.[15]

Counties exist as they do for a variety of reasons. The original goal of making county seats easily accessible by horseback is, of course, no longer pertinent. Other reasons are political. For example, wealthy landowners may have urged the legislature to create counties so that they could control county government and hence the amount of property taxes they might pay. Still, we must wonder if so many small counties are needed. The Jasper County situation suggests that even moderate-size counties by Texas standards may be too small to function adequately in unusual situations.

The Functions of County Government

What, then, are the main functions of Texas county government? Table 10.2 lists them. Like most other aspects of county government in Texas, these five primary functions are performed with great variation among the counties.

County road and bridge construction and maintenance have traditionally been such important functions of the commissioners' court that often county commissioners are called "road commissioners." County commissioners maintain more than one-half of the roads in the state.[16] There are roughly 134,000 miles of rural roadways and 17,000 rural bridges in Texas. Maintenance of these roads and bridges is a major cost for county government.[17] For example, a 20-foot-wide asphalt road for lightweight traffic costs a county $45,000 per mile to resurface; a road of the same width for heavy trucks costs about $100,000 per mile.[18] Although a 1947 law allowed counties to place the road system under the authority of a county engineer, in most counties roads and bridges remain one of the most important responsibilities of the commissioners.

Law enforcement is another important responsibility of county government. This job is undertaken by constables and by the sheriff. The sheriff is the chief law-enforcement officer within county government. In rural counties with few city police departments, the sheriff may be the major law-enforcement official in the county. In addition to law enforcement and the provision of deputies for the district and county courts, sheriffs are responsible for the county jail and the safety of prisoners. In many counties, operating a county jail is an expensive and major undertaking. On May 1, 2013, for example, Harris County was guarding and supervising 8,834 inmates in its county jail, Dallas County had 5,958 inmates in its jail, and Tarrant County had 3,096. On the other hand, 19 counties had no jails. Glasscock County had room for 12 inmates in its jail but had no inmates; Trinity County had room for 7 inmates but had 6 inmates. Real County had a jail capacity of 3 and had 1 inmate, and Terrell County had a capacity of 8 and had 1 inmate.[19]

TABLE 10.2

Primary Functions of County Government

- Construction and maintenance of county roads and bridges
- Law enforcement
- Dispute resolution
- Record-keeping
- Social services

Although the law-enforcement budget is approved by the county commissioners' court, sheriffs often have considerable influence in county government and develop their own law-enforcement styles. The sheriff of Montgomery County was the first sheriff in Texas to have an aerial drone at a cost of $220,000 until it rose into the air about 18 feet, went out of control, and crashed into the Sheriff's Department SWAT team armored vehicle.[20]

County attorneys and **district attorneys** also perform a law-enforcement role by prosecuting criminal cases. Usually, the district attorneys prosecute the more serious criminal cases in the district courts, whereas the county attorneys prosecute the lesser criminal cases in the county courts. In more urban counties, the offices of county attorney and district attorney may be combined into one office that is usually called the office of criminal district attorney.

Record-keeping is an important function of county government. **County clerks** keep vital statistics for the county and issue licenses; they maintain records for the commissioners' court and the county courts. Most important, the county clerk is responsible for records relating to property transactions. Sometimes the county clerk maintains election and voting records. If there is a **district clerk**, he or she maintains records for the district courts, though in small counties this office is combined with the office of the county clerk. Tax records are maintained by the **county tax assessor-collector**, who also collects taxes, though in the smaller counties the sheriff often performs this job. Although constitutional amendments have eliminated the office of county treasurer in many counties, where the office does exist, the treasurer is responsible for receiving and expending county funds. The **county auditor** now does much of the work of the county treasurer. There are now about 200 county auditors in Texas. Auditors are not elected; they are appointed by the county's district judges. Not only do they audit the county's funds, but in large counties they will often prepare the county budget for the commissioners' court.

Counties also have an important role in dispute resolution through their court systems. Civil law is a way to resolve disputes between people, and the justice of the peace court and the county and district courts deal with large numbers of civil disputes as well as criminal matters. County and district attorneys may also represent the interests of the county or state in disputes that involve governmental interests.

Finally, counties may perform a social service function. The social services provided vary from county to county. However, the most important social services involve emergency welfare assistance to individuals. This may include the provision of food, housing, rental assistance, or shelter to needy individuals. Larger counties have health departments to work on the prevention and control of communicable diseases. Some counties operate mental health services. Some counties provide parks, airports, fire protection, and sanitation facilities. One of the most important social services provided by counties is indigent health care.

Counties have control over law-enforcement budgets, but sheriffs often decide how the money gets spent. Pictured here is Montgomery County Sheriff's Department's $220,000 drone that quickly crashed because it was too heavy to fly.

county attorney county official who prosecutes lesser criminal cases in the county court

district attorney public official who prosecutes the more serious criminal cases in the district court

county clerk public official who is the main record-keeper of the county

district clerk public official who is the main record-keeper of district court documents

county tax assessor-collector public official who maintains the county tax records and collects the taxes owed to the county

county auditor public official, appointed by the district judges, who receives and disburses county funds; in large counties, this official also prepares the county budget

County Government in Perspective

County government occupies an important role in Texas local government, although the powers of county government are greatly restricted by the Texas legislature. One of the most notable features of Texas counties is their great variation in geographical size, in population, and even in county offices, duties of county

for critical analysis

Should county governments be merged into larger units? What would be the advantages and disadvantages of larger units than the current structure of county governments?

officials, and services provided by county government. Additionally, like state government, county government has a large number of elected county officials. Although this may limit the power of any one county official, it also produces disagreement, conflict, and difficulty in accomplishing objectives.

Many of Texas's counties are very small, possibly too small to meet the needs of Texans in the twenty-first century, although there is no serious effort to change the current structure of counties. Counties perform important and often expensive functions. Some of those functions of county government and the costs associated with them—for example, road and bridge construction and maintenance and jail construction and operation—are likely to increase significantly in the future.

● City Government in Texas

Describe the major types of city government in Texas

As of the 2010 Census, there were 1,221 municipalities in Texas, ranging in size from 27 residents in Corral City to nearly 2.1 million in Houston (see Table 10.3). Like county governments, municipal governments are creations of the state of Texas. In the early years of the Republic of Texas, the Texas Congress was responsible for enacting laws that incorporated cities. The number of urban areas grew in the state in the late nineteenth and early twentieth centuries, making the management of local affairs a growing burden on the state legislature. In 1912 the legislature passed the Home-Rule Charter Amendments that enabled cities of more than 5,000 inhabitants to adopt home-rule charters with a majority vote of qualified voters.

home-rule charter the rules under which a city operates; local governments have considerable independent governing power under these charters

Home-rule charters essentially lay down the rules under which a city will operate.[21] They provide for the form of government that operates in the city and specify the number of members serving on the city's governing body. They also may grant the governing body the power to annex land adjacent to the city as well as to set property tax rates up to $2.50 per $100 valuation. Home-rule cities are also constitutionally authorized to borrow money in ways not available to smaller municipal entities. Home-rule charters must be consistent with the state constitution and any other relevant statutory provisions. For example, the state has mandated that most city elections take place on a date provided by the Texas Election Code. City elections must be conducted under the general guidelines set by the state. Nevertheless, home rule in Texas has delegated enormous power to local city governments. According to a report by the Advisory Commission on Intergovernmental Relations, the Texas Constitution leaves cities more "home rule" than does any other state. There are now 335 home-rule cities in Texas.[22] Table 10.4 lists the 10 largest of these.

Cities and towns of fewer than 5,000 people are chartered by general statute, as was the case for all cities and towns prior to the 1912 home-rule amendments. These "general-law" cities and towns may act or organize themselves only as explicitly permitted by statutory law passed by the state legislature. The constitution also limits what they can do. For example, general-law cities may levy, assess, and collect taxes as authorized by statute. But the constitution sets a maximum property tax rate of $1.50 per $100 valuation, compared with $2.50 per $100 valuation for home-rule cities.

TABLE 10.3

Municipal Entities in Texas

SIZE	NUMBER
100,000 or more	28
50,000–99,999	30
10,000–49,999	157
5,000–9,999	115
Fewer than 5,000	891
Total	1,221

SOURCE: Calculated from www.texasalmanac.com/topics/government/government.

TABLE 10.4

The Largest Home-Rule Cities

NAME	2010 CENSUS POPULATION	2012 POPULATION ESTIMATES	FORM OF GOVERNMENT	FIRST CHARTER	PRESENT FORM ADOPTED
Houston	2,099,451	2,160,821	Mayor-council	1905	1994
San Antonio	1,327,407	1,382,951	Council-manager	1914	1951
Dallas	1,197,816	1,241,162	Council-manager	1889	1907
Austin	790,390	842,592	Council-manager	1919	1994
Fort Worth	741,206	777,992	Council-manager	1924	1985
El Paso	649,121	672,538	Council-manager	1873	2004
Arlington	365,438	375,600	Council-manager	1920	1990
Corpus Christi	305,215	312,195	Council-manager	1926	1993
Plano	259,841	272,068	Council-manager	1961	1993
Laredo	236,091	244,731	Council-manager	1848	1911

SOURCES: Compiled from *Texas Almanac 2006–2007* (Dallas: Dallas Morning News, 2006), 340–64; *Texas Almanac 2008–2009* (Dallas: Dallas Morning News, 2008), 8; Texas State Data Center; www.citypopulation.de/USA-Texas.html; City Charter of the City of Laredo as Amended (2010); City of El Paso website, www.elpasotexas.gov.; U.S. Census Bureau, "State and County QuickFacts," www.quickfacts.census.gov/qfd/states/48/484/464.html.

Politics at the local level is often politics at its most basic. Unlike in presidential elections, in which the issues may well involve questions of war and peace, or state elections, which may involve issues such as whether a state should have an income tax, in local elections the most pressing issue may well be potholes in the city streets. Although pothole repair may not seem earthshaking in the hierarchy of political concerns, it is exactly such an issue that most directly and routinely affects most people's lives, and thus it becomes a prime issue for discussion among candidates. As mundane as such concerns are, these are the fundamental issues in most local elections because they reflect the needs and expectations that residents have of local government.

Forms of Government in Texas Cities

Texas home-rule cities have had three major forms of city government: the mayor-council form, the commissioner form, and the council-manager form. The **mayor-council form of government** is the oldest. It consists of an elected mayor and city council. The mayor is usually elected from the city in an **at-large election**. The council may be elected either at large or from a series of **single-member districts**, or a mixture of the two. In the mayor-council form of government, the mayor is the chief executive officer of the city. He or she presides over council meetings and has a variety of appointment powers. The city council, meanwhile, serves as the legislative body in the city, passing local laws and watching over the executive departments.

There have been both strong mayor–council systems and weak ones, depending on the powers given to the mayor by the city charter or state statute. In the *strong mayor–council* variation, various executive powers, such as appointive and removal powers to boards and departments or veto powers, are concentrated in the

mayor-council form of government a form of city government in which the mayor is the chief executive and the city council is the legislative body; in the *strong mayor–council* variation, the mayor's powers enable him or her to control executive departments and the agenda of the city council; in the *weak mayor–council* variation, the mayor's power is more limited

at-large election an election in which officials are selected by voters of the entire geographical area, rather than from smaller districts within that area

single-member district an electorate that elects only one representative for each district

office of mayor. These powers enable the mayor to establish effective control over various executive departments in the city and to control the legislative agenda of the city council. In the *weak mayor–council* variation, these executive powers are much more limited, fragmenting power between the mayor and other elected or appointed officials.

In the 1990s the mayor-council form of government was the dominant form of government in most of the incorporated cities in Texas, particularly among general-law cities. However, among home-rule cities the mayor-council government was not popular. According to a 1995 survey of 284 home-rule cities conducted by the *Texas Almanac*, only 31 had adopted the mayor-council form of government.

A second form of city government found in Texas is the **commissioner form of government**.[23] Under the commissioner system, the city is run by a small commission, composed of between five and seven members generally elected at large. The commission acts in both a legislative and an executive capacity. As a group, commissioners enact laws for the city. Each commissioner is in charge of one of a variety of departments. One commissioner is also designated as the mayor to preside at meetings.

The commission plan was developed as a response to the devastating hurricane that hit Galveston in 1900, claiming an estimated 6,000 lives. It reflected a desire to bring good business practices to city government that would somehow escape the squabbles and inefficiency of traditional local government found in the mayor-council form. The commission plan was adopted by Houston in 1905 and by a number of other Texas cities in 1907, including Dallas, Fort Worth, and El Paso. Progressives across the country supported the plan and other reform principles often integrated with it, including nonpartisan elections, merit selection of employees, and such direct democracy techniques as the initiative, referendum, and recall. At its peak in 1918 the commission form was used by approximately

commissioner form of government a form of city government in which the city is run by a small group of elected commissioners who act in both legislative and executive capacities

The commissioner form of government was developed as a response to the devastating hurricane that hit Galveston in 1900.

How Extensive Are Texas's Local Governments?

Number of Local Governments in Each State, 2012

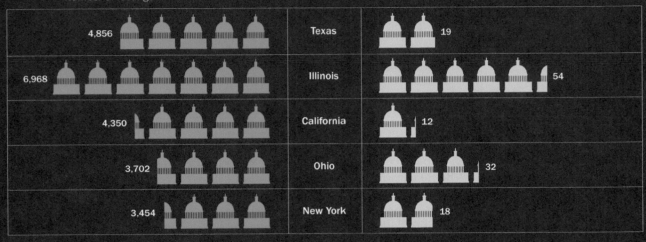

Number of local governments

4,856	Texas
6,968	Illinois
4,350	California
3,702	Ohio
3,454	New York

Number of local governments (per 100,000 people)

19	Texas
54	Illinois
12	California
32	Ohio
18	New York

	Total local govs.	Per 100K people		Total local govs.	Per 100K people		Total local govs.	Per 100K people		Total local govs.	Per 100K people		Total local govs.	Per 100K people
IL	6,968	54	MI	2,877	29	AK	1,543	53	TN	920	14	UT	613	22
PA	4,905	39	CO	2,818	55	OR	1,509	39	NM	854	41	NH	542	41
TX	4,856	19	IN	2,694	41	GA	1,365	14	MA	852	13	LA	530	12
CA	4,350	12	ND	2,666	390	NJ	1,344	15	ME	841	63	VA	497	6
KS	3,806	133	NE	2,581	140	KY	1,314	30	WY	795	140	MD	347	6
MO	3,752	62	SD	1,979	240	MT	1,240	124	VT	728	116	DE	338	37
OH	3,702	32	IA	1,939	63	AL	1,208	25	SC	681	15	NV	190	7
MN	3,633	68	OK	1,854	49	ID	1,161	73	AZ	659	10	AK	177	25
NY	3,454	18	WA	1,831	27	MS	991	33	WV	658	36	RI	134	13
WI	3,123	55	FL	1,554	8	NC	964	10	CT	644	18	HI	21	2

Like other states, Texas has many local governments, including county governments, school board districts, special districts, and municipal utility districts. One would expect that Texas's political culture would lead it to have fewer local governments than other states with traditions of more governmental involvement. Is this the case?

for critical analysis

1. What are some of the characteristics of states with large numbers of local governments?

2. Does the picture change when we factor in population? Which states have larger numbers of local governments per capita? What might explain these differences?

NOTE: Different sources provide different numbers of local governments, but Texas does have somewhat more than 4,800 local governments.

SOURCE: www.governing.com/gov-data/number-of-governments-by-state.html (accessed 2/20/14).

500 cities across the country and 75 cities in Texas. Following World War I, the number of commission-form cities decreased. By 2000 no city in Texas had a pure commission form of government, although 26 still claimed to have some variation of a commission-manager form of government.[24] In practice, none of the "commissioners" in these cities exercised executive control over specific city departments as envisioned in the original commission system. Instead, they functioned more like council members under the council-manager form of city government.[25]

The third form of city government found in Texas is the **council-manager form of government**.[26] As originally envisioned, a city council elected in at-large elections was to be the policy-making body. Council members generally received little or no pay and were intended to be publicly motivated citizens interested in serving the public good, rather than professional politicians. A mayor was selected from among the council members. The city manager was to be a professional public manager who served as the chief executive and administrative official in the city. As in the commissioner form of government, the goal of the council-manager form of government was twofold: to free local government from the seamier side of politics and to bring administrative expertise to local government.

In 1913, Amarillo was the first city to abandon the commissioner form of government for the council-manager system. In 1914, Taylor and Denton followed suit. By 1947 there were 47 council-manager systems in Texas. By the mid-1990s, 251 of the home-rule cities had council-manager systems. Across the United States, it has become the most popular form of government for cities of over 10,000 residents.

Today, council-manager systems vary across the state in a number of ways. The desire for professional administration of local government remains high. Most city managers have graduate degrees and are paid high salaries like other executive officers in the private sector. But a desire for more political accountability through traditional democratic processes has introduced some changes. The growing ethnic and racial diversity of some Texas cities has forced many political leaders to question the wisdom of freeing local government too much from democratic controls. In most cities, mayors now are elected at large from the population as a whole, rather than only from the council. Many cities also elect council members from single-member districts rather than only from at-large districts. Many see at-large districts as undercutting minority representation by diluting minority votes. Only when Dallas moved from an at-large council to a council elected from single-member districts in 1991 did minorities come to play a major role in the decision-making processes of city government. But most cities and towns under the council-manager system continue to view local political offices as part-time jobs. Mayoral and council salaries remain low. A few cities, such as Austin, offer considerably higher salaries. The demand for more democratic accountability in local government will likely continue to lead to more changes in the council-manager system of government across Texas. Balancing an efficient city government run by professionals with democratic political processes will continue to be a problem as Texas's metropolitan areas grow and diversify in the early twenty-first century.

A Tale of Five Cities

Houston Houston is the largest city in Texas, with over 2.1 million people. It has a strong mayor–council form of government. There are 16 elected officials in the city serving concurrent two-year terms, including a mayor, a controller, and 14 council members. The mayor serves as the chief executive official in the city and is the

council-manager form of government a form of city government in which public policies are developed by the city council and executive and administrative functions are assigned to a professional city manager

city's chief administrator and official representative. Much of the mayor's power stems from the authority to appoint department heads and people serving on advisory boards, subject to council approval. The mayor also presides over the city council with voting privileges. The 14-member council is a legislative body composed of five at-large seats and nine single-member district seats.

Unlike in most other cities, the city controller in Houston is an elected official.[27] The city controller, currently Ronald Green, is the city's chief financial officer. Besides investing city funds, conducting internal audits of city departments, and operating the city's financial management system, the controller is also responsible for certifying the availability of funds for city council initiatives. In the end, the office of the controller is both a professional position and a political position. Not surprisingly, the controller often comes into conflict with the mayor and the council over important policy issues.

Although local politics in Houston is nominally nonpartisan, in recent years it has taken on a partisan flavor. Houston's current mayor is Annise Parker, who serves as executive officer of the city. She is a well-known Democrat and is also a lesbian who supports gay marriage. Her call for legalizing gay marriage and her proclamation that Valentine's Day was Freedom to Marry Day have led to a political outcry among social conservatives including Republican leaders who claim that she is putting her personal political agenda ahead of the interests of Houston. Parker barely escaped a runoff in her election campaign in November 2011, and two incumbent city council members were defeated by opponents of gay marriage. Even after the election, the partisan furor over gay marriage has not died down in Houston.

San Antonio Recently, San Antonio has overtaken Dallas as the second-largest city in Texas. San Antonio has a council-manager form of government. The council is composed of members elected from 10 single-member districts on a nonpartisan basis. The mayor, currently Ivy R. Taylor, is the 11th member of the council and is selected at large. All members of the council serve for two-year terms and receive largely honorific salaries. The mayor's salary is a paltry $3,000 per year in addition

Pictured here are the mayors of Texas's two largest cities. Annise Parker (left) is the current mayor of Houston. She previously served as a member of the city council and as city controller. San Antonio mayor Ivy R. Taylor (right), was chosen in a special election by the city council in 2014 to replace former mayor Julian Castro, who was appointed to the position of Secretary of Housing and Urban Development in the Obama Administration.

to payment as a council member; other council members are paid $20 per meeting, not to exceed $1,040 per year. Members are subject to recall if 10 percent of the qualified voters in a district sign a petition of recall and a recall election is successful. The city charter also provides for initiatives and referendums that emerge from the voters.

The city manager in San Antonio serves at the pleasure of the council as the chief executive and administrative official in the city. He or she has wide-ranging appointment and removal authority over officers and employees in the administrative service of the city. The current city manager is Sheryl Sculley. Prior to becoming city manager, she was assistant city manager of Phoenix. She supervises the activities of all city departments, a budget of $2 billion, and 12,000 employees.

Dallas Dallas also operates under a council-manager form of government. For years, city politics had been dominated by the white business community. At-large nonpartisan elections tended to elect a council that was relatively united in its understanding of the problems facing the city and its vision of where the city should go. A bitter struggle in the late 1980s and early 1990s over rewriting the city charter divided the city along racial lines. The new charter, which went into effect in 1991, called for a 14-member council elected from single-member districts and a mayor elected at large. Members are limited to serving four 2-year terms consecutively. Under the new charter, membership on the council was transformed as a significant number of African Americans and Latinos were elected to the council.

As in other council-manager systems, the power of the mayor in Dallas is weak. The mayor—currently Mike Rawlings—presides over council meetings, creates council committees, and appoints members, chairs, and co-chairs. In many ways, however, the mayor is only first among equals on the council. The council as a whole is the legislative body for the city, approving budgets, determining the tax rate, and appointing key public officials, including the city manager, city attorney, city auditor, city secretary, municipal court judges, and various citizen boards and commissions. The city manager serves at the will of the council and is removable by a two-thirds vote of the council. As in San Antonio, the city manager's powers in Dallas are great. As the chief administrative officer, the city manager has the power to appoint and remove all heads of departments and subordinate officers and employees in the city, subject to civil service provisions. Despite the attempt to remove the city manager from the pressures of political life in Dallas, recent city managers have found themselves forced to accommodate the reality of an increasingly politicized city council. The political pressures emerging from Dallas's single-member district council may ultimately compel the city to reexamine the wisdom of retaining a council-manager system. As Dallas learned in the 1990s, efficient government and democratic governance are not as easy to balance as advocates of the council-manager system once thought.

One illustration of the push for change is that in 2001–02, each of the three major candidates for mayor suggested that the structure of city government needed reexamining. One of the mayoral candidates publicly commented on the need for more power to be in the hands of the mayor. A city council member argued that council members have so little power to set spending priorities or influence city staff that individual citizens do not see city government as a way to influence their lives. There has even been some discussion of the value of partisan elections in city races.

Mayor Mike Rawlings of Dallas was elected in 2011. He was previously the CEO of Pizza Hut.

Where Does Texas Spend Its Money?

State Expenditures by County, 2012

$0–25M	$25M–250M	$250M–500M	$500M–1B	$1B+

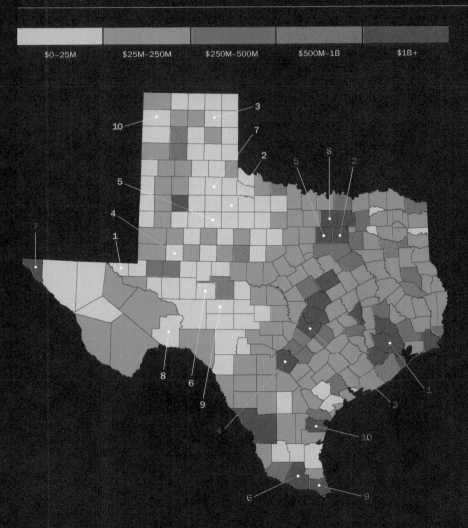

Top 10 counties (county seats)

1. Harris (Houston)	$15,863,264,716
2. Dallas (Dallas)	$12,890,306,321
3. Travis (Austin)	$8,048,586,713
4. Bexar (San Antonio)	$7,517,864,851
5. Tarrant (Fort Worth)	$6,678,436,744
6. Hidalgo (Edinburg)	$3,547,478,110
7. El Paso (El Paso)	$3,206,552,540
8. Denton (Denton)	$1,908,027,396
9. Cameron (Brownsville)	$1,786,468,683
10. Nueces (Corpus Christi)	$1,676,906,880

Bottom 10 counties (county seats)

1. Loving (Mentone)	$188,710
2. King (Guthrie)	$2,059,931
3. Roberts (Miami)	$2,871,832
4. Glasscock (Garden City)	$3,456,705
5. Kent (Jayton)	$3,519,166
6. Irion (Mertzon)	$3,871,967
7. Motley (Matador)	$3,941,857
8. Terrell (Sanderson)	$3,995,636
9. Schleicher (Eldorado)	$5,140,537
10. Hartley (Channing)	$5,257,381

Texas is a diverse state with 254 counties. Some counties in Texas are heavily populated, such as Harris County, which includes the seat of Houston and is the largest in the state. Other counties, however, such as Brewster, have small populations. We might expect the heavily populated counties to receive more state money, but do they?

for critical analysis

1. Are there major differences in funding between the largest counties in the state? For example, compare Harris (Houston), Dallas (Dallas), Travis (Austin), and Bexar (San Antonio).

2. Other than county size, what might help explain any differences in state funding?

SOURCE: Texas State Expenditures by County, Fiscal Year 2012: The Geography of State Spending www.texastransparency.org/State_Finance/Budget_Finance/Reports/Expenditures_by_County/ expbyco12/96-410-12.pdf (accessed 2/20/14).

Austin city manager Mark Ott (far left) and Austin mayor Lee Leffingwell (far right) announce transportation projects with U.S. transportation secretary Anthony Fox (center).

Austin Austin is the 11th most populous city in the United States and the 4th most populous city in Texas. It is the county seat of Travis County and is the state capital. In the November 2012 elections, Austinites adopted a plan by more than a 60 percent margin to change the method for selecting members of the city council. The system had been a mayor and a six-member city council. All seven of the officials were elected citywide. A city manager, Marc Ott, then served as chief administrative officer of the city. Austin continues to have a city manager; however, as of 2014 only the mayor is elected citywide. The 10 city council members are elected from single-member districts. Until this change, Austin was unusual in that it was the largest city in the United States that lacked a city council where at least some of the members were elected from geographic districts.[28]

Over the past 40 years, Austin voters had rejected district plans six times. This time, however, there was a strong grassroots movement favoring the 10-district plan with support from a broad coalition of groups such as the Travis County Republican Party and Hispanic groups. One important reason for the success of the proposal was that the issue appeared on the November ballot when there is a larger and more diverse group of voters than in the prior six elections when district plans were submitted in elections when turnout is less than November turnout.

A peculiar characteristic of the election was that another proposal was on the ballot which had been submitted by the mayor and city council that provided for eight city council seats to be elected through single-member districts, and the mayor and two other council seats to be elected citywide. Critics of that proposal claimed that the city council put that proposal on the ballot to confuse voters and keep the status quo by dooming both plans to failure. That proposal also gained a majority of the voters with about 51 percent approving. However, since the 10-district plan got about 60 percent of the vote, it was the proposal that was implemented.

The proposal required that the districts be drawn by a commission of citizens chosen through an application process that is overseen by the city auditor. The first elections under the new system were in 2014.[29]

El Paso El Paso, located in the far western part of the state, has a council-manager form of government with eight city council members chosen by single-member districts and a mayor who is elected at large. The mayor and council are elected in

Choosing City Council Members

City councils are the legislative bodies for municipalities in Texas. They are tasked with making laws that affect the residents of their city.

The number of city council members and the type of district that each council member represents vary from city to city. How a city elects council members—whether in at-large districts, from specific single-member districts, or by a combination of at-large and single-member districts—can affect representation and policy decisions.

Some cities employ an at-large system of electing city council members, in which each city council member is elected by the whole city, similar to the way the mayor is chosen. Other cities use single-member districts, such that city council members are elected by and represent different parts of the city rather than the city as a whole. Many cities have a hybrid system with some at-large members and others elected via a single-member district system. Each city decides how to elect its city council, and any changes must be implemented by voter approval of an amendment to the city charter (the city "constitution"). Until the U.S. Supreme Court's decision in June 2013 in *Shelby County, Ala. v. Holder*, the U.S. Department of Justice had to approve these changes in Texas (and other states subject to certain requirements of the Voting Rights Act) to make sure that they did not dilute the voting power of minorities.

Social science research seems to suggest that minorities fare better under a system of single-member districts, although this may not necessarily be the case in all cities. This research presupposes that minority

Bill Capener (left) and Ana Reyes (right) ran for a city council seat in a newly drawn district in Farmer's Branch. Reyes won, becoming the first Latina to hold a seat on the city council.

populations are concentrated in certain areas of the city, which makes it easier to draw districts ensuring a majority of minority voters. In one instance in Farmers Branch, Texas, minority citizens challenged the town's at-large system of electing city council members because they felt that it diluted their influence in the city. A federal judge later ordered the town to hold single-member district elections, giving Farmers Branch a realistic possibility of electing a Latino council member in the 37 percent Latino population town. It is also important to consider that minority groups might not form coalitions with other minority groups. For example, African Americans and Latinos might have distinct interests in some localities.

Advocates of the at-large approach argue that single-member district systems are more divisive, and say that city council members must represent the interests of the city as a whole rather than only their narrow neighborhood interests. They also point to research that shows that female candidates are more likely to win in cities with at-large districts. Which system is best for the representation of the city's residents?

critical thinking questions

1. What are the trade-offs of at-large versus single-member districts for city council elections?

2. What alternatives are there to at-large districts and single-member districts? What are their strengths and weaknesses?

Poverty and unemployment plague El Paso, and the city is trying to attract more jobs by developing the downtown area. Here, you can see the old city hall is being demolished. It is to be replaced by a new triple-A baseball park.

nonpartisan elections. The city manager, Joyce Wilson, reports to the elected mayor and city council.

Home to over 672,000 people, El Paso is on the border with Mexico, which makes the city a center for international trade. The military is also important to the El Paso economy because of the presence of Fort Bliss. El Paso has only a tiny African American population. In 2010 only 3.4 percent of the city's population was African American—far smaller than the proportion of African Americans statewide. However, 80.7 percent of the city's population is Latino, far larger than the overall proportion of Latinos in Texas.

The main problem facing El Paso is its poverty. The U.S. Census reports that 22.3 percent of its population is in poverty compared to 17.4 percent of the state as a whole. Median household income is $40,808 compared to $51,563 in Texas as a whole. The per capita income in El Paso is $19,262 compared to $25,809 statewide.[30]

What El Paso desperately needs are well-paying jobs. This explains the strong efforts being made by city government to attract business to El Paso and to make it easier to conduct business in the city.

Special Districts

special district a unit of local government that performs a single service, such as education or sanitation, within a limited geographic area

> **Examine the role of special districts in Texas government**

A **special district** is a unit of local government that performs a single service in a limited geographic area. These governments can solve problems that cross borders of existing units of government. Special districts can be created to serve an entire county, part of a county, all of two or more counties, or parts of two or more counties. The number of special districts has increased dramatically in the last 50 years. In the United States, the number increased by 400 percent.[31] In Texas, the number increased by more than 600 percent.[32] By the year 2002 there were more special districts than any other form of local government. There are now 2,309 special districts in Texas, not including school districts.[33]

Districts can be created to do almost anything that is legal. Some districts are formed to provide hospital care, others to furnish pure water to communities, still others to provide mosquito control—Texas has 13 mosquito control special districts[34]—navigation, flood control, sanitation, drainage, fire protection, ambulance services, and law enforcement. Some special districts can be very large—one, for example, manages Houston's two hospitals for the poor and uninsured and collects well over $500 million in property taxes every year. On the other hand, the North Fort Worth Water Control and Improvement District No. 1 collected a total of $85 in property taxes from its constitutents.[35]

Types of Special Districts

school district a specific type of special district that provides public education in a designated area

There are two types of special districts in Texas. The first is the **school district**, which consists of independent school districts in the state. These districts offer public education from pre-kindergarten through 12th grade. Almost all school districts offer the full range of educational opportunities; however, some small, rural schools provide education only through the 8th grade. Others limit their programs to the 6th grade, and still others end with the 4th grade. Those with limited offerings contract with nearby districts to complete the education of their students.

The second classification of special districts is the **nonschool special district**. Everything except the school districts is included in this category. Municipal utility districts, economic development corporations, hospital districts, and fire-prevention districts are the most common examples.

In addition to county taxes, for example, a property owner in Upshur County, Texas, will pay taxes to two special districts—the Union Grove Independent School District and the Emergency Services District No. 1 (fire protection). A property owner in Hopkins County, Texas, will pay to the Sulphur Springs Independent School District and to the Hopkins County Hospital District. A property owner in Collin County, Texas, will pay taxes to the Plano Independent School District and to the Collin College special district. One property owner in Houston pays taxes to the Houston Independent School District, the Harris County Department of Education, the Harris County Flood Control District, the Port of Houston Authority, the Harris County Hospital District, the Lone Star College System, Emergency Service District No. 13 (fire protection), and Emergency Service District No. 11 (EMS).

One problem is that sometimes local governmental officials work in relative obscurity, avoiding media and public scrutiny. This means that if they abuse their power, their behavior often takes longer to come to light. One example has been a recent scandal involving two of the five constables in Dallas County. Traditionally in Texas, the office of constable has been an elective office with limited duties. Constables have served civil court papers and have provided bailiffs for justices of the peace. However, some constables, such as those in Dallas County, transformed their offices into full-fledged police departments. Dallas County constables, for example, developed a traffic enforcement role. In Dallas County in 1995 no deputy constable positions were devoted to traffic enforcement; in 2010, 76 deputy constables in that county handled traffic enforcement. Constables also formed heavily armed, tactical units. They patrolled high-crime areas, shut down drug houses, arrested parents who were behind on child support, and cracked down on drug dealers selling "cheese" heroin to students. County commissioners not only approved some of the expanded activities of constables but also implemented new legal strategies to expand their law enforcement functions. Since constables are elected officials, they are not subject to much oversight by other public officials and instead function as law enforcement fiefdoms in larger counties in Texas.

In two constables' precincts in Dallas County, there have been problems with vehicles being impounded. These constables have impounded thousands of vehicles without requiring that the towing companies account for what happened to the vehicles. Subsequent investigations of the two constables have also identified issues such as complaints that deputy constables have been forced to work on unpaid security details and to sell raffle tickets to raise money for constables' re-election campaigns.[36] These problems, going on for years, have only recently caused county commissioners to reconsider the expanded role of constables.

nonschool special district any special district other than a school district; examples include municipal utility districts (MUDs) and hospital districts

School Districts

Every inch of land in Texas is part of a school district, and the state contains 1,265 school districts. Some districts in east and west Texas cover an entire county. In metropolitan counties, there may be a dozen or more districts. Each is governed by an elected board of trustees composed of five to nine members. The board employs a superintendent to oversee the daily operation of the district. On the recommendation of the superintendent, the trustees

- set overall policy for the school district
- adopt the budget for the district
- set the tax rate for the district (The maximum tax rate for a district is $1.04 for each $100 the property is worth. A rate higher than $1.04 requires voter approval.)
- select textbooks for classroom use
- hire principals, faculty, and support staff
- set the school calendar
- determine salaries and benefits for employees

Educating millions of students is a daunting task. By localizing public education, the state places much of the burden on the local school districts. This allows local residents to participate in governing the school districts. Unfortunately, few people vote in the elections to select members of the board of trustees. Even fewer individuals attend meetings of the school board.

Nonschool Special Districts

There are a vast number of types of special districts. Larger counties tend to have many different special districts. Dallas County, for example, has 13 nonschool special districts. Harris County is the record-holder for special districts in Texas. It contains a total of 436 nonschool special districts. Some of the most common are as follows.[37]

municipal utility district (MUD)
a special district that offers services such as electricity, water, sewage, and sanitation outside the city limits

Municipal Utility Districts Municipal utility districts (MUDs) offer electricity, water, sewer, and sanitation services outside the city limits. These governments might offer all utility services or only one or two, depending on the needs of the special district. Though MUDs are located throughout Texas, the vast majority are found in the Houston greater metropolitan area.

MUDs can be a financial blessing for developers. Entrepreneurs who build housing additions outside the city limits must furnish utilities to the homes they build, but few developers can afford to do this over a long period of time.

Banks and finance companies, legislators, and land developers maintain a warm and snug relationship with each other. Banks and finance companies willingly lend land developers millions of dollars to establish residential subdivisions, build new homes, and run water and sewer services to these houses. When a few houses are sold, the developer asks the residents to establish a MUD. Enabling the legislation is seldom a problem because of the close relationship between developers and local legislators.

Once the MUD is up and running, the board of directors sets a tax rate and determines how much to charge residents for its services. One of its first activities is to borrow money by issuing bonds. The bond proceeds are used to purchase the utilities from the developer, often at a premium. Using the proceeds from the sale of the utilities, the developer is able to repay loans. By establishing the MUD, residents agree to pay a property tax to retire the bonded indebtedness. In addition to the property tax, residents pay a monthly fee for the water, sewer, and sanitation services.

Community College Districts Community college districts are classified as nonschool special districts because they do not offer public education from pre-kindergarten through 12th grade. Community colleges offer postsecondary academic and vocational programs. They are governed by an elected board of regents. Residents of the district pay a property tax to the district. In return, residents pay lower tuition. The board employs a president or chancellor, who operates the college on a daily basis. The regents set policy on the recommendation of the president or chancellor. Among the regents' responsibilities are to

- set overall policy for the district
- set the tax rate
- set the cost of tuition and fees
- build new buildings and repair older ones
- hire teachers, counselors, administrators, and nonprofessional staff
- set the school calendar
- determine salaries and benefits for employees

Hospital, Emergency Services, and Flood Control Districts A number of counties have hospital districts that serve the poor and uninsured. These districts may collect payments from patients and government programs such as Medicaid for medical services, although it is necessary to supplement the costs of indigent medical care through the creation of hospital districts with taxing authority. Emergency services districts provide fire and are ambulance services to areas not served otherwise. The districts can be of varying size—Harris County has more than 30 emergency services districts, though most counties in Texas would contain only one or two such districts. A rural county, Delta County, for example, has only one emergency services district.[38] Flooding is seldom confined to a single county. Flood control districts are established to solve a multicounty problem.

Creating, Governing, and Paying for a Special District Special districts are created by voters of the area to be served. Creating a special district requires

- a petition signed by the residents of the area to be served, requesting the legislature to authorize an election to create a special district
- enabling legislation in the form of a law that authorizes a special election to create the district
- a majority positive vote of those voting in the special election

Most special districts are governed by boards elected by the voters of the district. The board of a school district is called the board of trustees, the governing board of a community college is often called the board of regents, and the governing boards of other special districts are usually known as boards of directors. Each board is the policy-making group for its district. The directors set the tax rate and establish rules and policy for the operation of the district. The district often employs an individual who runs the district on a day-to-day basis. **Property taxes** are the primary source of revenue for special districts. This was not always the case. In 1949 school districts received 80 percent of their income from the state, and the school dis-

property tax a tax based on an assessment of the value of one's property, which is used to fund the services provided by local governments, such as education

trict furnished 20 percent of necessary funds, primarily from property taxes. Today, property taxes constitute as much as 90 percent of revenues for some districts. The second-largest source of income is **user fees**. State and federal aid furnish the remainder of special district funding.

Property tax rates and actual user fees are set by governing boards. User fees are raised from providing goods and services. Water districts, for example, sell water, sewer, and possibly sanitation services.

Hospital districts set fees for room occupancy, medicine dispensed, use of surgical suites, X-rays taken and evaluated, nursing and laboratory service, and myriad other charges. The board of trustees of a school district sets the local property rate for taxes, which fund pre-kindergarten through 12th grade education. Tuition paid by in-district and out-of-district students, building fees, student fees, and technology and lab fees are determined by the board of regents of a community college district.

Hidden Governments Everyone in Texas lives in at least one special district, their school district. Most people live in several, have the opportunity to vote for people to represent them on the governing board of each district, and pay property taxes to these agencies of government. Yet few people are aware these agencies exist, thus their reputation as "**hidden governments**."

Special districts provide needed services in specific geographic areas. Existing governments may lack authority to provide the service or the necessary funds to finance the project. In theory, special districts are an example of democracy at work. Districts are created by a vote of the residents of the area to be served, and the districts' governing boards are elected by the voters. Board meetings, at which decisions on policy, taxing, and fees are made, are open for attendance by any interested residents. However, fewer than 10 percent of eligible voters cast ballots in special district elections, and fewer than 1 percent of district residents ever attend a board meeting.

Problems with Special Districts There is a potential for abuse in the creation of special districts. Many special districts were originally authorized by the Texas legislature to develop the economies of poor, rural counties. More recently, however, developers of large tracts of land began creating these districts to place the burden of developing the property's infrastructure on future owners of the property. In order to comply with the law, all the developers must do is create the district and hold an election where at least one short-term resident must vote. These short-term residents then approve bonds (interest-bearing financial instruments that are sold in financial markets to fund government projects) in the millions of dollars that must be paid for with the taxation of future homes and property owners. In the 1980s this kind of special district creation in Harris County led to defaults on bond issues after a housing bust.

In 2001 a major investigation of special districts created by developers in Dallas found unusual and questionable practices. Some developers drew district boundaries to exclude existing residents of an area. The developers then moved people into rent-free mobile homes shortly before the special district election. These newly established "residents" were the only ones eligible to vote in the election. After the election, the voters for the new district would often move away after approving large bond sales for the construction of roads, water lines, and sewers. Future homeowners in the area were then expected to pay for the bonds with property taxes on their homes. The investigation found that sometimes a single voter—and

always fewer than 10 voters—approved the bonded indebtedness that helped the developers create an infrastructure for their properties. In the Lantana subdivision near Flower Mound, for example, a family of three voted to authorize $277 million in bond sales by two water districts. That bond proposition rivals the biggest bond proposals by the city of Dallas.[39]

Similar schemes have been especially prevalent in Travis, Harris, and Denton counties. In 2006 developers in Denton County housed six people at below-market rents on property to be developed. These temporary residents were thus eligible to vote in a special tax-district election that would affect the taxation of thousands of future homeowners.[40]

In 2010 two voters in the Four Seasons Ranch Municipal Utility District No. 1 approved $292.5 million in bonds, including $138.5 million in bonds for water, sewer, and storm sewer systems and $154 million in roads. Recent special district elections near the Four Seasons Ranch district in Denton and Collin counties have authorized close to $1 billion in public debt.[41]

The pervasiveness of special districts is shown by one study of Texas special districts that address water issues. The study found that about 1,000 MUDs were engaged in supplying water; 48 special districts existed to deal with water drainage issues; 66 special districts existed solely to supply fresh water. Others had these purposes: 91 to conserve groundwater, 25 for irrigation, 46 to improve levees, 42 to manage municipal water, 26 to deal with navigation, 31 to deal with rivers. Fifty-five special utility districts dealt with general water issues; 221 were water control and improvement districts; and 18 were water improvement districts. Of course, this hodgepodge of special districts dealing with all aspects of water makes a coherent approach to statewide water policy virtually impossible.[42]

Special districts are among the least-studied areas of Texas politics, but their use as an instrument of private gain and their use by developers as a way to minimize their financial risks suggest the need for much greater scrutiny. Of course, developers may defend this system as a way to improve property and enhance the tax base of communities. On the other hand, the extent of enlistment of governmental taxing powers with little public scrutiny or accountability is disturbing. And if the huge bond issues floated by these entities default, thousands of people could suffer the financial consequences.

for critical analysis

Why are there so many special districts in Texas? Why don't cities and counties do the jobs of special districts?

Councils of Government (COGs)

council of government (COG)
a regional planning board composed of local elected officials and some private citizens from the same area

One of the greatest problems facing local governments in Texas today is coordination across legal boundaries. The Regional Planning Act of 1965 initially provided for the creation of regional **councils of government (COGs)** to promote coordination and planning across all local governments in a particular region. There are 24 regional councils in Texas today, each with its own bylaws or articles of agreement. The governing body of a regional council must consist of at least two-thirds of local elected officials of cities and counties and may include citizen members and representatives of other groups.

The basic responsibilities of regional councils include planning for the economic development of an area, helping local governments carry out regional projects, contracting with local governments to provide certain services, and reviewing applications for state and federal financial assistance. Originally, COGs focused considerable attention on meeting federal mandates for water and sewer provision, open space, and housing planning. More recently, activities have focused on comprehensive planning and service delivery in such policy areas as aging, employment and training, criminal justice, economic development, environmental quality, and transportation.[43] Figure 10.2 provides a map and listing of the 24 regional COGs in Texas.

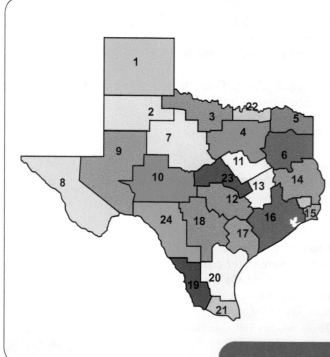

Region Name	Number
Alamo Area Council of Governments	18
Ark-Tex Council of Governments	5
Brazos Valley Council of Governments	13
Capital Area Council of Governments	12
Central Texas Council of Governments	23
Coastal Bend Council of Governments	20
Concho Valley Council of Governments	10
Deep East Texas Council of Governments	14
East Texas Council of Governments	6
Golden Crescent Regional Planning Commission	17
Heart of Texas Council of Governments	11
Houston-Galveston Area Council	16
Lower Rio Grande Valley Development Council	21
Middle Rio Grande Development Council	24
Nortex Regional Planning Commission	3
North Central Texas Council of Governments	4
Panhandle Regional Planning Commission	1
Permian Basin Regional Planning Commission	9
Rio Grande Council of Governments	8
South East Texas Regional Planning Commission	15
South Plains Association of Governments	2
South Texas Development Council	19
Texoma Council of Governments	22
West Central Texas Council of Governments	7

FIGURE 10.2
Regional Councils of Government in Texas

Financial Issues Facing Local Government

> **Examine the financial problems facing local government**

As noted earlier, there are many different forms of local government in Texas, including county governments, municipal governments, school districts, and special districts. These governments often raise money through special financial mechanisms based on their ability to tax. Among these financial mechanisms are capital appreciation bonds and local government pensions. Both raise important opportunities and problems for local government.

Capital Appreciation Bonds

A **capital appreciation bond (CAB)** is a type of security issued by municipalities. It is used primarily by school districts to raise revenue for development in times of rapid population growth.[44] This new financial instrument has been causing a great deal of controversy, especially in California and Texas—but despite the controversy, CABs are becoming more and more common in Texas. According to the nonpartisan group California Watch, "in Texas, 590 districts and other government entities have issued these bonds over the past six years—more than any other state."[45] Combined, Texas's local governments issued more than $2.3 billion in CABs in over 700 separate issuances between 2007 and 2011—debts that will eventually cost more than $20 billion to repay.[46] The per capita debt of Texas's state government ranks 45th in the nation. However, when local debt is taken into consideration, it jumps to the 15th-highest.[47]

When a municipality issues a traditional bond, it is obligated to make periodic interest payments to its bondholders. However, CABs are different; they are classified as "zero-coupon bonds."[48] The issuer of a zero-coupon bond pays back the initial investment and all accrued interest in one lump sum when the bond reaches maturity.[49] This lump sum, called the "maturity value," is the face value of the bond—typically a multiple of $5,000.[50] The bonds are sold to investors for significantly less than the maturity value. The difference between the maturity value and the price at which the bond is sold is called the "original issue discount"[51] and is the buyer's expected return on investment. However, CABs are distinct from typical zero-coupon bonds in an important way: the issue price, not the maturity value, is considered the principal. This means that the amount of debt that appears on the issuing government's balance sheet is much less than what it will actually owe when the bonds mature.[52] In California, many municipalities use this fact to borrow large amounts of money without exceeding their statutory debt limits.[53]

CABs are extremely long-term bonds. In many cases they do not mature until 40 years after they are issued.[54] For this entire time period, the issuer does not have to pay a dime to investors—meaning that local government officials can promise new education facilities to voters without raising taxes.[55] CABs are also very high yield. An analysis of the numbers provided by the *Austin American-Statesman* shows that Texas municipalities will owe, on average, nearly $9 for every $1 they have borrowed using CABs.[56] In extreme cases, the ratio of money owed to money borrowed can reach 35 to 1.[57] As with most municipal bonds, the interest accrued by capital appreciation bonds is tax exempt. Essentially what this all means is that

capital appreciation bond (CAB)
a long-term, high-interest-paying bond that pays off both principal and interest in one lump sum when the bond reaches maturity

the debt burden facing local government is considerably more than is found on the books.

Controversies over Capital Appreciation Bonds Most of the controversy about the use of capital appreciation bonds centers on two issues: the large amounts of debt taken on by the issuer and the relative unaccountability of elected officials and voters. Chuck DeVore, vice president of policy for the Texas Public Policy Foundation, is a vocal opponent of CABs for these reasons. He calls them "a tool that allows elected officials to enjoy the fruits of borrowed money while telling today's voters not to worry about the debt."[58] Texas senator Juan Hinojosa warns that "the buy-now, pay-later approach often results in crippling repayment obligations, with the repayment costs being greater than the benefits derived from the bond."[59] In the 2013 legislative session there were unsuccessful efforts to prohibit the use of CABs. Those who support CABs are concerned that prohibiting CABs will make it more difficult for school districts to keep pace with population growth.[60]

The dilemma of entities that use these bonds is well illustrated by the Anna Independent School District in Collin County. State law caps the school district tax rate on property, which is the primary funding source for public schools, yet Anna was undergoing tremendous growth as it was a rural school district that was becoming a suburban school district as the Dallas metropolitan area grew to the north. In 2002–03, Anna Independent School District had about 1,000 students; in 2012–13, it had about 2,500 students. By issuing CABs, Anna could build schools for its rapid growth, but since periodic interest payments are not required as they would be by traditional interest-bearing bonds, CABs do not count against the state cap on property taxes until the payment is due many years later. The state cap required that when school bonds are issued, they must be paid back at a tax rate that is not greater than 50 cents per $100 of assessed property value. In 2003, Anna's debt service tax rate was 13 cents, but by 2008 it had reached the 50-cent limit, which offered no additional bond funding unless CABs were used. When these bonds are repaid, Anna's taxpayers will have to pay back about five times the amount borrowed unless the bonds can be refinanced at a lower rate, but in the meantime Anna's schools can deal with the district's burgeoning growth.[61]

Over the next 40 years, California municipalities will have to pay back a combined $36 billion of CAB debt—on average 3.89 times as much as they borrowed.[62] The California State Assembly recently passed a measure placing new restrictions on CABs, including a maximum length of 25 years and a debt cap of 4 times the amount borrowed.[63] In Michigan, legislators have already taken more direct measures—they banned CABs outright in 1994.[64] Texas has not passed restriction on the bonds, and under the current bond financing structure CABs may be the only way that school districts can obtain the funding to pay for rapid growth, but the incautious use of CABs could have dire consequences for local government finances.

Local Government Pensions

Another area of concern with local government involves the cost and financial health of pension plans. Several municipal bankruptcies throughout the United States in the summer of 2012 brought attention to the instability of a number of state and local public pension plans. California cities have been particularly hard hit by the cost of local pensions. For example, in 2012, San Bernardino, California, failed to make a payment on $1 million in bonds that it had issued to support pensions. Two California cities claimed that their local employee pension costs were a major factor in their declarations of bankruptcy.[65]

Texas has 81 different local governmental pension plans that cover nearly 184,000 persons and that have net assets of over $28 billion. When a pension plan is fully funded and can meet all its obligations, it has a funded ratio of 100 percent. A rough rule (over which there is disagreement) is that a funded ratio of below 80 percent means that a pension plan is not fiscally healthy. Eighty-one percent of local pension plans in Texas have a funded ratio that is below 80 percent.[66] In 2014 and 2015 new standards will be put into effect for the valuation of public pension assets and liabilities. These new accounting standards will significantly reduce the funded ratios for many Texas public employee pension plans and will allow pension plans to operate with more unfunded liabilities, pushing more costs into the future.[67]

Pension Funding Controversies There are other measures of the financial stability of Texas public pension plans other than funded ratios, but those measures provide further support for the concern that there is a looming financial crisis in public pensions in the state. One other measure of financial stability is the amortization period for pensions. This is simply the length of time that is required to eliminate a pension plan's unfunded liabilities based on current contributions to the plan from employers and from active members of the pension plan. In 2012 the Texas Pension Review Board considered a plan with an amortization period of 40 years or more to be actuarially unsound. The Governmental Accounting Standards Board recommends that an amortization period be no more than 30 years. Fifty-eight of the public pension plans in Texas have an amortization period of less than 30 years, 12 have an amortization period of 31 to 40 years, and 19 have amortization periods of more than 40 years.[68] Houston's city workers have three major pension systems—Houston Police Officers Pension System, Houston Firefighters' Relief and Retirement Fund, and the Houston Municipal Employees Pension System. The police and firefighters' funds have funded ratios of 82.8 and 93.4 percent, respectively, which suggests sufficient funding to meet their obligations. However, the municipal employees fund has a funding ratio of 61.4 percent, which suggests this fund is in poor financial condition. Altogether, the three funds have unfunded liabilities of over $2.4 billion. Houston expects that its contributions to employee pensions will rise from $181 million, which is 10.9 percent of all city expenditures in 2007, to $394 million, or 17.1 percent of all city expenditures, by 2017.[69]

Fort Worth's Employees' Retirement Fund began having serious funding issues in the 1990s when the city's contributions to the fund were decreased while plan benefits were increased. Additionally investment returns to the fund were wiped out in the 2008 Great Recession. In 2011, Fort Worth's pension problems led to a reduction in benefits for new hires other than public safety workers that included increases in the minimum retirement age, reduction of the multiplier used to calculate benefits, elimination of cost-of-living adjustments, and removal of overtime earnings from benefit calculations. In spite of these reductions, Fort Worth's unfunded liability has increased from $431.7 million in 2010 to $748.2 million at the end of 2012.[70]

In comparison with private pension plans, local government retirement pensions can be remarkably generous. As an example, in Dallas after 32 years of service, some police and firefighters can receive pensions that are equal to 96 percent of their highest average annual pay. In some cases, it is possible to retire at 96 percent of annual pay in one's mid-50s and the pension payments would continue, along with annual increases, as long as the retiree lives.[71]

One aspect of local pension plans that has become very controversial and that has a huge effect on local budgets is the **Deferred Retirement Option Plan (DROP)**. With a DROP, a local employee who is eligible to retire can continue working. During this time, the employee's retirement benefits are deposited in a fund where the benefits draw interest until actual retirement when the DROP funds are withdrawn. DROP plans can have vastly negative consequences on local budgets when they allow for very early retirement ages, high interest rates, and cost-of-living adjustments. As an example, in 2012, Dallas had 3,014 employees with deferred retirement accounts. A major attraction of the DROP for Dallas police and fire employees is that it guarantees an 8 to 10 percent return on funds in the deferred retirement account at a time of very low interest payments from other sources. The average deferred retirement account balance in Dallas is about $347,000. The 20 oldest active police and fire department employees have an average of $1.3 million in their deferred retirement accounts. There have recently been benefit cuts for new hires, declines in the guaranteed interest rate, and increases in the employee contribution into the retirement system. Still, the system's unfunded liabilities amount to about $1.2 billion, and the return on investment by the system was only 0.3 percent.[72]

The Collin County judge has recently criticized Collin County employee pensions, arguing that the current pension system is too costly and a drain on the county budget. Collin County employees are part of the statewide plan, the Texas County and District Retirement System. Currently Collin County employees deposit 7 percent of their pay into the fund and the county matches that contribution with $2 for every $1 deposited. No matter what the market return, the county employees are guaranteed a 7 percent return per year. When investments of the pension money do not produce the 7 percent return, the county must make up the difference. By any standard, the pension system is very generous and, according to the county judge, so generous that it burdens taxpayers.[73]

The locally administered plans serve only 31 percent of local government pension members. About 400,000 county and municipal workers contribute to statewide plans for their pensions. Two of the largest statewide plans are the Texas County and District Retirement System (TCDRS) and the Texas Municipal Retirement System (TMRS). Both of these funds appear to be financially secure. The TCDRS, for example, has a funded ratio of 89 percent and the TMRS has a funded ratio of 85.1 percent. The biggest state plan is the Teacher Retirement System of Texas (TRS), which provides retirement pensions for Texas public school teachers, some state higher education teachers, and nonteaching staff. Its funding ratio is 82.7 percent. However, of the eight statewide retirement plans, even though six of them have funded ratios above 80 percent, four of the plans will run out of money with current contributions, benefits, and actuarial assumptions.[74]

Future Pension Policy Pensions have a huge effect on state, county, and local governments. And for some local governments, employee pensions have already become unmanageable. In 2011 in Houston, for example, the mayor tried to get legislation from the state that would allow the city a stronger role in setting pension benefits. However, the mayor was unsuccessful, in part because the municipal employees pension, the police pension, and the firefighters' pension plans in Houston spent at least $375,000 on lobbyists to oppose the mayor's effort.[75]

deferred retirement option plan (DROP) retirement plan in which local government employees who are eligible to retire have their retirement benefits deposited in an account in which the benefits draw interest until actual retirement. Some of these plans pay high interest and cost-of-living adjustments and may be coupled with very early retirement ages

A looming financial crisis for many local governments in Texas is its pension systems. It is likely that in the near future there will be increased efforts by cities to lower their pension liabilities and increased tension with employees who wish to keep their current benefits.

Some pension plans have already recognized that their plans were no longer economically viable and have instituted significant plan changes. Table 10.5 identifies the types of changes that are occurring in some pension plans.

One example of significant pension plan changes is the El Paso city retirement plan. Prior to September 1, 2011, normal retirement was age 55 if the employee had 10 years of credit with the pension system or age 60 with 7 years of credit, or any age with 30 years of credit. The employee pension was 2.5 percent of the employee's final wages times the years of pension credit. Final wages were calculated as the greater of average monthly gross earnings over the prior 3 years or average monthly base salary in the prior year or base salary for the month prior to retirement. After the pension changes were put into effect on September 1, 2011, normal retirement was age 60 with 7 years of credit or any age with 35 years of credit. The employee pension was calculated at 2.25 percent of final wages times the years of pension service credit and final wages which are calculated as the average monthly gross earnings over the prior three years.[76]

While those changes may seem trivial, those changes can significantly affect the pension received by an employee, and over large numbers of employees, the amounts of money can be dramatic. As an example, assume an El Paso city employee chooses to retire at age 60 with 25 years and 5 months of credited service with the city and that the employee's final wages were $2,000 per month. That employee's pension would be $1,270.85 per month, which is .025 times 25.417 times $2,000. Under the new plan, however, a 60-year-old employee with 25 years and 5 months of credited service with the city and the same final wages would receive .0225 times 25.417 times $2,000 or $1,143.76. Not only would the pension amount be less, but an employee could not begin normal retirement at 55 or at any age with 30 years of credit, and with fewer options to calculate the amount of final wages, it would be harder for the employee to actually have a final wage of $2,000 per month.[77]

The complex financial issues involved with providing pensions to local government workers may seem tiresome to students of politics. But they cut to the core of the problems facing government officials in the early twenty-first century. If local governments in Texas are to thrive in the coming decades, they must not be burdened with debts that cannot be paid.

TABLE 10.5

Options for Fully Funding Texas Public Employee Pension Plans

Increases in employee contributions to pensions

Increases in employer contributions to pensions

Formula for calculation of pension that is less favorable to employee

More years of employment required in calculation of pension

Increased retirement eligibility ages

SOURCE: State Pension Review Board, "2013 Guide to Public Retirement Systems in Texas" (2013).

for critical analysis

Why do local governments rely on bonds for fund projects? What advantage do capital appreciation bonds have in funding governmental projects? Why have public pensions become so controversial?

● Thinking Critically about Local Government

In this chapter, we have investigated the role of local government in Texas government and politics. In many ways, local government affects the average citizen's life much more than either the federal or the state government. Sadly, local government may not be functioning as well as we might hope. Part of the problem may lie in the conflicting demands we have come to place on it. On the one hand, Texans want local government of all kinds to provide an efficient delivery of services to all in a fair and equitable manner. On the other hand, Texans also want to keep local government under some sort of democratic control. But what sort of local controls are the best? The demands of efficiency and democracy are not easily balanced. The social, political, and economic changes of the last 20 years may spark a rethinking of local government in Texas for the first time since the early decades of the twentieth century. The disaster in West, Texas, that was discussed in the introduction was certainly an extreme case that reflected a major failure of regulation at the local governmental level, but that failure is not the only problem facing local government in the state. There are potential financial disasters facing local governments in their pension systems and in their method of borrowing money, and there is the fundamental question of whether the structure of local government in Texas at the county, municipal, and special district levels is adequate in providing necessary services for Texans.

County Government in Texas

Explain the importance of county government in Texas (pp. 312–20)

There are more counties in Texas than in any other state. County governance in Texas affects the lives of everyday Texans in ways ranging from hospital care to trash pickup.

Key Terms

county commissioners' court (p. 313)

county judge (p. 313)

county commissioner (p. 313)

constable (p. 314)

county attorney (p. 319)

district attorney (p. 319)

county clerk (p. 319)

district clerk (p. 319)

county tax assessor-collector (p. 319)

county auditor (p. 319)

Practice Quiz

1. Which of the following is *not* a type of local government found in Texas?
   a) city
   b) council of government
   c) county
   d) special district
   e) municipal

2. The basic governing body of a county is known as
   a) a council of government.
   b) a county council.

   c) a city-manager government.
   d) a county commissioners' court.
   e) a county governing committee.

3. How many counties are there in Texas?
   a) 25
   b) 56
   c) 110
   d) 254
   e) 500

4. All county commissioners' precincts must be equal in population according to
   a) Article 1 of the Texas Constitution.
   b) the Civil Rights Act of 1964.
   c) the Voting Rights Act of 1975.
   d) *Avery v. Midland County.*
   e) *Marbury v. Madison.*

5. A county judge
   a) only hears appellate cases from JP courts.
   b) is an appointive position from the governor.
   c) presides over the constitutional county court and the county commissioners' court.
   d) implements all the decisions of the Supreme Court affecting the county.
   e) judges juvenile cases.

6. Which county officials are responsible for the jail and the safety of the prisoners?
   a) sheriff
   b) county council
   c) county commissioners' court
   d) council of mayors
   e) city manager

City Government in Texas

Describe the major types of city government in Texas (pp. 320–30)

Municipalities in Texas vary in terms of how they are governed. Some cities have strong mayors who run the city, while other cities have weak mayors where the day-to-day running of the city is delegated to city managers. Mayors and city councils often decide issues that directly affect the lives of everyday people.

Key Terms

home-rule charter (p. 320)

mayor-council form of government (p. 321)

at-large election (p. 321)

single-member district (p. 321)

commissioner form of government (p. 322)

council-manager form of government (p. 324)

Practice Quiz

7. To adopt a home-rule charter, a city must have a minimum population of
   a) 201.
   b) 5,000.
   c) 10,000.
   d) 50,000.
   e) There is no minimum.

8. The two legal classifications of Texas cities are
   a) local and regional.
   b) general law and home rule.
   c) tax and nontax.
   d) charter and noncharter.
   e) big and small.

9. The form of city government that allows the mayor to establish control over most of the city's government is called the

   a) commissioner form of city government.
   b) council-manager form of city government.
   c) council of government form of city government.
   d) strong mayor–council form of city government.
   e) none of the above

10. A city controller
    a) works directly for the governor.
    b) controls and manages the election in a city.
    c) is a city's chief elected official who presides over the city council.
    d) is independent of all political control in a small statutory city.
    e) is a city's chief financial officer.

Special Districts

Examine the role of special districts in Texas government (pp. 330–36)

Special districts often span different cities and counties. They are tasked with operating such things as school districts or water utility districts. They have the authority to levy property taxes to fund the operation of services essential to the lives of many residents.

Key Terms

special district (p. 330)

school district (p. 330)

nonschool special district (p. 331)

municipal utility district (MUD) (p. 332)

property tax (p. 333)

user fee (p. 334)

hidden government (p. 334)

council of government (COG) (p. 336)

Practice Quiz

11. Which local government provides a single service not provided by any other local government?
    a) special district
    b) council of government
    c) police district
    d) city
    e) county

12. What are the two types of special districts found in Texas?
    a) school and nonschool
    b) home rule and general law
    c) tax and nontax
    d) statutory and constitutional
    e) none of the above

13. A special district
    a) must be limited to under 150,000 people.
    b) covers the entire state to provide a particular service.
    c) is a unit of local government that provides a special service to a limited geographic area.
    d) temporarily combines two congressional districts.
    e) none of the above

14. A MUD
    a) serves the needs of developers.
    b) is generally opposed by banks and real estate developers as being too expensive.
    c) provides ambulance service inside a city's geographic limits.
    d) delegates the setting of tax rates in a particular geographic area to the state legislature.
    e) provides funding for special districts.

15. Comprehensive planning and service delivery in a specific geographic area are the function of a
    a) special district.
    b) council of government.
    c) city.
    d) county.
    e) town.

Financial Issues Facing Local Government

Examine the financial problems facing local government (pp. 337–41)

Local government in Texas is facing a looming financial crisis as a result of widespread issuance of capital appreciation bonds, which allow funds to be raised in the present while interest and payments on the principal are paid far into the future, and the liabilities imposed on local government by generous retirement plans for governmental employees.

Key Terms

capital appreciation bond (CAB) (p. 337)

deferred retirement option plan (DROP) (p. 340)

Practice Quiz

16. Capital appreciation bonds
    a) are long-term bonds on which local governments pay back principal and interest on a yearly basis.
    b) are short-term bonds on which local governments borrow money for emergencies.
    c) are bonds on which interest is paid quarterly by local governments but the principal is not paid back for 40 years.
    d) are bonds on which principal and interest are not paid back until the end of a lengthy term while local governments can use the borrowed money immediately.
    e) create such long-term financial risks that they are illegal in Texas.

17. Some governmental employee retirement plans in Texas
    a) impose huge financial liabilities on government.
    b) need to be increased to support needy retired employees.
    c) have not kept up with inflation.
    d) will soon be merged into the Social Security retirement program.
    e) are so minimal that it is hard to recruit employees at the local level.

Recommended Websites

Individual State Descriptions
www.census.gov

Texas Association of Counties
www.county.org

Texas Local Government Code
www.statutes.legis.state.tx.us

U.S. Census Bureau, State and County QuickFacts
http://quickfacts.census.gov/qfd

In 2010 students at UT Austin protested against cuts in education spending and increases in tuition. As lawmakers work to balance the state budget, the decisions they make about taxes and spending affect all Texans.

Public Finance in Texas

11

WHY PUBLIC FINANCE MATTERS For college students, the state budget might appear to be pretty far removed from everyday life. Decisions made in Austin every two years may seem to have little to do with attending class, preparing for an exam, or getting everything in order for a timely graduation. But like it or not, the budgetary decisions made by legislators every two years affect students where they matter most: in the pocketbook.

In 2003 state political leaders found themselves staring at a $10 billion shortfall in the upcoming budget period. Mandated by the state constitution to maintain a balanced budget, they needed to find new and creative ways to close the budget gap without raising taxes. One method was to cut higher education funding.

Prior to 2003 tuition and fee rates for state universities had been set by the state legislature, and in Texas they tended to be low when compared to tuition in other states. Costs ranged from $2,870 per year at Texas A&M at Texarkana to $4,912 per year at the University of Texas (UT) at Austin. General revenues funded a large portion of the state university's education budget. In 2003, as a trade-off for a 2 percent cut in the higher education budget, the legislature gave the regents of the various state schools the authority to raise tuition to make up the difference.[1]

Tuition skyrocketed across the country in the first decade of the twenty-first century. Labor-intensive instruction and other high fixed expenditures fueled these increases. Texas higher education was not spared these inflationary pressures. Granted the discretion to increase tuition and fees by the legislature, universities across the state lined up to solve their own budget problems by raising tuition and fees on their students. Tuition and fees for Texas A&M at Texarkana rose 71 percent between 2003 and 2011 to $5,204 per year. At UT Austin, they rose 80 percent to $9,796 per year, and at UT Dallas, they rose 110 percent from $5,244 per year to $11,014 per year. Overall, the average cost of attending a four-year institution in Texas for a year rose 90 percent from $3,864 to $7,342. Although this was below the national average of $8,244 per year for an in-state public institution, higher education had become an expensive commodity in Texas.[2]

In response to the budget crisis of 2011, cuts in higher education were again made and pressures to increase tuition at most state institutions continued unabated.[3] The president of UT Austin had been locked in a struggle with the UT System Board of Regents over micromanaging higher education on a variety of issues in 2011. This conflict spilled over in the debate over how much students should pay to attend the university. While accepting the proposals from most member schools for increases in tuition and fees between 2 and 4 percent for the next budgetary period, the Board of Regents, all of whom were appointed by Governor Perry, turned down a UT Austin proposal to increase tuition for in-state undergraduates by 2.6 percent. To offset some of the lost revenues, the board allocated $6.6 million to UT Austin for the next two years out of the state's Permanent University Fund.

By the spring of 2014 the Texas economy was in full recovery. Increasing sales tax and oil and gas severance tax revenue meant that the budget was looking good for the upcoming legislative session in the spring of 2015. One might have thought that the legislature and various boards of regents would be more favorably disposed to new requests to raise tuition and fees at state universities, but that was far from the case. Demands across the state to hold the line on tuition increases continued to be popular inside and outside the state legislature. For example, in May of 2014, the UT System Board of Regents decided not to raise tuition for in-state students at all UT System institutions. Provisions were made to raise out-of-state tuition and to allow universities to approve optional four-year fixed tuition programs. But the message being sent to the universities was the same as when the budget was under stress: the board was not in the business of rubber-stamping universities' requests for higher tuition and fees. Like the decisions about the state budget facing legislators in Austin, tuition and fees decisions faced by university boards of regents remained deeply political.[4]

chapter goals

- Explain the purpose of the state budget and what is typically included (pp. 349–51)

- Describe the general pattern of state spending in Texas and where state revenue comes from (pp. 351–61)

- Describe how the money in the budget is organized into specific funds (pp. 361–66)

- Outline the constitutional provisions that affect how the state budget is made (pp. 366–68)

- Identify the major steps and players in making the state budget (pp. 369–72)

- Analyze major budget crises in Texas (pp. 372–77)

What Is the Budget?

Explain the purpose of the state budget and what is typically included

One of the most distinguishing characteristics about public finance in Texas is that the state constitution mandates that the legislature operate within a "balanced budget." On its face, the idea of a balanced budget is straightforward. A budget, according to *Webster's Dictionary*, is an "estimate of future financial income and outgo." A balanced budget would exist whenever the projected income from tax revenues is equal to or exceeds the projected expenditure. But public finance is a complicated business and the devil is in the details. There are actually a number of different ways to talk about the funds that constitute the "budget." One way to look at them is to divide them into the following five broad budgetary categories.[5]

- The **General Revenues Fund budget** is a nondedicated revenue account and is the state's primary operating fund. It is the place where most state taxes and fees flow. It also includes three educational funds (the Available School Fund, the State Textbook Fund, and the Foundation School Fund). Expenditures may be made directly from the nondedicated funds and may be transferred to special funds or accounts for allocation.

- The **General Revenue–Dedicated Funds budget** includes funds dedicated to specific purposes. In 1991, 200 special funds were brought into the General Revenue–Dedicated Funds Account as part of a budget reform and consolidation package. Other budget reforms and consolidation have taken place since then, the most recent being during the 2013 legislative session. This budget includes such funds as the State Parks Account and the college operating accounts (which hold tuition funds). Generally speaking, the legislature can appropriate money from these accounts only for their dedicated purposes. The balances in this budget are used to certify that the constitutional pay-as-you-go limits (discussed below) are being met.

- The **Federal Funds budget** includes all grants, payments, and reimbursements received from the federal government by state agencies and institutions.

- The **Other Funds budget** consists of all other funds flowing into the state treasury not included in the other methods of financing. These include, among other funds, the State Highway Fund, trust funds, and revenue held in certain local higher education accounts.

- The **All Funds budget** is the aggregate of all of the above budgets, referring to all spending that goes through agencies, including federal and state programs.

Appropriations from these funds for the period 2014–15 are shown in Table 11.1.

Some important things must be noted about this complicated system of public financing through these various budgets. First, the state budget involves huge amounts of money. Table 11.2 shows that for the 2014–15 biennium, more than $73.89 billion was appropriated for Health and Human Services activities (encompassing the

General Revenues Fund budget budget for a nondedicated revenue account that functions as the state's primary operating fund

General Revenue–Dedicated Funds budget budget composed of funds for dedicated revenues that target money for specific purposes

Federal Funds budget state budget that includes all grants, payments, and reimbursements received from the federal government by state agencies and institutions

Other Funds budget budget consisting of all other funds flowing into the state treasury that are not included in other state budgets; this includes the Texas Highway Fund, various trust funds operated by the state, and certain revenues held for local higher education accounts.

All Funds budget budget that aggregates all monies flowing into the state treasury and all state spending

TABLE 11.1

Texas Budgetary Funds Appropriated, 2014–15 (in billions of dollars)

General Revenues Fund budget	$94.977
General Revenue–Dedicated Funds budget	7.315
Federal Funds budget	68.716
Other Funds budget	31.153
All Funds budget	29.413

SOURCE: Legislative Budget Board, *Fiscal Size-Up: 2014–15 Biennium*, February 2014, pp. 3–8.

TABLE 11.2

Summary of All Funds State Budget Allocation by Biennium (in billions of dollars)

	2012–13	2014–15	PERCENTAGE CHANGE
Governmental functions	$4.92	$4.84	–1.6%
Health and human services	68.83	73.89	7.4
Education	75.77	74.20	–2.1
Judiciary	0.66	0.76	15.4
Public safety and criminal justice	11.71	11.68	–0.2
Natural resources	4.96	6.76	36.4
Business and economic development	22.86	26.29	15.0
Regulatory	0.70	1.29	82.9
General provisions	0.00	0.35	N/A
Legislature	0.35	0.36	3.1
Total all functions	**$190.75**	**$200.42**	**5.1%**

SOURCE: Legislative Budget Board, *Fiscal Size-Up: 2014–15 Biennium*, February 2014, p. 2.

Medicaid and Temporary Assistance for Needy Families programs). There were $74.2 billion appropriated for education, including $50.8 billion for public education and $17.94 billion for higher education, and $26.29 billion appropriated for business and economic development. Second, much of this money lies outside the direct control of the legislature. Trust funds and other dedicated funds exist for particular purposes and are hard to manipulate for other budgetary purposes. Legislators seeking to balance the budget are often left with relatively few places to cut expenditures. Given its large proportion of the General Revenues Fund budget, education is often at the top of the list. Third, federal expenditures have a very important role in shaping the overall direction of the state budget. The bulk of federal funds expenditures is in two areas: health and human services, and education. Strings are often attached to these monies. If legislators want federal dollars, they must spend state dollars first. Figure 11.1 highlights the increasingly important role that federal dollars have played in spending patterns in Texas. Unadjusted expenditures from the General Revenues Fund (state funds) have increased modestly between 1994–95 and 2014–15. But expenditures from the All Funds budget (which takes into account federal spending) have exploded during the same period. The pressure to maximize federal dollars flowing into Texas is one legislative goal. But legislators also desire to minimize state spending and not raise taxes.

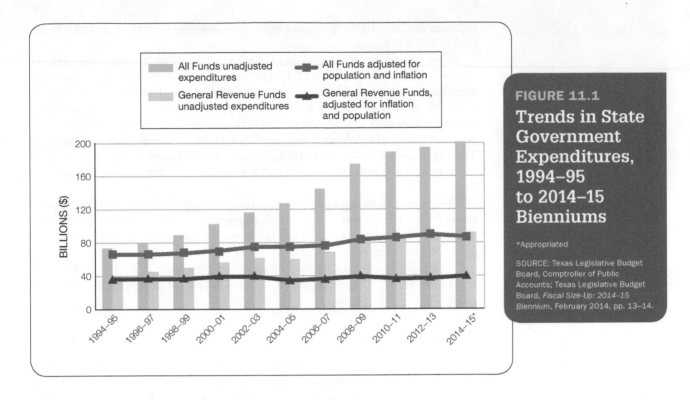

FIGURE 11.1

Trends in State Government Expenditures, 1994–95 to 2014–15 Bienniums

*Appropriated

SOURCE: Texas Legislative Budget Board, Comptroller of Public Accounts; Texas Legislative Budget Board, *Fiscal Size-Up: 2014–15 Biennium*, February 2014, pp. 13–14.

● Spending and Revenue in Texas

Describe the general pattern of state spending in Texas and where state revenue comes from

Texas has a reputation of being a "low service, low tax" state that seeks to maintain a favorable environment for business. In this section, we will look at the general pattern of state spending in Texas, as well as taxes and other sources of revenue in the state.

Trends in State Spending

For the most part, Texas's reputation as a low-spending state is well earned. On a variety of measures, Texas spends less than other states. One Texas Legislative Budget Board study found that among the 50 states, Texas ranked 46th on per capita state government expenditures. Texas's spending of $4,916 per person was far below the U.S. average of $6,433. On a per capita basis, Texas ranks 27th in educational spending, 44th in highway spending, 25th in hospital spending, and 41st in public welfare spending.[6] Conversely, Texas ranked high when compared to other states on the per capita federal dollars flowing into the state. In 2012, Texas took in $10,647 per capita from the federal government, ranking it 11th among the states, above the national state average of $8,844.[7]

The trend in overall spending reveals a similar story, particularly in recent years. As Figure 11.1 shows, in unadjusted dollars (that is, dollars spent not taking into account inflation or population increases), state spending in Texas rose from $39.959 billion in the 1994–95 biennium to $94.977 billion in the 2014–15 biennium. However, in real per capita dollars (that is, dollars spent controlling for inflation and population increases), state spending rose slightly from $39.959 billion to $40.973 billion.

When considering state and federal spending in Texas together (see the All Funds State Budget in Figure 11.1), the story is a little bit different. Unadjusted spending for all funds (state and federal) in Texas rose from $72.769 billion in 1994–95 to $200.421 billion in 2014–15. But in real per capita dollars, spending in the same periods rose from $72.769 billion to $86.461 billion. In other words, between the 1994–95 budget and the 2014–15 budget, real federal spending in Texas (per capita) increased by 18.9 percent while real state spending (per capita) increased only slightly, by 2.8 percent. There is a lot of federal money flowing into Texas.

The number of workers employed by Texas was smaller than that of many other states. In 2011 there were 124 state employees for every 10,000 people living in Texas. This figure was far below the U.S. state average of 140 state employees for every 10,000 state residents, ranking Texas 43rd among the 50 states. Interestingly, though, Texas ranked only a little behind New York at 41st with 125 state employees per 10,000 people, and ahead of California at 46th with 108 state employees per 10,000 people.[8]

Revenue in Texas

Spending and size of government are only part of Texas's "low service, low tax" reputation. The taxes that fund government are the other dimension. It is difficult to measure the state tax burden Texans face compared to that of citizens in other states. There are a variety of taxes that individuals can pay to the state government, including state income taxes, general state sales taxes, specific state sales taxes, local sales taxes, and property taxes. Moreover, some state taxes can be lower in one state but be offset by higher local taxes. Conversely, state taxes can be higher, offsetting lower local taxes.

After the legislature passes the biennial state budget, the state comptroller certifies the budget, confirming that it is within current revenue estimates for the period. Here, State Comptroller Susan Combs discusses the 2012–13 budget.

Who Pays the Highest State Taxes?

Texas is one of a handful of states that do not tax income. This means that Texans pay income taxes only to the federal government. Where does the state get its money? Through sales and property taxes, the state is able to fund roads, schools, prisons, and other needs. Critics of this approach argue that the poor pay a larger percentage of their incomes in states without income taxes. Proponents argue that businesses are attracted to Texas because it does not tax personal income.

Top State Income Tax Rates, 2014

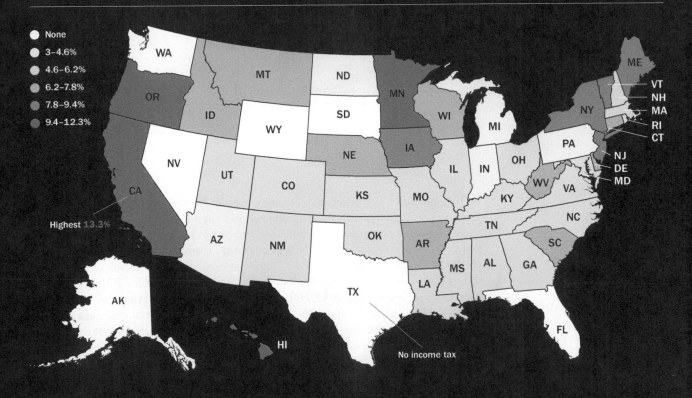

- None
- 3–4.6%
- 4.6–6.2%
- 6.2–7.8%
- 7.8–9.4%
- 9.4–12.3%

Highest 13.3%

No income tax

Number of States in Each Tax Bracket

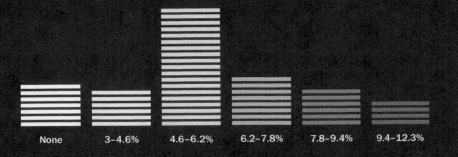

| None | 3–4.6% | 4.6–6.2% | 6.2–7.8% | 7.8–9.4% | 9.4–12.3% |

SOURCE: Tax Foundation, http://taxfoundation.org/blog/top-state-income-tax-rates-2014 (accessed 5/14/14).

TABLE 11.3

State Revenue Biennial Comparison, by Source, 2012–13 and 2014–15 Bienniums (in billions of dollars)

REVENUE	2012–13	2014–15*	PERCENTAGE CHANGE
Tax collections	$91.86	$98.75	7.5%
Federal receipts	65.45	73.92	12.9
Fees, fines, licenses, and penalties	15.51	16.46	6.1
Interest and investment income	2.28	2.18	−4.4
Lottery	3.72	3.15	−15.3
Land income	2.70	2.37	−12.2
Other revenue sources	12.15	11.31	−6.9
Total net revenue	$193.67	$208.14	7.5

*Appropriated monies.

SOURCE: Texas Legislative Budget Board, *Fiscal Size-Up: 2014–15 Biennium*, February 2014, p. 27.

Two measures are often used to compare tax burdens across states: state tax revenue per $1,000 of personal income and per capita state tax revenues. On both measures, Texas's low tax reputation seems to be well earned. In 2012, Texans paid $44.97 in state taxes for each $1,000 of personal income, ranking it 46th among the 50 states. This was well below the $59.29 national average in terms of per capita state tax revenue. A study by the Tax Foundation found that for 2011 per capita state taxes in Texas stood at $2,109, well below the $3,064 national average.[9]

Texas is one of seven states that still do not have a personal income tax. Two states, Tennessee and New Hampshire, only tax income from dividends and interest. There is a high sales tax in Texas of 6.25 percent, the 13th highest in the nation. Combined state and local sales taxes in the state can reach 8.25 percent. As we will see later in this chapter, there are a variety of other specific sales taxes that bring revenue into the state to fund government, including cigarettes, alcohol, and gasoline.

Although Texas state taxes are low compared with other states' taxes, local taxes are a different story. In 2011, Texas ranked 12th among the states in terms of property taxes paid per capita, at $1,393. When state and local taxes are taken together, however, Texas remains a low-tax state. Combined state and local taxes were $3,197 per capita in 2009, ranking Texas 45th in the nation. A 2011 study conducted by the Tax Foundation concluded that Texas had the 13th most business-friendly tax system.[10]

Government and public policy in Texas are funded from a variety of sources, including sales tax, severance taxes on oil and natural gas produced in the state, licensing income, interest and dividends, and federal aid (Table 11.3). In 2014–15, 47.4 percent of state revenues are expected to come from taxes of one sort or

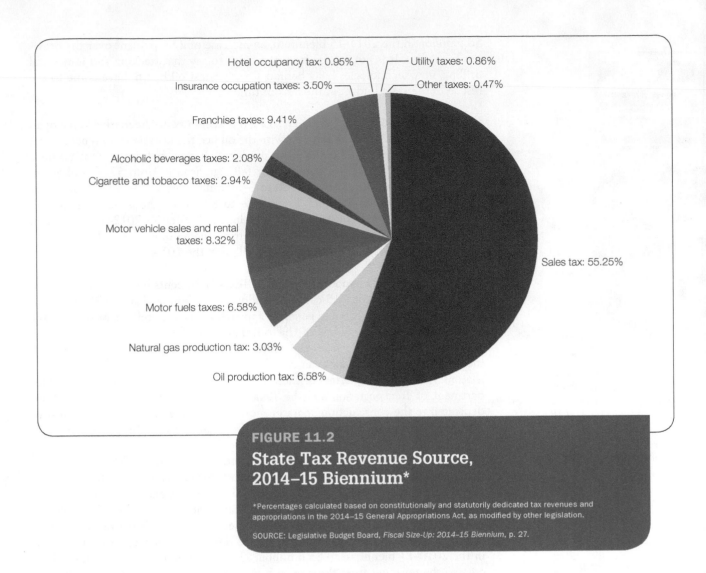

Hotel occupancy tax: 0.95%
Utility taxes: 0.86%
Insurance occupation taxes: 3.50%
Other taxes: 0.47%
Franchise taxes: 9.41%
Alcoholic beverages taxes: 2.08%
Cigarette and tobacco taxes: 2.94%
Motor vehicle sales and rental taxes: 8.32%
Sales tax: 55.25%
Motor fuels taxes: 6.58%
Natural gas production tax: 3.03%
Oil production tax: 6.58%

FIGURE 11.2

State Tax Revenue Source, 2014–15 Biennium*

*Percentages calculated based on constitutionally and statutorily dedicated tax revenues and appropriations in the 2014–15 General Appropriations Act, as modified by other legislation.

SOURCE: Legislative Budget Board, *Fiscal Size-Up: 2014–15 Biennium*, p. 27.

another. Many of these taxes are based on complex formulas. People often are unaware that they are paying them. But they are important sources of state revenue.

Sales Tax The most important single tax financing Texas government is the sales tax. Today, the sales tax in Texas is 6.25 percent of the retail sales price of tangible personal property and selected services. Together county, city, and metropolitan transit authorities are allowed to impose an additional 2 percent sales tax. For the 2014–15 biennium the sales tax is expected to account for 55.25 percent of the total tax collections in the state (see Figure 11.2).[11]

Oil Production and Regulation Taxes The oil severance tax is 4.6 percent of the market value of oil produced in the state. (There is also an oil regulation tax of three-sixteenths of one cent per barrel of oil produced in Texas.) The tax revenue from oil production fluctuates with the price of oil and the volume of oil produced in Texas. For 2013 the average price of oil per barrel was $91.99, and Texas produced 720 million barrels. Production for 2013 was up an astonishing 53.4 percent from 2012. Projected revenues from the oil severance tax are expected to rise to

The state of Texas collects a tax of 20 cents per gallon on motor fuels. The federal government collects an additional 18.4 cents per gallon, but Texans still pay less tax on gasoline than residents of many other states.

$6.5 billion in the 2014–15 biennium, an increase of 27.6 percent over the previous biennium. It is not too far from the truth to say that fracking and horizontal drilling, new technologies lying behind Texas's latest oil boom, have come to the rescue of the state budget in the nick of time.

Natural Gas Production Tax There is a 7.5 percent tax on the market value of all natural gas produced in the state. As with the oil tax, the tax raised from natural gas depends on the price and the amount produced. Revenues from natural gas have fluctuated considerably over time. They fell significantly from $734 million, or 6.9 percent of state revenues, in 1980 to $489 million, or a little more than 1 percent of state revenues, in 1997. Prices rose to $3.96 per thousand cubic feet in 2010 and $4.13 per thousand cubic feet in 2011. For the 2012–13 biennium, $3.03 billion flowed into the state treasury from the natural gas tax. That amount is projected to slightly decrease to $2.99 billion in the 2014–15 biennium.

Motor Fuels Tax The motor fuels tax in Texas is 20 cents per gallon of gasoline and diesel fuel. There is a 15-cents-per-gallon tax on liquefied gas. In 2014–15 the motor fuels tax is projected to generate approximately $6.5 billion, or 6.6 percent of all state revenues, far below the historical average of 10 to 12 percent.

The revenues flowing from the motor fuels tax are "dedicated" monies. This means that the tax revenues can only be used for purposes specified by the legislature. About three-quarters of these monies are appropriated to the Texas Department of Transportation and the Texas Department of Public Safety and are dedicated to the construction, maintenance, and policing of public roads. Most of the remaining one-quarter of the revenues are dedicated to public education.

Motor Vehicle Sales and Rentals and Manufactured Home Sales Tax There is a 6.25 percent tax on the sales price of all motor vehicles in the state. There is also a 10 percent tax on all rental vehicles up to 30 days and 6.25 percent thereafter. Newly manufactured homes are also taxed at 5 percent of 65 percent of the sale price. Because of the effects of the economic slowdown brought on by the Great Recession, motor vehicle sales and rental taxes declined by 5.6 percent in the 2010–11 biennium to $5.6 billion. The economic rebound in 2012–13 increased the revenues from these taxes by 32.6 percent, up to $7.4 billion. For the 2014–15 biennium, it is projected that tax revenues from this source will increase another 10.5 percent, up to $8.2 billion.

Franchise Tax The so-called franchise tax is imposed on all corporations in Texas. Prior to 2008 the tax was imposed on taxable capital and on earned surplus. The franchise tax became a "margins tax" based on the "taxable margin." The "taxable margin" is the lesser value derived from one of four methods of calculation: (1) 70 percent of total revenue, (2) total revenue minus cost of goods sold, (3) total revenue minus total compensation and benefits, or (4) total revenue minus $1 million. Most businesses pay a tax rate of 1 percent on their taxable margin, although a lower rate is available to businesses primarily in retail or wholesale trade. Some reforms aimed at small businesses were introduced into the franchise tax during the 2013 legislative session.

The goals of the legislature in reworking the franchise tax were to make it more difficult for corporations to escape the tax and to offset some of the costs of property tax reform. The Property Tax Relief Fund was established to take in excess revenue above and beyond the pre-2008 franchise tax amounts, which were put in the General Revenue Fund. There were some serious miscalculations, however, and the revenue generated was far less than expected. The $4.4 billion generated in 2009 was almost 30 percent less than originally forecast. Part of the budget crisis during the 2011 legislative session can be attributed to the miscalculation. As the economy recovered, so did the revenues produced by the franchise tax. For the 2012–13 biennium, tax receipts from the franchise tax rose to $9.36 billion. In 2013 alone, $4.8 billion came into the state from the tax, $2.8 billion allocated to the General Revenue Fund and $2 billion allocated to the Property Tax Relief Fund. The comptroller's franchise tax revenues are projected to decline slightly in 2014–15 to $9.3 billion.

Tobacco Taxes Texas imposes a variety of taxes on cigarettes and tobacco products. For example, every pack of 20 cigarettes has a $1.41 tax per pack and every pack of 25 cigarettes has a $1.76 tax per pack included in the purchase price. The tax on tobacco products like cigars, snuff, chewing tobacco, and smoking tobacco is based on the manufacturer's listed net weight. This tax was $1.22 per ounce in 2013. Approximately 87 percent of tobacco taxes are derived from cigarette sales, the remainder from other tobacco products. Revenues from these taxes are expected to total $2.9 billion for the 2014–15 biennium, a decrease of 4.0 percent from 2012–13.

Like the franchise tax reforms, increases in the tobacco taxes passed in 2006 were linked to property tax relief. Tax revenues generated by the tax rate in place before 2007 go directly into the General Revenues Fund. The excess above this amount goes into the Property Tax Relief Fund. A portion of the other tax increase on tobacco products put into effect in 2007 goes to a Physician Education Loan Repayment program. The remainder of the excess goes into the Property Tax Relief Fund.[12]

Alcoholic Beverage Taxes As with tobacco, a variety of taxes are imposed on alcoholic beverages. Some of these were increased during the 2013 legislative session. This tax took in $1.9 billion in the 2012–13 biennium and is expected to increase to $2.06 billion in the 2014–15 biennium.

Insurance Occupation Taxes A complex schedule of tax rates is applied to insurance premiums. For example, life, health, and accident insurance is taxed at the rate of 1.75 percent on gross premium receipts. In the 2014–15 biennium insurance premium taxes are expected to be $3.5 billion, up from $3.3 billion in the 2012–13 biennium.

Utility Taxes Utility tax revenue flows from three sources in Texas: First, there is a tax on gas, electric, and water utility gross receipts. Rates vary from 0.581 percent to 1.997 percent based on the size of the city population. There are also taxes posed on the gross receipts of public utilities and a gas utility pipeline tax. In 2014–15 it is estimated that the utility tax will take in $846.8 million, representing a 4.4 percent decline from the 2012–13 biennium.

Hotel and Motel Tax This state tax is 6 percent of the hotel and motel occupancy bill paid by the occupant. This tax revenue fell during the Great Recession but has rebounded along with the economic recovery over the past two years. It is expected to generate $937 million in the 2014–15 biennium, an 11.2 percent increase from the previous biennium.

Inheritance Tax Federal tax reforms in 2001 effectively eliminated the Texas inheritance tax by 2005. The law was scheduled to expire in 2012 along with other portions of the Bush tax cuts. The federal law was extended in 2011, meaning that there would be no inheritance tax collected in Texas for the 2014–15 biennium.

Other Taxes There are a small number of other taxes on such items as attorney services, cement, sulfur, coin-operated machines, and bingo rental receipts that are expected to generate $467.8 million for the 2014–15 biennium.

The Question of the Income Tax in Texas

regressive tax type of tax where the tax burden falls more heavily on lower-income individuals

Many commentators have complained that the tax system in Texas is too **regressive**.[13] By this they mean that the tax burden in the state falls more heavily on lower-income individuals. Sales and use taxes such as those found in Texas are generally considered to be regressive. Property taxes on individuals and businesses are generally considered to be somewhat regressive. Poor homeowners and renters generally pay more of their income in property taxes than do the wealthy.

progressive tax type of tax where the tax burden falls more heavily on upper-income individuals

There have been occasional calls for the institution of a state income tax in Texas. Supporters argue that not only is the income tax a more reliable source of revenue for the state, it can also be made fairer. Unlike sales and use taxes, which are applied equally to everyone whatever their income, income taxes can be made **progressive**. With a progressive income tax, people with lower income pay a lower tax rate than people with higher income. Progressive income taxes thus place a higher tax burden on the rich than on the poor. A 2013 study conducted by the Institute on Taxation and Economic Policy found that among the states Texas had the fifth most regressive tax system in the nation, behind Washington, Florida, South Dakota, and Tennessee. The study estimated that in Texas people with incomes at the bottom 20 percent paid 12.6 percent of their income in state and local taxes, while those with incomes in the upper 1 percent paid only 3.2 percent of their income in taxes.[14]

Few politicians have ever been willing to support an income tax. One of the attractive features of Texas to business has always been the absence of an income tax. It was not until the late 1980s and early 1990s that the first serious attempt to put a state income tax in place was undertaken. Responding to mounting budgetary pressures, the retiring lieutenant governor, Bill Hobby, came out in favor of an income tax in late 1989. Bob Bullock, Hobby's successor, announced in early 1991 that he would actively campaign for an income tax. A blue-ribbon panel chaired by former governor John Connally was charged with looking into new revenue sources for the state. The committee ended up recommending to the legislature both a corporate and a personal income tax, but not without generating an enormous amount of controversy.[15]

Chairman Connally himself opposed the income-tax recommendations, as did Governor Ann Richards. By the 1993 legislative session, Lieutenant Governor Bullock was backing off. Bullock proposed a constitutional amendment requiring voter approval of any personal income tax. Moreover, the amendment specified that funds raised under the personal income tax be used to support public education. The amendment quickly passed the 73rd legislature and was overwhelmingly

Who Pays the Most Taxes in Texas?

Taxes as a Percentage of Income in Texas, 2013*

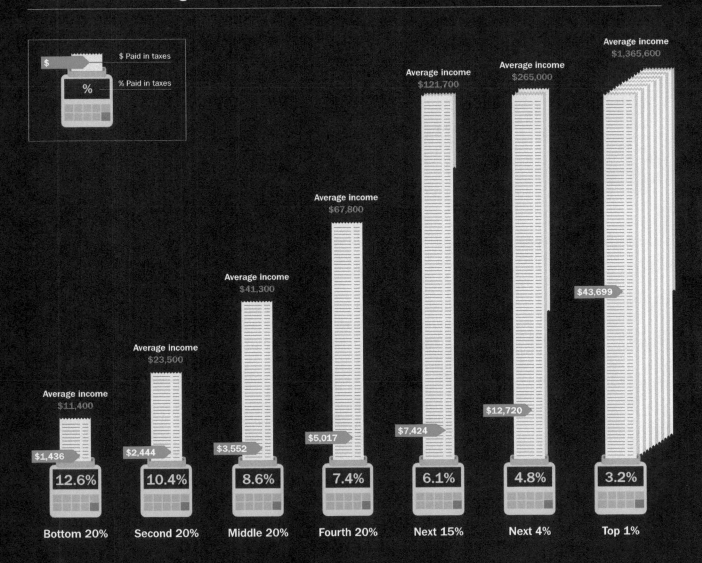

$ $ Paid in taxes

% % Paid in taxes

Average income $11,400	$1,436	**12.6%** Bottom 20%
Average income $23,500	$2,444	**10.4%** Second 20%
Average income $41,300	$3,552	**8.6%** Middle 20%
Average income $67,800	$5,017	**7.4%** Fourth 20%
Average income $121,700	$7,424	**6.1%** Next 15%
Average income $265,000	$12,720	**4.8%** Next 4%
Average income $1,365,600	$43,699	**3.2%** Top 1%

Texas has no state income tax, which does keep overall tax rates down. However, this means that the state's revenues come primarily from sales and property taxes. These taxes are regressive—those with less income pay a higher share of their income in taxes; those with higher incomes pay a lower share of their income in taxes.

for critical analysis

1. Which income groups benefit from Texas's state and local taxes? Which do not?

2. Most other states have income tax. Do you support a state income tax for Texas? What would be the advantages and disadvantages?

*Based on family income for non-elderly taxpayers

Source: Institute for Taxation and Economic Policy, www.itep.org/pdf/tx.pdf (accessed 3/6/14).

TABLE 11.4

Estimated State Revenue Collections, 2014–15 Biennium

Federal funds	35.5%
Sales tax	26.2
Other receipts	16.0
Motor vehicle sales and rental tax	3.1
Other taxes	5.1
Franchise tax	4.5
Motor fuels tax	3.1
Severance tax	4.6
Investment income	1.0

SOURCE: Legislative Budget Board, *Fiscal Size-Up: 2014–15 Biennium*, February 2014, p. 28.

matching funds federal monies going to a state based on state spending for a program

approved by voters on November 2, 1993. As this amendment effectively gave the electorate a veto over any proposal for an income tax, it is unlikely that Texans will have a personal income tax in the foreseeable future.

Other State Revenue

Next to taxes, the second-largest source of revenue for Texas is the federal government (see Table 11.4). Historically, Texas spends relatively little, compared with other states, for state-federal programs. As a result, the federal grants and **matching funds** (federal monies going to a state based on state spending for a program) also have been relatively low. Nevertheless, federal aid to Texas skyrocketed in the 1980s because of the expansion of transportation and human-services programs. For the 2014–15 biennium, federal funds accounted for $70.54 billion, about 35.5 percent of the total appropriations. Much of the increase in these federal funds in recent years can be attributed to Medicaid, a state-federal program providing funds to finance health care delivery to the poor.[16]

In addition to federal monies, there are a number of other revenue sources, as shown in Table 11.5, including interest income, licenses and fees, the sales of goods and services provided by the state, and land income. Two other sources in recent years have had a major impact on monies flowing into the state budget. A state lottery was passed by the state legislature and approved by the voters in 1991. Although the lottery was passed by voters overwhelmingly, attitudes about the appropriateness of using gambling as a source of state revenues are mixed. Some argue that the lottery unfairly takes money from people who can least afford it by fooling them into thinking that they, too, can strike it rich if only they have a little luck. Large numbers of people from all social classes continue to play the lottery. In 2013, 36.5 percent of Texans claimed that they had played a lottery game in the previous year. The median monthly dollar amount spent on any lottery game was $12.00. In 2013 the lottery took in $4.4 billion in sales, an increase of 4.4 percent from the previous year. Payouts to winners totaled $2.8 billion. After administrative expenses were paid, $1 billion was transferred to the Foundation School Account, $5.2 million was transferred to the Texas Veterans Commission, and $41.9 million of unclaimed prizes was transferred to the state. It is projected that over $2.1 billion will be available to transfer to the Foundation School Account in the 2014–15 biennium.[17]

A second major source of nontax revenue is a result of the settlement the state reached with tobacco companies in January 1998. Under the settlement, Texas would receive over $17.3 billion over the next 25 years and an additional $580 million every year thereafter from the tobacco industry. The largest payment—$3.3 billion—came up front, while the remainder was to be spread out over the remaining 25 years. Nationwide, states received a total of $246 billion in the final settlement reached with the tobacco industry. The Texas Comptroller's Office projects that Texas tobacco settlement receipts will total $916.5 million in 2014–15, down from the $959.3 million received in 2012–13. This drop is the result of a projected decline in cigarette sales.[18]

TABLE 11.5

Tax Collections Biennial Comparison by Source, 2012–13 and 2014–15 Bienniums (in billions of dollars)

	2012–13	2014–15	PERCENTAGE CHANGE
Sales tax	$50.14	$54.57	8.8%
Oil production taxes	5.09	6.50	27.6
Natural gas production tax	3.03	2.99	−1.2
Motor fuels tax	6.39	6.50	1.7
Motor vehicle sales and rental taxes	7.44	8.22	10.5
Franchise tax	9.36	9.30	−0.7
Cigarette and tobacco taxes	3.03	2.91	−4.0
Alcoholic beverage taxes	1.90	2.06	7.9
Insurance occupation taxes	3.26	3.47	6.3
Utility taxes	0.89	0.85	−4.4
Hotel occupancy tax	0.84	0.94	11.2
Inheritance tax	−0.01	0.00	−100.0
Other taxes	0.50	0.47	−6.2
Total tax collections	**$91.860**	**$98.755**	**7.5%**

NOTE: Biennial change and percentage change have been calculated on actual amounts before rounding in all tables and graphics in this chapter. Totals may not sum as a result of rounding.

SOURCE: Legislative Budget Board, *Fiscal Size-Up: 2014–15 Biennium*, February 2014, p. 27.

● State Funds

Describe how the money in the budget is organized into specific funds

Money comes into state coffers from a variety of sources and is dispersed in a wide range of activities. But money spent by the state doesn't just flow into and out of one pot. There are, in fact, 400 funds in the state treasury whose monies are directed to a wide variety of functions. Understanding how money flows into and out of these funds lies at the heart of mastering the state budget. We examine some of the most important funds here.

As previously mentioned, the **General Revenue Fund** consists of two parts: non-dedicated general revenue and general revenue–dedicated accounts. The nondedicated revenue is the state's primary operating fund and is the place where most state taxes and fees flow. In 1991, 200 special funds were brought into the General Revenue–Dedicated Funds account as part of a budget reform and consolidation

General Revenue Fund the state's primary operating fund

package. Expenditures may be made directly from the nondedicated funds and may be transferred to special funds or accounts for allocation.

The **Permanent School Fund (PSF)** was created in 1854 with a $2 million appropriation by the legislature to fund primary and secondary schools. The Constitution of 1876, along with subsequent acts, stipulated that certain lands and sales from these lands would constitute the PSF. The second-largest educational endowment in the country, the PSF is managed primarily by the state board of education. The fund distributes money to school districts across the state based on attendance and guarantees bonds issued by local school boards, enabling them to get lower interest rates in the bond markets. At the end of 2013 the fund was guaranteeing about $55.2 billion in school district bonds across the state.

How much money is available to public education through the PSF is determined by the State Board of Education by (1) taking into account the average market value of the fund for the preceding 16 fiscal quarters and (2) setting a distribution rate that does not jeopardize the likelihood that the fund can support future students at a similar rate. Issues of generational equity thus lie at the heart of managing the PSF. Future generations are not to be sacrificed to solve current budgetary shortfalls.

The value of this fund has fluctuated throughout the turbulent first decade of the twenty-first century, dropping to a little over $20 billion in 2009. At the end of 2013 the fund balance has recovered to $29 billion with a return on investment of approximately 10 percent. Distribution rates have ranged from 4.5 percent for the 2004–05 biennium to 2.5 percent for the 2010–11 biennium to an adopted rate of 3.3 percent for the 2014–15 biennium. Projections are that the PSF will yield approximately $1.6 billion to help fund public education in the 2014–15 biennium.[19]

The **Available School Fund (ASF)** is a dedicated fund established by the constitution for the support of public education in the state. The ASF is funded through distributions of the Permanent School Fund (mentioned above) and 25 percent of the state's motor fuels tax. The ASF also provides funds for another fund, the Instructions Materials Fund, that funds state purchases of instructional materials. Revenue flowing into the ASF for the 2012–14 biennium from the motor fuels tax and PSF together is projected to be $3.25 billion.

The **State Highway Fund** comes from a variety of sources, including motor vehicle registration fees, the federal highway fund, and the sales tax on motor lubricants. A significant portion of the motor fuels tax initially is deposited in the General Revenue Fund and then is allocated to the State Highway Fund. The purposes of the State Highway Fund are constructing, maintaining, and policing roadways in Texas and acquiring rights of way. An amendment to the constitution which will be voted on November 4, 2014, provides for diverting $1.2 billion of oil and gas tax revenue from the Rainy Day Fund into the State Highway Fund. Over $9.8 billion was allocated from this fund in the 2014–15 biennium, with more than 83 percent of the monies going to the Texas Department of Transportation.[20]

The **Economic Stabilization Fund (ESF)**, commonly known as the Rainy Day Fund, was established through constitutional amendment in 1988 to provide relief during times of financial distress. The fund is generated by a formula involving the base year of 1987. If collections from oil and gas taxes exceed the 1987 base year amount, 75 percent is transferred to the fund. Transfers are made in February by the comptroller. Half of any "unencumbered" general revenue, that is, revenue not already targeted for a specific purpose, also goes into the fund. The legislature has the authority to contribute additional funds but never has.

Under certain extraordinary circumstances, ESF monies can be appropriated only with a three-fifths vote of members of both houses of the legislature. These circumstances include when a budget deficit develops in a biennium or the comptroller estimates that revenue will decline from one biennium to the next. Money can also be appropriated from this fund for other purposes at any time with the support of two-thirds of present members in each house.

Few thought that large sums would accumulate in the fund. As noted in Table 11.6, the first transfer of funds from oil and gas tax revenues of $18.5 million took place in 1990. The ESF account balance was kept below $100 million until 2001, when deposits transferred into the account exceeded $700 million. In 2003 the ESF was depleted to help solve the impending $10 billion budget shortfall. In 2003 and 2005 the legislature appropriated ESF monies to a variety of agencies, including the Teachers' Retirement System, various health and human service agencies, the governor's office, and the Texas Education Agency. Rising tax revenues from oil and gas production in the first decade of the twenty-first century flooded the ESF with funds. By the end of fiscal year 2013 the Texas Rainy Day Fund had grown to over $6.17 billion. This was after expenditures to cover budget shortfalls of $3.2 billion in 2011 and $1.87 billion in 2013. This fund contained more cash than similar funds in any other state. Only Alaska, also awash in oil and gas revenues, had a fund that approached that of Texas. The debate over whether or how to use the Rainy Day Fund to close the budget shortfall was a major issue during the 2011 and 2013 legislative sessions, and likely will be so again whenever the economy falters and the state revenues decline.[21]

TABLE 11.6

Economic Stabilization Fund History, Fiscal Years 2004 to 2015 (in millions of dollars)

FISCAL YEAR	REVENUES	EXPENDITURES	ENDING BALANCE
2004	$358.1	$553.0	$365.6
2005	611.8	970.5	6.9
2006	926.5	508.2	405.2
2007	1,617.7	691.5	1,311.4
2008	3,114.5	90.5	4,355.4
2009	2,370.7	0.4	6,725.7
2010	966.9	0.0	7,692.6
2011	518.5	3,198.7	5,012.4
2012	1,121.0	0.0	6,133.4
2013	1,908.6	1,871.8	6,170.2
2014*	2,541.8	2,056.0	6,656.0
2015*	1,414.5	0.0	8,070.5

*Projected estimates.

SOURCE: Comptroller of Public Accounts.

What to Do with the Budget Surplus

Unlike the federal government, Texas state government cannot approve a budget deficit and must pass a balanced budget every two years. Discussion of the budget reached a fevered pitch during the 2010 legislative session, when Texas faced a budget shortfall because of the national recession and a serious shortfall in projected revenues from various taxes. Some Texans considered it a "rainy day" and urged the state government to tap the Rainy Day Fund for education and health services. Others believed that the fund should be preserved for the future and should be used only in extreme circumstances. In the end, Governor Perry decided to use the fund only sparingly in order to balance the state budget, instead implementing severe cuts in state spending on higher education, health care, and education.

In the 2015 legislative session, state lawmakers face a budget surplus instead of a budget shortfall. In other words, the state comptroller of public accounts predicts that the state will have approximately $11 billion to spend in the next budget cycle. This amounts to a substantial increase over the previous state budget. Why the surplus? Revenues from various sales taxes as well as the oil and gas severance taxes and the relatively recently revamped franchise tax have exceeded expectations as the economy has improved and unemployment has fallen.

How should state lawmakers deal with the budget surplus? On the one hand, some policy makers, such as Chuck DeVore of the Texas Public Policy Foundation, a conservative think tank in the state, argue that the surplus means that Texas taxpayers have overpaid the state and they should receive refunds. In particular, DeVore proposes creating what is called a Sales Tax Relief (STaR) fund which would allow state legislators to move any surplus money into an account allowing the comptroller of public accounts to temporarily cut state sales tax rates. He argues that this would

make possible a reduction of the state sales tax from 6.25 percent to 5.75 percent for approximately two years. Generally, Texas taxpayers pay no more than 8.25 percent on most items other than food and medicine because local governments can add to the state's baseline sales tax. Other conservatives have called for a reduction in the franchise tax.

On the other hand, Dick Lavine and Eva DeLuna Castro of the Center for Public Policy Priorities, a progressive think tank in Austin, argue that cuts to education and health care from the last session should be restored so that the state can better prepare for an uncertain economic future. Lavine and Castro argue that Texas is already a low-tax state that provides minimal funding to education, social services, and health care. In education, they argue, the student population continues to increase yet the need to hire more teachers is not being fulfilled. In addition, cuts in state funding do not occur in a vacuum. Many localities rely on property taxes to fund schools, and if state funding to schools decreases, local school boards have no option but to raise property taxes, thus increasing the tax burden through other channels, all while the state sits on over $8 billion in a "rainy day fund." In addition, liberals and conservatives have noted that transportation projects like the building and repair of roads and bridges may be underfunded to the tune of $5 billion.

DeVore counters that education money is spent not on the classroom but on bureaucratic overhead, and he points to the fact that the student-teacher ratio in Texas is better than the national average. He also contends that as the legislature spends more on new programs, a sense of entitlement will develop, making it difficult to make cuts later on during times of economic difficulty. Lavine and Castro, in turn, counter that Texas is simply not spending enough in real dollars given the state's rapid growth. With new residents on highways, in classrooms, and in hospitals, the state needs to maintain these public goods for future generations. Spending the same amount of money as we did when the state's population was smaller will not lead to a prosperous state.

What, then, should lawmakers do when deciding priorities for the next state budget?

critical thinking questions

1. How should policy makers deal with the projected budgetary surplus? Should taxes be cut or spending increased? If the latter, where should it be increased first?

2. What would be the budgetary consequences of replacing sales and franchise taxes with an income tax? Who would benefit? Who would lose?

To appreciate the importance of the operations of Texas's 400 funds and the complexity that they introduce into the budgetary process, one need only look at a few funds lying at the heart of higher education. Legislative goals are met through the creation of these funds and the allocation and reallocation of funds to and from them. Some funds, such as the Permanent University Trust Fund or the Higher Education Fund, were established to channel money directly to certain institutions of higher education. Others, like the National Research University Fund, operate in order to encourage universities to behave in certain ways and to achieve a specific set of legislative objectives.

The **Permanent University Trust Fund (PUF)** contributes to the support of most institutions in the University of Texas (UT) and Texas A&M University systems. Originally established in 1876 by a land grant of 1 million acres, the fund contains approximately 2.1 million acres in 24 west Texas counties. Under provisions in the state constitution, all surface lease income goes into the Available University Fund (AUF), a fund set up to distribute PUF monies. Mineral income and the proceeds from the sale of PUF lands go into PUF and are invested. In 1999 an amendment to the constitution authorized the UT Board of Regents to channel investment income into the AUF. Two-thirds of the monies going to AUF go to the UT system; one-third goes to the Texas A&M system. The first obligation of any income earned by PUF is to pay the debt service on outstanding PUF bonds. The estimated value of the PUF on June 30, 2013 was $14.4 billion.[22]

The **Higher Education Fund (HEF)** was established by a constitutional amendment for universities that did not have access to PUF monies. It is funded through the General Revenue Fund. Appropriations for the HEF are projected to be $525 million for the 2014–15 biennium. An advisory committee made up of member institutions provides input to the Texas Higher Education Coordinating Board, which in turn makes recommendations to the legislature for budgetary allocation to each school out of the HEF.

The **National Research University Fund (NRUF)** was established through a 2009 constitutional amendment to provide a source of funding for universities seeking to achieve national prominence as research institutions. Under the amendment, money was transferred from the HEF to the NRUF. UT Austin and Texas A&M are already considered to be national research institutions and therefore do not qualify for this fund. Eligibility criteria as well as distribution rules were established in 2011 by the legislature. An institution must be identified as an emerging research university by the Higher Education Coordinating Board and must expend at least $45 million in specifically defined types of research. In addition, universities must meet at least four of the following criteria to qualify: (1) maintain an endowment of at least $400 million in the two preceding academic years; (2) produce 200 Ph.D. degrees during the previous two years; (3) have a freshman class of high academic achievement; (4) be designated as a member of the Association of Research Libraries, have a Phi Beta Kappa Chapter, or be a member of Phi Kappa Phi; (5) have a certain number of tenured faculty who have demonstrated excellence by winning a Nobel Prize or other prestigious fellowships, or have been elected to one of the National Academies; and (6) have a demonstrable excellence in graduate education. In early 2014 the value of the fund was over $630 million.

In 2011 seven universities were designated as emerging research universities, each of which could have access to these funds if certain criteria were met. They were Texas Tech University, the University of Texas at Arlington, the University of Texas at Dallas, the University of Texas at El Paso, the University of Texas at San

Permanent University Trust Fund (PUF) fund established in 1876 and funded from the proceeds from land owned by the state; monies go to various universities in the University of Texas (UT) and Texas A&M systems

Higher Education Fund (HEF) state higher education fund for universities not having access to PUF monies

National Research University Fund (NRUF) fund established in 2009 to provide funding to universities seeking to achieve national prominence as research institutions

Antonio, the University of Houston, and the University of North Texas. In January 2012, Texas Tech and the University of Houston were identified by the Coordinating Board as being eligible to receive some of these NRUF monies subject to meeting a state audit.[23]

The Texas Constitution and the Budget

Outline the constitutional provisions that affect how the state budget is made

A number of constitutional factors affect the way the budget is made in Texas. Probably the biggest constraint on the budgetary process has to do with time limits. As noted in Figure 11.3, the legislature is compelled to write a two-year, or biennial, budget because of the constitutional provision that the legislature may meet in regular session only once every two years. One of the effects of this restricted time frame is to force government agencies to project their budgetary needs well in advance of any clear understanding of the particular problems they may be facing during the biennium. In addition, the legislature can meet for only 140 days in regular session. This seriously limits the amount of time that the legislature can spend analyzing the budget or developing innovative responses to pressing matters of public importance.

Another important factor is that a large portion of the biennial budget is dedicated for special purposes by federal law or by the Texas Constitution or state statute. These dedicated funds include federal monies earmarked for financing health care for the poor (Medicaid), as well as state funds for highways, education, teachers' retirement, and numerous other purposes. The purpose of dedicated funds is not difficult to understand. Supporters of particular programs want to create a stable revenue source for priority programs. But in protecting their own programs, supporters encourage other interests to do likewise, with the result that the legislature loses control of a large portion of the budget.

Finally, a number of specific constitutional provisions constrain the legislature's control of the budget.[24]

Article 3, Section 49a (Pay-as-You-Go Limit) portion of the Texas Constitution that requires the state to maintain a balanced budget

appropriations authorization by the legislature to a government agency or body to spend up to a particular amount of money

The Pay-as-You-Go Limit Article 3, Section 49a (Pay-as-You-Go Limit), of the Texas Constitution requires the state to maintain a balanced budget. All bills that get as far as **appropriations** in the legislative process must be sent to the comptroller of public accounts so the comptroller can certify that the bills are within available budget limit projections. One of the most important consequences of the pay-as-you-go limit is to put the comptroller at the heart of the budget process. In the summer of 2013 the comptroller certified that the 2014–15 General Appropriations Act and other appropriations acts passed during the 2013 session met the pay-as-you-go requirements. In December 2013 new estimates projected a budgetary surplus of $2.6 billion for the 2013–14 biennium. By June 2014 the projected surplus had risen to $3.6 billion, according to the comptroller.[25]

The Welfare Spending Limit Article 3, Section 51a, provides that the amount of money the state pays for assistance to or on behalf of needy dependent children and their caretakers shall not exceed 1 percent of the state budget in any biennium. This article sets a constitutional limit on the amount of money that the state may pay out to welfare beneficiaries under the Temporary Assistance for Needy Families program (TANF). The total state budget appropriated by the 83rd legislature

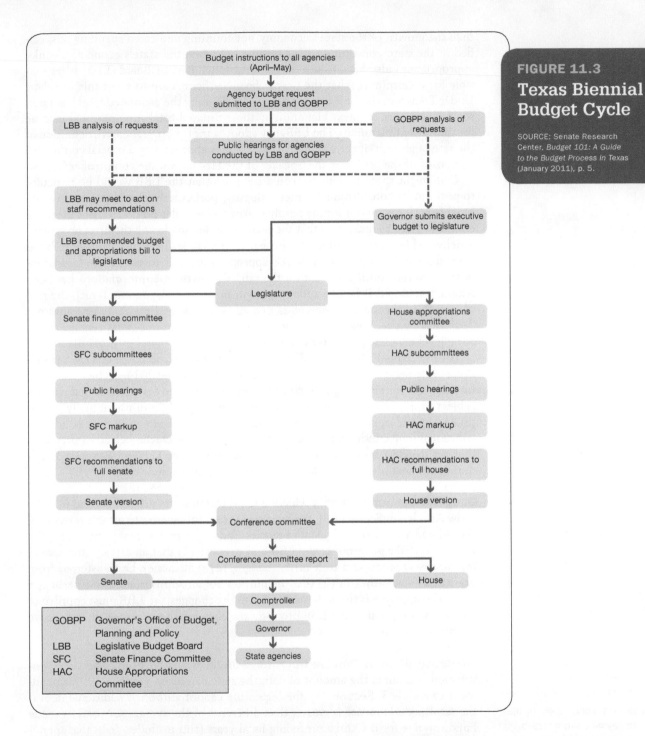

FIGURE 11.3

Texas Biennial Budget Cycle

SOURCE: Senate Research Center, *Budget 101: A Guide to the Budget Process in Texas* (January 2011), p. 5.

Budget instructions to all agencies (April–May)

Agency budget request submitted to LBB and GOBPP

LBB analysis of requests

GOBPP analysis of requests

Public hearings for agencies conducted by LBB and GOBPP

LBB may meet to act on staff recommendations

Governor submits executive budget to legislature

LBB recommended budget and appropriations bill to legislature

Legislature

Senate finance committee

House appropriations committee

SFC subcommittees

HAC subcommittees

Public hearings

Public hearings

SFC markup

HAC markup

SFC recommendations to full senate

HAC recommendations to full house

Senate version

House version

Conference committee

Conference committee report

Senate

House

Comptroller

Governor

State agencies

GOBPP	Governor's Office of Budget, Planning and Policy
LBB	Legislative Budget Board
SFC	Senate Finance Committee
HAC	House Appropriations Committee

was $200.4 billion, instituting a welfare spending limit of over $2 billion. State funds appropriated for TANF, however, were only $132.5 million, far below the 1 percent limit. State expenditures on Medicaid are not included in this spending limit.[26]

The Limit on the Growth of Certain Appropriations Article 8, Section 22, which was passed in 1978, specifies that the growth in appropriations cannot be more than the growth of the state's economy, not counting dedicated spending as specified in the state constitution. This means that when the state's economy shrinks, appropriations also have to shrink. The Legislative Budget Board (LBB) is responsible for determining what the proper financial figures are to meet this mandate. Under Texas law, the LBB determines this by dividing the estimated total state personal income for the next biennium by the estimated total state personal income for the current biennium. The LBB may adopt "a more comprehensive definition of the rate of growth" if the alternative definition is approved by a special committee composed of the governor, the Speaker of the House, and the comptroller.[27]

One might think that there would be times that the LBB would be reluctant to perform its constitutional duties. Adopting particularly dismal projections derived from the growth formula hardly makes one popular politically. But there are checks in place to make sure that the projections are made and the limit on growth is delivered in a timely fashion to the legislature. Under law, the LBB is prohibited from distributing the budget or the appropriations bill to either the legislature or the governor until this limit on the rate of growth of appropriations has been adopted. If the LBB fails to adopt a growth limit (and a spending limit), the rate of growth in the state's economy is treated as if it were zero. State revenues not dedicated by the Texas Constitution to particular functions must remain at the same level as in the previous biennium.

For the 2014–15 biennium, $85.2 billion was authorized under Article 8 provisions. Note that $200.4 billion of the state's budget for the 2014–15 biennium was funded with nontax revenue or constitutionally dedicated tax revenue and was not subject to the Article 8 spending limits. Since only $85 billion was actually appropriated by the legislature, that meant that the budget was within mandated constitutional limits. Indeed, rosy economic projections in December 2013 projected that up to $380.5 million could be appropriated from General Revenue Funds during the next biennium before the spending limit was reached.[28]

Budget-Execution Authority Under a constitutional amendment passed in 1985 (now Article 16, Section 69), the legislature was empowered to establish rules for the expenditure of funds by state agencies. Today this means that between legislative sessions, the governor or the LBB may propose (1) that an agency stop spending money appropriated to it in the budget, (2) that money be transferred from one agency to another, or (3) that the purpose for an appropriation to a particular agency be changed. If the governor proposes the changes, the LBB must approve or amend the proposal. If the LBB proposes the changes, the governor must approve or amend the proposal.

Limitation on Debt Payable from the General Revenue Fund The state constitution also limits the amount of debt the state can incur. Under a 1997 amendment to Article 3, Section 49j, the legislature cannot authorize additional debt if the resulting **debt service** is greater than 5 percent of the average General Revenue Fund revenue for the three preceding fiscal years (this excludes dedicated spending). Basically, Texas state debt cannot be more than 5 percent of state revenue.

One of the consequences of this constitutional debt limit is that compared to other states (as well as to the federal government), the Texas debt burden is relatively low. A 2012 Tax Foundation study calculated that Texas's per capita debt burden was $1,765. This contrasted with per capita debts of $6,956 in New York, $4,997 in Illinois, and $4,036 in California. Texas's per capita state debt was ranked 45th out of the 50 states.[29]

debt service money spent by the state to pay off debt; includes interest and principal payments

The Budgetary Process

Identify the major steps and players in making the state budget

In theory, Texas has a "dual-budget" system. This means that responsibility for preparing an initial draft of the budget is shared by the governor through the Governor's Office of Budget, Planning, and Policy (GOBPP) and the legislature through the LBB. In practice, the budget is primarily the responsibility of the legislature.

In 1967 the legislature designated the governor the chief planning officer of the state. The GOBPP was created in 1976, through the consolidation of an older agency, the Division of Planning Coordination, with the GOBPP. The GOBPP is responsible for advising the governor regarding fiscal matters. It prepares the governor's budget recommendations for the legislature and monitors state appropriations and operations. It also serves the governor in a variety of other capacities, including providing analysis on fiscal and economic matters and coordinating federal programs in the state as well as assisting in the operations of various regional and state planning councils.

Before 1949 there was little coordination in public budgeting. Financial procedures varied, and state agencies were funded by individual appropriations. In 1949 a law was enacted to establish the 10-member LBB, whose primary job would be to recommend appropriations for all agencies of state government. The board is chaired by the lieutenant governor. The vice chair is the Speaker of the House. Other members include the chairs of the House Appropriations Committee, the House Committee on Ways and Means, the Senate Finance Committee, and the Senate State Affairs Committee. Two additional members from the Senate and the House are chosen by the lieutenant governor and the Speaker, respectively.

The LBB appoints a budget director, who brings together budgeting requests from the various state agencies and prepares appropriations bills for them. Since 1973 the LBB has also been responsible for evaluating agency programs and developing estimates of the probable costs of implementing legislation introduced in a legislative session. The LBB's draft budget, not the governor's, is the basis for final legislation. Table 11.7 summarizes the duties of key players in the budgetary process.

Preparing and implementing a budget are complex matters. The budgetary process involves two stages. In the first stage, the LBB develops a draft budget based on requests supplied by state agencies. This draft budget follows a series of steps. First, strategic plans are developed by each agency. A strategic plan includes (1) a mission statement, (2) a statement about the goals of the agency, (3) a discussion of the population served by the agency, (4) an explanation of the means that will be used to achieve these goals, and (5) an identification of the measures to be used to assess the agency's success in meeting these goals. This information provides the basis for LBB funding recommendations for each agency. In the spring or early summer prior to the legislative session, the LBB sends out detailed Legislative Appropriation Request (LAR) instructions to the agencies. Hearings are then held by the LBB and by the GOBPP with each agency where the agency's strategic plan and LAR are discussed. LARs become the starting point for the appropriations bill that is prepared by the LBB. *Legislative Budget Estimates* is a publication of the LBB that contains information on the proposed appropriations bill, including expenditures for previous bienniums and proposed expenditures for the next biennium.[30]

While the draft budgets are being prepared, the comptroller's office prepares the Biennial Revenue Estimate (BRE). The BRE is a detailed forecast of the total

TABLE 11.7

Key Players in the Budgetary Process

The Legislative Budget Board (LBB)

1. adopts a constitutional spending limit

2. prepares a general appropriations bill

3. prepares agency performance reports

4. guides, reviews, and finalizes agency strategic plans

5. prepares fiscal notes regarding costs and impacts of proposed legislation

6. engages in "budget execution actions" in conjunction with the governor by transferring money from one assigned purpose to another purpose or to another agency

The governor and the Governor's Office of Budget, Planning, and Policy (GOBPP)

1. develop a strategic plan for the state

2. help to develop agency Legislative Appropriation Requests (LARs)

3. hold LAR hearings, often in conjunction with the legislature

4. deliver a governor's appropriations budget and a general appropriations bill at the beginning of the legislative session

5. exercise a line-item veto after an appropriations bill is passed by the legislature

6. engage in "budget execution actions" in conjunction with the LBB by transferring money from one assigned purpose to another purpose or to another agency

The comptroller of public accounts

1. submits a statement regarding the estimated anticipated revenues for the coming biennium

2. certifies that an appropriations bill is in balance with projected state revenues

3. collects state taxes

4. tracks 600 separate revenue and spending funds and makes sure that agencies stay within their budgets.

The state auditor's office develops independent audits of state agencies, including institutions of higher education. These audits are used to evaluate agencies.

revenue that the state is expected to take in over the next biennium. The Texas Constitution requires that the BRE contain "an itemized estimate of the anticipated revenue . . . to be credited during the succeeding biennium."[31] The BRE includes other information to assist legislators in the budget process, including (1) statements about the anticipated revenue from different sources, (2) an analysis of the economic outlook facing Texas and the nation, and (3) a detailed accounting of the funds in the state treasury. The comptroller effectively sets a ceiling on what the state legislature may spend. Although the legislature can override the comptroller's estimates with a four-fifths vote of each house, this has never happened. The BRE is updated by the comptroller when economic conditions change significantly and for special sessions of the legislature.[32]

The second stage of the budget process involves the legislative process. By the seventh day of each regular session, appropriations bills are submitted by the LBB to the House Appropriations Committee and the Senate Finance Committee.

Traditionally, the bills are introduced to these committees by their respective chairs, although any member may do so. The bills then work their way through the committee system of each house separately and are subject to hearings, debates, and revisions. This process of drafting the bill is referred to as a "markup." Final versions of the budget are prepared by the House Appropriations Committee and the Senate Finance Committee. Each house then votes on the bill. Differences between the two versions of the bill are reconciled in a conference committee.

The conference committee is composed of representatives from the Senate and the House. Senate members are selected by the lieutenant governor or the president pro tempore of the Senate. The senator sponsoring the bill, traditionally the chairman of the Senate Finance Committee, appoints the chair of the Senate conferees. At least two members from the Senate Finance Committee must sit on the conference committee. The Speaker of the House appoints all conferees from the House as well as the chair of the House conferees. Traditionally, Senate and House representatives alternate each session in chairing the conference committee.

Specific rules govern how disagreements between the Senate and House versions of the appropriations bills are to be handled.[33]

- Items that appear in both versions of the bill must be included in the final conference committee report.
- Items that appear in both versions of the bill with identical amounts allocated to them may not be changed by the committee.
- Items that appear in both versions of the bill with differing amounts allocated to them cannot be eliminated. The committee has the discretion to fund these items at a level not larger than the larger allocation or smaller than the smaller allocation.
- Items that appear in one version of the bill but not the other can be included or eliminated from the final bill subject to the discretion of the committee. However, no more money may be allocated to that item than is found in the original version of the bill.
- Items found in neither version of the bill may not be included in the final conference report. However, the conference committee has the discretion to propose the appropriation of money for bills that already have been passed by the legislature.

While constraining the discretionary authority of the committee to a degree, these rules still leave considerable room for political maneuvering on the part of the committee. Membership on this important committee is a highly prized commodity. Once the bill passes the conference committee, it is returned to both houses for final passage.

Under Article 3, Section 49a, of the Texas Constitution, the comptroller has the formal authority to "certify" the budget. This means that the comptroller confirms that the comptroller's office has analyzed the budget and concluded that it is within the current revenue estimates. For all intents and purposes, the budget is being declared balanced. If the general appropriations bill is not certified by the comptroller, it is returned to the house in which it originated. The legislature must then either decrease expenditures or raise revenues to make up the difference. According to provisions set out in Article 3, Section 49a, under conditions of "imperative public necessity" the legislature may with a four-fifths vote in each house decide to spend in excess of anticipated revenue.

After certification, the budget moves on to the governor, who can sign, not sign, or veto the entire bill or exercise the line-item veto. With the line-item veto, in particular, the governor has the power to unravel some of the compromises that legislators may have forged to get the bill through the committee system. The line-item veto also potentially gives the governor enormous power to limit expenditures in certain targeted areas. Of course, line-item vetoes exercised too vigorously in one session can come back to haunt the governor's legislative agenda in the next session.

The appropriations bill takes effect on September 1 in odd-numbered years. All agencies are bound by it. Monitoring agency compliance with the budget is the job of the LBB and the state auditor's office. The governor and LBB have the authority to execute the budget. This includes the power to shift funds between agency programs or between agencies if necessary when the legislature is not in session. This power to execute the budget is an important one. It has been a tool used by the governor and LBB to cope with the unanticipated shortfalls in the state budget by ordering state agencies to cut their expenditures in the middle of a biennium.

As noted in the chapter on the executive power, the governor is able to move funds from one account to another without permission of the LBB if he declares an emergency. Such a situation has only occurred once—in the summer of 2014—when Governor Perry declared an emergency and transferred funds to pay for the deployment of National Guard troops along the border with Mexico to cope with illegal immigration into Texas.

Budget Crises in Twenty-First-Century Texas

Analyze major budget crises in Texas

The 1970s and early 1980s were boom years for the Texas economy. Rising inflation coupled with high oil prices and rapid economic growth drove the economy forward.[34] Tax increases were unnecessary as tax revenues soared. The problem facing the legislature was not how to balance the budget, but how to spend revenue windfalls. There were no tax increases in Texas during this time.

The collapse of oil prices and a sputtering state economy in the mid-1980s, particularly severe in real estate and construction, brought on a budget crisis. As projected deficits mounted, tax increases became commonplace. Between 1985 and 1986, state tax collections fell. Income from the oil severance tax alone dropped 28 percent. Tax rates were increased, and the tax base was broadened in almost every year between 1984 and 1991.

As the state's economy turned around in the early 1990s, the budgetary situation brightened considerably. However, renewed budget surpluses did not bring a return to the spending patterns of the pre–oil crash years. Business and political leaders from both parties expressed an ongoing concern that taxes were becoming burdensome, perhaps placing Texas at a disadvantage with other states in trying to create a favorable environment for business. Additionally, a growing concern that state government was expanding too fast sparked demands for making government more efficient. With the recession beginning in 2008, all this changed. Over the next four years, political leaders in the state faced a series of budget crises that proliferated as the Great Recession worked its way through the economy and into the federal and state budgets.

The 2011 legislative session was a particularly difficult one.[35] From the outset, legislators knew that difficult budgetary choices would have to be faced. For two years, Texas had dodged the worst effects of the Great Recession. But in 2011 hard decisions were going to have to be made to balance the budget.

Two factors had delayed the full impact of the recession upon the Texas budget. First, LBB projections in January 2009 for tax revenues for the 2010–11 biennium grossly underestimated the impact that the recession would have upon tax revenues. The projection had anticipated a surplus of $2.1 billion in General Revenues and $3 billion set aside for property tax relief from the previous budget, making the 2010–11 financial outlook appear to be quite secure. But in reality the surpluses had evaporated, revealing the budget to be far too optimistic and exposing policy makers to some difficult decisions. Second, Texas had been initially protected from the worst of the recession by an infusion of federal funding. In an effort to fight the recession at the national level, the federal government instituted a surge of deficit spending under the American Recovery and Reinvestment Act passed in February 2009. This enabled the 2009 Texas legislature to appropriate $6.4 billion in federal funds to cover a projected General Revenues Fund gap and maintain educational and health and human services programs sponsored with the federal government. By the end of the 2010–11 biennium, the federal dollars coming into the state rose to $8 billion, largely as a result of higher-than-expected caseloads for Medicaid, as well as an expansion of that program through federal legislation.

The pressures on the budget continued unabated through 2009 and 2010. One of the chief effects of the Great Recession across the country was the sharp contraction in real estate prices.[36] Low interest rates supported by Federal Reserve policy along with loose credit standards had led to a "bubble" in real estate that had pushed up property values through the early years of the twenty-first century. The real estate bubble popped in 2008, bringing many banks to their knees as the value of their portfolios plunged with collapsing real estate prices. Banks turned to Washington for assistance and were ultimately bailed out by a massive intrusion of the federal government into the banking system.

A key component of the 2008 financial crisis was home foreclosures like this one in San Antonio. This crisis put intense strains on the Texas state budget.

Pressures to balance Texas's state budget often create difficult and controversial choices for legislators, like how much funding to provide for public schools.

Although Texas escaped the worst of the real estate collapse, largely because the real estate bubble had been more muted in Texas than elsewhere, credit tightened and property values declined across the state through 2007, 2008, and 2009. As property values declined, so did property tax revenues. What had been a banking crisis at the national level became a funding crisis at the state and local levels, particularly for schools, community colleges, and health districts where funding was based largely on property taxes. In addition, sales tax receipts in Texas fell for the first time in 2009 since 2003. Sales tax receipts fell each month from February 2009 to April 2010 in Texas.

By January 2011 the comptroller projected a $4.3 billion shortfall in general tax revenues against projected expenses for fiscal year 2011, the second year of the previous biennium. The deficit projections for the 2012–13 biennium were even worse, putting the shortfall in general tax revenue at around $17 billion. Taking into account increasing demands for Medicaid and school district funding put the general revenue shortfall for the coming biennium somewhere between $24 and $27 billion.

The Great Recession was not the only cause of the financial shortfall. There were also long-term structural problems facing the budget brought on by property tax reform. In 2006 the legislature required schools to reduce their school property tax rates by one-third. The reasons were complicated. The Texas Supreme Court had ruled in *West Orange Cove ISD v. Neeley* that school districts needed to have some "meaningful discretion" in the setting of property tax rates.[37] If all property tax rates were set at the maximum allowed under law, a situation found in many districts, the court concluded that a statewide property tax essentially would have been put into place, and this was a violation of the state constitution prohibiting such a statewide property tax. Lowering property tax rates was thus one way to bring the existing property tax into compliance with the court's ruling.

Lowering property tax rates, however, would have serious funding implications for public schools. In an effort to replace lost property tax revenues and maintain funding levels at the schools, the legislature also increased the state corporate franchise tax and the cigarette tax. The LBB calculated that lost revenue from the property tax cut would be $14.2 billion for the next 2014–15 biennium. Tax increases would bring in $8.3 billion. From the outset, there was thus a projected shortfall of $5.9 billion for the next 2013–14 biennium. Proponents argued that this shortfall would evaporate as new tax collections grew. Unfortunately, these optimistic predictions were wrong. The new taxes actually brought in $3.78 billion less than projected for 2008–09 and $5.13 billion less than anticipated for 2010–11. Thus, there was a structural deficit built into the budget from the property tax relief of $9.16 billion for 2008–09 and $9.95 billion for 2010–11. For 2012–13 the deficit from tax relief was projected to be $9.84 billion.

The initial response of state leaders to the impending fiscal shortfall was a call for immediate spending cuts in the current fiscal year. In January 2010 the governor, lieutenant governor, and Speaker of the House asked all state agencies and institutions of higher education to plan to reduce spending by 10 percent in fiscal year 2010 and 5 percent for fiscal year 2011. In December 2010 there was an additional 2.5 percent cut in spending. State leaders also drew upon the Economic Stabilization Fund (the Rainy Day Fund). Under a supplemental appropriations bill in 2011, the 2011 budget deficit thus was closed, $1.2 billion coming from reduced spending and $3.2 billion coming from the Rainy Day Fund (see Table 11.8).

But the bigger problem lay with the multibillion-dollar shortfall for the next biennium. Legislators had to agree exactly on what the deficit was, finally concluding that it was approximately $22.6 billion. How was this to be addressed? Conservative Republicans led by Governor Perry and Tea Party supporters rejected the idea that new taxes might be a solution. Instead they looked to spending cuts, payment deferments, and various "revenue enhancements" that would bring the budget back into balance. It took a special session of the legislature in June 2011 to finally pass the bill that brought the budget for 2012–13 back into balance. There were a few financial tricks used to balance the budget. For example, some taxpayers were required to speed up payments of various sales, alcohol, and motor fuels taxes so that the revenues would be received during this biennium rather than the next. The transfer of motor fuels tax receipts from the General Revenue Fund to the State Highway Fund was delayed, keeping money in this biennium. Payments to school districts for August 2013 were also deferred to September 2013, pushing another set of expenditures into the next biennium. Such budgetary sleights of hand can be done only once. But the hope was that the worst of the crisis would have passed by the time that these tactics became an issue in a future biennium.

The most important initiatives taken up to address the budget shortfall were spending cuts. Entitlement funding to public schools in the state was cut by $4 billion for the 2012–13 biennium. In addition, five months of the two-year Medicaid budget, approximately $4.3 billion, was not funded. On the face of it, one might think that a partially unfunded Medicaid proposal would not pass constitutional muster. But key legislators and the comptroller agreed to cover these unfunded Medicaid expenditures with either unexpected revenues or the remaining $7 billion in the Rainy Day Fund. They also agreed that this would meet the balanced budget requirement. Medicaid also underwent $1.8 billion in "cost containment savings." Ultimately, a total of $5 billion in new revenues was put into place along with $17.6 billion in cuts in expenditures (Table 11.9).

TABLE 11.8

Legislative Response to the 2011 Budgetary Shortfall during the 2011 Session (in billions of dollars)

Reduce spending during the 2010–11 biennium	$1.2
Tap Economic Stabilization Fund (Rainy Day Fund)	3.2

SOURCE: Legislative Budget Board, *Fiscal Size-Up: 2012–13 Biennium*, January 2012, p. 3.

TABLE 11.9

Legislative Response to the 2012–13 Biennium Deficit (in billions of dollars)

REVENUE SOLUTIONS	
Increased recurring revenues	$0.7
Created onetime revenues	1.4
Improved revenue estimate and other revenue	1.9
Made some funding contingent on improved revenue collection	1.0
Subtotal	5.0
SPENDING SOLUTIONS	
Reduced entitlement funding to local schools	4.0
Deferred 8/2013 payment to school districts until 9/2013	2.3
Medicaid cost containment	1.8
Underfunded Medicaid for 5 months in 2012	4.3
Reduced other spending in 2012–13	5.2
Subtotal	17.6
Total	**$22.6**

SOURCE: Legislative Budget Board, *Fiscal Size-Up: 2012–13 Biennium*, January 2012, p. 3.

On paper at least, the budget deficit had been addressed and political leaders had met their constitutional duties to balance the budget. Sales tax receipts began to recover from the depths of the recession throughout 2011 and into 2012. In June 2012, Comptroller Susan Combs reported that sales tax receipts were up 7 percent over the previous year and had increased every month for 12 months. The Texas economy was outperforming that of much of the nation, but not enough to cover a projected $4 billion budget shortfall for the 2012–13 biennium. There were also a number of school financing lawsuits in court that could potentially cost the state over $4 billion. In addition, state leaders had to figure out how to cover the onetime school payment delay and the Medicaid underfunding in the 2012–13 budget. But the biggest threat to a balanced budget did not lie in school funding or even in sales tax receipts. President Obama's federal reforms to health care presented new short-term and long-term spending commitments that could pose new and unanticipated challenges to the Texas budget in coming years.

Looking Beyond the Budget Crisis of 2011

The regular 2013 legislative session was smooth regarding budget matters, at least when compared to the 2011 session. Collegiality on budget matters was largely the result of Republican control of all branches of government coupled to a burgeoning state economy fueled by expanding job opportunities, rising housing prices, increased exports, and a resurgent oil and gas industry. Rosy budget projections for the next biennium offered legislators some wiggle room to do what they did best: cut taxes and increase spending on popular programs.

Public finance deeply affects the trade-offs in Texas's public policy. In 2013 the legislature compromised on a bill that would continue to fund highway construction (like this one in Sebastian) while still balancing the state budget.

During the 2013 session some modifications to the franchise tax were passed by the legislature, including modest tax cuts contingent upon the comptroller's certifying that the state will receive enough revenue to offset the proposed cuts. Also, a constitutional amendment was proposed during the regular session and passed by the voters in November 2013 providing the establishment of two new funds: the State Water Implementation Fund for Texas (SWIFT) and the State Water Implementation Revenue Fund for Texas (SWIRFT). The amendment also provided for a onetime transfer of Rainy Day Fund monies to support the financing of water supply projects in Texas through these funds.

Perhaps the most controversial budget issue dealt with by the legislature during the 2013 session centered upon transportation policy. How was the legislature going to pay for improving and expanding state highways, a cost that some experts put at up to $4 billion? Failing to pass a bill during the regular session and the first two special sessions in the summer of 2013, legislators finally brokered a compromise in the third special session. The financial mechanism that was established says much about the byzantine way in which budgetary matters often operate in the state. Under current law, 75 percent of funds raised above 1987 tax collection levels (which were $531.9 million for oil and $599.8 million for gas) was transferred from the General Revenue Fund to the Rainy Day Fund. The legislature sought to change this by proposing an amendment to the constitution (Article 3, Section 49g) taken before the voters on November 4, 2014. The amendment allowed half of this money (that is, half of the 75 percent above the 1987 levels) to still go to the Rainy Day Fund, but the other half would go to the State Highway Fund. There would be two provisos: first, certain statutory defined requirements would have to be met regarding the minimum funding of the Rainy Day Fund; second, the proposals for transferring money to the State Highway Fund would sunset in 2025. The amendment passed with 79.8 percent of the vote in favor.

Thinking Critically about Public Finance in Texas

Public finance in Texas will continue to be a troubling issue for political leaders in Texas. Revenues from the sales tax, severance taxes, and local property taxes are increasing once again. Confidence has grown among policy makers that the worst of the Great Recession is behind Texas. Despite this newfound optimism, state and local political leaders remain cautious in their projections about the future. There still remains uncertainty about the future course of the national and international economies. Texas's economy is tied inextricably to the booms and busts of the U.S. economy as well as the world economy. Moreover, the revenue mechanisms that support policy initiatives in Texas are sensitive and can move down quickly when the national and international economies falter. A declining economy can cut back on consumer spending, which affects the sales tax revenue. Falling housing prices can adversely affect property revenue. Falling prices for oil and natural gas can cut into severance revenues and undercut the revenue flowing into the Rainy Day Fund. Such are the rules that govern public finance in Texas in the early twenty-first century.

State budgetary policy ultimately depends on the successful implementation of a national recovery policy that works. Few leaders in the state, particularly Tea Party Republicans, are confident about the current direction of national economic policy. A looming national deficit with no solution in sight may lead to calls in Washington to push more responsibilities (and costs) onto the backs of the states, further exacerbating Texas's budgetary problems.

Four factors will continue to dominate public finance in Texas over the next biennium. First, economic conditions look favorable in the short run, assuring the state a healthy flow of revenues from its complex structure of state and local taxes. Second, there will be increased demands from the federal government for paying for expanded federal initiatives in health care (see Chapter 12). Third, increased population will lead to increased demands on state agencies for services ranging from health care to roads, to water, and to public education. All other things being equal, a larger population demands more from government, and that costs money. Fourth, there is a growing antigovernment feeling among portions of the population in Texas that state government is too big already. For Tea Partyers and other conservative Republicans, "No new taxes" is a successful mantra for winning office. Whether it will be a successful one for legislating and leading is another question. Navigating a passage between the rock of intensifying demands for expanded services and the hard place of "No new taxes" may be the most difficult problem legislators face in the foreseeable future.

What Is the Budget?

Explain the purpose of the state budget and what is typically included (pp. 349–51)

Texas is required to operate within a balanced budget. The budget can be considered in light of five revenue streams: the General Revenues Fund budget, the General Revenue–Dedicated Funds budget, the Federal Funds budget, the Other Funds budget, and the All Funds budget.

Key Terms

General Revenues Fund budget (p. 349)

General Revenue–Dedicated Funds budget (p. 349)

Federal Funds budget (p. 349)

Other Funds budget (p. 349)

All Funds budget (p. 349)

Spending and Revenue in Texas

Describe the general pattern of state spending in Texas and where state revenue comes from (pp. 351–61)

Texas spends less than the national average in a variety of policy areas, including education and highway spending. Although Texas does not have an income tax, it has one of the highest sales taxes in the nation. However, the per capita revenue from those sales taxes is among the lowest in the nation. Property taxes in Texas are among the highest in the nation. Among other important state taxes are the natural gas production tax and the oil production and regulation tax. Although a controversial issue in the past, a state income tax has little support either in the legislature or in the population as a whole. Texas also has on average fewer state employees per capita than other states.

Key Terms

regressive tax (p. 358)

progressive tax (p. 358)

matching funds (p. 360)

Practice Quiz

3. Texas has the reputation for being
    a) a low-service, low-tax state.
    b) a high-service, high-tax state.
    c) a low-service, high-tax state.
    d) a high-service, low-tax state.
    e) an average-service, average-tax state.

Practice Quiz

1. The Texas Constitution requires that the Texas budget must be
    a) balanced.
    b) approved by the governor's cabinet.
    c) funded only from sales taxes.
    d) approved by the governor, the legislature, and the state treasurer.
    e) funded only from federal grants.

2. Federal expenditures primarily affect the state budget in which two areas?
    a) energy and law enforcement
    b) health-human services and education
    c) business development and highways
    d) interstate highways and airports
    e) Medicare and transportation

4. The proportion of state employees to the population in Texas is
    a) far below the national average.
    b) far above the national average.
    c) right at the national average.
    d) exactly the same as in California.
    e) greater than in New York.

5. One major revenue source for Texas is the sales tax, which is
    a) 8.25 percent for state government and 2.25 percent for local government.
    b) 4.25 percent for state government and 2 percent for local government.
    c) 6.25 percent for state government and 2 percent for local government.
    d) 5 percent for state government and 1.25 percent for local government.
    e) none of the above

6. A Texas personal income tax
    a) used to exist but was repealed because of new taxes on oil production.
    b) would have to be approved by the voters, and the revenues from it would have to support public education.
    c) would have to be passed through a constitutional amendment.
    d) could only be imposed on incomes greater than $250,000 per year.
    e) would be unlikely to raise much revenue.

State Funds

Money flows into and out of a variety of over 400 different funds controlled by the state. Among the most important are the General Revenue Fund, the Permanent School Fund, the State Highway Fund, and the Economic Stabilization Fund (the Rainy Day Fund). The existence of these funds makes budgeting a complicated process.

Key Terms

General Revenue Fund (p. 361)

Permanent School Fund (PSF) (p. 362)

Available School Fund (ASF) (p. 362)

State Highway Fund (p. 362)

Economic Stabilization Fund (ESF) (p. 362)

Permanent University Trust Fund (PUF) (p. 365)

Higher Education Fund (HEF) (p. 365)

National Research University Fund (NRUF) (p. 365)

Practice Quiz

7. The Rainy Day Fund
   a) provides funds for flood victims.
   b) was designed to provide funding for the state during times of financial distress.
   c) contains only a small amount of state funds.
   d) is used to promote oil and gas development.
   e) can only be spent by the Texas comptroller.

8. The National Research University Fund
   a) pays for university-level research at all state universities.
   b) provides the funding for the University of Texas at Austin.
   c) funds Texas universities seeking national prominence as research institutions.
   d) only provides funds to universities with Nobel Prize winners.
   e) will not provide funds if more than 20 percent of students fail to graduate in four years.

The Texas Constitution and the Budget

There are many constitutional restrictions on the budget, including the requirement of a biennial budget, a pay-as-you-go limit, a welfare spending limit, a limit on the growth of some appropriations, rules on the spending of funds by state agencies, and limitations on debt payable from the general revenue fund. These restrictions play important roles in shaping the budget policy-making process.

Key Terms

Article 3, Section 49a (Pay-as-You-Go Limit) (p. 366)

appropriations (p. 366)

debt service (p. 368)

Practice Quiz

9. Which of the following is *not* a constitutional constraint on the budgetary process in Texas?
   a) the annual budget
   b) a welfare spending limit
   c) a pay-as-you-go limit
   d) a limitation on the debt payable from the General Revenue Fund
   e) All are constitutional limits.

10. What is meant by "the budget-execution authority"?
    a) the power to execute the laws of the land
    b) the legislature's power to establish rules for the expenditure of funds by state agencies
    c) the governor's power to veto the budget
    d) the LBB's power to create the budget for the judiciary in Texas
    e) none of the above

The Budgetary Process

In theory, Texas has a dual budget system with budgeting shared by the governor and the legislature. In reality, the budget is the responsibility of the legislature. There are a series of steps that the budget must go through to be passed by the legislature. Among the most important is the requirement that the Texas comptroller certify the budget as being balanced.

Practice Quiz

11. Who is the chief planning officer of the state of Texas?
    a) the lieutenant governor
    b) the Speaker of the House
    c) the comptroller
    d) the governor
    e) the state treasurer

12. The principal job of the Legislative Budget Board is
    a) to keep track of the expenses of the executive.
    b) to monitor the operations of the House.
    c) to raise taxes.
    d) to recommend appropriations for all agencies of state government.
    e) to conduct audits of state expenditures.

Budget Crises in Twenty-First-Century Texas

Texas has experienced a number of budgetary crises in the early years of the twenty-first century. Budgetary problems were exacerbated by property tax reforms and the Great Recession, which led to serious declines in revenue while the demands for services were increasing.

Practice Quiz

13. Which factors lie behind the budget crisis of 2011?
    a) the Great Recession and property tax reform
    b) declining oil and gas prices
    c) a burdensome income tax being implemented for the first time
    d) bipartisan government
    e) Obamacare

14. Which solution was put into place to address the budget crisis of 2011?
    a) instituting a state income tax
    b) speeding up the payments of various taxes on alcohol and motor fuels
    c) increasing the state sales tax
    d) allocating more money to elementary and secondary education
    e) increasing gasoline taxes

Recommended Websites

Texas Comptroller of Public Accounts
www.window.state.tx.us

Texas Legislative Budget Board
www.lbb.state.tx.us

General Appropriations for the 2014–15 Biennium
www.lbb.state.tx.us/Documents/GAA/General
_Appropriations_Act_2014-15.pdf

The Religious Viewpoints Antidiscrimination Act required Texas school districts to protect religious speech on campus, allowing students to express their faith in public. These students at Grapevine High School sang along with a Christian band at an event organized by the Christian organization Students Standing Strong.

Public Policy in Texas

WHAT PUBLIC POLICY DOES AND WHY IT MATTERS Like other states, Texas is involved in a broad range of public-policy initiatives. Some of these activities, such as criminal corrections or public education, are largely state responsibilities. Although the national government may contribute some funds and regulate various aspects of these public-policy areas, they remain for the most part the duty and responsibility of the state of Texas. Other public-policy areas, however, have involved considerable intermingling of state and federal government responsibilities. The balance of power between the state and federal governments in these areas has shifted over time.

Throughout the first decade of the twenty-first century, state policy makers in Texas waded through a variety of policy problems, including tax reform, educational testing, and criminal incarceration. Republican domination of both houses of the state legislature and the executive offices in the state ensured that a new conservative agenda would dominate policy debates across a variety of issues. Perhaps nothing captured this ideological orientation in public policy better than a new law that was passed during the 2007 session of the state legislature: the Religious Viewpoints Antidiscrimination Act.[1]

The law, which many claimed simply codified existing constitutional rulings by the federal courts, required Texas school districts to adopt a number of policies that would protect religious speech on campus. School districts were ordered to develop a neutral method for choosing student speakers at school events and graduation ceremonies, to ensure that religious-oriented clubs had the same access to school facilities as secular-oriented clubs, and to protect students who wished to express their religious beliefs in classroom assignments. The legislation did more than just give students permission to express their religious views in public schools; it also mandated the creation of a "limited public forum" for student speakers at public events that wouldn't discriminate against expressions of faith.

Social conservatives were ecstatic about the Religious Viewpoints Antidiscrimination Act, claiming that, at last, individual religious expression would be protected in the schools. Professional educators were somewhat hesitant in their praise for the bill, citing concerns about how the bill would be implemented and what it might mean for members of religious minorities. One commentator wrote for a law review that under the act "a student would be free to ask his or her fellow students to join in prayer to accept Jesus Christ as their personal savior so that they might have eternal life. Or a student would be free to tell his or her fellow students that Jesus was not God's son or that the Bible is a book of myths. Alternatively, a student might talk about why Catholics or Mormons are not Christians."[2] Far from solving the problems of religious discrimination, the act may unintentionally introduce religious bias and controversy into the classroom.

The Religious Viewpoints Antidiscrimination Act brings out two important truths about public policy in Texas. First, what goes on in Austin matters. The state legislature plays a major role in defining how public policy is conducted in the state. Second, public policy involves more than just introducing a bill in the legislature, passing it, and getting it signed. Laws also must be implemented. Implementation of policy by state agencies such as school boards is where the rubber meets the road in political life.

This chapter explores public-policy making in Texas across a variety of leading issue areas including public education, welfare, Medicaid, and water. In Chapter 13, we will explore criminal justice policy. We will begin with a discussion of the policy-making process and key concepts that shape political scientists' understanding of how public policy is made. We will then provide an overview of the problems confronting policy makers in these key areas and explain how political choices have shaped and continue to shape policy making in each case. We will also consider the current debates that are driving public policy in these areas.

chapter goals

- Describe the key steps and concepts in the policy-making process (pp. 384–87)

- Describe the major issues that have shaped education policy in Texas (pp. 387–97)

- Describe the state's role in addressing poverty and how it is affected by national policies (pp. 397–403)

- Explain why Medicaid in particular and health care policy in general have been so controversial in Texas (pp. 403–12)

- Consider the growing importance of policies related to water supplies in Texas (pp. 412–18)

● The Policy-Making Process

Describe the key steps and concepts in the policy-making process

In broadest terms, public policy refers to the outputs of governmental institutions. More narrowly, public policy can be defined as the expressed goals of a governmental body backed by incentives or sanctions.[3] Public policies can be found in laws passed by legislative bodies as well as in the rules, regulations, and orders from properly authorized public agencies. The incentives or sanctions can include a wide range of actions from subsidies encouraging individuals to act in a certain way to monetary penalties or admonitions to severe criminal penalties that punish people for engaging in particular actions.

One way that political scientists have approached the study of public policy is by focusing attention upon the different stages of the policy-making process, the political and administrative process through which governmental goals are identified, formulated, articulated into law, and evaluated.[4] The idea that there are stages of the policy-making process is not so much a step-by-step description or explicit roadmap of how public policy is made within institutions such as a legislature or a bureaucracy. Public policy is not made in a simple linear way. The real world of policy making is, in fact, much messier than a simple progression of stages moving neatly from one stage to another. In the real world, stages may overlap or even collapse into one another. Nevertheless, the idea that there are stages of the policy-making process has proven to be a useful analytical framework for understanding the various factors that go into the making of public policy.

Problem Identification The first stage is problem identification. Here society at large and actors in the political system develop an understanding of how we must think about and address a particular problem. Roger Cobb and Charles Elder refer to this set of ideas as a "systemic agenda" where all issues are "commonly perceived by members of the political community as meriting public attention and as involving matters within the legitimate jurisdiction of existing governmental authority."[5] This systemic agenda is used by citizens and policy makers as a conceptual framework to understand the nature of public problems and to shape and direct the way policy makers will develop public policy aimed at them. For example, if we view the problem of poverty being fundamentally one of limited income, we might conclude that the best solution is increasing welfare payments to the poor. However, if we consider the problem of poverty to be behavior that causes people to be poor such as unwillingness to work or poor job skills, we might conclude that policies directed toward encouraging work or subsidizing education are better courses of action. In the problem identification stage, our ideology—that is, our ideas, concepts, and visions about the way society works—plays a major role in defining public-policy making.

Policy Formulation Policy formulation is the second stage of the policy-making process. Here the more general ideas that we have about social and political problems become clarified and strategies for dealing with these specifically defined problems are developed. Policy formulation involves the detailed procedures in passing legislation as well as in making administrative rules and regulations. Here a kind of agenda setting—institutional agenda setting—takes place. As we noted in our earlier discussion of interest groups, one of the goals of interest groups is to gain access to policy discussions inside legislatures and agencies. Access provides interest groups with the opportunity to help set the institutional agenda in the policy formulation stage. Setting the agenda on what problems will be discussed, how these problems will be understood, and what concrete measures will be taken to address them lies at the heart of all policy formulation.

Implementation The third stage in the policy-making process is implementation. At this stage, the goals of public policy along with the incentives or sanctions to support them are put into effect by a particular government agency. Identifying the appropriate agency to implement a program is crucial at this stage. Similarly, budgetary policy plays a major role in the implementation stage and can determine the success or failure of a particular public policy. A well-formulated public policy can be dashed by poorly executed or poorly funded implementation.

As shown here, education policy involves the four key stages in the policy-making process. Clockwise from top left: A policy issue like school funding is identified. Politicians, like Wendy Davis, who filibustered a bill to lower school funding, create policies to address the issue. Bureaucrats implement policy changes (for example, adding more computers in classrooms). Finally, policies are evaluated and changes are considered. Here, the Texas Education Commissioner visits a school in Abilene.

Evaluation The fourth stage of the policy-making process is evaluation. At a certain point all public policies must be evaluated for their effectiveness. In the best of all possible worlds, good evaluation procedures would assess the stated goals of a particular policy against the actual outcomes of the implemented policy. Good evaluation would lead to a rethinking of the public policy in light of the problems being addressed and the solutions being formulated to address the problem. Similarly, good evaluation could lead to a rethinking of the strategies being used and the resources being committed to implementing the policy. Closing the loop between problem identification and program evaluation is one of the most difficult problems facing policy makers.

Some political scientists identify policy legitimation as another stage in the policy-making process. Legitimation—the establishment and recognition in the political community of the legality and constitutionality of a particular policy initiative—is probably better understood not as a separate stage but as something that takes place throughout the entire policy-making process. Legitimation can include a wide range of activities: open discussions of a problem in the press, committee investigations and oversight investigations, following the appropriate rules for passing a bill in the legislature or making a rule in an administrative agency, and judicial review of the policy. Establishing the legitimacy of a public policy throughout the various stages of the policy-making process is an essential part of any democratic political system.

Rationality in Policy Making

An often-stated goal of policy makers is to make public policy more rational and more efficient. **Rationality**, in this regard, generally refers to the idea that we have

rationality the idea in public-policy making that we have clearly identified goals and that we seek to achieve these goals in an optimal or efficient manner

clearly identified the goals that we wish to achieve and have formulated and implemented policies that address these problems in an optimal or efficient manner. Optimality or efficiency refers to the idea that policy will be developed that will maximize the outputs of government with a minimum commitment of resources. Given this commitment to rationality in policy making, people are often surprised by how irrational and inefficient public policy can seem in a democracy. Part of the problem lies in the fact that the policy-making process is highly complex. Writing reports, holding committee hearings, and passing legislation often involve political compromises that muddy the waters of policy making. Vagueness in the problem identification stage along with compromises made among competing parties in the policy formulation stage can work against the development of rational and efficient solutions to problems.

There are additional factors that tend to work against rationality and efficiency in the making of public policy. The first is the fact that governments tend to work incrementally. Neither legislators nor government agencies begin their work on a particular problem from ground zero every year. Year in and year out, there is a general agreement among policy makers on the nature of a public problem and on how it should be addressed. Unless measures are taken to compel agencies to reassess what they are doing and why, programs, policies, and budgets tend to grow incrementally from one policy cycle to another. And even when such measures are taken, as in the Sunset process, as discussed in Chapter 8, or major changes are initiated in the fundamental direction of public policy, incrementalism governs the decision-making process.

A second factor that tends to work against rational and efficient government is that policy makers and other politically active individuals may not behave strictly rationally or efficiently. The economist Herbert Simon has argued that individual rationality is limited by a number of factors, including the expense of getting information about a problem, the cognitive limitations of the human mind, and the time constraints that all individuals face in making a decision.[6] Policy makers' rationality may be a **"bounded rationality."** Rather than seeking to rationally understand everything that is involved in a particular policy problem or optimize every action taken to address this problem, they may actually simply seek to "satisfice." Essentially, satisficing means to reach a decision that is satisfactory rather than optimal to the individual. From the perspective of the policy process as a whole, satisficing by many individuals and groups can lead to less-than-rational and less-than-efficient public policy.

To appreciate the intricacies of policy making, we will turn to a discussion of four policy areas shaping political life in Texas: education, welfare, health care, and water.

bounded rationality the idea in policy making that decision makers may seek satisfactory solutions to problems that are not necessarily optimal or efficient

● Education Policy

Describe the major issues that have shaped education policy in Texas

Education is big business in Texas. For the 2014–15 biennium, $52.8 billion in state monies went to public education, 37 percent of all state spending. Local property taxes contributed an estimated $42.8 billion in revenue to local school districts. The federal government contributed an estimated $10.3 billion to fund a variety of programs including Child Nutrition Grants, No Child Left Behind Grants, disabilities funding, and other formula grants.[7]

There were over 5 million students enrolled in public schools in Texas in 2013, second only to California. Enrollments increased by 19.3 percent between 2003 and 2013, far above the 4.8 percent national increase. There are 1,025 regular school districts in Texas along with 202 charters operating 552 open-enrollment charter school campuses. Although funded with public monies, charter schools have been set up as an alternative to traditional public schools, often because the public schools have failed to meet the needs of certain groups of students. Charter schools are in many ways more flexible than public schools, but they must meet the standards set by the state for public schools.

Eight hundred and twenty-five state school districts and charters had fewer than 1,600 students in 2014. A large number of these school districts were small and in rural areas. Eighteen school districts enrolled over 50,000, 62 percent of all students in the state. The largest school districts are in Houston (203,354), Dallas (158,932), Cypress-Fairbanks in Harris County (110,013), and Northside in Bexar County (100,159).[8] Over 292,000 students graduated from Texas high schools in 2012.

State school districts employ almost 327,000 teachers, with an average salary of $48,373, well below the national average of $55,418. The race and ethnicity of teachers differ considerably from those of the student body in Texas: 64.4 percent of teachers are white, 22.5 percent are Latino, and 9.5 percent are African American. The districts also employ over 25,000 administrators and almost 65,000 professional support staff (such as counselors, librarians, and nurses). On top of that, they employ another 226,000 educational aides and auxiliary staff. Total staffing in elementary and secondary schools in Texas exceeds 643,000 people.[9]

The challenges facing educational policy in Texas are great, but a few stand out. First, Texas ranks 44th on public expenditures per enrolled student in 2012, spending $8,498 per pupil, well below the $10,834 national average. Second, the demographics are increasingly minority and disadvantaged. In 2013, 51.3 percent of students in Texas were Hispanic, 30 percent were white, 12.7 percent were African American, and 3.6 percent were Asian or Pacific Islander. Of these students, 16.9 percent had "limited English proficiency." In addition, 59 percent were considered to be "economically disadvantaged" (meaning they were poor), and 47.2 per-

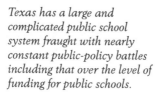

Texas has a large and complicated public school system fraught with nearly constant public-policy battles including that over the level of funding for public schools.

cent were consider to be "at risk" (meaning that given their circumstances, they are more likely to fail academically). Not surprisingly, these demographic characteristics often lead to lower performance on national and state tests. Third, there are high dropout rates in Texas. For example, in 2012 over 36,000 students dropped out of school. Dropout rates, particularly among Latinos and African Americans, affect other state and federal efforts to address the problem of poverty. To understand how policy makers are dealing with these challenges, we must look deeper into the making of educational policy since the founding of the state.

The debate over public education in Texas extends back to the break with Mexico.[10] One of the indictments of the Mexican regime contained in the Texas Declaration of Independence was that the government had failed to establish a public system of education. Later, the Constitution of the Republic of Texas required a public system of education, but a bill actually establishing a public school system did not pass the legislature until 1854.

Public education was to be financed with a special school fund that would use $2 million of the $10 million given to Texas by the U.S. government on Texas's admission to the Union to settle outstanding land claims in parts of what are now New Mexico, Colorado, and Oklahoma. Unfortunately, the fund was used for a variety of other purposes in the following years, including the purchase of railroad stock and the building of prisons. When Democrats returned to power following Reconstruction, an effort was made to protect the fund and commit its use solely to education. Under the Constitution of 1876, the Special School Fund became the Permanent School Fund, and restrictions were placed on how the money could be used and invested.[11] The Constitution of 1876 also had provisions to support public education through one-quarter of the occupation tax, a $1 poll tax, and local taxation.

Throughout much of the late nineteenth and early twentieth centuries, public education remained largely a local affair. Schools were funded by local taxes, and decisions such as what to teach and how long the school year would be were made at the local level. Many of the school systems were chronically short of funds, facing such problems as a shortage of supplies and textbooks, inadequate facilities, and poorly trained teachers. In 1949 the state legislature tried to address some of these problems by passing the **Gilmer-Aikin Laws**, under which school districts were consolidated into 2,900 administrative units, state equalization funding was provided to supplement local taxes, teachers' salaries were raised, and a minimum 175 teaching days school year was established. In addition, the laws established the Texas Education Agency (TEA), originally known as the State Department of Education, to supervise public education in the state.

The Gilmer-Aikin Laws also established bureaucratic institutions responsible for public education in the state. Previously, public education had been run by a state board of education, whose 9 members were appointed by the governor for six-year terms, and an elected state superintendent of public instruction. This was replaced by an elected 21-member board. The State Board of Education became the policy-making body for public education in the state, selecting budgets, establishing regulations for school accreditation, executing contracts for the purchase of textbooks, and investing in the Permanent School Fund. The board also had the power to appoint a commissioner of education, subject to confirmation by the Texas Senate. The commissioner of education served a four-year term and became the chief executive officer for the TEA. The TEA was responsible for setting standards for public schools, for supervising the public schools of the state, and for handling federal funds related to public education. For the next 50 years, educational

Gilmer-Aikin Laws education reform legislation passed in 1949 that supplemented local funding of education with public monies, raised teachers' salaries, mandated a minimum length for the school year, and provided for more state supervision of public education

policy in the state would work through the institutional framework established by the Gilmer-Aikin Laws.[12]

Since 1949 the State Board of Education has undergone occasional restructuring. Membership was expanded to 24 in 1973 and to 27 in 1981. Following a special legislative session, the board became a 15-member appointed body in 1984. But in 1988 it reverted to an elected body composed of 15 members serving four-year terms. Three issues have played a major role in shaping educational policy over the last 50 years: desegregation, equity in funding, and the search for educational excellence.

Desegregation

Few issues have troubled educational policy in Texas as much as desegregation. Segregation of the races was provided for under the Texas Constitution of 1876. In *Plessy v. Ferguson* (1896), the U.S. Supreme Court upheld the validity of state-imposed racial segregation through the now-infamous "separate but equal" doctrine. In Texas, as elsewhere across the South, segregated schools may have been separate, but they were far from equal. In the 1920s and '30s, for example, the length of the school term for black schools was only about four days shorter than that for white schools, but Texas spent an average of $3.39 less per student (about one-third less) on the education of African American students than on white students.[13]

The U.S. Supreme Court overturned *Plessy v. Ferguson* in the 1954 case *Brown v. Board of Education*, ruling that state-imposed segregation in schools violated the equal protection clause of the Fourteenth Amendment. School districts were ordered to desegregate their school systems "with all deliberate speed." In some cases, "all deliberate speed" was rapid. The San Antonio school district, for example, became one of the first school districts in the nation to comply with the Supreme Court's order. Other school districts in the state, such as Houston's, were much slower in implementing the Court's desegregation ruling.

The desegregation of public schools was hampered further by political opposition at both the local and state levels. In 1957 the Texas legislature passed laws encouraging school districts to resist federally ordered desegregation, although then-governor Price Daniel, Sr., chose to ignore such laws.[14] By the late 1960s legally segregated schools were largely a thing of the past. Nevertheless, de facto segregation remained a problem, particularly in urban areas with large minority populations. As in many other urban areas across the country, a large number of middle- and upper-income whites in Texas abandoned urban public school systems for suburban public schools or private schools.

Equity in the Public School System

Federal court cases such as *Brown v. Board of Education* played a major role in shaping educational policy regarding the desegregation of schools. Two other important court cases have affected education policy and politics in Texas over the last 30 years: *San Antonio v. Rodríguez* and *Edgewood ISD v. Kirby*.

San Antonio v. Rodríguez *San Antonio v. Rodríguez* was a landmark case involving the constitutionality of using property taxes to fund public schools.[15] At the heart of the case lay the question of the equitable funding of public schools. Lawyers for Rodríguez and seven other children in the poor Edgewood independent school

Who Attends School in Texas?

Total Public School Enrollment by Race, 2006–11

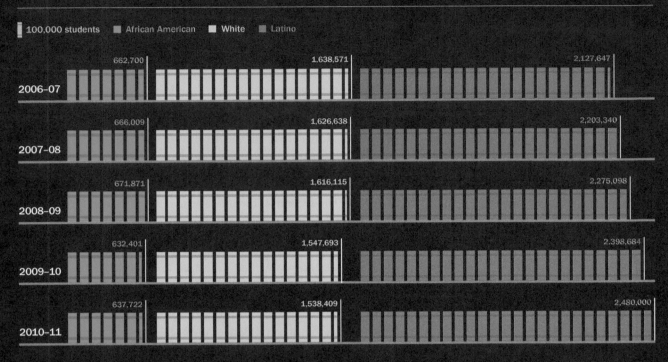

| 100,000 students | ■ African American | ■ White | ■ Latino |

	African American	White	Latino
2006–07	662,700	1,638,571	2,127,647
2007–08	666,009	1,626,638	2,203,340
2008–09	671,871	1,616,115	2,275,098
2009–10	632,401	1,547,693	2,398,684
2010–11	637,722	1,538,409	2,480,000

Public School Enrollment by Race vs. Texas State Population, 2011

African American
Enrollment
13%
State population
11%

White
Enrollment
31%
State population
47%

Latino
Enrollment
50%
State population
37%

The demographics in Texas are rapidly changing. The state is becoming more diverse and the population is growing, especially in major cities. As more people move to Texas, they bring their children, and the state is responsible for educating them in public schools. What are the demographics of Texas schoolchildren? What socioeconomic classes do they come from? Are Texas's schoolchildren representative of the population of the state as a whole?

for critical analysis

1. Which racial/ethnic group has seen the largest growth in Texas's public schools? What might account for this?

2. How does the growing number of children from lower socioeconomic backgrounds affect how education is delivered in Texas public schools?

district (ISD) in the San Antonio area argued that the current system of financing public schools in Texas was unfair. The Edgewood school district had one of the highest property tax rates in the country, but it could raise only $37 per pupil. Meanwhile the neighboring school district of Alamo Heights was able to raise $413 per pupil with a much lower property tax rate. The difference was that the value of the property subject to taxation in Alamo Heights far exceeded that in Edgewood. Equalizing educational funding would require Edgewood to tax at the rate of $5.76 per $100 of property value, while Alamo Heights could tax at a rate of $0.68 per $100 of property value.

A three-judge federal district court was impaneled to hear the case in January 1969. The district court initially delayed action, giving the 1971 Texas legislature time to address the funding issue. When the legislature failed to act during its regular session, the court took action. On December 23, 1971, it ruled that the Texas school finance system was unconstitutional under the **equal protection clause** of the Fourteenth Amendment to the U.S. Constitution. However, on appeal to the U.S. Supreme Court, the decision was overturned. On March 21, 1973, the Supreme Court ruled 5–4 that states such as Texas were not required to subsidize poorer school districts under the equal protection clause of the U.S. Constitution. The question of equity in public school funding would have to be addressed later in terms of Texas's state constitution and in Texas courts.

Edgewood ISD v. Kirby The second landmark case involving the financing of public schools was *Edgewood ISD v. Kirby*. Unlike *Rodriguez, Edgewood* considered whether the system of funding public schools through local property taxes fulfilled the Texas State Constitution's provisions on education. Much of the litigation over the next few years would center on Article 7, Section 1, of the 1876 Constitution, which read:

> A general diffusion of knowledge being essential to the preservation of the liberties and rights of the people, it shall be the duty of the Legislature of the State to establish and make suitable provision for the support and maintenance of an efficient system of free public schools.

A key constitutional issue would be exactly what constituted an "efficient system of free public schools."

On behalf of the Edgewood ISD, the Mexican American Legal Defense and Education Fund (MALDEF) sued William Kirby, the state commissioner of education, on May 23, 1984. Initially, only 8 districts were represented in the case. By the time the case was finally decided, 67 other school districts had joined the original plaintiffs. The plaintiffs argued that the state's reliance on local property taxes to fund public education discriminated against poor children by denying them equal opportunities in education. One month after the original case was filed, the legislature passed House Bill 72, a modest reform measure that increased state aid to poor districts. In 1985 plaintiffs filed an amended lawsuit, arguing that the legislature's action was far from satisfactory.

The amended case was heard early in 1987 by a state district judge, who ruled on April 29, 1987 in favor of the plaintiffs, calling for the institution of a new system of public school funding by September 1989.

The decision was reversed on appeal to the state appeals court in late 1988. But in a 9–0 decision, the Texas Supreme Court held that the funding system was, indeed, in violation of the state constitution. The court held that education was a fundamental right under the Texas Constitution and that the "glaring disparities" between rich and poor schools violated the efficiency clause of the constitution. In its ruling, the court did not demand "absolute equality" in per pupil spending. But it did require a standard of "substantially equal access to similar revenues per pupil at similar levels of tax effort."[16] It ordered the legislature to implement an equitable system by the 1990–91 school year.

The Texas Supreme Court's ruling touched off a political firestorm that swept through Texas politics throughout the 1990s and into the 2000s. Over the years, various courts held various funding provisions of public education to be unconstitutional. The legislature responded with various funding plans for public education. One was dubbed the "Robin Hood" plan because it transferred funds from rich to poor districts.

Unlike the U.S. Constitution, the Texas Constitution does specifically mention "education". Y'all were just barking up the wrong constitution in San Antonio v. Rodriguez.

stus.com

In San Antonio v. Rodríguez, *the U.S. Supreme Court based its ruling to uphold Texas's public school finance system on its reading of the federal constitution.* Edgewood ISD v. Kirby, *however, evaluated the constitutionality of the system in light of the provisions for education set forth in the Texas State Constitution, giving the Texas Supreme Court grounds to overturn the original unequal funding system.*

In November 2005 the Texas Supreme Court upheld a lower court ruling that the school districts lacked "meaningful discretion" in setting local maintenance and operation tax rates. In the court's opinion, too many districts were being forced to set tax rates at the maximum $1.50 per $100 valuation. Essentially, this meant that the school system was being financed by an unconstitutional state property tax. The court gave the legislature until June 1, 2006, to address the matter or the court would enjoin the state from distributing funding to the public school system.

It took three special sessions of the state legislature to craft a compromise and finally put constitutional concerns over the financing of public schools brought on by Robin Hood to rest. The final proposal cut property taxes by one-third and replaced lost revenues with money raised statewide by an expanded business tax and a new $1-per-pack tax on cigarettes. General revenue monies are now used to address some of the inequities of the property tax system.[17] Unfortunately, the compromise generated, at least in the short run, as many problems as it solved.

The Great Recession of 2008–09 brought a budget crisis to the 2011 legislative session that shook educational policy in Texas to its core. One of the principal ways that the 2011 legislature balanced the budget without raising taxes was by making severe cuts to the tune of $5.6 billion in elementary and secondary education funding. The cuts not only jeopardized many of the reform initiatives of the previous 20 years, but raised fundamental questions about fairness that had been resolved with the Edgewood decisions. Approximately $3.4 billion in educational funds from the state were restored during the 2013 legislative session, but many educational reformers believed that was not enough. School districts went to court arguing that the state was no longer meeting the demands for a fair and equitable school system laid down by the Texas Supreme Court. Judge John Dietz had ruled in February 2013 during the legislative session that the state had violated the constitution by underfunding schools during the 2011 session. He reopened the case after the $3.4 billion had been put back into the budget during the 2013 regular session. In the summer of 2014, Judge Dietz found the current funding system to be unconstitutional again. The legislature was going to have to reconsider, one more time, the whole issue of funding education constitutionally.[18]

Financing public education became a defining issue during the 2014 election campaigns. Republican candidate for governor Greg Abbott found himself as attorney general in the unenviable position of representing the state in the lawsuits that were claiming Texas was underfunding public education. Democratic candidate

Wendy Davis, meanwhile, staked out a position for increasing funding significantly. Davis, it must be noted, had filibustered the 2011 budget that had contained all the cuts.

The struggle to rework the funding mechanism for public education was only one dimension of educational policy in Texas in the 1980s and '90s. Concerns over the quality of education in the state and how best to promote educational excellence would also help to define educational policy in the early twenty-first century.

Educational Excellence and Accountability in Texas

The equity issue in public education had been touched off by litigation. Only when forced by the courts to rethink how schools were being funded was the legislature finally willing to act. A different set of factors has driven the debate over educational excellence and accountability.

The issue of education reform came to a head in the early 1980s in Texas. The Texas debate was actually part of a larger national debate over the state of education in the United States.[19] A 1983 report by the National Commission on Excellence in Education, *A Nation at Risk*, identified a number of crises that were beginning to grip the nation's educational system. Test scores were declining and functional illiteracy was on the rise. Students were simply not equipped with the intellectual skills required in the modern world. If steps were not taken soon to reform education in the United States, the report argued, the nation was at risk of falling behind other countries in the rapidly changing world of international competition.[20]

Educational reform was put on the state agenda when, at the end of the 1983 regular session, the legislature established the Select Committee on Public Education (SCOPE). SCOPE was created as a 22-member committee to which the governor would have only 5 appointees.[21] The remaining seats were filled by appointees made by the House and Senate leadership and by 3 members of the State Board of Education. The intent of the legislature in creating SCOPE was not only to figure out how to fund pay raises for teachers but also to evaluate the entire system of public education in the state.

One of the most important decisions made by Governor White was appointing the Dallas businessman Ross Perot to chair the committee. Perot had supported White's opponent in the 1982 gubernatorial race. It was felt that Perot's participation in the process would help broaden support for the committee across party lines as well as bring in needed support from the business community. At the time of his selection, however, few knew how important Perot would be to the process of educational reform. To the surprise of many, Perot took an active role in SCOPE, mobilizing the committee in private and public to take on what he considered abuses in the public education system.

Perot was particularly scornful of athletic programs and what he considered the misplaced priorities of the existing educational system. In the end, SCOPE presented 140 recommendations for reforming the Texas education system in its final report on April 19, 1984. Among the most controversial of the proposed reforms was "No Pass, No Play." Students who failed to earn a passing grade of 70 would be unable to participate in any extracurricular activities for the next grading period of six weeks. But "No Pass, No Play" was only the tip of the iceberg. Other reform proposals set new standards for students' attendance and performance; annual school performance reports and tighter accreditation standards, with schools that did not meet these higher standards losing state funds; a longer school year—

One means of encouraging educational excellence has been to allow students to transfer from low-performing to high-performing schools, thus promoting competition among the schools and allowing parents more choices.

from 175 to 180 days; and a professional career ladder for teachers, tying pay raises to performance.[22] In early July 1984 many of the reform proposals were put into place in a 266-page education reform bill, along with the necessary accompanying tax increases.

The so-called Perot reforms were but the first round in the debate over excellence and accountability in the public school system. A second round opened during the 1995 legislative session. As in the past, there was strong business and bipartisan support for reforms that supported increased accountability through testing. There were some important differences in the reform package finally signed by Republican governor George W. Bush. The Perot reforms had generally centralized control over education policy in the state. The Bush reforms, in contrast, gave more discretion to local school districts to achieve the educational goals the state was mandating. Some of the reforms put through were symbolic. The controversial "No Pass, No Play" rule was relaxed, cutting the period of nonparticipation from six to three weeks and lifting a ban on practicing while on scholastic probation. But other changes were more substantive. Local control of public schools was increased by limiting the power of the TEA. Local voters were empowered to adopt home charters that could free their school districts from many state requirements, including class-size caps at lower grades. The 1995 reforms also enabled students under certain circumstances to transfer from low-performing schools to high-performing schools in their districts, thus promoting competition among the schools by holding the schools accountable for the performance of their students.[23]

One of the most controversial aspects of the reform movement in public education in Texas was the development of statewide assessment standards. "Testing," as assessment came to be known, was first instituted in 1986 with the Texas Educational Assessment of Minimal Skills (TEAMS) exams. TEAMS sought to certify that students from all districts met certain minimum academic expectations. Students had to pass TEAMS to be eligible to receive a high school diploma. TEAMS was replaced with the Texas Assessment of Academic Skills (TAAS) test in 1990, which focused upon minimum academic skills in reading, writing, and math at grade 10. The implementation of Texas Assessment of Knowledge and Skills (TAKS) in 2003 pushed statewide testing across the state-mandated curriculum, requiring students to pass exit-level tests in English, math, science, and social studies. TAKS, in turn, was replaced by the State of Texas Assessments of Academic Readiness (STAAR), 15 end-of-course exams across the curriculum for grades 9 through 12 beginning in 2011. The idea was to have passing standards increased with subsequent administrations of the exam. Schools would be held accountable for their student performances. In the process, it was hoped that public education in Texas would ratchet upward in quality.

Unfortunately, high-minded expectations about reforming public schools through intensified testing and accountability were dashed as failure rates stayed stubbornly high. In 2012 the TEA reported passing rates on five of the STAAR end-of-course exams ranged from 87 percent in biology to 55 percent in English writing. Although failing students were allowed to retake the test, fears began to mount about the impact that failure rates would have on retention and graduation rates. In addition, a storm brewed up out of the classrooms as teachers and administrators complained about the growing need to teach to the test.[24]

Support among business and political elites for an expanded, intensified set of tests to reform public education collapsed during the 2013 legislative session. As

Testing has remained a controversial issue in Texas schools. Some say frequent testing will raise standards and student performance, while others say that it will lead to "teaching to the test."

we discussed in the introduction to Chapter 6, new groups with different interests emerged to challenge the consensus around accountability and testing that had driven educational reform policy for 25 years. Under House Bill 5, the state legislature cut the number of required end-of-course tests from 15 to 5. The idea of testing to promote academic excellence was not being abandoned completely, but it no longer held center stage for reformers. As State Senator Dan Patrick, the chair of the Senate Public Education Committee, noted, "By the elimination of 15 [tests] to 5 . . . that could save 40 or more days of testing, give teachers more time to teach, be innovative and creative."[25]

Education Policy in a New Era

One might have hoped that the educational reforms of the past 25 years would have ushered in an era of rising educational attainment in Texas in the first decade of the twenty-first century. Such was hardly the case. Despite the efforts of policy makers, teachers' salaries and overall state and local spending on public education remained low compared with those in other states as did graduation rates. In 2010 the average SAT scores in Texas were 481 in reading and 504 in math, compared with a national average of 1017 for the two tests together.[26] These scores represented a slight but ongoing drop in Texas test scores in the first decade of the twenty-first century.

Although the dropout rate in grades 7 through 12 has been declining since the 1990s, it remained high among minorities. For a few years at the turn of the century, scores on standardized tests such as the TAAS test improved across the state, sparking calls for the development of new assessment tests to hold teachers and schools more accountable. But with the implementation of more rigorous STAAR assessments, overall student performance stayed flat or fell on various tests. More disturbingly, there appeared to be a growing "achievement gap" where minorities and at-risk students failed at higher rates than whites in consecutive iterations of the tests.[27]

Vouchers and Charter Schools The perceived failure of educational reform efforts based on the ideas of testing and accountability led some to advocate new ideas in public education. One new idea—actually an old idea from the early '60s—being offered up by conservatives, particularly in the Tea Party wing of the Republican Party, is vouchers. The basic idea of vouchers is simple. Increase competition in the school system by letting funding follow the students. If the public school doesn't work, let parents and students opt out and take their funding with them.[28] Among the recurring criticisms of voucher-based reform is that middle- and upper-middle-income students will leave poorer students behind in poorly funded public schools.

An alternative to vouchers has been available to some in Texas through open-enrollment charter schools. Like vouchers, the idea of charter schools is to make more options available to parents and students, particularly in places where schools are underperforming. As part of a larger reform package, in 1995 the legislature authorized the establishment of charter schools, which would be given increased flexibility to deliver education to student populations with special needs. Working under their own charter and granted freedom to manage their own schools, charter schools operate under the Texas Education Agency and receive their own accountability ranking based on test scores. While they receive state monies, as of 2014 charter schools do not receive local tax revenue or, in most cases, funding for facilities. Charter schools are able to receive privately raised funds. There is a cap in Texas of 215 open-enrollment charters with about 460 campuses across the state. Approximately 154,000 students attend these schools. Significantly, there are approximately 101,000 on waiting lists seeking admission to the schools.[29]

The criticisms of charter schools resemble, in some ways, the criticism of vouchers. Opponents fear that charter schools will drain money from public schools. While serving the needs of their specially identified student bodies, they will distract attention away from the needs of other, possibly more needy groups. In addition, there is some concern that charter schools will not be able to meet the challenges of educating youth any better than traditional public schools.

Increased Funding A third alternative to current education policy is rather simple. Spend more money, a lot more money. Here the idea is that Texas schools fail us because they are woefully underfunded. Salaries of teachers are too low and state regulations of the curriculum and classroom are too great. Get the best teachers to be in the classroom and the problem of public education will be able to right itself. Vouchers and charter schools are seen as threats to this alternative.

New interest groups have emerged over the last two sessions of the Texas legislature to champion approaches to educational reform far different from the business-led bipartisan efforts of the Bush and Perry years that championed testing and accountability.[30] Groups like Texans for Educational Reform, Texans Deserve Great Schools, and Raise Your Hand Texas will change the direction of the debate on education policy in the future.

The 2014 election may prove to be a pivotal election for educational policy in the state. Both gubernatorial candidates articulated positions calling for reform. Republican candidate Abbott called for pre-K programs with lofty goals but smaller budgets. Democratic candidate Wendy Davis called for increases in spending. Not surprisingly, these proposed increases were branded as excessive by Abbott attack ads.

Interestingly, the public appears to be in favor of increased expenditures going to public education, but it splits along partisan lines. A poll conducted by the University of Texas in 2014 found that 74 percent of Texans believed that increasing pay to teachers would be an effective way of improving public education in Texas, including 87 percent of Democrats and 65 percent of Republicans. Even 52 percent of self-identified Tea Partyers supported increased pay to teachers as a way to improve public education. But when respondents were asked if increasing overall funding would be effective, a different story emerged. Eighty-nine percent of Democrats agreed that increased overall funding would improve public education, but only 51 percent of Republicans did. One of the problems facing policy makers in the future will be negotiating reform proposals amid a divided electorate.[31]

● Welfare Policy

Describe the state's role in addressing poverty and how it is affected by national policies

One long-term policy issue has been how to provide for the basic needs of poor people in Texas. This issue raises fundamental questions about the state's role in helping people in poverty and the extent to which national policies determine the state's response to the needs of poor people.

The Texas Department of Public Welfare was established in 1939 during the New Deal. This photo shows farmers receiving support from the government at the time.

Poverty in Texas

Poverty has never been a popular subject in Texas. The idea that some individuals have trouble taking care of themselves or meeting the basic needs of their families seems to fly in the face of Texas's individualistic culture. In light of the booming Texas economy, many policy makers may have hoped that the poverty problem would go away. It hasn't. Between 1990 and 1999 the percentage of Texans living in poverty fell from 15.9 percent to 15.0 percent, but it rose again during the Great Recession. In 2014, 17.4 percent of Texans (4,270,218 people) lived below the poverty line. In addition, in October 2013 a total of 3,651,344 people were enrolled in Medicaid, the federally financed, state-operated program providing medical services to low-income people. Poverty remains one of the most intractable problems facing the state.[32]

Policy makers define poverty in very specific terms. Poverty is the condition under which individuals or families do not have the resources to meet their basic needs, including food, shelter, health care, transportation, and clothing. The U.S. Department of Health and Human Services developed a "poverty index" in 1964. This index was revised in 1969 and 1980. The index calculates the consumption requirements of families based on their size and composition. The poverty index is adjusted every year to account for the rate of inflation. Although there is considerable controversy as to whether it adequately measures the minimal needs of a family, the poverty index is the generally accepted standard against which poverty is measured.

In 2014 the federal poverty guideline was $11,670 a year for one person and $4,060 a year for each additional person in the family. Over 26 percent of Latinos and 23.8 percent of African Americans in Texas are poor. Of those over age 65 in Texas, 11.4 percent are poor compared with 9.4 percent in the nation as a whole. Poverty among children under age 18 is much higher in Texas (24.8 percent) than in the United States as a whole (20.8 percent).

Texas uses these federal poverty guidelines to determine eligibility for a variety of social programs. For example, a family of three is eligible for reduced-price school meals if the family is at no more than 185 percent of the poverty level. A family of three is eligible for free school meals if the family is at no more than 130 percent of the poverty level, and is eligible for food stamps (the Supplemental Nutritional Assistance Program or SNAP) if the family is at no more than 130 percent of the poverty level.

Since 2003 the Texas Health and Human Services Commission (HHS) has been responsible for overseeing the state's health and human services system, including the Department of Family and Protective Services, the Department of Assistance and Rehabilitative Services, the Department of Aging and Disability Services, and the Department of State Health Services (see Table 12.1). HHS is responsible for coordinating, determining eligibility for, and administering the major welfare and antipoverty programs in Texas, including Temporary Assistance to Needy Families (TANF), a welfare program for families with dependent children; Medicaid (a state-federal program providing health coverage to the poor); SNAP; and other programs to address family violence, provide disaster relief, and settle refugees. The appropriated budget for HHS programs is over $73.9 billion, 38.9 percent of all state appropriations. HHS agencies employ over 55,000 state workers at more than 1,000 locations.[33]

Poverty is a complicated policy issue in Texas. There are more than 200 programs administered by HHS that are aimed at different problems related to poverty. We will now focus attention upon two of the most important initiatives aimed at addressing poverty in Texas: welfare and health care financing. Understanding how these programs evolved over time and the reforms that were put into place over the past 20 years will shed considerable light on public-policy making in the state.

Welfare in Texas, 1935–96

The origins of modern welfare policy lie in President Franklin Delano Roosevelt's **New Deal**.[34] Prior to the 1930s welfare was considered to be a state and local responsibility. The Great Depression overwhelmed many state and local welfare arrangements, causing the federal government to expand its role in addressing the needs of the poor and the unemployed. The Social Security Act of 1935 transformed the way in which welfare policy was implemented in the United States. Along with two social insurance programs (Old Age Insurance and Unemployment Insurance), the Social Security Act established a number of state-federal public assistance programs: Aid for Dependent Children (ADC, later **Aid to Families with Dependent Children or AFDC**), Old Age Assistance (OAA), and Aid for the Blind (AB). States administered and determined the benefit levels for these programs. In exchange for federal assistance in funding, state programs had to meet certain minimum federal guidelines.

The Department of Public Welfare was established in Texas in 1939 to run the state's various public assistance programs. It was to be supervised by a state board of welfare, composed of three members appointed by the governor for six-year terms. The board appointed an executive director who, in turn, was the chief administrative officer of the department.[35]

Through the early 1960s the basic strategy adopted by welfare-policy makers in Texas was to minimize the cost to the state while maximizing federal dollars. Some programs were expanded during these years. In 1950, ADC became AFDC as mothers were included in the program. Other new social-service programs were also added. Much of the initiative for the expansion of welfare came from the federal government. One of the major issues in Texas was the problem of the constitutional ceiling on welfare spending. This had to be raised from $35 million in 1945 to $52 million in 1961, and again to $60 million in 1963.[36]

Welfare policy in Texas was transformed fundamentally in the 1960s. Federal court decisions between 1968 and 1971 effectively ended a series of policies such as bans on men in the houses of mothers receiving welfare and residency requirements, both of which had been used by states to keep welfare rolls low. In 1965, Congress established **Medicaid**, a state-federal program to finance health care for the poor. President Lyndon Johnson's "War on Poverty" also expanded the number of social service programs available to the poor. Increasingly, it was argued, the solution to alleviating poverty was through expanded federal control over welfare programs.

In 1965 the Department of Public Welfare was authorized to work with the federal government's new antipoverty programs. The welfare ceiling was raised to $80 million in 1969. Among the welfare programs administered by the department were four public assistance programs: AFDC, Aid for the Blind, Aid to

---

TABLE 12.1

Agency Budgets for the 2014–15 Biennium

Health and Human Services Commission: $48.5 billion

Department of Aging and Disability Services: $13.8 billion

Department of Assistive and Rehabilitative Services: $1.3 billion

Department of Family and Protective Services: $6.5 billion

Department of State Health Services: $6.2 billion

SOURCE: Texas Legislative Budget Board, *Fiscal Size-Up: 2014–15 Biennium*, p. 161.

New Deal President Franklin Delano Roosevelt's 1930s programs to stimulate the national economy and provide relief to victims of the Great Depression

Aid to Families with Dependent Children (AFDC) a federally and state-financed program for children living with parents or relatives who fell below state standards of need; replaced in 1996 by TANF

Medicaid a federal and state program financing medical services to low-income people

In 2012, 3.6 million Texans participated in the food stamps program (now called SNAP), which allows low-income people to buy groceries with a special debit card. SNAP benefits are paid by the federal government, but the state and federal governments share administrative costs.

Supplemental Security Income (SSI) a national welfare program passed in 1972 that provides assistance to low-income elderly or disabled individuals; replaced the federal-state programs that had offered assistance to the blind, the permanently and totally disabled, and the aged

the Permanently and Totally Disabled, and Old Age Assistance. The latter three programs were taken over by the federal government in 1972 in the form of the new national **Supplemental Security Income (SSI)** program to provide assistance to individuals in need who have disabilities or are aged. Along with these programs, the department ran the Texas Medical Assistance Program (Medicaid), the national food stamp program, and a series of social-service programs.

In 1977 the Department of Public Welfare became the Department of Human Resources. It was renamed again in 1985 as the Texas Department of Human Services and then as the Health and Human Services Commission in 2003. The name reflected an ongoing desire on the part of policy makers to think of the agency less as a welfare agency and more as a service agency to the poor. By 1980 the department was reorganized to focus on the major client groups it served: families with children and aged and disabled people. In 1981 the constitutional ceiling on welfare spending was replaced with a more flexible standard. Instead of having a flat cap of $80 million, welfare expenditures could not exceed 1 percent of the total state budget.

Between 1967 and 1973 participation rates and welfare expenditures in Texas exploded. The number of children on AFDC during this time rose from 79,914 to 325,244, while the number of families on AFDC went from 23,509 to 120,254. Rates leveled off in the late 1970s, but they began to push upward again in the 1980s. Liberal attempts to reform welfare by nationalizing AFDC (turning the state-federal program into a national program like SSI) failed throughout the 1970s. Conservative attempts to compel welfare recipients to participate in job-training programs, such as the Work Incentive Program of 1967, had limited success. A frustrating political stalemate set in. Few were happy with welfare policy as then conducted. But no consensus had emerged as to what would be a better alternative. Meanwhile, welfare rolls expanded and expenditures continued to increase in both Texas and the nation.

The Idea of Dependency and Welfare Reform in the 1990s

By the mid-1980s a new critique of welfare programs had begun to emerge. At its heart lay the idea that the well-intentioned policies of the 1960s had backfired, creating a dysfunctional underclass of people dependent on welfare. Welfare programs such as AFDC may have helped people financially in the short run, but in the long run they had robbed people of the character traits and the moral values that would enable them to succeed in a market economy.[37] Observers believed that the skyrocketing rate of children born to poor, unwed mothers was in part the result of a perverse set of incentives created by welfare programs. Under the existing welfare system, at least to a point, the more children you had, the higher the welfare payment. Because some states did not provide welfare to families with fathers in the home, fathers were actually being encouraged to abandon their families so that the families might qualify for welfare. According to critics, the poor needed encouragement and proper incentives to become independent workers rather than have a permanent source of income from the state.

At the national level, the deadlock over welfare reform was broken with the passage of the Family Support Act in 1988. In the attempt to stem the rising tide of illegitimacy rates and single-parent families among the poor, the act mandated two-parent coverage for all state AFDC programs. It also established a number of new "workfare" programs whose goals were to get people off welfare and into the workforce. New standards were also developed requiring parents to participate in these workfare programs or lose their benefits.[38]

Much hyperbole surrounded the passage of the Family Support Act. Although the act did break new ground in formulating programs to help people make the transition from welfare to work, it also was an important expansion of the existing AFDC system. Far from declining, welfare roll expansion was unabated in the early 1990s. In Texas, this expansion was especially rapid. By 1994 an average 786,400 people were receiving AFDC in Texas. Total federal and state expenditures rose from $188.3 million in 1984 to $544.9 million in 1994. Food stamp costs also rose rapidly during this period, from $664.9 million to $2.2 billion. But AFDC and food stamps were only part of the problem. Medicaid was escalating at a rate of more than 20 percent a year. During the 1994–95 biennium, $18.6 billion in state and federal funds was being spent on Medicaid. Texas's share was 13 percent of the state budget, or $6.7 billion. Escalating costs of AFDC, food stamps, and Medicaid provided the backdrop to the welfare reforms that would be put into place by Texas policy makers in 1995.

Growing discontent over welfare policy across the country encouraged many states to seek waivers from federal regulations so that they too might experiment with welfare reform.[39] Some states sought to modify AFDC rules to eliminate some of the perverse incentive structures in the welfare system. Other states set caps on benefits and how long one could continue to receive welfare. Welfare became a state issue during the 1994 elections. As governor of Texas, George W. Bush echoed the ideas of conservative critics of the welfare system, arguing that the existing system was robbing people of their independence. Among the changes that he called for were

- strengthening child-support procedures and penalties
- imposing a two-year limit on benefits for recipients able to work
- requiring individuals receiving welfare to accept a state-sponsored job if after two years they were unable to find work
- creating new child-care and job-training programs
- requiring unwed mothers to live with their parents or grandparents
- moving family support systems from the state to the local level

Data released by the comptroller's office lent support to the Bush contention that there were serious problems with the existing system of welfare in Texas. Over one-quarter of all welfare recipients in 1993 were "long-term" recipients who had remained on the rolls for five years or more. The publication of *A Partnership for Independence: Welfare Reform in Texas*, by the office of the comptroller, John Sharp, a Democrat, helped to set the legislative agenda for the debate over welfare policy. Agreeing with other critics across the nation who were unhappy with the current state of welfare policy, the report documented how welfare often failed to help those most in need or to encourage those dependent on welfare to become independent of government largesse. Among the report's 100 proposals were many of the reforms that had been put into place by conservative reformers in other states or by the Bush gubernatorial administration.

A bipartisan legislative coalition ultimately supported major welfare reform in Texas. On May 26, 1995, the vote on House Bill 1863 was 128 to 9 in the House and 30 to 1 in the Senate. The law provided a number of "carrot and stick" incentives that sought to mold the character of welfare recipients in positive ways and wean them off welfare. Among the carrots were expanded education and job-training programs, as well as a select number of pilot studies involving transitional child care and medical benefits. Among the sticks were a limitation on benefits to 36 months, alimony for ex-spouses who couldn't support themselves, and the institution of a five-year ban on reapplying for benefits once benefits ran out. To implement the state reforms, Texas secured a waiver from the federal government that freed the state from various federal regulations regarding welfare programs. In granting the waivers to Texas and other states, the Clinton administration hoped to stimulate innovative reforms that might be duplicated elsewhere.

Texas was ahead of the welfare reform curve in 1995. In 1996, President Bill Clinton signed into law the most important reform in federal welfare policy since the New Deal. The Personal Responsibility and Work Opportunity Reconciliation Act essentially rethought the assumptions that had guided the expansion of welfare programs for 60 years. Under the legislation, AFDC, JOBS (a work-related training program), and the Emergency Assistance Program were combined into one block grant entitled **Temporary Assistance for Needy Families (TANF)**. As with the welfare reforms instituted in Texas and in other states across the country, the primary purpose of TANF was to make families self-sufficient by ending the cycle of dependency on government benefits. States such as Texas were given great flexibility in setting benefit levels, eligibility requirements, and other program details.

Temporary Assistance for Needy Families (TANF) a welfare program passed in 1996 to provide temporary assistance to families with needy children; replacing the AFDC program, TANF sought to make poor families self-sufficient and to give states greater flexibility in setting benefit levels, eligibility requirements, and other program details

Today in Texas, TANF provides temporary financial assistance to families with needy children when one or both of the parents are missing or disabled.[40] The TANF program provides a onetime $1,000 payment to individuals in certain crisis situations. To qualify, a recipient's income must be below 17 percent of the poverty income limit based on family size. In addition, the combined equity of the family may not exceed $2,000 ($3,000 for the elderly and disabled). People participating in TANF receive a monthly assistance payment based on the size of their family. They cannot receive benefits for more than 36 months. They are also eligible for Medicaid benefits, food stamps, and child day-care services. Unless legally exempt, recipients are also required to participate in an employment services program.

The maximum monthly grant available to a household of three under TANF is low, only $277 a month. For the 2014–15 biennium $187.7 million in grants will be distributed to under 100,000 recipients on average per month, close to 85 percent being children. Of this money, $131.9 million (70.2 percent) will be from state General Revenue Funds, $55.9 million from federal funds (29.8 percent).

Evaluating Welfare Reforms

The welfare reforms in Texas have been evaluated along two dimensions. First, they are measured in terms of the number of people receiving welfare assistance from the state. Success is determined by the degree to which the reforms help lower the number of welfare recipients in Texas. If the reforms do not decrease the welfare rolls, they likely will be considered a failure. A second measure of success is the degree to which the reforms help take people off welfare and move them into the workforce as productive, independent members of society.

Judged by changes in the number of people on welfare, the reforms appear to be a success. The average monthly number of people on welfare in Texas rose from a little more than half a million in 1989 to a peak of more than three-quarters of a million in 1994 but then began to fall in 1995. Time limits and work requirements were put into place by the state legislature in 1995, one year before similar measures were passed nationally by the U.S. Congress. The decline in the number of people on welfare continued over the next decade, falling to 155,895 people in 2006 and to approximately 100,000 in 2014.[41]

By a second measure—the number of people moving from welfare to work— indications are that the welfare reforms of 1995 are more mixed in their success. Studies by the Center for Public Priorities in Austin over the past decade have found that caseloads on TANF may have fallen, but child poverty was on the rise. Moreover, there were indications that people leaving the welfare rolls were not necessarily transitioning to work. Such problems were likely exacerbated by the economic downturn of the Great Recession that began in 2008.[42] Welfare reform in the 1990s took place under conditions of a booming economy and a rising demand for all types of labor. Jobs seemed to be available for people who were willing and able to work. But how will the new welfare policies respond to the economic problems of the early decades of the twenty-first century? Now that labor markets have tightened and jobs are difficult to find, will Texas policy makers be satisfied with the welfare reforms in place? How far will unemployment be allowed to go before policy makers demand that we reconsider the incentive structure created to get people off the public dole? These are questions that policy makers concerned with welfare reform will have to consider one day. Only then will we be able to have a more accurate evaluation of the welfare reforms of the mid-1990s.

Though poverty in Texas afflicts many different social groups, Latinos currently make up the majority of Texans living below the poverty line. The border counties in Texas are by far the poorest in the state.

Medicaid and Health Care Policy

Explain why Medicaid in particular and health care policy in general have been so controversial in Texas

Health insurance is a major policy problem facing Texas. In 2010 it was estimated that 6.2 million Texans (24.6 percent of the state population) were without insurance. This number was the highest percentage in the nation. Figure 12.1 shows the breakdown of this uninsured population by age group. Approximately 1.2 million children under age 18 (16.3 percent) were without insurance, far below the national average of 9.8 percent.[43] A report released by Rice University's Baker Institute in April 2014 found that the uninsured rate had only fallen slightly since the implementation of the first stages of the Affordable Care Act, a piece of federal legislation, dubbed Obamacare, that sought to address the uninsured problem across the nation. According to the report, the uninsured population had fallen to 23.5 percent. Still, over 5 million people were believed to have no health insurance in the state.[44]

Medicaid

Other than health insurance programs established for state employees, Texas's principal policy initiative regarding health care and health insurance is Medicaid, a health financing program closely linked to poverty programs. Medicaid, which provides for the health care of poor people, particularly poor children, is an especially

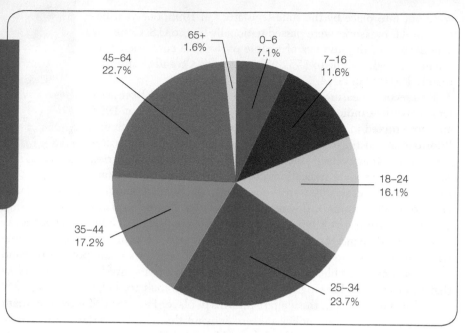

FIGURE 12.1

Texas's Uninsured Population by Age Group

SOURCE: Texas Health and Human Services Commission, *Texas Medicaid and CHIP in Perspective*, 9th ed. (January 2013), www.hhsc.state.tx.us/medicaid/about/PB/PinkBook.pdf, pp. 1–7.

Pie chart labels:
- 65+ 1.6%
- 0–6 7.1%
- 7–16 11.6%
- 18–24 16.1%
- 25–34 23.7%
- 35–44 17.2%
- 45–64 22.7%

costly program for the state. The caseload for Medicaid has exploded in recent years, pushed up by the Great Recession. Between 2008 and 2012 the caseload grew 26.8 percent, and it is expected to reach 4.2 million monthly clients by the end of the 2014–15 biennium. For the 2014–15 biennium a total of $56.2 billion of state and federal funds will be appropriated to Medicaid programs in Texas, an increase of $4.2 billion from the previous biennium. The program's costs have risen more quickly than the rate of inflation, which makes Medicaid increasingly burdensome for the state budget. Funding Medicaid is a major issue in the broader debate over the state and national governments' roles in providing health care.

Medicaid is a state-federal program that was established under the Social Security Amendments of 1965 as Title XIX of the Social Security Act. The Social Security Act requires that Texas and other states follow certain principles and meet certain standards if they are to receive federal funds. First, Medicaid services must be available on a statewide basis. Second, the same level of service must be available to all clients throughout the state. Children are entitled to a broader range of services than adults. Third, participants must be allowed to use any health provider who meets program standards. (Providers, of course, must be willing to accept Medicaid recipients.) Fourth, the amount, duration, and scope of medical services must be "sufficiently reasonable." Exactly what this constitutes is a problem, and Medicaid reimbursement rates tend to be much lower than those provided for under conventional private insurance plans. While Texas may limit the services provided to adult clients, it may not arbitrarily deny services for specific conditions or illnesses.

Federal law also allows states to be granted waivers from these principles to create programs directed toward particular clients. In this approach, federal Medicaid policy mirrors the initiatives in welfare policy by providing states more freedom of action in developing programs to serve clients. For example, Texas has been granted the authority to enroll clients in managed care programs. In traditional fee-for-service programs a doctor or a hospital provides a service directly to the patient and is paid a fee for that service. In the managed care organization (MCO) model, programs such as health maintenance organizations or doctor-hospital networks act as an intermediary between the patient and the doctor, and negotiate discounted fees for medical services. In addition, MCOs reimburse their member health care providers with a monthly payment, which is known as a capitation payment because it has a limit or "cap" based on medical expenses calculated for the average patient. The State of Texas Access Reform program (STAR) is the managed care program where the Health and Human Services Commission contracts with MCOs to provide health care in various areas to poor populations in Texas.

Another model, found primarily in rural areas in Texas, is now referred to as Traditional Medicaid. It is a noncapitated program enabling Medicaid recipients to receive medical home services from a primary care provider. As a noncapitated plan, it does not contain any average dollar amount per patient per month set by the state to pay for the cost of health care service. Primary care providers receive fee-for-service reimbursement and a small monthly management fee directly from the state. A recent initiative, Medicaid Rural Area STAR, has been implemented to provide managed care to clients in 164 mostly rural counties. The goal is to move rural clients away from traditional fee-for-service delivery as much as possible.

Managed care programs in Texas Medicaid have been growing in popularity since the early 1990s and became an essential part of cost containment measures instituted by the legislature over the next 20 years. In 1994, 2.9 percent of Texas Medicaid recipients were in state-sponsored managed care programs. By 2004 this participation had risen to 41.44 percent. By 2012 almost 78 percent of Medicaid recipients were in managed care programs.[45]

Medicaid Participation The initial goal of Medicaid in 1965 was to pay the medical bills of low-income individuals on public assistance. Over the last five decades, Medicaid has grown from a narrowly defined program targeting people on public assistance to a large, complex insurance program serving a variety of special groups. In the late 1980s and early 1990s Medicaid was expanded to include older adults not fully covered by Medicare (a federal medical insurance program funded through payroll taxes for persons age 65 and older), people with disabilities, and pregnant women. Individuals participating in TANF and SSI automatically qualify for Medicaid, as do others who meet these other criteria.

A variety of factors can affect an individual's eligibility to participate in Medicaid. People can go on and off Medicaid given their changing eligibility status. For example, eligibility can change when a parent or caregiver has a change in income or when a child is born. Eligibility also can change when a child reaches a certain age. For these reasons, there is significant fluctuation in Medicaid enrollment from month to month. However, one fact is strikingly clear: participation rates have gone up significantly in the first decade of the twenty-first century. Between 2001 and 2009 the average monthly Medicaid enrollment in Texas rose from 1.87 million people to 3.1 million.

The increase in participation is not caused by a rise in participation through Texas's principal public assistance program, the TANF program. As the number of monthly caseloads grew between 2001 and 2009 for Medicaid, the number of those eligible through the TANF actually decreased from approximately 500,000 to less than 350,000 in 2009. Although Medicaid and public assistance are still joined together, the close link between them that existed at the founding of Medicaid has largely been severed.

Figure 12.2 shows participation in Medicaid by age and ethnicity. Seventy-one percent of those on Medicaid are under the age of 20. Over 54 percent on Medicaid roles are Latino, 22 percent are white, and 17 percent are African American.

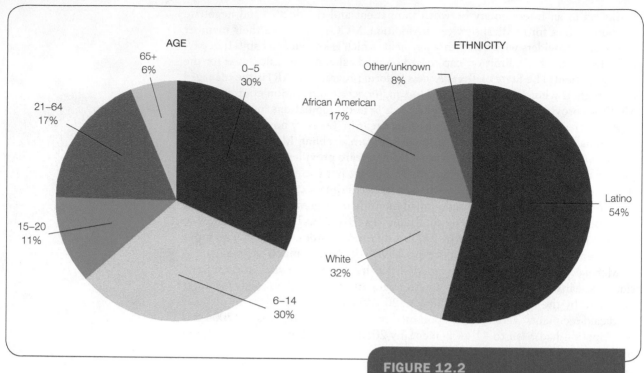

AGE

65+ 6%

21–64 17%

15–20 11%

0–5 30%

6–14 30%

ETHNICITY

Other/unknown 8%

African American 17%

White 32%

Latino 54%

FIGURE 12.2

Texas Medicaid Recipients by Age and Ethnicity

SOURCE: Texas Health and Human Services Commission, *Texas Medicaid and CHIP in Perspective*, 9th ed. (January 2013). www.hhsc.state.tx.us/medicaid/about/PB/PinkBook. pdf, pp. 5, 13–14.

Administration and Financing of Medicaid in Texas In Texas, Medicaid is administered through the Texas Health and Human Services Commission. At the federal level, the Centers for Medicare and Medicaid in the Department of Health and Human Services monitor Texas's Medicaid program and establish basic services, delivery, quality, funding, and eligibility standards. Through Medicaid, Texas and the federal government together pay for a variety of health care services for a number of low-income populations. The acute health care services paid for include physicians' bills, inpatient care in a hospital and outpatient care, and pharmacy, lab, and X-ray services. Medicaid also provides for selected long-term and support services, including home- and community-based services for the disabled, home-health and personal care, and nursing services (Figure 12.3).

The federal portion of the program is determined every year by comparing average state per capita income to the average national per capita income. Each state thus has its own FMAP (the federal medical assistance percentage). Poorer states receive more federal assistance for the program than richer states. In 2014 the FMAP for Texas was 58.69 percent, which means that 41.31 percent of all Medicaid expenditures were state funded.[46]

A related program to Medicaid is the Children's Health Insurance Program (CHIP), which provides coverage for children in families with incomes too high

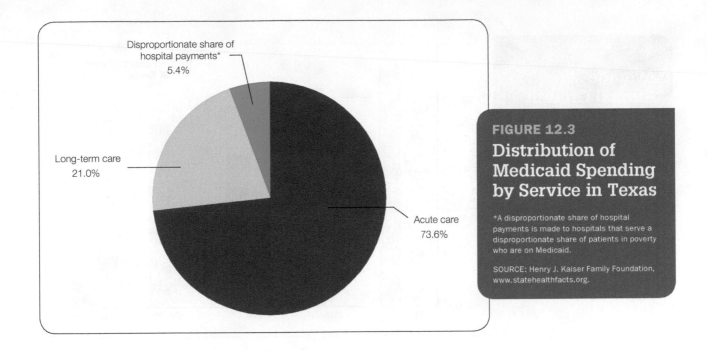

FIGURE 12.3

Distribution of Medicaid Spending by Service in Texas

Disproportionate share of hospital payments*
5.4%

Long-term care
21.0%

Acute care
73.6%

*A disproportionate share of hospital payments is made to hospitals that serve a disproportionate share of patients in poverty who are on Medicaid.

SOURCE: Henry J. Kaiser Family Foundation, www.statehealthfacts.org.

to qualify for Medicaid. Established in 1997 under Title XXI of the Social Security Act, CHIP is administered like Medicaid through the Centers for Medicare and Medicaid Services in the U.S. Department of Health and Human Services. The 2010 federal allocation to Texas for CHIP was more than $925 million. The average monthly caseload for CHIP was 497,666 in 2002. After falling to 312,101 in 2007 before the Great Recession, enrollment in CHIP has fluctuated between 500,000 in early 2010 and 600,000 in early 2013. Participation numbers were falling throughout the first half of 2014 as the economy continued to improve, dropping below 500,000 in April 2014. The bulk of the increase in Medicaid caseload in the 2014–15 biennium mentioned in Chapter 11 will come because of the transfer of children from CHIP to Medicaid under the Affordable Care Act.

Medicaid and CHIP expenditures have become an increasing part of both the national and state budgets. In 1996 the total Medicaid budget of both federal and state dollars was $8.2 billion. By 2009 this had risen to $22.8 billion. By 2009 federal expenditures on Medicaid and CHIP encompassed 7 percent of the $3.5 trillion federal budget.[47] For Texas in October 2013 the monthly enrollment on Medicaid had reached 3,651,344 people. Figure 12.4 shows the average increases in Medicaid spending between 1990 and 2012. Figure 12.5 shows the distribution of Medicaid payments across various enrollment groups.

Broader Health Care Issues in Texas

Medicaid policy is embedded in a larger national discussion over health care in America and the proper way to fund it. Numerous controversies divide the public and politicians at all levels of government. Is health care fundamentally a private or a public issue? How can exploding health care costs, including the costs of private health care insurance like Blue Cross/Blue Shield or public health care insurance like Medicare and Medicaid, be brought under control? Should individuals be compelled to purchase health care insurance? How much and what kind of

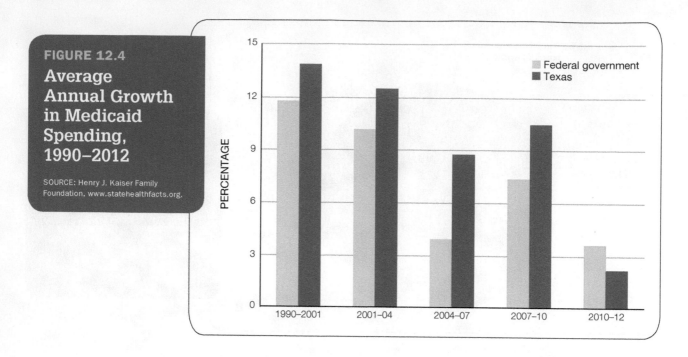

FIGURE 12.4

Average Annual Growth in Medicaid Spending, 1990–2012

SOURCE: Henry J. Kaiser Family Foundation, www.statehealthfacts.org.

insurance? Who should foot the bill for individuals who cannot afford to pay for private insurance? What is the proper role for the state and federal governments in the delivery of health care across the nation?

As in other state-federal programs, federal money for Medicaid is accompanied by federal rules and regulations with which the state must comply in order to maintain this funding. This sometimes breeds tremendous political controversy between the state and the federal government. One such controversy broke out in early 2012 over provisions relating to Texas's Medicaid Women's Health Program.[48]

The Medicaid Women's Health Program in Texas serves more than 100,000 women and is funded by $35 million from federal funds and $7 million from state funds. Through subsidized clinics located across the state, the program helps pay for birth control, health screening, and family exams for a select group of women on Medicaid. Planned Parenthood offers these services as well as abortion services at its various clinics across the state. Conservatives in Texas, including Governor Perry, were unhappy with any state monies being used to subsidize groups supporting abortion and moved to cut program funds from going to these clinics. But federal regulations clearly state that patients in the program, not state officials, decide where money from the program is spent.

By March 2012 an impasse had been reached. On one side were Governor Perry and the Republican-dominated state legislature, who ordered an end to Medicaid funding of Planned Parenthood clinics. On the other side were the federal government and supporters of Planned Parenthood, who insisted on strictly following federal rules and guidelines. Interestingly, some moderate Republicans, like Senator Kay Bailey Hutcheson, broke with the governor and backed Planned Parenthood in the dispute. By early March 2012 all federal funding of the Texas Women's Health Program had been pulled. Governor Perry claimed that he would find new funding for the program at the state level that would exclude Planned Parenthood.

In early May 2012 the issue became even more complicated. Eight Planned Parenthood clinics that did not provide abortion services sued the state, claiming

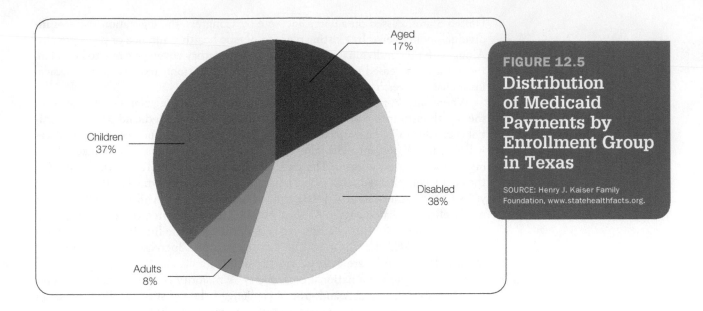

FIGURE 12.5

Distribution of Medicaid Payments by Enrollment Group in Texas

SOURCE: Henry J. Kaiser Family Foundation, www.statehealthfacts.org.

Aged
17%

Children
37%

Disabled
38%

Adults
8%

their rights to freedom of speech and freedom of association had been violated. A federal appeals court ruled on August 22, 2012 that Texas could ban Planned Parenthood from receiving funds. Texas solicitor general Jonathan Mitchell reiterated the state's opposition to providing taxpayer money "to entities that affiliate with abortion-promoting entities."[49] The conflict over the funding and administration of the Texas Women's Health Program signals the emergence of a new set of conflicts over Medicaid in Texas and a new round in the debate over the relationship between the national and the state government in the federal system. Cost, however, is the single most important issue confronting policy makers regarding Medicaid in Texas. Now encompassing more than 25 percent of state expenditures, Medicaid in Texas as in other states threatens to overwhelm the budget. In the spring of 2012, Texas comptroller Susan Combs began referring to Medicaid as "The Big Red," the program that was going to push an otherwise healthy state budget into the red. She claimed that by 2023 "Big Red is going to be over a third of state spending."[50] Medicaid expenditures, many mandated by the federal government, would begin to crowd out other forms of spending from the state budget.

Policy makers are forever looking for ways to make the program less costly. Two strategies have predominated over the past 20 years: first, to bring more efficiency into the program by expanding managed care initiatives across the state, and second, to institute cost controls and cutbacks to providers. Both efforts have had limited success, and at the same time have sparked concern over the quality of care being offered to Medicaid participants across the state. As cost containment efforts intensify, Texas policy makers inside and outside the legislature will be compelled to increase their monitoring of the delivery of the program.

The Affordable Care Act

In March 2010, Congress passed two bills, the Patient Protection and Affordable Care Act and the Health Care and Reconciliation Act of 2010, which together became known as the Affordable Care Act (ACA), often referred to as Obamacare. The passage of the ACA transformed the debate over health care policy in the

United States. Passed on a party line vote by Congress, the legislation requires in-dividuals not covered by existing plans to pursue health insurance or pay a penalty. Along with this "individual mandate," as the mandatory coverage came to be called, the act also increased coverage for preexisting conditions and expanded medical insurance to an estimated 30 million people.[51]

When fully implemented, the ACA is expected to bring significant change to the health insurance market in Texas as well as to Texas's Medicaid program.[52] Initial estimates in 2012 projected that under the ACA, insurance coverage in Texas will rise to 91 percent, with almost 40 percent of the remaining uninsured being undocumented persons. The expansion of Medicaid in Texas will be funded through a complicated set of subsidies based on family income. For the first three years of the expansion (2014–16), the federal government will cover all costs for newly eligible participants in Medicaid and CHIP. Thereafter, the percentage will slowly decline, committing Texas to a larger portion of the funding. The long-term effect of the ACA for Texas will be a budgetary one. Increased expenditures on Medicaid and health care in Texas are all but inevitable.

The ACA sparked a national controversy. A majority of the states and a number of private individuals and groups challenged the constitutionality of the act in court, focusing on the mandatory coverage provisions. For three days in March 2012 the U.S. Supreme Court held oral argument on the case, *National Federation of Independent Business v. Sebelius*. A complicated decision was delivered by a divided Court on June 28, 2012. Four liberal justices believed that most features of the ACA were constitutional. Four conservative justices countered that they were not. Representing the decisive vote, Chief Justice Roberts rejected the idea that people could be mandated or forced to buy insurance under Congress's power to regulate commerce, but he nevertheless concluded that a tax penalizing people who did not get medical insurance met constitutional muster. Regarding the expansion of Medicaid, he supported a conservative position, arguing that states could not be bullied into expanding medical insurance coverage for poorer segments of the population. Chief Justice Roberts wrote that for federalism to thrive, states had to have a meaningful and real choice as to whether or not they would participate in federally sponsored programs.

The complicated U.S. Supreme Court decision opened the door for a new round of political posturing around the health care issue in Texas. Governor Perry announced that Texas would refuse to participate in the expanded Medicaid program, giving up millions of federal dollars for not having to incur new financial responsibilities at the state level. The state legislature, supporting Governor Perry, has refused to expand Medicaid in Texas. An estimate by the Kaiser Family Foundation in 2014 concluded that over 1 million uninsured adults in Texas, 17 percent of the uninsured in the state, would not be brought under the ACA provisions to expand Medicaid because of Texas's actions (or inactions).[53] Perry also decided that the state would not go into the business of designing an insurance exchange in the state. Texas would let the federal government sell federally designed insurance policies in the state on its own.

As if things weren't complicated enough in the emerging discussion over what to do about Medicaid and health care coverage in Texas, a 2012 survey was released by the Texas Medical Association that found only 31 percent of Texas doctors were accepting new patients who relied on Medicaid for insurance coverage, down from 42 percent in 2012 and 67 percent in 2000. Low payment and excessive red tape were cited as the reasons for the declining acceptance of Medicaid as a form of medical insurance.[54] Further complicating matters, officials from the Texas Health

The Texas Sonogram Law

In 2011 the Texas legislature passed a law requiring doctors who perform abortions to provide a sonogram to women before carrying out the procedure. Abortion laws are among the most contentious social policies in the United States, and the Texas law garnered national attention. Conservative supporters of the sonogram policy passed it through the Texas legislature, and it was signed into law by former governor Rick Perry, who at the time was preparing his 2012 run for president. Opponents of the law immediately challenged it in court, arguing that it is unconstitutional given the U.S. Supreme Court's rulings in abortion cases since the landmark *Roe v. Wade* in 1973.

The law requires doctors to provide with the sonogram "a simultaneous verbal explanation of the results of the live, real-time sonogram images, including a medical description of the dimensions of the embryo or fetus, the presence of cardiac activity, and the presence of arms, legs, external members, and internal organs." Doctors are also required to make the fetus's heartbeat audible to the woman. Although the law does not require vaginal sonograms, which entail an invasive procedure of inserting a probe into the pregnant woman's vagina, some cases would require this type of sonogram, according to medical experts. Pregnant women affected by the law may choose not to view the sonogram, listen to the doctor's explanations, or listen to the heartbeat. However, doctors who refuse to comply with the law are subject to losing their licenses to practice medicine. Doctors are not required to perform the sonogram procedure for women who were impregnated as a result of rape or incest.

Proponents of Texas's new law argue that because abortion involves a nascent human life, efforts to make women think twice about going forward with an abortion should be implemented. They believe that the state has a compelling interest to protect the lives of what they consider to be human beings in the earliest stages of development. Supporters emphasize

that women can still go forward with a legal abortion if they so choose, but they should have full and complete information about the consequences of the decision they are making. They also argue that the procedure is constitutional because it does not prevent women from having abortions; it only makes them go through an additional step. The Court, they argue, has already upheld waiting periods and parental consent laws for abortion, and this law falls in the same vein.

Opponents of the new law argue that abortion is a constitutional right that has been protected by the Supreme Court and that, through forcing women to take the extra step of having a sonogram, the state is making it more difficult for women to exercise this right. They cite the Court's argument that no abortion law can place an undue burden on women who choose to obtain an abortion, and they note that the law makes women come into a medical office twice—once for the sonogram and again for the abortion after the 24-hour waiting period. In particular, opponents argue that vaginal ultrasounds invade a woman's privacy, as they necessarily involve an invasive procedure that women should not be required to endure. They also argue that the law violates doctors' First Amendment rights because it requires them to make statements and perform activities that are not medically necessary and that some women may not want.

Opponents sought a court ruling to delay the implementation of the law, but in February 2012, a federal district court judge refused to delay the law, deciding that the U.S. Court of Appeals for the Fifth Circuit, which includes Texas, had already ruled that the law was constitutional. In March 2014 the Fifth Circuit agreed with the district court judge and allowed the law to remain on the books. The U.S. Supreme Court also decided not to hear the challenge, which means that the law will remain in effect for the foreseeable future.

critical thinking questions

1. What are the trade-offs of this piece of legislation? Does it balance the rights of women and the interests of the state to protect fetuses?

2. Are there any possible compromises to this issue? If so, what would they look like?

and Human Services Commission released a new estimate of the costs of the ACA in Texas based upon new, more conservative assumptions about how quickly newly eligible people might apply to participate in the program. The new estimates were 42 percent less than the original ones. In July 2012 state officials believed that if Texas opted into the new ACA Medicaid programs, by 2023 the state would spend $15.6 billion of state money and bring in $100.1 billion of federal money. Despite these new projections, neither the Health and Human Services commissioner Tom Suehs nor Governor Perry believed that Texas should opt into the new ACA programs. Before Texas should participate in an expanded program, they believed the act should be "fixed" by Congress.[55]

The ACA is in effect, but it is unclear what that will mean for poorer Texans. Individuals will have to buy a health insurance package or pay a penalty on their federal income tax. Federal exchanges will be offering health insurance, but not with the assistance of Texas. The failure to opt into the expanded federal programs under ACA will mean a sizable portion of the poor population will continue to not have health insurance coverage, including undocumented persons whose health care was not addressed under the ACA. One thing is clear: few individuals are willing to argue that Texas has solved the problem of providing health care to the poor. In a report released by the federal Agency for Health Research and Quality in July 2012, Texas ranked dead last in health care services and delivery.[56]

● Water Policy

Consider the growing importance of policies related to water supplies in Texas

Water is the life blood of Texas. Access to plentiful water supplies over the past 100 years has been a necessary condition for a thriving economy and an expanding urban population in Texas. Approximately 59 percent of the water used in Texas comes from aquifers (underground pools of water), the vast majority of which (60 percent) is used in irrigation, particularly in the arid Panhandle region (Figure 12.6). The remainder comes from surface sources, including rivers and reservoirs. Twenty-seven percent of the state's water use is in municipal areas. Individual cities rely on various amounts of aquifer and surface water, but overall, aquifers are the source for more than one-third of the water consumed by metropolitan areas.

Texas's water consumption is projected to increase by 82 percent, from about 18 million acre-feet per year in 2010 to about 22 million acre-feet per year in 2060.[57] An acre-foot is a volume measurement used by water planners. It comprises an acre of area (66 feet × 660 feet) one foot deep.[58] At the same time, existing supplies under current systems of production and conservation are expected to decrease by 10 percent, largely as a result of the depletion of the Ogallala Aquifer in the Texas Panhandle and reduced reliance on the Gulf Coast Aquifer. By 2060 experts project that an additional 8.3 million acre-feet per year will be needed for the state to continue to thrive.

Formulating a coherent water policy in Texas to address these and other issues is difficult for many reasons. As noted in Chapter 1, Texas is a large state with a diverse climate. The water-related issues along the Gulf Coast in southeast Texas near Houston, which is subtropical and humid, are quite different from those in the high plains Panhandle, which is semiarid savanna, or in the El Paso desert. For

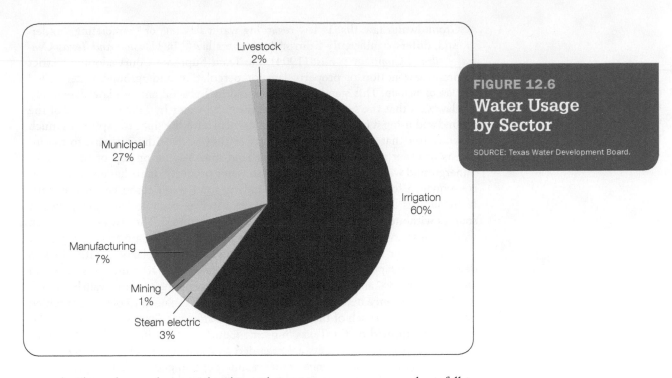

FIGURE 12.6
Water Usage by Sector

SOURCE: Texas Water Development Board.

Livestock 2%
Municipal 27%
Manufacturing 7%
Mining 1%
Steam electric 3%
Irrigation 60%

example, along the southeastern border with Louisiana, average annual rainfall is more than 80 inches per year, while near El Paso it is only 10 inches per year.[59] There are 15 major river basins and 8 coastal basins across the state, as well as 9 major and 21 minor aquifers.

Water policy is further complicated by the fact that various regions of the state have periodically experienced severe droughts and devastating floods. Throughout the twentieth century, reservoirs have been built to more effectively distribute water during times of shortage and to control flooding. In 1913, when the Texas Board of Water Engineers was established, there were only 8 major reservoirs in the state. By 1950 the number of major reservoirs had grown to 53. Today there are 188.[60]

Water Law in Texas

Underlying water policy in Texas is a complicated system of private property rights derived from three sources: Spanish law, traditional English common law, and statutory law. Texas law recognizes several legal classes of water rights for surface water and groundwater that are governed by different rules. Historically, these variations in the law have made the forging of water policy an arduous and at times a politically charged matter.

In 1967 the law covering surface water and relatively well-defined underground streams was clarified when the state legislature passed the Water Rights Adjudication Act. This legislation essentially merged the various water rights doctrines dating back to the nineteenth century into a unified water permit system. It requires individuals seeking water rights to file a claim with the Texas Commission on Environmental Quality (originally called the Texas Water Commission) before using the water. A complex administrative and judicial process was put into place that essentially grants water rights holders certificates of adjudicated water rights. The ability of the state to control and manage surface water use thus was greatly expanded by the 1967 act.[61]

Groundwater law, that is, law regarding water flowing, or "percolating," under-ground, differs significantly from surface water law.[62] In *Houston and Texas Cen-tral Railroad Company v. East* (1904), the Texas Supreme Court adopted a strict common law notion of property law for percolating underground water called the **law of capture**. This standard is also found in Texas oil and gas law. Essentially, the law says that the first person to "capture" the water by pumping it out of the ground and using it owns the water. Landowners have the right to capture as much groundwater that is under their property as they wish without regard to the in-terests of other property owners whose land may also lie on top of the pool of underground water. The rule of capture in water property rights has one important consequence for the development of underground water resources in the state. It encourages landowners to take as much water as possible from groundwater sources without considering the needs of other consumers. The law of capture can work against conservation efforts of private individuals who are trying to protect the water under their lands. It can also undercut efforts of planning authorities to develop a water plan for a particular area that takes into account the short-term and long-term availability of water as well as the competing uses for available water.

Finding a balance between the law of capture and the need to plan has troubled policy makers for much of the last 60 years. *Houston and Texas Central Railroad v. East* was reaffirmed by the Texas Supreme Court in 1955. In its ruling, the court stated that "percolating waters are regarded as the property of the owner of the surface who may, in the absence of malice, intercept, impede and appropriate such waters while they are on their premises, and make whatever use of them they please, regardless of the fact that use cuts off the flow of such waters to adjoining land and deprives the adjoining owner of their use." Nevertheless, the court also accepted the state's authority to regulate groundwater. In 1949 the state legisla-ture passed the Texas Groundwater Act, which created water districts to manage groundwater supply.

Today there are 99 groundwater districts in Texas with varying powers. The smallest district is the Red Sands Groundwater Conservation District in Hidalgo County, covering 31 square miles. The largest is the High Plains Underground Wa-ter District, covering 12,000 square miles over the Ogallala Aquifer. Generally, the groundwater districts are able to develop regulations to protect the water supply provided by groundwater sources, including rules that may restrict pumping, re-quire well permits, delineate well-spacing, and establish rates of water usage. The rules and regulations generated by these groundwater districts, however, can come into direct conflict with the law of capture, as we will see later.[63]

Planning Authorities and Water Policy

The history of water planning in Texas stretches back to the early twentieth cen-tury. A constitutional amendment in 1904 paved the way for the development of various agencies and authorities concerned with water planning. Among the most important innovations put into place by the state legislature in the early 1900s were drainage districts (1905); conservation and reclamation districts, later referred to as river authorities (1917); and water and control improvement districts (1925).

From 1950 to 1956 Texas experienced its worst drought in history. Every major urban area experienced the effect of the drought, many turning to emergency sup-plies and to rationing. In 1957 the drought was ended by heavy rains that resulted in the massive flooding of every major river and tributary in the state. Two hundred fifty-three of Texas's counties were declared disaster areas. Estimates were that the

law of capture the idea that the first person "to capture" water or oil by pumping it out of the ground and using it owns that water or oil

What Are the Trade-Offs in Texas Public Policy?

The contemporary Texas government tends to pass conservative policies (low taxes and lower levels of social services). The figures below show this in comparison to other states. Texas collects the sixth lowest share of taxes of any state. But when government lacks revenue, it cannot spend money to address social problems, such as providing health insurance to those who cannot afford it.

State Taxes (as a percentage of gross state product)

Sixth lowest state taxes
7.9%

7.0% ●●●●● 12.8%

Percentage without Health Insurance

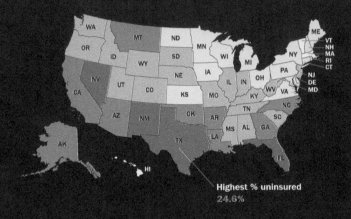

Highest % uninsured
24.6%

4.1% ●●●●● 24.6%

State Taxes Compared with Percentage Uninsured*

	Low Tax Rank	Uninsured Rank		Low Tax Rank	Uninsured Rank		Low Tax Rank	Uninsured Rank
Alaska	1	6	Georgia	18	5	Oregon	35	16
South Dakota	2	21	Colorado	19	26	Arkansas	36	7
Tennessee	3	25	Delaware	20	42	Hawaii	37	48
Louisiana	4	8	Virginia	21	33	Vermont	38	49
Wyoming	5	16	Utah	22	21	Maryland	39	34
Texas	6	1	Washington	23	27	Illinois	40	27
New Hampshire	7	37	Florida	24	4	Pennsylvania	41	37
Alabama	8	19	Kentucky	25	15	Maine	42	45
Nevada	9	2	Idaho	26	14	Massachusetts	43	50
South Carolina	10	23	Iowa	27	43	Minnesota	44	46
Arizona	11	10	Indiana	28	29	Rhode Island	45	35
New Mexico	12	3	Kansas	29	32	Wisconsin	46	44
Montana	13	9	Nebraska	30	30	California	47	11
Mississippi	14	18	Ohio	31	35	Connecticut	48	47
Oklahoma	15	12	West Virginia	32	20	New Jersey	49	24
North Dakota	16	39	Michigan	33	41	New York	50	40
Missouri	17	30	North Carolina	34	12			

*States with the same percentage of uninsured individuals have been given the same rank.

SOURCES:
Tax Data: 2010 tax data from TaxFoundation.org (accessed 3/7/14).
Uninsured Data: 2012 uninsured data from U.S. Census Bureau, Current Population Survey, Annual Social and Economic Supplements, www.census.gov (accessed 3/7/14).

for critical analysis

1. What appears to be the relationship between state taxes and insurance rates in a state?

2. When Obamacare is fully implemented, will the numbers of uninsured change? Why or why not?

drought had cost the state hundreds of millions of dollars. Damages from flooding were calculated to cost another $120 million. Calls for a more permanent planning and policy agency to direct and coordinate water policy came from all over the state.[64]

New agencies were established by the state in the 1960s to address various water issues. In 1977 the three major state water agencies (the TWDB, the TWRC, and the Water Quality Board) were combined into the Texas Department of Water Resources, whose job was to develop Texas's water resources, maintain the quality of water, and assure an equitable distribution of water rights. Sunset legislation in 1985 reorganized this single agency into two new agencies: a new Texas Water Commission and a new version of the Texas Water Development Board. Today, the TWDB is the state's primary water planning and financing agency. Enforcement of the state's environmental regulations regarding water is the job of the Texas Commission on Environmental Quality, an agency that resulted from the 1993 consolidation of the Texas Water Commission with the Texas Air Control Board.[65]

The TWDB is composed of a six-member board serving six-year terms with overlapping membership. Each member comes from a different part of the state. Since 1997, when the legislature passed an omnibus water planning law, the TWDB has had a number of important responsibilities, including the following:

- Supporting the development of 16 regional water plans
- Developing a state water plan every five years
- Providing financial assistance to local governments for (1) water supply and waste management projects, (2) flood protection and control projects, (3) agricultural water conservation projects, and (4) the creation of groundwater districts
- Administering the Texas Water Bank, which facilitates the transfer, sale, and lease of water and water rights throughout the state
- Administering the Texas Water Trust, which holds water rights for environmental flow maintenance purposes
- Data collection for the state's freshwater needs[66]

A number of strategies for meeting the short- and long-term water needs in the state were articulated in the 2012 State Water Plan. Two elements of the plan stand out. First, there is a notable focus on the importance of conservation. Policy makers agree that in the future water must be used more efficiently in Texas. One of the most important policies is a conservation strategy throughout all regions that seeks a more efficient use of current water supplies. Second, there is an emphasis on the importance of expanding and developing available surface water throughout Texas. The plan calls for the building of 26 new major reservoirs by 2060, each with a storage capacity of at least 5,000 acre-feet. Most of the proposed reservoirs would be along the Interstate Highway 35 corridor, where rainfall and runoff are more plentiful than in the western part of the state.[67] Another surface water recommendation is to build new pipeline infrastructure from existing sources to new points of use. Proposed construction includes a pipeline from Lake Palestine to Dallas and from Tarrant Regional Water District Lakes to Fort Worth. Such projects represent an important shift in existing water policy in some planning areas, as they shift the focus of water policy from flood control or hydroelectric power generation to the provision of water.

Groundwater strategies include the expansion of production by drilling more wells or building treatment plants for water quality. Conservation efforts also play a major part in groundwater initiatives, as some of the aquifers are experiencing overuse. The TWDB estimates that total groundwater supplies available to Texans will decline by 30 percent between 2010 and 2060. The Ogallala Aquifer (which runs from the Texas high plains up through western Kansas and into Nebraska) and the Edwards Aquifer (which runs along the Balcones fault line near San Antonio) are estimated to decline by 50 percent by 2060.

The total capital needs of funding these future initiatives proposed by regional water planning groups are estimated to be $53 billion, along with annual operating and maintenance costs. But cost is not the only challenge facing water policy makers. Some environmental groups in the state are opposed to the further expansion of the state reservoir system, arguing that the costs to the ecosystem of the state far outweigh the advantages provided by more water. On the other hand, some property owners, particularly in west Texas, are opposed to any new conservation restrictions or penalties put upon them by the state. Texas water law itself may be one of the most intractable problems that water planners may have to face in coming years.

On February 24, 2012, the Texas Supreme Court ruled on the case *The Edwards Aquifer Authority v. Burrell Day and Joel McDaniel*, which has important implications for future attempts to regulate water usage in Texas, particularly in those areas that rely heavily upon aquifers. The case involved two farmers who had applied to the Edwards Aquifer Authority for permission to pump 700 acre-feet per year of water to irrigate their 350-acre ranch in Van Ormy, a small town south of San Antonio. The farmers argued that they had rights to water from the aquifer based on their ownership of land above it. Maintaining that the farmers were unable to prove "historical use" of water from the aquifer, the authority granted them a permit for pumping only 14 acre-feet.

Writing for the 9–0 court majority, Justice Hecht ruled that using "historical use" as a criterion for granting a permit to pump water was a departure from the Texas Water Code. "Unquestionably," Hecht wrote, "the state is empowered to regulate groundwater production . . . [but] groundwater in place is owned by the landowner on the basis of oil and gas law."[68] Texas regulatory authorities thus had the power to reasonably regulate the use of water drawn from an aquifer in the public interest, but they may have to pay property owners with a stake in that water any damages that are incurred by the regulation.

The ruling sparked a firestorm of controversy among interested parties. Landowners celebrated the decision as vindication of their ownership of water under their lands. In contrast, state planning authorities and environmentalists were aghast at the implications that the case could have for their attempts to efficiently allocate and conserve water in Texas. The Texas Supreme Court's ruling raised an important question regarding water policy in Texas: Which policy-making body would dominate water policy in the foreseeable future in Texas? Would it be the courts working through judicial interpretations of the applicability of water property law? Or would it be the regulatory bodies whose job was to plan and to allocate water based on their assessment of available water supplies and the competing needs for water? Developing regulatory rules for the use of aquifer water that both protect property rights and promote the public interest through reasonable and efficient regulations will be a challenge facing these policy makers in years to come.[69]

A major step toward planning for water in the future took place in November 2013, when voters approved a constitutional amendment to create a $2.0 billion water fund. The bulk of the monies being directed to water policy came from a onetime transfer of money from the Rainy Day Fund to the State Water Implementation Fund for Texas (SWIFT). Proponents claimed that the two accounts

The drought of 2011 was the worst in the history of Texas. The drought extended into 2012, 2013, and 2014, threatening the state's prosperity, causing dust storms in the Texas panhandle (top), and drying lake beds throughout the state. Many of the state's cities were put on various levels of water emergencies that restricted use. Some smaller towns saw their water supplies drift down to 60 days and less.

could fund over $25 billion in water development projects over the next 50 years.

The basic idea behind this water initiative is that SWIFT projects would generate revenue that would go into another account (the State Water Implementation Revenue Fund for Texas or SWIRFT) that could be used to fund more water projects. Proposals for projects to be funded by the SWIFT and SWIRFT would come from regional water planning groups and could include such things as building new reservoirs, fixing pipes, and groundwater development. A number of provisos were attached to the legislation that put forward the constitutional amendment: 20 percent of the funds had to be directed to conservation and 10 percent would have to serve rural areas. Interestingly, concerns were raised about the fact that the agency managing the program, the Texas Water Development Board, might be too close to the governor given that the board would be appointed by him or her. The authorizing legislation thus established a separate committee to oversee how the SWIFT and SWIRFT funds are managed. The committee would be appointed by the Speaker of the House and the lieutenant governor and be composed of the comptroller, three state representatives, and three state senators. Planning for Texas's water future did not mean that traditional concerns over too much executive power in public policy matters would be ignored.[70]

● Thinking Critically about Public Policy in Texas

In this chapter, we examined various aspects of public-policy making in Texas. We focused particular attention on the complex issues that have driven policy making in public education, welfare, health care, and water policy. Looking at these matters with a critical eye demands that we pay attention to a number of key political questions: Who benefits by a particular public policy? Who pays for the policy? What ideas are used to justify or legitimate a particular program? How do particular public policies evolve and change over time to address new problems? How do they alter the relationship between individual citizens and the government that represents them in Austin?

In earlier chapters, we saw how the high-tech revolution transformed Texas's economy in the 1980s and '90s. We also traced how social and political changes have restructured the political party system in the state and the increasing power of the Republican Party. In this chapter, we have seen how many of these shifts resulted in important changes in public policy in the twentieth and twenty-first centuries. These policy changes are occurring as the Texas political economy moves from an oil, cattle, and cotton economy into an era of computers, high technology, and globalization. We can't be sure exactly where public policy in Texas will go in the next decade. We can be sure that new solutions will be required in the areas of welfare, education, health care, and water policy as the Texas political system tries to meet the challenges and opportunities of the twenty-first century.

In Chapter 13, we will explore one final area of public policy that differs in many ways from the four broad areas of public policy considered in this chapter. The criminal justice system in the state performs two of the most important functions of any state: maintaining order and policing society.

The Policy-Making Process

Describe the key steps and concepts in the policy-making process (pp. 384–87)

Public policies are the outcomes of governmental institutions. There are a number of stages in the policy-making process. One stage is problem identification, where political actors and society at large develop an understanding of a problem and how that problem can be addressed. The second stage in the process is policy formulation, where strategies for dealing with specifically defined problems are developed. The third stage is policy implementation, where the goals of public policy along with sanctions to support them are put into effect by a particular government agency. A fourth stage of the process is evaluation, where efforts are made to evaluate the effectiveness of a policy. Some political scientists argue that still another stage in the process is policy legitimation, where the legality of a particular policy initiative is determined.

Key Terms

rationality (p. 386)

bounded rationality (p. 387)

Practice Quiz

1. Satisficing means that policies are developed that
   a) are the optimal means of solving a problem.
   b) are satisfactory ways of solving a problem.
   c) are policies that will satisfy voters.
   d) are the easiest policies to adopt.
   e) are likely to be policies that satisfy the courts.

2. Among the factors that work against rationality and efficiency in the making of public policies is that
   a) politicians are more interested in votes than in effective policies.
   b) administrators of policies seek the easiest way of administering laws rather than rational or efficient ways.
   c) governments work incrementally.
   d) rational and efficient policies are too expensive to implement.
   e) government is inherently irrational and inefficient.

3. An example of policy legitimation is
   a) the Supreme Court upholds the constitutionality of a law.
   b) the president talks about an issue in his State of the Union Address.
   c) the governor talks about an issue in his State of the State Address.
   d) political scientists research the effectiveness of a law.
   e) The legislature does not repeal a law during the legislative session following its passage.

Education Policy

Describe the major issues that have shaped education policy in Texas (pp. 387–97)

One of the most important functions of state government is providing and funding public education. Under the Gilmer-Aikin Laws, Texas extended its control over financing and administering public education through local school districts. As in many southern states, segregation of public schools was a major problem that was not dealt with until federal courts forced Texas to desegregate in the 1950s and '60s. Equity in the funding of public education remains a major issue in Texas. State courts continue to play an important role in addressing the equity issue. Concerns over excellence and accountability in public education persist today.

Key Terms

Gilmer-Aikin Laws (p. 389)

equal protection clause (p. 392)

Practice Quiz

4. The Gilmer-Aikin Laws
   a) regulate schools in the Gilmer-Aikin ISD.
   b) were major educational reforms passed in 1949.
   c) established an office of elected state superintendent of public instruction.
   d) allowed for homeschooling of children.
   e) required that money raised from the poll tax be spent on public education.

5. State courts tried to address the issue of equity in the funding of public schools
   a) in the case of *Edgewood ISD v. Kirby*.
   b) in the case of *Brown v. Board of Education*.
   c) in the case of *San Antonio v. Rodríguez*.
   d) by appointing Ross Perot to recommend changes to the property tax in Texas.
   e) by abolishing the office of the State Board of Education.

6. Among the reforms in public education in Texas to improve the quality of education was
   a) "No Pass, No Play."
   b) "No Play, No Pass."
   c) a shorter school year.
   d) more flexible standards for accrediting schools.
   e) tying teacher pay raises to student grades.

Welfare Policy

Describe the state's role in addressing poverty and how it is affected by national policies (pp. 397–403)

Texas has large numbers of people living in poverty who have received governmental assistance since the New Deal when the Social Security Act of 1935 was passed. Texas's most important welfare program was AFDC. President Lyndon Johnson's War on Poverty expanded social welfare programs for the poor in the 1960s. But compared with other states, welfare benefits remained low in Texas. Concerns over the problem of welfare dependency led to major reforms at the national level in 1996 when AFDC was replaced with TANF. Since these reforms, welfare rolls have declined, although poverty has remained a chronic problem among a significant portion of the Texas population.

Key Terms

New Deal (p. 399)

Aid to Families with Dependent Children (AFDC) (p. 399)

Medicaid (p. 399)

Supplemental Security Income (SSI) (p. 400)

Temporary Assistance for Needy Families (TANF) (p. 402)

Practice Quiz

7. Poverty among those over age 65 and those under age 18 in Texas
   a) is almost nonexistent because of the welfare reforms of the 1990s.
   b) is at a level above the national average.
   c) is at a level below the national average.
   d) was largely eliminated by the Social Security Act of 1935.
   e) was largely eliminated by Lyndon Johnson's "War on Poverty."

8. The welfare reforms of the 1990s
   a) resulted from a belief that the welfare policies of the 1960s had failed.
   b) led to a 36-month limitation on welfare benefits in Texas.
   c) led to a five-year ban on reapplying for benefits once benefits ran out.
   d) expanded education and job-training programs.
   e) all of the above

9. Two presidents who had major roles in welfare policy are
   a) Franklin Delano Roosevelt and Lyndon B. Johnson.
   b) Dwight Eisenhower and Herbert Hoover.
   c) Harry Truman and John F. Kennedy.
   d) Woodrow Wilson and Franklin Delano Roosevelt.
   e) Lyndon B. Johnson and George H. W. Bush.

Medicaid and Health Care Policy

Explain why Medicaid in particular and health care policy in general have been so controversial in Texas (pp. 403–12)

One major welfare program that has become increasingly costly is Medicaid, a state-federal program that finances health care for the poor. Reforms instituted under the Obama administration have significantly expanded health care coverage for the poor. Texas, however, is not participat-

ing in that expansion. The rising cost of Medicaid is seen by many conservatives to be a growing threat to the financial integrity of the state's budget.

Practice Quiz

10. Which of the following statements is *true* about Medicaid in Texas?
    a) Medicaid is a program that was part of the New Deal.

b) Texas policy makers make all the major decisions regarding the principles and standards directing Medicaid in Texas. There is no federal oversight.

c) Texas can apply for a waiver with the federal government, enabling it to create programs directed toward particular clients.

d) Medicaid employs doctors and nurses as members of the Department of Health and Human Services hired to provide medical care to the poor.

e) Medicaid is funded entirely by the state.

11. Managed care programs
    a) are not found in the Texas Medicaid program.
    b) provide medical care to an increasing number of Medicaid clients in Texas.
    c) provide medical care to a small number of Medicaid clients in Texas.
    d) provide direct fee-for-service care for Medicaid recipients.
    e) have declined in popularity since the 1990s.

12. The Affordable Care Act
    a) was part of the War on Poverty.
    b) merged Medicare and Medicaid into a single program.
    c) will increase health insurance coverage to millions of Texans.
    d) was declared unconstitutional by the Texas Supreme Court.
    e) originated in the Texas legislature.

Water Policy

Consider the growing importance of policies related to water supplies in Texas (pp. 412–18)

A looming threat to Texas's further economic development is access to freshwater. Over the next 50 years, water consumption is expected to vastly increase while existing supplies may decrease. Current water law in Texas adds complexity to the development of rational water policies for the state.

Key Term

law of capture (p. 414)

Practice Quiz

13. Which of the following is *true*?
    a) Texas water consumption will decrease as the population expands.
    b) The idea of planning for future water provision has been rejected by the Texas state legislature as being too socialistic.
    c) Water law in Texas distinguishes between surface water and ground water.
    d) Providing water in Texas is primarily a federal responsibility.
    e) Current state water policies do not emphasize conservation.

14. The law rule of capture concerns
    a) property rights in underground percolating water.
    b) the right of the state to regulate rivers and estuaries.
    c) political control of the legislature by a particular policy interest.
    d) the Corps of Engineers' various attempts to direct the flow of the Rio Grande.
    e) the federal government's ability to override Texas water laws.

15. Which of the following is *true*?
    a) The Texas Supreme Court rejects the idea that the state can regulate *surface* water.
    b) Texas is empowered by the state constitution to seize without compensation an individual's right to use underground water.
    c) Aquifers provide a negligible supply of water to Texas.
    d) Attempts to regulate groundwater access frequently come into conflict with property rights.
    e) The Water Rights Adjudication Act of 1967 prohibits the state from regulating surface water permits.

Recommended Websites

Texas Education Agency
www.tea.state.tx.us

Texas Health and Human Services Commission
www.hhsc.state.tx.us

U.S. Medicaid Website
www.medicaid.gov

Texas Water Development Board
www.twdb.texas.gov

In 2011, Michael Morton was released from prison based on new DNA testing in his case. He served nearly 25 years in prison before another man was arrested for the crime. DNA evidence has revealed a series of wrongful convictions, raising questions about criminal justice in Texas.

Crime and Corrections Policy in Texas

13

WHY CORRECTIONS POLICY MATTERS On August 13, 1986, Christine Morton was beaten to death at her home in Austin. Her husband, Michael Morton, was charged with the murder and was prosecuted by Williamson County district attorney Ken Anderson. Michael received a life sentence for the murder, though he persisted in claiming his innocence and argued that some unknown intruder must have killed his wife after he had gone to work. The day after the murder, Christine's brother had found a bloodstained blue bandana near the crime scene, and he had turned it over to detectives. In 2005, Michael asked for DNA testing on several items including the blue bandana.

District Attorney Ken Anderson had by this time been appointed to a state district judgeship by Governor Rick Perry, who then appointed John Bradley, an assistant district attorney under Anderson, as the new district attorney. Bradley was known as a tough prosecutor, and he opposed the requests for DNA testing, claiming there was no way the testing would lead to some "mystery killer." Michael Morton's lawyers were, argued District Attorney Bradley, "grasping at straws." Morton's lawyers suspected that key evidence had been withheld in the case, and so they sought investigative materials in Morton's case. Bradley opposed those requests as well. In 2008, Bradley was forced to turn over the investigative materials, and Morton's defense lawyers discovered that Eric Morton, who was three years old at the time of his mother's murder, had seen the murder and described the killer as a "monster" who had red gloves and a big mustache. He also had said that the killer was not his father.

Defense lawyers discovered other information as well from the newly released files of the case. Police reports noted that there was a check to Christine that was cashed with a forged signature after her death, and there were also reports of fraudulent use of her credit card after her death. There were also neighbors' statements to police that a man was seen parked in a green van near the Morton home on several occasions before the murder. Contrary to a legal requirement that prosecutors share exculpatory materials, this information had not been provided to the defense lawyers.

Then, in 2010, DNA testing on the blue bandana was allowed. DNA was found on the bandana to belong to the victim, Christine, and to a man whose DNA was in a national database as a result of an arrest in California. That man was Mark Alan Norwood. On October 4, 2011, Michael Morton was released from prison—he had been convicted in 1987. Mark Alan Norwood was convicted of the murder of Christine Morton on March 27, 2013. He has also been indicted in another murder of a woman in 1988.

District Attorney Bradley was defeated for re-election in the Republican primary in 2012. His opponent, Williamson County Attorney Jana Duty, won with 55 percent of the vote and hammered Bradley for blocking the postconviction DNA testing for Morton. Bradley's resistance to that testing meant that Morton spent six additional years in prison.[1] Judge Ken Anderson was sentenced to 10 days in jail, a $500 fine, and 500 hours of community service for criminal contempt in telling the Morton trial judge that he had no evidence favorable to Morton.[2] He has also lost his judgeship and law license. Morton is free and will receive financial restitution from the state for the quarter century that he spent in prison for a murder he did not commit. He was present when the Texas legislature passed a bill, the Michael Morton Act, which establishes a uniform policy for district attorneys to make material that can help defendants' cases available to defense attorneys.[3]

The Morton case highlights several aspects of the criminal justice system in Texas and raises questions about how it works. The defeat of District Attorney Bradley at the polls, the punishment and disciplining of Judge Anderson, and the passage of the Michael Morton Act demonstrate in stark terms how important the fair operation of the criminal justice system is to all residents in the state of Texas. In this chapter we will look both at the basics of the criminal justice system and at recent issues related to criminal justice in Texas.[4]

chapter goals

- Identify the major classifications of crime under Texas law and the types of punishments that may be imposed (pp. 425–27)

- Outline the procedural steps that occur after a person is arrested (pp. 427–34)

- Describe prisons and corrections policy in Texas (pp. 434–45)

- Explain why Texas's criminal justice system is often controversial (pp. 445–50)

- Consider recent proposals to improve Texas's criminal justice system (pp. 450–51)

Categorizing Crime in Texas

Crimes, of course, have different levels of seriousness, and punishments vary according to the legislature's classification of the seriousness of the crime. In the Texas criminal justice system, crimes are classified as felonies or misdemeanors. Table 13.1 shows the punishment range for the various classifications of crime in Texas.

Identify the major classifications of crime under Texas law and the types of punishments that may be imposed

Felonies

A **felony** is a serious criminal offense that subjects a person to state prison punishment. Fines can be up to $10,000, and prison punishment can range from six months to the death penalty. The right to vote, to have a gun, or to have certain occupational licenses can also be taken away, although in Texas voting rights for felons are restored after the sentence has been fully discharged. The most serious felony is capital murder, for which the penalty can be death or life imprisonment without parole. The next most serious felony is a first degree felony, for which the punishment can be 5 to 99 years in a state prison and a possible fine of up to $10,000. First degree felonies include such crimes as aggravated assault on a public servant, aggravated kidnapping, aggravated sexual assault, and arson of a habitation. A crime defined as "aggravated" involves the use of some sort of weapon. A second degree felony is punished with a sentence of 2 to 20 years in state prison

felony a serious criminal offense, punishable by a prison sentence or a fine. A capital felony is punishable by death or a life sentence

---

TABLE 13.1

Classification of Crimes

FELONY CRIMES	PENALTIES*
Capital murder	Death or life without parole
First degree	5 to 99 years in state prison; fine up to $10,000
Second degree	2 to 20 years in state prison; fine up to $10,000
Third degree	2 to 10 years in state prison; fine up to $10,000
State jail	180 days to 2 years in a state jail; fine up to $10,000
MISDEMEANOR CRIMES	PENALTIES*
Class A	No more than 1 year in county jail; fine up to $4,000
Class B	No more than 180 days in county jail; fine up to $2,000
Class C	Fine up to $500

*In many cases, probation is a possible substitute for serving jail or prison time. If jail or prison time is imposed, it is possible to obtain parole or early release.

SOURCES: "Texas Criminal Laws & Penalties," Texas Criminal Defense Lawyer, www.mytexasdefenselawyer.com; Fred Dahr, "Crimes and Punishment in Texas State Court," www.texasdefenselaw.com.

While possession of a small amount of marijuana is a misdemeanor, possession of larger amounts and selling drugs are felonies. Here, a Fort Worth police captain holds a press conference on an investigation into a drug-dealing ring.

misdemeanor a minor criminal offense usually punishable by a small fine or short jail sentence

probation punishment where an offender is not imprisoned but remains in the community under specified rules and under the supervision of a probation officer

and a possible fine of up to $10,000. Second degree felonies include such crimes as arson, bigamy, bribery, robbery, sexual assault, manslaughter, and possession of 50 to 2,000 pounds of marijuana. A third degree felony is punished with a sentence of 2 to 10 years in state prison and a possible fine of up to $10,000. Examples of third degree felonies include a stalking conviction, a third driving while intoxicated (DWI) charge, or a third offense of violation of a protective order. The last category of felonies, state jail felonies, results in 180 days to 2 years in a state jail and a possible fine of up to $10,000. Examples of a state jail felony include burglary of a building, DWI with a child as a passenger, forgery of a check, and possession of less than one gram of a controlled substance.

Misdemeanors

Misdemeanors are less serious crimes, for which the fine is $4,000 or less and the sentence is up to one year in the county jail. No rights such as the right to vote, the right to possess a weapon, or the rights to have some occupational licenses are lost as a result of a misdemeanor conviction. There are three classes of misdemeanors. The most serious is a class A misdemeanor, for which the fine is not more than $4,000 and the sentence would not be more than one year in the county jail. Examples of class A misdemeanors include burglary of a vehicle, a second DWI offense, public lewdness, and possession of two to four ounces of marijuana. Class B misdemeanors are punishable with a sentence of up to 180 days in the county jail and a fine not to exceed $2,000. Examples of class B misdemeanors are prostitution, terrorist threats, a first DWI charge, criminal trespass, and possession of two ounces or less of marijuana. Finally, class C misdemeanors are punished with fines not to exceed $500 and involve such crimes as public intoxication, disorderly conduct, and a minor's possession of alcohol.

Punishing Crime

In some cases, the judge may allow **probation**, or community supervision, rather than a jail or prison sentence, especially if it is the defendant's first conviction. Probation is a suspension of the jail or prison sentence with the understanding that the defendant will meet certain requirements that are imposed by the court. These requirements usually include reporting to a probation officer on a regular basis, holding a steady job, paying fines or restitution, and abstaining from alcohol or drug use. Generally, community supervision can run up to 2 years for misdemeanors and up to 10 years for felonies, although if a probationer is compliant with the rules of community supervision, it is possible to obtain early release from probation after serving one-third of the term.[5]

Violation of probation requirements can result in being sent to jail or prison to serve out the remainder of the sentence behind bars. Often prosecutors know that people with lengthy probation sentences will find it difficult to comply with all of the requirements. So, in cases where they believe it will be difficult to get a conviction, they might agree to a plea bargain allowing community supervision for a long period. They expect that the defendant will violate probation and spend time in jail or prison.

People who are sentenced to prison may be released on **parole** after a period of time behind bars. This decision to grant parole is made by the Texas Board of Pardons and Paroles. The agency is composed of a chair and six board members. Members of the board serve six-year staggered terms. The board makes recommendations about state prisoners' sentences, clemency, parole, and supervision. In order for the governor to alter a prisoner's sentence, a majority of the board must support the change. The board also determines which prisoners are to be released on parole, determines conditions of parole, determines revocation of parole, and recommends clemency matters to the governor.

People serving time for capital crimes are not eligible for parole, and generally those convicted of other violent crimes must serve at least half their sentence before being considered for parole. People convicted of nonviolent crimes must serve at least one-fourth of their sentences or 15 years, whichever is less, before being considered for parole. A complex formula is used by the Board of Pardons and Paroles that considers the crime, when it was committed, the time served, and the behavior of the inmate, so that no simple rule generally applies to offenders. If a prisoner is granted parole, he or she must comply with the requirements imposed on the parole or, like probation violators, he or she can be sent to prison for the remainder of the sentence.[6]

There are also sentencing enhancements that increase sentences or increase the classification of the crime in certain circumstances. Previous convictions can be used to enhance the punishment for a crime. For example, a DWI offense is a class B misdemeanor, but a second DWI is a class A misdemeanor, and a third DWI is a third degree felony. That means, of course, that a second or third DWI conviction will result in more serious penalties than will the first DWI offense.

Texas enhances sentences for repeat felony offenders as well. If a person who commits a third degree felony has a prior felony conviction, that person is sentenced for a second degree felony. Similarly, a second degree felony is punished as a first degree felony if the person had a prior felony conviction. A person convicted of a third felony can be sentenced to life imprisonment based on a **"three strikes" provision** in the penal code, and in some cases, such as sexual assault cases, two felony convictions are sufficient for life imprisonment.

parole the conditional release of an offender who has served some prison time, under specified rules and under the supervision of a parole officer

"three strikes" provision a law that allows persons convicted of three felonies (or in some cases two felonies) to be sentenced to life imprisonment

● The Criminal Justice Process

Outline the procedural steps that occur after a person is arrested

There are several procedural steps that occur after a person is arrested and prior to the determination of guilt or innocence. In Texas, as in most other states, this process may take months or even years. The major procedural steps are listed below.

Arraignment and Posting Bail

Generally, when a person is arrested for a felony or misdemeanor and jailed rather than ticketed, he or she will be arraigned before a judge. At the arraignment, the charges will be explained to the accused, and he or she will be reminded of the due process rights—such as the right to remain silent and the right to an attorney. Generally, bail will be set at this point. In some cases, a date will be determined for the judge to review the charges against the defendant.

After being charged, a defendant may be released on bail. If the individual does not have enough money to post bail, he or she may make arrangements with a bail bondsman, who posts bail in exchange for a nonrefundable payment.

bail payment of money to the state as an assurance that an accused person who is released from jail pending trial will appear for trial; if the accused does not appear, the bail is forfeited

grand jury jury that determines whether sufficient evidence is available to justify a trial; grand juries do not rule on the accused's guilt or innocence

After being charged, a defendant may be released on bail until the trial. **Bail** is money that is provided by the defendant to assure his or her appearance in court. Usually, if a defendant does not show up for trial, the bail is forfeited. If the defendant appears as required, the bail money is returned. An individual may put up the entire sum for bail in order to be released from prison pending trial. Often, however, bail is more than the accused can pay, and so he or she will arrange with a bail bondsman to pay the bail in exchange for a nonrefundable payment that is often 10 percent of the amount but can be higher. A recent scandal involving bail bondsmen in Dallas County is leading to a reconsideration of how bail bonds are administered in that county. In Dallas, many bail bondsmen have had accused persons flee, but they have not forfeited the bail money for those persons. Additionally, many bail bondsmen can use property as security for their bonds and have gotten unusually high valuations on their property to support the bail bonds that they underwrite. This means that the property guaranteeing the bail does not actually equal the value of the bail, which means people are being released from jail for less than the amount of money that should be provided to guarantee their appearance at trial.

If a person cannot provide bail on the person's own or cannot pay a bondsman, the accused possibly can be released on personal recognizance, which is the accused's promise to appear. This process is most likely if the accused has ties in the community such as a family or employment and does not have a criminal record. If an accused person cannot provide bail, he or she usually will be held in jail pending the trial.

Grand Jury Indictment

Although the procedure can vary, generally after arraignment, a felony case will be presented to a **grand jury** which consists of 12 persons who will hear the case to determine if there is sufficient evidence to hold the accused for trial. Grand juries do not find people guilty of a crime, but instead will vote a "true bill," meaning that they find probable cause that an accused person has committed the crime, or they will return a "no bill," meaning that they did not find probable cause. A person would, of course, be held for trial only if a grand jury voted a "true bill." A grand jury indictment is far from conviction, as all a grand jury determines is the existence of probable cause and usually the grand jury's decision is based only on a presentation made by the prosecutor. In a trial, to find a person guilty, there must be a finding of guilt "beyond a reasonable doubt," which is a demanding standard of proof for a prosecutor. At a trial the defense is also heard and has the opportunity to cross-examine witnesses and present the defense's version of events. The major criticism of the grand jury is that it usually hears only what the prosecutor chooses to let it hear and that it serves as a "rubber stamp" for the prosecutor's decision.

Pretrial Hearings

After indictment for a felony, there will likely be a number of pretrial hearings in which the accused will formally plead guilty or not guilty, the trial is scheduled, and various motions may be presented such as motions to move the trial or motions to exclude certain evidence. These hearings vary in length but in most cases are quite brief. In a criminal trial, a common motion is one to exclude certain evidence on the grounds that the evidence was seized in violation of the Fourth Amendment to the U.S. Constitution, meaning that it was illegally seized. In these instances, the judge examines the facts of the seizure and determines whether the evidence was legally seized and therefore can be used at trial.

Although plea bargaining can occur even during a trial and even after a finding of guilt but before sentencing, the prosecution and the defense will often discuss a punishment in exchange for a guilty plea and reach an agreement before the trial.

Trial and Sentencing

If the case does go to trial, a defendant may waive the right to a jury trial and have the determination of guilt made by a judge. A jury trial may be waived in cases where a judge is perceived as more inclined to be favorable because of past decisions by the judge or because the crime is believed to be one that would inflame the emotions of jurors, resulting in less favorable treatment. A defendant may also have a jury trial but waive the right to sentencing by a jury so that the judge determines the sentence if there is a guilty verdict. In Texas, felony juries are composed of 12 people and misdemeanor juries are composed of 6. Decisions by criminal juries must be unanimous, and for both felonies and misdemeanors the standard of proof is "beyond a reasonable doubt." If the jury's decision in a felony case is not unanimous, the case results in a mistrial, and the prosecutor must decide whether to retry the defendant.

If the defendant is acquitted (found not guilty), the defendant is, of course, set free. If the defendant is found guilty, there will be a jail or prison sentence or probation and/or a fine. A defendant may appeal a determination of guilt, meaning that the defendant asks a higher court to reconsider the lower court's decision. Very minor criminal cases that are heard by municipal courts or by justice of the peace courts can be appealed to the county courts. More serious misdemeanors and felonies, however, are heard by county or district courts, and appeals from county courts or district courts will be to one of the 14 courts of appeal in Texas. An appeal beyond the Texas courts of appeal will be to the highest criminal court in Texas, the Texas Court of Criminal Appeals. In rare events where a question of U.S. constitutional or statutory law is raised, it may also be possible to appeal to the federal courts.

Does the Criminal Justice System Create Criminals?

In some cases, the requirements of the Texas criminal justice system can be quite burdensome on individuals. For some people, complying with the rules of the process can be difficult and even financially impossible. One common crime in Texas, especially among younger offenders, is possession of less than two ounces of marijuana. Although Travis County treats this crime as the equivalent of a typical traffic offense where the police officer tickets the offender, in other Texas counties offenders will be taken to a local jail to be held until the bond hearing and until they can make bail. Commonly, the bail on such a charge would be $500, which means that the full $500 will have to be posted with the county, or a bail bondsman will have to be retained for roughly a $50 nonrefundable fee. After bail is posted, the defendant will eventually have to go to trial in a county-court-at-law.

Some defendants hire an attorney, which may cost $1,000 to $3,000 for the entire process in this type of case; others may appear in court without an attorney. It would not be unusual for a first offense to result in at least a $500 fine plus court costs, a sentence of 30 hours of community service, a sentence of 15 hours in an approved drug education course, and nine months' probation where the defendant would pay a fee for each visit to the probation officer and any drug testing required by the probation officer. After court costs, probation costs, and the fine, the offender will probably have spent about $1,000 to $1,200, excluding legal fees.

While on probation, the offender will not be allowed to use drugs or alcohol and will be subject to testing. There will be a required visit with a drug counselor and regular trips to a probation officer. Travel will be restricted. If the offender is in compliance, he or she will probably get early release from probation. If not, probation could be full length and jail time is possible. Additionally, because this is a drug case, the driver's license of the offender will be suspended for six months. If driving is necessary for the offender, in order to be in compliance, the offender must go to court and obtain an occupational driver's license in order to drive to and from work or care for family matters. Filing this paperwork can easily cost nearly $300 not counting possible attorney's fees. Additionally, the offender will have to purchase an SR-22 automobile insurance policy for two years in order to drive legally. This is a high-risk insurance policy in which the insurance company reports directly to the state that the offender has automobile insurance coverage. This type of insurance can cost twice as much as a regular insurance policy. Thus, an arrest for possession of a marijuana cigarette can easily cost more than $5,000 to $7,000 overall in fines, court costs, insurance charges, probation fees, and attorney costs, not to mention time in jail after arrest and, if the marijuana was found in the offender's vehicle, towing and impoundment charges. Failure to comply with all probation requirements can lead to violation of probation and other criminal charges such as driving with a suspended license or driving without proper insurance.

The structure of the criminal justice process even for minor crimes such as a class B misdemeanor may deter future crimes because of the severity of punishment, but the cost and penalty structure also seems to encourage failure and further criminality by the offender.

Crime and Texas District Attorneys

Ordinarily when we think of the criminal justice system, we think of the police who make arrests and the Texas criminal courts that adjudicate those criminal cases. The most important actors in the Texas criminal justice system, however, are probably the prosecuting attorneys. Some counties have an elected county attorney whose office represents the state in misdemeanor criminal cases. The county attorney usually provides legal advice to the county commissioners as well, although generally the **county attorney** does not represent the county in civil cases. Counties with elected county attorneys also have elected **district attorneys**. They represent the state in felony cases. There are counties that have merged the offices of county and district attorney into a combined office that represents the state in both misdemeanor and felony cases. Often, when the offices of county and district attorney are merged, the combined office is called the office of the criminal district attorney.[7]

In the urban counties in Texas, the office of the district attorney is huge, encompassing several hundred lawyers, investigators, and support staff. In August 2014, Dallas County's District Attorney's office employed 242 prosecutors, 72 investiga-

county attorney an elected official in some counties who prosecutes misdemeanor cases

district attorney public official who prosecutes the more serious criminal cases in the district court

Susan Reed's Facebook page shows how candidates for district attorney must emphasize how they are "tough on crime." Reed is a Republican from Bexar County.

tors, and 128 support staff. In the most rural counties, the district attorney's office may be composed of only one or two lawyers. The head of every district attorney's office in Texas is an elected officer who runs under a party label. The term of office is four years. And as the chief prosecuting officer of the county or district, the district attorney has the responsibility for criminal prosecutions within the district attorney's jurisdiction. This means that the district attorneys generally campaign as officials who are "tough on crime," and they brag about high conviction rates. If they appear too lenient or their conviction rates are too low, political opponents will emerge who will accuse them of not doing their job appropriately. Because prosecutors often deal with people who have committed terrible crimes, they often see the worst aspects of humanity, and this also may lead to a "tough on crime" approach. A Parker County prosecutor wrote in a periodical widely read by other prosecutors of the mindset that prosecutors develop in the course of their work, "Like many of you, I've become jaded. The past nine years as a felony prosecutor has convinced me that an unending supply of humanity is willing to lie, cheat, steal, maim, or kill for the smallest reasons or for no reason at all. I had begun to think that my conscience could no longer be shocked, regardless of the facts and circumstances of any case I prosecuted."[8] Thus, the political pressures of the job coupled with the experiences one has in the job do not incline prosecutors to be sympathetic in their dealings with defendants.

Prosecutors must maintain high conviction rates in order to keep their positions. One way that high conviction rates are maintained is through plea bargaining. In a **plea bargain**, a prosecutor will meet with the accused or his lawyer and offer a sentence in exchange for a plea of guilty. The prosecutor's offer might involve reducing the charge, dropping some of the charges, or recommending a lighter sentence than the defendant might get at trial if found guilty. Plea bargaining is not only necessary politically for an elected district attorney to maintain high conviction rates but also crucial in managing the limited resources of the prosecutor's office and the courts. Prosecuting a case that goes to trial after a defendant pleads not guilty can cost thousands and even hundreds of thousands of dollars and uses

plea bargain a negotiated agreement in a criminal case in which a defendant agrees to plead guilty in return for the state's agreement to reduce the severity of the criminal charge or prison sentence the defendant is facing

up the time of employees. If plea bargaining were suddenly abandoned in Texas, the criminal justice system would quickly come to a halt as a result of a massive overflow of trials. There is often an incentive for defense lawyers to plea bargain as well. In many cases, defense lawyers can generate more income by representing numerous defendants (who often have limited resources) in plea negotiations than they can generate in a few time-consuming trials. And, of course, plea bargains can benefit defendants, even innocent defendants, in that they get an assured sentence that may be less than they would receive if they went to trial and were found guilty and sentenced by either a judge or a jury.

In almost all cases that involve plea bargaining, the judge with jurisdiction over the case will agree with the bargain made by the district attorney's office. For one thing, plea bargains reduce the crowded dockets of judges. Without a trial, the judge cannot be aware of the strengths and weaknesses of the state's case and so will generally recognize that the district attorney is in a far better position to determine the appropriate sentence.

The district attorney has prosecutorial discretion, which includes the power to charge or not charge a person with a crime. Even when a case is presented before a grand jury to determine if a criminal indictment should be issued, the grand jury is dependent on the prosecutor to present the evidence that may lead to an indictment, and a prosecutor has great discretion in choosing to go before a grand jury and in deciding to accept or not accept the decision of a particular grand jury. There have been several recent examples of the vast power of the district attorney in the state's criminal justice process. Prosecutors are powerful enough to even go after judges. In Collin County in late 2011, District Judge Suzanne Wooten was convicted of six counts of bribery, one count of money laundering, tampering with a government record, and engaging in an organized criminal activity. In order to get the indictment of Judge Wooten that led to her conviction, the district attorney had to go before at least six different grand juries. The first five grand juries did not decide to indict. It was an extraordinary example of prosecutors shopping for a grand jury that would finally indict someone they had targeted. After Wooten was convicted at trial, she faced the possibility of a 20-year sentence. Prosecutors then offered her a sentencing deal. She would get 10 years' probation, get a $10,000 fine, and have to do 1,000 hours of community service. She took the deal even though it meant that she also had to agree not to appeal the conviction, which protected the prosecution from an appeal and from further controversy over whether the case was tainted by local politics.[9]

In another case, a Dallas County judge held a prosecutor in contempt for not following a court order. The judge had ordered the prosecutor to hand over the criminal histories of police officers, and the assistant district attorney had objected, claiming the district attorney's office was not required to do so and that federal law prohibited that information from being provided to defense lawyers. The assistant district attorney who refused was confined by being ordered to remain in the courtroom. Later the judge suspended her decision to hold the assistant district attorney in contempt and agreed to hold a hearing about the matter. However, prior to the hearing, the district attorney's office began (though it later dropped) a grand jury investigation of the judge for official oppression. In still another Dallas County case the district attorney was found in contempt by a judge when the district attorney refused to testify about allegations that he had indicted a person on mortgage fraud charges as a favor to an influential lawyer who was in a dispute with that person over legal fees. The district attorney's contempt charges were dismissed, but he has begun a grand jury investigation of the judge who found him in contempt along with two other judges with whom the first judge consulted.[10] Most recently, the Dallas County district attorney has been accused of urging his assistant district attorneys to run for judgeships—at least six of them are running for state district judge and five of those are running against incumbent Democratic judges.[11] A clear message seems to be that even judges, who are commonly perceived as all-powerful within the legal process, should be cautious when dealing with the power of a district attorney.

In Harris County, a grand jury investigated the district attorney's office over allegations that assistant district attorneys who prosecute DWI cases knew about possible problems with the Houston Police Department's breath alcohol vehicles and violated the law by not telling defendants about those concerns. There had been charges that the breath alcohol tests conducted by the vehicles were not accurate because of overheating and electrical spikes. It was highly unusual for a grand jury to take on an investigation of a district attorney's office, but again, the power of the district attorney was evident in a report issued by the grand jury in 2012. The report claimed that the district attorney's office had investigated the grand jurors, two judges, and a political opponent of the district attorney. It also criticized a prosecutor for refusing to testify and the district attorney's office for "unexpected resistance." When the grand jury issued its one-page report criticizing the Harris County district attorney's office, the district attorney called a press conference and attacked the grand jury, claiming, "This politically motivated investigation, I would submit to you, is an outrage. It's an abuse of power and a corruption of the criminal justice system. For months our office has been hounded, and there have been a torrent of grand jury leaks."[12] When district attorneys can mobilize the power of the state to prosecute and attempt to intimidate judges and grand juries, it emphasizes their power in the criminal justice system and power over ordinary citizens they charge with wrongdoing.

assigned counsel private lawyers appointed by judges to provide legal representation for indigent defendants in serious criminal cases. The lawyer's fee is determined by and paid by the county

public defender salaried lawyer who is funded by the government or by grants who represents indigents in Texas in some counties or for some types of cases

Crime and Criminal Defense

Persons accused of crime may represent themselves or may retain a criminal defense lawyer to represent them. Since the famous Supreme Court case *Gideon v. Wainwright*, persons too poor to hire a lawyer have had a constitutional right to have an attorney appointed to represent them in serious cases. In Texas, that representation will generally be provided by **assigned counsel**—that is, the judge will appoint a lawyer to represent the indigent accused of crimes. However, in some counties in at least some types of cases, a **public defender** will represent an indigent. A public defender is a lawyer who is paid a salary by the government to represent indigents. With assigned counsel, usually judges appoint a private attorney on a case-by-case basis for a fee that varies according to the county and the legal service performed. One concern with the assigned counsel system is that the fee paid by counties may be so small that the assigned attorneys do not do an adequate job in representing their indigent client. The issue of the quality of representation provided to indigents in Texas, however, is an important one because large numbers of cases and substantial amounts of money are spent in providing this representation. Table 13.2 specifies the 2012 costs of indigent defense in the state and the numbers of cases involving indigents whose lawyers are paid by the state.

TABLE 13.2

Indigent Defense in Texas, 2013

State costs of indigent legal services	$217,068,685
Number of noncapital trials	191,558
Number of misdemeanor Felony trials	228,357
Juvenile hearings	48,114
Appeals	3,093
Capital cases	487

SOURCES: Texas Indigent Defense Commission, "Indigent Defense Data for Texas," www.tidc.tamu.edu/public.net.

Jim Bethke is executive director of the Texas Indigent Defense Commission. The commission helps counties maintain adequate legal services for criminal defendants in Texas with financial need.

With the use of assigned counsel, different counties have different fees that they pay lawyers. Some of those fees seem remarkably inadequate. As examples, Bexar County pays appointed counsel $75 an hour for trial work involving a state jail felony, $100 an hour for a second degree felony, and $125 an hour for a first degree felony. The first chair—the lead defense attorney—in a capital case in Bexar County gets $150 an hour for trial time. Harris County pays $300 a day for trial work in a state jail felony, $400 a day for a second degree felony, and $500 a day for a first degree felony. In capital cases a flat rate of $35,000 is paid. Hunt County pays $100 an hour, but in a capital case, the lead lawyer gets $110 an hour with a minimum payment for all trial work of $250.[13]

Public defenders are far rarer in Texas than are assigned counsel. However, there is a public defender program available for capital cases that is statewide and serves participating small and midsize counties. Altogether there are 19 public defender offices in Texas serving 140 counties. Most of these offices are regional in scope and most have specialized caseloads such as mentally ill defendants, rural areas, appeals, or juvenile defendants. Interestingly the public defender program for capital cases has been evaluated by comparing the program with assigned counsel in capital cases. Several interesting findings emerged from the study. For one thing, in rural areas of the state, there are few lawyers qualified to handle capital cases. In an area of Texas spanning over 80,000 square miles, for example, there are only 13 private lawyers qualified for capital cases. For such an area, death penalty specialists who are public defenders are particularly useful. Additionally, death penalty public defenders have the necessary support team that would be difficult to organize in the more rural and isolated parts of the state. For many smaller counties, the cost of death penalty cases is prohibitive—defense costs alone often exceed $100,000. Participating in a public defender program with death penalty specialists can greatly reduce costs for these counties. The public defenders were also more likely than assigned counsel to avoid a death penalty and were more likely than assigned counsel to get better dispositions for their clients overall.[14] Death penalty work is very specialized and complex, but the success of public defender programs over assigned counsel in death penalty cases suggests that an expansion of public defender programs in other areas may be beneficial to indigent defendants.

for critical analysis

To what extent is there a class bias in the criminal justice system where it is poor people who get convicted and go to prison? Are there checks on the power of district attorneys? Should there be?

● Crime, Corrections, and the Texas Prison System

Describe prisons and corrections policy in Texas

It has long been claimed that Texas does things in a big way. That is certainly true of its levels of crime and the way it deals with criminals. As of August 31, 2012, there were 152,303 offenders incarcerated in the state's prisons, state jails, and substance abuse facilities.[15] These numbers exclude those incarcerated in municipal and county facilities. In 2012 the average cost per day for each bed in the state's correctional facilities was $50.04.[16]

Who Is in Prison in Texas?

Prison Population in Texas by Race, 2012

■ % of Texas population ■ % of prison population

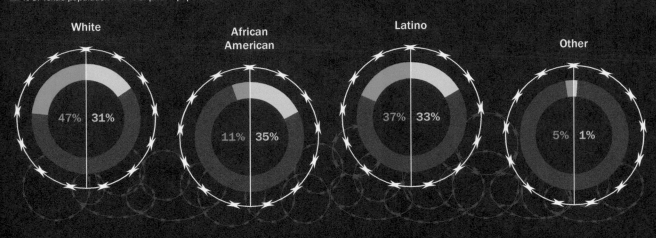

White
47% 31%

African American
11% 35%

Latino
37% 33%

Other
5% 1%

Death Row Population in Texas, 2013

% of Texas population   % of death row population   Total death row inmates

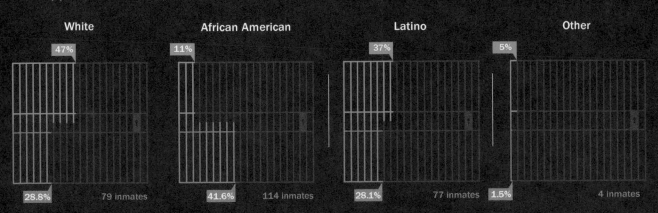

White
47%
28.8%   79 inmates

African American
11%
41.6%   114 inmates

Latino
37%
28.1%   77 inmates

Other
5%
1.5%   4 inmates

While Texas does not lead the nation in its incarceration rate, it is still the fifth highest in the United States. Who are the people in Texas's prisons? A disproportionately high number of African American men, for example, are serving in the state's prisons compared to their percentage of the population in the state. In fact, 7 out of every 10 prisoners in Texas is either African American or Latino.

SOURCES: Texas Department of Criminal Justice, Statistical Report 2012 (pages 10–11), www.tdcj.state.tx.us/documents/Statistical_Report_FY2012.pdf:
Texas Department of Criminal Justice, Gender and Racial Statistics of Death Row Offenders, www.tdcj.state.tx.us/death_row/dr_gender_racial_stats.html (accessed 5/16/14).

for critical analysis

1. The Texas population is 37% Latino, 11% African American, and 47% white. How does the Texas prison population compare?

2. What might help explain the racial/ethnic makeup of the prison population in Texas?

History of the Prison System

Shortly after Texas joined the Union, construction was authorized for a state penitentiary in Huntsville. The 225-cell facility opened in 1849. It confined prisoners in single cells at night and congregated inmates during the day to work in silence. From 1870 to 1883 the entire prison system was leased to private contractors who used the labor of inmates in exchange for providing maintenance and security for prisoners. After 1883 convicts in the Texas prison system were leased to railroads, planters, and others who provided the prisoners with food and clothing and paid a stipend to the state. These leasing arrangements were abandoned in 1910 as a result of scandals and abuses of the system.[17]

Although Texas moved to a state-run system, abuses continued. In 1924 an investigation of the system found cruel and brutal treatment of prisoners, inefficient management, and inadequate care of inmates. That investigation led to the creation of a state prison board, which supervised the work of a general prison manager. Still, however, the abuses continued. By the mid-1940s the Texas prison system was considered one of the worst in the United States. In 1974 the Joint Committee on Prison Reform submitted findings to the legislature that were very critical of the Texas prison system. The committee found fault with numerous aspects of the prison system's operation—from living and working conditions for inmates to classification of inmates to medical care to staff training. Still, no significant reforms were made to the system.[18]

The event that had the most dramatic effect on the operation of the Texas prison system in modern times was a federal court case, *Ruiz v. Estelle*.[19] Lawsuits filed by prisoners are nothing new. During the tenure of W. J. Estelle, Jr., the prison director from 1973 to 1983 and the defendant in the *Ruiz* case, prisoners filed 19,696 cases in the federal courts in Texas, a caseload amounting to about 20 percent of the federal court docket in Texas during that period.[20] However, the *Ruiz* case was

David Ruiz (right) and other Texas prison inmates filed a class-action lawsuit demanding stronger rights for prisoners. The case resulted in changes in how Texas prisons operated.

exceptional. It was a class-action suit on behalf of inmates that began in 1972, and it focused on issues of crowding in the system, security and supervision, health care, discipline, and access to the courts. In 1980 the federal court concluded that inmates' constitutionally guaranteed rights had been violated. Texas joined several other states in having its prison system declared unconstitutional.

The result was the appointment by the court of a special master, a court officer, to oversee the Texas prison system to eliminate the constitutional problems such as overcrowding, improper supervision of inmates, and improper care of inmates. There was a massive reform of the system, one that had to be imposed by the federal courts, because the state seemed unwilling or unable to reform its own prison system. Federal court supervision of the prison system ended in 2002.

For a long time, many in Texas government were resistant to federal court supervision of the prison system, arguing, for example, that the *Ruiz* decision involved federal court judicial activism and interfered with the rights of the state. In order to reduce the overcrowding in state prisons to comply with *Ruiz*, the state also encouraged the early release of prisoners, some of whom reentered society and committed more crimes. *Ruiz* did, however, help turn the criminal justice system into a major public policy issue in Texas.

The Prison System Today

The Texas prison system is operated by the Texas Department of Criminal Justice. This agency is run by a nine-member board that is appointed by the governor, and board members serve staggered six-year terms. The board hires an executive director to lead the sprawling agency, and it is responsible for developing the rules and regulations that govern the entire state prison system.[21]

There have been dramatic increases in the costs of prison construction and prison maintenance in Texas over time. Operating costs of Texas prisons rose from $147 million in 1982 to $609 million in 1990 to nearly $1.5 billion in 1996 and over $2.8 billion in 2008. In 2011 the total operating budget for the Texas Department of Criminal Justice was $3.06 billion. Despite a steady increase in prison operating costs, prison construction costs have varied from year to year. In 1982, $126 million was spent on prison construction, but in 1990 only $24 million was spent. The greatest period of prison construction was from 1991 through 1995. During those years, nearly $1.4 billion was spent on prison construction. In 2011 prison construction costs were $62.4 million.[22] In the wake of estimates in 2007 that Texas would need 17,000 new prison beds costing $1 billion by 2012, the Texas legislature increased the capacity of prison alternatives such as drug treatment and halfway homes, much cheaper alternatives to prison.[23]

Until 2007 when the Texas legislature began to seriously address alternatives to imprisonment, the state government had significantly increased the incarceration of offenders by building more prisons. In 2011, however, for the first time in Texas history, the state actually closed a prison—the century-old Central Unit in Sugarland. State leaders also announced plans to close three juvenile detention centers with its move toward rehabilitation, crime prevention, and cost-cutting. Two other prisons closed on August 31, 2013, the Dawson State Jail and the Mineral Wells Pre-Parole Transfer Facility.[24]

From 1976 to 1990 the rate of property crime in Texas rose 38 percent, and the violent crime rate rose 113 percent. During the same time period, prison expansion did not keep up with the increase in the crime rate. Instead, generous early-release

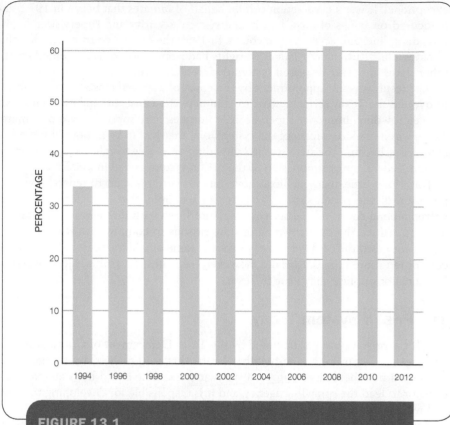

FIGURE 13.1

Percentage of Prison Sentence Served by Texas Inmates

SOURCES: Criminal Justice Policy Council, "Percentage of Prison Sentence Served for All Release Types, Fiscal Years 1994–2004"; Texas Department of Criminal Justice, Fiscal Year 2006 Statistical Report; Texas Department of Criminal Justice, Fiscal Year 2008 Statistical Report; Texas Department of Criminal Justice, "Fiscal Year 2011 Operating Budget and Fiscal Years 2012–2013 Legislative Appropriations Request," August 16, 2010. Texas Department of Criminal Justice, Fiscal Year 2012 Statistical Report.

policies were used to move prisoners out of jail to allow room for newly convicted inmates. With prison expansion, however, early-release policies were reduced. In 1990, for example, 38,000 prisoners were given early release from prison; however, even with a much larger prison population in 1997, only slightly more than 28,000 prisoners were given early release.[25] The steady lengthening of sentences is shown in Figure 13.1. In 1994 prisoners on average were released after serving one-third of their sentences. In 2012 prisoners were serving about 59.6 percent of their sentences before being released. Inmates at state jails served on average 98.5 percent of their sentences.[26]

As shown in Figure 13.2, the Texas prison population has soared, especially since about 1992. In 1980, at the time of the *Ruiz* case, the Texas prison population consisted of fewer than 30,000 inmates. A decade later, in 1990, there were slightly more than 49,000 inmates in Texas prisons. Only seven years later, in 1997,

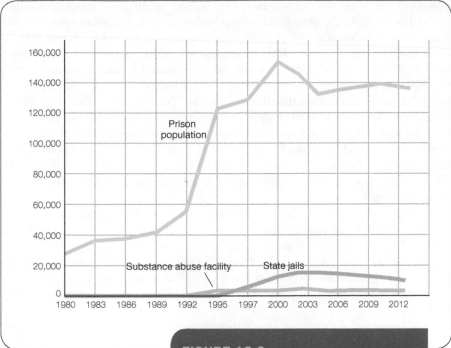

FIGURE 13.2

Texas Inmate Population, 1980–2012

SOURCES: Associated Texans Against Crime Annual Report, 1998; Texas Department of Criminal Justice, "Fiscal Year 2004 Statistics"; Criminal Justice Policy Council, "Texas Department of Criminal Justice State Incarcerated Population, Fiscal Years 1988–2002"; and Texas Department of Criminal Justice, 2006, 2008, 2010, and 2012 Statistical Report.

there were almost 130,000 inmates in state prisons. In 2000 the number of inmates in state prisons had jumped to over 150,000, dropping back to about 145,000 in 2002, to 139,316 in 2010, and to 137,095 in 2012. Put another way, there were more than 4.57 inmates in state prisons in 2012 for every inmate in state correctional facilities in 1980.[27]

For much of the 1980s the rates of violent and property crime in Texas were especially high. By the mid-1990s, however, those rates had dropped. Some observers argued that the reduction in the crime rate is caused by the increased incarceration of offenders.[28] There may also be other causes, however. Other analysts have suggested demographic change determines the size of the prison population. The most prison-prone group in society is males between the ages of 20 and 29. If that demographic group is large, then we would expect the prison population to also be large.[29] Indeed, 92.5 percent of Texas prisoners are male, and the average age of prisoners is 38.1 years.[30] Of course, changes in laws and treatment practices also affect the crime rate and the incarceration rate. Long sentences for habitual criminals, for example, are relatively new, as are long sentences for the use of a firearm in the commission of a crime.[31] The number of prison inmates per 100,000 population in Texas in 2012 was 601. The average for all states was 480. California and New York, the closest states in population to Texas, incarcerate 351 per 100,000 population and 276 per 100,000, respectively. Only Oklahoma with an incarceration rate of 648 per 100,000 population, Alabama with an incarceration rate of 650 per 100,000, Louisiana with an astronomical incarceration rate of 893 per 100,000 population, and Mississippi with an incarceration rate of 717 have a higher rate of incarceration than Texas. (See the "Texas and the Nation" graphic.) Texas had 10.4 percent of the nation's total state prison population in 2011. Neither the national government nor any other state had more inmates in its prison system than Texas.[32] In spite of its high rate of incarceration, Texas ranked high in crime. A study of crime rates nationwide found that Texas in 2011 ranked 38 in the United States in crime where a ranking of 1 is the least crime and 50 is the greatest crime ranking.[33]

As Figure 13.3 shows, Texas imprisons mostly violent offenders. In 2012, 55.3 percent of Texas inmates had been convicted of violent offenses and 16.1 percent had been convicted of property offenses. Nearly 17 percent of the inmate population was convicted of drug offenses.[34] Whether imprisonment for drug offenses is an appropriate remedy for the drug problem has been debated, but it is interesting to note that almost one in five people in Texas prisons are there because of drugs.

It is especially difficult for felons to gain legitimate employment after their release—so much so that the federal government offers a large tax credit to employers who will give jobs to people who have been convicted of a felony and have served their sentence. This difficulty in finding legal employment makes it more likely that former prisoners will commit further crimes. Another problem that inmates face once they leave prison is that the average sentence in a Texas prison is 19.3 years. After serving substantial time in prison, it is hard to readjust to life in the free world, and support structures such as family members have often died or removed the inmate from their lives. Still another difficulty is that 44.3 percent of inmates in Texas prisons do not have a high school diploma or GED and their

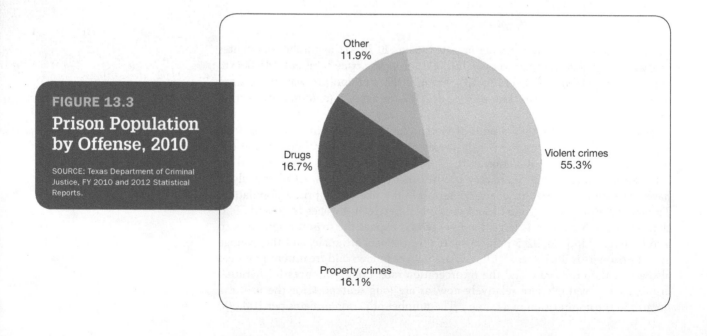

FIGURE 13.3

Prison Population by Offense, 2010

SOURCE: Texas Department of Criminal Justice, FY 2010 and 2012 Statistical Reports.

Other 11.9%

Drugs 16.7%

Violent crimes 55.3%

Property crimes 16.1%

How Does Criminal Justice in Texas Compare to Other States?

Incarceration Rate, 2012 (per 100,000 residents)

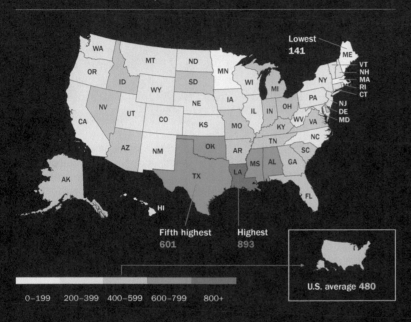

Lowest **141**

Fifth highest **601**

Highest **893**

0–199   200–399   400–599   600–799   800+

U.S. average **480**

The Texas criminal justice system is known for high incarceration rates. In 2012, 601 out of every 100,000 Texans were sentenced to time in prison, and rates in other recent years are similar. Texas is also known for its harsh punishment of criminals, especially the use of the death penalty. Since the U.S. Supreme Court reinstated the death penalty in 1976, Texas has executed 513 people: four times more than any other state.

Total Executions, 1976–2014

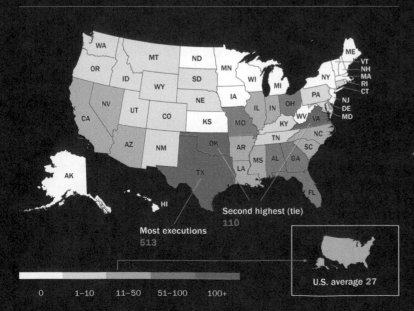

Second highest (tie) **110**

Most executions **513**

0   1–10   11–50   51–100   100+

U.S. average **27**

SOURCES: Incarceration rate: The Sentencing Project, www.sentencingproject.org/map/map.cfm
Total executions: Death Penalty Information Center, Number of Executions by State and Region since 1976, http://deathpenaltyinfo.org/number-executions-state-and-region-1976 (accessed 5/14/14).

for critical analysis

1. Which elements of Texas political culture or public opinion may contribute to the willingness to use the death penalty and to have high incarceration rates?

2. Examine the regional patterns on the two maps. Do certain regions of the country have higher incarceration rates and death penalty usage? What do you think explains these regional patterns?

Concealed Weapons on Campus

In January 2013, students at Lone Star College in North Harris County, Houston, were stunned when a gunman opened fire on the campus and injured four people. While this incident resulted from a dispute between two men and was not an indiscriminate act of violence, it nevertheless raised the contentious policy debate on whether concealed weapons should be allowed on Texas campuses. Just two years earlier, in May 2011, the Texas Senate had discussed legislation sponsored by Senator Jeff Wentworth (R–San Antonio) to allow the carrying of concealed handguns on public college campuses. Officials at the University of Texas and Texas A&M argued that they did not want the law to be implemented on their campuses. Some student groups organized on both sides of the issue. Eventually in 2013, the legislature passed a law allowing guns on campus if authorized by the campus and allowing guns to be stored in vehicles.

The politics of gun control continues to be a polarizing topic in the United States, as it involves tough trade-offs between liberty, public safety, public law, and collective security. Many people already have their minds made up on the subject of gun legislation and are unwilling to consider viewpoints different from their own. As the topic changes from laws regulating the constitutional "right to keep and bear arms" to laws expanding access to firearms and the "right to carry" firearms, the issue becomes even more controversial. These divergent viewpoints are evident in the reactions to tragic events such as shooting massacres.

On April 16, 2007, Seung-Hui Cho shot 49 people—killing 32—on the campus of Virginia Tech. In the aftermath of the shooting, police determined that Cho had illegally bought the firearms after having been declared mentally ill and "an imminent danger

to self or others" over one year prior to the shootings. As a result, a "mental health loophole" was identified in the firearms background check process, and federal and state governments passed legislation seeking to close the loophole.

Since the April 2007 Virginia Tech shooting, concealed carry advocates have expressed concerns about student safety, offering that students, faculty, and staff should have the right to carry weapons on college campuses. Proponents of carrying concealed handguns on college campuses have argued that firearms have not had a negative impact on learning; some point to Utah's 2004 concealed carry law, which allows the possession of weapons on college campuses and in student housing, as a model. However, while most people might agree that an individual has a right to self-defense in his or her own home, many dispute whether student housing on college campuses should be included.

Opponents of carrying concealed handguns on college campuses have argued that the presence of concealed weapons in a classroom would be disruptive to the learning environment and represent a safety hazard. They claim that the risk of an accidental or an intentional discharge on campus increases if more firearms are present. Moreover, opponents often contend that institutions of higher learning are not appropriate venues for any kind of weapon. They argue that concealed handgun carriers may lack the necessary training to defend themselves, let alone others, while proponents argue that with law enforcement several minutes away, concealed handgun carriers can potentially defend themselves and others.

Are college campuses with "gun-free zones" some of the safest places in Texas, or do they represent a prime place for criminal predators seeking easy unarmed prey in "victim zones"? Do more guns lead to more crime or enhance collective security? Would you feel more or less secure with the prospect that your fellow students may be legally concealing handguns?

critical thinking questions

1. If opponents and proponents of concealed weapons on campus cannot agree, how should lawmakers determine what policy to pass? Can you think of a compromise that might be proposed?

2. Do you think allowing concealed weapons would make your campus safer or less safe? Can you find any data that support your view?

average educational achievement is slightly less than 8 years.[35] That lack of education makes adjustment to life and legitimate employment outside of prison an extremely difficult experience.

For persons under community supervision who were convicted of felonies, from 2001 to 2012, the average percentage of persons whose community supervision was revoked was 15.2 percent. Almost everyone whose community supervision was revoked was sent to prison or state jail. In 2012 there were 44,608 new admissions to Texas prisons and 13,523 were persons whose community supervision was revoked. Of the 23,226 new admissions to state jails, 9,926 were persons whose community supervision was revoked. Of those revocations, about 45 percent were because of a new arrest or conviction. The rest were because of violations of rules of community supervision—such as consumption of alcohol or drugs or failure to make required payments.[36]

During the administration of Governor Ann Richards (1991–95), there was recognition that very large proportions of prisoners were involved with alcoholism, drug addiction, and drug-related crimes. An effort was made to create alcohol- and drug-abuse treatment programs within the prison system to help alleviate these problems, although the problems remain severe. In 2007 the Texas legislature again spent resources on prison alternatives, which have helped reduce the need for new prison construction.

The Death Penalty

Political scientists Paul Brace and Brent Boyea found that judges tend to affirm death penalty sentences in states where judges are elected and where there is strong public support for the death penalty.[37] This may explain why Texas appellate courts are so supportive of the death sentences imposed by juries at the trial court level. Texas judges are elected and polls show strong public support in Texas for the death penalty. One 2012 Texas poll, for example, showed that 73 percent of Texas voters either somewhat or strongly supported the death penalty and only 21 percent were opposed.[38] Texas has led the nation in the number of executions since the death penalty was reinstated in 1976. Of the top 15 counties in the United States that have issued death sentences since 1976, 9 of the counties have been in Texas (see Table 13.3).[39]

Since 1977 lethal injection has been the means for execution in Texas. The first execution by lethal injection was on December 7, 1982. Beginning in 1923 the state ordered that executions be carried out in Huntsville by electrocution. Prior to that time, each county was responsible for carrying out executions.[40] In March 2011, Texas replaced sodium thiopental with pentobarbital in the three-drug execution cocktail that is used for lethal injection. That was because the maker of sodium thiopental quit producing the drug after

TABLE 13.3

U.S. Counties with the Most Executions, 1976–2012

COUNTY (LARGEST CITY)	STATE	EXECUTIONS
Harris (Houston)	Texas	116
Dallas (Dallas)	Texas	50
Oklahoma City (Oklahoma City)	Oklahoma	38
Tarrant (Fort Worth)	Texas	37
Bexar (San Antonio)	Texas	36
Montgomery (Conroe)	Texas	16
Tulsa (Tulsa)	Oklahoma	15
Jefferson (Beaumont)	Texas	14
St. Louis (Florissant)	Missouri	13
St. Louis City (St. Louis)	Missouri	12
Brazos (College Station)	Texas	11
Maricopa (Phoenix)	Arizona	11
Nueces (Corpus Christi)	Texas	11
Pima (Tucson)	Arizona	11
Potter (Amarillo)	Texas	11

SOURCE: Data are from the Death Penalty Information Center, www.deathpenaltyinfo .org/executions-county.

In 1998, Karla Faye Tucker became the first woman executed in Texas since 1863. She was convicted of murder in 1983.

there were international protests over its use as an execution drug in the United States. Although there is controversy over this practice, at least for now Texas is using a single dose of pentobarbital because of drug shortages for the three-drug execution cocktail. Texas executed 515 people from 1976 through 2013. As of July 2013 there were 282 people on death row.[41] In Texas, one is subject to the death penalty for the murder of a public safety officer, fireman, or correctional employee; murder during commission of a kidnapping, burglary, robbery, aggravated rape, or arson; murder for hire; multiple murders; murder during a prison escape; murder by a prison inmate serving a life sentence; or murder of a child under the age of 6.

A stay on death row can be a lengthy one, even in Texas. The average time spent on death row prior to execution is 10.6 years, although the time varies considerably. One inmate under a death sentence waived his appeals and spent only a little more than eight months on death row prior to execution. On the other hand, David Lee Powell spent 31 years on death row prior to being executed in 2010.[42] A death sentence carried out in February 1998, however, initiated the greatest controversy over the death penalty. The case of Karla Faye Tucker, a convicted ax murderer, generated national demands for clemency. Tucker was widely believed to have undergone a religious conversion after her 1983 conviction. She was also attractive and articulate and was the first woman in modern times condemned to be executed in Texas. Supporters of her execution argued that her gender, appearance, articulateness, and possible religious conversion were irrelevant to the fact that she was a convicted murderer who should be treated like others in similar situations.

One of the issues involving the death penalty is whether all offenders are treated in the same way. There is a racial and ethnic disparity such that minorities, especially African Americans, are disproportionately represented on death row. Currently 110 death-row inmates are African American, 84 are Hispanic, 84 are white, and 4 are classified as "other."[43]

Since 1982, 225 whites have been executed, 187 African Americans, 86 Hispanics, and 2 of "other" racial and ethnic groups.[44] It may be that there is a bias in the criminal justice system such that minorities are disproportionately subject to the death penalty, although a counterargument is that the murder rate is higher among minorities. When the issue of whether there was racial bias in the imposition of the death penalty was presented to the U.S. Supreme Court, the Court refused to strike down the death penalty on the basis of statistical generalizations—essentially saying that there had to be evidence of racial bias in the imposition of the death penalty in the specific case presented to the Court.[45]

The Texas Board of Pardons and Paroles votes on clemency for death-row inmates. The board was originally considered to be a remedy for possible corruption in clemency granted by the governor. Prior to 1936 the governor essentially had unlimited power to grant clemency. This power was often abused, especially by Governor Miriam Ferguson, who granted 4,000 requests for commutations of sentences in 1922 alone. It was widely believed that payments were made for many of these acts of executive clemency. In reaction, a constitutional amendment was passed in

1936 that charged the board with giving the governor recommendations on clemency. Without such a recommendation, the governor can only grant a single 30-day reprieve. No other state so limits the powers of the governor.

In August 2007 the board recommended commutation of Kenneth Foster's sentence to be executed—only seven hours before Foster was scheduled to die. Governor Perry commuted Foster's sentence to life imprisonment about one hour later.[46] Foster's much-publicized case seemed to challenge two aspects of the death penalty in Texas: (1) Foster had been tried simultaneously with the other capital defendants rather than getting a separate trial, and (2) he was the getaway driver in the crime and not the actual shooter in the robbery and murder. Simultaneous trials with other defendants in murder cases can be a huge disadvantage for a defendant like Foster who was not the shooter but who is being tried with the shooter. Texas also has the law of parties—a person involved in a crime that leads to a murder is guilty of murder even though that person is not actually the person who committed the murder.

Though Texas has been called the nation's "Death Penalty Capital," in recent years the number of death penalties imposed in the state has dropped. One study of the Texas death penalty compared its imposition from 1992 to 1996 with its imposition from 2005 to 2009 and noted there was a 70 percent drop in death sentences. One explanation was a decline in capital murder convictions over this time period, and another was that beginning in 2005, Texas juries could impose a sentence of life without parole. Additionally, U.S. Supreme Court decisions now prevent execution of juveniles or the mentally retarded. The cost of death penalty prosecutions has greatly reduced death penalty prosecutions in all but the 12 largest counties. Finally, Harris County was the major county for imposing the death penalty in Texas. Because of changes in district attorneys there, scandal in the Houston crime lab, and improvements in the quality of capital defense work in Houston, there has been a huge drop in the imposition of the death penalty in Harris County.[47]

Kenneth Foster's father and wife celebrate after hearing that Governor Perry had commuted Foster's sentence only hours before Foster was to receive the death penalty. Foster was convicted of murder despite only driving the getaway car.

for critical analysis

Should prison be only for violent offenders? Will Texas ever eliminate the death penalty? Why or why not?

● The Integrity of the Texas Criminal Justice System

Explain why Texas's criminal justice system is often controversial

In recent years, numerous controversial issues and cases have raised questions about how criminal justice works in Texas. Earlier in the chapter we discussed concerns with prosecutorial abuses of power and with the difficulty some people may have in complying with the rules of the criminal justice process. Here, we consider whether aggressive use of the death penalty, wrongful convictions, and flawed evidence procedures are compromising the integrity of the criminal justice system. At the end of this section, we consider some of the reforms that have been attempted and proposed as ways to address concerns about criminal justice in Texas.

How Fair Is the Criminal Justice System?

Ideally, the criminal justice system should hold the guilty accountable and the innocent should be protected from punishment. That has not always been the case in Texas. There seem to be problems with fairness in the implementation of the death penalty, and there are a number of cases where overzealous police and prosecutors have punished innocent parties. The question is how common are those abuses and what, if anything, can be done about them.

The Death Penalty and Wrongful Convictions Texas has been more aggressive than any other state in imposing the death penalty. Yet as Texas continues to execute people, in 2000 Illinois suspended the death penalty after revelations of a number of wrongful convictions. New Jersey, North Carolina, and California are all considering moratoriums on the death penalty. Since 1989, 280 people wrongfully convicted of crimes in 34 states have been cleared as a result of DNA testing, including 17 people who served time on death row. The average prison time served by an exoneree was 13 years.[48] In the summer of 2005, Supreme Court Justice John Paul Stevens publicly noted that DNA evidence had shown that a number of death sentences had been erroneously imposed.[49]

This concern about the death penalty has even affected the internal dynamics of the Texas Court of Criminal Appeals, which is the state's court of last resort for death penalty appeals. Judge Tom Price challenged presiding judge Sharon Keller in the Republican primary in 2006 in part because he thought Judge Keller was too strict in her support of the decisions of trial courts in death penalty and other criminal cases. The Price-Keller primary battle reflected an emerging concern in Texas that the state has been too free in its imposition of the death penalty and too unquestioning of the evidence that leads to the imposition of criminal punishments.

Texas is the home of more verified wrongful convictions than any other state. As of July 12, 2013, 49 exonerations have occurred in Texas as a result of DNA testing.[50] Dallas County has emerged as the national leader in DNA exonerations of wrongfully convicted men. Twenty-four men in Dallas County were exonerated by DNA evidence.[51]

Problems with Police Procedures and Evidence Concerns about wrongful convictions are often related to the methods police and prosecutors use to convict suspects. One reason for the large number of DNA exonerations in Dallas County is simply that Dallas County has a policy of preserving physical evidence for lengthy periods of time, but others point to a pattern of convictions based on eyewitness identification with little or questionable forensic evidence. Many of the wrongfully convicted were prosecuted during the administration of District Attorney Henry Wade, whose office was known for high conviction rates. Critics claimed his office prized those high conviction rates above all else.[52]

Immediately after he became Dallas County district attorney in 2007, Craig Watkins did something no other Texas district attorney had ever done: he created a Conviction Integrity Unit in his office to investigate postconviction claims of actual innocence, to identify valid claims, and to then take appropriate action. Interestingly, with the exception of one case, every exoneration case that was investigated by the Conviction Integrity Unit involved mistaken eyewitness identification. At some point before their trial testimony, each eyewitness became certain that the innocent man was the criminal. In most cases, the innocent man was in the photo spread or the police lineup even though there was no specific reason to believe that he was the criminal. Being wrongly chosen in the lineup or photo spread by the eyewitness became the evidence against the innocent man. In many cases that was the only evidence against the innocent man, and in every case it was the most compelling evidence against him. That has led to a suggestion that there needs to be some minimum threshold of probability that those displayed in the photo spread or the lineup actually committed the crime. Additionally, it has been suggested that pretrial identification procedures be done in a way recognized by scientific best practices rather than in a haphazard, potentially unreliable way.[53] For example, with photo spreads, eyewitnesses are provided six photographs and asked if they recognize anyone in the photographs. However, sometimes those in the photographs are wearing distinguishing clothing or they are smiling or posed differently. One case examined by the Innocence Project of Texas, an organization that works on claims of innocence of those who have been imprisoned, involved a photo spread of six persons. A rape victim had told the police that the rapist was wearing a blue windbreaker. Only one person in the photo spread was wearing a blue windbreaker.

Johnny Pinchback celebrates after being freed from prison after serving 27 years. In 1984, Pinchback was convicted of aggravated sexual assault of two teenage girls, but DNA evidence cleared him in 2011. At the time, Pinchback was the twenty-second person to be exonerated through DNA testing in Dallas County since 2001.

There have also been problems with the handling of evidence sent to state and local crime labs. In 2002 the Houston Police Department Crime Laboratory was closed. An independent audit of the lab's DNA section had identified enormous problems. Analysts did not know how to do their jobs, and supervisors were also incompetent. There was no quality control system, and there were few standardized procedures. Other sections of the lab had problems as well, but the most serious were in the DNA section. Harris County sends more people to death row than any other county in America, and it had done thousands of other tests in non-death-penalty cases. All these tests were now placed in doubt. One of the first retests of the lab's work showed that a man who had been convicted of rape in 1998 at the age of 16 and had been given a 25-year sentence largely on the basis of DNA evidence was actually innocent. The problem with the lab was that as DNA technology changed, the analysts got no training in new methods, were overworked, and were following procedures inconsistently. Additionally, the lab was never inspected by an outside agency and did not seek accreditation. Nor were judges, prosecutors, and defense attorneys able to spot the lab's sloppy work—they had not kept up with DNA technology either. The lab's facilities were not conducive to good forensic science. The roof leaked over the DNA section of the crime lab, and the leaks were never patched. In 2001 when Tropical Storm Allison hit Houston, water poured through the roof, and DNA evidence in three dozen murder and rape cases was soaked. Bloody water was seen seeping out of evidence boxes.[54] DNA is often seen as the definitive proof of guilt or innocence in many serious crimes, but it is hardly definitive when the facilities are defective and the analysts are incompetent.

Another area of concern is the use of dog scent evidence to convict persons accused of crimes. Some prosecutors have claimed this evidence is as powerful as DNA evidence in supporting a conviction. This technique does not involve following a scent or picking out a package of drugs by trained dogs. Instead, it involves distinguishing different odors among people, identifying one odor, and then matching that odor to evidence obtained from a crime scene. A dog will be introduced to a scent sample collected at a crime scene. It will then be presented with a series of containers with similar scents—one taken from a suspect and others taken from other people matching the general description of the suspect. The dog will communicate to its handler if the first scent matches one of the scents in the containers. The handler will then testify that the dog accurately picked out the scent of a particular person or suspect. It is called a "scent lineup" and it has become a prosecution tool in Texas. The problem is that scent lineups are not reliable scientific evidence. Though some prosecutors in Texas have used them since the mid-1990s, defense lawyers have only recently successfully challenged them. The result is that the Innocence Project of Texas is now trying to identify persons in Texas who were convicted on the basis of scent lineups in the belief that this evidence is invalid and that those prisoners can be exonerated.[55]

The Willingham Case The case of Cameron Todd Willingham raises serious questions about whether questionable evidence led to the execution of an innocent man for the arson murders of his three children. In 1991, Willingham's three girls were killed in a fire at their home shortly before Christmas. Willingham was convicted of starting the fire that killed them. Even though he was offered a plea bargain of a life sentence, he refused the plea, claiming that he was innocent. Willingham was executed in 2004. His conviction was largely based on expert testimony that the fire was arson. To a great extent, that testimony was based on the opinion that the fire had burned so hot that a fire accelerant must have been used to start the fire. Additionally, forensic tests had found evidence of an accelerant on the front porch of the house. However, before Willingham was executed, a noted arson expert examined the case and prepared a report that showed that the fire patterns relied upon by the forensic experts who testified for the prosecution could have occurred without the presence of an accelerant and that the prosecution experts were relying on outdated information about the behavior of fire to reach their conclusions. That report was submitted to the Board of Pardons and Paroles, but the board rejected the plea for clemency.

After Willingham's execution, reporters for the *Chicago Tribune* investigated the case and asked three fire experts to examine the evidence. They concluded that the fire was not arson. Later, the Innocence Project of Texas asked four fire experts to review the Willingham case. They all agreed that the fire was not arson.

In 2005, Texas created a commission, the Texas Forensic Science Commission, to investigate claims of error or misconduct by forensic scientists. A fire scientist was hired by the commission to investigate the Willingham case and he too concluded there was no evidence that the fire was arson.[56] In September 2009, 48 hours prior to the review of the report by the Texas Forensic Science Commission, Governor Perry replaced the head of the commission and two of its members. The meeting of the commission was canceled as a result. Earlier, Governor Perry had expressed confidence in Willingham's guilt, called the critics of the original arson investigation "supposed experts," and said that he had not "seen anything that would cause me to think that the decision [to execute Willingham] was not correct."[57] The commission, however, did not drop the Willingham case, which remained under its review.

In July 2011, Attorney General Greg Abbott issued a ruling that restricted the further investigation of the Willingham case after a new commission chair showed greater interest in investigating the case. Nevertheless, cases of persons now in prison on arson charges are being reviewed by the Innocence Project to determine if their imprisonment resulted from bad arson science.[58]

The Tulia Drug Arrests Other widely publicized matters have also contributed to the questions raised about the adequacy of the Texas criminal justice system in protecting the innocent. One of those matters in particular became a national scandal—drug arrests in 1999 in Tulia, Texas. An undercover narcotics officer was responsible for the arrests of 47 persons in Tulia; 38 of them were black and made up about 20 percent of the black adults in the town. The defendants were zealously prosecuted. Though they were charged with possessing only small amounts of cocaine, the defendants, including those with no prior records, received long sentences—including one as long as 361 years. The undercover officer was supported by local authorities even as questions about his veracity mounted, and he was even named Officer of the Year in Texas. Doubts about the arrests and convictions, however, did not die. The officer never wore a wire, never videotaped his alleged drug buys, and was never observed by another officer. Indeed, most of his alleged drug buys had no corroboration at all.

Two and a half years after the last trials of the Tulia defendants, the undercover officer had been fired from two later narcotics assignments. It became clear that he had no undercover narcotics experience prior to coming to Tulia and that he had left jobs as a deputy sheriff in two other towns, leaving behind significant unpaid debts. One of the sheriffs who had employed him had filed criminal charges against him, which meant that he was indicted while working undercover in Tulia. Accusations were also made against him that he had racist attitudes as well as difficulties with telling the truth.

It eventually became clear that the Tulia drug busts were a massive miscarriage of justice. Thirty-five of the 47 defendants were pardoned by the governor; 9 had their charges dismissed prior to trial or were placed on deferred adjudication. One was a juvenile at the time of his alleged crime and so will not have an adult criminal record. The remaining 2 were sent to prison on probation violations. The disturbing factor is that without the efforts of a small number of concerned citizens, lawyers, and the press, this gross abuse of the criminal justice process would have remained undetected and unresolved.[59]

Nor was the Tulia affair the only major problem with drug arrests. In 2001 the Dallas Police Department agreed to pay an informant $1,000 per kilogram of confiscated drugs. Although the informant did know actual drug dealers, he realized they were dangerous, so he found harmless persons—Mexican immigrants and legal residents—on whom he could plant drugs. Apparently the informant also realized he could make more money with less risk if he passed off gypsum as cocaine. (Gypsum is a substance found in billiard-cue chalk.) Convictions on dozens of drug cases were obtained without even testing to see if the seized material contained real drugs. The informant was the Dallas Police Department's highest paid in 2001, earning more than $210,000 for the seizure of nearly 1,000 pounds of cocaine and amphetamines that turned out to be fake drugs. Twenty fake drug cases were multikilo seizures, and two were

Billy Wafer stands along Main Street in Tulia, Texas. Wafer was part of a large group of black Tulia residents who were arrested and imprisoned in a highly questionable 1999 drug sting. All of the people arrested were either pardoned or had their sentences greatly reduced.

Does Texas's criminal justice system need to be reformed? Some observers feel that, beyond problems with wrongful convictions, the emphasis on imprisonment and the large number of inmates in Texas are major concerns, though incarceration rates are declining.

the largest busts in the history of the Dallas police. Yet nothing seemed to arouse the suspicions of the police about the arrests. This scandal reached deep into the police department, where there was a lack of supervision of undercover officers and an extreme push for numbers in terms of amounts of drugs seized and number of arrests. The implausibility of some of the arrests is amazing: a lone mechanic working under his car, with no guns or cash seized; a drug buy on credit, according to the uncorroborated word of a confidential informant; and a seizure of 25 kilos of fake cocaine, for example. Nor did the district attorney's office escape blame: its policy was not to test seized drugs unless plea bargains failed and a case went to trial. When more than 80 of the drug cases were dismissed, Dallas district attorney Bill Hill went on television and insisted that many of those who were released were guilty. Were it not for the efforts of some criminal defense attorneys who were suspicious of the drug seizures, the Dallas Police Department might well still be seizing huge quantities of gypsum and paying its informant, and Texas might be sending innocent men and women to prison.[60]

● Reforms

Consider recent proposals to improve Texas's criminal justice system

Improvements in the Texas criminal justice system have occurred. Texas is no longer handling its crime problem solely by incarceration. The number of drug treatment programs has increased and there is greater emphasis on imprisonment as a last response to criminal behavior and more emphasis on community supervision such as requiring increased reporting to probation officers, community service, electronic monitoring of offenders, or mandatory treatment for alcohol or drug addiction as a first response. Parole supervision costs $4 a day for a prisoner as opposed to about $50 a day for incarceration. Probation costs are about 10 percent the cost of prison.[61]

The result has been a decline in prison construction and even the beginning of prison closings. Efforts are being made to compensate those who are wrongfully convicted. Texas has one of the most generous compensation systems in the nation for the wrongfully convicted. If a wrongfully convicted person waives his or her right to sue the state and is not convicted of further felonies after exoneration, he or she will receive a lump sum payment of $80,000 for each year wrongfully served in prison as well as an additional yearly payment during his or her lifetime that can amount to as much as $80,000 per year.

Some police departments are modifying their procedures for obtaining eyewitness evidence. For example, the Dallas Police Department has changed the way lineups are conducted so that the police officer administering the photographic lineup does not know who the actual suspect is, thus avoiding the police officer providing cues to the witness as to which photo to pick. Additionally, photos are now shown by many police departments sequentially rather than as a group. Research has shown that this helps prevent witnesses from comparing the photos and choosing the photo that most closely resembles the suspect rather than picking the suspect's picture. Prosecutors often call on scientific experts, such as arson investigators, to help prove their cases. However, fields such as arson science are rapidly evolving and sometimes the scientific theories that were once used to convict defendants in the past have now been debunked. For example, certain indicators that were once considered signs of arson are now known to appear in accidental fires.[62] A new Texas law makes it much easier for an inmate to challenge a conviction if it was based on bad science. As noted in the introduction, the Michael Morton Act has established a uniform system for district attorneys to provide exculpatory evidence to defense attorneys. Finally, some Texas district attorneys, most notably the district attorneys in Dallas county, have recognized the problem of wrongful conviction and have appointed prosecutors who review claims of wrongful convictions and who take a cooperative approach toward lawyers working with various innocence projects that exist to provide legal representation to people who claim they have been wrongfully convicted.

for critical analysis

Are wrongful convictions inevitable? Overall, is the Texas criminal justice process working as it should?

● Thinking Critically about Criminal Justice in Texas

Perhaps the criminal justice system in Texas works well. Overall, the previous examples may be exceptions to the rule. However, the documented problems with evidence, the Willingham case, the Tulia drug arrests, the Anthony Graves case, and the Michael Morton case discussed in the introduction to this chapter do raise questions about whether the criminal justice system in Texas is working as well as it should.

One of the issues facing Texas is the fairness of the process toward those accused of crime. Will Texas, for example, decide that there needs to be greater quality in the representation of people accused of crime so that the problems in the system can be identified and resolved before a person is convicted and imprisoned for a lengthy period? Dallas County district attorney Craig Watkins has received national acclaim by offering a new perspective on the role of a district attorney. Watkins sees the role of a prosecutor as not only convicting the guilty but also protecting the innocent charged with crime.

Texas is recognizing that the cost of imprisoning offenders is enormous and that there are alternatives to prison, especially for nonviolent offenders. The issue of the future will be whether Texas will continue pursuing alternatives to prison for offenders. On a related note, the death penalty has declined in its imposition in Texas. Will that pattern continue with urban counties reducing the imposition of the death penalty and with life without parole being increasingly seen as a reasonable alternative punishment? Finally, many states are reducing the penalties for some crimes such as possession of small amounts of marijuana. Will Texas join the national movement toward decriminalization? Crime and corrections have always been a major issue in Texas politics, and we may be on the cusp of major changes in this area.

Categorizing Crime in Texas

Identify the major classifications of crime under Texas law and the types of punishments that may be imposed (pp. 425–27)

Crimes are categorized along a number of dimensions. The more serious crimes are felonies. The less serious crimes are misdemeanors. Within each classification are various degrees of crime based upon the severity of the offenses. The more serious the crime, the greater are the penalties.

Key Terms

felony (p. 425)

misdemeanor (p. 426)

probation (p. 426)

parole (p. 427)

"three strikes" provision (p. 427)

Practice Quiz

1. The most serious crimes are classified as
   a) felonies.
   b) misdemeanors.
   c) trial-eligible crimes.
   d) grand jury felonies.
   e) county-court-at-law crimes.

2. Probation refers to
   a) a judge's initial term in office.
   b) a suspension of the jail or prison sentence.
   c) a court in the local state court system.
   d) release into the community after time in prison.
   e) failure to pay bail.

3. Which of the following is true?
   a) Parole is granted by the governor.
   b) Members of the Texas Board of Pardons and Paroles are elected by the legislature every two years.
   c) People convicted of capital crimes are not eligible for parole.
   d) The death penalty is required in all serious felonies.
   e) Texas does not enhance the sentence of repeat felony offenders.

The Criminal Justice Process

Outline the procedural steps that occur after a person is arrested (pp. 427–34)

There are a number of stages in the criminal justice process, including arrest, arraignment, possible posting of bail, possible grand jury indictment, pretrial hearings, and either plea bargaining or trial. If a person is found guilty, he or she will be sentenced, after which there may be appeals. Within this process, the most important actor is probably the district attorney, who is the key decision maker with regard to charging a suspect, presenting evidence to a grand jury, plea bargaining, or recommending a sentence to a jury or judge.

Key Terms

bail (p. 428)

grand jury (p. 428)

county attorney (p. 430)

district attorney (p. 430)

plea bargain (p. 431)

assigned counsel (p. 433)

public defender (p. 433)

Practice Quiz

4. Grand juries
   a) review all decisions made by a trial judge.
   b) determine if witnesses are telling the truth by voting "true bills" or "false bills."
   c) determine if there is probable cause to prosecute an individual for a crime.
   d) hear trials involving the death penalty.
   e) hear trials in district court.

5. District attorneys may have the most important roles in the criminal justice process because
   a) they have the power to charge people with crimes.
   b) they have the power to plea bargain with defendants.

c) they usually make the only presentation before grand juries.

d) all of the above

e) none of the above

6. Which of the following statements about plea bargaining is true?

a) Plea bargaining threatens to overwhelm the limited resources of a prosecutor's office.

b) Plea bargaining does not benefit defendants.

c) Plea bargains are made by defendants with district attorneys and agreed to by a judge.

d) Most Texas district attorneys oppose plea bargaining.

e) Most Texas criminal defense attorneys oppose plea bargaining.

7. Indigent defendants charged with serious crimes in Texas

a) must represent themselves.

b) are represented by private attorneys pro bono as part of their ethical obligation to help others.

c) most commonly are represented by public defenders.

d) most commonly are represented by judicially appointed private attorneys.

e) are usually represented by legal clinics at law schools.

Crime, Corrections, and the Texas Prison System

Describe prisons and corrections policy in Texas (pp. 434–45)

The Texas prison system is one of the largest in the nation. A major federal court decision (*Ruiz v. Estelle*) found serious overcrowding in the prison system. A series of reforms have been implemented to address the concerns raised by the decision. There has been an effort to lessen the number of people in prison through community supervision. While Texas remains the death penalty capital of the United States, fewer death penalties have been imposed recently than in earlier years.

Practice Quiz

8. The Texas prison system

a) was vastly affected by a federal court decision, *Ruiz v. Estelle*, that declared that the overcrowded system was unconstitutional.

b) holds mostly persons convicted of violent crimes.

c) is a very costly way of dealing with crime as opposed to community supervision such as drug and alcohol programs and probation and parole.

d) is beginning to contract in size after a long period of expansion.

e) All of the above are true of the Texas prison system.

9. The Texas Department of Criminal Justice

a) is run by a nine-member board appointed by the governor.

b) is run by an elected body.

c) runs the court system for felony murder.

d) establishes sentencing guidelines for crimes.

e) grants probation to those convicted of crimes.

10. The death penalty

a) is imposed in Texas for all murders.

b) has been imposed less frequently since Texas allowed juries to sentence a defendant to life without parole.

c) is carried out in the county where the crime occurred.

d) is carried out with an electric chair.

e) cannot be carried out without approval by the Texas Board of Pardons and Parole.

The Integrity of the Texas Criminal Justice System

> **Explain why Texas's criminal justice system is often controversial (pp. 445–50)**

Texas has had a significant number of people who have been wrongfully convicted. Numerous recent cases in which convictions were overturned have raised questions about the criminal justice system in Texas.

Practice Quiz

11. People have been wrongfully convicted in Texas because of
    a) police misconduct.
    b) bad or outdated forensic science.
    c) mistaken identifications.
    d) prosecutorial misconduct.
    e) All of the above are reasons for wrongful convictions.

12. An advance in which technology has conclusively proved the innocence of a large number of convicted people is
    a) drug testing.
    b) ballistics testing.
    c) DNA analysis.
    d) fire science.
    e) fingerprinting.

Reforms

> **Consider recent proposals to improve Texas's criminal justice system (pp. 450–51)**

Recent reforms that have been enacted may help reduce the number of wrongful convictions in Texas and improve the fairness of the criminal justice system. Reforms also may rely more on rehabilitation programs and less on incarceration as a solution to crime.

Practice Quiz

13. Reforms in the criminal justice process include
    a) financial compensation for people wrongfully convicted.
    b) changes to suspect lineups so that the police officer in charge of the lineup does not know who the actual suspect is.
    c) expanding drug treatment programs.
    d) showing photos in photo identifications to witnesses sequentially rather than at the same time to reduce the danger of witnesses comparing photos and choosing the one that best fits their memory of the assailant.
    e) All of the above are reforms to the criminal justice process.

14. Probation costs are
    a) about 10 percent of the cost of prison.
    b) 10 percent higher than the cost of prison.
    c) the same as the cost of prison.
    d) half the cost of prison.
    e) double the cost of prison.

Recommended Websites

Texas Criminal Justice Coalition
www.texascjc.org

Texas Department of Criminal Justice
www.tdcj.state.tx.us

Texas Coalition to Abolish the Death Penalty
www.tcadp.org

The Stand Down Texas Project
http://standdown.typepad.com

Innocence Project of Texas
http://ipoftexas.org

appendix

Here we include a series of documents that capture the nature of philosophical and practical problems the people of Texas confronted during their lengthy founding period. For each text we provide short introductions to guide the reader from the Texas Revolution, through statehood and the Civil War, to the Constitution of 1876. Copies of the various constitutions of Texas are available online at www.tarlton.law.utexas.edu/constitutions.

Texas Declaration of Independence (1836)

The Texas Declaration of Independence *was the product of the Convention of 1836.*[1] *Drawing upon John Locke's* Two Treatises of Government *(1689) and Thomas Jefferson's* Declaration of Independence *(1776) for inspiration, it lays out an explanation of the nature of government, lists the grievances that Texas's people hold against the Mexican government, and declares independence and the establishment of a new "free, sovereign, and independent Republic." Note the appeals to "the first law of nature, the right to self-preservation," "the inherent and inalienable right of the People to appeal to first principles," and the "sacred obligation" that people have to their posterity to create a government that will "secure their future wealth and happiness." In addition to presenting the Texas Constitution of 1836, the* Texas Declaration of Independence *lays down the republican principles that would define government and politics in Texas from 1836 to 1845, when Texas joined the United States of America.*

To the Public.

The undersigned, Plenipotentiaries from the Republic of Texas to the United States of America, respectfully present to the American People the unanimous DECLARATION OF INDEPENDENCE, made by the People of Texas in General Convention, on the 2d day of March, 1836; and, also, the CONSTITUTION framed by the same body.

ROBERT HAMILTON,
GEO. C. CHILDRESS.
WASHINGTON CITY, *May 22, 1836.*

Unanimous Declaration of Independence, by the Delegates of the People of Texas.

In General Convention, at the town of Washington, on the 2d day of March, 1836.

When a Government has ceased to protect the lives, liberty, and property of the People from whom its legitimate powers are derived, and for the advancement of whose happiness it was instituted, and so far from being a guarantee for the enjoyment of their inestimable and inalienable rights, becomes an instrument in the hands of evil rules for their oppression: when the Federal Republican Constitution of their country, which they have sworn to support, no longer has a substantial existence, and the whole nature of their Government has been forcibly changed, without their consent, from a restricted Federative Republic, composed of sovereign States, to a consolidated central military despotism, in which every interest is disregarded but that of the army and the priesthood, both the eternal enemies of civil liberty, the ever-ready minions of power, and the usual instruments of tyrants: when, long after

[1] "Unanimous Declaration of Independence, by the Delegates of the People of Texas," *Laws of the Republic of Texas, in Two Volumes* (Houston: Printed at the Office of the Telegraph, 1838), 1:3–4; Thomas W. Streeter, *Bibliography of Texas, 1795–1845* (5 vols.; Cambridge, MA: Harvard University Press, 1955–60). Errors in the original document are retained.

the spirit of the constitution has departed, moderation is at length so far lost by those in power, that even the semblance of freedom is removed, and the forms themselves of the Constitution discontinued; and so far from their petitions and remonstrances being regarded, the agents who bear them are thrown into dungeons and mercenary armies sent forth to force a new Government upon them at the point of the bayonet.

When, in consequence of such acts of malfeasance and abdication on the part of the Government, anarchy prevails, and civil society is dissolved into its original elements: in such a crisis, the first law of nature, the right of self-preservation, the inherent and inalienable right of the People to appeal to first principles, and take their political affairs into their own hands in extreme cases enjoins it as a right towards themselves, and a sacred obligation to their posterity, to abolish such Government, and create another in its stead, calculated to rescue them from impending dangers, and to secure their future welfare and happiness.

Nations, as well as individuals, are amenable for their acts to the public opinion of mankind. A statement of a part of our grievances is therefore submitted to an impartial world, in justification of the hazardous but unavoidable step now taken, of severing our political connexion with the Mexican People, and assuming an independent attitude among the nations of the earth.

The Mexican Government, by its colonization laws, invited and induced the Anglo-American population of Texas to colonize its wilderness, under the pledged faith of a written constitution, that they should continue to enjoy that constitutional liberty and republican Government to which they had been habituated in the land of their birth, the United States of America.

In this expectation they have been cruelly disappointed, inasmuch as the Mexican nation has acquiesced in the late changes made in the Government by General Antonio Lopez de Santa Ana, who, having overturned the Constitution of his country, now offers us the cruel alternative, either to abandon our homes, acquired by so many privations, or submit to the most intolerable of all tyranny, the combined despotism of the sword and the priesthood.

It hath sacrificed our welfare to the State of Coahuila, by which our interests have been continually depressed, through a jealous and partial course of legislation, carried on at a far-distant seat of Government, by a hostile majority, in an unknown tongue; and this too notwithstanding we have petitioned in the humblest terms for the establishment of a separate State Government, and have, in accordance with the provisions of the National Constitution, presented to the General Congress a Republican Constitution, which was, without just cause, contemptuously rejected.

It incarcerated in a dungeon, for a long time, one of our citizens, for no other cause but a zealous endeavor to procure the acceptance of our Constitution and the establishment of a State Government.

It has failed and refused to secure, on a firm basis, the right of trial by jury, that palladium of civil liberty and only safe guarantee for the life, liberty, and property of the citizen.

It has failed to establish any public system of education, although possessed of almost boundless resources, (the public domain,) and although it is an axiom in political science that, unless a People are educated and enlightened, it is idle to expect the continuance of civil liberty, or the capacity for self-government.

It has suffered the military commandants stationed among us to exercise arbitrary acts of oppression and tyranny, thus trampling upon the most sacred rights of the citizen, and rendering the military superior to the civil power.

It has dissolved by force of arms the State Congress of Coahuila and Texas, and obliged our Representatives to fly for their lives from the seat of Government, thus depriving us of the fundamental political right of representation.

It has demanded the surrender of a number of our citizens, and ordered military detachments to seize and carry them into the interior for trial; in contempt of the civil authorities, and in defiance of the laws and the Constitution

It has made piratical attacks upon our commerce by commissioning foreign desperadoes, and authorizing them to seize our vessels and convey the property of our citizens to far-distant ports for confiscation.

It denies us the right of worshipping the Almighty according to dictates of our own conscience, by the support of a national religion calculated to promote the temporal interests of its human functionaries rather than the glory of the true and living God.

It has demanded us to deliver up our arms, which are essential for our defence, the rightful property of freemen, and formidable only to tyrannical Governments.

It has invaded our country, both by sea and by land, with intent to lay waste our territory, and drive us from our homes; and has now a large mercenary army advancing, to carry on against us a war of extermination.

It has, through its emissaries, incited the merciless savage, with the tomahawk and scalping-knife, to massacre the inhabitants of our defenceless frontiers.

It has been, during the whole time of our connexion with it, the contemptible sport and victim of successive military revolutions, and hath continually exhibited every characteristic of a weak, corrupt, and tyrannical government.

These and other grievances were patiently borne by the People of Texas, until they reached that point at which forbearance ceases to be a virtue. They then took up arms in defence of the National Constitution. They appealed to their Mexican brethren for assistance. Their appeal has been made in vain: though months have elapsed, no sympathetic response has yet been heard from the interior. They are, therefore, forced to the melancholy conclusion that the Mexican People have acquiesced in the destruction of their liberty, and the substitution therefor of a military despotism; that they are unfit to be free, and incapable of self-government.

The necessity of self-preservation, therefore, now decrees our eternal political separation.

We, therefore, the Delegates, with plenary powers, of the People of Texas, in solemn Convention assembled, appealing to a candid world for the necessities of our condition, do hereby resolve and DECLARE that our political connexion with the Mexican nation has forever ended, and that the People of Texas do now constitute a FREE, SOVEREIGN, AND INDEPENDENT REPUBLIC, and are fully invested with all the rights and attributes which properly belong to independent States; and, conscious of the rectitude of our intentions, we fearlessly and confidently commit the issue to the decision of the Supreme Arbiter of the destinies of nations.

RICHARD ELLIS,
President.

C. B. Stewart,
Thomas Barnett, of Austin,
James Collinsworth,
Edwin Waller,
Asa Brigham
J. S. D. Byrom, of Brazoria,
Francisco Ruis,
Antonio Navaro,
Jesse B. Badgett, of Bexar,
Wm. D. Lacy,
Wm. Menifee, of Colorado,
James Gains,
M. B. Menard,
A. B. Hardin, of Liberty,
Baily Hardiman, of Matagorda,
J. W. Bunton,
Thos. J. Gazeley,

R. M. Coleman, of Mina,
Robert Potter,
Thos. J. Rusk,
Charles S. Taylor,
Jno. S. Roberts, of Nacogdoches
Robert Hamilton,
Collin McKinnee,
Alb. H. Lattimer, of Red River,
Martin Palmer,
W. Clark, jr., of Sabine,
John Fisher,
Matt. Caldwell, of Gonzales,
Wm. Motley, of Goliad,
L. de Zavala, of Harrisburg,
S. C. Robertson,
Geo. C. Childress, of Milam,
Steph. H. Everett,

Geo. W. Smith, of Jasper,
Elijah Stapp, of Jackson,
Claiborne West,
Wm. B. Scates, of Jefferson,
E. O. Legrand,
S. W. Blount, of San Augustine,
Syd. O. Bennington,
W. C. Crawford, of Shelby,
J. Power,
Sam. Houston,
David Thomas,
Edward Conrad, of Refugio,
John Turner, of San Patricio,
B. Briggs Goodrich,
G. W. Barnett,
James G. Swisher,
Jesse Grimes, of Washington.

Ordinance of Annexation Approved by the Texas Convention on July 4, 1845

The independent Republic of Texas ceased to exist in 1845 following the implementation of a new state constitution and Texas's formal admission into the Union as a state. Resolutions passed by the U.S. Congress stated the conditions under which Texas was to be admitted into the Union.[2] Note that the resolutions demand a republican form of government be adopted by the people through a constitutional convention (via a new constitution) and that the existing government consent to this action. Passage of this ordinance by the convention is an expression of the consent of the people of Texas to this new political configuration.

An Ordinance
Whereas,

the Congress of the United States of America has passed resolutions providing for the annexation of Texas to that Union, which resolutions were offered by the President of the United States on the first day of March, 1845; and

Whereas,

the President of the United States has submitted to Texas the first and second sections of said resolutions, as the basis upon which Texas may be admitted as one of the States of the said Union; and

Whereas,

the existing Government of the Republic of Texas, has assented to the proposals thus made,—the terms and conditions of which are as follows:

"Joint Resolutions for annexing Texas to the United States
Resolved by the Senate and House of Representatives of the United States of America in Congress assembled, That Congress doth consent that the territory properly included within and rightfully belonging to the Republic of Texas, may be erected into a new State to be called the State of Texas, with a republican form of government adopted by the people

of said Republic, by deputies in convention assembled, with the consent of the existing Government in order that the same may by admitted as one of the States of this Union.

2nd. And be it further resolved, That the foregoing consent of Congress is given upon the following conditions, to wit: First, said state to be formed, subject to the adjustment by this government of all questions of boundary that may arise with other governments,—and the Constitution thereof, with the proper evidence of its adoption by the people of said Republic of Texas, shall be transmitted to the President of the United States, to be laid before Congress for its final action on, or before the first day of January, one thousand eight hundred and forty-six. Second, said state when admitted into the Union, after ceding to the United States all public edifices, fortifications, barracks, ports and harbors, navy and navy yards, docks, magazines and armaments, and all other means pertaining to the public defense, belonging to the said Republic of Texas, shall retain funds, debts, taxes and dues of every kind which may belong to, or be due and owing to the said Republic; and shall also retain all the vacant and unappropriated lands lying within its limits, to be applied to the payment of the debts and liabilities of said Republic of Texas, and the residue of said lands, after discharging said debts and liabilities, to be disposed of as said State may direct; but in no event are said debts and liabilities to become a charge upon the Government of the United States. Third—New States of convenient size not exceeding four in number, in addition to said State of Texas and having sufficient population, may, hereafter by the consent of said State, be formed out of the territory thereof, which shall be entitled to admission under the provisions of the Federal Constitution; and such states as may be formed out of the territory lying south of thirty-six degrees thirty minutes north latitude, commonly known as the Missouri Compromise Line, shall be admitted into the Union, with or without slavery, as the people of each State, asking admission shall desire; and in such State or States as shall be formed out of said territory, north of said Missouri compromise Line, slavery, or involuntary servitude (except for crime) shall be prohibited."

Now in order to manifest the assent of the people of this Republic, as required in the above recited portions of said

[2] *Journals of the Constitution Convention of Texas, 1845* (Austin: Miner and Cruger, Printers to the Constitution, 1845), 367–70.

resolutions, we the deputies of the people of Texas, in convention assembled, in their name and by their authority, do ordain and declare, that we assent to and accept the proposals, conditions and guarantees, contained in the first and second sections of the Resolution of the Congress of the United States aforesaid.

In testimony whereof, we have hereunto subscribed our names

THOMAS J. RUSK
President

followed by 61 signatures

Attest
JAMES H. RAYMOND
Secretary of the Convention

Sam Houston's Address on Secession (1860) and Declaration of Causes (1861)

Texas joined the Union in 1845 and left it in 1861. Following the lead of other southern states after the election of Lincoln, Texas called a Secession Convention that met in January 1861. Despite the efforts of Governor Sam Houston to keep Texas in the Union, the convention passed an Ordinance of Secession on February 1 and a Declaration of Causes on February 2, 1861.[3] Texas joined the Confederacy as a state on March 1, 1861. Following a four-year conflict, as a practical matter the war ended in April 1865 with the surrender of Lee's Army of Northern Virginia. The last battle of the war (the Battle of Palmito Ranch) was fought May 12–13, 1865, near Brownsville.

Sam Houston's address captures the minority pro-Union position in Texas. A disciple of Andrew Jackson who rigorously opposed the attempts of South Carolina to reject the dominance of the national government during the Nullification Debates of the 1830s, Houston argued that leaving the Union was a dangerous action for the South. Note that Houston does not reject slavery as an institution but argues that the best way to defend Texans and Texas's interests is within the existing constitutional structure.

The Declaration of Causes presents the pro-secession argument in Texas, the one that ultimately carried the day. Note this document expresses the fear that southern proslavery states will become a minority in the Union. It also rejects the northern abolitionist contention that there is a "higher law" operating above the U.S. Constitution.

From Sam Houston's Address on Secession, Austin, Texas, 1860

. . . [I]n 1836, I volunteered to aid in transplanting American liberty to this soil, it was with the belief that the Constitution and the Union were to be perpetual blessings to the human race,—that the success of the experiment of our fathers was beyond dispute, and that whether under the banner of the Lone Star or that many-starred banner of the Union, I could

[3] Edwin Anderson Alderman, *Library of Southern History*, ed. Joel Chandler Harris (Atlanta: Martin and Hoyt, 1909).

point to the land of Washington, Jefferson, and Jackson, as the land blest beyond all other lands, where freedom would be eternal and Union unbroken. . . . Power, wealth, expansion, victory, have followed in its path, and yet the aegis of the Union has been broad enough to encompass all. Is not this worth perpetuating? Will you exchange this for all the hazards, the anarchy and carnage of civil war? Do you believe that it will be dissevered and no shock felt in society? You are asked to plunge into a revolution; but are you told how to get out of it? Not so; but it is to be a leap in the dark—a leap into an abyss, whose horrors would even fright the mad spirits of disunion who tempt you on.

. . . What is there that is free that we have not? Are our rights invaded and no Government ready to protect them? No! Are our institutions wrested from us and others foreign to our taste forced upon us? No! Is the right of free speech, a free press, or free suffrage taken from us? No! Has our property been taken from us and the Government failed to interpose when called upon? No, none of these! The rights of the States and the rights of individuals are still maintained. We have yet the Constitution, we have yet a judiciary, which has never been appealed to in vain—we have yet just laws and officers to administer them; and an army and navy, ready to maintain any and every constitutional right of the citizen. Whence then this clamor about disunion? Whence this cry of protection to property or disunion, when even the very loudest in the cry, declared under their Senatorial oaths, but a few months since, that no protection was necessary? Are we to sell reality for a phantom?

There is no longer a holy ground upon which the footsteps of the demagogue may not fall. One by one the sacred things placed by patriotic hands upon the altar of our liberties, have been torn down. The Declaration of our Independence is jeered at. The farewell counsels of Washington are derided. The charm of those historic names which make glorious our past has been broken, and now the Union is no longer held sacred, but made secondary to the success of party and the adoption of abstractions. We hear of secession—"peaceable secession." We are to believe that this people, whose progressive civilization has known no obstacles, but has already driven back one race and is fast Americanizing another, who have conquered armies and navies,—whose career has been onward and never has receded, be the step right or wrong, is at last quietly and calmly to be denationalized, to be rent into fragments, sanctioned by the Constitution, and there not only be none of the incidents of revolution, but amid peace and happiness we are to have freedom from abolition clamor, security to the institution of slavery, and a career of glory under a Southern Confederacy, which we can never attain in our present condition! When we deny the right of a State to secede, we are pointed to the resolves of chivalric South Carolina and other States; and are told, "Let them go out and you can not whip them back." My friends, there will be no necessity of whipping them back. They will soon whip themselves, and will not be worth whipping back. Deprived of the protection of the Union, of the aegis of the Constitution, they would soon dwindle into petty States, to be again rent in twain by dissensions or through the ambition of selfish chieftains, and would become a prey to foreign powers. They gravely talk of holding treaties with Great Britain and other foreign powers, and the great advantages which would arise to the South from separation are discussed. Treaties with Great Britain! Alliance with foreign powers! Have these men forgotten history? Look at Spanish America! Look at the condition of every petty State, which by alliance with Great Britain is subject to continual aggression! And yet, after picturing the rise and progress of Abolitionism, tracing it to the Wilberforce movement in England, and British influence in the North, showing that British gold has sustained and encouraged Northern fanaticism, we are told to be heedless of the consequences of disunion, for the advantages of British alliance would far over-estimate the loss of the Union!

. . . It is but natural that we all should desire the defeat of the Black Republican candidates. As Southern men, the fact that their party is based upon the one idea of opposition to our institutions, is enough to demand our efforts against them; but we have a broader, a more national cause of opposition to them. Their party is sectional. It is at war with those principles of equality and nationality upon which the Government is formed, and as much the foe of the Northern as of the Southern man. Its mission is to engender strife, to foster hatred between brethren, and to encourage the formation here of Southern sectional parties equally dangerous to Southern and Northern rights. The conservative energies of the country are called upon to take a stand now against the Northern sectional party, because its strength betokens success. Defeat and overthrow it, and the defeat and overthrow of Southern sectionalism is easy.

I come not here to speak in behalf of a united South against Lincoln. I appeal to the nation. I ask not the defeat of sectionalism by sectionalism, but by nationality. These men who talk of a united South, know well that it begets a united North. Talk of frightening the North into measures by threats of dissolving the Union! It is child's play and folly. It is all the Black Republican leaders want. American blood, North nor South, has not yet become so ignoble as to be chilled by threats. Strife begets strife, threat begets threat, and taunt begets taunt, and these disunionists know it. American blood brooks no such restraints as these men would put upon it. I would blush with shame for America, if I could believe that one vast portion of my countrymen had sunk so low that childish threats would intimidate them. . . .

The error has been that the South has met sectionalism by sectionalism. We want a Union basis, one broad enough to comprehend the good and true friends of the Constitution at the North. To hear Southern disunionists talk, you would think the majority of the Northern people were in this Black Republican party; but it is not so. They are in a minority, and it but needs a patriotic movement like that supported by the conservatives of Texas, to unite the divided opposition to that party there and overthrow it. . . .

I came not here to vindicate candidates or denounce them. They stand upon their records. If they are national, approve them; if they are sectional, condemn. Judge them by the principles they announce. Let past differences be forgotten in the determination to unite against sectionalism. I have differed with all three of the candidates; but whenever I see a man at this crisis coming boldly up to the defense of the Constitution of the country, and ready to maintain the Union against its foes, I will not permit old scores to prejudice me against him. Hence I am ready to vote the Union ticket, and if all the candidates occupy this national ground, my vote may be transferred to either of them. This is the way to put Mr. Lincoln down. Put him down constitutionally, by rallying the conservative forces and sacrificing men for the sake of principles.

But if, through division in the ranks of those opposed to Mr. Lincoln, he should be elected, we have no excuse for dissolving the Union. The Union is worth more than Mr. Lincoln, and if the battle is to be fought for the Constitution, let us fight it in the Union and for the sake of the Union. With a majority of the people in favor of the Constitution, shall we desert the Government and leave it in the hands of the minority? A new obligation will be imposed upon us, to guard the Constitution and to see that no infraction of it is attempted or permitted. If Mr. Lincoln administers the Government in accordance with the Constitution, our rights must be respected. If he does not, the Constitution has provided a remedy.

No tyrant or usurper can ever invade our rights so long as we are united. Let Mr. Lincoln attempt it, and his party will scatter like chaff before the storm of popular indignation which will burst forth from one end of the country to the other. Secession or revolution will not be justified until legal and constitutional means of redress have been tried, and I can not believe that the time will ever come when these will prove inadequate. . . .

Declaration of Causes: February 2, 1861[4]
A declaration of the causes which impel the State
of Texas to secede from the Federal Union.

The government of the United States, by certain joint resolutions, bearing date the 1st day of March, in the year A.D. 1845, proposed to the Republic of Texas, then a free, sovereign and independent nation, the annexation of the latter to the former as one of the co-equal States thereof,

The people of Texas, by deputies in convention assembled, on the fourth day of July of the same year, assented to and accepted said proposals and formed a constitution for the proposed State, upon which on the 29th day of December in the same year, said State was formally admitted into the Confederated Union.

Texas abandoned her separate national existence and consented to become one of the Confederated States to promote her welfare, insure domestic tranquility [sic] and secure more substantially the blessings of peace and liberty to her people. She was received into the confederacy with her own constitution, under the guarantee of the federal constitution and the compact of annexation, that she should enjoy these blessings. She was received as a commonwealth holding, maintaining and protecting the institution known as negro slavery—the servitude of the African to the white race within her limits—a relation that had existed from the first settlement of her wilderness by the white race, and which her people intended should exist in all future time. Her institutions and geographical position established the strongest ties between her and other slave-holding States of the confederacy. Those ties have been strengthened by association. But what has been the course of the government of the United States, and of the people and authorities of the non-slave-holding States, since our connection with them?

The controlling majority of the Federal Government, under various pretences and disguises, has so administered the same as to exclude the citizens of the Southern States, unless under odious and unconstitutional restrictions, from all the immense territory owned in common by all the States on the Pacific Ocean, for the avowed purpose of acquiring sufficient power in the common government to use it as a means of destroying the institutions of Texas and her sister slave-holding States.

By the disloyalty of the Northern States and their citizens and the imbecility of the Federal Government, infamous combinations of incendiaries and outlaws have been permitted in those States and the common territory of Kansas to trample upon the federal laws, to war upon the lives and property of Southern citizens in that territory, and finally, by violence and mob law, to usurp the possession of the same as exclusively the property of the Northern States.

The Federal Government, while but partially under the control of these our unnatural and sectional enemies, has for years almost entirely failed to protect the lives and property of the people of Texas against the Indian savages on our border, and more recently against the murderous forays of banditti from the neighboring territory of Mexico; and when our State government has expended large amounts for such purpose, the Federal Government has refused reimbursement therefor, thus rendering our condition more insecure and harrassing [sic] than it was during the existence of the Republic of Texas.

These and other wrongs we have patiently borne in the vain hope that a returning sense of justice and humanity would induce a different course of administration.

When we advert to the course of individual non-slaveholding States, and that [of] a majority of their citizens, our grievances assume far greater magnitude.

The States of Maine, Vermont, New Hampshire, Connecticut, Rhode Island, Massachusetts, New York, Pennsylvania, Ohio, Wisconsin, Michigan and Iowa, by solemn legislative enactments, have deliberately, directly or indirectly violated the 3rd clause of the 2nd section of the 4th article of the federal constitution, and laws passed in pursuance thereof; thereby annulling a material provision of the compact, designed by its framers to perpetuate amity between the members of the confederacy and to secure the rights of the slaveholding States in their domestic institutions—a provision founded in justice and wisdom, and without the enforcement of which the compact fails to accomplish the object of its creation. Some of those States have imposed high fines and degrading penalties upon any of their citizens or officers who may carry out in good faith that provision of the compact, or the federal laws enacted in accordance therewith.

In all the non-slave-holding States, in violation of that good faith and comity which should exist between entirely distinct nations, the people have formed themselves into a great sectional party, now strong enough in numbers to control the affairs of each of those States, based upon the unnatural feeling of hostility to these Southern States and their beneficent and patriarchal system of African slavery, proclaiming the debasing doctrine of the equality of all men, irrespective of race or color—a doctrine at war with nature, in opposition to the experience of mankind, and in violation of the plainest revelations of the Divine Law. They demand the abolition of negro slavery throughout the confederacy, the recognition of political equality between the white and the negro races, and avow their determination to press on their crusade against us, so long as a negro slave remains in these States.

For years past this abolition organization has been actively sowing the seeds of discord through the Union, and has rendered the federal congress the arena for spreading firebrands and hatred between the slave-holding and non-slave-holding States.

---

[4] Ernest William Winkler, ed., *Journal of the Secession Convention of Texas 1861, Edited from the Original in the Department of State by Ernest William Winkler, State Librarian* (Austin: Texas Library and Historical Commission, 1912), 61–65.

By consolidating their strength, they have placed the slave-holding States in a hopeless minority in the federal congress, and rendered representation of no avail in protecting Southern rights against their exactions and encroachments.

They have proclaimed, and at the ballot box sustained, the revolutionary doctrine that there is a "higher law" than the constitution and laws of our Federal Union, and virtually that they will disregard their oaths and trample upon our rights.

They have for years past encouraged and sustained lawless organizations to steal our slaves and prevent their recapture, and have repeatedly murdered Southern citizens while lawfully seeking their rendition.

They have invaded Southern soil and murdered unoffending citizens, and through the press their leading men and a fanatical pulpit have bestowed praise upon the actors and assassins in these crimes, while the governors of several of their States have refused to deliver parties implicated and indicted for participation in such offences, upon the legal demands of the States aggrieved.

They have, through the mails and hired emissaries, sent seditious pamphlets and papers among us to stir up servile insurrection and bring blood and carnage to our firesides.

They have sent hired emissaries among us to burn our towns and distribute arms and poison to our slaves for the same purpose.

They have impoverished the slave-holding States by unequal and partial legislation, thereby enriching themselves by draining our substance.

They have refused to vote appropriations for protecting Texas against ruthless savages, for the sole reason that she is a slave-holding State.

And, finally, by the combined sectional vote of the seventeen non-slave-holding States, they have elected as president and vice-president of the whole confederacy two men whose chief claims to such high positions are their approval of these long continued wrongs, and their pledges to continue them to the final consummation of these schemes for the ruin of the slave-holding States.

In view of these and many other facts, it is meet that our own views should be distinctly proclaimed.

We hold as undeniable truths that the governments of the various States, and of the confederacy itself, were established exclusively by the white race, for themselves and their posterity; that the African race had no agency in their establishment; that they were rightfully held and regarded as an inferior and dependent race, and in that condition only could their existence in this country be rendered beneficial or tolerable.

That in this free government all white men are and of right ought to be entitled to equal civil and political rights; that the servitude of the African race, as existing in these States, is mutually beneficial to both bond and free, and is abundantly authorized and justified by the experience of mankind, and the revealed will of the Almighty Creator, as recognized by all Christian nations; while the destruction of the existing relations between the two races, as advocated by our sectional enemies, would bring inevitable calamities upon both and desolation upon the fifteen slave-holding States.

By the secession of six of the slave-holding States, and the certainty that others will speedily do likewise, Texas has no alternative but to remain in an isolated connection with the North, or unite her destinies with the South.

For these and other reasons, solemnly asserting that the federal constitution has been violated and virtually abrogated by the several States named, seeing that the federal government is now passing under the control of our enemies to be diverted from the exalted objects of its creation to those of oppression and wrong, and realizing that our own State can no longer look for protection, but to God and her own sons—We the delegates of the people of Texas, in Convention assembled, have passed an ordinance dissolving all political connection with the government of the United States of America and the people thereof and confidently appeal to the intelligence and patriotism of the freemen of Texas to ratify the same at the ballot box, on the 23rd day of the present month.

Adopted in Convention on the 2nd day of Feby, in the year of our Lord one thousand eight hundred and sixty-one and of the independence of Texas the twenty-fifth.

Ordinance of Secession Null (1866) and *Texas v. White et al.* (1869)

Once the South and Texas had been defeated in the Civil War, the question arose as to the constitutional status of the secessionist states, including Texas. From the perspective of law and constitutional thought, had the southern states ever left the Union? Were the actions of state governments under the Confederacy legal or not? Two documents help clarify this issue.[5]

The ordinance declaring secession null and void answers these questions directly. By the expressed declaration of the Texas people in convention, the ordinance proclaims the 1861 act of secession to be null and void. Texas may have been in rebellion, but it never left the Union. Actions by the Confederate state of Texas thus were not legal.

The Texas v. White et al. *case answers this question further by exploring the legality of specific actions of the Confederate legislature in Texas. In 1850, Congress authorized $10 million in bonds to Texas. In 1862 the Confederate legislature authorized using the bonds for war supplies. In 1866, after the war, the Reconstruction government of Texas tried to reclaim the bonds on the grounds that the Confederate state government had illegally sold the bonds. Note the constitutional theory about the nature of the Union and the rebellion that is developed in the Chief Justice's opinion. The union established under the Articles of Convention and the U.S. Constitution is "perpetual" and "indissoluble." Once Texas joined the Union, Texas and Texans became part of this Union. Texas may have been in rebellion against the Union, but it had never left the Union. The actions of the Confederate government, like the act of secession, were thus null and void. The bonds thus had not been legally sold.*

An Ordinance, Declaring the Ordinance of Secession Null and Void (*March 15, 1866*)

Be it ordained by the people of Texas in Convention assembled, That we acknowledge the supremacy of the Constitution of the United States, and the laws passed in pursuance thereof;

and that an Ordinance adopted by a former Convention of the people of Texas on the 1st day of February, A.D. 1861, entitled "An Ordinance to Dissolve the Union between the State of Texas and the other States, united under the compact styled 'Constitution of the United States of America,'" be and the same is hereby declared null and void; and the right heretofore claimed by the State of Texas to secede from the Union, is hereby distinctly renounced. Passed 15th March, 1866.

From TEXAS v. WHITE ET AL. (1869)
Supreme Court of United States.

The CHIEF JUSTICE delivered the opinion of the court.

. . . If, therefore, it is true that the State of Texas was not at the time of filing this bill, or is not now, one of the United States, we have no jurisdiction of this suit, and it is our duty to dismiss it.

We are very sensible of the magnitude and importance of this question, of the interest it excites, and of the difficulty, not to say impossibility, of so disposing of it as to satisfy the conflicting judgments of men equally enlightened, equally upright, and equally patriotic. But we meet it in the case, and we must determine it in the exercise of our best judgment, under the guidance of the Constitution alone. . . .

. . . [T]he word . . . [*state is*] used in the clause which provides that the United States shall guarantee to every State in the Union a republican form of government, and shall protect each of them against invasion. . . .

The Republic of Texas was admitted into the Union, as a State, on the 27th of December, 1845. By this act the new State, and the people of the new State, were invested with all the rights, and became subject to all the responsibilities and duties of the original States under the Constitution.

From the date of admission, until 1861, the State was represented in the Congress of the United States by her senators and representatives, and her relations as a member of the Union remained unimpaired. In that year, acting upon the theory that the rights of a State under the Constitution might be renounced, and her obligations thrown off at pleasure, Texas undertook to sever the bond thus formed, and to break up her constitutional relations with the United States. . . .

---

[5] The Constitution of the State of Texas, as Amended by the Delegates in Convention Assembled, Austin, 1866 (Austin: Printed at the Southern Intelligencer Office, 1866), 32.

The governor and secretary of state, refusing to comply, were summarily ejected from office.

The members of the legislature, which had also adjourned and reassembled on the 18th of March, were more compliant. They took the oath, and proceeded on the 8th of April to provide by law for the choice of electors of president and vice-president of the Confederate States.

The representatives of the State in the Congress of the United States were withdrawn, and as soon as the seceded States became organized under a constitution, Texas sent senators and representatives to the Confederate Congress.

In all respects, so far as the object could be accomplished by ordinances of the convention, by acts of the legislature, and by votes of the citizens, the relations of Texas to the Union were broken up, and new relations to a new government were established for them.

The position thus assumed could only be maintained by arms, and Texas accordingly took part, with the other Confederate States, in the war of the rebellion, which these events made inevitable. During the whole of that war there was no governor, or judge, or any other State officer in Texas, who recognized the National authority. Nor was any officer of the United States permitted to exercise any authority whatever under the National government within the limits of the State, except under the immediate protection of the National military forces.

Did Texas, in consequence of these acts, cease to be a State? Or, if not, did the State cease to be a member of the Union? . . .

The Union of the States never was a purely artificial and arbitrary relation. It began among the Colonies, and grew out of common origin, mutual sympathies, kindred principles, similar interests, and geographical relations. It was confirmed and strengthened by the necessities of war, and received definite form, and character, and sanction from the Articles of Confederation. By these the Union was solemnly declared to "be perpetual." And when these Articles were found to be inadequate to the exigencies of the country, the Constitution was ordained "to form a more perfect Union." It is difficult to convey the idea of indissoluble unity more clearly than by these words. What can be indissoluble if a perpetual Union, made more perfect, is not? . . .

When, therefore, Texas became one of the United States, she entered into an indissoluble relation. All the obligations of perpetual union, and all the guaranties of republican government in the Union, attached at once to the State. The act which consummated her admission into the Union was something more than a compact; it was the incorporation of a new member into the political body. And it was final. The union between Texas and the other States was as complete, as perpetual, and as indissoluble as the union between the original States. There was no place for reconsideration, or revocation, except through revolution, or through consent of the States.

Considered therefore as transactions under the Constitution, the ordinance of secession, adopted by the convention and ratified by a majority of the citizens of Texas, and all the acts of her legislature intended to give effect to that ordinance, were absolutely null. They were utterly without operation in law. The obligations of the State, as a member of the Union, and of every citizen of the State, as a citizen of the United States, remained perfect and unimpaired. It certainly follows that the State did not cease to be a State, nor her citizens to be citizens of the Union. If this were otherwise, the State must have become foreign, and her citizens foreigners. The war must have ceased to be a war for the suppression of rebellion, and must have become a war for conquest and subjugation.

Our conclusion therefore is, that Texas continued to be a State, and a State of the Union, notwithstanding the transactions to which we have referred. And this conclusion, in our judgment, is not in conflict with any act or declaration of any department of the National government, but entirely in accordance with the whole series of such acts and declarations since the first outbreak of the rebellion. . . .

These new relations imposed new duties upon the United States. The first was that of suppressing the rebellion. The next was that of re-establishing the broken relations of the State with the Union. The first of these duties having been performed, the next necessarily engaged the attention of the National government.

The authority for the performance of the first had been found in the power to suppress insurrection and carry on war; for the performance of the second, authority was derived from the obligation of the United States to guarantee to every State in the Union a republican form of government. . . .

It follows that the title of the State was not divested by the act of the insurgent government in entering into this contract. . . .

From Governor Richard Coke Second Inaugural Address (1876)

Following the Civil War, Texas operated under two constitutions (the Constitution of 1866 and 1869). The return to power of the Democratic Party in the elections of 1872 and 1873 effectively ended reconstruction in Texas. A Constitutional Convention dominated by the Democrats in 1875 drafted a new constitution for the state that took effect in 1876.

Governor Richard Coke's second inaugural address in 1876 captures how many people thought of the new constitution. For Coke the 1876 Constitution was not meant to be a reworking of the earlier state constitutions. The people of Texas had become dissatisfied with the power granted to governmental institution over the last decade and were seeking to limit the powers and reach of government. The new constitution was to be unabashedly conservative in design and intent.

After years of trial and struggle, the people of Texas have at length inaugurated a government made in all its parts by themselves. Its faults and errors, as well as its blessings, have no uncertain paternity. The highest exercise of sovereign power of which a State in the American Union is capable, is that through which the people of Texas have swept out of existence the old government and enacted in its stead that which today has been put in operation in all its departments. Thus has a great revolution been accomplished, without violence or disorder, and with no other conflict than the attrition of opposing opinions in the field of argument and discussion, preparatory to the grand arbitrament of the peaceful ballot. . . . This is the sixth time in the history of Texas that this sovereign right has been exercised. . . .

In the more recently framed constitutions we plainly see a wide departure from the beaten track of constitutional structure, and in none of them is this more apparent than in the new Constitution of Texas.

The accepted theory of American constitutional government is that State constitutions are limitations upon, rather than grants of power; and, as a general rule, not without its exceptions, that powers not prohibited exist in State government. Hence, express prohibitions are necessary upon the powers the people would withhold from the State government, and as time and circumstances and experience suggest their wisdom, these restrictions upon the powers of government have multiplied in the more recently created instruments of fundamental law. Many causes have conspired to produce these great changes of constitutional theory, and prominent among them are the enormous amounts of capital concentrated in few hands, operating under charters which perpetuate its power; immense railroad systems, which drive off competition and monopolize the carrying trade of the country; the wonderful growth of towns and cities, whose immediate local governments are peculiarly subject to abuses and malign influences, general extravagance, and frequent corruptions of all departments of government, of late years becoming so alarming— all producing results which necessitate a clearer definition and closer guardianship of the rights of the people; and, for their protection, constitutional barriers not demanded by the conditions of society a quarter of a century ago.—

In this instrument we see mirrored the result of issues made in the politics of the State, in the halls of legislation, and in the primary assemblies of the people during the last decade; and we see faithfully reflected in its restrictions upon the power of government, as in its assertion of powers, the dangers of the past, a recurrence of which is so well guarded against in the future. The instrument presents in its fundamental and leading features a basis on which a government may be reared, eminently conservative of all the purposes for which government is instituted; adapted to a sound and healthy growth and development of the State. It may possibly be, in some respects too restrictive, but when such is the case, the error is on the safe side, and while temporary inconvenience may ensue, no permanent injury will result. . . .

The country and people whose welfare depends upon our deliberations and action need and expect a government light in its burdens, effective in administration, and certain in its securities for person and property. Naught else is necessary to ensure prosperity and continued progress and advancement. With such government the elements of greatness so abundant in the noble State we represent, in the hands of our intelligent adventurous and enterprising people, will combine, and evolve from the womb of the future a destiny of grander proportions than the most gorgeous dream of the enthusiast now pictures. . . .

Government of Texas Key Offices

	LEGISLATIVE BRANCH			
Name	**Party**	**District**	**City**	**Began serving**
Texas House of Representatives				
Gary Van Dever	Republican	1	Texarkana	2015
Dan Flynn	Republican	2	Canton	2003
Cecil Bell, Jr.	Republican	3	Magnolia	2013
Stuart Spitzer	Republican	4	Terrell	2015
Bryan Hughes	Republican	5	Mineola	2003
Matt Schaefer	Republican	6	Tyler	2013
David Simpson	Republican	7	Longview	2011
Byron Cook	Republican	8	Corsicana	2003
Chris Paddie	Republican	9	Marshall	2013
John Wray	Republican	10	Waxahachie	2015
Travis Clardy	Republican	11	Nacogdoches	2013
Kyle Kacal	Republican	12	College Station	2013
Lois W. Kolkhorst	Republican	13	Brenham	2001
John Raney	Republican	14	College Station	2011
Mark Keough	Republican	15	The Woodlands	2015
Will Metcalf	Republican	16	Conroe	2015
Tim Kleinschmidt	Republican	17	Lexington	2009
John Otto	Republican	18	Dayton	2005
James White	Republican	19	Woodville	2011
Marsha Farney	Republican	20	Georgetown	2013
Dade Phelan	Republican	21	Nederland	2015
Joe D. Deshotel	Democrat	22	Beaumont	1999
Wayne Faircloth	Republican	23	Galveston	2015
Dr. Greg Bonnen	Republican	24	Friendswood	2013
Dennis Bonnen	Republican	25	Angleton	1997
Rick Miller	Republican	26	Sugar Land	2013
Ron Reynolds	Democrat	27	Missouri City	2011
John Zerwas	Republican	28	Richmond	2007

(continued)

Name	Party	District	City	Began serving
Ed Thompson	Republican	29	Pearland	2013
Geanie Morrison	Republican	30	Victoria	1999
Ryan Guillen	Democrat	31	Rio Grande City	2003
Todd A. Hunter	Republican	32	Corpus Christi	1989
Scott Turner	Republican	33	Frisco	2013
Abel Herrero	Democrat	34	Robstown	2005
Oscar Longoria	Democrat	35	Mission	2013
Sergio Muñoz, Jr.	Democrat	36	Palmview	2011
René O. Oliveira	Democrat	37	Brownsville	1981
Eddie Lucio III	Democrat	38	Harlingen	2007
Armando Martinez	Democrat	39	Weslaco	2005
Terry Canales	Democrat	40	Edinburg	2013
R. D. "Bobby" Guerra	Democrat	41	Mission	2012
Richard Peña Raymond	Democrat	42	Laredo	1993
J. M. Lozano	Republican	43	Kingsville	2011
John Kuempel	Republican	44	Seguin	2010
Jason Isaac	Republican	45	Dripping Springs	2011
Dawnna Dukes	Democrat	46	Austin	1995
Paul Workman	Republican	47	Austin	2011
Donna Howard	Democrat	48	Austin	2006
Elliott Naishtat	Democrat	49	Austin	1991
Celia Israel	Democrat	50	Austin	2014
Eddie Rodriguez	Democrat	51	Austin	2003
Larry Gonzales	Republican	52	Round Rock	2011
Andrew Murr	Republican	53	Kerrville	2015
Jimmie Don Aycock	Republican	54	Killeen	2007
Molly S. White	Republican	55	Temple	2015
Charles "Doc" Anderson	Republican	56	Waco	2005
Trent Ashby	Republican	57	Lufkin	2013
Dewayne Burns	Republican	58	Burleson	2015
J. D. Sheffield	Republican	59	Gatesville	2013
Jim Keffer	Republican	60	Eastland	1997

(continued)

Name	Party	District	City	Began serving
Phil King	Republican	61	Weatherford	1999
Larry Phillips	Republican	62	Sherman	2003
Tan Parker	Republican	63	Flower Mound	2007
Myra Crownover	Republican	64	Denton	2000
Ron Simmons	Republican	65	Carrollton	2013
Matt Shaheen	Republican	66	Plano	2015
Jeff Leach	Republican	67	Plano	2013
Drew Springer, Jr.	Republican	68	Muenster	2013
James Frank	Republican	69	Wichita Falls	2013
Scott Sanford	Republican	70	McKinney	2013
Susan King	Republican	71	Abilene	2007
Drew Darby	Republican	72	San Angelo	2007
Doug Miller	Republican	73	New Braunfels	2009
Poncho Nevárez	Democrat	74	Eagle Pass	2013
Mary E. González	Democrat	75	Clint	2013
César Blanco	Democrat	76	El Paso	2015
Marisa Márquez	Democrat	77	El Paso	2009
Joseph E. Moody	Democrat	78	El Paso	2009
Joe C. Pickett	Democrat	79	El Paso	1995
Tracy O. King	Democrat	80	Batesville	1995
Brooks Landgraf	Republican	81	Odessa	2015
Tom Craddick	Republican	82	Midland	1969
Dustin Burrows	Republican	83	Lubbock	2015
John M. Frullo	Republican	84	Lubbock	2010
Phil Stephenson	Republican	85	Wharton	2013
John Smithee	Republican	86	Amarillo	1985
Walter "Four" Price	Republican	87	Amarillo	2011
Ken King	Republican	88	Canadian	2013
Jodie Laubenberg	Republican	89	Parker	2003
Ramon Romero, Jr.	Democrat	90	Fort Worth	2015
Stephanie Klick	Republican	91	Fort Worth	2013
Jonathan Stickland	Republican	92	Bedford	2013

(continued)

Name	Party	District	City	Began serving
Matt Krause	Republican	93	Fort Worth	2013
Troy Tinderholt	Republican	94	Arlington	2015
Nicole Collier	Democrat	95	Fort Worth	2013
Bill Zedler	Republican	96	Arlington	2003
Craig Goldman	Republican	97	Fort Worth	2013
Giovanni Capriglione	Republican	98	Southlake	2013
Charlie Geren	Republican	99	Fort Worth	2001
Eric Johnson	Democrat	100	Dallas	2010
Chris Turner	Democrat	101	Grand Prairie	2009
Linda Koop	Republican	102	Dallas	2015
Rafael Anchia	Democrat	103	Dallas	2005
Roberto Alonzo	Democrat	104	Dallas	1993
Rodney Anderson	Republican	105	Irving	2015
Pat Fallon	Republican	106	Frisco	2013
Kenneth Sheets	Republican	107	Dallas	2011
Morgan Meyer	Republican	108	Dallas	2015
Helen Giddings	Democrat	109	DeSoto	1993
Toni Rose	Democrat	110	Dallas	2013
Yvonne Davis	Democrat	111	Dallas	1993
Angie Chen Button	Republican	112	Richardson	2009
Cindy Burkett	Republican	113	Sunnyvale	2011
Jason Villalba	Republican	114	Dallas	2013
Matt Rinaldi	Republican	115	Coppell	2015
Trey Martinez Fischer	Democrat	116	San Antonio	2001
Rick Galindo	Republican	117	San Antonio	2015
Joe Farias	Democrat	118	San Antonio	2007
Roland Gutierrez	Democrat	119	San Antonio	2008
Ruth Jones McClendon	Democrat	120	San Antonio	1996
Joe Straus (Speaker of the House)	Republican	121	San Antonio	2005
Lyle Larson	Republican	122	San Antonio	2011
Mike Villarreal	Democrat	123	San Antonio	2000
José Menéndez	Democrat	124	San Antonio	2001

(continued)

Name	Party	District	City	Began serving
Justin Rodriguez	Democrat	125	San Antonio	2013
Patricia Harless	Republican	126	Spring	2007
Dan Huberty	Republican	127	Houston	2011
Wayne Smith	Republican	128	Baytown	2003
Dennis Paul	Republican	129	Houston	2015
Allen Fletcher	Republican	130	Cypress	2009
Alma Allen	Democrat	131	Houston	2005
Mike Schofield	Republican	132	Houston	2015
Jim Murphy	Republican	133	Houston	2007
Sarah Davis	Republican	134	West University Place	2011
Gary Elkins	Republican	135	Houston	1995
Tony Dale	Republican	136	Cedar Park	2013
Gene Wu	Democrat	137	Houston	2013
Dwayne Bohac	Republican	138	Houston	2003
Sylvester Turner	Democrat	139	Houston	1993
Armando Walle	Democrat	140	Houston	2009
Senfronia Thompson	Democrat	141	Houston	1993
Harold V. Dutton, Jr.	Democrat	142	Houston	1985
Ana Hernandez	Democrat	143	Houston	2005
Gilbert Peña	Republican	144	Houston	2015
Carol Alvarado	Democrat	145	Houston	2009
Borris Miles	Democrat	146	Houston	2007
Garnet Coleman	Democrat	147	Houston	1991
Jessica Farrar	Democrat	148	Houston	1995
Hubert Vo	Democrat	149	Houston	2005
Debbie Riddle	Republican	150	Tomball	2003
Texas Senate				
Brian Birdwell	Republican	22	Granbury	2010
Donna Campbell	Republican	25	New Braunfels	2013
Mike Dooling	Republican	16	Dallas	2015
Konni Burton	Republican	10	Fort Worth	2015
Bob Hall	Republican	2	Greenville	2015

(continued)

Name	Party	District	City	Began serving
Charles Perry	**Republican**	28	Lubbock	2014
Rodney Ellis	**Democrat**	13	Houston	1990
Kevin Eltife	**Republican**	1	Tyler	2004
Craig Estes	**Republican**	30	Wichita Falls	2001
Troy Fraser	**Republican**	24	Horseshoe Bay	1997
Sylvia Garcia	**Democrat**	6	Houston	2013
Kelly Hancock	**Republican**	9	North Richland Hills	2013
Undecided*		18	Katy	
Juan "Chuy" Hinojosa	**Democrat**	20	McAllen	2003
Joan Huffman	**Republican**	17	Houston	2008
Eddie Lucio, Jr.	**Democrat**	27	Brownsville	1991
Jane Nelson	**Republican**	12	Flower Mound	1993
Robert Nichols	**Republican**	3	Jacksonville	2007
Paul Bettencourt	**Republican**	7	Houston	2015
Van Taylor	**Republican**	8	McKinney	2015
José Rodríguez	**Democrat**	29	El Paso	2011
Charles Schwertner	**Republican**	5	Georgetown	2013
Kel Seliger	**Republican**	31	Amarillo	2004
Larry Taylor	**Republican**	11	Friendswood	2013
Carlos Uresti	**Democrat**	19	San Antonio	2007
Leticia Van de Putte	**Democrat**	26	San Antonio	1999
Kirk Watson	**Democrat**	14	Austin	2007
Royce West	**Democrat**	23	Dallas	1993
John Whitmire	**Democrat**	15	Houston	1983
Brandon Creighton	**Republican**	4	Conroe	2014
Judith Zaffirini	**Democrat**	21	Laredo	1987

*A special election will be held to replace Glenn Hegar, who resigned his Senate seat to take his position as Comptroller of Public Accounts.

(continued)

EXECUTIVE BRANCH				
Name	Party	District	City	Began serving
Governor				
Greg Abbott	**Republican**	Statewide		2015
Lieutenant Governor				
Dan Patrick	**Republican**	Statewide		2015
Attorney General				
Ken Paxton	**Republican**	Statewide		2015
Commissioner of the General Land Office				
George P. Bush	**Republican**	Statewide		2015
Comptroller of Public Accounts				
Glenn Hegar	**Republican**	Statewide		2015
Commissioner of Agriculture				
Sid Miller	**Republican**	Statewide		2015
Railroad Commission				
Ryan Sitton	**Republican**	Statewide		2015
David Porter	**Republican**	Statewide		2011
Christi Craddick (Chairman)	**Republican**	Statewide		2012
State Board of Education				
Martha Dominguez	**Democrat**	1	El Paso	2013
Ruben Cortez, Jr.	**Democrat**	2	Brownsville	2013
Marisa Perez	**Democrat**	3	San Antonio	2013
Lawrence A. Allen, Jr.	**Democrat**	4	Fresno	2005
Ken Mercer	**Republican**	5	San Antonio	2007
Donna Bahorich	**Republican**	6	Houston	2013
David Bradley	**Republican**	7	Beaumont	1997
Barbara Cargill (Chair)	**Republican**	8	The Woodlands	2005
Thomas Ratliff (Vice Chair)	**Republican**	9	Mount Pleasant	2011
Tom Maynard	**Republican**	10	Georgetown	2013

(continued)

Patricia Hardy	**Republican**	11	Fort Worth	2003
Geraldine Miller	**Republican**	12	Dallas	1984
Erika Beltran	**Democrat**	13	Dallas	2015
Sue Melton	**Republican**	14	Waco	2013
Marty Rowley	**Republican**	15	Amarillo	2013

JUDICIAL BRANCH

Name	Party	District	City	Began serving
Supreme Court of Texas				
Nathan Hecht (Chief Justice)	**Republican**	Statewide		1989
Don R. Willett	**Republican**	Statewide		2005
Debra Lehrmann	**Republican**	Statewide		2010
John Phillip Devine	**Republican**	Statewide		2012
Paul W. Green	**Republican**	Statewide		2004
Jeff Brown	**Republican**	Statewide		2013
Jeffrey S. Boyd	**Republican**	Statewide		2012
Phil Johnson	**Republican**	Statewide		2005
Eva Guzman	**Republican**	Statewide		2009
Court of Criminal Appeals				
Sharon Keller (Presiding Judge)	**Republican**	Statewide		1994
Lawrence Edward Meyers	**Republican**	Statewide		1992
Bert Richardson	**Republican**	Statewide		2015
Kevin Patrick Yeary	**Republican**	Statewide		2015
Cheryl Johnson	**Republican**	Statewide		1998
Michael E. Keasler	**Republican**	Statewide		1998
Barbara Parker Hervey	**Republican**	Statewide		2000
Elsa Alcala	**Republican**	Statewide		2011
David Newell	**Republican**	Statewide		2015

glossary

action by the governor the final step in the legislative process, during which the governor signs, vetoes, or refuses to sign a bill

agricultural commissioner elected state official who is primarily responsible for enforcing agricultural laws

Aid to Families with Dependent Children (AFDC) a federally and state-financed program for children living with parents or relatives who fell below state standards of need; replaced in 1996 by TANF

All Funds budget budget that aggregates all monies flowing into the state treasury and all state spending

answer the presentation of a defendant's defense against an allegation in a civil case

appointment the power of the chief executive, whether the president of the United States or the governor of a state, to appoint persons to office

appropriations authorization by the legislature to a government agency or body to spend up to a particular amount of money

Article 3, Section 49a (Pay-as-You-Go Limit) portion of the Texas Constitution that requires the state to maintain a balanced budget

assigned counsel private lawyers appointed by judges to provide legal representation for indigent defendants in serious criminal cases; the lawyer's fee is determined by and paid by the county

at-large election an election in which officials are selected by voters of the entire geographical area, rather than from smaller districts within that area

attorney general elected state official who serves as the state's chief civil lawyer

Available School Fund (ASF) dedicated fund established by the constitution for the support of public education in the state

bail payment of money to the state as an assurance that an accused person who is released from jail pending trial will appear for trial; if the accused does not appear, the bail is forfeited

bench trial a trial held without a jury and before only a judge

beyond a reasonable doubt the legal standard in criminal cases, which requires the prosecution to prove that a reasonable doubt of innocence does not exist

bicameral having a legislative assembly composed of two chambers or houses

biennial occurring every two years

bill a proposed law that has been sponsored by a member of the legislature and submitted to the clerk of the House or Senate

block grants federal grants that allow states considerable discretion on how funds are spent

Blue Dog Democrats another name for conservative Democrats, mostly from the South

bounded rationality the idea in policy making that decision makers may seek satisfactory solutions to problems that are not necessarily optimal or efficient

bundling the interest-group practice of combining campaign contributions from several sources into one larger contribution from the group, so as to increase the group's impact on the candidate

bureaucracy the complex structure of offices, tasks, rules, and principles of organization that are employed by all large-scale institutions to coordinate the work of their personnel

capital appreciation bond (CAB) a long-term, high-interest-paying bond that pays off both principal and interest in one lump sum when the bond reaches maturity

capital case a criminal case in which the death penalty is a possible punishment

categorical grants congressionally appropriated grants to states and localities on the condition that expenditures be limited to a problem or group specified by law

checks and balances the constitutional idea that overlapping power is given to different branches of government to limit the concentration of power in any one branch

civil law a branch of law that deals with disputes, usually between private individuals over relationships, obligations, and responsibility

closed primary a primary election in which only registered members of a particular political party can vote

coercive federalism federal policies that force states to change their policies to achieve national goals

commissioner form of government a form of city government in which the city is run by a small group of elected commissioners who act in both legislative and executive capacities

complaint the presentation of a grievance by the plaintiff in a civil case

comptroller elected state official who directs the collection of taxes and other revenues and estimates revenues for the budgeting process

concurrent resolution a resolution of interest to both chambers of the legislature and which must pass both the House and Senate and generally be signed by the governor

Confederacy the Confederate States of America, those southern states that seceded from the United States in late 1860 and 1861 and argued that the power of the states was more important than the power of the central government

conference committee a joint committee created to work out a compromise on House and Senate versions of a piece of legislation

consideration by standing committee the third step in the legislative process, during which a bill is killed, amended, or heard by a standing committee

constable precinct-level county official involved with serving legal papers and, in some counties, enforcing the law

constituent a person living in the district from which an official is elected

constitution the legal structure of a government, which establishes its power and authority as well as the limits on that power

contingent fee a fee paid to the lawyer in a civil case which is contingent on winning the case

cooperative federalism a type of federalism existing since the New Deal era in which grants-in-aid have been used to encourage states and localities (without commanding them) to pursue nationally defined goals; also known as "intergovernmental cooperation"

council of government (COG) a regional planning board composed of local elected officials and some private citizens from the same area

council-manager form of government a form of city government in which public policies are developed by the city council and executive and administrative functions are assigned to a professional city manager

county attorney county official who prosecutes lesser criminal cases in the county court

county auditor public official, appointed by the district judges, who receives and disburses county funds; in large counties, this official also prepares the county budget

county chair the county party official who heads the county executive committee

county clerk public official who is the main record-keeper of the county

county commissioner government official (four per county) on the county commissioners' court whose main duty is the construction and maintenance of roads and bridges

county commissioners' court the main governing body of each county; has the authority to set the county tax rate and budget

county convention a meeting held by a political party following its precinct conventions, for the purpose of electing delegates to its state convention

county courts the courts that exist in some counties that are presided over by county judges

county executive committee the party group, made up of a party's county chair and precinct chairs, that is responsible for running a county's primary elections and planning county conventions

county judge the person in each of Texas's 254 counties who presides over the county court and the county commissioners' court, with responsibility for the administration of county government; some county judges carry out judicial responsibilities

county tax assessor-collector public official who maintains the county tax records and collects the taxes owed to the county

courts of appeal the 14 intermediate-level appellate courts that hear appeals from district and county courts to determine whether the decisions of these lower courts followed legal principles and court procedures

criminal law the branch of law that regulates the conduct of individuals, defines crimes, and specifies punishment for criminal acts

dark money political money where the donors of the money do not have to be disclosed

debt service money spent by the state to pay off debt; includes interest and principal payments

deferred retirement option plan (DROP) retirement plan in which local government employees who are eligible to retire have their retirement benefits deposited in an account in which the benefits draw interest until actual retirement; some of these plans pay high interest and cost-of-living adjustments and may be coupled with very early retirement ages

directive and supervisory power the legislature's power over the executive branch; for example, the legislature determines the size of appropriations for state agencies

district attorney public official who prosecutes the more serious criminal cases in the district court

district clerk public official who is the main record-keeper of district court documents

district courts the major trial courts in Texas, which usually have general jurisdiction over a broad range of civil and criminal cases

Dixiecrats conservative Democrats who abandoned the national Democratic Party in the 1948 presidential election

dual federalism the system of government that prevailed in the United States from 1789 to 1937, in which most fundamental governmental powers were strictly separated between the federal and state governments

Duverger's Law the observation that in a single-member district system of electing representatives, a two-party system will emerge

early registration the requirement that a voter register long before the general election; in effect in Texas until 1971

early voting a procedure that allows voters to cast ballots during the two-week period before the regularly scheduled election date

Economic Stabilization Fund (ESF) fund established by constitutional amendment in 1988 to provide funds for the state during times of financial stress, commonly known as the Rainy Day Fund

electoral power the legislature's mandated role in counting returns in the elections for governor and lieutenant governor

elite a small group of people that dominates the political process

en banc referring to an appellate hearing with all judges participating

equal protection clause provision in the Fourteenth Amendment of the U.S. Constitution guaranteeing citizens the "equal protection of the laws"; this clause has been the basis for the civil rights of African Americans, women, and other groups

executive budget the state budget prepared and submitted by the governor to the legislature, which indicates the governor's spending priorities; the executive budget is overshadowed in terms of importance by the legislative budget

Federal Funds budget state budget that includes all grants, payments, and reimbursements received from the federal government by state agencies and institutions

federalism a system of government in which power is divided, by a constitution, between a central government and regional governments

felony a serious criminal offense, punishable by a prison sentence or a fine; a capital felony is punishable by death or a life sentence

filibuster a tactic used by members of the Senate to prevent action on legislation they oppose by continuously holding the floor and speaking until the majority backs down; once given the floor, senators have unlimited time to speak as long as they follow Senate rules, and it requires a vote of three-fifths of the Senate to end a filibuster

"first past the post" an election rule that states that the winner is the candidate who receives a plurality of the votes

floor action the fourth step in the legislative process, during which a bill referred by a standing committee is scheduled for floor debate by the Calendars Committee

free rider problem the incentive to benefit from others' work without making a contribution, which leads individuals in a collective action situation to refuse to work together

general bill a bill that applies to all people and/or property in the state

general election the election in which voters cast ballots to select public officials

General Revenue Fund the state's primary operating fund

General Revenue–Dedicated Funds budget budget composed of funds for dedicated revenues that target money for specific purposes

General Revenues Fund budget budget for a nondedicated revenue account that functions as the state's primary operating fund

Gilmer-Aikin Laws education reform legislation passed in 1949 that supplemented local funding of education with public monies, raised teachers' salaries, mandated a minimum length for the school year, and provided for more state supervision of public education

grand jury jury that determines whether sufficient evidence is available to justify a trial; grand juries do not rule on the accused's guilt or innocence

Grange a militant farmers' movement of the late nineteenth century that fought for improved conditions for farmers

hidden government a term that refers to special districts of which many citizens are unaware

Higher Education Fund (HEF) state higher education fund for universities not having access to PUF monies

home-rule charter the rules under which a city operates; local governments have considerable independent governing power under these charters

impeachment under the Texas Constitution, the formal charge by the House of Representatives that leads to trial in the Senate and possible removal of a state official

impresario an individual who promotes, organizes, or helps to finance a particular endeavor

independent state grounds allow states, usually under the state constitution, to expand rights beyond those provided by the U.S. Constitution

indictment a written statement issued by a grand jury that charges a suspect with a crime and states that a trial is warranted

individualistic political culture the belief that government should limit its role to providing order in society, so that citizens can pursue their economic self-interests

interest group an organization established to influence the government's programs and policies

interest-group capture government agency that serves the objectives of the interests that the agency is supposed to regulate

intermediate standard of review primarily used for classifications in the law based on sex; for the law to be constitutional the government must show important governmental objectives and the law must be substantially related to achievement of those objectives

introduction the first step in the legislative process, during which a member of the legislature gets an idea for a bill and files a copy of it with the clerk of the House or secretary of the Senate

investigative power the power, exercised by the House, the Senate, or both chambers jointly, to investigate problems facing the state

issue advocacy independent spending by individuals or interest groups on a campaign issue but not directly tied to a particular candidate

Jaybird Party after the white primary was ruled unconstitutional, this offshoot Democratic party preselected candidates for the Democratic primary and prohibited African Americans from participating

joint resolution a resolution, commonly a proposed amendment to the Texas Constitution or ratification of an amendment to the U.S. Constitution, that must pass both the House and Senate but which does not require the governor's signature

Judicial Campaign Fairness Act a judicial reform that places limits on judicial campaign contributions

judicial power the power of the House to impeach and of the Senate to convict members of the executive and judicial branches of state government

justice of the peace courts local trial courts with limited jurisdiction over small claims and very minor criminal misdemeanors

La Raza Unida Party political party formed in Texas in order to bring attention to the concerns of Mexican Americans

land commissioner elected state official who is the manager of most publicly owned lands

law of capture the idea that the first person "to capture" water or oil by pumping it out of the ground and using it owns that water or oil

layer-cake federalism a way of describing the system of dual federalism in which there is a division of responsibilities between the state and the national governments

legislative budget the state budget that is prepared and submitted by the Legislative Budget Board (LBB) and that is fully considered by the House and Senate

lieutenant governor the second-highest elected official in the state and president of the state Senate

limited government a principle of constitutional government; a government whose powers are defined and limited by a constitution

line-item veto the power of the executive to veto specific provisions (lines) of an appropriations bill passed by the legislature

lobbyist an individual employed by an interest group who tries to influence governmental decisions on behalf of that group

local bill a bill affecting only units of local government, such as a city, county, or special district

marble-cake federalism a way of describing federalism where the boundaries between the national government and state government have become blurred

matching funds federal monies going to a state based on state spending for a program

mayor-council form of government a form of city government in which the mayor is the chief executive and the city council is the legislative body; in the *strong mayor–council* variation, the mayor's powers enable him or her to control executive departments and the agenda of the city council; in the *weak mayor–council* variation, the mayor's power is more limited

Medicaid a federal and state program financing medical services to low-income people

merit selection a judicial reform under which judges would be nominated by a blue-ribbon committee, would be appointed by the governor, and, after a brief period in office, would run in a retention election

misdemeanor a minor criminal offense usually punishable by a small fine or short jail sentence

moralistic political culture the belief that government should be active in promoting the public good and that citizens should participate in politics and civic activities to ensure that good

motor voter law a national act, passed in 1993, that requires states to allow people to register to vote when applying for a driver's license

municipal courts local trial courts with limited jurisdiction over violations of city ordinances and very minor criminal misdemeanors

municipal utility district (MUD) a special district that offers services such as electricity, water, sewage, and sanitation outside the city limits

National Research University Fund (NRUF) fund established in 2009 to provide funding to universities seeking to achieve national prominence as research institutions

necessary and proper clause Article I, Section 8, of the U.S. Constitution; it provides Congress with the authority to make all laws "necessary and proper" to carry out its powers

New Deal President Franklin Delano Roosevelt's 1930s programs to stimulate the national economy and provide relief to victims of the Great Depression

New Federalism the attempts by Presidents Nixon and Reagan to return power to the states through block grants

Nineteenth Amendment ratified in 1919, amendment guaranteeing women the right to vote

nonschool special district any special district other than a school district; examples include municipal utility districts (MUDs) and hospital districts

North American Free Trade Agreement (NAFTA) trade treaty among the United States, Canada, and Mexico to lower and eliminate tariffs among the three countries

Occupy movement political movement aimed at limiting the influence of Wall Street and big corporations in American politics; created following government bailouts in 2008

one-person, one-vote principle the principle that all districts should have roughly equal populations

open primary a primary election in which any registered voter can participate in the contest, regardless of party affiliation

ordinance a regulation enacted by a city government each of Texas's incorporated cities and towns

Other Funds budget budget consisting of all other funds flowing into the state treasury that are not included in other state budgets; this includes the Texas Highway Fund, various trust funds operated by the state, and certain revenues held for local higher education accounts

parole the conditional release of an offender who has served some prison time, under specified rules and under the supervision of a parole officer

partisan polarization the degree to which Republicans have become more conservative and Democrats have become more liberal

patronage the resources available to higher officials, usually opportunities to make political appointments to offices and to confer grants, licenses, or special favors to supporters

per diem daily payment to a public official engaged in state business

Permanent School Fund (PSF) fund created in 1854 that provides monies for primary and secondary schools

Permanent University Trust Fund (PUF) fund established in 1876 and funded from the proceeds from land owned by the state; monies go to various universities in the University of Texas (UT) and Texas A&M systems

pigeonholing a step in the legislative process during which a bill is killed by the chair of the standing committee to which it was referred, as a result of his or her setting the bill aside and not bringing it before the committee

plea bargain negotiated agreement in a criminal case in which a defendant agrees to plead guilty in return for the state's agreement to reduce the severity of the criminal charge or prison sentence the defendant is facing

plural executive an executive branch in which power is fragmented because the election of statewide officeholders is independent of the election of the governor

political action committee (PAC) a private group that raises and distributes funds for use in election campaigns

political culture broadly shared values, beliefs, and attitudes about how the government should function and politics should operate; American political culture emphasizes the values of liberty, equality, and democracy

political socialization the introduction of individuals into the political culture; learning the underlying beliefs and values on which the political system is based

poll tax a state-imposed tax on voters as a prerequisite for voting; poll taxes were rendered unconstitutional in national elections by the Twenty-Fourth Amendment, and in state elections by the Supreme Court in 1966

post-adjournment veto a veto of a bill that occurs after the legislature adjourns, thus preventing the legislature from overriding it

precinct chair the local party official, elected in the party's primary election, who heads the precinct convention and serves on the party's county executive committee

precinct convention a meeting held by a political party to select delegates for the county convention and to submit resolutions to the party's state platform; precinct conventions are held on the day of the party's primary election and are open to anyone who voted in that election

precinct the most basic level of political organization at the local level

preclearance provision under Section 5 of the Voting Rights Act of 1965 requiring any changes to election procedures or district lines to be approved by the U.S. Department of Justice or the U.S. district court for the District of Columbia

preemption where the national government imposes its priorities and prevents the state from acting in a particular field

preponderance of the evidence the standard of proof in a civil jury case, by which the plaintiff must show that the defendant is more likely than not the cause of the harm suffered by the plaintiff

presidential Republicanism a voting pattern in which conservatives vote Democratic for state offices but Republican for presidential candidates

primary election a ballot vote in which citizens select a party's nominee for the general election

probation punishment where an offender is not imprisoned but remains in the community under specified rules and under the supervision of a probation officer

progressive tax type of tax where the tax burden falls more heavily on upper-income individuals

property tax a tax based on an assessment of the value of one's property, which is used to fund the services provided by local governments, such as education

proportional representation a multimember district system that allows each political party representation in proportion to its percentage of the total vote

provincialism a narrow, limited, and self-interested view of the world often associated with rural values and notions of limited government

public defender salaried lawyer who is funded by the government or by grants who represents indigents in Texas in some counties or for some types of cases

Radical Republicans a bloc of Republicans in the U.S. Congress who pushed through the adoption of black suffrage as well as an extended period of military occupation of the South following the Civil War

rational basis test presumes that the legal classification made by the government is constitutional; all the government must show is some rational justification for the law

rationality the idea in public-policy making that we have clearly identified goals and that we seek to achieve these goals in an optimal or efficient manner

reapportionment process that takes place every 10 years to determine how many congressional seats each state will receive, depending on population shifts

recognition the power to control floor debate by recognizing who can speak before the House and Senate

Reconstruction the period after the Civil War when much of the South was under military occupation

redistricting the process of redrawing election districts and redistributing legislative representatives in the Texas House, Texas Senate, and U.S. House; this process usually happens every 10 years to reflect shifts in population or in response to legal challenges in existing districts

referral the second step in the legislative process, during which a bill is assigned to the appropriate standing committee by the Speaker (for House bills) or the lieutenant governor (for Senate bills)

regressive tax type of tax where the tax burden falls more heavily on lower-income individuals

regular session the 140-day period, occurring only in odd-numbered years, during which the Texas legislature meets to consider and pass bills

republican government a representative democracy, a system of government in which power is derived from the people

resolution an expression of opinion on an issue by a legislative body

retention election an election in which voters decide whether to keep an incumbent in office by voting "yes" or "no" to retain the incumbent and where there is no opposing candidate

runoff primary a second primary election held between the two candidates who received the most votes in the first primary election if no candidate in the first primary election had received a majority

Sanford dictum held in *Gitlow v. New York* that the First Amendment right of free speech was a fundamental right that applied to the states

school district a specific type of special district that provides public education in a designated area

secretary of state state official, appointed by the governor, whose primary responsibility is administering elections

selective incorporation rights in the Bill of Rights that the Court believes are fundamental and are held to apply to the states as well as the national government because they are part of the "liberty" protected from state action in the Fourteenth Amendment

senatorial courtesy the practice whereby the president, before formally nominating a person for a federal judgeship, seeks the indication that senators from the candidate's own state support the nomination; in Texas, the practice whereby the governor seeks the indication that the senator from the candidate's home supports the nomination

"separate but equal" an interpretation of the equal protection clause of the Fourteenth Amendment that held that states could segregate races as long as equal facilities were provided; it was overturned in 1954

separation of powers the division of governmental power among several institutions that must cooperate in decision making

Shivercrat movement a movement led by the Texas governor Allan Shivers during the 1950s in which conservative Democrats in Texas supported Republican candidate Dwight Eisenhower for the presidency because many of those conservative Democrats believed that the national Democratic Party had become too liberal

simple resolution a resolution that concerns only the Texas House or Senate, such as the adoption of a rule or the appointment of an employee, and which does not require the governor's signature

single-member district an electorate that is allowed to elect only one representative for each district

sovereign possessing supreme political authority within a geographic area

Speaker the chief presiding officer of the House of Representatives; the Speaker is the most important party and House leader, and can influence the legislative agenda, the fate of individual pieces of legislation, and members' positions within the House

special bill a bill that gives an individual or corporation a special exemption from state law

special district a unit of local government that performs a single service, such as education or sanitation, within a limited geographic area

special election an election that is not held on a regularly scheduled basis; in Texas, a special election is called to fill a vacancy in office, to give approval for the state government to borrow money, or to ratify amendments to the Texas Constitution

special session a legislative session called by the governor that addresses an agenda set by him or her and that lasts no longer than 30 days

standing committee a permanent committee with the power to propose and write legislation that covers a particular subject, such as finance or agriculture

state chair and **vice chair** the top two state-level leaders in the party

state convention a party meeting held every two years for the purpose of nominating candidates for statewide office, adopting a platform, electing the party's leadership, and in presidential election years selecting delegates for the national convention and choosing presidential electors

state executive committee the committee responsible for governing a party's activities throughout the state

State Highway Fund fund that supports the construction, maintenance, and policing of roadways and acquires rights of way; funded through a variety of taxes such as motor vehicle registration fees, the federal highway fund, and the sales tax on motor lubricants

statutory county courts at law courts that tend to hear less serious cases than those heard by district courts

statutory probate courts specialized courts whose jurisdiction is limited to probate and guardianship matters

strict scrutiny the most rigorous equal protection standard; it requires that the government show a compelling state interest in order to successfully defend a law that makes certain classifications such as racial classifications; additionally, that classification must be one that is narrowly tailored by the least drastic means possible to achieve the government's objective

suffrage term referring to the right to vote

Sunset Advisory Commission (SAC) a commission created in 1975 for the purpose of reviewing the effectiveness of state agencies

Supplemental Security Income (SSI) a national welfare program passed in 1972 that provides assistance to low-income elderly or disabled individuals; replaced the federal-state programs that had offered assistance to the blind, the permanently and totally disabled, and the aged

supremacy clause Article VI of the U.S. Constitution, which states that the Constitution and laws passed by the national government and all treaties are the supreme law of the land and superior to all laws adopted by any state or any subdivision

Tea Party movement created after Barack Obama's election, a political movement that advocates lower government spending, lower taxes, and limited government

Temporary Assistance for Needy Families (TANF) a welfare program passed in 1996 to provide temporary assistance to families with needy children; replacing the AFDC program, TANF sought to make poor families self-sufficient and to give states greater flexibility in setting benefit levels, eligibility requirements, and other program details

Texas Court of Criminal Appeals the highest criminal court in Texas; consists of nine justices and has final state appellate authority over criminal cases

Texas Supreme Court the highest civil court in Texas; consists of nine justices and has final state appellate authority over civil cases

"three strikes" provision a law that allows persons convicted of three felonies (or in some cases two felonies) to be sentenced to life imprisonment

traditionalistic political culture the belief that government should be dominated by political elites and guided by tradition

tyranny according to James Madison, the concentration of power in any one branch of government

unfunded mandates federal requirements that states or local governments pay the costs of federal policies

unicameral comprising one body or house, as in a one-house legislature

urbanization the process by which people move from rural areas to cities

user fee a fee paid for public goods and services, such as water or sewage service

veto the governor's power to turn down legislation; can be overridden by a two-thirds vote of both the House and Senate

Voting Rights Act of 1965 important legislation passed in order to ensure that African Americans would be guaranteed the right to vote; renewed several times since 1965, the act also prevents the dilution of minority voting strength

white primary primary election in which only white voters are eligible to participate

endnotes

Chapter 1

1. Alan Rosenthal, "On Analyzing States," in *The Political Life of the American States*, ed. Alan Rosenthal and Maureen Moakley (New York: Praeger, 1984), 11–12.
2. Daniel Elazar, *American Federalism: A View from the States*, 2nd ed. (New York: Crowell, 1971), 84–126. See also John Kincaid, "Introduction," in *Political Culture, Public Policy and the American States*, ed. John Kincaid (Philadelphia: Center for the Study of Federalism, Institute for the Study of Human Issues, 1982), 1–24.
3. Rosenthal, "On Analyzing States," 13.
4. An excellent discussion of the problem of characterizing Texas political culture is found in Chandler Davidson, *Race and Class in Texas Politics* (Princeton, NJ: Princeton University Press, 1990), chap. 2.
5. The following is drawn from Texas State Historical Association, *Texas Almanac 2014–2015* (Denton: Texas State Historical Association, 2014), 78–84.
6. See Joseph A. Schumpeter, *Capitalism, Socialism, and Democracy*, 3rd ed. (New York: Harper & Brothers, 1950), chap. 6. For a discussion of the relationship between long-term economic transformation and political change at the national level, see Brian J. L. Berry, Euel Elliott, Edward J. Harpham, and Heja Kim, *The Rhythms of American Politics* (Lanham, MD: University Press of America, 1998).
7. The following is drawn from Karen Gerhardt Britton, Fred C. Elliott, and E. A. Miller, "Cotton Culture," *Handbook of Texas Online*.
8. See Cecil Harper, Jr., and E. Dale Odum, "Farm Tenancy," *Handbook of Texas Online*.
9. See Harper and Odum, "Farm Tenancy"; Texas State Historical Association, *Texas Almanac 2014–2015*, 687.
10. See T. C. Richardson and Harwood P. Hinton, "Ranching," *Handbook of Texas Online*.
11. See Texas State Historical Association, *Texas Almanac 2014–2015*, 687–88. Southern Plains Regional Office, United States Department of Agriculture, National Agriculture Statistics Service, "Texas Cotton Production," Issue No. PR-123-14. Austin: May 2014.
12. Texas State Historical Association, *Texas Almanac 2014–2015*, 683–84.
13. The following is drawn from Mary G. Ramos, "Oil and Texas: A Cultural History," Dallas Morning News, *Texas Almanac 2000–2001*, 29–35; Roger M. Olien, "Oil and Gas Industry," *Handbook of Texas Online*.
14. Ramos, "Oil and Texas," 31.
15. Olien, "Oil and Gas Industry."
16. See Texas Legislative Budget Board, *Fiscal Size-Up: 2014–15 Biennium* (2014), 28–29.
17. University of Texas Investment Management Company, *Permanent University Fund Semi-annual Report* (December 31, 2013).
18. Simone Sebastian, "New Data Show 'Meteoric' Rise of Texas Oil," fuelfix.com, December 3, 2013; see James Osborne, "Texas Oil Production Hits 2 Million Barrels a Day, the Most since 1986," *Dallas Morning News*, April 25, 2014. For a more detailed discussion of the new technology of fracking and its impact on the oil boom in Texas and the United States, see Russell Gold, *The Boom: How Fracking Ignited the American Energy Revolution and Changed the World* (New York: Simon & Schuster, 2014).
19. See *Manufacturing in Texas* (2013) at www.governor.state .tx.us/files/ecodev/Manufacturing_in_Texas and Texas State Comptroller, "Texas Gross State Product Detail—Calendar Years 1990–2040."
20. TechAmerica Foundation, *Tech Trade in the States: A State-by-State Overview of International Trade in Tech Goods* (2014), www.techamericafoundation.org/tech-trade-in-the-states; *Texas Almanac 2014–15*, 586.
21. Texas Center for Border Economic and Enterprise Development, texascenter.tamiv.edu
22. Standard and Poor's, "Twenty Years into NAFTA, Mexico and Texas Have Been the Two Main Beneficiaries of Increased Trade" (January 17, 2014), www.standardandpoors

.com/ratings/articles/en/us/?articleType=HTML&assetID=1245363256676.

23. See Robert E. Scott, "NAFTA's Legacy: Growing U.S. Trade Deficits Cost 682,900 Jobs," Economic Policy Institute (December 13, 2013), www.epi.org/publication/nafta-legacy-growing-us-trade-deficits-cost-682900-jobs/. See also Anil Kumar, "Did NAFTA Spur Texas Exports?" *Southwest Economy* 2 (March–April 2006), www.dallasfed.org/research/swe/2006/swe0602b.html (accessed 3/28/08); U.S. Department of Labor Employment & Training Administration, "Trade Adjustment Assistance: Number of Certified Workers by State"; Robert E. Scott, "Heading South: U.S.-Mexico Trade and Job Displacement after NAFTA," Economic Policy Institute (May 3, 2011), www.epi.org/publication/heading_south_u-s-mexico_trade_and_job_displacement_after_nafta1/.

24. U.S. Census Bureau, "State Exports for Texas 2013" and "State Imports for Texas 2013." See also Texas Economy Online Report from the Office of the Governor, "Overview of the Texas Economy" (June 2014).

25. Daniel Gross, "Lone Star: Why Texas Is Doing So Much Better Than the Rest of the Nation," *Slate*, April 19, 2010, www.slate.com/id/2250999 (accessed 7/7/10).

26. Texas Comptroller of Public Accounts, "Comptroller's Weekly Economic Outlook," *The Texas Economy, Economic Outlook* (May 21, 2014).

27. See Erica Grieder, *Big, Hot, Cheap, and Right: What America Can Learn from the Strange Genius of Texas* (New York: PublicAffairs, 2013). Some have argued that Texas characteristics cannot be duplicated by other states. See, for example, Elizabeth McNichol and Nicholas Johnson, "The Texas Economic Model: Hard for Other States to Follow and Not All It Seems," Center for Budget and Economic Priorities (April 3, 2012).

28. Bruce Wright, "Weathering the Storm," *Fiscal Notes*, April 2009, www.window.state.tx.us/comptrol/fnotes/fn0904/economy.html; D'Ann Petersen and Laila Assanie, "Texas Dodges Worst of Foreclosure Wars," Federal Reserve of Dallas (Dallas, 2009).

29. See Texas State Library and Archives Commission, "United States and Texas Populations 1850–2012," www.tsl.texas.gov/ref/abouttx/census.html.

30. See census data analysis on www.governing.com website: Governing Data, "State Population Estimates: 2013 Births, Deaths, Migration Totals," www.governing.com/gov-data/census/census-state-population-estimates-births-deaths-migration-totals-2013.html.

31. See Arnoldo De León, "Mexican Americans," *Handbook of Texas Online*.

32. See U.S. Census Bureau, "State & County QuickFacts," http://quickfacts.census.gov/qfd/states/48000.html; U.S. Census Bureau, 2010 Census; Sharon R. Ennis, Merarys Rios-Vargis, and Nora G. Albert, "The Hispanic Population: 2010," *2010 Census Briefs* (May 2011); Texas State Historical Association, *Texas Almanac 2014–2015*, 15.

33. See National Association of Latino Elected and Appointed Officials (NALEO), "2014 Latino Primary Profile: Texas," NALEO Educational Fund (2014), www.naleo.org/2014_Images/profiles/NEF-2014profile-TX-4.pdf.

34. See W. Marvin Dulaney, "African Americans," *Handbook of Texas Online*; Chandler Davidson, "African Americans and Politics," *Handbook of Texas Online*.

35. See U.S. Census Bureau, "The Asian Population," 2010 Census Briefs, www.census.gov/prod/cen2010/briefs/c2010br-11.pdf.

36. See Texas State Historical Association, *Texas Almanac 2014–2015* for county-by-county data. The Asian population of Texas counties can be found at www.indexmundi.com/facts/united-states/quick-facts/texas/asian-population-percentage#map.

37. U.S. Census Bureau, "Texas."

38. Bruce H. Webster, Jr., and Alemayehu Bishaw, "Income, Earnings, and Poverty Data from the 2006 American Community Survey," American Community Survey Reports, U.S. Census Bureau (August 2007); U.S. Census Bureau, Poverty 2007 and 2008 American Community Surveys (September 2009); U.S. Census Bureau, *Texas QuickFacts: 2009*; Alemayehu Bishaw, "Poverty: 2000–2012," U.S. Census Bureau, American Community Survey Briefs (September 2013).

39. The definition used to measure the urban/rural dichotomy has shifted over time. For a more detailed discussion, see U.S. Census Bureau, "2012 Census Urban Area FAQs" at www.census.gov/geo/reference/ua/uafaq.html.

40. The following is based on David G. McComb, "Urbanization," *Handbook of Texas Online*.

41. The following is drawn from David G. McComb, "Houston, Texas," *Handbook of Texas Online*.

42. Estimates are drawn from the U.S. Census Bureau, "State & County QuickFacts," http://quickfacts.census.gov/qfd/states/48/4827684.html.

43. The following is drawn from Jackie McElhaney and Michael V. Hazel, "Dallas, Texas," *Handbook of Texas Online*.

44. The following is drawn from Janet Schmelzer, "Fort Worth, Texas," *Handbook of Texas Online*.

45. The following is drawn from T. R. Fehrenbach, "San Antonio, Texas," *Handbook of Texas Online*.

46. Estimates are drawn from the U.S. Census Bureau, "State & County QuickFacts," http://quickfacts.census.gov/qfd/states/48/4865000.html.

Chapter 2

1. The following is drawn from Proposition 10, Deleting Constitutional References to County Office of Inspector of Hides and Animals, www.hro.house.state.tx.us/focus/prop80–10.pdf (accessed 3/31/08); Eric Aasen, "Round

'Em Up: Hide Inspectors Abolished," *Dallas Morning News*, November 8, 2007; John Council, "Richmond Lawyer Has Personal Stake in Hide Inspector Position," *Texas Lawyer*, November 2, 2007; Mark Lisheron, "Prop. 10 Would Abolish Office That No One Holds," *Austin American-Statesman*, October 15, 2007.

2. See Dick Smith, "Inspector of Hides and Animals," *Handbook of Texas Online*.

3. Donald E. Chipman, "Spanish Texas," *Handbook of Texas Online*; Donald E. Chipman, *Spanish Texas, 1519–1821* (Austin: University of Texas Press, 1992).

4. S. S. McKay, "Constitution of 1824," *Handbook of Texas Online*.

5. S. S. McKay, "Constitution of Coahuila and Texas," *Handbook of Texas Online*.

6. See Ralph W. Steen, "Convention of 1836," *Handbook of Texas Online*.

7. The following is drawn from Joe E. Ericson, "Constitution of the Republic of Texas," *Handbook of Texas Online*.

8. Randolph B. Campbell, "Slavery," *Handbook of Texas Online*.

9. For a brief summary of the war, see Eugene C. Barker and James W. Pohl, "Texas Revolution," *Handbook of Texas Online*.

10. S. S. McKay, "Constitution of 1845," *Handbook of Texas Online*.

11. The Texas Ordinance of Secession (February 2, 1861).

12. See Walter L. Buenger, "Secession Convention," *Handbook of Texas Online*; Walter L. Buenger, *Secession and the Union in Texas* (Austin: University of Texas Press, 1984).

13. See Claude Elliott, "Constitutional Convention of 1866," *Handbook of Texas Online*; S. McKay, "Constitution of 1866," *Handbook of Texas Online*; Charles W. Ramsdell, *Reconstruction in Texas* (New York: Columbia University Press, 1970).

14. See S. S. McKay, "Constitution of 1869," *Handbook of Texas Online*; Ramsdell, *Reconstruction in Texas*.

15. See John Walker Mauer, "Constitution Proposed in 1874," *Handbook of Texas Online*; John Walker Mauer, "State Constitutions in a Time of Crisis: The Case of the Texas Constitution of 1876," 68 *Texas Law Review* (June 1990): 1615–46.

16. Texas Legislative Council, *Amendments to the Texas Constitution since 1876* (Austin: March 1912).

17. For a further discussion, see George D. Braden et al., *The Constitution of the State of Texas: An Annotated and Comparative Analysis* (Austin: University of Texas Press, 1977), 707–10.

18. See Sam Kinch, Jr., "Sharpstown Stock-Fraud Scandal," *Handbook of Texas Online*; Charles Deaton, *The Year They Threw the Rascals Out* (Austin: Shoal Creek, 1973).

19. CBSDFW.com, "Texas Voters Approve 7 Constitutional Amendments," November 9, 2011, www.dfw.cbslocal.com/2011/11/09/texas-voters-approve-7-constitutional-amendments/.

Chapter 3

1. Anna M. Tinsley, "Former House Speaker Jim Wright Gets ID to Vote," *Fort Worth Star-Telegram*, November 4, 2013, www.star-telegram.com/2013/11/04/5305718/former-house-speaker-jim-wright.html (accessed 3/24/14).

2. Much of the material on Jim Wright is from James W. Riddlesperger, Jr., and Anthony Champagne, *Lone Star Leaders: Power and Personality in the Texas Congressional Delegation* (Fort Worth: Texas Christian University Press, 2011), 135–44.

3. This discussion is taken from David Brian Robertson, *Federalism and the Making of America* (New York: Routledge, 2012), 1–3.

4. Robertson, *Federalism and the Making of America*, 20–21.

5. Robertson, *Federalism and the Making of America*, 20–22.

6. Robertson, *Federalism and the Making of America*, 27.

7. Robertson, *Federalism and the Making of America*, 29–30.

8. Robertson, *Federalism and the Making of America*, 31.

9. *McCulloch v. Maryland*, 17 U.S. 316 (1819).

10. *Gibbons v. Ogden*, 22 U.S. 1, 2 (1824).

11. *Gibbons v. Ogden*, 22 U.S. 1, 2 (1824).

12. Robert F. Nagel, *The Implosion of American Federalism* (New York: Oxford University Press, 2001), 5.

13. *Texas v. White*, 74 U.S. 700 (1869).

14. *The Collector v. Day*, 78 U.S. 113, 124 (1870).

15. Morton Grodzins, *The American System*, ed. Daniel J. Elazar (Chicago: Rand McNally, 1966).

16. *Wickard v. Filburn*, 317 U.S. 111 (1942).

17. "Getting Stuck with the Check," *Bloomberg Businessweek*, www.businessweek.com/stories/1994-05-29/getting-stuck-with-the-check (accessed 3/24/14).

18. Sean Loughlin, "Local Government Fighting Unfunded Federal Mandates," *Herald-Journal*, November 6, 1993, www.news.google.com/newspaper?nid=1876&dat=19931106&id=tcfAAAAIBAJ&SJid=688EAAAAIBAJ&pg=5991,1336021.

19. Loughlin, "Local Government Fighting Unfunded Federal Mandates."

20. *Arizona v. Inter Tribal Council of Arizona, Inc.*, 570 U.S. __ (2013).

21. Jullian Reyfield, "Ted Cruz Measure Would Overturn SCOTUS on Voter Registration," *Salon*, June 17, 2013, www.salon.com/2013/06/17/ted_cruz_measure_would_overturn_scotus_on_voter_registration/ (accessed 3/24/14).

22. "State Officials Warn White House against Enforcing New Gun Regulations," FoxNews.com, January 15, 2013, www.foxnews.com/politics/2013/01/15/ore-sheriff-says-wont-enforce-new-gun-laws/ (accessed 3/24/14).

23. Sue Owen, "Greg Abbott Says He Has Sued Obama Administration 25 Times," PolitiFact Texas, May 10, 2013, www.politifact.com/texas/statements/2013/may/10/greg-abbott/greg-abbott-says-he-has-sued-obama-administration-/ (accessed 3/24/14).

24. Greg Abbott, "Lawsuits against Obama Are Taxpayer Bargain," dallasnews.com, September 25, 2012, www .dallasnews.com/opinion/latest-columns/20120925 -greg-abbott-lawsuits-against-obama-are-taxpayer -bargain.ece (accessed 3/24/14).

25. *Printz v. United States*, 521 U.S. 898, 935 (1997).

26. *Missouri Pacific Railway Co. v. Nebraska*, 106 U.S. 403 (1896), and *Chicago, Burlington & Quincy Railway Co. v. Chicago*, 166 U.S. 226 (1897).

27. *Gitlow v. People of State of New York*, 268 U.S. 652, 666 (1925).

28. *McDonald v. Chicago*, 561 U.S. 742.

29. *Sweatt v. Painter*, 339 U.S. 629 (1950).

30. *Brown v. Board of Education of Topeka*, 347 U.S. 483 (1954).

31. *DeLeon v. Perry*, 2014 WL 715741 (2014).

32. *Craig v. Boren*, 429 U.S. 190, 197 (1976).

33. *Plyler v. Doe*, 457 U.S. 202, 230 (1982).

34. *Shelby County, Ala. v. Holder*, 679 F3d 848, 858 (C.A.D.C., 2012).

35. *Shelby County, Ala. v. Holder*, Brief of the State of Texas as amicus curiae in support of Petitioner, Supreme Court of the United States (2013), p. 4.

36. *Shelby County, Ala. v. Holder*, Brief of the State of Texas, p. 2.

37. *Shelby County, Ala. v. Holder*, 2013 WL 3184629 (2013).

38. Keith G. Bentele and Erin E. O'Brien, "Jim Crow 2.0? Why States Consider and Adopt Restrictive Voter Access Policies," *Perspectives on Politics* 11 (2013): 1104.

39. Jill D. Weinberg, "Remaking Lawrence," 98 *Virginia Law Review in Brief* 61, 66 (2012).

40. *San Antonio v. Rodriguez*, 411 U.S. 1 (1973).

41. *Edgewood Independent School District v. Kirby*, 777 S.W.2d 391, 398 (Tex., 1989).

Chapter 4

1. Jeffrey M. Jones, "Special Report: Many States Shift Democratic during 2005," Gallup, January 23, 2006, www .gallup.com/poll/21004/Special-Report-Many-States -Shift-Democratic-During-2005.aspx (accessed 4/7/08).

2. Use of party affiliation as an ideological cue is discussed in Philip L. Dubois, *From Ballot to Bench* (Austin: University of Texas Press, 1980).

3. University of Texas/*Texas Tribune*, "Texas Statewide Survey," May 7–13, 2012, www.laits.utexas.edu/txp_media /html/poll/files/201205-summary.pdf (accessed 11/28/12).

4. University of Texas/*Texas Tribune*, "Texas Statewide Survey," February 15–24, 2013, www.texasresearchinstitute .org/poll/uttt-statewide-poll-february-2013.

5. University of Texas/*Texas Tribune*, "Texas Statewide Survey," 2012.

6. Quoted in Chandler Davidson, *Race and Class in Texas Politics* (Princeton, NJ: Princeton University Press, 1990), 198.

7. Davidson, *Race and Class in Texas Politic*, 24–25.

8. Jones, "Special Report: Many States Shift Democratic during 2005."

9. Pew Research Center for the People and the Press, "Fewer Voters Identify as Republicans," March 20, 2008, www .pewresearch.org/2008/03/20/fewer-voters-identify-as -republicans/.

10. Jeffrey M. Jones, "Party ID: Despite GOP Gains, Most States Remain Blue," Gallup Politics, February 1, 2010, www.gallup.com/poll/125450/party-affiliation-despite -gop-gains-states-remain-blue.aspx (accessed 11/29/12).

11. James R. Soukup, Clifton McClesky, and Harry Holloway, *Party and Factional Division in Texas* (Austin: University of Texas Press, 1964), 22.

12. Mark P. Jones, "Guest Column: The 2013 Texas House from Right to Left," *Texas Tribune*, October 15, 2013, www.texastribune.org/2013/10/15/guest-column-2013 -texas-house-right-left/.

13. Robert T. Garrett, "2 Major GOP Donors Show Rift in Party," *Dallas Morning News*, February 3, 2006, p. 2A.

14. Robert T. Garrett, "PAC's Late Aid Altered Races," *Dallas Morning News*, March 10, 2006, pp. 1A, 16A.

15. Dante Chinni and James Gimpel, *Our Patchwork Nation* (New York: Gotham, 2011).

16. Terri Langford, "District Judge Fends off Democratic Rival's Challenge," *Dallas Morning News*, November 9, 2000, p. 36A.

17. Anthony Champagne and Greg Thielemann, "Awareness of Trial Court Judges," *Judicature* 75 (1991): 271–72.

18. Anthony Champagne, "The Selection and Retention of Judges in Texas," 40 *Southwestern Law Journal* 80 (1986).

19. The lone Democratic survivor, Ron Chapman, became an appellate judge. Democratic judges who did not switch to the Republican Party were defeated.

20. Langford, "District Judge Fends off Democratic Rival's Challenge."

21. David Koenig, "Democrats' Dream Team Falters," *Laredo Morning Times*, November 10, 2002, pp. 1A, 19A.

22. Joe Holley, "Texas Dems Still Waiting for Latino Surge," chron.com, April 4, 2010, www.chron.com/news /houston-texas/article/Texas-Dems-still-waiting-for-Latino -surge-1711939.php.

23. In 1994 it was estimated that there were between 420,000 and 460,000 illegal immigrants in Texas. Many of those illegal immigrants were Hispanic. See Leon F. Bouvier and John L. Martin, "Shaping Texas: The Effects of Immigration, 1970–2020," Center for Immigration Studies, April 1995, www.cis.org/articles/1995/texas .html (accessed 4/7/08). The Federation for American Immigration Reform cites the Immigration and Naturalization Service for a January 2000 estimate that there were 1,041,000 illegal immigrants then in Texas. See their report, "Texas: Illegal Aliens," www.fairus.org/site

/PageServier?pagename=research_researchable (accessed 4/7/08). An April 2006 study by the Pew Hispanic Center estimated that between 1.4 and 1.6 million unauthorized individuals were living in Texas. Pew Hispanic Center, "Estimates of the Unauthorized Migrant Population for States Based on the March 2006 CPS, Fact Sheet: April 26, 2006," http://pewhispanic.org/files/factsheets/17.pdf (accessed 4/7/08). Jeff Salamon reports 10.8 million undocumented immigrants in the United States and 1.68 million in Texas. Jeff Salamon, "Everything You Ever Wanted to Know about Illegal Immigration (But Didn't Know Who to Ask)," *Texas Monthly*, November 2010.

24. Pew Research Hispanic Trends Project, "Latinos in the 2012 Election: Texas," October 1, 2012. See also U.S. Census Bureau, "The Diversifying Electorate—Voting Rates by Race and Hispanic Origin in 2012 (and Other Recent Elections)," May 2013.

Chapter 5

1. See Robert Draper, "The Legend of Wendy Davis," *New York Times Magazine*, February 16, 2014, pp. 18–25, 46–50.

2. Wayne Slater, "Strayhorn Gets Democratic Cash," *Dallas Morning News*, January 26, 2006, pp. 1A, 17A.

3. Pete Slover, "Independents' Day Is a Bid for the Ballot," *Dallas Morning News*, March 8, 2006, p. 14A.

4. Sam Acheson, *Joe Bailey: The Last Democrat* (New York: Macmillan, 1932), 354.

5. Joe Robert Baulch, "James B. Wells: State Economic and Political Leader" (Ph.D. diss., Texas Tech University, 1974), 358–59.

6. Sue Tolleson-Rinehart and Jeanie R. Stanley, *Claytie and the Lady: Ann Richards, Gender, and Politics in Texas* (Austin: University of Texas Press, 1994), 18–19.

7. O. Douglas Weeks, "The Texas-Mexican and the Politics of South Texas," *American Political Science Review* 224 (1930): 625–26; Anthony Champagne, "John Nance Garner," in *Masters of the House*, ed. Roger H. Davidson, Susan Webb Hammond, and Raymond W. Smock (Boulder, CO: Westview, 1998), 145–80.

8. *United States v. Texas*, 384 U.S. 155 (1966).

9. *Beare v. Smith*, 321 F. Supp. 1100 (1971).

10. *Kramer v. Union Free School District No. 15*, 395 U.S. 621 (1969); *Hill v. Stone*, 421 U.S. 289 (1975).

11. *Dunn v. Blumstein*, 405 U.S. 330 (1972).

12. *Newberry v. United States*, 256 U.S. 232 (1921).

13. *Nixon v. Herndon*, 273 U.S. 536 (1927).

14. *Nixon v. Condon*, 286 U.S. 73 (1932).

15. *Grovey v. Townsend*, 295 U.S. 45 (1935).

16. *Smith v. Allwright*, 321 U.S. 649 (1944).

17. *Terry v. Adams*, 345 U.S. 461 (1953).

18. Gary Scharrer, "Holder Issues Challenge to Texas on Voter Rights," chron.com, December 13, 2011, www.chron.com/news/article/Holder-issues-challenge-to-Texas-on-voter-rights-2401340.php.

19. National Conference of State Legislatures, "Voter Identification Requirements," April 30, 2014, www.ncsl.org/research/elections-and-campaigns/voter-id.aspx#details.

20. Texas Secretary of State, "Turnout and Voter Registration Figures, 1970–Current," www.sos.state.tx.us/elections/historical/70-92.shtml.

21. The motor voter law is a federal statute that requires states to allow voter registration when individuals apply for or renew their driver's licenses.

22. See U.S. Census Bureau, www.census.gov/hhes/www/socdemo/voting/publications/p20/2012/tables.html; and Texas Secretary of State, "Turnout and Voter Registration Figures, 1970–Current." It is important to recognize how easily different studies can produce different registration rates or voting rates for different racial and ethnic groups. The Texas secretary of state's office uses hard data on the number of registered voters and divides by an agreed-upon number of people in the voting-age population given by state and federal demographers. But the secretary of state's office has no information on how people from different racial and ethnic groups actually voted. The statistics cited here were based upon a survey done after the election asking individuals to self-identify their race or ethnicity, whether or not they were registered to vote, and if they voted. Registration rates and voting rates were built up from the survey rather than being based on hard data provided by outside authorities. Different methodological approaches to the same question can lead to different numbers without any of the numbers being "wrong."

23. Thomas R. Patterson, *The American Democracy* (New York: McGraw-Hill, 1999), 188.

24. Daniel Elazar, *American Federalism: A View from the States*, 2nd ed. (New York: Crowell, 1971).

25. Kevin Diaz, "Texas Latino Vote Splits," *Houston Chronicle*, November 6, 2014.

26. Donald R. Kinder and Lynn M. Sanders, *Divided by Color: Racial Politics and Democratic Ideals* (Chicago: University of Chicago Press, 1996).

27. University of Texas/*Texas Tribune*, "Texas Statewide Survey," February 1–7, 2010, www.laits.utexas.edu (accessed 12/18/12).

28. University of Texas/*Texas Tribune*, "Texas Statewide Survey," June 11–22, 2009, www.laits.utexas.edu (accessed 12/18/12).

29. University of Texas/*Texas Tribune*, "Texas Statewide Survey," May 14–20, 2010, www.laits.utexas.edu (accessed 12/18/12).

30. University of Texas/*Texas Tribune*, "Texas Statewide Survey," May 14–20, 2010, www.laits.utexas.edu (accessed 12/18/12).

31. University of Texas/*Texas Tribune*, "Texas Statewide Survey," February 2013, www.laits.utexas.edu.

32. University of Texas/*Texas Tribune*, "Texas Statewide Survey," May 11–18, 2011, www.laits.utexas.edu (accessed 12/18/12).

33. Julian Aguilar, "Abbott Defends Corruption Remarks, Border Security Plan," *Texas Tribune*, February 10, 2014, www.texastribune.org/2014/02/10/abbott-again-ties-public-corruption-third-world-co/. Jens Manuel Krogstad and Mark Hugo Lopez, "Hispanic Voters in the 2014 Election," Pew Research Hispanic Trends Project, November 7, 2014, www.pewhispanic.org/2014/11/07/hispanic-voters-in-the-2014-election/ (accessed 12/3/14).

34. Candidates in Texas Supreme Court races are affected by "friends and neighbors" voting, whereby voters tend to cast ballots for candidates from their home county or from neighboring counties. See Gregory Thielemann, "Local Advantage in Campaign Financing: Friends, Neighbors, and Their Money in Texas Supreme Court Elections," *Journal of Politics* 55 (1993): 472–78.

35. Roy A. Schotland, "Campaign Finance in Judicial Elections," 34 *Loyola of Los Angeles Law Review* 1508–12 (2001).

36. Alexa Ura, "Davis Renews Equal Pay Attack on Abbott," *Texas Tribune*, March 24, 2014, www.texastribune.org/2014/03/24/davis-renews-equal-pay-attack-abbott/.

Chapter 6

1. The above is drawn from Jeffrey Weiss, "How Texas' Testing Bubble Popped," *Dallas Morning News*, March 30, 2014; Jeffrey Weiss, "Looking into the 'Heart of the Vampire,'" *Dallas Morning News*, March 31, 2014; Jeffrey Weiss, "Testing System Shaken to Its Core," *Dallas Morning News*, April 1, 2014; Dax Gonzalez, "Finding the Funding," *Texas Lone Star*, August 2013; see also www.TAMSATX.org.

2. Mancur Olson, *The Logic of Collective Action: Public Goods and the Theory of Groups*, Harvard Economic Studies (Cambridge, MA: Harvard University Press, 1971).

3. James W. Lamare, *Texas Politics: Economics, Power and Policy*, 3rd ed. (St. Paul, MN: West, 1988), 82. See George Norris Green, *The Establishment in Texas Politics: The Primitive Years, 1938–1957* (Norman: University of Oklahoma Press, 1984).

4. Governor Rick Perry's schedule, Office of the Governor, September 15, 2010.

5. Jason Embry, "The Most Powerful Group in Texas Politics Has Wentworth in Its Sights," Statesman.com, December 7, 2011.

6. Texans for Public Justice, "Power Surge: TXU's Patronage Grid Plugs All but Seven Lawmakers," *Lobby Watch*, March 1, 2007.

7. Matt Stiles, "Lobbyist Gives 'Shocking' Gift to Lawmaker," *Texas Tribune*, February 15, 2010.

8. Steve McGonigle, "For Perry, Big Game Means Big Business—Trucking Lobby Paid for Governor's Private Jet to Rose Bowl," *Dallas Morning News*, December 12, 2006.

9. Matt Stiles and Chris Chang, "Texas Lobbying Directory Details Spending, Clients," *Texas Tribune*, March 15, 2011.

10. Emily Ramshaw and Marcus Funk, "For Some Dallas-Area Legislators, Donations Fund the Good Life," *Dallas Morning News*, February 1, 2009.

11. Texans for Public Justice, "Special Interests Paid Lobbyists," p. 1.

12. Texans for Public Justice, "Special Interests Paid Lobbyists."

13. Texans for Public Justice, "Special Interests Paid Lobbyists."

14. Texans for Public Justice, "Special Interests Paid Lobbyists."

15. Andy Pierrotti, "Lobbyist's Lavish Party," Kvue.com, February 21, 2013.

16. Texans for Public Justice, "Special Interests Paid Lobbyists Up to $328 Million in 2013 Session," p. 3.

17. Ross Ramsey, "Legislature Is a Training Ground for Lobbyists," *Texas Tribune*, June 10, 2010.

18. Ramsey, "Legislature Is a Training Ground."

19. Texans for Public Justice, "Ten New Lawmaker Retreads Merge into the 2009 Lobby," *Lobby Watch*, May 20, 2009.

20. Texans for Public Justice, "12 Republicans Flip from Legislature to the Lobby," April 23, 2013.

21. "Rick Perry's Former Staffers Made Millions as Lobbyists," *Huffington Post*, December 19, 2011.

22. "Rick Perry's Former Staffers."

23. Ramsey, "Legislature Is a Training Ground."

24. Texans for Public Justice, "Texas Revolvers: Public Officials Recast as Hired Guns" (1999).

25. Texans for Public Justice, "Special-Interests Spend Up to $180 Million on Lobby Services in 1999 Legislative Session," May 24, 1999.

26. Texans for Public Justice, "Money in PoliTex" (2008, 2010).

27. Anthony Champagne, "Campaign Contributions in Texas Supreme Court Races," *Crime, Law and Social Change* 17 (1992): 91–106.

28. Texans for Public Justice, "Texans for Lawsuit Reform Sustains Pricey Primary Hits," *Lobby Watch*, March 5, 2010; Julian Aguilar, "Primary Color: HD-43," *Texas Tribune*, February 26, 2010.

29. Embry, "Most Powerful Group."

30. National Institute on Money in State Politics.

31. National Institute on Money in State Politics.

32. Kristen Mack, "New Lawmakers Learn to Juggle Hectic Lives; Everybody—Lobbyists, Family—Wants a Moment of Their Time," *Houston Chronicle*, February 6, 2005, p. 1B.

33. Texans for Public Justice, "Texans for Lawsuit Reform."

34. Embry, "Most Powerful Group"; John W. Gonzalez,

"Campbell Upsets Wentworth for Texas Senate," *San Antonio Express-News*, August 1, 2012.

35. Texans for Public Justice, "Operation Vouchsafe: Dr. Leininger Injects $5 Million into Election; Many Candidates Fail on His Life Support," *Lobby Watch*, n.d.

36. Texans for Public Justice, "Texas PACs: 2012 Election Cycle Spending" (2013), p. 20.

37. Sunset Advisory Commission Staff Report, "Railroad Commission of Texas," November 2012, p. 12.

38. Public Citizen, "Drilling for Dollars: How Big Money Has a Big Influence at the Railroad Commission," (2010), p. 1.

39. Public Citizen, "Drilling for Dollars," p. 4.

40. National Institute on Money in Politics.

41. Sunset Advisory Commission, "Railroad Commission of Texas," p. 2.

42. Brett Shipp, "Attempt to Overhaul Texas Railroad Commission Fails, Again," WFAA.com, May 31, 2013.

43. Emily Ramshaw, "Fighting for Fair Warning—Man Who Lost Wife, Kids in Blaze Seeks Visual Smoke Alarms for Deaf," *Dallas Morning News*, April 17, 2009; "Tragedy Leads to Improved Fire Safety in Texas," National Association of the Deaf, July 1, 2009.

44. Regina Lawrence, Deborah Wise, and Emily Einsohn, *Texas Civic Health Index* (Austin: Annette Strauss Institute for Civic Life, 2013), 5–14.

45. Lawrence, Wise, and Einsohn, *Texas Civic Health Index*, 22.

Chapter 7

1. Chris Tomlinson, "Texas Abortion Bill: Republican Lawmakers Approve Tough New Restrictions," Huffington Post, June 24, 2013, www.huffingtonpost.com/2013/06/24/texas_abortion_bill_n_3488965.html.

2. State of Texas, "Senate Rules Adopted by 82nd Legislature" (January 19, 2011), pp. 8–12.

3. 83 S.J. 1 C.S. 303, remarks by Senator Williams.

4. Peter Weber, "Wendy Davis' Stunning Filibuster of a Texas Abortion Bill," The Week, June 26, 2013, www.theweek.com/article/index/246101/wendy-davis-confounding-filibuster-of-a-texas-abortion-bill.

5. Weber, "Wendy Davis' Stunning Filibuster."

6. 83 S.J.1 C.S. 297, 302-303, remarks by Lt. Governor Dewhurst and Senator Williams; Weber, "Wendy Davis' Stunning Filibuster."

7. 83 S.J. 1 C.S. 303.

8. Chris Tomlinson and Jim Vertuno, "Filibuster Broken, but Texas Abortion Law Fails to Pass," Christian Science Monitor, June 26, 2013, www.csmonitor.com/USA/Latest-news-filibuster-broken-but-Texas-abortion-law-fails-to-pass.

9. 83 S.J. 1 C.S. 305.

10. Mollie Reilly, "Leticia Van de Putte, Texas Legislator Slams Male Colleagues During Abortion Filibuster," Huffington Post, June 26, 2013, www.huffingtonpost.com/2013/06/26/leticia-van-de-putte_m_3500497.html.

11. Weber, "Wendy Davis' Stunning Filibuster."

12. 83 S.J. 1 C.S. 305.

13. Weber, "Wendy Davis' Stunning Filibuster."

14. "Senate Gives Tentative OK to Guns on Campuses," *Dallas Morning News*, May 20, 2009.

15. "Texas Bill to Allow Guns on Campus Rejected for Violating Constitutional Requirement," *Security Director News*, June 7, 2011.

16. "Texas Legislature Passes Record Number of Pro-Gun Bills but Key Items Remain as "Unfinished Business," NRA-ILA, June 5, 2013, www.nraila.org/legislation/state-legislation/2013/6/texas-legislature-passes-record-number-of-progun-bills-but-key-Itmes-remain-as-unfinished-business.aspx.

17. Ann Marie Kilday, "Equal Measure," *Dallas Morning News*, May 24, 2001, p. 31A.

18. Anthony Champagne and Rick Collis, "Texas," in *The Political Life of the American States*, ed. Alan Rosenthal and Maureen Moakley (New York: Praeger, 1984), 138.

19. Ross Ramsey, "Will Texas Lawmakers Cut Their Own Benefits?" *Texas Tribune*, March 11, 2011.

20. Ramsey, "Will Texas Lawmakers Cut."

21. "State Rep. Joe Driver of Garland Double-Billed for Travel," *Dallas Morning News*, August 16, 2010; "Garland Republican Joe Driver Pleads Guilty to Double-Dipping on Travel Reimbursements," *Dallas Morning News*, November 22, 2011.

22. Christy Hoppe, "At Home, Collecting Expense Pay," *Dallas Morning News*, June 19, 2013, pp. 1, 2A.

23. Texas Legislature, "Legislative Statistics," July 10, 2013.

24. "83rd Legislative Session Bills," *Texas Tribune*, www.texastribune.org/session/83R/bills.

25. Kelley Shannon, "Doctor Twice Honored by the Texas Legislature Registered as Sex Offender," *Sulphur Springs News-Telegram*, June 22, 2007, p. 1.

26. Frank M. Stewart, "Impeachment in Texas," *American Political Science Review* 24, no. 3 (August 1930): 652–58; George D. Braden et al., *The Constitution of the State Texas: An Annotated and Comparative Analysis* (Austin: University of Texas Press, 1977), 707–18.

27. Office of Governor Rick Perry, "Press Release," June 19, 2009.

28. Karen Brooks, "Craddick's Win May Cost Him," *Dallas Morning News*, May 27, 2007, p. 1.

29. Karen Brooks, "In 1877, Lawmakers Ran Republican Out of the Chair," *Dallas Morning News*, May 27, 2007, p. 26A.

30. Vince Leibowitz, "Texas Senate Republicans Trying to Dump Two-Thirds Voting Rule," *Capitol Annex*, January 14, 2009.

31. Terrence Stutz, "Texas Senate at Odds over Voter ID Legislation, Two-Thirds Rule," *Dallas Morning News*, January 14, 2009.

32. Joe Straus, letter to Sachi Dave, March 12, 2014.

33. Joe Straus, letter to Sachi Dave, March 12, 2014.

34. Paul Burka, "Partisanship Ranking: The Texas Tribune List," *Texas Monthly*, July 17, 2010.

35. Mark Jones, "Guest Column: The 2013 Texas House, from Right to Left," *Texas Tribune*, October 15, 2013.

36. Mark Jones, "Guest Column: The 2013 Texas Senate, from Left to Right," *Texas Tribune*, November 26, 2013.

37. Paul Starr, *Remedy and Reaction: The Peculiar American Struggle over Health Care Reform*, rev. ed. (New Haven: Yale University Press, 2013), 162–63.

38. *Baker v. Carr*, 369 U.S. 186 (1962); *Reynolds v. Sims*, 377 U.S. 533 (1964).

39. *Wesberry v. Sanders*, 376 U.S. 1 (1964).

40. Sam Attlesey, "Panel OKs Map Favoring GOP," *Dallas Morning News*, December 7, 2001.

41. The preceding is drawn from Sam Attlesey, "Taking Stock of the Fallout from Redistricting," *Dallas Morning News*, December 11, 2001; Terrance Stutz, "GOP Expecting to Grab the House," *Dallas Morning News*, January 3, 2002; Sam Attlesey, "Before Election, House Democrats Seeing Losses," *Dallas Morning News*, December 11, 2001.

42. Medill School of Journalism, "On the Docket: *League of United Latin American Citizens, Travis County, Jackson, Eddie and GI Forum of Texas v. Perry, Rick (Texas Gov.).*"

43. State Appellants' Brief in the Supreme Court of the United States, *LULAC v. Perry*.

44. Medill School of Journalism, "On the Docket."

45. Appellants' Brief, *LULAC v. Perry*.

46. See, generally, Steve Bickerstaff, *Lines in the Sand: Congressional Redistricting in Texas and the Downfall of Tom DeLay* (Austin: University of Texas Press, 2007).

47. "Texas Redistricting Battle Headed Back to Federal Courts," *Lubbock Avalanche-Journal*, June 21, 2013, www.lubbockonline.com/local-news/2013-06-21/texas-redistricting-battle-headed-back-federal-court#.Ud2xf21VjMA.

Chapter 8

1. Ross Ramsey, "A Weak Governor System, with a Strong Governor," *Texas Tribune*, July 8, 2013, www.texastribune.org/2013/08/weak-governor-system-strong-governor/.

2. Brian McCall, *The Power of the Texas Governor: Connally to Bush* (Austin: University of Texas Press, 2009).

3. Bruce Tomaso, "Adios to Memorable Moments, Achievements," *Dallas Morning News*, July 9, 2013, p. 9A.

4. See the discussion of gubernatorial power in Cheryl D. Young and John J. Hindera, "The Texas Governor: Weak or Strong?" in *Texas Politics: A Reader*, ed. Anthony Champagne and Edward J. Harpham (New York: W. W. Norton, 1998), 53.

5. Sam Kinch, in *Government by Consent—Texas, A Telecourse* (Dallas: Dallas County Community College District, 1990).

6. McCall, *Power of the Texas Governor*.

7. McCall, *Power of the Texas Governor*, 5.

8. McCall, *Power of the Texas Governor*, 131–39.

9. McCall, *Power of the Texas Governor*, 120.

10. Christy Hoppe and Robert T. Garrett, "How Deep Does Governor Dig into Issues?" *Dallas Morning News*, November 27, 2011, pp. 1, 30A.

11. Kinch, *Government*.

12. Polly Ross Hughes, "Farewell to a Yalie, Howdy to an Aggie," *Houston Chronicle*, December 14, 2000, p. 1A.

13. Hughes, "Farewell to a Yalie," p. 26A.

14. George Kuempel, "The Tab Texas Taxpayers Are Picking Up for Security Protection," *Dallas Morning News*, February 2, 2000, p. 25A.

15. William P. Hobby, in *Government by Consent—Texas, A Telecourse* (Dallas: Dallas County Community College District, 1990).

16. Christy Hoppe, "Lt. Gov. Rick Perry, Honoring the Economic Generators of Texas Tourism," *Dallas Morning News*, February 28, 2000, p. 13A.

17. Hoppe, "Lt. Gov. Rick Perry."

18. Hoppe and Garrett, "How Deep Does Governor Dig," p. 30A.

19. Steve McGonigle and James Drew, "Perry Stocks State Boards with Allies," *Dallas Morning News*, December 4, 2011, pp. 1, 32A.

20. James C. McKinley Jr., "Texas Governor Defends Shakeup of Commission," *New York Times*, October 2, 2009, p. A16.

21. Becca Aaronson, "House Panel Grills CPRIT Oversight Committee," My highplains.com, April 10, 2013, myhighplains.com/fulltext?nxd_id=359622.

22. Daniel Sylvia, "Cash, Cancer, and CPRIT," Hardhatters.com, June 6, 2013, www.hardhatters.com/2013/06/cash-cancer-and-cprit/.

23. Jacelyn Kaiser, "Peer Panel Implodes at Texas Cancer Research Agency," *Science Insider*, October 12, 2012, www.news.science.org/scienceinsider/2012/10/peer-panel-Implodes-at-texas-can.html.

24. "House Panel to Vote in May on UT Regent's Impeachment," dallasnews.com, April 24, 2014, www.dallasnews.com/news/state/headlines/20140424-texas-house-panel-to-vote=in-may-on-ut-regent-s-impeachment.ece; Reeve Hamilton, "How Will UT Regent Impeachment Probe Play Out?" *Texas Tribune*, September 25, 2013, www.texastribune.org/2013/09/25/what-will-impeachment-probe-look/.

25. Tim Eaton, "Insurance Commissioner on Her Way Out," *Austin American-Statesman*, May 24, 2013, www.statesman.com/news/news/inaurance-commissioner-announces-resignation/nX3JP/; "Perry Names Rathgeber

Insurance Commissioner," *Texas Tribune*, May 27, 2013, www.texastribune.org/2013/05-27-senator-kitzman-unlikely-win-confirmation/; Terrance Stutz, "Exclusive: Texas Insurance Commissioner Withheld Annual Profit Numbers to Boost Confirmation Case, Sources Say," dallasnews.com, May 28, 2013, www.dallasnews.com/news/politics/headlines/20130527-exclusive-texas-insurance-commissioner-withheld-annual-profit-numbers-to-boost-con.

26. See Texas Constitution Article XV Section 9. See also Janice C. May, *The Texas State Constitution* (Oxford: Oxford University Press, 2011), 376–77.

27. Legislative Reference Library of Texas, "Bill Statistics."

28. Aman Batheja and Jay Root, "Perry Issues More than Two Dozen Vetoes," *Texas Tribune*, June 14, 2013; Texas Legislature Online—Report, "Bills Vetoed by the Governor," 83rd Legislature, Regular Session, June 24, 2013, www.legis.state.tx.us/Reports/Report.aspx?LegSess=83R&id=vetoedbygov.

29. Batheja and Root, "Perry Issues More Than Two Dozen Vetoes."

30. Office of Governor Rick Perry, "Governor Perry Signs State Budget That Reduces GR by $1.6 Billion," press release, June 19, 2009.

31. Texas Legislative Library, Special Sessions of the Texas Legislature (2010).

32. Office of the Governor, "Gov. Perry Grants Clemency to Fourteen," December 21, 2012, www.governor.state.tx.us/news/press-release/18001/.

33. Young and Hindera, "Texas Governor: Weak or Strong?" 61.

34. Young and Hindera, "Texas Governor: Weak or Strong?" 61.

35. The above discussion was taken from Jim Yardley, "Public Lives: This Texan, Too, Has a Lot Riding on Bush's Campaign," *New York Times*, October 7, 2000, p. 9; Kathy Walt, "Texas Legislature; Jobs Well Done; Senators Give Perry High Marks after Starting Out with Low Expectation," *Houston Chronicle*, June 6, 1999, p. State 1.

36. Jim Yardley, "Public Lives: A Power in Texas Governing Finds Fault in Texas Politics," *New York Times*, June 9, 2001, p. A7.

37. Much of this material on the attorney general's office is taken from the website of the Attorney General of Texas Greg Abbott.

38. Much of this material on the Texas General Land Office is taken from the website of the Texas General Land Office.

39. Texas State Auditor's Office, "A Summary Report on Full-Time Equivalent State Employees for Fiscal Year 2004" and "A Summary Report on Full-Time Equivalent State Employees for Fiscal Year 2013," www.hr.sao.state.tx.us/publications/reports.aspx?type=FTE.

40. Christy Hoppe, "Perry's Appointees Give Him Unprecedented Hold on Texas—Longest-Serving Governor Spreads Pro-Business View," *Dallas Morning News*, December 19, 2008.

41. Hoppe, "Perry's Appointees Give Him Unprecedented Hold."

42. Christy Hoppe, "Perry Ousts Officials before Arson Hearing—He's Assailed as New Chair Delays Session on Flawed Case That Led to Execution," *Dallas Morning News*, October 1, 2009.

43. William McKenzie, "Rick Perry's Curious Ways—Governor's Strongman Tactics Are Hard to Comprehend amid a Heated Campaign, Says William McKenzie," *Dallas Morning News*, October 20, 2009.

44. Texas Conservative Coalition, "Senate Bill 14 (78R)," www.txcc.org/general-state-policy.

45. Bill Peacock, "Policy Perspective: Is the Free Market Working for the Texas Homeowners' Insurance Market?" Texas Public Policy Foundation, February 28, 2006.

46. Terrence Stutz, "State Farm Stiff-Arming Regulators," *Dallas Morning News*, April 14, 2010; Terrence Stutz, "State Farm near Top in Rates," *Dallas Morning News*, September 7, 2011, p. 1.

47. Terrence Stutz, "Legal Tactics Stall Insurance Reform," DallasNews.com, September 16, 2007.

48. Russell Shorto, "How Christian Were the Founders?" *New York Times Magazine*, p. MM32, February 14, 2010; Terrence Stutz, "Debate Continues over Social Studies," *Dallas Morning News*, March 11, 2010.

49. Morgan Smith, "Texas State Board of Education Races Could Get Ugly," *Texas Tribune*, November 7, 2011.

Chapter 9

1. Ralph Blumenthal, "Texas Judge Draws Outcry for Allowing an Execution," *New York Times*, October 25, 2007; Christy Hoppe, "Criminal Appeals Court Creates Emergency Filing System," *DallasNews.com*, November 6, 2007; "Texas Judge Fosters Tough-on-Crime Reputation," MSNBC, October 23, 2007; State Commission on Judicial Conduct, "Special Master's Findings of Fact, In Re: Honorable Sharon Keller, Presiding Judge of the Texas Court of Criminal Appeals" (January 20, 2010).

2. "Judge Who Refused Last-Minute Appeal Re-Elected," News 92 FM, November 6, 2012, www.news92fm.com/295422/judge-who-refused-last-minute-appeal-is-re-elected/.

3. "Keller Case Illustrates Why Prop. 9 Is So Necessary," *Dallas Morning News*, October 7, 2013, p. 12A.

4. Dave Lieber, "Justice May Be Easier to Access," *Dallas Morning News*, August 25, 2013, pp. B1, B6.

5. Texas Office of Court Administration, "Annual Statistical Report for the Texas Judiciary Fiscal Year 2012" (January 2013), p. 87.

6. Barbara Kirby, "Neighborhood Justice: Campaign Funding and Texas Justice of the Peace Courts," paper presented at the annual meeting of the Southern Political Science Association, New Orleans, Louisiana, January 3, 2007.

7. Ed Housewright, "Emotional Issues, Historical Pedigree," *Dallas Morning News*, April 9, 2001, p. 10A.

8. Texas Office of Court Administration, "Activity Report for Municipal Courts, September 1, 2008 to August 31, 2009."

9. Texas Office of Court Administration, "Annual Statistical Report for the Texas Judiciary Fiscal Year 2012."

10. Steve Thompson, "Toughen Up, City Officials Tell Judges," *Dallas Morning News*, August 2, 2012, pp. 1B, 7B.

11. Thomas Petzinger, Jr., *Oil and Honor: The Texaco-Pennzoil Wars* (New York: Putnam, 1987).

12. Task Force on Indigent Defense, "Evidence for the Feasibility of Public Defender Offices in Texas" (2006).

13. Mary Alice Robbins, "West Texas Plans Public Defender Office for Capital Cases," *Texas Lawyer*, August 20, 2007, pp. 1, 19; "New Public Defender for Capital Cases," *Tex Parte Blog*, October 16, 2007.

14. Ken Anderson, *Crime in Texas* (Austin: University of Texas Press, 1997), 40.

15. Anderson, *Crime in Texas*, 44. Nationally, 95 percent of felonies are plea-bargained.

16. Of the 79 judicial appointments made by Governor William Clements, only 6 were either African American or Hispanic. In contrast, one-third of Governor Ann Richards's judicial appointees were minorities. See Michael Totty, "Is This Any Way to Choose a Judge?" *Wall Street Journal*, August 3, 1994, pp. T1, T4.

17. Texas Office of Court Administration, "Profile of Appellate and Trial Judges as of September 1, 2009."

18. Anthony Champagne, "The Selection and Retention of Judges in Texas," 40 *Southwestern Law Journal* (1986): 78–79.

19. Texans for Public Justice, "Payola Justice: How Texas Supreme Court Justices Raise Money from Court Litigants" (1998).

20. From surveys conducted in 1998 jointly by the Texas Supreme Court, the Office of Court Administration, and the State Bar of Texas. See "Judging Texas Justice in the Court of Opinion," www.laits.utexas.edu/txp_media/html/just/features/0407_02/slide1.html.

21. L. Douglas Kiel, Carole Funk, and Anthony Champagne, "Two-Party Competition and Trial Court Elections in Texas," 77 *Judicature* (1994): 291.

22. Linda Campbell, "'H' as in Herasimchuk," *Fort Worth Star-Telegram*, December 6, 2001.

23. Mary Flood and Brian Rogers, "Why Some Harris County Judges Lost Not Entirely Clear," *Houston Chronicle*, November 6, 2008.

24. Eden Stiffman and Tristan Hallman, "Did Name Cost Justice in Race?" *Dallas Morning News*, August 2, 2012, p. 9A.

25. Elliott Slotnik, "Gender, Affirmative Action, and Recruitment to the Federal Bench," 14 *Golden Gate University Law Review* (1984): 524.

26. Texas Office of Court Administration, "Profile of Appellate and Trial Judges, September 1, 2012."

27. Barbara L. Graham, "Toward an Understanding of Judicial Diversity in American Courts," 10 *Michigan Journal of Race and Law* (2004): 178.

28. One report is that 90 percent of African American voters and 60 to 79 percent of Hispanic voters vote Democratic. See Ronald W. Chapman, "Judicial Roulette: Alternatives to Single-Member Districts as a Legal and Political Solution to Voting-Rights Challenges to At-Large Judicial Elections," 48 *SMU Law Review* (1995): 182.

29. The trial court opinion was unpublished.

30. *League of United Latin American Citizens v. Clements*, 902 F2d 293 (1990), and *League of United Latin American Citizens v. Clements*, 914 F2d 620 (1990).

31. *Houston Lawyers' Association v. Attorney General of Texas*, 501 U.S. 419 (1991).

32. *League of United Latin American Citizens Council v. Clements*, 999 F2d 831 (1993).

33. A discussion of the Bullock plan and the politics surrounding it is in Anthony Champagne, "Judicial Selection in Texas," in *Texas Politics: A Reader*, 2nd ed., ed. Anthony Champagne and Edward J. Harpham (New York: W. W. Norton, 1998), 99–103.

34. Susan Carbon and Larry Berkson, *Judicial Retention Elections in the United States* (Chicago: American Judicature Society, 1980), 21.

35. A discussion of these general systems of selection is found in Champagne, "Judicial Selection in Texas," 88–104.

36. Daniel Becker and Malia Reddick, *Judicial Selection Reform: Examples from Six States* (Chicago: American Judicature Society, 2003), 1–10.

37. Phil Hardberger, "Juries under Siege," 30 *St. Mary's Law Journal* (1998): 6–7.

38. "High Court Voting Patterns," *Texas Lawyer*, September 6, 1999, p. 5.

39. David A. Anderson, "Judicial Tort Reform in Texas," 26 *Review of Litigation* (2007): 7.

40. Lynne Liberato and Kent Rutter, "Reasons for Reversals in the Texas Courts of Appeals," *Houston Law Review* (2012): 993–1018.

41. Citizens' Commission on the Texas Judicial System, "Report and Recommendations: Into the Twenty-First Century" (1993), p. 3.

42. Texas Courts Online, "Trial Courts and Jurisdiction by County," www.courts.state.tx.us/courts/county.asp.

43. "Disciplinary Actions," *Texas Bar Journal* (April 2012): 331.

44. John McCormack, "Barratry Suit Names Corpus Lawyers," *San Antonio Express News*, December 9, 2011.

45. McCormack, "Barratry Suit."

46. Isiah Carey, "Lawyer Filed Reynolds Barratry Complaint," myfoxhouston.com, April 25, 2012.

47. Kari-Thomas Musselman, "Rep. Ron Reynolds Charged (again) With Barratry, Constituent Calls for Resignation," Burnt Orange Report, April 6, 2013, www.burntorange report.com/diary/13326/rep-ron-reynolds-charged -again-with-barratry-constituent-calls-for-resignation.

48. Data from the American Bar Association.

49. The material on the State Commission on Judicial Conduct is taken from the Staff Report of the Sunset Advisory Commission, "State Commission on Judicial Conduct" (March 2012).

50. State Commission on Judicial Conduct, FY2012 Annual Report, www.scjc.state.tx.us/pdf/rpts/AR-FY12.pdf.

51. State Commission on Judicial Conduct, "Public Warning Honorable William Adams County Court at Law Judge Rockport, Aransas County, Texas," www.scjc.state.tx.us /actions.asp.

52. Carson R. Guy, "Get Smart," 76 *Texas Bar Journal* (2013): 972, 976 and Cindy Horswell, "District Judge Resigns in Texting Case," *Houston Chronicle*, October 21, 2013.

Chapter 10

1. Randy Lee Loftis, "Texas Bans Fire Codes in 70% of Its Counties," *Dallas Morning News*, May 26, 2013, pp. 1, 12A–13A.

2. Dallas Morning News, *Texas Almanac 2009–2010* (Dallas: Dallas Morning News, 2008), 500; U.S. Census Bureau, *Lists & Structure of Government*; Texas State Historical Society, "Government," *Texas Almanac*, www.texas almanac.com/topics/government. Different sources provide varying numbers regarding municipal governments in Texas.

3. The two states that don't use counties as units of local government are Connecticut and Rhode Island. See Richard L. Cole and Delbert A. Taebel, *Texas: Politics and Public Policy* (Fort Worth: Harcourt Brace Jovanovich, 1987), 151.

4. Texas Association of Counties, "About Counties: County Government."

5. Texas Association of Counties, "About Counties."

6. Cole and Taebel, *Texas: Politics and Public Policy*, 152.

7. *Avery v. Midland County*, 390 U.S. 474 (1968).

8. Anthony Champagne and Rick Collis, "Texas," in *The Political Life of the American States*, ed. Alan Rosenthal and Maureen Moakley (Washington, DC: CQ Press, 1984), 140.

9. Texas State Data Center; U.S. Census Bureau, 2012 census estimates.

10. Brenda Rodriguez, "Loving and Losing in West Texas," *Dallas Morning News*, March 14, 2001, p. 21A.

11. Robert Bryce, "Trial's High Costs Tax Jasper Coffers," *Christian Science Monitor*, February 25, 1999, www .csmonitor.com/1999/0225/p2s1.html.

12. Russell Gold, "Counties Struggle with High Cost of Prosecuting Death-Penalty Cases," *Wall Street Journal*, January 9, 2002, p. B1.

13. "Capital Trial Could Be Costly for Franklin Co.," *Sulphur Springs News-Telegram*, June 27, 2007, p. 4.

14. Andrew Becker and G. W. Schultz, "Drug Busts Strain County Budget," *Dallas Morning News*, July 28, 2013, p. 10A.

15. Adam M. Gershowitz, "Statewide Capital Punishment: The Case for Eliminating Counties' Role in the Death Penalty," 63 *Vanderbilt Law Review* 8–9 (2010).

16. Cole and Taebel, *Texas: Politics and Public Policy*, 155.

17. Lawrence M. Crane, Nat Pinnoi, and Stephen W. Fuller, "Private Demand for Publicly Provided Goods: A Case Study of Rural Roads in Texas," *TAMRC Contemporary Market Issues Report No. CI-1-92* (1992).

18. Texas Association of Counties, "Debate Goes Back and Forth, Just like Overweight Trucks," www.county.org /resources/library/county-mag/county/124/bridgedebate .html.

19. Texas Commission on Jail Standards, "Abbreviated Population Report," May 1, 2013, www.tcjs.state.tx.us/docs /AbbreRptCurrent.pdf.; Texas Commission on Jail Standards, "Incarceration Rate Report—Highest to Lowest," May 1, 2013, www.tcjs.state.tx.us/docs/IncarcerationRate RptCurrent.pdf.

20. Julie Wilson, "Montgomery County Drone Launch a Major Failure," Liberty Beat, May 15, 2013, www.the libertybeat.com/montgomery-county-drone-launch -amajor-failure/.

21. Article 11, Section 5, of the Texas Constitution is concerned with home rule. For a further discussion of home rule in Texas, see Terrell Blodgett, *Texas Home Rule Charters* (Austin: Texas Municipal League, 1994); Terrell Blodgett, "Home Rule Charters," *Handbook of Texas Online*, www.tshaonline.org/handbook/online/articles/HH /mvhek.html (accessed 4/17/08).

22. Correspondence with Terrell Blodgett, Wednesday, February 3, 2000; *Texas Almanac 2009–2010*, 500–510.

23. The following is drawn from Bradley R. Rice, "Commission Form of City Government," *Handbook of Texas Online*.

24. Dallas Morning News, *Texas Almanac 1996–97* (Dallas: Dallas Morning News, 1995), 513.

25. Correspondence with Terrell Blodgett, Wednesday, February 3, 2000.

26. For a further discussion, see Terrell Blodgett, "Council-Manager Form of City Government," *Handbook of Texas Online*; Blodgett, *Texas Home Rule Charters*.

27. For a history of the Office of Controller in Houston, see the City of Houston Office of the City Controller, "Controller History," www.houstontx.gov/controller/history.html.

28. PolitiFact Texas, "Austin Group Says Austin Is the Biggest U.S. City Lacking City Council Members Elected from Geographic Districts," August 17, 2012, www.politifact.com/texas/statements/2012/aug/17/austinites-geographic-representation/austin-group-says-austin-biggest-us-city-lacking-c/

29. Sarah Coppola, "Grass-Roots Effort Drove Austin City Council District Plan to Victory, Observers Say," Austin American-Statesman, November 7, 2012, www.statesman.com/news/grass-roots-effort-drove-austin.

30. Taken from www.elpasotexas.gov and U.S. Census, "State & County QuickFacts," www.quickfacts.census.gov/qfd/states/48/4824000.html.

31. Jack C. Plano and Milton Greenberg, *The American Political Dictionary*, 10th ed. (Fort Worth: Harcourt, Brace, 1997).

32. *Texas Almanac and State Industrial Guide, 2000–2001* (Dallas: Dallas Morning News, 1999), 533; *Statistical Abstract of the United States* (Washington, DC: Bureau of the Census, 1998), 496.

33. Jennifer Peebles, "Growing Governments: How 'Special Districts' Spread across Texas with Limited Oversight and Accountability—but with Plenty of Power to tax," Texas Watchdog, February 15, 2011, www.texaswatchdog.org/2011/02/growing-governments-how-special-districts-spread-across-Texas-power-to-tax/1297796531.story; U.S. Census, "Number of Special Districts," Lists and Structure of Governments, www.census.gov/govs/go/number_of_special_districts_by_county.html.

34. Peebles, "Growing Governments."

35. Peebles, "Growing Governments."

36. Ed Timms and Kevin Krause, "Constables' Tickets Collect Funds, Critics," *Dallas Morning News*, October 25, 2009; Kevin Krause, "Commissioners OK Hiring Own Lawyer," *Dallas Morning News*, September 30, 2009; Kevin Krause, "Towed Cars Remain on Road to Nowhere," *Dallas Morning News*, September 18, 2009; Ed Timms and Kevin Krause, "Constables' Mission Has Changed," *Dallas Morning News*, October 26, 2009.

37. County Information Program, Texas Association of Counties. Data are for 2010.

38. County Information Program, Texas Association of Counties. Data are for 2010.

39. Brooks Egerton and Reese Dunklin, "Government by Developer," *Dallas Morning News*, June 10, 2001, p. 1A.

40. Peggy Heinkel-Wolfe, "Developers Still Using Renters to Create Special Tax Districts," *Dallas Morning News*, November 1, 2006, p. 1B.

41. Peggy Heinkel-Wolfe, "Bonds Approved with Blessing of 2 Voters," *Dallas Morning News*, November 22, 2010, p. B6.

42. Sara C. Galvan, "Wrestling with MUDs to Pin Down the Truth about Special Districts," 75 *Fordham Law Review* (2007): 3041–80.

43. See Texas Association of Regional Councils, "About TARC."

44. Chuck DeVore, "On Prohibiting the Issuance of Capital Appreciation Bonds: Testimony to the Senate Committee on Intergovernmental Relations," Texas Public Policy Foundation, March 20, 2013, www.texaspolicy.com/center/fiscal-policy/reports/prohibiting-issuance-capital-appreciation-bonds.

45. Trey Bundy and Shane Shifflet, "Controversial School Bonds Create 'Debt for the Next Generation,'" 31 California Watch, January 2013, http://californiawatch.org/k-12/controversial-school-bonds-create-debt-next-generation-18795.

46. Chuck DeVore, "On Prohibiting the Issuance of Capital Appreciation Bonds."

47. Chuck DeVore, "CAB Rides Can Be Extremely Costly," Austin American-Statesman, September 11, 2012, www.statesman.com/news/news/opinion/devore-cab-rides-can-be-extremely-costly/nSLLC/.

48. Municipal Securities Rulemaking Board, "Zero Coupon Bond," www.msrb.org/msrb1/glossary/view_def.asp?param=ZEROCOUPONBOND.

49. C. Taylor, "How Does a Capital Appreciation Bond Work?" Houston Chronicle, undated, http://smallbusiness.chron.com/capital-appreciation-bond-work-39357.html.

50. Municipal Securities Rulemaking Board, "Capital Appreciation Bond (CAB)," www.msrb.org/msrb1/glossary/view_def.asp?param=CAPITALAPPRECIATIONBOND.

51. Municipal Securities Rulemaking Board, "Original Issue Discount (O.I.D.)," www.msrb.org/msrb1/glossary/view_def.asp?[ara,=ORIGINALISSUEDISCOUNT.

52. James Estes, "Capital Appreciation Bonds: The Creation of a Toxic Waste Dump in Our Schools," Alpha Wealth Management, April, 2013, www.alpha-wealth.com/resources/publications/CAB-Paper.pdf

53. Estes, "Capital Appreciation Bonds."

54. Estes, "Capital Appreciation Bonds."

55. DeVore, "CAB Rides Can Be Extremely Costly."

56. DeVore, "On Prohibiting the Issuance of Capital Appreciation Bonds."

57. Keeley Webster, "Lockyer Challenges Poway CAB Advisors," Bond Buyer, Business Source Complete (2012), http://search.ebscohost.com.libproxy.utdallas.edu/login.aspx?direct=true&db=bth&AN=82740146&site=ehost-live.

58. DeVore, "CAB Rides Can Be Extremely Costly."

59. Richard Williamson, "Texas Seeks CAB Ban to Bar School Risk," *Bond Buyer*, March 21, 2013, p. 1.

60. Mike Ward, "Senate Approves Limit on Capital-Appreciation Bonds," Austin American-Statesman, April 9, 2013, www.statesman.com/news/news/senate-approves-limit-on-capital-appreciation-bond/nXG9h/.

61. Eva-Marie Ayala, "Anna ISD Used Costly Bonds to Cope," *Dallas Morning News*, June 16, 2013, p. 1.

62. Bundy and Shifflet, "Controversial School Bonds Create 'Debt.'"

63. Allison Fu, "State Assembly Passes Bill Aimed to Curtail School District Debt Burden," *Daily Californian*, April 10, 2013, www.dailycal.org/2013/04/09/state-assembly-passes-bill-aimed-to-curtail-debt-burden/

64. DeVore, "On Prohibiting the Issuance of Capital Appreciation Bonds."

65. Susan Combs, Texas Comptroller of Public Accounts, "Your Money and Pension Obligations" (2012), 4.

66. Combs, "Your Money and Pension Obligations," 3.

67. Combs, "Your Money and Pension Obligations," 14.

68. Combs, "Your Money and Pension Obligations," 6

69. Combs, "Your Money and Pension Obligations," 7.

70. Combs, "Your Money and Pension Obligations," 17.

71. Gary Jacobson, "Dallas Police and Fire Pension System Pursues High Returns," Dallas News, July 28, 2012, www.dallasnews.com/business/headlines/20120728-dallas-pol.

72. Jacobson, "Dallas Police and Fire Pension System."

73. Matthew Watkins, "Changes to Pension Plans Eyed," *Dallas Morning News*, September 7, 2013, pp. 1B, 6B.

74. Combs, "Your Money and Pension Obligations," 10–13.

75. Combs, "Your Money and Pension Obligations," 7, 10–13.

76. Comparison of El Paso City Employees' Pension Fund, "Summary Plan Description First Tier for Persons Whose Participation Date Is before September 1, 2011," with "Summary Plan Description Second Tier for Persons Whose Participation Date Is after September 1, 2011."

77. Comparison of El Paso City Employees' Pension Fund, "Summary Plan Description First Tier for Persons Whose Participation Date Is before September 1, 2011," with "Summary Plan Description Second Tier for Persons Whose Participation Date Is after September 1, 2011."

Chapter 11

1. Jeannie Kever, "As Texas Public College Tuition Rises, Legislators Feel the Heat," *Houston Chronicle*, July 10, 2008; Texas Higher Education Coordinating Board, "Tuition Set-Aside-House Bill 3013, 78th Texas Legislature," *Overview* (February 2010).

2. Texas Legislative Budget Board Staff, *Financing Higher Education in Texas: Legislative Primer*, as submitted to the 82nd Texas Legislature (January 2011); Texas Higher Education Coordinating Board, "Tuition Deregulation," *Overview* (March 2011).

3. Reeve Hamilton, "Texplainer: How Can I Get a $10,000 Degree?" *Texas Tribune*, March 29, 2012.

4. Minjae Park, "UT Regents Back Some Tuition Hikes, New Med Schools," *Texas Tribune*, May 3, 2012. See also Reeve Hamilton and Morgan Smith, "UT's Reform-Minded Chairman at the Center of Controversy," *Texas Tribune*, May 18, 2012; Reeve Hamilton, "For In-State Students, UT System Keeps Tuition Steady," *Texas Tribune*, May 20, 2014.

5. The following discussion is drawn from Texas Legislative Budget Board, *Fiscal Size-Up: 2014–15 Biennium* (2014), pp. 1–7.

6. Texas Legislative Budget Board, *Fiscal Size-Up: 2014–15 Biennium*, p. 58.

7. Texas Legislative Budget Board, *Fiscal Size-Up: 2014–15 Biennium*, p. 59.

8. Texas Legislative Budget Board, *Fiscal Size-Up: 2014–15 Biennium*, p. 60.

9. Texas Legislative Budget Board, *Fiscal Size-Up: 2014–15 Biennium*, p. 52. See also data provided by the Federation of Tax Administrators at www.taxadmin.org and Texas Public Policy Foundation at www.texasbudgetsource.com (accessed June 2014). See also tax burden rankings provided by the Tax Foundation at www.taxfoundation.org (accessed June 2014).

10. Information from the preceding two paragraphs is from Texas Legislative Budget Board, *Fiscal Size-Up: 2014–15 Biennium*, p. 55. Additional data on Texas are from the Tax Foundation at www.taxfoundation.org (accessed June 2014).

11. The following explanations and data on the various taxes in Texas are based on Texas Legislative Budget Board, *Fiscal Size-Up: 2014–15 Biennium*, pp. 29–32.

12. Texas Legislative Budget Board, *Fiscal Size-Up: 2014–15 Biennium*, pp. 30–31.

13. Carl David et al., *Who Pays? A Distributional Analysis of the Tax Systems in All 50 States*, 3rd ed. (Washington, DC: Institute on Taxation and Economic Policy, January 2013), pp. 4, 11–12.

14. David et al., *Who Pays?* p. 4; Susan Combs, Texas Comptroller of Public Accounts, *Tax Exemptions and Tax Incidence: A Report to the Governor and the 82nd Texas Legislature* (Austin: Texas Comptroller of Public Accounts, February 2011), pp. 41–42.

15. Clay Robinson, "Bullock Paints a Grim Picture/Says Income Tax Needed to Avert Financial Crisis," *Houston Chronicle*, March 12, 1991; Clay Robinson, "Bullock Plan May Open Door to Tax Battle," *Houston Chronicle*, March 2, 1993.

16. Texas Legislative Budget Board, *Fiscal Size-Up: 2014–15 Biennium*, p. 39; Senate Research Center, *Budget 101: A Guide to the Budget Process in Texas* (2013), pp. 34–35.

17. Texas Lottery Commission, "Demographic Survey of Texas Lottery Players 2009" (December 1, 2009), p. 11;

Office of the Texas Comptroller, "Window on State Government, Revenue by Source for Fiscal Year 2011," www.window.state.tx.us/taxbud/revenue.html; Texas Legislative Budget Board, *Fiscal Size-Up: 2014–15 Biennium*, p. 32.

18. James LeBas, "Who Wants to Be a Billionaire? Texas Spending Tobacco Money on Health Care, Endowments," Texas Comptroller of Public Accounts, *Fiscal Notes* (January 2000); Texas House of Representatives, House Research Organization, "State Finance Report No. 82-3" (March 11, 2011). The income projections are from Texas Legislative Budget Board, *Fiscal Size-Up: 2014–15 Biennium*, p. 32.

19. Michael E. McClellan, "Permanent School Fund," *Handbook of Texas Online*; Texas Educational Agency, "Permanent School Fund Hits Record High," February 6, 2014; Texas Legislative Budget Board, *Fiscal Size-Up: 2014–15 Biennium*, pp. 240–41.

20. Texas Legislative Budget Board, *Fiscal Size-Up: 2014–15 Biennium*, pp. 484–85.

21. Susan Combs, Texas Comptroller of Public Accounts, "Rainy Day Fund 101," *Fiscal Notes*, February 2011; Texas Legislative Budget Board, *Fiscal Size-Up: 2014–15 Biennium*, p. 27.

22. Texas Higher Education Coordinating Board, "Overview: Permanent University Fund (PUF)," Higher Education Fund (HEF) (December 2012); Texas Legislative Budget Board, *Fiscal Size-Up: 2014–15 Biennium*, pp. 309–14.

23. Texas Higher Education Coordinating Board, "National Research University Fund Eligibility: A Report to the Comptroller and the Texas Legislature," Higher Education Fund (HEF) (February 2012).

24. Texas Legislative Budget Board, *Texas Fact Book 2012* (Austin: State of Texas, 2012), p. 27; Texas Legislative Budget Board, *Fiscal Size-Up: 2014–15 Biennium*, pp. 12–13.

25. Texas Legislative Budget Board, *Fiscal Size-Up: 2014–15 Biennium*, p. 12; Robert T. Garrett, "State Sales Tax Receipts Grew by 8.5 Percent in May," *Dallasnews*, June 11, 2014.

26. Texas Legislative Budget Board, *Fiscal Size-Up: 2014–15 Biennium*, pp. 12–13.

27. The following is drawn from Senate Research Center, *Budget 101*, p. 29.

28. Senate Research Center, *Budget 101*, p. 29.

29. Texas Legislative Budget Board, *Fiscal Size-Up: 2014–15 Biennium*, p. 22; Tax Foundation, *Facts and Figures* (Washington, DC, 2014), Table 36.

30. See Senate Research Center, *Budget 101*, pp. 24–25.

31. Senate Research Center, *Budget 101*, p. 28.

32. See the discussion in Senate Research Center, *Budget 101*, p. 28.

33. See the discussion in Senate Research Center, *Budget 101*, pp. 34–35.

34. Bernard L. Weinstein, "Taxes in Texas," in *Texas Politics: A Reader*, ed. Anthony Champagne and Edward J. Harpham (New York: W.W. Norton, 1998), chap. 12.

35. The following discussion is drawn from Texas Legislative Budget Board, *Fiscal Size-Up: 2012–13 Biennium*; Texas Legislative Budget Board, *Texas Fact Book 2012* (Austin: State of Texas, 2012). The data for the following are drawn from Texas Legislative Budget Board, *Fiscal Size-Up: 2012–13 Biennium*; Robert T. Garrett, "Tension Rises over Future Cuts," *Dallas Morning News*, February 24, 2012, p. A1; Dave Montgomery and Anna M. Tinsley, "Texas Budget with $15 Billion in Cuts Clears Legislature," *Fort Worth Star-Telegram*, May 28, 2011; Ross Ramsey, "The End Game: Special Session Wraps Up Today," *Texas Tribune*, June 29, 2011. See also Robert T. Garrett, "Many Texas Politicians, Including Perry and White, Talk Little of $21 Billion Budget Gap," *Dallas Morning News*, September 12, 2010; Robert T. Garrett, "Budget Likely to Cut Deep," *Dallas Morning News*, October 24, 2010; Emily Ramshaw, "Legislators Consider Medicaid Withdrawal," *Texas Tribune*, November 7, 2010. See also Eugenio Aleman and Tyler B. Kruse, "Texas Budget: 2012–2013 Biennium," Wells Fargo Securities, June 24, 2011.

36. For a discussion of the factors lying behind the financial collapse and federal responses to it, see Simon Johnson and James Kwak, *13 Banks: The Wall Street Takeover and the Next Financial Meltdown* (New York: Pantheon Books, 2010); Roger Lowenstein, *The End of Wall Street* (New York: Penguin Press, 2010); David Wessel, *In Fed We Trust: Ben Bernanke's War on the Great Panic* (New York: Crown Business, 2009). See Texas Comptroller of Public Accounts, *Window on State Government*, May 2012 State Sales Tax Collections to General Revenue.

37. This discussion relies heavily upon Dick Lavine, "How to Fill the Hole in the Texas Revenue System," Center for Public Policy Priorities (February 2012).

Chapter 12

1. The following is drawn from Brandon Formby, "Schools Wrestling with Policies under New Religious Liberties Act," *Dallas Morning News*, August 27, 2007; Jenny Lacoste-Caputo, "Law on Religion in School Spurs Fear," *San Antonio Express-News*, July 25, 2007; Kelly Coghlan, "Religion Gets Equal Treatment," *Dallas Morning News*, September 6, 2007; Karen Brooks, "One State under God," *Dallas Morning News*, April 22, 2007; Wendy Gragg, "New State Law on Religious Expression in Schools Draws Mixed Reactions," *Waco Tribune-Herald*, August 9, 2007. The text of HB 3678 is available at www.capitol.state.tx.us/tlodocs/80R/billtext/html/HB03678F.htm (accessed 4/21/08).

2. See Texas Association of School Boards, "Legal Notes: An Open Mike." The quotation is from Melissa Rogers, "The Texas Religious Viewpoints Antidiscrimination Act and the Establishment Clause," 42 *University of California Davis Law Review* 939, 991–92 (2009).

3. See Benjamin Ginsberg, Theodore J. Lowi, Margaret Weir, Caroline Tolbert, Anthony Champagne, Edward J. Harpham, et al., *We The People: Texas Edition*, 9th ed. (New York: W. W. Norton, 2012), 643.

4. B. Guy Peters, *American Public Policy: Promise and Performance*, 9th ed. (Washington, DC: CQ Press, 2012), chaps. 2 and 3; Charles O. Jones, *An Introduction to the Study of Public Policy*, 3rd ed. (Monterey, CA: Brooks, Cole, 1984).

5. Roger Cobb and Charles Elder, *Participation in American Politics* (Baltimore: Johns Hopkins University Press, 1983), 85.

6. See Herbert Simon, "Bounded Rationality and Organizational Learning," *Organizational Science* 2, no. 1: 125–34; Kristen Renwick Monroe, *The Economic Approach to Politics: A Critical Reassessment of the Theory of Rational Action* (New York: HarperCollins, 1991).

7. See Texas Legislative Budget Board, *Fiscal Size-Up: 2014–15 Biennium* (Austin: State of Texas, 2014), 233, 242.

8. Texas State Historical Association, *Texas Almanac 2014–15* (Denton: Texas State Historical Association, 2014), 596. See Texas Education Agency, "Enrollment in Texas Public Schools 2012–13."

9. The data in this section are largely drawn from Texas Legislative Budget Board, *Fiscal Size-Up: 2014–15 Biennium*, 230–54. See also *Texas Tribune*, Public Education Data.

10. For a discussion of the history of public education in Texas from which the following is drawn, see Max Berger and Lee Wilborn, "Education," *Handbook of Texas Online*, www.tshaonline.org/handbook/online/articles/EE/khel.html (accessed 4/21/08); Dallas Morning News, "Public Schools," *Texas Almanac 2000–2001*, Millennium Edition (Dallas: Dallas Morning News, 1999), 533–54.

11. See Lewis B. Cooper, *The Permanent School Fund of Texas* (Fort Worth: Texas State Teachers Association, 1934); Michael E. McClellan, "Permanent School Fund," *Handbook of Texas Online*, www.tshaonline.org/hand book/online/articles/PP/khpl.html (accessed 4/21/08).

12. See Oscar Mauzy, "Gilmer-Aikin Laws," *Handbook of Texas Online*, www.tshaonline.org/handbook/online/articles/GG/mlgl.html (accessed 4/21/08); Dick Smith and Richard Allen Burns, "Texas Education Agency," *Handbook of Texas Online*, www.tshaonline.org/handbook/online/articles/TT/met2.html (accessed 4/21/08); Berger and Wilborn, "Education."

13. See Anna Victoria Wilson, "Education for African Americans," *Handbook of Texas Online*, www.tshaonline.org/handbook/online/articles/EE/kde2.html (accessed 4/21/08).

14. Arnoldo De León and Robert A. Calvert, "Segregation," *Handbook of Texas Online*, www.tshaonline.org/handbook/online/articles/SS/pksl.html (accessed 4/21/08).

15. The following discussion of the *Rodríguez* and *Edgewood* cases is drawn from Texas Legislative Budget Board Staff, "Financing Public Education in Texas: Kindergarten through Grade 12," *Legislative Handbook* (February 1999); Berger and Wilborn, "Education"; Cynthia E. Orozco, "Rodríguez v. San Antonio ISD," *Handbook of Texas Online*, www.tshaonline.org/handbook/online/articles/RR/jrrht.html (accessed 4/21/08); Teresa Palomo Acosta, "Edgewood ISD v. Kirby," *Handbook of Texas Online*, www.tshaonline.org/handbook/online/articles/EE/jre2.html (accessed 4/21/08).

16. See Texas Legislative Budget Board Staff, "Financing Public Education in Texas: Kindergarten through Grade 12," 26–27.

17. See Texas House of Representatives, House Research Organization, "Focus Report: Schools and Taxes" (May 25, 2007), www.house.state.tx.us/featured/schools&taxes79–13.pdf (accessed 4/21/08); Jason Embry, "Session Ends with Property Tax Cut," *Austin American-Statesman*, May 26, 2006.

18. Mark Wiggins, "Attorneys, Schools and 83rd Texas Legislature's Impact on Education," www.kvue.com; Morgan Smith, "Texas School Finance Trial Goes for Round Two," *Texas Tribune*, June 19, 2013; Terrance Stutz, "State Seeks to Remove School Finance Judge," *Dallas Morning News*, June 3, 2014, p. 3a.

19. See Clark D. Thomas, "Education Reform in Texas," in *Texas Politics*, ed. Anthony Champagne and Edward J. Harpham (New York: W. W. Norton, 1998), 213–32.

20. National Commission on Excellence in Education, *A Nation at Risk: The Imperative for Educational Reform* (Washington, DC: Department of Education, 1983).

21. See Thomas, "Education Reform in Texas," 218.

22. See Thomas, "Education Reform in Texas," 221.

23. See Thomas, "Education Reform in Texas," 231; Dallas Morning News, "Public Schools," *Texas Almanac 2000–2001*, Millennium Edition (Dallas: Dallas Morning News, 1999), 533. See also Terrence Stutz, "State's List Cites Sub-par Schools in Transfer Plan," *Dallas Morning News*, December 24, 1999, p. 1.

24. College Board, "Mean 2009 SAT Scores by State"; College Board, "2009 College-Bound Seniors Total Group Profile Report" (2009), p. 3. See also Texas Education Agency, "College Admissions Testing of Graduating Seniors in Texas High Schools, Class of 2010" (October 2011) and Texas Education Agency, "2010 Comprehensive Annual Report on Texas Public Schools" (Austin: 2010). See Joshua Benton, "Legislators Left Unanswered Questions on New State Tests," *Dallas Morning News*,

June 11, 2007, p. B1. See also Terrence Stutz, "Failing Tests, Passing Grades," *Dallas Morning News*, March 8, 2012, p. A1.

25. See Kate McGee, "Two Big Education Bills Gain Approval from Texas Legislature," KUTnews.org, May 27, 2013.

26. See footnote 24 for background and details.

27. See Legislative Budget Board, Fiscal Note, 83rd Legislative Regular Session (February 19, 2013). See also Texas Education Agency, "Initial STAAR Results Released," News. TEA (June 8, 2012); Jeffrey Weiss and Daniel Lathrop, "Low-Scoring Groups Slipping More," *Dallas Morning News*, June 9, 2014, pp. 1a and 8.

28. See Milton Friedman, *Capitalism and Freedom* (Chicago: University of Chicago, 1962).

29. Texas Association of Charter Schools, txcharterschools .org.

30. See the respective web sites of these organizations. See also Morgan Smith, "Education Reform Group Mobilizes for 2014 Elections," *Texas Tribune*, January 8, 2014.

31. See Jim Henson and Joshua Blank, "Polling Center: Threading the Needle on Education," *Texas Tribune*, April 10, 2014. See also University of Texas/Texas Tribune, "Texas Statewide Survey," February 2014 and earlier surveys.

32. Data from U.S. Bureau of the Census and Texas Health and Human Services Commission.

33. See Texas State Historical Association, *Texas Almanac 2014–15*, 497; Texas Legislative Budget Board, *Fiscal Size-Up: 2014–15 Biennium*, February 2014, 161–62.

34. The following is drawn from Edward J. Harpham, "Welfare Reform and the New Paternalism in Texas," in *Texas Politics*, ed. Champagne and Harpham, 233–49.

35. See Vivian Elizabeth Smyrl, "Texas Department of Human Services," *Handbook of Texas Online*, www.tsha online.org/handbook/online/articles/TT/mct6.html (accessed 4/23/08).

36. Harpham, "Welfare Reform and the New Paternalism in Texas," 238.

37. See Charles Murray, *Losing Ground: American Social Policy, 1950–1980* (New York: Basic Books, 1984).

38. For a discussion of these programs, see Lawrence Mead, *The New Politics of Poverty: The Nonworking Poor in America* (New York: Basic Books, 1992).

39. The following paragraphs are drawn from Harpham, "Welfare Reform and the New Paternalism in Texas," 244–47.

40. See Texas Legislative Budget Board, *Fiscal Size-Up: 2014–15 Biennium*, 221–22; Texas Health and Human Services Commission, "Temporary Assistance for Needy Families (TANF): Frequently Asked Questions," www .hhsc.state.tx.us/programs/TexasWorks/TANF-FAQ .html (accessed 4/23/08). See also Texas Health and Human Services Commission, "Presentation to the House Select Committeee on Human Services: HHSC Overview" (February 12, 2013).

41. See Texas Legislative Budget Board, *Fiscal Size-Up: 2014–15 Biennium*, 160. See Texas Workforce Investment Council, "Issues in Welfare to Work: A State of the Workforce Report on State Issues Arising from TANF Reauthorization" (December 2006), p. 11, www.governor .state.tx.us/divisions/twic/files/wfwissues.pdf (accessed 4/23/08); Texas Health and Human Services Commission, "Texas TANF and SNAP Enrollment Statistics," www.hhsc.state.tx.us/research/TANF_FS.asp.

42. The Center for Public Policy Priorities has produced many studies on the situation facing children in poverty in Texas. See, for example, Center for Public Policy Priorities, "TANF at 10: Has Welfare Reform Been a Success in Texas?" (August 22, 2006).

43. Texas Health and Human Services Commission, *Texas Medicaid and CHIP in Perspective*, 9th ed. (January 2013), www.hhsc.state.tx.us/medicaid/about/PB/PinkBook .pdf. Medicaid and Chip information and data for this section are taken from this document and from data for Texas on the Henry Kaiser Family Foundation website, www.statehealthfacts.org.

44. See Rice University's Baker Institute and the Episcopal Health Foundation, "Health Reform Monitoring Survey: Texas" (April 2014). See also Edgar Walters, "Report: Texas' Rate of Uninsured Dips Slightly," *Texas Tribune*, April 16, 2014.

45. See Texas Health and Human Services Commission, *Texas Medicaid*, chap. 1.

46. In 2015 there are two FMAPs calculated for Texas: the basic FMAP (58.05 percent) and the enhanced FMAP (70.64 percent), which is used for the CHIP program federal match. See Texas Health and Human Services Commission, *Texas Medicaid*, 5–16.

47. See Texas Health and Human Services Commission, *Texas Medicaid*, chap. 7, p. 2.

48. See Louis Radnofsky, "Texas Medicaid Funds Cut Over Planned Parenthood," *Wall Street Journal*, March 15, 2012; Emily Ramshaw and Thanh Tan, "The Storm Over Women's Health Care Had Been Brewing," *Texas Tribune*, March 23, 2012; Wade Goodwyn, "As Texas Cuts Funds, Planned Parenthood Fights Back," www.npr.com, May 7, 2012; Amanda Peterson Beadle, Thinkprogress .org, March 16, 2012; Sean Walsh, "Hutcheson Backs Planned Parenthood in Funding Dispute," *Dallas Morning News*, March 22, 2012.

49. Moni Basu, "Court Rules Texas Can Ban Planned Parenthood from Health Program," CNN U.S. (articles .cnn.com) August 22, 2012; "Judge Says Texas Not Allowed to Cut Funds to Planned Parenthood," www .foxnews.com, May 4, 2012.

50. See Nancy Flake, "Combs: Texas in Great Shape, but Watch out for Medicaid," *Cyprus Creek Mirror*, May 2,

2012. See also Kristie Avery, "Comptroller Warns of Medicaid Costs," *Texas Gazette*, www.susancombs.com/media/comptroller-warns-medicaid-costs.

51. In the Senate, 58 Democrats and 2 independents voted for the Patient Protection and Affordable Care Act. All 39 Republicans in the Senate were opposed. In the House of Representatives, the final vote was 219 to 212. All supporters of the bill were Democrats, with 34 Democrats and 178 Republicans opposing the bill.

52. See Texas Health and Human Services Commission, *Texas Medicaid*, chap. 3, for a further discussion of the impact of federal health care reforms on Texas.

53. See Kaiser Family Foundation, "How Will the Uninsured in Texas Fare under the Affordable Care Act?" at kff.org/medicaid.

54. "Fewer Texas Doctors Taking Medicaid Patients," *Dallas Morning News*, July 9, 2012.

55. Robert T. Garrett, "State Slashes Health Law Estimate," *Dallas Morning News*, July 13, 2012.

56. "Federal Scorecard Ranks Texas Last in Health Care," *Dallas Morning News*, July 6, 2012.

57. Peter G. George, Robert E. Mace, and Rima Petrossian, Aquifers of Texas, "Texas Development Board, Report 380" (July 2011).

58. An acre-foot is equal to 325,851.43 U.S. gallons. Planners typically assume that a suburban family will consume an acre-foot of water a year.

59. Texas Water Development Board, "Water for Texas 2012 State Water Plan" (January 2012), p. xii.

60. See Texas Water Development Board, "Water for Texas 2012," pp. 17–18.

61. See Otis W. Templer, "Water Law," *Handbook of Texas Online*; Otis W. Templer, "Water Rights Issues: Texas Water Rights Law; East Meets West," *Journal of Contemporary Water Research and Education* 85 (Spring 1991).

62. The following is drawn largely from Templer, "Water Law" and "Texas Water Rights." See also Terry L. Hadley, "Texas Water Commission," *Handbook of Texas Online*; Laurie E. Jasinski, "Texas Water Development Board," *Handbook of Texas Online*; Texas Water Development Board, "Water for Texas 2012," Executive Summary and chap. 1. See also Texas Water Development Board, "A Texan's Guide to Water and Water Rights Marketing"; Ronald Kaiser, *Handbook of Texas Water Law: Problems and Need Water Monograph No. 87-1* (College Station: Texas Water Resources Institute, Texas A&M University, 1987). We also thank Benedict Voit for his useful summary of water policy issues. See Benedict Voit, "Texas Water Policy for the 21st Century," unpublished paper, University of Texas at Dallas, April 10, 2008.

63. See Texas Water Development Board, "A Texan's Guide to Water."

64. Texas Water Development Board, "Water for Texas 2012," pp. 15–16.

65. See the historical timeline regarding environmental policy, Texas Commission on Environmental Quality, www.tceq.texas.gov.

66. See Texas Water Development Board, "About the Texas Water Development Board," www.txdb.texas.gov.

67. Texas Water Development Board, "Water for Texas 2012," p. 190.

68. See Kate Galbraith, "Texas Supreme Court Rules for Landowners in Water Case," *Texas Tribune*, February 24, 2012. See also Forrest Wilder, "The Texas Supreme Court Turns Water into a Landmark Groundwater Decision," *Texas Observer*, February 24, 2012; Chuck Lindell, "Supreme Court Delivers Major Water Ruling on Water Regulation," *Austin American Statesman*, February 24, 2012.

69. For a good discussion of some of these issues, see a five-part series published by the *Texas Tribune*: Neena Satija, "Beneath the Surface," *Texas Tribune*, November 19, 2013–January 19, 2014.

70. Michael Marks and Terence Henry, "Everything You Need to Know about Proposition 6, Texas' Water Fund," *State Impact: A Reporting Project of NPR Member Stations*, November 4, 2013.

Chapter 13

1. Jordan Smith, "WillCo D.A.: Duty Upsets Bradley," *Austin Chronicle*, June 1, 2012, www.austinchronicle.com/news/2012-06-01/wilso-d-a-duty-upsets-bradley/.

2. Claire Osborn, "Ken Anderson Begins Serving Jail Sentence in Michel Morton Case," statesman.com, November 13, 2013.

3. Will Weissert, "Bill Named for Michael Morton Passes House," May 13, 2013, www.kxan.com/dpp/news/texas-lege/bill-named-for-michael-morton-passes-house; "Perry Set to Sign Michael Morton Act," May 16, 2013, www.kxan.com/dpp/news/texas-lege/perry-set-to-sign-michael-morton-act.

4. This material is from Brandi Grissom, "In Deposition, Morton Prosecutor Can't Recall Details," *Texas Tribune*, November 30, 2011; Brandi Grissom, "A Tough Prosecutor Finds His Certitude Shaken by a Prisoner's Exoneration," *Texas Tribune*, November 18, 2011; Brandi Grissom and Benjamin Hasson, "Michael Morton: A Timeline," *Texas Tribune*, November 18, 2011.

5. Fred Dahr, "Crimes and Punishment in Texas State Court," www.texasdefenselaw.com; Texas Criminal Defense Lawyer, "Texas Criminal Laws and Penalties," www.mytexasdefenselawyer.com.

6. Texas Board of Pardons and Paroles, www.tdcj.state.tx.us/bpp/.

7. Information is from the Texas Association of Counties. The term *district attorney* will be used to encompass district attorneys, county attorneys, and criminal district attorneys.

8. Robert S. DuBoise and Kathleen Catania, "The Longest Sentence in Texas History," *The Prosecutor* (March–April 2009).

9. Valerie Wigglesworth, "Collin County District Judge Suzanne Wooten Found Guilty of Bribery," Dallasnews .com, November 22, 2011.

10. Jennifer Emily, "Grand Jury Subpoena Issued for Judge Who Held Dallas County DA Craig Watkins in Contempt," Dallasnews.com. September 24, 2013.

11. Jennifer Emily, "DA Accused of Pushing Staff to Run," *Dallas Morning News*, October 7, 2013, pp. 1, 2A.

12. Brian Rogers, "Grand Jury Won't Indict DA's Office, but Issues Strong Rebuke," *Houston Chronicle*, February 1, 2012.

13. Texas Indigent Defense Commission, "Indigent Defense Data for Texas," tidc.tamu.edu/public.net/Reports/Fee Documents.aspx.

14. Dottie Carmichael, "Judgement and Justice" (2013), pp. vii–x, www.txcourts.gov/tide/pdf/130607_FINAL .CapitalDefenderReport.pdf.

15. Texas Department of Criminal Justice, "Fiscal Year 2012 Statistical Report," www.tdcj.state.tx.us/documents /Statistical_Report_FY2012.pdf.

16. Legislative Budget Board, "Criminal Justice Uniform Cost Report: Fiscal Years 2010 to 2012" (2013), p.8, www .lbb.state.tx.us/Public Safety Criminal Justice/Uniform _Cost/Criminal_Justice_Uniform_Cost_Report_Fiscal _Years_2010_to_2012.pdf.

17. Harry Mika and Lawrence J. Redlinger, "Crime and Correction," in *Texas at the Crossroads*, ed. Anthony Champagne and Edward J. Harpham (College Station: Texas A&M University Press, 1987), 245–46.

18. Mika and Redlinger, "Crime and Correction," 245–46.

19. *Ruiz v. Estelle*, 503 F. Supp. 1265 (1980).

20. Mika and Redlinger, "Crime and Correction," 247.

21. Texas Department of Criminal Justice, "Texas Board of Criminal Justice," www.tdcj.state.tx.us/tbcj/index.html (accessed 8/30/12).

22. See Associated Texans against Crime, "Annual Report" (1998); Texas Department of Criminal Justice, "Fiscal Year 2011 Operating Budget and Fiscal Years 2010–2013 Legislative Appropriations Request" (August 16, 2010).

23. Marc A. Levin, "2009–2010 Legislator's Guide to the Issues" (November 2008), 1.

24. Robert Wilonsky, "Texas Department of Criminal Justice Says Dawson State Jail on the Shores of the Trinity River Will Close August 31," *Dallas Morning News*, June 11, 2013, http://cityhallblog.dallasnews.com/2013/06/texas -department-of-criminal-justice-says-dawson-state-jail -on-the-shores-of-the-trinity-river-will-close-august-31 .html/.

25. See Associated Texans against Crime, "Annual Report" (1998).

26. Texas Department of Criminal Justice, "Fiscal Year 2012 Statistical Report."

27. Texas Department of Criminal Justice, "Fiscal Year 2012 Statistical Report."

28. Texas Department of Criminal Justice, "Fiscal Year 2006 Statistical Summary" (December 2006).

29. Texas Department of Criminal Justice, "Fiscal Year 2010 Statistical Reports."

30. Department of Justice, "Bureau of Justice Statistics Bulletin: Prisoners in 2011" (2012), www.bis.gov.content /pub/pdf/p11.pdf; Texas Department of Criminal Justice, "Fiscal Year 2012 Statistical Report."

31. Texas State Historical Association, *Texas Almanac 2010– 2011* (2010), 482.

32. Department of Justice, "Bureau of Justice Statistics Bulletin: Prisoners in 2011" (2012).

33. Rachal Boba, "Crime State Rankings 2011: Crime across America" (Washington, DC: CQ Press, 2011), xxi.

34. Texas Department of Criminal Justice, "Fiscal Year 2012 Statistical Report."

35. Texas Department of Criminal Justice, "Fiscal Year 2012 Statistical Report."

36. Legislative Budget Board, "Statewide Criminal Justice Recidivism and Revocation Rates," www.lbb.state.tx.us /Public_Safety_Criminal_Justice/RecRev_Rates/State wide Criminal Justice Recidivism and Revocation Rates 2012.pdf.

37. Paul Brace and Brent D. Boyea, "State Public Opinion, the Death Penalty, and the Practice of Electing Judges," *American Journal of Political Science* (2008): 360–72.

38. Ross Ramsey, "UT/TT Poll: Texans Stand behind Death Penalty," *Texas Tribune*, May 24, 2012.

39. Data come from the Death Penalty Information Center, www.deathpenaltyinfo.org/executions-county.

40. Texas State Historical Association, *Texas Almanac 2010– 2011*, 482.

41. Texas Department of Criminal Justice, "Executed Offenders," www.tdcj.state.tx.us/death_row/dr_executed _offenders.html.

42. Texas Department of Criminal Justice, "Offenders on Death Row," www.tdcj.state.tx.us/death_row/dr _offenders_on_dr.html.

43. Texas Department of Criminal Justice, "Offenders on Death Row."

44. Texas Department of Criminal Justice, "Executions: December 7, 1982 through June 27, 2013," www.tdcj .state.tx.us/death_row/dr_executions_by_year.html.

45. Texas Department of Criminal Justice, "Executions, December 7, 1982 through March 16, 2010"; Texas Department of Criminal Justice, "Gender and Racial Statistics of Death Row Offenders"; *McClesky v. Kemp*, 481 U.S. 279 (1987).

46. "Gov. Perry Commutes Sentences of Man Scheduled to Die Thursday," ABC13, August 30, 2007.

47. David McCord, "What's Messing with Texas Death Sentences?" 43 *Texas Tech Law Review* 601–12 (2011).

48. The Innocence Project of Texas, "Facts on Post-Conviction DNA Exonerations."

49. "DNA Proving to Cut Both Ways on Death Penalty," *Dallas Morning News*, January 14, 2006, p. 10A.

50. The Innocence Project of Texas, "Texas Exonerations at a Glance."

51. The Innocence Project of Texas, "Texas Exonerations at a Glance."

52. Steve McGonigle, "Righting Wrongs," *Dallas Morning News*, January 22, 2007, p. 1; Jennifer Emily, "DA: Man Didn't Do '82 Rape," *Dallas Morning News*, September 17, 2007, p. 1B.

53. Mike Ware, "Dallas County Conviction Integrity Unit and the Importance of Getting It Right the First Time," 56 *New York Law School Law Review* 1034–50 (2011–2012).

54. Michael Hall, "Why Can't Steven Phillips Get a DNA Test?" *Texas Monthly*, January 2006.

55. Jeff Blackburn, "Dog Scent Lineups: A Junk Science Injustice," a special report by the Innocence Project of Texas (September 21, 2009).

56. David Grann, "Trial by Fire," *New Yorker*, September 7, 2009.

57. Jeff Carleton, "Cameron Todd Willingham: Texas Governor Dismisses 3 Commission Members Just 48 Hours before Arson Review," *Huffington Post*, September 30, 2009.

58. Allan Turner, "Abbott Ruling Limits Probe of Arson Case," *Houston Chronicle*, July 29, 2011.

59. See Nate Blakeslee, *Tulia: Race, Cocaine, and Corruption in a Small Texas Town* (New York: Public Affairs, 2005).

60. Paul Duggan, "'Sheetrock Scandal' Hits Dallas Police," *Washington Post*, January 18, 2002, p. 12.

61. "Texas and Mississippi: Reducing Prison Population, Saving Money, and Reducing Recidivism," *ABA Criminal Justice Section Parole & Probation*, www2.americanbar.org/sections/criminaljustice/CR203800/PublicDocuments/paroleandprobationsuccess.pdf.

62. Maurice Chammah, "Bill Addresses Changing Science in Criminal Appeals," *Texas Tribune*, February 4, 2013.

answer key

Chapter 1
1. B
2. A
3. C
4. D
5. B
6. D
7. E
8. A
9. E
10. C
11. B
12. C
13. A
14. A

Chapter 2
1. A
2. C
3. D
4. C
5. E
6. D
7. A
8. D
9. D
10. C
11. A
12. A
13. D
14. D
15. D

Chapter 3
1. C
2. C
3. A
4. B
5. B
6. A
7. A
8. C
9. A
10. C
11. B
12. A
13. A
14. B
15. C
16. E

Chapter 4
1. B
2. B
3. A
4. B
5. A
6. A
7. A
8. D
9. C
10. B
11. B
12. A

Chapter 5
1. C
2. C
3. D
4. E
5. C
6. C
7. A
8. A
9. A
10. C
11. C
12. A
13. D
14. B

Chapter 6
1. B
2. E
3. E
4. E
5. A
6. E
7. A
8. D
9. C
10. C
11. E
12. B
13. D
14. D
15. B
16. A

Chapter 7
1. A
2. A
3. D
4. B
5. E
6. B
7. C
8. B
9. D
10. D
11. C
12. A
13. D
14. A
15. A
16. D
17. B

Chapter 8
1. D
2. E
3. E
4. B
5. D
6. A
7. A
8. B
9. B
10. B
11. E
12. A
13. C
14. A
15. E

Chapter 9
1. C
2. C
3. C
4. B
5. B
6. A
7. E
8. D
9. E
10. E
11. E
12. A
13. A
14. A
15. C

Chapter 10
1. B
2. D
3. D
4. D
5. C
6. A
7. B
8. B
9. D
10. E
11. A
12. A
13. C
14. A
15. B
16. D
17. A

Chapter 11	Chapter 12	Chapter 13
1. A	1. B	1. A
2. B	2. C	2. B
3. A	3. A	3. C
4. A	4. B	4. C
5. C	5. A	5. D
6. B	6. A	6. C
7. B	7. B	7. D
8. C	8. E	8. E
9. A	9. A	9. A
10. B	10. C	10. B
11. D	11. B	11. E
12. D	12. C	12. C
13. A	13. C	13. E
14. B	14. A	14. A
	15. D	

photo credits

index

Page numbers in *italics* refer to figures, illustrations, and tables.

Voter Registration Information*

State	Registration Deadline before Election	Early Voting Permitted?	Identification Required to Vote?	More Information
Alabama	10 days	No	Photo ID requested	sos.state.al.us
Alaska	30 days	Yes	ID requested; photo not required	elections.alaska.gov
Arizona	29 days	Yes	ID required (nonphoto OK)	azsos.gov/election
Arkansas	30 days	Yes	ID requested; photo not required	sos.arkansas.gov
California	15 days	Yes	No	sos.ca.gov
Colorado	22 days; same-day registration permitted	Yes (all voting by mail)	ID requested; photo not required	sos.state.co.us
Connecticut	General election: in person, 7 days; by mail, 14 days Primary elections: in person, 1 day; by mail, 5 days	No	ID requested; photo not required	ct.gov/sots
Delaware	24 days	No	ID requested; photo not required	elections.delaware.gov
District of Columbia	30 days; same-day registration permitted	Yes	No	dcboee.org
Florida	29 days	Yes	Photo ID requested	election.dos.state.fl.us
Georgia	28 days	Yes	Photo ID required	sos.ga.gov
Hawaii	30 days	Yes	Photo ID requested	hawaii.gov/elections
Idaho	25 days; same-day registration permitted	Yes	Photo ID requested	idahovotes.gov
Illinois	27 days	Yes	No	elections.il.gov
Indiana	29 days	Yes	Photo ID required	in.gov/sos/elections
Iowa	10 days	Yes	No	sos.iowa.gov
Kansas	21 days	Yes	Photo ID required	kssos.org
Kentucky	28 days	No	ID requested; photo not required	elect.ky.gov
Louisiana	30 days	Yes	Photo ID requested	sos.la.gov
Maine	21 days; same-day registration permitted	Yes	No	maine.gov/sos
Maryland	21 days	Yes	No	elections.state.md.us
Massachusetts	20 days	No	No	www.sec.state.ma.us
Michigan	30 days	No	Photo ID requested	michigan.gov/sos
Minnesota	21 days	Yes	No	mnvotes.org
Mississippi	30 days	No	Photo ID required	sos.ms.gov
Missouri	Fourth Wednesday prior to election	No	ID requested; photo not required	sos.mo.gov

State	Registration Deadline before Election	Early Voting Permitted?	Identification Required to Vote?	More Information
Montana	30 days; same-day registration permitted	Yes	ID requested; photo not required	sos.mt.gov
Nebraska	In person: second Friday prior to election By mail: third Friday prior to election	Yes	No	www.sos.ne.gov
Nevada	In person: 21 days By mail: 31 days	Yes	No	nvsos.gov
New Hampshire	10 days; same-day registration permitted	No	ID requested; photo not required	sos.nh.gov
New Jersey	21 days	Yes	No	njelections.org
New Mexico	28 days	Yes	No	sos.state.nm.us
New York	25 days	No	No	www.elections.ny.gov
North Carolina	25 days	Yes	No	ncsbe.gov
North Dakota	No voter registration required	Yes	ID required (nonphoto OK)	vote.nd.gov
Ohio	30 days	Yes	ID required (nonphoto OK)	sos.state.oh.us
Oklahoma	24 days	Yes	ID requested; photo not required	ok.gov/elections
Oregon	21 days	Yes (all voting by mail)	No	sos.oregon.gov
Pennsylvania	30 days	No	No	www.votespa.com
Rhode Island	30 days	No	Photo ID requested	www.elections.state.ri.us
South Carolina	30 days	No	ID requested; photo not required	scvotes.org
South Dakota	15 days	Yes	Photo ID requested	sdsos.gov
Tennessee	30 days	Yes	Photo ID required	tn.gov/sos/election
Texas	30 days	Yes	Photo ID required	votetexas.gov
Utah	In person: 15 days By mail: 30 days	Yes	ID requested; photo not required	vote.utah.gov
Vermont	Wednesday before the election	Yes	No	www.sec.state.vt.us/elections
Virginia	22 days	No	Photo ID required	sbe.virginia.gov
Washington	In person: 8 days By mail: 30 days	Yes (all voting by mail)	ID requested; photo not required	sos.wa.gov/elections/myvote
West Virginia	21 days	Yes	No	sos.wv.gov
Wisconsin	Same-day registration permitted	Yes	No	sos.state.wi.us
Wyoming	14 days; same-day registration permitted	Yes	No	soswy.state.wy.us

*As of November 2014. Information collected from Project Vote Smart, votesmart.org/elections/voter-registration (accessed 11/4/14), and the National Conference of State Legislatures, www.ncsl.org/ (accessed 11/4/14). States often reevaluate the voting rules. Check the websites in the far right column to confirm current information.